ADRIENNE'S DICTIONARY

English/French

French in 32 Lessons
German in 32 Lessons
Spanish in 32 Lessons
Italian in 32 Lessons
Fast French
Gimmick I: Français parlé (previously published as Le Gimmick)
Gimmick I: gesprochenes Deutsch (previously published as Der Gimmick)
Gimmick I: Español hablado (previously published as El Gimmick)
Gimmick I: Italiano Parlato

ADRIENNE'S DICTIONARY

English/French

BY

ADRIENNE

W · W · Norton & Company
New York   London

Copyright © 1990 Editions La Decouverte
Copyright © 1988 Editions CARRERE as *Dictionnaire de L'Américain Parlé*
First American edition, 1991

Printed in the United States of America.

Manufacturing by The Courier Group.

Library of Congress Cataloging-in-Publication Data

Adrienne.
    [Dictionnaire de l'américain parlé. English]
    Adrienne's dictionary : English-French—1st American ed.
      p.   cm.
    Translation of: Dictionaire de l'américain parlé.
    Includes index.
1. English language—Spoken English—United States—Dictionaries—
French. 2. Americanisms—Dictionaries—French. I. Title.
PE2837.F7A368   1991
423'.41—dc20   91–8020

ISBN 0-393-02976-X

W. W. Norton & Company, Inc., 500 Fifth Avenue, New York, N.Y. 10110
W. W. Norton & Company, Ltd., 10 Coptic Street, London WC1A 1PU

1 2 3 4 5 6 7 8 9 0

With great gratitude to my assistants who survived this book with me:

SABINE BOSSAN
CLAIRE BEAUVILLARD

and to my long-standing collaborators:
PHILIPPE CARRE
ELISABETH HOPKINS

and to my principal reader: Peter Weissman
and to readers: Anne Kraatz and Barbara Tchertoff
with a special thank you to other members of my team : Anne Baudry, Marc Dondey, Sylvia Glassman and Agathe Logeart.

TO RAOUL WALLENBERG

"Confucius, the wisest of sages, once said the greatest reform would be to 'improve denominations'. A good dictionary is a tool for that purpose and, as such, promotes understanding among men. I congratulate you for undertaking this useful work."

Marguerite Yourcenar,
of the Académie française.
(Translated from the French)

TO MY READERS

THE GIMMICK

an unusual teacher

After teaching English to adults for many years in France I eventually put together a method published under the name of THE GIMMICK.
This innovative method was intended to give my students fluency in the spoken language and revolutionized the way English was being taught at that time.
My main concern was not for people to learn what they were supposed to say (approved by the purists and laid down in grammar books) but what is actually said.
This led me to reverse the usual teaching process : through continual practice in speaking the language, I progressively introduced theory to my students without forcing it on them.

My method is based on three main principles : gradually assimilating vocabulary through natural word association ; learning the specificity of the language through its idiomatic expressions ; and, most of all, mastering the number one problem of the English language : verbs and prepositions.
The GIMMICKS' success was living proof that my method fulfilled a need in people eager for a lively and dynamic learning experience. They were being taught Shakespearean English, whereas what they really wanted was to understand Woody Allen, *Newsweek,* and Bob Dylan.

Big Ben versus the Statue of Liberty? Preference has always been given to British over American English as a reference to correct language ; yet, it's obvious that American is the language of communications and the mass media, reflecting the pulse of the modern-day world.

The GIMMICK series was made up of several volumes, including thousands of words and expressions from the spoken language. My readers were the first to suggest classifying the contents of my different books in alphabetical order.

However, what started out as mere classification turned into a thorough inventory of the spoken language, taking into account the frequency with which different words are used. Thus, the necessity of a DICTIONARY OF THE SPOKEN LANGUAGE, and, of course, that language would be AMERICAN ENGLISH.

Under no account was this going to be a run-of-the-mill dictionary. I wanted it to be a reflection of my way of teaching, a lexicon and a book that was fun to read all at the same time. I had to rethink the very concept of a dictionary, working especially on the links between language and culture. After having worked so many years on this project, I hope to have attained my goal.

My purpose is to show you the way, step by step, word by word, jumping from one idiom to the next on an incredible journey through the American language as it is spoken today.

CHOICE OF WORDS
keep in step with the times

The way I selected the words and idioms for my book was by recalling the very same ones I myself had needed in French when I first came to Paris from my native Brooklyn, the ones I lacked in order to share the everyday life of French people, to understand movies, the radio, read newspapers, and keep in step with the times...

From literary chat to street talk, from yuppie lingo to slang, I've covered the whole scope of spoken language, without censoring anything. I know only too well that fluency in a language means being able to understand others and make oneself understood in any kind of situation.

Some people may be surprised at the lack of phonetics in my book. But, like most Americans, I've always enjoyed charming foreign accents — provided that they don't get in the way of people understanding each other. Phonetics has virtually disappeared as a basis for learning a foreign language. These days everybody is familiar with the rhythms and accents of American English through films and singers. Instead of cluttering my dictionary with a lot of information that is useless to the vast majority of my readers, I've thus been able to introduce several important aspects of the language.

FROM METHOD TO DICTIONARY
learning by association

"NO WORD IS AN ISLAND." Starting from this idea, I developed my own method of gradual assimilation of vocabulary through association : it's easier to learn several words at once if there's a logical link between them. That's the way we naturally think. I've applied this method to the dictionary, associating each word with its synonyms, antonyms, and other closely related words.

"NO WORD IS AN ISLAND." The variety of choices for translations in other dictionaries have often left me high and dry in understanding the real meaning of a word in a particular context. That's why giving a specific translation for each meaning of a word in the appropriate context is so important. Each time it was necessary, I've given examples for translations in order to make the meaning clearer, more precise and to show its usage.

I've tried to express the wealth inherent in both languages by finding the right partner for each word, according to its meaning, while keeping to the appropriate register.

There are a few words (crazy, rich, etc.) which are so important in the language, that they have a vast number of synonyms and associated words. Therefore, I decided to group them together and put them under headings in boxes to make them stand out more.

In that way, looking up the translation of a word becomes an opportunity for finding hidden treasure.

V&P'S
VERBS AND PREPOSITIONS

V&P'S are that astounding phenomenon of the English language whereby the meaning of a verb completely changes by adding a preposition to it. Traditional methods often neglect to teach this all-important aspect of our language.

Imagine a French person learning the words « to stand » and « up » translated as « être debout » and « vers le haut » ; this information won't be of any help to him or her in understanding what « to stand up to someone » (« tenir tête à quelqu'un »), « to stand up for someone » (« prendre le parti de quelqu'un »), and « to stand someone up » (« poser un lapin à quelqu'un ») mean.

Accordingly I've listed all the V&P usages for every verb and the different meanings that each accompanying preposition indicates.

Mastering the use of these wonderful little « tools » seems to me of the utmost importance to anyone who wants to know the ins and outs of the language.

CAUTION !
DANGER AHEAD !
beware of false friends!

Knowing WHAT A WORD IS is not always enough, you also have to know WHAT A WORD IS NOT. I've taken particular care in pointing out the numerous false friends that can trip you up in written translations or in conversations. I've listed all the cases in which a translation is no longer valid for a particular word due to a change of context or meaning. For instance, the words « cat » and « boss » are translated respectively as « chat » and « patron » ; however the French words don't always translate back the same way.

A skull and crossbones (☠) indicates that though « boss » is translated as « patron » when referring to your superior, the word « patron » in reference to sewing is translated as « pattern ».

Translating the idioms that make up the fabric of our two languages word for word is a dangerous affair. The skull and crossbones is designed to warn you of such pitfalls : though « cat » may mean « chat » it is impossible to use « cat » as the translation for « chat » in the expression « il n'y avait pas un chat » which means « there wasn't a soul ». By the same token, you can't translate « it's raining cats and dogs » by « il pleut des chats et des chiens », the correct translation being « il pleut des cordes ».

IDIOMS

Idioms give the language its special flavor and enable you to speak in a lively and easy manner. It's obviously important to be familiar with as many of these idioms as possible. Please don't try to count them ; the list is a mile long in my dictionary.

For each idiom I've given a translation and associated expressions, grouping them together in numerous cases so that the reader may familiarize him or herself with them and know when to use them.

CLASSIFICATION

Naturally I've used alphabetical order in classifying the entries in my dictionary.

As for idiomatic expressions, they're found under the first noun or adjective in the expression. Thus « to call a spade a spade » is at « spade », and « once in a blue moon » at « blue ».

The part of speech is also a factor in deciding the order of words with several entries, the order being : noun, adjective, verb, adverb, etc. Whenever necessary (frequence of use or importance of the word) this order has been changed.

SPELLING

In my dictionary, American English has been used as the reference for spelling.

The abbreviation (GB) points out differences between British and American English spellings.

(GB) also indicates specific British English usages.

GRAMMAR

I've always disliked teaching grammar for grammar's sake but such an important element of language had to be included in my dictionary. Therefore I've introduced basic grammatical rules whenever not knowing them might inhibit one's fluency.

The boxes serve to give concrete examples of specific usages, pitfalls, etc.

LAYOUT

The layout is intended to be as clear as possible and to enhance the particularity of each word, to make it stand out in all its wealth. The boxes throughout the dictionary were designed for this purpose.

Each entry appears in bold type and capital letters. Any translations or abbreviations in French are printed in italics.

Following each entry : the part of speech in parentheses, a French translation, preceded by a number when there are several meanings listed. Examples are indicated by colons. Then come associated words (synonyms are indicated by ⨀, antonyms by ≠) ; idioms ; false friends (indicated by a skull and crossbones ☠).

If the entry is a verb, idiomatic usages are listed, followed by the different meanings the verb has when accompanied by various prepositions.

NOW, IT'S YOUR TURN TO DO THE TALKING !

ADRIENNE

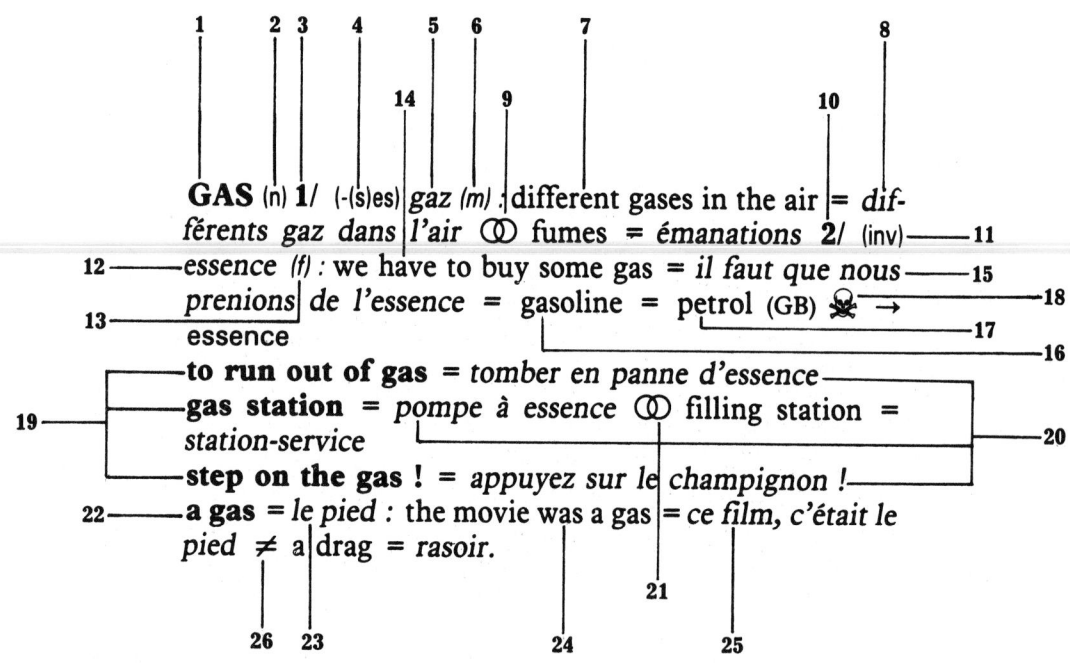

1 2 3 4 5 6 7 8

14 9 10

GAS (n) **1/** (-(s)es) *gaz (m)* : different gases in the air = *dif-*
férents gaz dans l'air ⓓ fumes = *émanations* **2/** (inv)———11

12———*essence (f)* : we have to buy some gas = *il faut que nous*———15

13———*prenions* de l'essence = gasoline = petrol (GB) ☠ →———18

essence ———17

———16

19———**to run out of gas** = *tomber en panne d'essence*———

gas station = *pompe à essence* ⓓ filling station =

station-service ———20

step on the gas ! = *appuyez sur le champignon !*———

22———**a gas** = *le pied* : the movie was a gas = *ce film, c'était le*

pied ≠ a drag = *rasoir.*

26 23 24 25

21

SAMPLE ARTICLE

1 entry
2 part of speech
3 first meaning of entry
4 irregular plural in first meaning
5 translation of first meaning
6 gender of French noun
7 example of first meaning
8 translation of first meaning
9 associated word and its translation
10 second meaning of entry
11 the entry is invariable (no plural) in this second meaning
12 translation of second meaning
13 gender of French noun
14 example of second meaning
15 translation of the example
16 « gasoline » can also be used in this second meaning
17 « petrol » is the British word in this sense
18 beware of the false friend : see the entry « essence »
19 idiomatic expressions
20 translations of the idiomatic expressions
21 associated expression and its translation
22 idiomatic use
23 translation of the idiomatic use
24 example of the idiomatic use
25 translation of the example
26 associated opposite and its translation

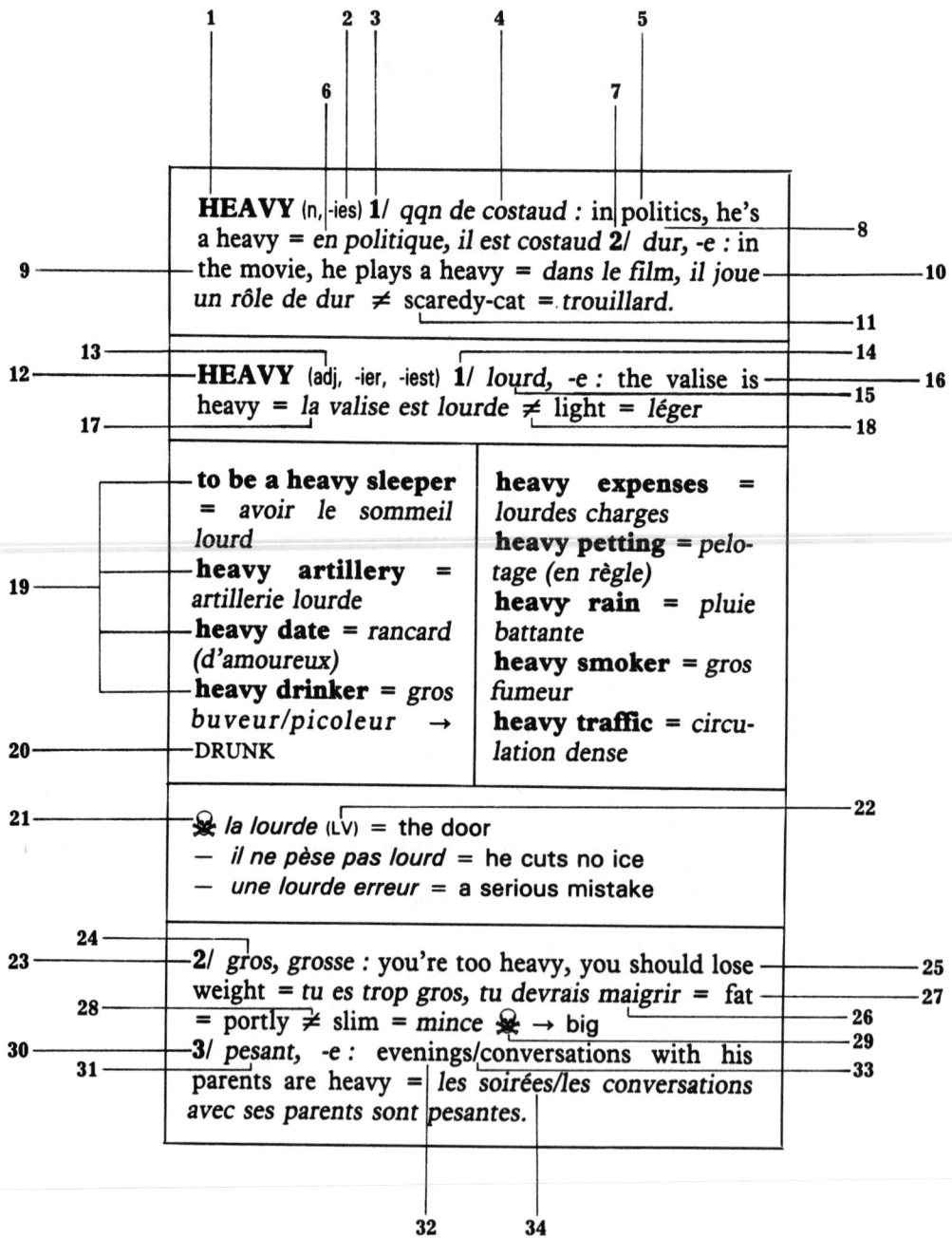

1   2 3   4   5

6   7

HEAVY (n, -ies) **1/** *qqn de costaud :* in politics, he's
a heavy = *en politique, il est costaud* **2/** *dur, -e :* in
the movie, he plays a heavy = *dans le film, il joue*
un rôle de dur ≠ scaredy-cat = *trouillard.*

8

9   10

11

13   14

12   **HEAVY** (adj, -ier, -iest) **1/** *lourd, -e :* the valise is   16

15

heavy = *la valise est lourde* ≠ light = *léger*

17   18

to be a heavy sleeper
= *avoir le sommeil*
lourd
heavy artillery =
artillerie lourde
heavy date = *rancard*
(d'amoureux)
heavy drinker = *gros*
buveur/picoleur →
DRUNK

heavy expenses =
lourdes charges
heavy petting = *pelo-*
tage (en règle)
heavy rain = *pluie*
battante
heavy smoker = *gros*
fumeur
heavy traffic = *circu-*
lation dense

19

20

22

21   ☠ *la lourde* (LV) = the door
— *il ne pèse pas lourd* = he cuts no ice
— *une lourde erreur* = a serious mistake

24

23   **2/** *gros, grosse :* you're too heavy, you should lose   25

28   weight = *tu es trop gros, tu devrais maigrir* = fat   27

= portly ≠ slim = *mince* ☠ → big   26

29

30   **3/** *pesant, -e :* evenings/conversations with his   33

31   parents are heavy = *les soirées/les conversations*
avec ses parents sont pesantes.

32   34

SAMPLE BOX

1. entry
2. part of speech, irregular plural (« -ies »)
3. first meaning of entry
4. translation of first meaning
5. example of first meaning
6. translation of the example
7. second meaning of entry
8. translation of second meaning, and its feminine form
9. example of second meaning
10. translation of the example
11. associated opposite and its translation
12. second entry
13. part of speech, irregular comparative and superlative (« -ier, -iest »)
14. first meaning of entry
15. translation of first meaning, and its feminine form
16. example of first meaning
17. translation of the example
18. antonym, and its translation
19. idiomatic expressions and uses, and their translations
20. for other synonyms of « heavy drinker » and associated terms, see the group « DRUNK »
21. false friends : where « lourd » is not translated by « heavy »
22. the register is not the same : « lourde » is slang, « door » is not
23. second meaning of entry
24. translation of second meaning, and its feminine form
25. example of second meaning
26. translation of the example
27. « fat » or « portly » can also be used in this second meaning
28. antonym and its translation
29. watch out for false friends ! see the entry « big », where these are listed
30. third meaning of the entry
31. translation of third meaning, and its feminine form
32. example of third meaning
33. « or »
34. translation of the example

SYMBOLS

=	before a translation (example : « cat = chat ») or an equivalent (example : « gas = essence = gasoline »)
:	introduces an example
⊕	synonym or associated term
≠	antonym or associated opposite
→	sends you to another entry. If followed by a word in small capitals, it sends you to a group (example : « nuts = dingue → CRAZY »)
←	the word is written the same in both languages (example : « permission = ← »)
☠	the skull and crossbones means « watch out, risk of confusion ! ». It is used when : 1) false friends exist. If followed by an arrow, these are listed under the entry mentioned 2) further explanation is needed about usage or meaning (example : « hot » and « warm ») 3) confusion is possible between two similar terms (example : « before » and « in front of ») 4) a grammatical explanation is needed (example : « must »)
1/ 2/ 3/	words often have several meanings, each meaning is indicated by a number
/	before an alternative term in an example or its translation
( )	what is in parentheses is optional or can be replaced

ABBREVIATIONS

(abbr)	abbreviation
(adj)	adjective
(adj, -ier, -iest)	adjective with comparative ending in « -ier », superlative in « -iest »
(adv)	adverb
(aux)	auxiliary
(comp)	comparative
(conj)	conjunction
(f)	feminine
(GB)	British English word or spelling
(+ ing)	progressive form (« -ing ») called for
(interj)	interjection or exclamation
(inv)	invariable noun : no plural, or plural form same as singular form
(LV)	« langue verte », a special slang, parallel language that is very used in French (example : « book = livre, bouquin (LV) »)
(m)	masculine
(m,f)	masculine and/or feminine
(n)	noun
(n, -ies)	noun ending in « y » whose plural ends in « -ies »
(n pl)	plural noun
(n pr)	proper noun
(n, teeth)	noun with irregular plural (here, « tooth »)
o.s.	oneself
(PEJ)	the translation given is pejorative or derogatory though the American word may not be
(pl)	plural
(prep)	preposition
(pron)	pronoun
qqch	quelque chose
qqn	quelqu'un
s.o.	someone
s.o.'s	someone's
stg	something
(superl)	superlative
(to, came, come)	irregular verb (« come ») which becomes « came » in the preterite and « come » in the past participle
(to, -ed)	regular verb with past endings in « -ed »

ADRIENNE'S DICTIONARY

English/French

A (art) *un, une* : a chair = *une chaise*, a book = *un livre* ⓪ some = *des*, the = *le, la, les*
a week/a day = *par semaine/jour* : it costs $ 10 a day = *cela coûte 10 dollars par jour*
☠ → one
— « a » *devant une consonne ou un « h » aspiré devient « an » devant une voyelle ou un « h » muet :* an egg = *un œuf*, an hour = *une heure*.

ABACK (adv) **to be taken aback** = *avoir le souffle coupé* ⓪ to be flabbergasted = *être bouche bée*.

ABANDON (n) *abandon (m)* : to make love with abandon = *faire l'amour avec abandon* ☠ *une maison laissée à l'abandon* = a totally neglected house.

ABANDON (to, -ed) *abandonner* : to abandon a child = *abandonner un enfant* ≠ to retain = *conserver* ☠ *j'abandonne !* = I give up !

ABANDONED (adj) *abandonné, -e* : an abandoned child = *un enfant abandonné*.

ABATE (to, -d) *s'apaiser* : the storm abated = *la tempête s'est apaisée* ☠ → to appease.

ABBREVIATION (n) *abréviation (f)* : Mr is the abbreviation for Mister = *M. est l'abréviation de Monsieur*.

ABC'S (n) *a.b.c. (m), b a ba (m)* : the abc's of business = *le b a ba des affaires*.

ABDICATE (to, -d) *abdiquer* : the king abdicated = *le roi a abdiqué*.

ABDOMEN (n) *abdomen (m)*.

ABDUCT (to, -ed) *enlever* : to abduct a child = *enlever un enfant* ⓪ to kidnap = *kidnapper* ☠ → to remove
ABDUCTION (n) *enlèvement (m)* ⓪ kidnapping = ←.

ABEYANCE (n) **in abeyance** = *en suspens* ⓪ pending = *en attente*.

ABHOR (to, -red) *abhorrer* ⓪ to detest = *détester* ≠ to adore = *adorer*.

ABIDE BY (to, abode or abided) *se conformer à* : to abide by a decision = *se conformer à une décision*.

ABILITY (n, -ies) *aptitude (f)* : a child's ability to learn languages easily = *l'aptitude d'un enfant à apprendre facilement les langues* = aptitude.

ABLE (adj) *capable* : an able veterinarian = *un vétérinaire capable* ≠ incompetent = *incompétent* ☠ → capable
to be able to = 1/ *pouvoir* : I won't be able to lend you the money = *je ne pourrai pas vous prêter l'argent* ☠ → can 2/ *être capable de* : I'm not able to lift both cases at once = *je ne suis pas capable de soulever les deux valises à la fois*.

ABNORMAL (adj) *anormal, -e* : abnormal behavior = *comportement anormal* ≠ normal = ←.

ABOARD (adv) *à bord* : to go aboard = *monter à bord* ≠ to go ashore = *descendre à terre*.

ABOLISH (to, -ed) *abolir* : to abolish a law = *abolir une loi* ⓪ to annul = *annuler*.

A-BOMB (n) *bombe (f) A*.

ABOMINABLE (adj) *abominable* : an abominable play = *une pièce abominable* ≠ wonderful = *merveilleux* → AWFUL.

ABORT (to, -ed) *avorter* : the plan/the woman aborted = *le projet/la femme a avorté*.

ABORTION (n) *avortement (m), I.V.G. (f), interruption (f) volontaire de grossesse* ⓪ pregnancy termination = *interruption de grossesse*
to have an abortion = *se faire avorter*.

ABORTIVE (adj) *avorté, -e* : an abortive attempt = *une tentative avortée*.

ABOUT (adv) *à peu près* : I have about two dollars = *j'ai à peu près deux dollars*, I've about finished = *j'ai à peu près fini* ⓪ almost = *presque*
to be about to = *être sur le point de* : we're about to go out = *nous sommes sur le point de sortir* ⓪ to be on the verge of = *être à deux doigts de*
☠ for the use of ''about'' after a verb, see the verb.

1

ABOUT (prep) *sur* : a film about orphans = *un film sur les orphelins* ☠ → on
how/what about (a coffee)? = *et si (on prenait un café) ?*
how about me? = *et moi alors ?*
to see/write about = *s'occuper de/écrire sur.*

ABOUT-FACE (n) **to do an about-face** = *faire volte-face* = to do a U-turn (GB) ⓪ to do a turnabout = *retourner sa veste.*

ABOVE (adj) *ci-dessus* : the above names = *les noms ci-dessus* ≠ below = *ci-dessous*

ABOVE (adv) *du dessus* : the apartment above = *l'appartement du dessus.*

ABOVE (prep) *au-dessus de* : the apartment above the store = *l'appartement au-dessus du magasin* ≠ below = *au-dessous de*
above all = *surtout* : she loves her parents, above all her father = *elle aime ses parents, surtout son père* ⓪ principally = *principalement*
☠ *vivre au-dessus de ses moyens* = to live beyond one's means.

ABOVEBOARD (adj) *sans équivoque* : his actions were honest and aboveboard = *ses actes étaient honnêtes et sans équivoque* ≠ underhanded = *dissimulé.*

ABRASIVE (adj) *corrosif, -ive* : an abrasive, feisty personality = *une personnalité corrosive et hargneuse* ⓪ virulent = ←.

ABREAST (adv) **to keep abreast (of the events)** = *se tenir au courant (des événements).*

ABRIDGE (to, -d) *abréger* : to abridge a text = *abréger un texte* ☠ *abrège !* = cut it short!

ABROAD (adv) *à l'étranger* : I'm going abroad this summer = *je vais à l'étranger cet été* ⓪ overseas = *outre-mer*
news from abroad = *des nouvelles de l'étranger.*

ABRUPT (adj) *abrupt, -e* : an abrupt answer = *une réponse abrupte* ⓪ curt = *brusque* **ABRUPTLY** (adv) *abruptement.*

ABSCESS (n) *abcès (m)* ⓪ pus = ← ☠ *crever l'abcès* = to let out resentment.

ABSCOND (to, -ed) *prendre la fuite* ⓪ to run away = *s'enfuir.*

ABSENCE (n) *absence (f)* : during his absence = *pendant son absence* ≠ presence = *présence*
absence makes the heart grow fonder = *loin des yeux, près du cœur.*

ABSENT (adj) *absent, -e* : five students were absent today = *il y avait cinq élèves absents aujourd'hui* ≠ present = *présent.*

ABSENT-MINDED (adj) *distrait, -e* : an absent-minded guy = *un type distrait* ⓪ in the clouds = *dans les nuages* ☠ *d'une oreille distraite* = with only half an ear.

ABSOLUTE (adj) 1/ *absolu, -e* : absolute power/confidence = *pouvoir absolu/confiance absolue* 2/ *véritable* : an absolute idiot/lie = *un véritable idiot/mensonge* ⓪ utter = *parfait* ☠ → real **ABSOLUTELY** (adv) *absolument* : you're absolutely wrong = *vous avez absolument tort* ☠ *il faut absolument qu'elle se fasse avorter* = she definitely has to get an abortion.

ABSORB (to, -ed) *absorber* : to absorb a company = *absorber une société*
to be absorbed in (one's work) = *être absorbé par (son travail)* ⓪ to be engrossed in = *être plongé dans* = to be immersed in.

ABSTAIN FROM (to, -ed) *s'abstenir de* : to abstain from smoking = *s'abstenir de fumer* ⓪ to refrain from = *se retenir de.*

ABSTENTION (n) *abstention (f)* : a vote with no abstentions = *un vote où il n'y a eu aucune abstention.*

ABSTRACT (adj) *abstrait, -e* : abstract painting = *peinture abstraite* ≠ concrete = *concret.*

ABSURD (adj) *absurde* : absurd remarks = *des remarques absurdes* ⓪ ridiculous = *ridicule* ≠ sensible = *sensé.*

ABSURDITY (n, -ies) *absurdité (f)* : the absurdity of living for money = *l'absurdité de vivre pour l'argent* ≠ wisdom = *sagesse* ☠ *absurdités que tout cela !* = hogwash !

ABUNDANCE (n) *abondance (f)* : an abundance of oil = *du pétrole en abondance* ≠ lack = *manque* ☠ *corne d'abondance* = horn of plenty.

ABUNDANT (adj) *abondant, -e* : oil is abundant in the Middle East = *le pétrole est abondant au Moyen-Orient* **ABUNDANTLY** (adv) *abondamment.*

ABUSE (n) *abus (m)* : drug abuse = *abus de drogues* ☠ *abus de confiance* = breach of trust.

ABUSE (to, -d) *abuser de* : to abuse a privilege = *abuser d'un privilège*
☠ *si je ne m'abuse* = if I'm not mistaken
— *je ne veux pas abuser de (votre gentillesse)* = I don't want to take advantage of (your kindness)
— *abuser qqn* = to deceive s.o.

ABUSIVE (adj) *injurieux, -euse* : abusive language = *langage injurieux* ☠ *une mère abusive* = a possessive mother.

ABYSS (n) *comble (m)* : to reach the abyss of despair = *atteindre le comble du désespoir.*

ACADEMIC (adj) 1/ *universitaire* : an academic career = *une carrière universitaire* 2/ *théorique* : the question is purely academic = *la question est purement théorique* = theoretical.

ACADEMY (n, -ies) *académie (f)* : art/dance academy = *académie de peinture/de danse.*

ACCELERATE (to, -d) *accélérer* : to accelerate production = *accélérer la production* ≠ to slow down = *ralentir.*

ACCENT (n) *accent (m)* : a good accent = *un bon accent* ⊚ drawl = *accent traînant*
☠ *mettre l'accent sur* = to lay emphasis on
— *des accents de (communisme)* = overtones of (communism).

ACCENTUATE (to, -d) *accentuer* : makeup accentuates her wrinkles = *le maquillage accentue ses rides* ⊚ to underline = *souligner.*

ACCEPT (to, -ed) *accepter* : to accept an invitation = *accepter une invitation* ⊚ to approve = *approuver* ≠ to refuse = *refuser* ☠ *il a accepté de m'aider* = he agreed to help me.

ACCEPTABLE (adj) *acceptable* : an acceptable offer = *une offre acceptable* ≠ unacceptable = *inacceptable.*

ACCESS (n, -es) *accès (m)* : I don't have access to the documents = *je n'ai pas accès aux documents* ☠ *un accès de toux* = a coughing fit
— *l'accès de l'immeuble* = the entry to the building.

ACCESSIBLE (adj) *accessible* : his films are not accessible to the general public = *ses films ne sont pas accessibles au grand public* ≠ inaccessible = *←.*

ACCESSORY (n, -ies) 1/ *accessoire (m)* : clothing accessories = *accessoires vestimentaires* ☠ *accessoires (théâtre)* = props 2/ *complice (m, f)* : letting him hide in her house made her an accessory = *elle s'est rendue complice en le laissant se cacher chez elle* ☠ → accomplice.

ACCIDENT (n) *accident (m)* : a car accident = *un accident de voiture* ⊚ calamity = *calamité*
by accident = *par accident* : I met him by accident = *je l'ai rencontré par accident* ≠ on purpose = *exprès* ☠ *un accident d'avion* = a plane crash
— *un accident de parcours* = a mishap.

ACCIDENTAL (adj) *accidentel, -elle* : an accidental meeting = *une rencontre accidentelle* ⊚ unexpected = *inattendu* ≠ deliberate = *délibéré* **ACCIDENTALLY** (adv) *accidentellement.*

ACCLAIM (n) **to win acclaim** = *recevoir des éloges* : his last play won critical acclaim = *sa dernière pièce a reçu les éloges de la critique* **ACCLAIM** (to, -ed) *acclamer* ≠ to boo = *huer.*

ACCLAMATION (n) *acclamation (f).*

ACCLIMATE TO (to, -d) *acclimater à* : I can't acclimate myself to cold weather = *je n'arrive pas à m'acclimater au temps froid* = to acclimatize to (GB) ⊚ to get used to = *s'habituer à.*

ACCOMMODATE (to, -d) *pouvoir accueillir* : the hotel accommodates forty people = *l'hôtel peut accueillir qua-*rante personnes ⊚ to have room for = *avoir de la place pour.*

ACCOMMODATING (adj) *accommodant, -e* : friendly accommodating neighbors = *des voisins gentils et accommodants* ⊚ obliging = *obligeant.*

ACCOMMODATIONS (n pl) *place (f)* : we couldn't find accommodations in a luxury hotel = *nous n'avons pas trouvé de place dans un hôtel de luxe* ☠ → place.

ACCOMPANY (to, -ied) *accompagner* ⊚ to go with = *aller avec*
to be accompanied by (his wife) = *être accompagné de (sa femme).*

ACCOMPLICE (n) *complice (m, f)* : he was one of the accomplices in the holdup = *il était un des complices du hold-up* ⊚ to be hand in glove with = *être de mèche avec* ☠ *en le cachant, il est devenu complice* = hiding him made him an accessory.

ACCOMPLISH (to, -ed) 1/ *faire* : we haven't accomplished anything today = *nous n'avons rien fait de la journée* ☠ → to do 2/ *accomplir* : she accomplished a lot in her lifetime = *elle a accompli beaucoup de choses au cours de sa vie* ⊚ to attain = *atteindre* ☠ *accomplir son devoir (envers sa famille)* = to do right (by one's family).

ACCOMPLISHED (adj) *accompli, -e* : an accomplished tennis player = *un joueur de tennis accompli* ⊚ talented = *de talent.*

ACCOMPLISHMENT (n) *tour (m) de force* : shooting the film in four weeks was an accomplishment = *ça a été un tour de force de tourner le film en quatre semaines* ⊚ feat = *prouesse.*

ACCORDANCE (n) **in accordance with (the law)** = *conformément à (la loi).*

ACCORDING TO (prep) *selon* : according to my husband she won't be elected = *selon mon mari elle ne sera pas élue* ⊚ following = *suivant*
☠ *selon toute apparence* = apparently
— *c'est selon* = it depends.

ACCORDINGLY (adv) *en conséquence* : she hates her in-laws and acts accordingly = *elle hait ses beaux-parents et agit en conséquence.*

ACCORDION (n) *accordéon (m)* : to play the accordion = *jouer de l'accordéon.*

ACCOUNT (n) 1/ *compte (m)* : a bank account = *un compte en banque* ☠ → count 2/ *compte rendu (m)* : he gave me an account of the meeting = *il m'a fait un compte rendu de la réunion* ⊚ summary = *sommaire*
account executive = *chef de produit* ⊚ adman = *publicitaire*
on account of = *en raison de* : we took the car on account of the rain = *nous avons pris la voiture en raison de la pluie* ⊚ because of = *à cause de*

on (my) account = *pour (moi)* : don't do it on my account = *ne le faites pas pour moi*

on no account = *en aucun cas* : on no account will I do it = *je ne le ferai en aucun cas* ⓪ in no way = *en aucune façon*

to take ≠ not to take into account = *prendre ≠ ne pas prendre en compte* : they took his age into account = *ils ont pris son âge en compte* ⓪ to allow for = *tenir compte de*

taking everything into account = *en fin de compte* : taking everything into account the trip wasn't too expensive = *en fin de compte le voyage n'était pas trop cher* ⓪ all in all = *l'un dans l'autre*

not taking into account = *sans compter* : not taking the food into account, it cost fifty dollars a day = *sans compter la nourriture, ça a coûté cinquante dollars par jour* ⓪ not taking into consideration = *sans prendre en considération*.

ACCOUNTANT (n) *comptable (m, f)* : to study to become an accountant = *faire des études de comptable* ⓪ CPA = *expert-comptable* **ACCOUNTING** (n) *comptabilité (f)* = bookkeeping ⓪ budget = ←.

ACCOUNT FOR (to, -ed) *expliquer* : I can't account for the missing money = *je ne peux pas expliquer la disparition de cet argent* ☠ → to explain

not to be accounted for = *manquer* : three P.O.W.'s aren't accounted for = *il manque trois prisonniers de guerre* = three P.O.W.'s are missing ☠ → to miss.

ACCUMULATE (to, -d) *(s')accumuler* : to accumulate wealth = *accumuler des richesses* ⓪ to amass = *amasser*.

ACCURACY (n) *exactitude (f)* : the accuracy of the report = *l'exactitude du rapport* ≠ inaccuracy = *inexactitude*.

ACCURATE (adj) *juste* : an accurate answer : *une réponse juste* ⓪ correct = ← ≠ inaccurate = *inexact* ☠ → just **ACCURATELY** (adv) *de façon juste, exactement*.

ACCUSATION (n) *accusation (f)* : a series of accusations against the mayor = *une série d'accusations portées contre le maire*
☠ *l'accusation a dit* = the prosecution said
— *une accusation de meurtre* = a murder charge.

ACCUSE (to, -d) *accuser* : he was accused of murder = *il a été accusé de meurtre* ⓪ to indict = *inculper* ≠ to vindicate = *innocenter*.

ACCUSED (n inv) **the accused** = *l'accusé* : all of the accused were guilty = *tous les accusés étaient coupables* ⓪ the defendant = *le prévenu*.

ACCUSTOMED (adj) **to be accustomed to + ing** = *être accoutumé à* : I'm not accustomed to going to bed so early = *je ne suis pas accoutumé à me coucher si tôt* **to get/become accustomed to** = *s'accoutumer à* ⓪ to get used to = *s'habituer à*.

AC/DC (adj) *ambivalent, -e* : he's not strictly gay, but

ac/dc = *il n'est pas uniquement homosexuel, mais ambivalent* ⓪ bi = ← ☠ → ambivalent.

ACE (n) **1/** as *(m)* : the ace of clubs = *l'as de trèfle* **2/** as *(m)* : he's an ace at cooking = *c'est un as en cuisine* ⓪ crackerjack = *crack*

an ace in the hole = *un atout en réserve*

to have an ace up one's sleeve = *avoir un atout dans sa manche*

to hold (all) the aces = *avoir tous les atouts dans son jeu* ⓪ to be in a strong bargaining position = *être en position de force*
☠ *passer (une question) à l'as* = to skip (a question).

ACHE (to, -d) *avoir mal* : to ache all over = *avoir mal partout* ⓪ to suffer = *souffrir*.

ACHES AND PAINS (n pl) *courbatures (f pl)*.

ACHIEVE (to, -d) *réaliser* : to achieve one's goal = *réaliser son but* ⓪ to accomplish = *accomplir* ☠ → to realize

what did you achieve by that ? = *ça t'a avancé à quoi ?* = what did you accomplish by that ?

ACHIEVEMENT (n) *exploit (m)* : shooting the movie in six weeks was an achievement = *ça a été un exploit de tourner le film en six semaines* ⓪ feat = *prouesse* ☠ → exploit.

ACHIEVER (n) *quelqu'un qui réussit* : children of divorced parents are often achievers = *les enfants de parents divorcés sont souvent de ceux qui réussissent* ⓪ winner = *gagnant*.

ACID (n) *acide (m)* ⓪ LSD = ←
to drop acid = *prendre de l'acide*.

ACID (adj) *acide* : an acid taste = *un goût acide* ≠ sweet = *sucré*

acid test = *épreuve décisive* ⓪ moment of truth = *moment de vérité*

acid rains = *pluies acides*.

ACKNOWLEDGE (to, -d) *reconnaître* : he acknowledged I was right = *il a reconnu que j'avais raison* ⓪ to admit = *admettre* ≠ to deny = *nier* ☠ → to recognize.

ACKNOWLEDGEMENT (n) **in acknowledgement of (your help)** = *en reconnaissance de (votre aide)*.

ACME (n) *faîte (m)* : the acme of his career = *le faîte de sa carrière* ⓪ peak = *apogée*.

ACNE (n) *acné (f)* ⓪ pimple = *bouton, blackhead = point noir*.

ACQUAINT (to, -ed) **to be acquainted with (the French medical system)** = *être familiarisé avec (le système médical français)*

to get acquainted = *faire connaissance* : we didn't have time to get acquainted = *nous n'avons pas eu le temps de faire connaissance*.

ACQUAINTANCE (n) *connaissance (f)* : he's not a

friend, just an acquaintance = *ce n'est pas un ami, mais une simple connaissance* ☠ → knowledge.

ACQUIESCE (to, -d) *acquiescer* : he was hard to convince, but he finally acquiesced = *il a été dur à convaincre, mais il a finalement acquiescé.*

ACQUIRE (to, -d) *acquérir* : to acquire a new car = *acquérir une nouvelle voiture* ⓪ to obtain = *obtenir.*

ACQUISITION (n) *acquisition* (f) ⓪ purchase = *achat.*

ACQUIT (to, -ted) *acquitter* : the Court acquitted him = *la Cour l'a acquitté* ⓪ to whitewash = *blanchir* ≠ to convict = *déclarer coupable*
to be acquitted = *être jugé non coupable* ☠ *s'acquitter d'une dette* = to pay off a debt.

ACQUITTAL (n) *acquittement* (m) ≠ indictment = *inculpation.*

ACRE (n) *acre* (m) = 0,4 hectare.

ACROBAT (n) *acrobate* (m, f) ⓪ trapeze artist = *trapéziste.*

ACROSS (prep) **across the street** = *de l'autre côté de la rue* ⓪ opposite = *en face de*
across from = *en face de* : they live across from us = *ils vivent en face de chez nous*
☠ for the use of "across" after a verb, see the verb.

ACROSS-THE-BOARD (adj) **an across-the-board (tax) increase** = *une hausse générale (des impôts).*

ACT (n) 1/ *acte* (m) : the three acts of the play = *les trois actes de la pièce* 2/ *comédie* (f) : her crying's all an act = *ses pleurs ne sont que de la comédie* ⓪ pretense = *faux-semblant* ☠ → comedy 3/ *numéro* (m) : the comedian's act was great = *le numéro du comédien était excellent* ☠ → number 4/ *acte* (m) : an act of kindness = *un acte de gentillesse*

caught in the act = *pris sur le fait* ⓪ red-handed = *la main dans le sac*	*partie* ⓪ to be in on it = *être dans le coup*
to crab s.o.'s act = *casser son coup à qqn* : he was trying to pick up the girl, but his friend crabbed his act = *il essayait de draguer la fille, mais son ami lui a cassé son coup*	**it's a hard/tough act to follow** = *il est difficile de prendre la relève* : his number's so extraordinary that it's a hard act to follow = *son numéro est si extraordinaire qu'il est difficile de prendre la relève*
to get into the act = *se mettre de la partie* : he's making a film and all his friends want to get into the act = *il fait un film et tous ses amis veulent se mettre de la*	**to get one's act together** = *se reprendre en main* : if he wants to win the election, he'd better get his act together = *s'il veut gagner les élections, il*

faut qu'il se reprenne en main = to get it together ⓪ to get a grip on o.s. = *se* | *maîtriser*
to put on an act = *jouer la comédie* ⓪ to put it on = *frimer*

☠ *acte de naissance* = birth certificate
— *faire acte d'autorité* = to put one's foot down
— *prendre acte de* = to take note of
— *un acte de vente* = a bill of sale
— *rédiger un acte de propriété* = to draw up a deed for the property.

ACT (to, -ed) 1/ *agir* : it's time to act = *il est temps d'agir* ⓪ to take action = *prendre des mesures* ☠ *de quoi s'agit-il ?* = what is it about ? 2/ *jouer* : she thinks she can act, but she's only a ham = *elle pense savoir jouer, mais ce n'est qu'une cabotine* ☠ → to play 3/ *avoir tout l'air d'être* : he acts happy = *il a tout l'air d'être heureux* ⓪ to seem = *sembler*

to act as = *faire office de* : my brother-in-law is acting as a lawyer = *mon beau-frère fait office d'avocat*
to act on = *agir sur* : noise acts on your nerves = *le bruit agit sur les nerfs*	**to act out** = *réaliser* : it's healthy to act out one's fantasies = *il est sain de réaliser ses fantasmes* ☠ → to realize
to act up = *faire des siennes* : my car's acting up = *ma voiture fait des siennes.*

ACTING (n) *jeu* (m) : his acting was superb = *son jeu était superbe* ☠ → game.

ACTING (adj) *par intérim* : the acting president = *le président par intérim* ⓪ temporary = *temporaire.*

ACTION (n) 1/ *action* (f) : the action takes place in London = *l'action se passe à Londres*, a woman of action = *une femme d'action* ☠ *une bonne action* = a good deed
— *acheter des actions* = to buy shares
2/ *du mouvement* (casino, racetrack, etc.) : there's a lot of action at the casino tonight = *il y a pas mal de mouvement au casino ce soir* ⓪ it's jumping = *ça bouge*
3/ *du sport* (fight) : on New York's West Side there's always a lot of action = *il y a toujours du sport dans le quartier ouest de New York*
4/ *de la baise* (screwing) : there was a lot of action at the party = *il y avait un max de baise à la soirée*

actions speak louder than words = *les actes pèsent plus que les mots*
to bring an action	**against** = *intenter une action en justice contre* ⓪ to bring to court = *traduire en justice*
killed in action = *tué*

au champ d'honneur
to see action = *se battre* : he saw action in Vietnam = *il s'est battu au Viêt-nam*
some of the action = *une part du gâteau* : the Mafia wants some of the action = *la Mafia*

veut sa part du gâteau
to take action = *prendre des mesures* : the government's going to take action to stop inflation = *le gouvernement va prendre des mesures pour arrêter l'inflation*.

ACTIVE (adj) *actif, -ive* : an active lover = *un amant actif* ≠ passive = *passif* ☙ *population active* = working population.

ACTIVIST (n) *activiste (m, f)* ⑩ extremist = *extrémiste*.

ACTIVITY (n, -ies) *activité (f)* : his business activities = *ses activités professionnelles* ⑩ occupation = ←.

ACTOR (n) *acteur (m)*, *comédien (m)* ⑩ tragedian = *tragédien*, ham = *cabotin* **ACTRESS** (n, es) *actrice (f)*, *comédienne (f)* ⑩ star = *vedette*, starlet = *starlette*.

ACTUAL (adj) **1/** *réel, -elle* : the actual benefit is less than you think = *le bénéfice réel est moindre que vous ne le pensez* ☙ → real
in actual fact (they're already divorced) = *de fait (ils sont déjà divorcés)* ⑩ as a matter of fact = *en fait*
2/ *même* : this is the actual house Bogart lived in = *c'est la maison même que Bogart a habitée* ☙ → same
— *mon travail actuel* = my present/current job.

ACTUALLY (adv) *en fait* : they say they're married, but actually they're not = *ils disent qu'ils sont mariés, mais en fait ils ne le sont pas* ⑩ in reality = *en réalité* ☙ *ils vivent actuellement à Paris* = they're presently/currently living in Paris.

ACUTE (adj) *aigu, -uë* : an acute pain = *une douleur aiguë*
☙ *une voix aiguë* = a high-pitched voice
— *une note aiguë* = a sharp note.

AD (n) → ADVERTISEMENT.

A.D. (adv) = Anno Domini = *après J.-C.* ≠ B.C. = *avant J.-C.*

ADAM (n) *Adam* ⑩ Eve = *Ève*
Adam's apple = *pomme d'Adam*
not to know s.o. from Adam = *ne connaître qqn ni d'Ève ni d'Adam*.

ADAMANT (adj) *intraitable* : I'm adamant about the kids not coming home late = *les enfants ne doivent pas rentrer tard, je suis intraitable sur ce point* ⑩ inflexible = ←.

ADAPT (to, -ed) *adapter* : the film was adapted from the novel = *le film a été adapté du roman*
to adapt o.s. to (a situation) = *s'adapter à (une situation)* ⑩ to acclimate o.s. to = *s'acclimater à*.

ADAPTATION (n) *adaptation (f)* : a period of adaptation = *une période d'adaptation*.

ADD (to, -ed) *ajouter* : I'd like to add something = *je voudrais ajouter quelque chose*
to add (6) and/to (20) = *ajouter (6) et/à (20)* ≠ to take (6) away from (20) = *ôter (6) de (20)*
to add to = *(s')ajouter à* : that only adds to our difficulties = *cela ne fait qu'ajouter à nos difficultés*
to add up = *additionner* : add the figures up = *additionnez les chiffres*
it doesn't add up = *il y a quelque chose qui cloche* ≠ **it all adds up** = *tout s'explique*
to add up to = 1/ *se résumer à* : it adds up to the fact that he wants a divorce = *ça se résume au fait qu'il demande le divorce* ⑩ to come to = *revenir à* 2/ *se chiffrer à* : how much does the bill add up to ? = *à combien se chiffre l'addition ?* ⑩ to amount to = *s'élever à*.

ADDED (adj) *de plus* : having the kids with us was an added problem = *c'était un problème de plus que d'avoir les gosses avec nous* ⑩ additional = *supplémentaire*.

ADDICT (n) *intoxiqué, -e* : a jazz/heroin addict = *un intoxiqué de jazz/d'héroïne* ⑩ junkie = *toxico*.

ADDICT (to, -ed) **to be addicted to (heroin)** = *être intoxiqué à (l'héroïne)* ⑩ to be hooked on = *être accroché à*.

ADDICTION (n) *dépendance (f)* : heroin addiction = *dépendance vis-à-vis de l'héroïne* ☙ → dependence.

ADDITION (n) *addition (f)* ≠ subtraction = *soustraction* ☙ *l'addition* = the check
in addition = *en plus* : he not only left his wife, but in addition took all the money = *non seulement il a quitté sa femme, mais en plus il a pris tout l'argent* ⑩ furthermore = *de plus*, to boot = *de surcroît*
in addition to = 1/ *en plus de* : in addition to toast, I want eggs = *en plus du pain grillé, je veux des œufs* ⑩ apart from = *à part* 2/ *non seulement ... mais en plus* : she's bright in addition to being pretty = *non seulement elle est jolie, mais en plus elle est intelligente* ⑩ also = *aussi*.

ADDITIONAL (adj) *supplémentaire* : do you have any additional questions ? = *est-ce que vous avez des questions supplémentaires ?* ⑩ further = *davantage de* ☙ → supplementary.

ADDRESS (n, -es) **1/** *adresse (f)* : give me your address = *donnez-moi votre adresse* ☙ *l'adresse* = skill **2/** *allocution (f)* : the President's address to Congress = *l'allocution du Président devant le Congrès* ⑩ speech = *discours*.

ADDRESS (to, -ed) **1/** *adresser* : to address a letter to s.o. = *adresser une lettre à qqn* ⑩ to send = *envoyer* ☙ *on m'a adressé à vous* = I was referred to you **2/** *s'adresser à* : to address a meeting = *s'adresser à une assemblée*.

ADEPT (adj) **adept at/in (backgammon)** = *expert au/en (jaquet)* ≠ inept = *incapable*.

ADEQUATE (adj) *suffisant, -e* : an adequate amount = *une quantité suffisante* ⓓ satisfactory = *satisfaisant* ☠ → sufficient
— *tenue adéquate* = appropriate clothes.

ADHERE TO (to, -d) *adhérer à* : to adhere to a cause = *adhérer à une cause* ⓓ to subscribe to = *souscrire à* ☠ *adhérer à un club* = to join a club.

ADJECTIVE (n) *adjectif (m)* ⓓ noun = *nom.*

ADJOURN (to, -ed) *interrompre ses activités* : Congress adjourned for a month = *le Congrès a interrompu ses activités pendant un mois* ⓓ to suspend = *suspendre* **to adjourn (a meeting)** = *lever (la séance)* ☠ *mon voyage a été ajourné* = my trip was postponed.

ADJUSTMENT (n) *adaptation (f)* : a difficult period of adjustment = *une difficile période d'adaptation* = adaptation.

ADJUST TO (to, -ed) *se faire à* : she can't adjust to living in the United States = *elle n'arrive pas à se faire à la vie aux États-Unis* ⓓ to adapt to = *s'adapter à.*

AD-LIB (to, -bed) *(faire) au pied levé* : the comic ad-libbed = *le comédien a fait son numéro au pied levé* ⓓ to improvise = *improviser.*

ADMAN (n, -men) *publicitaire (m)* **ADWOMAN** (n, -women) *publicitaire (f).*

ADMINISTRATION (n) *administration (f)* : the administration of the company = *l'administration de la société* ⓓ management = *gestion* **the (Roosevelt) administration** = *le gouvernement (Roosevelt)* ⓓ civil service = *fonction publique* ☠ *travailler dans l'administration* = to be a civil servant.

ADMINISTRATIVE (adj) *administratif, -ive* : I don't like administrative work = *je n'aime pas le travail administratif.*

ADMIRABLE (adj) *admirable* : an admirable cook = *une cuisinière admirable* → WONDERFUL.

ADMIRAL (n) *amiral (m)* ⓓ vice-admiral = *vice-amiral.*

ADMIRATION (n) *admiration (f)* : full of admiration for her mother = *pleine d'admiration pour sa mère* ≠ scorn = *mépris.*

ADMIRE (to, -d) *admirer* : she admires her teacher = *elle admire son professeur* ⓓ to respect = *respecter* ≠ to scorn = *mépriser.*

ADMIRER (n) *admirateur, -trice* : he's one of my mother's admirers = *c'est l'un des admirateurs de ma mère* ⓓ fan = ←.

ADMISSION (n) 1/ *admission (f)* : Jews were refused admission to the club = *on refusait aux Juifs l'admission au club* 2/ *entrée (f)* : admission to the park is one dollar = *l'entrée du parc coûte un dollar* ☠ → entrance.

ADMIT (to, -ted) 1/ *admettre* : I admit you're right = *j'admets que vous avez raison* ⓓ to avow = *avouer* ≠

to deny = *nier* 2/ *admettre* : no children admitted = *les enfants ne sont pas admis* ⓓ to allow = *permettre* **admitted to (Yale)** = *admis à (Yale)* ☠ *elle n'admet pas cela* = she doesn't accept that
— *admettons que ...* = let's say that ...

ADMITTANCE (n) **no admittance** = *entrée interdite* ⓓ entry = *entrée.*

ADMITTEDLY (adv) *de l'aveu général* : he was admittedly wrong = *de l'aveu général, il avait tort.*

ADO (n inv) *affaire (f)* : there was a whole ado about their divorce = *on a fait toute une affaire autour de leur divorce* ⓓ to-do = *embarras*, hullabaloo = *tapage* **much ado about nothing** = *beaucoup de bruit pour rien* ⓓ a tempest in a teapot = *une tempête dans un verre d'eau* ☠ → affair.

ADOLESCENCE (n) *adolescence (f)* ⓓ awkward age = *l'âge ingrat* **ADOLESCENT** (n) *adolescent, -e* ⓓ teenager = ←.

ADOPT (to, -ed) *adopter* : to adopt a child = *adopter un enfant* ≠ to reject = *rejeter* **ADOPTION** (n) *adoption (f).*

ADORABLE (adj) *adorable* : an adorable baby = *un bébé adorable* ⓓ cute = *mignon* **ADORATION** (n) *adoration (f).*

ADORE (to, -d) *adorer* : she adores her kids = *elle adore ses enfants* ≠ to detest = *détester* ☠ *adorer des idoles* = to worship idols.

ADRIFT (adv) *à la dérive* : the boat/their marriage is adrift = *le bateau/leur couple va à la dérive.*

ADULT (n) *adulte (m, f)* : adults only = *réservé aux adultes* ⓓ grown-up = *grande personne* ≠ child = *enfant* **adult education** = *formation continue.*

ADULTERY (n) *adultère (m)* ⓓ adulterer = *homme adultère*, adulteress = *femme adultère.*

ADVANCE (n) 1/ *avance (f)* : the advance of the troops = *l'avance des troupes* ⓓ progress = *progrès* 2/ *avance (f)* : can you give me a $ 100 advance ? = *pouvez-vous me faire une avance de 100 dollars ?* ⓓ loan = *prêt* **advance man** = *éclaireur* : the President's advance man = *l'éclaireur du Président* **great advances in (solar energy)** = *de gros progrès en matière (d'énergie solaire)* **in advance** = *d'avance* : to pay in advance = *payer d'avance* ⓓ beforehand = *au préalable* **to make advances to s.o.** = *faire des avances à qqn* ⓓ to make time with s.o. = *faire du gringue à qqn* ☠ *avoir de l'avance sur* = to have the edge on
— *je suis en avance* = I'm early
— *avoir une avance de 5 secondes dans une course* = to have a 5-second lead in a race.

ADVANCE (to, -d) 1/ *avancer* : the troops are advancing = *les troupes avancent* ≠ to draw back = *reculer* 2/ *avancer* : to advance a grand = *avancer mille dollars*

ⓐ to lend = *prêter* **3/** *avancer* : the work's advancing = *le travail avance* ⓐ to progress = *progresser*
☠ *avancer une théorie* = to put forward a theory
— *peux-tu avancer ta voiture ?* = could you move/pull up your car ?
— *là, tu t'avances !* = you're going out on a limb !
— *avancer (un rendez-vous)* = to move up (a date)
— *ma montre avance* = my watch's fast
— *est-ce que ça avance ?* = how are things coming along/coming on ?

ADVANCED (adj) *avancé, -e* : advanced ideas = *des idées avancées*
☠ *maintenant on est bien avancés !* = we're getting nowhere ! ,
— *d'un âge avancé* = quite elderly.

ADVANTAGE (n) *avantage* (m) : her diploma's a real advantage = *son diplôme est un avantage véritable* ⓐ asset = *atout* ≠ disadvantage = *désavantage*
to take advantage of = **1/** *profiter de* : take advantage of the good weather = *profitez du beau temps* **2/** *abuser de* : don't take advantage of my patience = *n'abusez pas de ma patience*
☠ *être à son avantage* = to be at one's best.

ADVANTAGEOUS (adj) *avantageux, -euse* : advantageous conditions = *des conditions avantageuses* ≠ disadvantageous = *désavantageux*.

ADVENTURE (n) *aventure* (f) : an adventure novel = *un roman d'aventure*
☠ *partir à l'aventure* = to take a trip and play it by ear
— *une aventure (sentimentale)* = a love affair.

ADVENTURER (n) *aventurier* (m) **ADVENTURESS** (n, -es) *aventurière* (f) **ADVENTUROUS** (adj) *aventureux, -euse* : an adventurous life = *une vie aventureuse* ≠ cautious = *circonspect*.

ADVERB (n) *adverbe* (m) ⓐ adjective = *adjectif*.

ADVERSARY (n, -ies) *adversaire* (m, f) : he's my worst adversary = *c'est mon pire adversaire* ⓐ opponent = *opposant*.

ADVERSE (adj) *néfaste* : to have an adverse effect on = *avoir un effet néfaste sur*.

ADVERSITY (n, -ies) *adversité* (f) ⓐ misfortune = *malchance*.

ADVERTISE (to, -d) *faire de la publicité* : to advertise a product = *faire de la publicité pour un produit*
to advertise for (a secretary) = *mettre une annonce pour (une secrétaire)*.

ADVERTISEMENT (n) **1/** *annonce* (f) *(publicitaire)* : a full page advertisement = *une annonce (publicitaire) d'une page* = ad ⓐ commercial = *spot publicitaire* **2/** *annonce* (f) : to place an advertisement for a job = *faire passer une annonce pour un emploi* = ad ☠ → announcement
classified ads = *petites annonces*.

ADVERTISING (n inv) **1/** *publicité* (f), *pub* (f) : the paper has a lot of advertising = *le journal contient beaucoup de publicité* ⓐ ads = *annonces* **2/** *la publicité* (f) : to work in advertising = *travailler dans la publicité* ⓐ PR = *relations publiques* ☠ → publicity
advertising agency = *agence de publicité*
advertising campaign = *campagne de publicité* ⓐ **Madison Avenue** = *quartier de New York où se trouvent les grandes agences de publicité*.

ADVICE (n inv) *conseils* (m pl) : can you give me some advice ? = *est-ce que vous pouvez me donner quelques conseils ?* ⓐ suggestion = ←
a piece of advice = *un conseil* : that was a good piece of advice = *c'était un bon conseil*
advice to the lovelorn = *courrier du cœur*
take my advice (and stop smoking) ! = *suis mes conseils (et arrête de fumer) !*
☠ *conseil d'administration* = board of directors
— *conseil municipal* = city council
— *conseil des ministres* = cabinet meeting
— *ingénieur-conseil* = consultant (engineer).

ADVISABLE (adj) *conseillé, -e* : it's advisable to use contraceptives = *il est conseillé d'utiliser des contraceptifs* ≠ ill-advised = *déconseillé*.

ADVISE (to, -d) **1/** *conseiller* : he's advising the President = *il conseille le Président*
to advise s.o. to (do stg) = *conseiller à qqn de (faire qqch)* ≠ **to advise s.o. against** = *déconseiller à qqn de* **2/** *aviser* : I'll advise you when he comes = *je vous aviserai de sa venue* ☠ *j'aviserai* = I'll give it some thought.

ADVISER (n) *conseiller, -ère* : legal adviser = *conseiller juridique* = advisor ⓐ mentor = ←.

ADVISORY (adj) *consultatif, -ive* : advisory committee = *comité consultatif*.

ADVOCATE (n) *partisan, -e* : an advocate of women's rights = *un partisan des droits de la femme* ≠ adversary = *adversaire* ☠ → partisan.

ADVOCATE (to, -d) *préconiser* : to advocate free abortion = *préconiser l'avortement libre* ⓐ to recommend = *recommander*.

AFFAIR (n) **1/** *affaire* (f) : what a sad affair ! = *quelle triste affaire !* ⓐ business = *histoire*
it's not your affair ! = *ce n'est pas ton affaire !* ⓐ mind your own business ! = *occupe-toi de tes affaires !*
☠ *se tirer d'affaire* = to get out of a jam
— *faire des affaires* = to do business
— *une affaire en or* = a fantastic bargain
— *ça fera l'affaire* = that'll do (the trick)
— *faire son affaire à qqn* = to bump s.o. off
— *une (bonne) affaire* = a (good) deal
— *c'est une autre affaire* = that's another story
— *monter une affaire* = to put a deal together
— *prends tes affaires !* = take your belongings/your things !
— *en faire toute une affaire* = to make a fuss/an ado

— *les Affaires étrangères* = the State Department
— *une affaire judiciaire* = a law case
2/ *aventure* *(f)* : my first affair was with a lawyer = *ma première aventure, c'était avec un avocat* ⓪ relationship = *liaison* ☠ → adventure.

AFFAIRS (n pl) *affaires* *(f pl)* : the son is taking care of all his father's affairs during his trip = *le fils s'occupe de tous les affaires de son père pendant son voyage.*

AFFECT (to, -ed) *affecter* : the news affected her = *la nouvelle l'a affectée* ☠ *être affecté à un poste à l'étranger* = to be assigned to a post abroad.

AFFECTATION (n) *affectation* *(f)* : her affectation bugs me = *son affectation me casse les pieds* ☠ *ma prochaine affectation* = my next post/appointment.

AFFECTED (adj) **affected manners** = *des manières affectées* ⓪ put-on = *maniéré* ≠ natural = *naturel.*

AFFECTION (n) *affection* *(f)* : his affection for his daughter = *son affection pour sa fille* ⓪ tenderness = *tendresse.*

AFFECTIONATE (adj) *affectueux, -euse* : an affectionate child = *un enfant affectueux* ⓪ cuddly = *câlin*
AFFECTIONATELY (adv) *affectueusement.*

AFFIDAVIT (n) *déclaration* *(f)* *écrite sous serment.*

AFFILIATE WITH (to, -d) (s')*affilier à* : affiliated with a French company = *affilié à une société française* ⓪ to associate with = *s'associer à.*

AFFINITY (n, -ies) *affinité* *(f)* ⓪ to be on the same wavelength = *être sur la même longueur d'ondes.*

AFFIRM (to, -ed) *affirmer* : I can't affirm he's cheating on her = *je ne peux pas affirmer qu'il la trompe* ⓪ to attest = *attester* ☠ *s'affirmer* = to assert o.s.

AFFIRMATIVE (adj) *affirmatif, -ive* : an affirmative answer = *une réponse affirmative* ≠ negative = *négatif.*

AFFLUENCE (n) *opulence* *(f)* : a period of great affluence = *une période de grande opulence* ☠ *heure d'affluence* = rush hour.

AFFLUENT (adj) *nanti, -e* : affluent nations = *les pays nantis* → RICH ≠ poor = *pauvre.*

AFFORD (to, -ed) **1/** *avoir les moyens de s'offrir* : we can't afford a new car = *nous n'avons pas les moyens de nous offrir une nouvelle voiture* **2/** *se permettre* : you're slim, you can afford a second piece of cake = *tu es mince, tu peux te permettre un second morceau de gâteau* ☠ → to permit
to afford to = **1/** *avoir les moyens de* : I can't afford to buy a car = *je n'ai pas les moyens d'acheter une voiture* **2/** *se permettre de* : I can't afford to lose this client = *je ne peux pas me permettre de perdre ce client.*

AFL-CIO (abbr) = American Federation of Labor - Congress of Industrial Organizations = *syndicat ouvrier majoritaire aux États-Unis.*

AFOUL (adv) **to run afoul of (the law)** = *avoir des démêlés avec (la justice).*

AFRAID (adj) **to be afraid** = *avoir peur* : the guy followed me but I wasn't afraid = *le type m'a suivie, mais je n'ai pas eu peur*
to be afraid of (dogs) = *avoir peur des (chiens)* ⓪ to fear = *craindre,* to be scared of = *être effrayé par*
I'm afraid (that) he's not here = *j'ai peur qu'il ne soit pas là* ⓪ I fear that = *je crains que.*

AFRESH (adv) = ANEW.

AFRICA (n) *Afrique* *(f)* **AFRICAN** (n, adj) *Africain, -e*

Algeria = *Algérie*	**Morocco** = *Maroc*
Angola = ←	**Mozambique** = ←
Cameroon = *Cameroun*	**Nigeria** = ←
	Rhodesia =
Chad = *Tchad*	*Rhodésie*
Congo = ←	**Senegal** = *Sénégal*
Egypt = *Égypte*	**Somali** = *Somalie*
Ethiopia = *Éthiopie*	**South Africa** = *Afrique*
Ivory Coast =	*du Sud*
Côte-d'Ivoire	**Sudan** = *Soudan*
Lybia = *Libye*	**Tunisia** = *Tunisie*
Kenya = ←	**Uganda** = *Ouganda*
Madagascar = ←	**Zaire** = *Zaïre.*

AFTER (adv) *après* : do it after ! = *faites-le après !* ⓪ later = *plus tard*
☠ for the use of "after" after a verb, see the verb.

AFTER (prep) **1/** *après* : we'll leave after dinner = *nous partirons après le dîner* ≠ before = *avant* **2/** *après* : you must put the adjective after the noun = *il faut mettre l'adjectif après le nom* ≠ in front of = *devant* **3/** *après* : after what he said to me, I don't want to see him again = *après ce qu'il m'a dit, je ne veux plus le revoir* ⓪ because of = *à cause de*
☠ *d'après (John)* = according to (John)
— *et après ?* = so what ?

AFTER (conj) *après que* : after he said that, he left = *après qu'il eut dit ça, il partit* ≠ before = *avant que*
after having (eaten, I left) = *après avoir (mangé, je suis parti).*

AFTEREFFECT (n) *suite* *(f)* : the aftereffects of the illness = *les suites de la maladie* ⓪ consequence = *conséquence* ☠ → suite.

AFTERMATH (n inv) *séquelles* *(f pl)* : the aftermath of war = *les séquelles de la guerre.*

AFTERNOON (n) *après-midi* *(m ou f)* : I'll see you this afternoon = *je vous verrai cet après-midi*
late ≠ **early afternoon** = *fin* ≠ *début d'après-midi.*

AFTERTASTE (n) *arrière-goût* *(m)* : a bitter aftertaste = *un arrière-goût amer.*

AFTERTHOUGHT (n) **to have afterthoughts about** = *se raviser au sujet de* : I've had afterthoughts about what I said = *je me suis ravisé au sujet de ce que j'ai dit.*

AFTERWARD(S) (adv) *ensuite* : we had dinner and afterward(s) went to the movies = *nous avons dîné et ensuite nous sommes allés au cinéma* ≠ beforehand = *au préalable.*

AGAIN (adv) *re-, encore* : I never saw him again = *je ne l'ai jamais revu,* he's written to me again = *il m'a encore écrit,* it's her again = *c'est encore elle* ⓪ once more = *encore une fois* ☠ → still
again and again = *maintes et maintes fois* : he asked me the same question again and again = *il m'a posé la même question maintes et maintes fois* ≠ once = *une fois*
not ... again = *ne ... plus* : I don't want to see him again = *je ne veux plus le voir*
to see s.o. again/to say again/etc. = *revoir qqn/redire/etc.*
again ! = *encore !*
what's (her name) again ? = *quel est (son nom) déjà ?*

AGAINST (prep) *contre* : I'm against capital punishment = *je suis contre la peine de mort,* stand against the wall = *mets-toi contre le mur*
☠ for the use of "against" after a verb, see the verb
— *je suis fâché contre toi* = I'm mad at you
— *la pilule contre le diaphragme* = the pill versus the diaphragm
— *à cent contre un qu'il va gagner* = it's a hundred to one he'll win
— *contre toute (attente, etc.)* = contrary to all (expectations, etc.)
— *contre nature* = unnatural.

AGE (n) *âge (m)* : at the age of eighteen = *à l'âge de dix-huit ans*
act your age ! = *ne sois pas gamin !*
ages ago = *il y a belle lurette* : she got married ages ago = *elle s'est mariée il y a belle lurette* ≠ recently = *récemment*
to be of age = *être majeur* ≠ underage = *qui n'a pas encore atteint sa majorité*
to come of age = *atteindre sa majorité*
for ages = *ça fait un bail* : I haven't seen him for ages = *ça fait un bail que je ne l'ai pas vu*
to look one's age = *paraître/faire son âge*
☠ *prendre de l'âge* = to be getting on in years
— *quel âge avez-vous ?* = how old are you ?

AGE (to, -d) *vieillir* : she's aging well = *elle vieillit bien* ≠ to be still spry = *être encore vert.*

AGED (n pl) *personnes (f pl) âgées* : the aged need our understanding = *les personnes âgées ont besoin de notre compréhension* ⓪ the elderly = *les gens âgés.*

AGENCY (n, -ies) *agence (f)* : a travel/press agency = *une agence de voyage/de presse.*

AGENDA (n) *ordre (m) du jour* : the agenda for the meeting = *l'ordre du jour de la réunion*
☠ *un agenda* = a diary.

AGENT (n) *agent (m)* : literary agent = *agent littéraire* ⓪ manager = ←
☠ *agent de change* = stockbroker
— *agent de police* = policeman
— *agent de liaison* = contact man.

AGGRAVATE (to, -d) **1/** *(s')aggraver* : his condition was aggravated by his drinking = *son état a été aggravé par la boisson* ≠ to improve = *s'améliorer* **2/** *agacer* : stop aggravating me ! = *arrête de m'agacer !* ⓪ to bug = *casser les pieds à.*

AGGRAVATING (adj) *agaçant, -e* : aggravating remarks = *des réflexions agaçantes* ⓪ irritating = *irritant.*

AGGRAVATION (n) *embêtement (m)* : her kids are nothing but aggravation = *ses gosses ne lui causent que des embêtements* ⓪ trouble = *ennui.*

AGGRESSIVE (adj) *agressif, -ive* : an aggressive attitude = *une attitude agressive* ⓪ hostile = ← **AGGRESSION** (n) *agression (f)* **AGGRESSOR** (n) *agresseur (m).*

AGHAST (adj) *frappé, -e d'horreur* : aghast at the poverty of the country = *frappé d'horreur devant la pauvreté du pays* ⓪ taken aback = *le souffle coupé.*

AGILE (adj) *agile* : an agile acrobat = *un acrobate agile* ⓪ limber = *souple,* dexterous = *adroit.*

AGO (adv) *il y a* : I saw him a year ago = *je l'ai vu il y a un an,* he came a few months/days ago = *il est venu il y a quelques mois/jours* ☠ *il y a deux hommes qui attendent là* = there are two men waiting here.

AGOG (adj) *en émoi* : the news left us agog = *la nouvelle nous a mis en émoi* ⓪ in a dither = *dans tout ses états.*

AGONY (n, -ies) *angoisse (f)* : the agony of waiting for the results of an exam = *l'angoisse d'attendre les résultats d'un examen* ⓪ worry = *inquiétude*
in agony = *dans les affres de la douleur*
to be in agony about stg = *être angoissé pour qqch* ⓪ to be in anguish about = *être dans l'angoisse de.*

AGREE (to, -d) *être d'accord* : does she agree ? = *est-ce qu'elle est d'accord ?* ⓪ to concur = *s'accorder* ≠ to disagree = *ne pas être d'accord*
to agree on (a price) = *convenir d'(un prix)*
to agree to (s.o.'s terms) = *être d'accord avec (les conditions de qqn)*
to agree with = *être d'accord avec* : I agree with you = *je suis d'accord avec vous*
not to agree with s.o. = *ne pas réussir à qqn* : Chinese food doesn't agree with me = *la cuisine chinoise ne me réussit pas.*

AGREEABLE (adj) *agréable* : an agreeable evening = *une soirée agréable* = pleasant ≠ disagreeable = *désa-*

gréable 🕱 *si je peux vous être agréable* = if I can help you in any way **AGREEABLY** (adv) *agréablement.*

AGREEMENT (n) *accord (m) :* there's an agreement between them that each one can take a lover = *il y a un accord entre eux : chacun peut prendre un amant*
to be in agreement with s.o. = *être d'accord avec qqn :* as for the project, I'm in agreement with you = *quant au projet, je suis d'accord avec vous*
to reach an agreement = *arriver à un accord.*

AGRICULTURE (n) *agriculture (f)* ⓪ crop = *récolte,* farmer = *agriculteur* **AGRICULTURAL** (adj) *agricole.*

AHEAD (adv) *qui mène :* their team's two points ahead = *leur équipe mène par deux points* 🕱 for the use of ''ahead'' after a verb, see the verb.

AHEAD (prep) **ahead of =** 1/ *devant :* walk ahead of me = *marche devant moi* = walk in front of me ≠ behind = *derrière* 🕱 → before 2/ *avant :* she arrived ahead of me = *elle est arrivée avant moi* = she arrived before me ≠ after = *après* 🕱 → before.

AID (n) *aide (f) :* aid to the poor = *l'aide aux pauvres* 🕱 *j'ai besoin d'aide* = I need some help
— *aide sociale* = welfare.

AID (to, -ed) *venir en aide à :* to aid the poor = *venir en aide aux pauvres* ⓪ to help = *aider.*

AIDE (n) *aide (m, f) :* a nurse's aide = *une aide infirmière* ⓪ helper = *assistant.*

AIDS (n) *SIDA (m) :* thousands are dying from AIDS = *des milliers de gens meurent du SIDA.*

AILING (adj) *souffrant, -e* ⓪ bedridden = *cloué au lit.*

AIM (n) *objectif (m) :* their aim is to do away with famine = *leur objectif est d'enrayer la famine* ⓪ goal = *but* 🕱 → objective
to take aim = *viser* ⓪ to fire = *tirer.*

AIM (to, -ed) **to aim at** = *viser :* to aim at the target = *viser la cible*
to aim (a gun) at s.o. = *pointer (un fusil) sur qqn*
to be aimed at = *viser :* the remark was aimed at me = *la remarque me visait*
to aim to = *viser à :* he's aiming to finish the film this month = *il vise à finir le film ce mois-ci* ⓪ to plan to = *projeter de*
🕱 *se sentir visé* = to take stg personally
— *je ne vise personne* = I'm not referring to anyone in particular.

AIN'T contraction *populaire de la forme négative de toutes les personnes de l'indicatif présent des verbes « to be » et « to have » :* I ain't going to do it = *j'vais pas le faire,* he ain't got money = *il a pas un rond.*

AIR (n) 1/ *air (m) :* polluted air = *air pollué*
air conditioning = *air conditionné*
Air Force = *Armée de l'air*
air raid = *raid aérien*

to be floating/walking on air = *nager dans le bonheur* ≠ to be down in the dumps = *être au trente-sixième dessous*
to be up in the air = *être en suspens :* our trip's up in the air = *notre voyage est en suspens* ≠ to be settled = *être réglé*
to clear the air = *détendre l'atmosphère :* perhaps if we have a talk, it'll clear the air = *peut-être que si nous avions une conversation, cela détendrait l'atmosphère*
to come up for air = *souffler :* there is so much work I hardly have time to come up for air = *il y a tant de travail que j'ai à peine le temps de souffler* 🕱 → to blow
to get some air = *aller prendre l'air* ⓪ to take a walk = *faire une promenade*
to live on air = *vivre de l'air du temps* → POOR
on the air = *sur les ondes :* the program's on the air = *l'émission passe sur les ondes* ⓪ on the radio = *à la radio*
2/ *air (m) :* an air of mystery = *un air de mystère*
to put on airs = *se donner de grands airs* ⓪ to show off = *faire de l'épate*
🕱 *avoir l'air (heureux)* = to look (happy)
— *un air de famille* = a family resemblance
— *tu me pompes l'air !* = stop bugging me !
— *menaces en l'air* = empty threats
— *ça n'a l'air de rien* = it looks easy
— *un air (chanson)* = a tune (song)
— *s'envoyer en l'air* = to make it with s.o.
— *ça a tout fichu en l'air* = it made a mess of everything.

AIR (to, -ed) *aérer :* to air a room = *aérer une pièce*
to air out = *essayer de dissiper :* let's air out the misunderstanding between us = *essayons de dissiper le malentendu qu'il y a entre nous* ⓪ to clear the air = *détendre l'atmosphère.*

AIRCRAFT (n) **aircraft industry** = *l'industrie aéronautique.*

AIRLIFT (n) *pont (m) aérien* ⓪ blockade = *blocus.*

AIRLINE (n) *compagnie (f) aérienne.*

AIRMAIL (n) **(by) airmail** = *par avion :* to send a letter (by) airmail = *envoyer une lettre par avion.*

AIRPLANE (n) *avion (m)* = plane.

AIRPORT (n) *aéroport (m)* ⓪ runway = *piste.*

AISLE (n) *couloir (m)* (plane, train), *allée (f)* (theater, church)
an aisle seat = *un siège côté couloir*
to lay them in the aisles = *faire un malheur :* the comic laid them in the aisles = *le comique a fait un malheur* ⓪ to go over with a bang = *remporter un gros succès*
🕱 *allée* → lane, *couloir* → hall.

AJAR (adj) *entrebâillé, -e :* the door's ajar = *la porte est entrebâillée.*

ALARM (n) *alarme (f)* : to give the alarm = *donner l'alarme*
an alarm clock = *un réveille-matin* Ⓓ a clock = *un réveil*
to pull the alarm = *tirer la sonnette d'alarme*
with alarm = *avec une vive inquiétude* : we view the chance of a nuclear war with alarm = *nous considérons avec une vive inquiétude le risque d'une guerre nucléaire.*

ALARM (to, -ed) *alarmer* : the news alarmed us = *la nouvelle nous a alarmés* Ⓓ to panic = *paniquer.*

ALARMING (adj) *alarmant, -e* : an alarming international situation = *une situation internationale alarmante* Ⓓ distressing = *consternant.*

ALAS ! (interj) *hélas !* → GOSH !

ALBUM (n) *album (m)* : picture album = *album de photos.*

ALCOHOL (n) *alcool (m)* : there was no alcohol at the party = *il n'y avait pas d'alcool à la soirée* ☠ *voulez-vous un petit alcool ?* = would you care for a liqueur ?

ALCOHOLIC (n) *alcoolique (m, f)* : she's in love with an alcoholic = *elle est amoureuse d'un alcoolique* Ⓓ A.A. = Alcoholics Anonymous = *les Alcooliques anonymes* → DRUNK.

ALCOHOLIC (adj) *alcoolisé, -e* : an alcoholic drink = *une boisson alcoolisée.*

ALCOVE (n) *alcôve (f).*

ALERT (n) *alerte (f)* : alerts during the war = *les alertes pendant la guerre*
on the alert = *en (état d')alerte* Ⓓ on the lookout = *aux aguets*
☠ *fausse alerte* = false alarm
— *alerte à la bombe* = bomb scare.

ALERT (adj) *alerte* (older people), *éveillé, -e* : her kids are alert = *ses enfants sont éveillés* Ⓓ bright = *vif.*

ALERT (to, -ed) *alerter* : to alert headquarters = *alerter le quartier général.*

ALGERIA (n) *Algérie (f)* **ALGERIAN** (n, adj) *Algérien, -enne.*

ALIAS (n, -es) *faux nom (m)* : he came into the country under an alias = *il est entré dans le pays sous un faux nom* Ⓓ assumed name = *nom d'emprunt.*

ALIBI (n) *alibi (m)* : a phony alibi = *un alibi bidon* Ⓓ excuse = ←.

ALIEN (n) *étranger, -ère (résident non naturalisé)* Ⓓ foreign national = *ressortissant d'un pays étranger*
alien card = *carte de résident étranger.*

ALIENATE (to, -d) *(s')aliéner* : her temper alienated all her friends = *son mauvais caractère a aliéné tous ses amis* Ⓓ to estrange = *éloigner.*

ALIGN (to, -ed) *s'aligner* : Hungary aligned itself with the U.S.S.R. = *la Hongrie s'est alignée sur l'URSS.*

ALIKE (adj) *semblable* : father and son are alike = *le père et le fils sont semblables* Ⓓ similar = *similaire*
to look alike = *se ressembler* : the two sisters look alike = *les deux sœurs se ressemblent* ☠ → to resemble ☠ *je n'ai rien dit de semblable* = I said nothing of the kind.

ALIKE (adv) *de la même manière* : to treat everyone alike = *traiter tout le monde de la même manière.*

ALIMONY (n, -ies) *pension (f) alimentaire* : she's getting ten thousand dollars in alimony = *elle touche une pension alimentaire de dix mille dollars.*

ALIVE (adj) *en vie* : the patient's still alive = *le malade est encore en vie* ≠ dead = *mort*
to skin s.o. alive = *avoir la peau de qqn* Ⓓ to get even = *se venger*
to take s.o. alive = *prendre qqn vivant.*

ALL (n) **to give one's all** = *se donner tout entier* : she gives her all to her work = *elle se donne tout entière à son travail.*

ALL (adj) *tout, -e, tous, toutes* : all men are different = *tous les hommes sont différents*, all her kids are grown-up = *tous ses enfants sont adultes* Ⓓ some = *quelques* ≠ each = *chaque*

all (day/week) = *toute la (journée/semaine)* **all (day/week) long** = *tout au long de la (journée/semaine)* **all good things must come to an end** = *les meilleures choses ont une fin* **all hands on deck !** = *tout le monde sur le pont !* **all hell's going to break loose (when he finds out) !** = *ça va barder (quand il l'apprendra) !* **all kinds of** = *toutes sortes de :*	all kinds of people/cars = *toutes sortes de gens/voitures* **all roads lead to Rome** = *tous les chemins mènent à Rome* **all smiles** = *tout sourires* **all the** = *tout le :* all the family came = *toute la famille est venue* Ⓓ part of = *une partie de* **all the time** = *tout le temps :* he was cheating on me all the time = *il me trompait tout le temps*	**all the way** = 1/ *tout le long du chemin :* she ran all the way = *elle a couru tout le long du chemin* 2/ *à fond :* everything she does, she does all the way = *tout ce qu'elle fait, elle le fait à fond* **all the world's a stage and all the men and women merely players** = *le monde entier est un théâtre ; et tous, hommes, femmes, ne sont que des acteurs* **all things considered (you're right)** = *tout bien considéré*

(vous avez raison)
all things being equal (we'll buy a new car next year) = toutes choses égales (nous achèterons une nouvelle voiture l'année prochaine)
all work and no play makes Jack a dull boy = le travail, rien que le travail, ça vous rend ennuyeux
all year round = tout le long de l'année = **all through the year**
almost/nearly/practically all (women use contraception) = presque toutes (les femmes utilisent des méthodes contraceptives)
and all that jazz = et patati et patata
at all costs = à tout prix : she's determined to get a divorce at all costs = elle est décidée à obtenir le divorce à tout prix = at any price
at all times = tout le temps : they're together at all times = ils sont tout le temps ensemble
to be all ears = être tout ouïe
to be all thumbs = être empoté = to be butterfingered
to be with s.o. all the way = être entièrement d'accord avec qqn : as for the plan, I'm with you all the way = quant au projet, je suis entièrement d'accord avec vous
beyond all doubt = sans nul doute : beyond all doubt he's the finest violinist today = sans nul doute, c'est le meilleur violoniste actuel
by all accounts (they're divorced) = d'après ce que l'on dit (ils sont divorcés) ① rumor has it = le bruit court que
by all odds = de très loin : he's by all odds the best filmmaker today = c'est de très loin le meilleur cinéaste actuel ① by far = de loin
don't put all your eggs in the same basket = ne mets pas

tous tes œufs dans le même panier ① a bird in the hand is worth two in the bush = un tiens vaut mieux que deux tu l'auras
for all... = malgré tout ... : for all the money he has, he isn't happy = malgré tout l'argent qu'il a, il n'est pas heureux
for all practical purposes = pour ainsi dire : for all practical purposes his career is over = sa carrière est pour ainsi dire terminée ① as good as = c'est tout comme
from all walks of life = de tous les horizons : people from all walks of life = des gens de tous les horizons
to go all the way = aller jusqu'au bout (en amour) : she was willing to pet but not to go all the way = elle voulait bien qu'ils se pelotent, mais elle ne voulait pas aller jusqu'au bout
to have all the time in the world = avoir tout son temps ≠ to be in a hurry = être pressé
in all fairness = en toute justice : in all fairness, you must admit he's right = en toute justice, il faut reconnaître qu'il a raison
in all likelihood = selon toute vraisemblance : in all likelihood he'll come late = selon toute vraisemblance, il arrivera en retard
in all probability = selon toute probabilité
in all seriousness = très sérieusement
to know all the answers = tout savoir : my son thinks he knows all the answers = mon fils croit tout savoir ① to be a wise guy = être un petit malin
it takes all sorts to make a world = il faut de tout pour faire un monde
not for all the tea in China = pas pour tout l'or du monde : I wouldn't sleep with him for all

the tea in China = je ne coucherais pas avec lui pour tout l'or du monde ① not on your life = jamais de la vie
not for all the world = pour rien au monde : I wouldn't go out with him for all the world = je ne sortirais avec lui pour rien au monde = not for anything
of all people = 1/ plus que quiconque : you, of all people, should have told me the truth = vous, plus que quiconque, auriez dû me dire la vérité 2/ il a fallu qu'(il) choisisse : she slept with John of all people = il a fallu qu'elle choisisse John pour baiser
of all things ! = par exemple ! → GOSH !
on all fours = à quatre pattes : to walk on all fours = marcher à quatre pattes
on all sides = de tous côtés
that makes all the difference in the world = ça fait une sacrée différence
to all appearances (they're happy) = selon toute apparence (ils sont heureux)
to all intents and purposes = virtuellement : their marriage is to all intents and purposes over = leur couple est virtuellement fichu ① for all practical purposes = pour ainsi dire
to end all ... = le plus ... qui puisse se faire : he made a blunder to end all blunders = il a fait la plus grosse gaffe qui puisse se faire
with all = avec tout : with all the money you earn, can't you afford a new car ? = avec tout l'argent que vous gagnez, vous ne pouvez pas vous offrir une nouvelle voiture ?
with all one's heart = de tout son cœur : I love him with all my heart = je l'aime de tout mon cœur
with all one's might = de toutes ses forces

— de toute beauté = most beautiful
— à toute vitesse/vapeur = at full speed
— à tout bout de champ = right, left and center
— en tout bien tout honneur = on the up and up
— en tout état de cause = whatever the case
— à tous les coups (elle sera en retard) = for sure (she'll be late)
— tout le monde = everyone
— manger à tous les râteliers = to run with the hare and hunt with the hounds

— *être dans tous ses états* = to be in a state	fuss about it
— *de toute manière/façon* = in any case	— *tous les deux jours* = every other day
— *toutes proportions gardées* = relatively speaking	— *toute vérité n'est pas bonne à dire* = what he doesn't know won't hurt him
— *et tout le bazar/le bataclan* = and the whole shebang/lot	— *à tout seigneur tout honneur* = you must give honor where honor is due
— *tous les combien ?* = how often ?	— *au tout début* = at the very beginning
— *en voir de toutes les couleurs* = to have a rough time of it	— *tous les deux* = both of them/us/you
— *examiner sous toutes les coutures* = to study from every angle	— *le Tout-Paris* = Paris café society
— *elle en a fait tout un plat* = she made a whole	— *à toute épreuve* = foolproof
	— *tout de suite* = immediately
	— *tous les 36 du mois* = once in a blue moon.

ALL (pron) *tout, -e, tous, toutes* : all were drowned = *tous se sont noyés* ⓪ some = *quelques-uns*

above all = *surtout* : they fight a lot, above all over money = *ils se disputent beaucoup, surtout à propos d'argent*

after all = *après tout* : you were right after all = *vous aviez raison après tout*

all aboard ! = *en voiture !* (car, train)/*tout le monde à bord !* (boat)

all I ask is (for you to be nice) = *tout ce que je demande, c'est (que vous soyez sympa)*

all in all = *l'un dans l'autre* : all in all the accident could have been worse = *l'un dans l'autre l'accident aurait pu être pire*

all's fair in love and war = *en amour comme à la guerre tous les coups sont permis*

all's quiet on the Western Front = *R.A.S./rien à signaler*

all's well that ends well = *tout est bien qui finit bien*

all that = *tout ce que* : all that I want is for my kids to be happy = *tout ce que je veux c'est que mes gosses soient heureux*

all that glitters isn't gold = *tout ce qui brille n'est pas or*

all told (it cost double) = *en tout (ça a coûté le double)*

all you have to do is (call) =

tout ce que vous avez à faire c'est de (téléphoner)

and all that = *et tout ce qui s'ensuit* : I don't like arguments, hassles and all that = *je n'aime pas les disputes, les emmerdes et tout ce qui s'ensuit*

and that's not all = *et ce n'est pas tout*

for all I care (he can drop dead) = *pour ce que j'en ai à foutre (il peut crever)* ⓪ I couldn't care less = *je n'en ai rien à faire*

for all I know = *(pour) autant que je sache* = as far as I know

for all one is worth = *de toutes ses forces* : I ran for all I was worth = *j'ai couru de toutes mes forces* ⓪ like crazy = *vachement*

for all that = *malgré cela* : she's wealthy but isn't happy for all that = *elle est riche, mais malgré cela elle n'est pas heureuse*

in all = *en tout* : in all it'll cost $ 20 = *cela coûtera en tout 20 dollars*

let it all hang out ! = *laisse pisser le mérinos !* ⓪ stay cool ! = *t'emballe pas !*

not as ... as all that = *pas si ...*

que ça : he isn't as rich as all that = *il n'est pas si riche que ça*

of all of them (she's the most intelligent) = *d'eux tous (c'est la plus intelligente)*

to take s.o. for all he's worth = *avoir qqn jusqu'au trognon* : she had a divorce and took him for all he was worth = *elle a divorcé et elle l'a eu jusqu'au trognon*

that crowns it all ! = *il ne manquait plus que ça !* → GOSH !

that's all ! = *c'est tout !* ⓪ that's enough ! = *ça suffit !*

that's all for now = *c'est tout pour l'instant*

that's all I ask ! = *c'est tout ce que je demande !*

that's all I needed ! = *il ne manquait plus que ça !*

(I'm going) that's all there is to it = *(je m'en vais) un point c'est tout*

when all's said and done = *tout compte fait* : when all's said and done, he's a nice guy = *tout compte fait, c'est un type sympa* ⓪ in the end = *finalement*

you can't win 'em all ! = *on ne peut pas gagner à tous les coups !* → THAT'S LIFE !

☠ *à tout casser* = at the most	— *il a tout du (flic)* = you can't miss taking him for (a cop)
— *pour tout dire* = to tell you the truth	— *un homme à tout faire* = a handyman
— *changer du tout au tout* = to change completely	— *c'est tout dire !* = need I say more !
— *tout un chacun* = everyone	— *risquer le tout pour le tout* = to go for broke
— *il a tout mangé* = he ate everything	— *on aura tout vu !* = that beats everything !
— *il est capable de tout* = he's capable of anything	

ALL (adv) *tout, tout à fait* : you're all dirty = *tu es tout sale*, you're all wrong = *vous avez tout à fait tort* ⓪ wholly = *entièrement*

all alone = *tout seul* : I was all alone last night = *j'étais toute seule hier soir* ≠ together = *ensemble*

all along = *dès le début* : I knew he was lying all along = *dès le début, j'ai su qu'il mentait* = **all the while**

all around = *tout autour* : I looked all around the room = *j'ai regardé tout autour de la pièce*

all at once = *tout d'un coup* : all at once we decided to go = *tout d'un coup nous avons décidé d'y aller* ⓌⒸ suddenly = *soudain*

all but = 1/ *peu s'en faut que* : he all but raped me = *peu s'en est fallu qu'il me viole* ⓌⒸ almost = *presque* 2/ *pour ainsi dire* : their marriage is all but over = *leur mariage est pour ainsi dire fichu*

all by oneself = *tout seul* : I did it all by myself = *je l'ai fait tout seul*

all in = *pompé* : after all that walking, I'm all in = *après cette longue marche, je suis pompé* ⓌⒸ shot = *claqué*, dead = *mort (de fatigue)*

all of = *un bon* : it costs all of a hundred dollars = *ça coûte une bonne centaine de dollars*

all of a sudden = *tout à coup* : all of a sudden he got angry = *tout à coup il s'est mis en colère* ⓌⒸ all at once = *tout d'un coup*

all over = *partout* : you can find that kind of thing all over = *vous pouvez trouver ce genre de chose partout*, all over France =

partout en France = everywhere ≠ nowhere = *nulle part*

all right = 1/ *d'accord* : all right, let's go ! = *d'accord, allons-y !* ⓌⒸ okay ! = *O.K. !* 2/ *moyen* : the film was all right = *le film était moyen* → AWFUL ☠ → average 3/ *pour sûr* : he's a jerk all right = *pour sûr, c'est un crétin* ⓌⒸ beyond all doubt = *sans aucun doute*

all right already ! = *laisse tomber !* ⓌⒸ that's enough ! = *ça suffit !*

all the more so = *a fortiori* : they've always been happy together, and all the more so since they have a lot of money = *ils ont toujours été heureux ensemble, et a fortiori depuis qu'ils ont beaucoup d'argent*

to be all for = *être tout à fait pour* : I'm all for having spare ribs tonight = *je suis tout à fait pour manger des travers de porc ce soir* ⓌⒸ to be keen on = *tenir beaucoup à*

to be all off = *ne pas y être du tout* : if you think I'm going to pay again, you're all off = *si tu crois que je vais encore payer, tu n'y es pas du tout* ⓌⒸ to be sadly mistaken = *se gourer complètement*

to be all over = 1/ *être la fin de tout* : it's all over if he finds out = *c'est la fin de tout s'il l'apprend* ⓌⒸ that's the ball game = *c'est la fin des haricots* 2/ *être complètement fini* : it's all over between Peter and his wife = *c'est complètement fini entre Peter et sa femme*

to be all over s.o. = *ne pas arrêter de peloter qqn* : he was all over me in the car = *dans la voiture, il n'arrêtait pas de me peloter*

she's her father all over = *c'est bien la fille de son père* ⓌⒸ she's the spitting image of her father = *c'est son père tout craché*

dressed all in (black) = *tout habillé en (noir)*

to go all out = 1/ *faire le maximum* : he went all out to help us = *il a fait le maximum pour nous aider* ⓌⒸ to do one's utmost = *faire tout son possible* 2/ *mettre les petits plats dans les grands* : they went all out for their daughter's wedding = *ils ont mis les petits plats dans les grands pour le mariage de leur fille* ≠ to skimp = *lésiner*

it's all right by me ! = *je n'ai rien contre !* ≠ no way ! = *je ne mange pas de ce pain-là !*

to be all right = *aller bien* : he was very ill but is all right now = *il a été très malade mais il va bien maintenant*

that's all right for you to say = *pour toi, c'est facile à dire*

not to be all there = *ne pas avoir toute sa tête* → CRAZY

that's all well and good but = *tout ça c'est bien beau, mais* ⓌⒸ that's very good but = *c'est bien joli, mais*

to walk all over s.o. = *marcher sur les pieds de qqn* : I won't let him walk all over me = *je ne le laisserai pas me marcher sur les pieds*

— ☠ *(je l'aime) tout court* = quite simply (I love him)

— *c'est tout juste si (j'ai réussi)* = I barely (succeeded)

— *c'est tout autre chose* = it's quite another matter

— *être tout feu tout flammes* = to be gung ho

— *à tout à l'heure !* = see you later !

— *tout au moins* ≠ *plus* = at the very least ≠ most

— *tout (drôle, jeune)* = ever so (funny, young)

— *tout de suite* = at once

— *il est tout à fait charmant* = he's quite charming

— *(je le ferai) tout à l'heure* = (I'll do it) in a little while

— *(je l'ai vu) tout à l'heure* = (I saw him) a little while ago

— *oui, tout à fait* = yes, indeed

— *c'est du tout cuit* = it's in the bag

— *tout en (marchant)* = while (walking)

— *tout droit* = straight ahead

— *les tout-petits* = the tots.

ALL-AROUND (adj) *complet, -ète* : an all-around athlete = *un athlète complet* ☠ → complete.

ALLEGED (adj) *présumé, -e* : alleged murderer/insanity = *meurtrier présumé/folie présumée.*

ALLERGY (n, -ies) *allergie (f)* ⓪ hay-fever = *rhume des foins* **ALLERGIC** (adj) *allergique.*

ALLEVIATE (to, -d) *alléger :* to alleviate the pain = *alléger la douleur* ⓪ to ease = *atténuer,* to relieve = *soulager.*

ALLEY (n) *ruelle (f) :* the guy was killed in the alley = *le type a été tué dans la ruelle*
alley cat = *chat de gouttière*
that's (right) up my alley = *c'est dans mes cordes.*

ALLIANCE (n) *alliance (f) :* the alliance between the two countries = *l'alliance entre les deux pays* ⓪ confederation = *confédération* ☠ *alliance (bague)* = wedding ring.

ALLIGATOR (n) *alligator (m) :* there are alligators in Miami = *il y a des alligators à Miami*
see ya' later alligator ! = *à la revoyure !* ⓪ in a while, crocodile ! = *à la prochaine !*

ALLOCATE (to, -d) *allouer :* to allocate funds = *allouer des fonds* ⓪ to allot = *attribuer.*

ALLOT (to, -ted) *attribuer :* each politician was allotted ten minutes to speak = *on avait attribué à chaque homme politique dix minutes de temps de parole* ⓪ to dole out = *distribuer au compte-gouttes* ☠ → to attribute.

ALL-OUT (adj) *tous azimuts* (offensive), *soutenu, -e* (effort) : an all-out military attack = *une attaque militaire tous azimuts,* an all-out effort = *un effort soutenu.*

ALLOW (to, -ed) *autoriser :* Russians are not allowed to travel abroad = *les Russes ne sont pas autorisés à voyager à l'étranger* ≠ to forbid = *interdire* ☠ → to authorize
allow me ! = *laisse-moi faire !*
to allow for = *tenir compte de :* you must allow for the extra expenses = *il faut tenir compte des dépenses supplémentaires* ⓪ to take into consideration = *prendre en considération*
allowing for (delays) = *si l'on tient compte des (retards)* ⓪ taking into account = *si l'on prend en compte*
to allow in = *laisser entrer :* they don't allow kids in sex shops = *on ne laisse pas les gosses entrer dans les sex-shops*
to allow s.o. (to) = *permettre à qqn (de) :* my folks don't allow me to smoke = *mes parents ne me permettent pas de fumer* ⓪ to let = *laisser.*

ALLOWANCE (n) *argent (m) de poche :* I give my kids an allowance = *je donne de l'argent de poche à mes gosses* = pocket money
to make allowances for the fact (that he lost his wife) = *être indulgent avec (lui) parce qu'(il a perdu sa femme)* ⓪ to take into consideration = *prendre en considération.*

ALL-TIME (adj) *sans précédent :* an all-time high ≠ low = *une hausse ≠ baisse sans précédent.*

ALLUDE TO (to, -d) *faire allusion à :* he alluded to his years in jail = *il a fait allusion à ses années de prison* ⓪ to refer to = *se référer à.*

ALLURE (n) *attrait (m) :* the allure of foreign countries = *l'attrait des pays étrangers* ⓪ charm = *charme* ☠ *elle a beaucoup d'allure* = she has a lot of class
— *à cette allure* = at this pace/tempo.

ALLUSION (n) **to make allusions to** = *faire allusion à.*

ALLY (n, -ies) *allié, -e* ≠ foe = *ennemi.*

ALMOST (adv) *presque :* it's almost 2 o'clock = *il est presque 2 heures* = nearly ⓪ just about = *quasiment*
almost always (late) = *presque toujours (en retard)*
almost never = *presque jamais :* we almost never watch TV = *nous ne regardons presque jamais la télé* ≠ frequently = *fréquemment*
almost + verb = *faillir :* I almost fell = *j'ai failli tomber.*

ALMS (n pl) *aumône (f) :* to give alms to the poor = *faire l'aumône aux pauvres.*

ALONE (adj) *seul, -e :* I was alone when he arrived = *j'étais seul quand il est arrivé* ≠ accompanied = *accompagné,* together = *ensemble*
leave me alone ! = *laisse-moi tranquille !* → BUZZ OFF !
☠ *la seule (personne)* = the only (person)
— *se sentir seul* = to feel lonely
— *il reste une seule (orange)* = there's only one (orange) left
— *pas un seul cas de SIDA* = not one solitary case of AIDS.

ALONE (adv) *seul, -e :* he did it alone = *il l'a fait seul* ⓪ all by himself = *tout seul*
to go it alone = *faire cavalier seul :* if you don't want to go into business with me, I'll go it alone = *si tu ne veux pas travailler avec moi, je ferai cavalier seul*
let alone = *sans parler de :* I'm having enough trouble with my boss, let alone my husband = *j'ai assez de problèmes avec mon patron, sans parler de ceux que j'ai avec mon mari.*

ALONG (prep) *le long de :* there were fruit stands along the road = *il y avait des étals de fruits le long de la route* ☠ for the use of ''along'' after a verb, see the verb.

ALONGSIDE (prep) *à côté de :* walk alongside me = *marche à côté de moi.*

ALOOF (adj) *distant, -e :* an aloof person = *une personne distante* = distant ⓪ reserved = *réservé.*

ALOUD (adv) *à haute voix :* say it aloud = *dis-le à haute voix* ≠ in a whisper = *tout bas*
to think aloud = *penser tout haut.*

ALPHABET (n) *alphabet (m)* ⓪ letter = *lettre* **ALPHABETICAL** (adj) *alphabétique :* alphabetical order = *ordre alphabétique* **ALPHABETICALLY** (adv) *alphabétiquement* **ALPHABETIZE** (to, -d) *alphabétiser.*

ALREADY (adv) *déjà* : has she already gone ? = *est-ce qu'elle est déjà partie ?* ≠ not yet = *pas encore*

yes, she has	=	*oui*
yes, she's **already** gone	=	*oui, elle est déjà partie*
no, **not yet**	=	*non, pas encore*
no, she **hasn't** gone **yet**	=	*non, elle n'est pas encore partie.*

ALSO (adv) *aussi* : he ate and I did also = *il a mangé et moi aussi* = too ≠ neither = *non plus* ☠ *aussi (riche) que* = as (rich) as.

ALTAR (n) *autel (m)* ⊕ choir = *chœur*.

ALTER (to, -ed) **1/** *modifier* : to alter one's way of thinking = *modifier sa façon de penser* ☠ → to modify **2/** *retoucher* : I have to have my dress altered = *il faut que je fasse retoucher ma robe.*

ALTERATION (n) *modification (f), retouche (f)* (dress) : to make alterations = *faire des modifications/des retouches.*

ALTERNATE (to, -d) *alterner* : to alternate the pill and the diaphragm = *alterner la pilule et le diaphragme* ⊕ to take turns at doing stg = *faire qqch à tour de rôle.*

ALTERNATIVE (n) **1/** *alternative (f)* (two choices only) : the alternative of giving in to her or losing her = *l'alternative de lui céder ou de la perdre* **2/** *possibilité (f)* : one of several alternatives = *une possibilité parmi d'autres* ⊕ option = ← ☠ → possibility **I had no alternative** = *je n'avais pas le choix.*

ALTHOUGH (conj) *quoique* : I'll work late although I'm tired = *je travaillerai tard quoique je sois fatigué* ⊕ though = *bien que.*

ALTITUDE (n) *altitude (f)* ⊕ height = *hauteur*.

ALTOGETHER (n) **in the altogether** = *dans le plus simple appareil* ⊕ in one's birthday suit = *en tenue d'Adam.*

ALTOGETHER (adv) **1/** *tout à fait* : you weren't altogether wrong about her = *vous n'aviez pas tout à fait tort à son sujet* ⊕ wholly = *totalement* **2/** *en tout* : altogether it'll cost a hundred dollars = *en tout, cela coûtera cent dollars.*

ALUMINUM (n) *aluminium (m)* = ← (GB) ⊕ tin = *fer-blanc.*

ALUMNUS (n, -ni) *ancien élève (m)* : they're Yale alumni = *ce sont d'anciens élèves de Yale* **ALUMNA** (n, -ae) *ancienne élève (f).*

ALWAYS (adv) *toujours* : I always eat a lot = *je mange toujours beaucoup* ≠ never = *jamais* ☠ *il est toujours marié* = he's still married — *toujours est-il que ...* = the fact still remains that ...

A.M. (adv) = ante meridiem = *du matin* : five a.m. = *cinq heures du matin* ≠ five p.m. = *cinq heures de l'après-midi/du soir.*

AMA (abbr) = American Medical Association = *Ordre des médecins* ⊕ A.B.A. = American Bar Association = *Ordre des avocats.*

AMASS (to, -ed) *amasser* : to amass a fortune = *amasser une fortune.*

AMATEUR (n, adj) *amateur (m)* : an amateur tennis player = *un joueur de tennis amateur* ⊕ dilettante = ← ≠ professional = *professionnel* ☠ *un amateur de (fromage)* = a (cheese) buff — *ne pas trouver d'amateurs* = to find no takers — *un comportement amateur* = an amateurish behavior.

AMATEURISH (adj) *amateur* : an amateurish behavior = *un comportement amateur.*

AMAZE (to, -d) *stupéfier* : his talent's going to amaze you = *son talent va vous stupéfier* ⊕ to flabbergast = *scier* **to be amazed at** = *être stupéfait de* : I was amazed at how much weight she had gained = *j'étais stupéfait de voir à quel point elle avait grossi.*

AMAZEMENT (n) *stupéfaction (f)* : to look at someone in amazement = *regarder quelqu'un avec stupéfaction.*

AMAZING (adj) *stupéfiant, -e* : an amazing tennis player = *un joueur de tennis stupéfiant* → WONDERFUL.

AMBASSADOR (n) *ambassadeur (m)* : he is the US ambassador to France = *il est l'ambassadeur des États-Unis en France* **AMBASSADRESS** (n, -es) *ambassadrice (f).*

AMBIDEXTROUS (adj) *ambidextre* ⊕ left-handed = *gaucher.*

AMBIGUITY (n, -ies) *ambiguïté (f)* : the ambiguity of the situation = *l'ambiguïté de la situation* ≠ clarity = *clarté.*

AMBIGUOUS (adj) *ambigu, -uë* : an ambiguous answer = *une réponse ambiguë* ≠ explicit = *explicite* **AMBIGUOUSLY** (adv) *de façon ambiguë.*

AMBITION (n) *ambition (f)* : my ambition is to make a million = *mon ambition, c'est de gagner un million* ⊕ goal = *but.*

AMBITIOUS (adj) *ambitieux, -euse* : an ambitious young man = *un jeune homme ambitieux* ⊕ driven = *qui en veut.*

AMBIVALENT (adj) *ambivalent, -e* : ambivalent feelings = *des sentiments ambivalents* ⊕ ambiguous = *ambigu* ☠ *être ambivalent* = to be ac/dc.

AMBULANCE (n) *ambulance (f)* ⊕ stretcher = *brancard* **ambulance chaser** = *avocat magouillant avec un médecin qui lui fournit sa clientèle parmi les urgences.*

AMBUSH (n, -es) *embuscade* (f) ⓒ trap = *piège*.

AMEND (n) **to make amends** = *faire amende honorable* ⓒ to make up for = *se racheter*.

AMEND (to, -ed) *amender* : to amend the Constitution = *amender la Constitution* ⓒ to rectify = *rectifier*.

AMENDMENT (n) *amendement* (m) : an amendment to the bill = *un amendement au projet de loi*.

AMERICA (n) *Amérique* (f) **AMERICAN** (n, adj) *Américain, -e* ⓒ Yankee = ←, Yank = *amerloque*.

AMIABLE (adj) *aimable* : an amiable girl = *une fille aimable* ⓒ nice = *sympa*.

AMISS (adv) **to go amiss** = *aller de travers* : since he left, everything has gone amiss = *depuis qu'il est parti tout va de travers*.
something's amiss = *il y a quelque chose qui cloche* ⓒ something's wrong = *il y a quelque chose qui ne va pas*.

AMMUNITION (n inv) *munitions* (f pl) : to sell ammunition to the enemy = *vendre des munitions à l'ennemi* ⓒ weapons = *armes*.

AMNESIA (n) *amnésie* (f) ≠ memory = *mémoire*.

AMNESTY (n, -ies) *amnistie* (f) : a general amnesty = *une amnistie générale* ⓒ pardon = *grâce*.

AMONG (prep) *parmi* : he's the only one I know among all these people = *c'est le seul que je connaisse parmi tous ces gens* ⓒ amid = *au milieu de*
we're among (friends) = *nous sommes entre (amis)*
among others = *entre autres* : you'll be able to play tennis and golf among others = *vous pourrez entre autres jouer au tennis et au golf*.

AMOUNT (n) **1/** *montant* (m) : the amount of the bill = *le montant de la facture* ⓒ total = ← **2/** *quantité* (f) : a large ≠ small amount of food = *une grande ≠ petite quantité de nourriture* → MANY 🕱 → quantity.

AMOUNT TO (to, -ed) **1/** *se monter à* : the bill amounted to a hundred dollars = *la facture se montait à cent dollars* ⓒ to come to = *se chiffrer à* **2/** *se résumer à* : it amounts to his wanting a divorce = *ça se résume au fait qu'il demande le divorce* ⓒ to boil down to = *se réduire à* **3/** *arriver à* : he'll never amount to anything = *il n'arrivera jamais à rien*.

AMPLE (adj) *largement assez de* : there's ample food for everyone = *il y a largement assez de nourriture pour tout le monde* 🕱 *une robe ample* = a loose dress.

AMPUTATE (to, -d) *amputer* : to amputate a leg = *amputer une jambe* = to cut off a leg.

AMUSE (to, -d) *amuser* : your criticisms don't amuse me = *vos critiques ne m'amusent pas*.
it amuses (me) to = *cela (m')amuse de* : it amuses me to see my son play with the cat = *ça m'amuse de voir mon fils jouer avec le chat*

🕱 *amusez-vous bien !* = have a good time !
— *nous nous sommes bien amusés* = we enjoyed ourselves.

AMUSEMENT (n) *amusement* (m) : to everyone's amusement = *à l'amusement général*
amusement park = *parc d'attractions*
for one's own amusement = *pour son plaisir personnel*.

AMUSING (adj) *amusant, -e* : an amusing remark = *une remarque amusante* ⓒ entertaining = *divertissant*.

AN (art) → A.

ANACHRONISM (n) *anachronisme* (m).

ANALYSIS (n, -ses) *analyse* (f) : I agree with your analysis of the situation = *je suis d'accord avec votre analyse de la situation*
to be in analysis = *être en analyse* ⓒ group therapy = *thérapie de groupe*
in the last/final analysis (you're right) = *en dernière analyse (vous avez raison)* ⓒ in the end = *en fin de compte*
🕱 *une analyse de sang* = a blood test.

ANALYST (n) *analyste* (m, f) : she slept with her analyst = *elle a couché avec son analyste* ⓒ psychiatrist = *psychiatre*.

ANALYTICAL (adj) *analytique*
an analytical mind = *un esprit d'analyse*.

ANALYZE (to, -d) *analyser* : to analyze the situation = *analyser la situation* = to analyse (GB) ⓒ to examine = *examiner*.

ANARCHIST (n) *anarchiste* (m, f), anar (m, f) (LV)
ANARCHY (n) *anarchie* (f) ≠ order = *ordre*.

ANATOMY (n, -ies) *anatomie* (f) ⓒ biology = *biologie*.

ANCESTOR (n) *ancêtre* (m, f) : French ancestors = *des ancêtres français* ⓒ forefathers = *aïeux*, family tree = *arbre généalogique*, ancestry = *ascendance*.

ANCHOR (n) *ancre* (f) : to cast anchor = *jeter l'ancre* ⓒ to moor = *amarrer*.

ANCHOR MAN (n, -men) *présentateur* (m) *de télévision*
ANCHOR WOMAN (n, -women) *présentatrice* (f) *de télévision*.

ANCHOVY (n, -ies) *anchois* (m) ⓒ herring = *hareng*.

ANCIENT (adj) **1/** *ancien, -enne* : I'm studying ancient history = *j'étudie l'histoire ancienne*
it's ancient history = *c'est de l'histoire ancienne* ⓒ let bygones be bygones = *le passé, c'est le passé*
🕱 *ancien combattant* = ex-serviceman/veteran
— *meubles anciens* = antique furniture
— *mon ancien professeur* = my former/old teacher
2/ *vieux, vieille comme Hérode* : his grandfather's ancient = *son grand-père est vieux comme Hérode*.

AND (conj) *et* : men and women = *les hommes et les femmes* ≠ neither men nor women = *ni les hommes ni les femmes*
and how ! = *et comment* ! : is he rich ? — and how ! = *est-il riche* ? — *et comment* ! ⓍⒹ you'd better believe it ! = *c'est le cas de le dire* !
and over = *et plus* : they admit kids of five and over = *ils admettent les enfants de cinq ans et plus* ≠ **and under** = *et moins*
and so ? = *et alors* ? ⓍⒹ so ? = *alors* ?
and so on and so forth = *et ainsi de suite/et patati et patata* ⓍⒹ et cetera = ←
and then again = *d'un autre côté* : he might come and then again he might not = *il se peut qu'il vienne, d'un autre côté il se peut qu'il ne vienne pas*
and then some = *et plus encore* : he earns millions of dollars and then some = *il gagne des millions de dollars et plus encore*
and then what ? = *et puis après* ?
and what have you ! = *et que sais-je encore* !
and what not = *et je ne sais quoi encore* : he's taking psychology, sociology and what not = *il fait de la psychologie, de la sociologie et je ne sais quoi encore*.

ANECDOTE (n) *anecdote* (f) : to tell anecdotes = *raconter des anecdotes* ⓍⒹ story = *histoire*.

ANEMIA (n) *anémie* (f).

ANESTHESIA (n) *anesthésie* (f) : local anesthesia = *anesthésie locale*.

ANESTHETIC (n) *anesthésique* (m) **ANESTHETIST** (n) *anesthésiste* (m, f).

ANEW (adv) **to do stg anew** = *se lancer dans un nouveau ...* : he is marrying anew = *il se lance dans un nouveau mariage* ⓍⒹ once again = *encore une fois*.

ANGEL (n) 1/ *ange* (m) ≠ devil = *diable* 2/ *ange* (m) : you were an angel to help me = *tu as été un ange de m'aider* ⓍⒹ doll = *amour*
☙ *un ange passe* = an awkward silence
— *être aux anges* = to be floating on air
3/ *mécène* (m) : a theater angel = *un mécène du théâtre* ⓍⒹ backer = *commanditaire*.

ANGELIC (adj) *angélique*.

ANGER (n) *colère* (f) : terrible things were said in anger = *des choses terribles ont été dites sous l'effet de la colère* ⓍⒹ rage = ←, wrath = *courroux*
☙ *être en colère* = to be angry
— *se mettre en colère* = to lose one's temper.

ANGER (to, -ed) *mettre en colère* : his reply angered me = *sa réponse m'a mis en colère* → ANGRY.

ANGLE (n) 1/ *angle* (m) : a right angle = *un angle droit*
from the angle of = *du point de vue de* : he's writing a novel from the angle of the murderer = *il écrit un roman du point de vue de l'assassin*
☙ *arrondir les angles* = to smooth things over
2/ *combine* (f) : we'll have to find an angle to get him to agree = *il va nous falloir trouver une combine pour qu'il accepte* ⓍⒹ scheme = *combinaison*.

ANGLO (n, adj) *Américain, -e de race blanche de toute provenance sauf l'Angleterre (Italiens, Juifs, Polonais, etc.)*.

ANGRY (adj, -ier, -iest) *en colère* : why are you so angry ? = *pourquoi êtes-vous si en colère* ?

GROUP : TO BE ANGRY = ÊTRE EN COLÈRE

to be angered by = *être mis en colère par*	**to be burning** = *bouillir de colère*	**to be galled** = *être horripilé*
to be angry (with) = *être en colère (contre)*	**to be burnt up** = *bouillir de colère*	**to get angry** = *se mettre en colère*
to be annoyed = *être énervé*	**to carry on** = *s'emporter*	**to get excited** = *s'exciter*
to be in a bad mood = *être de mauvaise humeur/de mauvais poil*	**to be cross with** = *être fâché contre*	**that got my goat** = *ça m'a échauffé les oreilles*
to blow one's cool = *se mettre en boule*	**to do a slow burn** = *avoir la moutarde qui vous monte au nez*	**to get one's back up** = *se hérisser*
to blow a fuse = *se mettre en pétard*	**to be enraged** = *être enragé*	**to get one's dander up** = *se mettre en rage*
to blow a gasket = *se mettre en rogne*	**to be exasperated** = *être exaspéré*	**that got my Irish up** = *j'ai pris la mouche*
to blow one's lid = *se fâcher tout rouge*	**to explode** = *exploser*	**to have/throw a fit** = *piquer une crise*
to blow one's stack = *piquer une colère*	**to be fit to be tied** = *être fou furieux*	**to have a low boiling point** = *être soupe au lait*
to blow one's top = *se mettre dans une colère noire*	**to flare up** = *éclater*	**to hit the ceiling** = *sauter au plafond*
to blow up = *éclater*	**to fly into a rage** = *se mettre en rage*	**to hit the roof** = *pousser une gueulante*
to be boiling = *être fumasse*	**to fly off the handle** = *sortir de ses gonds*	**to be hopping mad** = *être furax*
	to fume = *être furibard*	
	to be furious = *être furieux*	

to get hot under the collar = *prendre la mouche*	**to lose one's temper** = *se mettre en colère*	**to see red** = *voir rouge*
to be hotheaded = *avoir le sang chaud*	**to be mad** = *être très fâché*	**to be seething** = *être fou furieux*
to be hot-tempered = *être coléreux*	**to be miffed** = *être froissé*	**to be sore** = *être en pétard*
to be in a huff = *être en rogne*	**that made my blood boil** = *ça m'a fait bouillir (de colère)*	**to split a blood vessel** = *attraper un coup de sang*
to be incensed = *être horripilé*	**to be peeved** = *être froissé*	**to be steaming** = *être furax*
to be infuriated = *être furieux*	**I'm pissed off !** = *ça me fait chier !*	**to be teed off** = *être furibard*
to be irate = *être courroucé*	**to be quick-tempered** = *avoir la tête près du bonnet*	**to tick off** = *mettre en boule*
to be irked = *être contrarié*	**to be in a rage** = *être en rage*	**to be in a temper** = *être fou de rage*
to be irritated = *être irrité*	**to rage** = *fulminer*	**to be up in arms** = *être hors de soi*
to let go = *se déchaîner*	**to raise the devil** = *se mettre en boule*	**to be vexed** = *être contrarié*
to let loose = *se déchaîner*	**to rant and rave** = *tempêter*	**to be on the warpath** = *partir sur le sentier de la guerre*
to be livid = *être blême de colère*	**to be riled** = *être horripilé*	**to be worked up** = *être énervé.*

ANGUISH (n inv) *angoisse* *(f)* : only an orphan can feel such anguish = *il n'y a qu'un orphelin pour ressentir une angoisse pareille*
in anguish = *dans l'angoisse* : I was in anguish waiting for the results of the exam = *j'étais dans l'angoisse en attendant mes résultats d'examen* ⓪ upset = *inquiet.*

ANIMAL (n) *animal* *(m)* ⓪ beast = *bête*, Noah's ark = *arche de Noé* ☠ *animal domestique* = pet

alligator = ←	**hippopotamus** = *hippopotame*
ass = *âne*	
bear = *ours*	**horse** = *cheval*
bird = *oiseau*	**kangaroo** = *kangourou*
buffalo = *buffle/bison*	**leopard** = *léopard*
cat = *chat*	**lion** = ←
cow = *vache*	**monkey** = *singe*
deer = *daim/cerf*	**pig** = *cochon*
dog = *chien*	**reptile** = ←
elephant = *éléphant*	**rhinoceros** = *rhinocéros*
giraffe = *girafe*	**seal** = *phoque*
goat = *chèvre*	**tiger** = *tigre*
gorilla = *gorille*	**zebra** = *zèbre.*

ANIMATED (adj) *animé, -e* : an animated meeting = *une réunion animée* ≠ boring = *ennuyeux.*

ANIMOSITY (n) *animosité* *(f)* : full of animosity towards her family = *remplie d'animosité envers sa famille* ⓪ enmity = *inimitié* ≠ cordiality = *cordialité.*

ANKLE (n) *cheville* *(f)* : I twisted my ankle = *je me suis tordu la cheville* ⓪ calf = *mollet*
☠ *ne pas arriver à la cheville de qqn* = not to hold a candle to s.o.
— *avoir les chevilles qui enflent* = to be very self-satisfied
— *être en cheville avec qqn* = to be hand in glove with s.o.
— *la cheville ouvrière* = the kingpin.

ANNALS (n pl) *annales* *(f pl).*

ANNEX (n, -es) *annexe* *(f)* : the annex of a building = *l'annexe d'un immeuble* ⓪ wing = *aile* ☠ *annexe (texte de loi)* = rider (law text).

ANNEX (to, -ed) *annexer* : to annex a state = *annexer un État.*

ANNIHILATE (to, -d) *annihiler* : to annihilate the enemy = *annihiler l'ennemi* ⓪ to wipe out = *anéantir*
ANNIHILATION (n) *anéantissement* *(m).*

ANNIVERSARY (n, -ies) *anniversaire* *(m)* : their wedding anniversary = *leur anniversaire de mariage* ⓪ commemoration = *commémoration*, centenary = *centenaire* ☠ *mon anniversaire (naissance)* = my birthday.

ANNOUNCE (to, -d) *annoncer* : to announce one's retirement = *annoncer son départ à la retraite* ☠ *ça s'annonce bien* = it looks promising.

ANNOUNCEMENT (n) *annonce* *(f)* : the announcement of his death = *l'annonce de sa mort* ⓪ statement = *déclaration* ☠ *une annonce (pub)* = an advertisement/an ad.

ANNOY (to, -ed) 1/ *gêner* : their talking/smoking annoyed the others = *leur bavardage/fumée gênait les autres* ⓪ to bother ⓪ to irritate = *irriter* ☠ → to mind
I don't want to annoy you with (my problems) = *je ne veux pas vous ennuyer avec (mes problèmes)*
2/ *énerver* : I'm really annoyed that the hasn't called yet = *ça m'énerve vraiment qu'il n'ait pas encore appelé* → ANGRY ☠ *ne t'énerve pas !* = don't get excited !
to be annoyed with s.o. = *être fâché contre qqn*
what are you so annoyed about ? = *qu'est-ce qui t'énerve comme ça ?*

ANNOYANCE (n) *ennui* *(m)* : having to walk so far to get the bus is an annoyance ! = *quel ennui d'avoir tant à marcher pour prendre le bus !* ⓪ nuisance = *quelque chose d'empoisonnant* ☠ → boredom.

ANNOYING (adj) *énervant, -e* : any noise is annoying = *tout bruit est énervant* ⓪ irritating = *irritant.*

ANNUAL (adj) *annuel, -elle* : his annual European vacation = *ses vacances annuelles en Europe* = yearly ⓪ monthly = *mensuel* **ANNUALLY** (adv) *annuellement*.

ANNUL (to, -led) *annuler* : to annul a marriage = *annuler un mariage* ⓪ to nullify = *rendre nul* ☠ *annuler un contrat* = to void a contract — *annuler un voyage* = to cancel a trip.

ANNULMENT (n) *annulation (f)* : the annulment of a marriage = *l'annulation d'un mariage* ☠ *annulation (voyage)* = cancellation (trip).

ANONYMITY (n) *anonymat (m)* : the anonymity of city life = *l'anonymat de la vie en ville*.

ANONYMOUS (adj) *anonyme* : an anonymous letter = *une lettre anonyme* ☠ *une société anonyme* = a limited company.

ANOTHER (adj) *un, -e autre* : I would like another cup of coffee = *je voudrais une autre tasse de café* ⓪ one more = *encore un*
another day and age = *autres temps, autres mœurs*
another one = *un autre* : the coffee was good, give me another one = *le café était bon, donnez-m'en un autre*
another time = 1/ *une autre fois* : do it another time = *fais-le une autre fois* ⓪ again = *à nouveau* 2/ *une autre fois* : I can't talk to you now, I'll talk to you another time = *je ne peux pas vous parler maintenant, je vous parlerai une autre fois*
he has another think coming = *il peut toujours se brosser* : if he thinks I'm going to lend him money, he has another think coming ! = *s'il croit que je vais lui prêter de l'argent, il peut toujours se brosser !* ⓪ I have news for him ! = *il se fait des illusions !*

ANOTHER (pron) *un, -e autre* : can I have another ? = *est-ce que je peux en avoir un autre ?*
tell me another ! = *à d'autres !* → BUZZ OFF !

ANSWER (n) *réponse (f)* : who knows the answer ? = *qui connaît la réponse ?* ≠ question = ←
☠ *faire à qqn une réponse de Normand* = to give s.o. a song and a dance
— *il y a eu peu de réponse à l'appel du gouvernement* = there was little response to the government's call.

ANSWER (to, -ed) *répondre* : will you please answer me ! = *voulez-vous me répondre !* ⓪ to retort = *rétorquer* ≠ to ask = *demander*
to answer back = *répondre* : children should not answer back = *les enfants ne devraient pas répondre* = children shouldn't talk back

to answer for = *répondre de* : I'll answer for my brother = *je répondrai de mon frère* ⓪ to guarantee = *se porter garant de*
☠ *répondre à un besoin* = to fulfill a need.

ANT (n) *fourmi (f)* ⓪ grasshopper = *sauterelle*
to have ants in one's pants = *avoir la bougeotte*
☠ *j'ai des fourmis dans les jambes* = my legs fell asleep.

ANTAGONISM (n) *antagonisme (m)* ≠ agreement = *accord* **ANTAGONISTIC** (adj) *antagoniste* **ANTAGONIZE** (to, -d) *se mettre à dos* : she antagonized her in-laws with her remarks = *elle s'est mis ses beaux-parents à dos par ses remarques* ⓪ to put off = *rebuter*.

ANTE (n) **to raise up the ante** = *faire monter les enchères*.

ANTI- (pref) *anti-* : I'm anti-smoking = *je suis anti-tabac* ≠ pro- = ←.

ANTIBIOTIC (n) *antibiotique (m)* ⓪ penicillin = *pénicilline*.

ANTICIPATE (to, -d) 1/ *prévoir* : I'm anticipating problems = *je prévois des problèmes* ⓪ to expect = *s'attendre à* ☠ → to forecast 2/ *anticiper* (often intransitive in French) : let's not anticipate ! = *n'anticipons pas !*

ANTICS (n pl) *clowneries (f pl)* : enough of your antics ! = *arrête tes clowneries !* ⓪ monkey business = *singeries*.

ANTIQUE (n) *antiquité (f)* : an antique shop = *un magasin d'antiquités*, an antique dealer = *un antiquaire* **ANTIQUE** (adj) *ancien, -enne* : antique furniture = *meubles anciens* ≠ modern = *moderne* ☠ → ancient.

ANTI-SEMITE (n) *antisémite (m, f)* **ANTI-SEMITISM** (n) *antisémitisme (m)* ⓪ pogrom = ←.

ANUS (n) *anus (m)* ⓪ asshole = *trou du cul*.

ANXIETY (n, -ies) *anxiété (f)* : filled with anxiety = *rempli d'anxiété* ≠ serenity = *sérénité*.

ANXIOUS (adj) **to be anxious about (one's health)** = *être anxieux au sujet de (sa santé)* ⓪ to be worried about = *être inquiet de*
to be anxious to = *avoir hâte de* : I'm anxious to see him again = *j'ai hâte de le revoir* ⓪ to be eager to = *être désireux de*.

ANXIOUSLY (adv) *avec impatience* : we're anxiously waiting to hear from them = *nous attendons de leurs nouvelles avec impatience*.

ANY (adj) 1/ *du, de la, des* (forme interrogative et négative)
— do you have **any/some** cigarettes ? = *avez-vous des cigarettes ?*
— yes, I have **some** = *oui, j'en ai* — no, I **don't** have **any** = *non, je n'en ai pas*
2/ *n'importe quel, quelle* : any girl knows that = *n'importe quelle fille sait cela*, come any day = *viens n'importe quel jour*

any day of the week = *à tous les coups* : I'd rather eat Chinese food than pizza any day of the week = *à tous les coups je préfère la cuisine chinoise aux pizzas*
any other problem/question ? = *d'autres problèmes/questions ?*
any second/minute = *incessamment* : he'll come any second = *il va arriver incessamment* ⓪ shortly = *sous peu*
any which way = *à la va-comme-je-te-pousse* : he does his work any which way = *il fait son travail à la va-comme-je-te-pousse* ⓪ anyway at all = *n'importe comment*
at any moment = *à tout moment* : he's going to come at any moment = *il peut arriver à tout moment*

at any price = *à tout prix* : she wants to get divorced at any price = *elle veut divorcer à tout prix* ⓪ by hook or by crook = *coûte que coûte*
at any rate = *de toute façon* : the film wasn't great, but at any rate wasn't boring = *le film n'était pas terrible mais, de toute façon, il n'était pas ennuyeux* ⓪ anyway = *quand même*
by any chance = *(tout à fait) par hasard* : do you have cigarettes by any chance ? = *est-ce que (tout à fait) par hasard vous auriez des cigarettes ?*
for any little thing = *pour un oui pour un non* : she gets angry for any little thing = *elle se met en colère pour un oui pour un non*
to go to any lengths = *ne reculer devant rien* : he'd go to any

lengths to succeed = *il ne reculerait devant rien pour réussir* ⓪ to be capable of anything = *être capable de tout*
in any case = *en tout cas* : I'm tired and in any case, it's too cold to go out = *je suis fatigué et, en tout cas, il fait trop froid pour sortir* ⓪ anyhow = *de toute manière*
in any event = *de toute façon* : I'll come in any event = *je viendrai de toute façon* ⓪ nevertheless = *néanmoins*
in any way = *en quoi que ce soit* : can I help you in any way ? = *puis-je vous aider en quoi que ce soit ?*
not ... any = *pas de* : I don't have any money/problems = *je n'ai pas d'argent/de problèmes* ≠ a lot of = *beaucoup de.*

ANY (adv) *un peu* : does she feel any better ? = *est-ce qu'elle se sent un peu mieux ?*, did you sleep any ? = *est-ce que vous avez un peu dormi ?*

---

any more = *encore (de)* : do you want any more tea ? = *voulez-vous encore du thé ?*
not any = *pas du tout* : the film wasn't any good = *le film n'était pas bon du tout*
not ... any longer = *ne ...*

plus : she doesn't love him any longer = *elle ne l'aime plus* = she no longer loves him = she doesn't love him anymore
not ... any more = *ne ... pas ... plus* : I can't drink any more = *je ne peux pas boire plus*

not any more ... than = *pas plus ... que* : he isn't any more interesting than his brother = *il n'est pas plus intéressant que son frère*
that doesn't help things/matters any = *cela n'arrange rien.*

ANY (pron) *en* ≠ a few = *quelques,* a little = *un peu* ☠ → some
— there's a lot of food, do you want **any ?** = *il y a beaucoup à manger, en voulez-vous ?*
— yes, I want **some** = *oui, j'en veux* — no, I **don't** want **any** = *non, je n'en veux pas*

---

any of = 1/ *l'un de* : if any of you want to come, tell me = *si l'un de vous veut venir, dites-le-moi* 2/ *ceux/celles que* : you can take any of them = *prenez ceux/celles que vous voulez*
to get any = *se taper*

quelqu'un : did you get any last night ? = *tu t'es tapé quelqu'un hier soir ?* ⓪ to screw = *baiser*
hardly/scarcely/barely any = *presque pas* : she hardly/scarcely/barely has any money = *elle n'a presque pas d'argent*

I'm not having/buying any ! = *ça ne prend pas avec moi !* → BUZZ OFF !
not ... any = *n'en ... pas* : cigarettes ? I don't have any = *des cigarettes ? je n'en ai pas* ⓪ none = *aucun.*

ANYBODY (pron) = ANYONE.

ANYHOW (adv) *de toute manière* : I don't love him, and anyhow I don't want to get married = *je ne l'aime pas, et de toute manière je ne veux pas me marier* ⓪ anyway = *quand même.*

ANYMORE (adv) **not ... anymore** = *ne ... plus* : she doesn't live here anymore = *elle n'habite plus ici* = she doesn't live here any longer ≠ still = *encore.*

ANYONE (pron) 1/ *quelqu'un* = anybody
— did **anyone/anybody** call ? = *est-ce que quelqu'un a appelé ?*
— yes, **someone/somebody** called = *oui, quelqu'un a appelé*
— no, **no one/nobody** called = *non, personne n'a appelé*
anyone/anybody else = *quelqu'un d'autre* : do you know anyone else in New York ? = *connais-tu*

quelqu'un d'autre à New York ?
hardly/scarcely/barely anyone (came) = *presque personne (n'est venu)*
not anyone/anybody = *ne ... personne* : there isn't anyone/anybody here = *il n'y a personne ici* ⓒ no one = *personne* = nobody
2/ *n'importe qui* : you can come to the party with anyone/anybody = *tu peux venir à la soirée avec*

n'importe qui
it's anyone's/anybody's guess = *on n'en sait rien au juste* ⓒ who knows ? = *qui sait ?*
just anyone/anybody = *n'importe qui* : she didn't marry just anyone/anybody = *elle n'a pas épousé n'importe qui.*

ANYPLACE (adv) = ANYWHERE.

ANYTHING (pron) **1/** *quelque chose (forme interrogative et négative)*

— do you have **anything** to do tonight ? = *est-ce que vous avez quelque chose à faire ce soir ?*

— yes, I have **something** to do tonight = *oui, j'ai quelque chose à faire ce soir*

— no, I **don't** have **anything** to do tonight = *non, je n'ai rien à faire ce soir*

2/ *n'importe quoi* : I don't care what I eat, give me anything = *ce que je mange m'est égal, donnez-moi n'importe quoi*

---

anything but = *tout sauf* : she's anything but stupid = *elle est tout sauf stupide*
anything else = 1/ *autre chose* : do you want anything else ? = *est-ce que vous voulez autre chose ?* ⓒ something else = *quelque chose d'autre* 2/ *n'importe quoi d'autre* : I don't want milk, give me anything else = *je ne veux pas de lait, donnez-moi n'importe quoi d'autre*
anything goes = *tout est permis* : her mother isn't strict, anything goes = *sa mère n'est pas stricte, tout est permis*
anything (that) = *tout ce que* :

take anything (that) you want = *prenez tout ce que vous voulez*
anything you say = *comme vous voulez* : I agree to Chinese food, anything you say = *comme vous voulez ! je veux bien aller dans un restaurant chinois* = as you like
as ... as anything = *comme tout* : they're as rich as anything = *ils sont riches comme tout* → VERY
I couldn't ask for anything more = *je ne pouvais pas demander mieux*
I'd give anything to (know) = *je donnerais n'importe quoi pour (savoir)*

like anything = *vachement* : he drinks like anything = *il boit vachement* → VERY ☠ → damned
not ... anything = *rien* : he didn't eat anything = *il n'a rien mangé* = he ate nothing ≠ he ate something = *il a mangé quelque chose* ☠ → nothing
not ... anything more = *rien d'autre* : I don't want anything more = *je ne veux rien d'autre*
scarcely/barely/hardly anything = *presque rien* : I scarcely/barely/hardly understood anything he explained to me = *je n'ai presque rien compris de ce qu'il m'a expliqué.*

ANYTIME (adv) **1/** *n'importe quand* : come anytime = *venez n'importe quand* = come at any time **2/** *à tous les coups* : I can play as well as you anytime = *à tous les coups je joue aussi bien que toi* = any day of the week **3/** *si jamais* : anytime you need help, call me = *si jamais vous avez besoin d'aide, appelez-moi.*

ANYWAY (adv) **1/** *quand même* : I didn't want to go but I did anyway = *je ne voulais pas y aller, mais j'y suis allé quand même* ⓒ just the same = *tout de même* **2/** *enfin* : anyway, let me finish what I wanted to say = *enfin, laissez-moi finir ce que je voulais dire* ☠ *il est enfin venu* = he came at last **3/** *n'importe comment* : I'm tired and anyway it's too late to go out = *je suis fatigué, et n'importe comment il est trop tard pour sortir*
anyway (at all) = *n'importe comment* : she does her work anyway at all = *elle fait son travail n'importe comment*
anyway one looks at it (you're wrong) = *quel que soit l'angle sous lequel on voit les choses (vous avez tort)*
anyway you want = *comme vous voulez.*

ANYWHERE (adv) **1/** *n'importe où* : you can find a lighter like his anywhere = *vous pouvez trouver un briquet comme le sien n'importe où* = anyplace ⓒ everywhere = *partout* **2/** *quelque part* : can you get divorced anywhere in 24 hours ? = *est-ce que quelque part on peut divorcer en 24 heures ?* = anyplace ≠ nowhere = *nulle part*
— did you go **anywhere** today ? = *est-ce que tu es allé quelque part aujourd'hui ?*
— yes, I went **somewhere** = *oui, je suis allé quelque part*
— no, **I didn't** go **anywhere** = *non, je ne suis allé nulle part*

anywhere you want = *où vous voulez* : we can eat anywhere you want = *nous pouvons manger où vous voulez*
anywhere between

... and ... = *de ... à* : it will cost you anywhere between ten and twenty dollars = *ça vous coûtera de dix à vingt dollars*

not ... anywhere = *nulle part :* I couldn't find my lighter anywhere = *je n'ai pu trouver mon briquet nulle part* = I couldn't find my lighter anyplace
not anywhere as ... as = *loin de ... aussi ... que :* he isn't anywhere as bright as his sister = *il est loin d'être aussi intelligent que sa sœur*
not to get anywhere = 1/ *ne parvenir à rien :* he won't get anywhere in life = *il ne parviendra à rien dans la vie* = he'll get nowhere in life 2/ *n'avancer à rien :* his stupid advice didn't get me anywhere = *ses conseils stupides ne m'ont avancé à rien.*

A-ONE (adj) *hors ligne :* an A-one restaurant/poet = *un restaurant/poète hors ligne* → WONDERFUL.

APART FROM (prep) *à part :* apart from his lack of romanticism, he's a good husband = *à part son manque de romantisme, c'est un bon mari* ⓒ aside from = *mis à part*
☠ for the use of "apart" after a verb, see the verb.

APARTHEID (n) *apartheid (m)* ⓒ segregation = *ségrégation.*

APARTMENT (n) *appartement (m) :* our apartment has 6 rooms = *notre appartement a 6 pièces* = flat (GB) ⓒ house = *maison,* maintenance = *charges,* pad = *appart'*
apartment house = *immeuble (d'habitation)* ⓒ co-op = *copropriété* = condo.

APATHETIC (adj) *apathique :* an apathetic nature = *une nature apathique* ≠ dynamic = *dynamique*
APATHY (n) *apathie (f)* ≠ dynamism = *dynamisme.*

APE (n) *grand singe (m)* ⓒ monkey = *singe,* baboon = *babouin*
to go ape over = *être gaga de :* he goes ape over his baby = *il est gaga de son bébé* ⓒ to go crazy for = *s'emballer pour.*

APE (to, -d) *singer :* the comedian was aping the President = *le comédien singeait le Président* ⓒ to mimic = *imiter.*

APEX (n inv) *point (m) culminant :* the apex of her career = *le point culminant de sa carrière* ⓒ acme = *faîte.*

APHRODISIAC (n) *aphrodisiaque (m)* ≠ saltpeter = *bromure.*

APIECE (adv) 1/ *(la) pièce :* they cost ten dollars apiece = *ils coûtent dix dollars pièce* ⓒ for each = *chaque* 2/ *par personne :* the dinner will cost you ten dollars apiece = *le dîner vous coûtera dix dollars par personne* ⓒ a head = *par tête (de pipe).*

APOCALYPSE (n) *apocalypse (f)* ⓒ Judgment Day = *Jugement dernier.*

APOLOGIZE (to, -d) *s'excuser :* I apologize = *je m'excuse* ⓒ to be sorry = *être désolé* ☠ → to excuse

to apologize for = *s'excuser de :* I apologize for disturbing you = *je m'excuse de vous déranger*
to apologize to = *s'excuser auprès de :* apologize to your father for me = *excusez-moi auprès de votre père.*

APOLOGY (n, -ies) *excuse (f) :* give him my apologies = *faites-lui (toutes) mes excuses*
☠ → excuse
— *faire l'apologie de qqn* = to praise s.o.

APOSTROPHE (n) *apostrophe (f).*

APPAL(L) (to, -(l)ed) *effarer :* his language appalled me = *son langage m'a effaré* ⓒ to shock = *choquer*
to be appalled to (hear that news) = *être effaré d'(apprendre cette nouvelle).*

APPALLING (adj) *effarant, -e :* an appalling situation = *une situation effarante* ⓒ harrowing = *effroyable.*

APPARATUS (n, -es) *appareil (m) :* political/heating apparatus = *appareil politique/de chauffage* ⓒ device = *dispositif*
☠ *qui est à l'appareil ?* = who's calling ?
— *un appareil ménager* = a household appliance
— *appareil photo* = camera.

APPAREL (n) *habillement (m) :* men's apparel = *l'habillement masculin* ⓒ garment = *habit.*

APPARENT (adj) *apparent, -e :* an apparent calm = *un calme apparent* ⓒ supposed = *supposé*
apparent to s.o. = *manifeste pour qqn :* it was apparent to me that she was lying = *il était manifeste pour moi qu'elle mentait.*

APPARENTLY (adv) *apparemment :* they're apparently going to get married = *ils vont apparemment se marier* ⓒ obviously = *évidemment*
apparently so = *apparemment oui.*

APPEAL (n) 1/ *attrait (m) :* rock has a terrible appeal to young people = *le rock exerce un attrait énorme sur les jeunes* ⓒ fascination = *←* 2/ *appel (m)* ☠ → call
to make an appeal = *faire appel.*

APPEAL (to, -ed) *faire appel :* the defense will appeal the sentence = *la défense fera appel du jugement*
to appeal to = 1/ *attirer :* this guy doesn't appeal to me = *ce type ne m'attire pas* ☠ → to attract 2/ *tenter :* the idea doesn't appeal to me = *l'idée ne me tente pas* ☠ *c'est bien tentant !* = it's really tempting !
to appeal to (s.o.'s generosity) = *faire appel à (la générosité de qqn).*

APPEALING (adj) *séduisant, -e :* what an appealing outfit ! = *quel ensemble séduisant !* ⓒ attractive = *attrayant.*

APPEAR (to, -ed) 1/ *paraître :* she appears happy = *elle paraît heureuse* ⓒ to seem = *sembler* 2/ *paraître :* his article will appear tomorrow = *son article paraîtra demain* 3/ *apparaître :* she appears in the third act = *elle apparaît au troisième acte*

to appear to be = *paraître* : she appears to be sad = *elle paraît triste*
it appears so = *à ce qu'il paraît* ⓪ it seems that = *il semble que*
it appears to me that (they're happy) = *il me semble qu'(ils sont heureux)*
to appear in (court) = *comparaître devant (un tribunal)*
☠ *son livre vient de paraître* = his book just came out.

APPEARANCE (n) **1/** *apparence* (f) : a sloppy appearance = *une apparence négligée*
appearances are deceiving = *les apparences sont trompeuses* ⓪ looks are deceiving = *il ne faut pas se fier aux apparences*
to keep up appearances = *sauver les apparences*
☠ *en apparence, c'est facile, mais ...* = it appears to be easy, but ...
2/ *apparition* (f) : his appearance at the dinner surprised everyone = *son apparition au dîner a surpris tout le monde*
to put in an appearance = *faire une apparition*
☠ *avoir des apparitions* = to see things.

APPEASE (to, -d) *apaiser* : there was no way to appease the child = *il n'y avait aucun moyen d'apaiser l'enfant* = to placate ≠ to aggravate = *agacer*
☠ *s'apaiser (tension)* = to die down/to abate
— *pour apaiser la douleur* = to soothe the pain.

APPENDICITIS (n) *appendicite* (f).

APPENDIX (n, -es or -ices) *appendice* (m).

APPETITE (n) *appétit* (m) ≠ diet = *régime*
to have a good appetite = *avoir bon appétit* ⓪ to eat like a horse = *manger comme quatre*
to spoil s.o.'s appetite = *couper l'appétit à qqn*
to whet s.o.'s appetite = *mettre l'eau à la bouche de qqn*
to work up an appetite = *aiguiser son appétit*
☠ *l'appétit vient en mangeant* = the more you have the more you want.

APPETIZER (n) *hors-d'œuvre* (m) ≠ dessert = ←.

APPETIZING (adj) *appétissant, -e* : an appetizing dish = *un plat appétissant* ⓪ mouth-watering = *alléchant*.

APPLAUD (to, -ed) *applaudir* : no one applauded = *personne n'a applaudi* ≠ to boo = *huer*.

APPLAUSE (n pl) *applaudissements* (m pl) ≠ boos = *huées*.

APPLE (n) *pomme* (f) ⓪ apple tree = *pommier*, apple sauce = *compote de pommes*
(she's) the apple of (his) eye = *(il) tient à (elle) comme à la prunelle de ses yeux*
☠ *pomme de terre* = potato
— *tomber dans les pommes* = to pass out
— *c'est toujours ma pomme qui encaisse* = it's always yours truly who gets the worst of it.

APPLECART (n) **to upset the applecart** = *tout ficher par terre* : the police upset the applecart = *la police a tout fichu par terre.*

APPLE-PIE (adj) **in apple-pie order** = *parfaitement en ordre* ≠ in a mess = *en pagaille*.

APPLIANCE (n) *appareil* (m) : household appliances = *appareils ménagers* ☠ → apparatus.

APPLICANT (n) *postulant, -e* : there were ten applicants for the job = *il y avait dix postulants pour ce poste* ⓪ candidate = *candidat*.

APPLICATION (n) *application* (f) : the application of the law = *l'application de la loi*
application form = *formulaire d'inscription* : fill in the application form = *remplissez le formulaire d'inscription* ⓪ request = *requête*
to put in an application (for a job) = *faire une demande (pour un poste)*
☠ *mettre en application* = to implement.

APPLY (to, -ied) *appliquer* : apply the cream twice a day = *appliquez la crème deux fois par jour*
to apply for (a job) = *postuler (un emploi)* ⓪ to solicit = *solliciter*
to apply to = 1/ *s'appliquer à* : the rule applies to everyone = *la règle s'applique à tout le monde* 2/ *faire une demande d'admission* : to apply to Yale = *faire une demande d'admission à Yale*
☠ *appliquer la loi* = to enforce the law.

APPOINT (to, -ed) *nommer* : the Secretary of State is appointed by the President = *le secrétaire d'État est nommé par le Président* ⓪ to designate = *désigner* ☠ → to name.

APPOINTEE (n) *représentant, -e désigné, -e* : the labor union appointee to the federal conference = *le représentant désigné du syndicat à la conférence fédérale*
presidential appointee = *chargé de mission nommé par le président*.

APPOINTMENT (n) **1/** *rendez-vous* (m), *rencart* (m) (LV) : I have an appointment at 5 p.m. = *j'ai un rendez-vous à cinq heures du soir* ⓪ engagement = ← ☠ *un rendez-vous galant* = a rendezvous
by appointment = *sur rendez-vous*
to make an appointment = *prendre rendez-vous*
2/ *nomination* (f) : his appointment as Secretary of State = *sa nomination au poste de secrétaire d'État* ☠ → nomination.

APPRAISAL (n) *appréciation* (f) : the experts' appraisal = *l'appréciation des experts* ⓪ estimate = *estimation*.

APPRAISE (to, -d) *estimer la valeur de* : to have a diamond ring appraised = *faire estimer la valeur d'une bague en diamant*.

APPRECIATE (to, -d) **1/** *apprécier* : I appreciate your help = *j'apprécie votre aide* ⓪ to prize = *attacher du prix à* **2/** *se rendre compte* : I appreciate the danger of such a situation = *je me rends compte du danger d'une telle situation* ⓪ to be aware of = *avoir conscience de.*

APPRECIATIVE (adj) *reconnaissant, -e* : thank you for helping me, I'm most appreciative = *merci de m'avoir aidé, je vous en suis très reconnaissant* = grateful ⓪ pleased = *ravi.*

APPREHENSION (n) *appréhension* (f) : the idea of seeing him again fills me with apprehension = *l'idée de le revoir me remplit d'appréhension* ⓪ dread = *épouvante.*

APPREHENSIVE (adj) **to be apprehensive about** = *appréhender de/que* : she's apprehensive about the abortion = *elle appréhende de se faire avorter* ⓪ to dread = *redouter.*

APPRENTICE (n) *apprenti, -e* : the sorcerer's apprentice = *l'apprenti sorcier* ⓪ novice = ← **APPRENTICE-SHIP** (n) *apprentissage* (m).

APPROACH (n, -es) *approche* (f) : a very novel approach to the problem = *une approche très originale de la question.*

APPROACH (to, -ed) *approcher* : the enemy's approaching = *l'ennemi approche* ≠ to draw back = *reculer*
☠ *il approche de (la cinquantaine)* = he's nearing (fifty)
— *nous approchons du but* = we're nearly there
— *approche (la chaise du lit)* = move (the chair) near (the bed).

APPROBATION (n) *approbation* (f) : congressional approbation = *l'approbation du Congrès.*

APPROPRIATE (adj) *approprié, -e* : appropriate clothing = *tenue appropriée* ⓪ fitting = *de mise* ≠ inappropriate = *pas approprié.*

APPROVAL (n) *approbation* (f) : to have s.o.'s approval = *avoir l'approbation de qqn* ≠ disapproval = *désapprobation.*

APPROVE (to, -d) *approuver* : the bill was approved by Congress = *le projet de loi a été approuvé par le Congrès* ⓪ to sanction = *sanctionner* ≠ to disapprove = *désapprouver*
to approve of = *approuver* : I approve of my daughter living with a guy = *j'approuve ma fille de vivre avec un garçon* ≠ to disapprove of = *désapprouver.*

APPROVINGLY (adv) *d'un air approbateur* : he looked at me approvingly = *il m'a regardé d'un air approbateur.*

APPROXIMATE (adj) *approximatif, -ive* : the approximate price = *le prix approximatif* ≠ precise = *précis* **APPROXIMATELY** (adv) *approximativement* ⓪ more or less = *plus ou moins,* roughly = *en gros* **APPROXIMATION** (n) *approximation* (f).

APRICOT (n) *abricot* (m) ⓪ peach = *pêche.*

APRIL (n) *avril* (m) → MONTH
April fool's joke = *poisson d'avril*
April showers = *giboulées de mars.*

APRON (n) *tablier* (m) de cuisine ⓪ dishtowel = *torchon*
to be tied to (one's mother's) apron strings = *être toujours pendu aux jupes/jupons de (sa mère)* ☠ *rendre son tablier* = to give notice.

APROPOS (adv) *à propos* : apropos, what are you doing tonight ? = *à propos, qu'est-ce que vous faites ce soir ?*

APTITUDE (n) *aptitude* (f) : aptitude test = *test d'aptitude* ⓪ gift = *don.*

AQUARIUM (n) *aquarium* (m) ⓪ gold fish = *poisson rouge.*

ARAB (n) *Arabe* (m, f) ⓪ camel jockey = *bicot/bougnoul* **ARABIC** (adj) *arabe.*

ARBITRARY (adj) *arbitraire* : an arbitrary decision = *une décision arbitraire* ≠ well-thought-out = *bien réfléchi.*

ARBITRATE (to, -d) *arbitrer.*

ARBITRATOR (n) *arbitre* (m) : the arbitrator of the conflict = *l'arbitre du conflit* ☠ *arbitre (sports)* = referee/umpire.

A.R.C. (abbr) = American Red Cross = *Croix rouge américaine.*

ARCHAEOLOGY (n) *archéologie* (f) **ARCHAEOLOGIST** (n) *archéologue* (m, f).

ARCHERY (n) *tir* (m) *à l'arc* ⓪ bow = *arc.*

ARCHITECT (n) *architecte* (m, f) ⓪ city planner = *urbaniste* **ARCHITECTURE** (n) *architecture* (f).

ARCHIVES (n pl) *archives* (f pl) ⓪ file = *dossier.*

ARDENT (adj) *ardent, -e* : an ardent defender = *un ardent défenseur* ≠ lukewarm = *tiède.*

ARDUOUS (adj) *ardu, -e* ⓪ hard = *dur.*

AREA (n) *quartier* (m) : it's a nice/business area = *c'est un beau quartier/un quartier d'affaires* ☠ → quarter
in the area = 1/ *dans le coin* : I know a nice restaurant in the area = *je connais un restaurant sympa dans le coin* ⓪ in these parts = *dans les parages* 2/ *aux alentours de* : it will cost in the area of $ 20 = *ça coûtera aux alentours de 20 dollars.*
in the (New York) area = *dans la région de (New York).*

ARENA (n) *arène* (f) ⓪ stadium = *stade.*

ARGENTINA (n) *Argentine* (f) **ARGENTINE** (n, adj) *Argentin, -e.*

ARGUABLY (adv) *on peut soutenir que ...* : the country could arguably defend itself = *on peut soutenir que le pays saurait se défendre.*

ARGUE (to, -d) **1/** *se disputer* : they're always arguing about money = *ils sont toujours en train de se disputer à propos d'argent* ⓪ to have it out = *s'engueuler* ☠ → to dispute
— *arguer que* = to put forward the reason that
2/ *soutenir* : he argued the American currency wasn't strong enough = *il a soutenu que la monnaie américaine n'était pas assez forte* ⓪ to assert = *affirmer* ☠ → to support.

ARGUMENT (n) **1/** *dispute* (f) : we had an argument about the kids = *nous avons eu une dispute au sujet des enfants* ⓪ quarrel = *querelle*, row = *altercation* ☠ → dispute
to pick an argument = *chercher la dispute* ⓪ to pick a fight = *chercher la bagarre*
2/ *argument* (m) : your argument is poor = *votre argument est faible* ⓪ reasoning = *raisonnement*.

ARGUMENTATIVE (adj) *discutailleur, -euse* : in an argumentative mood = *d'humeur discutailleuse* ⓪ quarrelsome = *querelleur*.

ARID (adj) *aride* : arid land = *terre aride* ⓪ barren = *stérile*.

ARISE (to, arose, arisen) *se présenter* : if problems arise = *si des problèmes se présentent* ⓪ to crop up = *survenir*
to arise from = *provenir de* : problems arise from misunderstanding = *les problèmes proviennent de l'incompréhension* ⓪ to spring from = *découler de* ☠ → to present.

ARISTOCRACY (n, -ies) *aristocratie* (f) ⓪ nobility = *noblesse* **ARISTOCRAT** (n) *aristocrate* (m, f) ≠ commoner = *roturier* **ARISTOCRATIC** (adj) *aristocratique*.

ARITHMETIC (n) *arithmétique* (f) ⓪ algebra = *algèbre*.

ARM (n) *bras* (m) : my arms ache = *mes bras me font mal* ⓪ armpit = *aisselle*, elbow = *coude*
arm in arm = *bras dessus, bras dessous*
it cost an arm and a leg = *ça a coûté les yeux de la tête* ≠ I got it for a song = *je l'ai eu pour une bouchée de pain*
to keep s.o. at arm's length = *tenir qqn à distance* : she keeps me at arm's length = *elle me tient à distance*
to twist s.o.'s arm = *tirer l'oreille à qqn* : I had to twist his arm to get him to come = *il a fallu lui tirer l'oreille pour le faire venir*
☠ *les bras m'en tombent !* = I'm flabbergasted !
— *tomber sur qqn à bras raccourcis* = to attack s.o. violently
— *avoir le bras long* = to have pull
— *ça m'est resté sur les bras* = I'm stuck with it
— *baisser les bras* = to give up
— *rester les bras croisés* = to do nothing.

ARM (to, -ed) *armer* : to arm a country = *armer un pays* ⓪ to wage war = *faire la guerre*
to arm o.s. with (patience/courage) = *s'armer de (patience/courage)*.

ARMCHAIR (n) *fauteuil* (m) ⓪ chair = *chaise* ☠ *gagner dans un fauteuil* = to win hands down.

ARMED (adj) *armé, -e* : armed cops = *des flics armés* ≠ unarmed = *non armé*
armed forces = *forces armées*
armed robbery = *attaque à main armée* ⓪ holdup = hold-up.

ARMISTICE (n) *armistice* (m) ⓪ truce = *trève*.

ARMOR (n) *armure* (f) = armour (GB).

ARMORED (adj) *blindé, -e* : an armored car = *une voiture blindée*
☠ *porte blindée* = reinforced door
— *je suis blindée (contre ses remarques)* = I'm immune (to his remarks).

ARMS (n pl) *armes* (f pl) : to sell arms = *vendre des armes* = weapons ⓪ ammunition = *munitions*
arms race = *course aux armements*
to be up in arms = **1/** *partir en guerre* : they're up in arms over the nuclear plant = *ils partent en guerre contre la centrale nucléaire* **2/** *être hors de soi* : she's up in arms because her daughter's taking the pill = *elle est hors d'elle parce que sa fille prend la pilule* → ANGRY
☠ *une arme* = a weapon
— *une arme à feu* = a gun
— *à armes égales* = on equal ground
— *passer l'arme à gauche* = to kick the bucket.

ARMY (n, -ies) *armée* (f) : he's in the army = *il est à l'armée* ⓪ soldier = *soldat*, armed forces = *forces armées*, infantry/cavalry troops = *troupes d'infanterie/de cavalerie*, regiment = *régiment*, division = ←, reserves = *la réserve*, Air Force = *Armée de l'air*, marines = ← Navy = *la Marine*.

AROUND (adv) *actuellement* : he's the best filmmaker around = *c'est le meilleur cinéaste actuellement*
áround here (somewhere) = *(quelque part) par là* : the restaurant's around here somewhere = *le restaurant est quelque part par là* ⓪ nearby = *tout près*
☠ for the use of "around" after a verb, see the verb.

AROUND (prep) *autour de* : the garden around the house = *le jardin autour de la maison*, it costs around ten dollars = *ça coûte autour de dix dollars*
to be around 40 = *avoir environ 40 ans* = to be about 40.

AROUSE (to, -d) *éveiller* : to arouse s.o.'s curiosity = *éveiller la curiosité de qqn* ⓪ to excite = *exciter*.

AROUSED (adj) **to be aroused** = *être excité* : he was aroused after all this petting = *il était excité après ce pelotage en règle* ⓪ hot and bothered = *tout chose*.

ARRAIGN (to, -ed) *appeler à comparaître* ⓪ to bring to court = *traduire en justice*.

ARRANGE (to, -d) *arranger* : everything's arranged = *tout est arrangé* ⓪ to settle = *régler*

to arrange to (meet s.o.) = *s'arranger pour (rencontrer qqn)*
☠ *ça m'arrange mieux* = that suits me better
— *arranger (une voiture)* = to fix (a car).

ARRANGEMENT (n) *arrangement* (m) : the arrangement is that each one takes the kids every other weekend = *selon l'arrangement qu'ils ont conclu, chacun prend les enfants un week-end sur deux*
to make arrangements = *prendre des dispositions.*

ARRAY (n) **an array of (lovers)** = *une collection d'(amants)* → MANY.

ARREST (n) *arrestation* (f) : a first arrest = *une première arrestation* ≠ release = *libération*
to be under arrest = *être en état d'arrestation* ⓪ to be in custody = *être en garde à vue.*

ARREST (to, -ed) *arrêter* : to arrest a burglar = *arrêter un cambrioleur* ⓪ to nail = *choper*, to apprehend = *appréhender* ≠ to release = *relâcher* ☠ → to stop.

ARRIVAL (n) *arrivée* (f) ≠ departure = *départ* ☠ *ligne d'arrivée* = finish line.

ARRIVE (to, -d) *arriver* : to arrive on time = *arriver à l'heure* ⓪ to show up = *se pointer* ≠ to go away = *s'en aller*
☠ *j'arrive !* = coming !
— *je n'arrive pas à (le faire)* = I can't manage to (do it)
— *il arrive parfois que (je me trompe)* = it sometimes happens that (I'm wrong)
— *comment l'accident est-il arrivé ?* = how did the accident come about ?

ARROGANCE (n) *arrogance* (f) : the arrogance of his attitude = *l'arrogance de son attitude.*

ARROGANT (adj) *arrogant, -e* : an arrogant attitude = *une attitude arrogante* ≠ humble = ←.

ARROW (n) *flèche* (f) ⓪ dart = *fléchette*
☠ *monter en flèche* = to soar
— *partir en flèche* = to get off to a good start.

ARSENAL (n) *arsenal* (m) ⓪ arms = *armes.*

ARSENIC (n) *arsenic* (m) ⓪ poison = ←.

ARSON (n) *incendie* (m) *criminel* **ARSONIST** (n) *incendiaire* (m, f).

ART (n) *art* (m) : to study art = *faire des études d'art*
arts and crafts = *artisanat*
art director = *directeur artistique*
art for art's sake = *l'art pour l'art*
to have the art of = *avoir l'art de* : she has the art of getting on my nerves = *elle a l'art de me taper sur les nerfs* ⓪ to have the knack of = *avoir le chic pour*
☠ *arts ménagers* = home economics
— *cours d'art dramatique* = drama class.

ARTERY (n, -ies) *artère* (f) ⓪ blood circulation = *circulation du sang.*

ARTFUL (adj) *plein, -e d'habileté* : an artful lawyer = *un avocat plein d'habileté* ⓪ shrewd = *habile.*

ARTHRITIS (n) *arthrite* (f) ⓪ rheumatism = *rhumatisme.*

ARTICHOKE (n) *artichaut* (m) : artichoke hearts = *des cœurs d'artichaut.*

ARTICLE (n) 1/ *article* (m) : newspaper article = *article de journal* ⓪ cutting = *coupure* 2/ *article* (m) : to sell all kinds of articles = *vendre toute sorte d'articles* = item ⓪ object = *objet*
☠ *faire l'article* = to hawk
— *à l'article de la mort* = at death's door.

ARTICULATE (to, -d) *articuler* : to articulate clearly = *articuler clairement* ⓪ to pronounce = *prononcer.*

ARTIFICE (n) *artifice* (m) : an artifice to make the others think he was innocent = *un artifice pour faire croire aux autres qu'il était innocent.*

ARTIFICIAL (adj) *artificiel, -elle* : artificial flower/respiration = *fleur/respiration artificielle* ≠ real = *véritable.*

ARTILLERY (n) *artillerie* (f) : heavy artillery = *artillerie lourde.*

ARTIST (n) *artiste* (m, f) : Degas was an artist = *Degas était un artiste* ⓪ painter = *peintre*, sculptor = *sculpteur.*

ARTISTIC (adj) *artistique* (stg), *artiste* (s.o.) : artistic talent = *talent artistique*, artistic children = *des enfants artistes.*

ARTY (adj, -ier, -iest) *genre artiste* : an arty apartment = *un appartement genre artiste* ⓪ bohemian = *bohème.*

AS (conj) 1/ *comme* : as it's very cold, we'll stay in = *comme il fait très froid, nous resterons à !a maison* ⓪ given that = *étant donné que* 2/ *comme* : she lent me the money as she promised = *elle m'a prêté l'argent comme promis* 3/ *tandis que* : I caught sight of him as I crossed the street = *je l'ai aperçu tandis que je traversais la rue* ⓪ while = *pendant que*

as for = *quant à* : as for me, I don't agree = *quant à moi, je ne suis pas d'accord*	**as ... go** = *pour ...* : as shrinks go, he isn't expensive = *pour un psy, il n'est pas cher*	**as we go along** = *au fur et à mesure* : we'll go into the details as we go along = *nous verrons les détails au fur et à mesure*

as if/as though = *comme si* : she talked as if/as though she were angry = *elle parlait comme si elle était en colère*

as is = *tel quel* : I'll take it as is = *je le prendrai tel quel*

as it is = *en fait* : they're not thinking of having kids, as it is they might even get divorced = *ils ne pensent pas avoir d'enfants, en fait il se pourrait même qu'ils divorcent*

as it goes = *... déjà assez ... :* they're not thinking of getting married, as it goes, they're having trouble living together = *ils n'envisagent pas de se marier, ils ont déjà assez de mal à vivre ensemble*

as it were = *en quelque sorte* : they're living together, as it were = *ils vivent ensemble en quelque sorte* ◯◯ so to speak = *pour ainsi dire*

as such = *en tant que tel* : it's not money as such that's important = *ce n'est pas l'argent en tant que tel qui est important* ◯◯ in itself = *en soi*

as you know (we're having problems) = *comme vous le savez (nous avons des problèmes)*

as you like = *comme vous voulez* ◯◯ as you see fit = *comme bon vous semble*

☠ *comme ça ?* = like this ?
— *comme (elle est jolie) !* = how (pretty she is) !
— *comme ci comme ça* = so-so

— *c'est comme ça* = that's the way it is
— *(riche) comme tout* = (rich) like anything.

AS (adv) *comme* : I like suspense, as in spy movies = *j'aime le suspense, comme dans les films d'espionnage* ◯◯ for example = *par exemple*

---

as ... as = 1/ *aussi ... que* : are they as rich as they say ? = *sont-ils aussi riches qu'ils le disent ?* 2/ *bien que* : as tired as I am, I want to go out = *bien que je sois fatigué, j'ai envie de sortir*

as ... as can be = *comme tout* : it's as easy as can be = *c'est facile comme tout* → VERY

as ... as they come = *comme tout* : she's as pretty as they come = *elle est jolie comme tout* → VERY

as of = *à partir de* : as of today I stop smoking = *à partir d'aujourd'hui j'arrête de fumer* = from ... on

as usual = *comme d'habitude* : I'm getting up early tomorrow as usual = *je me lève tôt demain*

comme d'habitude ≠ for a change = *pour changer*

as to = *quant à* : as to whether I can go with you or not, I can't say yet = *quant à savoir si je peux venir avec vous ou non, je ne peux pas encore le dire* ◯◯ regarding = *au sujet de*

as well = *également* : he speaks French and English as well = *il parle français et également anglais* ☠ → equally

not as ... as = 1/ *pas aussi ... que* : she isn't as interesting as her brother = *elle n'est pas aussi intéressante que son frère* 2/ *pas si ... que* : it's not as late as that = *il n'est pas si tard que ça.*

AS (prep) *en tant que* : she came as my lawer = *elle est venue en tant que mon avocate.*

AS (pron) *comme* : he's a foreigner, as is obvious from his accent = *c'est un étranger, comme en témoigne son accent.*

ASCENT (n) *ascension (f)* ≠ decline = *déclin.*

ASH (n, -es) *cendre (f)* ◯◯ ashtray = *cendrier.*

ASHAMED (adj) **to be ashamed of (one's past)** = *avoir honte de (son passé)*
you ought to be ashamed of yourself ! = *tu devrais avoir honte !*

ASHCAN (n) *boîte (f) à ordures* ◯◯ garbage can = *poubelle*

ASHORE (adv) **to go ashore** = *descendre à terre.*

ASHTRAY (n) *cendrier (m)* ◯◯ butt = *mégot.*

ASIA (n) Asie *(f)* ◯◯ Middle East = *Proche-Orient*, Far East = *Extrême-Orient* **ASIAN** (n, adj) *Asiatique (m, f).*

Afghanistan = ←
Bangladesh = ←
Burma = *Birmanie*
Cambodia =. *Cambodge*
China = *Chine*
Hong Kong = ←
India = *Inde*
Indonesia = *Indonésie*
Japan = *Japon*
Korea = *Corée*

Laos = ←
Malaysia = *Malaisie*
Mongolia = *Mongolie*
Nepal = *Népal*
Pakistan = ←
Sri Lanka = ←
Taiwan = ←
Thailand = *Thaïlande*
Vietnam = *Viêt-nam*

ASIDE FROM (prep) *mis à part* : aside from his sister he has no family = *mis à part sa sœur, il n'a pas de famille* ◯◯ outside of = *en dehors de.*

ASININE (adj) *tarte* : an asinine idea = *une idée tarte* → STUPID.

ASK (to, -ed) *demander* : I'm going to ask him = *je vais le lui demander* ⓪ to inquire = *s'enquérir* ≠ to answer = *répondre*
to ask a question = *poser une question*
if you ask me (he's a bastard) = *si tu me demandes mon avis (je pense que c'est un salaud)*
he asked to be remembered to (your wife) = *il transmet son bon souvenir à (votre femme)*
who asked you ? = *je ne t'ai pas sonné !/on ne t'a pas demandé l'heure !*

to ask about = *demander des nouvelles de* : he asked about you = *il a demandé de vos nouvelles*
to ask about stg = *demander qqch* : I'll ask about the price = *je vais demander le prix* ⓪ to inquire about = *s'enquérir de*
to ask around = *demander autour de soi* : I don't know of a vacant apartment in the area, but I'll ask around = *je n'ai pas entendu parler d'appartement libre dans le coin, mais je vais demander autour de moi*
you asked for it ! = *tu l'as cherché !* ⓪ you've made your bed, now lie in it !* = *comme on fait son lit, on se couche !*

to ask s.o. for stg = *demander qqch à qqn* : ask your mother for some money = *demande de l'argent à ta mère*
to ask s.o. out = *demander à qqn de sortir avec soi* : that gal's cute, I'll ask her out = *cette fille est mignonne, je vais lui demander de sortir avec moi*
to ask s.o. to = 1/ *demander à qqn de* : he asked me to do it = *il m'a demandé de le faire* 2/ *inviter qqn à* : he asked me to the party = *il m'a invitée à la soirée*

☮ *je me demande si* = I wonder whether
— *ça demande du temps/du tact* = it requires time/tact.

ASKANCE (adv) **to look askance at** = *regarder d'un œil désapprobateur* ⓪ to frown on = *voir d'un mauvais œil.*

ASKING (n) **it can be had for the asking** = *il suffit de le demander.*

ASLEEP (adj) *endormi, -e* : I was asleep when you called = *j'étais endormi quand vous avez téléphoné* ⓪ sleeping = *qui dort* ≠ awake = *réveillé*
to be asleep on the job = *s'endormir sur son travail* ≠ to work like a horse = *se tuer au travail*
to be fast/sound asleep = *dormir à poings fermés* ⓪ to sleep soundly = *dormir profondément*
to fall asleep = *s'endormir* : I fell asleep while reading = *je me suis endormi en lisant* ≠ to wake up = *se réveiller*
my (legs) fell asleep = *j'ai des fourmis dans (les jambes).*

ASPARAGUS (n inv) *asperge (f)* ⓪ artichoke = *artichaut* ☮ *c'est une (grande) asperge* = she's a beanpole.

A.S.P.C.A. (abbr) = American Society for the Prevention of Cruelty to Animals = *Société protectrice des animaux (S.P.A.)* ⓪ pound = *fourrière.*

ASPECT (n) *aspect (m)* : one aspect of the problem = *un aspect du problème* ⓪ angle = ←
☮ *je n'aime pas l'aspect de ce restaurant* = I don't like the looks of this restaurant.

ASPIRE (to, -d) **to aspire to (a law career)** = *aspirer à (une carrière juridique)* ⓪ to set one's heart on = *tenir beaucoup à.*

ASPIRIN (n) *aspirine (f)* ⓪ headache = *mal de tête.*

ASS (n, -es) 1/ *cul (m)* : he has a big ass = *il a un gros cul* = arse (GB) ⓪ asshole = *trou du cul*
to fall on one's ass = *se casser la gueule*
you can kiss my ass ! = *va te faire enculer !* → BUZZ OFF !
to lick s.o.'s ass = *lécher le cul de qqn* : he's always licking the boss's ass = *il est toujours en train de lécher le cul du patron* ⓪ to brownnose = *faire de la lèche,* asskisser = *lèche-cul*
my ass ! = *mon cul !* → BUZZ OFF !
not to know one's ass from a hole in the ground/from one's elbow = *être con comme la lune/comme un balai* → STUPID
☮ *j'en ai ras le cul !* = I fucking had it !
— *tomber sur le cul* = to be fucking surprised
— *avoir du cul* = to be fucking lucky
— *cul sec !* = bottoms up !
— *être comme cul et chemise* = to be as thick as thieves
— *parler de cul* = to talk sex
2/ *con, conne* : what an ass he/she is ! = *quel con !/quelle conne !* → STUPID ☮ → con
to make an ass of o.s. = *faire le con* ⓪ to make a fool of o.s. = *se ridiculiser*
to make an ass of s.o. = *se foutre de la gueule de qqn*
3/ *âne, ânesse* = donkey
☮ *faire l'âne pour avoir du son* = to play dumb
— *on ne fait pas boire un âne qui n'a pas soif* = you can lead a horse to water, but you can't make him drink
— *bonnet d'âne* = dunce cap
— *têtu comme un âne* = stubborn as a mule.

ASSAIL (to, -ed) *assaillir* ⓪ to besiege = *assiéger*
to assail s.o. with (questions) = *assaillir qqn de (questions)*
☮ *être assailli de doutes* = to be riddled with doubts.

ASSASSIN (n) *assassin (m)* ⓪ murderer = *meurtrier*
ASSASSINATE (to, -d) *assassiner* : to assassinate a president = *assassiner un président* ⓪ to kill = *tuer* **ASSASSINATION** (n) *assassinat (m)* ⓪ murder = *meurtre.*

ASSAULT (n) *assaut (m)* ⓪ attack = *attaque*
assault and battery = *coups et blessures/voie de fait*
☮ *prendre d'assaut* = to take by storm

— *troupes d'assaut* = storm troops
— *char d'assaut* = tank.

ASSEMBLE (to, -d) *(s')assembler* : to assemble a crowd = *assembler une foule* ⑩ to gather = *rassembler*.

ASSEMBLY (n, -ies) *assemblée* (f) : an assembly of diplomats = *une assemblée de diplomates* ⑩ gathering = *réunion*
assembly line = *chaîne de montage* : to work on an assembly line = *travailler à la chaîne* ⑩ the daily grind = *métro, boulot, dodo*.

ASSERT (to, -ed) *soutenir* : the Senator asserted that nuclear plants weren't dangerous = *le sénateur a soutenu que les centrales nucléaires n'étaient pas dangereuses* ⑩ to affirm = *affirmer* ☠ ⇥ to support
to assert oneself = *s'affirmer* : he's always been too shy to assert himself = *il a toujours été trop timide pour s'affirmer* ☠ → to affirm.

ASSERTIVE (adj) *affirmé, -e* : an assertive personality = *une personnalité affirmée* ≠ timid = *timide*.

ASSESS (to, -ed) *estimer* : to assess the damages = *estimer le montant des dégâts* ⑩ to appraise = *apprécier* ☠ → to estimate.

ASSET (n) **1/** *atout* (m) : her intelligence is her chief asset = *son intelligence est son atout majeur* ☠ *atout (cartes)* = trump (cards) **2/** *actif* (m) : the principal asset of the company = *le principal actif de la société*
assets and liabilities = *l'actif et le passif*
☠ *c'est à son actif* = it's to his credit.

ASSHOLE (n) **1/** *trou* (m) *du cul* ⑩ anus = ← **2/** *connard, connasse* : that guy's a real asshole = *ce type-là est un vrai connard* → STUPID.

ASSIGN (to, -ed) **to be assigned to (night work)** = *être affecté au (travail de nuit)*.

ASSIMILATE (to, -d) *assimiler* : the country assimilated many immigrants = *le pays a assimilé beaucoup d'immigrants*, to assimilate new theories = *assimiler de nouvelles théories*.

ASSIST (to, -ed) *assister* : the head surgeon was assisted by two other doctors = *le chirurgien en chef était assisté de deux autres médecins* ⑩ to aid = *venir en aide à* ☠ *assister à un cours* = to attend/to sit in on a course.

ASSISTANCE (n) *assistance* (f) : to give assistance = *prêter assistance* ⑩ aid = *aide*
☠ *assistance sociale* = social work
— *assistance juridique* = legal aid
— *assistance publique* = welfare
— *l'assistance (le public)* = the audience.

ASSISTANT (n) *assistant, -e* : she's my assistant = *c'est mon assistante* ⑩ deputy = *adjoint*, right arm = *bras droit*.

ASSOCIATE (n) *associé, -e* ⑩ colleague = *collègue*.

ASSOCIATE (to, -d) *associer* : she associates fireworks

and war = *elle associe les feux d'artifice et la guerre* ⑩ to connect = *faire le rapprochement entre*
to associate with = *fréquenter* : he associates only with rich people = *il ne fréquente que des gens riches* ⑩ to hobnob with = *côtoyer* ☠ → to frequent
☠ *les deux États se sont associés* = the two States linked up

ASSOCIATION (n) *association* (f) ⑩ alliance = ←, league = *ligue*.

ASSORTED (adj) *un assortiment de* : assorted chocolates/fruit = *un assortiment de chocolats/de fruits* ⑩ various = *divers*.

ASSORTMENT (n) *assortiment* (m) (food), *choix* (m) : an assortment of chocolates = *un assortiment de chocolats*, an assortment of sweaters = *un choix de pulls* = choice ⑩ selection = *sélection*.

ASSUME (to, -d) *présumer* : I assume he'll agree = *je présume qu'il sera d'accord* ⑩ to presume ⑩ to suppose = *supposer*
assuming that (she'll agree) = *à supposer qu'(elle soit d'accord)*
let's assume that (I'm right) = *mettons que (j'aie raison)*
that's assuming a lot = *c'est beaucoup présumer*
☠ *il faut qu'elle s'assume* = she has to get it together
— *je ne peux pas assumer ses problèmes* = I can't deal with/handle/carry his problems
— *présumer* → to presume.

ASSUMPTION (n) *supposition* (f) : a false assumption = *une supposition fausse* = a false supposition
my assumption is that (they're going to get married) = *je suppose qu'(ils vont se marier)*
I'm going on the assumption that (she'll agree) = *je pars du principe qu'(elle sera d'accord)*.

ASSURANCE (n) **1/** *assurance* (f) : she lacks assurance = *elle manque d'assurance* ⑩ self-confidence = *confiance en soi* **2/** *assurance* (f) : I can give you no assurance that he'll help us = *je ne peux pas vous donner l'assurance qu'il va nous aider* ⑩ guarantee = *garantie*
☠ *prendre une assurance* = to take out insurance.

ASSURE (to, -d) **1/** *assurer* : I assure you he'll come = *je vous assure qu'il viendra* ⑩ to certify = *certifier* **2/** (GB) *assurer* = to insure
☠ *cela va assurer la victoire* = that will ensure victory
— *assurer son avenir* = to secure one's future
— *s'assurer que* = to make sure that.

ASTHMA (n) *asthme* (m) ⑩ allergy = *allergie*, fit = *crise*.

ASTONISH (to, -ed) *étonner* : his arrogance astonished me = *son arrogance m'a étonné* ⑩ to amaze = *stupéfier*
☠ *ça ne m'étonne pas* = it doesn't surprise me.

ASTONISHING (adj) *étonnant, -e* : an astonishing actress = *une actrice étonnante* → WONDERFUL.

ASTONISHMENT (n) *étonnement (m)* ↀ amazement = *stupéfaction.*

ASTOUND (to, -ed) *époustoufler :* his performance astounded me = *sa performance m'a époustouflé* ↀ to stupefy = *stupéfier* **ASTOUNDED** (adj) *époustouflé, -e* ↀ floored = *interdit* **ASTOUNDING** (adj) *époustouflant, -e :* an astounding performance = *une performance époustouflante* → WONDERFUL.

ASTRAY (adv) **to go astray** = *sortir du droit chemin :* all her kids went astray = *tous ses enfants sont sortis du droit chemin* ↀ to go wrong = *mal tourner*
to lead astray = *induire en erreur :* his reply led the inspector astray = *sa réponse a induit l'inspecteur en erreur.*

ASTROLOGY (n) *astrologie (f)* ↀ astrologer = *astrologue.*

ASTRONAUT (n) *astronaute (m, f)* ↀ spaceman = *cosmonaute,* spaceship = *vaisseau spatial.*

ASTRONOMER (n) *astronome (m, f)* **ASTRONOMY** (n) *astronomie (f).*

ASTUTE (adj) *astucieux, -euse :* an astute businessman = *un homme d'affaires astucieux* ↀ clever = *malin.*

ASYLUM (n) **1/** *asile (m)* ↀ refuge = ←
to seek asylum = *demander asile*
2/ *asile (m)* ↀ crazy house = *maison de fous.*

AT (prep) *à (au, à la) :* I was at the party also = *j'étais aussi à la soirée*

at all = *un tant soit peu :* was the movie interesting at all? = *est-ce que le film était un tant soit peu intéressant ?* ≠ not at all = *pas du tout*
at best ≠ **at worst** = *au mieux* ≠ *au pire*
at first = *d'abord*
at last = *enfin* ↀ finally = *finalement*
at least (ten dollars) = *au moins (dix dollars)*
at 6 o'clock/midnight = *à 6 heures/à minuit*
ↀ right away = *séance tenante* 2/ *à la fois :* I can't do two things at once = *je ne peux pas faire deux choses à la fois* ↀ simultaneously = *simultanément*
at the beauty parlor/doctor's = *chez le coiffeur/le docteur*
at home = *à la maison/chez soi*
at the office = *au bureau*
at s.o.'s. place = *chez qqn*
at war = *en guerre*
good ≠ **bad at (math)** = *bon* ≠ *mauvais en (maths)*
at once = 1/ *tout de suite :* do it at once = *faites-le tout de suite*

☠ for the use of "at" after a verb, see the verb — *à* → to.

ATHEIST (n) *athée (m, f)* ≠ agnostic = *agnostique,* believer = *croyant.*

ATHLETE (n) *athlète (m, f)* ↀ sportsman = *sportif.*

ATHLETIC (adj) **1/** *athlétique :* an athletic body = *un corps athlétique* **2/** *sportif, -ive :* my family's very athletic = *ma famille est très sportive* ☠ *journal sportif* = sports magazine.

ATHLETICS (n pl) *sport (m) :* she does a lot of athletics = *elle fait beaucoup de sport* ↀ track and field = *athlétisme* ☠ → sport.

ATMOSPHERE (n) **1/** *atmosphère (f) :* the atmosphere is polluted = *l'atmosphère est polluée* ☠ *détendre l'atmosphère* = to clear the air **2/** *ambiance (f) :* a good atmosphere at the party = *une bonne ambiance à la soirée.*

ATOM (n) *atome (m)* ↀ neutron = ←, electron = *électron* ☠ *avoir des atomes crochus avec qqn* = to click with s.o.

ATOMIC (adj) *atomique :* atomic bomb = *bombe atomique* = A-bomb.

ATONE FOR (to, -d) *racheter :* to atone for one's sins = *racheter ses péchés* ☠ → to make up for.

ATROCIOUS (adj) *atroce :* atrocious weather = *un temps atroce* → AWFUL ≠ wonderful = *merveilleux* ☠ *une douleur atroce* = an excruciating pain **ATROCITY** (n, -ies) *atrocité (f).*

ATTACH (to, -ed) **1/** *attacher :* they attached the prisoner's hands = *ils ont attaché les mains du prisonnier* ≠ to detach = *détacher*
to be attached to (one's parents) = *être attaché à (ses parents)* ↀ to be close to = *être proche de*
to attach value/importance to stg = *attacher de la valeur/de l'importance à qqch* ↀ to attribute to = *attribuer à*
☠ *s'attacher à des détails* = to dwell on details
— *attache ma robe* = fasten my dress
2/ *saisir :* they had to attach his salary to get what he owed = *ils ont dû saisir son salaire pour récupérer ce qu'il devait* ☠ → to seize.

ATTACHÉ CASE (n) *porte-documents (m), attaché-case (m)* ↀ briefcase = *serviette.*

ATTACK (n) **1/** *attaque (f) :* to prepare an attack = *préparer une attaque* ↀ offensive = ←, counterattack = *contre-attaque*
to be under attack = *être en butte aux attaques :* the budget's under attack = *le budget est en butte aux attaques*
2/ *attaque (f) :* a heart attack = *une attaque/une crise cardiaque* ↀ fit = *crise*
☠ *être d'attaque* = to feel one's oats.

ATTACK (to, -ed) **1/** *attaquer :* terrorists attacked the embassy = *des terroristes ont attaqué l'ambassade* ↀ to assail = *assaillir* ≠ to defend = *défendre* **2/** *s'attaquer* à : to attack a job = *s'attaquer à un travail* ⓪ to undertake = *entreprendre.*

ATTAIN (to, -ed) *parvenir à* : to attain one's goal = *parvenir à son but* ⓪ to achieve = *réaliser.*

ATTEMPT (n) *tentative (f)* ⓪ try = *essai.*

ATTEMPT TO (to, -ed) *tenter de* : he attempted to kill himself = *il a tenté de se tuer* ⓪ to try to = *essayer de.*

ATTEND (to, -ed) **1/** *assister à* : to attend a lecture = *assister à une conférence* **2/** *aller à* : to attend school = *aller à l'école* = to go to school
to attend to = *s'occuper de* : he'll attend to it next week = *il s'en occupera la semaine prochaine.*

ATTENTION (n) *attention (f)* : a lack of attention = *un manque d'attention*
attention ! = *garde-à-vous !*
to bring/call/draw attention to = *attirer l'attention sur*
to pay attention to = *prêter attention à* : they paid no attention to his remarks = *ils n'ont prêté aucune attention à ses remarques* ≠ to ignore = *passer outre à*
to stand at attention = *se mettre au garde-à-vous*
☠ *faire qqch avec attention* = to do stg with care
— *attention !* = watch out !

ATTENTIVE (adj) **1/** *attentif, -ive* : the class isn't very attentive today = *la classe n'est pas très attentive aujourd'hui* ≠ inattentive = *inattentif* ☠ *un conducteur attentif* = a careful driver **2/** *attentionné, -e* : an attentive husband = *un mari attentionné* ⓪ considerate = *prévenant.*

ATTENUATE (to, -d) *atténuer* ≠ to emphasize = *souligner.*

ATTEST TO (to, -ed) *témoigner de* : I can attest to his cruelty = *je peux témoigner de sa cruauté.*

ATTIC (n) *grenier (m)* ⓪ garret = *mansarde.*

ATTIRE (n) *tenue (f)* : extravagant attire = *tenue extravagante* ⓪ garb = *mise*
☠ *un peu de tenue !* = mind your manners !
— *tenue de soirée* = evening dress.

ATTITUDE (n) *attitude (f)* : an aggressive attitude = *une attitude agressive* ⓪ position = ←.

ATTORNEY (n) *avocat, -e* = lawyer ⓪ attorney-at-law = *avoué*
Attorney General = *ministre de la Justice/garde des Sceaux.*

ATTRACT (to, -ed) *attirer* : she attracts men = *elle attire les hommes* ≠ to repel = *repousser*
to be attracted to s.o. = *être attiré par qqn* : I'm attracted to tall men = *je suis attirée par les hommes grands* ≠ tall men don't appeal to me = *les hommes grands ne m'attirent pas*, to be turned off by = *être refroidi par*
☠ *s'attirer des ennuis* = to get into trouble

— *j'attire votre attention sur* = I call your attention to
— *ce comique attire les foules* = this comic draws crowds
— *l'idée ne m'attire pas* = the idea doesn't appeal to me.

ATTRACTION (n) **1/** *attraction (f)* : the show's main attraction = *l'attraction principale du spectacle* ⓪ number = *numéro* ☠ *parc d'attractions* = amusement park **2/** *attrait (m)* : power has a great attraction for him = *le pouvoir a beaucoup d'attrait pour lui.*

ATTRACTIVE (adj) *attrayant, -e (stg), attractif, -ive (stg), attirant, -e (s.o.)* : an attractive girl = *une fille attirante*, an attractive job = *un travail attrayant/attractif* ⓪ captivating = *captivant* ≠ unattractive = *peu attrayant/attirant.*

ATTRIBUTE TO (to, -d) *attribuer à* : he attributes his success to hard work = *il attribue son succès à un travail acharné* ⓪ to ascribe = *imputer* ☠ *on lui a attribué dix minutes de temps de parole* = he was allotted ten minutes to speak.

AUCTION (n) *vente (f) aux enchères* ⓪ the highest bidder = *le plus offrant* **AUCTION** (to, -ed) *vendre aux enchères.*

AUDACIOUS (adj) *audacieux, -euse* : an audacious idea = *une idée audacieuse* ⓪ bold = *hardi* **AUDACITY** (n, -ies) *audace (f).*

AUDIBLE (adj) *audible* : barely audible = *à peine audible.*

AUDIENCE (n) **1/** *audience (f)* : an audience with the President = *une audience avec le Président* ⓪ meeting = *entretien* ☠ *une audience (cour de justice)* = a hearing **2/** *auditoire (m), assistance (f)* : a large audience = *un large auditoire/une assistance nombreuse* ⓪ public = ← ☠ *assistance* → assistance.

AUDIOVISUAL (adj) *audiovisuel, -elle* : the audiovisual media = *les médias audiovisuels, l'audiovisuel.*

AUDITION (n) *audition (f)* : auditions will be held on Friday = *les auditions auront lieu vendredi* ☠ *audition des témoins* = hearing of witnesses
— *troubles de l'audition* = hearing problems.

AUDITION (to, -ed) *auditionner* : he's auditioning for the part = *il auditionne pour le rôle* ⓪ to try out = *passer une audition.*

AUDITORIUM (n) *auditorium (m)* ⓪ concert hall = *salle de concert.*

AUGMENT (to, -ed) *augmenter* : he's working overtime to augment his salary = *il fait des heures supplémentaires pour augmenter son salaire* ≠ to decrease = *diminuer*
☠ *je vais vous augmenter* = I'm going to give you a raise
— *augmenter (prix)* = to increase (prices).

AUGUST (n) *août (m)* → MONTH.

AUNT (n) *tante* (f) ⓓ auntie = *tata*
if my aunt had balls she'd be my uncle = *si ma tante en avait, elle s'appellerait mon oncle*
☠ *une tante (homosexuel)* = a pansy/fairy.

AUSTERE (adj) *austère* : austere living conditions = *des conditions de vie austères* ≠ frivolous = *frivole*.

AUSTRALIA (n) *Australie* (f) = Down Under **AUSTRALIAN** (n, adj) *Australien, -enne* = Aussie (LV).

AUSTRIA (n) *Autriche* (f) **AUSTRIAN** (n, adj) *Autrichien, -enne*.

AUTHENTIC (adj) *authentique* : authentic documents = *des documents authentiques* ⓓ true = *vrai* ≠ fake = *bidon*.

AUTHOR (n) *auteur* (m) **AUTHORESS** (n) *femme* (f) *auteur*
☠ *auteur dramatique* = playwright.

AUTHORITARIAN (adj) *autoritaire* : authoritarian parents = *des parents autoritaires* ⓓ tyrannical = *tyrannique*.

AUTHORITATIVE (adj) *qui fait autorité* : an authoritative report = *un rapport qui fait autorité*.

AUTHORITY (n, -ies) 1/ *autorité* (f) : parental authority = *autorité parentale* 2/ *autorité* (f) : he's an authority on art = *c'est une autorité en matière d'art*
public authorities = *les autorités*.

AUTHORIZATION (n) *autorisation* (f) ⓓ permission = ←. ≠ prohibition = ←.

AUTHORIZE (to, -d) *autoriser* : he was authorized to take the documents with him = *on l'a autorisé à emporter les documents* ⓓ to give the green light = *donner le feu vert*.
☠ *je ne me crois pas autorisé à ...* = I don't believe I'm entitled to ...
— *je ne suis pas autorisé à recevoir mes copains chez moi* = I'm not allowed to entertain my pals in my house.

AUTOBIOGRAPHY (n, -ies) *autobiographie* (f) ⓓ diary = *journal intime*.

AUTOGRAPH (n) *autographe* (m) ⓓ signature = ←.

AUTOMATIC (adj) *automatique* : automatic rifle/reaction = *fusil/réaction automatique* **AUTOMATICALLY** (adv) *automatiquement*.

AUTOMOBILE (n) *automobile* (f) ⓓ car = *voiture*.

AUTONOMOUS (adj) *autonome* : an autonomous country = *un pays autonome* ≠ dependent = *dépendant*.

AUTONOMY (n) *autonomie* (f) : the autonomy of a country = *l'autonomie d'un pays*.

AUTOPSY (n, -ies) *autopsie* (f) ⓓ morgue = ←.

AUTUMN (n) *automne* (m) = fall ⓓ Indian summer = *été indien* → SEASON.

AUXILIARY (adj) *auxiliaire* : auxiliary troops = *troupes auxiliaires*.

AVAIL (n) **to no avail** = *sans résultat* : our efforts were to no avail = *nos efforts sont restés sans résultat* ⓓ vain = ←.

AVAILABLE (adj) *disponible* : the new model won't be available till this fall = *le nouveau modèle ne sera pas disponible avant cet automne*.

AVALANCHE (n) *avalanche* (f) ⓓ earthquake = *tremblement de terre*.

AVENGE (to, -d) *venger* : to avenge a murder = *venger un meurtre* ☠ → to revenge.

AVENUE (n) *avenue* (f) ⓓ street = *rue*.

AVERAGE (n) *moyenne* (f) : an average of 100 people a night at the show = *une moyenne de 100 personnes par soirée au spectacle*
on the average = *en moyenne* : he smokes one pack of cigarettes a day on the average = *il fume en moyenne un paquet de cigarettes par jour*
above average = *au-dessus de la moyenne* : his intelligence is above average = *son intelligence est au-dessus de la moyenne*.

AVERAGE (adj) 1/ *moyen, -enne* : of average size = *de taille moyenne* ≠ exceptional = *exceptionnel* 2/ *moyen, -enne* : the film was average = *le film était moyen* → AWFUL
☠ *niveau moyen* = intermediate level
— *une entreprise moyenne* = a medium-sized company
— *les classes moyennes* = the middle class
— *le Moyen Âge* = Middle Ages.

AVERSION (n) *aversion* (f) : she has an aversion to sex = *elle a de l'aversion pour le sexe* ≠ taste = *goût*.

AVERT (to, -ed) *éviter* : to avert further problems = *éviter d'autres problèmes* ☠ → to avoid.

AVIATION (n) *aviation* (f) **AVIATOR** (n) *aviateur, -trice*.

AVID (adj) *fervent, -e* : an avid fan = *un fan fervent*.

AVOCADO (n, -es) *avocat* (m) : an avocado with shrimp sauce = *un avocat avec une sauce crevette* ☠ → lawyer.

AVOID (to, -ed) *éviter* : to avoid the question = *éviter la question* ⓓ to evade = *se dérober à*, to elude = *éluder*
☠ *éviter (des tracas) à qqn* = to spare s.o. (trouble)
— *éviter une voiture* = to avert a car.

AVOWED (adj) *juré, -e* : my avowed enemy = *mon ennemi juré*.

AWAIT (to, -ed) *attendre* : a marvelous dinner awaited them = *un dîner merveilleux les attendait* ☠ → to expect.

AWAKE (to, awoke, awoken or awaked) *(se) réveiller* : the letter awoke old memories = *la lettre a réveillé de vieux souvenirs* → TO WAKE.

AWAKE (adj) *réveillé, -e* : he isn't awake yet = *il n'est pas encore réveillé* ≠ sleeping = *en train de dormir*
to keep s.o. awake = *empêcher qqn de dormir* : the storm kept me awake all night = *la tempête m'a empêché de dormir toute la nuit.*

AWAKEN (to, -ed) *réveiller* : awakened by the noise = *réveillé par le bruit* → TO WAKE.

AWAKENING (n) *révélation (f)* : a sexual awakening = *une révélation sexuelle* ☠ → revelation.

AWARD (n) *récompense (f)* : to give out awards = *distribuer des récompenses* ⓧ prize = *prix* ☠ → reward.

AWARE (adj) *averti, -e* : an aware audience = *un public averti*
to be aware of = *être conscient de* : are you aware of the difficulty ? = *êtes-vous conscient de la difficulté ?* ≠ to be unaware of = *être inconscient de* = not to be aware of
to become aware of = *prendre conscience de.*

AWARENESS (n) *(prise (f) de) conscience (f)* : no awareness of what's going wrong in their couple = *aucune conscience de ce qui ne va pas dans leur couple.*

AWAY (adv) *pas là* : sorry, she's away for the moment = *désolé, elle n'est pas là pour l'instant*
(five miles) away = *à (huit kilomètres)*
☠ for the use of "away" after a verb, see the verb.

AWE (n) **in awe of** = *bouche bée devant* : he's in awe of his wife's accomplishments = *il est bouche bée devant les exploits de sa femme* ⓧ impressed with = *impressionné par.*

AWED (adj) **awed by (the beauty of the place)** = *impressionné par (la beauté de l'endroit)* ⓧ dazzled by = *ébloui par.*

AWESOME (adj) *impressionnant, -e* : an awesome amount of money = *une somme d'argent impressionnante* ⓧ mind-blowing = *renversant* ☠ → impressive.

AWFUL (adj) *affreux, -euse* : the movie was awful = *le film était affreux* ≠ wonderful = *merveilleux*

an awful lot of (money/problems) = *énormément d'(argent)/de (problèmes)* → MANY

I feel awful about (what I said) = *je suis navré d'(avoir dit ça)* ⓧ I feel sorry about = *je suis désolé de*

GROUP : AWFUL = AFFREUX

abominable = ←
all right = *moyen*
atrocious = *atroce*
average = *moyen*
bad = *mauvais*
bad news = *qui ne casse rien*
blah = *fadasse*
commonplace = *quelconque*
crappy = *merdique*
crummy = *moche*
deplorable = *déplorable*
disappointing = *décevant*
disgusting = *dégoûtant*
dreadful = *épouvantable*
fair = *pas terrible*
for the birds = *qui ne vaut rien*
foul = *infect*
frightful = *effroyable*
ghastly = *effroyable*
horrendous = *épouvantable*
horrible = ←
horrid = *atroce*
intolerable = *intolérable*

lamentable = ←
a loser = *un zéro*
lousy = *dégueulasse*
mediocre = *médiocre*
miserable = *abominable*
nauseating = *écœurant*
no big deal = *pas fameux*
no great shakes = *qui ne casse pas des briques*
no great thing = *qui ne vaut pas grand-chose*
nothing much = *pas grand-chose*
nothing in particular = *assez banal*
nothing to speak of = *pas terrible*
nothing special = *pas terrible*
nothing to write home about = *qui ne casse rien*
not much of anything = *qui ne vaut rien*
not so hot = *pas terrible*
ordinary = *ordinaire*

passable = ←
pathetic = *minable*
pedestrian = *plat*
pitiful = *pitoyable*
it's the pits = *c'est pas le pied*
repelling = *repoussant*
repulsive = *répugnant*
revolting = *révoltant*
rotten = *très moche*
run-of-the-mill = *très quelconque*
shitty = *merdique*
it smells = *c'est dégueu*
so-so = *comme ci, comme ça*
it stinks = *c'est chiant*
strictly from hunger = *une catastrophe*
it sucks = *c'est à chier*
terrible = *affreux*
vile = *infect*
it's a waste of time = *c'est une perte de temps*
wretched = *sale.*

AWFULLY (adv) *drôlement* : they're awfully rich/affected = *ils sont drôlement riches/affectés* ≠ not at all = *pas du tout* → VERY.

AWHILE (adv) *un moment* : why don't you stay awhile ? = *pourquoi ne restez-vous pas un moment ?* ⓧ for a bit = *un peu.*

AWKWARD (adj) *maladroit, -e* : an awkward answer = *une réponse maladroite* ⓐ clumsy = *gauche*
the awkward age = *l'âge ingrat*
an awkward time/silence/arrangement = *un moment/un silence/un arrangement un peu bizarre.*

AWOL (adj) = Absent Without Leave = *parti, -e sans permission* : 5 AWOL privates were found killed = *5 soldats partis sans permission ont été trouvés morts* ⓐ deserter = *déserteur.*

AWRY (adv) **to go awry** = *mal tourner :* their plans went awry = *leurs projets ont mal tourné* ⓐ to go amiss = *aller de travers.*

AX(E) (n) *hache (f)* ⓐ hatchet = *hachette*
to give s.o. the axe = *donner ses huit jours à qqn* ⓐ to oust = *vider*
to have an axe to grind = *avoir un compte à régler* ⓐ to settle scores = *régler ses comptes*
☠ *enterrer la hache de guerre* = to bury the hatchet.

BA (n) = Bachelor of Arts = *licence (f) (de lettres)* : I have a BA in English = *j'ai une licence d'anglais* ⓓ BS = *licence de sciences*, MA = *maîtrise*, PhD = *doctorat* ☠ → license.

BABE (n) *beauté (f)* : hi babe ! = *salut, beauté !* ⓓ kitten = *mon minou* ☠ → beauty
a babe in the woods = *une oie blanche* ⓓ she's wet behind the ears = *on lui pincerait le nez, il en sortirait du lait.*

BABY (n, -ies) **1/** *bébé (m)* ⓓ infant = *petit enfant*, bottle = *biberon*, diaper = *couche*, to nurse = *allaiter*, baby carriage = *landau* = pram (GB), cradle = *berceau*, playpen = *parc*, babyteeth = *dents de lait*
to cry like a baby = *pleurer à chaudes larmes* ⓓ to cry bitterly = *pleurer comme une Madeleine*

2/ *mon joli, ma jolie* : what do you want baby ? = *qu'est-ce que tu veux ma jolie ?* ⓓ sugar = *mon petit.*

BABY (to, -ied) *couver* : she babies her son too much = *elle couve trop son fils* ⓓ to mother = *materner* ☠ *couver qqn des yeux/du regard* = to eat s.o. up with one's eyes
— *couver une maladie* = to feel an illness coming on.

BABY-SIT (to, -ted) *faire du baby-sitting* **BABY-SITTER** (n) *baby-sitter (m, f)* **BABY-SITTING** (n) *baby-sitting (m)* ⓓ nanny = *gouvernante.*

BACHELOR (n) *célibataire (m) (homme)* : my brother's a bachelor = *mon frère est célibataire* ≠ a single woman = *une célibataire*
a confirmed bachelor = *un célibataire endurci.*

BACK (n) **1/** *dos (m)* : a straight back = *un dos droit* ⓓ backache = *mal de dos*, small of the back = *chute des reins*

to arch one's back = *faire le dos rond* : the cat arches its back = *le chat fait le dos rond* **to be on s.o.'s back** = *être sur le dos de qqn* **to break one's back** = *s'échiner* : he broke his back trying to finish his work on time = *il s'est échiné à essayer de finir son travail en temps voulu* ⓓ to take pains = *se donner de la peine* **to do stg behind s.o.'s back** = *faire qqch dans/derrière le dos de qqn* **get off my back !** = *fichez-moi la paix !* → BUZZ OFF !	**to get one's back up** = *se hérisser* → ANGRY **to know stg like the back of one's hand** = *connaître qqch comme sa poche* : I know Paris like the back of my hand = *je connais Paris comme ma poche* ⓓ to know stg inside out = *connaître qqch parfaitement* **to pat o.s. on the back** = *se féliciter de* : he patted himself on the back for picking up the prettiest girl = *il se félicitait d'avoir soulevé la plus jolie fille* ⓓ to sing one's own praises = *chanter ses propres louanges*	**to stab s.o. in the back** = *poignarder qqn dans le dos* **to talk about s.o. behind his back** = *casser du sucre sur le dos de qqn* ⓓ to speak ill of s.o. = *dire du mal de qqn* **to turn one's back on s.o.** = *tourner le dos à qqn* **with one's back to the wall** = *au pied du mur* **you scratch my back and I'll scratch yours** = *passe-moi la rhubarbe et je te passerai le séné* ⓓ one good turn deserves another = *c'est un échange de bons procédés*

☠ *ne rien avoir à se mettre sur le dos* = to have nothing to wear — *se mettre qqn à dos* = to antagonize s.o. — *ne pas y aller avec le dos de la cuiller* = not to	pull punches — *mettre qqch sur le dos de qqn* = to lay stg on s.o. — *tomber sur le dos de qqn* = to lace into s.o.

2/ arrière *(m)* : in the back of the car = *à l'arrière de la voiture* = in the rear of the car ☠ *assurer ses arrières* = to secure one's future
what's in the back of your mind ? = *qu'est-ce que tu as derrière la tête ?*
3/ verso *(m)* : write on the back = *écrivez au verso* ≠ front = *recto.*

BACK (adj) *arrière, de derrière* : back door = *porte arrière* (car) / *de derrière* (house) ☠ *arrière-grands-parents* = great grand-parents

a back number (magazine) = *un vieux numéro (magazine)*
back pay/taxes = *arriéré de salaire/d'impôts* ☠ *arriéré de travail* = backlog
no back talk ! = *pas de réplique !*

a back road = *une route départementale/secondaire*
in the back room = *dans les coulisses* : the choice of candidates is made by the men in the backroom = *le choix des candidats se fait dans les coulisses.*

BACK (adv) **back and forth** = *de long en large* : to walk back and forth on Broadway = *marcher de long en large sur Broadway*
to pace back and forth = *faire les cent pas* : he was pacing back and forth waiting for the results = *il faisait les cent pas en attendant les résultats*
☠ for the use of "back" after a verb, see the verb.

BACK (to, -ed) **1/** *appuyer* : to back a candidate = *appuyer un candidat* ⓪ to support = *soutenir*
☠ *s'appuyer sur* = to lean against
— *appuyer sur le bouton* = to press the button
2/ *soutenir financièrement* : who's backing his campaign ? = *qui soutient financièrement sa campagne ?* ⓪ to finance = *financer*

to back away = *reculer* : when the man approached her, she backed away = *quand l'homme s'est approché d'elle, elle a reculé* ⓪ to withdraw = *se retirer* ☠ → to move back
to be backed (up) by = *être accompagné par/à* : the singer's backed by a piano = *le chanteur est accompagné au piano*
to back down/off = *reculer* : the unions threatened to go on strike but backed down at the last minute = *les syndicats ont menacé de se mettre en grève, mais ils ont reculé au dernier moment* ⓪ to

sing small = *s'écraser* ☠ → to move back
to back out = *se défiler* : they backed out of the deal at the last moment = *ils se sont défilés au dernier moment* ⓪ to go back on = *revenir sur* ☠ → to march
to back up = 1/ *appuyer* : the tanks backed up the commandos = *les tanks appuyaient l'action des commandos*, I lied and she backed me up = *j'ai menti et elle m'a appuyé* ☠ → to back 2/ *reculer* : back up a bit ! = *recule un peu !* ☠ → to move back.

BACKBITING (n) *médisance (f)* : there's a lot of backbiting in the office = *les médisances vont bon train au bureau* ⓪ gossip = *commérage.*

BACKBONE (n) **1/** *épine (f) dorsale* ⓪ spine = *colonne vertébrale* **2/** *trempe (f)* : it takes backbone to be a dissident in the USSR = *il faut de la trempe pour être dissident en URSS* ⓪ pluck = *cran*
(he) has no backbone = *(il) n'a rien dans le ventre* ≠ he's got guts = *il a des tripes*
☠ *de la même trempe* = of the same ilk
— *flanquer une trempe à qqn* = to give s.o. a sound thrashing.

BACKBREAKING (adj) *éreintant, -e* : backbreaking work = *un travail éreintant* ⓪ exhausting = *épuisant.*

BACKER (n) *soutien (m) financier* : the backer of the play = *le soutien financier de la pièce* ⓪ sponsor = ←.

BACKFIRE (to, -d) *se retourner contre (l'auteur)* : our plan backfired = *notre projet s'est retourné contre nous* ⓪ to boomerang = *produire un effet de boomerang.*

BACKGAMMON (n) *backgammon (m), jaquet (m)* ⓪ chess = *échecs.*

BACKGROUND (n) **1/** *fond (m), arrière-plan (m)* : there were hills in the background = *il y avait des collines dans le fond/à l'arrière-plan* ⓪ backdrop = *toile de fond* ≠ foreground = *premier plan* ☠ *fond* → bottom
background music = *musique de fond*
to stay in the background = *rester à l'arrière-plan*
2/ *bagage (m), formation (f)* : a good professional background = *un bon bagage professionnel/une bonne formation professionnelle* ☠ → baggage, → formation
3/ *milieu (m)* : from a working-class background = *issu d'un milieu ouvrier* ☠ → middle.

BACKING (n) *appui (m)* : he has the backing of the leaders of the party = *il a l'appui des dirigeants du parti* ① support = *soutien*, endorsement = *aval*.

BACKLASH (n, -es) *retour (m) de bâton* : after his statement, there was a strong backlash from the feminists = *après sa déclaration, il y a eu un vif retour de bâton des féministes* ① reaction = *réaction*.

BACKLOG (n) *arriéré (m) de travail* : a huge backlog at the office = *un énorme arriéré de travail au bureau*.

BACKSEAT (n) **no backseat drivers !** = *tu veux conduire à ma place ?*
to take a backseat = *rester dans l'ombre* ① to stay in the background = *rester à l'arrière-plan*.

BACKSIDE (n) *postérieur (m)* : she has a big backside = *elle a un gros postérieur* ① rear end = *arrière-train*, ass = *cul*.

BACKSTAGE (adv) *dans les coulisses* : let's go backstage after the show = *allons dans les coulisses après le spectacle* ☙ *dans les coulisses (politique)* = behind the scenes.

BACKSTAIRS (n pl) *escalier (m) de service* ① fire escape = *escalier de secours*.

BACKTRACK (to, -ed) *faire marche/machine arrière* : the President backtracked on his promise to reduce taxes = *le Président a fait machine arrière quant à sa promesse de réduire les impôts*.

BACKWARD (adj) *arriéré, -e* : a backward child = *un enfant arriéré*, a backward country = *un pays arriéré* ≠ advanced = *avancé*.

BACKWARDS (adv) *en arrière* : don't look backwards = *ne regardez pas en arrière* ≠ forwards = *en avant* ☙ for the use of "backwards" after a verb, see the verb.

BACKWOODS (n pl) 1/ *fin fond (m) (du pays)* : there are still primitives in the backwoods = *il y a encore des populations primitives au fin fond du pays* 2/ *cambrousse (f)* : he comes from the backwoods = *il sort tout droit de sa cambrousse* ① Timbuktu = *Trifouillis-lès-Oies*.

BACKYARD (n) *jardin (m) (de derrière)* : kids were playing in the backyard = *des gosses jouaient dans le jardin (de derrière)* ① garden = *jardin*.

BACON (n) *bacon (m)* : eggs and bacon = *des œufs au bacon* ① fat = *lard*
to bring home the bacon = *faire bouillir la marmite*.

BACTERIA (n pl) *bactéries (f pl)* ① virus = ←, bacterium = *bactérie*.

BAD (n) **to go from bad to worse** = *aller de mal en pis* ≠ to get better and better = *aller de mieux en mieux*
to take the bad along with the good = *accepter les bons et les mauvais côtés de la vie* → THAT'S LIFE !

BAD (adj, worse, worst) 1/ *mauvais, -e (pire, le pire)* : a bad movie = *un mauvais film* ≠ good = *bon* → AWFUL

bad breath = *mauvaise haleine* **bad dream** = *cauchemar* **bad lot** = *mauvais sujet* **bad news** = *qui ne casse rien* : the film was bad news = *le film ne cassait rien* → AWFUL **to be bad at (tennis)** = *être mauvais au (tennis)* **to be bad for** = *être mauvais pour* : smoking's bad for your health = *c'est mauvais pour ta santé de fumer* ≠ to be good for = *être bon pour* **to be in bad way (health, business)** = *filer un mauvais coton* ① in bad ≠ great shape = *en mauvaise ≠ bonne posture*	**to come to a bad end** = *finir mal* **to feel bad (about having said that)** = *être navré (d'avoir dit ça)* = to feel rotten (about) **to get bad** = *se dégrader* : the situation's getting bad = *la situation se dégrade* ≠ to get better = *s'améliorer* ☙ → to degrade **to give a bad name** = *ruiner la réputation de* : drug dealing gave the place a bad name = *le trafic de drogue a ruiné la réputation de cet endroit* **to leave a bad taste in s.o.'s mouth** = *laisser un goût amer à*	qqn : his remark left a bad taste in my mouth = *sa réflexion m'a laissé un goût amer* **not bad (at all)** = *pas mal (du tout)* : the book wasn't bad at all = *le livre n'était pas mal du tout* ① all right = *moyen* **not so bad** = *pas trop mal* : how do you feel ? — not so bad ! = *comment te sens-tu ? — pas trop mal !* ① pretty good = *plutôt bien* **there's bad blood between them** = *ils ne peuvent pas se voir* ① there's no love lost between them = *ils ne peuvent pas s'encaisser*

☙ *un mauvais numéro* = a wrong number — *elle est mauvaise langue* = she has a sharp tongue — *se faire du mauvais sang* = to be worried sick — *passer un mauvais quart d'heure* = to have a rough time of it	— *tirer qqn d'un mauvais pas* = to get s.o. out of a jam — *faire contre mauvaise fortune bon cœur* = to grin and bear it — *mauvaise herbe* = weed

39

2/ *vilain, -e* : a bad child = *un vilain enfant* ≠ well-behaved = *qui se tient bien* ☠ → naughty
3/ *gros, grosse* : a bad cold = *un gros rhume*, a bad mistake = *une grosse faute* ☠ → big.

BAD (adv) *méchamment* : I want him bad = *j'ai méchamment envie de lui* → VERY ☠ → badly

bad(ly) off = *mal en point* : she's been bad(ly) off since her divorce = *elle est mal en point depuis son divorce* ≠ in great shape = *en pleine forme*
to go bad = *mal tourner* : all her kids went bad = *tous ses gosses ont mal tourné*

to have it bad (for s.o.) = *être fou de qqn* : they split up a year ago but she still has it bad (for him) = *ils ont rompu il y a un an, mais elle est encore folle de lui* Ⓦ to have s.o. in one's system = *avoir qqn dans la peau.*

BADGE (n) *badge (m), insigne (m)* (police) : a policeman's badge = *un insigne d'agent de police*, the delegates all wore badges = *tous les délégués portaient des badges.*

BADGER (to, -ed) *tarabuster* : stop badgering me with your questions = *ne me tarabustez plus avec vos questions* ⓌＯ to hock = *tanner.*

BADLY (adv) *mal* : he played badly = *il a mal joué* ≠ well = *bien*
to feel badly about stg = *être navré de qqch* = to feel bad about stg
you badly need (a haircut) = *vous avez grand besoin de (vous faire couper les cheveux)*
☠ *se trouver mal* = to faint
— *tu as mal écrit mon nom* = you wrote my name wrong
— *mal à l'aise* = ill at ease
— *mal en point* = in poor condition.

BADMINTON (n) *badminton (m)* : to play badminton = *jouer au badminton.*

BADMOUTH (to, -ed) *dire du mal de* : he's constantly badmouthing his in-laws = *il dit sans arrêt du mal de sa belle-famille* ⓌＯ to pan = *éreinter.*

BAD-TEMPERED (adj) *qui a mauvais caractère* = ill-tempered ≠ easygoing = *coulant.*

BAFFLE (to, -d) *dérouter* : the cops are baffled by the case = *les flics sont déroutés par cette affaire* ⓌＯ to bewilder = *plonger dans la perplexité* **BAFFLING** (adj) *déroutant, -e* ⓌＯ confusing = *embrouillant.*

BAG (n) *sac (m)* : I forgot my bag in the restaurant = *j'ai oublié mon sac au restaurant* ⓌＯ shoulder bag = *sac en bandoulière*, purse = *sac à main*
to walk out bag and baggage = *prendre ses cliques et ses claques*
bags of (dough) = *(du fric) à gogo* → MANY
bags under the eyes = *des poches sous les yeux*
to be a bag of bones = *être un sac d'os* ⓌＯ to be all skin and bones = *n'avoir que la peau et les os*
(drugs) are not my bag = *(la drogue,) c'est pas mon truc* = (drugs) are not my thing
in the bag = *dans le sac/du tout cuit* : the deal's in the

bag = *l'affaire est dans le sac / cette affaire, c'est du tout cuit*
to leave s.o. holding the bag = *faire porter le chapeau à qqn* : his partners took off and left him holding the bag = *ses partenaires se sont tirés et lui ont fait porter le chapeau* ⓌＯ to hang stg on s.o. = *faire porter la responsabilité de qqch à qqn*
☠ *dix sacs (cent francs)* = a hundred francs
— *mettre dans le même sac* = to lump together
— *vider son sac* = to tell s.o. what's on one's mind
— *mettre à sac* = to plunder
— *un sac de pommes de terre* = a sack of potatoes.

BAGGAGE (n inv) *bagages (m pl)* : my baggage was lost = *on a perdu mes bagages* = luggage ⓌＯ suitcase = *valise*
☠ *avoir un bon bagage* = to have a good working background
— *plier bagage* = to cut out/split.

BAGGY (adj, -ier, -iest) **baggy pants** = *un pantalon qui fait des poches.*

BAIL (n) *caution (f)* ⓌＯ parole = *liberté conditionnelle*
to be out on bail = *être en liberté sous caution/en liberté provisoire*
to jump bail = *profiter de sa liberté provisoire pour s'enfuir*
to put up bail (prison) = *payer la caution (prison)*
☠ *caution* → caution
— *un bail* = a lease.

BAIL OUT (to, -ed) **1/** *sauter (en parachute)* : the parachutists bailed out over the ocean = *les parachutistes ont sauté au-dessus de l'océan* ☠ → to jump **2/** *tirer d'affaire* : when he was in a jam his brother bailed him out = *quand il était dans le pétrin, son frère l'a tiré d'affaire.*

BAIT (n) *appât (m)* : they used the girl as bait to trap the gangster = *ils se sont servi de la fille comme appât pour prendre le gangster* ⓌＯ trap = *piège*
to swallow the bait = *mordre à l'hameçon* ⓌＯ to fall into the trap = *tomber dans le piège*
☠ *leur proposition était un appât* = their offer was a come-on.

BAIT (to, -ed) **to bait s.o.** = *chercher qqn* : if you continue baiting me, I'm going to get angry = *si tu continues* *à me chercher, je vais me fâcher* ☾☾ to tease = *taquiner.*

BAKE (to, -d) *cuire (au four)* : to bake a cake = *cuire un gâteau (au four)* ☾☾ to grill = *griller* ☠ → to cook.

BAKER (n) *boulanger, -ère* ☾☾ dough = *pâte* **a baker's dozen** = *treize à la douzaine.*

BAKERY (n, -ies) *boulangerie (f)* : an expensive bakery = *une boulangerie chère.*

BALANCE (n) *équilibre (m)* : I lost my balance = *j'ai perdu l'équilibre* **balance of payments** = *balance des paiements* ☾☾ GNP = *PNB* **balance of power** = *équilibre des pouvoirs* **balance sheet** = *bilan* ☠ → toll. ☠ *une balance* = a scale — *faire pencher la balance* = to tip the scales.

BALANCE (to, -d) *équilibrer* : to balance the budget = *équilibrer le budget* ☾☾ to counterbalance = *contrebalancer.*

BALCONY (n, -ies) *balcon (m)* ☾☾ terrace = *terrasse.*

BALD (adj, -er, -est) *chauve* : my husband's bald = *mon mari est chauve* **BALDNESS** (n) *calvitie (f).*

BALK (to, -ed) *regimber* : he balked at my suggestion = *il a regimbé devant ma suggestion* ☾☾ to crab = *rouspéter.*

BALL (n) 1/ *balle (f)*, *ballon (m)* (football, basketball), *boule (f)* (billiards, bowling) : a tennis/golf ball = *une balle de tennis/ de golf*, the player kicked the ball = *le joueur a donné un coup de pied dans le ballon*, the red ball touched the white ball = *la boule rouge a touché la boule blanche*

---

ball and chain = *boulet*
ball game = *match de base-ball*
to be on the ball = *être dégourdi* ☾☾ to be wide-awake = *être éveillé*
to carry the ball = *prendre l'affaire en main* : it's your turn to carry the ball = *c'est à vous de prendre l'affaire en main*
to have a ball = *bien se marrer* : we had a ball last night = *nous nous sommes bien marrés hier soir* ☾☾ to live it up = *faire les quatre cents coups*
it's your ball game ! = 1/ *à vous de jouer !*

= it's your move ! 2/ *c'est votre affaire* : don't ask me, it's your ball game ! = *ne me demandez rien, c'est votre affaire !*
that's another/a different ball game = *c'est une autre histoire* ☾☾ it's a horse of another color = *c'est une autre paire de manches*
to play ball (with) = *être de connivence avec* : the cops are playing ball with the Mafia = *les flics sont de connivence avec la Mafia*
to get/start the ball rolling = *ouvrir la discussion* : the President got the ball rolling by

---

asking direct questions = *le Président a ouvert la discussion en posant des questions directes* **that's the ball game !** = 1/ *c'est la fin des haricots !* : if he finds the truth out, that's the ball game ! = *s'il découvre la vérité, c'est la fin des haricots !* ☾☾ the jig's up = *les carottes sont cuites* 2/ *le tour est joué !* : I'm just put-

ting on the finishing touches and that's the ball game ! = *je mets la dernière touche et le tour est joué !* 3/ *les jeux sont faits !* : it's too late now you signed the contract ; that's the ball game ! = *il est trop tard maintenant que tu as signé le contrat, les jeux sont faits !* ☾☾ the die is cast = *les dés sont jetés*

☠ *ballon* → balloon
— *perdre la boule* = to go nuts
— *se mettre en boule* = to fly off the handle
— *saisir la balle au bond* = to seize the opportunity
— *un enfant de la balle* = a child from circus/showbiz family
— *(20) balles* = (20) francs
— *une balle (de revolver)* = a bullet
— *renvoyer la balle* = to answer tit for tat

2/ *bal (m)* : charity ball = *bal de bienfaisance* ☾☾ dinner dance = *dîner dansant.*

BALL (to, -ed) *baiser* : I came the first time we balled = *j'ai joui la première fois qu'on a baisé* = to fuck ☾☾ to bang = *baisouiller*
to ball up (the work) = *foutre (le travail) en l'air* = to fuck up ☾☾ to screw up = *foutre par terre.*

BALLET (n) *ballet (m)* ☾☾ ballerina = *ballerine*, to toe dance = *faire des pointes* ☠ *ballet rose/bleu* = prostitution of minor girls/boys

BALLOON (n) 1/ *ballon (m)* : he crossed the Channel in a balloon = *il a traversé la Manche en ballon* 2/ *ballon (m)(de baudruche)* : a red balloon = *un ballon de baudruche rouge* ☠ *avoir le ballon* = to be knocked up — *un ballon de football* = a football.

BALLOT (n) 1/ *bulletin (m) de vote* ☾☾ ballot box = *urne* 2/ *(tour (m) de) scrutin (m)* : elected on the first ballot = *élu au premier tour de scrutin* ☾☾ vote = ← ☠ *c'est un ballot* = he's a dumbbell.

BALLS (n pl) 1/ *couilles (f pl)* : she kicked him in the balls = *elle lui a donné un coup de pied dans les couilles* ☾☾ nuts = *roupettes*, rocks = *bourses*, testicles = *testicules*, family jewels = *bijoux de famille*, private parts = *les parties*, he's well-hung = *il est bien monté* **to break s.o.'s balls** = *les casser à qqn* : you're breaking my balls = *tu me les casses* **to have s.o. by the balls** = *avoir qqn à sa pogne* : my publisher has me by the balls = *mon éditeur m'a à sa pogne*

2/ *couilles (f pl)* : it took balls to do that ! = *il fallait des couilles pour faire ça !* ⓪ guts = *culot.*

BALLYHOO (n) *battage (m)*: a lot of ballyhoo over his last book = *beaucoup de battage autour de son dernier livre* ⓪ advertising = *publicité.*

BALONEY (n inv) **1/** *âneries (f pl)* : what you're saying's a lot of baloney ! = *ce que tu peux dire comme âneries !* ⓪ malarky = *balivernes,* fiddlesticks = *sornettes* **2/** *mortadelle (f)* : a baloney sandwich = *un sandwich à la mortadelle* ⓪ salami = ←.

BAN (to, -ned) *interdire* : to ban a film = *interdire un film* ⓪ to outlaw = *proscrire* ≠ to authorize = *autoriser* ☠ → to forbid.

BANAL (adj) *banal, -e* : a banal remark = *une remarque banale* ⓪ insipid = *insipide* ≠ novel = *original* ☠ *un (rhume) banal* = a common (cold).

BANANA (n) *banane (f)* ⓪ banana split = ←, banana tree = *bananier* ☠ *quelle banane !* = what a dummy !

BANANAS (adj) **you're bananas !** = *tu es timbré !* → CRAZY.

BAND (n) **1/** *petit orchestre (m),* fanfare *(f)* (municipal, military) : there's a great band at the club = *il y a un très bon petit orchestre au club* **2/** *bande (f)*: a band on my arm = *une bande autour de mon bras* **3/** *bande (f)*: a band of hoods = *une bande de voyous* = a gang of hoods **to beat the band** = *comme pas possible* : he drinks to beat the band = *il boit comme pas possible* ⓪ ever so much = *tant et plus*
☠ *bandes dessinées* = comic strips
— *bande sonore* = sound track
— *bande d'idiots !* = you idiots !
— *faire bande à part* = to be a loner
— *bande magnétique* = tape
— *apprendre par la bande* = to learn indirectly
— *lui et sa bande* = he and his crowd.

BANDAGE (n) *pansement (m)* ⓪ Band-Aid = *sparadrap.*

BANDIT (n) *bandit (m)* ⓪ highway robber = *bandit de grand chemin.*

BAND TOGETHER (to, -ed) *se liguer* : the citizens are banding together against the nuke = *les citoyens se liguent contre la centrale nucléaire* ⓪ to pull together = *joindre ses forces.*

BANDWAGON (n) **to jump on the bandwagon** = *prendre le train en marche* : now that he won the primary, everyone wants to jump on the bandwagon = *maintenant qu'il a gagné les primaires, tout le monde veut prendre le train en marche.*

BANE (n) *fléau (m)* : drinking's the bane of his existence = *l'alcoolisme est le fléau de son existence* ⓪ curse = *malédiction.*

BANG (n) **to get a bang out of** = *prendre son pied en* :

I got a bang out of seeing my first blue movie = *j'ai pris mon pied en voyant mon premier film porno* ⓪ to get a kick out of = *prendre plaisir à*
to go over with a bang = *faire un tabac* : the show went over with a bang = *le spectacle a fait un tabac* ≠ to lay an egg = *se casser la gueule*
to start off with a bang = *démarrer sur les chapeaux de roues* : the business started off with a bang = *l'affaire a démarré sur les chapeaux de roues* ≠ to fall on one's face = *se casser la figure*
a bang on (the head) = *un grand coup sur (la tête)* ⓪ slug = *marron.*

BANG ! (interj) *pan !* ⓪ ouch ! = *aïe !*

BANG (to, -ed) *cogner* : I banged my head = *je me suis cogné la tête* ☠ → to clobber
to bang up (a car) = *mettre (une voiture) en morceaux* ⓪ to bash up = *ratatiner.*

BANISH (to, -ed) *bannir* : to banish a political opponent = *bannir un opposant politique* ⓪ to expel = *expulser.*

BANK (n) **1/** *banque (f)* ⓪ safe = *coffre(-fort),* safe-deposit box = *coffre,* bankbook = *livret d'épargne,* checkbook = *carnet de chèques*
bank account = *compte en banque* ⓪ checking account = *compte-chèques,* savings account = *compte d'épargne,* savings bank = *caisse d'épargne,* deposit = *versement,* withdrawal = *retrait*
bank statement = *relevé de compte*
to break the bank = *faire sauter la banque* ⓪ to hit it big = *décrocher le gros lot*
☠ *la banque est une profession bien rémunérée* = banking is a profitable profession
2/ *berge (f),* rive *(f)*: the banks of the Thames = *les berges/rives de la Tamise,* left/right bank = *rive gauche/droite.*

BANKABLE (adj) *rentable* : the play isn't bankable = *la pièce n'est pas rentable.*

BANKER (n) *banquier, -ère* ⓪ financier = ←.

BANKING (n) *banque (f)*: banking attracts business school graduates = *la banque attire les diplômés des écoles de commerce* ☠ → bank.

BANK ON (to, -ed) *tabler sur* : we're banking on his approval = *nous tablons sur son approbation* ⓪ to rely on = *se reposer sur.*

BANKROLL (n) **to have/make a bankroll** = *avoir/se faire une galette* → RICH.

BANKROLL (to, -ed) *financer* : his campaign was bankrolled by his family = *sa campagne a été financée par sa famille* = to finance ⓪ to put up the money = *faire la mise de fonds.*

BANKRUPT (adj) **to go bankrupt** = *faire faillite* : his business went bankrupt the first year = *son affaire a fait faillite dès la première année* ⓪ to fold = *fermer boutique.*

BANKRUPTCY (n, -ies) *banqueroute (f), faillite (f) :* many bankruptcies during a depression = *de nombreuses faillites durant une dépression* ☠ *la faillite d'une politique* = the failure of a policy.

BANQUET (n) *banquet (m) :* a banquet in honor of the First Lady = *un banquet en l'honneur de la Première Dame* ① feast = *festin*.

BANTER (to, -ed) *badiner :* the star was bantering with the reporter = *la vedette badinait avec le journaliste* ① to josh = *galéjer* ☠ → to jest.

BAPTIZE (to, -d) *baptiser :* = to christen ① baptism = *baptême*.

BAR (n) 1/ *bar (m) :* to have a drink in a bar = *prendre un pot dans un bar* ① barman = ←
2/ *barreau (m) :* prison bars = *barreaux de prison*
behind bars = *derrière les barreaux* ① in jail = *en taule*
to belong to the bar = *appartenir au barreau*
to prepare for the bar = *préparer le concours d'avocat (le CAPA)*
3/ *barre (f) :* parallel bars = *barres parallèles*
☠ *la barre (bateau)* = the helm/the tiller (boat)
— *la barre des témoins* = the witness stand
— *avoir barre sur qqn* = to have the edge on s.o.

BAR (prep) **bar none** = *de tous :* it's the best restaurant bar none = *c'est le meilleur restaurant de tous.*

BAR (to, -red) **to bar s.o. from** = *exclure qqn de :* women are barred from certain professions = *les femmes sont exclues de certaines professions* ① to ban = *interdire.*

BARBARIAN (n) *barbare (m, f)* **BARBARIC** (adj) *barbare* **BARBAROUS** (adj) *barbare.*

BARBECUE (n) *barbecue (m)* ① picnic = *pique-nique.*

BARBER (n) *coiffeur (m) (hommes)* **BARBERSHOP** (n) *salon (m) de coiffure pour hommes.*

BARE (adj) *dénudé, -e :* a bare room = *une pièce dénudée,* bare legs = *des jambes dénudées*
the bare facts = *les faits bruts*
the bare necessities = *le strict nécessaire.*

BAREFOOT (adj, adv) *pieds nus :* to walk barefoot = *marcher pieds nus.*

BARELY (adv) *à peine :* barely enough money to cover expenses = *à peine assez d'argent pour couvrir les frais* = hardly ① just about = *tout juste.*

BARFLY (n, -ies) *pilier (m) de bistrot* → DRUNK.

BARGAIN (n) *affaire (f) :* this coat was a bargain = *ce manteau était une affaire* ① good deal = *bonne affaire*
into the bargain = *par-dessus le marché :* I have to work late and on Sundays into the bargain = *il faut que je travaille tard et le dimanche par-dessus le marché* ① in addition = *en plus*

to make a bargain = *conclure un marché* = to make a deal
☠ → affair.

BARGAIN (to, -ed) *marchander :* she bargained with the guy for a better price = *elle a marchandé avec le type pour obtenir un prix plus avantageux* ① to haggle over a price = *ergoter sur un prix*
I hadn't bargained on that = *je n'avais pas prévu ça* ① I didn't expect it = *je ne m'y attendais pas.*

BARGAINING (n) *marchandage (m) :* I don't like bargaining = *je n'aime pas le marchandage*
to be in a good/strong bargaining position = *être en position de force.*

BARGE (n) *péniche (f) :* they live on a barge = *ils vivent sur une péniche* ① tugboat = *remorqueur.*

BARGE IN (to, -d) *faire irruption :* to barge into a room = *faire irruption dans une pièce* ≠ to dash out = *sortir en trombe.*

BARK (n) *aboiement (m) :* the bark of a dog = *l'aboiement d'un chien*
his bark is worse than his bite = *chien qui aboie ne mord pas.*

BARK (to, -ed) *aboyer* ① to snarl = *grogner*
to bark at (the mailman) = *aboyer après (le facteur).*

BARMAN (n, -men) *barman (m)* = bartender **BARMAID** (n) *barmaid (f)* = bartender.

BARN (n) *grange (f) :* an old barn turned into a church = *une vieille grange convertie en église* ① stable = *écurie,* hay = *foin.*

BARNSTORM (to, -ed) *faire une tournée :* the candidate barnstormed through the West = *le candidat a fait une tournée dans l'Ouest* ① to stump = *faire une tournée électorale.*

BAROMETER (n) *baromètre (m)* ① thermometer = *thermomètre.*

BARON (n) *baron (m)* ① duke = *duc* **BARONESS** (n, -es) *baronne (f).*

BARRACKS (n pl) *caserne (f)* ① garrison = *garnison.*

BARREL (n) *tonneau (m)* ① cask = *barrique*
to have s.o. over a barrel = *mettre qqn au pied du mur* ① to corner s.o. = *coincer qqn*
a barrel of oil = *un baril de pétrole.*

BARREN (adj) *stérile :* a barren land = *une terre stérile*
☠ → sterile.

BARRICADE (n) *barricade (f)* ① riot = *émeute,* street fighting = *combats de rue.*

BARRIER (n) *barrière (f) :* a language barrier = *la barrière de la langue* ☠ *barrière* = fence.

BARRING (prep) *à moins de :* barring an unexpected event, we're leaving tomorrow = *à moins d'un événement inattendu, nous partons demain.*

BARRISTER (n) (GB) *avocat, -e (juridictions supérieures)* ⓪ solicitor = *avocat (juridictions inférieures)*.

BARTENDER (n) *barman (m), barmaid (f)*.

BARTER (to, -ed) *troquer* : to barter goods = *troquer des marchandises* ⓪ to exchange = *échanger*.

BASE (n) **1/** *base (f)* : American bases in Japan = *les bases américaines au Japon* ⓪ headquarters = *quartier général*
base rate = *taux de base*
to be off base = *être à côté de la plaque* : the person who told you that is off base = *celui qui vous a dit ça est à côté de la plaque* ⓪ to be all off = *ne pas y être du tout*
☠ *la base* = the rank and file
— *l'anglais de base* = basic English
— *la base de son argument* = the basis of his argument
— *base de lancement* = launching pad
2/ *socle (m)* : the base of the statue = *le socle de la statue* ⓪ pedestal = *piédestal*.

BASE (adj, -r, -st) *ignoble* : what a base thing to say ! = *c'était ignoble de dire ça !* ⓪ contemptible = *méprisable*.

BASEBALL (n) *base-ball (m)* ⓪ pitcher = *lanceur*, catcher = ←, bat = *batte*.

BASEMENT (n) *sous-sol (m)* : a small apartment in the basement = *un petit appartement en sous-sol* ≠ attic = *grenier*.

BASE ON (to, -d) **1/** *baser sur* : oil price is based on supply and demand = *le prix du pétrole est basé sur l'offre et la demande* **2/** *fonder sur* : I'm basing my judgment on what I read = *je fonde mon jugement sur ce que j'ai lu*.

BASH (n, -es) *raout (m)* : a bash at the White House = *un raout à la Maison-Blanche* ⓪ spread = *gueuleton*.

BASH (to, -ed) **to bash into (a tree)** = *heurter (un arbre)* ⓪ to smash into = *s'écraser contre* ☠ → to clash
to bash s.o. on (the head) = *assommer qqn* → TO HIT
to bash up (a car) = *mettre (une voiture) en bouillie* ⓪ to smash up = *bousiller*.

BASHFUL (adj) *timide* : a bashful child = *un enfant timide* = timid ⓪ reserved = *réservé*.

BASIC (adj) *de base* : a basic principle = *un principe de base*, basic English = *l'anglais de base* ⓪ elementary = *élémentaire*.

BASICALLY (adv) *au fond* : basically I agree with you, but I don't think you should do it = *au fond, je suis d'accord avec vous, mais je ne pense pas que vous devriez le faire* ⓪ fundamentally = *fondamentalement*.

BASIS (n, bases) *base (f)* : money is the basis of their relationship = *l'argent est à la base de leurs rapports* ⓪ key = *clef*

I'm going on the basis that (he'll agree) = *je pars du principe qu'(il sera d'accord)* ⓪ to take for granted = *tenir pour acquis*
no basis = *sans fondement* : there's no basis for your suspicions = *vos soupçons sont sans fondement* ☠ → base.

BASK (to, -ed) *lézarder* : to bask in the sun = *lézarder au soleil* ⓪ to sunbathe = *prendre un bain de soleil* ☠ → to crack.

BASKET (n) *panier (m)* : throw the papers in the basket = *jetez les papiers au panier* ⓪ straw = *paille* ☠ *jouer au basket* = to play basketball
— *panier à salade* = paddy wagon
— *panier percé* = spendthrift
— *panier de crabes* = rat race.

BASKETBALL (n) *basket(-ball) (m)* : he plays a lot of basketball = *il joue beaucoup au basket(-ball)*.

BASTARD (n) **1/** *salaud (m)* : she's married to a real bastard = *elle a épousé un vrai salaud*

bitch = *salope/garce*	**rat** = *sale type*
bugger (GB) = *ordure*	**rogue** = *gredin*
cocksucker = *enculé*	**scoundrel** = *scélérat*
crumb = *rosse*	**shit** = *salopard*
cunt = *sale connasse*	**skunk** = *saligaud*
fink = *sale type*	**so-and-so** = *chameau*
fuck = *salopard*	**s.o.b.** = *saligaud*
heel = *beau salaud*	**son of a bitch** = *fils de pute*
(little) shit = *petit morveux/merdeux*	**son of a gun** = *sale type*
louse = *fumier*	
mother (fucker) = *enculé*	**stinker** = *peau de vache*
prick = *ordure*	**swine** = *porc*

2/ *bâtard, -e* : the king's bastards = *les bâtards du roi* ⓪ illegitimate child = *enfant illégitime*.

BASTION (n) *bastion (m)* ⓪ fort = ←.

BAT (n) **1/** *batte (f)* : he hit him on the head with a bat = *il l'a frappé sur la tête avec une batte* ⓪ stick = *bâton*, baseball = *base-ball*
to go to bat for s.o. = *prendre fait et cause pour qqn* ⓪ to stand by = *soutenir*
in the bat of an eye = *en un tour de main* ⓪ in two shakes of a lamb's tail = *en deux coups de cuiller à pot*
(to answer) right off the bat = *(répondre) sur-le-champ* ⓪ at once = *tout de suite*
2/ *chauve-souris (f)* ⓪ owl = *hibou*
to have bats in the belfry = *avoir une araignée au plafond* → CRAZY
to run like a bat out of hell = *courir comme un dératé*

○ to run for one's life = *courir comme si on avait le diable à ses trousses.*

BATCH OF (n, -es) *plein de, fournée (f) de* (cookies) : a whole batch of people/papers/oranges = *tout plein de gens/de papiers/d'oranges,* a batch of freshly baked buns = *une fournée de petits pains juste sortis du four* → MANY.

BATH (n) *bain (m)* : to take a bath = *prendre un bain* ○ tub = *baignoire,* towel = *serviette* ☠ *être dans le bain* = to be in the swing of things
— *maillot de bain* = bathing suit
— *prendre un bain de foule* = to press the flesh.

BATHING SUIT (n) *maillot (m) de bain* ○ bikini = ←, one-piece bathing suit = *maillot une pièce,* beachrobe = *sortie de bain,* bathing cap = *bonnet de bain.*

BATHROBE (n) *robe (f) de chambre, peignoir (m)* ○ hostess gown = *robe d'intérieur.*

BATHROOM (n) 1/ *salle (f) de bains* : clean the bathroom = *nettoyez la salle de bains* ○ bathtub = *baignoire,* sink = *lavabo* 2/ *toilettes (f pl)* : where's the bathroom ? = *où sont les toilettes ?* ○ the john = *le petit coin* ☠ → toilet.

BATS (adj) *sonné, -e* : she's bats ! = *elle est sonnée !* → CRAZY
to be bats over s.o. = *en pincer pour qqn* ○ to be nuts about = *être dingue de.*

BATTALION (n) *bataillon (m)* ○ company = *compagnie.*

BATTER (to, -ed) *frapper à tour de bras* : he battered his wife = *il a frappé sa femme à tour de bras* → TO HIT.

BATTERY (n, -ies) *pile (f)* (radio), *batterie (f)* (car) ☠ *pile* → pile

— *il joue de la batterie* = he plays the drums
— *batterie de cuisine* = kitchen utensils.

BATTLE (n) *bataille (f)* ○ ambush = *embuscade,* skirmish = *escarmouche,* battlefield = *champ de bataille*
the battle against (inflation) = *la lutte contre (l'inflation)*
battle cry = *cri de guerre*
to fight a losing battle = *livrer une bataille perdue d'avance* ○ to fight City Hall = *se battre contre les moulins à vent*
it's a battle of wits = *(on) joue au plus fin* : it was a battle of wits getting him to sign the contract = *il a fallu jouer au plus fin pour lui faire signer le contrat* ☠ *les cheveux en bataille* = disheveled hair.

BATTLESHIP (n) *bâtiment (m), navire (m) de guerre.*

BATTY (adj, -ier, -iest) *givré, -e* : the guy's completely batty = *le type est complètement givré* → CRAZY.

BAWL (to, -ed) *brailler* ○ to blubber = *chialer,* to be a crybaby = *être pleurnicheur* ☠ → to holler
to bawl s.o. out = *enguirlander qqn* : he bawled me out when he discovered the truth = *il m'a enguirlandé quand il a découvert la vérité* → TO LAMBAST.

BAWLING OUT (n) *engueulade (f)* = dressing-down.

BAY (n) *baie (f)* ○ gulf = *golfe*
to keep s.o. at bay = *tenir qqn à distance* : the kidnappers kept the cops at bay for a week = *les kidnappers ont tenu les flics à distance pendant une semaine.*

BAZA(A)R (n) *bazar (m)* ○ market = *marché.*

BC (abbr) = Before Christ = *avant J.-C.* ○ AD = Anno Domini = *après J.-C.*

BE (to, was, been) *être* : are you married ? — no, I'm not, I'm single = *est-ce que vous êtes marié ? — non, je suis célibataire*

— I am	= I'm	= *je suis*	— I was		= *j'étais*
— you are	= you're	= *vous êtes/tu es*	— you were		= *vous étiez/tu étais*
— he/she/it is	= ...'s	= *il/elle est, c'est*	— he/she/it was		= *il/elle était, c'était*
— we are	= we're	= *nous sommes*	— we were		= *nous étions*
— you are	= you're	= *vous êtes*	— you were		= *vous étiez*
— they are	= they're	= *ils/elles sont*	— they were		= *ils/elles étaient*
— I am not	= I'm not	= *je ne suis pas*	— I was not	= wasn't	= *je n'étais pas*
— you are not	= aren't	= *vous n'êtes pas/ tu n'es pas*	— you were not	= weren't	= *vous n'étiez pas/ tu n'étais pas*
— he/she/it is not	= isn't	= *il/elle, ce n'est pas*	— he/she/it was not	= wasn't	= *il/elle/ce n'était pas*
— we are not	= aren't	= *nous ne sommes pas*	— we were not	= weren't	= *nous n'étions pas*
— you are not	= aren't	= *vous n'êtes pas*	— you were not	= weren't	= *vous n'étiez pas*
— they are not	= ·aren't	= *ils/elles/ce ne sont pas*	— they were not	= weren't	= *ils/elles n'étaient pas*

CONTINUOUS FORM	FUTURE	PASSIVE VOICE
TO BE + (...ING) = *être en train de* : — I'm eating = *je suis en train de manger* = *je mange* — I was eating when you called = *j'étais en train de manger quand vous avez appelé* = *je mangeais...*	— I will/shall be = *je serai* — you will be = *vous serez/ tu seras* — he/she will be = *il/elle sera* — we will/shall be = *nous serons* — you will be = *vous serez* — they will be = *ils seront*	— the book was written by him = *le livre a été écrit par lui* ☠ the passive voice is formed the same in both languages = *le passif se forme de la même manière dans les deux langues*

--- IF ---

— if I'm sick, I'll go to the doctor = *si je suis malade, j'irai chez le médecin*
— if I were sick, I'd go to the doctor = *si j'étais malade, j'irais chez le médecin*
— if I had been sick, I'd have gone ... = *si j'avais été malade, je serais allé ...*

--- TAGS = N'EST-CE PAS ---

— he's French, isn't he ? = *il est français, n'est-ce pas ?*
— you aren't English, are you ? = *vous n'êtes pas anglais, n'est-ce pas ?*

☠ *pour construire « n'est-ce pas », il faut : 1/ trouver l'auxiliaire (donné ou sous-entendu) de la proposition principale et son sujet 2/ lorsque l'auxiliaire est négatif, poser la question à l'affirmative et vice versa*

being that = *étant donné que* : being that I'm late, we'll have a quick snack = *étant donné que je suis en retard, nous mangerons un morceau rapidement* **to be it** = *être extra* : her sister's really it = *sa sœur est vraiment extra* ≠ the pits = *pas le pied* **be it only** = *ne serait-ce que* : I have to see you, be it only for a few minutes = *il faut que je vous voie, ne serait-ce que quelques minutes* **to be or not to be** = *être ou ne pas être* **be that as it may (we're divorcing)** = *quoi qu'il*	en soit (nous divorçons) **to have been** = *avoir été* : have you been to Chicago ? = *est-ce que vous avez été à Chicago ?* **how are you ?** = *comment allez-vous ?* ⓪ fine, thank you ; and you ? = *bien, merci, et vous ?* **it's windy/cold/hot** = *il fait du vent/froid/chaud* **that may be** = *c'est (bien) possible* ⓪ perhaps = *peut-être* **(two) and (two) are (four)** = *(deux) et (deux) font (quatre)*

to be afraid = *avoir peur* **to be ashamed** = *avoir honte* **to be cold** = *avoir froid* **to be hot** = *avoir chaud*	**to be hungry** = *avoir faim* **to be right** ≠ **wrong** = *avoir raison* ≠ *tort* **to be thirsty** = *avoir soif*	**to be used to** = *avoir l'habitude de* **to be (ten) years old** = *avoir (dix) ans*

☠ *je suis né à New York* = I **was** born in New York — *je suis marié depuis dix ans* = I **have been** married for ten years	— *il était une fois* = once upon a time — *j'y suis !* = I get it !

to be about = 1/ *s'agir de* : what's it about ? = *de quoi s'agit-il ?* 2/ *avoir/être à peu près* : she's about 40 = *elle a à peu près 40 ans* **to be about to** = *être sur le point de* : I'm about to leave = *je suis sur le point de partir* ⓪ to be on the verge of = *être à deux doigts de* **to be above** = *être au-dessus de* : he's above taking bribes = *les pots-de-vin, il est au-dessus de ça* **to be after** = 1/ *chercher* : what are you after ? = *qu'est-ce que vous cherchez ?* ☠ → to look for 2/ *rechercher* : the cops are after him = *les flics le recherchent* ☠ → to seek 3/ *ambitionner* : he's after	his boss's job = *il ambitionne le poste de son patron* ⓪ to be out for = *briguer* **to be against** = *être contre* : I'm against your idea = *je suis contre votre idée* ≠ to be for = *être pour* **to be ahead** = 1/ *avoir de l'avance sur* : America's ahead of Europe in technology = *l'Amérique a de l'avance sur l'Europe en matière de technologie* 2/ *mener (sport)* : which team's ahead ? = *quelle est l'équipe qui mène ?* ☠ → to lead **to be around** = *avoir/être environ* : he's around 40 = *il a environ 40 ans*, it's around 3 o'clock = *il est environ 3 heures*

to have been around = *ne pas être tombé de la dernière pluie* ⓞ not to be born yesterday = *ne pas être né d'hier*

to be at = 1/ *être à* (place), *chez* (s.o.) : he's at his office/at his mother's = *il est au bureau/chez sa mère* 2/ *en être* : she doesn't know where she's at with him = *elle ne sait pas où elle en est avec lui* 3/ *là où les choses bougent* : Los Angeles is where it's at for music = *c'est à Los Angeles que les choses bougent en matière de musique*

to be at it/stg again = *recommencer à* : she's at her drinking again = *elle recommence à boire*

to be good ≠ **bad at/in (math)** = *être bon* ≠ *mauvais en (maths)*

to be away = 1/ *être parti* : to be away for a week = *être parti une semaine* 2/ *être à* : it's 5 miles/2 hours away from here = *c'est à 8 kilomètres/2 heures d'ici*

to be back = *être de retour* : I'll be back in an hour = *je serai de retour dans une heure*

to be behind = 1/ *être derrière* : he's behind me = *il est derrière moi* ≠ to be in front of = *être devant* 2/ *être derrière* : who's behind it all ? = *qui est derrière tout ça ?* 3/ *avoir ... de retard* : their team's two points behind = *leur équipe a deux points de retard*

to be behind in = *avoir du retard dans* : I'm behind in my work = *j'ai du retard dans mon travail* ≠ to be ahead = *avoir de l'avance*

to be below = *être inférieur à* : this year's sales are below last year's = *les ventes de cette année sont inférieures à celles de l'année dernière*

to be beyond = 1/ *dépasser* : it's beyond me ! = *ça me dépasse !* ≠ I get it ! = *je pige !* ☠ → to overtake 2/ *être au-delà de* : the brothel's beyond the church = *le bordel est au-delà de l'église*

to be by = 1/ *être de* : who's this book by ? = *de qui est ce livre ?* 2/ *passer* : I'll be by at noon = *je passerai à midi* ☠ → to pass

to be down = 1/ *descendre* : I'll be down in a minute = *je descends dans une minute* ☠ → to descend 2/ *ne pas avoir le moral* : she's been really down since he jilted her = *elle n'a vraiment pas le moral depuis qu'il l'a plaquée* ⓞ to be low = *avoir la déprime*

to be down on s.o. = *battre froid à qqn* : I've been down on him since our last run-in = *je lui bats froid depuis notre dernière dispute* ≠ to be in s.o.'s good graces = *être dans les bonnes grâces de qqn*

to be down with (the flu) = *être au lit avec (la grippe)*

to be for = 1/ *être pour* : I'm for legal abortion = *je suis pour la légalisation de l'avortement* ≠ to be in opposition to = *être opposé à* 2/ *être fait pour* : my brother isn't for her = *mon frère n'est pas fait pour elle*

to be from = *être/venir de* : where are you from ? = *d'où êtes-vous ?*, the letter's from Rome = *la lettre vient de Rome*

to be in = 1/ *être là* : the boss isn't in = *le patron n'est pas là* ≠ to be out = *être sorti* 2/ *être in* : jeans are in = *les jeans sont in* ≠ old-fashioned = *démodé* 3/ *être au pouvoir* : Democrats have been in since 1976 = *les démocrates sont au pouvoir depuis 1976*

to be in for = 1/ *aller avoir* : you're in for trouble = *tu vas avoir des ennuis*, we're in for a storm = *nous allons avoir un orage* 2/ *en être de sa poche* : I was in for a grand = *j'en ai été de mille dollars de ma poche* 3/ *avoir à tirer* : he's in for 10 years = *il a 10 ans à tirer* ⓞ to do time = *faire de la taule*

to be in for it = *en prendre pour son grade* : if the boss finds out, you're in for it = *si le patron l'apprend, tu vas en prendre pour ton grade* ⓞ to catch it = *se faire attraper*

to be in it for = *avoir à y gagner* : what's in it for me ? = *qu'est-ce que j'ai à y gagner ?*

to be in stg for what one can get out of it = *être purement intéressé* : don't think she's doing you a favor, she's in it for what she can get out of it = *ne pense pas qu'elle te fait une fleur, elle est purement intéressée*

to be in on stg = *être dans le coup* : Harry's in on the deal = *Harry est dans le coup*

to be in stg together = *être logé à la même enseigne* : stop complaining, we're all in it together = *arrête de geindre, nous sommes tous logés à la même enseigne*

to be in with = *être bien avec* : she's in with the boss = *elle est bien avec le patron* ⓞ to be in s.o.'s good graces = *être dans les bonnes grâces de qqn*

to be into = *donner dans/être branché sur* : they're into bondage = *ils donnent dans/sont branchés sur le sado-masochisme*

to be of = *être de* : to be of Italian background = *être d'origine italienne*

to be off = 1/ *être éteint* : the TV's off = *la télé est éteinte* ≠ to be on = *être allumé* 2/ *être en congé* : I'm off today = *je suis en congé aujourd'hui* 3/ *être annulé* : the party's off = *la soirée est annulée* ≠ it's on = *ça tient toujours* 4/ *se sauver* : I'm late, I must be off = *je suis en retard, il faut que je me sauve* → TO LEAVE ☠ → to save 5/ *être faux* : your counting's off = *votre calcul est faux* 6/ *être cinglé* : he's a little off = *il est un peu cinglé* → CRAZY 7/ *ne plus vouloir de* : I'm off married men = *je ne veux plus d'hommes mariés* 8/ *être dans* : my birthday is a month off = *mon anniversaire est dans un mois* 9/ *être tout près de* : the store's off Madison Avenue = *le magasin est tout près de Madison Avenue*

(business) is off = *(les affaires) ne vont pas très fort*

to be on = 1/ *être allumé* : the lights are on = *les lumières sont allumées* ≠ to be out = *être éteint* 2/ *travailler* : I'm on Monday = *je travaille lundi* ≠ to be off = *être en congé* ☠ → to work 3/ *marcher* : the deal's on = *l'affaire marche* ☠ → to walk 4/ *être pour* : the meeting's on Friday = *la réunion est pour vendredi* 5/ *passer* (radio, TV) : what's on tonight ? = *qu'est-ce qu'on passe ce soir ?*, when is she on ? = *quand passe-t-elle ?* ☠ → to pass 6/ *se*

droguer à : to be on heroin = *se droguer à l'héroïne*
it's on (me) = *c'est (moi) qui paie* : dinner's on me = *c'est moi qui paie le dîner* ◑ it's my treat = *c'est moi qui régale*
you're on ! = *chiche* !
to be on to s.o. = 1/ *voir le manège de qqn* : I'm on to you = *je vois ton manège* ◑ to be wise to s.o. = *voir clair dans le jeu de qqn* 2/ *être au courant des faits et gestes de qqn* : the cops are on to him = *les flics sont au courant de tous ses faits et gestes*
to be out = 1/ *être sorti* : I'm sorry, the boss is out just now = *je suis désolé, le patron est sorti pour le moment* 2/ *être éteint* : the lights are out = *les lumières sont éteintes* ≠ to be on = *être allumé* 3/ *être démodé* : are minis out ? = *les mini-jupes sont-elles démodées ?* ≠ fashionable = *à la mode* 4/ *être sorti* : his book isn't yet out = *son livre n'est pas encore sorti* 5/ *être dans les vapes* : after a few drinks he was out = *après avoir bu quelques verres il était dans les vapes* ◑ to be high = *planer* 6/ *être fini* : we'll go before the week's out = *nous partirons avant que la semaine (ne) soit finie* 7/ *en être de sa poche* : I was out a grand = *j'en ai été de mille dollars de ma poche*
that's out ! = *c'est exclu !* ◑ out of the question = *hors de question*
to be out for = 1/ *briguer* : he's out for the presidency = *il brigue la présidence* ◑ to aspire to = *aspirer à* 2/ *vouloir la peau de* : the boss is out for you = *le patron veut ta peau*
to be out for what one can get = *prêcher pour son saint/sa paroisse* ◑ to act in one's own interest = *agir dans son propre intérêt*
to be out of (cigarettes) = *ne plus avoir de (cigarettes)* ◑ to lack = *manquer*
to be out of it = *être hors du coup* : his family's out of it = *sa famille est hors du coup* ≠ with it = *dans le coup*
to be out to = *chercher à* : to be out to get a better job = *chercher à obtenir un meilleur poste*
to be over = 1/ *être fini* : our love affair/the war is over = *notre liaison/la guerre est finie* 2/ *avoir plus de* : he's over fifty = *il a plus de cinquante ans*
to be through = 1/ *avoir terminé* : when will you be through ? = *quand aurez-vous terminé ?* ◑ to be finished = *avoir fini* 2/ *être fichu* : he's through in politics = *il est fichu en politique*, if he finds out, you're through = *s'il l'apprend, tu es fichu* ◑ your number's up = *ton compte est bon*
to be through with = *en avoir sa claque de* : I'm through with you ! = *j'en ai ma claque de toi !* ◑ to

be fed up with = *en avoir marre de*
to be to = *être pour* : what's he to you ? = *qu'est-ce qu'il est pour toi ?*
to be together = 1/ *être ensemble* : we were together last night = *nous étions ensemble hier soir* 2/ *être bien dans sa peau* : if he were more together, we'd be a great couple = *s'il était un peu mieux dans sa peau, nous ferions un couple formidable*
not to be together = *marcher à côté de ses pompes* : he hasn't been at all together since his wife split = *il marche complètement à côté de ses pompes depuis que sa femme s'est tirée* ◑ to be mixed up = *être paumé*
to be up = 1/ *être levé* : she isn't up yet = *elle n'est pas encore levée* ◑ awake = *réveillé* ≠ asleep = *endormi* 2/ *avoir le moral* : she's up these days = *elle a le moral en ce moment* ≠ to be down = *avoir la déprime* 3/ *être en hausse* : prices are up = *les prix sont en hausse* ≠ to go down = *baisser*
to be up against = *se heurter à* : we're up against serious problems = *nous nous heurtons à de sérieux problèmes*
to be up for = 1/ *être en taule pour* : he's up for ten years = *il est en taule pour dix ans* 2/ *être sur les rangs pour* : he's up for the presidency = *il est sur les rangs pour la présidence*
to be up on = *suivre de près* : she's up on modern art = *elle suit l'art moderne de près* ≠ not to know beans about = *n'entraver que dalle à*
to be up to = 1/ *être d'attaque pour* : I'm not up to going = *je ne suis pas d'attaque pour y aller* 2/ *fabriquer* : I don't like his silence, what's he up to ? = *je n'aime pas son silence, qu'est-ce qu'il fabrique ?* ☠ → to manufacture 3/ *devenir* : I haven't seen her a long time what's she up to ? = *je ne l'ai pas vue depuis longtemps, que devient-elle ?* ☠ → to become 4/ *être à la hauteur de* : he isn't up to the job = *il n'est pas à la hauteur de ce travail* ◑ to measure up = *faire le poids*
it's up to you (to decide) = *c'est à vous (de voir/de décider)*
to be with = 1/ *être à* : I'll be with you in a minute = *je suis à vous dans une minute* 2/ *suivre* : I'm with you = *je vous suis* ☠ → to follow
to be with it = *être dans le coup* : my parents aren't with it = *mes parents ne sont pas dans le coup* ◑ to be in = *être in*, to be hip = *être branché*
not to be with it = *marcher à côté de ses pompes* : since the divorce, he hasn't been with it at all = *il marche complètement à côté de ses pompes depuis son divorce.*

BEACH (n, -es) *plage (f)* : the landing beaches = *les plages du débarquement* ◑ sand = *sable*, beachwear = *vêtements de plage.*

BEAD (n) *perle (f) (de bois, verre, plastique, etc.)* : a pretty necklace of glass beads = *un joli collier de perles de verre* ☠ → pearl.

BE-ALL-AND-END-ALL (n) *l'alpha et l'oméga* : his work is the be-all-and-end-all of his life = *son travail est l'alpha et l'oméga de son existence.*

BEAM (n) 1/ *poutre (f)* : beams in the apartment = *des poutres apparentes dans l'appartement* 2/ *faisceau (m)* : a beam of light = *un faisceau de lumière* ◑ ray = *rayon.*

BEAN (n) *haricot* (m) ⊕ string bean = *haricot vert*
not to know beans about stg = *n'entraver que dalle à qqch* ≠ to know a lot about = *en savoir long sur*
to spill the beans = *manger le morceau* ⊕ to let the cat out of the bag = *vendre la mèche*
to work for beans = *travailler pour des prunes* ⊕ to work for peanuts = *travailler pour le roi de Prusse* ☠ *tu commences à me courir sur le haricot !* = you're a pain !

BEANPOLE (n) *asperge* (f) : she's a beanpole ! = *cette fille, quelle asperge !* ⊕ rod = *échalas* ☠ → asparagus.

BEAR (n) *ours* (m) : polar bear = *ours polaire* ⊕ bear cub = *ourson*, grizzly bear = *grizzly*
teddy bear = *nounours/ours en peluche*.

BEAR (to, bore, born) *supporter* : how can you bear his drinking ? = *comment peux-tu supporter qu'il boive tant ?* ☠ → to support
I can't bear her = *je ne peux pas la supporter* ⊕ I can't stomach her = *je ne peux pas la blairer*
to bear s.o. out = *donner raison à qqn* : the facts bore me out = *les faits m'ont donné raison*
to bear up = *tenir le coup* : she's bearing up well since her husband's death = *elle tient bien le coup depuis la mort de son mari* ⊕ to cope = *faire face*
bear with me ! = *ayez la patience de m'écouter jusqu'au bout !*

BEARD (n) *barbe* (f) : he's growing a beard = *il se fait pousser la barbe* ⊕ razor = *rasoir*, mustache = *moustache*, bearded = *barbu*, goatee = *barbiche/bouc* ☠ *quelle barbe !* = what a drag !
— *barbe à papa* = cotton candy
— *rire dans sa barbe* = to laugh up one's sleeve.

BEARING (n) **to have no bearing on (the subject)** = *n'avoir aucun rapport avec (le sujet)* = to have no connection with
to get ≠ **to lose one's bearings** = *s'y retrouver* ≠ *s'y perdre*.

BEAST (n) *bête* (f) ⊕ animal = ←
☠ *ma bête noire* = my pet peeve
— *il adore les bêtes* = he likes animals
— *être une bête de scène* = to have a great stage presence
— *tu es bête !* = you're a dummy !
— *bête de somme* = workhorse.

BEAT (n) **1/** *ronde* (f) : the cop's beat = *la ronde du flic* **2/** *rythme* (m) : the beat of the music = *le rythme de la musique* **3/** *battement* (m) : a heart beat = *un battement de cœur* ☠ *une heure de battement entre deux films* = an hour's pause between two films.

BEAT (adj) *crevé, -e* : after all that work I'm beat = *après tout ce travail, je suis crevé* ⊕ shot = *claqué*, bushed = *vidé* ☠ *un pneu crevé* = a flat tire.

BEAT (to, beat, beaten) **1/** *battre* : to beat a child = *battre un enfant* → TO HIT **2/** *battre* : that's the first time our

team was beaten = *c'est la première fois que notre équipe s'est fait battre* ⊕ to win = *gagner* **3/** *battre* : his last film beats all the others = *son dernier film bat tous les autres*
beat it ! = *fiche le camp !* → BUZZ OFF !
can you beat that ! = *ça alors !* → GOSH !
that beats all/everything ! = *c'est le comble !* → GOSH !
let's beat it ! = *fichons le camp !* → TO LEAVE
it beats me ! = *ça me dépasse !* : it beats me why he was so rude = *ça me dépasse qu'il ait été si grossier* ⊕ I don't get it = *je ne pige pas*
to beat s.o. to (it) = *devancer qqn* : I was going to ask you for a drink, but you beat me to it = *j'allais vous inviter à prendre un pot, mais vous m'avez devancé* ⊕ to jump the gun = *prendre de vitesse*
to beat up = *tabasser* : the kids beat up the old man = *les gosses ont tabassé le vieil homme* → TO HIT
☠ *battre la campagne* = to scour the countryside
— *battre les cartes* = to shuffle cards
— *se battre au Viêt-nam* = to fight/to see action in Vietnam
— *battre froid à qqn* = to give s.o. the cold shoulder
— *battre son plein* = to be in full swing
— *battre le fer pendant qu'il est chaud* = to strike while the iron is hot.

BEATING (n) *raclée* (f) ⊕ shellacking = *dérouillée*
to give s.o. a beating = *flanquer une raclée à qqn* → TO HIT
to take a beating = *prendre une raclée* : their team took a beating = *leur équipe a pris une raclée* ⊕ to fall on one's face = *se casser la figure*.

BEAT-UP (adj) *bousillé, -e* : my shoes are beat-up = *mes groles sont bousillées* ≠ brand-new = *flambant neuf*.

BEAU (n) *galant* (m) : my kid sister came with her beau = *ma petite sœur est venue avec son galant* ⊕ heartthrob = *amoureux*
☠ *un vieux beau* = an old dandy
— *le plus beau, c'est que ...* = the best part of the story is that ...
— *fais le beau !* = beg ! (dog).

BEAUTIFUL (adj) **1/** *beau, bel* (in front of a vowel), *belle* : a beautiful day/summer/cat = *une belle journée/un bel été/un beau chat* ≠ awful = *affreux* → WONDERFUL **2/** *beau, belle* : a beautiful woman = *une belle femme* ⊕ handsome = *beau*, pretty as a picture = *joli comme un cœur* ≠ ugly = *laid*
the beautiful people = *le beau monde* ⊕ the upper crust = *le gratin* ≠ the riffraff = *la canaille*
☠ *il a eu beau (expliquer)* = no matter how much he (explained)
— *ça me fait une belle jambe !* = what do I care !
— *être dans de beaux draps* = to be in hot water
— *un bel homme* = a handsome man
— *ma belle-mère* = my mother-in-law/stepmother
— *un beau parleur* = a smooth talker
— *un beau jour* = one day

— *c'est trop beau pour être vrai* = it's too good to be true

— *sois belle et tais-toi* = relax and enjoy it

— *il ne le fera pas pour tes beaux yeux* = he won't do it for nothing

— *faites de beaux rêves* = sleep tight

— *bel et bien* = really and truly

— *tout ça c'est bien beau, mais* = that's all very well and good but

— *au beau milieu de* = in the very middle of

— *une belle plante* = a good-looking tomato

— *je l'ai échappé belle* = it was a narrow escape

— *un beau (salaud)* = a damned (bastard).

BEAUTIFULLY (adv) *admirablement* : beautifully dressed = *admirablement habillé* ⓪ marvelously = *merveilleusement*.

BEAUTY (n, -ies) **1/** *beauté (f)* : the beauty of the sunset = *la beauté du coucher de soleil* ≠ ugliness = *laideur* **2/** *beauté (f)* : what a beauty she is ! = *quelle beauté !* ⓪ dream = *splendeur* ≠ dog = *boudin*

beauty is in the eye of the beholder = *il n'y a point de laides amours*

beauty and the beast = *la belle et la bête*

beauty contest = *concours de beauté*

beauty parlor/shop = *institut de beauté*

beauty spot = *grain de beauté*

I need my beauty sleep = *j'ai besoin de dormir pour récupérer*

☠ *gagner (un match) en beauté* = to win (a match) easily

— *être en beauté* = to look lovely

— *se refaire une beauté* = to freshen up

— *pour la beauté du geste* = for the sake of it

— *viens ici, beauté !* = comme here, babe !

BECAUSE (conj) *parce que* : she left him because he was cheating on her = *elle l'a quitté parce qu'il la trompait* ⓪ for = *car* ≠ why = *pourquoi*

because of = *à cause de* : we didn't get divorced because of the kids = *nous n'avons pas divorcé à cause des gosses* ⓪ owing to = *en raison de*.

BECK (n) **to be at s.o.'s beck and call** = *faire les quatre volontés de qqn* ⓪ to wait on s.o. hand and foot = *être aux petits soins pour qqn*.

BECOME (to, -came, -come) *devenir* : to become a doctor = *devenir médecin*

to become of = *devenir* : what will become of us ? = *qu'allons-nous devenir ?*

☠ *qu'est-ce que tu deviens ?* = what's up with you ?/what are you up to ?

— *c'est à devenir (fou)* = it's enough to drive you (crazy).

BECOMING (adj) *seyant, -e* : a becoming dress = *une robe seyante* ≠ unbecoming = *qui ne sied pas*.

BED (n) *lit (m)*, *pieu (m)* (LV) : a comfortable bed = *un lit confortable* ⓪ sheet = *drap*, blanket = *couverture*, pil-

low = *oreiller*, bedbug = *punaise*, bedside table = *table de nuit/de chevet*, bedspread = *couvre-lit*, mattress = *matelas*, bedtime = *l'heure de se coucher*

bed and board = *logé et nourri*

camp bed = *lit de camp*

double bed = *lit à deux places*

four-poster bed = *lit à colonnes/à baldaquin*

to go to bed = *aller au lit* : it's time to go to bed = *c'est l'heure d'aller au lit* ⓪ to sack out = *aller pioncer*

to go to bed with s.o. = *coucher avec qqn* : I went to bed with him the first time we met = *j'ai couché avec lui la première fois qu'on s'est rencontrés* ⓪ to have relations = *avoir des rapports*

to stay in bed = *rester au lit*

twin beds = *lits jumeaux*

it wasn't a bed of roses = *ce n'était pas marrant* ⓪ to have had a rough time of it = *en avoir vu de dures*

water bed = *matelas à eau*

you've made your bed, now lie in it = *comme on fait son lit, on se couche* ⓪ it's no use crying over spilt milk = *quand le vin est tiré il faut le boire*.

BEDFELLOWS (n pl) *drôle d'équipe (f)* : the underworld and the cops working together : strange bedfellows ! = *les flics et le milieu travaillant ensemble : drôle d'équipe !* ⓪ an odd couple = *un drôle de ménage*.

BEDRIDDEN (adj) *cloué, -e au lit* : bedridden with the flu = *cloué au lit par la grippe* ≠ up and around = *sur pied*.

BEDROOM (n) *chambre (f) à coucher* ⓪ bathroom = *salle de bains*.

BEE (n) *abeille (f)* : a bee sting = *une piqûre d'abeille* ⓪ honey = *miel*, beehive = *ruche*

to have a bee in one's bonnet = *avoir une idée fixe*.

BEEF (n) **1/** *(viande de) bœuf (m)* : beef stew = *ragoût de bœuf*

☠ *faire un effet bœuf* = to make quite an effect

— *saigner comme un bœuf* = to bleed like a pig

— *faire un bœuf* = to have a jam session

— *un bœuf (animal)* = an ox

2/ *(raison (f) de) rouspéter* : what's your beef ? = *pourquoi rouspétez-vous ?* ⓪ complaint = *plainte*.

BEEF (to, -ed) *rouspéter* : stop beefing all the time = *arrêtez de rouspéter tout le temps* ⓪ to bitch = *gueuler*, to go on about stg = *en faire une maladie*

to beef up (troops/personnel) = *amener des renforts de (troupes/personnel)*.

BEELINE (n) **to make a beeline for** = *filer tout droit vers* : I made a beeline for the sales = *il y avait des soldes, j'y ai filé tout droit* ⓪ to flock to = *aller en masse vers*.

BEER (n) *bière (f)* : I'll take a beer = *je prendrai une bière* ⓪ ale = ←, draft beer = *(bière à la) pression*.

BEET (n) *betterave (f)* ⓪ turnip = *navet*.

BEFORE (adv) **1/** *avant* : the night before = *la nuit avant*, I couldn't come before = *je n'ai pas pu venir avant* ≠ after = *après* **2/** *auparavant* : she's a teacher now, but she was a singer before = *elle est maintenant professeur, mais auparavant elle était chanteuse* ⑩ formerly = *jadis*.

BEFORE (prep) **1/** *avant* : before Christmas = *avant Noël* ≠ after = *après*, following = *à la suite de*
before then = *avant (cela)* : I'll see you before then = *je vous verrai avant (cela)*
before + ing = **1/** *avant de* : call her before going there = *appelle-la avant d'y aller* **2/** *plutôt que de* : I'd die before sleeping with him = *je préfère crever plutôt que de coucher avec lui* = rather than sleep with him
☠ he said it BEFORE me and IN FRONT OF his wife = *il l'a dit AVANT moi et DEVANT sa femme*
— *se pencher en avant* = to lean forward
— *avant tout* = above all
— *en avant !* = right on !
2/ *devant* : put the adjective before the noun = *placez l'adjectif devant le nom* = ahead of = in front of ≠ after = *après*
☠ *marchez devant moi* = walk in front of me
— *aller au-devant de* **1/** *gros ennuis* **2/** *qqn* = **1/** to let o.s. in for big problems **2/** to go on ahead to meet s.o.

BEFORE (conj) *avant que* : try to do it before I leave = *essaie de le faire avant que je (ne) parte* ≠ after = *après que*.

BEFOREHAND (adv) *au préalable* : I'll speak with him about it beforehand = *je lui en parlerai au préalable* ≠ subsequently = *subséquemment*.

BEFRIEND (to, -ed) *se lier d'amitié avec* : she befriended a young child in the hotel = *elle s'est liée d'amitié avec un petit enfant à l'hôtel* ⑩ to hit it off = *sympathiser*.

BEG (to, -ged) **1/** *prier* : don't make me beg you = *ne vous faites pas prier* ⑩ to entreat = *supplier*
to beg off = *prier d'excuser* : he said he would come, but begged off at the last moment = *il a dit qu'il viendrait, mais il nous a priés de l'excuser au dernier moment*
to beg s.o. to = *prier qqn de* : she begged me not to tell anyone = *elle m'a prié de ne le dire à personne*
I beg to differ with you = *je me permets de ne pas être d'accord avec vous*
2/ *mendier* : to beg in the streets = *mendier dans les rues* ⑩ to panhandle = *faire la manche*.

BEGGAR (n) *mendiant, -e* : there are a lot of beggars around Times Square = *il y a pas mal de mendiants autour de Times Square* ⑩ tramp = *vagabond*, bum = *clochard*

beggars can't be choosers = *faute de grives on mange des merles*.

BEGIN (to, began, begun) *commencer* : when will the meeting begin ? = *quand commencera la réunion ?* ≠ to end = *terminer*, to wind up = *boucler*
to begin to = *commencer à* : I'm beginning to understand = *je commence à comprendre*
to begin with = **1/** *commencer par* : their marriage began with money problems = *leur vie commune a commencé par des ennuis d'argent* **2/** *et d'abord* : I don't like him, to begin with he drinks too much = *je ne l'aime pas et d'abord, il boit trop* ⑩ for openers = *tout d'abord* **3/** *pour commencer* : let's have a shrimp cocktail to begin with = *pour commencer, prenons un cocktail de crevettes*
☠ *ça commence bien !* (ironical) = we're off to a good start !

BEGINNER (n) *débutant, -e* : beginner's class = *classe de débutants* ⑩ novice = *←* ≠ expert = *←*
it's beginners' luck ! = *aux innocents les mains pleines !*

BEGINNING (n) *commencement (m)* : the beginning of the book = *le commencement du livre* ⑩ start = *début* ≠ end = *fin*
at the (very) beginning = *(tout) au début* ≠ in the end = *à la fin*
from the beginning = *dès le commencement* ⑩ from the start = *dès le début*
from the beginning to the end = *du commencement jusqu'à la fin*.

BEGRUDGE (to, -d) **to begrudge s.o. stg** = *reprocher qqch à qqn* : I don't begrudge him his success = *je ne lui reproche pas son succès*.

BEHALF (n) **on behalf of** = *de la part de* : I'm calling on behalf of Peter = *j'appelle de la part de Pierre* ⑩ recommended by = *recommandé par*.

BEHAVE (to, -d) **1/** *se comporter* : that's no way to behave = *ce n'est pas une façon de se comporter* ☠ *comporter (des difficultés)* = to involve (difficulties) **2/** *se tenir* : the kids behaved well = *les enfants se sont bien tenus* ☠ → to hold
behave yourself ! = *tiens-toi bien !*

BEHAVIOR (n) *comportement (m)* = behaviour (GB).

BEHEAD (to, -ed) *décapiter* : the king and his family were beheaded = *le roi et sa famille ont été décapités* ⑩ to strangle = *étrangler*.

BEHIND (n) *derrière (m)* : a broad with a big behind = *une nana avec un gros derrière* ⑩ can = *derche*
☠ *le derrière de la maison* = the rear of the house
— *(porte) de derrière* = back (door).

BEHIND (adv) *derrière* : the kids stayed behind = *les gosses sont restés derrière*
to take s.o. from behind = *prendre qqn en levrette/par-derrière*

way/far behind (the others in math) = *très en retard sur (les autres en maths)*
☠ for the use of ''behind'' after a verb, see the verb.

BEHIND (prep) *derrière* : sit behind me = *asseyez-vous derrière moi* ≠ in front of = *devant*.

BEIGE (adj) *beige* : a beige coat = *un manteau beige* ⓪ off-white = *blanc cassé*.

BELATED (adj) *tardif, -ive* : my belated wishes = *mes vœux tardifs* ☠ *un printemps tardif* = a late spring.

BELCH (n, -es) *rot (m)* ⓪ hiccups = *hoquet.*

BELCH (to, -ed) *roter* ⓪ to burp = *faire un rototo.*

BELEAGUER (to, -ed) **to be beleaguered by** = *être déchiré par* : the party's beleaguered by internal dissensions = *le parti est déchiré par des conflits internes.*

BELGIUM (n) *Belgique (f)* **BELGIAN** (n, adj) *Belge (m, f).*

BELIE (to, -d) *démentir* : her spryness belies her age = *sa vivacité dément son âge* ☠ → to deny.

BELIEF (n) *croyance (f)* : a strong belief = *une forte croyance* ⓪ faith = *foi*
beyond belief = *c'est à ne pas le croire* : they're rich beyond belief = *ils sont riches, c'est à ne pas le croire* → VERY
it's my belief that = *je suis intimement convaincu que.*

BELIEVABLE (adj) *crédible* : a believable alibi = *un alibi crédible* ⓪ plausible = ←
it's just not believable = *ce n'est pas croyable* ⓪ unbelievable = *incroyable.*

BELIEVE (to, -d) 1/ *croire* : I believe you = *je te crois* 2/ *croire* : I believe he'll come = *je crois qu'il viendra* ⓪ to presume = *présumer* ≠ to doubt = *douter*
believe it or not = *aussi incroyable que cela puisse paraître*
I believe so = *je crois bien que oui* ≠ **I don't believe so** = *je crois que non*
I can hardly/scarcely believe it = *j'ai peine à le croire*
I could hardly believe my eyes/ears = *je n'en croyais pas mes yeux/oreilles*
would you believe it ! = *qui l'eût cru !* → GOSH !
to believe in (God/one's husband) = *croire en (Dieu/son mari)*
☠ *elle se croit jolie* = she thinks she's pretty
— *à l'en croire* = according to him.

BELIEVER (n) *croyant, -e* ⓪ churchgoer = *pratiquant, churchnut* = *grenouille de bénitier.*

BELITTLE (to, -d) *rabaisser* : he always belittles his wife = *il est toujours en train de rabaisser sa femme* ⓪ to disparage = *décrier*
☠ *rabaisser son caquet à qqn* = to take s.o. down a peg or two.

BELL (n) *cloche (f)* (church), *sonnette (f)* (door) = doorbell ⓪ chime = *carillon*, ring = *sonnerie*
it rings a bell = *ça me dit quelque chose*
☠ *sonner les cloches à qqn* = to let s.o. have it
— *qui n'entend qu'une cloche n'entend qu'un son* = one should hear both sides
— *quelle cloche !* = what a dummy !

BELLBOY (n) *chasseur (m), groom (m)* : the bellboy of the hotel = *le groom/le chasseur de l'hôtel* = bellhop
☠ *chasseur* → hunter, *groom* → groom.

BELLEVUE (n) *Charenton, Sainte-Anne* ⓪ nuthouse = *maison de fous.*

BELLICOSE (adj) *belliqueux, -euse* : he turns bellicose after three beers = *il devient belliqueux après trois bières* ≠ peaceful = *pacifique.*

BELLIGERENT (adj) *belliqueux, -euse* : a belligerent attitude = *une attitude belliqueuse* ⓪ feisty = *hargneux.*

BELLY (n, -ies) *ventre (m), bide (m)* (LV) : to have a big belly = *avoir un gros ventre/bide* ⓪ paunch = *panse*, tummy = *bidon*
☠ *ventre* → stomach
— *faire un bide* = to flop/to be a bomb.

BELLYACHE (to, -d) *ronchonner* : stop bellyaching ! = *arrête de ronchonner !* ⓪ to grumble = *grommeler.*

BELLYBUTTON (n) *nombril (m)* = navel
☠ *se prendre pour le nombril du monde* = to think one's God's gift.

BELLYFUL (n) **to have one's bellyful of stg/s.o.** = *en avoir plein les bottes de qqch/qqn* ⓪ to have had it = *en avoir plein le dos.*

BELONG (to, -ed) *être à sa place* : put it back where it belongs = *remets ça à sa place*
where does this belong ? = *où est-ce que je range ça ?*
to belong to = *appartenir à* : does this coat belong to you ? = *est-ce que ce manteau vous appartient ?*, the apartment belongs to me = *l'appartement m'appartient* ⓪ to be s.o.'s = *être à qqn* ☠ *il ne m'appartient pas de ...* = it's not for me to ...

BELONGINGS (n pl) **one's belongings** = *ses affaires* : he took all his belongings = *il a pris toutes ses affaires* ⓪ possessions = *biens.*

BELOVED (adj) *bien-aimé, -e* : my beloved wife = *ma femme bien-aimée.*

BELOW (adv) 1/ *du dessous, au-dessous* : the apartment below = *l'appartement du dessous*, they live below = *ils habitent au-dessous* ⓪ underneath = *en dessous* ≠ above = *au-dessus* 2/ *ci-dessous* : the names below = *les noms ci-dessous* ≠ above = *ci-dessus.*

BELOW (prep) *au-dessous de* : the family living below you = *la famille qui habite au-dessous de vous.*

BELT (n) *ceinture (f)* : leather belt = *ceinture de cuir* ⓪ waist = *taille*, buckle = *boucle*, suspenders = *bretelles*
chastity belt = *ceinture de chasteté*
to hit below the belt = *frapper au-dessous de la ceinture* ⓪ a low blow = *un coup bas*
safety/seat belt = *ceinture de sécurité*
to tighten one's belt = *se serrer la ceinture* → POOR
under one's belt = *à son actif* : she has two years of college under her belt = *elle a deux ans d'études supérieures à son actif* ⓪ behind her = *derrière elle.*

BELT (to, -ed) *flanquer un coup à* : he belted his wife = *il a flanqué un coup à sa femme* → TO HIT.

BELTING (n) **to give s.o. a belting** = *flanquer une correction à qqn* → TO HIT.

BENCH (n, -es) *banc (m)* : to sit on a bench = *s'asseoir sur un banc*
to sit on the bench = *être magistrat*
☠ *le banc des jurés* = the jury box
— *le banc des témoins* = the witness stand
— *un banc de poissons* = a school of fish.

BEND (to, bent, bent) *tordre, fléchir* (leg, knee), *plier* (arm) : you bent the can opener = *tu as tordu l'ouvre-boîte*, to bend one's arm/knee = *plier le bras/fléchir le genou*
to bend down = *se baisser* : I bent down to pick it up = *je me suis baissé pour le ramasser* ☠ → to lower
to be bent on = *être résolu à* : I'm bent on doing it now = *je suis résolu à le faire maintenant* ⓪ to be intent on = *avoir la ferme intention de*
to bend over backwards = *se mettre en quatre* : I bent over backwards to help them = *je me suis mis en quatre pour les aider* ⓪ to leave no stone unturned = *remuer ciel et terre*
☠ *plier* → to fold
— *tordre* → to twist
— *je n'ai pas réussi à le fléchir* = I couldn't get him to yield.

BENDER (n) **to go out on a bender** = *faire la bamboula* ⓪ to go on a binge = *faire la java.*

BENEATH (adv) **1/** *du dessous* : the floor beneath = *l'étage du dessous* ⓪ under = *sous* **2/** *en dessous* : they live beneath = *ils habitent en dessous* ⓪ below = *au-dessous.*

BENEATH (prep) **1/** *au-dessous de* : they live beneath us = *ils habitent au-dessous de chez nous* **2/** *indigne de* : it's beneath you to say that = *c'est indigne de vous de dire ça* = unworthy of.

BENEFICIAL (adj) *bénéfique* : sun is beneficial = *le soleil est bénéfique* ≠ harmful = *nuisible.*

BENEFIT (n) **1/** *allocation (f)* : unemployment benefits = *allocations de chômage* **2/** *gala (m) de bienfaisance* : a benefit for cancer research = *un gala de bienfaisance au profit de la recherche sur le cancer* **3/** *bienfait (m)* : the benefits of birth control = *les bienfaits de la contraception*
for s.o.'s benefit = *à l'intention de qqn* : she made the remark for your benefit = *elle a fait cette réflexion à ton intention*
for the benefit of (the kids) = *pour le bien des (enfants)*
the benefit of the doubt = *le bénéfice du doute*
☠ *les bénéfices d'une société* = the profits of a company.

BENEFIT (to, -ed) *profiter à* : the law benefits the wealthy = *la loi profite aux riches*
to benefit from = *profiter de* : you can benefit from my experience = *tu peux profiter de mon expérience.*

BENIGN (adj) *bénin, -igne* : a benign tumor = *une tumeur bénigne.*

BEQUEST (n) *legs (m)* ⓪ gift = *don, donation* = ←.

BERSERK (adj) **to go berserk** = *perdre la boule* : he went berserk and shot into the crowd = *il a perdu la boule et s'est mis à tirer sur la foule* → CRAZY.

BESIDE (prep) *à côté de* : sit beside me = *assieds-toi à côté de moi* = next to ⓪ near = *près de*
to be beside o.s. = *être dans tous ses états*
to be beside o.s. with (joy/anger) = *être fou de (joie/colère).*

BESIDES (adv) *en plus* : he works and writes poetry besides = *il travaille et, en plus, il écrit des poèmes* ⓪ what's more = *qui plus est.*

BESIDES (prep) *à part* : did anyone else come besides him ? = *est-ce que quelqu'un est venu à part lui ?* ⓪ in addition to = *en plus de.*

BESIEGE (to, -d) *assiéger* : to besiege a city = *assiéger une ville* ⓪ to assail = *assaillir.*

BEST (n) *le, la meilleur, -e ; le, la mieux* : which of his films is the best ? = *lequel de ses films est le mieux ?*, as a pianist she is the best = *comme pianiste, c'est la meilleure* ≠ the worst = *le pire/le plus mauvais*

all the best ! = *bonne chance !* **at best** = *au mieux* ≠ at worst = *au pire*	**to be at one's best** = *être au mieux de sa forme* ⓪ to be in great shape = *être en pleine forme*	**to be on the best of terms (with s.o.)** = *être au mieux (avec qqn)/être dans les meilleurs termes (avec qqn)* ≠ not to

be on speaking terms = *ne plus se parler*
to be the best of friends = *être les meilleurs amis du monde* ⓪ to be as thick as thieves = *être copains comme cochons*
to do one's best = *faire de son mieux* : I did my best to help = *j'ai fait de mon mieux pour aider* ⓪ to go all out = *faire le maximum*
to do stg to the best of one's ability = *faire qqch de son mieux*
to get the best of = *avoir raison de* : his last remark got the best of me = *sa dernière*

réflexion a eu raison de ma patience, their team got the best of ours = *leur équipe a eu raison de la nôtre*
to have the best of both worlds = *ne pas pouvoir rêver mieux* : living between Paris and New York, she has the best of both worlds = *elle vit entre Paris et New York, on ne peut rêver mieux*
let's hope for the best ! = *soyons optimistes !*
it's all for the best = *tout est pour le mieux*
to make the best of things = *tirer le meilleur parti des choses*

⓪ to grin and bear it = *faire contre mauvaise fortune bon cœur*
my best to (your wife) ! = *mes amitiés à (votre femme) !*
the best = *ce qu'il y a de mieux* : when he buys, he buys the best = *quand il achète, il achète ce qu'il y a de mieux*
to the best of my knowledge = *autant que je sache* ⓪ to my knowledge = *à ma connaissance*
to the best of my memory/ recollection = *autant que je me souvienne* ⓪ if my memory serves me right = *si j'ai bonne mémoire*

☠ *pour le meilleur et pour le pire* = for better or worse
— *un (léger) mieux* = a (slight) improvement

— *le mieux est l'ennemi du bien* = leave well enough alone.

BEST (adj) *meilleur, -e* : my best friend = *mon meilleur ami* ≠ worst = *pire* ☠ → better

---

best man = *témoin (homme)* ≠ maid of honor = *témoin (femme)* ☠ → witness
best seller = *best-seller* : his last book was a best seller = *son dernier livre a été un best-seller* ⓪ hit = *succès* ≠ flop = *bide*
best wishes = *meilleurs vœux* ⓪ Happy New Year = *bonne année*
it would be best to (tell him the truth) = *ce serait mieux de (lui dire la vérité)*

to put one's best foot forward = *se montrer sous son meilleur jour*
the best thing (to do is to leave) = *le mieux (c'est de partir)*
the best things in life are free = *le soleil brille pour tout le monde*
your best bet is to (go now) = *il vaut mieux que (tu y ailles maintenant).*

BEST (adv) *le mieux* : I like French cheese best = *ce sont les fromages français que j'aime le mieux*

---

you had best (tell him the truth) = *tu ferais mieux de (lui dire la vérité)*

you know best = *tu le sais mieux que moi.*

BESTOW (to, -ed) *octroyer* : to bestow a medal on s.o. = *octroyer une médaille à qqn.*

BET (n) *pari (m)* : to make a bet = *faire un pari* ⓪ wager = *gageure*
it's a good/sure bet that = *il y a gros à parier que* ≠ an off chance = *une petite chance*
☠ *tenir le pari* = to accept the challenge
— *c'est un pari politique* = it's a political gamble.

BET (to, bet, bet) *parier* : I bet he's wrong = *je parie qu'il a tort* ⓪ to wager on = *gager sur*
I'd bet anything that = *je parie tout ce que vous voulez que* ⓪ I bet my bottom dollar that = *je te fiche mon billet que*
I bet you can't ! = *je parie que non !* ⓪ you're on ! = *chiche !*

I'll bet you (two) to one = *je parie à (deux) contre un*
you bet ! = *je n'y manquerai pas !* ⓪ without fail = *sans faute*
you want to bet ? = *tu paries ?*
to bet on = 1/ *compter que/sur* : don't bet on his coming = *ne compte pas qu'il vienne/sur sa venue* ⓪ to expect to = *s'attendre à* 2/ *parier sur* : I always bet on number five = *je parie toujours sur le numéro cinq.*

BETRAY (to, -ed) *trahir* : to betray a friend = *trahir un ami* ⓪ to double-cross = *doubler*
☠ *ton sourire t'a trahi* = your smile gave you away
— *ma mémoire me trahit* = my memory's failing me.

BETRAYAL (n) *trahison (f)* ⓪ double-crossing = *double jeu* ☠ *haute trahison* = high treason.

BETTER (n) *meilleur, -e :* the better of the two = *le meilleur des deux* ≠ worse = *pire* ☠ → best

all the better ! = *tant mieux !* = **so much the better !** ≠ **too bad !** = *tant pis !*
for better or (for) worse = *pour le meilleur et pour le pire*
to get the better of (an opponent) = *l'emporter*

sur (un adversaire) ① **to get the best of** = *avoir raison de*
it's for the better ! = *tout est pour le mieux !*
the (spicier) the better = *plus c'est (épicé), meilleur c'est.*

BETTER (adj) *meilleur, -e, mieux* (attribute) : are you in a better mood ? = *est-ce que vous êtes de meilleure humeur ?,* he looks better = *il a l'air mieux* ≠ worse = *pire*

to be better = 1/ *aller mieux :* she's much better now = *elle va bien mieux maintenant* ≠ to be worse = *aller plus mal* 2/ *être mieux :* you're better without your mustache = *tu es mieux sans ta moustache*
better luck next time = *tant pis, ce sera pour une autre fois*
better ... than = *meilleur ... que :* he's a better lover than his brother = *c'est un meilleur amant que son frère*
to feel better = *se sentir mieux :* I feel much better

now = *je me sens beaucoup mieux maintenant*
it would be better if (you left) = *ce serait mieux si (vous partiez)*
it would be better to (leave now) = *ce serait mieux de (partir maintenant)*
I've seen better days = *j'ai connu des jours meilleurs* ① **there are better days ahead** = *après la pluie le beau temps*
my better half = *ma moitié*
(things) couldn't be better = *(les choses) ne pourraient aller mieux*

☠ *c'est mon meilleur ami* = he's my best friend (*"meilleur"* means both "better" and "best").

BETTER (adv) *mieux :* I understand him better since our last conversation = *je le comprends mieux depuis notre dernière conversation* ≠ worse = *plus mal*

to be better off = 1/ *être mieux :* he's better off with this wife than with the last one = *il est mieux avec cette femme-ci qu'avec la précédente* 2/ *être plus à l'aise :* they're better off than we are = *ils sont plus à l'aise que nous*
better and better = *de mieux en mieux* ≠ worse and worse = *de pire en pire*
better late than never = *mieux vaut tard que jamais*
better still/yet = *mieux encore :* I wish my wife would take a long vacation, or better still/yet ask for a divorce = *je souhaite que ma femme prenne de longues vacances, ou mieux encore, qu'elle demande le divorce*
better than = *mieux que :* I like him better than his brother = *je l'aime mieux que son frère*
had better = *ferait mieux de :* I had better go

before we fight again = *je ferais mieux de m'en aller avant que nous ne nous disputions encore* ① **ought to** = *devrait*
to know better = *le savoir :* you should have known better = *vous auriez dû le savoir*
(children) don't know any better = *(les enfants) ne sont pas responsables*
to like better = *aimer (le) mieux :* what do you like better, Scotch or vodka ? = *qu'est-ce que vous aimez le mieux, le whisky ou la vodka ?* ≠ to detest = *détester*
to think better of = *se raviser :* I was going to ask for a raise, but I thought better of it = *j'allais demander une augmentation, mais je me suis ravisé* ① **to change one's mind** = *changer d'avis*
you'd better believe it ! = *c'est le cas de le dire !*
① **you can say that again !** = *à qui le dites-vous !*

☠ *mieux vaut prévenir que guérir* = an ounce of prevention is worth a pound of cure

— *j'aimerais mieux ...* = I'd rather ...
— *je ne demande pas mieux* = that's all I ask.

BETWEEN (prep) *entre :* he sat between us = *il s'est assis entre nous,* come between two and four = *venez entre deux et quatre,* between my husband and the kids, I have little time for myself = *entre mon mari et les*

gosses, j'ai peu de temps à moi
between now and then = *d'ici là :* we'll see each other between now and then = *nous nous verrons d'ici là*
between you, me and the lamppost/gatepost (she

had an abortion) = *entre nous (elle s'est fait avorter)* ☠ *entre autres choses* = among other things
— *nous étions entre amis* = we were among friends.

BEVERAGE (n) *boisson (f)* : price of $ 20 will include a beverage = *la boisson est comprise dans le prix de 20 dollars* ☠ « beverage » *est moins employé que* « drink ».

BEWARE (to, -d) **beware of (the dog) !** = *attention au (chien) !/(chien méchant !)* ⓞ watch out ! = *faites attention !*

BEWILDER (to, -ed) *plonger dans la perplexité* : his statement bewildered the journalists = *sa déclaration a plongé les journalistes dans la perplexité* ⓞ to confuse = *embrouiller.*

BEWITCH (to, -ed) *ensorceler* : I was bewitched by her beauty = *sa beauté m'a ensorcelé* ⓞ to charm = *charmer.*

BEYOND (adv) *au-delà* : to see into the near future and beyond = *voir dans un avenir proche et au-delà* ☠ for the use of "beyond" after a verb, see the verb.

BEYOND (prep) *au-delà de* : the shop's beyond the post office = *le magasin est au-delà de la poste* ⓞ further than = *plus loin que.*

B-GIRL (n) *entraîneuse (f)* ⓞ hooker = *putain* ☠ → coach.

BI (adj) *bi* : lots of people are openly bi today = *beaucoup de gens ne se cachent pas d'être bi aujourd'hui* ⓞ to swing both ways = *marcher à voile et à vapeur.*

BIAS (n) *parti (m) pris* : that newspaper is full of bias =

ce journal est plein de parti pris ⓞ preconceived ideas = *idées préconçues.*

BIASED (adj) *de parti pris* : a biased judgment = *un jugement de parti pris* ⓞ tendentious = *tendancieux* ≠ unbiased = *sans parti pris.*

BIBLE (n) *Bible (f)* ⓞ Koran = *Coran*, New ≠ Old Testament = *Nouveau* ≠ *Ancien Testament*, Gospel = *Évangile*, biblical = *biblique*
Bible Belt = *états du sud des États-Unis à tendance baptiste ou presbytérienne et très attachés aux enseignements de la Bible.*

BICKER (to, -ed) *se chamailler* : stop bickering all the time ! = *arrêtez de vous chamailler tout le temps !* ⓞ to quarrel = *se quereller.*

BICYCLE (n) *bicyclette (f)* : he fell off his bicycle = *il est tombé de bicyclette* ⓞ bike = *vélo*, moped = *mobylette*, motorcycle = *motocyclette*, scooter = ←, handle bars = *guidon*, pedals = *pédales*, to bike = *faire du vélo* = to ride à bike.

BID (n) *offre (f)*, *enchère (f)* (auction) : the highest bid was a thousand dollars → *la plus grosse offre/enchère était de mille dollars* ☠ → offer, → bidding.

BID (to, bid, bid) *faire une offre/une enchère* : three companies bid for the contract = *trois sociétés ont fait une offre pour le contrat*, we bid $ 300 for this painting = *nous avons fait une enchère de 300 dollars pour ce tableau.*

BIDDING (n) *enchères (f pl)* : the bidding began at ten dollars = *les enchères ont commencé à dix dollars* ☠ *vente aux enchères* = auction sale.

BIG (adj, -ger, -gest) **1/** *grand, -e* : the coat's too big = *le manteau est trop grand*, the kids are big now = *les enfants sont grands maintenant*, a big city = *une grande ville* = large ⓞ gigantic = *gigantesque* ≠ small = *petit*, tiny = *minuscule* ☠ → great
2/ *gros, grosse* : a big mistake = *une grosse faute*, a big success = *un gros succès* ⓞ important = ←

☠ *je donnerais gros pour* = I'd give anything to	*sabots* = I have your number	lines
— *il y a gros à parier que* = it's a sure bet that	— *un gros rhume* = a bad cold	— *jouer gros jeu* = to play high stakes
— *c'est un peu gros* = that's a bit thick	— *un gros plan* = a close-up	— *en avoir gros sur le cœur* = to be heavy-hearted
— *je te vois venir avec tes gros*	— *décrocher le gros lot* = to hit the jackpot	— *il/elle est gros/grosse* = he/she's fat/heavy
	— *des gros mots* = dirty words	
	— *les gros titres* = the head-	

3/ *fort, -e* : a big woman = *une femme forte* ⓞ fat = *gros* ☠ → strong
4/ *qui a beaucoup de succès* : jeans are big this year (in the States) = *les jeans ont beaucoup de succès cette année (aux États-Unis)* ≠ out = *démodé*

---

to be big on = *raffoler de* : I'm not big on Chinese food = *je ne raffole pas de la cuisine chinoise* ≠ not to be much on = *ne pas être fou de*
to be big with = *avoir beaucoup de succès auprès de* : Chinese food's big with the Americans = *la cui-*

sine chinoise a beaucoup de succès auprès des Américains
I'd rather be a big fish in a little pond than a little fish in a big pond = *il vaut mieux être le premier dans son village que le second à Rome*

to be in the big time = *tenir le haut du pavé* : since his last record he's in the big time = *depuis son dernier disque il tient le haut du pavé*
to be too big for one's boots/breeches = *se croire sorti de la cuisse de Jupiter* ⓪ to think one's hot stuff = *se prendre pour le nombril du monde*
the Big Apple = New York City = *Manhattan*
big boss = *grand patron* : ask Joe, he's the big boss = *demandez à Joe, c'est lui le grand patron*
big cheese = *huile* : she's a big cheese (in the company) = *c'est une huile (dans l'entreprise)* ⓪ bigwig = *ténor* ☠ → oil
big deal ! = *et après* ! → GOSH !
big money = *beaucoup de fric* : they earn big money = *ils gagnent beaucoup de fric*
big name in = *grand nom de* : a big name in medicine = *un grand nom de la médecine* ⓪ big shot = *grand ponte*
big noise = *gros bonnet* : a big noise in politics = *un gros bonnet de la politique* ⓪ top banana = *grosse légume*
big shot = *grand ponte* : all the big shots of the party were at the dinner = *tous les grands pontes du parti participaient au dîner* ≠ small fry = *menu fretin*
big talk = *fanfaronnade* : everything he said yesterday was big talk = *tout ce qu'il a dit hier, c'était de la fanfaronnade*
big top = *chapiteau* ⓪ circus = *cirque*
big wheel = *grand manitou* : a big wheel in the party = *un grand manitou du parti* ≠ the fifth wheel = *la cinquième roue du carrosse*
we must speak softly and carry a big stick = *il faut que nous ayons une main de fer dans un gant de velours*
to go for in a big way = *s'enthousiasmer pour* : the public went for Piaf in a big way = *le public s'est enthousiasmé pour Piaf*
to have a big heart = *avoir un grand cœur*
to have a big stake in = *investir beaucoup dans* : the banks have a big stake in the aircraft industry = *les banques ont beaucoup investi dans l'industrie aéronautique*
no big deal = 1/ *pas de quoi fouetter un chat* : don't get excited, it's no big deal ! = *ne t'excite pas comme ça, il n'y a pas de quoi fouetter un chat* ! → THAT'S LIFE ! 2/ *pas fameux* : the play was no big deal = *la pièce n'était pas fameuse* → AWFUL
what's the big idea ? = *ça va pas, non ?* ⓪ who do you think you are ? = *pour qui te prends-tu ?* → GOSH !

BIG (adv) **to go over big** = *avoir un succès monstre* ≠ to come a cropper = *ramasser une gamelle*
to hit it big = *décrocher le gros lot* : he hit it big on the Stock Market = *il a décroché le gros lot à la Bourse*
to make it big = *bien réussir* : he made it big in the clothing industry = *il a bien réussi dans la* confection
to talk big = *fanfaronner* : he talks big but he didn't sleep with half the girls he claims to = *il fanfaronne mais il n'a pas couché avec la moitié des filles avec lesquelles il prétend l'avoir fait*
to think big = *voir grand* : in life you have to think big = *dans la vie il faut voir grand.*

BIGAMIST (n) bigame *(m, f)* **BIGAMY** (n) bigamie *(f)* ≠ monogamy = *monogamie.*

BIGGIE (n) gros bonnet *(m)* : he's a biggie in advertising = *c'est un gros bonnet de la publicité.*

BIGMOUTH (n) grande gueule *(f)* ⓪ loudmouth = *fort en gueule.*

BIGOT (n) sectaire *(m, f)* : her family are all bigots = *dans sa famille, ce sont tous des sectaires* ⓪ racist = *raciste* ☠ *un bigot* = a churchnut.

BIGOTED (adj) sectaire ≠ tolerant = *tolérant* **BIGOTRY** (n, -ies) sectarisme *(m).*

BIG-TIME (adj) *qui tient le haut du pavé* : a big-time crook = *un escroc qui tient le haut du pavé* ≠ small-time = *de petite envergure.*

BIGWIG (n) ténor *(m)* : the bigwigs of the party choose the candidate = *les ténors du parti choisissent le candidat* ⓪ big shot = *grand ponte*, honcho = *grosse légume.*

BIKE (n) vélo *(m)*, bécane *(f)* (LV) ⓪ moped = *mobylette* ☠ avoir un (petit) vélo = to have bats in the belfry.

BILATERAL (adj) bilatéral, -e : a bilateral decision = *une décision bilatérale.*

BILGE (n inv) idioties *(f pl)* : what bilge ! = *quelles idioties* ! ⓪ rot = *foutaises* ☠ *son idiotie dépasse les bornes* = her stupidity has no bounds.

BILINGUAL (adj) bilingue : a bilingual child = *un enfant bilingue* ⓪ trilingual = *trilingue.*

BILL (n) 1/ note *(f)* (restaurant), facture *(f)* (business) : may I have the bill, please ? = *est-ce que je peux avoir la note, s'il vous plaît ?*, send me the bill = *envoyez-moi la facture* ⓪ check = *addition* 2/ billet *(m)* : a ten-dollar bill = *un billet de dix dollars* 3/ projet *(m)* de loi : Congress passed the bill = *le Congrès a voté le projet de loi*
bill of exchange = *lettre de change*
a bill of goods = *des salades* : stop trying to sell me a bill of goods ! = *arrête d'essayer de me vendre tes salades* ! ⓪ salestalk = *boniment*
to fill the bill = *faire très bien l'affaire* : a good Scotch will fill the bill = *un bon whisky fera très bien l'affaire*

= a good Scotch will do the trick
to foot the bill = *payer la note* = to pick up the tab
to pad the bill = *saler la note*
post no bills = *défense d'afficher*
the Bill of Rights = *la Déclaration des droits de l'homme*
☠ *facture détaillée* = invoice
— *note* → note
— *billet* → ticket.

BILL (to, -ed) *facturer :* to be billed monthly = *être facturé au mois*
to bill and coo = *roucouler.*

BILLBOARD (n) *panneau (m) d'affichage :* billboards on the highway = *des panneaux d'affichage sur l'autoroute* ⚭ sign = *affiche.*

BILLION (n) *milliard (m),* billion *(m)* (GB) : a billion dollars = *un milliard de dollars* ☠ *un billion* = a trillion (US).

BILLIONAIRE (n) *milliardaire (m, f)* ⚭ trillionaire = *multimilliardaire.*

BIMONTHLY (adj) *bimensuel, -elle :* a bimonthly paper = *un journal bimensuel* ⚭ biweekly = *bihebdomadaire,* biyearly = *biannuel.*

BIND (n) **to be in a bind** = *être en mauvaise posture* ⚭ to be in hot water = *être dans de beaux draps.*

BIND (to, bound, bound) *lier :* they bound the hostages' hands = *ils ont lié les mains des otages* ⚭ to attach = *attacher*
to be bound by (a contract) = *être lié par (un contrat)*
☠ *se lier avec qqn* = to become friends with s.o.

BINGE (n) *débauche (f) :* a buying binge = *une débauche d'achats* ⚭ spree = *folie*
to go on a binge = *faire la java :* we went on a binge last night and got smashed = *on a fait la java hier soir et on a pris une cuite* ⚭ to go on a spree = *faire la bombe.*

BINOCULARS (n pl) *jumelles (f pl) :* to look through binoculars = *regarder avec des jumelles* ☠ → twin.

BIOGRAPHY (n, -ies) *biographie (f)* ⚭ autobiography = *autobiographie* **BIOGRAPHER** (n) *biographe (m, f).*

BIOLOGY (n) *biologie (f)* **BIOLOGIST** (n) *biologiste (m, f).*

BIPARTISAN (adj) *bipartite :* a bipartisan meeting = *une réunion bipartite.*

BIRD (n) *oiseau (m) :* some birds tell = *il y a des oiseaux qui parlent* ⚭ nest = *nid,* beak = *bec*

(blue) jay = *jais*	**duck** = *canard*
canary = *canari*	**eagle** = *aigle*
chicken = *poulet*	**falcon** = *faucon*
crow = *corbeau*	**goose** = *oie*
dove = *colombe*	**hawk** = *faucon*

---

hen = *poule*	**peacock** = *paon*	
lark = *alouette*	**pheasant** = *faisan*	
nightingale = *rossignol*	**pigeon** = ←	
ostrich = *autruche*	**robin** = *rouge-gorge*	
owl = *hibou/ chouette*	**sparrow** = *moineau*	
parakeet = *perruche*	**swallow** = *hirondelle*	
parrot = *perroquet*	**turkey** = *dinde*	

---

a bird in the hand is worth two in the bush = *un tiens vaut mieux que deux tu l'auras/il ne faut pas lâcher la proie pour l'ombre* ⚭ half a loaf is better than none ! = *c'est toujours ça de pris !*
birds of a feather flock together = *qui se ressemble s'assemble* ⚭ to be two of a kind = *être du même bois*
to eat like a bird = *avoir un appétit d'oiseau* ≠ to eat like a horse = *manger comme quatre*
for the birds = *qui ne vaut rien :* the movie was for the birds = *le film ne valait rien* → AWFUL
an odd/queer bird = *un drôle d'oiseau* ⚭ a queer duck = *un drôle de zigue*
(to tell children about) the birds and the bees = *(expliquer aux enfants que) les bébés ne naissent pas dans les choux* ⚭ the facts of life = *les choses de la vie*

☠ *être comme l'oiseau sur la branche* = to be in a precarious situation.

BIRTH (n) *naissance (f) :* birth certificate = *certificat/acte de naissance,* birth control = *contrôle des naissances* ⚭ birthplace = *lieu de naissance,* birthrate = *taux de natalité,* birthmark = *tache de vin*
to give birth to (a girl) = *donner naissance à/accoucher d'(une fille)*
(he's American) by birth = *(il est américain) de naissance.*

BIRTHDAY (n) *anniversaire (m) :* birthday party = *fête d'anniversaire*
in one's birthday suit = *dans la tenue d'Adam/d'Ève* ⚭ in the raw = *dans le plus simple appareil*
☠ → anniversary.

BISEXUAL (adj) *bisexuel, -elle* ⚭ to be ac/dc = *être ambivalent.*

BISHOP (n) *évêque (m)* ⚭ cardinal = ←, archbishop = *archevêque.*

BIT (n) **a bit** = *un peu :* the cake's good ; do you want a bit ? = *le gâteau est bon ; vous en voulez un peu ?* ⚭ a smatter-ing = *un petit peu* ≠ a great deal = *beaucoup*
a bit (drunk/hot) = *un peu (ivre/chaud)* ⚭ somewhat = *quelque*

peu
a bit of = *un peu de :* I could use a bit of help = *j'accepterais volontiers un peu d'aide* ≠ lots of = *beaucoup de*
a bit of a (liar/bastard) = *un tantinet (menteur/salaud)*
a bit part = *un rôle accessoire* ≠ leading part = *rôle principal*
a bit too (hot/sad) = *un peu trop (chaud/triste)*
bit by bit = *peu à peu* ⓪ step by step = *pas à pas*
to champ at the bit = *ronger son frein*
to do a whole bit = *faire tout un numéro*
to do one's bit = *faire sa part*
it's a bit much/thick ! = *c'est un peu raide/fort !*
just a bit = *un petit peu :* are you hungry ? — just a bit = *avez-vous faim ? — un petit peu* ⓪ sort of = *un peu*
not a bit = *pas du tout :* I'm not a bit in love with him = *je ne suis pas du tout amoureuse de lui*
(stay) a bit = *(reste) un peu* ⓪ for a while = *un moment.*

BITCH (n, -es) **1/** *salope (f),garce (f) :* what a bitch he married ! = *quelle salope/garce il a épousée !* → BASTARD
2/ *qqch d'emmerdant :* losing his job/getting a flat was a bitch = *c'était emmerdant de perdre son boulot/d'avoir crevé* ⓪ nightmare = *cauchemar.*

BITCH (to, -ed) *gueuler :* stop bitching about everything ! = *arrête de gueuler pour tout !* ⓪ to kick = *râler*
☠ *gueuler un nom* = to shout out a name.

BITCHY (adj, -ier, -iest) *salaud, salope :* it was a bitchy thing to do = *c'était salaud de faire ça* ⓪ low = *bas.*

BITE (n) **1/** *morsure (f)* (dog), *piqûre (f)* (insect) : a dog bite = *une morsure de chien,* a mosquito bite = *une piqûre de moustique* ☠ *piqûre* → sting
to have a bite = *manger un morceau* ⓪ a nosh = *un en-cas*
do you want a bite ? = *tu en veux un morceau ?*
to put the bite on s.o. for stg = *taper qqn de qqch :* he put the bite on me for a grand = *il m'a tapé de mille dollars* ≠ to lend = *prêter*
2/ *piquant (m) :* the novel lacks bite = *le roman manque de piquant*
to take the bite out of = *retirer tout le piquant de.*

BITE (to, bit, bitten) **1/** *mordre :* dogs bite = *les chiens mordent* ⓪ to gnaw = *ronger*
to be bitten by (jazz) = *être mordu de (jazz)*
to bite off more than one can chew = *avoir les yeux plus grands que le ventre*
☠ *mordre à l'hameçon* = to swallow the bait
2/ *marcher :* I tried to sell him a bill of goods, but he didn't bite = *j'ai voulu lui raconter des salades, mais il n'a pas marché* ☠ → to walk.

BITING (adj) *mordant, -e :* biting words = *paroles mordantes* ⓪ cutting = *cinglant.*

BITTER (adj) *amer, -ère :* a bitter woman/orange = *une femme/orange amère* ⓪ sour = *aigre*
bitter enemies = *ennemis mortels*
to the bitter end = *jusqu'au bout :* we had to remain at the dinner to the bitter end = *il a fallu que nous restions au dîner jusqu'au bout*
it's a bitter pill to swallow = *la pilule est dure à avaler.*

BITTERLY (adv) *amèrement :* bitterly disappointed = *amèrement déçu*
to cry bitterly = *pleurer comme une Madeleine* ⓪ to shed tears = *verser des larmes.*

BITTERNESS (n) *amertume (f).*

BITTERSWEET (adj) *aigre-doux, -douce :* bittersweet memories = *des souvenirs aigres-doux*
☠ *sauce aigre-douce* = sweet-and-sour sauce.

BIZARRE (adj) *bizarre :* a bizarre idea/guy = *une idée/un type bizarre* ⓪ peculiar = *insolite,* weird = *singulier.*

BLACK (n) **1/** *noir (m) :* dressed in black = *habillé en noir* ≠ white = *blanc*
in the black = *bénéficiaire :* the company's in the black = *la société est bénéficiaire* ≠ in the red = *déficitaire*
put it in black and white = *mettez ça noir sur blanc*
2/ *Noir, -e :* my favorite doctor is a black = *mon médecin préféré est un Noir* ⓪ negro = *nègre,* NAACP = *association de défense des Noirs,* nigger = *négro* ≠ honky = *sale Blanc*
☠ *avoir peur du noir* = to be afraid of the dark
— *broyer du noir* = to be down in the dumps
— *travailler au noir* = to do undeclared work.

BLACK (adj, -er, -est) **1/** *noir, -e :* a black shirt = *une chemise noire* ≠ white = *blanc*
black eye = *œil au beurre noir* ⓪ shiner = *œil poché*
black humor = *humour noir*
black magic = *magie noire*
black market = *marché noir*
black sheep = *brebis galeuse*
2/ *noir, -e :* black theater = *le théâtre noir,* the Black Panthers = *les Panthères noires,* black studies = *études de la civilisation noire*
☠ *être (complètement) noir* = to be smashed
— *chambre noire* = darkroom
— *blousons noirs* = Hell's Angels.

BLACK (adv) **to beat s.o. black and blue** = *rouer qqn de coups* ⓪ a black-and-blue mark = *un bleu* → TO HIT.

BLACKBALL (to, -ed) *blackbouler :* the club blackballed him = *le club l'a blackboulé* ⓪ to ostracize = *frapper d'ostracisme.*

BLACKBOARD (n) *tableau (m) noir :* to write on the blackboard = *écrire au tableau noir* ⓪ sponge = *éponge.*

BLACKLIST (to, -ed) *mettre à l'index/sur la liste noire.*

BLACKMAIL (n) *chantage* (m) **BLACKMAIL** (to, -ed) *faire chanter* **BLACKMAILER** (n) *maître chanteur* (m).

BLACKOUT (n) **1**/ *black-out* (m) ⓪ air raid = *raid aérien* **2**/ *black-out* (m) : a complete blackout on the scandal = *le black-out total sur le scandale* **3**/ *panne* (f) *d'électricité.*

BLACK OUT (to, -ed) *tourner de l'œil* : I blacked out from the heat = *j'ai tourné de l'œil à cause de la chaleur* ≠ to come to = *revenir à soi.*

BLAH (adj) *fadasse* : a blah personality = *une personnalité fadasse* ≠ exciting = *passionnant.*

BLAME (n) *blâme* (m) : we'll share the blame = *nous partagerons le blâme* ⓪ responsibility = *responsabilité*
to lay/put the blame on s.o. = *mettre la faute sur le dos de qqn* ⓪ to lay stg on s.o. = *rejeter qqch sur le dos de qqn*
to take the blame = *endosser la responsabilité.*

BLAME (to, -d) *blâmer* : I'm not blaming you = *je ne vous blâme pas*
don't blame me ! = *ne me faites pas de reproches !* =
I'm not to blame !
who's to blame ? = *à qui la faute ?*
you've no one to blame but yourself = *ne t'en prends qu'à toi-même*
to blame s.o. for stg = *reprocher qqch à qqn* : he blamed me for the mistake = *il m'a reproché cette erreur.*

BLAMELESS (adj) *irréprochable* **BLAMEWORTHY** (adj) *blâmable.*

BLAND (adj, -er, -est) *peu relevé, -e* (cooking), *sans relief* (personality) : bland food/personality = *nourriture peu relevée/personnalité sans relief* ⓪ flat = *fade.*

BLANK (n) *blanc* (m) : fill in the blanks = *remplissez les blancs* ☠ → white
to draw a blank = *avoir un trou de mémoire* ⓪ it slipped my mind = *ça m'est sorti de l'esprit.*

BLANK (adj, -er, -est) *vierge* : a blank paper/wall = *une feuille/un mur vierge* ⓪ empty = *vide*
a blank check = *un chèque en blanc*
☠ *elle est vierge* = she's a virgin.

BLANKET (n) *couverture* (f) ⓪ bedspread = *couvre-lit* ☠ *tirer la couverture à soi* = to steal the show
— *couverture (trafic)* = cover/front (dealings)
— *couverture (reportage)* = news coverage
— *couverture de livre* = book cover.

BLANKET (adj) **a blanket (increase)** = *une (augmentation) générale.*

BLASPHEMOUS (adj) *blasphématoire* ≠ sacred = *sacré* **BLASPHEMY** (n, -ies) *blasphème* (m) ⓪ sacrilege = *sacrilège.*

BLAST (n) **1**/ *raout* (m) : a blast at the White House = *un raout à la Maison-Blanche* **2**/ *explosion* (f) : a blast of

dynamite = *une explosion de dynamite* = explosion **3**/ *violente critique* (f) : the President's blast at the Senator = *la violente critique du sénateur par le Président.*

BLAST (to, -ed) *descendre en flammes* : he blasted the junior Senator = *il a descendu en flammes le jeune sénateur* → TO LAMBAST
blast it ! = *fichtre !* → GOSH !
to blast off = *mettre à feu* (fusée) ⓪ a blastoff = *une mise à feu.*

BLATANT (adj) *flagrant, -e* : a blatant lie = *un mensonge flagrant* ⓪ sheer = *pur* ☠ → flagrant.

BLAZE (n) *flambée* (f) ⓪ fire = *feu*
go to blazes ! = *du large !* → BUZZ OFF !
to run like blazes = *courir ventre à terre* ⓪ to run like a madman = *courir comme un fou*
☠ *une flambée des prix* = a jump in prices.

BLAZE (to, -d) *flamber* : the fire's blazing = *le feu flambe* ☠ *flamber (jeu)* = to gamble.

BLEACH (n, -es) *eau* (f) *de Javel* ⓪ starch = *amidon.*

BLEACH (to, -ed) *décolorer* : to bleach one's hair = *se décolorer les cheveux.*

BLEAK (adj, -er, -est) *gris, -e* : bleak weather/future = *temps/avenir gris* ⓪ drab = *terne,* dreary = *morne* ☠ → grey.

BLEED (to, bled, bled) *saigner* : the wound was bleeding = *la blessure saignait* ⓪ tourniquet = *garrot.*

BLEND (to, -ed) **1**/ *mélanger* : blend the ingredients = *mélangez les ingrédients* **2**/ *se marier* : the colors blend well = *les couleurs se marient bien* ≠ to clash = *jurer* ☠ → to marry.

BLESS (to, -ed) *bénir* ≠ to curse = *maudire*
bless you ! = **1**/ *à vos souhaits !/à vos amours !* ⓪ to sneeze = *éternuer* **2**/ *Dieu vous bénisse !* ⓪ God be with you ! = *Dieu vous accompagne !*

BLESSED (adj) *béni, -e* (des dieux) : a blessed life = *une vie bénie (des dieux)*
not to do a blessed thing = *ne pas en ficher une rame* ⓪ to twiddle one's thumbs = *se tourner les pouces*
a blessed event = *un heureux événement*
the Blessed Virgin = *la Sainte Vierge*
that blessed (car) = *cette sacrée (voiture).*

BLESSING (n) *bénédiction* (f) : the raise was a blessing = *cette augmentation a été une bénédiction* ⓪ godsend = *bienfait du ciel* ≠ curse = *malédiction*
to be a blessing in disguise = *avoir de la chance dans son malheur* ⓪ every cloud has a silver lining = *à quelque chose malheur est bon.*

BLIND (adj, -er, -est) *aveugle* : the child's blind = *l'enfant est aveugle* ⓪ blindness = *cécité,* seeing-eye dog = *chien d'aveugle,* blindman's buff = *colin-maillard*
blind as a bat = *myope comme une taupe*
blind date = *rendez-vous galant (entre deux personnes*

qui ne se connaissent pas) : my friends arranged a blind date and that's how I met my husband = *mes amis nous avaient arrangé un rendez-vous et c'est comme ça que j'ai rencontré mon mari* ⓓ to fix s.o. up = *organiser un rendez-vous pour qqn*
blind faith = *la foi du charbonnier*
it's the blind leading the lame = *c'est la fable de l'aveugle et du paralytique*
blind in one eye = *borgne*
(a) blind person = *(un) aveugle*.

BLINDER (n) **to have blinders on** = *avoir des œillères*.

BLINDFOLD (to, -ed) *bander les yeux de* : they blindfolded the hostage = *ils ont bandé les yeux de l'otage*.

BLINDLY (adv) **1/** *aveuglément* : to love s.o. blindly = *aimer qqn aveuglément* **2/** *à l'aveuglette* : to choose blindly = *choisir à l'aveuglette*.

BLINK (n) **on the blink** = *détraqué, -e* : my radio's on the blink = *ma radio est détraquée* ⓓ out of order = *en panne* ☠ → demented.

BLINK (to, -ed) *cligner des yeux* : the spotlight made me blink = *le spot m'a fait cligner des yeux*.

BLISS (n inv) *félicité (f), béatitude (f)* ≠ unhappiness = *malheur*.

BLISTER (n) *ampoule (f), cloque (f)* : a blister on one's hand = *une ampoule à la main* ☠ ampoule électrique = bulb.

BLIZZARD (n) *blizzard (m)* : the village was hit by a blizzard = *le village a été touché par le blizzard* ⓓ snowfall = *chute de neige*.

BLOATED (adj) *gonflé, -e* (stomach), *bouffi, -e* (face) ⓓ swollen = *enflé* ☠ *c'est gonflé (de sa part)* = it's nervy.

BLOCK (n) *rue (f)* : the bank's two blocks away = *la banque est à deux rues d'ici*, he lives on my block = *il habite dans ma rue* ☠ → street
to knock s.o.'s block off = *casser la figure à qqn* → TO HIT
(to run) around the block = *faire le tour du pâté de maisons (en courant)*.

BLOCK (to, -ed) **1/** *bloquer* : to block a bill = *bloquer un projet de loi*, the truck was blocking the street = *le camion bloquait la rue*
☠ *bloquer (salaires)* = to freeze (wages)
— *ma machine s'est bloquée* = my machine jammed
to be blocked up = *être bouché* : the sink's blocked up = *l'évier est bouché*
to block off = *barrer* : the cops blocked off the streets = *les flics ont barré les rues*
☠ *barrer (un mot)* = to cross out (a word)
— *se barrer* = to split
2/ *faire barrage* : the feminists are trying to block his election = *les féministes essaient de faire barrage à son élection*.

BLOCKADE (n) *blocus (m)* : to break the blockade = *forcer le blocus*.

BLOCKBUSTER (n) *grande réussite (f)* : his last movie is a blockbuster = *son dernier film est une grande réussite* ≠ a washout = *un bide intégral*.

BLOKE (n) (GB) *gars (m)* : he's a nice bloke = *c'est un gars sympa* ⓓ fellow = *type*.

BLOND(E) (n) *blond, -e* : she's a blonde = *c'est une blonde* ⓓ a redhead = *un roux* ☠ *une blonde (cigarette)* = a mild cigarette **BLOND** (adj) *blond, -e* : blond hair = *cheveux blonds*.

BLOOD (n) *sang (m)* : the body was lying in a pool of blood = *le cadavre gisait dans une mare de sang* ⓓ bloodshot eyes = *des yeux injectés de sang*
blood bank = *banque du sang*
blood clot = *caillot de sang*
blood group = *groupe sanguin*
blood poisoning = *septicémie*
blood pressure = *tension* : high ≠ low blood pressure = *hypertension* ≠ *hypotension* ☠ → tension
blood test = *analyse de sang*
blood ties = *liens du sang*
blood is thicker than water = *c'est la voix du sang*
it made my blood run cold = *ça m'a glacé le sang*
to sweat blood = *suer sang et eau* : I sweated blood with this work = *j'ai sué sang et eau sur ce travail* ⓓ it was like pulling teeth = *c'était la croix et la bannière*
you can't get blood from a stone = *la plus belle fille du monde ne peut donner que ce qu'elle a*
☠ *se ronger les sangs* = to be worried sick
— *bon sang !* = good Lord !

BLOODBATH (n) *bain (m) de sang* ⓓ bloodshed = *effusion de sang*.

BLOODTHIRSTY (adj) *sanguinaire* ⓓ cruel = ←.

BLOODY (adj, -ier, -est) **1/** *sanglant, -e* : a bloody battle = *une bataille sanglante*
bloody Mary = ← = *(vodka + jus de tomate)*
to yell bloody murder = *gueuler comme un putois* ⓓ to scream one's lungs out = *gueuler à pleins poumons* ☠ *un échec sanglant/une critique sanglante* = a devastating defeat/review
2/ (GB) *foutu, -e* = fucking ☠ → fucking.

BLOOM (to, -ed) **1/** *fleurir* : daffodils bloom in the spring = *les jonquilles fleurissent au printemps* ⓓ to blossom = *être en fleurs* **2/** *s'épanouir* : she's blooming with her husband = *elle s'épanouit avec son mari*.

BLOOPER (n) *bévue (f)* : the commentator's blooper cost him his job = *la bévue du commentateur lui a coûté son poste* ⓓ blunder = *gaffe*.

BLOT OUT (to, -ted) **to blot out (bad memories)** = *rayer (les mauvais souvenirs) de sa mémoire*.

BLOUSE (n) *chemisier (m), blouse (f)* : a silk blouse = *un chemisier/une blouse de soie* ⓓ shirt = *chemise* ☠ *blouse (de travail)* = smock.

BLOW

BLOW (n) **1/** *coup (m) :* a blow on the head = *un coup sur la tête* ① whack = *gnon* **2/** *coup (m) :* losing her job has been a terrible blow = *ça a été un coup terrible pour elle de perdre son boulot* ① shock = *choc*

to come to blows = *en venir aux mains* ① to be at each other's throat = *se bouffer le nez*	**to do a blow job** = *tailler une pipe* ① to go down on s.o. = *faire minette*

| ☠ *rendre coup pour coup* = to return like for like
— *il tient bien le coup* = he's holding up well
— *c'est le coup classique* = it's the same old story
— *en mettre un coup* = to really go at it
— *le coup a porté* = it struck home
— *boire un coup* = to have a drink
— *un coup de tête* = a sudden impulse
— *coups et blessures* = assault and battery
— *sur le coup de midi* = on the stroke of noon
— *coup de fusil* = 1/ shot 2/ expensive (clip joint)
— *tout à coup* = all of a sudden
— *coup de feu* = shot
— *coup de soleil* = sunburn
— *faire un coup* = to pull a job | — *il a raté son coup* = he struck out
— *tirer un coup* = to get one's rocks off
— *ça vaut le coup* = it's worth it
— *être dans le coup* = 1/ to be with it 2/ to be an accomplice
— *faire coup double* = to kill two birds with one stone
— *du même coup* = at the same time
— *du premier coup* = at the first try
— *tué sur le coup* = killed outright
— *coup de pied* = kick
— *coup de poing* = punch
— *coup de fouet* = uplift
— *coup de barre* 1/ sudden fatigue 2/ skyhigh prices
— *après coup j'ai pensé ...* = after I thought ...
— *coup sur coup* = one after the other | — *à coup sûr* = for sure
— *prendre un coup de vieux* = to age suddenly
— *risquer le coup* = to have a shot/a try
— *des coups durs* = hard knocks
— *avoir un coup dans le nez/ dans l'aile* = to be tipsy
— *coup de théâtre* = unexpected turn of events
— *coup fourré/de Jarnac* = stab in the back
— *coup de main* = helping hand
— *coup de veine* = stroke of luck
— *avoir un coup de pompe* = to be suddenly tired
— *un coup vite tiré* = a quick fuck/screw
— *coup d'envoi* = kickoff
— *coup de fil/de téléphone* = phone call. |

BLOW (to, blew, blown) **1/** *souffler :* the wind's blowing = *le vent souffle*

☠ *laissez-moi le temps de souffler* = let me catch my breath	— *souffler à qqn* = to prompt s.o. — *ça m'a soufflé* = I was taken aback

2/ *claquer :* he blew all the money in two years = *il a claqué tout l'argent en deux ans* ① to waste = *gaspiller* ☠ → to slam
3/ *ficher par terre :* you blew the interview = *tu as fichu l'entrevue par terre* ① to mess up = *ficher en l'air*
4/ *se casser :* let's blow ! = *on se casse !* → TO LEAVE ☠ → to break

| **to blow into** = *débarquer à/dans :* he blew into New York yesterday = *il a débarqué à New York hier* ① to show up = *rappliquer*
to blow out = *souffler :* he blew out the candles = *il a soufflé les bougies*
to blow over = *se calmer :* wait till things blow over = *attends que les choses se calment* ① to settle down = *se tasser* ☠ → to calm
to blow s.o. to stg = *payer qqch à qqn :* come on, we'll blow you to dinner = *venez, nous vous payons à dîner* | **to blow up** = 1/ *(faire) sauter :* the terrorists blow up the bridge = *les terroristes ont fait sauter le pont* 2/ *éclater :* my father blew up when I came home late = *mon père à éclaté parce que je suis rentré en retard à la maison* → ANGRY ☠ → to burst 3/ *grossir :* the press blew up the whole affair = *la presse a grossi toute l'affaire* ≠ to minimize = *minimiser* ☠ *grossir (prendre du poids)* = to put on weight 4/ *agrandir :* to blow up a photograph = *agrandir une photo* ☠ → to grow 5/ *gonfler :* to blow up a balloon = *gonfler un ballon* ☠ → to inflate. |

BLOWOUT (n) **1/** *nouba* (f) : they had a blow-out to celebrate their winning = *ils ont fait la nouba pour fêter leur victoire* ⓌⓉ spread = *gueuleton* **2/** *crevaison* (f) : a blowout on the highway = *une crevaison sur l'autoroute.*

BLOWUP (n) *agrandissement* (m) : the blowup of a photograph = *l'agrandissement d'une photo* = the enlargement of a photograph.

BLUBBER (to, -ed) *chialer* ⓌⓉ to be a crybaby = *être pleurnicheur.*

BLUE (n) *bleu* (m) : dressed in blue = *habillé en bleu*
to come out of the blue = *tomber du ciel* : the raise came out of the blue = *cette augmentation m'est tombée du ciel* ⓌⓉ out of nowhere = *arrivé comme par miracle* ☠ *un bleu (nouveau)* = a rookie
— *un bleu (sur le bras)* = a black-and-blue mark.

BLUE (adj, -r, -st) **1/** *bleu, -e* : a blue coat = *un manteau bleu* ⓌⓉ baby blue = *bleu layette,* navy blue = *bleu marine*
blue chip = *valeur sûre*
blue jeans = *blue-jean(s)*
blue laws = *lois puritaines (fermeture des bars le dimanche, etc.)*
blue movies = *films pornos*
blue ribbon = *premier prix* : their cattle won the blue ribbon = *leur bétail a gagné le premier prix*
once in a blue moon = *tous les trente-six du mois* : he visits his parents once in a blue moon = *il vient voir ses parents tous les trente-six du mois* ≠ all the time = *tout le temps*
to talk a blue streak = *avoir la langue bien pendue* ⓌⓉ to have the gift of gab = *avoir du bagou*
(to talk, etc.) till one's blue in the face = *se tuer à (dire, etc.)* : I told him till I was blue in the face that I wouldn't sleep with him = *je me suis tuée à lui dire que je ne coucherais pas avec lui*
☠ *un steak bleu* = a very rare steak
— *avoir une peur bleue de* = to have a great fear of
2/ *cafardeux, -euse* : I'm feeling blue this week = *je me sens cafardeuse cette semaine* ⓌⓉ down = *qui a la déprime.*

BLUE-COLLAR (adj) **blue-collar worker** = *col bleu* ⓌⓉ white-collar worker = *col blanc/employé.*

BLUEPRINT (n) *plans* (m pl) *détaillés* : the blueprint for the building/a new sales campaign = *les plans détaillés d'un immeuble/d'une nouvelle campagne de vente.*

BLUES (n inv) *blues* (m) : he plays the blues = *il fait du blues* ⓌⓉ jazz = ←
to have the blues = *avoir le cafard* ⓌⓉ to be down in the dumps = *être au trente-sixième dessous.*

BLUESTOCKING (n) *bas-bleu* (m).

BLUFF (n) *bluff* (m) : it's all bluff = *ce n'est que du bluff*
to call s.o.'s bluff = *dire chiche à qqn* : I said I would eat all the hamburgers he'd buy me and he called my

bluff = *j'ai dit que je mangerais tous les hamburgers qu'il m'achèterait, et il m'a dit chiche.*

BLUFF (to, -ed) *bluffer* : don't take his threats seriously, he's only bluffing = *ne prenez pas ses menaces au sérieux, il bluffe.*

BLUNDER (n) *gaffe* (f) : to make a blunder = *faire une gaffe* ⓌⓉ blooper = *boulette* ☠ → gaffe.

BLUNT (adj, -er, -est) **1/** *émoussé, -e* : a blunt knife = *un couteau émoussé* **2/** *brutal, -e* : a blunt answer = *une réponse brutale* ⓌⓉ brusque = ← ☠ → brutal.

BLUNTLY (adv) *sans ménagement* : he told me bluntly he thought I was a bitch = *il m'a dit sans ménagement qu'il pensait que j'étais une salope* ⓌⓉ point-blank = *de but en blanc.*

BLURRED (adj) *flou, -e* : a blurred picture = *une photo floue* ☠ → hazy.

BLUSH (to, -ed) *rougir* : why are you blushing ? = *pourquoi rougis-tu ?* ⓌⓉ to turn red = *piquer un fard* ≠ to turn pale = *pâlir.*

BOARD (n) **1/** *planche* (f) : a ten-inch board = *une planche de 25 cm*
☠ *brûler les planches* = to be a fantastic actor/actress
— *faire la planche* = to float (swimming)
2/ *conseil* (m) : the board's meeting tonight = *le conseil se réunit ce soir* ⓌⓉ committee = *comité* ☠ → advice
board of directors = *conseil d'administration* = board of trustees (institution)
board meeting = *réunion du conseil*
to go on board (a ship) = *monter à bord (d'un bateau).*

BOARD (to, -ed) *monter à bord* : to board a plane = *monter à bord d'un avion* ⓌⓉ to embark = *embarquer.*

BOARDER (n) *pensionnaire* (m, f) : they've always had boarders in their big house = *ils ont toujours eu des pensionnaires dans leur grande maison* ⓌⓉ boarding house = *pension de famille.*

BOARDING SCHOOL (n) *pensionnat* (m), *internat* (m) : I was sent to a co-ed boarding school = *on m'a envoyé dans un internat mixte.*

BOARDWALK (n) *les planches* (f pl) : the boardwalk in Atlantic City = *les planches d'Atlantic City* ☠ → board.

BOAST (to, -ed) *(se) vanter* : that's nothing to boast about = *il n'y a pas de quoi se vanter* ⓌⓉ to brag = *fanfaronner* ☠ *vanter qqn* = to speak highly of s.o.

BOAT (n) *bateau* (m) : we went by boat = *nous avons pris le bateau* ⓌⓉ helm = *barre,* mast = *mât,* oars = *rames,* sails = *voiles,* porthole = *hublot,* wreck = *épave*

barge = *péniche*	**ferry** = ← / *bac*
battleship = *cuirassé/*	**freighter** = *cargo*
âtiment de guerre	**gondola** = *gondole*
canoe = *canoë*	**houseboat** = *péniche*
dinghy = *youyou*	*(aménagée)*

craft = *embarcation*
lifeboat = *bateau de sauvetage*
liner = *paquebot*
motorboat = *hors-bord* = **speedboat**
(oil) tanker = *pétrolier*
rowboat = *barque/canot*
sailboat = *bateau à voile/voilier*
ship = *navire*
steamboat = *bateau à vapeur*
submarine = *sous-marin*
tugboat = *remorqueur*
vessel = *vaisseau*
yacht = ←

to get off the boat = *débarquer (de sa province)* : she talks like she just got off the boat = *elle parle comme si elle débarquait tout juste de sa province*
to miss the boat = *rater le coche* ⑩ to let the chance slip by = *laisser passer sa chance*
to rock the boat = *faire des remous* : if I were you, I wouldn't rock the boat = *si j'étais vous, je ne ferais pas de remous* ⑩ to make waves = *faire des vagues* ☠ *mener qqn en bateau* = to take s.o. for a ride — *un sujet bateau* = a trite subject.

BOBBY (n, -ies) (GB) *flic (m)* = cop.

BODY (n, -ies) *corps (m)*, *carrosserie (f)* (car) : the human body = *le corps humain*, a rusty car body = *une carrosserie de voiture rouillée*
they're just keeping body and soul together = *ils ont juste de quoi subsister* → POOR
☠ *le corps enseignant* = the teaching staff
— *prendre corps* = to take shape
— *se jeter à corps perdu dans* = to throw o.s. into.

BODYGUARD (n) *garde (m) du corps* : the industrialist and his bodyguards = *l'industriel et ses gardes du corps* ⑩ watchdog = *chien de garde*.

BOG (to, -ged) **to be/get bogged down** = *s'enliser* : the Geneva talks are bogged down = *les pourparlers de Genève s'enlisent*.

BOGEYMAN (n, -men) *croque-mitaine (m)*, *père (m) Fouettard* ⑩ sandman = *marchand de sable*.

BOGUS (adj) *faux, fausse, bidon* : a bogus ten-dollar note = *un faux billet de dix dollars*, bogus documents = *des documents bidon* ≠ real = *véritable* ☠ *faux* → false.

BOHEMIAN (n) *bohème (m, f)* ⑩ hippy = ← BOHE-MIAN (adj) *(de) bohème* : a bohemian life = *une vie de bohème* ⑩ kooky = *farfelu*.

BOIL (to, -ed) *(faire) bouillir* : to boil potatoes = *faire bouillir des pommes de terre*, the water's boiling = *l'eau bout* ⑩ to simmer = *cuire à feu doux*
to boil down to = *se réduire à* : their problems boil down to a lack of money = *leurs problèmes se réduisent à une question d'argent* ⑩ to come down to = *revenir à*
to boil over = *déborder* : the milk's boiling over = *le lait déborde* ☠ → to overflow
to be boiling = 1/ *crever de chaleur* : I'm boiling = *je crève de chaleur*, the room's boiling = *on crève de chaleur dans cette pièce* 2/ *être fumasse* : he's boiling over

the mistake = *il est fumasse à cause de cette erreur* → ANGRY
☠ *faire bouillir la marmite* = to bring home the bacon.

BOILER (n) *chaudière (f)* ⑩ central heating = *chauffage central*.

BOISTEROUS (adj) *tapageur, -euse* : a boisterous party = *une soirée tapageuse* ≠ calm = *calme* ☠ → flashy.

BOLD (adj, -er, -est) *hardi, -e* : a bold answer = *une réponse hardie* ⑩ brazen = *effronté*.

BOLLIX (to, -ed) *bâcler* : to bollix (up) a job = *bâcler un boulot* ⑩ to louse up = *ficher en l'air*.

BOLSTER (to, -ed) *soutenir* : you bolstered (up) my morale = *vous m'avez soutenu le moral* ⑩ to strengthen = *renforcer* ☠ → to support.

BOLT (n) **a bolt from the blue** = *qqch de totalement inattendu* : his failure was a bolt from the blue = *son échec était totalement inattendu*.

BOLT OUT (to, -ed) *sortir comme un ouragan* : he bolted out of the room = *il est sorti comme un ouragan de la pièce* ≠ to dash in = *entrer en trombe*.

BOMB (n) 1/ *bombe (f)* : neutron bomb = *bombe à neutrons*, A-bomb = *bombe A*, to drop bombs = *lâcher des bombes*, bomb shelter = *abri antiaérien*
bomb scare = *alerte à la bombe*
☠ *faire la bombe* = to go on a binge
2/ *bide (m)* : the play was a bomb = *la pièce a fait un bide* ⑩ bust = *fiasco* ☠ → belly.

BOMB (to, -ed) 1/ *bombarder* : to bomb a city = *bombarder une ville* ⑩ bombing = *bombardement*, bomber = *bombardier* ☠ → to bombard 2/ *foirer* : his last play bombed = *sa dernière pièce a foiré* ⑩ to come a cropper = *ramasser une gamelle* ≠ to be a hit = *avoir du succès* ☠ *foirer (un examen/un entretien)* = to botch (an exam/an interview).

BOMBARD (to, -ed) *bombarder* : to bombard with questions = *bombarder de questions* ☠ *bombarder une ville* = to bomb a city.

BOMBED (adj) *pété, -e* : bombed after five Scotches = *pété au bout de cinq whiskies* → DRUNK.

BOMBSHELL (n) *qqch qui fait l'effet d'une bombe* : his book was a political bombshell = *son livre a fait l'effet d'une bombe sur le plan politique*.

BONA FIDE (adj) *reconnu, -e authentique* : a bona fide Picasso piece of pottery = *une poterie de Picasso reconnue authentique*.

BONANZA (n) *don (m) du ciel* : the bonus was a bonanza = *cette prime a été un don du ciel*.

BOND (n) 1/ *bon (m)* : treasury bonds = *des bons du Trésor* ☠ *bon (essence)* = (gas) coupon 2/ *lien (m)* : the bonds of friendship = *les liens de l'amitié* ☠ → link.

BONDAGE (n) 1/ *servitude (f)* : the slaves were freed

from bondage = *les esclaves ont été libérés de leur servitude* ☠ *des servitudes* = constraints 2/ *sadomasochisme (m)* : she and her husband are into bondage = *elle et son mari donnent dans le sado-masochisme.*

BONE (n) *os (m), arête (f)* (fish) : the dog's gnawing the bone = *le chien ronge l'os,* a (fish) bone stuck in my throat = *une arête s'est plantée dans ma gorge*
bone of contention = *pomme de discorde*
to have a bone to pick with s.o. = *avoir qqch à régler avec qqn* ⊕ to have an axe to grind with s.o. = *avoir un compte à régler avec qqn*
to make no bones about stg = *ne pas y aller par quatre chemins* : he made no bones about saying what he thought = *il n'y est pas allé par quatre chemins pour dire ce qu'il pensait*
☠ *tomber sur un os* = to run into a snag.

BONE (to, -d) **to bone up on (French)** = *potasser (son français)* ⊕ to go over = *revoir.*

BONER (n) *bourde (f)* : to make a boner = *faire une bourde* ⊕ gaffe = ←.

BONFIRE (n) *feu (m) de joie* ⊕ firecracker = *pétard.*

BONUS (n, -es) *prime (f)* : as a bonus = *en prime* ☠ → premium.

BONY (adj, -ier, -iest) *osseux, -euse* ≠ corpulent = ←.

BOO (n) **not to say boo (the whole evening)** = *ne pas piper mot (de la soirée)* ≠ to talk a mile a minute = *ne pas avoir la langue dans sa poche.*

BOO (to, -ed) *huer* : the audience booed the comic = *le public a hué le comique* ⊕ to hiss = *siffler.*

BOOBS (n pl) *nénés (m pl)* ⊕ jugs = *lolos,* boobies = *roberts,* knockers = *nichons.*

BOOBY PRIZE (n) *prix (m) de consolation* : to win the booby prize = *gagner le prix de consolation.*

BOOBY TRAP (n) *attrape-nigaud (m)* ⊕ trick = *piège.*

BOOK (n) *livre (m), bouquin (m)* (LV) : I'm reading an interesting book = *je suis en train de lire un livre intéressant* ⊕ novel = *roman,* volume = ←, tome = ←, paperback = *livre broché,* hardcover = *livre relié,* bookcase = *bibliothèque,* bookends = *serre-livres,* book review = *critique littéraire,* galleys = *épreuves,* to proofread = *lire les épreuves,* to rewrite = *rewriter,* pocket book = *livre de poche,* guest book = *livre d'or,* textbook = *manuel,* bookmark = *signet*
to be in s.o.'s good ≠ bad books = *être ≠ ne pas être dans les petits papiers de qqn* ⊕ to be in s.o.'s good graces = *être dans les bonnes grâces de qqn*
to keep the books = *tenir les comptes*
don't judge a book by its cover = *l'habit ne fait pas le moine* ⊕ appearances are deceiving = *les apparences sont trompeuses*
to go by the book = *faire selon les règles*
in my book = *quant à moi* : he's O.K. in my book =

quant à moi, je le trouve bien ⊕ in my opinion = *à mon avis*
I know you like a book = *je te connais comme si je t'avais fait*
to throw the book at s.o. = *filer le maxi à qqn* : the judge threw the book at the rapist = *le juge a filé le maxi au violeur*
☠ *une livre (sterling/poids)* = a pound.

BOOK (to, -ed) 1/ *retenir* : to book seats = *retenir des places* ⊕ booking = *réservation,* booking office = *bureau de réservation* ☠ → to restrain
2/ *ficher* : the cop booked the guy for speeding = *le flic a fiché le type qu'il avait arrêté pour excès de vitesse* ☠ *je m'en fiche* = I don't give a darn
— *tu te fiches de moi ?* = who do you take me for ?
— *je n'ai rien fichu de la journée* = I didn't do a darn thing all day
— *tu t'es fichu dedans* = you're sadly mistaken.

BOOKIE (n) *bookmaker (m)* ≠ gambler = *joueur.*

BOOKKEEPER (n) *comptable (m, f)* = accountant.

BOOKKEEPING (n) *comptabilité (f)* ⊕ ledger = *grand livre.*

BOOKLET (n) *opuscule (m), brochure (f)* : the AMA put out a booklet on the dangers of smoking = *l'Ordre des médecins a sorti une brochure/un opuscule sur les dangers du tabac* ⊕ essay = *essai* ☠ → brochure.

BOOKSHELF (n, -ves) *rayon (m) de bibliothèque* ⊕ shelf = *étagère.*

BOOKSTORE (n) *librairie (f)* : this bookstore doesn't sell my book = *cette librairie ne vend pas mon livre* = bookshop (GB) ⊕ stationery store = *papeterie* ☠ → library.

BOOKWORM (n) *rat (m) de bibliothèque* ⊕ egghead = *grosse tête.*

BOOM (n) *boom (m)* : baby boom = *boom des naissances* ≠ drop = *chute.*

BOOM (to, -ed) *être en plein essor* : business is booming = *les affaires sont en plein essor* ⊕ to flourish = *être florissant.*

BOOMERANG (to, -ed) *faire un effet de boomerang* : their plan boomeranged = *leur projet a fait un effet de boomerang.*

BOON (n) *aubaine (f)* : the pill is a boon to women = *la pilule est une aubaine pour les femmes* ⊕ blessing = *bénédiction.*

BOOR (n) *ours (m) mal léché* ⊕ oaf = *mufle.*

BOOST (n) *relance (f)* : a boost in production = *une relance de la production* ≠ drop = *chute*
to give s.o. a boost = *remonter le moral à qqn.*

BOOST (to, -ed) *faire monter* (prices), *relancer* (production), *remonter* (morale) ⊕ to raise = *augmenter*

☠ *relancer (une conversation)* = to get (a conversation) going
— *il faut que je le relance* = I have to speak with him again about it
— *remonter* → to wind.

BOOT (n) *botte (f)* : he sleeps with his boots on = *il garde ses bottes pour dormir* ⓪ rubbers = *bottes de caoutchouc*
boot camp = *les classes* ⓪ barracks = *caserne*
to give s.o. the boot = *flanquer qqn dehors* ⓪ to give s.o. the axe = *donner ses huit jours à qqn*
to lick s.o.'s boots = *lécher les bottes de qqn* ⓪ to lick s.o.'s ass = *lécher le cul à qqn*
to boot = *de surcroît* : she asked for a raise and a vacation to boot = *elle a demandé une augmentation, et des vacances de surcroît* ⓪ into the bargain = *par-dessus le marché.*

BOOTH (n) *baraque (f) foraine* : the booths at the fair = *les baraques de la foire.*

BOOTLEG (to, -ged) *faire de la contrebande d'alcool* **BOOTLEGGER** (n) *bootlegger (m)* **BOOTLEGGING** (n) *contrebande (f) d'alcool* ⓪ prohibition = ←.

BOOTY (n, -ies) *butin (m)* : war booty = *butin de guerre* ⓪ looting = *pillage* ☠ *butin (cambrioleur)* = haul (burglar).

BOOZE (n) *gnôle (f)* : bring your own booze = *apportez votre gnôle* ⓪ schnapps = ←.

BOOZE (to, -d) *picoler* : we boozed all weekend = *on a picolé tout le week-end.*

BOOZER (n) *pochard, -e* : a family of boozers = *une famille de pochards* → DRUNK.

BORDER (n) *frontière (f)* : the French border = *la frontière française* ⓪ boundary line = *ligne de démarcation* ☠ → frontier.

BORDER (to, -ed) **to border on (the ridiculous)** = *friser (le ridicule)* ☠ → to frizz.

BORDERLINE (n) **to be on the borderline** = *être à la limite* : he isn't alcoholic but he's on the borderline = *il n'est pas alcoolique, mais il est à la limite*
a borderline case = *un cas limite.*

BORE (n) *qqn/qqch d'ennuyeux* : what a bore you are ! = *ce que tu peux être ennuyeux !*, it's a bore to have to spend one's vacation with one's family ! = *que c'est ennuyeux de devoir passer ses vacances avec sa famille !* ⓪ a drag = *rasoir.*

BORE (to, -d) *ennuyer, barber* (LV) : the play bored me = *la pièce m'a ennuyé*, you bore me = *vous m'ennuyez/me barbez* ≠ to thrill = *passionner*
☠ *je m'ennuie de vous* = I miss you
— *cela m'ennuie de vous dire que* = I hate to tell you that
— *je ne veux pas vous ennuyer* = I don't want to bother you

— *je suis ennuyé que* = I'm annoyed that.

BORED (adj) **to be bored** = *s'ennuyer* : I'm never bored with him = *je ne m'ennuie jamais avec lui,* are you bored ? = *est-ce que vous vous ennuyez ?* ☠ → to bore
to be bored to death = *s'ennuyer à mourir* ⓪ **to be bored stiff** = *s'ennuyer comme un rat mort,* **to be bored to tears** = *s'ennuyer à cent sous de l'heure.*

BOREDOM (n) *ennui (m)* : a life of boredom = *une vie d'ennui* ≠ pleasure = *plaisir*
☠ *avoir des ennuis* = to have headaches/trouble
— *quel ennui !* = what annoyance !

BORING (adj) *ennuyeux, -euse* : a boring teacher/job = *un professeur/travail ennuyeux* ⓪ dull = *assommant* ≠ thrilling = *captivant*
boring as hell = *ennuyeux comme la pluie/qui sue l'ennui.*

BORN (adj) **to be born** = *naître* : the baby will be born next month = *le bébé va naître le mois prochain*
I was born (in New York) = *je suis né (à New York)* ≠ to die = *mourir*
to be a born (pianist) = *être un (pianiste) né.*

BOROUGH (n) *quartier (m)* : the five boroughs of New York = *les cinq quartiers de New York* ⓪ ward = *secteur* ☠ → quarter.

BORROW (to, -ed) *emprunter* : to borrow ten dollars = *emprunter dix dollars* ≠ to lend = *prêter*
to borrow from = *emprunter à* : he borrowed ten dollars from his mother = *il a emprunté dix dollars à sa mère.*

BORSCHT BELT (n) *région de villégiature dans les Catskill Mountains (N.Y.), très fréquentée par les juifs et où de nombreux artistes firent leurs débuts.*

BOSOM (n) *poitrine (f)* : a big bosom = *une grosse poitrine* ⓪ breast = *sein* ☠ → chest.

BOSS (n, -es) *patron, -onne* : I was hired by the boss = *j'ai été engagé par le patron* ⓪ chief = *chef,* the person in charge = *le responsable* ≠ worker = *travailleur,* employee = *employé* ☠ *patron (robe)* = pattern (dress).

BOSS (to, -ed) *mener à la baguette* : he bosses his family about = *il mène sa famille à la baguette* ⓪ to rule with an iron hand = *mener avec une main de fer.*

BOSSY (adj, -ier, -iest) *qui aime commander* : his wife is very bossy = *sa femme aime commander* ⓪ authoritarian = *autoritaire.*

BOTCH (UP) (to, -ed) *saboter* : she botched (up) the work = *elle a saboté le boulot* ⓪ to bollix = *bâcler* ☠ → to sabotage.

BOTH (pron) *tous, toutes les deux* : both came = *ils sont venus tous les deux* ⓪ each one = *chacun*
both of (us) = *(nous) deux.*

BOTH (adj) *les deux* : both guys are French = *les deux types sont français*

to give it to s.o. with both barrels = *descendre qqn en flèche* → TO LAMBAST

to hear both sides = *entendre les deux sons de cloche*

to have both feet on the ground = *avoir les pieds sur terre* ⓓ to be down-to-earth = *être terre à terre*

you can't have it both ways = *il faut qu'une porte soit ouverte ou fermée*

to play both ends against the middle = *jouer sur les deux tableaux*

it works/cuts both ways = *c'est une arme à double tranchant* = what's good for the goose is good for the gander

to swing both ways = *marcher à voile et à vapeur* ⓓ to be ac/dc = *être ambivalent.*

BOTH (conj) **both ... and** = *à la fois ... et ... :* the play was successful both in England and France = *la pièce a eu du succès à la fois en Angleterre et en France* ⓓ as well ... as = *aussi bien ... que.*

BOTHER (n) *qqn/qqch d'embêtant :* the kids are a bother = *les gosses sont embêtants*

it's no bother = *ça ne me dérange pas.*

BOTHER (to, -ed) *embêter :* don't bother me while I'm working = *ne m'embête pas quand je travaille*, I don't want to bother you with my problems = *je ne veux pas vous embêter avec mes problèmes* ⓓ to disturb = *déranger*, to inconvenience = *importuner*

does it bother you if (I smoke) ? = *est-ce que ça vous dérange si (je fume) ?* = do you mind if (I smoke) ?

don't bother to (call) = *ce n'est pas la peine de (téléphoner)*

what's bothering you ? = *qu'est-ce qui ne va pas ?* ⓓ what's worrying you ? = *qu'est-ce qui t'inquiète ?*
☠ *je m'embête ici* = I'm bored here.

BOTHERSOME (adj) *énervant, -e* = annoying.

BOTTLE (n) **1/** *bouteille (f) :* a bottle of wine = *une bouteille de vin* ⓓ bottle opener = *ouvre-bouteilles*, glass = *verre*

to hit the bottle = *caresser la bouteille :* since his retirement he's been hitting the bottle = *depuis qu'il a pris sa retraite, il caresse la bouteille* → DRUNK
☠ *prendre de la bouteille* = to be getting on in years
2/ *biberon (m) :* the baby's bottle = *le biberon du bébé.*

BOTTLENECK (n) *bouchon (m) :* a bottleneck on the highway = *un bouchon sur l'autoroute* ⓓ bumper-to-bumper = *pare-chocs contre pare-chocs* ☠ *bouchon (bouteille)* = cork.

BOTTLE UP (to, -d) *contenir :* to bottle up one's anger = *contenir sa colère* ⓓ to hold back = *refouler* ☠ → to contain.

BOTTOM (n) **1/** *fond (m) :* the bottom of the well = *le fond du puits*

what's at the bottom of (the scandal) ? = *qu'y a-t-il derrière (ce scandale) ?*

to bet one's bottom dollar = *donner sa main à couper* ⓓ to stake one's own life on it = *en mettre sa main au feu*

bottoms up ! = *cul sec !* ⓓ here's looking at you ! = *à la bonne vôtre !*, down the hatch ! = *à vos amours !*

from the bottom of my heart = *du fond du cœur*

to get to the bottom of things = *aller au fond des choses*

to scrape the bottom of the barrel = *en être réduit à la dernière extrémité :* asking him to help is scraping the bottom of the barrel = *il faut en être réduit à la dernière extrémité pour lui demander de nous aider*

bottom line = *au bout du compte :* you said you loved me but the bottom line is that you never left your wife = *tu me disais que tu m'aimais, mais au bout du compte tu n'as jamais quitté ta femme*
☠ *un article de fond* = a leading article
— *au fond de soi* = deep down
— *au fond* = basically
— *les fonds* = the funds
— *faire qqch à fond* = to do stg thoroughly
— *musique de fond* = background music
— *racler les fonds de tiroir* = to scrape around for pennies
2/ *arrière-train (m)* (LV) : she has a big bottom = *elle a un gros arrière-train* ⓓ behind = *derrière*
3/ *bas (m) :* at the bottom of the page = *au bas de la page* ≠ top = *haut*
☠ *des bas* = stockings
— *bas de laine* = nestegg.

BOULEVARD (n) *boulevard (m)* ⓓ avenue = ←.

BOUNCE (to, -d) **1/** *être sans provision :* this check bounced = *ce chèque était sans provision* ⓓ to be overdrawn = *être à découvert* **2/** *flanquer à la porte :* bounced from the club = *flanqué à la porte du club* ⓓ to throw out = *vider*

to bounce back = *reprendre le dessus :* the economy bounced back = *l'économie a repris le dessus.*

BOUNCER (n) *videur (m)* ⓓ nightclub = *boîte de nuit.*

BOUND (n) **out of bounds** = *en dehors des limites.*

BOUND (adj) **bound for** = *à destination de :* a plane bound for New York = *un avion à destination de New York*

it's/he's bound to = *c'est forcé :* he's bound to call soon = *il va appeler bientôt, c'est forcé* ⓓ it's inevitable that = *il est inévitable que.*

BOUNDARY (n, -ies) *limite (f) :* the boundaries of medical science/of the country = *les limites de la médecine/du pays* ☠ → limit.

BOUQUET (n) *bouquet (m) :* a bouquet of flowers = *un bouquet de fleurs* ☠ *c'est le bouquet !* = that takes the cake !

BOW (n) *nœud (m) :* a bow in her hair = *un nœud dans les cheveux* ☠ → knot.

BOW (to, -ed) *s'incliner* : boys bow and girls curtsy = *les petits garçons s'inclinent et les petites filles font la révérence*
to bow out of (a dinner) = *s'excuser de ne pas pouvoir venir à (un dîner)*
to bow to (s.o.'s desires) = *s'incliner devant (les désirs de qqn).*

BOWELS (n pl) **to move one's bowels** = *aller à la selle* ⓪ to do number two = *faire la grosse commission.*

BOWERY (n) *quartier très pauvre de Manhattan caractérisé par ses hôtels borgnes et ses clochards.*

BOWL (n) *bol (m)* : a bowl of soup = *un bol de soupe*
not a bowl of cherries = *pas rose* : life with him wasn't all a bowl of cherries = *la vie avec lui n'était pas toujours rose* ⓪ not a bed of roses = *pas marrant*
🦋 *coup ≠ manque de bol* = lucky ≠ bad break
— *j'en ai ras le bol* = I'm fed up.

BOWL (to, -ed) *jouer au bowling* : do you know how to bowl ? = *vous savez jouer au bowling ?*
bowling alley = *piste de bowling* ⓪ pin = *quille*, ball = *boule*
to go bowling = *faire du bowling*
to bowl s.o. over = *laisser qqn interdit* : the news/her beauty bowled us over = *la nouvelle/sa beauté nous a laissés interdits* ⓪ to take aback = *couper le souffle.*

BOWLEGGED (adj) *qui a les jambes arquées* ≠ knock-kneed = *qui a les genoux en dedans.*

BOX (n, -es) *boîte (f)* : a box of chocolates = *une boîte de chocolats* ⓪ carton = ←
box office = 1/ *bureau de location* ⓪ seat = *place*, ticket = *billet* 2/ *qui fait recette/qui fait box office* : violence is box office today = *la violence fait recette aujourd'hui*
🦋 *boîte (de conserve)* = can
— *elle travaille pour une boîte américaine* = she works for an American company/firm
— *boîte de nuit* = nightclub
— *mettre qqn en boîte* = to pull s.o.'s leg.

BOX (to, -ed) *boxer* **BOXER** (n) *boxeur (m)* ⓪ boxing gloves = *gants de boxe*, wrestler = *lutteur*, trainer = *entraîneur.*

BOXING (n) *boxe (f)* : boxing's my favorite sport = *la boxe est mon sport préféré* ⓪ ring = ←
Boxing Day = *lendemain de Noël, jour férié en Grande-Bretagne.*

BOY (n) *garçon (m)* : my sister has two boys = *ma sœur a deux garçons* ⓪ lad = *jouvenceau* ≠ girl = *fille*
🦋 *garçon d'honneur* = groomsman
— *garçon de café* = waiter
— *garçon manqué* = tomboy.

BOYCOTT (n) *boycott (m)* **BOYCOTT** (to, -ed) *boycotter.*

BOYFRIEND (n) *petit ami (m)* : bring your boyfriend with you = *amène ton petit ami* ⓪ her guy = *son mec, beau* = *galant.*

BRA (n) *soutien-gorge (m)* : a padded bra = *un soutien-gorge rembourré.*

BRACE (n) *appareil (m) orthopédique* : she has a brace on her leg = *elle a un appareil orthopédique à la jambe.*

BRACE FOR (to, -d) *préparer à* : brace yourself for some bad news = *préparez-vous à de mauvaises nouvelles.*

BRACELET (n) *bracelet (m)* ⓪ chain = *chaîne*, charm = *breloque* 🦋 *bracelet-montre* = wristwatch.

BRACES (n pl) *appareil (m) dentaire* : braces to straighten her teeth = *un appareil pour lui redresser les dents.*

BRACKET (n) *tranche (f)* : high tax bracket = *tranche d'impôts élevée* 🦋 → slice
in brackets = *entre crochets* : put the sentence in brackets = *mettez la phrase entre crochets* ⓪ quotes = *guillemets.*

BRAG (to, -ged) *fanfaronner* : that's nothing to brag about = *il n'y a pas de quoi fanfaronner* **BRAGGART** (n) *fanfaron, -onne.*

BRAID (n) *natte (f)* : my hair isn't long enough for braids = *je n'ai pas les cheveux assez longs pour faire des nattes.*

BRAIN (n) 1/ *cerveau (m)* : a brain operation = *une opération du cerveau* ⓪ mind = *esprit*
brain concussion = *commotion cérébrale*
to beat s.o.'s brains out = *faire une grosse tête à qqn*
→ TO HIT
to blow one's brains out = *se faire sauter la cervelle*
she has brains = *elle n'est pas bête* ⓪ to be on the ball = *être dégourdi*
to pick s.o.'s brains = *harceler qqn de questions pour tirer profit de ses connaissances*
to rack one's brains = *se creuser la cervelle/les méninges*
2/ *cerveau (m)* : she's a brain = *c'est un cerveau* ⓪ intelligence = ←
brain drain = *exode des cerveaux*
brain trust = *brain-trust.*

BRAINCHILD (n, -children) *invention (f) personnelle* : this project's his brainchild = *ce projet est son invention personnelle.*

BRAINSTORM (n) *idée (f) lumineuse* ⓪ find = *trouvaille* **BRAINSTORMING** (n) *brainstorming (m)* : to have a brainstorming session = *avoir une séance de brainstorming.*

BRAINWASH (to, -ed) *faire un lavage de cerveau* **BRAINWASHING** (n) *lavage (m) de cerveau* ⓪ propaganda = *propagande.*

BRAINY (adj, -ier, -est) *intello* ≠ dumb = *bête.*

BRAKE (n) *frein (m)* : the car brakes = *les freins de la voiture* ≠ gas pedal = *accélérateur*

to put on the brakes = *freiner* ☠ → to curb ☠ *enthousiasme sans frein* = unbridled enthusiasm
— *ronger son frein* = to champ at the bit.

BRANCH (n, -es) **1/** *branche* *(f)* : the highest branch of the tree = *la plus haute branche de l'arbre* ⓒⓓ twig = *brindille* **2/** *branche* *(f)* : a branch of medicine = *une branche de la médecine*
☠ *scier la branche sur laquelle on est assis* = to cut one's own throat
— *dans quelle branche est-il ?* = what's his line ?
— *salut vieille branche !* = hi, old buddy !
3/ *succursale* *(f)* : we have a branch in Paris = *nous avons une succursale à Paris* ≠ head office = *siège social.*

BRANCH OUT (to, -ed) *étendre ses activités* : the record company's branching out into books = *la maison de disques étend ses activités en se lançant dans les livres.*

BRAND (n) *marque* *(f)* : brand mark = *marque de fabrique* = trade mark ☠ → mark.

BRAND-NEW (adj) *flambant neuf, neuve* : a brand-new car = *une voiture flambant neuve* ≠ used = *usagé.*

BRANDY (n, -ies) *cognac* *(m)* : he brought brandy to the party = *il a apporté du cognac à la soirée.*

BRASH (adj, -er, -est) *effronté, -e* : a brash answer = *une réponse effrontée* ⓒⓓ impertinent = ←.

BRASS (n, adj) *laiton* *(m)* : a brass candlestick = *un chandelier de laiton* ⓒⓓ bronze = ←.
the brasses = *les cuivres (orchestre)*
let's get down to brass tacks ! = *venons-en au fait !*

BRASSIERE (n) *soutien-gorge* *(m)* = bra.

BRAT (n) *sale gosse* *(m, f)* : her kids are brats = *ses enfants sont de sales gosses* ⓒⓓ holy terror = *enfant terrible.*

BRAVE (to, -d) *braver* : he braved the wrath of his in-laws = *il a bravé la colère de ses beaux-parents.*

BRAVE (adj, -r, -st) *brave* : a brave man = *un homme brave* ⓒⓓ heroic = *héroïque* ≠ yellow = *lâche* ☠ *un brave homme* = a nice guy **BRAVELY** (adj) *bravement* ⓒⓓ courageously = *courageusement* **BRAVERY** (n) *bravoure* *(f).*

BRAWL (n) *rixe* *(f)* : a brawl between two drunkards = *une rixe entre deux ivrognes* ⓒⓓ free-for-all = *foire d'empoigne.*

BRAWN (n) *muscle* *(m)* : he has brawn but no brains = *il a du muscle mais pas de cervelle* ☠ → muscle **BRAWNY** (adj, -ier, -iest) *musclé, -e* ⓒⓓ husky = *baraqué* ☠ *des méthodes musclées* = high-handed methods.

BRAZEN (adj) *effronté, -e* : a brazen answer = *une réponse effrontée* ⓒⓓ cheeky = *gonflé.*

BRAZIL (n) *Brésil* *(m)* **BRAZILIAN** (n, adj) *Brésilien, -enne.*

BREAD (n) **1/** *pain* *(m)* : a loaf of bread = *un pain/une miche de pain* ⓒⓓ slice = *tranche*, gingerbread = *pain d'épice*, rye bread = *pain de seigle*, wholewheat bread = *pain complet*, roll = *petit pain*
it's her bread and butter = *c'est son gagne-pain* ⓒⓓ to earn one's living = *gagner sa vie*
☠ *tu as du pain sur la planche* = you have your work cut out for you
— *je ne mange pas de ce pain-là* = I won't go along with that
— *manger son pain blanc le premier* = to begin with the best part
2/ *pognon* *(m)* (LV) : I don't have enough bread to buy a new car = *je n'ai pas assez de pognon pour acheter une nouvelle voiture* ⓒⓓ lettuce = *blé*, cabbage = *oseille.*

BREADLINE (n) *soupe* *(f)* *populaire* : the breadline during the depression = *la soupe populaire pendant la dépression* ⓒⓓ welfare = *aide sociale.*

BREADWINNER (n) *soutien* *(m)* *de famille* ⓒⓓ to bring home the bacon = *faire bouillir la marmite.*

BREAK (n) *pause* *(f)*, *break* *(m)* : it's time to take a break = *il est temps de faire une pause* ⓒⓓ respite = *répit* ☠ → pause

a lucky ≠ **bad break** = *un coup* ≠ *manque de bol* **give me a break !** = **1/** *donne-moi une chance !* : give me a break and let me play the part = *donnez-moi une chance de jouer le rôle* = give me a chance	**2/** *je t'en prie (arrête)* ! : give me a break and stop yelling at me ! = *je t'en prie, arrête de hurler après moi !* ⓒⓓ that's enough already ! = *ça suffit !* **those are the breaks !** = *ainsi vont les choses !* → THAT'S LIFE !

BREAK (to, broke, broken) **1/** *(se) casser* : you broke the dish = *tu as cassé le plat*, the glass broke = *le verre s'est cassé*, I broke my leg = *je me suis cassé la jambe* ⓒⓓ to crack = *fêler*, to smash = *fracasser*, to chip = *ébrécher*

☠ *on se casse !* = let's beat it !/let's blow ! — *ça ne casse rien* = it's no great shakes — *casser un jugement* = to quash/to reverse/to set aside/to overrule a judgment	— *elle ne s'est pas cassé* = she didn't kill himself over it — *casser les prix* = to slash prices

2/ *briser (la carrière et la réputation)* : his father-in-law threatened to break him if he left his wife = *son beau-père l'a menacé de briser sa carrière et sa réputation s'il quittait sa femme*
3/ *rompre* : to break a contract = *rompre un contrat*
☠ *rompre qqn aux affaires* = to break s.o. in
— *rompre (les relations)* = to break off (relations)

— *ils ont rompu* = they broke up
4/ *faire une pause* : let's break for an hour = *faisons une pause d'une heure*
5/ *(se) débloquer* : the situation will soon break = *la situation se débloquera bientôt*
☠ *tu débloques !* = you're flipping !
— *débloquer (des capitaux)* = to unfreeze (capital)

---

to break away from s.o. = *se détacher de qqn* ≠ to hold on to = *garder*
to break down = 1/ *tomber en panne* : his car broke down = *sa voiture est tombée en panne* ⓪ to conk out = *rendre l'âme* 2/ *craquer* : she held up through the illness but broke down when he died = *elle a tenu le coup pendant sa maladie, mais a craqué à sa mort* ☠ → to crack 3/ *décomposer/donner le décompte* (figures) : can you break the problem/figures down ? = *pourriez-vous décomposer tous les aspects du problème/me donner le décompte ?* ☠ *se décomposer (pourrir)* = to decay 4/ *défoncer* : to break down a door = *défoncer une porte* ☠ *se défoncer (drogues)* = to get stoned (drugs) 5/ *briser* : the questioning broke him down = *l'interrogatoire l'a brisé* 6/ *rester en plan* : the talks broke down = *les pourparlers sont restés en plan*
to break in = 1/ *interrompre* :

we were talking and he broke in = *nous étions en train de parler et il nous a interrompus* ☠ → to interrupt 2/ *entrer par effraction* : the burglars broke in and stole a fortune = *les cambrioleurs sont entrés par effraction et ont volé une fortune* ⓪ to burglarize = *cambrioler*
to break s.o./stg in = *roder qqn/qqch, briser* (shoes) : they're breaking the car/the new guy in = *ils sont en train de roder la voiture/le nouveau*
to break into = *entrer par effraction dans* : they broke into the house = *ils sont entrés dans la maison par effraction*
to break off = *rompre* : to break off diplomatic relations = *rompre les relations diplomatiques* ☠ → to break
to break out = 1/ *bourgeonner* : her face breaks out every time she has her period = *son visage bourgeonne chaque fois qu'elle a ses règles* 2/ *éclater* : war broke out in 1939 = *la guerre a éclaté en 1939* ☠ → to

burst
to break out of (prison, etc.) = *s'évader de (prison, etc.)* ⓪ to bust out = *jouer la fille de l'air*
to break up = 1/ *briser* : their marriage broke up after a year = *leur couple s'est brisé au bout d'un an* ⓪ to bust up = *péter* 2/ *briser* : her cat's death broke her up = *la mort de son chat l'a brisée* 3/ *se bidonner* : we were all broken up when he told us the story = *nous nous sommes tous bidonnés quand il nous a raconté l'histoire* ⓪ to split one's sides laughing = *se tenir les côtes* 4/ *prendre fin* : the party broke up at three = *la soirée a pris fin à trois heures du matin* 5/ *interrompre* : the cops broke up the fight = *les flics ont interrompu la bagarre* ☠ → to interrupt
to break with = *rompre avec* : the candidate broke with his party after the elections = *le candidat a rompu avec son parti après les élections.*

BREAKABLE (adj) *cassable* : breakable dishes = *vaisselle cassable* ≠ unbreakable = *incassable.*

BREAKDOWN (n) **1/** *panne (f)* : an electricity breakdown = *une panne d'électricité*
☠ *tomber en panne* = to break down
— *avoir une panne d'essence* = to turn out of gas
2/ *dépression (f)* : she had a breakdown = *elle a fait une dépression,* nervous breakdown = *dépression nerveuse* ☠ → depression
3/ *ventilation (f)* : give me a breakdown of the costs = *faites-moi une ventilation des coûts*
breakdown of law and order = *effondrement de l'ordre public.*

BREAKFAST (n) *petit déjeuner (m)* : continental or English breakfast = *petit déjeuner continental ou à l'anglaise.*

BREAK-IN (n) *effraction (f)* : that was the sixth break-in

in the area = *c'était la sixième effraction dans le quartier.*

BREAKNECK (adj) **at breakneck speed** = *à tombeau ouvert* ⓪ at full speed = *à toute vitesse.*

BREAKOUT (n) *évasion (f) de prison* = jailbreak.

BREAKTHROUGH (n) *percée (f)* : a technological breakthrough = *une percée technologique* ≠ stalemate = *impasse.*

BREAKUP (n) *rupture (f)* : the breakup of a marriage = *la rupture d'un couple* ☠ *rupture de contrat* = breach of contract.

BREAST (n) *sein (m)* ⓪ boobs = *nénés,* chest = *poitrine,* nipple = *mamelon,* to breast-feed = *nourrir au sein* ☠ *au sein du Congrès* = within Congress.

BREATH (n) *haleine (f)* : bad breath = *mauvaise haleine* ⓪ breathing = *respiration*

a breath of fresh air = *une bouffée d'air (pur)*
to catch one's breath = *reprendre haleine/son souffle*
don't hold your breath ! = *compte là-dessus et bois de l'eau (fraîche) !* → BUZZ OFF !
out of breath = *à bout de souffle/hors d'haleine*
save your breath ! = *pas la peine de gaspiller ta salive !* = **don't waste your breath !**
to take s.o.'s breath away = *couper le souffle à qqn* : her beauty takes your breath away = *elle est belle à vous couper le souffle*
☠ *le film m'a tenu en haleine* = the film kept me in suspense
— *travail de longue haleine* = long-term job.

BREATHE (to, -d) *respirer* : breathe deeply = *respirez profondément*
to breathe in ≠ **out** = *inspirer* ≠ *expirer* ☠ → to inspire, → to expire.

BREATHER (n) **to have a breather** = *avoir un moment de répit.*

BREATHING (n) *respiration (f)* : heavy breathing = *une respiration forte.*

BREATHLESS (adj) *essoufflé, -e* Ⓦ out of breath = *à bout de souffle.*

BREATHTAKING (adj) *à couper le souffle* : a breathtaking view = *une vue à vous couper le souffle* Ⓦ dazzling = *éblouissant.*

BREED (n) *race (f)* : a breed of cats = *une race de chats* ☠ → race **BREED** (to, bred, bred) *faire l'élevage de* : to breed horses = *faire l'élevage des chevaux* ⓌⒹ to raise = *élever* **BREEDER** (n)*éleveur, -euse.*

BREEDING (n) **1/** *bonnes manières (f pl)* : to lack breeding = *manquer de bonnes manières* **2/** *élevage (m)* : you need good land for breeding = *il faut une bonne terre pour faire de l'élevage.*

BREEZE (n) *brise (f)* ⓌⒹ wind = *vent*
(the test was) a breeze = *(l'examen était) bête comme chou* ⓌⒹ a cinch = *du gâteau*
to shoot the breeze = *parler de la pluie et du beau temps* ⓌⒹ to chew the fat = *discuter le bout de gras.*

BREEZE (to, -d) **to breeze through (an exam)** = *réussir (un examen) dans un fauteuil* ⓌⒹ to sail through = *réussir haut la main.*

BREW (to, -ed) *(faire) infuser* : to brew tea = *faire infuser du thé*
something's brewing = *il se mijote quelque chose* ⓌⒹ something's fishy = *il y a quelque chose de louche.*

BRIBE (n) *pot-de-vin (m)* : the veep was accused of taking bribes = *le vice-président était accusé d'accepter des pots-de-vin* ⓌⒹ kickback = *dessous-de-table* = payoff **BRIBE** (to, -d) *soudoyer* : he bribed the cops = *il a soudoyé les flics* ⓌⒹ to pay off = *arroser* **BRIBERY** (n)*corruption (f).*

BRICK (n) *brique (f)* : a brick wall = *un mur de briques*

☠ *ça coûtera une brique* = it'll cost a grand
— *ça ne casse pas des briques* = it's nothing to write home about.

BRIDE (n) *mariée (f)* ⓌⒹ bridesmaid = *demoiselle d'honneur*, newlyweds = *jeunes mariés*, bride-to-be = *future mariée* ☠ *il ne faut pas se plaindre que la mariée est trop belle* = don't complain that things are too good to be true.

BRIDGE (n) **1/** *pont (m)* : suspension bridge = *pont suspendu* ⓌⒹ drawbridge = *pont-levis*
to burn one's bridges = *brûler ses vaisseaux*
we'll cross that bridge when we come to it = *chaque chose en son temps* ⓌⒹ one thing at a time = *une chose à la fois*
☠ *ils lui ont fait un pont d'or* = they let him write his own ticket
— *faire le pont* = to link a weekend with a legal holiday (to take a long weekend)
— *se porter comme le Pont Neuf* = to be as fit as a fiddle
— *pont aérien* = airlift
— *le pont (bateau)* = the deck (ship)
2/ *bridge (m)* : to play bridge = *jouer au bridge* ⓌⒹ no trump = *sans atout*, dummy = *le mort*, bid = *annonce*, to double = *contrer*, a trick = *un pli.*

BRIEF (adj, -er, -est) *bref, -ève* : a brief letter = *une lettre brève* ≠ lengthy = *très long* ☠ bref ! = to cut a long story short !

BRIEF (to, -ed) **1/** *mettre au courant* : to brief s.o. about the situation = *mettre qqn au courant de la situation* **2/** *donner des instructions* : to brief a spy before a mission = *donner des instructions à un espion avant une mission.*

BRIEFCASE (n) *serviette (f), porte-documents (m)* ☠ *serviette* → towel.

BRIEFING (n) *briefing (m)* : there'll be a briefing for all the reporters = *un briefing sera fait pour tous les journalistes* ⓌⒹ rundown = *topo.*

BRIEFLY (adv) **1/** *brièvement* : tell me briefly what happened = *racontez-moi brièvement ce qui s'est passé* ⓌⒹ in a nutshell = *en deux mots* **2/** *très peu de temps* : he worked here briefly = *il a travaillé très peu de temps ici* ⓌⒹ a while = *un moment.*

BRIG (n) *cale (f)* : he spent all his navy days in the brig = *il a fait tout son temps dans la marine au fond de la cale* ⓌⒹ prison = ←.

BRIGHT (adj, -er, -est) **1/** *vif, vive* : a bright light = *une lumière vive* ⓌⒹ to brighten = *éclaircir*, dazzling = *éblouissant* **2/** *vif, vive* : she's very bright = *elle est très vive* ⓌⒹ smart = *intelligent* ≠ dumb = *bête*
what a bright idea ! = *quelle idée lumineuse !*
☠ *mort ou vif* = dead or alive
— *l'air est vif* = the air's brisk
— *(dire) de vive voix* = (to say) in person
— *vive (satisfaction)* = great (satisfaction).

BRILLIANCE (n) *brio (m)* : he exposed his ideas with brilliance = *il a exposé ses idées avec brio.*

BRILLIANT (adj) *brillant, -e* : a brilliant lawyer = *un*

avocat brillant ⓓ gifted = *doué* ≠ mediocre = *médiocre* ☠ *yeux/souliers brillants* = shiny eyes/shoes **BRILLIANTLY** (adv) *brillamment.*

BRIM (n) **filled to the brim** = *rempli à ras bord.*

BRING (to, brought, brought) *amener* (s.o.), *apporter* (stg) : bring him with you = *amenez-le avec vous*, bring me a coffee = *apportez-moi un café* ⓓ to take = *prendre*

☠ *il s'est amené à 10 heures* = he showed up at ten o'clock	— *qu'est-ce que ça t'apporte ?* = what good does that to you ?

to **bring about** = *occasionner* : the discovery of the pill brought about changes in women's lives = *la découverte de la pilule a occasionné des changements dans la vie des femmes* ⓓ to trigger off = *déclencher*
to **bring s.o. along** = *amener qqn* : bring him along with you = *amenez-le avec vous*
to **bring s.o. around** = *amener qqn à* : he brought me around to his way of thinking = *il m'a amené à sa façon de penser* ⓓ to persuade = *persuader*
to **bring s.o./stg back** = *ramener qqn/rapporter qqch* : bring the book back next week = *rapportez le livre la semaine prochaine*, bring the kids back at four = *ramenez les gosses à quatre heures* ≠ to come for = *venir chercher*
☠ *la ramener* = to talk big
— *se ramener* = to show up
— *se ramener à* = to come down to
— *rapporter* → to yield
to **bring down** = 1/ *faire tomber* : the army brought down the government = *l'armée a fait tomber le gouvernement* ⓓ to take over = *prendre le pouvoir* 2/ *faire baisser* : to bring down

prices = *faire baisser les prix* ≠ to boost = *faire monter*
to **bring in** = *rapporter* : the business brings in five grand a month = *l'affaire rapporte cinq mille dollars par mois* ☠ → to yield
to **bring s.o. into** = *mêler qqn à* : don't bring me into your family problems = *ne me mêlez pas à vos problèmes de famille* ⓓ to draw s.o. into = *embarquer qqn dans*
to **bring stg off** = *réussir son coup* : they brought the deal off nicely = *ils ont bien réussi leur coup*
to **bring it on o.s.** = *ne pas voler* : you brought it on yourself ! = *tu ne l'as pas volé !* ⓓ you have no one to thank but yourself ! = *tu ne peux t'en prendre qu'à toi-même !*
to **bring on** = *amener* : the flu brought on complications = *la grippe a amené des complications* ⓓ to set off = *entraîner*
to **bring out** = 1/ *sortir* : he'll bring out his first book next year = *il sortira son premier livre l'année prochaine* ⓓ to launch = *lancer* ☠ → to go out 2/ *faire ressortir* : to bring out an important point/the best in s.o. = *faire*

ressortir une chose importante/le meilleur côté de qqn
to **bring over** = *faire venir* : he was sent to Japan and he brought his family over = *il a été envoyé au Japon et il a fait venir sa famille*
to **bring s.o. to** = *ranimer qqn* : the nurse brought her to = *l'infirmière l'a ranimée* ⓓ to come to = *revenir à soi*
to **bring o.s. to** = *se résoudre à* : I couldn't bring myself to lie to her = *je n'ai pas pu me résoudre à lui mentir*
to **bring together** = *rapprocher* : the kids brought them together = *les gosses les ont rapprochés* ≠ to draw apart = *éloigner*
☠ *rapprochez votre chaise* = bring your chair nearer
— *se rapprocher* = to draw near
to **bring up** = 1/ *élever* : to bring up children = *élever des enfants* ☠ → to raise 2/ *rendre* : I brought up the dinner = *j'ai rendu mon dîner* ⓓ to vomit = *vomir* ☠ → to return 3/ *remettre sur le tapis* : don't bring up my divorce again = *ne remets pas encore mon divorce sur le tapis.*

BRINK (n) **on the brink of (war/tears)** = *à deux doigts de (la guerre/pleurer)* ⓓ about to = *sur le point de.*

BRISK (adj, -er, -est) *vif, vive* : the air's brisk = *l'air est vif* ⓓ cool = *frais* ☠ → bright.

BRISTLE (to, -d) *se hérisser* : she bristled at his remark = *elle s'est hérissée en entendant sa remarque* ⓓ to get one's Irish up = *s'exaspérer.*

BRITISH (adj) *britannique* **BRITISH** (n pl) *les Britanniques (m pl)* ⓓ the English = *les Anglais.*

BROACH (to, -ed) *aborder* : to broach a subject = *aborder un sujet* ☠ *aborder qqn* = to accost s.o./to come up to s.o. (in a street).

BROAD (n) *nana (f)* : she's a dynamite broad = *c'est une nana géniale* ⓓ chick = *pépée* ≠ guy = *mec.*

BROAD (adj, -er, -est) *large* : broad streets/shoulders = *rues/épaules larges* ⓓ to broaden = *élargir*
to **give s.o. a broad hint** = *faire un appel du pied à qqn* : she made a broad hint that I should leave them alone = *elle m'a fait un appel du pied pour que je les laisse seuls* ⓓ to make a hint = *faire des allusions*

broad jump = *saut en longueur*
in broad daylight = *en plein jour*
it's as broad as it's long = *c'est kif-kif* ⓪ **it all amounts to the same thing** = *ça revient au même.*

BROADCAST (n) *retransmission (f)* : the broadcast of the match = *la retransmission du match.*

BROADCAST (to, -cast, -cast) *diffuser, radiodiffuser* : the hearing was broadcast live = *l'audience a été diffusée en direct*
don't broadcast it ! = *ne le crie pas sur les toits !*

BROADLY (adv) **broadly speaking** = *en gros* ⓪ roughly speaking = *grosso modo.*

BROAD-MINDED (adj) *large d'esprit* : broad-minded parents = *des parents larges d'esprit* ⓪ liberal = *libéral.*

BROADWAY (n) *quartier des spectacles à New York* ⓪ off-Broadway = *spectacle d'avant-garde*, off-off Broadway = *genre de café-théâtre.*

BROCCOLI (n) *brocoli (m)* ⓪ cauliflower = *chou-fleur.*

BROCHURE (n) *prospectus (m)* : the hotel's brochure = *le prospectus de l'hôtel* ⓪ pamphlet = *opuscule* ☠ *une brochure* = a booklet.

BROIL (to, -ed) *(faire) griller* : to broil a chicken = *faire griller un poulet* ☠ → to grill **BROILER** (n) *gril (m).*

BROKE (adj, -r, -st) *fauché, -e* : I'm broke this month = *je suis fauché ce mois-ci* → POOR ≠ loaded = *plein aux as*
to go for broke = *risquer le tout pour le tout* ⓪ to stake all = *jouer son va-tout.*

BROKEN (adj) *brisé, -e (s.o.)*, *cassé, -e (stg)*, *rompu, -e (promise)* : a broken man = *un homme brisé*, a broken plate/machine = *une assiette/machine cassée*
to be like a broken record = *répéter qqch comme un disque rayé*
to speak broken (English) = *parler (anglais) comme une vache espagnole* ⓪ to murder (English) = *écorcher (l'anglais).*

BROKENHEARTED (adj) *qui a le cœur brisé.*

BROKER (n) *courtier (m)* : a wine broker = *un courtier en vins* ⓪ customer's man = *intermédiaire (Bourse).*

BRONCHITIS (n) *bronchite (f)* ⓪ pneumonia = *pneumonie.*

BRONZE (n) *bronze (m)* : a bronze statue = *une statue en bronze.*

BROOD (n) *smala (f)* : he came with all his brood = *il est venu avec toute sa smala* ⓪ tribe = *tribu.*

BROOD OVER (to, -ed) *ruminer* : stop brooding over your problems = *arrête de ruminer tes problèmes* ⓪ to mope = *se morfondre.*

BROOK (n) *cours (m) d'eau* ⓪ stream = *ruisseau.*

BROOKLYN (n) *district de New York, autrefois point*
d'arrivée des immigrants
he could sell you the Brooklyn bridge = *il pourrait vous vendre la tour Eiffel*
what has it got to do with the Brooklyn bridge ? = *rien à voir avec la choucroute !* ⓪ that has nothing to do with it = *ça n'a rien à voir.*

BROOM (n) *balai (m)* ⓪ to sweep = *balayer*
☠ *du balai !* = buzz off !
— *con comme un balai* = as dumb as they come.

BROTHEL (n) *bordel (m)* ⓪ bordello = *maison close*, whorehouse = *boxon*, trick = *passe*, madam = *mère maquerelle*, hooker = *putain*
☠ *quel bordel !* = what a fucking mess !
— *bordel !* = fuck it !

BROTHER (n) *frère (m)*, *frangin (m)* (LV) : my kid brother = *mon petit frère* ⓪ half brother = *demi-frère*, brother-in-law = *beau-frère*, brotherhood = *fraternité* ≠ sister = *sœur*
I'm not my brother's keeper = *je ne suis pas le gardien de mon frère.*

BROWN (n) *marron (m)* : I don't like brown = *je n'aime pas le marron*
☠ *flanquer un marron à qqn* = to slug s.o.
— *un marron* = a chestnut
— *tirer les marrons du feu pour qqn* = to do stg and let s.o. else take the credit.

BROWN (adj, -er, est) *brun (hair, eyes)*, *marron (clothes)* : brown hair = *cheveux bruns*, a brown coat = *un manteau marron* ⓪ chestnut brown = *châtain*
☠ *il est marron* = he was had
— *un avocat marron* = a shyster lawyer
— *une fille brune* = a brunette.

BROWNNOSE (to, -d) *faire de la lèche* ⓪ to lick s.o.'s boots = *lécher les bottes de qqn* **BROWNNOSER** (n) *lécheur, -euse* ⓪ bootlicker = *lèche-bottes.*

BROWNSTONE (n) *hôtel particulier new-yorkais en grès rouge* ⓪ townhouse = *hôtel particulier.*

BROWSE (to, -d) *regarder (en passant)* : I don't want to buy anything, I'm just browsing = *je ne veux rien acheter, je regarde juste (en passant).*
to browse through (a book) = *parcourir (un livre)* ⓪ to skim through = *lire en diagonale* ☠ *parcourir une distance* = to cover a distance.

BRUISE (n) *ecchymose (f)* : the child's body was covered with bruises = *le corps de l'enfant était couvert d'ecchymoses* ⓪ a black-and-blue mark = *un bleu* **BRUISE** (to, -d) *(se) faire un bleu* : to bruise one's arm = *se faire un bleu au bras.*

BRUNCH (n, -es) *brunch (m) (repas qui combine le petit déjeuner et le déjeuner).*

BRUNETTE (n) *brune (f)* ≠ blonde = ←.

BRUNT (n) **to bear the brunt of (s.o.'s anger)** = *subir le gros de (la colère de qqn).*

BRUSH (n, -es) *brosse* (f) ⓪ comb = *peigne*
to have a brush with (the police) = *avoir des démêlés avec (la police)*
☠ *passer la brosse à reluire* = to butter s.o. up.

BRUSH (to, -ed) *(se) brosser* : I brush my hair every day = *je me brosse les cheveux tous les jours* ⓪ to comb = *peigner*
to brush aside (a problem) = *écarter (un problème)*
☠ → to preclude
to brush off = *rembarrer* : the President brushed the diplomat off = *le Président a rembarré le diplomate* ⓪ to rebuff = *rabrouer*
to brush up = *réviser* : I'm brushing up my Spanish = *je révise mon espagnol* ⓪ to bone up = *potasser*
☠ → to revise
☠ *tu peux toujours te brosser* = you can whistle for it
— *brosser le tableau d'une situation* = to draw a picture of a situation.

BRUSH-OFF (n) **to give s.o. the brush-off** = *envoyer bouler qqn* : the guy tried to pick me up but I gave him the brush-off = *le type a essayé de me draguer mais je l'ai envoyé bouler* ⓪ to send s.o. packing = *envoyer qqn sur les roses.*

BRUSQUE (adj) *brusque* : brusque manners = *des manières brusques* = curt manners ☠ *un changement brusque* = a sudden change.

BRUSSELS SPROUT (n) *chou* (m) *de Bruxelles.*

BRUTAL (adj) *brutal, -e* : a brutal guy = *un type brutal* ⓪ cruel = ← ≠ gentle = *doux*
☠ *un arrêt brutal* = a sudden stop
— *une réponse brutale* = a blunt answer.

BRUTALITY (n, -ies) *brutalité* (f) ⓪ cruelty = *cruauté.*

BRUTALIZE (to, -d) *brutaliser* : to brutalize a prisoner = *brutaliser un prisonnier.*

BRUTALLY (adv) *brutalement.*

BUBBLE (n) *bulle* (f) : bubbles in champagne = *des bulles dans le champagne*
bubble bath = *bain moussant*
bubble gum = *chewing-gum*
☠ *se coincer la bulle* = to goof off
— *ça va chier des bulles* = all hell's going to break loose.

BUCK (n) *dollar* (m) ⓪ a grand = *une brique (mille dollars)*
to pass the buck = *refiler la responsabilité aux autres* : instead of making a decision he passed the buck = *au lieu de prendre une décision, il a refilé la responsabilité aux autres.*

BUCK (to, -ed) *s'opposer à* : Congress's trying to buck the President's decision = *le Congrès essaie de s'opposer à la décision du Président* ⓪ to resist = *résister à*
buck up ! = *courage !* ⓪ cheer up ! = *allez, allez !*

BUCKET (n) *seau* (m) : ice bucket = *seau à glace*

it's coming down in buckets = *il pleut à seaux* ⓪ it's coming down = *il tombe des cordes*
to kick the bucket = *passer l'arme à gauche* ⓪ to kick off = *casser sa pipe.*

BUCKLE (n) *boucle* (f) ⓪ belt = *ceinture* ☠ → curl.

BUCKLE DOWN (to, -d) *en mettre un coup* : we'd better buckle down if we want to finish next week = *il faut en mettre un coup si nous voulons finir la semaine prochaine* ⓪ to get down to it = *s'y mettre.*

BUD (n) *bourgeon* (m) ⓪ spring = *printemps*
to be nipped in the bud = *être étouffé dans l'œuf.*

BUDDING (adj) *en herbe* : a budding writer = *un écrivain en herbe* ⓪ promising = *prometteur.*

BUDDY (n, -ies) *pote* (m) : I'm with an old buddy = *je suis avec un vieux pote à moi* ⓪ bosom pals = *copains comme cochons*
listen, buddy ! = *écoute, bonhomme !*

BUDDY-BUDDY (adj) *copain copain* ⓪ to be as thick as thieves = *être comme cul et chemise.*

BUDGE (to, -d) *transiger* : once she's made up her mind, she won't budge = *une fois qu'elle s'est décidée, elle ne transige pas.*

BUDGET (n) *budget* (m) : balanced budget = *budget équilibré.*

BUFF (n) *mordu, -e* : a jazz buff = *un mordu de jazz* ⓪ bug = *passionné.*

BUFFALO (n, -es) *buffle* (m), *bison* (m).

BUFFER (n) *tampon* (m) : buffer zone = *zone tampon* ⓪ no man's land = ←.

BUFFET (n) *buffet* (m) : a delicious buffet = *un buffet délicieux* ⓪ appetizer = *hors-d'œuvre.*

BUG (n) 1/ *bestiole* (f) : the room was full of bugs = *la pièce était pleine de bestioles*
to pick up a bug = *attraper un microbe*
2/ *micro* (m) : bugs all over the embassy = *des micros dans toute l'ambassade* ☠ → mike
3/ *passionné, -e* : a camera bug = *un passionné de la photo* ⓪ fan = ← ☠ *un passionné* = s.o. very intense
4/ *dingo* (m) : a cleanliness bug = *un dingo de la propreté.*

BUG (to, -ged) 1/ *turlupiner* : his health is bugging him = *sa santé le turlupine* ⓪ to worry = *inquiéter* 2/ *casser les pieds à* : stop bugging me about it = *arrête de me casser les pieds avec ça* ⓪ to pester = *enquiquiner* 3/ *poser des micros (clandestins)* : the room's bugged = *on a posé des micros dans la pièce* ⓪ to wiretap = *mettre sur table d'écoute.*

BUGGER (to, -ed) *enculer* ⓪ to take from behind = *prendre en levrette* ☠ *va te faire enculer !* = fuck off !

BUGLE (n) *clairon* (m) ⓪ trumpet = *trompette.*

BUILD (to, built, built) *bâtir* : to build a house = *bâtir une maison* ⓪ to construct = *construire* ≠ to tear down = *abattre*

to build up = 1/ *bâtir* : he's building his business/clientele up = *il bâtit son affaire/sa clientèle* ⓪ to develop = *développer* 2/ *urbaniser* : to build up an area = *urbaniser une région* 3/ *monter* : tension's building up = *la tension monte* ⓪ to increase = *augmenter* ☠ → to rise

to build (things) up = *en rajouter* : the situation isn't that bad, you're building things up = *la situation n'est pas mauvaise à ce point-là, tu en rajoutes* ⓪ to magnify = *amplifier*

to build s.o. up = *vanter les mérites de qqn* : don't build up your sister like that, she isn't so gifted = *ne vante pas autant les mérites de ta sœur, elle n'est pas si douée que ça* ⓪ to enhance = *mettre en valeur*.

BUILDER (n) *entrepreneur* (m) *du bâtiment* ⓪ constructor = *constructeur*, architect = *architecte*.

BUILDING (n) *immeuble* (m), *bâtiment* (m), *building* (m) (modern, tall) : I live in a new building = *j'habite un immeuble neuf*, temples and houses are buildings = *les temples et les maisons sont des bâtiments* ⓪ edifice = *édifice*, skyscraper = *gratte-ciel*

to work in building = *travailler dans le bâtiment*.

BUILDUP (n) *renforcement* (m) : a buildup of forces/armament in the Middle East = *un renforcement des troupes/de l'armement au Moyen-Orient*

to give s.o. a buildup = *vanter les mérites de qqn*.

BUILT (adj) *bien fichu, -e* : his wife's really built = *sa femme est vraiment bien fichue* ⓪ well-developed = *bien fait*

she's built like a battleship = *elle est bien roulée* ⓪ she's well-stacked = *elle est bien foutue*.

BUILT-IN (adj) *encastré, -e* : a built-in TV = *une télé encastrée*.

BULB (n) *ampoule* (f) : buy a new bulb for the lamp = *achète une nouvelle ampoule pour la lampe* ☠ → blister.

BULGARIA (n) *Bulgarie* (f) **BULGARIAN** (n, adj) *Bulgare* (m, f).

BULGING (adj) *exorbité, -e* (eyes), *ballonné, -e* (stomach), *bombé, -e* (suitcase)

what's bulging out of your bag ? = *qu'est-ce qui dépasse de votre sac ?* = what's protruding out of your bag ?

BULK (n) *gros* (m) : to do the bulk of the work = *faire le gros du travail*

in bulk = *en vrac* : to buy in bulk = *acheter en vrac* ☠ *acheter en gros* = to buy wholesale
— *en gros, disons ...* = roughly, let's say ...

BULKY (adj, -ier, -iest) *volumineux, -euse* : a bulky package = *un paquet volumineux* ⓪ cumbersome = *encombrant*.

BULL (n) 1/ *taureau* (m) ⓪ bullfighter = *toréador*, bullfight = *corrida*

bull session = *bonne conversation* ⓪ rap = *discussion*

like a bull in a china shop = *comme un éléphant dans un magasin de porcelaine*

to shoot the bull = *tailler une bavette* ⓪ to shoot the breeze = *parler de la pluie et du beau temps*

to take the bull by the horns = *prendre le taureau par les cornes*

2/ *conneries* (f pl) = bullshit.

BULLET (n) *balle* (f) : stray bullet = *balle perdue* ⓪ blank = *balle à blanc*, slug = *pruneau*, cartridge = *cartouche* ☠ → ball

to sweat bullets = *suer sang et eau* ⓪ to knock o.s. out = *se crever*.

BULLETIN (n) *bulletin* (m) : news bulletin = *bulletin d'informations* ⓪ press release = *communiqué de presse*

bulletin board = *panneau d'affichage*
☠ *bulletin de vote* = ballot
— *bulletin météorologique* = weather report
— *bulletin de notes* = report card.

BULLETPROOF (adj) *pare-balles* : a bulletproof jacket/pane = *un gilet/une vitre pare-balles* ⓪ armored = *blindé*.

BULLFIGHT (n) *corrida* (f), *course* (f) *de taureaux* ☠ *quelle corrida pour être à l'heure !* = what a circus to get here in time !

BULL'S-EYE (n) **to hit the bull's-eye** = *faire mouche* ⓪ to hit the nail on the head = *taper dans le mille*.

BULLSHIT (n inv) *conneries* (f pl) : that' a lot of bullshit = *tout ça, ce sont des conneries !* = B.S. = bull ⓪ nonsense = *bêtises*, hogwash = *absurdités*

a bullshit artist = *un déconneur*
☠ *quelle connerie !* = what a fucking stupid thing !/what a foul-up !

BULLY (n, -ies) *brute* (f) ⓪ tyrant = *tyran*.

BULLY (to, -ied) *brutaliser* : big brothers often bully little ones = *les grands frères brutalisent souvent les petits* ⓪ to browbeat = *rudoyer*

bully for you ! = *grand bien te fasse !* ⓪ a lot I care ! = *je n'en ai rien à faire !*

BUM (n) 1/ *clochard, -e* : a bum on the Bowery = *un clochard du Bowery* ⓪ baglady = *clocharde*, panhandler = *mendigot* 2/ *bon, bonne à rien* : his sons are lazy bums = *ses fils sont des bons à rien et des feignants* ⓪ goof-off = *tire-au-flanc*.

BUM (adj) **a bum rap** = *une accusation bidon* : to be sent to prison on a bum rap = *être envoyé en prison sur une accusation bidon*

a bum deal = *un marché de dupes* : I got a bum deal on the contract = *ce contrat était un marché de dupes* ⓪ a low trick = *une vacherie*

bum steer = *tuyau crevé* : his tip for the third race was a bum steer = *son tuyau pour la troisième course, c'était un tuyau crevé* ≠ good lead = *bonne piste*.

BUM (to, -med) *taper :* can I bum a cigarette ? = *est-ce que je peux te taper une cigarette ?* = can I grub a cigarette ? → to hit

to bum around = *ne rien ficher :* to bum around all day = *ne rien ficher de la journée* ⓪ to goof off = *tirer au flanc*

to bum through (Europe) = *bourlinguer en (Europe)* ⓪ to drift = *vadrouiller.*

BUMMER (n) *sale truc (m) :* their divorce was a bummer for the kids = *leur divorce a été un sale truc pour les gosses* ⓪ bitch = *qqch d'emmerdant.*

BUMP (n) *bosse (f) :* a bump on my forehead = *une bosse au front,* a bump on the car = *une bosse sur la voiture*
bumps and grinds = *danse provocante (genre striptease)*
 avoir la bosse de = to have a good head for
— *avoir roulé sa bosse* = to have knocked around
— *bosse (dos)* = hump.

BUMP (to, -ed) *cogner :* to bump one's head = *se cogner la tête* → to clobber
to bump into = 1/ *rencontrer par hasard :* I bumped into her yesterday = *je l'ai rencontrée par hasard hier* ⓪ to run into = *tomber sur* 2/ *rentrer dans :* he bumped into a tree = *il est rentré dans un arbre* ⓪ to crash into = *percuter*
to bump s.o. off = *expédier qqn dans l'autre monde :* the gang bumped him off = *le gang l'a expédié dans l'autre monde* ⓪ to do in = *refroidir.*

BUMPER (n) *pare-chocs (m)* ⓪ headlights = *phares*
bumper-to-bumper = *pare-chocs contre pare-chocs*
bumper crop = *récolte exceptionnelle.*

BUMPY (adj, -ier, -iest) *cahoteux, -euse :* a bumpy road = *une route cahoteuse* ≠ smooth = *lisse.*

BUNCH (n, -es) *tout un tas :* a bunch of kids/cookies = *tout un tas de gosses/petits gâteaux* → MANY
the best/pick of the bunch = *la fine fleur* ⓪ the pick of the lot = *le dessus du panier.*

BUNDLE (n) *paquet (m) :* to carry heavy bundles = *porter des paquets lourds* ⓪ parcel = *colis* → pack
a bundle of nerves = *un paquet de nerfs*
to make/have a bundle = *se faire/avoir un magot :* he made a bundle on the Stock Market = *il s'est fait un magot en jouant à la Bourse* → RICH.

BUNDLE UP (to, -d) *s'emmitoufler :* bundle up, it's cold = *emmitoufle-toi, il fait froid* ⓪ to wrap up = *se couvrir.*

BUNGALOW (n) *bungalow (m)* ⓪ villa = ←.

BUNGLE (to, -d) *louper :* the Senator bungled his speech = *le sénateur a loupé son discours* ⓪ to fuck up = *foutre en l'air*
 louper son train = to miss one's train
— *louper sa vie* = to make a mess of one's life.

BUNK (n inv) *fadaises (f pl) :* what bunk ! = *quelles fadai-*

ses ! = bunkum ⓪ baloney = *âneries.*

BURDEN (n) *fardeau (m) :* her parents are a real burden to her = *ses parents sont un véritable fardeau pour elle* ⓪ charge = ←.

BURDEN WITH (to, -ed) *importuner avec :* I won't burden you with my problems = *je ne vais pas vous importuner avec mes problèmes* ⓪ to annoy with = *ennuyer avec.*

BUREAUCRACY (n, -ies) *bureaucratie (f)* **BUREAUCRAT** (n) *bureaucrate (m, f)* ⓪ civil servant = *fonctionnaire* **BUREAUCRATIC** (adj) *bureaucratique.*

BURGER (n) *hamburger (m)* = ←.

BURGLAR (n) *cambrioleur, -euse :* the burglars got away = *les cambrioleurs se sont enfuis* ⓪ safecracker = *perceur de coffre-fort*
burglar alarm = *sonnerie d'alarme.*

BURGLARY (n, -ies) *cambriolage (m)* ⓪ break-in = *vol avec effraction.*

BURIAL (n) *mise (f) en terre* ⓪ incineration = *incinération,* funeral = *enterrement.*

BURLESQUE (adj) *burlesque* ⓪ vaudeville = *vaudevillesque.*

BURN (n) *brûlure (f)* ⓪ skin graft = *greffe de peau.*

BURN (to, -ed or burnt) *brûler, cramer* (LV) : I burned my fingers = *je me suis brûlé les doigts,* I burned all his letters = *j'ai brûlé toutes ses lettres*
to be burning = *bouillir de colère* → ANGRY
to be burning to (be an actress) = *brûler de (devenir actrice)* ⓪ to yearn to = *désirer vivement*
to burn down/up = *détruire par le feu :* the school burned down/up = *l'école a été détruite par le feu*
to burn s.o. up = *faire bouillir qqn de colère :* his remark burned me up = *sa réflexion m'a fait bouillir (de colère)* → ANGRY
 tu brûles ! = you're getting warm !
— *brûler un feu rouge* = to run a red light.

BURP (n) *renvoi (m)* ⓪ belch = *rot* → dismissal
BURP (to, -ed) *faire un renvoi.*

BURST (to, burst, burst) *éclater :* the balloon burst = *le ballon a éclaté* ⓪ to explode = *exploser*
to burst into (the room) = *faire irruption dans (la pièce)* ⓪ to dash in = *entrer en trombe*
to burst out (crying/laughing) = *éclater (en sanglots/de rire)*
 éclater (colère) = to blow up/to flare up (anger)
— *la guerre a éclaté* = war broke out.

BURY (to, -ied) *enterrer :* they're burying him on Friday = *on l'enterre vendredi* ≠ to unearth = *déterrer*
buried and forgotten = *enterré depuis longtemps*
 il nous enterrera tous = he'll outlive all of us
— *enterrer (scandale)* = to hush up (scandal)
— *enterrer un projet de loi* = to kill a bill.

BUS (n, -es) *bus (m)*, *autobus (m)* : bus stop = *arrêt de bus*, busdriver = *conducteur de bus* ⊕ coach = *car*.

BUSH (n, -es) *buisson (m)* ⊕ shrub = *arbuste*
to beat around the bush = *tourner autour du pot* ≠ to get down to cases = *en venir au fait*.

BUSHED (adj) *vidé, -e* : boy, I'm bushed ! = *oh là là, je suis vidé !* ⊕ done in = *vanné*, dead = *mort de fatigue*.

BUSHEL (n) *boisseau (m)* : $ 5 a bushel = *5 dollars le boisseau*.

BUSINESS (n) 1/ (-es) *affaire (f)* : this is is his first business = *c'est sa première affaire* ⊕ trade = *commerce* ⚓ → affair 2/ (inv) *genre (m) de travail* : what's his business ? = *quel genre de travail fait-il ?* 3/ (inv) *les affaires (f pl)* ≠ leisure = *loisirs*

to be in business = *être dans les affaires*
to be in the book/film business = *être dans l'édition/le cinéma*
business is business = *les affaires sont les affaires*
business is good ≠ bad = *les affaires vont bien ≠ mal*
business school = *école de commerce*
to combine business with pleasure = *joindre l'utile à l'agréable*
to do business with (the French) = *faire des affaires avec (les Français)*
to give s.o. the business = *faire marcher qqn* : don't take him seriously, he's just giving you the business = *ne le prenez pas au sérieux, il vous fait marcher* ⊕ to pull s.o.'s leg = *mettre qqn en boîte*

(he) had no business (telling you that) = *ce n'était pas à (lui) de (vous dire ça)*
how's business ? = *comment vont les affaires ?*
it's business as usual = *le monde continue de tourner* : in spite of the strikes, it's business as usual = *malgré les grèves, le monde continue de tourner* → THAT'S LIFE !
let's get down to business = *passons aux choses sérieuses* ⊕ to get down to brass tacks = *en venir au fait*
to make it one's business to = *faire en sorte que* : make it your business to come on time = *faites en sorte d'arriver à l'heure* ⊕ to see to = *veiller à*
to mean business = *ne pas plaisanter* : you're not going to get a raise if your work isn't better, and I mean business = *vous*

n'aurez pas d'augmentation si vous ne travaillez pas mieux, et je ne plaisante pas
mind .your (own) business ! = *occupe-toi de tes affaires !* ⊕ stop meddling ! = *mêle-toi de ce qui te regarde !*
on business = *pour affaires* : he's in town on business = *il est en ville pour affaires*
to send s.o. about his business = *envoyer balader qqn* ⊕ to give s.o. his walking papers = *envoyer paître qqn*
to talk business = *parler affaires*
what business is it of yours ? = *est-ce que ça te regarde ?*
what's this business about (his wanting to retire) ? = *qu'est-ce que c'est que cette histoire, (il paraît qu'il veut démissionner) ?*

BUSINESSLIKE (adj) *sérieux, -euse (dans le travail/en affaires)* : when he works, he's very businesslike = *il est très sérieux dans le travail* ⊕ efficient = *efficace* ⚓ → serious.

BUSINESSMAN (n, -men) *homme (m) d'affaires* **BUSINESSWOMAN** (n, -women) *femme (f) d'affaires* ⊕ career girl = *femme qui fait carrière*.

BUSING (n) *ramassage scolaire visant à la déségrégation des écoles*.

BUSMAN (n, -men) **to take a busman's holiday** = *continuer à faire son métier pendant les vacances (chauffeur de bus qui conduit pendant ses vacances)*.

BUST (n) 1/ *fiasco (m)* : the play was a bust = *la pièce a été un fiasco* ⊕ washout = *bide* ≠ hit = *succès* 2/ *buste (m)* : to have a big bust = *avoir un buste imposant* ⊕ chest = *poitrine* 3/ *descente (f)* : a police bust = *une descente de police* ⚓ → descent 4/ *arrestation (f)* : his first bust since he's been dealing = *sa première arrestation depuis qu'il fait du trafic* ⚓ → arrest.

BUST (adj) *sans un rond* = busted → POOR
to go bust = *couler* : the business went bust = *l'affaire a coulé* ⊕ to go bankrupt = *faire faillite* ⚓ → to flow.

BUST (to, -ed) *coffrer* : that was the first time he was busted = *c'était la première fois qu'il se faisait coffrer* ⊕ to pull in = *embarquer*
(my watch) is busted = *(ma montre) est fichue* ⊕ to be broken = *être cassé*
to bust out = *jouer la fille de l'air* ⊕ to be on the run = *être en cavale*
to bust up = *péter entre* : my sister and her husband busted up = *ça a pété entre ma sœur et son mari* ⊕ to split up = *rompre*.

BUSTER (n) *mon vieux* : listen buster ! = *écoute, mon vieux !*

BUSY (adj, -ier, -iest) 1/ *occupé, -e* : the line's busy = *la ligne est occupée*, I can't talk too long I'm very busy = *je ne peux pas vous parler trop longtemps, je suis très occupé* ⚓ → occupied 2/ *pris, -e* : I'm busy tonight =

je suis pris ce soir ≠ free = *libre* **3/** *chargé, -e* : a busy month = *un mois chargé* ☠ → loaded
to be as busy as beavers = *s'activer comme des fourmis* ≠ to twiddle one's thumbs = *se tourner les pouces*
a busy street = *une rue passante.*

BUSYBODY (n, -ies) *mouche* (f) *du coche* ⓪ meddler = *qqn qui s'immisce dans les affaires des autres*, nosybody = *fouineur.*

BUT (prep) *sauf* : I'll eat anything but chicken = *je veux bien manger n'importe quoi, sauf du poulet* ⓪ except = *excepté.*

BUT (conj) **1/** *mais* : the course is boring but important = *le cours est ennuyeux mais important* ⓪ however = *cependant*, nevertheless = *néanmoins* ☠ *mais non !* = of course not ! **2/** *sauf* : she can do everything but cook = *elle sait tout faire sauf cuisiner* ⓪ besides = *à part*

but for = *n'était* : but for the kids, she would have committed suicide = *n'étaient les enfants, elle se serait suicidée* **there are no buts about it** = *il n'y a pas de mais* **but still** = *mais encore* : it's not expensive but still you have to have the money = *ce*	*n'est pas cher, mais encore faut-il avoir l'argent* **but then (again)** = *mais d'un autre côté* : you're not so smart, but then (again) I'm no genius either = *tu n'es pas si malin que ça, mais d'un autre côté, je ne suis pas non plus un génie.*

BUTCHER (n) *boucher, -ère* ⓪ butcher shop = *boucherie*, meat = *viande*, slaughterhouse = *abattoir.*

BUTCHER (to, -ed) *massacrer* : the terrorists butchered the hostages = *les terroristes ont massacré les otages* = to slaughter ⓪ to kill off = *exterminer* ☠ → to massacre.

BUTLER (n) *maître* (m) *d'hôtel* ⓪ valet = *valet de chambre.*

BUTT (n) *mégot* (m) : the ashtray's full of butts = *le cendrier est plein de mégots*
to be the butt of (jokes) = *être en butte aux (plaisanteries)* ⓪ to be the whipping boy = *être le souffre-douleur.*

BUTTER (n inv) *beurre* (m) : salted butter = *du beurre salé* ⓪ margarine = ←, cholesterol = *cholestérol*
butter wouldn't melt in her mouth = *elle est aimable comme une porte de prison* ⓪ a cold fish = *un pisse-froid*
☠ *ça va mettre du beurre dans les épinards* = it's gravy (extra money)
— *on ne peut pas avoir le beurre et l'argent du beurre* = you can't have your cake and eat it too

— *compter pour du beurre* = to cut no ice
— *œil au beurre noir* = black eye
— *il fait son beurre* = he's making a pile.

BUTTER (to, -ed) **to butter s.o. up** = *passer de la pommade à qqn* : he's buttering me up for a raise = *il me passe de la pommade pour que je l'augmente* ⓪ to lay it on = *en faire des tonnes.*

BUTTERBALL (n) *personne* (f) *rondelette* ⓪ plump = *rondouillard.*

BUTTERFINGERS (n inv) *empoté, -e* : what a butterfingers you are ! = *quel empoté tu fais !* ⓪ a clumsy person = *une personne gauche.*

BUTTERFLY (n, -ies) *papillon* (m) ⓪ caterpillar = *chenille*
to have butterflies in one's stomach = *avoir l'estomac noué*
☠ *minute papillon !* = just a minute !

BUTT IN (to, -ed) *ramener sa fraise* : don't butt in, it's none of your business ! = *ne ramène pas ta fraise, ce ne sont pas tes oignons !* ⓪ to interfere = *s'ingérer.*

BUTTOCKS (n pl) *fesses* (f pl) ⓪ rear end = *arrière-train*, can = *derche*
☠ *serrer les fesses* = to have the willies
— *film de fesses* = sexy movie.

BUTTON (n) *bouton* (m) : to sew a button = *coudre un bouton* ⓪ buttonhole = *boutonnière*
push the button = *appuyez sur le bouton*
☠ *bouton (visage)* = pimple
— *boutons de manchette* = cufflinks.

BUTTON (to, -ed) *boutonner* : to button one's coat = *boutonner son manteau* ≠ to unbutton = *déboutonner.*

BUTTRESS (to, -ed) *soutenir* : measures to buttress the automobile industry = *des mesures pour soutenir l'industrie automobile* ⓪ to prop up = *étayer* ☠ → to support.

BUXOM (adj) *plantureux, -euse* : a buxom blonde = *une blonde plantureuse* ⓪ stacked = *bien foutue* ☠ *un repas plantureux* = a copious meal.

BUY (n) *occasion* (f) : a good buy = *une bonne occasion* ⓪ bargain = *affaire* ☠ → occasion.

BUY (to, bought, bought) **1/** *acheter* : to buy a new car = *acheter une voiture neuve* ⓪ to acquire = *acquérir* ≠ to sell = *vendre* **2/** *acheter* : some politicians can be bought = *on peut acheter certains hommes politiques* ⓪ to bribe = *soudoyer*
I don't buy it ! = *je ne marche pas !* → BUZZ OFF !
I'll buy that ! = *c'est bon !* ≠ no way ! = *que dalle !*
I'll buy (you a drink) = *je (te) paie (un verre)*
to buy from = *acheter à* : I bought the car from my cousin = *j'ai acheté la voiture à mon cousin* ≠ to sell to = *vendre à*
to buy into (a business) = *acheter des parts d'(une affaire)*

to buy off = *acheter* : to buy off the referee = *acheter l'arbitre* ≠ **to be in the pay of** = *être à la solde de*
to buy (one's partner) out = *racheter les parts de (son associé)*
to buy up = *acheter en bloc* : to buy up all the shares = *acheter toutes les actions en bloc.*

BUYER (n) *acheteur, -euse* ⓒ buying agent = *commissionnaire d'achat.*

BUZZ (n, -es) *coup (m) de fil* : give me a buzz tonight = *passez-moi un coup de fil ce soir* = give me a call tonight.

BUZZ OFF ! (interj) *débarrasse le plancher* !

———— GROUP : BUZZ OFF ! = DÉBARRASSE LE PLANCHER ! ————

beat it ! = *fiche le camp* !
can it ! = *écrase* !
cool it ! = *mets-la en veilleuse* !
cut it out ! = *fiche-moi la paix* !
cut the comedy ! = *arrête ta comédie !/ton cirque* !
cut the jazz ! = *arrête tes salades* !
cut the shit ! = *arrête tes conneries* !
damn him ! = *qu'il aille au diable* ! = **darn him** !
don't bullshit me ! = *ne me raconte pas de conneries* !
I don't buy it ! = *je ne marche pas* !
don't give me that ! = *pour qui me prends-tu* ?
don't give me that routine ! = *arrête ton numéro* !
don't hand me that ! = *pour qui me prends-tu* ?
don't hold your breath ! = *compte là-dessus et bois de l'eau (fraîche)* !
drop dead ! = *et ta sœur* !
dry up ! = *écrase* !
fuck off ! = *va te faire foutre !/enculer* !
fuck you ! = *je t'emmerde !/tu m'emmerdes* !
get lost ! = *fiche-moi le camp* !
get off my case ! = *lâche-moi les baskets* !

get off it ! = *arrête ton char* !
get off my back ! = *fiche-moi la paix* !
get the fuck out ! = *va te faire foutre* !
get the hell out ! = *va te faire voir* !
get out ! = *sortez* !
go fly a kite ! = *va voir là-bas si j'y suis* !
go fuck a duck ! = *va te faire cuire un œuf* !
go jump in the lake ! = *du balai* !
go peddle your papers ! = *casse-toi* !
go to blazes ! = *du large* !
go to hell ! = *va au diable* !
I'm not having/buying any ! = *je ne marche pas* !
the hell with him ! = *qu'il aille se faire pendre ailleurs* !
keep your big mouth shut ! = *ferme ta grande gueule* !
knock it off ! = *ça va bien comme ça* !
leave me alone ! = *fichez-moi la paix* !
lay off ! = *foutez-moi la paix* !
my ass ! = *mon cul* !
my foot ! = *mon œil* !
off with you ! = *décampe* !
out ! = *oust !/dehors* !
none of your lip ! = *ferme ton clapet* ! = **button your lip** !

piss off ! = *va te faire voir* !
scram ! = *dégage* !
screw off ! = *foutez-moi la paix !/le camp* !
screw you ! = *tu me fais chier* !
shove it ! = *ta gueule* !
shut up ! = *ferme-la !/boucle-la* !
shut your trap ! = *ferme ton clapet* !
stick it ! = *va chier* !
tell me another ! = *à d'autres* ! = **tell it to the marines** !
tough shit ! = *je n'en ai rien à branler* !
up yours ! = *je t'emmerde* !
who are you trying to kid ? = *de qui se moque-t-on* ?
you bet your sweet ass ! = *et mon cul, c'est du poulet* ?
you can kiss my ass ! = *va te faire enculer (par les Grecs)* !
you can't sell that to me ! = *vous ne me ferez pas croire ça* !
you're full of it ! = *tu déconnes* !
you're full of shit ! = *tu ne dis que des conneries* !
you know where you can go ! = *va te faire voir* !
keep your big mouth shut ! = *ferme ta grande gueule* !

BY (prep) *par* : the book was written by a specialist = *le livre a été écrit par un spécialiste*

by ... = *d'ici ...* : we won't finish by Friday/5 o'clock = *nous n'aurons pas fini d'ici vendredi/5 heures*
... by ... = *... sur ...* : the room's 5 meters by 8 = *la pièce fait 5 mètres sur 8* 🐝 → on
a (book) by (Miller) = *un (livre) de (Miller)*

by + ing = *à force de* : she succeeded by working so hard = *elle a réussi à force de travailler avec acharnement*
by (oneself) = *(tout) seul* : I did it by myself = *je l'ai fait tout seul*
by and large = *dans l'ensemble* : by and large she works well

= *dans l'ensemble, elle travaille bien* = on the whole ⓒ overall = *en gros*
by car = *en voiture*
by chance = *par hasard* : would you have any cigarettes by chance ? = *est-ce que par hasard vous auriez des cigarettes* ?
by far = *de loin* : she's the wit-

79

tiest by far = *c'est de loin la plus spirituelle*

by heart = *par cœur*

by hundreds/thousands = *par centaines/milliers*

by mistake = *par erreur* : I did it by mistake = *je l'ai fait par erreur*

by name = *de nom*

by now = *à l'heure qu'il est* : he should be here by now = *à l'heure qu'il est, il devrait être là* ① already = *déjà*

by the by = *au fait* : by the by, where are you going on vacation ? = *au fait, où allez-vous en vacances ?*

by the day/hour/month = *à la journée/à l'heure/au mois* : paid

by the hour = *payé à l'heure*

by the way = *à propos* : by the way, how's your wife ? = *à propos, comment va votre femme ?*

by train/plane = *par le train/par avion*

sit/stand by (me) = *asseyez-vous/mettez-vous à côté de (moi)* = *beside*

☠ for the use of "by" after a verb, see the verb
— *par personne* = per person
— *par ici* = this way
— *par pitié !* = for pity's sake !

— *par bonté/curiosité* = out of kindness/curiosity
— *par contre* = on the other hand
— *par exemple* = for instance.

BYGONE (n) **let bygones be bygones** = *oublions le passé* ① to bury the hatchet = *enterrer la hache de guerre* **BYGONE** (adj) **in bygone days** = *jadis*.

BYE-BYE ! (interj) *salut !* = bye ! ① see you soon = *à bientôt*, hello = *bonjour* ☠ → salvation.

BYLINE (n) *signature (f) (d'un article)* : an article without a byline = *un article sans signature/un article non signé*.

BYPASS (to, -ed) **1/** *contourner* : to bypass a town = *contourner une ville* ☠ → to get around **2/** *court-circuiter* : the President bypassed Congress = *le Président a court-circuité le Congrès*.

BY-PRODUCT (n) *sous-produit (m)*.

BYSTANDER (n) *badaud, -e* : bystanders witnessed the accident = *des badauds ont été témoins de l'accident* ① passerby = *passant*.

CAB (n) taxi (m) : to hail a cab = héler un taxi **CABBY** (n, -ies) (chauffeur (m) de) taxi (m).

CABARET (n) cabaret (m) : a cabaret singer = un chanteur de cabaret ⟨D⟩ music hall = music-hall.

CABBAGE (n) chou (m) ⟨D⟩ cauliflower = chou-fleur, sauerkraut = choucroute
☠ faire chou blanc = to strike out
— rentrer dans le chou à qqn = to let s.o. have it
— mon chou = honey/sweetheart
— faire ses choux gras de = to go to town with.

CABIN (n) 1/ cabane (f) : a log cabin = une cabane en rondins ☠ mettre en cabane = to put in the pen
Uncle Tom's cabin = la case de l'oncle Tom
2/ cabine (f) : a cabin in a boat = une cabine de bateau ☠ cabine téléphonique = phone booth.

CABINET (n) conseil (m) des ministres : a cabinet meeting = une réunion du conseil des ministres
☠ cabinet d'un médecin/d'un avocat = doctor's/lawyer's office/practice
— aller aux cabinets = to go to the lavatory.

CABLE (n) câble (m) : to send a cable = envoyer un câble ⟨D⟩ wire = télégramme **CABLE** (to, -d) câbler : to cable home = câbler à la maison.

CACTUS (n) cactus (m) ⟨D⟩ desert = désert.

CAD (n) goujat (m) : what a cad he was ! = c'était un sacré goujat ! ⟨D⟩ oaf = mufle.

CAFÉ SOCIETY (n) le Tout-... : the café society of New York = le Tout-New York ⟨D⟩ jet set = ←, the upper crust = le gratin.

CAFETERIA (n) cafétéria (f) : to have lunch in a cafeteria = déjeuner dans une cafétéria ⟨D⟩ self-service = ←.

CAGE (n) cage (f) : marriage is no gilded cage = le mariage n'est pas une cage dorée.

CAG(E)Y (adj, -ier, -iest) dissimulé, -e : a cagey businessman = un homme d'affaires dissimulé ⟨D⟩ shrewd = habile ≠ upfront = droit.

CAHOOTS (n pl) **to be in cahoots with** = être de mèche avec : the cops are in cahoots with the Mafia = les flics sont de mèche avec la Mafia ⟨D⟩ to be hand in glove with = avoir partie liée avec.

CAIN (n) **to raise Cain** = faire un esclandre : when he discovered he had been had, he raised Cain = quand il s'est aperçu qu'on l'avait roulé, il a fait un esclandre ⟨D⟩ to raise a riot = pousser les hauts cris.

CAKE (n) gâteau (m) : to bake a cake = faire cuire un gâteau au four ⟨D⟩ icing = glaçage, brownie = gâteau au chocolat et aux noix, doughnut = (genre de) beignet, Danish pastry = (genre de) feuilleté
that takes the cake ! = c'est le pompon ! → GOSH !
you can't have your cake and eat it (too) = on ne peut pas avoir le beurre et l'argent du beurre ⟨D⟩ you can't have it both ways = il faut qu'une porte soit ouverte ou fermée
it's a piece of cake ! (GB) = c'est du gâteau !
☠ c'est du gâteau ! = it's a cinch !
— avoir sa part du gâteau = to get one's share
— un papa gâteau = a sugar daddy.

CALAMITY (n, -ies) calamité (f) ⟨D⟩ disaster = désastre .
Calamity Jane = Cassandre ⟨D⟩ worrywart = bileux.

CALCIUM (n) calcium (m).

CALCULATE (to, -d) calculer : to calculate the risk = calculer les risques ⟨D⟩ calculation = calcul, to estimate = estimer ≠ to miscalculate = mal calculer.

CALCULATING (adj) calculateur, -trice : a calculating mind = un esprit calculateur ⟨D⟩ scheming = intrigant.

CALCULATOR (n) calculatrice (f) : electronic calculator = calculatrice électronique.

CALENDER (n) calendrier (m) ⟨D⟩ date = ← ☠ un calendrier chargé = a heavy schedule.

CALF (n, -ves) mollet (m) : the dog bit his calf = le chien l'a mordu au mollet ⟨D⟩ knee = genou.

CALIBER (n) calibre (m) : lawyers of that caliber are hard to find = c'est dur de trouver des avocats de ce calibre ⟨D⟩ level = niveau.

CALL (n) coup (m) de téléphone/de fil, appel (m) : give her a call = donne-lui un coup de télé-

phone/de fil, there's a call for you = *il y a un appel pour vous*
call girl = ← ⚏ prostitute = *prostituée*
to make calls (doctor) = *faire des visites à domicile*
to give s.o. a call = *passer un coup de téléphone à qqn :* I'll give you a call tonight = *je vous passerai un coup de téléphone ce soir*
on call = *de garde :* Doctor Smith's on call this weekend = *le docteur Smith est de garde ce weekend*
☠ *faire appel (justice)* = to appeal
— *faire appel à qqn* = to ask for s.o.'s help
— *appel (d'offres)* = request (for bids)
— *faire un appel du pied* = to make an indirect hint
— *l'appel* = the roll call.

CALL (to, -ed) **1/** *appeler (téléphone) :* I'll call you tonight = *je vous appellerai ce soir* = to ring (GB) ⚏ to buzz = *passer un coup de fil* **2/** *appeler :* she's in the backyard, call her ! = *elle est dans la cour, appelle-la !* **3/** *traiter de :* he called me a liar ! = *il m'a traité de menteur !*
call (me) collect = *téléphonez(-moi) en PCV*
who's calling ? = *qui est à l'appareil ?*
they call him J.R. = *on l'appelle J.R.*
☠ *voilà qui s'appelle parler !* = now you're talking !
— *ils l'ont appelé Pierre* = they named him Peter
— *comment vous appelez-vous ?* = what's your name ?

to call s.o. back = *rappeler qqn :* I'll call you back later = *je vous rappellerai plus tard*
to call for = *exiger :* the problem calls for diplomacy = *le problème exige de la diplomatie* ☠ → to demand
to call for s.o. = *venir chercher qqn :* I'll call for you at ten = *je viendrai vous chercher à dix heures*
to call in = *faire venir :* they called in a specialist = *ils ont fait venir un spécialiste*
to call off = *décommander :* the meeting was called off = *la réunion a été décommandée* ⚏ to put off = *repousser*
to call on s.o. = *faire une visite à qqn :* we called on my old aunt last year = *nous avons fait une visite à ma vieille tante l'année dernière* ⚏ to visit = *rendre visite à*
to call s.o. over = *appeler qqn :* call him over, I want to speak to him = *appelez-le, je veux lui parler*
to call s.o. up = *passer un coup de téléphone à qqn :* call me up tonight = *passez-moi un coup de téléphone ce soir* = ring me up tonight (GB)
to be called up = *être appelé sous les drapeaux :* both brothers were called up the same year = *les deux frères ont été appelés sous les drapeaux la même année* ≠ to draft = *appeler sous les drapeaux.*

CALLING (n) vocation *(f) :* her calling to become a nun = *sa vocation de religieuse.*

CALLOUS (adj) *sans cœur :* a ruthless, callous businessman = *un homme d'affaires impitoyable et sans cœur* ⚏ hardhearted = *au cœur dur* ≠ sensitive = *sensible.*

CALM (n) *calme (m) :* the calm before the storm = *le calme avant la tempête* ⚏ tranquillity = *tranquillité,* serenity = *sérénité* ☠ *rétablir le calme* = to restore law and order.

CALM (adj, -er, -est) *calme :* don't be so excited, stay calm ! = *ne t'excite pas comme ça, reste calme !* ⚏ serene = *serein* ≠ upset = *bouleversé*
to be calm, cool and collected = *garder une parfaite égalité d'âme* ≠ to be all excited = *être dans tous ses états.*

CALM (to, -ed) *calmer :* to calm a child = *calmer un enfant*
to calm down = *se calmer :* calm down ! = *calme-toi !* = cool down ! ≠ to blow one's cool = *se mettre en boule*
☠ *la tempête s'est calmée* = the storm abated
— *ses excuses ont calmé le patron* = her excuses pacified the boss.

CALMLY (adv) *calmement* ≠ nervously = *nerveusement.*

CALORIE (n) *calorie (f)* ⚏ diet = *régime.*

CAMEL (n) *chameau (m) :* a caravan of camels = *une caravane de chameaux* ⚏ dromedary = *dromadaire*
camel jockey = *bougnoul / bicot*
☠ *quel chameau !* = what a so-and-so !
— *sobre comme un chameau* = cold sober.

CAMERA (n) *appareil (m) photo, caméra (f)* (movies) : I never take a trip without my camera = *je ne pars jamais en voyage sans mon appareil photo* ⚏ flash = ←, film = *pellicule.*

CAMERAMAN (n, -men) *cameraman (m), cadreur, -euse* ⚏ to shoot = *tourner.*

CAMOUFLAGE (n) *camouflage (m)* ⚏ disguise = *déguisement.*

CAMP (n) *camp (m) :* a refugee camp = *un camp de réfugiés* ☠ *fiche le camp !* = buzz off !
(summer) camp = *colonie de vacances*
camp counselor = *moniteur de colonie/de colo.*

CAMP (adj) *d'une originalité démesurée :* Sarah Bernhardt having a coffin as a bed is camp = *Sarah Bernhardt ayant un cercueil pour lit, c'est d'une originalité démesurée* ⚏ eccentric = *excentrique,* kooky = *farfelu.*

CAMP (to, -ed) **to go camping** = *faire du camping.*

CAMPAIGN (n) *campagne (f) :* electoral campaign = *campagne électorale,* advertising campaign = *campagne publicitaire* ⚏ crusade = *croisade*

☠ *aller à la campagne* = to go to the country
— *campagne (paysage)* = countryside.

CAMPAIGN (to, -ed) *faire campagne* : to campaign for equal rights = *faire campagne pour l'égalité des droits.*

CAMPHOR (n) *camphre (m)* ⃝⃝ mothball = *boule de naphtaline.*

CAMPUS (n, -es) *campus (m)* : to live on campus = *vivre sur le campus.*

CAN (n) *boîte (f)* : can opener = *ouvre-boîtes*, a can of string beans = *une boîte de haricots verts* = tin (GB) ⃝⃝ canned = *de conserve/en boîte* ☠ → box.

CAN (aux, could) **1/** *pouvoir* : can you come now ? *pouvez-vous venir maintenant ?*, I can't lift this suitcase = *je ne peux pas soulever cette valise* ⃝⃝ to be able to = *être capable de*

☠ *qu'est-ce que ça peut te faire ?* = what's it to you ?	— *il se peut qu'(il pleuve)* = it may (rain) — *je ne pourrai pas venir* = I won't be able to come

2/ *savoir* : can you drive ? = *savez-vous conduire ?* = do you know how to drive ? ☠ → to know

can I (smoke) ? = *est-ce que je peux (fumer) ?* ⃝⃝ **may I (smoke) ?** = *puis-je fumer ?* **can't/couldn't help (+ ing)** = *ne pas pouvoir s'empêcher de* : I couldn't help laughing = *je n'ai pas pu m'empêcher de rire*	**I could eat/drink something** = *je mangerais/boirais bien quelque chose* **you could have (told me)** = *vous auriez pu (me le dire)*

PRESENT	PAST	FUTURE
— I can/can't = *je peux/ne peux pas* — you can/can't = *vous pouvez/ne pouvez pas*	— I could = *je pouvais/j'ai pu* — you could = *vous pouviez/vous avez pu*	— I'll be able to = *je pourrai* — you'll be able to = *vous pourrez*

— he **thinks** he **can** do it = *il pense qu'il peut le faire*
— he **thought** he **could** do it = *il pensait qu'il pouvait/pourrait le faire*

☠ *l'auxiliaire « can » n'a pas d'infinitif.*

CAN (to, -ned) *virer* : he was canned last year = *il s'est fait virer l'année dernière* ⃝⃝ to sack = *saquer* ☠ → to veer.

CANADA (n) *Canada (m)* **CANADIAN** (n, adj) *Canadien, -enne.*

CANAL (n) *canal, -aux (m)* : the Panama canal = *le canal de Panama* ⃝⃝ waterway = *voie d'eau.*

CANARY (n, -ies) *canari (m)* ⃝⃝ bird = *oiseau.*

CANCEL (to, -(l)ed) *annuler* : to cancel a trip = *annuler un voyage* ⃝⃝ to call off = *décommander* ☠ → to annul.

CANCELLATION (n) *annulation (f)* : cancellation of the whole trip = *annulation totale du voyage* ≠ confirmation = ←.

CANCER (n) *cancer (m)* : breast cancer = *cancer du sein* ⃝⃝ tumor = *tumeur*, leukemia = *leucémie* **CANCEROUS** (adj) *cancéreux, -euse* : cancerous cells = *cellules cancéreuses.*

CANDID (adj) *(naïvement) direct, -e* : a candid answer = *une réponse (naïvement) directe* ⃝⃝ straightforward = *sans détours* ☠ *elle est candide* = she's wide-eyed.

CANDIDACY (n, -ies) *candidature (f)* : when will she announce her candidacy ? = *quand annoncera-t-elle sa candidature ?* = candidature (GB).

CANDIDATE (n) *candidat, -e* : who's the Democratic candidate ? = *qui est le candidat démocrate ?* ≠ incumbent = *(personne) en titre.*

CANDIDLY (adv) *avec une franchise un peu naïve.*

CANDLE (n) *bougie (f)* : buy some candles = *achète des bougies* ⃝⃝ wax = *cire*, candlestick = *bougeoir*
to burn the candle at both ends = *brûler la chandelle par les deux bouts* ⃝⃝ to live it up = *faire les quatre cents coups*

(he) can't hold a candle to (his sister) = *(il) n'arrive pas à la cheville de (sa sœur)* ⓪ he's no match for ... = *il ne fait pas le poids contre ...*

CANDLELIGHT (n) **(dinner) by candlelight** = *(dîner) aux chandelles.*

CANDY (n inv) *bonbons (m pl) :* buy me some candy, please = *achète-moi des bonbons, s'il te plaît* = sweets (GB) ⓪ chocolates = *chocolats*
to be like taking candy from a baby = *être un jeu d'enfant :* getting him to sign the contract was like taking candy from a baby = *ça a été un jeu d'enfant de lui faire signer le contrat*
a piece of candy = *un bonbon*
candy store = *genre de tabac-kiosque où l'on vend des bonbons, des journaux, des cigarettes, etc.*

CANE (n) *canne (f) :* to walk with a cane = *marcher avec une canne* ☠ *canne à pêche* = fishing rod.

CANNIBAL (n) *cannibale (m, f)* **CANNIBALISM** (n) *cannibalisme (m).*

CANNON (n) *canon (m)* ⓪ cannonball = *boulet de canon.*

CANNY (adj, -ier, -est) *habile :* a canny negotiator = *un négociateur habile* ⓪ cunning = *rusé.*

CANOE (n) *canoë (m)* ⓪ paddle = *pagaie.*

CANTALOUPE (n) *melon (m) (cantaloup).*

CANTEEN (n) *cantine (f) :* to have lunch at the canteen = *déjeuner à la cantine* ⓪ cafeteria = *cafétéria.*

CANVAS (n, -es) *toile (f) :* to paint on a canvas = *peindre sur toile*
☠ *se faire une toile* = to go see a flick
— *toile d'araignée* = spider's web
— *toile de fond* = background.

CANVASS (to, -ed) *faire du démarchage :* to canvass an area = *faire du démarchage dans une région.*

CAP (n) *casquette (f) :* do cops wear hats or caps ? = *les flics portent-ils des chapeaux ou des casquettes ?*

CAPABILITY (n, -ies) *capacité (f) :* America's seeking to buttress its nuclear capability = *l'Amérique cherche à renforcer sa capacité nucléaire* ☠ *une capacité de 100 places assises* = a seating capacity of 100.

CAPABLE (adj) *capable :* a very capable manager = *un gestionnaire très capable* ⓪ skillful = *habile* ≠ incapable = ←
to be capable of (killing s.o.) = *être capable de (tuer qqn)*
☠ *je ne suis pas capable de (vous expliquer)* = I'm not able to/I can't (explain it to you).

CAPACITY (n, -ies) **1/** *capacité (f) :* not to have the capacity to understand = *ne pas avoir la capacité de comprendre* ⓪ faculty = *faculté* **2/** *capacité (f) :* a seating

capacity of 10,000 = *une capacité de 10 000 places assises* ☠ → capability
filled to capacity = *rempli au maximum*
in (her) capacity as (adviser) = *en (sa) qualité de (conseillère).*

CAPE (n) *cape (f)* ⓪ hood = *capuchon*
☠ *rire sous cape* = to laugh up one's sleeve
— *roman de cape et d'épée* = cloak-and-dagger story.

CAPER (n) *fric-frac (m) :* the robbery of the crown jewels was the caper of the century = *le vol des bijoux de la couronne a été le fric-frac du siècle* ⓪ job = *coup.*

CAPITAL (n) **1/** *capital (m) :* who's going to put up the capital ? = *qui va avancer le capital ?* **2/** *capitale (f) :* Santiago is the capital of Chile = *Santiago est la capitale du Chili.*

CAPITAL (adj) *capital, -e :* it's of capital importance = *c'est d'une importance capitale* ≠ unimportant = *sans importance*
a capital letter = *une lettre majuscule* ≠ a small letter = *une lettre minuscule*
capital punishment = *peine de mort*
☠ *c'est capital (d'avoir le conseil d'un avocat)* = it's very important (to have a lawyer's advice).

CAPITALISM (n) *capitalisme (m)* ≠ socialism = *socialisme* **CAPITALIST** (n, adj) *capitaliste (m, f)* ≠ proletarian = *prolétaire.*

CAPITALIZE ON (to, -d) *tirer parti de :* to capitalize on one's contacts = *tirer parti de ses relations* ⓪ to make the most of = *profiter au maximum de.*

CAPITULATE (to, -d) *capituler :* the enemy capitulated = *l'ennemi a capitulé* ≠ to hold out = *tenir.*

CAPRICE (n) *caprice (m) :* her latest caprice cost him a small fortune = *son dernier caprice lui a coûté une petite fortune* ⓪ folly = *folie.*

CAPRICIOUS (adj) *capricieux, -euse :* a capricious personality = *un caractère capricieux* ⓪ unpredictable = *imprévisible.*

CAPSIZE (to, -d) *chavirer :* the boat capsized = *le bateau a chaviré* ⓪ to turn over = *se retourner* ☠ *la nouvelle m'a chaviré* = the news bowled me over.

CAPTAIN (n) **1/** *capitaine (m)* ⓪ corporal = *caporal,* commander = *commandant* **2/** *capitaine (m)* (boat) ⓪ crew = *équipage.*

CAPTION (n) *légende (f) :* I understood the drawing but not the caption = *j'ai compris le dessin mais pas la légende* ☠ → legend.

CAPTIVATE (to, -d) *captiver, subjuguer :* we were captivated by her beauty = *nous avons été subjugués par sa beauté* ☠ → to subjugate.

CAPTIVATING (adj) *captivant, -e :* a captivating book

= *un livre captivant* ⓐ appealing = *séduisant* ≠ boring = *ennuyeux*.

CAPTIVE (n) *captif, -ive* ⓐ prisoner = *prisonnier* **CAPTIVITY** (n) *captivité (f)*.

CAPTURE (to, -d) *capturer* : to capture a criminal = *capturer un criminel* ⓐ to arrest = *arrêter* ≠ to liberate = *libérer*.

CAR (n) *voiture (f)*, *bagnole (f)* (LV) : I'm going to buy a new car = *je vais acheter une nouvelle voiture/bagnole*, racing car = *voiture de course*, secondhand car = *voiture d'occasion*, hot rod = *bolide*, jalopy = *tire*

brake = *frein*	**car pool** = *entente entre automobilistes pour se transporter mutuellement et faire des économies*
bucket seat = *siège baquet*	
bumper = *pare-chocs*	
carburetor = *carburateur*	
to be car sick = *être malade en voiture*	**e x h a u s t** = *p o t d'échappement*
car wash = *lavage de voiture*	**to put in reverse** = *faire marche arrière*
choke = *starter*	**rearview mirror** = *rétroviseur*
clutch = *embrayage*	
convertible = *décapotable*	**right-of-way** = *priorité*
dashboard · = *tableau de bord*	**to run a light** = *brûler un feu*
driver's license = *permis de conduire*	**spark plug** = *bougie*
gasoline = *essence*	**(steering) wheel** = *volant*
gearshift = *changement de vitesses*	**taillight** = *feu arrière*
to honk = *klaxonner*	**tank** = *réservoir*
hood = *capote*	**ticket** = *contravention*
ignition key = *clef de contact*	**tire** = *pneu*
jack = *cric*	**traffic jam** = *embouteillage*
license plate = *plaque d'immatriculation*	**trunk** = *coffre*
	wheel = *roue*
	windshield = *parebrise*

☠ *en voiture !* = all aboard !
— *car (touristes)* = bus/coach (GB)
— *être rangé des voitures* = to be a stick-in-the-mud
— *voiture d'enfant* = baby carriage.

CARAMEL (n) *caramel (m)* ⓐ chocolate = *chocolat*.

CARAVAN (n) (GB) *caravane (f)* = van.

CARD (n) **1/** *carte (f)* : do you play cards ? = *est-ce que vous jouez aux cartes ?*, a pack of cards = *un jeu de car-*tes ⓐ to serve = *donner* = to deal, to cut = *couper*, a trick = *un pli*, a good hand = *une bonne main*, cardsharp = *tricheur professionnel (aux cartes)*, to wash the cards = *battre les cartes* = to shuffle, hearts = *cœur*, spades = *pique*, diamonds = *carreau*, clubs = *trèfle*
business/calling card = *carte de visite*
birthday card = *carte d'anniversaire*
card trick = *tour de cartes*
to be in the cards for s.o. = *être écrit pour qqn* : marriage wasn't in the cards for her = *il était écrit qu'elle ne devait pas se marier*
to hold the (winning) cards = *avoir tous les atouts dans son jeu*
to play one's cards right = *bien mener sa barque* : if you play your cards right, you'll get a raise = *si vous menez bien votre barque, vous aurez une augmentation*
to put one's cards on the table = *jouer cartes sur table* ⓐ to lay it on the line = *annoncer la couleur*
to read cards = *tirer les cartes*
to stack the cards = *corner les cartes* → TO HUSTLE
☠ *donner carte blanche à qqn* = to give s.o. a free hand
— *carte (routière)* = map
— *carte maritime* = chart
— *faire une carte de France* = to have wet dreams
— *brouiller les cartes* = to confuse the issue
— *carte de travail* = work permit
2/ *rigolo, -ote* : my brother's a card = *mon frère est un rigolo* ⓐ joker = *plaisantin*.

CARDBOARD (n) *carton (m)* : cardboard boxes = *des boîtes de carton*.

CARDIGAN (n) *cardigan (m)* ⓐ turtleneck = *col roulé*.

CARDINAL (n) *cardinal (m)* ⓐ the Pope = *le pape*.

CARE (n) *soin (m)* : to do something with care = *faire quelque chose avec soin* ☠ *je vous laisse le soin de* = I'll entrust you to

handle with care ! = *fragile !*	kids for an hour ? = *est-ce que vous pouvez vous occuper des gosses pendant une heure ?*
(in) care of = *aux bons soins de* : write me (in) care of Mr. Smith = *écrivez-moi aux bons soins de M. Smith*	
	take care of yourself ! = *prends bien soin de toi !*
she doesn't have a care in the world = *elle n'a aucun souci*	**she can take care of herself** = *elle peut se débrouiller toute seule*
take care ! = *bon courage !* ⓐ so long ! = *à bientôt !*	**take care of (your cold)** = *soigne (ton rhume)*
to take care of = *s'occuper de* : I'll take care of everything = *je m'occuperai de tout*, can you take care of the	**under the care of** = *dans les mains de* : under the care of the finest cancerologist = *dans les mains du meilleur cancérologue*.

CARE (to, -d) *se soucier de, ne pas être égal à :* nobody cares = *personne ne s'en soucie,* do you care if I come late ? = *est-ce que ça vous est égal si j'arrive tard ?,* no, I don't care = *oui, cela m'est égal,* yes, I care = *non, cela ne m'est pas égal*

I don't care ! = *ça m'est égal !* ⓒ it's all the same to me ! = *ça m'est complètement égal !*
what do I care ! = *ça me fait une belle jambe !* ⓒ I don't give a rap ! = *je m'en tamponne le coquillard !*
what do you care ? = *qu'est-ce que ça peut bien te faire ?*
who cares ! = *on s'en fiche !*
to care for = 1/ *désirer :* what would you care for ? = *que dé-* sirez-vous ? ☠ → to desire 2/ *soigner :* in that nursing home, he'll be properly cared for = *dans cette maison de repos, il sera bien soigné* 3/ *tenir à :* I care for her = *je tiens à elle,* I don't care for Chinese food = *je ne tiens pas à la cuisine chinoise* ⓒ to be fond of = *aimer*
to care to = *désirer :* would you care to go with us ? = *désirez-vous venir avec nous ?* ☠ → to desire.

CAREER (n) *carrière (f) :* a diplomatic career = *une carrière diplomatique*
a career girl/woman = *une fille/femme qui fait carrière*
☠ *(militaire) de carrière* = professional (soldier).

CAREFREE (adj) *insouciant, -e :* a carefree childhood = *une enfance insouciante* ⓒ lighthearted = *enjoué* ≠ uptight = *coincé.*

CAREFUL (adj) *soigné, -e* (stg), *soigneux, -euse* (s.o., stg) : careful work = *travail soigné,* a careful worker = *un ouvrier soigneux* ⓒ conscientious = *consciencieux* ≠ sloppy = *négligé*
be careful ! = *faites attention !* ⓒ look out ! = *attention !*
a careful driver = *un conducteur prudent*
☠ *il est très soigné* = he's well-groomed
— *une femme soigneuse* = 'a neat woman.

CAREFULLY (adv) *soigneusement :* read the contract carefully = *lisez soigneusement le contrat.*

CARELESS (adj) *peu soigné, -e* (stg), *peu soigneux, -euse* (s.o., stg) : a careless typist = *une dactylo peu soigneuse,* your work's careless = *votre travail est peu soigné* ⓒ negligent = *négligent,* slipshod = *brouillon* ≠ careful = *soigné/soigneux*
careless mistake = *faute d'inattention.*

CARELESSLY (adv) *sans soin.*

CARELESSNESS (n) *insouciance (f) :* her carelessness caused the accident = *son insouciance a provoqué l'accident* ⓒ neglect = *manque de soin.*

CARESS (n, -es) *caresse (f)* **CARESS** (to, -ed) *caresser :* she likes to be caressed = *elle aime être caressée*
☠ *caresser un chien* = to pet/stroke a dog
— *caresser une idée* = to toy with/to flirt with/to entertain an idea.

CARETAKER (n) *gardien, -enne (propriété) :* the caretaker of the estate = *le gardien de la propriété* ⓒ super = *concierge* ☠ → watchman
caretaker government = *gouvernement intérimaire.*

CARGO (n, -s or -es) *cargaison (f) :* a cargo of bananas = *une cargaison de bananes* ⓒ freight = *fret* ☠ *un cargo* = a freighter.

CARICATURE (n) *caricature (f) :* a cruel caricature = *une caricature cruelle* ⓒ takeoff = *pastiche.*

CARING (adj) *attentionné, -e :* a caring father = *un père attentionné* ⓒ sensitive = *sensible.*

CARNAGE (n) *carnage (m)* ⓒ genocide = *génocide.*

CARNATION (n) *œillet (m) :* a red carnation = *un œillet rouge* ⓒ flower = *fleur.*

CARNIVAL (n) *carnaval (m)* ⓒ festival = ←.

CARP (to, -ed) *trouver à redire :* he's always carping about my cooking = *il trouve toujours à redire à ma cuisine* ⓒ to bitch = *gueuler.*

CARPENTER (n) *menuisier (m) (charpentier) :* I must get a carpenter to build a closet = *il faut que je trouve un menuisier pour me faire un placard* ⓒ locksmith = *serrurier.*

CARPET (n) *moquette (f) :* a blue carpet = *une moquette bleue* ⓒ rug = *tapis,* vacuum cleaner = *aspirateur*
to call s.o. on the carpet = *passer un savon à qqn* → TO LAMBAST
to pull the carpet out from under s.o. = *couper l'herbe sous les pieds de qqn* ⓒ to steal the show = *voler la vedette.*

CARPETBAGGER (n) *Nordiste tirant profit du désordre régnant dans le Sud après la guerre de Sécession.*

CARRIAGE (n) *fiacre (m) :* carriages in the park = *des fiacres dans le parc* ⓒ coach = *carrosse.*

CARROT (n) *carotte (f) :* I eat a lot of carrots = *je mange beaucoup de carottes* ☠ *les carottes sont cuites !* = the jig's up !

CARRY (to, -ied) **1/** *porter :* can you carry my suitcase ? = *est-ce que tu peux me porter ma valise ?* ⓒ to lug = *transbahuter*

☠ *tout porte à croire que* = everything leads to think that — *bien se porter* = to be in good health — *porter la responsabilité de* = to bear the respon-	sibility for — *porter qqn disparu* = to report s.o. missing — *porter (des gants)* = to wear (gloves) — *portez-lui ça* = bring it to him

2/ *remporter (élections)* : Kennedy carried New York = *Kennedy a remporté les élections à New York* ☠ *remporter (ses affaires)* = to take back (one's things) **3/** *assumer* : I can't carry his problems too = *je ne peux pas aussi assumer ses problèmes* = I can't handle ... ☠ → to assume **4/** *faire* : the store doesn't carry children's clothing = *le magasin ne fait pas de vêtements pour enfants* ☠ → to do **5/** *transporter* : the boat was carrying immigrants = *le bateau transportait des immigrants* = the boat was transporting immigrants

to carry away = *emporter* : the storm carried away the roof = *la tempête a emporté le toit* ☠ *que le diable l'emporte !* = the devil with him ! — *un sandwich à emporter* = a sandwich to take out — *emporter (un livre)* = to take (a book) along — *l'emporter sur* = to prevail over **to be/get carried away** = *se laisser emporter* : don't get so	carried away ! = *ne t'emporte pas comme ça !* **to carry s.o. back to** = *replonger qqn dans* : that movie carried me back to my childhood = *ce film m'a replongé dans mon enfance* **to carry on** = 1/ *s'emporter* : what are you carrying on about ? = *pourquoi vous emportez-vous ?* → ANGRY 2/ *poursuivre* : carry on the good work ! = *votre travail est bon, poursuivez-le !*	☠ → to pursue **to carry on with** = *faire des frasques avec* : her husband's carrying on with the maid = *son mari fait des frasques avec la bonne* ⓪ to mess around with = *coucher avec* **to carry out** = *mettre à exécution* : the kidnappers carried out their threat = *les ravisseurs ont mis leur menace à exécution* ⓪ to execute = *exécuter.*

CARRYINGS-ON (n pl) *frasques (f pl)* : his carryings-on with his secretary = *ses frasques avec sa secrétaire* ⓪ monkey business = *histoires de fesses.*

CARRY-OVER (n) *reste (m)* : the complex is a carry-over from her childhood = *ce complexe est un reste de son enfance*
☠ *les restes* = the leftovers
— *le reste de* = the rest of

CART (n) **to put the cart before the horse** = *mettre la charrue avant les bœufs* ≠ one thing at a time = *chaque chose en son temps.*

CARTE BLANCHE (n) *carte (f) blanche* : to give s.o. carte blanche = *donner carte blanche à qqn* ⓪ to give

s.o. a free hand = *laisser les coudées franches à qqn.*

CARTOON (n) *dessin (m) animé, dessin (m) humoristique* : a cartoon on the front page of the newspaper = *un dessin humoristique en première page du journal*, a funny cartoon before the film = *un dessin animé marrant avant le film* ⓪ comics = *bandes dessinées* **CARTOONIST** (n) *dessinateur, -trice de bandes dessinées.*

CARVE (to, -d) *découper* : please will you carve the meat ? = *est-ce que tu peux découper la viande, s'il te plaît ?* ⓪ to cut = *couper* ☠ *découper (un article)* = to cut out (an article).

CASCADE (n) *cascade (f)* ⓪ cataract = *cataracte* ☠ *une cascade (dans un film)* = a stunt (in a film).

CASE (n) 1/ *cas (m)* : a complicated case = *un cas compliqué* 2/ *cas (m)* : you're a case ! = *tu es un cas !* ⓪ character = *original*	
☠ *c'est le cas de le dire !* = you said it ! — *le cas échéant* = if need be	— *faire peu de* ≠ *grand cas de* = to attach little ≠ great importance to

3/ *affaire (f)* : a lawyer's first case = *la première affaire d'un avocat* ⓪ litigation = *litige* ☠ → affair

as the case may be = *selon le cas* **a case of mistaken identity** = *une erreur sur la personne* **to crack a case** = *débrouiller une affaire* ⓪ to solve = *résoudre*	**to drop a case** = *renoncer à un procès* ≠ to sue = *poursuivre (en justice)* **get off my case !** = *lâche-moi les baskets !* → BUZZ OFF ! **to have** ≠ **not to have a case** = *avoir* ≠ *ne pas avoir de motif*	à poursuites : my lawyer told me I had no case = *mon avocat m'a dit que je n'avais aucun motif à poursuites* **if that's the case** = *si c'est le cas* **in case** = *au cas où* : let's take

<table>
<tr>
<td>

an umbrella in case it rains =
*prenons un parapluie au cas où
il pleuvrait* ⓪ if = *si*
in case of (fire) = *en cas
d'(incendie)*
in that case (get out !) = *dans
ce cas (fiche le camp !)*
just in case = *au cas où :* take
some money just in case =

</td>
<td>

*prends un peu d'argent au cas
où*
let's get down to cases =
venons-en au fait = let's get
down to brass tacks
to make a case = *présenter des
arguments :* she makes a good
case for capital punishment =
elle présente de bons arguments

</td>
<td>

en faveur de la peine de mort
(that's) a case in point =
*(c'est) un exemple type/un cas
de figure*
to try/hear a case = *entendre
une affaire*
to win one's case = *avoir/obte-
nir gain de cause.*

</td>
</tr>
</table>

CASH (n inv) (*argent (m)*) *liquide (m), cash (m) :* I don't
have any cash = *je n'ai pas d'argent liquide/de liquide,* I
gave him $ 500 cash = *je lui ai donné 500 dollars en
liquide/cash* ☠ → liquid
the cash register = *la caisse* ⓪ cashier = *caissier*
to pay cash = *payer comptant/cash* ⓪ to pay by check
= *payer par chèque*
to pay cash on the line/nail = *payer rubis sur l'ongle.*

CASHIER (n) *caissier, -ère :* the cashier is checking the
takings = *le caissier vérifie la recette* ☠ *caissier (banque)* = teller.

CASH IN ON (to, -ed) *tirer profit de :* his publisher's
trying to cash in on his suicide = *son éditeur essaie de
tirer profit de son suicide* ⓪ to capitalize on = *tirer
parti de.*

CASHMERE (n) *cachemire (m) :* a cashmere sweater =
un pull en cachemire ⓪ mohair = ←.

CASINO (n) *casino (m) :* to blow one's money in a casino
= *claquer son argent au casino* ⓪ gambler = *flambeur.*

CASSETTE (n) *cassette (f) :* a blank cassette = *une cassette vierge* ⓪ tape recorder = *magnétophone.*

CAST (n) **1/** *distribution (f) :* the film has a great cast =
le film a une distribution fantastique ☠ → distribution
2/ *plâtre (m) :* a cast on her leg = *une jambe dans le plâtre* ☠ → plaster **3/** *les gens de la troupe :* the cast got on
well = *les gens de la troupe se sont bien entendus.*

CAST (to, cast, cast) *faire la distribution (des rôles) :*
they're casting on Friday = *on fait la distribution des
rôles vendredi*
to cast aside (an old mistress) = *laisser tomber (une
ancienne maîtresse)* ⓪ to ditch = *larguer*
to cast off = *lever l'ancre/larguer les amarres*
cast iron = *fonte.*

CASTE (n) *caste (f) :* he belongs to the lowest caste = *il
appartient à la caste la plus basse* ⓪ class = *classe.*

CASTING (n) *distribution (f) :* they're going to do the
casting next month = *ils vont faire la distribution le
mois prochain* ☠ → distribution.

CASTLE (n) *château (m)* ⓪ fort = ←, ghost = *fantôme*
☠ *mener la vie de château* = to live the life of Riley.

CASUAL (adj) *décontracté, -e :* casual manners = *des
manières décontractées,* a casual dinner = *un dîner*

décontracté, he's very casual about the divorce = *il est
très décontracté quant au divorce* ⓪ cool = ← ≠ formal = *formaliste.*

CASUALLY (adv) *sans façons :* to entertain casually =
recevoir sans façons ≠ formally = *avec cérémonie.*

CASUALTY (n, -ies) *accidenté, -e* (accident), *perte (f)*
(war) : there were many casualties in the car crash = *il y
a eu de nombreux accidentés dans le carambolage,* there
were many casualties among the civilians = *il y a eu de
nombreuses pertes parmi les civils* ☠ *perte* → loss.

CAT (n) **1/** *chat, chatte :* what a beautiful cat ! =
quel beau chat ! ⓪ kitty = *minou* = pussy, pussy-
cat = *minet,* tomcat = *matou,* kitten = *chaton,*
alley cat = *chat de gouttière,* feline = *félin,* claw =
griffe, whiskers = *moustaches,* to meow = *miauler,* to purr = *ronronner,* litter = *litière*
it's the cat's meow ! = *c'est bath !* →
WONDERFUL
it's raining cats and dogs = *il tombe des hallebardes* ⓪ it's coming down in buckets = *il pleut à
seaux*
to let the cat out of the bag = *vendre la mèche*
⓪ to give the show away = *manger le morceau*
(to fight) like cats and dogs = *(s'entendre)
comme chien et chat* ≠ to get on like a house on
fire = *s'entendre comme larrons en foire*
to play cat and mouse = *jouer au chat et à la
souris*
the cat's got (his) tongue = *(il) a avalé sa langue*
when the cat's away, the mice will play =
quand le chat n'est pas là, les souris dansent

<table>
<tr>
<td>

☠ *il n'y a pas de quoi
fouetter un chat* =
that's nothing to make
such a fuss about
— *il n'y a pas un chat*
= there isn't a soul
— *appeler un chat un
chat* = to call a spade a
spade
— *avoir d'autres chats
à fouetter* = to have
other fish to fry
— *la chatte* = the cunt

</td>
<td>

— *avoir un chat dans
la gorge* = to have a
frog in one's throat
— *chat échaudé craint
l'eau froide* = once bit-
ten twice shy
— *jouer à chat* = to
play tag
— *il ne faut pas réveil-
ler le chat qui dort* = let
sleeping dogs lie
— *elle est très chatte*
= she's very kittenish

</td>
</tr>
</table>

2/ *mauvaise langue* (f) : she's a cat = *c'est une mauvaise langue* ⓪ gossip = *commère* **3/** *gus* (m) : he's a strange cat = *c'est un drôle de gus* ⓪ bloke = *gars.*

CATALOGUE (n) *catalogue* (m) : a catalogue of the new models = *un catalogue des nouveaux modèles* ⓪ brochure = *prospectus.*

CATALYST (n) *catalyseur* (m) : what will be the catalyst of World War III ? = *quel sera le catalyseur de la Troisième Guerre mondiale ?*

CATASTROPHE (n) *catastrophe* (f) : what a catastrophe ! = *quelle catastrophe !* ⓪ calamity = *calamité.*

CATASTROPHIC (adj) *catastrophique* : a catastrophic mistake = *une erreur catastrophique* ⓪ disastrous = *désastreux.*

CATCALL (n) *sifflet* (m) : catcalls from the audience = *les sifflets de l'assistance* ⓪ boos = *huées* ☠ → whistle.

CATCH (n, -es) *piège* (m) : his offer is too good to be true, where's the catch ? = *sa proposition est trop belle pour être vraie, où est le piège ?* ⓪ hitch = *hic* ☠ → trap
(he's) a good/great catch = *(c'est) un beau parti.*

CATCH (to, caught, caught) **1/** *attraper* : to catch a ball = *attraper un ballon* ≠ to throw = *lancer* ☠ *attraper (une contravention)* = to get (a ticket) **2/** *attraper* : to catch a train = *attraper un train* ≠ to miss = *rater* **3/** *attraper* : to catch a criminal = *attraper un criminel* ⓪ to capture = *capturer,* to nab = *pincer* **4/** *attraper* : to catch a cold = *attraper un rhume* **5/** *saisir* : I didn't catch what you said = *je n'ai pas saisi ce que vous avez dit* ⓪ to dig = *piger* ☠ → to seize **6/** *pouvoir voir* : did you catch his act when you were in Paris ? = *est-ce que vous avez pu voir son numéro quand vous étiez à Paris ?* **7/** *surprendre* : the teacher caught them smoking pot = *le professeur les a surpris en train de fumer de l'herbe* ☠ → to surprise

---

to catch s.o. napping = *prendre qqn en défaut* : the Senator was caught napping = *le sénateur a été pris en défaut* ⓪ to catch s.o. unawares = *prendre qqn de court* | **you won't catch (me) at it again** = *on ne (m')y reprendra plus*

---

to catch on = **1/** *piger* : do you catch on ? = *tu piges ?* ⓪ to get the drift of = *saisir le sens de* **2/** *avoir du succès* : C.B.'s caught on = *la C.B. a du succès* ⓪ to take = *prendre* ≠ to bomb = *foirer*
to be caught up in = *être pris dans* : the government was caught up in the scandal = *le gouvernement a été pris dans le scandale*

to catch up (with) = **1/** *rattraper (retard)* : I fell behind in my work and it's too late to catch up = *j'ai pris du retard dans mon travail et il est trop tard pour le rattraper* **2/** *rattraper* : I ran fast, but I couldn't catch up with him = *j'ai couru vite, mais je n'ai pas pu le rattraper* ☠ *rattraper le temps perdu* = to make up for lost time **3/** *payer cher* : you're smoking too much, it'll catch up with you = *tu fumes trop, tu le paieras cher*
to catch up on = *se remettre au courant de* : I'll have to catch up on what's happening in the world = *il va falloir que je me remette au courant de ce qui se passe dans le monde*
to be caught up in (traffic) = *être pris dans (les embouteillages).*

CATCHER (n) *catcher* (m), celui qui attrape la balle au base-ball.

CATCHING (adj) *contagieux, -euse* : the disease is catching = *la maladie est contagieuse* = the disease is contagious.

CATCHWORD (n) *mot* (m) *clé* : the catchword of the advertising campaign = *le mot clé de la campagne publicitaire* ⓪ slogan = ←.

CATCHY (adj, -ier, -iest) *facile à retenir* : a catchy melody = *une mélodie facile à retenir.*

CATEGORICAL (adj) *catégorique* : a categorical refusal = *un refus catégorique* ≠ ambiguous = *ambigu*
CATEGORICALLY (adv) *catégoriquement* : to say no categorically = *dire catégoriquement non.*

CATEGORY (n, -ies) *catégorie* (f) : three categories of rooms = *trois catégories de chambres* ⓪ group = *groupe.*

CATER (to, -ed) *être le traiteur* : who's catering the wedding ? = *quel est le traiteur pour le mariage ?*
to cater to = *chercher à satisfaire* : she caters to her boss hoping to get a raise = *elle cherche à satisfaire son patron dans l'espoir d'obtenir une augmentation*
(this restaurant) caters to (yuppies) = *(ce restaurant) cherche à attirer la clientèle (des yuppies)*
catered dinner = *dîner qui vient de chez le traiteur.*

CATERER (n) *traiteur* (m) ⓪ deli = *charcutier-traiteur.*

CATERPILLAR (n) *chenille* (f) ⓪ butterfly = *papillon.*

CATHEDRAL (n) *cathédrale* (f) : Gothic cathedrals = *des cathédrales gothiques* ① abbey = *abbaye.*

CATHOLIC (n, adj) *catholique* (m, f) : a Catholic newspaper = *un journal catholique* ① Catholicism = *catholicisme,* rosary = *chapelet,* priest = *prêtre* ☠ *ce n'est pas très catholique* = it's not very kosher.

CATNAP (n) *roupillon* (m) (LV) ① doze = *petit somme* **to take a catnap** = *piquer un roupillon.*

CAT-O'-NINE-TAILS (n) *martinet* (m).

CATSKILLS (n) **the Catskills/the Catskill Mountains** = *région montagneuse de l'État de New York où ont été lancés des chanteurs et acteurs (souvent juifs).*

CATTLE (n inv) *bétail* (m) : 50 heads of cattle = *50 têtes de bétail* ① herd = *troupeau.*

CATTY (adj, -ier, -iest) *médisant, -e* : a catty woman = *une femme médisante* ① malicious = *malveillant,* gossipy = *commère.*

CAUCASIAN (n, adj) *personne* (f) *de race blanche.*

CAUCUS (n, -es) *comité* (m) *électoral (d'un parti politique)* ① lobby = ←.

CAULIFLOWER (n) *chou-fleur* (m) ① artichoke = *artichaut.*

CAUSE (n) *cause* (f) : what was the cause of their strike ? = *quelle a été la cause de leur greve ?* ① reason = *raison*
the cause and effect = *la cause et l'effet*
and with (good) cause = *et pour cause*
to espouse a cause = *épouser une cause*
there's no cause to worry = *il n'y a pas lieu de s'inquiéter*
☠ *être en cause* = to be in question
— *à cause de* = because of.

CAUSE (to, -d) *causer* : what caused the accident ? = *qu'est-ce qui a causé l'accident ?* ① to lead to = *conduire à,* to trigger off = *déclencher* ☠ *causer (avec qqn)* = to chat (with s.o.).

CAUSTIC (adj) *caustique* : a caustic remark = *une remarque caustique* ① biting = *mordant,* scathing = *cinglant.*

CAUTION (n) **(to proceed) with caution** = *(agir) avec circonspection.*

CAUTIOUS (adj) *prudent, -e* : a cautious driver = *un conducteur prudent* = a careful driver ≠ reckless = *imprudent* **CAUTIOUSLY** (adv) *prudemment* : to advance cautiously = *avancer prudemment.*

CAVALRY (n, -ies) *cavalerie* (f) : the cavalry charged the tanks = *la cavalerie a attaqué les tanks.*

CAVE (n) *caverne* (f) ① cavemen = *hommes des cavernes*
☠ *de la cave au grenier* = in every nook and cranny

— *un cave* = someone "straight" (who doesn't belong to the underworld)
— *une cave* = a cellar.

CAVE IN (to, -d) *s'écrouler* : the stairs caved in = *l'escalier s'est écroulé* ① to give way = *céder* ☠ *être écroulé de rire* = to split one's sides laughing.

CAVIAR (n) *caviar* (m) ① roe = *laitance.*

CAVITY (n, -ies) *carie* (f) : a cavity in my tooth = *une carie dans ma dent* ① hole = *trou.*

CEASE (to, -d) *cesser* : when will their fighting cease ? = *quand cesseront-ils de se battre ?*

CEASE-FIRE (n) *cessez-le-feu* (m inv) ① armistice = ←.

CEASELESS (adj) *incessant, -e* : ceaseless quarreling = *des querelles incessantes* ① non-stop = ←.

CEILING (n) *plafond* (m) : the ceiling's high = *le plafond est haut* ≠ floor = *plancher,* ground = *sol*
to hit the ceiling = *sauter au plafond* : when he said that, she hit the ceiling = *quand il a dit ça, elle a sauté au plafond* → ANGRY.

CELEBRATE (to, -d) *célébrer* (official), *faire la fête* : to celebrate an anniversary = *célébrer un anniversaire,* let's go out tonight and celebrate ! = *ce soir, on sort et on fait la fête !*
let's celebrate ! = *ça s'arrose !*

CELEBRATED (adj) *célèbre* : a celebrated novelist = *un romancier célèbre* ≠ unknown = *inconnu.*

CELEBRATION (n) *célébration* (f), *fête* (f) : the celebration of their 50th wedding anniversary = *la célébration de leur 50e anniversaire de mariage* ① ceremony = *cérémonie*
that calls for a celebration ! = *on va fêter ça !* ① that calls for a drink ! = *ça s'arrose !*
☠ *Noël est un jour de fête* = Xmas is a holiday
— *fête des Mères* = Mothers' Day
— *ça va être ta fête !* = you're going to get it !
— *donner une fête* = to give a party.

CELEBRITY (n, -ies) *célébrité* (f) : celebrities are often recognized in the street = *on reconnaît souvent des célébrités dans la rue* ① public figure = *personnalité en vue.*

CELERY (n, -ies) *céleri* (m) ① celeriac = *céleri-rave.*

CELL (n) 1/ *cellule* (f) : prison cell = *cellule de prison* 2/ *cellule* (f) : body cell = *cellule du corps.*

CELLAR (n) *cave* (f) : there are rats in the cellar = *il y a des rats dans la cave* ① basement = *sous-sol* ☠ → cave.

CEMENT (n) *ciment* (m) : a cement wall = *un mur en ciment* ① concrete = *béton.*

CEMETERY (n, -ies) *cimetière* (m) : an animal cemetery = *un cimetière d'animaux* = graveyard ① tomb = *tombe.*

CENSOR (to, -ed) *censurer :* to censor a book = *censurer un livre* ⓪ to ban = *interdire.*

CENSORSHIP (n) *censure (f) :* to be against censorship = *être contre la censure* ≠ freedom of speech = *liberté de parole* ☠ *motion de censure* = motion of no confidence.

CENSUS (n, -es) *recensement (m) (démographique) :* population census = *recensement de la population* ⓪ poll = *sondage.*

CENT (n) *cent(ime) (m) :* there are a hundred cents in a dollar = *il y a cent cent(ime)s dans un dollar* = penny ⓪ dime = *10 cents*
not to have a (red) cent = *ne pas avoir un sou (vaillant)* → POOR.

CENTENARY (n, -ies) *centenaire (m) :* the centenary of the Statue of Liberty = *le centenaire de la Statue de la Liberté* = centennial ⓪ bicentennial = *bicentenaire.*

CENTER (n) *centre (m) :* the center of the room = *le centre de la pièce,* center of attraction = *centre d'attraction* = centre (GB) ≠ edge = *bord.*

CENTER ON (to, -ed) *centrer sur :* to center one's hopes on the new regime = *centrer ses espoirs sur le nouveau régime.*

CENTRAL (adj) *central, -e :* a central part of town = *un quartier central* ⓪ main = *principal* ≠ peripheral = *périphérique*
central heating = *chauffage central*
Central America = *Amérique centrale.*

CENTRALIZE (to, -d) *centraliser.*

CENTURY (n, -ies) *siècle (m) :* the twentieth century = *le vingtième siècle* ⓪ era = *ère*
for centuries = *depuis des siècles :* I haven't seen him for centuries = *je ne l'ai pas vu depuis des siècles.*

CERAMICS (n pl) *céramique (f).*

CEREAL (n inv) *céréales (f pl) :* I eat cereal every morning = *je mange des céréales tous les matins* ☠ *vendre des céréales à la Russie* = to sell grain to Russia.

CEREMONY (n, -ies) *cérémonie (f) :* a wedding ceremony = *une cérémonie de mariage* ⓪ ceremonial = *cérémonial,* ritual = *rituel*
let's not stand on ceremony ! = *ne faisons pas de façons !/de cérémonies !*
☠ *sans plus de cérémonie* = without further ado.

CERTAIN (adj) **1/** *certain, -e :* I was certain that you would agree = *j'étais certain que vous seriez d'accord* ⓪ positive = *sûr* ≠ uncertain = *pas certain*
for certain ! = *à coup sûr* ! = for sure !
for certain = *avec exactitude :* I don't know what it costs for certain = *je ne sais pas avec exactitude ce que cela coûte*
to make certain of stg = *s'assurer de qqch*

2/ *certain, -e :* a certain man = *un certain homme* ⓪ particular = *particulier*
☠ *une réponse certaine* = a definite answer
— *certaines personnes* = some people.

CERTAINLY (adv) *certainement :* certainly not = *certainement pas* ⓪ without a doubt = *sans aucun doute.*

CERTAINTY (n, -ies) *certitude (f) :* it's a certainty that he'll agree = *j'ai la certitude qu'il sera d'accord* ≠ doubt = *doute* ☠ *j'en ai la certitude* = I'm quite certain.

CERTIFICATE (n) *certificat (m) :* vaccination certificate = *certificat de vaccination.*

CERTIFY (to, -ied) *certifier :* we can certify that he's dead = *nous pouvons vous certifier qu'il est mort* ⓪ to attest = *attester.*

CESSATION (n) *cessation (f) :* cessation of hostilities = *cessation des hostilités.*

CHAIN (n) *chaîne (f) :* a gold chain = *une chaîne en or* ⓪ link = *maillon*
to be a chain smoker = *fumer cigarette sur cigarette* ⓪ to smoke like a chimney = *fumer comme une cheminée*
chain gang = *chaîne de forçats*
chain letter = *lettre (d'une chaîne)*
chain reaction = *réaction en chaîne*
chain store = *succursale d'une chaîne de magasins*
☠ *une chaîne de télé* = a TV channel
— *chaîne stéréo* = stereo set
— *chaîne de montage* = assembly line.

CHAIN-SMOKE (to, -d) *fumer comme un sapeur* ⓪ to be a chain smoker = *fumer cigarette sur cigarette.*

CHAIR (n) **1/** *chaise (f) :* there aren't enough chairs = *il n'y a pas assez de chaises* ⓪ armchair = *fauteuil,* rocking chair = *fauteuil à bascule,* sofa = ←, divan = ←, stool = *tabouret,* couch = *canapé,* deck chair = *transat*
to get the chair = *être condamné à la chaise électrique*
2/ *chaire (f) (university) :* a chair at the university = *une chaire d'université.*

CHAIRMAN (n, -men) *président (m) :* chairman of the board of directors = *président du conseil d'administration* ☠ → president **CHAIRWOMAN** (n, -women) *présidente (f)* **CHAIRPERSON** (n) *président, -e.*

CHALK (n inv) *craie (f) :* I wrote with a piece of chalk = *j'ai écrit avec une craie* ⓪ blackboard = *tableau noir.*

CHALK UP TO (to, -ed) *mettre sur le compte de :* you can chalk his success up to hard work = *on peut mettre son succès sur le compte d'un travail acharné.*

CHALLENGE (n) *défi (m),* challenge *(m) :* this work's a challenge = *ce travail est un défi/challenge* ⓪ provocation = ←
to accept the challenge = *relever le défi.*

CHALLENGE (to, -d) **to challenge s.o. to (a game of chess)** = *proposer à qqn (une partie d'échecs).*

CHALLENGER (n) *challenger (m)* ⓒ opponent = *adversaire.*

CHALLENGING (adj) *stimulant, -e :* challenging work = *un travail stimulant* = stimulating work.

CHAMBER (n) **chamber of commerce** = *chambre de commerce*
chamber music/orchestra = *musique/orchestre de chambre.*

CHAMPAGNE (n) *champagne (m) :* get the champagne ! = *va chercher le champagne !* ⓒ bubble = *bulle.*

CHAMPION (n) *champion, -onne :* a tennis champion = *un champion de tennis* = champ ⓒ ace = *as* ≠ loser = *perdant.*

CHAMPIONSHIP (n) *championnat (m)* ⓒ a sporting event = *une compétition.*

CHANCE (n) **1/** *chance (f) :* you have no chance of winning = *vous n'avez aucune chance de gagner*, give me another chance = *donnez-moi encore une chance*, there's a chance that he'll come tonight = *il y a une chance qu'il vienne ce soir* ⓒ possibility = *possibilité*

a/one chance in a million = *une chance sur mille* ⓒ not the ghost of a chance = *pas l'ombre d'une chance* **by chance** = *par hasard :* she got the job by chance = *elle a eu le poste par hasard* **chances are that (he'll come)** = *il y a des chances qu'(il vienne)* ⓒ it's a good bet that = *il y a gros à parier que* **a fat chance** = *pas la moindre chance :* he has a fat chance of winning = *il n'a pas la moindre chance de gagner* ⓒ a long shot = *très peu de chances* **a fighting chance** = *des chances raisonnables :* he has a fight-	ing chance of pulling through = *il a des chances raisonnables de s'en tirer* **a good/fair chance** = *de bonnes chances :* there's a good/fair chance she'll win = *elle a de bonnes chances de gagner* **it's the chance of a lifetime !** = *c'est la chance de sa vie !* **to leave nothing to chance** = *ne rien laisser au hasard* **not a chance !** = *aucune chance !* ⓒ no way ! = *que dalle !* **not to stand a (Chinaman's) chance** = *ne pas avoir la moindre chance* ≠ to be a sure thing = *être dans le sac*	**on the off chance that (he calls)** = *si par hasard (il téléphone)* **an out/off chance of (winning)** = *de faibles chances de (gagner)* **to stand a (good) chance of** = *avoir toutes les chances de* **that's the chance you'll have to take** = *c'est un risque à prendre* **there's very little chance that (he'll come)** = *il y a très peu de chances qu'(il vienne)* **you're taking chances** = *vous prenez des risques*

☠ *elle a de la chance* = she's lucky — *quelle chance !* = what luck ! — *bonne chance !* = good luck ! — *par chance ...* = fortunately/luckily	— *quelles sont ses chances ?* = what are his prospects ? — *pas de chance !* = rough luck !

2/ *occasion (f) :* he never misses the chance to criticize her = *il ne rate jamais une occasion de la critiquer* ☠ → occasion

you blew your chance ! = *tu as raté l'occasion !* **to jump at the chance** = *sauter sur l'occasion* ⓒ to seize the opportunity = *saisir l'occasion* **this is your chance to (make a lot of money)** = *c'est l'occasion pour vous de (gagner beaucoup*	*d'argent)* **when I get the chance** = *quand j'aurai un moment :* when I get the chance, I'll call you back = *quand j'aurai un moment, je vous rappellerai.*

CHANCE (adj) *fortuit, -e :* chance meeting = *rencontre fortuite* ⓒ accidental = *accidentel.*

CHANCE (to, -d) *risquer de :* I don't want to chance missing him = *je ne veux pas risquer de le rater* ⓒ to take a gamble = *risquer le coup*

chance it ! = *risque le coup !* **to chance on** = *avoir la chance de tomber sur :* I	chanced on an honest publisher = *j'ai eu la chance de tomber sur un éditeur honnête.*

CHANCELLOR (n) *chancelier (m)*
Chancellor of the Exchequer (GB) = *chancelier de l'Échiquier/ministre des Finances.*

CHANDELIER (n) *lustre (m) :* a crystal chandelier = *un lustre de cristal* ☠ *un chandelier* = a candlestick.

CHANGE (n) **1/** *changement (m) :* since her marriage what a change ! = *quel changement depuis son mariage !* ⓓ modification = ←
a change of clothes = *des vêtements de rechange*
change of life = *retour d'âge* ≠ puberty = *puberté*
a change of plans = *un changement de programme*
for a change = *pour changer :* 'smile for a change ! = *souris pour changer !*
to have a change of heart = *se raviser* ⓓ to change one's mind = *changer d'avis*
☠ *donner le change à qqn* = to put stg over on s.o.
— *changement de direction* = under new management
2/ (inv) *monnaie (f) :* I don't have any change = *je n'ai pas de monnaie,* keep the change = *gardez la monnaie*
☠ *monnaie de singe* = wooden nickels
— *monnaie forte* = hard currency
— *rendre à qqn la monnaie de sa pièce* = to pay s.o. back in kind
— *c'est monnaie courante* = it's a dime a dozen.

CHANGE (to, -d) **1/** *changer :* she has changed a lot = *elle a beaucoup changé* ⓓ to modify = *modifier* **2/** *se changer :* do you want to change before dinner ? = *voulez-vous aller vous changer avant le dîner ?* **3/** *changer de :* we had to change cars = *nous avons dû changer de voiture*
to change into = *(se) changer en :* the frog changed into a prince = *le crapaud s'est changé en prince*
☠ *pour changer* = for a change.

CHANGEABLE (adj) *changeant, -e* (s.o., stg), *variable* (stg) : changeable weather = *temps variable.*

CHANNEL (n) *chaîne (f) (de télévision) :* on the first channel = *sur la première chaîne* ☠ → chain
the (English) Channel = *la Manche*
to go through official/the usual channels = *passer par les voies officielles/habituelles.*

CHAOS (n) *chaos (m) :* the economy's in a state of chaos = *l'économie est en plein chaos* ⓓ havoc = *chambardement* ≠ harmony = *harmonie* **CHAOTIC** (adj) *chaotique :* a chaotic situation = *une situation chaotique* ≠ calm = *calme.*

CHAP (n) (GB) *type (m) :* he's a nice chap = *c'est un type sympa* ⓓ bloke = *gars* ≠ bird = *gonzesse* ☠ → type.

CHAPEL (n) *chapelle (f)* ⓓ cathedral = *cathédrale,* chaplain = *chapelain.*

CHAPERON (n) *chaperon (m) :* she never goes out without a chaperon = *elle ne sort jamais sans un chaperon* ⓓ a third party = *une tierce personne.*

CHAPTER (n) *chapitre (m) :* the first chapter's the best = *le premier chapitre est le meilleur* ⓓ table of contents = *table des matières* ☠ *assez sur ce chapitre !* = enough (about it) !

CHARACTER (n) **1/** *personnage (m) :* the main character in the play = *le personnage principal de la pièce* ☠ → personage
a character role/part = *un rôle de composition*
2/ *caractère (m) :* that shows his true character = *cela montre son véritable caractère* ⓓ nature = ←
it is in ≠ **out of character (for him to do it)** = *c'est* ≠ *ce n'est pas dans son caractère (de le faire)*
what a character (he is) ! = *(c'est) un drôle de numéro !* ⓓ what a queer fish ! = *quel drôle de coco !*

CHARACTERISTIC (n) *caractéristique (f)* ⓓ particularity = *particularité* **CHARACTERISTIC** (adj) *caractéristique :* jealousy is characteristic of insecure people = *la jalousie est caractéristique des gens insécurisés* ⓓ typical = *typique* **CHARACTERISTICALLY** (adv) *de façon caractéristique.*

CHARACTERIZE (to, -d) *caractériser :* jazz is characterized by irregular rhythms = *le jazz est caractérisé par des rythmes irréguliers.*

CHARCOAL (n) *charbon (m) de bois :* charcoal for the barbecue = *du charbon de bois pour le barbecue* ⓓ coal = *charbon.*

CHARGE (n) **1/** *accusation (f) :* what's the charge ? = *quelle est l'accusation ?,* a murder charge = *une accusation de meurtre* ⓓ indictment = *inculpation* ☠ → accusation **2/** *charge (f) :* a cavalry charge = *une charge de cavalerie* ☠ *les charges (publiques)* = (public) expenses **3/** *ce qu'il faut payer :* what's the charge ? = *combien faut-il payer ?*

to be in charge of (everything) = *avoir la charge de (tout)* ⓓ to run = *diriger*	**the charges against (him)** = *les charges retenues/les accusations portées contre (lui)*	**movies)** = *prendre son pied en (regardant les films pornos)* ⓓ
to bring a charge against s.o. = *porter plainte contre qqn*	**to dismiss charges** = *prononcer un arrêt de non-lieu*	to get a kick out of = *prendre du plaisir à*
a charge account = *un compte :* a charge account at Bloomingdale's = *un compte chez Bloomingdale*	**to drop the charges** = *retirer sa plainte* ⓓ to settle out of court = *régler à l'amiable* **to get a charge out of (porno**	**is there any charge ?** = *est-ce qu'il faut payer quelque chose ?* **there's no charge** = *il n'y a rien à payer* ⓓ it's free = *c'est gratuit*

| **to press charges** = *poursuivre en justice*
 I reversed the charges = *j'ai appelé en PCV* = I called collect | **to take charge of** = *prendre en charge* : he's taking charge of everything = *il prend tout en charge* | **who's in charge ?** = *qui est le responsable ?* |

CHARGE (to, -d) **1/** *faire payer* : how much did he charge you ? = *combien vous a-t-il fait payer ?* **2/** *mettre sur le compte de* : I don't have any money on me, charge it to me •= *je n'ai pas d'argent sur moi, mettez-le sur mon compte* **3/** *charger* : the troops charged = *les troupes ont chargé*

| **to charge s.o. for** = *faire payer qqn pour* : he didn't charge me for the phone call = *il ne m'a rien fait payer pour le coup de téléphone* | **to be charged with** = *être accusé de* : he was charged with murder = *il a été accusé de meurtre* ≠ to exonerate = *disculper* |

| ☠ *charger un camion* = to load a truck | — *je me chargerai de lui !* = I'll take care of him ! |

CHARISMA (n) *charisme (m)* : a Pope with charisma = *un pape avec du charisme* **CHARISMATIC** (adj) *charismatique* : a charismatic leader = *un chef charismatique.*

CHARITABLE (adj) *charitable.*

CHARITY (n, -ies) *charité (f)* : a charity sale = *une vente de charité* ⓓ alms = *aumône*, help = *secours*
charity begins at home = *charité bien ordonnée commence par soi-même*
out of charity = *par charité.*

CHARLATAN (n) *charlatan (m)* : the doctor's a charlatan = *le docteur est un charlatan* = the doctor's a quack ☠ *il dit qu'il est avocat mais c'est un charlatan* = he says he's a lawyer but he's a fake *(plus utilisé que « charlatan »)*:

CHARLEY HORSE (n) **to have a Charley horse** = *avoir des courbatures.*

CHARM (n) *charme (m)* : the charm of Greenwich Village = *le charme de Greenwich Village* ⓓ attractiveness = *séduction*
to break the charm = *rompre le charme*
charm bracelet = *bracelet à breloques*
like a charm = *à merveille* : the medicine worked like a charm = *le médicament a marché à merveille*
to turn on the charm = *faire son numéro de charme* : he always turns on the charm in front of the boss's wife = *il fait toujours son numéro de charme quand la femme du patron est là*
☠ *être sous le charme* = to be under the spell
— *se porter comme un charme* = to be as fit as a fiddle.

CHARM (to, -ed) *charmer* : I was charmed by her beauty = *j'ai été charmée par sa beauté* ⓓ to captivate = *captiver.*

CHARMING (adj) *charmant, -e* : a charming guy/evening = *un type charmant/une soirée charmante* ⓓ attractive = *attrayant*, enchanting = *enchanteur.*

CHART (n) *tableau (m)* : a chart showing the rise of inflation = *un tableau montrant la hausse de l'inflation* ⓓ diagram = *diagramme* ☠ → picture.

CHARTER (n) **1/** *(vol) charter (m)* : to take a charter to New York = *prendre un charter pour New York* **2/** *charte (f)* : a charter of political rights = *une charte des droits politiques.*

CHASE (n) *poursuite (f)* : a chase through streets = *une poursuite à travers les rues* ⓓ manhunt = *chasse à l'homme* ☠ → pursuit
to give chase to (a pickpocket) = *donner la chasse à (un pickpocket).*

CHASE (to, -d) *pourchasser* : the dog's chasing the cat = *le chien pourchasse le chat* ⓓ to run after = *courir après*, to pursue = *poursuivre*
I'm not chasing you ! = *je ne vous cours pas après !*
to chase away = *chasser* : he chased the dog/the child away = *il a chassé le chien/l'enfant* ☠ → to hunt
to chase s.o. out of = *chasser qqn de* : they chased me out of the room = *ils m'ont chassé de la pièce.*

CHASER (n) *verre de bière, de lait ou d'eau pris après une boisson très alcoolisée.*

CHASTE (adj) *chaste* ⓓ pure = *pur.*

CHASTISE (to, -d) *châtier* ⓓ to chide = *tancer.*

CHAT (n) *causerie (f)* : a fireside chat = *une causerie au coin du feu* ⓓ chitchat = *parlotte*, talk = *conversation.*

CHAT (to, -ted) *causer* : to chat hours and hours = *causer pendant des heures et des heures* ⓓ to gossip = *potiner* ☠ → to cause.

CHATTER (to, -ed) *jacasser* : to chatter all day = *jacasser toute la journée* ⓓ to cackle = *caqueter.*

CHATTERBOX (n, -es) *moulin (m) à paroles* ⓓ windbag = *pie-jacasse.*

CHAUFFEUR (n) *chauffeur (m)* : the ambassador's chauffeur = *le chauffeur de l'ambassadeur* ⓓ driver = *conducteur* ☠ *chauffeur de taxi* = taxi driver.

CHAUVINISM (n) *chauvinisme (m)* : French chauvinism = *le chauvinisme français* ⓓ patriotism = *patriotisme* **CHAUVINIST** (n, adj) *chauvin, -e.*

CHEAP (adj, -er, -est) **1/** *bon marché* : melons are cheap in summer = *les melons sont bon marché l'été* ⊕ for a song = *pour une bouchée de pain* ≠ expensive = *cher* **2/** *quelconque* : everything about her is cheap = *tout en elle est quelconque* ⊕ vulgar = *vulgaire* ⚰ → commonplace **3/** *pingre* : he's so cheap, he rarely leaves a tip = *il est très pingre, il laisse rarement un pourboire* ⊕ tight = *regardant* ≠ generous = *généreux* **4/** *de la camelote* : what a cheap watch ! = *cette montre, c'est de la camelote !* ⊕ shoddy = *de pacotille*.

CHEAPEN (to, -ed) *dévaloriser* : ugly furniture cheapens the place = *la laideur du mobilier dévalorise l'endroit* ≠ to improve = *améliorer* ⚰ *la monnaie se dévalorise* = the currency's depreciating.

CHEAPSKATE (n) *pignouf (m)* : don't be such a cheap-skate and leave a bigger tip = *ne sois pas si pignouf et laisse un plus gros pourboire* ⊕ tightwad = *grigou*.

CHEAT (n) *tricheur, -euse* : you're a cheat ! = *tu es un tricheur !* = cheater ⊕ swindler = *arnaqueur*.

CHEAT (to, -ed) *tricher* : you're cheating ! = *tu triches !* ⊕ cheating = *tricherie*
to cheat at (cards) = *tricher aux (cartes)*
to cheat on s.o. = *tromper qqn* : he's cheating on his wife = *il trompe sa femme* ≠ to be faithful to = *être fidèle à*
to cheat s.o. = *rouler qqn* : your pal cheated you = *ton copain t'a roulé* → TO HUSTLE
to cheat s.o. out of = *refaire qqn de* : he cheated me out of my share = *il m'a refait de ·ma part* → TO HUSTLE.

CHECK (n) **1/** *chèque (m)* : a blank check = *un chèque en blanc*, a bounced check = *un chèque sans provision/en bois*, to pay by check = *payer par chèque* = cheque (GB) ⊕ checkbook = *carnet de chèques* ≠ cash = *argent liquide* **2/** *addition (f)* : can I please have the check ? = *est-ce que je peux avoir l'addition, s'il vous plaît ?* ⊕ tab = *note* ⚰ → addition

a check on = *un frein à* : the Supreme Court is a check on Presidential abuse of power = *la Cour suprême est un frein à l'abus de pouvoir présidentiel* **checks and balances** = *l'équilibre des pouvoirs entre l'exécutif, le législatif et le judiciaire*	**to cash a check** = *donner du liquide contre un chèque* : I hope the bank can cash my check = *j'espère que la banque pourra me donner du liquide contre mon chèque* ⊕ to stop payment = *faire opposition* **to hold in check** = *tenir en bride* ≠ to give free rein = *laisser la bride sur le cou*.

CHECK (to, -ed) **1/** *vérifier* : check the list/if the door's locked = *vérifiez la liste/que la porte est fermée à clef* ⊕ to control = *contrôler* ⚰ « to check » *est plus dit que* « to verify » **2/** *refréner* : to check one's anger = *refréner sa colère* **3/** *cocher* : check the items you want = *cochez les articles que vous voulez* = check off the items you want
to check one's coat/one's luggage = *mettre son manteau au vestiaire/faire enregistrer ses bagages*

to check in ≠ **out** = *se faire enregistrer* ≠ *régler sa note* : if you check in at noon, you have to check out at noon = *si vous vous faites enregistrer à midi (à l'hôtel), vous devrez régler la note à midi* **to check (up) on** = *vérifier* : the cops are checking (up) on his	alibi = *les flics sont en train de vérifier son alibi* ⊕ to look into = *examiner* **to check out** = *se faire une idée sur* : we're going to check out the new singer = *on va se faire une idée sur le nouveau chanteur* **to check over** = *vérifier* :	check over the letter before it's typed = *vérifiez la lettre avant qu'elle soit tapée* **to check with** = *voir avec* : check with your mother ; if she agrees, it's O.K. with me = *vois avec ta mère ; si elle est d'accord, moi aussi*.

CHECK ! (interj) *d'ac !* : 5 o'clock ? — check ! = *5 heures ? — d'ac !* ⊕ okay ! = *O.K. !*

CHECKBOOK (n) *carnet (m) de chèques, chéquier (m)* : my checkbook was stolen = *on m'a volé mon carnet de chèques/mon chéquier* ⊕ a blank check = *un chèque en blanc*.

CHECKERS (n pl) *dames (f pl)* : to play checkers = *jouer aux dames* ⊕ checkerboard = *damier*, chess = *échecs*.

CHECKMATE (n) *échec (m) et mat* ⊕ stalemate = *impasse* **CHECKMATE** (to, -d) *mettre échec et mat*.

CHECKROOM (n) *vestiaire (m)* (clothes), *consigne (f)* (luggage)
⚰ *un vestiaire (sport)* = a locker
— *donner des consignes* = to give instructions.

CHECKUP (n) *check-up (m)* : to go for a checkup = *se faire faire un check-up* ⊕ physical = *bilan de santé*.

CHEEK (n) **1/** *joue (f)* : red cheeks = *des joues rouges* ⊕ high cheekbones = *pommettes saillantes*, rouge = *rouge*

à joues **2/** *aplomb (m)* : what cheek to answer like that ! = *quel aplomb de répondre comme ça !* ⓪ nerve = *toupet* ☠ *se remettre d'aplomb* = to get back on one's feet.

CHEEKY (adj, -ier, -iest) *qui ne manque pas d'aplomb* ⓪ impudent = ←.

CHEER (to, -ed) *faire une ovation* : they cheered the team = *ils ont fait une ovation à l'équipe* ⓪ to applaud = *applaudir*
to cheer up = *remonter le moral à* : let's go out for dinner, it'll cheer you up = *allons dîner dehors, ça te remontera le moral* ⓪ to pep up = *ragaillardir*
cheer up ! = *allez, courage !* ⓪ keep your chin up ! = *allez, du cran !*

CHEERFUL (adj) *réjoui, -e* : cheerful faces = *des mines réjouies* ⓪ jubilant = *épanoui*.

CHEERLEADER (n) *étudiante séduisante chargée d'animer les chants et slogans des supporters d'une équipe sportive universitaire*.

CHEERS (n pl) *vivats (m pl)* : cheers welcomed the singer = *des vivats ont accueilli le chanteur* ≠ boos = *huées*.

CHEERS ! (interj) *tchin-tchin !* ⓪ bottoms up ! = *à la bonne vôtre !*

CHEESE (n) *fromage (m)* : we eat a lot of cheese = *nous mangeons beaucoup de fromage*, cheeses from different countries = *des fromages de différents pays* ☠ *se faire un fromage* = to make a pile.

CHEESECAKE (n) **1/** (inv) *photo (f) de pin-up* : she started her career doing cheesecake = *elle a commencé sa carrière en faisant des photos de pin-up* **2/** *gâteau (m) au fromage blanc*.

CHEMICAL (n) *produit (m) chimique* : no chemicals are used in this bread = *il n'y a aucun produit chimique dans ce pain* **CHEMICAL** (adj) *chimique*.

CHEMIST (n) **1/** *chimiste (m, f)* ⓪ physicist = *physicien* **2/** (GB) *pharmacien, -enne* = druggist.

CHEMISTRY (n) **1/** *chimie (f)* : to study chemistry = *faire des études de chimie* ⓪ biology = *biologie* **2/** *question (f) de peau* : I don't know why I'm attracted to him ; it's chemistry = *je ne sais pas pourquoi il m'attire ; c'est une question de peau*.

CHERISH (to, -ed) *chérir* : to cherish one's parents = *chérir ses parents* ⓪ to adore = *adorer* ≠ to detest = *détester*.

CHERRY (n, -ies) **1/** *cerise (f)* : to eat cherries = *manger des cerises* ⓪ cherry tree = *cerisier*
that's the cherry on the sundae = *c'est le plus merveilleux* : the job's great and the cherry on the sundae is frequent trips abroad = *le boulot est formidable, et le plus merveilleux ce sont les fréquents déplacements à l'étranger* ⓪ the icing on the cake = *le plus beau* **2/** *fleur (f)* : she lost her cherry at 15 = *elle a perdu sa fleur à 15 ans* ⓪ virginity = *virginité* ☠ → flower.

CHESS (n inv) *échecs (m pl)* : to play chess = *jouer aux échecs* ⓪ chessboard = *échiquier*, checkmate = *échec et mat*, castle = *tour* = rook, queen = *reine*, king = *roi*, bishop = *fou*, knight = *cavalier*.

CHEST (n inv) *poitrine (f)* : to have chest pains = *avoir des douleurs à la poitrine*
to get stg off one's chest = *dire ce qu'on a sur le cœur* ⓪ to open up = *s'ouvrir* ☠ *une grosse poitrine* = a big bosom.

CHESTY (adj, -ier, -iest) *qui a une poitrine avantageuse* : a chesty broad = *une nana qui a une poitrine avantageuse* = busty ⓪ buxom = *qui a de la poitrine*.

CHEW (to, -ed) *mâcher* : chew your meat = *mâche ta viande* ⓪ to bite = *mordre*
to chew s.o. out = *tirer les oreilles à qqn* : the boss chewed his assistant out = *le patron a tiré les oreilles à son assistant* → TO LAMBAST
to chew over (an idea) = *ressasser (une idée)* ⓪ to mull over = *ruminer* ☠ *ne pas mâcher ses mots* = not to mince words.

CHIC (adj) *chic* : a chic dress = *une robe chic* ⓪ stylish = *élégant* ☠ *chic !* = swell !
— *un chic type* = a swell guy.

CHICANO (n) *résident ou citoyen américain d'origine mexicaine* ⓪ wetback = *ouvrier mexicain entré illégalement aux États-Unis*.

CHICK (n) *pépée (f)* : I don't like the chick he's going out with = *je n'aime pas la pépée avec laquelle il sort* ⓪ Jane = *Berthe*.

CHICKEN (n) **1/** *poulet (m)* : fried chicken = *poulet frit* ⓪ chick = *poussin*, hen = *poule*, drumstick = *pilon*, breast = *blanc*, wing = *aile*, wishbone = *bréchet*
chicken feed = *des clous* : he's working for chicken feed = *il travaille pour des clous* ⓪ for beans = *pour des prunes*
chicken pox = *la varicelle*
don't count your chickens before they're hatched = *il ne faut pas vendre la peau de l'ours avant de l'avoir tué* ⓪ a bird in the hand is worth two in the bush = *un tiens vaut mieux que deux tu l'auras*
to run around like a chicken without a head = *courir dans tous les sens*
which came first, the chicken or the egg ? = *qui fut le premier de l'œuf ou de la poule ?/c'est l'histoire de l'œuf et de la poule* ☠ *et mon cul, c'est du poulet ?* = you bet your sweet ass !
— *les poulets* = the fuzz
— *mon poulet* = sweetie
2/ *poule (f) mouillée* : don't be such a chicken = *ne sois pas poule mouillée à ce point* ⓪ scaredy-cat = *trouillard*.

CHICKEN (adj) *froussard, -e* : how chicken can you be ! = *ce que tu peux être froussard !* ≠ gutsy = *culotté*.

CHICKEN OUT (to, -ed) *se dégonfler* : he chickened out at the last minute = *il s'est dégonflé à la dernière minute* ⦾ to cop out = *se débiner.*

CHIDE (to, -d or chid) *tancer* : she chided me for the mistake = *elle m'a tancé pour l'erreur que j'avais faite* → TO LAMBAST.

CHIEF (n) *chef (m)* : the chief of the tribe = *le chef de la tribu* ⦾ leader = ←, commander = *commandant*
chief of police = *préfet de police*
chief of staff = *chef d'état-major*
chief of state = *chef d'État*
☠ *chef d'entreprise/de service* = manager of a company/head of a department
— *chef d'orchestre* = conductor (orchestra)
— *chef de famille* = head of the household
— *le chef (restaurant)* = the chef
— *le chef de file* = the leading member/the leader
— *rédacteur en chef* = senior editor.

CHIEF (adj) *principal, -e* : their chief complaint = *leur principale revendication* = principal ⦾ foremost = *de premier plan*
the chief cook and bottle-washer = *le factotum* ⦾ jack-of-all-trades = *homme/femme orchestre*
chief rabbi = *grand rabbin*
Chief Justice = *président de la cour suprême.*

CHIEFLY (adv) *principalement* : he writes chiefly novels = *il écrit principalement des romans* ⦾ largely = *dans une large mesure.*

CHILD (n, -ren) *enfant (m)*, *môme (m, f)* (LV) : I have 3 children = *j'ai 3 enfants* ⦾ kid = *gosse*, youngster = *gamin*, siblings = *frères et sœurs*, childless = *sans enfant*
child's play = *un jeu d'enfant* : getting him to agree was child's play = *ça a été un jeu d'enfant d'obtenir son accord* ⦾ kid stuff = *l'enfance de l'art*
☠ *elle attend un enfant* = she's expecting
— *enfant de chœur* = altar boy
— *un enfant terrible* = a holy terror.

CHILDBIRTH (n) **(to die) in childbirth** = *mourir en couches.*

CHILDHOOD (n) *enfance (f)* : she had a very happy childhood = *elle a eu une enfance très heureuse*
childhood friend = *ami d'enfance*
☠ *c'est l'enfance de l'art* = it's kid stuff.

CHILDISH (adj) *puéril, -e* : a childish answer = *une réponse puérile* = puerile ⦾ immature = ←.

CHILDLIKE (adj) *enfantin, -e* : a childlike innocence = *une innocence enfantine* ⦾ naive = *naïf* ☠ *c'est enfantin* = it's as easy as pie.

CHILL (n) **a chill (in the air)** = *un rafraîchissement (de l'air)*
to give s.o. the chills = *faire froid dans le dos à qqn* : the movie gave me the chills = *le film m'a fait froid dans le dos.*

CHILLY (adj, -ier, -est) *frisquet, -ette* : it's chilly today = *il fait frisquet aujourd'hui* ⦾ brisk = *vif* ≠ hot = *chaud.*

CHIME IN (to, -d) *ramener sa fraise* : stop chiming in ! = *arrête de ramener ta fraise !* ⦾ to put one's two cents in = *mettre son grain de sel.*

CHIMNEY (n) *cheminée (f)* ⦾ soot = *suie* ☠ *cheminée (intérieure)* = fireplace.

CHIMPANZEE (n) *chimpanzé (m)* ⦾ gorilla = *gorille.*

CHIN (n) *menton (m)* : double chin = *double menton*
keep your chin up ! = *allez, du cran !* ⦾ keep a stiff upper lip ! = *haut les cœurs !*

CHINA (n) *service (m) en porcelaine* : my in-laws gave us beautiful china for a wedding present = *mes beaux-parents nous ont offert un beau service en porcelaine comme cadeau de mariage* ⦾ silverware = *argenterie.*

CHINA (n) *Chine (f).*

CHINESE (n inv) *Chinois, -e* ⦾ chink = *chinetoque*, rickshaw = *pousse-pousse*
☠ *pour moi, c'est du chinois* = it's Greek to me
— *se polir le chinois* = to masturbate (man).

CHINESE (adj) *chinois, -e* : Chinese food = *la nourriture chinoise* ⦾ chopsticks = *baguettes*, Peking duck = *canard laqué*, egg roll = *pâté impérial*, spareribs = *travers de porc*, fried rice = *riz cantonais.*

CHIP (n) **he's a chip off the old block** = *c'est bien le fils de son père* ⦾ they're two of a kind = *ils sont du même bois*
in the chips = *en fonds* → RICH
when the chips are down = *quand tout va mal* : he's never there when the chips are down = *il n'est jamais là quand tout va mal*
to have a chip on one's shoulder = *en vouloir à l'humanité entière* ⦾ to have an axe to grind = *avoir un compte à régler.*

CHIP IN (to, -ped) *donner quelque chose* : we all chipped in to buy them a wedding present = *nous avons tous donné quelque chose pour leur acheter un cadeau de mariage* ⦾ to kick in = *participer.*

CHIROPRACTOR (n) *chiropracteur, -trice.*

CHISELER (n) *canaille (f)* : you can't trust that chiseler = *tu ne peux pas faire confiance à cette canaille* ⦾ sharpie = *aigrefin* ☠ *la canaille* = the riffraff.

CHISEL OUT OF (to, -ed) *carotter* : he chiseled me out of a grand = *il m'a carotté mille dollars* → TO HUSTLE.

CHOCOLATE (n) *chocolat (m)* : milk chocolate = *chocolat au lait* ☠ *être chocolat* = to be taken in **CHOCOLATE** (adj) *au chocolat* : chocolate cake/ice cream = *gâteau/glace au chocolat* ⦾ vanilla = *à la vanille.*

CHOICE (n) *choix (m)* : if there's no other choice = *s'il n'y a pas d'autre choix* ⦾ option = ←
take your choice ! = *faites votre choix !*

CHOICE (adj) *de (premier) choix* : choice meat/melons = *une viande/des melons de premier choix.*

CHOIR (n) *chœur (m)* : my sons sing in the church choir = *mes fils chantent dans le chœur de l'église* ○○ hymn = *hymne.*

CHOKE (to, -d) **1/** *étrangler* : let go, you're choking me ! = *lâche-moi, tu m'étrangles !* **2/** *étouffer* : the smoke made me choke = *j'étouffais à cause de la fumée*
to choke back (one's tears) = *contenir (ses larmes)* ○○
to hold back = *refouler* ☠ → to contain
to choke on (one's food) = *s'étouffer (en mangeant)* ○○ to suffocate = *suffoquer*
to be (all) choked up = *avoir la gorge nouée* ○○ to be moved = *être ému*
☠ *étouffer un scandale* = to hush up a scandal
— *ce ne sont pas les scrupules qui l'étouffent* = you can't say he's overscrupulous
— *étouffer une révolution* = to suppress/to quash a revolution
— *on étouffe !* = it's sweltering !
— *elle étouffe ses enfants (d'amour)* = she smothers her children (with her love).

CHOLERA (n) *choléra (m)* ○○ yellow fever = *fièvre jaune*, malaria = ←.

CHOOSE (to, chose, chosen) *choisir* : choose the one you want = *choisissez celui que vous voulez* = to pick ○○ to select = *sélectionner*
to choose to = *choisir de* : she chose to tell him the truth = *elle a choisi de lui dire la vérité.*

CHOOSY (adj, -ier, -iest) *difficile* : to be choosy about one's food = *être difficile pour la nourriture* ○○ fussy = *tatillon* ☠ → difficult.

CHOP (n) *côte (f)* : lamb chops = *côtes d'agneau*
to lick one's chops = *se lécher les babines* ≠ to whet s.o.'s appetite = *mettre l'eau à la bouche à qqn* ☠ → coast.

CHOPSTICKS (n pl) *baguettes (f pl)* : to eat with chopsticks = *manger avec des baguettes*
☠ *baguette magique* = magic wand
— *mener à la baguette* = to rule with an iron hand.

CHORE (n) *corvée (f)* : washing the dishes is a chore = *c'est une corvée de faire la vaisselle* ○○ job = *travail* ☠ *être de corvée de soupe* = to be on KP duty.

CHOREOGRAPHER (n) *chorégraphe (m, f)* **CHOREO-GRAPHY** (n, -ies) *chorégraphie (f).*

CHORUS (n, -es) *refrain (m)* : most ballads have choruses = *la plupart des ballades ont des refrains*
chorus boy/girl = boy/girl.

CHOW (n) *bouffe (f)* : the chow's lousy here = *la bouffe est dégueulasse ici* ○○ grub = *boustifaille.*

CHRIST (n) *Christ (m)* ○○ Messiah = *Messie*
for Christ's sake ! = *nom de Dieu !* → GOSH !

CHRIST ! (interj) *bon Dieu !* : Christ ! what the fuck are you doing ? = *bon Dieu ! qu'est-ce que tu glandes ?* → GOSH !

CHRISTEN (to, -ed) *baptiser* = to baptize.

CHRISTIAN (n, adj) *chrétien, -enne*
Christian Science = *la science chrétienne, religion fondée par Mary Baker Eddy au XIXᵉ siècle.*

CHRISTIANITY (n) *christianisme (m).*

CHRISTMAS (n) *Noël (m)* : I'm spending Christmas with my folks = *je passe Noël en famille* = Xmas ○○ Santa Claus = *Père Noël*
a Christmas card = *une carte de vœux*
Christmas Eve = *veille/réveillon de Noël*
Christmas tree = *arbre de Noël.*

CHROMOSOME (n) *chromosome (m)* ○○ cell = *cellule.*

CHRONIC (adj) *chronique* : a chronic disease/liar = *une maladie/un menteur chronique* ○○ habitual = *impénitent.*

CHRONICLE (n) *chronique (f)* ○○ memoirs = *mémoires.*

CHRONOLOGY (n, -ies) *chronologie (f)* : that's not the chronology of how things happened = *ce n'est pas la chronologie des événements.*

CHUBBY (adj, -ier, -iest) *joufflu, -e, potelé, -e* : a chubby baby = *un bébé joufflu/potelé* ○○ plump = *rondouillard* ≠ skinny = *maigre.*

CHUCK (to, -ed) *balancer* : to chuck a candidate = *balancer un candidat* ○○ to get rid of = *se débarrasser de* ☠ *se balancer* = to swing
— *je m'en balance* = I don't give a darn
— *balancer (hésiter)* = to vacillate.

CHUCKLE (to, -d) *glousser* : the girls were chuckling = *les filles gloussaient* ○○ to giggle = *rire bêtement.*

CHUG-A-LUG (to, -ged) *faire cul sec.*

CHUM (n) *pote (m)* : I met an old chum = *j'ai rencontré un vieux pote* = buddy ○○ pal = *copain.*

CHUMMY (adj) *copain, copine* : I'm chummy with my in-laws = *je suis très copain avec mes beaux-parents* ○○ buddy-buddy = *copain-copain.*

CHUMP (n) *gogo (m)* : what a chump he was to believe you ! = *quel gogo de t'avoir cru !* ○○ pigeon = ←.

CHUNK (n) *gros morceau (m)* : a chunk of cheese/meat = *un gros morceau de fromage/de viande* = a hunk of cheese/meat.

CHURCH (n, -es) *église (f)* : a gothic church = *une église gothique* ○○ abbey = *abbaye*, churchgoer = *pratiquant*, chapel = *chapelle*, cathedral = *cathédrale*, pulpit = *chaire*, pew = *banc d'église*, temple = ←.

CHUTZPA(H) (n inv) *culot (m)* : what chutzpah he had to ask me that ! = *quel culot il a eu de me demander ça !* ⓪ cheek = *aplomb.*

C.I.A. (n) = Central Intelligence Agency = *C.I.A. (f), services secrets américains* ⓪ secret agent = *agent secret*, FBI = *renseignements généraux.*

CIDER (n) *cidre (m)* : cider vinegar = *vinaigre de cidre* ⓪ apple = *pomme.*

CIGAR (n) *cigare (m)* ⓪ pipe = ←.

CIGARETTE (n) *cigarette (f)* : I smoke 50 cigarettes a day = *je fume 50 cigarettes par jour* ⓪ fag = *clope*, puff = *bouffée*, carton = *cartouche*, ashtray = *cendrier*, lighter = *briquet*, matches = *allumettes*, butt = *mégot*, drag = *taffe*, lung cancer = *cancer du poumon*, cigarette holder = *fume-cigarette*, cigarette case = *étui à cigarettes.*

CINCH (n) **it's a cinch !** = *c'est du gâteau !* : this work's a cinch ! = *ce travail, c'est du gâteau !* ⓪ it's a snap = *c'est enfantin.*

CINDERELLA (n) *Cendrillon (f)* ⓪ Snow White = *Blanche-Neige.*

CINEMA (n) *cinéma (m)* : American cinema is famous for its musical comedies = *le cinéma américain est réputé pour ses comédies musicales* ☠ *aller au cinéma* = to go to the movies.

CINNAMON (n) *cannelle (f)* : cinnamon cookies = *des biscuits à la cannelle.*

CIRCLE (n) *cercle (m)* : draw me a circle = *dessinez-moi un cercle* ≠ rectangle = ←
(her) circle of friends = *(son) cercle d'amis*
to go round in circles = *tourner en rond* ⓪ to get nowhere = *n'arriver à rien*
in (political) circles = *dans les milieux (politiques)*
in the (same) circles = *dans le (même) milieu* : we don't move in the same circles = *nous n'évoluons pas dans le même milieu.*

CIRCULATE (to, -d) *circuler* : blood circulates = *le sang circule* ⓪ to move = *bouger*
☠ *circulez !* = move on !
— *on circule difficilement* = there's a lot of traffic
— *il circule des histoires sur sa mort* = gossip about her death is going around.

CIRCULATION (n) 1/ *tirage (m)* : the newspaper has a circulation of 100 000 = *le journal a un tirage de 100 000 exemplaires*
☠ *tirage (photo)* = printing
— *tirage au sort* = drawing
— *du tirage entre les deux frères* = friction between the two brothers
2/ *circulation (f)* : blood circulation = *la circulation du sang*
in ≠ out of circulation = *dans le circuit ≠ hors circuit* : he's divorced and is in circulation again = *il est divorcé et il est à nouveau dans le circuit* ⓪ free = *libre*

☠ *il y a beaucoup de circulation à six heures* = there's a lot of traffic at six o'clock
— *libre circulation (des travailleurs)* = free movement (of workers).

CIRCUMCISE (to, -d) *circoncire.*

CIRCUMSPECT (adj) *circonspect, -e* ⓪ prudent = ←.

CIRCUMSTANCE (n) *circonstance (f)* : circumstances forced me to retire = *les circonstances m'ont forcé à prendre ma retraite* ⓪ event = *événement*
circumstances beyond our control = *des circonstances indépendantes de notre volonté*
under no circumstances (will I agree) = *en aucun cas (je ne serai d'accord)*
under the circumstances = *vu les circonstances* ⓪ in that case = *dans ce cas.*

CIRCUMSTANTIAL (adj) **circumstantial evidence** = *preuve indirecte.*

CIRCUMVENT (to, -ed) *tourner* (law, rule) : to circumvent the regulations = *tourner le règlement* ⓪ to get round = *contourner* ☠ → to turn.

CIRCUS (n, -es) *cirque (m)* : we're going to the circus on Friday = *nous allons au cirque vendredi* ⓪ the big top = *le grand chapiteau* ☠ *quel cirque !* = what a rigmarole !

CITIZEN (n) *citoyen, -enne* : a citizen of France = *un citoyen français* ⓪ subject = *sujet* ≠ stateless = *apatride* **CITIZENSHIP** (n) *citoyenneté (f)* : British citizenship = *la citoyenneté britannique* ⓪ nationality = *nationalité.*

CITY (n, -ies) (grande) *ville (f)* : to live in a city = *vivre dans une ville* ⓪ town = *petite ville*
city council = *conseil municipal*
city dweller = *citadin* ≠ hick = *plouc*
city hall = *hôtel de ville* ⓪ town hall = *mairie*
city life = *vie citadine/en ville*
city planner = *urbaniste* ⓪ city planning = *urbanisme*
you can't fight city hall = *on ne peut pas se battre contre les moulins à vent* → THAT'S LIFE !
☠ *"cité"* is less used in modern language
— *ville d'eaux* = spa
— *dîner en ville* = to go out for dinner.

CIVIC (adj) *civique* : civic duties = *devoirs civiques.*

CIVICS (n pl) *instruction (f) civique* : to study civics = *faire de l'instruction civique.*

CIVIL (adj) 1/ *civil, -e* : civil defense = *défense civile*, civil war = *guerre civile*
civil engineering = *travaux publics*
civil liberties = *libertés publiques*
civil rights = *droits civiques*
civil servant = *fonctionnaire*
2/ *civil, -e* : be civil to her = *soyez civil avec elle* ⓪ courteous = *courtois* ≠ uncivil = *incivil.*

CIVILIAN (n) *civil* (m) : no civilian's allowed on the base = *aucun civil n'est admis à l'intérieur de la base* ≠ soldier = *soldat* CIVILIAN (adj) **in civilian clothes** = *en civil* = in civvies.

CIVILIZATION (n) *civilisation* (f) : the Greek civilization = *la civilisation grecque* ⓓ culture = ←.

CIVILIZED (adj) *civilisé, -e* : a civilized world = *un monde civilisé* ⓓ cultivated = *cultivé* ≠ uncivilized = *non civilisé*.

CIVVIES (n pl) **in civvies** = *en civil*.

CLAD (adj) **to be clad in** = *être vêtu, -e de* : clad in a skimpy bikini = *vêtue d'un tout petit bikini*.

CLAIM (n) **1/** *(le fait de) prétendre* : the government's claim is that inflation is inevitable = *le gouvernement prétend que l'inflation est inévitable* **2/** *demande* (f) : the judge is considering his claim for custody of the children = *le juge examine sa demande de garde des enfants* ☠ → demand.

CLAIM (to, -ed) *prétendre* : he claims I'm wrong = *il prétend que j'ai tort* ⓓ to maintain = *maintenir*.

CLAM (n) *palourde* (f), *clam* (m) : clam chowder = *soupe épaisse au lait et aux palourdes/clams* ⓓ shellfish = *coquillages*.

CLAMOR (n) *levée* (f) *de boucliers* : a clamor went up in the assembly = *il y a eu une levée de boucliers dans l'assemblée* = clamour (GB) ⓓ outcry = *tollé*.

CLAMOR FOR (to, -ed) *réclamer à cor et à cri* : to clamor for lower taxes = *réclamer à cor et à cri des impôts moins lourds*.

CLAMP DOWN ON (to, -ed) *mettre le holà à* (stg), *serrer la vis à* (s.o.) : the government's clamping down on tax evasion = *le gouvernement met le holà à la fraude fiscale*, the parents decided to clamp down on their 18-year old daughter = *les parents ont décidé de serrer la vis à leur fille de 18 ans* ⓓ to get tough with = *durcir sa position face à*.

CLAM UP (to, -med) *la boucler* : he clammed up when she asked him about his affair = *il l'a bouclée quand elle lui a posé des questions sur sa liaison* ⓓ to shut up = *la fermer*.

CLAN (n) *clan* (m) ⓓ tribe = *tribu*.

CLANDESTINE (adj) *clandestin, -e* : a clandestine network = *un réseau clandestin* ☠ *un passager clandestin* = a stowaway.

CLAP (n inv) *chaude-pisse* (f), *chtouille* (f) (LV) : he picked up the clap in a second-rate brothel = *il a attrapé la chtouille/une chaude-pisse dans un bordel de second ordre* ⓓ syphilis = ←.

CLAP (to, -ped) *applaudir* : everyone clapped loudly = *tout le monde a applaudi très fort* = to applaud ≠ to hiss = *siffler*.

CLARIFY (to, -ied) *clarifier* : clarify your argument = *clarifiez votre argumentation* ≠ to obscure = *obscurcir*.

CLARINET (n) *clarinette* (f) ⓓ flute = *flûte*.

CLARITY (n) *clarté* (f) : the clarity of his style = *la clarté de son style* ⓓ purity = *pureté*.

CLASH (n, -es) *heurt* (m), *affrontement* (m) : a clash between unions and management = *un affrontement/heurt entre syndicats et patrons* ⓓ fight = *bagarre*.

CLASH (to, -ed) **1/** *se heurter* : the parties clashed over the new tax proposal = *les partis se sont heurtés au sujet de la nouvelle proposition de loi fiscale* ☠ *heurter qqn/un arbre* = to collide with/to bash into s.o./a tree — *se heurter à une opposition* = to run up against opposition **2/** *jurer* : her scarf clashes with her lipstick = *son écharpe jure avec son rouge à lèvres* ⓓ to jar = *détonner* ☠ → to swear.

CLASS (n, -es) **1/** *classe* (f) : a history class = *une classe d'histoire* ⓓ classroom = *salle de classe*, grade = *note* **2/** *classe* (f) : his wife has a lot of class = *sa femme a beaucoup de classe* ⓓ elegance = *élégance*, style = ← **3/** *classe* (f) : the working class = *la classe ouvrière* ⓓ category = *catégorie*
the class of (1981) = *la promotion de (1981)*
to be in a class by o.s. = *être hors concours* ⓓ to be one of a kind = *être unique en son genre*
class consciousness = *conscience de classe*
class war/struggle/conflict = *guerre/lutte/conflit des classes*
☠ *livre de classe* = school book — *aller en classe* = to go to school.

CLASS (to, -ed) *classer* : I class him among the best writers = *je le classe parmi les meilleurs écrivains* ☠ *classer (des fiches)* = to file (index cards) — *classer une question* = to shelve a question.

CLASSIC (n) *classique* (m) : this book's a classic = *ce livre est un classique*, the classics = *les classiques* ⓓ masterpiece = *chef-d'œuvre*.

CLASSIC (adj) *classique* : a classic coat/example = *un manteau/exemple classique* ⓓ traditional = *traditionnel*, typical = *typique*
☠ *musique classique* = classical music — *armes classiques* = conventional weapons.

CLASSICAL (adj) *classique* : a classical problem = *un problème classique* = classic ⓓ typical = *typique*
classical music = *musique classique*
☠ → classic.

CLASSIFICATION (n) *classification* (f) **CLASSIFY** (to, -ied) *classifier*
a classified document = *un document secret*.

CLASSY (adj, -ier, -iest) *qui a de la classe* : a classy suit = *un costume qui a de la classe* ≠ commonplace = *quelconque.*

CLAUSE (n) *clause (f)* : the clauses of a contract = *les clauses d'un contrat* ⓪ provision = *disposition.*

CLAW (n) *griffe (f), serre (f)* (bird) : the cat's claws = *les griffes du chat,* the eagle's claws = *les serres de l'aigle* ☠ *griffe (couturier)* = label (couture house)
— *tomber sous la griffe de qqn* = to fall into s.o.'s clutches
— *une serre (plantes)* = a hothouse.

CLAW (to, -ed) *labourer avec ses griffes.*

CLAY (n) *argile (f)* : a sculpture in clay = *une sculpture d'argile* ⓪ pottery = *poterie.*

CLEAN (adj, -er, -est) **1/** *propre* : a clean kitchen = *une cuisine propre* ⓪ spick-and-span = *d'une propreté éclatante* ≠ dirty = *sale* **2/** *blanc, blanche comme neige* : they checked his record, but he was clean = *ils ont vérifié son casier judiciaire, mais il était blanc comme neige*
as clean as a whistle = *propre comme un sou neuf*
a clean (joke) = *une (plaisanterie) convenable* ≠ a dirty joke = *une plaisanterie grossière*
a clean record = *un casier judiciaire vierge*
(to start) with a clean slate = *repartir complètement à zéro* : a new job, wife, city ; he's starting with a clean slate = *un nouveau boulot, une nouvelle femme, une nouvelle ville ; il repart complètement à zéro*
to give s.o. a clean bill of health = *donner à qqn un certificat de bonne conduite* ⓪ to clear = *blanchir*
to make a clean breast of = *faire son mea culpa*
to make a clean sweep = *faire table rase*
☠ *le chien/l'enfant est propre* = the dog's housebroken/the child's toilet-trained
— *sa propre fille* = her own daughter

— *voler de ses propres ailes* = to stand on one's own two feet
— *le sens propre* = the literal meaning.

CLEAN (adv) **to come clean** = *se mettre à table* ⓪ to talk = *parler.*

CLEAN (to, -ed) *nettoyer* : clean the kitchen = *nettoie la cuisine* ⓪ to scour = *récurer* ≠ to soil = *souiller*
to clean out = **1/** *nettoyer* : they cleaned out the safe = *ils ont nettoyé le coffre-fort* ⓪ to empty = *vider* **2/** *mettre sur la paille* : the drop in the Stock Market cleaned them out = *la chute de la Bourse les a mis sur la paille* → POOR
to clean up = **1/** *briquer* : I'm going to clean everything up this afternoon = *je vais tout briquer cet après-midi* ≠ to dirty = *salir* **2/** *faire son beurre* : he cleaned up on the Stock Market = *il a fait son beurre à la Bourse* ≠ to lose one's shirt = *perdre sa chemise* → RICH **3/** *épurer/retirer les mots vulgaires* (film, song) : to clean up the city/the government = *épurer la ville/le gouvernement,* you'd better clean up the first chapter if you want to be published = *vous feriez mieux de retirer les mots vulgaires du premier chapitre si vous voulez être publié.*

CLEAN-CUT (adj) *bon chic, bon genre* : a clean-cut young man = *un jeune homme bon chic, bon genre* ≠ rough-looking = *à la mine patibulaire,* preppie = *clean.*

CLEANER (n) *teinturier, -ère* : take your coat to the cleaner's = *porte ton manteau chez le teinturier* ⓪ laundry = *blanchisserie.*

CLEANING WOMAN (n, women) *femme (f) de ménage* ⓪ maid = *bonne* **CLEANING MAN** (n, men) *homme (m) de ménage.*

CLEANLINESS (n) *propreté (f)* : the cleanliness of the room = *la propreté de la pièce* ≠ filth = *crasse.*

CLEAR (adj, -er, -est) **1/** *clair, -e* : a clear answer = *une réponse claire* ≠ unclear = *pas clair,* hazy = *flou* **2/** *clair, -e* : a clear day/sky = *une journée claire/un ciel clair* ≠ misty = *brumeux* ☠ *bleu/gris clair* = light blue/gray .

to be as clear as mud = *être clair comme du jus de boudin* ≠ **as clear as daylight** = *clair comme le jour/comme de l'eau de roche*
a clear case of (murder) = *manifestement une affaire de (meurtre)*
a clear profit of ($ 50) = *un bénéfice net de (50 dollars)*
get that clear ! = *comprends bien ça !* ⓪ get that through your head ! = *mets-toi bien ça dans la tête !*

it's clear that (he's wrong) = *il est clair qu'(il a tort)*
to make it clear that = *bien préciser que* : she made it clear that she didn't want to go out with him = *elle a bien précisé qu'elle ne voulait pas sortir avec lui* ⓪ to specify = *spécifier*
out of a clear (blue) sky = *sans qu'on s'y attende* : my ex-lover called me out of a clear blue sky = *mon ex-amant m'a téléphoné sans que je m'y attende* ⓪ unexpectedly = *à l'improviste.*

CLEAR (adv) **to steer clear of** = *se tenir éloigné de* : I'm steering clear of him for the moment = *je me tiens éloigné de lui pour l'instant.*

CLEAR (to, -ed) **1/** *disculper* : to be cleared of charges = *être disculpé d'une accusation* ⓪ to acquit = *acquitter* ≠ to indict = *inculper* **2/** *toucher net* : to clear a grand a week = *toucher mille dollars nets par semaine* **3/** *(se) dégager* : clear the road ! = *dégagez la route !*, the sky's clearing = *le ciel se dégage*

☠ *allez, dégage !* = scram !
— *dégager (des corps)* = to dig out (bodies)

— *dégager qqn de toute responsabilité* = to relieve s.o. from all responsibility

to clear out = *prendre le large* → TO LEAVE
to clear up = 1/ *tirer au clair/éclaircir* : the mystery was cleared up = *le mystère a été éclairci*

⓪ to solve = *résoudre* 2/ *s'éclaircir* : the weather's clearing up = *le temps s'éclaircit* ☠ *s'éclaircir les cheveux* = to lighten one's hair.

CLEAR-CUT (adj) *bien net, nette* : a clear-cut answer = *une réponse bien nette* ⓪ explicit = *explicite* ≠ hazy = *flou*.

CLEARHEADED (adj) *à l'esprit clair* : a clearheaded politician = *un homme politique à l'esprit clair* ⓪ lucid = *lucide*.

CLEARING (n) *clairière (f)* : a picnic in a sunny clearing = *un pique-nique dans une clairière ensoleillée* ⓪ forest = *forêt*.

CLEARLY (adv) 1/ *manifestement* : you're clearly mistaken = *manifestement, vous vous trompez* ⓪ evidently = *de toute évidence* 2/ *clairement* : to explain something clearly = *expliquer quelque chose clairement*.

CLEMENCY (n, -ies) *clémence (f)* : to show clemency = *faire preuve de clémence* **CLEMENT** (adj) *clément, -e* : clement weather/judge = *temps/juge clément*.

CLENCH (to, -ed) *serrer* : I clenched his arm = *je lui ai serré le bras* ⓪ to grip = *agripper*
☠ *serrer la main* = to shake hands
— *serrez-vous* = move closer together
— *se serrer la ceinture* = to tighten one's belt
— *serrer qqn dans ses bras* = to hug s.o.

CLERGY (n, -ies) *clergé (m)* **CLERGYMAN** (n, -men) *ecclésiastique (m)* ⓪ minister = *ministre du culte*.

CLERICAL (adj) *de bureau* : clerical work = *travail de bureau* = office work.

CLERK (n) *employé, -e (de bureau), clerc (m)* (legal) : a bank clerk = *un employé de banque*, he's a clerk for a judge = *il est clerc chez un juge* ⓪ penpusher = *gratte-papier* ☠ → employee.

CLEVER (adj) *intelligent, -e, malin, -igne* : what a clever idea ! = *quelle idée intelligente !*, my lawyer's a little too clever = *mon avocat est un peu trop malin* ⓪ bright = *vif* ≠ dumb = *bête*
☠ *prendre un malin plaisir à* = to take a perverse pleasure in
— *une tumeur maligne* = a malignant tumor.

CLEVERLY (adv) *adroitement* : he answered very cleverly = *il a répondu très adroitement* ⓪ intelligently = *intelligemment* ☠ *(coudre) adroitement* = (to sew) skillfully.

CLICHÉ (n) *cliché (m), poncif (m)* : that women are the weaker sex is a cliché = *c'est un cliché/poncif de dire que les femmes sont le sexe faible* ☠ *cliché (photo)* = snapshot.

CLICK (to, -ed) 1/ *prendre* : his last song clicked and became a hit = *sa dernière chanson a pris et a fait un tube* ≠ to flop = *faire un four* ☠ → to take 2/ *accrocher* : we clicked right away = *on a tout de suite accroché* ⓪ to hit it off = *sympathiser* ☠ → to hang.

CLIENT (n) *client, -e* : a lawyer's/a shop's client = *le client d'un avocat/d'un magasin*.

CLIENTELE (n) *clientèle (f)* : a French clientele = *une clientèle française*.

CLIFF (n) *falaise (f)* : to fall off the cliff = *tomber du haut de la falaise* ⓪ slope = *pente*.

CLIMATE (n) *climat (m)* : a warm climate = *un climat chaud*.

CLIMAX (n, -es) *point (m) culminant* : the climax of his career = *le point culminant de sa carrière* = culmination ⓪ summit = *sommet*
to reach a climax = *avoir un orgasme*.

CLIMB (to, -ed) 1/ *grimper* : prices are climbing = *les prix grimpent* ⓪ to go up = *monter* 2/ *grimper* : to climb a tree = *grimper à un arbre* ⓪ to scale = *escalader*
to climb up ≠ **down (a ladder)** = *monter sur* ≠ *descendre d'(une échelle)*
to climb over (a wall) = *escalader (un mur)*.

CLINCH (to, -ed) *sceller* : to clinch a deal/an agreement = *sceller une affaire/un accord* ⓪ to settle = *régler*.

CLINCHER (n) *argument (m) massue* : the price was the clincher for buying the car = *le prix a été un argument massue pour l'achat de cette voiture* ⓪ deciding factor = *facteur décisif*.

CLINGING (adj) *collant, -e* : a clinging broad = *une nana collante* ⓪ leech = *sangsue*.

CLING TO (to, clung, clung) *se cramponner à* : she clings to her daughter = *elle se cramponne à sa fille* ⓞ to hang on to = *se raccrocher à.*

CLINIC (n) *clinique* (f) : she's in a private clinic = *elle est dans une clinique privée* ⓞ nursing home = *maison de santé.*

CLINICAL (adj) *froidement clinique* : don't be so clinical about love = *ne soyez pas si froidement clinique quand vous parlez d'amour.*

CLINK (n) **in the clink** = *au violon/à l'ombre* ⓞ behind bars = *derrière les barreaux,* in the can = *au gnouf.*

CLIP JOINT (n) *coup* (m) *de massue*: that restaurant's a clip joint = *ce restaurant, c'est le coup de massue* ⓞ tourist trap = *piège à touristes.*

CLIPPING (n) *coupure* (f) *de presse* = cutting (GB).

CLIQUE (n) *clique* (f) : snooty clique = *une clique de snobinards* ⓞ group = *groupe.*

CLITORIS (n) *clitoris* (m) ⓞ clit = *bouton.*

CLOAK (n) *grande cape* (f) ⓞ coat = *manteau.*

CLOAK-AND-DAGGER (adj) *de cape et d'épée* : a cloak-and-dagger story/film = *un roman/film de cape et d'épée.*

CLOAKROOM (n) *vestiaire* (m) = checkroom.

CLOBBER (to, ed) **1/** *cogner* : the gang clobbered the guy = *le gang a cogné le type* → TO HIT ☠ *se cogner (la tête)* = to bump/ to bang (one's head) **2/** *enfoncer* : their team clobbered ours = *leur équipe a enfoncé la nôtre* ⓞ to lick = *flanquer une piquette à* ☠ *enfonce-toi ça dans la tête/le crâne !* = get that into your head !
— *s'enfoncer dans le crime* = to sink into crime.

CLOCK (n) *pendule* (f) (big), *réveil* (m) : I have to buy a clock = *il faut que j'achète un réveil* ⓞ cuckoo clock = *coucou,* alarm clock = *réveille-matin,* clock radio = *radio-réveil,* watch = *montre,* grandfather clock = *horloge,* little ≠ big hand = *petite* ≠ *grande aiguille*
to sleep (a)round the clock = *faire le tour du cadran* ≠ not to sleep a wink = *ne pas fermer l'œil de la nuit*
there's no turning the clock back = *on ne peut pas revenir en arrière*
(to work) around the clock = *(travailler) 24 heures sur 24*
☠ *à son réveil* = when he wakes up.

CLOCK (to, -ed) *chronométer* : to clock a runner = *chronométrer un coureur*
to clock in ≠ **out** = *pointer* : to clock in at 9 a.m. and clock out at 4 p.m. = *pointer à 9 heures du matin et à 4 heures du soir* ☠ → to point.

CLOCKWISE (adv) *dans le sens des aiguilles d'une montre* ≠ counterclockwise = *dans le sens contraire des aiguilles d'une montre.*

CLOCKWORK (n) **to go like clockwork** = *marcher comme sur des roulettes* : the holdup went like clockwork = *le hold-up a marché comme sur des roulettes* ≠ to backfire = *se retourner contre son auteur.*

CLONE (n) *clone* (m) : she's looking for the clone of her first husband = *elle cherche le clone de son premier mari* ⓞ carbon copy = *copie conforme.*

CLOSE (n) **to draw/come to a close** = *toucher à sa fin* ⓞ to draw to an end = *tirer à sa fin.*

CLOSE (adj, -r, -st) **1/** *proche* : a close relative = *un proche parent,* the restaurant's very close = *le restaurant est très proche,* we were very close = *nous étions très proches* ≠ faraway = *lointain*
at close quarters = *à l'étroit*
to have a close brush with death = *frôler la mort*
it was a close call = *c'était de justesse*
very close friends = *amis intimes*
it was a close shave = *il était moins une* ⓞ it was a narrow escape = *on l'a échappé belle,* it was a near miss = *on a eu chaud*
2/ *serré, -e* : a close race/election = *une course/élection serrée* ☠ → tight.

CLOSE (adv) *près* : she lives close = *elle habite près* = she lives near ⓞ close by = *près d'ici*
to come close = *faillir* : he came close to winning = *il a failli gagner* = he almost won.

CLOSE (to, -d) *fermer* : close the door = *fermez la porte* = shut the door ☠ *ferme-la !* = shut up !
to close in on = *resserrer les mailles du filet autour de* : the cops are closing in on the gang = *les flics resserrent les mailles du filet autour du gang* ⓞ to make it hot for = *rendre la vie dure à*
to be closed to (new ideas) = *être fermé aux (idées nouvelles)*
to close up/down = *fermer (ses portes)* : the store closed up/down after two months = *le magasin a fermé ses portes au bout de deux mois* ≠ to open up = *ouvrir (ses portes)*
to close with = *terminer sur* : he closed his speech with a quotation = *il a terminé son discours sur une citation.*

CLOSED (adj) **closed hearing** = *huis clos*
closed session = *séance/audience à huis clos.*

CLOSEFISTED (adj) *près de ses sous* = tightfisted.

CLOSELY (adv) **to look at stg closely** = *regarder qqch de près*
we're closely related = *nous sommes proches parents.*

CLOSER (comp adj, adv) *le plus près* : who lives closer ? = *qui habite le plus près ?* = who lives nearer ?

CLOSEST (superl adj) *le, la plus proche* : she's my closest friend = *c'est mon amie la plus proche*, which bank is closest ? = *quelle est la banque la plus proche ?*

CLOSET (n) *placard (m)* : hang your coat in the closet = *mettez votre manteau dans le placard*
to come out of the closet = *sortir de l'ombre* : homosexuals are coming out of the closet = *les homosexuels sortent de l'ombre.*

CLOSET (adj) *honteux, -euse, non avoué, -e* : a closet homosexual = *un homosexuel honteux*
a closet communist = *un cryptocommuniste*
☠ → shameful.

CLOSE TO (prep) **1/** *près de* : sit close to me = *asseyez-vous près de moi* = near ≠ far from = *loin de* **2/** *au bord de* : close to tears = *au bord des larmes* = on the verge of tears.

CLOSE-UP (n) *gros plan (m)* : a close-up of her face = *un gros plan de son visage* ≠ full-length = *en pied.*

CLOTHES (n pl) *vêtements (m pl)*, *fringues (f pl)* (LV) : she wears expensive clothes = *elle porte des vêtements chers/des fringues chères* ⊙ apparel = *habillement*, duds = *frusques*
clothes don't make the man = *l'habit ne fait pas le moine.*

CLOTHESHORSE (n) *gravure (f) de mode* : his new wife's a real clotheshorse = *sa nouvelle femme est une véritable gravure de mode.*

CLOTHING (n inv) *vêtements (m pl)* : they gave the refugees food and clothing = *ils ont donné de la nourriture et des vêtements aux réfugiés* = clothes
a piece of clothing = *un vêtement.*

CLOUD (n) *nuage (m)* : clouds in the sky = *des nuages dans le ciel* ⊙ fog = *brouillard*, mist = *brume*
to be in the clouds = *être dans les nuages/dans la lune* ⊙ to daydream = *rêvasser*
every cloud has a silver lining = *à quelque chose malheur est bon*
to be on cloud nine = *être aux anges* ⊙ to be in seventh heaven = *être au septième ciel*
☠ *un nuage de (lait)* = a speck of (milk).

CLOUD OVER (to, -ed) *se couvrir* : the weather's clouding over = *le temps se couvre* ≠ to clear up = *s'éclaircir*
☠ → to cover.

CLOUDY (adj, -ier, -iest) *nuageux, -euse* : a cloudy sky = *un ciel nuageux* ⊙ overcast = *couvert*, misty = *brumeux.*

CLOUT (n inv) **to have** ≠ **not to have clout** = *peser* ≠ *ne pas peser lourd* : women don't have political clout = *les femmes ne pèsent pas lourd politiquement.*

CLOWN (n) *clown (m)* ⊙ buffoon = *bouffon.*

CLOWN AROUND (to, -ed) *faire le clown* ⊙ to horse around = *faire l'andouille.*

CLUB (n) **1/** *club (m)* : private club = *club privé* ⊙ club-house = ←
a club sandwich = *un sandwich club à deux étages*
join the club ! = *tu n'es pas le seul !* : you've had an abortion, join the club ! = *tu t'es fait avorter, tu n'es pas la seule !*
2/ *massue (f)*, *matraque (f)* : the cop was carrying a club = *le flic portait une matraque* ⊙ bludgeon = *gourdin.*

CLUE (n) *indice (m)* : the cops have a clue = *les flics ont un indice* ⊙ tip = *tuyau*
I don't have a clue = *je n'en ai pas la moindre idée* = I don't have the slightest idea
☠ *indice (des prix)* = (cost of living) index.

CLUE IN (to, -d) *mettre au parfum* : I can't imagine why they got divorced, clue me in = *je n'arrive pas à comprendre pourquoi ils ont divorcé, mets-moi au parfum* ⊙ fill me in = *affranchis-moi.*

CLUMSY (adj, -ier, -iest) *gauche* : a clumsy guy/excuse = *un type/une excuse gauche* ⊙ fumbling = *emprunté* ≠ graceful = *gracieux* ☠ → left.

CLUTCH (n) *embrayage (m)* ⊙ brake = *frein*
to fall into s.o.'s clutches = *tomber sous la griffe de qqn.*

CLUTCH (to, -ed) *s'agripper à* : to clutch the railing/the child = *s'agripper à la rampe/à l'enfant* ⊙ to grab = *empoigner.*

CLUTTERED (adj) *encombré, -e* : a cluttered table = *une table encombrée* ☠ *rues encombrées* = streets jammed with cars.

CO. (abbr) = COMPANY.

COACH (n, -es) **1/** *carrosse (m)* : Cinderella's coach = *le carrosse de Cendrillon* ⊙ stagecoach = *diligence* **2/** (GB) *car (m)* = bus **3/** *coach (m, f)* (cinema), *entraîneur, -euse* : a baseball coach = *un entraîneur de base-ball* ☠ *une entraîneuse (boîte de nuit)* = a B-girl.

COAGULATE (to, -d) *coaguler* ⊙ to curdle = *cailler.*

COAL (n) *charbon (m)* : tons of coal = *des tonnes de charbon* ⊙ mine = ←, soot = *suie*
to haul/take s.o. over the coals = *passer un savon à qqn* → TO LAMBAST
to bring/carry coals to Newcastle = *porter de l'eau à la rivière* ⊙ to waste one's time = *perdre son temps*
☠ *être sur des charbons ardents* = to be on pins and needles.

COALITION (n) *coalition (f)* : a coalition government = *un gouvernement de coalition* ⊙ alliance = ←.

COARSE (adj, -r, -st) *grossier, -ère* : coarse language = *langage grossier* ⊙ vulgar = *vulgaire* ≠ refined = *raffiné*
☠ *des enfants grossiers* = rude children

— *une erreur grossière* = a blatant mistake
— *ne sois pas si grossier* = don't be so rude
— *dessin grossier* = crude drawing.

COAST (n) *côte* (f) : we drove to the coast = *on est allé en voiture jusqu'à la côte* ① shore = *rivage*
coast guard = *garde-côte*
from coast to coast = *d'une côte à l'autre*
the coast is clear = *on a le champ libre*
☠ *une côte (corps)* = a rib
— *se tenir les côtes* = to split one's sides laughing
— *côte de porc/d'agneau* = pork/lamb chop
— *côte à côte* = side by side.

COAST ALONG (to, -ed) *laisser aller les choses* : I'm just coasting along waiting to see what will happen = *je laisse aller les choses pour voir ce qui va se passer* ① to take it easy = *ne pas s'en faire*.

COAT (n) 1/ *manteau* (m) : put on your coat = *mettez votre manteau* ① raincoat = *imperméable*, overcoat = *pardessus*, poncho = ←, lined = *doublé*, furlined = *fourré* ☠ *sous le manteau* = secretely 2/ *couche* (f) : two coats of polish = *deux couches de vernis* = two layers of polish ☠ → diaper.

COAX (to, -ed) **to coax s.o. to** = *insister gentiment pour que* : we had to coax him to make him come to our party = *il a fallu que nous insistions gentiment pour qu'il vienne à notre soirée.*

COCAINE (n) *cocaïne* (f) ① drugs = *de la drogue*, snow = *neige.*

COCK (n) *queue* (f) : a little ≠ big cock = *une petite ≠ grosse queue* ① tool = *instrument*, rod = *pine*, pecker = *dard*, prick = *bite*, whang = *quéquette*, dick = *braquemard* ≠ cunt = *chatte* ☠ → tail
cock sucker = *sale con* → BASTARD.

COCK-A-DOODLE-DOO (n) *cocorico* (m).

COCK-AND-BULL STORY (n, -ies) *histoire* (f) *à dormir debout.*

COCKEYED (adj) *maboul*, -e : you're cockeyed ! = *t'es maboul !* → CRAZY.

COCKER SPANIEL (n) *cocker* (m) ① dog = *chien.*

COCKROACH (n, -es) *cafard* (m) : the room was full of cockroaches = *la pièce était remplie de cafards* ① vermin = *vermine* ☠ *avoir le cafard* = to be blue.

COCKSURE (adj) *trop sûr*, -e : cocksure of himself = *trop sûr de lui* ≠ unsure = *pas sûr.*

COCKTAIL (n) *cocktail* (m) : do you want a cocktail ? = *voulez-vous un cocktail ?*
Molotov cocktail = *cocktail Molotov*
a cocktail party = *un cocktail.*

COCKY (adj, -ier, -iest) *puant*, -e : he's pretentious and cocky = *il est prétentieux et puant* ① arrogant = ← ☠ *odeur puante* = stinking smell.

COCONUT (n) *noix* (f) *de coco* : coconut ice cream = *glace à la noix de coco* ① mango = *mangue.*

C.O.D. (abbr) = Cash On Delivery = *payable à la livraison.*

CODE (n) *code* (m) : to break a code = *déchiffrer un code* ① rule = *règle* ☠ *code civil* = common law.

COED (n) *étudiante* (f) : he's making it with a young coed = *il se tape une jeune étudiante.*

CO-ED (adj) **co-ed schools** = *écoles mixtes* = co-educational schools.

COERCE INTO (to, -d) *contraindre à/de* : he was coerced into paying blackmail = *il a été contraint à/de céder au chantage* = he was compelled to pay blackmail.

COEXIST (to, -ed) *coexister* **COEXISTENCE** (n) *coexistence* (f).

COFFEE (n inv) *café* (m) : do you want a coffee ? = *est-ce que vous voulez un café ?* ① tea = *thé*, cream = *crème*, coffeepot = *cafetière*, percolator = *percolateur*
coffee break = *pause café*
coffee klatch = *causerie*
coffee shop = *café* : we'll eat lunch in a coffee shop = *nous déjeunerons dans un café*
black ≠ white coffee = *café noir ≠ crème*
coffee table = *table basse.*

COFFIN (n) *cercueil* (m) : the body's in the coffin = *le corps est dans le cercueil* = casket ① bier = *bière*, corpse = *cadavre.*

COG (n) **to be a cog in the wheel** = *n'être qu'un rouage (de la machine).*

COHERENT (adj) *cohérent*, -e : his speech wasn't coherent = *son discours n'était pas cohérent* ① clear = *clair* ≠ incoherent = *incohérent* ☠ *vous n'êtes pas cohérent* = you're not being consistent.

COHESION (n) *cohésion* (f).

COIN (n) *pièce* (f) *(de monnaie)* : a few coins for the tip = *quelques pièces de monnaie pour le pourboire* ① change = *monnaie* ☠ → room
to toss/flip a coin = *jouer à pile ou face.*

COINCIDE (to, -d) *coïncider* : his birthday coincides with mine = *son anniversaire coïncide avec le mien* ≠ to diverge = *diverger.*

COINCIDENCE (n) *coïncidence* (f) : what a coincidence ! = *quelle coïncidence !* ① change = *hasard.*

COINCIDENTAL (adj) *de/une pure coïncidence* : it was coincidental that we both were in the same hotel = *c'était une pure coïncidence de se retrouver tous les deux dans le même hôtel* ≠ intentional = *intentionnel*
COINCIDENTALLY (adv) *par (pure) coïncidence.*

COLD (n) *froid (m)* : we had to wait in the cold = *il a fallu que nous attendions dans le froid*

to have a cold = *avoir un rhume/être enrhumé* ⓪ to have the sniffles = *avoir la goutte au nez*, to have a sore throat = *avoir mal à la gorge*	**to leave s.o. out in the cold** = *laisser qqn en rade* ⓪ to leave s.o. high and dry = *laisser qqn en plan*
☠ *ça me fait froid dans le dos* = it gives me the shivers — *elle n'a pas froid aux yeux* = she's gutsy	— *nous sommes en froid* = we're not on speaking terms — *jeter un froid dans* = to put a damper on.

COLD (adj, -er, -est) **1/** *froid, -e* : cold weather = *temps froid* ⓪ ice-cold = *glacial*, chilly = *frisquet* ≠ sweltering = *étouffant* **2/** *froid, -e* : a cold personality = *une personnalité froide* ≠ warm = *chaleureux* ☠ *garder la tête froide* = to keep one's head

to be cold = *avoir froid* : I'm cold, are you ? = *j'ai froid, et vous ?* **to be a cold potato** = *être aimable comme une porte de prison* **to be out cold** = *être dans les vapes* ⓪ to pass out = *tomber dans les pommes* **to break out in a cold sweat** = *avoir des sueurs froides* ⓪ to be scared stiff = *ne pas en mener large*	**cold cuts** = *assiette anglaise* **a cold fish** = *un pisse-froid* **cold turkey** = *le fait de décrocher brutalement (drogue)* : when he gave up drugs, he did it cold turkey = *quand il a arrêté la drogue, il a décroché brutalement* ⓪ to have a monkey on one's back = *être en état de dépendance* **to get cold feet** = *se dégonfler* : he was going to ask for a raise but got cold feet = *il allait*	demander une augmentation mais il s'est dégonflé = to chicken out **to give s.o. the cold shoulder** = *recevoir qqn comme un chien dans un jeu de quilles* = to cold-shoulder s.o. ⓪ to give s.o. the brush-off = *envoyer bouler qqn* **it's colder than a witch's tit** = *on se caille les miches* **(to kill s.o.) in cold blood** = *(tuer qqn) de sang-froid.*

COLD-BLOODED (adj) *de sang-froid* : a cold-blooded murder = *un meurtre commis de sang-froid.*

COLDLY (adv) *froidement* : to answer coldly = *répondre froidement.*

COLESLAW (n) *salade (f) de chou cru* ⓪ Waldorf salad = *salade de céleri, pommes et noix.*

COLLABORATE (to, -d) *collaborer* : to collaborate with the enemy = *collaborer avec l'ennemi* ⓪ to cooperate = *coopérer* **COLLABORATION** (n) *collaboration (f).*

COLLABORATOR (n) **1/** *collaborateur, -trice* : she's his close collaborator = *c'est sa proche collaboratrice* ⓪ colleague = *collègue* **2/** *collaborateur, -trice, collabo (m, f)* : collaborators were tried at the end of the war = *les collaborateurs/les collabos ont été jugés à la fin de la guerre* ⓪ informer = *indicateur.*

COLLAPSE (n) *effondrement (m)* : the collapse of the dollar/the ceiling = *l'effondrement du dollar/du plafond* ⓪ caving-in = *écroulement* ☠ → crack-up.

COLLAPSE (to, -d) **1/** *s'effondrer* : he collapsed when he heard the news = *il s'est effondré en apprenant la nouvelle* ⓪ to fall apart = *s'écrouler* **2/** *s'effondrer* : the bridge collapsed = *le pont s'est effondré* ⓪ to cave in = *s'écrouler.*

COLLAR (n) **1/** *col (m)* : lipstick on his collar = *du rouge à lèvres sur son col* ⓪ neck = *cou* ☠ *col roulé* = turtleneck **2/** *collier (m)* : to put a collar on a dog = *mettre un collier à un chien* ☠ *un collier (bijou)* = a necklace.

COLLATERAL (n) *nantissement (m)* : he gave his stocks as collateral = *il a donné ses actions comme nantissement.*

COLLEAGUE (n) *collègue (m, f)* ⓪ fellow-worker = *camarade de travail.*

COLLECT (to, -ed) **1/** *collectionner* : to collect stamps = *collectionner les timbres* **2/** *recueillir* (funds), *ramasser* (garbage) : to collect information/funds = *recueillir des informations/des fonds*, garbage is collected at 6 a.m. = *les ordures sont ramassées à 6 heures du matin* ≠ to distribute = *distribuer*
the collected works of = *les œuvres complètes de* ☠ *se recueillir devant une tombe* = to pay one's last respects to s.o.
— *recueillir qqn* = to give shelter to s.o.
— *ramasser qqch par terre* = to pick up stg
— *ramasser du fric* = to take in money.

COLLECTION (n) *collection (f)* : a stamp collection = *une collection de timbres*
to take up a collection = *faire une quête/collecte.*

COLLECTIVE (adj) *collectif, -ive* : collective work = *travail collectif*
collective bargaining = *négociations syndicales.*

COLLECTOR (n) *collectionneur, -euse* : a collector of antique cars = *un collectionneur de vieilles voitures.*

COLLEGE (n) *faculté (f), fac (f)* (premières années) ⦿ university = *université*, BA = *licence*, MA = *maîtrise*, major ≠ minor = *matière principale* ≠ *secondaire* ☠ *faculté* → faculty
— *un collège* = a high school.

COLLIDE (to, -d) *entrer en collision* : the cars collided = *les voitures sont entrées en collision*
to collide with = *rentrer dans* : the truck collided with a car = *le camion est rentré dans une voiture* ⦿ to bash into = *heurter.*

COLLIE (n) *colley (m)* ⦿ dog = *chien.*

COLLISION (n) *collision (f)* : a car collision = *une collision entre voitures* ⦿ accident = ←.

COLLOQUIAL (adj) *familier, -ère* : a colloquial expression = *une expression familière* ☠ → familiar **COLLO-QUIALISM** (n) *expression (f) familière* ⦿ slang = *argot* **COLLOQUIALLY** (adv) *familièrement.*

COLLUSION (n) **in collusion with (the Mafia)** = *de mèche/d'intelligence avec (la Mafia).*

COLON (n) *deux-points (m inv)* ⦿ comma = *virgule.*

COLONEL (n) *colonel (m)* ⦿ lieutenant = ←, general = *général.*

COLONIST (n) *colon (m)* ⦿ colonial = ←.

COLONIZATION (n) *colonisation (f)* **COLONIZE** (to, -d) *coloniser* **COLONIZER** (n) *colonisateur, -trice.*

COLONY (n, -ies) *colonie (f)* : the English colonies = *les colonies anglaises* ☠ *colonie de vacances* = summer camp.

COLOR (n) *couleur (f)* : I like solid colors = *j'aime les couleurs unies* = colour (GB) ⦿ hue = *teinte*, pastel = ←, color-blind = *daltonien*

auburn = ←	*marine*
beige = ←	**orange** = ←
black = *noir*	**pink** = *rose*
blue = *bleu*	**purple** = *pourpre*
brown = *marron*	**red** = *rouge*
gray = *gris*	**violet** = ←
green = *vert*	**white** = *blanc*
navy blue = *bleu*	**yellow** = *jaune*

---

to succeed with flying colors = *réussir brillamment* ≠ to fall on one's face = *se casser la figure*

☠ *la couleur d'un journal* = the slant of a newspaper
— *annoncer la couleur* = to put one's cards on the table.

COLOR (to, -ed) *fausser* : his opinions are colored by his racism = *ses opinions sont faussées par son racisme* ☠ → to twist.

COLORED (adj) *teint, -e* : colored hair = *des cheveux teints*
colored people = *les gens de couleur* ⦿ black = *Noir*, mulatto = *mulâtre.*

COLORFUL (adj) *coloré, -e* (dress), *haut, -e en couleur* (personality) ≠ drab = *terne.*

COLOSSAL (adj) *colossal, -e* : a colossal mistake = *une erreur colossale* ⦿ gigantic = *gigantesque* ≠ tiny = *minuscule.*

COLOSSUS (n, -i or -es) *colosse (m)* ⦿ giant = *géant.*

COLUMN (n) **1/** *colonne (f)* : spinal column = *colonne vertébrale* **2/** *rubrique (f), chronique (f)* : sports column = *rubrique/chronique sportive.*

COLUMNIST (n) *chroniqueur, -euse* : Will is a well-known columnist = *Will est un chroniqueur célèbre.*

COMA (n) *coma (m)* : in a coma = *dans le coma* ⦿ critical condition = *état critique.*

COMB (n) *peigne (m)* : I lost my comb = *j'ai perdu mon peigne* ☠ *sale comme un peigne* = filthy dirty.

COMB (to, -ed) **1/** *peigner* : to comb one's hair = *se peigner les cheveux* ⦿ to tease = *crêper* **2/** *ratisser* : to comb an area = *ratisser un secteur* ⦿ to scour the countryside = *battre campagne.*

COMBAT (n) *combat (m)* : armed combat = *combat armé* ⦿ battle = *bataille.*

COMBINATION (n) *combinaison (f)* : the winning combination = *la combinaison gagnante*
☠ *ta combinaison dépasse* = your slip's showing
— *combinaison (travail)* = overalls
— *une combinaison louche* = a fishy scheme.

COMBINE (to, -d) *combiner* : brunch combines breakfast and lunch = *le brunch combine le petit déjeuner et le déjeuner* ⦿ to join = *joindre* ≠ to separate = *séparer*
☠ *combiner qqch pour sauver les otages* = to contrive a way to save the hostages.

COME (to, came, come) **1/** *venir* : when will you come ? = *quand viendrez-vous ?* ⓪ to show up = *se pointer* ≠ to go away = *s'en aller* ☠ *venir de* = to have just (*il vient de partir* = he (has) just left) **2/** *jouir* : I came the first time we made love = *j'ai joui la première fois que nous avons fait l'amour* ⓪ to have an orgasm = *avoir un orgasme*

☠ *jouir de la vie* = to enjoy life	— *jouir d'un privilège* = to benefit from a privilege

come and get it ! = *à table !*
come, come ! = *allons, allons !* → GOSH !
coming ! = *j'arrive !*
if it comes to that (I'll split) = *si on en arrive là (je me tire)*
to come = *à venir* : in the years to come = *dans les années à venir*, the best ≠ worst is yet to come = *le meilleur ≠ le pire reste à venir* ⓪ coming = *qui vient*
to come across as (shy) = *donner l'impression d'être (timide)*

to come and go = *aller et venir* : men come and go in her life = *les hommes vont et viennent dans sa vie*
to come running = *accourir*
to come to pass = *se concrétiser* ⓪ to come off = *se faire*
come to think of it (I'm getting paid tomorrow) = *maintenant que j'y pense (je vais être payé demain)*
(the knot/package) came undone = *(le nœud/le paquet) s'est défait*

to come about = *arriver* : how did the accident come about ? = *comment l'accident est-il arrivé ?* ⓪ to happen = *se passer* ☠ → to arrive
to come across = 1/ *tomber sur* : I came across some old letters = *je suis tombé sur de vieilles lettres* ⓪ to unearth = *déterrer* 2/ *passer* : she doesn't come across well on TV = *elle ne passe pas bien à la télé* ☠ → to pass 3/ *passer* : he tried to explain what he was doing but it didn't come across = *il a essayé d'expliquer ce qu'il faisait, mais le message n'est pas passé* ☠ → to pass
to come along = 1/ *avancer* : how are things coming along ? = *est-ce que ça avance ?* ☠ → to advance 2/ *venir (avec nous)* : we're going to the movies, do you want to come along ? = *nous allons au cinéma, est-ce que tu veux venir (avec nous) ?*
to come apart = *s'effondrer* : his alibi's coming apart = *son alibi s'effondre* = to collapse ≠ to hold up = *tenir*
to come (a)round to = 1/ *se ranger à* : he came around to my point of view = *il s'est rangé à mon avis* 2/ *venir* : why don't you come around to our place tonight ? = *pourquoi ne venez-vous pas à la maison ce soir ?*
to come at = *avancer vers* : the mugger came at me with a knife

= *mon agresseur s'est avancé vers moi avec un couteau* ⓪ to attack = *attaquer*
to come away (with the feeling that) = *rester (sur l'impression que)*
to come back = *revenir* : I'll come back early = *je reviendrai de bonne heure* ⓪ to go back = *retourner*
☠ *il est revenu sur (sa déclaration)* = he took back (his statement)
— *je n'en reviens pas !* = I can't get over it !
— *revenir à soi* = to come to
— *il a une tête qui ne me revient pas* = I can't take him
— *revenir à (son propriétaire)* = to revert to (one's owner)
it comes back to me now = *ça me revient maintenant*
to come before = 1/ *venir avant* : Monday comes before Tuesday = *lundi vient avant mardi* ≠ to come after = *venir après*, to follow = *suivre* 2/ *passer devant* : the abortion bill will come before Congress in the fall = *le projet de loi sur l'avortement passera devant le Congrès en automne* 3/ *passer avant* : her kids come before her husband = *ses gosses passent avant son mari*
to come between = *se mettre entre* : the kids came between them = *les gosses se sont mis entre eux*

to come by = *passer* : I'll be home later if you want to come by = *si vous voulez passer, je serai à la maison plus tard* ⓪ to visit = *rendre visite à* ☠ → to pass
to come down = 1/ *descendre* : he'll come down later = *il descendra tout à l'heure* ☠ → to descend 2/ *se dégriser* : with the press he got it'll take him time to come down = *il a eu des critiques tellement bonnes qu'il va lui falloir un certain temps pour se dégriser* 3/ *tomber des cordes* : take your umbrella, it's coming down ! = *prenez votre parapluie, il tombe des cordes !* ⓪ to rain = *pleuvoir* 4/ *baisser* : prices are coming down = *les prix baissent* ☠ → to lower 5/ *décompresser* : it took the hostages a long time to come down = *il a fallu longtemps aux otages pour décompresser*
to come down on s.o. = *s'en prendre à qqn* : the boss came down on his secretary for the mistake = *le patron s'en est pris à sa secrétaire pour l'erreur commise* → TO LAMBAST
it comes down to = *ça se réduit à* : it comes down to two alternatives = *ça se réduit à deux possibilités* ⓪ to amount to = *se résumer à*
when it comes down to it = *tout compte fait* : when it comes down to it, America's still a

great country = *tout compte fait, l'Amérique reste un pays formidable* ⓪ ultimately = *en fin de compte*

to come down with (pneumonia) = *être atteint de (pneumonie)* ⓪ to catch = *attraper*

to come from = *venir de* : she comes from Europe = *elle vient d'Europe* ⓪ to originate from = *être originaire de*

to come in = 1/ *entrer* : come in ! = *entrez !* ☠ → to enter 2/ *entrer en jeu* : that's where you come in = *c'est là que vous entrez en jeu* 3/ *exister en* : the car comes in brown = *la voiture existe en marron*

to come into (a lot of money) = *hériter de (beaucoup d'argent)* = to inherit (a lot of money) ≠ to leave = *laisser*

to come of stg = *donner* : what came of it ? = *qu'est-ce que ça a donné ?*, nothing came of it = *ça n'a rien donné* ☠ → to give

to come off = 1/ *partir* : the spots won't come off = *les taches ne partiront pas* ☠ → to leave 2/ *se faire* : the deal didn't come off = *l'affaire ne s'est pas faite* ⓪ to pan out = *se concrétiser* ☠ → to do

come off it ! = *allons, allons !*

to come on = 1/ *avancer* : how's your work coming on ? = *est-ce que votre travail avance ?* = how's your work coming along ? ☠ → to advance 2/ *donner l'impression* : he comes on really sure of himself = *il donne l'impression d'être vraiment sûr de lui*

come on ! = *allez !* : come on, hurry up ! = *allez, dépêche-toi !*

to come out = 1/ *sortir* : the book will come out next year = *le livre sortira l'année prochaine* ⓪ to publish = *éditer* ☠ → to go out 2/ *faire ses débuts dans le monde* : my sister's coming out next month = *ma sœur fera ses débuts dans le monde le mois*

prochain ⓪ a debutante = *une débutante* 3/ *partir* : this spot will never come out = *cette tache ne partira jamais* ☠ → to leave 4/ *sortir de l'ombre* : homosexuals are finally able to come out = *les homosexuels peuvent enfin sortir de l'ombre*

to come out for ≠ **against** = *se prononcer pour* ≠ *contre* : the Senator came out for ≠ against the bill = *le sénateur s'est prononcé pour* ≠ *contre le projet de loi*

to come out with = *sortir* : you never know what kids will come out with = *on ne sait jamais ce que les gosses vont vous sortir* ☠ → to go out

to come over = 1/ *venir* : do you want to come over tonight ? = *est-ce que vous voulez venir ce soir ?* 2/ *passer* : she comes over well on television = *elle passe bien à la télévision* ☠ → to pass

(I don't know) what came over him = *(je ne sais pas) ce qui lui a pris*

to come through = 1/ *tenir* : he promised but didn't come through = *il a promis mais il n'a pas tenu* ⓪ to keep one's word = *tenir parole* ☠ → to hold 2/ *se réaliser* : he was promised a better job, but it didn't come through = *on lui avait promis un meilleur poste, mais ça ne s'est pas réalisé* ⓪ to come off = *se faire* ☠ → to realize

to come to = 1/ *arriver à* : to come to an agreement/a decision = *arriver à un accord/une décision* 2/ *revenir à soi* : she fainted but came to very quickly = *elle s'est évanouie, mais elle est très vite revenue à elle* ≠ to pass out = *tomber dans les pommes* 3/ *venir à* : will you come to our party ? = *est-ce que vous viendrez à notre soirée ?* 4/ *donner* : his idea came to nothing = *son idée n'a rien donné* ⓪ to work

= *marcher* ☠ → to give 5/ *se chiffrer à* : the bill comes to $ 100 = *la facture se chiffre à 100 dollars* = the bill adds up to $ 100

when it comes to (music, they're the best in town) = *pour ce qui est de (la musique, c'est la meilleure adresse de la ville)*

to come up = 1/ *monter* : do you want to come up for a few minutes ? = *tu veux monter quelques minutes ?* ≠ to come down = *descendre* ☠ → to rise 2/ *venir sur le tapis* : that question will come up next week = *cette question viendra sur le tapis la semaine prochaine* 3/ *se présenter* : let me know if the problem comes up again = *faites-moi savoir si le problème se présente à nouveau* ⓪ to crop up = *survenir* ☠ → to present

to come up against (difficulties) = *buter sur (des difficultés)* ⓪ to run up against = *se heurter à*

to come up to = 1/ *être à la hauteur de* : his work doesn't come up to his brother's = *son travail n'est pas à la hauteur de celui de son frère* ⓪ not to hold a candle to = *ne pas arriver à la cheville de* 2/ *arriver à* : my guy's very short, he comes up to my shoulders = *mon mec est très petit, il m'arrive à l'épaule* 3/ *aborder* : a stranger came up to me = *un étranger m'a abordé* ☠ → to broach

to come up with = *trouver* : we came up with a good idea = *nous avons trouvé une bonne idée* ⓪ to dream up = *échafauder* ☠ → to find

to come with = *être servi avec* : what comes with the fish ? = *qu'est-ce qui est servi/ qu'est-ce qu'on sert avec le poisson ?* = what's the fish served with ?

COMEBACK (n) **1/** come-back (m), rentrée (f) (sur scène) : to make one's comeback = *faire sa rentrée/son come-back*
☠ *la rentrée des classes* = the reopening of school (in the fall)

— *avoir une rentrée d'argent* = to have money coming in
2/ *réplique* (f) : his comeback was quick and sarcastic = *sa réplique a été rapide et sarcastique* ⓪ riposte = ←
☠ *réplique (théâtre)* = line
— *réplique (d'un tableau)* = replica (of a picture).

COMEDIAN (n) *comique (m, f)* : the Marx Brothers were great comedians = *les Marx Brothers étaient de grands comiques* = comic ⓓ humorist = *humoriste* ☠ *un comédien* = an actor.

COMEDOWN (n) *régression (f)* : what a comedown for her to play a bit part after years of being a star = *quelle régression pour elle de jouer les utilités après avoir été une vedette pendant des années* ⓓ setback = *recul.*

COMEDY (n, -ies) *comédie (f)* : the play's a comedy = *la pièce est une comédie* ≠ tragedy = *tragédie*
comedy of errors = *malheureux concours de circonstances*
cut the comedy ! = *arrête ta comédie !/ton cirque !* → BUZZ OFF !
☠ *c'est de la comédie* = it's all an act
— *c'est toujours la même comédie* = it's always the same old story.

COME-ON (n) *appât (m)* : the offer of free tickets was just a come-on to make people come = *cette offre de billets gratuits n'était qu'un appât pour faire venir les gens* ⓓ trick = *piège* ☠ → bait.

COMEUPPANCE (n) **to get one's comeuppance** = *récolter ce qu'on a semé* ⓓ it served him right = *il l'a bien mérité.*

COMFORT (n) 1/ *confort (m)* : to like comfort = *aimer le confort* 2/ *réconfort (m)* : it's a comfort to know you care = *c'est un réconfort de savoir que vous vous sentez concernés* ⓓ solace = *consolation* **COMFORT** (to, -ed) *réconforter.*

COMFORTABLE (adj) 1/ *confortable* : a comfortable armchair = *un fauteuil confortable* ⓓ comfy = *douillet* ≠ uncomfortable = *inconfortable*
to feel comfortable with (one's in-laws) = *se sentir bien avec (ses beaux-parents)* ⓓ to feel at ease with = *se sentir à l'aise avec*
make yourself comfortable = *mettez-vous à l'aise* ⓓ make yourself at home = *faites comme chez vous*
2/ *à l'aise* : his inheritance left them quite comfortable = *son héritage les a mis à l'aise* → RICH.

COMFORTING (adj) *réconfortant, -e* : comforting news = *des nouvelles réconfortantes* ≠ unsettling = *déconcertant.*

COMIC (n) *comique (m, f)* = comedian ⓓ a fun guy = *un amuseur.*

COMIC (adj) *comique* : a comic act = *un numéro comique* ≠ dramatic = *dramatique*
comic book = *illustré*
comic strip = *bande dessinée*
to provide comic relief = *détendre l'atmosphère.*

COMICAL (adj) *cocasse* : it was comical to see the dog dressed up as a clown = *c'était cocasse de voir le chien déguisé en clown* ⓓ laughable = *risible*, droll = *rigolo.*

COMICS (n pl) *bandes (f pl) dessinées* ⓓ funnies = *B.D.*, caption = *légende*, balloon = *bulle.*

COMING (adj) *qui vient* : this coming Tuesday = *le mardi qui vient* ⓓ next = *prochain.*

COMMA (n) *virgule (f)* ⓓ semicolon = *point-virgule.*

COMMAND (n) **to obey commands** = *obéir aux ordres*
to take command = *prendre le commandement*
a good command of (Russian) = *une bonne maîtrise du (russe)*
who's in command ? = *qui commande ?* ⓓ who's at the helm ? = *qui est à la barre ?*
☠ *passer une commande* = to place an order
— *aux commandes (avion)* = at the controls (plane)
— *commande à distance* = remote control.

COMMAND (to, -ed) *commander* : he commands the first regiment = *il commande le premier régiment*
☠ *j'ai déjà commandé* = I've already ordered
— *le gouvernement a commandé la statue* = the government commissioned the statue.

COMMANDER (n) *commandant (m)* : the commander in chief = *le commandant en chef* ⓓ officer = *officier.*

COMMANDO (n, -es) *commando (m)* : the commando took five hostages = *le commando a pris cinq otages.*

COMMEMORATE (to, -d) *commémorer* ⓓ to honor = honorer **COMMEMORATION** (n) *commémoration (f).*

COMMENCEMENT (n) **commencement day** = *jour de la remise des diplômes.*

COMMEND (to, -ed) *faire l'éloge de* : he commended his staff for their help = *il a fait l'éloge de son équipe pour l'aide qu'elle lui avait apportée* ≠ to run down = *dénigrer.*

COMMENDABLE (adj) *digne d'éloge* : commendable behavior = *conduite digne d'éloge* ≠ shameful = *honteuse.*

COMMENT (n) *commentaire (m)* : I didn't ask for your comments = *je me passe de tes commentaires* ⓓ observation = ←
no comment ! = 1/ *sans commentaire !* 2/ *je n'ai rien à déclarer !*
☠ → commentary.

COMMENT (to, -ed) **to comment on** = *faire des commentaires sur* : the doctor refused to comment on her disease = *le médecin a refusé de faire des commentaires sur sa maladie.*

COMMENTARY (n, -ies) *commentaire (m)* : instructive commentaries = *des commentaires instructifs* ☠ *sans commentaire !* = no comment ! **COMMENTATOR** (n) *commentateur, -trice.*

COMMERCE (n) *commerce (m)* : commerce with other countries = *le commerce avec les autres pays* ⓓ export = *exportation* ☠ « commerce » *est moins employé que* « trade ».

COMMERCIAL (n) *spot (m) publicitaire* : TV commercials = *spots publicitaires télévisés* ⓪ advertising = *publicité.*

COMMERCIAL (adj) *commercial, -e* : a commercial film/failure = *un film/échec commercial* ≠ moneymaking = *rentable* ☠ *centre commercial* = shopping center.

COMMERCIALIZE (to, -d) *commercialiser* : pocket calculators have been widely commercialized = *les calculatrices de poche ont été commercialisées sur une grande échelle.*

COMMIE (n) *coco (m, f)* ⓪ a red = *un rouge.*

COMMISSION (n) **1/** *commission (f)* : a commission was appointed to investigate the situation = *une commission a été désignée pour analyser la situation* ⓪ delegation = *délégation* **2/** *commission (f)* : to work on a commission basis = *travailler à la commission*
out of commission = *hors d'état* : the car's out of commission = *la voiture est hors d'état* ⓪ out of order = *en panne*
☠ *faire les commissions* = to run errands
— *faire une commission à qqn* = to give s.o. a message.

COMMISSION (to, -ed) *commander* : the piece of sculpture was commissioned by the Mayor = *la sculpture a été commandée par le maire* ☠ → to command.

COMMIT (to, -ted) *commettre* : to commit a crime = *commettre un crime*
to be committed to (an asylum) = *être enfermé dans (un asile)*
to commit oneself = *s'engager* : the Senator refused to commit himself = *le sénateur a refusé de s'engager* ☠ → to engage
☠ *commettre sa réputation* = to endanger one's reputation
— *commettre une erreur* = to make a mistake.

COMMITMENT (n) *engagement (m)* : our commitment to developing countries = *notre engagement envers les pays en voie de développement* ☠ → engagement.

COMMITTEE (n) *comité (m)* : to form a committee = *former un comité* ⓪ commission = ←
to sit on a committee = *faire partie d'un comité.*

COMMODITY (n, -ies) *denrée (f)* : a nation with few commodities to export = *une nation qui a peu de denrées à exporter* ⓪ goods = *marchandises* ☠ *commodités de la vie moderne* = conveniences of modern life.

COMMON (n) **in common** = *en commun* : we have little in common = *nous avons peu de choses en commun.*

COMMON (adj) **1/** *courant, -e* : it's common to drink wine in France = *il est courant de boire du vin en France* ⓪ ordinary = *ordinaire* ≠ uncommon = *peu courant* ☠ → current **2/** *commun, -e* : his wife's very common = *sa femme est très commune* ≠ elegant = *élégante* **3/** *commun, -e* : we have a common history = *nous avons une histoire commune* ⓪ shared = *partagé*
common knowledge = *de notoriété publique*
common law = *droit coutumier*
the common man = *le commun des mortels* : is the common man racist ? = *est-ce que le commun des mortels est raciste ?*
Common Market = *Marché commun*
common sense = *sens commun/bon sens*
common stock = *action ordinaire* ≠ blue chip = *valeur sûre*
☠ *déclaration commune* = joint declaration
— *d'un commun accord* = unanimously.

COMMONER (n) *roturier, -ère* : the king married a commoner = *le roi a épousé une roturière* ≠ nobleman = *noble.*

COMMONLY (adv) *communément* : New York is commonly known as the Big Apple = *on surnomme communément New York la « Grosse Pomme »* ⓪ ordinarily = *ordinairement.*

COMMONPLACE (adj) **1/** *quelconque* : the restaurant was very commonplace = *le restaurant était très quelconque* → AWFUL **2/** *chose courante* : prostitution is commonplace everywhere = *la prostitution est partout chose courante* ⓪ pedestrian = *commun*
☠ *(prenez un exemple) quelconque* = (take) any (example)
— *elle est quelconque* = she's very plain/cheap.

COMMONWEALTH (n) *Commonwealth (m)* ⓪ British Empire = *l'Empire britannique.*

COMMOTION (n) *agitation (f)* : there was a tremendous commotion at the airport over the Pope's arrival = *il y avait une agitation fantastique à l'aéroport pour l'arrivée du pape* ⓪ uproar = *effervescence,* flap = *branle-bas*
to cause a commotion = *semer la perturbation* : her topless dress caused a commotion = *sa tenue topless a semé la perturbation*
☠ *commotion cérébrale* = (brain) concussion.

COMMUNE (n) *communauté (f)* : she's living in a Hare Krishna commune = *elle vit dans une communauté Hare Krishna* ⓪ sect = *secte* ☠ → community.

COMMUNICATE (to, -d) *communiquer* : when he gets angry, it's hard to communicate with him = *quand il est en colère, c'est dur de communiquer avec lui* ⓪ to transmit = *transmettre,* to impart = *faire part de* **COMMUNICATION** (n) *communication (f)* : there's a lack of communication between us = *il y a un manque de communication entre nous* **COMMUNICATIVE** (adj) *communicatif, -ive* : you're not very communicative today = *tu n'es pas très communicatif aujourd'hui.*

COMMUNIQUÉ (n) *communiqué (m)* : a communiqué published at the end of the summit meeting = *un communiqué publié à la fin de la conférence au sommet* ⓪ bulletin = ←.

COMMUNISM (n) *communisme (m)* ⓓ Marxism = *marxisme*, hammer and sickle = *la faucille et le marteau*, class struggle = *lutte des classes* ≠ capitalism = *capitalisme*.

COMMUNIST (n, adj) *communiste (m, f)* : he's a communist = *c'est un communiste* ⓓ a red = *un rouge*, commie = *coco*, proletarian = *prolétaire*, fellow traveler = *compagnon de route*, Marxist = *marxiste*.

COMMUNITY (n, -ies) *communauté (f)* : there's a large American community in Paris = *il y a une importante communauté américaine à Paris* ☠ *communauté (hippie)* = *commune*.

COMMUTE (to, -d) *habiter en banlieue et se rendre en ville pour son travail* : he lives in Connecticut and commutes to New York every day = *il habite le Connecticut et va à New York tous les jours* ⓓ to go back and forth = *faire la navette* **COMMUTER** (n) *banlieusard, -e (qui va travailler en ville)* ⓓ suburbs = *banlieue*.

COMPANION (n) *compagnon, compagne* : a pet is a good companion = *un animal domestique est un bon compagnon*.

COMPANIONSHIP (n) *compagnie (f)* : she's not looking for a husband, just for companionship = *elle ne cherche pas un mari, mais juste de la compagnie*.

COMPANY (n, -ies) **1/** *compagnie (f), société (f)* : an American company = *une compagnie/société américaine* ☠ *société* → society
2/ *compagnie (f)* : I like the company of children = *j'aime la compagnie des enfants*
to keep company = *(se) fréquenter* : they've been keeping company for a year = *ça fait un an qu'ils se fréquentent* ⓓ to go out with = *sortir avec* ☠ → to frequent
I'll keep you company = *je vous tiendrai compagnie*
a man is known by the company he keeps = *dis-moi qui tu hantes, je te dirai que tu es*
☠ *(Paul) et compagnie* = (Paul) and the others
— *fausser compagnie à qqn* = to give s.o. the slip
— *chercher de la compagnie* = to look for companionship
3/ *du monde* : we're having company tonight = *ce soir, nous avons du monde* ☠ *il y avait du monde* = there were a lot of people).

COMPARABLE (adj) *comparable* : items of comparable quality = *des articles de qualité comparable* ⓓ equivalent = *équivalent*.

COMPARATIVELY (adv) *comparativement* : comparatively speaking = *comparativement (parlant)*.

COMPARE (to, -d) *comparer* : you can't compare their personalities = *on ne peut pas comparer leurs personnalités*
compared with/to = *comparé à* : compared with/to New York, Paris is small = *comparé à New York, Paris est petit* ⓓ in comparison with = *en comparaison de*
you can't compare (the pill) with (the dia-

phragm) = *on ne peut pas comparer (la pilule) et (le diaphragme)*.

COMPARISON (n) *comparaison (f)* : I don't understand the comparison = *je ne comprends pas la comparaison* ⓓ analogy = *analogie*
in comparison with (New York, Paris is small) = *en comparaison de (New York, Paris est petit)*
there's no comparison between (the pill and the diaphragm) = *il n'y a aucune comparaison (possible) entre (la pilule et le diaphragme)*.

COMPARTMENT (n) *compartiment (m)* : to divide in 10 compartments = *diviser en 10 compartiments*.

COMPASS (n, -es) *boussole (f)*, *compas (m)* ☠ *perdre la boussole* = to go nuts.

COMPASSION (n) *compassion (f)* : to have compassion for s.o. = *avoir de la compassion pour qqn* ⓓ pity = *pitié*.

COMPASSIONATE (adj) *compatissant, -e* : a compassionate attitude = *une attitude compatissante* ⓓ merciful = *clément*.

COMPATIBILITY (n, -ies) *compatibilité (f)* : a lack of compatibility = *un manque de compatibilité* ≠ incompatibility = *incompatibilité*.

COMPATIBLE (adj) *compatible* : compatible ideas = *des idées compatibles* ≠ incompatible = ←.

COMPATRIOT (n) *compatriote (m, f)* ⓓ fellow citizen = *concitoyen*.

COMPEL TO (to, -led) *contraindre à* : what compelled you to tell him ? = *qu'est-ce qui vous a contraint à le lui dire ?* ⓓ to oblige to = *obliger à*.

COMPENSATE FOR (to, -d) *compenser* : nothing can compensate for the loss of a child = *rien ne peut compenser la perte d'un enfant* ⓓ to make up for = *rattraper* ☠ *compenser une perte (financière)* = to offset a loss.

COMPENSATION (n) **1/** *compensation (f)* : the only compensation when I'm out of work is that I can sleep late = *la seule compensation quand je suis au chômage, c'est que je peux dormir tard* **2/** *rémunération (f)* : the compensation does not match the responsibilities = *la rémunération n'est pas à la hauteur des responsabilités* ⓓ indemnity = *indemnité*, golden handshake = *prime substantielle de licenciement*.

COMPETE (to, -d) *se concurrencer* (people), *se faire concurrence* : the two sisters/companies are always competing = *les deux sœurs/sociétés sont toujours en train de se concurrencer/les deux sociétés se font toujours concurrence* ⓓ to vie for = *être en compétition*
to compete with = *faire concurrence à* : nobody can compete with the Americans for skyscrapers = *personne ne peut faire concurrence aux Américains pour les gratte-ciel*.

COMPETENCE (n) *compétence (f)* : that's beyond my competence = *ça dépasse ma compétence* ⑩ skill = *habileté.*

COMPETENT (adj) *compétent, -e* : a competent manager = *un gestionnaire compétent* ⑩ able = *capable* ≠ incompetent = *incompétent.*

COMPETITION (n) *compétition (f), concurrence (f)* : competition in the company is rough = *la concurrence est dure au sein de l'entreprise*, a competition to win a prize = *une compétition pour gagner un prix* ⑩ rivalry = *rivalité* 💀 *une compétition* = a sporting event.

COMPETITIVE (adj) **1/** *compétitif, -ive, concurrentiel, -elle* : competitive prices = *des prix compétitifs/concurrentiels* **2/** *qui a l'esprit de compétition* : my children are very competitive = *mes enfants ont l'esprit de compétition très développé.*

COMPETITOR (n) *concurrent, -e* ⑩ rival = ← 💀 *dix concurrents (course)* = ten contestants (race).

COMPILE (to, -d) *compiler* : to compile documents to write a book = *compiler des documents pour écrire un livre.*

COMPLAIN (to, -ed) *se plaindre* : why are you always complaining ? = *pourquoi êtes-vous toujours en train de vous plaindre ?* ⑩ to kick = *râler*, to bitch = *gueuler*
I can't complain = *je n'ai pas à/je ne peux pas me plaindre*
to complain about (the weather/the food) = *se plaindre du (temps)/de (la nourriture)*
💀 *je vous plains* = ·I feel sorry for you/I pity you.

COMPLAINT (n) *plainte (f)* : his complaints were unjustified = *ses plaintes étaient injustifiées* ⑩ kick = *raison de râler*
complaint department = *bureau des réclamations*
to lodge a complaint against (s.o./a shop) = *porter plainte contre (qqn/un magasin)* ⑩ to sue = *poursuivre en justice*
I've no complaint = *je n'ai pas lieu de me plaindre*
what's your complaint ? = *de quoi vous plaignez-vous ?*

COMPLETE (adj) **1/** *complet, -ète* : a complete mess/failure = *la pagaille complète/un échec complet* ⑩ entire = *entier*
to be complete opposites = *être aux antipodes* ⑩ they are as different as night and day = *c'est le jour et la nuit*
complete confidence/surprise = *confiance/surprise totale*
💀 *pain complet* = whole wheat bread
— *complet (hôtel)* = full (hotel)
— *(athlète) complet* = all-around (athlete)
2/ *achevé, -e* : a complete fool = *un imbécile achevé* ⑩ absolute = *parfait.*

COMPLETE (to, -d) **1/** *achever* : we completed the work yesterday = *nous avons achevé le travail hier* ⑩ to wind up = *boucler* ≠ to start = *démarrer* 💀 *achever qqn* =

to finish s.o. off **2/** *compléter* : this painting completes his collection = *ce tableau complète sa collection* 💀 *nos idées se complètent* = our ideas are complementary.

COMPLETELY (adj) *complètement* : completely mad = *complètement fou* ≠ in part = *en partie* → VERY.

COMPLETION (n) *achèvement (m)* : upon completion of the work = *à l'achèvement des travaux* ⑩ termination = *fin.*

COMPLEX (n, -es) *complexe (m)* : an industrial complex = *un complexe industriel*, a complex about her skin = *un complexe à cause de sa peau* = hang-up
inferiority ≠ **superiority complex** = *complexe d'infériorité* ≠ *de supériorité*
Œdipus complex = *complexe d'Œdipe.*

COMPLEX (adj) *complexe* : a complex case = *un cas complexe* ⑩ mixed-up = *embrouillé.*

COMPLEXION (n) *teint (m)* : a clear complexion = *un teint clair* ⑩ pimples = *boutons.*

COMPLEXITY (n, -ies) *complexité (f)* : the complexity of their relationship = *la complexité de leurs rapports* ≠ simplicity = *simplicité.*

COMPLIANCE (n) **in compliance with (the new regulations)** = *en conformité avec (le nouveau règlement).*

COMPLICATE (to, -d) *compliquer* : stop complicating everything = *arrête de tout compliquer* ⑩ to mix (things) up = *embrouiller (les choses).*

COMPLICATED (adj) *compliqué* : a complicated person/problem = *une personne compliquée/un problème compliqué* ⑩ complex = *complexe* ≠ simple = ←.

COMPLICATION (n) *complication (f)* : cancer with other complications = *un cancer avec d'autres complications.*

COMPLICITY (n, -ies) *complicité (f)* : robbery with the complicity of someone on the inside = *un vol avec la complicité de quelqu'un à l'intérieur* ⑩ connivance = *connivence.*

COMPLIMENT (n) *compliment (m)* : my compliments ! = *mes compliments !* ⑩ congratulations ! = *félicitations !*
to angle/fish for compliments = *faire l'âne pour avoir du son/chercher les compliments*
with the compliments of (the house) = *avec les compliments de (la maison).*

COMPLIMENT (to, -ed) **to compliment s.o. on stg** = *complimenter qqn pour qqch* : I compliment you on your work = *je vous complimente pour votre travail* ≠ to put down = *descendre.*

COMPLIMENTARY (adj) **1/** *flatteur, -euse* : a complimentary write-up = *une critique flatteuse* = a flattering write-up **2/** *à titre gracieux* : a complimentary ticket = *un billet offert à titre gracieux* ⑩ free = *gratuit.*

COMPLY WITH (to, -ied) *se conformer à* : you'll have to comply with the rules = *il faudra vous conformer aux règles* ⓪ to obey = *obéir.*

COMPONENT (n) *composant (m)* : the chemical compo-. nents of the product = *les composants chimiques du produit* ⓪ element = *élément.*

COMPORT (to, -ed) **to comport o.s. like** = *se comporter comme* : she comported herself like a slut = *elle s'est comportée comme une salope.*

COMPOSE (to, -d) *composer* : to compose an opera = *composer un opéra* ☠ *composer un numéro de téléphone* = to dial a phone number.

COMPOSER (n) *compositeur, -trice* ⓪ lyricist = *parolier.*

COMPOSITION (n) *composition (f)* : to study the composition of a metal = *étudier la composition d'un métal* ☠ *de bonne* ≠ *mauvaise composition* = easy ≠ hard to deal with.

COMPOSURE (n) **to lose one's composure** = *perdre son sang-froid.*

COMPREHEND (to, -ed) *comprendre* : we didn't comprehend the implication = *nous n'avons pas compris ce qui était sous-entendu* ⓪ to grasp = *saisir* ☠ « to comprehend » *est moins dit que* « to understand ».

COMPREHENSIBLE (adj) *compréhensible* ⓪ intelligible = ←

COMPREHENSION (n) *compréhension (f), entendement (m)* : that's beyond my comprehension = *cela dépasse ma compréhension/mon entendement.*

COMPREHENSIVE (adj) *détaillé, -e* : a comprehensive list/study = *une liste/étude détaillée* ⓪ exhaustive = *exhaustif* ☠ *il a été très compréhensif* = he was very understanding.

COMPRISE (to, -d) *comprendre* : the book comprises 12 chapters = *le livre comprend 12 chapitres* ☠ → to understand.

COMPROMISE (n) *compromis (m)* : in life, we often have to make compromises = *dans la vie, il faut souvent faire des compromis* ⓪ concession = ←.

COMPROMISE (to, -d) **1/** *compromettre* : his reputation's compromised = *sa réputation est compromise* ⓪ to endanger = *mettre en danger* **2/** faire des compromis : in marriage you have to compromise = *quand on est marié, il faut faire des compromis.*

COMPULSIVE (adj) *(qui fait qqch) de façon maladive* : a compulsive eater = *quelqu'un qui mange de façon maladive* ⓪ inveterate = *invétéré* **a compulsive liar** = *un mythomane.*

COMPULSIVELY (adv) *de façon maladive* : to talk/ smoke compulsively = *parler/fumer de façon maladive.*

COMPULSORY (adj) *obligatoire* : compulsory retirement = *retraite obligatoire* = obligatory ⓪ required = *requis.*

COMPUNCTION (n) *scrupule (m)* : he had no compunction about lying to her = *il n'a eu aucun scrupule à lui mentir* = he had no scruples about lying to her.

COMPUTER (n) *ordinateur (m)* : the computer is out of order = *l'ordinateur est en panne*	
byte = *octet*	**ware** = *logiciel*
computer science = *informatique*	**keyboard** = *clavier*
data base = *base de données*	**personal computer** = *micro-ordinateur*
data entry/input = *saisie de données*	**P.C.** = *micro*
diskette = *disquette* = **floppy**	**printer** = *imprimante*
hacker = *pirate informatique*	**office automation** = *bureautique*
hard-disk = *disque dur*	**screen** = *écran*
	storage = *mémoire*
hardware = *matériel informatique* ≠ **soft-**	**user-friendly** = *convivial*
	word processing = *traitement de texte.*

COMRADE (n) *camarade (m, f)* : comrades in the revolution = *camarades de la révolution* ⓪ colleague = *collègue* ☠ *la camarade de ma fille* = my daughter's chum.

CON (n) **1/** *arnaque (f)* : the business deal was a con = *cette affaire était une arnaque* ⓪ ripoff = *escroquerie* **2/** *taulard, -e* : cons have a hard time finding a job after prison ≤ *les taulards ont un mal fou à trouver du boulot en sortant de prison* ⓪ convict = *détenu*
a con artist = *un embobineur* : my publisher's a con artist = *mon éditeur est un embobineur* ⓪ swindler = *arnaqueur*
con game = *piège à cons/attrape-couillon* ⓪ swindle = *arnaque*
con job = *marché de dupes* ⓪ line = *baratin*
con man = *arnaqueur* = confidence man ⓪ wheeler-dealer = *brasseur d'affaires*
☠ *quel con !* = what an ass !
— *le con* = the cunt
— *(film) à la con* = shitty (movie)
— *il est con (comme la lune/comme un balai/comme ses pieds)* = he's an (absolute) ass.

CON (to, -ned) *arnaquer* : he conned the tourists = *il a arnaqué les touristes* → TO HUSTLE
to con s.o. into (doing stg) = *embobiner qqn pour (qu'il fasse qqch)*
to con out of = *escroquer de* : to con s.o. out of a grand = *escroquer qqn de mille dollars* → TO HUSTLE.

CONCEAL (to, -ed) *dissimuler* : he concealed a gun under his coat = *il a dissimulé un revolver sous son* manteau ⓪ to hide = *cacher* 🐝 *je ne me dissimule pas les difficultés* = I'm not trying to close my eyes to the difficulties.

CONCEDE (to, -d) *concéder* : he conceded that I was right = *il m'a concédé que j'avais raison* ⓪ to acknowledge = *reconnaître.*

CONCEIT (n) *suffisance (f)* : full of conceit = *plein de suffisance* ≠ humility = *humilité.*

CONCEITED (adj) *suffisant, -e* : a conceited guy = *un type suffisant* ⓪ pretentious = *prétentieux,* to think one's hot stuff = *se croire sorti de la cuisse de Jupiter* 🐝 → sufficient.

CONCEIVABLE (adj) *concevable* : it's not conceivable that she'll leave him and the kids = *il n'est pas concevable qu'elle les quitte, lui et les gosses* ≠ inconceivable = *inconcevable* **CONCEIVABLY** (adv) *de manière concevable.*

CONCEIVE (to, -d) **1/** *concevoir* : the housing project was poorly conceived = *le lotissement a été mal conçu* ⓪ to imagine = *imaginer*
I can't conceive of (his hitting her) = *je n'arrive pas à concevoir qu'(il la batte)*
2/ *concevoir* : I was conceived on my parents' wedding night = *j'ai été conçu dès la nuit de noces de mes parents* ⓪ to beget = *engendrer*
🐝 *le théâtre n'est pas conçu pour ...* = the theater isn't geared to ...
— *concevoir un moyen de* = to devise a way to.

CONCENTRATE (to, -d) *(se) concentrer* : I can't concentrate when you talk to me = *je ne peux pas me concentrer quand tu me parles* ⓪ to think = *réfléchir*
to concentrate on (what one's doing) = *se concentrer sur (ce qu'on fait).*

CONCENTRATION (n) *concentration (f)* : this book requires great concentration = *ce livre exige une grande concentration* ⓪ attention = ←
concentration camp = *camp de concentration.*

CONCEPT (n) *concept (m)* : a new publicity concept = *un nouveau concept publicitaire* ⓪ idea = *idée.*

CONCERN (n) **1/** (inv) *souci (m)* : her concern is that her children get a good education = *elle a le souci que ses enfants reçoivent une bonne éducation* 🐝 → worry
it's no concern of yours ! = *ce n'est pas votre affaire !* ⓪ it's no business of yours ! = *ce ne sont pas vos oignons !*
2/ *entreprise (f)* : small family-owned concerns = *de petites entreprises familiales* = small family-owned enterprises ⓪ firm = *firme.*

CONCERN (to, -ed) *concerner* : your problems don't concern me = *vos problèmes ne me concernent pas* ⓪ to interest = *intéresser*
as concerns (your salary) = *en ce qui concerne (votre salaire)*
to be concerned (that/about) = *se faire du souci (pour)* : I'm concerned that my father might be ill/I'm

concerned about my father's health = *je me fais du souci pour la santé de mon père* ⓪ to fret = *se tracasser.*

CONCERNED (adj) *concerné, -e* : concerned citizens = *les citoyens concernés* ≠ indifferent = *indifférent.*

CONCERNING (prep) *concernant, en ce qui concerne* : we have no information concerning his whereabouts = *nous n'avons aucune information concernant le lieu où il se trouve,* concerning your new job = *en ce qui concerne votre nouveau travail* ⓪ about = *au sujet de.*

CONCERT (n) *concert (m)* : to give a concert = *donner un concert* ⓪ recital = *récital*
concert hall = *salle de concert.*

CONCESSION (n) **1/** *concession (f)* : to make concessions = *faire des concessions* **2/** *concession (f)* : who has the Ford concession in France ? = *qui a la concession Ford en France ?* ⓪ franchise = *autorisation de vente.*

CONCILIATORY (adj) *conciliant, -e* : conciliatory remarks = *des remarques conciliantes.*

CONCISE (adj) *concis, -e* : a concise speech = *un discours concis* ≠ redundant = *redondant.*

CONCLUDE (to, -d) **1/** *conclure* : we concluded he was lying = *nous en avons conclu qu'il mentait* ⓪ to infer = *déduire* **2/** *conclure* : to conclude a commercial agreement = *conclure un accord commercial* ⓪ to wrap up = *tout régler.*

CONCLUSION (n) *conclusion (f)* : that's my conclusion = *c'est ma conclusion* ⓪ opinion = ←
to come to/to reach a conclusion = *en venir à une conclusion*
draw your (own) conclusions = *tirez-en vos (propres) conclusions*
don't jump to conclusions = *ne tirez pas de conclusions trop hâtives*
in conclusion = *en conclusion.*

CONCLUSIVE (adj) *concluant, -e* : a conclusive experiment = *une expérience concluante* ⓪ decisive = *décisif* ≠ inconclusive = *non concluant.*

CONCOCT (to, -ed) *inventer (de toutes pièces), concocter* : to concoct an excuse/a new dish = *inventer une excuse de toutes pièces/concocter un nouveau plat* ⓪ to dream up = *échafauder.*

CONCOCTION (n) *mixture (f)* : she cooks strange concoctions = *elle fait d'étranges mixtures* 🐝 → mixture.

CONCRETE (n) *béton (m)* : reinforced concrete = *béton armé* ⓪ mason = *maçon.*

CONCRETE (adj) *concret, -ète* : concrete propositions = *des propositions concrètes* ⓪ real = *réel* **CONCRETELY** (adv) *concrètement.*

CONCUBINE (n) *concubine (f)* ⓪ mistress = *maîtresse.*

CONCUR (to, -red) *s'accorder* : their opinions often concur = *leurs opinions s'accordent souvent* ≠ to differ =

différer ☠ *je vous l'accorde* = I grant you that.

CONDEMN (to, -ed) *condamner* : to condemn violence = *condamner la violence* ⓪ to decry = *décrier* ≠ to approve = *approuver*
to be condemned to (a life of poverty) = *être condamné à (une vie de misère)*
☠ *être condamné à (faire qqch)* = to be doomed to (do stg)
— *il a été condamné à (cinq ans)* = he was sentenced to (five years).

CONDENSE (to, -d) *condenser* : to condense an article = *condenser un article* ⓪ to abridge = *abréger* **CONDENSATION** (n) *condensation (f)*.

CONDESCEND (to, -ed) *condescendre* : to condescend to answer = *condescendre à répondre*.

CONDESCENDING (adj) *condescendant, -e* : a condescending attitude = *une attitude condescendante* ⓪ patronizing = *paternaliste*.

CONDITION (n) 1/ *condition (f)* : those are my conditions = *voilà mes conditions* 2/ *état (m)* : the patient's condition = *l'état du malade* ☠ → state
(a car/person) in good ≠ poor condition = *(une voiture) en bon ≠ mauvais état/(quelqu'un) en bonne ≠ mauvaise forme*
in ≠ out of condition = *en bonne ≠ mauvaise condition physique* : the tennis champion is in ≠ out of condition = *le champion de tennis est en bonne ≠ mauvaise condition physique*
on condition that = *à condition que* : I'll go with you on condition that you pay = *je viendrai avec vous à condition que vous payiez* ⓪ provided that = *pourvu que*
to have a (heart) condition = *être cardiaque*
under no condition = *en aucun cas*.

CONDITION (to, -ed) *conditionner* : we're all conditioned by our education = *nous sommes tous conditionnés par notre éducation*.

CONDITIONAL (n) *conditionnel (m)* **CONDITIONAL** (adj) *conditionnel, -elle*.

CONDOM (n) *préservatif (m)* ⓪ rubber = *capote*.

CONDOMINIUM (n) 1/ *copropriété (f)* : her building's a condominium = *son immeuble est en copropriété* = condo = co-op ⓪ high-rise = *tour*
☠ *les lois de propriétés sont moins sévères dans les « condominiums » que dans les « co-ops »*
2/ *appartement (m) en copropriété* : she bought a condominium = *elle a acheté un appartement en copropriété*.

CONDONE (to, -d) *excuser* : I don't condone his taking drugs = *je ne l'excuse pas de se droguer* ⓪ to pardon = *pardonner* ☠ → to excuse.

CONDUCIVE TO (adj) *qui conduit à* : a policy conducive to terrorism = *une politique qui conduit au terrorisme*.

CONDUCT (n) *conduite (f)* : outrageous conduct = *une*

conduite scandaleuse ⓪ behavior = *comportement*
☠ *conduite (parti)* = leadership (party)
— *conduite à gauche* = left-hand drive.

CONDUCT (to, -ed) *diriger* : to conduct an orchestra/an inquiry = *diriger un orchestre/une enquête* ☠ → to direct.

CONDUCTOR (n) *chef (m) d'orchestre* ⓪ baton = *baguette*.

CONFEDERATION (n) *confédération (f)* ⓪ federation = *fédération*.

CONFER (to, -red) *conférer* : to confer with one's adviser = *conférer avec son conseiller* ⓪ to discuss = *discuter*
to confer (a title) on = *conférer (un titre) à* = to bestow (a title) on.

CONFERENCE (n) *conférence (f)* : a conference on sexology = *une conférence sur la sexologie* ⓪ meeting = *réunion*, summit conference = *conférence au sommet*
to be in conference = *être en conférence*
☠ *faire une conférence* = to give a lecture.

CONFESS (to, -ed) *avouer, se confesser* (church) : the defendant confessed = *le prévenu a avoué* ⓪ to admit = *admettre*
to confess to (having murdered the woman) = *avouer (avoir assassiné la femme)*
☠ *s'avouer (vaincu)* = to admit (defeat).

CONFESSION (n) *aveu (m), confession (f)* (church) : the criminal's confession = *l'aveu du criminel*
to go to confession = *aller se confesser*.

CONFIDE IN (to, -d) *se confier à* : I confide in my father = *je me confie à mon père* ⓪ to open up to = *s'ouvrir à*
☠ *confier son chien/un secret à qqn* = to entrust s.o. with one's dog/a secret.

CONFIDENCE (n) 1/ *confiance (f)* : he inspires confidence = *il inspire confiance* = he inspires trust 2/ *confiance (f) en soi* : he lacks confidence = *il manque de confiance en lui* ⓪ assurance = ←
in confidence = *en confidence* : he told me that in confidence = *il me l'a dit en confidence*
to have confidence in s.o. = *avoir confiance en qqn* = to trust s.o.
☠ *fais-moi confiance !* = trust me !

CONFIDENT (adj) *qui a bon espoir de* : they're confident they're going to win = *ils ont bon espoir de gagner* **CONFIDENTLY** (adv) *avec confiance*.

CONFIDENTIAL (adj) *confidentiel, -elle* : a confidential letter = *une lettre confidentielle* ⓪ secret = ←
CONFIDENTIALLY (adv) *confidentiellement*.

CONFINE (to, -d) **to be confined to** = *être obligé de rester à* : she was confined to bed for a week = *elle a été obligée de rester au lit pendant une semaine*.

CONFIRM (to, -ed) *confirmer* : that confirms what I was saying = *cela confirme ce que je disais* ⓪ to corroborate

= corroborer ≠ to refute = *réfuter* CONFIRMATION (n) *confirmation (f)* : we're waiting for the President's confirmation = *nous attendons la confirmation du Président* ≠ denial = *démenti.*

CONFIRMED (adj) **a confirmed bachelor =** *un célibataire endurci*
a confirmed cook/sailor = *un cuisinier/marin expérimenté.*

CONFISCATE (to, -d) *confisquer* : to confiscate property = *confisquer la propriété* ≠ to restore = *restituer.*

CONFLICT (n) *conflit (m)* : armed conflict = *conflit armé*, endless conflicts between them = *des conflits sans fin entre eux* ⓓ pull = *tirage* ≠ agreement = *accord*
a conflict of interest = *un conflit d'intérêts.*

CONFLICT (to, -ed) *être contradictoire* : that conflicts with what they told me = *c'est contradictoire avec ce qu'ils m'ont dit* ≠ to concur = *s'accorder.*

CONFLICTING (adj) *contradictoire* : conflicting opinions/evidence = *des opinions/preuves contradictoires.*

CONFORM (to, -ed) *faire comme tout le monde* : when you're young there's tremendous pressure to conform = *quand vous êtes jeune, on exerce une très forte pression sur vous pour que vous fassiez comme tout le monde*
to conform to (regulations) = *se conformer aux (règlements)* ≠ to oppose to = *s'opposer à.*

CONFORMIST (n, adj) *conformiste (m, f)* : a family of conformists = *une famille de conformistes* ⓓ traditionalist = *traditionaliste* ≠ nonconformist = *nonconformiste.*

CONFORMITY (n, -ies) *conformisme (m)* : a life of conformity = *une vie de conformisme*
in conformity with (your opinions) = *conformément à (vos opinions)* ⓓ in accordance with = *en accord avec.*

CONFOUND (to, -ed) *confondre* : the police confounded the murderer = *la police a confondu le meurtrier* ⓓ to baffle = *dérouter* ☠ → to confuse.

CONFRONT (to, -ed) *affronter* : to confront serious problems = *affronter des problèmes sérieux* ⓓ to face = *être face à*
to be confronted with difficulties/the truth = *être confronté à des difficultés/la vérité.*

CONFRONTATION (n) *confrontation (f)* : confrontation of ideas = *confrontation d'idées.*

CONFUSE (to, -d) **1/** *embrouiller* : you're confusing me = *vous m'embrouillez* = you're mixing me up ⓓ to puzzle = *laisser perplexe*
to be confused = *s'embrouiller* : I'm confused = *je m'embrouille*
2/ *confondre* : don't confuse sex with love = *il ne faut pas confondre le sexe et l'amour*
☠ *tu confonds les deux frères* = you're mixing up the two brothers
— *confondre (un meurtrier)* = to confound (a murderer)

— *se confondre en (excuses)* = to fall over o.s. (apologizing).

CONFUSED (adj) *confus, -e* : what a confused situation ! = *quelle situation confuse !* ⓓ mixed-up = *embrouillé* ☠ *je suis confus* = I'm terribly sorry.

CONFUSION (n) *confusion (f)* : a great deal of confusion in the office = *pas mal de confusion au bureau* ⓓ disorder = *désordre*
☠ *une confusion dans les dates* = a mix-up in the dates.

CONGENIAL (adj) *qui attire la sympathie* : a congenial personality = *une personnalité qui attire la sympathie.*

CONGLOMERATE (n) *conglomérat (m)* ⓓ multinational company = *société multinationale.*

CONGRATULATE (to, -d) *féliciter* : I want to congratulate you = *je veux vous féliciter*
to congratulate s.o. on = *féliciter qqn de.*

CONGRATULATIONS (n pl) *félicitations (f pl)* : he sent his congratulations = *il a envoyé ses félicitations*
congratulations ! = *félicitations !* ⓓ kudos = *félicitations particulières.*

CONGREGATE (to, -d) *se rassembler* ⓓ to meet = *se réunir* ☠ → to gather.

CONGREGATION (n) *fidèles (m pl)* : the whole congregation turned against the priest = *tous les fidèles se sont retournés contre le prêtre* ⓓ churchgoer = *pratiquant.*

CONGRESS (n, -es) **1/** *Congrès (m)* : he's running for Congress = *il se présente au Congrès* ⓓ Senate = *Sénat*, House of Representatives = *Chambre des représentants* **2/** *congrès (m)* : a medical congress = *un congrès médical* ⓓ reunion = *réunion.*

CONGRESSMAN (n, -men) *parlementaire (m)*, membre *(m) du Congrès* **CONGRESSWOMAN** (n, -women) *parlementaire (f)* ⓓ Senator = *sénateur.*

CONJECTURE (n) *conjecture (f)* : based on conjecture = *fondé sur une conjecture.*

CONJUGATE (to, -d) *conjuguer* ☠ *nous avons conjugué nos efforts* = we combined our efforts.

CONJUNCTION (n) **in conjunction with =** *conjointement avec.*

CONK OUT (to, -ed) *rendre l'âme* : our car conked out = *notre voiture a rendu l'âme* ⓓ to be on the blink = *être déglingué.*

CONNECT (to, -ed) **1/** *relier* : the bridge connects the two cities = *le pont relie les deux villes* ⓓ to join = *joindre* ☠ *relier un livre* = to bind a book **2/** *faire le rapprochement entre* : I didn't connect the two people = *je n'ai pas fait le rapprochement entre les deux personnes* ⓓ to link = *faire le lien* **3/** *brancher* : the phone isn't connected = *le téléphone n'est pas branché* ☠ *ça me branche* = it turns me on
to be connected with = *1/ avoir un rapport avec* :

that's not connected with what I was saying = *cela n'a aucun rapport avec ce que je disais* ⓪ to be related to = *être lié à* 2/ *travailler avec* : are you connected with this company ? = *est-ce que vous travaillez avec cette société ?* ⓪ to work for = *travailler pour* 3/ *avoir un rapport avec* : how is he connected with the murder ? = *en quoi a-t-il un rapport avec le meurtre ?* ⓪ to be involved in = *être impliqué dans*

to connect with = 1/ *faire le rapport avec* : did you connect what I said with what I hinted at before ? = *est-ce que vous avez fait le rapport entre ce que j'ai dit et ce à quoi j'avais fait allusion avant ?* 2/ *passer* : can you please connect me with Mr. Wilson ? = *est-ce que vous pouvez me passer M. Wilson, s'il vous plaît ?* ☠ → to pass.

CONNECTION (n) 1/ *rapport* (m) : is there a connection between the pill and cancer ? = *y a-t-il un rapport entre la pilule et le cancer ?*, he has no connection with our New York office = *il n'a aucun rapport avec notre bureau de New York* ⓪ tie-in = *lien* ☠ → report

in connection with = *à propos de* : he wants to see you in connection with the new job = *il veut vous voir à propos du nouveau poste* ⓪ regarding = *au sujet de*

to make the connection = *faire le rapprochement* : when you said that, I didn't make the connection = *quand vous avez dit ça, je n'ai pas fait le rapprochement* 2/ *correspondance* (f) : there are great connections between Miami and New York = *il y a de bonnes correspondances entre Miami et New York* ⓪ link = *liaison* ☠ → correspondence.

CONNECTIONS (n pl) *relations* (f pl) : he has great connections in Washington = *il a d'importantes relations à Washington* ⓪ pull = *piston* ☠ → relations.

CONNIVING (adj) *intrigant, -e* : a conniving politician/woman = *un homme politique intrigant/une femme intrigante* ≠ straightforward = *sans détours* ☠ → intriguing.

CONNOISSEUR (n) *connaisseur, -euse* : a connoisseur of French wines = *un connaisseur en vins français* ⓪ expert = ←.

CONNOTATION (n) *connotation* (f) **CONNOTE** (to, -d) *comporter l'idée de,* : prostitution connotes brutality = *la prostitution comporte l'idée de brutalité.*

CONQUER (to, -ed) 1/ *conquérir* : to conquer enemy territory = *conquérir le territoire ennemi* ⓪ to make the conquest of = *faire la conquête de* 2/ *vaincre* : to conquer one's sexual fears = *vaincre ses craintes en matière de sexe* ⓪ to overcome = *surmonter* ☠ → to vanquish.

CONQUEROR (n) *conquérant, -e* ⓪ victor = *vainqueur.*

CONQUEST (n) *conquête* (f) : the conquest of the West = *la conquête de l'Ouest* ≠ defeat = *défaite.*

CONSCIENCE (n) *conscience* (f) : why is your conscience bothering you ? = *pourquoi votre conscience*

vous torture-t-elle ?

to ease one's conscience = *se déculpabiliser/soulager sa conscience* : he told his wife about the affair to ease his conscience = *il a parlé de son aventure à sa femme pour se déculpabiliser/pour soulager sa conscience*

to have a clear ≠ **guilty conscience** = *avoir* ≠ *ne pas avoir la conscience tranquille/avoir bonne* ≠ *mauvaise conscience*

☠ *conscience de classe* = class consciousness
— *avoir de la conscience professionnelle* = to be conscientious about one's work
— *avoir conscience de* = to be aware of
— *perdre* ≠ *reprendre conscience* = to lose ≠ to regain consciousness
— *objecteur de conscience* = conscientious objector.

CONSCIENTIOUS (adj) *consciencieux, -euse* : a conscientious secretary = *un secrétaire consciencieux* ≠ careless = *peu soigneux*
conscientious objector = *objecteur de conscience.*

CONSCIENTIOUSLY (adv) *consciencieusement* : to do one's work conscientiously = *faire consciencieusement son travail.*

CONSCIOUS (adj) *conscient, -e* : the patient's not conscious = *le malade n'est pas conscient*
to be conscious of = *être conscient de* : I wasn't conscious of their problems = *je n'étais pas conscient de leurs problèmes* ≠ to be unconscious of = *être inconscient de.*

CONSCIOUSLY (adv) *consciemment* : he consciously insulted me = *il m'a insulté consciemment* ≠ unconsciously = *inconsciemment.*

CONSCIOUSNESS (n) *conscience* (f) : consciousness of one's body = *la conscience de son corps*
to lose ≠ **to regain consciousness** = *perdre* ≠ *reprendre conscience/connaissance*
☠ → conscience.

CONSECUTIVE (adj) *consécutif, -ive* : two consecutive evenings = *deux soirées consécutives* ⓪ successive = *successif.*

CONSENSUS (n, -es) *consensus* (m) : the consensus was to support the candidate = *il y avait un consensus pour soutenir le candidat* ⓪ agreement = *accord.*

CONSENT (n) *consentement* (m) : I give you my consent = *je vous donne mon consentement* ≠ refusal = *refus.*

CONSENT (to, -ed) *consentir* : he finally consented to come = *il a finalement consenti à venir* ⓪ to acquiesce = *acquiescer* ☠ *consentir un prêt* = to grant a loan.

CONSEQUENCE (n) *conséquence* (f) : the consequences of the economic crisis = *les conséquences de la crise économique* ⓪ upshot = *aboutissement*
as a consequence = *en conséquence* ⓪ thus = *donc*
to face the consequences = *supporter les conséquences* ⓪ to pay the piper = *payer les pots cassés.*

CONSEQUENTLY (adv) *par conséquent* : the OPEC

countries have increased the cost of oil, and consequently the price of gas will go up = *les pays de l'OPEP ont augmenté le prix du pétrole, et par conséquent le prix de l'essence va augmenter* ⟨D⟩ therefore = *donc.*

CONSERVATION (n) *conservation* (f) : the conservation of forests = *la conservation des forêts* ≠ waste = *gaspillage*
conservation of energy = *les économies d'énergie.*

CONSERVATISM (n) *conservatisme* (m).

CONSERVATIVE (n) *conservateur, -trice* : in politics, he's a conservative = *en politique, c'est un conservateur* ⟨D⟩ reactionary = *réactionnaire* ☠ *conservateur (musée)* = curator.

CONSERVATIVE (adj) *conservateur, -trice* : a conservative policy/politician = *une politique conservatrice/un politicien conservateur* ≠ progressive = *progressiste*
the Conservative Party = *le Parti conservateur* ≠ the Labor Party = *le Parti travailliste.*

CONSERVE (to, -d) 1/ *préserver* : to conserve natural resources = *préserver les ressources naturelles* 2/ *conserver* : to conserve food by deep-freezing = *conserver des aliments par congélation*
☠ *j'ai conservé (mon sang-froid)* = I kept (my cool)
— *conserver (le contrôle d'une société)* = to retain (the control of a company)
— *ça ne se conservera pas* = it won't keep.

CONSIDER (to, -ed) 1/ *considérer* : I consider him a genius = *je le considère comme un génie* ⟨D⟩ to deem = *estimer* 2/ *envisager* : we're considering having another child = *nous envisageons d'avoir un autre enfant* ⟨D⟩ to think about = *penser* ☠ → to envisage
considering that (he's rich) = *étant donné qu'(il est riche)* ⟨D⟩ inasmuch as = *dans la mesure où*
if you consider (his age) = *si l'on considère (son âge)*
not considering (the price) = *sans considération du (prix).*

CONSIDERABLE (adj) *considérable* : a man of considerable importance = *un homme d'une importance considérable* ⟨D⟩ sizable = *de taille.*

CONSIDERABLY (adv) *considérablement* : it's considerably hotter today = *il fait considérablement plus chaud aujourd'hui* → VERY.

CONSIDERATE (adj) *prévenant, -e* : a considerate son = *un fils prévenant* ⟨D⟩ thoughtful = *attentionné*
to be very considerate of (other people) = *avoir beaucoup d'égards pour (les autres)*
that was very considerate of you = *c'était très gentil de ta part.*

CONSIDERATION (n) 1/ *considérations* (f pl) : after long consideration, he decided to run for Mayor = *après de longues considérations, il a décidé de se présenter aux municipales* 2/ *qqch qui entre en ligne de compte* : was money a consideration ? = *est-ce que l'argent entrait en ligne de compte ?* ⟨D⟩ concern = *souci* 3/ *considération* (f) : she has no consideration for her parents = *elle n'a aucune considération pour ses parents* ⟨D⟩ thoughtfulness = *prévenance*

give it some consideration = *prêtez-y attention* **out of consideration for (my parents)** = *par égard pour (mes parents)* **to take into consideration** = *prendre en considération* : the jury took the fact that it was his first offense into consideration = *le jury a pris en considération le fait que c'était son premier délit* ⟨D⟩ to take into account = *prendre en compte*	**taking** ≠ **not taking (her age) into consideration** = *si l'on prend (son âge) en considération* ≠ *sans prendre (son âge) en considération* ⟨D⟩ allowing for = *si l'on tient compte de* **taking everything into consideration (it's not expensive)** = *tout bien considéré (ce n'est pas cher)* = all things considered **(the project's) under consideration** = *(le projet est) à l'étude.*

CONSIST (to, -ed) **to consist in** = *consister en/dans* (stg), à (verb) : the problem consists in finding a rapid solution = *la difficulté consiste à trouver une solution rapide*
to consist of = *consister en* : the meal consists of three courses = *le repas consiste en trois plats* ⟨D⟩ to be made up of = *être fait de.*

CONSISTENCY (n, -ies) *cohérence* (f) : your analysis lacks consistency = *ton analyse manque de cohérence.*

CONSISTENT (adj) *cohérent, -e, conséquent, -e* : you're not being consistent = *vous n'êtes pas cohérent/conséquent* ⟨D⟩ logical = *logique* ≠ inconsistent = *inconséquent* ☠ → coherent.

CONSISTENTLY (adv) *systématiquement* : you're consistently wrong = *vous avez systématiquement tort* = you're systematically wrong.

CONSOLATION (n) *consolation* (f) : the second prize is no consolation = *ce n'est pas une consolation d'avoir eu le deuxième prix* ⟨D⟩ comfort = *réconfort* **CONSOLE** (to, -d) *consoler* : the idea that the accident could have been worse consoled me = *la pensée que l'accident aurait pu être pire m'a consolé* ⟨D⟩ to comfort = *réconforter.*

CONSOLIDATE (to, -d) *consolider* : to consolidate one's position = *consolider sa position.*

CONSOMMÉ (n) *consommé* (m) ⟨D⟩ soup = *soupe.*

CONSPICUOUS (adj) *qui ne passe pas inaperçu, -e* : conspicuous clothes = *des vêtements qui ne passent pas inaperçus* ≠ inconspicuous = *qui passe inaperçu*
to be conspicuous by one's absence = *briller par son absence.*

CONSPICUOUSLY (adv) *d'une façon peu discrète* : conspicuously dressed = *habillé d'une façon peu discrète.*

CONSPIRACY (n, -ies) *conspiration (f), conjuration (f)* : a conspiracy to overthrow the government = *une conspiration/conjuration pour renverser le gouvernement* ⟲ scheme = *machination* **CONSPIRATOR** (n) *conspirateur, -trice/conjuré, -e* ⟲ plotter = *comploteur.*

CONSPIRE (to, -d) *conspirer* : to conspire to overthrow the government = *conspirer pour renverser le gouvernement* ⟲ to plot = *comploter.*

CONSTANT (adj) *constant, -e, incessant, -e* : constant rain = *pluie constante,* our constant arguments = *nos disputes incessantes* ⟲ continual = *continuel* ≠ occasional = *occasionnel* **CONSTANTLY** (adv) *constamment* : he's constantly late = *il est constamment en retard* ⟲ always = *toujours.*

CONSTERNATION (n) *consternation (f)* : consternation on his face = *la consternation sur son visage.*

CONSTIPATION (n) *constipation (f)* ⟲ enema = *lavement,* laxative = *laxatif.*

CONSTITUENCY (n, -ies) *circonscription (f) électorale* : his constituency is against abortion = *dans sa circonscription, on est contre l'avortement* ⟲ electorate = *électorat.*

CONSTITUTE (to, -d) *constituer* : to constitute a committee = *constituer un comité* ☠ *se constituer prisonnier* = to give o.s. up.

CONSTITUTION (n) 1/ *constitution (f)* : the Constitution of the United States = *la Constitution des États-Unis* ⟲ law = *loi* 2/ *constitution (f)* : he's got a good ≠ poor constitution = *il est de constitution robuste* ≠ *faible.*

CONSTITUTIONAL (adj) *constitutionnel, -elle* : striking is a constitutional right = *la grève est un droit constitutionnel.*

CONSTRUCT (to, -ed) *construire* : we're constructing a new house = *nous sommes en train de construire une nouvelle maison* ⟲ to erect = *ériger* ≠ to demolish = *démolir* ☠ *la région se construit beaucoup* = the area is being built up.

CONSTRUCTION (n) *construction (f)* : what a strange construction ! = *quelle construction étrange !* ⟲ edifice = *édifice,* building = *immeuble* **under construction** = *en construction.*

CONSTRUCTIVE (adj) *constructif, -ive* : constructive remarks = *des remarques constructives* ≠ destructive = *destructeur.*

CONSUL (n) *consul (m)* ⟲ consular = *consulaire,* attaché = ← **CONSULATE** (n) *consulat (m)*

CONSULT (to, -ed) *consulter* : to consult a doctor/a lawyer = *consulter un médecin/un avocat* ⟲ to advise = *conseiller*
to consult with (the union leaders) = *consulter (les dirigeants syndicaux)* ⟲ to confer with = *conférer avec.*

CONSULTANT (n) *consultant, -e, expert (m)* : he's an established consultant = *c'est un consultant/expert établi* ⟲ adviser = *conseiller*
consultant engineer = *ingénieur-conseil.*

CONSULTATION (n) *consultation (f)* : the doctor's in consultation = *le médecin est en consultation* ⟲ appointment = *rendez-vous.*

CONSUME (to, -d) *consommer* : advertising makes people consume more = *la publicité pousse les gens à consommer plus* ⟲ to buy = *acheter* ☠ *consommer un mariage* = to consummate a marriage.

CONSUMER (n) *consommateur, -trice* : a world of docile consumers = *un monde de consommateurs dociles* ⟲ buyer = *acheteur* ≠ producer = *producteur*
consumer goods = *biens de consommation*
consumer society = *société de consommation* ⟲ waste = *gaspillage.*

CONSUMERISM (n) *consumérisme (m).*

CONSUMPTION (n) *consommation (f)* : an increase in gas consumption = *une augmentation de la consommation d'essence*
☠ *biens de consommation* = consumer goods
— *qui règle les consommations ?* = who pays for the drinks ?

CONTACT (n) *contact (m)* : he has great contacts in advertising = *il a d'excellents contacts dans la publicité* ⟲ connection = *relation*
contact lenses = *verres/lentilles de contact*
a contact man/woman = *un contact/un agent de liaison*
in contact with = *en contact avec* : she's in contact with many writers = *elle est en contact avec beaucoup d'écrivains*
she lost contact with (reality) = *elle a perdu tout contact avec (la réalité)*
to make contact = *entrer en contact* : the informer hasn't yet made contact with the police = *l'indicateur n'est pas encore entré en contact avec la police.*

CONTACT (to, -ed) *contacter* : I had his address, but I didn't contact him = *j'avais son adresse, mais je ne l'ai pas contacté* ⟲ to get in touch with = *prendre contact avec.*

CONTAGIOUS (adj) *contagieux, -euse* : a contagious laugh/disease = *un rire contagieux/une maladie contagieuse* ⟲ infectious = *infectieux.*

CONTAIN (to, -ed) *contenir* : how much milk does the bottle contain ? = *quelle quantité de lait la bouteille contient-elle ?* = how much milk does the bottle hold ? ☠ *l'avion contient dix personnes* = the plane holds ten persons

— *contenir ses larmes/sa colère* = to choke back one's tears/to bottle up one's anger.

CONTAINER (n) *conteneur (m)*, *récipient (m)* : furniture shipped in containers = *du mobilier acheminé par conteneurs*, put the water in this earthenware container = *mets l'eau dans ce récipient en terre* ⑩ containership = *porte-conteneurs.*

CONTAMINATE (to, -d) *contaminer* : all the water was contaminated = *toute l'eau était contaminée* ≠ to purify = *purifier* **CONTAMINATION** (n) *contamination (f).*

CONTEMPLATE (to, -d) *envisager* : I'm contemplating going on a trip = *j'envisage de faire un voyage* ⑩ to plan = *projeter* ☙ → to envisage.

CONTEMPLATION (n) **after long/much contemplation** = *après mûre réflexion.*

CONTEMPORARY (n, -ies) *contemporain, -e* : I don't like my contemporaries = *je n'aime pas mes contemporains* ⑩ peer = *pair.*

CONTEMPORARY (adj) *contemporain, -e* : contemporary architecture = *l'architecture contemporaine* ⑩ modern = *moderne*, present = *actuel.*

CONTEMPT (n inv) *dédain (m)* : I have nothing but contempt for him = *je n'ai que du dédain pour lui* ⑩ scorn = *mépris* ≠ admiration = ←
contempt of court = *outrage à magistrat*
to hold s.o. in contempt = *avoir le plus grand mépris pour qqn.*

CONTEMPTIBLE (adj) *méprisable* : a contemptible traitor = *un traître méprisable* ⑩ hateful = *haïssable* ≠ admirable = ←.

CONTEMPTUOUS (adj) *dédaigneux, -euse* : a contemptuous look = *un regard dédaigneux* ⑩ scornful = *méprisant.*

CONTEND (to, -ed) *soutenir* : the prisoner contended he had been tortured = *le prisonnier a soutenu qu'il avait été torturé* ⑩ to claim = *prétendre* ☙ → to support.

CONTENDER (n) *prétendant, -e au titre* ⑩ challenger = ←.

CONTENT (adj) *content, -e* : I'm content with your work = *je suis content de votre travail* = contented ⑩ thrilled = *ravi* ≠ discontent = *mécontent* ☙ *je suis très content* = I'm very glad/pleased
— *content de soi* = self-satisfied.

CONTENT (to, -ed) **to content o.s. with** = *se contenter de* : he contented himself with a week's vacation = *il s'est contenté d'une semaine de vacances.*

CONTENTION (n) **my contention is that (you're wrong)** = *je soutiens que (vous avez tort).*

CONTENTS (n pl) *contenu (m)* : the contents of a letter/suitcase = *le contenu d'une lettre/d'une valise.*

CONTEST (n) *concours (m)* : he won the contest = *il a*

gagné le concours ⑩ tournament = *tournoi*
☙ *concours de circonstances* = combination of circumstances
— *avec le concours de* = with the participation of.

CONTEST (to, -ed) *contester* : they contested the decision = *ils ont contesté la décision* ≠ to admit = *admettre.*

CONTESTANT (n) *concurrent, -e* : thirty contestants in the race = *trente concurrents dans la course* ☙ → competitor.

CONTEXT (n) *contexte (m)* : his remark was out of context = *il a fait une remarque hors du contexte.*

CONTINENT (n) *continent (m)* : on the continent = *sur le continent* ≠ island = *île.*

CONTINENTAL (adj) *très sophistiqué, -e* : her husband's very continental = *son mari est très sophistiqué* ⑩ cosmopolitan = *cosmopolite*
continental breakfast = *petit déjeuner à l'européenne.*

CONTINUAL (adj) *continuel, -elle* : continual interruptions/arguments = *des interruptions/des disputes continuelles* ⑩ uninterrupted = *ininterrompu.*

CONTINUALLY (adv) *continuellement* : she's continually complaining = *elle est continuellement en train de se plaindre.*

CONTINUATION (n) *continuation (f)* : the continuation of the work = *la continuation du travail* ⑩ sequel = *suite.*

CONTINUE (to, -d) *continuer* : I'm listening, continue ! = *je vous écoute, continuez !*
to continue (+ ing) = *continuer à/de* : he continued talking = *il continuait de parler* = to keep on (+ ing) ≠ to stop = *arrêter*
to be continued = *à suivre.*

CONTINUITY (n, -ies) *continuité (f)* : a lack of continuity = *un manque de continuité.*

CONTINUOUS (adj) *continu, -e* : continuous financial problems = *des problèmes financiers continus* ⑩ continual = *continuel*, endless = *sans fin*
continuous performance = *spectacle permanent*
☙ *la journée continue* = non-stop workday.

CONTINUOUSLY (adv) *continûment* : science is continuously progressing = *la science progresse continûment.*

CONTRACEPTION (n) *contraception (f)* : they discovered a new method of contraception = *on a découvert une nouvelle méthode de contraception* ⑩ birth control = *contrôle des naissances*, diaphragm = *diaphragme*, French letter = *préservatif* = condom, I.U.D. = intrauterine device = *stérilet* = coil = loop, the pill = *la pilule*, rubber = *capote*, chastity belt = *ceinture de chasteté* **CONTRACEPTIVE** (adj) *contraceptif, -ive.*

121

CONTRACT (n) *contrat (m)* : to sign a contract = *signer un contrat*
breach of contract = *rupture de contrat.*

CONTRACT (to, -ed) *contracter* : to contract syphilis = *contracter la syphilis.*

CONTRACTION (n) *contraction (f).*

CONTRACTOR (n) *entrepreneur (m)* : I have to find a contractor to get the work done on my new house = *il faut que je trouve un entrepreneur pour faire les travaux dans ma nouvelle maison.*

CONTRADICT (to, -ed) *contredire* : don't contradict me = *ne me contredis pas* ⓪ to deny = *démentir.*

CONTRADICTION (n) *contradiction (f)* : that's in contradiction with what he said yesterday = *c'est en contradiction avec ce qu'il a dit hier.*

CONTRADICTORY (adj) *contradictoire* : contradictory attitudes = *des attitudes contradictoires* ⓪ opposite = *opposé.*

CONTRAPTION (n) *engin (m)* : what's this contraption for ? = *à quoi sert cet engin ?* ⓪ gadget = ←.

CONTRARY (n, -ies) *contraire (m)* : it's just the contrary = *c'est exactement le contraire* ⓪ reverse = *inverse*
on the contrary = *au contraire* : I thought they were happy together, but on the contrary, they're splitting = *je pensais qu'ils étaient heureux ensemble, mais au contraire ils se séparent.*

CONTRARY (adj) **contrary to** = 1/ *contraire à* : it's contrary to the rules = *c'est contraire aux règles* ≠ in agreement with = *en accord avec* 2/ *contrairement à* : contrary to what he said = *contrairement à ce qu'il a dit*
☠ *(avis) contraires* = opposite (opinions).

CONTRAST (n) *contraste (m)* : the contrast between the rich and poor parts of the city = *le contraste entre les quartiers riches et les quartiers pauvres de la ville* ⓪ opposition = ←.

CONTRAST (to, -ed) *contraster* : the colors contrast = *les couleurs contrastent* ⓪ to oppose = *s'opposer.*

CONTRIBUTE (to, -d) *contribuer* : he contributed on the discovery = *il a contribué à la découverte* ⓪ to help = *aider* **CONTRIBUTION** (n) *contribution (f)* : to give a contribution to a good cause = *apporter sa contribution pour soutenir une cause juste* ⓪ donation = ← **CONTRIBUTOR** (n) *donateur, -trice.*

CONTRIVE (to, -d) *combiner* : we'll have to contrive a way to save the hostages = *il va falloir combiner quelque chose pour sauver les otages* ⓪ to concoct = *inventer (de toutes pièces)* ☠ → to combine.

CONTRIVED (adj) *un peu trop sophistiqué, -e* : the plot of the story was contrived = *la trame de l'histoire était un peu trop sophistiquée*
a contrived smile = *un sourire artificiel* ≠ natural = *naturel.*

CONTROL (n) *contrôle (m)* : I have no control over my husband = *je n'ai aucun contrôle sur mon mari*
to be in control of o.s. = *se contrôler* : when he drinks he isn't in control of himself = *quand il boit, il ne se contrôle plus*
at the controls (plane) = *aux commandes (avion)*
control tower = *tour de contrôle*
it's beyond my control = *c'est indépendant de ma volonté*
to lose control = *perdre le contrôle de soi*
who's in control ? = *qui est le responsable ?* = who's in charge ?
out of ≠ **under control** = *hors de contrôle* ≠ *bien en main* : the situation's out of ≠ under control = *la situation est hors de contrôle* ≠ *nous avons la situation bien en main*
☠ *contrôle (des billets)* = verification (of the tickets).

CONTROL (to, -led) *contrôler* : she controls her husband/her temper = *elle contrôle son mari/ses humeurs.*

CONTROVERSIAL (adj) *qui prête à controverse* : a controversial question = *une question qui prête à controverse* ⓪ polemical = *polémique.*

CONTROVERSY (n, -ies) *controverse (f)* : a controversy over the abortion problem = *une controverse sur le problème de l'avortement* ⓪ argument = *dispute.*

CONVALESCE (to, -d) *être en convalescence* ⓪ to recuperate = *récupérer* **CONVALESCENCE** (n) *convalescence (f)* : a long convalescence = *une longue convalescence* ≠ relapse = *rechute* **CONVALESCENT** (n, adj) *convalescent, -e* ⓪ nursing home = *maison de repos.*

CONVENE (to, -d) *se réunir* : Congress convenes next week = *le Congrès se réunit la semaine prochaine* = Congress meets next week ☠ → to reunite.

CONVENIENCE (n) *commodité (f)* : the convenience of owning a car = *la commodité d'avoir une voiture*
at your convenience = *à votre convenance* ⓪ when it suits you = *quand cela vous arrange*
☠ → commodity.

CONVENIENT (adj) *commode* : a convenient time/place = *une heure/un endroit commode* ⓪ good = *bon* ≠ inconvenient = *incommode* ☠ → handy **CONVENIENTLY** (adv) 1/ *commodément/par commodité* : he conveniently pretends not to have heard the remarks = *il prétend, par commodité, ne pas avoir entendu les remarques* 2/ *à un bon endroit* : conveniently seated/located = *assis/situé à un bon endroit.*

CONVENT (n) *couvent (m)* ⓪ monastery = *monastère*, nun = *religieuse.*

CONVENTION (n) 1/ *convention (f)* : the Democratic/Republican convention = *la convention démocrate/républicaine* ⓪ delegate = *délégué* 2/ *convention (f)* : most of the countries signed the convention = *la plupart des pays ont signé la convention* ⓪ treaty = *traité* 3/ *convention (f)* : getting married is a convention =

c'est une convention de se marier ⓐ tradition = ←
☙ *convention collective* = collective bargaining.

CONVENTIONAL (adj) *conventionnel, -elle* : a conventional education = *une éducation conventionnelle* ⓐ traditional = *traditionnel* ≠ unconventional = *non conventionnel*.

CONVERSATION (n) *conversation (f)* : we had an interesting conversation = *nous avons eu une conversation intéressante* ⓐ chat = *causette*
to bring the conversation around to = *amener la conversation sur*
to bring the conversation back to = *ramener la conversation sur*
to carry on a conversation = *tenir une conversation*
conversation piece = *objet de curiosité* : the antique clock is a conversation piece = *la vieille pendule est un objet de curiosité*
to keep the conversation going = *nourrir/alimenter/entretenir la conversation*
we're just making conversation = *nous parlons pour parler* ⓐ idle talk = *propos oiseux*
☙ *détourner la conversation* = to change the subject
— *elle a de la conversation* = she's a conversationalist.

CONVERSION (n) *conversion (f)* : conversion to Catholicism = *conversion au catholicisme*.

CONVERT (n) *converti, -e*.

CONVERT (to, -ed) *(se) convertir* : many Jews were forced to convert during the Spanish Inquisition = *beaucoup de juifs ont dû se convertir sous l'Inquisition espagnole*
to convert (the dining room) into (a bedroom) = *transformer (la salle à manger) en (chambre à coucher)*.

CONVERTIBLE (n) *décapotable (f)* : will convertibles make a comeback ? = *va-t-il y avoir un retour des décapotables ?*

CONVEY (to, -ed) *communiquer* : I couldn't convey my ideas to him = *je n'ai pas pu lui communiquer mes idées* = I couldn't communicate my ideas to him.

CONVEYANCE (n) **public conveyances** = *transports en commun* = public transportation.

CONVICT (n) *détenu, -e* : two convicts share a cell = *deux détenus partagent une cellule* ⓐ jailbird = *taulard*.

CONVICT (to, -ed) *déclarer coupable* : he was convicted of murder = *il a été déclaré coupable de meurtre* ≠ to be cleared = *être disculpé*.

CONVICTION (n) 1/ *conviction (f)* : his compliments lack conviction = *ses compliments manquent de conviction* 2/ *condamnation (f)* : a second conviction = *une seconde condamnation* ≠ acquittal = *acquittement* ☙ *condamnation à mort* = death sentence.

CONVINCE (to, -d) *convaincre* : he convinced me that he wasn't lying = *il m'a convaincu qu'il ne mentait pas*

ⓐ to persuade = *persuader* ≠ to talk s.o. out of = *dissuader qqn de*
to convince s.o. to = *convaincre qqn de* : he convinced me to help them = *il m'a convaincu de les aider*.

CONVINCED (adj) *convaincu, -e* : convinced that he was lying, I slapped him = *convaincue qu'il mentait, je l'ai giflé* ⓐ persuaded = *persuadé*.

CONVINCING (adj) *convaincant, -e* : your argument isn't convincing = *votre argument n'est pas convaincant* ⓐ valid = *valable*.

CONVOKE (to, -d) *convoquer* : to convoke a meeting = *convoquer une réunion* ⓐ to dissolve = *dissoudre* ☙ *convoquer qqn (au tribunal)* = to summon s.o. (to court).

CONVOY (n) *convoi (m)* : a convoy of trucks = *un convoi de camions* ⓐ escort = *escorte*.

CONVULSION (n) *convulsion (f)* : epileptic convulsions = *des convulsions épileptiques* ⓐ spasm = *spasme*.

COOK (n) *cuisinier, -ère* : I'm not a good cook = *je ne suis pas une bonne cuisinière* ⓐ chef = ←, cookbook = *livre de cuisine*, recipe = *recette*, cordon bleu = *cordon-bleu*
too many cooks spoil the broth = *trop de cuisiniers gâtent la sauce*
☙ *une cuisinière électrique* = an electric stove.

COOK (to, -ed) 1/ *faire la cuisine* : he likes to cook = *il aime faire la cuisine*, I cook every night for the whole family = *je fais tous les soirs la cuisine pour toute la famille* 2/ *(faire) cuire* : the chicken's cooking = *le poulet est en train de cuire*, I'm cooking a chicken = *je suis en train de faire cuire un poulet* ⓐ to roast = *rôtir*, to stew = *mijoter*
to cook up (an excuse) = *(se) forger (une excuse)* ⓐ to concoct = *inventer de toutes pièces*
☙ *on cuit là-dedans !* = it's boiling hot (in) here !
— *cuire au four* = to bake.

COOKED (adj) *cuit, -e* : cooked vegetables = *légumes cuits* ☙ *je suis cuit !* = my number's up !

COOKIE (n) *gâteau (m) sec* ⓐ biscuit = ←, cake = *gâteau*.

COOKING (n) *cuisine (f)* : what great cooking ! = *quelle cuisine délicieuse !* ☙ → kitchen
to do the cooking = *faire la cuisine*.

COOKOUT (n) *barbecue (m)* : we're having a cookout tonight = *ce soir, nous faisons un barbecue*.

COOL (n) **to blow one's cool** = *se mettre en boule* : the boss blew his cool = *le patron s'est mis en boule* → ANGRY
to keep ≠ **lose one's cool** = *garder* ≠ *perdre son sang-froid*.

COOL (adj, -er, -est) 1/ *cool* : Peter's a cool guy = *Pierre est un type cool* ⓐ loose = *relax* ≠ uptight = *coincé* 2/ *frais, fraîche* : a cool evening/drink = *une soirée/bois-*

son fraîche ≠ hot = *chaud* 💀 → fresh **3/** *extra* : what a cool movie ! = *quel film extra !* → WONDERFUL 💀 → *extra* **4/** *plutôt tiède* : a cool welcome = *un accueil plutôt tiède* ≠ enthusiastic = *enthousiaste*

to be as cool as a cucumber = *garder la tête froide*
to be cool to = 1/ *ne pas être chaud pour* : the Senate's cool to the project = *le Sénat n'est pas chaud pour le projet* ≠ to be all for = *être à cent pour cent pour* 2/ *battre froid* : she was very cool to me = *elle m'a battu froid*

a cool customer = *qqn de finaud* : my lawyer's a cool customer = *mon avocat est quelqu'un de finaud* ⓓ shrewdy = *qqn d'habile*

a cool (million) = *(un million) tout rond*

stay cool ! = *t'emballe pas !* ⓓ hold your horses ! = *minute papillon !*

COOL (adv) **to play it cool** = *y aller molo* : she played it cool with him at the beginning = *elle y est allée molo avec lui au début.*

COOL (to, -ed) *beaucoup diminuer* : their passion cooled = *leur passion a beaucoup diminué* ⓓ to wane = *être sur le déclin*

cool it ! = *mets-la en veilleuse !* → BUZZ OFF !

to cool down = *se calmer* : I'll tell you what to do when you cool down = *je vous dirai ce qu'il faut faire quand vous vous calmerez* 💀 → to calm

to cool off = *(se) rafraîchir* : have a glass of milk, it'll cool you off = *prenez un verre de lait, ça vous rafraîchira* 💀 → to freshen up.

COOP (n) **to fly the coop** = *prendre la clef des champs* ⓓ to escape from = *s'échapper de.*

CO-OP (n) **1/** *coopérative (f)* : a farmers' co-op = *une coopérative agricole* ⓓ association = ← **2/** *appartement (m) en copropriété* : he bought a co-op in New York = *il a acheté un appartement en copropriété à New York.*

COOPERATE (to, -d) *coopérer* : to cooperate with foreign countries = *coopérer avec des pays étrangers* ⓓ to participate = *participer* **COOPERATION** (n) *coopération (f)* : we need her cooperation = *nous avons besoin de sa coopération* ⓓ collaboration = ← 💀 *partir en coopération* = to be part of the French Peace Corps.

COOPERATIVE (n) *coopérative (f)* = co-op.

COOPERATIVE (adj) *coopératif, -ive* : thank you for being so cooperative = *merci d'avoir été si coopératif* ⓓ helpful = *serviable.*

COOP UP (to, -ed) *cloîtrer* : to be cooped up with pneumonia = *être cloîtré avec une pneumonie* ⓓ to be shut up = *être enfermé.*

COORDINATE (to, -d) *coordonner* : let's coordinate the work = *coordonnons le travail.*

COORDINATION (n) *coordination (f)* : your work lacks coordination = *votre travail manque de coordination* ⓓ organization = *organisation.*

COORDINATOR (n) *coordinateur, -trice* : the coordinator of the gala = *le coordinateur du gala* ⓓ organizer = *organisateur.*

COP (n) *flic (m)* : there are few female cops = *il y a peu de femmes flics* ⓓ meter maid = *contractuelle*, flatfoot = *condé*, the fuzz = *les poulets*, beat = *ronde*, motorcycle cop = *motard*, pig = *cogne*

to play cops and robbers = *jouer au gendarme et au voleur*

the cops are coming ! = *22, v'là les flics !*

COPE (to, -d) *faire face* : with all her kids she has a hard time coping = *avec tous ses gosses, elle a du mal à faire face*

to cope with = *faire face à* : I can't cope with his problems = *je ne peux pas faire face à ses problèmes* ⓓ to handle = *assumer*, to contend with = *affronter.*

COPIOUS (adj) *copieux, -euse* : a copious meal = *un repas copieux* ≠ frugal = ←, meager = *maigre.*

COP-OUT (n) *dérobade (f)* : her not coming at the last moment was a cop-out = *c'était une dérobade de ne pas venir au dernier moment.*

COP OUT (to, -ped) *se débiner* : he promised to help but copped out at the last moment = *il a promis de nous aider mais il s'est débiné au dernier moment* ⓓ to get cold feet = *se dégonfler* 💀 *débiner qqn* = to put s.o. down.

COPPER (n, adj) *cuivre (m)* : a copper pot = *une casserole en cuivre* ⓓ brass = *laiton* 💀 *les cuivres (orchestre)* = the brass (orchestra).

COPY (n inv) *texte (m) publicitaire* : I'm writing the copy for the ad = *je suis en train de rédiger le texte de l'annonce* **COPYWRITER** (n) *rédacteur, -trice en publicité.*

COPY (n, -ies) **1/** *copie (f)* : make three copies = *faites trois copies*
💀 *rendez vos copies* = hand in your papers
— *une pâle copie de* = a pale imitation of
2/ *exemplaire (m)* : a copy of Newsweek/Time = *un exemplaire de Newsweek/Time* ⓓ issue = *numéro*
to make (good) copy = *être un sujet en or* : sex scandals make good copy = *les affaires de mœurs sont des sujets en or.*

COPY (to, -ied) **1/** *copier* : she copies everything I do = *elle copie tout ce que je fais* ⓓ to imitate = *imiter* **2/** *recopier* : copy the poem on the board = *recopiez le poème au tableau*
to copy from = *copier sur* : he copied from my paper = *il a copié sur ma feuille.*

COPYCAT (n) *copieur, -euse* : you bought the same hat as mine, you copycat ! = *tu as acheté le même chapeau que moi, espèce de copieuse !* ⓓ follower = *mouton de Panurge.*

COPYRIGHT (n) *copyright (m)* **COPYRIGHT** (to, -ed) *obtenir le copyright de.*

CORAL (n, adj) *corail* *(m)* : a coral reef = *un récif de corail* ⊕ mother-of-pearl = *nacre.*

CORD (n) *cordon* *(m), grosse ficelle* *(f)* : I need some cord for the packages = *j'ai besoin de grosse ficelle pour les paquets* ⊕ rope = *corde* ☠ *tenir les cordons de la bourse* = to hold the purse strings.

CORDIAL (adj) *cordial, -e* : a cordial answer = *une réponse cordiale* ≠ unfriendly = *inamical.*

CORDIALITY (n) *cordialité* (f) **CORDIALLY** (adv) *cordialement.*

CORDUROY (n) *velours* *(m) côtelé* ⊕ material = *tissu.*

CORE (n) *noyau* *(m)* : the core of the matter = *le noyau du problème* ⊕ crux = *nœud* ☠ → pit
to the core = *jusqu'à la moelle* : she's a bitch to the core = *elle est salope jusqu'à la moelle* ⊕ a hundred percent = *à cent pour cent.*

CORK (n) *bouchon* *(m)* : this wine bottle has a bad cork = *cette bouteille de vin a un mauvais bouchon* ⊕ corkscrew = *tire-bouchon,* label = *étiquette* ☠ → bottleneck.

CORKER (n) *qqch de pas piqué des vers* : his answer was a corker = *sa réponse n'était pas piquée des vers* ⊕ humdinger = *truc super, lulu* = *qqch de pas piqué des hannetons.*

CORN (n inv) 1/ *maïs* *(m)* : do you like corn ? = *est-ce que vous aimez le maïs ?* ⊕ popcorn = *pop-corn*
corn on the cob = *maïs en épi*
corn beef = *corned-beef/singe* ⊕ pickle = *cornichon*
corn belt = *Midwest agricole* = *Iowa + Illinois + Ohio + Indiana + Kansas*
2/ *guimauve* (f) : what corn that movie was ! = *quelle guimauve, ce film !* ⊕ mush = *sensiblerie.*

CORNER (n) *coin* *(m)* : the four corners of the world = *les quatre coins du monde*
around the corner = *à deux pas* : I found a parking place around the corner = *j'ai trouvé une place pour me garer à deux pas*
go stand in a corner ! = *va au coin !*
to cut corners = *rogner sur tout* : they cut corners to make their trip cheaper = *ils rognent sur tout pour avoir un voyage moins cher*
to look at s.o. out of the corner of one's eye = *regarder qqn du coin de l'œil*
on the corner = *au coin* : I'll meet you on the corner = *je vous retrouverai au coin*
☠ *un coin sympa* = a nice place/area/spot/dive
— *(chercher) dans tous les coins* = (to look) all over the place
— *il est dans le coin* = he's in the area
— *ça m'en a bouché un coin* = it was mindblowing
— *(la pharmacie) du coin* = the neighborhood (drugstore).

CORNER (adj) *qui fait le coin* : the corner building = *l'immeuble qui fait le coin.*

CORNER (to, -ed) *coincer* : the journalist tried to get some information but he couldn't corner the Prime Minister = *le journaliste a essayé d'obtenir des renseignements, mais il n'a pas réussi à coincer le Premier ministre*
☠ *coincer un criminel* = to nail a criminal
— *(ma fermeture Éclair) est coincée* = (my zipper) is stuck.

CORNERSTONE (n) *pierre* (f) *angulaire* : the Constitution is the cornerstone of American democracy = *la Constitution est la pierre angulaire de la démocratie américaine* ⊕ keystone = *clef de voûte.*

CORNY (adj, -ier, -iest) *sentimentalo* : a corny film/guy = *un film/type sentimentalo* ⊕ schmaltzy = *plein de sentimentalisme.*

CORPORATE (adj) **corporate responsibility** = *responsabilité morale.*

CORPORATION (n) *société* (f) (commerciale) : she works for an important corporation = *elle travaille pour une société importante* ⊕ limited liability company = *société à responsabilité limitée,* multinational company = *multinationale*
☠ *une corporation* = a guild
— *société* → society.

CORPSE (n) *cadavre* *(m)* : the corpse was on the floor = *le cadavre était par terre* ⊕ stiff = *macchabée,* remains = *dépouille.*

CORRECT (adj) *correct, -e* : a correct answer = *une réponse correcte* ≠ incorrect = ←
that's correct ! = *c'est exact !* ⊕ that's right ! = *c'est ça !*
the correct time = *l'heure exacte*
you were correct in (saying that) = *vous aviez raison de (dire ça)*
☠ *correct en affaires* = square in business dealings.

CORRECT (to, -ed) *corriger* : he always corrects my mistakes in French = *il corrige toujours mes fautes de français* ⊕ to rectify = *rectifier*
correct me if I'm wrong, but ... = *dites-moi si je me trompe, mais ...*
☠ *corriger qqn* = to give s.o. a licking.

CORRECTION (n) *correction* (f) : he made several corrections = *il a fait plusieurs corrections* ⊕ rectification = ← ☠ *flanquer une correction à qqn* = to give s.o. a licking.

CORRECTLY (adv) *correctement* : she answered correctly = *elle a répondu correctement.*

CORRESPOND (to, -ed) *correspondre* : the two friends have corresponded for a long time = *les deux amis correspondent depuis longtemps* ⊕ to write = *écrire*
to correspond to/with = *correspondre à* : he didn't correspond to/with the image I had of him = *il ne correspondait pas à l'image que je me faisais de lui.*

CORRESPONDENCE (n) *correspondance* (f) : correspondence course = *cours par correspondance* ☠ *correspondance (train)* = connection (train).

CORRESPONDENT (n) *correspondant, -e, envoyé, -e* : he's a correspondent for the Times = *c'est un correspondant du Times* ⓓ journalist = *journaliste* ⚲ *un correspondant en France* = a pen pal in France.

CORRESPONDING (adj) *correspondant, -e* : most idioms have a corresponding idiom in other languages = *la plupart des expressions idiomatiques ont une expression correspondante dans les autres langues.*

CORRIDOR (n) *corridor* (m) : your room's at the end of the corridor = *votre chambre est au bout du corridor* ⓓ hall = *couloir.*

CORROBORATE (to, -d) *corroborer* : that corroborates what he said = *cela corrobore ce qu'il a dit* ≠ to contradict = *contredire.*

CORRUPT (adj) *corrompu, -e* : corrupt lawyers/politicians = *avocats/politiciens corrompus* ⓓ dishonest = *malhonnête* ≠ straight = *droit* **CORRUPT** (to, -ed) *corrompre* : too much power corrupts = *trop de pouvoir corrompt* ⓓ to debase = *abaisser* **CORRUPTION** (n) *corruption* (f) : corruption in political circles = *la corruption dans les milieux politiques* ⓓ bribery = *soudoiement.*

COSMETIC (n) *cosmétique* (m), *produit* (m) *de beauté* : to sell cosmetics = *vendre des cosmétiques/des produits de beauté* ⓓ makeup = *maquillage.*

COSMONAUT (n) *cosmonaute* (m, f) ⓓ astronaut = *astronaute.*

COSMOPOLITAN (adj) *cosmopolite* : a cosmopolitan city = *une ville cosmopolite* ⓓ international = ←, sophisticated = *sophistiqué.*

COST (n) *coût* (m) : the cost of the trip = *le coût du voyage* ⓓ price = *prix*
at cost = *à prix coûtant*
cost of living = *coût de la vie*
cost price = *prix coûtant/de revient* ⓓ list price = *tarif*
at all/any cost = *à tout prix.*

COST (to, cost, cost) *coûter* : how much does it cost ? = *combien ça coûte ?*, it costs too much = *ça coûte trop cher* ⓓ to pay = *payer.*

CO-STAR (to, -red) *se partager la vedette* : Taylor and Burton co-starred in the film = *Taylor et Burton se sont partagé la vedette de ce film* ⓓ to play opposite = *se donner la réplique.*

COSTLY (adj, -ier, -iest) *coûteux, -euse* : abortions are costly = *les avortements sont coûteux* ⓓ sky-high = *hors de prix* ≠ cheap = *bon marché.*

COSTUME (n) *costume* (m) : you must come in costume = *vous devez venir en costume* ⓓ fancy dress = *déguisement* ⚲ *un costume (deux pièces)* = a suit.

COSTUME (adj) *costumé, -e* : costume ball = *bal costumé*
costume jewelry = *bijoux fantaisie.*

COT (n) *lit* (m) *de camp* ⓓ bed = *lit.*

COTTAGE (n) *petite maison* (f) *de campagne, cottage* (m) : a cottage lost in the country = *une petite maison perdue dans la campagne* ⓓ villa = ←
cottage cheese = *fromage blanc*
thatched cottage = *chaumière*
cottage industry = *entreprise artisanale familiale.*

COTTON (n) *coton* (m) : a cotton dress = *une robe en coton* ⓓ material = *tissu*
cotton candy = *barbe à papa*
Cotton Belt = *États cotonniers du sud-est des États-Unis*
⚲ *c'est coton* = it's not easy
— *élever un enfant dans du coton* = to give a child a sheltered upbringing
— *avoir les jambes en coton* = to be on one's last legs
— *filer un mauvais coton* = to be in a bad way.

COUCH (n, -es) *divan* (m), *canapé* (m) : a comfortable couch = *un divan/canapé confortable* ⓓ armchair = *fauteuil*
casting couch = *droit de cuissage* : the day of the casting couch in Hollywood is over = *il n'y a plus de droit de cuissage à Hollywood.*

COUGH (n) *toux* (f) : I have a bad cough = *j'ai une mauvaise toux* ⓓ sore throat = *mal de gorge*, fit of coughing = *quinte de toux*, whooping cough = *coqueluche.*

COUGH (to, -ed) *tousser* : stop smoking ! you're coughing too much = *arrête de fumer ! tu tousses trop* ⓓ to clear one's throat = *se racler la gorge*
to cough up = *cracher* : he finally coughed up the money he owed me = *il a fini par cracher l'argent qu'il me devait* ⓓ to fork out = *abouler* ⚲ → to spit.

COUNCIL (n) *conseil* (m) : city council = *conseil municipal* ☠ → advice.

COUNSEL (n) 1/ *conseiller, -ère (juridique)* ⓓ solicitor (GB) = *avoué*
the counsel for the defense = *l'avocat de la défense*
2/ *conseil* (m) : invaluable counsel = *un conseil inestimable* ☠ « counsel » *est beaucoup moins employé que* « advice ».

COUNSEL(L)OR (n) 1/ *moniteur, -trice* : camp counselor = *moniteur de colonie de vacances* 2/ *avocat, -e* : the defense counselor is late = *l'avocat de la défense est en retard* = lawyer ⓓ counsel = *conseiller juridique.*

COUNT (n) 1/ *compte* (m) : the count's off = *le compte est faux*
to lose count = *ne plus savoir combien il y en a* : he's had so many wives that I have lost count = *il a eu tellement de femmes que je ne sais plus combien il y en a eu* ⚲ *tenir compte de* = to take into account

— *y trouver son compte* = to get stg out of stg
— *il a mis ça sur le compte de* = he put it down to
— *s'établir à son compte* = to go into business for o.s.
— *en fin de compte/au bout du compte* = in the end
— *un compte dans un magasin* = a charge account in a department store
— *je n'ai pas de comptes à te rendre* = I don't have to report to you
— *avoir un compte à régler* = to have a score to settle
— *se rendre compte* = to realize
— *un compte en banque* = a bank account
— *son compte est bon !* = his number's up !
— *être loin du compte* = to be way off
2/ *comte (m)* : the count of Monte Cristo = *le comte de Monte Cristo* = earl (GB) ⓓ countess = *comtesse*.

COUNT (to, -ed) **1/** *compter* : count the money = *comptez l'argent* ⓓ to add up = *additionner* **2/** *compter* : money counts = *l'argent compte*, she invited the people who count = *elle a invité les gens qui comptent*
not counting = *sans compter* : it will cost $ 10 not counting the tip = *ça coûtera 10 dollars sans compter le pourboire* ≠ including = *y compris*
to count against s.o. = *jouer contre qqn* : his record counts against him = *son casier judiciaire joue contre lui*
to count in = *compter dans* : he doesn't count in the company = *il ne compte pas dans l'entreprise*
count me in ≠ **out** = *je suis* ≠ *je ne suis pas des vôtres/j'en suis* ≠ *très peu pour moi*
to count on = *compter sur* : I'm counting on your help = *je compte sur votre aide* ⓓ to rely on = *se reposer sur*
to count to = *compter jusqu'à* : my son can count to ten = *mon fils sait compter jusqu'à dix*
☠ *que comptez-vous faire ?* = what do you intend to do ?

COUNTDOWN (n) *compte (m) à rebours* ⓓ zero hour = *l'heure H.*

COUNTER (n) *comptoir (m)*, *zinc (m)* (LV) : let's have a coffee at the counter = *prenons un café au comptoir/sur le zinc*
under the counter = *de la main à la main* : the agent asked to be paid under the counter = *l'agent a demandé à être payé de la main à la main* ⓓ under the table = *sous la table*.

COUNTER (adv) **to run counter to** = *aller à l'encontre de* : your suggestion runs counter to the rules = *votre suggestion va à l'encontre des règles* ⓓ to be opposed to = *s'opposer à*.

COUNTER (to, -ed) *contrer* : feminists are trying to counter widespread male chauvinism = *les féministes essaient de contrer une phallocratie trop répandue* ⓓ to oppose = *s'opposer à*.

COUNTERACT (to, -ed) *agir contre* : the government is trying to counteract the rise in oil prices = *le gouvernement essaie d'agir contre la hausse du prix du pétrole* ⓓ to neutralize = *neutraliser*.

COUNTERBALANCE (to, -d) *contrebalancer* : his generosity counterbalances his bad temper = *sa générosité contrebalance son mauvais caractère* ⓓ to offset = *compenser*.

COUNTERFEIT (adj) *faux, fausse* : counterfeit money = *fausse monnaie* ≠ genuine = *authentique* ☠ → false.

COUNTERFEIT (to, -ed) *contrefaire* **COUNTERFEITER** (n) *faux-monnayeur (m)* ⓓ forger = *faussaire*.

COUNTERPART (n) *homologue (m, f)* : he earns more than his counterpart in France = *il gagne plus que son homologue français* ⓓ equivalent = *équivalent*.

COUNTLESS (adj) *innombrable* : countless problems = *des problèmes innombrables* → MANY.

COUNTRY (n, -ies) **1/** *pays (m)* : I love my country = *j'aime mon pays* ⓓ State = *État*, homeland = *patrie* ☠ *avoir vu du pays* = to have been around
— *un vin de pays* = a local wine
— *pays de cocagne* = never-never land
2/ *campagne (f)* : I'm spending this weekend in the country = *je passe le week-end à la campagne* ⓓ backcountry = *arrière-pays*, countryside = *campagne (paysage)*, countryman = *campagnard* ≠ city = *ville* ☠ → campaign
country bumpkin = *cul-terreux* ⓓ hick = *plouc*, yokel = *bouseux*
country club = ←
country house = *maison de campagne*
developing ≠ **underdeveloped countries** = *pays en voie de développement* ≠ *pays sous-développés*.

COUNTRYSIDE (n) *campagne (f)* : the countryside's beautiful in the fall = *la campagne est belle en automne*
to scour the countryside = *battre la campagne* ☠ → campaign.

COUNTY (n, -ies) *comté (m)* ⓓ district = *département*.

COUP D'ÉTAT (n) *coup (m) d'État* ⓓ putsch = ←.

COUPLE (n) *couple (m)* : they're a good couple = *ils forment un bon couple* ⓓ twosome = *paire*
a couple of (drinks) = *quelques (verres)* = a few (drinks) ≠ several = *plusieurs*.

COUPLE OFF (to, -d) *se mettre par couples* : everybody coupled off at the party = *ils se sont tous mis par couples au cours de la soirée*.

COUPON (n) *bon (m)* : a coupon on each box = *un bon sur chaque boîte* ⓓ ticket = *billet* ☠ → bond.

COURAGE (n) *courage (m)* : a man of great courage = *un homme d'un grand courage* ⓓ backbone = *trempe* ≠ cowardice = *lâcheté*
to have the courage of one's convictions = *avoir le courage de ses opinions*
I don't have the courage to (tell him) = *je n'ai pas le courage de (le lui dire)*

to take one's courage in both hands = *prendre son courage à deux mains*
☠ *courage !* = keep smiling !
— *elle a beaucoup de courage* = she's got a lot of energy/will/guts.

COURAGEOUS (adj) *courageux, -euse* : a courageous speech/position = *un discours courageux/une position courageuse* ⊕ valiant = *vaillant* ≠ yellow = *trouillard*.

COURSE (n) **1/** *cours (m)* : she's taking a French course twice a week = *elle suit un cours de français deux fois par semaine*
course of action = *ligne de conduite* ⊕ policy = *politique*
in the course of (the year) = *au cours de (l'année)*
of course ! = *bien sûr !* ⊕ for sure = *à coup sûr* ≠ of course not = *bien sûr que non*
(things) must take their course = *il faut laisser (les choses) suivre leur cours*
crash/refresher course = *cours accéléré/de recyclage*
☠ *l'année en cours* = the present year
— *le cours de (l'or)* = the price of (gold)
— *un cours d'eau* = a river
— *une course* = a race
2/ *plat (m)* : main course = *plat principal* ☠ → dish.

COURT (n) **1/** *tribunal (m)* : my lawyer's in court this morning = *mon àvocat est au tribunal ce matin* ⊕ the bench = *le parquet*, lawyer = *avocat*, court-martial = *cour martiale*, courthouse = *palais de justice*, the dock = *le banc des accusés*
criminal court = *cour d'assises*
court of appeal = *cour d'appel*
juvenile court = *tribunal pour enfants*
Supreme Court = *Cour suprême*
(to settle) out of court = *régler à l'amiable* ≠ to bring an action = *intenter une action en justice*
to take/bring to court = *attaquer en justice* ≠ to drop charges = *retirer sa plainte*
2/ *court (m)* : tennis court = *court de tennis*
3/ *cour (f)* : royalty and the court = *la royauté et la cour*
☠ *faire la cour à qqn* = to court s.o.
— *cour (d'immeuble)* = courtyard.

COURT (to, -ed) **1/** *faire la cour à* : to court a girl/voters = *faire la cour à une fille/à ses électeurs* ⊕ to woo = *courtiser* **2/** *s'exposer à* : you're courting danger/trouble = *tu t'exposes à un danger/à des ennuis* ⊕ to look for = *chercher*.

COURTEOUS (adj) *courtois, -e* : a courteous letter = *une lettre courtoise* ⊕ amiable = *aimable* ≠ ill-mannered = *mal élevé*.

COURTESY (n, -ies) *courtoisie (f)* ≠ rudeness = *grossièreté*
by courtesy of (the American government) = *avec la permission/le concours (du gouvernement américain)*
a courtesy call = *une visite de politesse*.

COURTYARD (n) *cour (f) de l'immeuble* : no parking in the courtyard = *il est défendu de stationner dans la*

cour ⊕ yard = *jardin*.

COUSIN (n) *cousin, -e* : we're cousins = *nous sommes cousins* ⊕ first cousin = *cousin germain*, once/twice removed = *germain/issu de germain*.

COVER (n) **1/** *couverture (f)* : the cover of a book = *la couverture d'un livre* ☠ → blanket **2/** *couvercle (m)* : put the cover on the pot = *mets le couvercle sur la casserole* = put the lid on the pot **3/** *couverture (f)* : the store's a cover for drug dealing = *le magasin est une couverture pour le trafic de drogue* = the store's a front for drug dealing ☠ → blanket

cover charge = *droit d'entrée* **cover girl** = *cover-girl* ⊕ model = *mannequin*	**cover story** = *grand reportage faisant la couverture d'une revue* **take cover !** = *planquez-vous !/abritez-vous !*

COVER (to, -ed) **1/** *couvrir* : snow covered the garden = *la neige couvrait le jardin* **2/** *couvrir* : John's covering the elections/the riots = *John couvre les élections/les émeutes* ⊕ to write a lead article = *écrire un article de fond* **3/** *couvrir* (distance), *abattre* (work) : we covered five miles/a lot of work today = *nous avons couvert une distance de cinq miles/nous avons abattu pas mal de boulot aujourd'hui*

to cover (up) for s.o. = *couvrir qqn* : if the boss comes back, cover for me = *si le patron revient, couvre-moi* **to cover up** = **1/** *cacher* : he tried to cover up his shyness/his mistakes = *il a essayé de cacher sa*	*timidité/ses erreurs* ☠ → to hide **2/** *se couvrir* : it's cold outside, cover up ! = *il fait froid dehors, couvrez-vous !* ⊕ to bundle up = *s'emmitoufler* **to cover with** = *(re)couvrir de* : covered with leaves = *(re)couvert de feuilles*

☠ *abattre qqn* = to shoot s.o. down — *abattre une maison* = to pull down a house — *couvrir qqn de ridicule* = to make s.o. look ridiculous — *le temps se couvre* = the weather's clouding over.

COVERAGE (n) *couverture (f)* : the American elections got full ≠ scant coverage abroad = *il y a eu une bonne ≠ insuffisante couverture des élections américaines à l'étranger*
(insurance) coverage = *couverture (par l'assurance)* ☠ → blanket.

COVER-UP (n) *tentative (f) pour étouffer (une affaire)* : the journalist found out it was a cover-up = *le journa-*

liste a découvert qu'il s'agissait d'une tentative pour étouffer l'affaire.

COW (n) *vache (f)* ⓓ calf = *veau*, bull = *taureau*, udder = *pis*, heifer = *génisse*, to milk = *traire*, to moo = *meugler*
when the cows come home = *quand les poules auront des dents* ⓓ when hell freezes over = *à Pâques ou à la Trinité*
☠ *la vache !* = damn it !
— *tu es vache !* = you're rotten !
— *mort aux vaches !* = death to/kill the pigs !
— *considérer (une affaire) comme une vache à lait* = to milk (a business)
— *manger de la vache enragée* = to have a rough time of it financially
— *il pleut comme vache qui pisse* = it's raining cats and dogs
— *période de vaches maigres* = lean years.

COWARD (n) *lâche (m, f), couard, -e* : what a coward you are ! = *quel lâche tu fais !* ⓓ chicken = *poule mouillée*, poltroon = *poltron*.

COWARDICE (n) *lâcheté (f), couardise (f)* : what cowardice ! = *quelle lâcheté !* ≠ bravery = *bravoure*.

COWARDLY (adj) *lâche* : a cowardly attitude = *une attitude lâche* ⓓ pusillanimous = *pusillanime* ≠ courageous = *courageux* ☠ *une robe lâche* = a loose dress
COWARDLY (adv) *lâchement* : to act cowardly = *agir lâchement*.

COWBOY (n) *cow-boy (m)* : she's in love with a cowboy = *elle est amoureuse d'un cow-boy* ⓓ ranch = ←, cowgirl = *cow-girl*.

COY (adj, -er, -est) *coquin, -e* : he gave her a coy smile = *il lui a fait un sourire coquin* ⓓ mischievous = *espiègle*.

COZY (adj, -ier, -iest) *cosy, douillet, -ette* : a cozy apartment/restaurant = *un appartement douillet/un restaurant cosy* ⓓ quaint = *au charme vieillot*.

C.P.A. (abbr) = Certified Public Accountant = *expert-comptable (m, f)*.

CRAB (n) **1/** *crabe (m)* : crab soup = *soupe au crabe* ⓓ lobster = *homard* **2/** *rouspéteur, -euse* : you're always complaining, what a crab ! = *tu es toujours en train de te plaindre, quel rouspéteur !* ⓓ grouch = *grognon*.

CRAB (to, -bed) *rouspéter* : stop crabbing ! = *arrêtez de rouspéter !* ⓓ to grouse = *g"rincher* **CRABBY** (adj, -ier, -iest) *bougon, -onne* : in a crabby mood = *d'humeur bougonne* ⓓ grumpy = *grincheux*.

CRABS (n pl) *morpions (m pl)* : he has crabs = *il a des morpions* ⓓ the clap = *la chaude-pisse*.

CRACK (n) **1/** *fêlure (f), lézarde (f)* : a crack in the wall = *une lézarde sur le mur*, a crack in the vase = *la fêlure d'un vase* **2/** *vanne (f)* : what a nasty crack ! = *quelle méchante vanne !* ⓓ jab = *pointe*
to make cracks = *lancer des vannes*

to take a crack at (doing stg) = *essayer de (faire qqch).*

CRACK (adj) *crack* : a crack tennis player/businessman = *un crack au tennis/en affaires* ⓓ topflight = *de haut vol* ≠ third-rate = *de troisième ordre*
crack shot = *fin tireur* ⓓ good shot = *bon fusil*.

CRACK (to, -ed) **1/** *(se) fêler, (se) lézarder* (wall) : the glass/wall cracked = *le verre s'est fêlé/le mur s'est lézardé* ⓓ to split = *(se) fendre* ☠ *lézarder au soleil* = to bask in the sun **2/** *craquer* : she cracked under the pressure of the divorce = *elle a craqué sous le coup du divorce* ⓓ to break down = *faire une dépression* ☠ *leur couple a craqué* = they split up
to crack down on = *mettre le holà à* (stg), *s'attaquer à* (s.o.) : the cops are cracking down on drug smuggling = *les flics mettent le holà au trafic de drogue*, the government's cracking down on drug dealers = *le gouvernement s'attaque aux revendeurs de drogue*
to crack up = **1/** *craquer* : after the accident, he cracked up = *après l'accident, il a craqué* **2/** *se tordre de rire* : the joke cracked us up = *la blague nous a fait (nous) tordre de rire* ⓓ to break up = *se bidonner* **3/** *mettre en compote/en accordéon* : he cracked up the car = *il a mis la voiture en compote/en accordéon*
it wasn't all it was cracked up to be = *c'était surfait* ⓓ it didn't come up to expectations = *ça n'a pas répondu à l'attente*.

CRACKDOWN (n) *coup (m) de force* : a crackdown on drugs = *un coup de force contre la drogue*.

CRACKED (adj) **1/** *fêlé, -e* : you're cracked if you think I'll sleep with you ! = *si tu penses que je vais coucher avec toi, t'es un peu fêlé !* → CRAZY **2/** *fêlé, -e, lézardé, -e* (wall) : a cracked plate/wall = *une assiette fêlée/un mur lézardé*.

CRACKER (n) *biscuit (m) salé* : buy some crackers = *va acheter des biscuits (salés)* ⓓ cookie = *gâteau sec*.

CRACKERJACK (n) *crack (m)* : he's a crackerjack at bridge = *c'est un crack au bridge* ⓓ champion = ←.

CRACKPOT (n) *dingo (m)* : what a crackpot she married ! = *quel dingo elle a épousé !* ⓓ madman = *forcené*.

CRACK-UP (n) **1/** *carambolage (m)* : a crack-up on the highway = *un carambolage sur l'autoroute* ⓓ collision = ← **2/** *effondrement (m) (nerveux)* ⓓ nervous breakdown = *dépression nerveuse* ☠ *effondrement (prix)* = collapse (prices).

CRADLE (n) *berceau (m)* : Greece is the cradle of Western civilization = *la Grèce est le berceau de la civilisation occidentale*, a child's cradle = *le berceau d'un enfant*
to rob the cradle = *les prendre au berceau*.

CRAFT (n) *métier (m) artisanal* : pottery's a craft = *la poterie est un métier artisanal* ⓓ craftsman = *artisan*.

CRAFT (n inv) *bateau (m) /avion (m) de plaisance* : many small craft in the harbor = *beaucoup de petits bateaux de plaisance dans le port.*

CRAFTY (adj, -ier, -iest) *roublard, -e* : a crafty lawyer = *un avocat roublard* ⓓ sly = *sournois.*

CRAM (to, -med) *bachoter* : to cram for an exam = *bachoter pour un examen* ⓓ to study = *étudier*
to cram into = 1/ *bloquer sur* : the tour was crammed into a week = *le voyage était bloqué sur une semaine* 2/ *entasser dans* : they crammed everyone into the elevator = *ils ont entassé tout le monde dans l'ascenseur*
to be crammed with (people/papers) = *être bourré de (gens/papiers)* = to be loaded with ⓓ to be packed = *être plein à craquer.*

CRAMP (n) *crampe (f)* : a cramp in my leg = *une crampe à la jambe* ⓓ spasm = *spasme.*

CRAMPED (adj) *où l'on est à l'étroit* : a cramped apartment = *un appartement où l'on est à l'étroit.*

CRANBERRY (n, -ies) *airelle (f)* : stuffed turkey and cranberry sauce = *de la dinde farcie et de la sauce aux airelles* ⓓ corn bread = *pain à la farine de maïs*, pumpkin pie = *tarte au potiron*, pecan pie = *tarte aux pacanes.*

CRANK (n) *ronchonneur, -euse* : what a crank you are ! = *quel ronchonneur tu fais !* ⓓ crab = *grognon*
CRANKY (adj, -ier, -iest) *ronchon, -onne* : a cranky husband = *un mari ronchon* ⓓ cantankerous = *acariâtre.*

CRANK (adj) *de détraqué, -e* : a crank call = *un coup de téléphone de détraqué.*

CRAP (n inv) 1/ *saloperies (f pl)* : what's all this crap on the table ? = *qu'est-ce que c'est que toutes ces saloperies sur la table ?*, take your crap and let's go = *prends tes saloperies et allons-y* ⓓ junk = *machins* 2/ *de la merde* : his books/films are crap = *ses livres/films, c'est de la merde* ⓓ trash = *saletés*
cut the crap ! = *arrête tes conneries !* → BUZZ OFF !
a piece of crap = *de la merde* : the watch you bought is a piece of crap ! = *la montre que tu as achetée, c'est de la merde !* = the watch you bought is a piece of shit !
to take a crap = *chier un coup*
that's a lot of crap ! = *quelles conneries !*

CRAP ! (interj) *merde !* → GOSH !

CRAPPY (adj, -ier, -iest) *merdique* : a crappy watch = *une montre merdique* → AWFUL.

CRAPS (n pl) *jeu (m) de dés (genre de 421)* : to play craps = *jouer aux dés* ⓓ to gamble = *jouer.*

CRASH (n, -es) *accident (m)* : a car/plane crash = *un acci-* dent de voiture/d'avion ⓓ collision = ← ☠ → accident
Wall Street/Stock Market crash = *krach de Wall Street/krach boursier.*

CRASH (to, -ed) 1/ *s'écraser* : the plane crashed = *l'avion s'est écrasé* ⓓ a crash landing = *un atterrissage en catastrophe*
to crash into = *percuter (contre)* : the car crashed into a tree = *la voiture a percuté (contre) un arbre* ⓓ to collide with = *rentrer dans*
☠ *écraser (son adversaire)* = to wipe the floor with (one's opponent)
— *écrase !* = shut up !
— *se faire écraser* = to be run over
— *être écrasé de travail* = to be snowed under with work
— *écraser (une révolte)* = to crush/to squash (a revolt)
2/ *resquiller* : they weren't invited to the party but they crashed (in) = *ils n'étaient pas invités à la soirée, mais ils ont resquillé* = to gate-crash.

CRASS (adj) *crasse* : crass stupidity/vulgarity = *stupidité/vulgarité crasse* ⓓ gross = *grossier.*

CRATE (n) *caisse (f), cageot (m)* (fruit, vegetables) : oranges in crates = *des caisses/cageots d'oranges* ⓓ carton = ←
☠ *caisse d'épargne* = savings bank
— *la caisse* = the cash register.

CRATER (n) *cratère (m)* : the crater of a volcano = *le cratère d'un volcan.*

CRAVE (to, -d) **to crave for** = *mourir d'envie de* : I crave for a good Chinese dinner = *je meurs d'envie d'un bon dîner chinois* ⓓ to long for = *avoir très envie de.*

CRAVING (n) *envie (f) folle* : a craving for chocolate = *une envie folle de chocolat.*

CRAWL (n) *crawl (m)* : to do the crawl = *nager le crawl* ⓓ to float = *faire la planche.*

CRAWL (to, -ed) : *marcher à quatre pattes* : the baby crawls = *le bébé marche à quatre pattes* = the baby goes on all fours
to crawl with = *fourmiller de* : crawling with cops = *qui fourmille de flics* ⓓ to swarm with = *grouiller de.*

CRAYON (n) *crayon (m) de couleur* ⓓ pencil = *crayon.*

CRAZE (n) *engouement (m), toquade (f)* : roller-skating is the latest craze = *le patin à roulettes est la toquade du moment* ⓓ fad = *grande vogue.*

CRAZINESS (n inv) *folie (f)* : that's utter craziness ! = *c'est de la pure folie !* = madness ≠ wisdom = *sagesse*
☠ *la folie des grandeurs* = delusions of grandeur
— *faire des folies* = to go on a shopping spree
— *vous avez fait des folies !* = you shouldn't have !

CRAZY (adj, -ier, -iest) *fou, folle* : a crazy guy/idea = *un type fou/une idée folle* ≠ sane = *sain d'esprit*

to be crazy about (music/s.o.) = *être fou de (musique/qqn)* ⓓ to be wild about = *être dingue de*	≠ to be cool to = *ne pas être chaud pour* **to drive s.o. crazy** = *rendre qqn fou* : the kids are

driving me crazy = *les gosses me rendent fou* ⓄⒹ to drive s.o. wild = *faire tourner qqn en bourrique*
to go crazy for = *être fou de* : I go crazy for spare ribs = *je suis fou des travers de porc* ⓄⒹ to go nuts for = *être dingue de*

like **crazy** = *vachement* : he drinks like crazy = *il boit vachement* → VERY ☠ → damned
to run like crazy = *courir à toute allure* ⓄⒹ to run like mad = *courir comme un fou*

──────── GROUP : CRAZY = FOU ────────

bananas = *siphonné* **barmy** = *braque* = **bonkers** (GB) **batty** = *givré* **buggy** = *frappé* **cockeyed** = *maboul* **cracked** = *fêlé* **crackers** (GB) = *timbré* **crazed** = *barjot* **cuckoo** = *zinzin* **daft** = *sinoque* **demented** = *détraqué* **dotty** = *maboul* **far-gone** = *ravagé* **flipped** = *qui déménage* **freaked out** = *jeté* **to go berserk** = *perdre la boule* **to go haywire** = *perdre la boussole* **goofy** = *toqué* **to have bats in the belfry** = *avoir une araignée dans le plafond*	**to have a screw loose** = *avoir une case en moins* **insane** = *insensé* **loco** = *fada* **loony** = *marteau* **to lose one's marbles** = *perdre les pédales* **mad** = *fou* **mad as a hatter** = *qui travaille du chapeau* **mental** = *dérangé* **not all there** = *qui n'a pas toute sa tête* **not right/soft in the head** = *qui ne tourne pas rond (dans sa tête)* **nuts** = *dingue* **nutty** = *dingue* **nutty as a fruitcake** = *qui travaille du chapeau* **meshuga** = *dingue* **off** = *cinglé* **off one's nut** = *qui a une case vide/un grain*	**off one's rocker** = *qui a un petit vélo* **off-the-wall** = *timbré* **ought to have one's head examined** = *ça se soigne* **out of one's head** = *tombé sur la tête* **out of one's mind** = *qui a perdu l'esprit* = **not right in one's mind** **psycho** = *désaxé* **psychotic** = *psychotique* **raving lunatic** = *fou furieux* **screwy** = *dingo* **sick** = *malade* **stark raving mad** = *fou à lier* **to take leave of one's senses** = *perdre la raison* **touched** = *piqué* **unbalanced** = *déséquilibré* **w(h)acky** = *loufoque* **weird** = *taré* **zany** = *louf*

☠ *avoir le fou rire* = to be giddy
— *fou de (joie)* = beside o.s. with (joy)

— *pas folle la guêpe !* = she's nobody's fool !
— *un succès fou* = a tremendous success.

CREAM (n) *crème* (f) : do you take cream in your coffee ? = *est-ce que vous voulez de la crème dans votre café ?* ⓄⒹ creamy = *crémeux*, whipped cream = *crème fouettée*
the cream of the crop = *la fine fleur* ⓄⒹ the pick of the bunch = *le dessus du panier*
the cream of society = *la crème*
cream cheese = *fromage à tartiner*
☠ *un (café) crème* = a white coffee.

CREASE (n) *faux pli* (m) : a crease in her dress = *un faux pli à sa robe.*

CREASE (to, -d) *froisser* : you're creasing your dress = *vous êtes en train de froisser votre robe* ⓄⒹ to rumple = *chiffonner*
☠ *il est froissé* = he's peeved
— *se froisser (un muscle)* = to strain (a muscle).

CREATE (to, -d) **1/** *créer* : he created a new kind of gun = *il a créé une nouvelle sorte d'arme à feu* ⓄⒹ to invent = *inventer* **2/** *créer* : having a child creates a lot of problems = *ça crée pas mal de problèmes d'avoir un enfant* ⓄⒹ to trigger off = *déclencher.*

CREATION (n) *création* (f) : his latest creations = *ses dernières créations* ⓄⒹ work of art = *œuvre d'art.*

CREATIVE (adj) *créateur, -trice, créatif, -ive* (s.o.) : a creative person/mind = *une personne créative/un esprit créateur* ⓄⒹ inventive = *inventif.*

CREATIVITY (n, -ies) *créativité* (f) : a young artist full of creativity = *un jeune artiste plein de créativité.*

CREATOR (n) *créateur, -trice* ⓄⒹ inventor = *inventeur.*

CREATURE (n) *créature* (f) : Man and other creatures = *l'homme et les autres créatures* ⓄⒹ being = *être*
we're creatures of habit = *l'habitude est une seconde nature.*

CREDENTIALS (n pl) *aptitudes* (f pl) : he doesn't have the credentials to write a biography of de Gaulle = *il n'a pas les aptitudes pour écrire une biographie de De Gaulle*
to show one's credentials = *montrer patte blanche*
(the Ambassador's) credentials = *les lettres de créance (de l'ambassadeur).*

131

CREDIBILITY (n) **credibility gap** = *manque de crédibilité.*

CREDIBLE (adj) *crédible :* the statement wasn't credible = *sa déclaration n'était pas crédible* = believable ≠ incredible = *incroyable.*

CREDIT (n) **1/** *crédit (m) :* they don't give any credit = *ils ne font pas de crédit* 🐝 *nous n'avons pas les crédits nécessaires* = we don't have the necessary funds

to be a credit to = *faire honneur à :* she's a credit to the company = *elle fait honneur à l'entreprise*	*crédit de qqn :* I give him credit for apologizing = *il a présenté des excuses, c'est à porter à son crédit* 2/ croire
to buy on credit = *acheter à crédit* ≠ to pay cash = *acheter comptant*	*(qqch de qqn) :* I gave him credit for more sense than that = *je le croyais plus intelligent que ça*
credit card = *carte de crédit*	
credit squeeze = *restrictions de crédit*	**he took all the credit for himself** = *il s'en est attribué tout le mérite*
to get credit = *se voir attribuer le mérite :* she worked as hard as the boss but didn't get any credit = *elle a travaillé aussi dur que le patron, mais ne s'en est pas vu attribuer le mérite*	**to one's credit** = *à porter à son crédit/à mettre à son actif :* apologizing was to her credit = *ses excuses sont à porter à son crédit/à mettre à son actif*
to give s.o. credit for stg = 1/ *porter qqch au*	⓪ to her honor = *à son honneur*

2/ *unité (f) de valeur :* in most US universities you take 18 credits a term = *dans la plupart des universités américaines, il faut présenter 18 unités de valeur par trimestre.*

CREDIT (to, -ed) **to credit to** = *porter au crédit de :* the money was credited to my account = *l'argent a été porté au crédit de mon compte* ≠ to debit = *débiter*
to credit with = *attribuer à :* they credited her with the discovery = *on lui a attribué cette découverte* = she was credited with the discovery.

CREDITOR (n) *créancier, -ère :* to pay one's creditors back = *rembourser ses créanciers* ≠ debtor = *débiteur.*

CREDITS (n pl) *générique (m)* ⓪ film = ←.

CREDULOUS (adj) *crédule :* naive and credulous = *naïf et crédule* ≠ skeptical = *sceptique.*

CREED (n) *credo (m) :* justice for all is his creed = *la justice pour tous, c'est son credo* ⓪ belief = *croyance.*

CREEK (n) *crique (f) :* to fish in a creek = *pêcher dans une crique*
to be up the creek (without a paddle) = *être dans la panade :* he'll be up the creek when the boss finds out the truth = *il sera dans la panade quand le patron découvrira la vérité* ⓪ to be in hot water = *être dans de beaux draps.*

CREEP (n) *minable (m, f) :* his brother's really a creep = *son frère est vraiment un minable* ⓪ drip = *minus,* wimp = *pauvre type.*

CREEP (to, crept, crept) **to creep into** ≠ **out of** = *entrer* ≠ *sortir à pas de loup :* the robber crept into the house = *le voleur est entré à pas de loup dans la maison* ⓪ to tiptoe = *marcher sur la pointe des pieds.*

CREEPS (n pl) **the creeps** = *les jetons :* the horror film gave me the creeps = *le film d'épouvante m'a flanqué les jetons* ⓪ the heebie-jeebies = *les chocottes.*

CREEPY (adj, -ier, -iest) *qui flanque les jetons :* the cemetery was creepy = *le cimetière vous flanquait les jetons* ⓪ frightening = *effrayant.*

CREMATE (to, -d) *incinérer* **CREMATION** (n) *incinération (f)* **CREMATORY** (n, -ies) *(four) crématoire (m).*

CRESTFALLEN (adj) *déconfit, -e :* a crestfallen look = *un regard déconfit* ⓪ dejected = *abattu.*

CREW (n) *équipage (m) :* the plane's crew = *l'équipage de l'avion* ⓪ team = *équipe*
crew cut = *cheveux en brosse.*

CRIB (n) *lit (m) d'enfant :* the baby fell from his crib = *le bébé est tombé de son lit* ⓪ cradle = *berceau.*

CRIME (n) *crime (m) :* crime and punishment = *crime et châtiment* ⓪ felony = *forfait,* misdemeanor = *délit*
crime doesn't pay = *le crime ne paie pas* ⓪ poetic justice = *juste retour des choses*
it's a crime (to pay so much) = *c'est scandaleux (de payer aussi cher)* ⓪ it's a shame = *c'est une honte.*

CRIMINAL (n) *criminel, -elle :* a hangout for criminals = *un repaire de criminels* ⓪ murderer = *meurtrier,* gangster = ← **CRIMINALITY** (n) *criminalité (f).*

CRIMINAL (adj) *criminel, -elle :* criminal proceedings = *poursuites criminelles*
Criminal Investigation Department (GB) = C.I.D. = *Police judiciaire* = P.J.
criminal law = *droit pénal*
it's criminal to (waste so much) ! = *c'est criminel de (gaspiller autant)* !

CRINGE (to, -d) *avoir un mouvement de recul :* I cringed when he tried to kiss me = *j'ai eu un mouvement de recul quand il a essayé de m'embrasser* ⓪ to dodge = *se dérober.*

CRIPPLE (n) *infirme (m, f) :* he's been a cripple since birth = *il est infirme de naissance* ⓪ wheelchair = *fauteuil roulant.*

CRIPPLE (to, -d) **1/** *rendre infirme* : crippled in the war = *rendu infirme par la guerre* ⓓ to disable = *rendre impotent* **2/** *paralyser* : the strikes crippled the country = *les grèves ont paralysé le pays* = the strikes paralyzed the country.

CRISIS (n, -ses) *crise* (f) : endless international crises = *des crises internationales interminables* ⓓ turning point = *tournant*, conflict = *conflit*
☠ *piquer une crise* = to throw a fit
— *une crise de larmes* = a fit of tears
— *crise de confiance* = loss of confidence
— *crise cardiaque* = heart attack
— *crise de nerfs* = tantrum.

CRISP (adj, -er, -est) *croustillant, -e* : crisp bread/bacon = *pain/bacon croustillant* ⓓ brittle = *croquant* ☠ *des détails croustillants* = juicy details.

CRITERION (n, -s or -ia) *critère* (m) : my only criterion is quality = *la qualité est mon seul critère*.

CRITIC (n) *critique* (m, f) : the critic wrote a lousy review = *le critique a fait un papier dégueulasse* ☠ → criticism.

CRITICAL (adj) **1/** *critique* : a critical situation = *une situation critique* ⓓ grave = ←
on the critical list = *dans un état critique*
2/ (qui a l'esprit) *critique* : don't be so critical = *n'aie pas tant l'esprit critique/ne sois pas si critique* ≠ encouraging = *encourageant*.

CRITICALLY (adv) **critically ill** = *gravement malade*.

CRITICISM (n) *critique* (f) : I don't appreciate your constant criticisms = *je n'apprécie pas vos critiques incessantes*
☠ *un critique (de théâtre/littéraire)* = a (theater) critic/a (book) reviewer
— *de bonnes critiques* = good reviews/notices/write-ups/critiques.

CRITICIZE (to, -d) *critiquer* : stop criticizing everything = *arrête de tout critiquer* ⓓ to find fault with = *trouver à redire à*, to pan = *éreinter* ≠ to praise = *louer*.

CRITIQUE (n) *critique* (f) : the critique was lousy = *la critique était mauvaise* ☠ → criticism.

CROAK (to, -ed) *crever, claquer* : I hope he croaks = *j'espère qu'il va crever/claquer* ⓓ to kick the bucket = *passer l'arme à gauche*
☠ *claquer* → to slam
— *plutôt crever !* = I'd rather die !
— *je me suis crevé à faire les courses* = I knocked myself out shopping
— *crever un pneu* = to get a flat
— *tu me crèves le cœur* = you're breaking my heart
— *je crève d'ennui/de chaleur* = I'm dying of boredom/the heat.

CROCODILE (n) *crocodile* (m) : crocodile tears = *larmes de crocodile* ⓓ alligator = ←.

CRONY (n, -ies) *familier, -ère* : one of the President's cronies = *un des familiers du Président* ⓓ sidekick = *acolyte*.

CROOK (n) *escroc* (m) : publishers are often crooks = *les éditeurs sont souvent des escrocs* ⓓ hustler = *combinard*, swindler = *arnaqueur*.

CROOKED (adj) **1/** *de travers* (painting), *sinueux, -euse* (road) : the picture looks crooked = *le tableau paraît de travers*, a crooked mountain road = *une route de montagne sinueuse* **2/** *malhonnête* : many lawyers/politicians are crooked = *beaucoup d'avocats/d'hommes politiques sont malhonnêtes* = dishonest ⓓ corrupt = *corrompu* ≠ upright = *intègre*.

CROONER (n) *crooner* (m), *chanteur, -euse de charme*.

CROP (n) *récolte* (f) : the corn crop is poor = *la récolte de maïs est mauvaise* ⓓ yield = *rendement*.

CROPPER (n) **(her marriage) came a cropper** = *elle a ramassé une gamelle avec (son mariage)*.

CROP UP (to, -ped) *survenir* : let me know if the problem crops up again = *faites-moi savoir si ce problème survient à nouveau* ⓓ to spring up = *surgir*.

CROSS (n, -es) **1/** *croix* (f) : Christ on the cross = *le Christ sur la croix* ⓓ crucifix = ←
(this illness is) a cross to bear = *(cette maladie est) une vraie croix*
2/ *croix* (f) : put a cross next to the articles you want = *mettez une croix à côté des articles que vous désirez*
a cross between (a boxer and a cocker) = *un croisement entre (un boxer et un cocker)*
☠ *faire une croix sur qqch* = to kiss stg good-bye
— *c'est la croix et la bannière* = it's like pulling teeth.

CROSS (adj) **to be cross with** = *être fâché contre* : I'm cross with her for what she said = *je suis fâché contre elle à cause de ce qu'elle a dit* → ANGRY
a cross section of (the population) = *un échantillon de (la population)* ⓓ poll = *sondage*.

CROSS (to, -ed) **1/** *traverser* : to cross the street = *traverser la rue* ☠ *traverser une période difficile* = to go through a bad time **2/** *croiser* : to cross a boxer and a poodle = *croiser un boxer et un caniche* ☠ *je l'ai croisé hier* = I ran into him yesterday **3/** *(se) croiser* : where the roads cross = *là où les routes se croisent*, our letters crossed = *nos lettres se sont croisées*
to cross out = *barrer* : cross their names out = *barrez leurs noms* ⓓ to strike out = *rayer* ☠ → to block off
to cross s.o. up = *doubler qqn* : he crossed us up on the contract = *il nous a doublés pour le contrat* → TO HUSTLE ☠ → to double.

CROSS-COUNTRY (adj) **cross-country skiers** = *des skieurs de fond* ⓓ downhill skiers = *des skieurs de descente*.

CROSS-EXAMINE (to, -d) *faire (subir) un contre-interrogatoire* : the lawyer cross-examined the witness = *l'avocat a fait subir un contre-interrogatoire au témoin*

⟨D⟩ to give s.o. the third degreee = *mettre qqn sur la sellette* **CROSS-EXAMINATION** (n) *contre-interrogatoire (m)*.

CROSS-EYED (adj) *qui louche* : she's cross-eyed = *elle louche.*

CROSSING (n) *croisement (m)* : there's a drugstore at the crossing = *il y a une pharmacie au croisement.*

CROSS-LEGGED (adj, adv) *(assis, e) en tailleur* : she sat cross-legged = *elle s'est assise en tailleur.*

CROSS-PURPOSES (n pl) **to be talking at cross-purposes** = *avoir un dialogue de sourds*
to work at cross-purposes = *se contrecarrer dans le travail.*

CROSS-REFERENCE (n) *renvoi (m)* : a cross-reference to another book = *un renvoi à un autre livre* ☠ → dismissal.

CROSSROADS (n pl) *carrefour (m)* ⟨D⟩ intersection = ←, crossing = *croisement*
at the crossroads of (her life) = *au carrefour de (sa vie).*

CROSSWORD PUZZLE (n) *mots croisés (m pl).*

CROTCH (n, -es) **1/** *entrejambe (m)* : the crotch of the pants = *l'entrejambe du pantalon* **2/** *entre les jambes* : she grabbed his crotch = *elle l'a attrapé entre les jambes.*

CROW (n) *corneille (f)* ⟨D⟩ raven = *corbeau*, lark = *alouette*
as the crow flies = *à vol d'oiseau*
crow's feet = *pattes d'oie*
to eat crow = *en prendre pour son grade* : he's going to eat crow if his policy doesn't succeed = *il va en prendre pour son grade si sa politique échoue*
☠ *bayer aux corneilles* = to fiddle around.

CROWD (n) **1/** *foule (f)* : there was a crowd on the beach = *il y avait foule sur la plage* ⟨D⟩ a lot of people = *beaucoup de monde* **2/** *gens qui fréquentent/que fréquente* : I don't like my husband's/the club's crowd = *je n'aime pas les gens que fréquente mon mari/qui fréquentent le club*
(that restaurant) gets a good crowd = *(ce restaurant) est bien fréquenté*
the (Hollywood) crowd = *la faune d'(Hollywood).*

CROWD (to, -ed) **to crowd around** = *se masser autour de* : the groupies crowded around the singer = *les groupies se massaient autour du chanteur*
to crowd into (the train) = *s'entasser dans (le train).*

CROWDED (adj) *bondé, -e* : a crowded hotel/theater = *un hôtel/théâtre bondé* ⟨D⟩ packed = *plein à craquer.*

CROWN (n) *couronne (f)* ⟨D⟩ tiara = *tiare*, coronation = *couronnement*, diadem = *diadème*
the crown jewels = *les joyaux de la couronne*
crown prince = *prince héritier* ≠ **crown princess** = *princesse héritière.*

CROWN (to, -ed) *couronner* : to crown a king = *couronner un roi*
I'll crown him if (he lies to me again) ! = *je le tuerai s'(il me ment à nouveau)* ! = I'll kill him if ... !

CRUCIAL (adj) *crucial, -e* : the crucial moment = *le moment crucial* ⟨D⟩ decisive = *décisif.*

CRUCIFY (to, -ied) *crucifier* ⟨D⟩ crucifixion = ←.

CRUDE (adj, -r, -st) **1/** *cru, -e* : crude language = *langage cru* ⟨D⟩ rude = *grossier* ☠ → raw **2/** *rudimentaire* : crude drawing/dwelling = *dessin/habitation rudimentaire*
crude oil = *pétrole brut.*

CRUEL (adj, -er, -est) *cruel, -elle* : cruel parents = *des parents cruels* ⟨D⟩ ruthless = *impitoyable* ≠ merciful = *clément*
to be cruel to s.o. = *être cruel avec qqn*
that was cruel of you = *c'était cruel de votre part.*

CRUELTY (n, -ies) *cruauté (f)* : mental cruelty = *cruauté mentale* ⟨D⟩ meanness = *méchanceté.*

CRUISE (n) *croisière (f)* : to go on a cruise = *faire une croisière*
cruise missile = *missile de croisière.*

CRUISE (to, -d) **1/** *aller à sa vitesse de croisière* : the boat/plane is cruising = *le bateau/l'avion va à sa vitesse de croisière* **2/** *être en maraude* : taxis cruising in New York = *taxis en maraude à New York* **3/** *draguer* : I met guys cruising in Central Park = *j'ai rencontré des types qui draguaient à Central Park* ☠ *il l'a draguée dans un bar pour célibataires* = he picked her up in a singles bar **4/** *rouler sans but* : cars cruising on Saturday night = *des voitures qui roulent sans but le samedi soir.*

CRUMB (n) **1/** *miette (f)* : bread crumbs = *des miettes de pain* ⟨D⟩ crust = *croûte* **2/** *rosse (f)* : what a crumb he is ! = *quelle rosse !* → BASTARD.

CRUMBLE (to, -d) *émietter* (bread), *s'effriter* : the wall's crumbling = *le mur s'effrite* ⟨D⟩ to collapse = *s'effondrer.*

CRUMMY (adj, -ier, -iest) *moche* : what a crummy thing to say ! = *que c'est moche de dire une chose comme ça !* → AWFUL
to feel crummy = *se sentir patraque* ⟨D⟩ to feel like hell = *être mal fichu*
to feel crummy about = *se sentir morveux de* : I feel crummy about having lied to her = *je me sens morveux de lui avoir menti* ⟨D⟩ to feel shitty = *se sentir merdeux* ☠ *elle est moche* = she's very plain-looking.

CRUMPLE (to, -d) *chiffonner* : to crumple a dress/a piece of paper = *chiffonner une robe/un morceau de papier* ⟨D⟩ to crease = *froisser* ☠ *ça me chiffonne* = it's bugging me.

CRUNCH (n, -es) *restriction (f)* : economic crunch = *restriction économique* ⟨D⟩ pinch = *manque*

in a crunch = *le cas échéant* : in a crunch, I can borrow some money from my parents = *le cas échéant, je peux emprunter un peu d'argent à mes parents* ⓪ in a pinch = *en cas de force majeure* ⚹ → restriction.

CRUSADE (n) *croisade (f)* : a crusade against alcoholism = *une croisade contre l'alcoolisme*
the Crusades = *les croisades* ⓪ crusader = *croisé*.

CRUSH (n, -es) *béguin (m)* : adolescent crushes = *des béguins d'adolescent* ⓪ infatuation = *entichement*
to have a crush on = *avoir le béguin pour* ⓪ to be sweet on = *avoir un faible pour*.

CRUSH (to, -ed) **1/** *écraser* : the regime was crushed = *le régime a été écrasé* ⓪ to overthrow = *renverser* **2/** *écraser* : the car/body was crushed = *la voiture/le corps a été écrasé(e)* ⚹ → to crash.

CRUST (n) *croûte (f)* : I like the crust = *j'aime la croûte* ⚹ *casser la croûte* = to have a bite
— *une vieille croûte* = an old schnock
— *gagner sa croûte* = to earn one's keep.

CRUTCH (n, -es) **1/** *béquille (f)* : to walk with crutches = *marcher avec des béquilles* ⓪ cane = *canne* **2/** *support (m)* (s.o.), *béquille (f)* (stg) : his wife's his crutch = *sa femme est un support pour lui*, sleeping pills are his crutch = *les somnifères lui servent de béquilles* ⚹ → support.

CRUX (n, -es) **the crux of (the matter)** = *le nœud de (l'affaire)* ⓪ heart = *cœur*.

CRY (n, -ies) *cri (m)* : I heard the baby's cries = *j'ai entendu les cris du bébé* ⓪ yell = *hurlement*
to have a (good) cry = *pleurer un bon coup* ⓪ to cry one's eyes out = *pleurer toutes les larmes de son corps* ⚹ *le dernier cri* = the latest fashion.

CRY (to, -ied) **1/** *pleurer* : the baby cried all night = *le bébé a pleuré toute la nuit* ⓪ to sob = *sangloter*, to bawl = *brailler* **2/** *crier* : "come quick !", she cried = *« venez vite ! »*, a-t-elle crié ≠ to whisper = *chuchoter*
to be crying out for (help) = *réclamer de (l'aide) à grands cris*
to cry out with (pain) = *pousser un cri de (douleur)*
to cry over = *pleurer (sur)* : she's still crying over her dog's death = *elle pleure encore (sur) la mort de son chien*
⚹ *sans crier gare* = without warning
— *arrête de crier !* = stop shouting !

CRYBABY (n, -ies) *pleurnicheur, -euse* : what a crybaby you are ! = *quel pleurnicheur tu fais !* ⓪ pain in the neck = *casse-pieds*.

CRYSTAL (n, adj) *cristal (m)* : a crystal glass = *un verre en cristal* ⓪ glass = *verre*
crystal ball = *boule de cristal*.

CRYSTALLIZE (to, -d) *(se) cristalliser* : when love crystallizes = *quand l'amour se cristallise*.

CUB (n) *petit (m)* : the tigress and her cubs = *la tigresse et ses petits*, lion-cub = *lionceau*, bear cub = *ourson*
cub reporter = *journaliste débutant*.

CUBA (n) *Cuba (f)* **CUBAN** (n, adj) *Cubain, -e*.

CUBE (n) *cube (m)* ⓪ square = *carré*.

CUBISM (n) *cubisme (m)* ⓪ dadaism = *dadaïsme*
CUBIST (n, adj) *cubiste (m, f)*.

CUCKOLD (to, -ed) *cocufier* : he was cuckolded = *il était cocufié* ⓪ to cheat on s.o. = *tromper qqn*.

CUCKOO (adj) *zinzin* : all her family are cuckoo = *dans la famille, ils sont tous zinzins* → CRAZY.

CUCUMBER (n) *concombre (m)* : marinated cucumber = *du concombre mariné* = *cuke* ⓪ gherkin = *cornichon*.

CUDDLE (to, -d) *se pelotonner* : children like to cuddle (up) = *les enfants aiment se pelotonner* ⓪ to snuggle (up) = *se blottir*.

CUE (n) **to give s.o. the cue** = *donner le signal à qqn* : give me the cue when you want to leave = *donnez-moi le signal du départ*
to miss one's cue (theater) = *manquer sa réplique* ⓪ prompter = *souffleur*.

CUFF (n) *manchette (f), revers (m) de pantalon* : cuff links = *boutons de manchette*
off the cuff = *au pied levé* : he answered the journalists off the cuff = *il a répondu aux journalistes au pied levé* ⓪ impromptu = *à l'impromptu* ⚹ *manchette (journal)* = headlines.

CULMINATE IN (to, -d) *aboutir à* : the crisis culminated in the resignation of the Prime Minister = *la crise a abouti à la démission du Premier ministre* ⓪ to end in = *se solder par*.

CULPRIT (n) *fautif, -ive* : someone ate all my cookies, who's the culprit ? = *quelqu'un a mangé tous mes petits gâteaux, qui est le fautif ?* ⓪ the guilty party = *le coupable*.

CULT (n) *culte (m)* : the Elvis Presley cult = *le culte d'Elvis Presley*.

CULTIVATE (to, -d) *cultiver* : to cultivate one's land/one's mind = *cultiver sa terre/son esprit*.

CULTIVATED (adj) *cultivé, -e* : cultivated circles = *milieux cultivés* ⓪ refined = *raffiné*.

CULTURAL (adj) *culturel, -elle* : cultural activities = *activités culturelles*.

CULTURE (n) *culture (f)* : a man of great culture = *un homme d'une grande culture* ⓪ knowledge = *savoir* ⚹ *culture (des champs)* = farming.

CUMBERSOME (adj) *encombrant, -e* : a cumbersome package = *un paquet encombrant* ⓪ unwieldy = *peu maniable*.

CUNNING (adj) *rusé, -e* : a cunning businessman/lawyer = *un homme d'affaires/un avocat rusé* ⓪ artful = *plein de doigté*, conniving = *intrigant*.

CUNT (n) **1/** *con* (m) : a hairy cunt = *un con vachement poilu* ⓪ pussy = *chatte* ≠ prick = *bite* ☠ → con **2/** *sale connasse* (f) : he married a real cunt = *il a épousé une sale connasse* → BASTARD.

CUP (n) *tasse* (f) : give me a cup of coffee = *donnez-moi une tasse de café* ⓪ saucer = *soucoupe*
it's not my cup of tea = *ce n'est pas mon genre* ⓪ it's not my speed = *ce n'est pas mon truc*
☠ *boire la tasse* = to swallow a mouthful (swimming).

CUPBOARD (n) *placard* (m) : put the dishes in the cupboard = *range la vaisselle dans le placard* ⓪ shelf = *étagère*.

CURABLE (adj) *guérissable, curable* : a curable disease = *une maladie guérissable/curable* ≠ incurable = ←.

CURATOR (n) *conservateur, -trice* : the curator of the museum = *le conservateur du musée* ☠ → conservative.

CURB (n) *bordure* (f) *de trottoir* = kerb (GB) ⓪ gutter = *caniveau*.

CURB (to, -ed) *freiner* : efforts to curb inflation = *des efforts pour freiner l'inflation* ⓪ to control = *contrôler* ☠ *freiner (voiture)* = to put on the brakes.

CURDLE (to, -d) *cailler* : milk's sour when it curdles = *le lait qui caille devient sur* ☠ *on caille !* = we're freezing !

CURE (n) *remède* (m) : a cure for diabetes = *un remède au diabète* ⓪ treatment = *traitement*, healing = *guérison* ☠ → remedy
the cure is worse than the disease = *le remède est pire que le mal* ⓪ leave well enough alone = *le mieux est l'ennemi du bien*.

CURE (to, -d) *guérir* : cured of cancer/of my crush on him = *guéri du cancer/de mon béguin pour lui* ≠ to be stricken with = *être frappé par*.

CURE-ALL (n) *remède* (m) *miracle* : there's no cure-all for love = *il n'y a pas de remède miracle à l'amour* ⓪ panacea = *panacée*.

CURFEW (n) *couvre-feu* (m) : a ten o'clock curfew = *un couvre-feu à dix heures du soir* ⓪ air raid = *raid aérien*.

CURIO (n) *bibelot* (m) : I bought unusual curios in China = *j'ai acheté des bibelots insolites en Chine* ⓪ whatnot = *bricole*.

CURIOSITY (n inv) *curiosité* (f) : I'm dying of curiosity = *je meurs de curiosité* ≠ discretion = *discrétion*
curiosity killed the cat = *la curiosité est un vilain défaut*
out of curiosity = *par curiosité* : he asked the question out of curiosity = *il a posé la question par curiosité*.

CURIOUS (adj) **1/** *curieux, -euse* : don't be so curious about everything = *ne sois pas si curieux de tout* ≠ discreet = *discret*
curious to (know) = *curieux de (savoir)*
2/ *curieux, -euse* : what a curious thing to say ! = *que c'est curieux de dire ça !* ⓪ odd = *étrange*.

CURIOUSLY (adv) *curieusement* : curiously (enough) I felt I had met him before = *curieusement, j'avais le sentiment de l'avoir déjà rencontré*.

CURL (n) *boucle* (f) : the baby's curls = *les boucles du bébé* ⓪ spit curl = *accroche-cœur*
☠ *une boucle (ceinture)* = a buckle
— *une boucle d'oreille* = an earring
— *boucler la boucle* = to have come full circle.

CURL UP (to, -ed) *se rouler en boule* : I curled up on the sofa and went to sleep = *je me suis roulée en boule sur le sofa et je me suis endormie* ⓪ to cuddle up = *se pelotonner*.

CURLY (adj, -ier, -iest) *bouclé, -e* : curly hair = *des cheveux bouclés* ⓪ frizzy = *frisé*.

CURRENCY (n, -ies) *monnaie* (f) : the American currency = *la monnaie américaine* ☠ → change
foreign currency = *devise (étrangère)* ☠ → motto.

CURRENT (n) *courant* (m) : a strong current in the ocean = *un fort courant dans l'océan*, a current of public opinion = *un courant d'opinion*
☠ *dans le courant de l'année* = in the course of the year
— *mettre qqn au courant* = to bring s.o. up to date
— *le courant passe entre nous* = there are good vibes between us
— *la courante* = the runs
— *un courant d'air* = a draft.

CURRENT (adj) *actuel, -elle* : his current job/wife = *son boulot actuel/son actuelle femme* = present ≠ past = *ancien* ☠ → actual
current events = *l'actualité*
current issue = *dernier numéro*
the current year = *l'année en cours*.

CURRENTLY (adv) *actuellement* : they're currently living in New York = *actuellement, ils habitent New York* ⓪ at present = *à présent* ☠ → actually.

CURRICULUM (n, -s or -la) *programme* (m) *(scolaire)* : languages aren't on the curriculum = *les langues ne sont pas au programme* ⓪ syllabus = *programme (d'études)*
curriculum vitae = ← = *C.V.* = résumé
☠ → program.

CURRY (n, -ies) *curry* (m) : a curry sauce = *une sauce au curry* ⓪ spice = *épice*.

CURSE (n) *malédiction* (f) : there's a curse on the family = *il y a une malédiction sur la famille* ⓪ hex = *sort*, godsend = *bienfait du ciel*
curse word = *juron* ⓪ dirty word = *gros mot*
to have the curse = *avoir ses ourses* ⓪ it's that time of the month = *les Anglais ont débarqué*.

CURSE (to, -d) *dire des gros mots* : children shouldn't curse = *les enfants ne devraient pas dire de gros mots* ⓓ to swear = *jurer*
to be cursed with (a terrible disease) = *être affligé d'(une terrible maladie).*

CURSORY (adj) *superficiel, -elle* : a cursory review = *une critique superficielle* = superficial ≠ in-depth = *en profondeur.*

CURT (adj, -er, -est) *brusque* : a curt answer = *une réponse brusque* ⓓ succinct = *←* ☠ → *brusque.*

CURTAIL (to, -ed) *restreindre* : to curtail s.o.'s power/expenses = *restreindre le pouvoir de qqn/les dépenses* ≠ to augment = *augmenter.*

CURTAIN (n) *rideau (m)* : when the curtain goes up = *quand le rideau se lève* ⓓ drapes = *tentures*
a curtain call = *un rappel* ⓓ an encore = *un bis*
curtain raiser = *lever de rideau*
it'll be curtains for you (if she finds out the truth) = *tu es fait (si elle découvre la vérité)* ⓓ it'll be all over for you = *tu es fichu.*

CURTSY (to, -ied) *faire la révérence* : young girls rarely curtsy anymore = *les petites filles ne font quasiment plus la révérence.*

CURVE (n) *virage (m), courbe (f)* (chart) : a curve in the road = *un virage sur la route* ⓓ turn = *tournant*, bend = *coude.*

CURVES (n pl) *rondeurs (f pl)* : she has some curves ! = *elle a des rondeurs !*

CUSHION (n) *coussin (m)* : put the cushions on the bed = *mets les coussins sur le lit* ⓓ pillow = *oreiller.*

CUSHY (adj, -ier, -iest) *pénard, -e* : a cushy job = *un boulot pénard* ⓓ plum = *en or.*

CUSTARD (n) *crème (f) patissière.*

CUSTODIAN (n) *gardien, -enne (d'immeuble)* : ask the custodian = *demandez au gardien* ⓓ caretaker = *gardien (propriété)* ☠ → watchman.

CUSTODY (n inv) *garde (f) (des enfants)* : she got custody of the kids = *elle a obtenu la garde des gosses* ☠ → guard
to take into custody = *mettre en garde à vue* : the police took the man into custody = *la police a mis le type en garde à vue* ⓓ to be out on bail = *être en liberté provisoire.*

CUSTOM (n) *coutume (f)* : the customs of the country = *les coutumes du pays* ⓓ tradition = *←*, mores = *mœurs.*

CUSTOMARY (adj) *coutumier, -ère* : tipping is customary = *il est coutumier de laisser un pourboire* ≠ occasional = *occasionnel* **CUSTOMARILY** (adv) *habituellement* : we are customarily closed on Saturdays = *nous sommes habituellement fermés le samedi* ⓓ as a rule = *en règle générale.*

CUSTOMER (n) *client, -e* : she's our best customer = *c'est notre meilleure cliente* = client ≠ salesman = *vendeur*
customer's man = *agent de change* = stockbroker
odd/queer customer = *drôle de zigoto* ⓓ a queer duck = *un drôle de zigue*
a rough/tough customer = *un dur*
☠ *un « customer » achète un produit et non un service.*

CUSTOM-MADE (adj) *fait, -e sur mesure* : a custom-made suit = *un costume fait sur mesure* = tailor-made ≠ ready-made = *de confection.*

CUSTOMS (n pl) *douane (f)* ⓓ duty = *droit de douane*
customs officer = *douanier*
to pass customs = *passer la douane*
to clear customs = *franchir la douane.*

CUT (n) **1/** *coupe (f)* : I like the cut of your suit = *j'aime la coupe de votre costume*	
☠ *la coupe est pleine !* = that's enough already !	— *avoir qqn sous sa coupe* = to have s.o. under one's thumb
2/ *part (f) du gâteau* : he wants his cut = *il veut sa part du gâteau* ⓓ share = *part* **3/** *coupure (f)* : the text is too long, we must make cuts = *le texte est trop long, il faut faire des coupures* ☠ *coupure de journal* = newspaper clipping	
a cut above = *un cran au-dessus de* : the novel is a cut above the film = *le roman est un cran au-dessus du film* **a cut in (pay/prices)** = *une diminution de*	(salaire)/des (prix) ≠ increase = augmentation = raise **to make cuts about s.o.** = *envoyer des pointes à qqn.*
CUT (to, cut, cut) **1/** *(se) couper* : he cut the meat/his hand = *il a coupé la viande/il s'est coupé la main* ⓓ to prune = *tailler*, to chop = *hacher*, to slice = *couper en tranches*	

☠ *couper le souffle à qqn* = to take s.o.'s breath away
— *couper l'appétit à qqn* = to spoil s.o.'s appetite

— *tu n'y couperas pas !* = you won't get away with it !/it's inevitable !

2/ *sécher* : I cut all my classes yesterday = *j'ai séché tous mes cours hier* ⓪ to play hooky = *faire l'école buissonnière* ☠ → to dry

to cut across = *recouper* : support for gun control cuts across party lines = *le soutien à une politique de contrôle de la vente d'armes recoupe la ligne du parti*
to cut back = *réduire* : to cut back expenditure/production = *réduire les dépenses/la production* ≠ to up = *faire monter* ☠ → to reduce
to cut down = 1/ *réduire* : she smokes a lot but is trying to cut down = *elle fume beaucoup mais elle essaie de réduire*, the company's trying to cut its expenses down = *la société essaie de réduire ses dépenses* ⓪ to scale down = *réduire proportionnellement* ☠ → to reduce 2/ *couper* : to cut a tree down = *couper un arbre*
to cut down on = *réduire* : she's cutting down on cigarettes = *elle réduit les cigarettes* ≠ to increase = *augmenter* ☠ → to reduce
to cut in = 1/ *interrompre un couple en train de danser et prendre la place du cavalier* 2/ *couper la parole à* : when I'm talking, don't cut in ! = *quand je parle, ne me coupez pas la parole !* ⓪ to interrupt = *interrompre*
to cut s.o. in = *mettre qqn*

dans le coup : we'll cut you in the deal = *nous vous mettrons dans le coup* ≠ to cut s.o. out of = *frustrer qqn de*
to cut off = 1/ *couper* : to cut off supplies/electricity = *couper les vivres/l'électricité* ⓪ to stop = *arrêter* 2/ *amputer* : his leg was cut off = *sa jambe a été amputée* = his leg was amputated 3/ *faire une queue de poisson à* : the car cut off the truck = *la voiture a fait une queue de poisson au camion*
to cut s.o. off = *couper les vivres à qqn* : my parents cut me off (without a cent) = *mes parents m'ont coupé les vivres (sans me donner un sou)* ⓪ to disinherit = *déshériter*
to cut s.o. off from = *couper qqn de* : the war cut her off her friends = *la guerre l'a coupée de ses amis*
to be cut off = *être coupé* : we were talking on the phone and were cut off = *on était en communication et on a été coupés*
to cut out = 1/ *arrêter* : I cut out smoking/drinking = *j'ai arrêté de fumer/de boire* = to stop 2/ *décamper* : let's cut out of here ! = *décampons d'ici !* → TO LEAVE 3/ *supprimer* : cut out all the dirty words = *supprime*

tous les gros mots ⓪ to delete = *biffer* ☠ → to do away with
4/ *découper* : I cut out this article for you = *je vous ai découpé cet article*
cut it out ! = *fiche-moi la paix !* → BUZZ OFF !
to cut s.o. out of = *frustrer qqn de* : the gang cut him out of his share = *le gang l'a frustré de sa part* → TO HUSTLE
to be cut out for (+ noun)/to (+ verb) = *être fait pour* : I'm not cut out for that kind of job/to be a doctor = *je ne suis pas fait pour ce genre de boulot/pour être médecin*
to cut up = 1/ *couper en morceaux* : cut up the carrots = *coupez les carottes en morceaux* ⓪ to slice = *couper en tranches* 2/ *faire le guignol* : they started cutting up around midnight = *ils ont commencé à faire les guignols vers minuit* ⓪ to clown around = *faire le clown* 3/ *dire pis que pendre de* : the critics cut up his last play = *les critiques ont dit pis que pendre de sa dernière pièce* ⓪ to pull apart = *descendre en flammes*
to be cut up = *être accablé* : he was cut up when he lost his job = *il était accablé quand il a perdu son emploi.*

CUT-AND-DRIED (adj) *tout, -e fait, -e* : cut-and-dried speech/opinions = *un discours tout fait/opinions toutes faites.*

CUTBACK (n) *réduction (f)* : a cutback in production = *une réduction de la production* = reduction ≠ increase = *augmentation.*

CUTE (adj, -r, -st) *mignon, -onne* : a cute little boy = *un petit garçon mignon* ⓪ sweet = *délicieux*
don't be so cute ! = *ne fais pas le malin !*

CUTLET (n) *côtelette (f)* : lamb cutlets = *des côtelettes d'agneau* ⓪ chop = *côte.*

CUT-RATE (adj) *à prix réduit* : cut-rate stores = *des magasins à prix réduits* ⓪ discount = ←, marked down = *démarqué.*

CUTTHROAT (adj) *où l'on ne se fait pas de cadeau* : politics is cutthroat = *en politique, on ne se fait pas de cadeau* ⓪ dog-eat-dog = *l'homme est un loup pour l'homme*
cutthroat competition = *concurrence à mort.*

CUTTING (adj) *cinglant, -e* : cutting remarks = *des remarques cinglantes* ⓪ virulent = ←.

CUTUP (n) *pitre (m)* : Jack's a real cutup = *Jack est un vrai pitre* ⓒⒹ practical joker = *farceur.*

CYCLE (n) *cycle (m)* : an economic cycle = *un cycle économique* ⓒⒹ series = *série* **CYCLICAL** (adj) *cyclique.*

CYCLIST (n) *cycliste (m, f)* ⓒⒹ bike = *vélo.*

CYCLONE (n) *cyclone (m)* : the eye of the cyclone = *l'œil du cyclone* ⓒⒹ hurricane = *ouragan.*

CYNIC (n) *cynique (m, f)* ⓒⒹ pessimist = *pessimiste* **CYNICAL** (adj) *cynique* : don't be so cynical about life ! = *ne sois pas si cynique à propos de la vie !* ⓒⒹ skeptical = *sceptique* **CYNICISM** (n) *cynisme (m)* : your constant cynicism makes me sad = *ton cynisme permanent me rend triste.*

CYST (n) *kyste (m)* : she has a cyst on her left ovary = *elle a un kyste à l'ovaire gauche.*

CZAR (n) *tsar (m)* ⓒⒹ czarina = *tsarine*, emperor = *empereur.*

CZECHOSLOVAKIA (n) *Tchécoslovaquie (f)* **CZECH-OSLOVAK(IAN)** (n, adj) *Tchécoslovaque (m, f)* ⓒⒹ Czech = *Tchèque.*

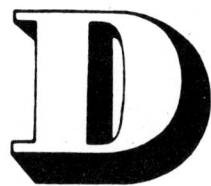

D.A. (abbr) = District Attorney = *procureur (m) de la République* ⟳ Attorney General = *ministre de la Justice.*

DABBLE (to, -d) **to dabble in (painting)** = *faire (de la peinture) en amateur.*

DAB ON (to, -bed) *tamponner (légèrement) :* to dab ether on the wound = *tamponner légèrement la blessure avec de l'éther.*

DACHSHUND (n) *teckel (m)* ⟳ dog = *chien.*

DADDY (n, -ies) *papa (m) :* hi daddy ! = *salut papa !* = dad ⟳ pa = *p'pa,* father = *père* ≠ mommy = *maman* = mom
☠ *faire qqch à la papa* = to do stg at snail's pace
— *le cinéma de papa* = old-fashioned.movies
— *faire l'amour à la papa* = to make love the man on the top.

DAFFODIL (n) *jonquille (f)* ⟳ flower = *fleur.*

DAFT (adj) *sinoque :* daft ideas = *des idées sinoques* → CRAZY.

DAGGER (n) *poignard (m) :* to murder s.o. with a dagger = *assassiner qqn avec un poignard* ⟳ sword = *épée*
to be at daggers drawn = *être à couteaux tirés* ⟳ they are at sixes and sevens = *le torchon brûle entre eux.*

DAILY (n, -ies) *quotidien (m) :* this newspaper's a daily = *ce journal est un quotidien* ⟳ weekly = *hebdomadaire.*

DAILY (adj) *quotidien, -enne :* daily problems/phone calls = *des problèmes/coups de téléphone quotidiens* ⟳ weekly = *hebdomadaire*
the daily grind = *le train-train quotidien/métro-boulot-dodo.*

DAILY (adv) *quotidiennement :* to come daily = *venir quotidiennement.*

DAINTY (adj, -ier, -iest) *délicat, -e :* a dainty piece of china = *une porcelaine délicate* ☠ → delicate.

DAIRY (adj) *laitier, -ère :.* dairy products = *des produits laitiers* ⟳ butter = *beurre,* cream = *crème,* cheese = *fromage.*

DAIS (n) *estrade (f) :* the President and the First Lady sat at the dais = *le Président et son épouse étaient assis sur l'estrade* ⟳ microphone = *micro* ☠ *un dais* = a canopy.

DAISY (n, -ies) *marguerite (f)* ⟳ marigold = *souci.*

DAM (n) *barrage (m) :* they're constructing a dam = *ils sont en train de construire un barrage* ⟳ reservoir = *réservoir* ☠ *barrage routier* = roadblock.

DAMAGE (n inv) *dommage (m)* (material), *dégâts (m pl) :* the storm caused a lot of damage = *la tempête a causé beaucoup de dommage/dégâts,* financial problems did a lot of damage to their marriage = *les problèmes d'argent ont fait beaucoup de dégâts dans leur ménage* ⟳ break-age = *casse* ☠ *c'est dommage !* = it's a shame !/it's a pity !

DAMAGE (to, -d) *endommager, nuire à* (psychological) : the storm damaged the roof = *la tempête a endommagé le toit,* the scandal damaged her reputation = *le scandale a nui à sa réputation* ⟳ to ruin = *gâcher,* to harm = *causer du tort à.*

DAMAGES (n pl) *dommages-intérêts (m pl) :* to pay 2 grand in damages = *payer deux mille dollars de dommages-intérêts*
what are the damages ? = *donnez-moi la douloureuse* ⟳ bill = *note.*

DAMAGING (adj) *nuisible :* a statement damaging to his campaign = *une déclaration nuisible à sa campagne* ⟳ detrimental = *néfaste.*

DAME (n) *gonzesse (f) :* what a gorgeous dame ! = *quelle superbe gonzesse !* ⟳ bird (GB) = *nénette*
☠ *jouer aux dames* = to play checkers
— *dame de cœur* = queen of hearts
— *une dame* = a lady.

DAMN (n) **I don't give a damn !** = *je m'en fiche !* ⟳ I don't give a hang ! = *je m'en bats l'œil !*

DAMN (to, -ed) *damner :* damned for one's sins = *damné pour ses péchés*
damn him ! = *qu'il aille au diable !* → BUZZ OFF !
damn it ! = *zut !* = **dammit !** ⟳ **I'll be damned if ... !** = *que le diable m'emporte si ... !* → GOSH !

DAMN = DAMNED (adj) *sacré, -e* : he's a damned fool ! = *c'est un sacré con !* ⓂⒹ darned = *fichu* 💀 → sacred.

DAMN = DAMNED (adv) *vachement* : he's a damned nice guy = *c'est un type vachement sympa* → VERY 💀 *j'aime vachement le chocolat* = I like chocolate like crazy/mad
— *je lis vachement !* = I read like anything/like nobody's business !

DAMNEDEST (n) to do one's damnedest (to help) = *faire l'impossible (pour aider)* ⓂⒹ to do one's utmost = *faire tout son possible.*

DAMP (adj, -er, est) *humide* : the laundry's damp = *le linge est humide* ⓂⒹ moist = *moite* 💀 → humid.

DAMPER (n) to put a damper on = *jeter un froid sur* : their fighting put a damper on the weekend = *leurs disputes ont jeté un froid sur le week-end.*

DANCE (n) 1/ *danse* (f) : the tango's a difficult dance = *le tango est une danse difficile* 2/ *soirée* (f) *dansante* : there's a big dance at the Ritz = *il y a une grande soirée dansante au Ritz* ⓂⒹ ball = *bal*, hop = *sauterie*, dinner dance = *dîner dansant*

	dancing
ballet = ←	
ballroom dancing = *danse de salon*	**fox-trot** = ←
choreography = *chorégraphie*	**rock'n'roll** = ←
dance floor = *piste de danse*	**rumba** = ←
	tango = ←
	tap dance = *claquettes*
a dance hall = *un*	**waltz** = *valse*

💀 *entrer dans la danse* = to come into the picture
— *mener la danse* = to run the show.

DANCE (to, -d) *danser* : we danced all night = *nous avons dansé toute la nuit.*

DANCER (n) *danseur, -euse* : my daughter's a dancer = *ma fille est danseuse* ⓂⒹ ballerina = *ballerine*, chorus boy/girl = *boy/girl*
💀 *danseuse étoile* = prima ballerina.

DANDRUFF (n inv) *pellicules* (f pl) : lots of dandruff on his shoulders = *beaucoup de pellicules sur ses épaules* 💀 *pellicule (film)* = film.

DANDY (n, -ies) *dandy* (m) : modern dandies wear jeans and furs = *les dandys modernes portent des jeans et des manteaux de fourrure* ⓂⒹ fop = *bellâtre*.

DANGER (n) *danger* (m) : my life's in danger = *ma vie est en danger* ⓂⒹ risk = *risque*
💀 *mettre en danger* = to endanger
— *un danger public* = a public menace.

DANGEROUS (adj) *dangereux, -euse* : a dangerous road = *une route dangereuse* ⓂⒹ precarious = *précaire* ≠ safe = *sûr* **DANGEROUSLY** (adv) *dangereusement* : to live dangerously = *vivre dangereusement.*

D.A.R. (abbr) = Daughters of the American Revolution = *association patriotique de droite composée des descendantes de la révolution américaine.*

DARE (n) I did it on a dare = *je l'ai fait par défi.*

DARE (to, -d) *oser* : how dare you say that ? = *comment osez-vous dire ça ?*
I dare you ! = *je t'en défie !* ⓂⒹ you're on ! = *chiche !*
to dare s.o. to (do stg) = *mettre qqn au défi de (faire qqch)* : he dared me to strip in the parking lot = *il m'a mis au défi de me mettre à poil dans le parking* ⓂⒹ to bet = *parier.*

DAREDEVIL (n) *casse-cou (m inv)* : daredevils on their motorbikes = *des casse-cou sur leurs motos* ≠ chicken = *poule mouillée.*

DARING (adj) *audacieux, -euse* : a daring thing to do = *une chose audacieuse à faire* = audacious ≠ cowardly = *lâche.*

DARK (n inv) *noir* (m) : children don't like to be alone in the dark = *les enfants n'aiment pas rester seuls dans le noir* 💀 → black
(to keep s.o.) in the dark = *(tenir qqn) dans la plus totale ignorance*
after dark = *la nuit venue.*

DARK (adj, -er, -est) 1/ *sombre* : a dark room = *une pièce sombre* ≠ light = *clair* 💀 → somber 2/ *foncé, -e* : dark brown/green = *marron/vert foncé* ≠ light = *clair*
dark horse = *gagnant inattendu et inconnu* ⓂⒹ outsider = ←
it's getting dark = *la nuit tombe.*

DARKEN (to, -ed) *assombrir* : our vacation was darkened by my father's death = *nos vacances ont été assombries par la mort de mon père*
to darken (a color) = *foncer (une couleur).*

DARKNESS (n) *ténèbres* (f pl) : hiding in the darkness = *caché dans les ténèbres* ⓂⒹ obscurity = *obscurité.*

DARKROOM (n) *chambre* (f) *noire* : he's developing a film in the darkroom = *il développe un film dans la chambre noire.*

DARLING (n) *chéri, -e* : come here, darling = *viens ici, chéri* ⓂⒹ honey = *mon chou*
the darling of (Paris) = *l'enfant chéri de (Paris).*

DARLING (adj) 1/ *chéri, -e* : my darling husband = *mon mari chéri* 2/ *adorable* : she's a darling little girl = *c'est une petite fille adorable* ⓂⒹ cute = *mignon.*

DARN (n) I don't give a darn ! = *je m'en moque !* ⓂⒹ it's no skin off my back ! = *je m'en moque comme de ma première chemise !*

DARN ! (interj) *flûte* ! = **darn it** ! → GOSH !

DARN (to, -ed) *repriser* : to darn socks = *repriser des chaussettes* ⓪ to mend = *raccommoder*
darn him ! = *qu'il aille au diable* ! = damn him ! → BUZZ OFF !
I'll be darned if (I'll help him) ! = *le diable m'emporte si (je l'aide)* ! → GOSH !

DARN = DARNED (adj) *fichu, -e* : you're a darn/darned fool ! = *tu es un fichu crétin* ! ⓪ bloody = *foutu* ☠ *elle est ≠ n'est pas bien fichue* = she is ≠ isn't well-built
— *elle est mal fichue* = she's feeling under the weather
— *elle est fichue comme l'as de pique* = she looks like little orphan Annie
— *je suis fichue* ! = I'm finished !

DARN = DARNED (adv) *bigrement* : you're darn/darned right ! = *vous avez bigrement raison* ! → VERY
you're darn tootin' ! = *et comment donc* ! : will I get even ? you're darn tootin' ! = *si je vais me venger ? et comment donc* !

DARNDEST (n) **to do one's darndest** = *faire l'impossible* = to do one's damnedest.

DART (n) *fléchette (f)* : to play darts = *jouer aux fléchettes* ⓪ English pub = *pub anglais.*

DASH (n, -es) *tiret (m)* ⓪ hyphen = *trait d'union*
a dash of (paprika) = *une pincée de (paprika)* ⓪ a touch of = *un brin de.*

DASH (to, -ed) **to dash in ≠ out** = *entrer ≠ sortir en trombe* ⓪ to zip in ≠ out = *entrer ≠ sortir en flèche.*

DASHING (adj) *fringant, -e* : a dashing young diplomat = *un jeune diplomate fringant* ⓪ stylish = *élégant.*

DATA (n pl) *données (f pl)* : there is/are not enough data available = *il n'y a pas assez de données connues* ⓪ information = ←
data processing = *traitement de données.*

DATE (n) **1/** *date (f)* : what's the date ? = *quelle est la date ?* ⓪ what's today ? = *quel jour sommes-nous ?*

| ☠ *cela fera date* = it will be remembered | — *date limite* = deadline |

2/ *rendez-vous (m) (galant)* : do you have a date tonight ? = *est-ce que tu as un rendez-vous (galant) ce soir ?* ⓪ tryst = *cinq à sept,* appointment = *rendez-vous* **3/** *personne avec qui l'on sort* : my date's French = *la personne avec qui je sors est française* **4/** *datte (f)* : to eat dates = *manger des dattes*

| **date of birth** = *date de naissance*
to keep up to date = *se tenir au courant* = to keep informed
to set the date = *fixer la date*
to date = *jusqu'ici* : no news | from her to date = *pas de nouvelles d'elle jusqu'ici* ⓪ up to now = *jusqu'à présent*
up to date ≠ out of date = **1/** *à jour ≠ pas à jour* : they brought the dictionary up to | date = *ils ont mis le dictionnaire à jour* **2/** *au courant ≠ pas au courant* : let me bring you up to date = *laissez-moi vous mettre au courant.* |

DATE (to, -d) **1/** *sortir avec* : she's dating a doctor = *elle sort avec un médecin* = she's going out with a doctor **2/** *dater* : the letter's dated December 2nd = *la lettre est datée du 2 décembre* ☠ *ça ne date pas d'hier* = it's been going on for a long time.

DATED (adj) *qui date* : dated methods = *des méthodes qui datent* ≠ up-to-the-minute = *le plus récent.*

DAUGHTER (n) *fille (f)* : they have three daughters = *ils ont trois filles* ⓪ daughter-in-law = *belle-fille* ≠ son = *fils* ☠ → girl.

DAUNT (to, -ed) *décontenancer* : I wasn't daunted by his remark = *sa remarque ne m'a pas décontenancé* ⓪ to disconcert = *déconcerter.*

DAUNTING (adj) *décourageant, -e* : a daunting reversal of strategy = *un revirement stratégique décourageant* = discouraging.

DAWDLE (to, -d) *lambiner* : to dawdle on the way to one's office = *lambiner sur le chemin du bureau* ≠ to hurry up = *se dépêcher.*

DAWN (n) *aube (f)* : to get up at dawn = *se lever à l'aube* ⓪ daybreak = *aurore* ≠ dusk = *crépuscule*
at the break/crack of dawn ≠ nightfall = *au lever/point du jour* ≠ *tombée du jour/de la nuit.*

DAWN ON (to, -ed) *venir à l'idée* : it didn't dawn on me that you wouldn't agree = *il ne m'était pas venu à l'idée que vous refuseriez* ⓪ it didn't enter my mind = *ça ne m'était pas venu à l'esprit.*

DAY (n) *jour (m)* : two days ago = *il y a deux jours* ⓪ week = *semaine*

(10 dollars) a day = *(dix dollars) par jour*
(I can do it) any day = *(je peux le faire) n'importe quand*
(to be paid) by the day = *(être payé) à la journée*
to carry the day = *remporter la victoire*
day after day = *jour après jour*
day and night = *jour et nuit* ⓪ night and day = *nuit et jour*
day in, day out (it's the same thing) = *jour après jour (c'est la même chose)*
day laborer = *journalier*
day nursery = *crèche/pouponnière*
day off = *jour de congé* : tomorrow's my day off = *demain, c'est mon jour de congé* ⓪ holiday = *jour férié*
day school = *externat* ≠ boarding school = *internat*
day student = *externe*
D-day = *le jour J*
during the day = *pendant la journée*

every day isn't a holiday = *ce n'est pas tous les jours dimanche*
Father's/Mother's Day = *fête des Pères/fête des Mères*
from day to day = *au jour le jour/sans souci du lendemain* : she lives from day to day = *elle vit au jour le jour*
his days are numbered = *ses jours sont comptés* ⓪ he's had it = *il est fichu*
in days gone by = *dans le temps*
in this day and age = *à notre époque* ⓪ nowadays = *de nos jours*
in those days (there were no cars) = *dans ce temps-là (il n'y avait pas de voitures)*
in (her) day = *à (son) époque* : she was very well-known in her day = *elle était très connue à son époque*
it's all in a day's work = *ça fait partie de la routine* → THAT'S LIFE !

let's call it a day ! = *à chaque jour suffit sa peine !*
that'll be the day ! = *je voudrais bien voir ça !*
the day after ≠ **the day before** = *le lendemain* ≠ *la veille*
the day after tomorrow = *après-demain* ≠ **the day before yesterday** = *avant-hier*
the day of reckoning = *le jour du Jugement dernier* = Judgment Day ⓪ the moment of truth = *le moment de vérité*
these days = *à l'heure actuelle* : there's a lot of unemployment these days = *il y a beaucoup de chômage à l'heure actuelle*
those were the days = *c'était le bon vieux temps*
to this day = *jusqu'à aujourd'hui* : he didn't know what really happened to this day = *jusqu'à aujourd'hui, il ne savait pas ce qui s'était vraiment passé*
what a beautiful day ! = *quelle belle journée !*

♟ *sous un jour (favorable)* = in a (good) light
— *mettre qqch à jour* = to bring stg up to date
— *être à jour* = to be up-to-date

— *vivre au jour le jour* = to live from hand to mouth
— *il fait encore jour* = it's still daylight
— *fixer un jour* = to set a date.

DAYDREAM (to, -ed) *rêvasser* : this child's always daydreaming = *cet enfant est toujours en train de rêvasser* ⓪ to be lost in one's thoughts = *être perdu dans ses pensées.*

DAYLIGHT (n) **it's still daylight** = *il fait encore jour*
(he's beginning) to see daylight = *(il commence à) y voir clair*
daylight saving time = *heure d'été*
to beat the (living) daylights out of s.o. = *frapper qqn comme un sourd* → TO HIT
to scare the (living) daylights out of s.o. = *flanquer la pétoche à qqn* ⓪ to give s.o. the creeps = *flanquer les jetons à qqn.*

DAYTIME (n) **during the daytime** = *pendant la journée.*

DAZE (n) **in a daze** = *dans un état second* : he walked in a daze = *il marchait dans un état second* ⓪ groggy = ←.

DAZE (to, -d) *abasourdir* : dazed by the news/the blow = *abasourdi par la nouvelle/le coup* ⓪ to floor = *laisser interdit.*

DAZZLE (to, -d) *éblouir* : dazzled by her beauty = *ébloui par sa beauté* **DAZZLING** (adj) *éblouissant, -e* : dazzling beauty = *beauté éblouissante* ⓪ striking = *frappant,* stunning = *superbe.*

D.C. (abbr) = District of Columbia.

DDT (n) *D.D.T. (m)* ⓪ insecticide = ←.

DEAD (n) **in the dead of (night)** = *au plus profond de (la nuit)*

the dead = *les morts*
to wake the dead = *réveiller les morts.*

DEAD (adj) 1/ *mort, -e* : her father's dead = *son père est mort* ⓪ defunct = *défunt* 2/ *mort, -e* : we walked so much, I'm dead ! = *on a tellement marché, je suis morte !* ⓪ beat = *crevé,* weary = *las*

as dead as a doornail = *raide mort* ⟁ **a stiff** = *un macchabée*

to be a dead duck = *être cuit :* I'm a dead duck if the teacher sees me cheating = *je suis cuit si le professeur me voit en train de tricher*

to be dead to the world = *dormir du sommeil du juste* ⟁ **to be sound asleep** = *dormir à poings fermés*

dead and buried = *mort et enterré*

(he's) dead from the neck up = *(il est) bête à manger du foin*

→ STUPID

dead end = *cul-de-sac :* the street's a dead end = *la rue est un cul-de-sac,* the talks are at a dead end = *les pourparlers sont dans un cul-de-sac*

it was a dead giveaway = *c'était cousu de fil blanc*

dead loss = *perte sèche*

dead men tell no tales = *morte la bête, mort le venin*

a dead ringer for = *le sosie de :* he's a dead ringer for Bogart = *c'est le sosie de Bogart* ⟁ **the picture of** = *le portrait de*

more dead than alive = *plus mort que vif*

over my dead body ! = *il faudra me passer sur le corps !* ⟁ **not on your life !** = *jamais de la vie !*

shot dead = *tué par balle*

wanted dead or alive = *recherché mort ou vif* ⟁ **ransom chaser** = *chasseur de primes*

he wouldn't be caught dead (in a gay club) = *pour rien au monde il ne voudrait qu'on le voie (dans une boîte d'homosexuels).*

DEAD (adv) **to be dead set against** ≠ **on (the new tax law)** = *être farouchement opposé à* ≠ *tenir absolument à (la nouvelle loi fiscale)*
I'm dead (serious) = *je suis tout ce qu'il y a de plus (sérieux)*

you're dead wrong = *vous êtes complètement à côté de la plaque*
to drop dead = *tomber raide mort :* he dropped dead on the tennis court = *il est tombé raide mort sur le court de tennis* ⟁ **to croak** = *crever*
drop dead ! = *et ta sœur !* → BUZZ OFF !

DEAD BEAT (adj) *harassé, -e :* I am dead beat after a five-mile run = *je suis harassée après une course de 8 kilomètres* ⟁ **exhausted** = *épuisé,* **dog-tired** = *flapi.*

DEAD-DRUNK (adj) *ivre mort, -e :* she went home dead-drunk = *elle est rentrée chez elle ivre morte* → DRUNK.

DEADLINE (n) *date (f) limite :* the deadline to finish the manuscript = *la date limite pour finir le manuscrit* ⟁ **time limit** = *délai.*

DEADLOCK (n) *impasse (f) :* the talks have reached a deadlock = *les pourparlers sont dans une impasse* ⟁ **standstill** = *point mort* ≠ **breakthrough** = *percée* ☠ *une impasse (rue)* = a dead-end street.

DEADLY (adj, -ier, -iest) *mortel, -elle :* what a deadly evening ! = *quelle soirée mortelle !* ≠ **exciting** = *passionnant* ☠ → mortal.

DEADPAN (adj) *impassible :* a deadpan expression = *une expression impassible* ⟁ **poker-faced** = *avec un visage de marbre.*

DEADWOOD (n inv) *poids (m) mort :* he's deadwood in the company = *c'est un poids mort dans l'entreprise.*

DEAF (adj, -er, -est) *sourd, -e, sourdingue* (LV) : he's deaf in one ear = *il est sourd d'une oreille* ⟁ **hard-of-hearing** = *dur d'oreille,* **deafness** = *surdité*

to be as deaf as a post = *être sourd comme un pot* = to be stone-deaf

deaf people = *les malentendants*

deaf and dumb = *sourd-muet* ⟁ **a deaf-mute** = *un sourd-muet*

to fall on deaf ears = *tomber dans l'oreille d'un sourd :* I hope that now my complaints won't fall on deaf ears = *j'espère que maintenant mes plaintes ne tomberont pas dans l'oreille d'un sourd* ⟁ **to talk to a wall** = *parler à un mur*

to turn a deaf ear to = *faire la sourde oreille à* ≠ **to pay attention to** = *prêter attention à* ☠ *une hostilité sourde* = a latent hostility.

DEAFENING (adj) *assourdissant, -e :* a deafening noise = *un bruit assourdissant* ⟁ **earsplitting** = *strident.*

DEAL (n) *affaire (f) :* they're offering you a good deal = *ils te proposent une bonne affaire* ☠ → affair

---

to close a deal = *conclure une affaire*
a good/great deal of = *énormément de* → MANY
it's a deal ! = *O.K. !/marché conclu !* ≠ **no soap !** = *que dalle !*

it's your deal ! = *c'est à vous de donner !*
let's make a deal ! = *faisons un marché !*
to make a whole/big deal about = *en faire une maladie :* don't make such a whole/big

deal about it ! = *n'en fais pas une (telle) maladie !* ⟁ **to make a fuss** = *faire des histoires*
to put a deal together = *monter une affaire :* he got ten percent for putting the deal together = *il a touché dix pour*

cent pour avoir monté l'affaire **the deal is (that you get ten percent on what you sell)** =	*notre arrangement est (que vous touchez dix pour cent de ce que vous vendez)*	**what's the deal ?** = *comment s'arrange-t-on ?* ⓪ **what's the setup ?** = *comment s'organise-t-on ?*

DEAL (to, dealt, dealt) **1/** *faire du trafic de drogue* : he's been dealing to pay for college and hasn't got caught yet = *il fait du trafic de drogue pour payer ses études et il ne s'est pas encore fait prendre* **2/** *donner* (cards) : whose turn is it to deal ? = *à qui est-ce de donner ?* ≠ to misdeal = *faire une mauvaise donne* 🕱 → to give

to deal with = **1/** *avoir affaire à* : I only deal with big shots = *je n'ai affaire qu'aux grands pontes* **2/** *s'occuper de* : I'll deal with him/that later = *je m'occuperai de lui/de ça plus tard* **3/** *faire face à* : I can't deal with his neuroses = *je ne peux pas faire*	*face à ses névroses* = to cope with ⓪ to handle = *assumer* **4/** *traiter de* : the movie deals with today's drug problems = *le film traite des problèmes actuels de la drogue.*

DEALER (n) *dealer (m)* (drugs), *négociant, -e* : he's the largest wine dealer in New York = *c'est le plus gros négociant en vins de New York,* even kids are dealers = *même les gosses sont (des) dealers.*

DEALINGS (n pl) *façons (f pl) d'agir* : shady ≠ honest business dealings = *des façons louches ≠ honnêtes d'agir en affaires.*

DEAN (n) *doyen, -enne* : the dean of the university = *le doyen de l'université* ⓪ head = *président*
to be on the dean's list = *être reçu avec mention.*

DEAR (n) *chéri, -e* : hurry up dear, or we'll be late = *dépêche-toi chéri, ou nous allons être en retard* = darling ⓪ honey = *mon chou*
dear me ! = *oh là !* = **oh dear !** → GOSH !

DEAR (adj, -er, -est) **1/** *cher, -ère* : dear Mr Smith = *cher M. Smith* **2/** (GB) *cher, -ère* : this restaurant's dear = *ce restaurant est cher* = expensive
Dear John letter = *lettre de rupture* ≠ love letter = *lettre d'amour*
she's very dear to me = *elle m'est très chère.*

DEATH (n) *mort (f)* : the accident caused ten deaths = *l'accident a causé la mort de dix personnes* ≠ life = *vie*

at death's door = *à l'article de la mort/à l'agonie* **to be on death row** = *être dans le quartier des condamnés à mort* **to bleed to death** = *saigner à mort* **death certificate** = *certificat de décès* **death penalty** = *peine de mort* ⓪ capital punishment = *peine capitale* **death rate** = *taux de mortalité* **death wish** = *pulsion de mort* **he'll be the death of me !** = *il me fera mourir !*	⓪ he's driving me crazy ! = *il me fait tourner en bourrique !* **to freeze to death** = *mourir de froid* **to put to death** = *mettre à mort* **sentenced to death** = *condamné à mort* **to sign one's death warrant** = *signer son propre arrêt de mort* **till death do us part** = *jusqu'à ce que la mort nous sépare*
🕱 *un mort* = a dead person — *un mort-né* = a stillborn child	— *la mort dans l'âme* = heartbrokenly — *le mort (bridge)* = dummy.

DEATHBED (n) **on one's deathbed** = *sur son lit de mort.*

DEATHLY (adv) *mortellement* : deathly wounded = *mortellement blessé* 🕱 → mortally.

DEBASE (to, -d) *(s')abaisser* : her vulgar language debases her = *elle s'abaisse en parlant vulgairement* ⓪ to degrade = *(se) dégrader* 🕱 *abaisser (levier/manette)* = to pull down (handle).

DEBATABLE (adj) *discutable* : whether the pill's better than the loop is debatable = *il est discutable que la pilule soit plus efficace que le stérilet* ⓪ questionable = *contestable* ≠ undeniable = *indéniable.*

DEBATE (n) *débat (m)* : a debate in Congress = *un débat au Congrès* ⓪ discussion = *←,* panel = *tribune* 🕱 *les débats d'un procès* = the proceedings of a trial.

DEBATE (to, -d) *débattre* : they're debating whether to go or not = *ils débattent pour s'ils y vont ou non* ⓪ to discuss = *discuter*
🕱 *débattre d'un prix* = to dicker over a price
— *se débattre avec* = to struggle with/against.

DEBAUCH (to, -ed) *débaucher* : to debauch young girls = *débaucher de jeunes filles* 🕱 *débaucher (travail)* = to lay off (work) **DEBAUCHED** (adj) *débauché, -e* : to lead a debauched life = *mener une vie débauchée* ⓪ wanton = *dévergondé.*

DEBILITATING (adj) *débilitant, -e :* a debilitating disease = *une maladie débilitante.*

DEBIT (n) *débit (m)* **DEBIT** (to, -ted) *débiter :* to debit an account = *débiter un compte* ≠ to credit = *créditer* ☠ *débiter (des mensonges, etc.)* = to utter (lies, etc.).

DEBRIEF (to, -ed) *(faire) faire un compte rendu :* to debrief an intelligence agent = *faire faire un compte rendu à un agent de renseignements.*

DEBRIS (n inv) *débris (m) :* the streets were full of debris = *les rues étaient pleines de débris* ◎ detritus = *détritus.*

DEBT (n) *dette (f) :* I always pay my debts = *je paie toujours mes dettes* ◎ debtor = *débiteur*
to be in debt = *être endetté*
to incur debts = *contracter des dettes.*

DEBUNK (to, -ed) *démystifier :* to debunk a legend = *démystifier une légende.*

DEBUTANTE (n) *débutante (f)* ◎ to make one's debut = *faire son entrée dans le monde* ☠ *une débutante* = a beginner.

DECADE (n) *décennie (f) :* a violent decade = *une décennie violente* ◎ century = *siècle* ☠ *une décade* = ten days.

DECADENCE (n) *décadence (f) :* she enjoys a life of decadence = *elle aime vivre dans la décadence* ◎ degradation = *dégradation* **DECADENT** (adj) *décadent, -e :* a decadent society = *une société décadente* ◎ declining = *déclinant.*

DECAY (n) *déclin (m) :* the decay of male supremacy = *le déclin de la suprématie masculine* ≠ apogee = *apogée* **DECAY** (to, -ed) *se délabrer :* teeth/houses decay = *les dents/maisons se délabrent* ◎ to rot = *pourrir.*

DECEASED (n) **the deceased** = *le(s) défunt(s).*

DECEIT (n) *duperie (f) :* he accused his lawyer of deceit = *il a accusé son avocat de duperie* ◎ deception = *tromperie,* duplicity = *duplicité.*

DECEITFUL (adj) *fourbe :* a deceitful businessman/answer = *un homme d'affaires/une réponse fourbe* ◎ devious = *tortueux.*

DECEIVE (to, -d) *abuser :* I'm very easy to deceive = *il est très facile de m'abuser* ◎ to betray = *trahir*
you're deceiving yourself = *vous vous faites des idées* ◎ you're kidding yourself = *vous vous faites de douces illusions*
☠ → to abuse.

DECEMBER (n) *décembre (m)* ◎ Xmas = *Noël* → MONTH.

DECENCY (n, -ies) *décence (f) :* out of common decency = *par simple décence* ≠ indecency = *indécence.*

DECENT (adj) *décent, -e :* a decent meal/salary = *un repas/salaire décent* ≠ indecent = *indécent*

it was decent of him (to help us) = *c'était chic de sa part de (nous aider).*

DECENTRALIZE (to, -d) *décentraliser* ≠ to centralize = *centraliser* **DECENTRALIZATION** (n) *décentralisation (f)* ≠ centralization = *centralisation.*

DECEPTION (n) *tromperie (f) :* it was a case of deception = *c'était une affaire de tromperie* ◎ cheating = *tricherie* ☠ *c'était une déception* = it was a letdown/a disappointment.

DECEPTIVE (adj) *mensonger, -ère :* deceptive publicity = *publicité mensongère* ◎ misleading = *trompeur.*

DECIDE (to, -d) *décider :* he can't decide where he wants to eat = *il n'arrive pas à décider où il veut manger* ◎ to conclude = *conclure*
decide ! = *décidez-vous !* = make up your mind !
to decide against (taking the pill) = *décider de ne pas (prendre la pilule)*
to decide on (the red one) = *se décider pour (le rouge)*
to decide to (leave) = *décider de (partir)*
☠ *décider qqn à faire qqch* = to talk s.o. into doing stg
— *il est décidé à (partir)* = he's determined to (leave).

DECIDED (adj) *très net, nette :* a decided change in his manner = *un changement d'attitude très net.*

DECIDEDLY (adv) *incontestablement :* he's decidedly a very stubborn guy = *c'est incontestablement un type très têtu.*

DECIPHER (to, -ed) *déchiffrer :* to decipher secret codes = *déchiffrer des codes secrets* ◎ to decode = *décoder.*

DECISION (n) *décision (f) :* that's my decision = *voici ma décision* ◎ conclusion = ←
to come to a decision = *parvenir à une décision*
to make a decision = *prendre une décision* ◎ to decide = *décider*
☠ *la décision du juge* = the judge's ruling.

DECISIVE (adj) *décisif, -ive :* a decisive step in the talks = *une étape décisive des pourparlers* ◎ capital = ←.

DECK (n) *pont (m)* (boat) : to go on deck = *monter sur le pont* ◎ hold = *cale*
clear the decks ! = *branle-bas de combat !*
a deck of cards = *un jeu de cartes*
hit the deck ! = *planque-toi !* ◎ take cover ! = *abritez-vous !*

DECK (to, -ed) **to be (all) decked out** = *être (bien) sapé, -e* ◎ to be (well) rigged out = *être (bien) fringué.*

DECLARATION (n) *déclaration (f) :* a declaration of war/independence = *une déclaration de guerre/d'indépendance* ◎ announcement = *annonce*
☠ *la Déclaration des droits de l'homme* = the Bill of rights
— *faire sa déclaration (d'amour)* = to propose
— *une déclaration (gouvernement)* = a statement.

DECLARE (to, -d) *déclarer* : war was declared = *la guerre a été déclarée* Ⓞ to announce = *annoncer*
I declare ! = *ma parole !* → GOSH !
anything to declare ? = *avez-vous quelque chose à déclarer ?*
☠ *il a été déclaré coupable* = he was pronounced guilty.

DECLINE (n) *déclin (m)* (empire, society, etc.), *diminution (f)* : the decline of the West = *le déclin de l'Occident*, the decline in unemployment = *la diminution du chômage* Ⓞ decrease = *baisse* ≠ rise = *montée/hausse*
on the decline = *sur le déclin.*

DECLINE (to, -d) **1/** *décliner* : to decline an invitation = *décliner une invitation* Ⓞ to turn down = *refuser* **2/** *décliner* : his health/influence is declining = *sa santé/son influence décline* Ⓞ to diminish = *diminuer.*

DECODE (to, -d) *décoder* : to decode a message = *décoder un message* Ⓞ to crack a code = *trouver la clé d'un code.*

DECOR (n) *décor (m)* : a modern decor = *un décor moderne*
☠ *rentrer dans le décor* = to crash/to smash into (a tree, etc.)
— *les décors (théâtre)* = the scenery (theater).

DECORATE (to, -d) *décorer* : to decorate an apartment = *décorer un appartement* Ⓞ to redecorate = *refaire* = to remodel **DECORATION** (n) *décoration (f)* **DECORATIVE** (adj) *décoratif, -ive* Ⓞ ornamental = *ornemental* **DECORATOR** (n) *décorateur, -trice* Ⓞ designer = *dessinateur.*

DECOY (n) *amorce (f)* : she was a police decoy = *elle a servi d'amorce à la police* Ⓞ bait = *appât* ☠ *l'amorce (des négociations)* = the first stages (of the negotiations).

DECREASE (n) *baisse (f)* : a decrease in the birthrate = *une baisse du taux de natalité* Ⓞ fall = *chute* ≠ increase = *augmentation* **DECREASE** (to, -d) *décroître* : racism is decreasing = *le racisme décroît* Ⓞ to diminish = *diminuer* ≠ to increase = *augmenter.*

DECREE (n) *décret (m)* : a government decree = *un décret du gouvernement* Ⓞ law = *loi* **DECREE** (to, -d) *décréter.*

DECREPIT (adj) *décrépit, -e* : a decrepit old man/building = *un vieil homme/immeuble décrépit.*

DEDICATE (to, -d) **1/** *consacrer* : to dedicate one's life to science = *consacrer sa vie à la science* ☠ *pouvez-vous me consacrer une heure ?* = can you spare me an hour ? **2/** *dédicacer* : to dedicate a book = *dédicacer un livre* Ⓞ to sign = *signer* **DEDICATION** (n) *dédicace (f).*

DEDICATED (adj) *qui se consacre entièrement à* : a dedicated scientist = *quelqu'un qui se consacre entièrement à la science.*

DEDUCE (to, -d) *déduire* : I deduced from what he said that they were really having problems = *j'ai déduit de ce*

qu'il a dit qu'ils avaient réellement des problèmes ☠ *déduire (cinq pour cent)* = to deduct (five percent).

DEDUCT (to, -ed) *déduire* : he deducted ten percent = *il a déduit dix pour cent* Ⓞ to subtract = *soustraire* ☠ → to deduce.

DEDUCTIBLE (adj) *déductible* : deductible expenses = *dépenses déductibles* ≠ taxable = *imposable.*

DEDUCTION (n) *déduction (f)* : tax deduction = *déduction d'impôts.*

DEED (n) **1/** *action (f)* : a good deed = *une bonne action* Ⓞ act = *acte* ☠ → action **2/** *acte (m)* : to draw up a deed for the property = *rédiger un acte de propriété* ☠ → act.

DEEJAY (n) *disc-jockey (m)* = disc jockey.

DEEM (to, -ed) *estimer* : I didn't deem it necessary = *je n'ai pas estimé (cela) nécessaire* Ⓞ to reckon = *croire* ☠ → to estimate.

DEEP (adj, -er, -est) **1/** *profond, -e* : a deep river = *une rivière profonde* ≠ shallow = *peu profond* **2/** *profond, -e* : sensitive and deep = *sensible et profond* Ⓞ intelligent = ← ≠ shallow = *peu profond* ☠ → profound
to be in deep water = *avoir des pépins* Ⓞ to be in a pickle = *être frais*
deep in (debt) = *(endetté) jusqu'au cou*
to go off the deep end = *perdre les pédales* : she went off the deep end when her husband died = *elle a perdu les pédales à la mort de son mari* Ⓞ to go to pieces = *s'effondrer*
take a deep breath ! = *respire profondément !*

DEEP (adv) *profond(ément)* : to dive deep = *plonger profond(ément)*
deep down (she hates her family) = *au tréfonds d'elle-même (elle déteste sa famille).*

DEEPLY (adv) *profondément* : deeply offended = *profondément offensé.*

DEEP-ROOTED (adj) *profondément enraciné, -e* : deep-rooted racism = *racisme profondément enraciné* Ⓞ ingrained = *ancré.*

DEEP-SEATED (adj) = DEEP-ROOTED.

DEER (n) *daim (m)* Ⓞ doe = *biche*, reindeer = *renne*, stag = *cerf* ☠ *un manteau de daim* = a suede coat.

DEFAMATORY (adj) *diffamatoire* : defamatory remarks = *des remarques diffamatoires.*

DEFAULT (n) **(to win) by default** = *(gagner) par défaut*
to be sentenced by default = *être condamné par contumace.*

DEFEAT (n) *défaite (f)* : he's never known defeat = *il n'a jamais connu la défaite* ≠ victory = *victoire* **DEFEAT** (to, -ed) *vaincre* : the army was defeated = *l'armée a été vaincue* Ⓞ to beat = *battre* ☠ → to vanquish.

DEFEATIST (n, adj) *défaitiste (m, f)* : don't be such a defeatist = *ne sois pas si défaitiste* ≠ optimist = *optimiste.*

DEFECT (n) *défaut (m)* : a technical defect = *un défaut technique* ⓪ imperfection = ←
☠ *son plus gros défaut est son caractère* = his biggest shortcoming is his temper
— *défaut (diamant)* = flaw (diamond).

DEFECT (to, -ed) **to defect from (a country)** = *déserter (un pays)* ☠ → to desert
to defect to = *passer à* : the scientist defected to the West = *le savant est passé à l'Ouest* ≠ to be exiled = *être exilé.*

DEFECTION (n) *défection (f)* ⓪ defector = *transfuge.*

DEFECTIVE (adj) *défectueux, -euse* : a defective machine = *une machine défectueuse* ⓪ faulty = *imparfait.*

DEFEND (to, -ed) *défendre* : a lawyer defends his client = *un avocat défend son client* ⓪ to protect = *protéger* ≠ to combat = *combattre*
☠ *je vous défends de ...* = I forbid you to ...
— *il se défend bien (aux cartes)* = he holds his own (at cards).

DEFENDANT (n) *prévenu, -e* : the defendant will now take the stand = *le prévenu a maintenant la parole* ≠ plaintiff = *plaignant.*

DEFENSE (n) *défense (f)* : a large defense budget = *un gros budget pour la Défense*
the defense rests its case = *la défense conclut son plaidoyer* ≠ the prosecution = *l'accusation*
in s.o.'s defense = *pour la défense de qqn* : I'll say this in her defense = *je dirai ceci pour sa défense*
to take s.o.'s defense = *prendre la défense de qqn*
☠ *défenses (éléphant)* = tusks.

DEFENSELESS (adj) *sans défense* : defenseless children = *des enfants sans défense* ⓪ vulnerable = *vulnérable.*

DEFENSIVE (n) *défensive (f)* : she's always on the defensive = *elle est toujours sur la défensive* ≠ attack = *attaque* **DEFENSIVE** (adj) *défensif, -ive* : defensive weapons = *armes défensives* ≠ offensive = *offensif.*

DEFER (to, -red) *différer* : the trial was deferred = *le procès a été différé* ⓪ to postpone = *remettre*
to defer to = *s'en remettre à* : we deferred to his experience = *nous nous en sommes remis à son expérience* ☠ → to differ.

DEFERENCE (n) **in deference to (her age)** = *par déférence pour (son âge)* ⓪ out of respect for = *par respect pour.*

DEFIANCE (n) **in defiance of the law** = *au mépris de la loi* ≠ in compliance with = *conformément à.*

DEFICIENCY (n, -ies) *déficience (f), carence (f)* (body) : a deficiency in the plan/iron = *une déficience du plan/une carence en fer.*

DEFICIENT (adj) **mentally deficient** = *débile mental* ⓪ retarded = *retardé.*

DEFICIT (n) *déficit (m)* : to show a deficit = *être en déficit* ≠ profit = ←.

DEFINE (to, -d) *définir* : to define a word = *définir un mot.*

DEFINITE (adj) *certain, -e* : it's definite that I'll go = *j'irai, c'est certain,* when will you give me a definite answer ? = *quand me donnerez-vous une réponse certaine ?* ≠ dubious = *douteux* ☠ → certain.

DEFINITELY (adv) *sans aucun doute* : she's definitely going to have an abortion = *elle va sans aucun doute se faire avorter* ⓪ for sure = *à coup sûr* ☠ *elle est partie définitivement* = she has left for good.

DEFINITION (n) *définition (f)* : what's the definition of a bastard ? = *quelle est la définition d'un salaud ?* ⓪ signification = ←.

DEFINITIVE (adj) *définitif, -ive* : his refusal was definitive = *son refus était définitif* ⓪ final = ←.

DEFLATION (n) *déflation (f)* : a period of deflation = *une période de déflation* ⓪ recession = *récession.*

DEFLOWER (to, -ed) *déflorer, dépuceler* : to deflower a girl = *déflorer/dépuceler une fille* ⓪ the cherry = *la fleur.*

DEFORM (to, -ed) *déformer* : you're deforming the meaning of the word = *vous déformez le sens du mot* ☠ *déformer les faits* = to distort the facts **DEFORMATION** (n) *déformation (f)* : a deformation of his theory = *une déformation de sa théorie.*

DEFORMED (adj) *difforme* : a deformed body = *un corps difforme* ⓪ disfigured = *défiguré.*

DEFORMITY (n, -ies) *difformité (f)* : a physical deformity = *une difformité physique.*

DEFROST (to, -ed) *décongeler* (food), *dégivrer* (fridge) : defrost the meat = *décongelez la viande* = thaw the meat, defrost the freezer = *dégivrez le congélateur* ≠ to freeze = *congeler.*

DEFT (adj, -er, -est) *adroit, -e* : a deft mechanic = *un mécanicien adroit* ⓪ dexterous = *habile* ≠ clumsy = *gauche.*

DEFUSE (to, d) *désamorcer* : the cops defused the bomb = *les flics ont désamorcé la bombe.*

DEFY (to, -ied) *défier* : your reasoning defies logic = *ton raisonnement défie la logique*
I defy you to (tell me the truth) = *je te défie de (me dire la vérité)*
☠ *je me défie de lui* = I distrust him.

DEGENERATE (n, adj) *(de) dégénéré, -e* : a degenerate life = *une vie de dégénéré* **DEGENERATE** (to, -d) *dégénérer* : a serious energy crisis could degenerate into a war = *une grave crise de l'énergie pourrait dégénérer en guerre* **DEGENERATION** (n) *dégénérescence (f).*

DEGRADE (to, -d) *(se) dégrader* : she degraded herself by lying like that = *elle s'est dégradée en mentant comme ça* ⓓ to demean = *s'avilir* ☠ *la situation/le temps se dégrade* = the situation/weather is deteriorating/getting bad.

DEGRADING (adj) *dégradant, -e* : a degrading job = *un boulot dégradant* ⓓ demeaning = *avilissant.*

DEGREE (n) 1/ *degré (m)* : ten degrees below normal = *dix degrés au-dessous de la normale* ⓓ temperature = *température* 2/ *degré (m)* : he has a limited degree of intelligence = *il a un degré d'intelligence limité* 3/ *diplôme (m)* : a law/BA degree = *une licence de droit/ de lettres* ☠ → diploma
to a (certain) degree = *jusqu'à un certain degré* : she's sensitive to a certain degree = *elle est sensible jusqu'à un certain degré* ⓓ to a certain extent = *dans une certaine mesure*
to such a degree that ... = *à tel degré que ...* ⓓ so much so that ... = *à telle enseigne que ...*
to what degree = *à quel point* : I don't know to what degree he loves her = *je ne sais pas à quel point il l'aime.*

DEHYDRATED (adj) *déshydraté, -e* : dehydrated by a long walk in the desert = *déshydraté par une longue marche dans le désert* ⓓ thirsty = *assoiffé.*

DEIGN TO (to, -ed) *daigner* : she didn't deign to answer = *elle n'a pas daigné répondre* ⓓ to condescend to = *condescendre à.*

DEJECTED (adj) *abattu, -e* : I'm feeling depressed, really dejected = *je me sens déprimé, vraiment abattu* ≠ in heaven = *aux anges.*

DELAY (n) *retard (m)* : there will be a two-hour delay before takeoff = *il y aura deux heures de retard au décollage*
without delay = *sans délai* ⓓ straightaway = *illico* ☠ *un retard dans la production* = a lag in production.

DELAY (to, -ed) *retarder* : I was delayed by the storm = *j'ai été retardé par l'orage*
☠ *ma montre retarde* = my watch is slow
— *tu retardes* = you're behind times
— *j'ai été retardé au bureau* = I was hung up at the office
— *retarder le développement de qqch* = to set back the development of stg.

DELEGATE (n) *délégué, -e* : he's a delegate to the UN = *il est délégué à l'ONU* ⓓ representative = *représentant* **DELEGATE** (to, -d) *déléguer* : to delegate one's powers = *déléguer ses pouvoirs* **DELEGATION** (n) *délégation (f)* : the German delegation = *la délégation allemande* ⓓ mission = ←.

DELETE (to, -d) *supprimer* : to delete a name from a list = *supprimer un nom d'une liste* ⓓ to strike it out = *biffer* ☠ → to do away with.

DELIBERATE (adj) *délibéré, -e* : a deliberate mistake = *une faute délibérée* ⓓ intentional = *intentionnel, intended = voulu.*

DELIBERATE (to, -d) *délibérer* : the jury's deliberating = *le jury est en train de délibérer* ⓓ to think through = *réfléchir.*

DELIBERATELY (adv) *délibérément* : he lied deliberately = *il a délibérément menti* ⓓ purposely = *à dessein.*

DELIBERATION (n) *délibération (f)* : after lengthy deliberations = *après de longues délibérations* ⓓ discussion = ←.

DELICACY (n, -ies) *mets (m) raffiné* : caviar's a delicacy = *le caviar est un mets raffiné* ⓓ treat = *régal.*

DELICATE (adj) *délicat, -e* : delicate health/features = *santé délicate/traits délicats* ⓓ fragile = ←
☠ *c'est très délicat (de lui parler de ça)* = it's very ticklish/tricky (to speak with him about that)
— *une porcelaine délicate* = dainty china.

DELICATESSEN = DELI (n) *charcutier-traiteur (m)* : there's a great delicatessen/deli on 56th Street = *il y a un très bon charcutier-traiteur sur la 56e Rue* ⓓ cold cuts = *viandes froides et charcuterie.*

DELICIOUS (adj) *délicieux, -euse* : a delicious meal = *un repas délicieux* ⓓ scrumptious = *exquis* ≠ inedible = *immangeable* ☠ *un enfant délicieux* = a delightful child.

DELIGHT (n) *délice (m)* : her children are a delight = *ses enfants sont un délice* ⓓ enchantment = *enchantement.*

DELIGHT (to, -ed) *faire grand plaisir à* : the dinner delighted us = *le dîner nous a fait grand plaisir* ≠ to displease = *déplaire*
to delight in (seeing one's grandchildren) = *prendre plaisir à (voir ses petits-enfants)* = to get a kick out of ≠ not to care for = *ne pas tenir à.*

DELIGHTED (adj) *enchanté, -e* : I'm delighted to go = *je suis enchanté d'y aller* ⓓ pleased = *ravi.*

DELIGHTFUL (adj) *délicieux, -euse* : what a delightful afternoon ! = *quelle après-midi délicieuse !* → WONDERFUL ☠ → delicious.

DELINQUENCY (n, -ies) *délinquance (f)* : frequent cases of delinquency = *de fréquents cas de délinquance* **DELINQUENT** (n) *délinquant, -e* : a home for delinquents = *une maison pour délinquants* ⓓ reformatory = *maison de redressement,* wayward children = *des enfants délinquants.*

DELIRIOUS (adj) **to be delirious** = *délirer* : the patient's delirious = *le malade délire.*

DELIRIUM (n) *délire* (m) : she was sweating in her delirium = *elle transpirait dans son délire* ☠ *une foule en délire* = a delirious crowd.

DELIVER (to, -ed) **1/** *livrer, distribuer* (mail) : your car will be delivered today = *votre voiture sera livrée aujourd'hui*, mail is delivered at 8 = *le courrier est distribué à 8 heures*
☠ *distribuer* → to distribute
— *se livrer* = to open up/to make confidences
— *le voleur s'est livré à la police* = the thief turned himself in/gave himself up
2/ *accoucher* : she delivered at 2 a.m. = *elle a accouché à 2 heures du matin* ⓓ to give birth to = *donner naissance à* ☠ *accouche !* = spit it out !
3/ *s'exécuter* : he promised but never delivered = *il a promis mais ne s'est jamais exécuté* ⓓ to come through = *tenir* ☠ → to execute
4/ *délivrer* : deliver us from evil ! = *délivrez-nous du mal !*
☠ *délivrer un prisonnier* = to release a prisoner
— *délivrer un passeport* = to issue a passport.

DELIVERY (n, -ies) **1/** *livraison* (f) : free delivery = *livraison gratuite* ⓓ deliveryman = *livreur* **2/** *accouchement* (m) : a difficult delivery = *un accouchement difficile* ⓓ cesarean = *césarienne*.

DELUDE (to, -d) **to delude o.s.** = *se leurrer* : stop deluding yourself and face the truth = *arrête de te leurrer et regarde la vérité en face* ⓓ to fool o.s. = *se faire des idées*.

DELUGE (n) *déluge* (m) : a deluge of letters = *un déluge de lettres* ⓓ flooding = *inondation*
☠ *déluge (pluie)* = downpour
— *après moi le déluge !* = I don't care what happens after I'm gone !

DELUSION (n) *psychose* (f) : she had the delusion that she was being followed = *sa psychose était de se croire suivie*
delusions of grandeur = *folie des grandeurs*
she's laboring under the delusion that (he's going to marry her) = *elle croit à tort qu'(il va l'épouser)*.

DELUXE (adj) *de luxe* : a deluxe model = *un modèle de luxe* ≠ sleazy = *de bas étage*.

DELVE INTO (to, -d) *fouiller dans* : to delve into s.o.'s personal life = *fouiller dans la vie privée de qqn* ⓓ to rake up = *remuer*.

DEMAGOG(UE) (n) *démagogue* (m, f) **DEMAGOGY** = **DEMAGOGUERY** (n, -ies) *démagogie* (f).

DEMAND (n) **1/** *exigence* (f), *revendication* (f) : the unions' demands = *les exigences/revendications syndicales* **2/** *demande* (f) : the demand for the pill is great = *il y a une grosse demande pour la pilule*
to be in (great) demand = *être (très) demandé* ⓓ to be sought after = *être recherché*
☠ *faire une demande* = to make a request/to apply

— *une demande en mariage* = a marriage proposal
— *examiner une demande* = to consider a claim.

DEMAND (to, -ed) *exiger* : the unions demanded new pay increases = *les syndicats ont exigé de nouvelles augmentations de salaire* ⓓ to insist on = *insister sur*
I demand to (see the boss) = *j'exige de (voir le patron)*
☠ *ce travail exige beaucoup de patience* = this work calls for a lot of patience.

DEMANDING (adj) *exigeant, -e* : my new husband/job is very demanding = *mon nouveau mari/boulot est très exigeant* ≠ easy = *facile*.

DEMEAN (to, -ed) *avilir* : work can be demeaning = *le travail peut être avilissant* ≠ to glorify = *glorifier*.

DEMENTED (adj) *détraqué, -e* : that guy's demented = *ce type est détraqué* → CRAZY ☠ *une voiture détraquée* = a car on the blink.

DEMOBILIZATION (n) *démobilisation* (f) : the demobilization of the troops = *la démobilisation des troupes* **DEMOBILIZE** (to, -d) *démobiliser*.

DEMOCRACY (n, -ies) *démocratie* (f) : democracy is the worst regime with the exception of all others (Churchill) = *la démocratie est le pire des régimes si l'on excepte tous les autres* ⓓ republic = *république* ≠ monarchy = *monarchie*, dictatorship = *dictature*.

DEMOCRAT (n) **1/** *démocrate* (m, f) : Lincoln was a great democrat = *Lincoln était un grand démocrate* ≠ fascist = *fasciste* **2/** *démocrate* (m, f) : Democrats are very powerful in New York = *les démocrates sont très puissants à New York* ⓓ Republican = *républicain*.

DEMOCRATIC (adj) *démocratique* : a democratic country = *un pays démocratique* ⓓ liberal = *libéral*
the Democratic Party = *le Parti démocrate* (*l'un des deux grands partis politiques des États-Unis, fondé en 1828*) ⓓ donkey = *âne (symbole)* ≠ Republican Party = *Parti républicain*.

DEMOCRATIZE (to, -d) *démocratiser*.

DEMOLISH (to, -ed) **1/** *démolir* : they demolished the building = *ils ont démoli l'immeuble* ⓓ to destroy = *détruire* ≠ to build = *bâtir* **2/** *démolir* : the critics demolished the play = *les critiques ont démoli la pièce* ≠ to praise = *louer* ☠ *se démolir (la santé)* = to ruin (one's health).

DEMOLITION (n) *démolition* (f) ≠ construction = ←.

DEMON (n) *démon* (m) : her children are demons = *ses enfants sont des démons* ≠ angel = *ange*
☠ *le démon de midi* = the seven-year itch
— *il a le démon du bridge* = bridge is his mania.

DEMONSTRATE (to, -d) **1/** *manifester* : the students demonstrated for peace = *les étudiants ont manifesté pour la paix* ⓓ to march = *défiler* ☠ → to manifest
2/ *démontrer* : doctors have demonstrated that smoking

causes cancer = *les médecins ont démontré que le tabac est cause de cancer* ⓪ to prove = *prouver* ☠ *ça démontre que vous aviez tort* = that shows you were wrong **3/** *faire la démonstration de* : he demonstrated how the machine works = *il a fait la démonstration du fonctionnement de la machine*.

DEMONSTRATION (n) **1/** *manifestation* (f) : a demonstration for peace = *une manifestation pour la paix* ⓪ demo = *manif*, riot = *émeute* ☠ → manifestation **2/** *démonstration* (f) : a demonstration of friendship = *une démonstration d'amitié*.

DEMONSTRATIVE (adj) *démonstratif, -ive* : she's emotional and demonstrative = *elle est émotive et démonstrative* ≠ withdrawn = *renfermé*.

DEMONSTRATOR (n) *manifestant, -e* : a crowd of demonstrators in the streets = *une foule de manifestants dans les rues* ⓪ rioter = *émeutier*.

DEMORALIZE (to, -d) *démoraliser* : the defeat demoralized the troops = *la défaite a démoralisé les troupes* ⓪ to discourage = *décourager* ≠ to pick up = *remonter (le moral)*.

DEMOTE (to, -d) *rétrograder* : he was demoted from captain to lieutenant = *il a été rétrogradé de capitaine à lieutenant* ≠ to promote = *promouvoir* **DEMOTION** (n) *rétrogradation* (f) ≠ promotion = ←.

DEN (n) **1/** *antre* (m) : the tiger's den = *l'antre du tigre* ⓪ lair = *tanière* **2/** *salle* (f) *de loisirs* : large houses have dens where you can watch TV and play games = *les grandes maisons ont des salles de loisirs où l'on peut regarder la télé et jouer à des jeux de société* **a den of thieves** = *un repaire de brigands* **a den of vice** = *un lieu de perdition*.

DENIAL (n) *démenti* (m) (official), *dénégation* (f) : a denial by the government = *un démenti du gouvernement*, the prisoner's denial = *les dénégations de l'accusé* ⓪ disavowal = *désaveu*.

DENMARK (n) *Danemark* (m) ⓪ Danish = *danois*, a Dane = *un Danois*.

DENOUNCE (to, -d) *dénoncer* : denounced to the cops = *dénoncé aux flics* ⓪ to betray = *trahir*.

DENSE (adj) **1/** *dense* : a dense population = *une population dense* ⓪ thick = *épais* **2/** *bouché, -e* : he's a bit dense = *il est un peu bouché* ≠ quick on the uptake = *qui a l'esprit vif* → STUPID ☠ *un évier bouché* = a blocked sink **DENSITY** (n, -ies) *densité* (f).

DENT (n) *petite bosse* (f) : why does your car have so many dents ? = *pourquoi ta voiture a-t-elle tant de petites bosses ?* **not to make a dent in** = *ne pas entamer* : we haven't made a dent in our work yet = *nous n'avons pas encore entamé notre travail*.

DENTIST (n) *dentiste* (m, f) : to go to the dentist = *aller*

chez le dentiste ⓪ toothache = *mal de dents*, drill = *fraise*.

DENY (to, -ied) *nier, démentir* (official) : I don't deny it = *je ne le nie pas*, the government denied the charge = *le gouvernement a démenti l'accusation* ≠ to affirm = *affirmer*, to avow = *avouer* ☠ *sa voix démentait son calme* = his voice belied his calm.

DEODORANT (n) *déodorant* (m) ⓪ to have b.o. = *sentir le fauve*.

DEPARTED (adj) **the departed** = *les défunts* = the defunct.

DEPARTMENT (n) *rayon* (m) (store), *service* (m) (company) : perfume department = *rayon parfumerie*, personnel/accounting department = *service du personnel/ de la comptabilité* **department store** = *grand magasin* **the French/English department (school)** = *la section de français/d'anglais (école)* **that's not my department** = *ce n'est pas mon rayon* ⓪ that's not within my abilities = *cela ne relève pas de ma compétence* ☠ *rayon* → ray, service → service.

DEPARTURE (n) *départ* (m) : departure time = *l'heure de départ* ⓪ embarkation = *embarquement* ☠ *il a pris un bon départ* = he's off to a good start.

DEPEND (to, -ed) *dépendre* : I'm not sure of going ; it depends = *je ne suis pas sûre d'y aller ; ça dépend* **to depend on** = **1/** *compter sur* : I'm depending on you to help me = *je compte sur vous pour m'aider* ⓪ to bank on = *tabler sur* **2/** *dépendre de* : everything depends on what he says = *tout dépend de ce qu'il va dire* ⓪ to hinge on = *reposer sur* **depending on whether (it rains or not)** = *suivant qu'(il pleut ou non)*.

DEPENDABLE (adj) *sur lequel, laquelle on peut compter* : a dependable secretary = *une secrétaire sur laquelle on peut compter* ⓪ reliable = *fiable* ≠ undependable = *sur lequel on ne peut pas compter*.

DEPENDENCE (n) *dépendance* (f) : the economic dependence of a country = *la dépendance économique d'un pays* ≠ autonomy = *autonomie* ☠ *les dépendances* = outbuildings — *dépendance (drogue)* = (drug) dependency/addiction.

DEPENDENT (n) *personne* (f) *à charge* : to support three dependents = *avoir trois personnes à charge*.

DEPENDENT (adj) *dépendant, -e* ≠ independent = *indépendant* **to be dependent on (one's parents)** = *être dépendant de (ses parents)*.

DEPICT (to, -ed) *dépeindre* : the film depicts life in Brooklyn in 1900 = *le film dépeint la vie à Brooklyn en 1900* ⓪ to portray = *faire le portrait de*.

DEPLETE (to, -d) *épuiser* : to deplete our supplies = *épuiser nos provisions* = to exhaust ≠ to refill = *regarnir*.

DEPLORABLE (adj) *déplorable* : a deplorable attitude = *une attitude déplorable* ≠ remarkable = *remarquable* → AWFUL.

DEPLORE (to, -d) *déplorer* : I deplore his tendency to lie = *je déplore sa tendance à mentir* ⓓ to regret = *regretter*.

DEPOPULATE (to, -d) *dépeupler* : wars depopulated whole areas = *les guerres ont dépeuplé des contrées entières* **DEPOPULATION** (n) *dépeuplement (m)*.

DEPORT (to, -ed) *expulser, déporter* (in camps) : Mexican workers are deported when found without working papers = *les travailleurs mexicains sont expulsés quand on les trouve sans carte de travail*, France deported most of its Jews → *la France a déporté la plupart de ses Juifs* ☠ *expulser* → to evict
— ''*déporter*'' specifically means to send to a concentration camp.

DEPORTATION (n) *déportation (f)*.

DEPOSE (to, -d) *déposer* : the Shah was deposed = *le shah a été déposé* ⓓ to overthrow = *renverser* ☠ *déposer qqn (en voiture)* = to drop s.o. off
— *déposer 100 dollars* = to deposit $ 100
— *déposer une plainte* = to lodge a complaint.

DEPOSIT (n) *arrhes (f pl)* : if you like the television set, why don't you leave a deposit ? = *si ce téléviseur vous plaît, pourquoi ne laissez-vous pas des arrhes ?* ⓓ down payment = *acompte*.

DEPOSIT (to, -ed) *déposer* : I deposited $ 1000 in my account = *j'ai déposé 1000 dollars sur mon compte* ≠ to withdraw = *retirer* ☠ → to depose.

DEPOSITION (n) *déposition (f)* : the witness' deposition = *la déposition du témoin* ⓓ testimony = *témoignage*.

DEPRAVED (adj) *dépravé, -e* : a depraved life = *une vie dépravée* ⓓ perverted = *perverti*.

DEPRECIATE (to, -d) *(se) déprécier* : the dollar's depreciating = *le dollar se déprécie* **DEPRECIATION** (n) *dépréciation (f)*.

DEPRESSED (adj) *déprimé, -e* : unhappy and depressed = *malheureux et déprimé* ⓓ low = *qui n'a pas le moral* ≠ up = *qui a le moral*.

DEPRESSING (adj) *déprimant, -e* : depressing news = *des nouvelles déprimantes* ⓓ saddening = *attristant* ≠ uplifting = *remontant*.

DEPRESSION (n) **1/** *dépression (f)* : an economic depression = *une dépression économique* ⓓ crash = krach **2/** *dépression (f)* : she went through a period of depression = *elle a traversé une période de dépression* ☠ *une dépression nerveuse* = a nervous breakdown.

DEPRIVE OF (to, -d) *priver (de)* : the war deprived him of a good education = *la guerre l'a privé d'une bonne éducation*
☠ *ne pas se priver de (critiquer)* = not to spare (criticism)
— *tu es privé de dessert !* = no dessert for you today !

DEPTH (n) *profondeur (f)* : the depth of his despair = *la profondeur de son désespoir* ≠ surface = ←
to be out of one's depth = *perdre pied (en classe)/ ne plus avoir pied (dans l'eau)*.

DEPUTY (n, -ies) *adjoint, -e* : deputy police inspector = *inspecteur de police adjoint* ⓓ aide = ← ☠ *un député* = a congressman/a representative of Congress.

DERELICT (n) *pauvre hère (m)* : derelicts sleeping in the subway = *de pauvres hères dormant dans le métro* ⓓ bum = *clochard*.

DERIVE FROM (to, -d) *tirer de* : she derives little satisfaction from her kids = *elle tire peu de satisfaction de ses gosses*.

DEROGATORY (adj) *péjoratif, -ive* : derogatory remarks = *des remarques péjoratives* ≠ flattering = *flatteur*.

DESCEND (to, -ed) *descendre* : to descend a mountain path = *descendre un sentier de montagne*
to descend from (an illustrious family) = *descendre d'(une famille illustre)*
☠ « to descend » *se dit beaucoup moins que* « to go down »
— *il m'a descendu en flammes* = he really put me down
— *descendre les bagages* = to take the luggage down
— *le gang l'a descendu* = the gang bumped him off
— *descendre dans un hôtel* = to stay in a hotel
— *je descends dans une minute* = I'll be down/come down in a minute
— *pour Times Square, descendez à la 42e Rue* = for Times Square, get off at 42nd Street
— *descends de là immédiatement !* = get down now !

DESCENDANT (n) *descendant, -e* : a descendant of George Washington = *un descendant de George Washington* ≠ ancestor = *ancêtre*.

DESCENT (n) *descente (f)* : the plane's beginning its descent = *l'avion commence sa descente*
of (Spanish) descent = *d'origine (espagnole)*
☠ *une descente de police* = a police raid/bust.

DESCRIBE (to, -d) *décrire* : I can't describe his vulgarity = *je ne peux pas décrire sa vulgarité* ⓓ to depict = *dépeindre*.

DESCRIPTION (n) *description (f)* : a description of the city = *une description de la ville*.

DESCRIPTIVE (adj) *descriptif, -ive* : a descriptive portrayal = *un portrait descriptif*.

153

DESEGREGATE (to, -d) *mettre fin à la déségrégation :* the university has been desegregated = *il a été mis fin à la déségrégation à l'Université.*

DESEGREGATION (n) *déségrégation (f) :* the desegregation of schools = *la déségrégation des écoles* ⓓ busing = *ramassage scolaire visant à la déségrégation* ≠ racism = *racisme.*

DESERT (n) *désert (m) :* the Gobi desert = *le désert de Gobi* ⓓ mirage = ←, oasis = ←, sand = *sable* ☠ *prêcher dans le désert* = to talk to a brick wall.

DESERT (to, -ed) **1/** *déserter :* the soldier deserted = *le soldat a déserté* ☠ *déserter un pays* = to defect from a country **2/** *abandonner :* to desert one's family = *abandonner sa famille* = to abandon **DESERTED** (adj) *désert(é), -e :* a deserted city/building = *une ville désert(é)e, un immeuble désert(é)* **DESERTER** (n) *déserteur (m)* ⓓ draft dodger = *insoumis,* conscientious objector = *objecteur de conscience.*

DESERVE (to, -d) *mériter :* she deserved the prize = *elle a mérité le prix* ☠ → to merit
(he hit her) and she deserved it ! = *(il l'a battue) et elle l'a bien mérité !* ⓓ she had it coming = *elle l'a bien voulu.*

DESERVEDLY (adv) *à bon droit :* he's deservedly considered a great writer = *il est considéré à bon droit comme un grand écrivain.*

DESIGN (n) **1/** *motif (m) :* a flowery design on the vase = *un motif fleuri sur le vase* ☠ → motive **2/** *conception (f) :* the design of the plane is revolutionary = *cet avion est de conception révolutionnaire* **3/** *plans (m pl) :* the design for our new house = *les plans de notre nouvelle maison* ⓓ blueprints = *plans détaillés* ☠ → plans
to have designs on = *avoir des visées sur :* he has designs on my sister = *il a des visées sur ma sœur* ⓓ to be out for = *briguer.*

DESIGN (to, -ed) *dessiner :* she designs her own clothes = *elle dessine elle-même ses vêtements* ⓓ to sketch = *faire le croquis* ☠ → to draw.

DESIGNATE (to, -d) **1/** *désigner :* he was designated for this particular job = *il a été désigné pour ce travail spécial* ⓓ to name = *nommer* **2/** *désigner :* an asterisk designates a footnote = *un astérisque désigne une note en bas de page*
☠ *désigner un candidat* = to nominate a candidate
— *vous me paraissez tout désigné pour ce travail* = you'll be perfect for this job.

DESIGNER (n) *dessinateur, -trice :* he's a top dress designer = *c'est un très grand dessinateur de mode* ⓓ inventor = *inventeur*
designer clothes = *vêtements haute couture*
☠ *un dessinateur* = a commercial artist/cartoonist.

DESIRABLE (adj) *désirable :* a desirable woman = *une femme désirable* ≠ undesirable = *indésirable.*

DESIRE (n) *désir (m) :* a desire for love/power = *un désir d'amour/de pouvoir* ⓓ want = *besoin,* craving = *envie folle* ☠ *tu prends tes désirs pour des réalités* = that's wishful thinking.

DESIRE (to, -d) *désirer :* give him whatever he desires = *donne-lui tout ce qu'il désire* ⓓ to crave = *mourir d'envie*
☠ *qu'est-ce que vous désirez ?* = what would you like ?/care for ? (« to desire » *est peu employé*)
— *est-ce que tu désires venir avec nous ?* = would you care to come with us ?

DESK (n) *bureau (m)* (office), *pupitre (m)* (school) : your picture's on my desk = *ta photo est sur mon bureau,* each student has a desk = *chaque élève a un pupitre* ☠ *bureau* → office.

DESOLATE (adj) *désolé, -e :* a desolate town = *une ville désolée* ⓓ forsaken = *abandonné,* deserted = *désert(é)* ☠ *je suis désolé* = I'm sorry.

DESPAIR (n) *désespoir (m) :* the refugees are filled with despair = *les réfugiés sont remplis de désespoir* ≠ hope = *espoir*
to be in despair = *être au désespoir* ⓓ to be in dismay = *être atterré* ≠ hopeful = *plein d'espoir*
out of despair = *par/de désespoir :* she committed suicide out of despair = *elle s'est suicidée par désespoir.*

DESPAIR (to, -ed) *désespérer :* don't despair = *ne désespérez pas* ⓓ to lose hope = *perdre l'espoir.*

DESPERATE (adj) **1/** *prêt, -e à tout :* a desperate criminal = *un criminel prêt à tout* ⓓ reckless = *imprudent* **2/** *désespéré, -e :* the situation's desperate = *la situation est désespérée* ⓓ hopeless = *sans espoir.*

DESPERATELY (adv) *désespérément :* desperately in need of food = *ayant désespérément besoin de manger.*

DESPERATION (n) **in desperation** = *en désespoir de cause :* he robbed the bank in desperation = *il a dévalisé la banque en désespoir de cause.*

DESPICABLE (adj) *abject, -e :* that was a despicable thing to do = *c'était abject de faire ça* ⓓ contemptible = *méprisable.*

DESPISE (to, -d) *exécrer :* I despise him = *je l'exècre* ⓓ to hate = *détester.*

DESPITE (prep) *en dépit de :* despite your criticisms, I'll still do it my way = *en dépit de vos critiques, je le ferai tout de même comme je l'entends* ⓓ regardless of = *peu importe.*

DESPONDENT (adj) *abattu, -e :* a despondent look = *un regard abattu* ≠ joyful = *joyeux.*

DESPOT (n) *despote (m) :* she is considered a despot by her family = *sa famille la considère comme un despote.*

DESSERT (n) *dessert (m) :* do you want dessert ? = *vous voulez un dessert ?* ⓓ pastry = *pâtisserie.*

DESTINATION (n) *destination* *(f)* : he left for an unknown destination = *il est parti pour une destination inconnue.*

DESTINE (to, -d) *destiner* : he was destined to play an important role in the history of his country = *il était destiné à jouer un rôle important dans l'histoire de son pays*
🕱 *(le coup) lui est destiné* = (the blow) is meant for him
— *destiner une somme d'argent à qqch* = to earmark a sum for stg.

DESTINY (n, -ies) *destinée* *(f)* : hers was a strange destiny = *quelle étrange destinée que la sienne* ⓓ fate = *destin.*

DESTITUTE (n, adj) *démuni, -e* : help for destitute refugees = *de l'aide pour des réfugiés démunis* ≠ wealthy = *fortuné* → POOR.

DESTROY (to, -ed) *détruire* : to destroy a city/marriage = *détruire une ville/un couple* ⓓ to ruin = *abîmer* ≠ to construct = *construire.*

DESTROYER (n) *escorteur* *(m)* *d'escadre* : the sub was chased by the destroyer = *le sous-marin a été pris en chasse par l'escorteur d'escadre* ⓓ carrier = *porte-avions.*

DESTRUCTION (n) *destruction* *(f)* ⓓ damage = *dégâts.*

DESTRUCTIVE (adj) *destructeur, -trice, destructif, -ive* (stg) : a destructive personality = *une personnalité destructrice*, destructive power = *pouvoir destructif.*

DESUETUDE (n) **to fall into desuetude** = *tomber en désuétude.*

DETACH (to, -ed) *détacher* : to detach troops = *détacher des troupes* ⓓ to send = *envoyer*
🕱 *se détacher (des autres)* = to stand out (from the others)
— *je ne pouvais détacher mes yeux de* = I could not take my eyes off
— *détacher le chien* = to untie the dog
— *une tuile s'est détachée* = a tile fell (from the roof).

DETACHED (adj) *détaché, -e* : a detached attitude = *une attitude détachée* ⓓ indifferent = *indifférent.*

DETACHMENT (n) *détachement* *(m).*

DETAIL (n) *détail* *(m)* : give me the details = *donnez-moi les détails* ⓓ data = *données*
to go into detail = *entrer dans les détails*
to tell in detail = *raconter en détail*
🕱 *(vendre) au détail* = (to sell) retail.

DETAILED (adj) *détaillé, -e* : a detailed report = *un rapport détaillé* ⓓ exhaustive = *exhaustif.*

DETAIN (to, -ed) *retenir* : detained by bad weather = *retenu par le mauvais temps* ⓓ to delay = *retarder*
to detain s.o. for questioning = *faire subir un interrogatoire à qqn*
🕱 → to restrain.

DETECT (to, -ed) *détecter* : to detect alcohol in the blood = *détecter de l'alcool dans le sang* ⓓ to find = *trouver.*

DETECTIVE (n) *détective* *(m)* : Sherlock Holmes was a great detective = *Sherlock Holmes était un grand détective* ⓓ private eye = *privé*, detective story = *roman policier.*

DETENTION (n) *détention* *(f)* : two months of detention = *deux mois de détention.*

DETER (to, -red) *détourner (de)* : does prison deter crime ? = *est-ce que la prison détourne du crime ?* ≠ to encourage = *encourager*
🕱 *détourner des fonds* = to misappropriate funds/to embezzle
— *se détourner* = to turn away
— *détourner (l'attention de qqn)* = to divert (s.o.'s attention)
— *détourner un avion* = to hijack/skyjack a plane.

DETERGENT (n) *détergent* *(m)* ⓓ cleansing powder = *lessive.*

DETERIORATE (to, -d) *se détériorer* : my health/the situation is deteriorating = *ma santé/la situation se détériore* ≠ to improve = *améliorer.*

DETERMINATION (n) *détermination* *(f)* : a person of great determination = *une personne d'une grande détermination* ≠ hesitation = *hésitation.*

DETERMINE (to, -d) *(se) déterminer* : the doctor couldn't determine why he had an attack = *le médecin n'a pas pu déterminer les raisons de son attaque* ⓓ to decide = *décider*
to be determined to (quit) = *être déterminé/décidé à (démissionner)*
🕱 *qu'est-ce qui vous a déterminé à (partir) ?* = what made you decide to (go) ?

DETERRENT (n) *arme* *(f)* *de dissuasion* : the atomic bomb is a deterrent = *la bombe atomique est une arme de dissuasion* **DETERRENT** (adj) *dissuasif, -ive* : a deterrent weapon = *une arme dissuasive* ⓓ cold war = *guerre froide.*

DETEST (to, -ed) *détester* : I detest my mother-in-law/string beans = *je déteste ma belle-mère/les haricots verts* = to hate ≠ to be fond of = *aimer bien.*

DETESTABLE (adj) *détestable* : a detestable habit = *une habitude détestable* ⓓ hateful = *haïssable* ≠ lovable = *adorable.*

DETHRONE (to, -d) *détrôner* : bourbon will never dethrone Scotch = *le bourbon ne détrônera jamais le whisky.*

DETOUR (n) *détour* *(m)* : to make a detour = *faire un détour* 🕱 *sans détour* = straightforward.

DETRACT FROM (to, -ed) *nuire à* : the dirt of the city detracts from its beauty = *la saleté de la ville nuit à sa beauté* ⓓ to ruin = *gâcher* ≠ to intensify = *intensifier.*

155

DETRIMENT (n) *détriment (m)* : to your detriment = *à votre détriment* ≠ advantage = *avantage* **DETRIMENTAL** (adj) *néfaste* : a detrimental influence = *une influence néfaste* = harmful ≠ beneficial = *bénéfique.*

DEVALUATE (to, -d) *dévaluer* : to devaluate the dollar = *dévaluer le dollar* ≠ to revaluate = *réévaluer* **DEVALUATION** (n) *dévaluation (f)* : the devaluation of the dollar = *la dévaluation du dollar* ≠ revaluation = *réévaluation.*

DEVASTATE (to, -d) *dévaster* : the bomb devastated the city = *la bombe a dévasté la ville* ⓓ to lay waste = *faire des ravages.*

DEVASTATING (adj) **1/** *bouleversant, -e* : it was a devastating experience to see him again = *c'était bouleversant de le revoir* **2/** *impitoyable* : a devastating attack on modern society = *une attaque impitoyable de la société moderne* ⓓ awful = *affreux.*

DEVELOP (to, -ed) **1/** *(se) développer* : the company's developing = *la société se développe* ⓓ to expand = *être en pleine expansion* **2/** *développer* : to develop films = *développer des films.*

DEVELOPING (adj) **developing countries** = *les pays en voie de développement* ⓓ underdeveloped = *sous-développé.*

DEVELOPMENT (n) **1/** *développement (m)* : are there any new developments in the case ? = *y a-t-il de nouveaux développements dans cette affaire ?* ⓓ event = *événement* ☠ *pays en voie de développement* = developing countries **2/** *grand ensemble (m)* : he lives in a modern development = *il habite un grand ensemble moderne* ⓓ housing project = *H.L.M.*

DEVICE (n) **1/** *dispositif (m)* : a device to open the door without a key = *un dispositif pour ouvrir la porte sans clef* ⓓ mechanism = *mécanisme* **2/** *truc (m)* : her complaining of cramps was a device to avoid going to school = *ses crampes d'estomac, c'était en fait un truc pour ne pas aller à l'école* ⓓ scheme = *combinaison* ☠ → thing.

DEVIL (n) *diable (m)* : my kids are devils = *mes enfants sont des diables* ⓓ demon = *démon*, Satan = ←
(to be caught) between the devil and the deep blue sea = *(être pris) entre le marteau et l'enclume* ⓓ (to be caught) in the middle = *(être coincé) entre les deux*
to give the devil his due = *rendre à César ce qui est à César* ⓓ to give s.o. credit = *rendre justice à qqn*
how the devil (did you do it) ? = *comment diable (avez-vous fait ça) ?*
speak of the devil ! = *quand on parle du loup, on en voit la queue !*
the devil's advocate = *l'avocat du diable*
the devil with him ! = *qu'il aille au diable !* → BUZZ OFF !
what the devil ! = *que diable !* → GOSH !
☠ *tirer le diable par la queue* = to live from hand to mouth

— *il habite au diable (vauvert)* = he lives miles away
— *le diable m'emporte si ...* = I'll be hanged if ...

DEVIL-MAY-CARE (adj) *je-m'en-foutiste* : a devil-may-care attitude towards life = *une attitude je-m'en-foutiste devant la vie* ⓓ carefree = *insouciant.*

DEVIOUS (adj) *tortueux, -euse* : a devious answer = *une réponse tortueuse* ≠ straightforward = *sans détour.*

DEVISE (to, -d) *concevoir* : she'll have to devise a way to see him without her parents' knowing = *il va falloir qu'elle conçoive un moyen de le voir sans que ses parents soient au courant* ⓓ to engineer = *machiner* ☠ → to conceive.

DEVOID OF (adj) *dénué, -e de* : he's devoid of tenderness = *il est dénué de tendresse* ⓓ wanting in = *dépourvu de.*

DEVOTED (adj) *dévoué, -e* : a devoted employee = *un employé dévoué* ⓓ loyal = ←.

DEVOTEE (n) *passionné, -e* : a music devotee = *un passionné de musique* ⓓ nut = *fana.*

DEVOTE TO (to, -d) **1/** *(se) dévouer à* : she's devoted to her kids = *elle est dévouée à ses enfants* **2/** *(se) vouer à* : to devote one's life to science = *vouer sa vie à la science* ⓓ to dedicate o.s. to = *se consacrer à.*

DEVOTION (n) *dévouement (m)* : her devotion to her mother = *son dévouement pour sa mère* ⓓ self-sacrifice = *abnégation.*

DEVOUR (to, -ed) *dévorer* : he devoured the meal = *il a dévoré le repas* ⓓ to gulp down = *engloutir*
to be devoured by (jealousy) = *être dévoré de (jalousie).*

DEVOUT (adj) *dévot, -e* : to come from a devout family = *venir d'une famille dévote* ⓓ pious = *pieux.*

DEW (n) *rosée (f)* : morning dew = *la rosée du matin* ⓓ frost = *givre.*

DIABETES (n) *diabète (m)* : she has diabetes = *elle a du diabète* ⓓ insulin = *insuline* **DIABETIC** (n, adj) *diabétique (m, f).*

DIAGNOSE (to, -d) *diagnostiquer* : it's a difficult case to diagnose = *c'est un cas difficile à diagnostiquer* **DIAGNOSIS** (n, -ses) *diagnostic (m)* : the diagnosis was wrong = *le diagnostic était mauvais.*

DIAGONAL (adj) *diagonal, -e* ⓓ horizontal = ←.

DIAGRAM (n) *diagramme (m)* (math), *schéma (m)* : a diagram on how to use the diaphragm = *un schéma montrant comment utiliser le diaphragme.*

DIAL (n) *cadran (m)* ⓓ dial tone = *tonalité.*

DIAL (to, -ed) *composer (un numéro de téléphone)* : for information dial "511" = *pour toute information composez le « 511 »* ☠ → to compose.

DIALECT (n) *dialecte (m)* : to speak a strange dialect = *parler un étrange dialecte* ⊕ vernacular = *jargon.*

DIALOGUE = DIALOG (n) *dialogue (m)* : there's no possible dialogue with him = *il n'y a aucun dialogue possible avec lui* ⊕ conversation = ← 💀 *c'est un dialogue de sourds* = we're talking at cross purposes.

DIAMOND (n) *diamant (m)* : diamonds are expensive = *les diamants sont chers* ⊕ carat = ←, ice = *diams,* rocks = *cailloux*
a diamond necklace = *une rivière de diamants*
to be a diamond in the rough = *être un diamant dans sa gangue.*

DIAPER (n) *couche (f)* : change the baby's diaper = *change la couche du bébé* = nappy (GB) ⊕ toilet trained = *propre*
💀 *couche de peinture* = coat/layer of paint
— *il en tient une couche* = he's dense/thick
— *les couches sociales* = social classes.

DIAPHRAGM (n) *diaphragme (m)* : she doesn't want to take the pill so she uses a diaphragm = *elle ne veut pas prendre la pilule, alors elle utilise un diaphragme* ⊕ I.U.D. = *stérilet.*

DIARRHEA (n) *diarrhée (f)* : to have diarrhea = *avoir la diarrhée* ⊕ Montezuma's revenge = *la courante* ≠ constipation = ←.

DIARY (n, -ies) *journal (m) intime* : do you keep a diary ? = *est-ce que vous tenez un journal ?* ⊕ memoirs = *Mémoires.*

DICE (n pl) *dés (m pl)* : throw the dice = *lance les dés* ⊕ a die = *un dé*
the dice are loaded = *les dés sont pipés* → TO HUSTLE.

DICEY (adj) **it was dicey !** = *ça a été tangent !*

DICK (n) *limier (m)* : to hire a dick = *engager un limier* ⊕ private eye = *privé.*

DICKER OVER (to, -ed) *débattre (de)* : to dicker over a price = *débattre (d')un prix* ⊕ to bargain = *marchander*
💀 *elle s'est débattue* = she fought to escape.

DICTATE (to, -d) *dicter* : to dictate a letter/orders = *dicter une lettre/des ordres.*

DICTATION (n) *dictée (f)* : a short dictation in each language class = *une courte dictée à chaque cours de langue*
she doesn't take dictation = *elle ne sait pas prendre en sténo.*

DICTATOR (n) *dictateur (m)* ⊕ tyrant = *tyran* **DICTATORSHIP** (n) *dictature (f)* : to live under a dictatorship = *vivre sous une dictature* ≠ democracy = *démocratie.*

DICTIONARY (n, -ies) *dictionnaire (m), dico (m)* (LV) : a bilingual dictionary = *un dictionnaire bilingue* ⊕ glossary = *glossaire*, lexicon = *lexique.*

DIE (n, dice) **the die is cast** = *les dés sont jetés/le sort en est jeté* → THAT'S LIFE !

DIE (to, -d) *mourir* : my husband died last year = *mon mari est mort l'année dernière* ⊕ to croak = *crever*, to kick off = *casser sa pipe*, to be six foot under = *manger les pissenlits par la racine*, to be at death's door = *être à l'article de la mort*
to die of (cancer) = *mourir d'(un cancer)*
to die down = *s'apaiser* : we'll make the trip once the country's problems die down = *nous ferons le voyage une fois que les problèmes intérieurs se seront apaisés* ⊕ to taper off = *s'atténuer* 💀 → to appease
to die off (race of animals) = *disparaître un à un (race d'animaux)*
to die out (custom) = *s'éteindre (coutume)* 💀 → to extinguish
to be dying to/for = *mourir d'envie de* : I'm dying to go = *je meurs d'envie d'y aller*, I'm dying for Chinese food = *je meurs d'envie de manger chinois*
💀 *c'est à mourir de rire* = it's a scream
— *je mourais (de peur)* = I was (frightened) to death
— *(je me suis ennuyé) à mourir* = (I was bored) to death.

DIEHARD (n) *jusqu'au-boutiste (m, f)* : the diehards of the party = *les jusqu'au-boutistes du parti* ≠ moderate = *modéré* **DIE-HARD** (adj) *à tout crin* : a die-hard conservative = *un conservateur à tout crin* ⊕ ardent = ←.

DIET (n) *régime (m) (alimentaire)* : a well-balanced diet = *un régime équilibré* ⊕ overweight = *trop gros*, underweight = *trop maigre* 💀 → regime
to go/to be on a diet = *se mettre/être au régime.*

DIET (to, -ed) *suivre un régime* : are you dieting ? = *suivez-vous un régime ?* ⊕ to fast = *jeûner.*

DIETITIAN (n) *diététicien, -enne* = dietician ⊕ nutritionist = *nutritionniste.*

DIFFER (to, -ed) 1/ *différer* : how do French men and American men differ ? = *en quoi les hommes français diffèrent-ils des hommes américains ?* 💀 *différer (procès)* = to defer/to postpone (lawsuit) 2/ *être en désaccord* : we rarely differ ; usually we see things eye to eye = *nous sommes rarement en désaccord ; habituellement nous voyons les choses de la même façon*
I don't want to differ with you but ... = *je ne veux pas vous contredire, mais ...*

DIFFERENCE (n) *différence (f)* : there's a slight difference between the two = *il y a une légère différence entre les deux* ≠ similarity = *similitude*
a difference of opinion = *un différend* : we had a difference of opinion = *nous avons eu un différend* ⊕ clash = *affrontement*
it makes no difference = *ça n'a pas d'importance* ⊕ it doesn't matter = *ça ne fait rien*
to split the difference = *couper la poire en deux*
to tell the difference = *faire la différence* : I can't tell the difference between the twins = *je ne peux pas*

faire la différence entre les jumeaux ⓪ to distinguish between = *distinguer*

what's the difference ? = *qu'importe ?* ⓪ it's all the same thing = *ça revient au même.*

DIFFERENT (adj) **1/** *différent, -e* : her children are very different = *ses enfants sont très différents* ⓪ dissimilar = *dissemblable* ≠ similar = *similaire* **2/** *différent, -e* : different people told me the same thing = *différentes personnes m'ont dit la même chose* ⓪ diverse = *divers* **3/** *peu commun, -e* : her clothes are very different = *ses vêtements sont peu communs* ≠ banal = ←

at different times = *à diverses reprises*

they're as different as night and day = *c'est le jour et la nuit*

she's very different from me = *elle est très différente de moi.*

DIFFERENTIATE (to, -d) *différencier* : I couldn't differentiate the original from the copy = *je ne pourrais pas différencier l'original de la copie.*

DIFFERENTLY (adv) *différemment* : we both reacted differently = *nous avons tous deux réagi différemment* ≠ identically = *identiquement.*

DIFFICULT (adj) *difficile* : a difficult question/child = *une question/un enfant difficile* ⓪ arduous = *ardu,* tough = *dur* ≠ easy = *facile,* a snap = *bête comme chou* ☠ *être difficile pour (la nourriture)* = to be choosy/finicky/fussy/picky about (food).

DIFFICULTY (n, -ies) *difficulté* (f) : to run up against difficulties = *se heurter à des difficultés* ⓪ problem = *problème.*

DIG (n) **1/** *fouille* (f) ⓪ archeology = *archéologie* ☠ *fouille (police)* = search

to go on a dig = *faire des fouilles*

2/ *pique* (f) : constant digs at her husband = *de constantes piques contre son mari* ⓪ cut = *pointe* ☠ *pique (cartes)* = spades (cards).

DIG (to, dug, dug) **1/** *creuser* : we dug a hole = *on a creusé un trou*

☠ *creuser une idée* = to develop an idea

— *ça creuse !* = it gives you an appetite !

— *se creuser la tête/la cervelle* = to rack one's brains **2/** *botter* : I don't dig jazz = *le jazz ne me botte pas* ⓪ to be crazy about = *être fou de* ≠ not to stand = *ne pas supporter* ☠ *botter le derrière de qqn* = to kick s.o. in the pants

dig ? = *pigé ?* ⓪ do you get it ? = *tu saisis ?*

dig in ! = *sers-toi !* ⓪ come and get it ! = *à table !*

to dig out = *dégager* : it took three days to dig the bodies out after the earthquake = *il a fallu trois jours pour dégager les corps après le séisme* ☠ → to clear

to dig up = *dénicher* : where did you dig up that old piano ? = *où avez-vous déniché ce vieux piano ?* ⓪ to unearth = *déterrer.*

DIGEST (n) *condensé* (m) : a digest of the report = *un condensé du rapport* ⓪ summary = *résumé.*

DIGEST (to, -ed) *digérer* : I can't digest fat = *je n'arrive pas à digérer la graisse* ⓪ to swallow = *avaler* **DIGESTION** (n) *digestion* (f) : digestion problems = *des problèmes de digestion.*

DIGNIFIED (adj) *digne* : a dignified old lady = *une vieille dame digne* ⓪ stately = *imposant* ☠ *cette remarque n'était pas digne de toi* = that remark wasn't worthy of you.

DIGNITARY (n, -ies) *dignitaire* (m) : church dignitaries = *des dignitaires ecclésiastiques* ⓪ big shot = *grand ponte.*

DIGNITY (n, -ies) *dignité* (f) : they surrendered with dignity = *ils se sont rendus avec dignité* ⓪ pride = *fierté.*

DIGRESS (to, -ed) *faire une digression* : stop digressing and get to the point = *cessez de faire des digressions et venez-en au fait* ⓪ to stray from the subject = *sortir du sujet* **DIGRESSION** (n) *digression* (f).

DIGS (n inv) *baraque* (f) (LV) : they're looking for new digs on the coast = *ils cherchent une nouvelle baraque sur la côte* ⓪ pad = *appart.*

DIKE (n) *digue* (f) : a dike to protect the land from floods = *une digue pour protéger la terre des inondations* ⓪ dam = *barrage.*

DILAPIDATED (adj) *délabré, -e* : a dilapidated building = *un immeuble délabré* ⓪ run-down = *mal entretenu* ≠ well-kept = *bien entretenu.*

DILDO (n) *godemiché* (m), *gode* (m) : do lesbians use dildos ? = *est-ce que les lesbiennes utilisent des godemichés ?*

DILEMMA (n) *dilemme* (m) : how are we going to get out of this dilemma ? = *comment réussirons-nous à sortir de ce dilemme ?* ⓪ predicament = *situation difficile.*

DILIGENCE (n) *diligence* (f) : to work with diligence = *travailler avec diligence* ☠ *la diligence est arrivée* = the stagecoach has arrived.

DILLYDALLY (to, -ied) *traînasser* ⓪ to waste one's time = *perdre son temps.*

DILUTE (to, -d) *diluer* : to dilute syrup in water = *diluer du sirop dans de l'eau* ⓪ to thin out = *délayer* ≠ to thicken = *épaissir.*

DIM (adj) *tamisé, -e* : dim lights = *lumières tamisées* ≠ bright = *vif*

to take a dim view of = *voir d'un mauvais œil* ⓪ to look askance at = *regarder d'un œil désapprobateur.*

DIME (n) *(pièce de) dix cents* : newspapers no longer cost a dime = *les journaux ne coûtent plus dix cents*

it's a dime a dozen = *ça court les rues* : bad doctors are a dime a dozen = *les mauvais docteurs, ça court les rues.*

DIMENSION (n) *dimension* (f) : the dimensions of the

room = *les dimensions de la pièce* ☠ *le problème a pris des dimensions importantes* = the problem's become a big one.

DIMINISH (to, -ed) *diminuer* : chances for peace are diminishing = *les possibilités de paix diminuent* ⓪ to taper off = *s'atténuer* ≠ to grow = *s'agrandir* ☠ *diminuer les prix* = to cut prices
— *la maladie l'a diminué* = his illness weakened him
— *sa fièvre diminue* = his fever is going down.

DIMINUTION (n) *diminution* (f).

DIMINUTIVE (adj) *tout, -e petit, -e* : a diminutive diamond on her ring = *un tout petit diamant sur sa bague.*

DIMPLE (n) *fossette* (f) : an adorable dimple on his chin = *une fossette délicieuse sur son menton* ⓪ cheek = *joue.*

DIMWIT (n) *nouille* (f) : what a dimwit you are ! = *quelle nouille tu fais !* → STUPID ☠ → noodle.

DIN (n) *vacarme* (m) : what a din the machine made ! = *quel vacarme faisait cette machine !* ⓪ racket = *raffut.*

DINE (to, -d) *dîner* : they dine at eight = *ils dînent à huit heures*
to dine in ≠ **out** = *dîner à la maison* ≠ *dehors/en ville* ☠ « to dine » *est beaucoup moins dit que* « to have dinner ».

DINER (n) *restaurant* (m) *bon marché et rapide, aménagé comme un wagon-restaurant.*

DINING ROOM (n) *salle* (f) *à manger* ⓪ room = *pièce.*

DINNER (n) *dîner* (m) : dinner's ready = *le dîner est prêt* ⓪ meal = *repas*
at dinner time = *à l'heure du dîner/au dîner*
dinner jacket = *tenue de soirée (hommes)* ⓪ tuxedo = *smoking*
to have dinner = *dîner* = to have supper.

DINOSAUR (n) *dinosaure* (m) ⓪ mammoth = *mammouth.*

DIP (n) *légère baisse* (f) : a dip in the Stock Market = *une légère baisse de la Bourse* ≠ upsurge = *flambée*
let's go for a dip ! = *si on allait faire trempette !*
(onion/curry) dip = *sauce (à l'oignon/au curry) accompagnant des légumes à croquer.*

DIP (to, -ped) *accuser une légère baisse* : the Stock Market dipped = *la Bourse a accusé une légère baisse* ≠ to climb = *grimper.*

DIPHTHERIA (n) *diphtérie* (f) ⓪ tetanus = *tétanos.*

DIPLOMA (n) *diplôme* (m) : she finally got her diploma = *elle a fini par avoir son diplôme* ⓪ high school diploma = *baccalauréat*, BA = *licence*, MA = *maîtrise*, PhD = *doctorat*
☠ *remise des diplômes* = graduation day
— *un diplôme en sciences politiques* = a degree in political science.

DIPLOMACY (n, -ies) *diplomatie* (f) : she lacks diplomacy = *elle manque de diplomatie* ⓪ tact = *←.*

DIPLOMAT (n) *diplomate* (m, f) : a bash for diplomats at the White House = *un raout pour les diplomates à la Maison-Blanche* ⓪ consul = *←.*

DIPLOMATIC (adj) 1/ *diplomate* : a diplomatic answer = *une réponse diplomate*, be diplomatic ! = *sois diplomate !* ⓪ tactful = *plein de tact* 2/ *diplomatique* : diplomatic immunity = *immunité diplomatique.*

DIRE (adj) **in dire need of (help)** = *qui a grand besoin d'(aide)*
in dire straits = *dans le plus grand dénuement* → POOR.

DIRECT (adj) *direct, -e* : a direct answer/flight = *une réponse directe/un vol direct* ≠ indirect = *←* ☠ *une émission en direct* = a live broadcast.

DIRECT (adv) **to fly direct (to New York)** = *prendre un vol direct (pour New York)* ⓪ without a stopover = *sans escale.*

DIRECT (to, -ed) 1/ *diriger* : he directs the company/the school = *il dirige la société/l'école* ⓪ to be the head of = *être le chef de* 2/ *mettre en scène* : that was the first movie that he directed = *c'était le premier film qu'il mettait en scène* ⓪ to produce = *produire*
can you direct me to (the nearest subway) ? = *pouvez-vous m'indiquer (le métro le plus proche) ?*
the remark was directed at you = *la remarque vous était destinée*
☠ *se diriger vers* = to head for
— *diriger un pays* = to rule/to run a country
— *diriger un orchestre* = to conduct an orchestra.

DIRECTION (n) *direction* (f) : walk in my direction = *marchez dans ma direction*
under the direction of = *sous la direction de*
☠ *être à la direction de* = to be in charge of
— *il faut que vous alliez voir la direction* = you'll have to see the management.

DIRECTIONS (n pl) *instructions* (f pl) : why didn't you follow my directions ? = *pourquoi n'avez-vous pas suivi mes instructions ?* = why didn't you follow my instructions ?
directions for use = *mode d'emploi.*

DIRECTIVE (n) *directive* (f) : directives from the President's office = *des directives provenant du bureau du Président* ⓪ instruction = *←.*

DIRECTLY (adv) *directement* : I went directly home after work = *je suis rentrée directement à la maison après le travail* ⓪ straight = *tout droit.*

DIRECTOR (n) 1/ *directeur, -trice* : the director of the company = *le directeur de la société* ⓪ chairman = *président*, manager = *administrateur*
☠ *directeur de journal* = (newspaper) editor
— *directeur commercial* = sales manager

159

— *directeur (d'école)* = principal/headmaster
2/ *metteur (m) en scène* : Fellini's a great director = *Fellini est un grand metteur en scène* ⑩ filmmaker = *cinéaste.*

DIRT (n inv) **1/** *saleté (f)* : look at all that dirt on your pants = *regarde-moi cette saleté sur ton pantalon* ≠ cleanliness = *propreté* ⚔ *acheter des saletés* = to buy trash **2/** *ragots (m pl)* : what's the latest dirt about his divorce ? = *quels sont les derniers ragots sur son divorce ?* ⑩ gossip = *commérages*
to treat s.o. like dirt = *traiter qqn comme un chien*
dirt cheap = *donné, -e* : this restaurant's dirt cheap = *ce restaurant est donné* ≠ sky-high = *hors de prix.*

DIRTY (adj, -ier, -iest) *sale* : why are you so dirty ? = *pourquoi es-tu si sale ?* ⑩ filthy = *crasseux* ≠ immaculate = *immaculé*
dirty joke = *plaisanterie cochonne* : he always tells dirty jokes = *il fait toujours des plaisanteries cochonnes* ⑩ sexy stories ⇐ *histoires de fesses*
to do the dirty work = *faire le sale boulot*
a dirty old man/woman = *un vieux vicieux/une vieille vicieuse* ⑩ flasher = *exhibitionniste*
dirty words = *gros mots*
to give s.o. a dirty look = *lancer un regard noir à qqn* ⑩ if looks could kill = *si les yeux pouvaient/si le regard pouvait tuer*
to have a dirty mind = *avoir l'esprit mal tourné*
to wash one's dirty linen in public = *laver son linge sale en public*
what a dirty trick ! = *quelle crasse !* ⑩ what a low trick ! = *quelle vacherie !*
⚔ *un sale (rhume)* = a wretched (cold)
— *un sale gosse* = a brat
— *avoir une sale gueule* = 1/ to look lousy 2/ to be rough-looking
— *sale (temps/type)* = lousy (weather/guy).

DIRTY (to, -ied) *salir.*

DISABLE (to, -d) *rendre impotent, -e* : disabled by rheumatism = *rendu impotent par les rhumatismes*
disabled war veterans = *invalides de guerre.*

DISABILITY (n, -ies) *invalidité (f)* : disability pension = *pension d'invalidité* ⑩ handicap = ←.

DISADVANTAGE (n) *désavantage (m)* : not being bilingual is a disadvantage = *c'est un désavantage de ne pas être bilingue* ⑩ drawback = *inconvénient* **DISADVANTAGEOUS** (adj) *désavantageux, -euse* ⑩ unfavorable = *défavorable.*

DISAGREE (to, -d) *ne pas être d'accord* : I disagree with you = *je ne suis pas d'accord avec vous* ⑩ to differ = *être en désaccord* ≠ to see eye to eye = *voir du même œil.*

DISAGREEABLE (adj) *désagréable* : a disagreeable smell = *une odeur désagréable* ⑩ unpleasant = *déplaisant* ≠ nice = *sympa.*

DISAGREEMENT (n) *désaccord (m)* : we had a disagreement = *nous étions en désaccord* ⑩ spat = *accrochage*, falling-out = *brouille.*

DISAPPEAR (to, -ed) *disparaître* : the money/her husband disappeared = *l'argent/son mari a disparu* ≠ to appear = *apparaître.*

DISAPPEARANCE (n) *disparition (f)* : the criminal's sudden disappearance = *la soudaine disparition du criminel* ≠ appearance = *apparition* ⚔ *depuis la disparition de sa femme* = since his wife's death.

DISAPPOINT (to, -ed) *décevoir, désappointer* : the film/you disappointed us = *le film nous a déçus/vous nous avez déçus* = to let down ≠ to satisfy = *satisfaire*
I'm disappointed in (you) = *(vous) me décevez.*

DISAPPOINTING (adj) *décevant, -e, désappointant, -e* : disappointing news = *une nouvelle décevante* → AWFUL.

DISAPPOINTMENT (n) *déception (f), désappointement (m)* : it was a big disappointment = *ça a été une grosse déception* = it was a big letdown.

DISAPPROVAL (n) *désapprobation (f)* : he showed his disapproval = *il a montré sa désapprobation* ⑩ reprobation = *réprobation.*

DISAPPROVE OF (to, -d) *désapprouver* : I disapprove of his behavior = *je désapprouve son comportement* ⑩ to condemn = *condamner.*

DISARM (to, -ed) *désarmer* : to disarm a gangster = *désarmer un gangster* ≠ to arm = *armer* ⚔ *je suis complètement désarmée !* = I'm at a loss !

DISARMAMENT (n) *désarmement (m)* : progressive disarmament = *un désarmement progressif* ≠ buildup = *renforcement de l'armement.*

DISARMING (adj) *désarmant, -e* : a disarming smile = *un sourire désarmant.*

DISASTER (n) *désastre (m)* : the play was a disaster = *cette pièce a été un désastre* **DISASTROUS** (adj) *désastreux, -euse* : disastrous results = *des résultats désastreux* ⑩ unfortunate = *malheureux.*

DISAVOW (to, -ed) *désavouer* : to disavow one's predecessors' policy = *désavouer la politique de ses prédécesseurs* **DISAVOWAL** (n) *désaveu (m).*

DISBAR (to, -red) *rayer du barreau* : he's not the first lawyer to be disbarred for taking bribes = *ce n'est pas le premier avocat à s'être fait rayer du barreau pour avoir accepté des pots-de-vin* ≠ to reinstate = *rétablir dans ses fonctions.*

DISCARD (to, -ed) *se défaire de* : to discard old clothes = *se défaire de vieux vêtements* ⑩ to get rid of = *se débarrasser de.*

DISCERNING (adj) *plein de discernement* : discerning critics = *des critiques pleins de discernement.*

DISCHARGE (n) *libération (f)* (army, prison), *sortie (f)* (hospital)

dishonorable ≠ **honorable discharge** = *renvoi de l'armée* ≠ *démobilisation honorable* ☠ → liberation, → exit.

DISCHARGE (to, -d) *libérer* (army), *laisser sortir* (hospital) ⓪ to release = *relâcher* (army)/*laisser sortir* (hospital) ☠ → to liberate.

DISCIPLE (n) *disciple (m, f)* : a disciple of Gandhi = *un disciple de Gandhi* ⓪ follower = *adepte*.

DISCIPLINE (n) *discipline (f)* : discipline is slackening = *la discipline se relâche* ⓪ authority = *autorité* **DISCIPLINE** (to, -d) *discipliner* : my kids are hard to discipline = *mes gosses sont durs à discipliner* ⓪ to train = *dresser*.

DISC JOCKEY (n) *disc-jockey (m)* = deejay = DJ.

DISCLOSE (to, -d) *dévoiler* : he disclosed the true identity of the author = *il a dévoilé la véritable identité de l'auteur* ⓪ to reveal = *révéler*, to make public = *rendre public* ☠ *dévoiler ses intentions/batteries* = to lay down one's hand.

DISCLOSURE (n) *révélation (f)* : startling disclosures = *des révélations renversantes* = startling revelations.

DISCOMFORT (n) *inconfort (m)* : we travelled in great discomfort = *nous avons voyagé dans le plus grand inconfort*.

DISCONCERT (to, -ed) *déconcerter* : disconcerted by his aggressive attitude = *déconcerté par son attitude agressive* ⓪ to fluster = *démonter*.

DISCONCERTING (adj) *déconcertant, -e* : disconcerting answers = *des réponses déconcertantes*.

DISCONNECT (to, -ed) *déconnecter* : disconnect the phone = *déconnectez le téléphone* ⓪ to pull out = *débrancher* ≠ to plug in = *brancher*.

DISCONTENTED (adj) *mécontent, -e* : discontented with his life = *mécontent de sa vie* ⓪ dissatisfied = *insatisfait*.

DISCONTINUE (to, -d) *interrompre* : she's going to discontinue her subscription = *elle va interrompre son abonnement* ⓪ to stop = *arrêter* ☠ → to interrupt.

DISCORD (n) *discorde (f)* : discord within the party = *discorde au sein du parti* ⓪ dissension = ← ≠ agreement = *accord*.

DISCOTHEQUE (n) *discothèque (f)* : what about going to a discotheque ? = *si on allait dans une discothèque ?*

DISCOUNT (n) *discount (m), remise (f)* : they give a discount of 10 percent on all cash sales = *ils font une remise de 10 pour cent sur tous les achats payés comptant* ⓪ deduction = *déduction*, abatement = *abattement*
a discount store = *un magasin de discount*
to sell at a discount = *vendre au rabais* ☠ *remise* → shed.

DISCOUNT (to, -ed) *ne pas prendre pour argent comptant* : he's really partial, you should discount what he says = *il est vraiment partial, il ne faut pas prendre ce qu'il dit pour argent comptant* ⓪ to take with a pinch of salt = *ne pas prendre au pied de la lettre*.

DISCOURAGE (to, -d) *décourager* : don't discourage him ! = *ne le découragez pas !* ⓪ to dishearten = *faire perdre courage* ≠ to encourage = *encourager*.

DISCOURSE (n) *discours (m)* : a solemn discourse = *un discours solennel* ⓪ allocution = ← ☠ *assez de discours !* = less talk and more action ! — « speech » *est plus employé que* « discourse ».

DISCOVER (to, -ed) 1/ *découvrir* : when was electricity discovered ? = *quand a-t-on découvert l'électricité ?* ⓪ to create = *créer* 2/ *découvrir* : I broke off when I discovered he was married = *j'ai rompu quand j'ai découvert qu'il était marié* ⓪ to find out = *apprendre*.

DISCOVERY (n, -ies) *découverte (f)* : a scientific discovery = *une découverte scientifique* ⓪ invention = ← ☠ *partir/aller à la découverte de* = to go searching for.

DISCREDIT (n inv) *discrédit (m)* : to throw discredit on s.o./on s.o.'s policy = *jeter le discrédit sur qqn/sur la politique de qqn* **DISCREDIT** (to, -ed) *discréditer* : discredited by his own lies = *discrédité par ses propres mensonges*.

DISCREET (adj) *discret, -ète* : a discreet lover = *un amant discret* ≠ indiscreet = *indiscret* **DISCREETLY** (adv) *discrètement*.

DISCREPANCY (n, -ies) *divergence (f)* : what a discrepancy between what she says and what she does ! = *quelle divergence entre ce qu'elle dit et ce qu'elle fait !* ⓪ difference = *différence*.

DISCRETION (n inv) *discrétion (f)* : a man of great discretion = *un homme d'une grande discrétion* ≠ indiscretion = *indiscrétion*
discretion is the better part of valor = *la parole est d'argent, mais le silence est d'or*
use discretion = *faites preuve de discrétion*
use your own discretion = *faites comme bon vous semblera*
☠ *(vin) à discrétion* = as much (wine) as you want.

DISCRIMINATE AGAINST (to, -d) *faire une discrimination à l'égard de* : to discriminate against women = *faire une discrimination à l'égard des femmes*.

DISCRIMINATION (n) *discrimination (f)* : racial/sexual discrimination = *discrimination raciale/de sexe* ⓪ segregation = *ségrégation* **DISCRIMINATORY** (adj) *discriminatoire* : discriminatory laws = *lois discriminatoires*.

DISCUSS (to, -ed) *discuter de* : I discussed it with him last night = *j'en ai discuté avec lui hier soir* ⓪ to talk over = *en parler* ☠ *je ne le discute pas* = I can't dispute that.

DISCUSSION (n) *discussion (f)* : an interesting discussion = *une discussion intéressante* ⑤ talk = *conversation*
it's up for discussion = *c'est à discuter*
☠ *discussion (sur l'heure du crime)* = dispute (over the time of the murder).

DISDAIN (n) *dédain (m)* : to have nothing but disdain for s.o. = *n'avoir que du dédain pour qqn* ≠ admiration = ←.

DISDAIN (to, -ed) **to disdain to (answer)** = *ne pas daigner (répondre)*.

DISEASE (n) *maladie (f)* : to catch a disease = *attraper une maladie* ⑤ infection = ←
☠ *en faire une maladie* = to make a federal case out of
— *la maladie de ma mère* = my mother's sickness/illness.

DISEMBARK (to, -ed) *débarquer* : the passengers disembarked = *les passagers ont débarqué* ⑤ to go ashore = *descendre à terre* ☠ *débarquer dans (une ville)* = to blow into (town).

DISFIGURE (to, -d) *défigurer* : disfigured by the accident = *défiguré par l'accident.*

DISGRACE (n) **to be a disgrace to (one's family)** = *être la honte de (sa famille)*
it's a disgrace to (pay so much) ! = *c'est une honte de (payer autant)* !
it's no disgrace to (be poor) = *il n'y a pas de honte à (être pauvre)*.

DISGRACE (to, -d) *déshonorer* : he disgraced his family = *il a déshonoré sa famille* = he dishonored his family.

DISGRACEFUL (adj) *qui fait honte* : disgraceful manners = *des manières qui font honte* ⑤ shameful = *honteux.*

DISGUISE (n) *déguisement (m)* : she wore a disguise = *elle portait un déguisement* ⑤ costume = ←.

DISGUISE (to, -d) *déguiser* : to disguise one's intentions = *déguiser ses intentions* ⑤ to hide = *cacher.*

DISGUST (n) *dégoût (m)* : his attitude fills me with disgust = *son attitude me remplit de dégoût* ⑤ repugnance = *répugnance.*

DISGUST (to, -ed) *dégoûter* : you disgust me ! = *tu me dégoûtes* ! ≠ to please = *plaire*
I'm disgusted with (him/his work) = *(il/son travail) me dégoûte*
☠ *le bruit m'a dégoûté des (boîtes de nuit)* = the noise turned me off (nightclubs).

DISGUSTING (adj) *dégoûtant, -e* : a disgusting smell = *une odeur dégoûtante* → AWFUL.

DISH (n, -es) *plat (m)* : it's a delicious dish = *c'est un plat délicieux*
to do the dishes = *faire la vaisselle/la plonge* (LV) = to do the washing-up (GB)

she's quite a dish ! = *quelle belle nénette* ! ⑤ a good-looking tomato = *une belle plante*
☠ *œufs au plat* = fried eggs
— *faire du plat à qqn* = to make up to s.o.
— *mettre les pieds dans le plat* = to put one's foot in it
— *plat du jour* = today's special
— *un repas composé de cinq plats* = a five-course meal.

DISH (to, -ed) **to dish it out** = *en dire des vertes et des pas mûres* → TO LAMBAST.

DISHEARTEN (to, -ed) *faire perdre courage* : his constant criticisms are disheartening = *ses critiques perpétuelles me font perdre courage* ⑤ to demoralize = *démoraliser.*

DISHEVEL(L)ED (adj) **dishevelled hair** = *des cheveux ébouriffés* ⑤ tousled = *en bataille.*

DISHONEST (adj) *malhonnête* : a dishonest guy = *un type malhonnête* ⑤ unprincipled = *peu scrupuleux* ≠ square = *carré* **DISHONESTY** (n, -ies) *malhonnêteté (f)* : I've never seen such dishonesty = *je n'ai jamais vu pareille malhonnêteté.*

DISHONOR (n) *déshonneur (m)* : he's a dishonor to the family = *il fait le déshonneur de la famille* **DISHONOR** (to, -ed) *déshonorer* : to dishonor one's family = *déshonorer sa famille* ⑤ to discredit = *discréditer* **DISHONORABLE** (adj) *déshonorant, -e* : a dishonorable deed = *un acte déshonorant* ⑤ shameful = *honteux.*

DISHRAG (n) *torchon (m)* : to dry dishes with a dishrag = *essuyer la vaisselle avec un torchon* = dishcloth/dish towel
to feel like a dishrag = *être sur les rotules* ⑤ to be on one's last legs = *être sur les genoux*
☠ *ton devoir est un vrai torchon* = your homework's a mess
— *le torchon brûle entre eux* = they're at sixes and sevens
— *il ne faut pas mélanger les torchons et les serviettes* = you can't speak about ... and ... in the same breath
— *le pire torchon du pays* = the worst rag in the country.

DISHWASHER (n) 1/ *plongeur, -euse* : he worked as a dishwasher = *il a travaillé comme plongeur* ⑤ cook = *cuisinier* ☠ → diver 2/ *lave-vaisselle (m)* ⑤ washing machine = *machine à laver.*

DISILLUSION (n) *désillusion (f)* ⑤ disenchantment = *désenchantement* **DISILLUSION** (to, -ed) *désillusionner* : to be disillusioned with politics = *être désillusionné par la politique* ⑤ to disappoint = *décevoir.*

DISINFORMATION (n) *désinformation (f)* ⑤ lie = *mensonge.*

DISINHERIT (to, -ed) *déshériter* : he disinherited his elder son = *il a déshérité son fils aîné* ≠ to leave = *léguer.*

162

DISINTEGRATE (to, -d) *désintégrer* : an empire/a rock disintegrates = *un empire/une roche se désintègre* ⓄⒹ to decay = *se délabrer.*

DISLIKE (n) *aversion (f)* : a dislike for foreigners = *une aversion pour les étrangers* ⓄⒹ distaste = *dégoût* ≠ fondness = *penchant*
to take a dislike to s.o. = *prendre qqn en grippe.*

DISLIKE (to, -d) *ne pas aimer* : I dislike her brother = *je n'aime pas son frère* ⓄⒹ to despise = *exécrer* ≠ to adore = *adorer.*

DISLOYAL (adj) *déloyal, -e* : a disloyal friend = *un ami déloyal* ⓄⒹ perfidious = *perfide* ☠ *concurrence déloyale* = unfair competition.

DISMAL (adj) *sinistre* : a dismal day/future = *un jour/avenir sinistre* ⓄⒹ bleak = *gris* ☠ → sinister.

DISMANTLE (to, -d) *démanteler* : to dismantle a terrorist network = *démanteler un réseau terroriste.*

DISMAY (n) **in dismay** = *atterré* : he looked at me in dismay = *il m'a regardé atterré*
it fills me with dismay (to think I have to have another abortion) = *je suis complètement atterrée (à l'idée de me faire avorter encore une fois).*

DISMAY (to, -ed) *atterrer* : he was dismayed to see his daughter drunk = *il était atterré de voir sa fille saoule* ⓄⒹ to appall = *effarer.*

DISMISS (to, -ed) *renvoyer* : dismissed from his job = *renvoyé de son boulot* ⓄⒹ to fire = *congédier* ≠ to hire = *engager*
☠ *renvoyer (un paquet)* = to send back/to return (a parcel)
— *renvoyer (élèves)* = to expel (students).

DISMISSAL (n) *renvoi (m)* : his dismissal triggered off a strike = *son renvoi a déclenché une grève* ⓄⒹ firing = *congédiement*
☠ *renvoi (rot)* = burp
— *renvoi (au bas de la page)* = footnote
— *renvoi à un autre livre* = cross-reference
— *renvoi (école)* = expulsion (school).

DISOBEDIENT (adj) *désobéissant, -e* : a disobedient child = *un enfant désobéissant* ⓄⒹ insubordinate = *insubordonné* **DISOBEY** (to, -ed) *désobéir* : to disobey orders = *désobéir aux ordres* ≠ to execute = *exécuter.*

DISORDER (n) *désordre (m)* : I've never seen such disorder ! = *je n'ai jamais vu un pareil désordre !* ≠ organization = *organisation* ☠ *des désordres ont éclaté dans la ville* = outbreaks have flared up in the city **DISORDERLY** (adj) *désordonné, -e* : a disorderly house = *une maison désordonnée* ⓄⒹ messy = *en pagaille.*

DISORGANIZED (adj) *mal organisé, -e* : a disorganized office = *un bureau mal organisé* ≠ organized = *organisé.*

DISORIENT (to, -ed) *désorienter* : I was disoriented by the change in time zones = *j'étais désorienté par le décalage horaire* ⓄⒹ to disconcert = *déconcerter.*

DISOWN (to, -ed) *renier* : he disowned his children = *il a renié ses enfants* ⓄⒹ to disinherit = *déshériter* ☠ *renier une action* = to repudiate/negate an action.

DISPARAGING (adj) *désobligeant, -e* : disparaging remarks = *des remarques désobligeantes* ⓄⒹ disagreeable = *désagréable.*

DISPATCH (n, -es) *dépêche (f)* : to send a dispatch = *envoyer une dépêche* ⓄⒹ remittance = *envoi.*

DISPERSE (to, -d) *(se) disperser* : the bystanders dispersed = *les badauds se sont dispersés* ☠ *se disperser trop* = to spread o.s. too thin.

DISPLAY (n) **a display of (jewelry/courage)** = *une exposition de (bijoux)/une manifestation de (courage)*
on display = *exposé* : the crown jewels are on display = *les bijoux de la couronne sont exposés.*

DISPLAY (to, -ed) **1/** *manifester* : he displayed great courage = *il a manifesté un grand courage* ⓄⒹ to show = *montrer* ☠ → to manifest **2/** *exposer* : the crown jewels are being displayed at the Tower of London = *les bijoux de la couronne sont exposés à la tour de Londres* ☠ → to expose.

DISPOSABLE (adj) *jetable* : disposable diapers = *des couches jetables.*

DISPOSAL (n) **I'm at your disposal** = *je suis à votre disposition.*

DISPOSE OF (to, -d) **1/** *se défaire de* : to dispose of old clothes = *se défaire de vieux vêtements* ⓄⒹ to chuck = *balancer* **2/** *disposer de* : you can dispose of your free time as you like = *vous pouvez disposer de votre temps libre comme vous le désirez.*

DISPOSITION (n) *naturel (m)* : a joyous disposition = *un naturel gai* ⓄⒹ temperament = *tempérament*
at s.o.'s disposition = *à la disposition de qqn* : our company's services are at your disposition = *les services de notre société sont à votre disposition*
to have a good ≠ **bad disposition** = *avoir bon* ≠ *mauvais caractère*
☠ *naturel* = natural
— *les dispositions de la loi* = the provisions of the law
— *elle a des dispositions pour la musique* = she has a bent for music
— *je suis à votre disposition* = I'm at your disposal
— *prendre ses dispositions* = to make arrangements
— *la disposition de l'appartement* = the layout of the apartment.

DISPROVE (to, -d) *réfuter* : his theory was disproved = *sa théorie a été réfutée* ≠ to confirm = *confirmer.*

DISPUTABLE (adj) *discutable* : a disputable statement/interpretation = *une déclaration/interprétation discutable* ≠ unquestionable = *indiscutable.*

DISPUTE (n) *discussion* (f) : there was a dispute over the time of the murder = *il y a eu discussion sur l'heure du crime*
☠ → discussion
— *une dispute avec sa femme* = an argument with his wife.

DISPUTE (to, -d) *discuter* : I don't dispute that = *je ne le discute pas* ⊚ to contest = *contester*
☠ *discuter* → to discuss
— *se disputer* = to argue
— *disputer un match* = to play a match.

DISQUALIFY (to, -ied) *disqualifier* : to disqualify a player = *disqualifier un joueur* ≠ to qualify = *qualifier.*

DISREGARD (to, -ed) *ne pas s'occuper de* : disregard what he said = *ne t'occupe pas de ce qu'il a dit* ⊚ to ignore = *passer outre*
disregarding (his temper) = *si on fait abstraction de (son mauvais caractère).*

DISREPAIR (n) **to be in a state of disrepair** = *avoir grand besoin de réparations.*

DISRUPT (to, -ed) *perturber* : the demonstrators disrupted the meeting = *les manifestants ont perturbé la réunion* ☠ → to perturb.

DISSATISFACTION (n inv) *insatisfaction* (f) : she expressed her dissatisfaction = *elle a exprimé son insatisfaction* ⊚ discontentment = *mécontentement.*

DISSATISFIED (adj) *insatisfait, -e* : dissatisfied customers = *des clients insatisfaits* ≠ content = ←.

DISSENSION (n inv) *dissension* (f) : dissension within the party = *des dissensions au sein du parti* ⊚ strife = *discorde* ≠ harmony = *harmonie.*

DISSENT (n inv) *profond désaccord* (m) : dissent over the neutron bomb = *un profond désaccord sur la bombe à neutrons.*

DISSERTATION (n) *dissertation* (f) (school), *mémoire* (m) (university) : a dissertation on Freud = *un mémoire sur Freud* ☠ → memory.

DISSIDENT (n, adj) *dissident, -e* : political dissidents = *des dissidents politiques* ≠ partisan = ←.

DISSIMILAR (adj) *dissemblable* : dissimilar attitudes = *des attitudes dissemblables* ≠ similar = *similaire.*

DISSOCIATE (to, -d) *dissocier* : to dissociate the politician from the man = *dissocier l'homme politique et l'homme* ⊚ to distinguish = *distinguer.*

DISSOLUTE (adj) *dissolu, -e* : a dissolute life = *une vie dissolue* ⊚ debauched = *débauché.*

DISSOLVE (to, -d) **1/** *dissoudre* : to dissolve Parliament = *dissoudre le Parlement* **2/** *se dissoudre* : the medicine dissolves in water = *ce médicament se dissout dans l'eau.*

DISSUADE (to, -d) *dissuader* : she dissuaded me from marrying him = *elle m'a dissuadée de l'épouser* ≠ to encourage = *encourager.*

DISTANCE (n) *distance* (f) : what's the distance between New York and Boston ? = *quelle distance y a-t-il entre New York et Boston ?*
at/from a distance = *de loin* : from a distance he looks like his brother = *de loin, il ressemble à son frère* ≠ close up = *tout près*
in the distance = *dans le lointain* : I saw a boat in the distance = *j'ai vu un bateau dans le lointain* ⊚ far off = *au loin*
to keep s.o. at a distance = *tenir qqn à distance*
to keep one's distance = *garder ses distances*
to view (things) from a distance = *considérer (les choses) avec du recul.*

DISTANT (adj) *distant, -e* : he's very distant with his friends = *il est très distant avec ses amis* ⊚ reserved = *réservé*
distant relatives = *des parents éloignés*
in the distant future = *dans un avenir lointain* ≠ in the near future = *dans un avenir proche.*

DISTASTE (n) *aversion* (f) : a distaste for traveling = *une aversion pour les voyages* ≠ liking = *goût.*

DISTINCT (adj) **1/** *distinct, -e* : two distinct problems = *deux problèmes distincts* ⊚ different = *différent* **2/** *distinct, -e* : a distinct smell of onion = *une odeur distincte d'oignon* ⊚ clear = *clair.*

DISTINCTION (n) *distinction* (f) : without distinction of race = *sans distinction de race* ⊚ difference = *différence*
to have the distinction of being (the best paid call girl in Paris) = *avoir le suprême honneur d'être (la call-girl la mieux payée de Paris).*

DISTINCTIVE (adj) *distinctif, -ive* ⊚ characteristic = *caractéristique.*

DISTINCTLY (adv) **1/** *distinctement* : speak distinctly = *parlez distinctement* **2/** *nettement* : he distinctly said he was going to leave = *il a nettement dit qu'il allait partir.*

DISTINGUISH (to, -ed) *distinguer* : she can't distinguish Klee from Miro = *elle ne sait pas distinguer Klee de Miro*
☠ *distinguer qqn parmi d'autres* = to single s.o. out
— *le chef s'est distingué* = the chef outdid himself
— *on ne peut pas distinguer les jumeaux* = you can't tell the twins apart.

DISTINGUISHED (adj) *distingué, -e* : a distinguished pianist = *un pianiste distingué* ⊚ well-known = *connu.*

DISTORT (to, -ed) *déformer* : you're distorting the facts = *vous déformez les faits* ⊚ to twist = *fausser*
(a face) distorted by pain/anger = *(un visage) déformé par la douleur/la colère*
☠ → to deform.

DISTRACT (to, -ed) *distraire* : I was distracted by the noise = *j'ai été distraite par le bruit* ⓓ to divert s.o.'s attention = *détourner l'attention de qqn.*

DISTRACTION (n) *distraction* (f) : there are many distractions in New York = *il y a de nombreuses distractions à New York* ⓓ amusement = ←
(her drinking) is driving me to distraction = *(son alcoolisme) me rend dingue* ⓓ it's driving me up the wall = *ça me rend chèvre.*

DISTRAUGHT (adj) *très anxieux, -euse* : distraught over her husband's operation = *très anxieuse pour l'opération de son mari* ⓓ frantic = *affolé.*

DISTRESS (n inv) *détresse* (f) : great moral distress = *une grande détresse morale* ⓓ misery = *souffrance.*

DISTRESS (to, -ed) *consterner* : it distresses me to see you like this = *ça me consterne de vous voir comme ça* ⓓ to upset = *bouleverser* **DISTRESSING** (adj) *consternant, -e* : distressing news = *des nouvelles consternantes* ⓓ upsetting = *bouleversant* ≠ reassuring = *rassurant.*

DISTRIBUTE (to, -d) *distribuer* : clothes were distributed to the refugees = *des vêtements ont été distribués aux réfugiés* = to give out ≠ to gather = *rassembler* 💀 *distribuer le courrier* = to deliver the mail
— *distribuer des prospectus* = to hand out/give out leaflets.

DISTRIBUTION (n) *distribution* (f) : distribution of money/food = *distribution d'argent/de nourriture* 💀 *la distribution (film)* = the cast (film)
— *faire la distribution (d'un film)* = to do the casting (of a film).

DISTRIBUTOR (n) *distributeur, -trice* : they've several distributors in Europe = *ils ont plusieurs distributeurs en Europe* ⓓ wholesaler = *grossiste* 💀 *distributeur automatique* = slot machine.

DISTRICT (n) *quartier* (m), *district* (m) : to live in a poor district = *vivre dans un quartier pauvre* ⓓ area = *région* 💀 → quarter
District Attorney = *procureur de la République* = D.A.

DISTRICT OF COLUMBIA (n) = D.C. = *territoire fédéral (ce n'est pas un État) correspondant à la ville de Washington, siège du gouvernement fédéral.*

DISTRUST (n) *défiance* (f) : distrust of publishers = *défiance à l'égard des éditeurs* ⓓ mistrust = *méfiance* **DISTRUST** (to, -ed) *se défier de* : to distrust one's partner = *se défier de son partenaire* ≠ to have confidence in = *avoir confiance en* **DISTRUSTFUL** (adj) *défiant, -e* : distrustful personality = *caractère défiant* ⓓ suspicious = *soupçonneux.*

DISTURB (to, -ed) *déranger* : am I disturbing you ? = *est-ce que je vous dérange ?* ⓓ to bother = *embêter*
it disturbs me to (think my parents might get divorced) = *ça me perturbe de (penser que mes parents*

pourraient divorcer) ⓓ it upsets me = *ça me bouleverse* 💀 *ne dérange pas mes livres* = don't upset my books.

DISTURBANCE (n) *perturbation* (f) : disturbances during the meeting = *des perturbations pendant le meeting*
disturbance of the peace = *tapage nocturne.*

DISTURBING (adj) *préoccupant, -e* : disturbing news = *des nouvelles préoccupantes* ⓓ troubling = *troublant.*

DITCH (n, -es) *fossé* (m) : the car fell into the ditch = *la voiture est tombée dans le fossé* ⓓ trench = *tranchée* 💀 *le fossé entre les générations* = the generation gap.

DITCH (to, -ed) *larguer* : she ditched the guy after a year = *elle a largué le type au bout d'un an* ⓓ to jilt = *plaquer*
💀 *larguer les amarres* = to cast off
— *je suis complètement largué* = I'm all mixed up.

DITHER (n inv) **in a dither** = *dans tous ses états* : she's in a dither because she lost her purse = *elle est dans tous ses états parce qu'elle a perdu son sac à main* ⓓ in a fluster = *agité.*

DITTO (adv) *idem* : he's fed up with the situation and ditto for me = *il en a marre de cette situation et idem pour moi* ⓓ likewise = *de même.*

DIVE (n) 1/ *plongeon* (m) : a perfect dive = *un plongeon parfait* ⓓ a belly dive = *un plat*, diving board = *plongeoir* 💀 *faire le plongeon* = to take the plunge 2/ *coin* (m), *boui-boui* (m) (food) : if you want to eat Italian food I know a nice dive on 52nd Street = *si tu veux manger italien, je connais un coin/boui-boui sympa sur la 52e Rue* ⓓ joint = *endroit/gargote* 💀 *coin* → corner.

DIVE (to, -d or dove) *plonger* : do you know how to dive ? = *est-ce que tu sais plonger ?* ⓓ to scuba-dive = *faire de la plongée sous-marine* 💀 → to plunge **DIVER** (n) *plongeur, -euse* 💀 *le plongeur (dans un restaurant)* = the dishwasher.

DIVERGE (to, -d) *diverger* : our ideas diverge in every respect = *nos idées divergent dans tous les domaines* ≠ to converge = *converger.*

DIVERSE (adj) *divers, -e* : a family of diverse interests = *une famille aux intérêts divers* ≠ identical = *identique* 💀 *frais divers* = miscellaneous/sundry expenses
— *diverses sortes de glaces* = various kinds of ice cream.

DIVERSIFY (to, -ied) *diversifier* : to diversify a country's exports = *diversifier les exportations d'un pays* ⓓ to vary = *varier.*

DIVERSION (n) *qqch pour (se) distraire* : tennis was a diversion from his studies = *il jouait au tennis pour se distraire de ses études.*

DIVERSITY (n, -ies) *diversité* (f) : a great diversity of exports/interests = *une grande diversité d'exportations/d'intérêts* ≠ uniformity = *uniformité.*

DIVERT (to, -ed) *détourner* : to divert s.o.'s attention/the traffic = *détourner l'attention de qqn/la circulation* ☠ → to deter.

DIVEST (to, -ed) *révoquer* : to divest a general = *révoquer un général* ⓪ to remove from = *destituer de* ☠ → to revoke.

DIVIDE (to, -d) *diviser* : racism is dividing the country = *le racisme est en train de diviser le pays*
divide (the money) between/among you = *partagez-vous (l'argent)*
divide (20) by (5) = *divisez (20) par (5)*
to divide and conquer = *diviser pour régner* ⓪ united we stand, divided we fall = *l'union fait la force*
to divide up (the profits) = *répartir (les bénéfices)*.

DIVIDEND (n) *dividende (m)* : to get dividends = *toucher des dividendes* ⓪ share = *action*, interest = *intérêt*.

DIVINE (adj) *divin, -e* : a divine actress/evening = *une actrice/soirée divine* → WONDERFUL ≠ horrible = ←.

DIVINITY (n, -ies) *divinité (f)* ⓪ God = *Dieu*.

DIVISION (n) *division (f)* : a division of the profits/the army = *une division des bénéfices/de l'armée*.

DIVORCE (n) *divorce (m)* : she decided to get a divorce = *elle a décidé d'obtenir le divorce* ⓪ legal separation = *séparation de corps*, alimony = *pension alimentaire*, custody = *garde des enfants*, palimony = *pension versée à un concubin*.

DIVORCE (to, -d) *divorcer* : she wants to divorce = *elle veut divorcer*

to divorce s.o. = *divorcer de/d'avec qqn* : when did he divorce his first wife ? = *quand a-t-il divorcé de/d'avec sa première femme ?*
to get divorced = *divorcer* : they're getting divorced = *ils sont en train de divorcer* ⓪ to split up = *se séparer*.

DIVORCED (adj) *divorcé, -e* : a club for divorced and single men = *un club pour hommes divorcés et célibataires*.

DIVORCEE (n) *divorcée (f)* : she's a rich divorcee = *c'est une riche divorcée* ⓪ widow = *veuve* ☠ *un divorcé* = a divorced man, *des divorcés* = divorced people.

DIVULGE (to, -d) *divulguer* : the terrorist who was caught refused to divulge the names of his friends = *le terroriste qui a été pris a refusé de divulguer les noms de ses amis* ⓪ to disclose = *dévoiler*.

DIVVY UP (to, -ied) *diviser* : the crooks divvied up the haul = *les escrocs ont divisé le butin* = the crooks divided up the haul.

DIZZY (adj, -ier, -iest) **1/** *qui a la tête qui tourne* : I'm dizzy after two drinks = *j'ai la tête qui tourne après deux verres* **2/** *étourdi, -e* : she's so dizzy she often forgets important things = *elle est tellement étourdie qu'elle oublie souvent des choses importantes* ⓪ scatterbrained = *tête de linotte*
(heights) make me dizzy = *(l'altitude) me donne le vertige*.

DIZZYING (adj) *qui donne le vertige* : listening to her lying is dizzying = *ça me donne le vertige d'entendre tous ses mensonges*.

TO DO/TO MAKE = FAIRE

DO (to, did, done) **1/** *faire* : what are you doing tonight ? = *qu'est-ce que vous faites ce soir ?*, I'm doing it now = *je le fais maintenant*, I've a lot to do = *j'ai beaucoup à faire*, don't do that ! = *ne fais pas ça !* **2/** *faire (dans la vie)* : what does he do ? = *que fait-il (dans la vie) ?* ⓪ what's his job ? = *quel est son boulot ?*

MAKE (to, made, made) **1/** *faire* : his company makes cars = *sa société fait des voitures* ⓪ to manufacture = *fabriquer* **2/** *gagner* : he makes $ 100 a week = *il gagne 100 dollars par semaine*, she doesn't make much = *elle ne gagne pas beaucoup* ⓪ to pull in = *se faire* ☠ → to win **3/** *rendre* : Scotch makes me sick = *le whisky me rend malade* ☠ → to return

---

DO AND MAKE — IDIOMS

do as I say but not as I do = *fais ce que je dis et non pas ce que je fais*
to do as one pleases = *n'en faire qu'à sa tête* : whatever you say, he always does as he pleases = *quoi que l'on dise, il n'en fait toujours qu'à sa tête*
do as you like = *faites comme vous voulez* = **do as you please**
do as you see fit = *faites comme bon vous semble*
to do stg behind s.o.'s back = *faire qqch derrière le dos de qqn*
to do one's best = *faire de son mieux* : I did my best to help him = *j'ai fait de mon mieux pour l'aider* ⓪ to do one's damnedest = *faire l'impossible*

to make s.o.'s acquaintance = *faire la connaissance de qqn*
to make s.o. angry = *mettre qqn hors de soi* : it makes me angry to have to work so hard = *ça me met hors de moi d'avoir à travailler si dur*
to make an appointment = *prendre rendez-vous*
to make the bed = *faire le lit*
to make believe = **1/** *faire croire* : he made me believe he was an actor = *il m'a fait croire qu'il était acteur* **2/** *faire comme si* : make believe we're rich ! = *fais comme si nous étions riches !* ⓪ to pretend = *faire semblant*
to make the best of things = *tirer le meilleur parti des choses*

to do one's bit = *y mettre du sien* : if a couple wants to last, each one has to do his bit = *si un couple veut durer, chacun doit y mettre du sien*

to do the books = *faire les comptes*

to do business = *faire des affaires* : he does a lot of business with the French = *il fait beaucoup d'affaires avec les Français*

to do the cooking = *faire la cuisine* : does your husband ever do the cooking ? = *est-ce que votre mari fait parfois la cuisine ?*

to do damage (to) = *causer des dégâts (à)* : the snow did damage to the crops = *la neige a causé des dégâts aux récoltes*

to do s.o. dirty = *faire une crasse à qqn*

to do the dirty work = *faire le sale boulot* : the boss asked me to fire his secretary ; I always have to do the dirty work = *le patron m'a demandé de renvoyer sa secrétaire ; c'est toujours moi qui fais le sale boulot*

to do the dishes = *faire la vaisselle/la plonge* (LV) = **to do the washing-up** (GB)

to do exercises = *faire des exercices* : I do exercises every morning = *je fais des exercices tous les matins*

to do s.o. a favor = *rendre (un) service à qqn/faire une fleur à qqn* : can you please do me a favor ? = *pourriez-vous me rendre un service ?*

(a hot drink) will do you good = *(une boisson chaude) vous fera du bien*

it wouldn't do you any harm (to get a haircut) = *ça ne te ferait pas de mal (de te faire couper les cheveux)*

to do one's homework = *faire ses devoirs* : my son's doing his homework = *mon fils fait ses devoirs*

to do the housework = *faire le ménage* : I have to do the housework today = *aujourd'hui, il faut que je fasse le ménage*

to do it = *le faire* : we did it twice last night = *on l'a fait deux fois la nuit dernière* ⓧ to screw = *baiser*

to do s.o. justice = *rendre justice à qqn* : your criticisms don't do him justice = *tes critiques ne lui rendent pas justice*

to do right by (one's family) = *bien se conduire avec (sa famille)*

to do the shopping = *faire les courses* : I do the shopping once a week = *je fais les courses une fois par semaine*

to do one's thing = *faire son truc* : in their family, everyone does his thing = *dans leur famille, chacun fait son truc*

to do time = *faire de la prison* : he did time in Sing Sing = *il a fait de la prison à Sing Sing*

do unto others as you would have others do unto you = *ne faites pas à autrui ce que vous ne voudriez pas qu'on vous fît*

to do one's utmost = *faire tout son possible* : I'll do my utmost to help her = *je ferai tout mon possible pour l'aider*

to make a big deal about = *en faire une maladie* : don't make a whole big deal about it ! = *n'en fais pas une maladie !* ⓧ to make a fuss = *faire des histoires*

to make a blunder/a faux pas/a slip = *faire une gaffe/un faux pas/un impair*

to make a check out to = *faire un chèque à l'ordre de* : who should I make the check out to ? = *à quel ordre dois-je faire le chèque ?*

to make a choice = *faire un choix*

to make it clear = *bien préciser* : he made it clear he wasn't resigning = *il a bien précisé qu'il ne démissionnait pas*

to make dinner = *faire le dîner*

to make do with = *faire avec (les moyens du bord)* : you'll have to make do with what you have = *il faudra que vous fassiez avec ce que vous avez/avec les moyens du bord*

to make s.o. do stg = *faire faire qqch à qqn* : he made me do it = *il me l'a fait faire*, he made me drink = *il m'a fait boire*

to make an effort = *faire un effort*

to make eyes at s.o. = *faire de l'œil à qqn*

to make a fool of o.s. = *se rendre ridicule*

to make a fortune/a killing/a bundle = *faire fortune/son beurre/sa pelote*

to make friends = *se faire des amis*

to make fun of s.o. = *se moquer de qqn* : don't make fun of me = *ne te moque pas de moi*

to make a fuss/a scene = *faire des histoires/une scène*

to make a go of (the business) = *faire une réussite de (l'affaire)*

to make good = *dédommager* : he'll make good the damage he caused = *il vous dédommagera du préjudice qu'il a causé*

to make good money = *gagner bien sa vie*

to make it = 1/ *réussir* : he's rich now ; he's really made it = *il est riche maintenant ; il a vraiment réussi* ⚥ → to succeed 2/ *l'avoir* : the train leaves in 10 minutes, I'll never make it = *le train part dans 10 minutes, je ne l'aurai jamais*

I can't make it (at 7/tonight) = *(7 heures/ce soir) ça ne me va pas*

to make it with s.o. = *s'envoyer en l'air avec qqn* : I never made it with a black guy = *je ne me suis jamais envoyée en l'air avec un Noir* ⓧ to sleep with = *coucher avec*

to make s.o. laugh/cry = *faire rire/pleurer qqn* : his book made us laugh/cry = *son livre nous a fait rire/pleurer*

make like/as if/as though (you didn't hear) = *faites comme si (vous n'aviez pas entendu)*

to make love = *faire l'amour*

to make a mess = *ficher la pagaille*

to make a mistake/an error = *se tromper/faire une erreur*

to make money = *se faire du fric* : he's really making money in the Stock Market = *il se fait beaucoup de fric en Bourse*

to do well to = *faire bien de* : you'd do well to study more = *tu ferais bien d'étudier plus*
to be doing well = 1/ *bien marcher* : he's doing well in school = *il marche bien à l'école* 2/ *aller bien* : he was operated last week and is doing well = *il a été opéré la semaine dernière et il va bien* 3/ *se faire du fric* : their business just opened and they're doing well = *leur affaire vient d'ouvrir, et ils se font du fric* ⓪ to make money = *gagner de l'argent*
how are you doing ? = *ça va ?* ⓪ what's new ? = *quoi de neuf ?*
to be done = *avoir terminé* : are you done yet ? = *est-ce que vous avez déjà terminé ?*, no, I'm not done yet = *non, je n'ai pas encore terminé* ⓪ to be finished = *avoir fini*
how do you do ? = *enchanté !* = pleased to meet you !
it's do or die = *c'est marche ou crève* = it's sink or swim
that'll do ! = *ça va !* ⓪ that's enough ! = *ça suffit !*
that isn't done = *cela ne se fait pas* ⓪ it's a crying shame = *c'est une honte*
that does it ! = *ça suffit !* ⓪ that's the limit ! = *c'est le comble !*
there is nothing/not anything to be done about it = *on ne peut rien y faire* ≠ **is there anything to be done about it ?** = *peut-on y faire quelque chose ?*
what can you do ! = *qu'y faire !* → THAT'S LIFE !
what do you do for a living ? = *que faites-vous dans la vie ?*
what's doing ? = *qu'est-ce que vous devenez ?* ⓪ what's cooking ? = *ça gaze ?*
that'll do the trick = *ça fera l'affaire !* ≠ that won't do = *ça n'ira pas*
what's done is done = *ce qui est fait est fait* → THAT'S LIFE !
will Saturday/$ 10 do ? = *est-ce que samedi/ 10 dollars ça ira ?*
we were doing (60 on the highway) = *nous faisions du (60 sur l'autoroute)*

to make noise = *faire du bruit*
to make an offer = *faire une offre* : make me an offer ! = *faites-moi une offre !*
to make a pig of o.s. = *se bâfrer*
to make plans = *faire des projets*
to make progress/headway = *faire des progrès*
to make a remark/a suggestion = *faire une remarque/une suggestion*
to make room for = *faire un peu de place pour* (stg) /*à* (s.o.) : could you make room for me ? = *pourriez-vous me faire un peu de place ?*
to make sense = *être raisonnable* : it makes sense to vote for her = *il est raisonnable de voter pour elle*
to make a speech = *faire un discours*
to make sure/certain = *s'assurer de* : make sure/certain that you get a receipt = *assurez-vous qu'on vous donne un reçu*
to make things/matters better ≠ **worse** = *pour arranger* ≠ *ne pas arranger les choses*
to make things hard/rough/tough on s.o. = *rendre les choses très difficiles pour qqn/mener la vie dure à qqn*
to make a trip = *faire un voyage* ⓪ to travel = *voyager*
did I make myself understood ? = *me suis-je bien fait comprendre ?*
make yourself at home ! = *faites comme chez vous !*
(2) and (2) make (4) = *(2) et (2) font (4)*
she'll make a (good lawyer) = *elle fera une (bonne avocate)*
that'll make it or break it = *cela décidera de tout* : their marriage is in trouble, having the baby will either make it or break it = *leur couple est en danger, le fait d'avoir cet enfant va décider de tout*
you can't make me ! = *vous ne pouvez pas m'y forcer !* : if I don't want to go, you can't make me ! = *si je ne veux pas y aller, vous ne pouvez pas m'y forcer !*
(meeting the star) made (the kids' vacation) = *ça a transformé (les vacances des gosses de rencontrer cette vedette)* ≠ to spoil = *gâcher*

— DO AND MAKE — VERBS + PREPOSITIONS

to do something about it = *y faire quelque chose* ≠ **not to do anything about it** = *ne rien y faire* : sorry, but I can't do anything about it = *désolé, mais je ne peux rien y faire*
to do away with = *supprimer* : to do away with capital punishment = *supprimer la peine de mort* ⓪ to abolish = *abolir*
⚐ *supprimer un nom d'une liste* = to delete a name from a list
— *supprimer (la cigarette)* = to cut out (cigarettes)
what can I do for you ? = *que puis-je faire pour vous ?*
to be done for = *être fichu* : if the boss finds out, I'm done for ! = *si le patron l'apprend, je suis fichu !* ⓪ I've had it ! = *je suis cuit !*

to make for = *se diriger vers* : we made for the house = *nous nous sommes dirigés vers la maison*
they're made for each other = *ils sont faits l'un pour l'autre*
made in (the US/France) = *fait aux (USA)/en (France)*
to be made of money = *être cousu d'or* → RICH
to make nothing/not to make anything of = *faire peu de cas de* : the boss made nothing of/didn't make anything of the mistake = *le patron a fait peu de cas de cette erreur*
what do you make of (what he said) ? = *que doit-on penser de (ce qu'il a dit) ?*
to make off/away with = *faire main basse sur* : he made off/away with the money = *il a fait main basse*

to do s.o. in = *refroidir qqn* : the gang did him in = *le gang l'a refroidi* ⓓ to shoot down = *abattre, to* zap = *trucider*

to be done in = *être vanné* : after all that work I'm done in = *après tout ce travail, je suis vanné* ⓓ to be beat = *être crevé*

to do s.o. out of stg = *gruger qqn de qqch* : they did him out of his share = *ils l'ont grugé de sa part* → TO HUSTLE

to do over = 1/ *refaire* : I'm doing my room over = *je refais ma chambre* ⓓ to redecorate = *redécorer* 2/ *refaire* : your homework isn't good ; do it over = *ton devoir n'est pas bon ; refais-le* ⓓ to begin again = *recommencer* ☠ → to redo

to do stg to s.o. = *faire qqch à qqn* : what did you do to your little brother ? = *qu'est-ce que tu as fait à ton petit frère ?*

to do with = *faire de* : what did you do with the money I gave you ? = *qu'avez-vous fait de l'argent que je vous ai donné ?*

to have to do with = *avoir à voir avec* : what does that have to do with it ? = *qu'est-ce que ça a à voir (avec ça) ?*, that has nothing to do with it = *ça n'a rien à voir (avec ça)* = that doesn't have anything to do with it, her job has something to do with handicapped children = *son travail a quelque chose à voir avec les enfants handicapés*

I could do with a drink/something to eat = *je boirais/mangerais bien quelque chose* ⓓ I feel like = *j'ai envie de*

what were you doing with (her husband) ? = *que faisiez-vous avec (son mari) ?*

to do without = *se passer de* : I can't do without him = *je ne peux pas me passer de lui*, I can't do without your advice = *je ne peux pas me passer de vos conseils*

sur l'argent ⓓ to pinch = *piquer*

to make out = 1/ *s'en sortir* : how is he making out in his new job ? = *comment s'en sort-il dans son nouveau boulot ?* ⓓ to get along = *marcher* 2/ *flirter* : the couples were making out at the party = *les couples flirtaient pendant la soirée* ⓓ to smooch = *se bécoter* 3/ *comprendre* : I can't make him/his writing out = *je ne le comprends pas/je ne comprends pas son écriture* = I can't understand ... ⓓ to decipher = *déchiffrer*

it's not as (hard) as you make it out = *ce n'est pas aussi (dur) que tu le prétends*

to make up = 1/ *se réconcilier* : they fought but made up after = *ils se sont disputés, mais ils se sont réconciliés après* ≠ to quarrel = *se quereller* ☠ → to reconcile 2/ *rattraper* : if you miss two days work you'll have to make them up = *si vous loupez deux jours de travail, vous devrez les rattraper* ☠ → to catch up 3/ *fabriquer* : she made the story up = *elle a fabriqué toute cette histoire* ⓓ to concoct = *forger* ☠ → to manufacture 4/ *se maquiller* : she makes up too much = *elle se maquille trop* ☠ *maquiller les comptes* = to doctor up the books — *maquiller la vérité* = to distort the truth

to make up for = *se racheter* : how can I make up for the trouble I've caused ? = *comment puis-je me racheter pour les ennuis que j'ai causés ?* ☠ *racheter (une affaire)* = to buy up (a business)

to make up to s.o. = 1/ *faire du plat à qqn* : Jack always makes up to the boss = *Jack est toujours en train de faire du plat au patron* ⓓ to butter up = *passer de la pommade* 2/ *(promettre de) remettre* : I know we were supposed to go away this weekend ; I promise I'll make it up to you = *je sais que nous étions censés partir ce week-end ; je te promets qu'on remettra ça*

☠ *il fait son droit/sa médecine* = he's studying law/medicine

— *faire une promenade* = to go for a walk

— *ne vous en faites pas !* = don't worry !

— *je ne m'y ferai jamais* = I'll never get used to it

— *il fait chaud/froid* = it's hot/cold

— *faire sa valise/ses bagages* = to pack one's bags

— *se faire engueuler/attraper* = to catch hell

— *nous ne faisons pas (ce genre de voiture)* = we don't handle (that kind of car)

— *ça fait longtemps/un bail/une paie que* = it's been a long time since

— *puis-je faire remarquer que ... ?* = may I point out that ... ?

— *combien ça fait ?* = how much is it ?

— *quel temps fait-il ?* = what's the weather like ?

— *tu me fais mal !* = you're hurting me !

— *tu ferais mieux de (partir maintenant)* = you'd be better off (leaving now)

— *cela ne s'est pas fait* = it didn't come off

— *faire venir un médecin* = to call in a doctor

— *faire peur* = to frighten

— *faire de la dépression* = to be depressive

— *fais attention !* = watch out !

— *faire connaissance de qqn* = to meet s.o.

— *faire confiance* = to trust

— *faire marcher qqn* = to pull

s.o.'s leg

— *se faire mille dollars* = to pull down/in $ 1,000

— *faire un voyage* = to take a trip

— *comment se fait-il que ... ?* = how is it that ... ?

— *faire un somme* = to take a nap

— *faire du vélo/bateau* = to go bicycling/boating

— *cela fait dix ans que (je suis marié)* = (I've been married) for ten years

— *cela ne fait rien* = it doesn't matter

— *il fait jeune/vieux* = he looks young/old

— *se faire couper les cheveux* = to have one's hair cut

DO — AUXILIAIRE

— **do you smoke ?** = *est-ce que vous fumez ?*
— yes, I do   — no, I don't
— yes, I smoke   — no, I don't smoke

— **did you smoke yesterday ?** = *avez-vous fumé hier ?*
— yes, I did   — no, I didn't
— yes, I smoked   — no, I didn't smoke
yesterday   yesterday

— I
— you } do/don't   — we do/don't
— he
— she } does/doesn't   — they do/don't

POUR INSISTER
— stay ! = *restez !*
— **do** stay ! = *restez, je vous en prie !*

DO — TAGS (N'EST-CE PAS ?)

— she smokes, doesn't she ? = *elle fume, n'est-ce pas ?*
— she doesn't smoke, does she ? = *elle ne fume pas, n'est-ce pas ?*

DO (n) **the dos and don'ts** = *les choses à faire et à ne pas faire :* the dos and don'ts of getting ahead in life = *les choses à faire et à ne pas faire pour se frayer un chemin dans la vie* ⓄⒹ the rules of the game = *les règles du jeu.*

MAKE (n) *marque (f) :* a make of car = *une marque de voiture ?* ☠ → mark
to be on the make = *être en chasse :* single guys are on the make Saturday night = *les célibataires sont en chasse le samedi soir.*

DOING (n) **that takes some doing !** = *il faut le faire !* → GOSH !
that's not my doing ! = *ce n'est pas mon fait !*
the doings of (the week/town) = *les événements de (la semaine/la ville).*

MAKING (n) **she has the makings of (a fine painter)** = *elle a l'étoffe d'(un bon peintre)* ⓄⒹ to be cut out for = *être fait pour*
that was the making of him = *c'est ce qui l'a fait* ≠ it was his undoing = *c'est ce qui a causé sa perte.*

DOCILE (adj) *docile :* a docile child/husband = *un enfant/mari docile* ⓄⒹ obedient = *obéissant* ≠ rebellious = *rebelle.*

DOCK (n) **1/** *dock (m) :* trouble on the docks = *des troubles sur les docks* ⓄⒹ wharf = *quai* **2/** *banc (m)des accu-* *sés :* the murderer was in the dock = *le meurtrier était sur le banc des accusés* ⓄⒹ witness-box = *barre des témoins.*

DOCKER (n) *docker (m) :* dockers' strike = *grève des dockers* ⓄⒹ longshoreman = *débardeur.*

DOCTOR (n) *docteur (m), médecin (m), toubib (m)* (LV) : I have a great doctor = *j'ai un excellent docteur/médecin* ⓄⒹ nurse = *infirmière*

chiropractor = *chiropracteur* **consulting doctor** = *médecin consultant* **dermatologist** = *dermatologue* **intern** = *interne* **medical doctor** = *docteur en médecine* = **MD**	**medical student** = *étudiant en médecine* **neurologist** = *neurologue* **physician** = *docteur en médecine* **psychiatrist** = *psychiatre* **quack** = *charlatan*	**resident** = *médecin stagiaire à l'hôpital* **shrink** = *psy* **specialist** = *spécialiste* **surgeon** = *chirurgien* **therapist** = *thérapeute* **veterinarian** = *vétérinaire*

doctor of law = *docteur en droit*
that's just what the doctor ordered ! = *c'est*

exactement ce qu'il me fallait ! ⓄⒹ that does the trick = *ça fait l'affaire.*

DOCTOR (UP) (to, -ed) *trafiquer :* they doctored (up) the Scotch = *ils ont trafiqué le whisky* ⓄⒹ to tamper with = *tripatouiller*
☠ *trafiquer (drogue)* = to deal (drugs)
— *qu'est-ce que tu trafiques ?* = what are you up to ?

DOCTORATE (n) *doctorat (m) :* he's doing a doctorate

in biology = *il fait un doctorat de biologie* ⓄⒹ MA = *maîtrise.*

DOCTRINE (n) *doctrine (f) :* the Monroe doctrine = *la doctrine Monroe* ⓄⒹ philosophy = *philosophie.*

DOCUMENT (n) *document (m) :* official documents =

des documents officiels ⓧ *archives* = ← **DOCUMENTA-TION** (n) *documentation (f)*.

DOCUMENTARY (n, -ies) *documentaire (m)* : a documentary on prostitution = *un documentaire sur la prostitution* ⓧ short = *court métrage*.

DOCUMENTED (adj) **a documented article** = *un article bien étayé*.

DODGE (to, -d) *se dérober à* : the President dodged the journalists' questions = *le Président s'est dérobé aux questions des journalistes* ⓧ to avoid = *éviter*.

DOER (n) *fonceur, -euse* : I've always been a doer = *j'ai toujours été une fonceuse* ⓧ dynamo = *force de la nature*.

DOG (n) *chien, chienne, clebs (m)* (LV) : I have to walk the dog = *je dois aller promener le chien*

to bark = *aboyer* **beg !** = *fais le beau !* **to bite** = *mordre* **boxer** = ← **cocker (spaniel)** = *cocker* **collar and leash** = *collier et laisse* **collie** = *colley* **dachshund** = *teckel* **doggy** = *toutou* **doghouse** = *niche* **dog show** = *exposition canine* **German shepherd** = *berger allemand*	**Great Dane** = *danois* **greyhound** = *lévrier* **to growl** = *gronder* **hound** = *chien (de chasse)* **hunting dog** = *chien de chasse* **Irish setter** = *setter irlandais* **kennel** = *chenil* **a litter** = *une portée* **mongrel** = *corniaud* **mutt** = *cabot* **muzzle** = *muselière* **pointer** = *chien d'arrêt* **pooch** = *clébard* **poodle** = *caniche*	**pound** = *fourrière* **puppy** = *chiot* **retriever** = ← **Seeing Eye dog** = *chien d'aveugle* **sit !** = *assis !* **to snarl** = *grogner* **to sniff** = *renifler* **spaniel** = *épagneul* **toy poodle** = *caniche nain* **a vet** = *un véto* **to wag its tail** = *remuer la queue* **watchdog** = *chien de garde*

to be going to the dogs = *être à la dérive* (s.o),*battre de l'aile* (stg) : the business/the house is going to the dogs = *l'affaire/la maison bat de l'aile*, he's going to the dogs = *il est à la dérive* ⓧ to be on the skids = *aller à vau-l'eau* **a dog's life** = *une vie de chien* ≠ the life of Riley = *une vie de coq en pâte* **every dog has its day** = *tout vient à point à qui sait attendre*	**to put on the dog** = *en mettre plein la vue* : whenever the rich part of the family comes, my parents put on the dog = *chaque fois que vient la partie la plus riche de la famille, mes parents lui en mettent plein la vue* ⓧ to show off = *faire de l'épate* **unleash** ≠ **call off the dogs !** = *lâchez* ≠ *rappelez les chiens !* **to work like a dog** = *travailler comme un forçat* ⓧ to sweat bullets = *suer sang et eau*
☠ *elle a du chien !* = she's got it ! — *entre chien et loup* = at twilight — *un temps de chien* = crummy weather — *une chienne n'y retrouverait pas ses petits* = the place is upside down — *se regarder en chiens de faïence* = to glare at one another	— *je lui garde un chien de ma chienne* = I have it in for him — *qui veut noyer son chien l'accuse de la rage* = anything can be justified — *recevoir qqn comme un chien dans un jeu de quilles* = to give s.o. the cold shoulder.

DOG (to, -ged) *talonner* : dogged by the cops/by endless problems = *talonné par les flics/par des problèmes sans fin* ⓧ to harass = *harceler*.

DOG-EAT-DOG (n, adj) *l'homme est un loup pour l'homme* : politics is dog-eat-dog = *en politique, l'homme est un loup pour l'homme* ⓧ ruthless = *impitoyable*.

DOGGED (adj) *opiniâtre* : a dogged resistance = *une résistance opiniâtre* ⓧ unremitting = *acharné*, unrelenting = *implacable* **DOGGEDLY** (adv) *opiniâtrement* : to resist doggedly = *résister opiniâtrement*.

DOGGIE BAG (n) *sac qui permet d'emporter ce qu'on n'a pas mangé au restaurant* : there is some chop suey left, give us a doggie bag = *il reste du chop suey, donnez-nous un sac pour les restes*.

DOGHOUSE (n) **to be in the doghouse** = *être en quarantaine* : I'm in the doghouse with the boss = *le patron m'a mis en quarantaine*.

DOGMA (n) *dogme (m)* : marxist dogma = *le dogme marxiste* ⓧ doctrine = ← **DOGMATIC** (adj) *dogmatique*.

DO-GOODER (n) *bienfaiteur, -trice (de l'humanité)* : a family of do-gooders = *une famille de bienfaiteurs (de l'humanité)* ⓪ good Samaritan = *bon samaritain.*

DOG-TIRED (adj) *flapi, -e* : dog-tired after the tennis match = *flapi après le match de tennis* ⓪ pooped = *raplapla.*

DO-IT-YOURSELF (adj) **a do-it-yourself shop** = *un magasin de bricolage.*

DOLDRUMS (n pl) **to be in the doldrums** = *être malheureux comme les pierres* ⓪ to be down in the dumps = *être au trente-sixième dessous.*

DOLE (n inv) **to be on the dole** = *être au chômage* ⓪ welfare = *aide sociale.*

DOLE OUT (to, -d) *distribuer au compte-gouttes* : the government doles out help to the poor = *le gouvernement distribue au compte-gouttes l'aide aux pauvres* ⓪ to ration = *rationner.*

DOLL (n) *poupée (f)* : I'm buying my daughter a doll for Christmas = *j'achète une poupée à ma fille pour Noël* ⓪ toy = *jouet*
you were a doll (to help) ! = *tu as été un amour (de m'aider)* ! ⓪ gem = *trésor.*

DOLLAR (n) *dollar (m)* : a dollar bill = *un billet d'un dollar* ⓪ greenback = *billet vert,* a ten-spot = *un billet de 10 dollars.*

DOLL UP (to, -ed) *se pomponner* : where are you going all dolled up like that ? = *où est-ce que vous allez pomponnée comme ça ?* ⓪ spruced up = *tiré à quatre épingles.*

DOLPHIN (n) *dauphin (m)* : the intelligence of dolphins = *l'intelligence des dauphins* ⓪ whale = *baleine* ☠ *dauphin (prince)* = crown prince.

DOMAIN (n) *domaine (m)* : progress in the domain of technology = *des progrès dans le domaine de la technologie* ⓪ sphere = *sphère*
it's not in my domain = *ce n'est pas de mon ressort* ⓪ it's not my field = *ce n'est pas mon domaine* ☠ *un domaine* = an estate
— *c'est dans le domaine du possible* = it's within the realm of possibility.

DOMESTIC (adj) **1/** *intérieur, -e* : domestic matters/flights = *affaires intérieures/vols intérieurs* ≠ foreign = *étranger* ☠ → interior **2/** *domestique* : problems in their domestic life = *les problèmes de leur vie domestique* ☠ *animal domestique* = pet animal.

DOMICILE (n) *domicile (m)* : what's your legal domicile ? = *quel est votre domicile légal ?* ⓪ residence = *résidence.*

DOMICILED (adj) **to be domiciled** = *être domicilié* ⓪ to be a resident = *être résident.*

DOMINANT (adj) *dominant, -e* : what's the dominant religion in the Middle East ? = *quelle est la religion dominante au Moyen-Orient ?* ⓪ main = *principal* ≠ subordinate = *subordonné.*

DOMINATE (to, -d) **1/** *dominer* : he dominates his kids = *il domine ses gosses* ⓪ to lord over = *régenter* **2/** *dominer* : skyscrapers dominate the city = *les gratte-ciel dominent la ville*
☠ *dominer son sujet* = to master one's subject
— *se dominer* = to get a hold of o.s.

DOMINATION (n) *domination (f)* ⓪ authority = *autorité.*

DOMINEERING (adj) *dominateur, -trice* : a domineering wife = *une épouse dominatrice* ⓪ authoritarian = *autoritaire.*

DONATE (to, -d) *faire un don* : all the toys were donated = *tous les jouets étaient des dons.*

DONATION (n) *donation (f)* : a donation for cancer research = *une donation à la recherche contre le cancer.*

DONKEY (n) *âne (m)* ⓪ mule = ← ☠ → ass.

DONOR (n) *donneur, -euse* : blood donor = *donneur de sang.*

DOODLE (to, -d) *faire des petits dessins* : the President doodles during cabinet meetings = *le Président fait des petits dessins pendant le conseil des ministres.*

DOOM (n) *perte (f)* : meeting him was her doom = *ça a été sa perte de le rencontrer* ⓪ downfall = *chute* ☠ → loss.

DOOM (to, -ed) **to be doomed** = *être voué à l'échec* : the marriage was doomed from the start = *depuis le début, leur couple était voué à l'échec.*

DOOMSDAY (n) *jour (m) du Jugement dernier* = Judgment Day
to put off till doomsday = *renvoyer aux calendes grecques.*

DOOR (n) *porte (f), lourde (f)* (LV) : open the door = *ouvre la porte* ⓪ doorknob = *bouton de porte,* bell = *sonnette,* threshold = *seuil,* doormat = *paillasson,* doorway = *portail*
the back ≠ **front door** = *la porte de derrière* ≠ *de devant*
to knock at the door = *frapper à la porte*
out of doors = *à l'extérieur, dehors* : we're eating out of doors tonight = *ce soir nous mangeons dehors* = we're eating outdoors tonight
to see/to show s.o. to the door = *raccompagner qqn à la porte* ⓪ to see s.o. out = *reconduire qqn*
to shut the door in s.o.'s face = *claquer la porte au nez de qqn*
don't slam the door ! = *ne claque pas la porte* !
☠ *les portes de la ville* = the city gates
— *écouter aux portes* = to eavesdrop
— *il faut commencer par balayer devant sa porte* = people who live in glass houses shouldn't throw stones

— *(se ménager) une porte de sortie* = (to leave o.s.) a way out
— *entrer par la petite ≠ grande porte* = to start at the bottom ≠ top
— *mettre qqn à la porte* = to throw s.o. out.

DOORMAN (n, -men) *portier (m)* : the doorman will get you a taxi = *le portier va vous appeler un taxi* ⓓ bellboy = *chasseur.*

DOOR-TO-DOOR (adj) *porte-à-porte (m)* : he's a door-to-door salesman = *il fait du porte-à-porte* = he peddles.

DOORWAY (n) **(standing) in the doorway** = *(debout,) dans l'encadrement de la porte* ⓓ doorstep = *le pas de la porte.*

DOPE (n) **1/** *dope (f), came (f)* : many kids take dope = *beaucoup d'enfants prennent de la came* ⓓ drugs = *drogues* **2/** *dessous (m pl)* : what's the dope on their divorce ? = *quels sont les dessous de leur divorce ?* ⓓ dirt = *ragots* ☠ → underwear **3/** *gourde (f)* : what a dope I am ! = *quelle gourde je suis !* → STUPID.

DOPE (to, -d) *droguer, doper* (horses/athletes) : they doped the young girl/horse = *ils ont drogué la jeune fille/ils ont dopé le cheval* = to drug.

DORMANT (adj) *qui dort, en sommeil* : a dormant project = *un projet en sommeil.*

DORMITORY (n, -ies) *dortoir (m)* : the dormitory is co-ed = *le dortoir est mixte* = the dorm is co-ed.

DOSE (n) *dose (f)* : I can take my mother-in-law in small doses = *j'arrive à supporter ma belle-mère à petites doses* ⓓ overdose = ←.

DOT (n) *point (m)* : a dot over an i = *un point sur un i* **on the dot** = *sonnante* : he came at nine on the dot = *il est venu à neuf heures sonnantes* ⓓ on the nose = *tapante* ☠ → point
— *une dot* = a dowry.

DOTE ON (to, -d) *être gaga de* : to dote on one's kids = *être gaga de ses gosses* ⓓ to pamper = *chouchouter.*

DOTTED (adj) **to sign on the dotted line** = *apposer sa signature* (papiers officiels, contrats) *sur la ligne pointillée.*

DOUBLE (n) *double (m)* : I'll pay you the double = *je vous paierai le double*
to be s.o.'s double = *être le portrait de qqn* : he's Bogart's double = *c'est le portrait de Bogart* ⓓ the spitting image = *le portrait tout craché*
on the double = *dare-dare* : you'd better get the letter to the boss on the double = *tu ferais bien d'apporter dare-dare la lettre au patron* ⓓ in nothing flat = *en moins de rien*, pronto = *illico*
☠ *le double d'une facture* = the copy of an invoice.

DOUBLE (adj) *double* : a double portion/chin = *une double portion/un double menton*

double agent = *agent double* ⓓ spy = *espion* **double bed** = *grand lit/lit à deux places* **double date** = *sortie à quatre (deux couples)* **double meaning/entendre** = *double sens* **double occupancy** = *sur la base de deux personnes par chambre* **double or nothing** = *quitte ou double* = double or quits (GB)	**double room** = *chambre pour deux* **double standard** = *deux poids, deux mesures* **to do a double take** = *faire un bond* : I did a double take when I saw his wife holding hands with another guy = *j'ai fait un bond quand j'ai vu sa femme main dans la main avec un autre type*

☠ *faire double emploi* = to be redundant
— *double nationalité* = dual nationality.

DOUBLE (adv) *(le) double (de)* : to earn double = *gagner le double,* to see double = *voir double.*

DOUBLE (to, -d) *doubler* : prices have doubled in 10 years = *les prix ont doublé en 10 ans* ⓓ to triple = *tripler*
to double as = *servir aussi de* : he's the cook but doubles as the chauffeur = *il est cuisinier mais sert aussi de chauffeur*
to double up = *se mettre à deux* : the rooms are filled, we'll have to double up = *les chambres sont pleines, il va falloir se mettre à deux*
to be doubled up with (pain/laughter) = *se tordre de (douleur/rire)*

☠ *doubler (classe)* = to take a class over — *doubler une voiture* = to pass a car — *doubler (manteau)* = to line (coat)	— *doubler qqn* = to double-cross s.o./to cross s.o. up — *doubler un film* = to dub a film.

DOUBLE-BREASTED (adj) *croisé, -e* : a double-breasted coat = *un manteau croisé.*

DOUBLE-CHECK (to, -ed) *revérifier* : to double-check a list = *revérifier une liste* ⓓ to verify = *vérifier.*

DOUBLE-CROSS (to, -ed) *doubler* : I trusted him but he double-crossed me = *je lui faisais confiance mais il m'a doublé* → TO HUSTLE ☠ → to double **DOUBLE-CROSSER** (n) *vendu, -e* : you're a lousy double-crosser ! = *tu es un sale vendu !* ⓓ turncoat = *faux frère.*

DOUBLE-DATE (to, -d) *sortir à quatre* : we double-dated last night = *nous sommes sortis à quatre hier soir.*

DOUBLE-DEALING (n) *double jeu* (m) : I don't appreciate his double-dealing = *je n'apprécie pas son double jeu* ⓪ duplicity = *duplicité* **DOUBLE-DEALER** (n) *qqn qui joue double jeu* : his partner's a double-dealer = *son associé joue double jeu* ⓪ con artist = *embobineur.*

DOUBLE-EDGED (adj) *à double tranchant* : a double-edged compliment = *un compliment à double tranchant.*

DOUBLE-PARK (to, -ed) *se garer en double file* : there was no place so I double-parked = *il n'y avait pas de place, alors je me suis garé en double file.*

DOUBLE-TALK (n) *charabia* (m) : his answer was double-talk = *sa réponse, c'était du charabia* ⓪ gibberish = *baragouin.*

DOUBT (n) *doute* (m) : we have doubts about his honesty = *nous avons des doutes sur son honnêteté* ≠ certainty = *certitude*

---

beyond doubt = *hors de doute* ⓪ undoubtedly = *indubitablement*
I have my doubts about that = *j'ai des doutes à ce sujet*
in doubt = 1/ *incertain* : the result is in doubt = *le résultat est incertain* 2/ *dans le doute* : I'm in doubt as to what to do = *je suis dans le doute quant à ce qu'il faut faire*

no doubt = *sans doute* : they're no doubt getting married soon = *ils vont sans doute se marier bientôt* ⓪ most likely = *très probablement*
there's no doubt about it = *cela ne fait aucun doute*
when in doubt, do nothing = *dans le doute, abstiens-toi*
without a doubt = *sans aucun doute* ⓪ for sure = *à coup sûr.*

DOUBT (to, -ed) 1/ *douter* : I doubt that he'll agree = *je doute qu'il soit d'accord* ≠ to be sure = *être sûr* 2/ *douter de* : I doubt his honesty = *je doute de son honnêteté* ⓪ to question = *mettre en question*
I doubt it = *j'en doute* ≠ **I don't doubt it** = *je n'en doute pas/je m'en doute*
👻 *est-ce que vous vous doutiez qu'il mentait ?* = did you think/guess/suspect that he was lying ?
— *il ne doute de rien !* = he's overconfident !
— *je m'en doutais !* = I thought/guessed as much !
— *il ne se doute de rien* = he doesn't suspect anything
— *je ne m'étais jamais douté que ...* = I never surmised that ...

DOUBTFUL (adj) *douteux, -euse* : it's doubtful whether he'll come tomorrow = *il est douteux qu'il vienne demain* ⓪ debatable = *discutable* ≠ sure = *sûr*

👻 *un personnage douteux* = a shifty/questionable character
— *une plaisanterie douteuse* = a joke in dubious taste.

DOUBTLESS (adv) *sans doute* : doubtless you're right, but still I want to check = *vous avez sans doute raison, mais je veux quand même vérifier* = doubtlessly ⓪ most likely = *très probablement.*

DOUCHE (n) douche (f) vaginale 👻 douche → shower.

DOUGH (n inv) 1/ *fric* (m) : can you lend me some dough till the end of the month ? = *est-ce que tu peux me prêter du fric jusqu'à la fin du mois ?* ⓪ cabbage = *oseille*, lettuce = *blé* 2/ *pâte* (f) : the baker uses dough to make bread = *le boulanger utilise de la pâte pour faire le pain* ⓪ yeast = *levure*
👻 *des pâtes* = pasta
— *pâte à papier* = pulp
— *pâte dentifrice* = toothpaste.

DOUGHNUT (n) (genre de) *beignet* (m) ⓪ cake = *gâteau.*

DOVE (n) *colombe* (f) : the doves are a minority in the Pentagon = *les colombes sont en minorité au Pentagone* ≠ hawk = *faucon.*

DOWDY (adj) *mal fagoté, -e* ⓪ slovenly = *débraillé.*

DOW-JONES AVERAGE/INDEX (n) *indice* (m) Dow Jones, *indice boursier américain basé sur le cours de certaines actions représentatives du marché.*

DOWN (adj) 1/ *déprimé, -e* : down because of the weather = *déprimé à cause du temps* ⓪ low = *qui n'a pas le moral* 2/ *en baisse* : sales/prices are down = *les ventes/les prix sont en baisse* ≠ up = *en hausse*

---

to be down in the dumps = *être au trente-sixième dessous* ≠ to be in seventh heaven = *être au septième ciel*
to be down on s.o. = *battre froid à qqn* ≠ to be in s.o.'s good books = *être dans les petits papiers de qqn*
to be down with (the

flu) = *être au lit avec (la grippe)*
don't kick (a man) when he's down = *on ne frappe pas (un homme) à terre*
a down payment (of $ 100) = *un acompte (de 100 dollars)*
(three) down, (two) to go = *(trois) de faits, encore (deux) à faire.*

DOWN (adv) **to pay ($ 500) down** = *payer (500 dollars) comptant* ≠ to pay in full = *payer entièrement*
down to = *jusqu'à* : everyone from the adults down to the smallest child was afraid = *tout le monde, des adultes jusqu'au plus petit enfant, avait peur*

down with (the government) ! = *à bas (le gouvernement)* !
☠ for the use of "down" after a verb, see the verb.

DOWN (prep) *en bas de* : their house is down the hill = *leur maison est en bas de la colline* ≠ up = *en haut de*
down the street = *au bout de la rue.*

DOWN (to, -ed) *écluser* : to down five Scotches = *écluser cinq whiskies* ⓪ to toss down = *descendre.*

DOWN-AND-OUT (adj) *dans la dèche* : we're not only broke, but truly down-and-out = *nous ne sommes pas seulement fauchés, mais réellement dans la dèche* → POOR.

DOWNBEAT (adj) *morose* : a downbeat view of the future = *une vision morose de l'avenir* ⓪ pessimistic = *pessimiste.*

DOWNCAST (adj) *abattu, -e* : a downcast look = *un regard abattu* ⓪ downhearted = *découragé.*

DOWNER (n) *qqch de déprimant* : listening to them argue was a downer = *c'était déprimant de les entendre se disputer.*

DOWNFALL (n) *chute (f)* : drugs were his downfall = *la drogue a entraîné sa chute* ⓪ ruin = *ruine* ☠ → fall.

DOWNGRADE (to, -d) *minimiser l'importance de, rétrograder* (job) : the government's downgrading the threat of a nuclear war = *le gouvernement minimise l'importance de la menace de guerre nucléaire*, the Colonel was downgraded in front of his men = *le colonel a été rétrogradé devant ses hommes* ≠ to exaggerate = *exagérer.*

DOWNHILL (adv) **to go downhill** = *être sur la pente descendante* (business), *être sur la mauvaise pente* : the business/his health is going downhill = *l'affaire est sur la pente descendante/sa santé est sur la mauvaise pente* ⓪ to go to the dogs = *battre de l'aile.*

DOWN-IN-THE-MOUTH (adj) *malheureux, -euse comme les pierres* = in the doldrums.

DOWNPOUR (n) *déluge (m)* : what a downpour this afternoon ! = *quel déluge cet après-midi !* ⓪ shower = *averse* ☠ → deluge.

DOWNRIGHT (adj) *achevé, -e* : a downright idiot = *un idiot achevé* ⓪ utter = *parfait* **DOWNRIGHT** (adv) *franchement* : downright crazy = *franchement fou* ⓪ really = *vraiment* ☠ → frankly.

DOWNSTAIRS (adv) *en bas* : wait for me downstairs = *attendez-moi en bas* ≠ upstairs = *en haut.*

DOWN-TO-EARTH (adj) *terre à terre* : she married a down-to-earth guy = *elle a épousé un type terre à terre* ⓪ realistic = *réaliste.*

DOWNTOWN (n, adv) *centre (m) ville* : to shop downtown = *faire des courses dans le centre ville* ≠ uptown = *quartier résidentiel.*

DOWNWARD (adj) *à la baisse* : a downward trend = *une tendance à la baisse* ≠ upward = *à la hausse.*

DOWRY (n, -ies) *dot (f)* : dowries are out = *les dots ne se font plus.*

DOZE (to, -d) *sommeiller* : he dozed for an hour = *il a sommeillé pendant une heure* ⓪ to take a nap = *faire un somme*
to doze off (while reading) = *s'assoupir (en lisant)* ⓪ to fall asleep = *s'endormir.*

DOZEN (n) *douzaine (f)* : give me a dozen = *donnez-m'en une douzaine*, half a dozen = *une demi-douzaine*
dozens of (times) = *des dizaines de (fois)* → MANY
☠ *il y a une douzaine d'années* = about twelve years ago.

DRAB (adj, -ber, -best) *terne* : a drab dress/life = *une robe/vie terne* ≠ bright = *vif*, exciting = *passionnant.*

DRAFT (n) **1/** *brouillon (m)* : to make a draft = *faire un brouillon* **2/** *courant (m) d'air* : a draft in the room = *un courant d'air dans la pièce* ⓪ drafty = *plein de courants d'air* **3/** *conscription (f)* (army) : there's no more draft in the United States = *il n'y a plus de conscription aux États-Unis* ⓪ draftee = *conscrit* ≠ AVF = All Volunteer Force = *armée de volontaires*
draft dodger = *insoumis* ⓪ conscientious objector = *objecteur de conscience*
draft board = *conseil de révision.*

DRAFT (to, -ed) **1/** *rédiger* : to draft a bill/a speech = *rédiger un projet de loi/un discours* ☠ → to word **2/** *appeler (sous les drapeaux)* : do they draft women ? = *est-ce qu'on appelle les femmes sous les drapeaux ?*

DRAG (n) *qqn/qqch de rasoir* : the party/he was a drag = *la soirée/il était rasoir* ⓪ a pain in the neck = *casse-pieds*
a drag show = *un spectacle de travelos*
(dressed) in drag = *(habillé) en travelo*
to take a drag = *prendre une taffe* ⓪ puff = *bouffée.*

DRAG (to, -ged) *traîner* : your coat's/the evening's dragging = *votre manteau/la soirée traîne*
to drag s.o. into = *entraîner qqn dans* : why did you drag me into it ? = *pourquoi m'as-tu entraîné là-dedans ?* ⓪ to bring into = *mêler à*
to drag stg out of s.o. = *arracher qqch à qqn* ⓪ to draw stg out of s.o. = *soutirer qqch à qqn*
to drag on = *traîner en longueur* : the meeting dragged on = *la réunion a traîné en longueur* ⓪ to be endless = *être interminable*
☠ *traîner (un mauvais rhume)* = not to be able to shake off (a bad cold)
— *elle laisse traîner ses affaires* = she leaves her things all over the place

— *traîner la jambe* = to walk with difficulty
— *traîner (avec une bande de voyous)* = to hang around (with a tough group).

DRAGON (n) *dragon (m)* : eaten by the dragon = *mangé par le dragon* ① monster = *monstre* ☠ *un dragon de vertu* = a paragon of virtue.

DRAIN (n) *qqch qui épuise* : our constant problems are a drain on my energy = *nos éternels problèmes épuisent mon énergie*
to be going down the drain = *aller à vau-l'eau* : because of the fire all my work/my efforts went down the drain = *à cause de l'incendie, tout mon travail est allé/tous mes efforts sont allés à vau-l'eau*
to throw (one's money/one's youth) down the drain = *ficher (son argent/sa jeunesse) en l'air*.

DRAIN (to, -ed) *pomper* : the argument drained me = *cette dispute m'a pompé*, the resources of the country are being drained = *on est en train de pomper les ressources du pays* ☠ → to pump.

DRAMA (n) *drame (m)* : the play's a drama = *la pièce est un drame* ① melodrama = *mélodrame*

to study drama = *faire de l'art dramatique* = to study dramatics
☠ *ça a tourné au drame* = it turned out tragically.

DRAMATIC (adj) *dramatique, théâtral, -e* (s.o.) : a dramatic speech/personality = *un discours dramatique/une personnalité théâtrale* ① tragic = *tragique*
don't be so dramatic ! = *ne dramatise pas tant !*

DRAMATICS (n pl) *art (m) dramatique* : she's studying dramatics = *elle fait de l'art dramatique*.

DRAMATIST (n) *dramaturge (m, f)* : Harold Pinter is a famous dramatist = *Harold Pinter est un célèbre dramaturge* ① playwright = *auteur dramatique*.

DRAMATIZE (to, -d) *dramatiser* : stop dramatizing everything = *arrête de tout dramatiser* ① to overdo it = *en faire trop*.

DRAPES (n pl) *doubles rideaux (m pl)*.

DRASTIC (adj) *radical, -e, drastique* : drastic changes/decisions = *des changements radicaux/des décisions radicales* = radical changes/decisions.
drastic measures = *des mesures draconiennes* ≠ halfway measures = *des demi-mesures*.

DRAW (n) *qqn/qqch qui attire du monde* : the new comic's a draw = *le nouveau comique attire du monde*

to be/end in a draw = *faire match nul* : the match was a draw = *ils ont fait match nul* ① to end in a tie = *terminer ex aequo* **to be quick on the draw** = *dégainer rapidement* **to beat s.o. to the draw** = *prendre qqn de*	*vitesse* : I was going to invite you to dinner, but you beat me to the draw = *j'allais vous inviter à dîner, mais vous m'avez pris de vitesse* ① to pull the carpet out from under s.o. = *couper l'herbe sous le pied de qqn*.

DRAW (to, drew, drawn) **1/** *dessiner* : draw me a sheep ! = *dessine-moi un mouton !* ① to sketch = *esquisser*

☠ *se dessiner (projets)* = to take shape (plans)	— *dessiner (plans/robes)* = to design (plans/dresses)

2/ *attirer* : the comic draws crowds = *le comique attire les foules* ☠ → to attract
3/ *tirer* : a cart drawn by a horse = *une charrette tirée par un cheval* ☠ *« to draw » est beaucoup moins employé que « to pull »*

to draw away/back = *avoir un mouvement de recul* : she drew away/back when he put his hand on her shoulder = *elle a eu un mouvement de recul quand il lui a mis la main sur l'épaule* **to be drawn into** = *se laisser embarquer dans* : I don't want to be drawn into your problems = *je ne veux pas me laisser embarquer dans vos histoires* ① to	drag into = *entraîner dans* ≠ to stay out of = *rester en dehors de* **to draw on (one's own experience)** = *faire appel à (son expérience personnelle)* **to draw out** = *faire traîner en longueur* : he drew the interview out = *il a fait traîner l'entretien en longueur* ① to protract = *faire traîner* **to draw stg out of s.o.** = *souti-*	*rer qqch à qqn* : to draw information out of s.o. = *soutirer des informations à qqn* ① to worm stg out of s.o. = *tirer les vers du nez à qqn* **to be drawn to (bright men)** = *être attiré par (les hommes brillants)* **to draw up** = *rédiger* : he drew up the contract = *il a rédigé le contrat* ☠ → to word.

DRAWBACK (n) *inconvénient (m)* : the price is a drawback = *le prix est un inconvénient* ① shortcoming = *défaut* ≠ advantage = *avantage* ☠ → inconvenience.

DRAWBRIDGE (n) *pont-levis (m)* : a drawbridge over the moat = *un pont-levis qui enjambait les douves* ① castle = *château*.

DRAWER (n) *tiroir* (m) : the drawer's full = *le tiroir est plein* ⓧ chest of drawers = *commode* ☠ *avoir un polichinelle dans le tiroir* = to be knocked up.

DRAWERS (n pl) *caleçon* (m) : my husband wears drawers = *mon mari porte des caleçons.*

DRAWING (n) **1/** *tirage* (m) au sort : the drawing's on Saturday = *le tirage au sort a lieu samedi* **2/** *dessin* (m) : make me a drawing ! = *fais-moi un dessin !* ⓧ print = *gravure,* charcoal = *fusain* ☠ *pas besoin de me faire un dessin !* = you don't have to draw a picture !
— *dessin animé* = cartoon.

DRAWL (n) *accent* (m) *traînant (du Sud)* : to speak with a drawl = *parler avec un accent traînant.*

DRAWN (adj) **to look drawn** = *avoir les traits tirés* ⓧ to look haggard = *avoir l'air hagard.*

DREAD (n) *épouvante* (f) : the idea of seeing his ex-wife fills him with dread = *l'idée de revoir son ex-femme le remplit d'épouvante* ⓧ terror = *terreur*
to live in dread of (the future) = *vivre dans la hantise de (l'avenir)*
☠ *film d'épouvante* = horror film.

DREAD (to, -ed) *redouter* : I dread seeing my in-laws again = *je redoute de revoir mes beaux-parents* ⓧ to apprehend = *appréhender*
I dread to think that ... = *je frémis à la pensée que ...*

DREADFUL (adj) *épouvantable* : dreadful weather = *temps épouvantable* → AWFUL ≠ wonderful = *merveilleux* **DREADFULLY** (adv) *terriblement* : dreadfully tired = *terriblement fatigué* → VERY.

DREAM (n) **1/** *rêve* (m) : a bad dream = *un mauvais rêve* ⓧ nightmare = *cauchemar*
to have a dream = *faire un rêve*
2/ *splendeur* (f) : her sister/house is a dream = *sa sœur/maison est une splendeur* ≠ nightmare = *cauchemar.*

DREAM (adj) *de rêve* : a dream apartment = *un appartement de rêve.*

DREAM (to, -ed or dreamt) *rêver* : I can dream, can't I ? = *je peux rêver, n'est-ce pas ?* ⓧ to daydream = *rêvasser*
I never dreamt that (he'd do that !) = *je ne me serais jamais douté qu'(il ferait ça !)* ⓧ I never suspected ... = *je n'aurais jamais soupçonné ...*
I wouldn't dream of (telling her) = *il ne me serait jamais venu à l'idée de (le lui dire)*
to dream up = *échafauder* : to dream up excuses = *échafauder des excuses* ⓧ to think up = *imaginer.*

DREAMBOAT (n) *type* (m) *splendide* : her husband's a dreamboat = *son mari est un type splendide* ≠ dog = *boudin.*

DREAMER (n) *rêveur, -euse* : not enough dreamers in the world = *pas assez de rêveurs dans le monde* ⓧ poet = *poète.*

DREAMWORLD (n) **to live in a dreamworld** = *vivre dans ses rêves* ⓧ to live in a world of one's own = *vivre dans un monde à soi.*

DREARY (adj, -ier, iest) *morne* : dreary weather/lives = *un temps morne/des vies mornes* ⓧ dismal = *sinistre.*

DRECK (n inv) *saloperies* (f pl) : he bought a lot of dreck at the flea market = *il a acheté un tas de saloperies au marché aux puces* ⓧ junk = *cochonneries* ☠ *faire des saloperies à qqn* = to do s.o. dirty.

DREGS (n pl) **the dregs of society** = *la lie de la société* ⓧ scum = *racaille.*

DRENCH (to, -ed) **to be drenched** = *se faire saucer* : what a downpour ! I'm drenched ! = *quel déluge ! je me suis fait saucer !* ⓧ to be wet through = *être trempé jusqu'aux os.*

DRESS (n, -es) *robe* (f) : I bought a new dress = *j'ai acheté une nouvelle robe*
dress designer = *modéliste*
dress rehearsal = *générale* ⓧ the opening night = *la première*
☠ *robe de chambre* = bathrobe/robe.

DRESS (to, -ed) *s'habiller* : I don't like the way she dresses = *je n'aime pas sa façon de s'habiller*
to be dressed to kill = *être sur son trente et un* ⓧ to be spruced up = *être tiré à quatre épingles*
to dress for = *s'habiller pour* : do we have to dress for dinner ? = *est-ce qu'il faut s'habiller pour le dîner ?*
to dress up = *broder* : when she told the story, she dressed it up = *elle a brodé en racontant l'histoire* ⓧ to build up = *en rajouter* ☠ *broder (robe)* = to embroider
to get dressed = *s'habiller* : you'd better get dressed ; it's getting late = *tu devrais t'habiller ; il se fait tard* ≠ to get undressed = *se déshabiller*
to get dressed up = *se mettre sur son trente et un* : on Sundays we get all dressed up and go to a restaurant = *le dimanche nous nous mettons tous sur notre trente et un et nous allons au restaurant* ⓧ to get dolled up = *se pomponner.*

DRESSER (n) *coiffeuse* (f) : a bed, a dresser and an armchair in the bedroom = *un lit, une coiffeuse et un fauteuil dans la chambre à coucher* ☠ → hairdresser.

DRESSING (n) *assaisonnement* (m) (salad) : this salad has a great dressing = *cette salade a un assaisonnement délicieux* ⓧ sauce = ←.

DRESSMAKER (n) *couturier, -ère* ⓧ seamstress = *retoucheuse.*

DRESSY (adj, -ier, -iest) *habillé, -e* : your outfit's too dressy = *ton ensemble est trop habillé* ≠ casual = *décontracté.*

DRIFT (n) *glissement* (m) : there's a drift to the left = *il y a un glissement à gauche*

I didn't get the drift of (what you were saying) = *je n'ai pas saisi le sens de (ce que vous étiez en train de dire)* ≠ I got it = *j'ai pigé.*

DRIFT (to, -ed) **1/** *ne pas arriver à se fixer* : he's been drifting since he dropped out of school = *il n'arrive pas à se fixer depuis qu'il a abandonné ses études* ⊕ to knock around = *rouler sa bosse* **2/** *dériver* : the boat's drifting = *le bateau dérive* **3/** *glisser* : the country's drifting left = *le pays est en train de glisser à gauche* ☠ → to slip
to drift apart = *s'éloigner* : our family was close but now we've drifted apart = *notre famille était proche, mais maintenant nous nous sommes éloignés les uns des autres* ≠ to come together = *se rapprocher* ☠ *s'éloigner du sujet* = to stray from the subject
to drift from (job) to (job) = *aller de (boulot) en (boulot)*
to drift into (war) = *glisser vers (la guerre).*

DRIFTER (n) *qqn à la dérive* : a lot of drifters on the West Coast = *beaucoup de gens à la dérive sur la côte Ouest.*

DRILL (n) **1/** *colle (f)* : a drill on verbs = *une colle sur les verbes* ⊕ exam = *examen* ☠ → glue **2/** *perceuse (f)* : an electric drill = *une perceuse électrique.*

DRILL (to, -ed) *forer* : to drill an oil well = *forer un puits de pétrole*
to drill in(to) = *se mettre dans la tête* : the importance of being a virgin was drilled into her = *on lui a mis dans la tête qu'il était important d'être vierge.*

DRINK (n) **1/** *boisson (f)* : I'd like a cool drink = *j'aimerais une boisson fraîche* ⊕ refreshment = *rafraîchissement* **2/** *verre (m)* (alcohol) : come in and have a drink ! = *viens prendre un verre !* ⊕ cocktail = ←, one for the road = *le coup de l'étrier*, a nightcap = *un dernier*

verre, hard liquor = *alcool fort*, after-dinner drink = *digestif*, apéritif = *apéritif* ☠ → glass
I could do with a drink = *je prendrais bien un verre* = **I could stand a drink**
hard ≠ **soft drink** = *boisson alcoolisée* ≠ *non alcoolisée*
to spike a drink = *corser une boisson*
that calls for a drink ! = *ça s'arrose !*

DRINK (to, drank, drunk) *boire* : you drink too much = *vous buvez trop*, the baby drinks his bottle = *le bébé boit son biberon* ⊕ to gulp down = *engloutir*
I'll drink to that ! = *je lève mon verre à cette occasion !*
to drink in (the beauty of the landscape/compliments) = *se délecter de (la beauté du paysage/compliments)* ⊕ to lap up = *boire comme du petit lait*
to drink out of (a glass) = *boire dans (un verre)*
to drink up = *vider son verre*
☠ *qui a bu boira* = a leopard doesn't change its spots
— *il y a à boire et à manger (dans son livre)* = there's both good and bad (in his book).

DRINKER (n) *buveur, -euse* : I've never been much of a drinker = *je n'ai jamais été un vrai buveur*
to be a good ≠ **bad drinker** = *avoir le vin gai* ≠ *mauvais* → DRUNK.

DRIP (n) *minus (m, f)* : her date's a drip = *le type avec qui elle sort est un minus* ⊕ nothing = *nullité.*

DRIP (to, -ped) *goutter* : the tap's dripping = *le robinet goutte* ⊕ to leak = *fuir*
I'm dripping = *je suis en eau* ⊕ I'm soaked = *je suis trempé.*

DRIP-DRY (adj) *qui ne se repasse pas* : drip-dry clothes = *des vêtements qui ne se repassent pas.*

DRIVE (n) **1/** *chemin (m) d'accès* : a drive leading to the house = *un chemin d'accès à la maison* **2/** *campagne (f)* : a drive to raise money for cancer = *une campagne pour collecter de l'argent pour le cancer* = a campaign to raise money for cancer ☠ → campaign	
it's a (four-hour) drive to (Miami) = *il y a (quatre heures) de voiture jusqu'à (Miami)* **it's a long** ≠ **short drive (from here to Washington)** = *il y a un long* ≠ *court trajet (d'ici à Washington)*	**she has a lot of drive** = *elle en veut* ⊕ she has a lot of ambition = *elle a beaucoup d'ambition* **let's go for a drive** = *allons faire un tour en voiture* ⊕ let's go for a spin = *allons faire une balade en voiture.*
DRIVE (to, drove, driven) **1/** *conduire* : can you drive ? = *est-ce que vous savez conduire ?*	
☠ *se conduire bien* ≠ *mal* = to behave well ≠ badly	— *conduire ses troupes* = to lead one's troops
2/ *aller en voiture* : do you want to walk or drive ? = *vous voulez y aller à pied ou en voiture ?*	
to be driven = *avoir le feu sacré*	**you're driving me mad/crazy** = *tu me rends fou*

what are you driving at ? = *où voulez-vous en venir ?* = what are you aiming at ?
to drive away = 1/ *faire fuir* : his temper drove her away = *son mauvais caractère l'a fait fuir* ⬭ to repel = *repousser* 2/ *démarrer* : he was furious and drove away without me = *il était furieux et a démarré sans moi* ☠ → to start
to drive back = 1/ *revenir en voiture* : we took the plane to Miami and drove back = *nous*

avons pris l'avion jusqu'à Miami et sommes revenus en voiture 2/ *refouler* : to drive back enemy troops = *refouler les troupes ennemies* ⬭ to beat back = *faire reculer* ☠ → to hold back
to drive by = *passer en voiture* : we didn't stop in Baltimore, just drove by = *nous ne nous sommes pas arrêtés à Baltimore, nous sommes juste passés en voiture*
to drive on = *continuer sa route* : he stopped the car for a

minute and then drove on = *il a arrêté la voiture un instant, puis a continué sa route*
to drive to (work) = *aller en voiture (au bureau)*
to drive s.o. to = *pousser qqn à* : his wife's cheating drove him to drink = *le fait que sa femme le trompe l'a poussé à boire*
to drive up = *faire monter* : to drive oil prices up = *faire monter le prix du pétrole* ⬭ to jack up = *faire grimper.*

DRIVE-IN (n) *drive-in (m), cinéma (m) de plein air.*

DRIVE-IN (adj) *où on est servi dans sa voiture* : a drive-in bank/restaurant = *une banque/un restaurant où on est servi dans sa voiture.*

DRIVEL (n inv) *inepties (f pl)* : I've never heard such drivel ! = *je n'ai jamais entendu de telles inepties !* ⬭ nonsense = *bêtises.*

DRIVER (n) *chauffeur (m), conducteur, -trice* (bus, train) : the driver's drunk = *le chauffeur/le conducteur est ivre* ≠ passenger = *passager*
driver's license = *permis de conduire*

to be in the driver's seat = *tenir les commandes* ☠ *chauffeur* → chauffeur.

DRIVEWAY (n) *allée (f) de garage.*

DRIVING (adj) **driving force** = *élément moteur* : he's the driving force of the party = *c'est l'élément moteur du parti* ⬭ mainstay = *pilier*
driving instructor = *moniteur d'auto-école*
driving lessons = *leçons de conduite*
driving license (GB) = *permis de conduire*
driving school = *auto-école.*

DRIZZLE (to, -d) *bruiner* : it's been drizzling all day = *il a bruiné toute la journée* ⬭ to rain = *pleuvoir.*

DROP (n) *goutte (f)* : just a drop of Scotch = *juste une goutte de whisky* ⬭ pinch = *pincée,* touch = *brin*

at the drop of a hat = *pour un oui, pour un non* : he gets angry at the drop of a hat = *il se met en colère pour un oui, pour un non* **a drop in (temperature/oil prices)** = *une chute de (la température/des prix du pétrole)* ≠ a rise in =	*une hausse de* **a drop in the bucket** = *une goutte d'eau dans la mer* **to have a drop too much** = *avoir un verre dans le nez* → DRUNK
☠ *se ressembler comme deux gouttes d'eau* = to be like two peas in a pod	— *c'est la goutte d'eau qui fait déborder le vase !* = that's the last straw ! — *avoir la goutte* = to have gout.

DROP (to, -ped) 1/ *faire tomber* : I dropped the book = *j'ai fait tomber le livre* 2/ *tomber* : the book/the temperature dropped = *le livre est tombé/la température est tombée* ☠ → to fall

to drop s.o. = *laisser tomber qqn* : she dropped him when she found out he was on drugs = *elle l'a laissé tomber quand elle s'est rendu compte qu'il se droguait* ⬭ to dump = *larguer*
to drop behind = *passer derrière* : France's steel production has dropped behind Germany's = *la production française*

d'acier est passée derrière celle de l'Allemagne ⬭ to lag behind = *être à la traîne*
to drop in (on) s.o. = *passer (à l'improviste) chez qqn* : let's drop in on Jane later ! = *si on passait chez Jane tout à l'heure ?*
to drop off = *ne pas cesser de diminuer* : sales have been dropping off = *les ventes n'ont pas*

cessé de diminuer
to drop s.o. off = *déposer qqn (en voiture)* : can you drop me off at the bank ? = *est-ce que vous pouvez me déposer à la banque ?* ⬭ to give s.o. a ride = *emmener qqn en voiture*
to drop out of = *laisser tomber* : he dropped out of school = *il a laissé tomber l'école*

DROPOUT (n) étudiant, -e qui abandonne ses études en cours d'année.

DROUGHT (n) sécheresse (f) : months of drought = des mois de sécheresse ≠ monsoon = mousson ☠ sécheresse (ton/style) = dryness/harshness (tone/style).

DROWN (to, -ed) (se) noyer : the child drowned = l'enfant s'est noyé

to drown out = noyer : his voice was drowned out by the noise = sa voix s'est noyée dans le bruit.

DROWSE (to, -d) somnoler : I drowsed during the lesson = j'ai somnolé pendant le cours ⓓ to doze = sommeiller.

DROWSY (adj, -ier, -iest) somnolent, -e : drowsy after a copious meal = somnolent après un repas copieux ⓓ tired = fatigué.

DRUG (n) drogue (f) : coffee's my drug = le café, c'est ma drogue

barbiturate = barbiturique **cocaine** = cocaïne **cold turkey** = le fait de décrocher brutalement **a dealer** = un dealer **dope** = came/dope **a downer** = un downer/un calmant **drug addict** = dro-	gué/toxicomane **drug addiction** = toxicomanie **a fix** = un fix **grass** = herbe **hard** ≠ **soft drugs** = drogues dures ≠ douces **hash** = hasch **head** = toxico **heroin** = héroïne	**horse** ≒ ← **junkie** = ← **marijuana** = ← **morphine** = ← **the narcs** = les stups **narcotics** = narcotiques/stupéfiants **opium** = ← **overdose** = **o.d.** = overdose **pot** = marie-jeanne	**a pothead** = un camé **to shoot up** = se shooter **snow** = neige/blanche **speed** = amphétamines **to take drugs** = se droguer **a trip** = un trip **uppers** = des excitants.

DRUG (to, -ged) droguer : they drugged the young girl = ils ont drogué la jeune fille ☠ elle se drogue = she takes drugs.

DRUGSTORE (n) pharmacie (f) : get some aspirin at the drugstore = va chercher de l'aspirine à la pharmacie ☠ "le drugstore" is a fun place which sells various items and includes a drugstore **DRUGGIST** (n) pharmacien, -enne.

DRUM (n) tambour (m) : a Tahitian drum = un tambour tahitien ⓓ drummer = joueur de tambour/batteur

to play the drums = jouer de la batterie ☠ une porte tambour = a revolving door.

DRUM (to, -med) **to drum into** = seriner : they drummed into her their ideas on education = ils lui ont seriné leurs idées sur l'éducation ⓓ to hammer away = rabâcher

to drum up = racoler : the sales will drum up business = les soldes vont racoler la clientèle ☠ → to solicit.

DRUNK (n) ivrogne, -esse : her husband's a drunk = son mari est un ivrogne = her husband's a drunkard → DRUNK.

DRUNK (adj, -er, -est) ivre, saoul, -e : I was drunk last night = j'étais saoul/ivre hier soir

— GROUP : DRUNK = IVRE, SAOUL —

an alcoholic = un alcoolique **a bad drinker** = qqn qui a le vin mauvais **a barfly** = un pilier de bistrot **to be blind** = être noir **to be bombed** = être pété **to booze (it up)** = picoler **a boozer** = un pochard **to be dead drunk** = être ivre mort **to drink like a fish** = boire comme un trou **to drink s.o. under the table** = faire rouler qqn sous la table **a drinking bout** = une beuve-	rie/une soûlerie **to be drunk** = être ivre/saoul **a drunk** = un ivrogne **a drunkard** = un ivrogne **to be drunk as a lord** = être saoul comme un Polonais **to feel like the morning after the night before** = avoir mal au cheveux **to be fond of one's drink/bottle** = avoir une bonne descente **to get drunk** = se saouler **to get loaded** = se beurrer/se bourrer	**to go barhopping** = faire la tournée des bars **to go to s.o.'s head** = monter à la tête de qqn **to hang one on** = prendre une cuite/se cuiter **to have a drop too much** = avoir un verre dans le nez **to have a hangover** = avoir la gueule de bois **to have one too many** = avoir bu un coup de trop **to have three sheets in the wind** = avoir du vent dans les voiles

a **heavy drinker** = *un gros buveur/un picoleur*
to be high = *être parti*
to be high as a kite = *avoir un coup dans l'aile/le nez*
to hit the bottle = *caresser la bouteille*
to be intoxicated = *être en état d'ivresse*
to like one's liquor = *avoir la dalle en pente*

to be lit up (GB) = *être éméché*
to be loaded = *être bourré*
a **lush** = *un sac à vin*
to be out = *être dans les vapes*
to be pie-eyed = *être rond (comme une queue de pelle/comme une bille)*
to be pissed = *être pété*
to be plastered = *être schlass*
to be potted = *être paf*
to be smashed = *être plein*

comme une outre/barrique
to be soused = *être beurré*
to be stoned = *être pinté*
to tie one on = *s'enivrer*
to be tight = *être gai*
a **tippler** = *un soûlographe*
to be tipsy = *être pompette*
a **wino** = *un poivrot*
to be zonked = *prendre une biture.*

DRY (adj, -ier, iest) *sec, sèche* : a dry climate = *un climat sec* ≠ wet = *mouillé*
dry dock = *cale sèche*
dry humor = *humour caustique* ≠ slapstick = *tarte à la crème*
dry ice = *neige carbonique*
dry run = *exercice simulé*
☠ *je suis à sec* = I'm broke
— *sec ou avec de la glace ?* = straight or on the rocks ?

DRY (adv) **to milk s.o. dry** = *saigner qqn à blanc* : she milked her lover dry = *elle a saigné son amant à blanc* ⓪ to milk = *considérer comme un vache à lait.*

DRY (to, -ied) *sécher* : my hair's drying = *mes cheveux sont en train de sécher*
dry up ! = *écrase !* → BUZZ OFF !
to dry up = *se tarir* : the river dried up = *la rivière s'est tarie* ☠ *sur ce sujet, il ne tarit pas* = on that subject, he doesn't stop
☠ *sécher ses cours* = to cut classes.

DRY-CLEAN (to, -ed) *nettoyer à sec* ⓪ dry-cleaner = *teinturier.*

DRYLY (adv) *sèchement* : to answer dryly = *répondre sèchement.*

DUAL (adj) *double* : dual nationality = *double nationalité* ☠ → double.

DUB (to, -bed) *doubler* : to dub a film = *doubler un film* ⓪ to subtitle = *sous-titrer* ☠ → to double **DUBBING** (n) *doublage (m)* ⓪ subtitle = *sous-titre.*

DUBIOUS (adj) *douteux, -euse* : dubious business transactions = *des transactions d'affaires douteuses* ⓪ fishy = *louche* ☠ → doubtful
I'm dubious about (our chances of winning) = *j'ai des doutes sur (nos chances de succès).*

DUCK (n) *canard (m)* : that restaurant has great duck = *ce restaurant fait un canard fabuleux* ⓪ duckling = *caneton*
go fuck a duck ! = *va te faire cuire un œuf !* → BUZZ OFF !
to take to stg like a duck takes to water = *mordre immédiatement à qqch* : she took to tennis like a duck takes to water = *elle a mordu immédiatement au tennis* ☠ *il fait un froid de canard* = it's ice-cold
— *un canard (journal)* = a newspaper.

DUCK (to, -ed) *esquiver* : to duck a blow/a question = *esquiver un coup/une question* ⓪ to hedge = *répondre à côté* ☠ *s'esquiver* = to sneak away.

DUD (n) *qqn/qqch à la noix* : the play was a dud = *c'était une pièce à la noix*, as a lover he's a dud = *c'est vraiment un amant à la noix* ≠ the cat's meow = *bath.*

DUDE (n) *citadin de l'Est (correspondant à Parigot)* ⓪ city dweller = *citadin* ≠ cowboy = *cow-boy.*

DUDS (n pl) *sapes (f pl), frusques (f pl)* : she always wears expensive duds = *elle porte toujours des sapes/frusques vachement chères.*

DUE (n) *dû (m)* : to claim one's due = *réclamer son dû* ⓪ right = *droit*
to take stg as one's due = *considérer qqch comme son dû.*

DUE (adj) *dû, due* : the bill's due on the fifth = *la facture est due le cinq* ⓪ payable = ←
due at = *prévu à/pour* : the plane's due at noon = *l'arrivée de l'avion est prévue à midi*
to be due to = *être dû à* : his success was due to years of hard work = *son succès était dû à des années de travail acharné*
to be due to (retire)/for (retirement) = *devoir en principe (prendre sa retraite)*
I'm due there = *on m'y attend*
in due course = *en temps utile* : you'll be promoted in due course = *vous serez promu en temps utile* ⓪ **in due time** = *en temps voulu*
with (all) due respect = *avec (tout) le respect que je vous (lui, etc.) dois.*

DUEL (n) *duel (m)* : a duel at dawn = *un duel à l'aube* ⓪ sword = *épée*, witness = *témoin.*

DUES (n pl) *cotisation (f)* : the club's dues = *la cotisation du club* = the club's membership fee.

DUET (n) *duo (m)* ⓪ solo = ←.

DUE TO (prep) **1/** *en raison de* : the meeting was put off due to the strikes = *la réunion a été reportée en raison des grèves* ⓪ because of = *à cause de* **2/** *grâce à* : due to his father's help, he finally got the job = *grâce à l'intervention de son père, il a finalement obtenu le poste* = thanks to ≠ in spite of = *malgré.*

DUKE (n) *duc (m)* ⓪ duchess = *duchesse.*

DULL (adj) *assommant, -e*: a dull film/guy = *un film/ type assommant* ≠ interesting = *intéressant* ☠ *ce que tu peux être assommant !* = you're a pain !

DULY (adv) *dûment*: duly authorized = *dûment autorisé*.

DUMB (adj, -er, -est) *bête*: I never saw such a dumb guy = *je n'ai jamais vu un type aussi bête* → STUPID ≠ smart = *intelligent*
he's as dumb as they come = *il est bête comme ses pieds* → STUPID
to be playing dumb = *faire celui qui ne sait rien*
to be struck dumb = *être sans voix*: she was struck dumb by surprise = *la surprise l'a laissée sans voix* ⓪ astounded = *époustouflé*
☠ *bête comme chou* = as easy as pie.

DUMBBELL (n) *ballot* (m): his new assistant's a dumbbell = *son nouvel assistant est un ballot* → STUPID.

DUMBFOUNDED (adj) *ahuri, -e*: I was too dumbfounded to answer = *j'étais trop ahuri pour répondre* ⓪ amazed = *stupéfié*.

DUMBWAITER (n) *monte-charge* (m): a dumbwaiter between the kitchen in the basement and the dining-room above = *un monte-charge entre la cuisine au sous-sol et la salle à manger au-dessus*.

DUMMY (n, -ies) 1/ *banane* (f): that's not what I said, dummy ! = *ce n'est pas ce que j'ai dit, banane !* → STUPID ☠ → banana 2/ *faux* (m): this gun's a dummy = *ce pistolet est un faux* ☠ → fake.

DUMP. (n) *endroit* (m) *pourri*: she lives in a dump = *elle habite un endroit pourri* ≠ palace = *palais*
city dump = *dépotoir municipal*.

DUMP (to, -ed) *flanquer dehors*: the party dumped him = *le parti l'a flanqué dehors* ⓪ to get rid of = *se débarrasser de*, to chuck = *balancer*.
to dump on = *cracher sur*: she's always dumping on her in-laws = *elle passe son temps à cracher sur sa belle-famille* ⓪ to put down = *débiner*.

DUMPY (adj, -ier, -iest) *boulot, -otte*: a short, dumpy guy = *un type petit et boulot* ≠ lanky = *efflanqué*.

DUNCE (n) *cancre* (m): a dunce in every class = *un cancre dans chaque classe* → STUPID
dunce cap = *bonnet d'âne*.

DUNE (n) *dune* (f): sand dune = *dune de sable* ⓪ desert = *désert*.

DUNGAREES (n pl) *jean* (m): what a sexy pair of dungarees ! = *quel jean sexy !* ⓪ overalls = *salopette*.

DUNGEON (n) *cachot* (m), *oubliettes* (f pl): slaves died in dungeons = *les esclaves mouraient dans des cachots/des oubliettes*.

DUNK (to, -ed) *tremper*: dunk your toast in the coffee = *trempe ton toast dans le café* ☠ → to soak.

DUPE (to, -d) *duper*: he duped his client = *il a dupé son client* → TO HUSTLE.

DUPLEX (n) *duplex* (m): to live in a duplex = *vivre dans un duplex* ⓪ townhouse = *hôtel particulier*.

DUPLICATE (n) *duplicata* (m): a duplicate of the contract = *un duplicata du contrat* ⓪ copy = *copie* **DUPLICATE** (to, -d) *faire un double*.

DUPLICITY (n, -ies) *duplicité* (f) ⓪ hypocrisy = *hypocrisie*.

DURABLE (adj) *durable*: a durable friendship = *une amitié durable* = a lasting friendship.

DURATION (n) *durée* (f): for the duration of the summer = *pour la durée de l'été*.

DURESS (n) **under duress** = *contraint et forcé*: I would only marry him under duress = *je ne l'épouserais que contrainte et forcée* ⓪ over my dead body = *il faudra me passer sur le corps*.

DURING (prep) *pendant, durant*: we watch TV during dinner = *on regarde la télé pendant/durant le dîner*
☠ *il a été marié pendant dix ans* = he was married for ten years
— *il est venu pendant que nous mangions* = he came while/as we were eating.

DUSK (n) *crépuscule* (m): we'll leave at dusk = *nous partirons au crépuscule* ⓪ nightfall = *tombée de la nuit*.

DUST (n) *poussière* (f): a lot of dust on the shelves = *beaucoup de poussière sur les étagères* ⓪ to dust = *épousseter* ☠ *30 dollars et des poussières* = 30-odd dollars.

DUTCH (n pl) **the Dutch** = *les Hollandais/les Néerlandais* ⓪ Dutchman = *Hollandais*, Dutchwoman = *Hollandaise*
to be in Dutch with (the teacher) = *ne pas être dans les bonnes grâces du (professeur)*.

DUTCH (adj) *hollandais, -e, néerlandais, -e*: he's Dutch = *il est hollandais/néerlandais*
Dutch treat = *chacun paie sa part*
to talk to s.o. like a Dutch uncle = *faire la morale à qqn* ⓪ to lecture = *sermonner*.

DUTCH (adv) **to go dutch** = *payer chacun sa part*: when I go out with my boyfriend, we go dutch = *quand je sors avec mon petit ami, chacun paie sa part* ≠ to treat s.o. = *inviter qqn*.

DUTIFUL (adj) *qui fait son devoir*: she is a dutiful daughter = *c'est une fille qui fait son devoir* ⓪ obedient = *obéissant*.

DUTY (n, -ies) *devoir* (m): it's almost a duty to have orgasms today = *c'est presque un devoir d'avoir des orgasmes aujourd'hui* ⓪ responsibility = *responsabilité*
to be on ≠ **off duty** = *être de service* ≠ *ne pas être de service/avoir quartier libre* (army)
duty free = *hors-taxe*

import ≠ **export duty** = *taxe à l'importation* ≠ *à l'exportation*

to pay duty (on the goods) = *payer des droits de douane (sur les marchandises)* ⓓ **tax** = *impôt*
☠ *devoir (école)* = homework.

DWARF (n, -s or -ves) *nain, -e :* Snow White and the Seven Dwarves = *Blanche-Neige et les sept nains* = midget ≠ giant = *géant*
☠ « *dwarf* » *est un nain difforme alors que* « midget » *est une très petite personne.*

DWELLING (n) *demeure (f) :* ssordid dwellings = *des demeures sordides* ⓓ lodgings = *logements.*

DWELL ON (to, -ed) *s'appesantir sur :* stop dwelling on your own problems so much = *cessez de vous appesantir autant sur vos problèmes personnels* ⓓ to mull over = *retourner dans sa tête.*

DWINDLE (to, -d) *décroître :* our supplies are dwindling = *nos réserves décroissent* ⓓ to diminish = *diminuer* ≠ to increase = *augmenter.*

DYE (n) *teinture (f) :* black dye = *teinture noire* **DYE** (to, -d) *teindre :* to dye one's hair = *se teindre les cheveux* ⓓ to color = *colorer.*

DYED-IN-THE-WOOL (adj) *bon teint :* a dyed-in-the-wool Republican = *un républicain bon teint* ⓓ die-hard = *jusqu'au-boutiste.*

DYKE (n) *gouine (f) :* a club for dykes = *un club de gouines* ≠ queer = *pédé*
bull dyke ≠ **butch dyke** = *lesbienne mec* ≠ *lesbienne julie.*

DYNAMIC (adj) *dynamique :* a dynamic person = *une personne dynamique* ⓓ enterprising = *entreprenant* ≠ lackadaisical = *indolent.*

DYNAMICS (n pl) *dynamique (f) :* who understands the dynamics of love ? = *qui comprend la dynamique de l'amour ?*

DYNAMISM (n) *dynamisme (m) :* she's full of dynamism = *elle est pleine de dynamisme* ⓓ get-up-and-go = *fougue.*

DYNAMITE (n) *dynamite (f) :* to blow up a bridge with dynamite = *faire sauter un pont à de la dynamite* **DYNAMITE** (to, -d) *dynamiter :* to dynamite a building = *dynamiter un immeuble.*

DYNAMITE (adj) *génial, -e :* his cooking/his broad is dynamite = *sa cuisine/sa nana est géniale* → WONDERFUL ≠ awful = *affreux.*

DYNAMO (n) *force (f) de la nature :* her brother's a dynamo = *son frère est une force de la nature* ⓓ live wire = *vif-argent.*

DYNASTY (n, -ies) *dynastie (f) :* the Rockfeller dynasty = *la dynastie Rockfeller* ⓓ clan = ←.

EACH (pron) *chacun, -e* : I have two brothers and each is divorced = *j'ai deux frères et chacun est divorcé* ≠ both = *tous les deux*

each and every one = *tout un chacun* **each of us** = *chacun de nous/d'entre nous* **each one** = *chacun* **to each his own** = *chacun ses goûts* ⓧ that's what makes for horse racing = *tous les goûts sont dans la*	nature **each other** = *se* : they often write to each other = *ils s'écrivent souvent* = they often write to one another, they love each other = *ils s'aiment* = they love one another ☠ → myself.

EACH (adv) *chacun, -e* : the books cost a dollar each = *les livres coûtent un dollar chacun* = the books cost a dollar apiece.

EACH (adj) *chaque* : each book has 200 pages = *chaque livre a 200 pages* ⓧ every = *tous les* ☠ *à chaque jour suffit sa peine* = let's call it a day
— *chaque chose en son temps* = everything in good time.

EAGER (adj) **eager to (help)** = *désireux d'(aider)* ⓧ gung ho = *tout feu tout flamme.*

EAGLE (n) *aigle (m)* ⓧ hawk = *faucon*, buzzard = *buse* ☠ *ce n'est pas un aigle* = he's no genius.

EAR (n) *oreille (f)* ⓧ deaf = *sourd*, eardrum = *tympan*, earache = *mal d'oreille*

to be coming out of one's ears = *sortir par les yeux* : this work's coming out of my ears = *ce travail me sort par les yeux* ⓧ I've had it = *j'en ai plein le dos* **to be up to one's ears**	**(in work)** = *avoir (du travail) à ne savoir qu'en faire* ⓧ to be swamped with = *être débordé de* **to be up to one's ears in debt** = *être endetté jusqu'au cou* → POOR

to bend s.o.'s ear = *casser les oreilles à qqn* ⓧ to harass = *harceler* **to chew/talk s.o.'s ears off** = *rebattre les oreilles à qqn* **my ears are burning** = *les oreilles me tintent* **to have an ear for** = *avoir de l'oreille* ≠ to be tone-deaf = *ne pas avoir d'oreille* **to keep one's ears open** = *ouvrir grand les oreilles* **to lend an ear** = *prê-*ter *l'oreille* ⓧ to listen = *écouter* **to prick up one's ears** = *dresser l'oreille* **to play it by ear** = *voir le moment venu* : let's not make plans, we'll play it by ear = *ne faisons pas de projet, nous verrons le moment venu* ⓧ to improvise = *improviser* **it went in one ear and out the other** = *cela lui est entré par une oreille et sorti par l'autre*

☠ *se faire tirer l'oreille* = to have to be begged to do stg
— *tu commences à m'échauffer les oreilles* = you're getting on my nerves.

EARLIEST (n) **at the earliest** = *au plus tôt* : she'll come Friday at the earliest = *elle arrivera vendredi au plus tôt.*

EARLY (adj, -ier, -iest) 1/ *en avance* : you're early today = *vous êtes en avance aujourd'hui* ≠ late = *en retard* 2/ *de bonne heure* : an early dinner = *un dîner de bonne heure* ≠ late = *tardif* **early bird** = *matinal* ≠ night owl = *oiseau de nuit* **the early bird catches the worm** = *l'avenir/le monde appartient à ceux qui se lèvent tôt* **early** ≠ **late riser** = *lève-tôt* ≠ *tard.*

EARLY (adv) 1/ *en avance* : he showed up two hours early = *il s'est pointé deux heures en avance* ≠ late = *en retard* 2/ *tôt, de bonne heure* : to get up early = *se lever de bonne heure/tôt* ≠ late = *tard* **early to bed, early to rise makes a man healthy, wealthy and wise** = *à qui se lève tôt matin, Dieu aide et prête main* ☠ *ce n'est pas trop tôt* = it's not too soon
— *tôt ou tard* = sooner or later.

EARMARK (to, -ed) **to be earmarked for =** *être destiné à* : these funds are earmarked for the purchase of more bombs = *cet argent est destiné à l'achat de bombes supplémentaires.*

EARN (to, -ed) **1/** *gagner* : to earn a lot of money = *gagner beaucoup d'argent* = to make a lot of money ☠ → to win **2/** *mériter* : you earned your vacation = *tu as mérité tes vacances* ☠ → to merit.

EARNEST (n) **in earnest =** *le plus sérieusement du monde* : he asked me in earnest to sleep with his wife = *il m'a demandé le plus sérieusement du monde de coucher avec sa femme.*

EARNEST (adj) *sérieux, -euse* : an earnest answer = *une réponse sérieuse* ⑩ sincere = *sincère* ☠ → serious.

EARNINGS (n pl) *gains (m pl)* : monthly earnings = *gains mensuels* ⑩ salary = *salaire* ☠ → gain.

EARPHONES (n pl) *écouteurs (m pl)* : his earphones glued to his ears = *ses écouteurs collés aux oreilles* ⑩ loudspeakers = *haut-parleurs.*

EARRING (n) *boucle (f) d'oreille* : gold earrings = *des boucles d'oreille en or* ⑩ pierced ear = *oreille percée.*

EARTH (n) **1/** *Terre (f)* : life on earth = *la vie sur Terre* ⑩ planet = *planète*, world = *monde* **2/** *terre (f)* : the vegetables were planted in rich earth = *les légumes ont été plantés dans une terre riche*
that'll bring him down to earth = *cela lui remettra les pieds sur terre*
to come down to earth = *revenir sur terre* ≠ to be in the clouds = *être dans les nuages*
where on earth (have you been) ? = *où diable (étiez-vous) ?*
why on earth (did you do that) ? = *pourquoi diable (avez-vous fait ça) ?*
☠ *acheter de la terre* = to buy land
— *tomber par terre* = to fall down
— *vouloir rentrer sous terre* = to want to hide one's head in shame
— *j'ai tout fichu par terre* = I blew.

EARTHLY (adj, -ier, -iest) **for no earthly reason =** *sans raison aucune* ≠ on purpose = *exprès.*

EARTHQUAKE (n) *tremblement (m) de terre* ⑩ tidal wave = *raz de marée.*

EARTHSHAKING (adj) *qui change le cours du monde* : the news isn't exactly earthshaking = *cette nouvelle ne va pas changer le cours du monde.*

EARTHY (adj, -ier, -iest) *rustique* (things), *sain, -e et décontract* (people).

EASE (n) **at ease =** *à l'aise* : I don't feel at ease with my in-laws = *je ne me sens pas à l'aise avec mes beaux-parents* ≠ ill at ease = *mal à l'aise*
at ease ! = *repos !* ≠ attention ! = *garde-à-vous !*
with ease = *aisément* : she won the race with ease = *elle a aisément gagné la course*
☠ *en prendre à son aise* = to be a little too offhand
— *être à l'aise (argent)* = to be well-off.

EASE (to, -ed) **to ease s.o. out (of his job) =** *évincer qqn (de son travail)* ⑩ to oust = *vider*
to ease up = *être plus calme* : I'll take a week off when business eases up = *je prendrai une semaine de vacances quand les affaires seront plus calmes.*

EASEL (n) *chevalet (m)* : an unfinished painting on the easel = *un tableau inachevé sur le chevalet* ⑩ canvas = *toile.*

EASILY (adv) **1/** *facilement* : I can finish in an hour easily = *je peux facilement finir en une heure* **2/** *de loin* : he's easily the richest guy here = *c'est de loin l'homme le plus riche d'ici.*

EAST (n, adj) *est (m)* ≠ West = *ouest*
(Lower) East Side = *quartier des immigrants pauvres à New York*
(Upper) East Side = *quartier résidentiel chic à New York.*

EASTER (n) *Pâques (f pl)* : Easter egg = *œuf de Pâques* ⑩ Passover = *la Pâque juive*
Easter Monday = *lundi de Pâques*
☠ *à Pâques ou à la Trinité* = in a month of Sundays.

EASTERN (adj) *de l'est* : Eastern Europe = *Europe de l'Est* ≠ Western = *de l'ouest*
Eastern Seaboard = *côte Est des États-Unis.*

EASY (adj, -ier, -iest) *facile* : the test was easy = *l'examen était facile* ⑩ kid stuff = *l'enfance de l'art*, a cinch = *du gâteau* ≠ hard = *dur* ☠ *une femme facile* = a loose woman

to be on easy street = *nager dans l'opulence* ⑩ → RICH **easy lay =** *marie-couche-toi-là* : she's an easy lay = *c'est une marie-couche-toi-là* ⑩ hot mamma = *qui a le feu aux fesses* **easy mark =** *proie facile* : teenagers are easy marks for pimps = *les adolescentes sont des*	*proies faciles pour les maquereaux* **easy money =** *argent gagné facilement* ⑩ to make a fast buck = *faire rapidement fortune* **easy pickings =** *un jeu d'enfant* : the widow's money was easy pickings for the gigolo = *ça a été un jeu d'enfant pour*	*le gigolo de piquer l'argent de la veuve* **easy to =** *facile à/facile de (+ phrase)* : his theory is easy to understand = *sa théorie est facile à comprendre*, it's easy to understand why ... = *il est facile de comprendre pourquoi ...* **it's as easy as pie =** *c'est facile*

comme bonjour ⓪ there's nothing to it = *c'est simple comme bonjour*
it's easier than falling off a log (GB) = *c'est facile comme tout*
it's no easy matter = *ce n'est pas rien* : getting you on the

phone is no easy matter = *pour t'avoir au téléphone, ce n'est pas rien* ⓪ it's like pulling teeth = *c'est la croix et la bannière*
nothing could be easier = *rien de plus facile* = **there isn't anything easier**
to take the easy way out =

choisir la solution de facilité : by asking her to fire him for you, you're taking the easy way out = *en lui demandant de le mettre à la porte à ta place, tu choisis la solution de facilité*
that's easy for you to (say) = *tu as beau jeu de (dire ça).*

EASY (adv) **to breathe easy/easily** = *respirer librement* ⓪ to be relieved = *être soulagé*
to come easy to = *être facile pour qqn* : learning languages comes easy to her = *il lui est facile d'apprendre des langues*
easy come, easy go = *ça va, ça vient* : money with him is easy come, easy go = *l'argent avec lui, ça va et ça vient*
easy does it ! = *doucement !* ⓪ nice and easy ! = *mollo !* ☠ → softly
to get off easy = *bien s'en sortir* : he only got 6 months ; he got off easy = *il en a juste pris pour 6 mois ; il s'en est bien sorti* ≠ to have a rough time of it = *en baver*

to go easy on = *y aller doucement (avec)* : go easy on the Scotch ! = *vas-y doucement avec le whisky !*
to have it easy = *se la couler douce* : he has it easy in his new job = *il se la coule douce dans son nouveau boulot* = he's got it made in his new job
it's easier said than done = *c'est plus facile à dire qu'à faire*
to take it/things easy = 1/ *ne pas faire grand-chose* : we're just taking it easy today = *aujourd'hui nous ne faisons pas grand-chose* ⓪ to goof off = *ne rien ficher* 2/ *ne pas se fatiguer* : his doctor told him to take it easy = *son médecin lui a dit de ne pas se fatiguer* ⓪ to rest = *se reposer*
take it easy ! = *du calme !* ⓪ stay loose ! = *ne te frappe pas !*

EASYGOING (adj) 1/ *coulant, -e* : an easygoing teacher/mother = *un professeur coulant/une mère coulante* 2/ *facile à vivre* : an easygoing woman = *une femme facile à vivre.*

EAT (to, ate, eaten) 1/ *manger, bouffer* (LV) : I eat a lot = *je mange/bouffe beaucoup* ⓪ to stuff o.s. = *s'empiffrer* ≠ to fast = *jeûner*
to eat (breakfast/lunch/dinner) = *prendre son (petit déjeuner/déjeuner/dîner)*
to eat in ≠ **out** = *dîner à la maison* ≠ *en ville* : we're eating in ≠ out tonight = *ce soir, nous dînons à la maison* ≠ *en ville/dehors* ⓪ to pig out = *s'inviter à bouffer quelque part*
to eat up = *bouffer* : the venture ate up all my money = *l'affaire a bouffé tout mon argent*
(he's so cute) I could eat him up = *(il est mignon) à croquer*
to be eaten up with (jealousy) = *être dévoré par (la jalousie)*
2/ *brouter* : to eat a woman = *brouter une femme* ≠ to do a blow job = *tailler une pipe* ☠ → to graze.

EATER (n) *mangeur, -euse* : to be a big ≠ small eater = *être* ≠ *ne pas être un gros mangeur.*

EAVESDROP (to, -ped) *écouter aux portes* **EAVESDROPPER** (n) *qqn qui écoute aux portes.*

ECCENTRIC (adj) *excentrique* : an eccentric person = *une personne excentrique* ⓪ kooky = *farfelu* ≠ conformist = *conformiste* **ECCENTRICITY** (n, -ies) *excentricité (f).*

ECHELON (n) *échelon (m)* : in the lower echelons = *dans les échelons inférieurs* ⓪ rank = *rang* ☠ *à l'échelon ministériel* = at a ministerial level.

ECHO (n, -es) *écho (m)* **ECHO** (to, -ed) *faire écho* ☠ *j'ai eu des échos que* = I got wind that — *les échos d'un journal* = news items.

ECOLOGICAL (adj) *écologique* : acid rains are an ecological problem = *les pluies acides sont un problème écologique* **ECOLOGIST** (n) *écologiste (m, f)* ⓪ the greens = *les Verts.*

ECOLOGY (n) *écologie (f)* ⓪ conservation = ← ≠ pollution = ←.

ECONOMIC (adj) *économique* : economic problems = *problèmes économiques*, economic policy = *politique économique* ☠ → economical.

ECONOMICAL (adj) 1/ *économique* : a small, economical car = *une petite voiture économique* ☠ *sanctions économiques* = economic sanctions 2/ *économe* : an economical househusband = *un homme d'intérieur économe* ≠ wasteful = *gaspilleur.*

ECONOMICS (n pl) *économie (f)* : to write books on economics = *écrire des livres d'économie* ☠ → economy **ECONOMIST** (n) *économiste (m, f).*

ECONOMIZE (to, -d) *économiser* : to economize gas = *économiser l'essence* ☠ *l'inflation est tellement rapide que je ne peux économiser que 100 F par semaine* = inflation is so high that I can only save 100 francs per week.

ECONOMY (n, -ies) *économie (f)* : a country's economy = *l'économie d'un pays*, planned economy = *économie planifiée/dirigisme*
☠ *faire des économies de bouts de chandelle* = to be penny-wise and pound-foolish
— *elle a dépensé toutes ses économies* = she spent all her savings
— *étudier l'économie* = to study economics.

ECSTASY (n, -ies) *extase (f)* : the ecstasy of an orgasm = *l'extase d'un orgasme*
in ecstasy = *absolument ravi* : she's in ecstasy about having a baby = *elle est absolument ravie d'avoir un enfant.*

ECSTATIC (adj) *absolument ravi, -e* : she's ecstatic at/about having a big wedding = *elle est absolument ravie d'avoir un grand mariage* ⓪ delighted = *ravi.*

ECZEMA (n) *eczéma (m)* ⓪ skin disease = *maladie de la peau.*

EDGE (n) *bord (m)* : the edge of the table = *le bord de la table*
to have the edge on (one's competitor) = *avoir l'avantage sur (son concurrent)* ⓪ to have the jump on = *prendre le pas sur*
on edge = *à bout (de nerfs)* ⓪ wound-up = *qui a les nerfs en pelote*
on the edge of (a breakdown) = *au bord de (la dépression)* ⓪ on the brink of = *à deux doigts de*
on the edges = *sur les bords* : he's gay on the edges = *il est homo sur les bords*
☠ *au bord de la mer* = at the seaside
— *être du même bord* ≠ *virer de bord (politique)* = to be on the same side ≠ to change sides (politics)
— *le bord d'un verre* = the rim of a glass
— *passer par-dessus bord* = to fall overboard.

EDGE OUT (to, -d) *mettre petit à petit à l'écart* : Smith was edged out of the company = *Smith a été petit à petit mis à l'écart de la société* ⓪ to ease out = *évincer.*

EDGY (adj, -ier, -iest) *à cran* ⓪ nervous = *nerveux.*

EDIBLE (adj) *mangeable* : her lunch was hardly edible = *son déjeuner était tout juste mangeable.*

EDICT (n) *édit (m)* ⓪ decree = *décret.*

EDIT (to, -ed) 1/ *remanier* : to edit a text = *remanier un texte* ☠ *remanier un gouvernement* = to shuffle a cabinet around 2/ *faire le montage* : to edit a film = *faire le montage d'un film*
☠ *éditer* = to publish.

EDITING (n) *remaniement (m)* (text), *montage (m)* (film)
☠ *remaniement ministériel* = cabinet shakeup.

EDITION (n) *édition (f)* : the morning edition = *l'édition du matin*
☠ *maison d'édition* = publishing company
— *travailler dans l'édition* = to work in publishing.

EDITOR (n) *rédacteur, -trice* : political editor = *rédacteur politique*, editor in chief = *rédacteur en chef* ⓪ an editorial = *un éditorial* ☠ *éditeur* = publisher.

EDITORIAL (n) *éditorial (m)* : a leftist editorial = *un éditorial de gauche* **EDITORIAL** (adj) *de la rédaction* : an editorial decision = *une décision de la rédaction*
editorial policy = *ligne politique d'un journal.*

EDUCATE (to, -d) *éduquer* : to educate the public = *éduquer le public* ⓪ to instruct = *instruire.*

EDUCATED (adj) *instruit, -e* : an educated grandfather = *un grand-père instruit* ⓪ cultivated = *cultivé*
to be educated (at Harvard) = *avoir fait ses études (à)/être diplômé (de Harvard)*
☠ *bien* ≠ *mal éduqué* = well- ≠ ill-bred.

EDUCATION (n) *éducation (f)* : a good education = *une bonne éducation*
continuing education = *formation permanente*
☠ *éducation (enfant)* = upbringing.

EDUCATOR (n) *éducateur, -trice* ⓪ pedagogue = *pédagogue* ≠ disciple = ←.

EEC (abbr) = European Economic Community = *C.E.E. (f)* = *Communauté économique européenne* ⓪ Common Market = *Marché commun.*

EEL (n) *anguille (f)* ⓪ sardine = ← ☠ *il y a anguille sous roche* = there's something fishy.

EERIE (adj, -r, -st) *inquiétant, -e* : eerie sounds in the night = *des bruits inquiétants dans la nuit* ⓪ troubling = *troublant* ☠ → worrisome.

EFFECT (n) *effet (m)* : what he said had no effect = *ce qu'il a dit n'a pas eu d'effet* ⓪ result = *résultat*
in effect = *en fait* : I thought he was lying and in effect he was = *je pensais qu'il mentait, et en fait c'est ce qu'il faisait* ⓪ for all practical purposes = *pour ainsi dire*
just for the effect = *pour voir l'effet que ça ferait* : she said that just for the effect = *elle a dit ça pour voir l'effet que ça ferait*
to no effect = *sans effet* : her words were to no effect = *ses paroles sont restées sans effet* ⓪ useless = *inutile*
to take effect = 1/ *prendre effet* (law) = **to go into effect** ⓪ to come into force = *entrer en vigueur* 2/ *faire de l'effet* : the medicine didn't take effect = *le médicament n'a pas fait d'effet*
to that effect = *de ce genre* : he called me a bitch, or something to that effect = *il m'a traitée de garce, ou de quelque chose de ce genre*
☠ *en effet* = indeed
— *il me fait l'effet d'(un faux jeton)* = he strikes me as being (a phony)
— *couper ses effets à qqn* = to steal s.o.'s thunder
— *c'est tout l'effet que ça te fait ?* = that's all it does to you ?

EFFECTIVE (adj) *efficace* : trying to understand a child is more effective than spanking = *il est plus efficace d'essayer de comprendre un enfant que de lui donner*

des fessées ⓪ valid = *valable* ≠ ineffective = *inefficace*
to become effective = *entrer en vigueur* (law)
☠ *(une secrétaire) efficace* = (an) efficient (secretary).

EFFEMINATE (adj) *efféminé, -e* : an effeminate guy =
un type efféminé ⓪ pretty boy = *mignon* ≠ mannish
= *hommasse.*

EFFICIENCY (n inv) *efficacité (f)* : she does the work
with great efficiency = *elle fait le travail avec une
grande efficacité* ≠ inefficiency = *inefficacité.*

EFFICIENT (adj) *efficace* : an efficient assistant = *une
assistante efficace* ⓪ able = *capable* ≠ inefficient =
inefficace ☠ → effective **EFFICIENTLY** (adv) *efficace-
ment.*

EFFIGY (n, -ies) **(he was burned) in effigy** = *(il a été
brûlé) en effigie.*

EFFORT (n) *effort (m)* ⓪ endeavor = *tentative*
to make an effort to (help) = *faire un effort pour
(aider)* ⓪ to try to = *essayer de.*

E.G. (abbr) *par exemple* : he goes in for sports, e.g. base-
ball, tennis, swimming and basketball = *il aime beaucoup le sport, par exemple le base-ball, le tennis, la natation et le basket-ball.*

EGG (n) *œuf (m)* ⓪ yolk ≠ white = *jaune* ≠ *blanc,*
shell = *coquille,* eggcup = *coquetier*

bacon and eggs = *œufs au bacon*	**hard-boiled** ≠ **soft-boiled egg** = *œuf dur* ≠ *à la coque*
scrambled eggs = *œufs brouillés*	
fried eggs = *œufs sur le plat*	**eggs sunny-side up/ over** = *œufs sur le plat/ retournés*

egg roll = *pâté impérial* ⓪ fried rice = *riz cantonais*
a good ≠ **bad egg** = *un chic* ≠ *sale type*
to lay an egg = 1/ *pondre un œuf:* the hen laid a gold-
en egg = *la poule a pondu un œuf d'or* 2/ *se casser la
gueule* : the play laid an egg = *la pièce s'est cassé la
gueule* ⓪ to fall on one's face = *se casser la figure* ≠ to
go over big = *avoir un succès fou*
☠ *être étouffé dans l'œuf* = to be nipped in the bud
— *va te faire cuire un œuf !* = go fly a kite !

EGGHEAD (n) *grosse tête (f),* fort, *-e en thème* : egg-
heads surrounding the Minister = *de grosses têtes
autour du ministre* ⓪ longhair = *intello.*

EGG ON (to, -ed) *inciter fortement* : she wanted to get a
divorce and her parents egged her on = *elle voulait le
divorce et ses parents l'y ont fortement incitée.*

EGGPLANT (n) *aubergine (f)* : stuffed eggplants = *des
aubergines farcies.*

EGO (n) 1/ *moi (m)* ⓪ superego = *surmoi* ≠ id = *ça*
2/ *amour-propre (m)* : the remark hurt his ego = *la
remarque a blessé son amour-propre*

ego trip = *qqch qui flatte la vanité* : going out with the
famous actress was an ego trip for him = *le fait de sortir
avec une actrice célèbre flattait sa vanité*
to have an inflated ego = *avoir la grosse tête.*

EGOCENTRIC (n, adj) *égocentrique (m, f)* ⓪ to think
one's the center of the world = *se prendre pour le nombril du monde.*

EGOISM (n) *égoïsme (m)* ⓪ egotism = *égotisme* ≠
altruism = *altruisme* **EGOIST** (n) *égoïste (m, f)* ⓪ egotist
= *égotiste,* narcissist = *narcissique* ≠ altruist =
altruiste **EGOISTIC** (adj) *égoïste* ⓪ self-centered =
égocentrique.

EGOTISM (n) *égotisme (m)* ≠ humility = *humilité.*

EGOTISTICAL (adj) *égotiste, content, -e de soi* : I don't
mean to be egotistical, but I think my work is pretty
good = *je ne veux pas paraître trop contente de moi
mais je trouve que j'ai fait du plutôt bon travail* ⓪ conceited = *suffisant.*

EGYPT (n) *Égypte (f)* **EGYPTIAN** (n, adj) *Égyptien, -enne*
EGYPTOLOGY (n) *égyptologie (f).*

EIGHT (n, adj) *huit (m)* : at eight o'clock = *à huit
heures* ⓪ eighth = *huitième*
to be behind the eight ball = *être en mauvaise posture* : if she doesn't pass the exam, she'll be behind the
eight ball = *si elle n'a pas son examen, elle sera en mauvaise posture* ⓪ to be in a jam = *être dans le pétrin.*

EIGHTEEN (n, adj) *dix-huit (m)* ⓪ eighteenth = *dix-
huitième.*

EIGHTY (n, -ies, adj) *quatre-vingt(s) (m)* ⓪ eightieth =
quatre-vingtième
the eighties = *les années quatre-vingt*
to be in one's eighties = *avoir quatre-vingts ans et
quelques* ⓪ to be eightyish = *avoir dans les quatre-
vingts ans.*

EITHER (adv) **not … either** = *non plus* : he
doesn't smoke and I don't either = *il ne fume pas
et moi non plus* = he doesn't smoke and neither do
I ≠ he smokes and I do too = *il fume et moi aussi*
not … (me) either = *(moi) non plus* = (me)
neither ≠ (me) too = *(moi) aussi.*

EITHER (conj) **either … or** = *ou bien … ou bien* :
either tell me the truth or get out ! = *ou bien tu me
dis la vérité ou bien tu fiches le camp !*
either … or else = *soit … soit* : either you agree,
or else quit ! = *soit tu es d'accord, soit tu démis-
sionnes !*

EITHER (pron) *l'un, -e ou l'autre* : I like both coats,
I'll take either = *j'aime les deux manteaux, je prendrai l'un ou l'autre*

either one = *soit l'un soit l'autre* **not ... either** = *ni l'un*	*ni l'autre* : I don't want either = *je ne veux ni l'un ni l'autre.*

EITHER (adj) *l'un, -e ou l'autre* : I can write with either hand = *je peux écrire avec l'une ou l'autre main*	

in either event = *dans un cas comme dans l'autre* : I don't know if I'm going or not, but in either event, I'll let you know = *je ne sais pas si je vais y aller ou non, mais dans un cas comme dans l'autre je vous tiendrai au courant* **not ... either** = *ni l'un ni l'autre* : I don't like either book = *je n'aime*	*ni l'un ni l'autre livre* **on either side** = *de chaque côté* : the Pope appeared with a body-guard on either side = *le pape est apparu avec un garde du corps de chaque côté/entre deux gardes du corps*, big trees on either side of the house = *de grands arbres de chaque côté de la maison.*

EJACULATE (to, -d) *éjaculer* ⓪ to jerk off = *se branler.*

EJECT (to, -ed) *éjecter* : ejected from the car = *éjecté de la voiture.*

EKE OUT (to, -d) *gagner tout juste* : to eke out one's living = *gagner tout juste sa vie.*

ELABORATE (adj) *élaboré, -e* : an elaborate hairdo/project = *une coiffure élaborée/un projet élaboré* ≠ plain = *tout simple.*

ELABORATE ON (to, -d) *développer* : please elaborate on your idea = *je vous prie de développer votre idée* ⓪ to go into = *creuser* ☠ → to develop.

ELAPSE (to, -d) *s'écouler* ⓪ to go by = *passer* ☠ *écouler (la marchandise)* = to sell off (the goods).

ELATED (adj) *rendu, -e fou, folle de joie* : elated by her wedding = *rendue folle de joie par son mariage* ⓪ overjoyed = *absolument ravi.*

ELBOW (n) *coude (m)* ⓪ funny bone = *petit juif*
to rub elbows with (the rich) = *coudoyer (les riches)* ⓪ to hobnob with = ↑*côtoyer*
☠ *se serrer les coudes* = to stick together
— *au coude à coude* = neck to neck.

ELDER (adj) *aîné, -e (de deux)* : my elder brother = *mon frère aîné* = older ≠ younger = *cadet* ☠ → eldest.

ELDERLY (adj) *assez âgé, -e* : her parents are elderly = *ses parents sont assez âgés* ≠ young = *jeune.*

ELDEST (n, adj) *aîné, -e (de plusieurs)* : their eldest son = *leur fils aîné*, he's the eldest = *il est l'aîné* ≠ youngest = *le plus jeune* ☠ *ma sœur aînée (de deux sœurs)* = my elder/older sister.

ELECT (to, -ed) *élire* : to elect a Senator = *élire un sénateur* ⓪ to reelect = *réélire.*

ELECTION (n) *élection (f)* ⓪ franchise = *droit de vote*, universal suffrage = *suffrage universel*, by-election = *élection partielle.*

ELECTORAL (adj) **electoral college** = *collège électoral (qui élit le Président et le vice-Président des États-Unis après avoir été désigné par les électeurs).*

ELECTORATE (n) *électorat (m), corps (m) électoral* ⓪ voters = *électeurs.*

ELECTRIC (adj) *électrique* : electric blanket/kettle = *couverture/bouilloire électrique*
the electric chair = *la chaise électrique* = the hot seat ⓪ guillotine = ←.

ELECTRICIAN (n) *électricien, -enne* ⓪ plumber = *plombier.*

ELECTRICITY (n, -ies) *électricité (f)* ⓪ blackout = *panne d'électricité.*

ELECTRIFYING (adj) *grisant, -e* : electrifying piece of news = *nouvelle grisante* ⓪ thrilling = *passionnant.*

ELECTROCUTE (to, -d) *électrocuter* ⓪ to put to death = *mettre à mort* **ELECTROCUTION** (n) *électrocution (f).*

ELECTRONIC (adj) *électronique* ⓪ nuclear = *nucléaire.*

ELEGANCE (n) *élégance (f)* ≠ vulgarity = *vulgarité* **ELEGANT** (adj) *élégant, -e* : an elegant outfit = *un ensemble élégant* ⓪ smart = ← ≠ inelegant = *inélégant* **ELEGANTLY** (adv) *élégamment.*

ELEGY (n, -ies) *élégie (f)* ⓪ poem = *poème.*

ELEMENT (n) *élément (m)* : she's a good element for the team = *c'est un bon élément dans l'équipe*
in ≠ out of one's element = *dans son élément* ≠ *pas dans son élément.*

ELEMENTARY (adj) *élémentaire* : it's an elementary problem = *c'est un problème élémentaire* ⓪ fundamental = *fondamental*
elementary school = *école primaire.*

ELEPHANT (n) *éléphant (m)* ⓪ ivory = *ivoire*, tusk = *défense*, trunk = *trompe* ☠ *comme un éléphant dans un magasin de porcelaine* = like a bull in a china shop.

ELEVATOR (n) *ascenseur (m)* = lift (GB) ⓪ dumbwaiter = *monte-plats* ☠ *renvoyer l'ascenseur* = to return a favor.

ELEVEN (n, adj) *onze (m).*

ELEVENTH (n, adj) *onzième (m, f)*
at the eleventh hour = *à la dernière minute.*

ELF (n) *elfe (m)* ⓪ imp = *lutin*, fairy = *fée.*

ELIGIBLE (adj) 1/ *non marié, -e* : she has three eligible brothers = *elle a trois frères qui ne sont pas mariés* ⓪ a

good catch = *un beau parti* **2/** *éligible* : you're eligible at the age of 21 = *vous êtes éligible à 21 ans*
eligible to (vote/retire) = *qui a droit au (vote)/à (prendre sa retraite).*

ELIMINATE (to, -d) *éliminer* ⓓ to get rid of = *se débarrasser de* ≠ to keep = *garder* **ELIMINATION** (n) *élimination (f).*

ELITE (n) *élite (f)* ⓦ the cream of the crop = *la crème* ☠ *tireur d'élite* = sharpshooter **ELITISM** (n) *élitisme (m)* **ELITIST** (n, adj) *élitiste (m, f).*

ELOPE (to, -d) *s'enfuir pour se marier en secret* ⓓ to tie the knot = *se mettre la corde au cou.*

ELOQUENCE (n) *éloquence (f)* **ELOQUENT** (adj) *éloquent, -e* ☠ *ces statistiques sont éloquentes* = these statistics speak for themselves.

ELSE (adj) *(d')autre* : what else could I do ? = *que pourrais-je faire d'autre ?*

anyone/anybody else = *quelqu'un d'autre* **anything/something else** = *quelque chose d'autre* **no one else** = *personne d'autre*	**nothing else** = *rien d'autre* **someone else** = *quelqu'un d'autre* **who else ?** = *qui d'autre ?*

ELSE (adv) **how else (can I do it) ?** = *comment (puis-je faire) autrement ?*
little else/not much else = *pas grand-chose d'autre*
what else ? = *quoi d'autre ?*
when else (can you come) ? = *à quel autre moment (pouvez-vous venir) ?*
where else (can we find a good restaurant) ? = *à quel autre endroit (pouvons-nous trouver un bon restaurant) ?*

ELSEWHERE (adv) *ailleurs* : look elsewhere = *regarde ailleurs* ⓓ somewhere else = *autre part* ☠ *être ailleurs* = to be in the clouds
— *nulle part ailleurs* = nowhere else
— *d'ailleurs* = as a matter of fact
— *par ailleurs* = on the other hand.

ELUDE (to, -d) *éluder* : to elude a question = *éluder une question* ⓓ to fence = *répondre par une pirouette.*

EMACIATED (adj) *émacié, -e* : emaciated face = *visage émacié* ⓓ scrawny = *maigrichon.*

EMANCIPATE (to, -d) *émanciper* : women were emancipated only recently = *les femmes n'ont été émancipées que récemment* **EMANCIPATION** (n) *émancipation (f).*

EMBARGO (n, -es) *embargo (m)* : an embargo on crude oil = *un embargo sur le pétrole brut* ⓓ seizure = *saisie.*

EMBARK (to, -ed) *embarquer* ≠ to disembark = *débarquer*
to embark on (a crazy scheme) = *s'embarquer dans/s'embringuer dans (une folle entreprise)* ⓓ to get mixed up in = *se trouver mêlé à*
☠ *être embarqué par les flics* = to be picked up by the cops.

EMBARRASS (to, -ed) *embarrasser* : dirty jokes embarrass me = *les plaisanteries cochonnes m'embarrassent* ⓓ to mortify = *mortifier*, to feel abashed = *se sentir déconcerté* ☠ *je suis bien embarrassé pour (lui répondre)* = I'm at a loss to (answer him).

EMBARRASSING (adj) *embarrassant, -e* : an embarrassing situation = *une situation embarrassante.*

EMBARRASSMENT (n) *embarras (m)* : imagine my embarrassment when I realized that my blouse was open = *imaginez mon embarras quand je me suis rendu compte que ma blouse était ouverte* ⓓ shame = *honte*
to be an embarrassment to (one's family) = *être la honte de (sa famille)*
to my embarrassment = *à mon grand embarras*
☠ *être dans l'embarras* = to be in a pickle
— *avoir l'embarras du choix* = to have a vast choice
— *que d'embarras !* = what a to-do !

EMBASSY (n, -ies) *ambassade (f)* : the American embassy = *l'ambassade des États-Unis* ⓓ ambassador = *ambassadeur*, consulate = *consulat*, mission = ←.

EMBELLISH (to, -ed) *embellir* : to embellish a story = *embellir une histoire* ⓓ to enhance = *mettre en valeur.*

EMBEZZLE (to, -d) *détourner des fonds* = *arnaquer* **EMBEZZLEMENT** (n) *détournement (m) de fonds* : charged with embezzlement = *accusé de détournement de fonds* ⓓ rip-off = *escroquerie.*

EMBLEM (n) *emblème (m)* ⓓ symbol = *symbole.*

EMBODY (to, -ied) *incarner* : a woman who embodies the ideal of feminism = *une femme qui incarne l'idéal du féminisme* ⓓ to personify = *personnifier.*

EMBROIDER (to, -ed) *broder* : I embroidered my blouse = *j'ai brodé mon chemisier* ☠ → to dress up **EMBROIDERY** (n, -ies) *broderie (f).*

EMBROIL (to, -ed) **to get/be embroiled in** = *se trouver mêlé à* : I don't want to get embroiled in the party's internal strife = *je ne veux pas me trouver mêlé aux querelles intestines du parti* ⓓ to be involved in = *être impliqué dans.*

EMBRYO (n) *embryon (m)* ⓓ fetus = *fœtus.*

EMCEE (n) *présentateur, -trice d'un spectacle* ⓓ master of ceremonies = *maître de cérémonie.*

EMERALD (n) *émeraude (f)* ⓓ sapphire = *saphir.*

EMERGE (to, -d) *émerger* : to emerge from a long silence = *émerger d'un long silence* ⓓ to come to the surface = *faire surface.*

EMERGENCY (n, -ies) **an emergency case** = *une urgence*
emergency exit = *sortie de secours*
emergency operation = *opération d'urgence*
in an emergency (call me) = *en cas d'urgence (appelez-moi)*
it's an emergency = *d'urgence* : I must see you, it's an emergency = *il faut que je vous voie d'urgence*
emergency ward = *salle des urgences.*

EMIGRANT (n) *émigrant, -e* ⓓ refugee = *réfugié* **EMIGRATE** (to, -d) *émigrer* ⓓ to expatriate = *s'expatrier* **EMIGRATION** (n) *émigration (f)* ⓓ migration = ←.

EMINENT (adj) *éminent, -e* : an eminent scientist = *un savant éminent* ⓓ distinguished = *distingué.*

EMISSARY (n, -ies) *émissaire (m)* : the sheikh's emissary = *l'émissaire du cheikh* ⓓ envoy = *envoyé.*

EMOTION (n) *émotion (f)* ⓓ feeling = *sentiment* **EMOTIONAL** (adj) 1/ *émotif, -ive* : I'm very emotional = *je suis très émotive* ⓓ sensitive = *sensible* 2/ *passionnel, -elle* : an emotional meeting = *une réunion passionnelle* ☙ *crime passionnel* = crime of passion.

EMPEROR (n) *empereur (m)* **EMPRESS** (n, -es) *impératrice (f).*

EMPHASIS (n, -ses) *accent (m)* : an emphasis on discipline = *l'accent mis sur la discipline*
to lay/place/put emphasis on = *mettre l'accent sur* : society is at last putting emphasis on human rights = *la société a met enfin l'accent sur les droits de l'homme* = to lay stress on ≠ to play down = *faire peu de cas de* ☙ → accent.

EMPHASIZE (to, -d) *souligner* : he emphasized the dangers of a nuclear war = *il a souligné les dangers d'une guerre nucléaire* = to underline ⓓ to stress = *mettre l'accent sur.*

EMPHATIC (adj) *formel, -elle* : he was emphatic about it = *il a été formel à ce sujet* ⓓ categorical = *catégorique*
☙ → formal
— *style emphatique* = pompous style.

EMPHATICALLY (adv) *énergiquement* : he most emphatically refused = *il a refusé très énergiquement.*

EMPIRE (n) *empire (m)* ⓓ colony = *colonie* ☙ *exercer un empire sur qqn* = to have a hold over s.o.

EMPLOY (to, -ed) 1/ *employer* : the boss prefers to employ foreigners = *le patron préfère employer des étrangers* ⓓ to hire = *engager* 2/ *employer* : to employ strange means = *employer de drôles de moyens* ⓓ to make use of = *se servir de*
☙ *s'employer à* = to go to great lengths to.

EMPLOYEE (n) *employé, -e* : the company has one thousand employees = *la société a mille employés* ⓓ

wage earner = *salarié* ☙ *un employé de banque* = a bank clerk.

EMPLOYER (n) *employeur, -euse* ⓓ boss = *patron.*

EMPLOYMENT (n) *emploi (m)* ≠ unemployment = *chômage*
to look for employment = *chercher du travail/ un emploi*
employment agency = *agence pour l'emploi*
☙ *mon emploi du temps* = my time schedule
— *l'emploi d'un mot* = the use of a word.

EMPOWER (to, -ed) **to be empowered to (sentence to death)** = *être investi du pouvoir de (condamner à mort).*

EMPTINESS (n) *vide (m)* : the emptiness of life without love = *le vide d'une vie sans amour* ⓓ nothing = *néant*
☙ *regarder dans le vide* = to stare off into space
— *faire le vide autour de soi* = to drive everyone away
— *sa mort a laissé un vide* = his death left a void
— *combler un vide* = to fill a vacuum.

EMPTY (adj, -ier, -iest) *vide* : an empty bottle/apartment = *une bouteille/un appartement vide* ≠ full = *plein.*

EMPTY (to, -ied) *vider* : to empty a bottle = *vider une bouteille* ≠ to fill = *remplir*
☙ *vider qqn* = to oust s.o./to throw s.o. out
— *vider les lieux* = to clear out the premises
— *(le voyage) m'a vidé* = (the trip) wore me out.

EMPTY-HANDED (adj) **to come back empty-handed** = *revenir les mains vides/bredouille* ⓓ to go on a wild-goose chase = *y aller pour des prunes.*

EMULATE (to, -d) *prendre exemple sur* : to emulate one's parents = *prendre exemple sur ses parents* **EMULATION** (n) *émulation (f).*

ENABLE TO (to, -d) *permettre de* : intensive lessons enabled me to learn quickly = *des cours intensifs m'ont permis d'apprendre rapidement.*

ENACT (to, -ed) *donner force de loi à* : to enact a bill = *donner force de loi à un texte* ⓓ to promulgate = *promulguer.*

ENAMEL (n) *émail (m) (émaux)* **ENAMEL** (to, -ed) *émailler* : an enameled bowl = *une coupe émaillée* ☙ *il émaille sa conversation de grossièretés* = he sprinkles his conversation with crude words.

ENCHANT (to, -ed) *enchanter* : we're enchanted with the idea = *nous sommes enchantés de l'idée* ☙ *je suis enchanté (de vous voir)* = I'm delighted (to see you) **ENCHANTING** (adj) *qui est un enchantement (s.o.), enchanteur, -eresse* : what an enchanting weekend ! = *quel week-end enchanteur !*, her little boy's enchanting = *son petit garçon est un enchantement !* ⓓ charming = *charmant.*

ENCIRCLE (to, -d) *encercler* : to encircle an area = *encercler un secteur* ⓓ to hem in = *cerner.*

ENCLOSE (to, -d) *joindre* : to enclose a check = *joindre un chèque* ⓄⒹ to include = *inclure* 💀 → to join **(letter) enclosed** = *(lettre) ci-jointe.*

ENCLOSURE (n) *pièce* (f) *jointe* : two enclosures with my letter = *deux pièces jointes à ma lettre.*

ENCORE (n) *bis* (m) ≠ boo = *huée* **to call for an encore** = *faire un rappel/crier bis.*

ENCOUNTER (n) *rencontre* (f) : an unexpected encounter = *une rencontre inattendue* **encounter group** = *groupe de rencontre* 💀 « encounter » *est moins utilisé dans le langage parlé que* « meeting »
— *aller à la rencontre de qqn* = to go on ahead to meet s.o.
— *faire la rencontre de qqn* = to make s.o.'s acquaintance.

ENCOUNTER (to, -ed) *rencontrer* : to encounter difficulties = *rencontrer des difficultés* ⓄⒹ to run into = *tomber sur* 💀 → to meet.

ENCOURAGE (to, -d) *encourager* : he wanted to be a violinist and his family encouraged him = *il voulait être violoniste et sa famille l'y a encouragé* ⓄⒹ to stimulate = *stimuler* ≠ to discourage = *décourager* **to encourage s.o. to (do stg)** = *encourager qqn à (faire qqch).*

ENCOURAGEMENT (n) *encouragement* (m) : my parents never gave me any encouragement = *mes parents ne m'ont jamais donné d'encouragement* **ENCOURAGING** (adj) *encourageant, -e* ≠ discouraging = *décourageant.*

ENCROACH ON (to, -ed) *empiéter sur* : the new bill encroaches on individual rights = *le nouveau projet de loi empiète sur les libertés individuelles.*

ENCYCLOPEDIA (n) *encyclopédie* (f) ⓄⒹ dictionary = *dictionnaire.*

END (n) **1/** *fin* (f) : the end of the year = *la fin de l'année* ≠ start = *début*

at the end = *à la fin* ≠ in the beginning = *au commencement* **at the end of (one's patience)** = *à bout de (patience)* **to come/to draw to an end** = *tirer à sa fin* ⓄⒹ to wind up = *prendre fin* **in the end (he decided to vote Republican)** = *finalement (il a décidé de voter républicain)* ⓄⒹ when all's said and done = *tout compte fait* 💀 → finally **no end** = *rudement* : I appreciate what you did for me no end	= *j'apprécie rudement ce que vous avez fait pour moi* 💀 → roughly **no end of** = *à n'en plus finir* : we had no end of trouble = *nous avons eu des ennuis à n'en plus finir* → MANY **on end** = *d'affilée* : she talked for hours on end = *elle a parlé (pendant) des heures d'affilée* **to put an end to (torture)** = *mettre fin à (la torture)* **that's the end of you !** = *c'en est fini de toi !* ⓄⒹ you've had it !	= *tu es fichu !* **the end** = *le fin du fin* : good champagne is the end = *un bon champagne, c'est le fin du fin* **the end justifies the means** = *la fin justifie les moyens* **to no end** = *qui ne sert à rien* : the talks were to no end = *les discussions n'ont servi à rien* ⓄⒹ to no avail = *sans effet* **you'll never hear the end of it !** = *vous n'avez pas fini d'en entendre parler !*

💀 *une fin tragique* = a tragic ending — *c'est la fin des haricots !* = that's the ball game ! — *il est arrivé à ses fins* = he got what he wanted	— *qui veut la fin veut les moyens* = that's the price one has to pay — *jouer au plus fin* = to try to outwit s.o.

2/ *bout* (m) : the house at the end of the street = *la maison au bout de la rue* ⓄⒹ extremity = *extrémité* 💀 → tip

to be at the end of one's rope = *être au bout du rouleau* ⓄⒹ not to know which way to turn = *ne plus savoir à quel saint se vouer* **at the end of the world** = *au bout du monde* ⓄⒹ in God's	country = *à Pétaouchnock* **he can't see any further than the end of his nose** = *il ne voit pas plus loin que le bout de son nez* **not to know which end is up** = *ne pas savoir sur quel pied*	danser ⓄⒹ to be at loose ends = *être déboussolé* **not to make ends meet** = *ne pas arriver à joindre les deux bouts* → POOR

3/ *partie* (f) : the advertising end of the business = *la partie publicité de l'affaire* ⓄⒹ side = *côté* 💀 → part
at/on my end = *de mon côté* : all's well at my end = *de mon côté, tout va bien* ⓄⒹ as for me = *quant à moi.*

END (to, -ed) *(se) terminer* : the movie ended early = *le film s'est terminé tôt* ⓒ to wind up = *prendre fin* ≠ to start = *commencer*

to end in a deadlock = *aboutir à une impasse* ⓒ to result in = *avoir pour résultat* **to end up (+ ing)** = *finir par* : she ended up (by) asking for a divorce = *elle a fini par demander le divorce* = she wound up asking for a divorce	**to end up (in jail)** = *finir (en prison)* ⓒ to land in = *atterrir en* ☠ → to finish **to end with** = *(se) terminer par* : the movie ended with a murder = *le film s'est terminé par un meurtre*

☠ *j'ai terminé le livre/mon travail hier soir* = I finished the book/my work last night.

END-ALL (n) *nec plus ultra (m)* : Dom Pérignon is the end-all in champagne = *le Dom Pérignon est le nec plus ultra en matière de champagne* ≠ the pits = *pas le pied.*

ENDANGER (to, -ed) *mettre en danger* : to endanger one's health = *mettre sa santé en danger* ⓒ to imperil = *mettre en péril.*

ENDEAVOR (n) *tentative (f)* : he made no endeavor to help us = *il n'a fait aucune tentative pour nous aider* = he made no attempt **ENDEAVOR TO** (to, -ed) *s'efforcer de* : he endeavored to help the refugees to find jobs = *il s'est efforcé d'aider les réfugiés à trouver du travail* ⓒ to attempt to = *tenter de.*

ENDING (n) *fin (f)* : a tragic ending = *une fin tragique* ⓒ conclusion = ← ☠ → end.

ENDLESS (adj) **1/** *interminable* : the film seemed endless = *le film semblait interminable* ⓒ never-ending = *qui n'en finit pas* **2/** *une infinité de* : endless problems = *une infinité de problèmes* → MANY **ENDLESSLY** (adv) *sans fin* ⓒ continually = *continuellement.*

ENDORSE (to, -d) *endosser* (check), *avaliser* (candidacy) ☠ *endosser une responsabilité* = to shoulder a responsibility.

ENDURANCE (n) *endurance (f)* ⓒ resistance = *résistance.*

ENDURE (to, -d) *endurer* : to endure awful sufferings = *endurer des souffrances atroces* ⓒ to undergo = *subir.*

ENDURING (adj) *durable* : an enduring friendship = *une amitié durable* ≈ lasting ≠ fleeting = *fugace.*

ENEMA (n) *lavement (m)* : he was given an enema before undergoing surgery = *on lui a fait un lavement avant de l'opérer.*

ENEMY (n, -ies) *ennemi, -e* = foe ⓒ adversary = *adversaire* ≠ ally = *allié.*

ENERGETIC (adj) *énergique* : energetic measures = *des mesures énergiques* **ENERGETICALLY** (adv) *énergiquement, avec énergie.*

ENERGY (n, -ies) *énergie (f)* : I feel full of energy = *je me sens pleine d'énergie* ⓒ go = *allant*, vitality = *vitalité* **energy crisis** = *crise de l'énergie*

☠ *(refuser) avec énergie* = (to refuse) energetically.

ENFORCE (to, -d) *faire observer* : not enough soldiers to enforce the truce = *pas assez de soldats pour faire observer la trêve* ☠ *je lui ai fait observer que ...* = I pointed out to her that ...

ENGAGE (to, -d) *engager* : to engage a new maid = *engager une nouvelle bonne* = to hire ≠ to fire = *congédier* **to be engaged to (a doctor)** = *être fiancée à (un médecin)* ⓒ to get hitched = *se mettre un fil à la patte* ☠ « to engage » *est moins utilisé que* « to hire »
 — *s'engager (dans l'armée)* = to join/to sign up
 — *ça n'engage à rien* = it does not commit you to anything
 — *un chanteur engagé* = a politically committed singer.

ENGAGEMENT (n) **1/** *fiançailles (f pl)* : she broke her engagement = *elle a rompu ses fiançailles*, engagement ring = *bague de fiançailles* **2/** *engagement (m)* ⓒ appointment = *rendez-vous*
 ☠ *sans engagement* = without any obligation
 — *engagement politique* = political commitment.

ENGAGING (adj) *engageant, -e* : an engaging smile = *un sourire engageant* ≠ standoffish = *rébarbatif.*

ENGINE (n) *moteur (m)* : the engine of a car = *le moteur d'une voiture*
 ☠ → motor
 — *un engin* = a device/contraption.

ENGINEER (n) *ingénieur (m)* : sound engineer = *ingénieur du son* **ENGINEERING** (n) *engineering (m), ingénierie (f)* : to study engineering = *étudier l'ingénierie/faire des études d'ingénieur.*

ENGINEER (to, -ed) *machiner* : to engineer a plot = *machiner un complot* ⓒ to contrive = *combiner.*

ENGLAND (n) *Angleterre (f)* ⓒ United Kingdom = *Royaume-Uni.*

ENGLISH (adj) *anglais, -e* : a young English girl = *une jeune fille anglaise* ⓒ British = *britannique.*

ENGLISH (n inv) **1/** *les Anglais, -es* : the English drive on the left = *les Anglais conduisent à gauche* ⓒ British = *Britanniques* **2/** *anglais (m)* : to speak English = *parler*

anglais **ENGLISHMAN** (n, -men) *Anglais (m)* ⓌⓄ limey = *angliche* **ENGLISHWOMAN** (n, -women) *Anglaise (f)*
☠ *filer à l'anglaise* = to take French leave
— *les Anglais ont débarqué* = to have the curse.

ENGRAVE (to, -d) *graver* : facts engraved in my memory = *des faits gravés dans ma mémoire* **ENGRAVER** (n) *graveur, -euse* **ENGRAVING** (n) *gravure (f)*.

ENGROSS (to, -ed) **to be engrossed in (a novel)** = *être complètement absorbé par (un roman)*.

ENHANCE (to, -d) *mettre en valeur* ≠ to detract from = *nuire à*.

ENIGMA (n) *énigme (f)* ⓌⓄ mystery = *mystère* ☠ *parler par énigmes* = to speak in riddles **ENIGMATIC** (adj) *énigmatique*.

ENJOY (to, -ed) **did you enjoy (this book) ?** = *est-ce que (ce livre) t'a plu ?/est-ce que tu as trouvé (ce livre) bien ?*
to enjoy (drinking) = *aimer bien (boire)*
to enjoy o.s. = *bien s'amuser* : enjoy yourself ! = *amusez-vous bien !* ⓌⓄ to have a ball = *bien se marrer* ≠ to be bored = *s'ennuyer*.

ENJOYABLE (adj) *agréable* : an enjoyable evening = *une soirée agréable* → WONDERFUL ☠ → agreeable.

ENJOYMENT (n) *plaisir (m)* : she gets no enjoyment from her children = *elle ne tire aucun plaisir de ses enfants* ☠ → pleasure.

ENLARGE (to, -d) *(s')agrandir* : to enlarge a photo = *agrandir une photo* ≠ to reduce = *réduire* ☠ → to grow
to enlarge on (an idea) = *approfondir (une idée)* ⓌⓄ to expand on = *développer*.

ENLARGEMENT (n) *agrandissement (m)* (photo).

ENLIGHTEN (to, -ed) *éclairer* ⓌⓄ to clue in = *mettre au parfum* ☠ → to light.

ENLIST (to, -ed) *s'enrôler* (army) ⓌⓄ to reenlist = *rempiler*, to sign up = *s'engager*.

ENLISTED MAN (n, men) *engagé* ≠ a draftee = *un appelé* **ENLISTED WOMAN** (n, women) *engagée (f)*.

ENLIVEN (to, -ed) *égayer* : his presence will enliven the meal = *sa présence va égayer le repas*.

ENMITY (n, -ies) *inimitié (f)* ⓌⓄ hostility = *hostilité*.

ENORMITY (n) *énormité (f)* : uttering enormities = *en proférant des énormités*.

ENORMOUS (adj) *énorme* : an enormous building = *un immeuble énorme* ⓌⓄ colossal = *←* ≠ teeny = *tout petit*
an enormous amount of (books/money) = *énormément de (livres)/d'(argent)* → MANY.

ENORMOUSLY (adv) *énormément, extrêmement* (+ adj) : you've changed enormously = *vous avez énor-*

-mément changé, they're enormously rich = *ils sont extrêmement riches* → VERY.

ENOUGH (n, pron) *assez* : do you have enough ? = *est-ce que vous en avez assez ?*	
enough and to spare = *à revendre* → MANY **enough to** = *assez pour* : I don't have enough to buy a car = *je n'ai pas assez pour acheter une voiture*	**to have (just) enough to live on** = *avoir (tout juste) de quoi vivre* → POOR **I've had enough !** = *j'en ai assez !* ⓌⓄ I'm fed up ! = *j'en ai ras le bol !*

ENOUGH (adj) *assez (de)* : is there enough coffee ? = *y a-t-il assez de café ?* ⓌⓄ sufficient = *suffisant* ≠ too much = *trop*.

ENOUGH (adv) *assez* : I'm not hungry enough to eat now = *je n'ai pas assez faim pour manger maintenant* ≠ not so much = *pas tant que ça* **enough already !** = *ça suffit !* ⓌⓄ cut it out ! = *arrête !* **oddly/strangely/curiously/funnily enough** = *chose curieuse* ☠ *il est assez (riche)* = he's quite/fairly (rich).

ENRAGED (adj) *rendu, -e fou, folle* : enraged by her refusal = *rendu fou par son refus* → ANGRY.

ENRAPTURED (adj) *transporté, -e* : an enraptured public = *un public transporté* ⓌⓄ fascinated = *fasciné*.

ENRICH (to, -ed) *enrichir* : to enrich one's vocabulary = *enrichir son vocabulaire*.

ENROL(L) IN (to, -(l)ed) *s'inscrire à* : to enrol in school = *s'inscrire à l'école*.

ENSUE (to, -d) *s'ensuivre* : a long love affair ensued = *une longue liaison s'en est suivie*.

ENSURE (to, -d) = TO INSURE.

ENTAIL (to, -ed) *entraîner* : putting the deal together entailed a lot of problems = *monter cette affaire a entraîné de nombreux problèmes* ⓌⓄ to mean = *vouloir dire* ☠ *s'entraîner (athlète)* = to work out.

ENTANGLED (adj) *emmêlé, -e* : entangled hair = *cheveux emmêlés*.

ENTER (to, -ed) *entrer (dans)* : he entered the room = *il est entré dans la pièce* = to go in ≠ to leave = *quitter* **(her age) did not enter into it** = *(son âge) n'y était pour rien*
to enter into (an agreement) = *conclure (un accord)* ☠ *entrez !* = come in !
— *faire entrer qqn* = to show s.o. in
— *je suis entré par la porte* = I got in through the door.

ENTERPRISE (n) **1/** *entreprise (f)* : a foreign-based enterprise = *une entreprise basée à l'étranger* = concern ⓪ business = *affaire* **2/** *entreprise (f)* : this new enterprise is too difficult for him = *cette nouvelle entreprise est trop difficile pour lui* = undertaking.

ENTERPRISING (adj) *entreprenant, -e* ⓪ full of initiative = *plein d'initiative*.

ENTERTAIN (to, -ed) **1/** *recevoir* : my wife and I are entertaining tonight = *ma femme et moi recevons ce soir* ⓪ to have company = *avoir du monde* ☠ → to receive **2/** *divertir* : the clown entertained the kids = *le clown a beaucoup diverti les gosses* **3/** *caresser* : we're entertaining the idea of buying a ranch = *nous caressons l'idée d'acheter un ranch* ⓪ to have in mind = *avoir en vue* ☠ → to caress.

ENTERTAINER (n) *artiste (m, f) de variétés* ⓪ singer = *chanteur*.

ENTERTAINING (adj) *divertissant, -e* : the show was entertaining = *le spectacle était divertissant* ≠ boring = *ennuyeux*.

ENTERTAINMENT (n) *spectacle (m)* : there's no entertainment at the club = *le club ne donne aucun spectacle* ☠ → spectacle.

ENTHRALLED (adj) *captivé, -e* : enthralled by a detective story = *captivée par un roman policier*.

ENTHUSIASM (n) *enthousiasme (m)* ⓪ ardor = *ardeur* ≠ indifference = *indifférence*.

ENTHUSIASTIC (adj) *enthousiaste* : enthusiastic reviews = *des critiques enthousiastes* ⓪ overenthusiastic = *trop enthousiaste*, gungho = *tout feu tout flamme* ≠ indifferent = *indifférent*
to be enthusiastic about (his new novel) = *être enthousiasmé par (son nouveau roman)*.

ENTHUSIASTICALLY (adv) *avec enthousiasme*.

ENTICING (adj) *séduisant, -e* : an enticing offer = *une offre séduisante* ⓪ tempting = *tentant*.

ENTIRE (adj) *(tout) entier, -ère* : I ate the entire cake = *j'ai mangé le gâteau tout entier* ⓪ whole = *entier* ☠ *elle est très entière* = she's very whole/absolute
— *pendant des heures entières* = for hours on end.

ENTIRELY (adv) *entièrement* : you're entirely right = *vous avez entièrement raison* ≠ partially = *partiellement* → VERY.

ENTITLE TO (to, -d) *donner droit à* : the invitation entitles you to 2 free drinks = *l'invitation vous donne droit à 2 boissons gratuites*.

ENTRANCE (n) *entrée (f)* ≠ exit = *sortie*
entrance exam = *examen d'entrée*
entrance fee = *droit d'entrée*
☠ *d'entrée de jeu* = from the outset
— *l'entrée en guerre* = entry into the war

— *avoir ses entrées* = to be well-introduced
— *comme entrée en matière* = as an introduction
— *l'entrée est gratuite* = admission is free
— *entrée des artistes* = stage door
— *entrée (repas)* = entrée/first dish.

ENTREAT (to, -ed) *supplier* : they entreated the terrorists to let the children go = *ils ont supplié les terroristes de libérer les enfants* ⓪ to beseech = *conjurer*.

ENTRÉE (n) *plat (m) principal* : fish for the entrée = *du poisson en plat principal* ⓪ appetizer = *hors-d'œuvre* ☠ *entrée* → entrance.

ENTREPRENEUR (n) *entrepreneur (m)* ⓪ wheeler-dealer = *brasseur d'affaires*.

ENTRY (n, -ies) **1/** *entrée (f)* : America's entry into the war = *l'entrée en guerre des Américains* **2/** *accès (m)* : entry to the building = *l'accès de l'immeuble* ⓪ entrance = *entrée* ☠ → access **3/** *entrée (f)* : 10,000 entries in the dictionary = *10 000 entrées dans le dictionnaire* ☠ → entrance.

ENUMERATE (to, -d) *énumérer* **ENUMERATION** (n) *énumération (f)*.

ENVELOPE (n) *enveloppe (f)* ⓪ stamp = *timbre*.

ENVIOUS (adj) *envieux, -euse* : she's envious of her sister's job = *elle est envieuse du poste de sa sœur* ⓪ green with envy = *vert d'envie*.

ENVIRONMENT (n) *environnement (m)* : an unhappy home environment = *un triste environnement familial* ⓪ milieu = ←.

ENVIRONMENTALIST (n) *écologiste (m, f)* = ecologist.

ENVISAGE (to, -d) *envisager* : we're all envisaging the possibility of a nuclear war = *nous envisageons tous la possibilité d'une guerre nucléaire* ☠ *j'envisage (d'y aller ce soir)* = I'm contemplating/considering (going there tonight).

ENVOY (n) *envoyé, -e* : the king's envoy = *l'envoyé du roi* ⓪ messenger = *messager* ☠ *un envoyé spécial* = a special reporter.

ENVY (n) *envie (f)* : her ring is the envy of all her friends = *sa bague fait l'envie de toutes ses amies*, feelings of envy = *des sentiments d'envie* ⓪ jealousy = *jalousie* ☠ *une envie de* = a longing for
— *j'ai envie de ...* = I feel like ...

ENVY (to, -ied) *envier* : he envies his sister = *il envie sa sœur* ⓪ to be jealous of = *jalouser*.

EPHEMERAL (adj) *éphémère* : ephemeral joy = *joie éphémère*.

EPIC (adj) *épique* : an epic novel = *un roman épique*.

EPIDEMIC (n) *épidémie (f)* : cholera epidemic = *une épidémie de choléra* ⓪ wave = *vague*.

EPILEPSY (n) *épilepsie (f)* ⓪ fit = *crise* **EPILEPTIC** (n, adj) *épileptique (m, f)*.

EPILOGUE (n) *épilogue (m)* : a sad epilogue to a happy vacation = *un triste épilogue à des vacances heureuses*.

EPISODE (n) *épisode (m)* ⓪ event = *événement*.

EPITAPH (n) *épitaphe (f)* ⓪ grave = *tombe*.

EPITOME (n) *exemple (m) même* : the epitome of stupidity/heroism = *l'exemple même de la stupidité/de l'héroïsme* ⓪ quintessence = *comble*.

EPITOMIZE (to, -d) *incarner* = to incarnate.

EPOCH (n) *époque (f)* ⓪ period = *période* ☠ *meubles d'époque* = period furniture
— *à cette époque-là* = at that time.

EQUAL (n) *égal, -e* : I don't feel he's my equal = *je n'ai pas l'impression qu'il soit mon égal* ⓪ peer = *pair*.

EQUAL (adj) *égal, -e* : problems of equal importance = *des problèmes d'égale importance* ⓪ equivalent = *équivalent*
equal time = *temps d'antenne équivalent*
to be ≠ not to be equal to (the job) = *être ≠ ne pas être de taille à (faire le travail)* ⓪ to be up to = *être à la hauteur de*
to be on equal footing with s.o. = *être sur un pied d'égalité avec qqn*
☠ *être égal à soi-même* = to be always the same
— *ça m'est égal* = I don't care
— *le sol n'est pas égal* = the floor is not even.

EQUAL (to, -(l)ed) *égaler* : my cooking doesn't equal hers = *ma cuisine n'égale pas la sienne* ⓪ to be up to = *être à la hauteur de*.

EQUALITY (n) *égalité (f)* : equality of the sexes = *l'égalité des sexes* ☠ *l'égalité des chances* = equal opportunity
— *être à égalité* = to be tied.

EQUALLY (adv) **1/** *également* : he treats his children equally = *il traite également tous ses enfants* ☠ *j'ai également ...* = I have ... as well **2/** *tout aussi bien* : the film can be appreciated equally by children = *le film peut tout aussi bien être aimé des enfants*.

EQUATOR (n) *équateur (m)* : to cross the equator = *passer l'équateur* ⓪ pole = *pôle* **EQUATORIAL** (adj) *équatorial, -e* : equatorial climate = *un climat équatorial*.

EQUIP (to, -ped) *équiper* : the office is equipped with the latest computers = *le bureau est équipé des derniers ordinateurs* ⓪ to outfit = *installer*
to be equipped to = *être équipé pour* : the hotel is equipped to handle conventions = *l'hôtel est équipé pour recevoir des séminaires* ⓪ to be geared to = *être conçu pour*
to be equipped for = *avoir les qualités nécessaires pour* : I'm not equipped for the job = *je n'ai pas les qualités nécessaires pour ce travail*.

EQUIPMENT (n) *équipement (m)* : the hospital lacks modern equipment = *l'hôpital manque d'équipement moderne* ⓪ gear = *attirail*.

EQUITY (n) *équité (f)* ≠ inequity = *inéquité*.

EQUIVALENT (n) *équivalent (m)* : that expression has no equivalent in French = *cette expression n'a pas d'équivalent en français*.

EQUIVALENT (adj) *équivalent, -e* : give me the equivalent amount in francs = *donnez-moi la somme équivalente en francs*
to be equivalent to = *équivaloir à* : that's equivalent to telling him to go to hell = *ça équivaut à lui dire d'aller au diable* = that's tantamount to.

EQUIVOCAL (adj) *équivoque* : an equivocal attitude = *une attitude équivoque* ⓪ ambiguous = *ambigu*.

ERA (n) *ère (f)* ⓪ epoch = *époque*.

ERASE (to, -d) *gommer* ⓪ to cross out = *barrer*.

ERASER (n) *gomme (f)* = rubber (GB)
☠ *à la gomme* = junky
— *mets la gomme !* = step on it !

ERECT (to, -ed) *ériger* : to erect a war memorial = *ériger un monument aux morts* ⓪ to build = *bâtir*.

ERECTION (n) *érection (f)* ⓪ to have a hard-on = *bander*.

ERODE (to, -d) *éroder* ⓪ to decay = *se dégrader*.

EROSION (n) *érosion (f)* ⓪ disintegration = *désintégration*.

EROTIC (adj) *érotique* : erotic literature = *littérature érotique* ⓪ sensual = *sensuel* **EROTICISM** (n) *érotisme (m)* ≠ pornography = *pornographie*.

ERR (to, -ed) *commettre des erreurs* : they erred in their statistics = *ils ont commis des erreurs dans leurs statistiques* ⓪ to be wrong = *avoir tort*.

ERRAND (n) *course (f)* : I have some errands to do = *j'ai quelques courses à faire* ☠ → race
errand boy = *garçon de courses/coursier*
to run errands = *faire des courses*.

ERRATIC (adj) *lunatique* : an erratic personality = *une personnalité lunatique* ⓪ capricious = *capricieux*.

ERRONEOUS (adj) *erroné, -e* : erroneous conclusions = *des conclusions erronées* ≠ accurate = *juste* **ERRONEOUSLY** (adv) *à tort* : they erroneously called me a leftist = *ils m'ont traité à tort de gauchiste*.

ERROR (n) *erreur (f)* : to make an error = *faire une erreur* ⓪ mistake = *faute*
to be in error = *être dans l'erreur* ⓪ to be mistaken = *se tromper*
☠ *par erreur* = by mistake
— *induire en erreur* = to mislead.

ERUDITE (adj) *érudit, -e* ① cultured = *cultivé*, bookish = *qui a une culture livresque.*

ERUPT (to, -ed) *entrer en éruption* : the volcano erupted = *le volcan est entré en éruption* **ERUPTION** (n) *éruption (f)* ⚕ *une éruption de boutons* = a rash.

ESCALATE (to, -d) *s'accroître* : the number of ski accidents is escalating = *le nombre d'accidents de ski s'accroît* ① to expand = *être en pleine expansion.*

ESCALATOR (n) *escalier (m) roulant* ① elevator = *ascenseur.*

ESCAPADE (n) *escapade (f)* ① adventure = *aventure.*

ESCAPE (n) **1/** *évasion (f)* : to plan an escape = *projeter une évasion* ① getaway = *fuite* **2/** *échappatoire (f)* : his job's an escape (from his marriage) = *son travail est une échappatoire (à sa vie privée)* ① release = *exutoire*
escape clause = *échappatoire (contrat)* ① out = *porte de sortie.*

ESCAPE (to, -d) **1/** *s'échapper* : three prisoners escaped = *trois prisonniers se sont échappés*
to escape from (prison) = *s'échapper de (prison)* ① to break out of = *s'évader de*, to abscond = *prendre la fuite*, to go over the wall = *faire le mur*
2/ *échapper à* : to escape punishment = *échapper à une punition* ① to avoid = *éviter*
⚕ *vous n'y échapperez pas !* = you won't get away with it !
— *je ne voulais pas dire ça, ça m'a échappé* = I didn't mean to say that, it just slipped out.

ESCORT (n) **1/** *chevalier (m) servant* : she never goes out without an escort = *elle ne sort jamais sans chevalier servant* ① chaperon = ← **2/** *escorte (f)* : a police escort = *une escorte de police* **ESCORT** (to, -ed) *escorter.*

ESKIMO (n) *esquimau, -de* ① igloo = ←.

ESPECIALLY (adv) **1/** *tout spécialement* : I especially like intelligent men = *j'aime tout spécialement les hommes intelligents* ① particularly = *particulièrement*, chiefly = *avant tout* **2/** *spécialement* : the dinner was prepared especially for you = *le dîner a été préparé spécialement pour toi*
especially as = *d'autant plus que* : I'm angry especially as it's not the first time he's lied to me = *je suis d'autant plus en colère que ce n'est pas la première fois qu'il m'a menti*
not especially = *pas spécialement* : do you like ice cream ? — not especially = *vous aimez les glaces ? — pas spécialement.*

ESPOUSE (to, -d) *épouser* : to espouse a cause = *épouser une cause* ⚕ → to marry.

ESSAY (n) *essai (m)* : an essay on torture = *un essai sur la torture* ① essayist = *essayiste*
⚕ *prendre qqn à l'essai* = to take s.o. on a trial basis
— *un essai* = a try/a go
— *un essai (football américain)* = a touchdown.

ESSENCE (n) *essence (f)* : the essence of the problem = *l'essence du problème*
in essence = *en réalité* : he talks rough, but in essence he's a softy = *il est brutal en paroles, mais en réalité, c'est un tendre* ① in truth = *en vérité*
the essence of = *le comble de* : the neutron bomb is the essence of man's madness = *la bombe à neutrons, c'est le comble de la folie humaine*
⚕ *essence* = gas/petrol (GB)/fuel.

ESSENTIAL (adj) *essentiel, -elle* : that's the essential difference between us = *c'est la différence essentielle entre nous* ① fundamental = *fondamental.*

ESSENTIALLY (adv) **1/** *essentiellement* : her writings are essentially feminist = *ses écrits sont essentiellement féministes* **2/** *au fond* : he loses his temper a lot, but is essentially a good father = *il se met souvent en colère, mais au fond c'est un bon père.*

ESTABLISH (to, -ed) **1/** *établir* : to establish a company = *établir une société* ① to found = *fonder* **2/** *établir* : the police established he was guilty = *la police a établi sa culpabilité* ① to demonstrate = *démontrer*
⚕ *établir un record* = to set a record
— *s'établir en Floride* = to settle in Florida.

ESTABLISHMENT (n) *établissement (m)* : it's a dirty establishment = *c'est un établissement malpropre*
the Establishment = *l'Establishment* ① the moral majority = *les gens bien pensants.*

ESTATE (n) **1/** *grande propriété (f)* : an estate in the country = *une grande propriété à la campagne* ① land = *terre* **2/** *biens (m pl)* : he left a large estate to his son = *il a laissé de nombreux biens à son fils* ① real estate = *biens immobiliers* ⚕ → possession.

ESTEEM (n) *estime (f)* : we have great esteem for her = *nous avons beaucoup d'estime pour elle* ≠ scorn = *mépris* **ESTEEM** (to, -ed) *estimer* : she's highly esteemed at work = *elle est très estimée à son travail* ≠ to scorn = *mépriser* ⚕ → to estimate.

ESTIMATE (n) *estimation (f)* : an estimate of the work to be done = *une estimation du travail à faire* ① price quotation = *devis* ⚕ → estimation.

ESTIMATE (to, -d) *estimer* : they estimated that 1,000 people would come = *ils ont estimé que 1 000 personnes viendraient*
⚕ *j'estime que ...* = I consider that ...
— *estimer beaucoup qqn* = to esteem s.o. highly
— *estimer le montant des dégâts* = to assess the damages.

ESTIMATION (n) **in my estimation (the fault is his)** = *à mon humble avis (c'est de sa faute)*
⚕ *estimation (prix)* = estimate (price).

ESTRANGE (to, -d) *éloigner* : her temper estranged her friends = *son mauvais caractère a éloigné ses amis* ⚕ → to drift apart.

ESTRANGED (adj) **to be estranged from (one's wife)** = *être séparé (de sa femme)* ⓓ to be divorced = *être divorcé*
his estranged wife = *son ex-femme.*

ETC (abbr) *etc.* ⓓ and so on and so forth = *et patati et patata, et cetera* = ←.

ETCHING (n) *eau-forte* (f)
come up and see my etchings = *viens voir mes estampes japonaises/mon compteur bleu* ⓓ your place or mine ? = *on va chez toi ou chez moi ?*

ETERNAL (adj) *éternel, -elle* : eternal hatred = *haine éternelle* ⓓ lasting = *durable* **ETERNALLY** (adv) *éternellement* ⓓ for ever and ever = *à tout jamais.*

ETERNITY (n) *éternité* (f) : I haven't seen him for an eternity = *je ne l'ai pas vu depuis une éternité* ⓓ infinity = *infini.*

ETHICAL (adj) *probe* : an ethical man = *un homme probe* ⓓ moral = ←.

ETHICS (n pl) *éthique* (f) ⓓ philosophy = *philosophie.*

ETHNIC (adj) *ethnique* : ethnic groups = *des groupes ethniques* **ETHNOLOGIST** (n) *ethnologue* (m, f) ⓓ anthropologist = *anthropologue* **ETHNOLOGY** (n) *ethnologie* (f) ⓓ anthropology = *anthropologie.*

ETYMOLOGY (n) *étymologie* (f) ⓓ lexicology = *lexicologie.*

EULOGY (n, -ies) *panégyrique* (m) ⓓ tribute = *hommage.*

EUNUCH (n) *eunuque* (m) : eunuchs watching his harem = *des eunuques qui gardaient son harem.*

EUPHEMISM (n) *euphémisme* (m) = understatement ⓓ figure of speech = *figure de style.*

EUROPE (n) *Europe* (f) ⓓ EEC = *C.E.E.* **EUROPEAN** (n, adj) *Européen, -enne* ⓓ Asian = *Asiatique*, African = *Africain.*

EUTHANASIA (n) *euthanasie* (f) = mercy killing.

EVACUATE (to, -d) *évacuer* : to evacuate troops = *évacuer des troupes* **EVACUATION** (n) *évacuation* (f).

EVADE (to, -d) *se dérober à* : to evade a question = *se dérober à une question* ⓓ to hedge = *répondre à côté*, to duck = *esquiver.*

EVALUATE (to, -d) *évaluer* : to evaluate one's chances = *évaluer ses chances* ⓓ to appraise = *apprécier la valeur de* **EVALUATION** (n) *évaluation* (f) ⓓ appraisal = *appréciation.*

EVAPORATE (to, -d) *s'évaporer* : the water evaporated = *l'eau s'est évaporée.*

EVASIVE (adj) *évasif, -ive* : an evasive answer = *une réponse évasive* ≠ direct = ←.

EVE (n) *veille* (f) : Christmas Eve = *la veille de Noël*

on the eve of (their wedding) = *à la veille de (leur mariage)* ≠ the night after = *la nuit suivante* ☠ *arriver la veille* = to arrive the day before
— *une longue veille* = a long vigil.

EVEN (adj) 1/ *égal, -e* : her work/the floor isn't even = *son travail/le sol n'est pas égal* ⓓ flat = *plat* ☠ → equal

to be even = *être quitte* : I got back and now we're even = *je me suis vengé et maintenant nous sommes quittes* **to be even with (the ground)** = *être au ras du (sol)* ⓓ to be flush with = *être au niveau de* **even money/odds** = *une chance sur deux* :	it's even money/odds that he is going to win = *il a une chance sur deux de gagner* **even** ≠ **odd number** = *chiffre pair* ≠ *impair* **even temper** = *caractère égal* **to get even with** = *se venger de* ⓓ to pay s.o. back = *faire payer à qqn*

2/ *tout rond* : I have $ 20 even = *j'ai 20 dollars tout rond* ≠ $ 20-odd = *20 dollars et des poussières.*

EVEN (adv) *même* : even adults cry = *même les adultes pleurent* ☠ *(aujourd'hui) même* = this very (day)

to break even = *rentrer dans ses fonds* : when will the business break even ? = *quand l'affaire rentrera-t-elle dans ses fonds ?* ⓓ to make a profit = *faire un bénéfice* **even more/-er** = *encore plus* ... : she's even nicer now = *elle est encore plus gentille maintenant*, even more intelligent = *encore plus intelligent* **even if/though** = *même si* : even if/though the car's expensive, I'll buy it = *j'achèterai cette voiture même si elle est chère*	**even more (of)** ... **than** = *encore plus* ... *que* : she's even more (of) a bitch than her sister = *elle est encore plus garce que sa sœur* **even so** = *quand même* : I know he's a bastard, but I love him even so = *je sais que c'est un salaud, mais je l'aime quand même* ⓓ anyhow = *de toute manière* **even then** = *toujours* : he gave me a discount, but even then I couldn't afford it = *il m'a fait une réduction, mais je ne pouvais toujours pas me l'offrir.*

EVENING (n) *soir* (m) : Monday evening = *lundi soir*
evening gown = *robe du soir*
evening school = *cours du soir* ⓓ adult education = *formation permanente*

in the evening = *le soir* ≠ in the morning = *le matin*
the evening before = *la veille au soir* ≠ **the evening after** = *le lendemain soir*
this evening = *ce soir* : we're eating at home this evening = *nous dînons à la maison ce soir* = we're eating at home tonight
a beautiful evening = *une belle soirée.*

EVENLY (adv) *de force égale* : they're evenly matched = *ils sont de force égale.*

EVEN OUT (to, -ed) *rétablir l'équilibre* : that will even things out = *ça rétablira l'équilibre.*

EVENT (n) **1/** *événement (m)* : the course of events = *le cours des événements* ⓪ occasion = ← **2/** *épreuve (f)* sportive : track event = *épreuve d'athlétisme*
in the event of (an emergency) = *au cas où (il y aurait une urgence)* = in case (there's an emergency).

EVEN-TEMPERED (adj) *d'humeur égale* ≠ bad-tempered = *qui a mauvais caractère.*

EVENTFUL (adj) **1/** *fertile en événements* : an eventful year = *une année fertile en événements* ≠ uneventful = *sans incidents* **2/** *mouvementé, -e* : an eventful day = *une journée mouvementée* ⓪ busy = *chargé* ☠ → hectic.

EVENTUAL (adj) *éventuel, -elle* : we'll share any eventual profit = *nous partagerons tout bénéfice éventuel* ☠ *un (client) éventuel* = a possible (customer).

EVENTUALITY (n, -ies) *éventualité (f)* : I'm ready for any eventuality = *je suis prête à toute éventualité.*

EVENTUALLY (adv) *en fin de compte* : we eventually made up = *en fin de compte nous nous sommes réconciliés* ⓪ in the end = *finalement* ☠ *éventuellement (on pourrait ...)* = (we could ...) perhaps.

EVER (adv) *jamais* : have you ever been to England ? = *êtes-vous jamais allé en Angleterre ?* ☠ → never

did you ever ! = *par exemple !* → GOSH! **ever since** = *depuis lors* : I had an abortion and I've been taking the pill ever since = *je me suis fait avorter et depuis lors je prends la pilule* **ever so (nice)** = *tellement (gentil)* → VERY **hardly/scarcely/ barely ever** = *ne ... presque jamais* : I hardly/barely/scarcely	ever smoke cigars = *je ne fume presque jamais le cigare* **is ... ever !** = *et comment donc !* : bright ? is he ever ! = *intelligent ? et comment donc !* ⓪ and how ! = *et comment !* **not ever** = *jamais* : I haven't ever smoked = *je n'ai jamais fumé* = I've never smoked ≠ sometimes = *quelquefois* ☠ → never.

EVERY (adj) *tous, toutes les* : every book on the shelf is in English = *tous les livres sur cette étagère sont en anglais* ⓪ all = *tous*, each = *chaque*

every bit as ... as = *tout aussi ... que* : every bit as nice as his brother = *tout aussi gentil que son frère* **every day** = *tous les jours* **every little bit helps** = *les petits ruisseaux font les grandes rivières* ⓪ little by little = *petit à petit* **every other/second day** = *tous les deux jours/un jour sur deux* **every other week** = *tous les quinze jours* ⓪	a week out of two = *une semaine sur deux* **every (single) time** = *chaque fois (sans exception)* **every so often** = *de temps à autre* : I go to the States every so often = *je vais aux États-Unis de temps à autre* **every Tom, Dick and Harry** = *le premier venu* : she sleeps with every Tom, Dick and Harry = *elle couche avec le premier venu.*

EVERYBODY (pron) → EVERYONE.

EVERYDAY (adj) *de tous les jours* : my everyday coat = *mon manteau de tous les jours.*

EVERYONE (pron) *tout le monde* : everyone loved him = *tout le monde l'aimait* = everybody ≠ no one = *personne*
everyone who is anyone = *le Gotha* : everyone who is anyone was at the party = *tout le Gotha assistait à cette soirée* ⓪ the upper crust = *le gratin.*

EVERYTHING (pron) *tout* : he ate everything = *il a tout mangé* ≠ nothing = *rien* ☠ → all

to be everything to s.o. = *être tout pour qqn* : his kids are everything to him = *ses enfants sont tout pour lui* **everything has its price** = *tout a un prix* ⓪ you get nothing for nothing = *on n'a rien sans rien* **everything considered** = *au bout du compte* : everything considered the divorce wasn't too hard on the kids = *au bout du compte le divorce n'a pas été trop dur pour les enfants* ⓪ all things	considered = *tout bien considéré* **everything and anything** = *tout et n'importe quoi* : the cat eats everything and anything = *le chat mange tout et n'importe quoi* **everything in good time** = *chaque chose en son temps* ⓪ one thing at a time = *une chose à la fois* **everything is relative** = *tout est relatif* **everything within reason** = *il ne faut pas exagérer* ≠ to push too far = *exagérer*

to talk of everything and anything = *parler de tout et de rien* ⓪ | to shoot the breeze = *parler de la pluie et du beau temps.*

EVERYWHERE (adv) *partout* : I looked everywhere = *j'ai cherché partout* ⓪ all around = *de tous côtés* ≠ nowhere = *nulle part*
everywhere else = *partout ailleurs.*

EVICT (to, -ed) *expulser* : evicted from the apartment = *expulsé de l'appartement* ⓪ to throw out = *jeter dehors* 💀 *expulser qqn (d'un pays)* = to deport s.o.

EVIDENCE (n inv) *preuves (f pl)* : his evidence was rejected by the court = *ses preuves ont été rejetées par le tribunal* ⓪ testimony = *témoignage*
a piece of evidence = *une preuve*
circumstancial evidence = *preuves indirectes*
to give evidence = *porter témoignage*
incriminating evidence = *pièces à conviction*
💀 → proof
— *rendez-vous à l'évidence !* = face the facts !
— *c'est l'évidence même* = it's perfectly obvious.

EVIDENT (adj) *évident, -e* : it was evident that he was lying = *il était évident qu'il mentait* ⓪ clear = *clair* ≠ disputable = *discutable* 💀 *ce n'est pas évident* = it's not so sure.

EVIDENTLY (adv) *de toute évidence* : he's evidently lying = *de toute évidence, il ment* ⓪ plainly = *manifestement.*

EVIL (n) *mal (m)* : work is a necessary evil = *le travail est un mal nécessaire*
💀 *dire du mal de qqn* = to speak ill of s.o.
— *avoir le mal de mer/du pays* = to be seasick/homesick
— *faire mal à qqn* = to hurt s.o.
— *j'ai eu beaucoup de mal/un mal fou à ...* = I had a lot of trouble to ...
— *mal de tête/à la gorge* = headache/sore throat
— *se donner du mal* = to take pains
— *prendre son mal en patience* = to tough it out.

EVIL (adj) *malveillant, -e* (thoughts), *malfaisant, -e* (person) ≠ good = *bon.*

EVOKE (to, -d) *évoquer* : to evoke the past = *évoquer le passé.*

EVOLUTION (n) *évolution (f)* : the evolution of events = *l'évolution des événements* ≠ status quo = *statu quo.*

EVOLVE (to, -d) *évoluer* : city life has evolved a great deal = *la vie en ville a pas mal évolué* ⓪ to change = *changer* 💀 *elle évolue dans les milieux huppés* = she moves in smart circles.

EX (n) **one's ex** = *son ex (-mari/-femme)* : I saw your ex last night = *j'ai vu ton ex hier soir.*

EX- (prefix) *ex-* : the ex-champion = *l'ex-champion* ⓪ former = *ancien.*

EXACERBATE (to, -d) *exacerber* : to exacerbate a conflict = *exacerber un conflit* ≠ to appease = *apaiser.*

EXACT (adj) **1/** *exact, -e* : an exact description = *une description exacte* ⓪ accurate = *juste* ≠ inexact = ←
2/ *exact, -e* : give me the exact details = *donnez-moi les détails exacts* ⓪ precise = *précis*
to be exact = *pour être précis* : it cost $ 10.50 to be exact = *ça a coûté 10,50 dollars, pour être précis*
💀 *il est toujours exact* = he's always on time
— *oui, c'est exact* = yes, that's correct.

EXACTING (adj) *astreignant, -e* : exacting work = *travail astreignant* ⓪ demanding = *exigeant.*

EXACTLY (adv) *exactement* : that's exactly what happened = *c'est exactement ce qui s'est passé* ⓪ precisely = *précisément.*

EXAGGERATE (to, -d) *exagérer* : when he says she's a hooker, he's exaggerating = *quand il dit que c'est une putain, il exagère* ⓪ to go too far = *y aller un peu fort* ≠ to understate = *minimiser.*

EXAGGERATION (n) *exagération (f)* ≠ understatement = *euphémisme.*

EXAM (n) *examen (m)* = examination ⓪ drill = *colle*
to pass ≠ **to fail an exam** = *réussir* ≠ *échouer à un examen*
to take an exam = *passer un examen* = to sit for an exam (GB).

EXAMINATION (n) **1/** *examen (m)* : she's studying for her French examination = *elle travaille son examen de français* = exam **2/** *examen (m)* : a medical examination = *un examen médical* ⓪ checkup = *check-up*
💀 *le problème est à l'examen* = the problem is under study.

EXAMINE (to, -d) *examiner* : to examine a patient/a report = *examiner un malade/un rapport* ⓪ to reexamine = *réexaminer.*

EXAMPLE (n) *exemple (m)* : give me an example = *donnez-moi un exemple* ⓪ case = *cas*
for example = *par exemple* = for instance
to hold s.o. up as an example = *prendre qqn pour exemple* : she holds her father up as an example = *elle prend son père pour exemple*
to set ≠ **to follow the example** = *montrer* ≠ *suivre l'exemple*
💀 *ça par exemple !* = I'll be darned !
— *être un exemple de (courage)* = to be a model of (courage).

EXASPERATE (to, -d) *exaspérer* : your attitude exasperates me = *votre attitude m'exaspère* → ANGRY.

EXASPERATING (adj) *exaspérant, -e* : this work's exasperating = *ce travail est exaspérant* ⓪ annoying = *ennuyeux* **EXASPERATION** (n) *exaspération (f).*

EXCAVATE (to, -d) *faire des fouilles* : they discovered a tomb while excavating = *ils ont découvert une tombe en faisant des fouilles* **EXCAVATION** (n) *excavation (f)* ⓓ dig = *fouilles*.

EXCEED (to, -ed) **1/** *excéder* : it won't exceed $ 100 = *cela n'excédera pas 100 dollars* ☠ *tu m'excèdes !* = you're a pain ! **2/** *dépasser* : to exceed a speed limit/s.o.'s hopes = *dépasser une limitation de vitesse/les espoirs de qqn* ☠ → to overtake.

EXCEEDINGLY (adv) *excessivement* : exceedingly expensive = *excessivement cher* = excessively expensive → VERY.

EXCEL IN (to, -led) *exceller en* : to excel in sports = *exceller en sport* ⓓ to be good at = *être bon en*.

EXCELLENCY (n, -ies) **Your Excellency** = *Votre Excellence*.

EXCELLENT (adj) *excellent, -e* : an excellent play = *une pièce excellente* → WONDERFUL ≠ no great shakes = *qui ne casse rien*.

EXCEPT (prep) *excepté* : everything was delicious except the dessert = *tout était délicieux excepté le dessert* ⓓ apart from = *à part*, save = *hormis*
except for = *excepté* : everyone was pleased except for me = *tout le monde était content excepté moi* ⓓ with the exception of = *à l'exception de*.

EXCEPT (conj) **1/** *si ce n'est (que)* : what can I do except agree ? = *que puis-je faire si ce n'est accepter ?* **2/** *excepté* : she can do everything, except type = *elle peut tout faire, excepté taper à la machine* ⓓ but = *sauf*
except if = *sauf si* : I won't do it except if you want me to = *je ne le ferai pas sauf si vous le voulez* ⓓ unless = *à moins que*.

EXCEPTING (prep) *exception faite de* : I like all his films excepting the first one = *j'aime tous ses films exception faite du premier*.

EXCEPTION (n) *exception (f)* : I'll make no exception = *je ne ferai pas d'exception* ≠ rule = *règle*
to take exception to = *récuser* ≠ to agree with = *être d'accord avec*
that's an exception to the rule = *c'est une exception à la règle*
the exception proves the rule = *c'est l'exception qui confirme la règle*
with the exception of (my husband) = *à l'exception de (mon mari)* ⓓ other than = *à part*
☠ *un (athlète) d'exception* = an outstanding (athlete).

EXCEPTIONAL (adj) *exceptionnel, -elle* : an exceptional quality = *une qualité exceptionnelle* → WONDERFUL ≠ average = *moyen* **EXCEPTIONALLY** (adv) *exceptionnellement* → VERY.

EXCERPT (n) *extrait (m)* : excerpts from his book published in the press = *des extraits de son livre publiés dans la presse* = extract.

EXCESS (n, -es) *excès (m)* : the excesses of the regime = *les excès du régime*
☠ *faire un excès de vitesse* = to pass the speed limit
— *(scrupuleux) à l'excès* = overly (scrupulous)
— *tomber d'un excès dans l'autre* = to go from one extreme to another.

EXCESS (adj) *en/de trop* : he jogs to get rid of his excess fat = *il fait du jogging pour se débarrasser de ses kilos en trop*
to be excess baggage = *être de trop* ⓓ to be in the way = *être importun*.

EXCESSIVE (adj) *excessif, -ive* : an excessive personality = *une personnalité excessive* ⓓ inordinate = *démesuré*, immoderate = *immodéré*.

EXCESSIVELY (adv) *excessivement* : excessively expensive = *excessivement cher* → VERY.

EXCHANGE (n) *échange (m)* : an exchange of prisoners = *un échange de prisonniers* ⓓ barter = *troc*
exchange rate = *taux de change*
in exchange for = *en échange de* ⓓ in return for = *en contrepartie de*
☠ *libre échange* = free trade.

EXCHANGE (to, -d) *échanger* : the store said I could exchange the coat = *le magasin a dit que je pouvais échanger le manteau*
to exchange for = *échanger contre* : to exchange a white one for a green one = *échanger un blanc contre un vert*.

EXCITABLE (adj) *excitable* ≠ even-tempered = *d'humeur égale*.

EXCITE (to, -d) **to be excited** = *être excité* : after all this necking, I'm all excited = *après toutes ces caresses, je suis tout excitée* ⓓ hot-and-bothered = *tout chose*
to be excited about (a trip) = *être excité par (un voyage)*.

EXCITED (adj) *excité, -e* : excited children waiting for Santa Claus = *des enfants excités qui attendaient le Père Noël*
don't get excited ! = **1/** *ne t'excite pas !* → ANGRY **2/** *ne t'en fais pas !* ⓓ don't worry ! = *ne t'inquiète pas !*

EXCITEMENT (n) *excitation (f)* : hey ! what's all the excitement about ? = *hé, qu'est-ce que c'est que toute cette excitation ?* ⓓ commotion = *agitation*, ado = *affaire*.

EXCITING (adj) *passionnant, -e* : an exciting trip = *un voyage passionnant* ≠ unexciting = *pas très excitant* ☠ *une fille excitante* = a sexy girl.

EXCLAIM (to, -ed) *s'exclamer* : "shit !", she exclaimed = *« merde ! » s'est-elle exclamée*.

EXCLAMATION (n) *exclamation (f)* ⓓ interjection = ←
exclamation mark = *point d'exclamation*.

EXCLUDE (to, -d) *exclure* : to exclude s.o. from a club = *exclure qqn d'un club* ⓐ to eliminate = *éliminer* ⓐ exclusion = ← ☠ *il est exclu que ...* = it's out of question that ...

EXCLUDING (prep) *à l'exclusion de* : 30 hostages excluding the pilots = *30 otages à l'exclusion des pilotes* ⓐ aside from = *mis à part.*

EXCLUSIVE (adj) **1/** *exclusif, -ive* : the exclusive right to film a novel = *le droit exclusif d'adapter un roman au cinéma* **2/** *sélect* : an exclusive area = *un quartier sélect* ⓐ snobbish = *snob* ☠ → select
exclusive of (drinks) = *à l'exclusion (des boissons).*

EXCLUSIVELY (adv) *exclusivement* : a club exclusively for women = *un club exclusivement pour les femmes.*

EXCOMMUNICATE (to, -d) *excommunier.*

EXCRUCIATING (adj) *atroce* : an excruciating dilemma = *un dilemme atroce* ⓐ acute = *aigu* ☠ → atrocious.

EXCURSION (n) *excursion (f)* : a day excursion to Monaco = *une journée d'excursion à Monaco* ⓐ trip = *voyage.*

EXCUSE (n) *excuse (f)* : he had no excuse for being late = *il n'avait aucune excuse pour son retard* ⓐ pretext = *prétexte*
to make excuses for s.o. = *chercher des excuses à qqn* : don't make excuses for your husband = *ne cherche pas d'excuses à ton mari*
☠ *faire ses excuses* = to apologize
— *des excuses par écrit* = a written apology.

EXCUSE (to, -d) *excuser* : please excuse my calling again = *je vous prie de m'excuser de vous téléphoner de nouveau* ⓐ to pardon = *pardonner*
excuse me ! = *excusez-moi !/je m'excuse !* ⓐ pardon me ! = *pardonnez-moi !*
to excuse s.o. for = *excuser qqn de* : excuse me for calling so late = *excusez-moi d'appeler si tard*
☠ *je ne l'excuse pas de se droguer* = I don't condone his taking drugs
— *excusez-moi auprès de (votre mère)* = apologize to (your mother) for me.

EXECUTE (to, -d) *exécuter* : to execute a prisoner = *exécuter un prisonnier* ⓐ to put to death = *mettre à mort*, to hang = *pendre*, to electrocute = *électrocuter*
to execute orders = *exécuter des ordres.*

EXECUTION (n) *exécution (f)* ⓐ firing squad = *peloton d'exécution* ☠ *mettre (une menace) à exécution* = to carry out (a threat).

EXECUTIONER (n) *bourreau (m)* ≠ victim = *victime* ☠ *bourreau de travail* = workaholic
— *bourreau des cœurs* = lady-killer.

EXECUTIVE (n) *cadre (m)* : he's an advertising executive = *il est cadre dans la publicité* ≠ white collar = *col blanc* ☠ → frame.

EXECUTOR (n) **executor of a will** = *exécuteur testamentaire.*

EXEMPLARY (adj) *exemplaire* : exemplary behavior = *conduite exemplaire.*

EXEMPT (adj) *exempté, -e* : exempt from the finals/military service = *exempté d'examens de fin d'année/de service militaire.*

EXEMPTION (n) *exemption (f)* : tax exemption = *exemption d'impôts.*

EXERCISE (n) *exercice (m)* : to do exercises every morning = *faire des exercices tous les matins*
☠ *exercice illégal d'une profession* = illegal practice of a profession
— *entrer en exercice* = to take office.

EXERCISE (to, -d) **1/** *faire de l'exercice* : I exercise to stay in form = *je fais de l'exercice pour rester en forme* ⓐ to work out = *s'entraîner* **2/** *user de* : to exercise one's rights/power = *user de son droit/pouvoir.*

EXERT (to, -ed) *exercer* : to exert pressure on s.o. = *exercer une pression sur qqn*
☠ *exercer le pouvoir* = to wield power
— *s'exercer à* = to practice.

EXHALE (to, -d) *exhaler* : to exhale the smoke = *exhaler la fumée* ≠ to inhale = *inhaler.*

EXHAUST (to, -ed) *épuiser* : we've exhausted our supplies = *nous avons épuisé nos réserves*
☠ *notre café s'épuise* = our coffee is running low
— *nos dernières provisions sont épuisées* = our last supplies gave out.

EXHAUSTED (adj) *épuisé, -e* : I feel exhausted = *je me sens épuisée* ⓐ tired = *fatigué*, washed-out = *lessivé*
☠ *un livre épuisé* = a book out of print.

EXHAUSTING (adj) *épuisant, -e* : an exhausting day = *une journée épuisante* ⓐ grueling = *exténuant.*

EXHAUSTION (n) *épuisement (m)* : trembling with exhaustion = *tremblante d'épuisement* ⓐ fatigue = ←.

EXHAUSTIVE (adj) *exhaustif, -ive* : an exhaustive list = *une liste exhaustive* ≠ superficial = *superficiel.*

EXHIBIT (n) **1/** *(petite) exposition (f)* : jewelry exhibit = *(petite) exposition de bijoux* ⓐ exhibition = *exposition* **2/** *pièce (f) à conviction* : exhibit A was the gun = *la pièce à conviction A était le pistolet.*

EXHIBIT (to, -ed) *exposer* : this is the first time his work has been exhibited = *c'est la première fois que son œuvre est exposée* ☠ → to expose.

EXHIBITION (n) *exposition (f)* : art/jewelry exhibition = *exposition d'art/de bijoux* ⓐ exhibitor = *exposant*
to make an exhibition of o.s. = *se donner en spectacle* ⓐ to make a fool of o.s. = *se rendre ridicule*

on exhibition = *exposé* : the jewels are on exhibition = *les bijoux sont exposés*
☠ → *exposition*.

EXHIBITIONISM (n) *exhibitionnisme* (m) **EXHIBITIONIST** (n) *exhibitionniste* (m, f) ⓄⒹ dirty old man = *vieux vicieux*.

EXHIBITOR (n) *exposant, -e* : 100 exhibitors at the show = *100 exposants au salon*.

EXHILARATING (adj) *stimulant, -e* : exhilarating work = *un travail stimulant*.

EXHUME (to, -d) *exhumer* : to exhume a corpse = *exhumer un cadavre* ≠ to bury = *enterrer*.

EXILE (n) *exil* (m) : to live in exile = *vivre en exil* ⓄⒹ banishment = *bannissement* **EXILE** (to, -d) *exiler* : to exile political opponents = *exiler des opposants politiques*.

EXIST (to, -ed) *exister* : such things exist = *de telles choses existent* ⓄⒹ to be = *être* ☠ *il existe de(s) ...* = there is/are ...

EXISTENCE (n) *existence* (f) : means of existence = *moyens d'existence*.

EXISTENTIALISM (n) *existentialisme* (m) **EXISTENTIALIST** (n) *existentialiste* (m, f).

EXIT (n) *sortie* (f) : where's the exit ? = *où est la sortie ?* ≠ way in = *entrée*
☠ *faire une sortie contre qqn* = to lace into s.o.
— *une sortie* = an outing
— *à sa sortie de l'hôpital* = upon his discharge from the hospital.

EXODUS (n) *exode* (m) ≠ arrival = *arrivée*.

EXONERATE (to, -d) *disculper* : the Senator was exonerated of charges of bribery = *le sénateur a été disculpé de toute accusation de corruption* ≠ to indict = *inculper*
☠ *exonérer d'impôts* = to exempt from taxes.

EXORBITANT (adj) *exorbitant, -e* : exorbitant prices = *des prix exorbitants* ⓄⒹ excessive = *excessif* ≠ moderate = *modéré*.

EXORCISE (to, -d) *exorciser* ≠ to bewitch = *ensorceler*.

EXOTIC (adj) *exotique* : exotic fruit = *des fruits exotiques* ≠ native = *indigène*.

EXPAND (to, -ed) **1/** *être en pleine expansion* : the car industry is expanding = *l'industrie automobile est en pleine expansion* ⓄⒹ to enlarge = *s'agrandir* **2/** *élargir* : the newspaper is expanding its activities = *le journal élargit ses activités*
to expand on (a theory) = *développer (une théorie)* = to enlarge on ☠ → to develop
☠ *élargir une robe* = to let out a dress
— *élargir une route* = to widen a road.

EXPANSION (n) *expansion* (f) : to be in full expansion = *être en pleine expansion* ⓄⒹ growth = *croissance*.

EXPATRIATE (n) *expatrié, -e* **EXPATRIATE** (to, -d) (*s'*)*expatrier* **EXPATRIATION** (n) *expatriation* (f).

EXPECT (to, -ed) **1/** *attendre* : we're expecting him for dinner = *nous l'attendons à dîner*, I'm expecting a letter soon = *j'attends bientôt une lettre* ☠ *attendez-moi !* = wait for me !
— *(un bon dîner) vous attend* = (a good dinner) is awaiting you
2/ *s'attendre à* : I'm expecting big problems = *je m'attends à de gros problèmes*, I don't know what to expect = *je ne sais pas à quoi m'attendre*

to be expecting = *attendre un enfant* ⓄⒹ to be in the family way = *attendre un heureux événement* **I expected it** ≠ **I didn't expect it** = *je m'y attendais* ≠ *je ne m'y attendais pas* **I expect so** = *je pense bien* = I think so **it was to be expected** = *il fallait s'y attendre* **to expect to** = *envisager de* : I expect to go to Europe this summer = *j'envisage d'aller en Europe cet été* ⓄⒹ to	plan to = *projeter de* **to expect s.o. to** = *s'attendre à ce que qqn* : we expected you to help us = *nous nous attendions à ce que vous nous aidiez*, don't expect me to lend you the money = *ne vous attendez pas à ce que je vous prête cet argent* **to expect too much of s.o.** = *trop attendre de qqn* **what do you expect me to do about it ?** = *que voulez-vous que j'y fasse ?*

3/ *imaginer* : I expect you're hungry ? = *j'imagine que vous devez avoir faim ?* = I imagine you're hungry ?

EXPECTATION (n) *espérance* (f) : great expectations for her children = *de grandes espérances pour ses enfants*
beyond all expectations = *au-delà de toute espérance*
to come up to expectations = *répondre à l'attente*
contrary to (all) expectations = *contrairement à toute attente*
☠ *perdre toute espérance* = to lose all hope
— *espérance de vie* = life expectancy.

EXPEDITE (to, -d) *accélérer* : to expedite the passage of a bill = *accélérer le passage d'un texte de loi* = to accelerate ≠ to slow down = *ralentir*.

EXPEDITION (n) *expédition* (f) ⓄⒹ trip = *voyage*.

EXPEL (to, -led) *renvoyer* : expelled from school = *renvoyé de l'école* ⓄⒹ to throw out = *vider* ☠ → to dismiss.

EXPENDITURE (n) *dépense* (f) : government expenditure = *dépenses publiques* ⓄⒹ expenses = *frais*

☠ *regarder à la dépense* = to watch one's money
— *l'université représente une grosse dépense* = college is quite an expense.

EXPENSE (n) *dépense* (f) : a big expense in a small budget = *une grosse dépense dans un petit budget* ⓪ cost = *coût* ☠ → expenditure
at little ≠ great expense = *à peu de* ≠ *à grands frais*
at one's own expense = *à ses propres frais*
at s.o.'s expense = *aux dépens de qqn*
at the expense of (his health) = *aux dépens de (sa santé)*
expense account = *note de frais*
the expense of (buying a new car) = *la dépense représentée par (l'achat d'une nouvelle voiture)*
to go to some expense = *se mettre en frais* ≠ to skimp = *lésiner*
to spare no expense = *ne pas reculer devant la dépense.*

EXPENSES (n pl) *frais* (m pl) : traveling expenses paid = *tous frais de voyage payés* ⓪ incidentals = *faux frais*
to meet expenses = *couvrir ses dépenses*
☠ *aux frais de la princesse* = on the house
— *rentrer dans ses frais* = to get one's money back
— *partager les frais* = to go dutch
— *faire les frais de* = to be the butt of
— *j'en ai été pour mes frais* = I got nothing out of it
— *frais généraux* = overheads.

EXPENSIVE (adj) *cher, chère* : an expensive hotel = *un hôtel cher* = dear (GB) ⓪ costly = *coûteux*, onerous = *onéreux*, to cost an arm and a leg = *coûter les yeux de la tête*, pricey = *chérot* ≠ inexpensive = *pas cher* ☠ → dear.

EXPERIENCE (n) 1/ *expérience* (f) : it was a terrible experience = *ça a été une expérience épouvantable* ⓪ ordeal = *épreuve* 2/ *expérience* (f) : a lot of business experience = *beaucoup d'expérience des affaires*
☠ *tenter l'expérience* = to try stg
— *faire une expérience (laboratoire)* = to do an experiment.

EXPERIENCE (to, -d) 1/ *éprouver* : what did you experience the first time you made love ? = *qu'avez-vous éprouvé la première fois que vous avez fait l'amour ?* ☠ *(ce travail) m'a beaucoup éprouvé* = (this work) took a lot out of me 2/ *connaître* : the country's experiencing great changes = *le pays connaît de grands changements* ☠ → to know.

EXPERIENCED (adj) *expérimenté, -e* : experienced workers = *des travailleurs expérimentés* ≠ inexperienced = *inexpérimenté.*

EXPERIMENT (n) *expérience* (f) : to do experiments on animals = *faire des expériences sur les animaux* ⓪ test = ← ☠ → experience.

EXPERIMENTAL (adj) *expérimental, -e* : experimental theater = *théâtre expérimental* ⓪ avant-garde = ←.

EXPERIMENT WITH (to, -ed) *expérimenter* : to experiment with a new vaccine = *expérimenter un nouveau vaccin.*

EXPERT (n) *expert, -e* : when it comes to tax evasion, he is an expert = *pour la fraude fiscale, c'est un expert* ⓪ connoisseur = *connaisseur*, specialist = *spécialiste* ≠ novice = ← ☠ *un expert comptable* = a certified public accountant.

EXPERT (adj) *expert, -e* : an expert typist = *une dactylo experte* ⓪ topflight = *de haut vol* ≠ inexperienced = *inexpérimenté.*

EXPIRE (to, -d) *expirer* : the contract expired on the tenth = *le contrat a expiré le dix* ☠ *expirer (respiration)* = to breathe out **EXPIRATION** (n) *expiration* (f) : expiration of a lease = *l'expiration d'un bail.*

EXPLAIN (to, -ed) *expliquer* : let me explain how to do it = *laissez-moi expliquer comment on fait* ⓪ to demonstrate = *faire la démonstration*
☠ *s'expliquer avec qqn* = to have it out with s.o.
— *ça s'explique !* = that figures !

EXPLANATION (n) *explication* (f) : I don't get your explanation = *je ne pige pas ton explication* ☠ *avoir une explication avec qqn* = to have it out with s.o.

EXPLANATORY (adj) *explicatif, -ive* : an explanatory prospectus = *une notice explicative.*

EXPLICIT (adj) *explicite* : a very explicit answer = *une réponse très explicite* ⓪ precise = *précis* ≠ ambiguous = *ambigu.*

EXPLODE (to, -d) 1/ *exploser* : the bomb exploded = *la bombe a explosé* ⓪ to go off = *partir* 2/ *exploser* : when she heard that she exploded = *quand elle a entendu ça, elle a explosé* → ANGRY.

EXPLOIT (n) *exploit* (m) : daring exploits = *des exploits audacieux* ⓪ adventure = *aventure*, accomplishment = *tour de force* ☠ *quel exploit !* = what an achievement !

EXPLOIT (to, -ed) *exploiter* : society exploits all of us = *la société nous exploite tous* ⓪ to take advantage of = *abuser de* **EXPLOITATION** (n) *exploitation* (f).

EXPLORE ((to, -d) *explorer* **EXPLORER** (n) *explorateur, -trice* **EXPLORATION** (n) *exploration* (f).

EXPLOSION (n) *explosion* (f) : population explosion = *explosion démographique.*

EXPLOSIVE (n) *explosif* (m) : explosives hidden in his cellar = *des explosifs cachés dans sa cave* ⓪ powder = *poudre* **EXPLOSIVE** (adj) *explosif, -ive* : an explosive situation = *une situation explosive.*

EXPONENT (n) **an exponent of (abortion)** = *un partisan de (l'avortement).*

EXPORT (n) *exportation* (f) : diamonds are the principal export = *les diamants représentent la principale exportation* ≠ import = *importation* **EXPORT** (to, -ed) *exporter*

205

≠ to import = *importer* **EXPORTER** (n) *exportateur, -trice* ≠ *importer* = *importateur*.

EXPOSE (to, -d) **1/** *exposer* : to be exposed to radiation = *être exposé aux radiations*
☠ *exposer clairement une situation* = to explain a set-up clearly
— *exposer (tableaux)* = to exhibit/to display (paintings)
2/ *révéler (au grand jour)* : to expose a scandal = *révéler un scandale (au grand jour)* ≠ to hush up = *passer sous silence*
to expose o.s. = *s'exhiber* : the man exposed himself in the street = *l'homme s'est exhibé dans la rue* ⓓ a flasher = *un exhibitionniste* ☠ *exhiber (sa richesse)* = to flaunt (one's wealth).

EXPOSITION (n) *exposition* (f) : art/car exposition = *exposition d'art/automobile* = exhibition ⓓ show = *salon* ☠ *exposition au soleil* = exposure to the sun.

EXPOSURE (n) **direct exposure (to modern methods)** = *expérience directe (des méthodes modernes)*.

EXPOUND ON (to, -ed) *expliciter* : to expound on a theory = *expliciter une théorie* ⓓ to expand on = *développer*.

EXPRESS (adj) *express* : an express train = *un train express* ⓓ fast = *rapide*
with/for the express purpose of = *avec l'intention avouée de*.

EXPRESS (to, -ed) *exprimer* : to express doubts = *exprimer des doutes* ⓓ to state = *énoncer*
to express o.s. = *s'exprimer* : he has trouble expressing himself = *il a du mal à s'exprimer*
☠ *si l'on peut s'exprimer ainsi* = if I can put it that way.

EXPRESSION (n) **1/** *expression* (f) : a sad expression = *une expression de tristesse* ⓓ look = *air* **2/** *expression* (f) : a slang expression = *une expression argotique*.

EXPRESSIVE (adj) *expressif, -ive* : an expressive face = *un visage expressif* ≠ inexpressive = *inexpressif*.

EXPRESSLY (adv) *expressément* : she told me expressly not to tell you = *elle m'a recommandé expressément de ne pas vous le dire*.

EXPRESSWAY (n) *voie* (f) *express* ⓓ motorway = *autoroute*.

EXPULSION (n) *expulsion* (f) ≠ admission = ←.

EXQUISITE (adj) *exquis, -e* : an exquisite woman/evening = *une femme/soirée exquise* ⓓ divine = *divin*.

EXTEND (to, -ed) *(s')étendre, prolonger* (time) : we extended our vacation = *nous avons prolongé nos vacances*, the beach extends for 5 miles = *la plage s'étend sur 8 kilomètres*
☠ *prolonger* → to prolong
— *se faire étendre* = to flunk (test)
— *s'étendre* = to stretch out/to lay down
— *s'étendre sur (un sujet)* = to elaborate on (a subject).

EXTENSION (n) *extension* (f) (building, powers), *appareil* (m) *supplémentaire* (phone), *prolongation* (f) (lease, contract).

EXTENSIVE (adj) *étendu, -e* : extensive vocabulary/damages = *vocabulaire étendu/des dégâts étendus* ≠ limited = *limité*
☠ *étendu sur le sol* = lying on the ground
— *bras étendus* = arms stretched out.

EXTENT (n) *étendue* (f) : the extent of the damages = *l'étendue des dégâts* ⓓ scope = *portée*
to a certain/some extent = *dans une certaine mesure* : he's right to a certain extent = *il a raison dans une certaine mesure* ⓓ in a way = *en un sens*
to a large/great extent = *pour une large part* ⓓ for the most part = *en grande partie*
to such an extent that = *à tel point que* ⓓ to such a degree that = *à tel degré que*
to the extent of = *au point de* : I agree with you, but not to the extent of spending so much money = *je suis d'accord avec vous, mais pas au point de dépenser tant d'argent*
to what extent = *dans quelle mesure* : I don't know to what extent he'll agree to help = *je ne sais pas dans quelle mesure il sera d'accord pour nous aider*.

EXTERIOR (n) *extérieur* (m) : the exterior of the house = *l'extérieur de la maison* ≠ interior = *intérieur*
on the exterior (he's cold) = *(il est) d'un abord (froid)*
☠ *tourner un film en extérieur* = to shoot a movie on location
— *dîner à l'extérieur* = to eat out.

EXTERMINATE (to, -d) *exterminer* : to exterminate cockroaches = *exterminer les cafards* ⓓ to annihilate = *annihiler* **EXTERMINATION** (n) *extermination* (f) ⓓ massacre = ←.

EXTERNAL (adj) *externe* : for external use = *usage externe* ≠ internal = *interne*.

EXTINCT (adj) *éteint, -e* : an extinct race = *une race éteinte* ≠ existing = *existant* ☠ *les lumières sont éteintes* = the lights are off **EXTINCTION** (n) *extinction* (f) : the slow extinction of whales = *la lente extinction des baleines* ⓓ disappearance = *disparition*.

EXTINGUISH (to, -ed) *éteindre* : to extinguish a fire = *éteindre un feu* ≠ to set on fire = *mettre le feu à*
☠ *s'éteindre (mourir)* = to pass away
— *éteindre (lumières)* = to switch off/to turn off/to put off (lights)
— *les lumières se sont éteintes* = the lights went off/out
— *cette coutume s'est éteinte* = the custom died out.

EXTOL (to, -led) *chanter les louanges de* ≠ to denigrate = *dénigrer*.

EXTORT (to, -ed) *extorquer* : he extorted money from her = *il lui a extorqué de l'argent* ⓓ to drag out = *arra-*

cher **EXTORTION** (n) *extorsion* (f) ① bribery = *corruption.*

EXTRA (n) **1/** *extra* (m), *supplément* (m) : there were a lot of extras on the trip = *il y avait beaucoup d'extras/de suppléments à payer pendant le voyage* ① incidental expenses = *frais accessoires* ☙ *supplément* → supplement **2/** *figurant, -e* : she's not a star, just an extra = *ce n'est pas une vedette, seulement une figurante* ① to have a walk-on part = *jouer les utilités.*

EXTRA (adj) *de plus* : I'm staying an extra week = *je reste une semaine de plus* ① additional = *supplémentaire*
no extra charge = *sans supplément*
☠ *extra !* = cool !

EXTRA (adv) *extra-* : extra long = *extra-long*
to charge ≠ **to pay extra** = *faire payer* ≠ *payer en supplément/en extra.*

EXTRACT (n) *extrait* (m) : extracts from H. Miller = *des extraits de H. Miller.*

EXTRACT (to, -ed) *extraire* : to extract perfume from plants = *extraire le parfum des plantes.*

EXTRACURRICULAR (adj) *extra-scolaire* : extracurricular activities = *des activités extra-scolaires.*

EXTRADITE (to, -d) *extrader* ① to turn back = *refouler* **EXTRADITION** (n) *extradition* (f).

EXTRAMARITAL (adj) *extra-conjugal, -e* : his extramarital affairs ruined their marriage = *ses aventures extra-conjugales ont détruit leur ménage.*

EXTRAORDINARILY (adv) *extraordinairement* : extraordinarily rich = *extraordinairement riche* → VERY.

EXTRAORDINARY (adj) *extraordinaire* : an extraordinary view/woman = *une vue/femme extraordinaire* ① amazing = *stupéfiant* ≠ ordinary = *ordinaire* ☙ *assemblée extraordinaire* = special session.

EXTRAVAGANCE (n) *extravagance* (f) ① folly = *folie* **EXTRAVAGANT** (adj) *extravagant, -e* : extravagant ideas = *des idées extravagantes* ① excessive = *excessif* ≠ reasonable = *raisonnable* **EXTRAVAGANTLY** (adv) *de façon extravagante.*

EXTRAVAGANZA (n) show (m) *à grand spectacle.*

EXTREME (n) *extrême* (m) : jealous to an extreme = *jaloux à l'extrême*
to carry to extremes = *pousser à l'extrême* ① to overdo it = *en faire trop.*

EXTREME (adj) *extrême* : the extreme right = *l'extrême droite* ≠ moderate = *modéré*
☙ *à l'extrême limite* = if really necessary
— *Extrême-Orient* = Far East.

EXTREMELY (adv) *extrêmement* : extremely nice = *extrêmement gentil* → VERY.

EXTREMIST (n) *extrémiste* (m, f) ≠ moderate = *modéré.*

EXTRICATE FROM (to, -d) *s'extirper de* : to extricate oneself from a bad situation = *s'extirper d'une situation difficile.*

EXTROVERT (n) *extraverti, -e* ≠ loner = *solitaire* **EXTROVERTED** (adj) *extraverti, -e* ≠ people-shy = *farouche.*

EXUBERANCE (n) *exubérance* (f) ≠ reserve = *réserve* **EXUBERANT** (adj) *exubérant, -e* : an exuberant personality = *une personnalité exubérante* ≠ reserved = *réservé.*

EYE (n) *œil* (m), eyes = *yeux* : you have beautiful eyes = *tu as de beaux yeux* ① peepers = *mirettes*, eyeball = *globe oculaire*, iris = ←, pupil = *pupille*, cornea = *cornée*, eyebrow = *sourcil*, eyelash = *cil*, retina = *rétine*, glasses = *lunettes*, contact lenses = *verres/lentilles de contact*, glass eye = *œil de verre*, eye shadow = *fard à paupières*, eyelid = *paupière*

an eye for an eye, a tooth for a tooth = *œil pour œil, dent pour dent* ≠ let bygones be bygones = *le passé, c'est le passé*
to be up to one's eyes in (work) = *être débordé de (travail)* ① to be swamped with = *être surchargé de*
to catch s.o.'s eye = *attirer l'attention de qqn* : the ring caught my eye = *la bague a attiré mon attention* ① to catch s.o.'s fancy = *taper dans l'œil de qqn*
I couldn't believe my eyes =

je n'en croyais pas mes yeux
to cry one's eyes out = *pleurer toutes les larmes de son corps* ① to cry bitterly = *pleurer comme une Madeleine*
to give s.o. the eye = *faire de l'œil à qqn* ① to look s.o. up and down = *déshabiller qqn du regard*
to have an eye for (putting colors together) = *avoir l'œil pour (assortir les couleurs)*
to have eyes only for (one's wife) = *n'avoir d'yeux que pour (sa femme)*
to have one's eyes on (a job)

= *avoir des vues sur (un poste)*
in my eyes = *à mes yeux* : in my eyes, it's important = *à mes yeux, c'est important* ① to my mind = *à mon sens*
in the eyes of the law = *au regard de la loi*
to keep an eye on = *avoir l'œil sur* ① to watch = *surveiller*
to keep one's eyes open/peeled = *ouvrir l'œil (et le bon)*
to knock s.o.'s eyes out = *en mettre plein la vue à qqn* : her jewels knocked their eyes out = *ses bijoux leur en ont mis plein la vue*

| to look s.o. (straight) in the eye = *regarder qqn (droit) dans les yeux*
to make (sheep's) eyes at s.o. = *faire les yeux doux à qqn* ⓄⒹ to make passes = *faire des avances*
my eye ! = *mon œil !* = my foot !
not to take one's eyes off s.o. = *ne pas quitter qqn des yeux* ⓄⒹ to stare at = *fixer* | to open s.o.'s eyes = *ouvrir les yeux à qqn* : the remark opened my eyes = *sa remarque m'a ouvert les yeux*
to see eye to eye = *voir les choses du même œil* ⓄⒹ to share s.o.'s opinion = *partager l'opinion de qqn*
I've never set/laid my eyes on him = *je ne l'ai jamais vu de ma vie* ⓄⒹ I don't know him from Adam = *je ne le connais ni d'Ève ni d'Adam* | to shut one's eyes to = *fermer les yeux sur* ⓄⒹ to look the other way = *pratiquer la politique de l'autruche*
there's more than meets the eye = *ce n'est pas aussi simple que cela en a l'air* ⓄⒹ there's something fishy = *il y a quelque chose de louche*
without batting an eye = *sans sourciller* ⓄⒹ without saying boo = *sans piper mot* |

| ☠ *je m'en bats l'œil* = I don't give a rap
— *tourner de l'œil* = to faint
— *(un repas) à l'œil* = (a meal) on the house
— *avoir les yeux plus grands que le ventre* = to bite off more than one can chew
— *ouvrir des yeux ronds* = to stare wide-eyed
— *voir qqch d'un bon ≠ d'un mauvais œil* = to see stg favorably ≠ unfavorably | — *ne pas fermer l'œil de la nuit* = not to sleep a wink
— *ça saute aux yeux/ça crève les yeux* = it's staring you in the face
— *coûter les yeux de la tête* = to cost an arm and a leg
— *se rincer l'œil* = to get an eyeful. |

EYE (to, -d) *reluquer* : the guy eyed the girl but didn't have the nerve to try to pick her up = *le type a reluqué la fille mais n'a pas eu le culot d'essayer de la draguer* ⓄⒹ to stare at = *fixer*.

EYEBROW (n) *sourcil (m)* ⓄⒹ tweezers = *pince à épiler*
to cause raised eyebrows = *faire du bruit dans les chaumières* : their affair caused raised eyebrows = *leur aventure a fait du bruit dans les chaumières* ⓄⒹ to cause a stir = *provoquer des remous*
☠ *froncer les sourcils* = to frown.

EYE-CATCHING (adj) *accrocheur, -euse* : an eyecatching advertisement = *une publicité accrocheuse* ⓄⒹ flashy = *tapageur*.

EYEFUL (n) **to get an eyeful** = *se rincer l'œil*.

EYEGLASSES (n pl) *lunettes (f pl)* = glasses.

EYELASH (n, -es) *cil (m)* ⓄⒹ mascara = ← / *rimmel*.

EYE-OPENER (n) **it was an eye-opener** = *ça m'a ouvert les yeux* : seeing them together was an eye-opener = *le fait de les voir ensemble m'a ouvert les yeux* = it opened my eyes ⓄⒹ it put me wise = *ça m'a mis la puce à l'oreille*.

EYESIGHT (n) *vue (f)* : his eyesight is poor = *il a une mauvaise vue* ☠ → view.

EYETOOTH (n, -teeth) **to give one's eyeteeth** = *donner cher* : I'd give my eyeteeth to know the truth = *je donnerais cher pour connaître la vérité* ⓄⒹ to give anything = *donner n'importe quoi*.

EYEWITNESS (n, -es) *témoin (m) oculaire* ⓄⒹ onlooker = *badaud*.

FABLE (n) *fable (f)* ⓒⓓ fairy tale = *conte de fées.*

FABRIC (n) *étoffe (f)* ⓒⓓ material = *tissu* ☠ *avoir l'étoffe d'(un écrivain)* = to have the makings of (a writer).

FABULOUS (adj) *fabuleux, -euse :* a fabulous movie = *un film fabuleux* → WONDERFUL ≠ horrible = ←

FABULOUSLY (adv) *fabuleusement :* fabulously intelligent = *fabuleusement intelligent* → VERY.

FACADE (n) *façade (f) :* the facade of the building = *la façade de l'immeuble.*

FACE (n) *visage (m), gueule (f)* (LV), *figure (f) :* a pretty face = *un joli visage* ⓒⓓ kisser = *bouille/frimousse,* baby-faced = *poupin*

---

to fall (flat) on one's face = *s'étendre de tout son long* ⓒⓓ to take a spill = *prendre une bûche*
to feed one's face = *s'en mettre plein la lampe/la gueule* ≠. to pick at one's food = *manger du bout des lèvres*
in the face of = *face à :* in the face of such opposition, he decided not to run = *face à une telle opposition, il a décidé de ne pas se présenter*
on the face of it = *à première vue :* the work looks easy on the face of it = *à première vue, le travail a l'air facile* ⓒⓓ offhand = *comme ça*
to s.o.'s face = *en face :* if you have something to say, say it to my face = *si vous avez quelque chose à dire, dites-le-moi en face*
to laugh in s.o.'s face = *rire au nez de qqn* ⓒⓓ to

make fun of = *se moquer de*
to lose ≠ **save face** = *perdre* ≠ *sauver la face*
to make a face = *faire la grimace :* when he saw the spinach, the child made a face = *l'enfant a fait la grimace en voyant les épinards*
to make faces = *faire des grimaces :* the clown made faces = *le clown a fait des grimaces*
to powder one's face = *se refaire une beauté*
it's staring you in the face = *ça (te) crève les yeux* ⓒⓓ it's self-evident = *ça va de soi*
to take at face value = *prendre pour argent comptant :* don't take what he says at face value = *ne prends pas ce qu'il dit pour argent comptant* ⓒⓓ to take with a grain of salt = *ne pas prendre au pied de la lettre*

☠ *figure* → figure
— *casser la gueule/la figure à qqn* = to beat s.o. up
— *ta gueule !* = shut up !

— *avoir de la gueule* = to have a lot of class
— *se jeter dans la gueule du loup* = to walk right into the trap

— *se saouler la gueule* = to get smashed
— *avoir la gueule de bois* = to have a hangover.

FACE (to, -d) 1/ *être en face de :* we're facing a serious economic crisis = *nous sommes en face d'une crise économique sérieuse* 2/ *faire face à :* she'll have to face the truth = *il lui faudra faire face à la vérité* 3/ *donner sur :* the room faces the sea = *la chambre donne sur la mer*

---

face me ! = *tournez-vous vers moi !*
to be facing (South) = *être exposé au (sud)*

let's face it = *regardons les choses en face :* he's a bastard, let's face it ! = *regardons les choses en face, c'est un salaud !*

---

to face up to = 1/ *se rendre à l'évidence :* he's lying, face up to it ! = *il faut se rendre à l'évidence, il ment !* ⓒⓓ to acknowledge = *reconnaître* 2/ *faire face à :* to face up to a difficult situation = *faire face*

à une situation difficile ⓒⓓ to come to grips with = *faire front à*
to be faced with (bankruptcy) = *devoir faire face à (une faillite).*

FACE-LIFT (n) *lifting (m)* : to have a face-lift = *se faire faire un lifting.*

FACET (n) *facette (f)* : his personality has many facets = *sa personnalité a des facettes multiples.*

FACETIOUS (adj) *persifleur, -euse* : facetious remarks = *des remarques persifleuses* ⓪ sarcastic = *sarcastique.*

FACILITATE (to, -d) *faciliter* : your attitude doesn't facilitate things = *votre attitude ne facilite pas les choses* ⓪ to simplify = *simplifier.*

FACILITY (n, -ies) **1/** *facilité (f)* : a facility for languages = *de la facilité pour les langues* ☠ *facilités de paiement* = easy credit terms **2/** *installation (f)* : the university has excellent facilities = *l'université a d'excellentes installations* **3/** *service (m) gracieux* : a bus to the beach is one of the facilities offered by the hotel = *une navette pour la plage est l'un des services gracieux offerts par l'hôtel.*

FACING (prep) *face à* : facing the sea = *face à la mer* ≠ behind = *derrière.*

FACT (n) *fait (m)* : tell me the facts = *donnez-moi les faits* ⓪ data = *données*
except for the fact that = *excepté que*
face the facts = *il faut se rendre à l'évidence* ≠ **stop running away from the facts** = *ne niez pas l'évidence*
a fact of life = *un fait inéluctable* : that children die of hunger everyday is a fact of life = *c'est un fait inéluctable qu'il y a tous les jours des enfants qui meurent de faim*
the facts of life = *les choses de la vie* : did you tell your daughter about the facts of life ? = *est-ce que vous avez parlé des choses de la vie à votre fille ?*
the fact (of the matter) is = *le fait est que* : the fact (of the matter) is, I'm fed up = *le fait est que j'en ai marre* ⓪ in point of fact = *en réalité*
the fact remains that (you're wrong) = *toujours est-il que (tu as tort)*
in fact = *en fait* : in fact, it cost less than I expected = *en fait, ça a coûté moins cher que je ne le pensais* ⓪ as a matter of fact ⓪ in reality = *en réalité*
I know it for a fact = *j'en suis sûr et certain*
to look the facts in the face = *regarder les choses en face* ≠ to kid o.s. = *se faire des illusions*
plus the fact that (he drinks) = *en plus du fait qu'(il boit)*
stick to the facts ! = *tenez-vous-en aux faits !*
☠ *prendre fait et cause pour qqn* = to go to bat for s.o.
— *pris sur le fait* = caught in the act
— *de ce fait* = thereby
— *ce n'est pas mon fait* = it's not my doing
— *aller droit au fait* = to get straight to the point
— *au fait* = by the way
— *faits divers* = news items.

FACTION (n) *faction (f)* ⓪ group = *groupe.*

FACTOR (n) *facteur (m)* : high oil prices are a big factor in inflation = *le prix élevé du pétrole est un important* facteur d'inflation ⓪ element = *élément* ☠ *le facteur* = the mailman.

FACTORY (n, -ies) *usine (f)* : a car factory = *une usine automobile* = works (GB) ⓪ mill = *fabrique*, assembly line = *chaîne*, foundry = *fonderie*
factory worker = *ouvrier (d'usine).*

FACULTY (n, -ies) **1/** *faculté (f)* : to be in possession of all one's faculties = *être en possession de toutes ses facultés* ⓪ ability = *capacité* ☠ *je vais à la faculté* = I go to college **2/** *corps (m) enseignant* : the school faculty = *le corps enseignant de l'école.*

FAD (n) *grande vogue (f)* : short skirts were a fad = *les jupes courtes étaient la grande vogue* ⓪ rage = ←.

FADE (to, -d) **1/** *(se) faner* (flowers), *passer* (colors, clothes) : the roses/your jeans have faded = *les roses se sont fanées/ton blue-jean a passé* ⓪ to wither = *se flétrir* ≠ to bloom = *fleurir* ☠ *passer* → to pass **2/** *s'estomper* : our love's fading = *notre amour s'estompe* ⓪ to disappear = *disparaître*
to fade away = *dépérir* : he's been fading away with this diet = *il dépérit avec ce régime.*

FADE-OUT (n) *fondu (m)* : the movie ends with a fade-out = *le film se termine sur un fondu.*

FAG (n) **1/** *pédale (f)* : a bar for fags = *un bar pour les pédales* ⓪ faggot = *tapette*, queer = *pédé*, gay = ← ☠ → pedal **2/** (GB) *clope (m)* : give me a fag = *donne-moi un clope* ⓪ weed = *sèche.*

FAGGOT (n) *tapette (f)* ≠ dyke = *gouine.*

FAIL (n) **without fail** = *sans faute* : I'll come without fail = *je viendrai sans faute* ⓪ as sure as shooting = *aussi sûr que deux et deux font quatre.*

FAIL (to, -ed) **1/** *échouer* : the project failed = *le projet a échoué* ⓪ to fall through = *tomber à l'eau* ≠ to succeed = *réussir* **2/** *échouer à* : to fail an exam = *échouer à un examen* ≠ to pass = *réussir*
to fail (s.o.) = *coller (qqn)* : the teacher failed most of his students = *le professeur a collé la plupart de ses étudiants*
to fail in (math) = *échouer en (maths)*
to fail to = *1/ ne pas arriver à* : society has failed to put an end to torture = *la société n'est pas arrivée à mettre fin à la torture 2/ omettre de* : he failed to call me back = *il a omis de me rappeler*
☠ *il a échoué à New York* = he wound up in New York.

FAILING (n) *travers (m)* : his lack of patience is his main failing = *son principal travers est le manque de patience* ⓪ weakness = *faiblesse* ☠ *travers de porc* = spareribs.

FAILURE (n) **1/** *échec (m)* : the play was a failure = *la pièce a été un échec* ≠ success = *succès*
☠ *échec et mat* = checkmate
— *tenir en échec* = to checkmate
— *les échecs* = chess

2/ *raté, -e* : to be a failure in life = *être un raté dans la vie* ⓪ loser = *perdant.*

FAINT (adj) *faible* : a faint chance = *une faible chance* ⓪ minute = *infime* ☠ → weak
I don't have the faintest chance/idea = *je n'ai pas la moindre chance/idée.*

FAINT (to, -ed) *s'évanouir* ⓪ to black out = *tourner de l'œil* ≠ to come to = *revenir à soi.*

FAINTHEARTED (adj) *pusillanime* ⓪ timorous = *timoré* ≠ fearless = *intrépide.*

FAIR (n) *foire* (f) : trade fair = *foire commerciale* ⓪ carnival = *carnaval*
(book) fair = *salon (du livre)*
☠ *faire la foire* = to go out on a bender
— *foire d'empoigne* = free-for-all.

FAIR (adj, -er, -est) **1/** *juste* : your criticism isn't fair = *votre critique n'est pas juste* ⓪ square = *correct*, equitable = *équitable* ≠ unfair = *injuste* ☠ → just **2/** *pas terrible* : the play was fair = *la pièce n'était pas terrible* → AWFUL **3/** *bon, bonne* : a fair amount of money = *une bonne somme d'argent*, a fair chance of success = *une bonne chance de réussir* ☠ → good **4/** *qui a les cheveux et le teint clairs* : her kids are all fair = *ses gosses ont tous les cheveux et le teint clairs*

fair enough (but) = *très bien (mais)* : you want to sleep with others, fair enough but I will too = *tu veux coucher avec d'autres, très bien mais je ferai de même* **fair play** = *fair-play* : the British are known for their fair play = *les Britanniques sont connus pour leur fair play* ≠ foul play = *magouillage* **(to be) fair and square** = *(jouer) franc*	*jeu* : he was fair and square with us = *il a joué franc jeu avec nous* ⓪ aboveboard = *sans équivoque* **the fair sex** = *le beau sexe* **to give s.o. a fair deal/a fair shake** = *être fair-play avec qqn* : the boss gave me a fair deal/a fair shake = *le patron a été fair-play avec moi* ≠ to play dirty = *faire des coups bas.*

FAIR-HAIRED BOY/GIRL (n) *poulain* (m) : the President's fair-haired boy/girl = *le poulain du Président* ⓪ pet = *chouchou* ☠ *un poulain* = a colt.

FAIRLY (adv) *assez* : a fairly difficult book = *un livre assez difficile* ⓪ somewhat = *quelque peu*
fairly good = *assez bon* : a fairly good businesswoman = *une assez bonne femme d'affaires* ⓪ pretty good = *plutôt bon*
fairly well = *assez bien* : he writes fairly well = *il écrit assez bien*
☠ → enough.

FAIR-WEATHER FRIENDS (n pl) *les amis des beaux jours.*

FAIRY (n, -ies) **1/** *fée* (f) : the good fairy = *la bonne fée* ⓪ witch = *sorcière*, magic wand = *baguette magique*
fairy tale = *conte de fées*
fairy godmother = *bonne fée*
2/ *tante* (f) : gays don't like being called fairies = *les gays n'aiment pas qu'on les traite de tantes* ⓪ queen = *grande folle* ≠ dyke = *gouine* ☠ → aunt.

FAITH (n) *foi* (f) : faith in God = *foi en Dieu* ⓪ creed = *credo* ≠ doubt = *doute*
I put no faith in (what he says) = *je n'ai aucune confiance en (ses paroles)*
☠ *il n'a ni foi ni loi* = he fears neither God nor man
— *ma foi !* = goodness !
— *être de mauvaise foi* = not to be square/upfront/straightforward.

FAITHFUL (adj) *fidèle* : a faithful lover = *un amant fidèle* ≠ unfaithful = *infidèle*
☠ *témoin/mémoire fidèle* = reliable witness/memory.

FAKE (n) **1/** *faux* (m) : the painting's a fake = *le tableau est un faux* ⓪ imitation = ←
☠ *prêcher le faux pour savoir le vrai* = to say purposely the opposite of something to find out the truth
— *s'inscrire en faux contre* = to take objection to
2/ *charlatan* (m) : gurus are often fakes = *les gourous sont souvent des charlatans* ⓪ fraud = *imposteur* ☠ → charlatan.

FAKE (adj) *faux, fausse* : fake diamonds/Rembrandts = *de faux diamants/faux Rembrandt* ⓪ phony = *bidon* ≠ real = *véritable* ☠ → false.

FAKE (to, -d) *faire semblant* : I thought he was sick but he was faking = *j'ai cru qu'il était malade, mais il faisait semblant* ⓪ to make believe = *faire comme si*
fake it ! = *fais semblant !* ⓪ bluff ! = *bluffe !*
to fake s.o. out = *avoir qqn* : I thought you had really lost your job, you faked me out ! = *j'ai cru que tu avais vraiment perdu ton boulot, tu m'as eu !* → TO HUSTLE.

FAKER (n) *fabulateur, -trice* ⓪ fake = *charlatan.*

FALL (n) **1/** *chute* (f) : a fall of the currency = *une chute de la monnaie* ⓪ decline = *diminution* ≠ jump = *hausse brutale* **2/** *automne* (m) : we'll see you in the fall = *nous vous verrons à l'automne* = autumn ⓪ season = *saison* **3/** *chute* (f) : the fall of the Roman Empire = *la chute de l'Empire romain* ⓪ decline = *déclin* ≠ ascension = ←
☠ *la chute des reins* = the small of the back

| fall guy = *tête de Turc* : when the whole business was over, he realized he'd been the fall guy = *quand* | *tout a été terminé, il a réalisé qu'il avait été la tête de Turc* ⓌⒹ scapegoat = *bouc émissaire* |

FALL (to, fell, fallen) **1/** *tomber* : I fell in the street = *je suis tombé dans la rue*, the book fell = *le livre est tombé* = the book dropped **2/** *chuter* : prices fell last month = *les prix ont chuté le mois dernier* ≠ to go down = *descendre* ≠ to increase = *augmenter* **3/** *tomber* : night's falling = *la nuit tombe*, the city fell = *la ville est tombée*

to **fall apart** = *se casser la figure* (relationship, coalition)/ *se déglinguer* (car) : their marriage/car is falling apart = *leur mariage est en train de se casser la figure/leur voiture est en train de se déglinguer*

to **fall back on** = *avoir recours à* : she can always fall back on her parents = *elle peut toujours avoir recours à ses parents* ⓌⒹ to turn to = *se tourner vers*

to **fall behind** = **1/** *prendre du retard* : I fell behind in my work = *j'ai pris du retard dans mon travail* ≠ to catch up = *rattraper* **2/** *rester à la traîne* : the others ran fast and he fell behind = *les autres couraient vite et il est resté à la traîne*

to **fall down** = **1/** *tomber par terre* : the pavement was slippery and I fell down = *le trottoir était glissant et je suis tombée (par terre)* ≠ to get up = *se relever* **2/** *s'écrouler* : the build-ing's falling down = *l'immeuble s'écroule* ⓌⒹ to collapse = *s'effondrer* ☠ → to cave in

to **fall for** = **1/** *s'amouracher de* : I fell for him on our first date = *je me suis amourachée de lui lors de notre premier rendez-vous* ⓌⒹ to flip over = *se toquer de* **2/** *tomber dans le panneau* : it was a lie but he fell for it = *c'était un mensonge mais il est tombé dans le panneau*

to **fall in(to)** = *tomber à/dans* : she fell in(to) the water and drowned = *elle est tombée à/dans l'eau et s'est noyée*

to **fall in with (a strange group)** = *se laisser entraîner par (une drôle de bande)*

to **fall off** = **1/** *être en baisse* : attendance/business is falling off = *le nombre d'entrées est/les affaires sont en baisse* ⓌⒹ to slow down = *ralentir* **2/** *tomber de* : he fell off the ladder = *il est tombé de l'échelle*

to **fall on** = *tomber* : Christmas falls on Monday = *Noël tombe un lundi*

to **fall on s.o. to** = *retomber sur qqn* : the boss didn't want to fire him, so it fell on me to do it = *le patron ne voulait pas le renvoyer lui-même, et la sale besogne est retombée sur moi*

to **fall over** = *en avoir le souffle coupé* : I fell over when he told me what happened = *j'en ai eu le souffle coupé quand il m'a raconté ce qui s'était passé* ⓌⒹ I couldn't get over it = *je n'en revenais pas*

to **fall over oneself** = *faire des ronds de jambe* : he fell (all) over himself to make a good impression on his in-laws = *il a fait des ronds de jambe pour faire bonne impression à ses beaux-parents*

to **fall through** = *tomber à l'eau* : our plans fell through = *nos projets sont tombés à l'eau* ≠ to work out = *marcher*

☠ *tomber sur qqn* = to run into s.o.
— *tomber bien* ≠ *mal* = to come at the right ≠ wrong time
— *être tombé sur la tête* = to be out of one's head
— *j'ai fait tomber le livre* = I dropped the book

— *tomber sur (un restaurant génial)* = to stumble on (a very good restaurant)
— *il tombe des hallebardes !* = it's raining cats and dogs !

FALLACIOUS (adj) *fallacieux, -euse* : fallacious reasoning = *raisonnement fallacieux* ⓌⒹ misleading = *trompeur*.

FALLEN (adj) *déchu, -e* : a fallen angel/woman = *un ange déchu/une femme déchue*.

FALLING-OUT (n) *brouille (f)* : that was our worst falling-out = *ça a été notre pire brouille* ⓌⒹ hassle = *engueulade*.

FALLOFF (n) *diminution (f)* : a falloff in imports = *une diminution des importations* ⓌⒹ decrease = *baisse*.

FALLOUT (n inv) *retombées (f pl)* : radioactive fallout = *retombées radioactives* ⓌⒹ aftermath = *séquelles*.

FALSE (adj) **1/** *faux, fausse* : false teeth = *fausses dents*

≠ real = *véritable*, genuine = *authentique* **2/** *faux, fausse* : what you're saying is false = *ce que vous dites est faux* ⓌⒹ wrong = *mauvais* ≠ so = *vrai*

false alarm = *fausse alerte*
☠ *chanter faux* = to sing off key
— *un faux (numéro)* = a wrong (number)
— *faire fausse route* = to bark up the wrong tree
— *faux frais* = incidental expenses
— *fausse couche* = miscarriage
— *un faux jeton* = a phony
— *fausse monnaie* = counterfeit money
— *fausse manœuvre* = wrong move
— *faire faux bond à qqn* = to stand s.o. up
— *un faux (tableau)* = a fake (painting).

FALSEHOOD (n) *contre-vérité (f)* ⓌⒹ lie = *mensonge* ≠ truth = *vérité*.

FALSIES (n pl) *faux seins (m pl)* ⓓ padded bra = *soutien-gorge rembourré.*

FALSIFY (to, -ied) *falsifier* : to falsify documents = *falsifier des documents* ⓓ to doctor up = *traficoter.*

FALTER (to, -ed) *chanceler* : once she's made up her mind she never falters in her determination = *une fois qu'elle a pris sa décision jamais sa détermination ne chancelle* ⓓ to waver = *tergiverser* ☠ *l'ivrogne a chancelé et est tombé* = the drunkard tottered and fell.

FAME (n) *renommée (f)* : keep the fame and give me the money = *garde la renommée et donne-moi l'argent* ⓓ celebrity = *célébrité*, renown = *renom.*

FAME (to, -d) **to be famed for (its wines)** = *être renommé pour (ses vins).*

FAMILIAR (adj) **1/** *familier, -ère* : a familiar place = *un endroit familier* ≠ unknown = *inconnu* **2/** *familier, -ère* : he's a little too familiar = *il est un peu trop familier* ⓓ forward = *envahissant*
to be familiar to = *être familier à* : his name is familiar to me = *son nom m'est familier*
to be familiar with (the subject) = *être au fait (de la question)*
to be on familiar grounds = *être en terrain connu*
to be on familiar terms = *être à tu et à toi*
☠ *le langage familier* = colloquial language.

FAMILIARITY (n, -ies) *familiarité (f)*
familiarity breeds contempt = *la familiarité engendre le mépris* ⓓ to keep one's distance = *garder ses distances.*

FAMILIARIZE (to, -d) *familiariser* : to familiarize oneself with a subject = *se familiariser avec un sujet* ⓓ to get used to = *s'habituer à.*

FAMILY (n, -ies) *famille (f)* : my family comes from Russia = *ma famille vient de Russie* ⓓ clan = ←, relatives = *des parents*, in-laws = *beaux-parents*, parents = ← = folks
to be in the family way = *attendre un heureux événement* ⓓ to be pregnant = *être enceinte*
family likeness = *air de famille*
family man/woman = *homme/femme d'intérieur*
family name = *nom de famille*
family planning = *planning familial*
family ties = *liens familiaux*
family tree = *arbre généalogique*
to run in the family = *être de famille* : blue eyes run in the family = *les yeux bleus sont de famille.*

FAMINE (n) *famine (f)* ≠ abundance = *abondance* ☠ *un salaire de famine* = a starvation salary.

FAMISHED (adj) *affamé, -e* : are you hungry ? — I'm famished ! = *tu as faim ? — je suis affamé !* ⓓ starving = *qui meurt de faim* ≠ satiated = *rassasié.*

FAMOUS (adj) *célèbre* : a famous actress = *une actrice célèbre* ⓓ notorious = *notoire* ≠ unknown = *inconnu*

to be famous for (one's cooking) = *être connu pour (sa cuisine)*
famous last word ! = *tu parles !* : we won't have another argument, famous last word ! = *nous ne nous disputerons plus, tu parles !* ⓓ that remains to be seen = *cela reste à voir*
☠ *(un dîner) fameux* = a great/smashing (dinner)
— *c'était pas fameux* = it wasn't all that great.

FAN (n) **1/** *fan (m, f)* : tennis fans = *les fans du tennis*, fan club = *club de fans* ⓓ fiend = *mordu*, admirer = *admirateur* **2/** *éventail (m)*, *ventilateur (m)* : it's hot, turn on the fan = *il fait chaud, mets le ventilateur*, she dropped her fan and gloves = *elle a laissé tomber son éventail et ses gants* ⓓ air conditioning = *air conditionné* ☠ *éventail des prix* = price range.

FANATIC (n) *fanatique (m, f)* : a religious fanatic = *un fanatique religieux* ⓓ zealot = *zélateur* ☠ *un fanatique de football* = a football fiend **FANATIC(AL)** (adj) *fanatique* **FANATICISM** (n) *fanatisme (m).*

FANCY (n, -ies) **to catch s.o's fancy** = *taper dans l'œil à qqn* : the coat caught my fancy = *le manteau m'a tapé dans l'œil*
to take a fancy to s.o. = *prendre qqn en affection* : he took a fancy to my daughter = *il a pris ma fille en affection.*

FANCY (adj, -ier, -iest) *habillé, -e* : a fancy dress to go to the White House = *une robe habillée pour se rendre à la Maison-Blanche* ⓓ elaborate = *élaboré* ≠ simple = ←
a fancy (apartment/restaurant) = *un (appartement/restaurant) cossu*
fancy prices = *prix faramineux* ≠ reasonable = *raisonnable.*

FANCY (to, -ied) *avoir envie de* : do you fancy a cup of tea ? = *avez-vous envie d'une tasse de thé ?*
fancy that ! = *tu t'imagines !* → GOSH !
to fancy o.s. (a writer) = *s'imaginer (être un écrivain).*

FANNY (n, -ies) *popotin (m)* : a friendly slap on her fanny = *une petite tape amicale sur le popotin* ⓓ buttocks = *fesses.*

FANTASIZE (to, -d) *fantasmer* : she fantasized about being whipped = *elle fantasmait sur le fait de se faire fouetter.*

FANTASTIC (adj) *fantastique* : a fantastic novel = *un roman fantastique* → WONDERFUL ≠ awful = *affreux* ☠ *le cinéma fantastique* = horror movies **FANTASTICALLY** (adv) *formidablement* : fantastically rich = *formidablement riche* → VERY.

FANTASY (n, -ies) **1/** *fantasme (m)* : fantasy or reality ? = *fantasme ou réalité ?*
(he lives) in a world of fantasy = *(il vit) sur sa propre comète*
sexual fantasies = *fantasmes sexuels*
2/ *fantaisie (f)* : a lot of fantasy in the decoration =

beaucoup de fantaisie dans la décoration ⓪ imagination = ←
💀 bijoux fantaisie = costume jewelry.

FAO (abbr) = Food and Agriculture Organization =

FAO (f) = Organisation des Nations unies pour l'alimentation et l'agriculture ⓪ UNCTAD = United Nations Conference on Trade and Development = Conférence des Nations unies sur le commerce et le développement = CNUCED.

FAR (adj, further or farther, furthest or farthest) lointain, -e : in the far past = dans un passé lointain ⓪ remote = reculé

---

a far cry from = un pâle reflet de : American cheeses are a far cry from French ones = les fromages américains sont un pâle reflet des fromages français

Far East = Extrême-Orient
the far right ≠ **left** = l'extrême droite ≠ gauche
Far West = ←
how far is it ? = c'est loin ?

FAR (adv) loin : her place is far from here = sa maison est loin d'ici ≠ around the corner = au coin

---

as far back as = aussi loin que : as far back as I can remember = aussi loin que je me souvienne
as far as I can tell = pour autant que je puisse en juger
as far as I am concerned (she's a bitch) = en ce qui me concerne (c'est une salope) ⓪ as for me = quant à moi
as far as I can remember = autant que je m'en souvienne
that's as far as it goes = cela ne va pas plus loin : we're friends but that's as far as it goes = nous sommes amis mais cela ne va pas plus loin
as far as I know (he isn't

married) = (pour) autant que je sache (il n'est pas marié)
as far as possible = dans la mesure du possible : I'll help you as far as possible = je vous aiderai dans la mesure du possible
far away = très loin : the restaurant's far away = le restaurant est très loin ≠ nearby = tout près
far and away = sans conteste : to be far and away the best student = être sans conteste le meilleur élève ⓪ by far = de loin
far apart = très éloigné : our ideas are far apart = nos idées

sont très éloignées
far be it from me to (criticize you) = loin de moi l'idée de (vous critiquer)
far from (stupid) = loin d'être (stupide)
far from it = loin de là : he's not the best filmmaker, far from it ! = ce n'est pas le meilleur cinéaste, loin de là !
I wouldn't go so/as far as to (say that) = je n'irai pas jusqu'à (dire ça)
far (+ comparative) = bien (plus) : I feel far better = je me sens bien mieux, I'm far more timid than my brother = je suis bien plus timide que mon frère

---

💀 (mon divorce ?), c'est loin ! = (my divorce ?), it was a long time ago !
— il revient de loin = it was a close call

— loin des yeux, loin du cœur = out of sight, out of mind
— au loin = in the distance.

FARAWAY (adj) éloigné, -e : faraway places = des endroits éloignés
faraway look = regard perdu dans le vague.

FARCE (n) farce (f) ⓪ burlesque = ←
💀 faire des farces = to play tricks
— farce (dinde) = stuffing (turkey).

FARCICAL (adj) grotesque ⓪ ridiculous = ridicule.

FARE (n) prix (m) du billet : plane fare = prix du billet d'avion
full ≠ **half fare** = plein ≠ demi-tarif.

FARE (to, -d) **how did you fare ?** = comment cela s'est-il passé (pour vous) ? ⓪ **we fared well** = ça s'est bien passé (pour nous).

FAREWELL (adj) d'adieux : farewell party = soirée

d'adieux **FAREWELL** ! (interj) adieu ! ⓪ so long ! = salut !, good-bye = au revoir.

FARFETCHED (adj) tiré, -e par les cheveux : a farfetched explanation = une explication tirée par les cheveux ⓪ far-out = dément.

FAR-FLUNG (adj) très étendu, -e : far-flung business contacts = des relations d'affaires très étendues ⓪ vast = vaste.

FARM (n) ferme (f) (small), exploitation (f) agricole ⓪ barn = grange
farm hand = ouvrier agricole.

FARMER (n) fermier, -ière, agriculteur, -trice ⓪ countryman = campagnard, hick = plouc, redneck = agriculteur sudiste.

FAR-OFF (adj) *lointain, -e* : far-off places = *endroits lointains* ≠ close-by = *tout près*
(their wedding) is far-off = *(leur mariage) n'est pas pour tout de suite.*

FAR-OUT (adj) *dément, -e* : far-out ideas = *des idées démentes* ① way-out = *délirant.*

FAR-REACHING (adj) *très étendu, -e* : a far-reaching influence = *une influence très étendue* ① spread-out = *étendu* ≠ limited = *limité.*

FARSIGHTED (adj) **1/** *presbyte* ≠ shortsighted = *myope* **2/** *prévoyant, -e* : a farsighted policy = *une politique prévoyante* ≠ shortsighted = *à courte vue.*

FART (n) *pet (m)* **FART** (to, -ed) *péter* ① to break/pass wind = *faire des vents*
☠ *il a pété sa montre* = he broke his watch
— *il est pété* = he's bombed.

FARTHER (adv) *plus loin* : I can't walk any farther = *je ne peux pas marcher plus loin* = I can't walk any further
☠ « farther » *est moins fréquemment utilisé que* « further ».

FARTHEST (adv) *le plus loin* : who can run farthest ? = *qui peut courir le plus loin ?* = who can run furthest ?

FASCINATE (to, -d) *fasciner* : I was fascinated by her intelligence = *son intelligence m'a fasciné* ① to charm = *charmer* **FASCINATING** (adj) *fascinant* : a fascinating story = *une histoire fascinante* ① captivating = *captivant* **FASCINATION** (n) *fascination (f)* ① spell = *envoûtement.*

FASCISM (n) *fascisme (m)* **FASCIST** (n, adj) *fasciste (m, f).*

FASHION (n) *mode (f)* : this year's fashion = *la mode de cette année* ① fad = *vogue* ☠ → mode
after a fashion = *tant bien que mal* : he speaks French after a fashion = *il parle français tant bien que mal* ① more or less = *plus ou moins* ≠ quite = *tout à fait*
fashion designer = *couturier/styliste*
fashion house = *maison de couture*
fashion plate = *gravure de mode* : he's married to a fashion plate = *il a épousé une gravure de mode*
fashion show = *défilé de mode*
in ≠ **out of fashion** = *à la mode* ≠ *passé de mode* ① outmoded = *désuet*
to set the fashion = *donner le la* ① to set the pace = *donner le rythme.*

FASHIONABLE (adj) *à la mode* : fashionable shops = *magasins à la mode* ① with it = *dans le coup* ≠ unfashionable = *passé de mode.*

FAST (adj, -er, -est) **1/** *rapide* : a fast car = *une voiture rapide* ≠ slow = *lent* ☠ → rapid **2/** *rapide en besogne* : I don't like going out with fast guys = *je n'aime pas sortir avec des types (un peu trop) rapides en besogne* ① to have roaming hands = *avoir les mains baladeuses* **3/** *qui avance* : my watch is fast = *ma montre avance* ≠ slow = *qui retarde*

a fast talker = *un baratineur*
fast food = *fast food/restauration rapide*
to pull a fast one = *blouser* : the salesman pulled a fast one on me with his line = *le vendeur m'a blousé avec son baratin* → TO HUSTLE
(life) on the fast track = *(vie) speedée.*

FAST (adv) *vite* : you eat too fast = *tu manges trop vite* = quickly ① on the double = *dare-dare*, in a flash = *en un éclair* ≠ slowly = *lentement*
to hold fast = *tenir bon* ≠ to give in = *céder*
(he) ran as fast as (his) legs could carry (him) = *(il) a couru à toutes jambes* ① to run for one's life = *courir comme si on avait le diable à ses trousses*
☠ *"vite"* isn't an adjective : a fast car = *une voiture rapide*
— *(il l'a fait)* vite fait, bien fait = (he did it) quickly and well
— *c'est vite dit* = it's easier said than done
— *vite !* = quick !

FAST (to, -ed) *jeûner* ≠ to feast = *faire un festin.*

FASTEN (to, -ed) *attacher* : fasten my dress = *attache ma robe* ≠ to unfasten = *détacher* ☠ → to attach.

FASTIDIOUS (adj) *minutieux, -euse* : fastidious work = *travail minutieux*
☠ *travail fastidieux* = dull work
— *une personne minutieuse* = a thorough person.

FAT (n) **1/** *matière (f) grasse* : to cook with a lot of fat = *mettre beaucoup de matière grasse dans sa cuisine* ① butter = *beurre* **2/** *graisse (f)* : a lot of fat around the waist = *beaucoup de graisse autour de la taille* ☠ → grease
to chew the fat = *discuter le bout de gras* ① to talk of everything and anything = *parler de tout et de rien*
to live off the fat of the land = *vivre de ses rentes* → RICH.

FAT (adj, -ter, -test) *gros, grosse* : a fat woman = *une grosse femme* ① plump = *rondouillard*, fleshy = *charnu* ≠ thin = *mince* ☠ → big
fat cat = *gros richard* : he was elected with the support of the fat cats = *il a été élu avec le soutien des gros richards*
a fat slob = *un gros lard* ① a pig = *un cochon.*

FATAL (adj) *fatal, -e* : a fatal decision/illness = *une décision/maladie fatale* ① mortal = *mortel*
☠ *c'était fatal* = it was inevitable
— *(une rencontre) fatale* = (a) fateful (meeting).

FATALISM (n) *fatalisme (m)* ① defeatism = *défaitisme* **FATALIST** (n) *fataliste (m, f)* **FATALISTIC** (adj) *fataliste* **FATALITY** (n, -ies) *fatalité (f).*

FATE (n) **1/** *sort (m)* : her fate was to die young = *son sort était de mourir jeune* ① lot = ← ☠ → sort
it's a fate worse than death = *c'est pire que la mort* **2/** *destin (m)* : that we met was fate = *c'était notre destin de nous rencontrer.*

FATED (adj) **fated to (fall in love with each other)** = *destinés à (tomber amoureux l'un de l'autre).*

FATEFUL (adj) *fatidique* : a fateful meeting = *une rencontre fatidique* ⊕ predestined = *prédestiné.*

FATHER (n) *père* (m) : my father's 64 = *mon père a 64 ans* ⊕ daddy = *papa*, my old man = *mon vieux*, father-in-law = *beau-père*, stepfather = *beau-père (remariage de la mère)*, foster father = *père adoptif*, fatherly = *paternel*, fatherhood = *paternité*, patriarch = *patriarche* **like father like son** = *tel père, tel fils*
☠ *père de famille* = family man
— *Smith père* = Smith senior
— *Père Noël* = Santa Claus.

FATHERLY (adj) *paternel, -elle* : fatherly advice = *des conseils paternels* ≠ motherly = *maternel.*

FATHOM (to, -ed) *arriver à comprendre* : I can't fathom why he left her = *je n'arrive pas à comprendre pourquoi il l'a quittée* = to figure out ⊕ to grasp = *saisir.*

FATIGUE (n) *fatigue* (f) ⊕ exhaustion = *épuisement* ☠ *tomber de fatigue* = to be ready to drop.

FATSO (n) *gros lard* (m) : listen, fatso ! = *écoute, gros lard !* ≠ beanpole = *grande perche.*

FATTEN (to, -ed) *engraisser* : to fatten pigs = *engraisser des porcs* ⊕ to force-feed = *gaver.*

FATTENING (adj) *qui fait grossir* : potatoes are fattening = *les pommes de terre font grossir.*

FATTY (adj, -ier, -est) *gras, grasse* : fatty food = *nourriture grasse* ≠ low-fat = *maigre*
☠ *faire la grasse matinée* = to sleep late
— *cheveux gras* = oily/greasy hair.

FAUCET (n) *robinet* (m) = tap.

FAULT (n) *faute* (f) : it's my fault = *c'est de ma faute* ⊕ responsibility = *responsabilité*, failing = *travers* **whose fault is it ?** = *à qui (est-ce) la faute ?* **we all have our faults** = *nous avons tous nos défauts* **through no fault of mine** = *vraiment pas ma faute* : if they didn't make up, it was through no fault of mine = *s'ils ne se sont pas réconciliés, ce n'est vraiment pas ma faute*
to find fault with = *trouver à redire à* ⊕ to run down = *dénigrer* ≠ to rave about = *s'enthousiasmer pour*
to a fault = *à l'excès* : generous to a fault = *généreux à l'excès* → VERY
☠ *faute de mieux* = for lack of better
— *faute d'impression* = misprint
— *faire une faute* = to make a mistake
— *sans faute* = without fail
— *faute de grives on mange des merles* = beggars can't be choosers.

FAULTY (adj, -ier, -iest) *défaillant, -e* : faulty reasoning = *raisonnement défaillant* ≠ flawless = *sans défaut.*

FAUX PAS (n) *faux pas* (m) ⊕ slip = *impair*, blooper = *boulette*
to make a faux pas = *faire un faux pas* ⊕ to make a blunder = *faire une gaffe.*

FAVOR (n) = **FAVOUR** (GB) **1/** *service* (m) : may I ask you a favor ? = *est-ce que je peux vous demander un service ?* ☠ → service **2/** *faveur* (f) : to win the teacher's favor = *gagner la faveur du professeur* ⊕ approval = *approbation*
to do s.o. a favor = *rendre (un) service à qqn/faire une fleur à qqn* : could you please do me a favor ? = *est-ce que vous pourriez me rendre un service ?*
you're not doing me any favors (by stopping smoking) = *cela ne me fait ni chaud ni froid (que tu arrêtes de fumer)*
to return the favor = *revaloir ça* : when I can, I'll return the favor = *quand je pourrai, je vous revaudrai ça* ⊕ one good turn deserves another = *c'est un échange de bons procédés*
in (your) favor = *en (votre) faveur* : it's in your favor that ... = *cela joue en votre faveur que ...*
in favor of (abortion) = *en faveur de (l'avortement)* ≠ against = *contre*
to be in ≠ out of s.o.'s favor = *avoir ≠ ne pas avoir la cote avec qqn*
☠ *traitement de faveur* = VIP treatment.

FAVORABLE (adj) *favorable* : a favorable report = *un rapport favorable* = favourable (GB) ⊕ auspicious = *propice* ≠ unfavorable = *défavorable* **FAVORABLY** (adv) *favorablement.*

FAVORITE (n) *favori, -ite* : my mother didn't have favorites = *ma mère n'avait pas de favoris* = favourite (GB) ⊕ pet = *chouchou* ☠ *porter des favoris* = to wear sideburns.

FAVORITE (adj) *favori, -ite* : my favorite actress/restaurant = *mon actrice favorite/mon restaurant favori* = favourite (GB) ⊕ pet = *préféré* **FAVORITISM** (n) *favoritisme* (m) ⊕ nepotism = *népotisme.*

FAZE (to, -d) **not to faze s.o.** = *ne pas démonter qqn* : his calling her a bitch did not faze her = *ça ne l'a pas démontée qu'il la traite de salope* ⊕ to daunt = *impressionner.*

FBI (abbr) = Federal Bureau of Investigation = *FBI* (m), *correspond à la DST et aux Renseignements généraux en France* ⊕ the Feds = *les agents du FBI.*

FEAR (n) *peur* (f), *crainte* (f) (psychological) : a fear of dogs = *la peur des chiens*, a fear of poverty/sex = *la crainte de la misère/du sexe* ⊕ dread = *hantise*
for fear that = *de peur que* = fearing that ⊕ lest = *de crainte que*
to put the fear of God into s.o. = *flanquer une sainte trouille à qqn* ⊕ to scare the daylights out of s.o. = *flanquer la pétoche à qqn*
☠ *avoir peur de* = to be afraid of

— *plus de peur que de mal* = more frightened than anything else
— *ça m'a fait peur* = it gave me a scare.

FEAR (to, -ed) *craindre* : he fears his boss = *il craint son patron* ⓓ to dread = *redouter*
I fear that (you're wrong) = *je crains que (tu n'aies tort)*

FEARFUL (adj) *peureux, -euse* : a fearful child = *un enfant peureux* **FEARLESS** (adj) *sans peur* **FEARLESSLY** (adv) *sans peur.*

FEASIBLE (adj) *faisable* : a feasible plan = *un projet faisable* ⓓ workable = *réalisable* ≠ unfeasible = *infaisable.*

FEAST (n) *festin (m)* : the meal was a feast = *le repas a été un festin* **FEAST** (to, -ed) *festoyer.*

FEAT (n) *prouesse (f)* : getting there so fast was a feat = *ça a été une prouesse d'arriver si vite* ⓓ exploit = ←.

FEATHER (n) *plume (f)* : a peacock's feather = *une plume de paon*
a feather in s.o.'s cap = *un bon point pour qqn* : getting a contract was a feather in his cap = *c'est un bon point pour lui d'avoir obtenu un contrat*
to knock s.o. over with a feather = *laisser qqn comme deux ronds de flan* : you could have knocked me with a feather when she said that = *quand elle a dit ça, j'en suis resté comme deux ronds de flan* ⓓ to knock s.o. for a loop = *laisser qqn baba*
☠ *j'y ai laissé des plumes* = I lost a lot on it
— *vivre de sa plume* = to live off one's writings
— *stylo à plume* = fountain pen
— *voler dans les plumes à qqn* = to let s.o. have it.

FEATHERWEIGHT (n) *poids (m) plume* ≠ heavyweight = *poids lourd.*

FEATURE (n) 1/ *trait (m)* : the main features of the plan = *les principaux traits du projet* ⓓ characteristic = *caractéristique* 2/ *trait (m)* : delicate features = *des traits délicats* ⓓ face = *visage* ☠ → trait
feature film = *long métrage* ≠ short = *court métrage*
feature story = *grand article.*

FEATURE (to, -d) *avoir pour vedette* : the show features Marilyn Monroe = *le spectacle a Marilyn Monroe pour vedette*
I don't feature (working late tonight) = *ça ne me chante pas de (travailler tard ce soir)* ⓓ I don't dig it = *ça ne me botte pas.*

FEBRUARY (n) *février (m)* ⓓ leap year = *année bissextile* → MONTH.

FEDERAL (adj) *fédéral, -e* : a federal government = *un gouvernement fédéral* ≠ regional = *régional*
Federal Bureau of Investigation = *FBI*
Federal Reserve System = *système bancaire américain*
to make a federal case out of = *faire une affaire d'État de* ⓓ to make a fuss = *faire des histoires.*

FEDERATION (n) *fédération (f)* ⓓ alliance = ←.

FEE (n) *honoraires (m pl)* (doctor, lawyer), *droits (m pl) d'inscription* (school) : the doctor's fee was high = *les honoraires du médecin étaient élevés*, what's the yearly fee ? = *à combien se montent les droits d'inscription annuels ?*

FEEBLE (adj) *faible* : a feeble excuse/old person = *une faible excuse/une vieille personne faible* ☠ → weak.

FEED (to, fed, fed) *donner à manger à* : to feed a baby/the cat = *donner à manger à un bébé/au chat* ⓓ to nourish = *nourrir*
to be fed up (with) = *en avoir ras le bol (de)* : I'm fed up with his criticisms = *j'en ai ras le bol de ses critiques* ⓓ to be sick of = *en avoir marre de* ≠ to be delighted with = *être ravi de.*

FEEDBACK (n) *réaction (f)*, *feed-back (m)* : I'm getting negative feedback about my idea = *je n'obtiens que des réactions négatives à mon idée* ⓓ remark = *remarque* ☠ *réaction* → reaction.

FEEL (n) **to have a feel for (music)** = *avoir le sens de (la musique)* ⓓ gift = *don.*

FEEL (to, felt, felt) 1/ *se sentir* (health, feelings) : how do you feel ? — I feel quite well = *comment vous sentez-vous ? — je me sens tout à fait bien*, I feel sad = *je me sens triste*
☠ *je ne peux pas la sentir* = I can't bear her
— *sentir (mauvais)* = to smell (bad)
2/ *ressentir* (feeling, reaction) : what did you feel when he told you he loved you ? = *qu'avez-vous ressenti lorsqu'il vous a dit qu'il vous aimait ?* ⓓ to experience = *éprouver* ☠ *elle est fatiguée, son travail s'en ressent* = she's tired and her work shows it
3/ *sentir* : he doesn't feel anything in his paralyzed arm = *il ne sent rien dans son bras paralysé*
4/ *toucher* : feel how soft this cashmere is = *touche comme ce cachemire est doux* ☠ → to touch

---

how does it feel (to be single again) ? = *quel effet cela fait-il (d'être à nouveau célibataire) ?*
I feel that (I'm right) = *je pense que (j'ai raison)*

---

to feel for s.o. = *plaindre qqn* : I feel for her having lost a child = *je la plains d'avoir perdu un enfant* ⓓ to sympathize = *compatir*
to feel s.o. out = *sonder qqn* : feel him out and let me know what he thinks = *essayez de le sonder et dites-moi ce qu'il pense* ⓓ sound him out
to feel out of it/things = *se sentir hors du coup* : I feel out of it with my kid sister's friends = *je me sens complètement hors du coup avec les amis de ma petite sœur*
to feel s.o. up = *peloter qqn* : she never lets me

feel her up = *elle ne me laisse jamais la peloter* ⓪ to paw = *tripoter*
to feel up to = *être en forme pour* : I don't feel up to taking a walk now = *je ne me sens pas en forme pour faire une promenade maintenant* ≠ to be out of sorts = *être mal en point.*

FEELER (n) **to put out feelers** = *sonder son entourage* : the President is putting out feelers about a new tax law = *le Président sonde son entourage à propos de la nouvelle loi fiscale* ⓪ to see how the land lies = *tâter le terrain.*

FEELING (n) *sentiment (m)* : her feelings towards him are ambiguous = *ses sentiments pour lui sont ambigus*
you have no feelings = *tu n'as pas de cœur* ≠ you're too sensitive = *tu es trop sensible*
I have a feeling that (she's not going to come) = *j'ai le sentiment qu'(elle ne viendra pas)*
to have a feeling for (words) = *avoir le sens des (mots)*
I don't want to hurt your feelings = *je ne veux pas vous blesser*
☙ → sentiment.

FEIGN (to, -ed) *feindre* : to feign illness = *feindre d'être malade* ⓪ to make believe = *faire comme si.*

FEISTY (adj, -ier, -iest) *hargneux, -euse* : a feisty nature = *une nature hargneuse* ⓪ abrasive = *corrosif.*

FELINE (n) *félin (m)* : cats and lions are felines = *les chats et les lions sont des félins.*

FELLOW (n) *type (m)* : he's a nice fellow = *c'est un type sympa* = chap (GB) ≠ broad = *nana* ☙ → type
fellow traveller = *compagnon de route* ⓪ commie = *coco*
fellow of (Oxford) = *titulaire d'un poste d'agrégé (lecteur, chercheur) à l'université (d'Oxford).*

FELLOWSHIP (n) *bourse (f) attribuée aux chercheurs avancés (écrivains, scientifiques, etc.)* : to obtain a fellowship for research work = *obtenir une bourse pour un travail de recherche* ⓪ scholarship, = *bourse.*

FELONY (n, -ies) *forfait (m)* ⓪ petty offense = *infraction mineure*
☙ *forfait (argent)* = lump sum
— *déclarer forfait* = to withdraw (from a race, an election, etc.).

FEMALE (n) *femelle (f)* (animal), *femme (f)* : the females stay in the nest = *les femelles restent dans le nid*, no females in the locker room = *le vestiaire est interdit aux femmes* ≠ male = *mâle* ☙ *femme* → woman.

FEMALE (adj) **1/** *femelle* (animal), *féminin, -e* : a female elephant = *un éléphant femelle*, a female team = *une équipe féminine* ≠ male = *mâle/masculin* ☙ *féminin* → feminine **2/** *très femme* : his broad's very female = *sa nana est très femme.*

FEMININE (adj) *féminin, -e* ≠ tomboyish = *garçon manqué* ☙ *une équipe féminine* = a female team.

FEMINISM (n) *féminisme (m)* ⓪ Women's lib = *MLF*, ERA = Equal Rights Amendment = *Amendement sur l'égalité des droits* ≠ male chauvinism = *phallocratie.*

FEMINIST (n, adj) *féministe (m, f)* ≠ sexist = *sexiste*, woman hater = *misogyne.*

FEMININITY (n) *féminité (f)* ≠ masculinity = *masculinité.*

FENCE (n) **1/** *clôture (f)* : a fence around the garden = *une clôture autour du jardin* ⓪ gate = *portail*
to sit on the fence = *ne pas se mouiller* : many UN countries are sitting on the fence as far as the Middle East problem is concerned = *beaucoup de pays de l'ONU ne se mouillent pas au sujet du Moyen-Orient* ☙ *la clôture d'une réunion* = the closing of a meeting **2/** *receleur, -euse* : a fence hides hot stuff = *un receleur cache de la marchandise volée.*

FENCE (to, -d) **1/** *faire de l'escrime* : she's learning how to fence = *elle apprend (à faire de) l'escrime* **2/** *répondre par des pirouettes* : to fence questions = *répondre à des questions par des pirouettes* ⓪ to hedge = *répondre à côté.*

FENCING (n) *escrime (f)* : a fencing champion = *un champion d'escrime* ⓪ martial arts = *arts martiaux.*

FEND (to, -ed) **to fend for o.s.** = *se dépatouiller tout seul* : she's been fending for herself since she was 13 = *elle se dépatouille toute seule depuis qu'elle a 13 ans* ⓪ to take care of o.s. = *se débrouiller tout seul.*

FENDER (n) *pare-chocs (m)* = bumper ⓪ lights = *feux de route.*

FEROCIOUS (adj) *féroce* : ferocious animals = *des animaux féroces* ⓪ wild = *sauvage* **FEROCITY** (n) *férocité (f).*

FERRY (n, -ies) *ferry (m), bac (m)* ☙ *le bac* = the French high school diploma.

FERTILE (adj) *fertile, fécond, -e* (person) : a fertile imagination/woman = *une imagination fertile/une femme féconde* ☙ *année fertile en événements* = eventful year.

FERTILITY (n) *fertilité (f).*

FERTILIZER (n) *engrais (m)* : chemical fertilizers = *des engrais chimiques* ⓪ manure = *fumier.*

FERVENT (adj) *fervent, -e* : a fervent believer/admirer = *un croyant/admirateur fervent* ⓪ ardent = ←.

FERVOR (n) *ferveur (f)* ⓪ ardor = *ardeur.*

FESTIVAL (n) *festival (m)* : a film festival = *un festival de cinéma.*

FESTIVITY (n, -ies) *festivité (f)* ⓪ celebration = *fête.*

FETCH (to, -ed) *(aller) chercher* : fetch the ball = *va chercher la balle.*

FETISH (n, -es) *objet (m) de fétichisme* : big tits are his fetish = *les gros nichons sont pour lui un objet de fétichisme* ☠ *un fétiche* = a lucky charm/a mascot.

FETUS (n, -es) *fœtus (m inv)* : experiments on fetuses = *des expériences sur les fœtus* ⓓ womb = *matrice*.

FEUD (n) *vendetta (f)* : a feud between two families = *une vendetta entre deux familles* ≠ friendship = *amitié*.

FEUDAL (adj) *féodal, -e* ⓓ medieval = *médiéval*.

FEVER (n) *fièvre (f)* : I had a high fever = *j'avais une forte fièvre* ⓓ temperature = *température*, pulse = *pouls* **FEVERISH** (adj) *fiévreux, -euse* ⓓ sickly = *maladif*.

FEW (n) a few = *quelques-uns, -unes* : if you have some cigarettes, give me a few = *si vous avez des cigarettes, donnez-m'en quelques-unes* ⓓ very little = *très peu* ≠ many = *beaucoup*
a few of (us) = *certains d'entre (nous)*
win a few, lose a few = *à la guerre comme à la guerre* → THAT'S LIFE !

FEW (pron) *peu* : all were invited but few came = *tous étaient invités mais peu sont venus*, few of his remarks were taken into consideration = *peu de ses remarques ont été prises en considération* ≠ many = *beaucoup*.

FEW (adj, -er, -est) *peu de (choses dénombrables)* : few eggs/people/books = *peu d'œufs/de gens/de livres* ⓓ little = *peu de (choses indénombrables)* ≠ many = *beaucoup de* = a lot of
a few = *quelques* : I know a few people in Paris = *je connais quelques personnes à Paris* = some ≠ many = *beaucoup*
few and far between = *rares et espacés* : nice days in winter are few and far between = *les beaux jours en hiver sont rares et espacés*
to be a man/woman of few words = *être quelqu'un qui parle peu*.

FEWER (adj) *moins de (choses dénombrables)* : fewer cars/problems = *moins de voitures/problèmes* ⓓ less than = *moins de (choses indénombrables)* ≠ more = *plus de*
no fewer than (20 people came) = *(il n'y avait) pas moins de (20 personnes)* ≠ no more than = *pas plus de*.

FIANCÉ (n) *fiancé (m)* ⓓ intended = *promis* **FIANCÉE** (n) *fiancée (f)*.

FIASCO (n) *fiasco (m)* : the attempt to rescue the hostages was a fiasco = *la tentative pour sauver les otages fut un fiasco* ≠ smash = *succès fracassant*.

FIB (n) *bobard (m)* ⓓ white lie = *pieux mensonge*.

FIB (to, -bed) *raconter des bobards* : stop fibbing ! = *arrête de raconter des bobards !* = stop telling fibs ! ⓓ to lie through one's teeth = *mentir comme un arracheur de dents*.

FICKLE (adj) *changeant, -e* : fickle voters = *électorat changeant* ⓓ capricious = *capricieux* ☠ *temps changeant* = unstable weather.

FICTION (n) *fiction (f)* ≠ nonfiction = *qui n'est pas de la fiction*
to write fiction = *écrire des romans*.

FICTITIOUS (adj) *fictif, -ive* : a fictitious character = *un personnage fictif* ≠ real = *réel*.

FIDDLE (to, -d) **to fiddle around** = *bayer aux corneilles* : stop fiddling around and get to work ! = *arrête de bayer aux corneilles et mets-toi au travail !*
to fiddle with = 1/ *tripoter* : stop fiddling with your hair = *arrête de tripoter tes cheveux* ☠ → to paw 2/ *tripatouiller* : to fiddle with the books = *tripatouiller les comptes*.

FIDDLESTICKS ! (interj) *sornettes !* ⓓ nonsense ! = *bêtises !*

FIDELITY (n, -ies) *fidélité (f)* ⓓ allegiance = *allégeance*.

FIDGET (to, -ed) *(s')agiter* : I can't take the picture if you don't stop fidgeting ! = *je ne peux pas te prendre en photo si tu t'agites comme ça !*

FIDGETY (adj) *agité, -e* : why are you so fidgety ? = *pourquoi êtes-vous si agité ?* ⓓ to have ants in one's pants = *avoir la bougeotte*
☠ *une mer agitée* = a rough sea
— *un esprit agité* = a febrile mind.

FIELD (n) 1/ *champ (m)* : to work in the fields = *travailler dans les champs*
(the press) had a field day with the (scandal) = *(le scandale) a fait le bonheur de (la presse)*
to play the field = *courir le jupon* : my brother's divorced again and is playing the field = *mon frère est de nouveau divorcé et il se remet à courir le jupon* ⓓ to be a free agent = *être libre comme l'air*
☠ *sur-le-champ* = on the spot
— *le champ est libre* = the coast is clear
— *être tué au champ d'honneur* = to be killed in action
— *champ de courses* = racetrack
2/ *domaine (m)* : he's well-known in his field = *il est connu dans son domaine* ⓓ job = *travail* ☠ → domain.

FIELDMAN (n, -men) *éclaireur, -euse* : the President's fieldman = *l'éclaireur du Président* = the President's advance man.

FIEND (n) *mordu, -e* : a football fiend = *un mordu de football* ⓓ freak = *dingue*.

FIERCE (adj, -r, -st) *féroce* : fierce competition = *concurrence féroce* ⓓ ruthless = *impitoyable*, violent = ←
FIERCELY (adv) *farouchement* : fiercely opposed to his policy = *farouchement opposé à sa politique* → VERY.

FIERY (adj, -ier, -iest) *fougueux, -euse* : a fiery redhead = *une rouquine fougueuse* ⓓ ardent = ←.

FIFTEEN (n, adj) *quinze (m)* : count to fifteen = *compte*

jusqu'à quinze ⬭ fifteenth =*quinzième*
☠ *dans quinze jours* = in a fortnight.

FIFTH (n, adj) *cinquième* *(m)* ⬭ five = *cinq*
to be the fifth wheel = *être la cinquième roue du carrosse* ⬭ to cut no ice = *compter pour du beurre*
fifth column = *cinquième colonne* ⬭ spying = *espionnage*
to take the fifth = *invoquer le cinquième amendement (refuser de témoigner, quand ce témoignage peut vous faire accuser).*

FIFTY (n, -ies, adj) *cinquante* *(m)* ⬭ fiftieth = *cinquantième*
the fifties = *les années cinquante*
to be in one's fifties = *avoir cinquante ans et quelques* ⬭ to be fiftyish = *avoir la cinquantaine.*

FIFTY-FIFTY (adj, adv) *moitié-moitié, fifty-fifty*
a fifty-fifty chance = *une chance sur deux*
to go fifty-fifty = *partager fifty-fifty* ⬭ to go halves = *faire moitié-moitié.*

FIG (n) *figue* *(f)* : dry figs = *figues sèches*
fig leaf = *feuille de vigne*
☠ *mi-figue, mi-raisin* = neither one thing, nor the other.

FIGHT (n) *bagarre* *(f)* : we had a fight last night = *nous avons eu une bagarre hier soir* ⬭ row = altercation, brawl = *rixe*
to pick a fight with s.o. = *chercher noise à qqn* ⬭ to pick a quarrel with s.o. = *chercher querelle à qqn*
to spoil for a fight = *chercher la bagarre* ⬭ to be looking for trouble = *chercher des ennuis*
to put up a (good) fight = *(bien) se défendre*
the fight against (cancer) = *la lutte contre (le cancer)* ⬭ battle = *bataille.*

FIGHT (to, fought, fought) **1/** *se bagarrer* : my sister and her husband always fight = *ma sœur et son mari sont toujours en train de se bagarrer* ≠ to get on like a house on fire = *s'entendre comme larrons en foire* **2/** *se battre* : the armies fought all night = *les armées se sont battues toute la nuit* ⬭ to wage war = *faire la guerre* ☠ → to beat
to fight (cancer) = *se battre contre (le cancer)*
to fight back = *rendre coup pour coup* : if someone hits you, fight back = *si quelqu'un te frappe, rends coup pour coup* ⬭ to counterattack = *contre-attaquer*
to fight for (better working conditions) = *se battre pour (de meilleures conditions de travail)*
he fought in (Vietnam) = *il s'est battu au (Viêt-nam)* ⬭ to serve in = *servir dans*
to fight off (the enemy) = *refouler (l'ennemi)* ⬭ to fend off = *repousser* ☠ → to hold back.

FIGHTER (n) **1/** *boxeur* *(m)* = boxer **2/** *lutteur, -euse* : he doesn't give up easily, he's a fighter = *il n'abandonne pas facilement la partie, c'est un lutteur* ⬭ dynamo = *battant* ☠ *lutteur (sport)* = wrestler.

FIGMENT (n) **a figment of (your) imagination** = *le*

fruit de (votre) imagination ⬭ completely made up = *inventé de toutes pièces.*

FIGURATIVE (adj) *figuré, -e* : in the figurative sense = *au sens figuré* ≠ literal = *littéral*
figurative art = *l'art figuratif.*

FIGURATIVELY (adv) *au figuré* ≠ literally = *littéralement.*

FIGURE (n) **1/** *ligne* *(f)* : she has a fantastic figure = *elle a une ligne fantastique* ⬭ body = *corps* ☠ → line **2/** *figure* *(f)* : an important figure in feminism = *une figure importante du féminisme* ⬭ personage = *personnage* ☠ *une jolie figure* = a pretty face **3/** *chiffre* *(m)* : his salary is in the six figures = *il a un salaire à six chiffres* ☠ *chiffre d'affaires* = turnover
to be good at figures = *être doué pour les chiffres*
to cut quite a figure = *faire bonne impression* ≠ **to cut a sorry figure** = *faire piètre figure*
father/mother figure = *l'image du père/de la mère*
a figure of speech = *une façon de s'exprimer.*

FIGURE (to, -d) *croire* : I never figured he would have cheated on her = *je n'aurais jamais cru qu'il la tromperait* ⬭ I never dreamed that = *je ne me serais jamais douté que*, I never reckoned that = *je n'aurais jamais imaginé que* ☠ → to believe
go figure ! = *va comprendre !*
how do you figure that ? = *comment expliquez-vous cela ?*
that figures ! ≠ **that doesn't figure !** = *cela s'explique !* ≠ *cela ne s'explique pas !*
to figure on = **1/** *s'attendre à* : I didn't figure on his getting so angry = *je ne m'attendais pas à ce qu'il se mette autant en colère* ⬭ to count on = *compter sur* **2/** *figurer sur* : her name figures on the list = *son nom figure sur la liste*
to figure out = *arriver à comprendre* : I can't figure out why he quit = *je n'arrive pas à comprendre pourquoi il a démissionné* ⬭ to make out = *comprendre.*

FIGUREHEAD (n) *potiche* *(f)* : the king's just a figurehead = *le roi n'est qu'une potiche* ⬭ puppet = *pantin.*

FILCH (to, -d) *chaparder* : the tourists filched all the ashtrays = *les touristes ont chapardé tous les cendriers* ⬭ to lift = *chiper.*

FILE (n) **1/** *dossier* *(m)* : to have files on private citizens = *avoir des dossiers sur des personnes privées* ⬭ index card = *fiche*
file cabinet = *fichier/classeur*
2/ *lime* *(f)* à ongles ⬭ nail scissors = *ciseaux à ongles.*

FILE (to, -d) **1/** *classer* : to file letters = *classer des lettres* ⬭ to catalogue = *cataloguer* ☠ → to class **2/** *limer* : to file one's nails = *se limer les ongles.*

FILIBUSTER (to, -ed) *faire de l'obstruction parlementaire* ⬭ to lobby = *faire pression.*

FILL (n) **to have one's fill of** = *en avoir jusque-là de* :

I've had my fill of listening to his problems = *j'en ai jusque-là de l'entendre parler de ses problèmes* ⓓ I've had it = *j'en ai plein le dos.*

FILL (to, -ed) *remplir* : to fill a bottle/a theater = *remplir une bouteille/un théâtre* ≠ to empty = *vider*
to fill in = *remplir* : to fill in a form = *remplir un formulaire* = **to fill out** ≠ to leave out = *laisser en blanc*
fill me in (on what happened) = *affranchis-moi (sur ce qui s'est passé)* ⓓ enlighten me = *éclaire ma lanterne*
to fill in for = *remplacer temporairement* : Pete's filling in for Tom till he gets out of the hospital = *Pete remplace Tom jusqu'à ce qu'il sorte de l'hôpital* ⓓ to stand in for = *suppléer*
fill 'er up ! = *faites le plein !*
to fill up = *(se) remplir* : the theater filled up quickly = *le théâtre s'est vite rempli*
☠ *remplir des conditions* = to fulfill conditions.

FILLING STATION (n) *station-service (f)* ⓓ gasoline = *essence.*

FILM (n) **1/** *film (m)* = movie = flick = motion picture

actor/actress = *acteur/actrice*	**lighting** = *éclairage*
blue movie = *film porno* = **skin flick**	**on location** = *en extérieur*
cameraman = ←	**producer** = *producteur*
character role = *rôle de composition*	**reel** = *bobine*
close-up = *gros plan*	**screen** = *écran*
credits = *générique*	**the set** = *le plateau*
director = *metteur en scène*	**script** = *scénario*
documentary = *documentaire*	**script girl** = *scripte*
to dub, dubbing = *doubler, doublage*	**scriptwriter** = *scénariste*
editing = *montage*	**to shoot** = *tourner*
extra = *figurant*	**a short** = *un court métrage*
feature film = *long métrage*	**silent film** ≠ **talkie** = *film muet* ≠ *parlant*
filmgoer = *cinéphile* = **moviegoer**	**slow motion** = *ralenti*
filmmaker = *cinéaste*	**snuff film** = *film avec un meurtre non simulé*
to go to the flicks = *aller au cinoche/se faire une toile*	**soundtrack** = *bande-son*
to go to the movies = *aller au ciné(ma)*	**special effects** = *effets spéciaux*
hard ≠ **soft core** = *porno dur* ≠ *doux*	**star** = *vedette*
leading lady ≠ **man** = *premier rôle féminin* ≠ *masculin*	**subtitle** = *sous-titre*
	super eight = *super-huit*
	usher, usherette = *placeur, ouvreuse*
	X-rated = *classé X*

2/ *pellicule (f)* : color ≠ black and white film = *pellicule couleur* ≠ *noir et blanc* ☠ → dandruff.

FILM (to, -ed) *filmer* : to film a play = *filmer une pièce* ⓓ to shoot = *tourner.*

FILTER (n) *filtre (m)* **FILTER** (to, -ed) *filtrer* : to filter water = *filtrer de l'eau* ☠ *filtrer les invités* = to screen the guests.

FILTH (n inv) **1/** *saleté (f)* : how can you read such filth ? = *comment pouvez-vous lire de telles saletés ?* = how can you read such trash ? ☠ → dirt **2/** *crasse (f)* : to live in filth = *vivre dans la crasse* ☠ *faire une crasse à qqn* = to do s.o. dirty.

FILTHY (adj, -ier, -iest) **1/** *crasseux, -euse* : a filthy room/child = *une pièce crasseuse/un enfant crasseux* ⓓ disgusting = *dégoûtant* **2/** *ordurier, -ère* : filthy film/language = *un film/langage ordurier*
filthy rich = *richissime* → RICH.

FINAGLE (to, -d) *ruser pour avoir* : to finagle free tickets = *ruser pour avoir des places gratuites* ⓓ to hustle = *se débrouiller pour avoir.*

FINAL (adj) **1/** *dernier, -ère, final, -e* : my final offer = *ma dernière proposition*, the final chapter = *le chapitre final* ≠ initial = ← ☠ *dernier* → last **2/** *définitif, -ive* : her decision's final = *sa décision est définitive*
that's final ! = *un point c'est tout !*
the final blow = *le coup de grâce*
he had the final say = *il a eu le dernier mot.*

FINALIST (n) *finaliste (m, f)* ⓓ finals = *finale.*

FINALLY (adv) *finalement* : he finally understood = *il a finalement compris* ⓓ at last = *enfin* ☠ *finalement, tu as eu raison d'accepter* = in the end, you were right to accept.

FINALS (n pl) **1/** *finale (f)* : the tennis finals = *la finale de tennis* ⓓ playoff = *la belle* **2/** *examen (m) de fin d'année* : the finals are in June = *les examens de fin d'année sont en juin.*

FINANCE (n) *finance (f)* : high finance = *haute finance* **FINANCE** (to, -d) *financer* : to finance a business = *financer une affaire* ⓓ to put up the money = *avancer les fonds*, to put a deal together = *monter une affaire.*

FINANCIAL (adj) *financier, -ère* : financial circles = *milieux financiers* ⓓ fiscal = *budgétaire* ☠ *le marché financier* = the money market.

FINANCIALLY (adv) *financièrement* : a financially interesting project = *un projet intéressant financièrement.*

FINANCIER (n) *financier (m)* ⓓ backer = *soutien financier.*

FIND (n) *trouvaille (f)* : their apartment's a find = *leur appartement est une trouvaille* ⓓ discovery = *découverte.*

FIND (to, found, found) *trouver* : where did you find your wallet ? = *où avez-vous trouvé votre portefeuille ?* ⊕ to dig up = *dégoter* ≠ to lose = *perdre*

to find o.s. = *se trouver* : she went to Europe for a year to find herself = *elle a passé un an en Europe pour se trouver*

to find guilty ≠ **innocent** = *déclarer coupable* ≠ *innocent*

to find out = 1/ *se renseigner* : I'm going to find out how much it costs = *je vais me renseigner sur le prix* 2/ *apprendre* : I found out he was married = *j'ai appris qu'il était marié* ⊕ to hear = *entendre dire* ☠ → to learn

☠ *vous trouvez ?* = do you think so ?

— *il se trouve qu'(il a tort)* = it so happens that (he's wrong)

— *où est-ce que ça se trouve ?* = where is it ?

— *je trouve que (tu as tort)* = I feel (you're wrong)

— *qu'est-ce qu'il lui trouve ?* = what does he see in her ?

— *il a trouvé la bonne solution* = he came up with the right answer.

FINDER (n) **finder's fee** = *commission* : he got a finder's fee for putting the deal together = *il a touché une commission pour avoir monté l'affaire* ⊕ percentage = *pourcentage* ☠ → commission

finders keepers, losers weepers = *trouver n'est pas voler.*

FINDINGS (n pl) *conclusions (f pl)* : the committee's findings = *les conclusions du comité* ⊕ result = *résultat* ☠ → conclusion.

FINE (n) *amende (f)* : to pay a $ 100 fine = *payer une amende de 100 dollars* ⊕ ticket = *contravention* ☠ *faire amende honorable* = to make amends.

FINE (adj, -r, -st) 1/ *très bon, bonne* : a fine writer = *un très bon écrivain* → WONDERFUL ≠ awful = *affreux* 2/ *fin, -e* : fine features = *des traits fins* ⊕ delicate = *délicat*

to feel fine ≠ **ill** = *se sentir bien* ≠ *malade*

fine and dandy = *on ne peut mieux* : everything's fine and dandy = *tout est on ne peut mieux* → WONDERFUL

fine arts = *les beaux arts*

that's a fine state of affairs ! = *c'est du joli !* → GOSH !

that's a fine how-do-you-do ! = *c'est du propre !* → GOSH !

that's (all) very fine but = *tout ça, c'est bien joli mais* ⊕ that's all well and good but = *tout ça, c'est bien beau mais*

☠ *un esprit fin* = a subtle mind

— *épicerie fine* = specialty foods

— *faire la fine bouche* = to turn one's nose up

— *la fine fleur* = the pick of the lot

— *au fin fond de (la Chine)* = in deepest (China)

— *c'est vraiment fin !* = that's really smart ! (sarcastic).

FINE (adv) *bien* : we're doing just fine = *nous nous débrouillons bien* ☠ → well

that suits me fine = *ça me convient parfaitement* ≠ no way = *que dalle.*

FINE ! (interj) *parfait !* ⊕ great ! = *formidable !*

FINESSE (n) *finesse (f)* ≠ awkwardness = *maladresse.*

FINE-TOOTH COMB (n) **to go over (the place) with a fine-tooth comb** = *passer (l'endroit) au peigne fin.*

FINGER (n) *doigt (m)* : a ring on her finger = *une bague à son doigt* ⊕ pinky = *petit doigt*, thumb = *pouce*, middle finger = *médium*, ring finger = *annulaire*, finger bowl = *rince-doigts*, knuckle = *articulation du doigt*

to have a finger in every pie = *manger à tous les râteliers*

to keep one's fingers crossed = *croiser les doigts* : I'm keeping my fingers crossed that you'll get the job = *je croise les doigts pour que tu aies le poste* ⊕ to touch wood = *toucher du bois*

not to lay a finger on = *ne pas lever la main sur* : he never laid a finger on the kids = *il n'a jamais levé la main sur les gosses* ≠ to beat black and blue = *rouer de coups*

not to lift a finger = *ne pas remuer le petit doigt* ≠ to lend a hand = *donner un coup de main*

to put one's finger on (a problem) = *mettre le doigt sur (un problème)*

to slip through s.o.'s fingers = *filer entre les doigts de qqn* : she let the chance of her life slip through her fingers = *elle a laissé la chance de sa vie lui filer entre les doigts*

to twist s.o. around one's (little) finger = *mener qqn par le bout du nez* ≠ to be at s.o.'s beck and call = *faire les quatre volontés de qqn*

to work one's fingers to the bone = *se tuer à la tâche* ≠ to goof off = *ne rien ficher*

☠ *un doigt de (whisky)* = a spot of (Scotch)

— *gagner les doigts dans le nez* = to win hands down

— *à un doigt de* = within an inch of

— *faire marcher qqn au doigt et à l'œil* = to make s.o. toe the line

— *s'en mordre les doigts* = to rue something

— *se fourrer le doigt dans l'œil* = to be all wet

— *doigt de pied* = toe

— *montrer du doigt* = to point to/out.

FINGERPRINT (n) *empreinte (f) digitale* ⊕ murderer = *assassin.*

FINGERTIP (n) **to one's fingertips** = *jusqu'au bout des ongles* : she's feminine to her fingertips = *elle est féminine jusqu'au bout des ongles* ≠ not a bit = *pas le moins du monde.*

FINICKY (adj) *difficile* : she's finicky about what she eats = *elle est difficile pour la nourriture* ⊕ particular = *exigeant* ☠ → difficult.

FINISH (to, -ed) *finir* : he finished his work = *il a fini son travail* ⊕ to end = *(se) terminer* ≠ to begin = *commencer*

to finish off = 1/ *achever* : the killer finished him off = *le tueur l'a achevé* ⓐ to shoot down = *abattre* ☠ → to complete 2/ *finir* : finish off the brandy = *finis le cognac* **to finish up** = *boucler* : we'll finish up the work tonight = *on bouclera le travail ce soir* ☠ → to wind up **to be finished** = 1/ *avoir fini* : are you finished ? = *est-ce que vous avez fini ?* 2/ *être fini* : everything's finished between them = *tout est fini entre eux* ⓐ through = *terminé*
to be finished with = *c'est fini* : I'm finished with him/cigarettes = *c'est fini, je ne veux plus de lui/je ne fume plus* ⓐ I'm fed up with = *j'en ai marre de* ☠ *je finirai bien par (le trouver)* = I'll end up (finding him)
— *ça finira bien* = it will turn out well
— *il finira mal* = he'll come to a bad end

— *il n'en finit pas de (parler)* = there's no end to his (talking).

FINISHED (adj) *fichu, -e* : if he finds out, I'm finished = *s'il apprend la vérité, je suis fichu* ⓐ I've had it = *je suis cuit* ☠ → darn.

FINK (n) *sale type* (m) : her brother's a fink = *son frère est un sale type* → BASTARD.

FINK OUT (to, -ed) *se défiler* : he said he would help me, but he finked out = *il a dit qu'il m'aiderait, mais il s'est défilé* ⓐ to cop out = *se débiner* ☠ → to march.

FINLAND (n) *Finlande* (f) **FINN** (n) *Finlandais, -e* **FINNISH** (adj) *finlandais, -e.*

FIRE (n) *feu* (m) (small), *incendie* (m) (arson, etc.) : a fire in the chimney = *un feu dans la cheminée*, a fire in the forest = *un incendie de forêt*, fire hydrant = *bouche d'incendie*, fire engine = *voiture de pompier*, fire insurance = *assurance-incendie*, fire alarm = *avertisseur d'incendie*, fire escape = *escalier de secours extérieur*, fire extinguisher = *extincteur* ⓐ bonfire = *feu de joie*, smoke = *fumée*, flame = *flamme*, arson = *incendie criminel*, fireproof = *ignifuge*

fire ! = *au feu !* **to catch fire** = *prendre feu* **to cease fire** = *cesser le feu* **to come under (heavy) fire** = *essuyer le feu* **on fire** = *en feu* ⓐ ablaze = *en flammes* **to open fire** = *ouvrir le feu*	**to play with fire** = *jouer avec le feu* ≠ to play it safe = *jouer sur du velours* **to set fire to/to set on fire** = *mettre le feu à* : the arsonist set fire to the building = *l'incendiaire a mis le feu à l'immeuble* = the arsonist set the building	on fire **under fire** = *sur la sellette* : the Senator's under fire for his racial remarks = *le sénateur est sur la sellette à propos de ses déclarations racistes*

☠ *péter le feu* = to be raring to go — *avez-vous du feu ?* = do you have a light ? — *feu rouge* ≠ *vert* = red ≠ green light — *les feux de la rampe* = limelight — *avoir le feu aux fesses/au cul* = to have hot pants	— *avoir le feu sacré* = to be driven — *n'y voir que du feu* = to be taken in — *il n'y a pas le feu !* = there's no rush ! — *donner le feu vert à qqn* = to give s.o. the green light — *ne pas faire long feu* = not to last long.

FIRE (to, -d) **1/** *congédier* : she fired her secretary = *elle a congédié sa secrétaire* ⓐ to lay off = *licencier*, to oust = *vider* ≠ to hire = *engager* **2/** *tirer* : to fire a shot = *tirer un coup de feu* ☠ → to pull

fire ! = *feu !* ⓐ shoot ! = *tirez !* **fire away !** = *allez-y !* : you have questions ? fire	away ! = *vous avez des questions ? allez-y !* ⓐ shoot ! = *dites !*

FIRECRACKER (n) *pétard* (m) ☠ *se mettre en pétard* = to throw a fit.

FIREFIGHTER (n) *pompier* (m), *femme* (f) *pompier* ⓐ fire engine = *voiture de pompier* ☠ *faire un pompier* = to do a blow job.

FIREMAN (n, -men) = firefighter.

FIREPLACE (n) *cheminée* (f) : asleep by the fireplace = *endormi au coin de la cheminée* ⓐ wood = *bois* ☠ → chimney.

FIREWORKS (n pl) *feu* (m) *d'artifice* ⓐ bonfire = *feu de joie.*

FIRM (n) *firme* (f) : a large French firm = *une grande firme française* ⓐ concern = *entreprise.*

FIRM (adj, -er, -est) *ferme* : be firm with the kids = *sois ferme avec les enfants*
to be a firm believer in = *croire dur comme fer à* ☠ *prison ferme* = prison without bail
— *discuter ferme* = to thrash out (subject)
— *tenir ferme* = to stand pat.

FIRMLY (adv) *fermement.*

FIRST (n) *premier, -ère* : she was the first to leave = *elle a été la première à partir* ≠ last = *dernier* ☙ *John et Harry sont jumeaux, le premie fait de la natation, le second du football* = John and Harry are twins, the former swims, the latter plays football

at first = *d'abord* : at first I thought he lied = *j'ai d'abord pensé qu'il mentait* ⓌⒹ initially = *initialement*
first come, first served = *premier arrivé, premier servi*
from the (very) first = *dès le début* : I knew he was lying from the very first = *j'ai compris dès le*

début *qu'il mentait* ⓌⒹ from the beginning = *au commencement*
if at first you don't succeed, try, try again = *cent fois sur le métier remettez votre ouvrage* ⓌⒹ practice makes perfect = *c'est en forgeant qu'on devient forgeron.*

FIRST (adj) *premier, -ère* : I fell in love the first time we met = *je suis tombé amoureux la première fois que nous nous sommes rencontrés* ≠ last = *dernier*

at first sight = *à première vue*
to be back at first base = *revenir au point de départ* : the contract fell through, we're back at first base = *le contrat a foiré, nous sommes donc revenus au point de départ* ≠ to be at home base = *arriver au but*
to cast the first stone = *jeter la première pierre*
first aid = *les premiers secours/soins*
first cousin = *cousin germain*
first floor = *rez-de-chaussée* = ground floor
first lady = *première dame/ épouse du Président*

first name = *prénom*
(love) in the first position = *(l'amour) à la papa* ⓌⒹ man on the top = *à la missionnaire*
the first step is the hardest = *il n'y a que le premier pas qui coûte*
first thing = *aussitôt* : he called me first thing = *il m'a appelé aussitôt*
first thing in the morning = *demain à la première heure* : I'll call you first thing in the morning = *je vous téléphonerai demain à la première heure*
first things first = *commençons par le commencement* =

let's begin by the beginning
first thing I know = *tout à coup* : I was walking along when first thing I know someone hit me = *je marchais quand tout à coup quelqu'un m'a frappé*
not to get to first base = *ramasser une veste* : he couldn't get to first base with the girl = *il a ramassé une veste avec la fille* ⓌⒹ to strike out = *faire chou blanc*
not to know the first thing about it = *ne pas en connaître le premier mot* ⓌⒹ not to know beans about = *n'entraver que dalle à*

☙ *premier rôle* = leading part
— *Premier ministre* = Prime Minister
— *première nouvelle !* = that's a new one to me !
— *du premier coup* = straight off

— *être aux premières loges* = to have ringside seats
— *s'en soucier comme de sa première chemise* = not to give a hang.

FIRST (adv) 1/ *d'abord* : first, let's eat ! = *mangeons d'abord !* ⓌⒹ firstly = *premièrement* 2/ *pour la première fois* : when did you first meet her ? = *quand l'avez-vous rencontrée pour la première fois ?* ≠ last = *pour la dernière fois*

first of all = *tout d'abord* ⓌⒹ to begin with = *pour commencer*
first and foremost = *avant toute chose*
first off = *primo* : first off tell me what happened

= *primo, raconte-moi ce qui s'est passé* ≠ lastly = *en dernier*
I'd (die) first ! = *plutôt (mourir) !* = I'd rather (die) !

FIRST-CLASS (adj) *de première classe* : a first-class cook/restaurant = *une cuisinière/un restaurant de première classe* → WONDERFUL ≠ crummy = *moche.*

FIRST-CLASS (adv) *en première classe* : to travel first-class = *voyager en première classe* ≠ second-class (train)/economy (plane) = *en seconde classe/en classe touriste.*

FIRSTHAND (adj, adv) *de source sûre* : I got the news firsthand = *je tiens cette information de source sûre* ≠ by hearsay = *par ouï-dire.*

FIRST-RATE (adj) *de premier ordre* : a first-rate hotel/lawyer = *un hôtel/avocat de premier ordre* → WONDERFUL ≠ second-rate = *de second ordre.*

FISCAL (adj) *fiscal, -e, budgétaire* : the fiscal year = *l'année fiscale/budgétaire.*

FISH (n, fish or -es) *poisson* (m) : we eat a lot of fish = *nous mangeons beaucoup de poisson* ⓌⒹ seafood = *fruits de mer*, aquarium = ←, fin = *nageoire*, bone = *arête*, shellfish = *crustacé(s)*

bass = *bar*	**pike** = *brochet*
eel = *anguille*	**plaice** = *carrelet*
fresh cod = *cabillaud*	**salt cod** = *morue*
haddock = ←	**salmon** = *saumon*
halibut = *flétan*	**sardine** = ←
herring = *hareng*	**skate** = *raie*
mackerel = *maquereau*	**sole** = ←
octopus = *pieuvre/poulpe*	**trout** = *truite*
	tuna fish = *thon*
	whitefish = *merlan*

to drink like a fish = *boire comme un trou* → DRUNK
to feel like a fish out of water = *ne pas être dans son élément* ≠ **to be in one's element** = *être dans son élément*
fish and chips (GB) = *poisson frit et frites*
a queer/odd fish = *un drôle de coco/pistolet* ⓪ **a queer duck** = *un drôle de zigoto*
that's neither fish nor fowl = *ce n'est ni chair ni poisson*

☠ *noyer le poisson* = to talk around the issue
— *poisson d'avril !* = April fool's joke !
— *engueuler qqn comme du poisson pourri* = to really let s.o. have it
— *être comme un poisson dans l'eau* = to be in one's element.

FISH (to, -ed) *pêcher* ⓪ **bait** = *appât*, **hook** = *hameçon*, **fishing rod** = *canne à pêche*, **fisherman** = *pêcheur*, **fishing net** = *filet*, **fishmonger** = *poissonnier*
to go fishing = *aller à la pêche*
☠ *où as-tu été pêcher ça ?* = where did you dig that up ?
— *pêcher* = to sin.

FISHING (n) *pêche* (f) : **the fishing industry** = *l'industrie de la pêche* ⓪ **hunting** = *chasse*.

FISHY (adj, -ier, -iest) *louche* : **his story sounds fishy** = *son histoire semble louche* ⓪ **not kosher** = *pas catholique* ☠ *affaires louches* = shady dealings.

FIST (n) *poing* (m) ⓪ **fistfight** = *combat aux poings*, **wrist** = *poignet* ☠ *dormir à poings fermés* = to sleep like a log.

FIT (n) *crise* (f) : **epileptic fit** = *crise d'épilepsie*
in a fit of anger = *dans un mouvement de colère*
fit of coughing = *quinte de toux*
by fits and starts = *par à-coups* : **the work progressed by fits and starts** = *le travail avançait par à-coups*
to have/throw a fit = *piquer une crise* : **the boss will have a fit when he sees the mistake** = *le patron va piquer une crise quand il s'apercevra de cette erreur* → ANGRY ☠ → crisis.

FIT (adj) *en forme* : **you look fit** = *vous avez l'air en forme* ⓪ **healthy** = *en bonne santé*

to be as fit as a fiddle = *se porter comme un charme/à merveille* ⓪ **to be in great shape** = *être en pleine forme*
to be fit for a king = *être un morceau de roi* ⓪ **choice piece** = *morceau de choix*
to be fit to be tied = *être fou furieux* → ANGRY
do as you see fit = *faites comme bon vous semble*
to keep fit = *se maintenir en forme*
not fit to be (a leader) = *qui n'a pas les compétences pour être (un chef)*
to see fit = *croire bon* : **he didn't see fit to apologize** = *il n'a pas cru bon de s'excuser.*

FIT (to, -ted) *aller à* (s.o.), *aller* (stg) : **this dress does not fit me** = *cette robe ne me va pas*, **this key doesn't fit** = *cette clé ne va pas* ☠ → to go
to fit in = 1/ *rentrer* : **all your clothes won't fit in the case** = *tous tes vêtements ne rentreront pas dans la valise* ☠ → to return 2/ *avoir à voir là-dedans* : **I understand your plan, but where do I fit in ?** = *je comprends votre plan, mais qu'est-ce que j'ai à voir là-dedans ?*
to fit in with = 1/ *ne pas détonner au milieu de* : **she doesn't fit in with her husband's friends** = *elle détonne au milieu des amis de son mari* 2/ *cadrer avec* : **what he said doesn't fit in with what she has said before** = *ce qu'il a dit ne cadre pas avec ce qu'elle avait dit auparavant* ⓪ **to jibe with** = *coller avec.*

FIVE (n, adj) *cinq* (m) : **five dollars** = *cinq dollars* ⓪ **fifteen** = *quinze*, **fifty** = *cinquante* ☠ *un cinq à sept* = an afternoon tryst.

FIX (n) 1/ (inv) *qqch de truqué* : **the game was a fix** = *le jeu était truqué* 2/ *fixe* (m) (drugs) : **heroin is $ 100 a fix** = *l'héroïne vaut cent dollars le fixe* ⓪ **shot** = *piqûre*
to be in a fix = *être dans le pétrin* ⓪ **to be in hot water** = *être dans de beaux draps.*

FIX (to, -ed) 1/ *fixer* : **to fix a time/date** = *fixer une heure/un rendez-vous* ⓪ **to establish** = *établir*
☠ *je ne serai pas fixé avant demain* = I won't be set till tomorrow
— *se fixer (quelque part)* = to settle down
— *fixer qqn (regard)* = to stare at s.o.
— *fixer ses conditions* = to lay down one's conditions
2/ *arranger* : **my wife fixed the car** = *ma femme a arrangé la voiture* ⓪ **to repair** = *réparer* ☠ → to arrange
3/ *préparer* : **to fix dinner/a sandwich** = *préparer le dîner/un sandwich* ☠ → to prepare
4/ *truquer* : **to fix an election/a horse race** = *truquer une élection/une course de chevaux* = **to rig**
☠ *truquer les cartes* = to stack the cards
— *truquer une photo* = to touch up a photograph
to fix it = *s'arranger* : **the boss fixed it so that I could take a long weekend** = *le patron s'est arrangé pour que je puisse prendre un long week-end*
that'll fix him ! = *c'est bien fait pour lui !* ⓪ **it serves him right !** = *il ne l'a pas volé !*
how are you fixed for (dough) ? = *où en êtes-vous au point de vue (fric) ?*
to be fixing to = *envisager de* : **I'm fixing to go tonight**

= *j'envisage d'y aller ce soir* ① to plan to = *projeter de*
to fix up = 1/ *préparer* : come on, I'll fix you up with a good Scotch = *allez, je vais te préparer un bon whisky* ☠ → to prepare 2/ *arranger* : everything's fixed up between them = *tout est arrangé entre eux* ① to be patched up = *être raccommodé* ☠ → to arrange
to fix s.o. up = *présenter qqn* : fix me up with your brother = *présentez-moi à votre frère* ① date = *rendez-vous*.

FIXED (adj) 1/ *fixe* : fixed salary = *salaire fixe* ☠ *c'est une idée fixe* = it's an obsession 2/ *truqué, -e* : fixed elections/races = *élections/courses truquées*.

FIXTURE (n) *qqn qui fait partie des meubles* : he's a fixture at the club = *au club, il fait partie des meubles*.

FIZZLE OUT (to, -d) *s'en aller en eau de boudin* : the movement's fizzling out = *le mouvement s'en va en eau de boudin*.

FLABBERGAST (to, -ed) *scier* : I was flabbergasted at the news = *j'ai été scié en entendant la nouvelle* ① to knock s.o. for a loop = *laisser qqn baba*, to be dumbfounded = *être ahuri* ☠ → to saw **FLABBERGASTING** (adj) *qui laisse baba*.

FLABBY (adj, -ier, -iest) *flasque* : fat and flabby = *gros et flasque* ≠ firm = *ferme*.

FLACK (n) *attaché, -e de presse* : he's one of the President's flacks = *c'est un des attachés de presse du Président* = he's one of the President's press agents.

FLAG (n) *drapeau* (m) : to salute the flag = *saluer le drapeau* ① banner = *bannière*, at half-mast = *en berne* ☠ *être appelé sous les drapeaux* = to be called up (military service).

FLAGRANT (adj) *flagrant, -e* : it's a flagrant lie = *c'est un mensonge flagrant* ① obvious = *évident* ☠ *être pris en flagrant délit* = to be caught in the act.

FLAIR (n) **to have a flair for (music/entertaining)** = *avoir des dons pour (la musique/recevoir)* ☠ *elle a du flair* = she's intuitive.

FLAK (n) *vive opposition* (f) : the proposition ran into flak = *la proposition a rencontré une vive opposition* ① opposition = ←.

FLAKY (adj, -ier, -iest) *foufou, fofolle* : scatterbrained and flaky = *tête de linotte et fofolle* ① kooky = *farfelu*.

FLAMBOYANT (adj) *voyant, -e* : flamboyant clothes = *vêtements voyants* = showy ① gaudy = *criard* ☠ *un ciel flamboyant* = a blazing sky.

FLAME (n) *flamme* (f) : in flames = *en flammes* ① blaze = *flambée*
to go up in flames = *s'enflammer* : the building went up in flames = *l'immeuble s'est enflammé* ① to blaze = *flamber* ☠ *s'enflammer pour qqch* = to go for stg.

FLANK (to, -ed) *flanquer* ① to surround = *entourer*

to be flanked by (bodyguards) = *être flanqué de (gardes du corps)*
☠ *flanquer un coup/la trouille à qqn* = to give s.o. a blow/the jitters.

FLAP (n) *branle-bas* (m inv) : the Pope's visit had the city in a flap = *la visite du pape a mis toute la ville en branle-bas* ① bustle = *remue-ménage*, uproar = *effervescence* ☠ *branle-bas de combat* = call to arms.

FLARE-UP (n) *poussée* (f) : a flare-up of fever/violence = *une poussée de fièvre/de violence* ① outburst = explosion.

FLARE UP (to, -d) *éclater* : he flared up hearing what had happened = *en entendant ce qui s'était passé, il a éclaté* → ANGRY ☠ → to burst.

FLASH (n, -es) 1/ *éclair* (m) : a flash of inspiration = *un éclair de génie* 2/ *flash* (m) : a news flash = *un flash d'information*
a flash (bulb) = *un flash (photo)*
a flash of lightning = *un éclair*
a flash in the pan = *un feu de paille* : his success was a flash in the pan = *son succès n'a été qu'un feu de paille*
in a flash = *en un éclair* : he prepared the dinner in a flash = *il a préparé le dîner en un éclair* ① in the bat of an eye = *en un tour de main*
☠ *des éclairs* = lightning
— *un éclair au chocolat* = a chocolate éclair.

FLASHBACK (n) *flash-back* (m), *retour* (m) *en arrière*.

FLASHER (n) *exhibitionniste* (m, f) : flashers in the subway = *des exhibitionnistes dans le métro* = exhibitionist.

FLASHLIGHT (n) *torche* (f) = torch (GB) ① pocket flashlight = *lampe de poche*, battery = *pile* ☠ → torch.

FLASHY (adj, -ier, -iest) *tapageur, -euse* : flashy clothes = *des vêtements tapageurs* ① showy = *voyant* ☠ *une soirée tapageuse* = a boisterous/rowdy party.

FLAT (n) 1/ (GB) *appartement* (m) = apartment 2/ *pneu* (m) *crevé* : we had a flat last night = *on a eu un pneu crevé hier soir/on a crevé (un pneu) hier soir* ① blowout = *crevaison*.

FLAT (adj, -ter, -test) *plat, -e* : a flat stomach/floor = *un ventre/sol plat* ① level = *nivelé*
to be flat on one's back = *être cloué au lit* ≠ up and around = *sur pied*
to be as flat as a board/pancake = *être plate comme une planche à pain/une limande* ≠ she's top-heavy = *il y a du monde au balcon*
flat rate/price = *prix fixe*
flat refusal = *refus net* ① categorical = *catégorique*
☠ *battre qqn à plate couture* = to lick the pants off of s.o.
— *être à plat* = to be exhausted
— *un style plat* = a pedestrian style.

FLAT (adv) *tout rond* : it costs $ 10 flat = *ça coûte 10 dollars tout rond*
to fall flat = *tomber à plat* (remark)/*tomber à l'eau* (project) : his joke fell flat = *sa plaisanterie est tombée à plat*, ours plans fell flat = *nos projets sont tombés à l'eau* ⓪ to lay an egg = *se casser la gueule*
flat broke = *complètement fauché/à sec* → POOR
in (five minutes) flat = *en (cinq minutes) pile*
to lay s.o. flat = *étendre qqn sur le carreau* : before he could say a word, the guy laid him flat = *avant qu'il ait pu dire un mot, le type l'a étendu sur le carreau* → TO HIT
to tell flat out = *dire carrément* : tell me flat out what you think = *dites-moi carrément ce que vous pensez* ⓪ to be frank = *être franc*.

FLATFOOT (n, -s) *condé* (m) ⓪ fuzz = *les poulets*, police = ←.

FLATLY (adv) *tout net* : he flatly refused = *il a refusé tout net* ⓪ categorically = *catégoriquement*.

FLATTEN (to, -ed) *étendre raide* : he flattened his opponent = *il a étendu raide son adversaire* → TO HIT.

FLATTER (to, -ed) *flatter* : I love it when you flatter me = *j'aime que vous me flattiez* ⓪ to butter up = *passer de la pommade à.*

FLATTERING (adj) *flatteur, -euse* : a flattering comparison = *une comparaison flatteuse* ⓪ laudatory = *élogieux* **FLATTERY** (n, -ies) *flatterie* (f) ≠ criticism = *critique.*

FLAUNT (to, -ed) *étaler* : to flaunt one's wealth/knowledge = *étaler sa fortune/ses connaissances* ⓪ to parade = *faire parade de*
☠ *étaler du beurre (sur un toast)* = to spread butter (on a piece of toast)
— *s'étaler (dans la rue)* = to fall down (in the street).

FLAVOR = **FLAVOUR** (GB) (n) **1/** *goût* (m) : spices will add flavor = *les épices ajouteront du goût* ☠ → taste **2/** *parfum* (m) : ice cream ? what flavor ? = *une glace ? quel parfum ?* ⓪ pistachio = *pistache*, coffee = *café*, chocolate = *chocolat*, vanilla = *vanille*, strawberry = *fraise*, cherry = *cerise* ☠ → perfume.

FLAW (n) *faille* (f) (reasoning), *défaut* (m) (precious stone) : a flaw in your reasoning = *une faille dans votre raisonnement*, a flaw in the diamond = *un défaut dans le diamant*
☠ *faille (mur)* = crack (wall)
— *défaut* → defect.

FLAWLESS (adj) *sans défaut* (diamond), *sans faille* (argument).

FLEA (n) *puce* (f) ⓪ bedbug = *punaise*
flea market = *marché aux puces*
☠ *secouer les puces à qqn* = to tell s.o. off
— *ça m'a mis la puce à l'oreille* = that set me wise
— *puce (d'ordinateur)* = (computer) chip.

FLEDGLING (adj) *néophyte* : a fledgling reporter = *un reporter néophyte* ≠ experienced = *expérimenté.*

FLEE (to, fled, fled) *fuir* : many Jews fled Europe in the thirties = *de nombreux juifs ont fui l'Europe dans les années trente* ⓪ to run away = *s'enfuir*
☠ *fuir les gens* = to shun people
— *fuir (robinet)* = to leak (tap).

FLEECE (to, -d) *plumer* : we got fleeced at the hotel = *on s'est fait plumer à l'hôtel* → TO HUSTLE.

FLEET (n) *flotte* (f) ⓪ ship = *bateau* ☠ *flotte* (LV) = 1/ rain 2/ water.

FLEETING (adj) *fugace* : a fleeting desire = *un désir fugace* ⓪ ephemeral = *éphémère.*

FLESH (n inv) *chair* (f) ⓪ skin = *peau*, carnal = *charnel*
in the flesh = *en chair et en os* ⓪ in person = *en personne*
to make s.o.'s flesh creep = *faire froid dans le dos à qqn* : the film made my flesh creep = *le film m'a fait froid dans le dos* ⓪ to give the shivers = *donner des frissons*
(a woman) with flesh = *(une femme) bien en chair.*

FLEXIBLE (adj) *flexible* (hours), *souple* (person) : flexible hours = *horaire flexible*, a flexible personality = *une personnalité souple* ≠ inflexible = ← ☠ *souple* → limber.

FLICK (n) *film* (m) = movie → FILM
to go to see a flick = *aller au cinoche.*

FLIER (n) **1/** *aviateur, -trice* = aviator ⓪ plane = *avion* **2/** *imprimé* (m) ⓪ handbill = *prospectus* ☠ *remplir un imprimé* = to fill in a form.

FLIGHT (n) *vol* (m) : to take the noon flight = *prendre le vol de midi*
to live (one) flight up ≠ **down** = *habiter (un) étage au-dessus* ≠ *au-dessous*
flight attendant = *steward/hôtesse de l'air*
☠ *un vol* = a robbery/a theft
— *attraper (une occasion) au vol* = to jump at (a chance)
— *vol à la tire* = shoplifting.

FLIGHTY (adj, -ier, -iest) *écervelé, -e* : she's flighty and superficial = *elle est écervelée et superficielle* ⓪ frivolous = *frivole.*

FLIMSY (adj, -ier, -iest) *trop léger, -ère* : flimsy material = *un matériau trop léger* ≠ sturdy = *robuste*
a flimsy excuse = *une piètre excuse.*

FLING (n) *amourette* (f) : she had a fling with her lawyer = *elle a eu une amourette avec son avocat* ⓪ passing fancy = *passade.*

FLIP (adj, -per, -pest) *cavalier, -ère* : a flip answer = *une réponse cavalière* ⓪ glib = *désinvolte.*

FLIP (to, -ped) *flipper* : he flipped when I said I was splitting = *il a flippé quand je lui ai dit que je me tirais* ⓪ to be taken aback = *avoir le souffle coupé*

to flip over/for = *se toquer de* : he flipped over/for my kid sister = *il s'est toqué de ma petite sœur*

to flip through = *survoler* : I flipped through the book = *j'ai survolé le livre* ⓪ to browse through = *parcourir* ☠ → to fly over.

FLIPPANT (adj) *cavalier, -ère* : a flippant remark = *une remarque cavalière* = flip ≠ uptight = *coincé*.

FLIRT (n) *aguicheur, -euse* : his wife's a flirt = *sa femme est une aguicheuse* ⓪ tease = *allumeuse*.

FLIRT WITH (to, -ed) *faire du charme à* : he was flirting with the boss's wife = *il faisait du charme à la femme du patron* ⓪ to make passes at = *faire des avances à*

to flirt with the idea (of visiting India) = *caresser l'idée (d'aller en Inde)*
☠ *flirter* = to neck.

FLIT (to, -ted) *papillonner* : to flit from guy to guy = *papillonner d'un type à l'autre*.

FLOAT (to, -ed) 1/ *faire la planche* : I can't swim, I can only float = *je ne sais pas nager, je ne sais que faire la planche* 2/ *flotter* : the dollar's floating = *le dollar flotte* ☠ *il flotte* = it's raining.

FLOCK (n) *troupeau (m) (petits animaux)* : a flock of geese/sheep = *un troupeau d'oies/de moutons* ⓪ herd = *troupeau*.

FLOCK TO (to, -ed) *aller en masse vers* : to flock to the sales = *aller en masse vers les soldes* ⓪ to rush to = *se ruer sur*.

FLOG (to, -ged) *flageller* ⓪ to whip = *fouetter*.

FLOOD (n) *inondation (f)* ⓪ overflowing = *débordement*.

FLOOD (to, -ed) *inonder* : the river flooded the city = *le fleuve a inondé la ville* = to inundate ⓪ to submerge = *submerger*

to be flooded with = *être inondé de* : Congress is flooded with protest letters = *le Congrès est inondé de lettres de protestation* ⓪ to be swamped with = *être submergé de*.

FLOODLIGHT (n) *projecteur (m)* ⓪ lighting = *éclairage*.

FLOOR (n) 1/ *plancher (m)* (wood), *sol (m)* : the kitchen floor = *le sol de la cuisine* ⓪ tiles = *carrelage*
floor show = *spectacle de cabaret*
to have the floor = *avoir la parole*
on the floor = *par terre*
to wipe the floor with s.o. = *battre qqn à plate couture* : the tennis champion wiped the floor with his opponent = *le champion de tennis a battu son adversaire à plate couture*
☠ *débarrasse le plancher !* = clear out !

2/ *étage (m)* : on the first floor = *au premier étage* ⓪ landing = *palier* ☠ → story.

FLOOR (to, -ed) *laisser interdit, -e* : his dirty language floored me = *son langage grossier m'a laissé interdit* ⓪ to flabbergast = *scier*.

FLOOZY (n, -ies) *pouffiasse (f)* ⓪ harlot = *fille de joie*, tart = *poule*.

FLOP (n) *four (m)* : what a flop ! = *quel four !* ⓪ turkey = *navet* ≠ hit = *succès* ☠ → oven

to be a flop = *faire un four* (play)/ *être un fiasco* : the play was a flop = *la pièce a fait un four*, the party was a flop = *cette soirée était un fiasco* ⓪ to lay an egg = *se casser la gueule*.

FLOP (to, -ped) *faire un four* : the play flopped = *la pièce a fait un four* ⓪ to fail = *échouer* ≠ to go over with a bang = *faire un tabac*.

FLOPHOUSE (n) *hôtel (m) borgne* ⓪ dive = *bouge*.

FLORIST (n) *fleuriste (m, f)* ⓪ florist store = *boutique de fleurs* = flower shop.

FLOUNDER (to, -ed) *patauger* : the new Cabinet's floundering = *le nouveau cabinet est en train de patauger* ☠ *patauger (dans l'eau)* = to wade.

FLOUR (n) *farine (f)* ⓪ baking powder = *levure*, yeast = *levain*, dough = *pâte*.

FLOURISH (to, -ed) *être florissant, -e* : the business is flourishing = *l'affaire est florissante* ⓪ to be in full expansion = *être en pleine expansion*.

FLOW (n) *flot (m)* : the flow of events = *le flot des événements*.

FLOW (to, -ed) *couler (à flots)* : wine was flowing = *le vin coulait à flots*
to flow over = *déborder* = to overflow
☠ *le bateau a coulé* = the boat sank/went under
— *l'affaire a coulé* = the business went bust/went under.

FLOWER (n) *fleur (f)* : what beautiful flowers ! = *quelles jolies fleurs !* ⓪ flowerpot = *pot de fleurs*, florist = *fleuriste*, bud = *bouton*, plant = *plante*, hothouse = *serre*, petal = *pétale*, stem = *tige*, corsage = *petit bouquet*, to flower = *fleurir*

African violet = *saint-paulia*	**honeysuckle** = *chèvrefeuille*
buttercup = *bouton-d'or*	**lilac** = *lilas*
carnation = *œillet*	**lily** = *lis*
daffodil = *jonquille*	**lily of the valley** = *muguet*
daisy = *marguerite*	**marigold** = *souci*
dandelion = *pissenlit*	**orchid** = *orchidée*
forget-me-not = *myosotis*	**peony** = *pivoine*
	rose = ←

sunflower = *tournesol* **tulip** = *tulipe* **violet** = *violette*	**water lily** = *nénuphar* **wisteria** = *glycine*

flower girl = *demoiselle d'honneur (petite fille)* ⓓ **bridesmaid** = *demoiselle d'honneur*

☙ *faire une fleur à qqn* = to do s.o. a favor
 — *fleur bleue* = romantic and sentimental
 — *dans la fleur de l'âge* = in the prime of life
 — *sa fleur* = her cherry
 — *s'envoyer des fleurs* = to sing one's own praises.

FLOWERY (adj) *fleuri, -e* : a flowery style = *un style fleuri* ☙ *une table fleurie* = a table covered with flowers.

FLU (n) *grippe (f)* : I have the flu = *j'ai la grippe* = influenza ☙ → *grippe*.

FLUCTUATE (to, -d) *fluctuer* : prices are fluctuating = *les prix fluctuent* ⓓ to vary = *varier* ≠ to stabilize = *se stabiliser.*

FLUENT (adj) **to speak fluent (French)** = *parler (français) couramment* **FLUENTLY** (adv) **to speak (French) fluently** = *parler (français) couramment.*

FLUID (adj) *fluide* ≠ solid = *solide* **FLUID** (n) *fluide (m).*

FLUKE (n) *coup (m) de hasard (heureux ou malheureux)* : the discovery was a fluke = *cette découverte a été un coup de hasard* ⓓ stroke of luck = *coup de chance.*

FLUNK (to, -ed) *être collé, -e à, recalé, -e à* : I flunked the test = *j'ai été collé/recalé à mon examen* ⓓ to fail = *échouer à.*

FLUNKY (n, -ies) *larbin (m)* : his assistant's just a flunky = *son assistant n'est qu'un larbin* ⓓ lackey = *laquais.*

FLURRY (n) **in a flurry** = *en état d'agitation* : the marriage is in a week and everybody is in a flurry = *le mariage est dans huit jours et tout le monde est en état d'agitation* ⓓ excited = *tout excité.*

FLUSH (to, -ed) *tirer la chasse d'eau* : he flushed the secret documents away = *il a tiré la chasse d'eau sur des documents secrets.*

FLUSTER (n) **in a fluster** = *en émoi* : she is in a fluster because her daughter is pregnant = *elle est en émoi car sa fille est enceinte* ⓓ all agog = *tout en émoi.*

FLUTE (n) *flûte (f)* ⓓ piccolo = ←, harmonica = ←, flutist = *flûtiste.*

FLUTTER (n) **in a flutter** = *en effervescence* : the city is in a flutter = *la ville est en effervescence* ⓓ in a flurry = *en émoi.*

FLY (n, -ies) **1/** *mouche (f)* ⓓ flypaper = *papier tue-mouches,* mosquito = *moustique*
 you catch more flies with honey than with vinegar = *on ne prend pas les mouches avec du vinaigre*
 a fly in the ointment = *une ombre au tableau* ⓓ hitch = *hic*
 he wouldn't hurt a fly = *il ne ferait pas de mal à une mouche* ⓓ to be as gentle as a lamb = *être doux comme un agneau*
 ☙ *on aurait entendu une mouche voler* = you could have heard a pin drop
 — *prendre la mouche* = to get hot under the collar
 — *faire mouche* = to hit the bull's-eye
 — *quelle mouche te pique ?* = what's eating you ?
 — *enculer les mouches* = to nitpick
 — *une mouche du coche* = a busybody
 2/ *braguette (f)* : he forgot to zip his fly = *il a oublié de fermer sa braguette* ⓓ zipper = *fermeture Éclair.*

FLY (to, flew, flown) *voler* : birds/planes fly = *les oiseaux/les avions volent* ⓓ to take off = *décoller* ≠ to land = *atterrir*
 let's fly ! = *filons !* : we're late, let's fly ! = *nous sommes en retard, filons !* → TO LEAVE
 to fly at = *tomber sur le poil de* : he flew at me when he saw my typing mistakes = *il m'est tombé sur le poil quand il a vu mes fautes de frappe* → TO LAMBAST
 to fly away = *s'envoler* : the bird flew away = *l'oiseau s'est envolé*
 to fly over (a country) = *survoler (un pays)* ☙ *survoler un livre* = to flip through a book
 to fly to = *prendre l'avion pour* : I'm flying to Paris Friday = *je prends l'avion pour Paris vendredi*
 ☙ *tu ne l'as pas volé* = you had it coming
 — *voler qqn* = to rob s.o.
 — *voler qqch* = to steal stg.

FLY-BY-NIGHT (adj) *véreux, -euse* : he got screwed because he was working for a fly-by-night company = *il s'est fait avoir en travaillant pour une société véreuse* ≠ reliable = *digne de confiance.*

FLYER (n) = FLIER.

FLYING SAUCER (n) *soucoupe (f) volante* ⓓ UFO = *OVNI.*

FLYNN (n) **to be in like Flynn** = *avoir partie gagnée* : if you can convince him to sign the contract, we're in like Flynn = *si vous pouvez le convaincre de signer le contrat, nous avons partie gagnée* ⓓ to be in the bag = *être dans le sac.*

FOAM (n) *écume (f)* : foam at the mouth = *l'écume aux lèvres* ⓓ froth = *mousse*
 foam rubber = *mousse (de polyester).*

FOCAL POINT (n) *point (m) central* : the focal point of the discussion = *le point central de la discussion.*

FOCUS (n) **in** ≠ **out of focus** = *au point* ≠ *pas au point* (camera).

FOCUS ON (to, -ed) *se focaliser sur* : to focus on one's own problems = *se focaliser sur ses problèmes personnels* ⓓ to concentrate on = *se concentrer sur.*

FOE (n) = ENEMY.

FOG (n) *brouillard* (m) : the fog caused a pile-up on the highway = *le brouillard a provoqué un carambolage sur l'autoroute* ◯D haze = *brume*
in a fog = *dans le brouillard* ◯D in a dither = *dans tous ses états.*

FOGGY (adj, -ier, -iest) *brumeux, -euse* ◯D cloudy = *nuageux.*

FOGGY BOTTOM (n) *équivalent du Quai d'Orsay* ◯D State Department = *Département d'État.*

FOIL (to, -ed) *déjouer* : the pilot foiled the skyjacking attempt = *le pilote a déjoué la tentative de détournement* ◯D to frustrate = *contrarier*, to undermine = *miner.*

FOLD (to, -ed) **1/** *plier* : to fold a sheet of paper = *plier une feuille de papier* ≠ to unfold = *déplier*
☠ *se plier aux ordres de qqn* = to bow to s.o.'s orders
— *faire plier qqn* = to make s.o. change his mind
— *plier le bras* = to bend one's arm
2/ *déposer son bilan* : their business folded = *leur affaire a déposé son bilan* ◯D to close up = *fermer ses portes.*

FOLDER (n) *chemise* (f) : put the contract in a folder = *mettez le contrat dans une chemise* ☠ → shirt.

FOLK (adj) *folklorique* : folk dances = *danses folkloriques*, folk music = *musique folklorique/folk*, folk singer = *chanteur folk.*

FOLKS (n pl) **1/** *parents* (m pl) : her folks are both French = *ses parents sont tous les deux français* = her parents are both French **2/** *les gars* (m pl) : what are you folks doing tonight ? = *eh les gars, qu'est-ce que vous faites ce soir ?* ◯D people = *les mecs.*

FOLLOW (to, -ed) **1/** *suivre* : you lead and I'll follow = *tu me conduis et je suivrai* ≠ to precede = *précéder* **2/** *suivre* : the cops followed him = *les flics l'ont suivi* ◯D to shadow = *prendre en filature* **3/** *suivre* : I don't follow you = *je ne vous suis pas* ◯D to get it = *saisir* **4/** *s'ensuivre* : it doesn't necessarily follow that she'll agree = *il ne s'ensuit pas nécessairement qu'elle sera d'accord*
(the service) will be followed by (a reception) = *(la cérémonie religieuse) sera suivie d'(une réception)*
(the system works) as follows = *(le système fonctionne) comme suit*

to follow through = *aller jusqu'au bout* : he has good ideas but never follows through = *il a de bonnes idées mais ne va jamais jusqu'au bout*
to follow up (on a suggestion) = *donner suite à (une suggestion)*
☠ *les jours se suivent et ne se ressemblent pas* = no two days are alike
— *faire suivre une lettre* = to forward a letter
— *à suivre* = to be continued
— *suivre un cours* = to take a course
— *suivre un régime* = to be on a diet.

FOLLOWER (n) **1/** *adepte* (m, f) : a guru and his followers = *un gourou et ses adeptes* **2/** *mouton* (m) de Panurge, *suiveur* (m) : a nation of followers = *une nation de suiveurs/de moutons de Panurge.*

FOLLOWING (n inv) *adeptes* (m, f pl) : the Church has a large following = *l'Église a beaucoup d'adeptes.*

FOLLOWING (adj) *suivant, -e* : the following night = *la nuit suivante* ≠ previous = *précédent.*

FOLLOWING (prep) *à la suite de* : following the ceremony, there was a big party = *à la suite de la cérémonie, il y a eu une grande soirée* ◯D after = *après.*

FOLLOW-UP (adj) **follow-up letter** = *lettre de relance* **follow-up visit** = *visite de contrôle.*

FOLLY (n, -ies) *folie* (f) : it's a folly to spend so much money on a car = *c'est de la folie de dépenser tant d'argent pour une voiture* ◯D sheer foolishness = *de la pure bêtise* ☠ → craziness.

FOND (adj) **to be fond of (dogs)** = *aimer bien (les chiens)* ≠ to be turned off by = *avoir horreur de*
to be fond of one's drink/bottle = *avoir une bonne descente* → DRUNK.

FONDLE (to, -d) *caresser* : he fondled her knee = *il caressait son genou* ☠ → to caress.

FONDLY (adv) *tendrement* : she looked at the child fondly = *elle a regardé tendrement l'enfant* = tenderly ◯D affectionately = *avec affection.*

FONDNESS (n) **to have a fondness for (candy)** = *affectionner (les bonbons).*

FOOD (n) *nourriture* (f) : is there enough food for ten ? = *est-ce qu'il y a assez de nourriture pour dix ?*
food poisoning = *intoxication alimentaire*
that's food for thought = *il y a là matière à réflexion.*

FOOL (n) *imbécile* (m, f) : what a fool ! = *quel imbécile !* → STUPID ☠ → imbecile

fools rush in where angels fear to tread = *(ces naïfs,) ils n'ont pas froid aux yeux* ◯D beginners' luck = *aux innocents les mains pleines*
to go on a fool's errand = *y aller pour des prunes* ◯D to go on a wild-goose chase = *y aller pour rien*
to live in a fool's paradise = *être un imbécile heureux* ◯D what he doesn't know won't hurt him = *toute vérité n'est pas bonne à dire*
to look like a fool = *avoir l'air fin*
to make a fool of o.s. = *se rendre ridicule* : you made a fool of yourself at the party = *tu t'es rendu ridicule à cette soirée*

to make a fool of s.o. = *tourner qqn en ridicule* : the boss made a fool of him at the meeting = *le patron l'a tourné en ridicule au cours de la réunion* ⓐ to deride s.o. = *tourner qqn en dérision* **to play the fool** = *faire l'imbécile* ⓐ to horse around = *faire l'andouille.*

FOOL (to, -ed) **1/** *plaisanter* : don't take him seriously, he was just fooling = *ne le prenez pas au sérieux, il ne faisait que plaisanter* = to joke ⓐ to kid = *blaguer* **2/** *bien avoir* : you really fooled me ! = *tu m'as bien eu !* → TO HUSTLE !

---

no fooling ! = *sans blague !* → GOSH !
to fool o.s. = *se faire des idées* : you're fooling yourself if you think he'll give you another raise = *tu te fais des idées si tu crois qu'il va te donner une autre augmentation* ⓐ to kid o.s. = *se faire des illusions*
to fool around = 1/ *faire l'imbécile*: stop fooling around ! = *arrête de faire l'imbécile !* ⓐ to clown around = *faire le clown* 2/ *ne pas ficher grand-chose* : we fooled around all day = *nous n'avons pas fichu grand-chose de la journée* 3/ *courir les filles/les hommes* : he's been fooling around since his marriage = *il court les filles depuis son*

mariage ⓐ to run around = *courir le jupon/les hommes*
to fool around with = *se taper (qqn)*: she's fooling around with her secretary = *elle se tape son secrétaire* ⓐ to carry on with = *s'envoyer*
to fool s.o. into = *faire croire à qqn* : he fooled me into believing he was rich = *il m'a fait croire qu'il était riche*
to fool with = *s'acoquiner avec* : I wouldn't fool with him if I were you = *si j'étais vous, je ne m'acoquinerais pas avec lui* ⓐ to mess with = *se frotter à.*

FOOLHARDY (adj) *téméraire :* a foolhardy project = *un projet téméraire* ≠ sensible = *sensé.*

FOOLISH (adj) *bête* : a foolish idea/boy = *une idée/un garçon bête* → STUPID ≠ intelligent = ← ☠ → dumb
FOOLISHLY (adv) *sottement* ⓐ stupidly = *stupidement.*

FOOLISHNESS (n inv) *bêtise (f)* : enough of this foolishness ! = *assez de bêtises !* ⓐ silliness = *sottise* ☠ *faire une bêtise* = to do stg stupid.

FOOLPROOF (adj) *infaillible :* a foolproof method = *une méthode infaillible* ☠ → infallible.

FOOT (n, feet) **1/** *pied (m) :* you have big feet = *tu as de grands pieds* ⓐ clubfoot = *pied bot*, paw = *patte*, corn = *cor*, dogs = *panards* (LV) **2/** *pied (m)* = 0,30 m : the room is three feet wide = *la pièce a trois pieds (un mètre) de large* ⓐ yard = ←

---

at the foot of (the mountain) = *au pied de (la montagne)*
to be back on one's feet = *être de nouveau sur pied* : give me six months to get back on my feet = *donnez-moi six mois pour être de nouveau sur pied*
to be falling off one's feet = *avoir les jambes en compote/en coton* : I'm so tired I'm falling off my feet = *je suis tellement fatigué que j'ai les jambes en compote* ⓐ to be washed-out = *être lessivé*
to get off on the right ≠ **wrong foot** = *partir du bon* ≠ *mauvais pied*
to get a foot in (a company) = *avoir un pied dans (une société)*

it knocked me off my feet ! = *les bras m'en sont tombés !* ⓐ it took my breath away = *ça m'a coupé le souffle*
to land on one's feet = *retomber sur ses pieds* : whatever happens to her, she always lands on her feet = *quoi qu'il lui arrive, elle retombe toujours sur ses pieds* ≠ to fall on one's face = *se casser la figure*
my foot ! = *mon œil !* → BUZZ OFF !
on foot = *à pied* : to go to school on foot = *aller en classe à pied* ≠ by car = *en voiture*
to put one's foot down = *faire acte d'autorité* : she likes to put her foot down = *elle aime faire acte d'autorité* ⓐ to lay down

the law = *faire la loi*
to put one's foot in it = *mettre les pieds dans le plat* ⓐ to make a faux pas = *faire un faux pas*
to sweep s.o. off his/her feet = *littéralement séduire qqn* : he swept her off her feet and they were married in a month = *il l'a littéralement séduite et au bout d'un mois ils étaient mariés* ⓐ to wine and dine = *faire une cour effrénée à*
to walk one's feet off = *être sur les rotules à force de marcher*
I wouldn't set a foot in (his house) = *plus question que je mette les pieds (chez lui) !*
to be five feet tall = *mesurer un mètre soixante-cinq*

☠ *jouer au foot* = to play soccer
— *c'est le pied !* = it's nifty !
— *prendre au pied de la lettre* = to take literally

— *prendre son pied* = 1/ to have an orgasm 2/ to enjoy oneself
— *faire du pied* = to play footsies

— *être sur un pied d'égalité* = to be on an equal footing
— *au pied levé* = off the cuff
— *ne pas savoir sur quel pied danser* = not to know which way to turn
— *perdre pied* = to lose one's footing
— *ne pas se laisser marcher sur les pieds* = not to let anyone step on one's toes

— *au pied du mur* = with one's back to the wall
— *faire des pieds et des mains* = to stand on one's head (to do stg)
— *ça lui fera les pieds* = that'll fix his wagon
— *mettre sur pied* = to set up
— *je suis pieds et poings liés* = my hands are tied
— *avoir le pied marin* = to be a good sailor
— *casser les pieds à qqn* = to bug s.o.

FOOTBALL (n) **1/** football *(m)* américain : to play football = *jouer au football*, footballer = *joueur de football* ⊗ quarter back = *arrière*, soccer = *football* **2/** *ballon (m) de football* ⊗ ball = *ballon*.

FOOTHOLD (n) **to get a foothold in** = *s'implanter dans* : the Republicans are getting a foothold in the South = *les républicains commencent à s'implanter dans le Sud* ⊗ to get a footing in = *prendre pied dans*.

FOOTING (n) **to get** ≠ **to lose one's footing** = *reprendre* ≠ *perdre pied* ☠ *le footing* = jogging.

FOOTLOOSE (adj) **to be footloose and fancyfree** = *être sans attaches* ⊗ to be a free agent = *être libre comme l'air*.

FOOTNOTE (n) *note (f) en bas de page* ⊗ cross-reference = *renvoi*.

FOOTPRINT (n) *empreinte (f) de pas* ⊗ fingerprint = *empreinte digitale*.

FOOTSIE (n) **to play footsies (with)** = *faire du pied (à)* ⊗ to make advances to = *faire des avances à*.

FOOTSTEPS (n pl) **to follow in s.o.'s footsteps** = *suivre les traces de qqn* : he's following in his father's footsteps = *il suit les traces de son père* ≠ to set an example = *donner l'exemple*.

FOR (prep) **1/** *pour* : it's for you = *c'est pour vous*, who's it for ? = *pour qui est-ce ?*	
for ever and ever = *à tout jamais* : I'll love you for ever and ever = *je t'aimerai à tout jamais*	**for always** = *(pour) toujours* : I'll love you for always = *je t'aimerai toujours* ⊗ forever = *à jamais*
for how long ? = *depuis combien de temps ?* : for how long have you been waiting ? = *depuis combien de temps attendez-vous ?*	**for ... to** = *pour que* : it's too difficult for me to do = *c'est trop difficile pour que je le fasse*
for once = *pour une fois* : you pick me up for once = *venez me chercher pour une fois*	**that's for (you) to (decide)** = *c'est à (vous) de (décider)*
	that's (gratitude) for you ! = *voilà (la reconnaissance) qu'on t'en a !*

2/ *depuis* : I've been working here for two months = *je travaille ici depuis deux mois*

for	**since**
— for six months/a year = *depuis six mois/un an*	— since Christmas/Easter = *depuis Noël/Pâques*
— for ten years = *depuis dix ans*	— since 1580 = *depuis 1580*

☠ for = *depuis (durée, période de temps)*
— since = *depuis (date précise)*

3/ *pendant* : I was married for ten years = *j'ai été mariée pendant dix ans* ☠ → during
4/ *pour* ⊗ so that = *afin que*

for + nom	**to + verbe**
— she called for an appointment = *elle a appelé pour prendre rendez-vous*	— she called to make an appointment = *elle a appelé pour prendre rendez-vous*

☠ *pour que* = so that
— *(15) pour cent* = (15) per cent
— *pour ce qui est de* = as regards to
— *et pour cause* = and with good reason
— *pour ainsi dire* = so to speak
— for the use of "for" after a verb, see the verb.

FOR (conj) *car* : she had to hurry for she was late = *elle a dû se dépêcher car elle était en retard* ⊗ because = *parce que*.

FORBID (to, -bade, -bidden) *interdire, défendre* : smoking and drinking were forbidden = *il était interdit/défendu de fumer et de boire* ≠ to allow = *permettre*
to forbid s.o. to = *interdire/défendre à qqn de* : I forbid you to speak to me like that = *je vous défends/interdis de me parler sur ce ton*
☠ *défendre* → to defend
— *interdire un film* = to ban a film.

FORBIDDEN (adj) *défendu, -e* : forbidden fruit/relationships = *fruit défendu/relations défendues*.

FORCE (n) force *(f)* : to use force = *utiliser la force* ⊗ might = *puissance* ≠ weakness = *faiblesse*
to come into force = *entrer en vigueur*
force of habit = *la force de l'habitude*
in force = *en force* : the journalists were there in force = *les journalistes étaient là en force*

to join forces = *faire cause commune* ⊕ **to hang together** = *se solidariser*

to resort to force = *recourir à la force*

to take by force = *prendre de force*

☠ *à force de (travail)* = by sheer (work)

— *c'est au-dessus de mes forces* = I'm not up to it

— *par la force des choses* = inevitably

— *quelle force !* = what strength !

— *la force publique* = authorities in charge of law and order

— *de gré ou de force* = willingly or not.

FORCE (to, -d) *forcer* : she'll do it if she wants to, don't force her ! = *elle le fera si elle en a envie, ne la force pas !* ⊕ **to coerce into** = *contraindre à*

to force s.o. out = *forcer qqn à partir* : the directors are trying to force him out = *les directeurs essaient de le forcer à partir* ⊕ **to oust** = *vider*

to force s.o. to do stg = *forcer qqn à faire qqch*

to be forced to do stg = *être forcé de faire qqch* ⊕ **to have to** = *devoir*

to force (a secret/a confession) from s.o. = *extorquer (un secret/un aveu) à qqn*

☠ *forcer le respect* = to command respect

— *forcer un coffre* = to crack/break open a safe

— *forcer la dose/la note* = to overdo it.

FORCED (adj) *forcé, -e* : forced landing = *atterrissage forcé*, forced labor camp = *camp de travaux forcés*, forced smile = *sourire forcé* ☠ *c'est forcé !* = it's inevitable !

FORCEFUL (adj) *puissant, -e* : a forceful argument = *un argument puissant* ⊕ **effective** = *efficace* ☠ *un médicament puissant* = a powerful/potent medicine.

FORCIBLY (adv) *par la force, de force* : he was forcibly fed = *on l'a nourri de force/par la force.*

FORECAST (n) *prévision (f)* : the weather forecast = *les prévisions météorologiques/la météo.*

FORECAST (to, -cast, -cast) *prévoir* : to forecast a cold winter = *prévoir un hiver froid* ⊕ **to prognosticate** = *pronostiquer*

☠ *qu'est-ce que vous avez prévu pour ce soir ?* = what have you got lined up/planned/scheduled for tonight ?

— *je prévois des problèmes* = I'm anticipating difficulties

— *prévoir (des changements)* = to anticipate/to foresee (changes).

FOREGO (to, -went, - gone) *renoncer à* : we'll have to forego lunch if you're in a hurry = *il va falloir renoncer à déjeuner si vous êtes pressé* ⊕ **to do without** = *se passer de.*

FOREGONE CONCLUSION (n) **it's a foregone conclusion** = *c'est couru (d'avance)* : her winning was a foregone conclusion = *elle a gagné, c'était couru.*

FOREGROUND (n) **in the foreground** = *au premier plan.*

FOREHEAD (n) *front (m)* : a receding forehead = *un front fuyant* ☠ → front.

FOREIGN (adj) *étranger, -ère* : foreign language = *langue étrangère*, foreign policy = *politique étrangère*, foreign affairs = *affaires étrangères* ≠ domestic = *intérieur*

foreign correspondent = *correspondant à l'étranger*

foreign aid = *aide extérieure*

the Foreign Legion = *la Légion étrangère*

Foreign Office (GB) = *ministère des Affaires étrangères*

foreign trade = *commerce extérieur*

☠ *ce sujet m'est totalement étranger* = I'm not at all familiar with the subject.

FOREIGNER (n) *étranger, -ère* : there are a lot of foreigners in New York during the summer = *il y a beaucoup d'étrangers à New York l'été* ⊕ **stranger** = *inconnu* ☠ *aller à l'étranger* = to go abroad.

FOREMAN (n, -men) *contremaître (m)* (factory), *premier juré (m)* (jury) : fired by the foreman = *mis à la porte par le contremaître* **FOREWOMAN** (n, -women) *femme (f) contremaître, femme (f) premier juré.*

FOREMOST (adj) *de premier plan* : a foremost historian = *un historien de premier plan* ≠ of minor importance = *d'importance mineure.*

FOREPLAY (n) *attouchements (m pl) préliminaires* : orgasms are rare without foreplay = *les orgasmes sont rares sans attouchements préliminaires.*

FORERUNNER (n) *précurseur (m)* : Baudelaire was a forerunner of symbolism = *Baudelaire a été un précurseur du symbolisme.*

FORESEE (to, -saw, -seen) *prévoir* : they didn't foresee the economic crisis = *ils n'avaient pas prévu la crise économique* ⊕ **to expect** = *s'attendre à* ☠ → to forecast.

FORESEEABLE (adj) *prévisible* : foreseeable problems = *des problèmes prévisibles*

in the foreseeable future = *dans un avenir proche.*

FORESHADOW (to, - ed) *laisser présager* : events foreshadowed the assassination = *les événements laissaient présager l'assassinat* ⊕ **to augur** = *augurer.*

FORESIGHT (n) *prévoyance (f)* : you're lacking foresight = *vous manquez de prévoyance* ≠ hindsight = *jugement a posteriori.*

FOREST (n) *forêt (f)* : a forest fire = *un incendie de forêt* ⊕ **woods** = *bois*, **tree** = *arbre*

not to be able to see the forest for the trees = *c'est l'arbre qui cache la forêt.*

FORESTALL (to, -ed) *retarder volontairement* : to forestall the decision by changing the subject = *retarder volontairement la décision en changeant de sujet.*

FORETELL (to, -told, -told) *présager* : who could have foretold the disaster ? = *qui aurait pu présager un tel désastre ?* ⊕ **to foresee** = *prévoir.*

FOREVER (adv) **1/** *à jamais* : I'll love you forever = *je t'aimerai à jamais* ⟲ eternally = *éternellement* **2/** *sans arrêt* : he's forever changing his mind = *il change sans arrêt d'avis.*

FOREWARN (to, -ed) **forewarned is forearmed** = *un homme averti en vaut deux.*

FOREWORD (n) *avant-propos (m)* ⟲ preface = *préface.*

FORFEIT (to, -ed) *perdre (à la suite d'une sanction)* : the deposit was forfeited because he didn't turn up = *les arrhes ont été perdues parce qu'il ne s'est pas présenté* ☠ → to lose.

FORGE (to, -d) *fabriquer un/des faux* : to forge a passport = *fabriquer un faux passeport*
to forge ahead = *aller de l'avant.*

FORGERY (n, -ies) *falsification (f), fabrication (f) de faux* : he's an expert at forgery = *c'est un expert en fabrication de faux.*

FORGET (to, forgot, forgotten) *oublier* : I forgot his address = *j'ai oublié son adresse* ≠ to remember = *se souvenir*
forget it ! = **1/** *laisse tomber !* : if you can't lend me the money, it doesn't matter, forget it ! = *si tu ne peux pas me prêter d'argent, ça ne fait rien, laisse tomber !* ⟲ too bad ! = *tant pis !* **2/** *tu peux toujours courir !* : if you think I'm going to give you more money, forget it ! = *si tu crois que je vais te donner plus d'argent, tu peux toujours courir !* ⟲ no deal ! = *je ne marche pas !*
I forgot about it ! = *j'ai complètement oublié !*
to forget to = *oublier de* : I forgot to tell you that I saw him again = *j'ai oublié de vous dire que je l'ai revu.*

FORGETFUL (adj) **how forgetful of me !** = *mais où ai-je donc la tête ?*

FORGIVE (to, -gave, -given) **to forgive s.o.** = *pardonner à qqn* : she never forgave him = *elle ne lui a jamais pardonné* ⟲ to excuse = *excuser* ≠ to bear a grudge = *garder rancune*
forgive and forget = *passons l'éponge* ⟲ let bygones be bygones = *le passé est le passé*
forgive me ! = *pardonnez-moi !*
I'll never forgive you for having said that/for that = *je ne vous pardonnerai jamais d'avoir dit cela/je ne vous le pardonnerai jamais.*

FORGIVING (adj) *indulgent, -e* : he's never been very forgiving = *il n'a jamais été très indulgent.*

FORK (n) *fourchette (f)* ⟲ knife = *couteau*, spoon = *cuiller*
a fork in the road = *une fourche sur la route* ☠ *une fourchette de prix* = a price margin.

FORK OUT (to, -ed) *abouler (LV)* : to fork out $ 100 = *abouler 100 dollars* ⟲ to ante up = *débourser.*

FORLORN (adj) *accablé, -e* : the forlorn faces of the refugee children = *le visage accablé de ces jeunes réfu-*giés ⟲ despondent = *prostré* ☠ *accablé de travail* = overwhelmed with work.

FORM (n) **1/** *forme (f)* : a human form = *une forme humaine* **2/** *forme (f)* : different forms of tyranny = *différentes formes de tyrannie* ⟲ sort = *sorte*
a form of speech = *une façon de parler* = a manner of speaking
to be in form = *être en forme* : the tennis player's in good form = *le joueur de tennis est en bonne forme* ☠ *faire qqch dans les formes* = to do stg in the proper way
— *prendre forme* = to take shape
— *je suis en (pleine) forme* = I'm in great shape
— *ça a la forme d'une étoile* = it is shaped like a star
3/ *formulaire (m)* : fill in the form, please = *remplissez ce formulaire, s'il vous plaît.*

FORM (to, -ed) *former* : to form a club = *former un club* ⟲ to create = *créer* ☠ *former (une secrétaire)* = to train (a secretary).

FORMAL (adj) *protocolaire* (dinner), *formel, -elle* (dinner), *habillé, -e* (clothes), *formaliste* (personality) : a formal dinner = *un dîner protocolaire/formel*, a formal dress = *une robe habillée*, her family's very formal = *sa famille est très formaliste* ⟲ ceremonious = *cérémonieux* ≠ informal = *décontracté* ☠ *un refus formel* = a definite/an emphatic refusal.

FORMALITY (n, -ies) *formalité (f)* : complex formalities = *des formalités compliquées* ⟲ procedure = *procédure.*

FORMALLY (adv) *officiellement* : the museum was formally opened today = *le musée a été officiellement ouvert aujourd'hui* ☠ *formellement interdit* = strictly forbidden.

FORMAT (n) **1/** *format (m)* : the format of the book = *le format du livre* ⟲ size = *taille* **2/** *formule (f)* : the format of the TV show has changed = *la formule de l'émission de télé a changé* ☠ → formula.

FORMATION (n) *formation (f)* : a rock formation = *une formation de roche*
☠ *formation professionnelle* = continuing adult education
— *une bonne formation* = a good (professional) background/training.

FORMATIVE (adj) **the formative years** = *les années de formation.*

FORMER (adj) *ancien, -enne* : the former Ambassador to Washington = *l'ancien ambassadeur à Washington* ⟲ ex = ← ☠ → ancient
the former ... the latter ... = *le premier ... le second ...* : the former suggestion was preferred to the latter = *la première suggestion a été préférée à la seconde* ☠ → first.

FORMERLY (adv) *autrefois* : gays were formerly considered crazy = *les homosexuels étaient autrefois consi-*

dérés comme fous ⟲ once upon a time = *il était une fois.*

FORMIDABLE (adj) *redoutable* : a formidable opponent = *un adversaire redoutable* ⟲ awesome = *impressionnant* ☠ *un livre formidable* = a terrific/great book.

FORMULA (n, -s or -ae) *formule* (f) : there's no formula for happiness = *il n'y a pas de formule pour être heureux* ⟲ method = *méthode* ☠ *une formule de politesse* = a standard polite phrase — *la formule de l'émission de télé* = the format of the TV show.

FORMULATE (to, -d) *formuler* : to formulate a doctrine = *formuler une doctrine.*

FORSAKE (to, -sook, -saken) *laisser tomber* : he never forsakes his friends = *il ne laisse jamais tomber ses amis* = to drop.

FORSAKEN (adj) *à l'abandon* : a forsaken house = *une maison à l'abandon.*

FORT (n) *fort* (m) ⟲ castle = *château (fort)*, fortress = *forteresse*
to hold the fort = *être fidèle au poste* : while he was sick, his secretary held the fort = *pendant sa maladie, sa secrétaire était fidèle au poste*
☠ *un fort en thème* = an egghead
— *avoir fort à faire* = to have one's hands full
— *ce n'est pas son fort* = it's not his forte.

FORTE (n) *fort* (m) : cooking isn't his forte = *la cuisine n'est pas son fort* ⟲ strong point = *point fort* ☠ → fort.

FORTHCOMING (adj) *à venir* : the forthcoming elections = *les élections à venir.*

FORTIFICATION (n) *fortification* (f) ⟲ moat = *douve.*

FORTIFY (to, -ied) *fortifier* : to fortify a city = *fortifier une ville* ⟲ to strengthen = *renforcer.*

FORTNIGHT (n) (GB) *quinze jours, une quinzaine de jours* : he's coming in a fortnight = *il arrive dans une quinzaine (de jours)/dans quinze jours* ☠ *une quinzaine de (personnes)* = about fifteen (people).

FORTUNATE (adj) *qui a de la chance* : you were fortunate to find your wallet = *vous avez eu de la chance de retrouver votre portefeuille* ≠ out of luck = *qui n'a pas de chance* **FORTUNATELY** (adv) *heureusement* ⟲ luckily = *par chance* ≠ unfortunately = *malheureusement.*

FORTUNE (n) **1/** *fortune* (f) : his father left him a fortune = *son père lui a laissé une fortune*
a fortune hunter = *un coureur de dot* ⟲ dowry = *dot*
to make a fortune = *gagner une fortune/faire fortune* → RICH
2/ *fortune* (f) : he had the good fortune to meet a wonderful woman = *il a eu la bonne fortune de rencontrer une femme merveilleuse* ⟲ luck = *chance*

to tell fortunes = *dire la bonne aventure* ⟲ to read cards = *tirer les cartes*
☠ *à la fortune du pot* = pot-luck.

FORTUNE-TELLER (n) *diseur, -euse de bonne aventure* ⟲ clairvoyant = *voyant (extralucide)*, crystal ball = *boule de cristal.*

FORTY (n, -ies, adj) *quarante* (m) : forty people = *quarante personnes* ⟲ fortieth = *quarantième*
in the forties = *dans les années quarante*
to be in one's forties = *avoir quarante ans et quelques* ⟲ to be fortyish = *avoir la quarantaine.*

FORUM (n) *forum* (m) : a boring forum on electronic music = *un forum ennuyeux sur la musique électronique* ⟲ symposium = ←.

FORWARD (adj) *envahissant, -e* : I'm too shy to get along with someone forward = *je suis trop timide pour bien m'entendre avec quelqu'un d'envahissant.*

FORWARD(S) (adv) *en avant* : step forward(s) = *faites un pas en avant* ≠ backwards = *en arrière*
☠ for the use of "forward(s)" after a verb, see the verb.

FORWARD (to, -ed) *faire suivre* (letter) : please forward my mail = *prière de faire suivre mon courrier* ⟲ to transmit = *transmettre.*

FOSSIL (n) *fossile* (m) ⟲ vestige = ←.

FOSTER (adj) *nourricier, -ère* : foster mother/father = *mère nourricière/père nourricier.*

FOUL (adj, -er, -est) *infect, -e* : foul weather = *temps infect*, foul smell = *odeur infecte* → AWFUL
foul language = *langage ordurier* ⟲ dirty words = *gros mots*
foul play = *qqch de pas très catholique* : there was some foul play in the election = *il y a eu quelque chose de pas très catholique dans les élections* ⟲ hanky-panky = *cuisine*
☠ *il est infect avec son petit frère* = he's rotten to his kid brother
— *ta soupe est infecte !* = your soup is revolting !

FOULMOUTHED (adj) *mal embouché, -e* : a foulmouthed individual = *un individu mal embouché* ⟲ coarse = *grossier.*

FOUL-UP (n) *connerie* (f) : the foul-up was due to lack of coordination = *la connerie venait du manque de coordination* ☠ → bullshit.

FOUL UP (to, -ed) *(faire) foirer* : he fouled everything up = *il a tout fait foirer* ⟲ to ball up = *foutre en l'air.*

FOUND (to, -ed) *fonder* : they founded the company in 1890 = *ils ont fondé l'entreprise en 1890* ⟲ to create = *créer* ☠ *fonder (une théorie) sur* = to base (a theory) on.

FOUNDATION (n) **1/** *fondation* (f) : to get a grant from the Ford foundation = *obtenir une bourse de la fondation Ford* **2/** *fondation* (f) : the foundations of the building = *les fondations de l'immeuble* **3/** *fondement* (m) :

your argument has no foundation = *votre argument est sans fondement.*

FOUNDER (n) *fondateur, -trice :* the founder of this university = *le fondateur de cette université* ⓪ creator = *créateur.*

FOUNDLING (n) *enfant trouvé, -e :* the nuns fed the foundling = *les religieuses ont nourri l'enfant trouvé* ⓪ orphan = *orphelin.*

FOUNTAIN (n) *fontaine (f)* ⓪ basin = *bassin*
fountain of youth = *fontaine de jouvence*
fountain pen = *stylo à plume* ⓪ ball point = *stylo à bille*
☠ *il ne faut pas dire « fontaine, je ne boirai pas de ton eau »* = never say never.

FOUR (n, adj) *quatre (m) :* two and two are four = *deux et deux font quatre* ⓪ fourteen = *quatorze,* fourteenth = *quatorzième,* fourth = *quatrième*
☠ *ne pas y aller par quatre chemins* = not to beat around the bush
— *un de ces quatre* = one of these days
— *se mettre en quatre* = to bend over backwards
— *manger comme quatre* = to eat like a horse
— *faire les quatre volontés de qqn* = to be at s.o.'s beck and call
— *dire à qqn ses quatre vérités* = to tell s.o. off
— *tiré à quatre épingles* = spruced up
— *couper les cheveux en quatre* = to split hairs
— *faire les quatre cents coups* = to paint the town red
— *entre quat'z-yeux* = between you, me and the lamppost.

FOUR-LETTER WORD (n) *gros mot (m)* (shit, fuck, etc.) : her father slaps her when she uses four-letter words = *son père la gifle quand elle utilise des gros mots* ⓪ dirty words = *mots grossiers.*

FOWL (n) *volaille (f)* ⓪ chicken = *poulet,* hen = *poule,* turkey = *dinde,* goose = *oie,* duck = *canard.*

FOX (n, -es) *renard (m)* ⓪ wolf = *loup.*

FOXY (adj, -ier, -iest) *futé, -e :* don't be foxy with me = *ne joue pas à la plus futée avec moi* ⓪ wily = *madré.*

FRACTION (n) *fraction (f) :* 2/3 is a fraction = *2/3 est une fraction* ⓪ part = *partie.*

FRACTURE (n) *fracture (f)* ⓪ cast = *plâtre.*

FRAGILE (adj) *fragile :* sensitive and fragile = *sensible et fragile* ⓪ frail = *frêle* ≠ robust = *robuste* **FRAGILITY** (n, -ies) *fragilité (f) :* the fragility of her personality = *la fragilité de sa personnalité.*

FRAGMENT (n) *fragment (m) :* scattered fragments of bones = *des fragments d'os éparpillés* ⓪ piece = *morceau* **FRAGMENTARY** (adj) *fragmentaire :* a very fragmentary knowledge of French = *une connaissance très fragmentaire du français* ⓪ partial = *partiel.*

FRAGRANCE (n) *odeur (m) :* the perfume has a nice fra-grance = *le parfum a une odeur agréable* ☠ → odor.

FRAIL (adj, -er, -est) *frêle :* a frail child = *un enfant frêle* ⓪ delicate = *délicat.*

FRAME (n) *cadre (m) :* a gilded frame = *un cadre doré*
frame of mind = *état d'esprit* ⓪ mood = *humeur*
frame of reference = *cadre de référence*
☠ *dans le cadre de (l'ONU)* = within the framework of (the UN)
— *un cadre (entreprise)* = an executive
— *ils travaillent dans un cadre agréable* = they work in pleasant surroundings
— *le cadre du roman* = the setting of the novel.

FRAME (to, -d) *monter un coup (contre) :* who framed you ? = *qui a monté le coup contre vous ?*
to be framed by (the cops) = *être coincé par un coup monté (des flics).*

FRAME-UP (n) *coup (m) monté :* the accusation was a frame-up = *l'accusation était un coup monté* ⓪ conspiracy = *conspiration.*

FRAMEWORK (n) *cadre (m) :* not within the framework of the Constitution = *pas dans le cadre de la Constitution* ☠ → frame.

FRANCE (n) France *(f)* ⓪ Eiffel Tower = *tour Eiffel.*

FRANCHISE (n) *franchise (f),* autorisation *(f)* de vente : he got the perfume franchise for Paris = *il a obtenu la franchise sur Paris pour les parfums*
☠ *sa franchise* = her frankness
— *en toute franchise* = honestly.

FRANCHISER (n) *concessionnaire (m),* franchiseur *(m).*

FRANK (adj, -er, -est) *franc, -che :* a frank answer = *une réponse franche* ⓪ straightforward = *sans détour* ≠ evasive = *évasif*
☠ *avoir les coudées franches* = to have a free hand
— *il joue franc jeu* = he's a square shooter/he's straight from the shoulder
— *zone franche* = duty-free area.

FRANKFURTER (n) *saucisse (f)* de Francfort := frank.

FRANKLY (adv) *franchement :* frankly, I don't agree = *franchement, je ne suis pas d'accord* ☠ *il est franchement désagréable* = he's downright disagreeable.

FRANKNESS (n) *franchise (f) :* I appreciate your frankness = *j'apprécie ta franchise* ☠ → franchise.

FRANTIC (adj) 1/ *affolé, -e :* when the child disappeared, she was frantic = *quand l'enfant a disparu, elle était affolée* ⓪ worried sick = *aux cent coups* 2/ *effréné, -e :* frantic letter-writing = *correspondance effrénée* ☠ *un enthousiasme effréné* = unbridled enthusiasm.

FRATERNITY (n, -ies) 1/ *club (m) d'étudiants :* my brother belongs to a fraternity = *mon frère fait partie d'un club d'étudiants* 2/ *fraternité (f)* = brotherhood **FRATERNAL** (adj) *fraternel, -elle.*

FRAUD (n) **1/** *fraude (f)* : election fraud = *fraude électorale* Ⓓ hanky-panky = *cuisine* ☠ *fraude fiscale* = tax evasion **2/** *imposteur (m)* : he says he's a prince but he's a fraud = *il se dit prince, mais c'est un imposteur* = impostor Ⓓ phony = *charlatan*
you're a fraud ! = *tu racontes n'importe quoi !*

FRAUDULENT (adj) *frauduleux, -euse* : fraudulent dealings = *des affaires frauduleuses* Ⓓ crooked = *malhonnête*.

FRAYED (adj) *effiloché, -e* : frayed clothing = *des vêtements effilochés* Ⓓ ragged = *loqueteux*.

FREAK (n) **1/** *dingue (m, f)* : a bridge/rock freak = *un dingue de bridge/rock* Ⓓ buff = *mordu* ☠ *c'est un dingue* = he's a crazy person **2/** *spécimen (m)* : her friends are all freaks = *tous ses amis sont des spécimens* Ⓓ oddball = *drôle de numéro* ☠ → specimen.

FREAK (adj, -er, -est) *bizarroïde* : a freak accident = *un accident bizarroïde* Ⓓ strange = *étrange*.

FREAK OUT (to, -ed) *flipper* : I freaked out when I heard they were divorcing = *j'ai flippé quand j'ai appris qu'ils divorçaient* Ⓓ to be thrown = *être retourné*.

FREAKY (adj, -ier, -iest) *bizarroïde* : freaky friends/tastes = *des amis/goûts bizarroïdes* = freakish Ⓓ kooky = *farfelu*.

FRECKLE (n) *tàche (f) de rousseur* Ⓓ beauty spot = *grain de beauté*.

FREE (adj, -r, -st) **1/** *gratuit, -e* : drinks are free = *les boissons sont gratuites* Ⓓ on the house = *aux frais de la princesse* ☠ → gratuitous **2/** *libre* : are you free tonight ? = *êtes-vous libre ce soir ?* ≠ tied up = *pris*, occupied = *occupé* **3/** *libre* : a free man = *un homme libre* Ⓓ independent = *indépendant* **4/** *libre* : her brother's free again = *son frère est de nouveau libre* Ⓓ single = *célibataire* ≠ married = *marié*

---

to be a free agent = *être libre comme l'air* ≠ to be tied down = *avoir des obligations*
to be free with (one's money) = *ne pas être avare de (son argent)*
free and easy = *décontracté* : he has a free and easy manner = *il a des manières décontractées* ≠ square = *guindé*
free enterprise = *libre entreprise*
to be free to (think what you want) = *être libre de (penser ce*

qu'on veut*)*
it's a free world ! = *on est en république !*
to be free with one's hand = *avoir la main leste* → TO HIT
free love = *amour libre*
to feel free to = *ne pas hésiter à* : if you need help, feel free to call = *si tu as besoin d'aide, n'hésite pas à m'appeler* = be my guest = *ne te gêne pas*
free of charge = *sans frais* Ⓓ gratis = ←
free on board =

franco à bord = FOB
free time = *temps libre* : I study piano in my free time = *j'apprends à jouer du piano pendant mon temps libre* Ⓓ leisure = *loisir*
for free = *gratuitement* : I get my meals for free = *j'ai mes repas gratuitement*
to give free rein to = **1/** *laisser la bride sur le cou à* : the boss gave free rein to his assistant = *le patron laissait à son assistant la bride sur le cou* **2/** *laisser libre cours à* : to give free rein to one's anger = *laisser libre cours à sa colère*
to have ≠ **give a free hand** = *avoir* ≠ *laisser carte blanche* ≠ to hold tight reins = *tenir la bride haute/courte*
to set free = *libérer* : they set the hostages free at midnight = *ils ont libéré les otages à minuit* Ⓓ to release = *relâcher* ☠ → to liberate.

FREE (adv) *gratuitement* : we got in free = *nous sommes entrés gratuitement*.

FREE (to, -d) *libérer* : they freed the hostages = *ils ont libéré les otages* ≠ to arrest = *arrêter*, to imprison = *emprisonner* ☠ → to liberate.

FREEDOM (n) *liberté (f)* : the slaves fought for their freedom = *les esclaves se sont battus pour leur liberté* ≠ bondage = *asservissement*
freedom of the press = *liberté de la presse*
freedom of speech = *liberté de parole*
☠ → liberty.

FREE-FOR-ALL (n) *foire (f) d'empoigne, mêlée (f) générale* : the meeting degenerated into a free-for-all = *la réunion a dégénéré en foire d'empoigne/en mêlée générale* Ⓓ fight = *bagarre*, rumble = *rififi*.

FREE-LANCE (adj) *en free-lance* : she does free-lance PR work = *elle travaille en free-lance dans les relations publiques* ≠ salaried = *salarié*.

FREE-LANCE (to, -d) *travailler en free-lance* : she was salaried but she's free-lancing now = *elle était salariée, mais maintenant elle travaille en free-lance* Ⓓ to be on one's own = *être à son compte*.

FREELOAD (to, -ed) *vivre aux crochets de* : he always freeloads on his family = *il vit toujours aux crochets de sa famille* Ⓓ to sponge off = *vivre en parasite* ≠ to pay one's way = *payer son écot* **FREELOADER** (n) *pique-assiette (m, f)* Ⓓ parasite = ←.

FREELY (adv) *librement* : to speak freely = *parler librement*.

FREEMASON (n) *franc-maçon (m)* Ⓓ lodge = *loge*.

FREETHINKER (n) *libre penseur (m)*.

FREEWHEELING (adj) *indiscipliné, -e* : freewheeling junior Senators = *de jeunes sénateurs indisciplinés* Ⓓ maverick = *franc-tireur*.

FREEZE (n) **a freeze on (prices)** = *un gel/blocage des (prix)*.

FREEZE (to, froze, frozen) **1/** *geler, congeler* (food) : to freeze food = *congeler de la nourriture*, the lake's frozen = *le lac est gelé* **2/** *geler* : to freeze prices = *geler les prix* ⓓ to block = *bloquer* **3/** *geler, cailler* (LV) : I'm freezing = *je gèle/je caille* ≠ to be boiling = *crever de chaleur*
to freeze over = *geler* : the lake freezes over every year = *le lac gèle tous les ans*.

FREEZER (n) *freezer (m), congélateur (m)* ⓓ refrigerator = *réfrigérateur*.

FREEZING (adj) **it's freezing** = *il gèle* ⓓ it's ice-cold = *il fait glacial*
I'm freezing ! = *je gèle !* ≠ **I'm boiling !** = *je crève de chaud !*
freezing temperatures = *des températures au-dessous de zéro*.

FREIGHT (n) *fret (m)*
freight car = *wagon de marchandises*.

FREIGHTER (n) *cargo (m)*.

FRENCH (n inv) **1/** *les Français, -es* : the French think a lot = *les Français pensent beaucoup* **2/** *français (m)* : to speak French = *parler français* **FRENCHMAN** (n, -men) *Français (m)* **FRENCHWOMAN** (n, -women) *Française (f)*.

FRENCH (adj) *français, -e* : French cheeses = *les fromages français*
French dressing = *vinaigrette*
French fries = *frites* = chips (GB)
French kiss = *patin* ⓓ soul kiss = *pelle* ☠ → skate
French tickler = *capote anglaise érotisée*
French toast = *pain perdu*
French windows = *porte-fenêtre* ⓓ bay window = *baie vitrée*
to take French leave = *filer à l'anglaise* → TO LEAVE
the French Riviera = *la Côte d'Azur*.

FRENZY (n, -ies) **in a frenzy** = *dans un état de frénésie*.

FREQUENCY (n, -ies) *fréquence (f)* : the frequency of holdups = *la fréquence des hold-up* ≠ rarity = *rareté*.

FREQUENT (adj) *fréquent, -e* : frequent visits/problems = *des visites fréquentes/des problèmes fréquents* ≠ infrequent = *peu fréquent*, rare = ← **FREQUENTLY** (adv) *fréquemment* : it frequently rains = *il pleut fréquemment* ⓓ often = *souvent* ≠ infrequently = *peu fréquemment*.

FREQUENT (to, -ed) *fréquenter* : we used to frequent brothels = *nous fréquentions les bordels* ⓓ to hang out in = *être toujours fourré dans*
☠ *fréquenter qqn* = to keep company with s.o.
— *nous ne fréquentons pas les mêmes gens* = we do not socialize with the same people.

FRESH (adj, -er, -est) **1/** *frais, fraîche* : fresh vegetables =

légumes frais ≠ canned = *en boîte*, fresh meat = *viande fraîche* ≠ spoiled = *avarié*
to feel fresh as a daisy = *être frais comme un gardon/une rose* ⓓ to be fit as a fiddle = *se porter comme un charme*
don't be fresh ! = *ne sois pas insolent !*
to make a fresh start = *repartir du bon pied*
fresh water = *eau douce* ≠ salt water = *eau de mer*
let's get some fresh air ! = *si on allait prendre l'air !*
☠ *(des amis) de fraîche date* = recent (friends)
— *me voilà frais !* = I'm in a pickle !
— *une soirée fraîche* = a cool evening
2/ *neuf, neuve* : a fresh approach = *une approche neuve* ⓓ modern = *moderne* ☠ → new.

FRESH (adv) **to be fresh out of (coffee)** = *venir de finir (le café)*.

FRESHEN UP (to, -ed) *se rafraîchir* : would you like to freshen up before dinner ? = *voulez-vous aller vous rafraîchir avant le dîner ?* ⓓ to powder one's nose = *se refaire une beauté*
☠ *se rafraîchir (boire)* = to cool off (drink)
— *rafraîchir la mémoire à qqn* = to refresh s.o.'s memory
— *se faire rafraîchir les cheveux* = to have one's hair trimmed.

FRESHMAN (n, -men) *étudiant, -e de première année, bizut (m, f)* (LV) : she's a freshman at Yale = *c'est une étudiante de première année à Yale* ≠ senior = *étudiant de dernière année*.

FRET (to, -ted) *se tracasser* : there's no reason to fret = *il n'y a aucune raison de vous tracasser* ⓓ to eat one's heart out = *se ronger les sangs*.

FREUDIAN (adj) *freudien, -enne*
freudian slip = *lapsus révélateur*.

FRICTION (n) *friction (f)* : there's a lot of friction between them = *il y a beaucoup de friction entre eux* ⓓ pull = *tirage*.

FRIDAY (n) *vendredi (m)* : Good Friday = *Vendredi saint* → WEEK
gal/guy Friday = *fille/garçon de bureau*.

FRIDGE (n) *frigo (m)* ⓓ icebox = *glacière*.

FRIED (adj) *frit, -e* : fried fish = *poisson frit* ⓓ baked = *cuit au four*.

FRIEND (n) *ami, -e* : a friend of mine = *un de mes amis* ⓓ buddy = *pote*, crony = *compère* ≠ enemy = *ennemi*
to make friends = *se faire des amis* : she doesn't make friends easily = *elle ne se fait pas facilement des amis*.

FRIENDLY (adj, -ier, -iest) *amical, -e* : friendly people = *des gens amicaux* ⓓ amiable = *aimable*, affable = ← ≠ unfriendly = *peu amical*
a friendly nation = *un pays ami*.

FRIENDSHIP (n) *amitié* (f) : a lifelong friendship = *une amitié qui dure toute la vie* ≠ enmity = *inimitié*
out of friendship = *par amitié* : he did it out of friendship = *il l'a fait par amitié*
to strike up a friendship = *se lier d'amitié* : we struck up a friendship on the beach = *nous nous sommes liés d'amitié sur la plage* ⓪ to hit it off = *sympathiser* ☠ *mes amitiés à* = my best regards to.

FRIGGING (adj) *foutu, -e* : what's this frigging mess ? = *qu'est-ce que c'est que cette foutue pagaille ?* ⓪ damned = *sacré* ☠ → fucking.

FRIGHT (n) what a fright you gave me ! = *tu m'as fait une de ces peurs !*
to look a fright = *avoir une tête à faire peur* ⓪ to look a sight = *avoir une sale tête*.

FRIGHTEN (to, -ed) *effrayer* : you frightened me = *tu m'as effrayé* ⓪ to scare the living daylights out of s.o. = *flanquer la pétoche à qqn*
to frighten away = *faire fuir* : the sirens frightened the burglars away = *les sirènes ont fait fuir les cambrioleurs.*

FRIGHTENED (adj) *effrayé, -e* : frightened by thunder = *effrayé par le tonnerre* ⓪ scared ⓪ terrified = *terrifié*
frightened to death = *mort de frayeur* ⓪ panic-stricken = *pris de panique*
he was more frightened than anything = *il a eu plus de peur que de mal.*

FRIGHTENING (adj) *effrayant, -e* : what a frightening experience ! = *quelle expérience effrayante !* ⓪ scary = *qui fait peur.*

FRIGHTFUL (adj) *effroyable* : frightful weather = *un temps effroyable* → AWFUL.

FRIGHTFULLY (adv) *effroyablement* : frightfully late/rich = *effroyablement tard/riche* → VERY.

FRIGID (adj) *frigide* : a frigid woman = *une femme frigide* ≠ hot number = *chaud lapin* **FRIGIDITY** (n) *frigidité* (f).

FRILLS (n pl) *fioritures* (f pl) : the flight was cheap but with no frills = *le voyage en avion était bon marché mais sans fioritures* ⓪ extras = ←.

FRINGE (n) **on the fringe of (society)** = *en marge de* (la société).

FRINGE (adj) *marginal, -e* : a fringe theater group = *une troupe de théâtre marginale* ☠ → marginal
fringe benefit = *avantage social* : the company offers health insurance as a fringe benefit = *la société offre une assurance-maladie comme avantage social.*

FRISK (to, -ed) *fouiller* (s.o.) : the cops frisked everyone in the place = *les flics ont fouillé tous ceux qui se trouvaient là*
☠ *fouiller une maison* = to search/go through a house
— *tu peux toujours te fouiller !* = you can whistle for it !

FRITZ (n, -es) *Fritz* (m, f) ⓪ Kraut = *Boche*
to be on the fritz = *être déglingué* : my car's on the fritz = *ma voiture est déglinguée* ⓪ to be out of order = *être en panne.*

FRIVOLOUS (adj) *frivole* : a frivolous life/person = *une vie/personne frivole* ⓪ shallow = *peu profond.*

FRIZZ (to, -ed) *friser* : my hair frizzes = *mes cheveux frisent* ⓪ to wave = *onduler*
☠ *friser l'accident* = to just miss having an accident
— *friser le ridicule* = to border on the ridiculous
— *friser la (quarantaine)* = to be pushing (forty).

FRIZZY (adj, -ier, -est) *frisé, -e* : frizzy hair = *cheveux frisés* ≠ straight = *raide.*

FROG (n) 1/ *grenouille* (f) ⓪ tadpole = *têtard*, toad = *crapaud*
to have a frog in one's throat = *avoir un chat dans la gorge* ⓪ a hoarse voice = *une voix enrouée*
☠ *une grenouille de bénitier* = a church nut
2/ *franchouillard, -e* : a lot of limeys, dagos and frogs = *beaucoup d'angliches, de ritals et de franchouillards* = Frenchy ⓪ Yankee = ←.

FROLIC (to, -ked) *batifoler* : a foal frolicking in the grass = *un poulain qui batifolait dans l'herbe* ⓪ to romp = *gambader.*

FROM (prep) *de* : to come from the States = *venir des États-Unis*, sick from eating too much = *malade d'avoir trop mangé*
from what he says (they're splitting) = *(ils se séparent) d'après ce qu'il dit* ⓪ according to = *selon*
from far off = *de loin* : I saw her from far off = *je l'ai vue de loin*
from ... on = *à partir de* : I'm on vacation from Monday on = *je suis en vacances à partir de lundi* ≠ until = *jusqu'à*
from now on = *à partir de maintenant* : from now on, I want to live apart on weekends = *à partir de maintenant, je veux qu'on vive séparés pendant les week-ends*
from ... to = *de ... à* : from one day to the other = *d'un jour à l'autre*
from ... up = *à partir de* : they cost from $ 20 up = *on en trouve à partir de 20 dollars* ≠ up to = *jusqu'à*
from then on = *à partir de là* : from then on, we had problems = *à partir de là, nous avons eu des problèmes*
☠ → of
— for the use of "from" after a verb, see the verb.

FRONT (n) 1/ *avant* (m) (car, plane), *devant* (m) : sit in the front of the car = *asseyez-vous à l'avant de la voiture*, the front of the house = *le devant de la maison* ☠ *prendre les devants* = to jump the gun
in front of = 1/ *devant* : sit in front of me = *assieds-toi devant moi*, wait for me in front of the house = *attends-moi devant la maison* ≠ behind = *derrière*
2/ *devant* : he said it in front of me = *il l'a dit devant moi* ≠ behind my back = *derrière mon dos*
the front = *le front* : killed on the front = *tué au front*

☠ *le front (partie de la tête)* = the forehead
— *avoir le front de ...* = to have the nerve to ...
— *faire front commun* = to join forces
— *faire front (aux difficultés)* = to face (difficulties)
2/ couverture *(f)* : the store's just a front for drug peddling = *le magasin n'est qu'une couverture pour le trafic de drogue* ☠ → blanket
3/ contenance *(f)* : her offhandedness is just a front = *sa désinvolture n'est qu'une contenance* ⓪ facade = *façade*, put-on = *frime* ☠ *perdre contenance* = to lose face
to put up a (good) front = *faire bonne figure* : they're broke now but they put up a front = *ils sont fauchés, mais ils font bonne figure.*

FRONT (adj) *de devant* : the front door = *la porte de devant* ≠ back = *de derrière*
front yard = *jardin devant la maison*
front porch = *auvent sur le devant de la maison*
to be splashed (all) over the front pages = *défrayer la chronique* ⓪ to make the headlines = *faire les gros titres*
to make the front page = *faire la une.*

FRONT (to, -ed) *servir de couverture* : the store fronts for the CIA = *le magasin sert de couverture à la CIA.*

FRONTIER (n) frontière *(f)* : the frontiers of science/America = *les frontières de la science/de l'Amérique* ⓪ customs = *douane.*

FROST (n) gel *(m)*, gelée *(f)* (blanche) : morning frost = *gel matinal*, frost on the lawn = *de la gelée blanche sur la pelouse* ⓪ frostbite = *engelure*
☠ *gelée de fraises* = strawberry jelly
— *(poulet) en gelée* = (chicken) in aspic
— *gel des prix* = price freeze.

FROSTBITE (n) engelure *(f)*
to die from frostbite = *mourir de froid* ⓪ frostbitten = *gelé*, hypothermia = *hypothermie.*

FROWN (to, -ed) *froncer les sourcils* : he frowned when I said that = *quand j'ai dit ça, il a froncé les sourcils*
to frown on = *voir d'un mauvais œil* : she frowns on her husband's drinking = *elle voit l'alcoolisme de son mari d'un mauvais œil* ≠ to approve of = *approuver.*

FROZEN (adj) gelé, -e : the lake's frozen = *le lac est gelé*

frozen food = *aliments surgelés* ≠ thawed = *décongelé.*

FRUGAL (adj) frugal, -e : a frugal meal = *un repas frugal* ⓪ austere = *austère.*

FRUIT (n) **1/** (inv) fruits *(m pl)* : do you like fruit ? = *est-ce que vous aimez les fruits ?* **a piece of fruit** = *un fruit*	
apple = *pomme* **apricot** = *abricot* **cherry** = *cerise* **grapefruit** = *pamplemousse* **lemon** = *citron* **nectarine** = *brugnon* **orange** = ← **peach** = *pêche*	**pear** = *poire* **pineapple** = *ananas* **plum** = *prune* **prune** = *pruneau* **strawberry** = *fraise* **tangerine** = *mandarine* **watermelon** = *pastèque*
☠ *fruits de mer* = seafood	— *un fruit sec* = a drip

2/ tapette *(f)* : her husband's a fruit = *son mari est une tapette* ⓪ fag = *pédale*, flit = *tantouse.*

FRUITFUL (adj) fructueux, -euse : fruitful talks = *des pourparlers fructueux* ⓪ beneficial = *bénéfique* ≠ unfruitful = *infructueux* ☠ *commerce fructueux* = profitable business.

FRUSTRATE (to, -d) **1/** *frustrer* : to feel frustrated in one's work = *se sentir frustré dans son travail*, I haven't made love for a week, I feel frustrated = *je n'ai pas fait l'amour depuis une semaine, je suis frustré* ≠ to fulfill = *combler* **2/** *contrarier* : his efforts to become a Senator were frustrated by his own party = *ses efforts pour devenir sénateur ont été contrariés par son propre parti* ⓪ to thwart = *contrecarrer* ☠ *son attitude me contrarie* = his attitude irks me/vexes me.

FRUSTRATING (adj) frustrant, -e : a frustrating day = *une journée frustrante* ⓪ infuriating = *excédant* ≠ satisfying = *satisfaisant* **FRUSTRATION** (n) frustration *(f)* : a feeling of frustration = *un sentiment de frustration* ⓪ disappointment = *déception.*

FRY (to, -ied) *faire frire* : to fry fish = *faire frire du poisson* ⓪ to brown = *faire revenir.*

FUCK (n) **1/** baiseur, -euse : he's a good fuck = *c'est un bon baiseur/il baise bien* = he's a good lay **2/** coup *(m)* : a quick fuck = *un coup vite tiré* ⓪ lay = *coucherie*, roll in the hay = *partie de jambes en l'air* ☠ → blow **3/** salopard *(m)* : what a fuck ! = *quel salopard !* → BASTARD	
get the fuck out ! = *va te faire foutre !* → BUZZ OFF ! **I don't give a fuck !** = *je n'en ai rien à foutre !* ⓪	I don't give a damn ! = *je m'en fous !* **what the fuck !** = *putain !* → GOSH **who gives a fuck !** = *qu'est-ce que ça peut foutre ?*

FUCK (to, -ed) *baiser* : the first time we fucked it was awful = *la première fois que nous avons baisé, c'était affreux* = the first time we screwed

I'm fucked = *je suis foutu !* = I'm screwed ⓪ you've had it ! = *tu es fichu !,* your number's up ! = *les carottes sont cuites !*
fuck it ! = *putain de merde !* → GOSH !

fuck you ! = *je t'emmerde !/tu m'emmerdes !* → BUZZ OFF !
to get fucked = *se faire baiser :* I got fucked on the deal = *je me suis fait baiser dans cette affaire*

to fuck around/off = 1/ *déconner :* stop fucking around ! = *arrête de déconner !* ⓪ to clown around = *faire le clown* 2/ *ne rien foutre :* we just fucked around all day = *on n'a rien foutu de la journée* 3/ *baiser à droite et à gauche :* she's been fucking around since her marriage = *elle baise à droite et à gauche depuis qu'elle est mariée*
to fuck around with = *se taper :* he's fucking around with his secretary = *il se tape sa secrétaire* ⓪ to screw around with = *sauter* ☠ → to hit
fuck off ! = *va te faire foutre !* → BUZZ OFF !
to fuck s.o. (over) = *baiser/couillonner qqn :* his

partner's fucking him over = *son partenaire est en train de le baiser/couillonner* → TO HUSTLE
to fuck up = 1/ *foutre en l'air :* you fucked everything up = *tu as tout foutu en l'air* ⓪ to foul up = *faire foirer* 2/ *foutre en l'air :* seeing a shrink fucked her up = *ça l'a foutue en l'air d'aller voir un psy* ⓪ to screw up = *foutre par terre* 3/ *foutre dedans :* your stupid advice fucked me up = *tes stupides conseils m'ont foutu dedans*
to fuck with s.o. = *se foutre de qqn :* don't fuck with me = *ne te fous pas de moi* ⓪ to screw with s.o.** = *se foutre de la gueule de qqn*

GROUP : TO FUCK, ETC. = BAISER, ETC.

AIDS = *SIDA*
to ball = *baiser* = **to screw**
balls/nuts = *les couilles/les roupettes*
to bang = *baisouiller*
to be ac/dc = *être ambivalent*
to be excited/turned on/ aroused = *être excité/troublé*
to be horny = *être en manque*
to be hot and bothered = *être tout chose*
bondage = *éducation anglaise/sado-maso .*
boobs/knockers/tits = *nénés/ doudounes/nichons*
to bugger/to ream/to rim = *enculer*
to have the clap = *avoir la chaude-pisse*
cock/tool/prick = *queue/ pine/bite*
to come = *jouir*
to copulate = *copuler*
cunt/pussy = *con/chatte*
dildo = *godemiché*
to do a blow job = *tailler une pipe* = **to give s.o. head** = *faire un pompier à qqn*
to do it = *le faire*
to do it the Greek way = *faire ça à la grecque*
to do everything but = *flirter sans aller jusqu'au bout*
to eat a woman = *brouter une femme*
to feel s.o. up = *peloter qqn*
the first position = *à la papa*
foreplay = *attouchements*
French/soul kiss = *patin/pelle*
gang bang = *viol collectif*

to get it off = *prendre son pied*
to get it on with s.o. = *s'envoyer en l'air avec qqn*
to get it up = *bander*
to get laid = *se faire sauter*
to get one's rocks off/one's nuts off = *tirer un coup/décharger*
to go all the way = *aller jusqu'au bout*
to go around the world = *faire feuille de rose*
to go down on s.o. = *faire minette (guys do)/ faire un pompier (girls do)*
to go limp = *débander*
(he's/she's) a good lay = *(il/elle) baise bien/(c'est) un bon coup*
a great screw = *un super baiseur* = **a great fuck**
a hand job = *une branlette*
to have a hard-on = *bander/avoir la trique*
to have intercourse = *avoir des rapports sexuels*
to have relations = *avoir des rapports* = **to have sex**
to hump = *culbuter*
a lesbian/dyke ≠ **a queer/ fag/fruit** = *une lesbienne/une gouine* ≠ *un pédé/une pédale/une tapette*
to make it = *s'envoyer en l'air*
to make love = *faire l'amour*
to masturbate/to jerk off (guys)/to play with o.s. = *se masturber/se branler/s'amuser en solitaire*
man on the top = *à la mission-*

naire = **in the missionary position**
to mount s.o. = *monter qqn*
to neck/to paw/to pet = *flirter/tripoter/peloter*
one-night stand = *aventure d'un soir*
oral sex = *caresses buccales*
orgasm = *orgasme*
to pick s.o. up = *draguer qqn*
a quickie = *un coup vite tiré*
to score with s.o. = *se faire qqn*
to be sexed-up = *avoir le feu aux fesses*
S.M. = *S.M.* ⓪ sado-masochism = *sadomasochisme*
to sock it to s.o. = *tringler qqn*
to sleep around = *coucher à droite et à gauche*
to sleep with s.o. = *coucher avec qqn*
sperm = *sperme/foutre*
to straddle s.o. = *chevaucher qqn*
to suck s.o. = *sucer qqn*
a swing = *une partouze*
to swing = *partouzer*
to swing both ways = *marcher à voile et à vapeur*
syphilis = ←
to take s.o. from behind = *prendre qqn en levrette*
to turn a trick = *faire une passe*
a two-couple swing = *une partie carrée*
well-hung = *bien monté*
to have wet dreams = *faire des rêves humides.*

FUCKED-UP (adj) *qui déconne (psychologiquement)* : fucked-up teenagers = *des jeunes qui déconnent* ① messed-up = *complètement paumé.*

FUCKING (adj) *foutu, -e, putain de* : I still haven't seen that fucking film = *je n'ai pas encore vu ce foutu film/ce putain de film* ① damned = *sacré*
you fucking (fool) ! = *espèce de (con)* !
☠ *tu es foutu* = you're fucked/screwed
— *un foutu (caractère)* = a lousy (disposition)
— *être mal foutu* = to feel lousy
— *elle est bien ≠ mal foutue* = she is ≠ isn't stacked.

FUCKING (adv) *putain ce que* : he's fucking rich ! = *putain ce qu'il est riche* ! → VERY.

FUDDY-DUDDY (adj) *vieux jeu* : fuddy-duddy parents = *des parents vieux jeu ≠ hep = à la page.*

FUEL (n) (GB) *essence* (f) = gas ☠ → essence
to add fuel to the fire = *jeter de l'huile sur le feu.*

FUEL (to, -ed) *alimenter* : his remarks fueled the dissension within the party = *ses réflexions ont alimenté les dissensions au sein du parti* ☠ *alimenter un malade/les ragots* = to feed a sick person/gossip.

FUGITIVE (n) *fugitif, -ive* : a fugitive from justice = *un fugitif au regard de la loi* ① escaped prisoner = *évadé.*

FULFIL(L) (to, -(l)ed) *combler* : motherhood didn't fulfill her = *la maternité ne l'a pas comblée* ① to satisfy = *satisfaire* ☠ *combler une lacune* = to bridge a gap.

FULL (adj) *plein, -e* : a full bottle = *une bouteille pleine* ① filled = *rempli,* packed = *plein à craquer*

I'm full ! = *je cale* ! ① satiated = *rassasié ≠* to be starving = *mourir de faim*
you're full of it ! = *tu déconnes* ! → BUZZ OFF !
to be full of laughs = *avoir le mot pour rire ≠* to be a killjoy = *être un rabat-joie*
full employment = *plein emploi ≠* unemployment = *chômage*
full of hope ≠ despair = *plein d'espoir ≠ de désespoir*
full moon = *pleine lune ≠* new moon = *nouvelle lune*
you're full of shit ! = *tu ne dis que des conneries* !
→ BUZZ OFF !
at full speed = *à toute vitesse ≠* at a snail's pace = *à un train de sénateur*
full steam ahead ! = *en avant toute* !
full support = *soutien total*
in full swing = *qui bat son plein* ① jumping = *en plein boum*
full time = *à temps complet* : to work full time = *travailler à temps complet* ① half-time = *à mi-temps ≠* part time = *à temps partiel*

☠ *être en pleine forme* = to be in top form
— *de plein gré* = of one's own will
— *puer à plein nez* = to stink to high heaven

— *en plein air* = in the open air
— *en pleine rue* = in the middle of the street
— *pleine saison* = high season
— *de plein fouet* = head-on
— *en mettre plein la vue* = to put it on
— *j'en ai plein le dos/les bottes/le cul* = I'm fed up
— *plein aux as* = filthy rich
— *plein de ressource* = resourceful

FULL-LENGTH (adj) *en pied* : a full-length portrait = *un portrait en pied.*

FULL-TIME (adj) *à plein temps* : a full-time job = *un travail à plein temps ≠* part-time = *à temps partiel.*

FULLY (adv) *entièrement* : I fully agree with you = *je suis entièrement d'accord avec vous* = I entirely agree with you.

FUMBLE (to, -d) *mener de façon maladroite* : he fumbled the job interview = *il a mené l'entretien d'embauche de façon maladroite* ① to bungle = *louper.*

FUME (n) *émanation* (f) *(toxique)* : fumes from the exhausts = *des émanations provenant des pots d'échappement.*

FUME (to, -d) *être furibard, -e* : Joe's late and the boss is fuming = *Joe est en retard et le patron est furibard* → ANGRY.

FUN (n inv) *qqch d'amusant* : the evening was a lot of fun = *la soirée était très amusante ≠* a drag = *rasoir*
fun and games = *folichon* : this work isn't fun and games = *ce travail n'est pas folichon*
for the fun of it = *histoire de rigoler* : I did it for the fun of it = *je l'ai fait histoire de rigoler* ① for a laugh = *pour rire*
now the fun begins ! = *que la fête commence* !
you're no fun ! = *tu n'es pas marrant* !
we had a lot of fun = *nous nous sommes bien amusés*
have fun ! = *amusez-vous bien* !
like fun ! = *tu rigoles* ! : give you money again ? like fun ! = *te redonner de l'argent ? tu rigoles* ! ① nothing doing ! = *rien à faire* !
to make fun of = *se moquer de* : stop making fun of me ! = *arrête de te moquer de moi* !
to poke fun at = *se payer la tête de.*

FUN (adj) *rigolo, -ote* : a fun restaurant/person = *un restaurant rigolo/une personne rigolote ≠* a drag = *rasoir*
fun furs/jewelry = *fourrures/bijoux fantaisie.*

FUNCTION (n) 1/ *fonction* (f) : what's his function in the company ? = *quelle est sa fonction dans l'entreprise* ? ① role = *rôle*
☠ *entrer en fonction* = to take office
— *la fonction publique* = the civil service .
2/ *réception* (f) *(officielle)* : several diplomatic functions to be attended every week = *plusieurs réceptions diplomatiques obligatoires par semaine.*

FUNCTION (to, -ed) *fonctionner* : the elevator doesn't function = *l'ascenseur ne fonctionne pas* ⓪ to work = *marcher* ≠ to be out of order = *être en panne.*

FUNCTIONAL (adj) *fonctionnel, -elle* : functional furniture = *meubles fonctionnels* ⓪ convenient = *commode.*

FUND (n) *fonds (m)* : there is a relief fund for the refugees = *il y a un fonds de secours pour les réfugiés.*

FUNDAMENTAL (adj) *fondamental, -e* : a fundamental right = *un droit fondamental* ⓪ basic = *de base* **FUNDAMENTALLY** (adv) *fondamentalement* : you're fundamentally mistaken = *tu as fondamentalement tort* ⓪ essentially = *essentiellement.*

FUNDAMENTALS (n pl) *notions (f pl) fondamentales* : the fundamentals of psychology = *les notions fondamentales de la psychologie.*

FUND-RAISING (adj) *pour récolter des fonds* : a fund-raising campaign = *une campagne pour récolter des fonds.*

FUNDS (n pl) *fonds (m pl)* : I don't have the funds to buy a new car = *je n'ai pas les fonds pour acheter une nouvelle voiture* ⓪ capital = ← ☠ *fond* → bottom.

FUNERAL (n) *obsèques (f pl), funérailles (f pl)* : the funeral will take place on Monday = *les obsèques auront lieu lundi*, several heads of state attended the King's funeral = *plusieurs chefs d'État ont assisté aux funérailles du roi* ⓪ coffin = *cercueil*, burial = *enterrement*, funeral parlor = *salon funéraire*, funeral march = *marche funèbre*, funeral procession = *cortège funèbre*, hearse = *corbillard*, cemetery = *cimetière*, to bury = *enterrer*, last rites = *derniers sacrements*, obituary = *notice nécrologique*, pallbearer = *qqn qui porte le cercueil*
it's your funeral ! = *c'est ton arrêt de mort !* : if the boss finds out, it's your funeral ! = *si le patron le découvre, c'est ton arrêt de mort !*

FUNK (n) **to be in a (blue) funk** = *être dans tous ses états* ⓪ to be in agony = *être angoissé.*

FUNKY (adj, -ier, -iest) *funky* : funky music = *musique funky* ⓪ jazz = ←.

FUNNIES (n pl) *bandes dessinées (f pl)* = comics ⓪ cartoon = *dessin animé.*

FUNNY (adj, -ier, -iest) **1/** *drôle, marrant, -e* (LV) : a funny story = *une histoire drôle/marrante* ⓪ a scream = *bidonnant*, comical = *comique*, droll = *rigolo* **2/** *drôle* : it was a funny kind of evening = *c'était une drôle de soirée* ⓪ strange = *étrange*, curious = *curieux*
to feel funny = *se sentir drôle* ⓪ to feel under the weather = *être mal fichu*
to feel funny about = *être gêné de* : I feel funny about asking her = *je suis gêné d'avoir à lui demander ça*
funny bone = *petit juif* ⓪ elbow = *coude*
funny business = *micmac* : funny business in the elections = *micmac électoral* ⓪ monkey business = *grenouillage*
funny farm = *maison de dingues* ⓪ nuthouse = *maison de fous*
the funny thing is ... = *ce qu'il y a de drôle, c'est ...* ☠ *une drôle de (patience)* = a helluva (patience).

FUR (n) *fourrure (f)* : fur coat = *manteau de fourrure*, fur lined = *doublé de fourrure* ⓪ skin = *peau*, mink = *vison*, seal = *phoque*, sable = *zibeline* **FURRIER** (n) *fourreur (m).*

FURIOUS (adj) *furieux, -euse* : furious strikers = *des grévistes furieux* → ANGRY
(I'll be) furious with (you if you don't come) = *(je serai) furieux contre (toi si tu ne viens pas).*

FURLOUGH (n) **on furlough** = *en permission* = on leave.

FURNACE (n) *fourneau (m)* ⓪ blast furnace = *haut fourneau.*

FURNISH (to, -ed) **1/** *meubler* : we're furnishing our apartment = *nous meublons notre appartement* ⓪ to decorate = *décorer* ☠ *meubler la conversation* = to keep the conversation going **2/** *fournir* : to furnish a good alibi = *fournir un bon alibi*
to furnish with = *fournir (en)* : the government is furnishing the troops with new guns = *le gouvernement fournit de nouveaux fusils aux troupes* = to supply with = to provide with
☠ *se fournir chez* = to get one's supplies at.

FURNISHED (adj) *meublé, -e* : furnished apartment = *appartement meublé* ≠ unfurnished = *non meublé.*

FURNISHINGS (n pl) *ameublement (m)* ⓪ decoration = *décoration.*

FURNITURE (n inv) *meubles (m pl)* : we bought our furniture in a department store = *nous avons acheté nos meubles dans un grand magasin*
a piece of furniture = *un meuble*
☠ *sauver les meubles* = to cut one's losses.

FUROR (n) *effervescence (f)* : the killing of the union leader caused a furor = *l'assassinat du dirigeant syndical a provoqué une grande effervescence* = furore (GB) ⓪ commotion = *agitation.*

FURTHER (adj) *davantage de* : I need further details = *j'ai besoin de davantage de détails* ⓪ supplementary = *supplémentaire*
for further information (write to) = *pour obtenir des renseignements complémentaires (écrivez à)*
until further notice = *jusqu'à nouvel ordre*
without further ado = *sans plus d'histoires.*

FURTHER (adv) **1/** *davantage* : I won't discuss it any further = *je n'en discuterai pas davantage* ☠ *en voulez-vous davantage ?* = do you want some more ? **2/** *plus loin* : I'm tired, I can't go further = *je suis fatigué, je ne peux pas aller plus loin* = I can't go farther.

FURTHERMORE (adv) *de plus* : he eats a lot and furthermore drinks like a fish = *il mange beaucoup et, de plus, il boit comme un trou* ① what's more = *qui plus est*.

FURY (n, -ies) *fureur (f)* : the fury of a jealous husband = *la fureur d'un mari jaloux* ① anger = *colère* ☠ *faire fureur* = to be the rage.

FUSE (n) *plomb (m)* : a fuse blew = *un plomb a sauté*
to blow a fuse = *se mettre en pétard* → ANGRY ☠ → lead.

FUSION (n) *fusion (f)* ☠ *fusion de sociétés* = merger.

FUSS (n inv) *histoire (f)* : all this fuss over my coming late = *toute cette histoire parce que je suis arrivée en retard* ① ado = *affaire,* flap = *branle-bas* ☠ → story
to make a fuss = 1/ *faire des histoires* : don't make such a fuss about it ! = *ne fais pas tant d'histoires pour ça !* ① to make a scene = *faire une scène* 2/ *se donner du mal* : yes, we can stay for dinner, but please don't make a fuss ! = *oui, nous pouvons rester dîner, mais je vous en prie ne vous donnez pas de mal !*

FUSS (to, -ed) **to fuss over s.o.** = *être aux petits soins pour qqn* ① to pamper = *choyer*.

FUSSBUDGET = FUSSPOT (n) *maniaque (m, f)*.

FUSSY (adj, -ier, -iest) 1/ *tarabiscoté, -e* : I don't like fussy clothes = *je n'aime pas les vêtements tarabiscotés* ≠ plain = *tout simple* 2/ *difficile* : don't be so fussy ! = *ne sois pas si difficile !* ① particular = *exigeant* ☠ → difficult
to be fussy about (food) = *être difficile pour (la nourriture)*.

FUTILE (adj) *vain, -e* : futile attempts = *vaines tentatives* ① useless = *inutile* ☠ *propos futiles* = frivolous words.

FUTILITY (n) *vanité (f)* : the futility of trying to end war = *la vanité de tenter de mettre fin à la guerre* ☠ *des futilités* = frivolities.

FUTURE (n) *futur (m)* (tense), *avenir (m)* : the future and the past = *le futur et le passé,* to have a brilliant future = *avoir un brillant avenir*

---

in the future = *à l'avenir* ① henceforth = *dorénavant*
in the distant ≠ **near future** = *dans un avenir lointain* ≠ *proche*
there's no future in (big cars) = *(les grosses voitures) n'ont aucun avenir*
who knows what the future holds ? = *qui sait ce que l'avenir nous réserve?* → THAT'S LIFE!

☠ *l'avenir appartient à ceux qui se lèvent tôt* = the early bird catches the worm.

FUTURE TENSE = LE FUTUR

— I'll = I will (shall)	— I won't (shan't)
— you'll = you will	— you won't
— he'll = he will	— he won't
— she'll = she will	— she won't
— we'll = we will (shall)	— we won't (shan't)
— they'll = they will	— they won't

☠ « shall/shan't » *sont plutôt anglais*

— will he come (tomorrow ?/next week ?/in a year ?) = *viendra-t-il (demain ?/la semaine prochaine ?/dans un an ?)*
— yes, he will = *oui*
— yes, he'll come tomorrow = *oui, il viendra demain*
— no, he won't = *non*
— no, he won't come tomorrow = *non, il ne viendra pas demain.*

FUTURE (adj) *futur, -e* : his future home/wife = *sa future maison/femme* ≠ past = *passé.*

FUZZ (n inv) **the fuzz** = *les poulets* : the fuzz are coming ! = *voilà les poulets !* ① police = ←.

FUZZY (adj, -ier, -iest) *flou, -e* (photo), *fumeux, -euse* (ideas) ☠ *flou* → hazy.

GAB (to, -bed) *papoter* : to gab all day = *papoter toute la journée* ⓪ to jabber = *jacasser.*

GADGET (n) *gadget (m)* : a kitchen full of gadgets = *une cuisine remplie de gadgets* ⓪ thing = *truc.*

GAFFE (n) *gaffe (f)*: to make a gaffe = *faire une gaffe/ gaffer* ⓪ blooper = *bévue* ☠ *fais gaffe !* = be careful !

GAG (n) **1/** *gag (m)* : a film full of gags = *un film rempli de gags* ⓪ joke = *blague* **2/** *bâillon (m)* : they put a gag over her mouth = *ils lui ont mis un bâillon sur la bouche.*

GAG (to, -ged) *bâillonner* : they tied and gagged him = *ils l'ont attaché et bâillonné*
to gag on (one's food) = *s'étrangler en (mangeant).*

GAGA (adj) **to be gaga about s.o.** = *être gaga de qqn* ⓪ to be bats over = *en pincer pour.*

GAIETY (n) *gaieté (f)* : a child's gaiety = *la gaieté d'un enfant* ⓪ mirth = *allégresse* ≠ sadness = *tristesse.*

GAIN (n) *gain (m)* : a gain of ten minutes = *un gain de dix minutes*
☠ *gains mensuels* = monthly earnings
— *obtenir gain de cause* = to win a case.

GAIN (to, -ed) *gagner* : you have nothing to gain by doing that = *vous n'avez rien à gagner en faisant ça* ≠ to lose = *perdre* ☠ → to win.

GAL (n) *fille (f)* : she's a nice gal = *c'est une fille sympa* ⓪ woman = *femme* ≠ fellow = *type* ☠ → girl.

GALA (n) *gala (m)* : I bought a new dress for the gala = *je me suis acheté une nouvelle robe pour le gala* ⓪ dinner dance = *dîner dansant.*

GALE (n) *rafale (f)* : strong gales = *de fortes rafales* ⓪ gust = *coup de vent/bourrasque.*

GALL (n) *impudence (f)* : what gall ! = *quelle impudence !* ⓪ cheek = *aplomb.*

GALL (to, -ed) *horripiler* : it galls me to lose = *ça m'horripile de perdre* → ANGRY.

GALLANT (adj) *galant, -e* : a gallant gesture = *un geste galant* ⓪ chivalrous = *chevaleresque.*

GALLBLADDER (n) *vésicule (f) biliaire.*

GALLERY (n, -ies) *galerie (f)* : art gallery = *galerie d'art*
to play to the gallery = *chercher à épater la galerie.*

GALLON (n) *gallon (m)* = *3,78 litres* : a gallon of gas = *3,78 litres d'essence.*

GALLOP (n) *galop (m)* ⓪ trot = ← **GALLOP** (to, -ed) *galoper* ⓪ to trot = *trotter.*

GALLOWS (n pl) *potence (f)* : condemned to the gallows = *condamné à la potence* ⓪ gibbet = *gibet.*

GALORE (adj) *à la pelle* : money galore = *de l'argent à la pelle* → MANY.

GALOSH (n, -es) *botte (f) de caoutchouc* : it's raining, put on your galoshes = *il pleut, mets tes bottes de caoutchouc.*

GAMBLE (n) **it's a gamble (whether he'll agree)** = *il y a un risque (qu'il ne soit pas d'accord)*
to take the gamble = *prendre le risque* : do you want to take the gamble ? = *est-ce que vous voulez prendre le risque ?*

GAMBLE (to, -d) *jouer, flamber* (LV) : her husband gambles a lot = *son mari joue/flambe pas mal* ⓪ roulette = ←, casino = ←
to gamble on (the fact that he'll get a raise) = *miser sur (le fait qu'il aura une augmentation)*
☠ *flamber* → to blaze, *jouer* → to play.

GAMBLER (n) *joueur, -euse* : I've always been a gambler = *j'ai toujours été (un) joueur* ⓪ high roller = *flambeur* ☠ *joueur* = player.

GAMBLING (n) *jeu (m) (d'argent)* : gambling isn't allowed in New York = *le jeu est interdit à New York* ⓪ casino = ← ☠ → game.

GAME (n) *jeu (m)* : chess is a difficult game = *les échecs sont un jeu difficile* ⓪ tag = *chat*, blindman's buff = *colin-maillard*, hide-and-seek = *cache-cache*

| **(you'll be) ahead of the game** = *ce sera* | *toujours ça de pris* : if you start studying for |

the exam now, you'll be ahead of the game = *si tu commences à réviser l'examen dès maintenant, ce sera toujours ça de pris*
to be on the game = *se prostituer :* she's been on the game since she was fifteen = *elle se prostitue depuis l'âge de quinze ans* = she's been hustling since she was fifteen
I beat him at his (own) game = *je l'ai battu à son propre jeu*
the game isn't worth the candle = *le jeu n'en vaut pas la chandelle*
the game's up ! = *c'est fichu !* ⓓ it's all over ! = *c'est la fin de tout !*
a game of (bridge/tennis) = *une partie de (bridge/tennis)*
let's not play games = *ne jouons pas à ce jeu-là*
to play the game = *jouer le jeu* ⓓ to go along with = *suivre*
what's his game ? = *à quel jeu joue-t-il ?*

☠ *ce qui est en jeu ...* = what's at stake ...
— *il aime le jeu* = he likes gambling
— *un jeu fantastique (théâtre)* = wonderful acting
— *c'est un jeu d'enfant* = it's child's play
— *un jeu de mots* = a play on words
— *les jeux sont faits* = the die is cast
— *faire le jeu de qqn* = to play into s.o.'s hands
— *entrer en jeu* = to come into the picture.

GAME (adj, -r, -st) *partant, -e :* we're going for a swim, are you game ? = *nous allons nous baigner, tu es partant ?* ≠ count me out = *je ne suis pas des vôtres.*

GAMUT (n) *gamme (f) :* the whole gamut of human misery = *toute la gamme des souffrances humaines* ☠ *gamme de couleurs* = range of colors.

GANG (n) 1/ *gang (m) :* a gang of teenagers killed the old lady = *un gang d'adolescents a tué la vieille dame*
gang bang = *viol collectif*
2/ *bande (f) :* the whole gang's into music = *toute la bande fait de la musique* ⓓ pals = *copains* ☠ → band.

GANGRENE (n) *gangrène (f)* ⓓ scurvy = *scorbut.*

GANGSTER (n) *gangster (m), malfaiteur (m) :* three gangsters killed during the holdup = *trois gangsters/malfaiteurs tués au cours du hold-up* ⓓ mobster = *truand.*

GANG UP ON (to, -ed) *faire bloc contre :* they ganged up on the youngest boy = *ils ont fait bloc contre le plus jeune* ⓓ to band together against = *se liguer contre.*

GAOL (n) (GB) = JAIL.

GAP (n) 1/ *fossé (m) :* a gap between rich and poor countries = *un fossé entre les pays riches et les pays pauvres,* a gap of 20 years between both wars = *un fossé de 20 ans entre les deux guerres* ⓓ hiatus = ← ☠ → ditch
to bridge a gap = *combler un fossé/un vide*
2/ *lacune (f) :* tremendous gaps in his knowledge =

d'énormes lacunes dans ses connaissances* ☠ *il y a une lacune dans la loi* = there's a loophole in the law.

GAPE AT (to, -d) *regarder avec des yeux ronds :* the child was gaping at the hooker = *l'enfant regardait la putain avec des yeux ronds* ⓓ to stare at = *fixer (des yeux).*

GARAGE (n) *garage (m) :* stop at the nearest garage for some gas = *arrête-toi au prochain garage pour prendre de l'essence* ⓓ gas station = *pompe à essence.*

GARBAGE (n inv) 1/ *ordures (f pl) :* garbage in the streets = *des ordures dans les rues* ⓓ refuse = *détritus*
garbage can = *poubelle*
garbage collector = *éboueur* = sanitation man
☠ *quelle ordure !* = what a prick !
2/ *qqch à la con :* his films are garbage = *il fait des films à la con* ⓓ nonsense = *bêtises,* hogwash = *absurdités.*

GARDEN (n) *jardin (m) (soigné et cultivé) :* we have beautiful flowers in the garden = *nous avons de belles fleurs dans le jardin* ⓓ flower = *fleur,* rake = *râteau,* hoe = *binette,* gardener = *jardinier*
garden party = *garden-party*
Garden of Eden = *jardin d'Éden*
to lead s.o. up the garden path = *faire prendre à qqn des vessies pour des lanternes* → TO HUSTLE
☠ → yard.

GARGLE (to, -d) *se gargariser* ⓓ mouthwash = *bain de bouche* ☠ *se gargariser de compliments* = to revel in compliments.

GARISH (adj) *tape-à-l'œil (inv) :* garish clothes = *des vêtements tape-à-l'œil* ⓓ gaudy = *criard,* chintzy = *clinquant.*

GARLIC (n inv) *ail (m) :* clove of garlic = *gousse d'ail,* a spicy garlic sauce = *une sauce à l'ail épicée.*

GARMENT (n) **Garment Center** = (7th Avenue) = *centre de la confection à New York (correspondant au Sentier à Paris)* ⓓ rag trade = *commerce des fringues.*

GARTER (n) *jarretière (f), jarretelle (f) :* my husband gave me a sexy garter = *mon mari m'a offert une jarretelle/une jarretière sexy* ⓓ garter belt = *porte-jarretelles,* stockings = *bas.*

GAS (n) 1/ (-(s)es) *gaz (m) :* different gases in the air = *différents gaz dans l'air* ⓓ fumes = *émanations* 2/ (inv) *essence (f) :* we have to buy some gas = *il faut que nous prenions de l'essence* = gasoline = petrol (GB) ☠· → essence
to run out of gas = *tomber en panne d'essence*
gas station = *pompe à essence* ⓓ filling station = *station-service*
step on the gas ! = *appuyez sur le champignon !*
a gas = *le pied :* the movie was a gas = *ce film, c'était le pied* ≠ a drag = *rasoir.*

GASOLINE (n) *essence (f)* = gas.

GASP (to, -ed) *être suffoqué, -e* : his parents gasped when he said "fuck it !" = *ses parents ont été suffoqués quand il a dit : « putain de merde ! »*

GATE (n) *portail (m)* : what does the sign on the gate say ? = *qu'y a-t-il d'écrit sur la plaque du portail ?* ⓧ entrance = *entrée*
to give s.o. the gate = *mettre qqn à la porte* ⓧ to give s.o. the axe = *donner ses huit jours à qqn.*

GATE-CRASH (to, -ed) *resquiller* : to gate-crash a party = *resquiller dans une soirée* **GATE-CRASHER** (n) *resquilleur, -euse.*

GATHER (to, -ed) **1/** *se rassembler* : people were gathering in the square = *les gens se rassemblaient sur la place* ⓧ to meet = *se retrouver* **2/** *rassembler* : gather your things ! = *rassemble tes affaires !* ⓧ to pick up = *ramasser*
as you probably gathered (we're having problems) = *vous vous doutiez sûrement que (nous avions des problèmes)*
from what I gather (they're divorced) = *d'après ce que j'ai compris (ils sont divorcés)*
I gather so = *je crois bien* ⓧ I assume so = *je présume*
I gather that (he's going to jilt her) = *j'ai cru comprendre qu'(il allait la plaquer)* ⓧ I reckon that = *je crois bien que,* I assume that = *je présume que*
☠ *rassembler ses idées* = to collect one's thoughts
— *rassembler tous les ouvriers* = to round up all the workers
— *elle est plus intelligente que toute sa famille rassemblée* = she's brighter than all her family put together.

GATHERING (n) *réunion (f)* : a family gathering = *une réunion de famille* ⓧ meeting = *rassemblement* ☠ → reunion.

GAUDY (adj, -ier, -iest) *criard, -e* : gaudy clothes = *des vêtements criards* ⓧ flashy = *tapageur.*

GAUNT (adj, -er, -est) *décharné, -e* : a gaunt face = *un visage décharné* ⓧ emaciated = *émacié.*

GAY (n) *homosexuel, -elle, homo* : a bar for gays = *un bar réservé aux homosexuels* ⓧ queer = *pédé,* dyke = *gouine* ≠ heterosexual = *hétérosexuel.*

GAY (adj, -er, -est) **1/** *gay, homosexuel, -elle* : New York has a large gay community = *il y a une importante communauté homosexuelle/gay à New York* ⓧ ac/dc = *ambivalent,* straight = *hétéro*
Gay Power = *Front homosexuel*
2/ *gai, -e* : a child's gay laughter = *le rire gai d'un enfant* ⓧ joyful = *réjoui,* lively = *plein de vie*
gay blade = *gai luron* ≠ sad sack = *gueule d'enterrement*
the Gay Nineties = *la Belle Époque*
☠ *être gai (ivre)* = to be tight
— *gai comme un pinson* = happy as a lark
— *c'est gai !* (sarcastic) = that's just swell !

GAZE AT (to, -d) *contempler* : to gaze at the beautiful

countryside = *contempler le superbe paysage* ⓧ to gawk at = *regarder avec des yeux de merlan frit.*

GEAR (n) **1/** *(inv) attirail (m)* : fishing/hunting gear = *attirail de pêche/de chasse* ⓧ paraphernalia = *bazar* **2/** *vitesse (f)* : gear box = *boîte de vitesses,* to shift gears = *changer de vitesse* ☠ → speed.

GEARED TO (adj) *conçu, -e pour* : high-rises are not geared to make life easy for the handicapped = *les tours ne sont pas conçues pour faciliter la vie des handicapés.*

GEE (WHIZ) ! (interj) *mince !* → GOSH !

GEEZER (n) *(vieux) schnock (m)* : what an old geezer she married ! = *quel vieux schnock elle a épousé !* ⓧ old fogey = *vieux croulant.*

GEISHA (n) *geisha (f)* : geishas singing at a Japanese stag party = *des geishas qui chantent à une soirée entre hommes au Japon.*

GEM (n) *pierre (f) précieuse* : gems on the crown = *des pierres précieuses sur la couronne* ⓧ stone = *pierre,* diamond = *diamant,* ruby = *rubis,* sapphire = *saphir,* emerald = *émeraude*
a gem = **1/** *qqch de pas piqué des hannetons* : the article was a gem = *l'article n'était pas piqué des hannetons* ⓧ a corker = *qqch de pas piqué des vers* **2/** *perle (s.o.)* : her maid's a gem = *sa bonne est une perle* ⓧ a wonder = *une vraie merveille* ☠ → pearl
the gem of (the exhibition) = *le clou de (l'exposition)*
you're a gem ! = *tu es un trésor !* ⓧ a sweetie pie = *un amour.*

GENDER (n) *genre (m)* : feminine/masculine/neuter gender = *genre féminin/masculin/neutre* ☠ → kind.

GENE (n) *gène (m)* : research being done on genes = *des recherches faites sur les gènes* ⓧ heredity = *hérédité*
☠ *il est sans-gêne* = he's a little too cool
— *où il y a de la gêne, il n'y a pas de plaisir* = feeling uptight kills all pleasure
— *être dans la gêne* = not to have much money.

GENERAL (n) *général (m)* : a four-star general = *un général quatre étoiles* ⓧ captain = *capitaine* ≠ private = *simple soldat*
in general = *en général* : the French in general don't drink milk = *en général, les Français ne boivent pas de lait* ⓧ usually = *habituellement*
☠ *la générale (théâtre)* = the dress rehearsal.

GENERAL (adj) *général, -e* : general discontent = *mécontentement général* ⓧ widespread = *largement répandu*
general assembly = *assemblée générale*
the general public = *le grand public.*

GENERALITY (n, -ies) *généralité (f)* : what you're saying is a generality = *ce que vous dites est une généralité* ≠ particularity = *particularité*
to speak in generalities = *dire des généralités.*

GENERALIZATION (n) *généralisation (f) :* that's just a generalization = *ce n'est qu'une généralisation.*

GENERALIZE (to, -d) *généraliser :* you're generalizing when you say that = *vous généralisez quand vous dites ça* ☠ *ça se généralise* = it is spreading.

GENERALLY (adj) *généralement :* we generally take our vacation in September = *nous prenons généralement nos vacances en septembre* ⓪ normally = *normalement*
generally speaking (my instincts are good) = *en général (mon instinct ne me trompe pas).*

GENERATE (to, -d) *engendrer :* publicity generates interest in products = *la publicité engendre un intérêt pour les produits* ⓪ to produce = *produire.*

GENERATION (n) *génération (f) :* the lost generation = *la génération perdue*
generation gap = *fossé entre les générations.*

GENEROSITY (n, -ies) *générosité (f) :* an act of great generosity = *un acte d'une grande générosité* ⓪ unselfishness = *désintéressement.*

GENEROUS (adj) *généreux, -euse :* a generous lover = *un amant généreux* ⓪ magnanimous = *magnanime* ≠ ungenerous = *peu généreux* **GENEROUSLY** (adv) *généreusement.*

GENETIC (adj) *génétique :* genetic engineering = *manipulations génétiques.*

GENITALS (n pl) *organes (m pl) génitaux, parties (f pl)* (LV) : an infection on his genitals = *une infection de ses organes génitaux.*

GENIUS (n, -es) *génie (m) :* a family of geniuses = *une famille de génies* ⓪ brain = *cerveau.*

GENOCIDE (n) *génocide (m) :* Hitler's genocide of the Jews = *le génocide des juifs par Hitler* ⓪ holocaust = *holocauste.*

GENTILE (n) *gentil (m), non-juif, -juive :* she married a gentile = *elle a épousé un non-juif/un gentil* ≠ Jewish = *juif.*

GENTLE (adj, -r, -st) *doux, douce :* a gentle manner/dog = *une manière douce/un chien doux* ⓪ tender = *tendre*
gentle as a lamb = *doux comme un agneau*
☠ → soft.

GENTLEMAN (n, -men) *monsieur (m) :* ladies and gentlemen = *mesdames et messieurs*
gentleman farmer = *gentleman-farmer*
gentleman's agreement = ←, *accord verbal qui engage les deux parties*
to be a gentleman = *être un gentleman*
☠ → mister.

GENTLY (adv) *avec/en douceur :* I comb my child's hair gently = *je coiffe mon enfant avec douceur.*

GENUINE (adj) *authentique :* a genuine Picasso = *un authentique Picasso* = authentic ≠ fake = *faux*
genuine leather = *cuir véritable.*

GENUINELY (adv) *véritablement :* she's genuinely sorry = *elle est véritablement désolée* → VERY.

GEOGRAPHY (n) *géographie (f) :* to study geography = *faire des études de géographie* ⓪ history = *histoire.*

GEOLOGIST (n) *géologue (m, f) :* she is a well-paid geologist = *c'est une géologue bien payée* ⓪ archeologist = *archéologue.*

GEOMETRY (n) *géométrie (f) :* plane/solid geometry = *géométrie plane/dans l'espace* ⓪ arithmetic = *arithmétique.*

GEORGE (n pr.) **by George !** = *nom d'un chien !* → GOSH !

GERM (n) *germe (m) :* germs in the air = *des germes dans l'air* ⓪ microbe = ←
germ warfare = *guerre bactériologique.*

GERMANY (n) *Allemagne (f)* **GERMAN** (n, adj) *Allemand, -e* ⓪ Kraut = *Boche,* Jerry = *Schleu,* Fritz = ←.

GERRYMANDER (to, -ed) *faire du charcutage électoral :* they won by gerrymandering = *ils ont gagné en faisant du charcutage électoral* ⓪ constituency = *circonscription.*

GESTICULATE (to, -d) *gesticuler :* she gesticulates a lot when she's excited = *elle gesticule beaucoup quand elle est excitée.*

GESTURE (n) *geste (m) :* a meaningful gesture = *un geste rempli de signification* ⓪ sign = *signe*
☠ *joindre le geste à la parole* = to suit the action to the word
— *s'exprimer par gestes* = to talk with one's hands.

GESTURE (to, -d) *faire un geste* ⓪ to wave = *faire un signe de la main.*

GET (to, got, got or gotten) **1/** *trouver :* where did you get that ? = *où avez-vous trouvé ça ?,* they got a new apartment = *ils ont trouvé un nouvel appartement* ☠ → to find **2/** *obtenir :* to get a raise/a degree = *obtenir une augmentation/un diplôme* ≠ to procure = *procurer* ☠ → to obtain **3/** *saisir :* I didn't get what you said = *je n'ai pas saisi ce que vous avez dit* ⓪ to catch on = *piger* ☠ → to seize **4/** *recevoir :* did you get my letter ? = *est-ce que vous avez reçu ma lettre ?* = did you receive my letter ? ☠ → to receive **5/** *aller chercher :* please get me a Scotch = *s'il vous plaît, allez me chercher un whisky,* get some bread for dinner = *va chercher du pain pour le dîner*

you don't get anything for nothing = *on n'a rien sans rien*

what does it get you ? = *qu'est-ce que ça vous apporte ?*

to get s.o. = *avoir qqn* : I couldn't get you last night (on the phone) = *je n'ai pas pu vous avoir hier soir (au téléphone)* ⓧ to reach = *joindre*

get cracking ! = *grouille-toi !* ⓧ get a move on ! = *magne-toi !*

to get (dressed, angry, tired, lost, etc.) = *s'(habiller), se (fâcher, fatiguer, perdre, etc.)*

to get going = *mettre en route* : it took two years to get the business going = *il a fallu deux ans pour mettre l'affaire en route*

let's get going (it's late) ! = *fichons le camp (il est tard) !* → TO LEAVE

to get it = 1/ *prendre* : when he gets home, he's going to get it = *quand il rentrera à la maison, qu'est-ce qu'il va prendre !* ⓧ to be in for it = *en prendre pour son grade* ☠ → to take 2/ *saisir* : I get it ! = *je saisis !* ⓧ to understand = *comprendre* ☠ → to seize

to get knocked up = *se faire engrosser* : she got knocked up when she was sixteen = *elle s'est fait engrosser à seize ans*

we aren't getting anywhere = *nous n'avançons pas* = **we're getting nowhere**

to get (stg) started = *démarrer (qqch)*: the meeting got started late = *le meeting a démarré tard*

get lost ! = *fiche-moi le camp !* → BUZZ OFF !

she's got it ! = *elle a du chien !* ⓧ she's a good-looking tomato ! = *c'est une belle plante !*

you've got me there ! = *tu m'as collé !* : who was the third President of the United States ? — I don't know, you've got me there ! = *qui était le troisième*

président des États-Unis ? — je ne sais, pas tu m'as collé !

to get (ten years) = *écoper (de) (dix ans)* ⓧ to be sentenced to = *être condamné à* ☠ *écoper pour qqn* = to take the rap for s.o.

to get there/to Paris/home = *arriver là-bas/à Paris/chez soi*

get this ! = *tenez-vous bien !* : get this ! he's been sleeping with his mother-in-law ! = *tenez-vous bien ! il couche avec sa belle-mère !* ⓧ listen to this ! = *écoutez-moi ça !*

to get what's coming = *n'avoir que ce qu'on mérite* : when she in turn takes a lover, he'll get what's coming to him ! = *si un jour elle prend un amant à son tour, il n'aura que ce qu'il mérite !* ⓧ to give s.o. a dose of his own medicine = *rendre à qqn la monnaie de sa pièce*

to get married/divorced = *se marier/divorcer*

he'll get his ! = *il ne l'emportera pas en paradis !* ⓧ he'll pay for it ! = *il me le paiera !*

he's got it made (in his new job) = *il se la coule douce (dans son nouveau boulot)* ⓧ he's sitting pretty = *il a la belle vie*

he's got what it takes (to be a singer) = *il a ce qu'il faut (pour être chanteur)*

I'll get him ! = *je l'aurai !* ⓧ I'll get back at him ! = *je me vengerai de lui !*

it gets me (that he lies so much !) = *ça me tape sur le système (qu'il mente comme ça !)* ⓧ it annoys me = *ça m'énerve*

when you get to know him = *quand on le connaît mieux* : he's nice when you get to know him = *il est sympa quand on le connaît mieux*

you got me ! = *je n'en sais rien !* ⓧ search me ! = *mystère et boule de gomme !*

---

to get stg across = *faire passer qqch* : he got his idea across = *il a fait passer son idée*

to get ahead = *faire son chemin* : she's the kind of gal who'll get ahead = *c'est le genre de fille qui fera son chemin* ≠ to fail = *échouer*

to get along = 1/ *se débrouiller* : how are you getting along ? = *comment vous débrouillez-vous ?* = how are you getting on ? ☠ → to manage 2/ *s'entendre* : I know the two of you will get along = *je sais que vous allez vous entendre tous les deux* ☠ → to hear

to get along on = *s'en sortir avec* : I don't know how they get along on so little money = *je ne sais pas comment ils s'en sortent avec si peu d'argent*

to get around = 1/ *se déplacer* : since she broke her leg, she's been having difficulty getting around = *elle éprouve des difficultés à se déplacer depuis qu'elle s'est cassé la jambe* ☠ → to shift 2/ *contourner* (law) : to get around the law = *contourner la loi* ⓧ to by-pass = *court-circuiter* ☠ *contourner une ville* = to go around a town 3/ *s'ébruiter* : it got around that they're sleeping together = *le fait qu'ils couchent ensemble s'est ébruité*

there's no getting around that = *il n'y a pas à tortiller* : we have to pay taxes, there's no getting around that = *il n'y a pas à tortiller, il faut payer ses impôts*

to get around to stg = *avoir*

un moment pour (faire) qqch : I'll do it when I get around to it = *je le ferai quand j'aurai un moment*

what are you getting at ? = *où voulez-vous en venir ?* = what are you driving at ?

to get away = 1/ *s'enfuir* : the gangsters got away = *les malfaiteurs se sont enfuis* ⓧ to escape = *s'échapper* 2/ *partir un peu* : are you going to be able to get away this summer ? = *est-ce que vous pourrez partir un peu cet été ?*

there's no getting away from it = *on ne peut pas le nier* : there's no getting away from the fact that smoking causes cancer = *on ne peut pas nier le fait que le tabac est cancérigène*

to get away with stg = *s'en*

sortir comme ça : you won't get away with it = *vous ne vous en sortirez pas comme ça* ⓓ you'll get what's coming to you = *tu n'auras que ce que tu mérites*

to get back = *rentrer* : when did you get back ? = *quand êtes-vous rentré ?* ☠ → to return

to get stg back = *récupérer qqch* : to get one's money/job back = *récupérer son argent/son boulot* ⓓ to recover = *retrouver*

to get back at s.o. = *avoir qqn au tournant* : I'll get back at him = *je l'aurai au tournant* ⓓ I'll get even with him = *je me vengerai de lui*

to get back to = *revenir à* : let's get back to what we were talking about = *revenons à ce que nous disions*

to get by = *s'en sortir* : don't worry about me, I'll always get by = *ne t'en fais pas pour moi, je m'en sortirai toujours* ⓓ to manage = *se débrouiller*

to get s.o. down = *ficher le moral de qqn par terre* : her remark/the rain got me down = *sa réflexion/la pluie m'a fichu le moral par terre* ⓓ to depress = *déprimer*

to get down from (a horse/a ladder) = *descendre d'(un cheval/une échelle)*

to get down to = *se mettre à* : let's get down to work = *mettons-nous au travail* ⓓ to go at it = *mettre les bouchées doubles*

to get in = 1/ *monter (dans)* : get in the car = *monte dans la voiture* ≠ to get out = *sortir de* ☠ → to rise 2/ *arriver* : what time does the train get in ? = *à quelle heure arrive le train ?* ☠ → to arrive 3/ *entrer* : if the door was locked how did you get in ? = *si la porte était fermée à clef, comment êtes-vous entré ?* ☠ → to enter 4/ *rentrer* : we got in late last night = *nous sommes rentrés tard hier soir* ☠ → to return 5/ *passer* : do you think the Republicans will get in next time ? = *est-ce que vous pensez que les républicains passeront la prochaine fois ?* ☠ → to pass

to get one's in = *en tirer vengeance* : I'll get mine in = *j'en tirerai vengeance* ⓓ to return like for like = *rendre la pareille*

to get in on stg = *profiter de qqch* : to get in on a scholarship program = *profiter d'une distribution de bourses*

to get into = 1/ *passer* : give me a minute to get into a dress = *donnez-moi une minute pour passer une robe* ⓓ to slip on = *enfiler* ☠ → to pass 2/ *entrer dans* : the movie was too difficult, I couldn't get into it = *le film était trop difficile, je n'ai pas pu entrer dedans*

I didn't know what I was getting into = *je ne savais pas dans quoi je fourrais les pieds*

what's got into you ? = *qu'est-ce qui vous prend ?*

to get off = 1/ *descendre (de)* : I got off the subway at Broadway = *je suis descendu du métro à Broadway* ≠ to get on = *monter* ☠ → to descend 2/ *s'en tirer* : he got off with a light sentence = *il s'en est tiré avec une peine légère* 3/ *arrêter de travailler* : what time do you get off ? = *à quelle heure arrêtez-vous de travailler ?*

to get (three weeks) off = *avoir (trois semaines) de congé/de libre*

where does he get off (talking to me like that) ? = *pour qui se prend-il (pour me parler comme ça) ?*

get off it ! = *arrête ton char !* → BUZZ OFF !

to get off on = *prendre son pied* : she gets off on rock music = *elle prend son pied avec la musique rock* ⓓ to dig = *botter*

to get on = 1/ *monter (dans)* : to get on the bus = *monter dans le bus* ≠ to get off = *descendre* ☠ → to rise 2/ *s'entendre* : we get on well = *nous nous entendons bien* ☠ → to hear 3/ *se débrouiller* : how are you getting on ? = *comment vous débrouillez-vous ?* ☠ → to manage

to be getting on = *prendre de l'âge* : his father's getting on = *son père prend de l'âge* ≠ to be

still spry = *être encore vert*

to get it on = *s'envoyer en l'air* : we got it on last night = *on s'est envoyé en l'air hier soir* ⓓ to screw = *baiser*

to get on to stg = *réussir à aborder qqch* : we didn't get on to what was really the matter = *on n'a pas réussi à aborder le vrai problème*

let's get on with it ! = *passons aux actes !* : we've wasted enough time, let's get on with it ! = *nous avons assez perdu de temps, passons aux actes !*

to get out = 1/ *sortir* : we get out at five = *nous sortons à cinq heures*, he got out of the hospital = *il est sorti de l'hôpital* ☠ → to go out 2/ *se savoir* : if it ever gets out that I told you, I'll be in trouble = *si jamais on sait que je vous l'ai dit, j'aurai des ennuis* ☠ → to know

to get out of stg = *se libérer de qqch* : I accepted his invitation and I can't get out of it now = *j'ai accepté son invitation et je ne peux plus m'en libérer*

what will you get out of it ? = *qu'est-ce que vous en retirerez ?*

get out (of here) ! = *sortez (d'ici) !*

to get out from under = *refaire surface* : I'm deep in debt and it'll take me months to get out from under = *je suis terriblement endetté et cela me prendra des mois pour refaire surface*

to get stg out of s.o. = *soutirer qqch à qqn* : I couldn't get any money/information out of him = *je n'ai pu lui soutirer aucun argent/aucun renseignement*

you get out of it what you put into it = *vous récoltez ce que vous avez semé*

to get over = *se remettre (de)* : to get over a cold/one's parents' death = *se remettre d'un rhume/de la mort de ses parents* ⓓ to recover = *se rétablir*

I can't get over it ! = *je n'en reviens pas !* ⓓ I was taken aback ! = *j'en ai eu le souffle coupé !*

to get stg over to s.o. = *faire comprendre qqch à qqn* : I couldn't get my idea over to Jack

= je n'ai pas pu faire comprendre mon idée à Jack

to get stg over with = en finir avec qqch : go to the doctor and get it over with = va voir le docteur et finis-en avec ça

to get through = finir : I won't be able to get through this translation today = je ne pourrai pas finir cette traduction aujourd'hui ☠ → to finish

to get stg through s.o. = avoir qqch par qqn : I got the job through my brother = j'ai eu le boulot par mon frère

to get through to s.o. = 1/ obtenir qqn : I called last night, but I couldn't get through to you = j'ai appelé hier soir, mais je n'ai pas pu vous obtenir 2/ faire entendre à qqn : I tried to convince her but I couldn't get through to her = j'ai essayé de la convaincre, mais je n'ai

rien pu lui faire entendre

to get to = arriver à : what time did you get to New York ? = à quelle heure êtes-vous arrivé à New York ?

to get to s.o. = atteindre profondément qqn : the poverty of India got to me = la pauvreté en Inde m'a profondément atteint ⓪ to affect = affecter

to get s.o. to = demander à qqn de : get him to help you = demande-lui de t'aider

to have got to = il faut que : I've got to go now = il faut que j'y aille maintenant

to get together = se voir : let's get together Friday = voyons-nous vendredi = to see each other ☠ → to see

to get it together = se reprendre en main : you'd better get it together and stop drinking so much = tu ferais mieux de te

reprendre en main et de ne pas boire tant ⓪ to get a grip on o.s. = se ressaisir

to get up = se lever : what time do you get up ? = à quelle heure vous levez-vous ? ≠ to go to sleep = aller se coucher ☠ → to raise

to get stg up = arranger qqch : what can we get up for the week-end ? = que peut-on arranger pour le week-end ?

to get it up = bander : the first time we made love he had trouble getting it up = la première fois qu'on a fait l'amour, il a eu du mal à bander ≠ to go limp = débander

to get with it = se mettre dans le coup : if you want to stay young, you'd better get with it ! = si tu veux rester jeune, il faut te mettre dans le coup !

GETAWAY (n) **to make a (quick) getaway** = prendre (rapidement) la fuite
a getaway car = une voiture pour s'évader.

GET-TOGETHER (n) petite réunion (f) : we're having a family get-together Saturday night = nous avons une petite réunion de famille samedi soir ⓪ party = soirée.

GETUP (n) accoutrement (m) : what a strange getup ! = quel accoutrement étrange ! ⓪ dress = tenue.

GET-UP-AND-GO (n) fougue (f) : she's full of get-up-and-go = elle est pleine de fougue ⓪ go = allant.

GHASTLY (adj, -ier, iest) effroyable : you look ghastly ! = tu as une tête effroyable ! → AWFUL.

GHETTO (n, -(e)s) ghetto (m) : he survived the Warsaw ghetto = il a survécu au ghetto de Varsovie ⓪ racism = racisme.

GHOST (n) fantôme (m), revenant (m) : I saw a ghost = j'ai vu un fantôme/un revenant ⓪ specter = spectre
you don't have a ghost of a chance = vous n'avez pas l'ombre d'une chance ≠ you have a slight chance = vous avez une faible chance
ghost town = ville fantôme
☠ tiens, un revenant ! = long time, no see !
— fantôme → phantom.

GHOSTWRITER (n) nègre (m) : his autobiography was written by a ghostwriter = son autobiographie a été écrite par un nègre ⓪ author = auteur ☠ → Negro.

GI (n) GI (m) ⓪ private = simple soldat.

GIANT (n) géant, -e : my brother's a giant ! = mon frère est un géant ! ≠ dwarf = nain.

GIANT (adj) (de) géant, -e : giant steps = des pas de géant ≠ tiny = minuscule.

GIBBERISH (n inv) baragouin (m) : enough of your gibberish ! = arrête ce baragouin ! ⓪ mumbo jumbo = galimatias.

GIBE (n) raillerie (f) : no gibes about my cooking = pas de railleries sur ma cuisine = jibe ⓪ sarcasm = sarcasme.

GIBE (to, -d) **to gibe at s.o. (because he stutters)** = railler qqn (parce qu'il bégaie) ⓪ to make fun of = se moquer de.

GIDDY (adj, -ier, -iest) qui a le fou rire : the children were so happy they were giddy = les enfants étaient tellement heureux qu'ils avaient le fou rire ⓪ punch-drunk = sonné.

GIFT (n) 1/ cadeau (m) : a birthday gift = un cadeau d'anniversaire ⓪ gift wrapping = papier cadeau ☠ il ne fait pas de cadeau = he's a tough customer 2/ don (m) : a gift for music = un don pour la musique ⓪ a feeling for = le sens de
to have the gift of gab = avoir du bagou ⓪ to talk a mile a minute = ne pas avoir la langue dans sa poche
don't look a gift horse in the mouth = à cheval donné on ne regarde pas les dents
☠ il a le don de m'énerver = he has the knack of getting on my nerves.

GIFTED (adj) doué, -e : a gifted musician = un musicien doué ⓪ talented = talentueux
gifted children = des (enfants) surdoués.

GIG (n) *courte représentation (f)* : the band's doing a gig in New York = *l'orchestre donne une courte représentation à New York.*

GIGANTIC (adj) *gigantesque* : a gigantic building = *un immeuble gigantesque* ⑩ huge = *immense.*

GIGGLE (n) *rire (m) bébête* **GIGGLE** (to, -d) *rire bêtement* : the girls were giggling = *les filles riaient bêtement* ⑩ to be giddy = *avoir le fou rire.*

GIGOLO (n) *gigolo (m)* : she's keeping a gigolo = *elle entretient un gigolo* ⑩ lover = *amant.*

GILT-EDGED (adj) **gilt-edged stocks** = *des valeurs en or* ⑩ blue-chip stocks = *des valeurs de père de famille.*

GIMMICK (n) *truc (m), astuce (f)* : the publicity campaign needs a good gimmick = *il faudrait trouver un bon truc/une bonne astuce pour lancer la campagne publicitaire* ⑩ find = *trouvaille*, device = *truc* ☠ *je ne saisis pas bien l'astuce* = I don't get the joke.

GIN (n) *gin (m)* : I'll have a gin straight = *je prendrai un gin sec* ⑩ vodka = ←
gin rummy = ←

GINGER (n) *gingembre (m)* : put some ginger in your curry sauce = *mettez du gingembre dans votre sauce au curry* ⑩ cinnamon = *cannelle.*

GIRAFFE (n) *girafe (f)* ⑩ zebra = *zèbre.*

GIRDLE (n) *gaine (f)* : girdles are out = *les gaines sont passées de mode* ⑩ garter belt = *porte-jarretelles.*

GIRL (n) *fille (f)* : there are 20 boys and 2 girls in the class = *il y a 20 garçons et 2 filles dans la classe* ⑩ lass = *jouvencelle*, maiden = *pucelle*, young lady = *demoiselle* ☠ *ma fille* = my daughter
— *jouer la fille de l'air* = to vanish into thin air
— *fille mère* = unwed mother
— *courir les filles* = to be on the make
— *c'est une fille sympa* = she's a nice gal
— *fille de joie* = harlot
— *vieille fille* = old maid.

GIRLFRIEND (n) 1/ *copine (f)* : she invited ten girlfriends to her birthday party = *elle a invité dix copines à son anniversaire* = pal ⑩ best friend = *meilleure amie* 2/ *petite amie (f)* : he came with his girlfriend = *il est venu avec sa petite amie* ≠ boyfriend = *petit ami.*

GIST (n) *sens (m) général* : I didn't get the gist of his speech = *je n'ai pas saisi le sens général de son discours* ⑩ drift = *sens.*

GIVE (to, gave, given) *donner, offrir* (gift) : give me the salt, please = *donnez-moi le sel, s'il vous plaît*, he gave me a watch for my birthday = *il m'a donné/offert une montre pour mon anniversaire*

dont give me that ! = *pour qui me prends-tu ?*
give or take ... = *à ... près* : we'll finish at the end of the month give or take a day or two = *à un ou deux jours près, nous aurons fini à la fin du mois*
to give s.o. stg to think about = *donner à qqn à réfléchir* : his remarks gave me something to think about = *ses remarques m'ont donné à réfléchir*
give ! = *raconte !* ⑩ spill it out ! = *accouche !*
what gives ? = *qu'est-ce qui se passe ?* = what's up ?

to give away = 1/ *donner* : why did you give your watch away ? = *pourquoi as-tu donné ta montre ?* 2/ *conduire à l'autel* : to give the bride away = *conduire la mariée à l'autel*
to give s.o. away = *trahir qqn* : she said she was American but her accent gave her away = *elle a dit qu'elle était américaine, mais son accent l'a trahie*
to give ... down = *verser (un acompte de) ...* : I gave ten dollars down = *j'ai versé (un acompte de) dix dollars* ⑩ to leave a deposit = *laisser des arrhes*
to give in = 1/ *céder* : I'm tired of always giving in to my husband = *j'en ai assez de toujours céder à mon mari* ⑩ to capitulate = *capituler* ☠ *le pont a cédé* = the bridge gave way

2/ *remettre* : give in your papers = *remettez vos copies* = hand in your papers ☠ → to postpone
to give it to s.o. = 1/ *engueuler qqn* : I was late and my mother really gave it to me = *j'étais en retard et ma mère m'a vraiment engueulé* → TO LAMBAST 2/ *tomber sur qqn à bras raccourcis* : the gang gave it to him = *le gang lui est tombé dessus à bras raccourcis* → TO HIT
to give s.o. stg off = *faire une remise à qqn* : he gave me ten percent off = *il m'a fait une remise de dix pour cent*
to give onto = *donner sur* : the apartment gives onto a park = *l'appartement donne sur un parc*
to give out = 1/ *distribuer* : the neo-Nazis are giving out anti-semitic leaflets = *les néo-nazis distribuent des tracts antisémi-*

tes = to hand out = to distribute ≠ to collect = *ramasser* 2/ *s'épuiser* : our supplies gave out = *nos réserves se sont épuisées* ☠ → to exhaust
to give stg back (to) = *rendre qqch (à)* : lend me your pen, I'll give it back to you later = *prête-moi ton stylo, je te le rendrai tout à l'heure*
to give up = 1/ *abandonner* : she gave up her career for her husband = *elle a abandonné sa carrière pour son mari*, the work is too difficult, I give up = *le travail est trop difficile, j'abandonne (la partie)* ⑩ to throw in the sponge = *jeter l'éponge* ☠ → to abandon 2/ *arrêter* : I gave up drinking = *j'ai arrêté de boire* ☠ → to stop
to give o.s. up = *se livrer* : he gave himself up to the cops = *il*

s'est livré aux flics ≠ to hold out = *tenir bon* 💀 → to deliver **I give up (tell me) !** = *je donne ma langue au chat (dis-*	*moi) !* ≠ take a guess ! = *devine !* = guess ! **to give up on s.o.** = *désespérer qqn :* you don't understand	anything, I give up on you ! = *vous ne comprenez rien, vous me désespérez !*

💀 *se donner de la peine/du mal pour* = to take a lot of trouble to — *qu'est-ce qu'on donne au cinéma ?* = what's playing at the movies ? — *je lui donne 50 ans* = I'd say he's fifty — *ils l'ont donné* = they ratted on him — *ça n'a rien donné ≠ ça a donné qqch* = nothing	came of it/it came to nothing ≠ something came of it — *se donner des airs* = to put on airs — *donner dans (le jazz)* = to be into (jazz) — *c'est à vous de donner (cartes)* = it's your turn to deal (cards) — *offrir* → to offer.

GIVE-AND-TAKE (n) **it's give-and-take** = *c'est donnant, donnant* ⓪ one good turn deserves another = *c'est un échange de bons procédés*.

GIVEAWAY (n) *preuve* (f) *manifeste :* his remark was a giveaway that he had stolen the money = *sa remarque était une preuve manifeste qu'il avait volé l'argent* ⓪ clue = *indice*.

GIVEN (adj) *étant donné :* given the present rate of inflation, we'll never be able to buy a house = *étant donné le taux actuel de l'inflation, nous ne pourrons jamais acheter de maison*
at a given time = *à un moment donné*
to be given to (drink) = *s'adonner à (la boisson)*
given that = *étant donné que :* given that the rain hasn't stopped, I'll stay in = *étant donné que la pluie n'a pas cessé, je reste à la maison* ⓪ since = *puisque*.

GIVING (adj) *qui se donne beaucoup :* a giving personality = *quelqu'un qui se donne beaucoup ≠* selfish = *égoïste*.

GLAD (adj, -der, -dest) *content, -e :* I'm glad that you came = *je suis content que tu sois venu* ⓪ delighted = *enchanté* 💀 → content
I'm glad to (meet you/see you again) = *je suis ravi de (faire votre connaissance/vous revoir)* ⓪ how do you do ?* = *enchanté !*

GLADIATOR (n) *gladiateur* (m) *:* gladiators often fought animals = *les gladiateurs combattaient souvent contre des animaux* ⓪ arena = *arène*.

GLADLY (adv) *volontiers :* I'll gladly help you = *je vous aiderai volontiers* ⓪ with pleasure = *avec plaisir* 💀 → willingly.

GLAMOR (n) *glamour* (m), *éclat* (m) *:* the glamor of Hollywood = *l'éclat/le glamour d'Hollywood* ⓪ brio = ← / *panache*, sparkle = *lustre*
💀 *voler en éclats* = to burst into smithereens
— *rire aux éclats* = to laugh heartily
— *faire un éclat* = to make a scandal
— *un éclat* = a chip/a splinter.

GLAMORIZE (to, -d) *embellir :* you're glamorizing what happened = *tu embellis ce qui s'est passé* ⓪ to enhance = *mettre en valeur*.

GLAMOROUS (adj) *plein, -e d'éclat :* a glamorous life = *une vie pleine d'éclat* ⓪ exciting = *passionnant*.

GLANCE (n) *coup* (m) *d'œil :* take a glance at this = *jettes-y un coup d'œil* ⓪ glimpse = *regard furtif*.

GLANCE (to, -d) *jeter un coup d'œil :* he glanced into the room and walked away = *il a jeté un coup d'œil dans la pièce et est parti*
to glance over (a report) = *jeter un coup d'œil sur (un rapport)* = to look over.

GLAND (n) *glande* (f) ⓪ organ = *organe*.

GLARE (n) **1/** *lumière* (f) *crue :* the glare of the headlights = *la lumière crue des phares* ⓪ glow = *lueur* **2/** *regard* (m) *irrité :* a glare in his eyes = *un regard irrité*.

GLARE (to, -d) *lancer un regard irrité :* he glared at me when I arrived late = *il m'a lancé un regard irrité quand je suis arrivé en retard* ⓪ to stare = *fixer (des yeux)*.

GLARING (adj) *criant, -e :* a glaring injustice = *une injustice criante* ⓪ flagrant = ←.

GLASS (n) **1/** (-es) *verre* (m) *:* a glass of milk = *un verre de lait* ⓪ coaster = *dessous de verre* **2/** (inv) *verre* (m) *:* is the vase made of glass ? = *est-ce que ce vase est en verre ?* ⓪ glassblower = *souffleur de verre*
a pane of glass = *une vitre*
💀 *verres de contact* = contact lenses
— *se noyer dans un verre d'eau* = to make too much out of stg
— *avoir un verre dans le nez* = to have had one too many
— *prendre un verre* = to have a drink.

GLASS (adj) *de/en verre :* a glass box = *une boîte en verre*.

GLASSES (n pl) *lunettes* (f pl) *:* to wear glasses = *porter des lunettes* = spectacles (GB) ⓪ binoculars = *jumelles*, sunglasses = *lunettes de soleil* = shades, contact lenses = *verres de contact*.

GLIB (adj, -ber, -best) *désinvolte :* a glib answer = *une réponse désinvolte* ⓪ flippant = *cavalier*.

GLIDE (to, -d) *planer :* a plane glides = *un avion plane* ⓪ glider = *planeur* 💀 *planer à (l'acide)* = to get high on/to be spaced out on (acid).

GLIMMER (n) *faible lueur (f)* : a glimmer of hope = *une faible lueur d'espoir* ⓓ gleam = *lueur* **GLIMMER** (to, -ed) *luire faiblement.*

GLIMPSE (n) *coup (m) d'œil* : take a glimpse at this = *jette un coup d'œil là-dessus* ⓓ peep = *regard rapide.*

GLISTEN (to, -ed) *chatoyer* : sun oil glistened on her tanned body = *l'huile solaire chatoyait sur son corps bronzé* ⓓ to glitter = *briller.*

GLITTER (to, -ed) *briller* : her jewels glitter = *ses bijoux brillent* ⓓ to sparkle = *étinceler* ☠ → to shine.

GLOAT (to, -ed) *jubiler* : he gloated over my mistakes = *il jubilait (à cause) de mes erreurs.*

GLOBAL (adj) *global, -e* : a global problem = *un problème global* ≠ partial = *partiel.*

GLOBE (n) *globe (m)* ⓓ sphere = *sphère.*

GLOBE-TROTTER (n) *globe-trotter (m, f)* ⓓ adventurer = *aventurier.*

GLOOM (n) *morosité (f)* : what gloom in this house ! = *quelle morosité dans cette maison !* ≠ joy = *joie.*

GLOOMY (adj, -ier, -iest) *lugubre* : a gloomy day/outlook = *une journée/un aspect lugubre* ⓓ sullen = *renfrogné* ≠ joyous = *joyeux*
Gloomy Gus = *ténébreux* : don't be such a Gloomy Gus = *ne sois pas si ténébreux* ≠ gay blade = *gai luron.*

GLORIFY (to, -ied) 1/ *glorifier* : to glorify God = *glorifier Dieu* ⓓ to praise = *louer* 2/ *porter aux nues* : she glorifies her husband = *elle porte son mari aux nues.*

GLORIOUS (adj) *glorieux, -euse* (weather), *sensationnel, -elle* : what a glorious evening ! = *quelle soirée sensationnelle !* → WONDERFUL.

GLORY (n inv) *gloire (f)* : for the glory of it = *pour la gloire* ⓓ fame = *renommée.*

GLOSSARY (n) *glossaire (m)* : a glossary at the end of the book = *un glossaire à la fin de l'ouvrage.*

GLOSS OVER (to, -ed) *glisser sur* : he glossed over my mistake = *il a glissé sur l'erreur que j'avais commise* ≠ to pick up = *relever.*

GLOVE (n) *gant (m)* : leather gloves = *des gants de cuir* ⓓ mitten = *moufle*
to fit like a glove = *aller comme un gant*
glove compartment = *boîte à gants*
☠ *gant de toilette* = washcloth.

GLOW (n) *lueur (f)* : a happy glow in her eyes = *une lueur de bonheur dans ses yeux* ⓓ glimmer = *faible lueur* ☠ *une lueur d'(intelligence)* = a flash of (intelligence).

GLOW (to, -ed) *être rayonnant, -e* : she's so happy she's glowing = *elle est rayonnante de bonheur.*

GLOWING (adj) *rayonnant, -e* : a glowing smile = *un sourire rayonnant*
in glowing terms = *en termes élogieux.*

GLUE (n inv) *colle (f) (forte)* : buy some glue for the chair = *achète de la colle pour la chaise*
☠ *vivre à la colle* = to shack up
— *une colle (examen)* = a drill.

GLUE (to, -d) **to be glued to (the television)** = *être collé à (la télévision).*

GLUM (adj, -mer, -mest) *maussade* : why do you look so glum ? = *pourquoi avez-vous l'air si maussade ?* ⓓ sullen = *renfrogné* ☠ *un temps maussade* = dreary weather.

GLUTTON (n) *glouton, -onne* : gluttons eat anything = *les gloutons mangent n'importe quoi*
a glutton for punishment = *un masochiste*
a glutton for work = *un bourreau de travail* = a workaholic.

G-MAN (n, -men) *agent (m) du FBI* ⓓ undercover agent = *agent infiltré.*

GNAW (to, -ed) *ronger* : to gnaw a bone = *ronger un os* ☠ *être rongé par les souvenirs* = to be plagued by memories
— *se ronger les ongles* = to bite one's nails.

GNP (abbr) = Gross National Product = *PNB (m)* = *Produit national brut.*

GO (n) **to have a go at** = *faire un essai* : have a go at it, it isn't so difficult = *faites un essai, ce n'est pas si difficile* ⓓ a shot = *un coup*
to be on the go = *être sur la brèche* : I've been on the go all day = *j'ai été sur la brèche toute la journée* ≠ to twiddle one's thumbs = *se tourner les* | *pouces*
to be full of go = *être plein d'allant* ⓓ to be full of pep = *avoir du pep*
to make a go of = *faire une réussite de* : she made a go of the business = *elle a fait une réussite de cette affaire* ≠ to fail = *échouer.*

GO (to, went, gone) 1/ *aller* : where are you going ? = *où allez-vous ?*, I'm going home = *je vais à la maison* ⓓ to come = *venir*, to show up = *se pointer*

☠ *cette robe me va* = that dress suits/fits me
— *ça va ?* = how are things ?
— *allons !* = come on !

— *y aller carrément* = not to pull punches
— *comment allez-vous ?* = how are you ?

2/ *se passer* : how dit it go ? = *comment cela s'est-il passé ?*, things went well = *ça s'est bien passé* ☠ → to pass

---

do you have to go ? = *tu veux aller aux toilettes ?* ① to go to the john = *aller au petit coin*
going, going, gone ! = *une fois, deux fois, trois fois, adjugé, vendu !*
who goes there ? = *qui va là ?*
to be going to (+ verb) = *aller (+ verbe)* : I'm going to quit smoking = *je vais arrêter de fumer*, they're going to write you soon = *ils vont bientôt vous écrire*, I was going to call you = *j'allais vous appeler*
to go far = 1/ *aller loin* : with her brains, she'll go far = *avec son intelligence, elle ira loin* 2/ *faire long feu* : money doesn't go far today = *aujourd'hui l'argent ne fait pas long feu*
how goes it ? = *ça va ?* ① how's tricks ? = *ça biche ?*
how's (your work) going ? = *ça marche (le travail) ?* ① how are things ? = *ça va ?*
I must be going = *il faut que j'y aille* → TO LEAVE
to go to sleep = *aller se coucher* ① to go to bed = aller au lit
it just goes to show you ! = *tu vois bien !* → THAT'S LIFE !
to go upstairs ≠ downstairs = *monter ≠ descendre les escaliers*
it goes without saying = *cela va sans dire* : it goes without saying that I'll help you = *je vous aiderai, cela va sans dire* ① obviously = *de toute évidence*
... to go = 1/ *à emporter* : sandwiches to go = *sandwiches à emporter* 2/ *encore à (faire, etc.)* : one finished, three to go = *un de fini, trois encore à faire*
to go and ... = *aller (faire)* : he went and told her the truth = *il est allé lui dire la vérité*
to go (crazy/mad/nuts/etc.) = *devenir (fou/dingue/etc.)* : when he heard that he went mad = *en entendant ça, il est devenu fou* ☠ → to become
where do we go from here ? = *et maintenant ?*
(her husband/this system) has got to go ! = *on l'a assez vu (son mari/ce système) !*

to go about stg = *s'y prendre* : you're going about it the wrong way = *vous vous y prenez mal*
to go after = *se battre pour avoir* : when she wants something, she goes after it = *quand elle veut quelque chose, elle se bat pour l'avoir*
to go against = *aller à l'encontre de* : giving advances goes against the company's policy = *le paiement d'avances va à l'encontre de la politique de l'entreprise*
to go ahead = 1/ *continuer* : they're against our project but we're going ahead anyway = *ils sont opposés à notre projet, mais nous continuons quand même*, go ahead ! = *continuez !* = to continue 2/ *passer devant* : I'll hold the door, you go ahead = *je vous tiens la porte, passez devant ≠* to walk behind = *marcher derrière*
to go after s.o. = *courir après qqn* : the police went after the robber but couldn't stop him = *la police a couru après le voleur, mais n'a pas pu l'arrêter*
to go along with = 1/ *aller avec* : if you're going shopping I'll go along with you = *si vous allez faire des courses, j'irai avec vous* ① to accompany = *accompagner* 2/ *suivre (le mouvement)* : the Senator didn't agree but he went along with the party = *le sénateur n'était pas d'accord, mais il a suivi le mouvement/le parti* 3/ *être d'accord avec* : I don't go along with your decision = *je ne suis pas d'accord avec votre décision*
to go around = *circuler* : a strange story about him is going around = *une histoire étrange circule à son sujet* ☠ → to circulate
you can't go around saying things like that = *on ne peut pas se permettre de dire des choses pareilles*
(is there enough coffee) to go around ? = *(est-ce qu'il y a assez de café) pour tout le monde ?*
to go at it = 1/ *ne pas y aller de main morte* : when he insulted/hit me he really went at it = *quand il m'a insulté/frappé, il n'y est pas allé de main morte* ① not to fool around = *ne pas plaisanter* 2/ *mettre les bouchées doubles* : she has to finish her work and is really going at it = *il faut qu'elle finisse son travail, et elle met les bouchées doubles* ① to peg away = *cravacher dur*
to go away = *s'en aller* : we're going away for the summer = *nous nous en allons pour l'été* → TO LEAVE ≠ to come back = *revenir*
go away ! = *va-t'en !*
to go back = *retourner* : don't go back there ! = *n'y retourne pas !* = don't return there ! ☠ → to return
there's no going back = *on ne peut pas revenir en arrière*
to go back on = *revenir sur* : he went back on his promise = *il est revenu sur sa promesse*
to go back to = *remonter à* : this style goes back to the twenties = *ce style remonte aux années 20*
to go backwards = *faire marche arrière ≠* **to go forwards** = *avancer* ☠ → to advance
to go beyond = *dépasser* : my raise in salary goes beyond what I was hoping for = *mon augmentation de salaire dépasse toutes mes espérances* ① to beat = *battre* ☠ → to overtake
to go by = 1/ *passer* : five years went by before I saw him again

= *cinq années ont passé avant que je ne le revoie* ☠ → to pass 2/ *se fier à* : I always go by my instincts/what she says = *je me fie toujours à mon instinct/à ce qu'elle dit* ⬭ to follow = *suivre* 3/ *utiliser* : she goes by her maiden name = *elle utilise son nom de jeune fille* ☠ → to utilize 4/ *y aller par* : we went by plane/train = *nous y sommes allés par avion/par le train* 5/ *passer par* : we drove to Washington and went by Philadelphia = *nous sommes allés en voiture à Washington en passant par Philadelphie*

to let (one's chance) go by = *laisser passer (sa chance)*

going by (her reaction, I don't think she'll come) = *à en juger par (sa réaction, je ne pense pas qu'elle viendra)*

to go down = 1/ *baisser* : prices aren't going down = *les prix ne baissent pas* ≠ to go up = *monter* ☠ → to lower 2/ *diminuer* : the swelling has gone down = *l'enflure a diminué* ☠ → to diminish

to go down on s.o. = *faire minette* (to women), *faire un pompier* (to men) : he never went down on his wife = *il n'a jamais fait minette à sa femme* ⬭ to eat = *brouter*

to go for = 1/ *aller chercher* : go for the doctor = *va chercher le docteur* ⬭ to call in = *faire venir* 2/ *botter* (LV)/*avoir des préférences pour* : he goes for blondes = *il a des préférences pour les blondes*, I don't go for your idea = *ton idée ne me botte pas* ⬭ to be fond of = *aimer bien* ☠ → to dig 3/ *être valable pour* : he should work better and that goes for all of you = *il devrait mieux travailler et ceci est valable pour vous tous* 4/ *attaquer* : the dog went for the guy = *le chien a attaqué le type* ☠ → to attack 5/ *partir pour* : the house went for $ 30 000 = *la maison est partie pour 30 000 dollars*

to go forward = *avancer* : the car was going forward when it hit the child = *la voiture avançait lorsqu'elle a heurté l'enfant*

≠ to go backward = *aller en arrière*

to go in = *entrer* : you can go in now = *vous pouvez entrer maintenant* ☠ → to enter

to go in for = *être féru de* : she goes in for sports/music = *elle est férue de sport/de musique*

to go into = 1/ *rentrer dans/à* : he's going into the family business/politics/the hospital = *il rentre dans l'entreprise familiale/la politique/à l'hôpital* 2/ *voir/s'occuper de* : we'll go into that next week = *nous verrons ça la semaine prochaine* = we'll see that next week ⬭ to enlarge on = *approfondir*

to go off = 1/ *se passer* : the party went off well = *la soirée s'est bien passée* ☠ → to pass 2/ *se déclencher* : the alarm went off at 4 a.m. = *l'alarme s'est déclenchée à 4 heures du matin* ⬭ to blow out = *exploser* ☠ → to trigger off 3/ *s'éteindre* : the lights went off = *les lumières se sont éteintes* = the lights went out ☠ → to extinguish

to go on = 1/ *s'appuyer sur* : the cops have no evidence to go on = *les flics n'ont aucune preuve sur laquelle s'appuyer* 2/ *continuer* : he went on talking = *il a continué à parler* = to keep on ≠ to stop = *arrêter* ☠ → to continue 3/ *durer* : their affair has been going on for months = *leur aventure dure depuis des mois* = their affair has lasted for months 4/ *passer (sur scène)* : the play begins at nine and she goes on at ten = *la pièce commence à neuf heures et elle passe à dix heures* ☠ → to pass 5/ *se rallumer* : the lights went on 2 hours later = *2 heures plus tard, les lumières se sont rallumées*

go on ! = *allez, allez !* : go on, I don't believe a word of it ! = *allez, allez, je n'en crois pas un mot !*

to be going on (60) = *aller sur (la soixantaine)*

to go on (and on) about stg = *insister lourdement sur qqch* : she went on (and on) about his drinking = *elle a insisté lourdement sur son alcoolisme* ⬭ to

make a federal case out of it = *en faire une affaire d'État*

to go on ahead = *partir devant* : go on ahead, I'll meet you later = *partez devant, je vous rejoindrai plus tard*

to be gone on s.o. = *en tenir pour qqn* : he's gone on my sister = *il en tient pour ma sœur* ⬭ to be hung up on s.o. = *avoir qqn dans la peau*, to have a crush on = *avoir le béguin pour*

what's going on ? = *qu'est-ce qui se passe ?* = what's up ?

what's going on between (them) ? = *qu'y a-t-il entre (eux) ?*

to go out = 1/ *sortir* : I'm going out tonight = *je sors ce soir* ≠ to stay in = *rester à la maison* ☠ *tu sais ce qu'il m'a sorti hier ?* = do you know what he came out with yesterday ?

— *sortir (un film)* = to bring out/to release (a film)

— *sortir de l'ordinaire* = to be out of the ordinary

— *sortir son portefeuille* = to take one's wallet out

— *le livre sortira en juin* = the book will come out in June

— *sortir (de l'hôpital)* = to get out (of the hospital)

— *vous ne vous en sortirez pas comme ça* = you won't get out of it like that

— *elle ne s'en sort pas avec si peu d'argent* = she can't get by on so little money

2/ *s'éteindre* : the lights went out during the storm = *l'électricité s'est éteinte pendant l'orage* ☠ → to extinguish 3/ *passer de mode* : padded shoulders went out in the forties and came back in the eighties = *les épaulettes sont passées de mode dans les années 40 et sont revenues à la mode dans les années 80*

to go out with s.o. = *sortir avec qqn* : she's going out with my brother = *elle sort avec mon frère* ⬭ to keep company with = *fréquenter*

to go over = 1/ *revoir* : to go over a report = *revoir un rapport* ☠ *revoir qqn* = to see s.o. again — *revoir (un jugement)* = to reconsider (a sentence)

2/ *avoir du succès* : did her talk go over well ? = *est-ce que sa conférence a eu du succès ?*

to go over to = *aller chez* : I'm going over to John's house = *je vais chez John*

to go through = 1/ *traverser* : to go through hard times = *traverser une période difficile* ⓪ to endure = *endurer* ☠ → to cross 2/ *aboutir* : the deal didn't go through = *l'affaire n'a pas abouti* ⓪ to materialize = *se matérialiser* ☠ *ça a abouti à ...* = it ended in ... 3/ *fouiller (dans)* : I went through all my drawers looking for some money = *j'ai fouillé (dans) tous mes tiroirs pour trouver de l'argent* ⓪ to rummage through = *farfouiller dans* ☠ → to frisk 4/ *dépenser facilement* : to go through a grand in a month = *dépenser facilement mille dollars en un mois* ⓪ to blow = *claquer*

to go through with = *aller jusqu'au bout* : she decided to have an abortion but she'll never go through with it = *elle a décidé de se faire avorter, mais*

jamais elle n'ira jusqu'au bout

to go to = *aller à* : to go to Paris/to the bank = *aller à Paris/à la banque*, the first prize went to an American = *le premier prix est allé à un Américain*

to go together = 1/ *aller ensemble* : those colors don't go together = *ces couleurs ne vont pas ensemble* ≠ to clash = *jurer* 2/ *sortir ensemble* : they've been going together for two years = *ils sortent ensemble depuis deux ans*

to go under = *couler* : the business went under = *l'affaire a coulé* ⓪ to fold = *déposer son bilan* ☠ → to flow

to go up = 1/ *monter* : the price of gas/the temperature is going up = *le prix de l'essence/la température monte* ≠ to fall = *chuter* ☠ → to rise 2/ *se construire* : many new buildings are going up = *beaucoup de nouveaux immeubles se construisent* ☠ → to construct

to go with = *aller avec* : the gloves go with the bag = *les gants vont avec le sac* ⓪ to match = *être assorti à*

to go with it = *évoluer avec son temps* : when you have three kids, you have to be able to go with it = *quand on a trois gosses, il faut évoluer avec son temps* ⓪ to keep up to date = *se tenir au courant*

to go with s.o. = *fréquenter qqn* : she's been going with a lawyer for a year = *elle fréquente un avocat depuis un an* ⓪ to go out with s.o. = *sortir avec qqn*

that doesn't go with me = *ça ne marche pas avec moi* : he wants me to be faithful while he screws around, that doesn't go with me = *il veut que je lui reste fidèle alors qu'il court le jupon, ça ne marche pas avec moi* ⓪ no way ! = *que dalle !*

not to go ... without = *ne pas passer ... sans* : he doesn't go a week without seeing his shrink = *il ne passe pas une semaine sans voir son psy*

to go without = *se passer de* : during the war, we went without butter = *nous nous sommes passé de beurre pendant la guerre* = to do without.

GOAD ON (to, -ed) *aiguillonner* : his desire for revenge goaded him on = *son désir de vengeance l'aiguillonnait* ⓪ to egg on = *inciter fortement.*

GO-AHEAD (n) *feu (m)vert* : he gave me the go-ahead = *il m'a donné le feu vert.*

GOAL (n) 1/ *but (m)* : my goal is to make a lot of money = *mon but, c'est de gagner beaucoup d'argent* ⓪ target = *cible* 2/ *but (m)* (sport) : that was the team's first goal = *ça a été le premier but de l'équipe* ⓪ goalie = *gardien de but* = goalkeeper, goalpost = *poteau* ☠ → purpose.

GOAT (n) *bouc (m)* (he-goat), *chèvre (f)* (she-goat) : to raise goats = *élever des chèvres* ⓪ kid = *chevreau*
to get s.o.'s goat = *échauffer les oreilles à qqn* : his racist remarks are beginning to get my goat = *ses réflexions racistes commencent à m'échauffer les oreilles* → ANGRY
☠ *il me rend chèvre* = he drives me crazy
— *ménager la chèvre et le chou* = to run with the hare and hunt with the hounds
— *un bouc (barbe)* = a goatee.

GOATEE (n)*barbiche (f), bouc (m)* : he has a goatee = *il porte le bouc* ☠ *bouc* → goat.

GOBBLE UP (to, -d) *ne faire qu'une bouchée de* : to gobble up a steak/a country = *ne faire qu'une bouchée d'un steak/d'un pays* ⓪ to swallow up = *engloutir.*

GO-BETWEEN (n) *trait (m) d'union* : he acted as a go-between for his divorced parents = *il était le trait d'union entre ses parents divorcés* ☠ *son nom s'écrit avec un trait d'union* = his name is spelt with a hyphen.

GOBS OF (n pl) *des tonnes de* : gobs of makeup/ice cream = *des tonnes de maquillage/de glace* → MANY.

GOD (n) *Dieu (m)* : do you believe in God ? = *est-ce que vous croyez en Dieu ?* ⓪ the Creator = *le Créateur*, Lord = *Seigneur*, goddess = *déesse*, Messiah = *Messie*, madonna = *madone*, apostle = *apôtre*, believer = *croyant*, the Almighty = *le Tout-Puissant*, the Holy Ghost = *le Saint-Esprit*, Allah = ←

for God's sake ! = *pour l'amour de Dieu !* → GOSH !
God be with you ! = *que Dieu soit avec vous !*

God bless you ! = 1/ *à vos souhaits !/à vos amours !* = Gesundheit ! 2/ *Dieu vous bénisse !*

God's country =

Pétaouchnock ① a long way off = *au diable vauvert*
God forbid ! = *à Dieu ne plaise !*
God help him ! = *Dieu lui vienne en aide !*
God helps those who help themselves = *aide-toi, le Ciel t'aidera*
God only knows ! = *Dieu seul le sait !* = heaven knows !
God save the Queen ! = *vive la reine !*
God willing = *si Dieu le veut* ① hopefully = es-pérons, Inch Allah = ←

it's God's honest truth = *c'est la vérité du bon Dieu* ① honest injun ! = *je te le jure !*
so help me God ! = *Dieu m'est témoin !* → GOSH !
thank God ! = *Dieu merci !*
he thinks he's God's gift = *il se croit sorti de la cuisse de Jupiter* ① he thinks he's hot stuff = *il se prend pour le nombril du monde*
with God's help = *avec l'aide de Dieu*

☠ *il vaut mieux s'adresser au bon Dieu qu'à ses saints* = it's better to go straight to the man at the top.

GODDAMN (n) **I don't give a goddamn !** = *je m'en fous !* ① I don't give a fuck ! = *je n'en ai rien à foutre !*

GODDAMN(ED) (adj) *espèce de :* you goddamn(ed) fool ! = *espèce d'imbécile !* ① fucking = *putain de*
GODDAMN(ED) (adv) *foutrement :* you're goddamn(ed) right = *vous avez foutrement raison.*

GODDAMNIT ! (interj) *nom de Dieu !* → GOSH !

GODFATHER (n) *parrain (m) :* my uncle's my godfather = *mon oncle est mon parrain* ① godchild = *filleul*
☠ *parrain (club)* = sponsor **GODMOTHER** (n) *marraine (f).*

GODFORSAKEN (adj) **a godforsaken place** = *un endroit paumé* ① remote = *reculé.*

GODSEND (n) *bienfait (m) du ciel :* the check was a god-send = *ce chèque a été un bienfait du ciel* ① boon = *aubaine* ≠ plague = *fléau.*

GOFER (n) *factotum (m) :* he works with a filmmaker but he's a gofer = *il travaille avec un cinéaste mais ce n'est qu'un factotum* ① assistant = ←, flunky = *larbin.*

GO-GETTER (n) *ambitieux, -euse :* a go-getter in business = *un ambitieux en affaires* ① pusher = *arriviste.*

GOING (n) **it's rough** ≠ **easy going** = *on avance difficilement* ≠ *facilement*
get out while the going's good = *essayez de bien tirer votre épingle du jeu*
when the going gets rough = *quand cela commence à* tourner au vinaigre : he split when the going got rough = *il s'est tiré quand ça a commencé à tourner au vinaigre.*

GOING (adj) **a going concern** = *une affaire qui marche* ① flourishing = *florissant*
going and coming = *qui n'a pas de porte de sortie :* my publishers have got me going and coming = *mes éditeurs ne m'ont pas laissé de porte de sortie*
the going rate = *le taux en vigueur.*

GOING-OVER (n) **(the car) needs a thorough going-over** = *(la voiture) a besoin d'être soigneusement révisée*
to give s.o. a (good) going-over = *passer qqn à tabac :* the gang gave him a good going-over = *le gang l'a passé à tabac* → TO HIT.

GOINGS-ON (n pl) *agissements (m pl) :* outrageous goings-on = *des agissements scandaleux* ① carryings-on = *frasques.*

GOLD (n inv) *or (m) :* solid gold = *or massif* ① silver = *argent,* gold-plated = *plaqué or,* gilded = *doré,* nugget = *pépite*
a gold digger = 1/ *chercheur d'or* 2/ *croqueuse de diamants :* he married a gold digger = *il a épousé une croqueuse de diamants* ① fortune hunter = *coureur de dot*
gold rush = *ruée vers l'or*
gold standard = *étalon-or*
☠ *rouler sur l'or* = to be rolling in money
— *une affaire en or* = a great bargain
— *à prix d'or* = for a very high price.

GOLDEN (adj) *doré, -e :* golden hair = *des cheveux dorés*
a golden opportunity = *une occasion en or* ≠ unfavorable = *défavorable*
the golden mean = *le juste milieu* = the happy medium
the golden rule = *la règle d'or*
☠ *une enfance dorée* = a gilded childhood.

GOLDFISH (n, -es) *poisson (m) rouge.*

GOLF (n) *golf (m) :* to play golf = *jouer au golf,* miniature golf = *golf miniature* ① caddie = ← **GOLFER** (n) *joueur, -euse de golf* ☠ *golfe* = gulf.

GOLLY ! (interj) *doux Jésus !* → GOSH !

GONDOLA (n) *gondole (f) :* gondolas racing on the canal = *des gondoles qui faisaient la course sur le canal* ① Chinese junk = *jonque chinoise.*

GONER (n) *qqn/qqch de fichu :* if the cancer spreads, he's a goner = *si le cancer s'étend, il est fichu* ① he's had it = *il est cuit.*

GOOD (n inv) **to be in good with s.o.** = *être bien vu de qqn :* she's in good with the boss = *elle est bien vue du patron* ① to be in s.o.'s good graces = *être dans les bonnes grâces de qqn*
it's no good (going now) = *ça ne sert à rien (d'y aller maintenant)*

(he's) no good = *(il est) mauvais* ⓪ he's as low as they come = *c'est le dernier des derniers*
to come to no good = *mal finir* : her son came to no good = *son fils a mal fini*
for good = *pour de bon* : I'm moving to New York for good = *je m'installe à New York pour de bon* ⓪ permanently = *de façon permanente*
for s.o.'s own good = *pour le bien de qqn* : I did it for your own good = *je l'ai fait pour ton bien*
a lot of good that does me ! = *ça me fait une belle jambe !* ≠ **that does me no good** = *ça ne me*

fait ni chaud ni froid
to do s.o. good = *faire du bien à qqn* : a long vacation would do me good = *de longues vacances me feraient du bien*
what's the good of (going now) ? = *à quoi bon (y aller maintenant)* ⓪ what's the point of ? = *à quoi ça rime ?*
good and evil = *le bien et le mal*
that's all for the good = *tout est pour le mieux* ⓪ all the better = *tant mieux.*

GOOD (adj, better, best) **1/** *bon, bonne* : a good book/meal = *un bon livre/repas* → WONDERFUL ≠ awful = *affreux* **2/** *sage* : the children were very good today = *les enfants ont été très sages aujourd'hui* ≠ bad = *vilain,* mischievous = *espiègle* ☠ → wise

---

a good (3 hours) = *(trois) bonnes (heures)*
to be as good as gold = *être sage comme une image*
to be as good as new = *être comme neuf*
to be as good as one's word = *n'avoir qu'une parole*
to be good and (mad) = *être bel et bien (en colère)* → VERY
be good enough to (let me know as soon as possible) = *soyez assez aimable pour (me le faire savoir dès que possible)*
to be in s.o.'s good graces = *être dans les bonnes grâces de qqn* ≠ to be in the doghouse = *être en quarantaine*
you're in good hands = *vous êtes en de bonnes mains*
to be off to a good start = *partir du bon pied* ⓪ to start off with a bang = *démarrer sur les chapeaux de roues*
to be on s.o.'s good side = *être dans les petits papiers de qqn* = to be in s.o.'s good books
to be onto a good thing = *être sur un bon coup* : with his new job, he's onto a good thing = *avec son nouveau boulot, il est sur un bon coup*
don't throw good money after bad = *il faut arrêter les frais*
for good measure = *pour faire bonne mesure* ⓪ just in case = *au cas où*
good at = *bon en* : good at English = *bon en anglais* ⓪ a wizard at = *un as en*
good clean fun = *bon enfant* : the trick was good clean fun = *la*

farce était bon enfant
good evening = *bonsoir* ≠
good morning = *bonjour*
good for = 1/ *bon pour* : smoking isn't good for you = *ce n'est pas bon pour vous de fumer* 2/ *à qui on peut faire confiance pour* : he's good for the money = *on peut lui faire confiance pour l'argent* 3/ *valable* : the ticket is good for a year = *le billet est valable un an* ☠ → valid
good for him ! = 1/ *tant mieux pour lui !* : he got another raise ? good for him ! = *il a obtenu une autre augmentation ? tant mieux pour lui !* 2/ *grand bien lui fasse !* : he wants to marry that bitch ? good for him ! = *il veut épouser cette salope ? grand bien lui fasse !*
good God ! = *bon Dieu !* ⓪
good grief ! = *bon sang (de bonsoir) !*, **good heavens !** = *ciel !*, **good Lord !** = *Seigneur !* → GOSH !
good luck ! = *bonne chance !*
good night ! = *bonne nuit !* ⓪ sleep tight ! = *fais de beaux rêves !*
good old (Jack) ! = *ce bon vieux (Jack) !*
good riddance ! = *bon débarras !*
it's a good thing (you lent me the money) = *heureusement (que vous m'avez prêté cet argent)*
good thinking ! = *bien vu !* ⓪ that's using your head ! = *y'en a là-dedans !*
to have a good head for (math/business) = *avoir la*

bosse des (maths/affaires) ⓪ to have a feeling for = *avoir le sens de*
to have a good laugh = *bien se marrer*
to have a good mind to = *avoir bien envie de* : I have a good mind to tell him what I think = *j'ai bien envie de lui dire ce que je pense*
to have a good thing going = *se la couler douce* : he has a good thing going with his rich wife/his new job = *il se la coule douce avec la fortune de sa femme/dans son nouveau boulot* = **to have it good**
have a good time ! = *amusez-vous bien !* = enjoy yourself !
he never had it so good ! = *ça n'a jamais été aussi bien pour lui !*
we had good times together = *nous avons passé de bons moments ensemble*
to hold good = *rester valable* : the contract holds good till the end of the month = *le contrat reste valable jusqu'à la fin du mois*
it's the good life ! = *c'est la belle vie !*
it's too good to be true = *c'est trop beau pour être vrai*
it's too much of a good thing ! = *trop, c'est trop !*
it will stand you in good stead = *ça vous rendra grand service* : languages will stand you in good stead with an international company = *les langues vous rendront grand service dans une société internationale*

ⓞ **to be of great use** = *être d'une grande utilité*
to make good = *dédommager* : I'll make good the money = *je vous dédommagerai pour l'argent* ⓞ **to make up for** = *se racheter pour*
to make good time (on the highway) = *bien rouler (sur l'autoroute)*
pretty good = *pas mal* : the movie was pretty good = *le film*

était pas mal → WONDERFUL
to talk a good game = *parler beaucoup* : he talks a good game but never acts = *il parle beaucoup mais il ne fait jamais rien*
that's good (enough) reason = *c'est une raison comme une autre*
the good guys and the bad guys = *les bons et les méchants*
those were the good old days = *c'était le bon vieux temps*

what's good for the goose is good for the gander = *il n'y a pas deux poids, deux mesures*
when I'm good and ready = *quand j'en aurai envie* : I'll do the dishes when I'm good and ready = *je ferai la vaisselle quand j'en aurai envie*
you can't keep a good man down = *un homme de valeur reprend toujours le dessus*

☠ *ah bon ?* = really ?
— *le bon numéro* = the right number
— *bonne année/bon anniversaire* = happy New Year/happy birthday
— *on lui donnerait le bon Dieu sans confession* = he's really clean-cut
— *il fait bon* = it's nice out
— *à bon entendeur, salut !* = a word to the wise is sufficient !
— *quel bon vent t'amène ?* = look who's here !
— *(les langues) vont bon train* = (tongues) are wagging
— *à bon chat bon rat* = I'll get mine in

— *garder qqch pour la bonne bouche* = to keep the best part till last
— *une bonne sœur* = a nun
— *avoir bon dos* = to be the fall guy
— *si j'ai bonne mémoire* = if my memory serves me right
— *les bons comptes font les bons amis* = short reckonings make long friends
— *de bon gré* = willingly
— *dire la bonne aventure* = to tell fortunes
— *faire bon ménage* = to get along well
— *une bonne pâte* = a sucker
— *à bon droit* = rightly so.

GOOD ! (interj) *bon !* : you have the money ? good ! = *vous avez l'argent ? bon !*

GOOD (adv) *bien* : to write good = *bien écrire* = to write well ☠ → well *(cet emploi représente un usage populaire incorrect)*

---

as good as = *c'est tout comme* : he as good as said yes = *il a dit oui, ou c'est tout comme* ⓞ **virtually** = *quasiment*

to give as good as one gets = *rendre à qqn la monnaie de sa pièce* ⓞ **to return like for like** = *rendre la pareille.*

GOOD-BYE (n) *au revoir (m)* : say good-bye to Granny = *dis au revoir à grand-mère* ⓞ so long ! = *salut !*
you can kiss it good-bye = *tu peux faire une croix dessus/tu peux en faire ton deuil*
you can say good-bye to it = *tu peux dire adieu à ça.*

GOOD-FOR-NOTHING (n) *bon, bonne à rien* : her husband's a good-for-nothing = *son mari est un bon à rien* ⓞ **schlep** = *crétin.*

GOOD-LOOKING (adj) *beau, belle* : what a good-looking girl/coat ! = *quelle belle fille/quel beau manteau !* ⓞ **stunning** = *sublime* ☠ → beautiful.

GOOD-NATURED (adj) *qui a une bonne nature* : a good-natured girl = *une fille qui a une bonne nature* ⓞ **good-tempered** = *qui a bon caractère.*

GOODNESS ! (interj) *fichtre !* → GOSH !
for goodness's sake ! = *nom de nom !* → GOSH !
my goodness ! = *mon Dieu !* → GOSH !
thank goodness ! = *Dieu merci !* = thank God !

GOODS (n pl) **(leather) goods** = *articles (de cuir)* ⓞ **wares** = *marchandises*
stolen goods = *marchandise volée*
to deliver the goods = *livrer la marchandise* : deliver the goods or we'll bump you off = *livre la marchandise ou on te zigouille*
to have the goods on s.o. = *avoir des preuves contre qqn* : the police have the goods on him = *la police a des preuves contre lui*
to be caught with the goods = *être pris en flagrant délit* ⓞ **to be caught in the act** = *être pris sur le fait.*

GOOD-TIME CHARLEY (n) *noceur (m)* : she wouldn't like to marry a good-time Charley = *elle n'aimerait pas épouser un noceur* ⓞ **pleasure-seeker** = *jouisseur.*

GOODWILL (n) 1/ *bonne volonté (f)* : he showed goodwill by making concessions = *il a fait preuve de bonne volonté en faisant des concessions* 2/ *pas-de-porte (m inv)* : the goodwill acquired by a company = *le pas-de-porte racheté par une société.*

GOODY ! (interj) *super* ! : lobster for dinner ? goody ! = *du homard au dîner ? super* ! ⓒ great = *formidable*.

GOODY-GOODY (n, goody-goodies) *petit, -e saint, -e* : it's no fun going out with a goody-goody = *ce n'est pas drôle de sortir avec un petit saint* ⓒ a prig = *qqn de bégueule*.

GOOF (n) *boulette* (f) : to make a goof = *faire une boulette* ⓒ a foul-up = *une connerie* ☠ → meatball.

GOOF (to, -ed) *se ficher dedans* : you goofed, man ! = *tu t'es fichu dedans, mon vieux !*
to goof off = *tirer au flanc* : he goofed off all day = *il a tiré au flanc toute la journée* ⓒ to muck about = *ne pas en ficher une rame* ≠ to go at it = *en mettre un coup*
to goof up = *ficher en l'air* : our plan was excellent, but you goofed it up = *notre plan était excellent mais tu as tout fichu en l'air* ⓒ to fuck up = *foutre en l'air*, to muck up = *saloper*.

GOOF-OFF (n) *tire-au-flanc* (m inv) : what a goof-off you are ! = *quel tire-au-flanc tu fais !* ⓒ screw-off = *tire-au-cul*.

GOOFY (adj, -ier, -iest) *bébête* : he's kind of goofy = *il est un peu bébête* → STUPID.

GOON (n) *niais, -e* : what a goon she married ! = *quel niais elle a épousé !* → STUPID.

GOOSE (n, geese) *oie* (f) ⓒ gander = *jars*

goose pimples = *chair de poule* = goose-flesh ⓒ the shakes = *la tremblote*

to kill the goose that lays the golden egg(s) = *tuer la poule aux œufs d'or* ⓒ to cut one's own throat = *scier la branche sur laquelle on est assis*
my goose is cooked = *je suis fait comme un rat* ⓒ my number's up = *mon compte est bon* ☠ *une oie blanche* = a babe in the woods.

GOOSE (to, -d) *mettre la main au panier à* : he goosed the maid = *il a mis la main au panier à la bonne*.

GOP (abbr) = Grand Old Party = Republican Party = *Parti républicain*.

GORGE (to, -d) **to gorge o.s. (on)** = *se gaver (de)* : we gorged ourselves on lobster = *on s'est gavé de homard* ≠ to nibble = *picorer*.

GORGEOUS (adj) *splendide* : gorgeous weather/girls = *un temps splendide/des filles splendides* → WONDERFUL ≠ horrible = ←.

GORILLA (n) 1/ *gorille* (m) ⓒ ape = *grand singe* 2/ *gorille* (m) : the President came with his gorillas = *le Président est venu avec ses gorilles* ⓒ bodyguard = *garde du corps*.

GORY (adj, -ier, -iest) *sanglant, -e* : the gory details = *les détails sanglants* ⓒ horrifying = *horrifiant* ☠ → bloody.

GOSH ! (interj) *oh là là* ! : gosh, what a blunder you made ! = *oh là là, quelle gaffe vous avez faite !*

———— GROUP : GOSH ! = OH LÀ LÀ ! ————

alas = *hélas !*
big deal ! = *et après !*
blast it ! = *fichtre !*
bless my soul ! = *mes aïeux !*
by George ! = *nom d'un chien !*
by Jove ! = *par Jupiter !*
can you beat that ! = *ça alors !*
Christ ! = *bon Dieu !*
come, come ! = *allons, allons !*
crap ! = *merde !*
damn it ! = *zut !* = **dammit** !
darn (it) ! = *flûte !*
dear me ! = *oh là !* = **(oh) dear** !
did you ever ! = *par exemple !*
doggone it ! = *sapristi !*
fancy that ! = *tu t'imagines !*
for Christ's sake ! = *nom de Dieu !*
for crying out loud ! = *bon sang !*
for God's sake ! = *pour l'amour de Dieu !*
for heaven's sake ! = *pour*

l'amour du ciel !
for goodness's sake ! = *nom de nom !*
for the life of me ! = *bon sang !*
for the love of God ! = *pour l'amour de Dieu !*
for the love of me ! = *ça alors !*
for the love of Mike ! = *pour l'amour du ciel !*
for Pete's sake ! = *nom d'une pipe !*
for pity's sake ! = *par pitié !*
fuck it ! = *putain de merde !*
gee whiz ! = *mince !*
God Almighty ! = *bon Dieu de bon Dieu !*
goddamnit ! = *nom de Dieu !*
good grief ! = *bon sang (de bonsoir) !*
golly ! = *doux Jésus !*
good God ! = *bon Dieu !*
good heavens ! = *ciel !*
good Lord ! = *Seigneur !*
goodness ! = *fichtre !*

gracious ! = *bonté divine !*
great guns ! = *bigre !*
hang it ! = *nom d'une pipe !*
heavens ! = *grand Dieu !*
heck ! = *mince !*
hell ! = *la barbe !*
holy cow ! = *bougre !*
holy mackerel ! = *saperlipopette !*
holy Moses ! = *saperlotte !*
holy shit ! = *bordel de merde !*
holy smoke ! = *nom d'un petit bonhomme !*
honest to God ! = *juré, craché !*
I declare ! = *ma parole !*
how about that ? = *tiens donc !*
I'll be damned if ... ! = *que le diable m'emporte si ... !*
I'll be darned if ... ! = *le diable m'emporte si ... !*
I'll be doggoned ! = *nom d'un petit bonhomme !*
I'll be hanged if ... ! = *je veux bien être pendu si ... !*

I never ! = *sapristi !* **Jesus !** = *nom de Dieu !* **Lord !** = *Seigneur !* = **my Lord !** **man !** = *eh ben !* **my goodness !** = *mon Dieu !* **(upon) my word !** = *ma parole !* **no fooling !** = *sans blague !* **no joking !** = *sans plaisanter !* **no kidding !** = *sans rigoler !* **no shit !** = *ben merde alors !* **nuts !** = *punaise !* **of all things !** = *par exemple !* **oh boy !** = *oh là là !* **oh shit !** = *merde alors !* **oh hell !** = *oh la vache !* **phew !** = *ouf !* **screw it !** = *bordel !* **shit !** = *merde !* **shucks !** = *oh mince alors !* **so !** = *eh bien !* **so help me !** = *je te jure !* **so help me God !** = *Dieu m'en soit témoin !* **that's all I needed !** = *il ne manquait plus que ça !*	**that beats all !/everything !** = *c'est le comble !* **that crowns it all !** = *il ne manquait plus que ça !* **that's a fine how-do-you-do !** = *c'est du propre !* **that's a fine state of affairs !** = *c'est du joli !* **that's going some !** = *c'est la meilleure !* **that's the limit !** = *c'est le bouquet !* **that's one for the books !** = *c'est pas piqué des hannetons !* **that's really something !** = *c'est vraiment quelque chose !* **that takes the cake !** = *c'est le pompon !* **that takes some doing !** = *il faut le faire !* **that tops it !** = *ça couronne le tout !* **well, I'll be !** = *diantre !* **what !** = *quoi !* **what's the big idea ?** = *ça ne va pas, non ?*	**what the dickens !** = *je vous demande un peu !* **what the deuce !** = *doux Jésus !* **what the devil !** = *que diable !* **what the fuck !** = *putain !* **what the heck !** = *que diable !* **what the hell !** = *bon Dieu !* **what do you know !** = *pas possible !* **what/who in the world !** = *pourquoi/qui diable !* **whew !** = *ouf !* **whoops !** = *hop là !* **well, well !** = *tiens donc !* **would you believe it !** = *qui l'eût cru !* **wow !** = *holà !* **you gotta be kidding !** = *tu veux rigoler !* **you're kidding !** = *tu blagues !/tu rigoles !* **you must be kidding !** = *tu veux rire !*

GOSPEL (n) *évangile (m)* : the Gospel tells us about the son of God = *l'évangile nous parle du fils de Dieu*
that's the Gospel truth = *parole d'évangile !*

GOSSIP (n) **1/** (inv) *commérages (m pl)*, *potins (m pl)* : some juicy gossip ! = *des commérages/potins juteux !*
a piece of gossip = *un commérage/un potin* ⓓ hearsay = *ouï-dire*, blabber = *cancans* ☠ *faire du potin* = to make noise
the gossip column = *la chronique mondaine/les échos* ⓓ gossip columnist = *échotier*
2/ *commère (f)* : she's a terrible gossip = *c'est une épouvantable commère* ⓓ yenta = *pipelette.*

GOSSIP (to, -ed) *commérer, potiner* : the two of them can gossip for hours = *ces deux-là peuvent potiner/commérer pendant des heures* ⓓ to blabber = *cancaner.*

GOTCHA ! (interj) *d'ac !* ⓓ Roger ! = *compris !*

GOULASH (n) *goulasch (m)* : goulash is a Hungarian beef stew = *le goulasch est un ragoût de bœuf hongrois* ⓓ borscht = *bortsch.*

GOURMET (n) *gourmet (m)* : my husband's a gourmet = *mon mari est un gourmet.*

GOVERN (to, -ed) *gouverner* : to govern a country = *gouverner un pays* ⓓ to reign = *régner* ☠ *gouverner un bateau* = to steer a ship.

GOVERNESS (n, -es) *gouvernante (f)* : a French governess = *une gouvernante française* ⓓ nanny = *nourrice.*

GOVERNMENT (n) *gouvernement (m)* : federal government = *gouvernement fédéral* ⓓ republic = *république* ☒ *le gouvernement (Roosevelt)* = the (Roosevelt) administration **GOVERNMENTAL** (adj) *gouvernemental, -e* : governmental policy = *politique gouvernementale.*

GOVERNOR (n) *gouverneur (m)* : governors are elected every six years = *les gouverneurs sont élus tous les six ans*
listen, governor ! (GB) = *écoute, mon vieux !*

GOWN (n) *robe (f) du soir* : a beautiful silk gown = *une belle robe du soir en soie* = evening gown ⓓ dress = *robe.*

GOY (n) *goy (m)* : she is Jewish but goes out only with goys = *elle est juive mais ne sort qu'avec des goys* ⓓ gentile = *gentil.*

GRAB (to, -bed) **1/** *saisir, empoigner* : he grabbed my arm/my bag = *il m'a empoigné le bras/il a saisi mon sac* ⓓ to grip = *agripper*
how does that grab you ? = *qu'est-ce que tu en dis ?* ⓓ how does that strike you ? = *qu'est-ce que tu en penses ?*
☠ *saisir→* to seize

2/ *manger sur le pouce* : we'll grab a sandwich before the play = *on mangera un sandwich sur le pouce avant la pièce* **3/** *se jeter sur* : she grabbed the best seat = *elle s'est jetée sur le meilleur siège.*

GRACE (n inv) *grâce (f)* : the grace of a ballerina = *la grâce d'une ballerine* ⓓ charm = *charme*
to fall from grace = *tomber en disgrâce* ≠ to be in

s.o.'s good books = *être dans les petits papiers de qqn*
to say grace = *dire le bénédicité/les grâces*
☠ *la grâce du Président* = the President's pardon
— *fais-moi grâce de tes critiques* = spare me your criticism
— *demander grâce* = to ask for mercy.

GRACEFUL (adj) *gracieux, -euse* : a graceful child = *un enfant gracieux* ≠ ungainly = *disgracieux* ☠ *à titre gracieux* = gratis **GRACEFULLY** (adv) *gracieusement*.

GRACIOUS (adj) *accueillant, -e* : she's a very gracious hostess = *c'est une hôtesse très accueillante* ⓓ hospitable = *hospitalier* **GRACIOUSLY** (adv) *avec bienveillance*.

GRACIOUS ! (interj) *bonté divine !* → GOSH !

GRAD (n) *diplômé, -e* = graduate.

GRADE (n) **1/** *note* (f) : she got good grades = *elle a eu de bonnes notes* = she got good marks ☠ → note **2/** *grade* (m) : the grade of captain = *le grade de capitaine* ⓓ rank = *rang* ☠ *en prendre pour son grade* = to eat crow **3/** *qualité* (f) : an inferior grade of beef = *une qualité inférieure de bœuf* ☠ → quality
to be in the (sixth) grade = *être en (sixième)*
grade school = *école primaire* = grammar school ⓓ high school = *lycée*
to make the grade = *y arriver* : he wanted the job but didn't make the grade = *il voulait le poste, mais il n'y est pas arrivé.*

GRADUAL (adj) *graduel, -elle* : a gradual change in his attitude = *un changement graduel dans son attitude* ⓓ progressive = *progressif* **GRADUALLY** (adv) *graduellement* : they gradually increased their prices = *ils ont graduellement augmenté leurs prix* ≠ all of a sudden = *subitement.*

GRADUATE (n) *diplômé, -e* : a Princeton graduate = *un diplômé de Princeton* ⓓ alumnus = *ancien élève* ≠ undergraduate = *étudiant non encore diplômé.*

GRADUATE (adj) *diplômé, -e* : graduate student = *étudiant diplômé* ≠ undergraduate = *non encore diplômé*
graduate school = *école supérieure/troisième cycle* (university).

GRADUATE (to, -d) *obtenir son diplôme* : my son will graduate next year = *mon fils aura son diplôme l'année prochaine* ⓓ graduation day = *jour de remise des diplômes, class of 1984* = *promotion de 1984.*

GRAFFITI (n pl) *graffiti* (m pl) : colorful graffiti on the subway trains = *des graffiti hauts en couleur sur les wagons de métro.*

GRAFT (n) **1/** *greffe* (f) : a skin graft = *une greffe de peau* ⓓ to graft = *greffer* ☠ *greffe du cœur* = heart transplant **2/** *politique des pots-de-vin* : the company used graft to land the contract = *la société a pratiqué une politique de pots-de-vin pour décrocher le contrat* ⓓ bribe = *pot-de-vin.*

GRAIN (n) **1/** *grain* (m) : a grain of rice = *un grain de riz* **2/** (inv) *céréales* (f pl) : America sells grain to the USSR = *les États-Unis vendent des céréales à l'URSS* ☠ → cereals
to go against s.o.'s grain = *aller contre la nature de qqn* : lying goes against my grain = *mentir va contre ma nature*
not a grain of truth (in what he told you) = *pas une once de vérité (dans ce qu'il vous a dit)*
☠ *une graine* = a seed
— *grain de beauté* = beauty spot
— *un grain de fantaisie* = a touch of fantasy
— *un grain (vent)* = a squall
— *un grain de café* = a coffee bean
— *veiller au grain* = to keep one's eyes open
— *il a un grain* = he's mad as a hatter
— *mettre son grain de sel* = to stick one's two cents in.

GRAMMAR (n) *grammaire* (f) : English grammar isn't hard = *la grammaire anglaise n'est pas dure* ⓓ grammarian = *grammairien*, grammatical = ←
grammar school = *école primaire.*

GRAND (n inv) *mille dollars* (m pl) : her ring cost two grand = *sa bague a coûté deux mille dollars.*

GRAND (adj, -er, -est) *épatant, -e* : a grand guy/evening = *un type épatant/une soirée épatante* → WONDERFUL ≠ awful = *affreux*
to feel grand = *se sentir merveilleusement bien*
grand piano = *piano à queue*
grand slam = *grand chelem.*

GRANDCHILD (n, -ren) *petit-fils* (m) = grandson, *petite-fille* (f) = granddaughter **GRANDCHILDREN** (n pl) *petits-enfants* (m pl) : they have three grandchildren = *ils ont trois petits-enfants.*

GRANDFATHER (n) *grand-père* (m) : my grandfather's 91 = *mon grand-père a 91 ans* ⓓ grandpa = *grandpapa*, gramps = *papi*
grandfather clock = *horloge.*

GRANDMOTHER (n) *grand-mère* (f) : my grandmother died last year = *ma grand-mère est morte l'année dernière* ⓓ granny = *mémé/mamie*, grandma = *grandmaman.*

GRANDPARENTS (n pl) *grands-parents* (m pl) : my grandparents live in New York = *mes grands-parents habitent New York.*

GRANDSTAND (n) *tribune* (f) : we watched the race from the grandstand = *nous avons assisté à la course de la tribune* ⓓ seat = *place*
to play to the grandstand = *(jouer) pour la galerie* =
to make a grandstand play : the politician objected strongly but he was only playing to the grandstand/making a grandstand play = *l'homme politique a fait de violentes objections mais c'était seulement pour la galerie*
☠ *une tribune* = a panel
— *la tribune (discours)* = the rostrum.

GRANT (n) **1/** *subvention* (f) : the theater got a grant from the government = *le théâtre a reçu une subvention de l'État* ⓐ aid = *aide* ☠ → subsidy **2/** *bourse* (f) : he got a grant to study a year in England = *il a obtenu une bourse pour faire un an d'études en Angleterre.*

GRANT (to, -ed) *accorder* : I grant you that a new car's a lot of money = *je vous accorde qu'une voiture neuve coûte cher* ⓐ to concede = *concéder* ☠ → to concur **granted that** = *à supposer que* : granted that he'll lend you the money, how will you ever manage to pay him back ? = *à supposer qu'il vous prête l'argent, comment pourrez-vous jamais le rembourser ?*

GRAPE (n) *raisin* (m) : the grapes of wrath = *les raisins de la colère* ⓐ bunch = *grappe* ☠ *raisins secs* = raisins.

GRAPEFRUIT (n) *pamplemousse* (m) : I'd like a grapefruit please = *je voudrais un pamplemousse, s'il vous plaît* ⓐ citrus fruit = *agrumes.*

GRAPEVINE (n) *téléphone* (m) *arabe* : we heard by the grapevine that they're splitting up = *on a su par le téléphone arabe qu'ils étaient en train de rompre* ⓐ by word of mouth = *de bouche à oreille.*

GRAPH (n) *graphique* (m) : a graph showing a decline in the birthrate = *un graphique montrant une diminution du taux de natalité* ⓐ chart = *tableau.*

GRAPHIC (adj) *par le menu* : a graphic description of the swing = *une description de la partouse par le menu* **graphic arts** = *les arts graphiques.*

GRAPPLE WITH (to, -d) *se débattre contre* : to grapple with a difficulty = *se débattre contre une difficulté* ⓐ to struggle with = *se battre avec.*

GRASP (n) **within s.o.'s grasp** = *à la portée de qqn* : power is within our grasp = *le pouvoir est à notre portée* **to have** ≠ **not to have a good grasp of the (situation)** = *bien* ≠ *mal saisir la (situation).*

GRASP (to, -ed) **1/** *saisir* : he grasped the chance = *il a saisi la chance* = he grabbed the chance **2/** *saisir* : I didn't grasp what you said = *je n'ai pas saisi ce que vous avez dit* ⓐ to catch on = *piger* ☠ → to seize.

GRASS (n) **1/** *herbe* (f) : to cut the grass = *couper l'herbe* ⓐ lawn = *pelouse* **the grass is always greener on the other side of the fence** = *l'herbe est toujours plus verte de l'autre côté de la barrière* **keep off the grass !** = *pelouse interdite !* **2/** *herbe* (f) : to smoke grass = *fumer de l'herbe* ⓐ marijuana = ← ☠ *(fines) herbes* = herbs — *couper l'herbe sous les pieds de qqn* = to pull the carpet out from under s.o. — *un écrivain en herbe* = a budding writer.

GRASSHOPPER (n) *sauterelle* (f) ⓐ cricket = *grillon.*

GRASS ROOTS (adj) *populaire régional, -e* : a grass roots movement = *un mouvement populaire régional.*

GRATEFUL (adj) *reconnaissant, -e* : thank you for helping my mother, I'm very grateful = *merci d'aider ma mère, je vous en suis très reconnaissant* ≠ ungrateful = *ingrat* **to be grateful to s.o. (for)** = *être reconnaissant à qqn (de)* : I'm very grateful to you for your help = *je vous suis très reconnaissant de l'aide que vous m'avez apportée* ⓐ to be indebted to s.o. = *avoir une dette envers qqn* **I would be grateful if you (came)** = *je vous serais reconnaissant de (venir)*

GRATE ON (to, -d) *courir sur le haricot à* : her voice grates on me = *sa voix me court sur le haricot* ⓐ to get on s.o.'s nerves = *taper sur les nerfs à qqn,* to bug = *casser les pieds à.*

GRATIFYING (adj) *gratifiant, -e* : the work wasn't very gratifying = *le travail n'était pas très gratifiant.*

GRATING (adj) *qui court sur le haricot* : a grating noise = *un bruit qui vous court sur le haricot* ≠ pleasant = *agréable.*

GRATIS (adj, adv) *gratis* : I got it gratis = *je l'ai eu gratis* ⓐ on the house = *aux frais de la maison.*

GRATITUDE (n) *reconnaissance* (f), *gratitude* (f) : she didn't show much gratitude = *elle n'a pas montré beaucoup de reconnaissance/de gratitude* ≠ ungratefulness = *ingratitude* ☠ *reconnaissance* → recognition.

GRATUITOUS (adj) *gratuit, -e* : an unpleasant gratuitous remark = *une réflexion désagréable et gratuite* ☠ *des boissons gratuites* = free drinks — *crime gratuit* = wanton killing.

GRAVE (n) *tombe* (f) : to dig a grave = *creuser une tombe* ⓐ cemetery = *cimetière,* gravedigger = *fossoyeur* **he'd turn over in his grave** = *il se retournerait dans sa tombe* : he'd turn over in his grave if he knew what his son is doing with his inheritance = *il se retournerait dans sa tombe s'il savait ce que son fils fait de l'héritage.*

GRAVE (adj, -r, -st) *grave* : a grave problem = *un problème grave* = serious ⓐ solemn = *solennel* ☠ *une voix grave* = a deep voice.

GRAVEYARD (n) *cimetière* (m) : corpses stolen from the graveyard = *des cadavres volés dans le cimetière* ⓐ gravestone = *pierre tombale* ☠ → cemetery.

GRAVITY (n inv) **1/** *gravitation* (f) : the law of gravity = *la loi de la gravitation* **2/** *gravité* (f) : the gravity of the situation = *la gravité de la situation.*

GRAVY (n) **1/** (-ies) *jus* (m) *de viande* : I like gravy on my potatoes = *j'aime le jus de viande sur les pommes de terre* ⓐ gravyboat = *saucière* **2/** (inv) *bénef* (m) : the money earned from the stocks is gravy = *l'argent gagné par les actions, c'est du bénef* ⓐ profit = ←.

GRAY (n) *gris (m)* : she wears a lot of gray = *elle porte beaucoup de gris* ⓓ black = *noir*.

GRAY (adj, -er, -est) *gris, -e* : a gray coat = *un manteau gris* = grey ⓓ black = *noir*
gray hair = *cheveux gris/cheveux blancs*
☠ *faire grise mine* = to pull a long face
— *un temps gris* = bleak weather
— *être un peu gris* = to be tipsy.

GRAY (to, -ed) *grisonner* : I'm only 30 and already graying = *je n'ai que trente ans et je grisonne déjà* = to turn gray.

GRAY MATTER (n) *matière (f) grise* : he uses his gray matter for computer programs = *il utilise sa matière grise sur des logiciels d'ordinateur*.

GRAZE (to, -d) **1/** *paître, brouter* : sheep are grazing = *les moutons paissent/broutent*
☠ *envoyer paître qqn* = to send s.o. packing
— *tu me les broutes !* = you're breaking my balls !
2/ *effleurer* : the bullet grazed his head = *la balle lui a effleuré la tête* ☠ → to skim.

GREASE (n inv) *graisse (f)* : there's too much grease in her cooking = *il y a trop de graisse dans sa cuisine* ⓓ oil = *huile* ☠ *avoir de la graisse autour de la taille* = to have fat around the waist.

GREASY (adj, -ier, -iest) *gras, grasse* (food, hair), *graisseux, -euse* (hand) : the French fries/his hands are greasy = *les frites sont grasses/il a les mains graisseuses* ☠ *gras* → fatty.

GREAT (adj, -er, -est) **1/** *grand, -e* : a great man/artist = *un grand homme/artiste* ⓓ eminent = *éminent* **2/** *formidable* : what a great movie/guy ! = *quel film/type formidable !* → WONDERFUL ≠ crummy = *moche* ☠ → formidable **3/** *grand, -e* : a great difference/great responsibilities = *une grande différence/de grandes responsabilités* ⓓ enormous = *énorme* ≠ small = *petit*

to feel great = *se sentir en pleine forme* ⓓ to feel like a million bucks = *être gonflé à bloc* **to go to great lengths** = *se donner beaucoup de mal* : he went to great lengths to get back at her = *il s'est donné beaucoup de mal pour se venger d'elle* ⓓ to put o.s. out = *se donner un mal de chien* **Great Britain** = *Grande-Bretagne* **a Great Dane** = *un danois (chien)* **a great deal** = *beaucoup* : he drinks a great deal = *il boit a great deal = il boit*	*beaucoup* ⓓ a hell of a lot = *un maximum* ≠ a bit = *un peu* ☠ → much **a great deal of** = *énormément de* : a great deal of money/free time = *énormément d'argent/de temps libre* → MANY ≠ a little bit = *un petit peu* **great minds think alike** = *les grands esprits se rencontrent* **to look great** = *avoir une mine superbe* **no great shakes** = *qui ne casse pas des briques* : the book was no great shakes = *ce livre ne cassait pas des briques* → AWFUL **no great thing** = *qui ne vaut*	*pas grand-chose* : the film was no great thing = *le film ne valait pas grand-chose* → AWFUL **he thinks he's great** = *il ne se prend pas pour rien* ⓓ he's conceited = *il est suffisant* **she's a great one for (telling other people what to do)** = *elle est très forte pour (dire aux autres ce qu'il faut faire)* **you're a great one to talk !** = *tu ne t'es pas regardé !* ⓓ people who live in glass houses shouldn't throw stones = *il faut commencer par balayer devant sa porte*

☠ *un homme grand* = a tall man — *une grande (pièce)* = a big/large (room) — *quand tu seras grand* = when you're grown up — *de grande envergure* = large-scale — *sortir le grand jeu* = to give s.o. the works — *une grande personne* = a grown-up — *au grand air* = in the open air — *monter sur ses grands chevaux* = to get on one's high horse	— *au grand jour* = in broad daylight — *vivre sur un grand pied* = to live high on the hog — *le grand monde* = high society — *il est grand temps que* = it's high time that — *un grand magasin* = a department store — *mon grand frère* = my big brother — *les grandes vacances* = the summer vacation — *les grands moyens* = drastic measures — *faire le grand écart* = to do the splits.

GREAT (adv) *merveilleusement* : everything's going great = *tout marche merveilleusement*.

GREAT ! (interj) *formidable !* : how about going out to dinner ? — great ! = *si on allait dîner au restaurant ? — formidable !* ⓓ swell ! = *chouette !*

GREAT-AUNT (n) *grand-tante (f)* **GREAT-UNCLE** (n) *grand-oncle (m)*.

GREATEST (n) **you're the greatest !** = *vous êtes le meilleur !*

he thinks he is the greatest = *il ne se prend pas pour de la petite bière* Ⓦ *he thinks he's hot stuff* = *il se prend pour le nombril du monde.*

GREAT-GRANDCHILD (n, -ren) *arrière-petit-fils (m)* = great-grandson, *arrière-petite-fille (f)* = great-granddaughter **GREAT-GRANDCHILDREN** (n pl) *arrière-petits-enfants (m pl).*

GREAT-GRANDFATHER (n) *arrière-grand-père (m).*

GREAT-GRANDMOTHER (n) *arrière-grand-mère (f).*

GREATLY (adv) *grandement* : greatly respected = *grandement respecté* → VERY.

GREECE (n) *Grèce (f)* ⓌMediterranean sea = *Méditerranée.*

GREED (n) *avidité (f)* : the revolting greed of some rich people = *l'avidité révoltante de certains riches* Ⓦ avarice = ←.

GREEDY (adj, -ier, -iest) *gourmand, -e* : don't be so greedy and accept 10 % = *ne sois pas si gourmand et accepte 10 %.*

GREEK (n, adj) *Grec, Grecque* : she married a Greek = *elle a épousé un Grec* Ⓦ Greece = *la Grèce*
it's all Greek to me ! = *c'est de l'hébreu/du chinois pour moi* ! Ⓦ what doubletalk ! = *quel charabia* !
☠ *va te faire enculer par les Grecs* ! = fuck you !

GREEN (n) *vert (m)* : she likes green = *elle aime le vert,* dark green = *vert foncé/vert bouteille*
the greens = *les verts* Ⓦ the ecologists = *les écologistes*
☠ *tu ferais bien de te mettre au vert* = take a holiday for a while
— *en avoir vu des vertes et des pas mûres* = to have been through rough times.

GREEN (adj, -er, -est) *vert, -e* Ⓦ red = *rouge*
green with (envy) = *vert de (jalousie)*
to give the green light = *donner le feu vert* = to give the go-ahead
to have a green thumb = *avoir la main verte*
☠ *il est encore vert* = he's still spry.

GREENHORN (n) *blanc-bec (m)* : he's new on the job, he's a greenhorn = *il est nouveau dans ce job, c'est un blanc-bec* ≠ old hand = *vieux de la vieille.*

GREENHOUSE (n) *serre (f)* : they have a greenhouse in the garden = *ils ont une serre dans le jardin.*

GREET (to, -ed) *accueillir* : the Pope was greeted by the President = *le pape a été accueilli par le Président* = the Pope was welcomed by the President.

GREETING (n) *salutation (f)* : to exchange friendly greetings = *échanger des salutations amicales*
greeting card = *carte de vœux*
Christmas/birthday greetings = *vœux de Noël/d'anniversaire*

☠ *recevez mes salutations distinguées* = sincerely yours.

GREGARIOUS (adj) *sociable* : my husband's very gregarious = *mon mari est très sociable* = sociable ≠ withdrawn = *renfermé.*

GRENADE (n) *grenade (f)* : to defuse a grenade = *désamorcer une grenade* Ⓦ Molotov cocktail = *cocktail Molotov.*

GREY (n, adj, -er, -est) = GRAY.

GREYHOUND (n) 1/ *lévrier (m), levrette (f)* : greyhound races in Florida = *des courses de lévriers en Floride* 2/ *car (m) (de la compagnie Greyhound)* : we took the Greyhound to Chicago = *nous avons pris le car pour Chicago.*

GRIEF (n inv) *douleur (f) (morale)* : filled with grief at his daughter's death = *rempli de douleur à la mort de sa fille* Ⓦ sorrow = *peine,* heartache = *chagrin*
☠ → pain
— grief → grievance.

GRIEVANCE (n) *grief (m)* : the grievances of the workers = *les griefs des ouvriers* Ⓦ kick = *raison de râler* ☠ *faire grief à qqn de qqch* = to hold stg against s.o.

GRIEVE (to, -d) *(s')affliger* : it grieves me to see you like this = *cela m'afflige de vous voir comme ça* Ⓦ to sadden = *attrister.*

GRILL (n) *gril (m)* : put the steak on the grill = *mettez le steak sur le gril* Ⓦ oven = *four.*

GRILL (to, -ed) *faire griller* : to grill a steak = *faire griller un steak* = to broil Ⓦ to roast = *rôtir*
☠ *je suis grillé* ! = my goose is cooked !
— *griller un feu (rouge)* = to pass a (red) light
— *faire griller du pain* = to toast bread
2/ *cuisiner* : the cops grilled him = *les flics l'ont cuisiné* Ⓦ to give the third degree = *mettre sur la sellette* ☠ *elle cuisine bien* = she cooks well.

GRIM (adj, -mer, -mest) *sombre* : a grim look/life = *un regard/une vie sombre* Ⓦ dreary = *morne,* dismal = *sinistre* ☠ → somber.

GRIMACE (n) *grimace (f)* : to make grimaces = *faire des grimaces* = to make faces.

GRIMACE (to, -d) *grimacer* : the pain was so strong that he grimaced = *la douleur a été si forte qu'il a grimacé.*

GRIN (n) *(large) sourire (m)* : a foolish grin = *un (large) sourire bête* Ⓦ smirk = *fin sourire*
wipe that grin off your face ! = *arrête de sourire bêtement comme ça* !

GRIN (to, -ned) *sourire jusqu'aux oreilles* : she grinned at the thought = *l'idée l'a fait sourire jusqu'aux oreilles*
you have to grin and bear it = *il faut faire contre mauvaise fortune bon cœur* → THAT'S LIFE !

GRIND (n) *sacré boulot (m)* : studying for the exams is a grind = *c'est un sacré boulot de préparer ses examens* ◍ drudgery = *travail pénible.*

GRIND (to, ground, ground) **to grind out** = 1/ *gagner difficilement :* he grinds out 300 dollars a week = *il gagne difficilement 300 dollars par semaine* 2/ *pondre laborieusement :* the playwright ground out three pages a day = *le dramaturge pondait laborieusement trois pages par jour.*

GRIP (n) *sac (m) de voyage :* take a small grip for the weekend = *prenez un petit sac de voyage pour le weekend* ◍ valise = ←
to come to grips with stg = *assumer qqch :* she has to come to grips with her family situation = *il faut qu'elle assume sa situation familiale* ◍ to cope with = *affronter*
to get a grip on oneself = *se maîtriser* ◍ to get it together = *se reprendre en main* ☠ → to master
to have a (good) grip of (the problem) = *(bien) maîtriser (le problème)*
to lose one's grip (on) = *perdre son emprise (sur) :* the dictator is losing his grip on the population = *le dictateur est en train de perdre son emprise sur la population.*

GRIP (to, -ped) *agripper :* to grip s.o.'s arm = *agripper le bras de qqn* ◍ to clutch = *s'agripper à.*

GRIPE (n) *raison (f) de rouspéter :* my main gripe is the salary = *je rouspète principalement à cause du salaire* = beef ◍ complaint = *plainte.*

GRIPE (to, -d) *rouspéter :* stop griping all the time ! = *arrête de rouspéter tout le temps !* ◍ to bellyache = *ronchonner.*

GRIPPE (n) *grippe (f) :* it's the third grippe I've had this winter = *c'est ma troisième grippe de l'hiver* = flu ◍ cold = *rhume* ☠ *prendre en grippe* = to take a dislike to.

GRIPPING (adj) *palpitant, -e :* a gripping film = *un film palpitant* ◍ exciting = *passionnant.*

GROAN (n) *gémissement (m) :* a painful groan = *un gémissement de douleur* **GROAN** (to, -ed) *gémir :* to groan with pain = *gémir de douleur* ◍ to moan = *geindre.*

GROCER (n) *épicier, -ère :* I went to the grocer's = *je suis allé chez l'épicier* ◍ groceries = *produits d'alimentation.*

GROCERY (n, -ies) **grocery (store)** = *épicerie :* there's a grocery store around the corner = *il y a une épicerie au coin de la rue.*

GROGGY (adj, -ier, -iest) *groggy (inv) :* the drink made me groggy = *le verre que j'ai bu m'a rendu groggy* ◍ dizzy = *qui a la tête qui tourne.*

GROOM (n) *marié (m) :* the groom was late = *le marié était en retard* ≠ bride = *mariée* ☠ *un groom* = a bellboy.

GROOVE ON (to, -d) *être friand, -e de :* to groove on

jazz = *être friand de jazz* ◍ to be big on = *raffoler de* ≠ can't bear = *ne pas pouvoir supporter.*

GROOVY (adj, -ier, -iest) *sensass :* a groovy place = *un endroit sensass* → WONDERFUL.

GROPE (to, -d) *tâtonner :* to grope in the dark = *tâtonner dans le noir* ◍ to feel one's way = *marcher à tâtons.*

GROSS (adj, -er, -est) *flagrant, -e :* a gross injustice = *une injustice flagrante* ◍ rank = *criant,* unmitigated = *absolu* ☠ → flagrant
gross benefit/salary = *bénéfice/salaire brut*
gross language = *langage grossier* ≠ refined = *raffiné.*

GROSS (to, -ed) *faire un bénéfice brut de :* the business grossed a million dollars = *l'affaire a fait un bénéfice net d'un million de dollars.*

GROTESQUE (adj) *grotesque :* that was a grotesque thing to say = *c'était grotesque de dire ça* ◍ absurd = *absurde,* ludicrous = *saugrenu* ☠ *c'est grotesque d'(avoir peur des chiens)* = it's ridiculous to (be afraid of dogs).

GROUCH (n, -es) *qqn de grognon :* don't be such a grouch = *ne sois pas si grognon* ◍ kvetch = *râleur.*

GROUCH (to, -ed) *grogner :* grouching again ? = *encore en train de grogner ?* ◍ to grouse = *grincher* ☠ *le chien grogne* = the dog is snarling.

GROUCHY (adj, -ier, -est) *grognon (inv) :* she is always grouchy = *elle est toujours grognon* ◍ crabby = *bougon.*

GROUND (n) *sol (m) :* to fall on the ground = *tomber sur le sol* ◍ earth = *terre* ☠ *sur le sol français* = on French soil

to break fresh/new ground = *tracer une nouvelle voie* ◍ to make a discovery = *faire une découverte* **to burn to the ground** = *brûler de fond en comble* **camping ground** = *terrain de camping* **to cover a lot of ground** = *parcourir du terrain (troops)/bien avancer (work)* **to cut the ground from under s.o.'s feet** = *couper l'herbe sous les pieds de qqn* ◍ to steal the show = *voler la vedette* **to gain** ≠ **to lose**	**ground** = *gagner* ≠ *perdre du terrain* **to get in on the ground floor** = *participer au démarrage d'une affaire :* the business today is earning a lot and he was lucky to get in on the ground floor = *l'affaire rapporte gros aujourd'hui et il a eu de la chance de participer à son démarrage* **not to get off the ground** = *ne même pas pouvoir démarrer :* our project didn't get off the ground = *notre projet n'a même pas pu démarrer* ◍ to be

nipped in the bud = être étouffé dans l'œuf
ground floor = rez-de-chaussée
ground rules = les règles du jeu
ground staff = personnel rampant
to stand one's

ground = ne pas céder de terrain ⓪ to stand pat = tenir ferme
to worship the ground s.o. walks on = faire de qqn son idole ⓪ to idealize = idéaliser.

GROUNDLESS (adj) sans fondement : his fears were groundless = ses craintes étaient sans fondement ≠ well-founded = fondé.

GROUNDS (n pl) **1/** motif (m) : adultery is still grounds for divorce = l'adultère est toujours un motif de divorce ⓪ reason = raison ☠ → motive
2/ fondement (m) : there are no grounds for his accusation = son accusation est sans fondement
on what grounds (is he suing you) ? = pour quel motif (vous poursuit-il) ?
3/ terrain (m) : the grounds around the house = le terrain autour de la maison
☠ terrain vague = vacant lot
— tâter le terrain = to see how the land lies
— préparer le terrain = to lay the groundwork
— chercher un terrain d'entente = to look for a compromise
— terrain de jeu = playground
— acheter du terrain = to buy some property/land
— terrain d'aviation = airfield
— aller sur le terrain = to go and check on the spot.

GROUNDWORK (n) **to lay the groundwork** = préparer le terrain.

GROUP (n) groupe (m) : group sex = amour en groupe, group therapy = thérapie de groupe.

GROUP (to, -ed) grouper : to group people = grouper les gens ≠ to disperse = disperser.

GROUPIE (n) groupie (f) : rock stars are often followed by groupies = les vedettes du rock sont souvent suivies de groupies ⓪ fan = ←.

GROUSE (to, -d) grincher : will you stop grousing ! = est-ce que tu pourrais arrêter de grincher ! ⓪ to belly-ache = ronchonner **GROUSER** (n) grincheux, -euse : my husband's a terrible grouser = mon mari est un terrible grincheux ⓪ crab = rouspéteur.

GROVEL (to, -led) ramper : I refuse to grovel before the boss = je refuse de ramper devant le patron ⓪ to toady = fayoter.

GROW (to, grew, grown) **1/** grandir (s.o.), pousser (hair, plants, etc.) : how you've grown ! = comme tu as grandi !, my hair's growing fast = mes cheveux poussent vite
to grow (vegetables/flowers) = faire pousser (des légumes/fleurs)

to grow on s.o. = gagner à être connu : his paintings grow on you = sa peinture gagne à être connue
she'll soon grow out of (her coat) = (le manteau) sera bientôt trop petit pour elle
she'll grow out of (her theater bug) = (son entichement pour le théâtre) lui passera
to grow up = grandir : he grew up in New York = il a grandi à New York ⓪ to grow old = vieillir
☠ ça la grandit = it makes her taller
— pousser → to push
2/ s'agrandir : the business is growing = l'affaire s'agrandit ⓪ to expand = être en pleine expansion ☠ agrandir une photo = to blow up a photograph.

GROWL (to, -ed) gronder : the dog's growling = le chien gronde ⓪ to bark = aboyer ☠ → to scold **GROWL** (n) grondement (m) ⓪ bark = aboiement ☠ grondement de tonnerre = roll of thunder.

GROWN-UP (n) grande personne (f) : a film for grown-ups only = un film pour les grandes personnes seulement ≠ kid = gosse.

GROWTH (n) **1/** croissance (f) : economic growth = la croissance économique ⓪ development = développement **2/** excroissance (f) : a growth on her leg = une excroissance à la jambe ⓪ lump = grosseur ☠ une excroissance de l'injustice sociale = an outgrowth of social injustice.

GRUB (n) boustifaille (f) : what lousy grub ! = quelle boustifaille infecte ! ⓪ eats = bouffe.

GRUB (to, -bed) piquer : to grub cigarettes/something to eat = piquer des cigarettes/quelque chose à manger ⓪ to scrounge = rabioter ☠ → to sting.

GRUBBY (adj, -ier, -iest) crado (inv), cradingue : grubby clothes = vêtements cradingues/crado ⓪ filthy = crasseux.

GRUDGE (n) rancune (f) : an old grudge = une vieille rancune ⓪ resentment = ressentiment
to bear a grudge against s.o. = garder rancune à qqn/avoir une dent contre qqn
☠ sans rancune ! = no hard feelings !

GRUDGINGLY (adv) à contrecœur : he did it grudgingly = il l'a fait à contrecœur ⓪ reluctantly = avec réticence.

GRUEL(L)ING (adj) exténuant, -e : this work's gruelling = ce travail est exténuant ⓪ trying = éprouvant.

GRUFF (adj, -er, -est) bourru, -e : gruff manners = des manières bourrues ⓪ rough = rude.

GRUMBLE (to, -d) bougonner : she grumbles all the time = elle bougonne tout le temps ⓪ to gripe = rouspéter.

GRUMPY (adj, -ier, -iest) grincheux, -euse : a grumpy husband = un mari grincheux ⓪ cantankerous = acariâtre.

GRUNT (n) grognement (m) **GRUNT** (to, -ed) pousser des grognements : he never speaks, he grunts = *il ne parle pas, il pousse des grognements.*

G-STRING (n) *cache-sexe (m)* : the stripteaser just wore a g-string = *la strip-teaseuse portait uniquement un cache-sexe.*

GUARANTEE (n) *garantie (f)* : a two-year guarantee = *une garantie de deux ans* = guaranty ☠ *c'est une garantie contre le vol* = it's a safeguard against robbery.

GUARANTEE (to, -d) *garantir :* the watch is guaranteed for two years = *la montre est garantie deux ans,* I guarantee he'll pay you back = *je vous garantis qu'il vous remboursera* Ⓞ to vouch for = *se porter garant de.*

GUARD (n) *garde (m)* : the king's guards = *les gardes du roi* Ⓞ bodyguard = *garde du corps,* sentry = *sentinelle*
to be on one's guard = *être sur ses gardes* Ⓞ to be wary = *se méfier*
to catch s.o. off guard = *prendre qqn au dépourvu* ≠ to be caught napping = *être pris en défaut*
on guard = *de garde* Ⓞ on duty = *de service*
(prison) guard = *gardien (de prison)*
☠ *chien de garde* = watchdog
— *prendre garde* = to watch out
— *la garde des enfants* = custody of the children
— *garde des Sceaux* = Secretary of Justice.

GUARD (to, -ed) *garder :* to guard a prisoner = *garder un prisonnier* Ⓞ to watch over = *surveiller*
to guard against = *se prémunir contre*
☠ *garder (enfants/magasin)* = to mind (kids/store)
— *garder le lit* = to be bedridden
— *garder rancune* = to bear a grudge
— *gardez-le pour vous* = keep it to yourself
— *elle garde le même poste depuis 10 ans* = she has held down/kept the same job for 10 years
— *garder des actions* = to hang on to stocks
— *le lait se garde deux jours* = milk will keep for two days
— *je te garde du gâteau* = I'll save you some cake.

GUARDIAN (n) *tuteur, -trice :* the child's guardian = *le tuteur de l'enfant* ≠ ward = *pupille*
guardian angel = *ange gardien.*

GUERRILLA (n) *guérillero (m)* : three guerrillas took control of the plane = *trois guérilleros se sont emparés de l'avion* Ⓞ rebel = *rebelle*
(urban) guerrilla warfare = *guérilla (urbaine).*

GUESS (n, -es) **my guess is that (he'll marry her)** = *à mon idée (il va l'épouser)* Ⓞ in my opinion = *à mon avis*
I'll give you (two) guesses ! = *devine un peu!/tu as droit à (deux) erreurs !*
take a guess ! = *devine !* = guess !
your guess is as good as mine = *je n'en sais pas plus que vous.*

GUESS (to, -ed) **1/** *deviner :* guess how old I am ! = *devinez quel âge j'ai !* **2/** *imaginer :* I guess he'll be late = *j'imagine qu'il sera en retard* Ⓞ to think = *penser* ☠ → to imagine

to keep s.o. guessing = *tenir qqn en haleine :* he keeps the press guessing about his candidacy = *il tient la presse en haleine au sujet de sa candidature*
I never guessed (she was gay) = *je n'aurais jamais deviné qu'(elle était homosexuelle)*
guess what ? = *tu sais quoi ?*
I guess so ! = *je suppose !* = I suppose so !
(I'll have to walk home,) I guess = *je suppose (qu'il va falloir que je rentre à pied).*

GUESSWORK (n) **it's just guesswork (but I think she'll win her case)** = *c'est juste une supposition (mais je pense qu'elle aura gain de cause).*

GUEST (n) *invité, -e :* to have guests for the weekend = *avoir des invités pour le week-end* Ⓞ guesthouse = *pension de famille* ≠ host = *hôte*
be my guest ! = *ne te gêne pas ! :* if you want to sleep with my husband, be my guest ! = *si tu veux coucher avec mon mari, ne te gêne pas !*
guest book = *livre d'or*
guest room = *chambre d'ami*
you're my guest ! = *vous êtes mon invité !/je vous invite !* Ⓞ it's my treat ! = *c'est moi qui régale !*
paying guest = *hôte payant.*

GUIDANCE (n) *orientation (f)* : she needs career guidance = *elle a besoin d'orientation pour sa carrière*
guidance counselor = *conseiller d'orientation.*

GUIDE (n) *guide (m, f)* : tourist guide = *guide pour touristes* Ⓞ sights = *curiosités*
a guide book = *un guide.*

GUIDE (to, -d) *guider :* he needs to be guided = *il a besoin d'être guidé* Ⓞ to lead = *conduire.*

GUIDELINES (n pl) *lignes directrices (f pl)* : the guidelines of his policy = *les lignes directrices de sa politique.*

GUILD (n) *g(u)ilde (f)* : the women's guild meets every second Tuesday = *la gilde des femmes se réunit un mardi sur deux* Ⓞ association = ←.

GUILE (n) *fourberie (f)* : the guiles of a scheming woman = *les fourberies d'une intrigante* Ⓞ cunning = *ruse.*

GUILELESS (adj) *sans malice :* she's candid and guileless = *elle est candide et sans malice* ≠ sly = *sournois.*

GUILLOTINE (n) *guillotine (f)* : the guillotine is no longer used in this country = *on ne se sert plus de la guillotine dans ce pays* Ⓞ to behead = *décapiter.*

GUILT (n inv) *culpabilité (f)* : he admitted his guilt = *il a avoué sa culpabilité* ≠ innocence = ←.

GUILTY (adj, -ier, -iest) *coupable :* he pleaded not guilty = *il a plaidé non coupable* Ⓞ at fault = *fautif* ≠ innocent = ←
to find s.o. guilty = *déclarer qqn coupable*
the guilty party = *le coupable* Ⓞ wrongdoer = *celui qui commet une infraction.*

GUINEA (n) *rital, -e* = wop.

GUINEA PIG (n) **1/** *cobaye (m)* : he was used as a guinea pig in an experiment = *il a servi de cobaye dans une expérience* **2/** *cochon (m) d'Inde* : the children forgot to feed the guinea pig = *les enfants ont oublié de nourrir le cochon d'Inde.*

GUITAR (n) *guitare (f)* : she plays the guitar = *elle joue de la guitare* ① guitarist = *guitariste*, violin = *violon*, banjo = ←.

GULF (n) *golfe (m)* : the Gulf of Mexico = *le golfe du Mexique* ☠ → golf.

GULLIBLE (adj) *jobard, -e* : how could you be so gullible as to believe the watch was gold ? = *comment as-tu pu être assez jobard pour croire que cette montre était en or ?* ① credulous = *crédule.*

GULP DOWN (to, -ed) *engloutir* : he gulped down three bottles of beer = *il a englouti trois bouteilles de bière* ① to toss down = *descendre*
☠ *engloutir une fortune dans* = to sink a fortune in
— *ce voyage a englouti toutes nos économies* = this trip swallowed up all our savings.

GUM (n) **1/** *chewing-gum (m)* ① bubble gum = *Malabar* **2/** *gencive (f)* : my gums bleed = *j'ai les gencives qui saignent* ① mouthwash = *bain de bouche.*

GUMPTION (n inv) *aplomb (m)* : it took a lot of gumption to say that = *il fallait beaucoup d'aplomb pour dire ça* ① chutzpah = *culot* ☠ → cheek.

GUN (n) *arme (f) à feu* : too many people own guns in the States = *il y a trop de gens qui possèdent une arme à feu aux États-Unis* ① pistol = *pistolet*, gat = *pétard*, rod = *flingue*, holster = *étui*, gunshot = *coup de feu*, gunpowder = *poudre*, shoot-out = *fusillade*, cartridge = *cartouche*, gunfire = *coups de feu*, revolver = ←, bullet = *balle*, handgun = *revolver de poche*, Saturday night special = *flingue de poche*
to go for one's gun = *dégainer* ① to fire = *tirer*
to carry a gun = *porter une arme*
gun moll = *femme gangster* : Bonnie was a gun moll = *Bonnie était une femme gangster* ① gangster = ←
gun license = *permis de port d'armes*
gun powder = *poudre à canon*
gunrunner = *trafiquant d'armes*
gunrunning = *trafic d'armes*
to jump the gun = 'prendre de vitesse : I wanted to ask you to dinner but you jumped the gun = *je voulais vous inviter à dîner, mais vous m'avez pris de vitesse*
to pull a gun = *braquer une arme à feu*
☠ *elle s'est braquée* = she got her back up
— *braquer une banque* = to hold up a bank
to stick to one's guns = *ne pas en démordre* ① not to budge an inch = *ne pas bouger d'un pouce.*

GUN (to, -ned) **to gun s.o. down** = *flinguer qqn* : the gang gunned him down = *le gang l'a flingué* ① to shoot down = *abattre*

to gun for = *avoir dans le collimateur* : the boss is gunning for you = *le patron vous a dans le collimateur.*

GUNFIRE (n inv) *coups (m pl) de feu* : gunfire was heard in the park = *on a entendu des coups de feu dans le parc* ① shoot-out = *fusillade.*

GUNG HO (adj) *tout feu tout flamme* : to be gung ho for an idea = *être tout feu tout flamme pour une idée* ≠ cool to = *pas très chaud pour.*

GUNMAN (n, -men) *homme (m) de main* : the Mafia and their gunmen = *la Mafia et ses hommes de main.*

GUNPOINT (n) **at gunpoint** = *en joue* : she was holding him at gunpoint = *elle le tenait en joue.*

GUNPOWDER (n) *poudre (f) à canon.*

GUNRUNNING (n) *trafic (m) d'armes* ① smuggling = *contrebande.*

GURGLE (to, -d) *glouglouter* : the baby gurgles in his bath = *le bébé glougloute dans sa baignoire.*

GURU (n) *gourou (m)* : gurus are often frauds = *les gourous sont souvent des charlatans* ① shrink = *psy*, master = *maître.*

GUSH (n) **a gush of feeling/blood** = *une effusion sentimentale/de sang.*

GUSH (to, -ed) *bêtifier* : to gush over a baby = *bêtifier sur un bébé.*

GUSHY (adj, -ier, -iest) *cucu(l) (inv)* : gushy love letters = *des lettres d'amour cucul* ① schmalzy = *plein de sentimentalisme.*

GUST (n) *rafale (f)* : a sudden gust of wind = *une rafale de vent soudaine* ① a squall = *un grain.*

GUSTO (n) **(to do stg) with gusto** = *(faire qqch) avec entrain.*

GUT (n) **a gut reaction** = *une réaction viscérale.*

GUT (to, -ted) *ne laisser debout que les murs* : the fire gutted the apartment = *l'incendie n'a laissé debout que les murs de l'appartement.*

GUTS (n pl) *culot (m)*, *tripes (f pl)* : he didn't have the guts to tell the boss off = *il n'a pas eu le culot/les tripes de dire au patron ce qu'il pensait* ① nerve = *toupet*, pluck = *cran*
he has no guts = *il n'a rien dans le ventre* ① he has no balls = *il n'a pas de couilles*
to hate s.o.'s guts = *ne pas pouvoir blairer qqn* ① not to stand the sight of = *ne pas pouvoir voir.*

GUTSY (adj, -ier, -iest) *culotté, -e* : that was a gutsy thing to do = *c'est culotté de faire ça* ① ballsy = *chiément gonflé*, brazen = *effronté.*

GUTTER (n) *caniveau (m)* : papers in the gutter = *des papiers dans le caniveau* ≠ sidewalk = *trottoir*
to come from the gutter = *sortir du ruisseau.*

GUY (n) *mec (m), type (m)* : she's going out with a great guy = *elle sort avec un mec/type formidable* ⓪ fellow = *type*, john = *gus* ≠ chick = *pépée* ☠ → type **what are you guys doing tonight ?** = *qu'est-ce que vous faites ce soir, les mecs ?* ⓪ what are you folks doing tonight ? = *qu'est-ce que vous faites ce soir, les gars ?*

GUZZLE (to, -d) *lamper* : he guzzled his wine noisily = *il a lampé son vin bruyamment* ⓪ to gulp down = *engloutir.*

GYM (n) **1/** *gymnase (m)* : I'll see you at 6 at the gym = *je te retrouve à 6 heures au gymnase* **2/** *gym (f)* : gym is her favorite class = *la gym est son cours préféré.*

GYMNASIUM (n, -a or -s) *gymnase (m)* : the volleyball game will be held in the gymnasium = *le match de volley aura lieu dans le gymnase* = gym.

GYMNASTICS (n pl) *gymnastique (f), gym (f)* : mental gymnastics = *gymnastique mentale/intellectuelle* ⓪ exercises = *exercices.*

GYNECOLOGIST (n) *gynécologue (m, f)* ⓪ obstetrician = *obstétricien*, midwife = *sage-femme.*

GYP (adj) **gyp joint** = *le coup de fusil* : don't eat there, it's really a gyp joint = *ne va pas manger là, c'est vraiment le coup de fusil* ⓪ tourist trap = *piège à touristes.*

GYP (to, -ped) *pigeonner* : he gypped me out of a dollar = *il m'a pigeonné d'un dollar* → TO HUSTLE.

GYPSY (n, -ies) *gitan, -e, romanichel, -elle.*

HABEAS CORPUS (n) *habeas corpus (m).*

HABIT (n) *habitude (f) :* smoking is a bad habit = *c'est une mauvaise habitude de fumer* ⓪ custom = *coutume.*

to be in the habit of = *être habitué à :* I'm in the habit of going to bed early = *je suis habitué à me coucher tôt* ⓪ to be accustomed to = *être accoutumé à* **to break o.s. of a habit** = *se défaire d'une habitude* **don't make it a habit of (coming late)** = *ne prends pas l'habitude d'(arriver en retard)*	**to get into the habit of** = *prendre l'habitude de :* I got into the habit of taking sleeping pills = *j'ai pris l'habitude de prendre des somnifères* ⓪ to get used to = *s'habituer à* **to kick the habit (of)** = *se désaccoutumer (de) :* I kicked the habit of smoking = *je me suis désaccoutumé du tabac*

☠ *avoir ses habitudes* = to have one's own little ways.

HABIT-FORMING (adj) *qui crée une accoutumance :* some medicines are habit-forming = *certains médicaments créent une accoutumance.*

HABITUAL (adj) **1/** *habituel, -elle :* a habitual gesture = *un geste habituel* ≠ occasional = *occasionnel* ☠ « *habitual* » *est moins employé que* « usual » **2/** *impénitent, -e :* a habitual drinker/liar = *un buveur/menteur impénitent* ⓪ inveterate = *invétéré.*

HABITUALLY (adj) *habituellement :* she's habitually late = *habituellement, elle est en retard* ⓪ customarily = *de coutume.*

HACKNEYED (adj) *rebattu, -e :* hackneyed ideas/ themes = *des idées rebattues/des thèmes rebattus* ⓪ old hat = *vieux jeu* ≠ fresh = *neuf.*

HAGGARD (adj) *hagard, -e :* a haggard expression = *une expression hagarde* ⓪ gaunt = *décharné.*

HAGGLE (to, -d) **to haggle over (a price)** = *ergoter sur (un prix)* ⓪ to dicker over = *débattre (de).*

HAIL (n) *grêle (f) :* the hail ruined the crop = *la grêle a détruit la récolte* ⓪ sleet = *neige fondue* **HAIL** (to, -ed) *grêler.*

HAIR (n inv) **1/** *cheveux (m pl), tifs (m pl)* (LV) : my hair is brown = *j'ai les cheveux bruns,* I had my hair cut = *je me suis fait couper les cheveux*

bald = *chauve* **bangs** = *frange/chiens* **barber** = *coiffeur* **beauty parlor** = *salon de coiffure* **at the beauty parlor** = *chez le coiffeur* = **at the hairdresser's** **blond** = ← **to blow** = *faire un brushing* **bobby pin** = *pince à cheveux/barrette* **braid** = *tresse*	**brunette** = *châtain* **brush** = *brosse* **brushing** = ← **chignon** = ← **comb** = *peigne* **comb-out** = *coup de peigne* **curler** = *bigoudi/rouleau* **dandruff** = *pellicule* **dryer** = *séchoir* **to dye** = *teindre* **fair-haired** = *aux cheveux clairs* **to frizz** = *friser*	**haircut** = *coupe de cheveux* **hairdo** = *coiffure* **hairnet** = *résille* **hairpiece** = *postiche* **hairpin** = *épingle à cheveux* **mane** = *crinière* **part** = *raie* **permanent** = *permanente* = **perm** **pigtail** = *natte* **ponytail** = *queue de cheval* **receding hairline** = *front dégarni*

redhead = *roux* **scalp** = *cuir chevelu* **to set** = *faire une mise en plis* **shampoo** = *shampooing*	**spray** = *laque* **to tease** = *crêper* **to trim** = *rafraîchir*	**wash and set** = *shampooing et mise en plis* **wave** = *ondulation* **wig** = *perruque*

to get in s.o.'s hair = *être dans les jambes de qqn* ⓧ to get on s.o.'s nerves = *taper sur les nerfs de qqn* **to let one's hair down** = *se décontracter* : after two drinks, she let her hair down = *après avoir bu deux verres, elle s'est décontractée* ⓧ to let off steam = *se défouler* **to lose one's hair** = *perdre ses cheveux* ⓧ to get bald = *devenir chauve* **that made my hair stand on end** = *ça m'a fait*	*dresser les cheveux sur la tête* ⓧ it scared the hell out of me = *ça m'a flanqué les foies* **stop splitting hairs** = *arrêtez de couper les cheveux en quatre/de chercher midi à quatorze heures* ⓧ stop nitpicking = *arrêtez de chercher la petite bête* **to tear one's hair out** = *s'arracher les cheveux* ≠ to keep one's cool = *garder son sang-froid* **to wash one's hair** = *se laver les cheveux/la tête* **who does your hair?** = *qui vous coiffe ?*

☠ *se faire des cheveux (blancs)* = to be worried sick — *c'est arrivé comme un cheveu sur la soupe* = it was bad timing	— *tiré par les cheveux* = farfetched — *il y a un cheveu* = there's a snag — *ne tenir qu'à un cheveu* = to hang by a thread — *avoir un cheveu sur la langue* = to have a lisp

2/ poil *(m)* : he has a lot of hair on his chest = *il a beaucoup de poil(s) sur la poitrine* ⓧ hairy = *poilu/velu*

☠ *avoir un poil dans la main* = to be workshy — *ne plus avoir un poil de sec* = to be scared stiff — *il m'est tombé sur le poil* = he laced into me — *reprendre du poil de la bête* = to get it together — *à poil* = bare-assed	— *au poil* = hunky-dory — *des gens de tout poil* = people from all walks of life — *être de bon* ≠ *mauvais poil* = to be in a good ≠ bad mood.

HAIRDO (n) *coiffure* (f) : a new hairdo = *une nouvelle coiffure* ⓧ cut = *coupe*.

HAIRDRESSER (n) *coiffeur, -euse (pour femmes)* : to go to the hairdresser's = *aller chez le coiffeur* ☠ *coiffeur (pour hommes)* = barber.

HAIR-RAISING (adj) *à faire dresser les cheveux sur la tête* : a hair-raising movie = *un film à vous faire dresser les cheveux sur la tête* ⓧ harrowing = *effroyable*.

HAIR(S)BREADTH (n) **(he lost) by a hair(s)-breadth** = *(il a perdu) d'un cheveu* ⓧ it was a close shave = *il était moins une*.

HAITI (n) *Haïti* (f) **HAITIAN** (n, adj) *Haïtien, -enne*.

HALF (n, -ves) *moitié* (f) : I'll give you half = *je vous en donnerai la moitié* ≠ whole = *tout*
my better/other half = *ma moitié* ⓧ my spouse = *mon épouse*
by halves = *à moitié* : she does nothing by halves = *elle ne fait rien à moitié* ≠ completely = *complètement*
to go halves = *faire moitié-moitié* ⓧ to go dutch = *payer sa part*
half an hour = *une demi-heure* : I'll be back in half an hour = *je serai de retour dans une demi-heure* ⓧ a quarter of an hour = *un quart d'heure*
(an hour) and a half = *(une heure) et demie*

that's half the battle = *le plus dur est fait*
in half = *en deux* : cut the apple in half = *coupez la pomme en deux*
(and) that's not the half of it ! = *(et) ce n'est pas tout !* = (and) that's not the whole story !
half a loaf is better than none = *c'est toujours ça de pris* ⓧ beggars can't be choosers = *faute de grives, on mange des merles*
half a dozen = *une demi-douzaine*
half past (nine) = *(neuf heures) et demie*.

HALF (adj) *demi-* : half measures = *demi-mesures*
half brother ≠ **sister** = *demi-frère* ≠ *-sœur*
a half hour = *une demi-heure*
half time = *mi-temps*.

HALF (adv) *à moitié, à demi* : she's half French = *elle est à moitié française* ≠ wholly = *entièrement*
to be half listening = *n'écouter que d'une oreille*
not half bad = *pas si mal* : the play wasn't half bad = *la pièce n'était pas si mal* ≠ nothing to write home about = *qui ne casse pas des briques*.

HALF-ASSED (adj) *à la con* : a half-assed job = *un boulot à la con* ⓧ crummy = *moche*.

HALF-BAKED (adj) *à la noix* : a half-baked lawyer = *un avocat à la noix* ⓧ two-bit = *à la manque*.

HALFHEARTED (adj) *sans conviction* : a halfhearted attempt = *une tentative faite sans conviction* **HALF-HEARTEDLY** (adv) *à contrecœur* : she accepted the job halfheartedly = *elle a accepté cet emploi à contrecœur.*

HALF-PINT (n) *demi-portion (f)* : screw off half-pint ! = *veux-tu me foutre le camp, espèce de demi-portion !* ⓪ shorty = *microbe.*

HALFWAY (adj) **to take halfway measures** = *prendre des demi-mesures.*

HALFWAY (adv) **halfway through** = *au milieu de* : we left halfway through the play = *nous sommes partis au milieu de la pièce*
to meet s.o. halfway = 1/ *couper la poire en deux* ⓪ to compromise = *faire un compromis* 2/ *rencontrer qqn à mi-chemin* : don't drive all the way to New York, let's meet halfway = *ne viens pas jusqu'à New York, rencontrons-nous à mi-chemin.*

HALF-WIT (n) *demeuré, -e* : his assistant's a half-wit = *son assistant est un demeuré* → STUPID.

HALL (n) 1/ *entrée (f)* : the telephone is in the hall = *le téléphone est dans l'entrée* ☠ → entrance 2/ *couloir (m)* : the children play ball in the hall = *les enfants jouent au ballon dans le couloir* ⓪ vestibule = *←*
☠ *le hall de l'hôtel* = the hotel lobby
— *couloir (train)* = aisle.

HALLMARK (n) *marque (f)* : flavor is the hallmark of a good wine = *la saveur est la marque d'un bon vin* ☠ → mark.

HALLOWEEN (n) *Halloween (f)*, *fête du 31 octobre où les enfants se déguisent en sorcières et fantômes* ⓪ pumpkin = *potiron.*

HALLUCINATION (n) *hallucination (f)* : to have hallu-cinations = *avoir des hallucinations* ⓪ illusion = *←.*

HALO (n) *auréole (f)*, halo *(m)* (moon) : an angel with a halo = *un ange avec une auréole*, a halo around the moon = *un halo autour de la lune.*

HALT (to, -ed) *stopper* : to halt production = *stopper la production* ⓪ to stop = *arrêter.*

HALTER (n) *bustier (m)* ⓪ top = *haut*
a halter top = *un débardeur.*

HAM (n) 1/ *jambon (m)* : ham and eggs = *des œufs au jambon* ⓪ bacon = *←* 2/ *cabot (m), cabotin, -e* : as an actor, he's a ham = *comme acteur, c'est un cabotin* ☠ *un cabot (chien)* = a mutt 3/ *radio-amateur (m)* ⓪ pirate station = *radio pirate.*

HAMBURGER (n) *hamburger (m)* ⓪ French fries = *frites.*

HAMMER (n) *marteau (m)* : get me a hammer ! = *va me chercher un marteau !* ⓪ pliers = *pince/tenailles*, screwdriver = *tournevis*, nail = *clou*
the hammer and sickle = *la faucille et le marteau*
☠ *t'es marteau !* = you're batty !

HAMMER (to, -ed) **to hammer away at (the same thing)** = *rabâcher toujours (la même chose)* ⓪ to harp on = *revenir sur.*

HAMMOCK (n) *hamac (m)* ⓪ nap = *somme.*

HAMPER (to, -ed) *gêner* : he was hampered by his lack of money/diplomas = *il a été gêné par le manque d'argent/de diplômes* ⓪ to thwart = *contrecarrer* ☠ → to mind.

HAMSTER (n) *hamster (m)* : five hamsters playing under his bed = *cinq hamsters en train de jouer sous son lit* ⓪ rabbit = *lapin.*

HAND (n) *main (f)* : take my hand = *prends ma main* ⓪ paw = *paluche/pince*, finger = *doigt*

at hand = *sous la main* ⓪ within reach = *à portée de la main*	soupe ⓪ to be ungrateful = *être ingrat*	ing ? = *peux-tu me donner un coup de main pour la peinture ?*
to ask for s.o.'s hand = *demander la main de qqn* ⓪ to pop the question = *faire sa déclaration*	**to change hands** = *changer de mains* : the land changed hands several times = *le terrain a changé de mains plusieurs fois*	⓪ **to give s.o. a helping hand** = *prêter main-forte à qqn* = **to lend s.o. a hand**
to be hand in glove with = *avoir partie liée avec* ⓪ to be in league with = *être de conni-vence avec*	**to eat out of s.o.'s hand** = *manger dans la main de qqn* ⓪ to be at s.o.'s beck and call = *faire les quatre volontés de qqn*	**to give s.o. a (big) hand** = *faire une ovation à qqn* ⓪ to applaud = *applaudir*
to be in s.o.'s hands = *être dans les mains de qqn* : you're in the hands of a good doctor/ lawyer = *vous êtes dans les mains d'un bon médecin/avocat*	**to fall into (enemy) hands** = *tomber entre les mains de (l'ennemi)*	**to go hand in hand** = *aller de pair* : that goes hand in hand with what I was saying = *ça va de pair avec ce que je disais*
to bite the hand that feeds one = *ne pas avoir la reconnais-sance du ventre/cracher dans la*	**to force s.o.'s hand** = *forcer la main à qqn* ⓪ to corner s.o. = *coincer qqn*	**a hand job** = *une branlette* ⓪ a blow job = *une pipe*
	to give s.o. a hand = *donner un coup de main à qqn* : can you give me a hand with the paint-	**hand luggage** = *bagages à main*
		hands off ! = *bas les pattes !*
		hands up ! = *haut les mains !*
		to have a hand in = *y être*

pour quelque chose : he had a hand in getting me a job = *il y est pour quelque chose si j'ai trouvé du travail* ⓪ to play a part in = *jouer un rôle dans*
in hand ≠ **out of hand** = *en main* ≠ *pas en main* : the situation's in ≠ out of hand = *nous avons* ≠ *nous n'avons pas la situation en main* ⓪ under control = *bien en main*
to have a (good) hand = *avoir une (bonne) main (cartes)*
to have one's hands full = *avoir fort à faire* ⓪ to have one's work cut out for one = *avoir du pain sur la planche*
to have roving hands = *avoir les mains baladeuses* ⓪ to paw = *tripoter*
to hold hands = *se tenir la main* : holding hands is romantic = *c'est romantique de se tenir la main* ⓪ to walk arm in arm = *marcher bras dessus, bras dessous*
to keep a hand in = *garder un pied dans* : he retired but he keeps a hand in the Stock Market = *il a pris sa retraite mais il garde un pied à la Bourse*

to lay one's hands on = 1/ *lever la main sur* : he never laid his hands on his kids = *il n'a jamais levé la main sur ses gosses* 2/ *mettre la main sur* : the guerrilla is buying all the arms he can lay his hands on = *le guérillero achète toutes les armes sur lesquelles il peut mettre la main* 3/ *faire main basse sur* : the Soviets would like to lay their hands on the Middle East oil fields = *les Soviétiques aimeraient bien faire main basse sur les gisements pétrolifères du Moyen-Orient*
to live from hand to mouth = *vivre au jour le jour* → POOR
to make money hand over fist = *gagner un fric fou* ≠ to lose one's shirt = *perdre sa chemise*
off ≠ **on one's hands** = *ne plus avoir* ≠ *avoir sur les bras* : with the kids off her hands, she can work again = *depuis qu'elle n'a plus les gosses sur les bras, elle peut retravailler*
on hand = *en stock* : we don't have the color you want on hand = *nous n'avons pas la couleur*

que vous voulez en stock
to overplay one's hand = *forcer la note* ⓪ to overdo it = *en faire trop*
to play right into s.o.'s hands = *faire le jeu de qqn* ⓪ to swallow the bait = *mordre à l'hameçon*
to shake hands = *(se) serrer la main*
to show/lay down one's hand = *abattre son jeu/ses cartes*
to take in hand = *prendre en main* : after the divorce she took her life in hand = *après son divorce elle a pris sa vie en main*
to throw in one's hand = *baisser les bras* ⓪ to give up = *abandonner (la partie)*
to wait on s.o.'s hand and foot = *être aux petits soins pour qqn* ≠ to twist s.o. around one's little finger = *mener qqn par le bout du nez*
to wash one's hands of (the problem) = *se laver les mains de (la question)*
to win stg hands down = *gagner qqch haut la main* ≠ to fall on one's face = *se casser la figure*

☠ *en venir aux mains* = to come to blows
— *être pris la main dans le sac* = to be caught red-handed
— *se faire la main* = to get the feel/the hang (of stg)
— *j'en mettrais ma main au feu* = I'd bet my bottom dollar
— *passer la main dans le dos de qqn* = to butter s.o. up
— *mettre la main au panier à qqn* = to goose s.o.

— *passer la main* = to step down
— *remettez-le-lui en main propre* = give it to him personally
— *main-d'œuvre* = manpower
— *avoir perdu la main* = to have lost the touch
— *ne pas y aller de main morte* = to really go at it
— *elle est en main* = she's going steady with s.o.
— *payer de la main à la main* = to pay under the counter.

HAND (to, -ed) *filer* (LV) : hand me the salt please = *file-moi le sel, s'il te plaît* ⓪ to pass = *passer* ☠ → to tail
don't hand me that ! = *pour qui me prends-tu ?* → BUZZ OFF !

---

to hand down = 1/ *transmettre* : the custom was handed down through the ages = *la coutume s'est transmise à travers les âges* ☠ → to transmit 2/ *rendre* : to hand down a verdict = *rendre un verdict* ☠ → to return
to hand in = *remettre* : hand in your papers = *remettez vos copies* ☠ → to postpone
to hand out = *distribuer* : hand out the papers please = *distribuez les copies, s'il vous plaît* ☠ →

to distribute
to hand over = *remettre* : hand the gun over ! = *remets-moi ton arme !*, to hand a criminal over to justice = *remettre un criminel à la justice* ☠ → to postpone
I have to hand it to you ! = *je vous tire mon chapeau !* ⓪ I have to give you credit = *je mets cela à votre crédit*.

HANDBAG (n) *sac (m) à main* = purse.

HANDBILL (n) *prospectus (m)* ⓪ flyer = *imprimé.*

HANDBOOK (n) *manuel (m) :* you'll find the instructions in the handbook = *vous trouverez les instructions dans le manuel* = manual.

HANDCUFFS (n pl) *menottes (f pl) :* put the handcuffs on him = *passez-lui les menottes* ⓪ gag = *bâillon* **HANDCUFF** (to, -ed) *passer les menottes à.*

HANDFUL (n) **a handful of (peanuts/people)** = *une poignée de (cacahuètes/gens)* ≠ a lot of = *beaucoup de* **to be a handful** = *donner du fil à retordre :* her kids are a handful = *ses gosses lui donnent du fil à retordre.*

HANDICAP (n) *handicap (m) :* not speaking languages is a handicap = *c'est un handicap de ne pas parler de langues étrangères* ⓪ disadvantage = *désavantage.*

HANDICAP (to, -ped) *handicaper :* he's handicapped by his lisp = *il est handicapé par son zézaiement.*

HANDICAPPED (n, adj) *handicapé, -e :* physically handicapped = *handicapé physique.*

HANDICRAFT (n) *artisanat (m) :* pottery is a handicraft = *la poterie est un artisanat.*

HANDKERCHIEF (n) *mouchoir (m)* = hanky ☠ *arriver dans un mouchoir* = to be a close finish.

HANDLE (n) **1/** *poignée (f)* (door), *manche (m)* (umbrella) **to fly off the handle** = *sortir de ses gonds* → ANGRY ☠ *une poignée de gens* = a handful of people — *une poignée de main* = a handshake — *manche* = sleeve **2/** *blase (m)* (LV) : what's your handle ? = *c'est quoi ton blase ?* ⓪ name = *nom.*

HANDLE (to, -d) **1/** *s'occuper de :* my lawyer handles all my business deals = *mon avocat s'occupe de toutes mes affaires* ⓪ to manage = *gérer* **2/** *faire face à :* I can't handle all his problems = *je n'arrive pas à faire face à tous ses problèmes* = to cope with ⓪ to carry = *assumer* **3/** *faire :* we don't handle secondhand cars = *nous ne faisons pas les voitures d'occasion* ⓪ to sell = *vendre* ☠ → to do **I'll handle it for you** = *je m'en occuperai à ta/votre place* **to handle s.o.** = *savoir prendre qqn :* she does not handle him well = *elle ne sait pas bien le prendre.*

HANDMADE (adj) *fait, -e main :* her clothes are hand-made = *ses vêtements sont faits main* ≠ mass-produced = *fait en série.*

HAND-ME-DOWN (n) *vêtement (m) donné :* his family was very poor and he always wore hand-me-downs = *sa famille était très pauvre et il a toujours porté des vêtements donnés.*

HANDOUT (n) *aumône (f) :* the beggar asked for a handout = *le mendiant demandait l'aumône* ⓪ charity = *charité.*

HANDPICK (to, -ed) *trier sur le volet :* she had hand-picked the guests for the dinner = *les invités qui participaient à son dîner étaient triés sur le volet* ⓪ to choose = *choisir.*

HANDSHAKE (n) *poignée (f) de main* ⓪ to shake hands = *(se) serrer la main.*

HANDS-OFF (adj) *de non-intervention :* a hands-off policy = *une politique de non-intervention.*

HANDSOME (adj) **1/** *beau (bel), belle :* a handsome man/outfit = *un bel homme/ensemble* ⓪ good-looking = *bien* ☠ → beautiful **2/** *coquet, -ette :* he earns a handsome salary = *il gagne un salaire coquet* ☠ *elle est coquette* = she's coquettish.

HANDSOMELY (adv) *très bien :* she's handsomely paid = *elle est très bien payée* = very well.

HANDWRITING (n) *écriture (f) :* I can't read her handwriting = *je ne peux pas lire son écriture* = writing ⓪ scribbling = *gribouillage,* graphology = *graphologie,* graphologist = *graphologue* **to see the handwriting on the wall** = *pressentir ce qui va se passer :* when the war broke out only a few Jews saw the handwriting on the wall = *quand la guerre a éclaté, quelques juifs seulement avaient pressenti ce qui allait se passer* ☠ *les écritures (comptes)* = the books — *les Écritures (saintes)* = the Scriptures.

HANDY (adj, -ier, -iest) *commode :* it's handy to have two telephones in the house = *c'est commode d'avoir deux téléphones chez soi* ⓪ practical = *pratique* **he's handy around the house** = *il est bricoleur* ⓪ a handyman = *un homme à tout faire* **to come in handy** = *s'avérer utile :* a flashlight can come in handy around the house = *une lampe électrique peut s'avérer utile dans la maison* ☠ *une heure commode* = a convenient time — *il n'est pas commode* = he isn't very easy to deal with.

HANG (n) **the hang of it** = *le coup de main :* playing the guitar is difficult ; I don't get the hang of it = *c'est difficile de jouer de la guitare ; je n'arrive pas à prendre le coup de main* ⓪ the feel for = *le sens de*

I don't give a hang ! = *je m'en bats l'œil !* ⓪ it's no skin off my back ! = *je m'en moque comme de ma première chemise !* I don't give a hoot ! = *je m'en moque !*

HANG (to, hung, hung (stg) or hanged, hanged (s.o.)) **1/** pendre : they hanged the prisoner = *ils ont pendu le prisonnier*, they hung their wet clothes = *ils ont pendu leurs vêtements mouillés* ⚐ hanging = *pendaison*, noose = *nœud coulant* ☠ *être pendu au téléphone* = not to get off the phone

hang it ! = *nom d'une pipe !* → GOSH !

⚐ **I'll be hanged if ... !** = *je veux bien être pendu si ... !* → GOSH !

2/ accrocher : we hung the picture over the fireplace = *nous avons accroché le tableau au-dessus de la cheminée*

☠ *accrocher (une voiture)* = to bump into (a car)
— *être accroché (drogue)* = to be hooked (drug)
— *tu peux toujours te l'accrocher* = you can whistle for it

— *s'accrocher avec qqn* = to quarrel with s.o.
— *accrocher l'œil* = to catch the eye
— *on a tout de suite accroché* = we clicked right away

to **hang around** = **1/** traîner : he's hanging around with a tough group = *il traîne avec une bande de voyous* **2/** traîner : the pickpockets hang around Broadway = *les pickpockets traînent autour de Broadway* ☠ → to drag
why don't you hang around for a while ? = *pourquoi ne restez-vous pas un peu ?*
hang in there ! = *accroche-toi !* ≠ give up ! = *laisse tomber !*
to **hang on** = **1/** être suspendu à : everything hangs on his decision = *tout est suspendu à sa décision* ⚐ to depend on = *dépendre de* **2/** tenir : can you hang on for another week ? = *est-ce que vous pouvez tenir encore une semaine ?* ⚐ to last = *durer* ☠ → to hold
hang on ! = **1/** *un instant !* ⚐ just a minute ! = *une minute !* **2/** *ne quittez pas !* ⚐ don't hang up ! = *ne raccrochez pas !*
to **hang on to (stg)** = *garder*

(qqch) : hang on to the stocks for a while = *gardez les actions encore un bout de temps* ☠ → to guard
to **hang out** = **1/** traînasser : we're not doing anything special, just hanging out = *on ne fait rien de spécial, on traînasse* ⚐ to screw around = *ne rien foutre* **2/** être (toujours) fourré : when she's in Paris, she always hangs out on the Left Bank = *quand elle est à Paris, elle est toujours fourrée sur la rive gauche* ⚐ to haunt = *hanter*
to **hang out with** = *traîner ses guêtres avec* : she hangs out with strange people = *elle traîne ses guêtres avec des gens étranges* ⚐ to knock around with = *fréquenter*
to **hang over** = *peser sur* : the threat of a nuclear war is hanging over us = *la menace d'une guerre nucléaire pèse sur nous*
to **hang together** = **1/** res-

ter solidaire : we must hang together if we want to win = *il faut rester solidaires si nous voulons gagner* ⚐ to throw in with = *se ranger du côté de* **2/** tenir debout : his story doesn't hang together = *son histoire ne tient pas debout*
to **hang up** = **1/** raccrocher : don't hang up ! = *ne raccrochez pas !* ⚐ hold the line ! = *restez en ligne !* ☠ *se raccrocher à (son mari)* = to cling to (one's husband) **2/** retarder : I was hung up at the office and I missed the party = *j'ai été retardé au bureau et j'ai raté la soirée* ☠ → to delay
to **be hung up on s.o.** = *avoir qqn dans la peau* : she's hung up on my brother = *elle a mon frère dans la peau* = she's stuck up on my brother
to **hang up on s.o.** = *raccrocher au nez de qqn* : she was so angry that she hung up on him = *elle était tellement en colère qu'elle lui a raccroché au nez.*

HANGAR (n) hangar (m) : the hangar is used to store my old furniture = *je me sers du hangar pour remiser mes vieux meubles* ⚐ barn = *grange*.

HANGER (n) portemanteau (m) : there's a hanger for your jacket = *il y a un portemanteau pour votre veste* ⚐ closet = *placard*.

HANGER-ON (n, hangers-on) pot (m) de colle : there are always hangers-on around stars = *il y a toujours des pots de colle dans l'entourage des vedettes* ⚐ leech = *sangsue*.

HANGMAN (n, -men) bourreau (m) (pour une pendaison) ☠ → executioner.

HANGOUT (n) fief (m) : now that I live in Paris this restaurant's my hangout = *maintenant que j'habite à Paris, ce restaurant est mon fief* ⚐ haunt = *lieu favori* ☠ → stronghold.

HANGOVER (n) gueule (f) de bois : I drank too much last night and I had a hangover this morning = *j'ai trop bu hier soir et ce matin j'avais la gueule de bois* → DRUNK.

HANG-UP (n) *complexe* (m) : he has a hang-up about his acne = *il a un complexe à cause de son acné* ☠ → complex.

HANKY-PANKY (n inv) **1/** *cuisine* (f) : hanky-panky during the elections = *cuisine électorale* ⓓ monkey business = *grenouillage* ☠ → kitchen **2/** *coucheries* (f pl) : a lot of extramarital hanky-panky = *beaucoup de coucheries en dehors du foyer conjugal* ⓓ sex = *sexe*.

HAPHAZARD (adj) *au petit bonheur (la chance)* : a haphazard choice = *un choix fait au petit bonheur (la chance)* **HAPHAZARDLY** (adv) *au petit bonheur (la chance)* : to choose haphazardly = *choisir au petit bonheur (la chance)*.

HAPLESS (adj) *infortuné, -e* : a hapless candidate = *un candidat infortuné* ⓓ unlucky = *qui n'a pas de chance*.

HAPPEN (to, -ed) *se passer* : when did it happen ? = *ça s'est passé quand ?* ⓓ to take place = *avoir lieu*
it so happens that (you're wrong) = *il se trouve que (vous avez tort)*
to happen to = **1/** *se trouver que* : I happen to be going there also = *il se trouve que j'y vais aussi* **2/** *par hasard* : do you happen to know why ? = *est-ce que par hasard vous savez pourquoi ?* **3/** *arriver à* : what happened to his sister ? = *qu'est-il arrivé à sa sœur ?* ☠ → to pass.

HAPPENING (n) **1/** *événement* (m) : her life's full of happenings = *elle a une vie remplie d'événements* = event **2/** *happening* (m) (theater) ⓓ episode = *épisode*.

HAPPILY (adv) *heureusement* : happily, he came on time = *heureusement, il est arrivé à l'heure* = fortunately ≠ unhappily = *malheureusement*
they lived happily for ever after = *ils (se marièrent,) furent heureux et eurent beaucoup d'enfants* ⓓ once upon a time = *il était une fois*.

HAPPINESS (n inv) *bonheur* (m) : I have rarely known such happiness = *j'ai rarement connu un tel bonheur* ⓓ bliss = *félicité* ≠ unhappiness = *malheur*
☠ *tu as trouvé ton bonheur ?* = did you find what you wanted ?
— *porter bonheur* = to bring luck.

HAPPY (adj, -ier, -iest) *heureux, -euse* : a happy family/woman = *une famille/femme heureuse* ⓓ joyous = *joyeux*, riding high = *aux anges* ≠ unhappy = *malheureux*
to be happy about = *être heureux de* : I'm happy about what you told me = *je suis heureux de ce que vous m'avez dit*
happy birthday ! = *heureux/joyeux anniversaire !*
happy ending = *heureux dénouement*
the happy few = *les quelques privilégiés/les « happy few »*
happy hunting ground = *paradis* : the flea market is a happy hunting ground for antique lovers = *le marché aux puces est le paradis des amateurs d'antiquités* ☠ → paradise
happy as a lark = *gai comme un pinson* ≠ down-in-the-mouth = *malheureux comme les pierres*
to find the happy medium = *trouver le juste milieu*
happy New Year ! = *bonne année !* ⓓ Merry Christmas ! = *Joyeux Noël !*
many happy returns of the day ! = *tous mes vœux !* ⓓ best wishes ! = *meilleurs vœux !*
happy to = *heureux de* : I'm happy to help you = *je suis heureux de vous aider*
☠ *un heureux événement* = a blessed event
— *encore heureux que tu ...* = thank God, you ...
— *heureux au jeu, malheureux en amour* = lucky at cards, unlucky in love.

HAPPY-GO-LUCKY (adj) **a happy-go-lucky guy/gal** = *un joyeux drille/une joyeuse luronne* ≠ gloomy gus = *ténébreux*.

HARASS (to, -ed) *harceler* : some of the crowd were harassing the speaker = *une partie de la foule harcelait l'orateur* ⓓ to bug = *casser les pieds à*, to needle = *asticoter*.

HARBINGER (n) *signe* (m) *annonciateur* : spring is a harbinger of happier days = *le printemps est un signe annonciateur de jours meilleurs* ⓓ precursor = *signe précurseur*.

HARBOR (n) *port* (m) : the ship's in the harbor = *le bateau est dans le port* = harbour (GB) ⓓ quay = *quai* ☠ → port.

HARD (n) **to have a hard on** = *bander* : he easily gets a hard on = *il bande facilement* ⓓ to have a stiff on = *avoir la trique* ☠ *bander une plaie* = to put a bandage on a wound.

HARD (adj, -er, -est) **1/** *dur, -e* : the bread's hard = *le pain est dur* ≠ soft = *mou* **2/** *dur, -e* : it's a very hard test/day = *c'est un examen très dur/une journée très dure* = tough ⓓ difficult = *difficile* ≠ child's play = *un jeu d'enfant* **3/** *dur, -e* : my boss is very hard = *mon patron est très dur* ⓓ callous = *sans cœur* ≠ gentle = *doux* ☠ *il est dur à la détente* = he is a tightwad

---

to be hard on = **1/** *être dur pour* : the divorce was hard on the kids = *le divorce a été dur pour les gosses* = the divorce	was tough on the kids **2/** *être très sévère avec* : you were very hard on him = *vous avez été très sévère avec lui*	**to do stg the hard way** = *choisir la difficulté* **don't give me a hard luck story !** = *arrête, tu vas me faire*

pleurer !
he drives a hard bargain = *il est dur en affaires* ⓓ he won't give you anything for nothing = *il ne fait pas de cadeau*
I find it hard to believe = *j'ai du mal à le croire*
hard cash = *espèces sonnantes et trébuchantes* ⓓ cash = *liquide*
hard core = *noyau dur* : the hard core of the party = *le noyau dur du parti*
hard egg = *dur à cuire* : what a hard egg you are ! = *quel dur à cuire tu fais !* ⓓ tough cookie = *coriace*
hard hat = *ouvrier (du bâtiment) conservateur* : the hard hats got into a fight with the students = *les ouvriers conservateurs et les étudiants se sont mis à se bagarrer*
hard knocks = *coups durs*

hard labor = *travaux forcés*
hard liquor = *alcool dur* ≠ soft drink = *boisson non alcoolisée*
hard ≠ **soft sell** = *vente forcée* ≠ *douce*
hard to come by = *dur à trouver* : an interesting, well-paid job is hard to come by = *un travail intéressant et bien payé, c'est dur à trouver*
it's hard to (tell him the truth) = *c'est dur de (lui dire la vérité)*
hard to swallow = *dur à avaler* : the news was hard to swallow = *la nouvelle a été dure à avaler*
hard worker = *bûcheur/bosseur* : Peter's a hard worker = *Peter est un bûcheur/un bosseur* ⓓ workaholic = *bourreau de travail* ≠ goof-off = *tire-au-flanc*

to have come up the hard way = *avoir eu la vie dure* ⓓ to have been to a school of hard knocks = *avoir été à rude école*
to learn the hard way = *apprendre à ses dépens* : she learns everything the hard way = *elle apprend tout à ses dépens*
to make (it) hard for s.o. = *mener la vie dure à qqn*
no hard feelings = *sans rancune* ⓓ let bygones be bygones = *le passé, c'est le passé*
to play hard to get = *jouer les intouchables* ≠ to put out for anyone = *passer à la casserole avec n'importe qui*
to take a hard line = *adopter une politique de fermeté* : the government took a hard line with the terrorists = *le gouvernement a adopté une politique de fermeté envers les terroristes.*

HARD (adv) *dur* : to work hard = *travailler dur* ☠ *croire dur comme fer à* = to be a staunch believer in

---

to be hard hit by (inflation) = *être durement frappé par (l'inflation)*
to be hard put to = *être bien embarrassé pour* : she was hard put to explain what happened = *elle était bien embarrassée pour expliquer ce qui s'était passé*
to be hard up = *être dans la mouise* : he's out of

work and hard up = *il est au chômage et dans la mouise* → POOR
to die hard = *avoir la vie dure* : racism dies hard = *le racisme a la vie dure* ⓓ to persist = *persister*
to take it hard = *mal vivre* : she took her second divorce very hard = *elle a très mal vécu son deuxième divorce.*

HARD-BOILED (adj) *dur, -e à cuire* : hard-boiled criminals = *des criminels durs à cuire* ⓓ tough = *coriace*
hard-boiled egg = *œuf dur* ≠ soft-boiled egg = *œuf à la coque.*

HARD-CORE (adj) X, hard-core *(inv)* : hard-core porn = *porno X/hard-core* ≠ soft-core = *soft.*

HARD-COVER (adj) *relié, -e* : hard-cover books cost double = *les livres reliés coûtent le double* ⓓ soft-cover = *broché.*

HARDEN (to, -ed) *durcir (stg)*, *endurcir (s.o.)* : life hardens you = *la vie vous endurcit*, freezing temperatures harden the soil = *le gel durcit le sol.*

HARD-LINER (n) *intransigeant, -e* : there are always hard-liners in a party = *il y a toujours des intransigeants dans un parti* ⓓ diehard = *jusqu'au-boutiste.*

HARDLY (adv) *à peine* : I hardly understood what she said = *j'ai à peine compris ce qu'elle disait* = scarcely
hardly ... than = *à peine ... que* : hardly had she closed

the door than the phone rang = *à peine avait-elle fermé la porte que le téléphone a sonné*
you can hardly expect (me to believe that) = *vous aurez du mal à (me faire croire ça).*

HARD-OF-HEARING (adj) *dur, -e d'oreille/de la feuille* (LV) : at 85, he is obviously hard-of-hearing = *à 85 ans, il est évidemment dur d'oreille.*

HARD-PRESSED (adj) *qui a du mal* : he is hard-pressed to give an explanation = *il a du mal à fournir une explication.*

HARDSHIP (n) *épreuve (f)* : a life of hardships = *une vie remplie d'épreuves* ≠ joy = *joie* ☠ → ordeal.

HARDWARE (n inv) **1/** *quincaillerie (f)* : the terrorists buy their hardware illegally = *les terroristes achètent leur quincaillerie illégalement* ⓓ arms = *armes*
hardware store = *quincaillerie*
2/ *matériel (m)* : the company manufactures the hardware but does not sell the software = *la société fabrique le matériel mais ne vend pas les logiciels* ⓓ computer = *ordinateur.*

HARDWORKING (adj) *bûcheur, -euse, bosseur, -euse* : a hardworking student = *un étudiant bûcheur* ⓓ industrious = *acharné (au travail)*, diligent = ←.

HARE (n) *lièvre (m)*, *hase (f)* ⓓ rabbit = *lapin*
to run with the hare and hunt with the hounds = *ménager la chèvre et le chou* ⓓ to play both ends against the middle = *jouer sur les deux tableaux* ☙ *soulever un lièvre* = to raise a tricky question
— *courir deux lièvres à la fois* = to be into two things at the same time.

HAREBRAINED (adj) *foufou, fofolle* : a harebrained idea = *une idée fofolle* ≠ sensible = *sensé*.

HAREM (n) *harem (m)* : the latest addition to his harem = *la dernière arrivée dans son harem* ⓓ eunuch = *eunuque*.

HARLOT (n) *fille (f) de joie* : he goes for harlots = *il aime les filles de joie* ⓓ whore = *pute*, lady of the night = *belle de nuit*.

HARM (n inv) **to do harm to** = *faire du mal à* (s.o.)/ *nuire à* (stg): his statements did a lot of harm to the party = *ses déclarations ont beaucoup nui au parti*, his attitude did a lot of harm to the children = *son attitude a fait beaucoup de mal aux enfants* ⓓ to hurt = *faire de la peine à* (s.o.)/ *faire du tort à* (stg)
it wouldn't do you any harm to (work more) = *ça ne vous ferait pas de mal de (travailler plus)*
he meant no harm by (saying that) = *il ne pensait pas à mal (en disant cela)*
there's no harm in (drinking a little) = *il n'y a pas de mal à (boire un peu)*.

HARM (to, -ed) **1/** *nuire à* : do it, it can't harm your career = *fais-le, cela ne peut pas nuire à ta carrière* ⓓ to hurt = *faire du tort à*
it won't harm you (to get up early) = *ça ne vous fera pas de mal (de vous lever tôt)*
2/ *blesser* : no one was harmed in the accident = *personne n'a été blessé dans l'accident* ☙ → to injure.

HARMLESS (adj) *inoffensif, -ive* : you can go out with my brother, he's harmless = *tu peux sortir avec mon frère, il est inoffensif* ≠ harmful = *nocif*.

HARMONICA (n) *harmonica (m)* ⓓ banjo = ←.

HARMONIOUS (adj) *harmonieux, -euse* : a harmonious couple = *un couple harmonieux* ⓓ melodious = *mélodieux*.

HARMONY (n, -ies) *harmonie (f)* ≠ discord = *discorde*
to live/work in (perfect) harmony = *vivre/travailler en (parfaite) harmonie*.

HARNESS (n, -es) *harnais (m)* : a leather harness = *un harnais de cuir* ⓓ yoke = *joug*.

HARP (n) *harpe (f)* : to play the harp = *jouer de la harpe* ⓓ harpist = *harpiste*.

HARP ON (to, -ed) *revenir sur* : she harped on the need

for free abortion = *elle est revenue sur la nécessité de la liberté de l'avortement* ⓓ to rehash = *rabâcher*.

HARROWING (adj) *effroyable* : a harrowing experience = *une expérience effroyable* ⓓ horrifying = *horrifiant*.

HARSH (adj, -er, -est) *rude* : a harsh winter/manner = *un hiver rude/des manières rudes* = rough ≠ mild = *doux* ☙ → rude.

HARVEST (n) *moisson (f)*, *cueillette (f)* (fruit) : a bad harvest = *une mauvaise moisson*, the fruit harvest = *la cueillette des fruits* ⓓ crop = *récolte*.

HAS-BEEN (n) *has-been (m, f)*, *vieille gloire (f)* : as an actor, he's a has-been = *cet acteur est un has-been/une vieille gloire*.

HASH (n) **1/** *hachis (m)* : hash for dinner = *du hachis pour le dîner* **2/** *hasch (m)* : to smoke hash = *fumer du hasch* ⓓ hashish = *ha(s)chisch*, grass = *herbe*.

HASSLE (n) **1/** *pépin (m)*, *emmerde (m)* (LV) : life is one hassle after another = *la vie est remplie de pépins/ d'emmerdes* ⓓ tsuris = *tracas*
it was a real hassle (to get through customs) = *ça a été toute une affaire (de passer la douane)* ≠ it was a snap = *c'était enfantin*
☙ *un pépin* (LV) = an umbrella
— *un pépin (fruit)* = a pip
2/ *engueulade (f)* : I'm fed up with the constant hassles between my parents = *j'en ai marre des engueulades permanentes entre mes parents* ⓓ row = *altercation*.

HASSLE (to, -d) *casser les pieds à* : stop hassling the waiter ! = *arrête de casser les pieds au serveur !* ⓓ to bother = *embêter*.

HASTE (n) *hâte (f)* ⓓ speed = *vitesse*
haste makes waste = *qui trop se hâte reste en chemin* ⓓ slowly but surely = *lentement mais sûrement* ☙ *j'ai hâte de partir* = I'm anxious to go.

HASTY (adj, -ier, -iest) *hâtif, -ive* : a hasty decision = *une décision hâtive* ⓓ slapdash = *à la va-vite*.

HAT (n) *chapeau (m)* : I never wore a hat = *je n'ai jamais porté de chapeau* ⓓ cap = *casquette*, top hat = *chapeau haut-de-forme*
I'll eat my hat (if he comes on time) ! = *(s'il arrive à l'heure) je me fais curé !* ⓓ I'd be astonished if = *ça m'étonnerait que*
keep it under your hat = *mets ça dans ta poche avec ton mouchoir par-dessus* ⓓ between you, me and the lamppost = *entre nous*
to pass the hat = *faire la quête*
I take my hat off to (you) = *je (vous) tire mon chapeau* ⓓ I give you credit = *je vous rends hommage*
you're talking through your hat = *vous parlez à tort et à travers* ⓓ that's a lot of hot air = *tout ça, c'est du vent*
to throw one's hat in the ring = *se mettre sur les rangs* : the Senator decided to throw his hat in the ring

and run for another term = *le sénateur a décidé de se mettre sur les rangs et de se représenter*

☠ *démarrer sur les chapeaux de roues* = to start off with a bang

— *il travaille du chapeau* = he's as nutty as a fruitcake

— *chapeau !* = well done !

— *faire porter le chapeau à qqn* = to leave s.o. holding the bag.

HATCH (n) **down the hatch !** = *à vos amours !* ⓪ here's mud in your eye ! = *à la tienne, Étienne !*

HATCHET (n) *hachette (f)*
to bury the hatchet = *enterrer la hache de guerre* ⓪ to smoke the peace pipe = *fumer le calumet de la paix* **hatchet man** = *homme de main* : the Mafia's/the President's hatchet man = *l'homme de main de la Mafia/du Président* ⓪ henchman = *sbire*.

HATE (n) *haine (f)* : full of hate = *rempli de haine* = hatred ≠ love = *amour*.

HATE (to, -d) *détester* (s.o., stg), *haïr* (s.o.) : I hate string beans = *je déteste les haricots verts*, I hate him = *je le hais/je le déteste* ⓪ to loathe = *exécrer* ≠ to cherish = *chérir*
I hate to tell you but (I don't agree) = *ça m'ennuie de vous dire ça mais (je ne suis pas d'accord)*
to hate (+ ing) = *avoir horreur de/détester* : I hate taking the subway = *j'ai horreur de/je déteste prendre le métro*.

HATEFUL (adj) *détestable* : what a hateful thing to say !

= *que c'est détestable de dire des choses comme ça !* ⓪ loathsome = *exécrable*.

HATRED (n) *haine (f)* : full of hatred for her parents = *remplie de haine pour ses parents* ⓪ loathing = *répugnance* ≠ adoration = ←.

HAUGHTY (adj, -ier, -iest) *hautain, -e* : snobbish and haughty = *snob et hautain* ⓪ high-and-mighty = *plein de morgue*.

HAUL (n) *butin (m)* : the gangsters got quite a haul = *les gangsters ont ramassé un beau butin* ⓪ robbery = *vol* **it's a long haul from here to the bank/to Texas** = *ça fait une bonne trotte d'ici à la banque/il y a un long chemin d'ici au Texas*
☠ → booty.

HAUL (to, -ed) *(se) coltiner* : we hauled the luggage to the station = *on s'est coltiné les bagages jusqu'à la gare* ⓪ to lug = *transbahuter*
to haul off and (hit s.o.) = *se mettre à (taper sur qqn)* → TO HIT
to haul into = *traîner devant* : he was hauled into court = *on l'a traîné devant les tribunaux*.

HAUNT (n) *lieu (m) favori* : the Ritz was Hemingway's haunt = *le Ritz était le lieu favori de Hemingway* ⓪ headquarters = *quartier général*.

HAUNT (to, -ed) 1/ *hanter* : my kids haunt nightclubs = *mes gosses hantent les boîtes de nuit* ⓪ to hang out in = *traîner dans* 2/ *hanter* : is the house haunted ? = *est-ce que la maison est hantée ?* ⓪ ghost = *fantôme*.

HAVE (to, had, had) 1/ *avoir* : she has a lot of money/enthusiasm = *elle a beaucoup d'argent/d'enthousiasme*

I have	= I've	= *j'ai*
you have	= you've	= *tu as/vous avez*
he } has		= *il*
she }		= *elle* } *a*
we have	= we've	= *nous avons*
they have	= they've	= *ils/elles ont*

have est le seul auxiliaire pour le present perfect :
j'ai vu = I've seen
je suis parti = I've left

does he have a car ? = has he a car ? (GB) = *est-ce qu'il a une voiture ?*

☠ *avoir froid* = to be cold
— *avoir soif* = to be thirsty
— *avoir faim* = to be hungry
— *avoir 10 ans* = to be 10 years old
— *avoir l'habitude de* = to be used to
— *avoir tort* ≠ *raison* = to be wrong ≠ right

— *vous l'avez eu au téléphone ?* = did you get him on the phone ?
— *(si le train part dans 10 minutes,) je ne l'aurai jamais* = (if the train leaves in 10 minutes,) I'll never make it
— *ce salaud, je l'aurai !* = this bastard, I'll get him !

2/ *prendre* : what will you have ? = *qu'est-ce que vous prendrez ?*, I'll have a coffee = *je prendrai un café*
☠ → to take

to be had = *se faire avoir* : you were had if you paid so much for such a piece of junk = *si tu as payé autant pour une telle saloperie, tu t'es fait avoir* ⓪ to be	screwed = *se faire baiser* **have a good time !** = *amusez-vous bien !* **I have it !** = *j'ai trouvé !* **to have got** = *avoir* : I haven't	got enough money = *je n'ai pas assez d'argent* **to have got to** = *avoir à* : I've got to leave now = *il faut que je m'en aille maintenant*

you had it coming ! = *vous l'avez voulu !* ⓄⒹ you asked for it ! = *tu l'as cherché !*
I've had it ! = *j'en ai plein le dos !* ⓄⒹ I'm sick and tired ! = *j'en ai par-dessus la tête !*
you've had it ! = *tu es cuit ! :* if your husband finds out you've cheated on him, you've had it ! = *si ton mari découvre que tu l'as trompé, tu es cuite !* ⓄⒹ your number's up ! = *ton compte est bon !*

to have a lot going for oneself = *avoir beaucoup pour soi :* she has a lot going for herself = *elle a beaucoup pour elle*
to have it made = *être peinard :* with her new job, she has it made = *avec son nouveau boulot, elle est peinarde*
to have stg (+ past part.) = *faire (faire) qqch :* I had my hair cut = *je me suis fait couper les cheveux,* I had a dress made = *je me suis fait faire une robe*

to have what it takes (to be a fine actress) = *avoir tout ce qu'il faut (pour être une bonne actrice)*
I have him where I want him = *je le tiens à ma merci*
I won't have it ! = *je ne le supporterai pas !* ⓄⒹ no way ! = *pas question !*
to have ... off = *avoir congé :* I have two weeks/Monday off = *j'ai deux semaines de congé/j'ai congé lundi*

---

to have against = *avoir contre :* what do you have against her/my idea ? = *qu'est-ce que vous avez contre elle/contre mon idée ?*
to have it in for s.o. = *en vouloir à qqn :* I have it in for the boss = *j'en veux au patron* ≠ to be even = *être quitte*
to have it out = *s'engueuler :* we really had it out last night ! = *on s'est vraiment engueulés hier soir !* ⓄⒹ to quarrel = *se quereller* ⚔ *engueuler qqn* = to give it to s.o.
to have on = 1/ *avoir sur soi :* when she opened the door she didn't have anything on = *quand elle a ouvert la porte, elle n'avait rien sur elle* ⓄⒹ to wear = *porter* 2/ *avoir sur :* the cops have nothing on him = *les flics n'ont rien sur lui* ⓄⒹ to have the goods on = *avoir des preuves contre* 3/ *avoir*

prévu : what do you have on for the weekend ? = *qu'est-ce que vous avez prévu pour le week-end ?*
to have s.o. over = *avoir qqn à la maison :* we're having friends over tonight = *nous avons des amis à la maison ce soir*
to have it (all) over = *être bien supérieur à :* French cheeses have it all over American ones = *les fromages français sont bien supérieurs aux fromages américains* ⓄⒹ to be miles ahead of = *être à cent coudées au-dessus de*
to have to do with = *avoir à voir avec :* does that have something/anything to do with it ? = *est-ce que ça a quelque chose à voir ?,* no, that has nothing to do with it = *non, ça n'a rien à voir* = no, it doesn't have anything to do with it.

TO HAVE TO : *falloir, devoir, avoir à, être obligé de* ⓄⒹ must = *il faut que*

do I have to go now ? = *faut-il que j'y aille maintenant ?/est-ce que je dois y aller maintenant ?*

— yes, you do = *oui, il le faut*
— yes, you have to go now = *oui, il faut que vous y alliez maintenant/vous devez y aller maintenant*

— no, you don't = *non, vous n'êtes pas obligé*
— no, you don't have to go now = *non, vous n'avez pas à/vous n'êtes pas obligé d'y aller maintenant*

	PRESENT		PAST
I have to		= *il faut que je parte/je dois partir maintenant*	**I had to** leave yesterday = *il fallait que je parte hier*
I must	leave now		
I've got to			
I ought to		= *je devrais partir maintenant*	**I ought to** / **I should** have left = *j'aurais dû partir*
I should			
I don't have to		= *je n'ai pas à partir/je ne suis pas obligé de partir maintenant*	**I didn't have to** leave yesterday = *je n'avais pas à partir/je n'étais pas obligé de partir hier*
I mustn't	leave now	= *il ne faut pas que je parte maintenant*	**I oughtn't to** / **I shouldn't** have left = *je n'aurais pas dû partir*
I oughtn't to		= *je ne devrais pas partir maintenant*	
I shouldn't			

USEFUL SENTENCES

— I really must leave = *il faut vraiment que je parte* — I'll have to leave tomorrow = *il faudra que je parte demain* — I would have had to have more money = *il aurait fallu que j'aie plus d'argent*	— you mustn't tell him = *il ne faut pas le lui dire* — I must have done it by mistake = *j'ai dû le faire par erreur* — I was supposed to come but I couldn't = *j'étais censé/je devais venir mais je n'ai pas pu*	— he must have been sick = *il a dû être malade* — we weren't supposed to tell him = *nous n'aurions pas dû/nous n'étions pas censés le lui dire*

☠ *devoir* → to owe — *il faut le faire !* = that takes some doing ! — *il m'a fallu (trois jours pour le faire)* = it took me	(three days to do it) — *(les gens) comme il faut* = the right kind of (people).

HAVEN (n) *havre (m)* : his country house is his haven = *sa maison de campagne est son havre* ⓪ shelter = *abri*.

HAVE-NOTS (n pl) *économiquement faibles (m pl), laissés-pour-compte (m pl)* : a continent of have-nots = *un continent de laissés-pour-compte* ⓪ outcast = *paria,* the downtrodden = *les opprimés*.

HAVES (n pl) *nantis (m pl)*.

HAVOC (n inv) *chambardement (m)* : there's great havoc in the country = *il y a un chambardement terrible dans le pays,* my life's/my room's in a state of havoc = *c'est le chambardement dans ma vie/dans ma chambre* ⓪ confusion = ←
to play havoc with = *faire des ravages sur* : the divorce played havoc with the kids = *le divorce a fait des ravages sur les gosses*.

HAWK (n) 1/ *faucon (m)* : the hawks aren't for signing the treaty = *les faucons ne sont pas pour la signature du traité* ⓪ warmonger = *belliciste* 2/ *faucon (m)* : the hawk is a bird of prey = *le faucon est un oiseau de proie* ⓪ vulture = *vautour*.

HAWK (to, -ed) *vendre à la sauvette* : he's hawking wallets on 42nd Street = *il vend des portefeuilles à la sauvette sur la 42e Rue* ⓪ to sell = *vendre*.

HAY (n) *foin (m)* : stacks of hay = *des meules de foin* ⓪ hayride = *promenade dans une charrette à foin*
hay fever = *rhume des foins*
to hit the hay = *se pieuter* : I'm tired, I'm going to hit the hay = *je suis fatigué, je vais me pieuter* ⓪ to go to sleep = *aller se coucher*
to make hay while the sun shines = *exploiter le filon* : the oil producing countries are making hay while

the sun shines = *les pays producteurs de pétrole exploitent le filon* ⓪ to feather one's nest = *faire son beurre* ☠ *faire du foin* = to kick up a row.

HAYWIRE (adj) *qui cafouille* : everything's haywire at the office = *tout cafouille au bureau* ⓪ mixed up = *embrouillé*
to go haywire = *perdre la boussole* : the guy went haywire and started shooting into the crowd = *le type a perdu la boussole et s'est mis à tirer dans la foule* → CRAZY.

HAZARD (n) *risque (m)* : a health hazard = *un risque pour la santé* ⓪ peril = *péril*
☠ « hazard » *est plus employé que* « risk »
— *jeu de hasard* = game of chance
— *au hasard* = at random
— *le hasard a fait/voulu que* = as chance would have it
— *par hasard* = by chance
— *le hasard fait bien les choses* = it's a lucky coincidence.

HAZARDOUS (adj) *risqué, -e, hasardeux, -euse* : a hazardous undertaking = *une entreprise risquée/hasardeuse* = risky ⓪ perilous = *périlleux*.

HAZY (adj, -ier, -iest) 1/ *brumeux, -euse* : the weather's hazy = *le temps est brumeux* ≠ clear = *clair* 2/ *flou, -e* : his ideas are hazy = *il a les idées floues* ⓪ nebulous = *nébuleux* ☠ *une photo floue* = a blurred/fuzzy photograph.

HE (pron) *il* : he's rich = *il est riche* → I
☠ *il pleut/il est cinq heures* = it's raining/it's five o'clock
— *ils* = they.

HEAD (n) 1/ *tête (f)* : he has a big head = *il a une grosse tête* ⓪ noodle = *ciboulot* 2/ *chef (m)* : the head of the company = *le chef d'entreprise* ⓪ director = *directeur* ☠ → chief 3/ *camé, -e* : there were lots of heads at the party = *il y avait beaucoup de camés à la soirée* ⓪ drug addict = *drogué*

a head = *par tête* : $ 10 a head = *10 dollars par tête*	**the head** = *les gogues* (LV) : to go to the head = *aller aux*	*gogues* **a head taller than** = *une tête*

284

de plus que : she's a head taller than her brother = *elle a une tête de plus que son frère*
at the head of (the company/class) = *à la tête de (l'entreprise/la classe)*
to bang one's head against a brick wall = *se taper la tête contre les murs* : keeping the class in order is like banging one's head against a brick wall = *maintenir l'ordre dans cette classe, c'est à se taper la tête contre les murs*
to be hanging over s.o.'s head = *être une épée de Damoclès au-dessus de la tête de qqn* : back taxes are hanging over her head = *la menace d'un rappel d'impôts est une épée de Damoclès au-dessus de sa tête*
to be head and shoulders above = *être à cent coudées au-dessus de* : his new book is head and shoulders above the last one = *son nouveau livre est à cent coudées au-dessus du précédent* ⓓ to have it all over = *être bien supérieur à*
to be head over heels in love (with) = *être éperdument amoureux (de)* ⓓ to be mad about = *être fou de*
to be over/above s.o.'s head = *être trop fort pour qqn* : this class is over/above my head = *cette classe est trop forte pour moi*
to bite/chew s.o.'s head off = *engueuler qqn comme du poisson pourri* : don't bite/chew my head off, I didn't make the mistake on purpose = *ce n'est pas la peine de m'engueuler comme du poisson pourri, cette faute, je ne l'ai pas faite exprès* → TO LAMBAST
I can't get (that idea) out of my head = *(cette idée) me trotte dans la tête* ⓓ to mull over = *retourner dans sa tête*
I can't make heads or tails of (what he's saying) = *(ce qu'il dit) n'a ni queue ni tête* ⓓ it's all Greek to me = *c'est de l'hébreu pour moi*
you can stand on your head and spit wooden nickels =

compte là-dessus et bois de l'eau fraîche ⓓ you should live so long = *tu peux toujours te brosser*
to come to a head = *devenir critique* : the situation will soon come to a head = *la situation va bientôt devenir critique*
don't trouble your head about it = *ne te casse pas la tête (à ce sujet)*
from head to foot = *de la tête aux pieds* : he was in black from head to foot = *il était en noir de la tête aux pieds*
get that into/through your head ! = *mets-toi/enfonce-toi bien ça dans la tête/dans le crâne !* ⓓ get that straight ! = *dis-toi bien ça !*
get your head together ! = *remets-toi !* ⓓ pull yourself together ! = *reprends-toi !*
to give s.o. head = *faire un pompier à qqn* : she never gave her husband head = *elle n'a jamais fait de pompier à son mari* = she never went down on her husband
to go over s.o.'s head = 1/ *passer au-dessus de la tête de qqn* : his remark went over my head = *sa réflexion m'est passée au-dessus de la tête* 2/ *passer par-dessus la tête de qqn* : he went over the foreman's head straight to the production manager = *il est passé par-dessus la tête du contremaître et est allé directement voir le chef de fabrication*
to go to s.o.'s head = *monter à la tête à qqn* : success/wine went to her head = *le succès/le vin lui est monté à la tête* → DRUNK
(she) has a good head on (her) shoulders = *(elle) a la tête sur les épaules*
to hang one's head in shame = *ne plus savoir où se mettre*
to have a swelled head = *avoir une/la grosse tête* ⓓ to think one's it = *ne pas se moucher du pied*
head cold = *rhume de cerveau*
my head's spinning = *j'ai la tête qui tourne* ⓓ I'm dizzy = *j'ai le vertige*

heads or tails = *pile ou face*
head start = *longueur d'avance* : I'll give you a head start in the race = *je vous donnerai une longueur d'avance dans la course* ⓓ lead = *avance*
to hold one's head high = *marcher la tête haute*
to keep one's head = *garder la tête froide* ⓓ to keep one's cool = *garder son sang-froid*
to keep one's head above water = *garder la tête hors de l'eau*
to laugh one's head off = *rire à gorge déployée* ⓓ to crack up = *se marrer*
let's put our heads together ! = *réfléchissons ensemble !*
he's not right in the head/ he's soft in the head = *ça ne tourne pas rond (dans sa tête)* → CRAZY
to stand on one's head = *faire des pieds et des mains* : I stood on my head trying to help her = *j'ai fait des pieds et des mains pour essayer de l'aider* ⓓ to bend over backwards = *se mettre en quatre*
to take it into one's head = *se mettre/se fourrer qqch dans la tête* : he took it into his head to quit his job = *il s'est mis/fourré dans la tête de quitter son boulot*
to talk one's head off = *ne pas cesser de parler* ⓓ to talk a blue streak = *avoir la langue bien pendue*
that's using your head ! = *il y en a là-dedans !* ⓓ you have something there ! = *c'est pas bête !*
to turn s.o.'s head = *tourner la tête à qqn* : success turned her head = *le succès lui a tourné la tête*
use your head ! = *réfléchis un peu !*
to win by a head = *gagner d'une tête* ≠ to win hands down = *gagner haut la main*
Head of Department = *chef de rayon* (store)/ *président de l'UER* (university) : Head of the French Department = *président de l'UER de français*
Head of State = *chef d'État*

☠ *se jeter à la tête de qqn* = to throw o.s. at s.o.
— *faire la tête* = to sulk
— *tenir tête à qqn* = to stand up to s.o.
— *j'en ai par-dessus la tête !* = I've had it !
— *je ne sais plus où donner de la tête* = I don't know if I'm coming or going
— *avoir la tête près du bonnet* = to be hot-tempered
— *tête de Turc* = whipping boy
— *une tête à claques* = an arrogant-looking person
— *n'en faire qu'à sa tête* = to do as one pleases
— *ça m'est sorti de la tête* = it slipped my mind
— *une idée qui me trotte dans la tête* = an idea that's been running through my mind
— *il a une bonne ≠ sale tête* = he's friendly ≠ rough-looking
— *faire une tête de six pieds de long/d'enterrement* = to pull a long face
— *avoir toute sa tête* = to have all one's faculties
— *quelle tête de mule/de lard !* = he's stubborn as a mule !
— *tête en l'air/tête de linotte* = absent-minded/scatterbrained
— *jurer sur la tête de (sa mère)* = to swear on a stack of bibles
— *se creuser la tête* = to rack one's brains
— *une tête brûlée* = a daredevil
— *elle lui a monté la tête contre moi* = she set him against me.

HEAD (adj) *principal, -e* : the head teacher = *le professeur principal* ☠ → principal
head office = *siège social* ⓓ parent company = *maison mère.*

HEAD (to, -ed) **1/** *être en tête de* : to head a list = *être en tête de liste* **2/** *se diriger vers* : they're heading North = *ils se dirigent vers le nord*

to head back = *rebrousser chemin* : it's late, let's head back ! = *il se fait tard, rebroussons chemin !* ≠ to set out = *se mettre en route*
to head for = *aller tout droit à* : she's heading for a breakdown = *elle va tout droit à la dépression*
to head off = *couper court à* : they managed to head off a split in the party = *ils ont réussi à couper court aux querelles du parti* ⓓ to avoid = *éviter.*

HEADACHE (n) **1/** *mal (m) de tête* : frequent headaches = *des maux de tête fréquents* ⓓ migraine = ←
I have a headache = *j'ai mal à la tête*
2/ *ennui (m)* : what a headache her kids are ! = *ses gosses, quel ennui !* ⓓ a pain = *qqch de pénible* ☠ → boredom.

HEADING (n) *titre (m)* : the heading of the chapter = *le titre du chapitre* = the title of the chapter ☠ → title.

HEADLIGHT (n) *phare (m)* : put on your headlights = *allume tes phares* ⓓ lights = *feux* ☠ *phare (mer)* = lighthouse.

HEADLINES (n pl) *manchette(s) (f (pl))*, *gros titres (m pl)* : did you see today's headlines ? = *est-ce que vous avez vu les gros titres/la manchette aujourd'hui ?*
to hit the headlines = *faire les gros titres* ⓓ to make the front pages = *faire la une.*

HEADLONG (adv) **to rush headlong into (trouble)** = *se ruer tête baissée vers (les ennuis).*

HEADMASTER (n) *directeur (m) (d'une école privée pour garçons)* : it's the headmaster's decision = *c'est la décision du directeur* **HEADMISTRESS** (n, -es) *directrice (f) (d'une école privée pour jeunes filles).*

HEAD-ON (adv) *de plein fouet* : the car crashed head-on into the tree = *la voiture a percuté l'arbre de plein fouet.*

HEADQUARTERS (n pl) *quartier (m) général* (army), *siège (m) social* (company) : US army's headquarters = *le quartier général de l'armée américaine.*

HEADSHRINKER (n) *psy (m, f)* = shrink.

HEADSTRONG (adj) *entêté, -e* : strong-willed and headstrong = *volontaire et entêté* ⓓ stubborn = *têtu.*

HEADWAITER (n) *maître (m) d'hôtel* = maître d'.

HEADWAY (n) **to make headway** = *faire des progrès* = to make progress.

HEADY (adj, -ier, -iest) *grisant, -e* : sudden success is heady = *un succès rapide, c'est grisant* ⓓ exciting = *excitant.*

HEAL (to, -ed) *cicatriser* : the wound's healing = *la blessure cicatrise.*

HEALTH (n inv) *santé (f)* : mental health = *santé mentale* ⓓ well-being = *bien-être* ≠ illness = *maladie*
to be in good ≠ **poor health** = *être en bonne* ≠ *mauvaise santé*
(good) health ! = *(à votre) santé !* ⓓ bottoms up ! = *à la bonne vôtre !*
☠ *respirer la santé* = to be as fit as a fiddle.

HEALTH (adj) **health food** = *produits diététiques* ⓓ organic food = *produits biologiques*
health insurance = *assurance maladie*
health resort = *station de cure.*

HEALTHY (adj, -ier, -iest) en *bonne santé* : my kids are healthy = *mes gosses sont en bonne santé* ⓪ in good shape = *en bonne forme* ≠ ill = *malade*.

HEAP (n) *tas* (m) : a heap of clothes on the bed = *un tas de vêtements sur le lit* ⓪ stack = *pile*
heaps of = *des tas de* : heaps of friends/fruit = *des tas d'amis/de fruits* → MANY ≠ a bit of = *un peu de*
☠ *grève sur le tas* = sit-down strike
— *apprendre (le métier) sur le tas* = to learn (the job) on the spot.

HEAR (to, heard, heard) **1/** entendre : did you hear what she said ? = *est-ce que vous avez entendu ce qu'elle a dit ?* ⓪ to overhear = *surprendre une conversation* **2/** *entendre dire* : I heard you're getting divorced = *j'ai entendu dire que vous divorciez* ⓪ rumor has it = *le bruit court que*

---

have you heard (the latest/the news) ? = *vous connaissez (la dernière/la nouvelle) ?*
you haven't heard anything yet ! = *et tu n'as encore rien entendu !* ⓪ that's not the half of it ! = *et ce n'est pas tout !*

---

to hear about = *entendre parler de* : have you heard about their accident ? = *avez-vous entendu parler de leur accident ?*
to hear from = **1/** *recevoir des nouvelles de* : I heard from him yesterday = *j'ai reçu de ses nouvelles hier* **2/** *avoir des nouvelles de* : if he doesn't pay me back, he'll hear from me ! = *s'il ne me rem-*

bourse pas, il va avoir de mes nouvelles ! ⓪ to get back on = *se venger de*
to hear of = *entendre parler de* : you say he's a great painter but I've never heard of him = *vous dites que c'est un grand peintre, mais je n'en ai jamais entendu parler*
I won't hear of it ! = *je ne veux pas en entendre parler !* ⓪ no way ! = *pas question !*
hear me out ! = *écoutez-moi jusqu'au bout !* ⓪ bear with me ! = *ayez la patience de m'écouter jusqu'au bout !*

☠ *qu'entendez-vous par là ?* = what do you mean by that ? — *faire entendre raison à qqn* = to make s.o. listen to reason	— *s'entendre sur qqch* = to agree on stg — *s'entendre (bien)* = to get on/along (well) — *à vous entendre* = listening to you.

HEARING (n) **1/** *audience* (f) : private ≠ public hearing = *audience privée* ≠ *publique* ☠ → audience **2/** *audition* (f) : poor hearing = *une audition médiocre* ☠ → audition
hearing aid = *appareil (acoustique)*.

HEARSAY (n inv) *ouï-dire* (m inv) : it's just hearsay, but I heard they're leaving Paris for good = *j'ai appris par ouï-dire qu'ils quittent Paris définitivement* ⓪ talk = *bruits*.

HEARSE (n) *corbillard* (m) : a hearse pulled by black horses = *un corbillard tiré par des chevaux noirs* ⓪ funeral = *funérailles*.

HEART (n) *cœur* (m) : she has a big heart = *elle a (un) grand cœur*, a weak heart = *un cœur fragile* ⓪ coronary = *infarctus*, heart transplant = *transplantation cardiaque*, pacemaker = *←/ stimulateur cardiaque*, heartbeat = *battement de cœur*, open-heart operation = *opération à cœur ouvert*

(a girl) after my (own) heart = *(une fille) selon mon cœur*
at heart = *au fond* : he acts tough, but he's a softy at heart = *il joue les durs, mais au fond c'est un tendre* ⓪ fundamentally = *fondamentalement*
to break s.o.'s heart = *briser le cœur de qqn*
by heart = *par cœur* : to know stg by heart = *connaître qqch par cœur* ⓪ from memory = *de mémoire*
cross my heart and hope to die ! = *croix de bois, croix de fer, si je mens, je vais en enfer !* ⓪ I swear on a stack of bibles that = *je jure mes grands dieux que*
to cry/weep one's heart out = *pleurer toutes les larmes de*

son corps ⓪ to cry bitterly = *pleurer comme une Madeleine*
to eat one's heart out = *se ronger les sangs* ⓪ to be worried sick = *être aux cent coups*
have a heart ! = *sois sympa !* ⓪ be a sport ! = *sois chic !*
to have one's heart in one's mouth = *ne pas en mener large* ⓪ to be scared silly = *avoir la pétoche*
to have one's heart in the right place = *avoir le cœur sur la main*
(his) heart is ≠ isn't in (his work) = *il a ≠ n'a pas le cœur à (son travail)*
my heart's pounding = *mon cœur bat à tout rompre*
heart attack = *crise cardiaque*
⓪ **to have a heart condition**

= *être cardiaque*
a heart of gold = *un cœur d'or*
(my) heart goes out to (her) = *(elle) a toute (ma) sympathie*
the heart of the matter = *le cœur/le vif du sujet*
a heart murmur = *un souffle au cœur*
my heart skipped a beat = *mon cœur s'est arrêté de battre*
heart and soul = *corps et âme* : she puts her heart and soul into her work = *elle se donne corps et âme à son travail*
in my heart of hearts = *au plus profond de mon cœur* ⓪ deep down = *au tréfonds de moi-même*
in the heart of (the city) = *en plein cœur de (la ville)* ⓪ in the midst of = *en plein*

not to have the heart to = *ne pas avoir le cœur de :* I didn't have the heart to tell her = *je n'ai pas eu le cœur de le lui dire* **to lose heart** ≠ **to take heart** = *perdre courage* ≠ *prendre courage* **to take stg to heart** = *prendre qqch à cœur :* she took the	criticisms to heart = *elle a pris ces critiques à cœur* **to one's heart's content** = *tout son soûl/tout son content* **to set one's heart on** = *vouloir vraiment :* I have my heart set on going to Europe = *je veux vraiment partir pour l'Europe*	**(he) wears (his) heart on (his) sleeve** = *tout se lit sur (son) visage* **with all my heart** = *de tout mon cœur :* I love my stepchildren with all my heart = *j'aime mes beaux-enfants de tout mon cœur*

☠ *avoir un cœur d'artichaut* = to fall in and out of love — *ça me soulève le cœur !* = it makes me sick ! — *avoir le cœur gros* = to be heavyhearted — *en avoir le cœur net* = to have a clear idea of what's going on	— *joli comme un cœur* = pretty as a picture — *avoir le cœur bien accroché* = to have solid nerves — *s'en donner à cœur joie* = to have a whale of a time.

HEARTACHE (n) *chagrin* (m) *:* her kids gave her nothing but heartache = *ses enfants ne lui causent que du chagrin* ⓪ anguish = *angoisse* ☠ *avoir un chagrin d'amour* = to have a disappointment in love.

HEARTBREAKING (adj) *à fendre l'âme :* what he said was heartbreaking = *ce qu'il a dit était à fendre l'âme* ⓪ heartrendering = *déchirant,* distressing = *consternant.*

HEARTBROKEN (adj) *qui a le cœur brisé :* she was heartbroken to have a miscarriage = *elle a eu le cœur brisé de faire une fausse couche* ≠ glad = *content.*

HEARTBURN (n inv) *brûlures* (f pl) *d'estomac :* spinach gives me heartburn = *les épinards me donnent des brûlures d'estomac* ⓪ indigestion = ←.

HEARTILY (adv) *de bon cœur :* she was laughing heartily = *elle riait de bon cœur.*

HEARTLESS (adj) *sans cœur :* a heartless father = *un père sans cœur* ⓪ cruel = ←.

HEARTS-AND-FLOWERS (n pl) *qqch à l'eau de rose :* all his movies are hearts-and-flowers = *tous ses films sont à l'eau de rose* ⓪ tearjerker = *histoire qui fait pleurer Margot,* corny = *sentimentalo.*

HEARTSICK (adj) *qui a la mort dans l'âme :* she was absolutely heartsick when she heard she was fired = *elle a eu la mort dans l'âme quand elle a appris qu'elle était renvoyée* ⓪ heavyhearted = *qui a le cœur gros.*

HEARTTHROB (n) *béguin* (m) *:* her latest heartthrob is French = *son dernier béguin est français* ⓪ sweetheart = *amoureux* ☠ *avoir le béguin pour* = to have a crush on.

HEART-TO-HEART (adj) *à cœur ouvert :* a heart-to-heart talk = *une conversation à cœur ouvert.*

HEARTY (adj, -ier, -iest) **a hearty laugh** = *un rire franc* **to be a hearty eater** = *avoir un bon coup de fourchette.*

HEAT (n inv) **1/** *chaleur* (f) *:* summer heat = *chaleur de l'été* ☠ → warmth
heat wave = *vague de chaleur/canicule*
in heat = *en chaleur/en chasse* ⓪ in rut = *en rut*
2/ *chauffage* (m) *:* is the heat on ? = *est-ce que le chauffage est allumé ?* ☠ *chauffage central* = central heating
the heat's on = *ça chauffe :* the heat's been on in the area since the two hookers were murdered = *ça chauffe dans le coin depuis que les deux putains ont été assassinées*
to turn the heat on = **1/** *mettre le chauffage :* it's cold, can you turn the heat on ? = *il fait froid, est-ce que vous pouvez mettre le chauffage ?* **2/** *faire pression sur :* feminists are turning the heat on different congressmen = *les féministes font pression sur différents parlementaires*
to turn on the heat = *resserrer les mailles du filet :* the cops are turning on the heat = *les flics sont en train de resserrer les mailles du filet.*

HEAT (to, -ed) **1/** *chauffer :* to heat a house = *chauffer une maison* ☠ *ça va chauffer !* = all hell's going to break loose ! **2/** *faire chauffer :* let's heat the soup = *faisons chauffer la soupe* ⓪ to warm up = *réchauffer.*

HEATED (adj) *enflammé, -e :* a heated discussion = *une discussion enflammée* ⓪ vehement = *véhément.*

HEATING (n) *chauffage* (m) *:* heating is more expensive than air conditioning = *le chauffage est plus cher que la climatisation* ☠ → heat.

HEAVEN (n) *paradis* (m) *:* heaven is being in love = *le paradis c'est d'être amoureux* ☠ → paradise
heaven help us ! = *le ciel nous en préserve !*
heaven knows ! = *Dieu seul le sait !* ⓪ who knows ? = *qui sait ?*
heavens ! = *grand Dieu !* ⓪ **for heaven's sake** = *pour l'amour du ciel !* → GOSH !
to move heaven and earth = *remuer ciel et terre* ⓪ to do one's utmost = *faire tout son possible*
thank heaven ! = *Dieu merci !*

HEAVENLY (adj) *divin, -e :* the dinner was heavenly = *le dîner était divin* = divine → WONDERFUL.

HEAVES (n inv) *haut-le-cœur (m inv) :* to have the heaves = *avoir des haut-le-cœur* ⓪ nausea = *nausée.*

HEAVILY (adv) *lourdement :* heavily taxed = *lourdement imposé* ≠ lightly = *légèrement* ☠ *se tromper lourdement* = to be sorely mistaken — *insister lourdement* = to rub it in.

HEAVY (n, -ies) 1/ *qqn de costaud :* in politics, he's a heavy = *en politique, il est costaud* 2/ *dur, -e :* in the movie, he plays a heavy = *dans le film, il joue un rôle de dur* ≠ scaredy-cat = *trouillard.*

HEAVY (adj, -ier, -iest) 1/ *lourd, -e :* the valise is heavy = *la valise est lourde* ≠ light = *léger*

to be a heavy sleeper = *avoir le sommeil lourd*	**heavy expenses** = *lourdes charges*
heavy artillery = *artillerie lourde*	**heavy petting** = *pelotage (en règle)*
heavy date = *rancard (d'amoureux)*	**heavy rain** = *pluie battante*
heavy drinker = *gros buveur/picoleur* → DRUNK	**heavy smoker** = *gros fumeur*
	heavy traffic = *circulation dense*

☠ *la lourde* (LV) = the door
— *il ne pèse pas lourd* = he cuts no ice
— *une lourde erreur* = a serious mistake

2/ *gros, grosse :* you're too heavy, you should lose weight = *tu es trop gros, tu devrais maigrir* = fat = *portly* ≠ slim = *mince* ☠ → big 3/ *pesant, -e :* evenings/conversations with his parents are heavy = *les soirées/les conversations avec ses parents sont pesantes.*

HEAVYSET (adj) *de forte constitution :* all her family's heavyset = *dans sa famille, ils ont tous une forte constitution* ≠ lanky = *efflanqué.*

HEAVYWEIGHT (n) 1/ *poids (m) lourd* ≠ lightweight = *poids léger,* middleweight = *poids moyen* ☠ → van 2/ *qqn de costaud :* if you need a lawyer, get a heavyweight = *si tu as besoin d'un avocat, prends-en un de costaud* ⓪ bigwig = *ténor.*

HECK (n) **a heck of a lot of (money/problems)** = *pas mal d'(argent)/de (problèmes)* → MANY **what the heck do I care !** = *je m'en balance !* ⓪ I don't give a hoot ! = *je m'en moque !* **what the heck !** = *que diable !* → GOSH ! **HECK !** (interj) *mince !* → GOSH !

HECKLE (to, -d) *chahuter :* the public heckled the speaker = *le public a chahuté l'orateur* ☠ *chahuter (classe)* = to make a rumpus.

HECTIC (adj) *mouvementé, -e :* what a hectic day ! = *quelle journée mouvementée !* ⓪ busy = *chargé.*

HEDGE (to, -d) *répondre à côté :* to hedge the journalists' questions = *répondre à côté des questions des journalistes* ⓪ to hem and haw = *atermoyer.*

HEEBIE-JEEBIES (n pl) *chocottes (f pl) :* to give s.o. the heebie-jeebies = *donner les chocottes à qqn* ⓪ the shakes = *la tremblote.*

HEED (to, -ed) *tenir compte de :* to heed s.o.'s advice = *tenir compte des conseils de qqn* ⓪ to listen to = *écouter.*

HEEL (n) 1/ *talon (m) :* Achilles' heel = *talon d'Achille* ⓪ ankle = *cheville* **to be on s.o.'s heels** = *être sur les talons/aux trousses de qqn :* the police are on his heels = *la police est sur ses talons/à ses trousses* ⓪ to shadow = *prendre en filature* **to bring s.o. to heel** = *mettre qqn au pas* **to cool one's heels** = *faire le pied de grue* **to take to one's heels** = *prendre ses jambes à son cou* → TO LEAVE 2/ *beau salaud (m) :* he's a heel with his wife = *c'est un beau salaud avec sa femme* → BASTARD.

HEFTY (adj, -ier, -iest) 1/ *râblé, e :* a sexy hefty guy = *un type râblé et sexy* ⓪ stocky = *trapu,* burly = *bien charpenté* 2/ *fort, -e :* a hefty increase = *une forte augmentation* ⓪ considerable = *considérable* ☠ → strong.

HEIGHT (n) *hauteur (f) :* at a height of three thousand feet = *à une hauteur de trois mille pieds* ≠ depth = *profondeur* **at/in the height of (the war/the summer)** = *en pleine (guerre)/en plein (été)* ⓪ in the middle of = *au milieu de* **the height of (stupidity)** = *le summum de (la stupidité)* ⓪ quintessence = *comble* ☠ *être à la hauteur (d'un travail)* = to be up to (a job).

HEIR (n) *héritier (m) :* he's the only heir to his father's fortune = *c'est le seul héritier de la fortune de son père* **heir apparent** = *héritier présomptif.*

HEIRESS (n, -es) *héritière (f) :* a rich heiress = *une riche héritière.*

HEIRLOOM (n) *objet (m) de famille (meuble, bijou) :* my watch is a family heirloom = *ma montre est un objet de famille.*

HEIST (n) *casse (m) :* to pull a heist = *faire un casse* ⓪ robbery = *vol* ☠ *qui paiera la casse ?* = who'll pay for the damage ?

HELICOPTER (n) *hélicoptère (m) :* doctors travelling by helicopter = *des médecins qui se déplacent en hélicoptère* = chopper.

HELL (n) enfer (m) : life with him was hell = *la vie avec lui, c'était l'enfer* ⓪ purgatory = *purgatoire* ≠ heaven = *paradis*

as hell = *sacrément* : rich as hell = *sacrément riche* → VERY

to beat the hell out of s.o. = *rentrer dans le chou/le lard à qqn* → TO HIT

to catch hell = *se faire engueuler* : if the boss finds the truth out, you'll catch hell = *si le patron découvre la vérité, tu vas te faire engueuler* ⓪ to be in for it = *en prendre pour son grade*

come hell or high water = *contre vents et marées* ⓪ no matter what = *coûte que coûte*

to feel like hell = *être mal fichu* ⓪ to feel lousy = *être mal foutu*

for the hell of it = *histoire de rire* : they beat up the old man for the hell of it = *ils ont roué le vieil homme de coups, histoire de rire* ⓪ for kicks = *pour se marrer*

get the hell out ! = *va te faire voir !* ⓪ go to hell ! = *va au diable !* → BUZZ OFF !

to give s.o. hell = *faire sa fête à qqn* : he's going to give you hell ! = *il va te faire ta fête !/ça va être ta fête !* → TO LAMBAST

to go through hell = *en baver* : they really went through hell during the war = *ils en ont vraiment bavé pendant la guerre* ⓪ to have a rough time of it =

en voir de dures

to be going to hell = *être foutu* : the company/my reputation is going to hell = *l'affaire/ma réputation est foutue* ⓪ to be going to the dogs = *battre de l'aile*

a hell of a = *un sacré* : a hell of a nice guy = *un sacré chic type* = a helluva ⓪ darned = *fichu*

a hell of a lot = *un max/un maximum* : he works a hell of a lot = *il travaille un max/un maximum* ⓪ plenty = *tout plein*

(to be) hell on earth = *(être) l'enfer* : our marriage was hell on earth = *notre ménage, c'était l'enfer* ⓪ not to be a bed of roses = *ne pas être marrant*

the hell with him ! = *qu'il aille se faire pendre ailleurs !* → BUZZ OFF !

the hell with it ! = *laisse tomber !* : if the car's too expensive, the hell with it ! = *si la voiture est trop chère, laisse tomber !* = if the car's too expensive, forget it !

hell's angels = *blousons noirs* ⓪ hood = *loulou*

like hell ! = *des clous !* : me pay for him ? like hell ! = *moi payer pour lui ? des clous !* ⓪ no soap ! = *que dalle !*

to look like hell = *avoir une sale gueule* ⓪ to look a sight = *avoir une sale tête*

to play hell with = *faire des ravages dans* : the pill played hell with my system = *la pilule a fait des ravages dans mon organisme*

to raise hell (about) = *faire du pétard (au sujet de)* ⓪ to make a scene = *faire une scène*

to run like hell = *courir comme un perdu* ⓪ to run like blazes = *courir ventre à terre*

to scare the hell out of s.o. = *flanquer les foies à qqn* ⓪ to scare the living daylights out of s.o.* = *flanquer la pétoche à qqn*

there'll be hell to pay (if he finds out) ! = *ça va barder (s'il l'apprend) !*

what the hell ! = *flûte !* : it's very expensive but what the hell ! = *c'est très cher, mais flûte !* ⓪ too bad ! = *tant pis !*

what the hell (are you doing here) ? = *bon Dieu (qu'est-ce que tu fais ici)* ? → GOSH !

when hell freezes over = *quand les poules auront des dents* ⓪ in a month of Sundays = *la semaine des quatre jeudis*

who the hell (does he think he is) ? = *bon Dieu (pour qui se prend-il)* ?

HELL ! (interj) *la barbe !* → GOSH !

oh hell ! = *oh la vache !* → GOSH !

HELLO ! (interj) *hello !, allô !* (phone) : hello ! how are you ? = *hello ! comment ça va ?* ⓪ hi ! = *salut !* ≠ good-bye ! = *au revoir !*
say hello to (your wife) = *dites bonjour à (votre femme) de ma part* ⓪ give my best to (your wife) = *mon meilleur souvenir à (votre femme)*.

HELLUVA (adj) **a helluva (jazz player)** = *un sacré (joueur de jazz)*.

HELM (n) **to be at the helm** = *être à la barre* ⓪ to steer = *barrer*.

HELMET (n) *casque (m)* ⓪ motorbike = *moto* ☠ *les casques bleus* = the UN troops
— *casque (musique)* = earphones.

HELP (n inv) **1/** *aide (f)* : I need help = *j'ai besoin d'aide* ⓪ assistance = ← ☠ → aid **2/** *domestiques (m pl)* : we have help at home = *nous avons des domestiques à la maison* ⓪ maid = *bonne* ☠ *un domestique* = a servant
can I be of any help ? = *est-ce que je peux être utile en quoi que ce soit ?*
to go for help = *aller chercher du secours*
he was of no help = *il n'a été d'aucune aide*
you're some help ! = *tu parles d'une aide !*

HELP ! (interj) *au secours !, à moi !*

HELP (to, -ed) *aider* : he tried to help you = *il a essayé de vous aider* ⓪ to assist = *assister*, to lend a hand = *prêter main-forte*
to help s.o. out = *dépanner qqn* : can you help me out

by lending me a hundred bucks ? = *est-ce que tu peux me dépanner en me prêtant cent dollars ?* ⓪ **to fix s.o. up** = *arranger qqn* ☠ *dépanner (une voiture)* = to fix (a car)

to help oneself to = *se servir* : help yourself to the mashed potatoes = *sers-toi de purée*

help yourself to some more ! = *reprenez-en !* = take a second helping !

it can't be helped ! = *on n'y peut rien !* → THAT'S LIFE !

I can't/couldn't help (laughing) = *je ne peux pas/ je n'ai pas pu m'empêcher de (rire)*.

HELPFUL (adj) **1/** *utile* : a helpful suggestion = *une suggestion utile* ≠ useless = *inutile* ☠ → useful **2/** *serviable* : thank you, you've been very helpful = *merci, vous avez été très serviable* ⓪ accommodating = *accommodant*.

HELPLESS (adj) *désarmé, -e* : helpless children/refugees = *des enfants/des réfugiés désarmés*

to be helpless to = *être impuissant à* : when he hit her, I was helpless to do anything about it = *quand il l'a frappée, j'ai été impuissant à faire quoi que ce soit*.

HELTER-SKELTER (adj, adv) *pêle-mêle* : the papers are scattered helter-skelter on the table = *les papiers sont pêle-mêle sur la table* = pell-mell ≠ in apple-pie order = *parfaitement en ordre*.

HEM (n) *ourlet (m)* ⓪ alteration = *retouche*.

HEM (to, -med) *faire un ourlet* ⓪ to sew = *coudre*

to hem and haw = *atermoyer* : when the journalist asked him a question, the President hemmed and hawed = *quand le journaliste lui a posé une question, le Président a atermoyé* ⓪ to shilly-shally = *ne pas se décider*

to hem in = *cerner* : hemmed in by the cops = *cernés par les flics* ⓪ to surround = *entourer* ☠ *cerner un problème* = to pinpoint/to hone in on a problem.

HE-MAN (n, -men) *beau mâle (m)* : she's not attracted to he-men = *elle n'est pas attirée par les beaux mâles* ⓪ pretty boy = *mignon*.

HEMISPHERE (n) *hémisphère (m)* ⓪ globe = ←.

HEMORRHAGE (n) *hémorragie (f)* ⓪ bleeding = *saignement*.

HEN (n) *poule (f)* : hens cackle = *les poules caquettent* ⓪ coop = *poulailler* ≠ cock = *coq*

mother/father hen = *mère/père poule*

hen party = *soirée entre filles* ≠ stag party = *soirée entre hommes*

☠ *quand les poules auront des dents* = when hell freezes over

— *la poule aux œufs d'or* = the goose that laid the golden egg

— *une poule* = a tart

— *se coucher avec les poules* = to go to bed early

— *une poule mouillée* = a chicken (coward).

HENCEFORTH (adv) *dorénavant* : we won't work on

Fridays henceforth = *dorénavant, nous ne travaillerons pas le vendredi* ⓪ from now on = *à partir de maintenant*.

HENCHMAN (n, -men) *sbire (m)* : the Mafia and their henchmen = *la Mafia et ses sbires* ⓪ gunman = *homme de main*.

HENPECKED (adj) *que l'on mène par le bout du nez* : henpecked husbands = *des maris que l'on mène par le bout du nez*.

HEP (adj) *à la page* : my brother's hep = *mon frère est à la page* ⓪ in = ← ≠ old hat = *vieux jeu*.

HER (pron) **1/** *la* (direct object) : I see her = *je la vois* → I **2/** *lui* (indirect object) : I spoke to her = *je lui ai parlé* ☠ → him

with/for her = *avec/pour elle*.

HER (adj) *son, sa, ses (à elle)* : her job = *son travail (à elle)*, her house = *sa maison (à elle)*, her feet = *ses pieds (à elle)* ≠ his = *son, sa, ses (à lui)* → MY.

HERBS (n pl) *(fines) herbes (f pl)* : plenty of herbs in the salad = *beaucoup d'herbes/de fines herbes dans la salade* ⓪ spices = *épices* ☠ → grass.

HERD (n) *troupeau (m)* : a herd of cattle = *un troupeau de bovins* ⓪ livestock = *cheptel*.

HERE (adv) *ici* : come here ! = *viens ici !* ≠ there = *là*, elsewhere = *ailleurs* ☠ *d'ici là* = by then

here comes (the train) = *voilà (le train)* **here it is !/she is !** = *le/la voici !* **here lies** = *ci-gît* **here's to you !** = *à la vôtre !* ⓪ bottoms up ! = *à la bonne vôtre* **here and there** = *ici et là* ⓪ all over the	place = *dans tous les coins* **to be here to stay** = *ne pas être près de disparaître* : women's lib is here to stay = *le MLF n'est pas près de disparaître* **look/see here !** = *écoutez-moi bien !*

HEREAFTER (n) *au-delà (m)* : I don't believe in a hereafter = *je ne crois pas en l'au-delà* ⓪ the afterlife = *la vie dans l'au-delà*.

HEREAFTER (adv) *désormais* : hereafter ask me before you take the car = *désormais demande-moi avant de prendre la voiture* ⓪ henceforth = *dorénavant*.

HEREDITARY (adj) *héréditaire* : a hereditary illness = *une maladie héréditaire* ⓪ congenital = *congénital*, to run in the family = *être de famille*.

HEREDITY (n, -ies) *hérédité (f)* : the influence of heredity = *l'influence de l'hérédité* ⓪ atavism = *atavisme*.

HERESY (n, -ies) *hérésie (f)* : what heresy ! = *quelle hérésie !* ⓪ sacrilege = *sacrilège*.

HERETIC (n, adj) *hérétique (m, f)* : heretics used to be burned = *autrefois on brûlait les hérétiques*.

HERITAGE (n) *héritage (m)* : our cultural heritage = *notre héritage culturel* ⓪ tradition = ←.

HERMIT (n) *ermite (m)* : to live like a hermit = *vivre comme un ermite* ⓪ recluse = *reclus*.

HERNIA (n) *hernie (f)* ⓪ appendicitis = *appendicite*.

HERO (n, -es) *héros (m)* : you're my hero ! = *vous êtes mon héros !* ≠ coward = *lâche*
hero sandwich = *super club sandwich*.

HEROIC (adj) *héroïque* : a heroic act = *un acte héroïque* ⓪ dauntless = *intrépide* ≠ cowardly = *lâche*
HEROICALLY (adv) *héroïquement*.

HEROIN (n) *héroïne (f)* : heroin sold to kids = *de l'héroïne vendue à des gosses* ⓪ drugs = *drogue* ☠ → heroine.

HEROINE (n) *héroïne (f)* : the heroine of the film = *l'héroïne du film* ⓪ the leading lady = *le principal rôle féminin* ☠ *héroïne (drogue)* = heroin.

HEROISM (n) *héroïsme (m)*.

HERRING (n) *hareng (m)* : smoked herring = *hareng fumé* ⓪ eel = *anguille*.

> **HERS** (pron) *le sien, les siens, la sienne, les siennes (à elle)* : this book's hers = *ce livre est le sien (à elle)*, these books are hers = *ces livres sont les siens (à elle)*, these shoes are hers = *ces chaussures sont les siennes (à elle)*.

> **HERSELF** (pron) *elle-même, se* (reflexive) : she did it by herself = *elle l'a fait elle-même*, she sees herself = *elle se voit* ≠ himself = *lui-même/se* → MYSELF.

HESITANT (adj) *qui hésite* : he asked me to work for him, but I'm hesitant = *il m'a demandé de travailler pour lui, mais j'hésite* ≠ determined = *déterminé*.

HESITATE (to, -d) *hésiter* : he answered without hesitating = *il a répondu sans hésiter* ⓪ to hem and haw = *atermoyer*, to procrastinate = *remettre à plus tard*
he who hesitates is lost = *la fortune sourit aux audacieux* ≠ to jump at the chance = *saisir l'occasion*.

HESITATINGLY (adv) *avec hésitation* : to answer hesitatingly = *répondre avec hésitation*.

HESITATION (n) *hésitation (f)* : without hesitation = *sans hésitation* ⓪ indecision = *indécision*.

HETEROSEXUAL (n, adj) *hétérosexuel, -elle* ⓪ straight = *hétéro*.

HEX (n, -es) *sort (m)*, *sortilège (m)* : there's a hex on my family = *il y a un sort sur ma famille* ⓪ jinx = *qqch qui porte malheur* ☠ → sort.

HEX (to, -ed) *jeter un sort à* : the witch hexed the young prince = *la sorcière a jeté un sort au jeune prince* ⓪ to jinx = *porter malheur à*.

HEY ! (interj) *dis donc !* : hey, can you get me a beer ? = *dis donc, tu peux m'apporter une bière ?*

HEYDAY (n) **in one's heyday** = *du temps de sa gloire* : she was the darling of New York in her heyday = *du temps de sa gloire, c'était l'enfant chérie de New York*.

HI ! (interj) *salut !, bonjour !* ≠ bye ! = *salut !/au revoir !*

HICCUPS (n pl) *hoquet (m)* : to have the hiccups = *avoir le hoquet* ⓪ to hiccup = *hoqueter*.

HICK (n) *plouc (m)* : she married a hick = *elle a épousé un plouc* ⓪ hillbilly = *péquenaud* ≠ city boy = *gars de la ville*.

HICKY (n, -ies) *suçon (m)* ⓪ French kiss = *palot*.

HIDE (to, hid, hidden or hid) 1/ *(se) cacher* : the kids are hiding in the cellar = *les gosses se cachent dans la cave* 2/ *cacher* : to hide one's feelings = *cacher ses sentiments* ≠ to reveal = *révéler*
to hide stg from s.o. = *cacher qqch à qqn* : he hid the truth from me = *il m'a caché la vérité* ⓪ to keep from = *dissimuler à*
to hide out = *se planquer* : they're hiding out in Baltimore = *ils se planquent à Baltimore* ⓪ to be on the run = *être en cavale* ☠ → to stash away
☠ *je ne m'en cache pas* = I make no secret of it
— *il cache bien son jeu* = he plays his cards close to the vest.

HIDE-AND-SEEK (n) **to play hide-and-seek** = *jouer à cache-cache* ⓪ blindman's buff = *colin-maillard*.

HIDEAWAY (n) *cachette (f)* : a hideaway for lovers = *une cachette pour amoureux* ⓪ retreat = *retraite* ☠ *en cachette* = on the sly.

HIDEOUS (adj) *hideux, -euse* : his sister's hideous = *sa sœur est hideuse* ⓪ ugly = *laid*.

HIDEOUT (n) *planque (f)* : the gang found a great hideout = *le gang a trouvé une planque géniale* ⓪ hiding place = *endroit pour se cacher* ☠ *une (bonne) planque (travail)* = a cushy job.

HIDING (n) **to go into hiding** = *entrer dans la clandestinité*
hiding place = *endroit pour se cacher*.

HIERARCHY (n, -ies) *hiérarchie (f)* ⓪ rank = *rang*.

HI-FI (n) *hi-fi (f)* = High Fidelity = *haute fidélité* ⓪ stereo = *stéréo*
a hi-fi set = *une chaîne hi-fi*.

HIGH (n) *sommet* *(m)* : production has hit a new high = *la production a atteint un nouveau sommet* **what a high (being in love)** ! = *quel pied (d'être amoureux)* ! ≠ what a bummer ! = *quel sale truc* ! ☠ → summit.

HIGH (adj, -er, -est) **1/** *haut, -e :* a very high ceiling/building = *un plafond/immeuble très haut* ≠ low = *bas*
2/ *élevé, -e :* their prices are very high = *leurs prix sont très élevés* ⓪ astronomical = *astronomique* ≠ low = *bas*, cheap = *bon marché*
☠ *bien* ≠ *mal élevé* = well- ≠ ill-behaved

— *des discussions élevées* = lofty discussions
3/ *parti, -e :* after one drink, I was a bit high = *j'ai bu un verre et j'étais un peu partie* → DRUNK
4/ *qui plane :* we smoked pot and really got high = *on a fumé de l'herbe et on a complètement plané* ⓪ stoned = *défoncé*

to be high as a kite = *avoir un coup dans l'aile/dans le nez* → DRUNK
to be in high spirits = *être plein d'entrain* ≠ to be down in the dumps = *être au trente-sixième dessous*
don't get on your high horse = *ne monte pas sur tes grands chevaux* ⓪ don't get your back up = *ne te hérisse pas*
to give s.o. the high sign = *donner le signal à qqn*
... high = *de haut :* the wall's six feet high = *le mur a 1,80 m de haut*

the highest bidder = *le plus offrant*
high chair = *chaise haute (d'enfant)* = baby chair
higher education = *enseignement supérieur*
high fever = *fièvre de cheval*
high jump = *saut en hauteur*
high mass = *grand-messe*
high point = *point fort :* the high point of his trip = *le point fort de son voyage*
high school = *lycée* ⓪ college = *collège*
high society = *haute société/la haute* (LV) ⓪ the upper crust =

le gratin
high spot = *grand moment :* the high spot of the evening = *le grand moment de la soirée*
how high (is the building) ? = *quelle est la hauteur de (l'immeuble)* ?
high treason = *haute trahison*
to hit the high spots = *faire la tournée des grands ducs* ⓪ to go out on the town = *faire la foire*
to play for high stakes = *jouer gros jeu*
to stink to high heaven = *schlinguer* (LV) / *cocoter* (LV)

☠ *pousser les hauts cris* = to let out a hue and cry
— *avoir la haute main sur* = to have total control of
— *à haute voix* = aloud
— *être haut en couleur* = to be colorful

— *(un ganster) de haut vol* = a big-time (gangster)
— *le haut lieu de l'édition* = the Mecca of publishing.

HIGH (adv, -er, -est) *haut :* the plane is flying higher than the bird = *l'avion vole plus haut que l'oiseau*

to aim high = *viser haut*
to be flying/riding high = *être aux anges* ≠ to be in the doldrums = *être malheureux comme les pierres*
to leave s.o. high and dry = *laisser qqn en plan :* he split and left her high and dry with the kids = *il l'a plaquée et l'a laissée en plan avec les gosses*

to live high = *vivre sur un grand pied*
from on high = *de haut/d'en haut :* we'll watch the demonstration from on high = *nous regarderons la manifestation d'en haut*
to look high and low = *chercher dans tous les coins :* I looked high and low for my bracelet = *j'ai cherché mon bracelet dans tous les coins*

☠ *gagner haut la main* = to win hands down
— *haut les mains !* = hands up !
— *péter plus haut que son cul* = to think one's hot shit

— *en haut* = upstairs
— *tomber de haut* = to have one's hopes dashed
— *regarder qqn de haut* = to look down on s.o.

HIGH-AND-MIGHTY (adj) *plein, -e de morgue* ⓪ uppity = *bêcheur*.

HIGHBALL (n) *whisky soda* *(m)* ⓪ straight Scotch = *whisky sec.*

HIGHBROW (n) *cérébral, -e :* my husband's friends are all highbrows = *tous les amis de mon mari sont des cérébraux* ⓪ intellectual = *intellectuel.*

HIGH-CLASS (adj) *de grand standing :* a high-class

hotel = *un hôtel de grand standing* ≠ low-class = *de bas étage.*

HIGHER-UP (n) *supérieur, -e* : ask your higher-up = *demandez à votre supérieur* ≠ underling = *subalterne.*

HIGHFALUTIN (adj) *prétentiard, -e* : highfalutin manners = *des manières prétentiardes* ⓒ pompous = *pompeux.*

HIGH-HANDED (adj) *musclé, -e* : high-handed methods = *des méthodes musclées* ⓒ authoritarian = *autoritaire* ☻ → brawny.

HIGH-LEVEL (adj) *de haut niveau* : high-level talks = *des conversations de haut niveau.*

HIGHLIGHT (n) **the highlight of (the evening)** = *le clou de (la soirée).*

HIGHLY (adv) *hautement* : highly qualified = *hautement qualifié* ⓒ expert = ←
to speak highly of s.o. = *recommander chaudement qqn.*

HIGHNESS (n, -es) **Your Highness** = *Votre Altesse.*

HIGH-PRESSURE (adj) **high-pressure salespeople** = *des vendeurs qui poussent à l'achat*
high-pressure work = *travail sous pression.*

HIGH-RISE (n) *tour (f)* : we live in a high-rise = *nous habitons (dans) une tour* ⓒ skyscraper = *gratte-ciel* ☻ → turn.

HIGH-STRUNG (adj) *hypernerveux, -euse* : she's temperamental and high-strung = *elle est colérique et hypernerveuse* ⓒ keyed up = *sur les nerfs.*

HIGHTAIL IT (to, -ed) *déguerpir* : if the cops come, let's hightail it ! = *si les flics arrivent, on déguerpit !* → TO LEAVE.

HIGH-TECH (adj) *de haute technologie* : high-tech industries = *les industries de haute technologie* = high-technology ⓒ robots = *la robotique* **HIGH-TECH** (n) *haute technologie (f).*

HIGHWAY (n) *autoroute (f)* : let's take the highway = *prenons l'autoroute* = motorway (GB) ⓒ turnpike = *autoroute à péage* ≠ back road = *route départementale*
highway robbery = 1/ *vol organisé* : this restaurant's highway robbery = *ce restaurant, c'est du vol organisé* ≠ dirt cheap = *donné* 2/ *vol de grand chemin* : highway robbery in the Far West = *vol de grand chemin au Far West* ⓒ bandit = ←.

HIJACK (to, -ed) *détourner* : to hijack a plane = *détourner un avion* ⓒ to take hostages = *prendre des otages* ☻ → to deter **HIJACKER** (n) *pirate (m) de l'air* ⓒ terrorist = *terroriste* **HIJACKING** (n) *détournement (m) d'avion.*

HIKE (n) 1/ *(forte) hausse (f)* : a hike in prices = *une (forte) hausse des prix* ⓒ increase = *augmentation* ≠ dip = *petite baisse* 2/ *randonnée (f) (à pied)* : a long hike

in the woods = *une longue randonnée dans les bois* ⓒ walk = *promenade.*

HIKE (UP) (to, -d) *augmenter fortement* : they hiked up their prices = *ils ont fortement augmenté leurs prix* ≠ to lower = *baisser.*

HILARIOUS (adj) *hilarant, -e* : the show was hilarious = *le spectacle était hilarant* ⓒ a roar = *poilant.*

HILL (n) *colline (f)* ⓒ hilly = *vallonné*
to be over the hill = *ne plus avoir vingt ans* ⓒ to be getting on in years = *prendre de l'âge*
the Hill = *le Congrès à Washington* : the President's having trouble with his friends on the Hill = *le Président a des ennuis avec ses amis du Congrès.*

HILLBILLY (n, -ies) *péquenaud, -e* : from a family of hillbillies = *d'une famille de péquenauds* ⓒ country bumpkin = *cul-terreux* ≠ dude = *gars de la ville.*

HILT (n) **to the hilt** = *jusqu'au cou* : in trouble to the hilt = *dans les ennuis jusqu'au cou.*

HIM (pron) **1/** *le* (direct object) : I can see him = *je le vois* **2/** *lui* (indirect object) : ask him = *demande-lui* → I
it's him = *c'est lui*
with/for him = *avec/pour lui*
☻ *c'est à lui* = it's his
— *demande-lui (femme)* = ask her.

HIMSELF (pron) *lui-même, se* (reflexive) : he did it himself = *il l'a fait lui-même,* he can't see himself = *il ne peut pas se voir* → MYSELF.

HINDER (to, -ed) *gêner* : his indecision is hindering our progress = *son indécision gêne notre progression* ⓒ to frustrate = *contrarier* ☻ → to mind.

HINDSIGHT (n) *jugement (m) à retardement, esprit (m) de l'escalier* : you should have told me before, now it's just hindsight = *vous auriez dû me le dire avant, maintenant ce n'est qu'un jugement à retardement* ⓒ to have an afterthought = *se raviser.*

HINGE ON (to, -d) *reposer sur* : everything hinges on his decision = *tout repose sur sa décision* ⓒ to turn on = *dépendre de.*

HINT (n) **to drop a hint** = *faire une allusion* ⓒ to insinuate = *insinuer*
to give a hint = *donner une indication* : I can't guess who's coming to dinner, give me a hint = *je n'arrive pas à deviner qui vient dîner, donne-moi une indication* ⓒ to give a clue = *donner un indice*
a hint of (vanilla/accent) = *une pointe de (vanille)/d'(accent)* ⓒ a dot of = *un soupçon de*
to take the hint = *comprendre l'allusion* : I said I was

tired and he took the hint and left = *j'ai dit que j'étais fatigué, il a compris l'allusion et il est parti*
she can't take a hint = *elle ne comprend pas à demi-mot.*

HINT (to, -ed) *laisser entendre* : he hinted he was going to retire = *il a laissé entendre qu'il allait prendre sa retraite* ⦾ to insinuate = *insinuer*
to hint at = *faire allusion à* : I didn't understand what she was hinting at = *je n'ai pas compris à quoi elle faisait allusion.*

HIP (n) *hanche (f)* : she broke her hip = *elle s'est cassé la hanche* ⦾ pelvis = *bassin.*

HIP (adj) *branché, -e* : her parents are really hip = *ses parents sont vachement branchés* ⦾ hep = *à la page* ≠ square = *vieux jeu.*

HIP HIP HURRAH ! (interj) *hip hip hip hourra !*

HIPPIE (n) *hippie (m, f)* : long-haired hippies = *des hippies aux cheveux longs* ⦾ backpacker = *personne qui voyage sac au dos*, beatnik = ←.

HIPPOPOTAMUS (n, -es) *hippopotame (m)* ⦾ giraffe = *girafe.*

HIRE (n) **(cars) for hire** = *location de (voitures).*

HIRE (to, -d) **1/** *engager* : they hired a new worker = *ils ont engagé un nouvel ouvrier* ⦾ to take on = *embaucher* ≠ to lay off = *licencier* ☠ → to engage **2/** *louer* : I'm going to hire a car/tuxedo for the day = *je vais louer une voiture/un smoking pour la journée* ☠ → to praise.

HIS (pron) *le sien, les siens, la sienne, les siennes (à lui)* : is it his car ? — yes, it's his = *est-ce que c'est sa voiture? — oui, c'est la sienne/à lui*, the shoes ? they're his = *les chaussures ? ce sont les siennes/elles sont à lui* → MY
☠ *faire des siennes* = to be up to one's old tricks
— *y mettre du sien* = to do one's bit
— *les siens* = her/his folks.

HIS (adj) *son/sa/ses (à lui)* : his mother = *sa mère (à lui)*, his book = *son livre (à lui)* ≠ her = *son/sa/ses (à elle)* → MY.

HISPANIC (n, adj) *Américain noir, blanc ou indien ayant pour origine un pays de langue espagnole. Le mot s'applique aux nouveaux immigrants aussi bien qu'à ceux installés depuis des siècles aux États-Unis.*

HISS (to, -ed) *siffler* : the audience hissed the speaker = *le public a sifflé l'orateur* ≠ to applaud = *applaudir* ☠ → to whistle.

HISTORICAL (adj) *historique* : historical research = *recherche historique* ⦾ mythological = *mythologique.*

HISTORY (n, -ies) *histoire (f)* : the history of a country = *l'histoire d'un pays* ⦾ historian = *historien*, records = *archives* ☠ → story
it's history in the making = *c'est l'histoire en marche*
to make history = *être historique* : Lindbergh's flight made history = *le vol de Lindbergh a été historique.*

HIT (n) **1/** *coup (m)* : a hit on the head = *un coup sur la tête* = a blow on the head ☠ → blow **2/** *gros succès (m)*, *tube (m)* (song) : his last song was a hit = *sa dernière chanson a fait un tube*, the play was a hit = *la pièce a remporté un gros succès* ⦾ winner = *qqch de chouette* ≠ bomb = *bide* ☠ → tube

hit list = *liste des gens à éliminer* : the terrorists' hit list included the Prime Minister = *la liste des gens à éliminer établie par les terroristes comprenait le Premier ministre*
hit man = *flingueur* : he's one of the Mafia's hit men = *c'est un des flingueurs de la Mafia* ⦾ hired killer = *tueur à gages*
hit parade = *hit-parade*
to make a hit = *avoir beaucoup de succès* : he really made a hit in his new suit = *il a eu beaucoup de succès dans son nouveau costume* ⦾ to be a sensation = *faire sensation*
to make a hit with = *faire une touche avec* : she made a hit with her fiancé's parents = *elle a fait une touche avec les parents de son fiancé* ⦾ to make a good impression on = *faire bonne impression à.*

HIT (to, hit, hit) **1/** *frapper, taper* (lightly) : we fought and he hit me = *nous nous sommes disputés et il m'a frappé*, Mommy, he hit me ! = *Maman, il m'a tapé !*

☠ *se taper la tête contre les murs* = to bang one's head against a brick wall	— *taper sur qqn* = to put s.o. down	— *te frappe pas !* = stay loose !
— *se taper (un gueuleton)* = to have (a feast)	— *se taper qqn* = to fuck around with s.o.	— *frapper (à la porte)* = to knock (at the door)
— *taper (une lettre)* = to type (a letter)	— *taper sur les nerfs* = to get on s.o.'s nerves	— *frapper le champagne* = to put the champagne on ice
	— *ça m'a frappé* = it struck me	

2/ *atteindre* : the bullet hit him = *la balle l'a atteint* ✎ → to reach **3/** *rentrer dans* : the car hit the tree = *la voiture est rentrée dans l'arbre* ⓓ to crash into = *percuter*

I hit (my head) = *je me suis cogné (la tête)*
to hit (the papers) = *parvenir (aux journaux)* : when the story hits the papers, all hell's going to break loose ! = *quand l'affaire parviendra aux journaux, ça va chauffer !* ⓓ to be the talk of the town = *faire couler beaucoup d'encre*
to hit back = *rendre coup pour coup* : if someone hits you, hit back = *si quelqu'un te frappe, rends coup pour coup*

to hit s.o. for = *taper qqn de* : he hit me for 100 bucks = *il m'a tapé de cent dollars* ≠ to lend to = *prêter à*
to hit it off = *sympathiser* : we hit it off immediately = *nous avons immédiatement sympathisé* ⓓ to take to s.o. = *se lier d'amitié avec qqn* ✎ → to sympathize
to hit on = *tomber sur* : we hit on a marvelous idea = *nous sommes tombés sur une idée géniale* ⓓ to think up = *imaginer*

─────── GROUP : TO HIT = FRAPPER, TAPER ───────

to bash s.o. (on the head) = *assommer qqn*
to batter = *frapper à tour de bras*
to be free with one's hand = *avoir la main leste*
to beat = *battre*
to beat black and blue = *rouer de coups*
to beat s.o.'s brains out = *faire une grosse tête à qqn*
to beat the hell out of s.o. = *rentrer dans le chou/dans le lard à qqn*
to beat the (living) daylights out of s.o. = *frapper qqn comme un sourd*
to beat to a pulp = *mettre en bouillie*
to beat/knock the shit out of s.o. = *casser la gueule à qqn*
to beat s.o. up = *tabasser qqn*
to belt = *flanquer un coup à*
to clobber = *cogner*
to flatten = *étendre raide*
to give a beating = *flanquer une raclée*

to give a belting = *flanquer une correction*
to give a clobbering = *flanquer une volée*
to give a (good) going-over = *passer à tabac*
to give it to s.o. = *tomber sur qqn à bras raccourcis*
to give s.o. a licking = *flanquer une déculottée à qqn*
to give a shellacking = *flanquer une dérouillée*
to give a (sound) thrashing = *flanquer une (bonne) trempe*
to give a whipping = *flanquer une pile*
to haul off and (hit s.o.) = *se mettre à (taper sur qqn)*
to kick = *donner un coup de pied à*
to kick s.o.'s ass = *flanquer un coup de pied au cul à qqn*
to kick s.o.'s face/teeth/head in = *démolir le portrait à qqn*
to knock about = *donner des coups à*
to knock s.o.'s block off =

casser la figure à qqn
to knock down = *envoyer à terre*
to knock out = *mettre K.O.*
to lay s.o. out = *étendre qqn sur le carreau* = **to lay s.o. flat**
to let s.o. have it = *faire sa fête à qqn*
to pin to the floor/ground = *clouer au sol*
to punch = *flanquer un coup de poing à*
to slam = *ficher une claque à*
to slap = *gifler*
to slug = *assommer*
to smack = *baffer*
to spank = *donner une fessée à* = **to give a spanking to**
to strike = *frapper*
to thrash = *rosser*
to wallop = *flanquer une trempe/une torgnole à*
to whack = *flanquer des gnons à*
to whip = *fouetter*
to work s.o. over = *passer qqn à tabac.*

HIT-AND-RUN (adj) *coupable de délit de fuite* : a hit-and-run driver = *un conducteur coupable de délit de fuite.*

HITCH (n, -es) **1/** *hic (m)* : the hitch is that my parents won't let me go = *le hic, c'est que mes parents ne me laisseront pas y aller* ⓓ snag = *os* **2/** *temps (m)* : a five-year hitch in the army = *un temps de cinq ans dans l'armée* ✎ → time.

HITCH (to, -ed) *faire du stop* : we hitched to California = *nous avons fait du stop jusqu'en Californie* ≠ to give s.o. a ride = *emmener qqn en voiture*
to get hitched = *se mettre un fil à la patte* ⓓ to tie the knot = *se mettre la corde au cou.*

HITCHHIKE (to, -d) *faire de l'auto-stop* ⓓ to bum a ride = *faire du stop* **HITCHHIKER** (n) *auto-stoppeur, -euse* ⓓ stowaway = *passager clandestin* **HITCHHIKING** (n) *auto-stop (m).*

HIT-OR-MISS (adj) *(fait) à la va-comme-je-te-pousse* : hit-or-miss work = *travail fait à la va-comme-je-te-pousse.*

HOARSE (adj, -r, -st) *enroué, -e* : the speaker was hoarse from talking too long = *l'orateur était enroué d'avoir parlé si longtemps.*

HOAX (n, -es) *canular (m)* : the bomb scare was a hoax =

l'alerte à la bombe était un canular ○○ *practical joke =* farce.

HOBBLE (to, -d) *clopiner :* the old man was hobbling = *le vieil homme clopinait* ○○ to limp = *boiter.*

HOBBY (n, -ies) *hobby (m), violon (m) d'Ingres* ○○ pastime = *passe-temps.*

HOBNOB (to, -bed) **to hobnob with (high society) =** *côtoyer (la haute société)* ○○ to mix with = *frayer avec.*

HOBO (n, -es or -s) *chemineau (m) :* a lot of hoboes during the Depression = *de nombreux chemineaux pendant la Dépression* ○○ bum = *clochard.*

HOCK (n) **in hock =** *au clou :* my watch is in hock = *ma montre est au clou* ○○ pawned = *au mont-de-piété.*

HOCK (to, -ed) **1/** *mettre au clou :* I hocked my watch = *j'ai mis ma montre au clou* ○○ to pawn = *mettre en gage* **2/** *tanner :* stop hocking me ! = *arrête de me tanner !* ○○ to bug = *casser les pieds à.*

HOCKEY (n) *hockey (m) :* field hockey = *hockey sur gazon,* ice hockey = *hockey sur glace,* hockey player = *hockeyeur.*

HOCUS-POCUS (n inv) *mystification (f) :* his speech was

a lot of hocus-pocus = *son discours n'était que mystification.*

HODGEPODGE (n inv) *fouillis (m) :* there was a hodgepodge of things on the bed = *il y avait un sacré fouillis sur le lit* ○○ hotchpotch ○○ potpourri = *pot-pourri.*

HOE (n) *binette (f) :* the hoe is rusty = *la binette est rouillée* ○○ rake = *râteau.*

HOG (n) *porc (m)* ○○ pig = *cochon* ☠ → pork
to live high on the hog = *mener grand train* ≠ to live from hand to mouth = *vivre au jour le jour.*

HOG (to, -ged) *accaparer :* to hog the conversation = *accaparer la conversation* ○○ to monopolize = *monopoliser* ☠ *accaparer le marché =* to corner the market.

HOGWASH (n inv) *absurdités (f pl) :* I've never heard such hogwash ! = *je n'ai jamais entendu de telles absurdités !* ○○ rot = *bêtises,* eyewash = *inepties* ☠ → absurdity.

HOIST (to, -ed) *hisser :* to hoist the flag = *hisser le drapeau* ○○ to lift = *soulever.*

HOKUM (n inv) *niaiseries (f pl) :* what he said was a lot of hokum = *il n'a dit que des niaiseries* ○○ baloney = *âneries.*

HOLD (n) **a hold over =** *une emprise sur :* when he lost his job, he lost his hold over her = *quand il a perdu son boulot, il a perdu son emprise sur elle* ○○ domination = ←
get a hold of that ! = *regarde-moi ça !*
to get hold of = **1/** *joindre :* where can I get hold of you ? = *où puis-je vous joindre ?* ☠ → to join **2/** *dénicher :* where can I get hold of a watch like yours ? = *où est-ce que je peux dénicher une montre comme la tienne ?* = where can I dig up a watch like yours ?* ○○ to scare up = *dégoter*
get hold of yourself ! = *domine-toi !* ○○ get a grasp of yourself ! = *maîtrise-toi !*
to take hold of = *s'emparer de :* he took hold of the rope = *il s'est emparé de la corde* ○○ to grasp = *saisir.*

HOLD (to, held, held) **1/** *tenir :* hold this ! = *tiens ça !* ○○ to take = *prendre,* to clasp = *serrer*

---

he held that (I was wrong) = *il a soutenu que (j'avais tort)* ○○ he maintained that = *il a maintenu que*

hold it ! = *minute papillon !* ○○ take it easy ! = *du calme !*
(my offer) still holds = *(ma proposition) tient toujours*

2/ *tenir debout :* your argument doesn't hold = *votre argument ne tient pas debout* ≠ to be groundless = *être sans fondement* **3/** *détenir :* they held him one night in jail = *ils l'ont détenu une nuit en prison* ○○ to keep in custody = *garder à vue* **4/** *contenir :* the bottle holds a quart = *la bouteille contient à peu près un litre* ☠ → to contain **5/** *tenir :* to hold a meeting/a conference = *tenir une réunion/une conférence* ○○ to convene = *se réunir* **6/** *tenir :* will the bridge hold ? = *est-ce que le pont tiendra ?,* I can hold for a week with this money = *je peux tenir pendant une semaine avec cet argent* ≠ to give way = *céder*

---

to hold stg against s.o. = *tenir rigueur à qqn de qqch :* I won't hold it against you = *je ne vous en tiendrai pas rigueur* ≠ to forgive = *pardonner*
to hold back = **1/** *refouler :* to

hold back one's anger/the crowd = *refouler sa colère/la foule* ☠ *refouler (troupes) =* to fight off/to drive back (troops) **2/** *retenir :* to hold back information = *retenir l'information* ☠ → to

restrain
to hold down = **1/** *garder :* she has held down the same job for 20 years = *elle a gardé la même place pendant 20 ans* ☠ → to guard **2/** *maintenir :* to hold

297

down prices = *maintenir les prix* 💀 → to maintain

to hold forth = *tenir de grands discours sur* : she held forth on the subject of racism = *elle a tenu de grands discours sur le racisme* ⓓ to go on and on about = *être intarissable sur*

to hold in = *retenir* : to hold in one's feelings = *retenir ses sentiments* ⓓ to repress = *réprimer* 💀 → to restrain

to hold off = 1/ *ne pas y avoir* : I hope the storm holds off = *j'espère qu'il n'y aura pas de tempête* 2/ *s'abstenir* : he held off from answering me = *il s'est abstenu de me répondre* 3/ *empêcher d'avancer* : they held off the enemy for days = *ils ont empêché l'ennemi d'avancer pendant des jours*

hold on ! = 1/ *minute papillon !* ⓓ hang on ! = *un instant !* 2/ *ne quittez pas !* ⓓ hold the line !* = *restez en ligne !*

to hold on = *tenir* : we'll have to hold on till help comes = *il va falloir que nous tenions jusqu'à ce que les secours arrivent* = to hang on

to hold on to = 1/ *arriver à garder* : he won't hold on to her =

il n'arrivera pas à la garder 2/ *se cramponner à* : hold on to me so you don't fall = *cramponne-toi à moi pour ne pas tomber*

to hold out = 1/ *tenir* : our money/supplies will hold out a month = *notre argent tiendra/nos réserves tiendront un mois* 2/ *se réserver* : to hold out for a better offer = *se réserver pour une meilleure proposition* ≠ to jump at = *sauter sur* 💀 → to reserve 3/ *tenir bon* : the army can hold out a week = *l'armée peut tenir bon une semaine* ≠ to yield = *céder*

to hold out on s.o. = *cacher son jeu à qqn* : tell us the truth, stop holding out on us = *dis-moi la vérité, ne nous cache plus ton jeu* ≠ to lay one's cards on the table = *jouer cartes sur table*

to hold over = 1/ *prolonger* : the play was a hit and was held over a month = *la pièce a fait un gros succès et a été prolongée un mois* = to prolong 2/ *permettre de tenir* : a thousand bucks will hold us over till my new job starts = *mille dollars nous permettront de tenir jusqu'à ce que commence mon nouveau boulot*

to hold s.o. to stg = *faire tenir*

qqch à qqn : I'll hold you to your promise = *je vous ferai tenir votre promesse*

to hold together = *bien tenir* : their marriage/the company held together all these years = *leur ménage/l'affaire a bien tenu pendant toutes ces années*

to hold up = 1/ *faire un hold-up* : to hold up a bank = *faire un hold-up dans une banque* ⓓ to do a job = *faire un coup* 2/ *soutenir* : the wall's held up by a beam = *le mur est soutenu par une poutre* 💀 → to support 3/ *tenir le coup* : how are you holding up ? = *comment tiens-tu le coup ?* = how are you bearing up ? 4/ *tenir en l'air* : hold up the picture so that everyone can see = *tenez le tableau en l'air pour que tout le monde puisse voir*

to hold s.o. up = *retenir qqn* : the rain held me up = *la pluie m'a retenu* ⓓ to delay = *retarder* 💀 → to restrain

that doesn't hold with me ! = *ça ne marche pas avec moi !* ⓓ tell it to the marines ! = *à d'autres !*

💀 *tenir à qqn* = to care for s.o.
— *se tenir debout/droit* = to be standing/straight
— *se tenir mal* ≠ *bien* = to misbehave ≠ to behave well
— *se tenir tranquille* = to keep quiet
— *ça tient à (son éducation)* = it can be explained by (his education)
— *tout se tient* = everything fits in
— *il tient de (son père)* = he takes after (his father)
— *tenir un journal/une promesse* = to keep a

diary/a promise
— *je ne savais pas à quoi m'en tenir* = I didn't know what to expect
— *tenez-vous-en aux faits !* = stick to the facts !
— *je tiens à faire ça* = I'm set on doing it
— *est-ce que vous pouvez tenir ?* = can you hang on ?/hold out ?
— *il avait promis mais il n'a pas tenu* = he had promised but he didn't come through.

HOLDING COMPANY (n, -ies) *holding (m ou f)* ⓓ trust = ←.

HOLDUP (n) *hold-up (m)* : the bank's third holdup = *le troisième hold-up à la banque* ⓓ break-in = *fric-frac*, heist = *casse*, theft = *vol*.

HOLE (n) 1/ *trou (m)* : a hole in my dress = *un trou à ma robe* 2/ *nid (m) à rats* : their apartment's a hole = *leur appartement est un nid à rats* ⓓ dump = *endroit pourri* **to be in a hole** = *être dans le pétrin* : if you can't lend me any money, I'll really be in a hole = *si tu ne peux pas me prêter d'argent, je serai vraiment dans le pétrin* ⓓ to be in a pickle = *être frais*

(I need your help) like a hole in the head ! = *(moi, avoir besoin d'aide ?) tu veux rire !*

to pick holes in (s.o.'s argument) = *relever les failles de (l'argumentation de qqn)* ⓓ to find fault with = *trouver à redire à*

💀 *trou d'air* = air pocket
— *avoir un trou de mémoire* = to draw a blank
— *boire comme un trou* = to drink like a fish
— *faire son trou* = to make one's mark
— *habiter un trou* = to live in a one-horse town.

HOLE-IN-THE-WALL (n) *nid (m) à rats* = hole.

HOLE UP (to, -d) *se terrer* : the crooks holed up in an abandoned farm = *les escrocs se sont terrés dans une ferme abandonnée* ⓓ to hide out = *se planquer.*

HOLIDAY (n) **1/** *jour (m) de fête, jour (m) férié :* banks are closed on holidays = *les banques sont fermées les jours de fête* ≠ workday = *jour ouvrable* **2/** vacances *(f pl)* (GB) = vacation.

HOLIER-THAN-THOU (adj) *de petit saint :* a holier-than-thou attitude = *une attitude de petit saint* ⓓ self-righteous = *moralisant.*

HOLLAND (n) *Hollande (f)* ⓓ the Netherlands = *les Pays-Bas,* the Dutch = *les Hollandais.*

HOLLER (to, -ed) *brailler :* "get out !" he hollered = « *sors d'ici ! » a-t-il braillé* ⓓ to shriek = *pousser des cris perçants* ≠ to whisper = *chuchoter* ☠ *le bébé braille* = the baby's wailing/bawling.

HOLLOW (adj) *creux, -euse :* hollow promises/logs = des promesses/des bûches creuses ☠ *heure/saison creuse* = off hour/season.

HOLOCAUST (n) *holocauste (m)* ⓓ apocalypse = ←.

HOLY (adj, -ier, -iest) *saint, -e :* a holy man = *un saint homme* ⓓ sacred = *sacré*
holy cow ! = *bougre !* ⓓ **holy mackerel !** = *saperlipopette !,* **holy Moses !** = *saperlotte !,* **holy shit !** = *bordel de merde !,* **holy smoke !** = *nom d'un petit bonhomme !* → GOSH !
Holy Ghost = *Saint-Esprit*
the Holy Land = *la Terre sainte*
a holy terror = *un enfant terrible* ⓓ kid = *gosse*
the Holy War = *la Guerre sainte*
☠ *une sainte nitouche* = a prig
— *à la saint-glinglin* = when hell freezes over
— *toute la sainte journée* = all day long
— *la Saint-Sylvestre* = New Year's eve.

HOMAGE (n) **to pay homage to** = *rendre hommage à.*

HOME (n) **1/** (inv) *chez soi :* we've been living in France for six months but home is New York = *nous habitons en France depuis six mois, mais chez nous c'est à New York* **2/** *foyer (m) :* orphans who have never known a home = *des orphelins qui n'ont jamais connu de foyer* ☠ *foyer d'infection* = source of infection

---

at home = **1/** *à la maison :* I left the kids at home = *j'ai laissé les gosses à la maison* **2/** *chez ses parents :* she's 25 but still living at home = *elle a 25 ans, mais elle habite toujours chez ses parents*
children's home = *home d'enfants*
to come from a broken home = *être issu d'un foyer désuni*

to feel at home = *se sentir (comme) chez soi :* I don't feel at home with my in-laws = *je ne me sens pas (comme) chez moi chez mes beaux-parents* ≠ to feel ill-at-ease = *se sentir mal à l'aise*
to hit home = *toucher au vif* ⓓ to hit a sore spot = *toucher le point sensible*

home sweet home ! = *qu'on est bien chez soi !*
to leave home = *quitter la maison :* he left home when he was 17 = *il a quitté la maison à 17 ans*
make yourself at home ! = *faites comme chez vous !*
nursing home = *maison de santé.*

HOME (adj) **to be at home base** = *arriver au but :* when the contract's signed, we'll be at home base = *quand le contrat sera signé, nous serons arrivés au but* ⓓ to be out of the woods = *être sorti de l'auberge*
home (cooking) = *(la bonne cuisine) familiale :*

there's nothing like home cooking = *rien ne vaut la bonne cuisine familiale*
home office = *siège social* = headquarters
Home Office (GB) = *ministère de l'Intérieur*
home port = *port d'attache.*

HOME (adv) **to bring home** = *faire comprendre :* the argument brought the truth home = *cet argument a fait comprendre la vérité*
to drive s.o. home = *raccompagner qqn (chez lui) :* can you drive me home ? = *est-ce que vous pouvez me raccompagner chez moi ?* = can you take me home ?
nothing to write home about = *qui ne casse pas des briques :* his last film was nothing to write home

about = *son dernier film ne cassait pas des briques* → AWFUL
to stay home = *rester à la maison :* we're staying home tonight = *ce soir, nous restons à la maison* ≠ to go out = *sortir*
to take home = *se faire ... net d'impôt :* she takes home $ 200 a week = *elle se fait 200 dollars net d'impôt par semaine*
I'll walk you home = *je vous raccompagne (à pied) chez vous* = **I'll take you home.**

HOMEBODY (n, -ies) *casanier, -ère* : my husband's a homebody = *mon mari est casanier* ≠ a good-time Charley = *un noceur.*

HOMECOMING (n) **to give a homecoming to s.o.** = *accueillir qqn en grande pompe* : his hometown gave him a homecoming when he came back from Vietnam = *sa ville natale l'a accueilli en grande pompe à son retour du Viêt-nam.*

HOMELESS (adj) *sans foyer* : homeless refugees = *des réfugiés sans foyer.*

HOMELY (adj, -ier, -iest) *au physique ingrat* : a homely girl = *une fille au physique ingrat* ⓓ ugly = *laid* ≠ lovely = *charmant.*

HOMEMADE (adj) *fait, -e maison* : homemade jam/clothes = *confiture faite maison/vêtements faits maison* ≠ store-bought = *acheté.*

HOMESICK (adj) *qui a le mal du pays* : when I'm abroad too long, I get homesick = *quand je reste trop longtemps à l'étranger, j'ai le mal du pays* ⓓ nostalgic = *nostalgique.*

HOMESTRETCH (n, -es) *dernière ligne (f) droite* : our project is reaching the homestretch = *notre projet est entré dans la dernière ligne droite* ⓓ the last lap = *la dernière étape.*

HOMETOWN (n) *ville (f) natale* : Chicago is her hometown = *Chicago, c'est sa ville natale.*

HOMEWORK (n) *devoir (m)* : I always do my homework = *je fais toujours mes devoirs* ☠ → duty.

HOMICIDE (n) *homicide (m)* : convicted of homicide = *inculpé d'homicide* ⓓ murder = *meurtre.*

HOMO (n) *homo (m, f)* : a club for homos = *un club d'homos* ⓓ fairy = *tante*, ac/dc = *à voile et à vapeur.*

HOMOGENEOUS (adj) *homogène* : a homogeneous class = *une classe homogène* ≠ heterogeneous = *hétérogène.*

HOMOSEXUAL (n, adj) *homosexuel, -elle* : defending the rights of homosexuals = *qui défend les droits des homosexuels* = gay ≠ heterosexual = *hétérosexuel.*

HONCHO (n) *grosse légume (f)* : advertising honchos = *les grosses légumes de la publicité* ⓓ big shot = *grand ponte.*

HONE IN ON (to, -d) *cerner* : to hone in on the issue = *cerner la question* ☠ → to hem in.

HONEST (adj) *honnête* : an honest lawyer/salesman = *un avocat/vendeur honnête* ⓓ on the level = *tout ce qu'il y a de plus sérieux*, ethical = *probe* ≠ crooked = *malhonnête* ☠ *résultat/prix honnête* = fair result/price
honest to God ! = *je le jure sur la tête de ma mère !*
honest injun ! = *je te le jure !* ⓓ cross my heart and hope to die = *croix de bois, croix de fer, si je mens, je vais en enfer !*

that's the honest truth = *c'est la pure vérité.*

HONESTLY (adv) *honnêtement* : I'm sorry, honestly = *honnêtement, je suis désolé* ⓓ sincerely = *sincèrement.*

HONESTY (n inv) *honnêteté (f)* : he's known for his honesty = *il est connu pour son honnêteté* ⓓ integrity = *intégrité* ≠ dishonesty = *malhonnêteté*
honesty's the best policy = *l'honnêteté est toujours récompensée.*

HONEY (n) 1/ *miel (m)* : I like honey in tea = *j'aime le miel dans le thé* ⓓ hive = *ruche* 2/ *mon chou, ma choute* : what do you want to do tonight, honey ? = *qu'est-ce que tu veux faire ce soir, mon chou ?* ⓓ kitten = *mon minou*, sweetie = *mon coco.*

HONEYMOON (n) *lune (f) de miel* : let's go on a second honeymoon = *partons pour une seconde lune de miel* ⓓ newlyweds = *jeunes mariés*, honeymooners = *jeunes mariés en voyage de noces.*

HONK (to, -ed) *klaxonner* ⓓ horn = *Klaxon.*

HONKY = HONKIE (n, -ies) *sale Blanc (m)* ⓓ the Man = *l'homme blanc* ≠ spade = *mal blanchi.*

HONKY-TONK (adj) *clinquant, -e* : the honky-tonk part of town = *les quartiers clinquants de la ville* ⓓ flashy = *tapageur.*

HONOR (n) *honneur (m)* : I have the honor to tell you that you're hired = *j'ai l'honneur de vous dire que vous êtes embauché* = honour (GB)

in honor of (her parents) = *en l'honneur de (ses parents)* **on my honor !** = *parole d'honneur !* ⓓ honest injun ! = *je te le jure !* **there's honor among thieves** = *les loups ne se mangent pas entre eux* ⓓ the rules of the	game = *les règles du jeu* **to what do I owe the honor ?** = *qu'est-ce qui me vaut cet honneur ?* **you must give honor where honor is due** = *à tout seigneur, tout honneur* ⓓ I give him credit = *je mets ça à son crédit*

☠ *c'est (tout) à votre honneur* = it's to your credit
— *en quel honneur ?* = by what right ?

HONOR (to, -ed) 1/ *honorer* : to honor s.o.'s memory = *honorer la mémoire de qqn* ☠ *cela t'honore* = it's to your credit
— *honorer (une femme)* = to service (a woman)
2/ *accepter* : to honor all credit cards = *accepter toutes les cartes de crédit* = to accept.

HONORABLE (adj) *honorable* : honorable results = *des résultats honorables* ≠ dishonorable = *déshonorant.*

HONORARY (adj) *honoraire* : an honorary member = *un membre honoraire.*

HONORS (n pl) **(to pass an exam) with honors** = *(réussir un examen) avec mention*
to do the honors = *faire les honneurs de la maison.*

HOOD (n) **1/** *loulou (m)* : hoods mugged the old lady = *des loulous ont agressé la vieille dame* Ⓞ hoodlum = *loubard*, reformatory = *centre d'éducation surveillée* **2/** *capuchon (m)* : a cape with a hood = *une cape avec un capuchon* **3/** *capot (m) de voiture* = *bonnet* (GB).

HOODLUM (n) *loubard, -e* : a group of hoodlums smashed the windows = *une bande de loubards a fracassé les vitrines* Ⓞ hooligan = *voyou*, gang = ←.

HOODWINK (to, -ed) *truander* : tourists are easy to hoodwink = *les touristes sont faciles à truander* → TO HUSTLE.

HOOEY (n inv) *sornettes (f pl)* : that's a lot of hooey ! = *que de sornettes !* Ⓞ bunk = *fadaises.*

HOOF (n, -ves) *sabot (m)* : the hooves of a horse = *les sabots d'un cheval* ☠ sabots *(chaussures)* = clogs.

HOOK (n) *patère (f)* : hang your coat on the hook = *accrochez votre manteau à la patère*
by hook or by crook = *coûte que coûte* Ⓞ at all costs = *à tout prix*
to fall hook, line and sinker = *gober le morceau* Ⓞ to walk into the trap = *tomber dans le panneau*
to get off the hook = *se dégager d'une obligation* : I promised to take my niece to the zoo and I can't get off the hook = *j'ai promis d'emmener ma nièce au zoo et je ne peux pas me dégager de cette obligation*
hook and eye = *agrafe* Ⓞ button = *bouton*
off the hook = *décroché* : the phone's off the hook = *le téléphone est décroché.*

HOOK (to, -ed) **1/** *accrocher* : the first time I heard Brel, I was hooked = *la première fois que j'ai entendu Brel, j'ai accroché* ☠ → to hang **2/** *mettre la main sur* : he hooked a beautiful girl = *il a mis la main sur une belle fille* **3/** *se prostituer* : even minors are hooking = *même les mineurs se prostituent* Ⓞ to trick = *faire des passes*
to be hooked on (heroin) = *être accroché à (l'héroïne)*
to get hooked = *se mettre la corde au cou* Ⓞ to get hitched = *se mettre un fil à la patte*
to hook up with = *avoir partie liée avec* : the French hooked up with the English to build the tunnel = *les Français ont partie liée avec les Anglais pour construire le tunnel* Ⓞ to pull together = *joindre ses efforts.*

HOOKER (n) *putain (f)* : there are lots of hookers around Times Square = *il y a beaucoup de putains autour de Times Square* Ⓞ courtesan = *courtisane*, trick = *passe*, madam = *mère maquerelle*, pimp = *maquereau*, harlot = *fille de joie*
☠ *ce putain de bouquin* = this fucking book
— *enfant/fils de putain* = s.o.b.
— *putain !* = screw it !/fuck it !

HOOKY (adv) **to play hooky** = *faire l'école buissonnière* Ⓞ to skip school = *sécher l'école.*

HOOLIGAN (n) *hooligan (m), voyou (m)* Ⓞ vandal = *vandale.*

HOOT (n) **I don't give a hoot !** = *je m'en moque !* Ⓞ what do I care ! = *ça me fait une belle jambe !*, I don't give a rap ! = *je m'en tamponne le coquillard !*

HOOTENANNY (n, -ies) *soirée (f) folk* Ⓞ Far West = ←.

HOP (n) *sauterie (f)* : there's a hop at the high school Saturday night = *il y a une sauterie au collège samedi soir* Ⓞ dance = *soirée dansante*
a hop, skip and jump = *à deux pas* : the bank is just a hop, skip and jump from here = *la banque est juste à deux pas d'ici* ≠ a long way off = *au diable.*

HOP (to, -ped) *sautiller* : rabbits hop = *les lapins sautillent* Ⓞ to jump = *sauter*
to hop down to (the bank) = *faire un saut à (la banque)* = to jump over to (the bank)
hop to it ! = *et que ça saute !* Ⓞ get a move on ! = *magne-toi !*

HOPE (n) *espoir (m)* : I'm full of hope = *je suis plein d'espoir* Ⓞ expectation = *espérance*

to dash s.o.'s hopes = *anéantir les espoirs de qqn*
don't give up (all) hope ! = *ne perdez pas (tout) espoir !*
to hope against hope = *espérer contre tout espoir*

in the hope that (I see you soon) = *dans l'espoir de (vous voir bientôt)*
to pin one's hopes on = *fonder ses espoirs sur*
to raise s.o.'s hopes = *donner de l'espoir à qqn.*

HOPE (to, -d) *espérer* : I hope you'll come = *j'espère que vous viendrez*, I hope to go Saturday = *j'espère y aller samedi* Ⓞ to wish = *souhaiter* ≠ to despair = *désespérer*

I hope so = *j'espère bien* ≠ **I hope not** = *j'espère que non*
hoping that (you'll write soon) = *en espérant (vous lire bientôt)*

to hope for = *espérer* : we're hoping for the best = *nous espérons que ça se passera au mieux.*

HOPEFUL (adj) *qui a bon espoir* : we're hopeful that he'll get the job = *nous avons bon espoir qu'il obtienne le poste* Ⓞ optimistic = *optimiste.*

HOPEFULLY (adv) *espérons (que)* : hopefully, there'll

be sun tomorrow = *espérons qu'il y aura du soleil demain.*

HOPELESS (adj) *sans espoir* : the situation's hopeless = *la situation est sans espoir*
a hopeless (liar) = *un (menteur) incorrigible* ⨀ chronic = *chronique.*

HORIZON (n) *horizon (m)* : new horizons = *de nouveaux horizons* ⨀ view = *vue.*

HORIZONTAL (adj) *horizontal, -e* ≠ vertical = ←.

HORMONE (n) *hormone (f)* : chicken fed on hormones = *du poulet nourri aux hormones* ⨀ gene = *gène.*

HORN (n) **1/** *cor (m)* : to play the horn = *sonner du cor* **2/** *corne (f)* : the horns of a bull = *les cornes d'un taureau* ☙ *il porte des cornes* = he's cuckolded **3/** *Klaxon (m)* : the horn doesn't work = *le Klaxon ne marche pas*
the horn of plenty = *la corne d'abondance*
to blow one's (own) horn = *s'envoyer des fleurs* ⨀ to pat o.s. on the back = *se féliciter.*

HORNET (n) *frelon (m)* ⨀ wasp = *guêpe*
to walk into the hornet's nest = *se fourrer dans un guêpier* ⨀ to fall into the trap = *tomber dans le piège.*

HORN IN (to, -ed) *ramener sa fraise* : we weren't speaking to him but he horned in = *nous ne lui parlions pas mais il a ramené sa fraise* ⨀ to stick one's two cents in = *mettre son grain de sel.*

HORNY (adj, -ier, -iest) *en manque (sexuel)* : a week without screwing and I'm horny = *une semaine sans baiser et je suis en manque* ⨀ oversexed = *complètement obsédé.*

HOROSCOPE (n) *horoscope (m)* : to read one's horoscope in the paper = *lire son horoscope dans le journal* ⨀ astrology = *astrologie.*

HORRENDOUS (adj) *épouvantable* : a horrendous experience = *une expérience épouvantable* = dreadful ≠ great = *formidable* → AWFUL.

HORRIBLE (adj) *horrible* : a horrible movie/dinner = *un film/un dîner horrible* → AWFUL ≠ wonderful = *merveilleux.*

HORRID (adj) *atroce* : horrid weather = *temps atroce* = atrocious → AWFUL ≠ great = *formidable.*

HORRIFY (to, -ied) *horrifier* : his remark horrified me = *sa remarque m'a horrifié* ⨀ to shock = *choquer* **HORRIFYING** (adj) *horrifiant, -e* : horrifying news = *des nouvelles horrifiantes* ⨀ frightening = *effrayant.*

HORROR (n) *horreur (f)* : the horrors of war = *les horreurs de la guerre* ⨀ dread = *épouvante*
horror film = *film d'horreur/d'épouvante*
☙ *j'ai horreur de prendre le métro* = I hate taking the subway.

HORSE (n) *cheval (m) (chevaux)* : what beautiful horses ! = *quels beaux chevaux !*

bridle = *bride*	**horse show** = *manifestation équestre*	**to ride bareback** = *monter à cru*
colt = *poulain*	**jockey** = ←	**to ride sidesaddle** = *monter en amazone*
to cover = *saillir*	**jumping** = *concours hippique*	**saddle** = *selle*
filly = *pouliche*	**mare** = *jument*	**stable** = *écurie*
foal = *(très jeune) poulain*	**nag** = *tocard/bourrin*	**stallion** = *étalon*
to foal = *mettre bas*	**to neigh** = *hennir*	**stirrup** = *étrier*
giddyep = *hue !*	**on horseback** = *à cheval*	**stud farm** = *haras*
to go horseback riding = *monter à cheval*	**pony** = *poney*	**thoroughbred** = *pur-sang*
harness = *harnais*	**racehorse** = *cheval de course*	**trotter** = *trotteur*
to hitch = *atteler*	**racetrack** = *champ de courses*	**turf** = ←
hoof = *sabot*	**reins** = *rênes*	**whoa !** = *holà !*
horseshoe = *fer à cheval*	**to ride** = *monter (à cheval)*	

I could eat a horse = *j'ai une faim de loup* ⨀ I'm ravenous = *je suis affamé*
to eat like a horse = *manger comme quatre* ⨀ to be a hearty eater = *avoir un bon coup de fourchette*
hold your horses ! = *minute papillon !* ⨀ take it easy ! = *du calme !*
horse doctor = *mauvais docteur* ⨀ charlatan = ←
I got it from the horse's mouth = *je le sais de source sûre* ≠ through the grapevine = *par le téléphone arabe*
to play the horses = *jouer aux courses*

that's a horse of another/a different color = *c'est une autre paire de manches* ⨀ that's another story = *c'est une autre histoire*
that's what makes for horseracing = *tous les goûts sont dans la nature/des goûts et des couleurs on ne discute pas* ⨀ it takes all kinds to make a world = *il faut de tout pour faire un monde*
you can lead a horse to water but you can't make it drink = *on ne saurait faire boire un âne qui n'a pas soif*

☠ *remède de cheval* = drastic remedy/strong medicine — *être à cheval sur (les principes)* = to be a stickler for (principles)	— *c'est son cheval de bataille* = it's his pet argument — *fièvre de cheval* = high fever — *cheval de retour* = old offender.

HORSE (to, -d) **to horse around** = *faire l'andouille* : stop horsing around and get to work = *arrête de faire l'andouille et mets-toi au travail* ⓓ to fool around = *faire l'imbécile.*

HORSERADISH (n) *raifort (m)* : horseradish with smoked mackerel = *du raifort avec du maquereau fumé* ⓓ mustard = *moutarde.*

HORSESHIT (n inv) *foutaises (f pl)* : that's a lot of horseshit ! = *tout ça, c'est des foutaises !* ⓓ bullshit = *conneries.*

HOSE (n) *tuyau (m) (d'arrosage)* : you can shower with the hose = *tu peux te doucher avec le tuyau (d'arrosage)* ⓓ to water = *arroser* ☠ → pipe.

HOSPITABLE (adj) *hospitalier, -ère* **HOSPITALITY** (n, -ies) *hospitalité (f).*

HOSPITAL (n) *hôpital (m), hosto (m)* (LV) : my wife's in the hospital = *ma femme est à l'hôpital* ⓓ clinic = *clinique,* infirmary = *infirmerie,* nursing home = *maison de santé,* sanatorium = ←, asylum = *asile,* orderly = *garçon de salle,* doctor = *médecin,* nurse = *infirmière* ☠ *c'est l'hôpital qui se fout de la charité* = it's the pot calling the kettle black.

HOSPITALIZE (to, -d) *hospitaliser.*

HOST (n) *hôte (m)* : our host got drunk = *notre hôte s'est saoulé* ⓓ hostess = *hôtesse*
a host of (problems) = *une foule de (problèmes)* → MANY
☠ *un hôte payant* = a paying guest
— *"hôte"* means both "host" and "guest".

HOSTAGE (n) *otage (m)* : will the hostages be soon released ? = *est-ce que les otages seront bientôt relâchés ?* ⓓ ransom = *rançon.*

HOSTESS (n, -es) *hôtesse (f)* : a charming hostess = *une hôtesse charmante*
hostess gown = *robe d'hôtesse* = dressing gown.

HOSTILE (adj) *hostile* : a hostile look/answer = *un regard/une réponse hostile* ⓓ antagonistic = *antagoniste* ≠ friendly = *amical* **HOSTILITY** (n, -ies) *hostilité (f)* : the hostility in his voice frightened me = *l'hostilité de sa voix m'a effrayé,* hostilities between the two families = *des hostilités entre les deux familles* ⓓ animosity = *animosité.*

HOT (n) **to have the hots for s.o.** = *bander pour qqn* : he has the hots for my sister = *il bande pour ma sœur* ⓓ to want to get into s.o.'s pants = *vouloir s'envoyer qqn.*

HOT (adj, -ter, -test) 1/ *(très) chaud, -e* : a very hot day = *une journée très (très) chaude* ⓓ sweltering = *étouffant,* red-hot = *brûlant* = piping hot = scorching, sizzling = *d'une chaleur torride,* torrid = *torride,* boiling = *cuisant* = baking ≠ cold = *froid* 2/ *relevé, -e* : her cooking's too hot for me = *sa cuisine est trop relevée pour moi* ⓓ spicy = *épicé* ≠ bland = *peu relevé* 3/ *tout excité, -e* : I'm hot from all that petting = *je suis tout excité après toutes ces caresses* ⓓ turned on = *troublé* 4/ *volé, -e* : hot goods = *marchandises volées,* a hot car = *une voiture volée* = stolen 5/ *en vogue* : jeans/rock groups are hot today = *les jeans/les groupes de rock sont en vogue aujourd'hui* ≠ out = *démodé*

to be hot = *avoir chaud* : I'm hot = *j'ai chaud* ≠ to be cold = *avoir froid*
to be a hot number = *avoir le feu aux fesses* ⓓ to be a good lay = *être un bon baiseur/une bonne baiseuse*
to be in hot water = *être dans de beaux draps* : to be in a spot = *être dans le pétrin*
to blow hot and cold = *souffler le chaud et le froid* : one day he's all excited about the project, and the next day, he's against it ; he blows hot and cold = *un jour il est enthousiasmé par le projet, le lendemain, il est contre ; il souffle le chaud et le froid* ⓓ to be capricious = *être capricieux*
don't get hot under the collar ! = *ne prends pas la mouche !* → ANGRY
to drop s.o. like a hot potato = *laisser tomber qqn comme une vieille chaussette* : he dropped his girlfriend like a hot potato = *il a laissé tomber sa petite amie comme une vieille chaussette* ⓓ to chuck = *balancer*
to feel hot and bothered = *se sentir tout chose* ⓓ to be all excited = *être tout excité*
to have hot pants = *être un chaud lapin*
hot air = *du vent* : what you're saying's a lot of hot air ! = *ce que tu dis, c'est du vent !* ⓓ

bullshit = *des conneries*
hot dog = *hot-dog* ⊙ frankfurter = *saucisse de Francfort*
the hot line = *le téléphone rouge*
hot plate = *réchaud*
hot rod = *bolide* ⊙ racing car = *voiture de course*
hot seat = *chaise électrique* = electric chair
hot spot = *point chaud* : the Middle East is a hot spot = *le Moyen-Orient est un point chaud*
hot stuff = *1/ le super-pied :*

that new rock group is hot stuff = *ce nouveau groupe de rock, c'est le super-pied* ⊙ wild = *dément* 2/ *qqn qui a du tempérament :* his broad's hot stuff = *sa nana a du tempérament*
hot tip = *bon tuyau* ≠ bum steer = *tuyau crevé*
it's hot (today) ! = *il fait chaud (aujourd'hui) !*
to make (things) hot for = *mener la vie dure à :* the cops are making things hot for the gang = *les flics mènent la vie dure au gang* ⊙ the heat's on = *ça*

chauffe
not so hot = *pas terrible :* the film wasn't so hot = *le film n'était pas terrible* → AWFUL ≠ great = *formidable*
to sell like hot cakes = *se vendre comme des petits pains* ≠ to be left on s.o.'s hands = *rester sur les bras de qqn*
to think one's hot stuff = *se prendre pour le nombril du monde* ⊙ to have a swelled head = *avoir la grosse tête*

☠ « hot » *et* « warm » *sont tous les deux traduits par chaud, mais* « warm » *est moins chaud que* « hot »
— *ça ne me fait ni chaud ni froid* = it's all the same to me

— *être chaud pour* ≠ *ne pas être chaud pour* = to be keen on ≠ to be cool to
— *pleurer à chaudes larmes* = to cry one's eyes out
— *j'ai eu chaud !* = it was a close call !

HOTEL (n) *hôtel* (m) : there are very few cheap hotels in New York = *il y a très peu d'hôtels bon marché à New York* ⊙ inn = *auberge*, room = *chambre*
☠ *hôtel particulier* = townhouse
— *hôtel de ville* = city hall.

HOTHEADED (adj) *emporté, -e* : he's a very hotheaded young man = *c'est un jeune homme très emporté* ≠ cool = ←.

HOTSHOT (adj) *hors pair* : a hotshot lawyer = *un avocat hors pair* ≠ two-bit = *à la manque.*

HOT-TEMPERED (adj) *coléreux, -euse* → ANGRY ≠ even-tempered = *d'humeur égale.*

HOUND (n) *chien* (m) *(de chasse)* = hunting dog.

HOUND (to, -ed) 1/ *s'acharner sur :* the journalists hounded her = *les journalistes se sont acharnés sur elle* ⊙ to harass = *harceler*
☠ *s'acharner sur (un travail)* = to slave at (a job)

— *s'acharner à vouloir ...* = to keep on trying ...
2/ *tanner :* stop hounding me about my smoking ! = *arrête de me tanner parce que je fume !* ⊙ to bug = *casser les pieds à.*

HOUR (n) *heure* (f) : it took an hour and a half = *ça a pris une heure et demie*
in an hour = 1/ *dans une heure* (future) : he'll be here in an hour = *il sera là dans une heure* 2/ *en une heure :* I did it in an hour = *je l'ai fait en une heure*
☠ quelle heure est-il ? = what time is it ?
— *il est cinq heures* = it's five o'clock
— *à son heure de gloire* = in her heyday
— *c'est l'heure !* = time's up !
— *je ne t'ai pas demandé l'heure qu'il était !* = mind your own business !
— *j'attends mon heure* = I'm biding my time
— *son heure a sonné* = his time has come
— *être à l'heure* = to be on time
— *il est (acteur) à ses heures* = he's a sometime (actor).

HOUSE (n) *maison* (f) : we live in a big house = *nous habitons une grande maison*, a two-family house = *une maison conçue pour deux familles*, split-level house = *maison à deux niveaux*, ranch house = *maison de plain-pied*, two-story house = *maison d'un étage (avec un rez-de-chaussée et un étage)* ⊙ houseboat = *péniche*, pavilion = *pavillon*, mansion = *belle demeure*, manor = *manoir*, digs = *baraque*

at my house = *chez moi* : the party's at my house = *la soirée a lieu chez moi*
to bring down the house = *faire un malheur :* the young singer brought down the house = *le jeune chanteur a fait un malheur* ≠ to be a flop = *faire un four*

to eat s.o. out of house and home = *dévaliser le frigidaire de qqn* ⊙ to eat like a horse = *manger comme quatre*
to get on like a house on fire = *s'entendre comme larrons en foire* ≠ to be at daggers drawn = *être à couteaux tirés*
House of Commons = *cham-*

bre des Communes ⊙ Parliament = *Parlement*
house of ill repute = *hôtel de passe/maison de tolérance* ⊙ brothel = *bordel*
House of Lords = *chambre des Lords*
House of Representatives = *chambre des Représentants* ⊙

Congress = *Congrès*
to keep house = *tenir le ménage/la maison*
man/lady of the house = *maître/maîtresse de maison*
on the house = *la tournée du*

patron : the drinks are on the house = *c'est la tournée du patron* Ⓞ scot-free = *à l'œil*
to play house = *jouer au papa et à la maman*
to play to an empty ≠ **a full**

house = *jouer devant des fauteuils vides/une salle vide* ≠ *jouer à guichets fermés*
under house arrest = *en résidence surveillée*

— ☠ *c'est une maison sérieuse* = it's a serious company
— *maison de repos* = rest home

— *maison de redressement* = reformatory (school)
— *(gâteau) fait maison* = home made (cake)
— *(rester) à la maison* = (to stay) home.

HOUSEBOAT (n) *péniche (f) aménagée* : to live on a houseboat = *vivre sur une péniche aménagée* Ⓞ sailboat = *voilier*.

HOUSEBROKEN (adj) *propre (animal)* : housebroken dog = *chien propre* ☠ → clean.

HOUSEHOLD (n) *maisonnée (f)* : there are nine people in our household = *nous sommes une maisonnée de neuf*
household goods = *produits ménagers*
household name = *nom connu de tout le monde* : Ralph Nader is a household name in the US = *Ralph Nader est (un nom) connu de tout le monde aux États-Unis*.

HOUSEKEEPER (n) *gouvernante (f)* : the priest married his housekeeper = *le prêtre a épousé sa gouvernante* Ⓞ maid = *bonne*.

HOUSEKEEPING (n) **to do the housekeeping** = *tenir la maison* : she does the housekeeping for the priest = *elle tient la maison du prêtre*.

HOUSEWARMING PARTY (n, -ies) *pendaison (f) de crémaillère*.

HOUSEWIFE (n, -wives) *femme (f) au foyer* : she dreams of being a housewife = *elle rêve d'être femme au foyer* Ⓞ homemaker = *ménagère*, househusband = *homme d'intérieur* ≠ career girl = *carriériste*.

HOUSEWORK (n) **to do the housework** = *faire le ménage* = to do the cleaning.

HOUSING (n inv) *logement (m)* : the problem of housing for refugees = *le problème du logement pour les réfugiés*
housing development = *lotissement*
housing project = *HLM*
housing shortage = *crise du logement*
☠ *je n'ai pas pu trouver de logement* = I couldn't find any lodgings.

HOVEL (n) *masure (f)* : they live in a hovel = *ils habitent une masure* Ⓞ dump = *endroit pourri*.

HOW (adv) *comment* : how can you say that ? = *comment pouvez-vous dire ça ?* ☠ *comment ?* = what did you say ?

how about ... ? = *et si ... ?* : how about a drink ? = *et si on prenait un verre ?* = what about a drink ?
how about it ? = *qu'en dites-vous ?*
how about that ! = *tiens donc !* → GOSH !
how are you ? = *comment allez-vous ?*
how can you tell (that they're not happy) ? = *comment pouvez-vous dire (qu'ils ne sont pas heureux) ?*
how come ? = *comment ça se fait ?* : she's quitting ? how come ? = *elle démissionne ? comment ça se fait ?*
how do you do ! = *enchanté !* Ⓞ pleased to meet you = *enchanté de faire votre connais-*

sance
how do you like (New York) ? = *comment trouvez-vous (New York) ?*
how else ... ? = *comment ... autrement ?* : if we don't take the train, how else can we go ? = *si nous ne prenons pas le train, comment pouvons-nous y aller autrement ?*
how ever ... ? = *comment peut-on ... ?* : how ever did she get such a great guy ? = *comment a-t-elle pu dénicher un type aussi formidable ?*
how far is it ? = *à quelle distance est-ce ?*
how is it ?/was it ? = *comment est-ce/était-ce ?*
how is it that ... ? = *comment se fait-il que ... ?*

how long = 1/ *combien de temps* : how long will it take ? = *combien de temps cela prendra-t-il ?*, (for) how long will you be here ? = *(pendant) combien de temps resterez-vous ?* 2/ *depuis combien de temps* : how long have you been here ? = *depuis combien de temps êtes-vous ici ?*
how many have you ? = *combien en avez-vous ?*
how much is it ? = *combien est-ce ?/ça fait ?* Ⓞ how much does it cost ? = *combien ça coûte ?*
how often ? = *tous les combien ?* : how often do you go to the movies ? = *tous les combien allez-vous au cinéma ?*
how (rich) he is ! = *ce qu'il est (riche) !* Ⓞ what a (rich guy) ! =

qu'est-ce qu'il est (riche) !
how so ? = *comment ça ? :* you don't want to go with us, how so ? = *comment ça, vous ne voulez pas venir avec nous ?*
how soon ? = *dans combien de temps ? :* how soon will you be ready ? = *dans combien de temps serez-vous prête ?*
how true ! = *c'est bien vrai !* ⓓ you're so right ! = *tu as cent fois raison !*

to know how to = *savoir :* she doesn't know how to drive/deal with children = *elle ne sait pas conduire/s'y prendre avec les enfants* ☠ → to know.

HOWEVER (adv) *cependant :* he's a bit selfish, however he's a nice guy = *il est un peu égoïste, cependant c'est un type sympa* ⓓ still = *quand même,* in spite of that = *malgré ça*
however (did she find out) ? = *comment diable (a-t-elle découvert la vérité) ? =* how in the world ... ?

HOWEVER (conj) **however much** = *avoir beau :* however much I study, I still don't understand = *j'ai beau travailler, je ne comprends toujours pas.*

HOWL (n) *qqch de tordant :* the play was a howl = *la pièce était tordante* ⓓ a riot = *qqch de désopilant* **HOWL** (to, -ed) *hurler de rire :* we howled at his jokes = *ses plaisanteries nous ont fait hurler de rire* ⓓ to guffaw = *s'esclaffer,* to be in stitches = *être plié en deux.*

HUBBUB (n inv) *brouhaha (m) :* there was a hubbub in Congress when the Senator stormed out = *il y a eu un sacré brouhaha au Congrès quand le sénateur a brusquement quitté la salle* ⓓ din = *vacarme.*

HUDDLE (n) *conciliabule (m) :* they went into a huddle to decide = *ils ont tenu (un) conciliabule pour prendre une décision* **HUDDLE** (to, -d) *tenir (un) conciliabule* ⓓ to confer = *conférer.*

HUE AND CRY (n inv) *levée (f) de boucliers :* a hue and cry against the new tax bill = *une levée de boucliers contre le nouveau projet de loi fiscale =* clamor.

HUG (n) **to give s.o. a hug** = *serrer qqn dans ses bras* **HUG** (to, -ged) *serrer dans ses bras :* he hugged his daughter = *il a serré sa fille dans ses bras* ⓓ to embrace = *étreindre.*

HUGE (adj, -r, -st) *immense :* a huge room/cake = *une chambre/un gâteau immense* ⓓ enormous = *énorme* ≠ small = *petit.*

HUH ? (interj) *hein ? :* you're coming tonight, huh ? = *tu viens ce soir, hein ?*

HULLABALOO (n inv) *tapage (m) :* a big press hullabaloo = *un grand tapage fait par la presse* ⓓ flap = *branle-bas.*

HUM (to, -med) *fredonner :* to hum a song = *fredonner une chanson.*

HUMAN (n) *humain (m).*

HUMAN (adj) *humain, -e :* it's human to cry = *il est humain de pleurer* ≠ inhuman = *inhumain*
human being = *être humain :* don't treat me like an animal, I'm a human being ! = *ne me traite pas comme un animal, je suis un être humain !*

☠ *les sciences humaines =* social sciences
— *il est très humain =* he's very humane.

HUMANE (adj) *humain, -e :* he's deeply humane = *il est profondément humain* ≠ inhumane = *inhumain* ☠ → human.

HUMANIST (n) *humaniste (m, f)* **HUMANITARIAN** (n) *qqn d'humain* **HUMANITARIAN** (adj) *humanitaire :* a humanitarian cause = *une cause humanitaire.*

HUMANITIES (n pl) **the humanities** = *les humanités.*

HUMANITY (n inv) **1/** *humanité (f) :* she's lacking humanity = *elle manque d'humanité* ⓓ charity = *charité* **2/** *humanité (f) :* the end of humanity = *la fin de l'humanité =* mankind.

HUMBLE (adj, -r, -st) *humble :* of humble origin = *d'une origine humble* ⓓ modest = *modeste* ≠ proud = *fier.*

HUMDRUM (adj) *routinier :* a humdrum life = *une vie routinière* ≠ boring = *ennuyeux.*

HUMID (adj) *humide :* New York's humid in the summer = *New York est humide l'été* ⓓ moist = *moite* ☠ *un linge humide =* a damp cloth
— *des rêves humides =* wet dreams
— *les yeux humides =* eyes filled with tears.

HUMIDITY (n, -ies) *humidité (f)* ⓓ moistness = *moiteur.*

HUMILIATE (to, -d) *humilier :* she gets her kicks humiliating him = *elle prend son pied en l'humiliant* ⓓ to belittle = *rabaisser* **HUMILIATING** (adj) *humiliant, -e :* a humiliating remark = *une réflexion humiliante* **HUMILIATION** (n) *humiliation (f)* ⓓ shame = *honte,* mortification = ←.

HUMILITY (n, -ies) *humilité (f) :* a lack of humility = *un manque d'humilité* ≠ pride = *orgueil.*

HUMOR (n) *humour (m) :* full of humor = *rempli d'humour =* humour (GB) ⓓ wit = *esprit*
I'm in no humor to (joke)/for (your jokes) = *je ne suis pas d'humeur à (plaisanter)/à entendre (tes plaisanteries)*
☠ *être de bonne* ≠ *mauvaise humeur =* to be in a good ≠ bad mood.

HUMOR (to, -ed) *ménager :* the President's humoring the feminists but isn't taking any serious measures = *le Président essaie de ménager les féministes, mais il ne prend aucune mesure sérieuse*
stop humoring me ! = *n'essaie pas de me ménager ! :*

don't tell me I look great if I don't ; stop humoring me ! = *ne me dis pas que j'ai l'air en forme si ce n'est pas vrai ; n'essaie pas de me ménager !*

HUMORIST (n) *humoriste (m, f)* ⓪ comedian = *comique.*

HUMOROUS (adj) *humoristique :* a humorous sketch = *un sketch humoristique* ⓪ comical = *cocasse,* witty = *spirituel.*

HUMP (n) *bosse (f) :* a camel's two humps = *les deux bosses d'un chameau* ☠ → bump
to be over the hump = *avoir doublé le cap* ⓪ to be at home base = *arriver au but.*

HUNCH (n, -es) *(petite) idée (f) :* the cops have a hunch that the murderer knew the family well = *les flics ont (la petite) idée que le meurtrier connaissait bien la famille* ⓪ suspicion = *soupçon*
to play a hunch = *agir par intuition.*

HUNCHBACK (n) *bossu, -e* ☠ *rire comme un bossu* = to laugh o.s. silly.

HUNDRED (n) **a hundred** = *cent :* a hundred dollars = *cent dollars,* five hundred kids = *cinq cents gosses* ⓪ a thousand = *mille*
hundreds (died) = *des centaines de personnes (sont mortes)*
hundreds of (people) = *des centaines de (gens)* → MANY ⓪ a hundred of = *une centaine de*
a hundred percent = *à cent pour cent :* you're a hundred percent right = *vous avez raison à cent pour cent* → VERY
☠ *être aux cent coups* = to be beside o.s. with worry
— *faire les cent pas* = to pace up and down (walking)
— *être à cent coudées au-dessus de* = to be head and shoulders above
— *être à cent lieues de se douter que* = to be far from thinking that.

HUNGARY (n) *Hongrie (f)* **HUNGARIAN** (n, adj) *Hongrois, -e* = Hunky (PEJ).

HUNGER (n) *faim (f), fringale (f)* (LV) : a hunger for love/power = *une faim d'amour/de pouvoir* ⓪ appetite = *appétit* ≠ famine = ←
to be dying of hunger = *mourir de faim* ⓪ to be starving = *crever de faim*
to be strictly from hunger = *ne pas voler haut :* his last book is strictly from hunger = *son dernier livre ne vole pas haut* → AWFUL
to go on a hunger strike = *faire une grève de la faim* ≠ to force-feed = *nourrir de force*
☠ *manger à sa faim* = to have enough to eat
— *rester sur sa faim* = to be left wanting
— *j'ai une faim de loup* = I could eat a horse.

HUNGER FOR (to, -ed) *avoir faim de :* she hungers for affection = *elle a faim d'affection* ⓪ to long for = *avoir très envie de.*

HUNGRY (adj, -ier, -iest) **to be hungry** = *avoir faim/la*

dalle (LV) / *la fringale* (LV) : I'm hungry, are you ? = *j'ai faim, et vous ?* ⓪ to be starving = *crever de faim* ≠ to be stuffed = *être gavé*
to be hungry for (news/love) ≐ *être avide de (nouvelles)/d'(amour)*
to go hungry = *n'avoir rien à se mettre sous la dent :* during the war, many people went hungry = *pendant la guerre, beaucoup de gens n'avaient rien à se mettre sous la dent.*

HUNK (n) **1/** *gros morceau (m) :* a hunk of cheese = *un gros morceau de fromage* ⓪ lump = *morceau* = morsel **2/** *qqn de canon :* she married a real hunk = *le type qu'elle a épousé est vraiment canon* ⓪ he-man = *beau mâle.*

HUNKY-DORY (adj) *au poil :* everything's hunky-dory = *tout est au poil* ⓪ fine and dandy = *on ne peut mieux.*

HUNT (n) *chasse (f) :* an elephant hunt = *une chasse à l'éléphant* ⓪ pursuit = *poursuite*
☠ *chasse gardée !* = private property !
— *permis de chasse* = hunting license
— *être en chasse (animaux)* = to be in heat
— *qui va à la chasse perd sa place* = stick around if you don't want to lose your place
— *prendre en chasse* = to chase.

HUNT (to, -ed) *chasser (à courré) :* to hunt deer = *chasser le cerf* ⓪ to shoot = *chasser (au fusil)*
to hunt for = **1/** *faire la chasse à :* the cops are hunting for criminals = *les flics font la chasse aux criminels* ⓪ to chase = *pourchasser* **2/** *être en quête de :* to hunt for a new job = *être en quête d'un nouveau poste* ⓪ to search for = *être à la recherche de*
to go hunting = *aller à la chasse*
hunting dog = *chien de chasse*
hunting season = *saison de la chasse*
☠ *je ne te chasse pas* = I'm not throwing you out.

HUNTER (n) *chasseur, -euse* ☠ *chasseur (hôtel)* ˙ = bellboy.

HUNTING (n inv) *chasse (f) :* she doesn't like hunting = *elle n'aime pas la chasse* ☠ → hunt.

HURDLE (n) **1/** *obstacle (m) :* I had to overcome a lot of hurdles before getting an abortion = *il a fallu que je surmonte pas mal d'obstacles avant de pouvoir me faire avorter* = obstacle ⓪ difficulty = *difficulté* ☠ → obstacle **2/** *haie (f) :* hurdle race = *course de haies* ☠ *haie (jardin)* = hedge.

HURL (to, -ed) *lancer à toute volée :* he hurled the bottle at me = *il m'a lancé la bouteille à toute volée* ⓪ to fling = *lancer.*

HURRICANE (n) *ouragan (m)* ⓪ tornado = *tornade.*

HURRIEDLY (adv) *précipitamment :* a special meeting was hurriedly organized = *une réunion spéciale a été précipitamment organisée.*

HURRY (n inv) **to be in a hurry** = *être pressé* = to be in a rush
I'm in no hurry to (leave) = *je ne suis pas pressé de (partir)*
there's no hurry = *rien ne presse* ⊛ take your time = *prenez votre temps*
what's the hurry ? = *ça ne presse pas !* ⊛ what's the rush ?* = *il n'y a pas le feu !*

HURRY (to, -ied) *se dépêcher* : if you want to be on time, you'd better hurry = *si tu veux être à l'heure, tu ferais bien de te dépêcher* ⊛ to hasten = *se hâter* ≠ to dilly-dally = *traînasser*
hurry up ! = *dépêchez-vous !* ⊛ get a move on ! = *magne-toi !*

HURT (to, hurt, hurt) **1/** *faire mal (à)* : does it hurt ? = *est-ce que ça fait mal ?*, don't hurt me ! = *ne me fais pas mal !* **2/** *faire du tort à* : the scandal hurt his reputation = *le scandale a fait du tort à sa réputation* ⊛ to damage = *nuire à* **3/** *blesser* : three people were hurt in the accident = *trois personnes ont été blessées dans l'accident* = three people were injured in the accident ☠ → to injure

(my leg) hurts (me) = *(ma jambe) me fait mal*	**to hurt oneself** = *se faire mal* : she didn't hurt herself = *elle ne s'est pas fait mal*

---

to hurt s.o. = *faire de la peine à qqn* : what you said hurt me = *ce que vous avez dit m'a fait de la peine* **it hurts me (to see her so unhappy)** = *ça me fait de la peine de (la voir si malheureuse)* ⊛ to pain = *peiner* **it won't hurt you to (get up earlier)** = *ça ne te fera pas de mal de (te lever plus tôt)*.

HUSBAND (n) *mari (m)*, *époux (m)* : I'd like you to meet my husband = *j'aimerais vous présenter mon mari/mon époux* ⊛ hubby = *petit mari*, married man = *homme marié*, spouse = *conjoint* ≠ wife = *femme/épouse*.

HUSH-HUSH (adj) *ultra-secret, -ète* : the meetings were hush-hush = *les réunions étaient ultra-secrètes* ⊛ confidential = *confidentiel*.

HUSH MONEY (n) *fonds (m pl) secrets pour acheter le silence de qqn* ⊛ slush fund = *caisse noire*.

HUSH UP (to, -ed) *enterrer* : they hushed up the scandal = *ils ont enterré le scandale* ≠ to play up = *monter en épingle* ☠ → to bury
hush up ! = *taisez-vous !* ⊛ shut up ! = *ferme-la !*

HUSKY (adj, -ier, -iest) **1/** *baraqué, -e* : a husky guy = *un type baraqué* ⊛ burly = *bien charpenté* **2/** *rauque* : a husky voice = *une voix rauque* ⊛ to have a frog in one's throat = *avoir un chat dans la gorge*.

HUSSY (n, -ies) *catin (f)* ⊛ trollop = *traînée*.

HUSTLE (to, -d) **1/** *faire des combines* : he's been on the street hustling since he was 14 = *depuis qu'il a 14 ans, il est dans les rues à faire ses (petites) combines*
2/ *se grouiller* : if we want to finish the work tonight, we'd better hustle = *si nous voulons finir ce boulot ce soir, nous ferions mieux de nous grouiller* ☠ *grouiller de (monde)* = to swarm with (people)
hustle it up ! = *grouillez-vous !* ⊛ get a move on ! = *magnez-vous !*
3/ *se prostituer* : she's hustling to pay for college = *elle se prostitue pour payer l'université* ⊛ to turn tricks = *faire des passes*
4/ *se débrouiller* : in show business, you really have to hustle = *dans le show-business, il faut savoir se débrouiller* ☠ → to manage

GROUP : TO HUSTLE = FAIRE DES COMBINES

to bamboozle = *entortiller*	**to do s.o. out of** = *gruger qqn de*	*au bluff*
to cheat s.o. = *rouler qqn*		**to pull a fast one on s.o.** = *blouser qqn*
to chisel s.o. out of = *carotter qqn de*	**to double-cross** = *doubler*	**to pull the wool over s.o.'s eyes** = *faire accroire à qqn/mystifier qqn*
to con s.o. = *arnaquer qqn*	**to dupe** = *duper*	
to con s.o. out of = *escroquer qqn de*	**to fake s.o. out** = *avoir qqn*	**to put stg over on s.o.** = *donner le change à qqn*
to cheat s.o. out of = *refaire qqn de*	**to fleece** = *plumer*	**to railroad s.o. into stg** = *brusquer qqn pour lui faire faire qqch*
to cross s.o. up = *doubler qqn*	**to fool s.o.** = *bien avoir qqn*	
to cut s.o. out = *frustrer qqn de*	**to fuck s.o. over** = *couillonner/baiser qqn*	**to rip s.o. off** = *escroquer qqn*
the dice are loaded = *les dés sont pipés*	**to gyp** = *pigeonner*	**to rope s.o. in** = *embobiner qqn*
to diddle = *entuber*	**to hoodwink** = *truander* **to lead s.o. up the garden path** = *faire prendre à qqn des vessies pour des lanternes* **to psych s.o. out** = *avoir qqn*	**to screw s.o.** = *baiser qqn*

to shift = *entuber* **to shit on s.o.** = *baiser qqn dans les grandes largeurs* **to shortchange** = *léser* **to soak s.o.** = *estamper qqn* **to stack the cards** = *corner les cartes* **to swindle** = *escroquer* = to sting* (GB)	**to take s.o. for a ride** = *mener qqn en bateau* **to take s.o. for all he's/she's worth** = *avoir qqn jusqu'au trognon* **to take s.o. in** = *berner qqn* **to take s.o. over** = *posséder qqn* **to take s.o. to the cleaner's** =	*rouler qqn dans la farine* **to trick s.o.** = *avoir qqn* **to trick s.o. out of** = *refaire qqn de* **to two-time s.o.** = *jouer double jeu avec qqn* **to wheel and deal** = *magouiller/brasser des affaires.*

HUSTLER (n) *débrouillard, -e, combinard, -e* (PEJ) : my brother's a real hustler = *mon frère est vraiment débrouillard*, you can be a hustler at any age = *on peut être combinard à n'importe quel âge* ○○ con man = *arnaqueur*, operator = *magouilleur*.

HUSTLING (n) *système D (m), débrouillardise (f), démerde (f)* (LV) : it takes a lot of hustling to put a deal together = *il faut pas mal de débrouillardise/démerde pour monter une affaire*.

HUT (n) *hutte (f)* ○○ shanty = *cabane*.

HYBRID (n) *hybride (m)* ○○ cross = *croisement*.

HYDRANT (n) *bouche (f) d'incendie* : parking is not allowed near hydrants = *le stationnement n'est pas autorisé près des bouches d'incendie*.

HYDROGEN (n) *hydrogène (m)* ○○ oxygen = *oxygène*.

HYGIENE (n) *hygiène (f)* : the lack of hygiene in the slums = *le manque d'hygiène dans les taudis*.

HYMEN (n) *hymen (m)* ○○ cherry = *fleur*.

HYMN (n) *hymne (m)* ○○ psalm = *psaume*.

HYPE (n inv) *battage (m) publicitaire* : media hype = *le battage publicitaire des médias* ○○ ado = *affaire*.

HYPER (prefix) *hyper* : hypersensitive = *hypersensible* → VERY.

HYPHEN (n) *trait (m) d'union* : a word with a hyphen = *un mot avec un trait d'union* ☠ → go-between.

HYPNOSIS (n, -es) *hypnose (f)* ○○ trance = *transe,*

hypnotic = *hypnotique* **HYPNOTIZE** (to, -d) *hypnotiser* : to hypnotize a patient = *hypnotiser un patient* ○○ hypnotism = *hypnotisme*, hypnotist = *hypnotiseur*.

HYPOCHONDRIAC (n) *hypocondriaque (m, f).*

HYPOCRISY (n, -ies) *hypocrisie (f)* : political hypocrisy = *hypocrisie politique* ≠ sincerity = *sincérité*.

HYPOCRITE (n) *hypocrite (m, f)* : don't be such a hypocrite, tell me what happened = *ne sois pas si hypocrite, dis-moi ce qui s'est passé* **HYPOCRITICAL** (adj) *hypocrite* : what a hypocritical thing to say ! = *que c'est hypocrite de dire ça !* ○○ two-faced = *faux jeton* ≠ sincere = *sincère*.

HYPOTHESIS (n, -ses) *hypothèse (f)* : a false hypothesis = *une hypothèse fausse* ○○ conjecture = ← ☠ *une hypothèse d'école* = a theoretical example.

HYPOTHETICAL (adj) *hypothétique* : his arrival remains hypothetical = *son arrivée reste hypothétique* ≠ certain = ←.

HYSTERIA (n) *hystérie (f)* : a case of hysteria = *un cas d'hystérie*.

HYSTERICAL (adj) 1/ *hystérique* : his wife's highstrung and hysterical = *sa femme est hypernerveuse et hystérique* 2/ *bidonnant, -e* : the movie was hysterical = *le film était bidonnant* ○○ funny = *drôle*.

HYSTERICS (n pl) *crise (f) d'hystérie* : she was in hysterics when I arrived = *elle était en pleine crise d'hystérie quand je suis arrivée*.

I (pron) *je* : I'm American = *je suis américain*	
SUBJECT	OBJECT/INDIRECT OBJECT
I = *je* **you** = *tu/vous* **she** = *elle* **he** = *il* **it** = *il/elle/ce/cela/ça/c'* **we** = *nous* **they** = *ils/elles*	**me** = *me/moi* **you** = *te/toi, vous* **her** = *la/lui* **him** = *le/lui* **it** = *le/la/lui* **us** = *nous* **them** = *les/leur/eux/ elles.*

ICE (n) **1/** *glace* (f) : would you like ice in your Scotch ? = *désirez-vous de la glace dans votre whisky ?*
to break the ice = *rompre la glace* : his joking broke the ice = *ses plaisanteries ont rompu la glace*
he could sell ice to the Eskimos in January = *il vous vendrait une voiture sans roues et sans moteur*
to cut no ice = *compter pour du beurre/des prunes* : he cuts no ice in the company = *il compte pour des prunes/du beurre au sein de l'entreprise* ⓪ to be small fry = *être du menu fretin*
ice cream = *glace* : I'd like an ice cream = *je voudrais une glace* ⓪ ice cream cone = *cornet*, flavor = *parfum*, whipped cream = *crème fouettée*
ice cube = *glaçon* ☠ → iceberg
ice hockey = *hockey sur glace*
to put on ice = *laisser en sommeil* : to put a project on ice = *laisser un projet en sommeil* ⓪ to put on the shelf = *mettre sur une voie de garage*
☠ *une glace (miroir)* = a mirror
— *il est de glace* = he's a cold fish
2/ *verglas* (m) : there's ice on the roads = *il y a du verglas sur les routes* ⓪ icy = *verglacé*.

ICEBERG (n) **1/** *iceberg* (m) : icebergs in the Antarctic = *des icebergs dans l'Antarctique* **2/** *glaçon* (m) : his broad's an iceberg = *sa nana est un vrai glaçon* ⓪ cold fish = *pisse-froid* ☠ *glaçon* = ice cube.

ICEBOX (n, -es) **to raid the icebox** = *dévaliser le frigo* : we were so hungry we raided the icebox = *nous avions tellement faim que nous avons dévalisé le frigo.*

ICE-COLD (adj) **1/** *glacé, -e* : ice-cold drinks = *des boissons glacées* ≠ lukewarm = *tiède* ☠ *je suis glacée* = I'm freezing **2/** *glacial, -e* : ice-cold weather = *un temps glacial* ≠ sweltering = *étouffant* ☠ *une voix glaciale* = an icy voice.

ICE-SKATE (n) *patin* (m) *à glace* **ICE-SKATE** (to, -d) *patiner (sur glace)* ⓪ to go ice-skating = *faire du patin à glace*, figure skating = *patinage artistique.*

ICING (n) *glaçage* (m) : chocolate icing = *glaçage au chocolat*
that's the icing on the cake ! = *c'est ça le plus beau !* : the job is great and the icing on the cake is going to Europe every year = *le boulot est chouette et le plus beau, c'est que nous allons en Europe tous les ans* ⓪ the end = *le fin du fin.*

ID (n) *pièce* (f) *d'identité* : the police wanted to see his ID = *la police voulait qu'il montre une pièce d'identité* ⓪ passport = *passeport.*

IDEA (n) *idée* (f) : odd ideas = *de drôles d'idées* ⓪ thought = *pensée*, notion = ←
don't get any ideas ! = *ne va pas te faire des idées !*
don't put any ideas into her head ! = *ne va pas lui donner des idées !*
I don't have the slightest/faintest/foggiest idea ! = *je n'en ai pas la moindre idée !*
I get the idea ! = *j'y suis !* ⓪ I catch on ! = *je pige !*
I have no idea ! = *je n'en ai pas la moindre idée !* ⓪ search me ! = *mystère et boule de gomme !*
I had an idea ≠ **no idea that (he was married)** = *j'avais* ≠ *je n'avais pas idée qu'(il était marié)*
an idea man/woman = *un homme/une femme qui a des idées* ⓪ brain trust = *brain-trust*
what's the idea (talking to your mother like that) ? = *qu'est-ce qui te prend (de parler à ta mère sur ce ton) ?*
☠ *rassembler ses idées* = to collect one's thoughts
— *fais à ton idée* = do as you like
— *on n'a pas idée de faire ça* = who would ever dream of doing that ?
— *avoir des idées noires* = to have gloomy thoughts
— *ça te changera les idées* = it will take your mind off of things
— *avoir les idées étroites* ≠ *larges* = to be narrow- ≠ broad-minded.

IDEAL (n) *idéal (m)* : she's my ideal (of what a woman should be) = *elle est mon idéal (de femme)* ① dream = *rêve.*

IDEAL (adj) *idéal, -e* : the ideal hour = *l'heure idéale* ① perfect = *parfait.*

IDEALISM (n) *idéalisme (m)* ≠ realism = *réalisme.*

IDEALIST (n) *idéaliste (m, f)* : you're really an idealist = *tu es vraiment un idéaliste* ≠ realist = *réaliste* **IDEAL-ISTIC** (adj) *idéaliste* ≠ realistic = *réaliste.*

IDEALIZE (to, -d) *idéaliser* : he idealizes his wife = *il idéalise sa femme* ≠ to belittle = *rabaisser.*

IDEALLY (adv) *idéalement, de manière idéale* : they're ideally matched = *ils sont idéalement assortis*
ideally speaking (we would only work five hours a day) = *l'idéal serait de (ne travailler que cinq heures par jour).*

IDENTICAL (adj) *identique* : identical houses = *des maisons identiques* ≠ different = *différent*
identical twins = *vrais jumeaux.*

IDENTIFICATION (n) *identification (f)* : the identification of a criminal = *l'identification d'un criminel*
identification papers = *papiers d'identité.*

IDENTIFY (to, -ied) *identifier* : to identify a murderer = *identifier un meurtrier* ① to recognize = *reconnaître*
to identify with s.o. = *s'identifier à qqn* : I identify with the character = *je m'identifie au personnage.*

IDENTITY (n, -ies) *identité (f)* : identity crisis = *crise d'identité* ⚹ *papiers d'identité* = identification papers.

IDEOLOGICAL (adj) *idéologique* **IDEOLOGY** (n, -ies) *idéologie (f)* : communism is an ideology = *le communisme est une idéologie* ① doctrine = ←.

IDIOM (n) *idiotisme (m), expression (f) idiomatique* : "to drink like a fish" is an idiom = « *boire comme un trou* » *est une expression idiomatique.*

IDIOMATIC (adj) *idiomatique* : idiomatic English = *l'anglais idiomatique* ① slang = *argot.*

IDIOSYNCRASY (n, -ies) *petite manie (f)* : eccentric and full of idiosyncrasies = *excentrique et plein de petites manies.*

IDIOT (n) *idiot, -e* : what an idiot you are ! = *quel idiot tu fais !* → STUPID ⚹ *arrête de faire l'idiot !* = stop fooling around ! **IDIOTIC** (adj) *complètement idiot, -e* : an idiotic idea = *une idée complètement idiote* → STUPID.

IDLE (adj, -r, -st) *oisif, -ive* : to lead an idle life = *mener une vie oisive* ≠ busy = *occupé*
idle talk = *propos oiseux* ① small talk = *propos de salon*
idle time is devil's time = *l'oisiveté/la paresse est mère de tous les vices.*

IDOL (n) *idole (f)* : Piaf became an idol = *Piaf est devenue une idole* ① god = *dieu.*

IDOLIZE (to, -d) *idolâtrer* : to idolize one's father = *idolâtrer son père* ① to put on a pedestal = *mettre sur un piédestal.*

IDYLL (n) *idylle (f)* : a short idyll with my teacher = *une courte idylle avec mon professeur* ① liaison = ←.

I.E. (abbr) *id est* = *c'est-à-dire* : it cost a lot of money, i.e. $ 50 = *ça a coûté pas mal d'argent, c'est-à-dire 50 dollars.*

IF (conj) **1/** *si* : do you know if she'll come ? = *est-ce que vous savez si elle viendra ?* = do you know whether she'll come ? **2/** *si* : if I have the money, I'll buy a car = *si j'ai de l'argent, j'achèterai une voiture* ① in case = *au cas où*

CONDITIONAL

if I have the money, I'll buy a car = *si j'ai de l'argent, j'achèterai une voiture*
if I had the money, I'd buy a car = *si j'avais de l'argent, j'achèterais une voiture*
if I had had the money, I would have bought a car = *si j'avais eu de l'argent, j'aurais acheté une voiture*

---

if and when = *si jamais* : if and when you need help, call me ! = *si jamais tu as besoin d'aide, appelle-moi !*
if any = *ni même si/si tant est que* : I don't know if they have one or two kids, if any = *je ne sais pas s'ils ont un ou deux enfants, si tant est qu'ils en aient/ni même s'ils en ont*
if anything = *c'est plutôt* : if anything, she should thank you = *c'est plutôt elle qui devrait vous remercier*
if anywhere = *si toutefois* : you'll find them on the left bank if anywhere = *vous les trouverez sur la rive gauche, si toutefois vous en trouvez*
if at all = *si toutefois* : he'll come late, if at all = *il arrivera tard, si toutefois il vient*
if I had to do it over again = *si c'était à refaire*

if I were you (I'd break off) = *si j'étais vous (je romprais)*
if not = *sinon* : try to see her, if not call = *essaie de la voir, sinon appelle-la* ① otherwise = *autrement*
if only = *si seulement* : if only you had told me the truth = *si seulement tu m'avais dit la vérité*
if so = *si c'est le cas* : I don't know if you're hungry, but if so let's go out and eat = *je ne sais pas si vous avez faim, mais si c'est le cas sortons dîner*
if that's how it is (don't come) = *dans ces conditions (ne venez pas)*
if there ever was one = *s'il en est/s'il en fut* : she's a bright girl if there ever was one = *c'est une fille intelligente s'il en est*

> 🐱 *si !* = yes ! (in response to negative question)
> — *ne cours pas si vite* = don't run so fast
> — *si bien que* = and as a result
> — *si on veut* = you could say that
> — *si (on prenait un café) ?* = what about (a coffee) ?
> — *si je ne me trompe* = unless I'm mistaken.

IGNORAMUS (n, -es) *ignare (m, f)* : what an ignoramus you are ! = *que tu es ignare !* → STUPID.

IGNORANCE (n) *ignorance (f)* ≠ knowledge = *savoir*
ignorance is bliss = *qui ne sait rien, de rien ne doute* ⓓ to be in a fool's paradise = *être un imbécile heureux*
ignorance of the law is no excuse = *nul n'est censé ignorer la loi* ⓓ law-abiding = *respectueux des lois.*

IGNORANT (adj) *ignorant, -e* : an ignorant guy = *un type ignorant* ⓓ illiterate = *illettré.*

IGNORE (to, -d) *ignorer* (s.o.), *passer outre à* (stg) : I ignored him at the party = *je l'ai ignoré pendant toute la soirée*, ignore his remarks = *passe outre à ses remarques* 🐱 *j'ignore si...* = I don't know whether...

ILK (n) **of that ilk** = *de cet acabit* : people of that ilk always get into trouble = *les gens de cet acabit ont toujours des ennuis.*

ILL (adj, worse, worst) *malade* : she's been ill for a week = *elle est malade depuis une semaine* = sick ⓓ in a bad way = *dans une mauvaise passe*, ailing = *souffrant* ≠ healthy = *en bonne santé*
ill effects = *méfaits* : the ill effects of alcohol = *les méfaits de l'alcool*
🐱 *sa tante malade* = her sick aunt.

ILL-ADVISED (adj) *déconseillé, -e* : it's ill-advised to drink a lot before driving = *il est déconseillé de boire beaucoup avant de conduire.*

ILL-AT-EASE (adj) *mal à l'aise* : I feel ill-at-ease with my in-laws = *je me sens mal à l'aise avec mes beaux-parents* ⓓ uncomfortable = *pas à l'aise.*

ILL-BRED (adj) *mal élevé, -e* : ill-bred children = *des enfants mal élevés* ≠ well-bred = *bien élevé.*

ILLEGAL (adj) *illégal, -e* : illegal dealings = *des procédés illégaux* ⓓ illicit = *illicite.*

ILLEGIBLE (adj) *illisible* : illegible handwriting = *une écriture illisible.*

ILLEGITIMATE (adj) *illégitime* : an illegitimate child = *un enfant illégitime* ≠ legitimate = *légitime.*

ILLICIT (adj) *illicite* ⓓ unlawful = *illégal.*

ILLITERATE (adj) *illettré, -e, analphabète* : too many people are still illiterate = *il y a encore trop de gens illettrés/analphabètes* ≠ erudite = *érudit.*

ILL-MANNERED (adj) *mal éduqué, -e* : ill-mannered children = *des enfants mal éduqués* ⓓ ill-bred = *mal élevé.*

ILLNESS (n, -es) *maladie (f)* : a mental illness = *une maladie mentale* ⓓ epidemic = *épidémie* 🐱 → disease.

ILLOGICAL (adj) *illogique* : illogical reasoning = *un raisonnement illogique* ≠ rational = *rationnel.*

ILLUSION (n) *illusion (f)* : optical illusion = *illusion d'optique* ⓓ delusion = *psychose*
to be under an illusion = *se bercer d'illusions* ⓓ to kid oneself = *se faire des illusions.*

ILLUSORY (adj) *illusoire* : illusory power = *pouvoir illusoire* ≠ real = *réel.*

ILLUSTRATE (to, -d) 1/ *illustrer* : that illustrates my point = *cela illustre mon propos* ⓓ to demonstrate = *démontrer* 2/ *illustrer* : to illustrate a book = *illustrer un livre* 🐱 *s'illustrer par* = to become known for.

ILLUSTRATION (n) 1/ *illustration (f)* : an illustration of his sense of humor = *une illustration de son sens de l'humour* ⓓ example = *exemple* 2/ *illustration (f)* : a book with beautiful illustrations = *un livre avec de belles illustrations* ⓓ picture = *image.*

ILLUSTRATOR (n) *illustrateur, -trice* : he's a well-known illustrator = *c'est un illustrateur célèbre.*

ILLUSTRIOUS (adj) *illustre* : an illustrious lawyer = *un illustre avocat* ⓓ noted = *réputé.*

IMAGE (n) 1/ *image (f)* : that's the image I have of him = *voilà l'image que je me fais de lui* ⓓ imagery = *imagerie* 2/ *image (f) de marque* : we have to think of our image = *il faut que nous pensions à notre image de marque*
the living/spitting image of (her father) = *le portrait tout craché de (son père)* ⓓ deadringer = *sosie* 🐱 *un livre d'images* = a picture book.

IMAGINABLE (adj) *imaginable* : the worst crime imaginable = *le pire crime imaginable* ≠ unimaginable = *inimaginable.*

IMAGINARY (adj) *imaginaire* : an imaginary world = *un monde imaginaire* ≠ real = *réel.*

IMAGINATION (n) *imagination (f)* : to lack imagination = *manquer d'imagination* ⓓ fantasy = *fantaisie*
it's your imagination ! = *c'est un effet de ton imagination !* ⓓ you're dreaming ! = *tu rêves !*

IMAGINATIVE (adj) *imaginatif, -ive* : you have to be imaginative in adversity = *dans l'adversité, il faut être imaginatif* ⓓ creative = *créatif.*

IMAGINE (to, -d) 1/ *imaginer* : I imagine she'll come = *j'imagine qu'elle viendra* ⓓ to presume = *présumer*
I imagine so = *j'imagine que oui*
imagine that ! = *tu t'imagines !*
you're imagining things ! = *tu te fais des idées !*
I can't imagine why (he hasn't called yet) = *je ne m'explique pas pourquoi (il n'a pas encore appelé)*

2/ s'imaginer : he imagines he's a great actor = *il s'imagine être un grand acteur* ⓪ to feel = *(se) trouver* ☠ *tu as imaginé ça tout seul ?* = did you think that up by yourself ?

IMBECILE (n) *imbécile (m, f)* → STUPID ☠ *faire l'imbécile* = to clown around.

IMF (abbr) = International Monetary Fund = *FMI (m)* = *Fonds monétaire international.*

IMITATE (to, -d) *imiter* : to imitate s.o.'s voice = *imiter la voix de qqn* ⓪ to ape = *singer.*

IMITATION (n) *imitation (f)* : he did an imitation of the President = *il a fait une imitation du Président* ⓪ take-off = *caricature.*

IMITATION (adj) *(d')imitation* : imitation leather = *imitation cuir* ⓪ fake = *faux.*

IMMACULATE (adj) *immaculé, -e* : her house is always immaculate = *sa maison est toujours immaculée* ≠ filthy = *crasseux.*

IMMATERIAL (adj) *sans importance* : it's immaterial whether he agrees or not = *c'est sans importance qu'il soit ou non d'accord*
(the cost) is immaterial to me = *(le prix) m'est indifférent.*

IMMATURE (adj) *immature* : an immature man = *un homme immature* ≠ adult = *adulte.*

IMMEDIATE (adj) *immédiat, -e* : an immediate answer = *une réponse immédiate* ⓪ direct = *←*
the immediate family = *la famille proche* ⓪ relatives = *membres de la famille*
in the immediate future = *dans l'immédiat* ⓪ in the near future = *dans un avenir proche.*

IMMEDIATELY (adv) *immédiatement* : come here immediately ! = *viens ici immédiatement !* ⓪ right away = *tout de suite* ≠ in a little while = *tout à l'heure.*

IMMENSE (adj) *immense* : an immense country = *un pays immense* ⓪ enormous = *énorme* ≠ tiny = *minuscule* **IMMENSELY** (adv) *immensément* : immensely rich = *immensément riche* → VERY **IMMENSITY** (n, -ies) *immensité (f).*

IMMIGRANT (n) *immigrant, -e* : immigrants often have a hard time finding jobs = *les immigrants ont souvent du mal à trouver du travail* ≠ emigrant = *émigrant.*

IMMIGRATE (to, -d) *immigrer* ≠ to emigrate = *émigrer* **IMMIGRATION** (n) *immigration (f)* ≠ emigration = *émigration.*

IMMINENT (adj) *imminent, -e* : her arrival is imminent = *son arrivée est imminente* ≠ remote = *éloigné.*

IMMOBILE (adj) *immobile* ⓪ inert = *inerte.*

IMMOBILIZE (to, -d) *immobiliser* : all my money is immobilized for the moment = *tout mon argent est immobilisé pour le moment.*

IMMODERATE (adj) *immodéré, -e* : an immoderate taste for Scotch = *un goût immodéré pour le whisky.*

IMMORAL (adj) *immoral, -e* : immoral behavior = *comportement immoral* ⓪ amoral = *←*, dissolute = *dissolu* **IMMORALITY** (n, -ies) *immoralité (f).*

IMMORTAL (adj) *immortel, -elle* : are gods immortal ? = *les dieux sont-ils immortels ?* ☠ *les immortels* = members of the French Academy **IMMORTALITY** (n) *immortalité (f)* **IMMORTALIZE** (to, -d) *immortaliser.*

IMMUNE (adj) *immunisé, -e* ⓪ vaccinated = *vacciné*
immune to (measles) = *immunisé contre (la rougeole).*

IMPACT (n) *impact (m)* : the impact of the press campaign = *l'impact de la campagne de presse* ⓪ effect = *effet.*

IMPAIR (to, -ed) *diminuer* : diaphragms don't impair women's pleasure = *le diaphragme ne diminue pas le plaisir féminin* ☠ → to diminish.

IMPARTIAL (adj) *impartial, -e* : an impartial witness = *un témoin impartial* ⓪ unbiased = *sans parti pris* **IMPARTIALITY** (n, -ies) *impartialité (f).*

IMPATIENCE (n) *impatience (f).*

IMPATIENT (adj) *impatient, -e* : how impatient you are ! = *que tu es impatient !* ⓪ impatiently = *impatiemment*
impatient to know = *impatient de savoir.*

IMPEACH (to, -ed) *mettre en accusation* : the President was impeached = *le Président a été mis en accusation* **IMPEACHMENT** (n) *mise (f) en accusation* ⓪ resignation = *démission.*

IMPECCABLE (adj) *impeccable* : impeccable English = *un anglais impeccable* ⓪ perfect = *parfait* ☠ *six heures ? impeccable !* = six o'clock ? just fine !

IMPEDE (to, -d) *entraver* : personal quarrels impeded the negotiations = *les querelles personnelles ont entravé les négociations* ⓪ to hinder = *gêner* **IMPEDIMENT** (n) *obstacle (m)* : his accent is an impediment to his career = *son accent est un obstacle pour sa carrière.*

IMPEL TO (to, -led) *pousser à* : what impelled you to tell her ? = *qu'est-ce qui vous a poussé à le lui dire ?* ⓪ to induce to = *décider à.*

IMPENDING (adj) *qui menace* : there's an impending revolution = *il y a une révolution qui menace* ⓪ imminent = *←.*

IMPERATIVE (adj) *impératif, -ive* : imperative needs = *des besoins impératifs* ⓪ urgent = *←*
it's imperative that (you lend me the money) = *il est absolument crucial pour moi que (vous me prêtiez cet argent).*

IMPERCEPTIBLE (adj) *imperceptible* : imperceptible changes = *des changements imperceptibles* ≠ perceptible = ←.

IMPERFECT (adj) *imparfait, -e* : an imperfect knowledge of history = *des connaissances imparfaites en histoire* ≠ excellent = ←.

IMPERFECTION (n) *imperfection* (f) : we all have our imperfections = *nous avons tous nos imperfections* ⑩ flaw = *défaut.*

IMPERIALISM (n) *impérialisme* (m) : cultural imperialism = *l'impérialisme culturel* ⑩ colonialism = *colonialisme* **IMPERIALIST** (n) *impérialiste* (m, f) ⑩ colonialist = *colonialiste* **IMPERIALIST(IC)** (adj) *impérialiste* : imperialist policy = *politique impérialiste.*

IMPERSONAL (adj) *impersonnel, -elle* : impersonal tone = *ton impersonnel.*

IMPERSONATE (to, -d) *faire une imitation de* : he impersonated the President = *il a fait une imitation du Président* ⑩ to imitate = *imiter.*

IMPERSONATION (n) *imitation* (f) : he does a good impersonation of the President = *il fait une bonne imitation du Président* = imitation **IMPERSONATOR** (n) *imitateur, -trice.*

IMPERTINENT (adj) *impertinent, -e* : an impertinent answer = *une réponse impertinente* ⑩ impudent = ←.

IMPERVIOUS (adj) **impervious to** = *imperméable à* : impervious to criticism = *imperméable aux critiques.*

IMPETUOUS (adj) *impétueux, -euse* : an impetuous child = *un enfant impétueux* ⑩ impulsive = *impulsif.*

IMPETUS (n, -es) *qqch qui stimule* : the promise of a new car is an impetus for her to work well at school = *la promesse d'une nouvelle voiture la stimule pour bien travailler en classe.*

IMPINGE ON (to, -d) *empiéter sur* : to impinge on s.o.'s rights = *empiéter sur les droits de qqn.*

IMPLEMENT (to, -ed) *mettre en œuvre* : to implement a platform/a plan = *mettre un programme/un projet en œuvre.*

IMPLICATE (to, -d) *impliquer*: he was implicated in the crime = *il était impliqué dans le crime* = he was involved in the crime
☠ *cela implique que* = that implies that
— *ça implique pas mal d'argent* = it involves a lot of money.

IMPLICATION (n) **1/** *implication* (f) : I didn't realize all the implications = *je ne me suis pas rendu compte de toutes les implications* **2/** *ce qui est sous-entendu* : the implication was that they were splitting = *il était sous-entendu qu'ils allaient se séparer.*

IMPLICIT (adj) *implicite* : an implicit agreement = *un accord implicite* ≠ explicit = *explicite.*

IMPLORE TO (to, -d) *implorer de* : I implore you to help us = *je vous implore de nous aider* ⑩ to beseech to = *conjurer de,* to beg to = *prier de.*

IMPLY (to, -ied) **1/** *impliquer* : getting a diploma implies a lot of work = *l'obtention d'un diplôme implique beaucoup de travail* ⑩ to mean = *vouloir dire* ☠ → to implicate **2/** *sous-entendre* : she implied that he was lying = *elle a sous-entendu qu'il mentait* ⑩ to hint = *laisser entendre.*

IMPOLITE (adj) *impoli, -e* : that was an impolite thing to say = *c'était impoli de dire ça* ⑩ rude = *grossier.*

IMPORT (n) *importation* (f) : Japanese imports = *importations japonaises* **IMPORT** (to, -ed) *importer* : they import most of their oil = *ils importent la majeure partie de leur pétrole*
☠ *ça importe peu* = it doesn't matter
— *n'importe qui* : anybody.

IMPORTANCE (n) *importance* (f) : the importance of love = *l'importance de l'amour*
it's of no importance = *ça n'a pas d'importance*
☠ *prendre de l'importance (entreprise)* = to branch out/to expand
— *(une ville) de cette importance* = (a city) of that size.

IMPORTANT (adj) **1/** *important, -e* : an important film = *un film important* ⑩ essential = *essentiel* ≠ unimportant = *peu important* **2/** *important, -e* : a very important man = *un homme très important* ⑩ influential = *influent* ≠ to cut no ice = *compter pour du beurre*
to be important to = *être important pour* : it's important to me that you come = *il est important pour moi que vous veniez* ≠ it's immaterial to me = *cela m'est indifférent.*

IMPORTED (adj) *importé, -e* : imported goods = *des marchandises importées* **IMPORTER** (n) *importateur, -trice.*

IMPOSE (to, -d) *imposer* : he imposed his decision = *il a imposé sa décision* ⑩ to dictate = *dicter*
to impose on s.o. = *s'imposer* : I don't want to impose on you = *je ne veux pas m'imposer* ⑩ to put out = *déranger*
☠ *imposer qqn lourdement* = to tax s.o. heavily
— *cela s'impose* = it's imperative.

IMPOSING (adj) *imposant, -e* : an imposing personality = *une personnalité imposante* ⑩ impressive = *impressionnant.*

IMPOSITION (n) *qqch qui importune* : I hope my staying isn't an imposition = *j'espère que je ne vous importune pas en restant.*

IMPOSSIBILITY (n, -ies) *impossibilité* (f) : the impossibility of being in two places at once = *l'impossibilité de se trouver à deux endroits en même temps.*

IMPOSSIBLE (n) **to do the impossible (to come)** =

faire l'impossible (pour venir) Ⓞ to do one's utmost = *faire tout son possible*
no one/nobody can do the impossible = *à l'impossible, nul n'est tenu* Ⓞ to move heaven and earth = *remuer ciel et terre.*

IMPOSSIBLE (adj) 1/ *impossible* : impossible goals = *des objectifs impossibles* ≠ feasible = *faisable*
it's impossible to (know) = *c'est impossible à (savoir) / de le (savoir)*
2/ *impossible* : impossible kids = *des gosses impossibles* Ⓞ rough = *dur.*

IMPOSSIBLY (adv) *incroyablement* : impossibly stupid = *incroyablement stupide* → VERY.

IMPOSTOR (n) *imposteur (m)* : he's just an impostor = *ce n'est qu'un imposteur* Ⓞ liar = *menteur.*

IMPOTENCE (n) *impuissance (f)* : the impotence of the government = *l'impuissance du gouvernement* ≠ power = *puissance.*

IMPOTENT (adj) *impuissant, -e* : an impotent government/husband = *un gouvernement/mari impuissant* ☠ *impuissant (à faire quoi que ce soit)* = helpless (to do anything).

IMPOVERISHED (adj) *appauvri, -e* : impoverished people = *des gens appauvris* → POOR.

IMPRACTICAL (adj) *irréalisable* : impractical ideas = *des idées irréalisables* ≠ impossible = ←.

IMPRESARIO (n) *imprésario (m)* : her impresario takes ten percent = *son imprésario prend dix pour cent* Ⓞ manager = ←.

IMPRESS (to, -ed) *impressionner* : don't brag, I'm not impressed = *ne te vante pas, ça ne m'impressionne pas*
to impress as = *donner l'impression de* : she impressed us as being very bright = *elle nous a donné l'impression d'être très intelligente*
to impress on = *faire bien comprendre à* : he tried to impress on them how dangerous the area was = *il a essayé de leur faire bien comprendre à quel point le coin était dangereux* Ⓞ to emphasize = *mettre l'accent sur*
to impress with = *impressionner par* : he impressed us with his perfect knowledge of the country = *il nous a impressionnés par sa parfaite connaissance du pays*
(we were) impressed by/with (her acting) = *(son jeu nous a) fait forte impression*

☠ *(sa colère) nous a impressionnés* = (his anger) awed/upset us.

IMPRESSION (n) *impression (f)* : it's just an impression I have = *c'est simplement une impression que j'ai*
I'm under the impression that (he's outphased) = *j'ai l'impression qu'(il est déphasé)*
to make a good ≠ **bad impression** = *faire bonne* ≠ *mauvaise impression* Ⓞ to be a sensation = *faire sensation*
☠ *impression (livre)* = printing (book).

IMPRESSIVE (adj) *impressionnant, -e* : an impressive sum = *une somme impressionnante* Ⓞ spectacular = *spectaculaire* ☠ *(son pouvoir) est impressionnant* = (his power) is awesome.

IMPRISON (to, -ed) *emprisonner* : this isn't the first time he's been imprisoned = *ce n'est pas la première fois qu'il est emprisonné* Ⓞ to incarcerate = *incarcérer,* to apprehend = *appréhender.*

IMPROBABLE (adj) *improbable* : an improbable victory = *une victoire improbable* ≠ likely = *vraisemblable.*

IMPROMPTU (adj) *impromptu, -e* : an impromptu speech/dinner = *un discours/dîner impromptu* Ⓞ improvised = *improvisé.*

IMPROVE (to, -d) *(s')améliorer* : her health/English is improving = *sa santé/son anglais s'améliore* Ⓞ to make progress = *faire des progrès* ≠ to worsen = *empirer*
to improve on stg = *améliorer qqch.*

IMPROVEMENT (n) *amélioration (f)* : an improvement in his work/health = *une amélioration de son travail/sa santé* Ⓞ recovery = *rétablissement.*

IMPROVISATION (n) *improvisation (f)* : the sketch was an improvisation = *le sketch était une improvisation* = ad-lib.

IMPROVISE (to, -d) *improviser* : his speech was improvised = *son discours était improvisé* ≠ to rehearse = *répéter.*

IMPUDENT (adj) *impudent, -e* : an impudent answer = *une réponse impudente* Ⓞ insolent = ←.

IMPULSE (n) *impulsion (f)* : I did it on impulse = *je l'ai fait par impulsion* Ⓞ instinct = ←.

IMPULSIVE (adj) *impulsif, -ive* : an impulsive child = *un enfant impulsif* Ⓞ spontaneous = *spontané.*

IN (n) *piston (m)* : a good in gets you an interesting job = *un bon piston permet d'obtenir un travail intéressant* Ⓞ connections = *relations*

to be on the in = *être dans le secret des dieux* ≠ to give s.o. the lowdown = *livrer à qqn le dessous des cartes*
to have ins in (the fashion world) = *avoir ses* entrées/être pistonné dans (le milieu de la mode)
to know the ins and outs = *connaître les tenants et les aboutissants* Ⓞ to know the whys and wherefores = *connaître le pourquoi et le comment.*

IN (prep) *dans* : put it in the box = *mettez-le dans la boîte* ⓪ inside = *à l'intérieur de*

in all = *en tout* : in all it cost
$ 1,000 = *en tout, ça a coûté
1 000 dollars*
in between = *entre les deux* : I
want the size in between = *je
veux la taille entre les deux*
in business = *dans les affaires*
in English = *en anglais*
in France/Germany/England = *en France/Allemagne/Angleterre* (feminine countries)
in good health = *en bonne
santé*
in itself = *en soi* : in itself, the
job wasn't very interesting = *en
soi, le travail n'était pas très
intéressant*
in many cases = *dans de nombreux cas*
in my opinion = *à mon avis*

in Paris/London/New York = *à Paris/Londres/New York* (cities)
in person = *en personne*
in power = *au pouvoir*
in prison = *en prison*
in school = *à l'école*
in so many years/days = *pendant tant d'années/de jours*
in the eighties = *dans les années quatre-vingt*
in 1984 = *en 1984*
in the morning/evening/afternoon = *le matin/le soir/l'après-midi*
in the office = *au bureau*
in the past ≠ **in the future** = *dans le passé* ≠ *à l'avenir*
in the rain/snow = *sous la
pluie/la neige*
in the shade = *à l'ombre*

in the spring/in the summer/in the fall/in the winter = *au printemps/en été/à l'automne/en hiver*
in the sun = *au soleil*
in the United States/in Japan = *aux États-Unis/au Japon* (masculine and plural countries)
in two hours = 1/ *en deux heures* : I can do it in two hours = *je peux le faire en deux heures* 2/ *dans deux heures* : I'll meet you in two hours = *je te retrouverai dans deux heures*
in years = *depuis des années* : I haven't seen her in years = *je ne l'ai pas vue depuis des années*
in your place = *à votre place*
in January/February = *en janvier/février*

⚵ *boire dans un verre* = to drink out of a glass
— *dans les (50 francs)* = about (50 francs)

— *entrer dans une pièce* = to go into a room.

IN (adv) 1/ *là* : is your dad in ? = *est-ce que ton papa est là ?*, no, he isn't in = *non, il n'est pas là* ≠ out = *sorti*
⚵ → there 2/ *in* : small cars are in = *les petites voitures sont in* ⓪ trendy = *dans le vent* ≠ old hat = *vieux jeu*

in and out = *parfaitement* : I know my husband/my business in and out = *je connais parfaitement mon mari/mon affaire* = inside out ⓪ to know like the back of one's hand = *connaître comme sa poche*

in that = *vu que* : I don't like to be with him, in that he's a racist = *je n'aime pas être avec lui, vu qu'il est raciste* ⓪ inasmuch as = *dans la mesure où*

⚵ for the use of "in" after a verb, see the verb.

IN (adj) 1/ *in* : it's the in restaurant = *c'est le restaurant in* ⓪ stylish = *à la mode* ≠ out = *passé de mode*
2/ *en place* : she belongs to the in group in Washington = *elle fait partie des gens en place à Washington.*

INACCURACY (n, -ies) *inexactitude* (f) : a book full of inaccuracies = *un livre plein d'inexactitudes* ⓪ error = *erreur.*

INACCURATE (adj) *inexact, -e* : an inaccurate answer = *une réponse inexacte* ≠ right = *bon* **INACCURATELY** (adv) *inexactement.*

INACTIVE (adj) *inactif, -ive* : he is never inactive for a long time = *il ne reste jamais longtemps inactif* ⓪ idle = *oisif.*

INADEQUATE (adj) *insuffisant, -e* : a 10 % tip is inade-

quate = *un pourboire de 10 %, c'est insuffisant* = insufficient ≠ adequate = *suffisant.*

INADVERTENTLY (adv) *par inadvertance* : I inadvertently told him the secret = *je lui ai dit le secret par inadvertance.*

INAPPROPRIATE (adj) *peu approprié, -e* : jeans used to be inappropriate for going out = *autrefois, les jeans étaient peu appropriés pour sortir* ⓪ unsuitable = *qui ne convient pas.*

INASMUCH AS (conj) *dans la mesure où* : they can't get

married inasmuch as he is already = *ils ne peuvent pas se marier, dans la mesure où il l'est déjà* ⓦ as = *comme.*

INAUGURATE (to, -d) *investir* (President, etc.), *inaugurer* (bridge, subway, etc.) ☠ *investir* → to invest.

INAUGURATION (n) *investiture* (f) (President), *inauguration* (f) (building) : the President's inauguration = *l'investiture du Président,* the inauguration of the new school = *l'inauguration de la nouvelle école.*

INBORN (adj) *inné, -e* : inborn laziness = *une paresse innée* ⓦ inherited = *hérité.*

INCAPABLE (adj) *incapable* : incapable of controling his temper = *incapable de contrôler ses humeurs.*

INCARNATE (to, -d) *incarner* : she incarnates my idea of a modern woman = *elle incarne, pour moi, la femme moderne* **INCARNATION** (n) *incarnation* (f).

INCENSE (to, -d) *horripiler* : his lying incenses me = *ses mensonges m'horripilent* → ANGRY.

INCENTIVE (n) *incitation* (f) : sales are an incentive to buy = *les soldes sont une incitation à l'achat* ☠ *incitation au meurtre* = incitement to kill.

INCEST (n) *inceste* (m) : the film's about incest = *c'est un film sur l'inceste* ⓦ Œdipus complex = *complexe d'Œdipe* **INCESTUOUS** (adj) *incestueux, -euse* : an incestuous relationship = *une relation incestueuse.*

INCH (n, -es) *2,54 cm* : ten inches of ribbon = *vingt-cinq centimètres de ruban* ⓦ foot = *0,30 m*
(to be) every inch (a woman) = *(être femme) jusqu'au bout des ongles* ⓦ to the core = *jusqu'à la moelle*
to fight s.o. every inch of the way = *combattre qqn pied à pied*
give him an inch and he'll take a mile/an ell = *donnez-lui-en long comme le doigt, et il en prendra long comme le bras*
not to give/to budge an inch = *ne pas céder d'un pouce* ⓦ to stand one's ground = *ne pas céder de terrain*
within an inch of (winning) = *à un cheveu de (gagner).*

INCIDENT (n) *incident* (m) : a minor incident = *un incident mineur* ⓦ episode = *épisode* ☠ *un voyage plein d'incidents* = a trip full of mishaps.

INCIDENTAL (adj) **incidental expenses** = *frais accessoires.*

INCIDENTALLY (adv) *au fait* : incidentally, can you lend me some money till next week ? = *au fait, peux-tu me prêter de l'argent jusqu'à la semaine prochaine ?* ⓦ by the way = *à propos.*

INCIDENTALS (n pl) *faux frais* (m pl) : there are always incidentals on a trip = *il y a toujours des faux frais au cours d'un voyage* ⓦ extras = ←.

INCITE TO (to, -d) *inciter à* : to incite the students to

riot = *inciter les étudiants à descendre dans la rue* ⓦ to stir up = *attiser* ☠ *ça vous incite à la dépense* = it encourages you to spend.

INCLINATION (n) *inclination* (f) : an inclination to drink = *une inclination à boire* ⓦ propensity = *propension.*

INCLINE (to, -d) **I'm inclined to (agree with you)** = *je suis enclin à (être d'accord avec vous).*

INCLUDE (to, -d) *inclure, comprendre* : the price includes drinks = *le prix inclut/comprend les boissons* ≠ to exclude = *exclure*
and that includes you ! = *et toi, y compris !* ☠ *comprendre* → to understand.

INCLUDED (adj) *compris, -e* : $ 100, breakfast included = *100 dollars, petit déjeuner compris.*

INCLUDING (prep) *y compris, inclus, -e* : we were forty including me = *nous étions quarante y compris moi/moi inclus*
not including = *non compris* : the dinner will cost $ 100 not including wine = *le dîner coûtera 100 dollars, vin non compris.*

INCLUSIVE (adj) *compris, -e* : the weekend will cost $ 200, all inclusive = *le week-end coûtera 200 dollars, tout compris.*

INCOGNITO (adv) *incognito* : to travel incognito = *voyager incognito* ⓦ clandestinely = *clandestinement.*

INCOHERENT (adj) *incohérent, -e* : an incoherent speech = *un discours incohérent* ⓦ muddled = *embrouillé.*

INCOME (n) *revenu* (m) : an income of $ 3,000 monthly = *un revenu de 3 000 dollars par mois* ⓦ earnings = *gains*
income tax = *impôt sur le revenu*
income tax return = *déclaration des revenus.*

INCOMING (adj) *qui entre en fonctions* : the incoming President = *le Président qui entre en fonctions* ≠ outgoing = *sortant.*

INCOMPARABLE (adj) *incomparable* : an incomparable lover = *un amant incomparable* → WONDERFUL ≠ run-of-the-mill = *quelconque.*

INCOMPATIBILITY (n, -ies) *incompatibilité* (f) *d'humeur* : they divorced on grounds of incompatibility = *ils ont divorcé pour incompatibilité d'humeur* **INCOMPATIBLE** (adj) *incompatible* : two incompatible personalities = *deux personnalités incompatibles.*

INCOMPETENT (adj) *incompétent, -e* : an incompetent manager = *un gestionnaire incompétent* ≠ qualified = *qualifié.*

INCOMPLETE (adj) *incomplet, -ète* : an incomplete list = *une liste incomplète* ⓦ unfinished = *inachevé.*

INCOMPREHENSIBLE (adj) *incompréhensible* : what

he did is incomprehensible = *ce qu'il a fait est incompréhensible* ⓪ obscure = *obscur*.

INCONCEIVABLE (adj) *inconcevable* : abortion would have been inconceivable to my grandmother = *l'avortement aurait été quelque chose d'inconcevable pour ma grand-mère* ⓪ incredible = *incroyable*.

INCONCLUSIVE (adj) *non concluant, -e* : inconclusive test results = *des résultats d'examen non concluants*.

INCONGRUOUS (adj) *incongru, -e* : incongruous remarks = *des remarques incongrues*.

INCONSIDERATE (adj) *sans égards* : he's inconsiderate toward his wife = *il est sans égards pour sa femme* ⓪ thoughtless = *peu attentionné*.

INCONSISTENT (adj) *inconséquent, -e* : inconsistent statements = *des déclarations inconséquentes*
to be inconsistent with = *ne pas concorder avec* : what you're saying now is inconsistent with what you said last week = *ce que vous êtes en train de dire ne concorde pas avec ce que vous disiez la semaine dernière*.

INCONSPICUOUS (adj) *qui passe inaperçu, -e* : inconspicuous clothing/personalities = *vêtements/personnalités qui passent inaperçu(e)s* ≠ striking = *frappant*.

INCONVENIENCE (n) *inconvénient (m)* : the inconveniences of using a diaphragm = *les inconvénients de l'utilisation du diaphragme*
☠ *si vous n'y voyez pas d'inconvénients* = if you have no objections
— *le prix est un inconvénient* = the price is a drawback.

INCONVENIENCE (to, -d) *importuner* : I don't want to inconvenience you by coming so late = *je ne veux pas vous importuner en arrivant si tard*.

INCONVENIENT (adj) *incommode* : it's an inconvenient hour = *c'est une heure incommode* ≠ suitable = *convenable*.

INCORPORATE (to, -d) **1/** *incorporer* : she incorporated my suggestion into her plan = *elle a incorporé ma suggestion à son plan* ≠ to exclude = *exclure* **2/** *se constituer en société* : he's incorporating his business = *il se constitue en société* ≠ to fold = *déposer son bilan*.

INCORRECT (adj) *incorrect, -e* : an incorrect answer/translation = *une réponse/traduction incorrecte* ⓪ inaccurate = *inexact* ☠ *être incorrect avec qqn* = to treat s.o. discourteously.

INCORRIGIBLE (adj) *incorrigible* : an incorrigible liar/pessimist = *un menteur/pessimiste incorrigible* ⓪ inveterate = *invétéré*.

INCORRUPTIBLE (adj) *incorruptible* : an incorruptible cop = *un flic incorruptible* ≠ unprincipled = *peu scrupuleux*.

INCREASE (n) *augmentation (f)* : an increase in crime = *une augmentation de la criminalité* ⓪ growth = *croissance* ≠ drop = *chute*

on the increase = *en hausse* ≠ on the decrease = *sur le déclin*
☠ *demander une augmentation* = to ask for a raise.

INCREASE (to, -d) *augmenter* : to increase taxes = *augmenter les impôts* ⓪ to expand = *étendre* ≠ to diminish = *diminuer* ☠ → to augment.

INCREASINGLY (adv) *de plus en plus* : increasingly dangerous work = *un travail de plus en plus dangereux*.

INCREDIBLE (adj) *incroyable* : incredible news = *des nouvelles incroyables* = unbelievable news → WONDERFUL.

INCREDIBLY (adv) *incroyablement* : incredibly pretty = *incroyablement jolie* → VERY.

INCREDULOUS (adj) *incrédule* : an incredulous look = *un regard incrédule*.

INCUMBENT (n) *(personne) en titre* : the democratic incumbent will probably win the election = *le (député) démocrate en titre sera probablement réélu* ⓪ officeholder = *titulaire*.

INCUMBENT (adj) *en exercice* : the incumbent President = *le Président en exercice* ⓪ incoming = *qui entre en fonctions*.

INDEBTED (adj) **to be indebted to s.o. for** = *avoir une dette envers qqn pour* : I'm indebted to you for your help = *j'ai une dette envers vous pour l'aide que vous m'avez apportée* ⓪ beholden to = *redevable à*.

INDECISION (n) *indécision (f)* : the President's indecision was fatal to the country = *l'indécision du Président a été fatale au pays*.

INDEED (adv) **1/** *vraiment* : he's indeed stupid = *il est vraiment stupide* ⓪ truly = *réellement* **2/** *en effet* : you said the restaurant was expensive and it was indeed = *vous m'aviez dit que le restaurant était cher, et en effet il l'était* ⓪ in fact = *en fait*.

INDEED ! (interj) *vraiment !* : my former husband and I have just remarried — indeed ! = *mon ex-mari et moi venons de nous remarier — vraiment !* = really ! ⓪ no kidding ! = *sans blague !*

INDEFINITE (adj) *indéfini, -e* : our plans are indefinite = *nos projets sont indéfinis* ⓪ uncertain = *incertain*.

INDEFINITELY (adv) *indéfiniment, à une date indéterminée* : the meeting was put off indefinitely = *la réunion a été remise à une date indéterminée*.

INDEMNIFY (to, -ied) *indemniser* : he was indemnified for his expenses = *il a été indemnisé pour ses dépenses* ⓪ to compensate = *compenser*.

INDEMNITY (n, -ies) *indemnité (f)* : indemnity for the damages = *indemnité pour les dégâts* ⓪ indemnification = *indemnisation* ☠ *indemnité de chômage* = unemployment compensation.

INDEPENDENCE (n) *indépendance (f)* : the independence of a country = *l'indépendance d'un pays* ⑩ autonomy = *autonomie*
Independence Day = *fête (nationale) de l'indépendance des USA, le 4 juillet.*

INDEPENDENT (adj) *indépendant, -e* : an independent nation = *une nation indépendante* ⑩ autonomous = *autonome,* sovereign = *souverain*
☠ *circonstances indépendantes de ma volonté* = circumstances beyond my will
— *travailleur indépendant* = self-employed person.

INDEPENDENTLY (adv) *en toute indépendance* : to act independently = *agir en toute indépendance.*

IN-DEPTH (adj) *approfondi, -e* : an in-depth study = *une étude approfondie* ≠ superficial = *superficiel.*

INDESCRIBABLE (adj) *indescriptible* : indescribable disorder = *un désordre indescriptible.*

INDEX (n, -es or -dices) **1/** *index (m)* : an alphabetical index at the end of the book = *un index alphabétique à la fin du livre* ⑩ glossary = *glossaire* ☠ *mettre à l'index* = to blacklist **2/** *indice (m)* : price index = *indice des prix* ☠ → clue.

INDIA (n) *Inde (f)* **INDIAN** (n, adj) *Indien, -enne*
in Indian file = *en file indienne* ⑩ in single file = *à la queue leu leu*
don't be an Indian giver ! = *donner, c'est donner, reprendre, c'est voler !*
Indian summer = *été indien/été de la Saint-Martin.*

INDICATE (to, -d) *indiquer* : high inflation indicates a weak economy = *une forte inflation indique une économie faible* ⑩ to suggest = *suggérer* ☠ *pourriez-vous m'indiquer (l'heure) ?* = could you tell me (the time) ?

INDICATION (n) *indication (f)* : inflation is an indication of a weak economy = *l'inflation est l'indication d'une économie faible* ⑩ sign = *signe*
an indication of (how much it will cost) = *une idée de (ce que ça coûtera)*
☠ *des indications sur* = information about.

INDICATIVE (adj) *révélateur, -trice* : stuttering is indicative of emotional problems = *le bégaiement est révélateur de problèmes émotionnels.*

INDICT (to, -ed) *inculper* : he was impeached but not indicted = *il a été mis en accusation mais pas inculpé* ⑩ to prosecute = *poursuivre en justice*
indicted for (murder) = *inculpé de (meurtre).*

INDICTMENT (n) *inculpation (f)* : murder indictment = *inculpation de meurtre* ⑩ impeachment = *mise en accusation.*

INDIFFERENCE (n) *indifférence (f)* : the indifference of most people to the plight of refugees = *l'indifférence de la plupart des gens face au sort dramatique des réfugiés* ≠ passion = *←.*

INDIFFERENT (adj) *indifférent, -e* : she's indifferent to others' needs = *elle est indifférente aux besoins des autres* ⑩ unconcerned = *insensible*
☠ *il m'est indifférent* = I don't care about him
— *ça m'est indifférent* = it's immaterial to me.

INDIGESTION (n) *indigestion (f)* : the oysters gave me indigestion = *les huîtres m'ont donné une indigestion* ⑩ stomachache = *mal à l'estomac.*

INDIGNANT (adj) *indigné, -e* : indignant at his suspicions = *indigné de ses soupçons* ⑩ scandalized = *scandalisé.*

INDIGNATION (n) *indignation (f)* : to stir up public indignation = *soulever l'indignation générale* ⑩ anger = *colère.*

INDIRECT (adj) *indirect, -e* : indirect lighting = *éclairage indirect.*

INDISCREET (adj) *indiscret, -ète* : an indiscreet remark = *une remarque indiscrète* ⑩ impolite = *impoli.*

INDISPENSABLE (adj) *indispensable* ⑩ necessary = *nécessaire* ≠ superfluous = *superflu.*

INDISPUTABLE (adj) *indiscutable* : indisputable proof = *preuve indiscutable* ≠ questionable = *contestable.*

INDIVIDUAL (n) *individu (m)* : the rights of the individual = *les droits de l'individu* ⑩ private person = *particulier.*

INDIVIDUAL (adj) *individuel, -elle* : individual portions = *portions individuelles* ≠ collective = *collectif* ☠ *une chambre individuelle* (hospital) = a private room.

INDIVIDUALIST (n) *individualiste (m, f)* : I'm from a family of individualists = *je suis issu d'une famille d'individualistes* ⑩ maverick = *franc-tireur.*

INDIVIDUALITY (n, -ies) **1/** *individualité (f)* ⑩ individual = *individu* **2/** *personnalité (f)* : many people lack individuality = *beaucoup de gens manquent de personnalité* = personality.

INDIVIDUALLY (adv) *individuellement* ≠ collectively = *collectivement.*

INDOCTRINATE (to, -d) *endoctriner* ⑩ to brainwash = *faire un lavage de cerveau* **INDOCTRINATION** (n) *endoctrinement (m).*

INDONESIA (n) *Indonésie (f)* **INDONESIAN** (n, adj) *Indonésien, -enne.*

INDOOR (adj) *(d')intérieur* : an indoor garden = *un jardin intérieur* ≠ outdoor = *en plein air*
indoor pool/court = *piscine couverte/court couvert*
indoor sports = *sport en chambre* ⑩ funny business = *bagatelle*
☠ → interior.

INDOORS (adv) *à l'intérieur* : let's eat indoors = *mangeons à l'intérieur* ⑩ inside = *dedans* ≠ outdoors = *à l'extérieur.*

INDUCE (to, -d) **to induce s.o. to** = *décider qqn à* : how can I induce you to accept my offer ? = *comment puis-je vous décider à accepter mon offre ?* ≠ to dissuade from = *dissuader de.*

INDUCEMENT (n) *incitation (f)* : the high salary was an inducement to take the job = *l'importance du salaire a été une incitation à accepter le poste* ≠ deterrent = *arme de dissuasion* ☠ → incentive.

INDULGE (to, -d) *tout passer à* : he indulges his kids = *il passe tout à ses gosses* ⊙ to pamper = *chouchouter.*

INDULGENCE (n) *indulgence (f)* : he lacks indulgence = *il manque d'indulgence.*

INDULGENT (adj) *indulgent, -e* : an indulgent father = *un père indulgent* ≠ stern = *strict* ☠ *(le juge) s'est montré indulgent* = (the judge) was lenient.

INDUSTRIAL (adj) *industriel, -elle* : an industrial area = *une région industrielle* ≠ agricultural = *agricole.*

INDUSTRIALIST (n) *industriel, -elle* : she married an industrialist = *elle a épousé un industriel* ⊙ capitalist = *capitaliste* **INDUSTRIALIZATION** (n) *industrialisation (f)* **INDUSTRIALIZE** (to, -d) *industrialiser* : to industrialize a country = *industrialiser un pays.*

INDUSTRIOUS (adj) *industrieux, -euse* : an industrious worker = *un ouvrier industrieux.*

INDUSTRY (n, -ies) *industrie (f)* : the construction industry = *l'industrie du bâtiment* ⊙ commerce = *←.*

INEFFECTIVE (adj) *inefficace* : ineffective laws = *des lois inefficaces* ☠ *une secrétaire inefficace* = an inefficient secretary.

INEFFICIENT (adj) *inefficace* : an inefficient manager = *un gestionnaire inefficace* ⊙ incapable = *← ☠ →* ineffective **INEFFICIENTLY** (adv) *inefficacement.*

INEPT (adj) **1/** *inepte* : an inept comparison = *une comparaison inepte* **2/** *peu habile* : an inept mechanic = *un mécanicien peu habile.*

INERT (adj) *inerte* ⊙ dead = *mort.*

INEVITABLE (adj) *inévitable, fatal, -e* : it was inevitable that they fall in love = *il était inévitable/fatal qu'ils tombent amoureux l'un de l'autre* ☠ *fatal →* fatal **INEVITABLY** (adv) *inévitablement* ⊙ unavoidably = *inéluctablement.*

INEXACT (adj) *inexact, -e* : an inexact statement = *une déclaration inexacte* ≠ correct = *←.*

INEXCUSABLE (adj) *inexcusable* : inexcusable rudeness = *une grossièreté inexcusable* ⊙ unpardonable = *impardonnable.*

INEXPENSIVE (adj) *pas cher, -ère* : an inexpensive dress = *une robe pas chère* ⊙ cheap = *bon marché* ≠ costly = *coûteux.*

INEXPERIENCED (adj) *inexpérimenté, -e* : an inexpe-rienced speaker = *un orateur inexpérimenté* ≠ seasoned = *chevronné.*

INFALLIBLE (adj) *infaillible* : no one's infallible = *personne n'est infaillible.*

INFAMOUS (adj) *tristement célèbre* : an infamous dicta-tor = *un dictateur tristement célèbre* ⊙ notorious = *notoire* ☠ *un restaurant infâme* = a vile restaurant.

INFANCY (n, -ies) *petite enfance (f)* : infancy is a fragile time in life = *la petite enfance est une période fragile de l'existence*
to be in one's infancy = *être tout petit* : he was in his infancy when his mother died = *il était tout petit à la mort de sa mère*
to be in its infancy = *en être à ses tous débuts* : solar energy is in its infancy = *l'énergie solaire en est à ses tous débuts.*

INFANT (n) *enfant (m, f)* en bas âge : she was just an infant when her parents split up = *elle n'était qu'une enfant en bas âge quand ses parents se sont séparés* ⊙ newborn = *nouveau-né.*

INFANTILE (adj) *infantile* (illness), *puéril, -e* (be-havior) : what an infantile attitude ! = *quelle attitude puérile !*
infantile paralysis = *poliomyélite* ⊙ polio = *←.*

INFANTRY (n, -ies) *infanterie (f)* ≠ cavalry = *cavalerie.*

INFATUATED (adj) **to be infatuated with** = *s'être entiché de* : he's infatuated with my kid sister = *il s'est entiché de ma sœur cadette* ⊙ to have a crush on = *avoir le béguin pour.*

INFATUATION (n) *entichement (m)* ⊙ passing fancy = *passade.*

INFECT (to, -ed) *infecter* : the wound was infected = *la plaie était infectée* ⊙ to contaminate = *contaminer* **INFECTION** (n) *infection (f).*

INFECTIOUS (adj) *infectieux, -euse* : an infectious disease = *une maladie infectieuse*
an infectious laugh = *un rire communicatif.*

INFER (to, -red) *déduire* : I inferred from what he said that they were splitting = *j'ai déduit de ce qu'il a dit qu'ils se séparaient* ⊙ to conclude = *conclure* ☠ → to deduce **INFERENCE** (n) *ce qu'on peut en déduire* : the inference is that they're divorcing = *on peut en déduire qu'ils vont divorcer.*

INFERIOR (adj) *inférieur, -e* : inferior quality = *qualité inférieure* ⊙ mediocre = *médiocre*
inferior to = *inférieur à*
☠ *inférieur à la normale* = below average.

INFERIORITY (n, -ies) *infériorité (f)* : inferiority com-plex = *complexe d'infériorité* ≠ superiority = *supério-rité.*

INFERNAL (adj) *infernal, -e* : infernal heat = *chaleur infernale* ⊙ unbearable = *insupportable*

🐾 *une douleur infernale* = an excruciating pain
— *tu es infernal !* = you're impossible !

INFIGHTING (n inv) *querelles (f pl) intestines* : there's a lot of infighting in the Cabinet = *il y a beaucoup de querelles intestines au sein du gouvernement* ⓪ bickering = *bisbille*.

INFILTRATE (to, -d) *s'infiltrer* : to infiltrate behind enemy lines = *s'infiltrer derrière les lignes ennemies* ⓪ to penetrate = *pénétrer* **INFILTRATION** (n) *infiltration* (f).

INFINITE (adj) *infini, -e* : an infinite capacity for loving = *une infinie capacité d'aimer* ⓪ immeasurable = *incommensurable* ≠ finite = *fini* **INFINITELY** (adv) *infiniment* : infinitely rich = *infiniment riche* → VERY.

INFIRMARY (n, -ies) *infirmerie (f)* : the school infirmary = *l'infirmerie de l'école*.

INFIRMITY (n, -ies) *infirmité (f)* : the infirmities of old age = *les infirmités de la vieillesse* ⓪ handicap = ←.

INFLAMMATION (n) *inflammation (f)* : an inflammation of a muscle = *l'inflammation d'un muscle* ⓪ swelling = *gonflement*.

INFLATE (to, -d) *gonfler* : to inflate a ball = *gonfler un ballon* ≠ to deflate = *dégonfler* 🐾 *gonfler un moteur* = to juice up/to soup up an engine.

INFLATION (n) *inflation (f)* ⓪ rise in prices = *hausse des prix* **INFLATIONARY** (adj) *inflationniste* : inflationary measures = *des mesures inflationnistes* ≠ deflationary = *déflationniste*.

INFLEXIBLE (adj) *inflexible* : an inflexible position = *une position inflexible* ⓪ rigid = *rigide*.

INFLICT (to, -ed) *infliger* : to inflict punishment on s.o. = *infliger une punition à qqn* ☠ *infliger une amende à* = to fine.

INFLUENCE (n) *influence (f)* : he has little influence in the party = *il a peu d'influence au sein du parti* ⓪ authority = *autorité*
under the influence of (drink) = *sous l'influence de* (la boisson).

INFLUENCE (to, -d) *influencer* : polls influence voters = *les sondages influencent les électeurs* ⓪ to sway = *influer sur*.

INFLUENTIAL (adj) *influent, -e* : he's very influential in the government = *il est très influent au gouvernement* ⓪ well-connected = *qui a ses entrées*.

INFLUENZA (n) *grippe (f)* : a bad case of influenza = *une mauvaise grippe* = flu ⓪ cold = *rhume* ☠ → *grippe*.

INFORM (to, -ed) *informer* : they're trying to inform the public of the widespread use of torture = *on essaie d'informer le public sur l'utilisation très répandue de la torture* ⓪ to let s.o. know = *faire savoir à qqn* ☠ *s'informer de* = to find out.

INFORMAL (adj) *informel, -elle* (meeting, talks), *sans cérémonie* (dinner, party), *sport* (clothes) : an informal dinner = *un dîner sans cérémonie* ⓪ casual = *décontracté* ≠ stuffy = *guindé*.

INFORMALLY (adv) *sans cérémonie, de façon simple* : to entertain informally = *recevoir sans cérémonie*, to dress informally = *s'habiller de façon simple*.

INFORMANT (n) *informateur, -trice* : the informant of the party = *l'informateur du parti* ⓪ spy = *espion*.

INFORMATION (n inv) *informations (f pl), renseignements (m pl)* : do you have any information about the killing ? = *avez-vous des informations/des renseignements sur le meurtre ?* ⓪ facts = *faits*
a piece of information = *une information/un renseignement*
for your information = *pour ta gouverne*
🐾 *les informations* = the news
— *traitement de l'information* = data processing
— *puis-je vous demander un renseignement ?* = may I ask you something ?
— *réseau de renseignements* = intelligence network.

INFORMATIVE (adj) *informatif, -ive* : informative advertising = *publicité informative*.

INFORMED (adj) *informé, -e* : an informed audience = *un public informé*.

INFORMER (n) *indicateur, -trice, délateur, -trice* : the gang bumped off the informer = *le gang a buté l'indicateur/le délateur* ⓪ stool pigeon = *indic*.

INFREQUENT (adj) *peu fréquent, -e* : infrequent meetings = *des réunions peu fréquentes* ⓪ rare = ←.

INFRINGE ON (to, -d) *empiéter sur* : to infringe on s.o.'s rights = *empiéter sur les droits de qqn*.

INFURIATE (to, -d) *rendre furieux, -euse* : what he said infuriated me = *ce qu'il a dit m'a rendu furieux* → ANGRY.

INGENIOUS (adj) *ingénieux, -euse* : an ingenious advertising campaign = *une campagne publicitaire ingénieuse* ⓪ clever = *intelligent*.

INGENUOUS (adj) *ingénu, -e* : an ingenuous young girl = *une jeune fille ingénue* ⓪ innocent = ←, naive = *naïf*.

INGRATIATE (to, -d) **to ingratiate o.s. with (the boss)** = *se faire bien voir du (patron)*.

INGREDIENT (n) *ingrédient (m)* : the ingredients for the cake = *les ingrédients pour le gâteau* ⓪ component = *composant*.

INHABITANT (n) *habitant, -e* : the inhabitants of New York = *les habitants de New York* ⓪ resident = *résident*.

INHABITED (adj) *habité, -e* : an inhabited house = *une*

maison habitée = lived-in ≠ uninhabited = *inhabité* ☠
un vaisseau spatial habité = a manned spaceship.

INHALE (to, -d) *inhaler, avaler la fumée* (cigarette) : she smokes but doesn't inhale = *elle fume, mais elle n'avale pas la fumée* ⓪ to breathe in = *inspirer.*

INHERENT (adj) *inhérent, -e* : problems inherent in marriage = *les problèmes inhérents au mariage* ⓪ intrinsic = *intrinsèque.*

INHERIT (to, -ed) *hériter* : he inherited a lot of money/his father's bad temper = *il a hérité beaucoup d'argent/le mauvais caractère de son père* ≠ to bequeath = *léguer.*

INHERITANCE (n) *héritage (m)* : this ring's an inheritance = *cette bague vient d'un héritage* ≠ bequest = *legs*
inheritance tax = *droits de succession*
☠ → *heritage.*

INHIBIT (to, -ed) *inhiber* : her husband inhibits her = *son mari l'inhibe* **INHIBITED** (adj) *inhibé, -e* : shy and inhibited = *timide et inhibé* **INHIBITION** (n) *inhibition (f)* : sexual inhibitions = *inhibitions sexuelles* ⓪ complex = *complexe.*

INHUMAN (adj) *inhumain, -e* : slavery is inhuman = *l'esclavage est inhumain* ⓪ heartless = *sans cœur.*

INITIAL (n) *initiale (f)* : my initials are C.B. = *mes initiales sont C.B.* **INITIAL** (adj) *initial, -e* : the initial text = *le texte initial* ⓪ original = ←.

INITIALLY (adv) *initialement* : initially we were going to fly to Europe, but we finally decided to go by boat = *initialement nous devions prendre l'avion pour l'Europe, mais finalement nous avons décidé de prendre le bateau.*

INITIATE (to, -d) **1/** *initier* : he initiated me to sex = *il m'a initiée au sexe* ⓪ to introduce to = *faire connaître* **2/** *amorcer* : to initiate new reforms = *amorcer de nouvelles réformes.*

INITIATION (n) *initiation (f)* ⓪ apprenticeship = *apprentissage.*

INITIATIVE (n) *initiative (f)* : on one's own initiative = *de sa propre initiative*, to take the initiative = *prendre l'initiative.*

INJECT (to, -ed) *apporter une note de* : to inject humor into a situation = *apporter une note d'humour à la situation.*

INJECTION (n) *injection (f)* : a penicillin injection = *une injection de pénicilline* ⓪ shot = *piqûre.*

INJURE (to, -d) *blesser* : three people were injured in the accident = *trois personnes ont été blessées dans l'accident*
☠ *injurier qqn* = to insult s.o.
— *ta remarque l'a blessé* = your remark hurt him

— *il a été blessé à la guerre* = he was wounded in the war.

INJURED (n) **the injured** = *les blessés* : the injured were taken to the hospital = *les blessés ont été transportés à l'hôpital* ⓪ a casualty = *un accidenté.*

INJURY (n, -ies) *blessure (f)* : injuries due to the accident = *blessures dues à l'accident.*

INJUSTICE (n) *injustice (f)* : the injustices of society = *les injustices de la société* ≠ equity = *équité*
to do s.o. an injustice = *commettre une injustice envers qqn.*

INK (n) *encre (f)* : ink spot = *tache d'encre* ⓪ inkwell = *encrier*, blotter = *buvard* ☠ *faire couler beaucoup d'encre* = to be the prime subject (press).

INKLING (n) **to have no inkling of (what happened)** = *ne pas avoir la moindre idée de (ce qui s'est passé).*

IN-LAWS (n pl) *beaux-parents (m pl)* : I'm crazy about my in-laws = *j'adore mes beaux-parents* ⓪ mother-in-law = *belle-mère*, father-in-law = *beau-père.*

INMATE (n) *interné, -e* (asylum), *détenu, -e* (prison), *malade (m, f)* (hospital).

INN (n) *auberge (f)* : an inn near the highway = *une auberge près de l'autoroute* ⓪ innkeeper = *aubergiste* ☠ *c'est l'auberge espagnole* = you get out of something what you put into it
— *on n'est pas sorti de l'auberge* = we're not yet out of the woods
— *auberge de jeunesse* = youth hostel.

INNATE (adj) *inné, -e* : an innate talent = *un talent inné* ⓪ natural = *naturel*, congenital = *congénital.*

INNER (adj) **inner feelings** = *sentiments intimes*
inner circle of friends = *cercle d'amis intimes.*

INNERMOST (adj) *le plus intime* : my innermost thoughts = *mes pensées les plus intimes.*

INNOCENCE (n) *innocence (f)* : the innocence of children = *l'innocence des enfants* ⓪ purity = *pureté.*

INNOCENT (n) *pur, -e* : my brother's an innocent = *mon frère est un pur*
☠ *un pur (en politique)* = a hard-liner
— *ne fais pas l'innocent* = don't play dumb
— *aux innocents les mains pleines* = beginners' luck.

INNOCENT (adj) **1/** *innocent, -e* : to be proved innocent = *être reconnu innocent* ⓪ cleared = *acquitté* **2/** *innocent, -e* : an innocent conversation = *une conversation innocente* ⓪ pure = *pur* **INNOCENTLY** (adv) *innocemment.*

INNOCUOUS (adj) *anodin, -e* : an innocuous personality = *une personnalité anodine* ⓪ insipid = *insipide.*

INNOVATE (to, -d) *innover* : to innovate a fashion = *innover une mode* **INNOVATION** (n) *innovation (f)* : the new boss made several innovations = *le nouveau patron a fait plusieurs innovations* **INNOVATOR** (n) *innovateur, -trice.*

INNUENDO (n, -es) *sous-entendu (m)* : sexual innuendoes = *des sous-entendus à connotation sexuelle* ⨁ *insinuation* = ←.

INOFFENSIVE (adj) *inoffensif, -ive* : an inoffensive remark = *une remarque inoffensive.*

INPUT (n) *input (m)* ≠ output = ←.

INQUEST (n) *enquête (f)* : a criminal inquest = *une enquête criminelle*
☠ *faire une enquête sur (les écoles)* = to make a survey on (schools)
— *commission d'enquête* = fact-finding committee
— *enquête (par sondage)* = opinion poll.

INQUIRE (to, -d) *s'enquérir* : the boss inquired whether my report was finished = *le patron s'est enquis de savoir si mon rapport était fini*
to inquire about = *s'enquérir de* : he inquired about her health = *il s'est enquis de sa santé* ⨁ to find out about = *se renseigner sur.*

INQUIRY (n, -ies) 1/ *enquête (f)* : an inquiry into the Mafia = *une enquête sur la Mafia* ⨁ investigation = ← ☠ → inquest 2/ *demande (f) de renseignements* : we received several inquiries = *nous avons reçu plusieurs demandes de renseignements*
to make inquiries = *prendre des renseignements*
inquiries should be addressed to (the desk) = *pour toute demande de renseignements, adressez-vous à (à la réception).*

INQUISITIVE (adj) *inquisiteur, -trice* : an inquisitive look = *un regard inquisiteur* ⨁ curious = *curieux.*

INROADS (n pl) **to make inroads** = *faire un pas en avant* : to make inroads towards peace = *faire un pas en avant vers la paix* ⨁ to make headway = *faire des progrès.*

INSANE (adj) *insensé, -e* : an insane idea = *une idée insensée* → CRAZY
insane asylum = *asile d'aliénés*
☠ → senseless.

INSANELY (adv) *follement* : insanely jealous = *follement jaloux* → VERY.

INSANITY (n) *démence (f)* : his insanity was a kind of schizophrenia = *sa démence était un genre de schizophrénie* ⨁ craziness = *folie.*

INSATIABLE (adj) *insatiable* : an insatiable appetite = *un appétit insatiable.*

INSCRIBE (to, -d) *inscrire* : it was inscribed in my memory = *c'était inscrit dans ma mémoire*
☠ *s'inscrire (université)* = to enroll/to register
— *inscrivez votre nom* = put down your name.

INSECT (n) *insecte (f)* : insect bite = *piqûre d'insecte* ⨁ bug = *bestiole,* insecticide = ←

ant = *fourmi*	**grasshopper** = *sauterelle*
bee = *abeille*	
beetle = *scarabée*	**ladybug** = *coccinelle*
bumblebee = *bourdon*	**louse** = *pou*
	midge = *moucheron*
caterpillar = *chenille*	**mosquito** = *moustique*
cockroach = *cafard*	
dragonfly = *libellule*	**moth** = *mite*
flea = *puce*	**spider** = *araignée*
fly = *mouche*	**wasp** = *guêpe.*

INSECURE (adj) 1/ *insécurisé, -e* : an insecure child = *un enfant insécurisé* ≠ self-confident = *qui a confiance en soi* 2/ *pas en sécurité* : he feels insecure in his job because of the company's financial problems = *il ne se sent pas en sécurité dans son travail à cause des problèmes financiers de l'entreprise.*

INSECURITY (n) *insécurité (f)* : a feeling of insecurity = *un sentiment d'insécurité.*

INSENSITIVE (adj) *insensible* : insensitive to other people's problems = *insensible aux problèmes des autres* ⨁ impervious = *imperméable.*

INSERT (to, -ed) *insérer* : to insert a few jokes in the play = *insérer quelques plaisanteries dans la pièce.*

INSIDE (n) *intérieur (m)* : wash the inside of the car = *lavez l'intérieur de la voiture* ≠ outside = *extérieur* ☠ → interior.

INSIDE (adj) *de l'intérieur* : an inside plot = *un complot de l'intérieur*
inside job = *coup monté avec une complicité de l'intérieur* : the robbery was an inside job = *le cambriolage était un coup monté avec une complicité de l'intérieur*
the inside story = *le fin mot de l'histoire* ⨁ the lowdown = *le dessous des cartes.*

INSIDE (adv) *dedans* : it's hot inside = *il fait chaud dedans* ≠ outside = *dehors*
inside out = *à l'envers* : my coat's inside out = *j'ai mis mon manteau à l'envers* ≠ right side out = *à l'endroit*
to know (New York) inside out = *connaître (New York) parfaitement*
to turn inside out = *mettre sens dessus dessous* : I turned the house inside out looking for my ring = *j'ai mis la maison sens dessus dessous pour retrouver ma bague*
☠ *tu t'es fichu dedans !* = you're all wet !

INSIDE (prep) *à l'intérieur de* : inside the box = *à l'intérieur de la boîte.*

INSIDER (n) *qqn de l'entourage* : the insiders say that the President has cancer = *les gens de son entourage* disent que le Président a un cancer ≠ outsider = qqn qui ne fait pas partie de l'entourage.

INSIDIOUS (adj) *insidieux, -euse :* insidious illness = *maladie insidieuse.*

INSIGHT (n) **1/** *éclaircissement (m) :* the report offers insights into the problem = *le rapport apporte des éclaircissements sur le problème* **2/** *perspicacité (f) :* a scientist of great insight = *un savant d'une grande perspicacité.*

INSIGNIFICANT (adj) *insignifiant, -e :* insignificant losses = *des pertes insignifiantes* ⓪ minor = *mineur.*

INSINCERE (adj) *pas sincère :* insincere flattery = *flatterie pas sincère* ⓪ hypocritical = *hypocrite.*

INSINUATE (to, -d) *insinuer :* she insinuated that he was too old for her = *elle insinuait qu'il était trop vieux pour elle* ⓪ to imply = *sous-entendre.*

INSINUATION (n) *insinuation (f) :* I resent your insinuations = *je n'apprécie pas du tout vos insinuations* ⓪ implication = *sous-entendu.*

INSIPID (adj) *insipide :* insipid personality/book = *personnalité/livre insipide* ⓪ prosaic = *prosaïque,* blah = *plat.*

INSIST (to, -ed) *insister :* I'll come if you insist = *si vous insistez je viendrai*
to insist on (+ ing) = *insister pour :* I insist on leaving now = *j'insiste pour partir maintenant*
(he) insists that (he's right) = *(il) soutient qu'(il a raison).*

INSISTENT (adj) *insistant, -e :* an insistent tone = *un ton insistant*
to be insistent that = *insister pour que :* he was insistent that I stay for dinner = *il a insisté pour que je reste dîner.*

INSOFAR AS (conj) *dans la mesure (où) :* I'll help you insofar as I can = *je vous aiderai dans la mesure du possible.*

INSOLENCE (n) *insolence (f) :* I won't put up with his insolence = *je ne tolérerai pas son insolence* ⓪ brazenness = *effronterie* **INSOLENT** (adj) *insolent, -e :* an insolent reply = *une réponse insolente* ⓪ bold = *hardi* ☠ *luxe insolent* = crass luxury.

INSOMNIA (n) *insomnie (f) :* I've always suffered from insomnia = *j'ai toujours souffert d'insomnie* ⓪ sleeping pill = *somnifère,* to count sheep = *compter les moutons.*

INSOMUCH AS (conj) = INASMUCH AS.

INSPECT (to, -ed) *inspecter :* to inspect troops = *inspecter des troupes* ⓪ to examine = *examiner* **INSPECTION** (n) inspection (f).

INSPECTOR (n) *inspecteur, -trice :* police inspector = *inspecteur de police.*

INSPIRATION (n) *inspiration (f) :* I have no inspiration for a song = *je n'ai pas d'inspiration pour écrire une chanson* ⓪ stimulus = *stimulant.*

INSPIRE (to, -d) *inspirer :* to inspire confidence = *inspirer confiance* ⓪ to incite = *inciter*
what inspired her to (do such an idiotic thing) ? = *qu'est-ce qui lui a pris de (faire une chose aussi stupide) ?*
☠ *inspirer (respiration)* = to breathe in.

INSTABILITY (n, -ies) *instabilité (f) :* the instability of the government = *l'instabilité gouvernementale.*

INSTALL (to, -ed) *installer :* to install air conditioning = *installer la climatisation* ⓪ to put in = *mettre en place*
☠ *nous nous installons dans le Midi* = we're settling down in the South of France
— *installez-vous* = make yourself comfortable
— *avant que l'hiver ne s'installe* = before winter sets in
— *installer (son fils, etc.)* = to set (one's son, etc.) up.

INSTALLMENT (n) *versement (m) :* to pay for a color TV in six installments = *payer une télé couleur en six versements* ⓪ deposit = *arrhes*
to buy on the installment plan = *acheter à tempérament.*

INSTANCE (n) *exemple (m) :* instances of police brutality = *des exemples de brutalité policière* ⓪ case = *cas*
for instance = *par exemple :* I'd like something to eat, for instance a hamburger = *j'aimerais quelque chose à manger, par exemple un hamburger* = for example
☠ *« instance » est moins utilisé que « example »*
— *exemple* → example
— *être en instance de divorce* = to be in the process of getting divorced.

INSTANT (n) *instant (m) :* it will only take an instant = *ça ne prendra qu'un instant* ⓪ second = *seconde*
☠ *un instant !* = hang on !
— *à l'instant* = a moment ago
— *dans un instant* = in a moment
— *pour l'instant* = for the moment
— *d'un instant à l'autre* = at any moment.

INSTANT (adj) *instantané, -e :* instant coffee = *café instantané* ☠ → instantaneous.

INSTANTANEOUS (adj) *instantané, -e :* an instantaneous reaction = *une réaction instantanée* ☠ *café instantané* = instant coffee.

INSTANTLY (adv) *instantanément :* I recognized him instantly = *je l'ai reconnu instantanément* ⓪ right away = *tout de suite.*

INSTEAD (adv) *à la place :* if you don't want tea, order coffee instead = *si vous ne voulez pas de thé, commandez du café à la place*
instead of = *au lieu de :* let's go today instead of Tuesday = *allons-y aujourd'hui au lieu de mardi* ⓪ rather than = *plutôt que.*

INSTIGATE (to, -d) *instiguer, pousser :* the dissidents instigated the students to riot = *les dissidents ont instigué/poussé les étudiants à descendre dans la rue* ⓀⒹ to incite = *inciter* ☠ → to push.

INSTIGATION (n) *instigation (f)*
at s.o.'s instigation = *à l'instigation de qqn.*

INSTIGATOR (n) *instigateur, -trice :* the instigators of the demonstration = *les instigateurs de la manifestation* ⓀⒹ troublemaker = *fauteur de troubles.*

INSTILL (to, -ed) *inculquer :* to instill honesty in one's children = *inculquer l'honnêteté à ses enfants.*

INSTINCT (n) *instinct (m) :* my instinct tells me he's a phony = *mon instinct me dit qu'il est bidon* ⓀⒹ reflex = *réflexe*
by instinct = *par instinct.*

INSTINCTIVE (adj) *instinctif, -ive* ≠ intentional = *intentionnel.*

INSTITUTE (n) *institut (m) :* language institute = *institut d'étude des langues* ⓀⒹ academy = *académie*
☠ *institut de beauté* = beauty parlor.

INSTITUTE (to, -d) *instituer :* to institute a new policy = *instituer une nouvelle politique* ⓀⒹ to establish = *établir.*

INSTITUTION (n) *institution (f) :* the institution of marriage = *l'institution du mariage* ⓀⒹ organization = *organisation.*

INSTITUTIONALIZE (to, -d) *institutionnaliser :* to institutionalize torture = *institutionnaliser la torture.*

INSTRUCT (to, -ed) *donner l'instruction (de) :* the general instructed the troops not to fire = *le général a donné aux troupes l'instruction de ne pas tirer* ⓀⒹ to order = *ordonner.*

INSTRUCTIONS (n pl) *instructions (f pl) :* she left her instructions = *elle a laissé ses instructions* ⓀⒹ order = *ordre*
instructions for use = *mode d'emploi.*

INSTRUCTIVE (adj) *instructif, -ive :* an instructive experience = *une expérience instructive* ⓀⒹ educational = *éducatif.*

INSTRUCTOR (n) *maître-assistant (m)* (university), *moniteur, -trice* (ski, driving) ⓀⒹ professor = *professeur.*

INSTRUMENT (n) *instrument (m) :* musical instruments = *instruments de musique* ☠ *instrument de travail* = working tool.

INSTRUMENTAL (adj) **to be instrumental in** = *contribuer à :* he was instrumental in getting the treaty signed = *il a contribué à la signature du traité* ≠ to have nothing to do with = *ne rien avoir à voir avec.*

INSUBORDINATE (adj) *insubordonné, -e :* insubordinate troops = *des troupes insubordonnées* ⓀⒹ rebellious = *rebelle.*

INSUFFERABLE (adj) *intolérable :* insufferable pretension = *une prétention intolérable.*

INSUFFICIENT (adj) *insuffisant, -e :* insufficient funds = *fonds insuffisants* ≠ enough = *assez de.*

INSULATE (to, -d) *isoler :* she insulated her apartment to save energy = *elle a isolé son appartement pour économiser l'énergie* ☠ → to isolate.

INSULIN (n) *insuline (f) :* a shot of insulin = *une piqûre d'insuline.*

INSULT (n) *insulte (f), injure (f) :* comparing me to him is an insult = *c'est une insulte/injure que de me comparer à lui* ⓀⒹ snub = *camouflet, offense* = ←
to add insult to injury = *porter l'insulte à son comble* ⓀⒹ to turn the knife in the wound = *retourner le couteau dans la plaie.*

INSULT (to, -ed) *insulter, injurier :* you insulted me by saying that = *vous m'avez insulté/injurié en disant cela* ⓀⒹ to offend = *offenser* ≠ to flatter = *flatter.*

INSULTING (adj) *insultant, -e, injurieux, -euse :* an insulting remark = *une remarque insultante/injurieuse* ≠ flattering = *flatteur.*

INSURANCE (n) *assurance (f) :* life/fire insurance = *assurance vie/incendie* ⓀⒹ coverage = *couverture*
insurance policy = *police d'assurance*
insurance premium = *prime d'assurance*
to take out an insurance = *souscrire une assurance*
☠ → assurance.

INSURE (to, -d) **1/** *assurer :* to insure one's jewels = *assurer ses bijoux* **2/** *assurer :* to insure victory = *assurer la victoire* = to ensure ⓀⒹ to guarantee = *garantir* ☠ → to assure.

INSURMOUNTABLE (adj) *insurmontable :* insurmountable difficulties = *des difficultés insurmontables.*

INSURRECTION (n) *insurrection (f) :* the workers' insurrection = *l'insurrection des ouvriers* ⓀⒹ uprising = *soulèvement.*

INTACT (adj) *intact, -e :* despite the scandal, her reputation was intact = *en dépit du scandale, sa réputation est restée intacte* ≠ damaged = *atteint.*

INTANGIBLE (adj) *intangible :* an intangible feeling of guilt = *un sentiment intangible de culpabilité.*

INTEGRAL (adj) *intégrant, -e :* the right to abortion is an integral part of the women's liberation platform = *le droit d'avorter fait partie intégrante du programme de libération des femmes*
☠ *un salaud intégral* = an utter/out-and-out bastard — *l'œuvre intégrale* = the complete works.

INTEGRATE (to, -d) **1/** *pratiquer la déségrégation :* to integrate schools in the South = *pratiquer la déségrégation dans les écoles du Sud* ≠ to segregate = *pratiquer la ségrégation* **2/** *intégrer :* we'll integrate your suggestion into our project = *nous allons intégrer votre suggestion dans notre projet.*

INTEGRATION (n) *déségrégation (f)* : school integration = *déségrégation des écoles* ≠ segregation = *ségrégation.*

INTEGRITY (n) *intégrité (f)* : she's a woman of great integrity = *c'est une femme d'une grande intégrité* ≠ corruption = ←.

INTELLECTUAL (n) *intellectuel, -elle* : the left bank is full of intellectuals = *la rive gauche est remplie d'intellectuels* ⓓ longhair = *intello,* intelligentsia = ←.

INTELLECTUAL (adj) *intellectuel, -elle* : an intellectual film = *un film intellectuel* ⓓ cultivated = *cultivé.*

INTELLIGENCE (n) *intelligence (f)* : the intelligence of dolphins = *l'intelligence des dauphins*
intelligence agent = *agent de renseignements*
intelligence service = *service de renseignements*
☠ *être d'intelligence avec qqn* = to be in cahoots with s.o.

INTELLIGENT (adj) *intelligent, -e* : an intelligent answer/person/film = *une réponse/personne intelligente/un film intelligent* ⓓ clever = *malin,* on the ball = *dégourdi* ≠ stupid = *stupide* **INTELLIGENTLY** (adv) *intelligemment.*

INTELLIGIBLE (adj) *intelligible* : an intelligible explanation = *une explication intelligible* ⓓ clear = *clair.*

INTEND (to, -ed) **to intend to** = *avoir l'intention de* : I intended to leave earlier = *j'avais l'intention de partir plus tôt* ⓓ to expect to = *envisager de*
to be intended for = *être destiné à* : the remark wasn't intended for you = *la réflexion ne vous était pas destinée* = to be meant for.

INTENDED (n) *futur, -e* : her intended is French = *son futur est français* ⓓ betrothed = *promis* ☠ → future.

INTENDED (adj) *voulu, -e* : an intended snub = *un camouflet voulu* ≠ unintended = *non voulu* ☠ *en temps voulu* = in due time.

INTENSE (adj) *intense* : intense heat = *chaleur intense,* an intense personality = *une personnalité intense* ⓓ extreme = *extrême.*

INTENSIFY (to, -ied) *intensifier* : we've intensified our efforts = *nous avons intensifié nos efforts* ⓓ to increase = *augmenter.*

INTENSITY (n, -ies) *intensité (f)* : the intensity of her look = *l'intensité de son regard.*

INTENSIVE (adj) *intensif, -ive* : intensive questioning/course = *interrogatoire/cours intensif.*

INTENT (n) *dessein (m)* : it wasn't my intent = *ce n'était pas mon dessein* ⓓ intention = ← ☠ *à dessein* = on purpose.

INTENT (adj) **to be intent on (losing weight)** = *avoir la ferme intention de (maigrir).*

INTENTION (n) *intention (f)* : what are your intentions ? = *quelles sont vos intentions ?* ⓓ purpose = *but.*

INTENTIONAL (adj) *intentionnel, -elle* : intentional cruelty = *cruauté intentionnelle* ⓓ voluntary = *volontaire* ≠ unintentional = *involontaire* **INTENTIONALLY** (adv) *intentionnellement* : he said it intentionally = *il l'a dit intentionnellement* ⓓ on purpose = *exprès* ≠ unintentionally = *involontairement.*

INTERACT (to, -ed) *agir l'un sur l'autre* : Congress and the President interact = *le Congrès et le Président agissent l'un sur l'autre* **INTERACTION** (n) *interaction (f), action (f) réciproque.*

INTERCEDE (to, -d) *intercéder* : to intercede on s.o.'s behalf = *intercéder en faveur de qqn.*

INTERCEPT (to, -ed) *intercepter* : to intercept a phone call = *intercepter un coup de téléphone.*

INTERCOURSE (n inv) *rapports (m pl) sexuels* : she first had intercourse when she was 15 = *elle a eu ses premiers rapports sexuels à 15 ans.*

INTEREST (n) **1/** *intérêt (m)* : he listened with interest = *il a écouté avec intérêt* **2/** *qqch qui intéresse* : girls are his only interest = *il n'y a que les filles qui l'intéressent,* what are your interests ? = *qu'est-ce qui vous intéresse ?* **3/** *intérêt (m)* : 10 percent interest = *un intérêt de 10 pour cent*

to be in s.o.'s interest to = *avoir intérêt à/être dans l'intérêt de qqn de* : it's in your interest to get on with the boss = *c'est dans votre intérêt de vous entendre avec le patron/vous avez intérêt à vous entendre avec le patron*
to have an interest in (a business) = *avoir des intérêts dans (une affaire)* ⓓ shares = *parts*
to have no interest (in girls) = *ne pas s'intéresser (aux filles)*
it's of no interest to me (whether he remarried or not) = *ça ne m'intéresse pas de (savoir s'il s'est remarié ou non)* ⓓ I couldn't care less = *je m'en fiche*
to look out for one's (own) interest = *veiller à ses (propres) intérêts*
to lose interest in = *perdre tout intérêt pour* : he lost interest in his work = *il a perdu tout intérêt pour son travail* ⓓ to become uninterested in = *se désintéresser de*
to take an interest in = *prendre de l'intérêt/un certain intérêt à.*

INTEREST (to, -ed) *intéresser* : your idea interests me = *votre idée m'intéresse,* does he interest you ? = *est-ce qu'il vous intéresse ?,* the film interested us = *le film nous a intéressés* ↀ to appeal to = *séduire* ≠ to leave s.o. cold = *laisser qqn froid*

to be interested = *intéresser qqn :* we're going to a Chinese restaurant, are you interested ? = *nous allons dans un restaurant chinois, ça t'intéresse ?*, no, I'm not interested = *non, cela ne m'intéresse pas*
to be interested in (+ noun) = 1/ *s'intéresser à :* are you interested in flying saucers ? = *est-ce que vous vous intéressez aux soucoupes volantes ?* 2/ *intéresser :* are you interested in him ? = *est-ce qu'il vous intéresse ?* ↀ to have a crush on = *avoir le béguin pour*
to be interested in (+ ing) = *intéresser qqn de :* are you interested in going with us ? = *est-ce que ça vous intéresse de venir avec nous ?*
the interested party = *l'intéressé* ≠ a third party = *un tiers*

☠ *être intéressé aux (bénéfices)* = to have a share in (the profits)
— *ils sont tous intéressés* = they're out for what they can get.

INTERESTING (adj) *intéressant, -e :* an interesting book/guy = *un livre/type intéressant* ↀ fascinating = *fascinant,* captivating = *captivant* ≠ boring = *ennuyeux,* a drag = *rasoir*
to make o.s. interesting = *se rendre intéressant* ↀ to put on airs = *se donner des airs.*

INTERFERE (to, -d) **to interfere in** = *s'ingérer dans :* she interferes in her son's life = *elle s'ingère dans la vie de son fils* ↀ to intervene in = *intervenir dans*
to interfere with = *nuire à :* her love life interferes with her work = *sa vie amoureuse nuit à son travail.*

INTERFERENCE (n) **1/** *ingérence (f) :* interference in the affairs of other countries = *ingérence dans les affaires d'autres pays* ≠ noninterference = *non-ingérence* **2/** *interférence (f) :* radio interference = *des interférences sur les ondes.*

INTERIM (n) **in the interim** = *dans l'intérim* ↀ in the meantime = *pendant ce temps-là.*

INTERIOR (n) *intérieur (m) :* the interior of the car is beige = *l'intérieur de la voiture est beige* ≠ outside = *extérieur*
☠ *un joli intérieur* = an attractive home
— *une femme/un homme d'intérieur* = a housewife/househusband.

INTERIOR (adj) *intérieur, -e :* interior decoration = *décoration intérieure* ↀ inside = *de l'intérieur*
interior decorator/designer = *décorateur*
☠ *politique intérieure* = domestic policy
— *jardin intérieur* = indoor garden.

INTERMEDIARY (n, -ies) *intermédiaire (m, f) :* to act as an intermediary = *servir d'intermédiaire* ↀ mediator = *médiateur*
☠ *par l'intermédiaire du (directeur)* = through (the director)
— *intermédiaire (affaires)* = middleman.

INTERMEDIATE (adj) *de niveau moyen :* an intermediate course = *un cours de niveau moyen* ≠ beginners' = *de débutants.*

INTERMINABLE (adj) *interminable :* an interminable meeting = *une réunion interminable* ↀ endless = *sans fin.*

INTERMISSION (n) *entracte (m) :* a ten-minute intermission = *un entracte de dix minutes* ↀ pause = ←.

INTERMITTENT (adj) *intermittent, -e :* intermittent rain = *pluie intermittente* ≠ continuous = *continuel*
INTERMITTENTLY (adv) *par intermittence.*

INTERN (n) *interne (m, f) des hôpitaux :* my sister's going out with an intern = *ma sœur sort avec un interne* ↀ internship = *internat,* medical student = *étudiant en médecine/carabin* ☠ *un interne (école)* = a boarder (school).

INTERNAL (adj) *interne :* an internal problem = *un problème interne* ≠ external = *externe*
Internal Revenue Service = *Direction générale des impôts.*

INTERNATIONAL (adj) *international, -e :* international law = *droit international* ≠ national = ←
International Monetary Fund = *Fonds monétaire international.*

INTERPRET (to, -ed) *interpréter :* he interpreted what I said the wrong way = *il a mal interprété ce que j'ai dit* ≠ to misinterpret = *mal interpréter*
to interpret for (a President) = *servir d'interprète à (un Président).*

INTERPRETATION (n) *interprétation (f) :* a wrong interpretation = *une fausse interprétation* ≠ misinterpretation = *mauvaise interprétation.*

INTERPRETER (n) *interprète (m, f) :* a Chinese interpreter = *un interprète chinois* ↀ translator = *traducteur.*

INTERROGATE (to, -d) *interroger :* to interrogate a prisoner = *interroger un prisonnier* ↀ to question = *questionner* ☠ *s'interroger sur* = to wonder about
INTERROGATOR (n) *interrogateur, -trice.*

INTERROGATION (n) *interrogatoire (m) :* police interrogation = *interrogatoire de police* ☠ *interrogation écrite* = written test.

INTERRUPT (to, -ed) **1/** *interrompre :* don't interrupt me when I'm speaking = *ne m'interrompez pas quand je parle* ↀ to chime in = *ramener sa fraise* **2/** *interrom-*

pre : the bus service is interrupted = *le service des bus est interrompu* ⓓ to suspend = *suspendre* ☠ *interrompre (ses études)* = to discontinue (school) — *interrompre une bagarre* = to break up a fight.

INTERRUPTION (n) *interruption* (f) : without interruption = *sans interruption* ⓓ suspension = ← ☠ *interruption volontaire de grossesse* = abortion.

INTERSECTION (n) *intersection* (f) : the intersection of two roads = *l'intersection de deux routes.*

INTERVAL (n) *intervalle* (m) : a two-year interval = *un intervalle de deux ans*
at intervals = *par intervalles* ⓓ from time to time = *de temps en temps* ☠ *dans l'intervalle* = in the meantime.

INTERVENE (to, -d) *intervenir* : if they fight, don't intervene = *s'ils se disputent, n'intervenez pas* ⓓ to meddle = *s'immiscer* ☠ *la TVA intervient dans le prix* = VAT affects the price — *un accord est intervenu* = an agreement was reached.

INTERVENTION (n) *intervention* (f) : her mother's constant interventions killed their marriage = *les interventions permanentes de sa mère ont brisé leur ménage* ≠ nonintervention = *non-intervention* ☠ *intervention chirurgicale* = surgical operation.

INTERVIEW (n) *entrevue* (f), *interview* (f) (press, TV) : a job interview = *une entrevue d'embauche*, a radio interview = *une interview à la radio* **INTERVIEW** (to, -ed) *interviewer.*

INTESTINE (n) *intestin* (m) ⓓ bowels = *boyaux.*

INTIMATE (adj) *intime* : intimate friends = *des amis intimes* ⓓ close = *proche.*

INTIMATE (to, -d) *laisser entendre* : he intimated that I was getting too fat = *il a laissé entendre que je devenais trop gros* ⓓ to insinuate = *insinuer.*

INTIMIDATE (to, -d) *intimider* : she intimidates her kids = *elle intimide ses gosses* ⓓ to terrorize = *terroriser.*

INTO (prep) *dans* : he walked into the room = *il est entré dans la pièce* ☠ → in — for the use of "into" after a verb, see the verb.

INTOLERABLE (adj) *intolérable* : intolerable bigotry = *sectarisme intolérable* → AWFUL.

INTOLERANCE (n) *intolérance* (f) **INTOLERANT** (adj) *intolérant, -e* ⓓ bigoted = *sectaire.*

INTOXICATED (adj) *en état d'ébriété* → DRUNK ☠ *intoxiqué par* = poisoned by.

INTOXICATING (adj) *enivrant, -e* : an intoxicating experience = *une expérience enivrante* ⓓ heady = *grisant.*

INTRICATE (adj) *compliqué, -e* : an intricate design = *un dessin compliqué* ⓓ elaborate = *élaboré* ☠ → complicated.

INTRIGUE (to, -d) *intriguer* : her silence intrigues me = *son silence m'intrigue.*

INTRIGUING (adj) *intrigant, -e* : an intriguing smile = *un sourire intrigant* ⓓ fascinating = *fascinant* ☠ *une femme intrigante* = a scheming/conniving woman.

INTRINSIC (adj) *intrinsèque* : he's of no intrinsic value = *il n'a aucune valeur intrinsèque* ⓓ basic = *de base.*

INTRODUCE (to, -d) **1/** *présenter* : he introduced us = *il nous a présentés* ☠ → to present **2/** *introduire* : to introduce a new product on the market = *introduire un nouveau produit sur le marché* ⓓ to launch = *lancer* ☠ *il s'est introduit dans la maison* = he broke into the house
to introduce s.o. to = **1/** *présenter qqn à* : he introduced me to his parents = *il m'a présentée à ses parents* **2/** *faire connaître* : he introduced me to sex = *il m'a fait connaître le sexe* ⓓ to turn on to = *brancher sur.*

INTRODUCTION (n) *introduction* (f) : the introduction to the book = *l'introduction du livre* ⓓ foreword = *avant-propos* ≠ conclusion = ←.

INTRODUCTORY (adj) *introductif, -ive* : an introductory course = *un cours introductif* ⓓ preliminary = *préliminaire.*

INTROSPECTION (n) *introspection* (f) : too much introspection cuts you off from others = *trop d'introspection vous coupe des autres* **INTROSPECTIVE** (adj) *introspectif, -ive.*

INTROVERT (n) *introverti, -e* : my brother's an introvert = *mon frère est un introverti* ≠ extrovert = *extraverti* **INTROVERTED** (adj) *intraverti, -e* : an introverted nature = *une nature introvertie* ≠ extroverted = *extraverti.*

INTRUDE IN (to, -d) *s'immiscer dans* : she tries to intrude in my private life = *elle essaie de s'immiscer dans ma vie privée* ⓓ to interfere in = *s'ingérer dans* **am I intruding ?** = *je vous dérange ?*

INTRUDER (n) *intrus, -e* : I felt like an intruder = *j'ai eu l'impression d'être un intrus* ⓓ busybody = *mouche du coche.*

INTRUSION (n) *intrusion* (f) : my mother-in-law's constant intrusions = *les intrusions permanentes de ma belle-mère* ⓓ interference = *ingérence.*

INTUITION (n) *intuition* (f) : feminine intuition = *l'intuition féminine* ⓓ sixth sense = *sixième sens.*

INTUITIVE (adj) *intuitif, -ive* : an intuitive woman = *une femme intuitive.*

INUNDATE (to, -d) **1/** *inonder* : the market's inundated with Japanese products = *le marché est inondé de produits japonais* ⓓ to submerge = *submerger* **2/** *inon-*

der : the village was inundated by the flood = *le village a été inondé par les crues.*

INVADE (to, -d) *envahir* : the enemy troops invaded the country = *les troupes ennemies ont envahi le pays* ⓪ to conquer = *conquérir.*

INVADER (n) *envahisseur (m)* : the invaders killed everyone in the village = *les envahisseurs ont tué tout le monde dans le village* ⓪ conqueror = *conquérant.*

INVALID (n, adj) *invalide (m, f)* : an invalid sister = *une sœur invalide* ⓪ cripple = *infirme.*

INVALIDATE (to, -d) *invalider* : to invalidate an election = *invalider une élection* ⓪ to nullify = *rendre nul.*

INVALUABLE (adj) *inestimable* : your help is invaluable = *votre aide est inestimable* ⓪ priceless = *sans prix.*

INVARIABLY (adv) *invariablement* : he's invariably wrong = *il a invariablement tort* ⓪ usually = *d'habitude.*

INVASION (n) *invasion (f)* : a military invasion = *une invasion militaire* ⓪ attack = *attaque, incursion = ←.*

INVEIGLE (to, -d) *ruser pour obtenir* : to inveigle a ticket = *ruser pour obtenir un billet* ⓪ to hustle = *se débrouiller pour avoir.*

INVENT (to, -ed) **1/** *inventer* : who invented the A-bomb ? = *qui a inventé la bombe A ?* ⓪ to discover = *découvrir* **2/** *inventer* : I just invented this story = *je viens d'inventer cette histoire* ⓪ to make up = *fabriquer.*

INVENTION (n) *invention (f)* : take out a patent for your invention = *fais breveter ton invention* ⓪ find = *trouvaille,* patent = *brevet d'invention.*

INVENTIVE (adj) *inventif, -ive* : he's so lazy he's become inventive = *il est tellement paresseux qu'il en est devenu inventif* ⓪ imaginative = *imaginatif.*

INVENTOR (n) *inventeur, -trice* : the inventors of the sewing machine = *les inventeurs de la machine à coudre* ⓪ discoverer = *découvreur.*

INVENTORY (n, -ies) *inventaire (m)* : we take an inventory once a year = *nous faisons l'inventaire une fois par an.*

INVEST (to, -ed) *investir, placer* : to invest money in a business = *investir/placer de l'argent dans une affaire* ⓪ to speculate = *spéculer*
☠ *investir (Président)* = to inaugurate (President)
— *elle a beaucoup investi dans son mariage* = she put a lot in her marriage
— *placer* → to place.

INVESTIGATE (to, -d) *enquêter sur* : to investigate a criminal case = *enquêter sur une affaire criminelle* ⓪ to delve into = *fouiller dans.*

INVESTIGATION (n) *investigation (f)* : police investigation = *investigation policière* ⓪ inquest = *enquête*
INVESTIGATOR (n) *enquêteur, -trice* ⓪ detective = *détective.*

INVESTMENT (n) *investissement (m), placement (m)* : gold is a very good investment = *l'or est un très bon investissement/placement* ⓪ stocks = *actions* = shares, capital = ←.

INVESTOR (n) *investisseur (m)* : small investors = *petits investisseurs* ⓪ shareholder = *actionnaire.*

INVETERATE (adj) *invétéré, -e* : an inveterate liar/boozer = *un menteur/poivrot invétéré* ⓪ hopeless = *incorrigible.*

INVIGORATING (adj) *revigorant, -e* : a good Scotch is invigorating = *un bon whisky est revigorant* ⓪ exhilarating = *stimulant.*

INVISIBLE (adj) *invisible* : ghosts are invisible = *les fantômes sont invisibles* ⓪ transparent = ←.

INVITATION (n) *invitation (f)* : an invitation to a party = *une invitation à une soirée* ⓪ announcement = *faire-part.*

INVITE (to, -d) **1/** *inviter* : who invited you ? = *qui vous a invité ?*
to invite over = *inviter (à la maison)* : I invited them over tonight = *je les ai invités ce soir (à la maison)*
to invite s.o. to (a party) = *inviter qqn à (une soirée)*
☠ *c'est moi qui invite* = it's my treat/I'm treating
2/ *courir après* : to invite trouble = *courir après les ennuis* ⓪ to look for = *chercher.*

INVITING (adj) *alléchant, -e* : an inviting offer = *une offre alléchante* ⓪ tempting = *tentant.*

INVOICE (n) *facture (f) détaillée* : to send an invoice = *envoyer une facture détaillée* ⓪ bill = *facture.*

INVOLUNTARY (adj) *involontaire* : an involuntary mistake = *une faute involontaire* ≠ deliberate = *délibéré.*

INVOLVE (to, -d) **1/** *impliquer* : how much work/money does it involve ? = *combien de travail/d'argent cela implique-t-il ?* ☠ → to implicate **2/** *mêler à* : don't involve me = *ne me mêlez pas à cela* **3/** *concerner* : the problem involves the whole family = *le problème concerne toute la famille* = to concern

to be involved in = 1/ *se donner à fond dans* : she's really involved in her work = *elle se donne vraiment à fond dans son travail* 2/ *être impliqué dans* :	three teenagers were involved in the murder = *trois adolescents étaient impliqués dans le meurtre* ⓪ to be mixed up in = *se trouver mêlé à*

> to be involved with =
> avoir une liaison avec
> qqn : it's the third time
> she's been involved
> with a married guy =
> c'est la troisième fois
> qu'elle a une liaison
>
> avec un homme marié
> Ⓞ to be in love with =
> être amoureux de
> **I don't want to get
> involved** = je ne veux
> pas me mêler de ça.

INVOLVED (adj) embrouillé, -e : an involved business = une affaire embrouillée.

IOU (abbr) = I owe you = reconnaissance (f) de dette : he gave me an IOU = il m'a donné une reconnaissance de dette.

IQ (abbr) = Intelligence Quotient = quotient (m) intellectuel = QI (m) : he has a low IQ = il a un faible QI.

IRAN (n) Iran (m) Ⓞ Persia = Perse **IRANIAN** (n, adj) Iranien, -enne Ⓞ Persian = Persan.

IRAQ (n) Irak (m) **IRAQI** (n, adj) Irakien, -enne.

IRELAND (n) Irlande (f).

IRISH (n, adj) Irlandais, -e = Paddy
to get one's Irish up = prendre la mouche : don't get your Irish up, I was just kidding = ne prends pas la mouche, je ne faisais que plaisanter → ANGRY.

IRK (to, -ed) contrarier : his attitude irked me = son attitude m'a contrarié → ANGRY ☠ → to frustrate.

IRON (n) 1/ fer (m) : an iron bar = une barre de fer, wrought iron = fer forgé, cast iron = fonte, iron ore = minerai de fer ☠ fer de lance = spearhead
to have many irons in the fire = avoir plusieurs fers au feu
iron constitution = santé de fer
iron curtain = rideau de fer
to rule with an iron hand = diriger avec une main de fer Ⓞ to crack the whip = serrer la vis
to strike while the iron is hot = battre le fer pendant qu'il est chaud Ⓞ to seize the opportunity = saisir l'occasion
2/ fer (m) à repasser : steam iron = fer à vapeur Ⓞ ironing board = planche à repasser.

IRON (to, -ed) repasser : to iron a shirt = repasser une chemise Ⓞ to starch = amidonner
to iron out (difficulties) = aplanir (les difficultés) Ⓞ to smooth things out = arrondir les angles
☠ tu peux toujours repasser ! = you can whistle for it !
— je repasserai demain = I'll come back tomorrow.

IRONIC(AL) (adj) ironique : an ironic remark = une remarque ironique Ⓞ mocking = moqueur **IRONICALLY** (adv) ironiquement.

IRONY (n, -ies) ironie (f) : a book full of irony = un livre rempli d'ironie Ⓞ satire = ← ☠ ironie du sort = quirk of fate.

IRRATIONAL (adj) irrationnel, -elle : irrational behavior = un comportement irrationnel Ⓞ absurd = absurde, wild = dément **IRRATIONALLY** (adv) irrationnellement.

IRREGULAR (adj) irrégulier, -ère : irregular verbs = verbes irréguliers Ⓞ abnormal = anormal ☠ l'ourlet est irrégulier = the hem's uneven **IRREGULARITY** (n, -ies) irrégularité (f) : the irregularities of the deliveries = les irrégularités des livraisons **IRREGULARLY** (adv) irrégulièrement.

IRRELEVANT (adj) hors de propos : irrelevant remarks = des remarques hors de propos Ⓞ beside the point = à côté de la question.

IRREPARABLE (adj) irréparable : an irreparable mistake = une faute irréparable.

IRRESISTIBLE (adj) irrésistible : an irresistible smile = un sourire irrésistible.

IRRESPECTIVE OF (adj) sans tenir compte de : irrespective of our differences = sans tenir compte de nos différences Ⓞ despite = malgré.

IRRESPONSIBLE (adj) irresponsable : irresponsible words = propos irresponsables.

IRREVERENT (adj) irrévérencieux, -euse : an irreverent attitude = une attitude irrévérencieuse.

IRREVOCABLE (adj) irrévocable : an irrevocable decision = une décision irrévocable.

IRRIGATE (to, -d) irriguer : to irrigate fields = irriguer des champs **IRRIGATION** (n) irrigation (f).

IRRITABLE (adj) irritable : why are you so irritable ? = qu'est-ce qui te rend si irritable ? Ⓞ testy = irascible.

IRRITATE (to, -d) irriter : irritated by his remarks = irrité par ses réflexions
to become irritated = s'irriter → ANGRY.

IRRITATING (adj) irritant, -e : irritating questions = des questions irritantes Ⓞ exasperating = exaspérant.

IRRITATION (n) irritation (f) : a skin irritation = une irritation de la peau Ⓞ inflammation = ←.

ISH (suffix) 1/ dans les : thirtyish = dans les trente ans 2/ vers les : at 8ish = vers les 8 heures 3/ -âtre : bluish = bleuâtre, greenish = verdâtre 4/ un peu : warmish = un peu chaud.

ISLAM (n) Islam (m) Ⓞ Mahomet = ←, the Koran = le Coran, imam = ←, ayatollah = ←, mullah = mollah **ISLAMIC** (adj) islamique.

ISLAND (n) île (f) : Manhattan's an island = Manhattan est une île Ⓞ peninsula = péninsule ≠ mainland = continent.

ISOLATE (to, -d) isoler : they isolated the prisoners = ils ont isolé les prisonniers ☠ isoler une maison = to insulate a house **ISOLATION** (n) isolement (m) : no one can live in complete isolation = *personne ne peut vivre dans un isolement complet.*

ISOLATIONISM (n) *isolationnisme (m)* ≠ interventionism = *interventionnisme* **ISOLATIONIST** (n) *isolationniste (m, f)* : the party's full of isolationists = *le parti est rempli d'isolationnistes* ≠ interventionist = *interventionniste.*

ISRAEL (n) *Israël (m)* **ISRAELI** (n, adj) *Israélien, -enne* ⓪ Israelite = *israélite,* the Hebrew people = *les Hébreux.*

ISSUE (n) **1/** *question (f)* : that's not the issue = *là n'est pas la question* ⓪ point = *problème* ☠ → question **2/** *numéro (m)* : the March issue = *le numéro de mars* ⓪ edition = *édition* ☠ → number
at issue = *(mis) en cause* : her competence isn't at issue = *sa compétence n'est pas en cause*
to cloud the issue = *brouiller les cartes*
to confuse/talk around the issue = *noyer le poisson*
to evade/avoid the issue = *chercher des faux-fuyants* ⓪ to elude the question = *éluder la question*
to make an issue (of) = *faire toute une affaire de* ⓪ to make a federal case out of = *faire une affaire d'État de*
that settles the issue ! = *la question est réglée !* ⓪ and that's that ! = *un point, c'est tout !*
to take issue with (what s.o. said) = *être en désaccord avec (ce que qqn a dit)* ≠ to be in agreement with = *être d'accord avec*
☠ *une heureuse issue* = a successful outcome.

ISSUE (to, -d) *délivrer* : to issue a passport = *délivrer un passeport* ☠ → to deliver.

IT (pron) **1/** (subject) *il, elle (choses, animaux)* : where's the car ? — it's in the street = *où est la voiture ? — elle est dans la rue,* where's my book ? — it's on the table = *où est mon livre ? — il est sur la table* → I ☠ *il* → he, *elle* → she

IT'S = IL FAIT	**IT'S = C'EST**
— it's cold = *il fait froid*	— it's hard ≠ easy = *c'est dur* ≠ *facile*
— it's hot = *il fait chaud*	— it's far ≠ near = *c'est loin* ≠ *près*
— it's nice out = *il fait beau dehors*	— it's me/it was her = *c'est moi/c'était elle*
— it's windy = *il fait du vent*	— it's Tuesday = *c'est/on est mardi*
	— it's winter = *c'est l'hiver*

---

it's (three) o'clock = *il est (trois) heures*
it's raining/snowing = *il pleut/il neige*
who/when/where is it ? = *qui est-ce ?/quand est-ce ?/où est-ce ?*

2/ (object) *le, la, l'* : do you see my car ? — yes, I see it = *est-ce que vous voyez ma voiture ? — oui, je la vois,* the dog ? I can't see it = *le chien ? je ne le vois pas*
what did he do with it ? = *qu'en a-t-il fait ?*

ITALY (n) *Italie (f)* **ITALIAN** (n, adj) *Italien, -enne* ⓪ wop = *rital.*

ITCH (n, -es) *démangeaison (f).*

ITCH (to, -ed) *démanger* : the rash itches = *cette éruption de boutons me démange* ⓪ to scratch = *gratter*
to be itching to/for = *démanger qqn de* : I'm itching to know what happened = *ça me démange de savoir ce qui s'est passé.*

ITEM (n) **1/** *article (m)* : to write an item for the paper = *écrire un article pour un journal* **2/** *article (m)* : ten items on the list = *dix articles sur la liste* ☠ → article.

ITEMIZE (to, -d) *faire le détail de* : to itemize expenses = *faire le détail des dépenses.*

ITINERARY (n, -ies) *itinéraire (m)* : a complicated itinerary = *un itinéraire compliqué* ⓪ route = ←.

ITS (adj) *son, sa, ses (choses, animaux)* : the dog's eating its meal = *le chien mange son repas*
☠ *son manteau* = his/her coat
— *sa mère* = his/her mother.

ITSELF (pron) **1/** *lui-même, elle-même (choses, animaux)* : life itself is difficult = *la vie elle-même est difficile*
☠ *lui-même (qqn)* = himself
— *elle-même (qqn)* = herself
2/ (reflexive) *se* : the dog's scratching itself = *le chien se gratte* → MYSELF.

IUD (abbr) = intrauterine device = *stérilet (m)* = coil = loop ⓪ the pill = *la pilule.*

IVORY (n, -ies) *ivoire (m)* : ivory bracelet = *bracelet d'ivoire* ⓪ tusks = *défenses*
ivory tower = *tour d'ivoire*
Ivory Coast = *Côte-d'Ivoire.*

IVY (n, -ies) *lierre (m)* : a wall covered with ivy = *un mur couvert de lierre* ⓪ Virginia creeper = *vigne vierge*
Ivy League Schools = *universités prestigieuses de la côte Est américaine (Harvard, Yale, Princeton, etc.).*

JAB (n) *pointe (f) :* she makes constant jabs at her husband = *elle envoie sans arrêt des pointes à son mari* ⦻ dig = *pique* ☠ → point.

JAB (to, -bed) *donner un coup à :* he jabbed me with his elbow = *il m'a donné un coup de coude.*

JACK (n) *valet (m) :* the jack of clubs = *le valet de trèfle* ☠ → valet.

JACKASS (n, -es) *couillon, -onne :* what a jackass you are ! = *quel couillon tu fais !* → STUPID.

JACKET (n) *veste (f) :* sports jacket = *veste de sport* ⦻ blazer = ←
☠ *retourner sa veste* = to do a turnabout
— *prendre une veste* = to take a beating (election)
— a vest = *un gilet.*

JACK-IN-THE-BOX (n) *diable (m) à ressort (qui sort d'une boîte).*

JACK-OF-ALL-TRADES (n) *homme/femme-orchestre.*

JACKPOT (n) **to hit the jackpot** = *décrocher le gros lot* ⦻ to strike it rich = *trouver le filon.*

JACK UP (to, -ed) *faire grimper :* to jack up prices = *faire grimper les prix* ⦻ to hike up = *augmenter fortement.*

JADE (n) *jade (m) :* a jade ring = *un anneau de jade.*

JADED (adj) *revenu, -e de tout :* a rich, jaded and perverted group of friends = *un groupe d'amis riches, revenus de tout et pervertis* ⦻ blasé = ←.

JAIL (n) *prison (f), taule (f)* (LV) : he's in jail for five years = *il est en prison pour cinq ans* ⦻ in solitary = *au cachot,* jailer = *geôlier,* guard = *garde.*

JAILBAIT (n) *adolescent, -e susceptible d'entraîner un cas de détournement de mineur.*

JAILBIRD (n) *taulard, -e* ⦻ con = *bagnard.*

JAILBREAK (n) *évasion (f) de prison* ⦻ escape = *évasion.*

JALOPY (n, -ies) *tire (f)* ⦻ automobile = ←.

JAM (n) **1/** *confiture (f) :* apricot jam = *confiture d'abricots* ⦻ jelly = *gelée* **2/** *encombrement (m) :* a jam on the highway = *de l'encombrement sur l'autoroute* ⦻ bottleneck = *bouchon*
to be in a jam = *être dans le pétrin* = to be in a fix
to have a jam session = *faire un bœuf.*

JAM (to, -med) *se bloquer :* my machine jammed = *ma machine s'est bloquée* ☠ → to block
to be jammed = *être bourré :* the theater was jammed = *le théâtre était bourré* ⦻ full = *plein*
to jam into = *s'entasser dans :* we jammed into the elevator = *nous nous sommes entassés dans l'ascenseur* ⦻ to crowd in = *entrer en foule.*

JANITOR (n) *homme (m) de ménage dans un immeuble* ⦻ handyman = *homme à tout faire.*

JANUARY (n) *janvier (m)* → MONTH.

JAP (abbr) = Jewish American Prince/Princess = *fils/fille à papa juif/juive.*

JAPAN (n) *Japon (m)* **JAPANESE** (n, adj) *Japonais -e* ⦻ Jap = ← ☠ *viens voir mes estampes japonaises* = come up and see my etchings.

JAR (n) *pot (m), bocal (m) :* a glass jar = *un bocal en verre,* a jar of jam = *un pot de confiture* ⦻ container = *récipient* ☠ *pot* → pot
to give s.o. a jar = *ficher un coup à qqn* = to give s.o. a jolt.

JAR (to, -red) *ébranler :* the news jarred her = *la nouvelle l'a ébranlée* ⦻ to jolt = *faire un coup à*
to jar with = *détonner avec :* pink jars with red = *le rose détonne avec le rouge* ≠ to go with = *aller avec.*

JARGON (n) *jargon (m) :* medical jargon = *jargon médical* ⦻ dialect = *dialecte.*

JAUNDICE (n) *jaunisse (f)* ⦻ yellow fever = *fièvre jaune* ☠ *en faire une jaunisse* = to make a federal case about something.

JAUNT (n) *virée (f) :* a quick jaunt to Spain = *une petite virée en Espagne* ⦻ pleasure trip = *voyage d'agrément.*

JAW (n) *mâchoire (f)* ⓪ throat = *gorge* ☠ *bâiller à se décrocher la mâchoire* = to yawn one's head off.

JAWBONE (to, -d) *exercer des pressions (verbales)* : the President's jawboning to get the law passed = *le Président exerce des pressions pour faire passer la loi.*

JAWBREAKER (n) *nom (m) à coucher dehors* : his name's a jawbreaker = *il a un nom à coucher dehors.*

JAYWALK (to, -ed) *traverser en dehors des clous* : you get a ticket for jaywalking in New York = *à New York on a une amende si l'on traverse en dehors des clous* ⓪ pedestrian = *piéton.*

JAZZ (n inv) **1/** *jazz (m)* : let's listen to some jazz tonight = *si on allait écouter du jazz ce soir ?* **2/** *histoire (f)* : what's this jazz about your wanting to split ? = *qu'est-ce que c'est que cette histoire, il paraît que tu veux te barrer ?* ☠ → story
cut the jazz ! = *arrête tes salades !* = **don't give me that jazz !** → BUZZ OFF !

JAZZ UP (to, -ed) *mettre une note de gaieté dans* : the apartment's gloomy, what can we do to jazz it up ? = *l'appartement est triste, que peut-on faire pour y mettre une note de gaieté ?* ⓪ to enliven = *égayer.*

JAZZY (adj, -ier, -iest) *tape-à-l'œil* : jazzy clothes = *des vêtements tape-à-l'œil* ⓪ splashy = *tapageur.*

JEALOUS (adj) *jaloux, -ouse* : jealous of her sister = *jalouse de sa sœur* ⓪ envious = *envieux* **JEALOUSY** (n, -ies) *jalousie (f)* ⓪ sour grapes = *les raisins sont trop verts.*

JEANS (n pl) *jean (m)* : your jeans are dirty = *ton jean est sale,* I bought two pairs of jeans = *j'ai acheté deux jeans* ⓪ slacks = *pantalon.*

JEEP (n) *Jeep (f)* ⓪ jalopy = *tire.*

JEER (n) *quolibet (m)* ⓪ gibe = *raillerie.*

JEER AT (to, -ed) *lancer des quolibets à* : the kids jeered at the drunkard = *les gosses lançaient des quolibets à l'ivrogne* ⓪ to gibe at = *se railler de,* to deride = *tourner en dérision.*

JELLY (n, -ies) *gelée (f)* : blackberry jelly = *gelée de mûres* ☠ → frost.

JEOPARDIZE (to, -d) *mettre en péril* : his drinking is jeopardizing his health = *son alcoolisme met sa santé en péril* ⓪ to endanger = *mettre en danger.*

JEOPARDY (n inv) **in jeopardy** = *en péril* : my life's in jeopardy = *ma vie est en péril* ⓪ endangered = *en danger.*

JERK (n) *crétin, -e* : my brother's a jerk = *mon frère est un crétin* → STUPID.

JERK OFF (to, -ed) *se branler* : he was jerking off in the john = *il se branlait dans les toilettes* ⓪ to play with o.s. = *s'amuser en solitaire* ☠ → to wobble.

JERKY (adj, -ier, -iest) *crétin, -e* : a jerky idea = *une idée crétine* → STUPID.

JEST (n) **in jest** = *sur le ton de la plaisanterie* : she said it in jest = *elle a dit ça sur le ton de la plaisanterie* ⓪ for laughs = *pour rire.*

JEST (to, -ed) *badiner* : don't get insulted, I was jesting = *ne t'offense pas, je badinais* ⓪ to joke = *plaisanter* ☠ *on ne badine pas avec (la loi)* = don't treat (the law) lightly.

JESUS (n) *Jésus* ⓪ Christ = ←.

JESUS ! (interj) *nom de Dieu !* → GOSH !

JET (n) *jet (m)* = jet plane
jet lag = *(troubles dus au) décalage horaire*
jet set = *jet-set* ⓪ the beautiful people = *le beau monde*
☠ *d'un seul jet* = in one sitting
— *premier jet* = first draft.

JET-BLACK (adj) *noir, -e comme jais* ⓪ snow-white = *blanc comme neige.*

JETTY (n, -ies) *jetée (f)* : a lighthouse at the end of the jetty = *un phare au bout de la jetée* ⓪ harbor = *port.*

JEW (n) *juif, juive* : the Wandering Jew = *le juif errant* ⓪ yid = *youpin* ≠ goy = ←.

JEWEL (n) *bijou (m), joyau (m)* ⓪ gems = *pierres précieuses* **JEWELER** (n) *bijoutier, -ère, joaillier, -ère.*

JEWELRY (n inv) *bijoux (m pl)* : she wears a lot of jewelry = *elle porte beaucoup de bijoux* ⓪ silver = *argent,* gold = *or,* diamond = *diamant,* ruby = *rubis,* broach = *broche,* ring = *bague,* bracelet = ←, necklace = *collier*
a piece of jewelry = *un bijou*
jewelry store = *bijouterie/joaillerie.*

JEWISH (adj) *juif, juive* ⓪ Hebrew = *Hébreu.*

JIBE (to, -d) *coller* : her new explanation doesn't jibe with what she said before = *sa nouvelle explication ne colle pas avec ce qu'elle avait dit avant* ⓪ to correspond = *correspondre* ☠ → to stick.

JIFFY (n) **in a jiffy** = *en un clin d'œil* : he did it in a jiffy = *il l'a fait en un clin d'œil* ⓪ in the twinkling of an eye = *en deux temps trois mouvements.*

JIG (n) **the jig's up !** = *les carottes sont cuites !* : the cops are coming, the jig's up ! = *les flics arrivent, les carottes sont cuites !* ⓪ the game's up ! = *c'est fichu !*

JILT (to, -ed) *plaquer* : she jilted him when she found out he was cheating = *elle l'a plaqué quand elle a découvert qu'il la trompait* ⓪ to dump = *larguer* ☠ *plaquer son boulot* = to walk out on one's job.

JIM CROW (adj) *ségrégationniste* : Jim Crow practices still exist in the South = *les pratiques ségrégationnistes existent toujours dans le sud des États-Unis.*

JINGLE (n) *refrain* (m) *publicitaire, jingle* (m) ⓒ commercial = *spot publicitaire.*

JINX (n, -es) *qqch qui porte malheur* : this car's a jinx = *cette voiture nous porte malheur* ⓒ curse = *malédiction.*

JITTERS (n pl) *frousse* (f) : going home in the dark gave me the jitters = *ça m'a flanqué la frousse de rentrer chez moi dans le noir* ⓒ the creeps = *les jetons.*

JITTERY (adj) *qui a la tremblote* ⓒ jumpy = *qui est une pile de nerfs.*

JOB (n) **1/** *job* (m), *travail* (m) : I lost my job = *j'ai perdu mon job/travail* ⓒ opening = *place disponible,* post = *poste* ☙ *travail* → work
to go job hunting = *faire les petites annonces*
to lie down on the job = *tirer au flanc* ≠ to keep one's nose to the grindstone = *travailler sans lever le nez*
it isn't my job (to do the dishes) = *ce n'est pas mon boulot de (faire la vaisselle)*
what a job (getting him to come) ! = *quelle affaire pour (le faire venir)* ! ⓒ undertaking = *entreprise* **2/** *coup* (m) : the hoodlums pulled the job when the house was empty = *les voyous ont fait le coup quand la maison était vide* ⓒ heist = *casse* ☙ → blow.

JOBBER (n) *sous-traitant* (m) ⓒ wholesaler = *grossiste.*

JOBLESS (adj) *sans emploi* ≠ employed = *qui a un emploi.*

JOCK (n) *athlète* (m, f) : he's a top French jock = *c'est un athlète français de haut niveau* = athlete ⓒ sportsman = *sportif.*

JOCKEY (n) *jockey* (m) ⓒ horse race = *course de chevaux.*

JOE BLOW (n pr) *M. Machin-Chose* ⓒ Mr. John Q. Public = *M. Tout-le-Monde.*

JOG (to, -ged) *faire du footing/du jogging* ⓒ to do push-ups = *faire des pompes*
to jog along = *aller cahin-caha.*

JOGGING (n) *footing* (m), *jogging* (m) ⓒ sneakers = *baskets,* jogger = ←.

JOHN (n inv) *petit coin* (m), *W.-C.* (m) : to go to the john = *aller au petit coin* = loo (GB) ⓒ toilet = *toilettes,* can = *gogues.*

JOHN DOE (n pr) *M. Dupont* ⓒ the man in the street = *l'homme de la rue.*

JOHN Q. PUBLIC (n pr) *M. Tout-le-Monde* ⓒ Mr. so-and-so = *M. Untel.*

JOIN (to, -ed) *adhérer (à)* (club, party), *s'engager (dans)* (army, navy) ⓒ to sign up = *s'inscrire* ☙ *adhérer* → to adhere, *engager* → to engage
to join s.o. = **1/** *rejoindre qqn* : will you join us later at the restaurant ? = *nous rejoindrez-vous plus tard au restaurant ?* **2/** *se joindre à qqn* : we want to create a club,

will you join us ? = *nous voulons créer un club, vous joindrez-vous à nous ?*
(I'm having a drink,) will you join me ? = *(je prends un verre,) tu m'accompagnes ?*
to join in = **1/** *se joindre à* : join in the debate = *joignez-vous au débat* **2/** *se mettre de la partie* : we all joined in to help = *nous nous sommes tous mis de la partie pour aider*
to join up = **1/** *s'enrôler* : he joined up as a private = *il s'est enrôlé comme simple soldat* **2/** *se joindre à* : they joined up with another firm to build the bridge = *ils se sont joints à une autre firme pour construire le pont* ☙ *où puis-je vous joindre ?* = where can I get hold of you/reach you ?
— *joindre (un chèque)* = to enclose (a check).

JOINT (n) **1/** *gargote* (f) (food), *endroit* (m) : it's a nice little joint and the food's good = *c'est une petite gargote/un endroit sympa, et la bouffe est bonne* ☙ *endroit* → place **2/** *joint* (m) : to smoke a joint = *fumer un joint* ⓒ pot = *de l'herbe*
to case the joint = *repérer les lieux* ⓒ to pull a job = *faire un coup*
out of joint = *qui ne correspond pas* : government policy is out of joint with its declared aims = *la politique gouvernementale ne correspond pas aux buts annoncés.*

JOINT (adj) *commun, -e* : a joint declaration = *une déclaration commune* ☙ → common
joint account = *compte joint*
joint owner = *copropriétaire* ⓒ joint ownership = *copropriété*
joint stock company = *société par actions.*

JOKE (n) *plaisanterie* (f), *blague* (f) : he told some very funny jokes = *il a dit des plaisanteries/des blagues très drôles*

a joke = **1/** *l'enfance de l'art* : the test was a joke = *cet examen, c'était l'enfance de l'art* ⓒ as easy as pie = *facile comme bonjour* **2/** *gratiné* : his last film was a joke = *son dernier film était gratiné* ⓒ a laugh = *de la rigolade,* a corker = *pas piqué des vers*
to be the joke of (one's family) = *être la risée de (sa famille)*
he can't take a joke = *il ne comprend pas la plaisanterie*
to carry the joke too far = *pousser la plaisanterie trop loin*

to crack jokes = *dire des plaisanteries*
for a joke = *pour s'amuser* : I said it for a joke = *j'ai dit ça pour m'amuser* ⓒ for the fun of it = *histoire de rigoler*
no joke = **1/** *sans blague* : you're getting married ? no joke ! = *tu te maries ? sans blague !* → GOSH ! **2/** *pas marrant* : war is no joke = *la guerre, ce n'est pas marrant*
to play a joke on s.o. = *faire une blague à qqn* ⓒ to play a prank on s.o. = *faire une niche à qqn*

> ☠ *prendre tout à la plaisanterie* = not to take anything seriously
> — *blague à part* = kidding aside
> — *faire une sale blague à qqn* = to play a dirty trick on s.o.

JOKE (to, -d) *plaisanter* : don't cry, I was just joking = *ne pleure pas, je plaisantais* ⓪ to kibitz = *blaguer*, to pull s.o.'s leg = *mettre qqn en boîte*
you're joking ! = *tu plaisantes ! :* rich, me ? you're joking ! = *moi, riche ? tu plaisantes !*
to joke about = *plaisanter avec :* don't joke about health = *ne plaisante pas avec ta santé.*

JOKER (n) **1/** *plaisantin, -e* ⓪ kibitzer = *blagueur*
2/ *joker (m)* ⓪ cards = *cartes.*

JOKING (n inv) *plaisanterie (f) :* a lot of joking at the meeting = *beaucoup de plaisanteries au cours de la réunion* = kidding around ⓪ shenanigans = *rigolade*
no joking ! = *sans plaisanter !* → GOSH !

JOKINGLY (adv) *en plaisantant :* he said it jokingly = *il a dit ça en plaisantant.*

JOLLY (adv) (GB) **a jolly (good lunch)** = *un bien (bon déjeuner)* → VERY.

JOLT (n) *cahot (m) :* the car started with a jolt = *la voiture a démarré dans un cahot* ⓪ jerk = *secousse*
it gave me a jolt = *ça m'a fichu un coup* ⓪ I was taken aback = *ça m'a coupé le souffle.*

JOLT (to, -ed) *donner un coup à :* the news jolted me = *la nouvelle m'a donné un coup* ⓪ to shock = *choquer.*

JONESES (n pl) **to keep up with the Joneses** = *ne pas vouloir être en reste (avec les voisins) :* the neighbors got a color TV so she wants one too ; she always keeps up with the Joneses = *les voisins ont acheté une télé couleur, alors elle en veut une aussi ; elle ne veut jamais être en reste.*

JORDAN (n) *Jordanie (f)* **JORDANIAN** (n, adj) *Jordanien, -enne.*

JOSH (to, -ed) *galéjer :* I wasn't serious, just joshing = *je n'étais pas sérieux, je galéjais* ⓪ to jest = *badiner.*

JOSTLE (to, -d) *bousculer :* jostled in the crowd = *bousculé dans la foule* ☠ *je ne veux pas vous bousculer* = I don't want to rush you.

JOT DOWN (to, -ted) *prendre note de :* to jot down a phone number = *prendre note d'un numéro de téléphone* ⓪ to note = *noter.*

JOURNAL (n) **1/** *journal (m) :* she kept a journal during her trip = *elle a tenu un journal pendant son voyage*
☠ *lire le journal* = to read the newspaper
— *journal parlé* = news broadcast
— *journal intime* = diary

2/ *revue (f) :* medical journal = *revue médicale* ☠ → revue.

JOURNALISM (n) *journalisme (m)* ⓪ newspaper = *journal* **JOURNALIST** (n) *journaliste (m, f) :* a print journalist = *un journaliste de la presse écrite* ⓪ reporter = ←.

JOURNEY (n) *trajet (m) :* a day's journey = *un trajet d'une journée*
☠ *c'est sur notre trajet* = it's on our way
— *un trajet de deux heures* = a two-hour ride.

JOY (n) *joie (f) :* what a joy to see you again ! = *quelle joie de vous revoir !* ⓪ glee = *allégresse* = mirth ≠ grief = *douleur*
to jump for joy = *sauter de joie*
☠ *se faire une joie de* = to be pleased to.

JOYOUS (adj) *joyeux, -euse :* a joyous evening = *une joyeuse soirée* = jolly (GB) ⓪ joyful = *réjoui*, jovial = ←, jubilant = *qui jubile*
☠ *joyeux Noël* = merry Christmas
— *un joyeux luron/drille* = a gay blade.

JOYRIDE (n) *partie (f) de plaisir :* this work's no joyride = *ce travail n'est pas une partie de plaisir.*

JUDGE (n) *juge (m) :* she's Supreme Court judge = *elle est juge à la Cour suprême* ⓪ jury = ←, lawyer = *avocat*, witness = *témoin*, bench = *parquet*
to be a good judge of (character) = *se tromper rarement sur (la personnalité des gens)*
you be the judge = *je vous laisse juge.*

JUDGE (to, -d) **1/** *juger :* to judge a case = *juger une affaire* ⓪ to try = *traduire en justice* **2/** *juger :* you're judging her too severely = *vous la jugez trop sévèrement*
judge for yourself ! = *à vous de juger !/jugez (par) vous-même !*
judging by (her attitude) = *à en juger par (son attitude)*
☠ *juger une situation* = to size up a situation
— *je ne juge pas ça utile* = I don't think it's useful
— *il sera jugé la semaine prochaine* = he'll be tried next week.

JUDGMENT (n) *jugement (m) :* you showed poor judgment = *vous avez montré peu de jugement*
don't pass judgment = *ne portez pas de jugement*
in my judgment (he's the best candidate) = *selon moi (c'est le meilleur candidat)* ⓪ in my opinion = *à mon avis*
Judgment Day = *le jour du Jugement dernier*
☠ *passer en jugement* = to stand trial
— *rendre un jugement* = to pass sentence.

JUDICIOUS (adj) *judicieux, -euse :* a judicious solution = *une solution judicieuse* ⓪ wise = *sage.*

JUDO (n) *judo (m)* ⓪ karate = *karaté.*

JUG (n) *cruche (f) :* an earthenware jug = *une cruche en* grès ⊕ pitcher = *pichet* ☠ *quelle cruche !* = what a numbskull !/schlemiel !

JUGGLE (to, -d) *jongler* **JUGGLER** (n) *jongleur, -euse.*

JUICE (n) *jus (m)* : orange juice = *jus d'orange*
☠ *jus de chaussette* = watery coffee
— *jus de viande* = gravy.

JUICE UP (to, -d) *gonfler* : to juice up a car = *gonfler un moteur* ⊕ hotrod = *bolide* ☠ → to inflate.

JUICY (adj, -ier, -iest) *juteux, -euse* : juicy orange/gossip = *orange juteuse/potins juteux* ⊕ choice tidbit = *histoire croustillante.*

JUKEBOX (n) *juke-box (m)* ⊕ record = *disque.*

JULY (n) *juillet (m)* → MONTH
the fourth of July = *le 4 juillet* (Independence Day).

JUMBLE (n) *fouillis (m)* : a jumble of clothes on the bed = *un fouillis de vêtements sur le lit* ⊕ hodgepodge = *méli-mélo.*

JUMBO (adj) *géant, -e* : jumbo olives = *des olives géantes* ☠ → giant
a jumbo jet = *un jumbo-jet.*

JUMP (n) **1/** *saut (m)* : a jump in the air = *un saut en l'air* ⊕ leap = *bond*
to give a jump = *sursauter* : she gave a jump when her ex walked into the restaurant = *elle a sursauté quand son ex-mari est entré dans le restaurant*
to have/get the jump on = *prendre le pas sur* : the Japanese are getting the jump on the Americans in the car industry = *les Japonais prennent le pas sur les Américains en matière d'industrie automobile*
jump rope = *corde à sauter* = skipping rope
☠ *faire le saut* = to take the plunge
— *faire un saut à/chez* = to run over to
2/ *hausse (f) brutale* : a jump in prices = *une hausse brutale des prix* ⊕ hike = *forte hausse* ≠ drop = *chute.*

JUMP (to, -ed) **1/** *sauter* : she jumped from the train = *elle a sauté du train* ⊕ to leap = *bondir*
to jump at (the chance) = *sauter sur (l'occasion)* ⊕ to seize = *saisir*
to jump down to/over to = *faire un saut à* : I'm going to jump down to the bank = *je vais faire un saut à la banque* ⊕ to skip over to = *faire un tour à*
to jump on s.o. = *sauter sur qqn* : don't jump on me, it's not my fault = *ne me saute pas dessus, ce n'est pas ma faute* → TO LAMBAST
to jump over (a fence) = *sauter par-dessus (une barrière)*
it's jumping (party/place) ! = *c'est vachement animé (soirée/endroit)* ! ⊕ it's swinging ! = *ça bouge !*
☠ *je la saute* = I'm starving
— *sauter une nana* = to lay a broad
— *sauter un repas/une ligne* = to skip a meal/a line
— *faire sauter un pont* = to blow up a bridge
2/ *faire un bond* : prices jumped = *les prix ont fait un bond* ⊕ to shoot up = *monter en flèche*

3/ *sursauter* : I jumped when I saw him = *j'ai sursauté quand je l'ai vu* ⊕ to be taken aback = *avoir le souffle coupé.*

JUMPING-OFF PLACE/POINT (n) *point (m) de départ.*

JUMPY (adj, -ier, -iest) *qui est un paquet de nerfs* : if she didn't smoke so much, she would not be so jumpy = *si elle ne fumait pas tant, elle ne serait pas un tel paquet de nerfs* ⊕ nervous = *nerveux.*

JUNCTURE (n) **at this juncture** = *dans la conjoncture actuelle* ⊕ at this stage of the game = *dans l'état actuel des choses.*

JUNE (n) *juin (m)* → MONTH.

JUNGLE (n) *jungle (f)* ⊕ swamp = *marécage.*

JUNIOR (n) **1/** *junior (m)* : clothes for juniors = *vêtements pour les juniors* **2/** *étudiant, -e de troisième année* ⊕ sophomore = *étudiant de seconde année*
one's junior = *le cadet de qqn* : she's ten years his junior = *elle est sa cadette de dix ans*
John Smith junior = *John Smith fils* ≠ senior = *père*
junior executive = *jeune cadre.*

JUNK (n inv) **1/** *de la cochonnerie* : her watch/the film is junk = *sa montre/le film, c'est de la cochonnerie* **2/** *cochonneries (f pl)* : the store sells a lot of junk = *ce magasin vend un tas de cochonneries* ⊕ crap = *merdes* ☠ *dire des cochonneries* = to talk dirty **3/** *machins (m pl)* : what's the junk on the table ? = *qu'est-ce que c'est que ces machins sur la table ?* ⊕ stuff = *trucs*
junk food = *cochonneries* : kids today eat a lot of junk food = *les enfants mangent beaucoup de cochonneries de nos jours* ≠ health food = *nourriture diététique*
a piece of junk = **1/** *de la cochonnerie* : my watch is a piece of junk = *ma montre, c'est de la cochonnerie* ⊕ a piece of shit = *de la merde* **2/** *machin (m)* : what's this piece of junk on the bed ? = *qu'est-ce que c'est que ce machin sur le lit ?* ⊕ thing = *truc.*

JUNK (to, -ed) *bazarder* : I junked my old clothes = *j'ai bazardé mes vieux vêtements* ⊕ to chuck = *balancer.*

JUNKET (n) *voyage (m) aux frais de la princesse* : the Senator went on a junket to China = *le sénateur a fait un voyage en Chine aux frais de la princesse* ⊕ jaunt = *virée.*

JUNKIE (n) **1/** *toxico (m, f), junkie (m, f)* ⊕ pothead = *camé* **2/** *fournisseur, -euse de drogue* ⊕ pusher = *revendeur.*

JUNKY (adj, -ier, -iest) *à la manque* : a junky car = *une voiture à la manque* ⊕ trashy = *de quatre sous.*

JURISDICTION (n) *juridiction (f)* : it's not within my jurisdiction = *ce n'est pas de ma juridiction* ⊕ authority = *autorité* ☠ *juridiction (tribunal)* = court.

JURIST (n) *juriste (m, f)* ⊕ lawyer = *avocat*, solicitor (GB) = *avoué.*

JURY (n, -ies) *jury (m)* : foreman of the jury = *président du jury* ① juror = *juré*
hung jury = *jury bloqué* : the votes of the jurors were six to six ; it was a hung jury = *les votes des jurés étaient six pour et six contre ; le jury était bloqué*
to stack a jury = *sélectionner partialement un jury*
☠ *jury d'un examen* = examining board
— *jury (télé)* = panel (TV).

JUST (adj) *juste* : a just punishment = *une punition juste* ① equitable = *équitable* ≠ unjust = *injuste*

☠ *l'heure/le mot juste* = the right time/word
— *(cette veste) est trop juste* = (this jacket) is too tight
— *tu n'es pas juste* = you're not fair
— *une réponse juste* = an accurate answer

— *à juste titre* = justifiably so
— *ramener les choses à leur juste valeur* = to bring things into proportion
— *le juste milieu* = the happy medium
— *juste retour des choses* = poetic justice.

JUST (adv) **1/** *juste* : that's just what I wanted = *c'est juste ce que je voulais,* it's just ten o'clock = *il est juste dix heures* ① exactly = *exactement* **2/** *tout simplement* : it was just wonderful/thrilling = *c'était tout simplement merveilleux/passionnant* ① really = *réellement* **3/** *juste* : he just drinks water = *il boit juste de l'eau* ① only = *seulement*

☠ *très juste !* = very true !
— *de quoi s'agit-il au juste ?* = what's it about exactly ?

— *chanter juste* = to sing in tune
— *ça a frappé juste* = it hit home

to be just (eating) = *être juste en train de (manger)*
to have just = *venir (juste) de* : we've just eaten = *on vient (juste) de manger* = we just ate
just about = 1/ *quasiment* : I have just about $ 20 = *j'ai quasiment 20 dollars,* he just about agreed = *il était quasiment d'accord* 2/ *faillir* : she just about died = *elle a failli mourir* ① nearly = *presque*
I just can't understand = *je n'arrive vraiment pas à comprendre*
just as = *juste au moment où* : just as I was leaving, he came in = *juste au moment où j'allais partir, il est entré*
just as ... as = *tout aussi ... que* : she's just as rich as I am = *elle est tout aussi riche que moi*
I'd/he'd just as soon = *j'aimerais/il aimerait autant* : I would just as soon go to the seaside this summer = *j'aimerais autant*

aller au bord de la mer cet été
just as well = 1/ *tant qu'à faire* : I'd just as well leave now = *tant qu'à faire, je pars maintenant* 2/ *tout aussi bien* : it's just as well that I didn't tell you before = *c'est tout aussi bien que je ne vous l'aie pas dit avant*
just fine ! = *impeccable !* : five o'clock ? just fine ! = *cinq heures ? impeccable !* ① great ! = *parfait !*
just imagine ! = *tu imagines !* : just imagine how rich they are ! = *tu imagines à quel point ils sont riches !*
just married = *jeunes mariés*
just might = *il se pourrait bien que* : I just might go to Europe this winter = *il se pourrait bien que j'aille en Europe cet hiver*
just missed = *avoir raté de peu* : the car just missed me = *la voiture m'a raté de peu,* I just missed the train = *j'ai raté le train de peu*

just now = *en ce moment* : I don't feel like going just now = *je n'ai pas envie d'y aller en ce moment*
just out (book, film) = *qui vient de sortir (livre, film)*
just over ≠ **under $ 100** = *un peu plus* ≠ *moins de 100 dollars*
just then = *juste à ce moment-là* : he came just then = *il est arrivé juste à ce moment-là* = right then
just think = *imagine un peu* : just think, in a month we'll be married ! = *imagine un peu : dans un mois nous serons mariés !*
just to = *juste pour* : she said that just to make you angry = *elle a dit ça juste pour te mettre en colère*
just wait ! = *attends un peu !*
just when (I was leaving) = *juste quand (je partais).*

JUSTICE (n) *justice (f)* : there's little justice in the world = *il y a peu de justice dans le monde* ≠ injustice = ←
to do justice to (a meal) = *faire honneur à (un repas)*
to do justice to s.o. = *avantager qqn* : this picture doesn't do her justice = *cette photo ne l'avantage pas* ☠ *avantager un candidat* = to favor a candidate

Justice of the Peace = *juge de paix (qui marie les gens = M. le maire)*
☠ *traduire qqn en justice* = to bring s.o. before the court.

JUSTIFIABLY (adv) *à juste titre* : she's justifiably angry

= *elle est en colère à juste titre*
justifiably so = *à juste titre :* she's proud of her children and justifiably so = *elle est fière de ses enfants et à juste titre.*

JUSTIFICATION (n) *justification (f)* ⓌⒹ reason = *raison.*

JUSTIFIED (adj) *justifié, -e :* justified criticism = *critique justifiée* ≠ unjustified = *injustifié*
to be justified in (thinking he was lying) = *avoir raison de (penser qu'il mentait).*

JUSTIFY (to, -ied) **1/** *justifier :* his fears were justified = *ses craintes étaient justifiées* ⓌⒹ to confirm = *confirmer* **2/** *justifier :* nothing justifies the use of torture = *rien ne justifie l'usage de la torture,* I don't have to justify my actions = *je n'ai pas à justifier mes actes* ⓌⒹ to warrant = *légitimer.*

JUVENILE (adj) *juvénile :* juvenile delinquency/delinquent = *délinquance/délinquant juvénile.*

JUXTAPOSE (to, -d) *juxtaposer* **JUXTAPOSITION** (n) *juxtaposition (f).*

KANGAROO (n) *kangourou (m)* ⓪ giraffe = *girafe*
kangaroo court = *tribunal irrégulier* : he was arrested
and tried by a kangaroo court = *il a été arrêté et jugé par
un tribunal irrégulier.*

KAPUT (adj) *kaput* : my car's kaput = *ma voiture est
kaput* ⓪ done for = *fichu.*

KARATE (n) *karaté (m)* ⓪ aikido = *aïkido.*

KEEN (adj, -er, -est) **to be keen on** = *aimer beaucoup* :
she's really keen on rock music = *elle aime vraiment
beaucoup la musique rock* ⓪ to be big on = *raffoler de*
I'm not keen on (going tonight) = *je ne suis pas très
chaud pour (y aller ce soir).*

KEEP (n) **to earn one's keep** = *gagner sa croûte
(en étant nourri et logé par qqn)* : he earns his keep
by doing our gardening = *il gagne sa croûte en faisant notre jardin* ⓪ to earn one's living = *gagner sa*
vie
for keeps = *pour de bon* : he gave me his bicycle
for keeps = *il m'a donné sa bicyclette pour de bon.*

KEEP (to, kept, kept) **1/** *garder* : if you like the book, keep it = *si vous aimez ce livre, gardez-le* ≠ to get rid of =
se débarrasser de **2/** *(se) garder* : milk keeps two days = *le lait se garde deux jours* ⓪ to conserve = *se conserver* ☠ → to guard **3/** *ranger* : where do you keep the Scotch ? = *où est-ce que vous rangez le whisky ?* ☠ →
to tidy

---

to keep abreast of (the news) = *suivre le cours de
(l'actualité)* ⓪ to keep up to date = *se tenir au
courant*
to keep s.o. dangling = *faire mariner qqn* ⓪ to
keep s.o. on tenterhooks = *mettre qqn au supplice*
to keep a diary/the books/a promise = *tenir un
journal intime/les comptes/une promesse*
keep me informed = *tenez-moi au courant* =
keep me posted

to keep (+ ing) = *continuer à/de* : keep talking
I'm listening = *continue de/à parler, je t'écoute*
keep to the right ≠ **to the left** = *tenez votre
droite* ≠ *votre gauche*
to keep s.o. waiting = *faire attendre qqn* : he kept
me waiting for an hour = *il m'a fait attendre une
heure*
that can keep = *ça peut attendre*

---

to keep after s.o. = *être sur le
dos de qqn* : she keeps after the
kids (about their marks) = *elle
est toujours sur le dos des gosses
(au sujet de leurs notes)* ⓪ to
hock s.o. = *tanner qqn*
to keep at = *s'acharner (sur)* :
even if you don't succeed the
first time, keep at it = *même si
vous n'y arrivez pas la première
fois, acharnez-vous*
to keep away from = *ne pas
s'approcher de* : you'd better

keep away from my young sister ! = *je te conseille de ne pas
t'approcher de ma petite sœur !*
keep back ! = *n'approchez
pas !* ⓪ move back ! = *reculez !*
to keep (prices) down =
empêcher (les prix) de monter
keep it down ! = *mets-la en
sourdine !* ⓪ hush ! = *chut !*
to keep from (+ ing) = *empêcher de (+ inf)* : I couldn't keep
her from telling him = *je n'ai
pas pu l'empêcher de le lui dire*

to keep stg from s.o. = *dissimuler qqch à qqn* : why did you
keep his death from me ? =
*pourquoi m'avez-vous dissimulé
sa mort ?*
to keep on (+ ing) = *continuer à/de* : he kept on talking =
il a continué de parler/à parler
⓪ to carry on = *poursuivre*
to keep on about = *ne pas cesser de harceler* : she keeps on
about his drinking = *elle
n'arrête pas de le harceler parce*

qu'il boit trop
to keep out (of) = *ne pas entrer (dans)* : keep out of my room ! = *n'entrez pas dans ma chambre !* ≠ to enter = *entrer*
to keep to o.s. = 1/ *rester tout seul dans son coin* : Peter always keeps to himself = *Peter reste toujours tout seul dans son coin* ⓪ to be a lone wolf = *faire bande à part* 2/ *garder pour soi* : keep the news to yourself = *gardez cette nouvelle pour vous* ≠ to let out = *dévoiler*

to keep together = *garder uni* : it was hard to keep families together during the war = *pendant la guerre, c'était dur de garder les familles unies*
to keep up = 1/ *entretenir* : to keep up one's English/a house = *entretenir son anglais/une maison* ⚠ → to maintain 2/ *continuer* : if the pressure keeps up, I'll crack = *si la tension continue, je vais craquer*, your work's very good, keep it up ! = *votre travail est excellent, continuez !*

= to continue ≠ to stop = *arrêter* 3/ *suivre* : you're walking too fast, I can't keep up (with you) = *vous marchez trop vite, je ne peux pas (vous) suivre* ⚠ → to follow 4/ *tenir éveillé* : the noise kept me up = *le bruit m'a tenu éveillé*
to keep up with = *se tenir au courant de* : I try to keep up with current events = *j'essaie de me tenir au courant de ce qui se passe* ≠ to be out of touch = *ne pas être dans le coup.*

KEEPING (n) **in** ≠ **out of keeping** = *de mise* ≠ *pas de mise* : her dress was in ≠ out of keeping with the occasion = *sa robe était* ≠ *n'était pas de mise (en cette occasion).*

KENNEL (n) *chenil (m)* ⓪ to breed = *élever.*

KENYA (n) *Kenya (m)* **KENYAN** (n, adj) *Kenyan, -e.*

KEPT (adj) *entretenu, -e* : a kept man/woman = *un homme entretenu/une femme entretenue.*

KETTLE (n) *bouilloire (f)* ⓪ teapot = *théière.*

KEY (n) 1/ *clef (f)* : the key to the door/to the problem = *la clef de la porte/du problème* ⓪ key ring = *porte-clefs*, locksmith = *serrurier*
key money = *pas-de-porte*
⚠ *prendre la clef des champs* = to cut out
— *fermer à clef* = to lock
2/ *corrigé (m)* : the key to the exercises is at the end of the book = *le corrigé des exercices est à la fin du livre*

to sing in ≠ **off key** = *chanter juste* ≠ *faux.*

KEY (adj) *clé* : the key problem/personage = *le problème/le personnage clé* ⓪ principal = ←.

KEYHOLE (n) *trou (m) de serrure* : to look/peep through the keyhole = *regarder/lorgner par le trou de la serrure* ⓪ lock = *serrure.*

KEYSTONE (n) *clef (f) de voûte* : the struggle for equal rights is the keystone of feminism = *le combat pour l'égalité des droits est la clef de voûte du féminisme.*

KEY UP (to, -ed) **to be keyed up** = *être sur les nerfs* ⓪ to be uptight = *être crispé.*

KIBITZ (to, -ed) *blaguer* : don't take it seriously, I was just kibitzing ! = *ne prenez pas ça au sérieux, je blaguais !* ⓪ to jest = *badiner* **KIBITZER** (n) *blagueur, -euse* : it's a serious card game, no kibitzers ! = *c'est une partie de cartes sérieuse, pas de blagueurs !*

KICK (n) 1/ *coup (m) de pied* : he gave the dog a kick = *il a donné un coup de pied au chien* 2/ *dada (m)* : tennis is her new kick = *le tennis, c'est son nouveau dada* ⓪ bug = *marotte* 3/ *raison (f) de râler* : what's your kick ? = *pourquoi râles-tu ?* ⓪ gripe = *raison de rouspéter*

for kicks = *pour se marrer* : the teenagers beat up the old man for kicks = *les adolescents ont battu le vieil homme pour se marrer* ⓪ for laughs = *pour rire*
a kick in the ass/in the pants = *un coup de pied au cul/au derrière*

to get a kick out of (cooking/one's grandchildren) = *prendre du plaisir à (faire la cuisine/voir ses petits-enfants)* ⓪ to enjoy = *trouver bien*
to get one's kicks from = *prendre son pied en* : they get their kicks from S-M = *ils prennent leur pied en ayant des rapports sadomasochistes.*

KICK (to, -ed) 1/ *donner un coup de pied à* : the kid kicked the dog = *le gosse a donné un coup de pied au chien* → TO HIT 2/ *râler* : stop kicking ! = *arrête de râler !* ⓪ to gripe = *rouspéter*

I could kick myself ! = *que je suis bête !* ⓪ I could kill myself ! = *je suis à tuer !*

---

to kick about = *râler à cause de* : he's always kicking about my cooking = *il est toujours en train de râler à cause de ma cuisine*
to kick around = 1/ *bourlinguer* : she kicked

around before getting married = *elle a bourlingué avant de se marier* ⓪ to drift = *ne pas se fixer* 2/ *discuter de* : it sounds like a good idea, come over and we'll kick it around = *cela semble être une*

bonne idée, venez et nous en discuterons
to kick in = *donner quelque chose* : we all kicked in to buy her a wedding gift = *nous avons tous donné quelque chose pour lui acheter un cadeau de mariage* ⓪ to shell out = *casquer*
to kick s.o.'s (face/teeth/head) in = *démolir le portrait à qqn* → TO HIT
to kick off = 1/ *donner le coup d'envoi* : they kicked the campaign off with a gala = *ils ont donné le coup d'envoi de la campagne par un gala* 2/ *casser*

sa *pipe* : he kicked off last week = *il a cassé sa pipe la semaine dernière* ⓪ to pass away = *décéder*
to kick s.o. out = *ficher qqn à la porte* : he was kicked out of three schools = *il a été fichu à la porte de trois écoles* ⓪ to oust = *vider*
to kick up = *ruer dans les brancards* : men are finally kicking up and demanding custody of the kids = *les hommes ruent enfin dans les brancards et exigent le droit à la garde des enfants.*

KICKBACK (n) *dessous-de-table (m)* : the mayor got a kickback on the contract = *le maire a touché un dessous-de-table pour le contrat.*

KICKOFF (n) *coup (m) d'envoi* : the kickoff of the campaign = *le coup d'envoi de la campagne* ⓪ launching = *lancement.*

KID (n) *gosse (m, f), mioche (m, f)* (LV) : my sister has four kids = *ma sœur a quatre gosses* ⓪ youngster = *gamin* brat = *sale gosse*
kid brother/sister = *frère cadet/sœur cadette* ≠ elder = *aîné*
to handle s.o. with kid gloves = *prendre des gants avec qqn*
kid stuff = *l'enfance de l'art* : getting him to sign the contract was kid stuff = *ça a été l'enfance de l'art de lui faire signer ce contrat* ≠ like pulling teeth = *la croix et la bannière.*

KID (to, -ded) *blaguer* : I was kidding when I said that = *je blaguais en disant ça* ⓪ to joke = *plaisanter*, to banter = *badiner*
to kid o.s. = *se faire de douces illusions* : you're kidding yourself if you think he'll agree = *tu te fais de douces illusions si tu penses qu'il va accepter* ⓪ to have illusions = *se faire des illusions*
you're kidding ! = *tu blagues !/tu rigoles !* ⓪ **you gotta be kidding !** = *tu parles !*, **you must be kidding !** = *tu veux rire !* → GOSH !
to kid around = *plaisanter* : stop kidding around, will you ? = *arrête de plaisanter, veux-tu ?* ⓪ to jest = *badiner*
(all) kidding aside (tell me what you think) = *blague à part (dites-moi ce que vous pensez)* ⓪ seriously = *sérieusement*
no kidding ! = *sans rigoler !* → GOSH !

KIDNAP (to, -(p)ed) *kidnapper* : to kidnap a diplomat = *kidnapper un diplomate* ⓪ to ransom = *rançonner* **KIDNAP(P)ER** (n) *ravisseur, -euse, kidnappeur, -euse* ≠ hostage = *otage* **KIDNAP(P)ING** (n) *kidnapping (m).*

KIDNEY (n) *rein (m)* (body), *rognon (m)* (food) : veal kidneys = *rognons de veau*, kidney graft = *greffe du rein* ⓪ gallbladder = *vésicule biliaire*
kidney stone = *calcul rénal*
☠ *avoir les reins solides* = to have solid backing.

KILL (to, -ed) 1/ *tuer* : the gang killed a cop = *le gang a tué un flic* = to murder ⓪ to slaughter = *massacrer*, to bump off = *expédier dans l'autre monde*
2/ *ficher en l'air* : lack of money killed their marriage = *le manque d'argent a fichu leur ménage en l'air*, bad acting killed the film = *le jeu minable des acteurs a fichu le film en l'air* ⓪ to ruin = *gâcher* = to spoil
3/ *enterrer* : the Senate killed the bill/the project = *le Sénat a enterré le projet de loi/le projet* ⓪ to veto = *opposer son veto à* ☠ → to bury
4/ *massacrer* : the critics killed the play = *les critiques ont massacré la pièce* ⓪ to pull apart = *démolir* ☠ → to massacre
5/ *tuer* : we killed the afternoon talking = *nous avons tué l'après-midi en bavardant*, I have four hours to kill = *j'ai quatre heures à tuer*
it kills me to (see him drink like that) = *ça me tue de (le voir boire comme ça)*
to kill off = *exterminer* : Hitler wanted to kill the Jews off = *Hitler voulait exterminer les juifs* = to exterminate ⓪ to wipe out = *anéantir.*

KILLER (n) *tueur, -euse* : the killer got away = *le tueur s'est enfui* ⓪ assassin = ←
hired killer = *tueur à gages* ⓪ gunman = *homme de main.*

KILLING (n) *meurtre (m)* : the third killing in the area = *le troisième meurtre dans le secteur* = the third murder in the area
to make a killing = *ramasser le paquet* → RICH.

KILLING (adj) *tuant, -e, crevant, -e* : this work's killing = *ce travail est tuant/crevant* ⓪ grueling = *exténuant.*

KILLJOY (n) *rabat-joie (m)* : everyone wants to go but you, you're really a killjoy = *tout le monde a envie d'y aller sauf toi, tu es vraiment un rabat-joie* ⓪ wet blanket = *bonnet de nuit.*

KILROY (n) **Kilroy was here** = *la petite souris est passée par là.*

KILTER (n) **out of kilter** = *déréglé* : the machine's out of kilter = *la machine est déréglée* ⓪ on the blink = *détraqué.*

KIND (n) *genre (m)* : he's not my kind of guy = *ce n'est pas mon genre d'homme* ⓢ sort = *sorte*
to pay s.o. back in kind = *rendre à qqn la monnaie de sa pièce* ⓢ to return like for like = *rendre la pareille*
kind of = *un peu* : I'm kind of cold = *j'ai un peu froid* ⓢ somewhat = *quelque peu*
☠ *ce n'est pas son genre de faire ça* = it's not like her to do that
— *le genre féminin* = the feminine gender
— *qqch dans le genre de* = stg in the line of
— *avoir bon ≠ mauvais genre* = to be clean-cut ≠ very vulgar.

KIND (adj, -er, -est) **to be kind to (animals/one's in-laws)** = *être bon avec (les animaux)/gentil avec (ses beaux-parents)*
it was kind of you to (send flowers) = *c'était très gentil de votre part de (nous envoyer des fleurs)*.

KINDERGARTEN (n) *jardin (m) d'enfants* ⓢ grammar school = *école primaire*.

KINDLY (adv) *gentiment* : to treat s.o. kindly = *traiter qqn gentiment*
would you kindly (close the door) ? = *voudriez-vous être assez aimable pour (fermer la porte) ?*
☠ *le travail avance gentiment* = the work's coming along nicely.

KINDNESS (n) *gentillesse (f)* : I will always remember his kindness = *je me rappellerai toujours sa gentillesse* ⓢ goodness = *bonté*
to kill s.o. with kindness = *agacer qqn par sa sollicitude* : stop looking after me, you're killing me with kindness = *ne t'occupe pas de moi comme ça, tu m'agaces avec ta sollicitude*.

KING (n) *roi (m)* : long live the king ! = *vive le roi !* ⓢ monarch = *monarque*, pretender = *prétendant*, coronation = *couronnement*, pharaoh = *pharaon*
to live like a king = *vivre comme un roi* → RICH
☠ *travailler pour le roi de Prusse* = to work for beans
— *le roi n'est pas son cousin* = he's really content with himself
— *tu es le roi des cons !* = you're a royal ass !

KINGDOM (n) *royaume (m)* : the United Kingdom = *le Royaume-Uni* ⓢ empire = ←
my kingdom for a horse = *mon royaume pour un cheval*
☠ *au royaume des aveugles, les borgnes sont rois* = everything's relative (talent, etc).

KINGPIN (n) *grand patron (m)* : he's the kingpin of television = *c'est le grand patron de la télévision* ⓢ top man = *grand manitou*.

KINK (n) **to get the kinks out of (a new machine/plan)** = *mettre (une nouvelle machine/un projet) au point* ⓢ to break in = *roder*.

KINKY (adj, -ier, -iest) *bizarroïde* : her husband likes kinky sex = *son mari aime les rapports sexuels bizarroïdes* ⓢ

far-out = *dément*.

KISS (n, -es) *baiser (m), bise (f)* : give me a kiss = *donne-moi un baiser/une bise* ⓢ peck = *bisou*, French kiss = *patin/palot*
kiss of death = *coup fatal* : the Mafia's support was the kiss of death for the candidate = *le soutien de la Mafia a porté un coup fatal au candidat*.

KISS (to, -ed) *embrasser* : kiss me ! = *embrasse-moi !* ⓢ to hug = *serrer dans ses bras*.

KISSER (n) *bouille (f)* : a punch on the kisser = *un coup de poing en pleine bouille* ⓢ mug = *tronche/trogne*.

KIT (n) *kit (m)* : the plane was made from a kit = *l'avion a été construit à partir d'un kit*
first-aid kit = *trousse de premiers soins*.

KITCHEN (n) *cuisine (f)* ⓢ kitchenette = ←, pots and pans = *batterie de cuisine*
kitchen cabinet = *cabinet personnel* ⓢ brain trust = *brain-trust*
(the burglars took) everything but the kitchen sink = *(les cambrioleurs ont) tout (emporté) sauf les murs*
☠ *livre de cuisine* = cookbook
— *la cuisine (politique)* = (political) monkey business/hanky-panky
— *la cuisine française* = French cooking.

KITE (n) *cerf-volant (m)* ⓢ balloon = *ballon*
go fly a kite ! = *va voir là-bas si j'y suis !* → BUZZ OFF !

KITTEN (n) *chaton (m)* ⓢ kitty = *minou*.

KLEPTOMANIA (n) *kleptomanie (f)* **KLEPTOMANIAC** (n, adj) *kleptomane (m, f)*.

KLUTZ (n) *godiche (f)* : what a klutz the new maid is ! = *quelle godiche, la nouvelle bonne !* ⓢ all thumbs = *empoté*.

KNACK (n) *coup (m) de main* : bowling/cooking is easy once you get the knack = *le bowling/la cuisine, c'est facile une fois qu'on a le coup de main*
you have the knack of (getting on my nerves) = *tu as le chic pour (me taper sur les nerfs)*.

KNAPSACK (n) *sac (m) à dos, havresac (m)* ⓢ duffel bag = *paquetage*.

KNEE (n) *genou (m)* ⓢ kneecap = *rotule*
to bring s.o. to his/her knees = *mettre qqn à genoux*
(to get) on one's knees = *(se mettre) à genoux*
☠ *être sur les genoux* = to be dead-tired
— *(le chat est) sur mes genoux* = (the cat's) on my lap.

KNEE-DEEP (adj) *jusqu'aux genoux* (water), *jusqu'au cou* (trouble, debt).

KNEE-HIGH (adj) **to be knee-high (to a grasshopper)** = *être haut comme trois pommes* ⓢ to be pint-sized = *être court sur pattes*.

KNEEL DOWN (to, knelt or kneeled) *s'agenouiller* : she knelt down to pray = *elle s'est agenouillée pour prier*.

KNICKKNACK (n) *bibelot (m)* : Chinese knickknacks = *des bibelots chinois* ⑩ whatnot = *bricole*.

KNIFE (n, -ves)*couteau (m)* : you forgot the knives = *tu as oublié les couteaux* ⑩ jackknife = *canif* = pocketknife
to turn the knife in the wound = *retourner le couteau dans la plaie* = to rub salt in s.o.'s wound
☠ *mettre le couteau sous la gorge de qqn* = to have s.o. over a barrel

— *être à couteaux tirés* = to be at daggers drawn.

KNIGHT (n) *chevalier (m)* ⑩ chivalry = *chevalerie*
☠ *chevalier d'industrie* = hustler
— *chevalier servant* = escort (for a woman).

KNIT (to, -ted or knit) *tricoter* : I don't know how to knit = *je ne sais pas tricoter* ⑩ knitting = *le tricot*, wool = *laine*, stitch = *maille*.

KNOCK (n) *coup (m)* : a knock on the head/door = *un coup sur la tête/à la porte* ⑩ tap = *tape* ☠ → blow.

KNOCK (to, -ed) **1/** *frapper* : someone knocked = *quelqu'un a frappé* ☠ → to hit **2/** *taper sur* : she's always knocking her husband = *elle est toujours en train de taper sur son mari* ⑩ to criticize = *critiquer*

---

don't knock it ! = *ce n'est pas à dédaigner ! :* $ 400 a week ; don't knock it ! = *400 dollars par semaine ; ce n'est pas à dédaigner !* ⑩ it's not to be sneezed at ! = *ne crache pas dessus !*

---

to knock about = *donner des coups à* : she knocks her kids about = *elle donne des coups à ses gosses* → TO HIT
to knock around = *rouler sa bosse* : she knocked around ten years before getting married = *elle a roulé sa bosse dix ans avant de se marier* ⑩ to have been around = *ne pas être tombé de la dernière pluie*
to knock around in = *pour (traîner à) la maison* : I'm keeping these shoes to knock around in* = *je garde ces chaussures pour (traîner à) la maison*
to knock at (the door/window) = *frapper à (la porte/fenêtre)*
to knock down = **1/** *envoyer à terre* : he knocked the guy down = *il a envoyé le type à terre* → TO HIT **2/** *faire tomber* : the bad weather knocked clothing prices down = *le mauvais temps a fait tomber les prix de l'habillement* ≠ to hike up = *augmenter fortement*
to knock off = **1/** *arrêter* : let's knock off at 4 ! = *arrêtons à 4 heures !* ☠ → to stop **2/** *buter* : the gang knocked him off = *le gang l'a buté* ⑩ to gun down = *descendre/flinguer* ☠ → to trip
knock it off ! = *ça va (bien) comme ça !* → BUZZ OFF !
to knock o.s. out = **1/** *se crever* : I knocked myself out shopping all day = *je me suis crevé à faire des courses toute la journée* ☠ → to croak **2/** *se décarcasser* : I knocked myself out trying to help you = *je me suis décarcassé à essayer de vous aider* ⑩ to go to a hell of a lot of trouble to = *se donner un mal de chien pour*
to knock out = **1/** *mettre K.-O.* : he knocked his opponent out* = *il a mis son adversaire K.-O.* → TO HIT **2/** *mettre K.-O.* : all that tennis playing knocked me out = *j'ai tellement joué au tennis que ça m'a mis K.-O.* ⑩ worn-out = *exténué*, done in = *vanné* **3/** *en mettre plein la vue à* : her engagement ring knocked them out = *sa bague de fiançailles leur en a mis plein la vue* ⑩ to impress = *impressionner*
to knock over = *renverser* : the car knocked the child over = *la voiture a renversé l'enfant* ☠ → to spill
to knock s.o. up = **1/** *engrosser qqn* : she's not the first girl he's knocked up = *ce n'est pas la première fille qu'il a engrossée* **2/** (GB) *réveiller qqn* = to wake s.o. up
to get knocked up = *se faire engrosser*.

KNOCKOUT (n) *K.-O. (m)* : the match ended in a knockout = *le match s'est terminé par un K.-O.*
a knockout = *du tonnerre* : his second wife's a knockout = *sa seconde femme est du tonnerre* ⑩ a dream = *une splendeur*.

KNOT (n) *nœud (m)* ⑩ string = *ficelle*
to tie the knot = *se mettre la corde au cou* ⑩ to take the plunge = *faire le plongeon*
☠ *le nœud du problème* = the core of the matter
— *nœud papillon* = bow tie.

KNOW (n) **in the know** = *au parfum* : ask Harry, he's in the know = *demande à Harry, il est au parfum* ⑩ to be on the in = *être dans le secret des dieux*.

KNOW (to, knew, known) *connaître (s.o., place)*, *savoir (stg, knowledge)*

— do you **know**	her family ? New York ? that restaurant ?	= est-ce que vous **connaissez**	sa famille ? New York ? ce restaurant ?
— do you **know**	if she'll come ? English ? how to drive ?	= est-ce que vous **savez**	si elle viendra ? (parler) l'anglais ? conduire ?

I didn't know what hit me ! = ça m'a fichu un coup ! ⓒ I was taken aback ! = j'en ai eu le souffle coupé !
I didn't know what to expect ! = je ne savais pas à quoi m'en tenir !
don't I know ! = je suis payé pour le savoir ! ⓒ you can say that again ! = à qui le dites-vous !
she doesn't know whether she's coming or going = elle ne sait plus où donner de la tête
do you know anything about it ? = est-ce que vous savez quelque chose à ce sujet ?, no, I know nothing about it = non, je n'en sais rien
how should I know ? = comment voulez-vous que je sache ?
you know where you can go ! = va te faire voir ! → BUZZ OFF !

to know how to = savoir : do you know how to drive ? = est-ce que vous savez conduire ?
he knows his (wines) = il s'y connaît en (vins)
you know what I mean ? = vous voyez ce que je veux dire ?
he doesn't know what it's (all) about = il ne sait pas de quoi il retourne ≠ he knows the score = il connaît la musique
you don't know what you're talking about = vous ne savez pas de quoi vous parlez
I knew you when = je t'ai vu naître : don't get so uppity ; I knew you when ! = ne joue pas les snobinards ; je t'ai vu naître !
you know it ! = tu parles ! ⓒ you bet your life ! = et comment donc !
not that I know = pas que je sache

you don't know what you're in for = vous ne savez pas où vous mettez les pieds ⓒ you don't know what you're getting into = vous ne savez pas où cela vous entraîne
(he has so much money) he doesn't know what to do with it = (il a de l'argent) à ne savoir qu'en faire
she ought to know ! = elle est bien placée pour le savoir !
what do you know ! = pas possible ! → GOSH !
what he doesn't know won't hurt him = toute vérité n'est pas bonne à dire ⓒ ignorance is bliss = qui ne sait rien, de rien ne se doute
who knows ! = qui sait ! ⓒ God only knows ! = Dieu seul le sait !

to know about = savoir : I don't want to know about it = je ne veux pas le savoir, I don't know about that = je n'en sais rien
to know stg backwards = connaître qqch comme sa poche (place), connaître/savoir parfaitement : to know Paris/a lesson backwards = connaître Paris comme sa poche/savoir parfaitement une leçon ⓒ to know pat = savoir sur le bout du doigt

to be known for = être connu pour : they're known for their hamburgers = ils sont connus pour leurs hamburgers
to know of = avoir entendu parler de : I don't know the guy personally, but I know of him = je ne connais pas le type personnellement, mais j'en ai entendu parler

☠ je l'ai connu en Italie au printemps = I met him in Italy in spring
— ça se saura = that will get out
— sachez bien que = bear in mind that
— savoir, c'est pouvoir = knowledge is power

— le parti connaît de profonds changements = the party's experiencing deep changes
— savez-vous nager/faire la cuisine ? = can you swim/cook ?

KNOWHOW (n) know-how (m) : American knowhow = le know-how américain ⓒ savoir-faire = ←.

KNOWING (n) **there's no knowing** = on ne peut pas (le) savoir.

KNOWINGLY (adv) sciemment : I didn't lie to you knowingly = je ne vous ai pas menti sciemment ⓒ deliberately = délibérément.

KNOW-IT-ALL (n) monsieur, madame, mademoiselle je-sais-tout : she's a real know-it-all = c'est une véritable mademoiselle je-sais-tout ⓒ wise guy = petit malin.

KNOWLEDGE (n inv) connaissance (f), savoir (m) : little

knowledge of the real world = *peu de connaissance du monde réel*, in spite of all his knowledge, he has no common sense = *malgré tout son savoir, il n'a aucun bon sens*

knowledge is power = *savoir, c'est pouvoir*
(not) to my knowledge = *(pas) à ma connaissance* ⓪ not that I know (of) = *pas que je sache*
without my knowledge = *à mon insu* : he left without my knowledge = *il est parti à mon insu*
☠ *prendre connaissance de* = to become acquainted with
— *faire la connaissance de qqn* = to make s.o.'s acquaintance
— *perdre connaissance* = to faint
— *c'est une connaissance* = he's an acquaintance.

KNUCKLE (to, -d) **to knuckle down** = *s'y mettre* : you'd better knuckle down if you want to pass the test = *tu ferais bien de t'y mettre si tu veux réussir l'examen* ⓪ to slave = *boulonner*
to knuckle under = *mettre les pouces* : management had to knuckle under to unions' demands = *la direction a dû mettre les pouces devant les exigences syndicales* ≠ not to give an inch = *ne pas céder d'un pouce*.

KOOK (n) *farfelu, -e* : she's married to a kook = *elle a épousé un farfelu* ⓪ oddball = *drôle de numéro* **KOOKY** (adj, -ier, -iest) *farfelu, -e* : a kooky idea/person = *une idée/personne farfelue* ⓪ wild = *dément*.

KOREA (n) *Corée (f)* **KOREAN** (n, adj) *Coréen, -enne*.

KOSHER (adj) *kasher* : kosher meat = *viande kasher*
not kosher = *pas catholique* : the deal wasn't very kosher = *le marché n'était pas très catholique* ≠ above-board = *sans équivoque*.

KOWTOW TO (to, -ed) *s'aplatir devant* : kowtowing to the boss won't help any = *cela n'aidera en rien de s'aplatir devant le patron* ⓪ to grovel before = *ramper devant*.

KP (abbr) **on KP duty** = *de corvée de soupe*.

KRAUT (n) *boche (m, f)* ⓪ Jerry = *schleu*.

KUDOS (n pl) *lauriers (m pl)* : she got a great deal of kudos for engineering his campaign = *elle a récolté tous les lauriers pour avoir organisé sa campagne* ☠ *se reposer sur ses lauriers* = to rest on one's laurels.

KU KLUX KLAN (n) *Ku Klux Klan (m)* = KKK.

KUWAIT (n) *Koweït (m)* **KUWAITI** (n, adj) *Koweïtien, -enne*.

KVETCH (n, -es) *râleur, -euse* : what a kvetch you are ! = *quel râleur tu fais !* ⓪ a pain in the neck = *un casse-pieds* **KVETCH** (to, -ed) *râler* : stop kvetching about everything = *arrête de râler pour tout* ⓪ to complain = *se plaindre*, to grouse = *grincher*.

LABEL (n) *étiquette (f), griffe (f) (haute couture)* ⓪ registered trademark = *marque déposée* ☠ *griffe* → claw, *étiquette* → tag.

LABEL (to, -(l)ed) *étiqueter* : he doesn't want to be labelled a revolutionary = *il ne veut pas être étiqueté comme révolutionnaire.*

LABOR = **LABOUR** (GB) (n inv) **1/** *travailleurs (m pl)* : there are problems between management and labor = *il y a des problèmes entre le patronat et les travailleurs* ⓪ workers = *ouvriers* **2/** *main-d'œuvre (f)* : immigrants are cheap labor = *les immigrants sont une main-d'œuvre bon marché*
to be in labor = *être en travail* ⓪ labor pains = *douleurs de l'enfantement*
Labor Day = *fête du travail aux États-Unis (premier lundi de septembre)*
labor leader = *dirigeant syndical*
Labour Party = *Parti travailliste* ≠ Conservative Party = *Parti conservateur*
labor union = *syndicat ouvrier.*

LABOR (to, -ed) *peiner* : they labored for days to find a solution = *ils ont peiné pendant des jours avant de trouver une solution* ☠ → to toil.

LABORATORY (n, -ies) *laboratoire (m)* : language laboratory = *laboratoire de langues* ⓪ lab = *labo.*

LABORIOUS (adj) *laborieux, -euse* ≠ a cinch = *du gâteau.*

LABORSAVING (adj) *qui économise du travail* : laborsaving devices = *des appareils qui économisent du travail.*

LABYRINTH (n) *labyrinthe (m)* ⓪ maze = *dédale.*

LACE (n) *dentelle (f)* : lace panties = *des slips en dentelle.*

LACE (to, -d) **to lace into** = *tancer (vertement)* : he laced into his secretary = *il a tancé (vertement) sa secrétaire* → TO LAMBAST
to lace with = *droguer avec* : to lace a drink with LSD = *droguer une boisson avec du LSD.*

LACK (n) *manque (m)* : a lack of money = *un manque d'argent* ⓪ deficiency = *carence* ≠ excess = *excès*

☠ *(état de) manque* = withdrawal symptoms
— *à la manque* = junky
— *manque de pot* = bad luck.

LACK (to, -ed) **to lack stg** = *manquer (de) qqch* : they lack the money to buy a car = *il leur manque l'argent pour acheter une voiture* ⓪ to need = *avoir besoin de*
to be lacking in (patience) = *manquer de (patience).*

LACKEY (n) *laquais (m)* : the President's lackeys = *les laquais du Président* ⓪ stooge = *valet.*

LACQUER (n) *laque (f)* ⓪ paint = *peinture* ☠ *laque (cheveux)* = hair spray.

LAD (n) *jouvenceau (m), puceau (m)* ⓪ man = *homme.*

LADDER (n) *échelle (f)* ⓪ stepladder = *escabeau* ☠ *à l'échelle nationale* = on a national scale.

LADEN (adj) **laden with (packages)** = *chargé de (paquets)* ⓪ weighed down with = *ployant sous.*

LADY (n, -ies) *dame (f)* : Daddy's talking with a very pretty lady = *papa parle avec une très jolie dame* ≠ gentleman = ← ☠ → dame
ladies and gentlemen = *mesdames et messieurs*
ladies' man = *homme à femmes* ⓪ Don Juan = ←, fast talker = *baratineur,* womanizer = *coureur.*

LADY-KILLER (n) *bourreau (m) des cœurs* = heartbreaker ≠ vamp = ←.

LAG (n) **1/** *décalage (m)* : there's a lag between women's rights and their actual status = *il y a un décalage entre les droits légaux des femmes et leur statut réel* ⓪ gap = *fossé* **2/** *retard (m)* : a lag in production = *un retard dans la production* ☠ → delay.

LAG BEHIND (to, -ged) *être à la traîne (derrière)* : France's GNP lags behind America's = *le PNB de la France est à la traîne derrière celui de l'Amérique* ⓪ to fall behind = *prendre du retard.*

LAID-BACK (adj) *décontracté, -e* : a laid-back way of doing business = *une façon décontractée de faire des affaires* ⓪ cool = ←.

LAKE (n) *lac (m)* : Lake Michigan = *le lac Michigan* ⓪ pond = *mare,* lagoon = *lagune*

go jump in the lake ! = *du balai !* → BUZZ OFF !
💀 *tomber dans le lac* = to go to the dogs.

LAM (n) **to be on the lam** = *être en fuite* : the gangsters are still on the lam = *les gangsters sont toujours en fuite* ⓪ to be at large = *courir toujours.*

LAMB (n) **1/** *agneau (m)* : to raise lambs = *élever des agneaux* **2/** (inv) *agneau (m)* : lamb chops = *côtelettes d'agneau*, leg of lamb = *gigot d'agneau.*

LAMBAST(E) (to, -(e)d) *tirer à boulets rouges sur* : the Senators lambasted the new budget proposal = *les sénateurs ont tiré à boulets rouges sur le nouveau budget qui leur était proposé*

——— GROUP : TO LAMBAST(E) = TIRER A BOULETS ROUGES SUR ———

to admonish = *admonester*	= *faire un sermon à qqn*	**to put s.o. in his place** = *remettre qqn à sa place*
to bawl out = *enguirlander*	**to give s.o. hell** = *faire sa fête à qqn*	**to rebuke** = *morigéner*
to bite/to chew s.o.'s head off = *engueuler qqn comme du poisson pourri*	**to give s.o. a piece of one's mind** = *dire à qqn sa façon de penser*	**to reprimand** = *réprimander*
to blast = *descendre (en flammes)*	**to give it to s.o.** = *engueuler qqn*	**to rip into** = *voler dans les plumes à*
to call s.o. down = *faire des remontrances à qqn*	**to give it to s.o. with both barrels** = *descendre qqn en flammes*	**to scold** = *gronder*
to call s.o. on the carpet = *passer un savon à qqn*	**to give s.o. what for** = *sonner les cloches à qqn*	**to shut s.o. up** = *clouer le bec à qqn*
to chew s.o. out = *tirer les oreilles à qqn*	**to haul/to rake over the coals** = *passer un savon à*	**to snap at s.o.** = *sauter sur qqn*
to chide = *tancer*	**to jump down s.o.'s throat** = *sauter sur qqn*	**to take it out on s.o.** = *passer sa colère sur qqn*
to come down on = *s'en prendre à*	**to jump on** = *sauter sur*	**to take s.o. to task** = *prendre qqn à partie*
to dish it out = *en dire des vertes et des pas mûres*	**to lace into** = *tancer vertement*	**to tear into** = *secouer les puces à*
to fly at = *tomber sur le poil à*	**to lash out at** = *s'en prendre à*	**to tell s.o. a thing or two** = *dire son fait à qqn*
to give s.o. a calling down/a dressing down/a bawling out = *passer un savon à qqn*	**to lay into** = *voler dans les plumes à*	**to tell s.o. off** = *dire ses quatre vérités à qqn*
to give s.o. the dickens = *frotter les oreilles à qqn*	**to let s.o. have it** = *engueuler qqn*	**to upbraid** = *faire des reproches à*
to give s.o. a good talking-to	**to pitch into** = *rentrer dedans*	**to yell at s.o.** = *crier après qqn.*

LAME (adj) **to be lame** = *boiter* : she's always been lame = *elle a toujours boité* ⓪ to be crippled = *être infirme*
a lame person = *un boiteux.*

LAME-DUCK (adj) **lame-duck President** = *Président non réélu, encore en exercice mais sans pouvoir réel entre les élections (novembre) et la prise de pouvoir effective (janvier) par son successeur.*

LAMENT (to, -ed) *déplorer* : I lament the fact that we're not getting along well anymore = *je déplore le fait que nous ne nous entendions plus bien* ⓪ to regret = *regretter* 💀 → to deplore.

LAMENTABLE (adj) *lamentable* → AWFUL.

LAMP (n) *lampe (f)* : bedside lamp = *lampe de chevet* ⓪ lampshade = *abat-jour*, bulb = *ampoule.*

LAMPPOST (n) *réverbère (m)* : the drunkard hit the lamppost = *l'ivrogne est rentré dans le réverbère.*

LAND (n) *terre (f)* : arid land = *terre aride* ⓪ soil = *sol*
a land of milk and honey = *un pays de cocagne*
to see how the land lies = *tâter le terrain* = to see the lay of the land
💀 → earth.

LAND (to, -ed) **1/** *atterrir* : the plane landed at ten = *l'avion a atterri à dix heures* ≠ to take off = *décoller*
to land in (jail) = *atterrir en (prison)* ⓪ to wind up in = *échouer en*
2/ *décrocher* : to land a job = *décrocher un boulot* ⓪ to get = *obtenir*
💀 *décrocher le téléphone* = to pick up the phone
— *vouloir décrocher la lune* = to shoot for the moon
3/ *débarquer* : the Allies landed in 1944 = *les alliés ont débarqué en 1944* 💀 → to disembark.

LANDING (n) **1/** *atterrissage (m)* : a smooth landing = *un atterrissage en douceur* ≠ takeoff = *décollage*
2/ *débarquement (m)* : the landing of the Americans in 1944 = *le débarquement des Américains en 1944* 💀

débarquement (passagers) = disembarkment **3/** *palier (m) :* we live at the same landing = *nous habitons sur le même palier* ⓓ next-door neighbor = *voisin de palier* **the landing beaches** = *les plages du débarquement* **a landing place** = *un point de chute :* to have a landing place in Paris = *avoir un point de chute à Paris* ⓓ *pied-à-terre* = ←.

LANDLADY (n, -ies) *propriétaire (f) (d'un immeuble)* ≠ tenant = *locataire* **LANDLORD** (n) *propriétaire (m) (d'un immeuble)*.

LANDLUBBER (n) *marin (m) d'eau douce* ⓓ sailor = *marin.*

LANDMARK (n) **1/** *événement (m) marquant :* the discovery of the pill is a landmark in women's liberation = *la découverte de la pilule est un événement marquant pour la libération de la femme* ⓓ milestone = *jalon important* **2/** *point (m) de repère :* the lighthouse is a landmark as you enter the harbor = *le phare est un point de repère quand on entre dans le port.*

LANDSCAPE (n) *paysage (m)* ⓓ view = *vue* **landscape painter** = *paysagiste.*

LANDSLIDE (n) **1/** *glissement (m) de terrain* ⓓ avalanche = ← **2/** *raz de marée (m) :* the election was a landslide = *ç'a été un raz de marée électoral* ⓓ overwhelming majority = *majorité écrasante* ☠ *un raz de marée* = a tidal wave.

LANE (n) *allée (f)* ⓓ path = *sentier* ☠ *allée (cinéma)* = aisle (movies) — *allées et venues* = comings and goings.

LANGUAGE (n) **1/** *langue (f) :* to speak a foreign language = *parler une langue étrangère* ☠ → tongue **2/** *langage (m) :* strong/dirty language = *langage violent/grossier* **to clear up one's language** = *châtier son langage.*

LANKY (adj, -ier, -iest) *efflanqué, -e :* a lanky guy = *un type efflanqué* ⓓ slender = *élancé* ≠ chubby = *joufflu.*

LANTERN (n) *lanterne (f)* ⓓ lamppost = *réverbère* ☠ *éclairer la lanterne de qqn* = to enlighten s.o. — *être la lanterne rouge* = to come in last.

LAP (n) **the first** ≠ **last lap (of the race/work)** = *le premier* ≠ *dernier tour (de la course) / la première* ≠ *dernière étape (du travail)* ⓓ the last stretch = *la dernière ligne droite* **to fall into s.o.'s lap** = *tomber tout rôti dans la bouche/le bec de qqn :* what luck ! everything fell into her

lap ! = *quelle veine ! tout lui est tombé tout rôti dans la bouche/le bec !* ≠ to have a rough time of it = *en baver* **to live in the lap of luxury** = *nager dans l'opulence* → RICH

on (my) lap = *sur (mes) genoux :* the cat's on my lap = *le chat est sur mes genoux.*

LAP (to, -ped) *laper* ⓓ to lick = *lécher* **to lap up** = *se délecter de :* she laps up his compliments = *elle se délecte de ses compliments.*

LAPEL (n) *revers (m) de veston :* a red carnation in his lapel = *un œillet rouge au revers de son veston.*

LAPSE (n) *laps (m) de temps :* after a lapse of two years = *après un laps de temps de deux années* ⓓ period = *période* **lapse of memory** = *trou de mémoire.*

LARCENY (n, -ies) *larcin (m)* ⓓ theft = *vol* **petty** ≠ **grand larceny** = *larcin* ≠ *vol qualifié.*

LARGE (n) **at large** = **1/** *qui court toujours :* the killer's at large = *le tueur court toujours* ⓓ on the run = *en cavale* **2/** *dans l'ensemble :* the country at large is for free abortion = *le pays dans son ensemble est pour l'avortement libre* ⓓ on the whole = *en gros.*

LARGE (adj, -r, -st) **1/** *grand, -e :* a large room = *une grande pièce,* your dress is too large = *ta robe est trop grande* ⓓ enormous = *énorme* ≠ tiny = *minuscule* ☠ → great **2/** *gros, grosse (amount) :* a large sum of money/ransom = *une grosse somme d'argent/rançon* ≠ small = *petit* ☠ → big ☠ *ne pas en mener large* = to be scared stiff — *au sens large* = in the broad sense — *large d'esprit* = broad-minded — *la rue est large* = the street's wide — *une interprétation large de la loi* = a loose interpretation of the law.

LARGELY (adv) *dans une large mesure :* my decision largely depends on what he says = *ma décision dépend dans une large mesure de ce qu'il va dire* ⓓ principally = *principalement.*

LARK (n) *alouette (f)* ⓓ swallow = *hirondelle* **to do stg for a lark** = *faire qqch pour se marrer* ⓓ for a laugh = *pour rire* ☠ *il attend que les alouettes lui tombent toutes rôties dans le bec* = he expects everything to fall into his lap.

LASH OUT AT (to, -ed) *s'en prendre à :* the Senator lashed out at the journalist = *le sénateur s'en est pris au journaliste* → TO LAMBAST.

LAST (n inv) *dernier, -ère :* he was the last to leave = *il a été le dernier à partir*

at last = *enfin :* at last, he showed up = *enfin, il s'est pointé* ⓓ eventually = *en fin de compte* ☠ *enfin !* = well, anyway ! **we haven't heard the last of it** = *on n'a pas fini*

d'en entendre parler **you have seen the last of me !** = *vous n'êtes pas près de me revoir !* ⓓ you won't catch me at it again ! = *on ne m'y reprendra plus !*

☠ *le (petit) dernier* = the youngest child
— *le dernier des derniers* = the lowest of the low
— *son premier mari était français, le dernier est* | *anglais* = her former husband was French, the latter's English.

LAST (adj) **1/** *dernier, -ère* : his last wife was French = *sa dernière femme était française* ≠ first = *premier*
2/ *dernier, -ère* : last Saturday = *samedi dernier* ≠ next = *prochain*

as a last resort = *en dernier ressort/recours* ⑩ **lastly** = *en dernier lieu*
at the last minute = *à la dernière minute*
to be down to one's last cent/penny = *ne plus avoir un centime* → POOR
to be on one's last legs = 1/ *être sur les genoux* ⑩ to be all in = *être pompé*, to be ready to drop = *ne plus tenir debout* 2/ *battre de l'aile* : their business is on its last legs = *leur affaire bat de l'aile* ⑩ to be on the rocks = *avoir du plomb dans l'aile*
the last ten years (have been very difficult) = *les dix dernières années (ont été très difficiles)*
to get last licks = *avoir qqn au tournant* : he's got me cornered

now but I'll get last licks = *il a réussi à me coincer, mais je l'aurai au tournant* ⑩ to get one's in = *avoir sa vengeance*
to have a last fling = *faire la java (avant de partir, de se marier, etc.)* ⑩ to paint the town red = *faire la bringue*
to have the last laugh = *rire le dernier* : I'll have the last laugh = *c'est moi qui rirai le dernier*
to have the last word = *avoir le dernier mot*
last name = *nom de famille*
last night = 1/ *hier soir* : I saw him last night = *je l'ai vu hier soir* ≠ tomorrow night = *demain soir* 2/ *cette nuit* : I slept well last night = *j'ai bien dormi cette nuit*
the last time = *la dernière*

fois : when was the last time you saw him ? = *quand l'as-tu vu pour la dernière fois ?*
last week/month = *la semaine dernière/le mois dernier*
last will and testament = *les dernières volontés* ⑩ will = *testament*
next to last = *avant-dernier* : we were next to last in line = *nous étions avant-derniers dans la file*
that's the last straw (that broke the camel's back) ! = *c'est la goutte d'eau qui fait déborder le vase !*
the last word = *le dernier cri* : it's the last word in women's fashion = *c'est le dernier cri en matière de mode féminine*

☠ *mettre la dernière main* = to put the finishing touches
— *ces derniers temps* = lately
— *dernier délai* = at the latest | — *je ne suis pas tombé de la dernière pluie* = I wasn't born yesterday
— *(alcoolique) au dernier degré* = an inveterate (alcoholic).

LAST (adv) **1/** *pour la dernière fois* : when did you see her last ? = *quand l'avez-vous vue pour la dernière fois ?* ≠ first = *d'abord* **2/** *en dernier* : he arrived last = *il est arrivé en dernier*

he who laughs last laughs longest = *rira bien qui rira le dernier* | **last but not least** = *dernière chose, mais pas la moindre.*

LAST (to, -ed) *durer* : her new affair won't last = *sa nouvelle aventure ne durera pas* ⑩ to continue = *continuer* ≠ to end = *se terminer*
to last for = *durer* : their marriage lasted for ten years = *leur mariage a duré dix ans.*

LASTING (adj) *durable* : a lasting love affair = *une liaison durable* ≠ ephemeral = *éphémère.*

LASTLY (adv) *en dernier lieu* : lastly, let me thank you all = *en dernier lieu, laissez-moi vous remercier tous* ≠ first off = *en premier lieu.*

LATCH (n, -es) *loquet (m)* ⑩ lock = *serrure.*

LATCH ONTO (to, -ed) *s'accrocher à* : she latched onto her husband's arm = *elle s'est accrochée au bras de son mari.*

LATE (adj, -r, -st) **1/** *en retard* : why are you so late ? = *pourquoi êtes-vous tellement en retard ?* ⑩ tardy ≈ *un peu en retard* ≠ on time = *à l'heure* **2/** *feu, -e* : my late husband = *feu mon mari*

to be in one's late fifties = *approcher de la (soixantaine)* **in the late (sixteenth century)** = *à la fin du (seizième siècle)*	**to keep late hours** = *être couche-tard* **late riser** = *lève-tard* ⓓ **night owl** = *oiseau de nuit* **in the late afternoon** = *tard dans l'après-midi.*

LATE (adv) **1/** *en retard* : he arrived late = *il est arrivé en retard*, the train left late = *le train est parti en retard* ≠ ahead of time = *en avance* **2/** *tard* : I went to bed late = *je suis allé me coucher tard* ≠ early = *tôt*

it's getting late = *il se fait tard* **it's too late now** = *c'est trop tard maintenant* ⓓ **what's done is done** = *ce qui est fait est fait*	**to sleep late** = *faire la grasse matinée* ≠ **to get up early** = *se lever tôt.*

LATELY (adv) *dernièrement* : I've been tired lately = *j'ai été fatigué dernièrement* ⓓ recently = *récemment.*

LATENT (adj) *latent, -e* : latent hostility = *une hostilité latente* ⓓ dormant = *en sommeil*
a latent homosexual = *un homosexuel qui s'ignore.*

LATER (adv) *plus tard* : I'll do it later = *je le ferai plus tard* ⓓ in a little while = *dans un moment*
later on = *plus tard* : we'll have kids later on = *nous aurons des gosses plus tard*
see you later ! = *à tout à l'heure !* ⓓ bye-bye ! = *salut !*

LATEST (n) **at the latest** = *au plus tard* : I'll call you Friday at the latest = *je vous appellerai vendredi au plus tard* ≠ at the earliest = *au plus tôt*
have you heard the latest ? = *tu connais la dernière ?*

LATEST (adj) **the latest fashion** = *la dernière mode*
the latest thing = *le dernier cri.*

LATIN (n, adj) *latin, -e* : to study Latin = *étudier le latin*
☠ *j'y perds mon latin* = I can't make head or tail of it.

LATIN AMERICA (n) *Amérique (f) latine*	
Argentina = *Argentine* **Bolivia** = *Bolivie* **Brazil** = *Brésil* **Chile** = *Chili* **Colombia** = *Colombie* **Costa Rica** = ← **Cuba** = ← **Ecuador** = *Équateur* **Guatemala** = ←	**Guyana** = *Guyane* **Honduras** = ← **Mexico** = *Mexique* **Nicaragua** = ← **Panama** = ← **Paraguay** = ← **Peru** = *Pérou* **El Salvador** = *Salvador* **Uruguay** = ← **Venezuela** = ←

LATTER (n) *le second, la seconde, le dernier, la dernière* : she likes swimming and tennis but prefers the latter = *elle aime la natation et le tennis mais elle préfère le second*, John and Jim are brothers ; the former's a teacher and the latter's a businessman = *John et Jim sont frères : le premier est professeur et le second/le dernier, homme d'affaires.*

LAUGH (n) *rire (m)* : a loud laugh = *un rire bruyant* ⓓ chuckle = *petit rire* ≠ sob = *sanglot*
for a laugh/for laughs = *pour rire* ⓓ for a joke = *pour rigoler*
the laugh's on (me) = *c'est (moi) qui fais les frais de la plaisanterie.*

LAUGH (to, -ed) *rire, rigoler* : he said something funny and I laughed = *il a dit quelque chose de drôle et j'ai ri/rigolé* ⓓ to crack up = *se tordre de rire*, to giggle = *rire bêtement* ≠ to cry = *pleurer*
don't make me laugh ! = *laisse-moi rire !* ⓓ you gotta be kidding ! = *tu parles !*
that's nothing to laugh about = *il n'y a pas de quoi rire* = **that isn't anything to laugh about**
to laugh at s.o. = *se moquer de qqn* : don't laugh at me = *ne te moque pas de moi* = to make fun of s.o. ⓓ to scoff at = *se railler de*
what are you laughing at ? = *de quoi/pourquoi riez-vous ?*
to laugh off = *écarter en riant* : he laughed the criticism off = *il a écarté la critique en riant* ≠ to take to heart = *prendre à cœur*
☠ *tu rigoles !* = like fun !
— *pour rigoler* = for fun
— *sans rigoler !* = no kidding !
— *et je ne rigole pas !* = I mean business !

LAUGHABLE (adj) *risible* : a laughable salary = *un salaire risible* ⓓ ridiculous = *ridicule*, farcical = *grotesque.*

LAUGHINGSTOCK (n) *risée (f)* : he was the laughingstock of the office = *il a été la risée de tout le bureau.*

LAUGHTER (n) *rire (m)* : children's laughter = *le rire des enfants*
to burst into laughter = *éclater de rire* ⓓ to crack up = *se marrer.*

LAUNCH (to, -ed) *lancer* : to launch a campaign = *lancer*

une campagne ⓪ to kick off = *donner le coup d'envoi* ☠ *lancer qqch* = to hurl/to toss stg
— *lancer des bombes* = to drop bombs.

LAUNCHING (n) *lancement (m)* : a successful launching = *un lancement réussi*
launching pad = *aire de lancement.*

LAUNDRY (n, -ies) **1/** *blanchisserie (f)* (place) ⓪ Laundromat = *laverie*, laundress = *blanchisseuse*, dry cleaning = *nettoyage à sec*, hamper = *panier à linge* **2/** *linge (m) (sale)* : there's a lot of laundry this week = *il y a beaucoup de linge sale cette semaine* ⓪ to launder = *nettoyer* ≠ linen = *linge propre* ☠ *laver son linge sale en famille* = not to wash one's dirty linen in public.

LAUREL (n) **to rest on one's laurels** = *se reposer sur ses lauriers.*

LAVATORY (n, -ies) *cabinets (m pl)* : where's the lavatory ? = *où sont les cabinets ?* ⓪ comfort station = *lieux d'aisances* ☠ → cabinet.

LAVISH (adj) *somptueux, -euse* : lavish apartment = *appartement somptueux* ⓪ posh = *rupin.*

LAVISH ON (to, -ed) *couvrir de* : he lavished gifts on her = *il l'a couverte de cadeaux.*

LAW (n) **1/** *loi (f)* ⓪ edict = *édit*, statute = *statut*
to break ≠ **to enforce the law** = *enfreindre* ≠ *appliquer la loi*
he's a law into himself = *il obéit à sa propre loi*
the law of diminishing returns = *la loi des rendements décroissants*
the law of the jungle = *la loi de la jungle*
the law of the land = *les lois du pays*
to lay down the law = *faire la loi* : he lays down the

law at home = *chez lui il fait la loi* ⓪ to rule the roost = *mener le jeu*
to maintain law and order = *maintenir l'ordre public*
to pass a law = *voter/passer une loi* : they passed the law = *ils ont voté la loi/la loi est passée*
to run afoul of the law = *se mettre hors la loi*
to take the law into one's own hands = *se faire justice soi-même*
there's no law against it = *ce n'est pas interdit par la loi*
2/ *droit (m)* : to study law = *faire du droit*, law student = *étudiant en droit*, criminal law = *droit pénal*, law school = *faculté de droit* ☠ → right.

LAW-ABIDING (adj) *respectueux, -euse des lois* : law-abiding citizens = *citoyens respectueux des lois.*

LAWFUL (adj) *légal, -e* : the lawful owner = *le propriétaire légal* ⓪ licit = *licite* ≠ unlawful = *illégal.*

LAWN (n) *pelouse (f)*, *gazon (m)* : lawn mower = *tondeuse à gazon* ⓪ garden = *jardin.*

LAWSUIT (n) *procès (m)* : to bring a lawsuit against s.o. = *intenter un procès à qqn* ⓪ litigation = *litige* ☠ *intenter un procès en divorce* = to institute divorce proceedings
— *faire un faux/mauvais procès à qqn* = to make unjustified criticisms of s.o.
— *le procès s'ouvre jeudi* = the trial starts on Thursday.

LAWYER (n) *avocat, -e* : trial lawyer = *avocat à la cour* ⓪ the bar = *le barreau*, disbarred = *radié de l'Ordre*
to retain a lawyer = *engager un avocat*
☠ *avocat (fruit)* = avocado
— *avocat du diable* = devil's advocate.

LAX (adj, -er, -est) *laxiste* ≠ strict = ←.

LAY (n) **1/** *coucherie (f)* : it was a quick lay = *ç'a été une petite coucherie* ⓪ bang = *coup* **2/** *baiseur, -euse* : she's a great lay = *c'est une bonne baiseuse* ⓪ hot number = *qui a le feu aux fesses*
to see the lay of the land = *tâter le terrain* ⓪ to send up a trial balloon = *envoyer un ballon d'essai.*

LAY (to, laid, laid) *sauter* : he's so horny he'd lay anyone = *il est tellement en manque qu'il sauterait n'importe qui*, she was the first girl he laid = *c'est la première fille qu'il ait sautée* ⓪ to screw = *baiser* ☠ → to jump

---

to be laid to rest = *être porté à sa dernière demeure* ⓪ here lies = *ci-gît*
to get laid = *se faire sauter* : she got laid for the

first time last night = *elle s'est fait sauter cette nuit pour la première fois* ⓪ to make it with s.o. = *s'envoyer qqn*

---

to lay down = *s'étendre* : why don't you lay down for a while ? = *pourquoi ne t'étends-tu pas quelques instants ?* ☠ → to extend
to lay into s.o. = *voler dans les plumes de qqn* → TO LAMBAST
to lay off = *licencier* : to lay off personnel = *licencier du personnel* ⓪ to dismiss = *renvoyer* ≠

to take on = *embaucher*
lay off ! = *fous-moi la paix !* → BUZZ OFF !
to lay it on = *en faire des tonnes* : he was trying to impress my parents and laid it on = *il essayait d'impressionner mes parents et il en a fait des tonnes* ⓪ to give s.o. a snow job = *faire du baratin à qqn*

to lay stg on s.o. = *rejeter qqch sur le dos de qqn* : don't lay your mistakes on me = *ne rejetez pas vos erreurs sur mon dos* ⓪ to blame s.o. for = *reprocher à qqn de*
to lay out = *débourser* : I laid out a hell of a lot of money = *j'ai déboursé vachement d'argent* ⓪ to advance = *avancer*

to be laid out = *être distribué :* their place is nicely laid out = *c'est bien distribué chez eux*

to be laid to = *être attribué à :* the economic crisis is laid to inflation = *la crise économique est attribuée à l'inflation*

to be laid up = *être alité :* laid up with the flu = *alité à cause de la grippe* ⓓ bedridden = *cloué au lit.*

LAY (adj) *profane :* a magazine for the lay public = *un magazine pour le public profane.*

LAYER (n) *couche (f) :* two layers of paint = *deux couches de peinture* ☠ → diaper.

LAYMAN (n, -men) *profane (m, f)* ≠ professional = *professionnel.*

LAYOFF (n) *licenciement (m) :* the strikes resulted in hundreds of layoffs = *les grèves se sont soldées par des centaines de licenciements* ≠ hiring = *embauche.*

LAYOUT (n) *disposition (f)* (apartment, city), *mise (f) en page* (book) ☠ *disposition* → disposition.

LAZE ABOUT/AROUND (to, -d) *paresser* ⓓ to loaf = *flemmarder.*

LAZINESS (n) *paresse (f)* ≠ energy = *énergie.*

LAZY (adj, -ier, -iest) *paresseux, -euse :* lazy students = *des étudiants paresseux* ⓓ indolent = ← ≠ hardworking = *bûcheur*
a lazy bum = *un fumiste* ⓓ goof-off = *tire-au-flanc.*

LAZYBONES (n inv) *fainéant, -e :* he's a lazybones = *c'est un fainéant.*

LEAD (n) **1/** *piste (f) :* the cops have a good lead = *les flics sont sur une bonne piste* ⓓ clue = *indice*
☠ *être sur la piste de qqn* = to be on s.o.'s tracks/trail
— *piste (envol)* = runway
— *piste de ski* = ski slope
2/ *rôle (m) principal :* the lead in the play = *le rôle principal de la pièce* ⓓ star = *vedette*
3/ *avance (f) :* a ten-minute lead = *une avance de dix minutes* ⓓ edge = *avantage* ☠ → advance
to be in the lead = *être en tête*
to follow s.o.'s lead = *suivre l'exemple de qqn*
to take the lead = *prendre la tête*
4/ *plomb (m)* ⓓ alloy = *alliage,* pewter = *étain*
☠ *sommeil de plomb* = heavy sleep
— *ne pas avoir de plomb dans la tête/cervelle* = to be light-headed
— *avoir du plomb dans l'aile* = to go downhill
— *les plombs* = the fuses
— *soldat de plomb* = tin soldier.

LEAD (to, led, led) **1/** *conduire :* I don't know the way, lead me = *je ne connais pas le chemin, conduisez-moi* ☠ → drive
2/ *mener :* what a life we lead ! = *quelle vie nous menons !*
3/ *mener :* his team is leading ours = *son équipe mène la nôtre*
☠ *mener une affaire* = to handle a deal

— *ça ne te mènera pas loin* = it won't get you far
4/ *être à la tête de :* to lead a political party = *être à la tête d'un parti politique*
to be led away by (soldiers) = *être emmené par (des soldats)*
to lead s.o. on = *donner de faux espoirs à qqn :* he always leads girls on = *il donne toujours de faux espoirs aux filles* ⓓ to put s.o. on = *se ficher de qqn*
to lead to = **1/** *amener à :* his remark led me to think that they were splitting = *sa remarque m'a amené à penser qu'ils allaient se séparer* **2/** *conduire à :* his policy led to inflation = *sa politique a conduit à l'inflation* ⓓ to bring about = *occasionner* **3/** *mener à :* where does the road lead to ? = *où mène cette route ?*
to lead to understand = *faire comprendre :* he led me to understand that he was quitting = *il m'a fait comprendre qu'il démissionnait*
to lead up to = **1/** *venir à :* what are you leading up to ? = *où voulez-vous en venir ?* ⓓ to hint at = *laisser entendre* **2/** *conduire à :* the events that led up to rebellion = *les événements qui ont conduit à la rébellion.*

LEADER (n) *leader (m) :* a party leader = *un leader de parti politique* ⓓ head = *chef,* ruler = *dirigeant* **LEADERSHIP** (n) *leadership (m).*

LEADING (adj) *de premier plan :* a leading newspaper/filmmaker = *un journal/cinéaste de premier plan* ≠ minor = *mineur*
leading article = *article de fond*
leading lady ≠ **man** = *principale vedette féminine* ≠ *masculine*
leading part = *rôle principal* ≠ extra = *figurant*
leading question = *question insidieuse* ⓓ tricky question = *question piège.*

LEAF (n, leaves) *feuille (f)* ⓓ fall = *automne*
☠ *être dur de la feuille* = to be hard-of-hearing
— *feuille de paie* = pay check.

LEAFLET (n) *prospectus (m)* ⓓ booklet = *fascicule.*

LEAF THROUGH (to, -ed) *feuilleter :* to leaf through a magazine = *feuilleter un magazine* ⓓ to browse through = *parcourir.*

LEAGUE (n) *ligue (f) :* the League of Nations = *la Ligue des nations* ⓓ alliance = ←
to be in league with = *être de connivence avec* ⓓ to be in cahoots with = *être de mèche avec*
to be in the same ≠ **in a different league** = *être* ≠ *ne pas être de la même force :* as bridge players we're not in the same league/we're in a different league = *nous ne sommes pas de la même force au bridge*

to be out of s.o.'s league = *ne pas faire le poids contre qqn* ≠ to be on equal footing with s.o. = *être sur un pied d'égalité avec qqn.*

LEAK (n) *fuite (f)* : a leak in the intelligence service/pipe = *une fuite dans le service de renseignements/dans le tuyau*
to take a leak = *pisser (un bock)* ⓪ to go to the john = *aller au petit coin*
☠ *prendre la fuite* = to make an escape.

LEAK (to, -ed) *fuir* : the tap's leaking = *le robinet fuit*
to leak out = *transpirer* : the news of their divorce leaked out = *la nouvelle de leur divorce a transpiré* ⓪ to get known = *se savoir* ☠ → to perspire
☠ → to flee.

LEAN (adj, -er, -est) *maigre* : lean meat = *viande maigre* ≠ fat = *gras* ☠ → meager
lean years = *période de vaches maigres* → POOR.

LEAN (to, -ed or leant) *pencher* : the tower of Pisa leans = *la tour de Pise penche* ⓪ to incline = *être incliné*
to lean against (a wall) = *s'appuyer contre (un mur)*
to lean forward ≠ **backward** = *se pencher en avant* ≠ *en arrière*
to lean on s.o. = *se reposer sur qqn* : in times of trouble she leans on her family = *dans les moments difficiles elle se repose sur sa famille* ⓪ to fall back on = *se rabattre sur*
to lean out of (the window) = *se pencher par (la fenêtre)*
to lean towards (the left) = *pencher vers (la gauche)*
☠ *je penche pour (cette solution)* = I'm rather for (this solution)
— *se pencher sur une question* = to examine a question.

LEANING (n) *tendance (f) à pencher vers* : far-right leanings = *tendances d'extrême droite.*

LEAP (n) *bond (m)* ⓪ leapfrog = *saute-mouton*
by leaps and bounds = *à pas de géant* : we're progressing by leaps and bounds = *nous progressons à pas de géant*
leap year = *année bissextile*
☠ *les prix ont fait un bond* = prices have soared
— *saisir une occasion au bond* = to leap at an opportunity.

LEAP (to, -ed or leapt) *bondir* : the cat leaped on the table = *le chat a bondi sur la table*
to leap at (the chance to go to China) = *saisir au bond (l'occasion d'aller en Chine)*
☠ *ça m'a fait bondir* = it made me wild.

LEARN (to, -ed or learnt) *apprendre* : I'm learning French = *j'apprends le français* ⓪ to study = *étudier*
☠ *vous ne m'apprenez rien* = you're not telling me anything
— *ça t'apprendra !* = it serves you right !
— *j'ai appris que ...* = I found out that ...
— *j'apprends à mes enfants à être polis* = I teach/train my children to be polite.

LEASE (n) *bail (m) (baux)* ⓪ rent = *loyer* ☠ *ça fait un bail que ...* = it's been ages since ...

LEASH (n, -es) *laisse (f)* : the dog's leash = *la laisse du chien* = lead (GB) ⓪ muzzle = *muselière*
to keep s.o. on a leash = *tenir qqn en laisse.*

LEAST (n) *le moins* : that's the least you can do = *c'est le moins que vous puissiez faire*
at least = *au moins* : it will take me at least a month = *cela me prendra au moins un mois* ≠ at most = *au plus*
at the (very) least = *au minimum* : at the very least it'll cost a grand = *ça coûtera au minimum mille dollars* ≠ at the most = *au plus*
not in the least = *pas le moins du monde* ⓪ in no way = *en aucune façon*
to say the least = *c'est le moins qu'on puisse dire*
that's the least of my worries = *c'est le cadet de mes soucis.*

LEAST (adj) *moindre* : I haven't the least desire to go = *je n'ai pas la moindre envie d'y aller*
not the least bit (intelligent) = *pas le moins du monde (intelligent)* ⓪ not at all = *pas du tout*
☠ *de deux maux il faut choisir le moindre* = you must choose the lesser of two evils.

LEAST (adv) *moins* : the least expensive book = *le livre le moins cher* ≠ most = *le plus*
least of all = *encore moins* : I don't like my husband's family, least of all his mother = *je n'aime pas la famille de mon mari, et sa mère encore moins*
when least expected = *quand on s'y attendait le moins* ⓪ unexpectedly = *à l'improviste.*

LEATHER (n) *cuir (m)* : patent leather = *cuir verni,* leather shoes = *chaussures en cuir* ⓪ kid = *chevreau*
to be into leather = *donner dans le « cuir »* : not only gays are into leather = *il n'y a pas que les homos qui donnent dans le « cuir »* ⓪ S-M = *sado-maso*
leather bars = *bars « cuir » (sado-maso).*

LEAVE (n) *congé (m),* permission *(f)* (army) : a ten-day leave from the army = *une permission (militaire) de dix jours,* the teacher has a two-week leave = *le professeur a un congé de deux semaines*	
to be on leave = *être en permission* (army)/ *être en congé* **to take leave (of s.o.)** = *prendre congé (de qqn)* →	TO LEAVE **to take leave of one's senses** = *perdre la raison* → CRAZY
☠ *permission* → permission — *donner son congé à qqn* = to give s.o. notice	— *congés payés* = paid vacation.

LEAVE (to, left, left) **1/** *partir* : what time do you want to leave ? = *à quelle heure veux-tu partir ?* ≠ to come = *venir*

☠ *on est bien partis !* (sarcastic) = we're off to a good start !
— *elle est un peu partie* = she's a bit tipsy
— *à partir de (maintenant)* = from (now) on

— *il est parti de rien* = he started from nothing
— *ces taches ne partiront pas* = these spots won't come off/come out

2/ *laisser* : leave me some money = *laissez-moi un peu d'argent*, I would like to leave a message = *je voudrais laisser un message* ☠ → to let
3/ *quitter* : what time did you leave him ? = *à quelle heure l'as-tu quitté ?*, I'm leaving France for good this year = *je quitte définitivement la France cette année* ☠ → to quit

there is/are left = *il reste* : there are ten days/dollars left = *il reste dix jours/dix dollars*

(I) have (two dollars) left = *il (me) reste (deux dollars)*

leave it at that ! = *restons-en là !*
to leave behind = 1/ *laisser derrière* : the long-distance runner left the others far behind = *le coureur de fond a laissé les autres loin derrière lui* 2/ *laisser* : they left the children behind in New York = *ils ont laissé les enfants à New York* ☠ → to let
where did I leave off ? = *où en étais-je resté ?* ① where were we ? = *où en étions-nous ?*
to leave out = *laisser tomber* : why don't you leave the second paragraph out ? = *pourquoi ne laissez-vous pas tomber le deuxième paragraphe ?* ≠ to include = *inclure*

leave (me) out of (it) = *laissez(-moi) en dehors de (tout cela)*
to leave to = *léguer à* : she left all her money to her sister = *elle a légué tout son argent à sa sœur* ≠ to come into = *hériter de*
leave it to me ! = *laisse-moi faire !* ① trust me ! = *fais-moi confiance !*
that leaves a lot to be desired = *ça laisse beaucoup à désirer*
to leave stg (up) to s.o. = *laisser à qqn le soin de* : I'll leave it (up) to you to choose a restaurant = *je vous laisse le soin de choisir un restaurant* ① it's up to you to = *c'est à vous de*

GROUP : TO LEAVE = PARTIR

to be off = *se sauver*
to be on one's way = *s'en aller*
let's beat it ! = *fichons le camp !*
to blow = *se casser*
to clear off = *se faire la malle*
to clear out = *prendre le large*
to cut out = *décamper*
to do a bunk = *prendre la tangente*
to fly = *filer*
let's get the show on the road = *si on mettait les bouts*
to give s.o. the slip = *fausser compagnie à qqn*

to go = *y aller*
to go away = *partir*
to go out = *sortir*
to hightail it = *déguerpir/détaler*
let's hit the road ! = *en route !*
to leave = *partir*
let's get going ! = *fichons le camp !*
I must be going ! = *il faut que j'y aille !*
to pack up and go = *prendre ses cliques et ses claques et partir*

to push off = *mettre les voiles*
to set out = *se mettre en route*
to shove off = *se tailler*
to skedaddle = *se carapater*
to skip out = *plier bagage*
to slip out = *s'éclipser*
to split = *se barrer/se tirer*
to take French leave = *filer à l'anglaise*
to take leave = *prendre congé*
to take off = *filer*
to take a powder = *prendre la poudre d'escampette*
to take to one's heels = *prendre ses jambes à son cou.*

LEBANON (n) *Liban (m)* **LEBANESE** (n, adj) *Libanais, -e.*

LECHER (n) *vicelard, -e* ① dirty old man = *vieux vicieux* **LECHEROUS** (adj) *vicieux, -euse, vicelard, -e* : a lecherous old woman = *une vieille vicelarde* ① licentious = *licencieux* ☠ *vicieux* → vicious.

LECTURE (n) *conférence (f)* : he's giving a lecture on Friday = *il fait une conférence vendredi* ① speech = *discours*, lecturer = *conférencier*

☠ → conference
— *la lecture (d'un livre)* = the reading (of a book).

LECTURE (to, -d) **1/** *sermonner* : stop lecturing me (about my drinking) ! = *arrête de me sermonner (parce que je bois) !* **2/** *faire une conférence* : he lectures at the university = *il fait des conférences à l'université.*

LEDGE (n) *rebord (m)* : the ledge of the window = *le rebord de la fenêtre* ① edge = *bord.*

LEDGER (n) *grand livre* (m) ⑩ balance sheet = *bilan.*

LEECH (n, -es) *sangsue* (f) : she sticks to you like a leech = *c'est une vraie sangsue* ≠ loner = *solitaire.*

LEERY (adj, -ier, -iest) **to be leery of** = *se méfier de* : I'm leery of him = *je me méfie de lui* ⑩ to be suspicious of = *être soupçonneux de.*

LEEWAY (n) **1/** *marge* (f) : it's one o'clock, if the plane leaves at three, we've plenty of leeway = *il est une heure, si l'avion part à trois heures nous avons une bonne marge* ☠ → margin **2/** *liberté* (f) *d'action* : her boss gives her a lot of leeway = *son patron lui laisse une grande liberté d'action* ⑩ a free hand = *les coudées franches.*

LEFT (n) *gauche* (f) : it's on your left = *c'est sur votre gauche* ≠ right = *droite.*

LEFT (adj) *gauche* : my left arm = *mon bras gauche* ≠ right = *droit* ☠ *tu es gauche* = you're clumsy
to be out in left field = *ne pas y être du tout* : if you think she'll sleep with you, you're out in left field = *si tu crois qu'elle va coucher avec toi, tu n'y es pas du tout* ⑩ to be off base = *être à côté de la plaque*
left bank = *rive gauche.*

LEFT (adv) *à gauche* : to turn/to vote left = *tourner/voter à gauche*
☠ *mettre (de l'argent) à gauche* = to put (money) away.

LEFT-HANDED (adj) *gaucher, -ère* : I'm left-handed = *je suis gaucher* ⑩ a lefty = *un gaucher* = a southpaw ≠ right-handed = *droitier*
a left-handed compliment = *un compliment empoisonné.*

LEFTIST (n) *homme/femme de gauche* = left-winger ≠ rightist = *homme/femme de droite* = right-winger
LEFTIST (adj) *de gauche* : leftist ideas = *des idées de gauche.*

LEFTOVERS (n pl) *restes* (m pl) : we're eating the leftovers tonight = *ce soir, nous mangeons les restes.*

LEG (n) *jambe* (f), *patte* (f) (animals) : she has nice legs = *elle a de jolies jambes* ⑩ gams = *guibolles/quilles*, foot = *pied*, calf = *mollet*, bow-legged = *qui a les jambes arquées*
not to have a leg to stand on = *ne rien avoir sur quoi se fonder* ⑩ to be groundless = *être sans fondements*
to pull s.o.'s leg = *mettre qqn en boîte* : I'm not serious, I'm just pulling your leg = *je ne parle pas sérieusement, je te mets en boîte* ⑩ to put s.o. on = *faire marcher qqn*
shake a leg ! = *remue-toi !* ⑩ get a move on ! = *magne-toi !*
to stretch one's legs = *se dégourdir les jambes*
☠ *prendre ses jambes à son cou* = to take to one's heels
— *tenir la jambe à qqn* = to bend s.o.'s ear
— *être dans les jambes de qqn* = to be under s.o.'s feet
— *traiter qqn par-dessus la jambe* = to slight s.o.
— *patte* → paw.

LEGACY (n, -ies) *legs* (m) ⑩ inheritance = *héritage.*

LEGAL (adj) *légal, -e* : is prostitution legal in the US ? = *est-ce que la prostitution est légale aux États-Unis ?* ≠ illegal = *illégal*
legal aid = *assistance judiciaire*
legal expenses = *frais de justice*
legal proceedings = *poursuites judiciaires*
legal separation = *séparation de corps*
legal tender = *cours légal.*

LEGALITY (n, -ies) *légalité* (f) ≠ illegality = *illégalité.*

LEGALIZE (to, -d) *légaliser* : to legalize abortion = *légaliser l'avortement* ⑩ to authorize = *autoriser.*

LEGALLY (adv) *légalement* : they're legally divorced = *ils sont légalement divorcés.*

LEGEND (n) *légende* (f) : Dracula's legend = *la légende de Dracula* ⑩ myth = *mythe* ☠ *la légende (sous les photos)* = the caption (under photographs).

LEGENDARY (adj) *légendaire* ⑩ mythical = *mythique.*

LEGIBLE (adj) *lisible* ≠ illegible = *illisible.*

LEGION (n) *légion* (f) : the Foreign Legion = *la Légion étrangère* ⑩ legionnaire = *légionnaire.*

LEGISLATION (n) *législation* (f) ⑩ law = *loi.*

LEGISLATIVE (adj) *législatif, -ive* : legislative powers = *pouvoirs législatifs* **LEGISLATOR** (n) *législateur, -trice* = lawmaker.

LEGISLATURE (n) *le législatif* ≠ the executive = *l'exécutif* ☠ *une législature* = a term (of Congress).

LEGITIMATE (adj) *légitime* : a legitimate complaint = *une plainte légitime* ⑩ sound = *valable* ☠ *légitime défense* = self-defense **LEGITIMATELY** (adv) *légitimement.*

LEGWORK (n) **to do the legwork** = *faire des démarches* : the journalist had a lot of legwork to do for his article = *le journaliste a dû faire de nombreuses démarches pour écrire son article.*

LEISURE (n inv) *loisir* (m) : the importance of leisure = *l'importance des loisirs* ⑩ spare time = *moments perdus*
at (your) leisure = *à votre convenance* : do it at (your) leisure = *faites-le à votre convenance.*

LEISURELY (adv) *sans se presser.*

LEITMOTIV (n) *leitmotiv* (m) ⑩ motto = *devise.*

LEMON (n) **1/** *citron* (m) : lemon juice = *jus de citron* ⑩ lime = *citron vert*, lemonade = *limonade*, orange = ← ☠ *presser qqn comme un citron* = to milk s.o. dry **2/** *rossignol* (m) : his car's a lemon = *sa voiture est un vrai rossignol* ⑩ a piece of junk = *de la cochonnerie* ☠ *un rossignol (oiseau)* = a nightingale.

LEND (to, lent, lent) *prêter* : I lent him a lot of money/I lent a lot of money to him = *je lui ai prêté beaucoup d'argent* ≠ to give back = *rendre*
to lend itself to = *se prêter à* : the law lends itself to ambiguous interpretations = *la loi se prête à des interprétations ambiguës*
☠ *prêter à rire* = to be laughable
— *prêter le flanc à la critique* = to lay o.s. open to criticism.

LENGTH (n) *longueur (f)* : what's the length of the table ? = *quelle est la longueur de la table ?* ≠ depth = *profondeur*
at length = *en long, en large et en travers* : he told me at length what had happened = *il m'a raconté ce qui s'était passé en long, en large et en travers* ⓓ in detail = *en détail*
☠ *à longueur de (temps)* = all the (time)
— *les longueurs d'un livre* = the boring parts of a book
— *traîner en longueur* = to drag on.

LENGTHEN (to, -ed) *(r)allonger* : to lengthen a skirt = *allonger une jupe* ≠ to shorten = *raccourcir* ☠ *s'allonger* = to lie down.

LENGTHWISE (adj, adv) *dans le sens de la longueur* = lengthways.

LENGTHY (adj, -ier, -iest) *très long, longue* : a lengthy answer = *une réponse très longue* ≠ short = *court.*

LENIENT (adj) *indulgent, -e* : a lenient teacher = *un professeur indulgent* ⓓ tolerant = *tolérant* ☠ → indulgent.

LENS (n, -es) *lentille (f)* : to wear lenses = *porter des lentilles*, the camera lens = *la lentille de l'appareil photo* ☠ *manger des lentilles* = to eat lentils.

LEOPARD (n) *léopard (m)* ⓓ jaguar = ←, cheetah = *guépard*
a leopard doesn't change its spots = *chassez le naturel, il revient au galop* ⓓ once (a thief) always (a thief) = *quand on est (voleur), c'est pour la vie.*

LEPER (n) *lépreux, -euse* **LEPROSY** (n) *lèpre (f).*

LESBIAN (n) *lesbienne (f)* ⓓ dyke = *gouine*, les = *gousse* ≠ fag = *pédale.*

LESS (n) *moins (m)* : I was fired for less = *j'ai été renvoyé pour moins (que ça)*

none the less = *ne... pas moins* : though very rich he's none the less a miser = *bien que très riche il n'en est pas moins avare* ⓓ nevertheless = *néanmoins*	**the less (I eat) the more (I lose weight)** = *moins (je mange), plus (je maigris)* **the less said the better** = *moins on en dit, mieux ça vaut* ⓓ silence is golden = *le silence est d'or.*

LESS (adj) *moins de (choses non dénombrables)* : less coffee/sugar = *moins de café/sucre* ⓓ fewer = *moins de (choses dénombrables)* ≠ more = *plus*

in less than no time = *en moins de rien* : I did it in less than no time = *je l'ai fait en moins de rien* ⓓ in no time = *en un rien de temps* **(I have) less and less (money)** = *(j'ai) de moins en moins d'(argent)* **less talk and more action !** = *assez de paroles, des actes !*	**less ... than** = *moins de ... que* : she has less dough than I thought = *elle a moins de fric que je ne pensais* **nothing/not anything less than** = *pas moins de/que* : he will accept nothing/he won't accept anything less than $ 500 = *il n'acceptera pas moins de 500 dollars.*

LESS (adv) *moins* : drink less and sleep more = *buvez moins et dormez plus* ≠ more = *plus*

I couldn't care less = *je n'en ai vraiment rien à faire* ⓓ I don't give a hang = *je m'en bats l'œil*, a lot I care = *je n'en ai rien à faire*	**less and less** = *de moins en moins* : I'm less and less in love with him = *je suis de moins en moins amoureuse de lui* ≠ more and more = *de plus en plus*	**less than** = *moins que* : she smokes less than I do = *elle fume moins que moi* ≠ more than = *plus que*

☠ *à moins de* = unless — *il était moins une* = it was a close call — *pas le moins du monde* = not in the least — *une heure moins le quart* = a quarter to one	— *au moins* = at least — *des enfants de dix ans et moins* = children of ten and under.

LESS (prep) *moins* : 6 less 4 equals 2 = *6 moins 4 égale 2* = minus ≠ plus = ←.

359

LESSEN (to, -ed) *amoindrir* : it lessened her chances of winning = *ça a amoindri ses chances de gagner* ⓓ to diminish = *diminuer* ☠ *la maladie l'a amoindri* = the illness weakened him.

LESSER (n) **the lesser of two evils** = *le moins mauvais* : as a candidate, he was the lesser of two evils = *c'était lui le moins mauvais des candidats.*

LESSON (n) *leçon* (f) : private lessons = *leçons particulières* ⓓ course = *cours*, fluency level = *cours de per-* fectionnement (langues), intermediate level = *cours de niveau moyen*, beginners' lessons = *cours de débutants* **I learned my lesson !** = *ça m'a donné une (bonne) leçon !* ⓓ I should have known better = *j'aurais dû le savoir*
to teach s.o. a lesson = *donner une leçon à qqn.*

LEST (conj) *de crainte de* : he didn't say what he thought lest he should be fired = *il n'a pas dit ce qu'il pensait de crainte d'être renvoyé.*

LET (to, let, let) *laisser* : he let me do it = *il m'a laissé le faire*, let me see what he wants = *laissez-moi voir ce qu'il veut* ⓓ to permit = *permettre* ≠ to prevent from = *empêcher de*

---

let (me/her) be ! = *laisse (-moi/-la) tranquille !*
to let believe = *laisser croire* : he let me believe he was single = *il m'a laissé croire qu'il était célibataire*
to let go = 1/ *lâcher* : let me go ! = *lâchez-moi !* ☠ *son cœur a lâché* = his heart went 2/ *relâcher* : the cops had to let the suspect go = *les flics ont dû relâcher le suspect* ≠ to hold = *retenir* ☠ → to release 3/ *licencier* : because of important losses, they let hundreds of workers go = *ils ont licencié des centaines d'ouvriers à cause de pertes importantes* ≠ to hire = *engager*
to let o.s. go = 1/ *se laisser aller* : since her husband's death she's let herself go = *depuis la mort de son mari elle se laisse aller* 2/ *se défouler* : he let him-* self go at the party = *il s'est défoulé à la soirée*
let it go at that ! = *laisse courir !* ⓓ **let it drop !** = *laisse tomber !*, **let it pass !** = *laissez passer !*
to let have = *laisser* : I'll let you have it for two grand = *je vous le laisserai pour deux mille dollars*
to let s.o. have it = 1/ *engueuler* : she was so angry that she let the kids have it = *elle était tellement en colère qu'elle a engueulé les enfants* → TO LAMBAST 2/ *faire sa fête à qqn* : the gangsters let him have it = *les gangsters lui ont fait sa fête* → TO HIT
let me have (some money/ sugar) = *file-moi (de l'argent/du sucre)*
to let s.o. know = *faire savoir à qqn* : let me know if you want to* come = *faites-moi savoir si vous voulez venir* ⓓ to keep s.o. informed = *tenir qqn au courant*
let it ride = *laisse courir pour le moment*
to let slip = *laisser échapper* : he let it slip that she was pregnant = *il a laissé échapper qu'elle était enceinte* ⓓ to drop a hint = *faire une allusion*
let me tell you something = *laissez-moi vous dire quelque chose*
(just) let him try ! = *qu'il essaie (pour voir) !*
to let (room) = *à louer (chambre)*
let's go !/let's eat ! = *allons-y !/ à table !*
let's take the car = *prenons la voiture*

---

to let down = *décevoir* : I'm sorry to let you down again = *je suis désolé de vous décevoir à nouveau* = I'm sorry to disappoint you again
to let s.o. in = *laisser entrer qqn* : they wouldn't let me in = *ils ne m'ont pas laissé entrer*
to let o.s. in for = *aller au-devant de* : you're letting yourself in for a lot of problems = *vous allez au-devant de gros ennuis* ⓓ to be in for = *aller avoir*
to let s.o. in on stg = *mettre qqn au parfum* : let me in on it = *mets-moi au parfum* ⓓ to give s.o. the lowdown = *montrer à qqn le dessous des cartes*
to be let off with = *s'en tirer avec* : he was let off with only a month = *il s'en est tiré avec seulement un mois de prison* ⓓ to get off with = *en être quitte pour*
don't let on that you know = *gardez ça pour vous*
to let out = 1/ *élargir* : I must let my dress out = *il faut que j'élargisse ma robe* ☠ → to expand 2/ *fer-* mer : school lets out for the summer = *l'école ferme l'été* ☠ → to close 3/ *dévoiler* : the papers let out that the Prime Minister had cancer = *les journaux ont dévoilé que le Premier ministre avait un cancer* ⓓ to divulge = *divulguer* ☠ → to disclose 4/ *laisser sortir* : let me out ! = *laissez-moi sortir !*, they let the pupils out at two = *ils laissent sortir les élèves à 2 heures*
that lets me out = *je ne fais pas l'affaire* : if you want someone who types, that lets me out = *si vous avez besoin de quelqu'un qui tape à la machine, je ne fais pas l'affaire*
to let up = *s'arrêter* : do you think the rain will let up soon ? = *croyez-vous que la pluie va s'arrêter bientôt ?* ⓓ to cease = *cesser* ☠ → to stop
without letting up = *sans arrêt(er)* : it's been raining/ I've been working for 10 hours without letting up = *ça fait dix heures qu'il pleut sans arrêt/que je travaille sans arrêter* = without stopping

---

> ☠ *laissez-moi rire !* = don't make me laugh !
> — *laisser tomber qqch/qqn* = to drop stg/s.o.
> — *(ce travail) laisse à désirer* = (this work) leaves a lot to be desired
> — *laissez-moi de l'argent/un message* = leave me

> some money/a message
> — *laisser entendre que* = to hint that
> — *il ne se laisse pas faire* = he's no pushover
> — *il a laissé les enfants à New York* = he left the kids behind in New York.

LETDOWN (n) *déception (f)* : not getting the part was a letdown = *ç'a été une déception de ne pas avoir le rôle* ☠ → deception.

LETHAL (adj) *mortel, -elle* : a lethal blow = *un coup mortel* ⓓ fatal = ← ☠ → mortal.

LETHARGIC (adj) *léthargique* ⓓ apathetic = *apathique*.

LETTER (n) **1/** *lettre (f)* : a registered letter = *une lettre recommandée* ⓓ letter box = *boîte aux lettres*, postcard = *carte postale*, airmail = *par avion*, letterhead = *en-tête*, stationery store = *papeterie*
to the letter = *à la lettre/au pied de la lettre* : I followed your instructions to the letter = *j'ai suivi vos instructions à la lettre/au pied de la lettre*

affectionately = *affectueusement*	**love and kisses** = *grosses bises*
(best) regards = *(bien) amicalement*	**respectfully** = *veuillez agréer l'expression de mes sentiments respectueux*
(my) best wishes = *(mes) amitiés*	
cordially = *cordialement*	**yours faithfully** = *recevez mes salutations distinguées*
kindest regards = *croyez à l'expression de mes meilleurs sentiments*	**yours truly** = *veuillez agréer l'expression de mes sentiments distingués* = **sincerly yours**
love = *je t'embrasse* = **fondly**	

2/ *lettre (f)* : 26 letters in the alphabet = *26 lettres dans l'alphabet*

☠ *passer comme une lettre à la poste* = to go smoothly
— *être (féministe) avant la lettre* = to be an early (feminist).

LETTERS (n pl) **a man/woman of letters** = *un homme/une femme de lettres.*

LETTUCE (n) *laitue (f)* ⓓ tomato = *tomate.*

LETUP (n) *relâche (f)* : there has been no letup in the rise of inflation = *l'inflation a progressé sans relâche* ⓓ stop = *arrêt* ☠ *relâche ce soir* = no performance tonight.

LEVEL (n) *niveau (m)* : the house is on two levels = *la maison est sur deux niveaux*, the lowest level of prices = *le niveau des prix le plus bas*

to be on a level with = *être au niveau de* : her work isn't on a level with that of the other secretaries = *son travail n'est pas au niveau de celui des autres secrétaires* ≠ to be no match for = *ne pas faire le poids contre*
are you on the level ? = *vous parlez sérieusement ?* ⓓ really ? = *vraiment ?*
on the level = *tout ce qu'il y a de plus sérieux* : you can trust him, he's on the level = *vous pouvez lui faire confiance, il est tout ce qu'il y a de plus sérieux*, his offer's on the level = *son offre est tout ce qu'il y a de plus sérieuse* ⓓ aboveboard = *sans équivoque*
to do one's level best = *faire de son mieux* ⓓ to do one's utmost = *faire tout son possible*
on the same ≠ **on a different level** = *au même niveau* ≠ *à un niveau différent*
☠ *niveau de vie* = standard of living.

LEVEL (adj) *nivelé, -e* : the ground's level = *le sol est nivelé* ⓓ even = *égal*
to be level with = *être au niveau de* : the pool's level with the ground = *la piscine est au niveau du sol* ⓓ to be even with = *être au ras de*
in a level voice = *d'une voix calme.*

LEVEL (to, -led) *raser* : to level a city = *raser une ville*
to level off = *plafonner* : inflation is levelling off = *l'inflation plafonne* ⓓ to stabilize = *se stabiliser*
to level with s.o. = *être franc avec qqn* ⓓ not to pull punches = *ne pas y aller avec le dos de la cuiller*
☠ → to raze.

LEVEL-HEADED (adj) *pondéré, -e* : a level-headed guy = *un type pondéré* ≠ impulsive = *impulsif.*

LEVER (n) *levier (m)* ⓓ controls = *commandes.*

LEVERAGE (n) *prise (f)* : I know he cheated on his expense account and I now have a lot of leverage on him = *je sais qu'il trichait sur ses notes de frais et j'ai maintenant une bonne prise sur lui* ☠ → plug.

LEWD (adj) *lubrique* : lewd songs = *des chansons lubriques* ⓓ licentious = *licencieux*, lascivious = *lascif.*

LIABILITIES (n pl) *passif (m)* : the liabilities of the company = *le passif de la société* ≠ assets = *actif.*

LIABLE (adj) **to be liable to** = *risquer de* : they're liable to come late = *ils risquent d'arriver tard* ⓓ they are likely to come late = *il est vraisemblable qu'ils arriveront tard.*

LIAISON (n) *liaison (f)* : she's having a liaison with her boss = *elle a une liaison avec son patron* ⓓ affair = *aventure*
liaison officer = *officier de liaison.*

LIAR (n)*menteur, -euse* : what a liar you are ! = *que tu es menteur !*

LIBEL (n) *diffamation* (f) : to sue s.o. for libel = *attaquer qqn en diffamation* ⟳ slander = *calomnie.*

LIBERAL (n)*libéral, -e* ≠ reactionary = *réactionnaire.*

LIBERAL (adj)*libéral, -e* : a liberal regime = *un régime libéral* ≠ totalitarian = *totalitaire*
liberal arts = *les arts libéraux*
☠ *personnes exerçant une profession libérale* = professional people.

LIBERATE (to, -d) *libérer* : Paris was liberated on the 25th of August 1944 = *Paris a été libéré le 25 août 1944*
☠ *libérer le passage* = to clear the way
— *je ne peux pas me libérer ce soir* = I can't get free this evening
— *libérer un prisonnier* = to release/to free a prisoner
— *libérer une chambre* = to vacate a room
— *libérer (de l'armée)* = to discharge.

LIBERATED (adj) *libéré, -e* : there are few liberated men/women = *il y a peu d'hommes libérés/de femmes libérées.*

LIBERATION (n) *libération* (f) : men's liberation = *la libération des hommes* ≠ enslavement = *asservissement*
☠ *en libération conditionnelle* = on parole
— *libération (de l'armée)* = discharge.

LIBERATOR (n) *libérateur, -trice* ≠ conqueror = *conquérant.*

LIBERTY (n, -ies) *liberté* (f) : I took the liberty of opening your mail = *j'ai pris la liberté d'ouvrir votre courrier*
at liberty to (do what you want) = *libre de (faire ce que vous voulez)*
liberty, equality, fraternity = *liberté, égalité, fraternité*
☠ *remettre en liberté* = to set free
— *en liberté provisoire* = out on bail
— *liberté de la presse/de parole* = freedom of the press/of speech
— *en liberté conditionnelle* = on parole.

LIBRARY (n, -ies) *bibliothèque* (f) ⟳ librarian = *bibliothécaire* ☠ *librairie* = bookstore.

LICENSE (n) *licence* (f) (business), *permis* (f) (driving, hunting), *bans* (m pl) (marriage) = licence (GB)
license plate = *plaque d'immatriculation* = number plate (GB)

☠ *permis* → permit
— *licence de lettres* = BA degree (in literature).

LICENTIOUS (adj) *licencieux, -euse* : licentious writings = *des écrits licencieux* ⟳ dissolute = *dissolu.*

LICK (to, -ed) **1/** *lécher* : the dog licked my hand = *le chien m'a léché la main* **2/** *flanquer une piquette à* : their team licked ours = *leur équipe nous a flanqué une piquette* ⟳ to give a beating = *flanquer une raclée à,* to cream = *écraser*
if you can't lick 'em, join 'em = *il faut savoir hurler avec les loups* ⟳ you can't fight city hall = *on ne peut se battre contre les moulins à vent.*

LICKING (n) **1/** *piquette* (f) : their team gave ours a good licking = *leur équipe nous a flanqué une bonne piquette* ⟳ beating = *raclée* **2/** *rossée* (f) : his father gave him a good licking = *son père lui a donné une bonne rossée* → TO HIT.

LID (n) *couvercle* (m) = cover
to blow one's lid off = *se fâcher tout rouge* → ANGRY
to blow the lid off = *étaler au grand jour* : the journalist blew the lid off the scandal = *le journaliste a étalé le scandale au grand jour.*

LIE (n) *mensonge* (m) : to tell lies = *raconter des mensonges* ⟳ fib = *bobard,* whopper = *gros mensonge,* bullshit = *des conneries*
a lie detector = *un détecteur de mensonges*
☠ *c'est vrai, ce mensonge ?* = are you kidding ?

LIE (to, -d) *mentir* ⟳ to fib = *raconter des bobards* ≠ to tell the truth = *dire la vérité*
to lie to s.o. = *mentir à qqn* : I'm fed up with your lying to me = *j'en ai ras le bol que tu me mentes.*

LIE (to, lay, lain) **(who knows) what lies ahead ?** = *qui sait ce que l'avenir nous réserve ?* → THAT'S LIFE !
to leave (a lot of cash) lying around = *laisser traîner (beaucoup d'argent)*
to lie down = *s'allonger* : I'm tired and want to lie down a while = *je suis fatigué et je veux m'allonger un instant* ⟳ to take a nap = *faire un somme* ☠ → to lengthen
to lie in = *résider dans* : the difficulty lies in getting a loan = *la difficulté réside dans l'obtention d'un prêt*
to be lying (on) = *être étendu (sur)* : the body was lying on the floor = *le corps était étendu sur le sol.*

LIEUTENANT (n) *lieutenant* (m) ⟳ captain = *capitaine.*

LIFE (n, lives) *vie* (f) : a happy life = *une vie heureuse* ⟳ existence = ←

for life = *à vie* : sentenced to prison for life = *condamné à la prison à vie* **for the life of me !** = *bon sang !* : for the life of me I don't	understand ! = *bon sang, je n'y comprends rien !* → GOSH ! **(to be) full of life** = *(être) plein de vie* ⟳ to be raring to go = *péter le feu*	**to get life** = *être condamné à perpétuité* **to lead the life of Riley** = *vivre comme un coq en pâte* ⟳ to be sitting pretty = *avoir la vie*

belle
late in life = *sur le tard* : to have kids late in life = *avoir des enfants sur le tard*
life expectancy = *espérance de vie* → **life span**
life imprisonment = *réclusion (criminelle) à perpétuité*
life insurance = *assurance-vie*
life jacket = *gilet de sauvetage*
the life of the party = *le boute-en-train* ≠ **a wet blanket** = *un bonnet de nuit*
life style = *style de vie*
(six) lives were lost = *cela a coûté (six) vies humaines*
not on your life ! = *jamais de la vie !* : lend you more money ? **not on your life !** = *vous prêter encore de l'argent ? jamais de la*

vie ! ⓪ **not for anything in the world** = *pour rien au monde*
I owe you my life = *je vous dois une fière chandelle* ⓪ **to be grateful** = *être reconnaissant*
to run for one's life = *courir comme si on avait le diable à ses trousses* ⓪ **to take to one's heels** = *prendre ses jambes à son cou*
to scare the life out of s.o. = *faire une peur terrible à qqn* ⓪ **to make s.o.'s blood run cold** = *glacer le sang à qqn*
to see life through rose-colored glasses = *voir la vie en rose* ≠ **to be a bird of ill omen** = *être un oiseau de malheur*
I'd stake my life on it = *j'en mettrais ma main au feu* ⓪ **I'd bet anything** = *je parie tout ce*

que tu veux
such is life = *la vie est ainsi faite* → THAT'S LIFE !
to take one's life in one's (own) hands = *prendre son courage à deux mains* : I'm going to take my life in my (own) hands and ask for a raise = *je vais prendre mon courage à deux mains et demander une augmentation*
to take one's (own) life = *attenter à ses jours* ⓪ **to commit suicide** = *se suicider*
that's life ! = *c'est la vie !*
you bet your life ! = *et comment donc !* ⓪ **you said a mouthful !** = *tu l'as dit bouffi !*

☸ *à la vie, à la mort* = till death do us part
— *enterrer sa vie de garçon* = to have a stag party (before one's marriage)
— *le coût de la vie* = the cost of living
— *être en vie* = to be alive

— *être entre la vie et la mort* = to be at death's door
— *mener une vie de patachon/de bâton de chaise* = to live it up
— *gagner sa vie* = to earn one's living

──────── **GROUP : THAT'S LIFE ! = C'EST LA VIE !** ────────

it's all in a day's work = *ça fait partie de la routine*
come what may = *advienne que pourra*
easy come, easy go = *ça va, ça vient*
to grin and bear it = *faire contre mauvaise fortune bon cœur*
here today, gone tomorrow = *on est bien peu de choses*
it can't be helped = *on n'y peut rien*
it doesn't surprise me = *ça ne m'étonne pas*
it's business as usual = *le monde continue de tourner*
it's just one of those things = *ça fait partie des choses qui arrivent*
it's no big deal = *il n'y a pas de quoi fouetter un chat*
it's the same old story/thing = *c'est toujours la même histoire/chanson/chose*
it was nice while it lasted = *les meilleures choses ont une fin*
never say never = *il ne faut pas dire « Fontaine, je ne boirai pas de ton eau »*
nothing lasts forever = *tout n'a qu'un temps*

so it goes = *ainsi va la vie*
such is life = *la vie est ainsi faite*
take things as they come = *prenez les choses comme elles viennent*
that just goes to show you = *tu vois bien*
that's the name of the game = *c'est dans l'ordre des choses*
that's par for the course = *ce n'est pas étonnant*
that's rough/tough ! = *dur ! dur !*
that's the way the ball bounces = *ainsi va la vie*
that's the way the cookie crumbles = *on ne fait pas d'omelette sans casser d'œufs*
that's the way it goes = *qu'est-ce que tu veux !*
that's the way things are = *c'est comme ça* = **that's how things are**
the best laid plans of mice and men oft go astray = *l'homme propose, Dieu dispose*
the die is cast = *le sort en est jeté/les dés sont jetés*
the rules of the game = *les règles du jeu*

these things happen = *ce sont des choses qui arrivent*
things are rough all over = *c'est dur pour tout le monde*
to take the bad along with the good = *accepter les bons et les mauvais côtés de la vie*
those are the breaks = *ainsi vont les choses*
time and tide wait for no man = *on n'arrête pas le temps qui passe*
too bad ! = *tant pis !*
what can you do ? = *qu'y faire ?*
what's done is done = *ce qui est fait est fait*
who knows what lies ahead ? = *qui sait ce que l'avenir nous réserve ?* = **who knows what the future holds ?**
who knows what tomorrow may bring ? = *qui sait de quoi demain sera fait ?*
win a few, lose a few = *à la guerre comme à la guerre*
you can't fight city hall = *c'est le pot de terre contre le pot de fer*
you never can tell = *on ne peut jamais savoir*

you can't win 'em all = *on ne peut pas gagner à tous les coups* **you have to take the rough** | **with the smooth** = *il faut prendre la vie comme elle vient* **you live and learn** = *on en* | *apprend tous les jours* **you never know** = *on ne sait jamais.*

LIFEGUARD (n) *sauveteur (m)* ⟲ artificial respiration = *respiration artificielle.*

LIFELONG (adj) *de toujours :* a lifelong friend = *un ami de toujours.*

LIFESAVER (n) *planche (f) de salut :* you're a lifesaver for lending me the money = *quand tu m'as prêté cet argent, tu as été ma planche de salut* ⟲ savior = *sauveur.*

LIFE-SIZE (adj) *grandeur nature*
I can get a life-size picture of (the President doing a striptease) = *(le Président en train de faire un strip-tease) j'imagine tout à fait le tableau* ⟲ I can just imagine it = *j'imagine bien.*

LIFETIME (n) *durée (f) de vie :* the average lifetime = *la durée moyenne de vie*
in (my grandfather's) lifetime = *du vivant de (mon grand-père)* ⟲ in s.o.'s time = *du temps de qqn.*

LIFT (n) (GB) *ascenseur (m)* = elevator
to give a lift = 1/ *donner un coup de fouet :* the drink/news gave me a lift = *ce verre/cette nouvelle m'a donné un coup de fouet* ⟲ to pep up = *ragaillardir* 2/ *déposer (en voiture) :* can you give me a lift downtown ? = *est-ce que vous pouvez me déposer en ville ?*

LIFT (to, -ed) 1/ *lever, soulever :* to lift an arm/a leg = *lever un bras/une jambe,* to lift a suitcase = *soulever une valise*
☠ *lever* → to raise
— *soulever une objection/question* = to raise an objection/a question
— *se soulever (rébellion)* = to rise up (rebellion)
2/ *chiper :* the kid lifted her pocketbook = *le gosse a chipé son sac* ⟲ to swipe = *faucher.*

LIFTOFF (n) *décollage (m), lancement (m) :* the liftoff of the missile = *le lancement du missile.*

LIGHT (n) *lumière (f), feu (m)* (car) : the lights are strong = *les lumières sont fortes* ⟲ lighting = *éclairage* ≠ darkness = *obscurité*

a light = *du feu :* do you have a light ? = *avez-vous du feu ?* ⟲ a lighter = *un briquet* **to bring to light** = *exposer au grand jour :* the newspaper brought the scandal to light = *le journal a exposé le scandale au grand jour* ⟲ to blow the lid off = *étaler au grand jour*	**to come to light** = *éclater au grand jour :* the scandal came to light thanks to a perseverant journalist = *le scandale a éclaté au grand jour grâce à un journaliste persévérant* ≠ to hush up = *étouffer* **to go out like a light** = *s'endormir comme*

différent
to see the light = *voir clair dans le jeu de qqn :* he thought he could fool me but I saw the light = *il a cru pouvoir me duper, mais j'ai vu clair dans son jeu*
in (the) light of = *à la lumière de :* in the light of recent events = *à la lumière des événements récents* ⟲ taking into account = *en tenant compte de*
lights out ! = *extinction des feux !*
to go through/to pass a light = *griller/brûler un feu rouge*
to see in the same ≠ **in a different light** = *voir sous le même jour* ≠ *sous un jour*

in a good ≠ **bad light** = *sous un bon* ≠ *mauvais jour*
to throw/to shed light on = *faire la lumière sur :* the investigating committee will throw/shed light on the matter = *la commission d'enquête fera la lumière sur cette affaire*

☠ *ce n'est pas une lumière* = he's no genius
— *il a des lumières sur* = he has knowledge about.

LIGHT (adj, -er, -est) 1/ *léger, -ère :* a light chair = *une chaise légère* ≠ heavy = *lourd* 2/ *clair, -e :* light blue = *bleu clair* ≠ dark = *foncé* ☠ → clear

light as a feather = *léger comme une plume* **light comedy** = *comédie légère* **light complexion** = *teint clair*	**light reading** = *lecture rapide* **to be a light sleeper** = *avoir le sommeil léger* ≠ to sleep like a log = *dormir comme un loir*

☠ *un léger goût d'ail* = a slight taste of garlic
— *thé léger* = weak tea
— *femme légère* = easy woman
— *(son article) est un peu léger* = (his article) is a little flimsy.

LIGHT (adv) **to make light of** = *traiter à la légère :* I made light of his arguments = *j'ai traité ses arguments à la légère* ⟲ to play down = *faire peu de cas de.*

LIGHT (to, lit or-ed) *allumer (lamp), éclairer (room) :* he lit the candle = *il a allumé la bougie,* the two lamps light the room well = *les deux lampes éclairent bien la pièce* ⟲ well-lit = *bien éclairé*
to light up = *s'éclairer :* the child's face lit up when he saw Santa Claus = *le visage de l'enfant s'est éclairé quand il a vu le Père Noël*

☠ *allumer (télé)* = to put on/switch on/turn on (TV)
— *éclairer qqn* = to enlighten s.o.

LIGHTEN (to, -ed) *éclaircir* : to lighten one's hair = *s'éclaircir les cheveux* ≠ to darken = *foncer* ☠ → to clear up.

LIGHTER (n) *briquet* (m) ⓓ matches = *allumettes*, ashtray = *cendrier*.

LIGHTHOUSE (n) *phare* (m) ⓓ pier = *jetée* ☠ → headlight.

LIGHTING (n) *éclairage* (m) : lighting effects = *effets d'éclairage*.

LIGHTLY (adv) **to get off lightly** = *en être quitte à bon compte* : the judge was lenient and the guy got off

lightly = *le juge a été indulgent et le type en a été quitte à bon compte*

to treat/take stg lightly = *traiter/prendre qqch à la légère*.

LIGHTNING (n inv) *éclairs* (m pl) : I'm afraid of lightning = *j'ai peur des éclairs* ⓓ thunderbolt = *foudre* ☠ → flash.

LIGHTWEIGHT (n) *poids* (m) *léger* ⓓ featherweight = *poids plume*.

LIK(E)ABLE (adj) *attachant, -e* : a likable guy = *un type attachant* ⓓ amiable = *aimable* ≠ disagreeable = *désagréable*.

LIKE (n) **to return like for like** = *rendre la pareille* ⓓ tit for tat = *un prêté pour un rendu*	**I've never seen the likes of (him/it)** = *je n'ai jamais vu quelqu'un/quelque chose de semblable*.

LIKE (to, -d) *aimer (bien)* : I like my brother but I love my husband = *j'aime bien mon frère, mais j'aime mon mari* ⓓ to be crazy about = *être fou de* ≠ to dislike = *ne pas aimer*

as you like = *comme vous voulez* **how do you like (my new coat) ?** = *comment trouvez-vous (mon nouveau manteau) ?* **how do you like that !** = *ben, dis donc !* **how would you like (a coffee) ?** = *que diriez-vous d'(un*	*café) ?* **I'd like (a coffee/to go)** = *je voudrais (un café/y aller)* **if you like** = *si vous voulez* : if you like, we'll go out for dinner tonight = *si vous voulez, nous dînerons dehors ce soir* **like it or lump it** = *que cela te plaise ou non*	**what would you like ?** = *qu'est-ce que vous aimeriez ?* **when/where you like** = *quand/où vous voudrez* **whether he likes it or not** = *que cela lui plaise ou non* ⓓ willingly or not = *bon gré, mal gré*
☠ *j'aimerais mieux y aller ce soir* = I'd rather go tonight — *aimer qqn* = to love s.o.	— *qui aime bien châtie bien* = spare the rod and spoil the child.	

LIKE (adv) *quoi* : they're having problems, like they're almost separated = *ils ont des problèmes, ils sont presque séparés, quoi*.

LIKE (prep) **1/** *comme* : you're like me = *tu es comme moi* ⓓ the same as = *pareil à* **2/** *comme* : arts, like painting and sculpture = *les arts, comme la peinture et la sculpture* ⓓ such as = *tel que*

to be anything/something like = *ressembler à* : is she anything/something like her mother ? = *est-ce qu'elle ressemble à sa mère ?*, no, she's nothing/not anything like her mother = *non, elle ne ressemble pas à sa mère* **to feel like** = *avoir envie de* : do you feel like a coffee ? = *est-ce que vous avez envie d'un café ?* ⓓ to care for = *désirer* **it looks like rain** = *on dirait qu'il va pleuvoir*	**to look like** = *ressembler à* : she looks like her mother = *elle ressemble à sa mère* **that's (just) like him !** = *ça lui ressemble (tout à fait) !* ≠ **that's not a bit like him** = *ça ne lui ressemble pas du tout* **what is ... like ?** = *comment est ... ?* : what is he like ? = *comment est-il ?* **what's it like out ?** = *quel temps fait-il ?* = what's the weather like ?

LIKE (conj) *comme* : it was like you said = *c'était comme vous l'aviez dit* = it was as you said ☠ → as

to act like = *agir comme (si)* : you acted like a fool = *tu as agi comme un imbécile*, she acted like she was angry = *elle a agi comme si elle était en colère* **like anything/like mad** = *vachement* : we ran like anything/like mad = *on a vachement couru* → VERY ☠ → damned	**it looks like** = *on dirait que* : it looks like it's going to rain = *on dirait qu'il va pleuvoir* = it looks as if it was going to rain = it looks like rain **to seem like** = *sembler être* : they seem like they're happy = *ils semblent être heureux*.

365

LIKELIHOOD (n) **there's little** ≠ **a strong likelihood that (he'll come)** = *il est peu* ≠ *très vraisemblable qu'(il vienne).*

LIKELY (adj) *vraisemblable* : it's likely that it's going to rain = *il est vraisemblable qu'il va pleuvoir* ⑩ the odds are that = *il y a des chances que* ≠ unlikely = *peu vraisemblable.*

LIKELY (adv) **most/very likely** = *très vraisemblablement* : he'll most/very likely be late = *il sera très vraisemblablement en retard*
not likely ! = *sûrement pas ! :* do you think he'll agree ? — not likely ! = *pensez-vous qu'il sera d'accord ? — sûrement pas !*

LIKEWISE (adv) *de même :* have a nice weekend ! — likewise ! = *passez un bon week-end ! — vous de même !*, I turned left and he did likewise = *j'ai tourné à gauche et il a fait de même.*

LIKING (n) **to take a liking to** = *se prendre de sympathie pour :* I took a liking to her brother = *je me suis pris de sympathie pour son frère* ⑩ to take a fancy to = *prendre en affection*
to one's liking = *à son goût.*

LIMB (n) *membre (m) :* to break a limb = *se casser un membre* ⑩ arm = *bras,* leg = *jambe* ☠ → member
(to leave) out on a limb = *(mettre) dans une situation délicate :* his refusal to help left me out on a limb = *son refus de m'aider m'a mis dans une situation délicate* ⑩ in a predicament = *dans une situation fâcheuse.*

LIMBER (adj, -er, -est) *souple :* a limber body = *un corps souple* ≠ stiff = *raide* ☠ *des horaires souples* = flexible

hours **LIMBER UP** (to, -ed) *s'échauffer :* to limber up before a dance class = *s'échauffer avant un cours de danse.*

LIMBO (n) **in limbo** = *entre parenthèses :* she's in limbo waiting for the divorce = *sa vie est entre parenthèses jusqu'à ce que le divorce soit prononcé.*

LIMELIGHT (n) **to be in the limelight** = *être sous les feux de la rampe* (show business), *être sur le devant de la scène* (politics) ⑩ to be in the spotlight = *être sous le feu des projecteurs.*

LIMEY (n) *angliche (m, f)* ⑩ frog = *franchouillard.*

LIMIT (n) *limite (f) :* the city limits = *les limites de la ville,* you have to know your own limits = *vous devez connaître vos propres limites*
off limits = *en dehors des limites autorisées*
that's the limit ! = *c'est le bouquet !* → GOSH !
☠ *cas limite* = borderline case
— *la date limite* = the deadline
— *dans une (certaine) limite* = to some extent
— *à la limite, on peut dire* = you could even say
— *les limites d'un pays* = the boundaries of a country.

LIMIT (to, -ed) *limiter :* to limit the speech to an hour = *limiter le discours à une heure* ≠ to extend = *prolonger.*

LIMITATION (n) *limitation (f)* ⑩ restriction = ← ☠ *limitation de vitesse* = speed limit.

LIMITED (adj) *limité, -e :* limited power = *pouvoir limité* ⑩ definite = *bien défini* ≠ unlimited = *illimité.*

LIMP (n) **to walk with a limp** = *marcher en boitant*
LIMP (to, -ed) *boiter.*

LIMPID (adj) *limpide* ≠ opaque = ←.

LINE (n) **1/** *ligne (f) :* a straight line = *une ligne droite* **2/** *baratin (m) :* he handed me some line = *il m'a fait un sacré baratin* ⑩ bill of goods = *salades* **3/** *queue (f) :* a long line at the movies = *une longue queue devant le cinéma* ☠ → tail **4/** *branche (f) :* what's his line ? = *dans quelle branche est-il ?* ⑩ field = *domaine* ☠ → branch **5/** *ligne (f) :* a line of cosmetics = *une ligne de produits de beauté*

along those lines = *dans cet ordre-là* **to be in line for (a promotion)** = *être sur les rangs pour (avoir une promotion)* **to draw the line** = *fixer une limite :* 4 Scotches, that's where I draw the line = *4 whiskies, c'est la limite que je me fixe* **drop me a line !** = *écris-moi un mot !* **to have a line on** = *avoir des tuyaux sur :* the cops have a line on him = *les flics ont des tuyaux sur lui* **hold the line !** = *restez en ligne !* ⑩ hang on ! = *ne quittez pas !* **to keep in line** = *faire marcher*	*droit :* she keeps her children in line = *elle fait marcher droit ses enfants* **(to know/learn) one's lines** = *(savoir/apprendre) son texte* **to lay it on the line** = *ne pas mâcher ses mots :* he told her what he thought and he really laid it on the line = *il lui a dit ce qu'il pensait et il n'a pas mâché ses mots* ⑩ not to pull punches = *ne pas y aller avec le dos de la cuiller* **to (make) toe the line** = *(faire) marcher droit* ⑩ to bring to heel = *mettre au pas* **not in line with** = *pas dans l'esprit de :* giving advances isn't in line with company policy =	*ce n'est pas dans l'esprit de la politique de l'entreprise de donner des avances* **on the line** = **1/** *en danger :* because of his being gay, his job's on the line = *il est en danger de perdre sa place parce qu'il est homosexuel* **2/** *en ligne/au bout du fil :* Sue's on the line = *Sue est en ligne/au bout du fil* ⑩ Sue speaking = *Sue à l'appareil* **out of line** = *pas de mise :* his remark was out of line = *sa réflexion n'était pas de mise* ⑩ out of place = *déplacé* **to read between the lines** = *lire entre les lignes* **to stand in line** = *faire la*

366

queue **to stay in line** = *se tenir à car-* *reau* : since the boss got angry, we've all been staying in line =	*depuis que le patron s'est fâché,* *nous nous tenons tous à carreau* **to take the line of least re-** **sistance** = *être partisan du*	*moindre effort* ⓓ to take the easy way = *choisir la solution de* *facilité*
☠ *prendre en ligne de compte* = to take into consideration		— *quelle ligne !* = what a figure !

LINE (to, -d) **to line up** = 1/ *(se) mettre en rang* ⓓ to stand in line = *faire la queue* 2/ *prévoir* : we've lined up some good musicians for the gala = *nous avons prévu de bons musiciens pour le gala* ⓓ to arrange for = *s'arranger pour que* ☠ → to forecast 3/ *avoir en vue* : what have you got lined up for the weekend ? = *qu'avez-vous en vue pour le week-end ?*

LINEN (n) *linge (m)* : put the linen in the closet = *mets le linge dans le placard* ☠ → laundry.

LINE-UP (n) *séance (f) d'identification d'un suspect.*

LINGER (to, -ed) *s'attarder* : we lingered at the airport after his plane took off = *nous nous sommes attardés à l'aéroport après le départ de son avion.*

LINGERIE (n) *lingerie (f)* ⓓ nightgown = *chemise de nuit.*

LINGO (n) *jargon (m)* : the medical lingo = *le jargon médical* ⓓ dialect = *dialecte.*

LINGUIST (n) *linguiste (m, f)* **LINGUISTIC** (adj) *linguistique* **LINGUISTICS** (n inv) *linguistique (f)* ⓓ philology = *philologie.*

LINING (n) *doublure (f)* : the coat's lining = *la doublure du manteau* ⓓ fur = *fourrure*, to line = *doubler* ☠ *une doublure (cinéma)* = an understudy.

LINK (n) 1/ *lien (m)* : there's no link between the two events = *il n'y a aucun lien entre les deux événements* ⓓ connection = *rapport* ☠ *les liens du sang/affectifs* = blood/emotional ties — *les liens du mariage* = the bonds of marriage 2/ *maillon (m)* : the links of a chain = *les maillons d'une chaîne*
missing link = *chaînon manquant.*

LINK (to, -ed) 1/ *faire le lien entre* : I didn't link the two events = *je n'ai pas fait le lien entre les deux événements* ⓓ to associate = *associer* 2/ *relier* : the bridge links the two banks = *le pont relie les deux rives* ☠ → to connect **to link to** = *lier à* : her resignation is linked to the scandal = *sa démission est liée au scandale* ⓓ to be connected to = *avoir rapport avec*
to link up (with) = *s'associer à* : they linked up with an European company = *ils se sont associés à une compagnie européenne* ⓓ to join up with = *se joindre à* **to link with** = *lier à* : her name was linked with his = *son nom à elle était lié au sien.*

LION (n) *lion (m)* **LIONESS** (n) *lionne (f)* ⓓ cub = *lionceau.*

LIP (n) *lèvre (f)* ⓓ to lip-read = *lire sur les lèvres*, mouth = *bouche*, harelip = *bec-de-lièvre*
none of your lip ! = *ferme ton clapet !* = **button your lip !** → BUZZ OFF !

to pay lip service to stg = *faire qqch du bout des lèvres* : his doctor advised him to stay in bed but he's paying lip service to the advice = *son médecin lui a recommandé de garder le lit mais il n'a accepté ce conseil que du bout des lèvres*
to smack one's lips = *se lécher les babines*
☠ *être suspendu aux lèvres de qqn* = to be hanging on s.o.'s every word.

LIPSTICK (n) *rouge (m) à lèvres* ⓓ rouge = *fard.*

LIQUID (n) *liquide (m)* : milk is a liquid = *le lait est un liquide* ☠ *du liquide* = cash.

LIQUIDATE (to, -d) 1/ *liquider* : to liquidate a company = *liquider une affaire* ⓓ to close shop = *fermer boutique* 2/ *liquider* : the gang liquidated the crook = *le gang a liquidé l'escroc* ⓓ to bump off = *expédier dans l'autre monde*, to rub out = *zigouiller.*

LIQUOR (n) *alcool (m)* : do you have any liquor in the house ? = *est-ce que vous avez des alcools dans la maison ?* ⓓ booze = *gnôle* ☠ → alcohol
to hold one's liquor = *tenir bien l'alcool* ⓓ to be a good drinker = *avoir le vin gai*
to like one's liquor = *lever le coude/avoir la dalle en pente* → DRUNK
liquor license = *licence d'exploitation d'un débit de boisson.*

LISP (n) *cheveu (m) sur la langue, zézaiement (m)* : she speaks with a lisp = *elle a un cheveu sur la langue* **LISP** (to, -ed) *zozoter* ⓓ to stutter = *bégayer.*

LIST (n) *liste (f)* : make a list of what you have to buy = *faites une liste de ce que vous devez acheter*
waiting list = *liste d'attente*
☠ *la liste d'un parti* = the party's ticket.

LISTEN (to, -ed) *écouter* : go ahead, I'm listening ! = *allez-y, j'écoute !* ⓓ to hear = *entendre*
to listen in on = *écouter* : the cops were listening in on their conversation = *les flics écoutaient leur conversation* ⓓ to wiretap = *brancher sur table d'écoute*
to listen to s.o. = *écouter qqn* : are you listening to me ? = *est-ce que vous m'écoutez ?* ≠ to turn a deaf ear = *faire la sourde oreille*
☠ *si je m'écoutais* = if I followed my own advice — *trop s'écouter* = to think too much about one's own problems.

LISTLESS (adj) *indolent, -e* ⓌⒹ *languid = languissant.*

LITERAL (adj) *littéral, -e* : the literal meaning = *le sens littéral/le sens propre* ≠ figurative = *figuré.*

LITERALLY (adv) *littéralement* : he's literally crazy = *il est littéralement fou*
literally speaking = *à proprement parler*
to take s.o. literally = *prendre qqn au pied de la lettre* : don't take him literally, he was just kidding = *ne le prends pas au pied de la lettre, il ne faisait que plaisanter.*

LITERARY (adj) *littéraire* : literary agent = *agent littéraire.*

LITERATE (adj) *lettré, -e* ≠ illiterate = *illettré.*

LITERATURE (n) *littérature (f)* : to study English literature = *étudier la littérature anglaise* ⓌⒹ letters = *les (belles) lettres.*

LITIGANT (n) *plaideur, -euse* ⓌⒹ plaintiff = *plaignant.*

LITIGATION (n) *litige (m)* ⓌⒹ lawsuit = *procès.*

LITTER (n) 1/ *portée (f)* : a litter of kittens = *une portée de chatons* ⓌⒹ to wean = *sevrer*
☠ *à portée de main* = within reach
— *c'est hors de ma portée* = it's beyond my scope
2/ (inv) *détritus (m pl)* : litter in the streets = *des détritus dans les rues* ⓌⒹ garbage = *ordures.*

LITTLE (n) **a little** = *un peu* : take a little = *prenez-en un peu*, stay a little = *restez un peu* ≠ a lot = *beaucoup*	**to get a little** = *s'envoyer en l'air* : did you get a little last night ? = *est-ce que tu t'es envoyé en l'air hier soir ?* ⓌⒹ to screw = *baiser*

☠ *pour un peu (il m'écrasait)* = (he) just missed (hitting me) — *écoute un peu* = listen to this — *il est un peu (menteur)* =	he's a bit of (a liar) — *peu importe* = never mind — *c'est peu dire* = that's the least you can say — *c'est peu (de choses)* à	demander = that's not much (to ask for) — *il s'en est fallu de peu* = it was touch and go.

LITTLE (adj, less, least) 1/ *petit, -e* : a little chair/woman = *une petite chaise/femme* = small ⓌⒹ tiny = *minuscule* ≠ big = *gros*
2/ *peu de (choses non dénombrables)* : she has little money/time = *elle a peu d'argent/de temps* ⓌⒹ few = *peu de (choses dénombrables)* ≠ a lot of = *beaucoup de*

a little ... = *un peu de ...* : do you want a little coffee ? = *voulez-vous un peu de café ?* = a bit of ⓌⒹ a drop of = *une goutte de*, a speck of = *un chouïa de* **a little bird(ie) told me so** = *mon petit doigt me l'a dit* **a little while ago** = *il y a un petit moment* : she left a little while ago = *elle est partie il y a un petit moment* ⓌⒹ not long ago = *il y a peu de temps*	**dressed like little orphan Annie** = *habillé/fagoté/ficelé comme l'as de pique* **in a little while** = *tout à l'heure* : I'll come in a little while = *je viendrai tout à l'heure* ⓌⒹ shortly = *sous peu* **very little** = *très peu de* : I've very little money = *j'ai très peu d'argent* ≠ loads of = *à gogo* **Little Red Riding Hood** = *le Petit Chaperon rouge*

☠ *poursuivre son petit bonhomme de chemin* = to jog along — *ne pas se prendre pour de la petite bière* = to think one's hot stuff — *mettre les petits plats dans les grands* = to go all out — *se vendre comme des petits pains* = to sell like hot cakes — *les petites annonces* = the classified ads — *être dans les petits papiers de qqn* = to be in s.o.'s good	books — *être aux petits soins pour qqn* = to fuss over s.o. — *aux petits oignons* = hunky-dory — *petit déjeuner* = breakfast — *il n'y a pas de petites économies* = every penny counts — *le monde est petit* = it's a small world — *boire du petit-lait* = to lap up — *petits-enfants* = grandchildren — *petit ami* = boyfriend	— *à la petite semaine* = halfbaked/crummy — *chercher la petite bête* = to nitpick — *le petit coin* = the john — *le petit écran* = TV — *être dans ses petits souliers* = to feel ill at ease — *parler petit nègre* = to speak pidgin French/English — *elle est plus petite que son mari* = she's shorter than her husband.

LITTLE (adv) *peu* : she eats little = *elle mange peu* ⓌⒹ less = *moins*, least = *le moins* ☠ *à peu près* = almost

a little more (coffee) ? = *un peu plus de (café) ?*
little by little = *petit à petit* ⓪ slow and steady = *lentement mais sûrement*
a little = *un peu* : I'm a little tired = *je suis un peu fatigué* ⓪ rather = *plutôt*

little more = *pas beaucoup plus* : I can do little more than try to help you = *je ne peux pas faire beaucoup plus qu'essayer de vous aider*
to make little of = *faire peu de cas de* ⓪ to make light of = *traiter à la légère.*

LIVE (to, -d) **1/** *habiter* : where do you live ? = *où habitez-vous ?* ⓪ to reside = *résider* ☠ *l'idée de la mort l'habite* = he's haunted by the idea of death
2/ *vivre* : Shakespeare lived in the 16th century = *Shakespeare a vécu au XVIᵉ siècle* ☠ *qui vivra verra* = whatever will be will be

---

live and let live = *soyez tolérant*

you live and learn = *on en apprend tous les jours*
→ THAT'S LIFE !

---

to live apart = *vivre séparés* : they've been living apart for a year = *ils vivent séparés depuis un an* = they've been estranged for a year
to live down = *poursuivre toute la vie* : he'll never live down the embarrassment of getting drunk in public = *la honte d'avoir été ivre en public le poursuivra toute sa vie*
to live for = *vivre pour* : she lives for her job = *elle vit pour son travail*
to live in = 1/ *habiter (à)* : she lives in New York = *elle habite (à) New York* 2/ *vivre à demeure* : their maid lives in = *leur bonne vit à demeure* ≠ to

live out = *vivre à l'extérieur*
to live off = *vivre de* : he lives off his writings = *il vit de sa plume*
to live on = *vivre de/avec* : I can't live on my salary = *je ne peux pas vivre avec/de mon salaire*
to live out = *passer* : she won't live out the year = *elle ne passera pas l'année* ☠ → to pass
to live through (two wars) = *avoir vécu (deux guerres)*
to live to (80) = *vivre jusqu'à (80 ans)*
to live together = *vivre ensemble* ⓪ to shack up = *être à la colle*

to live it up = *faire les quatre cents coups* : we lived it up last night = *nous avons fait les quatre cents coups hier soir* ⓪ to paint the town red = *faire la bringue*
to live up to = *se montrer à la hauteur de* : the restaurant didn't live up to its reputation = *le restaurant ne s'est pas montré à la hauteur de sa réputation* ⓪ to come up to (expectation) = *répondre à (l'attente)*
to live with = *vivre avec* : we have to live with the threat of a nuclear war = *nous devons vivre avec la menace d'une guerre nucléaire*, she lives with him = *elle vit avec lui.*

LIVE (adj) **1/** *vivant, -e* : a live animal = *un animal vivant* ⓪ alive = *en vie* ≠ dead = *mort*
live wire = *vif-argent* : my kid sister's a live wire = *ma sœur cadette, c'est du vif-argent* ⓪ fireball = *ouragan*

☠ *le malade est encore vivant* = the patient's still living

— *une description vivante* = a vivid description

2/ *en direct* : a live show = *un spectacle en direct* ≠ taped = *enregistré.*

LIVELIHOOD (n) *moyen (m) de subsistance* : he sells paintings for a livelihood = *son moyen de subsistance, c'est de vendre des tableaux* ⓪ bread and butter = *gagne-pain.*

LIVELY (adj, -ier, -iest) *plein, -e de vie* : a lively personality = *une personnalité pleine de vie* ⓪ perk = *guilleret* ≠ lethargic = *léthargique.*

LIVEN UP (to, -ed) *animer* : let's liven up the party ! = *animons un peu la soirée !* ⓪ to enliven = *égayer.*

LIVER (n) *foie (m)* : to eat liver = *manger du foie* ⓪ hepatitis = *hépatite*, gallbladder = *vésicule biliaire*, jaundice = *jaunisse* ☠ *avoir les foies* = to have the willies.

LIVESTOCK (n) *cheptel (m)* ⓪ cattle = *bétail.*

LIVID (adj) *blême de colère* → ANGRY.

LIVING (n) **to earn one's living** = *gagner sa vie* = **to make a living** ⓪ to make money = *gagner de l'argent*
for a living = *dans la vie* : what does he do for a living ? = *que fait-il dans la vie ?*
the living = *les vivants* ⓪ the survivors = *les survivants.*

LIVING (adj) *vivant, -e* : he was still living when the cops came = *il était encore vivant quand les flics sont arrivés*, the greatest living writer = *le plus grand écrivain encore vivant* ⓪ alive = *en vie* ☠ → live

living conditions = *conditions de vie*
the living end = *le super-pied* : doing nothing on the beach is the living end = *ne rien faire sur la plage, c'est le super-pied* ⓪ the end = *le fin du fin*
the living room = *le living-room* ⓪ den = *salle de séjour*
living quarters = *quartiers d'habitation*.

LOAD (n) *chargement* (m) : a load of coal = *un chargement de charbon*
get a load of him ! = *visez-le un peu !*
loads of = *à gogo/un tas de* (people) : loads of food = *de la nourriture à gogo* ≠ a sprinkling of = *un chouïa de* → MANY
take a load off your feet = *pose tes fesses* ⓪ take a seat = *prenez un siège*
that's a load off my mind = *ça m'ôte un poids de la conscience*.

LOAD (to, -ed) *charger* : to load a truck = *charger un camion* ≠ to unload = *décharger* ☠ → to charge.

LOADED (adj) 1/ *plein, -e aux as* : her in-laws are loaded = *ses beaux-parents sont pleins aux as* → RICH ≠ broke = *fauché* 2/ *bourré, -e* : three drinks and I was loaded = *après trois verres, j'étais bourré* → DRUNK ☠ *bourré (théâtre)* = packed 3/ *chargé, -e* : the gun was loaded = *le fusil était chargé* ☠ *une journée chargée* = a busy day
a loaded question = *une question chargée de sous-entendus*
to get loaded on (Scotch) = *se beurrer au (whisky)*
loaded (down) with (packages) = *chargé de (paquets)*
loaded with = *bourré de* : the Parliament's loaded with communists = *le Parlement est bourré de communistes*.

LOAF (to, -ed) *flemmarder* : we loafed all day = *nous avons flemmardé toute la journée* ⓪ to lounge = *se prélasser*, to loll = *fainéanter*.

LOAN (n) *prêt* (m) (you give), *emprunt* (m) (you get)
loan company = *caisse de crédit*
loan shark = *usurier*
on loan = *emprunté* : the paintings are on loan from the Washington Art Museum = *les tableaux ont été empruntés au musée de Washington*
to take out a loan = *faire un emprunt* ≠ **to give a loan** = *faire un prêt*
☠ *nom d'emprunt* = assumed name.

LOAN (to, -ed) *prêter* : to loan an art collection = *prêter une collection d'art* = to lend ⓪ to give = *donner* ☠ → to lend.

LO AND BEHOLD (interj) *voilà que* : I didn't think I would see him again, and then lo and behold I bumped into him yesterday = *je ne pensais pas le revoir, et voilà que je suis tombé sur lui hier*.

LOATH (adj) **to be loath to (borrow money)** = *répugner à (emprunter de l'argent)*.

LOATHE (to, -d) *exécrer* : I loathe my mother-in-law = *j'exècre ma belle-mère* ≠ to adore = *adorer*.

LOATHSOME (adj) *exécrable* ⓪ repulsive = *repoussant*.

LOBBY (n, -ies) 1/ *lobby* (m) : the gun lobby = *le lobby des marchands de canons* ⓪ pressure group = *groupe de pression* 2/ *hall* (m) : he was waiting in the lobby = *il attendait dans le hall* ⓪ vestibule = ←, groundfloor = *rez-de-chaussée* ☠ → hall.

LOBBY (to, -ied) *exercer des pressions* **LOBBYING** (n inv) *intrigues* (f) *de couloir* **LOBBYIST** (n) *membre* (m) *d'un groupe de pression* ⓪ politician = *homme politique*.

LOBSTER (n) *homard* (m) : steamed/broiled lobster = *homard cuit à la vapeur/grillé* ⓪ rock lobster = *langouste*.

LOCAL (adj) *local, -e* : local government = *administration locale*, local newspaper = *journal local* ⓪ regional = *régional*
local call = *appel local*
local train = *omnibus* ≠ express train = *train express*.

LOCALIZE (to, -d) *localiser* : to localize a tumor = *localiser une tumeur* ☠ *localiser une cachette* = to locate a hideout.

LOCALLY (adv) *localement* ⓪ regionally = *régionalement*.

LOCATE (to, -d) 1/ *localiser* : the cops located his hideout = *les flics ont localisé sa cachette* ⓪ to find = *trouver* ☠ → to localize 2/ *réussir à trouver* : when I was in New York I couldn't locate you = *quand j'étais à New York, je n'ai pas réussi à vous trouver*
to be located (in) = *se trouver (à)* : the company's located in Paris = *la société se trouve à Paris* ⓪ to be situated in = *être situé à*.

LOCATION (n) *emplacement* (m) : it's a good location for a factory = *c'est un bon emplacement pour une usine* ⓪ place = *endroit*
on location = *en extérieur* : the movie was shot on location in Spain = *le film a été tourné en extérieur en Espagne* ⓪ set = *plateau*.

LOCK (n) *serrure* (f) : safety lock = *serrure de sûreté* ⓪ locksmith = *serrurier*
lock, stock and barrel = *en bloc* : he sold the factory lock, stock and barrel = *il a vendu l'usine en bloc* ⓪ as a whole = *comme un tout*
to pick a lock = *crocheter une serrure* ⓪ to do a job = *faire un coup*.

LOCK (to, -ed) *fermer à clef* : lock the car = *fermez la voiture à clef* ⓪ to bolt = *verrouiller* ≠ to unlock = *ouvrir avec une clef*
to lock in ≠ **out** = *enfermer à l'intérieur* ≠ *dehors*
to lock up = 1/ *boucler* : the cops locked him up = *les flics l'ont bouclé* ⓪ to nab = *pincer* ≠ to let go = *relâcher* 2/ *boucler* : they locked up the house when they left = *ils ont bouclé la maison quand ils sont partis* ☠ → to wind up.

LOCKER (n) *vestiaire (m)* : each player has a locker = *chaque joueur a un vestiaire* ☠ → checkroom
locker room talk = *histoires de fesses* ⓪ cunt talk = *histoires de cul.*

LOCKOUT (n) *lock-out (m)* ⓪ strike = *grève.*

LOCO (adj) *fada* : her whole family's loco = *toute sa famille est fada* → CRAZY.

LODGINGS (n pl) *logement (m)* : to find lodgings = *trouver un logement* ⓪ lodger = *locataire* ☠ → housing.

LOFT (n) *loft (m)* ⓪ atelier = ←.

LOFTY (adj, -ier, -iest) *élevé, -e* : lofty goals = *des buts élevés* ≠ low = *bas* ☠ → high.

LOG (n) *bûche (f)* ⓪ saw = *scie*
log cabin = *cabane en rondins*
to sleep like a log = *dormir comme une souche/un loir* ⓪ to sleep around the clock = *faire le tour du cadran* ☠ *prendre une bûche* = to take a spill.

LOGBOOK (n) *livre (m) de bord* : to enter the course in the logbook = *noter la route suivie dans le livre de bord* ⓪ compass = *compas.*

LOGGERHEADS (n pl) **to be at loggerheads** = *être à couteaux tirés* = to be at daggers drawn.

LOGIC (n) *logique (f)* : there's no logic in what you're suggesting = *il n'y a aucune logique dans ce que vous suggérez* ⓪ reasoning = *raisonnement* **LOGICAL** (adj) *logique* ⓪ rational = *rationnel* ≠ illogical = *illogique* **LOGICALLY** (adv) *logiquement* ⓪ rationally = *rationnellement.*

LOITER (to, -ed) **no loitering** = *interdit aux rôdeurs.*

LOLLIPOP (n) *sucette (f)* ⓪ candy = *bonbon.*

LONDON (n) *Londres* ⓪ Londoner = *Londonien.*

LONE (adj) *solitaire* : a lone person on the beach = *une personne solitaire sur la plage*
a lone wolf = *quelqu'un qui fait bande à part* ≠ a good mixer = *quelqu'un de liant*
Lone Star State = *Texas.*

LONELINESS (n) *solitude (f)* : the loneliness of big cities = *la solitude des grandes villes.*

LONELY (adj, -ier, -iest) *seul, -e* : I live alone but rarely feel lonely = *je vis seul, mais je me sens rarement seul* ☠ → alone.

LONER (n) *solitaire (m,f)* : he's always been a loner = *il a toujours été un solitaire* ⓪ lone wolf = *quelqu'un qui fait bande à part* ☠ *course en solitaire (voile)* = solo race (sailing).

LONESOME (adj) *très seul, -e* : I feel lonesome without you = *je me sens très seul sans vous* ⓪ lonely = *seul.*

LONG (n) **before long** = *d'ici peu* : they're going to get married before long = *ils vont se marier d'ici peu* ⓪ shortly = *sous peu* ≠ in the distant future = *dans un avenir lointain*

for long = *longtemps* : we won't stay for long = *nous ne resterons pas longtemps*
the long and the short of it = *le fin mot de l'histoire*

☠ *le long du (fleuve)* = along (the river)
— *marcher de long en large* = to walk up and down
— *en savoir long* = to be in the know

— *expliquer qqch en long et en large* = to explain all the ins and outs of stg.

LONG (adj, -er, -est) *long, longue* : a long book/wait = *un long livre/une longue attente* ⓪ lengthy = *très long* ≠ short = *court*

---

at long last (she got pregnant) = *(elle a) fini par (tomber enceinte)* ⓪ finally = *finalement*
to be ... long = 1/ *durer* : the lesson was two hours long = *la leçon a duré deux heures* = to last 2/ *avoir ... de long* : it's three meters long = *ça a trois mètres de long*
to come a long way = *faire du chemin*
to cut a long story short = *bref* ⓪ in a word = *en un mot*
for a long time = *pendant longtemps* : he's been out of

work for a long time = *il a été sans travail pendant longtemps*
to go a long way(s) before = *ce n'est pas demain la veille* : you'll go a long way(s) before finding a singer like Garland = *ce n'est pas demain la veille qu'on retrouvera une chanteuse comme Garland*
to go a long way(s) towards = *faire un grand pas vers* : the new law goes a long ways towards resolving discrimination = *la nouvelle loi fait un grand pas vers la solution du problème de la discrimination*

in the long run = *à la longue* : he'll agree in the long run = *il finira par être d'accord à la longue*
it's a long story = *c'est une longue histoire*
it's been a long time = *ça fait bien longtemps*
it was a long time coming = *ça a mis longtemps à venir*
long johns = *caleçons longs*
a long shot = *très peu de chances* : his winning the election is a long shot = *il a très peu de chances de gagner les élections* ≠ in the bag = *dans le sac*

long time no see ! = *ça fait une paye qu'on ne s'est pas vus !* ⓪ look who's here ! = *quel bon vent t'amène ?*
a long way off = *au diable (vauvert)* : the restaurant's a long way off = *le restaurant est au diable (vauvert)* ⓪ far-off = *très loin*

not by a long shot = *tant s'en faut* : we're not finished, not by a long shot = *nous n'avons pas fini, tant s'en faut*
of long standing = *de longue date* : a friend of long standing = *un ami de longue date*
to pull a long face = *faire la tête* ⓪ to brood = *ruminer*

to take a long time = *prendre du temps* : this work took a long time = *ce travail a pris du temps*
to take a long time to (understand) = *mettre du temps à (comprendre)*
to take the long way around = *prendre le chemin des écoliers*

☠ *long comme un jour sans pain* = endless
— *trouver le temps long* = to find time hanging

heavy on one's hands
— *long métrage* = feature film.

LONG (adv) **1/** *longtemps* : it won't take me long to do it = *ça ne me prendra pas longtemps pour faire ça,* have you been here long ? = *ça fait longtemps que vous êtes là ?* **2/** *long, longue* : wait for me, I won't be long ! = *attends-moi, je ne serai pas longue !*

---

as long as = 1/ *aussi longtemps que/tant que* : as long as you're happy, I am = *aussi longtemps/tant que tu es heureux, je le suis* 2/ *du moment que* : you can borrow the car as long as you bring it back on time = *tu peux prendre la voiture du moment que tu me la rends à temps* ⓪ on the condition that = *à condition que*
to be long in = *être long à* : they weren't long in finding the killer = *ils n'ont pas été longs à trouver le tueur*
it hasn't been long since (we met) = *ça ne fait pas longtemps que (nous nous sommes rencontrés)*
to last long = *faire long feu* : she won't last long in

the job = *elle ne fera pas long feu dans ce travail*
long ago = *il y a longtemps* : they broke up long ago = *il y a longtemps qu'ils ont rompu* ≠ **not long ago** = *il n'y a pas longtemps*
long before ≠ **after** = *bien avant* ≠ *après* : I met him long before ≠ after you did = *je l'ai rencontré bien avant* ≠ *après vous*
long live (the king) ! = *vive (le roi) !*
long since = *depuis longtemps* : he's long since dead = *il est mort depuis longtemps*
you should live so long ! = *tu peux toujours te brosser !* ⓪ don't stand on a corner ! = *tu peux toujours courir !*

LONG-DISTANCE (adj) **a long-distance call** = *un appel à l'étranger/interurbain.*

LONG-DRAWN-OUT (adj) *qui s'éternise* : a long-drawn-out meeting = *une réunion qui s'éternise* ⓪ endless = *sans fin.*

LONGER (adv) **not ... any/no longer** = *ne ... plus* : she doesn't live here any longer = *elle n'habite plus ici* = she no longer lives here
not ... any/no longer than = *ne ... pas ... plus ... de/que* : I can't stay any longer than an hour = *je ne peux pas rester plus d'une heure* = I can stay no longer than an hour.

LONG FOR/TO (to, -ed) *avoir grande envie de* : I'm longing to be loved/for love = *j'ai grande envie d'être aimé/d'amour* ⓪ to hanker after = *aspirer à.*

LONGHAIR (n) *intello (m, f)* ⓪ highbrow = *cérébral.*

LONGING (n) *envie (f)* : a sudden longing to see him

again = *une envie soudaine de le revoir* ⓪ yearning = *aspiration* ☠ → envy.

LONG-RANGE (adj) **1/** *à long terme* : long-range plans = *des projets à long terme* ≠ short-term = *à court terme* **2/** *de longue portée* : long-range missiles = *des missiles de longue portée.*

LONGSHOREMAN (n, -men) *débardeur (m)* ⓪ docker = ← ☠ *débardeur (vêtement)* = sleeveless teeshirt.

LONGSTANDING (adj) *de longue date* : a long-standing friendship = *une amitié de longue date.*

LONG-TERM (adj) *à long terme* : a long-term loan = *un emprunt à long terme* ≠ short-term = *à court terme.*

LONG-WINDED (adj) *volubile* : a long-winded speaker = *un commentateur volubile* ⓪ loquacious = *loquace.*

LOO (n) (GB) *petit coin (m)* = john.

LOOK (n) *regard (m)* : a sad look = *un regard triste* ⓪ glance = *coup d'œil*, peek = *coup d'œil furtif* ☠ *au regard de la loi* = in the eyes of the law

---

by the look(s) of (him, I'd say he's an alcoholic) = *rien qu'à (le) voir, (je dirais qu'il est alcoolique)*

by the look(s) of things = *apparemment* : by the looks of things they'll be splitting soon = *apparemment, ils sont sur le point de se séparer*

if looks could kill = *(je) l'ai foudroyé du regard :* he was so furious when I made the blunder, if looks could kill ! = *il était tellement furieux quand j'ai fait cette gaffe qu'il m'a foudroyé du regard !*
let me have a look = *laissez-moi voir*
looks aren't everything = *la beauté, ce n'est pas tout dans la vie*
looks can be deceiving = *les apparences sont sou-* vent trompeuses ⓪ **still waters run deep** = *il n'est pire eau que l'eau qui dort*
(I don't like) the looks of (this place) = *(je n'aime pas) l'aspect de (cet endroit)*
to take a look at = *jeter un coup d'œil sur/à* = to glance at
what looks ! = *quelle gueule !*

LOOK (to, -ed) 1/ *regarder :* look ! a flying saucer ! = *regardez ! une soucoupe volante !* ⓪ to eye = *lorgner,* to gaze at = *contempler* ☠ → to watch
2/ *avoir l'air :* he looks tired/thirty = *il a l'air fatigué/d'avoir la trentaine* ⓪ to appear = *paraître*

---

it looks as if (you were wrong) = *on dirait que (vous avez tort)* = it looks like ...
look before you leap = *ne fonce pas dans le brouillard* ⓪ be careful = *fais attention*
look who's here ! = *quel bon vent t'amène ?*
look who's talking ! = *tu ne t'es pas regardé !* ⓪ you're a fine one to talk ! = *ça te va bien de dire ça !*
(things) look good ≠ **bad** = *(les choses) s'annoncent bien* ≠ *mal*
how do I look ? = *comment me trouvez-vous ?*

---

to look after s.o. = *surveiller qqn :* can you look after the kids for a couple of hours ? = *est-ce que vous pouvez surveiller les enfants pendant deux heures ?* ⓪ to keep an eye on = *avoir l'œil sur*
to look around = *se retourner :* I looked around and he was following me = *je me suis retournée et il me suivait* ☠ → to return
to look at = *regarder :* I'm looking at TV = *je regarde la télé,* look at me ! = *regardez-moi !*
he isn't much to look at = *il ne paie pas de mine* = **he's nothing to look at**
to look away = *détourner les yeux :* when I looked at her, she looked away = *quand je l'ai regardée, elle a détourné les yeux* ≠ to stare at = *fixer*
to look back ≠ **ahead** = *regarder en arrière* ≠ *devant :* don't look back, look ahead ! = *ne regarde pas en arrière, regarde devant toi !*
to look back on stg = *repenser à qqch :* she looks back on her marriage with bitterness = *elle repense à son mariage avec amertume*
to look down ≠ **up** = *baisser* ≠ *lever les yeux*
to look down on = *regarder de haut :* he looks down on his employees = *il regarde ses employés de haut* ⓪ to scorn = *mépriser*

to look for = *chercher :* I'm looking for a new job = *je cherche un nouveau boulot* ⓪ to seek = *rechercher*
☠ envoyer chercher qqn = to send for s.o.
— *qu'est-ce que tu cherches ?* = what are you after ?
— *va me chercher un café* = go and get me a coffee
— *elle se cherche* = she's trying to find herself
you're looking for it ! = *tu l'auras cherché !* = you're asking for it !
to look forward to = *attendre avec impatience :* thank you for your invitation, I'm looking forward to seeing you Saturday = *merci pour votre invitation, j'attends avec impatience de vous voir samedi*
to look in on = *passer voir :* the doctor will look in on you later = *le docteur passera vous voir plus tard*
to look into (a problem) = *examiner (un problème)* ⓪ to investigate = *enquêter sur* ☠ → to examine
to look on = *regarder faire :* the candidate was making a speech and his wife was looking on = *le candidat faisait un discours et sa femme le regardait faire*
to look out (of) = *regarder (par) :* look out of the window ! = *regarde par la fenêtre !*
look out ! = *attention !* ⓪ watch out ! = *fais gaffe !*
to look out for o.s. = *se*

débrouiller tout seul : I can look out for myself = *je peux me débrouiller tout seul*
to look out on = *donner sur :* the office looks out on the park = *le bureau donne sur le parc* = **to look onto**
to look over = *jeter un coup d'œil sur :* look the bill over = *jette un coup d'œil sur l'addition* ⓪ to check out = *vérifier*
to look through = 1/ *feuilleter :* to look through a book = *feuilleter un livre* = to leaf through 2/ *regarder par :* look through the window = *regarde par la fenêtre*
to look to = *se tourner vers :* he looks to his father for help = *il se tourne vers son père pour avoir de l'aide*
to look up = 1/ *aller mieux :* things are looking up = *ça va mieux* ⓪ to improve = *s'améliorer* 2/ *lever les yeux* ≠ to look down = *baisser les yeux* 3/ *faire signe à :* look me up if you come to Paris = *faites-moi signe si vous venez à Paris* ⓪ to get in touch with = *prendre contact avec* 4/ *chercher (dans le dictionnaire) :* to look up a word = *chercher un mot dans le dictionnaire*
to look s.o. up and down = *déshabiller qqn du regard* ⓪ to give s.o. the once-over = *jauger qqn d'un coup d'œil*
to look up to = *regarder avec admiration* ≠ to look down on = *regarder de haut.*

LOOK-ALIKE (n) *sosie (m)* : the star's look-alike = *le sosie de la star* ⓪ the spitting image = *le portrait tout craché*.

LOOKER (n) *beau gars (m), belle fille (f)* : what a looker his broad is ! = *quelle belle fille, sa nana !* ⓪ knockout = *merveille*.

LOOKOUT (n) **to be on the lookout** = 1/ *être aux aguets* : be on the lookout for the cops = *sois aux aguets pour voir si les flics arrivent* 2/ *être à la recherche de* : I'm on the lookout for a cheap used car = *je suis à la recherche d'une vieille voiture bon marché*.

LOOK-SEE (n) **to take a look-see** = *jeter un petit coup d'œil*.

LOOM (to, -ed) *se dessiner à l'horizon* : a depression's looming = *une dépression se dessine à l'horizon* ⓪ to threaten = *menacer*.

LOONY (adj, -ier, -iest) *marteau* : you're loony ! = *tu es complètement marteau !* → CRAZY
loony bin = *maison de dingues* = funny farm.

LOOP (n) *stérilet (m)* : she's stopped the pill for the loop = *elle a arrêté la pilule pour le stérilet*
to knock s.o. for a loop = *laisser qqn baba* : the news knocked me for a loop = *la nouvelle m'a laissé baba* ⓪ to bowl over = *laisser interdit*.

LOOPHOLE (n) *lacune (f)* : loopholes in the tax law = *des lacunes dans la loi fiscale* ⓪ escape clause = *clause échappatoire* ☠ → gap.

LOOSE (adj, -r, -st) 1/ *trop large* : my skirt's loose = *ma jupe est trop large* ≠ tight = *serré* 2/ *large* : a loose interpretation of the law = *une interprétation large de la loi* ☠ = large
at loose ends = *déboussolé* : he's been at loose ends since his wife left him = *il est déboussolé depuis que sa femme l'a quitté* ⓪ at sea = *à la dérive*
to let loose = *se déchaîner* : he got angry and let loose at everyone = *il s'est mis en colère et s'est déchaîné contre tout le monde* → ANGRY
☠ *déchaîner les cris/les rires* = to trigger off shouts/laughter
— *les gosses étaient déchaînés* = the kids ran riot
stay/hang loose ! = *te frappe pas !* ⓪ keep your head ! = *garde la tête froide !*

LOOSEN (to, -ed) *desserrer* : he loosened his belt = *il a desserré sa ceinture* ≠ to tighten = *serrer*
to loosen up = *se dégeler* : after a drink she loosened up = *après un verre elle s'est dégelée* ☠ → to thaw.

LOOT (n) *pèze (m)* : it's the end of the month and I don't have any loot left = *c'est la fin du mois et je n'ai plus de pèze* ⓪ bread = *pognon*.

LOOT (to, -ed) *piller* ⓪ to sack = *mettre à sac* **LOOTER** (n) *pillard, -e* ⓪ rioter = *émeutier* **LOOTING** (n) *pillage (m)* : there was a lot of looting during the riots = *il y a eu pas mal de pillage pendant les émeutes* ⓪ robbery = *vol*.

LOPSIDED (adj) *de travers* (painting), *bancal, -e* : the painting's lopsided = *le tableau est de travers*, his reasoning's lopsided = *son raisonnement est bancal*.

LOQUACIOUS (adj) *loquace* ⓪ verbose = *verbeux*.

LORD (n) *seigneur (m)* : the lord of the manor = *le seigneur du manoir*
to live like a lord = *vivre comme un pacha* → RICH
Lord knows what/who = *Dieu sait quoi/qui* = God knows what/who
lord (Byron/etc.) = *lord (Byron/etc.)*
the Lord = *le Seigneur* ⓪ the Savior = *le Sauveur*.

LORD ! (interj) *seigneur !* : Lord, she's beautiful ! = *seigneur, qu'elle est belle !* → GOSH !

LORD (to, -ed) **to lord it over** = *régenter* : as the boss's wife, she likes lording it over the others = *comme elle est la femme du patron, elle aime régenter les autres* ⓪ to boss = *mener à la baguette*.

LORRY (n, -ies) (GB) *camion (m)* = truck.

LOSE (to, lost, lost) 1/ *perdre, paumer* (LV) : he lost his book = *il a perdu son livre* ⓪ to mislay = *égarer* 2/ *perdre* : they lost the game = *ils ont perdu la partie* ⓪ to take a beating = *prendre une raclée* ≠ to win = *gagner* 3/ *perdre* : he lost his father = *il a perdu son père*
to be lost on s.o. = *passer au-dessus de la tête de qqn* : your remark was lost on him = *ta remarque lui est passée au-dessus de la tête*
☠ *ça te perdra* = it'll be your undoing
— *tu perds ton temps* = you're wasting your time
— *tu ne perds rien pour attendre* = I'll get mine in.

LOSER (n) 1/ *perdant, -e* : her brother's always been a loser = *son frère a toujours été un perdant* ≠ a winner = *un gagneur* 2/ (qqch qui est) *zéro* : his last movie was a loser = *son dernier film, c'était zéro* → AWFUL ≠ a winner = *qqch de chouette* 3/ *pauvre type/fille* : her husband's a loser = *son mari est un pauvre type* ⓪ schlepp = *minable*.

LOSS (n, -es) *perte (f)* : the loss of a child = *la perte d'un enfant* ≠ gain = ←
to be at a loss for words = *ne pas trouver ses mots*
to be at a loss to = *être bien embarrassé de* : I'm at a loss to explain to you why they split = *je serais bien embarrassé pour t'expliquer pourquoi ils ont rompu*
to cut one's losses = *limiter les dégâts* ≠ to get out while the going's good = *bien tirer son épingle du jeu*
he's no (great) loss ! = *ce n'est pas une (grosse) perte !*
☠ *le jeu a causé sa perte* = gambling was his undoing/his doom
— *de nombreuses pertes pendant la guerre* = many casualties during the war.

LOST (adj) *perdu, -e* : a lost cause = *une cause perdue*
a lost soul = *une âme en peine*
lost and found department = (*bureau des) objets trouvés*

to make up for lost time = *rattraper le temps perdu* ≠ to waste one's time = *perdre son temps* ☠ *à mes heures perdues* = in my spare time.

LOT (n) 1/ *lot (m)* : man's lot is self-destruction = *le lot de l'homme est de s'autodétruire* 2/ *lot (m)* : to sell land in lots = *vendre un terrain par lots* ⓪ parcel = *parcelle*

a lot = *beaucoup* : he drinks a lot = *il boit beaucoup* ≠ a bit = *un peu*	*ai rien à faire !* ⓪ I don't give a hang ! = *je m'en bats l'œil !*
a (strange) lot = *de (drôles) de gens* : what a strange lot her in-laws are !* = *ses beaux-parents sont vraiment de drôles de gens !*	**to draw lots** = *tirer à la courte paille/au sort* ⓪ to flip a coin = *tirer à pile ou face*
a lot (more interest-ing/happier) = *beau-coup (plus intéressant/ plus heureux)*	**to take a lot out of s.o.** = *beaucoup éprouver qqn* : the divorce took a lot out of her = *le divorce l'a beaucoup éprouvée* ⓪ to wipe s.o. out = *anéantir qqn*
a lot of = *beaucoup de* : he has a lot of money = *il a beaucoup d'argent* → MANY ≠ a bit of = *un peu de*	
a lot I care ! = *je n'en*	**that's saying a lot !** = *c'est beaucoup dire !* ⓪ you said it ! = *et comment !*
	what a lot of (money)! = *que d'(argent) !*

LOTS (n pl) *des tas* : do you have many ? — yes, lots = *est-ce que vous en avez beaucoup ? — oui, des tas* ≠ a few = *un peu*
lots of (kids) = *des tas de (gosses)* → MANY ≠ a few = *un peu*.

LOTS (adv) *drôlement* : lots happier/more interest-ing = *drôlement plus heureux/plus intéressant* ⓪ a great deal = *beaucoup*.

LOTION (n) *lotion (f)* : hair lotion = *lotion capillaire* ⓪ cream = *crème*.

LOTTERY (n, -ies) *loterie (f)* : a lottery ticket = *un billet de loterie* ⓪ drawing = *tirage*.

LOUD (adj, -er, -est) 1/ *fort, -e* : loud music = *de la musi-que forte* ≠ deafening = *assourdissant* ≠ soft = *doux* ☠ → strong 2/ *criard, -e* : loud clothes = *des vêtements criards* ⓪ showy = *voyant*.

LOUD (adv) *fort* : you're speaking too loud = *vous par-lez trop fort*
for crying out loud ! = *bon sang !* → GOSH !
out loud = *à haute voix* : say it out loud ! = *dites-le à haute voix !* ≠ in a whisper = *en chuchotant*
☠ *y aller fort* = to carry it too far
— *avoir fort à faire* = to have a lot to do
— *fort intéressant* = most interesting.

LOUDLY (adv) *fort* : he spoke loudly = *il parlait fort* ≠ softly = *doucement* ☠ → loud.

LOUDMOUTH (n) *fort, -e en gueule*.

LOUDSPEAKER (n) *haut-parleur (m)* ⓪ micro-phone = ←.

LOUNGE (n) *salon (m) (d'hôtel)* : if she's not upstairs, she must be in the lounge = *si elle n'est pas en haut, elle doit être au salon* ⓪ lobby = *hall*
☠ *salon de l'auto* = car show
— *salon (appartement)* = sitting-room.

LOUSE (n) *fumier (m)* : what a louse her husband is ! = *son mari, quel fumier !* → BASTARD ☠ → manure.

LOUSE UP (to, -d) *foutre par terre* : he loused everything up = *il a tout foutu par terre* ⓪ to ball up = *foutre en l'air*.

LOUSY (adj, -ier, -iest) *dégueulasse* : a lousy movie/meal = *un film/repas dégueulasse* → AWFUL ≠ great = *épatant*
to feel lousy = *être mal foutu* : I'm tired and feel lousy = *je suis fatiguée et je me sens mal foutue* ≠ to feel great = *se sentir en pleine forme*
to feel lousy about = *se sentir morveux pour* : I feel lousy about what happened = *je me sens morveux pour ce qui est arrivé* ⓪ to be sorry about = *être désolé de*
lousy with (bread/cops) = *pourri de (pognon)/qui grouille de (flics)*.

LOUT (n) *lourdaud (m)* ⓪ boor = *ours mal léché*, dolt = *balourd*.

LOVE (n) 1/ *amour (m)* : my first love = *mon pre-mier amour*, her love for children = *son amour des enfants* ⓪ friendship = *amitié*, crush = *béguin* ≠ hatred = *haine* ☠ *à vos amours !* = 1/ God bless you ! 2/ here's mud in your eye !

to be (madly) in love with = *être (éperdument) amoureux de* ⓪ to be stuck on = *avoir dans la peau*
to fall in and out of love = *avoir un cœur d'arti-chaut* ⓪ to flit = *papillonner*
to fall in love (with) = *tomber amoureux (de)* ⓪ to fall for = *s'amouracher de*
for the love of God !/Mike ! = *pour l'amour de Dieu !/du ciel !* → GOSH !
for the love of me ! = *ça alors !* : for the love of me, I can't understand ! = *ça alors, je ne comprends pas !* → GOSH !
give my love to = *bien des choses de ma part à* ⓪ my best to = *mes amitiés à*
love affair = *aventure (sentimentale)* ⓪ liaison = ←, fling = *amourette*
love at first sight = *coup de foudre*
love letter = *lettre d'amour/billet doux*
love life = *vie sentimentale*
how's your love life ? = *comment vont les amours ?*
to make love = *faire l'amour* ⓪ love-making = *ébats amoureux*

I don't work for the love of it = *je ne travaille pas pour le plaisir*
there's no love lost between (them) = *ils ne peuvent pas s'encaisser* ≠ **to be the best of friends** = *être les meilleurs amis du monde*
I won't do it for love nor money = *je ne le ferai à aucun prix*

2/ *mon chou* : **you're wrong, love** = *tu te trompes, mon chou* ⓒ **sugar** = *mon petit*.

LOVE (to, -d) *aimer* : **I love you** = *je t'aime* ⓒ **to be fond of** = *aimer bien* ≠ **to hate** = *détester* ☠ → **to like**
he loves me, he loves me not = *il m'aime un peu, beaucoup, passionnément, à la folie, pas du tout*
I'd love to (come) = *j'aimerais tellement (venir)*.

LOVEBIRDS (n pl) *tourtereaux* *(m pl)* = turtledoves ⓒ **to bill and coo** = *roucouler*.

LOVELY (adj) **1/** *charmant, -e* : **a lovely day/evening** = *une journée/soirée charmante* = **charming** ≠ **awful** = *affreux* → WONDERFUL **2/** *ravissant, -e* : **what a lovely girl !** = *quelle fille ravissante !* = **ravishing** ⓒ **beautiful** = *beau*.

LOVER (n) **1/** *amant, -e* : **my first lover was French** = *mon premier amant était français* ⓒ **friend** = *ami*, **flame** = *flirt* **2/** *amoureux, -euse* : **a nature lover** = *un amoureux de la nature* ⓒ **buff** = *mordu* ☠ *son amoureux* = **her sweetheart**.

LOVING (adj) *aimant, -e* : **loving parents** = *des parents aimants* ⓒ **sensitive** = *sensible*.

LOW (n) *niveau (m)/ point (m) (le plus) bas* : **the price of gold is at an all-time low** = *le prix de l'or est à son niveau/au point le plus bas*.

LOW (adj, -er, -est) **1/** *bas, basse* : **a low ceiling** = *un plafond bas*, **low prices** = *des prix bas* ≠ **high** = *haut*

---

to be at a low point = *être au creux de la vague* ⓒ **to be down in the dumps** = *être au trente-sixième dessous* **to be low man on the totem pole** = *être au bas de l'échelle* ⓒ **to be the fifth wheel** = *être la cinquième roue du carrosse*	**to be low on (money)** = *être à court d'(argent)* **to have a low boiling point** = *être soupe au lait* → ANGRY **to keep a low profile** = *ne pas se mettre sur le devant de la scène/ garder un profil bas*

2/ *bas, basse* : **what a low thing to have done !** = *que c'est bas d'avoir fait ça !* ⓒ **contemptible** = *méprisable* ≠ **noble** = ←

---

he's as low as they come = *c'est le dernier des derniers* = **he's the**	**lowest of the low** ⓒ **he's rotten to the core** = *il est pourri jusqu'à*

la moelle
low blow = *coup bas*
a low trick = *une vacherie* : **doing me out of my part was a low trick !** = *quelle vacherie de m'avoir supprimé ma part !*

☠ *au bas mot* = **at the very least**
— *les bas quartiers* = **the rough part of town**
— *de bas étage* = **sleazy/contemptible**

3/ *qui n'a pas le moral* ⓒ **blue** = *cafardeux* ≠ **up** = *qui a le moral*
to feel low = *ne pas avoir le moral* : **she's feeling low today** = *elle n'a pas le moral aujourd'hui* ⓒ **to be blue** = *avoir le cafard*.

LOW (adv) *bas* : **he spoke very low** = *il parlait très bas*
to lie low = *se tenir coi* : **the cops warned him to lie low** = *les flics lui ont dit de se tenir coi*
to be running low = *s'épuiser* : **our stocks are running low** = *nos stocks s'épuisent* ☠ → **to exhaust**
to sink low = *tomber bien bas*
☠ *bas les mains/pattes !* = **hands off !**

LOWBROW (n) *béotien, -enne* ≠ **highbrow** = *cérébral*.

LOWDOWN (n) *dessous (m) des cartes* : **to give/to know the lowdown** = *montrer/connaître le dessous des cartes* ⓒ **the dope** = *les dessous (de l'affaire)*.

LOWER (adj) *plus bas, basse* : **a lower price** = *un prix plus bas* ≠ **higher** = *plus haut*
lower class = *classe populaire* ⓒ **working class** = *classe ouvrière*
Lower East Side = *autrefois, quartier d'immigrants pauvres de Manhattan, foyer de la culture juive américaine (avec Brooklyn)*.

LOWER (to, -ed) *baisser* : **they're not going to lower prices** = *ils ne vont pas baisser les prix* ⓒ **to diminish** = *diminuer*, **to reduce** = *réduire*
I wouldn't lower myself to (calling him again) = *je ne m'abaisserais pas à (le rappeler)*
☠ *les prix baissent* = **prices are going down/coming down**
— *(ma mémoire) baisse* = **(my memory) is failing me**
— *se baisser pour ramasser qqch* = **to bend down to pick up stg.**

LOW-KEYED (adj) *mesuré, -e* : **a low-keyed statement/campaign** = *une déclaration/campagne mesurée*.

LOX (n) *saumon (m) fumé* = **smoked salmon** (GB).

LOYAL (adj) *loyal, -e* : **loyal ally** = *allié loyal* ⓒ **faithful** = *fidèle* ≠ **disloyal** = *déloyal*
loyal to (his friends) = *loyal envers (ses amis)*.

LOYALLY (adv) *loyalement* ⓒ **faithfully** = *fidèlement*.

LOYALTY (n, -ies) *loyauté (f)* ⓒ **fidelity** = *fidélité* ≠ **disloyalty** = *déloyauté*.

LUCID (adj) *lucide* ⓒ **aware** = *conscient*.

LUCK (n inv) *chance (f), pot (m)* (LV) : *what luck ! = quelle chance !/quel pot !* ⓐ break = *bol* ≠ misfortune = *malchance* ☠ → chance, → pot

as luck would have it = *comme le hasard fait bien les choses :* as luck would have it, the weather was beautiful = *comme le hasard fait bien les choses, il a fait beau* **bad ≠ good luck** = *déveine ≠ veine :* he lost his job, what bad luck ! = *il a perdu son travail, quelle déveine !* ☠ *veine* → vein **to be down on one's luck** = *avoir la poisse* ⓐ to be on a losing streak = *être en pleine série noire* **to be in ≠ out of luck** = *avoir du pot ≠ ne pas avoir de pot :* you were in luck finding such a great apartment = *tu as eu du*	*pot de trouver un appartement si chouette* **to bring luck** = *porter chance :* you brought me luck = *vous m'avez porté chance* **it's just my luck !** = *c'est bien ma chance !* **lots of luck !** = *bonne chance !* **= good luck !** **to push one's luck** = *tirer sur la corde :* you're pushing your luck asking for another raise so soon = *tu tires sur la corde en demandant une autre augmentation si rapidement* ⓐ to carry too far = *y aller fort* **rotten luck** = *tuile ≠ godsend = aubaine* ☠ → tile	**stroke of luck** = *coup de chance/pot ≠* a bitch = *qqch d'emmerdant* **tough luck !** = *pas de veine !* ⓐ too bad ! = *tant pis !* **what good luck !** = *quelle veine ! ≠* **what hard luck !** = *quel manque de veine !* **what lousy luck !** = *quelle guigne !* ⓐ what a bummer ! = *quel sale truc !* **wish me luck !** = *souhaitez-moi bonne chance !* **a run of good ≠ back luck** = *une période de chance ≠ déveine.*

LUCKY (adj, -ier, -iest) *qui a de la chance :* a lucky guy = *un type qui a de la chance ≠* unlucky = *qui n'a pas de chance*

to be lucky = *avoir de la chance :* we were lucky not to miss the train = *nous avons eu de la chance de ne pas rater le train* **to be born lucky** = *être né coiffé* **to thank one's lucky stars** = *remercier sa bonne étoile* **to hit it lucky** = *avoir un coup de pot* **how lucky !** = *quelle chance !* **lucky bastard/dog/stiff** = *sacré veinard*	**a lucky break** = *un coup de bol ≠* a bad break = *un manque de bol* **lucky charm** = *porte-bonheur* **lucky day** = *jour de chance* **lucky in cards, unlucky in love** = *heureux au jeu, malheureux en amour* **you don't know how lucky you are !** = *tu ne connais pas ta veine !*

LUCKILY (adv) *par chance :* luckily you were home when we came = *par chance, vous étiez chez vous quand nous sommes arrivés* ⓐ happily = *heureusement ≠* unluckily = *malheureusement.*

LUCRATIVE (adj) *lucratif, -ive :* a lucrative business = *une affaire lucrative* ⓐ moneymaking = *rentable* ☠ *une société à but non lucratif* = a nonprofit company.

LUDICROUS (adj) *saugrenu , -e :* a ludicrous situation = *une situation saugrenue* ⓐ preposterous = *abracadabrant.*

LUG (to, -ged) *transbahuter :* I had to lug my suitcase all the way to the station = *il a fallu que je transbahute ma valise jusqu'à la gare* ⓐ to schlepp = *trimballer.*

LUGGAGE (n inv) *bagages (m pl) :* the platform was filled with luggage = *le quai était couvert de bagages* ⓐ a piece of luggage = *un bagage,* suitcase = *valise* ☠ → baggage.

LUKEWARM (adj) *tiède :* the soup's lukewarm = *la soupe est tiède ≠* cool = *frais.*

LULL (n) *accalmie (f) :* a lull in the recession = *une accalmie dans la récession.*

LULLABY (n, -ies) *berceuse (f)* ⓐ fairy tale = *conte de fées.*

LUMBER (n inv) *bois (m) (planches)* ⓐ timber = *bois (de charpente),* lumberyard = *chantier de scierie,* lumberjack = *bûcheron* ☠ → wood.

LUMP (n) *motte (f)* (butter), *morceau (m)* (sugar), *bosse (f)* (head) ⓐ chunk = *gros morceau*
 to have a lump in one's throat = *avoir une boule dans la gorge/avoir la gorge serrée*
 lump sum = *somme forfaitaire/globale* ☠ *morceau* → piece, *bosse* → bump.

LUMP TOGETHER (to, -ed) *mettre en bloc :* lumping our resources together, we have 5 grand = *en mettant nos ressources en commun, nous avons 5 mille dollars.*

LUNATIC (n) *dément, -e :* he's a lunatic = *c'est un dément* ⓐ madman = *forcené*
 lunatic asylum = *asile d'aliénés.*

LUNCH (n, -es) *déjeuner (m)* : at what time is lunch ? = *à quelle heure est le déjeuner ?* ⊕ lunchtime = *heure du déjeuner*, meal = *repas*
to have lunch = *déjeuner* : we have lunch every day at noon = *nous déjeunons tous les jours à midi.*

LUNG (n) *poumon (m)* : lung cancer = *cancer du poumon.*

LURCH (n) **to leave s.o. in the lurch** = *laisser qqn le bec dans l'eau* : he took all the savings and left his wife in the lurch = *il est parti avec les économies et a laissé sa femme le bec dans l'eau* ⊕ to leave s.o. out on a limb = *mettre qqn dans une situation délicate.*

LURE (n) *leurre (m)* ⊕ bait = *appât* **LURE** (to, -d) *appâter* : lured by promises = *appâté par des promesses* ⊕ to entice = *allécher.*

LURID (adj) *macabre* : the lurid details of the story = *les détails macabres de l'histoire* ⊕ gruesome = *effroyable.*

LURK (to, -ed) *se tapir* : lurking behind the bushes = *tapi derrière les buissons* ⊕ to hide = *se cacher.*

LUSCIOUS (adj) *succulent, -e* : a luscious meal = *un repas succulent* ⊕ delicious = *délicieux* ≠ inedible = *immangeable.*

LUSH (n, -es) *sac (m) à vin* : her husband's a lush = *son mari est un sac à vin* → DRUNK ≠ teetotaler = *buveur d'eau.*

LUST (n) *passion (f) dévorante* : a lust for young boys/for power = *une passion dévorante pour les jeunes garçons/pour le pouvoir* ⊕ thirst = *soif* **LUST FOR** (to, -ed) *avoir une passion dévorante pour.*

LUXURIOUS (adj) *luxueux, -euse* : a luxurious apartment = *un appartement luxueux* ⊕ sumptuous = *somptueux* ≠ shabby = *miteux.*

LUXURY (n, -ies) *luxe (m)* : a life of luxury = *une vie de luxe* ≠ misery = *misère* ☠ *se payer le luxe de* = to indulge in.

LUXURY (adj) *de luxe* : a luxury hotel = *un hôtel de luxe* ⊕ opulent = *fastueux* ≠ crummy = *moche.*

LYNCH (to, -ed) *lyncher* ⊕ to string up = *pendre* **LYNCHING** (n) *lynchage (m)* ⊕ noose = *nœud coulant.*

LYRICIST (n) *parolier, -ère* ⊕ singer = *chanteur.*

LYRICS (n pl) *paroles (f pl) (d'une chanson)* : who wrote the lyrics ? = *qui a écrit les paroles ?* ☠ → word.

MA (abbr) = Master of Arts = *maîtrise (f) de lettres* ⓪ PhD = *doctorat*, MBA = Master in Business Administration = *diplôme d'études supérieures de commerce*.

MA BELL *compagnie privée de téléphone Bell (correspondant plus ou moins aux PTT)*.

MACHINE (n) *machine (f)* : sewing machine = *machine à coudre* ⓪ device = *dispositif*
machine gun = *mitrailleuse* ⓪ gun = *arme à feu* ☠ *machine à sous* = slot machine
— *machine à écrire* = typewriter.

MACHO (n) *macho (m)* : the man of my life was a macho = *l'homme de ma vie était un macho* ⓪ machismo = *machisme*, male chauvinist = *phallocrate*.

MAD (adj, -der, -dest) **1/** *fou, folle* : you're mad if you think I'm going to spend that kind of money ! = *vous êtes fou de penser que je vais dépenser une telle somme d'argent !* → CRAZY **2/** *fâché, -e* : she was mad when she found out the truth = *elle s'est fâchée quand elle a découvert la vérité* → ANGRY

to be hopping mad = *être furax* → ANGRY **to be mad about/for (Chinese food)** = *être fou de (cuisine chinoise)* ⓪ to be nuts about = *être dingue de* **to be mad as a hatter** = *travailler du chapeau* → CRAZY **to be mad at s.o.** = *être fâché contre qqn* : why are you mad at me ? = *pourquoi êtes-vous fâché contre moi ?* → ANGRY **to drive s.o. mad** =	*rendre qqn fou* : the kids are driving me mad = *les gosses me rendent fou* ⓪ to drive s.o. up the wall = *rendre qqn chèvre* **like mad** = *vachement* : he drinks like mad = *il boit vachement* → VERY ☠ → damned **to run like mad** = *courir à toute pompe* ⓪ to run like hell = *courir à bride abattue* **stark raving mad** = *fou à lier* → CRAZY.

MADAM (n) **1/** *madame (f)* : may I help you, madam ? = *puis-je vous aider, madame ?* ≠ sir = *monsieur* ☠ *madame Smith* = Mrs Smith

— *mesdames et messieurs* = ladies and gentlemen
2/ *mère (f) maquerelle, tenancière (f) de bordel* : she was a well-known madam = *c'était une mère maquerelle célèbre* ⓪ whorehouse = *boxon*.

MADDEN (to, -ed) *rendre fou, folle* : it maddens me to think that he's in jail = *ça me rend fou de penser qu'il est en prison* ⓪ it angers me to … = *ça me met en colère de …*

MADDENING (adj) *à rendre fou, folle* : maddening sloppiness = *une négligence à vous rendre fou* ⓪ exasperating = *exaspérant*.

MADE-TO-MEASURE (adj) *fait, -e sur mesure* = custom-made ≠ ready-to-wear = *prêt-à-porter*.

MADE-TO-ORDER (adj) *fait, -e sur commande, fait, -e sur mesure* (clothes) : made-to-order shoes = *des chaussures faites sur mesure*.

MADHOUSE (n) *maison (f) de fous* : to live in a madhouse = *vivre dans une maison de fous* ⓪ Bellevue = *Sainte-Anne/Charenton*.

MADISON AVENUE *centre du monde publicitaire américain à New York* ⓪ adman = *publicitaire*.

MADLY (adv) *à la folie* : to love s.o. madly = *aimer qqn à la folie* ⓪ wildly = *follement*.

MADMAN/MADWOMAN (n, -men/-women) *forcené, -e, fou, folle* : he was assassinated by a madman = *il a été assassiné par un fou/forcené* ⓪ mental case = *malade mental*
to run like a madman = *courir comme un fou* ⓪ to run like a bat out of hell = *courir comme un dératé* ☠ *maison de fous* = madhouse
— *plus on est de fous, plus on rit* = the more the merrier
— *(s'amuser) comme un fou* = (to enjoy o.s.) like crazy.

MADNESS (n) *démence (f)* : it's madness to spend so much for a coat = *c'est de la démence de dépenser autant pour un manteau* ⓪ craziness = *folie*.

MAFIA (n) *Mafia (f)* : the importance of the Mafia in US politics = *l'importance de la Mafia dans la politique américaine* ⓪ hired gun = *tueur à gages*.

MAGAZINE (n) *magazine (m), revue (f)* ⑩ periodical = *périodique*, quarterly = *publication trimestrielle*, weekly = *hebdomadaire* ☠ → *revue.*

MAGIC (n) *magie (f)* : to believe in magic = *croire à la magie* ⑩ witchcraft = *sorcellerie*, sleight of hand = *tour de passe-passe* **MAGICAL** (adj) *magique* : magical powers = *pouvoirs magiques.*

MAGICIAN (n) *magicien, -enne* ⑩ magic wand = *baguette magique.*

MAGISTRATE (n) *magistrat (m)* ⑩ judge = *juge.*

MAGNATE (n) *magnat (m)* : an oil magnate = *un magnat du pétrole* ⑩ baron = ←.

MAGNET (n) *aimant (m)* ⑩ compass = *boussole* **MAGNETIC** (adj) *magnétique* : magnetic field = *champ magnétique.*

MAGNIFICENT (adj) *magnifique* : a magnificent apartment = *un appartement magnifique* → WONDERFUL ≠ dreadful = *affreux* **MAGNIFICENTLY** (adv) *magnifiquement* : dressed magnificently = *magnifiquement habillé.*

MAGNIFY (to, -ied) *amplifier* : to magnify the seriousness of the situation = *amplifier la gravité de la situation* ⑩ to blow up = *grossir*, to heighten = *accroître.*

MAID (n) *bonne (f)* : we have a live-in maid = *nous avons une bonne à demeure* ⑩ chambermaid = *femme de chambre*, cleaning lady = *femme de ménage*
maid of honor = *témoin (femme)* ☠ → witness
☠ *il m'a à la bonne* = I'm in with him.

MAIDEN (adj) **maiden name** = *nom de jeune fille*
maiden voyage = *voyage inaugural.*

MAIL (n inv) *courrier (m)* : has the mail come yet ? = *le courrier est-il déjà arrivé ?* ⑩ the post office = *la poste*, mailbox = *boîte aux lettres*, zip code = *code postal*
by mail = *par la poste*
☠ *courrier du cœur* = advice to the lovelorn column
— *courrier des lecteurs* = letters to the editor.

MAIL (to, -ed) *mettre à la poste* : to mail a letter = *mettre une lettre à la poste* ⑩ to post = *poster.*

MAILMAN (n, -men) *facteur (m)* = postman (GB) ☠ → factor.

MAIL-ORDER HOUSE (n) *maison (f) de vente par correspondance.*

MAIM (to, -ed) *estropier* : maimed in the war = *estropié à la guerre* ⑩ to mutilate = *mutiler.*

MAIN (n) **in the main (I agree with you)** = *dans l'ensemble (je suis d'accord avec vous)* ⑩ for the most part = *en grande partie.*

MAIN (adj) *principal, -e* : money is my main problem = *l'argent est mon principal problème* ⑩ paramount = *de première (importance)*
main dish = *plat principal/de résistance*

main drag = *grande rue animée de la ville*
main floor = *rez-de-chaussée* = ground floor
main office = *bureau principal* ⑩ headquarters = *siège social*
the main thing is that ... = *le principal, c'est de...*

MAINLINE (to, -d) *se piquer (dans les veines)* : he's mainlining on heroin = *il se pique à l'héroïne* ⑩ to shoot up = *se shooter* ☠ → to sting.

MAINLY (adv) *surtout* : they eat mainly vegetables = *ils mangent surtout des légumes* ⑩ mostly = *principalement.*

MAINSTAY (n) *pilier (m)* : oil is the mainstay of the Middle East economy = *le pétrole est le pilier de l'économie du Moyen-Orient* ⑩ cornerstone = *pierre angulaire* ☠ → pillar.

MAINSTREAM (n) *idéologie (f) dominante* : the mainstream of our society = *l'idéologie dominante de notre société.*

MAINTAIN (to, -ed) **1/** *maintenir* : she maintains she's right = *elle maintient qu'elle a raison* ⑩ to assert = *affirmer*, to contend = *prétendre* **2/** *maintenir* : to maintain a certain speed = *maintenir une certaine allure* ☠ *maintenir une décision* = to uphold a decision
— *est-ce que le temps va se maintenir ?* = will the weather hold ?
3/ *entretenir* : they're so rich they maintain five residences = *ils sont assez riches pour entretenir cinq résidences*
☠ *s'entretenir avec qqn* = to have a talk with s.o.
— *entretenir une femme/un homme* = to keep a woman/a man
— *entretenir son anglais* = to keep up one's English.

MAINTENANCE (n) *entretien (m)* : the maintenance of the building = *l'entretien de l'immeuble* = the upkeep of the building
☠ *l'entretien d'une voiture* = the upkeep of a car
— *un entretien (conversation)* = a talk.

MAJESTIC (adj) *majestueux, -euse* : a majestic landscape = *un paysage majestueux* ⑩ stately = *imposant.*

MAJESTY (n, -ies) *majesté (f)* : yes, your Majesty = *oui, votre Majesté* ⑩ your Royal Highness = *votre Altesse royale.*

MAJOR (n) **1/** *matière (f) principale* : my major is psychology = *ma matière principale est la psychologie* ⑩ subject = *matière* **2/** *commandant (m)* : a major in the Air Force = *un commandant dans l'Armée de l'air* ⑩ captain = *capitaine*
☠ *le major (d'une promotion)* = the valedictorian (of a class).

MAJOR (adj) **1/** *majeur, -e* : a major problem = *un problème majeur* ⑩ big = *grand* ≠ minor = *mineur* ☠ *être majeur* = to be of age **2/** *de premier ordre* : a major poet = *un poète de premier ordre* ⑩ outstanding = *hors pair.*

MAJOR IN (to, -ed) *étudier comme matière principale :* he majored in chemistry = *il a étudié la chimie comme matière principale* ≠ to minor in = *étudier comme matière secondaire.*

MAJORITY (n, -ies) *majorité (f) :* the majority of people are lonely = *la majorité des gens sont seuls* ⓓ most of = *la plupart de*
majority rule = *gouvernement par la majorité*
to win by a narrow ≠ **an overwhelming majority** = *gagner d'une courte majorité* ≠ *par une majorité écrasante.*
☠ *atteindre sa majorité* = to come of age.

MAKE (to, made, made) → DO.

MAKE-BELIEVE (n, adj) *pour faire semblant :* don't be afraid, it's just make-believe = *n'aie pas peur, c'est juste pour faire semblant.*

MAKESHIFT (adj) *de fortune :* makeshift offices after the fire = *des bureaux de fortune après l'incendie* ⓓ provisional = *provisoire.*

MAKEUP (n) *maquillage (m) :* you wear too much makeup = *tu mets trop de maquillage* ⓓ powder = *poudre,* lipstick = *rouge à lèvres,* eye shadow = *ombre à paupières,* eyeliner = *eye-liner,* mascara = ←, foundation = *base*
the makeup of (the company) = *la composition de (l'entreprise).*

MAKINGS (n pl) **to have the makings of (a great writer)** = *avoir l'étoffe d'(un grand écrivain).*

MALARIA (n) *malaria (f), paludisme (m)* ⓓ cholera = *choléra.*

MALARKY (n inv) *balivernes (f pl) :* what you're saying's a lot of malarky = *ce que vous dites, ce sont des balivernes* ⓓ rot = *âneries,* rubbish = *sottises.*

MALE (n) **1/** *homme (m) :* no males allowed = *les hommes ne sont pas admis* = man ≠ female = *femme* ☠ → man **2/** *mâle (m) :* the dog's a male = *le chien est un mâle.*

MALE (adj) **1/** *mâle :* male elephants go off to die alone = *les éléphants mâles s'en vont mourir seuls* ≠ female = *femelle*
male chauvinism = *phallocratie*
male chauvinist (pig) = *(sale) phallocrate* ⓓ macho = ←
2/ *masculin, -e :* a male team = *une équipe masculine* ☠ → masculine.

MALICIOUS (adj) *malveillant, -e :* malicious rumors = *des rumeurs malveillantes* ⓓ bitchy = *salaud.*

MALIGNANT (adj) *malin, -igne :* a malignant tumor = *une tumeur maligne* ≠ benign = *bénin* ☠ → clever.

MALLEABLE (adj) *malléable :* a malleable personality = *une personnalité malléable* ⓓ flexible = ←, pliable = *maniable.*

MALNUTRITION (n) *malnutrition (f)* ⓓ undernourishment = *sous-alimentation.*

MALPRACTICE (n) *négligence (f) professionnelle (d'un médecin) :* malpractice suit = *procès pour négligence professionnelle.*

MAMMAL (n) *mammifère (m) :* whales are mammals = *les baleines sont des mammifères* ⓓ rodent = *rongeur.*

MAN (n, men) *homme (m) :* she married a very nice man = *elle a épousé un homme très sympa* ⓓ guy = *mec,* cat = *gus,* businessman = *homme d'affaires* ≠ woman = *femme.*

a man's home is his castle = *charbonnier est maître chez lui* **to be man and wife** = *être mari et femme* **every man for himself !** = *sauve qui peut !* **listen man !** = *écoute, mon vieux !* **the man who came to**	**dinner** = *celui qui s'incruste* **to a man** = *jusqu'au dernier :* they were killed to a man = *ils ont été tués jusqu'au dernier* **to see a man about a dog** = *aller au petit coin* ⓓ to go to the toilet = *aller aux toilettes*

☠ *un homme averti en vaut deux* = forewarned is forearmed
— *les hommes ne sont pas admis* = males are not allowed.

MAN ! (interj) *hé ben ! :* man, it's cold ! = *hé ben, il fait froid !* → GOSH !

MANAGE (to, -d) **1/** *gérer :* he manages a hotel = *il gère un hôtel* ⓓ to direct = *diriger* **2/** *se débrouiller :* now that she's divorced, she'll have to manage alone = *maintenant qu'elle est divorcée, il va falloir qu'elle se débrouille toute seule*
to manage on ($ 100 a week) = *se débrouiller avec (100 dollars par semaine)*
to manage to = 1/ *arriver à :* I finally managed to do it = *je suis finalement arrivée à le faire* 2/ *se débrouiller pour :* can you manage to come tonight ? = *est-ce que tu peux te débrouiller pour venir ce soir ?*
☠ *(dans le showbiz) il faut savoir se débrouiller* = (in show business) you really have to hustle
— *vous vous débrouillez ?* = how are you getting on/along ?

MANAGEMENT (n inv) *gestion (f) (d'une entreprise) :* poor management = *mauvaise gestion*
the management = *la direction :* speak with the management = *parlez-en à la direction.*

MANAGER (n) *manager (m) (sport, show biz), directeur, -trice :* the singer's manager = *le manager du chanteur,* I want to speak with the manager = *je veux parler au directeur* ⓓ impresario = *imprésario* ☠ → director.

MANDATE (n) *mandat (m)* : a political mandate = *un mandat politique*
☠ *mandat (argent)* = money order
— *mandat d'arrêt* = warrant for arrest
— *mandat de perquisition* = search warrant.

MANDATORY (adj) *obligatoire* : paying taxes is mandatory = *il est obligatoire de payer des impôts* = *obligatory* ≠ optional = *facultatif.*

MANEUVER (n) *manœuvre (f)* : a maneuver to get him to quit = *une manœuvre pour le faire démissionner* ⟳ tactic = *tactique* ☠ *un manœuvre* = an unskilled worker.

MANHOLE (n) *trou (m) d'homme* : a manhole into the engine room = *un trou d'homme qui mène à la salle des machines.*

MANHUNT (n) *chasse (f) à l'homme* ⟳ public enemy number one = *l'ennemi public numéro un.*

MANIA (n) 1/ *manie (f)* : a mania for cleanliness = *la manie de la propreté* ☠ *petites manies* = idiosyncrasies 2/ *démon (m)* : a mania for bridge = *le démon du bridge* ☠ → demon.

MANIAC (n) *maniaque (m, f)* : a dangerous maniac = *un dangereux maniaque* ⟳ madman = *forcené.*

MANIC-DEPRESSIVE (n, adj) *cyclothymique (m, f).*

MANICURE (n) *manucure (f)* ⟳ pedicure = *soin des pieds* **MANICURIST** (n) *manucure (m, f).*

MANIFEST (adj) *manifeste* : a manifest lie = *un mensonge manifeste* ⟳ obvious = *évident.*

MANIFEST (to, -ed) *manifester* : she manifested her disapproval = *elle a manifesté sa désapprobation* ⟳ to express = *exprimer*
☠ *manifester (dans les rues)* = to demonstrate (in the streets)
— *elle a manifesté beaucoup d'enthousiasme* = she displayed a lot of enthusiasm.

MANIFESTATION (n) *manifestation (f)* : a manifestation of friendship = *une manifestation d'amitié* ⟳ show = *démonstration* ☠ *manifestation (rues)* = demonstration.

MANIFESTO (n) *manifeste (m)* : the Communist Party manifesto = *le manifeste du Parti communiste* ⟳ proclamation = ←.

MANIPULATE (to, -d) *manipuler* : he was trying to manipulate me = *il essayait de me manipuler* ⟳ to maneuver = *manœuvrer* **MANIPULATION** (n) *manipulation (f).*

MANKIND (n) *genre (m) humain* : the end of mankind = *la fin du genre humain* ⟳ humanity = *humanité.*

MANLY (adj, -ier, -iest) *viril, -e* : sensitive and manly = *sensible et viril* = virile ≠ effeminate = *efféminé.*

MANNED (adj) *habité, -e* : a manned spaceship = *un vaisseau spatial habité* ☠ → inhabited.

MANNER (n) *manière (f)* : he looked at me in a strange manner = *il m'a regardé d'une drôle de manière* ⟳ way = *façon*
a (strange) manner of (speaking) = *une (drôle de) façon de (parler)*
in a manner of speaking = *façon de parler* : I could kill him, in a manner of speaking = *quand je dis que je pourrais le tuer, c'est une façon de parler*
☠ *à sa manière* = in her way
— *faire des manières* = to put on airs
— *d'une manière générale* = generally speaking
— *d'une manière ou d'une autre* = some way or another.

MANNERISM (n) *maniérisme (m)* ⟳ affectation = ←.

MANNERS (n pl) *manières (f pl)* : she has good manners = *elle a de bonnes manières* ⟳ behavior = *comportement.*

MANNISH (adj) *masculin, -e* : a mannish walk = *une démarche masculine* = masculine ☠ → masculine.

MANOR (n) *manoir (m)* ⟳ mansion = *belle demeure.*

MANPOWER (n) *main-d'œuvre (f)* : a lack of manpower = *un manque de main-d'œuvre* ⟳ staff = *personnel.*

MANSION (n) *belle demeure (f)* ⟳ castle = *château.*

MANSLAUGHTER (n) *homicide (m) involontaire* = second-degree murder.

MANUAL (n) *manuel (m)* : a bridge player's manual = *un manuel de bridge* ⟳ guide = ←.

MANUAL (adj) *manuel, -elle* : manual labor = *travail manuel.*

MANUFACTURE (to, -d) *fabriquer* : to manufacture cars = *fabriquer des voitures* ⟳ to make = *faire*
☠ *qu'est-ce que tu fabriques ?* = what are you up to ?
— *il a fabriqué cette histoire* = he made up the story.

MANUFACTURER (n) *fabricant, -e* ⟳ industrialist = *industriel* **MANUFACTURING** (n) *fabrication (f).*

MANURE (n) *fumier (m)* ⟳ dung = *crottin* ☠ *quel fumier !* = what a louse !

MANUSCRIPT (n) *manuscrit (m)* : to read a manuscript = *lire un manuscrit* ⟳ text = *texte.*

MANY (pron, adj) → MUCH		
GROUP : MANY = BEAUCOUP DE		
an array of = *une collection de* **an awful lot of** = *énormément de*	**bags of** = *à gogo* **barrels of** = *en veux-tu en voilà*	**a batch of** = *plein de* **a bevy of** = *une brochette de* **buckets of** = *à la pelle*

a **bunch of** = *un tas de*
countless = *innombrable*
dozens of = *des dizaines de*
endless = *une infinité de*
an **enormous amount of** = *énormément de*
enough and to spare = *à revendre*
ever so many = *je ne sais combien de*
a **flock of** = *une ribambelle de*
a **flow of** = *un flot de*
galore = *à la pelle*
gobs of = *des tonnes de*
a **good/great many** = *pas mal de*
a **good number of** = *un bon nombre de*
a **great deal of** = *énormément de*
a **great number of** = *un grand nombre de*
a **great/large quantity of** = *une grande quantité de*
heaps of = *des tas de*

a **heck of a lot of** = *pas mal de*
a **hell of a lot of/a helluva lot of** = *un max(imum) de*
a **herd of** = *un troupeau de*
a **host of** = *une foule de*
a **huge amount of** = *une grande quantité de*
hundreds of = *des centaines de*
loads of = *à gogo*
a **lot of** = *beaucoup de*
lots of = *des tas de*
masses of = *des masses de*
a **mess of** = *en pagaille*
millions of = *des millions de*
more than enough = *plus qu'assez*
more than (he) knows what to do with = *à ne plus savoir qu'en faire*
much = *beaucoup de*
a **multitude of** = *une multitude de*
no end of = *à n'en plus finir*
a **number of** = *un certain nombre de*

numerous = *nombreux*
oodles of = *à profusion*
piles of = *tout plein de*
plenty of = *plein de*
pots of = *en veux-tu en voilà*
quite a few = *pas mal de* =
quite a lot of
scads of = *à foison*
scores of = *un grand nombre de*
several = *plusieurs*
a **shitload of** = *une chiée de*
a **slew of** = *une flopée de*
stacks of = *des masses de*
a **stream of** = *un flot de*
a **string of** = *une suite de*
a **swarm of** = *un essaim de/une nuée de*
tons of = *des tonnes de*
umpteen = *des centaines de*
untold = *incalculable*
wads of = *à profusion*
a **wealth of** = *une profusion de*
a **whole lot of** = *tout plein de*
zillions of = *à l'infini.*

MAP (n)*carte* (f) : a map of the United States = *une carte des États-Unis* ⓪ graph = *graphique* ☠ → card
to put on the map = *rendre célèbre* : President Carter put Plains on the map = *le président Carter a rendu Plains célèbre.*

MAP OUT (to, -ped) *dessiner les grandes lignes de* : to map out a new policy = *dessiner les grandes lignes d'une nouvelle politique.*

MAR (to, -red) *gâter* : the building marred the view = *l'immeuble gâtait la vue* ⓪ to ruin = *gâcher* ☠ → to spoil.

MARATHON (n, adj) *marathon* (m) : a marathon debate = *un débat marathon.*

MARBLE (n, adj) *marbre* (m) : a marble statue = *une statue de marbre* ⓪ stone = *pierre.*

MARBLES (n pl) *billes* (f pl) : to play marbles = *jouer aux billes*
to lose one's marbles = *perdre les pédales* → CRAZY
☠ *je retire mes billes* = I'm pulling out
— *attaquer bille en tête* = to attack head-on.

MARCH (n inv) *mars* (m) → MONTH ☠ *les giboulées de mars* = April showers.

MARCH (n, -es) *défilé* (m) : the President watched the march = *le Président a assisté au défilé* ☠ *un défilé de mode* = a fashion show.

MARCH (to, -ed) *défiler* : the soldiers marched = *les soldats défilaient*
to march on (a city) = *marcher sur (une ville)*
☠ *se défiler* = to back out/to fink out

— *les gens ont défilé à l'exposition* = people streamed to the exhibition.

MARGIN (n) *marge* (f) : write in the margin = *écrivez dans la marge* ⓪ edge = *bord*
☠ *ça nous laisse de la marge pour manœuvrer* = that gives us room/leeway to maneuver
— *vivre en marge de la société* = to live on the fringe of society.

MARGINAL (adj) *marginal, -e* : a marginal life/problem = *une vie marginale/un problème marginal.*

MARIJUANA (n) *marijuana* (f) ⓪ drugs = *de la drogue.*

MARINE (n) *marine* (m) (US), *fusilier* (m) *marin* : he's in the marines = *il est dans les marines/fusiliers marins*
tell it to the marines ! = *à d'autres !* → BUZZ OFF !
☠ *la Marine* = the Navy.

MARIONETTE (n) *marionnette* (f) ⓪ puppet = *pantin.*

MARK (n) 1/ *marque* (f) : a mark on one's arm = *une marque sur le bras* ⓪ spot = *tache*
to leave one's mark on = *laisser son empreinte sur* : Picasso left his mark on modern painting = *Picasso a laissé son empreinte sur la peinture moderne* = to leave one's stamp on
to make one's mark = *s'imposer dans* : he made his mark in advertising = *il a réussi à s'imposer dans la publicité* ⓪ to make a name for o.s. = *se faire un nom*
on your mark, get set, go ! = *à vos marques, prêts, partez !* ⓪ off and running ! = *c'est parti !*
☠ *marque (de café)/marque (de voiture)* = brand (coffee)/make (car)
— *marque déposée* = (registered) trademark

— *la marque du génie* = the hallmark of genius
— *marque (sports)* = score
2/ note *(f)* : good marks = *de bonnes notes* = good grades ☠ → note.

MARK (to, -ed) **1/** *marquer* : the discovery of the pill marked the end of an era = *la découverte de la pilule a marqué la fin d'une époque*
☠ *marquer (un point)* = to score (a point)
— *marquez votre nom* = write your name down
2/ *noter* : he's marking the papers = *il note les copies* ☠ → to note
to be marked down ≠ **up** = *être démarqué* ≠ *augmenté* : the shoes were marked down ≠ up = *les chaussures ont été démarquées* ≠ *augmentées*.

MARKED (adj) *notable* : a marked improvement = *une amélioration notable* ⓪ obvious = *évident*.

MARKET (n) *marché (m)* : is there a market for home robots ? = *y a-t-il un marché pour les robots ménagers ?* ⓪ supply and demand = *l'offre et la demande*
bear ≠ **bull market** = *marché à la baisse* ≠ *à la hausse*
buyers' ≠ **sellers' market** = *marché des acheteurs* ≠ *des vendeurs*
to put on the market = *mettre sur le marché* ⓪ to come out = *sortir*
to corner the market = *accaparer le marché*
market research = *étude de marché*
to play the market = *jouer en Bourse*
☠ *marché conclu !* = it's a deal !
— *je vous mets le marché en main* = take it or leave it
— *par-dessus le marché* = on top of it
— *un marché de dupes* = a sucker deal.

MARKETING (n inv) *marketing (m)* : he works in marketing = *il travaille dans le marketing*
to do the marketing = *faire le marché* ⓪ to go to the market = *aller au marché*.

MARMALADE (n) *confiture (f) d'oranges, marmelade (f)* ⓪ jam = *confiture*.

MARRIAGE (n) *mariage (m)* : this is my first marriage = *c'est mon premier mariage*
marriage counselor = *conseiller conjugal*
marriage license = *certificat de mariage*
to rush into marriage = *vouloir se marier à tout prix*
☠ *je suis allé à leur mariage* = I went to their wedding.

MARRIED (adj) *marié, -e* : she always falls for married men = *elle tombe toujours amoureuse d'hommes mariés* ⓪ taken = *pris*
married life = *vie conjugale*.

MARRY (to, -ied) *épouser* : she married the boss's son = *elle a épousé le fils du patron* = to wed ≠ to divorce = *divorcer*
they're happily ≠ **unhappily married** = *ils sont heureux* ≠ *malheureux en ménage*
to get married = *se marier* : they're going to get married in June = *ils vont se marier en juin* ⓪ to get

hitched = *se mettre un fil à la patte*
to marry beneath o.s. = *faire une mésalliance*
to marry s.o. off = *marier qqn* : she wants to marry her older daughter off = *elle cherche à marier sa fille aînée*
☠ *(les couleurs) se marient bien* = (the colors) go well/blend together
— *épouser une cause* = to espouse a cause.

MARTIAL LAW (n) *loi (f) martiale*.

MARTIAN (n) *martien, -enne* ⓪ planet = *planète*.

MARTYR (n) *martyr, -e* : a martyr of the revolution = *un martyr de la révolution* ⓪ victim = *victime* ☠ *enfants martyrs* = battered children **MARTYRDOM** (n) *martyre (m)* : some terrorists seek martyrdom = *certains terroristes recherchent le martyre* ☠ *souffrir le martyre* = to be in great pain **MARTYRIZE** (to, -d) *martyriser*.

MARVEL (n) *merveille (f)* : as a cook he's a marvel = *comme cuisinier, c'est une merveille* ⓪ wonder = *miracle* ☠ *les sept merveilles du monde* = the seven wonders of the world.

MARVEL AT (to, -(l)ed) *s'émerveiller de* : we marvelled at his ability to speak Russian = *sa maîtrise du russe nous a émerveillés*.

MARVELOUS (adj) *merveilleux, -euse* : a marvelous lover = *un amant merveilleux* → WONDERFUL **MARVELOUSLY** (adv) *merveilleusement, à merveille*.

MASCARA (n) *mascara (m), rimmel (m)* ⓪ makeup = *maquillage*.

MASCOT (n) *mascotte (f)* : Snoopy's the mascot of the team = *Snoopy est la mascotte de l'équipe* ⓪ lucky charm = *porte-bonheur*.

MASCULINE (adj) *masculin, -e* : she goes for masculine, macho men = *elle apprécie beaucoup les hommes masculins et machos* ⓪ manly = *viril* ≠ feminine = *féminin* ☠ *l'équipe/la population masculine* = the male team/population **MASCULINITY** (n) *masculinité (f)*.

MASK (n) *masque (m)* : everyone wore a mask at the ball = *tout le monde portait un masque au bal* ☠ *jeter le masque* = to reveal one's true colors.

MASOCHISM (n) *masochisme (m)* ⓪ S-M = *sadomasochisme* **MASOCHIST** (n) *masochiste (m, f)* : her husband likes to be whipped ; he's a masochist = *son mari aime être fouetté ; c'est un masochiste* **MASOCHISTIC** (adj) *masochiste*.

MASON-DIXON LINE (n) *ligne imaginaire séparant les États sudistes des États nordistes des États-Unis*.

MASQUERADE (n) *mascarade (f)* : the political lawsuit was only a masquerade = *le procès politique n'était qu'une mascarade*
masquerade ball = *bal masqué*.

MASS (n, -es) **1/** *masse (f)* : a mass of clay = *une masse d'argile*

masses of (people) = *des masses de (gens)* → MANY
the masses = *les masses* ⓪ the common man = *le commun des mortels*
☠ *pas (marrant) des masses* = not very (funny)
— *tomber/s'écrouler comme une masse* = to slump down
— *masse monétaire* = money in circulation
— *s'endormir comme une masse* = to be out like a light
2/ *messe (f)* : to say mass = *dire la messe.*

MASS (adj) **mass media** = *mass media* ⓪ press = *presse*
mass production = *production de masse/fabrication en série.*

MASSACRE (n) *massacre (m)* ⓪ bloodbath = *bain de sang.*

MASSACRE (to, -d) *massacrer* : they massacred the hostages = *ils ont massacré les otages* ⓪ to exterminate = *exterminer*
☠ *massacrer une pièce* = to kill/criticize a play
— *massacrer (musique)* = to murder (music).

MASSAGE (n) *massage (m)* : can you give me a massage ? = *est-ce que vous pouvez me faire un massage ?* = rubdown **MASSAGE** (to, -d) *masser* : he massaged my back = *il m'a massé le dos* ☠ *se masser autour de qqn* = to crowd around s.o.

MASSIVE (adj) *massif, -ive* : massive support = *soutien massif* ☠ *or massif* = solid gold.

MASS-PRODUCE (to, -d) *fabriquer en (grande) série* : to mass-produce records = *fabriquer des disques en (grande) série* ≠ to make to order = *faire sur commande.*

MASTER (n) *maître (m)* : disciples and their master = *des disciples et leur maître* ⓪ virtuoso = *virtuose* ≠ apprentice = *apprenti*
Master of Arts/Science = *maîtrise de lettres/de sciences* ⓪ Bachelor of Arts = *licence de lettres*
master of ceremonies = *présentateur*
the master's touch = *la main/touche du maître*
☠ *être maître de* = to be in control of
— *Maître (Dupont)* = Mr (Dupont) lawyer
— *maître (d'école)* = schoolteacher.

MASTER (to, -ed) *maîtriser* : to master a skill = *maîtriser une discipline*
☠ *maîtrise-toi !* = get a grip on yourself !
— *maîtriser qqn* = to subdue s.o.

MASTERMIND (to, -ed) *être le cerveau de* : he masterminded the operation = *il a été le cerveau de l'opération* ⓪ to organize = *organiser.*

MASTERPIECE (n) *chef-d'œuvre (m)* : Rodin's Thinker is a masterpiece = *le Penseur de Rodin est un chef-d'œuvre* ⓪ work of art = *œuvre d'art.*

MASTURBATE (to, -d) *(se) masturber* : she can't go a week without masturbating = *elle ne peut pas passer une semaine sans se masturber* ⓪ to jerk off = *se bran-*

ler, to play with o.s. = *jouer en solitaire* **MASTURBATION** (n) *masturbation (f).*

MATCH (n, -es) **1/** *allumette (f)* : to strike a match = *craquer une allumette* ⓪ matchbox = *boîte d'allumettes*
2/ *match (m)* : a tennis match = *un match de tennis*
to be a good ≠ **bad match** = *être bien* ≠ *mal assorti* : as a couple they're a good match = *comme couple, ils sont bien assortis*
to be no match for = *ne pas faire le poids contre* : their team's no match for ours = *leur équipe ne fait pas le poids contre la nôtre*
to meet one's match = *trouver à qui parler* : she finally met her match in Peter = *elle a finalement trouvé à qui parler en Peter*
☠ *un match nul* = a draw
— *un match de foot* = a soccer game.

MATCH (to, -ed) *être assorti, -e à* : your shoes don't match your coat = *tes chaussures ne sont pas assorties à ton manteau*
can't match = *ne peut égaler* : I can't match their offer = *je ne peux pas égaler leur offre.*

MATCHLESS (adj) *sans pareil, -eille* : matchless luxury = *un luxe sans pareil* ⓪ unrivaled = *sans égal.*

MATCHMAKER (n) *marieur, -euse* : she likes to play matchmaker = *elle aime jouer les marieuses* ⓪ a good catch = *un beau parti.*

MATE (to, -d) *s'accoupler* : animals mate in the spring = *les animaux s'accouplent au printemps.*

MATERIAL (n) **1/** *tissu (m)* : I don't like this material = *je n'aime pas ce tissu* ⓪ cloth = *toile* ☠ → tissue	
burlap = *jute*	**lace** = *dentelle*
camel's hair = *poil de chameau*	**linen** = *lin*
cashmere = *cachemire*	**nylon** = ←
chiffon = *mousseline*	**organdy** = *organdi*
corduroy = *velours côtelé*	**rayon** = *rayonne*
cotton = *coton*	**satin** = ←
denim = *jean*	**silk** = *soie*
felt = *feutre*	**suede** = *daim*
flannel = *flanelle*	**taffeta** = *taffetas*
gabardine = ←	**terry cloth** = *tissu éponge*
jersey = ←	**tweed** = ←
	velvet = *velours*
	wool = *laine*
2/ *matière (f)* : the material for a new novel = *la matière d'un nouveau roman* ☠ → matter.	

MATERIALISM (n) *matérialisme (m)* **MATERIALIST** (n) *matérialiste (m, f)* **MATERIALISTIC** (adj) *matérialiste.*

MATERIALIZE (to, -d) *(se) matérialiser* : our projects didn't materialize = *nos projets ne se sont pas matérialisés* ⓪ to come to pass = *se concrétiser.*

MATERNAL

MATERNAL (adj) *maternel, -elle* : maternal instinct = *instinct maternel* ≠ paternal = *paternel*
☠ *langue maternelle* = mother tongue
— *école maternelle* = nursery school.

MATERNITY (n, adj) **maternity hospital** = *maternité* **maternity leave** = *congé de maternité.*

MATHEMATICAL (adj) *mathématique* **MATHEMATICALLY** (adv) *mathématiquement* **MATHEMATICIAN** (n) *mathématicien, -enne* **MATHEMATICS** (n pl) *mathémati-*

ques (f pl) : to study mathematics = *étudier les mathématiques* ⓪ math = ←, algebra = *algèbre*, geometry = *géométrie*, trigonometry = *trigonométrie.*

MATINEE (n) *matinée (f)* : there's a matinee daily = *ils jouent en matinée tous les jours* ⓪ performance = *représentation* ☠ *dans la matinée* = in the morning.

MATRIARCH (n) *femme (f) chef de tribu/de famille* **MATRIARCHY** (n, -ies) *matriarcat (m).*

MATRON (n) *matrone (f)* **MATRONLY** (adj) *de matrone.*

MATTER (n) 1/ *question (f)* : financial matters = *des questions financières* ⓪ affair = *affaire* ☠ → question
2/ *matière (f)* : there's matter in space = *il y a de la matière dans l'espace*

☠ *matières premières* = raw materials — *la matière d'un roman* = the material for a novel	— *matière principale* = major subject (school) — *matière grasse* = fat content
a matter of life and death = *une question de vie ou de mort* **as a matter of course** = *tout naturellement* : I ask my husband for his opinion as a matter of course = *je demande tout naturellement son avis à mon mari* ⓪ automatically = *automatiquement* **as a matter of fact** = *en fait* : have you seen her recently ? — as a matter of fact I saw her yesterday = *est-ce que vous l'avez vue récemment ? — en fait je l'ai vue hier* ⓪ in point of fact = *en réalité* **as matters stand now (we don't have the money for a new car)** = *dans l'état actuel des choses (nous n'avons pas l'argent pour acheter une nouvelle voiture)* ⓪ at this stage of the game = *à ce stade* **for that matter** = *d'ailleurs* : the diaphragm isn't sure ; for that matter the IUD isn't either = *le*	*diaphragme n'est pas sûr ; d'ailleurs le stérilet ne l'est pas non plus* ⓪ in actual fact = *en fait* **is anything/something the matter ?** = *est-ce qu'il y a quelque chose qui ne va pas ?* ≠ **no, nothing's the matter** = *non, il n'y a rien* **it's a matter of (days/hours)** = *c'est une question de (jours)/d'(heures)* **that's no laughing matter !** = *il n'y a pas de quoi rire !* **that's quite/altogether another matter !** = *c'est une tout autre affaire !* ⓪ that's quite another story ! = *c'est une tout autre histoire !* **what's the matter ?** = *qu'est-ce qu'il y a ?* ⓪ what's up ? = *qu'est-ce qui se passe ?* **what's the matter with him ?** = *qu'est-ce qu'il a ?*

MATTER (to, -ed) *importer* : the only thing that matters is health = *la seule chose qui importe, c'est la santé* ☠ → to import

it doesn't matter = *ça ne fait rien/peu importe* ⓪ it's of no importance = *ça n'a pas d'importance* ≠ **that matters** = *ça fait quelque chose*	**it doesn't matter to me** = *ça m'est égal* = I don't care.

MATTER-OF-FACT (adj) *comme si de rien n'était* : she was very matter-of-fact about her abortion = *elle a parlé de son avortement comme si de rien n'était* ⓪ glib = *désinvolte* **MATTER-OF-FACTLY** (adv) *comme si de rien n'était* : she answered his question matter-of-factly = *elle a répondu à sa question comme si de rien n'était.*

MATTRESS (n, -es) *matelas (m)* ⓪ bed = *lit.*

MATURE (adj) *mûr, -e* : young but very mature = *jeune mais très mûr* ⓪ mellow = *assagi* ≠ immature = ←
☠ *l'âge mûr* = middle age
— *un fruit mûr* = a ripe piece of fruit
— *après mûre réflexion* = after due consideration.

MATURE (to, -d) *mûrir* : he's matured a lot since I last

saw him = *il a beaucoup mûri depuis la dernière fois que je l'ai vu* ☠ *mûrir (fruit)* = to ripen (fruit).

MATURITY (n-, ies) 1/ *maturité (f) (s.o.)* : maturity of judgment = *maturité de jugement* 2/ *échéance (f) (policy)* : the maturity of a loan = *l'échéance d'un emprunt.*

MAUL (to, -ed) *lacérer* : the lion mauled its trainer = *le lion a lacéré son dompteur* ⓪ to mangle = *mutiler.*

MAVERICK (n) *franc-tireur (m)* : he's a political maverick = *en politique, c'est un franc-tireur* ⓪ lone wolf = *quelqu'un qui fait bande à part.*

MAXIM (n) *maxime (f)* ⓪ saying = *dicton.*

MAXIMUM (n) *maximum (m)* : he drinks a maximum of

5 Scotches a day = *il boit au maximum 5 whiskies par jour* ≠ minimum = ←
☠ *tirer le maximum de* = to get the most ouf of
— *faire le maximum* = to do one's utmost.

MAY (n inv) *mai* (m) → MONTH.

MAY (aux, might) **may I smoke ?** = *puis-je fumer ?*
ⓓ can I smoke ? = *est-ce que je peux fumer ?*
if I may say so = *si je puis dire*
it may rain = *il se peut qu'il pleuve*

MAY	MIGHT
he says that he may come = *il dit qu'il se* **peut** *qu'il vienne* **that well may be** = *cela se* **peut** *bien*	**he said that he might come** = *il a dit qu'il se* **pourrait** *qu'il vînt* **that well might be** = *cela se* **pourrait** *bien.*

MAYBE (adv) *peut-être* : maybe he'll come = *il viendra peut-être* = perhaps ⓓ probably = *probablement,* in all likelihood = *selon toute vraisemblance*
and I don't mean maybe ! = *et je ne plaisante pas !*
maybe, maybe not = *peut-être que oui, peut-être que non.*

MAYONNAISE (n) *mayonnaise* (f) ⓓ mustard = *moutarde.*

MAYOR (n) *maire* (m) ⓓ city hall = *mairie/hôtel de ville.*

MAZE (n) *dédale* (m) ⓓ labyrinth = *labyrinthe.*

MC (abbr) = master of ceremonies = *présentateur, -trice* = emcee.

MD (abbr) = medical doctor = *docteur* (m) *en médecine* = doctor of medicine.

ME (pron) **1/** *me* (object/indirect object) : she can't see me = *elle ne peut pas me voir,* he gives me ten francs = *il me donne dix francs*
2/ *moi* (imperative) : give me $ 10 ! = *donnez-moi 10 dollars !* → I
it's me = *c'est moi*
me too = *moi aussi*
with/for me = *avec/pour moi*
☠ *(cette voiture) est à moi* = (this car) is mine.

MEADOW (n) *pré* (m) : the cows in the meadow = *les vaches dans le pré* ⓓ field = *champ,* prairie = *la grande prairie.*

MEAGER (adj) *maigre* : a meager salary = *un maigre salaire* ⓓ paltry = *piètre*
☠ *elle est maigre* = she's skinny
— *viande maigre* = lean meat
— *un maigre repas* = a scanty meal.

MEAL (n) *repas* (m) : hot meals = *des repas chauds* ⓓ breakfast = *petit déjeuner,* lunch = *déjeuner,* dinner = *dîner* = supper, chow = *bouffe,* snack = *casse-croûte,* mealtime = *heure du repas*
a (good) meal ticket = *une (bonne) vache à lait* : she's not crazy about him, but he's a (good) meal ticket = *elle n'est pas folle de lui, mais c'est une (bonne) vache à lait.*

MEAN (adj, -er, -est) **1/** *méchant, -e* : why are you so mean ? = *pourquoi êtes-vous si méchant ?* ⓓ evil = *malfaisant,* nasty = *vilain* ≠ kind = *bon* **2/** *méchant, -e* : a mean tennis player = *un méchant joueur de tennis* ≠ lousy = *dégueulasse*
that's no mean accomplishment = *ce n'est pas une mince affaire*

☠ *un méchant rhume* = a nasty cold — *ce n'est pas bien méchant* = it's not too serious	— *une méchante langue* = a malicious person.

MEAN (to, meant, meant) **1/** *vouloir dire* : do you see what I mean ? = *vous voyez ce que je veux dire ?,* I said Sunday but I meant Saturday = *j'ai dit dimanche, mais je voulais dire samedi,* higher oil prices mean higher inflation = *une hausse du prix du pétrole, cela veut dire une augmentation de l'inflation grandissante*
2/ *parler sérieusement* : do you mean that ? = *est-ce que tu parles sérieusement ?,* yes, I mean it = *oui, je parle sérieusement* ≠ to kid around = *plaisanter*
3/ *vouloir dire* : what does this word mean ? = *qu'est-ce que veut dire ce mot ?* ⓓ to signify = *signifier,* to connote = *dénoter*

(not) to mean it = *(ne pas) faire exprès* : I'm sorry my remark hurt you, I didn't mean it = *je suis désolé que ma remarque vous ait blessé, je ne l'ai pas fait exprès* ≠ I meant it = *j'ai fait exprès* **I say exactly what I mean** = *je dis les choses comme je les pense*	**what do you mean by that ?** = *qu'entendez-vous par là ?* **without meaning it** = *sans le vouloir* **you don't mean it !** = *sans blague !* ⓓ no joke ! = *sans plaisanter !*

to be meant for = 1/ *être destiné à* : the flowers were meant for you = *les fleurs vous étaient destinées* 2/ *être fait pour* : they	were meant for each other = *ils étaient faits l'un pour l'autre* **to be meant to** = *être censé* : the remark wasn't meant to be	repeated/taken seriously = *cette remarque n'était pas censée être répétée/prise au sérieux* **does (his name) mean any-**

thing to you ? = *est-ce que (son nom) vous dit quelque chose ?*, **no, it doesn't mean anything to me** = *non, cela ne me dit rien* **to mean a lot to** = *compter énormément pour* : money/his

daughter means a lot to him = *l'argent/sa fille compte énormément pour lui* **to mean to** = 1/ *représenter pour* : what does he mean to you ? = *qu'est-ce qu'il représente pour vous ?* 2/ *avoir bien*

l'intention de : I meant to tell you but I forgot = *j'avais bien l'intention de te le dire, mais j'ai oublié* = to intend to **do you mean to say (she told you that) ?** = *vous voulez dire qu'(elle vous a dit ça) ?*

MEANING (n) *sens (m)* : what's the meaning of this word ? = *quel est le sens de ce mot ?* ⓪ *signification* = ←, gist = *sens général* ☠ → sense.

MEANINGFUL (adj) *qui a un sens* : a meaningful life = *une vie qui a un sens* ≠ meaningless = *qui n'a pas de sens*.

MEANS (n) 1/ (inv) *moyen (m)* : the pill's the surest means of contraception = *la pilule est le plus sûr moyen contraceptif* ⓪ way = *façon* 2/ (pl) *moyens (m pl)* : I don't have the means to buy a car = *je n'ai pas les moyens d'acheter une voiture* ⓪ funds = *fonds*

by all means = *je vous en prie* : may I use your phone ? — yes, by all means = *est-ce que je peux utiliser votre téléphone ? — oui, je vous en prie* **by means of (a rope)** = *au moyen d'(une corde)* **by any/whatever means** = *par tous les moyens* ⓪ by hook or by crook = *coûte que coûte* **by no means** = *en aucune façon* : she's by no means the most intelligent of the class = *ce n'est en*

aucune façon la plus intelligente de la classe **to have the means** = *avoir les moyens* → RICH **it's a means to an end** = *c'est un moyen d'arriver à ses fins* ⓪ the end justifies the means = *la fin justifie les moyens* **to live beyond one's means** = *vivre au-dessus de ses moyens* ⓪ to live high on the hog = *mener grand train*

☠ *le meilleur moyen de* = the best way to — *il y a un moyen de ...* = there is a way to ... — *j'ai perdu mes moyens* = I was completely

ruffled — *on fera avec les moyens du bord* = we'll make do with what we have.

MEANTIME (n) **in the meantime** = *pendant ce temps-là* : you work and I'll cook dinner in the meantime = *tu continues à travailler et pendant ce temps-là je prépare le dîner* ⓪ in the meanwhile = *entre-temps*.

MEANWHILE (n) **in the meanwhile** = *entre-temps* : go take a bath and in the meanwhile I'll call home = *va prendre un bain et entre-temps j'appelle à la maison*.

MEANWHILE (adv) *entre-temps, en attendant* : he'll come later, meanwhile let's have something to drink = *il va venir plus tard, entre-temps/en attendant buvons quelque chose*.

MEASLES (n inv) *rougeole (f)* : she came down with the measles = *elle a attrapé la rougeole* ⓪ German measles = *rubéole*, mumps = *oreillons*.

MEASLY (adj, -ier, -iest) *misérable* : a measly tip = *un pourboire misérable* ⓪ paltry = *piètre* ☠ → miserable.

MEASURE (n) *mesure (f)* : measures in favor of the poor = *des mesures en faveur des pauvres* **to take measures** = *prendre des mesures* = to take steps ☠ *être en mesure de* = to be in a position to — *dépasser la mesure* = to overdo it — *battre la mesure* = to beat time — *il n'a pas de mesure* = he has no sense of moderation — *dans la mesure du possible* = as far as possible.

MEASURE (to, -d) *mesurer* : measure the length of the room = *mesurez la longueur de la pièce* **to measure up to** = *être au niveau de* : she doesn't measure up to the company's standards = *elle n'est pas au niveau des critères de la société* ⓪ to be equal to = *être de taille à* ☠ *se mesurer à qqn* = to pit o.s. against s.o. — *combien mesurez-vous ?* = how tall are you ? — *mesurer ses paroles* = to weigh one's words.

MEASUREMENT (n) **what are her measurements ?** = *quelles sont ses mensurations ?* ⓪ bust = *poitrine*, waist = *taille*, hips = *hanches*.

MEAT (n) *viande (f)* : I eat a lot of meat = *je mange beaucoup de viande* ⓪ meatloaf = *pain de viande*, beef = *bœuf*, pork = *porc*, veal = *veau*, lamb = *agneau*, roast beef = *rosbif*, steak = ←, ham = *jambon*, rare = *saignant*, very rare = *bleu*, medium = *à point*, well-done = *bien cuit* **meat and potatoes man** = *homme popote*.

MEATBALL (n) *boulette (f) (de viande)* ☠ *boulette (gaffe)* = goof/blunder.

MEATY (adj, -ier, -iest) *étoffé, -e* : a meaty role = *un rôle étoffé* ≠ meager = *maigre*.

MECHANIC (n) *mécanicien, -enne* : a competent mechanic = *un mécanicien compétent* ⓪ repairman = *réparateur*.

MECHANICAL (adj) *mécanique* : his way of making love has become mechanical = *sa façon de faire l'amour est devenue mécanique* ⓪ automatic = *automatique* **MECHANICALLY** (adv) *machinalement* : she answered mechanically = *elle a répondu machinalement.*

MECHANICS (n inv) *mécanique* (f) : to study mechanics = *étudier la mécanique* 💀 *rouler des mécaniques* = to play the tough guy.

MECHANISM (n) *mécanisme* (m) : the mechanism of a clock = *le mécanisme d'une horloge.*

MEDAL (n) *médaille* (f) : a gold medal = *une médaille d'or* ⓪ prize = *prix.*

MEDDLE IN (to, -d) *s'immiscer dans* : to meddle in s.o.'s affairs = *s'immiscer dans les affaires de qqn* ⓪ to interfere in = *s'ingérer dans*
stop meddling ! = *mêle-toi de ce qui te regarde !* ⓪ it's none of your business ! = *ce ne sont pas tes oignons !*

MEDIA (n pl) → MEDIUM.

MEDIATE (to, -d) *servir de médiateur, -trice* : the Secretary of State mediated between Libya and Syria = *le ministre des Affaires étrangères a servi de médiateur entre la Libye et la Syrie.*

MEDIATION (n) *médiation* (f) **MEDIATOR** (n) *médiateur, -trice* ⓪ go-between = *intermédiaire.*

MEDICAID (n) *assurance maladie financée par le gouvernement fédéral, les États et les municipalités* ⓪ medicare = *assurance maladie pour le 3e âge financée par le seul gouvernement fédéral.*

MEDICAL (adj) *médical, -e* : medical expenses = *dépenses médicales,* medical examination = *examen médical*
medical school = *faculté/école de médecine*
medical student = *étudiant en médecine/carabin* (LV).

MEDICINE (n inv) 1/ *médicament* (m) : he takes a lot of medicine = *il prend beaucoup de médicaments* ⓪ medication = *médication,* pills = *comprimés* 2/ *médecine* (f) : he's studying medicine = *il fait (sa) médecine*
medicine cabinet = *armoire à pharmacie*
medicine man = *sorcier* ⓪ faith healer = *guérisseur* 💀 → witch doctor
💀 *docteur en médecine* = medical doctor/MD.
— *école de médecine* = medical school.

MEDIEVAL (adj) *médiéval, -e* : a medieval castle = *un château médiéval* ⓪ the Middle Ages = *le Moyen Âge.*

MEDIOCRE (adj) *médiocre* : a mediocre writer = *un écrivain médiocre* → AWFUL **MEDIOCRITY** (n, -ies) *médiocrité* (f).

MEDITATE (to, -d) *méditer* : gurus make money meditating = *les gourous gagnent de l'argent en méditant* ⓪ to cogitate = *cogiter* **MEDITATION** (n) *méditation* (f) ⓪ reflection = *réflexion* **MEDITATIVE** (adj) *méditatif, -ive.*

MEDITERRANEAN (adj) *méditerranéen, -enne* : the Mediterranean sea = *la (mer) Méditerranée.*

MEDIUM (n) 1/ (-ia) *média* (m) : television is an excellent medium for education = *la télévision est un excellent média pour l'éducation*
the media = *les médias* : the media are against the President = *les médias sont contre le Président*
2/ *médium* (m) ⓪ spirit = *esprit.*

MEDIUM (adj) 1/ *à point* : make my steak medium = *fais mon steak à point* ⓪ well-done = *bien cuit*
2/ *moyen, -enne* : medium height = *taille moyenne* 💀 → average.

MEDIUM-SIZED (adj) *de taille moyenne* : a medium-sized company/girl = *une entreprise/une fille de taille moyenne.*

MEEK (n, adj, -er, -est) *timoré, -e* : a meek personality = *une personnalité timorée* ≠ bold = *hardi*
the meek shall inherit the world = *bienheureux les faibles, car ils hériteront de la terre.*

MEEKLY (adv) *d'une façon timorée* : to answer meekly = *répondre d'une façon timorée.*

MEET (to, met, met) 1/ *rencontrer* : I met him last summer = *je l'ai rencontré l'été dernier* ⓪ to make s.o.'s acquaintance = *faire la connaissance de qqn,* to bump into = *rencontrer par hasard*
have you two already met ? = *est-ce que vous vous connaissez ?*
to meet with = *s'entretenir avec* : the President's meeting with the union leaders = *le Président s'entretient avec les dirigeants syndicaux* ⓪ to confer with = *conférer avec*
2/ *aller chercher* : is anyone meeting you at the airport ? = *est-ce que quelqu'un vient vous chercher à l'aéroport ?*
3/ *se réunir* : the committee's meeting on Tuesday = *le comité se réunit mardi* ⓪ to hold a meeting = *tenir une réunion* 💀 → to reunite
4/ *(se) retrouver* : we can meet at the Plazza = *on peut se retrouver au Plazza,* at what time should we meet ? = *à quelle heure faut-il se retrouver ?* 💀 → to recover
5/ *rencontrer* : to meet (with) difficulties = *rencontrer des difficultés* = to encounter.

MEETING (n) 1/ *meeting* (m) (political), *réunion* (f) : a church/political meeting on Friday = *une réunion paroissiale, une réunion/un meeting politique vendredi* ⓪ assembly = *assemblée,* agenda = *ordre du jour* 💀 → reunion 2/ *rencontre* (f) : our first meeting was very romantic = *notre première rencontre a été très romantique* 💀 → encounter
it's a meeting of the minds = *les grands esprits se rencontrent.*

MELANCHOLY (adj) *mélancolique* : melancholy music = *musique mélancolique.*

MELLOW (to, -ed) *s'assagir* : you've mellowed over the years = *vous vous êtes assagi avec les années* ⓪ to tone down = *s'adoucir.*

MELODRAMA (n) *mélodrame* (m) : the story's a melodrama = *c'est un mélodrame* ⓄⒹ soap opera = *soap*
MELODRAMATIC (adj) *mélodramatique.*

MELODY (n, -ies) *mélodie* (f) ⓄⒹ tune = *air.*

MELON (n) *melon* (m) ⓄⒹ watermelon = *pastèque,* cantaloupe = *cantaloup.*

MELT (to, -ed) *fondre* : the snow's melting = *la neige fond* ≠ to freeze = *geler*
☠ *fondre en larmes* = to burst into tears
— *l'argent lui fond dans les mains* = money burns a hole in his pocket.

MELTING POT (n) *creuset* (m) : the United States is a melting pot for all nationalities = *les États-Unis sont un creuset où se mêlent toutes les nationalités.*

MEMBER (n) *membre* (m) : a member of the party = *un membre du parti* ⓄⒹ adherent = *adhérent* ☠ *les membres du corps* = the limbs of the body.

MEMBERSHIP (n) 1/ *adhésion* (f) : to apply for membership = *faire une demande d'adhésion*
membership fee = *cotisation*
2/ *nombre* (m) *d'adhérents* : a membership of 300 = *un nombre d'adhérents de 300.*

MEMBRANE (n) *membrane* (f).

MEMO (n) *mémorandum* (m) : a memo from the President = *un mémorandum du Président* ⓄⒹ message = ←
memo pad = *bloc-notes.*

MEMOIRS (n pl) *Mémoires* (m pl) : to write one's memoirs = *écrire ses Mémoires* ⓄⒹ autobiography = *autobiographie* ☠ → memory.

MEMORABLE (adj) *mémorable* : a memorable evening = *une soirée mémorable* ⓄⒹ unforgettable = *inoubliable.*

MEMORANDUM (n, -s or -da) *mémorandum* (m) = memo.

MEMORIAL (n) *mémorial* (m) ⓄⒹ war = *guerre.*

MEMORIZE (to, -d) *apprendre par cœur* : to memorize a poem = *apprendre un poème par cœur* = to learn a poem by heart.

MEMORY (n, -ies) 1/ *mémoire* (f) : he has a good memory = *il a une bonne mémoire*
if my memory serves me right = *si j'ai bonne mémoire*
in memory of (the soldiers killed in the war) = *à la mémoire des (soldats tués à la guerre)*
to refresh s.o.'s memory = *rafraîchir la mémoire de qqn*
the memory of an elephant = *une mémoire d'éléphant*
☠ *un mémoire (sur Freud)* = a dissertation (on Freud)
— *écrire ses Mémoires* = to write one's memoirs
2/ *souvenir* (m) : childhood memories = *souvenirs d'enfance*

to bring back memories = *ranimer de vieux souvenirs*
☠ → souvenir.

MENACE (n) *menace* (f) : too much rain is a menace to the crops = *une pluie trop abondante est une menace pour les récoltes* ⓄⒹ danger = ←
you're a menace (to other drivers) = *vous êtes un danger (au volant)*
☠ *pas de menaces !* = no threats !

MENACE (to, -d) *menacer* : the whole area is menaced by a volcano = *toute la région est menacée par un volcan* ⓄⒹ to endanger = *mettre en danger* ☠ *menacer de tuer qqn* = to threaten to kill s.o.

MEND (to, -ed) *raccommoder, repriser* : to mend socks = *raccommoder/repriser des chaussettes* ☠ *nous nous sommes raccommodés* = we're good friends again.

MENIAL (adj) **menial job/work** = *basses besognes.*

MENOPAUSE (n) *ménopause* (f) ⓄⒹ change of life = *retour d'âge.*

MENSCH (n, -en) chic type (m) : what a mensch he is ! = *c'est vraiment un chic type !* ≠ crumb = *rosse.*

MENSTRUATE (to, -d) *avoir ses règles* ⓄⒹ menstrual period = *règles.*

MENTAL (adj) 1/ *mental, -e* : mental disorders = *troubles mentaux* 2/ *dérangé, -e* : they concluded the murderer was mental = *ils ont conclu que le meurtrier était dérangé* → CRAZY
a mental block = *un blocage psychologique*
a mental case = *un malade mental* ⓄⒹ nut = *dingue*
mental hospital = *hôpital psychiatrique.*

MENTALITY (n, -ies) *mentalité* (f) : you have the mentality of a four-year-old = *tu as la mentalité d'un gosse de quatre ans.*

MENTION (n) *mention* (f) : he made no mention of their personal problems = *il n'a fait aucune mention de leurs problèmes personnels* ☠ *réussir à un examen avec mention* = to pass an exam with honors.

MENTION (to, -ed) 1/ *mentionner* : his name was mentioned in the article = *son nom était mentionné dans l'article* ⓄⒹ to name = *nommer*
don't mention it ! = *il n'y a pas de quoi !* ⓄⒹ you're welcome ! = *je vous en prie !*
not to mention = *sans parler de* : the food was fabulous not to mention the company = *la nourriture était fabuleuse sans parler des gens qui étaient là* = to say nothing of the company
2/ *dire en passant* : they mentioned the fact that they were going to Europe this summer = *ils ont dit en passant qu'ils allaient en Europe cet été* ⓄⒹ to hint = *laisser entendre.*

MENTOR (n) mentor (m) ⓄⒹ guru = *gourou.*

MENU (n) menu (m) : today's menu = *le menu du jour* ☠

(raconter qqch) par le menu = (to tell stg) in minute detail.

MEOW (to, -ed) *miauler* : cats meow = *les chats miaulent* ① to purr = *ronronner* ≠ to bark = *aboyer*.

MERCENARY (n, -ies) *mercenaire (m)* ① hired killer = *tueur à gages*.

MERCHANDISE (n) *marchandise (f)* : merchandise of poor quality = *marchandise de qualité médiocre* ① commodities = *denrées*.

MERCHANT (n) *marchand, -e* : the Merchant of Venice = *le Marchand de Venise* ① shopkeeper = *commerçant* ☠ *marchand de sable* = sandman.

MERCIFUL (adj) *miséricordieux, -euse* : a merciful king = *un roi miséricordieux* **MERCILESS** (adj) *sans merci* : a merciless fight = *un combat sans merci* ① pitiless = *sans pitié*.

MERCURIAL (adj) *versatile* : a mercurial nature = *une nature versatile* ① changeable = *changeant* ☠ → versatile.

MERCY (n, -ies) **to ask for the mercy of (the court)** = *demander la clémence du (tribunal)*
to be at s.o.'s mercy = *être à la merci de qqn*
to beg ≠ **to show mercy** = *demander grâce* ≠ *se montrer clément*
mercy killing = *euthanasie* = euthanasia
mercy, mercy ! = *pitié, pitié !* ① have a heart ! = *grâce !*

MERE (adj) *ne ... que* : she's a mere child = *ce n'est qu'une enfant*, I have a mere hundred dollars = *je n'ai que cent dollars*
the mere sight of him (makes me sick) = *le simple fait de le voir (me rend malade)*.

MERELY (adv) *simplement* : I merely wanted to ask you a question = *je voulais simplement vous poser une question* = simply.

MERGE (to, -d) *fusionner* : our two companies merged = *nos deux sociétés ont fusionné* ① to amalgamate = *s'amalgamer* **MERGER** (n) *fusion (f)* : the merger of two companies = *la fusion de deux sociétés*.

MERIT (n) *mérite (m)* : a person of great merit = *une personne d'un grand mérite* ① worth = *valeur* ☠ *s'accorder tout le mérite de* = to take all the credit for.

MERIT (to, -ed) *mériter* : that merits our attention = *cela mérite notre attention*
☠ *il l'a bien mérité !* = that served him right !
— *ça mérite confirmation* = it requires confirmation
— *elle mérite ce qui se fait de mieux* = she rates/deserves the best.

MERMAID (n) *sirène (f)* ① Ulysses = *Ulysse* ☠ → siren.

MERRY (adj, -ier, -iest) *joyeux, -euse* : a little tight and very merry = *un peu bourré et très joyeux* ≠ gloomy = *lugubre* ☠ → joyous
Merry Christmas ! = *joyeux Noël !*

MERRY-GO-ROUND (n) *manège (m), chevaux de bois (m pl)* = roundabout
☠ *un manège d'équitation* = a riding school
— *je vois ton (petit) manège* = I'm on to you.

MESHUGA (adj) *dingue* : you're meshuga, man ! = *t'es dingue, mon vieux !* → CRAZY.

MESS (n, -es) *pagaille (f)* : look at this mess ! = *regarde-moi cette pagaille !*

to be a mess = 1/ *être la pagaille* : your room/the situation in Lebanon is a mess = *c'est la pagaille dans ta chambre/au Liban* 2/ *être un gâchis* (stg), *une loque* (s.o.) : what a mess their marriage is ! = *leur ménage, quel gâchis !*, since she's been drinking she's a mess = *c'est une loque depuis qu'elle boit*
to be in a mess = *être dans de beaux draps* : you'll be in a mess if he finds the truth out = *tu seras dans de beaux draps s'il découvre la vérité* ① to be in a fix = *être dans le pétrin*
I look a mess = *j'ai une sale tête*
to make a mess = *ficher la pagaille* : the kids made a mess in the kitchen = *les gosses ont fichu la pagaille dans la cuisine*
to make a mess of (one's marriage/work) = *ficher en l'air (son ménage/son travail)* ① to screw up = *foutre par terre*
a mess of (papers/clothes) = *(des papiers/des vêtements) en pagaille* → MANY.

MESS (to, -ed) **to mess around** = *ne pas ficher grand-chose* : what is he doing ? — he's just messing around = *qu'est-ce qu'il devient ? — il ne fiche pas grand-chose* ① to fiddle around = *bayer aux corneilles*
to mess around with = *coucher avec* : she's messing around with her brother-in-law = *elle couche avec son beau-frère* ① to play around with = *s'envoyer en l'air avec*
to mess up = *ficher en l'air* : she messed up her work/life = *elle a fichu son travail/sa vie en l'air* ① to fuck up = *foutre en l'air*
to mess with = *se frotter à* : don't mess with him ! = *ne vous frottez pas à lui !*

MESSAGE (n) *message (m), commission (f)* : can I leave a message ? = *est-ce que je peux laisser un message/une commission ?*
get the message ? = *tu piges le truc ?* ① catch on ? = *tu piges ?*
☠ → commission.

MESSED-UP (adj) *paumé, -e* : messed-up teenagers = *des adolescents paumés* ① out-of-it = *déphasé*.

MESSENGER (n) *messager, -ère* ⓪ errand boy = *garçon de courses.*

MESSY (adj, -ier, -iest) *en pagaille* (room), *désordonné, -e* (s.o.) : a messy room/person = *une chambre en pagaille/une personne désordonnée* ≠ neat = *net*
(firing people) is a messy business = *c'est un sale truc (d'avoir à renvoyer des gens)* ⓪ a bitch = *qqch d'emmerdant.*

METAL (n) *métal* *(m)* : iron and steel are metals = *le fer et l'acier sont des métaux* ⓪ alloy = *alliage,* foundry = *fonderie* **METALLIC** (adj) *métallique* **METALLURGY** (n) *métallurgie (f).*

METAMORPHOSIS (n, -oses) *métamorphose (f)* : she's so happy now, it's a real metamorphosis = *elle est tellement heureuse maintenant, c'est une véritable métamorphose* ⓪ transformation = ←.

METAPHOR (n) *métaphore (f)* : "the fall of his life" is a metaphor = *« l'automne de sa vie » est une métaphore* ⓪ simile = *comparaison,* allegory = *allégorie.*

METAPHYSICAL (adj) *métaphysique* : a metaphysical conversation = *une conversation métaphysique.*

METAPHYSICS (n inv) *métaphysique (f)* : to study metaphysics = *étudier la métaphysique.*

METEOR (n) *météore (m)* ⓪ shooting star = *étoile filante,* meteorite = *météorite.*

METER (n) **1/** *mètre (m)* : three meters long = *trois mètres de long* ⓪ yard = ← **2/** *compteur (m)* : gas meter = *compteur à gaz*
meter maid = *contractuelle*
☠ *viens voir mon compteur bleu* = come up and see my etchings.

METHOD (n) *méthode (f)* : a new method of contraception = *une nouvelle méthode contraceptive* ⓪ manner = *manière,* technique = ←
there's method in (her) madness = *ce n'est pas si bête que ça (ce qu'elle fait).*

METHODICAL (adj) *méthodique* : a methodical worker = *un travailleur méthodique* ⓪ orderly = *ordonné.*

METICULOUS (adj) *méticuleux, -euse* : meticulous work = *travail méticuleux* ⓪ careful = *soigneux.*

METRIC SYSTEM (n) *système (m) métrique.*

METROPOLITAN (adj) *de grande ville* : metropolitan life = *la vie dans une grande ville* ☠ *la France métropolitaine* = mainland France.

MEXICO (n) *Mexique (m)* **MEXICAN** (n, adj) *Mexicain, -e.*

MEZZANINE (n) *mezzanine (f), entresol (m)* ⓪ main floor = *rez-de-chaussée.*

MICKEY FINN (n) *boisson (f) droguée, casse-pattes (m)* (LV) : they gave the spy a Mickey Finn = *ils ont donné une boisson droguée à l'espion.*

MICROBE (n) *microbe (m)* : to catch a microbe = *choper un microbe* ⓪ bacteria = *bactéries* ☠ *écoute, microbe !* = listen, shorty !

MICROPHONE (n) *microphone (m)* : speak in the microphone = *parlez dans le microphone* ⓪ mike = *micro.*

MID (prefix) *(à la) mi-* : mid-May = *à la mi-mai.*

MIDDAY (n) *midi (m)* ≠ midnight = *minuit* ☠ → noon.

MIDDLE (n) *milieu (m)* : in the middle of the meeting/street = *au milieu de la réunion/rue* ⓪ center = *centre*
to be caught in the middle = *être coincé entre les deux* : when parents fight, kids are caught in the middle = *quand les parents se disputent, les gosses sont coincés entre les deux* ⓪ to be caught in the cross fire = *être pris entre deux feux*
in the middle of (reading) = *en pleine (lecture)*
right/smack in the middle of/in the very middle of = *en plein milieu de* : he came right/smack in the middle of dinner/in the very middle of dinner = *il est arrivé en plein milieu du dîner*
☠ *le milieu (pègre)* = the underworld
— *les milieux politiques* = political circles
— *un milieu ouvrier* = a working-class background/milieu.

MIDDLE (adj) **middle age** = *l'âge mur*
the Middle Ages = *le Moyen Âge* ⓪ the Dark Ages = *le haut Moyen Âge*
to have a middle age spread = *avoir de la brioche* ⓪ to have a stomach = *avoir du ventre*
middle class = *classes moyennes*
Middle East = *Proche-Orient*
middle name = *deuxième prénom*
lower ≠ **upper middle class** = *petite* ≠ *grande bourgeoisie.*

MIDDLE-AGED (adj) *d'âge mûr, entre deux âges* : a middle-aged lover = *un amant d'âge mûr* ⓪ fortyish = *qui a la quarantaine,* fiftyish = *qui a la cinquantaine.*

MIDDLEMAN (n, -men) *intermédiaire (m, f)* : the middleman buys from the producer and sells to a store = *l'intermédiaire achète au producteur et vend à un magasin* ☠ → intermediary.

MIDDLE-OF-THE-ROADER (n) *modéré, -e* : people vote for middle-of-the-roaders = *les gens votent pour les modérés* = moderate ⓪ centrist = *centriste.*

MIDGET (n) *nain, -e* ⓪ pygmy = *pygmée* ☠ → dwarf.

MIDNIGHT (n) *minuit (m)* : I left at midnight = *je suis partie à minuit*
to burn the midnight oil = *travailler tard dans la nuit* ⓪ to cram = *bachoter.*

MIDST (n) **to be in the midst of** = *être en train de* : we're in the midst of eating = *nous sommes en train de manger*

in the midst of (dinner) = *en plein (dîner)* Ⓞ right in the middle of = *en plein milieu de*
in our midst = *parmi nous.*

MIDWAY (adv) **midway between (New York and Miami)** = *à mi-chemin entre (New York et Miami).*

MIDWEST (n) *Midwest (m)* Ⓞ Rocky Mountains = *les Rocheuses.*

MIDWIFE (n, -wives) *sage-femme (f)* Ⓞ delivery = *accouchement*, obstetrician = *obstétricien.*

MIGHT (n) **(push) with all your might** = *(poussez) de toutes vos forces*
might makes right = *la raison du plus fort est toujours la meilleure* Ⓞ the law of the jungle = *la loi de la jungle.*

MIGHTY (adv) *bougrement* : mighty hungry = *qui a bougrement faim* → VERY.

MIGRAINE (n) *migraine (f)* : I have a terrible migraine = *j'ai une migraine terrible.*

MIGRANT WORKER (n) *travailleur, -euse émigré, -e.*

MIGRATE (to, -d) *migrer* : birds migrate = *les oiseaux migrent* **MIGRATION** (n) *migration (f).*

MIKE (n) *micro (m)* : speak in the mike = *parlez dans le micro* Ⓞ loudspeaker = *haut-parleur* ☠ *micros (dans une ambassade)* = bugs (in an embassy).

MILD (adj, -er, -est) *doux, douce* : mild weather = *temps doux* Ⓞ clement = *clément* ☠ → soft.

MILDLY (adv) **to put it mildly** = *et c'est un euphémisme* : New York is dangerous, to put it mildly = *New York est dangereux, et c'est un euphémisme* Ⓞ that's the least you can say = *c'est le moins qu'on puisse dire.*

MILE (n) *mile (m)(1,609 km)* : ten miles from here = *à dix miles d'ici* Ⓞ mileage = *kilométrage*, nautical mile = *mille marin (1,852 km)*
to be miles above = *être à cent coudées au-dessus de* : the play was miles above the film = *la pièce était à cent coudées au-dessus du film* Ⓞ to run circles around = *être bien supérieur à*
to be miles apart = *être aux antipodes* : our political opinions are miles apart = *nos opinions politiques sont aux antipodes* Ⓞ opposite extremes = *à l'opposé*
to be miles from anywhere = *être à perpète* : the restaurant's miles from anywhere = *le restaurant est à perpète* ≠ to be in the area = *être dans le coin*
to talk a mile a minute = *ne pas avoir la langue dans sa poche* Ⓞ to talk a blue streak = *avoir la langue bien pendue*
(to win ≠ to lose) by a mile = *(gagner ≠ perdre) de loin* : he won the race by a mile = *il a gagné la course, et de loin.*

MILESTONE (n) *jalon (m) important* : the desegregation ruling was a milestone in the American civil rights struggle = *les lois sur la déségrégation ont été un jalon impor-*

tant de la lutte pour les droits de l'homme aux États-Unis Ⓞ turning point = *tournant.*

MILITANT (n) *militant, -e* : a communist militant = *un militant communiste* Ⓞ activist = *activiste* **MILITANT** (adj) *militant, -e.*

MILITARY (adj) *militaire* : military academy = *école militaire*
military law = *code de justice militaire*
military police = *police militaire* = MP.

MILITATE (to, -d) *militer* : to militate in an extremist group = *militer dans un groupe extrémiste* Ⓞ to be committed = *être engagé.*

MILITIA (n) *milice (f)* Ⓞ police = ←.

MILK (n) *lait (m)* : do you want a glass of milk ? = *est-ce que vous voulez un verre de lait ?*, skim milk = *lait écrémé* Ⓞ milkman = *laitier*, buttermilk = *babeurre*
milk chocolate = *chocolat au lait*
milk shake = ←.

MILK (to, -ed) *considérer comme une vache à lait* (s.o.), *traire* (cow) : the brothers are milking the company = *les frères considèrent la société comme une vache à lait* Ⓞ to rip off = *escroquer.*

MILKY WAY (n) *voie (f) lactée* Ⓞ Big Dipper = *Grande Ourse.*

MILL (n) *moulin (m)* : water mill = *moulin à eau*
cotton/paper mill = *filature de coton/fabrique de papier*
to have been through the mill = *en avoir vu de toutes les couleurs* : she's nineteen but she's already been through the mill = *elle a dix-neuf ans, mais elle en a déjà vu de toutes les couleurs* Ⓞ to have a hard/rough time of it = *en voir de dures*
☠ *on y entre comme dans un moulin* = anyone can just walk in.

MILLION (n, adj) *million (m)* : he made a million on the Stock Market = *il s'est fait un million en Bourse* Ⓞ billion = *milliard*
to feel like a million (bucks) = *être en super forme* ≠ to feel under the weather = *être mal fichu*
millions (flew) = *des millions de personnes (ont fui)*
millions of = *des millions de* → MANY
to look like a million = *avoir une mine superbe* ≠ to look lousy = *avoir l'air mal foutu*
thanks a million ! = *merci mille fois !*

MILLIONAIRE (n) *millionnaire (m, f)* : she married a millionaire = *elle a épousé un millionnaire* Ⓞ multimillionaire = *multimillionnaire.*

MIME (n) *mime (m, f)* Ⓞ pantomime = ←.

MIMIC (to, -ked) *singer* : stop mimicking me ! = *arrête de me singer !* Ⓞ to imitate = *imiter.*

MINCEMEAT (n) **to make mincemeat of** = *réduire à néant* : he made mincemeat of my argument = *il a réduit mon argument à néant* Ⓞ to destroy = *détruire.*

MIND (n) *esprit (m)* : the human mind = *l'esprit humain* ⓒ intelligence = ← ☠ → spirit

to be/to go out of one's mind = *avoir perdu/perdre l'esprit* → CRAZY

to blow s.o.'s mind = *en boucher un coin à qqn* : the amount of money he earns blows my mind = *qu'il gagne autant d'argent, ça m'en bouche un coin* ⓒ to strike dumb = *laisser sans voix*

that calls/brings to mind (bitter memories) = *ça rappelle d'(amers souvenirs)*

to change one's mind = *changer d'avis* : he agreed to lend me the money but then changed his mind = *il avait accepté de me prêter cet argent, mais ensuite il a changé d'avis*

to come to mind = *venir à l'esprit* : it never came to my mind to ask for a raise = *il ne m'est jamais venu à l'esprit de demander une augmentation*

to cross/to enter s.o.'s mind = *effleurer l'esprit de qqn* : it never crossed/entered my mind that she would split = *ça ne m'aurait pas effleuré l'esprit qu'elle puisse se barrer*

to go over and over in one's mind = *tourner et retourner dans sa tête*

to have (half) a mind to = *avoir (presque) envie de* ⓒ to be inclined to = *être enclin à*

to have in mind = *penser à* : who do you have in mind for the job ? = *à qui pensez-vous pour ce poste ?* = to think about

have you lost your mind ? = *est-ce que vous avez perdu l'esprit ?*

it's mind over matter = *c'est la victoire de l'esprit sur la matière*

keep/bear in mind (that we're all only human) = *garde toujours à l'esprit (que nous ne sommes tous que des humains)*

keep your mind on your (work) = *concentrez-vous sur votre (travail)* ⓒ pay attention to = *faites attention à*

to make up one's mind = *se décider* : I don't know what to do ; I can't make up my mind = *je ne sais pas quoi faire ; je n'arrive pas à me décider* ⓒ to make a decision = *prendre une décision* ☠ → to decide

a mind reader = *quelqu'un qui lit dans les pensées (des autres)*

out of one's mind = *qui a perdu l'esprit* → CRAZY

to put one's mind to = *se mettre à* : I'm sure you can do it if you put your mind to it = *je suis sûre que tu peux le faire si tu t'y mets*

to run through s.o.'s mind = *venir à l'esprit de qqn* : it ran through my mind that perhaps I was wrong after all = *il m'est venu à l'esprit que j'avais peut-être tort après tout*

that'll put his mind at rest/at ease = *ça le tranquillisera*

to slip s.o.'s mind = *sortir de l'esprit de qqn* : his phone number slipped my mind = *son numéro de téléphone m'est sorti de l'esprit*

to speak one's mind = *dire ce qu'on pense* ≠ to pussyfoot = *atermoyer*

to stick in s.o.'s mind = *être gravé dans l'esprit de qqn* : for some reason her last remarks stuck in my mind = *pour une raison ou pour une autre, ses dernières paroles me sont restées gravées dans l'esprit*

to take s.o.'s mind off (stg) = *changer les idées à qqn* : do you want to go to the country for the day ? it will take your mind off things = *est-ce que vous voulez aller passer la journée à la campagne ? ça vous changera les idées*

that's a load/a weight off my mind = *ça m'ôte un (grand) poids de la conscience*

to my mind = *à mon sens* : to my mind you were wrong = *à mon sens vous aviez tort* ⓒ from my point of view = *de mon point de vue*

what's on your mind ? = *qu'est-ce qui vous préoccupe ?* ⓒ what's it about ? = *de quoi s'agit-il ?*

with this in mind = *dans cette perspective* ⓒ in this regard = *à cet égard*

it's weighing on my mind = *ça me préoccupe beaucoup*

a twisted/warped mind = *un esprit tordu/mal tourné*

she knows her own mind = *elle sait bien ce qu'elle veut*

I can't get him/it out of my mind = *je ne peux pas m'empêcher de penser à lui/d'y penser.*

MIND (to, -ed) 1/ *gêner* : do you mind if I smoke ? = *est-ce que ça vous gêne si je fume ?*, no, I don't mind = *non, ça ne me gêne pas*, yes, I mind = *oui, ça me gêne* ⓒ does it bother you if … ? = *est-ce que ça vous embête si je … ?*

☠ *ne te gêne pas !* = be my guest !
— *il ne s'est pas gêné pour …* = he didn't think anything of …

— *sa fumée gêne les autres* = his smoking annoys the others
— *il gêne notre travail* = he's hindering/hampering our work

---

2/ *garder* : can you mind the kids for me ? = *est-ce que tu peux me garder les gosses ?* ⓒ to look after = *surveiller* ☠ → to guard

> mind you ... = *remarquez ...* : she was right, mind you, but her attitude was still crummy = *elle avait raison, remarquez, mais son attitude est tout de même moche*
> don't mind me ! = *ne vous gênez pas pour moi !*

> mind (the steps) ! = *faites attention (aux marches) !*
> I wouldn't mind (a Scotch) = *j'aimerais bien (un whisky).*

MIND-BLOWING (adj) *renversant, -e* : mind-blowing news = *des nouvelles renversantes* ⓓ startling = *sidérant.*

MIND-BOGGLING (adj) *qui laisse rêveur, -euse* : a mind-boggling amount of money = *une somme d'argent qui laisse rêveur* ⓓ astounding = *époustouflant.*

MINE (n) *mine (f)* : a coal mine = *une mine de charbon* ⓓ pit = *puits de mine*
a mine of (information) = *une mine de (renseignements)*
☠ *faire mine de* = to pretend
— *avoir bonne ≠ mauvaise mine* = to look ≠ not to look well
— *faire une mine de six pieds de long* = to pull a long face
— *mine de rien (elle gagne pas mal d'argent)* = without seeming to (she earns a lot of money)
— *ne pas payer de mine* = not to be much to look at.

MINE (to, -d) *miner* : the enemy mined the road = *l'ennemi a miné la route*
☠ *miner les projets de qqn* = to undermine/to subvert s.o.'s plans
— *le chagrin le mine* = he's consumed with grief.

> **MINE** (pr poss) *le mien, la mienne, les miens, les miennes, à moi* : are they your shoes ? — yes, they're mine = *est-ce que ce sont tes chaussures ? — oui, ce sont les miennes/oui, elles sont à moi*, it's my book = *c'est mon livre*, it's mine = *c'est le mien/c'est à moi* → MY.

MINER (n) *mineur (m)* : ten miners were killed = *dix mineurs ont été tués* ☠ → minor.

MINERAL (n, adj) *minéral (m)* : quartz is a mineral = *le quartz est un minéral* ⓓ ore = *minerai.*

MINGLE WITH (to, -d) *se mêler à* : after his speech the President mingled with the crowd = *après son discours, le Président s'est mêlé à la foule.*

MINIATURE (adj) *miniature* : miniature soldiers = *des soldats miniatures* ⓓ tiny = *minuscule.*

MINIMIZE (to, -d) *minimiser* : to minimize the risks = *minimiser les risques* ≠ to magnify = *amplifier.*

MINIMUM (n, -a or -s) *minimum (m)* : a minimum of security = *un minimum de sécurité.*

MINIMUM (adj) *minimum* : minimum age = *âge minimum* ⓓ minimal = ←
minimum wage = *salaire minimum/SMIC.*

MINISTER (n) 1/ *ministre (m)* : a cabinet of fifteen ministers = *un gouvernement de quinze ministres*
☠ *ministre des Relations extérieures* = Secretary of State
— *ministre de la Justice* = Attorney General
— *ministre des Finances* = Secretary of the Treasury/Chancellor of the Exchequer (GB)
2/ *ministre (m) du culte* ⓓ pastor = *pasteur.*

MINISTRY (n, -ies) *ministère (m)* : Ministry of Health (GB) = *ministère de la Santé* = Health Department ☠ *ministère des Relations extérieures* = State Department/Foreign Office (GB).

MINK (n) *vison (m)* : a mink coat = *un manteau de vison* ⓓ sable = *zibeline*, ermine = *hermine.*

MINOR (n) 1/ *mineur, -e* : his girlfriend's still a minor = *sa petite amie est encore (une) mineure* ≠ of age = *majeur* ☠ *un mineur (mine)* = a miner 2/ *matière (f) secondaire* : sociology was my minor = *la sociologie était ma matière secondaire.*

MINOR (adj) *mineur,-e* : minor problems = *des problèmes mineurs* ⓓ lesser = *moindre* ≠ principal = ←
minor part/role (in a play) = *second rôle (dans une pièce)* ⓓ bit part = *rôle accessoire*
☠ *elle est mineure* = she's a minor.

MINOR IN (to, -ed) *prendre comme matière secondaire* : she's minoring in math = *elle a pris les maths comme matière secondaire.*

MINORITY (n, -ies) *minorité (f)* : racial minorities = *minorités raciales* ≠ majority = *majorité*
minority rights = *les droits des minorités*
☠ *mettre en minorité* = to defeat (vote).

MINT (n) *menthe (f)* : mint tea = *thé à la menthe* ⓓ peppermint = *menthe poivrée*
it costs a mint = *ça coûte les yeux de la tête* ≠ it's dirt cheap = *c'est donné*
to make a mint = *se faire un fric fou* : he made a mint on the Stock Market = *il s'est fait un fric fou à la Bourse* → RICH.

MINUS (prep) *en moins* : living together is marriage minus the red tape = *habiter ensemble, c'est le mariage avec la paperasserie en moins* ⓓ without = *sans*
(5) minus (3 equals 2) = *(5) moins (3 égale 2).*

MINUTE (n) *minute (f)* : there are sixty minutes in an hour = *il y a soixante minutes dans une heure*
in a minute = *dans une minute* : I'll be finished in a minute = *j'aurai fini dans une minute*
to make every minute count = *profiter de chaque instant de la vie*

the minute that (he found out) = *à l'instant où (il a découvert la vérité)*
wait a minute ! = *attends une minute !* = **just a minute !** ⑨ hold on ! = *minute papillon !*
I won't be a minute = *j'en ai pour une minute.*

MINUTE (adj) *infime* : minute particles = *des particules infimes* ⑨ tiny = *minuscule.*

MINUTES (n pl) *procès-verbal* (m) : the minutes of the meeting = *le procès-verbal de la réunion.*

MIRACLE (n) *miracle* (m) : it'll be a miracle if she pays you back = *ce sera un miracle si elle te rembourse* ⑨ marvel = *merveille*
to work miracles = *faire des miracles* : the medicine worked miracles = *le médicament a fait des miracles.*

MIRACULOUS (adj) *miraculeux, -euse* : a miraculous recovery = *une guérison miraculeuse* ⑨ supernatural = *surnaturel* **MIRACULOUSLY** (adv) *miraculeusement.*

MIRAGE (n) *mirage* (m) : a mirage in the desert = *un mirage dans le désert* ⑨ illusion = ←.

MIRROR (n) *miroir* (m), glace (f) : a large mirror in my room = *une grande glace/un grand miroir dans ma chambre*
☠ *glace* → ice
— *un miroir aux alouettes* = a deceptive lure.

MISADVENTURE (n) *mésaventure* (f) : the misadventures of Don Quixote = *les mésaventures de Don Quichotte* ⑨ misfortune = *infortune.*

MISAPPROPRIATE (to, -d) *détourner* : to misappropriate funds = *détourner des fonds* ⑨ to rip off = *escroquer* ☠ → to deter **MISAPPROPRIATION** (n) *détournement* (m) *de fonds.*

MISBEHAVE (to, -d) *se tenir mal* (kids) : the children misbehaved at dinner = *les enfants se sont mal tenus pendant le dîner* ≠ to behave = *se tenir (bien).*

MISCALCULATE (to, -d) *mal calculer* : we miscalculated the time we needed to finish the work = *nous avons mal calculé le temps qu'il nous fallait pour finir le travail* ⑨ to misjudge = *mal juger* **MISCALCULATION** (n) *mauvais calcul* (m).

MISCARRIAGE (n) *fausse couche* (f) : she had a second miscarriage = *elle a fait une deuxième fausse couche* ⑨ a premature baby = *un prématuré.*

MISCAST (to, -cast, -cast) *mal distribuer* (play), ne pas être fait pour (role) : the play was miscast = *la pièce était mal distribuée*, he was miscast in the role = *il n'était pas fait pour le rôle.*

MISCELLANEOUS (adj) *divers, -e* : miscellaneous expenses/articles = *frais/articles divers* ⑨ different = *différent* ☠ → diverse.

MISCHIEF (n) *espièglerie* (f) : her eyes are full of mischief = *ses yeux sont pleins d'espièglerie* ⑨ mischievousness = *malice.*

MISCHIEVOUS (adj) *espiègle, malicieux, -euse* : a mischievous child = *un enfant espiègle/malicieux* ⑨ naughty = *vilain.*

MISCONCEPTION (n) *idée* (f) *fausse* : he has misconceptions about the American way of life = *il se fait des idées fausses sur le mode de vie américain.*

MISCONSTRUE (to, -d) *mal interpréter* : the press misconstrued the President's statement = *la presse a mal interprété la déclaration du Président* ⑨ to misunderstand = *mal comprendre* **MISCONSTRUCTION** (n) *fausse interprétation* (f).

MISDEMEANOR (n) *délit* (m) : shoplifting's a misdemeanor = *le vol à l'étalage est un délit* = misdemeanour (GB) ⑨ petty offense = *infraction* ☠ *délit de fuite* = hit-and-run (driver).

MISER (n) *avare* (m, f) : her husband's a miser = *son mari est un avare* ⑨ tightwad = *grigou* ≠ spendthrift = *panier percé* **MISERLY** (adj) *avare* : miserly people = *des gens avares* ⑨ stingy = *radin* ☠ *avare de paroles* = sparing with words.

MISERABLE (adj) **1/** *malheureux, -euse (comme les pierres)* : she's miserable with her husband = *elle est malheureuse (comme les pierres) avec son mari* ⑨ down in the dumps = *au trente-sixième dessous* ≠ riding high = *aux anges* ☠ → unfortunate **2/** *abominable* : what a miserable day/weekend/failure ! = *quelle journée/quel week-end/quel échec abominable !* = abominable → AWFUL
to feel miserable = *être mal fichu* ≠ to be feeling one's oats = *avoir la pêche*
I feel miserable about it = *j'en suis vraiment navré* ⑨ I feel sorry = *je suis désolé*
to make s.o. miserable = *rendre la vie impossible à qqn* : our money problems are making me miserable = *nos problèmes d'argent me rendent la vie impossible* ☠ *des gens misérables* = poverty-stricken people
— *un pourboire misérable* = a measly tip.

MISERABLY (adv) *abominablement mal* : he played miserably today = *il a abominablement mal joué aujourd'hui* ⑨ badly = *mal.*

MISERY (n, -ies) *souffrance* (f) : she's so unhappy, she's never known such misery = *elle est terriblement malheureuse et n'a jamais connu une telle souffrance* ⑨ woe = *malheur*
to live in misery = *vivre dans la misère*
misery loves company = *il vaut mieux être deux pour pleurer*
to put (an animal) out of its misery = *abréger les souffrances (d'un animal)*
☠ → suffering
— *salaire de misère* = starvation wage/salary.

MISFIRE (to, -d) *faire long feu* : our plan misfired = *notre plan a fait long feu* ≠ to work well = *bien marcher.*

MISFIT (n) *inadapté, -e :* all societies produce misfits = *toutes les sociétés engendrent des inadaptés.*

MISFORTUNE (n)*infortune* (f) *:* his greatest misfortune was meeting his second wife = *sa plus grande infortune a été de rencontrer sa deuxième femme* ⅅ ill luck = *malchance.*

MISGIVING (n) **to have misgivings about** = *avoir des craintes sur :* she has misgivings about what his reaction will be = *elle a des craintes sur la réaction qu'il va avoir* ⅅ to doubt = *douter de.*

MISGUIDE (to, -d)*mettre sur une mauvaise route :* what he said misguided us = *ce qu'il a dit nous a mis sur une mauvaise route.*

MISHAP (n) *incident* (m) *:* a trip full of mishaps = *un voyage plein d'incidents* ⅅ misadventure = *mésaventure* ☠ → incident.

MISINFORM (to, -ed) *mal renseigner :* the congressmen were completely misinformed = *les sénateurs étaient tout à fait mal renseignés.*

MISINTERPRET (to, -ed) *mal interpréter :* you misinterpreted my remark = *vous avez mal interprété ma remarque* ⅅ to misunderstand = *mal comprendre* **MISINTERPRETATION** (n) *mauvaise interprétation* (f) *:* a misinterpretation of the facts = *une mauvaise interprétation des faits.*

MISJUDGE (to, -d) *mal juger, méjuger :* I misjudged him = *je l'ai mal jugé/méjugé* ≠ to size s.o. up = *jauger qqn.*

MISLAY (to, -laid) *égarer :* I mislaid my watch = *j'ai égaré ma montre* = I misplaced my watch ☠ *nous nous sommes égarés* = we got lost.

MISLEAD (to, -led) *induire en erreur :* the publicity misled them = *la publicité les a induits en erreur* ⅅ to misguide = *mettre sur une mauvaise route.*

MISLEADING (adj) *trompeur, -euse :* a misleading statement = *une déclaration trompeuse* ⅅ false = *faux.*

MISPLACE (to, -d) = TO MISLAY.

MISPRINT (n)*faute* (f)*d'impression :* a book full of misprints = *un livre plein de fautes d'impression* ⅅ typo = *coquille.*

MISPRONOUNCE (to, -d) *mal prononcer, écorcher :* he mispronounced my name = *il a mal prononcé/écorché mon nom.*

MISQUOTE (to, -d) *citer hors de propos :* they misquoted the President's statement = *ils ont cité la déclaration du Président hors de propos.*

MISREPRESENT (to, -ed) *donner une fausse idée de :* you're misrepresenting the feminist viewpoint/the facts = *vous donnez une fausse idée du point de vue des féministes/des faits* ⅅ to distort = *déformer.*

MISS (n, -es) *mademoiselle* (f), *Mlle :* Miss Jones = *mademoiselle/Mlle Jones* ⅅ Mrs = *Mme.*

MISS (n, -es) **a miss is as good as a mile** = *c'est le résultat qui compte.*

MISS (to, -ed) *manquer, rater :* you missed a good show/ the bus = *tu as manqué/raté un bon spectacle/l'autobus* **I miss my parents** = *mes parents me manquent* **my parents miss me** = *je manque à mes parents* **to (just) miss** = *manquer (de justesse) :* the car just missed me = *la voiture m'a manqué de justesse* **to miss by** = *manquer de :* the car missed me by an inch = *la voiture m'a manqué d'un poil* **to miss out on** = *manquer :* you missed out on a wonderful evening = *tu as manqué une merveilleuse soirée* ⅅ to let pass by = *laisser passer* ☠ *manquer de patience* = to lack patience — *il ne manquait plus que ça !* = that's all I needed ! — *je n'y manquerai pas* = without fail.

MISSILE (n)*missile* (m) *:* ground-to-air missile = *missile sol-air,* guided missile = *missile téléguidé* ⅅ rocket = *fusée,* cruise missile = *missile de croisière.*

MISSING (adj) *qui manque :* that's the missing part = *voilà la partie qui manque.*

MISSION (n) *mission* (f) *:* mission accomplished = *mission accomplie.*

MISSIONARY (n, -ies) *missionnaire* (m, f) ⅅ apostle = *apôtre.*

MISSIS (n) **the missis** = *la patronne :* I'll have to ask the missis = *il faudra que je demande à la patronne.*

MISSOURI (n) *Missouri* (m) **I'm from Missouri, show me !** = *je suis comme saint Thomas, je veux le voir pour y croire !*

MISSPELL (to, -ed or -spelt) *mal orthographier.*

MIST (n)*brume* (f) *:* morning mist = *brume matinale* ⅅ haze = *brume légère,* fog = *brouillard.*

MISTAKE (n) *faute* (f) *:* there are three mistakes in your letter = *il y a trois fautes dans ta lettre* ⅅ error = *erreur* **by mistake** = *par erreur :* I did it by mistake = *je l'ai fait par erreur* ≠ on purpose = *exprès* **it's a mistake to (think he'll agree)** = *c'est une erreur de (croire qu'il sera d'accord)* **to make a mistake** = *se tromper/faire erreur :* you're making a mistake = *vous vous trompez/vous faites erreur* ⅅ you're wrong = *vous avez tort,* you're all wet = *vous vous mettez le doigt dans l'œil* ☠ *tromper qqn* = to cheat on s.o. **make no mistake about it (I'm going whether you like it or not)** = *ne vous y trompez pas (j'y vais que cela vous plaise ou non)* ⅅ get this straight = *dites-vous bien ça* ☠ → fault.

MISTAKE (to, -took, -taken) **to mistake s.o. for s.o.** = *confondre qqn avec qqn d'autre :* I mistook her for her sister = *je l'ai confondue avec sa sœur* ⓪ to take s.o. for s.o. = *prendre qqn pour qqn d'autre.*

MISTAKEN (adj) **to be mistaken (about)** = *se tromper (sur)* : you're mistaken about him = *vous vous trompez sur lui.*

MISTER (n) *monsieur (m)* : Mister Smith = *monsieur Smith* ⓪ Mr = *M.*
Mister Charley = *l'homme blanc* = the Man
☠ *oui, monsieur !* = yes, sir !
— *(mesdames et) messieurs* = (ladies and) gentlemen.

MISTLETOE (n) *gui (m)* : to kiss under the mistletoe = *s'embrasser sous le gui* ⓪ New Year = *le Nouvel An.*

MISTRESS (n, -es) *maîtresse (f)* : a lot of married men have mistresses = *beaucoup d'hommes mariés ont des maîtresses* ⓪ kept woman = *femme entretenue* ≠ lover = *amant*
☠ *la maîtresse de maison* = the lady of the house
— *maîtresse (d'école)* = schoolteacher.

MISTRUST (to, -ed) *se méfier de* : I mistrust my own feelings = *je me méfie de mes propres sentiments* ⓪ to distrust = *se défier de* **MISTRUSTFUL** (adj)*défiant, -e.*

MISUNDERSTAND (to, -stood, -stood) *mal comprendre* : you misunderstood what I said = *vous avez mal compris ce que j'ai dit* ≠ to catch on = *saisir.*

MISUNDERSTANDING (n)*malentendu (m)* : there's a misunderstanding about the contract = *il y a un malentendu au sujet du contrat* ⓪ disagreement = *désaccord.*

MITIGATE (to, -d) *atténuer* : nothing can mitigate her suffering = *rien ne peut atténuer sa souffrance* ≠ to intensify = *intensifier* ☠ *atténuer (une peine)* = to lessen (a sentence).

MIX (to, -ed) *mélanger* : mix the salad = *mélangez la salade,* I can't mix people from my office and my personal friends = *je ne peux pas mélanger les gens de mon bureau et mes amis personnels*
not to mix = *ne pas coller* : her friends and mine don't mix = *ses amis et les miens, ça ne colle pas*
to mix well/easily = *se lier facilement* : invite him to the party, he mixes well/easily = *invite-le à ta soirée, il se lie facilement*
to mix up = 1/ *confondre* : I mixed the two brothers up = *j'ai confondu les deux frères* ☠ → to confuse 2/ *embrouiller* : you're mixing me up = *vous m'embrouillez,* I'm mixed up = *je m'embrouille,* don't mix me up = *ne m'embrouillez pas* ⓪ to baffle = *dérouter*
to be mixed up in = *se trouver mêlé à* : he's mixed up in the drug scandal = *il se trouve mêlé au scandale de drogue* ⓪ to be involved in = *se trouver impliqué dans*
to get mixed up with = *traîner avec* : she got mixed up with a strange lot of people = *elle traîne avec de drôles de gens*
to mix with = *se mêler à* : he mixed easily with all the other guests = *il s'est facilement mêlé aux autres invités* = to mingle with.

MIXED (adj) *mixte* : mixed marriage = *mariage mixte*
mixed feelings = *sentiments mitigés*
☠ *école mixte* = co-ed school
— *commission mixte* = joint committee.

MIXED-UP (adj) *déboussolé, -e* : she's a mixed-up teenager = *c'est une adolescente déboussolée* ⓪ messed-up = *paumé.*

MIXER (n) *quelqu'un de liant* : my brother's a good mixer = *mon frère est quelqu'un de très liant* ≠ people shy = *sauvage.*

MIXTURE (n)*mixture (f), mélange (m)* : he's a mixture of violent moods and extreme sensitivity = *il y a en lui un mélange de violence et d'extrême sensibilité* ⓪ combination = *combinaison* ☠ *quelle étrange mixture !* = what a strange concoction !

MIX-UP (n) *confusion (f)* : a mix-up in the dates = *une confusion dans les dates* ☠ → confusion.

MOAN (n) *geignement (m)* **MOAN** (to, -ed) *geindre* : the patient moaned all night = *le malade a geint toute la nuit* ⓪ to lament = *se lamenter* ☠ *arrête de geindre !* = stop whining !

MOAT (n) *douves (f pl)* : a moat around the fort = *des douves autour du fort* ⓪ drawbridge = *pont-levis.*

MOB (n) *foule (f)* : there was a mob at the movies/store = *il y avait foule au cinéma/magasin* = crowd ⓪ throng = *cohue*
mob rule = *la loi de la rue.*

MOB (to, -bed) *s'attrouper (autour de)* : the crowd mobbed the embassy = *la foule s'est attroupée autour de l'ambassade.*

MOBBED (adj) *bondé, -e* : the movie house was mobbed = *le cinéma était bondé* = crowded ⓪ jammed = *bourré à craquer.*

MOBILE (n)*mobile (m)* : Calder's mobiles = *les mobiles de Calder* ☠ *le mobile du crime* = the motive of the crime.

MOBILE (adj) *mobile* : in this job you must be very mobile = *dans ce travail, il faut être très mobile* ≠ immobile = ← **MOBILITY** (n, -ies) *mobilité (f)* ≠ immobility = *immobilité.*

MOBILIZATION (n) *mobilisation (f)* : the mobilization of all males of 16 and over = *la mobilisation de tous les hommes de 16 ans et plus* ≠ demobilization = *démobilisation* **MOBILIZE** (to, -d) *mobiliser* : to mobilize troops = *mobiliser des troupes* ⓪ to build up = *renforcer* ≠ to demobilize = *démobiliser.*

MOBSTER (n) *truand, -e* ⓪ gunman = *homme de main.*

MOCCASIN (n) *mocassin (m)* indien ⓪ loafers = *mocassins de cuir.*

MOCK (adj) *factice* : a mock trial = *un procès factice* ⓪ sham = *bidon*.

MOCK (to, -ed) *se moquer de* : don't mock crippled people = *ne te moque pas des infirmes* ⓪ to ridicule = *ridiculiser*
☠ *je m'en moque !* = I don't give a hoot !
— « to mock » *est beaucoup moins employé que* « to make fun of ».

MOCKERY (n, -ies) **a mockery of (justice)** = *une parodie de (justice)*.

MODE (n) *mode* (f) : the latest mode in men's wear = *la toute dernière mode en vêtements masculins*
☠ *mode d'emploi* = instructions for use
— *la mode* = fashion.

MODEL (n) 1/ *mannequin* (m) : she's the highest paid model today = *c'est le mannequin le plus payé actuellement* 2/ *modèle* (m) : the first model of the plane = *le premier modèle de l'avion* ⓪ prototype = ←
3/ *maquette* (f) : he's working on the model of our yacht = *il travaille à la maquette de notre voilier* ⓪ toy = *jouet*.

MODEL (adj) *modèle* : a model student = *un étudiant modèle*
a model apartment = *un appartement témoin*.

MODEL (to, -(l)ed) *être mannequin* : what does your sister do ? — she's modelling = *que fait votre sœur ? — elle est mannequin*
to be modelled on = *être (fait/construit/dessiné) sur le modèle de* : their modern art museum was modelled on one in New York = *leur musée d'art moderne a été construit sur le modèle d'un musée new-yorkais*.

MODERATE (adj) *modéré, -e* : moderate prices = *des prix modérés* ⓪ reasonable = *raisonnable* ≠ immoderate = *immodéré* **MODERATE** (n) *modéré, -e* : the moderates swung the elections = *les modérés ont fait basculer les élections* ⓪ liberal = *libéral* **MODERATE** (to, -d) *modérer* : to moderate one's position = *modérer sa position*.

MODERATELY (adv) *moyennement* : moderately interesting = *moyennement intéressant* ≠ extremely = *extrêmement*.

MODERATION (n) *modération* (f) : to advise moderation = *conseiller la modération* ≠ excess = *excès*
(to smoke) in moderation = *(fumer) modérément*.

MODERATOR (n) *meneur, -euse* : the moderator of the debate = *le meneur du débat* ☠ → ringleader.

MODERN (adj) *moderne* : a modern apartment = *un appartement moderne* ⓪ recent = *récent* ≠ ancient = *ancien*, archaic = *archaïque*
modern languages = *langues vivantes*.

MODERNIZATION (n) *modernisation* (f) **MODERNIZE** (to, -d) *moderniser* : to modernize an economy/a company = *moderniser une économie/une société* ⓪ to renovate = *rénover*.

MODEST (adj) *modeste* : don't be so modest ! = *ne soyez pas si modeste !* ⓪ unassuming = *sans prétention* ≠ vain = *vaniteux* **MODESTLY** (adv) *modestement*.

MODESTY (n, -ies) *modestie* (f) : false modesty = *fausse modestie* ≠ vanity = *vanité*.

MODIFICATION (n) *modification* (f) : to make modifications = *faire des modifications* ⓪ rectification = ←
MODIFY (to, -ied) *modifier* : they modified their position = *ils ont modifié leur position*.

MOGUL (n) *magnat* (m) : a press mogul = *un magnat de la presse* = magnate ⓪ big shot = *grand ponte*.

MOIST (adj, -er, -est) *moite* : moist hands = *des mains moites* ⓪ moisture = *humidité*, moistness = *moiteur*.

MOLD (n) *moule* (m) : the mold was broken after they made you = *le moule a été cassé après qu'on t'a fait* = mould (GB) ☠ *manger des moules* = to eat mussels.

MOLDY (adj, -ier, -iest) *moisi, -e* : moldy bread = *pain moisi* = mouldy (GB).

MOLE (n) *taupe* (f) : a CIA mole = *une taupe de la CIA* ⓪ double agent = *agent double*.

MOLECULE (n) *molécule* (f) ⓪ atom = *atome*.

MOLEST (to, -ed) *molester (sexuellement)* : she was molested in the subway = *elle s'est fait molester dans le métro* ⓪ to rape = *violer*.

MOLLIFY (to, -ied) *amadouer* : they mollified the terrorists by sending the ambassador to negotiate = *ils ont amadoué les terroristes en envoyant l'ambassadeur négocier* ⓪ to appease = *apaiser*.

MOMENT (n) *moment* (m) : let's stop a moment = *arrêtons-nous un moment* ⓪ instant = ←
at a moment's notice = *sur-le-champ* : be ready to leave at a moment's notice = *soyez prêts à partir sur-le-champ*
at that moment (the phone rang) = *à ce moment-là (le téléphone a sonné)* ⓪ just then = *juste à ce moment-là*
at the moment (they're living in New York) = *en ce moment (ils habitent New York)* ⓪ for the time being = *pour le moment*
in a moment = *dans un instant/moment* : I'll be with you in a moment = *je serai à vous dans un instant/un moment*
just a moment ! = *un petit instant !*
(just) a moment ago = *il y a un instant* : she left (just) a moment ago = *elle est partie il y a un instant*
the moment of truth = *le moment de vérité* ⓪ turning point = *tournant*
not for the moment = *pas pour l'instant/pas pour le moment* : do you want to have kids ? — no, not for the moment = *voulez-vous avoir des enfants ? — non, pas pour l'instant/pour le moment*

☠ *choisir son moment* = to choose one's time
— *au moment de (l'accident)* = when (the accident) happened
— *c'est le moment ou jamais* = it's now or never
— *du moment qu'il (est d'accord))* = as long as he (agrees)
— *ce n'est pas le moment de (dépenser tout notre argent)* = now is not the time (to spend all our money)
— *je ne l'ai pas vu depuis un moment* = I haven't seen him for some time
— *par moments* = every so often.

MOMENTARY (adj) *momentané, -e* : momentary financial problems = *des problèmes financiers momentanés* ⓓ *transient* = *passager* **MOMENTARILY** (adv) *momentanément.*

MOMENTOUS (adj) *très important, -e* : it was a momentous occasion = *c'était une occasion très importante* ⓓ *important* = ←.

MOMENTUM (n) **to gain/to gather** ≠ **to lose momentum** = *gagner* ≠ *perdre du terrain* : the abortion movement's gaining momentum = *le mouvement en faveur de l'avortement gagne du terrain.*

MOMMY (n, -ies) *maman (f)* = mummy (GB) ⓓ mom = *m'man.*

MONARCH (n) *monarque (m)* ⓓ ruler = *dirigeant.*

MONARCHY (n, -ies) *monarchie (f)* ⓓ monarchist = *monarchiste.*

MONASTERY (n, -ies) *monastère (m)* ⓓ abbey = *abbaye.*

MONDAY (n) *lundi (m)* → WEEK.

MONETARY (adj) *monétaire* : monetary policy/reserves = *politique monétaire/réserves monétaires* ☠ *marché/système monétaire* = money market/system.

MONEY (n, -ies) *argent (m)* : do you accept French money ? = *acceptez-vous l'argent français ?*, they have a lot of money = *ils ont beaucoup d'argent* ⓓ cabbage = *oseille*, bread = *pognon*, dough = *fric*, a buck = *un dollar*, a grand = *mille dollars*, coin = *pièce*, change = *monnaie*, cash = *argent liquide*, gelt = *des ronds*

to be in the money = *être en fonds* → RICH	*faire sa pelote* 2/ *rapporter de l'argent* : this investment's making money = *cet investissement rapporte de l'argent* 3/ *gagner* : how much money do you make in a month ? = *combien gagnez-vous par mois ?* ⓓ to pull in = *se faire* ☠ → to win	*prête qu'aux riches*
to be rolling in money = *rouler sur l'or* → RICH		**money makes the world go round** = *c'est l'argent qui fait tourner le monde*
to come into a lot of money = *faire un gros héritage*		**money order** = *mandat-poste*
to get one's money's worth = *en avoir pour son argent* : you get your money's worth in that restaurant = *on en a pour son argent dans ce restaurant*	**money burns a hole in my pocket** = *l'argent me fond dans les mains*	**money talks** = *l'argent ouvre bien des portes*
to have money to burn = *avoir de l'argent à jeter par les fenêtres* → RICH	**money comes easy (to him)** = *(il) a l'argent facile*	**put your money where your mouth is** = *les conseilleurs ne sont jamais les payeurs*
it doesn't hurt to have money = *abondance de biens ne nuit pas*	**money doesn't grow on trees** = *l'argent ne se ramasse pas sous le pas d'un cheval*	**to spend money like it's going out of style** = *claquer un fric fou*
to make/to earn (good) money = *gagner un fric fou*	**money has no smell** = *l'argent n'a pas d'odeur*	**there's money to be made in (advertising)** = *il y a de l'argent à gagner dans (la publicité)*
to make money = 1/ *gagner de l'argent* : disco singers are really making money = *les chanteurs disco gagnent un argent fou* ⓓ to make a pile =	**money isn't everything** = *l'argent ne fait pas le bonheur*	**to throw one's money around** = *dépenser son argent à droite et à gauche*
	money is the root of all evil = *l'argent est la source de tous les maux*	**to watch one's money** = *surveiller ses dépenses* ≠ to be a spendthrift = *être panier percé*
	money makes money = *on ne*	

☠ *argent (métal)* = silver — *son argent a fait des petits* = his investmen paid off handsomely — *argent liquide* = cash	— *prendre tout pour argent comptant* = to take everything for gospel truth — *monnaie* = change.

MONEYBAGS (n inv) *rupin (m)*, *richard, -e* : her father's a moneybags = *son père est un rupin/un richard* → RICH.

MONEYED (adj) *argenté, -e* : moneyed relatives = *des parents argentés* → RICH ☠ *cheveux argentés* = silvery hair.

400

MONEY-HUNGRY (adj) *assoiffé, -e d'argent.*

MONEYMAKER (n) *quelqu'un/quelque chose qui rapporte gros :* her guy/the company's a moneymaker = *son type/l'affaire rapporte gros.*

MONEYMAKING (adj) *rentable :* a moneymaking business = *une affaire rentable* ⓐ profitable = ←.

MONGREL (n) *corniaud (m) :* what a cute mongrel ! = *quel adorable corniaud !* ⓐ dog = *chien* ☠ *espèce de corniaud !* = you nitwit !

MONITOR (to, -ed) *contrôler par monitoring :* to monitor s.o.'s heartbeats = *contrôler le rythme cardiaque de qqn par monitoring.*

MONK (n) *moine (m)* ⓐ monastery = *monastère.*

MONKEY (n) *singe (m)* ⓐ ape = *grand singe,* chimpanzee = *chimpanzé*
to have a monkey on one's back = *être en état de dépendance* ⓐ to be hooked = *être accroché*
monkey business = 1/ *grenouillage :* a lot of monkey business in the elections = *pas mal de grenouillage pendant les élections* ⓐ shenanigans = *magouillage* 2/ *singeries :* stop your monkey business and get your work done ! = *arrête tes singeries et mets-toi au travail !* ⓐ shenanigans = *rigolade* 3/ *histoires de fesses/la bagatelle :* all he thinks about is monkey business = *il ne pense qu'aux histoires de fesses/qu'à la bagatelle* ⓐ sleeping around = *coucheries*
to throw a monkey wrench into = *mettre des bâtons dans les roues (pour) :* he threw a monkey wrench into our plans = *il nous a mis des bâtons dans les roues (pour nos projets)* ⓐ to undermine = *miner*
☠ *on n'apprend pas à un vieux singe à faire des grimaces* = you can't teach an old dog new tricks.

MONOGAMY (n) *monogamie (f)* ⓐ monogamous = *monogame* ≠ polygamy = *polygamie.*

MONOLOG(UE) (n) *monologue (m)* ⓐ soliloquy = *soliloque* ≠ dialogue = ←.

MONOPOLIZE (to, -d) *monopoliser :* to monopolize the conversation = *monopoliser la conversation.*

MONOPOLY (n, -ies) *monopole (m) :* a state monopoly = *un monopole d'État* ⓐ cartel = ←.

MONOTONOUS (adj) *monotone :* a monotonous life = *une vie monotone* ⓐ humdrum = *monocorde* ≠ entertaining = *divertissant.*

MONOTONY (n) *monotonie (f) :* the monotony of the work = *la monotonie du travail* ≠ diversity = *diversité.*

MONSTER (n) *monstre (m) :* people who beat animals are monsters = *les gens qui battent les animaux sont des monstres* ⓐ beast = *bête*
☠ *tu es un monstre d'égoïsme* = you're wildly selfish
— *monstre sacré* = superstar.

MONSTROSITY (n, -ies) *monstruosité (f) :* the new museum's a monstrosity = *le nouveau musée est une monstruosité.*

MONSTROUS (adj) *monstrueux, -euse :* a monstrous crime = *un crime monstrueux* ⓐ atrocious = *atroce.*

MONTEZUMA'S REVENGE (n) *la tourista* ⓐ the shits = *la chiasse,* the runs = *la courante.*

MONTH (n) *mois (m) :* there are twelve months in a year = *il y a douze mois dans une année* ⓐ day = *jour*

January = *janvier* **February** = *février* **March** = *mars* **April** = *avril* **May** = *mai* **June** = *juin* **July** = *juillet* **August** = *août*	**September** = *septembre* **October** = *octobre* **November** = *novembre* **December** = *décembre*

in a month of Sundays = *la semaine des quatre jeudis.*

MONTHLY (adj) *mensuel, -elle :* monthly payment/salary = *paiement/salaire mensuel* **MONTHLY** (adv) *mensuellement :* we're paid monthly = *nous sommes payés mensuellement* ⓐ by the month = *au mois.*

MONUMENT (n) *monument (m) :* an ancient monument = *un monument ancien* ⓐ statue = ←.

MONUMENTAL (adj) *monumental, -e :* a monumental mistake = *une faute monumentale* ⓐ colossal = ←.

MOOCH (to, -ed) *taper qqch à qqn :* can I mooch a cigarette ? = *est-ce que je peux vous taper une cigarette ?* = can I grub a cigarette ? **MOOCHER** (n) *tapeur, -euse* ⓐ sponger = *parasite.*

MOOD (n) **to be in a good** ≠ **bad mood** = *être de bonne* ≠ *de mauvaise humeur/de bon* ≠ *mauvais poil* → ANGRY
to be ≠ **not to be in the mood for/to** = *dire à qqn* ≠ *ne rien dire à qqn :* I'm not in the mood for pizza/to go to an Italian restaurant = *ça ne me dit rien d'aller manger une pizza/d'aller dans un restaurant italien* ⓐ to feel like = *avoir envie de*
to be in no mood for (kidding around) = *ne pas être d'humeur à (plaisanter).*

MOODY (adj, -ier, -iest) *d'humeur changeante :* temperamental and moody = *coléreux et d'humeur changeante* ⓐ erratic = *lunatique.*

MOOLAH (n) *flouse (m) :* can you lend me some moolah ? = *peux-tu me prêter du flouse ?* ⓐ bread = *pognon,* loot = *pèze.*

MOON (n) *lune (f) :* there's a full moon tonight = *c'est la pleine lune ce soir* ⓐ half-moon = *demi-lune,* moonlight = *clair de lune,* eclipse = *éclipse* ☠ *être dans la lune* = to be in the clouds.

MOONLIGHT (to, -ed) *faire un travail (souvent au noir) en plus de son travail habituel pour arriver à joindre les deux bouts :* my husband is a teacher but moonlights as a taxi driver on weekends = *mon mari est professeur mais il travaille en plus comme chauffeur de taxi les week-ends pour arriver à joindre les deux bouts.*

MOOT POINT (n) *question (f) controversée :* whether abortions are moral or not is a moot point = *savoir si l'avortement est moral ou non est une question controversée.*

MOP (n) *balai (m) à franges* ⓓ broom = *balai* **MOP** (to, -ped) *laver par terre avec un balai à franges.*

MOPE (to, -d) *se morfondre :* since he jilted her she's sitting around moping = *depuis qu'il l'a plaquée, elle reste là à se morfondre* ⓓ to be dejected = *être abattu.*

MORAL (n) *morale (f) :* the moral of the story = *la morale de l'histoire* ☠ *faire la morale* = to preach.

MORAL (adj) *moral, -e :* a moral victory/man = *une victoire morale/un homme moral* ≠ immoral = ←.

MORALE (n) *moral (m) :* the team's morale is low = *le moral de l'équipe est bas*
to boost s.o.'s morale = *remonter le moral de qqn* ⓓ to pep up = *ragaillardir*
☠ *avoir le moral à zéro* = to be down in the dumps.

MORALIST (n) *moraliste (m, f).*

MORALITY (n) *moralité (f) :* is there any morality left in this world ? = *y a-t-il encore de la moralité dans ce monde ?* ≠ immorality = *immoralité.*

MORALIZE (to, -d) **stop moralizing !** = *arrête de me faire la morale !*

MORALLY (adv) *moralement :* morally committed = *engagé moralement.*

MORALS (n pl) *moralité (f) :* she has no morals = *elle n'a aucune moralité* ⓓ ethics = *éthique.*

MORATORIUM (n) *moratoire (m)* (debts), *coup (m) d'arrêt :* a moratorium on rearmament = *un coup d'arrêt au réarmement.*

MORBID (adj) *morbide :* a rather morbid sense of humor = *un sens de l'humour plutôt morbide* ⓓ gruesome = *macabre* **MORBIDITY** (n, -ies) *morbidité (f).*

MORE (pron) *plus :* she's never happy, she always wants more = *elle n'est jamais contente, elle en veut toujours plus* ≠ less = *moins*

to get more than one asked for/bargained for = *ne pas en demander tant :* he loves kids, but five is more than he asked for/bargained for = *il aime les gosses, mais cinq c'est plus qu'il n'en demandait* **more than ...** = *plus de ... :* dinner took me more than two hours to cook = *il m'a fallu plus de deux heures pour préparer le*	dîner **need I say more !** = *c'est tout dire !* **to taste like more** = *avoir un goût de revenez-y* **that's more than I expected** = *c'est plus que je n'(en) attendais* **that's more than I had hoped for** = *je n'en espérais pas tant*	**the more (I see him), the less (I love him)** = *plus (je le vois), moins (je l'aime)* ≠ **the more (I see him), the more (I love him)** = *plus (je le vois), plus (je l'aime)* **the more, the merrier** = *plus on est de fous, plus on rit* ≠ the fewer, the better = *moins on est, mieux ça vaut.*

MORE (adj) *plus de :* I need more money = *j'ai besoin de plus d'argent* ⓓ additional = *supplémentaire*

more power to him ! = *tant mieux pour lui !* **how many more (years) ?** = *encore combien d'(années) ?* **more (bread) ?** = *(veux-tu) encore du (pain) ?*	**not ... any more/no more** = *(ne) ... plus de :* I don't have any more money = *je n'ai plus d'argent* = I have no more money.

MORE (adv) 1/ *plus :* you should work/rest more = *vous devriez travailler/vous reposer plus*
2/ *plus (surtout pour les adjectifs de trois syllabes et davantage) :* what he does is even more interesting/horrible = *ce qu'il fait est encore plus intéressant/horrible*

more and more (in love) = *de plus en plus (amoureux)* ≠ less and less = *de moins en moins* **more (you eat) more (you want to eat)** = *plus (on mange), plus (on a envie de man-*	*ger)* ≠ less ... less ... = *moins ... moins ...* **(we argue) more often than not** = *le plus souvent (nous nous disputons)* ⓓ most of the time = *la plupart du temps*	**more or less** = 1/ *plus ou moins :* they've more or less decided to get divorced = *ils ont plus ou moins décidé de divorcer* ⓓ to all intents and purposes = *virtuellement* 2/ *de plus*

ou de moins : an hour/ten dollars more or less doesn't matter = *une heure/dix dollars de plus ou de moins, ça ne fait rien*
more ... than = *plus ... que* :

she's more intelligent than her brother = *elle est plus intelligente que son frère*
more than enough (coffee/ problems) = *plus qu'assez de*

(café/problèmes) → MANY
that's more like it ! = *j'aime mieux ça!* ⌒⌒ now you're talking ! = *voilà ce qui s'appelle parler !*

☠ *plus (petit/riche/jeune)* = smaller/richer/younger *(adjectifs de une ou deux syllabes)*
— *10 dollars au plus* = $ 10 at the utmost
— *c'est plus fort que moi* = I can't help it

— *(deux) plus (deux font quatre)* = (two) plus (two are four)
— *il va plus mal aujourd'hui* = he's worse today.

MOREOVER (adv) *du reste* : it's expensive and moreover it's poor quality = *c'est cher et du reste c'est de mauvaise qualité* ⌒⌒ furthermore = *de plus.*

MORGUE (n) *morgue (f)* ⌒⌒ corpse = *cadavre* ☠ *avoir de la morgue* = to be arrogant.

MORMON (n) *mormon, -one* ⌒⌒ the Latter-Day Saints = *les saints du dernier jour.*

MORNING (n) *matin (m)* : I drink coffee every morning = *je bois du café tous les matins* ⌒⌒ afternoon = *après-midi*
to feel like the morning after the night before = *avoir mal aux cheveux* → DRUNK
in the morning = 1/ *le matin* : I take a shower in the morning = *je prends une douche le matin* 2/ *dans la matinée* : I'll call you in the morning = *je t'appellerai dans la matinée*
the morning after = *le lendemain matin*
what a (beautiful) morning ! ≠ *quelle (belle) matinée !*

MORNING (adj) *du matin* : a morning paper = *un journal du matin* ≠ evening = *du soir.*

MOROCCO (n) *Maroc (m)* **MOROCCAN** (n, adj) *Marocain, -e.*

MORON (n) *patate (f)* : what a moron you are ! = *quelle patate !* → STUPID
☠ *une patate* = a spud
— *en avoir gros/lourd sur la patate* = to be heavy-hearted.

MOROSE (adj) *morose* : worn-out and morose = *épuisé et morose* ⌒⌒ glum = *maussade.*

MORPHINE (n) *morphine (f)* ⌒⌒ heroin = *héroïne.*

MORSE CODE (n) *(code) morse (m).*

MORSEL (n) *morceau (m), parcelle (f)* : morsels of information/food = *des parcelles d'information/des morceaux d'aliment* ☠ *morceau* → piece.

MORTAL (n) *mortel, -elle* : death is the lot of all mortals = *la mort est le lot de tous les mortels.*

MORTAL (adj) *mortel, -elle* : we're all mortal = *nous sommes tous mortels* ≠ immortal = *immortel*
mortal enemies = *des ennemis mortels*
mortal sin = *péché mortel*

☠ *une soirée mortelle* = a deadly evening
— *une injection mortelle* = a lethal injection.

MORTALITY (n, -ies) *mortalité (f)* : mortality rate = *taux de mortalité.*

MORTALLY (adv) *mortellement* : mortally wounded = *mortellement blessé* ☠ *mortellement malade* = deathly sick.

MORTGAGE (to, -d) *hypothéquer* : to mortgage one's house = *hypothéquer sa maison* **MORTGAGE** (n) *hypothèque (f)* : to take out a mortgage on a house = *grever une maison d'une hypothèque* ⌒⌒ bank loan = *prêt bancaire.*

MORTIFY (to, -ied) *mortifier* : I was mortified when I realized my blunder = *j'ai été mortifié quand je me suis rendu compte de ma gaffe* ⌒⌒ to humiliate = *humilier* **MORTIFYING** (adj) *mortifiant, -e* : a mortifying experience = *une expérience mortifiante* ⌒⌒ humiliating = *humiliant.*

MOSLEM (n) *musulman, -e* = Muslim ⌒⌒ mosque = *mosquée,* Islam = ←, mollah = ←, Koran = *Coran.*

MOSQUITO (n, -s or -es) *moustique (m)* : a mosquito bite = *une piqûre de moustique* ⌒⌒ bee = *abeille,* wasp = *guêpe* ☠ *un moustique (personne)* = a peanut (person).

MOST (pron) *la plupart* : some women aren't feminists but most are = *certaines femmes ne sont pas féministes, mais la plupart le sont*

at (the very) most = *à tout casser* : it will cost $ 10 at the very most = *ça coûtera 10 dollars à tout casser* ≠ at the very least = *au minimum*
to make the most of = *profiter au maximum de* : it's wonderful that you're going on the trip, make the most of it ! = *c'est merveil-*

leux que vous fassiez ce voyage, profitez-en au maximum !
most of the time = *la plupart du temps* : we fight most of the time = *nous nous disputons la plupart du temps* ≠ rarely = *rarement*
most of us/the books = *la plupart d'entre nous/la plupart des livres.*

MOST (adj) *la plupart de* : most people like wine = *la plupart des gens aiment le vin*

for the most part (you're right) = *(vous avez raison) en grande partie* ① *by and large* = *dans l'ensemble*
the most ... = *la plus grande quantité de ... que :* that's the most beer he's ever drunk = *c'est la plus grande quantité de bière qu'il ait jamais bue.*

MOST (adv) 1/ *le plus :* what did you like most ? = *qu'avez-vous aimé le plus ?* ≠ least = *le moins* 2/ *fort :* I'm most grateful/happy = *je suis fort reconnaissant/heureux* → VERY ☠ → loud

the most (interesting/expensive/intelligent) = *le plus (intéressant/cher/intelligent)*
most likely = *très vraisemblablement :* he's most likely coming = *il viendra très vraisemblablement* ① **most certainly** = *très certainement*
to be on the most wanted list = *avoir sa tête mise à prix*

☠ *le plus (petit/riche/jeune)* = the (smallest/richest/youngest) *(adjectifs de une ou deux syllabes)*
— *le plus tôt sera le mieux* = the sooner the better
— *le plus tôt possible* = as soon as possible.

MOSTLY (adv) *principalement :* there were mostly men at the meeting = *il y avait principalement des hommes à la réunion* = principally ① especially = *tout spécialement.*

MOTEL (n) *motel (m) :* motels are often near highways = *les motels sont souvent près des autoroutes* ① hotel = *hôtel.*

MOTH (n) *mite (f) :* a moth-eaten fur = *une fourrure mangée aux mites* ① mothballs = *boules de naphtaline.*

MOTHER (n) *mère (f) :* he lost his mother = *il a perdu sa mère* ① mommy = *maman,* ma = *m'man,* the old lady = *la vieille,* motherhood = *maternité,* matriarchy = *matriarcat*
mother (fucker) = *enculé :* the mother (fucker) walked out when she was pregnant = *cet enculé s'est tiré quand elle a été enceinte* → BASTARD
mother's helper = *jeune fille au pair*
mother goose = *ma mère l'oie*
mother Nature = *Dame Nature*
Mother Superior = *mère supérieure* ≠ novice = ←
mother tongue = *langue maternelle.*

MOTHER-FUCKING (adj) *bordel de :* mother-fucking weather ! = *bordel de temps !* ① fucking = *putain de.*

MOTHER-IN-LAW (n) *belle-mère (f) :* I'm crazy about my mother-in-law = *j'adore ma belle-mère* ≠ daughter-in-law = *belle-fille,* son-in-law = *gendre.*

MOTHER-OF-PEARL (adj) *nacré, -e.*

MOTIF (n) *motif (m) :* the motif of the wallpaper = *le motif du papier peint* = design ☠ → motive.

MOTION (n) *motion (f) :* a motion to kill the bill = *une motion pour enterrer le projet de loi* ① vote = ←
to go through the motions = *faire machinalement :* he doesn't like to have sex with her and just goes through the motions = *il n'aime pas coucher avec elle et le fait machinalement*
motion picture = *film (de cinéma)*
to set in motion = *être le point de départ de :* kidnappings set in motion a wave of terrorism = *les kidnappings ont été le point de départ d'une vague de terrorisme.*

MOTION (to, -ed) *faire signe (à) :* he motioned me to sit down = *il m'a fait signe de m'asseoir.*

MOTIONLESS (adj) **(to sit) motionless** = *(être assis) sans bouger.*

MOTIVATE (to, -d) *motiver :* he won't do anything if he's not motivated = *il ne fera rien s'il n'est pas motivé* ① to inspire = *inspirer* **MOTIVATION** (n) *motivation (f) :* he lacks motivation = *il manque de motivation.*

MOTIVE (n) *mobile (m)* (crime), *motif (m) :* the third killing with no apparent motive = *le troisième meurtre sans mobile apparent,* what was the motive behind his quitting ? = *quel a été le motif de son départ ?* ① purpose = *but*
☠ *mobile* → mobile
— *les motifs du divorce* = the grounds for divorce
— *les motifs d'une robe* = the design of a dress
— *le motif du papier peint* = the wallpaper's motif/design.

MOTLEY (adj) *bigarré, -e :* a motley crowd = *une foule bigarrée.*

MOTOR (n) *moteur (m) :* the boat's motor = *le moteur du bateau* = engine ☠ *être le moteur de qqch* = to be the driving force of stg.

MOTORCYCLE (n) *moto (f)* ① motorbike = *mobylette,* bike = *bécane.*

MOTORIST (n) *automobiliste (m, f) :* the aggressivity of motorists = *l'agressivité des automobilistes* ① driver = *conducteur.*

MOTORWAY (n) (GB) *autoroute (f)* = highway.

MOTTO (n, -s or -es) *devise (f) :* "never say never" is my motto = « *il ne faut pas dire : fontaine je ne boirai pas de ton eau », telle est ma devise* ① adage = ←, saying = *dicton* ☠ *devise étrangère* = foreign currency.

MOUNT (to, -ed) *monter :* opposition's mounting = *l'opposition monte* = to rise ☠ → to rise
to mount up (to) = *s'accumuler :* expenses are mounting up = *les dépenses s'accumulent* ① to increase = *augmenter* ☠ → to accumulate.

MOUNTAIN (n) *montagne (f) :* to climb a mountain =

escalader une montagne ⑅ cliff = *falaise*, hill = *colline*, peak = *pic*, crest = *cime*, mountainous = *montagneux*
mountain climber = *alpiniste* = mountaineer
mountain range = *chaîne de montagnes*
to make a mountain out of a molehill = *se faire une montagne de quelque chose* ⑅ to make a federal case out of = *faire une affaire d'État de*
☠ *montagnes russes* = roller coaster.

MOURN (to, -ed) *porter le deuil* : Piaf was mourned by all of France = *toute la France a porté le deuil de Piaf*
MOURNER (n) *personne (f) en deuil* ⑅ the bereaved = *la famille du disparu.*

MOURNING (n) **to be in mourning** = *être en deuil* : the whole country is in mourning = *tout le pays est en deuil* ⑅ half-mast = *en berne.*

MOUSE (n, mice) *souris (f)* : mice in the cellar = *des souris dans la cave* ⑅ mousetrap = *souricière* ≠ cat = *chat*
☠ *une jolie souris* = a cute chick.

MOUTH (n) *bouche (f)* : don't speak with your mouth full = *ne parle pas la bouche pleine* ⑅ throat = *gorge*
keep your (big) mouth shut ! = *ferme ta (grande) gueule !* → BUZZ OFF !

to make s.o.'s mouth water = *faire venir l'eau à la bouche de qqn* : chocolate cakes make my mouth water = *les gâteaux au chocolat me font venir l'eau à la bouche* ⑅ to lick one's chops = *se lécher les babines*
out of mouths of babes (and sucklings comes forth the truth) = *la vérité sort de la bouche des enfants*
to shoot one's mouth off = *débloquer à pleins tubes* = **to pop off the mouth**
you should have kept your mouth shut ! = *vous avez perdu une belle occasion de vous taire !*
☠ *bouche bée* = stunned
— *(motus et) bouche cousue* = mum's the word.

MOUTHFUL (n) *bouchée (f)* : I can't eat another mouthful = *je ne peux pas avaler une bouchée de plus*
you said a mouthful ! = *tu l'as dit bouffi !* ⑅ you can say that again ! = *à qui le dis-tu !*
☠ *il n'en a fait qu'une bouchée* = she was a pushover for him
— *pour une bouchée de pain* = for a song
— *mettre les bouchées doubles* = to slave away.

MOUTHPIECE (n) *bavard, -e* (LV) : he's the Mafia's mouthpiece = *c'est le bavard de la Mafia* ⑅ attorney = *avocat* ☠ *quel bavard !* = what a talkative person !

MOVE (n) **1/** *déménagement (m)* : it's our third move in five years = *c'est notre troisième déménagement en cinq ans* **2/** *ce qu'on fait* : what's our next move ? = *qu'est-ce qu'on fait ensuite ?* ⑅ maneuver = *manœuvre*

a move in the right ≠ **wrong direction** = *un pas dans la bonne* ≠ *mauvaise direction* **get a move on !** = *magne-toi !* ⑅ snap it up ! = *active !*	**a good** ≠ **bad move** = *une bonne* ≠ *mauvaise manœuvre* **it's your move !** = *à vous de jouer !*

MOVE (to, -d) **1/** *bouger* : don't move ! = *ne bougez pas !* ⑅ to fidget = *s'agiter* ☠ *les prix n'ont pas bougé* = prices have remained the same **2/** *déménager* : we're moving next week = *nous déménageons la semaine prochaine* ⑅ movers = *déménageurs* ☠ *tu déménages complètement !* = you're nuts ! **3/** *émouvoir* : I was deeply moved by the movie = *le film m'a profondément ému* ⑅ to touch = *toucher*

move it ! = *remue-toi le popotin !* **to move that** = *proposer que* : he moved that the meeting be adjourned = *il a proposé que la réunion*	*soit ajournée* **nobody move !** = *que personne ne bouge !* ⑅ stick 'em up ! = *haut les mains !*

---

to move about/around = *se déplacer* : he moves about/around with difficulty = *il se déplace avec difficulté* ☠ → to shift **to move along/on** = *circuler* : the cops told the crowd to move along/on = *les flics ont dit à la foule de circuler* ☠ → to circulate **to move back** = *reculer* : don't crowd around ; move back ! = *ne vous agglutinez pas ; reculez !* ☠ *reculer un mariage* = to postpone a wedding	— *reculer (voiture)* = to back up (car) — *les syndicats ont reculé* = the unions backed off/down — *reculer pour mieux sauter* = to stoop to conquer — *ne pas reculer devant* = not to shrink from **to move in (interesting circles)** = *évoluer dans (des milieux intéressants)* **to move in** ≠ **out** = *emménager* ≠ *déménager* : we're moving in ≠ out today = *nous emménageons* ≠ *déménageons aujourd'hui*	**move over !** = *poussez-vous !* **to move to** = *inciter à* : what moved you to ask that ? = *qu'est-ce qui vous a incité à demander ça ?* ⑅ to urge to = *pousser à* **to be moved to (tears)** = *être ému aux (larmes)* **to move towards** = *avancer vers* : the world isn't moving towards peace = *le monde n'avance pas vers la paix* **to move up (a date)** = *avancer (une date)* ☠ → to advance.

MOVEMENT (n) *mouvement (m)* : the labor movement = *le mouvement ouvrier*, a lot of movement in the art world = *beaucoup de mouvement dans le monde des arts*
🐑 *dans un mouvement de colère* = in a fit of temper
— *premier mouvement* = first impulse
— *suivre le mouvement* = to follow suit.

MOVIE (n) *film (m)* : what a great movie ! = *quel film extra !* → FILM
to go to the movies = *aller au cinéma* = to go to the cinema (GB).

MOVING (adj) *émouvant, -e* : a moving speech = *un discours émouvant* ⓌⒹ *poignant* = ←.

MOW (to, -ed) *tondre* : to mow the lawn = *tondre la*

pelouse ⓌⒹ lawn mower = *tondeuse à gazon* 🐑 *tondre (moutons)* = to shear (sheep).

MP (abbr) **1/** Military Police = *police (f) militaire* ⓌⒹ patrol = *patrouille* **2/** Member of Parliament (GB) = *parlementaire (m, f)*.

MR (abbr) *M.* : Mr Walker = *M. Walker* ⓌⒹ Messrs = *MM.*
Mr Right = *l'homme idéal* : she's still waiting for Mr Right = *elle attend encore l'homme idéal* ⓌⒹ prince charming = *prince charmant*.

MRS (abbr) *Mme* : Mrs Jones = *Mme Jones*.

MS (abbr) *contraction proposée par les féministes pour remplacer « Miss » et « Mrs »*.

MUCH/MANY = BEAUCOUP DE = A LOT OF → MANY

MUCH (adj) *beaucoup de (choses non dénombrables)* : much money = *beaucoup d'argent*, much work to do = *beaucoup de travail à faire* ⓌⒹ a great deal of = *beaucoup/énormément de* ≠ a little = *un peu de*
as much (money) as (we need) = *autant d'(argent) que (nous en avons besoin)*
how much ? = *combien ?* : how much milk do you want ? = *combien de lait voulez-vous ?/quelle quantité de lait voulez-vous ?*
not much (Scotch left) = *pas beaucoup de (whisky qui reste)*
not so much (sugar) = *pas tant de (sucre)*
so much = *tant de/tellement de* : he drank so much wine that he was sick all evening = *il a bu tant/tellement de vin qu'il a été malade toute la soirée*
that much (time/money) = *tant de/tellement de (temps)/d'(argent)*
too much (coffee) = *trop de (café)*
much more (food) than usual = *bien plus de (nourriture) que d'habitude*
how much time (did it take) ? = *combien de temps (cela a-t-il pris) ?*
much of = *une grande partie de* : they live in New York much of the year = *ils vivent à New York une grande partie de l'année*
that doesn't make much difference = *cela ne fait pas une grande différence*.

MANY (adj) *beaucoup de (choses dénombrables)* : many things = *beaucoup de choses*, many people = *beaucoup de gens*, many times = *beaucoup de fois* ⓌⒹ numerous = *nombreux*, a lot of = *beaucoup de* ≠ few = *peu*
as many (beers) as (you want) = *autant de (bières) que (vous voulez)*
how many ? = *combien ?* : how many cigarettes do you smoke a day ? = *combien de cigarettes fumez-vous par jour ?*
not many (cigarettes left) = *pas beaucoup de (cigarettes qui restent)*
not so many (kids) = *pas tant de (gosses)*
so many = *tant de/tellement de* : so many people came that there wasn't enough room = *tant de personnes sont venues qu'il n'y avait pas assez de place*
that many (books/years) = *tant de/tellement de (livres)/d'(années)*
too many (problems) = *trop de (problèmes)*
many more (problems) than usual = *bien plus de (problèmes) que d'habitude*
how many times ? = *combien de fois ?*
for many a (year/day) = *pendant bien des (années/jours)*
many a (woman· takes the pill) = *plus d'une (femme prend la pilule)*
many (years/months) ago = *il y a bien des (années/ mois)*.

MUCH (pron) *beaucoup* : there's much to see in Moscow = *il y a beaucoup à voir à Moscou* ≠ little = *peu*
much of (what he says is wrong) = *beaucoup de (ce qu'il dit est faux)* ⓌⒹ for the most part = *en grande partie*
(she's) not much of a (writer) = *(elle) n'a pas grand-chose d'un (écrivain)* ≠ to have the makings of = *avoir l'étoffe de*
this much = *ceci* : I'll say this much for him, at least he tries = *je dirai ceci en sa faveur, au moins il essaie*.

MANY (pron) *beaucoup* : many disagreed with me = *beaucoup n'étaient pas d'accord avec moi* ≠ few = *peu*
many of (her friends have had abortions) = *beaucoup de (ses amies se sont fait avorter)* ≠ none of = *aucun de*
many of us = *beaucoup d'entre nous* ⓌⒹ most of us = *la plupart d'entre nous*
a great/good many = *pas mal de* : we've been having a great/good many problems lately = *nous avons eu pas mal de problèmes dernièrement* ⓌⒹ an awful lot of = *énormément de*.

MUCH (adv) *beaucoup :* I don't like pizza much = *je n'aime pas beaucoup les pizzas*

as much as you want/like = *autant que vous voulez :* drink as much as you want/like = *buvez autant que vous voulez*
much as = *bien que :* much as I would like to come with you, I can't = *bien que j'aie très envie de venir avec vous, je ne peux pas* ꝏ although = *quoique*
how much is it ? = *combien est-ce ?/combien ça fait ?*
much better ≠ worse = *bien mieux ≠ pire/plus mal :* he's much better ≠ worse now = *il se porte bien mieux ≠ bien plus mal maintenant*
much less = *et encore moins :* I can barely speak French, much less write it = *j'arrive à peine à parler français et encore moins à l'écrire*
much like = *presque comme :* yours is much like mine = *le vôtre est presque comme le mien*
much (+ er)/much more = *beaucoup plus :* much prettier/happier/richer = *beaucoup plus joli/heureux/riche,* much more intelligent/serious = *beaucoup plus intelligent/sérieux* ≠ **much less** = *beaucoup moins*
much to (my surprise) = *à (ma) grande (surprise)*
I'd much rather (go now) = *je préférerais de beaucoup (y aller maintenant)*
I thought as much = *c'est bien ce que je pensais* ꝏ that doesn't surprise me = *cela ne me surprend pas*
I'm not much for (jazz) = *je ne raffole pas du (jazz)* ꝏ I'm not crazy about = *je ne suis pas fou de*
there's nothing much we can do/say = *il n'y a pas grand-chose à faire/dire* = **there isn't anything much we can do/say**

☠ *le plus souvent on utilise* « a lot » *à la place de* « much »

— *c'est déjà beaucoup* = that's already something.

MUCKRAKE (to, -d) *fouiller la merde :* a muckraking journalist = *un journaliste qui fouille la merde* **MUCKRAKER** (n) *fouille-merde (m).*

MUD (n) *boue (f) :* my boots are covered with mud = *mes bottes sont couvertes de boue* ꝏ muddy = *boueux*
to drag through the mud = *traîner dans la boue*
here's mud in your eye ! = *à la tienne (Étienne) !* ꝏ cheers ! = *tchin-tchin !*

MUDDLE THROUGH (to, -d) *s'en sortir tant bien que mal :* I don't understand much at school, but I expect to muddle through = *je ne comprends pas grand-chose à l'école, mais j'espère m'en sortir tant bien que mal* ꝏ to struggle with = *avoir beaucoup de mal avec.*

MUDSLINGING (n inv) *basses attaques (f pl) :* a campaign full of mudslinging = *une campagne qui n'a pas manqué de basses attaques* ꝏ slander = *calomnie.*

MUFF (to, -ed) *faire foirer :* you muffed the interview = *tu as fait foirer l'interview* ꝏ to goof up = *ficher en l'air.*

MUFFIN (n) *muffin (m)* ꝏ bun = *petit pain rond.*

MUFFLER (n) *cache-nez (m inv)* ꝏ scarf = *écharpe.*

MUG (n) **1/** *chope (f) :* a mug of beer = *une chope de bière* **2/** *trogne (f), tronche (f)* (LV) : what an ugly mug he's got ! = *il a vraiment une sale trogne/tronche !*

MUG (to, -ged) *agresser :* she was mugged on the way home = *elle a été agressée en rentrant chez elle* ꝏ to assault = *assaillir* ☠ *agresser (psychologiquement)* = to attack s.o. (psychologically) **MUGGER** (n) *agresseur (m) :* the muggers were teenagers = *les agresseurs étaient des adolescents* ꝏ hoodlum = *voyou* ☠ *agresseur (guerre)* = aggressor (war) **MUGGING** (n) *agression (f) :* muggings in the subway = *des agressions dans le métro* ꝏ assault and battery = *voies de fait* ☠ *agression (verbale)* = (verbal) attack.

MULATTO (n, -es) *mulâtre (m, f)* ꝏ half-breed = *métis/sang-mêlé.*

MULE (n) *mulet (m), mule (f)* ꝏ ass = *âne.*

MULISH (adj) *buté, -e* ꝏ stubborn = *têtu.*

MULL OVER (to, -ed) *ruminer :* I'm mulling over his proposal = *je suis en train de ruminer sa proposition* ꝏ to ponder = *songer,* to muse = *être pensif.*

MULTICOLORED (adj) *multicolore.*

MULTILATERAL (adj) *multilatéral, -e :* multilateral talks = *des entretiens multilatéraux* ꝏ bilateral = *bilatéral.*

MULTIMILLIONAIRE (n) *multimillionnaire (m, f).*

MULTIPLE (adj) *multiple :* multiple possibilities = *des possibilités multiples* ≠ unique = ←
multiple sclerosis = *sclérose en plaques.*

MULTIPLICATION (n) *multiplication (f) :* multiplication table = *table de multiplication* ꝏ addition = ← ≠ division = ←, subtraction = *soustraction* **MULTIPLY** (to, -ied) *multiplier* ≠ to divide = *diviser.*

MULTITUDE (n) *multitude (f) :* a multitude of problems = *une multitude de problèmes* → MANY.

MUM (n) **mum's the word** = *motus et bouche cousue* ꝏ between you, me and the lamppost = *entre nous.*

MUMBLE (to, -d) *marmonner :* stop mumbling and speak clearly = *arrête de marmonner et parle distinctement* ꝏ to mutter = *marmotter.*

MUMMY (n, -ies) *momie (f)* ⓒ sarcophagus = *sarcophage*.

MUMPS (n inv) *oreillons (m pl)* : my daughter has the mumps = *ma fille a les oreillons* ⓒ chicken pox = *varicelle*, scarlet fever = *scarlatine*.

MUNCH (to, -ed) *mastiquer* ⓒ to chew = *mâcher*.

MUNDANE (adj) *tout, -e banal, -e* : the mundane matters of daily administration = *les affaires toutes banales de l'administration au quotidien*.

MUNICIPAL (adj) *municipal, -e* : municipal workers = *employés municipaux* ⓒ municipality = *municipalité*
☠ *élections municipales* = local elections
— *conseil municipal* = city council.

MURDER (n) 1/ *meurtre (m)* : every 24 minutes a murder is committed in the US = *toutes les vingt-quatre minutes un meurtre est commis aux États-Unis* ⓒ crime = ←, homicide = ←, life imprisonment = *réclusion à perpétuité*
to get away with murder = *en profiter largement* : when the teacher's away, the kids get away with murder = *quand le professeur n'est pas là, les enfants en profitent largement*
first-degree murder = *homicide volontaire* = **willful murder** ≠ manslaughter = *homicide involontaire*
premeditated murder = *meurtre avec préméditation*
second-degree murder = *homicide involontaire*
2/ *un cauchemar* : the exams were murder = *les examens ont été un cauchemar* ≠ a gas = *le pied*.

MURDER (to, -ed) 1/ *tuer* : he murdered his wife and children = *il a tué femme et enfants* = to kill ⓒ to assassinate = *assassiner*, to knock off = *buter* ☠ → to kill 2/ *écorcher* (language), *massacrer* (music) : she murders French/Mozart = *elle écorche le français/elle massacre Mozart* ☠ *massacrer* → to massacre.

MURDERER (n) *meurtrier (m)* : they haven't found the murderer = *ils n'ont pas retrouvé le meurtrier* ⓒ murderess = *meurtrière*, killer = *tueur*, hired killer = *tueur à gages*.

MURKY (adj, -ier, -iest) *trouble* : murky waters = *des eaux troubles* ≠ clear = *clair*
☠ *une vue trouble* = blurred vision
— *pêcher en eau trouble* = to fish in troubled waters.

MURMUR (n) *murmure (m)* : a murmur arose in the crowd = *un murmure s'est élevé dans la foule* ⓒ mumble = *marmonnement* **MURMUR** (to, -ed) *murmurer* ⓒ to mumble = *marmonner*.

MUSCLE (n) *muscle (m)* : I pulled a muscle = *je me suis froissé un muscle* ⓒ ligament = ←.

MUSCLE IN (to, -d) *marcher sur les plates-bandes de* : he was trying to pick up the girl but his best friend muscled in = *il essayait de draguer cette fille, mais son meilleur ami a marché sur ses plates-bandes* ⓒ to encroach on = *empiéter sur*.

MUSCULAR (adj) *musclé, -e* : a muscular body = *un corps musclé* ⓒ burly = *charpenté* ☠ → brawny.

MUSE (n) *muse (f)* : Beatrice was Dante's muse = *Béatrice était la muse de Dante* ⓒ poet = *poète*.

MUSEUM (n) *musée (m)* : the Museum of Modern Art = *le Musée d'art moderne* ⓒ art gallery = *galerie d'art*.

MUSH (n inv) *sensiblerie (f)* : his films are full of mush = *ses films sont pleins de sensiblerie* ⓒ hearts-and-flowers = *quelque chose à l'eau de rose*.

MUSHROOM (n) *champignon (m)* ⓒ truffle = *truffe*
☠ *appuyer sur le champignon* = to step on the gas.

MUSHROOM (to, -ed) *pousser comme des champignons* : shopping centers are mushrooming all over the country = *les centres commerciaux poussent comme des champignons dans tout le pays*.

MUSHY (adj, -ier, -iest) *plein, -e de sensiblerie* : a mushy film = *un film plein de sensiblerie* ⓒ soppy = *cucul*.

MUSIC (n) *musique (f)* : I often listen to music = *j'écoute souvent de la musique*, dinner music = *musique d'ambiance*, classical music = *musique classique*
to face the music = *payer les pots cassés* ⓒ to face the consequences = *supporter les conséquences*
music hall = *music-hall*
music lover = *mélomane*
☠ *connaître la musique* = to know the score.

MUSICAL (adj) *musical, -e* : musical comedy = *comédie musicale*
musical instruments = *instruments de musique*.

MUSICIAN (n) *musicien, -enne* : she's married to a musician = *elle a épousé un musicien*.

MUST (n) *must (m)* : the last Woody Allen movie is a must = *le dernier film de Woody Allen est un must* ⓒ necessity = *nécessité*.

MUST (aux) *il faut que* : I must go now = *il faut que j'y aille maintenant* → TO HAVE TO
must be/must have been = *doit être/a dû être* : she isn't here ; she must be sick = *elle n'est pas là* ; *elle doit être malade*, she didn't come ; she must have been sick = *elle n'est pas venue ; elle a dû être malade*
mustn't = *il ne faut pas (que)* : you mustn't smoke in the subway = *il ne faut pas fumer dans le métro*
☠ « must » *ne s'emploie qu'au présent*.

MUSTACHE (n) *moustache (f)* : my husband has a mustache = *mon mari a une moustache* ⓒ sideburns = *favoris*, goatee = *bouc* ☠ *les moustaches du chat* = the cat's whiskers.

MUSTARD (n inv) *moutarde (f)* : different kinds of mustard = *différentes sortes de moutarde* ⓒ ketchup = ←

☠ *la moutarde lui monte au nez* = he's getting hot under the collar.

MUSTER (UP) (to, -ed) **to muster (up) one's courage/strength** = *rassembler son courage/ses forces*.

MUSTY (adj, -ier, -iest) *qui sent le renfermé* : a musty room = *une pièce qui sent le renfermé* ⓪ moldy = *moisi*.

MUTE (n) *muet, muette* **MUTE** (adj) *muet, muette* : a mute child = *un enfant muet* ⓪ deaf = *sourd*, autistic = *autiste*
☠ *un film muet* = a silent movie
— *sourd et muet* = deaf and dumb
— *il est resté muet comme une carpe* = he didn't say boo.

MUTILATE (to, -d) *mutiler* : mutilated by the bomb = *mutilé par la bombe* ⓪ to disable = *rendre invalide*.

MUTINY (n, -ies) *mutinerie* *(f)* : the mutiny of the Potemkine = *la mutinerie du Potemkine* ⓪ rebellion = *rébel-lion*, insurrection = ←, mutineer = *mutiné/mutin*.

MUTT (n) *cabot* *(m)* : a cute mutt = *un cabot adorable* ⓪ dog = *chien* ☠ → ham.

MUTTER (to, -ed) *marmotter* : "she's a bitch", he muttered = *« c'est une salope », a-t-il marmotté* ⓪ to murmur = *murmurer*.

MUTTON (n) *(viande de) mouton* *(m)* ⓪ lamb = *agneau* ☠ → sheep.

MUTUAL (adj) *mutuel, -elle* : mutual respect/love = *respect/amour mutuel* ⓪ reciprocal = *réciproque*
the feeling's/it's mutual = *c'est réciproque* : I can't stand her and the feeling's/it's mutual = *je ne peux pas la voir et c'est réciproque*
mutual fund = *SICAV*
mutual insurance = *mutuelle*.

MUTUALLY (adv) *mutuellement* ⓪ one another = *l'un l'autre*.

MUZZLE (n) *muselière* *(f)* ⓪ to bite = *mordre*.

MY (adj poss) *mon, ma, mes (à moi)*

my = *mon, ma, mes (à moi)* : my apartment = *mon appartement (à moi)*, my wife = *ma femme (à moi)*, these are my children = *ce sont mes enfants (à moi)* → **mine** = *le mien, la mienne, les miens, les miennes (à moi)* : this book is mine = *ce livre est le mien (à moi)*, these shoes are mine = *ces chaussures sont les miennes (à moi)*

your = *ton, ta, tes (à toi)/votre, vos (à vous)* : that's your coat = *c'est ton/votre manteau (à toi/à vous)*, those are your papers = *ce sont tes/vos papiers (à toi/à vous)* → **yours** = *le tien, la tienne, les tiens, les tiennes (à toi)/le/la vôtre, les vôtres (à vous)* : these books are yours = *ces livres sont les tiens/les vôtres (à toi/à vous)*

his = *son, sa, ses (à lui)* : his wife = *sa femme (à lui)*, his shoes = *ses chaussures (à lui)*, his coat = *son manteau (à lui)* → **his** = *le sien, la sienne, les siens, les siennes (à lui)* : those kids are his = *ces gosses sont les siens (à lui)*

her = *son, sa, ses (à elle)* : her husband = *son mari (à elle)*, her kids = *ses gosses (à elle)*, her doll = *sa poupée (à elle)* → **hers** = *le sien, la sienne, les siens, les siennes (à elle)* : that coat's hers = *ce manteau-là est le sien (à elle)*

its = *son, sa, ses (animaux, choses)* : its lid = *son couvercle*, its tail = *sa queue*, its paws = *ses pattes* → **its** = *le sien, la sienne, les siens, les siennes (animaux, choses)*

our = *notre, nos (à nous)* : our books = *nos livres (à nous)*, our car = *notre voiture (à nous)* → **ours** = *le/la nôtre, les nôtres (à nous)* : this house is ours = *cette maison est la nôtre (à nous)*

their = *leur(s) (à eux/à elles)* : it's their car = *c'est leur voiture (à eux/à elles)* → **theirs** = *le/la leur, les leurs (à eux/à elles)* : that car's theirs = *cette voiture est la leur (à eux)*

☠ in French the possessive adjective agrees with the noun following : **her** bag = *son sac (à elle)* ; **his** wife = *sa femme (à lui)*.

MYSELF (pron) **1/** *moi-même* : I did it myself = *je l'ai fait moi-même* ⓪ he wrote it himself = *il l'a écrit lui-même*

myself = *moi-même*
yourself = *toi-même/vous-même*
himself = *lui-même*
herself = *elle-même*

itself = *lui-même/elle-même* (choses, animaux)
ourselves = *nous-mêmes*
yourselves = *vous-mêmes*
themselves = *eux-mêmes/elles-mêmes*

2/ (reflexive form)*me* : I can see myself in the mirror = *je me vois dans la glace* ⓓ she's looking at herself = *elle se regarde*

myself	= *me*		💀 most often the reflexive form, as the French use
yourself	= *te/vous*		it, doesn't exist in English/*la forme réfléchie, cou-*
himself	= *se*		*rante en français, est rare en anglais*
herself	= *se*		— *je me lave* = I'm
itself	= *se*		— *tu te laves* = you're
ourselves	= *nous*		— *il/elle se lave* = he's/she's
yourselves	= *vous*		— *on se lave* = one's washing/getting washed
themselves	= *se*		— *nous nous lavons* = we're
			— *vous vous lavez* = you're
			— *ils/elles se lavent* = they're

—————— 💀 SOME FRENCH REFLEXIVE VERBS AND THEIR TRANSLATIONS ——————

— *se lever* = to get up	— *se décider* = to make up one's mind	— *se souvenir de* = to remember
— *se promener* = to take a walk	— *s'en aller* = to go	— *se coucher* = to go to bed
— *se tromper* = to make a mistake	— *s'excuser* = to apologize	— *s'attendre à* = to expect
— *s'amuser* = to have a good time	— *se rappeler* = to remember	— *se réveiller* = to wake up
— *s'appeler* = to be called	— *se moquer de* = to make fun of	— *se laver* = to get washed
— *s'arrêter* = to stop	— *se foutre de* = not to give a shit about	— *s'habiller* = to get dressed
		— *se demander* = to wonder
		— *se dépêcher* = to hurry
		— *se reposer* = to rest

3/ (after an imperative or a preposition) *moi* : I took a photograph of myself eating = *j'ai pris une photo de moi en train de manger* ⓓ look at yourself ! = *regarde-toi !/regardez-vous !*

myself	= *moi*	**himself**	= *lui, le*	**ourselves**	= *nous*
yourself	= *toi/vous*	**herself**	= *elle, la*	**yourselves**	= *vous*
		itself	= *lui/elle, le/la*	**themselves**	= *eux/elles, les.*

MYSTERIOUS (adj) *mystérieux, -euse* : a mysterious look = *un regard mystérieux* ⓓ puzzling = *incompréhensible* **MYSTERIOUSLY** (adv) *mystérieusement.*

MYSTERY (n, -ies) *mystère (m)* : you ask me why they split up ; it's a real mystery = *tu me demandes pourquoi ils ont rompu ; c'est un vrai mystère*
💀 *mystère et boule de gomme !* = search me !
— *c'est un mystère pour moi que ...* = it's a puzzle for me why ...

MYSTICAL (adj) *mystique* : a mystical ideal = *un idéal mystique.*

MYSTIFY (to, -ied) *laisser perplexe* : his answer mystified me = *sa réponse m'a laissé perplexe* = his answer puzzled me 💀 *mystifier qqn* = to hoodwink s.o.

MYTH (n) *mythe (m)* : the myth of Orpheus = *le mythe d'Orphée* ⓓ fable = ←.

MYTHICAL (adj) *mythique* : a mythical animal = *un animal mythique.*

MYTHOLOGY (n, -ies) *mythologie (f).*

NAACP (abbr) = National Association for the Advancement of Colored People = *Association nationale pour l'insertion des personnes de couleur.*

NAB (to, -bed) *pincer* : to nab a pickpocket = *pincer un pickpocket* ⓪ to collar = *mettre la main au collet à,* to nail = *choper* ☠ → to pinch.

NAG (to, -ged) *bassiner* : she's always nagging her husband = *elle est toujours en train de bassiner son mari* ⓪ to hock = *tanner.*

NAIL (n) **1/** *ongle (m)* : I broke a nail = *je me suis cassé un ongle* ⓪ hangnail = *envie,* cuticle = *cuticule,* polish = *vernis,* remover = *dissolvant*
to bite one's nails = *se ronger les ongles*
2/ *clou (m)* ⓪ hammer = *marteau*
to be hard/tough as nails = *être coriace* ⓪ to be hard-boiled = *être dur à cuire*
to hit the nail on the head = *taper dans le mille* ≠ to be way-off = *être loin du compte*
☠ *ça ne vaut pas un clou* = it's worthless
— *le clou du spectacle* = the highlight of the show.

NAIL DOWN (to, -ed) *faire préciser à* : I couldn't nail him down to a date = *je n'ai pas pu lui faire préciser une date* ≠ to beat around the bush = *tourner autour du pot.*

NAIVE (adj) *naïf, -ïve* : a naive remark/girl = *une remarque/fille naïve* ⓪ credulous = *crédule,* guileless = *candide.*

NAKED (adj) *nu, -e* : she opened the door completely naked = *elle a ouvert la porte complètement nue* = nude ⓪ bare-assed = *les fesses à l'air* ≠ dressed = *habillé*
to go naked = *se promener tout nu*
the naked truth = *la vérité toute nue*
to the naked eye = *à l'œil nu*
☠ *pieds nus* = barefoot.

NAME (n) *nom (m)* : my name is Jane = *mon nom est Jane*

alias = *faux nom*	*nom d'emprunt*
assumed name =	**Christian name** =

nom de baptême
first name = *prénom* = **given name**
full name = *nom et prénom*
handle = *blase*
last name = *nom de famille*
maiden name = *nom de jeune fille*

middle name = *deuxième prénom*
nickname = *sobriquet*
pen name = *nom de plume*
pet name = *surnom*
pseudonym = *pseudonyme*
stage name = *nom de scène*

to call s.o.'s name(s) = *traiter qqn de tous les noms*
to have a good ≠ **bad name (in the company)** = *avoir bonne* ≠ *mauvaise réputation (dans l'entreprise)*
his name's mud (with my parents) = *il est mal vu (de mes parents)*
in name only = *si on peut dire* : they're married in name only = *ils sont mariés si on peut dire*
in s.o.'s name = *au nom de qqn* : the house is in my name = *la maison est à mon nom*
to go under the name of (one's husband) = *prendre le nom de (son mari)*
to know s.o. by name = *connaître qqn de nom*
to make a name for oneself (in advertising) = *se faire un nom (dans la publicité)*
I'm not mentioning any names = *je ne nomme personne*
name brand = *grande marque*
not to have a penny/a cent to one's name = *ne pas avoir un radis/un rond* → POOR ≠ to be in the money = *être en fonds*
open up in the name of the law ! = *au nom de la loi, ouvrez !*
(I'll do it) or my name's mud = *(je le ferai) ou je ne m'appelle plus ...*
that's the name of the game = *c'est dans l'ordre des choses* → THAT'S LIFE !
what's your name ? = *comment vous appelez-vous ?/quel est votre nom ?*
your name escapes me = *votre nom m'échappe*

☠ *un nom (propre)* = a (proper) noun
— *nom de Dieu !/nom d'un chien !* = good God !

NAME (to, -d) **1/** *nommer* : she was named chairwoman = *elle a été nommée présidente* = to appoint ⊕ to choose = *choisir* **2/** *appeler* : they named their son Charles = *ils ont appelé leur fils Charles* ☠ → to call **3/** *nommer* : can you name three writers who committed suicide ? = *pouvez-vous me nommer trois écrivains qui se sont suicidés ?*

name a (price/day) = *dites un (prix/jour)*
to name s.o. after = *donner à qqn le nom de* : he's named after his uncle = *on lui a donné le nom de son oncle.*

NAME-DROPPER (n) *poseur, -euse (qui laisse tomber des noms de gens connus pour épater la galerie)* ⊕ social climber = *quelqu'un qui cherche à se faire des relations.*

NAMELY (adv) *notamment* : we're having many problems, namely financial = *nous avons beaucoup de problèmes, notamment des problèmes financiers* ⊕ for instance = *par exemple.*

NAP (n) *somme (m)* ⊕ catnap = *roupillon, siesta* = *sieste* ☠ → sum
to take a nap = *faire un somme* ⊕ to get some shut-eye = *piquer un roupillon.*

NAP (to, -ped) *faire un somme* = to take a nap ⊕ to drowse = *somnoler.*

NAPKIN (n) **1/** *serviette (f) de table* : ask the waiter for a napkin = *demande une serviette au garçon* ☠ → towel **2/** *serviette (f) hygiénique* ⊕ period = *règles.*

NARCISSISM (n) *narcissisme (m)* **NARCISSIST** (n) *narcisse (m)* **NARCISSISTIC** (adj) *narcissique.*

NARCOTIC (n) *narcotique (m)* : to take narcotics = *prendre des narcotiques*
Narcotics Bureau = *brigade des stupéfiants.*

NARRATE (to, -d) *narrer* ⊕ to tell = *raconter* **NARRATIVE** (n) *narration (f)* **NARRATOR** (n) *narrateur, -trice.*

NARROW (adj, -er, -est) *étroit, -e* : a narrow alley = *une ruelle étroite* ≠ broad = *large*
it was a narrow escape ! = *on l'a échappé belle !* ⊕ it was touch-and-go = *c'était de justesse*
☠ *être à l'étroit* = to be cramped.

NARROW (to, -ed) **to narrow stg down to** = *limiter qqch à* : the party had to narrow its choice down to two candidates = *le parti a dû limiter son choix à deux candidats.*

NARROWLY (adv) *de peu* : the bullet narrowly missed him = *la balle l'a manqué de peu.*

NARROW-MINDED (adj) *étroit, -e d'esprit* : a narrow-minded and petty person = *une personne étroite d'esprit et mesquine* ≠ broad-minded = *large d'esprit.*

NASTY (adj, -ier, -iest) **1/** *vilain, -e* : nasty weather = *un vilain temps* ≠ great = *épatant* ☠ → naughty **2/** *méchant, -e* : a nasty remark = *une réflexion méchante* ⊕ bitchy = *salaud* ☠ → mean.

NATION (n) *nation (f)* ⊕ country = *pays.*

NATIONAL (n) *ressortissant, -e* : a French national = *un ressortissant français* ⊕ citizen = *citoyen.*

NATIONAL (adj) *national, -e* : a national anthem/holiday = *un hymne national/une fête nationale* ≠ local = ←
the National Guard = *la Garde nationale*
☠ *route nationale* = main road.

NATIONALISM (n) *nationalisme (m).*

NATIONALITY (n, -ies) *nationalité (f)* : she has French nationality = *elle a la nationalité française.*

NATIONALIZE (to, -d) *nationaliser* **NATIONALIZATION** (n) *nationalisation (f).*

NATIONWIDE (adj) *dans l'ensemble du pays, à l'échelle nationale* : a nationwide problem = *un problème à l'échelle nationale.*

NATIVE (n) *autochtone (m, f), indigène (m, f)* : many natives still live in huts = *beaucoup d'autochtones/d'indigènes vivent encore dans des cases* ⊕ locals = *les gens du pays*
to be a native of (Paris) = *être né à (Paris).*

NATIVE (adj) **1/** *natal, -e* : native land/language = *terre/langue natale* **2/** *du pays* : native customs/dish = *coutumes/plat du pays*
to go native = *adopter les coutumes locales.*

NATO (abbr) = North Atlantic Treaty Organization = OTAN = *Organisation du traité de l'Atlantique nord.*

NATURAL (n) **to be a natural for (a part)** = *être taillé pour (un rôle)*
☠ *un bon naturel* = a good disposition
— *chassez le naturel il revient au galop* = a leopard doesn't change its spots.

NATURAL (adj) **1/** *naturel, -elle* : she isn't very natural when she's with her in-laws = *elle n'est pas très naturelle quand elle est avec ses beaux-parents* ≠ unnatural = *pas naturel* **2/** *naturel, -elle* : it's natural for you to think that = *il est naturel que vous pensiez ça* ≠ strange = *étrange* **3/** *naturel, -elle* : natural blond hair = *des cheveux blonds naturels* ≠ artificial = *artificiel*
to die a natural death = *mourir de mort naturelle/de sa belle mort*
a natural ability = *une capacité naturelle*
natural childbirth = *accouchement naturel*
natural resources = *ressources naturelles*
☠ *un enfant naturel* = a child born out of wedlock.

NATURALIZE (to, -d) *naturaliser.*

NATURALLY (adv) *naturellement* : naturally I'll help you = *naturellement je vous aiderai* ⊕ of course = *bien sûr*

(being a bitch) comes naturally (to her) = *(elle) est naturellement (salope).*

NATURE (n) **1/** *nature (f)* : he has a good nature = *il a une bonne nature* ① personality = *personnalité* **2/** *nature (f)* : a nature lover = *un amoureux de la nature* ☠ *thé nature* = plain tea
— *il a disparu dans la nature* = he vanished into thin air
— *grandeur nature* = life-size
— *nature morte* = still life (painting)
— *payer en nature* = to pay in kind.

NAUGHT (n) (GB) = ZERO.

NAUGHTY (adj, -ier, -iest) *vilain, -e* : a naughty boy = *un vilain garçon* ≠ obedient = *obéissant*, good = *sage* ☠ *un vilain rhume* = a nasty cold.

NAUSEATE (to, -d) *écœurer* : her ways nauseate me = *ses façons d'agir m'écœurent* **NAUSEATING** (adj) *écœurant, -e* : a nauseating smell = *une odeur écœurante* → AWFUL.

NAUSEOUS (adj) **to feel nauseous** = *se sentir nauséeux/avoir la nausée.*

NAVAL (adj) *naval, -e* : naval base = *base navale* ☠ *chantier naval* = shipyard.

NAVIGATE (to, -d) *naviguer* ① to steer = *barrer.*

NAVIGATION (n) *navigation (f)* **NAVIGATOR** (n) *navigateur (m).*

NAVY (n, -ies) *marine (f)* : he's in the Navy = *il est dans la Marine* ① Army = *Armée de terre*
navy blue = *bleu marine*
navy yard = *chantier naval et arsenal (maritime)* ☠ → marine.

NAZI (n) *nazi, -e* ① fascist = *fasciste*, concentration camp = *camp de concentration* **NAZISM** (n) *nazisme (m).*

NEAR (adj, -er, -est) *proche* : Christmas is near = *Noël est proche*
the Near East = *le Proche-Orient*
☠ *je suis proche de mon père* = I'm close to my father.

NEAR (prep) *près de* : sit near me = *assieds-toi près de moi* = close to ≠ far from = *loin de*
to move near = *approcher* : move the chair near the bed = *approche la chaise du lit* ☠ → to approach
near here = *près d'ici*
I wouldn't go near (him/drugs) = *je ne me frotterais pas à (lui) / je ne toucherais pas à (la drogue)*
no one can come near him (at tennis) = *(au tennis) il n'y a personne qui lui arrive à la cheville.*

NEAR (adv) *près* : she lives very near = *elle habite tout près* = close ① nearby = *tout près* ≠ far = *loin*

---

to draw near = *se rapprocher* : the enemy is drawing near = *l'ennemi se rapproche* ☠ → to bring together
to come very near to (being fired) = *être sur le point d'être (renvoyé)*
not anywhere/nowhere near = **1/** *tant s'en faut* : it costs nowhere near $ 10 = *ça ne coûte pas 10 dollars, tant s'en faut* = it doesn't cost anywhere near $ 10, her cooking comes nowhere near mine = *sa cuisine ne vaut pas la mienne, tant s'en faut* : her cooking doesn't come anywhere near mine **2/** *pas tout près* : she lives nowhere near here = *elle n'habite pas tout près d'ici* = she doesn't live anywhere near here.

NEAR (to, -ed) *approcher de* : our work's nearing completion = *notre travail approche de sa fin.*

NEARBY (adj, adv) *tout près* : they live nearby = *ils habitent tout près* = close-by ≠ far off = *très loin.*

NEARER (comp adv) *plus près* : she lives nearer to me than you do = *elle habite plus près de chez moi que vous* = closer ≠ further = *plus loin*
nearer and nearer = *de plus en plus près* : he came nearer and nearer = *il venait de plus en plus près* = closer and closer
don't come any nearer ! = *n'approchez pas !*

NEAREST (superl adj) *(qui est) le plus proche* : the nearest restaurant is Italian = *le restaurant le plus proche est italien* = closest
the nearest thing to (democracy) = *ce qui se rapproche le plus de (la démocratie).*

NEAREST (superl adv) *le plus près* : she lives (the) nearest = *c'est elle qui habite le plus près.*

NEARLY (adv) *presque* : I've nearly finished = *j'ai presque fini* ① just about = *quasiment*
not nearly as ... as = *loin d'être aussi ... que* : he's not nearly as bright as his brother = *il est loin d'être aussi intelligent que son frère*
nearly (+ verb) = *faillir* : he nearly died in the accident = *il a failli mourir dans l'accident.*

NEAR-MISS (n) **to be a near-miss** = *être manqué de peu* : the launching was a near-miss = *le lancement a été manqué de peu.*

NEARSIGHTED (adj) *myope* = shortsighted ≠ farsighted = *presbyte* ☠ *myope comme une taupe* = blind as a bat.

NEAT (adj, -er, -est) **1/** *net, nette* (stg), *soigneux, -euse* (s.o.) : a neat room = *une chambre nette*, she's very neat = *elle est très soigneuse* ① orderly = *ordonné* ≠ sloppy = *négligé* ☠ *net* → net, *soigneux* → careful **2/** *sympa* : a neat guy/place = *un type/un endroit sympa* → WONDERFUL ≠ crummy = *moche.*

NEBBISH (n, -es) *pauvre type (m), pauvre fille (f)* : how can she go out with such a nebbish ? = *comment peut-elle sortir avec un pauvre type pareil ?* ⓒ creep = *minable.*

NEBULOUS (adj) *nébuleux, -euse* : nebulous projects = *des projets nébuleux* ⓒ vague = *←.*

NECESSARILY (adv) *nécessairement* : that's not necessarily so = *ce n'est pas nécessairement vrai.*

NECESSARY (adj) *nécessaire* : necessary repairs = *des réparations nécessaires* ⓒ essential = *essentiel ≠* unnecessary = *pas nécessaire*
to do whatever is necessary = *faire le nécessaire*
if necessary = *si (c'est) nécessaire* ⓒ if need be = *si besoin est*
a necessary evil = *un mal nécessaire*
was it necessary for you to say that ? = *était-ce vraiment nécessaire de dire ça ?*

NECESSITATE (to, -d) *nécessiter* : this work necessitates a lot of patience = *ce travail nécessite beaucoup de patience* ⓒ to entail = *entraîner.*

NECESSITY (n, -ies) *nécessité (f)* ⓒ requirement = *exigence*
necessity is the mother ot invention = *nécessité est mère d'invention*
of necessity = *par la force des choses* : their marriage must of necessity be put off = *leur mariage doit être repoussé par la force des choses*
(to do stg) out of necessity = *(faire qqch) par nécessité.*

NECK (n) *cou (m)* ⓒ nape of the neck = *nuque*	
to be up to one's neck in (work) = *crouler sous le travail* ⓒ swamped with = *être débordé de* **to break one's neck** = *se démener* : I broke my neck trying to help him = *je me suis démené pour essayer de l'aider* **to break s.o.'s neck** = *tordre le cou à qqn* : I'll break his neck for taking the money = *je vais lui tordre le cou pour avoir volé l'argent* **you'll get it in the neck !** = *tu vas en prendre pour ton grade !* ⓒ I'll get mine in ! = *tu ne l'emporte-*	*ras pas en paradis !* **in this neck of the woods** = *dans les parages* ⓒ in the area = *dans le coin* **neck and neck** = *au coude à coude* : the race was neck and neck = *la course était au coude à coude* ⓒ photo finish = *au finish* **to save one's neck** = *sauver sa peau/sa tête* **to stick one's neck out** = *se mouiller* : he stuck his neck out to stick up for me = *il s'est mouillé pour prendre ma défense* ☠ *se mouiller* = to get wet **to win by a neck** = *gagner d'une encolure.*

NECK (to, -ed) *flirter* : we watched TV and necked = *on flirtait en regardant la télé* ⓒ to smooch = *se bécoter* ☠ → to flirt with.

NECKING (n inv) *papouilles (f pl)* : a lot of necking at the party = *beaucoup de papouilles à cette soirée.*

NECKLACE (n) *collier (m)* : a pearl necklace = *un collier de perles* ⓒ bracelet = *← ☠ →* collar.

NEED (n) *besoin (m)* : my need for love = *mon besoin d'amour* ⓒ necessity = *nécessité*	
if need be = *si besoin est* ⓒ in a crunch = *le cas échéant* **to be badly in need of (money/help)** = *avoir méchamment besoin d'(argent/aide)*	**in need** = *dans le besoin* : families in need = *familles dans le besoin* → POOR **there's no need to (go there)** = *on n'a pas besoin (d'y aller)*

☠ *pour les besoins de la cause* = for the sake of argument.

NEED (to, -ed) *avoir besoin de* : I don't need a lot of money = *je n'ai pas besoin de beaucoup d'argent* ⓒ to want = *vouloir*	
you needn't (rush) = *ce n'est pas la peine de (vous presser)* **to need to** = *avoir besoin de* : I need to rest = *j'ai besoin de me reposer* **not to need to** = *ne*	*pas avoir besoin de* : you didn't need to tell him = *tu n'avais pas besoin de le lui dire* ⓒ you didn't have to tell him = *tu n'avais pas à le lui dire.*

NEEDLE (n) 1/ *aiguille (f)* : knitting needles = *aiguilles à tricoter* ⓒ thread = *fil*, sewing = *couture*
it's like looking for a needle in a haystack = *autant chercher une aiguille dans une botte de foin*
☠ *aiguilles (montre)* = hands (watch)
2/ *piqûre (f)* : the junkie gives himself daily needles = *le camé se fait des piqûres tous les jours* ⓒ injection = *← ☠ →* sting.

NEEDLE (to, -d) *asticoter* : stop needling him (about his smoking) = *arrête de l'asticoter (parce qu'il fume)* ⓒ to nag = *bassiner.*

NEEDLESS (adj) **needless to say** = *inutile de dire* ⓒ it goes without saying = *cela va sans dire.*

NEEDLESSLY (adv) *inutilement* : let's not fight needlessly = *ne nous battons pas inutilement.*

NEEDY (n inv) **the needy** = *les nécessiteux* ⓒ the have-nots = *les économiquement faibles.*

NEGATE (to, -d) *renier* : her present position negates her previous feminism = *par sa situation actuelle elle renie son féminisme passé* ☠ → to disown.

NEGATION (n) *négation (f)* : his criticisms were a negation of my personality = *ses critiques étaient une négation de ma personnalité ≠* affirmation = *←.*

NEGATIVE (adj) *négatif, -ive* : don't be so negative about everything ! = *ne sois pas si négatif !* ≠ positive = *positif* **NEGATIVELY** (adv) *négativement.*

NEGLECT (n) *manque (m) de soin* : her neglect of the house/the children = *son manque de soin pour la maison/les enfants.*

NEGLECT (to, -ed) *négliger* : he has too much work and neglects his children = *il a trop de travail et néglige ses enfants*
to neglect to = *négliger de* : he neglected to tell me = *il a négligé de me le dire*
☠ *son offre n'est pas à négliger* = his offer isn't to be sneezed at
— *ne rien négliger pour retrouver qqn* = to leave no stone unturned to find s.o.

NEGLIGENCE (n) *négligence (f)* : criminal negligence = *négligence criminelle.*

NEGLIGENT (adj) *négligent, -e* : negligent in his work = *négligent dans le travail.*

NEGLIGIBLE (adj) *négligeable* : negligible costs = *des frais négligeables* ≠ significant = *considérable.*

NEGOTIATE (to, -d) *négocier* : to negotiate a contract = *négocier un contrat* **NEGOTIATION** (n) *négociation (f)* ⓪ talks = *pourparlers* **NEGOTIATOR** (n) *négociateur, -trice.*

NEGRESS (n, -es) *négresse (f).*

NEGRO (n, -es) *nègre (m)* ⓪ Uncle Tom = *Noir fayot avec les Blancs*, nigger = *négro*, colored people = *gens de couleur* ≠ honky = *sale·Blanc* = whity ☠ *un nègre (écrivain)* = a ghostwriter
— *travailler comme un nègre* = to work like a dog.

NEIGHBOR (n) *voisin, -e* : we're neighbors = *nous sommes voisins*, nextdoor neighbors = *voisins d'à côté* = neighbour (GB).

NEIGHBORHOOD (n) *quartier (m)* : I live in a bad neighborhood = *j'habite un sale quartier* = neighbourhood (GB) ☠ → quarter
in the neighborhood = 1/ *dans le voisinage* : she lives in the neighborhood = *elle habite dans le voisinage* ⓪ in this neck of the woods = *dans les parages* 2/ *aux environs de* : in the neighborhood of $ 10 = *aux environs de 10 dollars* ⓪ around = *autour de.*

NEITHER (pron) *ni l'un, -e ni l'autre* : which one do you want ? — neither ! = *lequel voulez-vous ? — ni l'un ni l'autre !*
neither of (us/the two) = *aucun d'entre (nous)/aucun des (deux).*

NEITHER (adj) *ni l'un, -e ni l'autre des deux* : neither man interests me = *ni l'un ni l'autre des deux hommes ne m'intéresse.*

NEITHER (adv, conj) *non plus* : the kids didn't eat and neither did I = *les gosses n'ont pas mangé et moi non plus* = the kids didn't eat and I didn't either ≠ too = *aussi*

me neither = *moi non plus* ≠ me too = *moi aussi* **that's neither here nor there** = *c'est sans importance* **neither ... nor/or ...**	= *ni ... ni ...* : the natives can neither read nor/or write = *les autochtones ne savent ni lire ni écrire* ☠ *ni vu ni connu* = without anybody noticing.

NEPHEW (n) *neveu (m)* ≠ uncle = *oncle.*

NEPOTISM (n) *népotisme (m)* ⓪ pull = *piston.*

NERVE (n) *nerf (m)* : nerves of steel = *des nerfs d'acier*
to get on s.o.'s nerves = *taper sur les nerfs de qqn* : she gets on my nerves = *elle me tape sur les nerfs* ⓪ to be a pain in the neck = *être casse-pieds*
to have the nerve to = *avoir le toupet de* : he had the nerve to steal money from his own mother = *il a eu le toupet de voler de l'argent à sa propre mère*
to lose one's nerve = *se dégonfler* ☠ → to chicken out
☠ *avoir du nerf* ≠ *manquer de nerf* = to have ≠ to lack spunk
— *avoir les nerfs à fleur de peau* = to be overly sensitive.

NERVE-RACKING (adj) *éprouvant, -e pour les nerfs* : a nerve-racking afternoon with the kids = *une après-midi avec les enfants éprouvante pour les nerfs* ⓪ annoying = *énervant.*

NERVOUS (adj) *nerveux, -euse* : why are you so nervous ? = *pourquoi êtes-vous si nerveux ?* ⓪ on edge = *à bout de nerfs*, keyed up = *sur les nerfs*, burnt-out = *stressé*
to have a nervous breakdown = *faire une dépression nerveuse*
a nervous wreck = *une pile de nerfs*
you're making me nervous = *tu me rends nerveux* : stop walking up and down, you're making me nervous = *arrête de faire les cent pas, tu me rends nerveux.*

NERVOUSLY (adv) *nerveusement* ≠ quietly = *tranquillement.*

NERVY (adj, -ier, -iest) *gonflé, -e* : that was a nervy thing to say ! = *c'était gonflé de dire ça !* ⓪ gutsy = *culotté* ☠ → bloated.

NEST (n) *nid (m)* ⓪ egg = *œuf*
to feather one's nest = *faire son beurre* ⓪ to make a pile = *faire sa pelote*
nest egg = *bas de laine* ⓪ economies = *économies.*

NET (n) *filet (m)* : to work without a net = *travailler sans filet.*

NET (adj) *net, nette* : net income = *revenu net*
the net result = *le résultat final*
☠ *une chambre nette* = a neat room
— *un refus net* = a flat refusal
— *net d'impôt* = tax-exempt.

NET (to, -ted) *faire un bénéfice net de* : we netted 100 grand = *nous avons fait un bénéfice net de 100 000 dollars* ≠ to gross = *faire un bénéfice brut de*.

NETHERLANDS (n pl) *Pays-Bas (m pl)* ⊙ Holland = *Hollande*, the Dutch = *les Hollandais*.

NETTLE (n) *ortie (f)* ⊙ weed = *mauvaise herbe*.

NETWORK (n) **1/** *réseau (m)* : the crime network = *le réseau du crime* **2/** *grande chaîne (f)* (TV) : three large American networks = *trois grandes chaînes américaines* ⊙ the media = *les médias*.

NEUROLOGIST (n) *neurologue (m, f)* **NEUROLOGY** (n) *neurologie (f)*.

NEUROSIS (n, -ses) *névrose (f)* ⊙ hang-up = *complexe*.

NEUROTIC (n) *névrosé, -e* **NEUROTIC** (adj) *névrosé, -e* : why is he so neurotic ? = *pourquoi est-il si névrosé ?* ⊙ psychotic = *psychopathe*.

NEUTRAL (adj) *neutre* : a neutral position = *une position neutre* ⊙ impartial = ←.

NEUTRALITY (n) *neutralité (f)* : Swiss neutrality = *la neutralité suisse*.

NEUTRALIZE (to, -d) *neutraliser* : only ideas can neutralize ideas = *les idées ne peuvent être neutralisées que par des idées* ⊙ to offset = *compenser*.

NEVER (adv) **1/** *ne ... jamais* : he'll never come = *il ne viendra jamais* = he won't ever come ≠ always = *toujours* **2/** *jamais* : will you sleep with me ? — never ! = *est-ce que tu coucheras avec moi ? — jamais !* ≠ sometimes = *parfois*

I never ! = *sapristi !* → GOSH ! **never again !** = *plus jamais !* **never have I (eaten so much)** = *jamais je n'ai (tant mangé)* **never mind !** = *peu importe !* : if you can't lend me the money, never mind, I'll ask someone else = *si tu ne peux pas me prêter l'argent, peu importe, je demanderai à quelqu'un d'autre* ⊙ it doesn't matter = *ça ne fait rien*	**never say die !** = *il ne faut jamais désespérer !* **never so much as** = *même pas* : he never so much as offered to pay for the abortion = *il n'a même pas proposé de payer l'avortement* **never say never** = *il ne faut pas dire « fontaine, je ne boirai pas de ton eau »* → THAT'S LIFE ! **never you mind !** = *t'occupe !* ⊙ mind your own business ! = *mêle-toi de tes affaires !* **you never can tell !**

= on ne sait jamais ! = **you never know !** →	THAT'S LIFE !

☠ *jamais de la vie !* = not on your life !
— *êtes-vous jamais allé en France ?* = have you ever been to France ?
— *jamais deux sans trois* = things happen in threes.

NEVER-NEVER LAND (n) *pays (m) de rêve*.

NEVERTHELESS (adv) *néanmoins* : he's a bastard, but I love him nevertheless = *c'est un salaud, mais néanmoins je l'aime* ⊙ in any case = *en tout cas*, however = *cependant*.

NEW (adj, -er, -est) **1/** *neuf, neuve* : his car isn't second-hand, it's new = *sa voiture n'est pas une voiture d'occasion, elle est neuve* ≠ old = *vieux*
☠ *remettre à neuf* = to renovate
— *le neuf avril* = the ninth of April
— *neuf (bouteilles)* = nine (bottles)
2/ *nouveau, nouvel* (in front of a vowel), *-elle* : I met her new husband/lover = *j'ai rencontré son nouveau mari/nouvel amant* ≠ old = *ancien*
☠ *à nouveau* = again
— *jusqu'à nouvel ordre* = till further notice.

to be new at (this job) = *être nouveau dans (ce travail)* **to feel like a new man/woman** = *se sentir un autre homme/une autre femme* **to have a new lease on life** = *jeter un regard nouveau sur la vie* **the New Testament** = *le Nouveau Testament* **the New World** = *le Nouveau Monde* **New Year** = *la nouvelle année*	**New Year's Eve** = *la Saint-Sylvestre* **New York** = New York = the Big Apple ⊙ New Yorker = *New-Yorkais* **that's a new one on/to me !** = *on en apprend tous les jours !* **that's nothing new !** = *ce n'est pas nouveau !* = **that's not anything new !** **to turn (over) a new leaf** = *tourner la page* **under new management** = *changement de direction*

NEWBORN (adj) *nouveau-né, -e* : a newborn child = *un enfant nouveau-né*.

NEWCOMER (n) *nouveau venu, nouvelle venue* : he's a newcomer at the office = *c'est un nouveau venu au bureau* ≠ old hand = *vieux routier*.

NEWLYWEDS (n pl) *jeunes mariés (m pl)* ⊙ honeymooners = *jeunes mariés en voyage de noces*.

NEWS (n inv) *nouvelle (f), nouvelles (f pl)* : that's good news ! = *c'est une bonne nouvelle !/ce sont de bonnes nouvelles !*, I've some good ≠ bad news for you = *j'ai de bonnes ≠ mauvaises nouvelles pour vous*
the news = *les informations/les nouvelles* : the news is

on every night at ten = *les nouvelles/informations sont présentées tous les soirs à dix heures* ⓪ news agency = *agence de presse*, current events = *l'actualité*
to break the news to s.o. = *annoncer la nouvelle à qqn*
to have news from s.o. = *avoir des nouvelles de qqn* : I haven't had any news from him for a long time = *je n'ai pas eu de nouvelles de lui depuis longtemps*
I have news for him ! = *il se fait des illusions ! :* if he thinks I'm going to lend him money again, I have news for him ! = *s'il croit que je vais encore lui prêter de l'argent, il se fait des illusions !* ⓪ he's sadly mistaken = *il se trompe lourdement*
it's news = *c'est un événement :* when the President sneezes, it's news = *quand le Président éternue, c'est un événement*
news clippings = *coupures de presse*
news items = *faits divers*
no news is good news = *pas de nouvelles, bonnes nouvelles*
the news of the day = *les nouvelles/les informations de la journée*
that's news to me ! = *première nouvelle !*
a (fascinating) piece of news = *une nouvelle (fascinante)*
☠ *il écrit des nouvelles* = he writes short stories
— *demander des nouvelles de qqn* = to ask about s.o.
— *vous m'en direz des nouvelles* = I'm sure you'll like it
— *il va avoir de mes nouvelles* = that's not the end of it
— *c'est une nouvelle* = she/it is a new one.

NEWSCAST (n) *informations (f pl)* (radio, TV), *actualités (f pl)* (TV) **NEWSCASTER** (n) *présentateur, -trice du journal télévisé.*

NEWSPAPER (n) *journal (m), canard (m)* (LV) : to read the newspaper ! = *lire le journal !* ☠ → journal, → duck

by-line article = *article signé*	*liste*
classified ads = *petites annonces*	**leading article** = *article de fond*
clipping = *coupure*	**magazine** = ←
column = *rubrique*	**newsboy** = *jeune vendeur de journaux*
columnist = *chroniqueur*	**newspaperman/newspaperwoman** = *journaliste*
comic strips = *bandes dessinées*	**newsstand** = *kiosque à journaux*
correspondent = *correspondant*	**the press** = *la presse*
editor = *rédacteur*	**press conference** = *conférence de presse*
front page = *la une*	**rag** = *feuille de chou*
gazette = ←	**reporter** = ←
heading = *manchette*	**scoop** = ←
headline = *gros titre*	**sports page** = *page des sports*
journalism = *journalisme*	**tabloid** = *tabloïd.*
journalist = *journa-*	

NEWSWORTHY (adj) *intéressant, -e à signaler :* a newsworthy event = *un événement intéressant à signaler.*

NEXT (adj) *prochain, -e :* next week = *la semaine prochaine* ⓪ the following week = *la semaine suivante*

next ! = *au suivant !*	*ensuite ?*
next of kin = *les plus proches parents*	**who's next ?** = *à qui le tour ?*
the next day = *le lendemain*	**within the next ...** = *dans les ... qui viennent :* the town will be built within the next five years = *la ville sera construite dans les cinq années qui viennent.*
the next morning = *le lendemain matin*	
(the) next time = *la prochaine fois*	
what's next ? = *et*	

NEXT (adv) 1/ *ensuite :* what will we do next ? = *qu'allons-nous faire ensuite ?* ⓪ after = *après* 2/ *la prochaine fois, re- :* when will I see you next ? = *quand vous verrai-je la prochaine fois ?/quand est-ce que je vous revois ?* ⓪ again = *de nouveau* **next best** = *à défaut, le mieux ... :* the next best thing would be to accept his offer = *à défaut, le mieux serait d'accepter son offre.*

NEXT-DOOR (adj) *d'à côté :* this is our next-door neighbor = *voici notre voisin d'à côté.*

NEXT-DOOR (adv) *(d')à côté :* she lives next-door (to me) = *elle habite à côté (de chez moi)*, the guy next-door is really cute = *le type d'à côté est vraiment mignon.*

NEXT TO (prep) 1/ *à côté de :* sit next to me = *asseyez-vous à côté de moi* ≠ far from = *loin de* 2/ *juste après :* next to Chinese food, I like pizza best = *juste après la cuisine chinoise, ce sont les pizzas que je préfère* 3/ *pratiquement :* it's next to impossible = *c'est pratiquement impossible* ⓪ almost = *presque.*

NIBBLE (to, -d) *grignoter :* to nibble chocolate = *grignoter du chocolat* ⓪ to pick at = *picorer.*

NICE (adj, -r, -st) 1/ *gentil, -ille :* how nice you are ! = *que tu es gentille !* ⓪ kind = *bon* ≠ mean = *méchant* 2/ *sympathique, gentil, -ille :* what a nice family/little restaurant ! = *quelle gentille famille/quel gentil petit restaurant !, quelle famille sympathique/quel sympathique petit restaurant !* → WONDERFUL 3/ *joli, -e :* a nice coat = *un joli manteau* ≠ ugly = *laid* ☠ → pretty
to be nice to s.o. = *être gentil avec qqn :* he was very nice to me = *il a été très gentil avec moi*
it's nice to see you = *ça (me) fait plaisir de vous voir*
it was nice while it lasted = *les meilleures choses ont une fin* → THAT'S LIFE !
nice and easy ! = *mollo !* = easy does it ! ⓪ stay cool ! = *t'emballe pas !*
nice and (warm) = *agréablement (chaud)* → VERY

nice going ! = *chapeau !*
that was nice of him ! = *c'était gentil de sa part !*

NICELY (adv) *doucement* : the patient's doing nicely = *le malade se remet doucement* ☠ → softly.

NICETIES (n pl) *agréments (m pl)* : the niceties of city life = *les agréments de la vie en ville.*

NICK (n) **in the nick of time** = *à point nommé* : you came in the nick of time = *vous êtes arrivés à point nommé* ⓪ just in time = *à temps.*

NICK (to, -ed) (GB) *barboter* : he nicked my watch = *il m'a barboté ma montre* ⓪ to swipe = *faucher.*

NICKEL (n) *(pièce (f) de) 5 cents* : it costs a nickel = *ça coûte 5 cents* ⓪ dime = *10 cents.*

NICKNAME (n) *sobriquet (m)* ⓪ pet name = *surnom.*

NIECE (n) *nièce (f)* ≠ nephew = *neveu.*

NIFTY (adj, -ier, -iest) *super (inv)* : a nifty house = *une maison super* = super → WONDERFUL ≠ crummy = *moche.*

NIGGARDLY (adj) *pingre* ⓪ stingy = *radin.*

NIGGER (n) *négro, négresse* ⓪ spade = *mal blanchi,* darkie = *bamboula* ≠ the Man = *l'homme blanc.*

NIGHT (n) *nuit (f)* : during the night = *pendant la nuit* ⓪ evening = *soir*

at night = *la nuit* : he works at night = *il travaille la nuit* ⓪ **by night** = *de nuit*	**night owl** = *oiseau de nuit* ≠ early bird = *lève-tôt*
to make a night of it = *faire la noce* ⓪ to live it up = *faire les quatre cents coups*	**night person** = *noctambule*
	night school = *école/cours du soir*
night and day = *nuit et jour* : I think of him night and day = *je pense à lui nuit et jour*	**night shift** = *équipe de nuit*
	night watchman = *gardien de nuit*
	to work nights = *travailler la nuit*

☠ *cette nuit* = 1/ last night 2/ tonight
— *bonnet de nuit* = wet blanket
— *depuis la nuit des temps* = since time immemorial
— *la nuit porte conseil* = sleep on it.

NIGHTCAP (n) *dernier verre (m) avant d'aller se coucher.*

NIGHTCLUB (n) *boîte (f) de nuit* ⓪ nightspot = *boîte.*

NIGHTFALL (n) *tombée (f) de la nuit* ≠ daybreak = *point du jour.*

NIGHTGOWN (n) *chemise (f) de nuit* ⓪ négligé = *déshabillé.*

NIGHTMARE (n) *cauchemar (m)* : I had a nightmare last night = *j'ai fait un cauchemar cette nuit* ⓪ bad dream = *mauvais rêve.*

NIMBLE (adj, -r, -st) *preste* : nimble fingers = *des doigts prestes* ⓪ agile = ←.

NINCOMPOOP (adj) *nigaud, -e* → STUPID.

NINE (n, adj) *neuf (m)* : he's coming at nine o'clock = *il vient à neuf heures* ⓪ ninth = *neuvième,* nineteen = *dix-neuf*
to be dressed to the nines = *être sur son trente et un* ⓪ to be in one's Sunday's best = *avoir mis ses habits du dimanche.*

NINETY (n, -ies, adj) *quatre-vingt-dix (m)* ⓪ ninetieth = *quatre-vingt-dixième*
the nineties = *les années quatre-vingt-dix.*

NINNY (n, -ies) *bêta, bêtasse* → STUPID.

NIPPLE (n) *mamelon (m)* ⓪ tit = *téton.*

NITPICK (to, -ed) *chercher la petite bête, enculer les mouches* (LV) : if you don't stop nitpicking, we'll never finish = *si tu cherches toujours la petite bête, nous n'aurons jamais fini* ⓪ to quibble = *ergoter.*

NITWIT (n) *corniaud (m)* → STUPID ☠ → mongrel.

NO (n, -es) *non (m)* : the noes have it = *les nons l'emportent*

I won't take no for an answer = *il n'y a pas de non qui tienne.*

NO (adj) 1/ *ne ... pas de* : I have no money = *je n'ai pas d'argent* = I don't have any money ≠ some = *quelque* 2/ *aucun, -e* : no child likes to be beaten = *aucun enfant n'aime être battu*

to be no ... = *ne rien avoir d'un ...* : he's no writer = *il n'a rien d'un écrivain*	**nothing doing !** = *rien à faire !*	**no matter how !** = *peu importe comment !* : I'll get the money no matter how ! = *j'aurai l'argent, peu importe comment !*
in no time = *en un rien de temps*	**no ifs and buts** = *il n'y a pas de mais* ⓪ there are no two ways about it = *il n'y a pas à tortiller*	
no deal ! = *je ne marche pas !*	**no (man) is an island** = *personne ne peut vivre coupé des autres*	**no matter how you slice it/you look at it (he should not have hit her)** = *quoi qu'il*
no dice ! = *des clous !*		
no go ! = *pas question !* ⓪		

en soit (il n'aurait pas dû la frapper) **no matter what** = de toute façon : I'm going no matter what = j'y vais de toute façon ⑩ in any case = en tout cas **no matter what happens** = quoi qu'il arrive **no matter which** = n'importe lequel	**no matter who** = n'importe qui **no one** = personne : no one agrees with me = personne n'est d'accord avec moi = nobody ≠ somebody = quelqu'un **no smoking/parking !** = défense de fumer/de stationner ! **no way !** = que dalle ! = **no soap !** ≠ roger ! = d'ac !	**there's no knowing/saying/ telling** = on ne peut pas savoir/dire **there's no pleasing him** = il n'y a jamais moyen de le satisfaire **no ... whatever** = ne ... pas du tout : they have no money whatever = ils n'ont pas du tout d'argent.

NO (adv) *non* : no, you can't come with me = *non, vous ne pouvez pas venir avec moi* ⑩ nope = *ben non* ≠ yes = *oui*

no later than (yesterday) = pas plus tard qu'(hier) ≠ **no earlier than** = pas plus tôt que **no less** = rien que ça : he wants me to pay for the abortion no less = il veut que je paye l'avortement, rien que ça ⑩ to top it off = pour couronner le tout **no less than** = 1/ rien moins que : no less than the President himself = rien moins que le Président lui-même 2/ pas moins de : no less than 100 people = pas moins de 100 personnes **no more** = ne ... plus : he'll come no more = il ne viendra plus = he won't come any more **no more (Scotch for you) ?** = (vous ne voulez) plus de (whisky) ?	**no more than (20 people)** = pas plus de (20 personnes) **no sooner ... than** = à peine ... que : no sooner had I come in than the phone rang = à peine étais-je entrée que le téléphone a sonné **no sooner said than done** = aussitôt dit aussitôt fait **no worse** ≠ **better than** = pas pire ≠ mieux que : the film's no worse than the novel = le film n'est pas pire que le roman **no yet** = par-dessus le marché : he made love with the maid and in my bed no yet = il a fait l'amour avec la bonne et dans mon lit par-dessus le marché

☠ *non seulement* = not only — *elle a tort, non ?* = she's wrong, isn't she ?	— *j'ai peur que non* = I'm afraid not — *je crois que non* = I don't believe so.

NOBEL PRIZE (n) *prix Nobel (m)* : Nobel Peace Prize = *prix Nobel de la paix.*

NOBLE (adj, -r, -st) *noble* : a noble ideal = *un noble idéal* ⑩ lofty = *élevé.*

NOBODY (n, -ies) **to be a nobody** = *n'être rien du tout* : in films he's a nobody = *dans le cinéma, il n'est rien du tout* ≠ to be someone = *être quelqu'un.*

NOBODY (pron) *personne* : nobody came = *personne n'est venu*, there was nobody = *il n'y avait personne* = no one ≠ someone = *quelqu'un* → person
like nobody's business = *vachement* : he lies like nobody's business = *il ment vachement* → VERY ☠ → damned
nobody else = *personne d'autre* : if he can't help, nobody else can = *s'il ne peut pas vous aider, personne d'autre ne le peut* = no one else ≠ someone else = *quelqu'un d'autre*
(she's) nobody's fool = *pas folle, la guêpe !* ⑩ she wasn't born yesterday = *elle n'est pas née d'hier.*

NOD (n) *hochement (m) de tête* **NOD** (to, -ded) *hocher la tête.*

NOGGIN (n) *caboche (f)* ⑩ noodle = *ciboulot.*

NO-HOLDS-BARRED (adv) **1/** *tous les coups sont permis* : a fight, no-holds-barred = *une bagarre où tous*

les coups sont permis **2/** en mettant le paquet : they gave a wedding party, no-holds-barred = *ils ont donné une réception de mariage en y mettant le paquet.*

NOISE (n) *bruit (m)* : the kids made a lot of noise = *les gosses ont fait beaucoup de bruit* ⑩ din = *vacarme*, racket = *raffut*
☠ *le bruit court que* = rumor has it that
— *beaucoup de bruit pour rien* = much ado about nothing
— *le livre a fait du bruit* = the book caused a big stir.

NOISY (adj, -ier, -iest) *bruyant, -e* : a noisy meeting = *une réunion bruyante* ⑩ boisterous = *tapageur.*

NOMAD (n) *nomade (m, f)* ⑩ wanderer = *errant.*

NO-MAN'S-LAND (n) *no man's land (m).*

NOMINAL (adj) *nominal, -e* : a nominal sum = *une somme nominale*
the nominal (head) = *le (chef) nominal.*

NOMINATE (to, -d) *désigner* : to nominate a candidate = *désigner un candidat* ⑩ to elect = *élire* ☠ → to designate.

NOMINATION (n) *proposition (f) de candidature* : his nomination for the presidency = *la proposition de sa candidature pour la présidence* ⑩ election = *élection* ☠

sa nomination (comme ambassadeur) = his appointment (as ambassador).

NOMINEE (n) *personne (f) désignée* ⓪ candidate = *candidat.*

NONCHALANT (adj) *détaché, -e* : she appeared very nonchalant about her divorce = *elle s'est montrée très détachée au sujet de son divorce* ☠ *elle est nonchalante* = she's laid-back.

NONCOMMITTAL (adj) *qui n'engage à rien* : a noncommittal answer = *une réponse qui n'engage à rien*
he was noncommittal = *il ne s'est pas beaucoup engagé.*

NONCONFORMIST (adj) *non-conformiste* ⓪ bohemian = *bohème,* offbeat = *fantaisiste.*

NONDESCRIPT (adj) *falot, -e* (s.o.), *terne* : a nondescript personality = *une personnalité falote,* a nondescript way of dressing = *une façon terne de s'habiller.*

NONE (pron) *aucun, -e* : how many guests came ? — none = *combien d'invités sont venus ? — aucun* ☠ → no

I have none = *je n'en ai aucun* ⓪ I don't have any = *je n'en ai pas* **it's none of your business** = *ce ne sont pas tes oignons* **none of** = *aucun de* : none of us understood = *aucun de nous n'a compris,* none of the books are interesting =	*aucun des livres n'est intéressant* **next to none** = 1/ *incomparable* : her cooking's next to none = *sa cuisine est incomparable* → WONDERFUL 2/ *pratiquement aucun* : how many are left ? — next to none = *combien en reste-t-il ? — pratiquement aucun.*

NONE (adv) **he's none the better** ≠ **the worse for it** = *il ne s'en porte pas mieux* ≠ *plus mal pour autant*
none too (soon/intelligent) = *pas trop (tôt/intelligent).*

NONETHELESS (adv) *toutefois* : it's expensive, nonetheless I'll buy it = *c'est cher, toutefois je vais l'acheter* ⓪ all the same = *tout de même,* nevertheless = *néanmoins.*

NONEXISTENT (adj) *inexistant, -e* : nonexistent problems = *des problèmes inexistants* ≠ real = *réel.*

NONINTERVENTION (n) *non-intervention (f)* ⓪ noninterference = *non-ingérence.*

NO-NONSENSE (adj) *qui ne plaisante pas* : a no-nonsense boss = *un patron qui ne plaisante pas.*

NONPRODUCTIVE (adj) *improductif, -ive* : nonproductive investment = *investissement improductif.*

NONPROFIT (adj) *sans but lucratif* : a nonprofit organization = *une organisation sans but lucratif* ⓪ benevolent = *bénévole.*

NONSENSE (n inv) *bêtises (f pl)* : what nonsense to say you're going to kill her ! = *quelles bêtises quand tu dis que tu vas la tuer !* ⓪ bunk = *fadaises*
I won't stand for any nonsense = *je ne me laisserai pas faire*
to talk nonsense = *dire des bêtises*
☠ → foolishness.

NONSMOKER (n) *non-fumeur, -euse* ⓪ nondrinker = *qqn qui ne boit pas.*

NONSTOP (adj) *non-stop* : a nonstop flight = *un vol non stop* **NONSTOP** (adv) *non stop, sans arrêt* : to fly nonstop = *prendre un vol non stop,* to talk/work nonstop = *parler/travailler sans arrêt.*

NONVIOLENT (adj) *non violent, -e* : a nonviolent demonstration = *une manifestation non violente* ⓪ pacific = *pacifiste.*

NOODLE (n) *nouille (f)* ⓪ pasta = *pâtes* ☠ *quelle nouille !* = what a dimwit !

NOOK (n) **to look in every nook and cranny** = *chercher dans tous les coins et recoins* ⓪ to look high and low = *chercher dans tous les coins.*

NOON (n) *midi (m)* : we'll eat at noon = *nous mangerons à midi* ⓪ lunchtime = *heure du déjeuner* ☠ *chercher midi à quatorze heures* = to complicate things.

NOOSE (n) *nœud (m) coulant* ⓪ rope = *corde.*

NOPE (adv) *ben non* ≠ yeah = *ouais.*

NOR (conj) **1/** *d'ailleurs* : we don't have a dog, nor do I want one = *nous n'avons pas de chien et d'ailleurs je n'en veux pas* **2/** *non plus* : she doesn't smoke, nor do I = *elle ne fume pas et moi non plus.*

NORM (n) *norme (f)* : the national norm is 1.5 children by family = *au niveau national, la norme est de 1,5 enfant par famille* ⓪ rule = *règle.*

NORMAL (n) *normale (f)* ⓪ average = *moyenne*
above ≠ **below normal (intelligence)** = *(intelligence) au-dessus* ≠ *au-dessous de la normale.*

NORMAL (adj) *normal, -e* : a normal attitude = *une attitude normale* ⓪ natural = *naturel* ≠ abnormal = *anormal*
it's normal to (love one's children) = *c'est normal d'(aimer ses enfants).*

NORMALIZE (to, -d) *normaliser* : to normalize relations between countries = *normaliser les relations entre pays* **NORMALIZATION** (n) *normalisation (f).*

NORMALLY (adv) *normalement* : I normally don't eat breakfast = *normalement, je ne prends pas de petit déjeuner* ⓪ usually = *habituellement.*

NORTH (n) *nord (m)* ⓪ Northeast = *nord-est,* Northwest = *nord-ouest* ≠ South = *sud* ☠ *perdre le nord* = to go batty.

NORTH (adj) *(du) Nord* : North America/North Africa

= *Amérique du Nord/Afrique du Nord*
North Pole = *pôle Nord.*

NORTHERN (adj) *du Nord, nordique* ⊕ Southern =

du Sud **NORTHERNER** (n) *nordiste (USA)/nordique (m, f).*

NORWAY (n) *Norvège (f)* **NORWEGIAN** (n, adj) *Norvégien, -enne.*

NOSE (n) *nez (m)* (people), *museau (m)* (animals) : a broken nose = *un nez cassé* ⊕ schnozzle = *pif*, nozzle = *blair*, snout = *tarin*

---

to blow one's nose = *se moucher*
by a nose = *d'un cheveu* : he won by a nose = *il a gagné d'un cheveu* ⊕ neck and neck = *au coude à coude*
to cut off one's nose to spite one's face = *tendre les verges pour se faire fouetter* ⊕ to cut one's own throat = *scier la branche sur laquelle on est assis*
flat nose = *nez épaté*
follow your nose ! = *continuez tout droit !*
to have a nose for (bargains) = *avoir le nez (creux) pour (les affaires)*
hooked nose = *nez crochu*
to keep one's nose clean = *se tenir à carreau* : the cops told him to keep his nose clean = *les flics lui ont dit de se tenir à carreau* ⊕ to stay out of trouble = *se garder des ennuis*
to keep one's nose to the grind(stone) = *travailler sans lever le nez* ≠ to twiddle one's

thumbs = *se tourner les pouces*
to lead s.o. by the nose = *mener qqn par le bout du nez* ≠ to be at s.o.'s beck and call = *faire les quatre volontés de qqn*
to look down one's nose at = *regarder de haut*
my nose is bleeding = *je saigne du nez*
my nose is running = *j'ai le nez qui coule*
on the nose = *tapante* : five o'clock on the nose = *cinq heures tapantes* ⊕ sharp = *pile*
to pay through the nose = *c'est le coup de fusil/de barre* ⊕ to cost an arm and a leg = *coûter les yeux de la tête*
to pick one's nose = *se curer le nez*
to poke/to stick one's nose into (s.o.'s business) = *fourrer son nez dans (les affaires de qqn)* ⊕ to mix in = *se mêler de*
to powder one's nose = *se refaire une beauté* ⊕ to wash up = *faire un brin de toilette*

pug nose = *nez en pied de marmite/nez camus*
snub nose = *nez retroussé*
to speak through one's nose = *parler du nez*
stuffed nose = *nez bouché*
to thumb one's nose at = 1/ *faire un pied de nez à* 2/ *faire fi de* : she thumbs her nose at the doctor's advice = *elle fait fi des conseils du médecin* ≠ to take into consideration = *prendre en considération*
to turn up one's nose at = *faire la grimace devant* : kids turn up their nose at spinach = *les enfants font la grimace devant les épinards* ≠ to go for = *adorer*
turned-up nose = *nez en trompette*
(right) under s.o.'s nose = *(juste) sous le nez de qqn* : he stole the money (right) under my nose = *il a volé l'argent (juste) sous mon nez*

☙ *se bouffer le nez* = to fight like cats and dogs
— *se casser le nez* = to go somewhere for nothing (because nobody's there)
— *fermer la porte/rire au nez de qqn* = to slam the door/to laugh in s.o.'s face
— *on lui presserait le nez, il en sortirait du lait* = he's still wet behind the ears
— *nez à nez* = face to face

— *ça se voit comme le nez au milieu de la figure* = it's staring you in the face
— *ça te pend au nez* = it'll catch up with you
— *depuis deux jours, il n'a pas mis le nez dehors* = he hasn't set a foot outside for two days
— *l'affaire lui est passée sous le nez* = the deal slipped through his fingers.

NOSH (n, -es) *en-cas (m)* : what about a nosh ? = *que diriez-vous d'un petit en-cas ?* ⊕ snack = *morceau* **NOSH** (to, -ed) *casser la croûte* ⊕ to nibble = *grignoter.*
NOSTALGIA (n) *nostalgie (f)* **NOSTALGIC** (adj) *nostalgique.*

NOSTRIL (n) *narine (f)* ⊕ nose = *nez.*
NOSY (adj, -ier, -iest) *qui fourre son nez partout* : my mother-in-law is a bit nosy = *ma belle-mère a tendance à fourrer son nez partout* = nosey ⊕ inquisitive = *inquisiteur.*

NOT (adv) 1/ *ne ... pas* : I'm not hungry = *je n'ai pas faim* 2/ *pas* : she's French, not American = *elle est française, pas américaine*, certainly not = *certainement pas*

I'm afraid not = *j'ai peur que non*
I hope/think/believe not = *j'espère/je pense/je crois que non*

not (all) that = *pas tant que ça* : I'm not all that fond of my in-laws = *je n'aime pas mes beaux-parents tant que ça*
not anymore/not any longer

= *ne ... plus* : she doesn't live here anymore/any longer = *elle n'habite plus ici*
not at all = 1/ *de rien* : thank you — not at all ! = *merci — de*

rien ! **2/** *pas du tout :* I don't love him at all = *je ne l'aime pas du tout,* do you love him ? — not at all ! = *vous l'aimez ? — pas du tout !* **not enough** = *pas assez* **not even** = *même pas :* she didn't even say hello = *elle n'a même pas dit bonjour* **not like** = *pas comme :* things are not like before = *ce n'est pas comme avant* **that's not like (you)** = *cela ne (vous) ressemble pas* **not long after** = *peu de temps*	*après* = shortly after **not me !** = *pas moi !* **not much !** = *tu parles ! :* they're not rich — not much ! = *ils ne sont pas riches — tu parles !* **not only** = *pas seulement :* he's not only my lawyer, he's also my lover = *ce n'est pas seulement mon avocat, c'est aussi mon amant* **not that** = *non pas que :* not that you're wrong = *non pas que vous ayez tort* **not that I care/it matters** =	*ce n'est pas que ça me fasse quelque chose/que ça ait beaucoup d'importance* **not the least** = *pas le moins du monde :* he's not the least intelligent = *il n'est pas intelligent le moins du monde* **not to** = *de ne pas :* he told me not to come = *il m'a dit de ne pas venir* **not without** = *non sans :* he finished his work not without difficulty = *il a fini son travail non sans difficulté*

☠ *j'ai pas mal de problèmes* = I have quite a lot of problems	— *pas possible !* = no kidding !

NOTABLE (adj) *notable :* notable success/progress = *succès/progrès notable.*

NOTABLY (adv) *notamment :* many important people were at the dinner, notably the Prime Minister = *beaucoup de personnes haut placées participaient au dîner, notamment le Premier ministre* ⓪ for example = *par exemple.*

NOTARIZE (to, -d) *authentifier :* to notarize a document = *authentifier un document.*

NOTARY PUBLIC (n) *quelqu'un qui authentifie les actes rapidement et pour des sommes dérisoires* ☠ *un notaire* = a lawyer specialized in questions of inheritance, real estate problems, etc.

NOTE (n) **1/** *note (f) :* to speak without notes = *parler sans notes* **2/** *petit mot (m) :* this is just a note to thank you = *(c'est) juste un petit mot pour vous remercier* ⓪ letter = *lettre* **3/** *note (f) :* a note of mystery = *une note de mystère*

to compare notes = *échanger ses impressions*
to take note of (what he said) = *prendre (bonne) note de (ce qu'il a dit)*
to take notes = *prendre des notes*
☠ *notes (école)* = (school) grades/marks
— *note de frais* = expense account
— *la note* = the tab/the bill.

NOTE (to, -d) *noter :* note that it's important = *notez que c'est important* ⓪ to notice = *remarquer*
to note down = *mettre par écrit :* I noted down my impressions = *j'ai mis mes impressions par écrit* ⓪ to write down = *marquer*
☠ *noter (copies)* = to mark (papers).

NOTED (adj) *réputé, -e :* a noted scientist = *un savant réputé* ⓪ eminent = *éminent* ☠ → reputed.

NOTEWORTHY (adj) *digne d'attention :* the only noteworthy item in today's news = *la seule nouvelle digne d'attention aujourd'hui.*

NOTHING (n) *nullité (f) :* her husband's a nothing = *son mari est une nullité* ⓪ creep = *minable.*	

NOTHING (pron) *rien :* she ate nothing = *elle n'a rien mangé* = she didn't eat anything ≠ something = *quelque chose*	

a nothing kind of = *de rien du tout :* she's married to a nothing kind of guy = *elle est mariée à un type de rien du tout* **as if nothing was the matter** = *comme si de rien n'était* **to be nothing to s.o.** = *n'être rien pour qqn :* she's nothing to him = *elle n'est rien pour lui/elle ne lui est rien* **for nothing** = **1/** *pour rien :* I got it for nothing = *je l'ai eu pour rien* **2/** *pour rien :* he	knows his wines, he's not French for nothing = *il s'y connaît en vin, il n'est pas français pour rien* **to go for nothing** = *y aller pour rien* ⓪ to return empty-handed = *revenir bredouille* **to have nothing on** = **1/** *ne rien avoir sur le dos* ⓪ without a stitch on = *tout nu* **2/** *ne rien avoir à envier :* her brother has nothing on her for brains = *elle n'a rien à envier à son frère*	*quant à l'intelligence* **(he) knows from nothing** = *(il) ne sait rien de rien* **next to nothing** = *trois fois rien :* she earns next to nothing = *elle gagne trois fois rien* ≠ a lot = *beaucoup* **nothing but** = *ne ... que :* he does nothing but work = *il ne fait que travailler* ⓪ all he does is ... = *tout ce qu'il fait, c'est ...* **nothing doing !** = *rien à faire ! :* lend you some money ?*

nothing doing ! = *te prêter de l'argent ? rien à faire !* ⓪ no way ! = *que dalle !*
nothing else = *rien d'autre :* she's interested in nothing else but money = *elle ne s'intéresse à rien d'autre qu'à l'argent* = not ... anything else ≠ something else = *autre chose*
nothing hurts but the truth = *il n'y a que la vérité qui blesse*
(he's) nothing if not (rich) = *(il) est tout sauf (pauvre)*
nothing's further from my mind = *loin de moi cette idée*
nothing lasts forever = *tout n'a qu'un temps* → THAT'S LIFE !
nothing like (a good Scotch) = *rien de tel qu'(un bon whisky)*

nothing much = *pas grand-chose :* the book was nothing much = *le livre ne valait pas grand-chose* → AWFUL
nothing of the sort = *rien de tel*
nothing short of (real vengeance will satisfy him) = *il n'y a qu'(une vraie vengeance qui puisse le satisfaire)*
nothing succeeds like success = *on ne prête qu'aux riches/il pleut toujours où c'est mouillé*
nothing ventured nothing gained = *qui ne risque rien n'a rien*
to say nothing of = *sans parler de :* he's got a lot of money, to say nothing of his wife's wealth

= *il a beaucoup d'argent, sans parler de la fortune de sa femme*
that's nothing compared to (what he earns) = *ce n'est rien comparé à (ce qu'il gagne)*
there's nothing to worry about = *il n'y a pas de quoi s'inquiéter*
there's nothing in/to it = *c'est simple comme bonjour* ⓪ it's kid stuff = *c'est l'enfance de l'art*
think nothing of it = *n'en parlons plus* ⓪ thank you = *merci*
to think nothing of (spending a weekend together) = *trouver tout naturel de (passer un week-end ensemble)*

☠ *il n'en est rien* = it isn't true
— *elle n'a rien d'une (imbécile)* = she's no (fool)
— *ça ne me dit rien qui vaille* = it doesn't appeal to me
— *rien que d'y penser* = just thinking about it

— *il n'arrivera à rien* = he won't amount to anything
— *il ne faut jurer de rien* = never say never
— *ça ne fait rien* = it doesn't matter.

NOTHING (adv) **in nothing flat** = *en un rien de temps* ⓪ in two shakes of a lamb's tail = *en deux coups de cuiller à pot*, in the twinkling of an eye = *en deux temps trois mouvements*

nothing unusual = *rien de surprenant :* his sleeping out is nothing unusual = *le fait qu'il découche n'a rien de surprenant* ≠ surprising = *surprenant.*

NOTICE (n) 1/ *avis (m) :* there's a notice on the bulletin board = *il y a un avis sur le tableau d'affichage* ⓪ announcement = *annonce* ☠ → opinion 2/ *préavis (m) :* when they fired you did they give you notice ? = *quand ils vous ont licencié, vous ont-ils donné un préavis ?* ☠ *appeler avec préavis* = to call person to person
at ... notice = *dans un délai de :* can you be ready to leave at an hour's notice ? = *pourrez-vous être prêt à partir dans un délai d'une heure ?*
to give notice = *donner son congé* ⓪ to quit = *donner sa démission*
to give s.o. notice = *donner son congé à qqn* ⓪ to fire = *congédier*
to serve notice that = *faire savoir que*
to sit up and take notice = *prendre bonne note :* when the President speaks, the whole company sits up and takes notice = *quand le Président dit quelque chose, tout le monde en prend bonne note* ⓪ to be all ears = *être tout ouïe*
to take no notice of = *ne pas prêter attention à* ≠ to pay attention to = *prêter attention à*
without notice = *sans avis/sans préavis*
☠ *notice explicative* = directions for use.

NOTICE (to, -d) *remarquer :* he didn't notice my new dress = *il n'a pas remarqué ma nouvelle robe*, did you notice she was pregnant ? = *est-ce que vous avez remar-*

qué qu'elle était enceinte ? ⓪ to see = *voir* ☠ → to remark.

NOTICEABLE (adj) *sensible :* noticeable improvement = *des progrès sensibles* ☠ → sensible **NOTICEABLY** (adv) *sensiblement :* she's noticeably better = *elle va sensiblement mieux.*

NOTICES (n pl) *critiques (f pl) :* the play got good ≠ bad notices = *la pièce a eu de bonnes ≠ mauvaises critiques* ⓪ a review = *une critique* ☠ → criticism.

NOTIFICATION (n) *notification (f)* ⓪ notice = *avis.*

NOTIFY (to, -ied) *signaler :* notify the police = *signalez-le à la police* ⓪ to advise = *aviser.*

NOTION (n) 1/ *notion (f) :* notions of French = *des notions de français*, no notion of time = *aucune notion du temps* 2/ *idée (f) :* you have a strange notion of feminism = *vous vous faites une drôle d'idée du féminisme* ⓪ concept = ← ☠ → idea.

NOTORIETY (n) *notoriété (f)* ⓪ fame = *renommée.*

NOTORIOUS (adj) *notoire :* a notorious criminal = *un criminel notoire* ⓪ well-known = *connu* **NOTORIOUSLY** (adv) *notoirement.*

NOTWITHSTANDING (prep) *nonobstant* : notwithstanding the price = *nonobstant le prix* ⓪ in spite of = *malgré*.

NOUN (n) *nom (m)* : proper noun = *nom propre* ⓪ substantive = *substantif*, pronoun = *pronom* ☠ → name.

NOURISH (to, -ed) *nourrir* : to nourish hopes = *nourrir des espoirs* **NOURISHING** (adj) *nourrissant, -e* : a nourishing meal = *un repas nourrissant* **NOURISHMENT** (n) *aliments (m pl)*.

NOVEL (n) *roman (m)* : to write a novel = *écrire un roman* ⓪ fiction = ←, thriller = *roman policier*, short story = *nouvelle*, prologue = ←, epilogue = *épilogue* ☠ *c'est un roman fleuve* = it's a whole saga.

NOVEL (adj) *original, -e* : a novel idea = *une idée originale* ☠ → original.

NOVELIST (n) *romancier, -ère* ⓪ author = *auteur*.

NOVELTY (n, -ies) *nouveauté (f)* : a novelty shop = *une boutique de nouveautés*.

NOVEMBER (n) *novembre (m)* → MONTH.

NOVICE (n) *novice (m, f)* : a novice in politics = *un novice en politique* ⓪ fledgling = *néophyte* ≠ a pro = *un pro*.

NOW (adv) *maintenant* : do it now = *faites-le maintenant* ⓪ at present = *à présent*

now and again = *de temps à autre* : I think about you now and again = *je pense à vous de temps à autre* = **(every) now and then** ≠ from time to time = *de temps en temps* **now or never** = *maintenant ou jamais* : if you want to have a	baby, it's now or never = *si tu veux avoir un enfant, c'est maintenant ou jamais* **now then** = *bon alors* : now then where were we ? = *bon alors, où en étions-nous ?* **now you're talking !** = *voilà qui s'appelle parler !*

NOW (conj) **now that** = *maintenant que* : now that we've eaten, let's go to the movies = *maintenant que nous avons mangé, allons au cinéma*.

NOWADAYS (adv) *de nos jours* : everyone uses a contraceptive nowadays = *tout le monde utilise un contraceptif de nos jours* ≠ in days gone by = *dans le temps*.

NOWHERE (n) **to appear from nowhere** = *sortir du néant*
out of nowhere = *comme un cheveu sur la soupe* : his remark came out of nowhere = *sa remarque est arrivée comme un cheveu sur la soupe* ⓪ out of the clear blue sky = *comme tombé du ciel*.

NOWHERE (adv) *nulle part* : nowhere in America =

---

nulle part en Amérique = not anywhere in America ≠ somewhere = *quelque part*
to get nowhere = *ne mener à rien* : lying will get you nowhere = *mentir ne te mènera à rien*
we're getting nowhere fast = *on n'avance pas* ⓪ we're going around in circles = *on tourne en rond*
nowhere as ... as = *bien moins ... que* : he's nowhere as bright as his brother = *il est bien moins intelligent que son frère*
(there's) nowhere else = *nulle part ailleurs* : there's nowhere else where you can find it = *tu ne peux en trouver nulle part ailleurs*.

NTH (adj) *énième* : to the nth degree = *au énième degré*.

NUANCE (n) *nuance (f)* ⓪ subtility = *subtilité*.

NUCLEAR (adj) *nucléaire* : nuclear energy = *énergie nucléaire*, nuclear waste = *déchets nucléaires*, nuclear family = *famille nucléaire*
nuclear plant = *centrale nucléaire* = nuke.

NUCLEUS (n, -ei) *noyau (m)* : the nucleus of an atom/the President's staff = *le noyau d'un atome/de l'équipe présidentielle* ☠ → pit.

NUDE (n) *nu (m)* : a Manet nude = *un nu de Manet*.

NUDE (adj) *nu, -e* ⓪ in one's birthday suit = *en costume d'Adam/d'Ève* ≠ clothed = *vêtu* ☠ → naked.

NUDISM (n) *nudisme (m)*, *naturisme (m)* ⓪ nudist camp = *camp de nudistes/de naturistes*.

NUDGE (to, -d) *pousser du coude* ⓪ to poke = *donner un coup de coude*.

NUDNICK (n) *empoisonneur, -euse* : what a nudnick you are ! = *quel empoisonneur !* ⓪ pest = *enquiquineur*.

NUISANCE (n) *quelqu'un/quelque chose d'empoisonnant* : don't be such a nuisance ! = *ne sois pas si empoisonnant !* ⓪ pain in the neck = *casse-pieds*.

NUKE (n) *centrale (f) nucléaire* ⓪ nuclear energy = *énergie nucléaire*.

NULL (adj) **null and void** = *nul et non avenu*.

NULLIFY (to, -ied) *rendre nul* : to nullify a treaty = *rendre un traité nul* ⓪ to void = *rendre nul et de nul effet*.

NUMB (adj, -er, -est) *engourdi, -e* : my legs are numb = *mes jambes sont engourdies* ⓪ stiff = *raide* **NUMBNESS** (n) *engourdissement (m)*.

NUMBER (n) **1/** *nombre (m)* : 45 is a number = *45 est un nombre* ⓪ figure = *chiffre* **2/** *numéro (m)* : give me your (phone) number = *donnez-moi votre numéro (de téléphone)*, she lives at number 20 = *elle habite au numéro 20* **3/** *numéro (m)* : her guy's a weird number = *son mec est un drôle de numéro* ⓪ queer fish = *drôle de coco*, freak = *spécimen* **4/** *numéro (m)* : an interesting comic number = *un numéro comique intéressant* = act ⓪ show = *spectacle*

to do a number on s.o. = *se ficher de qqn* ⓪ to take s.o. for a ride = *mener qqn en bateau*
to do one's number = *faire son numéro*
a good/great number of (people) = *un grand nombre de (gens)* → MANY
to have s.o.'s number = *connaître son bonhomme :* he won't fool me again, I have his number = *il ne m'aura pas une deuxième fois, je connais mon bonhomme* ⓪ to be on to s.o. = *voir le manège de qqn*
to look out for number one = *s'occuper de bibi/de sa petite personne*
a number of = *un certain nombre de :* we're having a number of problems = *nous avons un certain nombre de problèmes*
number one = *petite commission :* to do number one = *faire sa petite commission* ≠ **number two** = *grosse commission*
your number's up = *ton compte est bon !* ⓪ it's all over ! = *c'est fichu !*
☠ *le numéro de janvier* = the January issue.

NUMBER (to, -ed) **to number among** = *compter parmi :* I number him among my closest friends = *je le compte parmi mes amis les plus intimes.*

NUMEROUS (adj) *nombreux, -euse :* numerous people/problems = *de nombreuses personnes/de nombreux problèmes* → MANY ☠ *famille nombreuse* = family with 3 or more children.

NUMSKULL (n) *cruche (f)* → STUPID ☠ → jug.

NUN (n) *nonne (f), religieuse (f), bonne sœur (f)* ⓪ sister = *sœur,* Mother Superior = *mère supérieure.*

NURSE (n) *infirmier, -ère* ⓪ hospital attendant = *aide-soignant,* orderly = *garçon de salle,* RN = *infirmière diplômée* = registered nurse.

NURSE (to, -d) *allaiter :* to nurse one's baby = *allaiter son bébé.*

NURSERY (n, -ies) **nursery school** = *maternelle* ⓪ kindergarten = *jardin d'enfants*
nursery rhyme = *comptine.*

NUT (n) **1/** *noix (f)* ⓪ hazelnut = *noisette,* peanut = *cacahuète,* coconut = *noix de coco,* walnut = *noix,* chestnut = *châtaigne/marron,* almond = *amande,* nutcracker = *casse-noix*
to be a hard/tough nut to crack = *être difficile à cerner* ⓪ what makes him run ? = *qu'est-ce qui le fait courir ?*
☠ *quelle noix !* = what a dummy !
— *(un écrivain) à la noix* = (a) two-bit (writer)
2/ *fana (m, f) :* a bridge nut = *un fana de bridge* ⓪ buff = *mordu*
3/ *dingue (m, f) :* her husband's a nut = *son mari est un dingue* ⓪ a screwball = *un louftingue*
to be off one's nut = *avoir un grain* → CRAZY.

NUTHOUSE (n) *maison (f) de fous* ⓪ loony bin = *maison de dingues.*

NUTRITION (n) *nutrition (f)* **NUTRITIOUS** (adj) *nutritif, -ive.*

NUTS (adj) *dingue :* Christ ! are you nuts ! = *bon Dieu ! t'es dingue !* → CRAZY
to be nuts about = *être dingue de :* she's nuts about him = *elle est dingue de lui*
☠ *un argent dingue* = a hell of a lot of money.

NUTSHELL (n) **in a nutshell** = *en deux mots :* that's my idea in a nutshell = *en deux mots, voilà mon idée* ⓪ to cut a long story short = *bref.*

NUTTY (adj, -ier, -iest) *dingue :* a nutty idea = *une idée dingue* → CRAZY
to be nutty about = *être toqué de :* she's nutty about him/music = *elle est toquée de lui/musique* ⓪ to be mad about = *être fou de*
to be nutty as a fruitcake = *travailler du chapeau* → CRAZY.

NYLON (n) *Nylon (m)* ⓪ acetate = *acétate.*

NYMPHO (n) *nymphomane (f)* = nymphomaniac ⓪ red-hot mama = *femme qui a le feu au cul.*

OAF (n) *rustre* (m), *mufle* (m) : she's married to a real oaf = *elle est mariée à un véritable rustre/mufle* ⓓ lout = *lourdaud* **OAFISH** (adj) *rustre* : oafish manners = *des manières rustres* ⓓ brutish = *de malappris.*

OAK (n) *chêne* (m) : oaks in the forest = *des chênes dans la forêt.*

OAR (n) *aviron* (m) ⓓ oarsman = *rameur.*

OASIS (n, -ses) *oasis* (f) ⓓ mirage = ←.

OATH (n) *serment* (m) : under oath = *sous serment* ⓓ affidavit = *déclaration sous serment*
to take an oath = *prêter serment.*

OATS (n pl) **to be feeling one's oats** = *avoir la pêche* ⓓ to feel like a million bucks = *être gonflé à bloc.*

OBEDIENCE (n) *obéissance* (f) ⓓ submission = *soumission* ≠ disobedience = *désobéissance.*

OBEDIENT (adj) *obéissant, -e* : an obedient child = *un enfant obéissant* ≠ disobedient = *désobéissant* **OBEDIENTLY** (adv) *avec obéissance.*

OBESE (adj) *obèse* ⓓ portly = *qui a de l'embonpoint* ≠ skinny = *maigrichon* **OBESITY** (n) *obésité* (f).

OBEY (to, -ed) *obéir* : obey your parents = *obéis à tes parents* ≠ to disobey = *désobéir.*

OBITUARY (n, -ies) *notice* (f) *nécrologique* : the obituary column = *la rubrique nécrologique.*

OBJECT (n) **1/** *objet* (m) : various objects on the table = *divers objets sur la table* ⓓ thing = *chose* **2/** *objet* (m) : what's the object of all this ? = *quel est l'objet de tout cela ?* ⓓ purpose = *but*
direct ≠ **indirect object** = *complément d'objet direct* ≠ *indirect*
no object = *qui ne compte pas* : money/price is no object = *l'argent/le prix ne compte pas*
☠ *(bureau des) objets trouvés* = lost and found department
— *la question est sans objet* = the question is purposeless.

OBJECT (to, -ed) *objecter* : Jack objected that the hotel was too expensive = *Jack a objecté que l'hôtel était trop cher*
to object to = *s'opposer à* : I object to his coming home so late = *je m'oppose à ce qu'il rentre si tard à la maison* ⓓ to disapprove of = *désapprouver*
I wouldn't object to (having a drink) = *je ne serais pas contre (le fait de prendre un verre).*

OBJECTION (n) *objection* (f) : I have no objection to leaving now = *je ne vois aucune objection à ce que nous partions maintenant.*

OBJECTIONABLE (adj) *désobligeant, -e* : an objectionable remark = *une remarque désobligeante* ⓓ distasteful = *déplaisant.*

OBJECTIVE (n) *objectif* (m) : his objective is to make a million dollars = *son objectif est de se faire un million de dollars* ⓓ goal = *but* ☠ *objectif (appareil photo)* = (camera) lens.

OBJECTIVE (adj) *objectif, -ive* : an objective judge = *un juge objectif* ≠ subjective = *subjectif* **OBJECTIVELY** (adv) *en toute objectivité* : objectively speaking = *pour parler en toute objectivité.*

OBJECTIVITY (n) *objectivité* (f) : you're lacking in objectivity = *vous manquez d'objectivité.*

OBLIGATION (n) *obligation* (f) ⓓ duty = *devoir*
to be under (no) obligation to = *(ne pas) être dans l'obligation de*
without obligation = *sans obligation*
☠ *des obligations* = bonds.

OBLIGATORY (adj) *obligatoire* : paying fines is obligatory = *il est obligatoire de payer ses amendes* ⓓ mandatory = *de rigueur.*

OBLIGE (to, -d) *rendre service* : he's always ready to oblige = *il est toujours prêt à rendre service*
much obliged (for your help) = *merci mille fois (de votre aide)* ⓓ thank you = *merci*
to oblige to = *obliger à* : her PR job obliges her to smile all the time = *son travail dans les relations publiques l'oblige à sourire tout le temps*
☠ *obliger qqn à faire qqch* = to compel s.o. to do stg

427

— *je suis ≠ ne suis pas obligé d'y aller* = I have ≠ don't have to go *(plus employé que « to be obliged to »).*

OBLIGING (adj) *obligeant, -e :* a very obliging travel agent = *un agent de voyages très obligeant* ⓪ helpful = *serviable.*

OBLIVION (n) **to pass/to fall into oblivion** = *tomber dans l'oubli :* his book fell/passed into oblivion = *son livre est tombé dans l'oubli.*

OBLIVIOUS TO (adj) *pas conscient, -e de :* he was oblivious to my problems/the risk = *il n'était pas conscient de mes problèmes/du risque* ≠ aware of = *conscient de.*

OBNOXIOUS (adj) *odieux, -euse :* an obnoxious guy = *un mec odieux* ⓪ repugnant = *répugnant* ☠ → odious.

OBSCENE (adj) *obscène :* obscene language = *langage obscène* ⓪ bawdy = *paillard,* risqué = *osé,* scabrous = *scabreux* **OBSCENITY** (n, -ies) *obscénité (f).*

OBSCURE (adj) **1/** *obscur, -e :* the meaning was obscure = *la signification était obscure* **2/** *obscur, -e :* an obscure author = *un auteur obscur* ≠ well-known = *connu* **OBSCURITY** (n, -ies) *obscurité (f).*

OBSERVANT (adj) *observateur, -trice :* actors must be observant = *les acteurs doivent être observateurs* ⓪ perspective = *perspicace.*

OBSERVATION (n) *observation (f) :* the doctor's observations = *les observations du médecin* ⓪ remark = *remarque*
under observation = *sous observation*
☠ *faire des observations à qqn* = to reprimand s.o.

OBSERVE (to, -d) **1/** *observer :* I'm not participating, just observing = *je ne participe pas, je ne fais qu'observer* ⓪ to watch = *regarder* **2/** *faire remarquer :* "she's pregnant", he observed = *« elle est enceinte », a-t-il fait remarquer* ⓪ to note = *noter* **3/** *observer :* to observe the regulations = *observer le règlement* ⓪ to comply with = *se conformer à* ☠ *faire observer qqch à qqn* = to point stg out to s.o.

OBSERVER (n) *observateur, -trice :* he went to the swing as an observer = *il est allé à la partouze en observateur.*

OBSESS (to, -ed) *obséder :* I'm obsessed by the threat of a nuclear war = *je suis obsédé par la menace d'une guerre nucléaire.*

OBSESSION (n) *obsession (f) :* death had become an obsession with him = *la mort était devenue une obsession pour lui* ⓪ idée fixe = ←, fixation = ←.

OBSESSIVE (adj) *obsessionnel, -elle :* obsessive guilt feelings = *des sentiments obsessionnels de culpabilité* ⓪ compulsive = *maladif.*

OBSOLETE (adj) *périmé, -e :* obsolete methods/equipment = *méthodes périmées/équipement périmé* ⓪ outmoded = *désuet* ☠ *mon passeport/billet d'avion est périmé* = my passport/plane ticket isn't valid any longer.

OBSTACLE (n) *obstacle (m) :* to overcome an obstacle = *surmonter un obstacle* ⓪ hindrance = *gêne,* difficulty = *difficulté*
☠ *je n'y vois pas d'obstacle* = I see no objection
— *faire obstacle à* = to counter.

OBSTETRICIAN (n) *obstétricien, -enne, accoucheur, -euse* ⓪ delivery = *accouchement.*

OBSTINATE (adj) *obstiné, -e :* you're so obstinate ! = *tu es tellement obstiné !* ⓪ stubborn = *têtu* ≠ flexible = *souple.*

OBSTRUCT (to, -ed) **1/** *obstruer :* buildings obstruct the view = *des immeubles obstruent la vue* ⓪ to block = *bloquer* **2/** *faire obstacle à :* to obstruct progress = *faire obstacle au progrès* ⓪ to impede = *entraver.*

OBSTRUCTION (n) **obstruction of justice** = *entrave à la justice*
☠ *faire de l'obstruction parlementaire* = to filibuster.

OBTAIN (to, -ed) *obtenir :* to obtain a law degree = *obtenir une licence en droit* = to get ⓪ to procure = *procurer*
☠ *j'ai obtenu de ...* = I managed to .../I got to ...
— *obtenir des voix* = to poll votes
— *« to obtain »* est beaucoup moins employé que *« to get ».*

OBTUSE (adj) *obtus, -e :* an obtuse guy = *un type obtus* ≠ bright = *vif.*

OBVIOUS (adj) *évident, -e :* it's obvious that he's lying = *il est évident qu'il ment* ⓪ clear = *clair* ☠ → evident.

OBVIOUSLY (adv) *de toute évidence :* obviously, you didn't understand what I said = *de toute évidence, vous n'avez pas compris ce que j'ai dit* ⓪ clearly = *manifestement*
obviously not = *évidemment non* ⓪ of course not = *bien sûr que non.*

OCCASION (n) **1/** *occasion (f) :* I don't have the occasion to see him much = *je n'ai pas l'occasion de le voir souvent* = opportunity
2/ *circonstance (f) :* a wedding is no occasion to be sad = *un mariage n'est pas une circonstance où l'on est triste* ☠ → circumstance
to fit the occasion = *être de circonstance*
on occasion = *de temps à autre :* she sees her relatives on occasion = *elle voit sa famille de temps à autre* ⓪ from time to time = *de temps en temps*
on several/different occasions = *à plusieurs/différentes occasions*
to rise to/to be equal to the occasion = *se montrer à la hauteur de la situation*
should the occasion arise = *le cas échéant*
should the occasion present itself = *si l'occasion se présente*
I want to take this occasion to (thank you) = *je profite de cette occasion pour (vous remercier)*

☠ *une occasion (affaire)* = a buy
— *d'occasion* = secondhand
— *j'ai perdu une belle/bonne occasion de me taire* = I should have kept my big mouth shut
— *il ne rate jamais une occasion de la critiquer* = he never misses a chance to criticize her.

OCCASIONAL (adj) *occasionnel, -elle* (visits), *à l'occasion* (s.o.) : occasional visits = *des visites occasionnelles,* she has an occasional lover = *elle prend un amant à l'occasion* ⓪ sporadic = *sporadique.*

OCCASIONALLY (adv) *de temps à autre, occasionnellement* : she drinks wine occasionally = *elle boit du vin de temps à autre* ⓪ sometimes = *quelquefois.*

OCCIDENT (n) **the Occident** = *l'Occident* ≠ the Orient = *l'Orient.*

OCCUPANT (n) *occupant, -e* : who are the new occupants of the house ? = *qui sont les nouveaux occupants de la maison ?* ⓪ tenant = *locataire* ☠ *les occupants d'un pays* = the occupying forces.

OCCUPATION (n) 1/ *occupation* (f) : she has to find an occupation = *il faut qu'elle se trouve une occupation* ⓪ profession = ← 2/ *occupation* (f) : the German occupation = *l'occupation allemande* ⓪ invasion = ←.

OCCUPATIONAL (adj) **occupational hazards** = *les risques du métier*
occupational therapy = *rééducation.*

OCCUPY (to, -ied) 1/ *occuper* : read this, it'll occupy you = *lisez ça, ça vous occupera* 2/ *occuper* : the workers occupied the factory = *les ouvriers ont occupé l'usine* ⓪ to demonstrate = *manifester*
to occupy o.s. with stg = *s'occuper en faisant qqch* : she occupies herself with piano lessons = *elle s'occupe en prenant des leçons de piano*
☠ *t'occupe !* = never you mind !
— *s'occuper de* = to take care of
— *la ligne est occupée* = the line's busy.

OCCUR (to, -red) *se produire* : when did the accident occur ? = *quand l'accident s'est-il produit ?* ⓪ to happen = *arriver* ☠ → to produce
that never occurred to me = *ça ne m'était jamais venu à l'idée* ⓪ it never crossed my mind = *ça ne m'a jamais effleuré l'esprit.*

OCEAN (n) *océan* (m) : Indian/Atlantic/Pacific Ocean = *océan Indien/Atlantique/Pacifique* ⓪ lake = *lac.*

O'CLOCK (adv) **it's (5) o'clock** = *il est (5) heures*
at (6) o'clock = *à (6) heures.*

OCTOBER (n) *octobre* (m) → MONTH.

OCTOPUS (n, -es) *pieuvre* (f), *poulpe* (m) ⓪ tentacle = *tentacule.*

ODD (adj, -er, -est) *étrange* : what an odd guy/idea ! = *quel type étrange !/quelle idée étrange !* = strange ⓪ bizarre = ←
an odd number = *un chiffre impair* ≠ even = *pair*

to be the odd man out = *faire tintin/être celui qui doit se passer de...* : there are 12 chairs and 13 people, you're the odd man out = *il y a 12 chaises et 13 personnes, tu devras faire tintin/te passer de chaise*
odd jobs = *des petits boulots.*

-ODD (adj) *et quelques* : 20-odd dollars/years = *20 dollars/années et quelques.*

ODDBALL (n) *drôle de numéro* (m) ⓪ a queer bird = *un drôle d'oiseau,* a case = *un cas.*

ODDITY (n, -ies) *chose* (f) *singulière* : a happy marriage is an oddity = *un mariage heureux, c'est une chose singulière* ⓪ anomaly = *anomalie.*

ODDLY (adv) *étrangement* : to behave oddly = *se conduire étrangement.*

ODDS (n pl) **the odds are that (he'll win)** = *(il a) toutes les chances de (gagner)*
against all/heavy/great odds = *contre toute attente* : he won the election against all/great/heavy odds = *contre toute attente il a gagné les élections*
to be at odds with (one's parents' political ideas) = *être en contradiction avec (les idées politiques de ses parents)*
to buck the odds = *avoir peu de chances de gagner* : the ecologists are bucking the odds in the election = *dans cette élection, les écologistes ont peu de chances de gagner*
odds and ends = 1/ *bric-à-brac* (m) : they sell odds and ends at the flea market = *on vend du bric-à-brac au marché aux puces* 2/ *petits trucs* (m pl) : I have a lot of odds and ends to do tomorrow = *j'ai beaucoup de petits trucs à faire demain*
the odds are (two) to (one) = *la cote est à (deux) contre (un).*

ODDS-ON (adj) **the odds-on favorite** = *le grand favori* : the Democrat candidate is the odds-on favorite = *le candidat démocrate est le grand favori.*

ODE (n) *ode* (f) ⓪ ballad = *ballade.*

ODIOUS (adj) *odieux, -euse* : an odious thing to do = *une chose odieuse à faire* ≠ adorable = ← ☠ *un type odieux* = an obnoxious guy.

ODOR (n) *odeur* (f) : a fishy odor = *une odeur de poisson* ☠ *j'aime cette odeur* = I like this smell
— *ce parfum a une bonne odeur* = this perfume has a nice fragrance.

ODYSSEY (n) *odyssée* (f) ⓪ journey = *voyage.*

OECD (abbr) = Organization for Economic Cooperation and Development = *OCDE = Organisation de coopération et de développement économiques.*

OF (prep) *de, d' (du, de la, des)* : a piece of cake = *un morceau de gâteau,* the door of the house = *la porte de la maison,* he died of cancer = *il est mort d'un cancer*

of (mine/ours) = *à (moi/nous)* : a friend of mine/ours = *un ami à moi/nous*
of late = *ces derniers temps* : I haven't seen him of late = *je ne l'ai pas vu ces derniers temps* ⓌⒺ lately = *dernièrement*
of the = *du, de la, des* : the door of the car = *la porte de la voiture* = the car's door

the (1st) of (May) = *le (1er) (mai)*
... of (us/them) = *... d'entre (nous/eux)* : two of us want to go = *deux d'entre nous veulent y aller*
how (kind/nice) of you ! = *c'est vraiment (gentil) de votre part !*
(it's ten) of (seven) = *(il est sept heures) moins (dix)*

☠ *venir de France* = to come from France
— *la voiture de Jean* = John's car
— *loin de ≠ près de* = far from ≠ near
— *c'est de Sartre* = it's by Sartre
— *(cinq) de plus* = (five) more
— *avez-vous du feu ?* = do you have a light ?
— *autour de* = around
— *avoir l'intention de* = to intend to
— *tâcher/oublier de* = to try to/to forget to
— *à deux heures du matin* = at two in the morning
— *il vit de (sa plume)* = he lives by (his writings)
— *cela dépend de vous* = it depends on you
— *de 10 à 20 personnes* = from 10 to 20 people
— *sauter de joie* = to leap for joy
— *un train de nuit* = a night train
— *demander à qqn de* = to ask s.o. to
— *changer de vêtements* = to change clothes
— *accompagné de* = accompanied by
— *de l'argent* = some money
— *à vous de jouer* = it's your turn
— *traiter qqn de menteur* = to call s.o. a liar
— *se servir de* = to use
— for the use of "of" after a verb, see the verb.

OFF (adj) **1/** *annulé, -e* : the trip/dinner is off = *le voyage/dîner est annulé*
2/ *qui a congé* : he'll be off on Tuesday = *il a congé mardi*
3/ *éteint, -e* : the lights are off = *les lumières sont éteintes* ≠ lit = *allumé* ☠ → extinct
4/ *qui marche mal* : business/sales are off = *les affaires/les ventes marchent mal*
an off year/month = *une mauvaise année/un mauvais mois.*

OFF (adv) **a ... off** = *dans un/une ... :* my birthday's a week off = *mon anniversaire est dans une semaine*
it's my day/my week off = *c'est mon jour/ma semaine de congé*

---

off again, on again = *avec des hauts et des bas :* our love affair lasted off again, on again for ten years = *notre liaison a duré dix ans avec des hauts et des*

bas
off and on = *de temps à autre* = on and off
off and running ! = *c'est parti !*
off with you ! = *décampe !* → BUZZ OFF !

OFF (prep) **(20 percent) off** = *une réduction de (vingt pour cent)* = a reduction of (20 percent).

☠ for the use of "off" after a verb, see the verb.

OFFBEAT (adj) *fantaisiste* : an offbeat style/guy = *un style/type fantaisiste* ⓌⒺ kooky = *farfelu* ≠ conventional = *conventionnel.*

OFF-BROADWAY (adj) **an off-Broadway play** = *un spectacle genre café-théâtre.*

OFF-COLOR (adj) *grivois, -e* : off-color jokes = *des plaisanteries grivoises* ⓌⒺ juicy = *croustillant,* risqué = *osé.*

OFFEND (to, -ed) *offenser* : did what he said offend you ? = *est-ce que ce qu'il a dit vous a offensé ?* ⓌⒺ to hurt = *faire de la peine à*
to be offended by (a remark) = *être vexé/offusqué par (une remarque).*

OFFENSE (n) *infraction (f)* : it's his first offense = *c'est sa première infraction* = offence (GB) ⓌⒺ felony = *forfait*
I meant no offense = *je ne voulais pas vous offenser*
to take offense at stg = *s'offusquer de qqch.*

OFFENSIVE (n) *offensive (f)* ≠ defensive = *défensive*
to take the offensive = *passer à l'offensive.*

OFFENSIVE (adj) **1/** *offensif, -ive* : offensive weapons = *armes offensives* **2/** *offensant, -e* : an offensive remark = *une remarque offensante* ≠ flattering = *flatteur.*

OFFER (n) *offre (f)* : they made me an offer I couldn't refuse = *ils m'ont fait une offre que je ne pouvais pas refuser*
☠ *offre (enchères)* = bid (auction sale)
— *l'offre et la demande* = supply and demand.

OFFER (to, -ed) *offrir* : he offered me a thousand dollars for the car = *il m'a offert mille dollars pour la voiture* ⓌⒺ to propose = *proposer*
to offer to (help) = *offrir d'(aider)*
☠ *deux possibilités s'offrent à nous* = we've got two possibilities
— *je vais m'offrir ...* = I'm going to treat myself to ...
— *je lui ai offert une bague pour son anniversaire* = I gave her a ring for her birthday.

OFFERING (n) *offrande (f)* ⓌⒺ sacrifice = ←.

OFFHAND (ED) (adj) *désinvolte :* she was very offhand-ed about her abortion = *elle était très désinvolte au sujet de son avortement* ⓓ casual = *décontracté.*

OFFHAND (adv) *comme ça :* I can't tell you offhand how much it costs = *je ne peux pas vous dire comme ça combien ça coûte* = off the top of my head.

OFFHANDEDLY (adv) *sur un ton désinvolte :* she was talking about her four husbands very offhandedly = *elle parlait sur un ton désinvolte de ses quatre maris.*

OFFICE (n) *bureau* *(m) :* come to my office at 5 = *viens à mon bureau à 5 heures*

to be at the office = *être au bureau* ⓓ **to be in one's office** = *être dans son bureau* **to be in office** = *être en fonction* **doctor's/lawyer's office** = *cabinet médical/d'avocat* **office boy/girl** = *garçon/fille de bureau*	**office hours** = *heures de bureau* **office work** = *travail de bureau* **to run for office** = *se présenter (à une élection)* ☠ → to present **to take office** = *entrer en fonction* **office worker** = *employé de bureau*

☠ *bureau de vote* = polling station
— *un bureau (table)* = a desk
— *un bureau (pièce)* = a study
— *faire office de* = to act as
— *l'office* = the pantry.

OFFICEHOLDER (n) *titulaire (m, f) d'un poste.*

OFFICER (n) **1/** *agent (m) de police* ⓓ cop = *flic* **2/** *officier (m)* (army) ≠ noncommissioned officer = *sous-officier*
excuse me, officer! = *excusez-moi, monsieur l'agent !*

OFFICIAL (n) *officiel, -elle :* a reception for the officials = *une réception pour les officiels* ⓓ VIP = *personnage de marque.*

OFFICIAL (adj) *officiel, -elle :* an official statement = *une déclaration officielle* ≠ unofficial = *officieux* **OFFICIALLY** (adv) *officiellement :* officially they're still married = *officiellement ils sont toujours mariés* ≠ unofficially = *officieusement.*

OFFING (n) **in the offing** = *en perspective :* there's no job for me in the offing = *il n'y a pas de boulot pour moi en perspective.*

OFF-SEASON (n) *morte saison (f)* ≠ peak season = *pleine saison* **OFF-SEASON** (adv) *hors saison :* it's cheaper to travel off-season = *c'est moins cher de voyager hors saison.*

OFFSET (to, -set, -set) *compenser :* to offset losses = *com-* penser *des pertes* ⓓ to counteract = *agir contre* ☠ → to compensate.

OFFSHORE (adj) *off shore :* offshore drilling = *forage off shore.*

OFFSPRING (n) *progéniture (f)* ⓓ scion = *descendant* = ←.

OFF-THE-WALL (adj) *timbré, -e :* an off-the-wall person = *une personne timbrée* → CRAZY.

OFTEN (adv) *souvent :* I often think of you = *je pense souvent à vous* ⓓ frequently = *fréquemment* ≠ rarely = *rarement*
as often as not = *assez souvent :* you're right as often as not = *vous avez assez souvent raison* ⓓ most of the time = *la plupart du temps*
how often? = *tous les combien ? :* how often do you take French lessons ? = *vous prenez des cours de français tous les combien ?*

OGLE (to, -d) *lorgner :* to ogle men in the street = *lorgner les hommes dans la rue* ⓓ to eye = *reluquer.*

OGRE (n) *ogre (m)* ⓓ beast = *bête.*

OH ! (interj) *oh !* ⓓ ouch ! = *aïe !*

OIL (n) **1/** *huile (f) :* oil and vinegar = *de l'huile et du vinaigre*
an oil painting = *une peinture à l'huile*
☠ *une huile* = a big cheese
— *jeter de l'huile sur le feu* = to add fuel to the fire
2/ *pétrole (m) :* oil crisis = *crise du pétrole* ⓓ OPEC = OPEP
oil company = *compagnie pétrolière*
oil slick = *marée noire*
to strike oil = *trouver le filon* = to hit pay dirt.

OILY (adj, -ier, -iest) *gras, grasse :* oily hair/skin = *cheveux gras/peau grasse* ⓓ greasy = *graisseux* ☠ → fatty.

OINTMENT (n) *onguent (m)* ⓓ pommade = ←, salve = *baume.*

OK = OKAY.

OKAY (n) *accord (m) :* he gave his okay = *il a donné son accord* = he gave his OK ☠ → agreement.

OKAY (adj) **1/** *qui va (bien) :* how are you today ? — okay ! = *comment ça va aujourd'hui ? — ça va (bien) !,* things are okay = *les choses vont bien* **2/** *pas mal :* the movie was okay = *le film était pas mal* ⓓ no great shakes = *qui ne casse pas des briques*
it's okay for (young girls to take the pill) = *ça ne pose pas de problème que (les jeunes filles prennent la pilule)*
it's okay ≠ it's not okay with me = *je suis d'accord* ≠ *je ne suis pas d'accord.*

OKAY (adv) *convenablement :* the car runs okay = *la voiture marche convenablement* = OK ⓓ well = *bien.*

OKAY (to, -ed) *dire O.K. à* : he okayed the project = *il a dit O.K. au projet* = he OK'd the project ≠ to kill = *enterrer.*

OKAY ! (interj) *O.K. !* ⓪ fine ! = *parfait !,* roger ! = *d'ac !* ≠ no go ! = *pas question !*

OLD (n inv) **the old** = *les vieux :* his last movie appeals to both the young and the old = *son dernier film plaît autant aux jeunes qu'aux vieux* ⓪ the aged = *les personnes âgées,* senior citizens = *le troisième âge* ☠ *mes vieux* = my old man and my old lady.

OLD (adj, -er, -est) **1/** *vieux, vieille :* my mother's old = *ma mère est vieille* ⓪ elderly = *assez âgé* ≠ still spry = *encore vert,* young = *jeune*
2/ *vieux, vieille :* old shoes = *de vieilles chaussures* ≠ new = *neuf*
☠ *il ne fera pas de vieux os* = he's not long for this world
— *un vieux garçon* = a confirmed bachelor
3/ *ancien, -enne :* my old teacher/apartment = *mon ancien professeur/appartement* = former ≠ present = *actuel* ☠ → ancient

---

to be as old as the hills = *être vieux comme le monde*	= *vieux avant l'âge*
to be old hat = *être vieux jeu* ≠ to be hip = *être branché*	**old enough to (dress o.s.)** = *assez grand pour (s'habiller tout seul)*
one is only as old as one feels = *on est vieux si on se sent vieux/la vieillesse est un état d'esprit*	**old flame** = *ancien flirt* ⓪ heartthrob = *amoureux*
to be 10 (years/days) old = *avoir 10 (ans/jours)*	**old fogey** = *vieux croulant*
to be too old to = *être trop vieux pour*	**old hag** = *vieille chouette* = **old bag**
for old times' sake = *en souvenir du bon vieux temps*	**old hand** = *vieux de la vieille* ≠ novice = ←
to get/grow old = *vieillir :* my father's getting/growing old = *mon père vieillit* = to age ⓪ to get on = *prendre de l'âge*	**the old lady** = *la vieille* ≠ **the old man** = *le vieux*
how old are you ? = *quel âge as-tu ?,* I'm five = *j'ai cinq ans*	**old maid** = *vieille fille* = spinster ⓪ single = *célibataire*
in the old days = *dans le temps*	**old man** = *vieille branche :* how are you old man ? = *comment ça va, vieille branche ?*
old age = *vieillesse*	**old offender** = *cheval de retour* ⓪ recidivist = *récidiviste*
old before one's time	**old people** = *les vieux :* a home for old people = *une maison de vieux* ⓪ the aged = *les personnes âgées*

Old Testament = *Ancien Testament*	*remèdes de bonne femme.*
old wives' tales =	

OLDER (comp adj) **1/** *plus âgé, -e* (s.o.), *plus vieux/plus vieille* (stg) : she's older than I am = *elle est plus âgée que moi,* my car's older than yours = *ma voiture est plus vieille que la vôtre* ≠ younger = *plus jeune* **2/** *aîné, -e :* I want you to meet my older brother = *je voudrais vous présenter mon frère aîné* = elder ≠ younger = *cadet* ☠ → eldest.

OLDEST (superl adj) *le plus âgé/la plus âgée* (s.o.), *le plus vieux/la plus vieille* (stg) : the oldest child = *le plus âgé des enfants,* the oldest family/company in Europe = *la famille/société la plus vieille d'Europe* ⓪ eldest = *aîné.*

OLD-FASHIONED (adj) *démodé, -e :* old-fashioned ideas/dresses = *des idées/robes démodées* ⓪ old hat = *vieux jeu* ≠ up-to-date = *au goût du jour.*

OLD-TIMER (n) **1/** *vieux routier* (m) ⓪ old hand = *vieux de la vieille* **2/** *vieux, vieille :* a home for old-timers = *un asile de vieux.*

OLIVE (n) *olive* (f) : olive tree = *olivier,* olive oil = *huile d'olive.*

OLYMPIC GAMES (n pl) *jeux olympiques* (m pl) = Olympics ⓪ world championship = *championnat du monde.*

OMELET (n) *omelette* (f) ⓪ scrambled eggs = *œufs brouillés* ☠ *on ne fait pas d'omelette sans casser des œufs* = nothing ventured nothing gained.

OMEN (n) *présage* (m), *augure* (m) : good ≠ bad omen = *bon* ≠ *mauvais présage/augure.*

OMINOUS (adj) *qui ne présage rien de bon* : an ominous silence = *un silence qui ne présage rien de bon* ⓪ threatening = *menaçant.*

OMISSION (n) *omission* (f) : many omissions in the list = *beaucoup d'omissions sur la liste.*

OMIT (to, -ted) *omettre* : omit this name = *omettez ce nom* ⓪ to leave out = *laisser tomber* ☠ *omettre un détail* = to overlook a detail.

OMNIPOTENT (adj) *omnipotent, -e :* an omnipotent ruler = *un dirigeant omnipotent* ⓪ almighty = *tout-puissant.*

OMNIPRESENT (adj) *omniprésent, -e :* omnipresent poverty = *une pauvreté omniprésente.*

ON (adj) **1/** *allumé, -e :* is the TV on ? = *est-ce que la télé est allumée ?* ≠ off = *éteint* **2/** *qui marche :* the deal/the dishwasher is on = *l'affaire/le lave-vaisselle marche.*

ON (adv) **on ahead** = *en avant* : go on ahead, I'll lock the door = *partez en avant, je ferme la porte à clé*
on and off = *de temps à autre* : he works on and off = *il travaille de temps à autre* ⓒⓓ from time to time = *de temps en temps*
on and on = *sans arrêt* : to talk on and on = *parler sans arrêt* ⓒⓓ endlessly = *sans cesse.*

ON (prep) **1/** *sur* : the book's on the table = *le livre est sur la table* ⓒⓓ over = *au-dessus de* ≠ underneath = *en dessous de* **2/** *sur* : a book on Henry Miller = *un livre sur Henry Miller* = about ⓒⓓ concerning = *concernant*

on average = *en moyenne*	*premier étage*
on business = *pour affaires*	**on the radio/on TV** = *à la radio/à la télé*
on duty = *de service*	**on time** = *à l'heure*
on Monday = *lundi*	**on the train/plane** = *dans le train/dans l'avion*
on Mondays = *le lundi*	
on the first floor = *au*	**on vacation** = *en vacances*

☠ for the use of "on" after a verb, see the verb
— *(faute) sur (faute)* = one (mistake) after another
— *(5 mètres) sur (8)* = (5 meters) by (8)
— *(un jour) sur (cinq)* = (one day) out of/in (five)
— *(vous avez tort) sur ce point* = (you're wrong) about that.

ON-AGAIN-OFF-AGAIN (adj) *qui a des hauts et des bas* : their love affair is an on-again-off-again business = *leur liaison a des hauts et des bas.*

ONCE (adv) **1/** *une fois* : I only met her once = *je ne l'ai rencontrée qu'une fois* ⓒⓓ twice = *deux fois* **2/** *dans le temps* : they were rich once = *dans le temps ils étaient riches* ⓒⓓ formerly = *autrefois*

(just) this once = *(juste) pour cette fois*	**once bitten twice shy** = *chat échaudé craint l'eau froide* ⓒⓓ to learn the hard way = *apprendre à ses dépens*
once a (bastard) always a (bastard) = *lorsqu'on est un (salaud), c'est pour la vie* ⓒⓓ a leopard doesn't change its spots = *chassez le naturel, il revient au galop*	**once in a while** = *une fois de temps en temps* ≠ time and again = *maintes et maintes fois*
once again = *encore une fois* ⓒⓓ another time = *une autre fois*	**once is enough** = *ça suffit comme ça*
once and for all = *une fois pour toutes* ⓒⓓ for the last time = *pour la dernière fois*	**once more** = *encore une fois*
	once a week/month = *une fois par semaine/mois.*

ONCE (conj) *une fois que* : once he split, she began to feel more together = *une fois qu'il s'est barré, elle a commencé à se sentir mieux dans sa peau*
at once = **1/** *tout de suite* : do it at once = *faites-le tout de suite* ⓒⓓ right away = *séance tenante* **2/** *à la fois* : I can't do two things at once = *je ne peux pas faire deux choses à la fois* ⓒⓓ simultaneously = *simultanément*
once too often = *une fois de trop.*

ONCE-OVER (n) **to give the once-over** = *jauger d'un coup d'œil* : he gave the girl/report the once-over = *il a jaugé la fille/le rapport d'un coup d'œil.*

ONE (n) *un, une* : I only want one = *je n'en veux qu'un* ⓒⓓ two = *deux*, three = *trois*

to be at one with oneself = *être en paix avec soi-même*
to be one in a million = *être l'oiseau rare/le merle blanc*
to go s.o. one better = *faire encore mieux que qqn* : he screwed two broads at the swing, but she went him one better and made it with all the guys = *il s'est tapé deux nanas à la partouze, mais elle a fait encore mieux que lui en se tapant tous les mecs*
to hang one on = *prendre une cuite/se cuiter* → DRUNK
to have one too many = *boire un coup de trop* : he had one too many last night = *il avait bu un coup de trop hier soir* → DRUNK
one and only = *cher et tendre* : John's my one and only = *c'est John mon cher et tendre* ⓒⓓ be-loved = *bien-aimé*
one doesn't rule out the other = *l'un n'empêche pas l'autre*
one for the road = *le coup de l'étrier* ⓒⓓ chaser = *pousse-café*
one in (ten) = *un sur (dix)* = one out of (ten)
that's one for the books ! = *c'est pas piqué des hannetons !* → GOSH !
they really put one over you = *ils vous ont vraiment eu* ⓒⓓ they took you in = *ils vous ont berné*
to tie one on = *s'enivrer* → DRUNK ≠ to be a teetotaler = *être un buveur d'eau*
when you've seen one, you've seen them all = *une fois qu'on en a vu un, on les a tous vus*
you're one up on me ! = *vous en savez plus que moi !*

🕱 *je veux un café* = I want a coffee
— *un jour sur deux* = every other day
— *à la une* = in the headlines
— *un type t'a appelé* = some guy called you

— *sans faire ni une ni deux* = without beating around the bush
— *l'un et l'autre* = both of them.

ONE (adj) **1/** *un, une* : one lover at a time = *un amant à la fois*, call me one evening = *appelle-moi un soir*
2/ *unique* : she's the one person who can do it = *c'est l'unique personne qui puisse le faire* 🕱 → unique

---

at one time = *dans le temps* : she was an actress at one time = *elle a été actrice dans le temps* ⑩ formerly = *autrefois*
for one thing (I love him) and for another thing (he's rich) = *d'une part (je l'aime) et d'autre part (il est riche)*
to go from one extreme to the other = *tomber d'un excès dans l'autre*
to have one foot in the grave = *avoir un pied dans la tombe* ⑩ to be six foot under = *manger les pissenlits par la racine*
in one go = *d'un seul coup* : I did all the ironing in one go = *j'ai fait tout le repassage d'un seul coup*
in one sitting = *d'un seul jet* : she wrote the short story in one sitting = *elle a écrit la nouvelle d'un seul jet*
it's been one damn thing after the other = *ça n'a pas*

arrêté de la journée
it goes in one ear and out of the other = *ça rentre par une oreille et ça ressort par l'autre*
to jump from one thing/ subject to another = *sauter/passer du coq à l'âne*
not one (guy helped us) = *pas un (type ne nous a aidés)*
on (the) one hand ... , on the other hand ... = *d'un côté ..., d'un autre côté ...* : on (the) one hand the job's very hard, but on the other hand the salary's fantastic = *d'un côté le boulot est très dur, mais d'un autre côté le salaire est formidable*
one day = *un jour* : I saw her one day last year = *je l'ai vue, un jour de l'année dernière*
one good turn deserves another = *c'est un échange de bons procédés* ⑩ one hand feeds the other = *on se renvoie l'ascenseur*

one man's meat is another man's poison = *le bonheur des uns fait le malheur des autres*
one more time = *encore une fois* ⑩ again = *à nouveau*
one thing at a time = *une chose à la fois*
one thing leading to another = *de fil en aiguille*
one way or another = *d'une façon ou d'une autre* : I'll get him to come one way or another = *je le ferai venir d'une façon ou d'une autre*
taking one thing with another = *à tout prendre* : taking one thing with another the job isn't too bad = *à tout prendre, le boulot n'est pas trop mal*
there's more than one way to skin a cat = *il y a plus d'une façon de s'y prendre/il y a mille façons d'y arriver.*

ONE (pron) **1/** *un, une* : would you like one ? = *est-ce que vous en voulez une ?* 🕱 « one » *après un adjectif ne se traduit pas* : I want the red one = *je veux la rouge*
2/ *on* : one shouldn't do that = *on ne devrait pas faire ça* 🕱 *cet emploi est rare en anglais.*

---

to be one of a kind = *être unique en son genre*
to be one too many = *être de trop* : he was one too many at the dinner = *il était de trop au dîner*
he's one of the boys = *il est un des nôtres*
I for one = *pour ma part* : I for one don't understand what you're talking about = *pour ma part, je ne comprends pas de quoi vous parlez* ⑩ as for me = *quant à moi*
it's just one of those things = *ça fait partie des choses qui arrivent* → THAT'S LIFE !
it takes one to know one = *tu*

ne t'es pas regardé ⑩ it's the pot calling the kettle black = *c'est la paille et la poutre*
not to be one to/for = *ne pas être du genre à* : I'm not one to tell other people what to do = *je ne suis pas du genre à dire aux autres ce qu'il faut faire*
one after the other = *l'un après l'autre*
one another = *l'un l'autre* : they love one another = *ils s'aiment l'un l'autre*
one by one = *un par un*
one of my friends = *l'un de mes amis*
one of them/us = *l'un d'entre eux/nous*

one of these (fine) days = *un de ces quatre (matins)/un de ces jours* ⑩ one day or another = *un jour ou l'autre*
the one = *celui/celle* : that's the one I want = *c'est celui que je veux*
he's the one who (can tell you) = *c'est lui qui (pourra vous le dire)*
the one about = *celle sur* : have you heard the one about pregnant women ? = *avez-vous entendu celle sur les femmes enceintes ?*
this ≠ that one = *celui-ci/celle-ci ≠ celui-là/celle-là* : do you want this one or that one ? =

voulez-vous celui-ci ou celui-là ? **to one another** = *se* : they often speak to one another = *ils se parlent souvent* → MYSELF
you're a fine/great one to talk ! = *ça te va bien de dire ça !* ↀ speak for yourself ! = *parle pour toi !*

☠ *on n'en sait rien* = nobody knows
— *on y va !* = let's go !
— *on dit que ...* = it's said/they say that ...
— *on frappe (porte)* = someone's knocking.

ONE-ARMED BANDIT (n) *machine (f) à sous.*

ONE-HORSE TOWN (n) *trou (m)* : he lives in a one-horse town = *il vit dans un trou* ☠ → hole.

ONE-MAN/WOMAN SHOW (n) *one-man/-woman-show (m).*

ONE-NIGHT STAND (n) **1/** *représentation (f) unique* : the theater troupe is performing one-night stands across the country = *la troupe théâtrale donne des représentations uniques à travers le pays* **2/** *aventure (f) d'un soir* : he's had a lot of one-night stands since his divorce = *il a eu de nombreuses aventures d'un soir depuis son divorce.*

ONES (pron pl) **the ones** = *ceux/celles* : those are the ones I want = *ce sont ceux-là que je veux/voilà ceux que je veux*
which ones ? = *lesquels ?*
☠ « ones » *ne se traduit pas après un adjectif* : give me the red ones please = *donnez-moi les rouges, s'il vous plaît*
— *je prendrai ceux-ci* ≠ *ceux-là* = I'll take these ≠ those *(on ne dit pas :* these ones, those ones).

ONESELF (pron) *soi-même* : one shouldn't think only of oneself = *on ne devrait pas penser qu'à soi-même.*

ONE-SIDED (adj) *partisan, -e* : a one-sided interpretation = *une interprétation partisane* ↀ prejudiced = *de parti pris* ☠ *être partisan de* = to be in favor of.

ONETIME (adj) *ancien, -enne* : a onetime actress = *une ancienne actrice* ☠ → ancient.

ONE-TRACK (adj) **to have a one-track mind** = *ne penser qu'à ça.*

ONE-UP (to, -ped) *damer le pion à* : Japanese technology has one-upped European technology = *la technologie japonaise a damé le pion à la technologie européenne* ↀ to get the better of = *l'emporter sur.*

ONE-UPMANSHIP (n) *rivalité (f) permanente* : between him and his wife everything is one-upmanship = *entre lui et sa femme, tout est l'objet d'une rivalité permanente.*

ONE-WAY (adj) *à sens unique* : a one-way friendship = *une amitié à sens unique,* a one-way street = *une rue à sens unique*
one-way ticket = *(billet) aller (simple)* ≠ round trip = *aller-retour.*

ONION (n) *oignon (m)* : onion soup = *soupe à l'oignon* ↀ garlic = *ail,* scallion = *échalote* ☠ *ce ne sont pas vos oignons* = it's none of your business.

ONLOOKER (n) *badaud (m)* = bystander ↀ spectator = *spectateur.*

ONLY (adj) *seul, -e* : my only hope/problem = *mon seul espoir/problème* ↀ sole = *unique* ≠ several = *plusieurs* ☠ → alone
only child = *enfant unique*
the only one = *le seul* : he's the only one who understands = *il est le seul qui comprenne.*

ONLY (adv) *seulement, ne ... que* : I have only ten dollars = *j'ai seulement dix dollars/je n'ai que dix dollars* ↀ quite simply = *tout bonnement*
it's only too true ! = *ce n'est que trop vrai !* ↀ it's so true ! = *c'est tellement vrai !*
(he's) only just (arrived) = *(il) vient tout juste (d'arriver)*
only (yesterday/last year) = *pas plus tard que (hier/l'année dernière)* ≠ ages ago = *il y a belle lurette*
only (he knows) = *(lui) seul (le sait)*
only too ... = *ne ... que trop* : I'm only too happy to help = *je ne suis que trop heureuse de vous aider,* I know him only too well = *je ne le connais que trop bien.*

ONLY (conj) *seulement* : I'd like to buy a new car only it costs too much = *je voudrais m'acheter une nouvelle voiture, seulement ça coûte trop cher* ↀ except = *si ce n'est que.*

ONWARD(S) (adv) **to go/walk onward(s)** = *poursuivre son chemin.*

OODLES (n pl) **oodles of (money/apples)** = *(de l'argent/des pommes) à profusion* → MANY.

OOMPH (n) *punch (m)* : rested and full of oomph = *reposé et plein de punch* ↀ go = *allant.*

OOPS ! (interj) *houp !* : oops ! I almost dropped the book = *houp ! j'ai failli laisser tomber le livre.*

OOPS-A-DAISY ! (interj) *hop là !*

OOZE (to, -d) *suinter* : pus was oozing out of the wound = *le pus suintait de la blessure.*

OPAL (n) *opale (f)* ↀ opal-colored = *opalin.*

OPAQUE (adj) *opaque* : opaque glass = *verre opaque.*

OPEC (abbr) = Organization of Petroleum Exporting Countries = *OPEP* = *Organisation des pays exportateurs de pétrole.*

OPEN (n) **to bring out in the open** = *faire éclater au grand jour* : the scandal was brought out in the open = *le scandale a éclaté au grand jour*
out in the open = *de notoriété publique* : his homosexuality is out in the open = *son homosexualité est de notoriété publique*
to sleep out in the open = *dormir à la belle étoile.*

OPEN (adj) **1/** *ouvert, -e* : the door's open = *la porte est ouverte* ① wide-open = *grand ouvert* ≠ *ajar* = *entrebâillé* **2/** *ouvert, -e* : an open mind/personality = *un esprit ouvert/une personnalité ouverte* **3/** *disponible* : the job isn't open anymore = *le poste n'est plus disponible* ☠ → available

---

an open book = *sans mystère* : her life's an open book = *sa vie est sans mystère*	**open about** = *qui ne se cache pas de* : he's very open about his homosexuality = *il ne se cache pas de son homosexualité*
to break open (a safe) = *forcer (un coffre)* ☠ → to force	**open house** = *porte ouverte*
it's open to question = *cela se discute* ① it's debatable = *c'est discutable*	**open on (Saturdays)** = *ouvert le (samedi)*
to lay o.s. open to = *prêter le flanc à* : you laid yourself open to his criticisms = *vous avez prêté le flanc à ses critiques* ① you asked for it = *vous l'avez cherché*	**open secret** = *secret de polichinelle*
	open to (new ideas) = *ouvert à (de nouvelles idées)*
to leave (the matter) open = *ne pas trancher (la question)*	**open to the public** = *ouvert au public*
	(to welcome) with open arms = *(accueillir) à bras ouverts*

OPEN (to, -ed) **1/** *ouvrir* : open the door ! = *ouvre la porte* ! ☠ *ouvrir l'appétit* = to work up an appetite **2/** *débuter* : the play opens in a week = *la pièce débute dans une semaine* ≠ to close = *se terminer* ☠ → to start off
to open up = **1/** *s'ouvrir* : she opened up and told me what was wrong = *elle s'est ouverte à moi et m'a dit ce qui n'allait pas* **2/** *ouvrir* : the new store opened up last week = *ce nouveau magasin a ouvert la semaine dernière*
to open with = *commencer par* : the movie opens with a murder = *le film commence par un meurtre.*

OPEN-AIR (adj) *en plein air* : an open-air concert = *un concert en plein air* ≠ indoors = *à l'intérieur.*

OPEN-AND-SHUT (adj) **an open-and-shut case (of murder)** = *une affaire (de meurtre) vite classée.*

OPEN-END(ED) (adj) *d'une durée illimitée*

---

an open-ended discussion = *une discussion libre.*

OPENERS (n pl) **for openers** = *tout d'abord* : for openers, I think you were wrong to tell her the truth = *tout d'abord, je trouve que vous avez eu tort de lui dire la vérité.*

OPENING (n) **1/** *ouverture (f)* : the opening of the factory = *l'ouverture de l'usine* ≠ closing = *fermeture*
opening night = *première* = premiere
☠ *ouverture (opéra)* = overture
— *l'ouverture des hostilités* = the outbreak of hostilities
— *ouverture d'esprit* = open-mindedness
— *heures d'ouverture* = working hours
2/ *poste (m) disponible* : is there an opening for a secretary ? = *y a-t-il un poste de secrétaire disponible ?*

OPENLY (adv) *ouvertement* : she talked openly of her problems = *elle a parlé ouvertement de ses problèmes.*

OPEN-MINDED (adj) *à l'esprit ouvert* ≠ narrow-minded = *étroit d'esprit.*

OPERA (n) *opéra (m)* : comic opera = *opéra comique* ① light opera = *opérette* = operetta.

OPERATE (to, -d) **1/** *opérer* : the surgeon will operate today = *le chirurgien opérera aujourd'hui*
to be operated = *se faire opérer/passer sur le billard* (LV) : she'll be operated on Monday = *elle se fait opérer lundi*
☠ *opérer (changements)* = to bring about (changes)
2/ *fonctionner* : that's not how I operate = *ce n'est pas comme ça que je fonctionne* ☠ → to function
3/ *faire fonctionner* : do you know how to operate this machine ? = *savez-vous faire fonctionner cette machine ?*
to operate in = *opérer à* : the gang operates in Chicago = *le gang opère à Chicago.*

OPERATION (n) *opération (f)* : to undergo an operation = *subir une opération* ① anesthesia = *anesthésie,* operating room = *salle d'opération.*
to put ≠ **to come into operation** = *mettre* ≠ *être mis en application (rule, law) / en service (machine)*
☠ *opérations de Bourse* = exchange transactions
— *opération publicitaire* = publicity campaign.

OPERATIONAL (adj) *opérationnel, -elle* : the new plan isn't operational yet = *le nouveau plan n'est pas encore opérationnel.*

OPERATIVE (adj) *en service* : the machine's operative = *la machine est en service.*

OPERATOR (n) **1/** *standardiste (m, f)* : the operator cut us off = *le standardiste nous a coupés* **2/** *magouilleur, -euse* : her brother's a real operator, almost a crook = *son frère est un vrai magouilleur, presque un escroc* ① con artist = *embobineur,* confidence man = *aigrefin.*

OPINION (n) *opinion (f), avis (m)* : I'd like to have your opinion = *j'aimerais avoir votre opinion/avis* ① convic-

tion = ←
to be of the opinion that ... = *être d'avis que...*
to have a high ≠ low opinion of = *avoir une bonne ≠ mauvaise opinion de*
in my opinion = *à mon avis* ⓪ to my mind = *à mon sens*
in the opinion of (the specialists) = *d'après (les spécialistes)* ⓪ according to = *selon*
opinion poll = *sondage d'opinion*
☠ *un avis (affiché)* = a notice
— *changer d'avis* = to change one's mind
— *deux avis valent mieux qu'un* = two heads are better than none.

OPINIONATED (adj) *qui a des opinions arrêtées* ⓪ dogmatic = *dogmatique.*

OPIUM (n) *opium (m)* ⓪ heroin = *héroïne.*

OPPONENT (n) *opposant, -e* (politics), *adversaire (m, f)* : opponents of the regime = *des opposants au régime* ≠ ally = *allié.*

OPPORTUNIST (n) *opportuniste (m, f)* ⓪ wheeler-dealer = *magouilleur.*

OPPORTUNITY (n, -ies) *occasion (f)* : a marvelous opportunity = *une occasion merveilleuse* ⓪ possibility = *possibilité* ☠ → occasion
to have the opportunity to = *avoir l'occasion de* : I didn't have the opportunity to tell him yet = *je n'ai pas encore eu l'occasion de le lui dire*
to seize the opportunity ≠ to let the opportunity slip by = *saisir ≠ laisser passer l'occasion.*

OPPOSE (to, -d) *s'opposer à* : the town's inhabitants are opposed to the construction of the nuke = *les habitants de la ville sont opposés à la construction de la centrale nucléaire* ≠ to be for = *être pour*
as opposed to what ? = *par opposition à quoi ?*
☠ *rien ne s'y oppose* = there's nothing against it
— *opposer une résistance* = to put up a fight.

OPPOSITE (n) *opposé (m)* : is old age the opposite of youth ? = *est-ce que la vieillesse est l'opposé de la jeunesse ?* ⓪ contrary = *contraire*
just the opposite = *tout l'opposé* : she's just the opposite of her husband = *elle est tout l'opposé de son mari*
opposites attract = *les contraires s'attirent.*

OPPOSITE (adj) *opposé, -e* : the opposite sex = *le sexe opposé* ≠ identical = *identique*
I'm going the opposite way = *je vais dans la direction opposée.*

OPPOSITE (prep) *en face de* : I live opposite the bank = *j'habite en face de la banque*
to play opposite s.o. = *donner la réplique à qqn* : has Schields ever played opposite Hoffman ? = *Schields a-t-elle jamais donné la réplique à Hoffman ?*

OPPOSITION (n) *opposition (f)* : there's strong opposition to the project = *il y a une forte opposition au projet*

☠ *faire opposition à (une décision)* = to oppose (a decision)
— *être en opposition avec qqn* = to be at variance with s.o.
— *faire opposition à un chèque* = to stop a check.

OPPRESS (to, -ed) *opprimer* : to oppress minority groups = *opprimer les groupes minoritaires* ⓪ to subjugate = *subjuguer* **OPPRESSION** (n) oppression *(f)* ⓪ tyranny = *tyrannie.*

OPPRESSIVE (adj) **1/** *oppressif, -ive* : oppressive laws = *lois oppressives* ⓪ tyrannical = *tyrannique* **2/** *oppressant, -e* : an oppressive atmosphere = *une atmosphère oppressante* ⓪ dismal = *sinistre.*

OPPRESSOR (n) *oppresseur (m)* ⓪ tyrant = *tyran.*

OPT FOR (to, -ed) *opter pour* ⓪ to choose = *choisir.*

OPTICIAN (n) *opticien, -enne* ⓪ glasses = *lunettes.*

OPTIMISM (n) *optimisme (m)* ≠ pessimism = *pessimisme* **OPTIMIST** (n) *optimiste (m, f)* ≠ worrywart = *bilieux.*

OPTIMISTIC (adj) *optimiste* : I'm not optimistic about my future = *je ne suis pas optimiste pour mon avenir* ≠ pessimistic = *pessimiste* **OPTIMISTICALLY** (adv) *avec optimisme.*

OPTION (n) **1/** *alternative (f)*, *option (f)* : there's no other option = *il n'y a pas d'autre alternative/option* ☠ → alternative **2/** *option (f)* : they took an option on the book = *ils ont pris une option sur le livre*
to have no option = *ne pas avoir le choix*
what are your options ? = *qu'avez-vous la possibilité de faire ?*

OPTIONAL (adj) *facultatif, -ive* : optional homework = *devoir facultatif* ≠ compulsory = *obligatoire.*

OPULENCE (n) *opulence (f)* ⓪ riches = *richesses.*

OPULENT (adj) *fastueux, -euse* : an opulent apartment = *un appartement fastueux* ≠ squalid = *sordide* ☠ *les familles opulentes* = affluent families.

OR (conj) *ou* : coffee or tea ? = *du café ou du thé ?*
or else = **1/** *ou bien* : eat or else go to sleep = *mange ou bien va te coucher* **2/** *sans quoi* : tell her or else I will = *dis-lui, sans quoi je le ferai* ⓪ if not = *sinon*
or longer = *ou plus* : I can stay an hour or longer = *je peux rester une heure ou plus*
or so = *à peu près* : I have $ 10 or so = *j'ai à peu près 10 dollars* ⓪ about = *environ*
or something = *ou quelque chose comme ça* : he's a lawyer or something = *il est avocat ou quelque chose comme ça*
or what = *ou quoi* : will she call or what ? = *elle va appeler ou quoi ?*
☠ *où (est-elle) ?* = where (is she) ?

ORAL (adj) *oral, -e* : an oral contraceptive/message = *un contraceptif/message oral*
oral sex = *caresses buccales* : during the 20 years of their marriage, they never had oral sex = *pendant leurs 20 années de mariage, ils n'ont jamais pratiqué les caresses buccales* ① fellatio = *fellation*, cunnilingus = ←, to suck = *sucer.*

ORALLY (adv) *oralement* (to say), *par voie orale* (medicine).

ORALS (n pl) *oral (m)* : to fail one's orals = *rater son oral.*

ORANGE (n) *orange (f)* : fresh orange juice = *orange pressée* ① grapefruit = *pamplemousse.*

ORATOR (n) *orateur, -trice* : the orator stammered = *l'orateur bafouillait* ① rhetoric = *rhétorique.*

ORBIT (n) *orbite (f)* **ORBIT** (to, -ed) *graviter autour de.*

ORCHARD (n) *verger (m)* ① vineyard = *vigne.*

ORCHESTRA (n) *orchestre (m)* : a jazz orchestra = *un orchestre de jazz* ① band = *petit orchestre*, conductor = *chef d'orchestre.*

ORCHID (n) *orchidée (f)* ① camelia = *camélia.*

ORDAIN (to, -ed) 1/ *décréter* = to decree 2/ *ordonner* : to ordain a priest = *ordonner un prêtre* ☠ → to order.

ORDEAL (n) *(rude) épreuve (f)* : getting divorced was an ordeal = *divorcer a été une rude épreuve* ① torture = *supplice*
☠ *j'ai une épreuve vendredi* = I've got a test on Friday
— *mettre (la patience de qqn) à l'épreuve* = to try (s.o.'s patience)
— *une vie remplie d'épreuves* = a life of hardships
— *épreuves (livre)* = galley proofs (book).

ORDER (n) 1/ *ordre (m)* : my husband likes to give orders = *mon mari aime donner des ordres* ① directives = ← 2/ *commande (f)* : to place an order = *passer une commande* ☠ → command 3/ *ordre (m)* : I don't like order = *je n'aime pas l'ordre* ≠ confusion = ←

by order of (the police) = *sur ordre de (la police)*	I'm working overtime in order to buy a new car = *je fais des heures supplémentaires afin d'acheter une nouvelle voiture* ① so as to = *de façon à*
in order = *tout indiqué* : an apology is in order = *des excuses sembleraient tout indiquées*	
in order ≠ **out of order** = *en ordre* ≠ *pas en ordre*	**to keep order** = *maintenir l'ordre*
in order of (importance) = *par ordre d'(importance)*	**to obey orders** = *obéir aux ordres*
in order to = *afin de* :	**on order** = *commandé* : the books are on order = *les livres sont commandés*

the order of the day = *l'ordre du jour*	**to put in order** = *remettre de l'ordre dans* : I'm putting my office in order = *je remets de l'ordre dans mon bureau* ① to tidy up = *ranger*
out of order = *en panne* : the elevator's out of order = *l'ascenseur est en panne* ≠ working = *qui marche*	

☠ *c'est dans l'ordre des choses* = it's in the nature of things
— *l'Ordre des avocats* = the bar.

ORDER (to, -ed) 1/ *commander* : to order a meal/a book = *commander un repas/un livre* ☠ → to command
2/ *ordonner* : the mullah ordered the prisoner to be flogged = *le mollah a ordonné que le prisonnier soit flagellé*
to order about/around = *donner des ordres à droite et à gauche* ① to lord over = *régenter*
to order s.o. to = *ordonner à qqn de* : I ordered him to leave = *je lui ai ordonné de partir*
☠ *ordonner un prêtre* = to ordain a priest.

ORDERLY (n, -ies) *garçon (m) de salle* : he's an orderly in the hospital = *il est garçon de salle à l'hôpital.*

ORDERLY (adj) *ordonné, -e* : a very orderly person = *une personne très ordonnée* ≠ disorderly = *désordonné*
☠ *une chambre ordonnée* = a tidy room.

ORDINARILY (adv) *d'ordinaire* : ordinarily, he isn't late = *d'ordinaire, il n'est pas en retard* ① generally = *généralement.*

ORDINARY (n, -ies) **out of the ordinary** = *qui sort de l'ordinaire* : this restaurant's really out of the ordinary = *ce restaurant sort vraiment de l'ordinaire* ① unusual = *inhabituel.*

ORDINARY (adj) 1/ *ordinaire* : the film was very ordinary = *le film était très ordinaire* ≠ exceptional = *exceptionnel* → AWFUL 2/ *habituel, -elle* : the ordinary hours = *l'horaire habituel* ☠ → habitual.

ORGAN (n) 1/ *orgue (m)*, *orgues (f pl)* : to play the organ = *jouer de l'orgue* 2/ *organe (m)* : body organs = *les organes du corps.*

ORGANDY (n, -ies) *organdi (m)* : an organdy dress = *une robe en organdi.*

ORGANIC (adj) *organique* : organic chemistry = *chimie organique.*

ORGANISM (n) *organisme (m)* ① body = *corps* ☠ *organisme international* = international organization.

ORGANIZATION (n) 1/ *organisation (f)*, *organisme (m)* : UNESCO is an international organization =

l'UNESCO est une organisation internationale ⑤ *asso-ciation* = ← ☠ *organisme* → organism **2/** *organisation (f)* : our work lacks organization = *notre travail manque d'organisation* ≠ disorganization = *désorganisation.*

ORGANIZE (to, -d) *organiser* : to organize a party = *organiser une soirée* ⑤ to arrange = *arranger.*

ORGANIZED (adj) *organisé, -e* : organized crime = *crime organisé*
organized labor = *main-d'œuvre syndiquée*
☠ *voyage organisé* = package tour.

ORGANIZER (n) *organisateur, -trice* : the organizer of the ball/meeting = *l'organisateur du bal/de la réunion.*

ORGASM (n) *orgasme (m)* : to have an orgasm = *avoir un orgasme* ⑤ to come = *jouir.*

ORGY (n, -ies) *orgie (f)* ⑤ swing = *partouze*, debauch = *débauche.*

ORIENT (n) *Orient (m)* ☠ *Moyen/Proche-Orient* = Middle/Near East.

ORIENT (to, -ed) *orienter* : research is oriented today towards problems of pollution = *la recherche est orientée actuellement vers les problèmes de pollution* ⑤ to direct = *diriger* ☠ *s'orienter* = to get one's bearings.

ORIENTAL (adj) *oriental, -e* : oriental cooking = *cuisine orientale* ≠ occidental = ←.

ORIGIN (n) *origine (f)* : of Russian origin = *d'origine russe* ⑤ source = ← ☠ *à l'origine (ils étaient amis)* = in the beginning (they were friends).

ORIGINAL (n) *original (m)* : the painting's an original = *le tableau est un original* ≠ copy = *copie* ☠ *son père est un original* = her father's a character.

ORIGINAL (adj) *original, -e* : an original idea/hairdo = *une idée/coiffure originale* ⑤ creative = *créatif* ≠ run-of-the-mill = *quelconque*
☠ *édition originale* = first edition
— *une bague originale* = an unusual ring
— *une personne originale* = a kooky person.

ORIGINALITY (n, -ies) *originalité (f)* : a film full of originality = *un film plein d'originalité* ≠ banality = *banalité.*

ORIGINALLY (adv) *à l'origine* : he's from London originally = *à l'origine, il est londonien* ⑤ at first = *au début.*

ORNAMENT (n) *ornement (m)* : the ornaments of a dress = *les ornements d'une robe* ⑤ decoration = *décoration* **ORNAMENTAL** (adj) *ornemental, -e.*

ORPHAN (n) *orphelin, -e* ⑤ orphanage = *orphelinat*, adopted child = *enfant adopté*, foster parents = *parents adoptifs.*

ORTHODOX (adj) *orthodoxe* : orthodox Jews = *Juifs orthodoxes*

not very orthodox = *pas très orthodoxe* ⑤ not very kosher = *pas très catholique.*

OSCAR (n) *Oscar (m)* ⑤ César = ←.

OSCILLATE (to, -d) *osciller* : France is oscillating between the right and the left = *la France oscille entre la droite et la gauche* ⑤ to hesitate = *hésiter.*

OSTENSIBLY (adv) *soi-disant* : he quit ostensibly for health reasons = *il a démissionné soi-disant pour raisons de santé.*

OSTENTATIOUS (adj) *tape-à-l'œil, ostentatoire* : an ostentatious decoration = *une décoration tape-à-l'œil* ⑤ showy = *voyant.*

OSTRACIZE (to, -d) *frapper d'ostracisme* : ostracized for being an unwed mother = *frappée d'ostracisme parce qu'elle était fille mère* ⑤ to blacklist = *mettre sur la liste noire.*

OSTRICH (n, -es) *autruche (f)* ⑤ bird = *oiseau.*

OTHER (n) *autre (m, f)* : some have money but others don't = *certains ont de l'argent mais d'autres n'en ont pas*

the others = *les autres* : when are the others coming ? = *quand arrivent les autres ?*

☠ *à d'autres !* = tell it to the Marines ! — *j'en veux un autre*	= I want another one — *j'en ai vu d'autres* = I've seen worse.

OTHER (adj) *autre* : she married the other brother = *elle a épousé l'autre frère* ⑤ another = *un autre* ≠ same = *même*

among other things = *entre autres choses*	**pays well** = *le travail est dur, par contre/en revanche c'est bien payé* ⑤ however = *cependant*
to have other fish to fry = *avoir d'autres chats à fouetter*	
in other words = *autrement dit*	**the other day** = *l'autre jour*
to look the other way = *pratiquer la politique de l'autruche* : he's cheating but she looks the other way = *il la trompe, mais elle pratique la politique de l'autruche*	**the other side of (the street)** = *l'autre côté de (la rue)*
	the other side of the picture/coin = *le revers de la médaille*
no other = *pas d'autre* : I have no other coat = *je n'ai pas d'autre manteau*	**it's the other way around** = *c'est tout le contraire*
	to see how the other half lives = *voir comment vivent les autres*
on the other hand = *par contre/en revanche* : the job's hard, but on the other hand it	**to turn the other cheek** = *tendre l'autre joue*

OTHER

green outfit = *elle s'est acheté un magnifique ensemble vert*
☣ *dans l'ensemble* = on the whole
— *(grand) ensemble* = housing complex
2/ *unité* (f) : their outfit is on the front = *leur unité est au front* ☠ → unit
3/ *entreprise* (f) : he works for a dynamic outfit = *il travaille pour une entreprise dynamique* ⊚ association = ← ☠ → enterprise.

OUTGOING (adj) 1/ *liant, -e* : an outgoing personality = *une personnalité liante* ⊚ friendly = *amical* ≠ withdrawn = *renfermé* 2/ *sortant, -e* : the outgoing mayor = *le maire sortant* ≠ incumbent = *en titre.*

OUTGROWTH (n) *excroissance* (f) : terrorism is an outgrowth of social injustice = *le terrorisme est une excroissance de l'injustice sociale* ☠ → growth.

OUTHOUSE (n) *cabinets* (m pl) *extérieurs* ⊚ toilet = W.-C.

OUTING (n) *sortie* (f) : the club's annual outing = *la sortie annuelle du club* ⊚ excursion = ← ☠ → exit.

OUTLANDISH (adj) *bizarroïde* : outlandish ideas = *des idées bizarroïdes* ⊚ ludicrous = *saugrenu,* farfetched = *tiré par les cheveux.*

OUTLAW (n) *hors-la-loi* (m), *proscrit, -e* : a gang of outlaws robbed the bank = *une bande de hors-la-loi a dévalisé la banque.*

OUTLAW (to, -ed) *proscrire* : to outlaw drugs = *proscrire la drogue* ≠ to legalize = *légaliser.*

OUTLAY (n) *mise* (f) *de fonds* : to get back one's outlay = *récupérer sa mise* ⊚ investment = *investissement.*

OUTLET (n) 1/ *débouché* (m) : his company's looking for outlets in Europe = *sa société cherche des débouchés en Europe* 2/ *exutoire* (m) : football is an outlet for his aggression = *le football est un exutoire à son agressivité* ⊚ escape = *échappatoire* 3/ *point* (m) *de vente* : they have three outlets in the city = *ils ont trois points de vente dans la ville* ⊚ shop = *magasin.*

OUTLINE (n) 1/ *aperçu* (m) : give me a quick outline of what he said = *donne-moi un aperçu rapide de ce qu'il a dit* ⊚ rundown = *topo,* synopsis = ← 2/ *contour* (m) : I couldn't see the building, just the outline = *je ne pouvais pas voir l'immeuble, seulement ses contours*
the broad outlines/general outline = *les grandes lignes/les grands traits.*

OUTLIVE (to, -d) *survivre à* : she outlived him by five years = *elle lui a survécu cinq ans*
you'll outlive us all ! = *tu nous enterreras tous !*

OUTLOOK (n) 1/ *façon* (f) *de voir les choses* : a pessimistic outlook = *une façon pessimiste de voir les choses* ⊚ point of view = *point de vue* 2/ *perspectives* (f pl) : what is the outlook for the economy ? = *quelles sont les perspectives économiques ?* ☠ → perspective.

OUTLYING (adj) **the outlying suburbs** = *la grande banlieue.*

OUTMODED (adj) *désuet, -ète* : an outmoded expression = *une expression désuète* ⊚ out-of-date = *passé de mode.*

OUTNUMBER (to, -ed) *surpasser en nombre* : girls outnumbered boys = *les filles surpassaient les garçons en nombre.*

OUT-OF-DATE (adj) *passé, -e de mode* (clothes) ⊚ old-fashioned = *démodé.*

OUT-OF-IT (adj) *qui n'est pas dans le coup* : an out-of-it guy/part of the country = *un garçon/une partie du pays qui n'est pas dans le coup* ⊚ old hat = *vieux jeu.*

OUT-OF-THE-WAY (adj) *(situé, -e) au diable (vauvert)* : an out-of-the-way restaurant = *un restaurant au diable vauvert* ⊚ remote = *éloigné.*

OUTPUT (n) 1/ *production* (f) : the country's steel output = *la production nationale d'acier* ☠ → production
2/ *rendement* (m) : a worker's yearly output = *le rendement annuel d'un ouvrier*
☣ *rendement (argent)* = yield (money)
— *la loi des rendements décroissants* = law of diminishing returns.

OUTRAGE (n) **what an outrage (to pay so much) !** = *quel scandale (de payer autant) !*
☣ *outrage à la pudeur* = indecent behavior
— *outrage à magistrat* = contempt of Court
— *c'est un outrage à sa mémoire* = it's an insult to his memory
— *les outrages du temps* = the ravages of time.

OUTRAGE (to, -d) **to be outraged by (s.o.'s attitude)** = *être outré par (l'attitude de qqn).*

OUTRAGEOUS (adj) *scandaleux, -euse* : outrageous prices = *des prix scandaleux* = scandalous ≠ reasonable = *raisonnable.*

OUTRAGEOUSLY (adv) *outrageusement, horriblement* : she's outrageously vulgar = *elle est horriblement vulgaire* → VERY.

OUTRIGHT (adj) *très net, nette* : an outright lie/refusal = *un mensonge/refus très net* ⊚ sheer = *pur.*

OUTRIGHT (adv) *carrément* : I told him outright what I thought = *je lui ai carrément dit ce que je pensais* ⊚ frankly = *franchement* ☣ *vous avez carrément tort* = you're plain wrong.

OUTSELL (to, -sold, -sold) *vendre plus que* : our competitors are outselling us = *nos concurrents vendent plus que nous.*

OUTSET (n) **from the outset** = *dès le départ* : they were enemies from the outset = *ils étaient ennemis dès le départ* ⊚ from the beginning = *dès le commencement.*

441

OUTSIDE (n) *extérieur (m)* : we have to paint the outside of the house = *il faut que nous peignons l'extérieur de la maison* ≠ inside = *intérieur* ☠ → exterior
on the outside (he looks tough/the house is pretty) = *extérieurement (il a l'air dur/la maison est jolie)* ☠ → outwardly.

OUTSIDE (adj) *extérieur, -e* : the outside wall = *le mur extérieur*, outside influences = *des influences extérieures* ☠ → outward.

OUTSIDE (adv) *dehors* : let's go outside = *allons dehors* ≠ inside = *dedans* ☠ *dehors !* = get out !

OUTSIDE (prep) **outside of** = *en dehors de* : outside of sex, we have nothing in common = *en dehors du cul, nous n'avons rien de commun* ⓪ apart from = *à part* ☠ *en dehors de (moi)* = other than (me).

OUTSIDER (n) 1/ *outsider (m)* : he was the outsider in the race = *c'était l'outsider de la course* ≠ the odds-on favorite = *le grand favori* 2/ *étranger, -ère* : small-town inhabitants often mistrust outsiders = *les habitants des petites villes se méfient souvent des étrangers* ☠ → foreigner.

OUTSKIRTS (n pl) **on the outskirts** = *dans les faubourgs* ⓪ outlying area = *périphérie*.

OUTSMART (to, -ed) *être plus malin, -igne que* : he thinks he can outsmart everyone = *il se croit plus malin que tout le monde* ⓪ to one-up = *damer le pion à*.

OUTSPOKEN (adj) *qui a son franc-parler* : an outspoken literary agent = *un agent littéraire qui a son franc-parler* ⓪ forthright = *direct*.

OUTSTANDING (adj) 1/ *hors pair* : an outstanding cook = *un cuisinier hors pair* → WONDERFUL 2/ *en souffrance* : outstanding bills = *des factures en souffrance* ⓪ unpaid = *impayé*.

OUTWARD (adj) *extérieur, -e* : an outward sign of wealth = *un signe extérieur de richesse*
☠ *commerce extérieur* = foreign trade
— *le monde extérieur* = the outside world.

OUTWARDLY (adv) *extérieurement* : outwardly she looks happy, but ... = *extérieurement, elle a l'air heureuse, mais ...* ≠ inwardly = *intérieurement* ☠ *extérieurement, la maison est jolie* = on the outside, the house is pretty.

OUTWEIGH (to, -ed) *passer avant* : money outweighs all his other aspirations = *chez lui, l'argent passe avant toute autre aspiration*.

OUTWIT (to, -ted) *se montrer plus malin, -igne que* : the kids outwitted the teacher = *les enfants se sont montrés plus malins que le professeur* ⓪ to foil = *déjouer*.

OVAL (adj) *oval, -e* : an oval mirror = *une glace ovale* ⓪ round = *rond*
the Oval Room = *le bureau du président des États-Unis*.

OVATION (n) *ovation (f)* ⓪ curtain call = *rappel*.

OVEN (n) *four (m)* ⓪ stove = *cuisinière*
☠ *il fait noir comme dans un four* = it's pitch-black
— *la pièce a été un four* = the play was a flop
— *cuire au four* = to bake
— *je ne peux pas être au four et au moulin* = I can't do two things at once.

OVER (adj) *fini, -e* : our love affair/the lesson is over = *notre liaison/la leçon est finie* ≠ beginning = *qui commence*
over and done with = *classé, -e* : the problem's over and done with = *le problème est classé* ⓪ dead and buried = *mort et enterré*
☠ *un idiot fini* = a regular/thorough fool.

OVER (adv) *re-* : do/write it over = *refaites-le/réécrivez-le* ⓪ again = *de nouveau*

over again = *re-* : say it over again = *redis-le* **over and over** = *ne pas cesser de* : he repeated the same thing over and over = *il ne cessait*	*de répéter la même chose* ⓪ again and again = *maintes et maintes fois* **over here** = *par ici* ≠ **over there** = *là-bas*.

OVER (prep) 1/ *plus de* : it costs over $ 100 = *ça coûte plus de 100 dollars*, we divorced over ten years ago = *nous avons divorcé il y a plus de dix ans* ≠ less than = *moins de* 2/ *au cours de* : over the summer/the five past years = *au cours de l'été/des cinq dernières années* ⓪ during = *pendant* 3/ *par rapport à* : a ten-per-cent increase over last year = *une hausse de dix pour cent par rapport à l'année dernière* 4/ *au-dessus de* : they live right over us = *ils habitent juste au-dessus de chez nous*, we hung the painting over the fireplace = *nous avons accroché le tableau au-dessus de la cheminée* ≠ below = *au-dessous de*

over and above = *plus que ... et de loin* : they gave me over and above what I asked for = *ils m'ont donné plus que je n'avais demandé et de loin* ≠ less than = *moins que*

☠ for the use of ''over'' after a verb, see the verb.

OVERACT (to, -ed) *en faire trop (en jouant)* : many actors overact = *beaucoup d'acteurs en font trop (en jouant).*

OVERALL (adj) *global, -e* : overall expenses = *frais globaux* **OVERALL** (adv) *globalement* : overall his last film wasn't so bad = *globalement, son dernier film n'était pas si mauvais* ⓪ all in all = *l'un dans l'autre.*

OVERALLS (n pl) *salopette (f) (homme)* ⓪ jumper = *salopette (femme)*, jump suit = *combinaison.*

OVERBEARING (adj) *impérieux, -euse* : an overbearing personality = *un caractère impérieux* ⓪ authoritarian = *autoritaire* ☣ *un besoin impérieux* = an urgent need.

OVERBOARD (adv) *par-dessus bord* : to fall overboard = *tomber par-dessus bord*
(man) overboard ! = *(un homme) à la mer !*
to go overboard = *dépasser la mesure* ⓪ to carry it too far = *dépasser les bornes.*

OVERCHARGE (to, -d) *pratiquer des prix exorbitants* : this restaurant overcharges = *ce restaurant pratique des prix exorbitants.*

OVERCOAT (n) *pardessus (m)* ⓪ coat = *manteau.*

OVERCOME (to, -came, -come) *surmonter* : I overcame my jealousy = *j'ai surmonté ma jalousie* ⓪ to get the better of = *l'emporter sur* ☣ → to surmount
to be overcome by (grief/fear) = *succomber au (chagrin)/à (la peur).*

OVERDO (to, -did, -done) *en faire trop* : you are overdoing the macho number = *tu en fais trop dans ton numéro de macho* ⓪ to push it = *pousser un peu.*

OVERDOSE (n) *overdose (f)* : to die of an overdose = *mourir d'une overdose.*

OVERESTIMATE (to, -d) *surestimer* : to overestimate one's abilities = *surestimer ses capacités* ≠ to underestimate = *sous-estimer.*

OVERFAMILIAR (adj) *trop sans-gêne* : a forward and overfamiliar guy = *un type envahissant et trop sans-gêne.*

OVERFLOW (to, -ed) *déborder* : the river's overflowing = *le fleuve déborde* ☣ *le lait déborde* = the milk's boiling over.

OVERHAUL (to, -ed) *réviser* : to overhaul an engine = *réviser un moteur* ☣ → to revise **OVERHAULING** (n) *révision (f)* ☣ → revision.

OVERHEAD (n inv) *frais (m pl) généraux* ⓪ overall expenses = *frais globaux.*

OVERHEAR (to, -heard) *surprendre* : I overheard their conversation = *j'ai surpris leur conversation* ⓪ to eavesdrop = *écouter aux portes* ☣ → to surprise.

OVERJOYED (adj) to be overjoyed = *être absolument ravi* : she was overjoyed to be working again = *elle était absolument ravie de recommencer à travailler* ⓪ thrilled = *ravi.*

OVERKILL (n) *effet (m) de saturation* : the advertising campaign was a case of overkill = *la campagne publicitaire a provoqué un effet de saturation.*

OVERLAP (to, -ped) *se chevaucher* : our time schedules are overlapping = *nos emplois du temps se chevauchent.*

OVERLOAD (to, -ed) *surcharger* : I overloaded the washing machine = *j'ai surchargé la machine à laver* ⓪ to load = *charger.*

OVERLOOK (to, -ed) **1/** *passer dessus/sur* : if he says something nasty, overlook it ! = *s'il dit quelque chose de méchant, passe dessus !* ⓪ to disregard = *ne pas s'occuper de* **2/** *omettre* : that's a point/detail that I overlooked = *c'est un point/détail que j'ai omis de signaler* ☣ → to omit **3/** *avoir vue sur* : our room overlooks the beach = *notre chambre a vue sur la plage*
don't overlook the fact that (it can be dangerous) = *n'oubliez pas que (cela peut être dangereux).*

OVERLY (adv) *par trop* : overly ambitious = *par trop ambitieux* ⓪ too = *trop.*

OVERNIGHT (adv) *du jour au lendemain* : he became famous overnight = *il est devenu célèbre du jour au lendemain* ⓪ from one day to the next = *d'un jour à l'autre*
to stay overnight = *passer la nuit* : I went to visit my aunt and stayed overnight = *je suis allé rendre visite à ma tante et j'ai passé la nuit chez elle.*

OVERPLAY (to, -ed) *grossir* : the newspaper overplayed the story = *le journal a grossi toute l'histoire* ≠ to underplay = *minimiser* ☣ → to blow up.

OVERPOPULATED (adj) *surpeuplé, -e* : an overpopulated country = *un pays surpeuplé* ≠ underpopulated = *sous-peuplé.*

OVERPOWER (to, -ed) *terrasser* : to overpower an enemy = *terrasser un ennemi* ⓪ to subdue = *maîtriser.*

OVERPOWERING (adj) *écrasant, -e* : an overpowering personality = *une personnalité écrasante* ☣ → overwhelming.

OVERRATE (to, -d) *surestimer* : you're overrating his talent = *tu surestimes son talent* = to overestimate ⓪ to exaggerate = *exagérer*
to be overrated = *être surfait* : in my opinion, the play was overrated = *à mon avis, cette pièce était surfaite.*

OVERRIDE (to, -rode, -ridden) *passer outre à* : the committee overrode the chairman's decision = *le comité a passé outre à la décision du président.*

OVERRIDING (adj) *prépondérant, -e* : the overriding danger/importance = *le danger prépondérant/l'importance prépondérante* ⓪ primary = *primordial* ☣ *jouer un rôle prépondérant* = to play an important role.

OVERRULE (to, -d) **1/** *casser* : to overrule a verdict = *casser un verdict* ☠ → to break **2/** *prévaloir sur* : the President's decision overruled the committee's = *la décision du Président a prévalu sur celle de la commission.*

OVERRUN (to, -ran, -run) *envahir* : the place was overrun by rats/tourists = *l'endroit était envahi par les rats/touristes* ⓪ to be swamped with = *grouiller de* ☠ → to invade.

OVERSEAS (adv) *outre-mer* : the first division was sent overseas = *la première division a été envoyée outre-mer.*

OVERSEE (to, -saw, -seen) *surveiller* : I'm overseeing the work = *je surveille le travail* ⓪ to supervise = *superviser* ☠ → to watch.

OVERSEXED (adj) *complètement obsédé, -e* ⓪ hot stuff = *qui a du tempérament.*

OVERSHADOW (to, -ed) **1/** *assombrir* : the fear of death overshadowed his old age = *la peur de la mort a assombri sa vieillesse* **2/** *éclipser* : his last novel overshadows all his others = *son dernier roman éclipse tous les autres* ☠ → to upstage.

OVERSIGHT (n) *oubli* (m) : not calling you back was an oversight = *si je ne vous ai pas rappelé, c'était un oubli* ☠ *tomber dans l'oubli* = to fall into oblivion.

OVERSLEEP (to, -slept, -slept) *se réveiller trop tard* : I'm late because I overslept this morning = *je suis en retard parce que je me suis réveillée trop tard ce matin.*

OVERSTATEMENT (n) *exagération* (f) *pure et simple* : to say that all men are macho is an overstatement = *dire que tous les hommes sont machos, c'est de l'exagération pure et simple* ⓪ exaggeration = *exagération.*

OVERSTEP (to, -ped) *outrepasser* : to overstep one's authority = *outrepasser son autorité* ⓪ to exceed = *excéder.*

OVERT (adj) *non dissimulé, -e* : overt hostility = *une hostilité non dissimulée* ≠ covert = *sous-jacent* **OVERTLY** (adv) *de façon non dissimulée.*

OVERTAKE (to, -took, -taken) *dépasser* : their car overtook ours = *leur voiture nous a dépassés* ☠ *ça me dépasse !* = it's beyond (me) !/it tops it off ! — *il y a quelque chose qui dépasse* = something's protruding/sticking out — *votre jupon dépasse* = your slip's showing — *dépasser une limitation de vitesse* = to exceed a speed limit.

OVERTHROW (to, -threw, -thrown) *renverser* : to overthrow a government = *renverser un gouvernement* ⓪ to topple = *faire chuter* ☠ → to spill.

OVERTIME (adv) *heures* (f pl) *supplémentaires* : to work overtime = *faire des heures supplémentaires* ⓪ to moonlight = *travailler au noir.*

OVERTONE (n) *accent* (m) : hostile overtones = *des accents d'hostilité* ☠ → accent.

OVERTURE (n) *ouverture* (f) : the overture of an opera = *l'ouverture d'un opéra*, peace overtures = *des ouvertures de paix* ☠ → opening. **to make overtures** = *faire des propositions* : he's making overtures to the boss's wife = *il fait des propositions à la femme du patron.*

OVERTURN (to, -ed) **1/** *se retourner* : the truck/boat overturned = *le camion/le bateau s'est retourné* ⓪ to capsize = *chavirer* ☠ → to return **2/** *faire tomber* : to overturn a government = *faire tomber un gouvernement* ⓪ to overthrow = *renverser.*

OVERWEIGHT (adj) **1/** *trop gros, grosse* : her husband's overweight = *son mari est trop gros* ⓪ obese = *obèse* ≠ underweight = *trop maigre* **2/** *en excédent* : our luggage was 2 pounds overweight = *nous avions 1 kilo de bagages en excédent.*

OVERWHELM (to, -ed) **1/** *accabler* : all these worries are overwhelming me = *tous ces soucis m'accablent* **2/** *écraser* : our troops were overwhelmed = *nos troupes ont été écrasées* ☠ → to crash **to be overwhelmed by** = **1/** *être très touché de* : I was overwhelmed by his goodness = *j'ai été très touché de sa bonté* **2/** *être accablé par* : to be overwhelmed by s.o.'s death = *être accablé par la mort de qqn* **to be overwhelmed with** = *être accablé de* : I'm overwhelmed with work/problems = *je suis accablé de travail/de problèmes.*

OVERWHELMING (adj) *écrasant, -e* : an overwhelming defeat/majority = *une défaite/majorité écrasante* ☠ *une personnalité écrasante* = an overpowering personality.

OVERWROUGHT (adj) *à bout de nerfs* : exhausted and overwrought parents = *des parents épuisés et à bout de nerfs* ⓪ wound up = *sur les nerfs.*

OWE (to, -d) *devoir* : I owe you $ 100 = *je vous dois 100 dollars* **to owe to** = *devoir à* : he owes his success to hard work = *il doit son succès à un travail acharné* **to owe it to oneself to** = *mériter de* : you owe it to yourself to take a vacation = *vous méritez de prendre des vacances* ☠ *comme il se doit* = as is right — *je dois (y aller demain)* = I have to (go tomorrow) — *vous devriez y aller* = you should/ought to go.

OWING TO (prep) *en raison de* : owing to the strike, all mail's late = *en raison des grèves, tout le courrier a du retard* ⓪ due to = *par suite de.*

OWL (n) *chouette* (f), *hibou* (m) ⓪ bat = *chauve-souris* ☠ *une vieille chouette* = an old hag — *chouette !* = great !

OZONE

OWN (pron) **to be on one's own** = 1/ *être tout seul* : I'm on my own this weekend = *je suis tout seul ce week-end* ⓪ alone = *seul* 2/ *être à son compte* : he's in advertising and is on his own = *il travaille à son compte dans la publicité* 3/ *se débrouiller tout seul* : she's been on her own since she's 15 = *elle se débrouille toute seule depuis qu'elle a 15 ans*, you're on your own ! = *débrouille-toi tout seul !*
to come into one's own = *se réaliser* : she hasn't yet come into her own as a painter = *elle ne s'est pas encore réalisée en tant que peintre* ⓪ to make a name for o.s. = *se faire un nom* ☠ → to realize
to get one's own back = *prendre sa revanche* ⓪ to get one's in = *avoir sa vengeance*

to hold one's own = *bien se défendre* : I can hold my own at tennis = *ie me défends bien au tennis* ⓪ to be good at = *être bon en*
to make it on one's own = *se faire tout seul* : her father's famous, but she made it on her own = *son père est célèbre, mais elle s'est faite toute seule*
of one's own = 1/ *de son côté* : her husband's rich but she has money of her own = *son mari est riche, mais elle a de l'argent de son côté* 2/ *son propre* : she has a car of her own = *elle a sa propre voiture* 3/ *bien à soi* : she has a charm of her own = *elle a un charme bien à elle*
on one's own = *tout seul* : she decided on her own = *elle a décidé toute seule.*

OWN (adj) *propre* : my own car/money = *ma propre voiture/mon propre argent* ☠ → clean

at your own risk = *à vos risques et périls*
to be left to one's own devices = *être livré à soi-même*
he can stew in his own juice = *il peut cuire/mariner dans son jus*
to dig one's own grave = *creuser sa propre tombe*
to give s.o. a taste/dose of his own medicine = *rendre à qqn la monnaie de sa pièce*
in my own good time = *quand bon me semblera* : I'll do it in my own good time = *je le*

ferai quand bon me semblera
in one's own right = *par soi-même* : her father's famous, but she's well-known in her own right = *son père est célèbre, mais elle est connue par elle-même*
to know one's own mind = *savoir ce qu'on veut*
of one's own accord = *de son propre gré* ⓪ willingly = *de bon gré*
of his own free will = *de son propre gré*
one's own ... = *... soi-même* :

she does her own shopping = *elle fait ses courses elle-même*
one's own flesh and blood = *la chair de sa chair* ⓪ kin = *les siens*
to paddle one's own canoe = *mener seul sa barque*
to stand on one's own (two) feet = *voler de ses propres ailes* ≠ to be tied to one's mother's apron strings = *être accroché aux jupes de sa mère*
to take one's own life = *se donner la mort.*

OWN (to, -ed) *être propriétaire de* : they own their car = *ils sont propriétaires de leur voiture* ☠ → to possess

who owns (this car) ? = *à qui appartient (cette voiture) ?* = who does (this car) belong to ?
you don't own me ! = *je ne t'appartiens pas !*
to own up = *avouer* : it's important that you own

up and apologize = *il est important que tu avoues et que tu t'excuses* ⓪ to make a clean breast = *faire son mea culpa* ☠ → to confess.

OWNER (n) *propriétaire (m, f)* : who's the car's owner ? = *qui est le propriétaire de cette voiture ?* ☠ → proprietor.

OX (n, -en) *bœuf (m)* ⓪ bull = *taureau* ☠ → beef.

OXYGEN (n) *oxygène (m)* ⓪ ozone = ←.

OYSTER (n) *huître (f)* ⓪ seafood = *fruits de mer.*

OZONE (n) *ozone (m)* ⓪ atmosphere = *atmosphère.*

PACE (n) *allure* (f) : he walked at a rapid pace = *il mar-chait à vive allure* ⓧ rhythm = *rythme*
to keep pace with = *suivre le rythme de* : supply can't keep pace with demand = *l'offre ne peut pas suivre le rythme de la demande*
to put s.o. through the paces = *faire faire ses preuves à qqn*
to set the pace = *donner le ton* = to set the tone
☠ → allure.

PACE (to, -d) **to pace up and down** = *faire les cent pas* : the students were pacing up and down waiting for the results = *les étudiants faisaient les cent pas en atten-dant les résultats.*

PACEMAKER (n) *pacemaker* (m), *stimulateur* (m) *cardia-que* ⓧ open-heart surgery = *chirurgie à cœur ouvert.*

PACESETTER (n) *locomotive* (f) : he's a pacesetter in the fashion world = *c'est une locomotive dans le monde de la mode* ⓧ leader = ← ☠ *locomotive (train)* = *locomotive.*

PACIFIC (adj) **the Pacific Ocean** = *l'océan Pacifique.*

PACIFIST (n) *pacifiste* (m, f) : even pacifists demon-strated = *même les pacifistes ont manifesté* ⓧ con-scientious objector = *objecteur de conscience* **PACIFISM** (n) *pacifisme* (m).

PACIFY (to, -ied) *calmer, pacifier* (country) : his apol-ogies pacified the boss = *ses excuses ont calmé le patron* ⓧ to soothe = *apaiser* ≠ to anger = *mettre en colère* ☠ → to calm.

PACK (n) *paquet* (m), *meute* (f) (wolves, dogs) : a pack of cigarettes = *un paquet de cigarettes*
a pack of lies = *un tissu de mensonges*
☠ *mettre le paquet* = to go all out
— *gagner un paquet* = to make a bundle
— *envoyer un paquet* = to send a package/bundle
— *un paquet de nerfs/d'os* = a bag of nerves/bones.

PACK (to, -ed) *faire ses valises/ses bagages* : I have to pack tonight = *il faut que je fasse mes valises/mes baga-ges ce soir* ≠ to unpack = *défaire ses valises/ses bagages*
to be packed = *être plein à craquer* : the theater/suit-case was packed = *le théâtre/la valise était plein(e) à cra-quer* ⓧ to be jammed = *être bourré*

to pack (them) in = *faire salle comble* : the show's packing them in = *le spectacle fait salle comble* ⓧ to be a sellout = *jouer à guichets fermés*
to pack into = 1/ *condenser en* : the European trip was packed into ten days = *le voyage en Europe a été con-densé en dix jours* 2/ *s'entasser dans* : people pack into the subway during rush hours = *les gens s'entassent dans le métro aux heures d'affluence* = people pile into the subway during rush hours
to pack off = *expédier* : she packs her kids off to her mother's every summer = *tous les étés, elle expédie ses gosses chez sa mère* ☠ → to ship
to pack up and go = *prendre ses cliques et ses claques et partir* : she packed up and went to California = *elle a pris ses cliques et ses claques et est partie pour la Cali-fornie* → TO LEAVE.

PACKAGE (n) *paquet* (m) : send the package airmail = *envoyez le paquet par avion* ⓧ parcel = *colis*
package deal = *règlement global* : the unions agreed to a package deal = *les syndicats ont accepté un règlement global*
package tour = *voyage organisé* : our trip was a package tour = *nous sommes partis en voyage organisé* ☠ → pack.

PACT (n) *pacte* (m) : to sign a pact = *signer un pacte* ⓧ deal = *arrangement.*

PAD (n) 1/ *bloc* (m) : I need a pad to take notes = *j'ai besoin d'un bloc pour prendre des notes* ⓧ notebook = *carnet*
☠ *(les féministes) en bloc* = (feminists) as a whole
— *acheter en bloc* = to buy in bulk
— *faire bloc contre* = to unite against
2/ *appart'* (m) : she's got a fantastic pad in Miami = *elle a un super appart' à Miami* ⓧ house = *maison.*

PAD (to, -ded) 1/ *faire du remplissage* : to pad a book = *faire du remplissage dans un livre* 2/ *saler* : to pad a bill/an expense account = *saler une addition/une note de frais.*

PADDING (n) *remplissage* (m) : it's a big book, but there's a lot of padding = *c'est un gros livre, mais il y a beaucoup de remplissage* ⓧ yakety-yak = *blabla.*

447

PADDY WAGON (n) *panier (m) à salade* : they hauled the rioters off in the paddy wagon = *ils ont embarqué les émeutiers dans le panier à salade* ⊕ patrol car = *voiture de patrouille.*

PAGAN (n, adj) *païen, -enne* = heathen **PAGANISM** (n) *paganisme (m).*

PAGE (n) *page (f)* : page 47 is missing = *il manque la page 47* ⊕ leaf = *feuille*
☠ *tourner la page* = to turn over a new leaf
— *la page des affaires (du « Times »)* = the business section (of the "Times")
— *être à la page* = to be hep.

PAID (adj) *payé, -e* : highly paid = *très bien payé* ≠ unpaid = *impayé*
paid holidays/vacation = *congés payés.*

PAID-UP (adj) *entièrement payé, -e* : paid-up bills = *des factures entièrement payées* = paid for.

PAIL (n) *seau (m)* : a pail of water = *un seau d'eau* = a bucket of water ☠ → bucket.

PAIN (n) *douleur (f)* : I have a pain in my back = *j'ai une douleur dans le dos* ⊕ ache = *mal* ≠ painkiller = *calmant*
to be a pain = *être pénible* : this work's/you're a pain ! = *ce travail est/tu es pénible !* ⊕ a nuisance = *empoisonnant*
to be in great pain = *souffrir beaucoup*
you give me a pain ! = *tu me cours sur le haricot !* ⊕ you're getting on my nerves ! = *tu me tapes sur les nerfs !*
a pain in the ass = *un emmerdeur/quelqu'un/quelque chose d'emmerdant/de chiant* : what a pain in the ass you are ! = *quel emmerdeur !/ce que tu es emmerdant/chiant !*, this work's a pain in the ass = *ce travail est emmerdant/chiant*
a pain in the neck = *quelqu'un/quelque chose de casse-pieds* : you're/this work's a pain in the neck = *vous êtes/ce travail est casse-pieds*
to take (great) pains = *se donner du mal* : she took (great) pains with this work = *elle s'est donné du mal pour ce travail* ⊕ to go to a lot of trouble = *se donner beaucoup de mal*
to writhe in pain = *se tordre de douleur* : he was hit and writhed in pain = *il a été touché et s'est tordu de douleur.*

PAIN (to, -ed) **it pains me to (see you like that)** = *ça me peine de (vous voir comme ça)* ≠ I enjoy ... = *ça me plaît de ...*

PAINFUL (adj) *douloureux, -euse* (wound), *pénible* : a painful subject = *un sujet pénible* ☠ *ce que tu es pénible ! = you're a pain !*

PAINFULLY (adv) *si ... que ça fait peine à voir* : she's painfully shy = *elle est si timide que ça fait peine à voir*
it's painfully clear that (he'll refuse) = *il n'est que trop clair qu'(il va refuser).*

PAINKILLER (n) *calmant (m)* : I need a painkiller = *j'ai besoin d'un calmant* ⊕ analgesic = *analgésique.*

PAINLESS (adj) **1/** *indolore* : X-rays are painless = *les rayons X sont indolores* **2/** *sans problèmes* : a painless way to lose weight/to break up = *comment maigrir/rompre sans problèmes.*

PAINSTAKING (adj) *assidu, -e* : painstaking research = *une recherche assidue* ⊕ careful = *soigneux.*

PAINT (n) *peinture (f)* : a coat of paint = *une couche de peinture* ⊕ paintbrush = *pinceau*
☠ *une peinture* = a painting
— *je ne peux pas le voir en peinture* = I can't stand him.

PAINT (to, -ed) *peindre* : he started painting at 50 = *il a commencé à peindre à 50 ans* ⊕ to draw = *dessiner*, to dabble = *barbouiller.*

PAINTER (n) *peintre (m, f)* : Picasso was a great painter = *Picasso était un grand peintre* ⊕ sculptor = *sculpteur.*

PAINTING (n) **1/** *peinture (f)* : an oil painting = *une peinture à l'huile* ⊕ canvas = *toile*, frame = *cadre*, lithography = *lithographie*, watercolor = *aquarelle* **2/** (inv) *peinture (f)* : I have to do some painting = *j'ai de la peinture à faire* ☠ → paint.

PAIR (n) *paire (f)* : a pair of gloves = *une paire de gants* ⊕ two = *deux*
a pair of jeans/slacks = *un jean/un pantalon*
what a pair of (fools) ! = *quelle paire d'(imbéciles) !*
☠ *ses pairs* = his peers
— *aller de pair* = to go hand in hand
— *se faire la paire* = to make a getaway.

PAIR OFF (to, -ed) *se mettre deux par deux* : the kids paired off and went looking for the dog = *les gosses se sont mis deux par deux pour chercher le chien.*

PAJAMAS (n pl) *pyjama (m)* : I never wear pajamas = *je ne mets jamais de pyjama* = pyjamas (GB) ⊕ nightgown = *chemise de nuit*, bathrobe = *robe de chambre.*

PAKISTAN (n) *Pakistan (m)* **PAKISTANI** (n, adj) *Pakistanais, -e.*

PAL (n) *copain, copine* : Joe's a pal of mine = *Joe est un de mes copains* ⊕ buddy = *pote*, friend = *ami*
to be great pals = *être très copains* ⊕ to get on like a house on fire = *s'entendre comme larrons en foire.*

PALACE (n) *palais (m)* : kings built palaces = *les rois construisaient des palais* ⊕ castle = *château*
☠ *le palais Bourbon* = the French National Assembly
— *palais de justice* = court.

PAL AROUND (to, -led) *copiner* : our kids pal around together = *nos gosses copinent ensemble* ⊕ to hang out together = *être toujours fourrés ensemble.*

PALE (adj, -r, -st) *pâle* : a pale complexion = *un teint pâle* ⊕ palish = *pâlot*, sallow = *cireux*, ashen = *terreux* ≠ flushed = *tout rouge* ☠ *une pâle imitation de* = a poor copy of.

PALEFACE (n) *visage pâle* (m) ≠ Indian = *Indien*.

PALIMONY (n inv) *pension* (f) *versée à un concubin après séparation.*

PALLBEARER (n) *personne qui porte le cercueil* ⓒ *funeral procession* = *cortège funèbre.*

PALM (n) *paume* (f) : the palm of the hand = *la paume de la main*
to grease s.o.'s palm = *graisser la patte à qqn* ⓒ to slip s.o. stg = *glisser un billet à qqn*
to have s.o. in the palm of one's hand = *faire ce qu'on veut de qqn* ⓒ to twist s.o. around one's little finger = *mener qqn par le bout du nez*
palm tree = *palmier.*

PALM (to, -ed) **to palm stg off on s.o.** = *refiler qqch à qqn* : he palmed the stolen watches off on the tourists = *il a refilé les montres volées aux touristes.*

PALSY-WALSY (adj) *comme cul et chemise* : he's palsy-walsy with the Mafia = *il est comme cul et chemise avec la Mafia* ⓒ bosom pals = *copains comme cochons.*

PALTRY (adj, -ier, -iest) *piètre* : she earns a paltry $ 200 a week = *elle gagne la piètre somme de 200 dollars par semaine* ⓒ trivial = *insignifiant*
☠ *faire piètre figure* = to cut a sorry figure
— *un piètre écrivain* = an unexceptional writer.

PAMPER (to, -ed) *chouchouter, choyer* : she pampers her children = *elle chouchoute/choie ses enfants* ⓒ to coddle = *dorloter*, to spoil = *gâter.*

PAMPHLET (n) *pamphlet* (m) (political), *opuscule* (m) : the government published a pamphlet on the dangers of smoking = *le gouvernement a publié un opuscule sur les dangers du tabac* ⓒ booklet = *fascicule.*

PAN (n) *poêle* (f) : frying pan = *poêle à frire*
to jump out of the frying pan into the fire = *tomber de Charybde en Scylla* ⓒ to go from bad to worse = *aller de mal en pis.*

PAN (to, -ned) *éreinter* : the critics panned the play = *les critiques ont éreinté la pièce* ⓒ to kill = *massacrer*
to pan out = *se concrétiser* : our plan didn't pan out = *notre projet ne s'est pas concrétisé* ⓒ to take shape = *prendre forme*
☠ *ce travail m'éreinte* = this work exhausts me.

PANACEA (n) *panacée* (f) : there's no panacea for inflation = *il n'y a pas de panacée contre l'inflation.*

PANCAKE (n) *pancake* (m) (genre de crêpe qu'on mange au petit déjeuner) ⓒ maple syrup = *sirop d'érable.*

PANEL (n) 1/ *tribune* (f) (discussion), *jury* (m) (game) : there were ten members on the panel = *il y avait dix participants à la tribune/dix personnes dans le jury* ⓒ panelist = *membre d'une tribune/d'un jury* ☠ *tribune* → grandstand, *jury* → jury
2/ *panneau* (m) : oak panels = *des panneaux en chêne*

a panel discussion = *une tribune* ⓒ symposium = ←
☠ *tomber dans le panneau* = to fall into the trap
— *panneau de signalisation* = traffic sign.

PANG (n) *tiraillement* (m) : pangs of jealousy = *les tiraillements de la jalousie*, hunger pangs = *les tiraillements de la faim* ☠ *des tiraillements entre le Sénat et le Congrès* = pull/friction between Senate and Congress.

PANIC (n) *panique* (f) : the bomb scare caused a terrible panic = *l'alerte à la bombe a causé une panique terrible* ⓒ dread = *épouvante*
don't push the panic button ! = *pas de panique !* ⓒ stay cool ! = *t'emballe pas !*
a panic = *quelque chose d'impayable* : the film was a panic ! = *le film était impayable !* ⓒ a riot = *quelque chose de désopilant.*

PANIC (to, -ked) *paniquer* : people panicked when the fire started = *les gens ont paniqué quand l'incendie s'est déclaré* ≠ to keep one's cool = *garder son sang-froid.*

PANICKY (adj) *paniqué, -e* : panicky before exams = *paniqué avant les examens* ⓒ frightened = *effrayé*, frantic = *affolé.*

PANIC-STRICKEN (adj) *pris, -e de panique* : the refugees were panic-stricken = *les réfugiés étaient pris de panique* ⓒ terrified = *terrifié.*

PANOPLY (n, -ies) *panoplie* (f), *superbe collection* (f) : a panoply of revolvers = *une panoplie de revolvers*, a panoply of antique dolls = *une superbe collection de poupées anciennes.*

PANORAMA (n) *panorama* (m) ⓒ view = *vue.*

PANSY (n, -ies) *tante* (f) : a bar for pansies = *un bar de tantes* ⓒ queer = *pédé*, fruit = *tapette* ☠ → aunt.

PANT (to, -ed) *haleter* : he was panting when he reached the top of the stairs = *il est arrivé haletant en haut de l'escalier* ⓒ to be out of breath = *être à bout de souffle.*

PANTHER (n) *panthère* (f) ⓒ jaguar = ←.

PANTIES (n pl) *(petite) culotte* (f) : sexy panties = *une (petite) culotte sexy* ⓒ underpants = *slip*
☠ *porter la culotte* = to wear the pants
— *ne rien avoir dans la culotte* = to have no balls.

PANTOMIME (n) *pantomime* (f) : a play in pantomime = *une (pièce de) pantomime* ⓒ mime = ←.

PANTRY (n, -ies) *garde-manger* (m).

PANTS (n pl) *pantalon* (m), *futal* (m) (LV) : I like your pants = *j'aime bien ton pantalon/ton futal* = slacks ⓒ dungarees = *jean*
to be caught with one's pants down = *être surpris dans une situation terriblement gênante* ⓒ to be caught unawares = *être pris de court*
to kid the pants off of s.o. = *mettre qqn en boîte* ⓒ to tease = *taquiner*
to lick the pants off of s.o. = *flanquer une déculottée*

à qqn/battre qqn à plate couture ⓄⒹ to give s.o. a licking = *flanquer une raclée à qqn*
a pair of pants = *un pantalon*
a pants suit = *un tailleur-pantalon* = a pantsuit
to want to get into s.o.'s pants = *vouloir s'envoyer qqn* ⓄⒹ to want to make s.o. = *vouloir se faire qqn*
to wear the pants = *porter la culotte* ⓄⒹ to run the show = *mener la danse.*

PAPER (n) **1/** *papier (m)* : I have to write a letter, do you have some paper ? = *il faut que j'écrive une lettre, est-ce que vous avez du papier ?*, wrapping paper = *papier d'emballage*, writing paper = *papier à lettres*, carbon (paper) = *(papier) carbone*, a sheet of paper = *une feuille de papier* ⓄⒹ cardboard = *carton*, paperweight = *presse-papiers*, stationery store = *papeterie* ☠ *être réglé comme du papier à musique* = to go like clockwork **2/** *journal (m)* : I haven't read today's paper yet = *je n'ai pas encore lu le journal (d'aujourd'hui)* = I haven't read today's newspaper yet ☠ → journal
go peddle your papers ! = *va aux fraises !* → BUZZ OFF !
it isn't worth the paper it's written on = *c'est du papier gâché*
on paper = *sur le papier* : the idea seems good on paper = *sur le papier, l'idée semble bonne*
paper clip = *trombone*
paper plates/glasses = *assiettes/verres en carton*
paper work = *paperasserie*
paper money = *papier-monnaie*
show me your papers ! = *montrez-moi vos papiers !*

PAPERBACK (n) *livre (m)* broché, *livre (m)* de poche : paperbacks are cheap = *les livres brochés sont bon marché* ≠ hardcover = *livre relié.*

PAR (n) **above** ≠ **below par** = *au-dessus* ≠ *au-dessous de la moyenne* : his test results are above ≠ below par = *ses résultats d'examen sont au-dessus* ≠ *au-dessous de la moyenne*
on a par with = *sur un pied d'égalité* : American wine isn't yet on a par with French wine = *les vins américains et les vins français ne sont pas encore sur un pied d'égalité.*

PAR (adj) **to be par for** = *(faire) en moyenne* : a mistake a day is par for her work = *elle fait en moyenne une faute par jour dans son travail*
that's par for the course = *ce n'est pas étonnant* → THAT'S LIFE !

PARACHUTE (n) *parachute (m)* : to tear one's parachute = *déchirer son parachute* **PARACHUTE** (to, -d) *parachuter* : they parachuted food to the refugees = *ils ont parachuté des vivres aux réfugiés* ⓄⒹ to airlift = *faire un pont aérien.*

PARADE (n) *parade (f)* : let's watch the parade = *allons voir la parade* ⓄⒹ march = *défilé.*

PARADISE (n) *paradis (m)* : life is no paradise = *la vie n'est pas un paradis* ≠ hell = *enfer*

☠ *vous ne l'emporterez pas en paradis !* = you won't get away with it !/I'll get mine in !
— *aller au paradis* = to go to heaven.

PARADOX (n, -es) *paradoxe (m)* : a nonviolent person killing his mother is a paradox = *c'est un paradoxe de tuer sa mère quand on est non-violent* ⓄⒹ contradiction = ← **PARADOXICAL** (adj) *paradoxal, -e* **PARADOXICALLY** (adv) *paradoxalement.*

PARAGRAPH (n) *paragraphe (m)* : leave out the second paragraph = *supprimez le second paragraphe* ⓄⒹ chapter = *chapitre.*

PARAKEET (n) *perruche (f)* ⓄⒹ parrot = *perroquet.*

PARALLEL (n) *parallèle (m)* : to draw a parallel between the two cases = *établir un parallèle entre les deux cas*
without parallel = *sans pareil* : stupidity without parallel = *une stupidité sans pareille.*

PARALYSIS (n, -es) *paralysie (f)* : paralysis of the economy = *paralysie de l'économie* **PARALYZE** (to, -d) *paralyser* : stage fright paralyzed me = *le trac m'a paralysé* ⓄⒹ to immobilize = *immobiliser* **PARALYZING** (adj) *paralysant, -e*, qui paralyse : a paralyzing strike = *une grève qui paralyse tout* = a crippling strike, paralyzing fear = *une peur paralysante.*

PARAMOUNT (adj) *de tout, -e premier, -ère* : of paramount importance = *de toute première importance* ⓄⒹ fundamental = *fondamental.*

PARANOIA (n) *paranoïa (f)* ⓄⒹ schizophrenia = *schizophrénie* **PARANOIAC** (n) *paranoïaque (m, f)* ⓄⒹ schizophrenic = *schizophrène* **PARANOID** (adj) *paranoïaque, parano* : you're too paranoid ! no one's following you ! = *vous êtes trop paranoïaque/parano ! personne ne vous suit !*

PARAPHERNALIA (n inv) *bazar (m)* : he brought along all his diving paraphernalia = *il a apporté tout son bazar de plongée* ⓄⒹ junk = *machins* ☠ *quel bazar !* = what a mess !

PARASITE (n) *parasite (m)* : stars are surrounded by parasites = *les vedettes sont entourées de parasites* ⓄⒹ leech = *sangsue* ☠ *parasites (radio)* = static (radio).

PARCEL (n) *colis (m)* : lots of parcels at Christmastime = *beaucoup de colis à l'époque de Noël* ⓄⒹ package = *paquet.*

PARDON (n) *grâce (f)* : Presidential pardon = *grâce présidentielle* ☠ → grace
I beg your pardon = *je vous demande pardon* ⓄⒹ I'm sorry = *je suis désolé.*

PARDON (to, -ed) **1/** *gracier* : the President pardoned the murderer = *le Président a gracié le meurtrier* ⓄⒹ to absolve = *absoudre* **2/** *pardonner* : I'll never pardon you = *je ne vous pardonnerai jamais*
pardon me for (being late) = *pardonnez-moi d'(être en retard)*
☠ « to pardon » *est moins employé que* « to forgive ».

PARENT (n) *parent (m)* : my parents live in Iowa = *mes parents habitent dans l'Iowa* ⓓ father = *père*, mother = *mère*
parent company = *société mère*
☠ *un parent éloigné/pauvre* = a distant/poor relative.

PARENTAL (adj) *parental, -e* : parental authority = *autorité parentale.*

PARENTHESIS (n, -es) *parenthèse (f)* : to put a sentence into parentheses = *mettre une phrase entre parenthèses* ⓓ brackets = *crochets*
☠ *entre parenthèses ...* = incidentally ...
— *ouvrir une parenthèse* = to digress from the subject.

PARIS (n) *Paris* **PARISIAN** (n, adj) *Parisien, -enne.*

PARISH (n, -es) *paroisse (f)* : parish priest = *curé de la paroisse* ⓓ parishioner = *paroissien.*

PARK (n) *parc (m)* : a national park = *un parc national* ⓓ garden = *jardin* ☠ *parc (pour enfants)* = playpen.

PARK (to, -ed) *(se) garer* : where can I park the car ? = *où est-ce que je peux garer la voiture ?* ⓓ to double-park = *se garer en double file* ☠ *gare à toi si ...* = you'd better watch it if ...

PARKING (n inv) *(le fait de) se garer* : there's easy parking near the restaurant = *on peut se garer facilement près du restaurant*
no parking = *stationnement interdit*
a parking place/spot = *une place (pour se garer)*
parking ticket = contravention (pour stationnement interdit)
a parking lot = *un parking.*

PARLEY (n) *pourparlers (m pl)* : peace parleys = *des pourparlers de paix* ⓓ conference = *conférence*, round table = *table ronde.*

PARLIAMENT (n) *parlement (m)* : a member of Parliament = *un membre du Parlement.*

PARODY (n, -ies) *parodie (f)* : a parody of justice = *une parodie de justice* ⓓ caricature = ←.

PAROLE (n) **on parole** = *en liberté conditionnelle* ⓓ time off for good behavior = *remise de peine (pour bonne conduite)* **PAROLE** (to, -d) *mettre en liberté conditionnelle.*

PARROT (n) *perroquet (m)* : parrots talk = *les perroquets parlent* ⓓ canary = *canari.*

PARRY (to, -ied) *se dérober à* : to parry a question = *se dérober à une question* ⓓ to duck = *esquiver.*

PART (n) **1/** *partie (f)* : (a) part of the work is done = *une partie du travail est faite*, what part of the US do you like best ? = *quelle partie des États-Unis préférez-vous ?* ⓓ piece = *morceau* ≠ the whole = *le tout*

☠ *les deux parties sont d'accord* = both parties agree
— *une partie de football* = a football game/match
— *la partie civile* = the plaintiff
— *abandonner la partie* = to throw in one's hand
— *prendre qqn à partie* = to take s.o. to task

— *avoir partie liée avec qqn* = to be hand in glove with s.o.
— *une partie carrée* = a two-couple swing
— *ce n'est que partie remise* = I'll take a rain check on it
— *une partie de jambes en l'air* = a roll in the hay
— *ce n'est pas une partie de plaisir* = it's no joyride

2/ *rôle (m)* : she got the part = *elle a obtenu le rôle* ⓓ to try out = *auditionner* ☠ → role

to be part and parcel of = *faire partie intégrante de* : ambition is part and parcel of politics = *l'ambition fait partie intégrante de la politique*
to be part of the family = *faire partie de la famille*
for my part = *pour ma part* : for my part, I prefer a pizza = *pour ma part, je préfère une pizza* ⓓ as for me = *quant à moi*
to do one's part = *y mettre du sien* : everyone must do his part = *tout le monde doit y mettre du sien* ⓓ to give a helping hand = *prêter main-forte*
to play a ≠ **no part in** = *jouer*

un rôle ≠ *ne pas jouer de rôle dans* : he played a ≠ no part in the coup d'état = *il a joué un rôle* ≠ *il n'a pas joué de rôle dans le coup d'État* ⓓ to be instrumental in = *contribuer à*
in part = *en partie* : that's true in part = *c'est vrai en partie* ≠ totally = *totalement*
in this part of (the country) = *dans cette partie du (pays)*
in these parts = *dans les parages* : she lives in these parts = *elle habite dans les parages* ⓓ in the area = *dans le coin*
one's part = *sa part* : don't forget to give me my part = *n'oublie pas de me donner ma*

part ⓓ my cut = *ma part du gâteau*
to look the part = *avoir le physique de l'emploi*
part of (the year) = *une partie de (l'année)*
to take part in (the debate) = *prendre part au (débat)* ⓓ to participate in = *participer à*
to take s.o.'s part = *prendre le parti de qqn* : she always takes her mother's part = *elle prend toujours le parti de sa mère* ⓓ to be on s.o.'s side = *être du côté de qqn*
I want no part of (the whole thing) = *je ne veux pas être mêlé à (tout ceci).*

| **PART** (adj) **part owner** = *copropriétaire* : he's part owner of the firm = *il est copropriétaire de l'entreprise* | **part time** = (*à*) *temps partiel* : to work part time = *travailler à temps partiel* ≠ full time = (*à*) *temps plein/complet.* |

PART (adv) *en partie* : to be part French = *être en partie français.*

PART (to, -ed) *se quitter* : we parted friends = *nous nous sommes quittés amis* ☠ → to quit
to part with = *se défaire de* : she hates to part with her old furniture = *ça l'ennuie de se défaire de ses vieux meubles.*

PARTAKE IN/OF (to, -d) *participer à* : to partake of/in a meal/a legacy = *participer à un repas/un héritage.*

PARTIAL (adj) **1/** *partial, -e* : try not to be partial = *essayez de ne pas être partial* ① biased = *de parti pris* ≠ impartial = ← ☠ *une opinion partiale* = a biased opinion **2/** *partiel, -elle* : partial payment/success = *paiement/succès partiel* ≠ complete = *complet*
to be partial to (French wines) = *avoir une préférence marquée pour (les vins français)* ① to have a soft spot for = *avoir un faible pour*
☠ *élections partielles* = by-elections
— *travail à temps partiel* = part-time work.

PARTIALITY (n, -ies) *partialité (f)* : to show partiality = *faire preuve de partialité.*

PARTIALLY (adv) *partiellement* : I was partially wrong, I know = *je sais, j'avais partiellement tort* ① in part = *en partie.*

PARTICIPANT (n) *participant, -e* : ten participants in the debate = *dix participants au débat* ① contestant = *concurrent.*

PARTICIPATE IN (to, -d) *participer à* : 10 people participated in the debate = *10 personnes ont participé au débat* ① to contribute to = *contribuer à.*

PARTICIPATION (n inv) *participation (f)* : with the participation of his friends, he put the deal together = *il a monté l'affaire avec la participation de ses amis* ① collaboration = ←
☠ *participation électorale* = election turnout
— *participation aux bénéfices* = profit sharing.

PARTICIPLE (n) *participe (m)* : present/past participle = *participe présent/passé.*

PARTICULAR (n) **in particular** = *en particulier* : I like Italian food, pizza in particular = *j'aime la cuisine italienne, en particulier la pizza* ① notably = *notamment.*

PARTICULAR (adj) *particulier, -ère* : to listen with particular interest = *écouter avec un intérêt particulier*, no particular reason = *aucune raison particulière* ① special = *spécial*
to be particular about = *être exigeant sur le choix de* : she's particular about what she eats/who she sleeps with = *elle est exigeante sur le choix de ce qu'elle mange/de ses amants* ① picky = *difficile*

☠ *amitiés particulières* = "special" friendships (homosexual)
— *leçon particulière* = private lesson.

PARTICULARITY (n, -ies) *particularité (f)* : the new model has several particularities = *le nouveau modèle a plusieurs particularités* ① feature = *trait.*

PARTICULARLY (adv) *particulièrement* : I'm particularly tired today = *je suis particulièrement fatigué aujourd'hui* ① specially = *spécialement.*

PARTICULARS (n pl) **the particulars** = *des précisions* : give me the particulars = *donnez-moi des précisions* ① details = *détails.*

PARTISAN (n) *partisan (m)* : partisans of the revolution = *les partisans de la révolution* ① adherent = *adhérent* ≠ adversary = *adversaire*
☠ *il est partisan du moindre effort* = he's always looking out for the easy way
— *un partisan de* = an advocate/a proponent of.

PARTITION (n) *partition (f)* : the partition of Poland = *la partition de la Pologne* ① division = ← ☠ *partition (musique)* = score (music) **PARTITION** (to, -ed) *partager* : to partition a country = *partager un pays* ① to divide = *diviser* ☠ → to share.

PARTLY (adv) *en partie* : you were partly responsible = *vous étiez en partie responsable* = you were responsible in part.

PARTNER (n) *associé, -e* (business), *partenaire (m, f)* : a bridge partner = *un partenaire au bridge*, he's starting a new business and needs a partner = *il démarre une nouvelle affaire et a besoin d'un associé* **PARTNERSHIP** (n) association (f).

PARTS (n pl) *pièces (f pl)* : plane parts = *des pièces d'avion* ☠ → room.

PART-TIME (adj) *à temps partiel* : a part-time job = *un boulot à temps partiel* ≠ full-time = *à temps complet.*

PARTY (n, -ies) **1/** *soirée (f)* : we're giving a party on Saturday = *nous donnons une soirée samedi* ① wingding = *pince-fesses* ☠ → evening
2/ *parti (m)* : there are two major political parties in the United States = *il y a deux grands partis politiques aux États-Unis*
☠ *tirer parti de* = to take advantage of

— *un (beau) parti* = a (good) catch
— *prendre parti* = to take sides
— *prendre le parti de qqn* = to take s.o.'s part
— *être de parti pris* = to be biased
— *en prendre son parti* = to resign o.s.

3/ *partie (f)* : both parties must sign the contract = *les deux parties doivent signer le contrat* ☠ → part
to be a party to = *être complice de :* I won't be a party to it = *je ne veux pas en être complice* ≠ not to get involved in = *ne pas se mêler de*
party boy/girl = *fêtard, -e* ⓪ good-time Charley = *noceur*
party line = *ligne de téléphone commune :* there are

barely any more party lines in the United States = *il n'y a pratiquement plus de lignes de téléphone communes aux États-Unis*
party pooper = *tue-joie* ⓪ killjoy = *rabat-joie.*

PARTY (adj) *de soirée :* party clothes = *habits de soirée* ≠ casual = *décontracté*
party politics = *politique partisane/de parti.*

PARTY (to, -ied) *faire la fête :* when we were in New York we partied till the wee hours = *quand on était à New York, on faisait la fête jusqu'au petit matin* ⓪ to have a ball = *bien se marrer.*

PASS (n, -es) **1/** *perme (f) :* the privates got a two-day pass = *les deuxième classe ont eu une perme de deux jours* ⓪ a leave = *une permission* **2/** *laissez-passer (m inv) :* you'll need a pass to get into the building = *vous aurez besoin d'un laissez-passer pour entrer dans l'immeuble.*

---

to make passes at s.o. = *faire des avances à qqn* = to make advances to s.o. ⓪ to make a play for s.o. = *essayer de draguer qqn.*

PASS (to, -ed) **1/** *passer :* summer passed quickly = *l'été a passé vite,* I was in the street and a very pretty girl passed = *j'étais dans la rue et une très jolie fille est passée* **2/** *faire passer :* to pass a law = *faire passer une loi* ⓪ to vote = *voter* **3/** *doubler :* their car passed ours = *leur voiture nous a doublés* ⓪ to overtake = *dépasser* ☠ → to double **4/** *réussir :* I passed the exam = *j'ai réussi l'examen* ≠ to flunk = *être recalé à* ☠ → to succeed **5/** *passer :* pass me the sugar/salt = *passe-moi le sucre/sel* ⓪ give me = *donne-moi*

---

to pass away = *décéder :* he passed away last year = *il est décédé l'année dernière* ⓪ to go the way of all flesh = *rendre l'âme*
to pass by = **1/** *passer à côté de :* she feels that love passed her by = *elle a le sentiment qu'elle est passée à côté de l'amour* **2/** *passer :* I'll pass by later = *je passerai tout à l'heure*
to pass down = *se passer :* that tradition has been passed down over centuries = *cette tradition s'est passée de siècle en siècle* ⓪ to hand down = *se transmettre*
to pass for = *passer pour :* his wife looks so young she could pass for his daughter = *sa femme a l'air tellement jeune qu'elle pourrait passer pour sa fille* ⓪ to be considered as = *être considéré comme*
to pass o.s. off as = *se faire passer pour :* he passes himself off as a prince = *il se fait passer pour un*

prince ⓪ to make believe = *faire croire*
to pass out = **1/** *tomber dans les pommes :* after 10 drinks, she passed out = *après avoir bu 10 verres, elle est tombée dans les pommes* ⓪ to black out = *tourner de l'œil* **2/** *faire une distribution de :* they passed out coffee = *ils ont fait une distribution de café*
to pass over = *passer sur :* I'll pass over that remark = *je passerai sur cette remarque* ≠ to pick up = *relever*
to pass through = *être de passage (dans) :* we're not going to stay in Miami, we're just passing through = *nous n'allons pas rester à Miami, nous sommes juste de passage* ≠ to stay = *rester*
to pass up = *laisser passer :* you passed up a good opportunity = *vous avez laissé passer une bonne occasion* ⓪ to miss out on = *manquer*

☠ *ça s'est passé hier* = it happened yesterday
— *je m'en passerai* = I'll do/live without it
— *j'en passe (et des meilleures)* = I'll spare you the rest
— *comment cela s'est-il passé ?* = how did it go ?
— *je suis passé par là aussi* = I went through that too
— *cela passe avant tout* = that comes first
— *est-ce que tu peux me passer*

2 dollars ? = can you spare $ 2 ?
— *passer un examen* = to take an exam
— *passer une robe* = **1/** to get into a dress **2/** to try a dress on
— *il lui passe tout* = he always gives in to her
— *à quelle heure passe le film ?* = what time is the movie on ?/does the movie go on ?
— *passons !* = skip it !
— *se passer bien* ≠ *mal* = to

go well/fare well ≠ not to go well
— *passer prendre qqn* = to pick s.o. up
— *pouvez-vous me passer M. Smith ?* = can you connect me with Mr Smith ?
— *passer une commande* = to place an order
— *le message n'est pas passé* = the message didn't come across
— *tout son argent passe en*

| films = all his money goes into movies
— *passer sur beaucoup de choses* = to overlook a lot of things
— *ça lui a vite passé* = it wore off quickly
— *passer de mode* = to go out | of fashion
— *qu'est-ce qui se passe ?* = what's going on ?
— *passer son temps à dormir* = to spend one's time sleeping
— *passer une bonne soirée* = to have a nice evening | — *il passe bien à la télé* = he comes across/over well on TV
— *si vous avez le temps, passez* = if you have the time, stop by/come by
— *les démocrates sont passés* = the Democrats got in. |

PASSABLE (adj) *passable* : passable grades = *des notes passables* → AWFUL.

PASSAGE (n) *passage (m)* : a passage in a book = *un passage dans un livre* ⓒ extract = *extrait*
to book passage = *réserver une place (bateau)*
💀 *être de passage* = to be passing through
— *passage interdit* = no entry
— *un passage à vide* = a very low point.

PASSÉ (adj) *passé, -e de mode* : is rock and roll passé ? = *le rock and roll est-il passé de mode ?* ⓒ old-fashioned = *démodé* ≠ trendy = *à la page*.

PASSENGER (n) *passager, -ère* : all the passengers were killed in the crash = *tous les passagers ont été tués dans l'accident* ⓒ traveler = *voyageur* 💀 *passager clandestin* = stowaway.

PASSER-BY (n, passers-by) *passant, -e* : three passers-by were hit by bullets = *trois passants ont été touchés par des balles* ⓒ onlooker = *badaud*.

PASSING (adj) **passing grades** = *des notes qui permettent de passer (dans la classe supérieure)*
a passing fancy = *une passade* ⓒ love affair = *aventure sentimentale*.

PASSION (n inv) *passion (f)* : a marriage that never knew passion = *un ménage qui n'a jamais connu la passion* ⓒ emotion = *émotion*.

PASSIONATE (adj) 1/ *passionné, -e* : a passionate interest in politics = *un intérêt passionné pour la politique*, the debate was passionate = *le débat était passionné* 2/ *(qui a un tempérament) passionné, -e* : a passionate lover = *un amant passionné* ⓒ hot stuff = *qui a du tempérament*
💀 *elle aime les gens passionnés* = she likes very vibrant people
— *elle est passionnée de tennis* = she has a passion for tennis.

PASSIONATELY (adv) *passionnément* : she loves him passionately = *elle l'aime passionnément* ⓒ fanatically = *fanatiquement*.

PASSIVE (adj) *passif, -ive* : a passive personality = *une personnalité passive* ⓒ submissive = *soumis* **PASSIVELY** (adv) *passivement* : she obeyed passively = *elle a obéi passivement* **PASSIVITY** (n) *passivité (f)* : her passivity killed their relationship = *sa passivité a fichu en l'air leurs rapports*.

PASSKEY (n) *passe-partout (m inv)*, *passe (m)* = skeleton key 💀 *passe* → trick.

PASSOVER (n) *Pâque (f) juive*.

PASSPORT (n) *passeport (m)* : to deliver a passport = *délivrer un passeport*.

PASSWORD (n) *mot (m) de passe* : "Inch Allah" is the password = *le mot de passe est « Inch Allah »*.

PAST (n) *passé (m)* : her past is full of mystery = *son passé est entouré de mystère*	
in the past = *dans le passé* : they were friends in the past = *dans le passé, ils étaient amis* ≠ in the future = *à l'avenir*	**don't rake up the past** = *ne remuez pas le passé* ⓒ let sleeping dogs lie = *il ne faut pas réveiller le chat qui dort*.

PAST (adj) 1/ *passé, -e* : forget our past problems = *oublions nos problèmes passés* ≠ current = *actuel* 💀 *passé de mode* = passé 2/ *ancien, -enne* : the past mayor = *l'ancien maire* = the former mayor 💀 → ancient **for the past ten years** = *ces dix dernières années*.

PAST (prep) *passé* : the post office is two blocks past the hotel = *passé l'hôtel, la poste est à deux rues* ⓒ beyond = *au-delà de*

it's (ten) past (three) = *il est (trois) heures (dix)* ⓒ **it's (a quarter) past (four)** = *il est (quatre) heures et (quart)* **he's past forty** = *il a quarante ans passés* ≠ he's	not yet forty = *il n'a pas encore quarante ans* **I wouldn't put it past him !** = *je l'en crois tout à fait capable !* ⓒ it's just like him = *c'est bien lui*.

PAST (adv) **they drove/ran past him** = *ils l'ont dépassé en voiture/en courant*

THE PAST TENSE = LE PASSÉ COMPOSÉ (ET LE PASSÉ SIMPLE) : *il se forme, pour les verbes réguliers, en ajoutant « ed » à l'infinitif du verbe, et s'emploie pour un passé fini et précisé (par opposition au present perfect)*

I		j'ai		I		je n'ai pas	
you		tu as/vous avez		you		tu n'as/vous n'avez pas	
he/she	talked =	il/elle a		he/she	didn't talk =	il/elle n'a pas	
we		nous avons	parlé	we		nous n'avons pas	parlé
they		ils/elles ont		they		ils/elles n'ont pas	

— SYSTEM —

— did you talk to him { yesterday ? / a week ago ? / last year ? }
— yes, I did = *oui*
— yes, I talked to him yesterday = *oui, je lui ai parlé hier*

= *lui avez-vous parlé* { *hier ? / il y a une semaine ? / l'année dernière ?* }
— no, I didn't = *non*
— no, I didn't talk to him yesterday = *non, je ne lui ai pas parlé hier.*

PASTE (n inv) *colle (f) blanche* : buy some paste for the stamps = *achetez de la colle blanche pour les timbres*
PASTE (to, -d) *coller* : paste the stamps on the envelope = *colle les timbres sur l'enveloppe* = stick the stamps on the envelope ☠ → to stick.

PASTEL (n, adj) *pastel (m)* : pastel green = *vert pastel.*

PASTIME (n) *passe-temps (m inv), marotte (f)* : bridge is his pastime = *le bridge est son passe-temps/sa marotte* ⓪ bag = *truc.*

PASTOR (n) *pasteur (m)* ⓪ priest = *prêtre.*

PASTRAMI (n) *épaule (f) de bœuf fumée.*

PASTRY (n inv) *pâtisseries (f pl)* : buy some pastry = *achetez des pâtisseries* ⓪ cake = *gâteau*
a pastry shop = *une pâtisserie.*

PASTURE (n) *pâturage (m)* ⓪ meadow = *prairie*
to put s.o. out to pasture = *envoyer qqn planter ses choux* ⓪ to put s.o. on the shelf = *mettre qqn sur une voie de garage.*

PAT (adj) *tout, -e fait, -e* : there's no pat answer to the problem of world hunger = *il n'y a pas de réponse toute faite au problème de la faim dans le monde*
to have stg (down) pat = *connaître/savoir qqch sur le bout du doigt* : she has her French lesson down pat = *elle sait sa leçon de français sur le bout du doigt* ⓪ to know by heart = *savoir par cœur*
to stand pat = *tenir ferme* ≠ to give way = *céder.*

PAT (to, -ted) *tapoter* : he patted the dog on the head = *il a tapoté le chien sur la tête* ⓪ to stroke = *flatter (de la main).*

PATCH (n, -es) *pièce (f)* : I sewed a patch on your jeans = *j'ai cousu une pièce à ton jean* ⓪ patchwork = *←* ☠ → room.

PATCH UP (to, -ed) **to be patched up** = *s'être arrangé* : are things patched up between them ? = *est-ce que les choses se sont arrangées entre eux ?* ⓪ to make peace = *faire la paix.*

PATENT (n) *brevet (m) d'invention* : inventors take out patents = *les inventeurs prennent des brevets d'invention* ⓪ royalties = *droits d'auteur*
patent leather = *cuir verni.*

PATERNAL (adj) *paternel, -elle* = fatherly.

PATH (n) *sentier (m)* : the path is too narrow for horses = *le sentier est trop étroit pour le passage des chevaux* ⓪ way = *chemin*
our paths crossed = *nos chemins se sont croisés* ≠ it was a parting of the ways = *nous avons pris des chemins différents*
☠ *suivre les sentiers battus* = to follow hackneyed ways
— *hors des sentiers battus* = off the beaten track.

PATHETIC (adj) 1/ *pathétique* : it's pathetic to see children begging in the streets = *c'est pathétique de voir des enfants mendier dans les rues* ⓪ pitiful = *pitoyable* 2/ *minable* : a pathetic salary/play = *un salaire/une pièce minable* → AWFUL.

PATHETICALLY (adv) *d'une façon minable* : he writes pathetically = *il écrit d'une façon minable.*

PATHFINDER (n) 1/ *pionnier (m)* : a pathfinder in nuclear research = *un pionnier en recherche nucléaire* = a trailblazer ☠ → pioneer 2/ *éclaireur, -euse* : the tribe's pathfinder = *l'éclaireur de la tribu.*

PATHOLOGICAL (adj) *pathologique* : a pathological liar = *un menteur pathologique* ⓪ compulsive = *maladif.*

PATHOS (n) *pathos (m)* : there are passages of the book full of pathos = *il y a des passages pleins de pathos dans le livre.*

PATIENCE (n) *patience (f)* : to lose patience = *perdre patience* ≠ impatience = *←*
to have the patience of Job = *avoir une patience d'ange* ≠ to be quick-tempered = *avoir la tête près du bonnet*

to try s.o.'s patience = *mettre la patience de qqn à l'épreuve.*

PATIENT (n) *patient, -e, malade (m, f)* : the doctor has seen six patients today = *le docteur a vu six patients/ malades aujourd'hui* ☠ *un malade imaginaire* = a hypochondriac.

PATIENT (adj) *patient, -e* : a patient teacher = *un professeur patient* ≠ impatient = ←.

PATIENTLY (adv) *patiemment* : wait patiently = *attendez patiemment* ≠ impatiently = *impatiemment.*

PATIO (n) *patio (m)* Ⓦ terrace = *terrasse.*

PATRIARCH (n) *patriarche (m)* : the patriarch of the family = *le patriarche de la famille* **PATRIARCHAL** (adj) *patriarcal, -e* **PATRIARCHY** (n, -ies) *patriarcat (m).*

PATRIOT (n) *patriote (m, f)* : you can be a draft dodger and a patriot = *on peut être un insoumis et un patriote* ⓌＤ chauvinist = *chauvin* **PATRIOTIC** (adj) *patriotique* **PATRIOTISM** (n) *patriotisme (m).*

PATROL (n) *patrouille (f)* : patrol car = *voiture de patrouille* = squad car, to be on patrol = *être de patrouille.*

PATROL (to, -led) *patrouiller (dans)* : the cops are patrolling the area = *les flics patrouillent dans le secteur* ⓌＤ to make one's rounds = *faire sa ronde.*

PATROLMAN (n, -men) *agent (m) de police qui patrouille* ⓌＤ cop = *flic.*

PATRON (n) *protecteur (m)* : a patron of the arts = *un protecteur des arts* ⓌＤ patroness = *protectrice* **a (regular) patron** = *un client (régulier)* ⓌＤ a customer = *un client* ☠ → protector.

PATRONAGE (n) *clientélisme (m)* : political patronage = *clientélisme politique* ⓌＤ nepotism = *népotisme* **under the patronage of** = *sous le patronage de.*

PATRONIZE (to, -d) *être paternaliste* : stop patronizing me ! = *arrête d'être paternaliste avec moi !* **PATRONIZING** (adj) *paternaliste* : a patronizing attitude = *une attitude paternaliste.*

PATSY (n, -ies) *dindon (m) de la farce* : to be the patsy = *être le dindon de la farce* ⓌＤ chump = *gogo.*

PATTERN (n) **1/** *processus (m), schéma (m)* : there's a pattern in her marriage failures = *ses échecs conjugaux suivent toujours le même processus/schéma* ☠ → process **2/** *patron (m)* : a dress pattern = *le patron d'une robe* ☠ → boss.

PATTERN ON (to, -ed) *prendre modèle sur* : the museum was patterned on the one in Berlin = *pour construire le musée, on a pris modèle sur celui de Berlin.*

PAUPER (n) *indigent, -e* : breadlines for paupers = *la soupe populaire pour les indigents* ⓌＤ the needy = *les nécessiteux.*

PAUSE (n) *pause (f)* : a ten-minute pause for refreshments = *une pause de dix minutes pour prendre des rafraîchissements* ⓌＤ respite = *répit* ☠ *pause-café* = coffee break **PAUSE** (to, -d) *faire une pause* : let's pause for coffee = *si on faisait une pause pour prendre un café.*

PAVEMENT (n) *trottoir (m)* : walk on the pavement = *marchez sur le trottoir* = walk on the sidewalk ☠ *faire le trottoir* = to be a streetwalker.

PAW (n) *patte (f)* : the cat hurt its paw = *le chat s'est fait mal à la patte* ⓌＤ claw = *griffe*, hoof = *sabot*
☠ *des pattes (cheveux)* = sideburns
— *les pattes (chien)* = the legs (dog)
— *pattes de mouche* = scribbling
— *marcher à quatre pattes* = to walk on all fours
— *tirer dans les pattes de qqn* = to make things difficult for s.o.
— *montrer patte blanche* = to show one's credentials (to get into a place)
— *graisser la patte à qqn* = to grease s.o.'s palm.

PAW (to, -ed) *tripoter* : I don't like to be pawed = *je n'aime pas qu'on me tripote* ⓌＤ to neck = *flirter* ☠ *arrête de te tripoter les cheveux* = stop fiddling with your hair.

PAWN (n) *pion (m)* : we're just pawns in his hands = *nous ne sommes que des pions dans ses mains* **pawn ticket** = *reconnaissance du mont-de-piété* ☠ *damer le pion à qqn* = to one-up s.o.

PAWN (to, -ed) *mettre en gage/au mont-de-piété* : I pawned my gold watch = *j'ai mis ma montre en or en gage/au mont-de-piété* ⓌＤ pawnbroker = *prêteur sur gages*, pawnshop = *mont-de-piété/bureau d'un prêteur sur gages.*

PAY (n) *paye (f)*, *paie (f)* : he's complaining about the pay = *il se plaint de la paye* ⓌＤ wages = *salaire*, income = *revenu*, payday = *jour de paye*	
to be in the pay of = *être à la solde de* : the cops are in the pay of the local Mafia = *les flics sont à la solde de la Mafia locale* **the pay's good** ≠ **bad** = *c'est bien* ≠ *mal payé* **to hit pay dirt** = *voir ses efforts couronnés de suc-*	*cès* : after months of research, they hit pay dirt = *après des mois de recherche, ils ont vu leurs efforts couronnés de succès* ⓌＤ to hit the jackpot = *décrocher le gros lot*
☠ *la paye d'une société* = the payroll of a company	— *ça fait une paye que...* = it's been ages since...

456

PAY (adj) *payant, -e* : pay phone/toilets = *téléphone payant/toilettes payantes.*

PAY (to, paid, paid) *payer* : I'll pay you later = *je vous paierai plus tard,* the job pays well = *le boulot paie bien* **to pay as one goes** = *payer au fur et à mesure*

☠ *je te paie un verre* = I'll buy you a drink	— *il est payé pour le savoir* = he learned that the hard way
to pay back = 1/ *rendre (son argent)* : I'll pay you back next week = *je vous rendrai votre argent la semaine prochaine* 2/ *rendre la monnaie de sa pièce* : I'll pay you back (for what you did) ! = *je te rendrai la monnaie de ta pièce !* ⓒ to get back at = *avoir au tournant* **to pay by the (day/month)** = *payer à la (journée)/au (mois)* **to pay stg down** = *verser un acompte* : we paid $ 100 down for the TV = *nous avons versé un acompte de 100 dollars pour la télé* ≠ to pay cash = *payer cash* **to pay for** = 1/ *payer* : how much did you pay for it ? = *combien l'avez-vous payé ?* 2/ *payer* : he'll	pay for it ! = *il va me le payer !* ⓒ he won't get away with it ! = *il ne s'en sortira pas comme ça !,* we're paying for a not-too-cold winter with a rainy spring = *nous payons un hiver pas trop froid par un printemps pluvieux* **to pay off** = 1/ *s'acquitter de* : I'm paying my debts off = *je m'acquitte de mes dettes* ⓒ to settle up = *régler* 2/ *arroser* : the nightclub pays off the cops = *la boîte de nuit arrose les flics* ⓒ to grease s.o.'s palm = *graisser la patte à qqn* ☠ → to water 3/ *être payant* : the investment didn't pay off = *l'investissement n'a pas été payant* **it doesn't pay to (be nice to him)** = *ça ne paie pas d'(être sympa avec lui).*

PAYDAY (n) *jour (m) de (la) paye* : broken until payday = *fauché jusqu'au jour de la paye.*

PAYMENT (n) *paiement (m)* : cash payment = *paiement comptant.*

PAYOFF (n) *dessous-de-table (m inv)* : some of the Senators accepted payoffs = *certains sénateurs ont accepté des dessous-de-table* ⓒ payola = *bakchich* **the payoff was (that they fired him)** = *le résultat, c'est qu'(ils l'ont renvoyé)* ⓒ the outcome = *l'issue.*

PAYOLA (n inv) *bakchich (m)* : there's a lot of payola in politics = *on pratique pas mal le bakchich en politique* ⓒ bribe = *pot-de-vin.*

PAYROLL (n) *paie (f), paye (f)* : the gangsters stole the payroll = *les gangsters ont volé la paye* ☠ → pay **on the payroll** = *dans l'ensemble du personnel* : they have few women on the payroll = *il y a peu de femmes dans l'ensemble du personnel.*

PEA (n) *pois (m)* : green peas = *petits pois* ⓒ string beans = *haricots verts,* pod = *cosse* ☠ *(une robe) à pois* = dots (on a dress).

PEACE (n inv) *paix (f)* : a period of peace = *une période de paix* ≠ war = *guerre* **to be at peace with oneself** = *être en paix avec soi-même* **to disturb the peace** = *troubler la paix/le silence* **to hold one's peace** = *garder le silence* **to keep the peace** = *maintenir l'ordre* **to make peace** = *faire la paix* **the Peace Corps** = *les coopérants* **peace of mind** = *tranquillité d'esprit* **(to smoke) the peace pipe** = *(fumer) le calumet de la paix*

speak now or forever hold your peace = *qui ne dit mot consent* **I want peace and quiet !** = *je veux avoir la paix !* ☠ *fichez-moi la paix !* = leave me alone !

PEACEFUL (adj) 1/ *pacifique* : peaceful uses of atomic energy = *les usages pacifiques de l'énergie atomique* ≠ belligerent = *belliqueux* 2/ *paisible* : a peaceful afternoon = *un après-midi paisible* ⓒ calm = *calme.*

PEACEMAKER (n) *pacificateur, -trice* ≠ troublemaker = *fauteur de troubles.*

PEACH (n, -es) *pêche (f)* : peach sherbet = *sorbet à la pêche* ⓒ peach tree = *pêcher,* fruit = *fruits* **you're a peach (to help me)** = *tu es un chou (de m'aider)* ⓒ a doll = *un amour* ☠ *avoir la pêche* = to be in great form — *aller à la pêche* = to go fishing.

PEACOCK (n) *paon (m)* ⓒ peahen = *paonne.*

PEAK (n) *sommet (m), pic (m)* : the peaks of the mountains are covered with snow = *les sommets des montagnes sont couverts de neige* ☠ → summit **at its peak** = *à son apogée* : fascism at its peak = *le fascisme à son apogée* **at the peak of (his fame)** = *à l'apogée/au sommet de (sa gloire)* ⓒ pinnacle = *pinacle* **peak hour** = *heure de pointe* **peak season** = *pleine saison* ≠ low season = *saison creuse* **to reach a peak** = *atteindre un sommet/son apogée.*

PEANUT (n) 1/ *cacahuète (f)* : peanut butter = *beurre de cacahuète* **no (remarks) from the peanut gallery !** = *on ne t'a* *pas sonné !* ⓸ mind your own business ! = *occupe-toi de tes affaires !*

to work for peanuts = *travailler pour le roi de Prusse* ⓸ to work for chicken feed = *travailler pour des clous* 2/ *moustique (m) :* she's too tall to go out with such a peanut = *elle est trop grande pour sortir avec ce moustique* ⓸ peewee = *nabot* ☠ → mosquito.

PEAR (n) *poire (f) :* pear sherbet = *sorbet à la poire* ⓸ pear tree = *poirier,* fruit = *fruits* ☠ *il a abordé le sujet entre la poire et le fromage* = he broached the subject over coffee
— *couper la poire en deux* = to split the difference
— *poire à injection* = douche bag
— *quelle poire !* = what a sucker !
— *garder une poire pour la soif* = to keep stg for a rainy day.

PEAR (n) *poire (f) :* pear sherbet = *sorbet à la poire* ⓸ pear tree = *poirier,* fruit = *fruits*
pearl = *nacre*
to cast pearls before swine = *jeter des perles aux pourceaux*
☠ *vous êtes une perle !* = you're a gem !

PEASANT (n) *paysan, -anne :* my grandparents were peasants = *mes grands-parents étaient des paysans* ⓸ farmer = *fermier* ≠ city dweller = *citadin* **PEASANTRY** (n, -ies) *paysannerie (f).*

PEBBLE (n) *caillou (m), galet (m)* (beach) : pebbles on the road/beach = *des cailloux sur la route/des galets sur la plage* ⓸ sand = *sable.*

PECAN (n) *pacane (f) :* pecan pie = *tarte aux pacanes* ⓸ pumpkin pie = *tarte au potiron.*

PECKER (n) **it's like pulling your pecker !** = *c'est comme si tu pissais dans un violon !* ⓸ you're wasting your time ! = *tu perds ton temps !*

PECULIAR (adj) *curieux, -euse :* what a peculiar idea ! = *quelle idée curieuse !* ⓸ queer = *bizarre* **PECULIARITY** (n, -ies) *particularité (f)* **PECULIARLY** (adv) *curieusement :* peculiarly dressed = *curieusement habillé.*

PEDAGOG(UE) (n) *pédagogue (m, f)* **PEDAGOGIC** (adj) *pédagogique* **PEDAGOGY** (n, -ies) *pédagogie (f)* ⓸ education = *éducation.*

PEDAL (n) *pédale (f) :* the pedals of a bike = *les pédales d'un vélo*
☠ *une pédale (homo)* = a fag
— *perdre les pédales* = to lose control.

PEDANT (n) *pédant, -e* **PEDANTIC** (adj) *pédant, -e :* a pedantic tone = *un ton pédant.*

PEDDLE (to, -d) *colporter :* to peddle scarfs on the streets = *colporter des foulards dans les rues* **PEDDLER** (n) *colporteur, -euse, vendeur, -euse à la sauvette :* peddlers on Times Square = *les colporteurs/vendeurs à la sauvette de Times Square.*

PEDESTAL (n) **to put s.o. on a pedestal** = *mettre qqn sur un piédestal.*

PEDESTRIAN (n) *piéton, -onne :* pedestrians are killed daily = *il y a tous les jours des piétons qui se font tuer* **pedestrian crossing** = *passage clouté.*

PEDESTRIAN (adj) *plat, -e :* a pedestrian style = *un style plat* → AWFUL ☠ → flat.

PEDIATRICIAN (n) *pédiatre (m, f)* **PEDIATRICS** (n inv) *pédiatrie (f).*

PEDICURE (n) *soin (m) / beauté (f) des pieds.*

PEDIGREE (n, adj) *pedigree (m) :* a pedigree dog = *un chien à pedigree* ⓸ purebred = *de pure race.*

PEE (to, -d) faire *pipi :* I have to pee = *il faut que je fasse pipi* ⓸ to piss = *pisser.*

PEEK (n) *coup (m) d'œil rapide :* can I take a peek ? = *est-ce que je peux jeter un coup d'œil rapide ?* ⓸ peep = *coup d'œil furtif.*

PEEL (to, -ed) 1/ *peler :* my skin's peeling = *j'ai la peau qui pèle* ⓸ sunburn = *coup de soleil* 2/ *éplucher :* to peel potatoes = *éplucher des pommes de terre.*

PEEPING (adj) **peeping Tom** = *petit voyeur* ≠ exhibitionist = *exhibitionniste.*

PEER (n) 1/ *pair (m) :* scientists accepted him as their peer = *les savants l'ont accepté comme leur pair* ⓸ colleague = *collègue* ☠ → pair 2/ *quelqu'un de son âge :* he doesn't go out with his peers = *il ne sort pas avec les gens de son âge*
(his) peer group = *les gens de (son) âge.*

PEER (to, -ed) *scruter du regard :* she was peering at him through her thick glasses = *elle le scrutait du regard à travers ses épaisses lunettes.*

PEEVE (to, -d) *froisser :* she'll be peeved if you don't come = *elle sera froissée si vous ne venez pas* → ANGRY ☠ → to crease.

PEG (n) **to take s.o. down a peg (or two)** = *rabattre son caquet à qqn* ⓸ to put s.o. in his place = *remettre qqn à sa place.*

PEG AWAY (to, -ged) *cravacher dur :* he's pegging away at his studies = *il cravache dur pour ses études* ⓸ to plug away = *bûcher.*

PELL-MELL (adv) *pêle-mêle :* she threw the papers pell-mell on the bed = *elle a jeté les papiers pêle-mêle sur le lit* ⓸ upside down = *sens dessus dessous.*

PELVIS (n, -es or -ves) *bassin (m)* ⓸ haunch = *hanche.*

PEN (n) 1/ *stylo (m) :* I always write with a pen = *j'écris toujours avec un stylo,* ball-point pen = *stylo à bille* ⓸ pencil = *crayon,* refill = *recharge*
pen pal = *correspondant :* my little sister has a pen pal in Paris = *ma petite sœur a un correspondant à Paris* ☠ → correspondent

pen name = *nom de plume*
2/ *cabane (f)* : he's doing five years in the pen = *il est en train de tirer cinq ans en cabane* ⓪ jail = *taule* ☠ → cabin.

PENALIZE (to, -d) *pénaliser* : he was penalized for cheating = *il a été pénalisé pour avoir triché* ⓪ to punish = *punir.*

PENALTY (n, -ies) **1/** *fâcheuse conséquence (f)* : getting pregnant was the penalty for not using a contraceptive = *elle est tombée enceinte, fâcheuse conséquence de n'avoir pas utilisé de contraceptif* **2/** *pénalité (f), penalty (m)* (sport) : a penalty kick = *un coup de pied de pénalité.*

PENCHANT (n) *penchant (m)* : a penchant for young girls = *un penchant pour les filles jeunes* ⓪ liking = *goût.*

PENCIL (n) *crayon (m)* : I need a pencil to write with = *j'ai besoin d'un crayon pour écrire* ⓪ eraser = *gomme* ☠ *crayon de couleur* = crayon.

PENDING (adj) *en attente* : the case is pending = *l'affaire est en attente* ≠ settled = *réglé.*

PENDING (prep) *dans l'attente de* : pending his decision = *dans l'attente de sa décision* ⓪ awaiting = *en attendant.*

PENETRATE (to, -d) *pénétrer* : the troops penetrated into enemy territory = *les troupes ont pénétré en territoire ennemi* ⓪ to enter = *entrer (dans)*
(I told him, but) it didn't penetrate ! = *(je le lui ai dit, mais) ça ne l'a pas marqué !* ⓪ it went in one ear and out the other = *c'est entré par une oreille et sorti par l'autre*
☠ *des voleurs ont pénétré dans la maison* = burglars broke into the house.

PENETRATING (adj) *pénétrant, -e* : a penetrating mind = *un esprit pénétrant* ⓪ discerning = *qui a du discernement,* clear-sighted = *perspicace.*

PENETRATION (n) *pénétration (f)* : they petted but there was no penetration = *ils se sont pelotés mais il n'y a pas eu pénétration.*

PENGUIN (n) *pingouin (m)* ⓪ seal = *phoque.*

PENICILLIN (n) *pénicilline (f)* : Fleming discovered penicillin = *Fleming a découvert la pénicilline.*

PENINSULA (n) *péninsule (f)* ⓪ continent = ←.

PENIS (n, -nes or -es) *pénis (m), verge (f)* ⓪ cock = *queue,* balls = *couilles* ☠ *vous donnez des verges pour vous faire fouetter* = you're cutting your nose to spite your face.

PENITENTIARY (n, -ies) *pénitencier (m)* : he's been in the penitentiary for five years = *ça fait cinq ans qu'il est au pénitencier* ⓪ reformatory = *maison de correction,* pen = *cabane.*

PENNILESS (adj) *sans le sou* : penniless friends = *des amis sans le sou* → POOR.

PENNY (n, -ies) *penny (m)* : there are a hundred pennies in a dollar = *il y a cent pennies dans un dollar* ⓪ nickel = 5 cents
not to have a penny = *ne pas avoir un sou (en poche)* → POOR
a penny for your thoughts = *dis-moi à quoi tu penses*
a penny pincher = *un grippe-sou* ⓪ cheapskate = *pignouf, miser* = *avare*
to pinch pennies = *être près de ses sous* : I don't think they'll go to a restaurant, they're pinching pennies = *je ne pense pas qu'ils iront au restaurant, ils sont près de leurs sous.*

PENNY-WISE (adj) **to be penny-wise and pound-foolish** = *faire des économies de bouts de chandelle.*

PENPUSHER (n) *gratte-papier (m)* : he hasn't an important job, he's just a penpusher = *il n'a pas un poste important, ce n'est qu'un gratte-papier* ⓪ gofer = *factotum.*

PENSION (n) *retraite (f)* : he has a very small pension = *il a une toute petite retraite*
pension fund = *caisse de retraite*
☠ *retraite* → retreat
— *pension complète* = room and board
— *pension alimentaire* = alimony
— *pension (école)/pension de famille* = boarding school/house.

PENSIVE (adj) *pensif, -ive* : in a pensive mood = *d'humeur pensive* ⓪ meditative = *méditatif.*

PENTAGON (n) *Pentagone (m)* (ministère de la Défense aux États-Unis).

PENTHOUSE (n) *appartement (m) au dernier étage d'un immeuble* ⓪ duplex = ←.

PENT-UP (adj) *contenu, -e* : pent-up feelings = *des sentiments contenus* ≠ expressed = *exprimé.*

PENURY (n, -ies) *pénurie (f)* : a penury of gasoline = *une pénurie d'essence* ⓪ lack = *manque.*

PEOPLE (n) **1/** (inv) *personnes (f pl), gens (m pl)* : seven people came = *sept personnes sont venues,* many people told me the same thing = *beaucoup de gens/de nombreuses personnes m'ont dit la même chose* ⓪ a person = *une personne*
☠ *les gens de lettres* = the literati
— *les gens du monde* = high society
— *personne* → person
2/ *peuple (m)* : the peoples of the world = *les peuples du monde,* the American people = *le peuple américain*
a lot of people = *du monde/beaucoup de monde* : there were a lot of people at the meeting = *il y avait du monde/beaucoup de monde à la réunion* ⓪ a crowd = *une foule*
the people's choice = *le choix du peuple*
people shy = *sauvage* : she's people shy = *elle est sauvage* ⓪ a loner = *un solitaire* ☠ → savage
people who live in glass houses shouldn't throw stones = *il faut commencer par balayer devant sa porte*

ⓧ it's the pot calling the kettle black = *c'est la poêle qui se moque du chaudron*
what are you people (doing tonight) ? = *qu'est-ce que vous (faites ce soir) les mecs ?* = what are you guys (doing tonight) ?
young/old people = *les jeunes/les vieux*
what will people say ? = *que vont dire les gens ?*
you can fool some of the people all the time and all of the people some of the time but you can't fool all of the people all of the time = *faut pas prendre les enfants du bon Dieu pour des canards sauvages.*

PEP (n inv) *pep (m)* : she's full of pep = *elle a du pep* ⓧ energy = *énergie*
pep talk = *paroles d'encouragement.*

PEPPER (n) *poivre (m)* : the steak needs more pepper = *il faut plus de poivre sur le steak* ⓧ mustard = *moutarde*
green ≠ **red pepper** = *poivron vert* ≠ *rouge.*

PEP UP (to, -ped) *ragaillardir (s.o.), mettre de l'entrain dans* : his jokes will pep you/the party up = *ses plaisanteries vont vous ragaillardir/mettront de l'entrain dans la soirée* ⓧ to pick up = *remonter (s.o.)/faire repartir.*

PER (prep) *par* : it costs $ 10 per person = *ça coûte 10 dollars par personne* ☠ → by
per capita = *par tête* : per capita income = *revenu par tête*
per diem (expenses) = *(frais) à la journée*
per se = *en soi* : the film isn't bad per se, but it's not his best = *le film n'est pas mauvais en soi, mais ce n'est pas ce qu'il a fait de mieux*
(50 miles) per hour = *(80 kilomètres) à l'heure.*

PERCEIVE (to, -d) *percevoir* : we couldn't perceive any difference = *nous n'avons pu percevoir aucune différence* ⓧ to notice = *remarquer* ☠ *percevoir des impôts* = to collect taxes.

PERCENT (adj) *pour cent* : a ten percent raise = *une augmentation de dix pour cent.*

PERCENTAGE (n) *pourcentage (m)* : to get a percentage of the profits = *toucher un pourcentage sur les bénéfices.*

PERCEPTIBLE (adj) *perceptible* : a hardly perceptible difference = *une différence à peine perceptible.*

PERCEPTIVE (adj) *perspicace* : perceptive remarks = *des remarques perspicaces* ⓧ penetrating = *pénétrant.*

PERFECT (adj) 1/ *parfait, -e* : your work's perfect = *votre travail est parfait* ⓧ excellent = ← ≠ imperfect = *imparfait* 2/ *parfait, -e* : he's a perfect fool ! = *c'est un parfait imbécile !* ⓧ sheer = *pur* ☠ *filer le parfait amour* = to be regular lovebirds.

PERFECT (to, -ed) *(se) perfectionner* : she's perfecting her English/the system = *elle perfectionne son anglais/le système* ⓧ to improve = *améliorer.*

PERFECTION (n) *perfection (f)* : perfection is impossible = *la perfection n'existe pas* ≠ imperfection = ←.

PERFECTIONIST (n) *perfectionniste (m, f)* : you're too much of a perfectionist = *vous êtes trop perfectionniste* ⓧ a stickler for = *une personne à cheval sur.*

PERFECTLY (adv) *parfaitement* : you're perfectly right = *vous avez parfaitement raison* ⓧ altogether = *tout à fait* ☠ tu le quittes ? — *parfaitement !* = you're leaving him ? — that's right !/absolutely !

PERFORM (to, -ed) *donner une représentation* : they're performing for the President = *ils donnent une représentation pour le Président.*

PERFORMANCE (n) 1/ *représentation (f)* : there are two performances on Sundays = *il y a deux représentations le dimanche* ☠ → representation 2/ *performance (f)* : disappointed in the performance of the new plane = *déçu par la performance du nouvel avion* **PERFORMER** (n) *artiste (m, f)* : he's a brilliant performer = *c'est un grand artiste* ⓧ entertainer = *artiste de variétés.*

PERFUME (n) *parfum (m)* : a French perfume = *un parfum français* ⓧ toilet water = *eau de toilette*, scent = *senteur*
☠ *être au parfum* = to be in the know
— *parfum (glace)* = flavor (ice cream).

PERHAPS (adv) *peut-être* : do you think you'll come ? — I don't know, perhaps = *est-ce que vous pensez venir ? — je ne sais pas, peut-être* = maybe ⓧ possibly = *cela se pourrait*, very likely = *très vraisemblablement*
perhaps not = *peut-être pas/que non.*

PERIL (n) *péril (m)* : to face many perils = *faire face à de nombreux périls* ⓧ danger = ←
☠ *mettre sa vie en péril* = to jeopardize one's life
— *à vos risques et périls* = at your own risk.

PERILOUS (adj) *périlleux, -euse* : a perilous undertaking = *une entreprise périlleuse* ⓧ risky = *risqué.*

PERIOD (n) 1/ *point (m)* : every sentence ends with a period = *toute phrase se termine par un point* = full stop (GB) ⓧ comma = *virgule* ☠ → point 2/ *règles (f pl)* : I have my period = *j'ai mes règles* ⓧ the curse = *les ourses* ☠ → rule 3/ *période (f)* : a period of two months = *une période de deux mois* ⓧ space = *espace*
period ! = *point final !* : I don't want to go, period ! = *je ne veux pas y aller, point final !* ⓧ that's all there is to it ! = *un point c'est tout !*
period furniture = *meubles d'époque.*

PERIODIC(AL) (adj) *périodique* : periodic fits of jealousy = *des crises de jalousie périodiques* ⓧ cyclic = *cyclique* **PERIODICALLY** (adv) *périodiquement.*

PERIODICAL (n) *périodique (m)* : the magazine's a periodical = *ce magazine est un périodique.*

PERIPHERAL (adj) *annexe* : a peripheral problem = *un problème annexe* ⓧ supplementary = *supplémentaire.*

PERISH (to, -ed) *périr* : ten people perished in the fire = *dix personnes ont péri dans l'incendie* ⊘ to die = *mourir.*

PERISHABLE (adj) *périssable* : perishable goods = *denrées périssables* ≠ imperishable = *impérissable.*

PERJURE (to, -d) **to perjure o.s.** = *se parjurer.*

PERJURY (n, -ies) *parjure (m)* : to commit perjury = *commettre un parjure* ⊘ false testimony = *faux témoignage.*

PERK (n) *à-côté (m)* : the company offers many perks, such as free lunch, cheap trips, etc. = *travailler dans cette société comporte de nombreux à-côtés tels que des repas gratuits, des voyages bon marché, etc.* ⊘ advantage = *avantage* ☠ → sideline.

PERK UP (to, -ed) *(se) requinquer* : a coffee will perk you up = *un café vous requinquera* ⊘ to pep up = *ragaillardir.*

PERMANENCE (n) *permanence (f)* : she's frightened by the permanence of marriage = *elle est effrayée par la permanence du mariage* ⊘ durability = *durabilité* ☠ *assurer une permanence* = to always have s.o. on duty.

PERMANENT (adj) *permanent, -e* : a permanent job = *un travail permanent* ≠ temporary = *temporaire.*

PERMANENTLY (adv) *en permanence* : they plan to live in New York permanently = *ils projettent d'habiter New York en permanence* ≠ temporarily = *temporairement.*

PERMISSION (n inv) *permission (f)* : you have to ask the teacher's permission = *il faut demander la permission du professeur* ⊘ consent = *consentement* ☠ *une permission (armée)* = a leave (army).

PERMISSIVE (adj) *permissif, -ive* : a permissive society = *une société permissive* ⊘ tolerant = *tolérant.*

PERMIT (n) *permis (m)* : a building permit = *un permis de construire* ⊘ authorization = *autorisation* ☠ *permis de conduire* = driving license.

PERMIT (to, -ted) *permettre* : smoking isn't permitted = *il n'est pas permis de fumer* = to allow ≠ to forbid = *défendre*
to permit to = *permettre de* : they didn't permit us to take pictures in the museum = *on ne nous a pas permis de prendre des photos dans le musée*
☠ *il se permet bien des choses* = he takes a few too many liberties
— *si je puis me permettre* = if I may say so
— *je ne peux pas me le permettre* = I can't afford it
— *ça lui a permis de prendre des vacances* = it enabled him to take a vacation.

PERPENDICULAR (adj) *perpendiculaire* : perpendicular lines = *lignes perpendiculaires* ⊘ horizontal = ← ≠ parallel = *parallèle.*

PERPETUAL (adj) *perpétuel, -elle* : perpetual lies = *des mensonges perpétuels* ⊘ constant = ← **PERPETUALLY** (adv) *perpétuellement* : perpetually sleepy/sick = *perpétuellement endormi/malade* ⊘ constantly = *constamment.*

PERPETUATE (to, -d) *perpétuer* : to perpetuate a tradition = *perpétuer une tradition.*

PERPLEX (to, -ed) *rendre perplexe* : I'm perplexed by his letter = *sa lettre me rend perplexe* ⊘ to confuse = *embrouiller.*

PERSECUTE (to, -d) *persécuter* : to persecute Jews/the Blacks = *persécuter les juifs/Noirs* ⊘ to martyrize = *martyriser* **PERSECUTION** (n) *persécution (f)* : the persecution of Jews/Blacks = *la persécution des juifs/Noirs* ⊘ oppression = ←.

PERSEVERANCE (n) *persévérance (f)* : you can't succeed without perseverance = *on ne peut pas réussir sans persévérance* ⊘ tenacity = *ténacité* **PERSEVERE** (to, -d) *persévérer* : you must persevere in your efforts = *il faut persévérer dans vos efforts* ⊘ to hold on = *tenir bon.*

PERSIST (to, -ed) *persister* : her headache persisted = *son mal de tête a persisté* ⊘ to continue = *continuer,* persistence = *persistance*
to persist in = *persister à* : he persists in thinking he's right = *il persiste à penser qu'il a raison* ⊘ to continue to = *continuer à.*

PERSISTENT (adj) *persistant, -e* : persistent rain = *pluie persistante* ⊘ relentless = *implacable* **PERSISTENTLY** (adj) *avec persistance.*

PERSON (n) *personne (f)* : she was the only person who understood me = *c'est la seule personne qui m'ait compris* ⊘ individual = *individu*
to call person-to-person = *appeler avec préavis*
in person = *en personne* : I never met a star in person = *je n'ai jamais rencontré une vedette en personne* ⊘ as big as life = *en chair et en os*
☠ *sans nommer personne* = without naming anyone
— *trois personnes* = three people *(plus dit que « three persons »)*
— *personne ne (l'a vu)* = nobody/no one (saw him)
— *j'ai payé de ma personne* = it took its toll on me.

PERSONABLE (adj) *affable* : a personable salesman = *un vendeur affable* ≠ standoffish = *rébarbatif.*

PERSONAGE (n) *personnage (m)* : he's a very important personage = *c'est un personnage très important* ⊘ personality = *personnalité* ☠ *la pièce a 10 personnages* = the play has 10 characters.

PERSONAL (adj) *personnel, -elle* : personal problems = *des problèmes personnels* ≠ impersonal = *impersonnel*
don't be so personal ! = *on n'a pas gardé les cochons ensemble !* ⊘ you're taking too many liberties ! = *vous prenez bien des libertés !*
personal appearance = *apparition en public.*

PERSONALITY (n, -ies) **1/** *personnalité (f)* : she has a lot of personality = *elle a beaucoup de personnalité* ⓪ character = *caractère* **2/** *personnalité (f)* : a political personality = *une personnalité politique* ⓪ a name = *un nom.*

PERSONALIZED (adj) *personnalisé, -e* : personalized service = *service personnalisé.*

PERSONALLY (adv) *personnellement* : personally I don't agree = *personnellement, je ne suis pas d'accord* ⓪ as for me = *quant à moi.*

PERSONIFICATION (n) *personnification (f)* : you're the personification of laziness = *tu es la personnification même de la paresse* ⓪ embodiment = *incarnation* **PERSONIFY** (to, -ied) *personnifier* : she personifies the independence of the modern woman = *elle personnifie l'indépendance de la femme moderne* ⓪ to incarnate = *incarner.*

PERSONNEL (n pl) *personnel (m)* : the personnel voted for the strike = *le personnel a voté la grève* ⓪ manpower = *main-d'œuvre*
personnel department = *direction du personnel*
☠ *dix femmes dans le personnel* = ten women on the staff.

PERSPECTIVE (n) *perspective (f)* : a new perspective on the problem = *une nouvelle perspective du problème* ⓪ point of view = *point de vue*
in ≠ **out of perspective** = *tel que c'est* ≠ *sous un faux jour* : she sees the situation in ≠ out of perspective = *elle voit la situation telle qu'elle est* ≠ *sous un faux jour*
☠ *de tristes perspectives* = a bleak outlook/prospect.

PERSPIRATION (n) *transpiration (f)* ⓪ sweat = *sueur* **PERSPIRE** (to, -d) *transpirer* : it's very healthy to perspire = *c'est très sain de transpirer* ⓪ to sweat = *suer* ☠ *la nouvelle a transpiré* = the news leaked out.

PERSUADE (to, -d) *persuader* : it's your father you have to persuade, not me = *c'est ton père qu'il faut persuader, pas moi* ⓪ to talk s.o. into = *arriver à persuader qqn de* ≠ to dissuade = *dissuader*
to persuade s.o. to (do stg) = *persuader qqn de (faire qqch).*

PERSUASION (n) *persuasion (f)* : the power of persuasion = *le pouvoir de persuasion* ⓪ conviction = *←*
PERSUASIVE (adj) *persuasif, -ive* : a persuasive personality = *une personnalité persuasive* ⓪ convincing = *convaincant.*

PERT (adj, -er, -est) *pimpant, -e* : he's dating a slim pert woman = *il sort avec une femme mince et pimpante* ⓪ sprightly = *guilleret.*

PERTAIN TO (to, -ed) *se rapporter à* : problems pertaining to nuclear energy = *des problèmes se rapportant à l'énergie nucléaire* ⓪ to relate to = *avoir un lien avec.*

PERTINENT (adj) *pertinent, -e* : pertinent questions = des questions pertinentes ≠ irrelevant = *hors de propos.*

PERTURB (to, -ed) *perturber* : he was perturbed by the news = *il a été perturbé par la nouvelle*
☠ *ça me perturbe de ...* = it disturbs me to ...
— *perturber (une réunion)* = to disrupt (a meeting).

PERU (n) *Pérou (m)* **PERUVIAN** (n, adj) *Péruvien, -enne.*

PERUSE (to, -ed) *lire attentivement* : to peruse a report = *lire attentivement un rapport* ≠ to leaf through = *feuilleter.*

PERVADE (to, -d) *se répandre dans, imprégner* : fear pervaded the country = *la peur s'est répandue dans le pays*, pessimism pervades his writings = *le pessimisme imprègne ses écrits.*

PERVASIVE (adj) *de plus en plus répandu, -e* : pervasive violence/use of drugs = *une violence de plus en plus répandue/un usage de la drogue de plus en plus répandu* ⓪ widespread = *largement répandu.*

PERVERSE (adj) *pervers, -e* : a perverse way of looking at things = *une façon perverse de voir les choses* ⓪ twisted = *tordu.*

PERVERSION (n) *perversion (f)* : sexual perversions = *perversions sexuelles* ⓪ vice = *←.*

PERVERT (n) *pervers, -e* : only a pervert asks a girl to do such things = *il n'y a qu'un pervers pour demander des choses pareilles à une fille* ⓪ sex fiend = *obsédé sexuel*, degenerate = *dégénéré* **PERVERT** (to, -ed) *pervertir* : to pervert young people = *pervertir les jeunes* ⓪ to debauch = *débaucher* **PERVERTED** (adj) *perverti, -e* : debauched and perverted = *débauché et perverti* ≠ wholesome = *sain.*

PESSIMISM (n) *pessimisme (m)* : filled with pessimism = *plein de pessimisme* ⓪ defeatism = *défaitisme* **PESSIMIST** (n) *pessimiste (m, f)* ⓪ defeatist = *défaitiste* **PESSIMISTIC** (adj) *pessimiste* : pessimistic views = *des vues pessimistes* ⓪ cynical = *cynique.*

PEST (n) *enquiquineur, -euse* : what a pest you are ! = *quel enquiquineur !* ⓪ a pain in the neck = *un casse-pieds.*

PESTER (to, -ed) *enquiquiner* : stop pestering me and let me work ! = *arrête de m'enquiquiner et laisse-moi travailler !* ⓪ to annoy = *énerver*, to nag = *bassiner.*

PET (n) **1/** *animal (m) domestique* : we always had pets = *nous avons toujours eu des animaux domestiques* ⓪ dog = *chien*, cat = *chat* **2/** *chouchou, -te* : he's the teacher's pet = *c'est le chouchou du prof* ⓪ darling = *enfant chéri.*

PET (adj) *domestique* : a pet monkey = *un singe domestique* ≠ wild = *sauvage*
his pet complaint = *son grand sujet de plainte*
pet name = *surnom*
pet peeve = *bête noire*

pet shop = *magasin d'animaux*
pet subject/argument = *cheval de bataille*
pet theory = *grande théorie*
☠ → domestic.

PET (to, -ted) **1/** *peloter* : they were petting in the back of the car = *ils se pelotaient à l'arrière de la voiture* ⓓ to neck = *flirter* **2/** *caresser* : to pet a cat = *caresser un chat* ☠ → to caress.

PETAL (n) *pétale (m)* : the petals of a flower = *les pétales d'une fleur.*

PETE (n) **for Pete's sake !** = *nom d'une pipe !* → GOSH !

PETER OUT (to, -ed) *diminuer peu à peu* : our enthusiasm petered out = *notre enthousiasme a peu à peu diminué* ⓓ to taper off = *s'atténuer.*

PETITION (n) *pétition (f)* : to sign a petition = *signer une pétition* **PETITION** (to, -ed) *faire une pétition* : to petition for better working conditions = *faire une pétition pour obtenir de meilleures conditions de travail* ⓓ to appeal = *faire appel.*

PETRIFY (to, -ied) *pétrifier* : the noise petrified me = *le bruit m'a pétrifié* ≠ to be scared stiff = *ne pas en mener large.*

PETROL (n inv) (GB) = GAS.

PETROLEUM (n) *pétrole (m) (brut)* : to refine petroleum = *raffiner du pétrole.*

PETTY (adj, -ier, -iest) **1/** *sans importance* : petty considerations = *des considérations sans importance* ⓓ minor = *mineur* **2/** *mesquin, -e* : don't be so petty ! = *ne sois pas si mesquin !* ≠ magnanimous = *magnanime*
petty cash = *petite/menue monnaie*
petty crook = *petite frappe/escroc à la petite semaine*
petty expenses = *menus frais.*

PHALLIC (adj) *phallique* : a phallic symbol = *un symbole phallique.*

PHANTASM (n) *phantasme (m)* : he lives between reality and phantasm = *il vit entre la réalité et le phantasme* ☠ → fantasy.

PHANTOM (n) *fantôme (m)* : I never met her husband, he must be a phantom = *je n'ai jamais rencontré son mari, ce doit être un fantôme* ⓓ specter = *spectre* ☠ *ville fantôme* = ghost town
— *un cabinet fantôme* = a shadow cabinet.

PHARMACIST (n) *pharmacien, -enne* = druggist.

PHARMACY (n, -ies) *pharmacie (f)* : I have a prescription to pick up at the pharmacy = *j'ai une ordonnance à prendre à la pharmacie* = drugstore = chemist (GB) ⓓ pharmaceutical = *pharmaceutique.*

PHASE (n) **1/** *phase (f)* : the first phase of the experiment = *la première phase de l'expérience* ⓓ stage = *étape* **2/** *aspect (m)* : several phases of the problem = *plusieurs aspects du problème* ☠ → aspect.

PHASE OUT (to, -d) *supprimer progressivement* : to phase out troops/a product = *supprimer progressivement des troupes/un produit* ⓓ to stop = *arrêter.*

PHD (n) *doctorat (m) d'État, agrégation (f)* : he has a PhD in biology = *il a un doctorat d'État/l'agrégation en/de biologie* ⓓ thesis = *thèse.*

PHEASANT (n) *faisan (m)* ⓓ hen pheasant = *poule faisane.*

PHENOMENAL (adj) *phénoménal, -e* : phenomenal prices/talent = *des prix phénoménaux/un talent phénoménal* → WONDERFUL **PHENOMENALLY** (adv) *phénoménalement* : they're phenomenally rich = *ils sont phénoménalement riches* → VERY.

PHENOMENON (n, -na) *phénomène (m)* : psychological phenomena = *des phénomènes psychologiques* ⓓ wonder = *prodige.*

PHEW ! (interj) *ouf !* → GOSH !

PHI BETA KAPPA (n) *association honorifique américaine qui, depuis 1776, choisit ses membres selon le haut niveau de leurs diplômes.*

PHILANDERER (n) *cavaleur (m)* : some congressmen are noted philanderers = *certains parlementaires sont des cavaleurs notoires* ⓓ ladies' man = *homme à femmes.*

PHILANTHROPIC (adj) *philanthropique* : a philanthropic association = *une association philanthropique* **PHILANTHROPIST** (n) *philanthrope (m, f)* ⓓ do-gooder = *bienfaiteur de l'humanité* ≠ misanthropist = *misanthrope* **PHILANTHROPY** (n, -ies) *philanthropie (f).*

PHILOSOPHER (n) *philosophe (m, f)* ⓓ thinker = *penseur* **PHILOSOPHICAL** (adj) *philosophique (stg), philosophe (s.o.)* : a philosophical essay = *un essai philosophique*, be a bit more philosophical ! = *sois un peu plus philosophe !* **PHILOSOPHICALLY** (adv) *philosophiquement* : to react philosophically = *réagir philosophiquement* **PHILOSOPHY** (n, -ies) *philosophie (f)* : to study philosophy = *faire des études de philosophie* ⓓ to philosophize = *philosopher.*

PHOBIA (n) *phobie (f)* : a phobia about snakes = *la phobie des serpents* ⓓ dread = *épouvante.*

PHONE (n) *téléphone (m)* : can I use the phone ? = *puis-je utiliser votre téléphone ?* ⓓ intercom = *interphone* ☠ → telephone
phone book = *annuaire/bottin*
phone booth = *cabine téléphonique*
phone call = *coup de fil* : were there any phone calls for me today ? = *est-ce qu'il y a eu des coups de fil pour moi aujourd'hui ?*

PHONE (to, -d) *téléphoner* : can you phone me tomorrow ? = *est-ce que vous pouvez me téléphoner demain ?* ⓓ to call = *appeler.*

PHONETICS (n inv) *phonétique (f)* ⓓ pronunciation = *prononciation.*

PHONOGRAPH (n) *phonographe* *(m)* : the phonograph's broken = *le phonographe est cassé* ⓓ pick-up = ←.

PHONY (n, -ies) *quelqu'un de bidon* : what a phony guy ! = *quel mec bidon !* ⓓ fake = *charlatan.*

PHONY (adj, -ier, -iest) 1/ *bidon* : a phony excuse/charge = *une excuse/accusation bidon* ≠ serious = *sérieux* 2/ *en toc* : a phony diamond = *un diamant en toc* ⓓ false = *faux.*

PHOOEY ! (interj) *beurk !* ≠ yummy = *miam, miam.*

PHOTO (n) *photo* *(f)* : I have a great photo of you on vacation = *j'ai une photo géniale de toi en vacances* ⓓ photograph = *photographie*
a photo finish = *photo-finish* : the race was a photo finish = *il y a eu photo-finish pour la course* ⓓ a draw = *un match nul.*

PHOTOCOPY (n, -ies) *photocopie* *(f)* : make five photocopies = *faites-en cinq photocopies* ⓓ duplicate = *duplicata* **PHOTOCOPY** (to, -ied) *photocopier.*

PHOTOGENIC (adj) *photogénique* : a photogenic face = *un visage photogénique.*

PHOTOGRAPH (n) *photographie* *(f)* : photographs of their marriage = *des photographies de leur mariage* ⓓ picture = *photo* = ←, blowup = *agrandissement*, snapshot = *cliché*, camera = *appareil photo*, movie camera = *caméra* **PHOTOGRAPH** (to, -ed) *photographier* **PHOTOGRAPHER** (n) *photographe* *(m, f)* : my brother's a photographer = *mon frère est photographe* ⓓ cameraman = ←.

PHOTOGRAPHIC (adj) *photographique* : a photographic memory = *une mémoire photographique.*

PHRASE (n) *locution* *(f)* : "on behalf of " is a phrase = « *de la part de* » *est une locution* ⓓ expression = ← ☠ *une phrase* = a sentence.

PHYSICAL (n) *bilan* *(m)* *de santé* : to go for a physical = *se faire faire un bilan de santé* ⓓ examination = *examen.*

PHYSICAL (adj) *physique* : physical education = *éducation physique*, physical culture = *culture physique*, physical fitness = *forme physique.*

PHYSICALLY (adv) *physiquement* : it's physically impossible = *c'est physiquement impossible.*

PHYSICIAN (n) *médecin* *(m)*, *docteur* *(m)* *en médecine* : physicians rarely go on strike = *les médecins se mettent rarement en grève* ⓓ surgeon = *chirurgien* ☠ *un physicien* = a physicist.

PHYSICIST (n) *physicien, -enne* : Newton was a great physicist = *Newton était un grand physicien* ⓓ scientist = *scientifique.*

PHYSICS (n inv) *physique* *(f)* : physics was my minor = *la physique était ma matière secondaire* ⓓ chemistry = *chimie*
☠ *avoir le physique de l'emploi* = to look the part
— *avoir un physique agréable* = to be good-looking.

PIANO (n) *piano* *(m)* : to play the piano = *jouer du piano* ⓓ grand piano = *piano à queue*, upright piano = *piano droit*, baby grand = *crapaud*, pianist = *pianiste*, keyboard = *clavier*, key = *touche*, sonata = *sonate*, organ = *orgue*, harpsichord = *clavecin*, harmonium = ←.

PICAYUNE (adj) *mesquin, -e* : picayune criticisms = *des critiques mesquines.*

PICK (n) **the pick of the lot** = *le dessus du panier* ⓓ the cream of the crop = *la fine fleur*	**take your pick** = *faites votre choix* = take your choice.

PICK (to, -ed) *choisir* : you can pick whichever you want = *vous pouvez choisir celui que vous voulez* = to choose

to pick and choose = *faire le difficile pour choisir* : when she goes to the market she picks and chooses = *quand elle va au marché, elle fait la diffi-*	*cile pour choisir* ⓓ to be choosy = *être difficile* **to pick (flowers/fruit)** = *cueillir (des fleurs/des fruits)*

to pick at = *picorer* : she's always picking at her food = *elle est toujours en train de picorer* ≠ to eat like a horse = *manger comme quatre* **to pick on s.o.** = *chercher des poux dans la tête de qqn* : he's always picking on his kid brother = *il est toujours en train de chercher des poux dans la tête de son petit frère* ⓓ to bug = *casser les pieds à*	**to pick out** = *choisir* : pick out the one you want = *choisissez celui que vous voulez* **to pick s.o. up** = 1/ *draguer* : she picked him up in a bar = *elle l'a dragué dans un bar* 2/ *passer prendre* : I'll pick you up at 6 = *je passe te prendre à 6 heures* 3/ *remonter* : this large Scotch will pick me up = *ce bon whisky va me remonter* ⓓ to perk up = *requinquer* ☠ → to	wind up 4/ *cueillir* : the cops picked him up at the station = *les flics l'ont cueilli à la gare* ⓓ to nab = *pincer* 5/ *recueillir* : the boat picked up the survivors = *le bateau a recueilli les survivants* ☠ → to collect **to pick stg up** = 1/ *apprendre* : where did you pick up your English ? = *où avez-vous appris l'anglais ?* ☠ → to learn 2/ *attraper (maladie)* : to pick up the

measles = *attraper la rougeole* ☠ → to catch 3/ *dégoter* (LV) : I picked this ring up in New York = *j'ai dégoté cette bague à New York* ⓪ to dig up = *dénicher* 4/ *ramasser* : my watch fell, can you pick it up ? = *ma montre est tombée, pouvez-vous la ramasser ?* 5/ *décrocher (téléphone)* : the phone's ringing, pick it up ! = *le téléphone sonne, va décrocher !* ≠ to hang up = *raccrocher* ☠ → to land 6/ *relever* : he made a sarcastic remark but no one picked it up = *il a fait une remarque sarcastique mais personne ne l'a relevée* ☠ *relever qqn de ses fonctions* = to relieve s.o. from office 7/ *lever, soulever* : I can't pick up my arm/suitcase = *je ne peux pas lever/soulever mon bras/ma valise* ☠ *lever* → to raise, *soulever* → to lift

(business) is picking up = *les affaires repartent* ⓪ to improve = *s'améliorer*
to pick up and go = *faire ses valises (et partir)* : they were forced to pick up and go after their land was seized = *ils ont été forcés de faire leurs valises et de partir après la saisie de leur terre* → TO LEAVE
to pick up the tab/the bill = *payer la note/l'addition.*

PICKET (n) **picket line** = *piquet de grève* : the employees are on strike, don't cross picket lines = *les employés sont en grève, ne franchissez pas !es piquets de grève* ≠ strikebreaker = *briseur de grève* **PICKET** (to, -ed) *barrer l'accès par des piquets de grève* : the workers are picketing the factory = *les ouvriers barrent l'accès de l'usine par des piquets de grève.*

PICKLE (n) *cornichon (m)* : I love pickles with ham = *j'aime les cornichons avec le jambon* ⓪ mustard = *moutarde*
to be in a pickle = *être frais* : we'll be in a pickle if he finds the truth out = *nous serons frais s'il découvre la vérité* ⓪ to be in a jam = *être dans le pétrin* ☠ *quel cornichon !* = what a nitwit !

PICK-ME-UP (n) *remontant (m)* : a stiff Scotch is a great pick-me-up = *un whisky bien tassé est un bon remontant.*

PICKPOCKET (n) *pickpocket (m), voleur, -euse à la tire* : watch out for pickpockets ! = *attention aux pickpockets/aux voleurs à la tire !* ⓪ shoplifter = *voleur à l'étalage.*

PICKUP (n) *quelqu'un qu'on a dragué* : the girl he's with is a pickup he met in a bar = *la fille avec laquelle il est, il l'a draguée dans un bar.*

PICKY (adj, -ier, -iest) *difficile* : don't be so picky ! = *ne sois pas si difficile !* = don't be so choosy !
a picky eater = *quelqu'un de difficile pour la nourriture*
☠ → difficult.

PICNIC (n) *pique-nique (m)* : let's go on a picnic today ! = *si on faisait un pique-nique aujourd'hui !*
it's no picnic ! = *ce n'est pas de la tarte !* : it was no picnic working for him ! = *ce n'était pas de la tarte de travailler pour lui !* ⓪ it's no joyride ! = *ce n'est pas une partie de plaisir !*

PICTURE (n) 1/ *tableau (m)* : a beautiful picture = *un beau tableau* ⓪ painting = *peinture*

☠ *un tableau noir* = a blackboard — *(analyser) un tableau* = (to analyze) a chart — *tableau de bord* ≠ dashboard	— *gagner sur tous les tableaux* = to win all the way down the line

2/ *film (m)* : "Gone with the wind" is a great picture = *« Autant en emporte le vent » est un grand film* → FILM
3/ *photo (f)* : it's a lovely day to take pictures = *c'est un jour idéal pour prendre des photos*
4/ *tableau (m)* : a grim picture of the future = *un sombre tableau de l'avenir* ⓪ description = ←
5/ *image (f)* : children's books often have pictures = *les livres d'enfants ont souvent des images* ⓪ drawing = *dessin* ☠ → image

to be the picture of health = *respirer la santé* ≠ to be in poor health = *être en mauvaise santé* **(he's) the picture of (his father)** = *(c'est) le portrait de (son père)* ⓪ the spitting image of (his father) = *(son père) tout craché* **where do I come into the picture ?** = *quand est-ce que j'entre en jeu ?* **to enter the picture** = *entrer en ligne de compte* :	the price doesn't enter the picture = *le prix n'entre pas en ligne de compte* **do I have to draw you a picture ?** = *est-ce qu'il faut que je te fasse un dessin ?* ⓪ get it ? = *pigé ?* **get the picture ?** = *vu ?* ⓪ get the message ? = *tu piges le truc ?* **to go to the pictures** = *aller au cinéma* **picture window** = *baie vitrée.*

PICTURE (to, -d) *imaginer (le tableau)* : I can just picture the boss doing a striptease ! = *le patron en train de faire un strip-tease, j'imagine (le tableau) !*

PICTURESQUE (adj) *pittoresque* : a picturesque port = *un port pittoresque* ≠ drab = *plat*.

PIDGIN ENGLISH (n) *petit nègre (m)* : to speak pidgin English = *parler petit nègre* ⓪ to speak broken English = *parler anglais comme une vache espagnole*.

PIE (n) *tarte (f) tourte (f)* : cherry pie = *tarte aux cerises*, pumpkin pie = *tarte au potiron*, meat pie = *tourte à la viande*
☠ *une idée tarte* = an asinine idea
— *tarte à la crème* = slapstick
— *c'est pas de la tarte !* = it's no picnic !

PIECE (n) *morceau (m)* : a piece of meat = *un morceau de viande* ⓪ chunk = *gros morceau* ≠ whole = *le tout*

to break into pieces = *(se) casser en mille morceaux* : the vase broke into pieces = *le vase s'est cassé en mille morceaux* **to be paid by the piece** = *être payé à la pièce* **to fall to pieces** = *tomber en ruine* : your car's falling to pieces = *votre voiture tombe en ruine* ⓪ to fall apart = *se déglinguer* **to give s.o. a piece of one's mind** = *dire à qqn sa façon de penser* → TO LAMBAST	**to go to pieces** = *être dans un triste état* : she went to pieces after her husband's death = *elle était dans un triste état après la mort de son mari* **a (nice) piece of ass/tail** = *un (joli) petit cul* **a piece of (furniture/clothing/advice/toast/fruit/candy/luggage)** = *un (meuble/vêtement/conseil/toast/fruit/bonbon/bagage)* **a piece of cake** = *une part de gâteau*	**a piece of paper** = *un papier* ⓪ a scrap of paper = *un bout de papier* **to say one's piece** = *dire ce qu'on a à dire* : now I've said my piece, I'll shut up ! = *maintenant que j'ai dit ce que j'avais à dire, je la ferme !* **to tear to pieces** = *dire pis que pendre de* : the critics tore the play/the actors to pieces = *les critiques ont dit pis que pendre de la pièce/des acteurs* ⓪ to find fault with = *trouver à redire à*
☠ *manger le morceau* = to give the show away — *manger un morceau* = to have a bite — *emporter le morceau* = to carry the day	— *morceaux choisis* = selected tidbits — *gober le morceau* = to fall hook, line and sinker — *pièce* → room.	

PIECE (to, -d) **to piece together** = *reconstituer* : the cops were able to piece the facts together = *les flics ont pu reconstituer les faits*.

PIE-EYED (adj) *rond, -e (comme une queue de pelle/comme une bille)* : he was pie-eyed after two Scotches = *il était rond (comme une queue de pelle/comme une bille) après deux whiskies* → DRUNK ☠ → round.

PIER (n) *jetée (f)* : they meet every night on the pier = *ils se donnent rendez-vous tous les soirs sur la jetée* ⓪ dock = *bassin*.

PIERCE (to, -d) *percer* : she's going to have her ears pierced = *elle va se faire percer les oreilles* ⓪ to penetrate = *pénétrer* ☠ *il est en train de percer* = he's making a name for himself.

PIETY (n, -ies) *piété (f)* : a man of great piety = *un homme d'une grande piété* ⓪ devotion = *dévotion*.

PIG (n) 1/ *cochon (m)* ⓪ swine = *porc*, sow = *truie*, boar = *sanglier* 2/ *cochon, -onne* : you eat like a pig ! = *tu manges comme un cochon !*
to bleed like a pig = *saigner comme un bœuf*
kill the pigs ! = *mort aux vaches !*
to make a pig of oneself = *se goinfrer* : she made a pig of herself at the dinner = *elle s'est goinfrée au dîner*
to sweat like a pig = *suer à grosses gouttes*

☠ *copains comme cochons* = bosom pals
— *on n'a pas gardé les cochons ensemble !* = don't be so personal !

PIGEON (n) *pigeon (m)* ⓪ dove = *colombe* ☠ *quel pigeon !* = what a sucker !

PIGGYBACK (adv) **to carry (a child) piggyback** = *porter (un enfant) sur son dos*.

PIGGY BANK (n) *tirelire (f)* : I broke my piggy bank to buy daddy's present = *j'ai cassé ma tirelire pour acheter le cadeau de papa*.

PIGHEADED (adj) *qui a une tête de lard/de cochon* : what a pigheaded guy ! = *quelle tête de lard/de cochon !* ⓪ mulish = *buté*.

PIGSTY (n, -ies) *porcherie (f)* : her apartment's a real pigsty = *son appartement est une vraie porcherie* ⓪ shithole = *merdier*.

PIGTAIL (n) *queue (f) de cheval* ⓪ bun = *chignon*.

PILE (n) *pile (f)* : a pile of books = *une pile de livres* ⓪ heap = *tas*
to have/make a pile = *avoir/se faire une pelote* → RICH

piles of (money/work to do) = *un monceau d'(argent)/de (travail à faire)* → MANY
- ☠ *(6 heures) pile* = (6 o'clock) sharp
- — *s'arrêter pile* = to stop dead in one's tracks
- — *tu tombes pile* = you came at the right moment
- — *piles (radio)* = battery (radio)
- — *flanquer une pile à qqn* = to give s.o. a whipping
- — *pile ou face ?* = heads or tails ?

PILE (to, -d) *empiler* : pile the books on the shelf = *empilez les livres sur l'étagère* ⓓ to heap = *entasser*
to pile into = *s'entasser dans* : we piled into the subway = *nous nous sommes entassés dans le métro* = we jammed into the subway
to pile it on = *en faire des tonnes* : he was trying to impress her and really piled it on = *il essayait de l'impressionner et il en a vraiment fait des tonnes* ⓓ to lay it on thick = *y aller fort*
to pile up = *(s')entasser* : my work is/bills are piling up = *mon travail s'entasse/les factures s'entassent* ⓓ to accumulate = *s'accumuler* ☠ *s'entasser dans le métro* = to crowd into the subway.

PILGRIM (n) *pèlerin (m)* : pilgrims going to Mecca = *les pèlerins qui se rendent à La Mecque* **PILGRIMAGE** (n) *pèlerinage (m)*.

PILL (n) *pilule (f), comprimé (m)* : take a pill every two hours = *prenez une pilule/un comprimé toutes les deux heures* ⓓ tablet = *cachet*, sedative = *sédatif*, prescription = *ordonnance*, pillbox = *boîte à pilules*
to be on the pill = *prendre la pilule* ⓓ to have an abortion = *se faire avorter*
to gild/sweeten the pill = *dorer la pilule*.

PILLAGE (n) *pillage (m)* : the pillage of the city = *le pillage de la ville* ⓓ sack = *sac* **PILLAGE** (to, -d) *piller* : they pillaged the town = *ils ont pillé la ville* ⓓ to ravage = *ravager*.

PILLAR (n) *pilier (m)* : pillars in a church = *les piliers d'une église* ☠ *pilier de bistrot* = barfly.

PILLOW (n) *oreiller (m)* : I can't sleep without a pillow = *je ne peux pas dormir sans oreiller* ⓓ pillowcase = *taie d'oreiller*
pillow fight = *bataille de polochons*.

PILOT (n) *pilote (m)* : the hijacker shot the pilot = *le pirate de l'air a tiré sur le pilote* ⓓ aviator = *aviateur* **PILOT** (to, -ed) *piloter* : the robot pilots the plane = *le robot pilote l'avion* **PILOT** (adj) **a pilot show** = *une émission pilote (télé)*.

PIMP (n) *souteneur (m), maquereau (m)* : her pimp takes half of all the tricks = *son maquereau/souteneur prend la moitié de toutes ses passes* ⓓ ponce (GB) = *proxénète*, mack = *mac*, madam = *mère maquerelle* ☠ *maquereau (poisson)* = mackerel.

PIMPLE (n) *bouton (m)* : lots of pimples on her face = *un visage couvert de boutons* ⓓ wart = *verrue*, blemish = *tache*, birthmark = *tache de naissance* ☠ → button.

PIN (n) *épingle (f)* : he stuck me with a pin = *il m'a piqué avec une épingle* ⓓ safety pin = *épingle de nourrice*, hairpin = *épingle à cheveux*
to be on pins and needles = *être sur des charbons ardents* ≠ to breathe easy = *respirer librement*
pin money = *argent de poche* = pocket money
you could have heard a pin drop = *on aurait entendu une mouche voler* ⓓ there is an awkward silence = *un ange passe*
☠ *monter qqch en épingle* = to play up a story
— *tirer son épingle du jeu* = to get out while the going's good.

PIN (to, -ned) **to be pinned** = *être presque fiancé, -e (une coutume américaine veut que le garçon donne à sa petite amie son épingle de club d'étudiants en témoignage de leur amour)* : she's pinned to the head of the tennis team = *elle est presque fiancée au capitaine de l'équipe de tennis* ⓓ to be engaged to = *être fiancé à*
to pin s.o. down = *faire préciser à qqn* : I tried to find out his opinion on abortion, but I couldn't pin him down = *j'ai essayé de savoir quelle était sa position sur l'avortement, mais je n'ai pas pu la lui faire préciser*
to pin stg on s.o. = *faire porter la responsabilité de qqch à qqn* : the cops tried to pin the murder on the Mafia = *les flics ont essayé de faire porter la responsabilité du meurtre à la Mafia* ⓓ to lay stg on s.o. = *rejeter qqch sur le dos de qqn*
to pin s.o. to the ground/floor = *clouer qqn au sol* : the wrestler pinned his opponent to the ground/floor = *le lutteur a cloué son adversaire au sol* → TO HIT.

PINBALL MACHINE (n) *flipper (m)* ⓓ one-armed bandit = *machine à sous*.

PINCH (n, -es) **to feel the pinch** = *être dans la gêne* : money's running low, we're feeling the pinch = *l'argent commence à manquer, nous sommes dans la gêne* → POOR
in a pinch = *au besoin* : I can lend you the money in a pinch = *au besoin, je peux vous prêter l'argent* ⓓ if need be = *si besoin est* ⓓ **at a pinch** = *s'il le faut*
a pinch of (curry) = *une pincée de (curry)* ⓓ a touch of = *un brin de*.

PINCH (to, -ed) **1/** *pincer* : he's 80 and still pinching girls = *il a 80 ans et continue à pincer les filles* ☠ *en pincer pour qqn* = to be hung up on s.o. **2/** *piquer* : the kids pinched some oranges = *les gosses ont piqué des oranges* ⓓ to filch = *chaparder* ☠ → to sting **3/** *pincer* : the cops pinched him = *les flics l'ont pincé* ⓓ to collar = *mettre la main au collet à*.

PINCH-HIT FOR (to, -hit, -hit) *suppléer* : his assistant pinch-hits for the boss when he's sick = *son assistant supplée le patron quand il est malade* ⓓ to substitute = *remplacer* ☠ *suppléer un manque de* = to make up for a lack of.

PINEAPPLE (n) *ananas (m)* : fresh pineapple = *ananas frais* ⓓ grapefruit = *pamplemousse*.

PING-PONG (n) *ping-pong (m)* : I play a lot of ping-pong = *je joue beaucoup au ping-pong* ◯ table tennis = *tennis de table.*

PINK (adj, -er, -est) **1/** *rose* : a pink dress = *une robe rose* ◯ red = *rouge*
shocking pink = *rose indien*
to be tickled pink = *être aux anges* : she was tickled pink to have a little girl = *elle était aux anges d'avoir une petite fille* ≠ to be down in the dumps = *être au trente-sixième dessous*
☠ *voir la vie en rose* = to see life through rose-colored glasses
— *une période rose* = an upbeat time
2/ *gauchisant, -e* : the paper has a pink slant = *le journal a une orientation gauchisante* ◯ red = *rouge.*

PINNACLE (n) *pinacle (m)* : he's reached the pinnacle of his career = *il est monté au pinacle* ◯ acme = *faîte*, apogee = *apogée* ☠ *porter au pinacle* = to praise to the skies.

PINPOINT (to, -ed) *bien définir* : the doctor's trying to pinpoint the exact nature of the disease = *le médecin essaye de bien définir la nature exacte du mal* ◯ to explain = *expliquer.*

PINT (n) *demi-litre (m)* : a pint of milk = *un demi-litre de lait* ◯ quart = *litre.*

PINUP (n) *pin-up (f inv)* : he married a real pinup = *il a épousé une vraie pin-up.*

PIONEER (n) *pionnier, -ère* : the pioneers of the Far West = *les pionniers du Far West* ☠ *un pionnier de la mode* = a trailblazer in fashion.

PIOUS (adj) *pieux, -euse* : a pious family = *une famille pieuse* ≠ impious = *impie* ☠ *un pieux mensonge* = a white lie.

PIPE (n) **1/** *pipe (f)* : to smoke a pipe = *fumer une pipe* ◯ cigarette = ←
pipe dream = *rêves fumeux* : his fame and fortune turned out to be pipe dream = *quand il parlait de renommée et de fortune, c'étaient des rêves fumeux* ◯ castles in Spain = *châteaux en Espagne*
put that in your pipe and smoke it ! = *mets ça dans ta poche et ton mouchoir par-dessus !*
☠ *casser sa pipe* = to kick the bucket
— *(trois francs) par tête de pipe* = (three francs) a head
— *tailler une pipe* = to do a blow job
— *se fendre la pipe* = to split one's sides laughing
2/ *tuyau (m)* : there's a leak in the pipe = *il y a une fuite dans le tuyau* ◯ tap = *robinet*
☠ *tuyau (d'arrosage)* = hose
— *un tuyau crevé* = a bum steer
— *un bon tuyau* = a good tip.

PIPE DOWN (to, -d) **pipe down !** = *taisez-vous !* = hush up !

PIPER (n) **to pay the piper** = *payer les pots cassés* = to face the music.

PIRATE (n) *pirate (m)* : there were few female pirates = *il y a eu peu de femmes pirates* ◯ piracy = *piraterie*
pirate station = *radio pirate*
☠ *pirate de l'air* = hijacker.

PISS (to, -ed) *pisser* : I want to piss = *je veux pisser* ◯ to shit = *chier*
to piss s.o. off = *faire chier qqn* : his remarks pissed me off = *ses remarques m'ont fait chier* → ANGRY
piss off ! = *va te faire voir !* → BUZZ OFF !
☠ *laisse pisser le mérinos !* = let it all hang out !

PISTACHIO (n) *pistache (f)* : pistachio ice cream = *glace à la pistache* ◯ almond = *amande.*

PISTOL (n) *pistolet (m)* : they're selling pocket pistols = *ils vendent des pistolets de poche* ◯ bullet = *balle* ☠ *un drôle de pistolet* = an oddball.

PIT (n) **1/** *fosse (f)* : to fall into a pit = *tomber dans une fosse* ◯ hole = *trou* **2/** *noyau (m)* : a peach pit = *un noyau de pêche*
☠ *le noyau dur (du parti)* = the hard core of (the party)
— *le noyau de l'atome* = the nucleus of the atom.

PIT AGAINST (to, -ted) *(se) mesurer à* : he pitted his wit against his opponent's = *il a mesuré son esprit à celui de son adversaire* ◯ to rival = *rivaliser avec.*

PITCH (n, -es) *boniment (m)* : the salesman's pitch = *le boniment du vendeur* ◯ line = *baratin*
(violence) reached a pitch = *(la violence) a atteint un degré élevé.*

PITCH (to, -ed) *être lanceur (base-ball)* : he pitched for the Dodgers = *il était lanceur dans l'équipe des Dodgers* ◯ pitcher = *lanceur*
to pitch in = *mettre la main à la pâte* : if everyone pitches in, we can finish quickly = *si tout le monde met la main à la pâte, nous pouvons finir vite* ◯ to lend a hand = *donner un coup de main.*

PITCH-BLACK (adj) *noir, -e comme de la suie/comme dans un four* : it's pitch-black inside = *il fait noir comme dans un four/c'est noir comme de la suie à l'intérieur* ≠ snow-white = *blanc comme neige.*

PITFALL (n) *embûche (f)* : the pitfalls of the French language = *les embûches de la langue française* ◯ peril = *péril.*

PITIFUL (adj) *pitoyable* : pitiful working conditions = *des conditions de travail pitoyables* → AWFUL.

PITILESS (adj) *sans pitié* : a pitiless boss/king = *un patron/un roi sans pitié* ◯ cruel = ←.

PITS (n pl) **it's/he's the pits !** = *c'est pas le pied !* ≠ it's the greatest ! = *c'est super-chouette !* → AWFUL.

PITTANCE (n) **to work for a pittance** = *travailler pour un salaire de misère.*

PITY (n, -ies) *pitié (f)* : do you feel only pity for me ? = *est-ce que tu ne ressens que de la pitié pour moi ?* ◯ mercy = *grâce*

for pity's sake ! = *par pitié !* → GOSH !
it's a pity ! = *c'est dommage !* ⓐ it's too bad ! = *c'est navrant !*
out of pity = *par pitié :* he did it out of pity = *il l'a fait par pitié*
what a pity ! = *quel dommage !*

PITY (to, -ied) *plaindre :* I pity people who have to get up early = *je plains les gens qui doivent se lever tôt*
I pity you ! = *je te plains !/j'ai pitié de toi !* ☠ → to complain.

PIZZA (n) *pizza* (f) : I don't like pizza = *je n'aime pas la pizza.*

PIZZAZZ (n inv) *piquant* (m) : she's got beauty and pizzazz = *elle est belle et a du piquant* ⓐ panache = ←.

PLACATE (to, -d) *apaiser :* she was furious and he did nothing to placate her = *elle était furieuse et il n'a rien fait pour l'apaiser* ≠ to infuriate = *rendre furieux* ☠ → to appease.

PLACE (n) 1/ *endroit* (m) : this is a nice place = *c'est un endroit sympa* ⓐ spot = *coin*, dive = *coin/boui-boui* ☠ *à l'endroit* = on the right side 2/ *place* (f) : save me a place = *gardez-moi une place* ⓐ seat = *siège* 3/ *place* (f) : there's a place open for a secretary = *il y a une place disponible pour une secrétaire* ⓐ post = *poste* 4/ *maison* (f) : they have a beautiful place in the country = *ils ont une belle maison à la campagne* ☠ → house

---

all over the place = *dans tous les coins :* there were cops all over the place = *il y avait des flics dans tous les coins* ⓐ everywhere = *partout*
to change places = *changer de place :* I can't see, let's change places = *je ne vois rien, changeons de place*
to fall into place = *devenir clair :* after his explanation, everything fell into place = *après son explication, tout est devenu clair*
to go places = *avoir un bel avenir :* with her brains, she'll go places = *avec son intelligence, elle a un bel avenir* ⓐ to go far = *aller loin*
in first/second place = *en premier/second lieu* ⓐ first of all = *tout d'abord*
in its place ≠ **out of place** = *à sa place* ≠ *pas à sa place :* nothing's in its place = *rien n'est à sa place* = everything's out of place
in place of = *à la place de :* I'll have salad in place of French

fries = *je prendrai de la salade à la place des frites* ⓐ instead of = *au lieu de*
in your place (I wouldn't do it) = *à votre place (je ne le ferais pas)* ⓐ if I were you = *si j'étais vous*
it's not your place to (tell her) = *ce n'est pas à vous de (le lui dire)*
to know one's place = *savoir rester à sa place :* my husband accuses me of not knowing my place = *mon mari m'accuse de ne pas savoir rester à ma place*
(my) place = *chez (moi) :* let's go to my place = *allons chez moi*
out of place = 1/ *pas à sa place :* she felt out of place with her husband's family = *elle ne se sentait pas à sa place dans la famille de son mari* ⓐ ill-at-ease = *mal à l'aise* 2/ *déplacé :* his remark was out of place = *sa remarque était déplacée* ⓐ out of keeping = *pas de mise*
a place in the sun = *une place au soleil*

put yourself in my place ! = *mettez-vous à ma place !*
to put s.o. in his place = *remettre qqn à sa place :* my answer put him in his place = *ma réponse l'a remis à sa place* → TO LAMBAST
to take place = *avoir lieu :* the talks will take place next month = *les pourparlers auront lieu le mois prochain* ⓐ to occur = *se produire*
to take s.o.'s place = *prendre la place de qqn :* no one can take the place of a dead parent = *personne ne peut prendre la place d'un parent disparu* ⓐ to replace = *remplacer*
to tear the place apart = *tout mettre à sac :* the gang tore the place apart = *le gang a tout mis à sac* ⓐ to turn upside down = *mettre sens dessus dessous*
there's no place like home ! = *on n'est vraiment bien que chez soi !*
your place or mine ? = *(tu veux qu'on aille) chez toi ou chez moi ?*

☠ *sur place* = on the spot
— *ne pas tenir en place* = to be restless
— *place aux jeunes !* = make way for the young !
— *une place (dans une ville)* = a square (in a city)

— *places de théâtre* = theater tickets/seats
— *place financière* = money market
— *il n'y a pas de place* = there's no room/space.

PLACE (to, -d) 1/ *placer :* he placed his chair near mine = *il a placé sa chaise près de la mienne* ⓐ to set = *poser*

☠ *placer de l'argent* = to invest money
— *je n'ai pas pu en placer une* = I couldn't get a word in edgeways

— *nous étions placés au premier rang* = we were seated in the first row
— *placer (des espions)* = to plant (spies)

2/ *situer* : when I saw her again, I couldn't place her at first = *quand je l'ai revue, je ne suis pas arrivé à la situer tout de suite* 💀 → to situate
3/ *passer* : to place an order = *passer une commande* 💀 → to pass
4/ *se placer* : the American runner placed second in the race = *le coureur américain s'est placé second dans la course.*

PLACID (adj) *placide* : a placid look/child/dog = *un regard/un enfant/un chien placide* ⓪ peaceful = *paisible.*

PLAGIARIZE (to, -d) *plagier* : she plagiarized the original text = *elle a plagié le texte original* ⓪ to copy = *copier* **PLAGIARISM** (n) *plagiat* *(m).*

PLAGUE (n) **1/** *peste* *(f)* : millions died of the plague = *des millions de gens sont morts de la peste* ⓪ epidemic = *épidémie*

to avoid s.o. like the plague = *fuir qqn comme la peste*
2/ *fléau* *(m)* : terrorists are a plague to modern society = *les terroristes sont un fléau pour la société moderne* ⓪ calamity = *calamité.*

PLAGUE (to, -d) *ronger* : he's plagued by the memory of his years in Auschwitz = *il est rongé par le souvenir de ses années à Auschwitz* ⓪ to haunt = *hanter* 💀 → to gnaw.

PLAID (n) *plaid* *(m)*, *(tissu) écossais* *(m)* : a plaid skirt = *une jupe en tissu écossais/une jupe écossaise.*

PLAIN (adj, -er, -est) **1/** *(très) simple* : a very plain coat/apartment = *un manteau/appartement très simple* ⓪ ordinary = *ordinaire* ≠ fancy = *fantaisie* 💀 → simple **2/** *clair, -e* : give me a plain answer = *donnez-moi une réponse claire*, it's plain that he's cheating on her = *il est clair qu'il la trompe* = it's clear that ... ⓪ clear-cut = *bien net* ≠ hazy = *flou* 💀 → clear **3/** *quelconque* : she's very plain = *elle est très quelconque* ⓪ homely = *au physique ingrat* ≠ attractive = *attirant* 💀 → commonplace **4/** *pur, -e et simple* : plain stupidity ! = *de la stupidité pure et simple !* ⓪ pure = *pur*, utter = *parfait.*

in plain English = *en bon anglais* : I told him in plain English to buzz off = *je lui ai dit en bon anglais de ficher le camp* ⓪ **in plain language** = *en langage clair*, in no uncertain terms = *en des termes on ne peut plus clairs*

it's as plain as can be = *c'est aussi clair que possible* ≠ it's as clear as mud = *c'est clair comme du jus de chique*
it's as plain as the nose on your face = *ça se voit comme le nez au milieu de la figure* ⓪ it's staring you in the face = *ça*

te crève les yeux
to make it plain that = *bien faire comprendre que* : she made it plain that she was quitting = *elle a bien fait comprendre qu'elle donnait sa démission* = to make it clear that.

PLAIN (adv) *tout simplement* : it's plain crazy to do that = *c'est tout simplement idiot de faire ça.*

PLAINCLOTHESMAN (n, -men) *policier* *(m)* *en civil* ⓪ cop = *flic.*

PLAINLY (adv) **1/** *simplement* : she was dressed very plainly = *elle était très simplement vêtue* = she was dressed very simply **2/** *clairement* : write your name and address very plainly = *écrivez vos nom et adresse très clairement*, I told her very plainly what I thought = *je lui ai dit très clairement ce que je pensais.*

PLAINSPOKEN (adj) *qui a son franc-parler* : a plainspoken guy = *un type qui a son franc-parler* ≠ evasive = *évasif.*

PLAINTIFF (n) *plaignant, -e* : the plaintiff sued for damages = *le plaignant a attaqué en justice pour obtenir des dommages-intérêts* ≠ the accused = *l'accusé.*

PLAN (n) **1/** *projet* *(m)* : what are your plans for the weekend ? = *quels sont vos projets pour le week-end ?* 💀 → project **2/** *plan* *(m)* : a plan of attack = *un plan d'attaque*

⓪ stratagem = *stratagème*
the best laid plans of mice and men oft go astray = *l'homme propose, Dieu dispose* → THAT'S LIFE !
European plan = *prix de la chambre* ≠ **American plan** = *pension complète*
💀 *laisser qqn en plan* = to leave s.o. in the lurch
— *au second plan* = of secondary importance
— *sur le plan (politique)* = (politically) speaking.

PLAN (to, -ned) *mettre sur pied* : he planned the trip carefully = *il a soigneusement mis le voyage sur pied* ⓪ to organize = *organiser*
to plan ahead = *s'y prendre à l'avance* : if you're going to have a party, you have to plan ahead = *si vous voulez donner une soirée, il faut que vous vous y preniez à l'avance*
to plan on = *projeter de* : I'm planning on taking vacation in the fall = *je projette de prendre des vacances à l'automne*
to plan to = *projeter de* : we're planning to go to New

York this summer = *nous projetons d'aller à New York cet été* ⬭ to intend to = *avoir l'intention de.*

PLANE (n) *avion (m) :* a big plane = *un gros avion* = airplane ⬭ runway = *piste,* flight = *vol,* air pocket = *trou d'air,* cockpit = ←, helicopter = *hélicoptère,* pilot = *pilote,* flight attendant = *steward/hôtesse de l'air,* aviation = ←, propeller = *hélice,* to land = *atterrir* ≠ to take off = *décoller* ☠ *par avion (courrier)* = airmail.

PLANET (n) *planète (f) :* there's little sign of life on other planets = *il y a peu de signes de vie sur les autres planètes* ⬭ star = *étoile.*

PLANT (n) 1/ *plante (f) :* do you talk to your plants ? = *est-ce que vous parlez à vos plantes ?* ⬭ flowerpot = *pot de fleurs,* ivy = *lierre* 2/ *usine (f) :* an automobile plant = *une usine de construction automobile* = factory ⬭ mill = *fabrique* 3/ *agent (m) de renseignements :* the secretary turned out to be a KGB plant = *la secrétaire s'est révélée être un agent de renseignements du KGB* ⬭ spy = *espion* 4/ *coup (m) monté :* the drugs found in their car were a police plant = *si on a trouvé de la drogue dans leur voiture, c'était un coup monté de la police.*

PLANT (to, -ed) 1/ *placer :* to plant spies in an embassy = *placer des espions dans une ambassade* ☠ → to place 2/ *planter :* to plant flowers/a tree = *planter des fleurs/un arbre*
☠ *se planter à (un examen)* = to flunk (an exam)
— *il m'a planté là* = he walked out on me right there and then
— *il s'est planté devant moi* = he plunked himself down in front of me.

PLANTATION (n) *plantation (f) :* a banana plantation = *une plantation de bananes* ⬭ planter = *planteur.*

PLASTER (n) *plâtre (m) :* a wall made of plaster = *un mur en plâtre* ⬭ cement = *ciment*
☠ *un bras dans le plâtre* = a cast on her arm
— *essuyer les plâtres* = 1/ to be the first to live in a brand-new place 2/ to be a trailblazer at one's own expense.

PLASTERED (adj) *schlass :* plastered on tequila = *schlass à la tequila* → DRUNK ≠ cold sober = *sobre comme un chameau.*

PLASTIC (n inv) *plastique (m) :* I don't like the feel of plastic = *je n'aime pas le contact du plastique.*

PLASTIC (adj) *en plastique :* a plastic glass = *un verre en plastique*
plastic surgery = *chirurgie esthétique*
plastic money = *les cartes de crédit.*

PLATE (n) *assiette (f) :* the plate's broken = *l'assiette est cassée* ⬭ glass = *verre* ☠ *je ne suis pas dans mon assiette* = I don't feel like my usual self.

PLATFORM (n) 1/ *programme (m) :* the party's platform = *le programme du parti* ⬭ ticket = *liste (électorale)* ☠ → program 2/ *estrade (f) :* the platform collapsed = *l'estrade s'est écroulée* 3/ *quai (m) :* the train departs from platform 3 = *le train part du quai 3* ☠ → wharf.

PLATINUM (n) *platine (m)* ☠ *une platine* = a turntable.

PLATITUDE (n) *platitude (f) :* a speech full of platitudes = *un discours rempli de platitudes* ⬭ cliché = ←.

PLATONIC (adj) *platonique :* platonic love = *amour platonique* ≠ sexual = *sexuel.*

PLAUSIBLE (adj) *plausible :* a plausible excuse = *une excuse plausible* ⬭ credible = *crédible.*

PLAY (n) *pièce (f) :* have you seen Pinter's last play ? = *est-ce que vous avez vu la dernière pièce de Pinter ?* ⬭ drama = *drame,* comedy = *comédie* ☠ → room

to come into play = *jouer :* other aspects of the question came into play = *d'autres aspects du problème ont joué* ⬭ to enter the picture = *entrer en ligne de compte* **to give heavy** ≠ **little play to** = *faire grand* ≠ *peu de cas de :* newspapers gave heavy ≠ little play to the story = *les journaux ont fait grand cas* ≠ *peu*	de cas de cette histoire ⬭ to pass over = *passer sur* **to make a play for** = *faire du gringue à :* he made a play for the boss's wife = *il a fait du gringue à la femme du patron* ⬭ to give s.o. a line = *faire du baratin à qqn* **a play on words** = *un jeu de mots* ⬭ spoonerism = *contrepèterie.*

PLAY (to, -ed) 1/ *jouer :* the kids are playing in the garden = *les enfants jouent dans le jardin* ⬭ to romp = *gambader,* to have fun = *s'amuser* 2/ *(se) jouer :* what's playing next week ? = *qu'est-ce qu'on joue la semaine prochaine ?,* she plays Nora = *elle joue Nora*
to play tennis/cards/piano = *jouer au tennis/aux cartes/du piano*

to play along with s.o. = *jouer le jeu de qqn :* play along with him till we find out what he really wants = *joue son jeu jusqu'à ce que nous trouvions ce qu'il veut vraiment* ⬭ to go	along with s.o. = *suivre qqn* **to play around** = *courir le jupon/les hommes :* he/she has been playing around since their marriage = *il/elle court le jupon/les hommes depuis leur*	mariage ⬭ to fool around = *courir les filles/les hommes* **to play around with** = *s'envoyer en l'air avec :* he's playing around with his secretary = *il s'envoie en l'air avec sa*

secrétaire ⚐ to fool around with = *se taper*
to play at (being a macho) = *jouer au (macho)*
to play down (a scandal) = *faire peu de cas d'(un scandale)* ≠ **to play up** = *monter en épingle*
to play off (against) = *monter (l'un) contre (l'autre) :* she always tries to play her mother off against her father = *elle*

essaie sans cesse de monter sa mère contre son père
to play on (s.o.'s feelings) = *jouer sur (les sentiments de qqn)*
to be played out = *(se) jouer :* everything will be played out in the coming weeks = *tout se jouera dans les semaines qui viennent*
to play up to s.o. = *chercher à se faire bien voir de qqn* ⚐ to butter up = *passer de la pom-*

made à
to play with o.s. = *jouer en solitaire*
to play with (one's food) = *manger du bout des lèvres* ⚐ to toy with (one's food) = *manger du bout des dents*
to play with (an idea) = *caresser (une idée)* ⚐ to toy with = *nourrir* ☠ → to caress

---

☠ *son mari joue* = her husband gambles
— *à vous de jouer* = it's your move
— *cela joue contre vous* = it isn't in your favor

— *jouer sa réputation sur* = to stake one's reputation on
— *cela ne joue pas* = it doesn't enter the picture.

PLAYBACK (n) *play-back (m) :* she didn't sing live, it was playback = *elle n'a pas chanté en direct, c'était du play-back.*

PLAYBILL (n) *programme (m) (de théâtre)* = theater program.

PLAYBOY (n) *play-boy (m) :* her guy's a real playboy = *son mec est un vrai play-boy* ⚐ wolf = *dragueur.*

PLAYER (n) *joueur, -euse :* a tennis player = *un joueur de tennis* ⚐ team = *équipe*
☠ *être bon* ≠ *mauvais joueur* = to be a good ≠ poor sport
— *joueur (argent)* = gambler.

PLAYFUL (adj) *joueur, -euse :* a playful little cat/girl = *une petite chatte/fille joueuse* ⚐ sprightful = *folâtre.*

PLAYGROUND (n) *terrain (m) de jeu :* the playground's closed on weekends = *le terrain de jeu est fermé le week-end* ⚐ recreation yard = *cour de récréation.*

PLAY-OFF (n) *finale (f) :* the play-offs are this week = *les finales ont lieu cette semaine* ⚐ cup = *coupe.*

PLAYTHING (n) *joujou (m) :* I'm not your plaything = *je ne suis pas ton joujou.*

PLAYTIME (n) *moment (m) de récréation :* my kids never have enough playtime = *mes gosses n'ont jamais assez de moments de récréation.*

PLAYWRIGHT (n) *auteur (m) dramatique :* he's a good playwright = *c'est un bon auteur dramatique* ⚐ scriptwriter = *scénariste.*

PLEA (n) *supplication (f) :* he beat the child in spite of his wife's pleas = *il a battu l'enfant en dépit des supplications de sa femme*
to cop a plea = *reconnaître un crime moins grave que celui qu'on a commis pour bénéficier d'une peine plus légère.*

PLEAD (to, -ed) *plaider :* to plead not guilty = *plaider non coupable*

to plead with s.o. to = *supplier qqn de :* she pleaded with him to stay = *elle l'a supplié de rester* ⚐ to beg s.o. to = *prier qqn de.*

PLEASANT (adj) *agréable :* a pleasant trip = *un voyage agréable* → WONDERFUL ≠ crummy = *moche* ☠ → agreeable.

PLEASE ! (interj) *s'il vous plaît ! :* give me the ketchup, please ! = *donnez-moi le ketchup, s'il vous plaît !* ≠ thank you ! = *merci !*

PLEASE (to, -d) **to please s.o.** = 1/ *faire plaisir à qqn :* I only did it to please you = *je l'ai fait uniquement pour vous faire plaisir* 2/ *plaire à qqn :* she wears sexy underwear to please her husband = *elle met des sous-vêtements sexy pour plaire à son mari*
hard ≠ **easy to please** = *difficile* ≠ *facile à contenter*
please yourself ! = *faites comme il vous plaira !* ⚐ suit yourself ! = *comme vous voudrez !*
to be pleased to = *avoir le plaisir de :* I'm pleased to tell you that you got the job = *j'ai le plaisir de vous annoncer que vous avez obtenu le poste*, we're pleased to inform you that ... = *nous avons le plaisir de vous annoncer que ...* ≠ to be sorry to = *être désolé de*
pleased to meet you ! = *enchanté (de faire/d'avoir fait votre connaissance) !* ⚐ glad to meet you ! = *ravi (de vous rencontrer) !*

PLEASED (adj) *content, -e :* we're pleased you came = *nous sommes contents que vous soyez venu* ⚐ thrilled = *ravi* ≠ displeased = *pas content*
to be pleased with (o.s./s.o.'s work) = *être content de (soi/du travail de qqn)* ⚐ to be satisfied with = *être satisfait de*
☠ → content.

PLEASING (adj) *plaisant, -e :* a pleasing personality = *un caractère plaisant* ≠ unpleasant = *déplaisant.*

PLEASURE (n) *plaisir (m) :* the pleasures of life = *les plaisirs de la vie* ≠ displeasure = *déplaisir*
pleasure trip = *voyage d'agrément* ≠ business trip = *voyage d'affaires*

it's my pleasure ! = *tout le plaisir est pour moi !* = **the pleasure is mine !**
its a pleasure to (see you again) = *c'est une joie de (vous revoir)*
to take pleasure in (one's grandchildren) = *prendre plaisir à (voir ses petits-enfants)* = to delight in
with pleasure = *avec plaisir* : will you have a Scotch ? — with pleasure ! = *prendrez-vous un whisky ? — avec plaisir !* ⓪ willingly = *volontiers*
☠ *pour vous faire plaisir* = to make you happy
— *faites-moi le plaisir de venir* = would you be so kind as to come.

PLEAT (n) *pli (m)* : a skirt with pleats = *une jupe à plis* ⓪ flounce = *volant*
☠ *faire un pli (cartes)* = to take a trick
— *prendre le pli* = to get into the habit
— *ça ne fait pas un pli* = there's no doubt about it.

PLEBISCITE (n) *plébiscite (m)* **PLEBISCITE** (to, -d) *plébisciter.*

PLEDGE (n) *gage (m)* : as a pledge of friendship = *en gage d'amitié* ☠ *des gages élevés* = high wages.

PLEDGE (to, -d) *s'engager à donner* : he pledged $ 100 to charity = *il s'est engagé à donner 100 dollars aux bonnes œuvres* ⓪ to promise = *promettre.*

PLENTY (n) **plenty of** = *plein de* : plenty of money/coffee = *plein d'argent/de café* → MANY.

PLENTY (pron) *plein* : do you need money ? — no, I have plenty (of money) = *as-tu besoin d'argent ? — non, j'en ai plein* ≠ a bit = *un peu.*

PLENTY (adv) *très très* : they're plenty rich = *ils sont très très riches* → VERY.

PLEURISY (n, -ies) *pleurésie (f).*

PLIERS (n pl) *pinces (f pl), tenailles (f pl)* ⓪ scissors = *ciseaux.*

PLIGHT (n inv) *situation (f) critique* : the plight of the refugees = *la situation critique des réfugiés* ⓪ predicament = *situation difficile.*

PLOD AHEAD (to, -ded) *avancer laborieusement* : he's plodding ahead with his book = *il avance laborieusement dans son livre* ⓪ to peg away = *cravacher dur.*

PLOT (n) 1/ *complot (m)* : a plot to overthrow the regime = *un complot pour renverser le régime* ⓪ conspiracy = *conspiration* 2/ *intrigue (f)* : the plot of the play = *l'intrigue de la pièce* ⓪ framework = *trame.*

PLOT (to, -ted) *comploter* : they're plotting a revolution = *ils complotent une révolution* ⓪ to scheme = *manigancer*
to plot to (overthrow the government) = *comploter pour (renverser le gouvernement).*

PLOW (to, -ed) *labourer* : the farmer's plowing his field = *l'agriculteur laboure son champ* = to plough (GB) ⓪ to sow = *semer.*

PLOY (n) *biais (m)* : the kidnapping was a ploy to get money from the government = *l'enlèvement était un biais pour soutirer de l'argent au gouvernement* ⓪ device = *truc*, trick = *ruse.*

PLUCK (n inv) *cran (m)* : you need pluck to be an acrobat = *il faut du cran pour être acrobate* ⓪ courage = ← ☠ *être à cran* = to be on edge.

PLUG (n) *prise (f)(mâle)* ⓪ socket = *prise (femelle)*
to give s.o. a plug = *faire de la pub à/pour* : he gave my book a plug in his column = *il a fait de la pub pour mon livre dans son article*
☠ *avoir prise sur qqn* = to have a hold over s.o./to have leverage on s.o.
— *la prise (d'une ville)* = the capture of (a city)
— *prise de pouvoir* = takeover
— *être aux prises avec qqn* = to be at odds with s.o.
— *une prise de bec* = a run-in
— *prise de vues (film)* = take (film).

PLUG (n) *(prise) (f)(mâle)* ⓪ socket = *prise (femelle)*
plug his new movie = *il passe à la télé pour faire de la pub pour son nouveau film* ⓪ to promote = *promouvoir*
to plug away at = *bûcher* : he's plugging away at his studies = *il bûche pour terminer ses études* ⓪ to slave away = *boulonner*
plug in (the iron) = *branchez (le fer)* ≠ take out = *débranchez.*

PLUM (n) *prune (f)* : a ripe plum = *une prune mûre*
(her new job's) a plum = *(elle a un nouveau boulot) en or* ≠ a nightmare = *un cauchemar*
☠ → *prune.*

PLUMBER (n) *plombier (m)* : her sister's a plumber = *sa sœur est plombier* ⓪ plumbing = *plomberie.*

PLUMMET (to, -ed) *descendre brusquement* : prices plummeted = *les prix ont descendu brusquement* ≠ to soar = *monter en flèche.*

PLUMP (adj, -er, -est) *rondouillard, -e* : he likes his women plump = *il aime les femmes rondouillardes* ≠ scrawny = *maigrichon.*

PLUNDER (to, -ed) *piller* : the troops plundered the village = *les troupes ont pillé le village* ⓪ to ransack = *saccager.*

PLUNGE (n) *dégringolade (f)* : a plunge in the stock market = *une dégringolade des cours de la Bourse* ⓪ collapse = *effondrement*
to take the plunge = *faire le plongeon/sauter le pas.*

PLUNGE (to, -d) *s'effondrer brutalement* : the stock market plunged = *la Bourse s'est brutalement effondrée* ≠ to dip = *accuser une légère baisse*
to plunge into (a new job/the water) = *se plonger dans (un nouveau travail)/plonger dans (l'eau).*

PLUNK DOWN (to, -ed) 1/ *s'affaler* : he plunked down in the armchair = *il s'est affalé dans le fauteuil* 2/ *met-*

tre sur la table : to plunk down a grand = *mettre mille dollars sur la table.*

PLURAL (n) *pluriel* (m) : "teeth" is the plural of "tooth" = « *dents* » *est le pluriel de* « *dent* » ≠ singular = *singulier.*

PLURALITY (n, -ies) *pluralité* (f) : a plurality of votes = *la pluralité des votes* ⓪ pluralism = *pluralisme.*

PLUS (n, -es or -ses) *quelque chose en prime* : the unexpected nice weather was a plus = *nous avons eu du beau temps en prime* ≠ disadvantage = *désavantage.*

PLUS (prep) **1/** *plus* : one plus three equals four = *un plus trois égale quatre* ⓪ and = *et* ☠ → more **2/** *en plus de* : she has brains plus beauty = *en plus de la beauté, elle a l'intelligence* ≠ minus = *en moins.*

PLUSH (adj, -er, -est) *fastueux, -euse* : a plush apartment = *un appartement fastueux* ⓪ luxurious = *luxueux* ≠ seedy = *miteux.*

PLY (to, -ied) **to ply s.o. with (questions/drinks)** = *presser qqn de (questions)/ne pas arrêter de (remplir le verre de) qqn.*

P.M. (adv) *du soir, de l'après-midi* : he's coming at 2 p.m./8 p.m. = *il vient à 2 heures de l'après-midi/8 heures du soir* ⓪ in the late afternoon = *tard dans l'après-midi.*

PNEUMONIA (n) *pneumonie* (f) : I had pneumonia last winter = *j'ai eu une pneumonie l'hiver dernier* ⓪ flu = *grippe.*

POACH (to, -ed) *braconner* : arrested for poaching = *arrêté pour avoir braconné.*

POB (abbr) = Post-Office Box = *boîte postale* = B.P.

POCKET (n) *poche* (f) : my wallet's in my pocket = *mon portefeuille est dans ma poche*
to go through s.o.'s pockets = *faire les poches de qqn*
to have s.o. in one's pocket = *avoir qqn dans sa poche* ⓪ to have s.o. eating out of one's hand = *avoir qqn qui vous mange dans la main*
☠ *mets ça dans ta poche et ton mouchoir par-dessus !* = put that in your pipe and smoke it !
— *connaître comme sa poche* = to know in and out
— *des poches sous les yeux* = bags under the eyes
— *c'est dans la poche !* = it's in the bag !
— *ne pas avoir la langue/les yeux dans sa poche* = to be talkative/observant.

POCKET (adj) *de poche* : a pocket camera/dictionary = *un appareil photo/dictionnaire de poche* ⓪ mini = ←
pocket money = *argent de poche.*

POCKET (to, -ed) *empocher* : I left a tip for the waiter, but his boss pocketed it = *j'ai laissé un pourboire au garçon, mais c'est le patron qui l'a empoché* ⓪ to swipe = *faucher.*

POCKETBOOK (n) **1/** *livre* (m) *de poche* : pocketbooks are cheaper = *les livres de poche sont moins chers* ⓪ paperback = *livre broché* **2/** *sac* (m) *à main* : she lost her pocketbook = *elle a perdu son sac à main* = handbag.

PODIUM (n) *podium* (m) ⓪ platform = *estrade.*

POEM (n) *poème* (m) : he writes love poems = *il écrit des poèmes d'amour* ≠ prose = ← **POET** (n) *poète* (m) : Rimbaud was a great French poet = *Rimbaud était un grand poète français* **POETESS** (n, -es) *poétesse* (f).

POETIC (adj) *poétique* : a poetic style = *un style poétique* ⓪ lyric = *lyrique*
poetic justice = *juste retour des choses.*

POETRY (n inv) *poésie* (f) : he writes poetry = *il écrit de la poésie* ⓪ verse = *vers*
poetry reading = *lecture de poèmes.*

POGROM (n) *pogrom(e)* (m) : millions of Jews fled pogroms = *des millions de juifs ont fui les pogroms* ⓪ ghetto = ←.

POIGNANT (adj) *poignant, -e* : a poignant story = *une histoire poignante* ⓪ touching = *touchant.*

POINT (n) **1/** *point* (m) : their team is one point ahead = *leur équipe mène d'un point*	
☠ *point de repère* = landmark — *un point noir* = a blackhead — *point* = period/full stop — *point d'interrogation* = question mark — *point virgule* = semicolon — *un point, c'est tout !* = that's all there is to it ! — *au point mort* = at a standstill — *à quel point ?* = to what degree ? — *faire le point* = to sum up/to take stock — *à point nommé* = in the nick of time	— *point de vente* = sales outlet — *mettre au point* = to perfect — *point chaud/sensible* = hot/sore spot — *un point sur le i* = a dot on the i — *faut-il que je vous mette les points sur les i ?* = do I have to spell things out ? — *être sur le point de (partir)* = to be about to (leave) — *(steak) à point* = medium (steak) — *point de suture* = stitch
2/ *pointe* (f) : the point of a knife = *la pointe d'un couteau*	
☠ *marcher sur la pointe des pieds* = to tiptoe — *(une entreprise) de pointe* = a leading	(enterprise) — *heures de pointe* = peak hours

— *pointe (vanne)* = cut/jab (crack)
— *être à la pointe de (la mode)* = to be up with (the latest fashion)

— *une pointe (d'accent/d'ail)* = a hint (of an accent/garlic)

at that point = *à ce moment-là* : at that point he walked in = *à ce moment-là, il est entré*
to be back at the starting point = *être revenu au point de départ*
get/come to the point ! = *venez-en au fait !* ⊕ stop beating around the bush ! = *arrêtez de tourner autour du pot !*
good ≠ bad point = *bon ≠ mauvais côté* : we all have our good ≠ bad points = *nous avons tous nos bons ≠ mauvais côtés*
I've reached the point where (I'm fed up) = *j'en suis arrivé au point où (j'en ai marre)*
in point of fact = *en réalité* : I thought I was right, but in point of fact I wasn't = *je pensais avoir raison, mais en réalité j'avais tort* ⊕ in fact = *en fait*
to labor the point = *revenir encore sur la même chose*
to make a point (of) = *ne pas manquer (de)* : he made a point of insulting her = *il n'a pas manqué de l'insulter*
to make one's point = *se faire comprendre* : did I make my point ? = *est-ce que je me suis bien fait comprendre ?*

I missed ≠ got the point = *je n'ai pas saisi ≠ j'ai saisi le truc*
on the point of (quitting) = *près de (démissionner)*
(from my) point of view = *(de mon) point de vue* ⊕ (to my) way of thinking = *(à mon) avis*
the point of no return = *le point de non-retour*
stick to the point ! = *ne vous écartez pas du sujet !*
that's beside the point = *c'est à côté de la question* ⊕ that's not what it's about = *il ne s'agit pas de cela*, that has nothing to do with it = *ça n'a rien à voir*
that's not the point ! = *il ne s'agit pas de ça !* ⊕ that's not the question ! = *là n'est pas la question !*
that's a point well taken = *vous avez bien fait de relever cela*
that's stretching the point ! = *vous forcez la note/la dose !* ⊕ you're carrying things too far ! = *vous dépassez les bornes !*
that's the (whole) point ! = *justement !* = **that's just the point !**
to the point = *tout à fait à propos* : her remark was to the

point = *sa remarque était tout à fait à propos* ⊕ pertinent = ←
to the point (where) = *au point de* : he became angry to the point where he started hitting her = *il s'est mis en colère au point de la frapper*
the turning point = *le tournant* : the turning point of the match/the war = *le tournant du match/de la guerre*
up to a point = *jusqu'à un certain point* : I agree with you up to a point = *je suis d'accord avec vous jusqu'à un certain point* ⊕ to some extent = *dans une certaine mesure*
my weak ≠ strong point = *mon point faible ≠ fort* : that's my weak point = *c'est mon point faible*
what's the point of it ? = *à quoi ça rime ?* ⊕ what's the use of it ? = *à quoi ça sert ?* ≠ **there's no point in (telling her)** = *ça ne rime à rien de (le lui dire)*
what's your point ? = *où voulez-vous en venir ?*
you have a point ! = *c'est pas bête !*

POINT (to, -ed) pointer : the arrow points left = *la flèche pointe vers la gauche*

to point out = 1/ *désigner du doigt* : the guide pointed out the most famous paintings = *le guide nous a désigné du doigt les toiles les plus célèbres* ⊕ to show = *montrer* 2/ *faire remarquer* : he pointed out that it wasn't the first time the problem had arisen = *il a fait remarquer que ce n'était pas la pre-*

mière fois que le problème se posait ⊕ to underline = *souligner*
to point to = 1/ *montrer du doigt* : point to the one you want = *montre du doigt celui que tu veux* 2/ *laisser supposer* : everything points to her guilt = *tout laisse supposer qu'elle est coupable*

🏭 *pointer (usine)* = to clock in/out

— *il s'est pointé à 6 heures* = he showed (up) at 6 o'clock.

POINT-BLANK (adv) *à brûle-pourpoint* : he asked her point-blank how old she was = *il lui a demandé son âge à brûle-pourpoint* ⊕ right off = *d'emblée*
to fire point-blank = *tirer à bout portant*.

POINTERS (n pl) **to give s.o. (some) pointers** = *donner des conseils pratiques à qqn* : can you give me some pointers on how to make a soufflé ? = *pouvez-vous me donner quelques conseils (pratiques) sur la manière de réussir un soufflé ?* ≠ **to pick up pointers** = *glaner*

des conseils pratiques.

POINTLESS (adj) *qui ne sert à rien* : it's pointless to leave now = *ça ne sert à rien de partir maintenant* ⊕ useless = *inutile*.

POISE (n inv) *allure* (f) *(et assurance)* : she has a lot of poise for a 15-year-old = *elle a beaucoup d'allure et d'assurance pour une fille de 15 ans* ⊕ bearing = *maintien*.

POISON (n) *poison (m)* : arsenic is a poison = *l'arsenic est un poison* ⓓ poisonous = *toxique*

poison ivy = *sumac vénéneux*

poison-pen letter = *lettre anonyme*

☠ *c'est un vrai poison !* = she's a plague !

POISON (to, -ed) *empoisonner* : he poisoned his mother = *il a empoisonné sa mère* ☠ *empoisonner (la vie de qqn)* = to make (s.o.'s life) miserable **POISONOUS** (adj) *venimeux, -euse* (snake), *toxique* (food).

POKE (to, -d) *donner un coup de coude* : he poked me in the ribs = *il m'a donné un coup de coude dans les côtes.*

POKER (n) *poker (m)* : to play poker = *jouer au poker* ⓓ craps = *dés.*

POKER-FACED (adj) *(au visage) de marbre* : the murderer remained poker-faced throughout the proceedings = *le meurtrier a gardé un visage de marbre tout au long du procès* ⓓ straight-faced = *au visage sérieux.*

POLAND (n) *Pologne (f)* **POLE** (n) *Polonais, -e* ⓓ Polack = *polack (m, f), polaque (m, f)* ☠ *soûl comme un Polonais* = drunk as a lord **POLISH** (adj) *polonais, -e.*

POLE (n) *poteau (m)* : telephone pole = *poteau téléphonique*

North ≠ South Pole = *Pôle Nord ≠ Sud*

we're poles apart = *nous sommes aux antipodes*

☠ *pôle d'attraction* = center of attraction

— *se faire coiffer (au poteau)* = to lose by a hairsbreadth.

POLEMIC (n) *polémique (f)* : a polemic over abortion = *une polémique sur l'avortement* ⓓ debate = *débat.*

POLICE (n pl) *police (f)* : the police are stuck with the case = *dans cette affaire, la police patauge* ⓓ vice squad = *brigade mondaine*

police car = *voiture de police*

police commissioner = *commissaire de police*

police dog = *chien policier*

police headquarters = *préfecture de police*

police inspector = *inspecteur de police*

police officer = *officier/agent de police*

police state = *État policier*

police station = *commissariat/poste de police*

police precinct = *circonscription administrative*

police story = *histoire policière/polar*

☠ *police judiciaire* = Criminal Investigation Department

— *police (d'assurance)* = (insurance) policy.

POLICE (to, -d) *faire régner l'ordre* : to police an area = *faire régner l'ordre dans un quartier.*

POLICEMAN (n, -men) *policier (m), gendarme (m)* : the gangsters killed three policemen = *les gangsters ont tué trois policiers/gendarmes* ⓓ cop = *flic*, officer = *agent (de police)*, constable (GB) = *gardien de la paix*, plain-clothesman = *policier en civil* ☠ *jouer au gendarme et au voleur* = to play cops and robbers **POLICEWOMAN** (n, -women) *femme (f) agent.*

POLICY (n, -ies) *politique (f)* : the government's eco-nomic policy = *la politique économique du gouverne-ment* ⓓ strategy = *stratégie*

to take out a policy = *souscrire une police (d'assurance)*

☠ → politics.

POLIO (n) *polio (f)* : he had polio when he was a child = *il a eu la polio quand il était petit* ⓓ infantile paralysis = *poliomyélite* = poliomyelitis.

POLISH (n, -es) 1/ *vernis (m)* (nails), *cirage (m)* (shoes) : I don't like nails without polish = *je n'aime pas les ongles sans vernis*

☠ *être dans le cirage* = to be in a fog

— *un vernis de (sophistication)* = a veneer of (sophistication)

2/ *raffinement (m)* : she has a great deal of polish = *elle a beaucoup de raffinement* ⓓ class = *classe.*

POLISH (to, -ed) *polir* (silver), *cirer* (shoes, furniture) ⓓ to varnish = *vernir*

to polish off = *faire un sort à* : let's polish off the Scotch/the chicken = *si on faisait un sort à ce whisky/poulet* ⓓ to finish off = *finir*

to polish up = *se remettre à* : I have to polish up my English = *il faut que je me remette à l'anglais* ⓓ to brush up = *réviser.*

POLISHED (adj) a polished (performance) = *(une représentation) de grand professionnel.*

POLITE (adj) *poli, -e* : polite children = *des enfants polis* ⓓ well-bred = *bien élevé ≠ impolite = impoli* **POLITELY** (adv) *poliment* : answer his letter politely = *répondez poliment à sa lettre* ⓓ courteously = *courtoisement* **POLITENESS** (n) *politesse (f)* : a lack of politeness = *un manque de politesse ≠ rudeness = grossièreté* ☠ *brûler la politesse* = to take French leave.

POLITICAL (adj) *politique* : a political party = *un parti politique*, political science = *science politique ≠ apolitical = apolitique* ☠ *un homme/une femme politique* = a politician **POLITICALLY** (adv) *politiquement* : politically speaking = *politiquement parlant.*

POLITICIAN (n) *homme/femme politique, politicien, -enne* : not all politicians take bribes = *tous les hommes/toutes les femmes politiques ne touchent pas de pots-de-vin* ⓓ pol = *politicard.*

POLITICIZE (to, -d) *politiser* : to politicize the women's movement = *politiser le mouvement féministe.*

POLITICKING (n inv) *approche (f) politique* : there's constant politicking in feminist circles = *on a constamment une approche politique dans les cercles féministes.*

POLITICS (n inv) *politique (f)* : she's never taken any interest in politics = *elle ne s'est jamais intéressée à la politique*

☠ *la politique étrangère* = foreign policy

— *pratiquer la politique de l'autruche* = to look the other way.

POLL (n) *sondage (m)* : opinion poll = *sondage d'opinion*

476

to go to the polls = *aller aux urnes* ⓒ ballot box = *urne.*

POLL (to, -ed) *obtenir* : the candidate polled a minority of votes = *le candidat n'a pas obtenu la majorité des suffrages* ☠ → to obtain.

POLLUTE (to, -d) *polluer* : most rivers are polluted = *la plupart des rivières sont polluées* ⓒ to contaminate = *contaminer* **POLLUTION** (n) *pollution (f)* : air pollution = *pollution atmosphérique* ≠ purification = ←.

POMP (n) *pompe (f)* : a ceremony of pomp and show = *une cérémonie empreinte de pompe et de spectaculaire* ☠ → pump.

POMPOUS (adj) *pompeux, -euse* : a pompous way of speaking = *une façon pompeuse de parler* ⓒ stuffy = *guindé.*

PONCHO (n) *poncho (m)* ⓒ cape = ←.

POND (n) *étang (m), mare (f)* : to go wading in a pond = *aller patauger dans une mare/un étang* ⓒ brook = *cours d'eau* ☠ *une mare de sang* = a pool of blood.

PONDER (to, -ed) *songer à* : he pondered his decision carefully = *il a beaucoup songé à la décision qu'il allait prendre* ⓒ to meditate = *méditer.*

PONY (n, -ies) *poney (m)* : there are ponies in Central Park = *il y a des poneys à Central Park* ⓒ horse = *cheval.*

POODLE (n) *caniche (m)* : she has a toy poodle = *elle a un caniche nain* ⓒ dog = *chien.*

POOH-POOH (to, -ed) *cracher sur* : she pooh-poohed my idea = *elle a craché sur mon idée* ≠ to praise = *louer.*

POOL (n) *piscine (f)* : I prefer to swim in a pool = *je préfère nager dans une piscine* = swimming pool
a pool of blood = *une mare de sang*
a (typing) pool = *un pool de (dactylos)*
to play pool = *jouer au billard américain* ⓒ pool table = *table de billard*, poolroom = *salle de billard*, to play billiards = *jouer au billard*
☠ *la piscine* = the company (CIA).

POOL (to, -ed) *mettre en commun* : we pooled our resources to take a trip to Europe = *nous avons mis nos ressources en commun pour faire un voyage en Europe.*

POOPED (adj) *raplapla* : pooped after a day's work = *raplapla après une journée de travail* ⓒ shot = *claqué*, worn-out = *exténué.*

POOR (n inv) **the poor** = *les pauvres* ⓒ the destitute = *les démunis*, poorhouse = *asile pour indigents* ≠ the rich = *les riches.*

POOR (adj, -er, -est) **1/** *pauvre* : a poor man = *un homme pauvre* ≠ rich = *riche*
2/ *assez mauvais, -e* : poor results = *d'assez mauvais résultats* ≠ excellent = ←

poor (little) me ! = *pauvre de moi !*
poor thing ! = *le/la pauvre !*
poor soul/devil = *pauvre bougre/diable*

to be poor at (math) = *être assez mauvais en (maths)*

GROUP : POOR = PAUVRE

to be broke = *être fauché* **to be bust(ed)** = *être sans le rond* **to be cleaned out** = *être sur la paille* **to be destitute** = *être démuni* **to be down-and-out** = *être dans la dèche* **to be down to one's bottom dollar** = *manger de la vache enragée* **to be down to one's last cent/penny** = *ne plus avoir un centime* **to be flat broke** = *être complètement à sec* **to be hard-pressed** = *être aux abois* **to be hard up** = *être dans la mouise*	**to be impoverished** = *être appauvri* **to be indigent** = *être indigent* **to be in dire straits** = *être aux abois* **to be in need** = *être dans le besoin* **to be in the red** = *être en déficit* **to feel the pinch** = *être dans la gêne* **to go through rough/hard times** = *tirer le diable par la queue* **to have just enough to live on** = *avoir tout juste de quoi vivre* **lean years** = *période de vaches maigres* **to live from hand to mouth** = *vivre au jour le jour*	**to live on air** = *vivre de l'air du temps* **not to have a cent/penny to one's name** = *ne pas avoir un radis/un rond* **not to have a (red) cent** = *ne pas avoir un sou (vaillant)* **not to have a penny** = *ne pas avoir un sou (en poche)* **not to make ends meet** = *ne pas arriver à joindre les deux bouts* **to be on one's uppers** (GB) = *tirer le diable par la queue* **to be penniless** = *être sans le sou* **to be as poor as a church mouse** = *être pauvre comme Job* **to be poverty-stricken** = *être*

miséreux/misérable **to be short of (money)** = *être à court d'(argent)* **to be stone-broke** = *être fau-*	*ché comme les blés* **to be strapped** = *être à sec* **to tighten one's belt** = *se serrer la ceinture*	**to be up to one's ears in debt** = *être endetté jusqu'au cou* **to be wiped out** = *être ratissé.*

POORLY (adv) *assez mal :* he writes poorly = *il écrit assez mal* ≠ marvelously = *merveilleusement.*

POP (adj) *pop :* pop art/music = *art/musique pop.*

POP (to, -ped) **to pop down to (the bank)** = *faire un saut à (la banque)* = to hop down
to pop in = *passer rapidement :* I just popped in to say hello = *je passais juste rapidement vous dire bonjour* ⓈⓈ to drop in = *passer à l'improviste*
to pop up = 1/ *faire son apparition :* S-M houses popped up all over the country = *des maisons spéciales pour sadomasochistes ont fait leur apparition dans tout le pays* ⓈⓈ to appear = *apparaître* 2/ *se poser :* let me know if the problem pops up again = *faites-moi savoir si le problème se pose à nouveau* ⓈⓈ to arise = *se présenter*
☠ → to pose.

POPE (n) *pape (m) :* the pope lives in the Vatican = *le pape habite le Vatican* ⓈⓈ the Holy Father = *le Saint-Père,* his Holiness = *sa Sainteté.*

POPULAR (adj) **1/** *très apprécié -e, populaire :* my daughter's very popular at the office = *ma fille est très appréciée/populaire à son bureau* ≠ unpopular = *impopulaire* ☠ *(quartier) populaire* = working-class (area)
2/ *à la mode :* red is popular this year = *le rouge est à la mode cette année* ⓈⓈ in = ←.

POPULARITY (n, -ies) *popularité (f) :* the popularity of the President = *la popularité du Président.*

POPULATE (to, -d) *peupler :* Japan is densely populated = *le Japon est très peuplé.*

POPULATION (n) *population (f) :* what's the population of New York ? = *quelle est la population de New York ?*
population growth = *croissance démographique.*

PORCELAIN (n) *porcelaine (f) :* a porcelain doll = *une poupée de porcelaine* ⓈⓈ china = *service en porcelaine.*

PORE OVER (to, -d) *se plonger dans :* to pore over one's books = *se plonger dans ses livres* ⓈⓈ to be absorbed in = *être absorbé par.*

PORK (n inv) *porc (m) :* pork chops = *côtes de porc*
☠ *porc (animal)* = hog
— *manger comme un porc* = to eat like a pig
— *peau de porc* = pigskin
— *quel porc !* = what a swine !

PORK-BARRELING (n) *mesures gouvernementales à but électoral (profitant aux régions, aux États), électoralisme (m) :* some congressmen are noted for their pork-barreling = *certains parlementaires sont connus pour leur électoralisme.*

PORN (n) *porno (m) :* he writes porn = *il écrit du porno.*

PORNOGRAPHIC (adj) *pornographique :* pornographic movies = *des films pornographiques* ⓈⓈ blue = *porno,* skin flick = *film de fesses,* chicken porn = *porno avec des mineurs.*

PORNOGRAPHY (n, -ies) *pornographie (f) :* what's the difference between pornography and eroticism ? = *quelle est la différence entre la pornographie et l'érotisme ?* ⓈⓈ hard-core = ←, soft-core = *porno doux,* X-rated = *pour adultes.*

PORT (n) *port (m) :* many boats in the port = *de nombreux bateaux dans le port* = harbor ⓈⓈ pier = *jetée*
☠ *le port d'armes est interdit* = carrying a gun is forbidden.

PORTABLE (adj) *portatif, -ive :* a portable TV/typewriter = *une télé/machine à écrire portative.*

PORTER (n) *porteur (m) :* get the porter for the luggage = *allez chercher le porteur pour les bagages.*

PORTION (n) *portion (f) :* a portion of spaghetti = *une portion de spaghetti,* side portion = *petite portion.*

PORTRAIT (n) *portrait (m) :* a full-length portrait = *un portrait en pied*
☠ *c'est le portrait de son père* = he's the picture of his father
— *abîmer le portrait à qqn* = to work s.o. over
— *dresser le portrait (de qqch)* = to portray (stg)/to give a portrayal (of stg).

PORTRAY (to, -ed) *brosser le tableau de* (stg) : the novelist portrays the misery of India = *le romancier brosse le tableau de la misère en Inde* ⓈⓈ to describe = *décrire*
to portray as = *présenter comme :* they portrayed the dictator as an idealist = *ils ont présenté le dictateur comme un idéaliste.*

PORTRAYAL (n) *portrait (m) :* Hemingway's portrayal of life in Paris = *le portrait par Hemingway de la vie à Paris* ☠ → portrait.

PORTUGAL (n) *Portugal (m)* **PORTUGUESE** (n, adj) *Portugais, -e* ☠ *avoir les portugaises ensablées* (LV) = to be stone-deaf.

POSE (to, -d) *poser :* that poses a problem = *cela pose un problème*
to pose as (a cop) = *se faire passer pour (un flic)* ⓈⓈ to pretend to be = *faire semblant d'être*
☠ *pose ça !* = put it down !
— *poser une question* = to ask a question
— *si le problème se pose* = if the problem pops up.

POSH (adj, -er, -est) *rupin, -e :* a posh hotel = *un hôtel rupin* ⓈⓈ ritzy = *cossu.*

POSITION (n) **1/** *position* *(f)* : what's the Senator's position on abortion ? = *quelle est la position du sénateur sur l'avortement ?* ⓒⓓ point of view = *point de vue* **2/** *situation* *(f)* : she's looking for a position in the bank = *elle cherche une situation dans la banque* ⓒⓓ job = *travail* ☠ → situation **3/** *position* *(f)* : what's the boat's position ? = *quelle est la position du bateau ?* **4/** *position* *(f)* : you're putting me in an awkward position = *vous me mettez dans une position embarrassante*
to be in a position to (help) = *être en mesure d'(aider)*
in your position = *à votre place* = in your place
☠ *rester sur ses positions* = to stand one's ground.

POSITIVE (adj) **1/** *sûr, -e* : I'm positive he won't come = *je suis sûr qu'il ne viendra pas* ⓒⓓ definite = *certain* ≠ unsure = *pas sûr* ☠ → sure **2/** *positif, -ive* : she's a very positive person = *c'est une personne très positive* ⓒⓓ optimistic = *optimiste* **3/** *véritable* : he's a positive genius = *c'est un véritable génie* ⓒⓓ downright = *achevé* **POSITIVELY** (adv) *absolument* : she's positively charming = *elle est absolument charmante* = she's absolutely charming ⓒⓓ undoubtedly = *indubitablement* ☠ → absolutely.

POSSESS (to, -ed) *posséder* : she was taken but never possessed = *elle a été prise mais jamais possédée* ⓒⓓ to have = *avoir*
what possessed you to (act so foolishly) ? = *qu'est-ce qui vous a pris d'(agir aussi bêtement) ?*
☠ *posséder deux maisons* = to own two houses (*beaucoup plus dit que « to possess »*)
— *je me suis fait posséder* = I was taken in.

POSSESSION (n) *bien* *(m)* : my cat's my most valuable possession = *mon chat est mon bien le plus précieux*
in my possession = *en ma possession* : the will's in my possession = *le testament est en ma possession*
☠ *biens immobiliers* = real estate
— *mener à bien (un projet)* = to bring off (a project) successfully
— *penser du bien de* = to think highly of
— *ça vous fera du bien* = it will do you good.

POSSESSIVE (adj) *possessif, -ive* : a possessive husband = *un mari possessif* ⓒⓓ jealous = *jaloux*.

POSSIBILITY (n, -ies) *possibilité* *(f)* : there's no possibility that he'll come tonight = *il n'y a aucune possibilité qu'il vienne ce soir* ⓒⓓ likelihood = *vraisemblance* ☠ *si j'en ai la possibilité* = if it's possible for me.

POSSIBLE (adj) *possible* : it's just not possible for me to come = *il ne m'est pas du tout possible de venir* ⓒⓓ probable = ← ≠ impossible = ←.

POSSIBLY (adv) **1/** *cela se pourrait* : could you come tomorrow ? — possibly ! = *pourriez-vous venir demain ? — cela se pourrait !* ⓒⓓ in all likelihood = *selon toute vraisemblance*, maybe = *peut-être* **2/** *ce qui est possible* : do whatever you possibly can = *faites ce qu'il vous est possible de faire*, I can't possibly come tonight = *il ne m'est pas possible de venir ce soir*.

POST (n) **1/** (inv) (GB) *courrier* *(m)* = mail
the post office = *la poste/le bureau de poste* ⓒⓓ mailbox = *boîte aux lettres*
2/ *poste* *(m)* : a diplomatic post = *un poste diplomatique* ⓒⓓ position = *situation*
☠ *poste de télévision* = television set
— *poste de police* = police station
— *chercher un poste* = to look for a job.

POST (to, -ed) **1/** *poster* : to post a letter = *poster une lettre* ⓒⓓ to mail = *mettre à la poste*, postage = *affranchissement* **2/** *poster* : three soldiers were posted at the gate = *trois soldats étaient postés à l'entrée* ⓒⓓ to be on guard = *être de garde*.

POST (pref) *post-* : the postimpressionists = *les postimpressionnistes.*

POSTCARD (n) *carte* *(f)* *postale.*

POSTER (n) *poster* *(m)*, *affiche* *(f)* : a Toulouse-Lautrec poster = *une affiche/un poster de Toulouse-Lautrec* ⓒⓓ sign = *enseigne* ☠ *tenir l'affiche* = to be playing.

POSTERITY (n inv) *postérité* *(f)* : his writings will be judged by posterity = *ses écrits seront jugés par la postérité* ⓒⓓ immortality = *immortalité.*

POSTHUMOUS (adj) *posthume* : posthumous recognition = *reconnaissance posthume.*

POSTPONE (to, -d) *remettre* : the meeting was postponed = *la réunion a été remise* ⓒⓓ to put off = *repousser*
☠ *remettre qqn à sa place* = to put s.o. in his place
— *se remettre (maladie)* = to get over (illness)
— *remettre (une copie/son arme)* = to hand/to give in (a paper)/to hand over (one's gun).

POSTURE (n) *posture* *(f)* : poor posture can lead to spinal problems = *une mauvaise posture peut entraîner des problèmes vertébraux.*

POSTWAR (adj) *d'après-guerre* : postwar economic problems = *les problèmes économiques d'après-guerre.*

POT (n) **1/** *casserole* *(f)* : put the spaghetti in the pot = *mets les spaghetti dans la casserole* ⓒⓓ potholder = *gant de cuisine*, pan = *poêle* **2/** *marie* *(f)* *(-jeanne)* : to smoke pot = *fumer de la marie* ⓒⓓ drug = *drogue*
to go to pot = *aller à la dérive* : his business is going to pot = *son affaire va à la dérive* ⓒⓓ to be going to the dogs = *battre de l'aile*
it's the pot calling the kettle black = *c'est la paille et la poutre/c'est la poêle qui se moque du chaudron/c'est l'hôpital qui se moque de la charité* ⓒⓓ look who's talking ! = *tu ne t'es pas regardé !*
shit or get off the pot ! = *(tu te décides) oui ou merde ?*
a watched pot never boils = *patience et longueur de temps font plus que force ni que rage*
☠ *(pour avoir le boulot) il a fallu qu'elle passe à la casserole* = she had to put out (to get the job)
— *un pot de colle* = a hanger-on

— *prendre un pot* = to have a drink
— *avoir du pot* = to be lucky
— *découvrir le pot aux roses* = to uncover the truth
— *quel pot !* = what luck !
— *payer les pots cassés* = to pay the piper
— *sourd comme un pot* = deaf as a post
— *c'est le pot de terre contre le pot de fer* = it's an un-equal fight
— *tourner autour du pot* = to beat around the bush
— *un pot de confiture* = a jar of jam.

POTATO (n, -es) *pomme de terre (f)* : I eat a lot of potatoes = *je mange beaucoup de pommes de terre*, to peel potatoes = *éplucher des pommes de terre* ① spud = *patate*, French fries = *frites*, baked potatoes = *pommes de terre en robe des champs/au four*, mashed potatoes = *purée*, potato chips = *chips*.

POTBELLIED (adj) *bedonnant, -e* : potbellied husbands aren't sexy = *les maris bedonnants ne sont pas sexy*.

POTBELLY (n, -ies) *bedaine (f)* : to have a potbelly = *avoir de la bedaine* ① to have a middle age spread = *avoir de la brioche*.

POTENT (adj) *puissant, -e* : a potent medicine = *un médicament puissant* ① strong = *fort* ☠ → forceful.

POTENTIAL (n) *potentiel (m)* : a writer with great potential = *un écrivain qui a un gros potentiel* **POTENTIAL** (adj) *potentiel, -elle, en puissance* : a potential champion = *un champion potentiel/en puissance* ① latent = ← **POTENTIALITY** (n, -ies) *potentialité (f)* **POTENTIALLY** (adv) *potentiellement*.

POTLUCK (n) **to take potluck** = *manger à la fortune du pot*.

POSTSHOT (n) **to take a potshot (at)** = *jeter une pierre dans le jardin (de)* : the Democratic candidate took a potshot at his opponent on TV = *au cours d'une émission télévisée, le candidat démocrate a jeté une pierre dans le jardin de son adversaire* ① a crack = *une vanne*.

POTTED (adj) *paf* : potted after two drinks = *paf après deux verres* → DRUNK.

POTTERY (n, -ies) *poterie (f)* : beautiful painted pottery = *de la belle poterie peinte* ① potter = *potier*, ceramics = *céramique*.

POULTRY (n inv) *volaille (f)* : hens, chickens, ducks are poultry = *les poules, les poulets, les canards sont de la volaille* = fowl ① game = *gibier*.

POUNCE ON (to, -d) **1/** *bondir sur* : the lion pounced on its prey = *le lion a bondi sur sa proie* **2/** *sauter sur* : the teacher pounces on every mistake I make = *le prof saute sur toutes les fautes que je fais*.

POUND (n) **1/** *livre (sterling) (f)* : the blouse costs ten pounds = *le chemisier coûte dix livres* **2/** *livre (f) (453 g)* : a pound of oranges = *une livre d'oranges* ☠ → book **3/** *fourrière (f)* : we adopted a beautiful mutt at the

pound = *nous avons adopté un adorable cabot à la fourrière*.

POUND (to, -ed) *frapper à coups redoublés* : he pounded on the door = *il a frappé à coups redoublés sur la porte*.

POUR (to, -ed) **1/** *pleuvoir à verse* : it poured all day = *il a plu à verse toute la journée* ① to rain = *pleuvoir* **2/** *verser* : pour me some Scotch = *verse-moi un peu de whisky* ☠ *verser (des arrhes)* = to give (a deposit)
to pour into = **1/** *engloutir dans* : he poured a fortune into the business = *il a englouti une fortune dans l'affaire* **2/** *affluer* : letters/people are pouring into the office = *les lettres/les gens affluent au bureau*
to be poured into (one's slacks) = *être très moulé dans (son pantalon)* ≠ to swim in = *flotter dans*
to pour it on = *y aller fort* : when he flatters the boss he really pours it on = *quand il flatte le patron, il y va vraiment fort* ① to lay it on = *en faire des tonnes*.

POUT (to, -ed) *faire la moue* : when I said I didn't want to make love, he pouted = *quand j'ai dit que je ne voulais pas faire l'amour, il a fait la moue* ① to sulk = *bouder*.

POVERTY (n inv) *pauvreté (f)* : the poverty of some African countries = *la pauvreté de certains pays africains* ① want = *besoin* ≠ affluence = *abondance*.

POVERTY-STRICKEN (adj) *miséreux, -euse, misérable* : poverty-stricken families = *des familles miséreuses/misérables* → POOR ≠ rolling in money = *qui roule sur l'or* ☠ *misérable* → miserable.

POW (abbr) = Prisoner of War = *prisonnier (m) de guerre* : 3 POWs were missing = *il manquait 3 prisonniers de guerre* ① hostage = *otage*.

POWDER (n) *poudre (f)* : to put powder on one's nose = *se mettre de la poudre sur le nez* ① compact = *poudrier*
powder keg = *poudrière*
powder puff = *houpette*
powder room = *toilettes pour dames*
to take a powder = *prendre la poudre d'escampette* → TO LEAVE
☠ *il n'a pas inventé la poudre* = he won't set the world on fire.

POWER (n) **1/** *pouvoir (m)* : he's after power = *il court après le pouvoir*, the President's powers = *les pouvoirs du Président* ☠ *les pouvoirs publics* = the government **2/** *puissance (f)* : the power of love/the engine = *la puissance de l'amour/du moteur* ① force = ←
to come to power = *accéder au pouvoir*
in power = *au pouvoir* : the government in power = *le gouvernement au pouvoir*
in my power = *en mon pouvoir* : I'll do everything in my power to help you = *je ferai tout ce qui est en mon pouvoir pour vous aider*
power of attorney = *procuration*
the power behind the throne = *l'éminence grise*
purchasing power = *pouvoir d'achat*

the staying power (of the generals) = *le maintien au pouvoir (des généraux)*.

POWERFUL (adj) *puissant, -e* : a powerful drug = *un médicament puissant* ⓓ all-powerful = *tout-puissant* ≠ powerless = *impuissant* ☠ → forceful.

POWWOW (n) *conseil (m) de guerre* : a powwow between the two leaders = *un conseil de guerre entre les deux dirigeants* ⓓ talks = *pourparlers*.

PR (abbr) = public relations = *relations publiques (f pl)* : she does interesting PR work = *elle fait un travail de relations publiques intéressant*.

PRACTICAL (adj) *pratique* : umbrellas are practical = *les parapluies sont pratiques* ⓓ judicious = *judicieux* ≠ impractical = *pas pratique*
practical joke = *farce* ⓓ **practical joker** = *farceur*
practical nurse = *garde-malade*.

PRACTICALLY (adv) *pratiquement* : you're practically as tall as I am = *vous êtes pratiquement aussi grand que moi* ⓓ nearly = *presque*.

PRACTICE (n) 1/ *pratique (f)* : you need some practice = *vous avez besoin de pratique* ⓓ training = *entraînement*
in practice = *en pratique* : bowling looks easy, but in practice it isn't = *ça a l'air facile de faire du bowling, mais en pratique, ça ne l'est pas* ≠ in theory = *en théorie*
to make a practice of = *se faire une règle de* : don't make a practice of coming late = *ne vous faites pas une règle d'arriver en retard* ⓓ to make a habit of = *prendre l'habitude de*
to be out of ≠ **in practice** = *manquer d'entraînement* ≠ *avoir de l'entraînement / manquer de pratique* ≠ *avoir de la pratique* (language)
practice makes perfect = *c'est en forgeant qu'on devient forgeron*
to put into practice = *mettre en pratique*
2/ *cabinet (m)* : the new doctor/lawyer has a large practice = *le nouveau médecin/le nouvel avocat a un cabinet important* ☠ → cabinet.

PRACTICE (to, -d) 1/ *s'exercer* : he practices on the piano everyday = *il s'exerce au piano tous les jours* = to practise (GB) ⓓ to work out = *s'entraîner* 2/ *exercer* : to practice law = *exercer la profession de juriste*
practice what you preach = *commence par donner l'exemple* ⓓ do as I say but not as I do = *fais ce que je dis, non pas ce que je fais*
☠ → to exert.

PRACTICING (adj) *en exercice* (profession), *pratiquant, -e* (religion) : a practicing doctor/Catholic = *un médecin en exercice/un catholique pratiquant*.

PRAGMATIC (adj) *pragmatique* : Americans are pragmatic = *les Américains sont pragmatiques* ≠ unrealistic = *irréaliste* **PRAGMATISM** (n) *pragmatisme (m)* : the pragmatism of the business world = *le pragmatisme du monde des affaires* **PRAGMATIST** (n) *pragmatique (m, f)*.

PRAISE (n inv) *louanges (f pl), éloges (m pl)* : I love praise = *j'aime les louanges/les éloges* ≠ criticism = *critique*
to sing s.o.'s praises = *chanter les louanges de qqn* ≠ to find fault with = *trouver à redire à*.

PRAISE (to, -d) *louer, faire des louanges* : don't praise me, pay me ! = *ne me faites pas de louanges, payez-moi !* ⓓ to laud = *louanger*, to acclaim = *acclamer*, to extol = *prôner* ☠ *louer un appartement* = to rent/let/hire an apartment.

PRAISEWORTHY (adj) *digne d'éloges* : a praiseworthy deed = *une action digne d'éloges* ⓓ deserving = *méritoire*.

PRANK (n) **to play a prank on s.o.** = *faire une niche à qqn* **PRANKSTER** (n) *farceur, -euse*.

PRAY (to, -ed) *prier* : to pray for peace in the world = *prier pour la paix dans le monde* ⓓ prayer = *prière* ☠ *je vous prie de ...* = would you please ...
— *il aime se faire prier* = he likes to have his arm twisted.

PRAYER (n) *prière (f)* : my daughter says her prayers every evening = *ma fille dit ses prières tous les soirs* ⓓ meditation = *méditation*
☠ *prière (demande)* = request
— *prière de (payer comptant)* = please (pay cash).

PREACH (to, -ed) 1/ *faire la morale* : stop preaching about my drinking = *arrête de me faire la morale parce que je bois* 2/ *prêcher* : priests preach = *les prêtres prêchent* ⓓ preacher = *prédicateur*, sermon = ←.

PRECARIOUS (adj) *précaire* : a precarious situation = *une situation précaire* ⓓ risky = *risqué* ☠ *santé précaire* = delicate health.

PRECAUTION (n) *précaution (f)* : he took the precaution of using a rubber = *il a pris la précaution de mettre une capote* ⓓ prudence = ← ☠ *agir avec précaution* = to proceed with caution.

PRECEDE (to, -d) *précéder* : the President entered the room preceded by his bodyguards = *le Président est entré dans la pièce précédé de ses gardes du corps*.

PRECEDENCE (n) **to take precedence over** = *passer en priorité* : that item takes precedence over the others on the agenda = *cette question passe en priorité à l'ordre du jour*.

PRECEDENT (n) *précédent (m)* : to set a precedent = *créer un précédent*, without precedent = *sans précédent*.

PRECEDING (adj) *précédent, -e* : the preceding day = *le jour précédent* ≠ following = *suivant* ☠ *son précédent mari* = her previous husband.

PRECINCT (n) *circonscription (f)* : to vote by precincts = *voter dans le cadre de la circonscription*, police precinct = *circonscription administrative*.

PRECIOUS (adj) 1/ *précieux, -euse* : precious gems/friends = *pierres précieuses/amis précieux* ⓪ invaluable = *inestimable* 2/ *adorable* : what a precious child ! = *quel enfant adorable !* = adorable ⓪ cute = *mignon*.

PRECIPITATE (to, -d) *précipiter* : events precipitated his resignation = *les événements ont précipité sa démission* ⓪ to accelerate = *accélérer*
☙ *se précipiter dans* = to rush into
— *les événements se sont précipités* = events happened in rapid succession.

PRECISE (adj) *précis, -e* : precise indications = *des indications précises* ⓪ specific = *spécifique* ≠ imprecise = *imprécis*.

PRECISELY (adv) 1/ *au juste* : what kind of work is he doing precisely ? = *qu'est-ce qu'il fait comme travail au juste ?* 2/ *précisément* : so you think I lied ? — precisely ! = *ainsi vous pensez que j'ai menti ? — précisément !*

PRECISION (n) *précision* (f) : her work lacks precision = *son travail manque de précision* ⓪ exactness = *exactitude* ☙ *donnez-moi des précisions* = give me the particulars.

PRECLUDE (to, -d) *écarter* : the taking of hostages precluded all possibility of compromise = *la prise d'otages a écarté toute possibilité de compromis*
☙ *écarter la foule* = to clear away the crowd
— *s'écarter du (sujet)* = to stray from (the subject).

PRECOCIOUS (adj) *précoce* : a precocious child = *un enfant précoce* ≠ retarded = *attardé*.

PRECONCEIVED (adj) *préconçu, -e* : preconceived ideas = *des idées préconçues* ⓪ biased = *de parti pris*.

PRECURSOR (n) *précurseur* (m) : Corot was the precursor of impressionism = *Corot a été le précurseur de l'impressionnisme*.

PREDATOR (n) *prédateur* (m) : man is the worst predator = *l'homme est le pire des prédateurs* **PREDATORY** (adj) *prédateur, -trice*.

PREDECESSOR (n) *prédécesseur* (m) : the Prime Minister greeted his predecessor = *le Premier ministre a salué son prédécesseur* ≠ successor = *successeur*.

PREDICAMENT (n) **(to be) in a predicament** = *(être) dans une situation difficile* ⓪ to be in hot water = *être dans de beaux draps*
what a predicament ! = *quel dilemme !*

PREDICT (to, -ed) *prédire* : I predict they're going to get married = *je vous prédis qu'ils vont se marier* ⓪ to foresee = *prévoir*, to prognosticate = *pronostiquer*.

PREDICTABLE (adj) *prévisible* : his reaction was predictable = *sa réaction était prévisible* ≠ unpredictable = *imprévisible* **PREDICTABLY** (adv) *comme c'était à prévoir* : predictably, the motion was defeated = *comme c'était à prévoir, la motion n'a pas été votée*.

PREDICTION (n) *prédiction* (f) : fortune-tellers make predictions = *les diseuses de bonne aventure font des prédictions* ⓪ forecast = *prévision*.

PREDISPOSE (to, -d) *prédisposer* : smoking predisposes you to cancer = *le tabac vous prédispose au cancer* ≠ to be prone to = *être sujet à*.

PREDOMINANCE (n) *prédominance* (f) : a predominance of Catholics in France = *une prédominance des catholiques en France*.

PREDOMINANT (adj) *prédominant, -e* : money is their predominant problem = *l'argent est pour eux le problème prédominant* **PREDOMINANTLY** (adv) *essentiellement* : the people there were predominantly foreigners = *les gens qui étaient là étaient essentiellement des étrangers*.

PREFAB (n) **prefab housing** = *logements préfabriqués/en préfabriqué*.

PREFACE (n) *préface* (f) : the book had no preface = *le livre n'avait pas de préface* ⓪ prologue = ←, introduction = ←.

PREFER (to, -ed) *préférer* : which color do you prefer ? = *quelle est la couleur que vous préférez ?* ⓪ to opt for = *opter pour*, to favor = *favoriser*
to prefer to = *préférer* : I prefer to go now = *je préfère y aller maintenant*
to prefer ... to = *préférer ... à* : I prefer Mahler to Strauss = *je préfère Mahler à Strauss* ⓪ to like better = *aimer mieux*.

PREFERABLE (adj) *préférable* : it's preferable to go by plane = *il est préférable d'y aller par avion* ⓪ better = *mieux* **PREFERABLY** (adv) *de préférence*.

PREFERENCE (n) *préférence* (f) : she has a preference for young men = *elle a une préférence pour les hommes jeunes* ⓪ predilection = *prédilection*.

PREFERENTIAL TREATMENT (n) *traitement* (m) *de faveur*.

PREFIX (n) *préfixe* (m) : "under-" is a prefix = « *sous-* » *est un préfixe*.

PREGNANCY (n, -ies) *grossesse* (f) : a nine-month pregnancy is too long ! = *une grossesse de neuf mois, c'est trop long !*

PREGNANT (adj) *enceinte* : she's three months pregnant = *elle est enceinte de trois mois* ⓪ expectant mother = *future mère*, to be expecting = *attendre un bébé*, to be knocked up = *être en cloque*, maternity dress = *robe de grossesse*.

PREHISTORIC(AL) (adj) *préhistorique* : prehistoric times/man = *les temps préhistoriques/l'homme préhistorique*.

PREJUDICE (n) *préjugé* (m) : racial prejudice = *préjugé racial* ⓪ bias = *parti pris*.

PREJUDICED (adj) **1/** *de parti pris* : a prejudiced judgment = *un jugement de parti pris* ① partial = ←
2/ *raciste* : her family's prejudiced = *sa famille est raciste* = racist.

PREJUDICIAL (adj) *préjudiciable* : prejudicial remarks = *des remarques préjudiciables.*

PRELIMINARY (n, -ies) *préliminaire (m)* : let's get rid of the preliminaries and get to work as soon as possible = *débarrassons-nous des préliminaires et mettons-nous au travail aussi vite que possible* **PRELIMINARY** (adj) *préliminaire* : preliminary exams = *examens préliminaires.*

PRELUDE (n) *prélude (m)* : the arms race is a prelude to the Third World War = *la course aux armements est un prélude à la troisième guerre mondiale* ① introduction = ←.

PREMATURE (adj) *prématuré, -e* : a premature baby/death = *un bébé prématuré/une mort prématurée.*

PREMEDITATED (adj) *prémédité, -e* : premeditated murder = *un meurtre prémédité* ① planned = *prévu* ≠ unpremeditated = *non prémédité.*

PREMIERE (n) *première (f)* : the play's premiere = *la première de la pièce* ① preview = *avant-première.*

PREMISE (n) *ce que l'on suppose, prémisse (f)* : her premise is that her husband is going to agree to divorce = *elle suppose que son mari sera d'accord pour divorcer*
I'm going on the premise (that he'll agree) = *je pars du principe (qu'il sera d'accord)* ① I take for granted = *je tiens pour acquis.*

PREMISES (n pl) *locaux (m pl)* : no smoking on the premises = *interdiction de fumer dans les locaux.*

PREMIUM (n) *prime (f)* : a week off as a premium for her excellent report = *une semaine de congé en prime pour son excellent rapport*
at a premium = *rare et cher* : apartments with terraces are at a premium = *les appartements avec terrasses sont rares et chers*
☠ *prime de fin d'année* = Christmas bonus.

PREMONITION (n) *prémonition (f)* : she had a premonition that she was going to have an accident = *elle a eu la prémonition qu'elle allait avoir un accident* ① presentiment = *pressentiment.*

PREOCCUPY (to, -ied) *préoccuper* : she's very preoccupied with her children's future = *elle est très préoccupée par l'avenir de ses enfants.*

PREPAID (adj) *payé, -e d'avance* : a prepaid delivery = *une livraison payée d'avance.*

PREPARATION (n) *préparation (f)* : this experiment requires long preparation = *cette expérience demande une longue préparation.*

PREPARATIONS (n pl) *préparatifs (m pl)* : preparations for the election/the wedding = *les préparatifs de l'élection/du mariage.*

PREPARE (to, -d) *préparer* : who's going to prepare the dinner ? = *qui va préparer le dîner ?*
prepare yourself for (a shock) = *préparez-vous à (avoir un choc)* ① steel yourself against = *cuirassez-vous contre*
to be prepared to = *être disposé à* : I'm prepared to help you = *je suis disposé à vous aider* ① to be ready to = *être prêt à*
☠ *je prépare (Harvard)* = I'm trying for (Harvard)
— *prépare-toi vite, j'ai faim !* = you'd better get ready, I'm hungry !

PREPONDERANT (adj) *prépondérant, -e* : she played a preponderant role = *elle a joué un rôle prépondérant.*

PREPOSITION (n) *préposition (f)* : "with" is a preposition = *« avec » est une préposition* ① conjunction = *conjonction.*

PREPOSTEROUS (adj) *démentiel, -elle* : what a preposterous thing to say ! = *c'est démentiel de dire un truc comme ça !* ① outlandish = *bizarroïde*, far-out = *dément.*

PREREQUISITE (n) *condition (f) préalable* : patience is a prerequisite for raising children = *la patience est une condition préalable pour pouvoir élever des enfants* ① sine qua non = *condition sine qua non.*

PREROGATIVE (n) *prérogative (f)* : the President has the prerogative of pardoning criminals = *le Président a la prérogative d'accorder la grâce aux criminels* ① right = *droit*
that's my prerogative ! = *c'est mon droit !* : if I want to spend all my money on records, that's my prerogative ! = *si je veux dépenser tout mon argent en disques, c'est mon droit !*

PRESCRIBE (to, -d) *prescrire* : the doctor prescribed some rest = *le médecin a prescrit du repos* **PRESCRIPTION** (n) *ordonnance (f)* : a prescription for penicillin = *une ordonnance pour avoir de la pénicilline.*

PRESENCE (n) *présence (f)* : she has great stage presence = *elle a beaucoup de présence sur scène*, your presence is requested = *votre présence est souhaitée*
presence of mind = *présence d'esprit.*

PRESENT (n) **1/** *présent (m)* : live life in the present ! = *vivez au présent !* ≠ future = *avenir*
2/ *cadeau (m)* : she gave me a beautiful present = *elle m'a fait un beau cadeau* = a beautiful gift ☠ → gift

at present = *à présent* : they're living in New York at present = *à présent, ils habitent New York* ① just now = *en ce moment*	**for the present** = *pour le moment* : let's not discuss it anymore for the present = *n'en discutons plus pour le moment* = for the moment.

PRESENT (adj) **1/** *présent, -e* : he was present at the meeting = *il était présent à la réunion*
2/ *actuel, -elle* : my present husband = *mon mari actuel* ≠ past = *ancien* ☠ → actual

in the present case = *dans le cas présent*	present company excepted = *excepté ceux qui sont présents*

───── **THE PRESENT TENSE = LE PRÉSENT** ─────

— do I (you, we, they) speak English ?	= *est-ce que je parle (tu parles/vous parlez, nous parlons, ils/elles parlent) anglais ?*
— yes, **I do**	= *oui*
— yes, I speak English	= *oui, je parle anglais*
— no, I **don't**	= *non*
no, I don't speak English	= *non, je ne parle pas anglais*
— does he/she speak English ?	= *est-ce qu'il/elle parle anglais ?*
— yes, **he/she does**	= *oui*
yes, he/she speaks English	= *oui, il/elle parle anglais*
— no, **he/she doesn't**	= *non*
no, he/she doesn't speak English	= *non, il/elle ne parle pas anglais*

☠ beware ! the French present can be translated in three different ways = *attention au présent en français : on peut le traduire de trois façons différentes :*	— *il parle* ... { he (often) speaks / he's speaking (now) / he has spoken (for two hours)

───── **THE PRESENT PERFECT = LE PASSÉ COMPOSÉ OU LE PRÉSENT** ─────

1/ *se traduit par le passé composé (ou passé simple)*

— have you ever been married ?	= *est-ce que vous avez déjà été marié ?*
— yes, I have = *oui*	— no, I haven't = *non*
— yes, I've been married = *oui, j'ai été marié*	— no, I haven't ever been married = *non, je n'ai jamais été marié*

☠ *ce premier emploi du* present perfect, *qui se traduit par le passé composé (ou par le passé simple), est utilisé pour un passé indéfini (le temps n'est pas précisé). On dit : « I've often been to New York », MAIS : « I went to New York last year » (emploi du* past tense *pour un passé précisé)*

2/ *se traduit par le* **présent**

— have you lived here for ten years ?	= *habitez-vous ici depuis dix ans ?*
— yes, I have = *oui*	— no, I haven't = *non*
— yes, I've lived here for ten years = *oui, j'habite ici depuis dix ans/cela fait dix ans que j'habite ici*	— no, I haven't lived here for ten years = *non, je n'habite pas ici depuis dix ans/cela ne fait pas dix ans que j'habite ici*

☠ *ce deuxième emploi du* present perfect, *qui se traduit par le présent, fait passer bien des nuits blanches ! (Il est utilisé pour une action commencée dans le passé et qui se poursuit).*

PRESENT (to, -ed) *présenter* : the movie house presents a new film every week = *le cinéma présente un nouveau film toutes les semaines*

to present s.o. to = *présenter qqn à* : may I present my wife to you ? = *puis-je vous présenter ma femme ?* = to introduce s.o. to	to be presented with (a gold medal) = *recevoir (la médaille d'or)* ☠ → to receive

☠ *les choses se présentent mal* ≠ *bien* = the situation looks ≠ doesn't look bad — *se présenter à (une élection)* = to run for (office) — *présenter son passeport* = to show one's passport	— *se présenter à un examen* = to take/sit for an exam — *si quelque chose se présente* = if something arises/turns up/comes up — *présenter un projet de loi* = to introduce a bill.

PRESENTABLE (adj) *présentable* ≠ unpresentable = *qui n'est pas présentable.*

PRESENTATION (n) *remise* (f) : the presentation of the Oscars = *la remise des Oscars* 💀 → shed.

PRESENT-DAY (adj) *d'aujourd'hui* : present-day methods = *les méthodes d'aujourd'hui* ⓓ current = *actuel.*

PRESENTIMENT (n) *pressentiment* (m) : I had a presentiment that I was going to have an accident = *j'avais le pressentiment que j'allais avoir un accident* ⓓ foreboding = *mauvais pressentiment.*

PRESENTLY (adv) *en ce moment* : he's presently working on a novel = *en ce moment, il travaille sur un roman* ⓓ currently = *actuellement.*

PRESERVATION (n) *préservation* (f) : the preservation of natural resources = *la préservation des ressources naturelles* ⓓ conservation = ←.

PRESERVE (to, -d) *préserver* : to preserve the institution of the family = *préserver l'institution de la famille* ⓓ to conserve = *conserver.*

PRESIDE OVER (to, -d) *présider* : the judge presided over the meeting = *le juge a présidé la réunion.*

PRESIDENCY (n, -ies) *présidence* (f) : during his presidency = *pendant sa présidence.*

PRESIDENT (n) *président, -e* (country, business), *P.-D.G.* (m) (business only) : who will be the next President ? = *qui sera le prochain Président/P.-D.G. ?* ⓓ vice-president = *vice-président,* ruler = *dirigeant* 💀 *le président du jury* = the foreman of the jury — *le président du conseil d'administration* = the chairman of the board.

PRESIDENTIAL (adj) *présidentiel, -elle* : the presidential seal = *le sceau présidentiel.*

PRESS (n inv) **the press** = *la presse* : the power of the press = *le pouvoir de la presse* ⓓ the media = *les médias*
to go to press = *mettre sous presse*
to have a good ≠ **bad press** = *avoir bonne* ≠ *mauvaise presse*
press agency = *agence de presse*
press agent = *attaché de presse*
press conference = *conférence de presse*
press release = *communiqué de presse.*

PRESS (to, -ed) **1/** *appuyer* : press the button = *appuyez sur le bouton* 💀 → to back
to press s.o. for stg = *faire pression sur qqn pour qqch* : the unions are pressing the government for reforms = *les syndicats font pression sur le gouvernement pour obtenir des réformes*
to press s.o. to/for = *presser qqn de* : he pressed me to explain/for an explanation = *il m'a pressé de m'expliquer/de lui donner une explication*

2/ *repasser* : press your skirt = *repassez votre jupe* = iron your skirt 💀 → to iron.

PRESSING (adj) *pressant, -e* : pressing matters to take care of = *des affaires pressantes dont il faut s'occuper* ⓓ critical = *critique.*

PRESSURE (n) *pression* (f) : the pressure of modern life = *la pression de la vie moderne* ⓓ tension = ←
pressure cooker = *Cocotte-Minute*
pressure group = *groupe de pression*
to put pressure on s.o. = *exercer une pression sur qqn* : they put pressure on the Senator to defend the bill = *ils ont exercé une pression sur le sénateur pour qu'il défende le projet de loi* ⓓ to prevail on s.o. = *persuader qqn*
under pressure = *sous pression* : we work under pressure = *nous travaillons sous pression.*

PRESSURE (to, -d) *faire pression sur* : he pressured me to lend him money = *il a fait pression sur moi pour que je lui prête de l'argent* ⓓ to compel to = *contraindre à.*

PRESTIGE (n) *prestige* (m) : the prestige of winning the Nobel Prize = *le prestige d'avoir le prix Nobel* **PRESTIGIOUS** (adj) *prestigieux, -euse* : a prestigious position = *une fonction prestigieuse* ⓓ renowned = *renommé.*

PRESTO (adv) *illico presto* ⓓ right away = *tout de suite.*

PRESUMABLY (adv) *en principe* : presumably, they'll marry one day = *en principe, ils se marieront un jour* ⓓ apparently = *apparemment.*

PRESUME (to, -d) *présumer* : he presumes every one agrees with him = *il présume que tout le monde est de son avis* ⓓ to guess = *imaginer*
I presume so = *je présume* ⓓ I suppose so = *je suppose*
I wouldn't presume to (know your kids better than you do) = *loin de moi la prétention de (connaître vos enfants mieux que vous)*
presumed dead = *tenu pour mort.*

PRESUMPTION (n) *ce qu'on pense* : his presumption that I was going to sleep with him was false = *il avait tort de penser que j'allais coucher avec lui.*

PRESUMPTUOUS (adj) *présomptueux, -euse* : a presumptuous attitude = *une attitude présomptueuse* ⓓ brash = *effronté.*

PRESUPPOSE (to, -d) *présupposer* : such a decision presupposes that the pros and cons have been weighed up = *une telle décision présuppose qu'on a pesé le pour et le contre.*

PRETEND (to, -ed) *faire semblant* : pretend you're dead/happy = *fais semblant d'être mort/heureux* ⓓ to feign = *feindre*
to pretend to = *prétendre* : I don't pretend to know everything = *je ne prétends pas tout savoir*
💀 *il prétend qu'(il ne m'a pas vu)* = he claims (he didn't see me).

PRETENDER (n) *prétendant, -e* : the pretender to the throne = *le prétendant au trône* ☙ *son prétendant* = her future husband.

PRETENSE (n) *prétention (f)* : he has no pretense of being a writer = *il n'a pas la prétention d'être un écrivain* ☙ → pretension.

PRETENSION (n) *prétention (f)* : literary pretension = *prétention littéraire* ⓪ ambition = ← ☙ *sans prétention* = without pretense.

PRETENTIOUS (adj) *prétentieux, -euse* : a pretentious girl = *une fille prétentieuse* ≠ modest = *modeste*.

PRETEXT (n) *prétexte (m)* : on the pretext that = *sous prétexte que* ⓪ reason = *raison* ☙ *sous aucun prétexte* = under no circumstances.

PRETTY (adj, -ier, -iest) *joli, -e* : a pretty woman = *une jolie femme* ⓪ cute = *mignon*, lovely = *charmant* ≠ plain = *quelconque* ☙ *faire le joli cœur* = to sweet-talk

to be sitting pretty = *avoir la vie belle* ⓪ to have it good = *se la couler douce* **to cost a pretty penny** = *coûter pas mal d'argent* ≠ to be dirt	cheap = *être donné* **a pretty boy** = *un mignon* ⓪ a fairy = *une tante* **as pretty as a picture** = *jolie comme un cœur*.

PRETTY (adv) *drôlement* : I'm pretty hungry = *j'ai drôlement faim*, she's pretty rich = *elle est drôlement riche* → VERY

to feel pretty good = *se sentir plutôt bien* ≠ to feel lousy = *être mal foutu* **pretty nearly (finished)** = *(fini) à peu de chose près*	**pretty much** = *à peu près* : that's pretty much what I expected = *c'est à peu près ce à quoi je m'attendais* ⓪ practically = *pratiquement*.

PREVAIL (to, -ed) *prévaloir* : his opinion prevailed = *son opinion a prévalu* ⓪ to triumph = *triompher* **to prevail on s.o. to do stg** = *persuader qqn de faire qqch* : he prevailed on me to help his son = *il m'a persuadé d'aider son fils* ⓪ to call on = *faire appel à.*

PREVAILING (adj) *qui prévaut* : the prevailing economic doctrine = *la doctrine économique qui prévaut* ⓪ general = *général.*

PREVALENT (adj) *répandu, -e* : the use of the pill is prevalent among teenagers = *l'usage de la pilule est répandu chez les adolescentes* ⓪ widespread = *largement répandu.*

PREVENT (to, -ed) *empêcher* : nothing can prevent another world war = *rien ne peut empêcher une autre guerre mondiale* **to prevent from** = *empêcher de* : you can't prevent me from seeing him = *vous ne pouvez pas m'empêcher de le voir* ≠ to authorize = *autoriser* ☙ *je n'ai pas pu m'empêcher de (rire)* = I couldn't help (laughing).

PREVENTION (n) *prévention (f)* : the prevention of a disease = *la prévention d'une maladie.*

PREVENTIVE (adj) *préventif, -ive* : preventive treatment = *traitement préventif* **preventive detention** = *détention préventive.*

PREVIEW (n) *avant-première (f)* : the preview of a film = *l'avant-première d'un film* ⓪ a private screening = *une projection privée.*

PREVIOUS (adj) *précédent, -e* : the previous month = *le mois précédent*, her previous husband = *son précédent mari* ≠ next = *prochain* **(she had) no previous experience** = *(elle n'avait) aucune expérience préalable* ☙ → preceding.

PREVIOUSLY (adv) *précédemment* : I hadn't met him previously = *je ne l'avais pas rencontré précédemment* ⓪ formerly = *autrefois.*

PREWAR (adj) *d'avant-guerre* : prewar economies = *les économies d'avant-guerre* ≠ postwar = *d'après-guerre.*

PREY (n) *proie (f)* : baby seals are easy prey = *les bébés phoques sont des proies faciles* ≠ predator = *prédateur* ☙ *lâcher la proie pour l'ombre* = to give up stg given for what might be **PREY ON** (to, -ed) *faire sa proie de* : pushers prey on adolescents = *les revendeurs de drogue font leur proie des adolescents.*

PRICE (n) *prix (m inv)* : what's the price of the car ? = *quel est le prix de la voiture ?* ⓪ cost = *coût*

asking price = *prix demandé* **ceiling price** = *prix plafond* **closing price** = *prix de clôture* **cost price** = *prix coûtant/de revient* **going price** = *prix en cours/pratiqué* **list price** = *prix de vente*	**price control** = *contrôle des prix* **price-fixing** = *alignement (illégal) des prix* **price freeze/freezing** = *blocage/gel des prix* **price tag** = *étiquette* **price war** = *guerre des prix*	**to quote a price** = *proposer un prix* **at a reduced price** = *au rabais* retail ≠ **wholesale price** = *prix de détail* ≠ *de gros* **selling price** = *prix de vente* **to slash/cut prices** = *casser les prix*

(but) at what price ! = *(mais) à quel prix* ! : I got the contract, but at what price ! = *j'ai eu le contrat, mais à quel prix* ! **to pay the price** = *payer le prix*	**there's a price on his head** = *sa tête est mise à prix* **you can't put a price on (love)** = *(l'amour) n'a pas de prix*
☠ *prix Nobel* = Nobel Prize	— *(si tu n'es pas content) c'est le même prix* ! = (if you're not happy) I couldn't care less !

PRICELESS (adj) 1/ *(d'une valeur) inestimable* : a priceless painting = *une peinture (d'une valeur) inestimable* ① valuable = *de grande valeur* 2/ *impayable* : his jokes are priceless = *ses plaisanteries sont impayables* ① amusing = *amusant*.

PRICEY (adj, -ier, -iest) *chérot, -e* : it's a pricey restaurant = *c'est un restaurant chérot* ≠ dirt cheap = *donné*.

PRICK (n) 1/ *bite (f)* : a small prick = *une petite bite* ① cock = *queue* 2/ *ordure (f)* : she's married to a real prick = *elle a épousé une véritable ordure* → BASTARD ☠ → garbage.

PRIDE (n) *orgueil (m), fierté (f)* : you have no pride = *vous n'avez aucun orgueil/aucune fierté* ① self-esteem = *amour-propre*
his pride was hurt = *son orgueil a été blessé/en a pris un coup*
pride and joy = *grande fierté* : she's her parents' pride and joy = *elle fait la grande fierté de ses parents*
to swallow one's pride = *ravaler son orgueil*
to take pride in = *tirer vanité de* : he takes pride in his wife's career = *il tire vanité de la carrière de sa femme* ① to glory in = *se glorifier de*.

PRIDE (to, -d) **to pride o.s. on** = *s'enorgueillir de* : he prides himself on his writing ability = *il s'enorgueillit de ses capacités littéraires* ≠ to be ashamed of = *avoir honte de*.

PRIEST (n) *prêtre (m)* : to ordain a priest = *ordonner un prêtre* ① priestess = *prêtresse*, prelate = *prélat*, clergy = *clergé*, clergyman = *ecclésiastique*.

PRIG (n) *bégueule (f)* : her sister's a prig = *sa sœur est une bégueule* **PRIGGISH** (adj) *bégueule* : a priggish family = *une famille bégueule* ① prim = *comme il faut*.

PRIM (adj, -mer, -mest) *comme il faut* : she's too prim and square for me = *je la trouve trop comme il faut et vieux jeu* ① straitlaced = *collet monté* ≠ debauched = *débauché*.

PRIMARILY (adv) *avant tout* : she's primarily a writer = *c'est avant tout un écrivain* ① chiefly = *principalement*.

PRIMARY (n, -ies) *primaire (f)* : the primaries will start in the spring = *les primaires commenceront au printemps*.

PRIMARY (adj) *primordial, -e* : lack of money was the primary reason for their marriage failure = *la raison primordiale de leur échec conjugal, c'est le manque d'argent* ≠ secondary = *secondaire*
primary school = *école primaire*.

PRIME (n) **to be in one's prime** = *être dans la fleur de l'âge* ① **to be in the prime of life** = *être dans la force de l'âge* ≠ **to have passed one's prime** = *ne plus être de la première jeunesse* ① to be over the hill = *ne plus avoir vingt ans*.

PRIME (adj) *primordial, -e* : a prime factor = *un facteur primordial* ① chief = *principal*
prime cause = *cause première*
Prime Minister = *Premier ministre*
prime rate = *taux de base*
prime time = *heures de grande écoute*.

PRIMITIVE (adj) *primitif, -ive* : primitive art = *art primitif*, primitive societies = *sociétés primitives* ≠ advanced = *avancé*.

PRINCE (n) *prince (m)* : prince charming = *prince charmant* **PRINCELY** (adj) *princier, -ère*.

PRINCESS (n, -es) *princesse (f)* : the princess married a commoner = *la princesse a épousé un roturier*.

PRINCIPAL (n) *principal (m), directeur, -trice (école)* : the school principal = *le principal/directeur de l'école* ① teacher = *enseignant*
☠ *c'est le principal* ! = that's the main thing !
— *directeur* → director.

PRINCIPAL (adj) *principal, -e* : the principal problem = *le problème principal* ① capital = ←
☠ *le personnage principal* = the main character
— *le professeur principal* = the head teacher.

PRINCIPALLY (adv) *principalement* : a film principally for children = *un film principalement destiné aux enfants* ① mainly = *surtout*.

PRINCIPLE (n) *principe (m)* : the principles of physics = *les principes de la physique*
a man/woman of principles = *un homme/une femme à principes*
(stealing is) against his principles = *c'est contraire à ses principes (de voler)*
in principle = *dans son principe* : they accepted the plan in principle = *ils ont accepté le projet dans son principe*
☠ *en principe, il vient demain* = he's presumably coming tomorrow
— *partir du principe que* = to go on the assumption that.

PRINT (n) **1/** (inv) *caractères* (m pl) *d'imprimerie* : the print is too small to read easily = *les caractères sont trop petits pour qu'on puisse les lire facilement*
(the book) is out of print = *(le livre) est épuisé*
in print = *imprimé* : don't believe everything you see in print = *ne croyez pas tout ce que vous voyez imprimé*
read the small/fine print (before signing) = *lisez les petits caractères/toutes les clauses (avant de signer)*
2/ *gravure* (f) : beautiful prints from China = *de belles gravures chinoises.*

PRINT (to, -ed) **1/** *publier* : his first novel was never printed = *son premier roman n'a jamais été publié*, all the papers printed the story = *tous les journaux ont publié cette histoire* = to publish **2/** *imprimer* : to print handbills/books = *imprimer des prospectus/des livres* **3/** *écrire en lettres d'imprimerie* : print your name = *écrivez votre nom en lettres d'imprimerie* ⓞ to write in block letters = *écrire en lettres majuscules*
a print dress = *une robe imprimée*
printed matter = *des imprimés.*

PRINTABLE (adj) *imprimable* : Henry Miller's first works were not considered printable in puritanical America = *l'Amérique puritaine a jugé que les premières œuvres de Henry Miller n'étaient pas imprimables* ⓞ publishable = *publiable.*

PRINTER (n) **1/** *imprimeur* (m) : my publisher has a very good printer = *mon éditeur a un très bon imprimeur* **2/** *imprimante* (f) : a screen, a keyboard and a printer = *un écran, un clavier et une imprimante* ⓞ computer = *ordinateur.*

PRINTING (n) *impression* (f) : the first printing of his book = *la première impression de son livre* ⓞ reprinting = *réimpression* ☠ → impression.

PRIOR (adj) **(he was invited but he had) a prior appointment** = *(il était invité mais il avait) déjà un rendez-vous.*

PRIORITY (n, -ies) *priorité* (f) : housing must be given priority this year = *cette année, on doit donner la priorité au programme de logement*
to take priority over = *avoir la priorité sur* ⓞ to take precedence over = *passer en priorité.*

PRIOR TO (prep) *avant (de)* : prior to his resignation = *avant de donner sa démission* ≠ following = *à la suite de.*

PRISON (n) *prison* (f) : they put him in prison = *ils l'ont mis en prison* ⓞ in the brig = *aux fers*, in the stir = *en taule*, in the can = *au gnouf*, penitentiary = *pénitencier*, reformatory = *maison de correction*
prison yard = *cour de prison.*

PRISONER (n) *prisonnier, -ère* : many prisoners were tortured = *beaucoup de prisonniers ont été torturés* ⓞ convict = *détenu*, lifer = *condamné à perpétuité*
prisoner of war = *prisonnier de guerre* = POW
to take prisoner = *faire prisonnier.*

PRISSY (adj, -ier, -iest) *pimbêche* : she's too prissy for me = *je la trouve trop pimbêche* ⓞ prim = *comme il faut.*

PRISTINE (adj) *nickel* : a pristine kitchen = *une cuisine nickel* ⓞ spick-and-span = *d'une propreté éclatante.*

PRIVACY (n inv) *intimité* (f) : there's no privacy in wards = *on n'a aucune intimité dans les salles communes*
in the privacy of (your own home) = *dans l'intimité du (foyer).*

PRIVATE (n) *simple soldat* (m) : he's a private in the army = *il est simple soldat dans l'armée* = buck private ⓞ rookie = *bleu*
in private = *en privé* : I'll tell you in private = *je vous le dirai en privé* ⓞ secretly = *secrètement.*

PRIVATE (adj) **1/** *privé, -e* : a private school = *une école privée* **2/** *personnel, -elle* : what I have to tell you is very private = *ce que j'ai à vous dire est très personnel* = personal ≠ impersonal = *impersonnel*
private citizen = *simple citoyen*
private detective = *détective privé* ⓞ **a private eye** = *un privé* ⓞ sleuth = *limier*
private income = *rente*
private lessons = *leçons particulières/cours particuliers*
private parts = *les parties*
private person = *quelqu'un de sauvage* ⓞ a loner = *un solitaire*
private property = *chasse gardée* : Jane's his private property = *Jane est sa chasse gardée*
private enterprise = *entreprise privée*
private secretary = *secrétaire particulière*
private visit = *visite privée.*

PRIVATION (n) *privation* (f) : to have known want and privation = *avoir connu le besoin et la privation.*

PRIVILEGE (n) *privilège* (m) : the privileges of the upper classes = *les privilèges des classes supérieures* ⓞ right = *droit*
it will be a privilege to (work with you) = *ce sera un privilège de (travailler avec vous).*

PRIVILEGED (adj) *privilégié, -e* : privileged nations = *les nations privilégiées* ≠ underprivileged = *défavorisé.*

PRIVY (n, -ies) *toilettes* (f pl) *extérieures* : there were privies at camp = *il y avait des toilettes extérieures à la colonie* ⓞ outhouse = *cabinets extérieurs.*

PRIZE (n) *prix* (m inv) : to win first prize = *gagner le premier prix* ☠ → price.

PRIZE (adj) *de concours* : prize cattle = *bétail de concours*
prize idiot/fool = *idiot/imbécile de première.*

PRIZEFIGHT (n) *match* (m) *de boxe* ⓞ boxing = *boxe.*

PRIZEWINNING (adj) *primé, -e* : a prizewinning book/novel = *un livre/un roman primé.*

PRO (n) *pro* *(m, f)* : a golf pro = *un pro du golf* ≠ amateur = ←
to weigh the pros and the cons = *peser le pour et le contre.*

PRO- (prefix) *pro-* : pro-American = *pro-américain* ⓪ for = *pour.*

PROBABILITY (n, -ies) *probabilité* *(f)* : the probability of a nuclear war = *la probabilité d'une guerre nucléaire* ⓪ eventuality = *éventualité*
in all probability = *selon toute probabilité* ⓪ in all likelihood = *selon toute vraisemblance.*

PROBABLE (adj) *probable* : it's probable that he'll come = *il est probable qu'il viendra* ≠ improbable = ←, dubious = *douteux.*

PROBABLY (adv) *probablement* : he's probably coming = *il va probablement venir* ⓪ in all probability = *selon toute probabilité.*

PROBATION (n) **on probation** = *en liberté provisoire* ⓪ on parole = *en liberté conditionnelle.*

PROBE (n) *enquête* *(f)* *approfondie* : the President demanded a probe into drugs in high schools = *le Président a exigé que l'on fasse une enquête approfondie sur la drogue dans les collèges* ⓪ investigation = ← **PROBE** (to, -d) *sonder* : psychiatrists are probing the mysteries of the mind = *les psychiatres sondent les mystères de l'esprit* ⓪ to dig into = *approfondir* ☠ *sonder qqn* = to sound s.o. out/to feel s.o. out.

PROBLEM (n) *problème* *(m)* : she's having a lot of problems with her kids = *elle a beaucoup de problèmes avec ses gosses* ⓪ trouble = *ennui.*

PROBLEM (adj) *à problèmes* : a problem child = *un enfant à problèmes.*

PROBLEMATIC(AL) (adj) *problématique* : a problematic situation = *une situation problématique.*

PROCEDURE (n) *procédure* *(f)* : that's the procedure to follow to get a visa = *voilà la procédure à suivre pour obtenir un visa* ⓪ way = *manière* ☠ *procédure de divorce* = divorce proceedings.

PROCEED (to, -ed) *poursuivre* : I don't want to interrupt you, please proceed = *je ne veux pas vous interrompre, je vous en prie poursuivez* ⓪ to continue = *continuer* ☠ → to pursue
to proceed to = *se mettre à* : he proceeded to tell the boss what he thought of him = *il s'est mis à dire au patron ce qu'il pensait de lui.*

PROCEEDINGS (n pl) *procédure* *(f)* : court proceedings = *procédure judiciaire,* divorce proceedings = *procédure de divorce* ☠ → procedure
to start/take proceedings against s.o. = *engager des poursuites contre qqn* ⓪ to bring to court = *attaquer en justice.*

PROCEEDS (n pl) *produit* *(m)* : the proceeds of the gala will go to charity = *le produit de la soirée de gala sera versé à des œuvres charitables* ☠ → product.

PROCESS (n, -es) **1/** *processus* *(m)* : curing cancer is a slow process = *la guérison du cancer est un long processus* ☠ *un processus (psychologique)* = a pattern **2/** *procédé* *(m)* : to develop a new process = *inventer un nouveau procédé* ☠ *suivre le bon* ≠ *mauvais procédé* = to follow the right ≠ wrong procedure
to be in the process of (getting a divorce) = *être en passe de (divorcer)* ⓪ to be getting (a divorce) = *être en train de (divorcer).*

PROCLAIM (to, -ed) *proclamer* : he was proclaimed the winner = *il a été proclamé vainqueur* ⓪ to declare = *déclarer* ☠ *proclamer (les résultats d'une élection)* = to announce (the results of a vote) **PROCLAMATION** (n) *proclamation* *(f)* : a proclamation of independence = *une proclamation d'indépendance* ⓪ statement = *déclaration.*

PROCRASTINATE (to, -d) *remettre au lendemain* : stop procrastinating and do what you have to do now = *arrêtez de remettre sans cesse au lendemain et faites ce que vous avez à faire maintenant* ⓪ to put off = *repousser.*

PROCURE (to, -d) *(se) procurer* : my lawyer procured the documents I needed = *mon avocat s'est procuré les documents dont j'avais besoin* ⓪ to acquire = *acquérir.*

PROD (to, -ded) *aiguillonner* : my son needs to be prodded to work = *il faut aiguillonner mon fils pour qu'il travaille* ⓪ to urge = *pousser.*

PRODIGAL (adj) *prodigue* : the prodigal daughter = *la fille prodigue.*

PRODIGIOUS (adj) *prodigieux, -euse* : a prodigious actor = *un acteur prodigieux* → WONDERFUL ☠ *(une fortune) prodigieuse* = (a) phenomenal (fortune).

PRODUCE (to, -d) **1/** *produire* : to produce a film = *produire un film* ⓪ to direct = *mettre en scène/réaliser* **2/** *produire* : the factory can produce a thousand cars a day = *l'usine peut produire mille voitures par jour* ⓪ to manufacture = *fabriquer* ☠ *cela ne s'est jamais produit* = it never occurred/came about.

PRODUCER (n) *producteur, -trice* : he's both producer and director = *il est à la fois producteur et metteur en scène.*

PRODUCT (n) *produit* *(m)* : corn is the country's leading product = *le maïs est le principal produit du pays* ☠ *produits de consommation* = consumer goods — *le produit d'une vente* = the proceeds of a sale.

PRODUCTION (n) *production* *(f)* : production is down this month = *la production est en baisse ce mois-ci,* cost of production = *coût de production*
to make a (big) production out of = *faire tout un plat de* ⓪ to make a mountain out of a molehill = *(se) faire une montagne de qqch.*

PRODUCTIVE (adj) *productif, -ive* : productive methods = *des méthodes productives* ≠ unproductive = *improductif.*

PRODUCTIVITY (n, -ies) *productivité (f)* : the productivity of an industry = *la productivité d'une industrie* ⊕ output = *rendement.*

PROFANE (n, adj) *profane (m, f)* : profane writings = *des écrits profanes.*

PROFESS (to, -ed) *professer* : he professes great love for his wife = *il professe un grand amour pour sa femme.*

PROFESSED (adj) *avoué, -e* : a professed communist = *un communiste avoué.*

PROFESSION (n) *profession (f), métier (m)* : what's your profession ? = *quelle est votre profession ?/quel est votre métier ?* ⊕ job = *travail*
☠ *métier manuel* = trade
— *avoir du métier* ≠ *manquer de métier* = to have ≠ to lack experience
— *métier à tisser* = weaving loom.

PROFESSIONAL (n) *professionnel, -elle* : the football player turned professional = *le joueur de football est passé professionnel* ⊕ pro = ←, expert = ←.

PROFESSIONAL (adj) *professionnel, -elle* : a professional tennis player = *un joueur de tennis professionnel* ⊕ experienced = *expérimenté* ≠ amateur = ←.

PROFESSIONALLY (adj) *professionnellement.*

PROFESSOR (n) *professeur (m), prof (m) (université)* : professor of history = *professeur d'histoire (à l'université)* ⊕ schoolteacher = *professeur (de collège/lycée).*

PROFILE (n) *profil (m)* : what's the profile of the ideal candidate ? = *quel est le profil du candidat idéal ?*

PROFIT (n) *profit (m), bénéfice (m)* : there was no profit = *il n'y a eu aucun profit/bénéfice* ≠ loss = *perte*
gross ≠ **net profit** = *bénéfice brut* ≠ *net*
to make a profit = *faire un profit/un bénéfice*
profit margin = *marge bénéficiaire*
profit sharing = *participation aux bénéfices*
to show a profit = *montrer un bénéfice/être bénéficiaire*
☠ *mettre qqch à profit* = to make the most out of stg
— *passer aux profits et pertes* = to write off as a dead loss
— *bénéfice* → benefit.

PROFIT (to, -ed) *profiter* : no one profits from the new tax law = *la nouvelle loi fiscale ne profite à personne*
☠ *profiter de (la gentillesse de qqn)* = to take advantage of (s.o.'s kindness)
— *profiter d'(une bourse)* = to get in on (a scholarship program).

PROFITABLE (adj) *qui rapporte* : a profitable business = *une affaire qui rapporte* ⊕ lucrative = *lucratif* ☠ *(un conseil) profitable* = (a) beneficial (piece of advice).

PROFOUND (adj) *profond, -e* : profound thoughts = *des pensées profondes* ≠ shallow = *peu profond*
☠ *un puits profond* = a deep well
— *la raison profonde* = the underlying reason.

PROFOUNDLY (adv) *profondément* : profoundly affected = *profondément affecté* ☠ *plonger profondément* = to dive deeply.

PROFUSION (n) *profusion (f)* ⊕ abundance = *abondance* ☠ *à profusion* = wads of.

PROGNOSIS (n, -ses) *pronostic (m)* : a pessimistic prognosis = *un pronostic pessimiste* ⊕ diagnosis = *diagnostic* ☠ *pronostic (courses)* = racing forecast.

PROGRAM (n) 1/ *émission (f)* : "Dallas" is my favorite program = *« Dallas » est mon émission préférée* 2/ *programme (m)* : what's your program for the summer ? = *quel est votre programme pour l'été ?*
☠ *programme politique* = political platform
— *le programme des études* = the syllabus
— *le français n'est pas au programme* = French is not on the curriculum.

PROGRAM (to, -med) *programmer* : all our lives are programmed by society = *toutes nos vies sont programmées par la société* **PROGRAMMER** (n) *programmeur, -euse.*

PROGRESS (n inv) *progrès (m)* : there's been a lot of progress in his work = *il y a eu beaucoup de progrès dans son travail* ⊕ improvement = *amélioration*
to make progress = *faire des progrès.*

PROGRESS (to, -ed) *progresser* : our work's progressing = *notre travail progresse* ≠ to regress = *régresser* ☠ *l'ennemi progresse* = the enemy's advancing.

PROGRESSIVE (n) *progressiste (m, f)* : he's a progressive in politics = *en politique, c'est un progressiste* ≠ reactionary = *réactionnaire.*

PROGRESSIVE (adj) 1/ *progressif, -ive* : lessons of progressive difficulty = *des leçons d'une difficulté progressive* 2/ *progressiste* : progressive ideas = *des idées progressistes* ≠ reactionary = *réactionnaire* **PROGRESSIVELY** (adv) *progressivement.*

PROHIBIT (to, -ed) *interdire (prohiber)* : it's prohibited to hire immigrants who don't have working papers = *il est interdit d'embaucher des immigrés qui n'ont pas de carte de travail,* her height prohibits her becoming a model = *sa taille lui interdit de devenir mannequin,* to prohibit the sale of liquor = *prohiber/interdire la vente d'alcool* ⊕ to ban = *interdire*
(smoking) is prohibited = *il est interdit de (fumer)* no (smoking) ⊕ forbidden = *défendu*
☠ *« to prohibit » est moins employé que « to forbid ».*

PROHIBITION (n) *prohibition (f)* : Prohibition began in 1920 and ended in 1933 = *la Prohibition a commencé en 1920 et s'est achevée en 1933.*

PROHIBITIVE (adj) *prohibitif, -ive* : prohibitive prices = *des prix prohibitifs* ≠ reasonable = *raisonnable.*

PROJECT (n) *projet (m)* : he presented his project to the boss = *il a présenté son projet au patron* ⚃ undertaking = *entreprise*
☠ *quels sont vos projets ?* = what are your plans ?
— *projet de loi* = bill.

PROJECT (to, -ed) *projeter* : you're projecting your own feeling of guilt onto me = *tu projettes sur moi ton propre sentiment de culpabilité*
you're projecting again ! = *arrête de te mettre à ma place !*
☠ *je projette d'y aller* = I plan to go there
— *projeter des diapositives* = to show slides.

PROJECTION (n) *projection (f)* : that's a projection of your own feelings = *c'est une projection de vos propres sentiments* ☠ *projection privée* = private screening.

PROLETARIAN (n, adj) *prolétaire (m, f)* : of proletarian background = *d'origine prolétaire* ⚃ prole = *prolo.*

PROLETARIAT (n) *prolétariat (m)* : to belong to the proletariat = *appartenir au prolétariat* ⚃ working class = *classe ouvrière* ≠ capitalist = *capitaliste.*

PROLIFIC (adj) *prolifique* : a prolific writer = *un écrivain prolifique* ⚃ fertile = *fécond.*

PROLOG(UE) (n) *prologue (m)* : the novel's prologue = *le prologue du roman* ⚃ foreword = *avant-propos* ≠ epilogue = *épilogue.*

PROLONG (to, -ed) *prolonger* : to prolong one's stay = *prolonger son séjour* ⚃ to lengthen = *rallonger.*

PROLONGATION (n) *prolongation (f)* : prolongation of life = *la prolongation de la vie.*

PROM (n) **(senior) prom** = *bal de fin d'année (des étudiants de dernière année)* ⚃ hop = *sauterie.*

PROMINENT (adj) 1/ *éminent, -e* : a prominent scientist = *un éminent savant* ⚃ well-known = *connu* 2/ *proéminent, -e* : a prominent nose = *un nez proéminent.*

PROMISCUITY (n inv) *liberté (f) des mœurs* : promiscuity in universities = *la liberté des mœurs dans les universités* ☠ *promiscuité avec (des drogués)* = close contact with (drug addicts).

PROMISCUOUS (adj) *très libre sur le plan des mœurs* : she has always led a promiscuous life = *elle a toujours mené une vie très libre sur le plan des mœurs* ≠ prudish = *prude.*

PROMISE (n) *promesse (f)* : don't forget your promise = *n'oubliez pas votre promesse* ⚃ word of honor = *parole d'honneur*
to break a promise = *manquer à une promesse*
to keep one's promise = *tenir sa promesse*
to make a promise = *faire une promesse*
a promise is a promise = *chose promise, chose due*
promises, promises = *des promesses, toujours des promesses et rien que des promesses .*

to show promise as (a writer) = *être prometteur comme (écrivain).*

PROMISE (to, -d) *promettre* : I promised my daughter a dog = *j'ai promis un chien à ma fille* ⚃ to give one's word = *donner sa parole*
to promise to (help) = *promettre d'(aider).*

PROMISING (adj) *prometteur, -euse* : a promising actor = *un acteur prometteur* ⚃ up-and-coming = *qui a le vent en poupe.*

PROMOTE (to, -d) 1/ *promouvoir* : he was recently promoted = *il a été récemment promu* ⚃ to upgrade = *monter en grade* ≠ to strip of rank = *dégrader* 2/ *promouvoir* : to promote a new product = *promouvoir un nouveau produit* ⚃ to push = *faire du battage pour* 3/ *encourager* : he promotes good relations between our two countries = *il encourage les bonnes relations entre nos deux pays*
to promote to (general) = *promouvoir (général).*

PROMOTER (n) *promoteur, -trice* : he was the promoter of the project = *c'était le promoteur du projet.*

PROMOTION (n) *promotion (f)* : he doesn't have the slightest chance of promotion = *il n'a pas la moindre chance de promotion* ☠ *la promotion de 1980* = the (graduating) class of 1980.

PROMPT (adj, -er, -est) *prompt, -e* : a prompt answer = *une prompte réponse* ⚃ quick = *rapide.*

PROMPTLY (adv) *promptement* : to be served promptly = *être servi promptement.*

PROMPT TO (to, -ed) *inciter à* : the report prompted Amnesty International to act = *le rapport a incité Amnesty International à agir* ⚃ to push = *pousser.*

PROMULGATE (to, -d) *promulguer* **PROMULGATION** (n) *promulgation (f)* : the promulgation of the law = *la promulgation de la loi.*

PRONE (adj) **(accident) prone** = *sujet aux (accidents)*
to be prone to (periods of depression) = *être sujet à (des périodes de dépression)* ⚃ to tend to = *avoir tendance à.*

PRONOUN (n) *pronom (m)* : a relative pronoun = *un pronom relatif.*

PRONOUNCE (to, -d) 1/ *prononcer* : to pronounce a word the wrong way = *mal prononcer un mot* ≠ to mispronounce = *mal prononcer*
☠ *se prononcer pour* ≠ *contre* = to come out/to speak out for ≠ against
— *prononcer un discours* = to make a speech
2/ *déclarer* : the judge pronounced him guilty = *le juge l'a déclaré coupable* ☠ → to declare.

PRONOUNCED (adj) *prononcé, -e* : a pronounced accent = *un accent prononcé* ⚃ marked = *marqué.*

PRONOUNCEMENT (n) *déclaration (f) officielle* ⚃ statement = *déclaration.*

PRONUNCIATION (n) *prononciation* (f) : poor pronunciation = *une mauvaise prononciation* ☠ *défaut de prononciation* = speech defect.

PROOF (n) *preuve* (f) : the cops have no proof = *les flics n'ont aucune preuve* ⓪ testimony = *témoignage*
the proof of the pudding is in the eating = *c'est aux fruits qu'on reconnaît l'arbre/c'est au pied du mur qu'on connaît le maçon* ⓪ moment of truth = *moment de vérité*
the proofs = *les épreuves* : the author's correcting the proofs = *l'auteur corrige les épreuves* = the galleys ☠ *faire ses preuves* = to prove oneself
— *faire preuve de (courage)* = to display (courage)
— *preuve par présomption* = circumstancial evidence.

PROOFREAD (to, -read, -read) *corriger les épreuves de* : I'm proofreading his novel = *je corrige les épreuves de son roman* **PROOFREADER** (n) *correcteur, -trice (d'épreuves)* : the proofreader found many misprints = *le correcteur a trouvé de nombreuses coquilles.*

PROP (n) *accessoire* (m) *(théâtre)* : the scenery and the props = *le décor et les accessoires* ☠ → accessory.

PROPAGANDA (n) *propagande* (f) : Soviet propaganda = *propagande soviétique* ⓪ publicity = *publicité.*

PROPAGATE (to, -d) *propager* : to propagate a rumor = *propager une rumeur.*

PROPELLER (n) *hélice* (f) ⓪ helicopter = *hélicoptère*
a propeller plane = *un avion à hélices.*

PROPER (adj) **1/** *(très) convenable* : he comes from a very proper family = *il vient d'une famille très convenable* ≠ improper = *pas convenable* **2/** *qui convient* : to get the proper form, I had to go back again and again = *pour avoir le formulaire qui convenait, j'ai dû y retourner un nombre de fois incalculable* ≠ improper = *impropre.*

PROPERLY (adv) *convenablement* : properly dressed = *convenablement vêtu/habillé.*

PROPERTY (n) **1/** (inv) *terrain* (m) : property in New York is worth a fortune = *le terrain à New York vaut une fortune* ⓪ real estate = *propriété foncière* ☠ → grounds
a piece of property = *un terrain*
2/ (inv) *biens* (m pl) : many Jews lost all their property during the last war = *beaucoup de juifs ont perdu tous leurs biens pendant la dernière guerre* ☠ → possession **3/** (-ies) *propriété* (f) : the properties of a gas = *les propriétés d'un gaz* ☠ *une grande propriété* = a large estate.

PROPHECY (n, -ies) *prophétie* (f) : his prophecy didn't come true = *sa prophétie ne s'est pas réalisée.*

PROPHESY (to, -ied) *prophétiser* **PROPHET** (n) *prophète* (m) : the Old Testament prophets = *les prophètes de l'Ancien Testament* ⓪ seer = *voyant*, soothsayer = *devin.*

PROPONENT (n) *partisan* (m) : a proponent of free abortion = *un partisan de l'avortement libre* ≠ adversary = *adversaire* ☠ → partisan.

PROPORTION (n) *proportion* (f) : the proportion of Blacks to Whites in Washington is one to one = *la proportion des Noirs par rapport aux Blancs à Washington est de un pour un* ⓪ percentage = *pourcentage*
in proportion to = *en proportion de* : what he earns is little in proportion to what he spends = *il gagne peu en proportion de ce qu'il dépense* ⓪ in relation to = *par rapport à*
out of proportion = *disproportionné* : a $ 50 raise a week is out of proportion = *une augmentation de 50 dollars par semaine est disproportionnée* ≠ in proportion = *proportionné.*

PROPORTIONAL (adj) *proportionnel, -elle* : the fine will be proportional to the misdemeanor = *l'amende sera proportionnelle à l'infraction* **PROPORTIONALLY** (adv) *proportionnellement.*

PROPORTIONATE (adj) *proportionné, -e* : the punishment was proportionate to the crime = *le châtiment a été proportionné au crime* ≠ disproportionate = *disproportionné.*

PROPOSAL (n) **1/** *proposition* (f) : the Senator's proposal = *la proposition du sénateur* ⓪ plan = *projet* ☠ → proposition **2/** *demande* (f) *en mariage* : I got my first proposal when I was sixteen = *j'ai reçu ma première demande en mariage à seize ans.*

PROPOSE (to, -d) *proposer* : he proposed that we go with him = *il nous a proposé d'y aller avec lui* ⓪ to recommend = *recommander*
to propose to s.o. = *demander qqn en mariage* : he proposed to her last night = *il l'a demandée en mariage hier soir* ⓪ to ask for s.o.'s hand = *demander la main de qqn*
☠ *proposer de l'argent/un poste* = to offer money/a job.

PROPOSITION (n) **1/** *proposition* (f) *(malhonnête)* : he was making propositions to a very young girl = *il faisait des propositions à une très jeune fille*
☠ *proposition de loi* = bill
— *la proposition du sénateur* = the Senator's proposal **2/** *affaire* (f) : love is often a painful proposition = *l'amour est souvent une affaire douloureuse* ☠ → affair
that's quite a proposition ! = *ce n'est pas une mince affaire !*

PROPOSITION (to, -ed) *faire des propositions malhonnêtes* : he propositioned me at the party = *il m'a fait des propositions malhonnêtes pendant la soirée* ⓪ to give s.o. a line = *faire du baratin à qqn.*

PROPRIETOR (n) *propriétaire* (m, f), *proprio* (m, f) (LV) : the proprietor of the brothel = *le propriétaire du bordel*
☠ *qui est le propriétaire (du chien) ?* = who's (the dog's) owner ?

PROP UP (to, -ped) *étayer* : they reformed the system to prop up the economy = *on a réformé le système pour étayer l'économie* ⓪ to reinforce = *renforcer.*

PROSAIC (adj) *prosaïque* : a prosaic task = *une tâche prosaïque* ⊕ dull = *terne*.

PROSE (n) *prose* (f) : to write in prose = *écrire en prose* ≠ verse = *vers*.

PROSECUTE (to, -d) *poursuivre en justice* : to be prosecuted for fraud = *être poursuivi en justice pour fraude* ⊕ to bring action = *intenter une action en justice* **the prosecuting attorney** = *le procureur*.

PROSECUTION (n inv) *accusation* (f) : the prosecution has strong arguments = *l'accusation a de puissants arguments* ≠ defense = *défense* ⚔ → accusation.

PROSECUTOR (n) **the prosecutor (lost the case)** = *l'accusation (a perdu le procès)* ≠ the defendant = *le prévenu*.

PROSPECT (n) *perspective* (f) : the prospect of seeing him again makes me nervous = *la perspective de le revoir me rend nerveux* ⚔ → perspective **in prospect** = *en perspective* : I've got a good job in prospect = *j'ai un bon boulot en perspective* ⊕ in mind = *en vue*.

PROSPECT (to, -ed) *prospecter* : to prospect for gold = *prospecter pour trouver de l'or* ⊕ to canvass = *faire du démarchage*.

PROSPECTIVE (adj) *futur, -e* : she's a prospective congresswoman = *elle est un futur député*.

PROSPECTS (n pl) *chances* (f pl) : what are his prospects of getting a new job ? = *quelles sont ses chances de trouver un nouveau poste ?* ⊕ hope = *espoir* ⚔ → chance.

PROSPECTUS (n, -es) *prospectus* (m) : a prospectus on a new computer = *un prospectus sur un nouvel ordinateur* ⊕ catalogue = ←.

PROSPER (to, -ed) *prospérer* : business is prospering = *les affaires prospèrent* ⊕ to boom = *être en plein essor* ≠ to go down the drain = *aller à vau-l'eau* **PROSPERITY** (n inv) *prospérité* (f) : a period of prosperity = *une période de prospérité* **PROSPEROUS** (adj) *prospère* : a prosperous country = *un pays prospère* ⊕ thriving = *florissant*, blooming = *en plein essor*.

PROSTITUTE (n) *prostituée* (f) : prostitutes in the streets = *des prostituées dans les rues* ⊕ streetwalker = *péripatéticienne*, harlot = *fille de joie*, tart = *poule*, courtesan = *courtisane*, brothel = *bordel* ≠ pimp = *maquereau*, John = *mec à putes*.

PROSTITUTION (n) *prostitution* (f) : the shameful prostitution of teenagers = *l'infâme prostitution des adolescents* ⊕ to be on the game = *se prostituer*.

PROTAGONIST (n) *protagoniste* (m, f) : the protagonists of history = *les protagonistes de l'histoire*.

PROTECT (to, -ed) *protéger* : he wanted to protect his little sister = *il voulait protéger sa petite sœur* ⊕ to guard = *garder* ≠ to assail = *assaillir*.

PROTECTION (n) *protection* (f) : safety belts are for your own protection = *les ceintures de sécurité sont faites pour votre protection* ⊕ security = *sécurité*.

PROTECTIVE (adj) *protecteur, -trice* : a protective lover = *un amant protecteur*.

PROTECTOR (n) *protecteur, -trice* : pimps are supposed to be protectors = *les maquereaux sont censés être des protecteurs* ⚔ *protecteur des arts* = patron of the arts.

PROTÉGÉ (n) *protégé* (m) : the boss's protégé = *le protégé du patron* ≠ patron = *protecteur* **PROTÉGÉE** (n) *protégée* (f).

PROTEIN (n) *protéine* (f) : cereals rich in protein = *des céréales riches en protéines* ⊕ vitamin = *vitamine*.

PROTEST (n) *protestation* (f) : the workers signed a protest = *les ouvriers ont signé une protestation* ⊕ objection = ←.

PROTEST (to, -ed) *protester* : the government is raising taxes and the masses are protesting = *le gouvernement lève des impôts et les masses protestent* ⊕ to object = *faire des objections*.

PROTESTANT (n, adj) *protestant, -e* : a Protestant family = *une famille protestante* ⊕ WASP = White Anglo-Saxon and Protestant = *blanc, anglo-saxon et protestant*, pastor = *pasteur*, minister = *ministre du culte*.

PROTOCOL (n) *protocole* (m) : diplomatic protocol = *le protocole diplomatique* ⊕ etiquette = *étiquette*.

PROTOTYPE (n) *prototype* (m) : the prototype of the new plane = *le prototype du nouvel avion* ⊕ mock-up = *maquette*.

PROTRACT (to, -ed) *faire traîner* : the labor negotiations were protracted till the next morning = *on a fait traîner les négociations syndicales jusqu'au lendemain matin* ⊕ to prolong = *prolonger*.

PROTRUDE (to, -d) *dépasser* : something is protruding from the package = *il y a quelque chose qui dépasse du paquet* ⊕ to bulge = *ressortir* ⚔ → to overtake.

PROUD (adj, -er, -est) *fier, -ère* : proud parents = *des parents fiers* ⊕ arrogant = ←, supercilious = *dédaigneux* ≠ humble = ←
to be proud as a peacock = *être fier comme Artaban* ≠ full of shame = *tout honteux*
to be proud of (one's daughter) = *être fier de (sa fille)* ≠ to be ashamed of = *avoir honte de*
to be proud to (announce one's marriage) = *être fier d'(annoncer son mariage)*
⚔ *je te dois une fière chandelle* = I'm greatly indebted to you.

PROUDLY (adv) *fièrement* : she spoke proudly of her child = *elle parlait fièrement de son enfant*.

PROVE (to, -d, -d or -proven) *prouver* : can the cops prove he killed her ? = *est-ce que les flics peuvent prouver qu'il l'a tuée ?* ≠ to disprove = *réfuter*
to prove oneself = *faire ses preuves*
to prove to be = *se révéler être* : the project proved to be too expensive = *le projet s'est révélé être trop cher* ⓪ to turn out to be = *s'avérer.*

PROVERB (n) *proverbe (m)* : "God helps those who help themselves" is a proverb = *« aide-toi, le Ciel t'aidera » est un proverbe* ⓪ maxim = *maxime.*

PROVIDE (to, -d) 1/ *fournir* : the hotel provides free soap = *l'hôtel fournit gratuitement le savon* = to supply ⓪ to give = *donner* ☠ → to furnish 2/ *stipuler* : the law provides that all children must go to school = *la loi stipule que tous les enfants doivent aller à l'école*
to provide for s.o. = *pourvoir aux besoins de qqn* : who's providing for the kids ? = *qui pourvoit aux besoins des enfants ?* ⓪ to support = *subvenir aux besoins de.*

PROVIDED (conj) *pourvu que* : provided it doesn't cost too much, we can go away this week = *pourvu que ça ne coûte pas trop cher, nous pouvons partir cette semaine* = providing ⓪ on the condition that = *à condition que.*

PROVIDENCE (n inv) *providence (f)* : saved by providence = *sauvé par la providence* ⓪ fate = *destin.*

PROVIDING (conj) = PROVIDED.

PROVIDER (n) *soutien (m) de famille* : he's a good lover but not a good provider = *c'est un bon amant, mais pas un bon soutien de famille.*

PROVINCE (n) *province (f)* : the French provinces = *les provinces françaises.*

PROVISION (n) 1/ *provision (f)* : food provisions = *des provisions de nourriture* ⓪ reserves = *réserves* 2/ *disposition (f)* : according to the provisions of the treaty = *selon les dispositions du traité* ☠ → disposition
with the provision that = *à condition que*
☠ *chèque sans provision* = overdrawn check
— *« provision » est surtout employé pour les vivres, sinon on emploie « supply ».*

PROVISIONAL (adj) *provisoire* : a provisional cabinet = *un gouvernement provisoire* ⓪ temporary = *temporaire* **PROVISIONALLY** (adv) *provisoirement.*

PROVISO (n) **with the proviso that** = *à condition que.*

PROVOCATIVE (adj) *provocant, -e* : a provocative dress/remark = *une robe/remarque provocante* ≠ discreet = *discrète.*

PROVOKE (to, -d) *provoquer* : he said that to provoke you = *il a dit ça pour vous provoquer* ⓪ to annoy = *embêter* ☠ *provoquer la guerre* = to bring on/to precipitate war.

PROWL (n) **(singles) on the prowl** = *(des célibataires) en quête d'aventures.*

PROWL (to, -ed) *rôder (dans)* : thieves prowling the streets = *des voleurs qui rôdent dans les rues* ☠ *roder une voiture* = to break a car in **PROWLER** (n) *rôdeur, -euse* : prowlers in the night = *des rôdeurs dans la nuit.*

PROXY (n, -ies) **to vote by proxy** = *voter par procuration.*

PRUDE (n) *prude (f)* : she's too much of a prude to go to see a blue movie = *elle est bien trop prude pour aller voir un film porno* ⓪ prig = *quelqu'un de bégueule.*

PRUDENT (adj) *prudent, -e* : a prudent investment/man = *un investissement/homme prudent* ≠ reckless = *imprudent* **PRUDENCE** (n) *prudence (f).*

PRUDISH (adj) *prude* : prudish parents = *des parents prudes* ⓪ prissy = *pimbêche.*

PRUNE (n) *pruneau (m)* : prunes with cream = *des pruneaux à la crème*
☠ *une prune* = a plum
— *travailler/y aller pour des prunes* = to work for peanuts/to go for nothing
— *pruneau (balle)* = slug (bullet).

PRURIENT (adj) *lascif, -ive* : a prurient lover = *un amant lascif* ⓪ lewd = *lubrique.*

PRY INTO (to, -ied) *fourrer son nez dans* : my mother-in-law always pries into our affairs = *ma belle-mère est toujours en train de fourrer son nez dans nos affaires* ⓪ to meddle in = *s'immiscer dans.*

P'S AND Q'S (n pl) **to watch/to mind one's p's and q's** = *faire attention à ce qu'on dit* : mind your p's and q's at the dinner tonight = *fais attention à ce que tu dis au dîner ce soir.*

PSEUDO- (prefix) *pseudo-* : a pseudobiography = *une pseudobiographie.*

PSEUDONYM (n) *pseudonyme (m)* : to use a pseudonym = *utiliser un pseudonyme* ⓪ pen name = *nom de plume.*

PSYCHEDELIC (adj) *psychédélique* : psychedelic music = *musique psychédélique.*

PSYCHIATRIST (n) *psychiatre (m, f)* : today everyone has a dentist, a lawyer and a psychiatrist = *aujourd'hui tout le monde a son dentiste, son avocat et son psychiatre* ⓪ shrink = *psy, psychologist* = *psychologue.*

PSYCHIATRY (n inv) *psychiatrie (f)* : different schools of psychiatry = *différentes écoles de psychiatrie* ⓪ shock therapy = *électrochocs, psychiatric* = *psychiatrique.*

PSYCHIC (adj) *psychique* : psychic powers = *forces psychiques* ⓪ mental = ←.

PSYCHO (n, adj) *désaxé, -e* : he's a real psycho = *c'est un véritable désaxé* → CRAZY.

PSYCHOANALYSIS (n, -ses) *psychanalyse (f)* : it's her third year in psychoanalysis = *c'est sa troisième année de psychanalyse.*

PSYCHOANALYST (n) *psychanalyste (m, f)* : my psychoanalyst needs a psychoanalyst = *mon psychanalyste a besoin d'un psychanalyste* ⓪ psychiatrist = *psychiatre*, guru = *gourou*, couch = *divan*.

PSYCHOANALYZE (to, -d) *psychanalyser* : she was psychoanalyzed by Lacan = *elle a été psychanalysée par Lacan* ⓪ to analyze = *analyser*.

PSYCHOLOGICAL (adj) *psychologique* : psychological warfare = *guerre psychologique*, psychological problems = *problèmes psychologiques* ⓪ psychosomatic = *psychosomatique* ≠ physical = *physique* **PSYCHOLOGICALLY** (adv) *psychologiquement*.

PSYCHOLOGIST (n) *psychologue (m, f)* : my son's seeing the school's psychologist = *mon fils voit le psychologue de l'école* ⓪ psychoanalyst = *psychanalyste*.

PSYCHOLOGY (n, -ies) *psychologie (f)* : she's studying psychology = *elle étudie la psychologie*.

PSYCHOPATH (n) *psychopathe (m, f)* : assassinated by a psychopath = *assassiné par un psychopathe* ⓪ madman = *dément*.

PSYCHOSIS (n, -ses) *psychose (f)* : war psychosis = *psychose de la guerre* ⓪ neurosis = *névrose*.

PSYCHOSOMATIC (adj) *psychosomatique* : his illness is psychosomatic = *il a une maladie psychosomatique*.

PSYCHOTIC (n, adj) *psychotique (m, f)* : psychotic behavior = *comportement psychotique* → CRAZY.

PSYCH OUT (to, -ed) *avoir au psychique/au bluff* : as a chess player he's famous for psyching out his opponents = *c'est un joueur d'échecs connu pour avoir ses adversaires au psychique/au bluff* → TO HUSTLE.

PTA (abbr) = Parent-Teacher Association = *association de parents d'élèves*.

PUB (n) *pub (m)* : a charming English pub = *un charmant pub anglais* ⓪ bar = ← 💀 *la pub* = publicity.

PUBERTY (n, -ies) *puberté (f)* : the age of puberty = *l'âge de la puberté* ⓪ period = *règles*, pimples = *boutons*.

PUBLIC (n) *public (m)* : the public was listening attentively = *le public écoutait attentivement* ⓪ spectator = *spectateur*
in public = *en public* : they never hold hands in public = *ils ne se tiennent jamais la main en public*.

PUBLIC (adj) *public, -ique* : a public garden = *un jardin public* ≠ private = *privé*
to be in the public eye = *être en vue* ⓪ to be in the limelight = *être sous les feux de la rampe*
to go public = *être coté en Bourse* : their company will go public in the fall = *leur entreprise sera cotée en Bourse à l'automne*
to make public = *rendre public*

(you're) a public danger = *(tu es) un danger public* ⓪ a menace = *un danger*
public enemy number one = *l'ennemi public numéro un*
public holiday = *jour férié*
public library = *bibliothèque municipale*
public opinion = *opinion publique*
public prosecutor = *procureur de la République/ avocat général/ministère public*
public relations = PR = *relations publiques* : my daughter wants to do public relations work = *ma fille veut travailler dans les relations publiques*
public school = *collège d'État* (US) / *collège privé* (GB)
public transportation = *transports en commun*
public utilities = *services publics*
public works = *travaux publics*.

PUBLICATION (n) *publication (f)* : a monthly publication = *une publication mensuelle* ⓪ periodical = *périodique*.

PUBLICIST (n) *publicitaire (m, f)* = adman/adwoman.

PUBLICITY (n, -ies) *publicité (f)*, *pub (f)* : his book got very little publicity = *on a fait très peu de publicité/pub pour son livre* ⓪ promotion = ←
publicity agent = *agent de publicité* ⓪ adman = *publicitaire*
publicity campaign = *campagne de publicité/pub*
publicity hounds = *assoiffés de pub(licité)* : actresses are publicity hounds = *les actrices sont assoiffées de pub(licité)*
💀 *publicité télévisée* = TV commercials
— *agence de publicité* = advertising agency
— *faire de la publicité* = to advertise
— *travailler dans la publicité* = to work in advertising
— *pub* → pub.

PUBLICIZE (to, -d) *faire de la publicité pour* : to publicize a new product = *faire de la publicité pour un nouveau produit*.

PUBLICLY (adv) *publiquement* : he publicly stated that he was going to resign = *il a déclaré publiquement qu'il allait démissionner*.

PUBLISH (to, -ed) *publier, éditer* (books) : the book will be published in the fall = *le livre sera publié/édité à l'automne* ⓪ to bring out = *sortir* 💀 *éditer* → to edit
PUBLISHER (n) *éditeur, -trice* : big publishers are sharks = *les gros éditeurs sont des requins* **PUBLISHING** (n) *édition (f)* : my brother works in publishing = *mon frère travaille dans l'édition* 💀 → edition.

PUDDLE (n) *flaque (f)* : puddles of rainwater = *des flaques d'eau (de pluie)* ⓪ mud = *boue*.

PUERILE (adj) *puéril, -e* : a puerile attitude = *une attitude puérile* ⓪ immature = ←.

PUFF (n) *bouffée (f)* : a puff of pot can't do you any harm = *une bouffée de marie ne peut pas vous faire de mal* ⓪ grass = *herbe*, tobacco = *tabac* 💀 *une bouffée d'air frais* = a breath of fresh air.

PUFF UP (to, -ed) *boursoufler* : a face puffed up from drink = *un visage boursouflé par l'alcool* ⓪ to swell up = *enfler.*

PUKE (to, -d) *dégueuler* : the guy puked all over the place = *le type a dégueulé partout* ⓪ to barf = *dégobiller.*

PULL (n inv) **to have pull (in the administration)** = *être influent (dans l'administration)* ⓪ to know the right people = *avoir le bras long.*

PULL (to, -ed) *tirer* : don't push the door, pull it ! = *ne poussez pas la porte, tirez-la !* ≠ to push = *pousser* **what are you trying to pull ?** = *qu'est-ce que vous manigancez ?*

---

to pull stg apart = *démolir qqch* : the reviewer pulled the book apart = *le critique a démoli le livre* ⓪ to knock = *taper sur* ☠ → to demolish

to pull away from = *se dégager de* : he grabbed her and she couldn't pull away from him = *il l'a attrapée et elle n'a pas pu se dégager*

to pull down = 1/ *abattre* : to pull down a building = *abattre un immeuble* ≠ to put up = *construire* ☠ → to cover 2/ *se faire* : I didn't know he pulled down $ 1 000 a week = *je ne savais qu'il faisait 1 000 dollars par semaine* ⓪ to earn = *gagner* ☠ → to do

to pull for = *être du côté de* : we're pulling for you = *nous sommes de votre côté* ⓪ to root for = *soutenir*

to pull in = 1/ *se faire* : he pulls in a grand each week = *il se fait mille dollars par semaine* ⓪ to rake in = *ramasser à la pelle* ☠ → to do 2/ *entrer en gare* : the train's pulling in = *le*

train entre en gare ≠ to pull out = *sortir de gare*

to pull s.o. in = *embarquer qqn* : the cops pulled the guy in for questioning = *les flics ont embarqué le type pour l'interroger* ⓪ to pick up = *cueillir, to capture = capturer*

to pull stg off = *réussir son coup* : if you can pull that deal off, you'll be a millionaire = *si tu réussis ce coup, tu seras millionnaire*

to pull out = 1/ *sortir de (la) gare* : the train's pulling out = *le train sort de gare* 2/ *se replier* : the troops are pulling out = *les troupes se replient* ⓪ to withdraw = *se retirer* ☠ *se replier sur soi-même* = to withdraw into oneself 3/ *retirer ses billes* : that deal sounds shady, I'm pulling out = *cette affaire me paraît louche, je retire mes billes*

to pull stg out of = *tirer qqch de* : the magician pulled a rabbit out of his hat = *le magicien a tiré un lapin de son chapeau*

to pull over = *se ranger sur le côté* : the policeman told us to pull over = *l'agent de police nous a dit de nous ranger sur le côté*

to pull through = *s'en tirer* : it's a serious operation, they don't know if he'll pull through = *c'est une opération grave, on ne sait pas s'il s'en tirera*

to pull together = *agir de concert* : if we all pull together, we can finish on time = *si nous agissons tous de concert, nous pouvons finir à temps* ⓪ to co-operate = *coopérer*

to pull o.s. together = *se reprendre* : pull yourself together, don't let the kids see you like that = *reprenez-vous, ne laissez pas les enfants vous voir dans cet état* ⓪ to get it together = *se reprendre en main* ☠ → to recapture

to pull up = *ranger* : pull your car up on the side of the road = *rangez votre voiture sur le bas-côté* ☠ → to tidy up

---

☠ *le film a été tiré d'un livre* = the film was taken from a book
— *tirez-en vos propres conclusions* = draw your own conclusions
— *tirer six mois de prison* = to be sent up for six months
— *deux ans à tirer* = two years to go

— *tirer (pistolet)* = to shoot (gun)
— *il n'y a pas grand-chose à en tirer* = there's not much to be got out of it
— *tirer les cartes* = to read cards
— *se tirer* = to shove off/to split
— *tirer à sa fin* = to draw to an end.

PULLOVER (n) *pull-over* (m), *pull* (m) : a cashmere pullover = *un pull-over/un pull en cachemire* ⓪ turtleneck = *col roulé.*

PULP (n) **to beat s.o. to a pulp** = *mettre qqn en bouillie* → TO HIT.

PULPIT (n) *chaire* (f) ⓪ preacher = *prédicateur.*

PULSE (n) *pouls* (m) : to take s.o.'s pulse = *prendre le pouls de qqn.*

PULVERIZE (to, -d) *pulvériser* : to pulverize an area = *pulvériser une région* ⓪ to destroy = *détruire.*

PUMP (n) *pompe* (f) : a pump to draw water = *une pompe pour tirer de l'eau*
☠ *des pompes* (LV) = shoes
— *les pompes funèbres* = funeral parlor
— *faire des pompes* = to do push-ups
— *en grande pompe* = with great pomp and circumstances.

PUMP (to, -ed) *pomper* : to pump water = *pomper de l'eau*

to pump s.o. (for) = *essayer de faire parler qqn (pour)* : he pumped her for information = *il a essayé de la faire parler pour obtenir des renseignements* ⊕ to draw stg out of s.o. = *soutirer qqch à qqn*
to pump money into = *mettre de l'argent dans* : they pumped a fortune into the business = *ils ont mis une fortune dans l'affaire* ⊕ to invest = *investir*
☠ *nos disputes me pompent* = our arguments are draining me.

PUMPKIN (n) *citrouille (f), potiron (m)* : pumpkin pie = *tarte au potiron.*

PUN (n) *calembour (m)* : to make a pun = *faire un calembour* ⊕ play on words = *jeu de mots.*

PUNCH (n, -es) **1/** *coup (m) de poing* : a punch on the nose = *un coup de poing sur le nez* ⊕ wallop = *châtaigne* **2/** *punch (m)* : she has a lot of punch = *elle a beaucoup de punch* ⊕ pep = ← **3/** *punch (m)* : a lime and coconut punch = *un punch au citron vert et à la noix de coco*

to beat s.o. to the punch = *prendre les devants* : I was just going to invite you to dinner, but you beat me to the punch = *j'allais justement vous inviter à dîner mais vous avez pris les devants* ⊕ to beat s.o. to the draw = *prendre qqn de vitesse*
not to pull punches = *ne pas y aller avec le dos de la cuillère* : he said what he thought and didn't pull punches = *il a dit ce qu'il pensait et n'y est pas allé avec le dos de la cuillère* ⊕ not to mince words = *ne pas mâcher ses mots*
punch line = *l'astuce finale* : I didn't understand the punch line (of the joke) = *je n'ai pas compris l'astuce finale (de l'histoire).*

PUNCH (to, -ed) *flanquer un coup de poing* : he punched him in the face = *il lui a flanqué un coup de poing dans la figure* → TO HIT.

PUNCH-DRUNK (adj) *sonné, -e* : after the six-hour exam we were a little punch-drunk = *après cet examen de six heures, nous étions un peu sonnés* ⊕ groggy = ←
☠ *elle a 50 ans bien sonnés* = she's well past 50 — *elle est sonnée* = she's bats (crazy).

PUNCTUAL (adj) *ponctuel, -elle* : come at 6 a.m. and be punctual = *venez à 6 heures du matin et soyez ponctuel* ≠ late = *en retard* **PUNCTUALLY** (adv) *ponctuellement.*

PUNCTUATION (n) *ponctuation (f)* : your punctuation's wrong = *votre ponctuation est mauvaise*

apostrophe = ←	**hyphen** = *trait d'union*
brackets = *crochets*	**period** = *point* = full stop (GB)
colon = *deux-points*	
comma = *virgule*	**parenthesis** = *parenthèse*
dash = *tiret*	
exclamation mark = *point d'exclamation*	**question mark** = *point d'interrogation*

quotation marks = *guillemets* = **quotes**	**semicolon** = *point-virgule.*

PUNISH (to, -ed) *punir* : when my wife's angry she refuses to have sex to punish me = *quand ma femme est fâchée, elle refuse de faire l'amour pour me punir* ⊕ to chastise = *châtier.*

PUNISHABLE (adj) **punishable by** = *passible de* : a crime punishable by death = *un crime passible de la peine de mort.*

PUNISHMENT (n) *punition (f)* : to mete out punishment = *infliger une punition* ⊕ chastisement = *châtiment* ≠ reward = *récompense.*

PUNK (n) *petit, -e merdeux, -euse* : get out, punk ! = *sors d'ici, petit merdeux !* ⊕ snot = *petit morveux*
punk music = *musique punk.*

PUNY (adj, -ier, -iest) *chétif, -ive* : she married a puny little guy = *elle a épousé un type petit et chétif* ≠ stocky = *trapu*, hefty = *râblé.*

PUPIL (n) *élève (m, f)* : twenty pupils in a class = *vingt élèves par classe* ⊕ schoolchildren = *écoliers* ≠ teacher = *professeur.*

PUPPET (n) **1/** *marionnette (f)* : a puppet show = *un spectacle de marionnettes* ⊕ Punch-and-Judy show = *guignol* **2/** *pantin (m)* : he carries no weight at all, he's just a puppet = *il n'a aucun poids, ce n'est qu'un pantin*
puppet government = *gouvernement fantoche.*

PUPPY (n, -ies) *chiot (m)* : a litter of five puppies = *une portée de cinq chiots* ⊕ kitten = *chaton*
puppy love = *amour(ette) de jeunesse* ⊕ turtledoves = *tourtereaux.*

PURCHASE (n) *achat (m)* : a tax on all purchases = *une taxe sur tous les achats* ☠ *faire des achats* = to go shopping.

PURCHASE (to, -d) *faire l'achat de* : the company purchased a new computer = *la société a fait l'achat d'un nouvel ordinateur* ⊕ to buy = *acheter.*

PURE (adj, -r, -st) **1/** *pur, -e* : pure wool/stupidity = *de la pure laine/stupidité* ⊕ absolute = *total* ≠ mixed = *mélangé* **2/** *pur, -e* : she's wide-eyed and pure = *elle est pure et candide* ⊕ ingenuous = *ingénu*, chaste = ←
it's pure luck (that he was home) = *c'est vraiment un coup de chance (qu'il ait été chez lui)*
☠ *pur (de ligne)* = sleek.

PUREBRED (n, adj) *de race* : a purebred horse = *un cheval de race* ⊕ thoroughbred = *pur-sang.*

PURELY (adv) *purement* ⊕ solely = *uniquement*
purely and simply = *purement et simplement* : he was lying purely and simply = *il mentait purement et simplement* ⊕ well and good = *bel et bien.*

PURGE (n) *purge (f)* : a purge after the putsch = *une purge après le putsch.*

PURGE (to, -d) *faire une purge dans :* to purge the government = *faire une purge dans le gouvernement* ⓪ to get rid of = *se débarrasser de.*

PURIFY (to, -ied) *purifier :* to purify the air = *purifier l'air.*

PURITAN (n) *puritain, -e :* puritans don't go to swings = *les puritains ne font pas de partouzes* ⓪ goody-goody = *petit saint* **PURITANICAL** (adj) *puritain, -e :* puritanical conformism = *conformisme puritain* ⓪ self-righteous = *moralisant.*

PURPLE (n, adj) *pourpre (m) :* a purple cloak = *une cape pourpre* ⓪ scarlet = *écarlate.*

PURPOSE (n) *but (m) :* what's the purpose of your trip ? = *quel est le but de votre voyage ?* ⓪ aim = *objectif* **for the (set) purpose of** = *dans le but (précis) de :* for the set purpose of meeting with him = *dans le but précis de le rencontrer* ⓪ with the intention of = *dans l'intention de* **for what purpose ?** = *dans quel but ?* ⓪ why ? = *pourquoi ?* **on purpose** = *exprès :* he said that on purpose to get me angry = *il a dit ça exprès pour me mettre en colère* ⓪ by design = *à dessein* ≠ accidentally = *accidentellement* **to serve its purpose** = *faire l'affaire* = to do the trick **what's the purpose of (telling him) ?** = *à quoi ça sert de (le lui dire) ?* ☠ *son seul but est de se marier* = his only goal is to get married — *un but (football)* = a goal

— *aller droit au but* = to get straight to the point
— *dire qqch de but en blanc* = to say stg point-blank.

PURPOSELY (adv) *exprès :* he lied purposely = *il a menti exprès* ⓪ designedly = *à dessein.*

PURR (to, -ed) *ronronner :* my cat purrs when you pet him = *mon chat ronronne quand on le caresse* ≠ to bark = *aboyer.*

PURSE (n) *sac (m) à main :* I lost my purse = *j'ai perdu mon sac à main* ⓪ pocketbook ⓪ change purse = *porte-monnaie* **to hold the purse strings** = *tenir les cordons de la bourse* ⓪ to wear the pants = *porter la culotte.*

PURSUE (to, -d) *poursuivre :* to pursue a career/a criminal = *poursuivre une carrière/un criminel* ⓪ to follow = *suivre* ☠ *cette idée me poursuit* = that idea is haunting me — *poursuivre en justice* = to sue — *poursuivez !* = proceed ! — *poursuivez votre travail* = carry on with your work.

PURSUIT (n) *poursuite (f) :* the pursuit of happiness = *la poursuite du bonheur* ☠ *une poursuite dans les rues* = a chase in the streets — *engager des poursuites (judiciaires) contre qqn* = to take legal action against s.o. — *la poursuite des négociations* = the continuation/ follow-up of the negotiations.

PUS (n) *pus (m) :* there was pus in the wound = *il y avait du pus dans la plaie* ⓪ infection = ←.

PUSH (n, -es) **1/** *coup (m) de collier :* a final push to finish this work = *un dernier coup de collier pour finir ce travail* ⓪ effort = ← **2/** *dynamisme (m) :* you need a lot of push to get ahead = *il faut beaucoup de dynamisme pour réussir* ⓪ energy = *énergie,* to have a lot of drive = *en vouloir* **3/** *courant (m) :* there's a push towards more liberal abortion laws → *il y a un courant en faveur de lois plus libérales concernant l'avortement* ⓪ campaign = *campagne* ☠ → current

| **when push comes to shove** = *le moment venu :* he promised to help, but when push came to shove he copped out = *il avait promis de nous aider, mais* | *le moment venu il s'est défilé* ⓪ when it comes down to it = *tout compte fait.* |

PUSH (to, -ed) **1/** *pousser :* push the door shut = *pousse la porte* ≠ to pull = *tirer*

| ☠ *sa barbe pousse* = his beard is growing — *pousser (un cri/une gueulante)* = to let out (a yell) | — *pousser la gentillesse jusqu'à* = to be so kind as to — *les gosses poussent vite* = kids shoot up quickly |

2/ *faire la promo(tion) de :* he went on TV to push his book = *il est passé à la télévision pour faire la promo de son livre* ⓪ to plug = *faire de la pub pour* **3/** *faire pression sur :* stop pushing me, let me do what I want = *cessez de faire pression sur moi, laissez-moi faire ce que je veux*

| **to be pushing (40)** = *friser (la quarantaine)* **to push a button** = *pousser un bouton/appuyer sur un bouton* | **that's pushing it !** = *tu pousses un peu !* ⓪ that's stretching it ! = *tu charries !* **to push (drugs)** = *revendre (de la drogue)* ⓪ to deal = *faire du trafic* |

to push s.o. about/around = *jouer au petit chef avec qqn :* stop pushing your brother about/around = *arrête de jouer au petit chef avec ton frère* ⓪ to bully = *brutaliser* **to push s.o. away** = *repousser qqn :* he went to kiss me but I pushed him away = *il allait m'embrasser, mais je l'ai repoussé* **to push (the enemy) back** = *repousser (l'ennemi)* ☠ → to repel	**to push s.o. into** = *pousser qqn à (faire) :* his mother pushed him into teaching = *sa mère l'a poussé à faire de l'enseignement* **to push for** = *faire pression pour :* the unions are pushing for higher wages = *les syndicats font pression pour obtenir une hausse des salaires* **to push off** = *mettre les voiles :* it's time to push off = *il est temps de mettre les voiles* → TO LEAVE **to push stg through** = *réussir*	*à faire passer qqch :* they pushed the bill through Congress = *ils ont réussi à faire passer le projet de loi au Congrès* **to push s.o. to** = *pousser qqn à :* he pushed me to do it = *il m'a poussé à le faire* ≠ to discourage from = *décourager de* **to push stg up** = *faire monter qqch :* frequent oil price rises push prices up = *les fréquentes hausses du prix du pétrole font monter les prix* ≠ **to push stg down** = *faire baisser qqch.*

PUSHER (n) 1/ *revendeur, -euse :* a drug pusher = *un revendeur de drogue* ⓪ dealer = ← ≠ drug addict = *toxicomane* ☠ *revendeur (biens)* = jobber 2/ *arriviste (m, f) :* the young sales manager is a pusher = *le jeune directeur des ventes est un arriviste* ⓪ young Turk = *jeune loup.*

PUSHOVER (n) **(my father) was a pushover for (the salesman)** = *(le vendeur) n'a fait qu'une bouchée (de mon père).*

PUSH-UP (n) **to do push-ups (every morning)** = *faire des pompes (tous les matins).*

PUSHY (adj, -ier, -iest) *qui se met en avant :* he's ambitious and pushy = *il est ambitieux et il se met toujours en avant* ⓪ aggressive = *agressif.*

PUSSY (n, -ies) 1/ *minou (m) :* a shaven pussy = *un minou rasé* ⓪ cunt = *chatte* ≠ cock = *pine* 2/ *minou (m),* minet, -ette : a nice little pussy = *un gentil petit minet/minou* ⓪ cat = *chat* ☠ *un minet (garçon)* = a pretty boy, *une minette* = a flaky gal
— *mon minet/mon minou* = honey.

PUSSYFOOT (to, -ed) *tourner autour du pot :* when he was asked his opinion about abortion, he pussyfooted = *quand on lui a demandé son avis sur l'avortement, il a tourné autour du pot* ⓪ to hem and haw = *atermoyer,* to avoid the issue = *chercher des faux-fuyants.*

PUT (to, put, put) *mettre :* put the book on the table = *mettez le livre sur la table* ⓪ to place = *placer*	
how can I put it ? = *comment dire ? :* he's, how can I put it, not really skin and bones but terribly thin = *il n'a pas, comment dire, que la peau et les os, mais il est terriblement mince* **let me put it another way** = *en d'autres termes*	**put up or shut up !** = *soit vous agissez, soit vous la fermez !* ⓪ shit or get off the pot ! = *tu te décides, oui ou merde ?* **that's putting it (strongly)** = *c'est aller un peu (loin)*

to put stg above = *mettre qqch au-dessus de :* he puts honor above money = *il met l'honneur au-dessus de l'argent* **to put stg across** = *faire comprendre qqch :* I couldn't put my ideas across = *je n'ai pas pu faire comprendre mes idées* **to put stg aside** = *mettre qqch de côté :* I put aside a bit of money every month = *je mets chaque mois un peu d'argent de côté* **to put stg away** = 1/ *ranger qqch :* put your things away = *range tes affaires* ☠ → to tidy up 2/ *mettre qqch à gauche :* infla-	tion is so high they can't put a lot of money away = *l'inflation est tellement forte qu'ils ne peuvent pas mettre beaucoup d'argent à gauche* ⓪ to save = *épargner* **to put stg back** = *remettre qqch (à sa place) :* please, put the glass back where it should be = *s'il te plaît, remets le verre où il devrait être* **to put down** = *réprimer :* they put down the revolution = *ils ont réprimé la révolution* ⓪ to quell = *mater* **to put s.o. down** = *débiner qqn :* she's always putting her	husband down = *elle est toujours en train de débiner son mari* ⓪ to knock = *taper sur* ☠ → to cop out **to put ... down** = *verser un acompte de ... :* I have put ten dollars down = *j'ai versé un acompte de dix dollars* **to put stg down** = 1/ *poser qqch :* put that knife down ! = *posez ce couteau !* ☠ → to pose 2/ *inscrire qqch :* could you put my name down ? = *pourriez-vous inscrire mon nom ?* ☠ → to inscribe **to put stg down to** = *mettre qqch sur le compte de :* you can

put his mistakes down to his absent-mindedness = *ses erreurs sont à mettre sur le compte de son étourderie*

to put forward = *parler de* : his name was put forward for vice-president = *on parle de lui comme vice-président*

to put s.o./stg in = 1/ *mettre qqn/qqch dans/en* : put your wallet in your pocket = *mettez votre portefeuille dans votre poche*, did they put him in jail just for that ? = *ils l'ont mis en prison juste pour ça ?*, he put a lot of money in the deal = *il a mis beaucoup d'argent dans l'affaire* 2/ *mettre ... à* : she put years in her book = *elle a mis des années à écrire son livre*

to put in for (membership) = *faire une demande d'(adhésion)*

to put into = *investir dans* : she puts a lot into her marriage = *elle investit beaucoup dans sa vie de couple* ☠ → to invest

to put off = 1/ *éteindre* : put off the lights = *éteins les lumières* ☠ → to extinguish 2/ *repousser* : the meeting was put off = *la réunion a été repoussée* ⓪ to defer = *différer* ☠ → to repel

to put s.o. off = *rebuter qqn* : his looks put me off = *son aspect m'a rebuté*, the noise in the apartment put me off = *le bruit dans l'appartement m'a rebuté* ⓪ to turn off = *refroidir*

to put on = 1/ *mettre/allumer* : put on the TV/radio = *mets/allume la télé/radio* 2/ *mettre* : put on your green dress = *mettez votre robe verte* 3/ *prendre* : she put on ten pounds = *elle a pris cinq kilos* ☠ → to take 4/ *monter* : when are they putting on the play ? = *quand montent-ils la pièce ?* ☠ → to rise

to put it on = *frimer* : the way she dresses, she really puts it on = *avec sa façon de s'habiller,* elle frime vraiment ⓪ to talk big = *se faire mousser*

to put s.o. on = *faire marcher qqn* : stop putting me on ; I don't believe a word ! = *arrêtez de me faire marcher ; je n'en crois pas un mot !* ⓪ to poke fun at = *se payer la tête de*

to put s.o. onto stg/s.o. = *faire connaître qqch/qqn à qqn* : he put me onto a great Chinese restaurant = *il m'a fait connaître un restaurant chinois génial* ⓪ to steer s.o. to = *aiguiller qqn sur*

to put out = 1/ *éteindre* : it took all day to put the fire out = *il a fallu toute la journée pour éteindre l'incendie* ☠ → to extinguish 2/ *faire paraître* : the government put out a pamphlet on the danger of smoking = *le gouvernement a fait paraître une brochure sur les dangers du tabac*

to put o.s. out = *se donner un mal de chien* : he put himself out trying to help me = *il s'est donné un mal de chien pour essayer de m'aider* = to go out of one's way

to put s.o. out = *déranger qqn* : I don't want to put you out by coming so late = *je ne veux pas vous déranger en venant si tard* ⓪ to bother = *embêter* ☠ → to disturb

to put out for = *passer à la casserole* : she put out for the whole team = *elle est passée à la casserole avec toute l'équipe* ⓪ to make it with s.o. = *s'envoyer en l'air avec qqn*

to put over = *faire passer* : he couldn't put his ideas over = *il n'a pas réussi à faire passer ses idées* ⓪ to put across = *faire comprendre*

to put stg over on s.o. = *donner le change à qqn* : it's easy to put something over on her = *c'est facile de lui donner le change* → TO HUSTLE

to put s.o. through = *payer à qqn* : she's putting her kid sister through college = *elle paye des études supérieures à sa petite sœur*

to put s.o. through to s.o. = *passer qqn à qqn* : please put me through to Mr. Walker = *s'il vous plaît, passez-moi M. Walker*

... put together = *... réuni* : I know better than all my family put together = *je le sais mieux que toute ma famille réunie*

to put stg together = 1/ *former qqch* : they're putting a new team/band/government together = *ils forment une nouvelle équipe/un nouvel orchestre/un nouveau gouvernement* ☠ → to form 2/ *assembler* (puzzle), *réunir* (evidence) : to put a puzzle together = *assembler les pièces d'un puzzle*, the cops are putting all the evidence together = *les flics sont en train de réunir toutes les preuves*

to put up = 1/ *faire la mise de fonds* : who's going to put up the money ? = *qui va faire la mise de fonds ?* ⓪ to invest = *investir* 2/ *opposer* : they put up a strong resistance = *ils ont opposé une forte résistance* ☠ → to oppose 3/ *construire* : they're putting up a lot of new buildings = *ils construisent beaucoup de nouveaux immeubles* ⓪ to erect = *ériger* ☠ → to construct

to put s.o. up = *héberger qqn* : can you put me up for the night ? = *est-ce que vous pouvez m'héberger pour la nuit ?*

put 'em up ! = *les mains en l'air !*

to put s.o. up to = *pousser qqn à* : it's not my fault, he put me up to it = *ce n'est pas de ma faute, il m'y a poussé*

to put up with = *supporter* : I won't put up with it ! = *je ne supporterai pas ça !* ⓪ to tolerate = *tolérer* ☠ → to support

---

☠ *j'ai mis deux jours* = it took me two days
— *mettre la table* = to set the table
— *se mettre au (travail)* = to get down to (work)
— *mettez-vous ici !* = sit/stand there !

— *se mettre à pleurer/pleuvoir* = to start crying/raining
— *mettre au monde* = to bring into the world
— *mettre un disque* = to play a record.

PUT-DOWN (n) *remise (f) en place* : after that put-down, he didn't want to see her again = *après cette remise en place, il ne voulait plus la revoir* ⓒ cut = *pointe.*

PUT-ON (n) *frime (f)* : it's all a put-on ! = *tout ça, c'est de la frime !* ⓒ show = *esbroufe.*

PUTSCH (n, -es) *putsch (m)* : a putsch in South America = *un putsch en Amérique du Sud* ⓒ revolution = *révolution.*

PUTTER AROUND (to, -ed) *faire des bricoles :* he puttered around the house all day = *il a fait des bricoles dans la maison toute la journée.*

PUTTY (adj, -ier, -iest) **to be putty in s.o.'s hands** = *faire tout ce que veut qqn :* the boss is putty in her hands = *le patron fait tout ce qu'elle veut* ⓒ to have in one's pocket = *avoir dans sa poche.*

PUT-UP JOB (n) *machination (f) :* the drug arrest was a put-up job = *son arrestation pour trafic de drogue était une machination* ⓒ frame-up = *coup monté.*

PUZZLE (n) 1/ *puzzle (m) :* to buy a puzzle for a child = *acheter un puzzle pour un enfant* 2/ *mystère (m) :* it's a puzzle to me why they got married so soon = *c'est un mystère pour moi qu'ils se soient mariés si vite* ⓒ enigma = *énigme* 🙞 → mystery **PUZZLE** (to, -d) *laisser perplexe :* his silence puzzles me = *son silence me laisse perplexe* ⓒ to bewilder = *plonger dans la perplexité* **PUZZLING** (adj) *qui laisse perplexe :* a puzzling attitude = *une attitude qui laisse perplexe.*

PX (n) *économat (m) militaire américain.*

PYGMY (n, -ies) *pygmée (m)* ⓒ aborigine = *aborigène.*

PYJAMAS (n pl) (GB) *pyjama (m)* = pajamas.

PYRAMID (n) *pyramide (f) :* pyramids in Egypt = *des pyramides en Égypte.*

QT (n) **on the qt** = *en cachette :* because he was married, they had to meet on the qt = *ils devaient se voir en cachette parce qu'il était marié* ⓧ in secret = *en secret.*

QUACK (n) *charlatan (m) :* that doctor's a quack = *ce médecin est un charlatan* ⓧ horse doctor = *mauvais docteur* ☠ → charlatan.

QUADRUPLE (to, -d) *quadrupler :* our rent quadrupled when we moved = *notre loyer a quadruplé quand nous avons déménagé* ⓧ to double = *doubler.*

QUADRUPLET (n) *quadruplé, -e* ⓧ triplet = *triplé.*

QUAINT (adj, -er, -est) *au charme vieillot :* a quaint restaurant = *un restaurant au charme vieillot* ⓧ picturesque = *pittoresque.*

QUAKER (n) *quaker (m, f)* ⓧ Mormon = ←.

QUALIFICATION (n) *qualification (f) :* she has the necessary qualifications for the job = *elle a les qualifications nécessaires pour le poste*
with ≠ without qualification = *avec des ≠ sans réserves.*

QUALIFIED (adj) *qualifié, -e :* a highly qualified secretary = *une secrétaire hautement qualifiée* ⓧ able = *capable* ☠ *ouvrier qualifié* = skilled worker.

QUALIFY (to, -ied) *nuancer :* let me qualify my statement = *laissez-moi nuancer ma déclaration*
to qualify for = 1/ *avoir les qualifications requises pour* (job) 2/ *se qualifier pour* (finals)
that doesn't qualify you to (criticize him) = *vous n'avez pas qualité pour (le critiquer)* ⓧ that doesn't entitle you to = *ça ne vous donne pas le droit de.*

QUALITY (n, -ies) **1/** *qualité (f) :* the finest quality cashmere = *un cachemire de la meilleure qualité* ⓧ value = *valeur* **2/** *qualité (f) :* he has a lot of qualities = *il a beaucoup de qualités* ⓧ virtue = *vertu*
☠ *en sa qualité d'avocate* = in her capacity of lawyer — *vous n'avez pas qualité pour ...* = that doesn't qualify you to ...

QUALM (n) **1/** *scrupule (m) :* I have qualms about lying to him = *j'ai des scrupules à lui mentir* ☠ → scruple **2/** *hésitation (f) :* she has no qualms about her daughter's taking the pill = *elle a fait prendre la pilule à sa fille sans aucune hésitation.*

QUANDARY (n, -ies) **to be in a quandary** = *être dans l'embarras :* I'm in a quandary about what to do = *je suis dans l'embarras pour agir* ⓧ to be in a hole = *être dans le pétrin.*

QUANTITY (n, -ies) *quantité (f) :* I know it needs seasoning, but I don't know what quantity = *je sais que ça a besoin d'assaisonnement, mais je ne sais pas en quelle quantité*
a large/great quantity of (beer) = *une grande quantité de (bière)* → MANY
☠ *elle en a une quantité* = she has an enormous amount (of them).

QUARANTINE (n) *quarantaine (f) :* to put in quarantine = *mettre en quarantaine* ☠ *être mis en quarantaine (psychologiquement)* = to be in the doghouse **QUARANTINE** (to, -d) *mettre en quarantaine* ⓧ to isolate = *isoler.*

QUARREL (n) *querelle (f) :* a lovers' quarrel = *une querelle d'amoureux* ⓧ run-in = *prise de bec,* squabble = *chamaillerie*
to pick a quarrel = *chercher querelle* ⓧ to pick an argument = *chercher la dispute*
☠ *vider une querelle avec qqn* = to have it out with s.o. — *querelles partisanes* = infighting.

QUARREL (to, -(l)ed) *(se) quereller :* they're always quarrelling = *ils sont toujours en train de se quereller* ⓧ to argue = *se disputer* ≠ to get on well = *bien s'entendre* **QUARRELSOME** (adj) *querelleur, -euse :* feisty and quarrelsome = *hargneux et querelleur* ⓧ belligerent = *belliqueux,* pugnacious = *pugnace.*

QUART (n) *0,946 litre* ⓧ gallon = *3,785 litres.*

QUARTER (n) **1/** *(pièce (f) de) 25 cents* ⓧ dime = *10 cents*
2/ *quart (m) :* he ate a quarter of the cake = *il a mangé un quart du gâteau* ⓧ half = *la moitié*
a quarter to ≠ past (ten) = *(dix heures) moins le quart ≠ et quart*
a quarter of an hour = *un quart d'heure*
☠ *(comprendre) au quart de tour* = (to understand) straight off

3/ *quartier (m)* : the Italian quarter of the city = *le quartier italien de la ville* = area ① part = *partie*
☠ *quartier réservé* = red-light district
— *vivre dans un quartier agréable* = to live in a pleasant neighborhood
— *avoir quartier libre* = to be off duty
— *quartier général* = headquarters
4/ *trimestre (m)* : the results for the last quarter = *les résultats du dernier trimestre.*

QUARTERLY (adj) *trimestriel, -elle* ① biyearly = *semestriel.*

QUARTZ (n) *quartz (m)* : quartz watch = *montre à quartz.*

QUASH (to, -ed) **1/** *étouffer* : to quash a rebellion = *étouffer une rébellion* ① to subdue = *maîtriser* ☠ → to choke **2/** *casser* : to quash a verdict = *casser un verdict* ☠ → to break.

QUASI (adv) *quasi, quasiment* : I'm quasi certain that you're wrong = *je suis quasiment sûr que vous avez tort.*

QUEEN (n) *reine (f)* : the queen of hearts = *la reine de cœur*, the queen mother = *la reine mère*

a **screaming queen** = *une grande folle* ① fag = *pédale.*

QUEER (n) *pédé (m)* : this bar's only for queers = *c'est un bar réservé aux pédés* ① homo = ←, flit = *tantouse* ≠ lesbian = *lesbienne.*

QUEER (adj, -er, -est) **1/** *bizarre* : queer ideas = *des idées bizarres* ① strange = *étrange*
a **queer duck** = *un drôle de zigoto* ① an oddball = *un drôle de numéro*
2/ *pédé* : her brother's queer = *son frère est pédé* ① gay = ←.

QUELL (to, -ed) *mater* : to quell a revolt = *mater une révolte* ≠ to foment = *fomenter*
☠ *mater (regarder)* = to peep
— *mater qqn* = to bring s.o. to heel.

QUERY (n, -ies) *demande (f) d'information* : queries about the product = *des demandes d'information sur le produit.*

QUEST (n) **in quest of (the truth)** = *en quête de (la vérité).*

QUESTION (n) *question (f)* : does anyone have questions ? = *est-ce que quelqu'un a des questions ?* ①
inquiry = *demande* ≠ answer = *réponse*

to ask a question = *poser une question* : can I ask you a question ? = *puis-je vous poser une question ?* **ask me no questions I'll tell you no lies** = *la curiosité est un vilain défaut* **to beg the question** = *tourner le problème* **to call/bring into question** = *remettre en question* : we are not calling her integrity into question = *nous ne remettons pas son intégrité en question* **in question** = 1/ *en question* : his honesty isn't in question =	*son honnêteté n'est pas en question* 2/ *en question* : look at the chapter in question = *regardez le chapitre en question* **it's a question of (money)** = *c'est une question d'(argent)* **question mark** = *point d'interrogation* **to pop the question** = *faire sa déclaration* ① to propose = *faire sa demande en mariage* **that's another question** = *c'est une autre affaire/question* **that's out of the question !** = *c'est hors de question !* **that's the question !** = *là est*	la question ! **there's no question about it** = *ça ne fait aucun doute* : there's something wrong, there's no question about it = *il y a quelque chose qui ne va pas, ça ne fait aucun doute* = there's no doubt about it **without question** = *incontestablement* : he's without question the most sensitive guy I know = *c'est incontestablement le type le plus sensible que je connaisse* ① without a doubt = *sans aucun doute*

☠ *pour des questions financières* = for financial matters — *question boulot, ça va* = as far as my job's concerned, it's O.K.	— *il est question de la jeunesse dans son article* = his article deals with youth — *je me pose des questions* = I'm wondering.

QUESTION (to, -ed) **1/** *questionner* : the cops questioned him = *les flics l'ont questionné* ① to grill = *cuisiner* **2/** *se poser des questions sur* : I question his honesty = *je me pose des questions sur son honnêteté* ① to contest = *contester.*

QUESTIONABLE (adj) *contestable* : questionable activities = *des activités contestables* ① dubious = *douteux.*

QUESTIONING (n) *interrogatoire (m)* : the suspect was brought in for questioning = *on a fait entrer le suspect pour l'interrogatoire* ☠ → interrogation.

QUESTIONNAIRE (n) *questionnaire (m)* : fill in the questionnaire = *remplissez le questionnaire* ⓪ form = *formulaire*.

QUEUE (n) (GB) *queue (f)* = line ☠ *tail*.

QUEUE (to, -d) (GB) **to queue (up)** = *faire la queue* = to stand in line.

QUIBBLE (to, -d) **to quibble about** = *ergoter/pinailler* : it's such a tiny amount, let's not quibble about it ! = *il s'agit d'une somme si infime, n'ergotons pas !/ne pinaillons pas !*

to quibble over = *ergoter/pinailler sur* : they're quibbling over the precise meaning of this word = *ils ergotent/ils pinaillent sur le sens précis de ce mot*.

QUICK (n) **to cut s.o. to the quick** = *piquer qqn au vif* ⓪ to hit the sore spot = *toucher le point sensible*.

QUICK (adj, -er, -est) **1/** *rapide* : a quick divorce/mind = *un divorce/un esprit rapide* ⓪ swift = *prompt* ☠ → rapid **2/** *vif, vive* : her children are very quick = *ses enfants sont très vifs* = bright ≠ dumb = *bête* ☠ → bright

to be quick on the trigger = *avoir la gâchette facile*.

QUICKIE (n) *coup (m) vite tiré* : how about a quickie before dinner ? = *si on tirait un coup vite fait avant le dîner ?* ⓪ one-night stand = *aventure d'un soir*.

QUICKLY (adv) *vite* : don't eat so quickly = *ne mangez pas si vite* = quick ⓪ rapidly = *rapidement* ☠ → fast.

QUICKSAND (n) *sable(s) (m (pl)) mouvant(s)* ⓪ swamp = *marécage*.

QUICK-TEMPERED (adj) *qui a la tête près du bonnet* : a quick-tempered boss = *un patron qui a la tête près du bonnet* → ANGRY.

QUICK-WITTED (adj) *qui a l'esprit vif* : quick-witted children = *des enfants qui ont l'esprit vif* ≠ slow on the uptake = *qui a l'esprit lent*.

QUIET (adj, -er, -est) *tranquille* : a quiet dinner/street = *un dîner/une rue tranquille* ⓪ calm = *calme*
be quiet ! = *restez tranquille !* ⓪ hush up ! = *taisez-vous !*
keep it quiet ! = *que cela reste entre nous !*
☠ *tu peux dormir tranquille/soyez tranquille* = you can sleep in peace/don't worry
— *laisse-moi tranquille !* = leave me alone !
— *avoir la conscience tranquille* = to have a clear conscience.

QUIET DOWN (to, -ed) *se calmer* : quiet down, please ! = *calmez-vous, s'il vous plaît !* = calm down, please ! ☠ → to calm.

QUIETLY (adv) *tranquillement* ⓪ calmly = *calmement*.

QUINTESSENCE (n) **the quintessence of (elegance)** = *le comble de (l'élégance)* ⓪ embodiment = *personnification*.

QUIP (n) *boutade (f)* ⓪ crack = *vanne* **QUIP** (to, -ped) *faire une boutade* : he quipped that he'd rather be a house-husband than a businessman = *il a fait une boutade en disant qu'il préférerait être un homme au foyer plutôt qu'un homme d'affaires* ⓪ to scoff = *railler*.

QUIRK (n) *bizarrerie (f)* : eccentric and full of quirks = *excentrique et plein de bizarreries*
quirk of fate = *caprice du destin* : our meeting was a quirk of fate = *notre rencontre a été un caprice du destin*.

QUIT (to, quit, quit) **1/** *donner sa démission* : I quit last week = *j'ai donné ma démission la semaine dernière* ⓪ to resign = *démissionner*
2/ *s'arrêter* : let's quit at four today = *arrêtons-nous à quatre heures aujourd'hui* ☠ → to stop
quit it ! = *arrêtez !* = stop it !
quit while you're ahead = *arrêtez pendant que vous avez le vent en poupe* ⓪ get out while the going's good = *tirez votre épingle du jeu*
3/ *quitter* : she quit school at 16 = *elle a quitté l'école à 16 ans*
☠ *j'ai quitté mon bureau à dix heures* = I left my office at ten
— *ne pas quitter des yeux/du regard* = not to take one's eyes off
— *ne quittez pas ! (téléphone)* = hold on ! (phone)
— *nous nous sommes quittés amis* = we parted friends.

QUITE (adv) **1/** *tout à fait* : you're quite right = *vous avez tout à fait raison*, I quite agree with you = *je suis tout à fait d'accord avec vous* → VERY
2/ *assez* : it's quite expensive = *c'est assez cher* ⓪ somewhat = *quelque peu* ☠ → enough
quite a few/a lot of (problems) = *pas mal de (problèmes)* → MANY
quite a bit = *pas mal* : he drinks quite a bit = *il boit pas mal*
quite simply = *tout bonnement* : you're quite simply wrong = *vous avez tout bonnement tort* → VERY
he's quite (a cook) ! = *quel (cuisinier) !*

QUITS (adj) **to call it quits** = *en rester là* : let's call it quits for today ! = *restons-en là pour aujourd'hui !*, after 5 years of marriage they decided to call it quits = *après 5 ans de mariage, ils ont décidé d'en rester là*.

QUITTER (n) *lâcheur, -euse* : don't be a quitter ! = *ne sois pas un lâcheur !*

QUIVER (to, -ed) *frémir* : his voice quivered = *sa voix a frémi* ⓪ to tremble = *trembler* ☠ → to shudder.

QUIZ (n, -zes) *interro (f)* : a quiz on verbs = *une interro sur les verbes* ⓪ drill = *colle*
quiz kid = *enfant prodige* = whiz kid
quiz show = *jeu télévisé*.

QUOTA (n) *quota (m)* : the US have a quota on immigration = *les USA ont un quota d'immigration* ⓪ percentage = *pourcentage*.

QUOTATION (n) *citation* *(f)* : a quotation from the Bible = *une citation extraite de la Bible* = a quote **quotation marks** = *guillemets*.

QUOTE (to, -d) *citer* : to quote an author/a text = *citer un auteur/un texte* ≠ to misquote = *citer hors de propos*

☠ *citer (devant une cour)* = to subpoena

— *citer qqn en exemple* = to hold s.o. up as an example.

RABBI (n) *rabbin* (m) : chief rabbi = *grand rabbin* ⓒⓓ temple = ←.

RABBIT (n) *lapin, -e* : a fairy tale about rabbits = *un conte de fées sur les lapins* ⓒⓓ bunny = *jeune lapin,* hare = *lièvre*
☠ *un chaud lapin* = a hot number
— *poser un lapin à qqn* = to stand s.o. up.

RABIES (n inv) *rage* (f) : you can die from rabies = *on peut mourir de la rage* ☠ → rage.

RACCOON (n) *raton* (m) *laveur* ⓒⓓ polecat = *putois.*

RACE (n) **1/** *course* (f) : he won the race = *il a gagné la course* ⓒⓓ contest = *concours*
it's a race against the clock = *c'est une course contre la montre*
☠ *faire des courses* = to run errands/to go shopping
— *être dans la course* = to be in the running
— *jouer aux courses* = to play the horses
— *course d'obstacles* = steeplechase
2/ *race* (f) : the Caucasian race = *la race caucasienne*
☠ *un chien de race* = a pedigree dog
— *une race de chiens* = a breed of dogs.

RACE (to, -d) **to race s.o.** = *faire la course avec qqn* : I'll race you to the house = *je fais la course avec toi jusqu'à la maison.*

RACES (n pl) *courses* (f pl) : I've never been to the races = *je ne suis jamais allé aux courses* ⓒⓓ to bet = *parier.*

RACETRACK (n) *champ* (m) *de courses.*

RACIAL (adj) *racial, -e* : racial problems = *des problèmes raciaux* ⓒⓓ ethnic = *ethnique.*

RACISM (n) *racisme* (m) : racism reared its ugly head = *le racisme est réapparu dans toute sa laideur* ⓒⓓ prejudice = *préjugé racial,* antisemitism = *antisémitisme,* apartheid = ← **RACIST** (n, adj) *raciste* (m, f) : a racist newspaper = *un journal raciste.*

RACKET (n) **1/** *racket* (m) : prostitution's a racket = *la prostitution est un racket* ⓒⓓ Mafia = ← ☠ *leur argent provient du racket* = their money comes from racketeering **2/** *raffut* (m) : what a racket you made last night !

= *qu'est-ce que tu as fait comme raffut hier soir !* ⓒⓓ rumpus = *boucan,* bedlam = *chambard,* pandemonium = *tohu-bohu.*

RACKETEER (n) *racketteur* (m) : prostitution's in the hands of racketeers = *la prostitution est aux mains des racketteurs* ⓒⓓ crook = *escroc* **RACKETEERING** (n) *racket* (m) : their money comes from racketeering = *leur argent provient du racket* ☠ → racket.

RACY (adj, -ier, -iest) *piquant, -e* : racy jokes = *des histoires piquantes* ⓒⓓ spicy = *salé* ☠ *sauce piquante* = spicy sauce.

RADAR (n) *radar* (m) : planes detected by radar = *des avions détectés au radar.*

RADIANT (adj) *radieux, -euse* : a radiant bride = *une mariée radieuse* ≠ glum = *maussade.*

RADIATION (n) *radiation* (f) : nuclear radiation = *radiation nucléaire* ⓒⓓ X-rays = *des rayons X.*

RADIATOR (n) *radiateur* (m) ⓒⓓ central heating = *chauffage central.*

RADICAL (n) *extrémiste* (m, f) : radicals are for drastic changes = *les extrémistes sont pour des changements radicaux* = extremist ⓒⓓ radicalism = *extrémisme* ≠ moderate = *modéré* ☠ *un radical* = a Centrist.

RADICAL (adj) *radical, -e* : radical changes = *des changements radicaux* ⓒⓓ fundamental = *fondamental* ≠ superficial = *superficiel*
the radical left/right = *l'extrême gauche/droite.*

RADICALIZE (to, -d) *se radicaliser* : women's lib has become radicalized = *le mouvement de libération de la femme s'est radicalisé.*

RADICALLY (adv) *radicalement* : radically different = *radicalement différent* ⓒⓓ completely = *complètement.*

RADIO (n) *radio* (f) : turn the radio on = *allume la radio* ⓒⓓ wireless = *TSF,* TV = *télé,* earphones = *écouteurs,* walkman = *Walkman/baladeur*
on the radio = *à la radio*
☠ *se faire faire une radio du bras* = to have one's arm X-rayed.

RADIOACTIVE (adj) *radioactif, -ive* **RADIOACTIVITY** (n inv) *radioactivité (f)* ⓞ nuclear plant = *centrale nucléaire.*

RADISH (n, -es) *radis (m) :* two bunches of radishes = *deux bottes de radis* ⓞ horseradish = *raifort* ☠ *je n'ai pas un radis* = I don't have a cent.

RADIUM (n) *radium (m)* ⓞ uranium = ←.

RADIUS (n, -i or -es) **within a radius of (thirty miles)** = *dans un rayon de (quarante kilomètres).*

RAFFLE (n) *tombola (f) :* a raffle ticket = *un billet de tombola* ⓞ lottery = *loterie.*

RAFT (n) *radeau (m)* ⓞ lifeboat = *bateau de sauvetage.*

RAG (n) **1/** *chiffon (m) :* to dust with a rag = *épousseter avec un chiffon* **2/** *torchon (m) :* it's the worst rag in the country = *c'est le pire torchon du pays* ⓞ newspaper = *journal* ☠ → dishrag
to chew the rag = *parler de choses et d'autres* ⓞ to shoot the breeze = *parler de la pluie et du beau temps*
to go from rags to riches = *partir de rien et devenir riche* ⓞ to make it = *réussir*
in rags = *en haillons*
the rag trade = *la friperie :* he works in the rag trade = *il travaille dans la friperie.*

RAGE (n) **to be (all) the rage** = *faire fureur :* walkmans are (all) the rage = *les Walkmans font fureur* ⓞ to be the craze = *être en vogue*
to fly into a rage = *se mettre en rage* → ANGRY
the rage to live = *la rage de vivre*
☠ *une rage de dents* = a raging toothache
— *la rage (maladie)* = rabies
— *ce n'est pas de l'amour, c'est de la rage* = it's not love, it's pure madness.

RAGE (to, -d) *faire rage :* the fire was raging = *l'incendie faisait rage.*

RAGGED (adj) *loqueteux, -euse :* ragged clothing = *des vêtements loqueteux* ⓞ threadbare = *élimé*
to run s.o. ragged = *mettre qqn sur les genoux :* taking care of the kids is running me ragged = *ça me met sur les genoux de m'occuper des gosses* ⓞ to knock s.o. out = *mettre qqn K.-O.*

RAID (n) *raid (m), descente (f) (de police) :* an air raid = *un raid aérien,* the cops made a raid on the casino = *les flics ont fait une descente au casino* ⓞ roundup = *rafle,* foray = *razzia* ☠ → descent.

RAID (to, -ed) *faire un raid :* they raided the village = *ils ont fait un raid sur le village* ⓞ to plunder = *piller.*

RAIL (n) *rail (m)* ⓞ track = *voie ferrée*
(to ship) by rail = *(envoyer) par le rail/par le chemin de fer.*

RAILROAD (n) *chemin de fer (m)* = railway (GB) ⓞ train = ←

railroad station = *gare ferroviaire*
railroad crossing = *passage à niveau.*

RAILROAD (to, -ed) **to railroad s.o. into stg** = *brusquer qqn pour lui faire faire qqch :* he was railroaded into working on a commission basis = *on l'a brusqué pour qu'il accepte de travailler à la commission uniquement* → TO HUSTLE
to railroad through = *faire voter (après un débat insuffisant) :* they railroaded the bill through the Senate = *le gouvernement a fait voter le projet de loi au Sénat en escamotant le débat.*

RAIN (n) *pluie (f), flotte (f)* (LV) : another day of rain = *un autre jour de pluie/flotte* ⓞ shower = *averse,* downpour = *déluge,* April shower = *giboulée de mars,* drizzle = *bruine,* raindrop = *goutte de pluie,* raincoat = *imperméable,* umbrella = *parapluie*
rain or shine = *qu'il pleuve ou qu'il vente*
to take a rain check = *n'être que partie remise :* I can't come tonight, but I'll take a rain check = *je ne peux pas venir ce soir, mais ce n'est que partie remise*
(to walk) in the rain = *(marcher) sous la pluie*
☠ *après la pluie, le beau temps* = the calm after the storm
— *ennuyeux comme la pluie* = as boring as hell
— *il fait la pluie et le beau temps* = he runs the show
— *parler de la pluie et du beau temps* = to shoot the breeze
— *flotte* → fleet.

RAIN (to, -ed) *pleuvoir, flotter* (LV) : it's going to rain tomorrow = *il va pleuvoir/flotter demain* ⓞ to pour = *pleuvoir à verse,* to teem = *pleuvoir à torrents,* to come down in buckets = *pleuvoir à seaux,* it's raining cats and dogs = *il tombe des hallebardes,* it's coming down = *il tombe des cordes* ≠ to drizzle = *bruiner,* to trickle = *pleuvoter* ☠ *flotter* → to float
to be rained out = *être annulé à cause de la pluie :* the match was rained out = *le match a été annulé à cause de la pluie* ⓞ to be cancelled = *être annulé*
when it rains it pours = *un malheur/bonheur n'arrive jamais seul.*

RAINBOW (n) *arc-en-ciel (m).*

RAINCOAT (n) *imperméable (m) :* I forgot my raincoat = *j'ai oublié mon imperméable* ⓞ galoshes = *bottes de caoutchouc.*

RAINY (adj, -ier, -iest) *pluvieux, -euse :* rainy weather = *un temps pluvieux* ≠ sunny = *ensoleillé*
to set stg aside for a rainy day = *garder une poire pour la soif* ⓞ to save up = *faire des économies.*

RAISE (n) *augmentation (f) :* I'm going to ask the boss for a raise = *je vais demander une augmentation au patron* = rise (GB) ≠ decrease = *baisse* ☠ → increase.

RAISE (to, -d) **1/** *augmenter :* to raise prices = *augmenter les prix* ≠ to lower = *baisser* ☠ → to augment **2/** *lever :* raise your arm = *levez le bras* = to lift ≠ to put down = *baisser*

☠ *lever la séance* = to adjourn a meeting
— *levez-vous !* = stand up !
— *il se lève (tôt)* = he gets up/rises (early)
3/ élever : to raise children/horses = *élever des enfants/des chevaux*
☠ *la facture s'élevait à* = the bill came to
— *s'élever contre* = to rise up against
4/ réunir : to raise money/funds = *réunir une somme d'argent/des fonds* ⓪ to collect = *recueillir* ☠ → to reunite.
5/ soulever : to raise an objection/a question = *soulever une objection/une question* ☠ → to lift.

RAISINS (n pl) *raisins (m pl) secs* ⓪ grapes = *raisin.*

RAKE IN (to, -d) *ramasser :* they raked in a grand during the weekend = *ils ont ramassé mille dollars pendant le week-end* ⓪ to pull in = *se faire* ☠ → to collect.

RAKE-OFF (n) *dessous-de-table (m inv) :* politicians often get rake-offs on government contracts = *les hommes politiques touchent souvent des dessous-de-table sur les contrats de l'État* ⓪ commission = *←,* payola = *bakchich.*

RALLY (n, -ies) **1/** *rassemblement (m) :* a political rally = *un rassemblement politique* ☠ *le rassemblement (de plusieurs documents)* = the gathering (of several documents) **2/** *reprise (f) :* a stock market rally = *une reprise de la Bourse* ☠ → rerun.

RALLY (to, -ied) *(se) rallier :* in times of crisis, the country rallies around the President = *en temps de crise, le pays se rallie au Président* ☠ *rallier qqn à une cause* = to win s.o. over to a cause.

RAMBLE (to, -d) **to ramble on** = *discourir :* he didn't stick to the point, he just rambled on = *il n'a fait que discourir sans s'en tenir au sujet.*

RAMBUNCTIOUS (adj) *déchaîné, -e :* rambunctious kids = *des gosses déchaînés* ⓪ noisy = *bruyant.*

RAMIFICATION (n) *ramification (f) :* the bill's ramifications = *les ramifications du projet de loi* **RAMIFY** (to, -ied) *(se) ramifier.*

RAM INTO (to, -med) *emboutir :* to ram into a wall = *emboutir un mur* ⓪ to smash into = *s'écraser contre.*

RAMPAGE (n) **on a rampage** = *qui se déchaîne :* the murderer went on a rampage = *le meurtrier s'est déchaîné* ⓪ to go berserk = *perdre la boule.*

RAMPANT (adj) *extrêmement répandu, -e :* rampant use of drugs = *usage extrêmement répandu de drogues* **rampant inflation** = *inflation rampante.*

RANCH (n, -es) *ranch (m) :* I lived on a ranch in Texas = *j'ai vécu dans un ranch au Texas* ⓪ rancher = *propriétaire d'un ranch.*

RANCID (adj) *rance :* rancid butter = *beurre rance* ≠ fresh = *frais.*

RANDOM (n) **at random** = *au hasard :* she chose at random = *elle a choisi au hasard* ⓪ haphazardly = *au petit bonheur la chance.*

RANGE (n) *gamme (f) :* a range of colors/prices = *une gamme de couleurs/de prix* ☠ → gamut
within ≠ **outside s.o.'s range** = *à la portée* ≠ *hors de la portée de qqn :* playing tennis with a champion is within ≠ outside my range = *c'est à ma portée* ≠ *hors de ma portée de jouer au tennis avec un champion.*

RANK (n) *rang (m) :* what's his rank in the army ? = *quel est son rang dans l'armée ?*
to pull rank = *se prévaloir de sa position auprès de qqn (pour obtenir un avantage) :* he pulled rank to get good seats = *il s'est prévalu de sa position pour obtenir de bonnes places*
the rank and file = *la base* (politics)/ *les employés* (business) : the rank and file of the party are for nationalized medicine = *la base du parti est pour une médecine nationalisée* ⓪ the common man/woman = *le commun des mortels*
to rise from the ranks = *sortir du rang*
☠ *un rang de (fauteuils)* = a row of (seats)
— *en rang d'oignons* = in single file
— *ne pas être sur le même rang que* = not to be in the same league with
— *être sur les rangs* = to be in the running
— *elle est rentrée dans le rang* = she's back in line.

RANK (to, -ed) **to rank among** = *ranger parmi :* they rank him among the greatest poets = *on le range parmi les plus grands poètes*
to rank as = *considérer comme :* I rank him as a great writer = *je le considère comme un grand écrivain.*

RANSACK (to, -ed) **1/** *saccager :* the soldiers ransacked the town = *les soldats ont saccagé la ville* ⓪ to pillage = *piller* **2/** *fouiller de fond en comble :* I ransacked the room looking for my wallet = *j'ai fouillé la pièce de fond en comble pour trouver mon portefeuille* ⓪ to go through = *fouiller dans.*

RANSOM (n) *rançon (f) :* to ask for a high ransom = *demander une forte rançon* ⓪ kidnapper = *ravisseur* ☠ *la rançon de la gloire* = the price of fame.

RANT (to, -ed) *déblatérer :* the madman was ranting = *le fou était en train de déblatérer* ⓪ to rave = *divaguer*
to rant and rave = *tempêter* → ANGRY.

RAP (n) **1/** discussion (f) : last night's rap lasted till two o'clock in the morning = *la discussion d'hier soir a duré jusqu'à deux heures du matin* ⓪ chat = *causette* ☠ → discussion
2/ accusation (f) : a murder rap = *une accusation de meurtre* ☠ → accusation
to beat the rap = *s'en tirer :* he was accused of smuggling but beat the rap = *il était accusé de contrebande mais il s'en est tiré* ≠ to be found guilty = *être reconnu coupable*
to take the rap for s.o. = *écoper pour qqn :* he took the rap for his brother = *il a écopé pour son frère* ⓪ to be the scapegoat = *être le bouc émissaire.*

RAP (to, -ped) *bavarder* : we rapped till past midnight = *nous avons bavardé jusqu'à minuit passé* ⊕ to shoot the bull = *tailler une bavette.*

RAPE (n) *viol* (m) : new laws on rape = *de nouvelles lois concernant le viol* ⊕ gang bang = *viol collectif* **RAPE** (to, -d) *violer* : the guy who raped her was sentenced to five years = *le type qui l'a violée a été condamné à cinq ans de prison* ⊕ to assault = *violenter* ☠ *violer la loi* = to violate the law **RAPIST** (n) *violeur* (m).

RAPID (adj) *rapide* : rapid progress/recovery = *des progrès rapides/un rétablissement rapide* = quick ≠ slow = *lent* ☠ *une voiture rapide* = a fast car.

RAPIDITY (n) *rapidité* (f) ≠ slowness = *lenteur.*

RAPIDLY (adv) *rapidement* : to walk rapidly = *marcher rapidement* ≠ leisurely = *en prenant son temps.*

RAPTURE (n) *ravissement* (m) : the rapture of an orgasm = *le ravissement d'un orgasme* ⊕ ecstasy = *extase.*

RARE (adj, -r, -st) 1/ *rare* : sunny days are rare = *les journées ensoleillées sont rares* ⊕ exceptional = *exceptionnel* ≠ usual = *habituel* ☠ *tu te fais rare* = I don't see you much around any more 2/ *saignant, -e* : I like my meat rare = *j'aime la viande saignante* ⊕ very rare = *bleu* ≠ medium = *à point.*

RARELY (adv) *rarement* : she rarely shows up on time = *elle se pointe rarement à l'heure* ≠ usually = *habituellement.*

RARING (adj) **to be raring to go** = *péter le feu* ⊕ to feel one's oats = *avoir la pêche.*

RARITY (n, -ies) *rareté* (f) : the rarity of real happiness = *la rareté du bonheur absolu.*

RASCAL (n) *polisson, -e* : her kids are little rascals = *ses gosses sont de petits polissons* ⊕ scamp = *galopin,* brat = *sale gosse.*

RASH (adj, -er, -est) *inconsidéré, -e* : a rash decision = *une décision inconsidérée* ⊕ hasty = *hâtif* ≠ thought-out = *réfléchi.*

RASH (n, -es) *éruption* (f) *de boutons* ⊕ pimple = *bouton,* hives = *urticaire.*

RASPBERRY (n, -ies) *framboise* (f) : raspberry jam = *confiture de framboises* ⊕ strawberry = *fraise.*

RAT (n) 1/ *rat, -e* : there are rats in the cellar = *il y a des rats dans la cave* ⊕ mouse = *souris,* rodent = *rongeur* **a rat race** = *un panier de crabes* : advertising's a rat race = *le monde de la publicité est un panier de crabes* ⊕ dog eat dog = *l'homme est un loup pour l'homme* **I smell a rat** = *il y a anguille sous roche* ⊕ there's something fishy = *il y a quelque chose de louche* ☠ *rat de bibliothèque* = bookworm
— *un (petit) rat* = a young ballet dancer
— *s'ennuyer comme un rat mort* = to be bored stiff
— *il est fait comme un rat* = his number's up

2/ *sale type* (m) : she's married to a rat = *elle est mariée à un sale type* → BASTARD.

RATE (n) *tarif* (m) : this hotel's rates are too high = *les tarifs de cet hôtel sont trop élevés* ⊕ price = *prix*
at this rate = *à ce train-là* : at this rate we'll never finish = *à ce train-là nous ne finirons jamais* ⊕ at this pace = *à cette allure*
rate of exchange = *taux de change*
☠ → tariff.

RATE (to, -d) *mériter* : I rate the best ! = *je mérite ce qu'il y a de mieux !* = I deserve the best !
to be rated among/as = *compter parmi/être considéré comme* : he's rated among our best filmmakers/he's rated as one of our best filmmakers = *il compte parmi nos meilleurs cinéastes/il est considéré comme l'un de nos meilleurs cinéastes*
to rate with = *avoir la cote auprès de* : she rates with the boss = *elle a la cote auprès du patron* ⊕ to be in s.o.'s good books = *être dans les petits papiers de qqn*
☠ → to merit.

RATHER (adv) *plutôt* : the play was rather interesting = *la pièce était plutôt intéressante* ⊕ quite = *assez*

I'd rather not = *j'aimerais mieux pas* **I'd rather ... than** = *j'aimerais mieux ... que* : I'd rather go now than later = *j'aimerais mieux y aller maintenant que plus tard* ⊕ **I'd prefer ... than** = *je préférerais ... que*	**rather like** = *plutôt comme* : he's rather like his brother = *il est plutôt comme son frère* **rather than** = *plutôt que* : rather than eat in, let's go out = *si on sortait, plutôt que de manger à la maison.*

RATIFICATION (n) *ratification* (f) : the ratification of the treaty = *la ratification du traité* ≠ veto = *veto* **RATIFY** (to, -ied) *ratifier* : to ratify a treaty = *ratifier un traité* ≠ to veto = *opposer un veto à.*

RATIO (n) *rapport* (m) *numérique* : what's the ratio of Blacks to Whites in Washington ? = *quel est le rapport numérique entre Noirs et Blancs à Washington ?* ⊕ proportion = ← ☠ → report.

RATION (to, -ed) *rationner* : to ration gas = *rationner l'essence.*

RATIONAL (adj) *rationnel, -elle* : you're not being rational = *vous n'êtes pas rationnel* ⊕ reasonable = *raisonnable* ≠ irrational = *irrationnel.*

RATIONALE (n) *argumentation* (f) : what's the rationale behind your decision ? = *quelle est l'argumentation qui sous-tend votre décision ?* ⊕ reasoning = *raisonnement.*

RATIONALIZATION (n) *tentative* (f) *de justification :*

everything he said is a rationalization = *ses propos n'étaient qu'une tentative de justification.*

RATIONALIZE (to, -d) *tenter de (se) justifier* : stop rationalizing and admit you were wrong = *ne tentez plus de vous justifier et admettez que vous avez eu tort.*

RATIONS (n pl) *rations (f pl)* : gas/sugar rations = *des rations d'essence/de sucre.*

RAT ON (to, -ted) *donner* : he ratted on the gang = *il a donné le gang* ⓪ to denounce = *dénoncer* ☠ → to give.

RATTLE (to, -d) *dérouter* : his question rattled me = *sa question m'a dérouté* ⓪ to faze = *démonter.*

RATTLESNAKE (n) *serpent (m) à sonnettes, crotale (m)* ⓪ cobra = ←.

RAUNCHY (adj, -ier, -iest) *cochon, -onne* : a raunchy joke = *une plaisanterie cochonne* ⓪ porn = *porno,* salacious = *salace* ☠ → smutty.

RAVAGES (n pl) *ravages (m pl)* : the ravages of time/war = *les ravages du temps/de la guerre.*

RAVE (adj, -r, -st) **rave notices/reviews** = *critiques dithyrambiques* ⓪ enthusiastic = *enthousiaste.*

RAVE (to, -d) *divaguer* : the patient's raving = *le malade divague* ⓪ to be delirious = *délirer*
to rave about = *s'enthousiasmer pour* : the critics raved about his last play = *les critiques se sont enthousiasmés pour sa dernière pièce* ≠ to put down = *débiner.*

RAVENOUS (adj) *affamé, -e* : when are we going to eat ? I'm ravenous ! = *quand allons-nous manger ? je suis affamé !* = famished ⓪ hungry = *qui a faim.*

RAVING (adj) **a raving lunatic** = *un fou furieux* → CRAZY.

RAVISHING (adj) *ravissant, -e* : a ravishing young girl/dress = *une jeune fille/une robe ravissante* ⓪ stunning = *sublime.*

RAW (adj, -er, -est) *cru, -e* : cats eat raw meat = *les chats mangent de la viande crue* ≠ cooked = *cuit*
a raw deal = *un marché de dupes* : he got a raw deal from his boss = *son patron lui a proposé un marché de dupes* ≠ to give s.o. a fair shake = *être fair-play avec qqn*
raw material = *matière première* ≠ by-product = *sous-produit*
☠ *lumière crue* = harsh light
— *langage cru* = crude language.

RAW (n) **in the raw** = *dans le plus simple appareil* = in the altogether ⓪ without a stitch on = *tout nu.*

RAY (n) *rayon (m)* : a ray of light/hope = *un rayon de lumière/d'espoir* ⓪ gleam = *lueur*
☠ *ce n'est pas mon rayon* = it's not within my sphere
— *dans un rayon de* = within a radius of
— *rayon (magasin)* = department (store).

RAZE (to, -d) *raser* : Berlin was razed in 1944 = *Berlin a été rasé en 1944* ⓪ to destroy = *détruire*
☠ *ça/il me rase !* = it's/he's a bore !
— *se raser* = to shave
— *raser les murs* = to hug the wall.

RAZOR (n) *rasoir (m)* : electric razor = *rasoir électrique,* razor blade = *lame de rasoir* ⓪ to shave = *se raser* ☠ *c'est rasoir !* = what a drag !

RE (prep) *au sujet de* : I'm writing re our last conversation = *je vous écris au sujet de notre dernière conversation* ⓪ with reference to = *en référence à.*

REACH (n) **to be in** ≠ **out of/beyond s.o.'s reach** = *être à la portée* ≠ *hors de la portée de qqn.*

REACH (to, -ed) **1/** *atteindre* : the shelf's too high, I can't reach it = *l'étagère est trop haute, je n'arrive pas à l'atteindre* ☠ *être atteint par (une balle/maladie)* = to be hit by (a bullet)/to be stricken by (a disease)
2/ *joindre* : I called but I couldn't reach you = *j'ai appelé mais je n'ai pas pu vous joindre* ⓪ to get in touch with = *prendre contact avec* ☠ → to join
3/ *parvenir à* : when the letter reaches him, it'll be too late = *quand la lettre lui parviendra, il sera trop tard,* to reach an agreement = *parvenir à un accord* ☠ *parvenir à faire qqch* = to manage to do stg
4/ *arriver à* : what time did you reach the coast ? = *à quelle heure êtes-vous arrivé à la côte ?*

REACT (to, -ed) *réagir* : he reacted poorly = *il a mal réagi* ⓪ he took it poorly = *il l'a mal pris* ☠ *il n'a pas réagi au traitement* = he didn't respond to the treatment.

REACTION (n) *réaction (f)* : I wonder what her reaction will be = *je me demande quelle sera sa réaction.*

REACTIONARY (n, -ies) *réactionnaire (m, f)* ≠ radical = *extrémiste (de gauche)* **REACTIONARY** (adj) *réactionnaire* : a reactionary policy = *une politique réactionnaire* ⓪ conservative = *conservateur.*

READ (to, read, read) *lire* : did you read his last novel ? = *est-ce que vous avez lu son dernier roman ?* ⓪ to peruse = *lire attentivement* ≠ to leaf through = *feuilleter*
to read about = *lire au sujet de* : did you read anything about the nuclear accident ? = *as-tu lu quelque chose sur l'accident nucléaire ?*
to read into = *voir dans* : you've read more into what he said than what he really meant = *vous avez vu dans ses propos plus que ce qu'il a vraiment voulu dire*
to read (a contract) over = *relire (un contrat)*
to read through = *lire d'un bout à l'autre* : read through the contract before you sign it = *lisez le contrat d'un bout à l'autre avant de le signer*
to read up on (new developments) = *(lire pour) se tenir au courant (des derniers développements).*

READER (n) *lecteur, -trice* : I receive a lot of letters from readers = *je reçois beaucoup de lettres de lecteurs.*

READERSHIP (n) *(nombre (m) de) lecteurs (m pl), lectorat (m) :* the magazine has a readership of 100 000 = *le magazine a 100 000 lecteurs.*

READING (n) *lecture (f) :* she enjoys reading = *elle aime la lecture* 💀 → lecture.

READJUST (to, -ed) *(se) (ré)adapter :* to readjust to a new job/marriage = *s'adapter à un nouveau boulot/se réadapter au mariage* **READJUSTMENT** (n) *(ré)adaptation (f).*

READY (adj, -ier, -iest) *prêt, -e :* are you ready ? — no, I'll be ready in an hour = *êtes-vous prêt ? — non, je serai prêt dans une heure*
I'm ready to drop ! = *je ne tiens plus debout ! / je ne tiens plus sur mes quilles !* ⓓ dead = *mort (de fatigue),* dead beat = *harassé*
to get ready = *se préparer :* it's time, you'd better get ready = *c'est l'heure, tu ferais mieux de te préparer* 💀 → to prepare
ready cash/money = *argent liquide (disponible)*
ready to = *prêt à :* I'm ready to help you = *je suis prêt à vous aider* ⓓ willing to = *disposé à*
(the film/book is) ready to roll = *(le film/livre est) fin prêt.*

READY (adv) **I'm ready willing and able** = *je ne demande pas mieux* ⓓ I'm game = *je suis partant.*

READY-TO-WEAR (n inv) *prêt-à-porter (m)* ⓓ ready-made clothes = *vêtements de confection* ≠ custom-made clothes = *vêtements faits sur mesure.*

REAL (n) **for real** = *pour de vrai :* I can't believe you're for real = *je n'arrive pas à te croire pour de vrai,* for real ? = *pour de vrai ?*

REAL (adj) 1/ *réel, -elle :* it's a real story = *c'est une histoire réelle* ⓓ genuine = *authentique*
real estate = *biens immobiliers (propriété foncière) :* he has a lot of real estate in the South = *il a pas mal de biens immobiliers dans le Sud* ⓓ land = *terre*
real estate agent = *agent immobilier*
the real McCoy = *quelque chose d'authentique :* the Picasso's the real McCoy = *le Picasso est authentique* 💀 *frais/bénéfices réels* = actual costs/profits
2/ *véritable :* a real diamond/Picasso = *un véritable diamant/Picasso* ≠ phony = *faux.*

REAL (adv) *rudement :* a real interesting guy = *un type rudement intéressant* → VERY 💀 → roughly.

REALISM (n) *réalisme (m) :* his films are noted for their realism = *ses films sont connus pour leur réalisme* ≠ idealism = *idéalisme.*

REALIST (n) *réaliste (m, f) :* my husband's too much of a realist = *mon mari est trop réaliste* ⓓ pragmatist = *pragmatique* ≠ dreamer = *rêveur.*

REALISTIC (adj) *réaliste :* we have to be realistic : we can't afford a third child = *il faux être réaliste : on ne peut pas se payer le luxe d'un troisième enfant* ≠ unrealistic = *peu réaliste* **REALISTICALLY** (adv) *de façon réaliste :* to think realistically = *voir les choses de façon réaliste.*

REALITY (n, -ies) *réalité (f) :* his remark brought me back to reality = *sa remarque m'a ramené à la réalité* ≠ fiction = ←
in reality (she's timid) = *en réalité (elle est timide)* ⓓ in truth = *en vérité*
💀 *la réalité dépasse la fiction* = truth is stranger than fiction.

REALIZATION (n) *ce dont on se rend compte :* he came to the realization that she was cheating on him = *il a fini par se rendre compte qu'elle le trompait*
💀 *c'est une superbe réalisation* = it's a magnificent achievement
— *la réalisation de ce film est de ...* = the film was directed by ...

REALIZE (to, -d) *se rendre compte de, réaliser :* do you realize how rich he is ? = *est-ce que vous vous rendez compte à quel point il est riche ?,* I didn't realize how unhappy she had been with him = *je ne m'étais pas rendu compte à quel point elle était malheureuse avec lui* ⓓ to become aware of = *prendre conscience de*
💀 *il n'a jamais pu réaliser son objectif* = he could never do/make/achieve/accomplish his objective
— *elle n'a jamais pu se réaliser* = she never came into her own
— *réaliser ses phantasmes* = to act out one's fantasies
— *ça ne s'est jamais réalisé* = it never came through/true.

REALLY (adv) *vraiment :* I'm really hungry = *j'ai vraiment faim* → VERY ≠ not at all = *pas du tout*
not really (rich) = *pas vraiment (riche)*
really and truly = *vraiment très :* he's really and truly a bastard = *il est vraiment très salaud* ⓓ purely and simply = *purement et simplement* → VERY
really ? = *vraiment ?* ⓓ no kidding ! = *sans rigoler !/sans blague !*

REALM (n) *domaine (m) :* it's beyond the realm of possibility = *ce n'est pas dans le domaine du possible* 💀 → domain.

REALTOR (n) *agent (m) immobilier* = real estate agent.

REANIMATE (to, -d) *ranimer, réanimer (medical) :* to reanimate a patient = *réanimer un malade* 💀 *ranimer une vieille coutume* = to revive an old costum **REANIMATION** (n) *ranimation (f), réanimation (f)* (medical).

REAP (to, -ed) *récolter :* to reap a profit = *récolter un bénéfice* 💀 *il a récolté ce qu'il méritait* = he got what he deserved.

REAPPEAR (to, -ed) *reparaître, réapparaître :* he reappeared in public after a long absence = *il a reparu/est réapparu en public après une longue absence.*

REAR (n) *arrière (m)* (car, bus), *derrière (m)* (house) : move to the rear of the bus = *avancez à l'arrière du bus* = move to the back of the bus ≠ front = *avant*

to bring up the rear = *fermer la marche*
from the rear (she looks like her mother) = *de dos (on dirait sa mère)*
☸ *arrière* → back, *derrière* → behind.

REAR (adj) *de derrière* : the rear entrance/door = *l'entrée/la porte de derrière* = back ≠ front = *de devant*

rear end = *arrière-train* : what a rear end she has ! = *elle a un de ces arrière-trains !* ⓓ behind = *derrière*
rear guard = *arrière-garde*
rear window = *glace arrière* (car) / *fenêtre sur cour.*

REARMAMENT (n) *réarmement* (m) ≠ disarmament = *désarmement.*

REASON (n) *raison* (f) : what reason did he give you ? = *quelle raison t'a-t-il donnée ?* ⓓ motive = *motif*

all the more reason ! = *raison de plus !* **to bring s.o. to reason** = *faire entendre raison à qqn* **for no (good) reason** = *sans aucune raison (valable)* : he quit for no good reason = *il est parti sans aucune raison valable* **for reasons of my own** = *pour des raisons personnelles* **for some/one reason or other** = *pour une raison ou pour une autre* **for reasons best known to herself (she didn't see him again)** = *pour des raisons con-*	*nues d'elle seule/pour des raisons qui lui sont personnelles (elle ne l'a pas revu)* **to have reasons to think that (someone won't come)** = *avoir des raisons de penser que (quelqu'un ne viendra pas)* **he won't listen to reason** = *il ne veut pas entendre raison* **that's the reason why (I split)** = *c'est la raison pour laquelle (je me suis barrée)* **that stands to reason** = *ça tombe sous le sens* ⓓ that goes without saying = *cela va sans dire*	**there is/we have every reason to believe that (he'll agree with us)** = *il y a/nous avons toutes les raisons de croire/tout porte à croire qu'(il sera d'accord avec nous)* **(and) with reason** = *(et) pour cause* : the boss is very angry and with reason = *le patron est furieux et pour cause* **within reason** = *dans la limite du raisonnable* : I'll pay your price within reason = *votre prix sera le mien, dans la limite du raisonnable*

☸ *(les événements) vous ont donné raison* = (events) proved you were right — *avoir raison* = to be right	— *en raison de (la pluie)* = owing to (the rain) — *se faire une raison* = to resign oneself — *avoir raison de qqn* = to get the best of s.o.

REASON (to, -ed) **to reason with s.o.** = *raisonner qqn* : she was so angry I couldn't reason with her = *elle était tellement en colère que je n'ai pas pu la raisonner* ≠ to listen to reason = *entendre raison.*

REASONABLE (adj) *raisonnable* : a reasonable person/claim = *quelqu'un de raisonnable/une demande raisonnable* ⓓ sensible = *sensé* ≠ unreasonable = *déraisonnable* **REASONABLY** (adv) *moyennement* : reasonably intelligent = *moyennement intelligent* ⓓ fairly = *assez.*

REASONING (n) *raisonnement* (m) : I don't agree with your reasoning = *je ne suis pas d'accord avec votre raisonnement* ⓓ way of thinking = *façon de penser.*

REASSURE (to, -d) *rassurer* : her gentleness reassured the child = *sa douceur a rassuré l'enfant* ⓓ to comfort = *réconforter* ☸ *rassurez-vous (je ne dirai rien)* = rest assured (I won't say anything) **REASSURING** (adj) *rassurant, -e* : a reassuring letter/mother = *une lettre/mère rassurante* ⓓ comforting = *réconfortant* ≠ alarming = *alarmant.*

REBATE (n) *ristourne* (f) : the car company is giving a $ 100 rebate on each car = *la firme automobile fait une ristourne de 100 dollars sur chaque voiture.*

REBEL (n) *rebelle* (m, f) : the rebels were arrested = *les rebelles ont été arrêtés* ⓓ insurgent = *insurgé* **REBEL** (to, -led) *se rebeller* : to rebel against authority = *se rebeller contre l'autorité* ⓓ to rise up = *se soulever.*

REBELLION (n) *rébellion* (f) : a student rebellion = *une rébellion estudiantine* ⓓ revolt = *révolte.*

REBELLIOUS (adj) *rebelle* : rebellious children = *des enfants rebelles* ≠ obedient = *obéissant.*

REBIRTH (n) *renaissance* (f) : the rebirth of Islam = *la renaissance de l'Islam.*

REBOUND (n) **on the rebound** = *par dépit* : she dropped him and he married his ex-mistress on the rebound = *elle l'a laissé tomber et il a épousé son ex-maîtresse par dépit.*

REBUFF (n) *rebuffade* (f) ⓓ snub = *camouflet* **REBUFF** (to, -ed) *repousser* : I rebuffed his advances/friendship = *j'ai repoussé ses avances/son amitié* ⓓ to snub = *snober* ☸ → to repel.

REBUILD (to, -built, -built) *reconstruire* : to rebuild an area = *reconstruire une région.*

REBUKE (to, -d) *morigéner* : the President rebuked the Prime Minister for his statement = *le Président a morigéné le Premier ministre au sujet de sa déclaration* → TO LAMBAST.

REBUTTAL (n) *réfutation (f)* : the defense offered no rebuttal = *la défense n'a apporté aucune réfutation* ⓕ denial = *démenti.*

RECALL (to, -ed) **1/** *se rappeler* : I couldn't recall his name = *je n'arrivais pas à me rappeler son nom* ⓕ to recollect = *se remémorer* **2/** *rappeler* (s.o.), *retirer de la circulation* (stg) : the ambassadors/cars were recalled = *les ambassadeurs ont été rappelés/les voitures ont été retirées de la circulation*
☠ *tu me rappelles ma mère* = you remind me of my mother
— *rappelle-moi de le faire* = remind me to do it
— *rappeler son chien* = to call off one's dog
— *rappeler qqn (téléphone)* = to call s.o. back (phone).

RECAPITULATE (to, -d) *récapituler* : let's recapitulate the different possibilities = *récapitulons les différentes possibilités* ⓕ to sum up = *résumer* **RECAPITULATION** (n) *récapitulation (f)* : a recapitulation of what happened = *une récapitulation de ce qui s'est passé* ⓕ synopsis = *compte rendu.*

RECAPTURE (to, -d) *reprendre* : the enemy recaptured the city = *l'ennemi a repris la ville*
☠ *ils ne le reprendront pas* = they won't take it back
— *reprendre une robe* = to take a dress in
— *on ne m'y reprendra plus !* = you won't catch me at it again !
— *reprendre (ses esprits)* = to regain (consciousness)
— *reprendre ses études* = to resume one's studies
— *l'économie a repris* = the economy bounced back
— *reprendre une scène* = to run through a scene
— *se reprendre* = to pull o.s. together
— *reprendre qqn* = to tell s.o. off
— *reprenez-en !* = help yourself to some more !

RECEIPT (n) *reçu (m)* : can I have a receipt ? = *est-ce que je peux avoir un reçu ?*
to acknowledge receipt of (a letter) = *accuser réception d'(une lettre)*
upon receipt of (your letter) = *dès réception de (votre lettre).*

RECEIVE (to, -d) *recevoir* : to receive a letter/a package = *recevoir une lettre/un paquet* = to get a letter/a package ≠ to send = *envoyer*
☠ *ils reçoivent souvent* = they often entertain/have guests
— *il a été reçu (à son examen)* = he passed (his exam).

RECENT (adj) *récent, -e* : a recent trip = *un voyage récent* ≠ old = *ancien*
in recent years = *ces dernières années* : I haven't seen him in recent years = *je ne l'ai pas vu ces dernières années.*

RECENTLY (adv) *récemment* : we met recently = *nous nous sommes rencontrés récemment* ⓕ a short time ago = *il y a peu de temps,* not long ago = *il n'y a pas longtemps.*

RECEPTION (n) **1/** *réception (f)* : a wedding reception = *une réception de mariage* ⓕ cocktail party = *cocktail*
☠ *accuser réception de* = to acknowledge receipt of
2/ *accueil (m)* : the book got a favorable reception = *le livre a reçu un accueil favorable* ☠ → welcome
reception desk = *réception (hôtel).*

RECEPTIONIST (n) *réceptionniste (m, f)* ⓕ switchboard operator = *standardiste.*

RECEPTIVE (adj) *réceptif, -ive* : receptive to new ideas = *réceptif aux idées nouvelles* ≠ indifferent = *indifférent.*

RECESS (n, -es) *récréation (f)* = recreation
congressional recess = *vacances parlementaires.*

RECESSION (n) *récession (f)* : an economic recession = *une récession économique* ≠ expansion = ←.

RECIPE (n) *recette (f)* : a curry recipe = *une recette de curry* ⓕ cookbook = *livre de cuisine*
☠ *faire recette* = to pack them in
— *la recette (théâtre)* = the take (theater).

RECIPIENT (n) *bénéficiaire (m, f)* : the recipient of the scholarship = *le bénéficiaire de la bourse.*

RECIPROCAL (adj) *réciproque* : a reciprocal hatred = *une haine réciproque* ⓕ bilateral = *bilatéral.*

RECIPROCATE (to, -d) *rendre la pareille* : she did me a favor and I reciprocated = *elle m'a rendu un service et je lui ai rendu la pareille* ⓕ to return the favor = *renvoyer l'ascenseur.*

RECIPROCITY (n) *réciprocité (f)* : reciprocity between nations = *la réciprocité entre les nations.*

RECITAL (n) *récital (m)* : to give a recital = *donner un récital* ⓕ festival = ←.

RECITATION (n) *récitation (f)* : the recitation of a poem = *la récitation d'un poème.*

RECITE (to, -d) *réciter* : to recite a poem = *réciter un poème.*

RECKLESS (adj) *imprudent, -e* : a reckless driver = *un conducteur imprudent* ⓕ rash = *inconsidéré* ≠ sensible = *sensé.*

RECKON (to, -ed) *croire bien* : I reckon they're going to get married soon = *je crois bien qu'ils ne vont pas tarder à se marier* ⓕ to guess = *imaginer*
(he's a man) to be reckoned with = *(c'est un homme) avec lequel il faut compter.*

RECLUSE (n) *reclus, -e* : to live like a recluse = *vivre en reclus* ⓕ loner = *solitaire.*

RECOGNITION (n) *reconnaissance (f)*: he got no recognition for his efforts = *on ne lui a eu aucune reconnaissance pour les efforts qu'il a faits*
☠ *ne pas avoir de reconnaissance / la reconnaissance du ventre* = to have no gratitude/to bite the hand that feeds one
— *une reconnaissance de dette* = an IOU.

RECOGNIZE (to, -d) *reconnaître* : she was so tanned I hardly recognized her = *elle était si bronzée que je l'ai à peine reconnue* ⓓ to know s.o. on sight = *connaître qqn de vue*
☠ *reconnaître un enfant* = to acknowledge a child
— *je reconnais que (tu as raison)* = I admit (you're right)
— *reconnaître qqn coupable* = to find s.o. guilty
— *je te reconnais bien là !* = that's just like you !

RECOLLECT (to, -ed) *se remémorer* : I can't recollect where I met him = *je n'arrive pas à me remémorer où je l'ai rencontré* ⓓ to remember = *se souvenir*
as far as I can recollect = *autant que je me souvienne*
☠ *se remémorer le passé* = to reminisce about the past.

RECOLLECTION (n) **to have no recollection of (having met someone)** = *ne pas avoir souvenir d'(avoir rencontré quelqu'un).*

RECOMMEND (to, -ed) *recommander* : can you recommend a good doctor ? = *est-ce que vous pouvez me recommander un bon médecin ?*

RECOMMENDATION (n) *recommandation (f)* : what's your recommendation ? = *quelle recommandation me faites-vous ?* ⓓ advice = *conseils.*

RECOMPENSE (n) *dédommagement (m)* : $ 1 000 in recompense = *1 000 dollars de dédommagement* ☠ *récompense* → reward.

RECOMPENSE (to, -d) *dédommager* : the insurance company will recompense the firm for all damages = *la compagnie d'assurances dédommagera la société pour tous les dégâts subis.*

RECONCILE (to, -d) *concilier* : try to reconcile your differences = *essayez de concilier vos différences*
to reconcile o.s. to = *se faire à l'idée de :* I've reconciled myself to not seeing him again = *je me suis fait à l'idée de ne plus le revoir* ⓓ to resign o.s. to = *se résigner à*
to reconcile ... with = *concilier ... avec :* how can she reconcile her getting an abortion with her religious ideas ? = *comment peut-elle concilier le fait de se faire avorter avec ses convictions religieuses ?*
☠ *nous nous sommes réconciliés* = we made up (plus utilisé que « to reconcile »).

RECONCILIATION (n) *conciliation (f).*

RECONSIDER (to, -ed) *reconsidérer* : I hope you'll reconsider your position = *j'espère que vous allez reconsidérer votre position* ⓓ to think over = *bien réfléchir.*

RECONSTRUCT (to, -ed) *reconstituer, reconstruire* (city) : to reconstruct a crime = *reconstituer un crime,* they reconstructed Berlin = *on a reconstruit Berlin* = to rebuild.

RECORD (n) **1/** *disque (m)* : to listen to records = *écouter des disques* ⓓ compact disc = *disque compact*

to cut a record = *enregistrer un disque* **long-playing** ≠ **short-playing record** = *33 tours* ≠ *45 tours*	**to play/put on records** = *mettre des disques* **record player** = *tourne-disques/électrophone* ⓓ phonograph = *phonographe*

2/ *casier (m) judiciaire* : he's only sixteen and already has a record = *il n'a que seize ans et il a déjà un casier judiciaire*
3/ *dossier (m)* : the journalist asked to see the government's records = *le journaliste a demandé à voir les dossiers du gouvernement* = file
4/ *bilan (m)* : the Senator's record is good = *le bilan du sénateur est positif* ☠ → toll
5/ *record (m)* : the world record = *le record du monde*

for the record = *pour ta gouverne* : just for the record, let me say your ideas are crummy = *pour ta gouverne, laisse-moi te dire que tes idées ne sont pas géniales* **to hold/set/break a record** = *détenir/établir/battre un record* **off the record** ≠ **on the record** = *à titre officieux* ≠ *à titre officiel* : the President made this statement off ≠ on the record = *le Président a fait*	*cette déclaration à titre officieux* ≠ *officiel* **keep a record of (your expenses)** = *gardez trace de (vos dépenses)* **to set the record straight** = *mettre les choses au point* : let me set the record straight and say I only hit her after she hit me = *mettons les choses au point, je l'ai frappée après qu'elle m'a frappé* ⓓ to straighten out = *remettre les pendules à l'heure.*

RECORD (adj) *record* : a record year/speed = *une année/une vitesse record.*

RECORD (to, -ed) *enregistrer* : the singer's recording today = *le chanteur enregistre aujourd'hui*

☠ *il n'a pas enregistré ce que je lui ai dit* = what I told him didn't register — *faire enregistrer ses bagages* = to check one's	luggage — *enregistrer (une conversation)* = to tape (a conversation).

RECORDED (adj) *enregistré, -e* : recorded music = *musique enregistrée* ⓪ playback = *en play-back*, recording studio = *studio d'enregistrement*.

RECOUP (to, -ed) **to recoup (an advance)** = *récupérer (une avance)* = to get back (an advance) ☠ → to recuperate.

RECOVER (to, -ed) **1/** *se rétablir* : she got pneumonia but recovered quickly = *elle a eu une pneumonie mais elle s'est vite rétablie* ⓪ to be up and about = *être sur pied*
☠ *rétablir l'ordre public* = to restore law and order
— *rétablir (la vérité)* = to reestablish (the truth)
2/ *retrouver* : he recovered his watch = *il a retrouvé sa montre* ≠ to lose = *perdre*
☠ *retrouver ses forces* = to regain one's forces
— *se retrouver dans la même position* = to find o.s. back in the same position
— *je vous retrouverai (à la gare)* = I'll meet you (at the station)
— *s'y retrouver* = 1/ to get one's bearings 2/ to get more than one's money back.

RECOVERY (n, -ies) *rétablissement (m)* : I wish you a quick recovery = *je vous souhaite un prompt rétablissement* ≠ relapse = *rechute*.

RECREATION (n) *récréation (f), récré (f)* : children get milk during recreation = *on donne du lait aux enfants pendant la récréation*, recreation yard = *cour de récréation/de récré*.

RECRUIT (n) *recrue (f)* : new recruits = *de nouvelles recrues* ⓪ rookie = *bleu* ≠ an old-timer = *un vieux routier* **RECRUIT** (to, -ed) *recruter* : they're recruiting new members = *ils recrutent de nouveaux membres* ⓪ to enlist = *enrôler* **RECRUITMENT** (n) *recrutement (m)*.

RECTANGLE (n) *rectangle (m)* ⓪ square = *carré* **RECTANGULAR** (adj) *rectangulaire*.

RECTIFICATION (n) *rectification (f)* : the text needs rectifications = *le texte a besoin de rectifications* ⓪ change = *changement* **RECTIFY** (to, -ied) *rectifier* : the Senator rectified his statement = *le sénateur a rectifié sa déclaration* ⓪ to revise = *réviser*.

RECUPERATE (to, -d) *récupérer* : she's been sick for months and it will be hard for her to recuperate = *cela fait des mois qu'elle est malade et elle aura du mal à récupérer* recuperation = *récupération*
☠ *ses idées ont été récupérées par son parti* = his ideas were co-opted by his party
— *récupérer (une avance)* = to recoup (an advance).

RECURRENT (adj) *qui se répète* : recurrent nightmares/strikes = *des cauchemars/des grèves qui se répètent* ⓪ intermittent = ←.

RECURRING (adj) *périodique* : a recurring dream = *un rêve périodique* = periodical ⓪ intermittent = ←.

RECYCLE (to, -d) *recycler* : to recycle glass = *recycler le verre* **RECYCLING** (n) *recyclage (m)*.

RED (n) **1/** *rouge (m)* : she wears a lot of red = *elle s'habille souvent en rouge* ⓪ orange = ← **2/** *rouge (m, f)* : a government full of reds = *un gouvernement plein de rouges* ⓪ leftist = *homme/femme de gauche*
in the red = *en déficit/déficitaire* : the company's in the red = *la société est en déficit/déficitaire* → POOR
to see red = *voir rouge* : when his son began to curse, he saw red = *il a vu rouge quand son fils s'est mis à jurer* → ANGRY
☠ *rouge à lèvres/à joues* = lipstick/rouge.

RED (adj, -der, -dest) *rouge* : a red coat = *un manteau rouge* ⓪ reddish = *rougeâtre*
to be as red as a beet = *être rouge comme une tomate/une pivoine/une écrevisse*
the Red Cross = *la Croix-Rouge*
red hair = *cheveux roux*
red herring = *faux-fuyant* : the President's statement was a red herring = *la déclaration du Président n'était qu'un faux-fuyant*
red tape = *tracasseries administratives* ⓪ paperwork = *paperasserie*
to roll out the red carpet = *dérouler le tapis rouge*
to turn red = *devenir rouge/cramoisi*.

RED-BLOODED (adj) **a red-blooded (American)** = *un grand gaillard (d'Américain)*.

RED-CARPET (adj) **(to get) the red-carpet treatment** = *(être reçu) en grande pompe* : heads of state usually get the red-carpet treatment = *les chefs d'État sont généralement reçus en grande pompe*.

REDECORATE (to, -d) *repeindre* : I'm redecorating my apartment = *je repeins mon appartement* ⓪ to redo = *refaire*.

REDEEMING (adj) **a redeeming quality** = *quelque chose qui rachète* : if you're a bastard, being good in bed is hardly a redeeming quality = *quand on est un salaud, ça vous rachète à peine d'être bon au lit*.

REDEMPTION (n) **without redemption** = *sans rémission*.

RED-HANDED (adj) **to catch s.o. red-handed** = *prendre qqn la main dans le sac* ⓪ to catch s.o. with the goods = *prendre qqn en flagrant délit*.

REDHEAD (n) *roux, rousse, rouquin, -e* : he has a weak spot for redheads = *il a un faible pour les rousses/les rouquines* ⓪ brunette = *brune*, carrottop = *poil de carotte*.

RED-HOT (adj) *brûlant, -e* ≠ ice-cold = *glacial*.

RED-LETTER DAY (n) *jour (m) à marquer d'une pierre blanche* : the day we got divorced was a red-letter day = *le jour de notre divorce était à marquer d'une pierre blanche* ⓪ milestone = *jalon important*.

RED-LIGHT DISTRICT (n) *quartier (m) chaud/réservé* ⓊⒹ brothel = *bordel*, hooker = *putain*.

REDNECK (n) *agriculteur (m) sudiste, bouseux (m)* (PEJ) : the redneck territory = *le territoire des agriculteurs sudistes* ⓊⒹ hick = *plouc*.

REDO (to, -did, -done) *refaire* : we're redoing the house = *nous refaisons la maison* = to do over ⓊⒹ to renovate = *rénover*
☠ *on ne me refera pas* = you won't make me over
— *se refaire une santé* = to get back one's health
— *si c'était à refaire* = if I had to do it over again
— *j'ai été refait* = I've been taken in.

REDRESS (to, -ed) *redresser* : to redress the situation = *redresser la situation*.

REDSKIN (n) *peau-rouge (m, f)* ≠ paleface = *visage pâle*.

REDUCE (to, -d) 1/ *réduire* : to reduce one's expenses = *réduire ses dépenses* ≠ to increase = *augmenter*
to be reduced to (begging) = *en être réduit à (mendier)*
☠ *le problème se réduit à ...* = the problem boils down to ...
— *elle fume beaucoup mais elle essaie de réduire* = she smokes a lot but she's trying to cut down
2/ *mincir* : I won't have dessert, I'm trying to reduce = *je ne prendrai pas de dessert, j'essaie de mincir* ≠ to put on weight = *prendre du poids*.

REDUCTION (n) *réduction (f)* : a reduction in taxes/prices = *une réduction d'impôts/de prix* ≠ increase = *augmentation*.

REDUNDANT (adj) *redondant, -e* : a redundant speech = *un discours redondant* ⓊⒹ repetitive = *répétitif*.

REEFER (n) *joint (m)* ⓊⒹ pot = *de l'herbe*.

REEK OF (to, -ed) *sentir à plein nez* : to reek of garlic = *sentir l'ail à plein nez*.

REFEREE (n) *arbitre (m, f)* (boxing, argument) ⓊⒹ umpire = *arbitre* (baseball, soccer), judge = *juge* ☠ → arbitrator.

REFERENCE (n) 1/ *référence (f)* : he has good references = *il a de bonnes références* ⓊⒹ recommendation = *recommandation* 2/ *référence (f)* : the author's many references to psychiatry = *les nombreuses références de l'auteur à la psychiatrie*
in/with reference to (your letter) = *en référence à/en ce qui concerne (votre lettre)* ⓊⒹ in connection with = *à propos de*
to make reference to = *faire allusion à* : he made no reference to his divorce/the accident = *il n'a fait aucune allusion à son divorce/à l'accident*.

REFERENDUM (n, -s or -a) *référendum (m)* ⓊⒹ plebiscite = *plébiscite*.

REFER TO (to, -red) 1/ *faire allusion à* : were you refer-ring to what I said ? = *est-ce que vous faisiez allusion à ce que j'ai dit ?* ⓊⒹ to imply = *sous-entendre* 2/ *envoyer chez* : he referred me to a good lawyer = *il m'a envoyé chez un bon avocat* ⓊⒹ to recommend = *recommander* 3/ *se référer à* : he referred to the Constitution/to the present economic crisis = *il s'est référé à la Constitution/à la crise économique actuelle* 4/ *soumettre à* : the question was referred to an international court = *la question a été soumise à une cour internationale*
to refer to s.o. as = *parler de qqn comme de* : don't refer to my husband as a crook = *ne parlez pas de mon mari comme d'un escroc* ⓊⒹ to call s.o. stg = *traiter qqn de qqch*.

REFILL (to, -ed) *(r)emplir à nouveau* (glass), recharger (lighter) : to refill a glass = *remplir à nouveau un verre*.

REFINED (adj) *raffiné, -e* : elegant and refined = *élégant et raffiné* ⓊⒹ polished = *policé*.

REFINERY (n, -ies) *raffinerie (f)* : oil refinery = *raffinerie de pétrole*.

REFLECT (to, -ed) *refléter* : his remarks reflect his insensitivity = *ses réflexions reflètent son insensibilité*
to reflect on = 1/ *rejaillir sur* : her constant digs at her husband reflect on the state of their marriage = *les vannes qu'elle envoie sans arrêt à son mari rejaillissent sur leur ménage* 2/ *réfléchir à* : let me reflect on it = *laisse-moi y réfléchir* = let me think it over.

REFLECTION (n) *réflexion (f)* : after much reflection = *après mûre réflexion*
☠ *faire des réflexions désagréables* = to make unpleasant remarks
— *ça mérite réflexion* = it's worth thinking over
— *réflexion faite* = on second thought.

REFLEX (n, -es) *réflexe (m)* : a conditioned reflex = *un réflexe conditionné* ⓊⒹ impulse = *impulsion*.

REFORM (n) *réforme (f)* : social/land reform = *réforme sociale/agraire* ⓊⒹ amendment = *amendement*
reform school = *maison de correction* = reformatory.

REFORM (to, -ed) *réformer* : you'll never reform society = *tu ne réformeras jamais la société* ☠ *réformer (service militaire)* = to declare unfit for (military service).

REFORMATORY (n, -ies) *maison (f) de correction, centre (m) d'éducation surveillée* ⓊⒹ juvenile delinquent = *délinquant juvénile*.

REFRAIN FROM (to, -ed) *s'abstenir de* : refrain from smoking = *abstenez-vous de fumer*.

REFRESHING (adj) *rafraîchissant, -e* : a refreshing drink = *une boisson rafraîchissante*
it's refreshing to (meet idealists) = *ça fait plaisir de (rencontrer des idéalistes)*.

REFRESHMENTS (n pl) *rafraîchissements (m pl)* : refreshments will be served = *des rafraîchissements vont être servis* ⓊⒹ beverage = *boisson*.

REFRIGERATOR (n) *réfrigérateur (m), Frigidaire (m)* ⓪ fridge = *frigo.*

REFUGE (n) *refuge (m)* : my apartment/lover is my refuge = *mon appartement/mon amant est mon refuge* ⓪ haven = *havre*
to take refuge = *se réfugier* : they took refuge in the embassy = *ils se sont réfugiés à l'ambassade.*

REFUGEE (n) *réfugié, -e* : political refugee = *réfugié politique*, refugee camp = *camp de réfugiés.*

REFUND (n) *remboursement (m)* : I asked for a refund because the coat was torn = *j'ai demandé le rembourse-ment parce que le manteau était déchiré* ≠ deposit = *arrhes* **REFUND** (to, -ed) *rembourser* : they refused to refund my deposit = *ils ont refusé de me rembourser mes arrhes* ⓪ to return = *rendre* ☠ → to reimburse.

REFURBISH (to, -ed) *remettre à neuf* ⓪ to restore = *restaurer.*

REFUSAL (n) *refus (m)* : my refusal shocked everyone = *mon refus a choqué tout le monde* ≠ acceptance = *acceptation*
☠ *essuyer un refus* = to strike out/to be turned down
— *ce n'est pas de refus !* = you won't have to ask me twice !

REFUSE (to, -d) *refuser* : to refuse an invitation = *refu-ser une invitation* ⓪ to decline = *décliner*
to refuse to = *refuser de* : he refused to help us = *il a refusé de nous aider* ≠ to be willing to = *être disposé à*
☠ *il ne se refuse rien* = he's self-indulgent
— *être refusé à un examen* = to fail an exam.

REFUTE (to, -d) *réfuter* : he refuted my theory/argu-ment = *il a réfuté ma théorie/mon argument* ≠ to prove = *prouver* **REFUTATION** (n) *réfutation (f).*

REGAIN (to, -ed) *recouvrer* : he regained his health = *il a recouvré la santé* ⓪ to recover = *retrouver.*

REGARD (n) **give my best regards to (your wife)** = *faites (toutes) mes amitiés à (votre femme)*
he has a high ≠ **no regard for (his wife)** = *il a beaucoup d'estime* ≠ *il n'a aucune estime pour (sa femme)*
in this regard = *à cet égard*
out of regard for (his parents) = *par égard pour (ses parents)*
with/in regard to (your letter) = *pour ce qui concerne (votre lettre)* ⓪ concerning = *en ce qui concerne*
without regard to (the cost) = *sans considéra-tion du (prix).*

REGARD (to, -ed) **to regard as** = *considérer comme* : I don't regard my colleagues as close friends = *je ne considère pas mes collègues comme des amis intimes*

---

as regards = *en ce qui concerne* : as regards what he told you, I just don't agree = *en ce qui concerne ce qu'il vous a dit, je ne suis tout simplement pas d'accord* = regarding what he told you ⓪ as to = *quant à.*

REGARDING (prep) *en ce qui concerne* : regarding your contract, you just have to sign it = *en ce qui con-cerne votre contrat, vous n'avez plus qu'à le signer* ⓪ concerning = *concernant.*

REGARDLESS (adv) *quand même* : he doesn't want me to go with him, but I'll go regardless = *il ne veut pas que je vienne avec lui, mais j'irai quand même* ⓪ never-theless = *néanmoins.*

REGARDLESS OF (prep) *peu importe* : regardless of the price, I'll buy it = *peu importe le prix, je l'achèterai* ⓪ in spite of = *malgré*, irrespective of = *sans tenir compte de.*

REGENT (n) *régent, -e* : the regent of the kingdom = *le régent du royaume.*

REGIME (n) *régime (m)* : a tyrannical regime = *un régime tyrannique* ⓪ system = *système*
☠ *suivre un régime* = to be on a diet
— *aller à un régime de croisière* = to cruise along.

REGIMENT (n) *régiment (m)* ⓪ battalion = *bataillon.*

REGION (n) *région (f)* : an agricultural region = *une région agricole* ⓪ district = *quartier*
in the region of ($ 100) = *dans les (100 dollars)* ⓪ about = *environ*
☠ *elle habite dans la région de New York* = she lives in the New York area.

REGIONAL (adj) *régional, -e* : regional news = *actuali-tés régionales* ≠ national = ←.

REGISTER (n) *registre (m)* : to sign the register = *signer le registre* ⓪ reception desk = *réception (hôtel).*

REGISTER (to, -ed) *s'inscrire* : you must register for school this week = *il faut que tu t'inscrives à l'école cette semaine*
it didn't register = *(je) ne l'ai pas enregistré* : he told me his name, but it didn't register = *il m'a dit son nom, mais je ne l'ai pas enregistré* ⓪ it didn't penetrate = *ça ne m'a pas marqué*
☠ → to inscribe.

REGISTRATION (n) *inscription (f)* : registration fee = *droits d'inscription.*

REGRESS (to, -ed) *régresser* **REGRESSION** (n) *régression (f)* : her regression to the state of a child = *sa régression au stade infantile.*

REGRET (n) *regret (m)* : I have no regrets = *je n'ai pas de regrets* ⓪ remorse = *remords*
(much/greatly) to my regret = *à mon (grand) regret.*

REGRET (to, -ted) *regretter* : I regretted having said that = *j'ai regretté d'avoir dit ça,* you won't regret it = *vous ne le regretterez pas* ⓓ to be sorry = *être désolé,* to rue = *regretter amèrement*
I regret to tell you that (you're fired) = *j'ai le regret de vous dire que (vous êtes renvoyé)*
☠ *je regrette infiniment* = I'm terribly sorry.

REGRETTABLE (adj) *regrettable* : a regrettable mistake = *une faute regrettable* ⓓ deplorable = *déplorable.*

REGULAR (n) *habitué, -e* : he's a regular here = *c'est un habitué de la maison* ⓓ client = ←.

REGULAR (adj) **1/** *régulier, -ère* : he doesn't have a regular job with regular hours = *il n'a pas de travail régulier avec des horaires réguliers* ⓓ normal = ← ≠ irregular = *irrégulier*
☠ *il est très régulier* = he's aboveboard
— *une augmentation régulière de l'inflation* = a steady rise in inflation
2/ *habituel, -elle* : he's not my regular doctor = *ce n'est pas mon médecin habituel* = usual ⓓ customary = *coutumier*
3/ *fini, -e* : you're a regular fool ! = *tu es un idiot fini !* ⓓ thorough = *intégral* ☠ → over.

REGULARITY (n inv) *régularité (f)* : they make love once a week with regularity = *ils font l'amour une fois par semaine avec régularité* **REGULARLY** (adv) *régulièrement* : he comes regularly at 8 = *il arrive régulièrement à 8 heures* ⓓ generally = *généralement* ≠ irregularly = *irrégulièrement.*

REGULARIZE (to, -d) *régulariser* : to regularize a situation = *régulariser une situation.*

REGULATE (to, -d) *régler* : to regulate a machine = *régler une machine* ⓓ to adjust = *ajuster* ☠ → to settle.

REGULATION (n) *règlement (m)* : regulations concerning drug offenders = *les règlements concernant les criminels de la drogue.*

REHABILITATE (to, -d) *réhabiliter* **REHABILITATION** (n) *réhabilitation (f).*

REHASH (to, -ed) *rabâcher* : stop rehashing the same argument all the time = *ne rabâche pas sans cesse le même argument* ⓓ to reiterate = *réitérer.*

REHEARSAL (n) *répétition (f)* : there won't be any rehearsal tomorrow = *il n'y aura pas de répétition demain* ☠ → repetition **REHEARSE** (to, -d) *répéter* : they're rehearsing tonight = *ils répètent ce soir* ⓓ to run through = *reprendre* ☠ → to repeat.

REIGN (n) *règne (m)* : the reign of Henry IV = *le règne d'Henri IV.*

REIGN (to, -ed) *régner* : he reigned for only ten years = *il n'a régné que dix ans*

☠ *la confiance règne !* = that's confidence ! (sarcastic)
— *la peur règne dans la ville* = fear is stalking the city.

REIMBURSE (to, -d) *rembourser* : I'll reimburse you for the taxi = *je vous rembourserai le taxi* ⓓ to pay back = *rendre l'argent de*
☠ *ils ont refusé de me rembourser mes arrhes* = they refused to refund my deposit
— *rembourser un prêt* = to repay a loan.

REIN (n) *rêne (m)* : hold the reins ! = *tiens les rênes !* ⓓ bridle = *bride.*

REINCARNATE (to, -d) *réincarner* : to be reincarnated as a cat = *se réincarner en chat* ⓓ to resuscitate = *ressusciter* **REINCARNATION** (n) *réincarnation (f).*

REINFORCE (to, -d) *renforcer* : that reinforces my suspicions/my hopes = *ça renforce mes soupçons/mes espérances* **REINFORCEMENT** (n) *renfort (m).*

REITERATE (to, -d) *réitérer* : he reiterated his question = *il a réitéré sa question* ⓓ to repeat = *répéter.*

REJECT (to, -ed) *rejeter* : the proposal was rejected = *la proposition a été rejetée* ⓓ to turn down = *refuser* ≠ to accept = *accepter*
☠ *rejeter (la responsabilité sur qqn)* = to lay (the responsibility on s.o.)
— *rejeter (un parti)* = to repudiate (a party)
— *rejeter un projet de loi* = to vote a bill down.

REJOICE (to, -d) *se réjouir* : it's no time for rejoicing = *ce n'est pas le moment de se réjouir.*

REJUVENATE (to, -d) *rajeunir* : his new hairstyle rejuvenates him = *sa nouvelle coiffure le rajeunit* ≠ to age = *vieillir.*

RELEGATE (to, -d) **to be relegated to (a lower job)** = *être relégué à (un poste inférieur).*

RELAPSE (n) *rechute (f)* : the patient had another relapse = *la patiente a fait une nouvelle rechute* **RELAPSE** (to, -d) *rechuter.*

RELATE (to, -d) **1/** *relater* : he related how hard it was to get a job in New York = *il a relaté combien il était dur de trouver du travail à New York* **2/** *faire le lien entre* : how do you relate both ideas ? = *comment faites-vous le lien entre les deux idées ?*
to relate to = **1/** *se sentir concerné par* (problems) : I can't relate to my daughter's problems = *je n'arrive pas à me sentir concerné par les problèmes de ma fille* **2/** *communiquer avec* (s.o.) : I can't relate to my daughter's friends = *je n'arrive pas à communiquer avec les amis de ma fille*
to be related = **1/** *avoir un rapport* : the two problems/murders aren't related = *les deux problèmes/meurtres n'ont pas de rapport* ≠ to be unrelated = *n'avoir aucun rapport* **2/** *être parent* : we're not related = *nous ne sommes pas parents*
to be related to s.o. = *avoir un lien de parenté avec qqn* : is he related to you ? = *est-ce qu'il a un lien de parenté avec vous ?* ⓓ to be relatives = *être parents.*

RELATION (n) 1/ *relation (f)* : he's a business relation = *c'est une relation d'affaires* 2/ *relation (f)* : is there a relation between the two facts ? = *est-ce qu'il y a une relation entre les deux faits ?* ⓪ connection = *rapport*
in relation to = *au sujet de* : the boss wants to see you in relation to the missing money = *le patron veut vous voir au sujet de l'argent disparu* ⓪ regarding = *en ce qui concerne*
that has no relation to (what I was saying) = *ça n'a aucun rapport avec (ce que je disais)* ⓪ that has nothing to do with = *ça n'a rien à voir avec.*

RELATIONS (n pl) *relations (f pl)* : international/business relations = *relations internationales/d'affaires* ⓪ contact = ←
to have relations = *avoir des rapports* ⓪ to make love = *faire l'amour*
☠ *elle a beaucoup de relations* = she has a lot of connections
— *de bonnes ≠ mauvaises relations avec (sa mère)* = a good ≠ bad relationship with (her mother).

RELATIONSHIP (n) 1/ *relations (f pl)*, *rapports (m pl)* : she has a good relationship with her parents = *elle a de bonnes relations/de bons rapports avec ses parents* ⓪ affinity = *affinité* ☠ → relations, → report 2/ *liaison (f)* : this is her first relationship with a married man = *c'est sa première liaison avec un homme marié* ⓪ love affair = *aventure* 3/ *rapport (m)* : don't you see the relationship between high interest rates and inflation ? = *vous ne voyez pas le rapport entre l'inflation et des taux d'intérêt élevés ?* ⓪ association = ←.

RELATIVE (n) *membre (m) de la famille, parent, -e* : most of my relatives live in New York = *la plupart des membres de ma famille/de mes parents habitent New York* ☠ → parent.

RELATIVE (adj) *relatif, -ive* : the importance of money is relative = *l'importance de l'argent est relative* ≠ absolute = *absolu* **RELATIVELY** (adv) *relativement* : they're relatively happy = *ils sont relativement heureux* ⓪ more or less = *plus ou moins.*

RELAX (to, -ed) *se relaxer* : have a drink and relax = *prends un verre et relaxe-toi* ⓪ to unwind = *se détendre*
relax and enjoy it = *sois belle et tais-toi*
relax ! = *du calme !* ⓪ **relax Max !** = *relax, Max !*, don't get excited ! = *ne t'excite pas !*
to feel relaxed with (one's in-laws) = *être décontracté avec (ses beaux-parents).*

RELAXATION (n) *relaxation (f)* : little time for relaxation = *peu de temps pour la relaxation.*

RELEASE (n) *remise (f) en liberté* : the terrorist demanded the release of all political prisoners = *les terroristes ont exigé la remise en liberté de tous les prisonniers politiques* ⓪ liberation = *libération*
(press) release = *communiqué (de presse).*

RELEASE (to, -d) 1/ *relâcher* (prison), *laisser sortir* (hos-

pital) : to release hostages = *relâcher les otages* ⓪ to free = *libérer* ☠ *les affaires se relâchent* = business is slackening 2/ *sortir* (film), *communiquer* (information) : when will the film be released ? = *quand le film sortira-t-il ?* ☠ *sortir* → to go out.

RELENT (to, -ed) *se laisser fléchir* : the boss relented and agreed to a raise = *le patron s'est laissé fléchir et a accepté de m'accorder une augmentation* ⓪ to yield = *céder.*

RELENTLESS (adj) *implacable* : relentless criticisms = *des critiques implacables* ⓪ ruthless = *impitoyable* **RELENTLESSLY** (adv) *implacablement.*

RELEVANT (adj) *pertinent, -e* : relevant remarks/indications = *des réflexions/indications pertinentes* ≠ irrelevant = *hors de propos.*

RELIABLE (adj) *fiable* : a reliable friend/company = *un ami/une entreprise fiable* ⓪ trustworthy = *digne de confiance* ≠ undependable = *sur qui l'on ne peut pas compter.*

RELIC (n) *relique (f)* : a relic from the civil war = *une relique de la guerre civile.*

RELIEF (n) *soulagement (m)* : what a relief ! = *quel soulagement !* ⓪ whew ! = *ouf !*
it's a relief to (know you can lend me the money) = *c'est un soulagement de (savoir que tu peux me prêter cet argent)*
on relief = *qui dépend de l'aide publique (pour vivre)* ⓪ the breadline = *la soupe populaire.*

RELIEVE (to, -d) *soulager* : the medicine will relieve the pain = *le médicament soulagera la douleur* ⓪ to soothe = *apaiser* ≠ to aggravate = *aggraver*
to relieve oneself = *se soulager* ⓪ to go to the john = *aller au petit coin*
to relieve s.o. (from duty) = *relever qqn (de ses fonctions)* ⓪ to strip of = *dépouiller de.*

RELIGION (n) *religion (f)* : what's your religion ? = *quelle est votre religion ?* ⓪ belief = *croyance*, opium of the people = *opium du peuple*, faith = *foi*, Catholicism = *catholicisme*, Protestantism = *protestantisme*, Islam = ←, Judaism = *judaïsme*, Buddhism = *bouddhisme*, Hinduism = *hindouisme* ☠ *entrer en religion* = to become a nun/a monk.

RELIGIOUS (adj) *religieux, -euse* : religious life = *vie religieuse* ⓪ pious = *pieux*, secular = *laïc* ☠ *un religieux/une religieuse* = a priest, a monk/a nun.

RELINQUISH (to, -ed) *renoncer à* : he relinquished his right to the property = *il a renoncé à ses droits sur la propriété* ⓪ to abandon = *abandonner.*

RELISH (n, -es) *condiment (m)* ⓪ spice = *épice.*

RELISH (to, ed) *se réjouir de* : I don't relish going out tonight = *ça ne me réjouit pas de sortir ce soir* ⓪ to dig = *botter.*

RELOCATE (to, -d) *transplanter* : the offices were relocated in the suburbs = *les bureaux ont été transplantés en banlieue* ⅅ to transfer = *transférer* ☠ → to transplant.

RELUCTANCE (n) *réticence* (f) : with great reluctance = *avec une grande réticence* ☠ → reticence.

RELUCTANT (adj) *réticent, -e* : a reluctant yes = *un oui réticent*
to be reluctant to (help) = *être réticent pour (aider)* ☠ → reticent.

RELUCTANTLY (adv) *avec réticence* : he agreed reluctantly = *il a donné son accord avec réticence* ≠ willingly = *volontiers*, readily = *de bon cœur*.

RELY ON (to, -ied) 1/ *se reposer sur* : I'm relying on you to help me/to lend me the money = *je me repose sur vous pour m'aider/pour me prêter de l'argent* ⅅ to count on = *compter sur* 2/ *se fier à* : I can't rely on what he says = *je ne peux pas me fier à ce qu'il dit* ≠ to mistrust = *se méfier de*.

REMAIN (to, -ed) *rester* : little remained of Berlin after the war = *il ne restait pas grand-chose de Berlin après la guerre*
it still remains that (he was right) = *il n'en reste pas moins qu'(il avait raison)* ⅅ nevertheless = *néanmoins*
that remains to be seen = *cela reste à voir*
to remain at (home) = *rester à (la maison)*
☠ *où en étiez-vous resté ? (travail)* = where did you leave off ? (work)
— *il en reste (deux)* = there are (two) left
— *rester sur une mauvaise impression* = to be left with a bad impression
— *je suis resté une semaine* = I stayed a week
— *restez tranquille !* = keep quiet !

REMAINDER (n) *restant* (m) : I ate most of the cake and gave the remainder to my neighbor = *j'ai mangé la majeure partie du gâteau et j'ai donné le restant à ma voisine* ⅅ rest = *reste*.

REMAINS (n pl) *dépouille* (f) : the remains of the body = *la dépouille mortelle*.

REMAKE (n) *remake* (m) : the remake of a film = *le remake d'un film* ⅅ rerun = *reprise*.

REMARK (n) *remarque* (f), *réflexion* (f) : to make mean remarks = *faire des remarques/des réflexions méchantes* ⅅ comment = *commentaire*, crack = *vanne* ☠ → reflection.

REMARK (to, -ed) *remarquer* : "you're tired" he remarked = *« vous êtes fatigué », a-t-il remarqué* ⅅ to observe = *faire remarquer*
☠ *je n'ai pas remarqué* = I didn't notice
— *remarquez (elle a peut-être raison)* = mind you (she's probably right).

REMARKABLE (adj) *remarquable* : a remarkable ballet = *un ballet remarquable* → WONDERFUL.

REMARKABLY (adv) *remarquablement* : to write remarkably well = *écrire remarquablement bien* → VERY.

REMARRY (to, -ied) *se remarier* : she remarried six months after her husband died = *elle s'est remariée six mois après la mort de son mari*.

REMEDY (n, -ies) *remède* (m) : there's no remedy for love = *il n'y a pas de remède à l'amour* ⅅ treatment = *traitement*
☠ *remèdes de bonne femme* = old wives' tales
— *remède contre le cancer* = cure against cancer.

REMEDY (to, -ied) *remédier à* : the situation was remedied = *on a remédié à la situation*.

REMEMBER (to, -ed) *se souvenir de* : do you remember me ? = *est-ce que vous vous souvenez de moi ?*, no, I don't remember you = *non, je ne me souviens pas de vous* ⅅ to recall = *se rappeler* ≠ to draw a blank = *avoir un trou*
if I remember right/correctly = *si je me souviens bien* ⅅ if my memory serves me right = *si j'ai bonne mémoire*
remember me to (your wife) = *rappelez-moi au bon souvenir de (votre femme)* ⅅ my regards to = *faites mes amitiés à*.

REMIND (to, -ed) **that reminds me, (what happened to the money I lent you ?)** = *au fait, (où est passé l'argent que je vous ai prêté ?)* ⅅ apropos = *à propos*
to remind s.o. of ... = *rappeler ... à qqn* : he reminds me of my first lover = *il me rappelle mon premier amant* ⅅ to make s.o. think of = *faire penser qqn à*
to remind s.o. to = *rappeler à qqn de* : remind me to go tomorrow = *rappelle-moi d'y aller demain* ≠ to remember = *se souvenir de*.

REMINDER (n) *quelque chose qui rappelle* : seeing the photographs was a reminder of her childhood = *ça lui a rappelé son enfance de regarder ces photos*.

REMINISCE (to, -d) *se remémorer* : yesterday I ran into an old pal, and we reminisced about our school years = *hier, j'ai rencontré par hasard un vieux copain et on s'est remémoré nos années d'école* ⅅ to remember = *se souvenir* ☠ → to recollect.

REMORSE (n inv) *remords* (m) : filled with remorse = *rempli de remords* ⅅ guilt = *culpabilité* **REMORSEFUL** (adj) *plein, -e de remords*.

REMOTE (adj, -r, -st) *reculé, -e* : they live in a remote part of Africa = *ils habitent un coin reculé d'Afrique* ⅅ distant = ← ≠ close = *proche*
remote control = *contrôle à distance/télécommande*
chances are remote that (I'll come) = *il y a très peu de chances que (je vienne)*.

REMOTELY (adv) *de très loin* : I'm not even remotely interested in him = *même de très loin, il ne m'intéresse pas*.

REMOVE (to, -d) *enlever* : she removed her coat = *elle a enlevé son manteau* ⓪ to take off = *ôter*
to be removed from (office) = *être destitué de (ses fonctions)* ⓪ to relieve = *relever*
☠ *enlever qqch à qqn* = to take stg away from s.o.
— *enlever (un enfant)* = to abduct (a child).

REMUNERATE (to, -d) *rémunérer* : he wasn't remunerated for his training period = *il n'a pas été rémunéré pour son stage* ⓪ to pay = *payer* **REMUNERATION** (n) *rémunération (f)* : a low remuneration = *une faible rémunération* **REMUNERATIVE** (adj) *rémunérateur, -trice* : highly remunerative work = *un travail très rémunérateur* ⓪ lucrative = *lucratif.*

RENDEZVOUS (n) *rendez-vous (m) d'amoureux* : a rendezvous with my lover = *un rendez-vous d'amoureux avec mon amant* ⓪ date = *rendez-vous galant.*

RENEGADE (n) *renégat (m)* : they shot the renegades = *ils ont fusillé les renégats* ⓪ traitor = *traître.*

RENEGE (to, -d) *se dédire* : he agreed to the contract but then reneged (on it) = *il était d'accord pour le contrat mais ensuite il s'est dédit* ⓪ to back out = *se défiler*, to welsh on = *se dérober à.*

RENEW (to, -ed) *renouveler* : to renew a contract/a subscription = *renouveler un contrat/un abonnement.*

RENOUNCE (to, -d) *renoncer à* : to renounce a claim = *renoncer à une revendication* ⓪ to give up = *abandonner* ≠ to keep = *garder*
☠ *renoncer à fumer* = to give up smoking
— *renoncer à son déjeuner* = to forgo lunch.

RENOVATE (to, -d) *rénover* : to renovate a building = *rénover un immeuble* ⓪ to restore = *restaurer*, to revamp = *retaper* **RENOVATION** (n) *rénovation (f)* ⓪ restoration = *restauration.*

RENOWNED (adj) *renommé, -e* : a renowned actress = *une actrice renommée* ⓪ illustrious = *illustre.*

RENT (n) *loyer (m)* : the rent is too high = *le loyer est trop élevé* ⓪ landlord = *propriétaire*, tenant = *locataire*
(room) for rent = *(chambre) à louer* = (room) to let (GB) ⓪ for sale = *à vendre*
rent control = *contrôle des loyers.*

RENT (to, -ed) *louer* : I decided to rent and not to buy = *j'ai décidé de louer et non d'acheter* ☠ → to praise.

REOPEN (to, -d) *rouvrir* : the shop will reopen next week = *le magasin rouvrira la semaine prochaine.*

REORGANIZATION (n) *réorganisation (f)* **REORGANIZE** (to, -d) *réorganiser* : they're reorganizing the company = *ils réorganisent la société* ⓪ to organize = *organiser.*

REP (n) *représentant, -e* : all reps work on a commission basis = *tous les représentants travaillent à la commission* ⓪ salesman = *vendeur* ☠ → representative.

REPAIR (n) *réparation (f)* : too many repairs to be made = *trop de réparations à faire*
beyond repair = *irréparable* : your watch is beyond repair = *votre montre est irréparable* = irreparable
☠ → reparations.

REPAIR (to, -ed) *réparer* : they repaired the engine = *ils ont réparé le moteur* ⓪ to patch up = *rafistoler* ≠ to break = *casser* ☠ *réparer un tort/les dégâts* = to right a wrong/to make good the damages.

REPARATIONS (n pl) *réparations (f pl)* : war reparations = *réparations de guerre* ☠ *réparations (voiture)* = repairs (car).

REPATRIATE (to, -d) *rapatrier* : to repatriate the hostages = *rapatrier les otages* ≠ to exile = *exiler.*

REPAY (to, -paid, -paid) *rembourser* : we're repaying the loan = *nous remboursons l'emprunt* ☠ → to reimburse
how can I ever repay you ? = *comment pourrais-je jamais te rendre tout ce que tu as fait pour moi ?*

REPEAL (to, -ed) *abroger* : the law was repealed = *la loi a été abrogée* ⓪ to nullify = *rendre nul.*

REPEAT (to, - led) *répéter* : could you repeat that please ? = *pourriez-vous répéter ça, s'il vous plaît ?* ⓪ to rehash = *rabâcher* ☠ *répéter une pièce* = to rehearse a play.

REPEATED (adj) *répété, -e* : repeated criticisms = *des critiques répétées* ≠ sole = *unique.*

REPEATEDLY (adv) *à plusieurs reprises* : he repeatedly criticized me = *il m'a critiqué à plusieurs reprises.*

REPEL (to, -led) **1/** *repousser* : his breath repels me = *son haleine me repousse* ⓪ to repulse = *répugner*
2/ *repousser* : to repel an attack = *repousser une attaque* ⓪ to drive back = *refouler*
☠ *repousser les avances de qqn* = to rebuff s.o.'s advances
— *repousser (à plus tard)* = to postpone/put off
— *repousser une accusation* = to deny a charge
— *repousser qqn* = to push s.o. away.

REPELLENT (adj) *repoussant, -e* : a repellent odor = *une odeur repoussante* ⓪ obnoxious = *odieux.*

REPENT (to, -ed) *se repentir* : sinners repent ! = *pécheurs, repentez-vous !* ⓪ to atone = *expier.*

REPERCUSSION (n) *répercussion (f)* : the repercussions of his speech were disastrous = *les répercussions de son discours ont été désastreuses* ⓪ fallout = *retombées.*

REPERTORY (n, -ies) *répertoire (m)* : the theater group's repertory = *le répertoire de la troupe de théâtre.*

REPETITION (n) *répétition (f)* : his second marriage is a repetition of his first one = *son second mariage n'est qu'une répétition du premier* ☠ *répétition d'une pièce* = rehearsal of a play.

REPETITIOUS (adj) *répétitif, -ive* : a repetitious boring speech = *un discours répétitif et ennuyeux* = a repetitive boring speech.

REPLACE (to, -d) *remplacer*: she's replacing our teacher who's sick = *elle remplace notre professeur qui est malade* ⓪ to fill in for = *remplacer temporairement*
REPLACEMENT (n) *remplaçant, -e*: she's her replacement = *c'est sa remplaçante.*

REPLICA (n) *réplique* (f): the vase is a replica of the original = *le vase est une réplique de l'original* ⓪ reproduction = ← ☠ → comeback.

REPLY (n, -ies) *réponse* (f): the ad got many replies = *on a reçu beaucoup de réponses à cette annonce,* a funny reply = *une réponse drôle* ⓪ retort = *repartie*
in reply to (your letter) = *en réponse à (votre lettre)* ☠ → answer.

REPLY (to, -ied) *répliquer*: "that's none of your business!" he replied: = « *ce ne sont pas tes oignons!* » *a-t-il répliqué.*

REPORT (n) *rapport* (m): to make a report = *faire un rapport* ⓪ account = *compte rendu*
☠ *le rapport numérique entre Noirs et Blancs* = the ratio of Blacks to Whites
— *je ne vois pas le rapport* = I don't see the connection/the relationship
— *un rapport de cinq pour cent* = a five-percent yield/return
— *avoir de bons rapports avec* = to have a good relationship with
— *avoir des rapports (sexuels)* = to have (sexual) relations.

REPORT (to, -ed) *signaler*: the paper reported ten soldiers were killed = *le journal a signalé que dix soldats avaient été tués*
to report to = *signaler à*: you'd better report the robbery to the police = *vous feriez mieux de signaler le vol à la police*
to report s.o. to = *dénoncer qqn à*: if you do it again, I'll report you to the boss = *si vous recommencez, je vous dénonce au patron*
to report to (the office at ten) = *se présenter au (bureau à dix heures)*
☠ *je voudrais vous signaler que ...* = I'd like to point out that ...

REPORTEDLY (adv) *on dit que*: they're reportedly having trouble again = *on dit qu'ils ont de nouveau des ennuis* ⓪ supposedly = *soi-disant.*

REPORTER (n) *reporter* (m): a roving reporter = *un reporter volant* ⓪ newspaper = *journal.*

REPREHENSIBLE (adj) *répréhensible*: a reprehensible mistake = *une faute répréhensible.*

REPRESENT (to, -ed) 1/ *représenter*: he represents the company in Europe = *il représente la société en Europe* 2/ *représenter*: what does the picture represent? = *que représente le tableau?* ⓪ to depict = *dépeindre*

☠ *se représenter aux élections* = to run for office again
— *il représente beaucoup pour moi* = he means a lot to me
— *si le problème se représente* = if the problem comes up again.

REPRESENTATION (n) *représentation* (f): the representation of a country in the UN = *la représentation d'un pays à l'ONU* ☠ *une représentation (spectacle)* = a performance.

REPRESENTATIVE (n) 1/ *représentant, -e*: each group sent a representative = *chaque groupe a envoyé un représentant* ☠ *représentant (de commerce)* = (traveling) salesman/rep 2/ *député* (m): the representative from Ohio = *le député de l'Ohio* ☠ → deputy.

REPRESENTATIVE (adj) *représentatif, -ive*: Lennon was representative of a whole generation = *Lennon était représentatif de toute une génération* ⓪ typical = *typique* ≠ unrepresentative = *pas représentatif.*

REPRESS (to, -ed) 1/ *réprimer*: to repress a revolution = *réprimer une révolution* ⓪ to subdue = *maîtriser* 2/ *réprimer*: to repress tears/laughter = *réprimer ses larmes/un rire* ⓪ to hold back = *refouler.*

REPRESSED (adj) *refoulé, -e*: a repressed personality = *une personnalité refoulée* ⓪ uptight = *coincé.*

REPRESSION (n) *répression* (f): government repression = *répression gouvernementale.*

REPRESSIVE (adj) *répressif, -ive*: a repressive political regime = *un régime politique répressif* ≠ liberal = *libéral.*

REPRIEVE (n) *sursis* (m) **REPRIEVE** (to, -d) *surseoir à l'exécution de*: the prisoner will be reprieved = *on va surseoir à l'exécution du prisonnier.*

REPRIMAND (n) *réprimande* (f) **REPRIMAND** (to, -ed) *réprimander*: he was reprimanded by the boss = *le patron l'a réprimandé* → TO LAMBAST.

REPRISAL (n) *représailles* (f pl): the country's fearing reprisals = *le pays craint des représailles* ⓪ revenge = *revanche*
in reprisal = *en représailles*: they killed the hostage in reprisal = *ils ont tué l'otage en représailles.*

REPROACH (n, -es) **above/beyond reproach** = *au-dessus de tout reproche.*

REPROACH (to, -ed) *reprocher*: he reproached me for having made the mistake = *il m'a reproché de m'être trompé* ⓪ to reprove = *réprouver*
☠ *qu'est-ce que tu reproches à ce livre?* = what's wrong with this book?
— *reprocher qqch à qqn* = to begrudge s.o. stg.

REPRODUCE (to, -d) *se reproduire*: some animals can reproduce in zoos = *certains animaux peuvent se reproduire dans les zoos* ☠ *se reproduire (événement)* = to happen again.

REPRODUCTION (n) *reproduction* (f) : the reproduction's as good as the original = *la reproduction est aussi bonne que l'original* ⓓ copy = *copie*.

REPTILE (n) *reptile* (m) ⓓ snake = *serpent*, crocodile = ←, alligator = ←, lizard = *lézard*.

REPUBLIC (n) *république* (f) : France is a republic = *la France est une république* ≠ monarchy = *monarchie* ☠ *on est en république !* = it's a free world !

REPUBLICAN (n, adj) *républicain, -e* : the Republicans won the election = *les républicains ont gagné l'élection* ≠ Democrat = *démocrate*
Republican Party = *Parti républicain (fondé en 1854, l'un des deux grands partis politiques aux États-Unis)* = Grand Old Party/GOP ⓓ elephant = *éléphant (symbole)*.

REPUDIATE (to, -d) *répudier* (s.o.), *rejeter* (party) : he repudiated the party and its platform = *il a rejeté le parti et son programme* ⓓ to deny = *renier* ☠ → to reject.

REPUGNANT (adj) *répugnant, -e* : repugnant manners/language = *des manières répugnantes/un langage répugnant* ⓓ revolting = *révoltant*
to be repugnant to = *répugner à* : the idea of making love with him is repugnant to me = *l'idée de faire l'amour avec lui me répugne.*

REPULSE (to, -d) *répugner à* : he repulses women = *il répugne aux femmes* ⓓ to disgust = *dégoûter* ☠ *je répugne à (boire de l'alcool)* = I loathe (drinking alcohol)
REPULSION (n inv) *répulsion* (f) : a physical repulsion towards her husband = *une répulsion physique pour son mari.*

REPULSIVE (adj) *repoussant, -e* : a repulsive guy = *un type repoussant* → AWFUL.

REPUTABLE (adj) *qui a bonne réputation* : a reputable company = *une société qui a bonne réputation* ⓓ respectable = ←.

REPUTATION (n) *réputation* (f) : she has the reputation of being a shrewd lawyer = *elle a la réputation d'être une avocate habile*
to live up to (one's) reputation = *être à la hauteur de sa réputation* ≠ not to be all (one is) cracked up to be = *ne pas répondre à l'attente.*

REPUTED (adj) *présumé, -e* : he's the reputed head of the Mafia = *c'est le chef présumé de la Mafia* ⓓ supposed = *prétendu*
the reputed father of the child = *le père putatif de l'enfant*
it's reputed to be (the best restaurant) = *(ce restaurant) est réputé être (le meilleur)*
☠ *un avocat réputé* = a noted lawyer.

REPUTEDLY (adv) *d'après ce qu'on dit* : this is reputedly the best restaurant in town = *d'après ce qu'on dit, c'est le meilleur restaurant de la ville.*

REQUEST (n) *requête* (f) : can I make a request ? = *puis-je faire une requête ?* ⓓ demand = *exigence*.

REQUEST (to, -ed) *demander* : a majority of Congressmen requested a special commission = *la majorité des membres du Congrès ont demandé une commission spéciale*
you're requested to (stay seated) = *vous êtes priés de (rester assis).*

REQUIRE (to, -d) 1/ *requérir* : the job requires the knowledge of a foreign language = *le poste requiert la connaissance d'une langue étrangère* ⓓ to necessitate = *nécessiter* ☠ *requérir la peine de mort* = to demand the death sentence 2/ *avoir besoin de* : what other monies will you require ? = *de quels autres fonds aurez-vous besoin ?* = to need.

REQUIREMENT (n) *condition* (f) *requise* : the knowledge of a foreign language is a requirement = *la connaissance d'une langue étrangère est la condition requise*
what are your (salary) requirements ? = *quelles sont vos exigences en matière de (salaire) ?*

RERUN (n) *reprise* (f) : that movie house only shows reruns = *ce cinéma ne donne que des reprises*
☠ *à différentes/plusieurs reprises* = at different/several times
— *la reprise du travail* = the return to work
— *reprise (économique)* = rally/revival
— *faire des reprises* = to mend.

RESCIND (to, -ed) *résilier* (contract), *rapporter* (law) : to rescind a contract = *résilier un contrat* ⓓ to invalidate = *invalider* ☠ *rapporter* → to yield.

RESCUE (n) **to come to s.o.'s rescue** = *venir à la rescousse de qqn.*

RESCUE (to, -d) *secourir (et sauver)* : they rescued everyone from the fire = *ils ont secouru tous ceux qui étaient pris dans l'incendie* ⓓ to save = *sauver* **RESCUER** (n) *sauveteur* (m).

RESEARCH (n, -es) *recherche* (f) : medical research = *la recherche médicale*
research worker = *chercheur*
☠ *à la recherche d'un appartement* = in search of an apartment.

RESEMBLANCE (n) *ressemblance* (f) : a striking resemblance = *une ressemblance frappante* ≠ difference = *différence.*

RESEMBLE (to, -d) *ressembler à* : she resembles her mother = *elle ressemble à sa mère* ⓓ to take after = *tenir de*, to be the spitting image of = *être le portrait tout craché de* ☠ *cela ne te ressemble pas de mentir* = it's not like you to tell a lie.

RESENT (to, -ed) *ne pas apprécier (du tout)* : I resented his taking Peter instead of me = *je n'ai pas apprécié (du tout) qu'il emmène Peter à ma place*, I resent what you said = *je n'apprécie pas (du tout) ce que vous avez dit*

RESENTFUL (adj) *plein, -e de ressentiment* **RESENTMENT** (n) *ressentiment (m)* : strong resentment towards his ex-wife = *un fort ressentiment à l'égard de son ex-femme* ⓓ spite = *dépit.*

RESERVATION (n) *réservation (f)* = booking (GB)
to have reservations about (s.o.'s honesty) = *émettre des réserves quant à (l'honnêteté de qqn)*
to make reservations = *faire/prendre des réservations*
without reservation = *sans réserve* : he agreed to the project without reservation = *il a accepté le projet sans réserve.*

RESERVE (n) *réserve (f)* : reserves of oil = *des réserves de pétrole* ⓓ stock = ←
without reserve = *sans réserve* : he told us what he thought without reserve = *il nous a dit ce qu'il pensait sans réserve*
in reserve = *en réserve* : plenty of food in reserve = *plein de nourriture en réserve* ⓓ in stock = *en stock* ☠ *émettre des réserves quant à* = to have reservations about.

RESERVE (to, -d) *réserver* : they reserved a table for tonight = *ils ont réservé une table pour ce soir* ⓓ to book = *retenir,* to make a reservation = *faire une réservation* ☠ *se réserver (en attendant mieux)* = to hold out (for a better offer).

RESERVED (adj) **1/** *réservé, -e* : a reserved personality = *une personnalité réservée* ≠ expansive = *expansif* **2/** *réservé, -e* : reserved seats/tables = *places/tables réservées* ≠ free = *libre.*

RESERVES (n pl) **(my brother's in) the reserves** = *(mon frère est dans) la réserve* ⓓ in the army = *à l'armée.*

RESERVOIR (n) *réservoir (m)* : a full reservoir = *un réservoir plein* ☠ *réservoir (voiture)* = tank (car).

RESIDE IN (to, -d) *résider à* : she resides in New York = *elle réside à New York* ⓓ to live in = *habiter,* to dwell in = *demeurer à.*

RESIDENCE (n) *résidence (f)* : a winter residence in Florida = *une résidence d'hiver en Floride* ⓓ house = *maison*
☠ *en résidence surveillée* = under house arrest
— *résidence secondaire* = weekend house.

RESIDENT (n) **1/** *résident, -e (étranger, -ère)* : she's a resident in France = *elle est résidente (étrangère) en France* ⓓ national = *ressortissant* **2/** *médecin (m) stagiaire* : he's a resident at Bellevue = *il est médecin stagiaire à Bellevue.*

RESIDENTIAL (adj) *résidentiel, -elle* : to live in a residential area = *habiter un quartier résidentiel.*

RESIGN (to, -ed) *démissionner* : do you think he's going to resign ? = *est-ce que vous pensez qu'il va démissionner ?* ⓓ to give notice = *donner son congé* ≠ to lay off = *licencier*

to resign oneself (to) = *se résigner (à)/prendre son parti de* : he resigned himself to living with a woman he didn't love = *il s'est résigné à/il a pris son parti de vivre avec une femme qu'il n'aimait pas*
☠ *comme père, il a complètement démissionné* = as a father, he totally abdicated.

RESIGNATION (n) **1/** *résignation (f)* : he accepted the news with resignation = *il a accepté la nouvelle avec résignation* ⓓ fatalism = *fatalisme* **2/** *démission (f)* : he offered his resignation = *il a donné sa démission* ⓓ notice = *congé.*

RESIST (to, -ed) **1/** *résister à* : I can't resist his blue eyes = *je ne peux pas résister à ses yeux bleus* **2/** *résister* : when they captured the prisoner, he didn't resist = *quand ils ont capturé le prisonnier, il n'a pas résisté* ≠ to struggle = *lutter* ☠ *résister à la douleur* = to withstand pain.

RESISTANCE (n) *résistance (f)* : he lacks resistance = *il manque de résistance*
the Resistance = *la Résistance* : he was a member of the French Resistance during World War II = *il était membre de la Résistance en France pendant la Seconde Guerre mondiale* ⓓ underground = *maquis.*

RESISTANT (adj) *résistant, -e* : a resistant material = *un matériau résistant.*

RESOLUTE (adj) *résolu, -e* : he was resolute in his decision = *il était résolu à s'en tenir à sa décision* ⓓ obstinate = *obstiné.*

RESOLUTION (n) *résolution (f)* : to lack resolution = *manquer de résolution,* New Year's resolutions = *les résolutions de début d'année* ⓓ decision = *décision.*

RESOLVE (to, -d) **1/** *résoudre* : our society is trying to find ways to resolve racial problems = *notre société essaie de trouver des moyens de résoudre les problèmes raciaux* ☠ → to solve **2/** *décider* : Congress resolved that taxes wouldn't be raised = *le Congrès a décidé que les impôts ne seraient pas augmentés*
to resolve to = *se résoudre à* : I resolved to quit smoking = *je me suis résolu à ne plus fumer* ⓓ to decide to = *décider de.*

RESORT (n) **resort area** = *station de vacances.*

RESORT TO (to, -ed) *avoir recours à* : to resort to violence = *avoir recours à la violence.*

RESOURCE (n) *ressource (f)* : oil resources = *ressources en pétrole* ⓓ wealth = *richesse.*

RESOURCEFUL (adj) *plein, -e de ressources, débrouillard, -e* : a resourceful politician/guy = *un politicien/type plein de ressources/débrouillard* ⓓ clever = *malin.*

RESPECT (n) *respect (m)* : she has a lot of respect for her parents = *elle a beaucoup de respect pour ses parents* ⓓ admiration = ←
in every respect = *à tous égards* : I find him hard to

get along with in every respect = *je trouve qu'il est dur de s'entendre avec lui à tous égards*
in this respect = *à cet égard* : the pay's good, and in this respect, I can't complain = *c'est bien payé et, à cet égard, je n'ai pas à me plaindre*
in many/some respects = *à bien des égards/à certains égards* : she's very much like her mother in many respects = *à bien des égards, elle ressemble beaucoup à sa mère*
to pay one's respects (to) = *présenter ses respects (à)*
with respect to (our last conversation) = *pour ce qui est de (notre dernière conversation)* ⓪ regarding = *en ce qui concerne*
out of respect for (your father) = *par respect pour (votre père)*
without respect to (age/sex/etc.) = *sans considération d'(âge)/de (sexe/etc.)*
☠ *tenir qqn en respect (avec un fusil)* = to keep (a gun) pointed at s.o.

RESPECT (to, -ed) *respecter* : to respect one's parents = *respecter ses parents* ⓪ to look up to = *regarder avec admiration* ≠ to scorn = *mépriser* ☠ *faire respecter la loi* = to enforce the law.

RESPECTABLE (adj) *respectable* : a respectable salary = *un salaire respectable* ⓪ honorable = ←.

RESPECTFUL (adj) *respectueux, -euse* : a respectful attitude = *une attitude respectueuse* ≠ disrespectful = *irrespectueux* **RESPECTFULLY** (adv) *respectueusement.*

RESPECTIVE (adj) *respectif, -ive* : the two brothers came with their respective wives = *les deux frères sont venus avec leurs femmes respectives* **RESPECTIVELY** (adv) *respectivement* : the biggest raises were given to Jack and Joe respectively = *on a donné les plus fortes augmentations respectivement à Jack et à Joe.*

RESPITE (n) *répit (m)* : we worked for ten hours with no respite = *nous avons travaillé dix heures sans répit* ⓪ breather = *moment de répit.*

RESPLENDENT (adj) *resplendissant, -e* ⓪ shining = *brillant.*

RESPOND (to, -ed) *répondre* : 300 people responded = *300 personnes ont répondu* = to answer
to respond to (a certain treatment) = *réagir à (un certain traitement)*
☠ « to respond » *est moins employé que « to answer ».*

RESPONSE (n) *réponse (f)* : the government asked for volunteers but there was little response = *le gouvernement a demandé des volontaires mais il y a eu peu de réponse, few responses to the ad = *peu de réponses à l'annonce*
in response to (your last letter) = *en réponse à (votre dernière lettre)*
☠ → answer.

RESPONSIBILITY (n, -ies) *responsabilité (f)* : that's some responsibility ! = *c'est une sacrée responsabilité !*

it's not my responsibility ! = *je n'en suis pas responsable !*

RESPONSIBLE (adj) *responsable* : a responsible girl/worker = *une fille/un ouvrier responsable* ⓪ trustworthy = *digne de confiance* ≠ irresponsible = *irresponsable*
to be responsible for (a mistake) = *être responsable d'(une faute)*
to hold s.o. responsible for = *tenir qqn responsable de*
☠ *la personne responsable* = the person in charge.

RESPONSIVE (adj) *qui réagit* : the public wasn't responsive = *le public ne réagissait pas* ≠ indifferent = *indifférent.*

REST (n) *repos (m)* : I need a long rest = *j'ai besoin d'un long repos* ⓪ nap = *somme*
for the rest (it's up to you) = *pour le reste (c'est à vous de voir)*
the rest = *le reste/les autres* (people) : she ate a big part of the cake and I ate the rest = *elle a mangé une grosse part du gâteau et j'ai mangé le reste, some of us went by plane and the rest took the boat = *certains d'entre nous sont partis en avion et les autres ont pris le bateau*
rest home = *maison de repos*
the rest room = *les lavabos* ⓪ the lavatory = *les cabinets.*

REST (to, -ed) *se reposer* : I want to rest this afternoon = *je veux me reposer cet après-midi* ⓪ to take it easy = *ne pas se fatiguer*, to take a nap = *faire un somme*
rest assured that (I'll tell you as soon as I know) = *soyez assuré que (je vous le dirai dès que je le saurai)* ⓪ you can be sure that = *vous pouvez être sûr que*
he won't rest till (he finds his daughter's murderer) = *il n'aura de cesse qu'il (n'ait retrouvé le meurtrier de sa fille)*
☠ *rester* → to stay
— *se reposer sur qqn* = to rely on s.o.

RESTAURANT (n) *restaurant (m)* : an expensive restaurant = *un restaurant cher* ⓪ inn = *auberge*, automat = *self*, snack bar = *snack-bar*
restaurant owner = *restaurateur.*

RESTFUL (adj) *reposant, -e* : a restful atmosphere = *une atmosphère reposante* ⓪ peaceful = *paisible.*

RESTITUTION (n) *restitution (f)* : the restitution of a property = *la restitution d'un bien.*

RESTLESS (adj) *qui ne tient pas en place* : a restless child = *un enfant qui ne tient pas en place* ⓪ fidgety = *agité.*

RESTORATION (n) *restauration (f)* : the restoration of the building = *la restauration de l'immeuble* ⓪ renewal = *remise à neuf.*

RESTORE (to, -d) *restaurer* : the building was restored = *l'immeuble a été restauré*
to restore to = *restituer à* : the house was restored to

its owners = *la maison a été restituée à ses propriétaires* ⓄⒹ to return to = *rendre à* ☠ *se restaurer* = to have something to eat.

RESTRAIN (to, -ed) *retenir* : to restrain one's anger = *retenir sa colère* ⓄⒹ to curb = *freiner* ☠ *retenir (information)* = to hold back (information) — *votre proposition a retenu notre attention* = your proposal is being taken into consideration — *retenir ses sentiments* = to hold in one's feelings — *se retenir de (fumer)* = to refrain from (smoking) — *il ne retient pas grand-chose* = he retains little — *retenir (des billets)* = to book (tickets) — *je ne veux pas vous retenir* = I don't want to hold you up/to detain you — *retenir (salaire)* = to hold back (salary)/to withhold.

RESTRAINT (n) *retenue* (f) : she talked without restraint = *elle a parlé sans retenue.*

RESTRICT (to, -ed) *restreindre* : there's a bill proposing to restrict the President's powers = *il y a un projet de loi proposant de restreindre les pouvoirs du Président* ⓄⒹ to limit = *limiter*
to be restricted to (members) = *être exclusivement réservé aux (membres)*
☠ *se restreindre* = to cut down (one's expenses/food/etc.).

RESTRICTION (n) *restriction* (f) : there's no restriction on liquor = *il n'y a aucune restriction sur les alcools* ☠ *consentir avec quelques restrictions* = to agree with reservation — *restriction économique* = economic crunch.

RESTRICTIVE (adj) *restrictif, -ive.*

RESULT (n) *résultat* (m) : inflation is partly the result of the oil crisis = *l'inflation est en partie le résultat de la crise du pétrole* ⓄⒹ outcome = *issue* ≠ cause = ←
as a result = *résultat* : I'm broke and as a result I had to cancel my trip = *je suis fauché et, résultat, j'ai dû annuler mon voyage* ⓄⒹ consequently = *par conséquent*
as a result of = *à la suite de* : he was fired as a result of his continual mistakes = *il a été renvoyé à la suite de ses erreurs continuelles*
to get results = *obtenir des résultats* : they're getting good results with the new contraceptive method = *ils obtiennent de bons résultats avec la nouvelle méthode contraceptive*
with the result that (he quit) = *et, résultat, (il a démissionné).*

RESULT (to, -ed) **to result from** = *résulter de* : their problems result from being broke all the time = *leurs problèmes résultent du fait qu'ils sont tout le temps fauchés*
to result in = *avoir pour résultat* : the case resulted in a change of the law = *le procès a eu pour résultat une modification de la loi* ⓄⒹ to wind up = *finir par.*

RESUME (to, -d) *reprendre* : to resume one's work =

reprendre son travail ≠ to interrupt = *interrompre* ☠ → to recapture.

RÉSUMÉ (n) 1/ *résumé* (m) : give me a résumé of the meeting = *faites-moi un résumé de la réunion* ⓄⒹ recapitulation = *récapitulation* 2/ *curriculum vitae* (m) : send us your résumé = *envoyez-nous votre curriculum vitae.*

RESURFACE (to, -d) *refaire surface* : he resurfaced in the South of France = *il a refait surface dans le midi de la France* ⓄⒹ to reappear = *réapparaître.*

RESURRECT (to, -ed) *ressusciter* **RESURRECTION** (n) *résurrection* (f).

RETAIL (adv) *au détail* : they sell TVs retail = *ils vendent des télés au détail* ≠ wholesale = *en gros* **RETAILER** (n) *détaillant, -e* ≠ wholesaler = *grossiste.*

RETAIN (to, -ed) 1/ *conserver* : to retain the control of a company = *conserver le contrôle d'une entreprise* ⓄⒹ to keep = *garder* ☠ → to conserve 2/ *retenir* : he reads quickly but retains little = *il lit vite mais ne retient pas grand-chose* ☠ → to restrain **RETAINER** (n) *acompte* (m) *provisionnel (versé à un avocat).*

RETALIATE (to, -d) *riposter* : the government retaliated by tightening censorship = *le gouvernement a riposté en renforçant la censure* ⓄⒹ to get even = *se venger,* to return like for like = *rendre la pareille* **RETALIATION** (n) *riposte* (f) : the terrorists killed the hostages in retaliation = *en riposte, les terroristes ont tué les otages* ⓄⒹ reprisal = *représailles.*

RETARDED (adj) *attardé, -e, retardé, -e* : one of their children is retarded = *l'un de leurs enfants est attardé/retardé* ⓄⒹ backward = *arriéré,* Mongolian child = *enfant mongolien.*

RETCH (to, -ed) *essayer de se faire vomir* ⓄⒹ to puke = *dégueuler.*

RETICENCE (n) *réticence* (f) : she said what she thought without reticence = *elle a dit ce qu'elle pensait sans réticence* ☠ *avec beaucoup de réticence* = with great reluctance.

RETICENT (adj) *réticent, -e* : speak frankly, don't be reticent = *parlez franchement, ne soyez pas réticent* ⓄⒹ reserved = *réservé* ☠ *il était réticent pour signer le contrat* = he was reluctant to sign the contract.

RETIRE (to, -d) 1/ *prendre sa retraite* : he's going to retire next June = *il prendra sa retraite en juin prochain* ⓄⒹ to resign = *démissionner* 2/ *se retirer* : to retire early = *se retirer de bonne heure* ⓄⒹ to go to sleep = *aller se coucher* ☠ → to withdraw.

RETIRED (adj) *retraité, -e* : a retired doctor = *un médecin retraité* ≠ working = *en activité.*

RETIREMENT (n) *retraite* (f) : to enjoy one's retirement = *profiter de sa retraite* ⓄⒹ pension = ← /*retraite*
in retirement = *à la retraite*
☠ → retreat.

RETIRING (adj) *replié, -e sur soi* : a retiring personality = *une personnalité repliée sur elle-même* ⓪ withdrawn = *renfermé*.

RETORT (n) *répartie* (f) : a quick retort = *une répartie vive* ⓪ comeback = *réplique*.

RETORT (to, -ed) *rétorquer* : "why should I be the one to pay all the time ?" he retorted = « *pourquoi serais-je toujours le seul à payer ?* » *a-t-il rétorqué* ≠ to query = *interroger*.

RETRACT (to, -ed) *(se) rétracter* : the Senator retracted the statement = *le sénateur s'est rétracté* ⓪ to withdraw = *retirer*.

RETREAT (n) *retraite* (f) : the army's retreat = *la retraite de l'armée* ≠ attack = *attaque*
to beat a retreat = *battre en retraite*
☠ *prendre sa retraite* = to retire
— *la retraite* = retirement (pension).

RETREAT (to, -ed) *battre en retraite* : the army retreated = *l'armée a battu en retraite* ≠ to advance = *avancer*.

RETROACTIVE (adj) *rétroactif, -ive* : contract riders are usually not retroactive = *les avenants à un contrat ne sont généralement pas rétroactifs*.

RETROSPECT (n) **in retrospect** = *rétrospectivement* : I realized in retrospect I was wrong = *rétrospectivement, je me suis rendu compte que j'avais tort*.

RETURN (n) **1/** *retour* (m) : the return of the hostages = *le retour des otages*, on his return from England = *à son retour d'Angleterre*	
☠ *être sur le retour* = to be past one's prime — *retour d'âge* = change of life	— *retour de bâton* = backlash — *retour en arrière* = flashback
2/ *rapport* (m) : investments with a good return = *placements d'un bon rapport* ⓪ profit = *bénéfice* ☠ → report	
election returns = *le résultat des élections* **in return** = *en retour/en contrepartie* : what did	you get in return ? = *qu'est-ce que vous avez eu en retour/en contrepartie ?*
RETURN (adj) *de retour* : the return trip was rough = *le voyage de retour a été dur*	
return address = *adresse de l'expéditeur* **by return mail** = *par retour du courrier* **return match** = *match retour*	**return ticket** (GB) = *aller-retour* = round-trip ticket.
RETURN (to, -ed) **1/** *rentrer* : he returned after the meeting = *il est rentré après la réunion* ⓪ to come back = *revenir*	
☠ *la valise ne rentre pas dans le coffre* = the suitcase doesn't fit in the trunk — *ils se sont rentrés dedans* = they crashed	— *rentrer (le ventre)* = to pull in (one's stomach) — *ça ne rentre pas* = it doesn't sink in — *rentrer à l'hôpital* = to go into hospital
2/ *retourner* : he returned to get his coat = *il est retourné chercher son manteau* = to go back **to return to (Paris)** = *retourner à (Paris)*	
☠ *retournez-vous !* = turn/look around ! — *laissez-moi (le temps de) me retourner* = let me catch my breath — *la nouvelle l'a complètement retournée* = the news threw her completely	— *la voiture s'est retournée* = the car turned over/overturned — *il sait de quoi il retourne* = he knows what's what — *son plan s'est retourné contre lui* = his plan turned against him/backfired
3/ *rendre* : don't forget to return my book = *n'oublie pas de me rendre mon livre* ⓪ to bring back = *rapporter*	
☠ *ça l'a rendue (heureuse)* = it made her (happy) — *se rendre à (Paris)* = to go to (Paris) — *rendre (un repas)* = to bring up (a meal)	— *je vous rendrai l'argent la semaine prochaine* = I'll pay you back next week — *se rendre* = to surrender — *rendre un verdict* = to hand down a verdict.

REUNION (n) *réunion (f)* : a school reunion = *une réunion d'anciens élèves* ⓪ assembly = *assemblée* ☠ *une réunion (syndicale)* = a (union) meeting — *une réunion de famille* = a family gathering.

REUNITE (to, -d) *réunir* : the family was reunited = *la famille était réunie* ≠ to separate = *séparer* ☠ *réunir (de l'argent)* = to raise (money) — *le Parlement se réunit demain* = Parliament meets/convenes tomorrow.

REVAMP (to, -ed) *retaper* : to revamp an old house = *retaper une vieille maison.*

REVEAL (to, -ed) *révéler* : to reveal a secret = *révéler un secret* ⓪ to debunk = *démystifier* ≠ to conceal = *dissimuler* ☠ *se révéler être (difficile)* = to turn out to be (difficult).

REVELATION (n) *révélation (f)* : that young actress is the revelation of the season = *cette jeune actrice est la révélation de la saison.*

REVEL IN (to, -(l)ed) *tirer une grande satisfaction de* : he revels in his success = *il tire une grande satisfaction de son succès* ⓪ to delight in = *prendre plaisir à.*

REVENGE (n) *revanche (f)* : he cheated on me, but I'll have my revenge = *il m'a trompée, mais j'aurai ma revanche* ☠ vengeance = ←
to get one's revenge = *prendre sa revanche* ⓪ to get even = *se venger* ☠ *revanche (match)* = return match.

REVENGE (to, -d) *venger* : he revenged his brother's murder = *il a vengé le meurtre de son frère* ☠ *se venger* = to get even.

REVENGEFUL (adj) *vengeur, -eresse* : a revengeful bitter woman = *une femme amère et vengeresse* ⓪ vindictive = *vindicatif.*

REVENUE (n) *revenu (m)* : over a third of the government's revenue goes for arms = *plus d'un tiers du revenu de l'État sert à acheter des armes* ☠ *mon revenu* = my income.

REVEREND (n) *révérend (m)* ⓪ pastor = *pasteur.*

REVERSAL (n) *revirement (m)* : a reversal of attitude = *un revirement d'attitude* ☠ *un revirement d'opinion* = a change of mind.

REVERSE (n) *inverse (m)* : he said one thing but did just the reverse = *il a dit une chose, mais il a fait exactement l'inverse* ⓪ opposite = *opposé.*

REVERSE (adj) **the reverse side** = *l'envers (coat)/ le revers (coin).*

REVERSE (to, -d) **1/** *casser* : the Supreme Court reversed the sentence = *la Cour suprême a cassé le jugement* ☠ → to break **2/** *inverser* : reverse the order of the two paragraphs = *inversez l'ordre des deux paragraphes.*

REVERSIBLE (adj) *réversible* : a reversible coat = *un manteau réversible.*

REVERT TO (to, -ed) *revenir à* : when she dies, the property reverts to her husband = *à sa mort, la propriété reviendra à son mari.*

REVIEW (n) **1/** *critique (f)* : the play got a bad review in the "Post" = *la pièce a eu une mauvaise critique dans le « Post »* = write-up ☠ → criticism **2/** *révision (f)* : a review of last week's lesson = *une révision de la leçon de la semaine dernière* ☠ → revision **3/** *revue (f)* : a new medical review = *une nouvelle revue médicale* ☠ → revue.

REVIEW (to, -ed) **1/** *faire la critique (de)* : to review a play = *faire la critique d'une pièce* ⓪ to write up = *faire un article sur* **2/** *réviser* : I have to review last week's lesson = *il faut que je révise la leçon de la semaine dernière*, the case is going to be reviewed = *l'affaire va être révisée* ☠ → to revise **3/** *passer en revue* : the President reviewed the troops = *le Président a passé les troupes en revue* ⓪ to inspect = *faire l'inspection de.*

REVIEWER (n) *critique (m, f) (littéraire)* : the reviewer blasted the book = *le critique a descendu le livre* ⓪ a review = *une critique* ☠ → criticism.

REVISE (to, -d) *réviser* : they revised the original edition = *ils ont révisé l'édition originale* ⓪ to correct = *corriger* ☠ *réviser (un procès)* = to review (a lawsuit) — *réviser une voiture* = to overhaul a car.

REVISION (n) *révision (f)* : this text needs a good revision = *ce texte a besoin d'une bonne révision* ☠ *révision (voiture)* = overhauling (car) — *révision d'une leçon* = review of a lesson.

REVIVAL (n) *renouveau (m)* (arts), *reprise (f)* (economy, play) ☠ *reprise* → rerun.

REVIVE (to, -d) *ranimer* : the patient was revived = *le patient a été ranimé* ⓪ to regain consciousness = *reprendre connaissance* ☠ → to reanimate.

REVOCATION (n) *révocation (f).*

REVOKE (to, -d) *révoquer* (decree), *retirer* (license) : his driver's license was revoked = *on lui a retiré son permis de conduire* ☠ *retirer* → to withdraw — *révoquer un général* = to divest a general.

REVOLT (n) *révolte (f)* : a peasant revolt = *une révolte de paysans* ⓪ revolution = *révolution*, uprising = *soulèvement.*

REVOLT (to, -ed) *se révolter* : kids often revolt against their parents = *les enfants se révoltent souvent contre leurs parents* ⓪ to rebel = *se rebeller*
to revolt s.o. = *révolter qqn* : his attitude revolts me = *son attitude me révolte* ⓪ to sicken s.o. = *écœurer qqn.*

REVOLTING (adj) *révoltant, -e* : revolting language = *un langage révoltant* → AWFUL.

REVOLUTION (n) *révolution (f)* : a revolution in the country/in the theater = *une révolution dans le pays/dans le théâtre* ⚭ coup d'état = *coup d'État*, rebellion = *rébellion*.

REVOLUTIONARY (adj) *révolutionnaire* : revolutionary ideas/methods = *des idées/des méthodes révolutionnaires* ≠ conservative = *conservateur* **REVOLUTIONARY** (n, -ies) *révolutionnaire (m, f)* ≠ reactionary = *réactionnaire*.

REVOLUTIONIZE (to, -d) *révolutionner* : to revolutionize birth control methods = *révolutionner les méthodes de contrôle des naissances*.

REVOLVE AROUND (to, -d) *tourner autour de* : her life revolves around her job = *sa vie tourne autour de son travail*.

REVOLVER (n) *revolver (m)* ⚭ rifle = *carabine*.

REVOLVING DOOR (n) *porte (f) à tambour*.

REVUE (n) *revue (f)* : the club has two revues nightly = *le club présente deux revues par soirée* ⚭ show = *spectacle* ☠ *une revue (magazine)* = a magazine/a review.

REVULSION (n) *répugnance (f)* : he fills me with revulsion = *je n'ai que de la répugnance pour lui* ⚭ disgust = *dégoût*.

REWARD (n) *récompense (f)* : a reward for returning the lost dog = *une récompense pour avoir ramené le chien perdu* ⚭ prize = *prix* ☠ *récompense (pour héroïsme)* = award (for heroism) **REWARD** (to, -ed) *récompenser*.

REWARDING (adj) *enrichissant, -e* : rewarding work = *travail enrichissant* ⚭ gratifying = *gratifiant*.

REWRITE (to, -wrote, -written) *réécrire* : to rewrite a text = *réécrire un texte* **REWRITING** (n) *rewriting (m), réécriture (f)*.

RHETORIC (n) *rhétorique (f)* **RHETORICAL** (adj) *rhétorique* : a rhetorical question = *une question rhétorique*.

RHEUMATISM (n) *rhumatisme (m)* : to have/suffer from rheumatism = *avoir des rhumatismes/souffrir de rhumatismes* **RHEUMATIC** (adj) *rhumatisant, -e*.

RHINOCEROS (n) *rhinocéros (m)* ⚭ crocodile = ←.

RHODESIA (n) *Rhodésie (f)* **RHODESIAN** (n, adj) *Rhodésien, -enne*.

RHYME (n) **without rhyme or reason** = *sans rime ni raison*.

RHYME (to, -d) *rimer* : funny rhymes with sunny = « funny » *rime avec* « sunny » ☠ *à quoi ça rime ?* = what's the point of it ?

RHYTHM (n) *rythme (m)* : the music has got a great rhythm = *la musique a beaucoup de rythme* ☠ *à ce rythme* = at this pace.

RIB (n) *côte (f)* : he broke three ribs in the accident = *il s'est cassé trois côtes dans l'accident* ☠ → coast.

RIB (to, -bed) *charrier* : my friends rib me because I'm afraid of taking the pill = *mes amis me charrient parce que j'ai peur de prendre la pilule* ⚭ to tease = *taquiner* ☠ *charrier (une valise)* = to haul (a suitcase) — *tu charries !* = you're stretching it !

RIBBON (n) *ruban (m)* : a ribbon in her hair = *un ruban dans ses cheveux* ⚭ braid = *galon*.

RICE (n) *riz (m)* : vegetarians eat a lot of rice = *les végétariens mangent beaucoup de riz* ⚭ rice field = *rizière*.

RICH (n inv) **the rich** = *les riches* ≠ the poor = *les pauvres*.

RICH (adj, -er, -est) *riche* : a rich man = *un homme riche* ≠ poor = *pauvre*

——— GROUP : RICH = RICHE ———

to be affluent = *être nanti*	**to be moneyed** = *être argenté*	**to have/make a bankroll** = *avoir/se faire une galette*
to be in the chips = *être en fonds*	**to be a moneybags** = *être un rupin/un richard*	**to have/make a bundle** = *avoir/se faire un magot*
to be comfortable = *être à l'aise*	**to be rolling in money** = *rouler sur l'or*	**to have/make a fortune** = *avoir de la fortune/gagner une fortune, faire fortune*
to be on easy street = *nager dans l'opulence*	**to be stinking rich** = *puer le fric*	
to be filthy rich = *être richissime*	**to be wealthy** = *être très aisé*	**to have the means** = *avoir les moyens*
to be flush = *être bourré de fric*	**to be well-fixed** = *être fortuné*	**to have money** = *avoir de l'argent*
to be loaded = *être plein aux as*	**to be well-heeled** = *être plein aux as*	**to have money to burn** = *avoir de l'argent à jeter par les fenêtres*
to be made of money = *être cousu d'or*	**to be well-off** = *être aisé*	
to be in the money = *être en fonds*	**to be well-to-do** = *être à son aise*	**to have more money than one knows what to do with** =
	to clean up = *faire son beurre*	
	to get rich = *s'enrichir*	

avoir de l'argent à ne plus savoir qu'en faire	to have the wherewithal = avoir de quoi	to live like a lord = vivre comme un pacha
to have/make a pile = avoir/se faire une pelote	**to live off the fat of the land** = vivre de ses rentes	**to make a killing** = ramasser le paquet
to have pots of money = être riche comme Crésus	**to live in the lap of luxury** = nager dans l'opulence	**to make a mint** = se faire un fric fou
to have the ways and means = avoir les moyens	**to live like a king** = vivre comme un roi	**to strike it rich** = trouver le filon.

RICHNESS (n inv) *richesse (f) :* the richness of his style/language = *la richesse de son style/de sa langue* ☠ → wealth.

RICKETS (n pl) *rachitisme (m)*
to have rickets = *être rachitique.*

RID (to, -ded or rid, rid) **to rid of** = *débarrasser de :* can we rid the world of famine ? = *peut-on débarrasser le monde de la famine ?*
to get rid of = *se débarrasser de :* get rid of him !/of all these newspapers ! = *débarrassez-vous de lui !/de tous ces journaux !* ⓪ to junk = *bazarder,* to dispose of = *se défaire de* ☠ *débarrasser la table* = to clear the table.

RIDDEN (adj) **ridden by (fears/guilt)** = *hanté par (ses craintes/sa culpabilité).*

RIDDLE (n) *devinette (f)* ⓪ enigma = *énigme*
to talk in riddles = *parler par énigmes.*

RIDDLE (to, -d) **to be riddled with (bullets/doubts)** = *être criblé de (balles)/être rempli de (doutes)* ⓪ to be loaded with = *être bourré de.*

RIDE (n) *trajet (m) :* it's a two-hour ride from the airport to town = *il y a un trajet de deux heures (en voiture) de l'aéroport à la ville* ☠ → journey
to bum/thumb a ride = *faire du stop :* it's hard to bum/thumb a ride in the city = *c'est dur de faire du stop en ville*
can you give me a ride (to the bank) ? = *est-ce que vous pouvez m'emmener en voiture (à la banque) ?* ⓪ to give a lift = *déposer en voiture*
to go along for the ride = *(juste) accompagner qqn :* I don't want to buy anything but I'll go along for the ride = *je ne veux rien acheter, mais je vais juste vous accompagner*
to go for a ride = *faire une promenade en voiture*
to take s.o. for a ride = *mener qqn en bateau :* how could have you believed him ? he really took you for a ride ! = *comment avez-vous pu le croire ? il vous a vraiment mené en bateau !* → TO HUSTLE.

RIDE (to, rode, ridden) **1/** *monter :* when I'm in the country, I ride every day = *quand je suis à la campagne, je monte tous les jours* ⓪ to go horseback riding = *monter à cheval* ☠ → to rise **2/** *aller en voiture :* do you ride to work ? = *est-ce que vous allez au travail en voiture ?* ⓪ to drive = *conduire*

to ride (a bike/a motorcycle) = *faire de (la bicyclette/moto)*
to ride s.o. = *tourmenter qqn :* she's always riding him because he doesn't earn enough money = *elle est toujours en train de le tourmenter parce qu'il ne gagne pas assez d'argent* ⓪ to bug = *casser les pieds à*
(to be) riding on = *(être) en jeu sur :* I have a lot of money riding on that horse/that contract = *j'ai beaucoup d'argent en jeu sur ce cheval/contrat* ⓪ to stake everything = *jouer son va-tout*
to ride out (the crisis) = *traverser (la crise) sans trop de dégâts* ⓪ to weather the storm = *traverser la tempête.*

RIDER (n) **1/** *cavalier, -ère :* Jane was an excellent rider at 6 = *à 6 ans, Jane était une excellente cavalière* ⓪ saddle = *selle* **2/** *annexe (f)* (bill), *avenant (m)* (contract) ⓪ clause = *←* ☠ *→* annex.

RIDICULE (to, -d) *ridiculiser :* he ridiculed my accent = *il a ridiculisé mon accent* ⓪ to make fun of = *se moquer de,* to deride = *tourner en dérision* ☠ *se ridiculiser* = to make a fool of o.s.

RIDICULOUS (adj) *ridicule :* a ridiculous idea = *une idée ridicule* ⓪ farfetched = *tiré par les cheveux* ≠ sensible = *sensé* **RIDICULOUSLY** (adv) *ridiculement :* ridiculously dressed/expensive = *ridiculement habillé/cher.*

RIFFRAFF (n inv) **the riffraff** = *la canaille :* he hangs around with the riffraff = *il traîne avec la canaille* ⓪ rabble = *populace.*

RIFLE (n) *carabine (f), fusil (m) :* he was shot dead with a rifle = *il a été tué avec une carabine/un fusil* ⓪ gun = *arme à feu* ☠ *changer son fusil d'épaule* = to change one's tactics.

RIFLE (to, -d) *piller, dévaliser :* our hotel room was rifled = *notre chambre d'hôtel a été pillée/dévalisée* ⓪ to rob = *voler.*

RIFT (n) *différend (m) :* there are many rifts within the party = *il y a de nombreux différends à l'intérieur du parti* ⓪ disagreement = *désaccord.*

RIG (to, -ged) *truquer :* the elections were rigged = *les élections ont été truquées* = the elections were fixed
to be rigged out in (jeans and a mink coat) = *être fringué avec (un jean et un manteau de vison)* ⓪ to be clad in = *être vêtu de*
☠ → to fix.

RIGHT (n) **1/** *droit* (m) : the right to vote = *le droit de vote*

by what right ? = *de quel droit ?* **to know right from wrong** = *distinguer le bien du mal*	**you had a right to** ≠ **you had no right to (do that)** = *vous aviez le droit de* ≠ *vous n'aviez pas le droit de (faire ça)*
☠ *faire des études de droit* = to study law	— *droit de douane* = customs duty

2/ *droite* (f) : to drive on the right = *conduire à droite,* the right voted against gun control = *la droite a voté contre la limitation des ventes d'armes* ≠ the left = *la gauche*
on your right = *à votre droite* : there's a bank on your right = *il y a une banque à votre droite.*

RIGHT (adj) **1/** *bon, bonne* : the right answer/decision/number = *la bonne réponse/décision/le bon numéro*
Ⓓ correct = ← ≠ erroneous = *erroné* ☠ → good
2/ *droit, -e* : a right angle = *un angle droit,* my right arm = *mon bras droit,* the right bank = *la rive droite*

☠ *tiens-toi droit !* = stand straight ! — *une veste droite* = a single-breasted jacket	— *une personne droite* = a very aboveboard person

at the right moment = *au bon moment*
to be right = *avoir raison* : I'm sorry, you were right = *je suis désolé, vous aviez raison* ≠ to be wrong = *avoir tort*
he was right to (tell him) = *il a eu raison de (le lui dire)* = **he was right in (telling him)**
right for s.o. = *qu'il faut à qqn* : she isn't the right girl for him/it isn't the right class for me = *ce n'est pas la fille qu'il lui faut/ce n'est pas la classe qu'il me faut* Ⓓ to be made for = *être fait pour*
to do the right thing by (one's family) = *faire ce qu'il faut pour (sa famille)*
I don't feel right about (going alone) = *ça me gêne d'(y aller tout seul)*
I'd give my right arm (to go to Europe this Summer) = *je vendrais mon âme au diable (pour aller en Europe cet été)* Ⓓ I'd give anything = *je donnerais n'importe quoi*
is that right ? = *c'est vrai ?* Ⓓ really ? = *vraiment ?*
to know the right people = *avoir le bras long* Ⓓ to be well-connected = *avoir des relations*
(lying) is not right = *ce n'est pas bien de (mentir)*
no one in his right mind (would have spent so much) ! = *quelqu'un de normalement constitué (n'aurait pas dépensé autant) !*
right ? = *n'est-ce pas ?* : you agree with me, right ? = *vous êtes d'accord avec moi, n'est-ce pas ?* Ⓓ isn't that so ? = *pas vrai ?*
right you are ! = *vous avez bien raison !*
the right arm = *le bras droit* : he's the President's right arm = *c'est le bras droit du Président* Ⓓ deputy = *adjoint*
the right kind of people = *les gens comme il faut*
the right man in the right place = *l'homme qu'il faut à la place qu'il faut/l'homme de la situation*
to set/put things/the situation right = *remettre les choses en ordre*
that's right ! = *c'est (bien) ça !* ≠ that's not it ! = *ce n'est pas ça !*

RIGHT (adv) *comme il faut* : her kids behave right = *ses gosses se conduisent comme il faut*

I didn't get (his name) right = *je n'ai pas bien compris (son nom)*
it served him right ! = *il ne l'a pas volé !/c'est bien fait pour lui !* Ⓓ he deserved it ! = *il l'a bien mérité !*
I'll be right with you ! = *je suis à vous immédiatement !*
it's right in front of you = *c'est droit devant vous*
right after = *juste après* : we had dinner and went home right after = *nous avons dîné et nous sommes rentrés à la maison juste après* ≠ **right before** = *juste avant*
right and left = *à droite et à gauche* : he's making money right and left = *il gagne de l'argent à droite et à gauche*
right at (the beginning) = *tout au (début)*
right here ! = *(juste) ici !* : where are you ? — right here ! = *où êtes-vous ? — (juste) ici !*
right, left and center = *de tous côtés/dans tous les azimuts* : there were cops right, left and center = *il y avait des flics dans tous les azimuts/de tous côtés*
right now/away = *séance tenante* : do it right now/away ! = *faites-le séance tenante !* Ⓓ straightaway = *illico*
right off = *d'emblée* : she said right off that she was a hooker = *elle a dit d'emblée qu'elle était putain* Ⓓ straight out = *tout de go*
right on ! = *en avant !* Ⓓ full steam ahead ! = *en avant toute !*
right then = *là-dessus* : I walked in, and right then the

phone rang = *je suis rentrée, et là-dessus le téléphone a son-*	né ① at that moment = *à ce moment-là*	**(turn) right** ! = *(tournez à droite !* ≠ *(turn) left* ! = *(tournez) à gauche*

RIGHT ! (interj) *d'accord !* : six o'clock, right ! = *à six heures, d'accord !* = all right ! ① gotcha ! = *vu !*

RIGHTEOUS (adj) *bien pensant, -e* : a righteous attitude towards prostitution = *une attitude bien pensante à l'égard de la prostitution* ① goody-goody = *de petit saint.*

RIGHTFUL (adj) *qui est dû à qqn* : give me my rightful share = *donnez-moi la part qui m'est due*
the rightful owner = *le propriétaire légitime.*

RIGHT-HANDED (adj) *droitier, -ère* : I'm right-handed = *je suis droitier* ≠ a southpaw = *un gaucher* = a lefty.

RIGHTLY (adv) *au juste* : I can't rightly say = *je ne saurai dire au juste*
rightly or wrongly = *à tort ou à raison* : we believe rightly or wrongly that a nuclear war won't happen = *nous croyons à tort ou à raison qu'il n'y aura pas de guerre nucléaire*
rightly so = *à bon droit* : he was furious and rightly so = *il était furieux et à bon droit* ① justifiably so = *à juste titre.*

RIGHTS (n pl) *droits (m pl)* : women's rights = *les droits des femmes,* the rights of the film were sold for two million = *les droits du film se sont vendus deux millions*
to be within one's rights = *être dans son droit*
☠ *droits d'auteur* = royalties
— *droits de succession* = inheritance tax
— *droits d'inscription* = registration fee.

RIGHT-WINGER (n) *homme (m) /femme (f) de droite* ① reactionary = *réactionnaire.*

RIGID (adj) *rigide* : rigid principles = *des principes rigides* ≠ flexible = ← **RIGIDITY** (n) *rigidité (f).*

RIGMAROLE (n) *cirque (m)* : what a rigmarole to get a visa ! = *quel cirque pour obtenir un visa !* ☠ → circus.

RIGOR (n) *rigueur (f)* : the rigors of winter = *les rigueurs de l'hiver*
☠ *tenir rigueur à qqn de qqch* = to hold stg against s.o.
— *de rigueur* = obligatory.

RIGOROUS (adj) *rigoureux, -euse* : rigourous laws/reasoning = *des lois rigoureuses/un raisonnement rigoureux.*

RILE (to, -d) *horripiler* : his attitude riles me = *son attitude m'horripile* → ANGRY.

RIM (n) *bord (m)* : the rim of the glass = *le bord du verre* ☠ → edge.

RING (n) **1/** *bague (f)* : a diamond ring = *une bague de diamants* ① bracelet = ← **2/** *réseau (m)* : a spy/prostitution ring = *un réseau d'espionnage/de prostitution* = a spy/prostitution network **3/** *ring (m)* : boxing ring = *ring de boxe*

give me a ring tonight (GB) = *passe-moi un coup de téléphone ce soir* ① give me a buzz = *passe-moi un coup de fil*
to have rings under one's eyes = *avoir les yeux cernés/des cernes* ① to have bags under one's eyes = *avoir des poches sous les yeux*
to run rings around = *être mille fois supérieur à* : his work runs rings around yours = *son travail est mille fois supérieur au tien* ① to be superior to = *être supérieur à.*

RING (to, rang, rung) **1/** *sonner* : the phone rang = *le téléphone a sonné* ≠ to answer = *répondre* ☠ *on ne t'a pas sonné !* = mind your own business ! **2/** (GB) *appeler* : ring me tonight = *appelez-moi ce soir* = call me tonight ☠ → to call
to ring s.o. back (GB) = *rappeler qqn* = to call s.o. back
to ring off (GB) = *raccrocher* : I have to ring off = *il faut que je raccroche* = I have to hang up ☠ → to hang up
to ring s.o. up (GB) = *passer un coup de téléphone à qqn* = to call s.o. up.

RINGLEADER (n) *meneur, -euse* : the ringleader of the rebellion = *le meneur de la rébellion* ① instigator = *instigateur,* agitator = *agitateur* ☠ *le meneur de jeu* = the moderator (in a debate).

RINGSIDE SEAT (n) **to have ringside seats** = *être aux premières loges.*

RINK (n) *patinoire (f)* ① skating = *patinage.*

RINSE (to, -d) *rincer* : I rinsed the sweater twice = *j'ai rincé le pull deux fois* ① to wring = *essorer* ☠ *se rincer la dalle* = to wet one's whistle.

RIOT (n) **1/** *émeute (f)* : hundreds of people were hurt during the riots = *des centaines de gens ont été blessés pendant les émeutes* ① street fighting = *combats de rue*
to raise a riot = *pousser les hauts cris* : my father raised a riot when the waiter brought the food all cold = *mon père a poussé les hauts cris quand le garçon a apporté le plat complètement froid* ① to raise hell = *faire du pétard*
riot squad = *brigade anticasseurs*
to run riot = *se déchaîner* : the kids ran riot when the teacher left the room = *les gosses se sont déchaînés lorsque le professeur a quitté la classe* ☠ → to let loose **2/** *quelque chose de désopilant* : the movie was a riot = *le film était désopilant* ① it was a scream = *c'était bidonnant.*

RIOTER (n) *émeutier, -ère* : many of the rioters were adolescents = *beaucoup d'émeutiers étaient des adolescents* ① insurgent = *insurgé.*

RIP (n) *déchirure (f)* : a rip in your dress = *une déchirure à votre robe* = tear.

RIP (to, -ped) *déchirer* : I ripped my blouse = *j'ai déchiré mon chemisier* ≠ to mend = *raccommoder*
to rip apart = *descendre en flammes* : the critic ripped the play apart = *le critique a descendu la pièce en flammes* ⟳ to find fault with = *trouver à redire à*
to rip off = *escroquer* : my lawyer really ripped me off = *mon avocat m'a vraiment escroqué* → TO HUSTLE
to rip up = *déchirer* : I ripped up the letter = *j'ai déchiré la lettre* = to tear up
☠ *déchirer (un pays)* = to tear (a country) apart.

RIPE (adj, -r, -st) *mûr, -e* : a ripe peach = *une pêche mûre* ⟳ ripened = *mûri*, overripe = *blet* ≠ green = *vert* ☠ → mature.

RIPOFF (n) *escroquerie (f)* : the contract was a ripoff = *le contrat était une escroquerie* ⟳ swindle = *arnaque*.

RISE (n) **a rise in (prices/temperature)** = *une hausse des (prix)/de la (température)* ⟳ increase = *augmentation* ≠ fall = *chute*
to get a rise out of s.o. = *faire bondir qqn* : he said that to get a rise out of me = *il a dit ça pour me faire bondir*
to give rise to = *donner lieu à* : feminism gave rise to a new awareness of the self = *le féminisme a donné lieu à une nouvelle conscience de soi* ⟳ to lead to = *conduire à*
the rise of (fascism) = *la montée du (fascisme)*.

RISE (to, rose, risen) 1/ *se lever* : he rises early = *il se lève tôt* = to get up ☠ → to raise 2/ *monter* : gas prices are rising = *le prix de l'essence monte* ⟳ to ascend = *s'élever* ≠ to fall = *chuter*
to rise up = *se soulever* : the whole population rose up = *toute la population s'est soulevée* ⟳ to take up arms = *prendre les armes* ☠ → to lift
☠ *monter dans (un bus)* = to get into/on (a bus)
— *il l'a monté contre moi* = he turned him against me
— *l'addition se monte à 10 dollars* = the bill amounts to $ 10
— *monter (à cheval)* = to ride (on horseback)
— *monter (affaire/club/etc.)* = to put (a deal/club/etc.) together
— *tu veux monter quelques minutes ?* = do you want to come up a few minutes ?
— *monter une pièce* = to put a play on
— *faire monter son dîner* = to have dinner sent up
— *montez ! (voiture)* = get in !

RISING (n) *soulèvement (m)* : a rising in the South = *un soulèvement dans le Sud* ⟳ rebellion = *rébellion*.

RISING (adj) *qui monte* : a rising novelist = *un romancier qui monte* ⟳ promising = *prometteur*.

RISK (n) *risque (m)* : with the pill there's little risk of getting pregnant = *avec la pilule il y a peu de risques de tomber enceinte* ⟳ peril = *péril*

at the risk of (seeming naive/shocking you) = *au risque de (paraître naïf/vous choquer)*
there's a risk (of fire) = *il y a un risque (d'incendie)*
to run/take the risk of (getting pregnant) = *courir/prendre le risque de (tomber enceinte)*
☠ *c'est un risque à prendre* = it's a chance you'll have to take
— *les risques du métier* = professional hazards.

RISK (to, -ed) *risquer* : to risk one's life = *risquer sa vie* ⟳ to jeopardize = *mettre en péril*
☠ *risquer une question* = to venture a question
— *vous risquez d'(arriver trop tard)* = you run the chance of (getting there too late)
— *qui ne risque rien n'a rien* = nothing ventured, nothing gained.

RISKY (adj, -ier, -iest) *risqué, -e* : making love without using a contraceptive is a risky business = *c'est risqué de faire l'amour sans contraceptif* ⟳ dangerous = *dangereux* ☠ a risqué joke = *une plaisanterie grivoise*.

RISQUÉ (adj) *grivois, -e* : he tells risqué jokes = *il fait des plaisanteries grivoises* ⟳ dirty = *cochon*, daring = *osé* ☠ *risqué* → riskey.

RITE (n) *rite (m)* : circumcision is a rite = *la circoncision est un rite* ⟳ ceremony = *cérémonie*.

RITUAL (n) *rituel (m)* : Christmas ritual = *le rituel de Noël* **RITUAL** (adj) *rituel, -elle* : a ritual celebration = *une fête rituelle*.

RITZY (adj, -ier, -iest) *cossu, -e* : a ritzy apartment = *un appartement cossu* ≠ seedy = *miteux*.

RIVAL (n) *rival, -e* : in fashion he has no rival = *dans le domaine de la mode, il n'a pas de rival* ⟳ adversary = *adversaire* **RIVAL** (adj) *rival, -e* : two rival companies = *deux sociétés rivales* ⟳ competing = *concurrent* **RIVAL** (to, -(l)ed) *rivaliser avec* : the diaphragm can't rival the pill = *le diaphragme ne peut pas rivaliser avec la pilule*.

RIVALRY (n, -ies) *rivalité (f)* : rivalry between the two brothers = *rivalité entre les deux frères*.

RIVER (n) *rivière (f)*, *fleuve (m)* : to fish in the river = *pêcher dans la rivière* ⟳ upstream = *en amont*, downstream = *en aval*
he'd sell (his mother) down the river = *il vendrait (sa propre mère)*
☠ *rivière de diamants* = diamond necklace
— *discours-/roman-fleuve* = endless speech/novel.

ROAD (n) *route (f)* : is this the road to Connecticut ? = *est-ce que c'est la route du Connecticut ?* ⟳ roadworks = *travaux (publics)*, street = *rue* ☠ → route
let's hit the road ! = *en route !* → TO LEAVE
on the road = *en tournée* : the show's on the road = *le spectacle est en tournée*
the road to hell is paved with good intentions = *l'enfer est pavé de bonnes intentions*.

ROADBLOCK (n) *barrage (m) routier* : he crashed into a

roadblock set up by the police = *il est venu s'écraser contre un barrage routier monté par la police.*

ROAM (to, -ed) *baguenauder* : we roamed around the left bank this afternoon = *nous avons baguenaudé sur la rive gauche cet après-midi* ⓪ to stroll = *se balader.*

ROAR (to, -ed) **1/** *se tordre de rire* : we roared at his jokes = *on s'est tordu de rire en écoutant ses blagues* ⓪ to howl = *hurler de rire*, to have a good laugh = *bien se marrer* **2/** *rugir* : lions roar = *les lions rugissent* ⓪ a roar = *un rugissement.*

ROAST (adj) *rôti, -e* : roast chicken = *poulet rôti* = roasted chicken.

ROAST (to, -ed) *(faire) rôtir* : roast the chicken ! = *fais rôtir le poulet !* ⓪ to bake = *cuire au four* **to roast in (the sun)** = *se rôtir au (soleil).*

ROB (to, -bed) *voler, dévaliser* (bank) : they robbed the bank again last week = *la banque a de nouveau été dévalisée la semaine dernière*, he robbed my bag ! = *il a volé mon sac !* ⓪ to swipe = *faucher*, to burglarize = *cambrioler*
☠ *dévaliser un magasin* = to buy up everything
— *voler* → to fly.

ROBBER (n) *voleur, -euse* : the robbers were caught red-handed = *les voleurs ont été pris la main dans le sac* ⓪ burglar = *cambrioleur*, hooligan = *voyou*
☠ *voleur à la tire* = shoplifter
— *au voleur !* = stop, thief !

ROBBERY (n, -ies) *vol* (m) : another robbery in the building ! = *encore un vol dans l'immeuble !* ⓪ burglary = *cambriolage*, holdup = *hold-up* ☠ → flight.

ROBE (n) *robe* (f) de chambre = bathrobe ⓪ beachrobe = *robe de plage* ☠ *robe* → dress.

ROBOT (n) *robot* (m) : a robot to do the housework = *un robot pour faire les travaux ménagers.*

ROBUST (adj) *robuste* : robust health = *santé robuste* ≠ delicate = *délicat*
☠ *un appétit robuste* = a hearty appetite
— *une table robuste* = a sturdy table.

ROCK (n) **1/** *grosse pierre* (f) : the kids were throwing rocks at the blind man = *les gosses lançaient de grosses pierres à l'aveugle* ⓪ stone = *pierre* **2/** *roche* (f) : geologists study rocks = *les géologues étudient les roches* ⓪ boulder = *rocher*
to be on the rocks = *avoir du plomb dans l'aile* : his business/his marriage is on the rocks = *son affaire/son ménage a du plomb dans l'aile* ⓪ to go to pot = *être à la dérive*
rock garden = *rocaille/jardin de rochers*
rock and roll = ← = rock'n'roll ⓪ funky music = *musique funky*
(Scotch) on the rocks = *(whisky) avec de la glace* ≠ straight = *sec.*

ROCK (to, -ed) *bercer* : to rock a baby = *bercer un bébé*

⓪ lullaby = *berceuse* ☠ *se bercer d'illusions* = to kid o.s.

ROCK-BOTTOM (adj) *le plus bas, la plus basse* : rock-bottom prices = *les prix les plus bas* ≠ sky-high = *hors de prix.*

ROCKER (n) **to be off one's rocker** = *avoir un petit vélo* → CRAZY.

ROCKET (n) *fusée* (f) : to launch a rocket = *lancer une fusée* ⓪ spaceship = *vaisseau spatial*, launching pad = *rampe de lancement.*

ROCKING CHAIR (n) *rocking-chair* (m), *fauteuil* (m) *à bascule.*

ROCKY (adj, -ier, -iest) **1/** *dans une mauvaise passe* : our business is in a rocky financial situation = *notre affaire est dans une mauvaise passe sur le plan financier* ⓪ to go to the dogs = *battre de l'aile* **2/** *rocailleux, -euse* : a rocky road = *une route rocailleuse*
the Rocky Mountains = *les (montagnes) Rocheuses.*

ROD (n) *flingue* (m) : the burglar pulled a rod = *le cambrioleur a sorti un flingue* ⓪ gun = *arme à feu*
spare the rod and spoil the child = *qui aime bien châtie bien.*

RODENT (n) *rongeur* (m) ⓪ rabbit = *lapin.*

RODEO (n) *rodéo* (m) ⓪ cowboy = *cow-boy.*

ROGER ! (interj) *d'ac !* ≠ no way ! = *pas question !*

ROGUE (n) *gredin* (m) : the Mafia's full of rogues = *la Mafia est pleine de gredins* → BASTARD.

ROLE (n) *rôle* (m) : he plays the role of Hamlet/peacemaker = *il joue le rôle d'Hamlet/il a un rôle de pacificateur* ☠ *un rôle de composition* = a character part.

ROLL (n) **1/** *petit pain* (m) = bun **2/** *rouleau* (m) : a roll of paper = *un rouleau de papier*
the roll call = *l'appel*
a roll in the hay = *une partie de jambes en l'air* ⓪ to screw = *baiser*
☠ *rouleau (cheveux)* = roller (hair).

ROLL (to, -ed) *rouler* : the ball rolled = *le ballon a roulé*
☠ *ils l'ont roulé* = they conned him
— *ça roule bien* = traffic's good
— *il roule très vite* = he drives very fast.

ROLLER (n) *rouleau* (m), *bigoudi* (m) : to set one's hair with rollers = *se faire une mise en plis avec des rouleaux/des bigoudis* ⓪ hair clip = *pince à cheveux*
roller coaster = *montagnes russes*
roller skates = *patins à roulettes* ⓪ to roller-skate = *faire du patin à roulettes*
☠ *rouleau* → roll.

ROLY-POLY (adj) *grassouillet, -ette* : a roly-poly wife = *une femme grassouillette* ⓪ plump = *dodu.*

ROMANCE (n) *histoire* (f) *d'amour* : our romance was short-lived = *notre histoire d'amour n'a pas duré long-*

temps ⓪ idyll = *idylle* ☠ *une romance* = a sentimental song.

ROMANIA (n) *Roumanie (f)* = Rumania **ROMANIAN** (n, adj) *Roumain, -e* = Rumanian.

ROMANTIC (n) *romantique (m, f)* : what a romantic you are ! = *quel romantique tu fais !* ⓪ sentimental = ←
ROMANTIC (adj) *romantique* : a romantic place/girl = *un endroit/une fille romantique* ⓪ mushy = *plein de sensiblerie.*

ROMANTICIZE (to, -d) *romancer* : she romanticizes her childhood = *elle romance son enfance* ⓪ to view through rose-colored glasses = *voir en rose.*

ROME (n) *Rome* ⓪ Roman = *Romain*
Rome wasn't built in a day = *Rome ne s'est pas faite en un jour* ⓪ slow but steady = *qui veut voyager loin ménage sa monture*
when in Rome do what the Romans do = *à Rome il faut vivre comme à Rome.*

ROMEO (n) *Roméo (m), Don Juan (m)* : my husband is a real Romeo = *mon mari est un vrai Don Juan* ⓪ Casanova = ←.

ROOF (n) *toit (m)* : I hear someone on the roof = *j'entends quelqu'un sur le toit* ⓪ shingles = *bardeaux,* tiles = *tuiles,* slates = *ardoises*
to hit the roof = *pousser une gueulante* → ANGRY
he's without a roof over his head = *il est sans toit* ⓪ he's homeless = *il est sans foyer.*

ROOFTOP (n) **to cry from the rooftops** = *crier sur (tous) les toits.*

ROOKIE (n) *bleu (m)* (army), *nouvelle recrue (f)* (police) ≠ veteran = *vétéran* ☠ → blue.

ROOM (n) *pièce (f)* : our apartment has six rooms = *notre appartement a six pièces*

bathroom = *salle de bains*	hommes)
ballroom = *salle de bal*	**living room** = *living (-room)/salle de séjour*
bedroom = *chambre à coucher*	**master bedroom** = *chambre principale*
cloakroom = *vestiaire*	**pantry** = *garde-manger*
communicating rooms = *chambres communicantes*	**room and board** = *pension complète*
den = *salle de loisirs*	**room service** = *service des chambres*
dining room = *salle à manger*	**single** ≠ **double room** = *chambre pour une personne* ≠ *deux personnes*
dressing room = *cabinet de toilette*	
guest/spare room = *chambre d'amis*	**sitting room** = *salon*
kitchen = *cuisine*	**study** = *bureau*
ladies'/men's room = *toilettes (femmes/*	**waiting room** = *salle d'attente*

---

in (one's) room = *dans (sa) chambre* : Jane's in her room = *Jane est dans sa chambre*

☠ *une pièce (de Brecht)* = a play (by Brecht)
— *des pièces (de rechange)* = (spare) parts
— *une pièce (de monnaie)* = a coin
— *pièces à conviction* = incriminating evidence
— *payé à la pièce* = paid by the piece
— *coudre une pièce* = to sew on a patch

2/ (inv) *place (f)* : there is/isn't enough room = *il y a* ≠ *il n'y a pas assez de place* ☠ → place
to make room = *faire un peu de place*
there's (still) room for improvement = *ça laisse (encore) à désirer.*

ROOMING HOUSE (n) *pension (f) de famille* ⓪ roomer = *pensionnaire.*

ROOMMATE (n) *compagnon, compagne de chambre* : my roommate's gay but we don't have any problems = *mon compagnon de chambre est homosexuel mais nous n'avons pas de problèmes.*

ROOM WITH (to, -ed) *partager une chambre avec* : my daughter is rooming with a French girl = *ma fille partage une chambre avec une Française.*

ROOMY (adj, -ier, -iest) *spacieux, -euse* : a roomy apartment = *un appartement spacieux* = a spacious apartment.

ROOST (n) **to rule the roost** = *faire la pluie et le beau temps* ⓪ to run the show = *mener la danse.*

ROOSTER (n) *coq (m)* = cock ⓪ cock-a-doodle-do = *cocorico* ≠ hen = *poule*
☠ *passer du coq à l'âne* = to jump from one subject to another
— *un jeune coq* = a young upstart
— *être comme un coq en pâte* = to lead the life of Riley.

ROOT (n) *racine (f)* : her roots are in Russia = *ses racines sont en Russie* ⓪ origin = *origine*
to be at the root of = *être la raison fondamentale de* : money's at the root of their problems = *l'argent est la raison fondamentale de leurs problèmes* ⓪ to be at the origin of = *être à l'origine de*
to get to the root of (the problem) = *aller à la racine du (problème).*

ROOT FOR (to, -ed) *soutenir* : what team are you rooting for ? = *quelle équipe soutenez-vous ?* ⓪ to be for = *être pour* ☠ → to support.

ROPE (n) *corde (m)* : to tie s.o.'s hands with rope = *attacher les mains de qqn avec de la corde* ⓪ string = *ficelle*
give her enough rope and she'll hang herself = *elle tisse la corde pour se pendre* ⓪ to be one's (own) worst enemy = *être son (propre) pire ennemi*
to jump/skip rope = *sauter à la corde.*

to know the ropes = *connaître les ficelles* ⓪ **to know the score** = *connaître la musique*
☠ *se mettre la corde au cou* = to get hitched
— *avoir plus d'une corde à son arc* = to have more than one string to one's bow
— *ce n'est pas dans mes cordes* = that's not my line
— *il ne vaut pas la corde pour le pendre* = he's the lowest of the low
— *toucher la corde sensible* = to hit home
— *usé jusqu'à la corde* = threadbare
— *vous tirez trop sur la corde* = you're carrying things too far
— *il tombe des cordes* = it's raining cats and dogs.

ROPE (to, -d) **to rope s.o. in(to)** = *embobiner qqn pour* : I got roped into helping him = *il m'a embobiné pour que je l'aide* → TO HUSTLE
to rope off (an area) = *barrer les rues (d'un quartier)*.

ROSARY (n, -ies) *chapelet (m)* ⓪ *missal = missel.*

ROSE (n) *rose (f)* : long-stemmed roses = *des roses à longues tiges* ⓪ *thorn = épine*
☠ *être frais comme une rose* = to be as fresh as a daisy
— *envoyer qqn sur les roses* = to send s.o. packing.

ROT (n inv) *âneries (f pl)* : that's a lot of rot ! = *ce ne sont que des âneries !* = *baloney* ⓪ *horseshit = foutaises.*

ROT (to, -ted) *pourrir* : the meat will rot if you don't put it in the refrigerator = *la viande va pourrir si vous ne la mettez pas dans le réfrigérateur* ⓪ to spoil = *se gâter.*

ROTATE (to, -d) 1/ *alterner* : the actors rotated roles = *les acteurs alternaient les rôles* = to alternate ⓪ to exchange = *échanger* 2/ *pivoter* : the Earth rotates on its axis = *la Terre pivote sur son axe.*

ROTTEN (adj) 1/ *pourri, -e* : the meat's rotten = *la viande est pourrie* ⓪ spoiled = *gâté* 2/ *très moche* : the film/the restaurant was rotten = *le film/le restaurant était très moche* ≠ swell = *chouette* → AWFUL
to feel rotten = *se sentir mal fichu* ≠ to be in great shape = *être en pleine forme*
to feel rotten about stg = *être navré de qqch* : I feel rotten about not being able to lend you the money = *je suis navré de ne pas pouvoir vous prêter cet argent* ⓪ to be sorry about = *être désolé de*
he's rotten to the core = *il est pourri jusqu'à la moelle*
it was a rotten thing to say = *c'était vache de dire ça.*

ROUGE (n) *rouge (m) (à joues)* : to put rouge on one's cheeks = *se mettre du rouge sur les joues* ☠ → red.

ROUGH (n) **to take the rough with the smooth** = *prendre la vie comme elle vient* → THAT'S LIFE !

ROUGH (adj, -er, -est) 1/ *rude* : a rough day/life = *une rude journée/une vie rude* = a tough day/life ☠ → rude
2/ *dur, -e* : the test was rough = *l'examen était dur* = the test was hard ≠ as easy as pie = *facile comme bonjour* ☠ → hard 3/ *rugueux, -euse* : a rough skin/material = *une peau rugueuse/un tissu rugueux* 4/ *assez brutal,*

-e : boys are rough = *les garçons sont assez brutaux* ≠ tender = *tendre*
to be rough on s.o. = 1/ *être un coup dur pour qqn* : the divorce was rough on the kids = *le divorce a été un coup dur pour les gosses* ⓪ to be hard on = *être dur pour* 2/ *être dur avec qqn* : the boss is rough on me = *le patron est dur avec moi*
it's rough to (live with a guy you no longer love) = *c'est dur de (vivre avec un type qu'on n'aime plus)* = it's tough to
a rough idea = *une idée approximative*
a rough neighborhood = *un quartier dangereux*
rough language = *langage grossier*
a rough sketch = *une ébauche*
at a rough guess = *à vue de nez*
that's rough ! = *dur, dur !* → THAT'S LIFE !

ROUGH (to, -ed) **to rough it** = *vivre à la dure* : he roughed it during his vacation = *il a vécu à la dure pendant ses vacances*
to rough s.o. up = *malmener qqn* : the cops roughed him up = *les flics l'ont malmené* → TO HIT.

ROUGHHOUSE (adj) **no roughhouse stuff !** = *pas de grabuge ici !* ⓪ no rumble ! = *pas de rififi !*
roughhouse tactics = *la manière forte.*

ROUGHLY (adv) 1/ *en gros* : I'd say roughly a hundred people came = *je dirais qu'en gros une centaine de personnes sont venues* ⓪ round = *environ*
roughly speaking = *grosso modo* : roughly speaking, I'd say it will cost $ 100 = *grosso modo, je dirais que ça va coûter 100 dollars*
2/ *rudement* : he treated her roughly = *il l'a traitée rudement* ☠ *j'ai rudement apprécié ce que vous avez fait* = I appreciated what you did no end.

ROUGHNECK (n) *brute (f) (épaisse)* ⓪ ruffian = *vaurien.*

ROUGHSHOD (adj) **to ride roughshod over** = *traiter sans ménagement* : he rides roughshod over the other people in his office = *il traite les autres personnes de son bureau sans ménagement.*

ROUND (n) *round (m)* : the fight was over after three rounds = *le combat s'est terminé après trois rounds*
to make one's rounds = *faire sa ronde (guard)/faire sa tournée (mailman)*
a round of (talks/meetings) = *une série de (conversations/réunions)*
this round's on me ! = *c'est ma tournée !*

ROUND (adj) *rond, -e* : a round ball = *un ballon rond* ⓪ circular = *circulaire*
(to hold) a round table = *(tenir) une table ronde*
☠ *rond (comme une bille)* = pie-eyed
— *ça ne tourne pas rond* = it isn't going so well.

ROUND (prep, adv) → AROUND.

ROUND (to, -ed) **to round off (a sum)** = *arrondir (une somme d'argent)*
to round up = 1/ *rafler* : the cops rounded up everyone

= *les flics ont raflé tout le monde* ☠ *rafler (tous les prix)* = to walk off with (all the prizes) 2/ *rassembler* : he rounded up all the men = *il a rassemblé tous les hommes* ☠ → to gather.

ROUNDABOUT (adj) *détourné, -e* : a roundabout route/answer = *une route/réponse détournée* ≠ straightforward = *sans détours*.

ROUND-SHOULDERED (adj) *voûté, -e* : a round-shouldered old man = *un vieil homme voûté* ⓪ hunchbacked = *bossu*.

ROUND-TRIP TICKET (n) *billet (m) aller-retour* ≠ one-way ticket = *aller simple*.

ROUNDUP (n) *rafle (f)* : a roundup of criminals = *une rafle de criminels*.

ROUTE (n) *route (f)* : what's the shortest route to Washington ? = *quelle est la route la plus courte pour aller à Washington ?* ⓪ way = *chemin*
☠ *se mettre en route* = to set out
— *faire route ensemble* = to go a piece of the way together
— *la route du succès* = the road to success.

ROUTINE (n) 1/ *routine (f)* : nothing kills like routine = *rien ne tue comme la routine* ⓪ habit = *habitude* 2/ *numéro (m)* : a dance routine = *un numéro de danse* = a dance number ☠ → number
don't give me that routine ! = *arrête ton numéro !* → BUZZ OFF !

ROUTINE (adj) *de routine* : a routine checkup = *un contrôle de routine* ⓪ regular = *régulier*.

ROW (n) 1/ (inv) *tapage (m)* : what a row the neighbors are making ! = *les voisins font un de ces tapages !* ⓪ racket = *raffut* 2/ *altercation (f)* : she had a row with her young brother = *elle a eu une altercation avec son jeune frère* ⓪ run-in = *prise de bec* 3/ *rang (m)* : to sit in the first row = *s'asseoir au premier rang* ☠ → rank
a row of (houses) = *une rangée de (maisons)*
(four times) in a row = *(quatre fois) d'affilée*
to raise/kick up a row = *faire du foin* ⓪ to raise a riot = *pousser les hauts cris*.

ROW (to, -ed) *ramer* : I'm too tired to row = *je suis trop fatigué pour ramer* ⓪ rowing boat = *bateau à rames*, oars = *rames* ☠ *pour arriver dans le showbiz, il faut ramer* = to succeed in showbiz, you must go at it.

ROWDY (adj, -ier, -iest) *tapageur, -euse* : a rowdy party = *une soirée tapageuse* ⓪ noisy = *bruyant* ☠ → flashy.

ROYAL (adj) *royal, -e* : the royal family = *la famille royale* **ROYALLY** (adv) *royalement* : they entertained us royally = *ils nous ont reçus royalement*.

ROYALIST (n, adj) *royaliste (m, f)*.

ROYALTY (n, -ies) 1/ *droits d'auteur (m pl)* (book), redevance *(f)* /royalties *(f pl)* (patent, oil well) : he gets a ten percent royalty on each book = *il touche dix pour cent de droits d'auteur sur chaque livre* 2/ (inv) *royauté (f)* : French royalty = *la royauté française*.

RUB (n) **the rub is that (it costs too much)** = *le hic, c'est que (ça coûte trop cher)* ⓪ snag = *os*.

RUB (to, -bed) *frotter* : please rub my back = *frotte-moi le dos, s'il te plaît*
don't rub it in ! = *n'insistez pas aussi lourdement !* ⓪ let it drop ! = *laissez tomber !*
to rub off onto s.o. = *déteindre sur qqn* : after ten years of marriage, her bad temper rubbed off onto him = *après dix ans de mariage, son mauvais caractère a déteint sur lui* ⓪ to leave one's mark on = *laisser son empreinte sur*
to rub s.o. out = *zigouiller qqn* : the gang rubbed him out = *le gang l'a zigouillé* ⓪ to do in = *refroidir*
☠ *ne vous y frottez pas !* = don't get mixed up in it !
— *ne vous frottez pas à lui !* = don't tangle with him !
— *frotter le plancher* = to scrub the floor.

RUBBER (n) 1/ *caoutchouc (m)* : made of rubber = *en caoutchouc* 2/ *capote (f) anglaise* : my husband uses rubbers = *mon mari utilise des capotes anglaises* ⓪ pill = *pilule*
a rubber band = *un élastique*.

RUBBERS (n pl) *bottes (f pl) en caoutchouc* : to wear rubbers = *porter des bottes en caoutchouc* = to wear galoshes.

RUBBISH (n inv) 1/ *sottises (f pl)* : what you're saying's a lot of rubbish ! = *tu racontes des sottises !* ⓪ nonsense = *bêtises*, hooey = *sornettes* ☠ *faire des sottises* = to act foolishly 2/ (GB) *détritus (m)* : the streets are filled with rubbish = *les rues sont pleines de détritus* ⓪ garbage = *ordures*.

RUBDOWN (n) *massage (m)* : to give s.o. a rubdown = *faire un massage à qqn* = to give s.o. a massage.

RUBY (n, -ies) *rubis (m)* : a ruby ring = *une bague en rubis* ⓪ emerald = *émeraude* ☠ *payer rubis sur l'ongle* = to pay cash on the nail.

RUDE (adj, -r, -st) *grossier, -ère* : rude children = *des enfants grossiers* ⓪ rudeness = *grossièreté* ≠ well-mannered = *bien éduqué*, courteous = *courtois*
don't be rude to (your mother) = *ne sois pas grossier avec (ta mère)*
to have a rude awakening = *avoir un réveil pénible*
☠ *grossier* → coarse
— *une rude journée/un rude hiver* = a rough day/harsh winter
— *avoir été à rude école* = to have been to the school of hard knocks.

RUDELY (adv) *grossièrement* : to answer rudely = *répondre grossièrement* ⓪ impolitely = *impoliment*
☠ *expliquer grossièrement qqch* = to explain stg roughly
— *se tromper grossièrement* = to be sadly mistaken.

RUDIMENTARY (adj) *rudimentaire* : rudimentary knowledge of the problem = *une connaissance rudimentaire de la question.*

RUE (to, -d) *regretter amèrement* : you'll rue telling her = *vous regretterez amèrement de le lui avoir dit* ⊙ to lament = *déplorer.*

RUFFIAN (n) *vaurien, -enne* : her bag was stolen by a gang of ruffians = *une bande de vauriens lui a volé son sac* ⊙ hoodlum = *loubard.*

RUG (n) *tapis (m)* : a thick green rug = *un épais tapis vert* ⊙ linoleum = ←, carpet sweeper = *balai mécanique*, wall-to-wall carpeting = *moquette*
to pull the rug out from under s.o. = *couper l'herbe sous les pieds de qqn* ⊙ to steal s.o.'s thunder = *couper ses effets à qqn*
☠ *mettre (un sujet) sur le tapis* = to bring (a subject) up.

RUGBY (n, -ies) *rugby (m)* : to play rugby = *jouer au rugby.*

RUGGED (adj) *buriné, -e* : he has rugged features = *il a des traits burinés* ⊙ craggy = *taillé à coups de hache* ≠ fragile = ←.

RUIN (n) 1/ *ruine (f)* : the ruins of Rome = *les ruines de Rome* ⊙ destruction = ← 2/ *ruine (f)* : drink was the ruin of the two brothers = *l'alcoolisme a été la ruine des deux frères* ⊙ undoing = *perte* ☠ *c'est la ruine !* = it's ruinous !

RUIN (to, -ed) 1/ *ruiner* : the stock market crash ruined him = *le krach boursier l'a ruiné* ⊙ to wipe out = *ratisser* 2/ *gâcher* : the bad weather ruined our trip = *le mauvais temps a gâché notre voyage* = to spoil ≠ to make = *transformer* ☠ → to spoil.

RUINOUS (adj) *ruineux, -euse* : the rent is ruinous = *le loyer est ruineux* ⊙ expensive = *cher.*

RULE (n) *règle (f)* : you have to follow the rules = *il faut suivre les règles* ⊙ regulation = *règlement*
as a rule (he comes on time) = *en règle générale (il arrive à l'heure)* ⊙ more often than not = *le plus souvent*
to do stg by the rules = *faire qqch en suivant la règle*
(to follow) the rules and regulations = *(suivre) le règlement*

it's against the rules = *c'est contraire aux règles*
the rule of (Hitler) = *le règne de (Hitler)*
the rules of the game = *les règles du jeu* → THAT'S LIFE !
☠ *avoir ses règles* = to have one's period
— *mettre les choses en règle* = to put things in order
— *une règle (mesure)* = a ruler.

RULE (to, -d) *diriger* : to rule a country = *diriger un pays* ⊙ to govern = *gouverner*, to command = *commander*
(the judge) ruled that (the company must pay for damages) = *(le juge) a décidé que (l'entreprise devait payer les dommages)* ⊙ to judge = *juger*
to rule stg out = *écarter qqch* : rule that possibility out = *écartez cette possibilité*, murder was ruled out = *l'éventualité du meurtre a été écartée* ≠ to take into consideration = *prendre en considération*
☠ → to direct.

RULER (n) 1/ *règle (f)* : to draw a line with a ruler = *tirer un trait avec une règle* ☠ → rule 2/ *dirigeant, -e* : a people and its rulers = *un peuple et ses dirigeants* ⊙ chief of State = *chef d'État*, sovereign = *souverain*
☠ *dirigeant (parti politique)* = leader
— *dirigeant (entreprise)* = manager.

RULING (n) *décision (f)* : that was the judge's ruling = *telle a été la décision du juge* ☠ → decision.

RULING (adj) **the ruling party/classes** = *le parti au pouvoir/les classes dirigeantes.*

RUM (n) *rhum (m)* ⊙ punch = ←.

RUMBLE (n) *rififi (m)* : nightly rumbles on the West Side = *du rififi toutes les nuits dans le quartier ouest* ⊙ brawl = *rixe.*

RUMMAGE SALE (n) *vente (f) de charité* ⊙ jumble sale = *braderie.*

RUMMAGE THROUGH (to, -d) *farfouiller dans* : to rummage through a drawer = *farfouiller dans un tiroir.*

RUMOR (n) *rumeur (f)* : that's just a rumor = *ce n'est qu'une rumeur* = rumour (GB) ⊙ hearsay = *ouï-dire*
rumor has it that (he's dead) = *le bruit court qu'(il est mort)* ⊙ it's said that = *on dit que.*

RUMPUS (n inv) *boucan (m)* : to make a rumpus = *faire du boucan* ⊙ row = *tapage.*

RUN (n) **to be on the run** = 1/ *être en cavale* : the three gangsters are still on the run = *les trois gangsters sont toujours en cavale* ⊙ to be on the lam = *être en fuite* 2/ *être sur la brèche* : I've been on the run since the morning = *je suis sur la brèche depuis ce matin*
to give s.o. a run for his money = *en donner à qqn pour son argent* : the football match was great, it gave us a run for our money = *le match de foot était super, on en a eu pour notre argent*
to have the run of (the place) = *être le roi de*

(*l'endroit*) : the dog has the run of the hotel = *le chien est le roi de l'hôtel*
to have a run in one's stocking = *avoir une maille filée/une échelle à un bas* = to have a ladder in one's stocking (GB)
the play had a short ≠ **long run** = *la pièce n'a pas tenu* ≠ *a tenu longtemps l'affiche*
a run of (nice ≠ **bad weather)** = *une période de (beau* ≠ *mauvais temps)*
a run on (sugar/the pound) = *une ruée sur (le sucre/la livre).*

RUN (to, ran, run) **1/** *courir* : he runs in the park every day = *il court dans le parc tous les jours* ⓪ to jog = *faire du footing* ≠ to walk = *marcher*

(he wants) to run before he can walk = *(il veut) voler avant d'avoir des ailes* ⓪ to put the cart before the horse = *mettre la charrue avant les bœufs*	**my nose/the water is running** = *j'ai le nez qui coule/l'eau coule* **what makes him run ?** = *qu'est-ce qui le fait courir ?*
☠ *tu peux toujours courir !* = you can whistle for it ! — *laisse courir !* = let it drop !	— *courir à (sa perte)* = to be heading for (disaster) — *courir sa chance* = to try one's luck

2/ *diriger* : to run a business = *diriger une affaire* ⓪ to manage = *gérer* ☠ → to direct
3/ *se présenter* : is he running or not ? = *est-ce qu'il se présente ou pas ?* ⓪ to be a candidate = *être candidat* ☠ → to present
4/ *marcher* : are the buses/trains running today ? = *est-ce que les bus/les trains marchent aujourd'hui ?* ☠ → to walk
5/ *faire paraître* : the papers ran the story on the first page = *les journaux ont fait paraître l'affaire en première page* ⓪ to publish = *publier*
6/ *déteindre* : this color runs = *cette couleur déteint* ☠ *déteindre sur qqn* = ro rub off onto s.o.
7/ *tenir l'affiche* : the play's been running for two years = *la pièce tient l'affiche depuis deux ans* ⓪ to play = *se jouer*

to run across = 1/ *tomber sur* : I ran across an old Garland record = *je suis tombée sur un vieux disque de Garland* 2/ *traverser en courant* : he was hit by a car when he ran across the street = *il a été heurté par une voiture alors qu'il traversait la rue en courant*
to run after = *courir après* : she ran after her husband/the guy who stole her bag = *elle a couru après son mari/le type qui lui avait volé son sac* ⓪ to pursue = *poursuivre*
to run around = *courir le jupon/les hommes* : being married doesn't stop him/her from running around = *le fait d'être marié(e) ne l'empêche pas de courir le jupon/les hommes* = to play around ≠ to be faithful = *être fidèle*
to run away from (home/school) = *faire une fugue (maison/école)* ⓪ to fly the coop = *prendre la clef des champs*
to run away with = 1/ *(se laisser) emporter par* : his enthusiasm ran away with him = *il s'est laissé emporter par son enthousiasme* 2/ *gagner dans un fauteuil* : their team ran away with the title = *leur équipe a gagné le titre dans un fauteuil* ⓪ to win hands down = *gagner*

haut la main
to run down = 1/ *renverser* : he was run down by a truck = *il a été renversé par un camion* ⓪ to run over = *écraser* ☠ → to spill 2/ *dénigrer* : she's always running her husband down = *elle est toujours en train de dénigrer son mari* ⓪ to put down = *débiner*
to run for = *se présenter à* : to run for President = *se présenter à la présidence*
run for it ! = *22, v'là les flics !* = the cops are coming !
to run s.o. in = *emmener qqn au poste* : the cops ran him in = *les flics l'ont emmené au poste* ⓪ to lock up = *boucler*
to run in ≠ **out** = *entrer* ≠ *sortir en courant* : he ran into ≠ out of the room = *il est entré en courant dans* ≠ *sorti en courant de la pièce* ⓪ to barge in = *faire irruption dans*
to run into = 1/ *tomber sur* : I ran into him on Broadway = *je suis tombé sur lui à Broadway* = to run across ⓪ to bump into = *rencontrer par hasard* 2/ *se heurter à* : to run into problems = *se heurter à des problèmes* ⓪ to meet with = *rencontrer* 3/ *s'élever à* : the repairs ran into thousands of dollars = *les réparations se sont élevées à des mil-

liers de dollars
to run off = *tirer à* : to run off a thousand copies = *tirer à mille exemplaires* ⓪ to print = *imprimer*
to run off with s.o. = *partir avec qqn* : she ran off with her husband's best friend = *elle est partie avec le meilleur ami de son mari*
to run out = *se terminer* : my subscription runs out next spring = *mon abonnement se termine au printemps prochain* ⓪ to expire = *expirer* ☠ → to end
to run out of = *manquer de* : we're running out of money = *nous manquons d'argent*, what will we do when money runs out ? = *que ferons-nous quand l'argent commencera à manquer ?*
to run out on = *laisser tomber* : she ran out on him = *elle l'a laissé tomber* ⓪ to jilt = *plaquer*
to run over = 1/ *déborder* : the river's running over = *le fleuve déborde* ☠ → to overflow 2/ *écraser* : to be run over by a car = *se faire écraser par une voiture* ☠ → to crash 3/ *durer plus de* : the speech ran over an hour = *le discours a duré plus d'une heure* 4/ *revoir* : let's run

over the figures again = *revoyons les chiffres encore une fois* = let's go over the figures again ☠ → to go over

to run over to = *faire un saut à :* to run over to the bank = *faire un saut à la banque* = to pop down to

to run through = 1/ *dilapi-der :* to run through a fortune = *dilapider une fortune* ① to blow = *claquer* 2/ *reprendre (entière-ment) :* to run through a scene/a list = *reprendre entièrement une scène/une liste* ☠ → to recapture

to run up = *laisser s'amonce-ler :* to run up bills/debts = *lais-*

ser *s'amonceler les factures/les dettes*

to run up against = *se heurter à :* he ran up against heavy oppo-sition/many problems = *il s'est heurté à une forte opposition/à de nombreux problèmes* ① to be faced with = *être en face de.*

RUNAROUND (n) **to give s.o. the runaround** = *lais-ser qqn dans le vague :* I asked him for a definite yes, but he gave me the runaround = *je lui ai demandé de me donner un oui définitif, mais il m'a laissé dans le vague* ① to give s.o. a song and a dance = *raconter des salades à qqn.*

RUNDOWN (n) *topo (m) :* his assistant gave us a run-down on the conference = *son assistant nous a fait un topo sur la conférence* ① synopsis = *compte rendu.*

RUN-DOWN (adj) 1/ *à plat :* I feel sick and run-down = *je me sens malade et à plat* ① pooped = *raplapla,* done in = *vanné* 2/ *mal entretenu, -e :* a run-down house = *une maison mal entretenue* ≠ well-kept = *bien entre-tenu.*

RUN-IN (n) *prise (f) de bec :* to have a run-in with one's parents = *avoir une prise de bec avec ses parents* ① falling-out = *brouille.*

RUNNER (n) *coureur, -euse :* a long-distance runner = *un coureur de fond*
☠ *coureur de dot* = fortune hunter
— *coureur automobile* = racing driver
— *un coureur (de filles)* = a Romeo/a womanizer.

RUNNER-UP (n) *second, -e :* he was the runner-up in the race = *il était second de la course* ① booby prize = *prix de consolation* ☠ → second.

RUNNING (n) **to be in** ≠ **out of the running** = *être* ≠ *ne plus être dans la course.*

RUNNING (adj) **for (8) days running** = *(8) jours consécutifs*
running battle = *point de litige*
running water = *eau courante*
running mate = *colistier.*

RUNOFF (n) *deuxième tour (m)* (election), *finale (f)* (race) : the runoff will be next week = *le deuxième tour/la finale aura lieu la semaine prochaine.*

RUN-OF-THE-MILL (adj) *très quelconque :* a run-of-the-mill restaurant = *un restaurant très quelconque* → AWFUL.

RUNS (n pl) **to have the runs** = *avoir la courante* ① to have diarrhea = *avoir la diarrhée.*

RUNT (n) *avorton (m) :* what a runt she married ! = *quel avorton elle a épousé !* ① squirt = *petit morveux,* shorty = *microbe.*

RUNWAY (n) *piste (f) d'atterrissage* ① control tower = *tour de contrôle.*

RURAL (adj) *rural, -e :* rural life = *la vie rurale* ① city = *citadin.*

RUSE (n) *ruse (f) :* it was a ruse to get money from him = *c'était une ruse pour lui soutirer de l'argent* ① ploy = *biais.*

RUSH (n, -es) *bousculade (f), rush (m) :* the big Christmas rush = *la grande bousculade de Noël*
to be in a rush = *être pressé :* I'm in a rush, tell me what you want = *je suis pressé, dites-moi ce que vous voulez* ≠ to have plenty of time = *avoir tout son temps*
what's the rush ? = *il n'y a pas le feu !* ① hold your horses ! = *minute papillon !*

RUSH (adj) **rush hour** = *heure d'affluence* ① peak time = *heure de pointe*
rush job = *travail fait à la va-vite*
to give (a girl) a rush act = *faire du rentre-dedans à (une fille).*

RUSH (to, -ed) *se presser :* there's no need to rush = *ce n'est pas la peine de se presser* ① to hurry = *se dépê-cher* ☠ → to squeeze
don't rush me ! = *ne me brusquez pas !*
to rush a fraternity/sorority = *poser sa candidature pour un club d'étudiants/d'étudiantes*
to rush in ≠ **out** = *se précipiter à l'intérieur* ≠ *à l'extérieur :* he rushed into ≠ out of the room = *il s'est précipité à l'intérieur* ≠ *à l'extérieur de la pièce*
to rush to = *se précipiter à :* my father was sick and I rushed to New York to see him = *mon père était malade et je me suis précipité à New York pour le voir* ≠ to wait = *attendre*
to rush s.o. to (hospital) = *transporter qqn d'urgence à (l'hôpital)*
to rush through = *faire à la hâte :* we rushed through dinner = *nous avons dîné à la hâte.*

RUSHES (n pl) *rushes (m pl) :* I saw the rushes and I think it's a good film = *j'ai vu les rushes, et je pense que c'est un bon film.*

RUSSIA (n) *Russie (f)* **RUSSIAN** (n, adj) *Russe (m, f) :* Russian roulette = *roulette russe.*

RUST (n) *rouille (f)* **RUST** (to, -ed) *rouiller.*

RUSTIC (adj) *rustique :* rustic furniture = *meubles rus-tiques* ≠ modern = *moderne.*

RUSTY (adj, -ier, -iest) *rouillé, -e :* the gate/my English is rusty = *le portail/mon anglais est rouillé.*

RUT (n) **to be in a rut** = *s'encroûter :* since they're married and both working, they're in a rut = *depuis qu'ils sont mariés et qu'ils travaillent tous les deux, ils s'encroûtent.*

RUTHLESS (adj) *impitoyable :* a ruthless businessman = *un homme d'affaires impitoyable* Ⓞ pitiless = *sans pitié,* bloodthirsty = *sanguinaire* **RUTHLESSLY** (adv) *impitoyablement.*

RYE (n) *seigle (m) :* rye bread = *pain de seigle* Ⓞ wholewheat bread = *pain complet.*

SABBATICAL YEAR (n) *année (f) sabbatique.*

SABLE (n) *zibeline (f) :* a sable coat = *un manteau de zibeline.*

SABOTAGE (n) *sabotage (m) :* a case of sabotage = *un cas de sabotage* ⓒ saboteur = ← **SABOTAGE** (to, -d) *saboter :* they sabotaged our efforts = *ils ont saboté nos efforts* ☠ *il a saboté le boulot* = he botched up the job.

SACK (n) *sac (m) :* a sack of potatoes = *un sac de pommes de terre* ☠ → bag
to hit the sack = *aller au plumard* ⓒ to sack out = *aller pioncer*

SACK (to, -ed) **1/** *mettre à sac :* the entire area was sacked = *la région tout entière a été mise à sac* ⓒ to plunder = *piller* **2/** *sacquer :* he was sacked after a week = *on l'a sacqué au bout d'une semaine* ⓒ to oust = *vider* ≠ to take on = *embaucher* ☠ *je ne peux pas le sacquer* = I can't stand him
to sack out = *aller pioncer :* it's time to sack out = *c'est l'heure d'aller pioncer* ⓒ to hit the hay = *aller se pieuter.*

SACRED (adj) *sacré, -e :* parents are sacred = *les parents, c'est sacré* ≠ profane = ←
☠ *tu as une sacrée veine !* = you're damn lucky !
— *tu es un sacré imbécile !* = you're a damned fool !

SACRIFICE (n) *sacrifice (m) :* we make too many sacrifices = *nous faisons trop de sacrifices*
to sell at a sacrifice = *vendre à des prix sacrifiés.*

SACRIFICE (to, -d) *sacrifier :* she sacrificed her career to raise her children = *elle a sacrifié sa carrière pour élever ses enfants.*

SACRILEGE (n) *sacrilège (m) :* it would be a sacrilege to replace the park by a high-rise = *ce serait un sacrilège de remplacer le parc par une tour.*

SAD (adj, -der, -dest) *triste :* why are you so sad ? = *pourquoi êtes-vous si triste ?* ⓒ downcast = *abattu* ≠ happy = *heureux*
to be a sad sack = *faire une gueule d'enterrement :* her husband's a sad sack = *son mari fait une gueule d'enterrement* ⓒ a gloomy gus = *un ténébreux* ☠ *faire triste mine* = to cut a sorry figure.

SADDEN (to, -ed) *attrister :* it saddens me to see her so unhappy = *ça m'attriste de la voir si malheureuse* ⓒ to depress = *déprimer* ≠ to fill with joy = *remplir de joie.*

SADDLE (n) *selle (f) :* I ride without a saddle = *je monte sans selle* ⓒ reins = *rênes,* harness = *harnais.*

SADDLE (to, -d) **to be saddled with** = *avoir sur le dos :* he's saddled with responsibilities = *il a des tas de responsabilités sur le dos* ⓒ to be loaded with = *être bourré de.*

SADISM (n) *sadisme (m)* ⓒ masochism = *masochisme* **SADIST** (n) *sadique (m, f) :* her husband's a sadist = *son mari est un sadique* ⓒ masochist = *masochiste* **SADISTIC** (adj) *sadique :* a sadistic husband = *un mari sadique* ⓒ masochistic = *masochiste.*

SADLY (adv) *tristement :* she looked at him very sadly = *elle l'a regardé très tristement*
to be sadly mistaken = *se tromper lourdement* ⓒ to be all wet = *se mettre le doigt dans l'œil.*

SADNESS (n inv) *tristesse (f) :* what sadness in her eyes ! = *quelle tristesse dans ses yeux !* ≠ joy = *joie.*

SADOMASOCHISM (n) *sadomasochisme (m) :* many couples are into sadomasochism = *nombreux sont les couples qui donnent dans le sadomasochisme* = S-M.

SAFARI (n) *safari (m) :* we're going on a safari = *nous allons faire un safari* ⓒ jungle = ←.

SAFE (n) *coffre-fort (m) :* he has a safe in his office = *il a un coffre-fort dans son bureau* ⓒ safe-deposit box = *coffre (banque)*
to crack a safe = *percer un coffre(-fort).*

SAFE (adj, -r, -st) **1/** *sauf, sauve :* all the passengers are safe = *tous les passagers sont saufs* ≠ in danger = *en danger* **2/** *sûr, -e :* a safe investment = *un investissement sûr,* a safe part of town = *un quartier sûr* ≠ precarious = *précaire,* risky = *risqué* ☠ → sure
to be on the safe side (let's take more money) = *pour plus de sûreté (prenons plus d'argent)*
in a safe place = *en lieu sûr*
to play it safe = *jouer sur du velours* ≠ to take chances = *prendre des risques*
safe and sound = *sain et sauf.*

SAFECRACKER (n) *perceur, -euse de coffres-forts* : Holtz is a well-known safecracker = *Holtz est un célèbre perceur de coffres-forts* ⓓ thief = *voleur.*

SAFEGUARD (n) *garantie (f), sauvegarde (f)* : it's a safeguard against unemployment = *c'est une garantie/une sauvegarde contre le chômage* ☠ → guarantee.

SAFEGUARD (to, -ed) *sauvegarder* : to safeguard one's virginity = *sauvegarder sa virginité* ⓓ to defend = *défendre.*

SAFEKEEPING (n) **for safekeeping** = *pour plus de sécurité* : put the policies in the safe-deposit box for safekeeping = *pour plus de sécurité, mettez les polices d'assurance dans un coffre à la banque.*

SAFETY (n, -ies) *sécurité (f)* : we're responsible for the safety of the children = *nous sommes responsables de la sécurité des enfants*
for safety's sake = *par mesure de sécurité*
safety pin = *épingle de nourrice/sûreté*
safety valve = *soupape de sûreté*
☠ → security.

SAG (to, -ged) *s'affaisser* : her breasts sag = *ses seins s'affaissent* ☠ *s'affaisser dans un fauteuil* = to slump into a chair.

SAGA (n) *saga (f)* : the story of her three marriages is a whole saga = *l'histoire de ses trois mariages, c'est une vraie saga* ⓓ epic = *épopée.*

SAIL (n) *voile (f)* : one of the sails is torn = *une des voiles est déchirée* ⓓ sailboat = *bateau à voiles/voilier*
☠ *marcher à voile et à vapeur* = to swing both ways
— *on met les voiles !* = let's split !
— *faire de la voile* = to go sailing
— *un voile* = a veil.

SAIL (to, -ed) **to go sailing** = *faire de la voile* : we went sailing in the bay for a week = *nous avons fait de la voile dans la baie pendant une semaine*
to sail through (a test) = *réussir (un examen) haut la main* ⓓ to waltz through = *réussir les doigts dans le nez.*

SAILING (n inv) *voile (f) (sport)* : do you like sailing ? = *aimez-vous la voile ?* ⓓ sailboat = *voilier*
to be plain/smooth sailing = *marcher comme sur des roulettes* : the exam was plain/smooth sailing = *l'examen a marché comme sur des roulettes* ≠ to hit a snag = *tomber sur un os*
☠ → sail.

SAILOR (n) *marin (m)* : she married a sailor = *elle a épousé un marin* ⓓ seaman = *matelot*, marine = ← ☠ *marin d'eau douce* = landlubber.

SAINT (n) *saint, -e* : my husband's a saint = *mon mari est un saint*
☠ *prêcher pour son saint* = to look out for one's own interest
— *ne plus savoir à quel saint se vouer* = not to know which way to turn.

SAKE (n) **for (my) sake** = *pour (moi)* : do it for my sake = *faites-le pour moi*
for the sake of appearances = *pour sauver les apparences*
for the sake of argument = *pour les besoins de la cause*
just for the sake of it = *juste comme ça* ⓓ for the fun of it = *histoire de rigoler.*

SALAD (n) *salade (f)* : I'd like a salad with my steak = *j'aimerais une salade avec mon steak*, tossed salad = *salade composée* ⓓ salad bowl = *saladier*, dressing = *assaisonnement*, lettuce = *laitue*, coleslaw = *salade de chou cru*
☠ *arrête tes salades !* = cut the jazz !
— *quelle salade !* = what a mix-up !

SALAMI (n) *salami (m) (saucisson sec)* : a salami sandwich = *un sandwich au salami* ⓓ sausage = *saucisse.*

SALARIED (adj) *salarié, -e* : salaried work/workers = *travail salarié/travailleurs salariés.*

SALARY (n, -ies) *salaire (m), cachet (m) (show business)* : to earn a high salary = *avoir un salaire élevé*, a performer's salary = *le cachet d'un artiste* ⓓ pay = *paye*, stipend = *traitement*, fee = *honoraires*
☠ *cachet* → tablet
— *gel des/conflit sur les salaires* = wage freeze/dispute.

SALE (n) 1/ *vente (f)* : the salesman made his first sale = *le vendeur a fait sa première vente* ≠ purchase = *achat* 2/ *soldes (m pl)* : there's a fantastic sale at Sak's today = *il y a des soldes fantastiques à Sak's aujourd'hui* ⓓ clearance sale = *liquidation*
to be on sale = *être en solde* : their skirts are on sale = *leurs jupes sont en solde*
for sale = *en vente/à vendre*
sales talk = *argument(s) de vente* ⓓ pitch = *boniment*
sales tax = *taxe à l'achat*
sales manager = *directeur des ventes*
sales department = *service commercial*
sales rep = *représentant*
☠ *être à la solde de qqn* = to be in the pay of s.o.
— *le solde d'un compte* = the balance of an account.

SALESMAN (n, -men) *vendeur (m)* : a dynamic salesman = *un vendeur dynamique*
traveling salesman = *voyageur de commerce/VRP*
☠ *est-il vendeur (de son appartement) ?* = is he selling (his apartment) ?
— *acheteurs et vendeurs* = buyers and sellers.

SALESWOMAN (n, -women) *vendeuse (f).*

SALIVA (n) *salive (f)* ⓓ spit = *crachat* ☠ *user sa salive pour rien* = to waste one's breath.

SALLOW (adj, -er, -est) *cireux, -euse* : a sallow complexion = *un teint cireux* ⓓ pallid = *blême.*

SALMON (n) *saumon (m)* : smoked salmon = *saumon fumé* = lox ⓓ tuna = *thon.*

SALOON (n) *saloon (m)* : saloons in the Far West = *les saloons du Far West* ⓪ bar = ←.

SALT (n) *sel (m)* : the steak needs more salt = *le steak manque de sel* ⓪ salty = *salé*, pepper = *poivre*
to be worth one's salt = *valoir le pain qu'on mange* : his lawyer isn't worth his salt = *son avocat ne vaut pas le pain qu'il mange*
the salt of the earth = *le sel de la terre*
to take stg with a grain/pinch of salt = *ne pas prendre qqch au pied de la lettre*
smelling salts = *des sels.*

SALT (abbr) = Strategic Arms Limitation Talks = *Entretiens sur la limitation des armements stratégiques* ⓪ North-South dialogue = *dialogue Nord-Sud.*

SALTPETER (n) *bromure (m)* : soldiers are often given saltpeter = *on donne souvent du bromure aux soldats* ≠ Spanish fly = *poudre de corne de rhinocéros.*

SALUTE (to, -d) *saluer* : the soldiers saluted = *les soldats ont salué.* ⓪ to be standing at attention = *être au garde-à-vous*
☠ *salue-le pour moi !* = say hello to him !
— *saluer (artistes)* = to bow to the public.

SALVAGE (to, -d) *sauver* : we salvaged what we could from the wreck = *nous avons sauvé ce que nous avons pu de l'épave* ☠ → to save.

SALVATION (n) *salut (m)* : falling in love was his salvation = *ça a été son salut de tomber amoureux*
Salvation Army = *Armée du salut*
☠ *un salut* = a salute.

SAME (adj) *même* : we're in the same class = *nous sommes dans la même classe* ⓪ identical = *identique* ≠ different = *différent*

at the same time = 1/ *en même temps* : she knits and watches TV at the same time = *elle tricote et regarde la télé en même temps* ⓪ at once = *à la fois* 2/ *en même temps* : she has a bad temper but at the same time is a lovely person = *elle a mauvais caractère, mais en même temps c'est quelqu'un de charmant* ⓪ yet = *pourtant*
to be in the same boat = *être dans la même galère* ⓪ to be in it together = *être logés à la même enseigne*
by the same token = *par la même occasion* : sure buying an

apartment's a lot of money but by the same token, it's a good investment = *bien sûr que cela coûte cher d'acheter un appartement, mais par la même occasion, c'est un bon investissement*
it all comes down/amounts to the same thing = *ça revient au même* ⓪ it's as broad as it's long = *c'est kif-kif*
it's the same old story/thing ! = *c'est toujours la même histoire/chanson !* → THAT'S LIFE !
the same ... as = *le même ... que* : the same turtleneck as mine = *le même col roulé que le mien*

the same ... that = *le même ... que* : she wore the same dress that you did = *elle portait la même robe que vous*
to see (it) the same way = *voir de la même manière* : I'm afraid we don't see things the same way = *j'ai bien peur que nous ne voyions pas les choses de la même manière*
you can't talk about (French wines) and (American wines) in the same breath = *il ne faut pas mélanger les torchons et les serviettes ni comparer (les vins français) aux (vins américains)*

☠ *le jour même* = this very day
— *être à mettre dans le même panier/sac* = to be two of a kind

— *c'est la maison même où je suis né* = it's the actual house where I was born.

SAME (adv) **same as** = *exactement comme* : I have a temper same as everyone else = *j'ai mon caractère, exactement comme tout le monde* ⓪ as = *comme.*

SAME (pron) **all/just the same** = *tout de même* : I love him all/just the same = *je l'aime tout de même* ⓪ anyhow = *de toute manière*
it's all the same to me = *ça m'est complètement égal* ⓪ what do I care ? = *ça me fait une belle jambe*
much the same = *inchangé* : his condition is much the same = *son état est inchangé*
same as usual = *comme d'habitude*
same for = *la même chose pour* : you're having coffee ? same for me ! = *vous prenez un café ? la même chose pour moi !*
same here ! = *moi aussi !* : I'll have a Scotch ! —

same here ! = *je prendrai un whisky ! — moi aussi !*
same to you ! = *vous de même !* : Merry Christmas ! — same to you ! = *Joyeux Noël ! — vous de même !*
the same = *pareil* : my husband will have a Scotch and I'll take the same = *mon mari prendra un whisky et je prendrai pareil*
☠ *je n'ai rien fait de pareil* = I didn't do anything of the kind
— *une cruauté sans pareille* = a cruelty without parallel
— *c'est du pareil au même* = it's six of one, half a dozen of another

> — *en pareil cas* = if such is the case
> — *rendre la pareille à qqn* = to return it
> **(just) the same as** = *(exactement) le même que :*
> he's (just) the same as before = *il est (exactement) le même qu'avant*
> **(I'll do) the same for you some time !** = *à charge de revanche !* ⓓ I'll return the favor = *je vous revaudrai ça*

> **it's the same with** = *il en est de même pour :*
> things are bad for you, it's the same with me = *les choses vont mal pour vous, il en est de même pour moi*
> **to feel the same about** = *voir de la même façon :*
> I feel the same about it as you do = *je vois les choses de la même façon que vous*
> **thank you all the same** = *merci quand même.*

SAMPLE (n) *échantillon (m) :* free sample = *échantillon gratuit.*

SAMPLING (n) *échantillonnage (m) :* a recent sampling of voters = *un échantillonnage récent d'électeurs* ⓓ survey = *enquête.*

SANATORIUM (n) *sana(torium) (m) :* a sanatorium in the Alps = *un sana(torium) dans les Alpes* ⓓ asylum = *asile.*

SANCTION (n) *sanction (f) :* economic sanctions = *des sanctions économiques* ⓓ punishment = *punition* **SANCTION** (to, -ed) *sanctionner :* to sanction a country for the violation of international rules = *sanctionner un pays pour la violation des règles internationales.*

SANCTUARY (n, -ies) *sanctuaire (m) :* a bird sanctuary = *un sanctuaire pour les oiseaux* ⓓ church = *église.*

SAND (n) *sable (m) :* to lie on the sand = *être étendu sur le sable* ⓓ sandy = *sablonneux,* dune = ←.

SANDAL (n) *sandale (f) :* to wear sandals = *porter des sandales* ⓓ shoe = *chaussure.*

SANDMAN (n, -men) *marchand de sable (m)* ⓓ bogeyman = *Père Fouettard.*

SANDWICH (n, -es) *sandwich (m) :* I'll make you a ham sandwich = *je vais vous faire un sandwich au jambon* ⓓ hero sandwich = *super-club sandwich,* snack = *casse-croûte.*

SANE (adj, -r, -st) *sain, -e (d'esprit) :* it was a sane reaction = *c'était une saine réaction* ≠ insane = *insensé.*

SANITY (n, -ies) *équilibre (m) mental :* he's losing his sanity being around you = *il est en train de perdre son équilibre mental à votre contact* ≠ insanity = *démence.*

SANTA CLAUS (n) *Père Noël (m) :* I still believe in Santa Claus = *je crois toujours au Père Noël* ⓓ Saint Nick = *Saint Nicolas,* chimney = *cheminée.*

SAP (n) *jobard, -e :* you were a sap to believe her = *tu as été un vrai jobard de la croire* ⓓ sucker = *bonne poire.*

SAP (to, -ped) *saper :* your constant criticisms are sapping my morale = *vos critiques continuelles me sapent le moral* ⓓ to undermine = *miner.*

SAPPHIRE (n) *saphir (m) :* a sapphire surrounded by diamonds = *un saphir entouré de diamants* ⓓ amethyst = *améthyste.*

SARCASM (n) *sarcasme (m) :* spare me your sarcasms = *épargnez-moi vos sarcasmes* ⓓ irony = *ironie* **SARCASTIC** (adj) *sarcastique :* don't be so sarcastic = *ne soyez pas si sarcastique* ⓓ sardonic = *sardonique.*

SARDINE (n) *sardine (f) :* a can of sardines = *une boîte de sardines* ⓓ tuna = *thon.*

SASSY (adj, -ier, -iest) *outrecuidant, -e :* a sassy answer = *une réponse outrecuidante* = saucy ⓓ impudent = ←.

SATELLITE (n) *satellite (m) :* the program was broadcast by satellite = *l'émission a été retransmise par satellite* ⓓ rocket = *fusée.*

SATIATED (adj) *rassasié, -e* ⓓ stuffed = *gavé.*

SATIN (n, adj) *(de/en) satin (m) :* satine underwear = *des dessous en satin* ⓓ sateen = *satinette.*

SATIRE (n) *satire (f) :* his play's a violent satire against society = *sa pièce est une violente satire de la société* ⓓ mockery = *parodie* **SATIRICAL** (adj) *satirique* ⓓ ironic = *ironique* **SATIRIZE** (to, -d) *faire la satire de :* this novel satirizes life in Washington = *ce roman fait la satire de la vie à Washington* ⓓ to do a takeoff of = *faire une caricature de.*

SATISFACTION (n) *satisfaction (f) :* a feeling of satisfaction = *un sentiment de satisfaction* ⓓ contentment = *contentement*
to get satisfaction out of (one's work) = *tirer satisfaction de (son travail)* ⓓ to take pleasure in = *prendre plaisir à.*

SATISFACTORY (adj) *satisfaisant, -e :* satisfactory results = *des résultats satisfaisants* ⓓ acceptable = ← **SATISFACTORILY** (adv) *d'une façon satisfaisante.*

SATISFIED (adj) *satisfait, -e :* satisfied clients = *des clients satisfaits* ≠ dissatisfied = *insatisfait.*

SATISFY (to, -ied) *satisfaire :* she satisfies his need for a victim = *elle satisfait son besoin d'avoir une victime*
to be satisfied with (one's work) = *être satisfait de (son travail)* ⓓ tickled pink = *aux anges.*

SATISFYING (adj) *qui apporte des satisfactions :* satisfying work = *un travail qui apporte des satisfactions* ⓓ gratifying = *gratifiant* ≠ dissatisfying = *peu satisfaisant.*

SATURATE (to, -d) *saturer :* the highway's always saturated at 6 p.m. = *l'autoroute est toujours saturée à 6 heures du soir* ⓓ to fill = *remplir.*

SATURDAY (n) *samedi* (m) : I'll see you on Saturday = *je vous verrai samedi* ⓓ Sabbath = *sabbat* → WEEK.

SAUCE (n) *sauce* (f) : a delicious sauce = *une sauce délicieuse* ⓓ sauceboat = *saucière*, gravy = *jus de viande* ☠ *à quelle sauce sera-t-il mangé ?* = what's in store for him ?

SAUCER (n) *soucoupe* (f) : a cup and saucer = *une tasse et une soucoupe*
flying saucer = *soucoupe volante* ⓓ UFO = *OVNI.*

SAUCY (adj, -ier, -iest) = SASSY.

SAUDI ARABIA (n) *Arabie Saoudite* (f) ⓓ sheikh = *cheikh.*

SAUERKRAUT (n) *choucroute* (f) : I love sauerkraut with sausages = *j'adore la choucroute avec des saucisses.*

SAUNA (n) *sauna* (m) ⓓ steam bath = *bain de vapeur.*

SAUSAGE (n) *saucisse* (f) : scrambled eggs with sausages = *des œufs brouillés avec des saucisses* ⓓ hot dog = *hot-dog.*

SAVAGE (n) *sauvage* (m, f) : they lived among savages = *ils ont vécu parmi les sauvages* ⓓ tribe = *tribu.*

SAVAGE (adj) *sauvage* : a savage attack = *une attaque sauvage* ⓓ fierce = *féroce*
☠ *un animal sauvage* = a wild animal
— *elle est très sauvage* = she's people shy
— *une grève sauvage* = a wildcat strike
— *camping sauvage* = unauthorized camping.

SAVE (to, -d) **1/** *sauver* : the doctor saved him = *le docteur l'a sauvé*
☠ *il est tard, je me sauve* = it's late, I must be off
— *le chat s'est sauvé* = the cat ran away
— *sauve qui peut !* = every man for himself !
— *sauver qqch (d'un naufrage)* = to salvage stg (from a wreck)
2/ *économiser* : if you buy five of them, you'll save ten bucks = *si vous en achetez cinq, vous économiserez dix dollars*, with my salary, I can hardly save $ 50 a month = *avec mon salaire, je peux à peine économiser 50 dollars par mois* ≠ to spend = *dépenser* ☠ → to economize
3/ *garder* : I'm saving the cake for later = *je garde le gâteau pour plus tard* ☠ → to guard.
it will save us (2 hours/$ 20) = *cela va nous faire gagner (2 heures/20 dollars)*
to save s.o. from = *sauver qqn de* : save me from myself = *sauvez-moi de moi-même*
to save up = *faire des économies* : she's saving up to buy a new car = *elle fait des économies pour acheter une nouvelle voiture.*

SAVE (prep) *hormis* : they have little in common save their hatred of the boss = *ils ont peu de choses en commun, hormis la haine de leur patron* ⓓ but = *sauf.*

SAVING (n) *économie* (f) : a saving of three percent = *une économie de trois pour cent.*

SAVING (adj) **(his sense of humor) is his saving grace** = *c'est (son sens de l'humour) qui le sauve.*

SAVINGS (n pl) *économies* (f pl) : their savings amount to little = *leurs économies se montent à peu de chose* ⓓ nest egg = *bas de laine*
savings account = *compte d'épargne*
savings bank = *caisse d'épargne.*

SAVIOR (n) **the Savior** = *le Sauveur* = the Saviour (GB) ⓓ God = *Dieu.*

SAVORY (adj) *savoureux, -euse* : a savory sauce = *une sauce savoureuse* ≠ tasteless = *sans goût.*

SAVVY (n, -ies) *sens* (m) : he has a lot of political savvy = *il a beaucoup de sens politique* ⓓ knowhow = *knowhow/savoir faire* ☠ → sense.

SAW (n) *scie* (f) : electric saw = *scie électrique* ⓓ sawdust = *sciure* **SAW** (to, -ed, -ed or sawn) *scier* : to saw a log = *scier une bûche* ☠ *ça m'a scié* = I was flabbergasted.

SAXOPHONE (n) *saxo(phone)* (m) ⓓ clarinet = *clarinette.*

SAY (n) **to have one's say** ≠ **to have no say in the matter** = *avoir son mot à dire/avoir voix au chapitre* ≠ *ne pas avoir voix au chapitre.*

SAY (to, said, said) *dire* : "I'm tired" she said = *« je suis fatiguée »*, *dit-elle*, the radio said it was going to snow = *la radio a dit qu'il allait neiger*

———— TO SAY = DIRE = TO TELL ————

(discours indirect, avec complément d'objet)	(discours direct)
— he said **to** { me / you / him/her / us / them } that he was tired	— he told { me / you / him/her / us / them } that he was tired

I'd say (he's fifty) = *je dirais qu'(il a cinquante ans)*	**I should say no !** = *absolument pas !*	**I should say so !** = *et comment donc !*

that's not for me to say = *ce n'est pas moi qui peux le dire* **it's said that (the president will retire soon)** = *on dit que (le président va bientôt prendre sa retraite)* **let's say (a hundred dollars)** = *disons (cent dollars)* **say when** = *vous m'arrêtez : I'll pour the Scotch, say when* = *je verse le whisky, vous m'ar-*	*rêtez* **says who ?** = *sur les ordres de qui ? : I have to type that again, says who ?* = *il faut que je retape ça, et sur les ordres de qui ?* **there's no saying (when he'll come)** = *on ne peut pas dire (quand il arrivera)* **what do you say ?** = *qu'en dites-vous ?*	**what he says goes** = *c'est lui le patron* **you can say that again !** = *à qui le dites-vous !* ① *you know it !* = *tu parles !* **you don't say !** = *pas possible !* ① *you're so right* = *vous avez cent fois raison* **you said it !** = *tu l'as dit (bouffi) !*

say no more about it ! = *n'en parlons plus !* **that doesn't say much for (his intelligence)** = *ça en dit long sur (son intelligence)* **there's a lot to be said for (this policy)** = *(cette*	*politique) peut se défendre* **what would you say to (a stiff Scotch) ?** = *que diriez-vous d'(un whisky bien tassé) ?* ① *how about ... ?* = *et si ... ?*

☠ *dire du bien ≠ du mal de qqn* = to speak well ≠ ill of s.o. — *on dirait qu'(il va neiger)* = it looks like (it's going to snow) — *dis donc !* = hey ! — *cela vous dit (d'aller voir ce film) ?* = would you like (to see this film) ? — *qu'est-ce qui me dit que ... ?* = how do I know whether ... ?	— *puisque je vous le dis !* = you can take that from me ! — *j'ai entendu dire que ...* = I heard that ... — *dire un secret* = to tell a secret — *je me suis dit que ...* = I thought that ... — *comment dire ?* = how can I put it ? — *cela me dit quelque chose* = it rings a bell ≠ *cela ne me dit rien* = it doesn't ring a bell.

SAYING (n) *dicton* (m) : "once bitten twice shy" is a saying = « *chat échaudé craint l'eau froide* » *est un dicton* ① proverb = *proverbe*
as the saying goes = *comme dit le proverbe* ① as they say = *comme on dit.*

SAY-SO (n) **on (his lawyer's) say-so** = *sur les dires de (son avocat).*

SCADS (n pl) **scads of (money)** = *(de l'argent) à foison* → MANY.

SCALD (to, -ed) *ébouillanter* : I scalded my hand in hot water = *je me suis ébouillanté la main avec de l'eau brûlante* ① to scorch = *cramer.*

SCALE (n) *balance* (f) : to weigh oneself on the scale(s) = *se peser sur la balance*
on a large ≠ small scale = *sur une grande ≠ petite échelle*
to tip the scale(s) = *faire pencher la balance*
☠ → balance.

SCALE DOWN (to, -d) *réduire proportionnellement* : to scale down federal expenses = *réduire proportionnellement les dépenses de l'État* ① to cut back = *réduire.*

SCALLION (n) *échalote* (f) ① garlic = *ail.*

SCALLOP (n) *coquille* (f) *Saint-Jacques* ① shellfish = *coquillages.*

SCALP (n) *cuir* (m) *chevelu, scalp* (m) : he shaves his scalp = *il se rase le cuir chevelu* ① skull = *crâne,* dandruff = *pellicule.*

SCAM (n) *scandale* (m) *financier* : the latest scam in Washington = *le dernier scandale financier à Washington* ① swindle = *escroquerie.*

SCAN (to, -ned) *parcourir des yeux* : to scan a report = *parcourir un rapport des yeux* ① to peruse = *lire attentivement.*

SCANDAL (n) *scandale* (m) : sex scandals in Washington = *des scandales sexuels à Washington* ① fuss = *histoire*
it's a scandal that (we're paid so little) = *c'est un scandale que (nous soyons si mal payés)* ① it's a disgrace that = *c'est une honte que.*

SCANDALIZE (to, -d) *scandaliser* : she scandalizes her family with her vocabulary = *elle scandalise sa famille avec son vocabulaire* ① to shock = *choquer.*

SCANDALOUS (adj) *scandaleux, -euse* : scandalous behavior = *comportement scandaleux* ① shocking = *choquant.*

SCANDINAVIA (n) *Scandinavie* (f) ① Sweden = *Suède,* Norway = *Norvège,* Denmark = *Danemark,* Finland = *Finlande,* Iceland = *Islande* **SCANDINAVIAN** (n, adj) *Scandinave* (m, f).

SCANTY (adj, -ier, -iest) *maigre* : a scanty dinner = *un maigre dîner ≠* abundant = *abondant* ☠ → meager.

SCAPEGOAT (n) *bouc* (m) *émissaire* : everyone needs a scapegoat = *tout le monde a besoin d'un bouc émissaire* ① patsy = *dindon de la farce.*

SCAR (n) *cicatrice* *(f)* : a scar on my leg = *une cicatrice à la jambe* ⒹⒹ gash = *balafre*.

SCARCE (adj, -r, -st) *peu abondant, -e* : meat was scarce during the war = *la viande était peu abondante pendant la guerre* ⒹⒹ rare = ←
to make oneself scarce = *se faire oublier* : mom's mad, make yourself scarce ! = *maman est furieuse, fais-toi oublier !* ⒹⒹ to lie low = *se tenir coi*.

SCARCELY (adv) *à peine* : I scarcely have money left = *il me reste à peine d'argent* = hardly ⒹⒹ almost = *presque*
scarcely ever = *presque jamais*.

SCARCITY (n, -ies) *rareté* *(f)* : the scarcity of oil in Europe = *la rareté du pétrole en Europe* ≠ surplus = ←
there's a scarcity of (motivated students at the university) = *il y a peu d'(étudiants motivés à l'université)*.

SCARE (n) **you gave me such a scare !** = *tu m'as fait une de ces peurs !* ⒹⒹ fright = *frayeur*.

SCARE (to, -d) **to scare s.o.** = *faire peur à qqn* : the big dog scared me = *le gros chien m'a fait peur* ⒹⒹ to frighten = *effrayer*
to scare away/off = *faire fuir* : the dogs/the exorbitant prices scared me away/off = *les chiens/les prix exorbitants m'ont fait fuir*
to scare up = *dégoter* : can you scare up $ 100 for me ? = *est-ce que tu peux me dégoter 100 dollars ?* ⒹⒹ to dig up = *dénicher*
to be scared (to) = *avoir peur (de)* : I'm scared to stay alone at night = *j'ai peur de rester seule la nuit*
to be scared out of one's wits = *avoir une de ces frousses* ⒹⒹ **I was scared shitless** = *je les mouillais/je les avais à zéro* ⒹⒹ **to be scared silly** = *avoir la pétoche* ⒹⒹ **to be scared stiff** = *ne pas en mener large* ⒹⒹ to have the willies = *avoir la trouille* ⒹⒹ **to be scared to death** = *avoir une peur bleue* ⒹⒹ to have the jitters = *avoir la frousse*.

SCARECROW (n) **1/** *épouvantail* *(m)* : the scarecrow frightened the birds away = *l'épouvantail a fait fuir les oiseaux* **2/** *squelette* *(m)* ambulant : you've lost so much weight that you look like a scarecrow = *tu as tellement maigri que tu ressembles à un squelette ambulant* ≠ a butterball = *quelqu'un de rondelet*.

SCARED (adj) *effrayé, -e* : scared children = *des enfants effrayés* ⒹⒹ afraid = *qui a peur*.

SCAREDY-CAT (n) *trouillard, -e* : don't be such a scaredy-cat ! = *ne sois pas si trouillard !* ⒹⒹ fraidy-cat = *pétochard*.

SCARF (n, -ves) *écharpe* *(f)*, *foulard* *(m)* : I have scarves of every color = *j'ai des écharpes/des foulards de toutes les couleurs* ⒹⒹ kerchief = *fichu*.

SCARLET (n, adj) *écarlate* *(f)* : a scarlet cloak = *une cape écarlate* ⒹⒹ violet = ←
scarlet fever = *scarlatine*.

SCARY (adj, -ier, -iest) *qui fait peur* : a scary story = *une histoire qui fait peur* ⒹⒹ hair-raising = *à faire dresser les cheveux sur la tête*.

SCATHING (adj) *foudroyant, -e* : a scathing answer/attack = *une réponse/attaque foudroyante* ⒹⒹ stinging = *cuisant* ☠ *un succès foudroyant* = a terrific success.

SCATTER (to, -ed) *éparpiller* : papers were scattered on the desk = *il y avait des papiers éparpillés sur le bureau* ⒹⒹ to spread = *répandre* ☠ *ne vous éparpillez pas trop* = don't spread yourself too thin.

SCATTERBRAIN (n) *tête* *(f)* de linotte : he married a real scatterbrain = *il a épousé une vraie tête de linotte*
SCATTERBRAINED (adj) *étourdi, -e* : she's scatterbrained, she forgets her purse everywhere = *elle est étourdie, elle oublie son sac partout* ⒹⒹ harebrained = *foufou*.

SCENARIO (n) *scénario* *(m)* : all love stories have the same scenario = *toutes les histoires d'amour ont le même scénario* ⒹⒹ script = ←.

SCENE (n) *scène* *(f)* : she's acting in the next scene = *elle joue dans la scène suivante* ⒹⒹ act = *acte*
to appear on the scene = *entrer en scène* ⒹⒹ to come into the picture = *entrer en jeu*
(drugs) aren't my scene = *(la drogue,) ce n'est pas mon truc* ⒹⒹ it's not my cup of tea = *ce n'est pas mon genre*
(her family/the divorce) is a bad scene = *(sa famille/le divorce,) c'est quelque chose d'affreux*
behind the scenes = *dans les coulisses*
to make a scene = *faire une scène* ⒹⒹ to raise Cain = *faire un esclandre*
to make the scene = *se mettre dans le bain* : when I go to New York, I make the scene = *quand je vais à New York, je me mets dans le bain*
on the (political) scene = *sur la scène (politique)*
the scene of the crime/the accident = *le lieu du crime/de l'accident*
☠ *scène de ménage* = domestic fight
— *metteur en scène* = director
— *scène (dans un théâtre)* = stage.

SCENERY (n inv) **1/** *paysage* *(m)* : the beautiful scenery of the Rocky Mountains = *le beau paysage des montagnes Rocheuses* ⒹⒹ countryside = *campagne* **2/** *décors* *(m pl)* : the scenery is ready for the play = *les décors de la pièce sont prêts* ⒹⒹ stage = *scène*, scenic = *scénique* ☠ → decor.

SCENT (n inv) *odeur* *(f)* agréable : a scent of perfume/lilacs = *une odeur agréable de parfum/de lilas*
to follow the scent (of the killer) = *suivre la piste (du meurtrier)*
to throw s.o. off the scent = *brouiller les pistes pour qqn*.

SCHEDULE (n) **1/** *emploi* *(m)* du temps, *planning* *(m)* : I have a heavy schedule this week = *j'ai un emploi du*

temps chargé cette semaine, the factory's schedule = *le planning de la société* ⓪ program = *programme* **2/** *horaire (m)* : the train's schedule = *l'horaire du train* = the train's timetable
to be ahead of ≠ **behind schedule** = *être en avance* ≠ *en retard sur son planning*
on schedule = *à l'heure* : the rocket was launched on schedule = *la fusée a été lancée à l'heure* ≠ late = *en retard.*

SCHEDULE FOR (to, -d) *prévoir pour* : the conference was scheduled for the end of the month = *la conférence était prévue pour la fin du mois* ⓪ to program = *programmer.*

SCHEME (n)**1/** *combinaison (f)* : a scheme to make a lot of money = *une combinaison pour gagner beaucoup d'argent* ⓪ plan = ← ☠ → combination **2/** *machination (f)* : a scheme to get the control of the company/the government = *une machination pour prendre le contrôle de la société/du gouvernement* ⓪ plot = *complot.*

SCHEME (to, -d) *manigancer* : politicians are always scheming = *les politiciens sont toujours en train de manigancer quelque chose*, what are you scheming now ? = *qu'est-ce que tu manigances à présent ?* ⓪ to contrive = *combiner*, to hatch = *ourdir.*

SCHEMING (adj) *intrigant, -e* : a scheming lover = *un amant intrigant* ⓪ sly = *sournois* ☠ → intriguing.

SCHISM (n) *schisme (m)* : a schism in the Church = *un schisme au sein de l'Église* ⓪ split = *scission.*

SCHIZOPHRENIA (n) *schizophrénie (f)* **SCHIZO (PHRENIC)** (n) *schizophrène (m, f)* : you almost have to be a schizo(phrenic) to survive in New York today = *il faut presque être schizophrène pour survivre à New York aujourd'hui* **SCHIZOPHRENIC = SCHIZOID** (adj) *schizophrène* : a schizophrenic/schizoid personality = *une personnalité schizophrène.*

SCHLEMIEL (n) *cruche (f)* : she married a schlemiel = *elle a épousé une cruche* → STUPID ☠ → jug.

SCHLEP (n) *crétin, -e* : what a schlep he is ! = *quel crétin !* → STUPID.

SCHLEPP (n) *trotte (f)* : it's quite a schlepp from here to the bank = *ça fait une bonne trotte d'ici à la banque* = haul.

SCHLEPP (to, -ed) *trimballer* : I had to schlepp my luggage back and forth = *il a fallu que je trimballe mes bagages à l'aller et au retour* ⓪ to haul = *se coltiner.*

SCHLIMAZEL (n) *andouille (f)* : what a schlimazel you've been to believe him ! = *quelle andouille tu as été de le croire !* → STUPID.

SCHLOCK (n inv) *truc (m) (en toc)* : the store sells a lot of schlock = *ce magasin vend des tas de trucs en toc* ⓪ junk = *de la cochonnerie* **SCHLOCK** (adj) *en/de toc* : schlock watches = *des montres en toc.*

SCHMALTZ (n inv) *sentimentalisme (m)* : a film full of schmaltz = *un film plein de sentimentalisme* ⓪ gush = *effusion.*

SCHMALTZY (adj, -ier, -iest) *cucul* : a schmaltzy film = *un film cucul* = mushy ⓪ sentimental = ←.

SCHMOE (n) *andouille (f)* : what a schmoe you've been to believe her ! = *quelle andouille tu as été de la croire !* → STUPID.

SCHMUCK (n) *dernier, -ère des cons, connes* : you were a schmuck not to realize they were married = *tu es le dernier des cons de ne pas t'être rendu compte qu'ils étaient mariés* → STUPID.

SCHNAPPS (n) *schnaps (m)* : it's time for some schnapps = *c'est le moment de boire un peu de schnaps* ⓪ whisky = ←.

SCHNOOK (n) *schnock (m)* : my boss is a real schnook = *mon patron est un vrai schnock* → STUPID.

SCHOLAR (n) *savant (m)* : scholars from the Western world met to discuss the danger of a nuclear war = *des savants du monde occidental se sont réunis pour discuter du danger d'une guerre nucléaire* ⓪ highbrow = *cérébral*
I'm no scholar ! = *je ne suis pas un érudit !*

SCHOLARLY (adj) *savant, -e* : a scholarly work = *un ouvrage savant* ⓪ erudite = *érudit.*

SCHOLARSHIP (n) *bourse (f)(d'études ou de recherche)* : she got a scholarship to Yale = *elle a obtenu une bourse pour entrer à Yale* ⓪ grant = *subvention* ☠ *la Bourse* = the stock market.

SCHOOL (n) *école (f)* : my kids like school = *mes enfants aiment l'école*

academy = *académie* **boarding school** = *internat/ pensionnat* **business school** = *école de commerce* **classroom** = *(salle de) classe* **co-ed school** = *école mixte* **college** = *université (quatre premières années)*	**day school** = *externat* **driving school** = *auto-école* **elementary schoolteacher** = *instituteur/institutrice* **the faculty** = *le corps enseignant* = **the teaching staff** **finishing school** = *école de jeunes filles (où on leur apprend leur rôle social)*	**grade** = *note* = **mark** **grade/elementary school** = *école primaire* **graduate school** = *école de spécialisation après les quatre premières années d'université* **high school** = *lycée* **law school** = *faculté de droit* **medical school** = *faculté de*

médecine **kindergarten** = *jardin d'enfants* **nursery school** = *(école) maternelle* **prep school** = *école privée (très chère)* **the principal** = *le proviseur* **professor** = *professeur d'université* **public** ≠ **private school** = *école publique ≠ privée*	**public school** (GB) = *école privée (très chère)* **report card** = *bulletin scolaire* **schoolboy/schoolgirl** = *écolier/écolière* **school bus** = *car de ramassage scolaire* **schoolmaster/schoolmistress** = *maître/maîtresse d'école* **schoolwork** = *travail scolaire* **school year** = *année scolaire* = **academic year**	**schooling** = *scolarité* **summer school** = *cours d'été* **Sunday school** = *catéchisme/école du dimanche* **student** = *étudiant* **teacher** = *professeur (lycée)* **trade school** = *collège technique* **university** = *université* **vocational school** = *école professionnelle privée*

to go to school = 1/ *aller à l'école* : it's time to go to school = *c'est l'heure d'aller à l'école* 2/ *faire ses études* : her children are going to school in America = *ses enfants font leurs études en Amérique*	**to have been to the school of hard knocks** = *avoir été à rude école* ① to go through hell = *en baver* **to stay in after school** = *être en retenue*
☠ *faire l'école buissonnière* = to play hooky	— *être à bonne école* = to be in good hands.

SCIENCE (n) *science (f)* : making love is not a science = *faire l'amour n'est pas une science*
science-fiction = *science-fiction* ① scifi = *S.F.*

SCIENTIFIC (adj) *scientifique* : a scientific program = *un programme scientifique* **SCIENTIFICALLY** (adv) *scientifiquement.*

SCIENTIST (n) *scientifique (m, f), homme/femme de science* : a world congress of scientists = *un congrès mondial de scientifiques/d'hommes de science* ① research = *recherche*, lab = *labo.*

SCISSORS (n pl) *ciseaux (m pl)* : your scissors don't cut well = *vos ciseaux ne coupent pas bien* ① shears = *cisailles/sécateur*
a pair of scissors = *une paire de ciseaux.*

SCOFF (to, -ed) *railler* : she scoffed at my suggestion = *elle a raillé ma suggestion* ① to flout = *faire fi de*, to snicker = *ricaner.*

SCOLD (to, -ed) *gronder* : to scold a child = *gronder un enfant* → TO LAMBAST ☠ *gronder (chien)* = to growl.

SCOOP (n) *scoop (m)* : his story on the assassination attempt was a scoop = *son papier sur la tentative d'assassinat était un scoop* ① newspaper = *journal.*

SCOOTER (n) *scooter (m)* ① bike = *vélo.*

SCOPE (n inv) *portée (f)* : what's the scope of the book/law ? = *quelle est la portée de ce livre/de cette loi ?*
it's beyond my scope = *ce n'est pas à ma portée* ① it's not my department = *ce n'est pas mon rayon*
the scope of (her activities) = *l'étendue de (ses activités)* ① the gamut of = *la gamme de* ☠ → litter.

SCORCH (to, -ed) *roussir* : the lawn/my shirt is scorched = *la pelouse/ma chemise est roussie* ① to burn = *brûler.*

SCORE (n) *score (m)* : what's the score now ? = *où en est le score ?* ① point = *←*, scoreboard = *tableau d'affichage*

to keep score = *tenir la marque* **to know the score** = *connaître la musique* ① not to have been born yesterday = *ne pas être né d'hier* **on that score** = *à ce sujet* : on that score, you have nothing to worry about = *vous n'avez rien à craindre à ce sujet* **scores of (people)** = *un grand nombre de*	(gens) → MANY **to settle a score** = *régler son compte à qqn* : I have a score to settle with her = *j'ai un compte à régler avec elle* ≠ to be even = *être quitte* **what's the score (on their divorce) ?** = *qu'est-ce qui se passe (pour leur divorce) ?* ① what's the lowdown ? = *quel est le dessous des cartes ?*

SCORE (to, -d) *marquer* : our team finally scored = *notre équipe a fini par marquer* ☠ → to mark
to score with s.o. = 1/ *se tailler un beau succès avec qqn* : she scored with my parents = *elle s'est taillé un beau succès avec mes parents* ① to make a hit with = *avoir beaucoup de succès auprès de* 2/ *se faire qqn* : he scored with the girl the first night = *il s'est fait la fille le premier soir* ① to seduce = *séduire.*

SCORN (n inv) *mépris (m)* : they have nothing but scorn for him = *ils n'ont que du mépris pour lui* ≠ respect = *←* **SCORN** (to, -ed) *mépriser* : she scorned my offer = *elle a méprisé ma proposition* ① to disdain = *dédaigner*, to snub = *snober* **SCORNFUL** (adj) *méprisant, -e* : a scornful reply = *une réplique méprisante* ① disdainful = *dédaigneux.*

SCOTCH (n, -es) *whisky (m), scotch (m)* : would you like a Scotch ? = *voulez-vous un whisky/un scotch ?*
Scotch tape = *du Scotch/de l'adhésif.*

SCOT-FREE (adj) *sans condamnation* : he was guilty but got off scot-free = *il était coupable, mais il s'en est tiré sans condamnation.*

SCOTLAND (n) *Écosse (f)* **SCOTTISH** (adj) *écossais, -e* ⓪ kilt = ←, bagpipe = *cornemuse* **SCOT** (n) *Écossais, -e.*

SCOTLAND YARD (n) *police criminelle de Londres (correspond au Quai des Orfèvres en France)* ⓪ Interpol = ←.

SCOUNDREL (n) *scélérat, -e* : the scoundrel left his wife with three young kids = *ce scélérat a plaqué sa femme et ses trois jeunes enfants* → BASTARD.

SCOUT (n) **boy/girl scout** = *boy-/girl-scout, éclaireur/éclaireuse, guide*
scout's honor ! = *juré ! craché !*

SCOUT AROUND FOR (to, -ed) *être à la recherche de* : I've been scouting around for a secondhand TV = *je suis à la recherche d'une télé d'occasion* = to be on the lookout for.

SCOWL (to, -ed) *se renfrogner* : she scowled when he said he was too tired to go out = *elle s'est renfrognée quand il a dit qu'il était trop fatigué pour sortir* ⓪ to frown = *froncer les sourcils* **SCOWL** (n) *mine (f) renfrognée.*

SCRAM ! (interj) *dégage !* → BUZZ OFF !

SCRAMBLE (to, -d) *se précipiter* : the kids scrambled onto the school bus = *les gosses se sont précipités pour monter dans le car de ramassage scolaire.*

SCRAP (n) *accrochage (m)* : I had a scrap with my parents = *j'ai eu un accrochage avec mes parents* ⓪ brawl = *rixe*
scrap of paper = *bout de papier*
☠ *un accrochage (voiture)* = a minor collision.

SCRAP (to, -ped) *mettre au rebut* : she scrapped her old TV = *elle a mis sa vieille télé au rebut* ⓪ to junk = *bazarder.*

SCRAPBOOK (n) *album (m) de photos.*

SCRAPE (to, -d) *(s')érafler* : I scraped my knee = *je me suis éraflé le genou* ⓪ to cut = *couper*
to scrape up/together = *arriver à réunir* : he scraped up/together enough money to go to Europe = *il est arrivé à réunir assez d'argent pour aller en Europe* ⓪ to raise = *réunir.*

SCRATCH (n, -es) *égratignure (f)* : a scratch on my hand = *une égratignure à la main*

to get out of (an accident) without a scratch = *se tirer d'(un accident) sans une égratignure* ⓪ it was a narrow escape = *on l'a échappé belle*
(to start) from scratch = *(commencer) à partir de rien.*

SCRATCH (to, -ed) **1/** *griffer* (s.o., animal), *égratigner* : the cat scratched my hand = *le chat m'a griffé la main*, I scratched my arm on the tree = *je me suis griffé/égratigné le bras à l'arbre* ⓪ to claw = *labourer avec ses griffes* **2/** *se gratter* : to scratch one's head = *se gratter la tête* ⓪ to tickle = *chatouiller* ☠ *ça gratte* = it itches
to scratch out = *sucrer* : scratch out my name from the list = *sucre mon nom de la liste* ⓪ to delete = *biffer*
☠ *se sucrer (money)* = to be on the take
— *sucrer (aliment)* = to put sugar on.

SCRAWL (n) *griffonnage (m)* : can you read this scrawl ? = *est-ce que vous pouvez lire ce griffonnage ?* **SCRAWL** (to, -ed) *griffonner* : he scrawled his name on the bottom of the page = *il a griffonné son nom au bas de la page* ⓪ to scribble = *gribouiller.*

SCRAWNY (adj, -ier, -iest) *maigrichon, -onne* : a scrawny child = *un enfant maigrichon* ⓪ lanky = *efflanqué* ≠ stout = *costaud.*

SCREAM (n) *hurlement (m)* : her screams scared the burglars away = *ses hurlements ont fait fuir les cambrioleurs* ⓪ shriek = *cri perçant*
a scream = *quelque chose de bidonnant* : the movie was a scream = *le film était bidonnant* ⓪ a roar = *quelque chose de poilant*, killing = *à mourir de rire*, a howl = *quelque chose de tordant.*

SCREAM (to, -ed) *hurler* : she always screams at the children = *elle est toujours en train de hurler après les enfants* ⓪ to shriek = *pousser des cris perçants*, to holler = *brailler* ☠ *hurler de rire* = to howl.

SCREEN (n) **1/** *écran (m)* : the screen is very small = *l'écran est très petit*
screen test = *essai filmé*
☠ *porter à l'écran* = to make a film of
2/ *paravent (m)* : there's a screen between the two rooms = *il y a un paravent entre les deux pièces* ⓪ partition = *cloison.*

SCREEN (to, -ed) *filtrer* : his deputy screens all his visitors = *son adjoint filtre tous les visiteurs* ☠ → to filter.

SCREENING (n) *projection (f)* : private screening = *projection privée* ⓪ showing = *exposition.*

SCREENPLAY (n) *scénario (m) de film* : who wrote the screenplay ? = *qui a écrit le scénario ?*

SCREENWRITER (n) *dialoguiste (m, f)* ⓪ scriptwriter = *scénariste.*

SCREW (n) **1/** *coup (m)* : what about a quick screw ? = *qu'est-ce que tu dirais de tirer un coup vite fait ?* ⓪ quickie = *coup vite tiré* ☠ → blow
what a great screw ! = *quel super baiseur !* = what a great fuck !

2/ *vis (f)* : buy some screws to put up the curtain rod = *achète des vis pour monter la tringle à rideaux* ⓪
screwdriver = *tournevis*
☠ *serrer la vis* = to crack the whip

---

he has a screw loose = *il a une case en moins* →
CRAZY
to put the screws on = *forcer la main à* : they put

the screws on me to get me to sign the contract = *ils m'ont forcé la main pour que je signe le contrat* ⓪
to put the pressure on = *exercer une pression sur.*

SCREW (to, -ed) **1/** *baiser* : the first time we screwed was fantastic = *la première fois qu'on a baisé, ça a été fantastique* = to fuck ⓪ to make it = *s'envoyer en l'air* **2/** *baiser* : I was screwed in the deal = *je me suis fait baiser dans l'histoire* → TO HUSTLE

---

to be screwed = *être foutu* : we're screwed if he finds out = *nous sommes foutus s'il l'apprend* ⓪
the jig's up = *les carottes sont cuites*

screw it ! = *bordel !* → GOSH !
screw you ! = *tu me fais chier !* ⓪ **screw off !** = *fous-moi la paix !/le camp !* → BUZZ OFF !

---

to screw around = **1/** *ne rien foutre* : he spent the whole day screwing around = *il n'a rien foutu de toute la journée* = to fuck around ⓪ to goof off = *tirer au flanc* **2/** *coucher à droite et à gauche* : since he got married he's been screwing around = *il couche à droite et à gauche depuis qu'il est marié* ⓪ to fool around = *courir les filles* **3/** *faire le con/le zouave* : stop screwing around ! = *arrête de faire le*

con !/le zouave ! ⓪ to horse around = *faire l'andouille*, to fuck around = *déconner*
to get screwed on (a deal) = *se faire baiser dans (une affaire)*
to screw up = *foutre en l'air* : you screwed up the deal by telling him what I was going to do = *tu as tout foutu en l'air en lui disant ce que j'allais faire* = to fuck up.

SCREWBALL (n) *quelqu'un de louftingue* : what a screwball you are ! = *t'es complètement louftingue !* ⓪ a wacko = *un dingo.*

SCREWED-UP (adj) *qui déconne* : screwed-up teenagers = *des adolescents qui déconnent* = fucked-up ⓪ not to be together = *marcher à côté de ses pompes.*

SCREW-OFF (n) *tire-au-cul (m)* : he's a screw-off who never works = *c'est un tire-au-cul qui ne travaille jamais* = fuck-off.

SCREWY (adj, -ier, -iest) *dingo* : a screwy broad/idea = *une nana/une idée complètement dingo* → CRAZY.

SCRIBBLE (to, -d) *gribouiller, faire des pattes de mouche* : she doesn't write, she scribbles = *elle n'écrit pas, elle gribouille/elle fait des pattes de mouche.*

SCRIMP (to, -ed) *rogner sur tout* : we're scrimping on everything to go to Europe for the summer = *nous rognons sur tout pour pouvoir aller en Europe cet été* ⓪ to pinch pennies = *regarder à la dépense.*

SCRIPT (n) *script (m)* ⓪ scriptwriter = *scénariste* **script boy/girl** = *script/scripte.*

SCROUNGE (to, -d) *quémander à droite et à gauche* : beggars have to scrounge to survive = *les mendiants doivent quémander à droite et à gauche pour survivre* ⓪ to grub = *taper.*

SCRUB (to, -bed) *frotter (avec de l'eau)* : go scrub your face = *va te frotter le visage avec de l'eau* ⓪ to scour = *récurer* ☠ → to rub.

SCRUFFY (adj, -ier, -iest) *débraillé, -e* : my kids always look scruffy = *mes gosses ont toujours l'air débraillés* ⓪ grubby = *crado.*

SCRUMPTIOUS (adj) *succulent, -e* : a scrumptious meal = *un repas succulent* = luscious.

SCRUPLE (n) *scrupule (m)* : she has no scruples = *elle n'a aucun scrupule* ☠ *je n'ai aucun scrupule à lui mentir* = I have no qualms about lying to him.

SCRUPULOUS (adj) *scrupuleux, -euse* : scrupulous work = *un travail scrupuleux* ⓪ careful = *soigné.*

SCRUTINIZE (to, -d) *examiner dans les moindres détails* : to scrutinize a passport = *examiner un passeport dans les moindres détails* ⓪ to scan = *parcourir des yeux* **SCRUTINY** (n, -ies) *examen (m) approfondi.*

SCUFFLE (n) *échauffourée (f)* : a scuffle between cops and hoodlums = *une échauffourée entre des flics et des voyous* ⓪ clash = *affrontement.*

SCULPT (to, -ed) *sculpter, faire de la sculpture* **SCULP-TOR** (n) *sculpteur (m)* : my brother's a sculptor = *mon frère est sculpteur* ⓪ sculptress = *femme sculpteur.*

SCULPTURE (n) *sculpture (f)* : a showing of his recent sculptures = *une exposition de ses dernières sculptures* ⓪ painting = *peinture* ☠ *sculpture sur bois* = wood carving.

SCUM (n inv) *rebut (m) de la société* : such a family comes from scum = *ce genre de famille, c'est le rebut de la société* ⓪ riffraff = *canaille*, hoi polloi = *populo* ≠ elite = *élite.*

SEA (n) *mer (f)* : the sea's rough today = *la mer est mauvaise aujourd'hui* ⓪ ocean = *océan*, shore = *rivage*, seaside = *bord de la mer* = seashore, sea gull = *mouette*, seaweed = *algue*
at sea = *à la dérive* : I'm completely at sea since he has gone = *je suis complètement à la dérive depuis qu'il est parti* ⓪ not to know which way to turn = *ne plus savoir à quel saint se vouer*
☠ *(un homme) à la mer* = (man) overboard
— *ce n'est pas la mer à boire* = it's no big deal.

SEAFOOD (n inv) *fruits (m pl) de mer* : a seafood restaurant = *un restaurant de fruits de mer* ⓪ shrimp = *crevette*, crab = *crabe*, lobster = *homard*, clam = *clam/palourde*, mussel = *moule*, oyster = *huître*, scallop = *coquille Saint-Jacques*, shellfish = *coquillages*.

SEAL (n) *phoque (m)* : trained seals = *des phoques savants* ⓪ porpoise = *marsouin*
the (presidential) seal = *le sceau (présidentiel)*.

SEAM (n) *couture (f)* : your seam is coming undone = *votre couture se défait* ⓪ hem = *ourlet*
to come apart at the seams = *craquer de toutes parts* : his alibi is coming apart at the seams = *son alibi craque de toutes parts* ≠ to hold up = *tenir*
☠ *travailler dans la couture* = to work in fashion
— *un cours de couture* = a sewing class.

SEAMSTRESS (n, -es) *retoucheuse (f)* : the seamstress can shorten the dress for you = *la retoucheuse peut vous raccourcir la robe* ⓪ alteration = *retouche*.

SEAMY (adj, -ier, -iest) *peu reluisant, -e* : the seamy side of the trade = *le côté peu reluisant de la profession* ⓪ seedy = *miteux*.

SÉANCE (n) *séance (f)* : a recording/matinée séance = *une séance d'enregistrement/en matinée*
☠ *séance tenante* = then and there
— *une séance d'enregistrement* = a recording session
— *la séance (film)* = the time when (the film) goes on
— *ouvrir* ≠ *lever la séance* = to open ≠ to adjourn the meeting.

SEARCH (n, -es) **1/** *fouille (f)* : a police search = *une fouille de la police* ☠ → dig **2/** *recherches (f pl)* : a search for the missing child = *des recherches pour retrouver l'enfant perdu* ☠ → research
in search of (a house) = *à la recherche d'(une maison)*
search warrant = *mandat de perquisition*.

SEARCH (to, -ed) *fouiller* : the cops searched the apartment/the guy = *les flics ont fouillé l'appartement/le type*
search me ! = *mystère et boule de gomme !* ⓪ who knows ! = *qui sait !*
to search for (a new apartment) = *être à la recherche d'(un nouvel appartement)* ⓪ to look for = *chercher*
☠ → to frisk.

SEASICK (adj) **to be seasick** = *avoir le mal de mer* ⓪ landlubber = *marin d'eau douce* ≠ sea dog = *(vieux) loup de mer*.

SEASIDE (n) *bord (m) de (la) mer* : he grew up near the seaside = *il a grandi au bord de la mer* ⓪ shore = *rivage*.

SEASON (n) *saison (f)* : the rainy season = *la saison des pluies* ⓪ spring = *printemps*, summer = *été*, fall = *automne*, winter = *hiver*
high ≠ **low season** = *pleine saison* ≠ *saison creuse*
in ≠ **out of season** = *en saison* ≠ *hors saison*
mating season = *saison des amours*
Season's Greetings ! = *tous mes vœux !* ⓪ best wishes = *meilleurs vœux*
season ticket (theater, train, etc.) = *carte d'abonnement (théâtre, train, etc.)*.

SEASON (to, -ed) *assaisonner* : the salad is not seasoned yet = *la salade n'est pas encore assaisonnée* ⓪ to spice = *épicer*.

SEASONAL (adj) **1/** *de saison* : seasonal weather = *un temps de saison* **2/** *saisonnier, -ère* : seasonal workers = *travailleurs saisonniers*.

SEASONED (adj) *chevronné, -e* : a seasoned reporter = *un reporter chevronné* ⓪ experienced = *expérimenté* ≠ beginner = *débutant*.

SEASONING (n) *assaisonnement (m)* : there's no seasoning on the meat = *il n'y a pas d'assaisonnement sur la viande* ⓪ dressing = *assaisonnement de salade*, spice = *épice*.

SEAT (n) **1/** *siège (m)* : do you want a seat ? = *désirez-vous un siège ?* ⓪ chair = *chaise* ☠ → siège
seat belt = *ceinture de sécurité*
fasten ≠ **unfasten your seat belts** = *attachez* ≠ *détachez vos ceintures*
the seat of government = *le siège du gouvernement*
take a seat ! = *prenez un siège !* ⓪ sit down ! = *asseyez-vous !*
2/ *place (f)* : two seats for the play = *deux places pour la pièce* ☠ → place.

SEAT (to, -ed) *avoir ... places* : the theater seats five hundred people = *le théâtre a cinq cents places*
to be seated (in the first row) = *être placé (au premier rang)*
please, be seated = *veuillez vous asseoir*
remain seated ! = *restez assis !*

SECEDE (to, -d) *faire sécession* : the Southern states seceded = *les États du sud ont fait sécession* **SECESSION** (n) *sécession (f)*.

SECLUDE (to, -d) *tenir à l'écart* : he secludes himself to write = *il se tient à l'écart pour écrire* ⓪ to isolate = *isoler*.

SECLUDED (adj) *retiré, -e* : a secluded cottage = *une maison de campagne retirée* ⓪ lonely = *seul*.

SECLUSION (n) **to live in seclusion** = *vivre retiré du monde*.

SECOND (n) **1/** *seconde* *(f)* : there are sixty seconds in a minute = *il y a soixante secondes dans une minute* ☠ *voyager en seconde* = to travel second-class

in a second = *dans une seconde* : I'll be with you in a second = *je suis à vous dans une seconde* ⓓ in a moment = *dans un instant*

just a second ! = *une petite seconde !* ⓓ wait a minute ! = *attendez une minute !*

2/ *second, -e, deuxième* *(m, f)* : he was the second to call = *il était le second/le deuxième à appeler*

☠ *le premier ..., le second ...* = the former ..., the latter ...

— *le second (dans une compétition)* = the runner-up (in a contest).

SECOND (adj) *second, -e, deuxième* : sit in the second row = *asseyez-vous au second/deuxième rang*

to be in one's second childhood = *être retombé en enfance* **second nature** = *seconde nature* **give me a second chance** = *donnez-moi encore une chance* **to have second thoughts** = *se poser des questions* : I was going to sleep with John, but after Peter's phone call I had second thoughts = *j'allais coucher avec John, mais après le coup de télé-*	*phone de Peter je me suis posé des questions* ⓓ to have reservations = *émettre des réserves* **on second thought** = *à la réflexion/réflexion faite* : on second thought, I won't go = *à la réflexion/réflexion faite, je n'irai pas* **second fiddle** = *sous-fifre* : to play second fiddle to the boss = *être le sous-fifre du patron* ⓓ underling = *subalterne*	**second to none** = *à nul autre pareil* : their cooking is second to none = *leur cuisine est à nulle autre pareille* → WONDERFUL ≠ a far cry from = *un pâle reflet de* **second wind** = *second souffle* **to take second helping** = *se resservir* : take a second helping of chocolate ice cream = *resservez-vous de glace au chocolat* ⓓ seconds = *du rab*

☠ *au second plan* = in the background
— *être dans un état second* = to be in a trance-like state

— *deuxième bureau* = intelligence service
— *un deuxième classe* = a (buck) private.

SECOND (to, -ed) *soutenir* (motion, bill) : the President seconded the bill = *le Président a soutenu le projet de loi* ☠ → to support.

SECONDARY (adj) *secondaire* : that's of secondary importance = *c'est d'une importance secondaire* ≠ major = *majeur*.

SECOND-BEST (adj) *deuxième meilleur, -e* : he's our second-best actor = *c'est notre deuxième meilleur acteur*.

SECOND-CLASS (adj) *de seconde classe* : second-class entertainment = *un spectacle de seconde classe* ⓓ mediocre = *médiocre*.

SECOND-CLASS (adv) *en seconde/deuxième classe* : I always travel second-class = *je voyage toujours en seconde/deuxième classe*.

SECONDHAND (adj) *d'occasion* : a secondhand car = *une voiture d'occasion* ≠ brand-new = *flambant neuf*
SECONDHAND (adv) *d'occasion* : he bought the car secondhand = *il a acheté la voiture d'occasion*.

SECONDLY (adv) *deuxièmement* : firstly the work's too hard, and secondly it isn't paid enough = *premièrement le travail est trop dur, et deuxièmement il n'est pas assez payé* ⓓ in second place = *en second lieu*.

SECOND-RATE (adj) *de second ordre* : a second-rate writer/restaurant = *un écrivain/restaurant de second ordre* ⓓ two-bit = *à la manque*.

SECONDS (n pl) *articles (m pl) démarqués* : the shirts you bought were seconds = *les chemises que vous avez achetées étaient des articles démarqués*.

SECRECY (n, -ies) *secret (m)* : he was tried in complete secrecy = *il a été jugé dans le plus grand secret* ☠ → secret.

SECRET (n) *secret (m)* : she can't keep a secret = *elle ne sait pas garder un secret*
in secret = *en secret* : the party was organized in secret = *la soirée a été organisée en secret* ⓓ on the sly = *en douce*
☠ *être dans le secret des dieux* = to be on the in
— *(juger qqn) en grand secret* = (to try s.o.) in complete secrecy
— *au secret (prison)* = in solitary.

SECRET (adj) *secret, -ète* : they have a secret meeting place = *ils ont un lieu de rendez-vous secret* ⓓ clandestine = *clandestin*, covert = *en sous-main*
secret agent = *agent secret*
secret ballot = *scrutin secret*

Secret Service = *services secrets*
secret door = *porte dérobée*
☠ *elle est très secrète* = she's very secretive.

SECRETARIAL (adj) *de secrétariat* : a secretarial job = *un travail de secrétariat/du secrétariat.*

SECRETARY (n, -ies) *secrétaire (m, f)* : I just hired a new secretary = *je viens d'engager une nouvelle secrétaire* ⑩ typist = *dactylo,* stenotypist = *sténotypiste,* typewriter = *machine à écrire*
executive/bilingual secretary = *secrétaire de direction/bilingue*
Secretary of States = *secrétaire d'État/ministre des Affaires étrangères*
☠ *secrétaire général* = 1/ head (political party) 2/ vice-president (company).

SECRETE (to, -d) *sécréter* **SECRETION** (n) *sécrétion (f).*

SECRETIVE (adj) *secret, -ète* : she's very secretive about her private life = *elle est très secrète sur sa vie privée* ☠ → secret.

SECRETLY (adv) *secrètement* : the two spies secretly met in London = *les deux espions se sont secrètement rencontrés à Londres* ⑩ on the qt = *en cachette.*

SECT (n) *secte (f)* : my son belongs to a sect = *mon fils appartient à une secte* ⑩ guru = *gourou.*

SECTARIAN (adj) *sectaire* : a sectarian attitude = *une attitude sectaire.*

SECTION (n) 1/ *partie (f)* : a section of the city/population/country = *une partie de la ville/de la population/du pays* = a part of ... ☠ → part 2/ *section (f)* : the commercial section of the embassy = *la section commerciale de l'ambassade*

the (sports) section (of the paper) = *la page (des sports) (du journal).*

SECTOR (n) *secteur (m)* : the private sector of industry = *le secteur privé de l'industrie.*

SECULAR (adj) *laïc, laïque* : secular education = *éducation laïque.*

SECURE (adj) *en sécurité, sécurisé, -e* : I feel very secure with him = *je me sens très en sécurité/sécurisé avec lui* ≠ insecure = *insécurisé.*

SECURITIES (n pl) *valeurs (f pl), titres (m.pl)* : my parents bought government securities = *mes parents ont acheté des valeurs/des titres d'État* ⑩ bond = *bon* ☠ *valeur* → value, *titres* → title.

SECURITY (n, -ies) *sécurité (f)* : a need for love and security = *un besoin d'amour et de sécurité* ≠ insecurity = *insécurité*
☠ *je me sens en sécurité (moralement)* = I feel safe/secure
— *ceinture de sécurité* = seat/safety belt.

SEDATE (adj) *posé, -e* : a sedate personality = *un caractère posé* ≠ excitable = ←, fiery = *fougueux.*

SEDATIVE (n) *sédatif (m)* : my doctor gave me sedatives = *mon médecin m'a donné des sédatifs* ⑩ sleeping pill = *somnifère,* under sedation = *sous sédatif.*

SEDUCE (to, -d) *séduire* : I let him think he seduced me = *je lui ai laissé croire qu'il m'avait séduite* ⑩ to deflower = *dépuceler* ☠ *l'idée m'a séduit* = the idea appealed to me **SEDUCTION** (n) *séduction (f)* : his power of seduction = *son pouvoir de séduction.*

SEE (to, saw, seen) *voir* : I (can) see you = *je vous vois* ⑩ to look at = *regarder*

as I see it = *à ce qu'il me semble* **I just don't see (modern art)** = *je trouve que (l'art moderne) n'a rien de terrible* **I've seen enough of him !** = *je l'ai assez vu !* **it has to be seen to be believed** = *il faut le voir pour le croire* **let's see !** = *voyons voir !* **I could see it coming !** = *je l'ai vu venir !* ⑩ I foresaw it = *je l'avais prévu* **see if I care !** = *je m'en fiche pas mal !* ⑩ I don't give a damn !* = *je m'en fiche comme de l'an quarante !* **seeing is believing** = *voir, c'est croire* **see ya !** = *ciao !* ⑩ so long ! = *salut !*	**see you around !** = *à un de ces quatre !* ⑩ see you soon ! = *à bientôt !* **(if he does that,) he'll see what I'm made of** = *(s'il fait ça,) il va voir de quel bois je me chauffe* **see what I mean ?** = *vous voyez ce que je veux dire ?* **see that (he comes on time)** = *veillez à ce qu'(il arrive à l'heure)* **that's not how I see it** = *je ne vois pas les choses sous le même angle/comme ça* **we'll see** = *on verra* **to see s.o.** = *sortir avec qqn* : she's been seeing him for a year = *elle sort avec lui depuis un an* = to date

to see about = *s'occuper de* : will you please see about it ? = *est-ce que vous pourrez vous en occuper, s'il vous plaît ?* ⑩ to tend to = *prendre soin de*	**to see again** = *revoir* : I saw him again last week = *je l'ai revu la semaine dernière* ☠ → to go over **(if you don't believe me,) see**	**for yourself !** = *(si tu ne me crois pas,) vois par toi-même !* **to see in s.o.** = *trouver à qqn* : what does he see in her ? = *qu'est-ce qu'il lui trouve ?*

to see much/a lot of s.o. = *voir beaucoup qqn* : we don't see much of each other = *nous ne nous voyons pas beaucoup*
to see s.o. off = *accompagner qqn* : I went to the airport to see him off = *je suis allé l'accompagner à l'aéroport*
to see s.o. out = *reconduire qqn* : I'll see you out = *je vais vous reconduire* ≠ to show in = *faire entrer* ☠ *reconduire un contrat/un bail* = to renew a contract/a lease

to see through = 1/ *être transparent* : move, I can't see through you = *ôte-toi de là, tu n'es pas transparent*, I can see through your blouse = *ta blouse est transparente* 2/ *ne pas être dupe* : it was some line, but I saw through it = *c'était un sacré baratin, mais je n'ai pas été dupe*
not to see through it = *n'y voir que du feu*
to see s.o. through stg = *soutenir qqn tout le temps de/pendant qqch* : I saw my brother through his divorce = *j'ai soutenu mon frère tout le temps de son divorce/pendant tout son divorce*
to see stg through = *aller jusqu'au bout de qqch* : I began this work and I'll see it through = *j'ai commencé ce boulot et j'irai jusqu'au bout*
to see to it = *veiller à* : I'll see to it that he writes to you = *je veillerai à ce qu'il vous écrive* ⓄⒹ to take care of = *prendre soin de*

☠ *ça ne s'est jamais vu* = it's unheard of
— *ça n'a rien à voir* = that has nothing to do with it
— *voyons !* = come on !
— *tu vois ça !* = imagine that !/can you beat it !
— *essayez voir !* = just try !
— *vu !* = gotcha !

— *je l'ai vu naître* = I knew him when he was so high
— *je ne peux pas le voir* = I can't stand him
— *va voir ailleurs/là-bas si j'y suis* = go fly a kite
— *à le voir ...* = by the look of him ...

SEED (n) *graine (f)* : sunflower seeds = *des graines de tournesol*
☠ *en prendre de la graine* = to pick up pointers
— *casser la graine* = to have a bite.

SEEDY (adj, -ier, -iest) *mal famé, -e* : the seedy part of town = *le quartier mal famé* ⓄⒹ squalid = *sordide* ≠ lavish = *somptueux*.

SEEING (conj) **seeing that** = *vu que* : seeing that you all want to eat Chinese food, it's okay with me = *vu que vous voulez tous manger chinois, je suis d'accord*.

SEEK (to, sought, sought) *rechercher* : to seek a solution = *rechercher une solution* ⓄⒹ to search for = *être à la recherche de*
seek and you shall find = *cherchez et vous trouverez* ⓄⒹ God helps those who help themselves = *aide-toi, le ciel t'aidera*
to be sought after = *être recherché* : apartments with terraces in New York are much sought after = *à New York, les appartements avec terrasse sont très recherchés* ⓄⒹ to be in fashion = *être à la mode* ≠ passé = *passé de mode*
to seek out (the company of men) = *rechercher (la compagnie des hommes)*
☠ *les flics le recherchent* = the cops are after him/want him.

SEEM (to, -ed) *sembler* : you seem tired = *vous semblez fatigué* ⓄⒹ to look = *avoir l'air*
it seems that (he's going to resign) = *il semble qu'(il soit sur le point de démissionner)* ⓄⒹ it looks like = *on dirait que*
so it seems = *il semble bien* : are they splitting up ? — so it seems = *est-ce qu'ils se séparent ? — il semble bien* ⓄⒹ one would think so = *il faut le croire*
things are not what they seem = *les choses ne sont pas ce qu'elles semblent être*

you don't seem to realize (how much it will cost) = *vous ne semblez pas vous rendre compte (du prix que ça va coûter)*.

SEEMINGLY (adv) *à ce qu'il semble* : she's seemingly happy with him = *à ce qu'il semble, elle est heureuse avec lui* ⓄⒹ apparently = *apparemment*.

SEETHE (to, -d) *être fou furieux, folle furieuse* : her father was seething when he found out about the stolen money = *son père était fou furieux quand il a découvert qu'elle avait pris l'argent* → ANGRY.

SEGMENT (n) **a segment of (the population)** = *une partie de (la population)* ⓄⒹ a fraction = *une fraction*.

SEGREGATE (to, -d) *faire une ségrégation (raciale) entre* : black children were segregated from white children = *on a fait une ségrégation entre les enfants noirs et les enfants blancs* ⓄⒹ to discriminate = *faire une discrimination entre* **SEGREGATED** (adj) *ségrégué, -e* : there are still segregated schools in the South = *il y a encore des écoles ségréguées dans le Sud*.

SEGREGATION (n) *ségrégation (f)* : does segregation still exist ? = *est-ce que la ségrégation existe encore ?* ≠ desegregation = *déségrégation* **SEGREGATIONIST** (n) *ségrégationniste (m, f)*.

SEIZE (to, -d) 1/ *saisir* : he seized my arm = *il m'a saisi le bras* ⓄⒹ to grab = *empoigner*, to take hold of = *s'emparer de* 2/ *saisir* : the customs officers seized the goods = *les douaniers ont saisi la marchandise* ⓄⒹ to confiscate = *confisquer*
☠ *tu saisis ?* = do you get it ?
— *saisir un tribunal d'une affaire* = to bring a case to court
— *saisir (un salaire)* = to attach (a salary)
— *je n'ai pas saisi ce que tu as dit* = I didn't catch what you said.

SEIZURE (n) *saisie (f)* : the seizure of the apartment = *la saisie de l'appartement* ⓪ confiscation = ←
heart/epileptic seizure = *crise cardiaque/d'épilepsie.*

SELDOM (adv) *rarement* : he seldom comes these days = *il vient rarement en ce moment* = rarely ≠ frequently = *fréquemment.*

SELECT (adj) *sélect* : a select group of people = *un groupe de gens sélect* ⓪ choice = *de choix.*

SELECT (to, -ed) *sélectionner* : select the one you want = *sélectionnez celui que vous voulez* ⓪ to handpick = *trier sur le volet,* to opt for = *opter pour.*

SELECTION (n) *sélection (f)* : a good selection of colors = *une bonne sélection de couleurs* ⓪ choice = *choix.*

SELECTIVE (adj) *sélectif, -ive* : selective recruitment = *recrutement sélectif.*

SELF-ASSURED (adj) *sûr, -e de soi* : a self-assured girl = *une fille sûre d'elle* ≠ insecure = *insécurisé.*

SELF-CENTERED (adj) *égocentrique* : an egotistical self-centered person = *une personne égotiste et égocentrique.*

SELF-CONFIDENCE (n) *confiance (f) en soi* : she lacks self-confidence = *elle manque de confiance en elle* **SELF-CONFIDENT** (adj) *confiant, -e en soi* ⓪ self-assured = *sûr de soi.*

SELF-CONSCIOUS (adj) *complexé, -e* : she's very self-conscious about her acne = *elle est très complexée à cause de son acné* ≠ cool = ← **SELF-CONSCIOUSLY** (adv) *d'une façon complexée, timidement* : she answered very self-consciously = *elle a répondu très timidement.*

SELF-CONTROL (n) *maîtrise (f) de soi* : when I make love, I lose self-control = *quand je fais l'amour, je n'ai plus aucune maîtrise de moi* ⓪ sangfroid = *sang-froid.*

SELF-DEFENSE (n) **in self-defense** = *en état de légitime défense* : she shot the rapist in self-defense = *elle a tiré sur le violeur en état de légitime défense* ⓪ second-degree murder = *homicide involontaire.*

SELF-DESTRUCTIVE (adj) *autodestructeur, -trice* : love is often a self-destructive passion = *l'amour est souvent une passion autodestructrice.*

SELF-DETERMINATION (n) *autodétermination (f).*

SELF-EFFACING (adj) *qui s'efface* : modest and self-effacing = *modeste et qui s'efface* ⓪ humble = ←.

SELF-EMPLOYED (adj) *qui travaille à son compte* : she's self-employed and doesn't have much time for herself = *elle travaille à son compte et n'a pas beaucoup de temps à elle* ⓪ free-lance = *en free-lance.*

SELF-ESTEEM (n) *amour-propre (m)* : people and nations must have self-esteem = *les gens comme les nations doivent avoir de l'amour-propre* ⓪ self-respect = *respect de soi-même.*

SELF-EVIDENT (adj) **a self-evident truth** = *une vérité de La Palice.*

SELF-IMPORTANCE (n) *suffisance (f)* : she's filled with self-importance = *elle est pleine de suffisance* = conceit ≠ humility = *humilité* **SELF-IMPORTANT** (adj) *plein de soi-même.*

SELF-IMPOSED (adj) *que l'on s'impose* : self-imposed sacrifice = *un sacrifice que l'on s'impose.*

SELF-INDULGENT (adj) *qui ne se refuse rien* : he's selfish and self-indulgent = *il est égoïste et ne se refuse rien.*

SELFISH (adj) *égoïste* : a selfish husband = *un mari égoïste* ≠ unselfish = *pas égoïste,* generous = *généreux* **SELFISHLY** (adv) *égoïstement* **SELFISHNESS** (n) *égoïsme (m)* : what selfishness ! = *quel égoïsme !*

SELFLESS (adj) *désintéressé, -e* : a father's selfless love for his children = *l'amour désintéressé d'un père pour ses enfants* ⓪ unselfish = *pas égoïste* ⚹ *elle est désintéressée dans l'affaire* = she has no financial stake in the business.

SELF-MADE (adj) *qui s'est fait, -e tout, -e seul, -e* : a self-made railroad tycoon = *un magnat des chemins de fer qui s'est fait tout seul*
self-made man/woman = *autodidacte/self-made-man* ⓪ self-taught = *qui a tout appris tout seul.*

SELF-PORTRAIT (n) *autoportrait (m)* : Van Gogh's self-portrait = *l'autoportrait de Van Gogh.*

SELF-PRESERVATION (n) *instinct (m) de conservation* : she has no sense of self-preservation = *elle n'a aucun instinct de conservation.*

SELF-RESPECT (n) *respect (m) de soi-même* : you have no self-respect = *vous n'avez aucun respect de vous-même* ⓪ pride = *fierté.*

SELF-RESPECTING (adj) *qui se respecte* : a self-respecting lawyer would say that = *c'est ce que dirait un avocat qui se respecte.*

SELF-RIGHTEOUS (adj) *moralisant, -e* : the self-righteous majority = *la majorité moralisante* ⓪ sanctimonious = *moralisateur.*

SELF-SACRIFICE (n) *sacrifice (m) personnel, abnégation (f)*
to make self-sacrifices for (one's family) = *faire des sacrifices (personnels) pour (sa famille)/se sacrifier pour (sa famille).*

SELF-SATISFIED (adj) *content, -e de soi* : a self-satisfied man = *un homme content de lui.*

SELF-SERVICE (n) *libre-service (m), self-service (m)* : the restaurant/supermarket is a self-service = *le restaurant/supermarché est un livre-service/self-service.*

SELF-SUFFICIENT (adj) *qui se suffit à soi-même* : my kids are self-sufficient = *mes enfants se suffisent à eux-mêmes* ≠ dependent = *dépendant.*

SELF-TAUGHT (adj) *qui a tout appris tout, -e seul, -e :* a self-taught potter = *un potier qui a tout appris tout seul.*

SELL (to, sold, sold) *(se) vendre :* I'm trying to sell my car = *j'essaie de vendre ma voiture,* her books sell well = *ses livres se vendent bien* ⓓ to resell = *revendre,* to put up for sale = *mettre en vente,* to hawk = *vendre à la sauvette,* to peddle = *colporter* ≠ to buy = *acheter*
you can't sell that to me ! = *vous ne me ferez pas croire ça !* → BUZZ OFF !
to sell for = *se vendre (pour) :* the car sold for ten thousand francs = *la voiture s'est vendue (pour) dix mille francs*
to sell off = *solder :* they're selling off the winter collection = *ils soldent la collection d'hiver* ☠ *se solder par (une impasse)* = to end in (a deadlock)
to sell out = *se laisser acheter :* the union is afraid its leader will sell out = *le syndicat a peur que son leader ne se laisse acheter*
to be sold out = *être épuisé :* on the first day the book was sold out = *le livre fut épuisé dès le premier jour.*

SELLER (n) *vendeur, -euse :* the seller gets a percentage = *le vendeur touche un pourcentage* ≠ buyer = *acheteur* ☠ → salesman.

SEMBLANCE (n) *semblant (m) :* he didn't even have a semblance of remorse = *il n'avait pas même un semblant de remords* ☠ *faire semblant* = to make believe.

SEMESTER (n) *semestre (m) :* she took physics the first semester = *elle a pris la physique au premier semestre* ⓓ school year = *année scolaire.*

SEMICOLON (n) *point-virgule (m)* ⓓ colon = *deux-points.*

SEMINAR (n) *séminaire (m) :* a seminar on Freud = *un séminaire sur Freud* ⓓ conference = *conférence* ☠ *séminaire (prêtres)* = seminary.

SEMINARY (n, -ies) *séminaire (m)* ⓓ seminarian = *séminariste* ☠ → seminar.

SENATE (n) *Sénat (m) :* the bill is going before the Senate = *le projet de loi passe devant le Sénat* ⓓ House of Representatives = *Chambre des représentants/des députés* **SENATOR** (n) *sénateur (m) :* the Senator from New York = *le sénateur de New York* ⓓ Representative = *député.*

SEND (to, sent, sent) *envoyer :* I still have the first letter you sent me = *j'ai encore la première lettre que vous m'avez envoyée,* they sent their kids to a private school = *ils ont envoyé leurs gosses dans une école privée* ⓓ to dispatch = *expédier*

to send back = *renvoyer :* he sent her letter back = *il lui a renvoyé sa lettre* ☠ → to dismiss
to send for (the doctor) = *envoyer chercher (le médecin)* ⓓ to go for = *aller chercher*
to send s.o. packing = *envoyer qqn sur les roses* ⓓ **to send s.o. about one's business** = *envoyer qqn balader*
to send s.o. up = *coffrer qqn :* he was sent up for ten years = *il a été coffré pendant dix ans* ≠ to get = *écoper*
to have (dinner) sent up = *faire monter (son dîner)* ☠ *s'envoyer (un scotch)* = to toss down (a Scotch)
— *je me suis envoyé tout le travail* = I had to do all the work
— *s'envoyer une nana* = to make a broad
— *envoie-moi une cigarette* = toss me a cigarette.

SEND-OFF (n) **to give s.o. a send-off** = *faire ses adieux à qqn* ≠ homecoming = *retour.*

SENILE (adj) *sénile :* senile behavior = *un comportement sénile* ≠ still spry = *encore vert* **SENILITY** (n, -ies) *sénilité (f) :* precocious senility = *sénilité précoce.*

SENIOR (n) *étudiant, -e de dernière année :* he teaches seniors only = *il n'enseigne qu'aux étudiants de dernière année* ≠ junior = *étudiant de troisième année*
s.o.'s senior = *l'aîné de qqn :* she's five years my senior = *elle est mon aînée de cinq ans* ≠ s.o.'s junior = *le cadet de qqn.*

SENIOR (adj) **the senior (member of the club)** = *le (membre) le plus ancien (du club)*
(Smith) Senior = *(Smith) père*
senior executive = *cadre supérieur*
senior officer = *officier supérieur*
senior partner = *principal associé*
senior Senator = *doyen de l'Assemblée.*

SENIORITY (n, -ies) *ancienneté (f) :* seniority in Congress = *l'ancienneté au Congrès.*

SENSATION (n) *sensation (f)* (physical), *sentiment (m) :* I had the sensation he was lying = *j'avais le sentiment qu'il mentait,* I had the sensation that I was going to fall = *j'avais la sensation que j'allais tomber*
to be/create a sensation = *faire sensation :* she was/created a sensation in her new dress = *elle a fait sensation dans sa nouvelle robe*
☠ *journal à sensation* = scandal sheet
— *sentiment* → sentiment.

SENSATIONAL (adj) *sensationnel, -elle :* a sensational movie = *un film sensationnel* → WONDERFUL ≠ horrible = *←.*

SENSATIONALISM (n) *sensationnel (m) :* bad journalism is based on sensationalism = *le mauvais journalisme est fondé sur le sensationnel.*

SENSE (n) *sens (m) :* a very strong sense of family = *un sens très fort de la famille*

to come to one's senses = *retrouver son bon sens*	*ramener qqn à la raison* ⓓ to reason with s.o. = *raisonner qqn*	**to have a sixth sense** = *avoir un sixième sens*
to bring s.o. to senses =	**the five senses** = *les cinq sens*	**(she has no) sense of direc-**

tion = (elle n'a pas) le sens de l'orientation
in a sense = en un sens : you're right in a sense, but I'm too fed up to apologize = en un sens, vous avez raison, mais j'en ai trop marre pour faire des excuses ⊕ in a way = d'une certaine façon
to make sense = avoir un sens : what you're saying doesn't make sense = ce que vous dites n'a pas de sens ⊕ to

be logical = être logique
to make sense out of = comprendre qqch à : I couldn't make sense out of what he was saying = je n'ai rien compris à ce qu'il disait
to lose (all) sense of proportion/time = perdre le sens de la mesure/la notion du temps
to knock some sense into s.o. = mettre du plomb dans la cervelle à qqn
a sense of humor = le sens de

l'humour
there's no sense in it = ça n'a pas de sens ⊕ there's no point in it = ça ne rime à rien
what's the sense of (doing that) ? = à quoi ça rime de (faire ça) ? ⊕ what's the use of ? = à quoi ça sert de ?
you should have more sense than that = vous devriez avoir plus de bon sens ⊕ you should have known better = vous auriez dû le savoir

---

☠ aller dans le même sens que qqn/abonder dans le sens de qqn = to think along similar lines to s.o.
— une rue à sens unique = a one-way street
— il a un grand sens de la politique = he has a great political savvy
— avoir du sens pratique = to be pragmatic

— double sens = double meaning
— dans le bon sens = in the right direction
— le sens d'un mot = the meaning of a word
— à mon sens = to my way of thinking
— ça tombe sous le sens = that goes without saying.

SENSE (to, -d) pressentir : she sensed the danger of the situation = elle a pressenti le danger de la situation ⊕ to feel = sentir.

SENSELESS (adj) insensé, -e : a senseless killing = un meurtre insensé ⊕ foolish = bête
it's senseless to (ask him) = ça ne rime à rien de (lui demander)
☠ tu es insensé ! = you're insane !

SENSIBLE (adj) sensé, -e : that's a sensible thing to do ! = voilà une chose sensée ! ⊕ rational = rationnel ≠ foolish = bête
be sensible ! = sois raisonnable !
☠ une fille sensible = a sensitive girl
— un progrès sensible = noticeable progress
— le Congrès a été sensible au projet de loi du Président = Congress was responsive to the President's bill.

SENSIBLY (adv) de façon sensée : you acted very sensibly = vous avez agi de façon très sensée.

SENSITIVE (adj) sensible : a sensitive child = un enfant sensible ≠ insensitive = insensible = unfeeling, hard-boiled = dur à cuire
to be sensitive about = être susceptible au sujet de : he's very sensitive about his weight = il est très susceptible au sujet de son poids ⊕ oversensitive = hypersensible
to be sensitive to = être sensible à : she's very sensitive to others = elle est très sensible aux autres ≠ indifferent to = indifférent à
☠ → sensible.

SENSUAL (adj) sensuel, -elle : sensual lips = des lèvres sensuelles ⊕ carnal = charnel **SENSUALITY** (n, -ies) sensualité (f) : Marilyn Monroe had great sensuality = Marilyn Monroe avait une grande sensualité.

SENSUOUS (adj) sensuel, -elle : felines are sensuous animals = les félins sont des animaux sensuels ⊕ voluptuous = voluptueux.

SENTENCE (n) 1/ phrase (f) : does a sentence begin with a capital and end with a period ? = est-ce qu'une phrase commence par une majuscule et se termine par un point ? 2/ sentence (f) : a very light sentence = une sentence très légère ⊕ judgment = jugement
a sentence of (3 months) = une condamnation de (3 mois)
to pass sentence = prononcer une sentence ⊕ to rule = décider
suspended sentence = condamnation avec sursis.

SENTENCE (to, -d) prononcer une sentence : when is he going to be sentenced ? = quand va-t-on prononcer la sentence ?
to sentence to (five years/the death penalty) = condamner à (cinq ans de prison/la peine de mort) ≠ to get off with = en être quitte pour.

SENTIMENT (n) sentiment (m) : there's no sentiment in politics = en politique, on ne fait pas de sentiment
☠ un sentiment de (culpabilité) = a feeling of (guilt)
— j'ai le sentiment que = I have the feeling/sensation that
— veuillez agréer (l'expression de) mes sentiments distingués = yours truly.

SENTIMENTAL (adj) sentimental, -e : a sentimental lover = un amant sentimental ⊕ nostalgic = nostalgique ☠ ma vie sentimentale = my love life **SENTIMENTALITY** (n, -ies) sentimentalité (f) : a movie full of sentimentality = un film plein de sentimentalité ⊕ mawkishness = sensiblerie, corn = guimauve.

SEPARATE (to, -d) 1/ se séparer : they separated after two years = ils se sont séparés au bout de deux ans ⊕ to divorce = divorcer 2/ séparer : you have to separate the two problems = il faut séparer les deux problèmes ⊕ to divide = *diviser* ☠ *rien ne les sépare* = they're in perfect agreement.

SEPARATE (adj) *séparé, -e* : give us separate checks, please = *donnez-nous des additions séparées, s'il vous plaît* ⓪ distinct = ←
to keep separate rooms = *faire chambre à part*
under separate cover = *sous pli séparé* ≠ herewith = *ci-joint*
we went our separate ways = *nous avons pris des chemins différents*.

SEPARATELY (adv) *séparément* : we sleep separately = *nous dormons séparément*.

SEPARATION (n) *séparation* (f) : the separation of Church and State = *la séparation de l'Église et de l'État* ⓪ division = ←.

SEPTEMBER (n) *septembre* (m) → MONTH.

SEQUEL (n) *suite* (f) : he's writing a sequel to his first novel = *il est en train d'écrire une suite à son premier roman* ☠ → *suite*.

SEQUENCE (n) *séquence* (f) : we're shooting the first sequence today = *nous tournons la première séquence aujourd'hui* ⓪ episode = *épisode*
the sequence of events = *la suite des événements*.

SEQUIN (n) *paillette* (f) : a sequin dress = *une robe à paillettes*.

SERENADE (n) *sérénade* (f) ⓪ ballad = *ballade*.

SERENE (adj) *serein, -e* : a serene old man = *un vieil homme serein* ⓪ peaceful = *paisible* **SERENELY** (adv) *sereinement*.

SERENITY (n, -ies) *sérénité* (f) : passion knows no serenity = *la passion ne connaît pas la sérénité* ⓪ peace = *paix*.

SERF (n) *serf* (m) ⓪ serfdom = *servage*.

SERGEANT (n) *sergent* (m) ⓪ private = *simple soldat*.

SERIAL (n) *feuilleton* (m) : a TV serial = *un feuilleton télévisé*.

SERIES (n inv) *série* (f) : a series of problems = *une série de problèmes* ⓪ sequence = *suite*
in series = *en série* : things happen in series = *les choses arrivent en série*
☠ *série noire* = streak of bad luck
— *production en série* = mass production.

SERIOUS (adj) 1/ *sérieux, -euse* : are you serious about your offer ? = *êtes-vous sérieux quand vous me proposez ça ?* ⓪ sincere = *sincère* 2/ *grave* : a serious accident = *un grave accident* ≠ trivial = *insignifiant* ☠ → *grave*
to give serious thought to = *réfléchir sérieusement à*
it's serious business = *c'est du sérieux* ≠ shenanigans = *de la rigolade*.

SERIOUSLY (adv) *sérieusement* : he said it very

seriously = *il a dit ça très sérieusement* ≠ casually = *sans façons*
to take stg seriously = *prendre qqch au sérieux*.

SERIOUSNESS (n) 1/ *gravité* (f) : the seriousness of the situation = *la gravité de la situation* = gravity 2/ *sérieux* (m) : when you guys talk, what seriousness ! = *les gars, quel sérieux quand vous parlez !*
☠ *garder son sérieux* = to keep a straight face
— *prendre au sérieux* = to take seriously.

SERMON (n) *sermon* (m) : the priest's sermon = *le sermon du prêtre*.

SERUM (n, -s or -ra) *sérum* (m) : truth serum = *sérum de vérité* ⓪ vaccine = *vaccin*.

SERVANT (n) *domestique* (m, f) : few people still have servants = *peu de gens ont encore des domestiques* ⓪ help = *les domestiques*.

SERVE (to, -d) *servir* : who served you ? = *qui vous a servi ?*, at what time is dinner served ? = *à quelle heure sert-on le dîner ?* ⓪ to wait on = *s'occuper de*

---

dinner's served ! = *le dîner est servi !/à table !*
to serve (... years) = *purger (... ans)* : he served three years and then was put on probation = *il a purgé trois ans et a ensuite été mis en liberté conditionnelle*
to serve as = *servir de* : my maid serves as my secretary = *ma bonne me sert de secrétaire* ⓪ to act as = *faire office de*

---

to serve in (the army) = *servir dans (l'armée)* **to serve on (a jury)** = *faire partie d'(un jury)* **to be served with** = *être servi avec* : what's	the chicken served with ? = *avec quoi servez-vous le poulet ?/qu'est-ce qu'il y a comme garniture avec le poulet ?*

☠ *ça ne sert à rien* = it's of no use
— *servez-vous !* = help yourself !
— *à quoi ça sert de (se plaindre) ?* = what's the use of (complaining) ?

SERVICE (n) *service* (m) : the restaurant's service is terrible = *le service de ce restaurant est épouvantable*
can I be of service ? = *est-ce que je peux être utile ?*
in the service = *au service (militaire)/sous les drapeaux* ⓪ in the army = *à l'armée*
out of service = *hors de service* ⓪ out of order = *en panne*
service station = *station-service* ⓪ gas station = *poste à essence*
services will be held (in the church) = *il y aura un office (à l'église)*
☠ *service compris* = tip included
— *pouvez-vous me rendre un service ?* = can you do me a favor ?

— *le service de presse/le service comptabilité* = the press department/the accounting department
— *être de service* = to be on duty.

SERVICE (to, -d) *honorer* : he services the old lady so as not to pay the rent = *il honore la vieille pour ne pas payer le loyer* ⓓ to screw = *baiser* ☠ → to honor.

SERVICEMAN (n, -men) *militaire (m)* : a club for servicemen = *un club de militaires* **SERVICEWOMAN** (n, -women) *femme (f) militaire.*

SERVILE (adj) *servile* : she's submissive and servile = *elle est soumise et servile.*

SESSION (n) *séance (f)* : a recording session = *une séance d'enregistrement* ☠ → séance
I had some session with (my husband) = *j'ai eu une explication avec (mon mari)* ⓓ to quarrel with = *se quereller avec*
in session = *en session* : Congress is in session = *le Parlement est en session.*

SET (n) **a chess/TV/hi-fi set** = *un jeu d'échecs/un poste de télé/une chaîne hi-fi* **on the set** = *sur le plateau* : the director's on the set = *le réalisateur est sur le plateau*	**a set of dishes** = *un service de table* **a set of friends** = *un groupe d'amis* **(shampoo and) set** = *(shampooing et) mise en plis.*

SET (adj) *fixe* : set prices/hours = *prix/heures fixes* = fixed ⓓ established = *établi* ☠ → fixed

all set ! = *fin prêt !* : I'm all set, let's go ! = *je suis fin prête, allons-y !* **to be set in one's ways** = *manquer de souplesse* : she's a typical spinster, she's set in her ways = *c'est la vieille fille type, elle manque de souplesse*	**to be set on** = *tenir à* : I'm set on going abroad this summer with my family = *je tiens à partir à l'étranger cet été avec ma famille* **set ideas** = *idées toutes faites* **set phrase** = *expression consacrée/toute faite.*

SET (to, set, set) *fixer* : to set a date = *fixer une date* ⓓ to agree on = *convenir de* ☠ → to fix

to set s.o. against s.o. = *monter qqn contre qqn* : he set her against her mother = *il l'a montée contre sa mère* **to set aside** = *casser* : to set aside a judgment = *casser un jugement* ⓓ to nullify = *annuler* ☠ → to break **to set stg aside** = *laisser qqch de côté* : he set his book aside to play with the kids = *il a laissé son livre de côté pour jouer avec les gosses* **setting aside (the fact that)** = *en faisant abstraction (du fait que)* ⓓ apart from = *à part* **to set stg back** = *retarder qqch* : the strikes set our production back = *les grèves ont retardé notre production* ⓓ to hinder = *gêner* ☠ → to delay **to set in** = *s'installer* : before winter sets in = *avant que l'hiver s'installe* ☠ → to install **to be set in** = *se situer dans* : the film was set in the Middle	Ages = *le film se situait au Moyen Âge* **to set off** = *déclencher* : inflation set off the economic crisis = *l'inflation a déclenché la crise économique* = to trigger off ⓓ to bring about = *occasionner* ☠ → to trigger off **to set stg off** = *mettre qqch en valeur* : black velvet sets the diamond off = *le velours noir met en valeur le diamant* ⓓ to show off = *faire ressortir* **to set out** = *se mettre en route* : we set out at dawn = *nous nous sommes mis en route à l'aube* → TO LEAVE **to set out to** = *entreprendre de* : she set out to get her first husband back = *elle a entrepris de récupérer son premier mari* **to set to (work)** = *se mettre au (travail)* **to set up** = *créer, implanter* (factory) : to set up a committee/a factory in Kenya = *créer*	*un comité/implanter une usine au Kenya* ⓓ to establish = *établir* ☠ *s'implanter (politique)* = to get a foothold in **to set s.o. up** = *installer qqn* : Jane's parents set him up when he married her = *les parents de Jane l'ont installé quand il l'a épousée* ☠ → to install **to set stg up** = *arranger qqch* : can you set an appointment up for Saturday ? = *est-ce que vous pouvez m'arranger un rendez-vous pour samedi ?* = can you arrange an appointment for Saturday ? ☠ → to arrange **to set o.s. up as (an authority)** = *prétendre être (une autorité)* **to set s.o. up for stg** = *monter (un coup) contre qqn* : they set the Senator up for the scandal = *ils ont monté le scandale contre le sénateur* ⓓ to trump up = *forger de toutes pièces.*

SETBACK (n) **1/** *revers (m)* : the army suffered a setback = *l'armée a subi un revers*
☠ *revers (tennis)* = backhand
— *le revers de la médaille* = the other side of the picture/coin

2/ *recul (m)* : this new law was a setback for civil liberties = *cette nouvelle loi a marqué un recul des libertés publiques*
☠ *un mouvement de recul* = a backward movement
— *être en recul* = to be in recession

— *prendre du recul* = to look at things more objectively
— *un recul de la production* = a decline in production.

SETTING (n) *monture* (f) (ring), *cadre* (m) (story) : an old story in a new setting = *une vieille histoire dans un cadre neuf* ☠ *cadre* → frame.

SETTLE (to, -d) **1/** *régler* : the problem will be settled before June = *le problème sera réglé avant juin*
that settles it ! = *c'est réglé !*
☠ *régler par chèque* = to pay by check
— *régler une machine* = to regulate a machine
2/ *trancher* : we don't agree ; let's ask him and he'll settle it = *nous ne sommes pas d'accord ; demandons-lui et il tranchera* ☠ → to slice
3/ *s'établir* : where did the Pilgrims settle ? = *où les pèlerins se sont-ils établis ?* ☠ → to establish

---

to settle down = **1/** *se tasser* : we won't make the trip till the political situation settles down = *nous ne ferons le voyage que lorsque la situation politique se sera tassée* ⓪ to clear up = *s'éclaircir* ☠ *se tasser dans le métro* = to squeeze into the subway **2/** *se ranger* : when are you going to get married and settle down ? = *quand vas-tu te marier et te ranger ?* ☠ → to tidy up
to settle for = *se contenter de* : I won't settle for being a housewife = *je ne me contenterai* pas d'être une femme au foyer
to settle in = *s'installer en* : to settle in California = *s'installer en Californie*
to settle on = *fixer son choix sur* : we settled on the red one = *nous avons fixé notre choix sur le rouge* ⓪ to decide on = *se décider pour*
to settle up = *faire ses comptes* : you owe me money, I owe you money, let's settle up ! = *vous me devez de l'argent, je vous dois de l'argent, faisons nos comptes !*

SETTLED (adj) *posé, -e* : a settled personality = *une personnalité posée* ⓪ calm = *calme*.

SETTLEMENT (n) **1/** *règlement* (m) : a cash settlement = *un règlement en espèces*
☠ *un règlement de comptes* = a settling of (the) scores
— *suivre le règlement* = to follow the rules and regulations
2/ *colonie* (f) *de peuplement* : new settlements on the West bank = *de nouvelles colonies de peuplement sur la rive ouest*.

SETTLER (n) *colon* (m) : the first settlers were Dutch = *les premiers colons étaient hollandais* ⓪ colonist = *colonialiste*.

SETUP (n) *organisation* (f) : the company has a tremendous setup in Europe = *la société a une organisation fantastique en Europe*
what's the setup ? = *comment s'organise-t-on ?*

SEVEN (n, adj) *sept* (m) : he came at seven o'clock = *il est arrivé à sept heures* ⓪ seventeen = *dix-sept*, seventeenth = *dix-septième*, seventh = *septième*
to be in seventh heaven = *être au septième ciel* ⓪ to be riding high = *être aux anges*
Seventh Avenue = *centre de la confection à New York* = Garment Center
the seven wonders of the world = *les Sept Merveilles du monde*.

SEVENTY (n, -ies, adj) *soixante-dix* (m) ⓪ seventieth = *soixante-dixième*
to be in one's seventies = *avoir soixante-dix ans et quelques* ⓪ to be seventyish = *être dans sa soixante-dixième année*
the seventies = *les années soixante-dix*.

SEVEN-YEAR ITCH (n) *période* (f) *de lassitude après quelques années de mariage, démon* (m) *de midi*.

SEVER (to, -ed) *cesser* : the two countries severed diplomatic relations = *les deux pays ont cessé toutes relations diplomatiques* ⓪ to break off = *rompre*.

SEVERAL (adj) *plusieurs* : several times = *plusieurs fois* ≠ a few = *quelques* → MANY.

SEVERE (adj) **1/** *sévère* : a severe criticism/winter = *une critique/un hiver sévère* ⓪ harsh = *rude* ≠ clement = *clément* **2/** *grave* : a severe increase in unemployment = *une grave augmentation du chômage* ☠ → grave **SEVERELY** (adv) *gravement* : severely wounded = *gravement blessé*.

SEVERITY (n, -ies) *sévérité* (f) : he treated his students with severity = *il traitait ses élèves avec sévérité*.

SEW (to, -ed, -ed or sewn) *coudre* : few men know how to sew = *il a y peu d'hommes qui savent coudre* ⓪ to embroider = *broder*, thimble = *dé à coudre*, needle = *aiguille*, to mend = *raccommoder*, sewing machine = *machine à coudre*
to sew up = *mener à bonne fin* : we sewed up the deal quickly = *nous avons rapidement mené l'affaire à bonne fin* ⓪ to wind up = *boucler*.

SEWER (n) *égout* (m) : he hid in a sewer during the war = *il s'est caché dans un égout pendant la guerre*.

SEWING (n) *couture* (f) : I hate sewing = *je déteste la couture* ☠ → seam.

SEX (n, -es) **1/** (inv) *sexe* (m), *cul* (m) (LV) : all he talks about is sex = *il ne sait parler que de cul*, he's only interested in sex = *il ne s'intéresse qu'au sexe/qu'au cul* ⓪ monkey business = *la bagatelle* ☠ *cul* = ass **2/** *sexe* (m) : both sexes can do most jobs = *la plupart des métiers sont accessibles aux deux sexes* **3/** (inv) *amour* (m) (sexuel/physique) : she always thought sex was wrong = *elle a toujours pensé que l'amour sexuel/physique était une mauvaise chose* ☠ → love
female ≠ **male sex** = *sexe fêminin* ≠ *masculin*
to have sex = *avoir des rapports sexuels* : the first time she had sex, she was fifteen = *la première fois qu'elle a*

eu des rapports sexuels, elle avait quinze ans ⓪ to make love = *faire l'amour*

sex appeal = *sex-appeal* ⓪ attraction = *attrait*
sex drive = *appétit sexuel*
a sex kitten = *une vraie chatte* : he's married to a sex kitten = *il a épousé une vraie chatte*
sex maniac/fiend = *obsédé sexuel*
sex organs = *organes sexuels*
sex outside marriage = *rapports extraconjugaux*
sex shop = *sex-shop*
sex symbol = *sex-symbol*
☠ *elle a saisi son sexe* = she grabbed his crotch
— *un petit sexe* = a small organ.

SEXED-UP (adj) *qui a le feu aux fesses* : I feel sexed-up tonight = *ce soir, j'ai le feu aux fesses* ⓪ hot and bothered = *tout chose*.

SEXISM (n) *sexisme (m)* **SEXIST** (n, adj) *sexiste (m, f)* : a sexist pig = *un sale sexiste* ⓪ male chauvinist pig = *phallocrate*.

SEXOLOGIST (n) *sexologue (m, f)* **SEXOLOGY** (n) *sexologie (f)*.

SEXPOT (n) *fille (f) bandante* : he's married to a sexpot = *il a épousé une fille vachement bandante* ⓪ hot mamma = *nympho*.

SEXUAL (adj) *sexuel, -elle* : sexual problems = *problèmes sexuels* ≠ asexual = *asexuel* = sexless **SEXUALITY** (n) *sexualité (f)*.

SEXY (adj, -ier, -iest) *sexy* : a sexy broad/dress = *une nana/une robe sexy* ⓪ erotic = *érotique*.

SHABBY (adj, -ier, -iest) *miteux, -euse* : shabby houses/clothes = *des maisons miteuses/des vêtements miteux* ⓪ seedy = *peu reluisant* ≠ posh = *rupin* **SHABBILY** (adv) *miteusement*.

SHACK (n) *cahute (f)* : a lot of poor people still live in shacks = *il y a encore pas mal de gens pauvres qui vivent dans des cahutes* ⓪ hut = *hutte*.

SHACK UP (to, -ed) *vivre à la colle* : they've been shacking up for a year = *ils vivent à la colle depuis un an* ⓪ to sleep together = *coucher ensemble*.

SHADE (n) **1/** *ombre (f)* : let's sit in the shade = *asseyons-nous à l'ombre* ≠ sun = *soleil*
a shade of (mauve) = *une ombre de (mauve)*
☠ *il est à l'ombre (prison)* = he's in the clink
— *il n'y a pas l'ombre d'un doute* = it's beyond the shadow of a doubt
— *pas l'ombre d'une chance* = not the ghost of a chance
— *il a peur de son ombre* = he's afraid of his shadow
— *il y a une ombre au tableau* = there's a fly in the ointment
2/ *store (m)* : pull down the shades = *tirez les stores* ⓪ shutter = *volet*.

SHADOW (n) *ombre (f)* : he's afraid of his shadow = *il a peur de son ombre*

it's beyond the shadow of a doubt = *il n'y a pas l'ombre d'un doute* ⓪ it's a sure thing = *c'est chose sûre*
to have shadows under one's eyes = *avoir les yeux cernés*
☠ → shade.

SHADOW (to, -ed) *prendre en filature* : the cops are shadowing him = *les flics l'ont pris en filature* ⓪ to dog = *talonner*.

SHADY (adj, -ier, -iest) *louche* : shady dealings = *des affaires louches* ≠ aboveboard = *sans équivoque* ☠ → fishy.

SHAFT (to, -ed) *entuber* : he was shafted by his partner = *il s'est fait entuber par son associé* → TO HUSTLE.

SHAGGY-DOG STORY (n, -ies) *histoire (f) à dormir debout*.

SHAKE (to, shook, shaken) **1/** *secouer* : shake the bottle = *secouez la bouteille* ⓪ to mix = *mélanger* **2/** *secouer* : the news really shook us = *la nouvelle nous a vraiment secoués* ⓪ to jar = *ébranler* ☠ *secoue-toi !* = get yourself together ! **3/** *trembler* : to shake from the cold = *trembler de froid* = to tremble ⓪ to shudder = *frémir*
let's shake on it ! = *topez là !* ⓪ it's a deal ! = *marché conclu !*
to shake s.o. down = *faire cracher qqn* : they tried to shake the Senator down = *ils ont essayé de faire cracher le sénateur* ⓪ to blackmail = *faire chanter*
to shake s.o. off = *semer qqn* : he followed me till I was able to shake him off = *il m'a suivi jusqu'à ce que j'arrive à le semer*
to shake off = *se défaire de* : I can't shake off this sore throat = *je n'arrive pas à me défaire de ce mal de gorge* ⓪ to get rid of = *se débarrasser de*
to shake s.o. up = *secouer qqn* : the news of his death shook us up = *la nouvelle de sa mort nous a secoués* ⓪ to upset = *bouleverser*.

SHAKEDOWN (n) *extorsion (f) de fonds* : the Mafia's shakedown of the casinos = *l'extorsion de fonds de la Mafia sur tous les casinos*.

SHAKES (n pl) **to have the shakes** = *avoir la tremblote* ⓪ that gives me the chills = *ça me fait froid dans le dos*.

SHAKEUP (n) *grand remaniement (m)* (cabinet), *vaste mouvement (m)* (personnel) : a shakeup in the government/in the company = *un grand remaniement au gouvernement/un vaste mouvement de personnel dans la société* ⓪ upheaval = *bouleversement*.

SHAKY (adj, -ier, -iest) **1/** *tremblant, -e* (hands), *branlant, -e* (table, government) **2/** *faiblard, -e* : the charges against her are shaky = *les accusations portées contre elle sont faiblardes* ⓪ precarious = *précaire*
to be on shaky ground = *être sur un terrain glissant*.

SHALLOW (adj) *peu profond, -e, sans profondeur* : a shallow river/personality = *une rivière peu profonde/*

une personnalité sans profondeur ⑩ superficial = *superficiel.*

SHAM (n) *simulacre* (m) : the trial/the election was a sham = *ça a été un simulacre de procès/d'élection* ⑩ parody = *parodie.*

SHAMBLES (n inv) *capharnaüm* (m) : your room is in shambles = *c'est le capharnaüm dans ta chambre* ⑩ havoc = *chambardement*, mess = *pagaille.*

SHAME (n) *honte* (f) : I felt no shame telling him I was a lesbian = *je n'ai éprouvé aucune honte à lui dire que j'étais lesbienne*
it's a crying shame ! = *c'est une honte !*
it's a shame (you can't come) = *c'est dommage (que vous ne puissiez pas venir)*
to put to shame = *faire honte à* : her playing put the others to shame = *son jeu a fait honte aux autres*
shame on you ! = *tu n'as pas honte !*
☠ *avoir honte* = to be ashamed
— *ce n'est pas une honte d'être pauvre* = it's no disgrace to be poor.

SHAMEFUL (adj) *honteux, -euse* : shameful behavior = *comportement honteux* ⑩ scandalous = *scandaleux* ☠ *un homosexuel honteux* = a closet homosexual
— *j'étais honteux d'avoir fait ça* = I was ashamed to have done that.

SHAMELESS (adj) *éhonté, -e* : shameless lying = *mensonge éhonté* ⑩ brazen = *effronté.*

SHAMPOO (n) *shampooing* (m) : a shampoo and set = *un shampooing et une mise en plis.*

SHANTYTOWN (n) *bidonville* (m) : shantytowns at the edge of the city = *des bidonvilles à la périphérie de la ville* ⑩ skid row = *les bas-fonds.*

SHAPE (n) **1/** *forme* (f) : in the shape of a snowman = *en forme de bonhomme de neige* ☠ → form
to be in good ≠ **bad shape** = *être* ≠ *ne pas être en forme* (people) / *marcher bien* ≠ *mal* : she/the business is in good shape = *elle est en forme/l'affaire marche bien*
to be in ≠ **out of shape** = *avoir* ≠ *ne pas avoir la forme*
to keep in shape = *se maintenir en forme*
to take shape = *prendre forme* : our plans are taking shape = *nos projets prennent forme* ⑩ to materialize = *se matérialiser*
2/ *silhouette* (f) : she has a great shape = *elle a une très belle silhouette* ⑩ figure = *ligne.*

SHAPELESS (adj) *informe* : a shapeless garment = *un habit informe* ⑩ misshapen = *difforme.*

SHAPELY (adj, -ier, -iest) *bien fait, -e* : a shapely broad = *une nana bien faite* ⑩ built like a battleship = *bien roulé*, well-built = *bien bâti.*

SHAPE UP (to, -d) *prendre forme* : the plan/team is shaping up = *le projet/l'équipe prend forme* ⑩ the plan/team is taking shape

shape up or ship out ! = *il faut vous soumettre ou vous démettre !/ou tu te tiens à carreau ou tu te tires !*

SHARE (n) **1/** *action* (f) : he has shares in the company = *il possède des actions dans la société* ⑩ treasury bond = *bon du Trésor* ☠ → action
2/ *part* (f) : you didn't give me my share = *vous ne m'avez pas donné ma part* ⑩ capital = ←
☠ *faire la part du feu* = to cut one's losses
— *faire la part des choses* = to sort things out
— *de la part de (Joe)* = on behalf of (Joe).

SHARE (to, -d) *partager* : we'll share the cake/profits = *nous allons partager le gâteau/les bénéfices* ⑩ to divide = *diviser* ☠ *partager un pays* = to partition a country.

SHAREHOLDER (n) *actionnaire* (m, f) : all the shareholders get a dividend = *tous les actionnaires touchent des dividendes.*

SHARK (n) *requin* (m) : all businessmen are sharks = *tous les hommes d'affaires sont des requins*, waters full of sharks = *des eaux grouillantes de requins.*

SHARP (adj, -er, -est) **1/** *pointu, -e* : a sharp knife = *un couteau pointu* ≠ blunt = *émoussé*
to have a sharp tongue = *avoir la langue bien affilée/acérée*
2/ *très astucieux, -euse* : her kids are sharp = *ses gosses sont très astucieux*, a sharp businessman = *un homme d'affaires très astucieux* ⑩ clever = *malin*
he's as sharp as a tack = *rien ne lui échappe* ⑩ he's on the ball = *il est dégourdi*
a sharp dresser = *quelqu'un de chicos*
a sharp pain = *une douleur vive* ⑩ acute = *aiguë*
a sharp rise (in prices) = *une brusque hausse (des prix).*

SHARP (adv) **at (five o'clock) sharp** = *à (cinq heures) pile.*

SHARPEN (to, -ed) *aiguiser* : to sharpen one's mind = *aiguiser son esprit.*

SHARPIE = SHARPY (n, -ies) *aigrefin* (m) ⑩ con man = *affairiste.*

SHARPSHOOTER (n) *tireur* (m) *d'élite* : his bodyguards are sharpshooters = *ses gardes du corps sont des tireurs d'élite* ⑩ crack shot = *fin tireur.*

SHATTER (to, -ed) *voler en éclats* : the glass fell and shattered = *le verre est tombé a volé en éclats* ⑩ to break = *se casser*
to be shattered by (the news) = *être anéanti par (la nouvelle)* ⑩ to be devastated = *être bouleversé.*

SHAVE (n) *rasage* (m), *le fait de se raser* : I need a good shave = *j'ai bien besoin de me raser* ⑩ razor = *rasoir*
SHAVE (to, -d, -d or shaven) *(se) raser* : most men shave every day = *la plupart des hommes se rasent tous les jours* ☠ → to raze.

SHAWL (n) *châle* (m) : to knit a shawl = *tricoter un châle* ⑩ scarf = *écharpe.*

SHE (pron) *elle* : she told me she was sick = *elle m'a dit qu'elle était malade* → I
☠ *c'est elle* = it's her
— *c'est à elle* = it's hers
— *elles ont tort* = they're wrong
— *avec elles* = with them.

SHED (n) *remise* (f) : there's a shed in the garden = *il y a une remise dans le jardin* ⚭ shack = *cahute*
☠ *remise de dix pour cent* = a discount of ten percent
— *remise des Oscars* = presentation of the Oscars
— *remise (décision)* = postponement.

SHEEP (n inv) *mouton* (m) : the sheep are grazing = *les moutons paissent* ⚭ lamb = *agneau*, shepherd = *berger*, to shear = *tondre*
to make sheep's eyes at = *faire les yeux doux à*
☠ *revenons à nos moutons* = let's get back to the subject
— *un mouton (traître)* = a stoolie
— *un mouton de Panurge* = a follower
— *un mouton à cinq pattes* = a very unusual person or thing
— *ragoût de mouton* = mutton stew.

SHEEPISH (adj) *penaud, -e* : a sheepish look = *un regard penaud* ⚭ embarrassed = *embarrassé*.

SHEER (adj, -er, -est) 1/ *pur, -e* : it's sheer stupidity/madness = *c'est de la pure stupidité/folie* ⚭ utter = *parfait* 2/ *presque transparent, -e* : a sheer blouse = *une blouse presque transparente* ⚭ transparent = ←
by sheer (hard work) = *à force de (travail)* ⚭ by dint of = *uniquement grâce à*
in ≠ out of sheer desperation (he rented a car) = *en désespoir de cause (il a loué une voiture)*.

SHEET (n) *drap* (m) : the sheets are dirty = *les draps sont sales* ⚭ blanket = *couverture*
a sheet of paper = *une feuille de papier* ⚭ a piece of paper = *un bout de papier*.

SHEIKH (n) *cheikh* (m) ⚭ emir = *émir*.

SHELF (n, -ves) *étagère* (f) : put the book on the bottom shelf = *posez le livre sur l'étagère du bas* ⚭ bookcase = *bibliothèque*
to put s.o. on the shelf = *mettre qqn sur une voie de garage* : he's too young to be put on the shelf = *il est trop jeune pour être mis sur une voie de garage*.

SHELL (n) 1/ *coquille* (f) (egg, nut, etc.), *carapace* (f) (turtle, lobster, etc.)
to come out of one's shell = *sortir de sa coquille* 2/ *obus* (m) : the shell exploded in the garden = *l'obus a explosé dans le jardin* ⚭ mortar = *mortier*.

SHELLACKING (n) *dérouillée* (f) : what a shellacking his father gave him ! = *son père lui a flanqué une de ces dérouillées !* → TO HIT.

SHELLFISH (n inv) *crustacés* (m pl), *coquillages* (m pl) : shellfish for dinner = *des crustacés pour le dîner*.

SHELL OUT (to, -ed) *casquer* : we all shelled out five dollars to buy her a birthday present = *nous avons tous casqué cinq dollars pour lui acheter un cadeau d'anniversaire* ⚭ to cough up = *cracher*.

SHELTER (n inv) *abri* (m) : it was raining and we looked for shelter = *il pleuvait et nous avons cherché un abri*
to give s.o. shelter = *donner asile à qqn*
to take shelter = *se mettre à l'abri*
☠ *ils sont sans abri* = they're without a roof over their heads.

SHELTER (to, -ed) *(s')abriter* : the telephone booth sheltered us from the rain = *la cabine téléphonique nous a abrités de la pluie* ⚭ to protect = *protéger*.

SHELTERED (adj) *bien protégé, -e* : a sheltered life = *une vie bien protégée* ⚭ protected = *protégé*.

SHELVE (to, -d) *laisser en suspens* : Congress shelved the bill = *le Congrès a laissé le projet de loi en suspens* ⚭ to put on ice = *laisser en sommeil*.

SHENANIGANS (n pl) 1/ *coucheries* (f pl) : shenanigans at the office between the boss and his secretaries = *des coucheries au bureau entre le patron et ses secrétaires* ⚭ monkey business = *la bagatelle* 2/ *magouillage* (m) : a lot of shenanigans during the elections = *pas mal de magouillages au cours des élections* ⚭ hanky-panky = *cuisine* 3/ *rigolade* (f) : a lot of shenanigans in the classroom when the teacher went out = *une grosse rigolade dans la classe quand le professeur est sorti* ⚭ antics = *clowneries*
☠ *c'est de la rigolade !* = it isn't true !
— *prendre qqch à la rigolade* = not to take stg seriously.

SHEPHERD (n) *berger* : she fell in love with a shepherd = *elle est tombée amoureuse d'un berger* ⚭ herd = *troupeau* **SHEPHERDESS** (n, -es) *bergère* (f).

SHERIFF (n) *shérif* (m) : the sheriff of Dallas = *le shérif de Dallas* ≠ outlaw = *hors-la-loi*.

SHIELD (n) *bouclier* (m) : knights used shields for protection = *les chevaliers utilisaient des boucliers pour se protéger* ⚭ armor = *armure*.

SHIELD (to, -ed) *protéger* : she tries to shield her children from realities = *elle essaie de protéger ses enfants des réalités* = to protect.

SHIFT (n) 1/ *roulement* (m) : each shift is four hours = *on travaille par roulements de quatre heures* 2/ *équipe* (f) *de travail* : each shift works eight hours = *chaque équipe travaille huit heures*
day/night shift = *équipe de jour/de nuit*.

SHIFT (to, -ed) *changer (de place)* : it's cold here, let's shift = *il fait froid ici, changeons de place*
to shift around = *déplacer* : we shifted the furniture around = *nous avons déplacé les meubles* ☠ *il se déplace difficilement* = he gets around/moves about with difficulty

to shift for oneself = *être autonome* : he's been shifting for himself since the age of fifteen = *il est autonome depuis qu'il a quinze ans* ⓓ to be on one's own = *se débrouiller tout seul.*

SHIFTY (adj, -ier, -iest) *douteux, -euse* : a shifty character = *un personnage douteux* ⓓ sly = *sournois* ☠ → doubtful.

SHIKSA (n) *goy (fille)* : he married a shiksa = *il a épousé une goy* ≠ shegetz = *goy (garçon).*

SHINDIG (n) *raout (m)* : there's a big shindig at the White House = *il y a un grand raout à la Maison-Blanche* = bash ⓓ blowout = *nouba.*

SHINE (n) **to take a shine to** = *avoir à la bonne* : my brother took a shine to you = *mon frère t'a à la bonne* ⓓ to be sweet on = *avoir un faible pour.*

SHINE (to, -d, -d (stg) or shone, shone) *(faire) briller* : the sun's shining = *le soleil brille,* to shine one's shoes = *faire briller ses chaussures* ⓓ to beam = *resplendir,* to shimmer = *miroiter,* to glisten = *chatoyer,* to gleam = *reluire*
☠ *tout ce qui brille n'est pas or* = all that glitters isn't gold
— *briller par son absence* = to be conspicuous by one's absence
— *il ne brille pas en maths* = math isn't his strong point
— *le besoin de briller* = the need to be brilliant/to stand out.

SHINGLE (n) *bardeau (m)* : shingles on the roofs = *des toits de bardeaux* ⓓ tile = *tuile.*

SHINY (adj, -ier, -iest) *brillant, -e* : shiny paper = *papier brillant* ≠ mat = ← ☠ → brilliant.

SHIP (n) *navire (m)* : the ship sank = *le navire a coulé* ⓓ shipwreck = *naufrage,* shipyard = *chantier naval,* shipment = *embarquement,* shipowner = *armateur,* porthole = *hublot*
to give up the ship = *abandonner le navire*

to jump ship = *déserter le navire*
when my ship comes in = *quand j'aurai hérité de mon oncle d'Amérique* : I'll buy you a splendid house when my ship comes in = *je t'achèterai une maison splendide quand j'aurai hérité de mon oncle d'Amérique* ⓓ every dog has its day = *tout vient à point à qui sait attendre.*

SHIP (to, -ped) *expédier* : we shipped the goods last week = *nous avons expédié la marchandise la semaine dernière* ⓓ to send = *envoyer*
☠ *on a expédié le poulet* = we polished off the chicken
— *expédier des troupes* = to dispatch troops
— *elle expédie ses gosses chez sa mère* = she packs her kids off to her mother's.

SHIPSHAPE (adj) *impec* : in shipshape order = *dans un ordre impec* ≠ messy = *pagailleux.*

SHIPWRECK (n) *naufrage (m)* ⓓ wrecker = *naufrageur.*

SHIRK (to, -ed) *se soustraire à* : to shirk one's responsibilities = *se soustraire à ses responsabilités* ⓓ to avoid = *éviter.*

SHIRT (n) *chemise (f)* : a black shirt = *une chemise noire* ⓓ blouse = *chemisier*
he'd give the shirt off his back = *il donnerait sa chemise*
in one's shirt sleeves = *en manches/bras de chemise*
keep your shirt on ! = *doucement !* ⓓ just a minute ! = *une minute !*
to lose one's shirt = *y laisser sa chemise* ≠ to make a pile = *se faire une petite pelote*
to be a stuffed shirt = *avoir avalé un parapluie* : what a stuffed shirt he is ! = *celui-là, il a avalé un parapluie !* ≠ a cool cat = *un mec cool*
☠ *chemise (bureau)* = folder
— *changer (d'avis) comme de chemise* = to change (one's mind) continually
— *chemise de nuit* = nightgown.

SHIT (n) **1/** (inv) *merde (f)* : I stepped into some shit = *j'ai marché dans une merde* ⓓ dropping = *crotte,* manure = *fumier,* number two = *grosse commission,* to do one's duty = *faire caca,* excrement = *excrément*
2/ (inv) *merde (f)* : what's all this shit on the bed ? = *qu'est-ce que c'est que toute cette merde sur le lit ?* ⓓ junk = *cochonneries*
3/ *salopard, salope* : she's married to a real shit = *elle a épousé un véritable salopard* → BASTARD

to be up shit creek (without a paddle) = *être dans la merde (jusqu'au cou)*
cut the shit, man ! = *arrête tes conneries, mon vieux !* → BUZZ OFF !
I don't give a shit ! = *je n'en ai rien à branler !* ⓓ I don't give a fuck ! = *je n'en ai rien à foutre !,* I don't give a damn ! = *je m'en fiche !*
to have the shits = *avoir la chiasse* ⓓ to have the runs = *avoir la courante*
to knock/beat the shit out of s.o. = *casser la gueule à qqn* → TO HIT

no shit ! = *ben merde alors !* : so you're finally getting married, no shit ! = *alors finalement tu te maries, ben merde alors !* → GOSH !
oh shit ! = *merde alors !* → GOSH !
a piece of shit = *de la merde* : this watch is a piece of shit = *cette montre, c'est de la merde* ⓓ a piece of dreck = *de la saloperie*
to scare the shit out of = *foutre la trouille à* : the noise scared the shit out of me = *le bruit m'a foutu la trouille* ⓓ to scare the pants off s.o. = *faire trembler qqn dans sa culotte*

shit list = *liste noire de merde :* I'm on the boss's shit list = *je suis sur la liste noire de merde du patron*
that's a lot of shit ! = *ce sont des conneries !* = that's a lot of bullshit !

to treat s.o. like shit = *traiter qqn comme de la merde*
when the shit hits the fan = *ça va chier (des bulles)*
who gives a shit ? = *qu'est-ce que ça peut foutre ?*

SHIT (to, shit or shat) *chier :* I have to go shit = *il faut que j'aille chier* ⅅ to take a shit = *chier un coup,* to defecate = *déféquer*
to shit on s.o. = *baiser qqn dans les grandes largeurs* → TO HUSTLE

☠ *ça va chier* = when the shit hits the fan

— *tu me fais chier !* = you're a pain in the ass !

SHITHOLE (n) *merdier (m) :* this place is a real shithole = *cet endroit est un vrai merdier* ⅅ fucking mess = *bordel*
to be in a shithole = *être dans un merdier* ⅅ to be in a mess = *être dans de beaux draps.*

SHITLOAD (n) **a shitload of (problems)** = *une chiée de (problèmes)* → MANY.

SHITTY (adj, -ier, -iest) **1/** *merdique :* a shitty film = *un film merdique* → AWFUL **2/** *salaud :* that was a shitty thing to say = *c'était salaud de dire ça* ⅅ lousy = *dégueulasse,* ratty = *vache*
to feel shitty = *être mal foutu :* I feel shitty today = *je suis mal foutu aujourd'hui* ⅅ to feel like hell = *être mal fichu*
to feel shitty about = *se sentir merdeux de :* I feel shitty about not having been able to help them = *je me sens merdeux de n'avoir pas réussi à les aider* ⅅ to feel lousy = *se sentir morveux.*

SHIVER (to, -ed) *frissonner, grelotter :* it's so cold, I'm shivering = *il fait tellement froid que je frissonne/grelotte* ⅅ to shake = *trembler,* to quiver = *frémir.*

SHIVERS (n pl) **to give s.o. the shivers** = *donner des frissons à qqn :* the movie gave me the shivers = *le film m'a donné des frissons* ⅅ the shakes = *la tremblote.*

SHOCK (n) *choc (m) :* the news was a shock = *cette nouvelle a été un choc,* the shock of the accident = *le choc de l'accident* ⅅ jolt = *coup* **SHOCK** (to, -ed) *choquer :* his attitude shocked me = *son attitude m'a choqué* ⅅ to startle = *sidérer.*

SHOCKING (adj) *choquant, -e :* a shocking remark = *une remarque choquante* ⅅ startling = *sidérant.*

SHODDY (adj, -ier, -iest) *de pacotille :* shoddy jewelry = *des bijoux de pacotille* ⅅ trashy = *de quatre sous.*

SHOE (n) *chaussure (f), pompe (f)* (LV) : I like your shoes = *j'aime vos chaussures* ⅅ sneakers = *tennis/baskets,* sandals = *sandales,* boots = *bottes,* loafers = *mocassins,* shoehorn = *chausse-pied,* shoelace = *lacet,* shoemaker = *cordonnier,* shoe polish = *cirage,* clogs = *sabots,* shoe size = *pointure,* flats = *talons plats,* mules = *←,* high heels = *talons hauts*
I wouldn't like to be in her shoes = *je n'aimerais pas être à sa place*
if the shoe fits, wear it ! = *qui se sent morveux, (qu'il) se mouche !* ⅅ a word to the wise is sufficient ! = *à bon entendeur, salut !*
the shoe is on the other foot = *les rôles sont inversés* ☠ *trouver chaussure à son pied* = to find one's match.

SHOESTRING (n) **on a shoestring** = *avec trois fois rien :* we started the partnership on a shoestring = *nous avons commencé notre association avec trois fois rien.*

SHOO AWAY (to, -ed) *faire partir :* Tom shooed the dog away = *Tom a fait partir le chien* ⅅ to chase away = *chasser.*

SHOO-IN (n) *gagnant, -e d'avance :* as a candidate, he's a shoo-in = *comme candidat, il est gagnant d'avance* ⅅ winner = *gagnant.*

SHOOT (to, shot, shot) **1/** *tirer :* who taught you to shoot ? = *qui vous a appris à tirer ?* ☠ → to pull **2/** *claquer :* to shoot a fortune in two months = *claquer une fortune en deux mois* ⅅ to spend = *dépenser* ☠ → to slam **3/** *tourner :* to shoot a film = *tourner un film* ⅅ on location = *en extérieur* ☠ → to turn **4/** *fusiller* (s.o.), *tirer sur :* they don't hang prisoners, they shoot them = *ils ne pendent pas les prisonniers, ils les fusillent,* he shot the rabbit = *il a tiré sur le lapin*

I could shoot you ! = *je pourrais te tuer !*
shoot ! = *parlez !/posez vos questions !* (press conference) : I'm listening ! shoot ! = *je vous écoute,*

parlez !/posez vos questions ! ⅅ go ahead ! = *allez-y !*

---

to shoot at s.o. = *tirer sur qqn :* the cops shot at the terrorists = *les flics ont tiré sur les terroristes* = to fire at s.o. ⅅ to draw a gun = *sortir une arme*
to shoot back = *riposter :* the President shot back

that he would maintain his policy = *le Président a riposté qu'il maintiendrait sa politique* ⅅ to retort = *rétorquer*
to shoot down = *abattre :* his plane was shot down

---

in the Far East = *son avion a été abattu en Extrême-Orient* ⓐ to down = *descendre* ☠ → to cover

to shoot stg down = *descendre qqch* : Congress shot the bill down = *le Congrès a descendu le projet de loi* ⓐ to kill = *massacrer*

to shoot up = 1/ *pousser* : her children shoot up

quickly = *ses enfants poussent vite* ☠ → to push 2/ *se shooter* : the junkies often use old needles to shoot up = *les camés utilisent souvent des seringues usagées pour se shooter* ⓐ drug = *drogue* 3/ *monter en flèche* : prices shot up = *les prix ont monté en flèche* ≠ to plummet = *descendre brusquement.*

SHOOTING (n) *tournage* (m) : five weeks of shooting = *cinq semaines de tournage.*

SHOOTOUT (n) *fusillade* (f) : a shootout on 5th Avenue = *une fusillade sur la 5e Avenue.*

SHOP (n) *(petit) magasin* (m), *boutique* (f) : I bought it in the shop around the corner = *je l'ai acheté dans le magasin/la boutique au coin de la rue* = boutique ⓐ store = *(grand) magasin*

to close shop = *fermer boutique* ⓐ to fold = *déposer son bilan*

closed ≠ **open shop** = *usine où les syndicats ont* ≠ *n'ont pas le monopole de l'embauche*

to talk shop = *parler boutique* ⓐ to talk business = *parler affaires.*

SHOP (to, -ped) *faire les magasins* : I'm shopping for a gift for my mother = *je fais les magasins pour trouver un cadeau pour ma mère*

to go shopping = *faire des courses* ⓐ to go window-shopping = *faire du lèche-vitrines*

to shop around = *comparer les prix* : we're shopping around for a powerful hi-fi set = *nous sommes en train de comparer les prix pour acheter une chaîne stéréo puissante.*

SHOPKEEPER (n) *commerçant, -e* : there are few shopkeepers left in New York = *il reste peu de commerçants à New York.*

SHOPLIFT (to, -ed) *voler à l'étalage* : she was caught shoplifting = *elle a été prise en train de voler à l'étalage* ⓐ to make off with = *faire main basse sur* **SHOPLIFTER** (n) *voleur, -euse à l'étalage.*

SHOPPING (n inv) *courses* (f pl) : do you have any shopping to do this afternoon ? = *est-ce que vous avez des courses à faire cet après-midi ?*

shopping center = *centre commercial* ☠ → race.

SHORE (n) *rivage* (m) : let's walk on the shore = *allons nous promener sur le rivage* ⓐ bank = *rive/berge*, offshore = *off-shore*

to hug the shore = *longer la côte* ⓐ oil slick = *marée noire*

let's go to the shore ! = *si on allait au bord de la mer ?*

SHORE UP (to, -d) *consolider* : the government took measures to shore up the economy = *le gouvernement a pris des mesures pour consolider l'économie* ⓐ to bolster = *soutenir* ☠ → to consolidate.

SHORT (n) *court métrage* (m) : a moving short on the massacre of baby seals = *un court métrage émouvant sur le massacre des bébés phoques* ⓐ film = ←

---

for short = *(comme) diminutif* : his name is Alexander but they call him Alex for short = *son nom est Alexandre mais son diminutif est Alex*

in short = *bref* : in short they finally got divorced = *bref, ils ont finalement divorcé* = to cut a long story short.

SHORT (adj, -er, -est) **1/** *petit, -e* : he's very short = *il est très petit* ≠ tall = *grand* ☠ → little **2/** *court, -e* : a short trip = *un court voyage* ⓐ brief = *bref*

☠ *tourner court* = to come to a sudden end
— *prendre de court* = to catch unawares

— *tirer à la courte paille* = to draw lots

---

we're ($ 100) short = *il nous manque (100 dollars)*

you're (a little) short on (patience) = *vous manquez (un peu) de (patience)*

to get the short end of the stick/deal = *sortir perdant de quelque chose* : you got the short end of the stick in the deal = *vous êtes sorti perdant de cette affaire* ≠ to get the lion's share = *se tailler la part du lion*

you have a short memory =

vous avez la mémoire courte

to make short work of = *liquider en vitesse* : let's make short work of the job and go out to eat = *liquidons le boulot en vitesse et allons manger* ⓐ to finish off = *finir*

on such short notice = *dans un délai si bref* : I can't make dinner for ten people on such short notice = *je ne peux pas préparer un dîner pour dix personnes dans un délai si bref*

short circuit = *court-circuit*

short for = *l'abréviation de* : UN is short for United Nations = *l'ONU est l'abréviation de l'Organisation des Nations unies* ⓐ initials = *sigle*

short of (money) = *à court d'(argent)*

a short story = *une nouvelle* : she wrote a lot of short stories = *elle a écrit beaucoup de nouvelles* ⓐ an essay = *un essai* ☠ → news.

SHORT (adv) **to cut short** = *écourter* : I cut my trip/speech short = *j'ai écourté mon voyage/mon discours*
to fall short (of) = *être loin derrière* : this year's production falls short of last year's = *la production de cette année est loin derrière celle de l'année dernière*
I'll make it short and sweet = *parlons peu, mais parlons bien*
to run short = *commencer à manquer de* : we're

running short of money/cigarettes = *nous commençons à manquer d'argent/de cigarettes* ⓓ to run low = *s'épuiser*
to sell short = *vendre à découvert*
to sell s.o. short = *sous-estimer qqn* : don't sell her short, she's a fabulous actress = *ne la sous-estimez pas, c'est une actrice fabuleuse*
short of = *à part* : short of killing, there's little he wouldn't do to get money = *à part tuer, il reculerait devant peu de choses pour obtenir de l'argent.*

SHORTAGE (n) *pénurie (f)* : a shortage of manpower = *une pénurie de main-d'œuvre* ⓓ lack = *manque.*

SHORTCHANGE (to, -d) *léser* : he was shortchanged in the deal = *il a été lésé dans l'affaire* → TO HUSTLE ☠ *léser qqn de ses droits* = to encroach on s.o.'s rights.

SHORT-CIRCUIT (to, -ed) *court-circuiter* : he short-circuited the sales manager and asked the big boss directly = *il a court-circuité le directeur des ventes et a demandé directement au grand patron.*

SHORTCOMING (n) *défaut (m)* : his biggest short-coming is his stinginess = *son plus gros défaut, c'est l'avarice* ⓓ failing = *travers* ☠ → defect.

SHORTCUT (n) *raccourci (m)* : to take a shortcut = *prendre un raccourci* ≠ the long way around = *le chemin des écoliers.*

SHORTEN (to, -ed) *raccourcir* : to shorten a dress/a trip = *raccourcir une robe/un voyage* ≠ to extend = *étendre.*

SHORTHAND (n) *sténo(graphie) (f)* : to take shorthand = *prendre en sténo*
shorthand typist = *sténodactylo.*

SHORTHANDED (adj) *à court de personnel* : it's vacation time and we're shorthanded = *c'est la période des vacances et nous sommes à court de personnel.*

SHORT-LIVED (adj) *éphémère* : a short-lived romance = *une aventure sentimentale éphémère* ⓓ momentary = *momentané* ≠ everlasting = *qui dure toujours.*

SHORTLY (adv) *sous peu* : he's coming shortly = *il va arriver sous peu* ⓓ soon = *bientôt*
shortly before = *peu avant* : I met my husband shortly before the war broke out = *j'ai rencontré mon mari peu avant que la guerre éclate.*

SHORT-RANGE (adj) *à court terme* : short-range planning = *planification à court terme.*

SHORTS (n pl) **1/** *short (m)* : what sexy shorts ! = *quel short sexy !* **2/** *caleçon (m) américain* : when he opened the door he was in shorts = *quand il a ouvert la porte, il était en caleçon américain* ⓓ drawers = *caleçon*, jockstrap = *suspensoir.*

SHORTSIGHTED (adj) *à courte vue* : a shortsighted policy = *une politique à courte vue* ≠ clear-sighted = *clairvoyant.*

SHORT-TEMPERED (adj) *soupe au lait* : don't be so short-tempered = *ne sois pas si soupe au lait* ≠ easygoing = *coulant.*

SHORT-TERM (adj) *à court terme* : short-term policy = *politique à court terme.*

SHORTY (n, -ies) *microbe (m)* : listen, shorty, shut up ! = *dis donc, microbe, tu vas la fermer !* ⓓ shrimp = *nabot* ☠ → microbe.

SHOT (n) **1/** *coup (m) de feu* : the terrorists fired shots into the crowd = *les terroristes ont tiré des coups de feu dans la foule* ⓓ bullet = *balle* **2/** *piqûre (f)* : the doctor gave me a shot = *le docteur m'a fait une piqûre* ⓓ needle = *aiguille*, intravenous = *intraveineuse* ☠ → sting **3/** *prise (f) de vues* (photo) : that's a good shot of the house = *c'est une bonne prise de vues de la maison*
to call the shots = *mener le jeu* : in their family, his mother calls the shots = *dans leur famille, c'est sa mère qui mène le jeu* ⓓ to rule the roost = *faire la pluie et le beau temps*
have a shot ! = *tentez le coup !* ⓓ try ! = *essayez !*
it's a shot in the dark = *je dis ça au pif* : it's a shot in the dark, but I think you can fly round trip to Paris for $ 800 = *je dis ça au pif, mais je pense que vous pouvez prendre l'avion pour Paris aller-retour pour 800 dollars*
a shot in the arm = *un coup de fouet* : the news was a shot in the arm = *la nouvelle m'a donné un coup de fouet* = an uplift ⓓ pick-me-up = *remontant*
a shot of (Scotch) = *un coup de (whisky)* ⓓ a speck of = *un chouïa de.*

SHOT (adj) **1/** *claqué, -e* : after all that lovemaking, I'm shot = *après avoir tant fait l'amour, je suis claqué* ⓓ run-down = *à plat* **2/** *bousillé, -e* : my car/health is shot = *ma voiture/ma santé est bousillée*
to be shot to hell = *être foutu en l'air* : our plans were shot to hell = *nos projets ont été foutus en l'air.*

SHOTGUN (adj) **shotgun wedding** = *mariage précipité.*

SHOULD (aux) *devrais* : you shouldn't eat so much = *vous ne devriez pas manger autant* → TO HAVE TO
it should be (time to go) = *ce devrait être (l'heure d'y aller)*

should have = *aurais dû* : you should have told me = *vous auriez dû me le dire*
should (he come, tell me) = *au cas où (il viendrait, dites-le-moi).*

SHOULDER (n) *épaule (f)* : he dislocated his shoulder = *il s'est démis l'épaule* ⓓ hunchback = *bossu,* round-shouldered = *voûté,* shoulder blade = *omoplate*
to cry on s.o.'s shoulder = *pleurer sur l'épaule de qqn* ≠ to comfort = *réconforter*
to put one's shoulder to the wheel = *s'atteler à la tâche* ⓓ to go at it = *mettre les bouchées doubles*
to rub shoulders with = *coudoyer* : he rubs shoulders with the big wheels = *il coudoie les huiles* ⓓ to hobnob with = *côtoyer*
shoulder bag = *sac en bandoulière*
to shrug one's shoulders = *hausser les épaules*
straight from the shoulder = *sans détour* : I told him straight from the shoulder what I thought = *je lui ai dit sans détour ce que je pensais.*

SHOUT (to, -ed) *crier* : stop shouting, I can hear you ! = *arrête de crier, je t'entends très bien !* ⓓ to bellow = *beugler,* to scream = *hurler*
to shout s.o. down = *étouffer la voix de qqn* : the opposition shouted him down = *l'opposition a étouffé sa voix*

to shout at = *crier après* : she keeps shouting at the kids = *elle est toujours en train de crier après les gosses*
to shout for (help) = *crier au (secours)*
☠ → to cry.

SHOVE (to, -d) *pousser* : don't shove, there's room for everyone = *ne poussez pas, il y a de la place pour tout le monde* = to push ⓓ to scramble = *se bousculer*
shove it ! = *ta gueule !* → BUZZ OFF !
to shove around = *houspiller* : his wife always shoves him around = *sa femme passe son temps à le houspiller* ⓓ to bully = *brutaliser*
to shove stg into (one's pocket/a drawer) = *fourrer qqch dans (sa poche/un tiroir)*
to shove off = *se tailler* : let's shove off ! = *taillons-nous !* → TO LEAVE
☠ *tailler un crayon* = to sharpen a pencil
— *tailler une bavette* = to shoot the breeze
shove over = *poussez-vous !* = move over !
☠ → to push.

SHOVEL (n) *pelle (f)* : the kid's crying because he lost his shovel = *le gosse pleure parce qu'il a perdu sa pelle* ⓓ pail = *seau*
☠ *ramasser une pelle* = to fall on one's face
— *(des gosses) à la pelle* = (kids) galore
— *rouler une pelle* = to give a soul kiss.

SHOW (n) *spectacle (m)* : what time does the show begin ? = *à quelle heure commence le spectacle ?* ⓓ performance = *représentation* ☠ → spectacle

car/plane show = *Salon de l'auto/de l'aviation*
cat/dog/art show = *exposition de chats/canine/de peinture*
to give the show away = *manger le morceau* = to spill the beans
it's a show ! = *c'est de la frime !* : it's a show for the relatives ! = *c'est de la frime pour épater les siens !*
let's get the show on the road ! = *si on mettait les bouts ?* → TO LEAVE
to run the show = *mener la danse* ⓓ to call the

shots = *mener le jeu*
a show of hands = *un vote à main levée*
show business/biz = *le monde du spectacle/le show-business, le show-biz*
to steal the show = *voler la vedette* ⓓ to steal s.o.'s thunder = *couper son effet à qqn*
to stop the show = *casser la baraque* : she stopped the show with her comic number = *elle a cassé la baraque avec son numéro comique* ⓓ to lay them in the aisles = *faire un malheur*
a show of force = *une démonstration de force.*

SHOW (to, -ed, -ed or shown) **1/** *montrer* : show me pictures of the baby = *montrez-moi des photos du bébé,* she showed me how to do it = *elle m'a montré comment le faire* ⓓ to indicate = *indiquer* ☠ *il s'est montré sympa* = he turned out to be nice **2/** *se pointer* : he promised to come but didn't show = *il a promis de venir, mais il ne s'est pas pointé* ⓓ to come = *venir* ☠ → to point

and it shows ! = *et ça se voit !* : I shaved very quickly, and it shows ! = *je me suis rasé très vite, et ça se voit !*

(my fear) showed = *(ma peur) se voyait*
that'll show him ! = *ça lui fera les pieds !* ⓓ that served him right ! = *c'est bien fait pour lui !*

to show s.o. (a)round = *faire visiter à qqn* : my assistant will show you around = *mon assistant vous fera visiter*
he has nothing to show for it = *il n'est pas plus avancé pour autant* ⓓ it was a waste of time

= *c'était du temps perdu*
what does he have to show for it ? = *à quoi ça l'a avancé ?*
to show s.o. in ≠ **out** = *faire entrer* ≠ *reconduire qqn* : the butler showed me in ≠ out = *le valet de chambre m'a fait entrer*

≠ *m'a reconduit*
to show stg off = *faire ressortir qqch* : the black velvet shows the diamond off = *le velours noir fait ressortir le diamant*
to show off = *faire de l'épate/de l'esbroufe* : stop show-

ing off ! what a snob you are ! = *quel snob ! arrête de faire de l'épate/de l'esbroufe !* ① **to lay it on** = *en faire des tonnes*
to show through = *se voir à travers* : your brassiere shows through your blouse = *ton soutien-gorge se voit à travers*

ton chemisier
to show up = 1/ *ressortir :* her wrinkles showed up in the sunlight = *ses rides ressortaient dans la lumière du soleil*
☠ *ressortir une vieille histoire* = to drag up an old story
— *faire ressortir un fait* = to

dwell on a fact
— *ça, je te le ressortirai ! =* I won't forget to tell you the same thing !
2/ *se pointer :* he showed up rather late = *il s'est pointé assez tard* ① to turn up = *se radiner* ☠ → to point.

SHOWCASE (n) *vitrine* (f) : off-Broadway is a showcase for new talent = *le théâtre off-Broadway est une vitrine pour les nouveaux talents* ☠ → window.

SHOWDOWN (n) *épreuve* (f) *de force :* there's going to be a showdown between the President and Congress = *il va y avoir une épreuve de force entre le Président et le Congrès.*

SHOWER (n) 1/ *douche* (f) : I'm going to take a shower = *je vais prendre une douche* ① bath = *bain*
☠ *quelle douche froide !* = what a terrible letdown !
— *avec lui, c'est la douche écossaise !* = he runs hot and cold !
2/ *averse* (f) : heavy showers in spring = *de grosses averses au printemps* ① heavy rain = *pluie battante*
3/ *fête* (f) *au cours de laquelle on donne des cadeaux à la future mariée :* my sister's getting married in two weeks and we're giving her a shower Saturday = *ma sœur se marie dans deux semaines et on lui fait une fête samedi.*

SHOWER (to, -ed) *se doucher :* I shower every morning = *je me douche tous les matins* ① to take a shower = *prendre une douche*
to shower (gifts) on s.o. = *couvrir qqn de (cadeaux).*

SHOWING (n) **to make a good ≠ poor showing** = *faire une bonne ≠ mauvaise prestation.*

SHOWOFF (n) *crâneur, -euse, m'as-tu-vu* (m, f) : what a showoff you are ! = *quel crâneur/quel m'as-tu-vu tu fais !* ① braggart = *fanfaron.*

SHOWROOM (n) *salle* (f) *d'exposition.*

SHOWSTOPPER (n) *clou* (m) *de la soirée :* his act was the showstopper = *son numéro était le clou de la soirée* ≠ a flop = *le bide.*

SHOWY (adj, -ier, -iest) *voyant, -e :* showy clothes = *des vêtements voyants* ① garish = *tape-à-l'œil.*

SHRAPNEL (n) *éclats* (m pl) *d'obus* ① shell = *obus.*

SHRED (n) **in shreds** = *en lambeaux :* his clothes were in shreds = *ses vêtements étaient en lambeaux* ① in tatters = *en loques.*

SHREW (n) *mégère* (f) : "the Taming of the Shrew" = « *la Mégère apprivoisée* » ① battle-ax = *harpie.*

SHREWD (adj, -er, -est) *habile :* a shrewd lawyer = *un avocat habile* ① foxy = *futé* ≠ gullible = *jobard* ☠ *habile (de ses mains)* = skil(l)ful **SHREWDY** (n, -ies) *quelqu'un d'habile :* her boss is a shrewdy = *son patron est quelqu'un d'habile* ① a wise guy = *un malin.*

SHRIEK (n) *cri* (m) *perçant :* shrieks in the night = *des cris perçants dans la nuit* ① yell = *gueulante,* screech = *cri aigu* **SHRIEK** (to, -ed) *pousser des cris perçants :* stop shrieking ! = *arrête de pousser ces cris perçants !* ① to yell = *gueuler.*

SHRILL (adj, -er, -est) *suraigu, -uë :* a shrill voice = *une voix suraiguë.*

SHRIMP (n) 1/ *crevette* (f) : I'll have a shrimp cocktail = *je prendrai un cocktail de crevettes* ① seafood = *fruits de mer* 2/ *nabot* (m) : her guy's a shrimp = *son mec est un nabot* ① a peanut = *un moustique,* half-pint = *demi-portion.*

SHRINE (n) *lieu saint* (m) : to profane a shrine = *profaner un lieu saint* ① sanctuary = *sanctuaire.*

SHRINK (n) *psy* (m, f) : she's been screwing with her shrink = *elle baise avec son psy* = headshrinker ① psychoanalyst = *psychanalyste.*

SHRINK (to, shrank, shrunk) *rétrécir :* does this material shrink ? = *est-ce que ce tissu rétrécit ?* ① to shrivel = *se ratatiner.*

SHRUB (n) *arbuste* (m) : shrubs around the house = *des arbustes autour de la maison* ① tree = *arbre,* hedge = *haie.*

SHRUG (to, -ged) *hausser les épaules :* when she made the remark, he just shrugged = *quand elle dit ça, il juste haussé les épaules*
to shrug off = *ne pas relever :* he shrugged off her sarcasms = *il n'a pas relevé ses sarcasmes* ≠ to pick up = *relever.*

SHTICK (n) *numéro* (m) : he does a great shtick about dogs = *il fait un numéro extra sur les chiens* ① sketch = ← ☠ → number.

SHUCKS ! (interj) *oh mince alors !* → GOSH !

SHUDDER (to, -ed) *frémir :* I shuddered at the idea of making love with him = *j'ai frémi à l'idée de faire l'amour avec lui* ① to shiver = *frissonner* ☠ *sa voix frémissait* = his voice was quivering.

SHUFFLE (to, -d) 1/ *battre :* shuffle the cards = *battez les cartes* ☠ → to beat 2/ *remanier :* the President shuffled his cabinet (around) = *le Président a remanié son gouvernement* ① to shake up = *remanier complètement* ☠ → to edit.

SHUN (to, -ned) *fuir :* she shuns her family = *elle fuit sa famille* ① to avoid = *éviter* ☠ → to flee.

SHUT (to, shut, shut) *fermer* : shut the door ! = *fermez la porte !* ≠ to open = *ouvrir* ☠ → to close

to shut down = *fermer* : a lot of business have shut down because of the economic situation = *beaucoup d'entreprises ont fermé à cause de la situation économique* ⓪ to close down = *fermer ses portes* ≠ to open up = *ouvrir* ☠ → to close

to shut off = *couper* : the electricity was shut off = *l'électricité était coupée* = to cut off ≠ to turn on = *brancher* ☠ → to cut

shut up ! = *ferme-la !* → BUZZ OFF !

to shut s.o. up = *clouer le bec à qqn* : my remark shut him up = *ma remarque lui a cloué le bec.*

SHUTDOWN (n) *fermeture* (f) : the factory shutdown = *la fermeture de l'usine* ≠ reopening = *réouverture* ☠ *fermeture Éclair* = zipper
— *heures de fermeture* = closing times.

SHUTEYE (n) **to get some shuteye** = *piquer un roupillon* : I'm tired, I'm going to get some shuteye = *je suis fatigué, je vais piquer un roupillon* ⓪ to hit the sack = *aller au plumard.*

SHUTTER (n) *volet* (m) : close the shutters = *ferme les volets* ⓪ curtain = *rideau* ☠ *trier sur le volet* = to handpick.

SHUTTLE (n) *navette* (f) : there's a shuttle between New York and Boston = *il y a une navette entre New York et Boston* **SHUTTLE** (to, -d) *faire la navette* : he shuttles back and forth between Boston and New York = *il fait la navette entre Boston et New York.*

SHY (adj, -ier or -er, -iest or -est) *timide* : I've always been shy = *j'ai toujours été timide* ⓪ reserved = *réservé*, meek = *timoré* ≠ sociable = ← **SHYLY** (adv) *timidement* **SHYNESS** (n) *timidité* (f).

SHY AWAY (FROM) (to, -ied) *répugner à* : she shies away from her in-laws = *elle répugne à voir sa belle-famille.*

SHYSTER (n) *avocat* (m) *marron* : don't go to see him,

he's a real shyster = *ne va pas le voir, c'est vraiment un avocat marron* ⓪ half-baked lawyer = *avocat à la noix.*

SICK (adj, -er, -est) *malade* : I feel sick = *je me sens malade* ⓪ not to feel like one's usual self = *ne pas être dans son assiette* ≠ well = *bien* ☠ → ill

to be sick at heart = *en être malade* : when her dog died, she was sick at heart = *quand son chien est mort, elle en a été malade* ≠ to be delighted = *être enchanté*

to be sick of = *en avoir marre de* : I'm really sick of you ! = *j'en ai vraiment marre de toi !* ⓪ to be through with = *en avoir sa claque de*

to be sick and tired of = *en avoir par-dessus la tête de* : I'm sick and tired of listening to his lies = *j'en ai par-dessus la tête d'entendre ses mensonges* ⓪ to have had enough = *en avoir assez*

I feel sick about (getting divorced) = *ça me fait mal au cœur de (divorcer)*

to make s.o. sick = *rendre qqn malade* : his attitude makes me sick = *son attitude me rend malade* ⓪ to nauseate = *écœurer*

sick humor = *humour grinçant*

sick leave = *congé de maladie*

sick pay = *indemnités de maladie*

a sick person = *un malade*

you're sick, man ! = *t'es malade, mon vieux !* → CRAZY.

SICKEN (to, -ed) *rendre malade* : it sickens me to see you in this state = *ça me rend malade de vous voir dans cet état* ≠ to delight = *faire grand plaisir à.*

SICKENING (adj) *écœurant, -e* : sickening indifference = *indifférence écœurante* ⓪ obnoxious = *odieux.*

SICKLY (adj) *maladif, -ive* : a sickly complexion = *un teint maladif* ⓪ pale = *pâle* ≠ wholesome = *sain.*

SICKNESS (n, -es) *maladie* (f) : a strange sickness = *une maladie étrange* ≠ illness

owing to sickness = *pour cause de maladie* ☠ → disease.

SIDE (n) *côté* (m) : the store's on the other side of the street = *le magasin est de l'autre côté de la rue*

to be on s.o.'s side = *être du côté de qqn* : they're on our side = *ils sont de notre côté* **to have a ... side** = *avoir un côté ...* : he has a mean side = *il a un côté méchant* **(a pain) in one's side** = *(une douleur) au côté* **to know which side one's bread is buttered** = *savoir de quel côté sa tartine est beurrée/savoir où est son intérêt* **not to leave s.o.'s side** = *ne pas lâcher qqn d'une semelle* : he didn't leave my side all evening = *il ne m'a pas lâché*	*d'une semelle de toute la soirée* **on one's mother's** ≠ **father's side** = *du côté de sa mère* ≠ *de son père* : he's Russian on his father's side = *il est russe du côté de son père* **on the right** ≠ **wrong side** = *à l'endroit* ≠ *à l'envers* : your sweater is on the right ≠ wrong side = *tu as mis ton chandail à l'endroit* ≠ *à l'envers* **on the side** = 1/ *comme à-côté* : she works full time and does some typing on the side = *elle travaille à plein-temps, et fait un peu de frappe comme*	*à-côté* 2/ *comme garniture* : the steak comes with spinach on the side = *le steak est servi avec des épinards comme garniture* **on the ... side** = *plutôt ...* : we felt the price was on the high side = *nous avons eu l'impression que le prix était plutôt élevé* **s.o.'s side** = *la version de qqn* : that's what he told you, now listen to my side = *c'est ce qu'il vous a dit, maintenant écoutez ma version* **one's better** ≠ **worse side** = *son meilleur* ≠ *pire côté* **side by side** = *côte à côte*

to split one's sides (with laughing) = *se tenir les côtes (de rire)* ⓒ **to crack up** = *se marrer comme une baleine*
to take sides = *prendre parti* : when two people are arguing,

it's better not to take sides = *quand deux personnes se disputent, il vaut mieux ne pas prendre parti*
there are many sides to (the problem) = *il y a plusieurs*

aspects du (problème)
whose side are you ? = *dans quel camp êtes-vous ?* ⓒ who are you siding with = *de quel côté vous rangez-vous ?*

☠ *d'un autre côté* = on the other hand
— *par certains côtés* = in some ways
— *c'est tout à côté* = it's very close/near
— *assieds-toi à côté de moi* = sit next to me
— *laisser de côté* = to set aside

— *côté argent ...* = moneywise ...
— *mettre (de l'argent) de côté* = to put (money) aside
— *ce n'est rien à côté de ce qu'il a dit* = it's nothing compared to what he said.

SIDE (adj) **a side dish of (spaghetti)** = *une petite portion de (spaghetti)*

side effects = *effets secondaires*
side street = *rue latérale.*

SIDE WITH (to, -d) *se ranger du côté de* : my mother always sides with my father = *ma mère se range toujours du côté de mon père* ⓒ to back up = *appuyer.*

SIDEBURNS (n pl) *favoris (m pl), rouflaquettes (f pl)* : Presley had great sideburns = *Presley avait des favoris/rouflaquettes terribles.*

SIDEKICK (n) *acolyte (m, f)* : he's one of the President's sidekicks = *c'est l'un des acolytes du Président* ⓒ pal = *copain.*

SIDELINE (n) *à-côté (m)* : he does photography as a sideline = *il fait de la photo comme à-côté* ≠ full-time job = *travail à plein-temps*
to be on the sidelines = *être sur la touche* : the top player was hurt and was put on the sidelines = *le meilleur joueur a été blessé et on l'a mis sur la touche* ☠ *les à-côtés du métier* = the perks of the job.

SIDESPLITTING (adj) *à se tenir les côtes* : sidesplitting jokes = *des plaisanteries à se tenir les côtes* ⓒ a howl = *désopilant.*

SIDESTEP (to, -ped) *esquiver* : the President tried to sidestep the journalists' questions = *le Président a essayé d'esquiver les questions des journalistes* = to duck ⓒ to dodge = *se dérober à* ☠ → to duck.

SIDETRACK (to, -ed) *(faire) dévier du sujet* : stop sidetracking and get to the point = *arrêtez de dévier du sujet et venez-en au fait* ≠ to stick to = *s'en tenir à.*

SIDEWALK (n) *trottoir (m)* : we walked on the sidewalk = *nous marchions sur le trottoir* ⓒ curb = *bordure de trottoir* ☠ → pavement.

SIDEWAYS = **SIDEWISE** (adv) *de côté* : to look sideways/sidewise = *regarder de côté.*

SIEGE (n) *siège (m)* : the siege of Troy = *le siège de Troie* ⓒ blockade = *blocus*
to lay siege to (a city) = *faire le siège d'(une ville)*
☠ *le siège social* = the company headquarters
— *prenez un siège !* = take a seat !

SIGH (n) *soupir (m)* : a sigh of relief = *un soupir de soulagement* ☠ *rendre le dernier soupir* = to take one's last breath.

SIGH (to, -ed) *soupirer* : he sighed from exasperation = *l'exaspération l'a fait soupirer* ☠ *soupirer après* = to yearn for.

SIGHT (n) **1/** *spectacle (m)* : the familiar sight of hookers in Times Square = *le spectacle familier des putains à Times Square* ☠ → spectacle **2/** *vue (f)* : her sight's poor = *elle a une mauvaise vue* ☠ → view

---

(the house) is a sight = *(la maison) fait peur à voir*
to buy stg sight unseen = *acheter qqch chat en poche*
to catch sight of s.o. = *apercevoir qqn* : I just caught sight of him = *je viens de l'apercevoir* ⓒ to glimpse = *entrevoir*
don't lose sight of (the fact that he's young) = *ne perdez pas de vue (le fait qu'il est jeune)*
in sight = *en vue* : I have no job in sight = *je n'ai pas de boulot en vue*
to know s.o. on sight = *reconnaître qqn en le voyant* : don't worry, I'll know you on sight = *ne*

vous en faites pas, je vous reconnaîtrai en vous voyant
to let s.o. out of one's sight = *quitter qqn des yeux* : he's so jealous he never lets her out of his sight = *il est tellement jaloux qu'il ne la quitte jamais des yeux*
to lose one's sight = *perdre la vue* ⓒ to become blind = *devenir aveugle*
to lose sight of (one's friends) = *perdre (ses amis) de vue*
not to bear/stand the sight of s.o. = *ne pas pouvoir voir qqn* : I can't bear/stand the sight of her =

je ne peux pas la voir ⓪ not to stomach s.o. = *ne pas pouvoir blairer qqn*
out of sight ! = *dément ! :* the movie was out of sight ! = *le film était dément !* → WONDERFUL ≠ crummy = *moche*
out of sight, out of mind = *loin des yeux, loin du cœur* ≠ absence makes the heart grow fonder = *loin des yeux, près du cœur*

to see the sights of (a city) = *voir les principaux sites/les curiosités d'(une ville)* ⓪ to go sightseeing = *faire du tourisme*
to shoot on sight = *tirer à vue :* the orders were to shoot on sight = *on avait ordre de tirer à vue*
you're a sight for sore eyes = *tu fais plaisir à voir*
you look a sight ! = *tu as une sale tête !* ⓪ you look a mess ! = *tu es affreux !*

SIGHTSEEING (n inv) **to go sightseeing =** *faire du tourisme :* we went sightseeing all day = *nous avons fait du tourisme toute la journée.*

SIGN (n) **1/** *signe (m) :* language is made of signs = *le langage est fait de signes*
sign language = *langage des sourds-muets*
a sign of = *un signe de :* is spitting blood a sign of cancer ? = *quand on crache le sang, est-ce un signe de cancer ?*
that's a good ≠ **bad sign** = *c'est bon* ≠ *mauvais signe*
2/ *pancarte (f), panneau (m) :* signs along the highway = *des panneaux sur l'autoroute,* there's a sign for an apartment to rent in the building = *il y a une pancarte pour un appartement à louer dans l'immeuble* ⓪ notice = *avis* ☠ *panneau* → panel
neon sign = *enseigne au néon*
traffic/road sign = *panneau de signalisation/indicateur.*

SIGN (to, -ed) *signer :* I forgot to sign the letter = *j'ai oublié de signer la lettre*
to sign away (one's rights) = *céder (ses droits) par écrit* ⓪ to relinquish = *renoncer à*
to sign off = *rendre l'antenne*
to sign up (in the army) = *s'engager (dans l'armée)* ⓪ to join up = *s'enrôler* ☠ → to engage
☠ *ça, c'est signé (Papa)* = that's (Daddy) all over.

SIGNAL (n) *signal (m) :* when I give you the signal, let's go ! = *quand je vous donnerai le signal, on partira !* ⓪ indication = ← **SIGNAL** (to, -ed) *faire signe de :* the cop signaled us to stop = *le flic nous a fait signe de nous arrêter* ⓪ to give s.o. the high sign = *donner à qqn le signal.*

SIGNATURE (n) *signature (f) :* I can't read his signature = *je n'arrive pas à lire sa signature.*

SIGNIFICANCE (n) *signification (f) :* I think that's of great significance = *je pense que ça a une grande signification* ⓪ importance = ← ≠ insignificance = *insignifiance.*

SIGNIFICANT (adj) **1/** *significatif, -ive :* don't think what he said was significant of anything = *ne pensez pas que ces propos soient significatifs de quoi que ce soit* ≠ insignificant = *insignifiant* **2/** *considérable :* a significant increase in the abortion rate = *une hausse considérable du taux d'avortement* ⓪ noticeable = *sensible.*

SIGNIFY (to, -ied) *signifier :* the letter signified that they

were going to get married soon = *la lettre signifiait qu'ils allaient bientôt se marier* ⓪ to mean = *vouloir dire* ☠ *qu'est-ce que ça signifie ?* = what does that mean ?

SILENCE (n) *silence (m) :* the doorbell broke the silence = *la sonnette a rompu le silence* ⓪ stillness = *tranquillité* ≠ noise = *bruit*
silence is golden = *le silence est d'or*
silence means consent = *qui ne dit mot consent*
☠ *passer sous silence* = to hush up.

SILENCE (to, -d) *faire taire :* his answer silenced the opposition = *sa réponse a fait taire l'opposition.*

SILENT (adj, -er, -est) *silencieux, -euse :* classes are never silent = *une classe n'est jamais silencieuse* ⓪ quiet = *tranquille* ≠ noisy = *bruyant*
be silent ! = *taisez-vous !* = hush up !
silent movie = *film muet* ⓪ film = ←
silent partner = *commanditaire.*

SILENTLY (adv) *silencieusement, en silence :* to work silently = *travailler silencieusement/en silence.*

SILK (n, adj) *(de/en) soie (f) :* a silk blouse = *un chemisier de soie* **SILKY** (adj, -ier, -iest) *soyeux, -euse.*

SILK-STOCKING (adj) *huppé, -e :* a silk-stocking neighborhood = *un voisinage huppé* ⓪ posh = *rupin.*

SILLY (adj, -ier, -iest) *sot, sotte :* how silly it was to make such a remark ! = *comme c'était sot de faire une réflexion pareille* ⓪ silliness = *sottise* ≠ sensible = *sensé* → STUPID ☠ *il n'y a pas de sot métier* = every kind of work has its value.

SILVER (n inv, adj) *(de/en) argent (m) :* a silver bracelet = *un bracelet en argent* ⓪ silver-plated = *plaqué argent,* platinum = *platine*
to be born with a silver spoon in one's mouth = *être né avec une cuiller d'argent dans la bouche/être né coiffé* ≠ to come from the wrong side of the tracks = *venir de la zone*
on a silver platter = *sur un plateau :* everything was given to him on a silver platter = *on lui a toujours tout apporté sur un plateau*
silver wedding anniversary = *noces d'argent*
☠ → money.

SILVERWARE (n) *argenterie (f) :* my in-laws gave us silverware for our wedding = *mes beaux-parents nous ont donné de l'argenterie pour notre mariage.*

SIMILAR (adj) *similaire* : the two products are very similar = *les deux produits sont très similaires* ⓒ comparable = ← ≠ unlike = *qui ne se ressemblent pas.*

SIMILARITY (n, -ies) *similitude (f)* : little similarity between the two parties = *peu de similitude entre les deux partis* ⓒ resemblance = *ressemblance.*

SIMMER (to, -ed) *mijoter* : the stew's simmering = *le ragoût mijote* ⓒ to cook = *cuire*
to simmer down = *être/devenir plus calme* : I'll go to the Middle East as soon as the situation simmers down = *j'irai au Moyen-Orient dès que la situation sera plus calme* ⓒ to settle down = *se tasser*
🕱 *il se mijote quelque chose* = something's brewing
— *qu'est-ce qu'il mijote ?* = what's he cooking up ?

SIMPLE (adj, -r, -st) **1/** *simple* : the exam was very simple = *l'examen était très simple* ⓒ easy = *facile* ≠ difficult = *difficile* **2/** *simple* : simple people/clothes = *des gens/des vêtements simples* ≠ complex = *complexe*
for the simple reason that (we have nothing in common) = *pour la bonne/simple raison que (nous n'avons rien de commun)*
🕱 *un simple soldat* = a buck private
— *dans le plus simple appareil* = in the altogether
— *un aller simple* = a one-way ticket.

SIMPLE-MINDED (adj) *naïf* : simple-minded reasoning = *raisonnement naïf* → STUPID.

SIMPLETON (n) *nigaud, -e* : he's no simpleton = *ce n'est pas un nigaud* → STUPID.

SIMPLICITY (n inv) *simplicité (f)* : a man of great simplicity = *un homme d'une grande simplicité.*

SIMPLIFICATION (n) *simplification (f)* : that's an extreme simplification of the problem = *c'est une simplification extrême du problème* ⓒ oversimplification = *simplification excessive.*

SIMPLIFY (to, -ied) *simplifier* : to simplify a question = *simplifier une question* ≠ to complicate = *compliquer.*

SIMPLISTIC (adj) *simpliste* : your reasoning's simplistic = *votre raisonnement est simpliste* ≠ complex = *complexe.*

SIMPLY (adv) **1/** *tout simplement* : the dinner was simply delicious = *le dîner était tout simplement délicieux* → VERY **2/** *simplement* : she dresses very simply = *elle s'habille très simplement* = plainly ≠ fancy = *avec fantaisie* **3/** *simplement* : he helped me simply because he was getting paid for it = *il m'a aidé simplement parce qu'il était payé pour ça* ⓒ only = *seulement*
simply to = *uniquement pour* : I said that simply to get his reaction = *j'ai dit ça uniquement pour provoquer une réaction de sa part.*

SIMULATE (to, -d) *simuler* : to simulate indifference = *simuler l'indifférence* ⓒ to feign = *feindre.*

SIMULTANEOUS (adj) *simultané, -e* : the simultaneous launching of the book and the film = *le lancement*

simultané du livre et du film **SIMULTANEOUSLY** (adv) *simultanément.*

SIN (n) *péché (m)* : sex is a beloved sin = *c'est un bien doux péché de faire l'amour* ⓒ vice = ← ≠ redemption = *rédemption*
it's a sin to (put ketchup on good meat) = *c'est un crime de (mettre du ketchup sur une bonne viande)* ⓒ it's a shame to = *c'est une honte de*
to live in sin = *vivre dans le péché*
🕱 *mon péché mignon* = my weak spot.

SINCE (prep) *depuis* : he's been here since noon = *il est ici depuis midi*	
SINCE *(date/début d'une action)* — since Monday = *depuis lundi* — since this summer = *depuis cet été* — since 1980 = *depuis 1980*	**FOR** *(durée)* — for three days = *depuis trois jours* — for eight months = *depuis huit mois* — for a few years = *depuis quelques années*
since then = *depuis lors* **since when ?** = *depuis quand ?* : they're divorced ? since when ? = *ils sont divorcés ? depuis quand ?*	
SINCE (conj) **1/** *(depuis) que* : it's been a long time since I moved = *il y a longtemps que j'ai déménagé* **2/** *puisque* : since you're here, stay for dinner = *puisque vous êtes là, restez pour dîner* ⓒ as = *comme.*	
SINCE (adv) *depuis* : she was here last summer and I haven't seen her since = *elle était là l'été dernier et je ne l'ai pas vue depuis.*	

SINCERE (adj, -r, -st) *sincère* : his answer wasn't sincere = *sa réponse n'était pas sincère* ⓒ honest = *honnête* ≠ insincere = *pas sincère.*

SINCERELY (adv) *sincèrement* : I'm sincerely sorry = *je suis sincèrement désolé* ⓒ honestly = *honnêtement.*

SINCERITY (n) *sincérité (f)* : in all sincerity = *en toute sincérité.*

SING (to, sang or sung, sung) **1/** *chanter* : she sings beautifully = *elle chante merveilleusement bien* ⓒ to hum = *fredonner*
🕱 *si ça vous chante* = if you feel like it
— *faire chanter qqn* = to blackmail s.o.
2/ *se mettre à table* : the crook sang and the whole gang was nabbed = *l'escroc s'est mis à table et tout le gang s'est fait pincer* ⓒ to squeal = *moucharder.*

SINGER (n) *chanteur, -euse* : he's a well-known singer = *c'est un chanteur connu* ⓒ crooner = ←/*chanteur de charme*, soprano = ←, mezzo = ←, contralto = ←, tenor = *ténor*, baritone = *baryton*, bass = *basse*, vocalist = *chanteur de groupe.*

SINGLE (n) *45 tours (m) :* his last single was a hit = *son dernier 45 tours a fait un tube.*

SINGLE (adj) *célibataire :* my sister's/brother's single = *ma sœur/mon frère est célibataire* ① eligible = *recherché* ≠ married = *marié*
not a single ... = *pas un seul ... :* not a single person understood me = *il n'y en a pas un seul qui m'ait compris*
single mother/father = *mère/père célibataire* ①
unwed mother = *fille mère*
single-parent family = *famille monoparentale*
in single file = *à la queue leu leu.*

SINGLE-BREASTED (adj) *droit, -e :* a single-breasted jacket = *une veste droite* ≠ double-breasted = *croisé* ☠ → right.

SINGLE-HANDED (adj, adv) *de ses mains :* he built the boat single-handed = *il a construit le bateau de ses mains* ① without help = *sans aide.*

SINGLE OUT (to, -d) *distinguer, s'en prendre particulièrement à :* of all secretaries, the boss singled Jane out = *entre toutes les secrétaires, le patron a distingué Jane,* everyone in the class made the same mistake but the teacher singled me out = *tout le monde dans la classe a fait la même faute, mais le professeur s'en est pris particulièrement à moi* ☠ → to distinguish.

SINGLES (n pl) *célibataires (m, f pl), solos (m, f pl) :* there were only singles at the party = *il n'y avait que des célibataires à la soirée,* a singles' bar = *un bar pour solos/célibataires* ① a bachelor = *un célibataire,* a single woman = *une célibataire*
ladies'/men's singles = *simple dames/messieurs.*

SING SING (n) *Sing Sing (prison d'État de New York).*

SINGULAR (n) *singulier (m) :* what's the singular of "crises" ? = *quel est le singulier de « crises » ?*

SINGULAR (adj) *singulier, -ère :* a singular noun = *un nom singulier* ≠ plural = *pluriel.*

SINISTER (adj) *sinistre :* a sinister personality = *une personnalité sinistre* ① gloomy = *lugubre* ☠ *une journée sinistre* = a dismal day.

SINK (n) *évier (m)* (kitchen), *lavabo (m)* (bathroom) : the sink's dirty = *l'évier/le lavabo est sale* ☠ *les lavabos* = the lavatory.

SINK (to, sank or sunk, sunk) *sombrer :* the boat sank = *le bateau a sombré* ① to go under = *couler*
to sink in = *rentrer :* I repeated my advice again and again but it didn't sink in = *j'ai répété maintes fois mes conseils, mais ce n'est pas rentré* → to return
to sink (money) into = *engloutir de (l'argent) dans :* he sank a fortune into the business = *il a englouti une fortune dans cette affaire* ① to put in = *mettre dans*
sink or swim = *marche ou crève* ① moment of truth = *moment de vérité*
☠ *sa raison a sombré* = his mind gave away.

SINUS (n, -es) *sinus (m)* ① sinusitis = *sinusite.*

SIP (n) *petite gorgée (f) :* it's delicious, take a sip = *c'est délicieux, prenez-en une petite gorgée* **SIP** (to, -ped) *boire à petites gorgées :* don't gulp your milk like that, sip it ! = *n'engloutis pas ton lait comme ça, bois-le à petites gorgées !*

SIR (n) *monsieur (m) :* yes, sir = *oui, monsieur,* dear sir = *cher monsieur* ≠ lady = *madame* ☠ → mister.

SIREN (n) *sirène (f) :* the police car's siren = *la sirène de la voiture de police* ☠ *une jolie sirène* = a lovely mermaid.

SISSY (n, -ies) *froussard, -e :* don't be such a sissy = *ne sois pas si froussard* ① scaredy-cat = *trouillard.*

SISTER (n) *sœur (f), frangine (f)* (LV) : my kid sister's very sexy = *ma petite sœur est très sexy* ① half sister = *demi-sœur,* sister-in-law = *belle-sœur* ☠ *et ta sœur !* = you can shove it !

SIT (to, sat, sat) *s'asseoir :* come sit near me = *viens t'asseoir à côté de moi*
to be sitting = *être assis :* they've been sitting here at this wedding dinner for hours = *ça fait des heures qu'ils sont assis là, à ce repas de noces*

to sit down = *s'asseoir :* sit down please = *asseyez-vous s'il vous plaît* ≠ to get up = *se lever* **to sit for (a portrait)** = *poser pour (un portrait)* **to sit in for** = *remplacer :* he sat in for the Prime Minister = *il a remplacé le Premier ministre* ① to fill in for = *remplacer temporairement* **to sit in on** = *assister à :* no visitors are allowed to sit in on	the classes = *aucun visiteur n'est autorisé à assister aux cours* ① to audit = *être auditeur libre* **to sit on** = 1/ *laisser dormir :* Congress is sitting on the bill = *le Congrès laisse dormir le projet de loi* ① to put on ice = *laisser en sommeil* 2/ *être assis sur :* he was sitting on the bed = *il était assis sur le lit* 3/ *siéger dans/à :* to sit on a committee =	*siéger dans un comité* **to sit stg out** = *ne pas participer à qqch :* I'll sit this dance out = *je ne participerai pas à cette danse* **to sit through stg** = *rester jusqu'à la fin de qqch :* we sat through the whole performance = *nous sommes restés jusqu'à la fin de la représentation* **sit up !** = *redressez-vous !* ≠ lie down ! = *allongez-vous !*

SITCOM (n) *mélo* *(m)* (TV) : the intellectual level of sit-coms on American TV is for thirteen-year-olds = *les mélos qui passent à la télé américaine correspondent au niveau intellectuel d'un gosse de treize ans* ⓪ melo-drama = *mélodrame*.

SITE (n) *site* *(m)* : a wonderful site for a restaurant = *un site merveilleux pour un restaurant* ⓪ place = *endroit*.

SIT-IN (n) *sit-in* *(m)*, *occupation* *(f)* *des locaux* : an ecologist sit-in at city hall = *un sit-in des écologistes à l'hôtel de ville*.

SITTER (n) *baby-sitter* *(m, f)* = ←.

SITTING DUCK (n) *cible* *(f)* *rêvée* : the President was a sitting duck for the killer = *le Président faisait une cible rêvée pour le tueur* ⓪ easy prey = *proie facile*.

SITUATE (to, -d) *situer* : the store is well situated = *le magasin est bien situé* ⓪ to locate = *localiser*, to place = *placer*
☠ *je n'arrive pas à le situer* = I can't place him
— *l'action se situe à Hollywood* = the action is set in Hollywood.

SITUATION (n) *situation* *(f)* : he's taking advantage of the situation = *il profite de la situation* ⓪ state of affairs = *état des choses*
☠ *être en situation de* = to be in a position to
— *l'homme de la situation* = the right man in the right place.

SIX (n, -es, adj) *six* *(m)* : there were six of us = *nous étions six* ⓪ sixth = *sixième*, sixty = *soixante*, sixtieth = *soixantième*
at sixes and sevens = *le torchon brûle* : my colleague and I are at sixes and sevens = *le torchon brûle entre mon collègue et moi* ≠ to see eye to eye = *voir (les choses) du même œil*
to be six foot under = *manger les pissenlits par la racine* ⓪ to kick off = *casser sa pipe*
it's six of one, half a dozen of the other = *c'est blanc bonnet et bonnet blanc* ⓪ it's as broad as it's long = *c'est kif-kif*.

SIXTEEN (n, adj) *seize* *(m)* ⓪ sixteenth = *seizième*.

SIXTY (n, -ies, adj) *soixante* *(m)* : there were sixty people at the swing = *il y avait soixante personnes à la partouse*
to be in one's sixties = *avoir soixante ans et quelques* ⓪ to be sixtyish = *avoir la soixantaine*
the sixties = *les années soixante*
that's the sixty-four dollar question ! = *c'est la question à mille francs !*

SIZE (n) *taille* *(f)* (clothes/room), *pointure* *(f)* (shoes) : what's your size ? = *quelle est votre taille/pointure ?* ⓪ dimension = ←
to cut s.o. down to size = *rabattre le caquet à qqn* : that remark cut him down to size = *cette réflexion lui a rabattu le caquet* ⓪ to shut s.o. up = *clouer le bec à qqn*
that's about the size of it ! = *voilà où en sont les choses !* : I'll get fired if I don't show up on time, that's about the size of it !* = *je serai renvoyé si je ne me pointe pas à l'heure, voilà où en sont les choses !*
try that on for size ! = *et toc !* : if you screw around, I will too ; try that on for size ! = *si tu couches à droite et à gauche, j'en ferai autant ; et toc !*
☠ *être de taille à* = to be up to
— *taille (de guêpe)* = (very small) waist.

SIZ(E)ABLE (adj) *de taille* : she has a sizeable income = *elle a un revenu de taille* ≠ meager = *maigre*.

SIZE UP (to, -d) *jauger* : she sizes people up very quickly = *elle jauge les gens très vite* ⓪ to judge = *juger*.

SIZZLE (to, -d) *grésiller* : the steak's sizzling in the pan = *le steak grésille dans la poêle*
sizzling weather = *temps étouffant*.

SKATE (n) *patin* *(m)* : I'm getting new skates for Christmas = *je vais avoir de nouveaux patins à Noël* ⓪ roller skates = *patins à roulettes*, ice skates = *patins à glace*, skating rink = *patinoire* ☠ *rouler un patin* = to give a French kiss.

SKATE (to, -d) *patiner* ⓪ to go skating = *faire du patin*, to go ice-skating = *faire du patin à glace* ☠ *la voiture patine* = the car's skidding.

SKATER (n) *patineur, -euse*.

SKEDADDLE (to, -d) *se carapater* : when the cops came he skedaddled = *quand les flics sont arrivés, il s'est carapaté* → TO LEAVE.

SKELETON (n) *squelette* *(m)* : you're so thin you look like a skeleton = *vous êtes tellement mince que vous avez l'air d'un squelette*
(every family) has a skeleton in the closet = *(toute famille) a un cadavre dans le placard*
skeleton key = *passe-partout* = passkey
skeleton staff = *personnel réduit au minimum*.

SKEPTIC (n) *sceptique* *(m, f)* : the pessimism of some skeptics = *le pessimisme de quelques sceptiques* ⓪ cynic = *cynique* **SKEPTICAL** (adj) *sceptique* : don't be so skeptical about everything ! = *ne soyez donc pas toujours si sceptique !* ≠ confident = *qui a bon espoir* **SKEPTICISM** (n) *scepticisme* *(m)*.

SKETCH (n, -es) 1/ *croquis* *(m)*, *ébauche* *(f)* (painting) : I don't understand ; draw me a sketch = *je ne comprends pas ; faites-moi un croquis*, he made several sketches before beginning the painting = *il a fait plusieurs ébauches avant de commencer le tableau* ⓪ drawing = *dessin* 2/ *sketch* *(m)* : there are some very funny sketches in the play = *il y a quelques sketches très drôles dans la pièce* ⓪ act = *acte*.

SKETCHY (adj, -ier, -iest) *sommaire* : a sketchy article on the situation in the Middle East = *un article sommaire sur la situation au Moyen-Orient* ≠ in-depth = *approfondi*.

SKI (n) *ski* *(m)* : ski instructor = *moniteur de ski* ⓪ slope

= *piste*, skier = *skieur*, cross-country skiing = *ski de fond/de randonnée*
ski lift = *remonte-pente/tire-fesses*
ski resort = *station de sports d'hiver.*

SKI (to, -ed) *skier* : I'm learning how to ski = *j'apprends à skier*
to go skiing = *aller faire du ski* : we go skiing in Vermont every Christmas = *tous les ans à Noël, nous allons faire du ski dans le Vermont.*

SKID (to, -ded) *déraper* : the car skidded on the ice = *la voiture a dérapé sur le verglas* ⓪ to glide = *glisser.*

SKID ROW (n) *bas-fonds (m pl)* : to be born on skid row = *venir des bas-fonds* ⓪ the wrong side of the tracks = *la zone.*

SKIDS (n pl) **to be on the skids** = *être sur une pente savonneuse* : their marriage is on the skids = *leur ménage est sur une pente savonneuse* ⓪ to go downhill = *être sur la pente descendante.*

SKILL (n) **1/** *habileté (f)* : being a surgeon demands great skill = *ça exige une grande habileté d'être chirurgien* ⓪ deftness = *adresse* **2/** *compétence (f)* : what skill do you have other than typing ? = *quelles compétences avez-vous à part savoir taper à la machine ?* ⓪ knowledge = *savoir/connaissance.*

SKILLED (adj) *qualifié, -e* : a skilled surgeon/mechanic = *un chirurgien/un mécanicien qualifié* ⓪ experienced = *expérimenté*, proficient = *compétent*
a skilled worker = *un ouvrier qualifié.*

SKIL(L)FUL (adj) *adroit, -e* : a skillful lawyer for the defense = *un avocat de la défense adroit* ⓪ expert = ←
≠ inept = *peu habile* **SKIL(L)FULLY** (adv) *adroitement.*

SKIM (to, -med) *effleurer* : the bullet skimmed his face = *la balle lui a effleuré le visage*
to skim through (the paper/a book) = *lire (le journal/un livre) en diagonale* ⓪ to flip through = *survoler*
☠ *effleurer (un sujet)* = to touch on (a subject)
— *ça ne m'a pas effleuré* = it didn't occur to me.

SKIMP ON (to, -ed) *lésiner sur* : they gave their daughter a big wedding but skimped on the food = *ils ont fait un grand mariage pour leur fille, mais ils ont lésiné sur le buffet.*

SKIMPY (adj, -ier, -iest) *chiche* : a skimpy dinner = *un dîner chiche* ⓪ meager = *maigre* ☠ *il est chiche* = he's tight.

SKIN (n) *peau (f)* : what beautiful skin you have ! = *quelle belle peau vous avez !* ⓪ complexion = *teint*, facial = *nettoyage de peau*, pimples = *boutons*, acne = *acné*, rash = *éruption*, pigment = ←
to be out for s.o.'s skin = *vouloir la peau de qqn* ⓪ to gun for s.o. = *avoir qqn dans le collimateur*
by the skin of one's teeth = *de justesse* : she passed the exam by the skin of her teeth = *elle a réussi l'examen de justesse* ⓪ by a hairsbreadth = *d'un cheveu*
to have s.o. under one's skin = *avoir qqn dans la*

peau ⓪ to be in love with = *être amoureux de*
to have a thick ≠ **thin skin** = *avoir la peau dure* ≠ *avoir l'épiderme sensible*
to get under s.o.'s skin = *courir sur le haricot à qqn* : you're getting under my skin ! = *tu me cours sur le haricot !*
it's no skin off my back ! = *je m'en moque comme de ma première chemise !* ⓪ I don't give a rap ! = *je m'en tamponne le coquillard !*
to be (all) skin and bones = *(n')avoir (que) la peau et/sur les os* ⓪ to be bony = *être osseux*
to jump out of one's skin = *avoir une peur bleue* : I jumped out of my skin when I heard the noise = *j'ai eu une peur bleue en entendant ce bruit*
to save one's skin = *sauver sa peau*
skin diving = *plongée sous-marine*
a skin flick = *un film de fesses* ⓪ porn = *porno*
☠ *une vieille peau* = an old hag
— *coûter la peau des fesses* = to cost a fucking fortune
— *faire peau neuve* = to turn over a new leaf
— *être bien dans sa peau* = to have it together
— *quelle peau de vache !* = what a stinker !
— *il ne faut pas vendre la peau de l'ours avant de l'avoir tué* = don't count your chickens before they're hatched
— *entrer dans la peau de qqn* = to put o.s. in s.o.'s shoes
— *il finira par y laisser sa peau* = it's going to be the end of him
— *risquer sa peau* = to risk one's life.

SKINFLINT (n) *pingre (m, f)* : don't be such a skinflint and buy her some flowers = *ne sois pas si pingre et achète-lui des fleurs* ⓪ penny pincher = *grippe-sou.*

SKINNY (adj, -ier, -iest) *maigre* : she's always been skinny = *elle a toujours été maigre* ⓪ bony = *osseux*, gangling = *dégingandé* ≠ heavy = *gros* ☠ → meager.

SKINNY-DIP (to, -ped) **to go skinny-dipping** = *se baigner tout nu.*

SKINTIGHT (adj) *moulant, -e* : skintight slacks = *pantalon moulant* ⓪ closefitting = *ajusté.*

SKIP (to, -ped) *sauter* : we skipped breakfast this morning = *nous avons sauté le petit déjeuner ce matin*, skip the next page = *sautez la page suivante* ☠ → to jump
skip it ! = *laisse tomber !*
to skip out = *plier bagages* : the cops came to get him at the hotel but he had already skipped out = *les flics sont venus le chercher à l'hôtel mais il avait déjà plié bagages* → TO LEAVE.

SKIPPER (n) *capitaine (m)* : all boats have skippers = *tous les bateaux ont un capitaine* = captain.

SKIRMISH (n, -es) *escarmouche (f)* : a skirmish with the police = *une escarmouche avec la police* ⓪ scuffle = *échauffourée.*

SKIRT (n) *jupe (f)* : she's wearing a pleated skirt = *elle porte une jupe plissée* ⓪ mini = *mini-jupe*, kilt = ←, wraparound skirt = *jupe portefeuille*, maxi = *maxi-jupe*

☙ *être pendu aux jupes de sa mère* = to be tied to one's mother's apron strings.

SKIT (n) *saynète (f)* : a very funny skit about hookers = *une saynète très drôle sur les putains* ⓪ sketch = ←.

SKULL (n) *crâne (m)* : a camel skull found in the desert = *un crâne de chameau trouvé dans le désert* ⓪ brain = *cerveau*
skull and crossbones = *tête de mort*
☙ *mets-toi ça dans le crâne !* = get that into your head !
— *bourrer le crâne à qqn* = to hammer stg into s.o.'s head.

SKUNK (n) 1/ *saligaud (m)* : what a skunk you are ! = *tu es un beau saligaud !* → BASTARD 2/ *putois (m)* ⓪ racoon = *raton laveur* ☙ *crier comme un putois* = to yell bloody murder.

SKY (n, -ies) *ciel (m)* : what a clear sky ! = *quel ciel dégagé !* ⓪ the Big ≠ Little Dipper = *la Grande ≠ Petite Ourse*, the Milky Way = *la Voie lactée*, cosmos = ←
sky blue = *bleu ciel* ≠ navy blue = *bleu marine*
the sky's the limit ! = *il n'y a pas de limite !*
☙ *être au ciel/au septième ciel* = to be in heaven/in seventh heaven
— *ciel !* = heavens !
— *aide-toi, le Ciel t'aidera* = God helps those who help themselves
— *remuer ciel et terre* = to move heaven and earth
— *ce chèque m'est tombé du ciel* = this check was a bolt out of the blue
— *à ciel ouvert* = in the open.

SKY-HIGH (adj) *hors de prix* : gas is sky-high today = *l'essence est hors de prix aujourd'hui* ≠ moderate = *modéré*, cheap = *bon marché*
sky-high prices = *des prix exorbitants*.

SKYJACK (to, -ed) *détourner (avion)* : three men skyjacked the plane = *trois hommes ont détourné l'avion* = to hijack ☙ → to deter **SKYJACKER** (n) *pirate (m) de l'air* : more and more skyjackers on international lines = *de plus en plus de pirates de l'air sur les lignes internationales* ⓪ terrorist = *terroriste*.

SKYLINE (n) *ligne (f) d'horizon, front (m) de mer* : New York has a beautiful skyline = *New York a un superbe front de mer*.

SKYROCKET (to, -ed) *monter en flèche* : prices are skyrocketing = *les prix montent en flèche* ≠ to plummet = *descendre brusquement*.

SKYSCRAPER (n) *gratte-ciel (m)* : we live in a skyscraper = *nous habitons un gratte-ciel* ⓪ tower = *tour* ≠ townhouse = *hôtel particulier*.

SLAB (n) **a slab of (meat)** = *une pièce de (viande)*.

SLACK (adj, -er, -est) *trop laxiste, qui marche au ralenti (business)* : slack gun control laws = *des lois trop laxistes sur le contrôle des armes*, business is slack = *les affaires marchent au ralenti* ⓪ sluggish = *calme*

the **slack season** = *la morte-saison* ⓪ the off-season = *la saison creuse*.

SLACKEN (to, -ed) *marcher au ralenti* : business is slackening (off) = *les affaires marchent au ralenti* ⓪ to slow down = *ralentir*.

SLACKS (n pl) *pantalon (m)* : what beautiful slacks you're wearing ! = *quel beau pantalon tu as !* = pants = trousers
a pair of slacks = *un pantalon*.

SLAM (n) *claque (f)* : he gave her a slam = *il lui a donné une claque* ⓪ wallop = *châtaigne*
☙ *j'en ai ma claque !* = I've had it !
— *prendre ses cliques et ses claques* = to pack up (and go)
— *un claque* = a cathouse.

SLAM (to, -med) 1/ *claquer* : to slam the door = *claquer la porte* ⓪ to shut = *fermer*, to bang = *cogner*
☙ *claquer (mourir)* = to croak
— *claquer du fric* = to blow/shoot money
2/ *flanquer une claque à* : she slammed the kid = *elle a flanqué une claque au gosse* → TO HIT.

SLANDER (n) *calomnie (f)* : this article is just slander = *cet article n'est que calomnie* ⓪ defamation = *diffamation* **SLANDER** (to, -ed) *calomnier* : the court ruled that his article slandered the Mayor = *le tribunal a décidé que son article calomniait le maire* ⓪ to defame = *diffamer*.

SLANDEROUS (adj) *calomnieux, -euse* : slanderous lies = *des mensonges calomnieux* ⓪ libelous = *diffamatoire* = defamatory.

SLANG (n) *argot (m)* : I use a lot of slang = *j'utilise beaucoup l'argot* ⓪ dirty words = *gros mots*.

SLANT (n) **a ... slant** = *une orientation ...* : the newspaper has a leftist slant = *le journal a une orientation de gauche* ⓪ leaning = *tendance*.

SLANT (to, -ed) 1/ *être incliné, -e* : the picture/the roof slants = *le tableau/le toit est incliné* 2/ *présenter avec parti pris* : Russia slants all the news = *la Russie présente toute les informations avec parti pris*.

SLAP (n) *gifle (f)* : a slap on the face = *une gifle dans la figure* ⓪ slam = *claque*, crack = *tarte*
to be a slap in the face = *faire l'effet d'une gifle* ⓪ a put-down = *une remise en place*.

SLAP (to, -ped) *gifler* : I was so angry I slapped him = *j'étais tellement en colère que je l'ai giflé* → TO HIT.

SLAPHAPPY (adj, -ier, -iest) *bêtement heureux, -euse* : I was slaphappy when I found out I was pregnant = *j'étais bêtement heureuse quand j'ai découvert que j'étais enceinte* ⓪ elated = *exalté*.

SLAPSTICK (n) *tarte à la crème (f)* : no one can beat Groucho Marx's slapsticks = *en matière de tarte à la crème, Groucho Marx est imbattable*.

SLASH (n, -es) *balafre* *(f)* : he had a slash on his face = *il avait une balafre sur la joue* ⓓ cut = *coupure*.

SLATE (to, -d) **to be slated for** = 1/ *être proposé pour* : he's slated for the governorship = *il est proposé pour le poste de gouverneur* ⓓ to be designated for = *être désigné pour* 2/ *être prévu pour* : the elections are slated for April = *les élections sont prévues pour avril* ⓓ to be scheduled for = *être programmé pour*.

SLAUGHTER (n) *massacre* *(m)* : the terrible slaughter of the American Indians = *le terrible massacre des Indiens d'Amérique* ⓓ carnage = ←, butchery = *boucherie*.

SLAUGHTER (to, -ed) *massacrer* : to slaughter prisoners = *massacrer des prisonniers* = to massacre ⓓ to slay = *tuer* ☠ → to massacre.

SLAUGHTERHOUSE (n) *abattoir* *(m)* : horses taken to the slaughterhouse = *des chevaux emmenés à l'abattoir*.

SLAVE (n) *esclave* *(m, f)* : there are still slaves in the world = *il y a encore des esclaves dans le monde* ⓓ serf = ← ≠ master = *maître*
to be a slave to (one's work) = *être esclave de (son travail)*
to work like a slave = *travailler comme un nègre* ≠ not to do a blessed thing = *ne pas en ficher une rame*.

SLAVE (adj) **slave driver** = *esclavagiste/négrier* ⓓ taskmaster = *tyran dans le travail*

slave labor = *main-d'œuvre d'esclaves*
slave trade = *commerce des esclaves/traite des Noirs*.

SLAVE (to, -d) *boulonner (comme un dingue)* : he's been slaving for months to finish his thesis = *il boulonne (comme un dingue) depuis des mois pour finir sa thèse* ⓓ to labor = *peiner* ≠ to laze about = *paresser*.

SLAVERY (n, -ies) *esclavage* *(m)* : slavery has been abolished = *l'esclavage a été aboli* ⓓ serfdom = *servage*, bondage = *servitude* ☠ *réduire en esclavage* = to enslave.

SLAY (to, slew, slain) 1/ *tuer sauvagement* : three men were slain in the subway = *trois hommes ont été sauvagement tués dans le métro* ⓓ to kill = *tuer* 2/ *faire marrer* : her jokes slay me = *ses plaisanteries me font marrer* ⓓ it's sidesplitting = *c'est à se tenir les côtes*.

SLEAZY (adj, -ier, -iest) 1/ *de bas étage* : a sleazy hotel = *un hôtel de bas étage* ⓓ seedy = *mal famé* 2/ *de pacotille* : a sleazy watch = *une montre de pacotille* = shoddy.

SLED (n) *luge* *(f)* : it's your turn to take the sled up the hill = *c'est à ton tour de remonter la luge* ⓓ sleigh = *traîneau*.

SLEEK (adj, -er, -est) 1/ *mielleux, -euse* : sleek manners = *des manières mielleuses* ⓓ slick = *doucereux* 2/ *pur, -e (de ligne)* : the sleek lines of the car = *les lignes pures de la voiture* ⓓ streamlined = *aux lignes pures* ☠ → pure.

SLEEP (n) *sommeil* *(m)* : I need some sleep = *j'ai besoin de sommeil* ⓓ nap = *somme*

to catch up on one's sleep = *rattraper des heures de sommeil* **my (legs) went to sleep** = *j'ai (les jambes) engourdies* ⓓ my (legs) fell asleep = *j'ai des fourmis dans (les jambes)* **to put s.o. to sleep** = *endormir qqn* : his conversa-	tion put me to sleep = *sa conversation m'a endormi* ⓓ to be boring = *être ennuyeux* ☠ → to fall asleep **to put (a dog) to sleep** = *piquer (un chien)* ☠ → to sting **to walk in one's sleep** = *être somnambule* = to sleepwalk ⓓ a sleepwalker = *un somnambule*
☠ *la maladie du sommeil* = sleeping sickness — *avoir sommeil* = to feel sleepy	— *tomber de sommeil* = to be ready to drop — *avoir le sommeil léger* = to be a light sleeper.

SLEEP (to, slept, slept) *dormir* : I love to sleep = *j'adore dormir* ⓓ to oversleep = *dormir trop longtemps*, to doze = *sommeiller*, to yawn = *bâiller*, to snooze = *roupiller*

to go to sleep = *(aller) se coucher* : we went to sleep early = *nous sommes allés nous coucher de bonne heure* ⓓ to go to bed = *aller au lit*, to beddy-bye = *aller faire dodo*, to hit the hay = *aller se pieuter*	**to sleep soundly** = *dormir profondément* : I was sleeping so soundly I didn't hear the noise = *je dormais si profondément que je n'ai pas entendu le bruit* ≠ to be a light sleeper = *avoir le sommeil léger*

to sleep around = *coucher à droite et à gauche* : she's been sleeping around since her marriage = *elle couche à droite et à gauche depuis son mariage* ⓓ to play around = *courir les fil-*	les/les hommes **to sleep in** = *faire la grasse matinée* = to sleep late **to sleep it off** = *cuver son vin* : we drank a lot last night and Harry's still sleeping it off =	*nous avons beaucoup bu hier soir et Harry est encore en train de cuver son vin* ⓓ to have a hangover = *avoir la gueule de bois* **sleep on it** ! = *la nuit porte*

conseil ! : let me know tomorrow, sleep on it ! = faites-le-moi savoir demain, la nuit porte conseil ! ⓿ think it over ! = réfléchissez-y bien !
to sleep out = découcher : when he heard his daughter had slept out last night, he smiled =

il a souri quand il a appris que sa fille avait découché la nuit dernière
I slept through (the movie) = j'ai dormi pendant tout (le film)
to sleep together = coucher ensemble : they've been sleeping together for a year = ça fait un

an qu'ils couchent ensemble ⓿ to screw = baiser
to sleep with s.o. = coucher avec qqn : he's sleeping with his secretary = il couche avec sa secrétaire ⓿ to make s.o. = se faire qqn, to get it on with s.o. = se taper qqn.

SLEEPER (n) succès (m) inattendu : this film was the sleeper of the year = ce film a été le succès inattendu de l'année ⓿ hit = gros succès.

SLEEP-IN (adj) nourri, -e et logé, -e : a sleep-in maid = une bonne nourrie et logée ≠ who lives out = qui habite à l'extérieur.

SLEEPING (adj) **let sleeping dogs lie** = il ne faut pas réveiller le chat qui dort ⓿ leave well enough alone = le mieux est l'ennemi du bien
sleeping bag = sac de couchage
Sleeping Beauty = la Belle au Bois dormant
sleeping car = wagon-lit ⓿ sleeping berth = couchette
sleeping partner = associé commanditaire
sleeping pill = somnifère
sleeping sickness = maladie du sommeil.

SLEEPLESS (adj) **a sleepless night** = une nuit blanche.

SLEEPWALK (to, -ed) être somnambule : I used to sleepwalk when I was young = j'étais somnambule quand j'étais jeune **SLEEPWALKER** (n) somnambule (m, f) **SLEEPWALKING** (n) somnambulisme (m).

SLEEPY (adj, -ier, -iest) **to be sleepy** = avoir sommeil ⓿ to be drowsy = être somnolent.

SLEET (n) neige (f) fondue ⓿ ice = verglas.

SLEEVE (n) manche (f) : short ≠ long sleeves = manches courtes ≠ longues ⓿ sleeveless = sans manches
to have something up one's sleeve = avoir quelque chose derrière la tête : be careful with him, I'm sure he has something up his sleeve = fais attention avec lui, je suis sûr qu'il a quelque chose derrière la tête
to laugh up one's sleeve = rire sous cape ⓿ to be giddy = avoir le fou rire
to roll up one's sleeves = retrousser ses manches
☠ la Manche = the Channel
— avoir qqn dans sa manche = to have s.o. at one's disposal
— faire la manche = to beg
— (la première) manche = (the first) lap
— le manche (d'un balai) = the handle (of a broom)
— faire qqch/se débrouiller comme un manche = to do stg awkwardly
— jeter le manche après la cognée = to give up in despair
— ça branle dans le manche = we're in a shaky position.

SLEIGHT OF HAND (n) tour (m) de passe-passe : political sleight of hand = tour de passe-passe politique ⓿ magic = magie.

SLENDER (adj) élancé, -e : a slender woman = une femme élancée ⓿ thin = mince ≠ dumpy = boulot.

SLEUTH (n) limier (m) : they hired a sleuth to find out who killed their daughter = ils ont engagé un limier pour retrouver celui qui avait tué leur fille ⓿ detective = détective.

SLEW (n) **a slew of (children)** = une floppée d'(enfants) → MANY.

SLICE (n) tranche (f) : a slice of bread/meat = une tranche de pain/viande
☠ s'en payer une tranche = to have the time of one's life
— tranche d'impôts = tax bracket.

SLICE (to, -d) couper en tranches, trancher : he slices the bread = il coupe le pain en tranches ⓿ to carve = découper ☠ trancher une question = to settle a question.

SLICK (adj, -er, -est) 1/ léché, -e : a slick magazine = un magazine léché ⓿ sophisticated = sophistiqué
2/ mielleux, -euse : a slick guy = un type mielleux ⓿ suave = ←
a slick lawyer = un avocat retors
a slick customer = une fine mouche.

SLIDE (n) diapositive (f) ⓿ photograph = photographie.

SLIDE (to, slid, slid) glisser : I slid the record under the door = j'ai glissé le dossier sous la porte
sliding doors = portes coulissantes
sliding scale = échelle mobile
☠ → to slip.

SLIGHT (n) affront (m) : the President's not receiving the head of state was a slight = le Président a fait un affront au chef d'Etat en refusant de le recevoir ⓿ insult = insulte.

SLIGHT (to, -ed) traiter par-dessus la jambe : the President slighted the diplomat = le Président a traité le diplomate par-dessus la jambe ⓿ to snub = snober.

SLIGHT (adj, -er, -est) léger, -ère : a slight improvement = une légère amélioration ⓿ faint = faible ≠ sizable = de taille
not in the slightest = pas le moins du monde : are you

hungry ? — not in the slightest = *est-ce que vous avez faim ? — pas le moins du monde*
a slight chance/possibility = *une faible chance/possibilité*
☠ → light.

SLIGHTLY (adv) *légèrement* : I feel slightly better = *je me sens légèrement mieux* ⓪ a bit = *un peu*.

SLIM (adj, -mer, -mest) *mince* : it's not easy to stay slim = *ce n'est pas facile de rester mince* ⓪ svelte = *← ≠* plump = *rondouillard*
a slim chance = *une chance très mince* ⓪ a slight chance = *une faible chance*
☠ → thin.

SLIMY (adj, -ier, -iest) *visqueux, -euse* : slimy liquid = *un liquide visqueux*.

SLING (n) **(his arm's) in a sling** = *(il a le bras) en écharpe* ⓪ a cast on (his arm) = *(le bras) dans le plâtre*.

SLING (to, slung, slung) *lancer* : the demonstrators slung stones at the cops = *les manifestants ont lancé des pierres aux flics* ⓪ to throw = *jeter* ☠ → to launch.

SLIP (n) **1/** *impair* (m) : what a slip you made ! = *quel impair vous avez commis !* ⓪ blunder = *gaffe* **2/** *jupon* (m), *combinaison* (f) : your slip's showing = *ton jupon/ta combinaison dépasse* ⓪ petticoat = *jupon long, pinafore* = *tablier*
Freudian slip = *lapsus (révélateur)*
to give s.o. the slip = *fausser compagnie à qqn* → TO LEAVE
a slip of the tongue = *un lapsus/la langue qui fourche* : her slip of the tongue cost her her job = *c'est un lapsus qui lui a coûté son emploi*
a slip of a (woman) = *un petit bout de (femme)*
☠ *combinaison* → combination
— *courir le jupon* = to run around
— *être pendu aux jupons de sa mère* = to be tied to one's mother's apron strings
— *un slip* = pants.

SLIP (to, -ped) *glisser* : I slipped on the kitchen floor = *j'ai glissé sur le sol de la cuisine* ⓪ to fall down = *tomber par terre*
to slip s.o. stg = *glisser qqch à qqn* : slip the waiter a buck and we'll get a good table = *glisse un dollar au serveur et nous aurons une bonne table* ⓪ to tip = *donner un pourboire à*
to let (one's chance) slip by = *laisser échapper (sa chance)* ⓪ to pass up = *laisser passer*
to slip into = *glisser dans* : I slipped some money into her pocket = *je lui ai glissé de l'argent dans la poche*
to slip on/into = *enfiler* : just a minute, I'll slip on/into a pair of jeans = *une minute, j'enfile un jean*
to slip out = **1/** *s'éclipser* : he slipped out of the meeting = *il s'est éclipsé de la réunion* → TO LEAVE ☠ → to upstage **2/** *(laisser) échapper* : I didn't mean to say that, it just slipped out = *je ne voulais pas dire ça, ça m'a échappé* ☠ → to escape

to slip past/by = *passer en douce devant* : he slipped past/by the guard = *il est passé en douce devant le garde*
to slip up = *faire une bourde* : he slipped up badly forgetting to put her name in the program = *il a fait une grosse bourde en oubliant de mentionner son nom dans le programme* ⓪ to screw up = *déconner*
☠ *le pays a glissé à gauche* = the country drifted left
— *glisser (qqch sous une porte)* = to slide (stg under a door).

SLIPPER (n) *pantoufle* (f) : old slippers are the best slippers = *les vieilles pantoufles sont les meilleures* ⓪ stay-at-home = *pantouflard*.

SLIPPERY (adj) *glissant, -e* : a slippery road = *une route glissante* ⓪ icy = *verglacé* ☠ *être sur un terrain glissant* = to be on shaky ground.

SLIPSHOD (adj) *brouillon, -onne* : slipshod work = *un travail brouillon* ⓪ careful = *soigné*.

SLIPUP (n) *bavure* (f) : one more slipup and you're fired = *encore une bavure et vous êtes renvoyé* ⓪ mistake = *faute*.

SLIT (n) *fente* (f) : a slit in the back of her skirt = *une fente au dos de sa jupe* ☠ → slot.

SLOB (n) *gros* (m) *plein de soupe* : she married a fat slob = *elle a épousé un gros plein de soupe*.

SLOGAN (n) *slogan* (m) : free abortion for all was a feminist slogan = *l'avortement libre pour toutes était un slogan féministe* ⓪ catchphrase = *devise*.

SLOPE (n) *piste* (f) *(ski)* : many slopes were closed because of the avalanche = *beaucoup de pistes étaient fermées à cause de l'avalanche* ⓪ ski lift = *tire-fesses* ☠ → lead.

SLOPPY (adj, -ier, -iest) *négligé, -e* : her work's/he's so sloppy = *son travail/il est vraiment négligé* ⓪ slipshod = *brouillon*, slovenly = *débraillé*.

SLOT (n) *fente* (f) : put the money in the slot = *mettez l'argent dans la fente* ⓪ hole = *trou*
slot machine = **1/** *distributeur automatique* : slot machines in the subway = *des distributeurs automatiques dans le métro* **2/** *machine à sous* : slot machines in Las Vegas = *les machines à sous de Las Vegas*
☠ *fente (d'une jupe)* = slit (in a skirt).

SLOUCH (to, -ed) *avoir la tête dans les épaules* : he doesn't sit straight, he slouches = *il ne se tient pas droit, il a la tête dans les épaules* ⓪ to stoop = *avoir le dos voûté*.

SLOVENLY (adj, adv) *(de façon) débraillé, -e* : slovenly dressed = *dans une tenue débraillée ≠* neat(ly) = *net*.

SLOW (adj, -er, -est) *lent, -e* : what a slow train ! = *que ce train est lent !*, a slow child = *un enfant lent ≠* quick = *rapide*
to do a slow burn = *avoir la moutarde qui vous monte au nez* → ANGRY

in slow motion = *au ralenti (film)*
(business) is slow = *(les affaires) marchent au ralenti* ≠ hectic = *mouvementé*
(20 minutes) slow = *qui retarde de (20 minutes)* ≠ (20 minutes) fast = *qui avance de (20 minutes)*
slow but steady (progress) = *(des progrès) lents mais sûrs*
you're as slow as molasses in January = *tu avances comme une tortue* ⊙ to go at a snail's pace = *avancer à une allure d'escargot.*

SLOW (adv, -er, -est) *lentement* : you're driving so slow ! = *vous conduisez si lentement !*
to go slow = *y aller doucement* : the doctor told me to go slow = *le docteur m'a dit d'y aller doucement.*

SLOWDOWN (n) *ralentissement (m)* : a slowdown in production = *un ralentissement de la production.*

SLOW DOWN (to, -ed) *ralentir* : you're driving too quickly, you'd better slow down = *vous conduisez trop vite, vous feriez mieux de ralentir.*

SLOWLY (adv) *lentement* : we're slowly advancing towards our goal = *nous avançons lentement vers notre but* ≠ rapidly = *rapidement*
slowly but surely = *lentement mais sûrement.*

SLOWNESS (n, -es) *lenteur (f)* : the slowness of her recovery = *la lenteur de sa guérison.*

SLOWPOKE (n) *traînard, -e* : what a slowpoke you are ! = *quel traînard !* ⊙ dawdler = *lambin,* lazybones = *fainéant.*

SLUG (n) *pruneau (m)* : killed by a slug in the heart = *tué d'un pruneau en plein cœur* ☠ → prune
a slug of (whisky) = *un coup de (whisky)* ⊙ a shot of = *un doigt de.*

SLUG (to, -ged) *assommer* : her husband slugged the guy = *son mari a assommé le type* → TO HIT ☠ *la nouvelle m'a assommé* = the news stunned me.

SLUGGISH (adj) **1/** *mou, molle* : this student is sluggish = *cet étudiant est mou* ⊙ lethargic = *léthargique* ≠ dynamic = *dynamique* ☠ → soft **2/** *calme* : business is sluggish = *les affaires sont calmes* ☠ → calm.

SLUM (n) **the slums** = *la zone* : she lives in the slums = *elle habite la zone* ⊙ shantytown = *bidonville,* housing project = *HLM*
a slum area = *une zone de taudis* : much of the Bronx is now a slum area = *le Bronx est en grande partie une zone de taudis.*

SLUM (to, -med) **to go slumming** = *s'encanailler* : she likes to go slumming = *elle aime s'encanailler* ⊙ to paint the town red = *faire la bringue.*

SLUMP (n) *baisse (f) brutale* : a slump in the stock market = *une baisse brutale de la Bourse* ≠ jump = *hausse brutale.*

SLUMP (to, -ed) *baisser brutalement* : business has

slumped = *les affaires ont brutalement baissé* ⊙ to fall off = *être en baisse*
to slump over = *s'affaisser* : he was hit by a bullet and slumped over = *il a été touché par une balle et s'est affaissé*
to slump to (the floor) = *s'affaisser sur (le sol).*

SLUR (n) *basse attaque (f) personnelle* : the campaign was full of slurs = *les basses attaques personnelles se sont multipliées pendant toute la campagne* ⊙ mud-slinging = *basses attaques*
a slur on (s.o.'s reputation) = *une atteinte portée à (la réputation de qqn)* ⊙ libel = *diffamation.*

SLUSH FUND (n) *caisse (f) noire* : a slush fund for bribes = *une caisse noire pour les pots-de-vin* ⊙ payoff = *dessous-de-table.*

SLUT (n) *traînée (f)* : he's always been attracted by sluts = *il a toujours été attiré par des traînées* = tramp ⊙ hussy = *catin* ☠ → tramp.

SLY (adj, -er or -ier, -est or -iest) *sournois, -e* : a sly politician = *un politicien sournois* ⊙ cunning = *rusé,* wily ≠ retors ≠ aboveboard = *sans équivoque*
to be (as) sly as a fox = *être rusé comme un renard/malin comme un singe*
on the sly = *à la dérobée/en douce* : she's going out with a married man on the sly = *elle sort à la dérobée/en douce avec un homme marié* ⊙ on the qt = *en cachette*
a sly fox = *un fin renard.*

S-M (n) *S.M. (m)* : are more gays into S-M than straights are ? = *est-ce que les homos donnent plus dans le S.M. que les hétéros ?* ⊙ sadomasochism = *sadomasochisme*
S-MER (n) *sadomaso (m, f).*

SMACK (n) *claque (f), baffe (f) (LV)* : I was so angry I gave him a hell of a smack = *j'étais tellement en colère que je lui ai flanqué une bonne claque/baffe* ⊙ slap = *gifle,* wham = *taloche* ☠ *claque* → slam

SMACK (to, -ed) *donner une claque à* : she smacked him on his behind = *elle lui a donné une claque sur les fesses* → TO HIT
to smack of = *sentir à plein nez* : the deal smacks of monkey business = *l'affaire sent le grenouillage à plein nez.*

SMALL (adj, -er, -est) *petit, -e* : a small car = *une petite auto* ⊙ tiny = *minuscule* ≠ enormous = *énorme* ☠ → little

to be small fry = *être du menu fretin* : in advertising, he's small fry = *dans la publicité, c'est du menu fretin* ≠ to be a big cheese = *être une huile* **to be small potatoes** = *compter pour des*	prunes : as literary agents, they're small potatoes = *comme agents littéraires, ils comptent pour des prunes* ≠ to be in the big = *tenir le haut du pavé* **it's a small world** = *le monde est petit*

to feel small = *ne pas être fier* : I felt small when I realized I hadn't sent her a birthday card = *je n'étais pas fier quand je me suis rendu compte que je ne lui avais pas envoyé de carte pour son anniversaire* ① to be ashamed = *avoir honte*
small talk = *banalités/propos de salon* ① to be just making conversation = *parler pour parler.*

SMALL (adv) **to sing small** = *se faire tout petit* : he had to sing small after he was proved wrong = *il a dû se faire tout petit après qu'on eut prouvé qu'il avait tort* ① to eat crow = *en prendre pour son grade.*

SMALLPOX (n inv) *variole* (f) : is smallpox contagious ? = *est-ce que la variole est contagieuse ?* ① chickenpox = *varicelle.*

SMALL-TIME (adj) *sans envergure* : a small-time crook = *un escroc sans envergure* ① two-bit = *à la manque.*

SMART (adj, -er, -est) 1/ *intelligent, -e* : smart kids = *des gosses intelligents* ① brilliant = *brillant* 2/ smart : it's a very smart shirt = *c'est une chemise très smart* ① chic = ←, sharp = *chicos* 3/ *malin, -igne* : don't try to be too smart = *n'essaie pas de jouer au plus malin* ① crafty = *roublard* ☠ → clever
smart aleck = *gros malin* ① a know-it-all = *un monsieur je-sais-tout*
smart ass = *connard, connasse* : don't be such a smart ass ! = *ne fais pas le connard/la connasse !* ① wise guy = *petit malin*
smart card = *carte à puce/à mémoire*
a smart cookie = *un petit futé* ≠ a babe in the woods = *une oie blanche*
a smart idea = *une idée de génie* ① a bright idea = *une idée lumineuse.*

SMARTEN UP (to, -ed) *dessiller les yeux à* : his wife had been screwing around for ten years before he smartened up = *sa femme couche à droite et à gauche depuis dix ans et ses yeux se sont enfin dessillés* ① to get wise to = *ouvrir les yeux sur.*

SMARTLY (adv) *de façon smart* : smartly dressed = *habillé de façon smart* ① elegantly = *élégamment.*

SMARTY-PANTS (n inv) *gros malin, grosse maligne* : don't be such a smarty-pants = *ne fais pas le gros malin* = smart aleck.

SMASH (n, -es) *succès* (m) *fracassant* : his last play was a smash = *sa dernière pièce a été un succès fracassant* ① hit = *gros succès* ≠ dud = *quelque chose à la noix.*

SMASH (adj) **smash hit** = *succès fou* : his record was a smash hit = *son disque a eu un succès fou.*

SMASH (to, -ed) *(se) fracasser* : the plate fell and smashed = *l'assiette est tombée et s'est fracassée* ① to shatter = *voler en éclats*
to smash into = *s'écraser contre* : they smashed into a wall = *ils se sont écrasés contre un mur* ① to bump into = *rentrer dans*
to smash up = *mettre en bouillie* : my son smashed up the car = *mon fils a mis la voiture en bouillie* ① to bang up = *mettre en morceaux.*

SMASHED (adj) *plein, -e comme une outre/comme une barrique* : we were all smashed at the end of the party = *nous étions tous pleins comme des outres/des barriques à la fin de la soirée* → DRUNK.

SMASHING (adj) *fameux, -euse* : a smashing dinner = *un dîner fameux* → WONDERFUL ☠ → famous.

SMASHUP (n) *carambolage* (m) : there was a smashup on the highway = *il y a eu un carambolage sur l'autoroute* ① collision = ←.

SMATTERING (n) **a smattering of (German)** = *quelques notions d'(allemand).*

SMEAR (n) **smear campaign** = *campagne de dénigrement.*

SMEAR (to, -ed) 1/ *salir, entacher* (reputation) : his coat was smeared = *son manteau a été sali,* the rumors smeared his reputation = *ces rumeurs ont sali/entaché sa réputation* ① to slander = *calomnier* ☠ se salir les mains = to dirty one's hands 2/ *graisser la patte à* : you have to smear the agent to get the apartment = *si vous voulez cet appartement, il faut graisser la patte à l'agent immobilier* ① to bribe = *soudoyer.*

SMELL (n) *odeur* (f) : a smell of roses/chocolate = *une odeur de roses/de chocolat* ① aroma = *arôme* ☠ → odor.

SMELL (to, smelt, smelt) *sentir* : this perfume smells good = *ce parfum sent bon,* she smelt the fish to see if it was still good = *elle a senti le poisson pour voir s'il était encore bon* ① to stink = *puer*
it smells ! = *c'est dégueu !* → AWFUL
to smell trouble/danger = *flairer des ennuis/un danger*
☠ → to feel.

SMELLY (adj, -ier, -iest) *malodorant, -e* : smelly feet = *des pieds malodorants.*

SMILE (n) *sourire* (m) : a warm smile = *un sourire chaleureux* ① grin = *sourire jusqu'aux oreilles*
I'll wipe that smile off your face ! = *je vais te faire passer l'envie de sourire !*

SMILE (to, -d) *sourire* : she often smiles = *elle sourit souvent* ≠ to frown = *froncer les sourcils*
keep smiling ! = *gardez le sourire !*
to smile at s.o. = *sourire à qqn* : he smiled at the teacher = *il a souri au professeur*
☠ *ça ne me sourit pas* = it doesn't appeal to me
— *tout lui sourit* = everything's going his way.

SMIRK (n) *fin sourire* (m) : he answered with a smirk = *il a répondu avec un fin sourire* ① sneer = *ricanement méchant.*

SMIRK (to, -ed) *avoir un fin sourire* : she smirked when he asked her her age = *elle a eu un fin sourire quand il lui a demandé son âge* ⊙ to sneer = *ricaner méchamment*.

SMITTEN (adj) **to be smitten** = *être toqué* : the first time he met my sister, he was smitten = *la première fois qu'il a rencontré ma sœur, il en a été toqué* ⊙ to have a crush on = *avoir le béguin pour*.

SMOCK (n) *blouse (f) (de travail)* : she wears a smock when she works = *elle porte une blouse quand elle travaille* ⊙ overalls = *salopette* ☠ → blouse.

SMOG (n inv) *brouillard (m) mêlé de fumée* : overwhelming smog in California = *un épais brouillard mêlé de fumée au-dessus de la Californie* ⊙ fog = *brouillard*, smoke = *fumée*, pollution = ←.

SMOKE (n) *fumée (f)* : the room's full of smoke = *la pièce est remplie de fumée* ⊙ fire = *feu*
to go up in smoke = *s'en aller en fumée* : our trip projects went up in smoke = *nos projets de voyage s'en sont allés en fumée*
where there's smoke, there's fire = *il n'y a pas de fumée sans feu* = there's no smoke without fire.

SMOKE (to, -d) *fumer* : do you mind if I smoke ? = *est-ce que cela vous gêne si je fume ?* ⊙ to chain-smoke = *fumer comme un sapeur* **SMOKER** (n) *fumeur, -euse* : a heavy smoker = *un grand fumeur* ≠ nonsmoker = *non fumeur*.

SMOKY (adj, -ier, -iest) *enfumé, -e* : a smoky apartment = *un appartement enfumé* ⊙ stuffy = *mal aéré*.

SMOOCH (to, -ed) *se bécoter* : we used to smooch at the movies = *on se bécotait au cinéma* ⊙ to pet = *se peloter*.

SMOOTH (adj, -er, -est) **1/** *en douceur* : the flight was very smooth = *le vol s'est passé en douceur* ≠ rough = *dur* **2/** *doucereux, -euse* : he's very sophisticated and very smooth = *il est très sophistiqué et très doucereux* ⊙ slick = *mielleux* **3/** *lisse* : your skin's so smooth = *ta peau est tellement lisse* ≠ rough = *rugueux*
a smooth talker = *un beau parleur* ⊙ a line = *du baratin*.

SMOOTHLY (adv) *en douceur* : everything went smoothly = *tout s'est passé en douceur* ≠ to go amiss = *aller de travers*.

SMOOTH OVER (to, -ed) *arrondir les angles* : her parents are always arguing and she tries to smooth things over = *ses parents sont toujours en train de se disputer et elle essaie d'arrondir les angles*.

SMOTHER (to, -ed) *étouffer* : she smothers her kids with love = *elle étouffe ses gosses d'amour*, the blanket smothered the baby = *la couverture a étouffé le bébé* ⊙ to asphyxiate = *asphyxier* ☠ → to choke.

SMUG (adj, -ger, -gest) *fat* : conceited and smug = *suffisant et fat* ⊙ complacent = *complaisant*, smugly = *avec fatuité*.

SMUGGLE (to, -d) *passer en contrebande/en fraude* : to smuggle guns = *passer des fusils en contrebande/en fraude* ⊙ to run = *faire passer*
to smuggle in ≠ **out** = *faire entrer* ≠ *sortir en contrebande/en fraude* : they smuggled heroin in(to) the country = *ils ont fait entrer de l'héroïne en contrebande/en fraude dans le pays*, the family was smuggled out of East Berlin = *on a fait sortir la famille en fraude de Berlin-Est*.

SMUGGLER (n) *contrebandier, -ère* : there are child smugglers = *il y a des enfants contrebandiers* ⊙ runner = *passeur*, black marketeer = *quelqu'un qui fait du marché noir* **SMUGGLING** (n) *contrebande (f)* ⊙ black market = *marché noir* ☠ *contrebande d'alcool* = bootlegging.

SMUT (n inv) *cochonneries (f pl)* : that paper/film is full of smut = *ce journal/film est plein de cochonneries* ⊙ obscenity = *obscénité* **SMUTTY** (adj, -ier, -iest) *cochon, -onne* : a smutty movie = *un film cochon* ⊙ raunchy = *obscène* ☠ *le dîner n'était pas cochon* = the dinner wasn't bad.

SNACK (n) *casse-croûte (m), en-cas (m)* : a coffee and a ham sandwich make a good snack = *un café et un sandwich au jambon, ça fait un bon casse-croûte/en-cas*
to have a snack = *casser la croûte* ⊙ to have a bite = *manger un morceau*
snack bar = *snack(-bar)*.

SNAG (n) *os (m)* : it's a high salary but the snag is that you have to work at night = *le salaire est élevé, mais l'os, c'est qu'il faut travailler la nuit* ⊙ catch = *piège*, a fly in the ointment = *l'ombre au tableau* ☠ → bone.

SNAIL (n) *escargot (m)* : let's have snails to begin with = *si on prenait des escargots pour commencer* ⊙ slug = *limace*
to go at a snail's pace = *avancer à une allure d'escargot* ≠ to hustle up = *se grouiller*.

SNAKE (n) *serpent (m)* : to be afraid of snakes = *avoir peur des serpents* ⊙ snakebite = *morsure de serpent*, rattlesnake = *serpent à sonnettes*, boa = ←, viper = *vipère*, python = ←, cobra = ←
the Snake = *le serpent monétaire*.

SNAP (n) **a snap** = *quelque chose d'enfantin* : the test was a snap = *l'examen était enfantin* ⊙ a breeze = *bête comme chou* ≠ no picnic = *pas de la tarte*.

SNAP (adj) **a snap decision** = *une décision prise sur un coup de tête* ⊙ hasty = *hâtif*.

SNAP (to, -ped) **1/** *répliquer sèchement* : when I asked him about his family problems he snapped that it was none of my business = *quand je lui ai parlé de ses problèmes familiaux, il a sèchement répliqué que ce n'étaient pas mes oignons* **2/** *casser net* : the rope snapped = *la corde a cassé net* ⊙ to break = *casser*

586

to snap at = 1/ *montrer les dents à* : the dog snapped at me = *le chien m'a montré les dents* ⓓ to bite = *mordre* 2/ *sauter sur* : when he said that, she snapped at him = *quand il a dit ça, elle lui a sauté dessus* → TO LAMBAST 3/ *se jeter sur* : he snapped at the opportunity = *il s'est jeté sur l'occasion* ⓓ to leap at = *saisir au bond*

snap out of it ! = *secoue-toi !* ⓓ get hold of yourself ! = *domine-toi !*

to snap up = *s'arracher* : the women snapped up all the articles on sale = *les femmes s'arrachaient les articles en solde* ✥ → to yank out

snap it up ! = *active !* ≠ take your own sweet time ! = *prends tout ton temps !*

SNAPPY (adj, -ier, -iest) **a snappy dresser** = *quelqu'un qui s'habille à la dernière mode*

make it snappy ! = *et que ça saute !* ⓓ hurry up ! = *dépêche-toi !*

SNAPSHOT (n) *cliché (m)* : we took a lot of snapshots of your daughter = *nous avons fait beaucoup de clichés de votre fille* ⓓ photo = *← ✥ → cliché.*

SNARE (n) *collet (m)* (animal), *piège (m)* ✥ → trap **SNARE** (to, -d) *prendre au collet/au piège* : to snare rabbits/terrorists = *prendre des lapins au collet/des terroristes au piège.*

SNATCH (to, -ed) *arracher* : he snatched my bag from my hands = *il m'a arraché mon sac des mains* ⓓ to seize = *saisir* ✥ → to yank out.

SNAZZY (adj, -ier, -iest) *bien fringué, -e* : snazzy girls = *des filles bien fringuées* ⓓ stylish = *chic.*

SNEAK (n) *traître (m, f)* : you did it when I was out, little sneak = *tu as fait ça quand je n'étais pas là, petit traître* ⓓ little rascal = *petit polisson* ✥ → traitor.

SNEAK (to, -ed) *(faire) en catimini* : to sneak a drink = *boire en catimini*

to sneak in ≠ **out of (the room)** = *entrer dans* ≠ *sortir de (la pièce) en catimini/subrepticement*

to sneak up on = *être traître* : Scotch sneaks up on you = *le whisky est traître.*

SNEAKERS (n pl) *baskets (m pl), tennis (m pl)* : your sneakers have holes in them = *tu as des trous à tes baskets/tennis* ✥ → tennis.

SNEAKY (adj, -ier, -iest) *(qui agit en) traître* : he's a sneaky child = *c'est un petit traître* ⓓ sly = *sournois* ≠ upfront = *franc.*

SNEER (n) *ricanement (m) méprisant* : the sneers of the schoolchildren = *les ricanements méprisants des écoliers* ⓓ taunt = *raillerie.*

SNEER AT (to, -ed) *ricaner (avec mépris) de* : they sneered at the new invention/at crippled people = *ils ont ricané avec mépris de la nouvelle invention/des infirmes* ⓓ to taunt = *railler.*

SNEEZE (to, -d) *éternuer* : pepper makes me sneeze = *le poivre me fait éternuer* ⓓ God bless you ! = *à vos souhaits !*

(his offer) is not to be sneezed at = *(sa proposition) n'est pas à dédaigner/il ne faut pas cracher sur (sa proposition).*

SNIDE (adj, -r, -st) *narquois, -e* : a snide remark = *une réflexion narquoise* ⓓ insinuating = *plein d'insinuations.*

SNIFF (to, -ed) *renifler* : some dogs sniff everything = *certains chiens reniflent tout* ⓓ to sneeze = *éternuer.*

SNIFFLES (n pl) **to have the sniffles** = *avoir la goutte au nez/avoir attrapé froid* ⓓ to have a cold = *avoir un rhume.*

SNIPE (to, -d) *canarder* : he sniped at the crowd = *il a canardé la foule* ⓓ to shoot at = *tirer sur* **SNIPER** (n) *tireur (m) embusqué/isolé.*

SNITCH (n, -es) *caf(e)teur, -euse* : my kid brother was a snitch = *mon petit frère était un caf(e)teur* ⓓ stoolie = *mouchard* **SNITCH** (to, -ed) *caf(e)ter* : why did you snitch ? = *pourquoi as-tu caf(e)té ?* ⓓ to tattle = *rapporter.*

SNOB (n) *snob (m, f)* : a family of snobs = *une famille de snobs* ⓓ snobbery = *snobisme.*

SNOBBISH (adj) *snob* : she's haughty and snobbish = *elle est hautaine et snob* ⓓ snooty = *snobinard.*

SNOOP INTO (to, -ed) *fouiner dans* : don't snoop into my private problems = *ne fouinez pas dans mes problèmes personnels* ⓓ to pry into (s.o.'s business) = *fourrer son nez dans (les affaires de qqn).*

SNOOTY (adj, -ier, -iest) *snobinard, -e* : snooty kids = *des gosses snobinards* ⓓ high-and-mighty = *plein de morgue.*

SNOOZE (to, -d) *roupiller* : let's snooze a little ! = *si on roupillait un peu !* ⓓ to take a nap = *faire un somme.*

SNORE (to, -d) *ronfler* : men who snore are not for me = *je n'aime pas les hommes qui ronflent.*

SNOT (n) *morveux, -euse* : a little snot = *un petit morveux* ⓓ brat = *sale gosse.*

SNOTTY (adj, -ier, -iest) *morveux, -euse* : a lot of snotty kids at the club = *pas mal de petits morveux au club* ✥ *qui se sent morveux, qu'il se mouche* = if the shoe fits, wear it.

SNOW (n) *neige (f)* : there's a lot of snow in New York in winter = *il y a beaucoup de neige à New York en hiver* ⓓ snowflake = *flocon de neige*, snowball = *boule de neige*, snowman = *bonhomme de neige*, snowstorm = *tempête de neige*

to give s.o. a snow job = *faire un baratin pas possible à qqn* : he gave me a real snow job = *il m'a vraiment fait un baratin pas possible* ⓓ to give s.o. a line = *faire du baratin à qqn*

snow bunny = *pin-up des neiges/de sports d'hiver (qui fait tout sauf du ski)*

Snow White = *Blanche-Neige* ⓪ Little Red Riding Hood = *le Petit Chaperon rouge.*

SNOW (to, -ed) *neiger* : it hasn't snowed yet this winter = *il n'a pas encore neigé cet hiver* ⓪ to hail = *grêler,* to freeze = *geler*
to be snowed under = 1/ *être débordé* : I'm snowed under with work/invitations = *je suis débordé de travail/d'invitations* 2/ *être sous la neige* : the car/house is snowed under = *la voiture/maison est sous la neige*
to snow s.o. = *baratiner qqn* : he tried to snow me into thinking he was a count = *il m'a baratiné pour me faire croire qu'il était comte* ⓪ to take s.o. for a ride = *mener qqn en bateau.*

SNOWBALL (to, -ed) *faire boule de neige* : our problems snowballed = *nos problèmes ont fait boule de neige.*

SNUB (n) *camouflet (f)* : the President's refusal to see him was a real snub = *le refus du Président de le recevoir a été un véritable camouflet* ⓪ slight = *affront.*

SNUB (to, -bed) *snober* : she snubs her husband's secretary = *elle snobe la secrétaire de son mari* ⓪ to brush off = *rembarrer.*

SNUFF (to, -ed) *sniffer* : to snuff coke = *sniffer de la coco.*

SNUG (adj, -ger, -gest) **to be as snug as a bug in a rug** = *être douillettement installé* ⓪ to be comfortable = *être installé confortablement.*

SNUGGLE (UP) (to, -d) *se blottir* : I snuggled up to him = *je me suis blottie contre lui.*

SO (adv) **1/** *si, tellement* : she's so happy with him = *elle est si/tellement heureuse avec lui,* it's not so difficult = *ce n'est pas si/tellement difficile* = it isn't that difficult → VERY 🐾 *si* → if
2/ *alors* : so tell me what happened ! = *alors, dites-moi ce qui s'est passé !,* so let's eat ! = *alors, mangeons !* ⓪ therefore = *donc*
3/ *tellement, tant* : I love him so ! = *je l'aime tellement/tant !*

🐾 *tant s'en faut* = far from it	— *tant qu'à faire allons au cinéma* = we might as well go to the movies
— *tant bien que mal* = after a fashion	
— *tant et plus* = enough and to spare	— *tant que (je vivrai)* = as long as (I live)

so am I !/so do I !/so did I !/etc. = *moi aussi !* : she's in a hurry — so am I ! = *elle est pressée — moi aussi !,* she travels a lot — so do I ! = *elle voyage beaucoup — moi aussi !,* she made a mistake — so did I ! = *elle a fait une erreur — moi aussi !* ≠ I'm not either !/I don't either !/I didn't either ! = *moi non plus !*
so as to = *de façon à* : she spoke slowly so as to make herself clearly understood = *elle a parlé lentement de façon à se faire bien comprendre*
so (kind) as to = *assez (gentil) pour* : would you be so kind as to bring some more water ? = *voulez-vous être assez gentil pour rapporter de l'eau ?*
so be it ! = *soit !*
so far = *jusque-là* : we haven't had any problems so far =

jusque-là nous n'avons eu aucun problème ⓪ to date = *jusqu'ici*
so far so good = *jusqu'ici ça va*
so help me ! = *je te jure !* → GOSH !
I am so !/I did so !/I will so ! = *si (je le suis/je l'ai fait/je le ferai) !*
so it goes = *ainsi va la vie* → THAT'S LIFE !
so it seems = *il semble bien*
so long ! = *salut !* ⓪ see you later, alligator ! = *à la revoyure !*
so many = *tant/tellement (de)* : she's got so many problems = *elle a tant/tellement de problèmes*
so much = *tellement/tant* : she'd like to see you so much = *elle aimerait tellement vous voir*
so much happier (with her second husband) = *tellement plus heureuse (avec son second mari)*

so much for that ! = *voilà qui est réglé !*
so much more (intelligent/comfortable) = *tellement plus (intelligent/à l'aise)*
so soon = *si tôt* : why are you leaving so soon ? = *pourquoi partez-vous si tôt ?*
so ... that = *si ... que* : I'm so tired that I could sleep for a week = *je suis si fatigué que je pourrais dormir pendant une semaine*
so there ! = *et toc !*
so to speak = *pour ainsi dire* = for all practical purposes
so very = *vraiment très* : she's so very rich = *elle est vraiment très riche* → VERY
not so ... as (GB) = *pas aussi ... que* : she's not so stupid as you think = *elle n'est pas aussi stupide que vous le pensez* = she's not as stupid as you think.

SO (adj) **it's so** ≠ **it isn't so** = *c'est vrai* ≠ *ce n'est pas vrai* : is it so they're going to divorce ? — yes, it's so ≠ no, it isn't so = *est-ce que c'est vrai qu'ils vont divorcer ? — oui, c'est vrai* ≠ *non, ce n'est pas vrai*
is that so ? = *pas possible !* : he's getting divorced

for the fifth time, is that so ? = *il divorce pour la cinquième fois ? pas possible !*
isn't that so ? = *pas vrai ?/n'est-ce pas ?* : he's going to be the Republican candidate, isn't that so ? = *ce sera lui le candidat républicain, pas vrai ?/n'est-ce pas ?*

just so = *comme il faut* : their house is always just so = *leur maison est toujours tenue comme il faut*	**this/that being so** = *les choses étant ce qu'elles sont.*

SO (pron) **I believe so/I think so** = *je crois bien/je pense bien.*

SO ! (interj) *alors !* : so ! you decided to come ! = *alors ! vous avez décidé de venir !*

SO (conj) **1/** *alors* : I'm tired, so I'm going to bed = *je suis fatigué, alors je vais me coucher* ⓓ thus = *donc* **2/** *afin que* : be quiet so I can sleep = *reste tranquille afin que je puisse dormir*

so that = *afin que* : finish your work so that we can go out to eat = *finissez votre travail afin que nous puissions aller manger* ⓓ in order to = *afin de*	**so what ?** = *et après ?* : they're living together, so what ? = *ils vivent ensemble, et après ?* ⓓ a lot I care ! = *ça me fait une belle jambe !*

SOAK (to, -ed) **1/** *estamper* : his lawyer soaked him = *son avocat l'a estampé* → TO HUSTLE **2/** *tremper* : let the sweater soak = *laissez tremper le pull*
to get soaked = *se faire tremper* ⓓ to get soused = *se faire saucer*
☠ *avoir trempé dans (une affaire louche)* = to have been involved in (shady dealings)
— *tremper son toast dans son café* = to dunk one's toast in one's coffee.

SO-AND-SO (n, so-and-sos) *chameau* (m) : what a so-and-so her brother is ! = *son frère, quel chameau !* → BASTARD
Mr. so-and-so = *M. Untel* ⓓ Mr. John Doe = *M. Dupont*
☠ → camel.

SOAP (n inv) *savon* (m) : don't forget to buy some soap = *n'oublie pas d'acheter du savon* ⓓ cake of soap = *savonnette*, soap dish = *porte-savon*, cleanser = *produit d'entretien*, soapy = *savonneux*, suds = *mousse*
soap opera = *mélo* : the serial is a soap opera for young girls = *ce feuilleton est un mélo pour jeunes filles* ⓓ hearts-and-flowers = *quelque chose à l'eau de rose*
☠ *passer un savon à qqn* = to give s.o. a dressing-down/calling-down.

SOAPBOX (n, -es) **to get on one's soapbox** = *repartir sur son cheval de bataille* : he's on his soapbox about the bad effects of smoking = *il est reparti sur son cheval de bataille : les effets nocifs du tabac.*

SOAR (to, -ed) *monter en flèche* : prices have soared = *les prix ont monté en flèche* ≠ to drop = *tomber.*

SOB (to, -bed) *sangloter* : stop sobbing ! = *arrête de sangloter !* ⓓ to weep = *pleurer à chaudes larmes* ≠ to laugh = *rire*
what a sob story ! = *quelle histoire larmoyante !* ⓓ a tearjerker = *une histoire pour faire pleurer Margot.*

S.O.B. (n) *saligaud* (m) : she's going out with a real s.o.b. = *elle sort avec un véritable saligaud* → BASTARD.

SOBER (adj) **1/** *sobre* : he's usually sober = *en général, il est sobre* ≠ drunk = *ivre* **2/** *sobre* : sober colors = *des couleurs sobres* ≠ gaudy = *criard.*

SOBER UP (to, -ed) *dessoûler* : a stiff coffee will sober you up = *un café fort te dessoûlera* ⓓ to sleep it off = *cuver son vin.*

SO-CALLED (adj) *soi-disant* : so-called friends = *de soi-disant amis* ⓓ alleged = *présumé.*

SOCCER (n) *football* (m) : to play soccer = *jouer au football.*

SOCIABLE (adj) *sociable* : my husband's very sociable = *mon mari est très sociable* ⓓ friendly = *amical* ≠ unsociable = *peu sociable*, a good mixer = *quelqu'un de liant.*

SOCIAL (n) *petite fête* (f) : there's a church social Saturday = *il y a une petite fête à la paroisse samedi* ⓓ dance = *soirée dansante.*

SOCIAL (adj) *social, -e* : we're all social animals = *nous sommes tous des animaux sociaux* ≠ individual = *individuel*
social climber = *arriviste* : his wife's a social climber = *sa femme est une arriviste* = arrivist ⓓ parvenu = ←
social life = *vie mondaine* : he has a very busy social life = *il a une vie mondaine bien remplie*
social reform = *réforme sociale*
social register = *le Bottin mondain* ⓓ the Who's Who = *le Who's Who*
social security = *sécurité sociale*
social status = *statut social/standing* : she's very aware of her social status = *elle attache beaucoup d'importance à son statut social/standing* ☠ → standing
social studies = *sciences sociales*
social work = *assistance sociale* ⓓ **social worker** = *assistante sociale.*

SOCIALISM (n) *socialisme* (m) : there are many kinds of socialism = *il y a beaucoup de formes de socialisme* ⓓ Welfare State = *État providence*, communism = *communisme.*

SOCIALIST (n, adj) *socialiste* (m, f) : are you a socialist ? = *est-ce que vous êtes socialiste ?* ⓓ communist = *communiste.*

SOCIALITE (n) *mondain, -e* : socialites spend their time at parties = *les mondains passent leur temps dans les soirées* ⓓ jet set = ←.

SOCIALIZE (to, -ed) **to socialize with** = *fréquenter* :
she doesn't socialize with people at work = *elle ne fréquente pas les gens de son bureau* ⓪ to hobnob with =
côtoyer ☠ → to frequent
socialized medicine = *médecine étatisée.*

SOCIETY (n, -ies) *société (f)* : are all societies violent ? =
est-ce que toutes les sociétés sont violentes ? ☠ *une
société (entreprise)* = a company.

SOCIOLOGICAL (adj) *sociologique* : a sociological
study = *une étude sociologique* **SOCIOLOGIST** (n) *sociolo-
gue (m, f)* ⓪ ethnologist = *ethnologue* **SOCIOLOGY** (n, -ies)
sociologie (f), socio (f) : to study sociology = *faire des études de sociologie* ⓪ anthropology = *anthropologie.*

SOCK (n) *chaussette (f)* : your socks are dirty = *tes chaussettes sont sales*
a sock in the mouth = *une beigne dans la figure*
☠ *laisser tomber qqn comme une vieille chaussette/
comme une chaussette sale* = to drop s.o. like a hot
potato.

SOCKET (n) *orbite (m)* : the eye was torn out of its socket
= *l'œil avait été arraché de son orbite* ⓪ eye = *œil.*

SODA (n) *soda (m)* ⓪ milk shake = ←
soda jerk = *garçon au comptoir.*

SODOMY (n inv) *sodomie (f)* : the pleasure of sodomy =
le plaisir de la sodomie **SODOMIZE** (to, -d) *sodomiser.*

SOFA (n) *sofa (m)* : she was sitting on the sofa = *elle était
assise sur le sofa* ⓪ couch = *divan.*

SOFT (adj, -er, -est) 1/ *doux, douce* : what soft material/
skin ! = *quel tissu doux/quelle peau douce !* ≠ rough =
rugueux
☠ *doux (comme un agneau)* = gentle (as a lamb)
— *c'est de la folie douce* = it's sheer madness
— *en douce* = on the sly
— *faire les yeux doux à qqn* = to make sheep's eyes at
s.o.
— *se la couler douce* = to have it easy
— *un temps doux* = a mild weather
2/ *mou, molle* : the butter's soft = *le beurre est mou* ⓪
malleable = *malléable*
a soft job = *une planque* ⓪ a plum = *un truc en or*
a soft spot = *un faible* : Scotch is my soft spot = *le*

whisky, c'est mon faible
a soft touch = *quelqu'un de facile à taper* ≠ moocher
= *tapeur*
☠ *un gouvernement mou* = a lax government
— *elle est molle (comme une chiffe)* = she's sluggish.

SOFT-COVER (adj) *broché, -e* : a soft-cover book = *un
livre broché* ⓪ pocketbook = *livre de poche.*

SOFTEN (to, -ed) *adoucir* : a Scotch will soften the shock
= *un whisky adoucira le choc* ≠ to harden = *durcir*
SOFTENER (n) *adoucisseur (m).*

SOFT-HEARTED (adj) *au cœur tendre* : a soft-hearted
father = *un père au cœur tendre* ≠ ruthless =
impitoyable.

SOFTLY (adv) *doucement* : talk softly = *parlez doucement*
☠ *les affaires vont doucement* = business is slack
— *doucement avec le whisky* = easy with the Scotch
— *doucement les basses !* = keep your shirt on !

SOFT-SOAP (to, -ed) *passer de la pommade à* : I have to
soft-soap my father to get some money = *pour obtenir
de l'argent de mon père, je dois lui passer de la pommade* ⓪ to lay it on (thick) = *en faire des tonnes.*

SOFTWARE (n inv) *logiciel (m), software (m)* : programs
are the software of computers = *les programmes forment le software/le logiciel des ordinateurs.*

SOFTY = SOFTIE (n, -ies) *tendre (m, f)* : don't be afraid
of her, she's a softy/a softie = *n'aie pas peur d'elle, c'est
une tendre* ≠ hard egg = *dur à cuire.*

SOGGY (adj, -ier, -iest) *ramolli, -e* : the toast is soggy = *le
toast est ramolli.*

SOIL (n) *sol (m)* : the soil is rich = *le sol est riche* ⓪
earth = *terre* ☠ → ground.

SOIL (to, -ed) *souiller* : I soiled my dress = *j'ai souillé ma
robe* ⓪ to stain = *tacher*, to dirty = *salir.*

SOLACE (n) *consolation (f)* : he's taking solace in the fact
she isn't happier than he is = *il trouve une consolation
dans le fait qu'elle n'est pas plus heureuse que lui* ⓪
relief = *soulagement.*

SOLAR (adj) *solaire* : solar energy = *énergie solaire.*

SOLDIER (n) *soldat (m)* : soldiers were marching in the streets = *des soldats défilaient dans les rues*

barracks = *caserne*	jecteur de conscience	**fatigues** = *treillis*
battalion = *bataillon*	**court-martial** = *cour martiale*	**firing squad** = *peloton d'exé-*
boot camp = *les classes*	**deserter** = *déserteur*	*cution*
buck private = *bidasse* (LV)/	**dog tag** = *plaque d'identité*	**GI** = *GI/soldat américain*
troufion (LV) / *seconde classe*	**the draft** = *la conscription* ⓪	**knapsack** = *havresac*
captain = *capitaine*	**the call-up** = *l'appel sous les*	**KP duty** = *corvée de patates*
commissioned officer = *offi-*	*drapeaux*	**major** = *commandant*
cier	**to enlist** = *s'enrôler*	**marine** = *marine/fusilier ma-*
company = *compagnie*	**enlisted man/woman** = *un*	*rin*
conscientious objector = *ob-*	*engagé/une engagée*	**mercenary** = *mercenaire*

noncommissioned officer = *sous-officier*	**rookie** = *bleu*	**troops** = *troupes*
a PFC = a Private First Class = *un première classe*	**sentry** = *sentinelle*	**veteran** = *ancien combattant*
	sergeant = *sergent*	**war** = *guerre*
a private = *un simple soldat*	**serviceman/woman** = *militaire (homme/femme)*	**woman soldier** = *femme soldat.*
recruit = *recrue*	**squadron** = *escadron*	

SOLE (adj) **the sole (country to maintain capital punishment)** = *l'unique (pays à avoir conservé la peine de mort)*
sole heir = *légataire universel.*

SOLELY (adv) *uniquement* : he works solely for money = *il travaille uniquement pour l'argent* ⓈⒹ exclusively = *exclusivement.*

SOLEMN (adj, -er, -est) *solennel, -elle* : a solemn speech = *un discours solennel* ⓈⒹ serious = *sérieux* **SOLEMNITY** (n, -ies) *solennité (f)* **SOLEMNLY** (adv) *solennellement.*

SOLICIT (to, -ed) 1/ *racoler* : hookers aren't allowed to solicit in the streets = *les putains ne sont pas autorisées à racoler dans les rues* ☠ *racoler la clientèle* = to drum up business 2/ *solliciter* : he solicited aid from the state = *il a sollicité l'aide de l'État* ⓈⒹ to ask = *demander* ☠ *elle est très sollicitée* = she's very much in demand.

SOLICITOR (n) (GB) *avocat, -e (auprès des juridictions inférieures)* = lawyer.

SOLID (adj, -er, -est) 1/ *solide* : solid cement = *ciment solide* ≠ liquid = *liquide* 2/ *solide* : her parents are both solid people = *ses parents sont tous les deux solides* ≠ fragile = ←
solid gold/silver = *or/argent massif* ⓈⒹ plated = *plaqué*
solid red/blue/yellow = *rouge/bleu/jaune uni* : a solid red coat = *un manteau rouge uni*
(four) solid (hours) = *(quatre heures) d'affilée*
☠ *un solide allié* = a steadfast ally.

SOLIDARITY (n, -ies) *solidarité (f)* : solidarity of a couple/family = *la solidarité d'un couple/d'une famille* ⓈⒹ unity = *unité.*

SOLIDIFY (to, -ied) *(se) solidifier* ≠ to liquefy = *se liquéfier.*

SOLITARY (n, -ies) **in solitary** = *au cachot* ⓈⒹ in the clink = *à l'ombre.*

SOLITARY (adj) *seul, -e* : not one solitary case of smallpox = *pas un seul cas de variole*
solitary confinement = *régime cellulaire*
☠ → alone.

SOLITUDE (n) *solitude (f)* : who doesn't suffer from solitude ? = *qui ne souffre pas de la solitude ?* ⓈⒹ isolation = *isolement.*

SOLO (n, -i or -s) *solo (m)* : a piano solo = *un solo de piano* ≠ duo = ←.

SOLO (adj) *en solitaire* : a solo flight = *un vol en solitaire.*

SOLUTION (n) *solution (f)* : I don't see any solution to the problem = *je ne vois aucune solution au problème* ⓈⒹ explanation = *explication.*

SOLVE (to, -d) *résoudre* : that's a very difficult problem to solve = *c'est un problème très difficile à résoudre* ⓈⒹ to explain = *expliquer*
☠ *se résoudre à …* = to bring o.s. to …
— « to resolve » *existe mais est beaucoup moins employé dans ce sens.*

SOLVENCY (n, -ies) *solvabilité (f)* : the company's solvency = *la solvabilité de la société* ≠ insolvency = *insolvabilité* **SOLVENT** (adj) *solvable* : our company isn't solvent any longer = *notre société n'est plus solvable* ≠ insolvent = *insolvable.*

SOMBER (adj) *sombre* : a somber outlook = *un aspect sombre* ⓈⒹ gloomy = *lugubre*
☠ *une sombre histoire* = a grim story
— *une pièce sombre* = a dark room.

SOME (adj) 1/ *du, de la, des* : have you some butter ?/money ?/problems ? = *est-ce que vous avez du beurre ?/de l'argent ?/des problèmes ?*
2/ *certains, certaines* : some men are interesting = *certains hommes sont intéressants* ≠ no = *aucun* ☠ → certain
3/ *un, une* : some guy called you = *un type t'a appelé*, there must be some explanation = *il doit y avoir une explication* ☠ → one

by some means or other = *d'une façon ou d'une autre*	*dans (un livre) ou un autre*	**day (or other)** = *je le trouverai un jour (ou l'autre)*
for some time = *depuis un bon moment* : I haven't seen him for some time = *je ne l'ai pas vu depuis un bon moment*	**in some ways** = *par certains côtés* : in some ways, you're right = *par certains côtés, vous avez raison*	**some more** = *encore (de)* : do you want some more coffee ? = *est-ce que vous voulez encore du café ?*, yes, I'll have some more = *oui, j'en prendrais bien*
in some (book) or other =	**some day (or other)** = *un jour (ou l'autre)* : I'll find him some	

encore **(call me) some other time** = *(appelez-moi) à un autre* *moment* **some such thing** = *quelque* *chose de ce genre* **some time** = *à un moment* *donné* : I saw her some time last	year = *je l'ai vue à un moment* *donné l'année dernière* **some time ago** = *il y a long-* *temps* ⓪ ages ago = *il y a un* *bail* **some way or other** = *d'une* *manière ou d'une autre* : I'll get a job some way or other =	*j'aurai un boulot d'une manière* *ou d'une autre* ⓪ one way or another = *d'une façon ou d'une* *autre* **that was some movie !/idea !** = *ça, c'est un film !/une idée !* ⓪ what a film !/idea ! = *quel* *film !/quelle idée !*

SOME (pron) **1/** *en* : if you have any coffee, give me some = *si vous avez du café, donnez-m'en*

————————————— SYSTÈME —————————————

do you have some money ? = *est-ce que vous avez de l'argent ?*

— yes, I have some = *oui, j'en ai* —— — no, I don't have any = *non, je n'en ai pas*

☠ *je vous en parlerai* = I'll talk to you about it — *je m'en souviens* = I remember that — *j'en doute* = I doubt it — *j'en reviens* = I just come from there — *j'en ai assez !/marre !* = I've had enough !/I've had it !	— *j'en ai pour une heure* = it'll take me an hour — *je n'en ai pas* = I don't have any — *voilà où en sont les choses* = that's how things stand at present — *(une intelligence) comme on en rencontre peu* = (intelligence) like you seldom find

2/ *quelques-uns, -unes* : some like his last movie = *quelques-uns aiment son dernier film*

some (agreed), some (didn't) = *certains (sont* *d'accord), d'autre (non)* **some of them (are interesting)** = *certains*	*d'entre eux (sont intéressants)* **some of what (you said was right)** = *une partie* *de (ce que vous avez dit était juste)* = part of.

SOME (adv) **1/** *quelque* : some seventy people = *quelque soixante-dix personnes* ⓪ about = *à peu près*
2/ *un peu* : he drinks some = *il boit un peu* = a bit

you have to go some to (find someone as dumb **as he is)** = *il faut se lever de bonne heure pour* *(trouver quelqu'un d'aussi bête que lui)*	**that's going some !** = *c'est la meilleure !* → GOSH !

☠ *(10 dollars) et quelques* = (10 dollars) something — *quelque peu (fier)* = somewhat (proud)	— *je n'ai que quelques minutes* = I only have a few minutes.

SOMEBODY (pron) = SOMEONE.

SOMEDAY (adv) *un beau jour* : there may be peace in the world someday = *peut-être qu'un beau jour il y aura la paix dans le monde* ⓪ one of these days = *un de ces jours.*

SOMEHOW (adv) **1/** *d'une façon ou d'une autre* : I'll do it somehow = *je le ferai d'une façon ou d'une autre* ⓪ by some means = *de quelque manière que ce soit*
2/ *pour une raison ou pour une autre* : somehow she strikes me as strange = *pour une raison ou pour une autre elle me semble étrange*
somehow or other = *d'une façon ou d'une autre* ⓪ some way or other = *d'une manière ou d'une autre.*

SOMEONE (pron) *quelqu'un* : there's someone waiting for you = *il y a quelqu'un qui vous attend* = somebody ≠ no one/nobody = *personne*
someone else = *quelqu'un d'autre*

————————————— SYSTÈME —————————————

did you meet }	**someone/somebody ?** **anyone/anybody ?**

= *est-ce que vous avez rencontré quelqu'un ?*

— yes, I met someone = *oui, j'ai rencontré* *quelqu'un* = yes, I met somebody	— no, I didn't meet anyone = *non, je n'ai* *rencontré personne* = no, I didn't meet any- body = I met no one/nobody.

SOMEPLACE (adv) = SOMEWHERE.

SOMERSAULT (n) *galipette* (f) : the kids were doing somersaults in the sand = *les gosses faisaient des galipettes dans le sable* ⓪ to stand on one's hands = *faire le poirier.*

SOMETHING (pron) *quelque chose* ≠ nothing = *rien* = not ... anything

SYSTÈME

did you buy **something ?/anything ?** = *est-ce que vous avez acheté quelque chose ?*
— yes, I bought something = *oui, j'ai acheté quel-que chose*

— no, I didn't buy anything = *non, je n'ai rien acheté* = no, I bought nothing

she's got a certain something = *elle a un petit je ne sais quoi*
... something = *... et quel-ques* : it costs $ 100 something = *ça coûte 100 dollars et quel-ques*, the plane lands at five something = *l'avion atterrit à cinq heures et quelques*
something else = 1/ *autre chose* : do you want something else ? = *est-ce que vous voulez autre chose ?* 2/ *du tonnerre* : Marilyn Monroe was something else = *Marilyn Monroe était du tonnerre* → WONDERFUL
something's got to give = *il faut que quelque chose se passe* : the talks are at a stalemate,

something's got to give = *les pourparlers sont dans une impasse, il faut que quelque chose se passe*
something or other = *je ne sais quoi* : I ate something or other that didn't agree with me = *j'ai mangé je ne sais quoi qui ne m'a pas réussi*
something's rotten in the State of Denmark = *il y a quelque chose de pourri au royaume de Danemark (de France)*
something tells me (they're having problems again) = *quelque chose me dit (qu'ils ont de nouveau des problèmes)*

that's (really) something ! = *c'est (vraiment) quelque chose !*
something like that = *quel-que chose dans ce genre* : he said he was going to the bank or something like that = *il a dit qu'il allait à la banque ou quel-que chose dans ce genre*
there's something about him (I don't like) = *il y a quelque chose en lui (que je n'aime pas)*
there's something in/to that ! = *c'est pas bête ! =* **you've got something there ! you want to make something of it ?** = *et ta sœur ?*

SOMETHING (adv) **to be something like** = *avoir quelque chose de* : he's something like Brando = *il a quelque chose de Brando*

to have something like = *avoir quelque chose comme* : the book has something like 200 pages = *le livre a quelque chose comme 200 pages.*

SOMETIME (adj) **a sometime (singer)** = *quelqu'un qui a été (chanteur) à l'occasion* ⓪ would-be = *prétendu.*

SOMETIME (adv) *au cours de* : I'll see you sometime next week = *je vous verrai au cours de la semaine pro-chaine*, sometime last winter = *au cours de l'hiver der-nier* ⓪ during = *pendant*
sometime or other = *à un moment ou à un autre* : we'll go sometime or other next week = *nous irons à un moment ou à un autre la semaine prochaine* ⓪ someday = *un beau jour*
sometime soon = *très prochainement* : call me back sometime soon = *rappelez-moi très prochainement* ⓪ very soon = *très bientôt.*

SOMETIMES (adv) *quelquefois* : we sometimes make love in the morning = *nous faisons quelquefois l'amour le matin* ⓪ at times = *parfois*
sometimes (he's nasty) sometimes (he's nice) = *parfois (il est désagréable), parfois (il est sympa).*

SOMEWAY(S) (adv) *d'une manière ou d'une autre* : I'll get the money someway(s) = *j'aurai l'argent d'une manière ou d'une autre* ⓪ somehow = *d'une façon ou d'une autre.*

SOMEWHAT (adv) *quelque peu* : he's somewhat stupid = *il est quelque peu stupide* ⓪ rather = *plutôt*, very = *très.*

SOMEWHERE (adv) **1/** *quelque part* : you'll find him somewhere in New York = *vous le trouverez quelque part dans New York* = someplace ≠ nowhere = *nulle part* **2/** *un endroit (où)* : he's looking for somewhere to live = *il cherche un endroit où habiter*, we went some-where expensive last night = *nous sommes allés dans un endroit cher hier soir*
it must be somewhere near here = *ce doit être dans le coin* ⓪ **it's somewhere around here** = *c'est quel-que part par là* = it's around here somewhere
somewhere along the line/the way = *à un moment donné* : somewhere along the line/the way they decided they weren't made for each other = *à un moment donné, ils ont décidé qu'ils n'étaient pas faits l'un pour l'autre*
somewhere around = *dans/vers les* : he's somewhere around forty = *il a dans les quarante ans*, it's somewhere around noon = *il est dans les midi/vers midi*
somewhere near (San Francisco) = *quelque part près de (San Francisco)* ≠ far away from = *très loin de*
somewhere else = *autre part* : don't buy it here, you'll find it cheaper somewhere else = *n'achetez pas ça ici, vous en trouverez de moins cher autre part.*

SON (n) *fils (m)* : I have two sons = *j'ai deux fils* ⓪ son-in-law = *gendre*, stepson = *beau-fils*, sonny = *fiston*
son of a bitch ! = *fils de pute !* → BASTARD
son of a gun ! = *sale type !* → BASTARD
☠ *fils à papa* = prep school type.

SONG (n) *chanson (f)* : this is my favorite song = *c'est ma chanson préférée* ⓪ ballad = *ballade*, anthem = *hymne*, lullaby = *berceuse*, serenade = *sérénade*, melody = *mélodie*, singing = *chant*, spiritual = ←, chorus = *refrain*, stanza = *strophe*, couplet = ←, psalm = *psaume*, record = *disque*
for a song = *pour une bouchée de pain* : I bought the painting for a song = *j'ai acheté ce tableau pour une bouchée de pain* ⓪ dirt cheap = *donné*
to give s.o. a song and a dance = *raconter des salades à qqn* : the journalist asked him a straight question but the Senator gave him a song and a dance = *le journaliste lui avait posé une question directe, mais le sénateur lui a raconté des salades* ⓪ to avoid the issue = *chercher des faux-fuyants*
☠ *je connais la chanson !* = I know the tune !
— *c'est toujours la même chanson !* = it's the same old story !

SOON (adv) *bientôt* : we'll eat soon = *nous allons bientôt manger* ⓪ in a while = *tout à l'heure*, in the near future = *dans un avenir proche*

as soon as = *dès que/aussitôt que* : tell me as soon as he comes = *préviens-moi dès qu'il/aussitôt qu'il arrive* ⓪ when = *quand* **as soon as possible** = *dès que possible*	**see you soon !** = *à bientôt !* ⓪ see you ! = *ciao !* **soon after** = *peu après* : his wife died in September and he died soon after = *sa femme est morte en septembre et il est mort peu après.*

SOONER (adv comp) *plus tôt* : you should have told me sooner = *vous auriez dû me le dire plus tôt* ≠ later = *plus tard*

I'd sooner (go now) than (later) = *j'aimerais mieux (y aller maintenant) que (plus tard)* **sooner or later** = *tôt ou tard* : he'll pay you back sooner or later = *il vous remboursera tôt*	*ou tard* **sooner ... than** = *plutôt que* : I'd sooner sleep with a stranger in the street than with you = *je coucherais plutôt avec un inconnu rencontré dans la rue qu'avec toi.*

SOOT (n) *suie (f)* : a face full of soot = *un visage couvert de suie.*

SOOTHE (to, -d) *apaiser* : to soothe a pain = *apaiser une douleur* ⓪ to calm = *calmer* ☠ → to appease.

SOPHISTICATED (adj) *sophistiqué, -e* : a sophisticated man/system = *un homme/un système sophistiqué* ⓪ refined = *raffiné* ≠ hickish = *plouc* ☠ "*sophistiqué*" in French is sometimes pejorative **SOPHISTICATION** (n) *sophistication (f).*

SOPHOMORE (n) *étudiant, -e de seconde année* : he's a sophomore at Yale = *il est en seconde année à Yale* ≠ freshman = *étudiant de première année.*

SOPRANO (n) *soprano (m, f)* ≠ contralto = ←.

SORDID (adj) *sordide* : a very sordid homelife = *des conditions de vie très sordides* ⓪ seedy = *miteux* ☠ *tu es sordide !* = you're really vile !
— *le côté sordide de la vie* = the seamy side of life.

SORE (adj, -r, -st) **1/** *en pétard* : what are you so sore about ? = *qu'est-ce qui t'a mis tellement en pétard ?* → ANGRY **2/** *endolori, -e* : my finger's sore = *mon doigt est endolori* ⓪ painful = *douloureux*
a sore spot/subject = *un point/sujet sensible* : don't talk to him about his divorce, it's a sore subject/spot = *ne lui parlez pas de son divorce, c'est un sujet/point sensible*
sore throat = *mal de gorge.*

SORORITY (n, -ies) *club d'étudiantes à l'université* ≠ fraternity = *club d'étudiants.*

SORROW (n inv) *peine (f)* : her death caused us great sorrow = *sa mort nous a causé beaucoup de peine* ⓪ woe = *malheur*, sadness = *tristesse* ≠ joy = *joie*
to drown one's sorrows = *noyer son chagrin dans l'alcool*
☠ *se donner de la peine* = to go to a lot of trouble
— *la peine capitale* = the death penalty
— *sans peine* ≠ *à grand peine* = easily ≠ with great difficulty
— *une peine de 3 mois* = a sentence of 3 months
— *c'est peine perdue* = it's a waste of time
— *ça n'en vaut pas la peine* = it isn't worth it.

SORRY (adj, -ier, -iest) *désolé, -e* : I'm sorry about that = *j'en suis désolé* ⓪ apologetic = *qui se confond en excuses*
to be sorry to = *être désolé de* : I'm sorry to tell you that you're wrong = *je suis désolé de te dire que tu as tort*
to be in a sorry state = *être en piteux état*
to feel sorry for s.o. = *plaindre qqn* : I really feel sorry for her = *je la plains vraiment*
sorry ! = *pardon !* ⓪ excuse me ! = *excusez-moi !*
you'll be sorry ! = *tu vas le regretter !*
☠ → desolate.

SORT (n) *sorte (f)* : what sort of man is he ? = *quelle sorte d'homme est-ce ?* ⓪ type = ←
my sort of = *le genre de .. qui me plaît* : she's my sort of girl = *c'est le genre de fille qui me plaît*
of sorts = *qui passe pour* : she's an actress of sorts = *elle passe pour être actrice*
out of sorts = *pas dans son assiette* : she's been feeling out of sorts lately = *dernièrement, elle n'était pas dans son assiette* ⓪ under the weather = *mal fichu*
sort of = **1/** *en quelque sorte* : he's sort of happy/a poet = *il est heureux/c'est un poète en quelque sorte* ⓪ kind of = *un peu* **2/** *comme ci comme ça* : did you like the book ? — sort of = *est-ce que vous avez aimé le livre ?*

comme ci comme ça

☠ *le sort (d'un homme)* = (a man's) fate

— *faisons un sort à ce gâteau* = let's polish off this cake

— *tirer au sort* = to draw lots

— *le sort en est jeté* = the die is cast

— *jeter un sort sur* = to cast a spell/to throw a hex on

— *faites en sorte que* = make sure that.

SORT OUT (to, -ed) **1/** *trier :* he sorted out his old love letters = *il a trié ses vieilles lettres d'amour* ⓐ to file = *classer* **2/** *mettre de l'ordre dans :* what you're writing is far too complicated, let's try to sort things out = *ce que vous écrivez est bien trop compliqué, essayons d'y mettre un peu d'ordre* ⓐ to settle = *régler.*

SOS (n) *SOS (m) :* I sent a SOS = *j'ai envoyé un SOS* = Mayday.

SO-SO (adj, adv) *comme ci comme ça, couci-couça :* he's a so-so lover = *comme amant, il est comme ci comme ça/couci-couça.*

SOUL (n) *âme (f) :* Faust sold his soul to the devil = *Faust a vendu son âme au diable* ⓐ spirit = *esprit*

not a soul = *pas un chat :* there was not a soul in the streets = *il n'y avait pas un chat dans les rues* ⓐ not a living thing = *pas âme qui vive*

a (trusting) soul = *un être (confiant)*

☠ *être l'âme damnée de qqn* = to be s.o.'s henchman

— *rendre l'âme* = to go the way of all flesh

— *à fendre l'âme* = heartbreaking.

SOUL (adj) *soul, qui se réfère à l'héritage (culture, tradition) des Noirs américains :* soul food/music = *nourriture/musique soul*

soul brother/sister = *frère/sœur de couleur*

soul mate = *âme sœur :* we meet few soul mates in life = *on rencontre peu d'âmes sœurs dans la vie.*

SOUL-SEARCHING (n) *nombrilisme (m) :* your constant soul-searching is ruining our relationship = *ton nombrilisme permanent est en train de ruiner nos rapports* ⓐ introspection = ←.

SOUND (n) *son (m) :* my cat recognizes the sound of my voice = *mon chat reconnaît le son de ma voix* ⓐ noise = *bruit,* soundproof = *insonore*

I don't like the sound of it = *ça ne me dit rien qui vaille* ⓐ there's something fishy = *il y a quelque chose de louche*

sound barrier = *mur du son*

sound effects = *effets sonores/bruitage*

sound film = *film parlant*

sound track = *bande-son.*

SOUND (to, -ed) *avoir l'air :* she sounds happy/intelligent/interested = *elle a l'air heureux/intelligent/intéressé* ⓐ to seem = *sembler*

it sounds as if (they're having trouble) = *ils ont l'air d'(avoir des ennuis)*

to sound off on/about = *faire de grands discours sur :* he sounded off on/about the danger of nuclear war = *il a*

fait de grands discours sur les dangers d'une guerre nucléaire

to sound s.o. out = *sonder qqn :* sound them out and see if they can lend us money = *sondez-les et voyez s'ils peuvent nous prêter de l'argent* = to feel s.o. out.

SOUND (adj, -er, -est) *valable :* sound investment/reasoning = *investissement/raisonnement valable* = valid ⓐ rational = *rationnel* ≠ unsound = *peu sûr* ☠ → valid.

SOUNDING BOARD (n) *banc (m) d'essai :* polls are a sounding board for public opinion = *les sondages sont des bancs d'essai pour connaître l'opinion publique.*

SOUP (n) *soupe (f), potage (m) :* vegetable soup = *soupe de légumes* ⓐ broth = *bouillon,* chowder = *sorte de soupe de poissons*

from soup to nuts = *du début à la fin :* the dinner was delicious from soup to nuts = *ce dîner était délicieux du début à la fin*

soup's on ! = *à la soupe !/à table !*

☠ *être trempé comme une soupe* = to be soaking wet

— *cracher dans la soupe* = to bite the hand that feeds one

— *la soupe populaire* = the breadline

— *être soupe au lait* = to be hot-tempered.

SOUP UP (to, -ed) *gonfler :* to soup up an engine = *gonfler un moteur* = to juice up ☠ → to inflate.

SOUR (adj, -er, -est) *aigre :* a sour taste = *un goût aigre* ≠ sweet = *sucré*

to end on a sour note = *se terminer sur une note amère :* the meeting ended on a sour note = *la réunion s'est terminée sur une note amère*

sour grapes = *les raisins sont trop verts*

sour milk = *lait tourné* ≠ fresh = *frais*

to turn sour = *tourner à l'aigre/au vinaigre :* their relationship turned sour = *leurs rapports ont tourné à l'aigre/au vinaigre*

☠ *des paroles aigres* = bitter words.

SOURCE (n) **1/** *source (f) :* money is the source of all our problems = *l'argent est la source de tous nos problèmes* ⓐ cause = ← **2/** *source (f) :* from an official source = *de source autorisée/officielle*

☠ *ça coule de source* = that goes without saying

— *retour aux sources* = return to the simple life

— *source (vive)* = spring (water).

SOUR (to, -ed) *s'aigrir :* our relations have soured = *nos rapports se sont aigris*

to sour on = *prendre en grippe :* after a few years I soured on my in-laws/New York = *après quelques années, j'ai pris mes beaux-parents/New York en grippe.*

SOURPUSS (n, -es) *bougon, -onne :* how could I have married such a sourpuss ? = *comment aurais-je pu épouser un tel bougon ?* ⓐ grouser = *grognon,* grumbler = *grincheux,* crank = *ronchonneur.*

SOUSE (to, -d) **to be soused** = *être beurré (comme un petit Lu) :* I really was soused last night = *j'étais vraiment beurré (comme un petit Lu) hier soir* → DRUNK.

595

SOUTH (n) *sud (m)* : to live in the South = *habiter dans le Sud* ⓐ southwest = *sud-ouest*, southeast = *sud-est* **the South of France** = *le Midi.*

SOUTH (adj) *(du) sud* : South Africa = *Afrique du Sud* **SOUTHERN** (adj) *du sud* : Southern Ireland = *Irlande du Sud* ≠ western = *de l'ouest.*

SOUTHERNER (n) *sudiste (m, f)* (US), *méridional, -e* ≠ northerner = *nordiste/nordique.*

SOUTHPAW (n) *gaucher, -ère* : both my kids are southpaws = *mes deux enfants sont des gauchers.*

SOUVENIR (n) *souvenir (m)* : we bought a lot of souvenirs in Florence = *nous avons acheté beaucoup de souvenirs à Florence* = memento ☠ *ne pas avoir le souvenir de* = to have no recollection of.

SOVEREIGN (n) *souverain, -e* : the sovereigns of 12 countries were at the wedding = *les souverains de 12 pays assistaient au mariage* ⓐ monarch = *monarque.*

SOVEREIGN (adj) *souverain, -e* : a sovereign state = *un État souverain* ⓐ autonomous = *autonome* ☠ *avoir un souverain mépris pour qqch/qqn* = to hold stg/s.o. in supreme contempt **SOVEREIGNTY** (n, -ies) *souveraineté (f).*

SOVIET (adj) *soviétique* : Soviet Union = *Union soviétique*, Soviet army = *armée soviétique* ☠ *un Soviétique* = a Russian **SOVIETS** (n pl) *Soviétiques (m pl).*

SOW (to, -ed, -ed or sown) *semer* : to sow seeds/discord/discontent = *semer des graines/la discorde/le mécontentement* ☠ *semer qqn* = to shake s.o. off.

SOYBEAN (n) *soja (m)* ⓐ tofu = ←.

SPA (n) *ville (f) d'eau, station (f) thermale* ⓐ health resort = *station de cure.*

SPACE (n) 1/ (inv) *place (f)* : there's not enough space for the bed = *il n'y a pas assez de place pour le lit* = room ☠ → place 2/ (inv) *espace (m)* : to travel in space = *voyager dans l'espace* ⓐ meteor = *météore*, spaceman = *astronaute*, outer space = *cosmos*, spaceship = *vaisseau spatial*, space shuttle = *navette spatiale* 3/ (inv) *liberté (f)* : my marriage didn't give me enough space of my own = *mon mariage ne m'a pas laissé assez de liberté* ☠ → liberty 4/ *espace (m)* : in the space of five minutes = *en l'espace de cinq minutes* **space age** = *ère spatiale.*

SPACED OUT (adj) *défoncé, -e* : spaced out on snow = *défoncé à la neige* ⓐ high = *qui plane.*

SPACEY (adj) *évaporé, -e* : a spacey broad = *une nana évaporée* ⓐ kooky = *farfelu.*

SPACIOUS (adj) *spacieux, -euse* : a spacious apartment = *un appartement spacieux* ≠ cramped = *à l'étroit.*

SPADE (n) *bamboula (m)* : she's married to a spade = *elle est mariée à un bamboula* ⓐ darkie = *mal blanchi* ≠ white trash = *les petits Blancs* **to call a spade a spade** = *appeler un chat un*

chat/appeler les choses par leur nom ⓐ to speak frankly = *parler franchement*
(to bid) spades = *(annoncer) pique*
in spades = *au centuple* : I'll get back in spades = *je me vengerai au centuple* ☠ *faire la bamboula* = to go out on a bender.

SPAGHETTI (n inv) *spaghetti (m)* : we eat a lot of spaghetti = *nous mangeons beaucoup de spaghetti* ⓐ pasta = *pâtes*, noodle = *nouille*, macaroni = ←, ravioli = ←, grated cheese = *fromage râpé*, meatballs = *boulettes.*

SPAIN (n) *Espagne (f)* : we're going to Spain this summer = *cet été, nous allons en Espagne.*

SPAN (n) **in the span of (an hour)** = *en l'espace d'(une heure).*

SPAN (to, -ned) *couvrir* : the film spanned most of our century = *le film couvrait la majeure partie de notre siècle* ☠ → to cover.

SPANIARD (n) *Espagnol, -e* ⓐ Spain = *Espagne.*

SPANISH (adj) *espagnol, -e* : Spanish tourists = *des touristes espagnols*
Spanish fly = *poudre de corne de rhinocéros* ⓐ aphrodisiac = *aphrodisiaque.*

SPANK (to, -ed) *donner une fessée à* : I rarely spank my children = *je donne rarement des fessées à mes enfants* → TO HIT **SPANKING** (n) *fessée (f)* : you're going to get a spanking if you don't stop that = *tu vas avoir une fessée si tu n'arrêtes pas* → TO HIT.

SPARE (adj, -r, -st) **spare parts** = *pièces de rechange*
spare room = *chambre d'ami*
spare ticket = *billet en plus/de rab*
spare time/cash = *temps/argent disponible*
spare tire = *roue de secours/pneu de rechange.*

SPARE (to, -d) 1/ *épargner* : spare me the bullshit, will you ! = *épargne-moi tes conneries, tu veux !*, all were killed, no one was spared = *tout le monde a été tué, personne n'a été épargné* ☠ *nous épargnons 1 000 dollars par mois* = we save $ 1 000 a month 2/ *lésiner sur* : don't spare the sugar = *ne lésinez pas sur le sucre*
can you spare ten dollars/ten minutes ? = *est-ce que tu peux me passer dix dollars ?/me consacrer dix minutes ?*
... to spare = *... de rab* : I don't have any cigarettes to spare = *je n'ai pas de cigarettes de rab.*

SPARERIBS (n pl) *travers (m pl) de porc* ⓐ fried rice = *riz cantonais.*

SPARK (n) *étincelle (f)* : sparks from the fire = *des étincelles provenant du feu*
a spark plug = *un vif-argent* : she's married to a spark plug = *elle a épousé un vif-argent* ⓐ the life of the party = *un boute-en-train.*

SPARKLE (to, -d) *étinceler* : her diamond sparkles = *son diamant étincelle* ⓐ to gleam = *luire*, to beam = *resplendir.*

SPARROW (n) *moineau (m)* : the old lady was throwing bread crumbs to the sparrows = *la vieille dame jetait des miettes de pain aux moineaux.*

SPARSE (adj, -r, -st) *clairsemé, -e* : a sparse population = *une population clairsemée* ≠ dense = ←.

SPASM (n) *spasme (m)* : stomach spasms = *des spasmes à l'estomac* ⓒⒹ convulsion = ←.

SPAT (n) *fâcherie (f)* : frequent spats between my parents = *des fâcheries fréquentes entre mes parents* ⓒⒹ scrap = accrochage, quarrel = *querelle.*

SPEAK (to, spoke, spoken) *parler* : do you speak English ? = *est-ce que vous parlez anglais ?* ⓒⒹ to rap = *bavarder* ☠ → to talk

---

don't speak too soon = *ne parlez pas trop vite* : I think I'll get a raise, but I don't want to speak too soon = *je pense que je vais avoir une augmentation, mais je ne veux pas parler trop vite*
who's speaking ? = *qui est à l'appareil ?* ⓒⒹ John speaking = *John à l'appareil*

---

to speak about = *parler de* : he never speaks about his first wife = *il ne parle jamais de sa première femme*
to speak at = *prendre la parole à* : the Senator will speak at the dinner = *le sénateur prendra la parole au dîner* ⓒⒹ to have the floor = *avoir la parole*, to make a speech = *faire un discours*
to speak for o.s. = 1/ *parler pour soi* : that's not my opinion, speak for yourself !* = *ce n'est pas mon avis, parlez pour vous !* 2/ *parler de soi-même* : the facts speak for themselves = *les faits parlent d'eux-mêmes*

to speak of = *pour ainsi dire* : he has no money to speak of = *il n'a pour ainsi dire pas d'argent*
not to speak of = *sans parler de* : he's got a sensual mouth not to speak of his beautiful blue eyes = *il a une bouche sensuelle, sans parler de ses beaux yeux bleus*
nothing much/not anything to speak of = *pas terrible* : the film wasn't anything/was nothing much to speak of = *le film n'était pas terrible* → AWFUL
to speak ill ≠ **well/highly of s.o.** = *dire du mal* ≠ *du bien/le plus grand bien de qqn*

speaking of (hookers, she's the best in town) = *en parlant de (putains, c'est la meilleure de la ville)*
to speak out = *dire ce qu'on a sur le cœur* : don't be afraid, speak out ! = *n'ayez pas peur, dites ce que vous avez sur le cœur !* ⓒⒹ to speak one's mind = *dire ce qu'on pense*
to speak to (the director) = *parler au (directeur)* = to talk to
speak up ! = *parlez plus fort !*
to speak with = *parler à* : can I speak with Mr Smith, please ? = *pourrais-je parler à M. Smith, s'il vous plaît ?*

SPEAKEASY (n, -ies) *bar clandestin des années vingt, du temps de la prohibition aux Etats-Unis.*

SPEAKER (n) *conférencier, -ère* : the speaker was drunk and stammered = *le conférencier était ivre et bégayait* ⓒⒹ orator = *orateur*
the Speaker of the House = *le speaker de la Chambre.*

SPEAKING (adj) **English-speaking** = *anglophone* ≠ **French-speaking** = *francophone* : they're looking for English-speaking/French-speaking teachers = *ils cherchent des professeurs anglophones/francophones.*

SPEAR (n) *lance (f)* : some tribes still use spears = *certaines tribus utilisent encore des lances* ⓒⒹ sword = *épée.*

SPEARHEAD (n) *fer (m) de lance* : an agressive advertising campaign was the spearhead of his commercial policy = *une campagne de publicité agressive était le fer de lance de sa politique commerciale.*

SPECIAL (adj) 1/ *spécial, -e* : she has to wear special glasses = *il faut qu'elle porte des lunettes spéciales* ⓒⒹ specific = *spécifique* 2/ *particulier, -ère* : today's a very special day, it's my birthday = *aujourd'hui, c'est un jour particulier, c'est mon anniversaire*

someone/something special = *quelqu'un/quelque chose en particulier*
nothing/not anything special = *pas terrible* : the play was nothing/wasn't anything special = *la pièce n'était pas terrible* → AWFUL
special agent = *agent spécial*
special correspondent = *envoyé spécial*
a special session of (Congress) = *une séance extraordinaire du (Congrès)*
a very special person = *quelqu'un qui m'est très cher*
a special delivery letter = *une lettre express*
what's so special about him/that ? = *qu'est-ce qu'il/qu'est-ce que ça a de spécial ?*

SPECIALIST (n) *spécialiste (m, f)* : a lung specialist = *un spécialiste des poumons* ≠ amateur = ←.

SPECIALIZATION (n) *spécialisation (f)* : there's more and more specialization in medicine = *il y a de plus en plus de spécialisation en médecine.*

SPECIALIZE (to, -d) *(se) spécialiser* : to specialize in psychiatry = *se spécialiser en psychiatrie.*

SPECIALLY (adv) = ESPECIALLY.

SPECIALTY (n, -ies) *spécialité (f)* : spareribs are their specialty = *les travers de porc sont leur spécialité* ⓒⒹ domain = *domaine.*

SPECIES (n inv) *espèce (f)* : that species is now extinct = *cette espèce est maintenant éteinte* ⓓ sort = *sorte* ☠ *espèces sonnantes et trébuchantes* = hard cash
— *l'espèce humaine* = mankind
— *un cas d'espèce* = a case in point
— *espèce d'(andouille)* ! = damned (fool) !

SPECIFIC (adj) **1/** *spécifique* : specific problems = *des problèmes spécifiques* ⓓ particular = *particulier* **2/** *précis, -e* : be specific ! = *soyez précis !* = precise ⓓ explicit = *explicite* **SPECIFICALLY** (adv) *spécifiquement* : films specifically for kids = *des films spécifiquement pour les gosses* ⓓ especially = *tout spécialement*.

SPECIFY (to, -ied) *spécifier* : she didn't specify what she wanted = *elle n'a pas spécifié ce qu'elle voulait* ⓓ to mention = *dire en passant,* to name = *mentionner*.

SPECIMEN (n) *spécimen (m)* : here's a specimen of her handwriting = *voici un spécimen de son écriture* ⓓ sample = *échantillon*
a (urine) specimen = *un échantillon (d'urine)*
☠ *tous ses amis sont des spécimens* = all her friends are freaks
— *quel spécimen !* = what a weirdo !

SPECK (n) **a speck of (curry)** = *un chouïa de (curry)* ⓓ a hint of = *une pointe de*.

SPECTACLE (n) *spectacle (m)* : this outdoor ballet was a lavish spectacle = *ce ballet en plein air était un spectacle somptueux*
to make a spectacle of o.s. = *se donner en spectacle* ⓓ to make a fool of o.s. = *se rendre ridicule*
☠ *il n'y a pas de spectacle dans ce club* = there's no entertainment/show in this club
— *le spectacle familier des mendiants* = the familiar sight of beggars.

SPECTACLES (n pl) (GB) *lunettes (f pl)* = glasses.

SPECTACULAR (adj) *spectaculaire* : a spectacular performance = *une performance spectaculaire* → WONDERFUL.

SPECTATOR (n) *spectateur, -trice* : in life, he's a spectator = *dans la vie, c'est un spectateur* ⓓ bystander = *badaud*.

SPECTER (n) *spectre (m)* : the specter of terrorism = *le spectre du terrorisme*.

SPECULATE (to, -d) *spéculer* : he speculated that the government would fall within the year = *il spéculait sur la chute du gouvernement avant la fin de l'année*
to speculate in (diamonds) = *spéculer sur (les diamants)*.

SPECULATION (n) *spéculation (f)* : speculation on Wall Street = *la spéculation à Wall Street*.

SPEECH (n, -es) **1/** *discours (m)* : did you listen to the President's speech ? = *est-ce que vous avez écouté le discours du Président ?* ⓓ fireside talk = *causerie au coin du feu* ☠ → discourse **2/** *façon (f) de parler* : you can tell from his speech that he is from New York = *on sait qu'il est de New York à sa façon de parler* ⓓ elocution = *élocution*
to give a speech = *faire un discours*
speech defects/problems = *défauts/problèmes d'élocution*.

SPEECHLESS (adj) *qui reste muet, -ette* : I was speechless when I heard that = *je suis resté muet en entendant ça* ⓓ voiceless = *sans voix*
speechless with (fear) = *muet de (peur)* ⓓ dumbfounded = *ahuri*.

SPEED (n) **1/** *vitesse (f)* : the speed of light = *la vitesse de la lumière*
speed limit = *limitation de vitesse*
☠ *partir en vitesse* = to leave in a hurry
— *changer de vitesse (voiture)* = to switch gears
— *être en perte de vitesse* = to gain momentum
2/ (inv) *amphétamines (f pl)* : he's into speed = *il prend des amphétamines* ⓓ drug = *drogue*
that is ≠ that isn't my speed = *c'est ≠ ce n'est pas mon truc* : don't invite Jack to the swing, that isn't his speed = *n'invite pas Jack à la partouse, ce n'est pas son truc* = that isn't his bag.

SPEED (to, -ed or sped) *faire des excès de vitesse* : he was speeding on the highway = *il faisait des excès de vitesse sur l'autoroute* ⓓ to step on the gas = *appuyer sur le champignon*
to speed up (mail delivery) = *activer (la distribution du courrier)* ≠ to slow down = *ralentir* ☠ *active !* = snap it up !

SPEEDING (n) *excès (m) de vitesse* : he was arrested for speeding = *il a été arrêté pour excès de vitesse*
a speeding ticket = *une contravention pour excès de vitesse*.

SPEEDY (adj, -ier, -iest) *rapide* : a speedy answer/recovery = *une réponse/une guérison rapide* = a rapid answer/recovery ⓓ swift = *prompt* ☠ → rapid.

SPELL (n) *charme (m)* : I'm under his spell = *je suis sous son charme* ⓓ enchantment = *enchantement*
a breathing spell = *le temps de souffler* ⓓ respite = *répit*
to cast a spell over s.o. = *envoûter qqn* ⓓ to bewitch = *ensorceler*
a hot ≠ cold spell = *une vague de chaleur ≠ de froid*
the spell is broken = *le charme est rompu*
☠ → charm.

SPELL (to, -ed or spelt) *épeler* : spell your name = *épelez votre nom*
how do you spell it ? = *comment l'épelez-vous ?/comment ça s'écrit ?*
do I have to spell it out ? = *est-ce qu'il faut que je vous mette les points sur les i ?* ⓓ do I have to draw you a picture ? = *tu veux que je te fasse un dessin ?*
to spell trouble/disaster = *laisser augurer des ennuis/un désastre* ⓓ to mean = *vouloir dire*.

598

SPELLBOUND (adj) *envoûté, -e* : the audience was held spellbound by his acting = *l'auditoire était comme envoûté par son jeu* ⓄⒹ fascinated = *fasciné*.

SPELLING (n) *orthographe* (f) : ten spelling mistakes = *dix fautes d'orthographe*
spelling bee = *test en orthographe*.

SPEND (to, spent, spent) **1/** *dépenser* : we spent a lot of money last month = *nous avons dépensé beaucoup d'argent le mois dernier* ⓄⒹ to blow = *claquer* ≠ to put away = *mettre à gauche* 💀 *se dépenser* = to wear o.s. out **2/** *passer* : he spends a lot of time with his family = *il passe beaucoup de temps en famille* 💀 → to pass
SPENDER (n) *quelqu'un de dépensier* : he's a big spender = *il est très dépensier* ≠ tightwad = *grigou*.

SPENDTHRIFT (n) *panier* (m) *percé* : she's always been a spendthrift = *elle a toujours été panier percé* ≠ penny pincher = *grippe-sou*.

SPERM (n) *sperme* (m), *foutre* (m) (LV) : sperm bank = *banque du sperme* ⓄⒹ ejaculation = *éjaculation*, semen = *semence*.

SPHERE (n) *domaine* (m) : someone notable in the sphere of culture = *quelqu'un de connu dans le domaine de la culture* 💀 → domain
sphere of influence = *sphère d'influence*.

SPHINX (n, -es) *sphinx* (m) ⓄⒹ pyramid = *pyramide*.

SPIC = SPIK (n) *latino* (m, f) (PEJ) ⓄⒹ Puerto Rican = *Portoricain*.

SPICE (n) *épice* (f) : put some more spice in it = *mettez un peu plus d'épices* ⓄⒹ condiment = ←, oregano = *origan*, cinnamon = *cannelle*, curry = ←, paprika = ←, bayleaf = *laurier*, thyme = *thym*.

SPICK-AND-SPAN (adj) *d'une propreté éclatante* : the kitchen's spick-and-span = *la cuisine est d'une propreté éclatante* ⓄⒹ immaculate = *immaculé*.

SPICY (adj, -ier, -iest) **1/** *épicé, -e* : the chicken's too spicy = *le poulet est trop épicé* ⓄⒹ peppery = *poivré*, pungent = *piquant* ≠ bland = *peu relevé* **2/** *salé, -e* : a spicy story = *une histoire salée* ⓄⒹ off-color = *grivois* 💀 *c'est trop salé* = it's too salted
— *des prix salés* = stiff prices.

SPIDER (n) *araignée* (f) : she's afraid of spiders = *elle a peur des araignées* ⓄⒹ web = *toile* 💀 *avoir une araignée dans le/au plafond* = to have bats in the belfry.

SPIEL (n inv) *boniment* (m) : don't give me that spiel ! = *arrête ton boniment !* ⓄⒹ line = *baratin*.

SPIKE (to, -d) *corser* : to spike a coffee/a drink = *corser un café/une boisson* 💀 *l'affaire se corse* = the deal's getting serious.

SPILL (n) **to take a spill** = *(se) prendre une bûche* ⓄⒹ to take a fall = *faire une chute*.

SPILL (to, -ed or spilt) **1/** *renverser* : I spilled the milk = *j'ai renversé le lait* ⓄⒹ to pour = *verser*
💀 *la nouvelle m'a renversé* = the news stunned me
— *le verre s'est renversé* = the glass tipped over
— *se faire renverser (par une voiture)* = to be knocked over/run down (by a car)
— *renverser un gouvernement* = to overthrow/overturn a government
2/ *vendre la mèche* : who spilled the story to the cops ? = *qui a vendu la mèche aux flics ?* ⓄⒹ to leak = *transpirer*.

SPIN (n) **to go for a spin** = *aller faire une balade (en voiture)* ⓄⒹ to go for a ride = *aller faire une promenade (en voiture)*.

SPIN (to, -ned) *tournoyer* : the top's spinning = *la toupie tournoie* ⓄⒹ to whirl = *tourbillonner*.

SPINACH (n inv) *épinards* (m pl) : I don't like spinach = *je n'aime pas les épinards*.

SPINE (n) *colonne* (f) *vertébrale* : she's seeing a chiropractor for her spine = *elle voit un chiropracteur pour sa colonne vertébrale* = spinal column ⓄⒹ vertebrate = *vertébré*.

SPINELESS (adj) *sans caractère* : she's married to a spineless fool = *elle a épousé un imbécile sans caractère* ⓄⒹ yellow = *pleutre* ≠ firm = *ferme*.

SPINOFF (n) *application* (f) *secondaire* : microprocessing is a spinoff of the space program = *la microprogrammation est une application secondaire du programme spatial* ⓄⒹ by-product = *sous-produit*.

SPINSTER (n) *vieille fille* (f) : you're only a spinster if you feel like a spinster = *on n'est vieille fille que si l'on se sent vieille fille* ⓄⒹ single = *célibataire*.

SPIRIT (n) *esprit* (m) : good team spirit = *bon esprit d'équipe*
💀 *il a de l'esprit/il est plein d'esprit* = he's witty/full of wit
— *l'esprit de l'escalier* = hindsight
— *les grands esprits se rencontrent* = great minds think alike
— *perdre ≠ reprendre ses esprits* = to lose ≠ to regain consciousness
— *venir à l'esprit* = to come to mind
— *avoir l'esprit ailleurs* = to be lost in one's thoughts
— *avoir l'esprit tranquille* = to set one's mind at ease
— *avoir l'esprit lent ≠ rapide* = to be slow-witted ≠ quick-witted
— *avoir l'esprit d'observation* = to be very observant
— *l'esprit humain* = the human mind.

SPIRITS (n pl) *liqueur* (f) ⓄⒹ schnapps = *schnaps*
in high ≠ low spirits = *qui a ≠ qui n'a pas le moral* ⓄⒹ in a good ≠ bad mood = *de bonne ≠ mauvaise humeur*.

SPIRITUAL (adj) *spirituel, -elle* : spiritual life = *vie spirituelle* ≠ earthy = *terre à terre*.

SPIT (to, spit or spat) *cracher* : to spit blood = *cracher le sang*

spit it out ! = *crache-le* ! ⓪ **out with it** ! = *accouche* !

to spit in (s.o.'s face) = *cracher à (la figure de qqn)* ☠ *cracher (argent)* = to cough up (money)

— *il ne faut pas cracher dessus* = it's not to be sneezed at

— *cracher sur une idée* = to pooh-pooh an idea.

SPITE (n) **in spite of** = *malgré* : we went out in spite of the rain = *nous sommes sortis malgré la pluie*, in spite of the fact that = *malgré le fait que* ⓪ despite = *en dépit de* ☠ *malgré moi* = against my will

out of spite = *par dépit* : she did it out of spite = *elle l'a fait par dépit* ≠ no hard feelings = *sans rancune.*

SPITEFUL (adj) *rancunier, -ère* : a spiteful nature = *une nature rancunière* ⓪ vindictive = *vindicatif.*

SPLASH (n, -es) **to make a splash** = *faire du bruit* : their divorce made a splash in the papers = *leur divorce a fait du bruit dans les journaux.*

SPLASH (to, -ed) **1/** *éclabousser* : the bus splashed water all over me = *le bus m'a complètement éclaboussé* ☠ *le scandale a éclaboussé toute la famille* = the scandal brought disgrace upon the whole family **2/** *asperger* : I splash my face with cold water every morning = *tous les matins, je m'asperge le visage d'eau froide*

to splash down = *amerrir* : the spaceship splashed down in the Pacific = *le vaisseau spatial a amerri dans le Pacifique.*

SPLASHDOWN (n) *amerrissage (m)* : the spaceship's splashdown = *l'amerrissage du vaisseau spatial* ⓪ landing = *atterrissage.*

SPLASHY (adj, -ier, -iest) *tapageur, -euse* : splashy clothes = *des vêtements tapageurs* = flashy clothes ☠ → flashy.

SPLATTER (to, -ed) *éclabousser* = to splash.

SPLENDID (adj) *splendide* : what a splendid day ! = *quelle journée splendide* ! → WONDERFUL **SPLENDIDLY** (adv) *d'une façon splendide.*

SPLENDOR (n) *splendeur (f)* : the splendor of the landscape = *la splendeur du paysage* ⓪ magnificence = ← ☠ *cette fille, c'est une splendeur* = this girl's a dream.

SPLINTER (n) *écharde (f)* (wood) : a splinter in my finger = *une écharde dans le doigt.*

SPLINTER (adj) **splinter group** = *groupe dissident.*

SPLIT (n) *scission (f)* : a split in the party = *une scission dans le parti* ≠ merger = *fusion*

to do the split = *faire le grand écart.*

SPLIT (to, split, split) *se barrer, se tirer* : it's late, I'm going to split = *il est tard, je vais me tirer/me barrer* → TO LEAVE ☠ *barrer* → to block off, *tirer* → to pull **2/** *scinder* : the issue split the party = *le problème a scindé le parti* ⓪ to divide = *diviser* **3/** *diviser* : we'll split what-ever money he'll give = *quel que soit l'argent qu'il nous donne, nous le diviserons* ⓪ to share = *partager* **4/** *(se) fendre* : my pants split = *mon pantalon s'est fendu* ⓪ to rip = *(se) déchirer* ☠ *il ne s'est pas fendu* = he didn't exactly break his back

to be split on (a question) = *être divisé sur (une question)*

to split up = *se séparer* : my sister and her husband split up last month = *ma sœur et son mari se sont séparés le mois dernier* ≠ to make up = *se réconcilier* ☠ → to separate.

SPLIT (adj) **to come from a split home** = *être issu d'un foyer désuni*

in a split second = *en une fraction de seconde* : the accident happened in a split second = *l'accident est arrivé en une fraction de seconde* ⓪ before you could say Jack Robinson = *avant d'avoir pu dire ouf*

split peas = *pois cassés*

split personality = *dédoublement de la personnalité.*

SPLITTING (adj) **splitting headache** = *mal de tête insupportable.*

SPLITUP (n) *rupture (f)* : their splitup was hard on the kids = *leur rupture a été dure pour les gosses* = their breakup was hard on the kids ⓪ divorce = ← ☠ → breakup.

SPLURGE (to, -d) *faire des folies* : we went to an expensive restaurant and splurged = *nous avons fait des folies en allant dans un restaurant cher* ≠ to skimp = *lésiner.*

SPOIL (n, adj) **spoil system** = *système des dépouilles* ⓪ nepotism = *népotisme*

the spoils of (the war) = *les dépouilles de (la guerre)* ⓪ booty = *butin.*

SPOIL (to, -ed or spoilt) **1/** *gâter* : you spoil your children = *vous gâtez vos enfants* ⓪ to fuss over = *être aux petits soins pour*

☠ *(le temps) se gâte* = (the weather) is turning bad

— *gâter la vue* = to mar the view

2/ *gâcher* : you/the rain spoiled everything = *vous avez/la pluie a tout gâché* = to ruin ⓪ to wreck = *foutre en l'air*

☠ *gâcher de l'argent* = to squander money

— *tu gâches ta vie* = you're making a mess of your life

3/ *se gâter* : meat's going to spoil in this heat = *la viande va se gâter avec cette chaleur* ⓪ to go bad = *s'avarier (meat) / tourner (milk).*

SPOILSPORT (n) *trouble-fête (m, f)* : you never want to go out, what a spoilsport you are ! = *tu ne veux jamais sortir, ce que tu peux être trouble-fête* ! ⓪ killjoy = *rabat-joie.*

SPOKESMAN (n, -men) *porte-parole (m inv)* : the government's spokesman = *le porte-parole du gouvernement* ⓪ go-between = *intermédiaire* **SPOKESWOMAN** (n, -women) *porte-parole (m inv).*

SPONGE (n) *éponge (f)* : I spilled water on the floor, give me a sponge = *j'ai renversé de l'eau par terre, donnez-moi une éponge*

to throw in/up the sponge = *jeter l'éponge* : come on, this is no time to throw in/up the sponge = *allez, ce n'est pas le moment de jeter l'éponge* ⓪ to throw in one's hand = *baisser les bras*
☠ *passons l'éponge* = let bygones be bygones
— *serviette-éponge* = terry towel.

SPONGE (to, -d) **to sponge (cigarettes) from s.o.** = *taper (des cigarettes) à qqn* : to mooch
to sponge of s.o. = *vivre en parasite de qqn* : he always sponged of his friends = *il a toujours vécu en parasite de ses amis.*

SPONGER (n) *parasite (m)* : stars are surrounded by spongers = *les vedettes sont entourées de parasites* ⓪ freeloader = *pique-assiette* ☠ → parasite.

SPONSOR (n) *sponsor (m)* (TV, etc.), *parrain (m), marraine (f)* (club, etc.) : the sponsor of a TV show = *le sponsor d'une émission télévisée*, you need two sponsors to get into the club = *il vous faut deux parrains pour entrer dans ce club* ☠ *parrain* → godfather.

SPONSOR (to, -ed) *sponsoriser, parrainer* : his company's sponsoring the show/the scholarship = *sa société sponsorise l'émission/parraine cette bourse.*

SPONTANEITY (n) *spontanéité (f)* : we're so conditioned that we often lack spontaneity = *nous sommes tellement conditionnés que nous manquons souvent de spontanéité* **SPONTANEOUS** (adj) *spontané, -e* : a spontaneous reaction = *une réaction spontanée* ⓪ instinctive = *instinctif* ≠ premeditated = *prémédité* **SPONTANEOUSLY** (adv) *spontanément.*

SPOOF (n) *parodie (f)* : the sketch is a spoof of campus life = *le sketch est une parodie de la vie sur un campus* = parody.

SPOOF (to, -ed) *parodier* : to spoof life in Washington = *parodier la vie à Washington* ⓪ to imitate = *imiter*, to do a takeoff = *faire un pastiche.*

SPOOK (n) *barbouze (f)* : the autobiography of a spook = *l'autobiographie d'une barbouze* ⓪ mole = *taupe.*

SPOOKY (adj, -ier, -iest) *qui donne le frisson* : the haunted house was spooky = *la maison hantée vous donnait le frisson* ⓪ scary = *effrayant*, eerie = *inquiétant.*

SPOON (n) *cuillère (f)* : give me a spoon please = *donnez-moi une cuillère, s'il vous plaît* ⓪ tablespoon = *cuillère à soupe*, teaspoon = *cuillère à dessert/à café*, spoonful = *cuillerée.*

SPORADIC (adj) *sporadique* : sporadic arguments = *des disputes sporadiques* ⓪ infrequent = *peu fréquent.*

SPORT (n) *sport (m)* : when sex becomes a sport, we're in trouble = *quand l'amour devient un sport, il y a quelque chose qui ne va pas* ⓪ game = *jeu*, activity = *activité*
to be a good ≠ **poor sport** = *être bon* ≠ *mauvais joueur*

be a sport (do the dishes) = *sois sympa (fais la vaisselle)*
☠ *il va y avoir du sport* = all hell's going to break loose.

SPORT (to, -ed) *arborer* : the last time I saw her, she was sporting an enormous diamond = *la dernière fois que je l'ai vue, elle arborait un énorme diamant.*

SPORTS (n pl) *le sport* : sports are important in USSR = *le sport est important en URSS*
to go in for sports = *aimer le sport*
winter sports = *les sports d'hiver.*

SPORTS (adj) *(de) sport* : sports car = *voiture de sport*, sports jacket/skirt = *veste/jupe sport.*

SPORTSMAN (n, -men) *sportif (m)* ⓪ athlete = *athlète* **SPORTSWOMAN** (n, -women) *sportive (f).*

SPORTSWEAR (n inv) *vêtements (m pl) de sport* : even her sportswear is sexy = *même ses vêtements de sport sont sexy* ⓪ casual clothes = *vêtements sport.*

SPORTSWRITER (n) *journaliste sportif, -ive.*

SPOT (n) 1/ *tache (f)* : a spot on my dress = *une tache sur ma robe* = a stain on my dress ☠ → stain 2/ *coin (m)* : I know a nice spot where we can eat = *je connais un coin sympa où nous pouvons manger* ⓪ location = *emplacement* ☠ → corner 3/ *poste (m)* : we can find a spot for you in the Middle East = *nous pouvons vous trouver un poste au Moyen-Orient* ⓪ job = *travail* ☠ → post

to be in a (tight/tough) spot = *être dans le pétrin* : now he knows I made the mistake, I'm really in a spot = *maintenant qu'il sait que c'est moi qui ai commis l'erreur, je suis vraiment dans le pétrin* ⓪ to be in a pickle = *être frais*

to hit the spot = *faire le bonheur de quelqu'un* : this stiff Scotch hits the spot = *ce whisky bien tassé va faire mon bonheur* ⓪ that's just what the doctor ordered = *c'est exactement ce qu'il me fallait*

to make a spot check = *faire une vérification au hasard*

the very/exact spot (where the accident happened) = *le lieu exact (de l'accident)*
on the spot = 1/ *sur place* : the hotel's remote but you have everything you need on the spot = *l'hôtel est isolé, mais vous avez tout ce dont vous avez besoin sur place* 2/ *sur-le-champ* : she decided on the spot to leave him = *elle a décidé de le quitter sur-le-champ* ⓪ immediately = *immédiatement*
☠ *un spot (lumière)* = a spotlight
— *un spot publicitaire* = a commercial.

SPOT (to, -ted) *repérer* : I spotted him in the store = *je l'ai repéré dans le magasin* ⓪ to identify = *identifier* ☠ *se repérer dans une ville* = to find one's bearings in a city.

SPOTLIGHT (n) *spot (m)* : spotlights in the garden = *des spots dans le jardin* ⓪ floodlight = *projecteur*
to be in the spotlight = *être sous les feux des projecteurs* : as a Senator's wife, she never liked to be in the

spotlight = *quand elle était femme de sénateur, elle n'a jamais aimé être sous les feux des projecteurs.*

SPOUSE (n) *conjoint, -e* : I'd like you to meet my spouse = *j'aimerais vous présenter mon conjoint.*

SPRAIN (to, -ed) *se faire une entorse à* : I sprained my ankle = *je me suis fait une entorse à la cheville* ① to strain = *se froisser (un muscle).*

SPRAWL OUT (to, -ed) *(s')affaler* : when I walked in, he was sprawled out on the bed = *quand je suis entré, il était affalé sur le lit.*

SPRAY (to, -ed) *vaporiser, laquer* (hair), *pulvériser* (crops) : to spray one's hair/crops = *vaporiser ses cheveux/se laquer les cheveux/pulvériser les récoltes* ① to sprinkle = *asperger/saupoudrer* ☠ *pulvériser un record* = to smash a record **SPRAY** (n) *laque* (f).

SPREAD (n) 1/ *grand reportage* (m) : there was a spread on the sex scandal = *il y a eu un grand reportage sur le scandale de mœurs* ① scoop = ← 2/ *gueuleton* (m) : what a spread she made ! = *quel gueuleton elle a fait !* ① feast = *festin* 3/ *grosse propriété* (f) : a spread in Texas = *une grosse propriété au Texas* ① stretch of land = *étendue de terrain*
the spread of the (disease/communism) = *l'extension de (la maladie)/du (communisme)* ① propagation = ←.

SPREAD (to, spread, spread) *se répandre* : the news spread throughout the country very quickly = *la nouvelle s'est très vite répandue dans tout le pays* ① to propagate = *se propager*
to spread on = *étaler sur* : to spread jam on a toast = *étaler de la confiture sur une tartine grillée* ① to cover with = *couvrir de*
to spread out = *(s')étendre* : the company's spreading out (its operations) = *la société s'étend/étend ses opérations* ① to boom = *être en plein essor*
to spread over = *étaler* : I spread the payments over two years = *j'étale les paiements sur deux ans*
to spread to = *s'étendre à* : the strikes spread to other countries = *les grèves se sont étendues aux autres pays.*

SPREE (n) **to go on a spree** = *faire la bombe* : the guys went on a spree last night = *hier soir, les garçons ont fait la bombe* ① to go on a bender = *faire la bamboula*
a shopping spree = *une folie d'achats.*

SPRING (n) 1/ *printemps* (m) : I always fall in love in spring = *je tombe toujours amoureuse au printemps* ① season = *saison*
no spring chicken = *qui n'a plus ses jambes de vingt ans* ① to have passed one's time = *ne plus être de la première jeunesse*
spring cleaning = *grand nettoyage de printemps*
2/ *source* (f) : water from a spring = *l'eau d'une source* ① stream = *ruisseau* ☠ → source
3/ *ressort* (m) : the springs of the bed = *les ressorts du lit* ☠ *avoir du* ≠ *manquer de ressort* = to be ≠ not to be dynamic

— *être du ressort de* = to be within the competence of
— *en dernier ressort* = in the last resort.

SPRING (to, sprang, sprung) *faire sortir de prison* : his lawyer was able to spring him = *son avocat a réussi à le faire sortir de prison* ≠ to lock s.o. up = *boucler qqn*
to spring from = *découler de* : her constant remarks spring from her concern to see her daughter happy = *c'est de son désir de voir sa fille heureuse que découlent ses réflexions permanentes* ① to stem from = *être issu de*
to spring up = *surgir brusquement* : a lot of businesses have sprung up in the suburbs = *de nombreux commerces ont brusquement surgi en banlieue* ① to arise = *se présenter.*

SPRINGBOARD (n) *tremplin* (m) : he uses the job as a springboard for his political ambitions = *son boulot lui sert de tremplin pour assouvir ses ambitions politiques* ① jumping-off place = *point de départ.*

SPRINKLE (to, -d) *asperger* (water), *saupoudrer* (powder, sugar, etc.) : to sprinkle sugar on the cake = *saupoudrer le gâteau de sucre* ① to scatter = *éparpiller*
sprinkled with (slang) = *émaillé d'(argot).*

SPRINKLING (n) **a sprinkling of (French/salt)** = *un tout petit peu de (français/sel)* ① a dot of = *un soupçon de.*

SPROUT (to, -ed) *pousser vite* : the grass sprouted = *l'herbe a poussé vite* ① to blossom = *fleurir.*

SPRUCE UP (to, -d) **to be spruced up** = *être tiré à quatre épingles* : he's spruced up and ready to go out = *il est tiré à quatre épingles et prêt à sortir* ① to be dressed up = *être sur son trente et un.*

SPRY (adj, -er or -ier, -est or -iest) *vert, -e* : he's still spry = *il est encore vert* ① still going strong = *encore bien portant* ☠ → green.

SPUD (n) *patate* (f) ① French fries = *frites.*

SPUNK (n inv) *nerf* (m) : she has a lot of spunk = *elle a beaucoup de nerf* ① pluck = *cran* ☠ → nerve **SPUNKY** (adj, -ier, -iest) *qui a du nerf.*

SPUR (n) *éperon* (m) : the spurs on his boots = *les éperons de ses bottes*
on the spur of the moment = *sous l'impulsion du moment* : we decided to go out on the spur of the moment = *nous avons décidé de sortir sous l'impulsion du moment* ① impulsively = *de façon impulsive.*

SPURN (to, -ed) *rejeter avec mépris* : she spurned his advances = *elle a rejeté ses avances avec mépris* ① to repel = *repousser.*

SPUR ON (to, -red) *éperonner* : his need for power spurred him on = *son besoin de pouvoir l'éperonnait* ① to goad on = *aiguillonner.*

SPY (n, -ies) *espion, -onne* : the spies were all Hungarian = *les espions étaient tous hongrois* ① secret agent = *agent secret*, mole = *taupe*, spook = *sous-marin.*

SPY (to, -ied) *faire de l'espionnage* : he's spying for the Russians = *il fait de l'espionnage pour le compte des Russes*

to spy on = *espionner* : she's spying on her husband = *elle espionne son mari* ⓄⒹ to keep an eye on = *avoir l'œil sur.*

SPYING (n inv) *espionnage (m)* : imprisoned for spying = *emprisonné pour espionnage.*

SQUABBLE (n) *chamaillerie (f)* : a squabble with my husband = *une chamaillerie avec mon mari* ⓄⒹ spat = *fâcherie* **SQUABBLE** (to, -d) *se chamailler* : she's always squabbling with her sister = *elle est toujours en train de se chamailler avec sa sœur* ⓄⒹ to quarrel = *se quereller.*

SQUAD (n) **firing squad** = *peloton d'exécution*
squad car = *voiture de patrouille* ⓄⒹ paddy wagon = *panier à salade.*

SQUADRON (n) *escadron (m), escadrille (f)* (aviation) : the squadrons of death = *les escadrons de la mort.*

SQUALID (adj) *sordide* : squalid living conditions = *des conditions de vie sordides* ⓄⒹ shabby = *miteux* ≠ sumptuous = *somptueux* ⚔ → sordid.

SQUALOR (n) *misère (f) noire* : the squalor of slums = *la misère noire des taudis.*

SQUANDER (to, -ed) *dilapider* : he squandered his inheritance = *il a dilapidé son héritage* ≠ to put away = *mettre à gauche.*

SQUARE (n) 1/ *carré (m)* : draw me a square = *dessine-moi un carré* ≠ circle = *cercle* ⚔ *un carré d'as* = four aces 2/ *place (f)* : Washington Square = *la place Washington* ⚔ → place
now we're back to square one = *nous revoilà au point de départ.*

SQUARE (adj, -r, -st) 1/ *vieux jeu* : I come from a very square family = *je suis issu d'une famille très vieux jeu* ≠ hep = *à la page* 2/ *carré, -e* : a square table = *une table carrée* ⚔ *une personnalité carrée* = a straight personality
square dance = *quadrille*
a square deal = *une affaire honnête* ≠ a raw deal = *un marché de dupes*
square meal = *repas complet*
square meter = *mètre carré*
square root = *racine carrée*
a square shooter = *quelqu'un qui joue franc jeu*
it's like trying to put a square peg in a round hole = *c'est la quadrature du cercle.*

SQUARE (to, -d) **to square away** = *régler* : we're trying to square things away before the weekend = *nous sommes en train d'essayer de régler le problème avant le week-end* ⚔ → to settle
to square up = *régler la facture* : let's square up and split = *réglons la facture et tirons-nous*
to square with = *cadrer avec* : his alibi doesn't square

with what the others said = *son alibi ne cadre pas avec ce que les autres ont dit.*

SQUASH (to, -ed) *écraser* : the team/the revolution was squashed = *l'équipe/la révolution a été écrasée* ⓄⒹ to put down = *réprimer* ⚔ → to crash
to squash s.o. = *clouer le bec à qqn* : her remark squashed him = *sa remarque lui a cloué le bec* ⓄⒹ to put s.o. down = *remettre qqn à sa place.*

SQUAT (adj, -ter, -test) *ramassé, -e* : he's squat but sexy = *il est ramassé mais sexy* ⓄⒹ stocky = *trapu* ≠ lanky = *efflanqué.*

SQUAT (to, -ted) 1/ *s'accroupir* : there were no seats so we squatted on the floor = *il n'y avait pas de sièges, alors nous nous sommes accroupis par terre* ⓄⒹ to sit cross-legged = *s'asseoir en tailleur* 2/ *squatter, squattériser* : they squatted in the deserted building = *ils ont squatté/squattérisé l'immeuble désert.*

SQUATTER (n) *squatter (m, f)* : squatters took over the building = *des squatters ont pris possession de l'immeuble* ⓄⒹ to squat = *squatter.*

SQUEAK (to, -ed) *grincer* : the door squeaked = *la porte a grincé.*

SQUEALER (n) *mouchard, -e* : you're a lousy squealer ! = *tu es un sale mouchard !* ⓄⒹ stool pigeon = *indic.*

SQUEAL ON (to, -ed) *moucharder* : he squealed on his kid brother = *il a mouchardé son frère cadet* ⓄⒹ to snitch = *cafeter.*

SQUEAMISH (adj) *facilement dégoûté, -e* : blood makes me squeamish = *je suis facilement dégoûté à la vue du sang* ⓄⒹ nauseated = *écœuré*, offended = *offusqué.*

SQUEEZE (n) **to put the squeeze on** = *exercer des pressions sur* : in order to get his bill through Congress, the President put the squeeze on the Republican Senators = *pour faire passer son projet de loi, le Président a exercé des pressions sur les sénateurs républicains.*

SQUEEZE (to, -d) *presser* : to squeeze an orange = *presser une orange*
to squeeze into (the subway) = *se tasser dans (le métro)* ⓄⒹ to pile into = *s'entasser dans*
to squeeze out of = *pressurer* : the government squeezes everything out of us they can = *l'État nous pressure autant qu'il le peut* ⓄⒹ to extort from = *extorquer à*
to squeeze through (the door) = *pouvoir à peine passer par (la porte)*
⚔ *se presser* = to rush
— *presser de questions* = to ply with questions.

SQUELCH (to, -ed) *clouer le bec à* : he squelched him with his arguments = *il lui a cloué le bec avec ses arguments.*

SQUINT (to, -ed) *plisser les yeux* : the sun made him squint = *le soleil lui faisait plisser des yeux.*

SQUIRM (to, -ed) **to make s.o. squirm** = *mettre qqn au supplice* : the defense lawyer's going to make him squirm at the stand = *l'avocat de la défense va le mettre au supplice quand il sera à la barre des témoins.*

SQUIRREL (n) *écureuil (m) :* squirrels in Central Park = *des écureuils à Central Park* ⓓ acorn = *gland.*

SQUIRT (n) *petit, -e morveux, -euse :* get out of my way, squirt ! = *tire-toi de là, espèce de petit morveux !* ⓓ peanut = *moustique.*

STAB (n) **have a stab at it !** = *tente le coup !* ⓓ attempt = *tentative*
a stab in the back = *un coup de Jarnac/un coup de poignard dans le dos*
to make a stab at stg = *s'essayer à qqch.*

STAB (to, -bed) *poignarder :* he was stabbed by a stranger = *il a été poignardé par un inconnu* ⓓ to strangle = *étrangler.*

STABILITY (n) *stabilité (f) :* the stability of the economy = *la stabilité de l'économie* ≠ instability = *instabilité.*

STABILIZE (to, -d) *stabiliser :* to stabilize the cost of living = *stabiliser le coût de la vie* ⓓ to maintain = *maintenir.*

STABLE (n) *écurie (f) :* horses in the stable = *des chevaux à l'écurie.*

STABLE (adj, -r, -st) *stable :* a stable government = *un gouvernement stable* ≠ unstable = *instable.*

STACK (n) *pile (f) :* a stack of papers = *une pile de papiers* ☠ → pile
to blow one's stack = *piquer une colère :* the boss blew his stack when he noticed the mistake = *le patron a piqué une colère quand il s'est aperçu de l'erreur* → ANGRY
stacks of = *des masses de :* stacks of papers on the table = *des masses de papiers sur la table* → MANY
I swear on a stack of bibles ! = *je le jure sur ce que j'ai de plus cher !* ⓓ honest to God ! = *je le jure sur la tête de ma mère !*

STACK (to, -ed) *mettre en pile :* stack the books on the table = *mets les livres en pile sur la table* ⓓ to pile = *empiler*
to be stacking against = *jouer contre :* it's not a great time for me, everything seems to be stacking against me = *je ne suis pas dans une période faste, tout semble jouer contre moi*
to stack up against = *supporter la comparaison avec :* he can't stack up against the ten other players = *il ne supporte pas la comparaison avec les dix autres joueurs.*

STACKED (adj) *bien roulée :* she's really stacked = *elle est vraiment bien roulée* ⓓ well-built = *bien bâtie,* curvaceous = *gironde.*

STADIUM (n, -ia or -s) *stade (m) :* the new stadium sits 50 000 = *le nouveau stade a 50 000 places* ☠ *à ce stade* = at this stage of the game.

STAFF (n) *personnel (m) :* they have a very small staff = *ils ont très peu de personnel*
to be on the staff = *faire partie du personnel :* we have too few blacks on the staff = *nous avons trop peu de Noirs parmi le personnel*
☠ → personnel.

STAG (adj) **a stag dinner/party** = *un dîner/une soirée entre hommes.*

STAG (adv) **to go stag** = *aller quelque part en célibataire :* we're all going stag to the party = *nous allons tous en célibataires à cette soirée.*

STAGE (n) 1/ *scène (f) :* she left the stage and started a new career in films = *elle a quitté la scène et a démarré une carrière cinématographique* ⓓ stagehand = *machiniste* ☠ → scene
2/ *étape (f) :* this is a new stage in our relationship = *c'est une nouvelle étape de nos relations*
☠ *brûler les étapes* = to shoot ahead
a stage = *une période :* his hippy dressing was just a stage = *il a eu une période où il s'est habillé en hippy*
at this stage of the game = *à ce stade*
to go on the stage = *monter sur scène/sur les planches/faire du théâtre*
to set the stage = *ouvrir la voie :* the talks with the President set the stage for the signing of the treaty = *les pourparlers avec le Président ont ouvert la voie à la signature du traité*
stage door = *entrée des artistes*
stage fright = *le trac* ⓓ to have butterflies in one's stomach = *avoir l'estomac noué*
stage manager = *régisseur*
stage name = *nom de scène*
☠ *un stage de formation* = a training course.

STAGECOACH (n, -es) *diligence (f) :* the Daltons attacked stagecoaches = *les Dalton attaquaient les diligences* ⓓ carriage = *fiacre* ☠ → diligence.

STAGESTRUCK (adj) *mordu, -e de théâtre :* stagestruck youngsters = *des gamins mordus de théâtre.*

STAGGER (to, -ed) 1/ *tituber :* the drunk was staggering = *l'ivrogne titubait* ⓓ to totter = *chanceler* 2/ *échelonner :* to stagger vacations/lunch hours = *échelonner les départs en vacances/les heures de déjeuner* ⓓ to spread over = *étaler.*

STAGGERING (adj) *renversant, -e :* a staggering confession = *une confession renversante* ⓓ startling = *sidérant.*

STAGING (n) *mise (f) en scène (théâtre) :* her staging of Hamlet was revolutionary = *sa mise en scène de Hamlet était révolutionnaire.*

STAGNANT (adj) *stagnant, -e :* a stagnant economy = *une économie stagnante* ⓓ static = *statique.*

STAGNATE (to, -d) *stagner :* our work isn't advancing, we're just stagnating = *notre travail n'avance pas, on stagne* ≠ to progress = *progresser.*

STAID (adj) *collet monté* : a staid family = *une famille collet monté* ⓓ stuffy = *guindé*.

STAIN (n) *tache* (f) : a stain on the mattress/his reputation = *une tache sur le matelas/sa réputation* ☠ *une tâche* = a task
— *taches de rousseur* = freckles
— *faire tache d'huile* = to spread like wildfire.

STAIN (to, -ed) *tacher* : you stained your jacket = *vous avez taché votre veste* ⓓ to dirty = *salir* ☠ *tâche de venir* = try to come.

STAIRS (n pl) the stairs = *l'escalier* : we were tired and walked up the stairs very slowly = *nous étions fatigués et nous avons monté l'escalier très lentement* ⓓ upstairs = *en haut*, downstairs = *en bas*, banister = *rampe*, landing = *palier*, elevator = *ascenseur*, fire escape = *escalier de secours*, stairway/staircase/flight of stairs = *cage d'escalier* ☠ *escalier roulant* = escalator
to push s.o. down the stairs = *pousser qqn dans l'escalier*
to run up ≠ down the stairs = *monter ≠ descendre les marches/l'escalier en courant/quatre à quatre*.

STAKE (n) *enjeu* (m) : the stakes were high = *l'enjeu était élevé* ⓓ ante = *mise*
at stake = *en jeu* : his reputation's at stake = *sa réputation est en jeu*, I have a lot at stake = *il y a beaucoup de choses en jeu pour moi* ⓓ in question = *en question*
to have a stake in (the business) = *être intéressé à (l'affaire)*
to pull up stakes = *emporter tout ce qu'on a* : my parents pulled up stakes and went to California = *mes parents ont emporté tout ce qu'ils avaient et sont partis pour la Californie.*

STAKE (to, -d) to stake everything on = *jouer son va-tout avec* : he's going to stake everything on that investment = *il va jouer son va-tout avec ce placement* ⓓ to stake one's all = *risquer le tout pour le tout*
to stake on = *jouer sur* : he's staking his career on the deal = *il joue sa carrière sur cette affaire* ⓓ to jeopardize = *mettre en péril*
to stake s.o. to stg = *payer qqch à qqn* : I'm broke, can you stake me to dinner ? = *je suis fauché, est-ce que tu peux me payer à dîner ?* ⓓ to treat s.o. to stg = *offrir qqch à qqn.*

STALE (adj, -r, -st) 1/ *rassis, -e* : the bread's stale = *le pain est rassis* ⓓ moldy = *moisi ≠ fresh = frais* 2/ *qui manque de pratique* : my piano playing is a little stale = *je manque de pratique·au piano*

stale jokes = *des plaisanteries éculées* ⓓ hackneyed = *rebattu*.

STALEMATE (n) *impasse* (f) : the talks have reached a stalemate = *les pourparlers sont dans une impasse* ⓓ standstill = *point mort* ☠ → deadlock.

STALK (to, -ed) 1/ *traquer* : pimps stalking young girls = *des maquereaux traquant les jeunes filles* ⓓ to pursue = *poursuivre* 2/ *régner* : fear was stalking = *la peur régnait* ⓓ to haunt = *hanter* ☠ → to reign.

STALL (n) *éventaire* (m), *étalage* (m) : a stall in a fair/market = *un éventaire/un étalage dans une foire/au marché* ⓓ booth = *baraque (foraine)* ☠ *faire étalage de ses connaissances* = to show off one's knowledge.

STALL (to, -ed) 1/ *atermoyer* : stop stalling and give me an answer = *cessez d'atermoyer et donnez-moi une réponse* ⓓ to temporize = *temporiser* 2/ *caler* : the car stalls when it's cold = *la voiture cale quand il fait froid* ⓓ starter = ← ☠ *je cale (repas)* = I'm full (eating).

STALLION (n) *étalon* (m) ⓓ horse = *cheval* ☠ *étalon or* = gold exchange standard.

STAMINA (n) *endurance* (f) : she lacks the stamina to be an athlete = *elle manque d'endurance pour être une athlète* ⓓ perseverance = *persévérance*.

STAMMER (to, -ed) *bredouiller* : he stammered his apologies = *il a bredouillé des excuses* ⓓ to stutter = *bafouiller*.

STAMP (n) *timbre* (m) : don't forget to buy some stamps = *n'oubliez pas d'acheter des timbres* ⓓ stamp collecting = *philatélie*, postage = *affranchissement*
to leave one's stamp on = *laisser son empreinte sur* : after six years, he left his stamp on her = *au bout de six ans, il a laissé son empreinte sur elle*
the stamp of genius = *le sceau du génie*.

STAMP (to, -ed) to stamp on (the ground/floor) = *trépigner/taper des pieds (par terre)*
to stamp out = *juguler* : they're trying to stamp out prostitution = *ils essaient de juguler la prostitution*
to stamp out of (a meeting) = *sortir (d'une réunion) en trépignant*.

STAMPEDE (n) *débandade* (f) : a stampede of horses = *une débandade de chevaux* ☠ *tout va à la débandade* = everything's going to hell.

STAMPING GROUND (n) *terrain* (m) *de prédilection* : Monaco is the Jet Set's favorite stamping ground = *Monaco est le terrain de prédilection de la jet-set* ⓓ haunt = *lieu favori*.

STAND (n) 1/ *position* (f) : the feminists are criticizing his stand on abortion = *les féministes critiquent sa position sur l'avortement* ⓓ attitude = ← ☠ → position
2/ *stand* (m) : a stand at the fair = *un stand de foire* ⓓ stall = *éventaire*

| to take ≠ not to take a stand = *prendre ≠ ne pas prendre position* | (will the witness) take the stand ? = *(est-ce que le témoin peut) venir à la barre ?* |

STAND (to, stood, stood) 1/ *être debout* : everyone stood but I sat = *tout le monde était debout, mais j'étais assise* ≠ to sit = *être assis* 2/ *se mettre debout* : will everyone please stand ? = *est-ce que tout le monde peut se mettre debout ?* ⓪ to stand up = *se lever*

as things/matters stand = *au point où en sont les choses* ⓪ things being as they are = *les choses étant ce qu'elles sont*
to be standing = *être debout* : they were all standing when I walked in = *ils étaient tous debout quand je suis entré*
I stand corrected = *je reconnais mon erreur*
I can't stand him ! = *je ne peux pas le supporter !* ⓪ I can't take him ! = *je ne peux pas l'encaisser !*

≠ I enjoy him = *je l'aime bien*
I could stand (a drink) = *je prendrais bien (un verre)* ⓪ I wouldn't object to (a drink) = *je ne serais pas contre (quelque chose à boire)*
I'll stand you (a drink) = *je vous invite à (prendre un pot)* ⓪ to stake s.o. to stg = *payer qqch à qqn*
(my offer) still stands = *(mon offre) tient toujours*
where do I stand ? = *où est-ce que j'en suis ?*

to stand back = *reculer* : stand back and let the firemen work = *reculez et laissez travailler les pompiers* ☠ → to move back
to stand by = 1/ *se tenir prêt* : doctors are standing by in case of an emergency operation = *les médecins se tiennent prêts en cas d'opération urgente* 2/ *ne rien faire* : everyone stood by as the girl was attacked in the subway = *personne n'a rien fait quand on a attaqué la fille dans le métro*
to stand by s.o. = *ne pas laisser tomber qqn* : she stood by her husband throughout the scandal = *elle n'a pas laissé tomber son mari durant tout le scandale* ≠ to walk out on s.o. = *plaquer qqn*
I stand by what I said = *je m'en tiens à ce que j'ai dit*
to stand down = *se désister* : the boss is standing down in favor of his son = *le patron se désiste en faveur de son fils* ⓪ to resign = *démissionner*
to stand for = *représenter* : the initials EEC stand for European Economic Community = *le sigle CEE représente* : Commu-

nauté économique européenne, I don't like tyrants and what they stand for = *je n'aime pas les tyrans et ce qu'ils représentent* = to represent ⓪ to symbolize = *symboliser* ☠ → to represent
not to stand for = *ne pas supporter* : I won't stand for that ! = *je ne supporterai pas ça !* ⓪ to tolerate = *tolérer*
to stand in for s.o. = *remplacer qqn* : his assistant is standing in for him = *son assistant le remplace* ⓪ to pinch-hit for = *suppléer*
to stand on = *avoir une position sur* : where does he stand on women's rights ? = *quelle est sa position sur les droits des femmes ?*
to stand out = *se détacher* : he's so tall he stands out in a crowd = *il est si grand qu'il se détache de la foule* ≠ to be inconspicuous = *passer inaperçu* ☠ → to detach
to stand to = *risquer de* : his wife stands to lose a fortune in the deal = *sa femme risque de perdre une fortune dans l'affaire* ⓪ she might ... = *elle pourrait bien ...*

to stand up = *se lever* : stand up ! = *levez-vous !* ≠ to sit down = *s'asseoir* ☠ → to raise
to stand s.o. up = *poser un lapin à qqn* : we had a date but he stood me up = *nous avions rendez-vous mais il m'a posé un lapin* ⓪ not to show up = *ne pas se pointer*
to stand up in (court) = *être valable au (tribunal)* : his testimony won't stand up in court = *son témoignage ne sera pas valable au tribunal* ⓪ to hold up = *tenir le coup*
to stand up for s.o. = *prendre le parti de qqn* : he always stands up for his wife = *il prend toujours le parti de sa femme* ⓪ to back up = *soutenir*
to stand up for (one's rights) = *défendre (ses droits)*
to stand up to s.o. = *tenir tête à qqn* : she's too afraid to stand up to her husband = *elle a bien trop peur pour tenir tête à son mari* ⓪ to answer back = *répondre*
where do you stand with him ? = *où est-ce que vous en êtes avec lui ?*

STANDARD (n) *valeur (f)* : her parents set strict standards = *ses parents ont des valeurs strictes* ⓪ criterion = *critère* ☠ → value
to have high ≠ **low standards** = *être* ≠ *ne pas être difficile* : she doesn't sleep with anyone, she has high standards = *elle ne couche pas avec n'importe qui, elle est difficile*
standard of living = *niveau de vie*
manufacturing standards = *normes de fabrication* ☠ *le standard ne répond pas* = the switchboard doesn't answer.

STANDARD (adj) *standard (machine, etc.), courant, -e* : a standard model/size = *un modèle standard/une taille courante* ☠ → current
it's standard practice to (take the pill today) = *c'est pratique courante de (prendre la pilule de nos jours)* ⓪ it's typical = *c'est typique*
that's standard for him ! = *il fait ça couramment !*

STANDARDIZE (to, -d) *standardiser* : to standardize models = *standardiser les modèles* **STANDARDIZATION** (n) *standardisation (f)*.

STANDBY (n) *quelqu'un sur la liste d'attente* : we'll put your name down but there are already standbys = *on va inscrire votre nom mais il y a déjà des gens sur la liste d'attente.*

STANDBY (adj) **standby list** = *liste d'attente.*

STAND-IN (n) *remplaçant, -e* : he's the stand-in for the Mayor = *c'est le remplaçant du maire.*

STANDING (n) *position* (f) : a high standing in his profession/hometown = *une position importante dans sa profession/dans sa ville* ① reputation = *réputation* ☠ *le standing* = social status — *un immeuble de standing* = a luxury building — *position* → position.

STANDING (adj) **to give s.o. a standing ovation** = *se lever pour faire une ovation à qqn* **to have a standing invitation** = *être toujours le bienvenu* **to remain standing** = *rester debout* **standing army** = *armée permanente* **standing joke** = *plaisanterie classique* **standing orders** = *ordres formels* **standing room** = *place debout.*

STANDOFFISH (adj) *rébarbatif, -ive* : I don't like her husband, he's standoffish = *je n'aime pas son mari, il est rébarbatif.*

STANDPOINT (n) *point* (m) *de vue* : from a feminist standpoint, his remarks were very macho = *d'un point de vue féministe, ses remarques étaient très machos* = viewpoint.

STANDSTILL (n) *point* (m) *mort* : the talks are at a standstill = *les pourparlers sont au point mort* ≠ breakthrough = *percée.*

STANZA (n) *strophe* (f) : I don't remember the first stanza = *je ne me rappelle pas la première strophe.*

STAPLE (n) *produit* (m) *de base* : wheat is a staple in the USSR = *le blé est un produit de base en URSS.*

STAPLE (adj) *de base* : staple articles = *produits de base* ① standard = *courant.*

STAPLER (n) *agrafeuse* (f) : where's the stapler ? = *où*

est l'agrafeuse ? ① paper staple = *agrafe*, clip = *trombone.*

STAR (n) **1/** *étoile* (f) : the sky's full of stars = *le ciel est plein d'étoiles* **2/** *vedette* (f), star (f) : everyone in films wants to be a star = *au cinéma, tout le monde veut être une vedette/une star* ① superstar = ← ≠ a bit player = *quelqu'un qui joue les utilités* **to see stars** = *voir trente-six chandelles* ① to black out = *tourner de l'œil* **shooting star** = *étoile filante* **the Stars and Stripes** = *la bannière étoilée* = the Star-Spangled Banner ☠ *vedette américaine* = curtain raiser — *être en vedette* = to be in the spotlight.

STAR (adj) *vedette* : the star player = *le joueur vedette.*

STAR (to, -red) *avoir pour vedette* : the film starred Marilyn Monroe = *le film avait Marilyn Monroe pour vedette* **to star in** = *être la vedette de* : Gable starred in this movie = *Gable était la vedette de ce film.*

STARCH (n) *amidon* (m) : put a little starch in the water = *mettez un peu d'amidon dans l'eau* **STARCH** (to, -ed) *amidonner.*

STARDOM (n) *vedettariat* (m) : she finally reached stardom = *elle a finalement atteint le vedettariat* ① star system = *star-système.*

STARE (to, -d) *fixer (des yeux)* : it's impolite to stare = *c'est impoli de fixer les gens* ① to look s.o. up and down = *déshabiller qqn du regard* **to stare at** = *fixer* : why are you staring at me ? = *pourquoi me fixez-vous ?* ☠ → to fix.

STARK-NAKED (adj) *à poil* : he was stark-naked when I opened the door = *il était à poil quand j'ai ouvert la porte* ① in one's birthday suit = *dans la tenue d'Ève/d'Adam.*

STARLET (n) *starlette* (f) : directors are surrounded by starlets = *les metteurs en scène sont entourés de starlettes.*

STARRY-EYED (adj) *qui est l'innocence même* : a starry-eyed young girl = *une jeune fille qui est l'innocence même* ≠ jaded = *revenu de tout.*

START (n) *début* (m) : we missed the start of the movie = *nous avons raté le début du film* ① outset = *départ* ≠ finish = fin ☠ *il n'en est plus à ses débuts* = he's no novice

at the start (of the race/war) = *au début de (la course/la guerre)* **for a start** = *d'abord* : I have a lot of things to tell you, for a start I'd like to apologize for the way I acted = *j'ai beaucoup de choses à vous dire, d'abord je*	*voudrais vous présenter mes excuses pour la façon dont j'ai agi* **from the start** = *dès le début* : we've had problems from the start = *nous avons eu des problèmes dès le début* ① from the outset = *dès le départ*	**to give s.o. a start** = *faire sursauter qqn* : the noise gave us a start = *le bruit nous a fait sursauter* ① to give a jolt = *ficher un coup* **to wake up with a start** = *se réveiller en sursaut.*

START (to, -ed) **1/** *commencer* : what time does the movie start ? = *à quelle heure commence le film ?* = what time does the movie begin ? ≠ to finish = *finir* ☠ → to begin
2/ *démarrer* : my car won't start = *ma voiture ne démarre pas,* he started the fight = *il a démarré la bagarre* ☠ *il a démarré sans moi* = he drove away without me

---

(are you trying) to start something ? = *tu me cherches (noise)* ? ⓪ you're picking an argument = *tu cherches la dispute*	**to start (+ ing)** = *commencer à* : we'll start working at ten = *nous commencerons à travailler à dix heures*

---

let's start again ! = *recommençons !* **to start off** = *débuter* : she started off in journalism as a reporter in a small paper = *elle a débuté dans le journalisme comme reporter d'un petit journal* ☠ *la pièce débute lundi* = the play opens on Monday **to start on** = *commencer :*	we'll start on the work next week = *nous commencerons le travail la semaine prochaine* **to start out** = *démarrer* : we started out with a great deal of optimism = *nous avons démarré avec pas mal d'optimisme* **to start to** = *commencer à* : she started to cry = *elle a commencé à pleurer*	**to start up (a business)** = *démarrer (une affaire)* **to start with** = 1/ *pour commencer* : I'll have a shrimp cocktail to start with = *pour commencer, je prendrai un cocktail de crevettes* 2/ *d'abord* : to start with, I think you're wrong = *d'abord, je pense que vous avez tort.*

STARTERS (n pl) **for starters** = *tout d'abord* : for starters, let me tell you why I think your mother's a busybody = *tout d'abord, laisse-moi te dire pourquoi je pense que ta mère est une mouche du coche* = for openers ⓪ to begin with = *pour commencer.*

STARTLE (to, -d) *faire sursauter* : the noise startled me = *le bruit m'a fait sursauter*
I was startled to (see them together) = *j'étais sidéré de (les voir ensemble).*

STARTLING (adj) *sidérant, -e* : startling news/situation = *une nouvelle/situation sidérante* ⓪ surprising = *surprenant.*

STARVATION (n) *inanition* (f) : children dying of starvation = *des enfants mourant d'inanition* ⓪ famine = ←
to be on a starvation diet = *suivre un régime draconien*
starvation wages = *salaire de famine.*

STARVE (to, -d) *souffrir de la faim* : millions of people in the world are starving = *des millions de gens dans le monde souffrent de la faim* ≠ to feed = *donner à manger à*
I'm starving ! = *je suis affamé !* = **I'm starved !** ⓪ I could eat a horse = *j'ai une faim de loup*
to be starving for (tenderness) = *être en mal de (tendresse)* ⓪ to crave = *mourir d'envie de*
to starve to death = *mourir de faim.*

STASH (AWAY) (to, -ed) *planquer* : to stash (away) money = *planquer de l'argent* ⓪ to hide = *cacher*
☠ *planquer qqn* = to hide s.o.
— *se planquer* = to hide out.

STATE (n) **1/** *état* (m) : the business's in a state of confusion = *l'affaire est dans un état de grande confusion* ⓪ condition = *condition/état* **2/** *État* (m) : matters of state = *des affaires d'État,* state college = *collège d'État*
don't get yourself into such a state ! = *ne vous mettez pas dans un état pareil !* ⓪ **to be in a state** = *être dans tous ses états*
to lie in state = *être exposé* : the body's lying in state = *le corps est exposé*
to give state's evidence = *dénoncer ses complices (pour atténuer sa propre culpabilité)*
state of affairs = *état des choses*
State Department = *Département d'État*
the States = *les États-Unis* ⓪ America = *l'Amérique*
the State of New York = *l'État de New York*
state visit = *visite officielle*
state trooper = *CRS*
☠ *hors d'état* = out of order
— *je ne suis pas en état de faire ce travail* = I'm not up to doing this work
— *son état est grave* = his condition is serious
— *état d'âme* = mood
— *état civil* = legal status
— *faire état de* = to put forward.

STATE (to, -d) *énoncer clairement* : they told him to state his name and address = *ils lui ont demandé d'énoncer clairement son nom et son adresse* ⓪ to announce = *annoncer.*

STATEMENT (n) *déclaration* (f) : the White House issued a statement = *la Maison-Blanche a fait une déclaration* ⓪ word = *mot* ☠ → declaration.

STATESMAN (n, -men) *homme* (m) *d'État* : another statesman was assassinated = *il y a encore un homme d'État qui a été assassiné* ⓪ politician = *homme politique* **STATESWOMAN** (n, -women) *femme* (f) *chef d'État.*

STATIC (n inv) *parasites* (m pl) (radio), *friture* (f) (phone) : a lot of static on the radio/phone = *beaucoup de parasites à la radio/de friture sur la ligne*

608

☠ → parasite
— *une friture* = fried fish.

STATIC (adj) *statique* : a static economy = *une écono-mie statique* ≠ moving = *qui bouge*, evolving = *qui évolue*.

STATION (n) **1/** *gare (f)* : can you pick me up at the station ? = *est-ce que vous pouvez venir me chercher à la gare ?* ⓪ train = ← **2/** *station (f)* : we get off at the next station = *nous descendons à la prochaine station* ⓪ stop = *arrêt* ☠ *station balnéaire/de sports d'hiver* = seaside/ski resort
radio station = *station de radio*
station wagon = *break* : the station wagon holds a lot of baggage = *le break contient beaucoup de bagages.*

STATION (to, -ed) *baser* : his unit was stationed in the Far East = *son unité était basée en Extrême-Orient.*

STATIONARY (adj) *stationnaire* : the situation's stationary now = *la situation est stationnaire maintenant* ⓪ immobile = ←.

STATIONERY (n, -ies) *papier et enveloppes* : I bought some stationery to write my friends = *j'ai acheté du papier et des enveloppes pour écrire à mes amis*, White House's stationery = *papier et enveloppes à en-tête de la Maison-Blanche* ⓪ writing paper = *papier à lettres*
stationery store = *papeterie* ⓪ bookstore = *librairie.*

STATISTICS (n pl) *statistiques (f pl)* : the statistics showed you were right = *les statistiques ont montré que vous aviez raison* ⓪ statistician = *statisticien*, figures = *chiffres.*

STATUE (n) *statue (f)* : Rodin's magnificent statues = *les magnifiques statues de Rodin* ⓪ sculpture = ←
the Statue of Liberty = *la Statue de la Liberté (dans le port de New York, don de la France en 1886, créée par Bartholdi).*

STATURE (n) *stature (f)*, *envergure (f)* : a filmmaker of great stature = *un cinéaste de grande envergure* ⓪ quality = *qualité* ☠ *une offensive de grande envergure* = a large-scale offensive.

STATUS (n, -es) **1/** *statut (m)* : the legal status of a foreigner = *le statut d'étranger* ☠ *statut (loi)* = statute **2/** *situation (f)* : what's the economic status of the immigrants ? = *quelle est la situation économique des immigrants ?* = situation ☠ → situation **3/** *prestige (m)* : he has status in the company = *il a du prestige dans la société* ⓪ rank = *rang*
status symbol = *signe extérieur de richesse*
status quo = *statu quo.*

STAUNCH (adj, -er, -est) *à toute épreuve* : a staunch friend/supporter = *un ami/un supporter à toute épreuve* ⓪ steadfast = *solide*
to be a staunch believer (in communism) = *croire dur comme fer au (communisme)*
to be a staunch defender of = *être un ardent défenseur de.*

STAY (n) *séjour (m)* : a week's stay = *un séjour d'une semaine* ⓪ vacation = *vacances*
(to grant) a stay of execution = *(accorder) un sursis d'exécution.*

STAY (to, -ed) *rester* : I stayed a week in Paris = *je suis resté une semaine à Paris*, how long did you stay ? = *combien de temps êtes-vous resté ?* ☠ → to remain
stay put ! = *ne bougez pas !* ⓪ keep still ! = *tenez-vous tranquille !*

---

to stay at = **1/** *rester chez (s.o.)/à* (somewhere) : we stayed at home/at my mother's = *nous sommes restés à la maison/chez ma mère* **2/** *descendre à* (hotel) : I always stay at the Ritz = *je descends toujours au Ritz*
to stay away from s.o. = *éviter qqn* : why are you staying away from me ? = *pourquoi m'évitez-vous ?*
to stay behind = *rester à la maison* : I went to London and my kids stayed behind = *je suis allé à Londres et mes gosses sont restés à la maison*
to stay for = *rester pour/à* : do you want to stay for lunch ? = *est-ce que vous voulez rester pour le déjeuner ?/à déjeuner ?*
to stay in = *rester chez soi* : we stayed in last night = *nous sommes restés chez nous hier soir*
to stay on = *rester encore* : we decided to stay on till Christmas = *nous avons décidé de rester encore jusqu'à Noël*
to stay out = *ne pas rentrer* : we stayed out till four a.m. = *nous ne sommes pas rentrés avant quatre*

heures du matin ⓪ to sleep out = *découcher*
to stay out of = **1/** *ne pas entrer dans* : stay out of the room ! = *n'entrez pas dans la pièce !* **2/** *rester à l'écart (de)* : if they begin to fight, stay out of it ! = *s'ils commencent à se battre, restez à l'écart !* ≠ to meddle in = *s'immiscer dans*
to stay over = *rester dormir* : do you want to stay over ? = *est-ce que vous voulez rester dormir ici ?* ⓪ to spend the night = *passer la nuit*
to stay through = *rester* : we're going to stay in Rome through the winter = *nous allons rester à Rome tout l'hiver* ☠ → to remain
to stay up = *veiller* : I stayed up too late last night = *j'ai veillé trop tard la nuit dernière*
☠ *veiller sur qqn/ses intérêts* = to look after s.o./one's interests
— *veiller à ce que ...* = to see to ...
to stay with = *habiter chez* : she's not at the hotel, she's staying with friends = *elle n'est pas à l'hôtel, elle habite chez des amis.*

STAY-AT-HOME (n) *pantouflard, -e* : she's married to a stay-at-home = *elle a épousé un pantouflard* ⑩ homebody = *casanier.*

STEADFAST (adj) *solide* : a steadfast ally = *un allié solide* ⑩ unwavering = *inébranlable* ☠ → solid.

STEADY (adj, -ier, -iest) **1**/ *stable* : the table isn't steady = *la table n'est pas stable* ≠ shaky = *chancelant* **2**/ *régulier, -ère* : a steady rise in inflation/a steady job = *une hausse régulière de l'inflation/un travail régulier* ☠ → regular **3**/ *sûr, -e* : steady hands = *des mains sûres* ≠ shaky = *tremblant* ☠ → sure.

STEADY (adv) **to go steady with** = *sortir régulièrement avec* : my daughter's going steady with a law student = *ma fille sort régulièrement avec un étudiant en droit* ⑩ to date = *sortir avec.*

STEAK (n inv) *steak (m), bifteck (m)* : let's have steak tonight = *si on mangeait des steaks ce soir* ⑩ chopped meat = *viande hachée,* sirloin = *faux-filet,* rib roast = *côte de bœuf,* steakhouse = *steak-house/restaurant de grillades* ☠ *gagner son bifteck* = to earn one's bread and butter.

STEAL (n) **a steal** = *une occase* : the watch was a steal at a hundred dollars = *à cent dollars, cette montre, c'était une occase* ⑩ a (good) buy = *une bonne affaire* ☠ *profiter de l'occase* = to make the most of stg — *d'occase* = secondhand.

STEAL (to, stole, stolen) *voler* : he stole my bag = *il m'a volé mon sac* ⑩ to make off with = *faire main basse sur* **to steal from** = *voler à/dérober à* : he stole a watch from my mother = *il a volé une montre à ma mère* ⑩ to pinch = *piquer* ☠ → to fly — *on dit « to steal stg »* = *voler qqch, mais « to rob s.o. »* = *voler qqn.*

STEAM (n inv) *vapeur (f), buée (f)* (window) : steam from the iron/on the window = *la vapeur du fer à repasser/de la buée sur la vitre* ⑩ mist = *brume,* steamboat = *bateau à vapeur* **to blow off/let off steam** = *se défouler* : after a month of hard work, I feel like letting off/blowing off some steam = *après un mois de travail pénible, j'ai envie de me défouler* ⑩ to unwind = *se détendre* **steam bath** = *bain de vapeur.*

STEAM (to, -ed) **to be steaming** = *être furax* : he was steaming over the mistake = *il était furax à cause de cette faute* → ANGRY.

STEAMY (adj, -ier, -iest) *embué, -e* : a steamy window = *une vitre embuée.*

STEEL (n inv) *acier (m)* : stainless steel = *acier inoxydable* ⑩ iron = *fer,* steelworks = *aciérie.*

STEEL ONESELF AGAINST (to, -ed) *se cuirasser pour/contre* : he steeled himself against falling in love again = *il s'est cuirassé pour ne pas retomber amoureux* ⑩ to harden o.s. = *s'endurcir.*

STEEP (adj, -er, -est) **1**/ *escarpé, -e* : the slope is steep = *la pente est escarpée* ≠ flat = *plat* **2**/ *élevé, -e* : prices are steep = *les prix sont élevés* = prices are high ⑩ exorbitant = ← ≠ low = *bas* ☠ → high.

STEER (to, -ed) *gouverner* : to steer a boat = *gouverner un bateau* ☠ → to govern **to steer s.o. to** = *aiguiller qqn sur* : he steered me to a good wholesale shop = *il m'a aiguillé sur un bon magasin de gros* ⑩ to introduce = *faire connaître.*

STEM (n) *tige (f)* : the stem of a flower = *la tige d'une fleur* ⑩ trunk = *tronc.*

STEM FROM (to, -med) *être issu, -e de* : the strikes stem from the economic crisis = *les grèves sont issues de la crise économique* ⑩ to come from = *venir de.*

STENCH (n, -es) *puanteur (f)* : a terrible stench from the junkyard = *une terrible puanteur venant du dépotoir* ⑩ odor = *mauvaise odeur.*

STENCIL (n) *stencil (m)* ⑩ photocopy = *photocopie.*

STENOGRAPHER (n) *sténographe (m, f)* **STENOGRAPHY** (n) *sténo(graphie) (f)* : do you take stenography ? = *est-ce que vous savez prendre en sténo(graphie) ?* → shorthand.

STEP (n) **1**/ *pas (m)* : a step forward = *un pas en avant*	
☠ *rouler au pas* = to drive at a snail's pace — *ça ne se trouve pas sous le pas d'un cheval* = you won't find it easily — *mettre qqn au pas* = to bring s.o. to heel	— *marquer le pas* = to mark time — *un pas de clerc* = a blunder — *à pas de loup* = stealthily — *sauter le pas* = to take the plunge
2/ *ce qu'on fait* : what's the next step ? = *qu'est-ce qu'on fait ensuite ?* **3**/ *marche (f)* : I tripped on the steps = *j'ai trébuché sur les marches* ⑩ landing = *palier*	
☠ *aimer la marche* = to be fond of walking — *ouvrir la marche* = to lead the way — *en marche* = in motion — *la marche d'une entreprise* = the running of an enterprise	— *c'est la marche à suivre* = it's the procedure to follow — *mettre en marche* = to start up — *faire marche arrière* = to backtrack — *marche arrière (sur une voiture)* = reverse (car)

to keep step with = *suivre le rythme/garder la cadence de* : Europeans have problems keeping step with the Americans = *les Européens ont du mal à garder la cadence/à suivre le rythme des Américains* **out of step** = *pas dans le ton* : she was out of step with the rest of the company = *elle n'était pas dans le ton de cette assemblée* **a step in the right direction** = *un pas dans la bonne direction*	**step by step** = *pas à pas* **to take a step forward** ≠ **backward** = *faire un pas en avant* ≠ *en arrière* **to take steps** = *prendre des mesures* : the government had to take steps to end inflation = *le gouvernement a dû prendre des mesures pour juguler l'inflation* **watch your step !** = *regarde où tu mets les pieds !* ⓪ watch out ! = *fais gaffe !*	

STEP (to, -ped) **to step down** = *se retirer* : the President stepped down after the scandal = *le Président s'est retiré après le scandale* = the President withdrew after the scandal ⓪ to retire = *prendre sa retraite* ☠ → to withdraw **to step forward** ≠ **back** = *faire un pas en avant* ≠ *en arrière* **to step in** = 1/ *s'interposer* : Jack stepped in to prevent the argument from getting out of hand = *Jack s'est interposé pour empêcher la discussion de dégé-*	*nérer* ⓪ to intervene = *intervenir* 2/ *marcher dans* : she stepped in a puddle = *elle a marché dans une flaque d'eau* **step on it !** = *mets la gomme !* : tell the driver to step on it = *dis au conducteur de mettre la gomme* ⓪ hurry up ! = *dépêche-toi !* **to step on s.o.** = *écraser qqn* : she'd step on anyone to get ahead = *elle écraserait tout le monde pour arriver* ⓪ she'd stop at nothing = *rien ne la ferait reculer* **to step out** = 1/ *faire la fête* :	we're stepping out tonight = *ce soir, on fait la fête* ⓪ to go out = *sortir* 2/ *s'absenter* : Mr. Smith has stepped out for a few minutes = *M. Smith s'est absenté quelques minutes* ☠ *s'absenter pour affaires* = to go away on business **to step over (a body)** = *enjamber (un corps)* **to step up (production)** = *accélérer (la production)* = to accelerate ⓪ to speed up = *activer* ≠ to put on the brake = *freiner.*

STEPBROTHER (n) *demi-frère* (m) = half brother **STEPSISTER** (n) *demi-sœur* (f) = half sister.

STEPCHILD (n, -ren) *beau-fils* (m), *belle-fille* (f) (*beaux-enfants*) : she never got on well with her stepchildren = *elle ne s'est jamais bien entendue avec ses beaux-enfants* ⓪ foster child = *enfant adoptif* **STEPDAUGHTER** (n) *belle-fille* (f) ☠ *belle-fille (femme du fils)* = daughter-in-law **STEPSON** (n) *beau-fils* (m).

STEPPARENT (n) *beau-père* (m), *belle-mère* (f) (*beaux-parents*) : he hates his stepparents = *il déteste ses beaux-parents* ⓪ foster parents = *parents nourriciers* **STEPFATHER** (n) *beau-père* (m) **STEPMOTHER** (n) *belle-mère* (f).

STEPPINGSTONE (n) *tremplin* (m) : this position is a steppingstone for the Presidency = *cette situation est un tremplin pour la présidence* ⓪ a means = *un moyen.*

STEREO (n) *stéréo* (f) ⓪ record player = *électrophone.*

STEREOTYPE (n) *stéréotype* (m) : the good guys and the bad guys are movie stereotypes = *les bons et les méchants sont des stéréotypes cinématographiques* ⓪ cliché = ←.

STERILE (adj) *stérile* : a sterile woman/environment/writer = *une femme/un environnement/un écrivain stérile* ≠ fertile = *fertile/fécond* ☠ terre stérile = barren land **STERILITY** (n, -ies) *stérilité* (f) ≠ fecundity = *fécondité* **STERILIZATION** (n) *stérilisation* (f) **STERILIZE** (to, -d) *stériliser* : are the bottles sterilized ? = *est-ce que les biberons sont stérilisés ?*

STERN (adj, -er, -est) *strict, -e* : she's stern with her children = *elle est stricte avec ses enfants* ⓪ severe = *sévère* ≠ lenient = *indulgent* ☠ → strict.

STEW (n) *ragoût* (m) : beef stew = *ragoût de bœuf.*

STEW OVER (to, -ed) *être tenaillé par* : he's stewing over his problems = *ses problèmes le tenaillent.*

STEWARD (n) *steward* (m) = flight attendant **STEWARD-ESS** (n, -es) *hôtesse* (f) de l'air.

STICK (n) *bâton* (m) : he hit the dog with a stick = *il a frappé le chien avec un bâton* ⓪ cane = *canne*	
to come from the sticks = *venir de la cambrousse* ⓪ to come from Timbuktu = *venir de Trifouillis-les-Oies*	**sticks and stones will hurt my bones, but names will never harm me** = *la bave du crapaud n'atteint pas la blanche colombe*
☠ *mettre des bâtons dans les roues* = to throw in a monkey wrench — *avoir une conversation à bâtons rompus* = to	have a rambling conversation — *mener une vie de bâton de chaise* = to lead a gay life.

STICK (to, stuck, stuck) **1/** *coller, attacher* (cooking) : stick the stamps on the envelope = *collez les timbres sur l'enveloppe,* the eggs stuck to the pan = *les œufs ont collé/attaché à la poêle*

☠ *j'ai été collé à l'examen* = I flunked the exam
— *ça ne colle pas* = it doesn't jibe

— *coller qqn* = to cling to s.o.
— *attacher* → to attach

2/ *piquer :* I stuck my finger with a pin = *je me suis piqué le doigt avec une épingle* ⓪ to cut = *couper* ☠ → to sting

to be stuck = *être bloqué :* the door's/the elevator's stuck = *la porte est bloquée/l'ascenseur est bloqué* **I'm stuck** = *je sèche :* can you help me, I'm stuck = *je sèche, est-ce que vous pouvez m'aider ?* = I'm stumped

to make stg stick = *étayer qqch :* they can't make the charge stick = *ils ne peuvent pas étayer cette accusation* **stick it !** = *va chier !* → BUZZ OFF !

stick around ! = *reste ! :* why don't you stick around a while ? = *pourquoi ne restez-vous pas un moment ?* ≠ get out ! = *sortez !*
to stick by s.o. = *soutenir qqn :* she stuck by her husband when the press attacked him = *elle a soutenu son mari quand la presse l'a attaqué* ⓪ to stand by = *ne pas laisser tomber*
to stick by = *ne pas démordre de :* the witness stuck by his first story = *le témoin n'a pas voulu démordre de sa première version*
to stick in = *coller dans :* stick it in the closet = *colle ça dans le placard*
to be stuck in (the elevator) = *être coincé dans (l'ascenseur)*
to be stuck on s.o. = *avoir qqn dans la peau :* John's stuck on my sister = *John a ma sœur dans la peau* ⓪ to be smitten = *être toqué*

to stick out of = *sortir de :* what's sticking out of your pocket ? = *qu'est-ce qui sort de votre poche ?* ⓪ to protrude = *dépasser*
to stick it out = *tenir jusqu'au bout :* I hate this work but I must stick it out = *je déteste ce travail, mais il faut que je tienne jusqu'au bout*
to stick to = 1/ *s'en tenir à :* stick to what he says = *tenez-vous-en à ce qu'il dit* 2/ *s'accrocher à :* if you start learning tennis, you must stick to it = *quand on apprend à jouer au tennis, il faut s'accrocher*
to stick together = *se serrer les coudes :* the two brothers stuck together = *les deux frères se sont serré les coudes* ⓪ to band together = *se liguer*
to stick up = *attaquer à main armée :* to stick up a bank = *attaquer une banque à main*

armée ⓪ to do/pull a job = *faire un coup*
stick 'em up ! = *haut les mains !*
to stick up for (what one thinks) = *défendre avec acharnement (ce qu'on pense)*
to stick up for s.o. = *prendre la défense de qqn :* my grandmother always sticks up for my younger brother = *ma grand-mère prend toujours la défense de mon frère cadet* ⓪ to side with s.o. = *se ranger du côté de qqn*
to stick s.o. with stg = *coller qqch à qqn :* they tried to stick me with the bill = *ils ont essayé de me coller l'addition*
to be stuck with s.o./stg = *avoir qqn/qqch qui vous reste sur les bras :* I bought it on sale and I'm stuck with it = *j'ai acheté ça en solde et ça me reste sur les bras.*

STICK-IN-THE-MUD (n) *quelqu'un d'encroûté :* I never met such a stick-in-the-mud = *je n'ai jamais rencontré quelqu'un d'aussi encroûté* ≠ a gay blade = *un gai luron.*

STICKLER (n) **to be a stickler for (cleanliness)** = *être à cheval sur (la propreté)* ⓪ to be a bug for = *être un maniaque de.*

STICK-TO-ITIVENESS (n) *opiniâtreté (f) :* this work demands stick-to-itiveness = *ce travail exige de l'opiniâtreté* ⓪ perseverance = *persévérance.*

STICKUP (n) *attaque (f) à main armée :* another stickup in the bank = *encore une attaque à main armée à la banque* ⓪ holdup = *hold-up.*

STICKY (adj, -ier, -iest) **1/** *épineux, -euse :* a sticky problem = *un problème épineux* ⓪ delicate = *délicat* **2/** *poisseux, -euse :* sticky hands = *des mains poisseuses* ⓪ viscous = *visqueux*
to be sticky about = *être pointilleux sur :* the boss is sticky about our coming on time = *le patron est pointilleux sur la ponctualité.*

STIFF (n) *macchabée (m) :* the stiff was found in the river = *on a trouvé le macchabée dans le fleuve* ⓪ cadaver = *cadavre.*

STIFF (adj, -er, -est) **1/** *raide :* my legs are stiff = *j'ai les jambes raides* ⓪ rigid = *rigide*
☠ *sur la corde raide* = on a tightrope
— *c'est un peu raide !* = that's a bit thick !
— *tomber raide (mort)* = to drop dead
2/ *guindé, -e :* a stiff style/personality = *un style*

guindé/une personnalité guindée ≠ *cool* = ←
keep a stiff upper lip ! = *haut les cœurs !* ⓓ buck
up ! = *courage !*
stiff prices = *des prix salés*
a stiff whisky = *un whisky bien tassé.*

STIFLING (adj) *étouffant, -e :* a stifling home life = *une
vie de famille étouffante* ⓓ oppressive = *oppressant.*

STIGMA (n) *tare (f) :* the stigma of being hunchbacked =
la tare d'être bossu ⓓ disgrace = *honte.*

STILL (n) **the still of (the evening)** = *la tranquillité du (soir).*

STILL (adj, -er, -est) **to be/keep still** = *rester tranquille :* the teacher told us to be/keep still = *le professeur nous a dit de rester tranquilles* ⓓ to hush
up = *se taire*
stand still ! = *ne bougez pas !* : if you take pictures
you have to stand still = *quand on prend des pho-*

tos, il ne faut pas bouger
still life = *nature morte :* he only paints still lives
= *il ne peint que des natures mortes*
still waters run deep = *il n'est pire eau que l'eau
qui dort* ⓓ appearances are deceiving = *les apparences sont trompeuses.*

STILL (adv) **1/** *encore, toujours :* are they still married ? = *sont-ils encore/toujours mariés ?,* he's still a child
= *c'est encore/toujours un enfant,* I still haven't called him = *je ne l'ai toujours pas/pas encore appelé*

☠ *pas encore* = not yet
— *faites-le encore* = do it again
— *quoi encore ?* = what else ?

— *en voulez-vous encore ?* = do you want some
more ?
— *toujours* → always

2/ *quand même :* he's a bastard but still she loves him = *c'est un salaud mais elle l'aime quand même* ⓓ just
the same = *tout de même,* anyhow = *de toute manière*

still and all = *malgré tout ça :* he beats her,
doesn't give her any money but still and all she loves
him = *il la bat, ne lui donne pas d'argent mais mal-*

gré tout ça, elle l'aime
still more ≠ **less (expensive)** = *encore plus* ≠
moins (cher).

STILL (conj) *quand même :* I know he's intelligent, still he bores me = *je sais qu'il est intelligent, mais il
m'ennuie quand même* ⓓ nevertheless = *néanmoins.*

STILLBORN (adj) *mort-né, -e :* a stillborn child = *un
enfant mort-né* ⓓ aborted = *avorté.*

STILTED (adj) *emprunté, -e :* a stilted literary style =
un style littéraire emprunté ⓓ pretentious = *prétentieux.*

STIMULANT (n) *excitant (m) :* coffee's a stimulant = *le
café est un excitant* ☠ *un stimulant (pour accepter un
travail)* = a stimulus (to accept a job).

STIMULATE (to, -d) *stimuler :* to stimulate sales = *stimuler les ventes* ⓓ to provoke = *provoquer* **STIMU-
LATING** (adj) *stimulant, -e :* a stimulating conversation =
une conversation stimulante ≠ disheartening = *décourageant.*

STIMULATION (n) *stimulation (f) :* intellectual stimulation = *stimulation intellectuelle.*

STIMULUS (n, -i) *stimulant (m) :* a job promotion is a
good stimulus = *la perspective d'une promotion est un
bon stimulant* ⓓ incentive = *incitation* ☠ → stimulant.

STING (n) *piqûre (f) :* a bee sting = *une piqûre d'abeille*
ⓓ bite = *morsure* ☠ *piqûre (avec une seringue)* =
shot/needle.

STING (to, stung, stung) *piquer :* bees sting = *les abeilles
piquent* ⓓ to bite = *mordre*
☠ *piquer qqch* = to pinch/grab stg
— *piquer (animal)* = to put to sleep (pet)
— *se piquer avec une épingle* = to stick o.s. with a pin
— *se piquer (drogue)* = to mainline
— *se piquer de qqch* = to pride oneself on stg
— *piquer la curiosité de qqn* = to arouse s.o.'s
curiosity.

STINGY (adj, -ier, -iest) *radin, -e :* a stingy lover = *un
amant radin* ⓓ tight = *regardant,* tightfisted = *près de
ses sous* ≠ generous = *généreux.*

STINK (n) *odeur (f) infecte :* the stink of decaying corpses
= *l'odeur infecte de cadavres en décomposition* ⓓ bad
smell = *mauvaise odeur,* stench = *puanteur*
to make a stink = *faire du grabuge :* he made a stink
about the bill = *il a fait du grabuge à cause de l'addition*
ⓓ to kick up a row = *faire du foin.*

STINK (to, stank or stunk, stunk) **1/** *puer :* the room stinks =
la chambre pue ⓓ to stink to high heaven = *schlinguer,*
to smell of = *sentir à plein nez* **2/** *être chiant, -e :* the
movie stank = *le film était chiant* → AWFUL
to stink with (money) = *puer (le fric).*

STINKER (n) *peau* (f) *de vache* : he's a stinker not to lend me the money = *c'est une peau de vache de ne pas me prêter cet argent* → BASTARD.

STINT (n) **to do a stint in (the army)** = *faire un temps dans (l'armée).*

STIPULATE (to, -d) *stipuler* : the contract stipulates that ... = *le contrat stipule que...* ① to specify = *spécifier* **STIPULATION** (n) *stipulation* (f) : worrisome stipulations in the contract = *des stipulations ennuyeuses dans le contrat* ① condition = ←.

STIR (n) **to create a stir** = *provoquer des remous* : the scandal created a stir in Congress = *le scandale a provoqué des remous au Congrès* ① to-do = *embarras* **in stir** = *en taule* : he was raped doing time in stir = *il a été violé quand il était en taule* ① in the clink = *à l'ombre.*

STIR (to, -red) **1/** *remuer* : to stir one's coffee = *remuer son café* ① to mix = *mélanger* **2/** *remuer* : the audience was stirred by her appeal = *son appel a remué l'assistance* ① to move = *émouvoir* ☠ *ne pas remuer le petit doigt* = not to raise a finger

— *remue-toi !* = get a move on !
— *le chien remue la queue* = the dog wags its tail
3/ *bouger* : he showered abuse on his in-laws but no one stirred = *il a insulté ses beaux-parents, mais personne n'a bougé*
☠ → to move
— *dans ce sens, « to stir » est moins employé que « to move ».*

STITCH (n, -es) *point* (m) *de suture* : ten stitches in the forehead = *dix points de suture au front*
(not) to do a stitch of work = *(ne pas) faire le moindre travail* : they refused to do a stitch of work till they get a raise = *ils ont refusé de faire le moindre travail jusqu'à ce qu'ils obtiennent une augmentation* ① to twiddle one's thumbs = *se tourner les pouces*
without a stitch on = *nu comme un ver* : he opened the door without a stitch on = *il a ouvert la porte nu comme un ver* ① stark-naked = *à poil*
to be in stitches = *être plié en deux* ① to burst into laughter = *éclater de rire*
a stitch in time saves nine = *mieux vaut prévenir que guérir* = an ounce of prevention is worth a pound of cure.

STOCK (n) **1/** *stock* (m) : she's trying to sell her old stock = *elle essaie de vendre ses vieux stocks* ① supply = *approvisionnement*
2/ *valeurs* (f pl) : he bought stocks for his grandchildren = *il a acheté des valeurs pour ses petits-enfants* ① dividends = *dividendes*, stockholder = *actionnaire*, stockbroker = *agent de change* ☠ → value

to do stock = *faire partie d'un groupe théâtral qui part en tournée pendant l'été* : she did a lot of stock in Boston = *elle a souvent fait du théâtre estival à Boston* **in stock** ≠ **out of stock** = *en stock* ≠ *en rupture de stock* **of good** ≠ **bad stock** = *de bonne* ≠ *mauvaise souche* ① of	**blue blood** = *qui a du sang bleu/noble* **to play the stock market** = *jouer à la Bourse/boursicoter* **to put stock in** = *avoir foi en* : I can't put stock in what he says = *je ne peux pas avoir foi en ce qu'il dit* ① to trust = *se fier à* **stock crash** = *krach boursier* **the stock market** = *la Bourse*	= **the stock exchange** **to take stock** = **1/** *faire l'inventaire* : the store's taking stock this week = *le magasin fait l'inventaire cette semaine* **2/** *faire le bilan* : having divorced again, it's time to take stock of the situation = *après un second divorce, il est temps de faire le bilan de la situation.*

STOCK (adj) *classique* : a stock joke/answer/argument = *une plaisanterie/une réponse/un argument classique* ① standard = *courant* ☠ → classic
stock company = *groupe théâtral estival qui reprend en tournée des spectacles théâtraux et musicaux connus.*

STOCK (to, -ed) *avoir en stock, stocker* : we don't stock this item = *nous n'avons pas cet article en stock*
to stock up on = *stocker* : we're stocking up on Scotch = *nous stockons du whisky.*

STOCKADE (n) *palissade* (f) : the car crashed into the stockade = *la voiture a enfoncé la palissade* ① barricade = ←.

STOCKBROKER (n) *agent* (m) *de change* : I told my stockbrokers to sell some of my stocks = *j'ai demandé à mes agents de change de vendre quelques-unes de mes valeurs* ① broker = *courtier.*

STOCKHOLDER (n) *actionnaire* (m, f) : a bulletin went

out to all the stockholders = *un bulletin a été envoyé à tous les actionnaires* ① investor = *investisseur.*

STOCKING (n) *bas* (m) : stockings with a red garter = *des bas avec une jarretière rouge* ① tights/pantyhose = *collant*, run = *maille filée* ☠ → bottom.

STOCK-IN-TRADE (n) *grande spécialité* (f) : sarcastic articles are his stock-in-trade = *les articles sarcastiques sont sa grande spécialité.*

STOCKY (adj, -ier, -iest) *trapu, -e* : I'm attracted to stocky guys = *je suis attirée par les types trapus* ⓪ stout = *costaud* ≠ slender = *élancé* ☠ *un problème trapu* = a really rough problem.

STOIC (adj) *stoïque* : a stoic attitude = *une attitude stoïque* ⓪ impassive = *impassible*.

STOMACH (n) *ventre* (m), *estomac* (m) : he sleeps on his stomach = *il dort sur le ventre* ⓪ abdomen = ←, paunch = *panse/brioche*
my stomach thinks my throat's cut = *j'ai l'estomac dans les talons* ⓪ I'm famished = *je suis affamé*
stomach troubles = *troubles gastriques* ≠ a cast-iron stomach = *un estomac d'autruche*
☠ *il n'a rien dans le ventre* = he's yellow.

STOMACH (to, -ed) **not to stomach** = *ne pas piffer* : I can't stomach him = *je ne peux pas le piffer* ⓪ not to stand = *ne pas pouvoir supporter*.

STOMACHACHE (n) *mal* (m) *d'estomac* : being with my in-laws gives me a stomachache = *ça me fait mal à l'estomac d'être avec mes beaux-parents* ⓪ bellyache = *mal de ventre*.

STONE (n) *pierre* (f) : the kids threw stones at the dog = *les gosses lançaient des pierres au chien* ⓪ pebble = *caillou/galet*
to leave no stone unturned = *remuer ciel et terre* ⓪ to break one's back = *s'échiner*
a rolling stone gathers no moss = *pierre qui roule n'amasse pas mousse*
the Stone Age = *l'âge de la pierre*
a stone's throw = *à deux pas* : my bank's a stone's throw from my office = *ma banque est à deux pas de mon bureau* = my bank's a hop, skip and jump from my office
☠ *on ne peut pas lui jeter la pierre* = you can't blame him
— *pierre d'achoppement* = stumbling block
— *jeter une pierre dans le jardin de qqn* = to take a swipe at s.o.
— *malheureux comme les pierres* = very unhappy
— *jour à marquer d'une pierre blanche* = red-letter day
— *pierre précieuse* = gem.

STONE-BROKE (adj) *fauché, -e comme les blés* : I've often been stone-broke = *j'ai souvent été fauché comme les blés* → POOR ≠ filthy rich = *richissime*.

STONED (adj) 1/ *pinté, -e* : after three drinks I was completely stoned = *après trois verres, j'étais complètement pinté* → DRUNK 2/ *défoncé, -e* : she got stoned on snow = *elle s'est défoncée à la neige* ⓪ to be out = *être dans les vapes*.

STONE-DEAF (adj) *sourd, -e comme un pot* : speak louder, he's stone-deaf = *parlez plus fort, il est sourd comme un pot* ⓪ hard-of-hearing = *dur d'oreille/de la feuille*.

STONEWALL (to, -ed) *opposer une fin de non-recevoir*

à : Congress stonewalled the bill = *le Congrès a opposé une fin de non-recevoir au projet de loi* ⓪ to filibuster = *faire de l'obstruction parlementaire*.

STOOL (n) *tabouret* (m) : we have no chairs in the kitchen, just stools = *nous n'avons pas de chaises dans la cuisine, que des tabourets* ⓪ bench = *banc*.

STOOLIE (n) *mouton* (m) : don't tell him anything, he's a stoolie = *ne lui dites rien, c'est un mouton* ⓪ tattle-tale = *rapporteur* ☠ → sheep.

STOOL PIGEON (n) *indic* (m) ⓪ stoolie = *mouton*.

STOOP (to, -ed) **to stoop to** = *se baisser pour* : she stooped to pick up the book = *elle s'est baissée pour ramasser le livre* ⓪ to lean to = *se pencher pour*
I wouldn't stoop to (answer him) = *je ne m'abaisserai pas à (lui répondre)* = I wouldn't lower myself to.

STOP (n) *arrêt* (m) : where is the next ? = *où est le prochain arrêt ?*
to put a stop to = *mettre un terme à* : she put a stop to his drinking = *elle a mis un terme à son alcoolisme* ⓪ to put an end to = *mettre fin à*
☠ *marquer un (temps d') arrêt* = to pause
— *mandat d'arrêt* = arrest warrant
— *arrêt (tribunal)* = judgment
— *arrêt de travail* = sick leave
— *faire du stop* = to hitch.

STOP (to, -ped) *arrêter* : we'll stop at six = *nous arrêterons à six heures* ⓪ to cease = *cesser* ≠ to keep on = *continuer*
he'll stop at nothing = *rien ne l'arrêtera* = **he won't stop at anything**
to stop by = *passer* : if you have time, stop by = *si vous avez le temps, passez* ⓪ to pop in = *ne faire que passer* ☠ → to pass
to stop s.o. from = *empêcher qqn de* : I couldn't stop her from coming/talking to him = *je n'ai pas pu l'empêcher de venir/de lui parler* = to keep s.o. from
to stop (+ ing) = *arrêter de (+ infinitif)* : I stopped smoking = *j'ai arrêté de fumer* = to cut out (+ ing)
to stop off/over = *faire une étape à* : on our way back to the coast, we stopped off/over in Washington for a few days = *en rentrant sur la côte, nous avons fait une étape de quelques jours à Washington*
to stop over = *faire escale* : we stopped over in London on our way back to the States = *nous avons fait escale à Londres en rentrant aux États-Unis*
to be stopped up = *être bouché* : the sink's stopped up = *l'évier est bouché*
☠ *arrêter une date* = to fix a date
— *arrêter un criminel* = to arrest a criminal.

STOPGAP (adj) *bouche-trou* : stopgap measures = *des mesures bouche-trous* ⓪ temporary = *temporaire*.

STOP-OFF = STOPOVER (n) *escale* (f) : the flight has one stop-off/stopover = *il y a une escale durant le vol*.

STOPWATCH (n, -es) *chronomètre* (m) : the coach uses a stopwatch = *l'entraîneur utilise un chronomètre*.

STORAGE (n) **in storage** = *entreposé* : all my furniture's in storage = *tous mes meubles sont entreposés* ⓪ in cold storage = *mis de côté en attendant.*

STORE (n) *magasin* (m) : let's go to the store and buy lots of things = *allons au magasin acheter plein de choses* ⓪ boutique = ←, department store = *grand magasin*
he doesn't know what's in store for him = *il ne sait pas ce qui l'attend*
to set store on = *faire grand cas de* : he sets store on what his parents say = *il fait grand cas de ce que disent ses parents* ⓪ to put stock in = *avoir foi en*
☠ *faire les magasins* = to go shopping
— *un store* = a shade.

STOREKEEPER (n) *commerçant, -e* : storekeepers are victims of constant robbery = *les commerçants sont constamment victimes de vols* = shopkeeper.

STORK (n) *cigogne* (f) : did the stork bring you ? = *est-ce que c'est la cigogne qui t'a apporté ?*

STORM (n) *orage* (m) : there was a terrible storm last night = *il y a eu un orage terrible hier soir* ⓪ tempest = *tempête*, hurricane = *ouragan*, thunder = *tonnerre*, lightning = *éclairs*
to raise a storm = *piquer une crise* : he raised a storm when he got the bill = *il a piqué une crise quand il a reçu la facture* ⓪ to make a stink = *faire du grabuge*
storm troops = *troupes d'assaut*
to take stg by storm = 1/ *faire un malheur* : the comedian took the public by storm = *le comique a fait un malheur* ≠ to lay an egg = *se casser la gueule* 2/ *prendre d'assaut* : the people took the Bastille by storm = *le peuple a pris la Bastille d'assaut*
(to talk) up a storm = *(discuter) à bâtons rompus* : we talked up a storm last night = *nous avons discuté à bâtons rompus hier soir*
to weather the storm = *traverser la tempête* ⓪ to be over the hump = *avoir doublé le cap.*

STORM (to, -ed) *faire de l'orage* : it stormed all day = *il a fait de l'orage toute la journée* ⓪ to rain = *pleuvoir*
to storm out of (a meeting) = *quitter (une réunion) comme un ouragan* ⓪ to stamp out of = *sortir en trépignant de.*

STORMY (adj, -ier, -iest) *orageux, -euse* : a stormy relationship = *des relations orageuses* ⓪ tumultuous = *tumultueux*
a stormy meeting = *une réunion houleuse.*

STORY (n, -ies) 1/ *étage* (m) : the building has five stories = *l'immeuble a cinq étages* = the building has five floors ☠ *il habite au deuxième étage* = he lives on the second floor
2/ *histoire* (f) : tell me a story = *raconte-moi une histoire*, shaggy-dog story = *histoire-fleuve* ⓪ tale = *conte*, storybook = *recueil d'histoires*
so the story goes = *d'après ce qu'on dit* : when she was a teenager, she heard the voice of God, so the story goes = *d'après ce qu'on dit, elle a entendu la voix de Dieu quand elle était adolescente*
that's another/a different story = *c'est une autre histoire*
what's the story ? = *de quoi s'agit-il ? :* I heard there's a new birth control pill, what's the story ? = *j'ai entendu parler d'une nouvelle pilule contraceptive, de quoi s'agit-il ?*
when the story breaks = *quand l'affaire éclatera* ⓪ when this gets out = *quand ça se saura*
☠ *c'est une fille à histoires* = nothing's ever simple with her
— *histoire de rire* = just for laughs
— *étudier l'histoire* = to study history
— *le plus (beau) de l'histoire, c'est que ...* = what's extraordinary about the whole thing is ...
— *quelle histoire !* = what a fuss !
— *avoir des histoires avec (la police)* = to be in trouble with (the police)
— *c'est l'histoire de quelques jours* = it's a question of a few days
— *qu'est-ce que c'est que cette histoire ?* = what's this jazz about ?
3/ *reportage* (m) : she did a good story on children in blue films = *elle a fait un bon reportage sur les films porno avec des enfants* ⓪ coverage = *couverture*, paper = *papier.*

STOUT (adj, -er, -est) *costaud* : a stout guy = *un type costaud* ⓪ heavy = *lourd*, plump = *rondouillard* ≠ slender = *élancé* ☠ *costaud en maths* = good at math.

STOVE (n) *cuisinière* (f) : why don't you clean the stove ? = *pourquoi ne nettoyez-vous pas la cuisinière ?* ⓪ grill = *gril* ☠ → cook.

STOWAWAY (n) *passager, -ère clandestin, -e* : a stowaway was found in the lifeboat = *on a trouvé un passager clandestin dans le bateau de sauvetage* ⓪ intruder = *intrus.*

STRAIGHT (n) *hétéro* (m, f) : a lot of straights in New York are into S-M = *il y a pas mal d'hétéros à New York qui donnent dans le sadomasochisme* ≠ gay = *homosexuel*, homo = ←
to follow the straight and narrow = *suivre le droit chemin* ≠ to go astray = *sortir du droit chemin.*

STRAIGHT (adj, -er, -est) 1/ *droit, -e* : a straight line = *une ligne droite* ≠ crooked = *sinueux*
2/ *hétéro* : his two brothers are gay but he's straight = *ses deux frères sont homosexuels, mais il est hétéro* ≠ queer = *pédé*
3/ *droit, -e* : he's always been very straight in all our business transactions = *il a toujours été très droit au cours de nos transactions commerciales* ⓪ up-front = *clair et net* ≠ underhand = *fourbe* ☠ → right

for (six hours/days) straight = *pendant (six heures/jours) de suite* ⓪ consecutive = *consécutif*
to keep a straight face = *garder son sérieux* ⓪ to keep an impassive face = *garder un visage impassible*
a straight answer = *une réponse franche* : why don't you give me a straight answer for a change ? = *pourquoi ne me faites-vous pas une réponse franche, pour changer ?* ≠ to give s.o. a song and a dance = *raconter des salades à qqn*
straight hair = *cheveux raides* ≠ curly hair = *cheveux bouclés*
straight man = *faire-valoir* : Harpo was Groucho's straight man = *Harpo était le faire-valoir de Groucho*
a straight Scotch = *un whisky sec* : I'd like a straight Scotch = *je voudrais un whisky sec* = a neat Scotch (GB).

STRAIGHT (adv) *droit* : stand straight ! = *tiens-toi droit !* ☠ → right

---

I can't think straight = *je n'arrive pas à mettre de l'ordre dans mes idées*
get this straight ! = *dites-le-vous bien !* : I said no and I mean no, get this straight ! = *j'ai dit non, et c'est non, dites-le-vous bien !* ⓪ get it clear ! = *comprenez bien ça !*
give it to me straight ! = *dites-le-moi sans détour !* ⓪ don't beat around the bush = *ne tournez pas autour du pot*
to go straight (home) = *rentrer directement (à la maison)*

to go straight = *rentrer dans le droit chemin* : he decided to go straight after a year in prison = *après un an de prison, il a décidé de rentrer dans le droit chemin* ⓪ to go astray = *sortir du droit chemin*
let's get things straight ! = *mettons les choses au clair !* ⓪ let's set the record straight ! = *réglons tout ça !*
let me set you straight (he was the one who hit you, not me) = *détrompez-vous (c'est lui qui vous a frappé, pas moi)*

to play it straight (down the line) = *jouer franc jeu* ⓪ to lay it on the line = *ne pas mâcher ses mots*
straight ahead = *tout droit* : the museum's straight ahead = *pour le musée, c'est tout droit*
straight away = *illico* : do it straight away = *faites-le illico* ⓪ at once = *tout de suite*
straight out/off = *tout de go* : she said straight out she was a hooker = *elle a dit tout de go qu'elle était putain* ⓪ point-blank = *à brûle-pourpoint*.

STRAIGHTEN (to, -ed) **to straighten out** = 1/ *mettre en ordre* : I have to straighten out a lot of things before I can take a few days off = *il faut que je mette un certain nombre de choses en ordre avant de prendre quelques jours de congé* ⓪ to settle = *régler* 2/ *remettre les pendules à l'heure* : I'm not going to sign his crummy contract and I'll straighten him out = *je ne vais pas signer son contrat pourri et je vais remettre les pendules à l'heure*
to straighten up (a room/the house) = *remettre de l'ordre dans (une pièce/la maison)* ⓪ to tidy up = *ranger*.

STRAIGHTFORWARD (adj) *sans détour* (stg), *très direct, -e* : to give a straightforward answer = *faire une réponse sans détour*, she's always been straightforward = *elle a toujours été très directe* ⓪ outspoken = *qui a son franc-parler*.

STRAIGHT-FROM-THE-SHOULDER (adj) *sans ambages* : a straight-from-the-shoulder answer = *une réponse sans ambages* ≠ devious = *tortueux*.

STRAIN (n) **to put a (great) strain on** = *mettre à rude épreuve* : the lack of money put a great strain on their marriage = *le manque d'argent a mis leur ménage à rude épreuve*.

STRAIN (to, -ed) *(se) froisser (un muscle)* : she strained herself picking up the box = *elle s'est froissé un muscle en ramassant la boîte* ⓪ to pull = *claquer*

don't strain yourself ! = *surtout, ne te foule pas !* ☠ → to crease.

STRAINED (adj) *tendu, -e* : a strained relationship = *des relations tendues* = tense.

STRAINER (n) *passoire (f)* : a strainer for spaghetti = *une passoire pour égoutter les spaghetti*.

STRAIT (n) *détroit (m)* : the Strait of Gilbraltar = *le détroit de Gibraltar*
the Strait of Dover = *le Pas-de-Calais*.

STRAITJACKET (n) *camisole (f) de force* : they put him in a straitjacket = *ils lui ont mis la camisole de force* ⓪ nuthouse = *maison de fous*.

STRAITLACED (adj) *collet monté* : a straitlaced family = *une famille collet monté* ⓪ priggish = *bégueule*, uptight = *coincé*.

STRAND (to, -ed) **to be stranded** = *être en rade* : stranded in Paris without a passport = *en rade à Paris sans passeport*.

STRANGE (adj, -r, -st) *étrange* : what a strange thing to say ! = *que c'est étrange de dire ça !* ⓪ peculiar = *curieux* ≠ normal = ←.

STRANGER (n) *inconnu, -e* : he's a perfect stranger = *c'est un parfait inconnu* ≠ acquaintance = *connaissance* ☠ *une (donnée) inconnue* = an unknown factor
— *un étranger* = a foreigner.

STRANGLE (to, -d) *étrangler* : she strangled her baby = *elle a étranglé son bébé* ① to choke = *étouffer* ☠ *s'étrangler en mangeant* = to gag on one's food.

STRAP (n) *courroie (f), bandoulière (f)* (bag), *bretelle (f)* : the strap of my bag/my bra is broken = *la courroie/la bandoulière de mon sac est cassée/la bretelle de mon soutien-gorge est cassée* ① belt = *ceinture,* whip = *fouet.*

STRAP (to, -ped) **to be strapped** = *être à sec* : I'm strapped this month = *je suis à sec ce mois-ci* → POOR.

STRAPPING (adj) *mastoc* : a strapping guy = *un type mastoc* ① stocky = *trapu.*

STRATAGEM (n) *stratagème (m)* : he used a stratagem to get into the house = *il a usé d'un stratagème pour pénétrer dans la maison.*

STRATEGIC (adj) *stratégique* : strategic weapons = *armes stratégiques.*

STRATEGY (n, -ies) *stratégie (f)* : you chose the wrong strategy = *vous avez choisi la mauvaise stratégie* ① stratagem = *stratagème,* ploy = *biais.*

STRAW (n) *paille (f)* : to drink with a straw = *boire avec une paille* ① hay = *foin*
to clutch at straws = *se raccrocher à toutes les branches*
to draw straws = *tirer à la courte paille*
☠ *sur la paille* = stone-broke
— *une paille !* = peanuts !
— *il voit la paille qui est dans l'œil de son voisin et ne voit pas la poutre dans le sien* = it's the pot calling the kettle black.

STRAW (n) *paille (f)* : to drink with a straw = *boire avec une paille* ① hay = *foin*
straw man = *homme de paille* ① figurehead = *potiche*
straw mattress = *paillasse.*

STRAWBERRY (n, -ies) *fraise (f)* : wild strawberries = *fraises des bois* ① cherry = *cerise*
strawberry blonde = *quelqu'un qui a les cheveux d'un blond vénitien*
☠ *va aux fraises !* = go fly a kite !
— *arrête de ramener ta fraise* = don't stick your two cents in
— *envoyer qqn aux fraises* = to send s.o. packing.

STRAY (adj) *errant, -e* : a stray dog = *un chien errant* ① lost = *perdu.*

STRAY (to, -ed) *faire des écarts* : after two years of marriage, he's beginning to stray = *après deux ans de mariage, il commence à faire des écarts*
to stray from (the subject/the main road) = *s'écarter du (sujet)/de (la route principale).*

STREAK (n) *mèche (f)* : yellow streaks in her hair = *des mèches jaunes dans les cheveux*
to be in a winning ≠ losing streak = *être dans une*
bonne ≠ mauvaise passe
to have a (mean/stubborn) streak = *avoir une certaine propension à être (méchant/têtu)*
a streak of good ≠ bad luck = *une série de coups de pot ≠ de déveines.*

STREAM (n) *ruisseau (m)* : we waded across the stream = *nous avons pataugé en traversant le ruisseau* ① river = *rivière*
a stream of (cars) = *un flot de (voitures)* → MANY
a stream of consciousness = *une association d'idées*
☠ *sortir du ruisseau* = to get out of the gutter.

STREAM (to, -ed) *entrer à flots* : sun streamed into the room = *le soleil est entré à flots dans la chambre.*

STREAMLINE (to, -d) *rationaliser* : they're streamlining the organization = *ils rationalisent l'organisation* ① to modernize = *moderniser* ☠ *tenter de rationaliser* = to try to rationalize.

STREAMLINED (adj) 1/ *aux lignes pures* : a streamlined car = *une voiture aux lignes pures* ① sophisticated = *sophistiqué* 2/ *rationalisé, -e* : streamlined methods = *des méthodes rationalisées* ① modernized = *modernisé.*

STREET (n) *rue (f)* : to cross the street = *traverser la rue* ① streetlight = *réverbère*
main street = *rue principale/grand-rue*
street fighting = *combats de rue*
street floor = *rez-de-chaussée*
the man ≠ woman in the street = *l'homme ≠ la femme de la rue*
to walk the streets = *faire le trottoir/le tapin* ① to be on the game = *se prostituer*
☠ *les ouvriers sont descendus dans la rue* = workers demonstrated
— *c'est à deux rues d'ici* = it's two blocks further
— *être à la rue* = to be homeless
— *ça court les rues* = it's a dime a dozen.

STREETCAR (n) *tramway (m)* : there aren't any more streetcars in New York = *il n'y a plus de tramways à New York* = tram (GB) ① trolley = *trolleybus.*

STREET SMART (n) *gosse (m, f) à l'école de la rue* : a lot of street smarts are better armed for the realities of life than sheltered kids = *les gosses à l'école de la rue sont souvent mieux armés pour affronter les réalités de la vie que les enfants protégés.*

STREET-SMART (adj) *à l'école de la rue* : street-smart, he's already a wheeler-dealer = *à l'école de la rue, c'est déjà un magouilleur.*

STREETWALKER (n) *péripatéticienne (f)* : there are many streetwalkers in Times Square = *il y a beaucoup de péripatéticiennes à Times Square* ① whore = *pute,* lady of the night = *belle de nuit.*

STREETWISE (adj) *à l'école de la rue* : kids born in slums become streetwise very quickly = *les gosses nés dans des taudis sont très vite à l'école de la rue.*

STRENGTH (n) *force* (f) : the strength of the economy = *la force de l'économie* ⓪ power = *puissance*
to get one's strength back = *recouvrer ses forces*
on the strength of = *sur la foi de* : he was hired on the strength of his college record = *il a été engagé sur la foi de ses diplômes* ⓪ on the basis of = *sur la base de* ☠ → force.

STRENGTHEN (to, -ed) *renforcer* : that strengthened our position = *ça a renforcé notre position* ⓪ to consolidate = *consolider*.

STRENUOUS (adj) *exténuant, -e* : strenuous work = *un travail exténuant* ⓪ exhausting = *épuisant*, laborious = *laborieux*.

STRESS (n, -es) *stress* (m) : noise can cause stress = *le bruit peut être une cause de stress* ⓪ tension = ←
to lay stress on = *mettre l'accent sur* : he lays no stress on good manners = *il ne met pas l'accent sur les bonnes manières* ⓪ to call attention to = *attirer l'attention sur* ≠ to play down = *faire peu de cas de*.

STRESS (to, -ed) *insister sur* : to stress the need for new contraception = *insister sur le besoin d'une nouvelle contraception* ⓪ to underscore = *souligner*.

STRETCH (n, -es) *étendue* (f) : a long stretch of beach = *une longue étendue de plage*
at a stretch = *d'affilée* : she typed for ten hours at a stretch = *elle a tapé à la machine dix heures d'affilée* ⓪ in one go = *d'un seul coup*
by no stretch of the imagination can I (picture him doing a striptease) = *même avec un gros effort d'imagination, je ne peux pas (l'imaginer en train de faire un strip-tease)*
to do a (five-year) stretch = *purger une peine de (cinq ans)* ⓪ a sentence of = *une condamnation de*
the last/final stretch = *la dernière ligne droite*.

STRETCH (to, -ed) *(s')étirer* : get up and stretch ! = *levez-vous et étirez-vous !* ⓪ to extend = *s'étendre*

to stretch the truth/the rules = *s'arranger avec la vérité/les règles*
you're stretching it ! = *tu charries !* ⓪ you're going too far ! = *tu y vas un peu fort !*
to stretch for = *s'étendre sur* : the beach stretches for miles = *la plage s'étend sur des kilomètres*
to stretch out = *s'étendre* : I'm tired and want to stretch out for a while = *je suis fatigué et je veux m'étendre un moment* ⓪ to lie down = *s'allonger* ☠ → to extend
to stretch over = *durer (pendant)* : their love stretched over ten years = *leur amour a duré (pendant) dix ans*.

STRETCHER (n) *civière* (f), *brancard* (m) : he was carried out on a stretcher = *on l'a emmené sur un brancard/une civière* ⓪ accident = ← ☠ *ruer dans les brancards* = to kick up.

STRICT (adj, -er, -est) *strict, -e* : strict orders/parents = *des ordres/parents stricts* ⓪ severe = *sévère* ≠ lax = *laxiste*
to be strict about = *être strict sur* : the boss is very strict about our coming on time = *le patron est très strict sur la ponctualité*
in strict confidence = *en confidence*
☠ *le strict nécessaire* = the bare minimum.

STRICTLY (adv) *strictement* : strictly forbidden = *strictement interdit* ⓪ absolutely = *absolument*
strictly speaking (she isn't a hooker) = *(ce n'est pas une putain) à proprement parler* ⓪ roughly speaking = *grosso modo*.

STRIDE (n) **to take stg in one's stride** = *prendre qqch avec sérénité* : she took the loss of her job in her stride = *elle a pris la perte de son emploi avec sérénité* ⓪ to resign oneself to = *se résigner à*.

STRIFE (n) *discorde* (f) : there's a lot of strife in the party = *il y a pas mal de discorde au sein du parti* = discord ⓪ conflict = *conflit*.

STRIKE (n) *grève* (f) : the unions called a strike for the following week = *les syndicats ont appelé à la grève la semaine suivante*

close ≠ **open shop** = *usine où les syndicats ont* ≠ *n'ont pas de monopole d'embauche*	faim	*grève* ⓪ scab = *jaune*
to cross the picket line = *franchir le piquet de grève*	**lockout** = *lock-out*	**sympathy strike** = *grève de solidarité/de soutien* = **sympathetic strike**
general strike = *grève générale*	**on strike** = *en grève*	**union** = *syndicat*
to go on strike = *se mettre en grève*	**sit-down strike** = *grève sur le tas*	**to walk out** = *débrayer*
hunger strike = *grève de la*	**sit-in** = ←	**wildcat strike** = *grève sauvage*
	slowdown strike = *grève perlée* = go-slow (GB)	**work stoppage** = *arrêt de travail*
	a striker = *un gréviste*	**work-to-rule** = *grève du zèle*.
	strikebreaker = *briseur de*	

STRIKE (to, struck, struck or stricken) **1/** *faire (la) grève* : the workers are planning to strike = *les ouvriers envisagent de faire (la) grève*
2/ *frapper* : did he ever strike you ? = *est-ce qu'il t'a jamais frappé ?* → TO HIT ☠ → to hit

it strikes me that (they're not very happy) = j'ai l'impression qu'(ils ne sont pas très heureux) ⓪ it seems to me that = *il me semble que*	how does it strike you ? = *qu'est-ce que tu en penses ?* ⓪ how about it ? = *qu'en dites-vous ?*
to be struck by (her beauty/a disease) = *être frappé par (sa beauté/la maladie)* to strike for (better pay) = *faire la grève pour (obtenir un meilleur salaire)* to strike on = *trouver* : they struck on a new means of contraception = *ils ont trouvé un nouveau moyen de contraception* = to hit on ☠ → to find to strike out = 1/ *rayer* : strike her name out =	*rayez son nom* ⓪ to X out = *raturer* ☠ *rayer une table* = to scratch a table — *rayer qqn/une ville (de la carte)* = to eliminate s.o./to wipe out a city (from the map) — *rayer de sa mémoire* = to blot out 2/ *faire chou blanc* : he tried to pick up my sister but he struck out = *il a essayé de draguer ma sœur mais il a fait chou blanc* ⓪ to bomb = *foirer.*

STRIKEBREAKER (n) *briseur, -euse de grève.*

STRIKER (n) *gréviste (m, f)* : the strikers won't be paid = *les grévistes ne seront pas payés.*

STRIKING (adj) *frappant, -e* : a striking similarity = *une similitude frappante* ⓪ breathtaking = *à vous couper le souffle,* startling = *sidérant.*

STRING (n) *ficelle (f)* : he tied the package with string = *il a attaché le paquet avec de la ficelle* ⓪ cord = *grosse ficelle,* twine = *ficelle résistante*
to keep s.o. on the string = *faire languir qqn* : he's been keeping her on the string for years = *il la fait languir depuis des années* ⓪ to keep s.o. on tenterhooks = *tenir qqn en haleine*
to pull strings = *jouer de ses relations* : he pulled strings to get a construction license = *il a joué de ses relations pour obtenir un permis de construire* ⓪ to know the right people = *avoir le bras long*
string beans = *haricots verts* ⓪ lima beans = *haricots blancs*
a string of pearls = *un collier de perles*
a string of (sex shops on the street) = *une suite dè (sex-shops dans la rue)* → MANY
the strings (of an orchestra/a guitar) = *les cordes (d'un orchestre/d'une guitare)*
with no strings attached = *sans conditions* : his offer was with no strings attached = *il m'a fait une offre sans conditions*
☠ *les ficelles du métier* = the tricks of the trade
— *connaître les ficelles* = to know what's what/to know the ropes
— *tenir les ficelles* = to run the show.

STRING (to, strung, strung) **to string along** = *faire mariner* : they've been talking about marriage for years, he keeps stringing her along = *ils parlent mariage depuis des années et il ne cesse de la faire mariner*
to string up = *pendre haut et court* : he was strung up at dawn = *il a été pendu haut et court à l'aube.*

STRINGENT (adj) **stringent laws/rules** = *des lois/des règles rigoureuses* ⓪ severe = *sévère.*

STRINGER (n) *pigiste (m, f)* : he's a stringer for the "Times" = *il est pigiste au « Times »* ⓪ free lance = *quelqu'un qui travaille en free-lance.*

STRIP (to, -ped) 1/ *se mettre à poil* : he stripped in the subway = *il s'est mis à poil dans le métro* ⓪ to peel = *se ficher à poil* 2/ *tout rafler dans* : the robbers stripped the apartment = *les voleurs ont tout raflé dans l'appartement* ⓪ to break in = *entrer par effraction*
to strip s.o. of (his/her powers) = *dépouiller qqn de (ses pouvoirs)* ⓪ to divest = *révoquer.*

STRIPE (n) 1/ *raie (f),* rayure *(f)* : white and blue stripes = *des raies/des rayures blanches et bleues* ☠ *raie (cheveux)* = part (hair) 2/ *galon (m)* : the soldier got his first stripes = *le soldat a reçu ses premiers galons* ☠ *prendre du galon* = to be promoted.

STRIPED (adj) *rayé, -e* : a striped shirt = *une chemise rayée* ⓪ checkered = *à carreaux.*

STRIPPER (n) *strip-teaseur, -euse* : male strippers are the thing = *les strip-teaseurs, c'est super.*

STRIPTEASE (n) *strip-tease (m)* : Pigalle offers far-out striptease shows = *à Pigalle, on trouve des spectacles de strip-tease déments* ⓪ nudie show = *revue de nu.*

STRIVE TO (to, strove, striven) *s'efforcer de* : we're striving to find a solution = *nous nous efforçons de trouver une solution* ⓪ to try to = *essayer de.*

STROKE (n) *attaque (f)* : he had his first stroke at forty = *il a eu sa première attaque à quarante ans* ⓪ heart attack = *crise cardiaque*
a stroke of genius = *un trait de génie*
a stroke of luck = *un coup de chance*
on the stroke of (ten) = *sur le coup de (dix heures)* ⓪ on the dot (of ten) = *à (dix heures) sonnantes*
☠ → attack.

STROKE (to, -d) *caresser* : to stroke a cat = *caresser un chat* ☠ → to caress.

STROLL (n) *balade (f)* : a stroll in Central Park = *une balade à Central Park* ⓪ hike = *randonnée*
to go for a stroll = *faire une balade/aller se balader* ⓪ to get some air = *prendre l'air.*

STROLL (to, -ed) *se balader* : we strolled along on Fifth Avenue = *nous nous sommes baladés sur la 5e Avenue* ⓪ to meander = *vadrouiller.*

STRONG (adj, -er, -est) *fort, -e* : a strong guy/coffee = *un type/un café fort* ⊙ powerful = *puissant*
strong language = *un langage violent*
strong as an ox = *fort comme un Turc*
☒ *c'est plus fort que moi* = I can't help it
— *la musique est trop forte* = the music's too loud
— *une forte augmentation* = a hefty increase
— *être fort en maths* = to be good at math
— *une femme forte/un homme fort* = a big woman/man
— *un fort en thème* = an egghead.

STRONG (adv) **to be still going strong** = *être encore bien portant* : he's no spring chicken, but he's still going strong = *il n'est plus tout jeune, mais il est toujours bien portant* ⊙ to be as old as the hills = *être vieux comme le monde*
to come on strong = 1/ *faire une forte impression* : he went for the interview and came on strong = *il a fait une forte impression au cours de l'interview* 2/ *y aller fort* : he tried to pick me up and he came on strong = *il a essayé de me draguer et il y est allé fort* ⊙ to overdo it = *en faire des tonnes.*

STRONG-ARM (adj) **strong-arm methods** = *la méthode forte.*

STRONGHOLD (n) *fief (m)* : the South is the stronghold of the Ku Klux Klan = *le Sud est le fief du Ku Klux Klan* ☒ *ce restaurant est son fief* = this restaurant is his hangout.

STRONGLY (adv) *fortement* : he strongly advised me to see a doctor = *il m'a fortement conseillé de voir un médecin*
I feel very strongly about it = *j'y attache une grande importance* ≠ I don't care about it = *cela m'est égal.*

STRONG-MINDED (adj) *qui sait ce qu'il veut* : he's a strong-minded guy = *c'est un type qui sait ce qu'il veut* ≠ weak-minded = *faible.*

STRONG-WILLED (adj) *qui a de la volonté* : he's stubborn and strong-willed = *il est têtu et il a de la volonté* ⊙ willful = *volontaire.*

STRUCTURAL (adj) *structurel, -elle* : structural changes = *des changements structurels.*

STRUCTURE (n) *structure (f)* : the structure of modern economy = *la structure de l'économie moderne* ⊙ organization = *organisation.*

STRUGGLE (n) *lutte (f)* : it's been a hell of a struggle to get him to agree = *ça a été une sacrée lutte pour obtenir son accord* ⊙ undertaking = *entreprise* ☒ *la lutte* = wrestling.

STRUGGLE (to, -d) *lutter* : most of us struggle to survive = *la plupart d'entre nous luttent pour survivre*
to struggle to = *se battre pour* : we have to struggle to make a living = *il faut se battre pour gagner sa vie* ⊙ to strive to = *s'efforcer de*
to struggle with (a problem/the cops) = *se battre*

contre *(un problème/les flics)* ⊙ to wrestle with = *être aux prises avec.*

STUBBORN (adj) *têtu, -e* : stop being so stubborn ! = *ne soyez pas si têtu !* ⊙ pigheaded = *tête de lard*, to stick to one's guns = *ne pas en démordre*
to be as stubborn as a mule = *être têtu comme une mule/avoir une tête de mule.*

STUCK-UP (adj) *snob* : a stuck-up family = *une famille snob* ⊙ conceited = *prétentieux.*

STUD (n) *étalon (m)* : he's not big on brains but he's a good stud = *il n'est pas terrible intellectuellement, mais c'est un bon étalon* ⊙ a great fuck = *un super-baiseur* ≠ eunuch = *eunuque.*

STUDENT (n) *étudiant, -e* : medical/law student = *étudiant en médecine/droit* ⊙ pupil = *élève* ≠ teacher = *professeur*
student unrest = *agitation estudiantine.*

STUDIO (n) *studio (m)* : my sister lives in a studio = *ma sœur habite un studio* ⊙ loft = ←.

STUDIOUS (adj) *studieux, -euse* : a studious child = *un enfant studieux* ⊙ assiduous = *assidu.*

STUDY (n, -ies) 1/ *étude (f)* : studies have been made of women having children after forty = *on a fait des études sur les femmes qui ont des enfants après quarante ans* ☒ *une étude d'avocat* = a lawyer's office
— *faire ses études* = to go to school
2/ *cabinet (m) de travail, bureau (m)* : he works mornings in his study = *il travaille le matin dans son bureau/cabinet de travail* ⊙ library = *bibliothèque* ☒ → office.

STUDY (to, -ied) *étudier, faire des études de* : my son's studying engineering = *mon fils fait des études d'ingénierie/étudie l'ingénierie* ⊙ to brush up = *réviser*
to study for (a test) = *préparer (un examen)* ⊙ to burn the midnight oil = *travailler tard dans la nuit.*

STUFF (n inv) *trucs (m pl)* : what's this stuff on the table ? = *qu'est-ce que c'est que ces trucs sur la table ?*, I bought a lot of stuff at the flea market = *j'ai acheté pas mal de trucs au marché aux puces* = a lot of things ☒ → thing
do your stuff ! = *montre ce que tu sais faire !*
to know one's stuff = *connaître son affaire* : he's a lawyer and he knows his stuff = *il est avocat et il connaît son affaire* ⊙ to have the knowhow = *avoir du savoir-faire*
that's the stuff ! = *bien dit !/bien fait !*
that's the stuff (actors) are made of = *voilà l'étoffe dont sont faits (les acteurs)*
what's all this stuff about (her taking drugs) ? = *qu'est-ce que c'est que cette histoire (il paraît qu'elle se drogue) ?*

STUFF (to, -ed) *bourrer* (cushions), *empailler* (dead animals), *farcir* (turkey, etc.)
to stuff oneself = *s'empiffrer* : you'd lose weight if you stopped stuffing yourself = *tu maigrirais si tu arrêtais de*

t'empiffrer ① to gorge oneself = *se gaver*
to stuff stg into (one's pocket) = *fourrer qqch dans (sa poche)*
to be stuffed = *être gavé* : I ate too much, I'm stuffed = *j'ai trop mangé, je suis gavé* ① I'm full = *je cale*, I'm satiated = *je suis rassasié*
to be stuffed with = *être bourré de* : the drawer's stuffed with a lot of junk = *le tiroir est bourré de saloperies* ① to be jam-packed = *être plein à craquer* ☠ *il faut se le farcir !* = you have to be able to put up with him !
— *bourrer le crâne à qqn* = to brainwash s.o.
— *je me suis farci tout le boulot* = I did all the work.

STUFFING (n) *farce (f)* : the stuffing was delicious = *la farce était délicieuse* ☠ → farce.

STUFFY (adj, -ier, -iest) **1/** *vieux jeu* : what a stuffy guy ! = *ce qu'il est vieux jeu, ce type !* ① straitlaced = *collet monté*, boring = *ennuyeux* **2/** *mal aéré, -e* : a stuffy room = *une pièce mal aérée*.

STUMBLE (to, -d) *trébucher* : I was a little tipsy and stumbled down the stairs = *j'étais un peu éméché et j'ai trébuché en descendant l'escalier* ① to trip = *buter*
to stumble on/upon = *tomber sur* : we stumbled on/upon a charming little restaurant = *nous sommes tombés sur un petit restaurant charmant*
stumbling block = *pierre d'achoppement*.

STUMP (to, -ed) **1/** *faire une tournée électorale* : he's stumping the East before the primaries = *il fait une tournée électorale dans l'Est avant les primaires* ① to campaign = *faire campagne* **2/** *rendre perplexe* : the police are stumped by the case = *l'affaire rend la police perplexe* ① to baffle = *dérouter*
I'm stumped ! = *je sèche !* ≠ I get it ! = *je saisis !*

STUN (to, -ned) *abasourdir* : the news of their divorce stunned me = *la nouvelle de leur divorce m'a abasourdi* ① to startle = *sidérer*.

STUNNING (adj) **1/** *abasourdissant, -e* : a stunning victory = *une victoire abasourdissante* ① impressive = *impressionnant* **2/** *sublime* : what a stunning woman ! = *quelle femme sublime !* ① gorgeous = *splendide*.

STUNT (n) *coup (m) d'épate* : that was just a publicity stunt = *ce n'était qu'un coup d'épate publicitaire*, it was just a stunt to get attention = *ce n'était qu'un coup d'épate pour attirer l'attention* ① act = *numéro*
stunt man/woman = *cascadeur/cascadeuse* ① daredevil = *casse-cou*.

STUPEFY (to, -ied) *stupéfier* : his language stupefied us = *son langage nous a stupéfiés* ① to dumbfound = *souffler* **STUPEFYING** (adj) *stupéfiant, -e* : stupefying intelligence = *une intelligence stupéfiante* ① surprising = *surprenant* **STUPEFACTION** (n) *stupéfaction (f)*.

STUPENDOUS (adj) *époustouflant, -e* : a stupendous salary = *un salaire époustouflant* → WONDERFUL.

STUPID (adj) *stupide* : a stupid answer/person = *une réponse/personne stupide* ≠ intelligent = ←

—————— GROUP : STUPID = STUPIDE ——————

to be asinine = *être tarte*	*benêt*	*un balai/comme la lune*
an ass = *un con*	**a fool** = *un imbécile*	**a numskull** = *une cruche* = **a**
an asshole = *un connard*	**to be foolish** = *être bête*	**schlemiel**
to be a birdbrain = *avoir une cervelle d'oiseau*	**a goof** = *une bécasse*	**a schlep** = *un crétin*
a blockhead = *un cornichon*	**to be goofy** = *être bébête*	**a schlimazel** = *une andouille*
a boob = *un ahuri*	**a goon** = *un niais*	**a schmoe** = *une andouille*
a clot = *un ballot*	**a half-wit** = *un demeuré*	**a schmuck** = *le dernier des cons*
to be dead from the neck up = *être bête à manger du foin/en tenir une couche*	**an idiot** = *un idiot*	**a schnook** = *un schnock*
	to be idiotic = *être complètement idiot*	**a shithead** = *un trouduc*
a deadhead = *un abruti*	**an ignoramus** = *un ignare*	**to be silly** = *être sot*
dense = *bouché*	**an imbecile** = *un imbécile*	**a silly goose** = *une bécasse*
a dimwit = *une nouille*	**a jackass** = *un couillon*	**to be simple-minded** = *être simple d'esprit*
a dolt = *une andouille*	**a jerk** = *un crétin*	**a simpleton** = *quelqu'un de simplet*
a dope = *une gourde*	**to be jerky** = *être crétin*	
to be dumb = *être bête*	**a lamebrain** = *un âne bâté*	**a stupid idiot** = *une espèce d'idiot*
to be as dumb as they come = *être bête comme ses pieds*	**a moron** = *une patate*	**to be a bit thick** = *être un peu bouché*
a dumbbell = *un ballot*	**a nincompoop** = *un nigaud*	**a twirp** (GB) = *un abruti*.
a dummy = *une banane*	**a ninny** = *un bêta, une bêtasse*	
a dunce = *un cancre*	**a nitwit** = *un corniaud*	
to be feeble-minded = *être*	**not to know one's ass from one's elbow/from a hole in the ground** = *être con comme*	

STUPIDITY (n inv) *stupidité (f)* : what stupidity ! = *quelle stupidité !* ① foolishness = *bêtise*.

STUPIDLY (adv) *stupidement* : to act stupidly = *agir stupidement*.

STUPOR (n) *stupeur (f)* : in a state of stupor = *dans un état de stupeur* ⓪ numbness = *torpeur.*

STURDY (adj, -ier, -iest) *robuste* : a sturdy construction = *une construction robuste* ⓪ strong = *fort* ☠ → robust.

STUTTER (to, -ed) *bégayer* : her younger son stutters = *son plus jeune fils bégaie* ⓪ to stammer = *bredouiller.*

STYLE (n) *style (m)* : she has a lot of style = *elle a beaucoup de style,* a writer's style = *le style d'un écrivain*
to do things in style = *faire les choses bien/avec classe* ≠ to skimp = *lésiner*
to cramp s.o.'s style = *couper les moyens à qqn* : he was trying to pick up the broad and his brother was cramping his style = *il essayait de draguer la fille et son frère lui coupait tous ses moyens*
to live in style = *vivre sur un grand pied* ⓪ to live high on the hog = *mener grand train*
☠ *meubles de style* = period furniture.

STYLISH (adj) *qui a du chic* : stylish clothes = *des vêtements qui ont du chic* ⓪ fashionable = *à la mode* ≠ unstylish = *qui n'a pas de chic.*

STYLIST (n) *styliste (m, f)* : a stylist for children = *un styliste pour enfants.*

STYMIE (to, -d) *contrarier* : our projects were stymied = *nos projets ont été contrariés* = our projects were frustrated ⓪ to thwart = *entraver* ☠ → to frustrate.

SUAVE (adj, -r, -st) *suave* : suave manners = *des manières suaves* ⓪ put-on = *affecté.*

SUB (n) = SUBMARINE.

SUB (to, -bed) *assurer l'intérim* : she's subbing for our regular teacher = *elle assure l'intérim de notre professeur habituel* ⓪ to substitute = *remplacer.*

SUBCONSCIOUS (n) *subconscient (m)* : who understands what goes on in our subconscious ? = *qui comprend ce qui se passe dans notre subconscient ?*

SUBCONSCIOUS (adj) *subconscient, -e* : subconscious desire = *désir subconscient* ⓪ unconscious = *inconscient.*

SUBDIVIDE (to, -d) *(se) subdiviser* : the property will be subdivided into small lots = *la propriété sera subdivisée en petits lots* ≠ to multiply = *(se) multiplier.*

SUBDUE (to, -d) *maîtriser* : to subdue a prisoner = *maîtriser un prisonnier* ⓪ to subjugate = *subjuguer*
to be subdued = *s'être bien calmé* : he's more subdued since his wife left him = *il s'est bien calmé depuis que sa femme l'a plaqué* ☠ → to master.

SUBJECT (n) 1/ *sujet (m)* : the subject of the film/the book = *le sujet du film/du livre* ☠ *sujet de mécontentement* = cause for displeasure — *un mauvais sujet* = a bad lot
2/ *matière (f)* : I took five subjects this year = *j'ai pris*

cinq *matières cette année* ⓪ course = *cours* ☠ → matter
3/ *sujet (m)* : the subject of the sentence = *le sujet de la phrase* ≠ object = *complément d'objet*
4/ *sujet (m)* : to rule over one's subjects = *régner sur ses sujets* ⓪ national = *ressortissant*
let's get back to the subject = *revenons à nos moutons*
(food is her) favorite subject = *(la bouffe est son) sujet de conversation préféré*
stop changing the subject = *ne détournez pas la conversation*
to stray from the subject = *sortir du sujet* ≠ **to stick to the subject** = *s'en tenir au sujet*
while we're on the subject = *pendant qu'on y est.*

SUBJECTIVE (adj) *subjectif, -ive* : a subjective opinion = *une opinion subjective* ≠ objective = *objectif.*

SUBJECT TO (adj) 1/ *soumis, -e à* : the goods are subject to an important tax = *les marchandises sont soumises à une forte taxe* 2/ *sujet, -ette à* : subject to headaches = *sujet aux maux de tête* ⓪ inclined to = *enclin à.*

SUBJECT TO (to, -ed) *soumettre à* : I won't subject myself to that kind of treatment = *je ne me soumettrai pas à ce genre de traitement* ⓪ to expose to = *exposer à.*

SUBJUGATE (to, -d) *subjuguer* : to subjugate a people = *subjuguer un peuple* ⓪ to dominate = *dominer* ☠ *être subjugué par qqn* = to be captivated by s.o.

SUBJUNCTIVE (n) *subjonctif (m)* : the subjunctive mode = *le subjonctif.*

SUBLET (n) *sous-location (f)* : there are no sublets in my buildings = *il n'y a pas de sous-locations dans mon immeuble* **SUBLET** (to, -let, -let) *sous-louer* : I'm trying to sublet my apartment for the summer = *je suis en train d'essayer de sous-louer mon appartement pour l'été* ⓪ to rent = *louer.*

SUBLIMATE (to, -d) *sublimer* : to sublimate one's desires = *sublimer ses désirs* **SUBLIMATION** (n) *sublimation (f).*

SUBLIME (adj) *sublime* : a sublime evening = *une soirée sublime* → WONDERFUL ≠ miserable = *minable.*

SUBLIMINAL (adj) **subliminal advertising** = *publicité insidieuse.*

SUBMACHINE GUN (n) *mitraillette (f)* : the terrorists had submachine guns = *les terroristes avaient des mitraillettes* ⓪ machine gun = *mitrailleuse.*

SUBMARINE (n) *sous-marin (m)* : a nuclear submarine = *un sous-marin nucléaire* = sub ☠ *un sous-marin (services secrets)* = a spook.

SUBMERGE (to, -d) *submerger* : the village was submerged by the melting snow = *le village a été submergé par la fonte des neiges*
submerged in (letters) = *submergé de (lettres)*
☠ *submergé de travail* = swamped with work.

SUBMISSIVE (adj) *soumis, -e* : a submissive nature = *une nature soumise* ≠ rebellious = *rebelle* ☙ *soumis à l'impôt* = subject to taxation.

SUBMIT (to, -ted) *soumettre* : to submit a new project to the committee = *soumettre un nouveau projet au comité.*

SUBNORMAL (adj) *au-dessous de la normale* : subnormal intelligence = *intelligence au-dessous de la normale* ≠ superior = *supérieur.*

SUBORDINATE (n) *subordonné, -e* : his subordinates hate his guts = *ses subordonnés ne peuvent pas le blairer* ⑩ underling = *subalterne.*

SUBORDINATE (adj) *subordonné, -e* : my agreement is subordinate to his = *mon accord est subordonné au sien* **SUBORDINATION** (n) *subordination (f)* ≠ autonomy = *autonomie.*

SUBPOENA (n) *assignation (f) (à comparaître)* ⑩ writ of habeas corpus = *writ d'habeas corpus.*

SUBPOENA (to, -ed) *assigner (à comparaître)* : he was subpoenaed to appear = *il a été assigné à comparaître.*

SUB ROSA (adv) *sous le manteau* : he was paid sub rosa = *on l'a payé sous le manteau* ⑩ on the qt = *en cachette.*

SUBSCRIBER (n) *abonné, -e* : most of our subscribers are women = *la plupart de nos abonnés sont des femmes* ⑩ readership = *lecteurs.*

SUBSCRIBE TO (to, -d) **1/** *souscrire à* : I subscribe to your ideas = *je souscris à vos idées* ☙ *souscrire une assurance/à un emprunt* = to take out an insurance/a loan **2/** *s'abonner à* : to subscribe to a magazine = *s'abonner à un magazine.*

SUBSCRIPTION (n) *abonnement (m)* : a year's subscription to the "Times" = *un abonnement d'un an au « Times »* ☙ *abonnement (théâtre)* = season ticket.

SUBSEQUENT (adj) *suivant, -e* : his first movie was a hit but the subsequent one was a disaster = *son premier film a été un succès, mais le suivant a été un vrai désastre* ≠ previous = *précédent* **SUBSEQUENTLY** (adv) *à la suite de quoi* : he lost his job and subsequently committed suicide = *il a perdu son travail, à la suite de quoi il s'est suicidé.*

SUBSERVIENT (adj) *servile* : a subservient attitude = *une attitude servile.*

SUBSIDE (to, -d) *disparaître* : tension between us has subsided = *la tension entre nous a disparu* ⑩ to wane = *décroître.*

SUBSIDIARY (n, -ies) *filiale (f)* : subsidiaries and parent company = *les filiales et la maison mère* ⑩ branch = *succursale.*

SUBSIDIZE (to, -d) *subventionner* : the city refuses to subsidize the new theater = *la ville refuse de subventionner le nouveau théâtre.*

SUBSIDY (n, -ies) *subvention (f)* : the theater got a thousand-dollar subsidy = *le théâtre a reçu une subvention de mille dollars* ⑩ aid = *aide* ☙ *subvention (études/recherches)* = grant.

SUBSIST (to, -ed) *subsister* : her doubts subsisted = *ses doutes ont subsisté* ⑩ to persist = *persister*
to subsist on (bread and water) = *subsister au (pain et à l'eau).*

SUBSTANCE (n) *substance (f)* : a sticky substance = *une substance poisseuse* ⑩ texture = ←
in substance = *en substance* : that's in substance what I think = *voilà, en substance, ce que je pense* ⑩ fundamentally = *fondamentalement*
to lack substance = *manquer de consistance* : the film/he lacks substance = *le film/il manque de consistance.*

SUBSTANDARD (adj) *de qualité inférieure* : substandard product = *produit de qualité inférieure.*

SUBSTANTIAL (adj) *substantiel, -elle* : a substantial sum = *une somme substantielle* ≠ meager = *maigre* **SUBSTANTIALLY** (adv) *substantiellement* : her work has substantially improved = *son travail s'est substantiellement amélioré.*

SUBSTANTIATE (to, -d) *établir le bien-fondé de* : to substantiate a charge = *établir le bien-fondé d'une accusation* ⑩ to prove = *prouver.*

SUBSTITUTE (n) *substitut (m)* : there's no substitute for love = *il n'y a pas de substitut de l'amour*
the substitute teacher = *le professeur remplaçant*
a substitute for (sugar) = *un succédané (du sucre).*

SUBSTITUTE (to, -d) **to substitute for (the regular teacher)** = *remplacer (le professeur habituel)* ⑩ to fill in for = *remplacer temporairement* **SUBSTITUTION** (n) *substitution (f).*

SUBTERFUGE (n) *subterfuge (m)* : he uses all kinds of subterfuges to get what he wants = *il utilise toutes sortes de subterfuges pour obtenir ce qu'il veut* ⑩ scheme = *manigance.*

SUBTITLE (n) *sous-titre (m)* : I don't like films with subtitles = *je n'aime pas les films avec des sous-titres* ⑩ credits = *générique.*

SUBTLE (adj, -r, -st) *subtil, -e* : a subtle difference/remark = *une différence/remarque subtile* ⑩ shrewd = *habile.*

SUBTLETY (n, -ies) *subtilité (f)* : the subtlety of love/language = *la subtilité de l'amour/de la langue.*

SUBTLY (adv) *subtilement* : he subtly implied that my cooking was bad = *il a subtilement sous-entendu que je faisais mal la cuisine.*

SUBTRACT (to, -ed) **to subtract (twenty) from (thirty)** = *soustraire (vingt) de (trente)* ≠ to add =

additionner ☠ *se soustraire à des questions/à la justice* = to elude questions/justice **SUBTRACTION** (n) *soustraction (f).*

SUBURB (n) *banlieue (f)* : there are many poor suburbs around the city = *il y a beaucoup de banlieues pauvres autour de la ville* ⓪ outskirts = *faubourgs* **to live in the suburbs** = *vivre en banlieue.*

SUBURBAN (adj) *de banlieue* : the boredom of suburban life = *l'ennui de la vie de banlieue.*

SUBURBANITE (n) *banlieusard, -e* : suburbanites in morning trains = *les banlieusards dans les trains du matin* ≠ city dweller = *citadin.*

SUBURBIA (n) *la banlieue* : the film depicts the life of frustrated housewives in suburbia = *le film dépeint la vie de ménagères frustrées en banlieue.*

SUBVERSIVE (adj) *subversif, -ive* : subversive ideas = *des idées subversives* ⓪ revolutionary = *révolutionnaire.*

SUBVERT (to, -ed) *miner* : divorce is subverting the institution of marriage = *le divorce est en train de miner l'institution du mariage* ☠ → to mine.

SUBWAY (n) *métro (m)* : there are pleasanter places than the New York subway = *il y a des endroits plus agréables que le métro de New York* = tube (GB) ⓪ bus = ←.

SUCCEED (to, -ed) *réussir* : he tried hard but didn't succeed = *il s'est donné beaucoup de mal, mais il n'a pas réussi* ⓪ to come off = *se faire,* to go over with a bang = *remporter un gros succès* ≠ to fall flat = *tomber à plat* **to succeed s.o. as** = *succéder à qqn comme* : Reagan succeeded Carter as President = *Reagan a succédé à Carter comme Président* **to succeed in** = *réussir* : he succeeded in getting the job = *il a réussi à obtenir le poste* ⓪ to manage to = *arriver à* ☠ *il a réussi son examen* = he passed his exam — *tout lui réussit* = everything comes easy to him — *les épices ne me réussissent pas* = spices don't agree with me.

SUCCESS (n, -es) *succès (m), réussite (f)* : this was a big success = *ça a été un gros succès/une grande réussite* ⓪ triumph = *triomphe* ≠ bust = *fiasco* **to make a success of (one's business)** = *faire une réussite de (son affaire)* **success story** = *réussite exemplaire* **without success** = *sans succès* ⓪ to no avail = *sans résultat* ☠ *sa robe a eu beaucoup de succès* = her dress made a hit — *un auteur/un film à succès* = a bestselling author/a box-office movie — *une réussite (cartes)* = a game of solitaire.

SUCCESSFUL (adj) *qui réussit* : a successful businesswoman/lawyer = *une femme d'affaires/un avocat qui réussit* ≠ unsuccessful = *qui ne réussit pas* **not to be successful** = *ne pas réussir/ne pas avoir de succès* : I tried to convince him but I was not successful = *j'ai essayé de le convaincre, mais je n'ai pas réussi,* the play wasn't successful = *la pièce n'a pas eu de succès* ⓪ to bomb = *foirer* **to be successful in** = *réussir dans* : she was successful in advertising = *elle a réussi dans la publicité* **a successful book/film** = *un livre/un film à succès.*

SUCCESSFULLY (adv) *avec succès* : she successfully completed her PhD = *elle a terminé son doctorat avec succès.*

SUCCESSION (n) *succession (f)* : a succession of problems = *une succession de problèmes* ⓪ series = *série* ☠ *prendre la succession (à la tête d'une affaire)* = to take over (a business).

SUCCESSIVE (adj) *successif, -ive* : three successive marriages = *trois mariages successifs* **SUCCESSIVELY** (adv) *successivement.*

SUCCESSOR (n) *successeur (m)* : the Prime Minister's successor = *le successeur du Premier ministre* ⓪ heir = *héritier.*

SUCCINCT (adj) *succinct, -e* : a succinct report = *un rapport succinct* ⓪ concise = *concis.*

SUCCUMB (to, -ed) **to succumb to (temptation)** = *succomber à (la tentation).*

SUCH (pron) **as such** = *en tant que tel* : I'm your wife, and as such have a right to decide also = *je suis ta femme, et en tant que telle j'ai aussi le droit de décider.*

SUCH (adj) *tel, telle* : that's such bullshit ! = *c'est d'une telle connerie !* ☠ *tel père tel fils* = like father like son

in such cases = *en pareil cas* : what would you do in such cases ? = *que feriez-vous en pareil cas ?* **in such a way that** = *de telle sorte que* : he said it in such a way that I couldn't be offended = *il l'a dit de telle sorte que je*	*ne puisse pas être offensé* **no such thing** = *rien de tel* : I said no such thing = *je n'ai rien dit de tel* **on such and such a day** = *tel et tel jour* **such a thing** = *une chose pareille* : I never heard of such a	thing ! = *je n'ai jamais entendu parler d'une chose pareille !* **such and such** = *tel et tel* : we went to such and such place = *nous sommes allés à tel et tel endroit* **such a lot of (problems)** = *tant de (problèmes)*

| **such ... as that** = *à ce point* : I didn't think he was such a fool as that = *je ne pensais pas qu'il était bête à ce point* | **not such ... as that** = *pas ... à ce point* : he isn't such a pain in the neck as that = *il n'est pas casse-pieds à ce point* | **there are no such things as (flying saucers)** = *(les soucoupes volantes) n'existent pas.* |

SUCH (adv) *tellement* : we had such nasty weather ! = *nous avons eu un temps tellement mauvais !* ☠ *il est tellement stupide que ...* = he's so stupid that ...

| **such a (+ adj)** = *tellement* : he's such a nice guy = *c'est un type tellement sympa*, it's such a nice day = *c'est une tellement belle journée* | **such as** = *tel que* : I love modern painters such as Klee and Miro = *j'aime les peintres modernes tels que Klee et Miro.* |

SUCK (to, -ed) *sucer* : to suck a man/a woman/a lollipop = *sucer un homme/une femme/une sucette* ⓪ to do a blow job = *tailler une pipe*, to french a woman = *brouter une femme*
it sucks ! = *c'est à chier !* → AWFUL
to suck (a man) off = *sucer (un homme) à fond.*

SUCKER (n) *(bonne) poire (f)* : you were a sucker to lend her money = *tu es une (bonne) poire de lui avoir prêté de l'argent* ⓪ chump = *gogo*
there's a sucker born every minute ! = *il y aura toujours des gogos !*

SUDDEN (adj) *soudain, -e* : a sudden downpour = *une averse soudaine* ⓪ unexpected = *inattendu* **SUDDENLY** (adv) *soudain(ement), subitement* : he suddenly got angry = *soudain(ement) il s'est mis en colère/il s'est mis subitement en colère* ⓪ all of a sudden = *tout à coup.*

SUDDENNESS (n) *soudaineté (f)* : the suddenness of his death = *la soudaineté de sa mort.*

SUE (to, -d) *poursuivre en justice* : she's suing the doctor for malpractice = *elle poursuit le médecin en justice pour négligence professionnelle* ⓪ to take to court = *attaquer en justice.*

SUEDE (n) *daim (m)* : suede shoes = *chaussures en daim* ⓪ felt = *feutre*, leather = *cuir* ☠ → deer.

SUFFER (to, -ed) *souffrir* : I suffered a lot when he left = *j'ai beaucoup souffert quand il est parti* ⓪ to endure = *endurer* ☠ *je ne peux pas le souffrir* = I can't stand him.

SUFFERING (n) *souffrance (f)* : the world's full of suffering = *le monde est rempli de souffrance* ⓪ torment = *tourment* ☠ *mettre fin aux souffrances de qqn* = to put s.o. out of his misery.

SUFFICE (to, -d) *suffire* : a brief note should suffice = *une note brève devrait suffire* ⓪ to be enough = *être assez*
it suffices to say that ... = *il suffit de dire que ...* : it suffices to say that it's too expensive for the company = *il suffit de dire que c'est trop cher pour la société*
☠ *suffire à ses propres besoins* = to be self-sufficient
— *il suffit que vous lui téléphoniez* = all you have to do is to call him
— *ça suffit !* = that's enough !

SUFFICIENT (adj) *suffisant, -e* : a sufficient amount of money = *une somme d'argent suffisante* = adequate ≠ insufficient = *insuffisant* ☠ *qqn de suffisant* = a conceited person **SUFFICIENTLY** (adv) *suffisamment* : are you sufficiently rested ? = *vous êtes-vous suffisamment reposé ?*

SUFFIX (n, -es) *suffixe (m)* ≠ prefix = *préfixe.*

SUFFOCATE (to, -d) *suffoquer* : it's so hot I'm suffocating = *il fait tellement chaud que je suffoque* ⓪ to smother = *étouffer* ☠ *j'ai été suffoqué par son histoire* = I was staggered by his story.

SUFFRAGE (n) *suffrage (m)* : universal suffrage = *suffrage universel* ⓪ vote = *←*, franchise = *droit de vote.*

SUFFRAGETTE (n) *suffragette (f)* : a demonstration of suffragettes = *une manifestation de suffragettes* ⓪ feminist = *féministe.*

SUGAR (n) **1/** *sucre (m)* : there's too much sugar in the cake = *il y a trop de sucre dans le gâteau*, I'll take two sugars please = *je prendrai deux sucres, s'il vous plaît* ⓪ sugary = *sucré*, saccharin = *saccharine*, sugar bowl = *sucrier*, sugarcane = *canne à sucre*
a lump of sugar = *un morceau de sucre*
sugar daddy = *papa gâteau* ⓪ a meal ticket = *une vache à lait*
☠ *casser du sucre sur le dos de qqn* = to criticize s.o. behind his back
— *être tout sucre tout miel* = to be all sweetness **2/** *mon petit, ma petite* : what do you want to do, sugar ? = *qu'est-ce que tu veux faire, mon petit/ma petite ?* ⓪ angel = *mon ange.*

SUGGEST (to, -ed) *suggérer* : what do you suggest ? = *qu'est-ce que vous suggérez ?* ⓪ to propose = *proposer.*

SUGGESTION (n) *suggestion (f)* : what a wild suggestion ! = *quelle suggestion démente !* ⓪ proposal = *proposition.*

SUGGESTIVE (adj) *suggestif, -ive* : a suggestive remark = *une remarque suggestive* ⓪ risqué = *grivois* **SUGGESTIVELY** (adv) *d'une façon suggestive* : he looked at me suggestively = *il m'a regardé d'une façon suggestive.*

SUICIDAL (adj) *suicidaire* : depressed and suicidal = *déprimé et suicidaire* ⓪ at the end of one's rope = *au bout du rouleau.*

SUICIDE (n) *suicide (m)* : was it murder or suicide ? = *est-ce qu'il s'agissait d'un meurtre ou d'un suicide ?* ⓍⒹ kamikaze = ←
to commit suicide = *se suicider* : her younger sister committed suicide = *sa sœur cadette s'est suicidée* ⓍⒹ to blow one's brains out = *se faire sauter la cervelle*
suicide attempt = *tentative de suicide.*

SUIT (n) **1/** *procès (m)* : he's a great lawyer but he has lost a suit yet = *c'est un grand avocat, mais il a pourtant perdu un procès* = lawsuit
to bring suit = *intenter un procès*
to follow suit = *suivre le mouvement* : the rank and file decided to strike and the union's leaders followed suit = *la base a décidé de faire grève et les leaders syndicaux ont suivi le mouvement*
2/ *tailleur (m)* (ladies), *costume (m)* (men) : she wears a lot of suits to work = *elle se met souvent en tailleur pour aller travailler* ⓍⒹ single-breasted = *droit*, double-breasted = *croisé*, lapel = *revers (veste)*, cuff = *revers (pantalon)*
☠ *tailleur* → tailor
— *costume* → costume
3/ *maillot (m)* : you've got the sexiest suit I've ever seen = *tu as le maillot le plus sexy que j'aie jamais vu* ⓍⒹ bathing suit = *maillot de bain.*

SUIT (to, -ed) *convenir* : will three o'clock suit you ? = *est-ce que trois heures vous convient ?* ⓍⒹ to be OK for = *être O.K. pour*
it suits me to a T/tee = *ça me va tout à fait* = **that suits me fine**
(red) doesn't suit you = *(le rouge) ne vous va pas*
suit yourself = *comme vous voudrez* ⓍⒹ do as you please = *faites comme bon vous semble*
to be suited to = *convenir pour* : he isn't suited to the job = *il ne convient pas pour le poste*
☠ *convenir d'(une date)* = to agree on/to (a date)
— *il a convenu que ...* = he acknowledged that ...

SUITABLE (adj) *convenable* : your jeans aren't suitable for the occasion = *ton jean n'est pas convenable pour la circonstance* ⓍⒹ appropriate = *approprié* ≠ unsuitable = *qui ne convient pas* ☠ *un salaire convenable* = a decent salary.

SUITCASE (n) *valise (f)* : my suitcase was lost = *on a perdu ma valise* ⓍⒹ grip = *sac de voyage*, trunk = *malle* ☠ → *valise.*

SUITE (n) *suite (f)* : the bridal suite = *la suite des jeunes mariés*
☠ *à la suite de la mort de sa mère* = after his mother's death
— *donner suite à* = to follow
— *la suite des événements* = the following events/the sequence of events
— *les suites* = the aftereffects
— *par la suite* = later on
— *ça n'a pas eu de suites* = it had no repercussions
— *comme suite à ma lettre* = further to my letter
— *à la suite de ça* = as a result

— *la suite de (l'histoire)* = the sequel of (the story)
— *(trois fois) de suite* = (three times) in a row
— *prendre la suite* = to succeed/take over
— *de la suite dans les idées* = great singleness of purpose.

SUITED (adj) *convenant* : food suited to his diet = *une alimentation convenant à son régime* ⓍⒹ adapted = *adapté.*

SUITOR (n) *soupirant (m)* : my sister's suitor = *le soupirant de ma sœur* ⓍⒹ beau = *galant.*

SULK (to, -ed) *bouder* : what are you sulking about ? = *pourquoi boudez-vous ?* ⓍⒹ to pull a long face = *faire la tête* ☠ *bouder l'offre de qqn* = to take no account of s.o.'s offer.

SULKY (adj, -ier, -iest) *boudeur, -euse* : a sulky child = *un enfant boudeur* ⓍⒹ sullen = *renfrogné.*

SULLEN (adj) *renfrogné, -e* : depressed and sullen = *déprimé et renfrogné* ⓍⒹ morose = ← ≠ cheerful = *réjoui.*

SULTRY (adj, -ier, -iest) *aguichant, -e, aguicheur, -euse* : a sultry voice = *une voix aguichante/aguicheuse* ⓍⒹ sensual = *sensuel.*

SUM (n) *somme (f)* : that's a very large sum of money = *c'est une très grosse somme d'argent* ⓍⒹ total = ←
in sum = *en somme* : in sum, you don't agree = *en somme, vous n'êtes pas d'accord* ⓍⒹ in a nutshell = *en deux mots*
☠ *faire un somme* = to take a nap.

SUMMARIZE (to, -d) *résumer* : can you summarize the situation for me ? = *pouvez-vous me résumer la situation ?* ⓍⒹ to recapitulate = *récapituler* ☠ *ça se résume au fait que ...* = it boils down to the fact that ...

SUMMARY (n, -ies) *résumé (m)* : give me a summary of the situation = *faites-moi un résumé de la situation* = résumé ⓍⒹ briefing = ←.

SUMMER (n) *été (m)* : what are you doing for the summer ? = *que faites-vous cet été ?* ⓍⒹ summertime = *saison d'été* ≠ winter = *hiver*
summer camp = *colonie de vacances*
summer resort = *station de vacances*
summer stock = *groupe théâtral qui part en tournée pendant l'été.*

SUMMING-UP (n) *point (m)* : a summing-up of the last few days' events = *le point sur les événements de ces derniers jours* ⓍⒹ résumé = ←.

SUMMIT (n) *sommet (m)* : the summits of joy = *les sommets de la joie* ⓍⒹ acme = *faîte*
summit meeting = *rencontre au sommet*
☠ *l'inflation a atteint un nouveau sommet* = inflation has reached a new high.

SUMMON (to, -ed) *convoquer* : the Secretary of State summoned the French ambassador = *le secrétaire d'État a convoqué l'ambassadeur de France*

to summon s.o. to (appear in court) = *citer/assigner qqn (à comparaître)*
to summon up (one's courage/strength) = *rassembler tout (son courage)/toutes (ses forces)*
☠ → to convoke.

SUMMONS (n inv) *sommation (f)* : a summons to appear in court = *une sommation à comparaître* ⊕ defendant = *prévenu.*

SUMPTUOUS (adj) *somptueux, -euse* : a sumptuous apartment = *un appartement somptueux* → WONDERFUL.

SUM UP (to, -med) *résumer* : it's hard to sum up the situation = *c'est dur de résumer la situation* = it's hard to summarize the situation ☠ → to summarize.

SUN (n) *soleil (m)* : the sun's shining = *le soleil brille* ⊕ sunlamp = *lampe solaire*, tan = *bronzage*
to get some sun = *prendre le soleil* ⊕ to take a sunbath = *prendre un bain de soleil*
to soak up the sun = *se dorer au soleil*
the sun rises ≠ **sets/goes down** = *le soleil se lève* ≠ *se couche*
under the sun = *au monde/qui soit* : they have the most beautiful house under the sun = *ils ont la plus belle maison qui soit/il n'y a pas au monde de plus belle maison que la leur*
Sun Belt = *États du Sud américain réputés pour leur climat ensoleillé.*

SUNBURN (n) *coup (m) de soleil* : bad sunburn on my back = *un sale coup de soleil sur le dos* ⊕ sunstroke = *insolation*, suntan lotion = *crème solaire.*

SUNDAE (n) *sundae (m)* : a chocolate sundae = *un sundae chocolat* ⊕ soda = ←.

SUNDAY (n) *dimanche (m)* : I always sleep late on Sundays = *je fais toujours la grasse matinée le dimanche* → WEEK
Sunday driver/painter = *conducteur/peintre du dimanche*
Sunday school = *école du dimanche/catéchisme*
to be in one's Sunday best = *être endimanché/avoir mis ses habits du dimanche* ⊕ to get dressed up = *se mettre sur son trente et un.*

SUNDRY (adj) *divers, -e* : sundry problems = *divers problèmes* ⊕ several = *plusieurs* ☠ → diverse.

SUNGLASSES (n pl) *lunettes (f pl) de soleil* : I never wear sunglasses = *je ne porte jamais de lunettes de soleil.*

SUNNY (adj, -ier-, -iest) *ensoleillé, -e* : a sunny day = *une journée ensoleillée* ≠ cloudy = *nuageux*
it's sunny = *il y a du soleil.*

SUNNY-SIDE UP (adj) *sur le plat* : I'll have two eggs sunny-side up = *je prendrai deux œufs sur le plat* ≠ eggs over = *œufs sur le plat retournés.*

SUNRISE (n) *lever (m) de/du soleil* : they started working before sunrise = *ils ont commencé à travailler avant*

le lever du soleil ⊕ dawn = *aube* ≠ nightfall = *la tombée de la nuit.*

SUNSET (n) *coucher (m) de/du soleil* : what a beautiful sunset ! = *quel beau coucher de soleil !* ⊕ dusk = *crépuscule.*

SUNSHINE (n) *(lumière (f) du) soleil (m)* : what we need is a little sunshine = *ce qu'il nous faut, c'est un peu de soleil.*

SUPER (n) = SUPERINTENDENT.

SUPER (adj) *super* : the party was super = *la soirée était super* → WONDERFUL ≠ crummy = *moche.*

SUPER (adv) *super-* : he's super rich = *il est super-riche* → VERY.

SUPERB (adj) *superbe* : a superb view = *une vue superbe* → WONDERFUL ≠ horrid = *atroce.*

SUPERFICIAL (adj) *superficiel, -elle* : a superficial wound/personality = *une blessure/une personnalité superficielle* ≠ deep = *profond* **SUPERFICIALITY** (n) *superficialité (f)* **SUPERFICIALLY** (adv) *superficiellement.*

SUPERFLUOUS (adj) *superflu, -e* : any other argument is superfluous = *tout autre argument est superflu* ≠ essential = *essentiel.*

SUPERHUMAN (adj) *surhumain, -e* : a superhuman undertaking = *une entreprise surhumaine* ⊕ extraordinary = *extraordinaire.*

SUPERINTENDENT (n) *gardien, -enne, concierge (m, f)* : the superintendent will fix your air conditioner = *le gardien va vous réparer votre climatiseur* = super ⊕ custodian = *gardien d'immeuble*
☠ *gardien* → watchman
— *quelle concierge !* = what a gossip !

SUPERIOR (n) *supérieur, -e* : talk to your superior about it = *parlez-en à votre supérieur* = higher-up ⊕ boss = *patron* ≠ subordinate = *subordonné.*

SUPERIOR (adj) *supérieur, -e* : don't act so superior ! = *ne prenez pas ces airs supérieurs !* ⊕ haughty = *hautain* ≠ inferior = *inférieur*
superior to = *supérieur à* : American meat's superior to French meat = *la viande américaine est supérieure à la viande française.*

SUPERIORITY (n) *supériorité (f)* : he's convinced of his superiority = *il est convaincu de sa supériorité*
superiority complex = *complexe de supériorité.*

SUPERLATIVE (adj) *suprême* : superlative indifference = *indifférence suprême.*

SUPERMARKET (n) *supermarché (m)* : supermarkets are cheaper = *les supermarchés sont moins chers* ⊕ shopping center/mall = *centre commercial*, department store = *grand magasin.*

SUPERNATURAL (adj) *surnaturel, -elle* : supernatural powers = *des pouvoirs surnaturels* ⊕ magic = *magi-*

que, miraculous = *miraculeux.*

SUPERPOWER (n) *superpuissance (f)* : a summit of the two superpowers = *un sommet entre les deux superpuissances* ≠ satellite = ←.

SUPERSEDE (to, -d) *prendre la place de* : the United States superseded England as a superpower = *les États-Unis ont pris la place de l'Angleterre comme superpuissance.*

SUPERSONIC (adj) *supersonique* : a supersonic flight = *un vol supersonique.*

SUPERSTAR (n) *superstar (f), monstre sacré (m)* : Elvis was a superstar = *Elvis était une superstar* ⓓ idol = *idole.*

SUPERSTITION (n) *superstition (f)* : touching wood is a superstition = *c'est une superstition de toucher du bois.*

SUPERSTITIOUS (adj) *superstitieux, -euse* : he's so superstitious he would never walk under a ladder = *il est tellement superstitieux qu'il ne passerait jamais sous une échelle.*

SUPERVISE (to, -d) *superviser* : who's supervising the work ? = *qui supervise le travail ?* ⓓ to direct = *diriger.*

SUPERVISION (n) *surveillance (f)* : the kids need supervision in their work = *les gosses ont besoin de surveillance dans leur travail*
☠ *les flics le gardent sous surveillance* = the cops are keeping a tab on him
— *sous surveillance médicale* = under medical surveillance.

SUPERVISOR (n) *surveillant, -e* : the supervisor is unpopular with the workers = *le surveillant est très mal vu des ouvriers* ⓓ manager = *directeur.*

SUPERVISORY (adj) *de surveillance* : supervisory methods = *méthodes de surveillance.*

SUPPER (n) *dîner (m)* : supper's at eight = *le dîner est à huit heures* = dinner ⓓ meal = *repas,* suppertime = *l'heure du dîner* ☠ *un souper* = a late evening meal.

SUPPLANT (to, -ed) *supplanter* : the sheriff's deputy is trying to supplant him = *l'adjoint du shérif essaie de le supplanter* ⓓ to replace = *remplacer.*

SUPPLEMENT (n) *supplément (m)* : diet supplement = *supplément de régime* ⓓ appendix = *appendice* ☠ *payer un supplément* = to pay a surcharge/an extra charge.

SUPPLEMENT (to, -ed) *arrondir* : he supplements his income typing on weekends = *il arrondit ses revenus en faisant de la dactylo le week-end.*

SUPPLEMENTARY (adj) *supplémentaire* : supplementary income = *revenu supplémentaire* ⓓ complementary = *complémentaire*
☠ *heures supplémentaires* = overtime

— *est-ce qu'il y a des dépenses supplémentaires ?* = are there any additional expenses ?

SUPPLIER (n) *fournisseur, -euse* : the restaurant has a French supplier = *le restaurant a un fournisseur français* ≠ client = ←.

SUPPLY (n, -ies) *approvisionnement (m), provision (f)* : our supplies are running low = *notre approvisionnement s'épuise/nos provisions s'épuisent*
(office) supplies = *fournitures (de bureau)*
supply and demand = *l'offre et la demande*
☠ *provision* → provision.

SUPPLY (to, -ied) *fournir* : the hotel supplies soap = *l'hôtel fournit le savon* = to provide ⓓ to give = *donner* ☠ → to furnish.

SUPPORT (n) *soutien (m)* : he has the support of his family/the party = *il a le soutien de sa famille/du parti* ⓓ help = *aide*
☠ *soutien de famille* = breadwinner
— *sa fille est un support pour lui* = his daughter is a crutch for him
— *support publicitaire* = advertising medium.

SUPPORT (to, -ed) 1/ *subvenir aux besoins de* : he supports both his ex-wives = *il subvient aux besoins de ses deux ex-femmes* ⓓ to have (two) dependents = *avoir (deux) personnes à charge* 2/ *soutenir* : the Senator supports free abortion = *le sénateur soutient la liberté de l'avortement* ⓓ to struggle for = *lutter pour*
to support oneself = *subvenir à ses propres besoins* : how does he support himself ? = *comment subvient-il à ses propres besoins ?*
☠ *elle soutient que ...* = she contends/asserts/argues that ...
— *sa famille la soutient* = her family is standing by her/is seeing her through
— *tu m'as soutenu le moral* = you bolstered up my morale
— *le balcon est soutenu par une poutre* = the balcony is held up by a beam
— *nos rêves nous soutiennent* = our dreams sustain us
— *soutenir une motion* = to second a motion
— *supporter une équipe* = to root for a team
— *je ne peux pas le supporter* = I can't stand him/bear him/put up with him.

SUPPORTABLE (adj) *supportable* : taxes are reaching a point where they are no longer supportable = *les impôts atteignent un niveau tel qu'ils ne sont plus supportables* ≠ unbearable = *insupportable.*

SUPPORTER (n) *supporter (m)* : an active supporter of women's rights = *un supporter actif des droits de la femme* ⓓ adherent = *adhérent.*

SUPPORTIVE (adj) *qui soutient* : he's supportive of his wife's career = *il soutient la carrière de sa femme* ≠ critical = *critique.*

SUPPOSE (to, -d) *supposer, croire* (interrogative and negative form) : I suppose she'll come = *je suppose qu'elle viendra,* do you suppose she'll come ? = *est-ce* que vous croyez qu'elle viendra ? Ⓦ to reckon = croire bien, to guess = imaginer

I don't suppose (he'll agree) = je ne crois pas (qu'il sera d'accord)

what do you suppose (he'll do) ? = que croyez-vous (qu'il va faire) ?

suppose (she dies) = et si (elle mourait)

suppose (he doesn't agree) = supposons qu'(il ne soit pas d'accord)

I suppose so ! = je suppose ! ⓌI believe so ! = je crois bien ! ≠ **I don't suppose so !** = je ne crois pas !

to be supposed to = être censé : don't tell her I dropped by, I'm supposed to be at the office = ne lui dis pas que je suis passé, je suis censé être au bureau

you're not supposed to (smoke in the subway) = on n'a pas le droit de (fumer dans le métro)

it's supposed to (snow this weekend) = on suppose qu'(il va neiger ce week-end).

SUPPOSED (adj) prétendu, -e : his supposed talent is very meager = son prétendu talent est très maigre Ⓦso-called = soi-disant.

SUPPOSEDLY (adv) soi-disant : she left early supposedly to go to the doctor = elle est partie tôt soi-disant pour aller chez le médecin Ⓦpresumably = en principe.

SUPPOSING (conj) à supposer que : supposing it rains = à supposer qu'il pleuve Ⓦin the event that = au cas où.

SUPPOSITION (n) supposition (f) : it's just a supposition of course = bien sûr, ce n'est qu'une supposition Ⓦhypothesis = hypothèse

on the supposition that = à supposer que

the supposition is that (he killed his wife) = on suppose qu'(il a tué sa femme).

SUPPRESS (to, -ed) étouffer : to suppress a desire/a rebellion = étouffer un désir/une rébellion Ⓦto repress = réprimer ☠ → to choke.

SUPREMACY (n, -ies) suprématie (f) : nuclear supremacy = suprématie nucléaire Ⓦdomination = ←

SUPREME (adj) suprême : supreme courage = courage suprême Ⓦunbelievable = incroyable

the Supreme Court = la Cour suprême.

SURCHARGE (n) supplément (m) à payer : there's a surcharge on gasoline = il y a un supplément à payer pour l'essence.

SURE (adj, -r, -st) sûr, -e : are you sure he'll come ? = est-ce que vous êtes sûr qu'il viendra ? Ⓦcertain = ← ≠ unsure = peu sûr

as sure as shooting = aussi sûr que deux et deux font quatre	**I'm not so sure** = je n'en suis pas si sûr Ⓦ I doubt it = j'en doute	**a sure thing** = quelque chose de sûr et certain : his reelection is a sure thing = sa réélection est
to be sure of oneself = être sûr de soi : he's always so sure of himself = il est toujours tellement sûr de lui	**to make sure** = s'assurer : make sure you take the right bus = assurez-vous que vous prenez le bon bus ☠ → to assure	sûre et certaine ≠ dubious = douteux
be sure to (call me tonight) = ne manquez pas de (m'appeler ce soir)	**sure thing !** = entendu ! : don't forget to call me tonight ! — sure thing ! = n'oubliez pas de m'appeler ce soir ! — entendu ! Ⓦroger ! = compris !	**sure to (arrive late)** = sûr d'(arriver en retard) Ⓦbound to = forcé de
I'm sure of it ! = j'en suis sûr !		**that's a sure sign (that it's going to rain)** = c'est le signe infaillible (qu'il va pleuvoir)
as sure as my name's ... = aussi sûr que je m'appelle ...		

☠ un investissement sûr/une route sûre = a safe investment/road	— une main sûre = a steady hand.

SURE (adv) 1/ bien entendu : sure, I'll have a Scotch ! = bien entendu, je vais prendre un whisky ! Ⓦof course = bien sûr 2/ archi- : it's sure cold out = il fait archifroid dehors → VERY

to be sure = c'est certain : she's bright to be sure, but she has a lousy temper = elle est intelligente, c'est certain, mais elle a un sale caractère	**for sure** = à coup sûr : for sure he's telling the truth = à coup sûr il dit la vérité Ⓦcertainly = certainement
(and) sure enough = effectivement : I thought it would rain, and sure enough it did = je pensais qu'il allait pleuvoir et effectivement il a plu Ⓦin fact = en fait	**that's for sure !** = c'est sûr ! : it's expensive, that's for sure ! = c'est cher, c'est sûr ! Ⓦthere's no doubt about it = il n'y a aucun doute.

SUREFIRE (adj) *qui marche à tous les coups* : a surefire scheme = *une combine qui marche à tous les coups.*

SURELY (adv) *sûrement* : surely he didn't say that = *il n'a sûrement pas dit ça* Ⓞ most assuredly = *assurément* ≠ perhaps = *peut-être.*

SURF (to, -ed) **to go surfing** = *faire du surf* Ⓞ surf-board = *planche de surf,* windsurf = *planche à voile.*

SURFACE (n) *surface (f)* : the surface of the lake = *la surface du lac*
on the surface (he's nice) = *en surface/au premier abord (il est sympa)*
not to scratch the surface = *ne pas effleurer* : we've not scratched the surface of the question yet = *nous n'avons pas effleuré la question jusqu'ici*
surface area = *superficie.*

SURFACE (to, -d) *faire surface* : her psychological problems are surfacing = *ses problèmes psychologiques font surface* Ⓞ to emerge = *émerger.*

SURGE (n) *vague (f)* : a surge of immigrants/opposition = *une vague d'immigration/d'opposition* ☠ → wave.

SURGEON (n) *chirurgien, -enne* : she's a good surgeon = *c'est une bonne chirurgienne* Ⓞ operation = *opération,* operation table = *table d'opération.*

SURGERY (n, -ies) *chirurgie (f)* : open-heart surgery = *chirurgie à cœur ouvert* Ⓞ anesthesia = *anesthésie.*

SURLY (adj, -ier, -iest) *revêche* : a surly personality = *une personnalité revêche* Ⓞ a cold fish = *un pisse-froid.*

SURMISE (to, -d) *se douter* : I never surmised they were not happy = *je ne m'étais jamais douté qu'ils n'étaient pas heureux* Ⓞ to conjecture = *conjecturer* ☠ → to doubt.

SURMOUNT (to, -ed) *surmonter* : problems impossible to surmount = *des problèmes impossibles à surmonter* Ⓞ to get on top of = *venir à bout de* ☠ *surmonter sa jalousie/sa timidité* = to overcome one's jealousy/timidity.

SURPASS (to, -ed) *surpasser* : he surpasses all the writers of his time = *il surpasse tous les écrivains de son temps* Ⓞ to go beyond = *dépasser.*

SURPLUS (n, -es) *surplus (m)* : a surplus of wheat = *un surplus de blé* ≠ shortage = *pénurie.*

SURPRISE (n) *surprise (f)* : the gift he gave me was a big surprise = *son cadeau a vraiment été une surprise* Ⓞ shock = *choc*
much to (my) surprise = *à (ma) grande surprise*
to take by surprise = *prendre par surprise* Ⓞ to be unexpected = *être inattendu*
surprise attack = *attaque-surprise*
surprise party = *surprise-partie.*

SURPRISE (to, -d) *surprendre* : the news surprised me = *la nouvelle m'a surpris,* what surprises me is how young she looks = *ce qui me surprend, c'est qu'elle ait*

l'air si jeune Ⓞ to stupefy = *stupéfier,* to flabbergast = *scier*
to be surprised at (his attitude) = *être surpris de (son attitude)*
that doesn't surprise me ! = *ça ne me surprend pas !/ça ne m'étonne pas !* → THAT'S LIFE !
☠ *surprendre une conversation* = to overhear a conversation
— *le professeur les a surpris en train de fumer* = the teacher caught them smoking.

SURPRISING (adj) *surprenant, -e* : that's not surprising = *ça n'a rien de surprenant* Ⓞ astonishing = *étonnant,* incredible = *incroyable,* mindblowing = *renversant*
SURPRISINGLY (adv) *étonnamment* : he looks surprisingly young for his age = *il a l'air étonnamment jeune pour son âge.*

SURREALISM (n) *surréalisme (m)* **SURREALIST** (n, adj) *surréaliste (m, f).*

SURRENDER (n) *reddition (f)* : their surrender was unexpected = *leur reddition était inattendue* Ⓞ capitulation = ← **SURRENDER** (to, -ed) 1/ *se rendre* : the guerillas surrendered = *les guérilleros se sont rendus* ≠ to hold out = *tenir bon* ☠ → to return 2/ *renoncer à* : I surrendered my citizenship = *j'ai renoncé à ma nationalité* Ⓞ to abandon = *abandonner.*

SURROGATE (adj) *qui tient lieu de* : he's a surrogate father for her six children = *il tient lieu de père à ses six enfants*
surrogate mother = *mère porteuse.*

SURROUND (to, -ed) *entourer* : the cops surrounded the house = *les flics ont entouré la maison* Ⓞ to encircle = *encercler*
to be surrounded by = *être entouré de* : Israël is surrounded by enemies = *Israël est entouré d'ennemis*
to surround o.s. with = *s'entourer de* : he surrounds himself with intelligent friends = *il s'entoure d'amis intelligents*
☠ *ses amis l'entouraient* = his friends were with/around him.

SURROUNDING (adj) *environnant, -e* : the surrounding country = *le pays environnant.*

SURROUNDINGS (n pl) *cadre (m)* : the ugliness of the surroundings = *la laideur du cadre* Ⓞ environment = *environnement* ☠ → frame.

SURVEY (n) *étude (f)* : to make a survey about unwed mothers = *faire une étude sur les mères célibataires* Ⓞ poll = *sondage.*

SURVIVAL (n) *survie (f)* : we're all concerned with our own survival = *nous sommes tous concernés par notre propre survie* Ⓞ extinction = ←
survival of the fittest = *sélection naturelle* Ⓞ Darwinism = *darwinisme.*

SURVIVE (to, -d) *survivre* : ten people survived = *dix personnes ont survécu* ≠ to perish = *périr.*

SURVIVOR (n) *survivant, -e / rescapé, -e* : there were no survivors = *il n'y a eu aucun survivant/rescapé* ⟲ the wounded = *les blessés*.

SUSCEPTIBLE (adj) **susceptible to** = *sensible à* : she's susceptible to the charm of older men = *elle est sensible au charme des hommes plus âgés* ☠ *elle est susceptible* = she's touchy.

SUSPECT (n) *suspect, -e* : he's the prime suspect = *c'est le suspect numéro un* ⟲ murder = *meurtre*.

SUSPECT (adj) *suspect, -e* : her sudden kindness is suspect = *sa gentillesse soudaine est suspecte* ☠ *un type suspect* = a suspicious-looking guy.

SUSPECT (to, -ed) *soupçonner* : the cops suspect the maid = *les flics soupçonnent la bonne*
I suspected as much = *je m'en doutais*.

SUSPEND (to, -ed) *suspendre* : the court will be suspended until tomorrow at nine = *l'audience est suspendue jusqu'à demain matin neuf heures* ⟲ to stop = *arrêter*
to be suspended from (school/the bar) = *être renvoyé de (l'école) / rayé du (barreau)*
☠ *suspendre la séance* = to adjourn the meeting.

SUSPENDERS (n pl) *bretelles (f pl)* : few men wear suspenders nowadays = *aujourd'hui, il y a peu d'hommes qui portent des bretelles* ⟲ garters = *jarretelles*.

SUSPENSE (n) *suspense (m)* : Hitchcock's films were full of suspense = *les films d'Hitchcock étaient remplis de suspense*
to keep s.o. in suspense = *tenir qqn en haleine*.

SUSPICION (n) *soupçon (m)* : the suspicions of a jealous wife = *les soupçons d'une femme jalouse* ⟲ doubt = *doute*
I have a suspicion that (they're sleeping together) = *quelque chose me dit qu'(ils couchent ensemble)*
on the suspicion of (murder) = *soupçonné de (meurtre)*
under ≠ **above suspicion** = *suspect ≠ au-dessus de tout soupçon*
☠ *un soupçon de (crème)* = a drop of (cream).

SUSPICIOUS (adj) 1/ *suspect, -e* : a suspicious-looking character = *un personnage qui a l'air suspect* ⟲ doubtful = *douteux* ☠ → suspect 2/ *soupçonneux, -euse* : his wife became suspicious when he began getting home late every night = *sa femme est devenue soupçonneuse quand il a commencé à rentrer tard tous les soirs* ≠ trusting = *qui fait confiance*.

SUSPICIOUSLY (adv) *avec méfiance* : he looked at me suspiciously = *il m'a regardé avec méfiance*.

SUSTAIN (to, -ed) *soutenir* : our dreams sustain us = *nos rêves nous soutiennent* ⟲ to keep up = *entretenir* ☠ → to support.

SWAGGER (to, -ed) *plastronner* : he swaggered in front of women = *il plastronnait devant les femmes* ⟲ to show off = *faire de l'épate*.

SWALLOW (to, -ed) 1/ *avaler* : to swallow a glass of water = *avaler un verre d'eau* ⟲ a swallow = *une gorgée* 2/ *gober* : he swallowed the whole story = *il a gobé toute l'histoire* ⟲ to believe = *croire*
to swallow up = *engloutir* : this business has swallowed up all my savings = *cette affaire a englouti toutes mes économies* ⟲ to eat up = *bouffer* ☠ → to gulp down.

SWAMP (n) *marais (m)* : eaten by an alligator in a swamp = *dévoré par un alligator dans un marais* ⟲ marsh = *marécage*.

SWAMP (to, -ed) **to be swamped with (work/mail)** = *être submergé de (travail/courrier)* ⟲ to be snowed under = *être débordé de*.

SWAMPY (adj, -ier, -iest) *marécageux, -euse* : a swampy area = *une région marécageuse*.

SWAN (n) *cygne (m)* : the grace of swans = *la grâce des cygnes* ⟲ duck = *canard*
swan song = *le chant du cygne*.

SWANKY (adj, -ier, -iest) *cossu, -e* : a swanky apartment = *un appartement cossu* ⟲ posh = *rupin* ≠ seedy = *miteux*.

SWAP (to, -ped) *échanger* : let's swap husbands for the weekend ! = *si on échangeait nos maris pour le weekend ?* ⟲ to barter = *troquer*.

SWAPPING (n) **wife/husband swapping** = *échangisme*.

SWARM (n) *essaim (m)* (bees), *nuée (f)* : a swarm of tourists = *une nuée de touristes* → MANY.

SWARM WITH (to, -ed) *grouiller de* : the place was swarming with tourists = *l'endroit grouillait de touristes* ⟲ to be flooded with = *être inondé de*.

SWASTIKA (n) *svastika (m), croix (f) gammée* ≠ yellow star = *étoile jaune*.

SWAY (to, -ed) *influer sur* : the President's last speech on TV swayed a lot of voters = *le dernier discours télévisé du Président a influé sur beaucoup d'électeurs* ⟲ to affect = *affecter*.

SWEAR (to, swore, sworn) 1/ *jurer* : I swear I'm not lying = *je jure que je ne mens pas* ⟲ to promise = *promettre* 2/ *jurer* : don't swear in front of the kids = *ne jurez pas devant les gosses* ⟲ swearword = *juron*
to swear by = *ne jurer que par* : he swears by his shrink = *il ne jure que par son psy*
to swear off (drinking) = *jurer de ne plus (boire)*
to swear to = *jurer* : I can't swear to it, but I think he'll lend you the money = *je ne peux pas le jurer, mais je pense qu'il vous prêtera l'argent*
I swear ! = *je le jure !* ≠ **I wouldn't swear to it !** = *je n'en jurerais pas !*

to be sworn in = *prêter serment* : the President of the United States is sworn in January = *le président des États-Unis prête serment au mois de janvier* ☠ *les couleurs jurent* = the colors clash.

SWEAT (n) *sueur* (f) : to be covered with sweat = *être couvert de sueur*
no sweat ! = *pas de problème !* : my brother can introduce you to a good lawyer, no sweat ! = *mon frère peut vous présenter un bon avocat, pas de problème !*
sweat shirt = *sweat-shirt.*

SWEAT (to, sweat or -ed) *suer* : it's so hot we're sweating = *il fait tellement chaud qu'on sue*
to sweat it out = *prendre son mal en patience* : you'll have to sweat it out till your test result comes in = *il va falloir prendre ton mal en patience jusqu'à ce que tu aies tes résultats d'examen*
to sweat over = *trimer sur* : we've been sweating over this work for months = *ça fait des mois que nous trimons sur ce boulot* ⑩ to knock o.s. out = *se crever* ☠ *tu me fais suer* = you're a pain in the neck — *on se fait suer* = what a drag.

SWEATER (n) *chandail* (m) : I just bought a new sweater = *je viens d'acheter un nouveau chandail* ⑩ turtleneck = *col roulé*, V neck = *col en V*, cardigan = ←.

SWEATSHOP (n) *entreprise* (f) *où les ouvriers sont exploités/où l'on fait suer le burnous* : the owner is running a sweatshop = *dans cette entreprise le propriétaire fait suer le burnous.*

SWEATY (adj, -ier, -iest) *en sueur* : sweaty after jogging = *en sueur après le jogging* ⑩ sticky = *poisseux.*

SWEDEN (n) *Suède* (f) **SWEDISH** (n, adj) *Suédois, -e.*

SWEEP (to, swept, swept) *balayer* : sweep the kitchen floor = *balayez le sol de la cuisine* ⑩ a broom = *un balai.*

SWEEPING (adj) *à grande échelle* : sweeping reforms = *des réformes à grande échelle* ⑩ extensive = *étendu*
sweeping generalization = *généralisation hâtive.*

SWEEPSTAKE(S) (n) *sweepstake* (m) : to win the sweepstakes = *gagner le sweepstake* ⑩ lottery = *loterie*, raffle ticket = *billet de tombola.*

SWEET (adj, -er, -est) **1/** *sucré, -e* : the chocolate cake was too sweet = *le gâteau au chocolat était trop sucré* ≠ bitter = *amer* **2/** *mignon, -onne* : a sweet child = *un enfant mignon* ⑩ adorable = ←
to be sweet on = *avoir un faible pour* : he's sweet on his secretary = *il a un faible pour sa secrétaire* ⑩ to be smitten on = *être toqué de*
to have a sweet tooth = *être bec sucré/porté sur les douceurs*
it'll be sweet revenge ! = *la vengeance est un plat qui se mange froid !*
it was sweet of you (to help) = *c'était très gentil à vous (de nous aider)*
sweet dreams ! = *fais de beaux rêves !* ⑩ good night ! = *bonne nuit !*

sweet potato = *patate douce*
sweet pepper = *poivron doux*
take your (own) sweet time ! = *prends tout ton temps !* ≠ hurry up ! = *dépêche-toi !*
you bet your sweet ass ! = *et mon cul, c'est du poulet ?* → BUZZ OFF !

SWEET-AND-SOUR (adj) *aigre-doux, -douce* : sweet-and-sour sauce = *une sauce aigre-douce* ⑩ spicy = *épicé* ☠ → bittersweet.

SWEETHEART (n) **1/** *amoureux, -euse* : she met one of her old sweethearts = *elle a rencontré un de ses amoureux d'autrefois* ⑩ beau = *galant*, boyfriend = *petit ami*, flame = *flirt* **2/** *chou, choute* : be a sweetheart and help me = *sois un chou et aide-moi* ⑩ angel = *ange* ☠ → cabbage.

SWEETIE PIE (n) *amour* (m) : my father's a sweetie pie = *mon père est un amour* ≠ a monster = *un monstre* ☠ → love.

SWEETS (n pl) (GB) *bonbons* (m pl) = candy.

SWEET-TALK (to, -ed) *flagorner* : he sweet-talked the boss into a raise = *il a flagorné le patron pour obtenir une augmentation* ⑩ to soft-soap = *passer de la pommade à.*

SWELL (adj, -er, -est) *chouette* : a swell movie/guy = *un film/un type chouette* → WONDERFUL ≠ crummy = *moche.*

SWELL (to, -ed, -ed or swollen) *enfler* : my ankle's swelling (up) = *ma cheville enfle* ⑩ to puff up = *(se) boursoufler*
to swell with pride = *se gonfler d'orgueil.*

SWELL ! (interj) *chouette !* ⑩ fine ! = *parfait !*

SWELLING (n) *enflure* (f), *gonflement* (m) : a swelling on her breast = *un gonflement au sein.*

SWELTERING (adj) *étouffant, -e* : a sweltering month of August = *un mois d'août étouffant* ⑩ burning = *brûlant* = sizzling, scorching = *bouillant*, it's baking = *on se croirait dans un four.*

SWERVE (to, -d) *faire une embardée* : the car swerved to avoid the drunkard = *la voiture a fait une embardée pour éviter l'ivrogne* ⑩ to put on the brakes = *freiner.*

SWIFT (adj, -er, -est) *prompt, -e* : a swift answer = *une réponse prompte* ⑩ fast = *rapide* **SWIFTLY** (adv) *promptement.*

SWIM (n) **to go for a swim** = *aller se baigner* : let's go for a swim = *si on allait se baigner* ⑩ to go for a dip = *aller faire trempette*
in the swim = *dans le bain* : we're finally getting in the swim (of things) = *on est enfin dans le bain* ≠ out of it = *pas dans le coup.*

SWIM (to, swam, swum) *nager* : do you know how to swim ? = *est-ce que vous savez nager ?* ⑩ to dive =

plonger, to float = *faire la planche* ≠ to drown = *se noyer*
to swim across (the Channel) = *traverser (la Manche) à la nage*
to go swimming = *aller se baigner* : let's go swimming = *si on allait se baigner* = to go bathing (GB).

SWIMMER (n) *nageur, -euse* : an Olympic swimmer = *un nageur/une nageuse olympique* ⑩ diver = *plongeur.*

SWIMMING (n) *natation (f)* : my sister does a lot of swimming = *ma sœur fait beaucoup de natation* ⑩ breaststroke = *brasse,* butterfly (breaststroke) = *brasse papillon,* crawl = ←
swimming pool = *piscine.*

SWINDLE (n) *escroquerie (f)* : the deal was a real swindle = *l'affaire était une véritable escroquerie* ⑩ con = *arnaque,* fraud = *fraude.*

SWINDLE (to, -d) *escroquer* : he swindled the company out of a hundred grand = *il a escroqué la société d'une centaine de milliers de dollars* → TO HUSTLE.

SWINDLER (n) *escroc (m)* : he's a swindler, not a killer = *c'est un escroc, pas un tueur* ⑩ hustler = *combinard,* con(fidence) man = *arnaqueur.*

SWINE (n inv) *porc (m)* : what a swine he is ! = *quel porc !* → BASTARD ☠ → pork.

SWING (n) **1/** *balançoire (f)* : there are swings in the yard for kids = *il y a des balançoires pour les gosses dans la cour* ⑩ seesaw = *bascule* **2/** *partouse (f)* : a small swing = *une petite partouse* ⑩ group sex = *sexe en groupe,* a two-couple swing/a foursome = *une partie carrée*
to get into the swing of things = *se mettre dans le bain* : when I go to New York, I like to get into the swing of things = *quand je suis à New York, j'aime me mettre dans le bain* ⑩ to be with it = *être dans le coup*
a swing to the left/right = *un revirement à gauche/à droite.*

SWING (to, swang, swung) **1/** *balancer, swinguer* : New York swings at any hour = *ça balance/ça swingue tout le temps à New York* ≠ to be out of it = *être hors du coup* ☠ → to chuck **2/** *partouser* : they began swinging long before their marriage = *ils ont commencé à partouser bien avant leur mariage* **3/** *se balancer* : monkeys swing in trees = *les singes se balancent dans les arbres* ☠ → to chuck
to swing stg = *se débrouiller pour obtenir qqch* : I'll swing two tickets for you = *je vais me débrouiller pour vous obtenir deux billets* ⑩ to finagle = *ruser pour avoir*
to swing (an election) = *truquer (une élection).*

SWINGER (n) **1/** *partouseur, -euse* : when they reached fourty they became swingers = *c'est à la quarantaine qu'ils sont devenus partouseurs* **2/** *quelqu'un dans le coup* : they are no deadheads, they're swingers ! = *ce ne sont pas des encroûtés, ils sont dans le coup !* ≠ square = *vieux jeu.*

SWINGING (adj) *qui bouge* : New York is a swinging town = *New York est une ville qui bouge* ≠ dull = *assommant.*

SWIPE (n) **to take a swipe at s.o.** = *jeter une pierre dans le jardin de qqn* : the Senator took a swipe at the President during his TV interview = *au cours de son entretien télévisé, le sénateur a jeté une pierre dans le jardin du Président* ⑩ to take a dig at = *lancer une pique à.*

SWIPE (to, -d) *faucher* : she swiped a watch = *elle a fauché une montre* ⑩ to make off with = *faire main basse sur.*

SWITCH (n, -es) **1/** *changement (m)* : a switch in policy = *un changement de politique* ☠ → change **2/** *interrupteur (m)* : where's the switch ? = *où est l'interrupteur ?*

SWITCH (to, -ed) *changer* : let's switch places ! = *changeons de place !* = let's change places ! ☠ → to change
to switch on ≠ **off** = *allumer* ≠ *éteindre (la lumière)* ☠ *allumer* → to light, *éteindre* → to extinguish.

SWITCHBOARD (n) *standard (m)* : switchboard operator = *standardiste* ⑩ telephone operator = *téléphoniste* ☠ → standard.

SWITZERLAND (n) *Suisse (f)* **SWISS** (n) *Suisse, Suissesse* **SWISS** (adj) *suisse* ☠ *boire en suisse* = to drink alone.

SWOON (to, -ed) *se pâmer* : his fans swooned when he sang = *ses fans se sont pâmés quand il s'est mis à chanter.*

SWORD (n) *épée (f)* : a blood-stained sword = *une épée tachée de sang* ⑩ saber = *sabre*
to cross swords with s.o. = *croiser le fer/rompre des lances avec qqn*
☠ *mettre à qqn l'épée dans les reins* = to prod s.o. without respite.

SYLLABLE (n) *syllabe (f)* : the word table has two syllables = *le mot table a deux syllabes* ⑩ vowel = *voyelle.*

SYLLABUS (n, -es or -bi) *programme (m) (scolaire)* : languages aren't in this year's syllabus = *les langues ne font pas partie du programme de cette année* ☠ → program.

SYMBOL (n) *symbole (m)* : a symbol of peace = *un symbole de paix* ⑩ sign = *signe* **SYMBOLIC(AL)** (adj) *symbolique* : a symbolic dream = *un rêve symbolique* **SYMBOLICALLY** (adv) *symboliquement* **SYMBOLIZE** (to, -d) *symboliser* : the drawing symbolizes the Judgment Day = *le dessin symbolise le Jugement dernier* ⑩ to represent = *représenter.*

SYMMETRY (n, -ies) *symétrie (f)* : I like symmetry = *j'aime la symétrie* **SYMMETRICAL** (adj) *symétrique.*

SYMPATHETIC (adj) *qui compatit à* : I'm sympathetic to his problems = *je compatis à ses problèmes* ⑩ understanding = *compréhensif.*

SYMPATHETICALLY (adv) *avec compassion* : I listened sympathetically = *je l'ai écouté avec compassion.*

SYMPATHIZE (to, -d) *compatir* : she lost her dog and I do sympathize with her = *elle a perdu son chien, et vraiment je compatis* ⓒ to commiserate = *s'apitoyer* ☠ *nous avons sympathisé* = we hit it off.

SYMPATHIZER (n) *sympathisant, -e* : communist sympathizers = *des sympathisants communistes* ⓒ supporter = ←.

SYMPATHY (n, -ies) **1/** *indulgence* (f) : I have no sympathy for him = *je n'ai aucune indulgence à son égard* ⓒ pity = *pitié* **2/** *sympathie* (f) : she has leftist sympathies = *elle a des sympathies de gauche*
my deepest sympathies = *toutes mes condoléances/je suis de tout cœur avec vous*
☠ *se prendre de sympathie pour* = to take a liking to.

SYMPHONY (n, -ies) *symphonie* (f) : Beethoven's ninth symphony = *la neuvième symphonie de Beethoven* ⓒ concerto = ←.

SYMPOSIUM (n, -s or -ia) *symposium* (m) : a symposium on mental diseases = *un symposium sur les maladies mentales* ⓒ conference = *conférence.*

SYMPTOM (n) *symptôme* (m) : he's showing symptoms of senility = *il présente des symptômes de sénilité* **SYMPTOMATIC** (adj) *symptomatique.*

SYNAGOGUE (n) *synagogue* (f) : the synagogue was attacked = *on a attaqué la synagogue* ⓒ temple = ←, rabbi = *rabbin.*

SYNCHRONIZE (to, -d) *synchroniser* : the film was badly synchronized = *le film était mal synchronisé* **SYNCHRONIZATION** (n) *synchronisation* (f).

SYNDICATE (n) *syndicat* (m) : a syndicate of real estate companies = *un syndicat de sociétés immobilières* ⓒ cartel = ← ☠ *un syndicat (ouvrier)* = a (labor) union.

SYNDICATE (to, -d) **to be syndicated** = *avoir le même article publié dans différents journaux* : his column is syndicated across the country = *sa chronique est publiée dans différents journaux.*

SYNONYM (n) *synonyme* (m) : "wealthy" and "rich" are synonyms = « *aisé* » *et* « *riche* » *sont synonymes* ≠ antonym = *antonyme.*

SYNONYMOUS (adj) *synonyme* : being rich is synonymous with having the freedom to do what you want = *être riche est synonyme de pouvoir faire ce qu'on veut.*

SYNOPSIS (n, -es) *synopsis* (m) (films), *compte rendu* (m) : a synopsis of the film/of the recent news = *un synopsis du film/un compte rendu des dernières nouvelles* ⓒ summary = *résumé*, script = ←.

SYNTAX (n, -es) *syntaxe* (f) ⓒ rhetoric = *rhétorique.*

SYNTHESIS (n, -es) *synthèse* (f) : he made a synthesis of the report = *il a fait la synthèse du rapport.*

SYNTHETIC (n, adj) *synthétique* (m) : synthetic materials = *des tissus synthétiques.*

SYPHILIS (n) *syphilis* (f) ⓒ VD = Venereal Disease = *maladie vénérienne*, crabs = *morpions*, gonorrhea = *blennorragie.*

SYRIA (n) *Syrie* (f) **SYRIAN** (n, adj) *Syrien, -enne.*

SYRINGE (n) *seringue* (f) : a disposable syringe = *une seringue à jeter* ⓒ needle = *aiguille.*

SYRUP (n) *sirop* (m) : cough syrup = *sirop contre la toux* ⓒ juice = *jus.*

SYSTEM (n) *système* (m) : a very good system = *un très bon système* ⓒ method = *méthode*
to get stg out of one's system = *se libérer de qqch* : she got her desire to act out of her system = *elle s'est libérée de son désir de jouer la comédie*
to have s.o. in one's system = *avoir qqn dans la peau* : we split two years ago but I still have him in my system = *ça fait deux ans que nous nous sommes séparés mais je l'ai toujours dans la peau* ⓒ to be in love with s.o. = *être amoureux de qqn*
☠ *le système D* = hustling
— *il me tape sur le système* = he gets on my nerves.

SYSTEMATIC (adj) *systématique* : systematic hostility = *une hostilité systématique* **SYSTEMATICALLY** (adv) *systématiquement* **SYSTEMATIZE** (to, -d) *systématiser* : the philosopher tried to systematize his thought = *le philosophe a essayé de systématiser sa pensée.*

TAB (n) *note* *(f)* : put the drinks on my tab = *mettez les boissons sur ma note* ⓪ the damages = *la douloureuse*
to keep tabs on s.o. = *avoir qqn à l'œil* : he keeps tabs on his wife = *il a sa femme à l'œil*
to pick up the tab = *payer (la note)* : he picked up the tab for all of us = *il a payé pour tout le monde*
☠ → note.

TABLE (n) *table* *(f)* : a formica table = *une table en formica*, table mat = *set de table* ⓪ tablecloth = *nappe*, napkin = *serviette*
to crawl under the table = *rentrer sous terre* : I was so embarrassed I wanted to crawl under the table = *j'étais tellement embarrassée que j'aurais voulu rentrer sous terre*
I can drink you under the table ! = *tu rouleras sous la table avant moi ! je tiens mieux l'alcool que toi !*
to set ≠ clear the table = *mettre ≠ débarrasser la table*
table of contents = *table des matières*
table tennis = *tennis de table*
to turn the tables on s.o. = *renverser les rôles* : he's been cheating on her for a long time, but now she's taken a lover and turned the tables on him = *il la trompe depuis longtemps, mais maintenant elle a pris un amant et elle a renversé les rôles*
under the table = *sous la table* : the brothel owner pays the cops under the table = *le patron du bordel paie les flics sous la table* ⓪ sub rosa = *sous le manteau*
☠ *se mettre à table* = to come clean/to sing
— *être sur table d'écoute* = to be wiretapped
— *faire table rase* = to make a clean sweep
— *à table* = soup's on !

TABLE (to, -d) **to table (a bill)** = *reporter le débat (sur un projet de loi)*.

TABLE-HOP (to, -ped) *aller de table en table* : he table-hopped all night = *il est allé de table en table toute la soirée*.

TABLESPOON (n) *cuillère* *(f)* *à soupe* ⓪ tablespoonful = *cuillerée à soupe*.

TABLET (n) *cachet* *(m)* : take two tablets every 4 hours = *prenez deux cachets toutes les 4 heures* ⓪ drops = *gouttes*

☠ *blanc comme un cachet d'aspirine* = as white as a sheet
— *le cachet d'un artiste* = a performer's salary
— *avoir du cachet* = to have a lot of class (restaurant, house, etc.).

TABLOID (n) *(journal) tabloïd* *(m)* : this tabloid focuses on sensational news = *ce tabloïd ne donne que les informations à scandale* ⓪ newspaper = *journal*.

TABOO (n, adj) *tabou* *(m)* : for some people sex is taboo = *pour certaines personnes, le sexe est tabou*.

TACIT (adj) *tacite* : his tacit consent = *son consentement tacite* ≠ expressed = *exprimé*.

TACITURN (adj) *taciturne* : a taciturn personality = *une personnalité taciturne* ⓪ morose = ←.

TACK (n) *punaise* *(f)* = thumbtack ⓪ nail = *clou* ☠ *une punaise (insecte)* = a bug.

TACKLE (to, -d) *s'attaquer à* : to tackle the drug problem = *s'attaquer au problème de la drogue* ⓪ to deal with = *traiter de*.

TACKY (adj, -ier, -iest) **1/** *clinquant, -e* : tacky jewelry = *des bijoux clinquants* ⓪ gaudy = *criard*, chintzy = *de pacotille* **2/** *miteux, -euse* : the tacky part of town = *les quartiers miteux de la ville* ≠ ritzy = *rupin*.

TACT (n inv) *tact* *(m)* : your answer lacked tact = *votre réponse manquait de tact* ⓪ delicacy = *délicatesse*
TACTFUL (adj) *plein, -e de tact* ≠ tactless = *sans tact*.

TACTICAL (adj) *tactique* : a tactical advantage = *un avantage tactique* ⓪ strategic = *stratégique*.

TACTICS (n pl) *tactique* *(f)* : I don't agree with your tactics = *je ne suis pas d'accord avec votre tactique* ⓪ course of action = *ligne de conduite*
to change one's tactics = *changer de tactique*.

TAFFETA (n) *taffetas* *(m)* ⓪ silk = *soie*.

TAG (n) *étiquette* *(f)* : the price is on the tag = *le prix est sur l'étiquette* ⓪ label = *griffe* (clothes)
to play tag = *jouer à chat*
☠ *(ne me dites pas que je suis à gauche,)* j'*aime pas les étiquettes* = (don't call me a leftist) I don't like labels.

TAG ALONG (to, -ged) *être pendu, -e aux basques de :* wherever she goes, her kid sister wants to tag along = *où qu'elle aille, sa petite sœur est toujours pendue à ses basques.*

TAIL (n) *queue (f) :* I walked on the dog's tail = *j'ai marché sur la queue du chien*
the tail end = *juste/tout à la fin :* we came at the tail end of his speech = *nous sommes arrivés tout à la fin de son discours,* we saw the tail end of the news = *nous avons juste vu la fin des nouvelles* ≠ the beginning = *le début*
the dog's wagging its tail = *le chien remue la queue*
with one's tail between one's legs = *la queue entre les jambes/la queue basse*
to put a tail on (a suspect) = *faire filer (un suspect)*
☠ *à la queue leu leu* = in single file
— *sa queue (homme)* = his cock (man)
— *piano à queue* = grand piano
— *faire une queue de poisson à qqn* = to cut s.o. off (car)
— *faire la queue* = to stand in line
— *finir en queue de poisson* = to fizzle out
— *tenir la queue de la poêle* = to run the show
— *la queue du train* = the rear of the train.

TAIL (to, -ed) *filer :* the cops are tailing him = *les flics le filent* Ⓞ to shadow = *prendre en filature,* to be on s.o.'s heels = *être sur les talons de qqn*
☠ *file-moi le sel* = hand me the salt
— *je file !* = I'm off !/I'm taking off !

TAILLIGHT (n) *feu (m) arrière :* it's foggy, check your taillights ! = *il y a du brouillard, vérifie tes feux arrière* ≠ headlight = *phare.*

TAILOR (n) *tailleur (m) :* my grandfather was a tailor = *mon grand-père était tailleur* Ⓞ dressmaker = *couturier*
☠ *un tailleur* = a woman's suit
— *s'asseoir en tailleur* = to sit cross-legged.

TAILORED (adj) *ultra-classique :* he always wears tailored clothes = *il a toujours des vêtements ultra-classiques.*

TAILS (n pl) *queue (f) de pie :* all the men wore tails = *tous les hommes étaient en queue de pie* Ⓞ tux = *smoking.*

TAILSPIN (n) **to send into a tailspin** = *ficher en l'air :* the news sent her into a tailspin = *la nouvelle l'a fichue en l'air.*

TAKE (n) **1/** *recette (f) :* what was last night's take ? = *quelle a été la recette hier soir ?* Ⓞ profit = *bénéfice* ☠ → recipe **2/** *prise (f) (de vues) :* ten takes were needed to shoot the scene = *il a fallu dix prises (de vues) pour tourner la scène* ☠ → plug

to be on the take = *se sucrer :* the cops on this beat are on the take = *les flics de cette ronde en profitent pour se sucrer* ≠ to be incorruptible = *être incorruptible* ☠ → to scratch out

the take = *la prise :* I wonder why they pulled the job, the take being so small = *je me demande pourquoi ils ont fait le fric-frac, la prise n'étant pas bien grosse* Ⓞ haul = *butin* ☠ → plug.

TAKE (to, took, taken) **1/** *prendre, emmener (s.o.) :* take an umbrella/the bus = *prends un parapluie/le bus,* take your brother = *emmène ton frère*
2/ *prendre :* that fad never took here = *cette mode n'a jamais pris ici* Ⓞ to work = *marcher*

to take an exam/a test = *passer un examen* Ⓞ to pass =*réussir*
to take (French/biology/ballet) = *faire (du français/de la biologie/de la danse classique)*
I can't take you anywhere ! = *tu n'es pas sortable !*
I can't take him ! = *je ne peux pas l'encaisser !* Ⓞ I can't bear him ! = *je ne peux pas le supporter !*
to take stg lying down = *encaisser qqch sans rien dire*
to take it = *encaisser :* whatever his wife says, he takes it = *quoi que sa femme lui dise, il encaisse* ☠ *encaisser un chèque* = to cash a check
take it or leave it ! = *c'est à prendre ou à laisser !*
I can take it or leave it : Chinese food ? I can take it or leave it ! = *la cuisine chinoise ? j'aime bien, mais sans plus !*
I take it that (you don't agree) =*je suppose que*

(vous n'êtes pas d'accord) Ⓞ I assume that = *je présume que*
to be taken = **1/** *se faire avoir :* how do you know you're not being taken ? = *comment savez-vous que vous n'êtes pas en train de vous faire avoir ?* ≠ to rip s.o. off = *escroquer qqn* **2/** *être pris :* the seat's taken = *la place est prise*
how did she take it ? = *comment l'a-t-elle pris ?*
I can't take it anymore ! = *je ne peux plus supporter ça !* Ⓞ I've had it ! =*j'en ai ras le bol !*
it takes (courage/patience) = *ça demande (du courage/de la patience)*
it'll take (an hour) = *ça prendra (une heure)* Ⓞ **how long will it take ?** = *ça prendra combien de temps ?*
to take stg well ≠ **badly** = *prendre bien* ≠ *mal qqch :* she took the news very well ≠ badly = *elle a très bien* ≠ *mal pris la nouvelle*

to be taken aback = *avoir le souffle coupé* : I was taken aback when he told me to pay = *ça m'a coupé le souffle quand il m'a dit de payer* ○ to be flabbergasted = *être scié*

to take after s.o. = *tenir de qqn* : she takes after her father = *elle tient de son père* ○ to be like = *ressembler à*

to take along = *emmener* (s.o.), *emporter* (stg) : take him along ! = *emmène-le !*, take your bathing suit along = *emporte ton maillot de bain* ☠ *emporter* → to carry away

to take apart = *démonter* : to take a puzzle apart = *démonter un puzzle* ≠ to put together = *assembler* ☠ *ne pas se démonter* = not to be fazed

to take s.o. aside = *prendre qqn à part* : he took me aside and told me the truth = *il m'a pris à part et m'a dit la vérité*

to take away = *enlever* : the child was taken away from his mother because she hit him = *l'enfant a été enlevé à sa mère parce qu'elle le battait*, the bill took away all the pleasure = *l'addition nous a enlevé tout plaisir* ☠ → to remove

take away (20) from (60) = *enlevez (20) de (60)*

to take stg back = 1/ *rapporter qqch* : I don't like the coat, I'm going to take it back = *je n'aime pas le manteau, je vais le rapporter* 2/ *reprendre qqch* (store) : I don't know if the store will take the coat back = *je ne sais pas si le magasin reprendra le manteau* 3/ *retirer qqch* : that was a mean thing to say, take it back ! = *retire ce que tu viens de dire, c'est méchant !*

that takes me back to (my youth) = *ça me rappelle (ma jeunesse)*

to take stg down = 1/ *noter qqch* : take his name down = *notez son nom* ○ to put down = *inscrire* ☠ → to note 2/ *enlever qqch* : take the picture down = *enlevez le tableau* ☠ → to remove

to take s.o. for = *prendre qqn pour* : I took him for his brother

= *je l'ai pris pour son frère*

who do you take me for ? = *pour qui me prends-tu ?*

to take stg for granted = *tenir qqch pour acquis* : I take it for granted that he'll agree = *je tiens pour acquis qu'il sera d'accord* ○ to go on the assumption that = *prendre pour acquis que*

to take s.o. for granted = *considérer qqn comme faisant partie des meubles* : he takes his wife for granted = *il considère sa femme comme faisant partie des meubles*

to be taken from = *être tiré de* : a film taken from a Tolstoy novel* = *un film tiré d'un roman de Tolstoï*

to take stg from = *prendre qqch à* : he took the candy from the child = *il a pris le bonbon à l'enfant*

take it from there ! = *faites le reste !* : you just introduce us and I'll take it from there = *présentez-nous seulement et je ferai le reste*

you can take it from me (abortions are no fun) ! = *croyez-en ma vieille expérience (ce n'est pas drôle de se faire avorter) !*

to take in = *se faire* : the restaurant took in a grand over the weekend = *le restaurant s'est fait mille dollars dans le week-end* ☠ → to do

to take stg in = *reprendre qqch* : the dress needs to be taken in = *cette robe a besoin d'être reprise*

to take s.o. in = 1/ *recueillir qqn* : they took the child in = *ils ont recueilli l'enfant* 2/ *berner qqn* : I'm easily taken in = *je me laisse facilement berner* → TO HUSTLE

to take off = 1/ *décoller* : what time does your plane take off ? = *à quelle heure votre avion décolle-t-il ?* 2/ *filer* : it's late, let's take off ! = *il est tard, il faut que nous filions !* → TO LEAVE ☠ → to tail 3/ *perdre* : he took off five pounds in a week = *il a perdu deux kilos et demi en*

une semaine = he lost five pounds in a week ≠ to put on = *prendre* ☠ → to lose

to take stg off = *ôter qqch* : why don't you take your coat off and stay for a while ? = *pourquoi n'ôtez-vous pas votre manteau et ne restez-vous pas un petit moment ?* ≠ to put on = *mettre*

to take ... off = *prendre ... de congé* : I took five days off = *j'ai pris cinq jours de congé*

to take on = *prendre* : the lawyer's too busy to take on any more clients = *l'avocat est trop occupé pour prendre plus de clients*

to take s.o. on = 1/ *embaucher qqn* : they took 5 new men on = *ils ont embauché 5 nouveaux* ≠ to oust = *vider* 2/ *attendre qqn de pied ferme* : I'll take him on any time = *son heure sera la mienne ; je l'attends de pied ferme*

to take out = *souscrire* : she took out an insurance policy = *elle a souscrit une police d'assurances* ☠ → to subscribe to

to take s.o. out = *sortir (avec) qqn* : who is he taking out tonight ? = *(avec) qui sort-il ce soir ?*

to take stg out = 1/ *sortir qqch* : he took his wallet out of his pocket = *il a sorti son portefeuille de sa poche* 2/ *ôter qqch* : this paragraph is bad, take it out ! = *ce paragraphe est mauvais, ôtez-le !* ☠ *ôte-toi de là !* = move !

... to take out = *... à emporter* : Chinese food to take out = *cuisine chinoise à emporter*

to take it out on s.o. = *passer sa colère sur qqn* : I don't care what your boss did, don't take it out on me ! = *je ne veux pas savoir ce que ton patron t'a fait, ne passe pas ta colère sur moi !* → TO LAMBAST

to take over = 1/ *prendre le pouvoir* : when the President died, the army took over = *quand le Président est mort, l'armée a pris le pouvoir* ○ to overthrow = *renverser* 2/ *prendre la suite/la relève* : when his father retires, he'll take over = quand son père partira à la retraite, il prendra la suite/la relève 3/ prendre le contrôle de : to take over another company = prendre le contrôle d'une autre société

to take stg over = redoubler en : she has to take French over next year = elle devra redoubler en français l'année prochaine ⦿ to repeat = redoubler

to take s.o. over = posséder qqn : his partners took him over = ses associés l'ont possédé → TO HUSTLE

to take s.o. round = faire visiter à qqn : I'll take you round when you come to New York = je vous ferai visiter New York quand vous viendrez

to take (the bus) to (work) = prendre (le bus) pour (aller travailler)

to take to (drink) = se mettre à (boire)

to take to s.o. = se prendre de sympathie pour qqn : I took to him right away = je me suis tout de suite pris de sympathie pour lui

to take stg to s.o. = porter qqch à qqn : take this to your father = porte ça à ton père

to take s.o. to = emmener qqn à/chez : I have to take my son to the doctor = il faut que j'emmène mon fils chez le docteur

to take stg up = examiner une question : we'll take that up next week = nous examinerons cette question la semaine prochaine

to take up = 1/ prendre : the bed takes up too much room = le lit prend trop de place 2/ commencer (à apprendre): she decided to take up painting/driving = elle a décidé de commencer la peinture/à apprendre à conduire

to take up with s.o. = se mettre avec : my sister took up with

a lawyer = ma sœur s'est mise avec un avocat ⦿ to go out with = sortir avec

to take s.o. up on stg = accepter volontiers : thank you for your invitation, I'll take you up on it = merci pour votre invitation, j'accepte volontiers

to be taken up with = être pris par : she won't come, she's taken up with her work = elle ne viendra pas, elle est prise par son travail

to take upon o.s. to = (faire) de soi-même : she took it upon herself to tell him what happened = elle lui a dit d'elle-même ce qui était arrivé

you can't take it with you ! = tu ne l'emporteras pas en paradis !

to be taken with = être épris de : he's taken with my sister = il est épris de ma sœur ⦿ to be infatuated with = être entiché de

---

☠ qu'est-ce qu'il va prendre ! = he's going to get it !
— qu'est-ce qui vous prend ? = what's gotten into you ?
— prendre un verre/un café = to have a drink/a coffee
— on ne m'y prendra plus ! = you won't catch me at it again !
— il a pris cinq kilos = he put on

eleven pounds
— ça ne prend pas ! = I don't buy it !
— savoir s'y prendre = to know how to go about stg
— prendre (une décision) = to make (a decision)
— pour qui se prend-il ? = who does he think he is ?

— en prendre pour dix ans = to get ten years
— s'en prendre à qqn = to hold s.o. responsible
— s'y prendre bien ≠ mal = to go about stg the right ≠ wrong way
— sa dernière chanson a bien pris = his last song clicked.

TAKE-HOME PAY (n) salaire (m) net (après impôts) : how much is your take-home pay ? = quel est votre salaire net ?

TAKEOFF (n) 1/ décollage (m) : the takeoff's at midnight = le décollage est à minuit ≠ landing = atterrissage 2/ pastiche (m) : he does a takeoff on famous politicians = il fait le pastiche d'hommes politiques célèbres ⦿ parody = parodie.

TAKEOVER (n) 1/ prise (f) de pouvoir : a takeover by the generals = une prise de pouvoir par les généraux ⦿ uprising = soulèvement, putsch = ← 2/ rachat (m) : economic crises led to numerous takeovers of troubled companies = les crises économiques ont entraîné de nombreux rachats d'entreprises en difficulté
a takeover bid = une offre publique d'achat.

TAKER (n) preneur, -euse : are there any takers for my offer ? = y a-t-il preneur pour l'offre que j'ai faite ? ⦿ purchaser = acquéreur.

TALE (n) 1/ récit (m) : tales of torture = des récits de torture ⦿ story = histoire 2/ bobard (m) : don't tell me any more tales ! = ne me racontez plus de bobards ! ⦿ falsehood = contrevérité.

TALENT (n) talent (m) : a painter of great talent = un peintre de grand talent ⦿ gift = don
talent scout = dénicheur de talents.

TALENTED (adj) talentueux, -euse : a talented filmmaker = un cinéaste talentueux ⦿ of genius = de génie.

TALK (n) 1/ conversation (f) : we had an interesting talk last night = nous avons eu une conversation intéressante hier soir ⦿ rap = discussion ☠ → conversation
2/ exposé (m) : an interesting talk on drugs = un exposé sur la drogue intéressant ⦿ lecture = conférence

to be the talk of the town = *faire couler beaucoup d'encre* : their couple's the talk of the town = *leur couple fait couler beaucoup d'encre* ⓪ to be splashed all over the front pages = *défrayer la chronique*

to have a talk with s.o. = *avoir une conversation/s'entretenir avec qqn*

it's just talk ! = 1/ *ce n'est que du blabla !* : she says she's a hooker, but it's just talk ! = *elle dit qu'elle est putain, mais ce n'est que du blabla !* ⓪

it's hot air = *c'est du vent* 2/ *ce ne sont que des racontars !* : the President is getting divorced ? it's just talk ! = *le Président va divorcer ? ce ne sont que des racontars !* ⓪ gossip = *commérages*

talk is cheap = *ça ne coûte rien de parler*

talk show = *entretien télévisé*

there's a lot of talk about (a nuclear war/his divorce) = *on a beaucoup parlé d'(une guerre nucléaire)/de (son divorce).*

TALK (to, -ed) 1/ *parler* : we talked all evening = *nous avons parlé toute la soirée* ⓪ to gab = *papoter*, to converse = *converser*, to shoot the breeze = *parler de la pluie et du beau temps* 2/ *parler* : the gangster talked and gave the show away = *le gangster a parlé et il a vendu la mèche* ⓪ to sing = *se mettre à table*

---

to talk about = *parler de* : we were just talking about you = *nous étions justement en train de parler de vous*

I don't know what you're talking about ! = *je ne sais pas de quoi vous parlez !*

to talk around = *tourner autour du pot* : stop talking around my question and answer = *cessez de tourner autour du pot et répondez à ma question* ⓪ to avoid the issue = *chercher des faux-fuyants*

to talk back = *répondre* : when your mother says something, don't talk back = *quand ta mère*

dit quelque chose, ne réponds pas = to answer back ☙ → to answer

to talk down to s.o. = *traiter qqn de haut* ⓪ to patronize = *être paternaliste*

to talk s.o. into ≠ **out of stg** = *arriver à persuader* ≠ *dissuader qqn de* : I talked him into ≠ out of coming = *je suis arrivé à le persuader* ≠ *dissuader de venir*

to talk of = *parler de* : all she talks of is sex = *elle ne parle que de cul*

to talk stg over = *parler de qqch* : let's talk it over tonight =

parlons-en ce soir ⓪ to thrash out stg = *débattre de qqch*

to talk to o.s. = *parler tout seul* : she's always talking to herself = *elle parle toujours toute seule*

to talk to s.o. = *parler à qqn* : I can't talk to you now I'll call you back = *je ne peux pas vous parler maintenant, je vous rappellerai*

not to talk to s.o. = *ne rien dire à qqn* : his last paintings don't talk to me = *ses dernières œuvres ne me disent rien* ⓪ I don't feature them = *ça ne me chante pas*

☙ *est-ce que vous parlez anglais ?* = do you speak English ?

— *je ne veux plus en entendre parler !* = I don't want to hear any more about it !

— *tu parles !* = you're telling me !

— *est-ce que tu parles sérieusement ?* = do you really mean it ?

TALKATIVE (adj) *bavard, -e* : a very talkative guy = *un type très bavard* ⓪ loquacious = *loquace.*

TALKIE (n) *film (m) parlant* : talkies came in 1927 = *les films parlants datent de 1927* ≠ silent movie = *film muet.*

TALKING-TO (n) **to give s.o. a (good) talking-to** = *faire un sermon à qqn* → TO LAMBAST.

TALKS (n pl) *pourparlers (m pl)* : talks between the two countries = *des pourparlers entre les deux pays* ⓪ conference = *conférence.*

TALL (adj, -er, -est) *grand, -e* : a tall man/building = *un homme grand/un grand immeuble* ≠ short = *petit*
to be (6 feet) tall = *mesurer (1,80 m)* ⓪ **how tall are you ?** = *combien mesurez-vous ?* ☙ → to measure
tall tale = *histoire à dormir debout* ⓪ yarn = *craques*
that's a tall order ! = *c'est beaucoup demander !*
☙ → great.

TAME (adj, -r, -st) *apprivoisé, -e* : a tame lion = *un lion apprivoisé* ≠ ferocious = *féroce.*

TAME (to, -d) *apprivoiser* : he's a playboy but I'll tame him ! = *c'est un play-boy, mais je l'apprivoiserai !* ⓪ to train = *dresser.*

TAMPER (to, -ed) **to tamper with (the election returns)** = *tripatouiller (le résultat des élections)* ⓪ to rig = *truquer.*

TAN (n) *bronzage (m)* : what a beautiful tan ! = *quel beau bronzage !* ⓪ sunburn = *coup de soleil*, skin cancer = *cancer de la peau* **TANNED** (adj) *bronzé, -e* : tanned legs = *des jambes bronzées.*

TANGERINE (n) *mandarine (f)* ⓪ orange = ←.

TANGIBLE (adj) *tangible* : no tangible proof was presented = *aucune preuve tangible n'a été avancée* ≠ intangible = ←.

TANGLE (n) *embrouillamini (m)* : the case is a terrible tangle = *cette affaire est un embrouillamini terrible.*

TANGLED (adj) *enchevêtré, -e* : tangled reasoning = *un raisonnement enchevêtré* ⑩ entangled = *emmêlé.*

TANGLE WITH (to, -d) *se colleter avec* : he's a tough customer, I wouldn't tangle with him if I were you = *c'est un dur, je n'essaierais pas de me colleter avec lui si j'étais à ta place* ⑩ to mess with = *se frotter à.*

TANK (n) *char (m)(d'assaut), tank (m), blindé (m)* : Russian tanks on the border = *des chars/tanks/blindés russes à la frontière* ☠ *arrête ton char !* = get off it !

TANTAMOUNT (adj) **to be tantamount to** = *équivaloir à* : what he said was tantamount to a confession = *ce qu'il a dit équivalait à une confession* ⑩ to amount to = *se résumer à.*

TANTRUM (n) *crise (f) de rage* : to throw a tantrum = *piquer une crise de rage* ⑩ to be a crybaby = *être pleurnicheur.*

TAP (n) **1/** *tape (f)* : a tap on the shoulder = *une tape sur l'épaule* **2/** *robinet (m)* : the tap's leaking = *le robinet fuit*
on tap = *à qui l'on peut faire appel* : she has some very good lawyers on tap = *elle a quelques très bons avocats à qui elle peut faire appel*
tap dancing = *les claquettes.*

TAP (to, -ped) **1/** *mettre sur table d'écoute* : the embassy's phone is tapped = *le téléphone de l'ambassade a été mis sur table d'écoute* ⑩ to bug = *poser des micros dans/chez* **2/** *faire appel à* : he was tapped for the chairmanship = *on a fait appel à lui pour la présidence,* society is tapping sources of solar energy = *la société fait appel à l'énergie solaire*
to tap on (the shoulder) = *taper sur (l'épaule).*

TAPE (n) *bande (f) (magnétique)* : a blank tape = *une bande magnétique vierge* ⑩ cassette = ← ☠ → band
tape recorder = *magnétophone.*

TAPE (to, -d) *enregistrer* : I taped the interview = *j'ai enregistré l'interview* ☠ → to record.

TAPER OFF (to, -ed) *diminuer petit à petit* : inflation's tapering off = *l'inflation diminue petit à petit* ⑩ to dwindle = *décroître.*

TAPESTRY (n, -ies) *tapisserie (f)* : an Aubusson tapestry = *une tapisserie d'Aubusson* ⑩ weaving = *tissage* ☠ *faire tapisserie* = to be a wallflower.

TAR (n) *goudron (m)* ⑩ asphalt = *asphalte.*

TARGET (n) *cible (f)* : our target is to sell 100 cars a week = *notre cible est de vendre 100 voitures par semaine* ⑩ purpose = but
to be on target = *ne pas dévier de sa trajectoire* : the spaceship's on target = *le vaisseau spatial ne dévie pas de sa trajectoire.*

TARIFF (n) **1/** *tarif (m)* : what are the hotel tariffs ? = *quels sont les tarifs de l'hôtel ?* **2/** *tarif (m) douanier* : a tariff on steel imports = *un tarif douanier pour les importations d'acier*
☠ *plein tarif* = full fare
— *tarif du médecin* = doctor's rate.

TARNISH (to, -ed) *ternir* : tarnished silver/reputation = *argent terni/réputation ternie* ⑩ to sully = *galvauder.*

TART (adj, -er, -est) *acerbe* : lengthy tart criticism = *une critique longue et acerbe* ⑩ biting = *mordant.*

TASK (n) *tâche (f)* : endless household tasks = *des tâches ménagères interminables* ⑩ chore = *corvée*
to take s.o. to task = *prendre qqn à partie* → TO LAMBAST
☠ *une tache* = a stain.

TASKMASTER (n) *(vrai) tyran (m)* : my boss is a real taskmaster = *mon patron est un vrai tyran.*

TASTE (n) **1/** *goût (m)* : the meat has a funny taste = *la viande a un drôle de goût* **2/** *goût (m)* : she has very good taste = *elle a beaucoup de goût* ⑩ elegance = *élégance*
do you want a taste ? = *vous voulez goûter ?* ⑩ do you want a bite ? = *vous en voulez un morceau ?*
in bad ≠ good taste = *de mauvais ≠ bon goût*
once you've had a taste of (independence, it's hard to be married) = *une fois qu'on a goûté à (l'indépendance, c'est dur d'être marié)*
a taste for (hot rods) = *le goût des (bolides)* ≠ an allergy to = *une allergie à*
☠ *des goûts et des couleurs, on ne discute pas* = that's what makes for horseracing.

TASTE (to, -d) *goûter* : taste this delicious sauce = *goûtez cette sauce délicieuse* ⑩ to try = *essayer*
it tastes very good = *ça a très bon goût*
to taste like (honey) = *avoir le goût de (miel)/avoir le même goût que (le miel).*

TASTEFUL (adj) *de bon goût* : tasteful decoration = *un décor de bon goût.*

TASTELESS (adj) *sans saveur* (food), *de mauvais goût* : this meat's tasteless = *cette viande est sans saveur,* tasteless decoration = *un décor de mauvais goût.*

TASTY (adj, -ier, -iest) *qui a du goût* : a tasty dish = *un plat qui a du goût.*

TATTERED (adj) *en lambeaux* : tattered clothing = *des vêtements en lambeaux.*

TATTLE (to, -d) *rapporter* : little kids often tattle = *les petits enfants rapportent souvent* ⑩ to squeal on = *moucharder* ☠ → to yield.

TATTLETALE (n) *rapporteur, -euse* : my brother's a real tattletale = *mon frère est un sacré rapporteur* ⑩ snitch = *cafeteur.*

TATTOO (n) *tatouage (m)* : a tattoo on his arm = *un tatouage sur le bras* **TATTOO** (to, -ed) *tatouer.*

TAUNT (to, -ed) *railler* : the kids taunted the blind man

= *les gosses ont raillé l'aveugle* ⊕ to jeer = *lancer des quolibets à* **TAUNT** (n) *raillerie* (f) ⊕ jeer = *quolibet.*

TAUT (adj, -er, -est) *crispé, -e* : a taut face = *un visage crispé.*

TAX (n, -es) *impôt* (m) (income), *taxe* (f) (product) : we all have to pay taxes alas ! = *tout le monde doit payer des impôts, hélas !*

deductible = *déductible*	**tax evasion** = *fraude fiscale*
to file taxes = *faire/remplir sa déclaration d'impôts*	**tax-exempt** = *exonéré d'impôt*
income tax = *impôt sur le revenu*	**tax exemption** = *exonération d'impôt*
inheritance tax = *droits de succession*	**tax-free** = *détaxé*
Internal Revenue Service = *le fisc* = IRS	**tax haven** = *paradis fiscal*
to levy taxes = *lever des impôts*	**taxpayer** = *contribuable*
property tax = *impôt foncier*	**tax return** = *déclaration/feuille d'impôts*
tax collector = *percepteur*	**tax shelter** = *échappatoire fiscale*
taxable = *imposable*	**value-added tax** = *taxe à la valeur ajoutée* = VAT = TVA
tax deduction = *déduction d'impôt*	**withholding tax** = *impôt retenu à la source.*

TAX (to, -ed) *imposer* (income), *taxer* (product) : our incomes are heavily taxed = *nos revenus sont lourdement imposés*, all imports are taxed = *toutes les importations sont taxées*
to be taxing = *être éprouvant* : the trip's too taxing for a man of his age = *le voyage est trop éprouvant pour un homme de son âge*
☠ *imposer* → to impose
— *taxer qqn d'infidélité* = to accuse s.o. of being unfaithful.

TAXI (n) *taxi* (m) : it isn't easy to get a taxi at lunchtime = *ce n'est pas facile d'avoir un taxi à l'heure du déjeuner* = cab ⊕ cruising = *en maraude*, meter = *compteur*
taxi driver = *chauffeur de taxi* ⊕ cabby = *taxi.*

TB (abbr) = tuberculosis = *tuberculose* (f).

TEA (n) *thé* (m) : I'll have tea with sugar, please = *je prendrai un thé sucré, s'il vous plaît*, tea bag = *sachet de thé* ⊕ teapot = *théière*, tearoom = *salon de thé.*

TEACH (to, taught, taught) *enseigner* : he taught history at Cornell = *il enseignait l'histoire à Cornell* ≠ to learn = *apprendre*
that will teach you ! = *ça t'apprendra !* ⊕ once bitten, twice shy = *chat échaudé craint l'eau froide*

to teach s.o. to = *apprendre à qqn à* : my husband's teaching me to drive = *mon mari m'apprend à conduire.*

TEACHER (n) *professeur* (m) : she's an English teacher = *elle est professeur d'anglais* ⊕ school = *école.*

TEACHING (n) *enseignement* (m) : I'm going into teaching = *je vais me lancer dans l'enseignement.*

TEAM (n) *équipe* (f) : I'm on the tennis team = *j'appartiens à l'équipe de tennis* ⊕ teamwork = *travail d'équipe*, teammate = *coéquipier* ☠ *équipe de nuit* = night shift.

TEAMSTER (n) *routier* (m) *syndiqué*
the Teamsters' Union = *le syndicat des camionneurs.*

TEAM UP (to, -ed) *faire équipe* : the French teamed up with the British to build the Concorde = *les Français ont fait équipe avec les Anglais pour construire le Concorde* ⊕ to band together = *se liguer.*

TEAPOT (n) *théière* (f) ⊕ coffee pot = *cafetière.*

TEAR (n) *larme* (f) : tears of joy = *des larmes de joie*
in tears = *en larmes*
to burst into tears = *fondre en larmes* ⊕ to cry like a baby = *pleurer à chaudes larmes*
to be near tears = *être au bord des larmes*
tear gas = *gaz lacrymogène*
☠ *avoir la larme facile* = to cry easily
— *une larme de (whisky)* = a drop of (whisky).

TEAR (to, tore, torn) *déchirer* : I tore my dress = *j'ai déchiré ma robe* = I ripped my dress ☠ → to rip
to tear apart = *déchirer* : the country's torn apart by war = *le pays est déchiré par la guerre*, their divorce's tearing the kids apart = *leur divorce est en train de déchirer les gosses* ☠ → to rip
to tear o.s. away = *s'arracher* : it was so interesting that I couldn't tear myself away = *c'était si intéressant que je n'ai pas pu m'en arracher* ☠ → to yank out
to be torn between (both parents) = *être tiraillé entre (ses deux parents)*
to tear down (building) = *démolir (immeuble)* ⊕ to pull down = *abattre* ☠ → to demolish
to tear into s.o. = *secouer les puces à qqn* → TO LAMBAST
to tear out = *arracher* : tear out the page = *arrachez la page* ⊕ to cut out = *découper* ☠ → to yank out
to tear up = *déchirer (en mille morceaux)* : after I read the letter, I tore it up = *après avoir lu la lettre, je l'ai déchirée* = to rip up.

TEARFUL (adj) *rempli, -e de larmes* : tearful eyes = *les yeux remplis de larmes.*

TEARJERKER (n) *histoire* (f) *à faire pleurer Margot* : his movies are always tearjerkers = *ses films sont toujours des histoires à faire pleurer Margot* ⊕ soap opera = *mélo.*

TEASE (n) *allumeuse* (f) : a tease tries to get men excited = *une allumeuse essaie d'exciter les hommes* ⊕ hot stuff = *quelqu'un qui a du tempérament.*

TEASE (to, -d) *taquiner* : I'm just teasing you = *c'est juste pour te taquiner* ⓪ to needle = *asticoter*, to put s.o. on = *faire marcher qqn*
to tease s.o. about = *taquiner qqn au sujet de* : don't tease him about his accent = *ne le taquinez pas au sujet de son accent.*

TECHNICAL (adj) *technique* : technical college = *collège technique* **TECHNICALLY** (adv) *techniquement* : it's just not possible technically = *ce n'est tout simplement pas possible techniquement.*

TECHNICALITY (n, -ies) *détail* (m) *technique* : that's a mere technicality = *c'est un simple détail technique.*

TECHNICIAN (n) *technicien, -enne* : to train technicians = *former des techniciens* ⓪ expert = ←.

TECHNIQUE (n) *technique* (f) : a great technique in bed = *une grande technique au lit* ⓪ manner = *manière*, tactics = *tactique.*

TECHNOCRAT (n) *technocrate* (m, f) : technocrats run the country = *les technocrates dirigent le pays* ⓪ technocracy = *technocratie.*

TECHNOLOGICAL (adj) *technologique* : tremendous technological progress = *des progrès technologiques énormes* **TECHNOLOGIST** (n) *technologue* (m, f) **TECHNOLOGY** (n, -ies) *technologie* (f) : modern technologies = *les technologies modernes*, high technology = *haute technologie.*

TEDIOUS (adj) *fastidieux, -euse* : tedious work = *travail fastidieux* ⓪ boring = *ennuyeux.*

TEED OFF (adj) **to be teed off** = *être furibard* : the boss is teed off because we've all come in late = *le patron est furibard parce que nous sommes tous arrivés en retard* → ANGRY.

TEEM (to, -ed) *pleuvoir à torrents* : it's been teeming all day = *il a plu à torrents toute la journée* ⓪ to rain = *pleuvoir*
to be teeming with = *fourmiller de* : the place was teeming with cops = *l'endroit fourmillait de flics* ⓪ to be swarming with = *grouiller de.*

TEENAGER (n) *teenager* (m, f) : teenagers robbed the bank = *ce sont des teenagers qui ont dévalisé la banque* ⓪ youngster = *gamin.*

TEENS (n pl) **to be in one's teens** = *être à l'âge ingrat.*

TEE SHIRT (n) = T-SHIRT.

TEETOTALER (n) *buveur, -euse d'eau* : he became a teetotaler after his accident = *c'est un buveur d'eau depuis son accident.*

TELEGRAM (n) *télégramme* (m) : to send a telegram = *envoyer un télégramme* ⓪ cable = *câble*, dispatch = *dépêche.*

TELEGRAPH (n) *télégraphe* (m) **TELEGRAPH** (to, -ed) *télégraphier* : to telegraph a message = *télégraphier un message.*

TELEPHONE (n) *téléphone* (m) = phone ⓪ answering service = *abonnés absents*, bad connection = *friture*, information = *renseignements*, switchboard operator = *standardiste*, phone book/directory = *annuaire*, toll-free number = *numéro vert*
to be on the telephone = *être au téléphone*
telephone operator = *opérateur, opératrice*
telephone booth = *cabine téléphonique*
☠ *téléphone rouge* = hot line
— *le téléphone arabe* = the grapevine.

TELESCOPE (n) *télescope* (m) : can you see the stars through the telescope ? = *est-ce que tu vois les étoiles dans le télescope ?*

TELEVISION (n) *télévision* (f) : I watch television late at night = *je regarde la télévision tard le soir* ⓪ the tube = *le petit écran*, TV = *télé*, commercial = *spot publicitaire*, television set = *poste de télévision*, remote control = *télécommande*, channel = *chaîne*, black and white = *noir et blanc*, a portable = *une télévision portative/un téléviseur portatif*, idiot card = *téléprompteur*, TV dinner = *plateau télé*, sponsor = ←, anchorman/woman = *présentateur/présentatrice des informations*, color television = *télévision (en) couleurs*, on television = *à la télévision*, prime time = *heure de grande écoute*, docudrama = *fiction documentaire*, prerecorded = *préenregistré/en différé* ≠ live = *en direct.*

TELL (to, told, told) *dire* : tell me what you think = *dites-moi ce que vous pensez*, don't tell me he didn't do it ! = *ne me dites pas qu'il ne l'a pas fait !* ⓪ to state = *énoncer*, to relate = *relater* ☠ → to say

I can tell (by his letters that he loves her) = *je vois bien (d'après ses lettres qu'il l'aime)* **how can you tell (when it's cooked) ?** = *comment savez-vous que (c'est cuit) ?* **to begin to tell** = *commencer à se faire sentir* : the austerity measures are beginning to tell = *les mesures d'austérité commencent à se faire sentir*	**I'll tell you what (you lend me the money and I'll treat you to dinner)** = *tu sais quoi ? (tu me prêtes l'argent et je t'invite à dîner)* **tell it like it is !** = *dites les choses comme elles sont !* **I told you so !** = *je te l'avais bien dit !* **I told him where to get off** = *je lui ai dit d'aller se faire voir*	⓪ **I told him where to go** = *je l'ai envoyé paître* ⓪ I gave him his walking papers = *je l'ai envoyé promener* **to tell a joke/a story** = *raconter une plaisanterie/une histoire* **who can tell ?** = *qui peut (le) dire ?* ⓪ who knows ? = *qui sait ?* **you're telling me !** = *à qui le dis-tu !*

---

to tell s.o. about stg = *raconter qqch à qqn* : tell me about it = *racontez-moi ça*
to tell ... apart = *distinguer* : I can't tell the twins apart =*je n'arrive pas à distinguer les jumelles* ☠ → to distinguish
to tell ... from ... = *distinguer ... de ...* : there's no way to tell him from his brother = *il n'y a pas moyen de le distinguer de son frère*
you couldn't tell from (his voice that he was drunk) = *on ne pouvait pas dire d'après (sa voix qu'il était ivre)*

to tell s.o. on = *cafarder qqn* : Tom's always telling on his older brother = *Tom est toujours en train de cafarder son frère aîné* ⓓ to tattle = *rapporter*
to tell s.o. off = *dire ses quatre vérités à qqn* : I'm so angry I'm going to tell him off when I see him = *je suis tellement fâché que je vais lui dire ses quatre vérités quand je le verrai* → TO LAMBAST
to tell s.o. to = *dire à qqn de* : he told me not to tell her he had told me* = *il m'a dit de ne pas lui dire qu'il me l'avait dit.*

TELLER (n) *caissier, -ière (banque)* : two tellers were killed in the robbery = *deux caissiers ont été tués au cours du hold-up* ☠ → cashier.

TELLTALE (adj) *qui trahit* : wrinkles are telltale signs of age = *les rides sont des signes qui trahissent l'âge.*

TEMPER (n) *mauvais caractère (m)* : what a temper she has ! = *ce qu'elle a mauvais caractère !* ⓓ nature = ←
to lose one's temper = *se mettre en colère* → ANGRY.

TEMPERAMENT (n) *tempérament (m)* : she couldn't be a doctor, she hasn't got the temperament for it = *elle ne pourrait pas être médecin, elle n'en a pas le tempérament*
☠ *acheter à tempérament* = to buy on the instalment plan/on time
− *elle a du tempérament* = she's hot stuff.

TEMPERAMENTAL (adj) *qui a ses humeurs* : a temperamental child = *un enfant qui a ses humeurs* ⓓ capricious = *capricieux.*

TEMPERATURE (n) *température (f)* : what's the temperature outside ? = *quelle température fait-il dehors ?* ⓓ thermometer = *thermomètre* ☠ *prendre la température (d'un groupe)* = to sound out (a group).

TEMPEST (n) *tempête (f)* : a tempest off the Pacific coast = *une tempête au large de la côte Pacifique* ⓓ storm = *orage*
a tempest in a teapot = *une tempête dans un verre d'eau* ⓓ to make a mountain out of a molehill = *se faire une montagne de quelque chose.*

TEMPLE (n) *temple (m)* : to profane a temple = *profaner un temple* ⓓ church = *église.*

TEMPO (n) *tempo (m)* (music), *allure (f)* : who can keep up with this tempo ? = *qui peut suivre ce tempo/cette allure ?* ⓓ rhythm = *rythme*, cadence = ← ☠ → allure.

TEMPORARILY (adj) *temporairement* : temporarily out of work = *temporairement sans travail* ⓓ momentarily = *momentanément*, for the time being = *pour le moment.*

TEMPORARY (adj) *temporaire* : a temporary job = *un travail temporaire* ⓓ momentary = *momentané* ≠ lasting = *durable.*

TEMPT (to, -ed) *tenter* : don't tempt her ! = *ne la tente pas !* ⓓ to entice = *allécher*
to be tempted to (tell him to fuck off) = *être tenté de (lui dire d'aller se faire foutre)*
☠ → to appeal.

TEMPTATION (n) *tentation (f)* : I can't resist the temptation = *je ne peux pas résister à la tentation* ⓓ inducement = *incitation.*

TEMPTING (adj) *tentant, -e* : a tempting offer = *une offre tentante* ⓓ enticing = *alléchant* ≠ repelling = *repoussant.*

TEN (n, adj) *dix (m)* : it's ten o'clock = *il est dix heures* ⓓ tenth = *dixième*
about ten (people) = *une dizaine de (personnes)*
the Ten Commandments = *les Dix Commandements*
☠ *ça vaut dix* = that takes the cake
− *ne rien faire de ses dix doigts* = to goof off.

TENACIOUS (adj) *tenace* : a tenacious struggle to survive = *une lutte tenace pour survivre* ⓓ obstinate = *obstiné.*

TENACITY (n) *ténacité (f)* : to work with tenacity = *travailler avec ténacité* ⓓ obstination = ←.

TENANT (n) *locataire (m, f)* : he married her tenant = *il a épousé sa locataire* ⓓ proprietor = *propriétaire*, resident = *résident*, boarder = *pensionnaire.*

TENDENCY (n, -ies) *tendance (f)* : racist tendencies = *des tendances racistes* ⓓ current = *courant* ☠ → trend.

TENDER (adj, -er, -est) **1/** *tendre* : the meat's tender = *la viande est tendre* ≠ hard = *dur* **2/** *tendre* : tender words = *des mots tendres* ⓓ affectionate = *affectueux* ☠ *dès ma plus tendre enfance* = from my earliest youth.

TENDERFOOT (n, -s) *novice (m, f)* : he's still a tenderfoot = *c'est encore un novice* ⓓ newcomer = *nouveau venu.*

TENDERHEARTED (adj) *au cœur tendre* ≠ hardhearted = *qui a le cœur dur.*

TENDERLY (adv) *tendrement.*

TENDERNESS (n) *tendresse (f)* ≠ brutality = *brutalité.*

TEND TO (to, -ed) **1/** *avoir tendance à :* I tend to agree with you = *j'ai tendance à être de votre avis* Ⓧ to be inclined to = *être enclin à* **2/** *prendre soin de :* I'll tend to it = *j'en prendrai soin* Ⓧ to see to = *veiller à.*

TENEMENT (n) *immeuble* (m) *misérable :* she was raised in a tenement on the West Side = *elle a été élevée dans un immeuble misérable du quartier Ouest* Ⓧ slum = *taudis.*

TENNIS (n) *tennis* (m) *:* tennis court = *court de tennis* Ⓧ racket = *raquette,* net = *filet,* love-15 = *zéro à 15,* 40-all = *40 partout,* (mixed) doubles = *double (mixte),* singles = *simple,* forehand = *coup droit,* backhand = *revers,* service = ← ☠ *porter des tennis* = to wear sneakers.

TENSE (n) *temps* (m) *:* present/past tense = *temps présent/passé* ☠ → time.

TENSE (adj, -r, -st) *tendu, -e :* a tense atmosphere = *une atmosphère tendue* Ⓧ nervous = *nerveux* ≠ cool = ←.

TENSE UP (to, -d) **to be tensed up** = *être tendu :* he was all tensed up after his conversation with the shrink = *il était très tendu après sa conversation avec le psy* ≠ to be relaxed = *être détendu.*

TENSION (n) *tension* (f) *:* there's incredible tension between them = *il y a une tension incroyable entre eux* Ⓧ stress = ← ☠ *tension (artérielle)* = blood pressure.

TENT (n) *tente* (f) *:* a tent that sleeps four = *une tente pour quatre personnes* Ⓧ camping = ←, to pitch camp = *planter la tente,* sleeping bag = *sac de couchage,* to sleep outdoors = *dormir à la belle étoile.*

TENTATIVE (adj) *pas arrêté, -e :* our plans are very tentative = *nos projets ne sont pas très arrêtés* Ⓧ uncertain = *pas certain.*

TENTATIVELY (adv) *provisoirement :* they're tentatively living in New York = *ils habitent provisoirement à New York.*

TENTERHOOK (n) **on tenterhooks** = *au supplice :* not knowing if John will marry her leaves me on tenterhooks =*ça me met au supplice de ne pas savoir si John va l'épouser.*

TENUOUS (adj) *ténu, -e* ≠ solid = *solide.*

TENURE (n) **to have tenure** = *obtenir sa titularisation* (teachers) : she now has tenure, after ten years of teaching in this university = *elle a enfin obtenu sa titularisation, après avoir enseigné dix ans dans cette université.*

TERM (n) *terme* (m) *:* "input" is an economic term = « input » *est un terme économique*
term of office = *longueur d'un mandat (électif)*
the (fall) term = *le semestre (d'automne)* = the semester
☠ *avant terme* = premature
— *en d'autres termes* = in other words

— *mettre un terme à* = to put an end to
— *mener à (bon) terme* = to bring to a successful conclusion.

TERMINAL (n) *terminal* (m) *:* the computer terminal = *le terminal de l'ordinateur* Ⓧ keyboard = *clavier,* screen = *écran,* program = *logiciel.*

TERMINAL (adj) *dans sa phase terminale :* a terminal disease = *une maladie dans sa phase terminale.*

TERMINATE (to, -d) (se) *terminer :* the lease terminates next year = *le bail se termine l'année prochaine* ≠ to start = *commencer.*

TERMINOLOGY (n, -ies) *terminologie* (f) *:* computer terminology = *terminologie informatique.*

TERMITE (n) *termite* (m) *:* termites ruin wood = *les termites abîment le bois.*

TERMS (n pl) *termes* (m pl) *:* they accept the terms of the contract = *ils acceptent les termes du contrat* Ⓧ conditions = ←
to be on good ≠ **bad terms** = *être* ≠ *ne pas être en bons termes* Ⓧ to be down on s.o. = *battre froid à qqn*
to come to terms = *arriver à un accord :* the two companies finally came to terms = *les deux entreprises ont fini par arriver à un accord*
to come to terms with = *prendre son parti de :* she hasn't yet come to terms with her husband's death = *elle n'a pas encore pris son parti de la mort de son mari* Ⓧ to accept = *accepter*
in terms of (money, the job's interesting) = *sur le plan de (l'argent, le boulot est intéressant)* Ⓧ with regard to = *pour ce qui concerne*
on my own terms = *à mes propres conditions*
not to be on speaking terms =*ne plus s'adresser la parole* Ⓧ to be at daggers drawn = *être à couteaux tirés*
to speak of s.o. in glowing terms = *parler de qqn en termes élogieux.*

TERRACE (n) *terrasse* (f) *:* an apartment with a terrace = *un appartement avec une terrasse* ☠ *asseyons-nous à la terrasse (café)* = let's sit outside.

TERRIBLE (adj) *terrible* (accident, etc.), *affreux, -euse :* a terrible book/film = *un livre/film affreux,* a terrible catastrophe = *une terrible catastrophe* → AWFUL ≠ great = *épatant*
to feel terrible about = *être navré de :* I feel terrible about having lied to him = *je suis navré de lui avoir menti* Ⓧ to feel lousy about = *se sentir morveux de* ☠ *c'est un mec terrible* = he's a terrific guy.

TERRIBLY (adv) *terriblement :* terribly poor = *terriblement pauvre* → VERY.

TERRIFIC (adj) **1/** *terrible :* a terrific play = *une pièce terrible* → WONDERFUL **2/** *terrible :* a terrific fortune = *une fortune terrible* Ⓧ considerable = *considérable* ☠ → terrible.

TERRIFICALLY (adv) *terriblement :* he's terrifically wealthy = *il est terriblement riche* → VERY.

TERRIFY (to, -ied) *terrifier* : the dog terrified the child = *le chien a terrifié l'enfant* ⓌⒹ to frighten = *effrayer*.

TERRIFYING (adj) *terrifiant, -e* : a terrifying experience = *une expérience terrifiante* ⓌⒹ frightening = *effrayant*.

TERRITORY (n, -ies) *territoire (m)* : occupied territories = *territoires occupés* ⓌⒹ state = *État*.

TERROR (n) *terreur (f)* : she lives in terror of her husband = *elle vit dans la terreur de son mari* ⓌⒹ fear = *peur*.

TERRORISM (n) *terrorisme (m)* : a wave of terrorism = *une vague de terrorisme* **TERRORIST** (n) *terroriste (m, f)* : terrorists kidnapped the ambassador = *des terroristes ont kidnappé l'ambassadeur* ⓌⒹ commando = ← ≠ hostage = *otage*.

TERRORIZE (to, -d) *terroriser* : he terrorizes his kids = *il terrorise ses gosses* ⓌⒹ to terrify = *terrifier*.

TERSE (adj) *laconique* : a terse answer = *une réponse laconique* ⓌⒹ concise = *concis*.

TEST (n) *épreuve (f)* (school only), *test (m)* (psycho, experiments) : we have tests at the end of the term = *nous avons des épreuves à la fin du semestre*, laboratory tests on dogs = *des tests de laboratoire sur les chiens*
to pass a test = *réussir une épreuve*
to take a test = *passer une épreuve*
test flight = *vol d'essai*
test tube = *éprouvette*
(urine) test = *analyse (d'urine)*.

TEST (to, -ed) *tester* : the teacher gives drills to test the students' knowledge = *le professeur fait passer des colles pour tester les connaissances des étudiants* ⓌⒹ to try = *éprouver*
you're just testing me ! = *vous prêchez le faux pour savoir le vrai !*

TESTICLE (n) *testicule (m)* ⓌⒹ penis = *pénis*.

TESTIFY (to, -ied) *témoigner* : he testified against his brother = *il a témoigné contre son frère* ⓌⒹ to give evidence = *porter témoignage* 🙎 *témoigner de l'intérêt/son amitié* = to show interest/one's friendship.

TESTIMONY (n, -ies) *témoignage (m)* : his testimony was all a lie = *son témoignage n'était que mensonge* 🙎 *en témoignage de (notre amitié)* = as a token of (our friendship)
— *témoignage oculaire* = eyewitness account.

TEST-TUBE BABY (n, -ies) *bébé (m) éprouvette*.

TESTY (adj, -ier, -iest) *irascible* : don't be so testy ! = *ne soyez pas si irascible !* ⓌⒹ feisty = *hargneux*.

TEXAS (n) *Texas (m)* = Lone Star State.

TEXT (n) *texte (m)* : the text is beautifully written = *le texte est merveilleusement écrit* ⓌⒹ speech = *discours*

🙎 *ne pas savoir son texte* = not to know one's lines
— *dans le texte* = in the original.

TEXTBOOK (n) *livre (m) (de classe)* : a geography textbook = *un livre de géographie* ⓌⒹ manual = *manuel*.

TEXTILE (n) *textile (m)* : imported textiles = *des textiles importés* ⓌⒹ material = *tissu*.

TEXTURE (n) *texture (f)* : a smooth texture = *une texture lisse* ⓌⒹ structure = ←.

THAILAND (n) *Thaïlande (f)* **THAI** (n, adj) *Thaïlandais, -e, Thaï, -e*.

THAN (conj) **more** ≠ **less than** = *plus* ≠ *moins que* : I like John more than his brother = *j'aime mieux John que son frère*
(better) than ever = *(meilleur) que jamais*
than usual = *que d'habitude* : he's later than usual = *il est plus en retard que d'habitude*.

THANK (to, -ed) *remercier* : I want to thank you for what you've done = *je veux vous remercier pour ce que vous avez fait*
I can't thank you enough = *je ne pourrai jamais assez vous remercier*
you have no one to thank but yourself ! = *tu ne peux t'en prendre qu'à toi-même !* ⓌⒹ it serves you right ! = *c'est bien fait pour toi !*
thank you very much ! = *merci beaucoup !*
no, thank you = *non, merci*
thank you = *merci*
to thank s.o. for (a lovely evening) = *remercier qqn pour (une charmante soirée)*
🙎 *remercier sa secrétaire* = to fire one's secretary.

THANKFUL (adj) *reconnaissant, -e* : I'm very thankful for your help = *je vous suis très reconnaissant de m'avoir aidé* ⓌⒹ grateful
you ought to be thankful that (no one was hurt) = *estimez-vous heureux (que personne n'ait été blessé)*.

THANKLESS (adj) **a thankless (job)** = *(une tâche) ingrate*.

THANKS (n pl) *remerciements (m pl)* : I want to express my thanks and my gratitude = *je veux vous exprimer mes remerciements et ma gratitude*
is that all the thanks I get ? = *c'est comme ça qu'on me remercie ?*
many thanks = *tous mes remerciements* ≠ you're welcome = *il n'y a pas de quoi*
thanks for (your help) = *merci de (votre aide)*
thanks for nothing ! = *je ne te dis pas merci !*
thanks a lot = *merci tout plein*
thanks to = *grâce à* : thanks to his help we got the loan we needed = *grâce à son aide nous avons obtenu l'emprunt dont nous avions besoin*.

THANKS ! (interj) *merci !* = thank you !

THANKSGIVING DAY (n) *4e jeudi de novembre, fête d'action de grâces (où l'on mange traditionnellement de la dinde)*.

647

THAT (adj, those) *ce, cette... (-là)* : this book and that pencil = *ce livre(-ci) et ce crayon(-là)* → THIS.

THAT (pron, those) 1/ *cela, ça* : did you see that ? = *est-ce que vous avez vu ça ?* → THIS
2/ *qui, que (pour remplacer* who/which*)* : here's the money that I owe you = *voici l'argent que je vous dois* = which I owe you, he's the guy that called her = *c'est le type qui l'a appelée* = who called her

☠ *que puis-je faire ?* = what can I do ?
— *plus intelligent que ...* = more intelligent than ...

— *qui est là ?* = who is it ?

about that = *de cela/de ça* : don't talk about that = *ne parlez pas de ça/cela*
at that = 1/ *en effet* : it might be less expensive at that = *en effet, ça pourrait être moins cher* 2/ *de surcroît* : yes, he's divorced and three times at that = *oui, il est divorcé, et trois fois de surcroît* ⊙ even = *même*
after that ≠ **before that** = *après ça* ≠ *avant ça* : what happened after ≠ before that ? = *qu'est-ce qui est arrivé après ≠ avant ça ?*
just like that ! = *comme ça !* : she quit, just like that ! = *elle*

est partie, comme ça !
that's (her husband) = *c'est (son mari)*
that's it ! = 1/ *c'est ça !* ≠ that's not it ! = *ce n'est pas ça !* 2/ *ça y est !* : one more page and that's it ! = *encore une page et ça y est !* 3/ *c'est tout !* : I'll give you $ 10 and that's it ! = *je vous donnerai 10 dollars et c'est tout !*
that's how it is ! = *c'est comme ça !*
the (day/month/year) that = *le (jour/mois)/l'(année) où* : the day that we met = *le jour où nous nous sommes rencontrés* = the day when we met

that being said = *ceci/cela (étant) dit*
that's why = *c'est pourquoi* : that's why they got divorced = *c'est pourquoi ils ont divorcé* ⊙ this is the reason why = *c'est la raison pour laquelle*
that's that ! = *un point c'est tout !* : I said no, and that's that ! = *j'ai dit non, un point c'est tout !* ⊙ period ! = *point final !*
that's very (interesting/expensive) = *c'est très (intéressant/cher).*

THAT (adv) *si* : is it that difficult ? = *est-ce que c'est si difficile ?*, it isn't that far = *ce n'est pas si loin* ☠ → so
that much = *à ce point* : she would kill for him, she loves him that much = *elle tuerait pour lui, elle l'aime à ce point.*

THAT (conj) *que* : I'm sorry that you can't come = *je suis désolé que vous ne puissiez pas venir,* he said that he was sorry = *il a dit qu'il était désolé.*

THAW (to, -ed) *dégeler, décongeler* (food) : the meat's thawing = *la viande est en train de décongeler* ⊙ to melt = *fondre*
☠ *dégeler l'atmosphère* = to break up the ice
— *elle s'est dégelée* = she loosened up.

THE (art) *le, la, les* : the book = *le livre,* the chair = *la chaise,* the guys = *les mecs* ⊙ a = *un, une.*

THEATER (n) *théâtre (m)* : there are lots of theaters on Broadway = *il y a des tas de théâtres à Broadway* = theatre (GB) ⊙ stage = *scène,* play = *pièce,* actor = *acteur,* actress = *actrice,* director = *metteur en scène*
to go to the theater = *aller au théâtre*
☠ *c'est du théâtre !* = it's just playacting !

THEATERGOER (n) *quelqu'un qui va beaucoup au théâtre* ⊙ moviegoer = *cinéphile.*

THEATRICAL (adj) *théâtral, -e* : a theatrical way of speaking = *une façon théâtrale de parler* ⊙ melodramatic = *mélodramatique.*

THEFT (n) *vol (m)* : numerous thefts in department stores = *de nombreux vols dans les grands magasins* ⊙ job = *coup,* burglary = *cambriolage* ☠ → flight.

THEIR (adj) *leur(s) (à eux/à elles)* : their car = *leur voiture (à eux),* their friends = *leurs amis (à eux)* → MY ☠ *je le leur ai dit* = I told them about it.

THEIRS (pron) *le, la leur, les leurs (à eux/à elles)* : those kids are theirs = *ces gosses sont les leurs,* we bought our house last year, when did they buy theirs ? = *nous avons acheté notre maison l'année dernière, quand ont-ils acheté la leur ?*
it's theirs = *c'est à eux/à elles.*

THEM (pron) 1/ *les* (direct object) : do you see them ? = *est-ce que vous les voyez ?* 2/ *leur* (indirect objet) : give them a drink = *donnez-leur un verre* → I ☠ → their
(no one) of them = *(aucun) d'entre eux*
that's them = *ce sont eux/elles*
with/for them = *avec/pour eux, elles.*

THEME (n) *thème* (m) : what was the theme of the film ? = *quel était le thème du film ?* ⓐ subject = *sujet*
theme song = *cheval de bataille* : his theme song is that women should stay home and take care of the kids = *son cheval de bataille, c'est que les femmes devraient rester à la maison et s'occuper des enfants* ⓐ leitmotiv = ←
♨ *thème (traduction)* = translation from mother tongue to other languages.

THEMSELVES (pron) *eux-mêmes, elles-mêmes, se* (reflexive) : they did it themselves = *ils l'ont fait eux-mêmes*, they can see themselves in the mirror = *ils peuvent se voir dans la glace* → MYSELF.

THEN (adv) **1/** *alors* : we lived in New York then = *nous habitions alors New York* ⓐ at that time = *à cette époque-là*
♨ *il a démissionné, alors il cherche un autre boulot* = he quit, so he's looking for another job
— *alors que* = whereas
— *(et) alors ?* = so what ?
2/ *puis* : we ate, then we made love = *nous avons mangé, puis nous avons fait l'amour* ⓐ next = *ensuite*
3/ *alors* : if it's too difficult, then don't do it = *si c'est trop difficile, alors ne le faites pas* ⓐ therefore = *donc*
(right) then and there = *séance tenante* : they bought the car (right) then and there = *ils ont acheté la voiture séance tenante* ⓐ on the spot = *sur-le-champ*.

THEORETICAL (adj) *théorique* : a theoretical problem = *un problème théorique* ≠ practical = *pratique* **THEORETICALLY** (adv) *théoriquement* : that's possible theoretically = *théoriquement, c'est possible*.

THEORY (n, -ies) *théorie* (f) : I don't agree with your theory = *je ne suis pas d'accord avec votre théorie* ⓐ hypothesis = *hypothèse*
in theory (it sounds easy enough) = *en théorie (ça a l'air assez facile)*.

THERAPIST (n) *thérapeute* (m, f) ⓐ doctor = *docteur*.

THERAPY (n, -ies) *thérapie* (f) : doctors have discovered a new therapy for treating handicapped children = *les médecins ont découvert une nouvelle thérapie pour soigner les enfants handicapés*
to be in therapy = *suivre une psychothérapie* : she's been in therapy for three years = *elle suit une psychothérapie depuis trois ans*.

THERE (adv) *là* : put your coat there = *mettez votre manteau là*, sit there = *asseyez-vous là* ⓐ over there = *là-bas*
do something, don't just sit/stand there ! = *ne reste pas assis/planté là, fais quelque chose !*
to go there = *y aller* : the bank ? I'm going there this afternoon = *la banque ? j'y vais cet après-midi*
put it there ! = *tope-là !* ⓐ it's a deal ! = *marché conclu !*
there and back (it takes an hour) = *aller et retour (il faut une heure)*
there is/there are = *il y a* : there is only one man in the room = *il n'y a qu'un homme dans la pièce*, there are many people here = *il y a beaucoup de gens ici*, is there anyone who understands me ? = *y a-t-il quelqu'un qui me comprenne ?*
there's (Daddy) ! = *voilà (Papa) !*
there's no stopping her = *il n'y a pas moyen de l'arrêter*
there's no telling = *on ne peut pas dire*
there seems (to be something wrong) = *il semble qu'il y ait (quelque chose qui cloche)*
there ! there ! (don't worry) ! = *allons ! allons ! (ne t'inquiète pas) !*
♨ *il y a (deux ans)* = (two years) ago
— *restons-en là !* = let's call it quits !
— *loin de là* = far from it
— *les choses en sont là* = that's where things are at
— *c'est là qu'est le problème* = therein lies the problem.

THEREABOUTS (adv) *à peu près* : it's noon or thereabouts = *il est à peu près midi*.

THEREAFTER (adv) *peu après* : he died and she died soon thereafter = *il est mort et elle est morte peu après*.

THEREBY (adv) *de ce fait* : to restore and thereby save the monument = *restaurer, et de ce fait sauver le monument*.

THEREFORE (adv) *donc* : I think, therefore I am = *je pense, donc je suis* ⓐ hence = *de ce fait*
♨ *allons donc !* = come on !
— *dis donc !* = hey !

THEREIN (adv) *là* : therein lies the problem = *c'est là qu'est le problème* ♨ → there.

THERMOMETER (n) *thermomètre* (m) : the thermometer is broken = *le thermomètre est cassé* ⓐ mercury = *mercure*.

THERMOSTAT (n) *thermostat* (m).

THESAURUS (n, -i or -es) *dictionnaire* (m) *de synonymes* ⓐ lexicon = *lexique*.

THESE (pron, adj) → THIS.

THESIS (n, -ses) **1/** *thèse* (f) : he defended the thesis that ... = *il a défendu la thèse suivante ...* ≠ antithesis = *antithèse* **2/** *thèse* (f) : to write a thesis on Baudelaire = *faire une thèse sur Baudelaire*.

THEY (pron pl) *ils, elles* : they had dinner at the White House = *ils/elles ont dîné à la Maison-Blanche*, they're rich = *ils/elles sont riches* → I
they say (she's rich) = *on dit (qu'elle est riche)*.

THICK (n) **in the thick of (the fight)** = *au plus fort de (la mêlée)* ⓐ in the middle of = *en plein*
through thick and thin = *à travers les moments difficiles* : his wife stuck with him through thick and thin = *sa femme l'a soutenu à travers les moments difficiles* ⓐ come hell or high water = *contre vents et marées*.

THICK (adj, -er, -est) *épais, -aisse* : a thick book/sauce = *un livre épais/une sauce épaisse* ≠ thin = *mince*
he's a bit thick = *il est légèrement bouché* → STUPID
to be (2 inches) thick = *avoir (5 cm)´ d'épaisseur*
to be as thick as thieves = *être comme cul et chemise* ⟲ to get on like a house on fire = *s'entendre comme larrons en foire*
to lay it on thick = *y aller fort* : he began complimenting her and laid it on thick = *il lui a fait des compliments et y est allé fort*
a thick accent = *un fort accent.*

THICKEN (to, -ed) *(s') épaissir* : to thicken a sauce = *épaissir une sauce*
(the plot) thickens = *(l'histoire) se corse.*

THICKNESS (n, -es) *épaisseur (f)* : the thickness of the wall = *l'épaisseur du mur* ☠ *un mètre d'épaisseur* = one-meter thick.

THICK-SKINNED (adj) *qui a le cuir épais* : a pimp has to be thick-skinned = *il faut qu'un maquereau ait le cuir épais* ⟲ hardboiled = *dur à cuire.*

THIEF (n, thieves) *voleur, -euse* : three thieves calmly walked into the bank and held it up = *trois voleurs sont entrés calmement dans la banque et ont fait un hold-up* ⟲ swindler = *escroc*, pickpocket = ←

stop thief ! = *au voleur !*
☠ → robber.

THIGH (n) *cuisse (f)* : her husband loves her fat thighs = *son mari aime ses grosses cuisses* ⟲ leg = *jambe*
☠ *des cuisses de grenouille* = frogs' legs
— *se croire sorti de la cuisse de Jupiter* = to think one's God's gift
— *elle a la cuisse légère* = she puts out for anyone.

THIN (adj, -ner, -nest) *mince* : he likes thin broads = *il aime les filles minces* = slim ≠ stocky = *trapu, corpulent* = ←
to be thin as a nail/a board = *être maigre comme un clou/mince comme un fil* ⟲ to be a bag of bones = *être un sac d'os*
to spread o.s. too thin = *se disperser trop* : you're spreading yourself too thin and you won't do anything good = *tu te disperses trop et tu ne feras rien de bien*
to vanish into thin air = *s'évanouir dans la nature*
you're skating on thin ice = *vous marchez sur une poudrière* ⟲ you're on shaky ground = *vous êtes sur un terrain glissant*
☠ *un mince espoir* = a slender hope
— *mince !* = gee whiz !
— *ce n'est pas une mince affaire !* = that takes some doing !

THING (n) *chose (f), truc (m)* : I have so many things to do = *j'ai tant de choses/trucs à faire*, what's this thing ? = *qu'est-ce que c'est que ce truc ?* ⟲ contraption = *engin*, thingamagig = *bidule*, gizmo = *machin*

to do one's thing = *faire son truc* : don't worry about what they say, just do your thing = *ne t'inquiète pas de ce qu'ils disent, fais ton truc*
he doesn't miss a thing = *rien ne lui échappe*
to have a thing about (flying/spiders) = *avoir la phobie de (l'avion)/des (araignées)*
to have a thing for s.o. = *s'être entiché de qqn* : she has a thing for my brother = *elle s'est entichée de mon frère* ⟲ to have a crush on = *avoir le béguin pour*
to hear things = *entendre des voix*
it's a thing of the past = *c'est une vieille histoire*
how are things (with you) ? = *comment ça va ?* ⟲ what's new ? = *quoi de neuf ?*
it was ≠ it wasn't the thing to do/say = *c'était vraiment la chose à faire/à dire ≠ à ne pas faire/dire*

one's thing = *son truc* : drugs aren't my thing = *la drogue, c'est pas mon truc* ⟲ my style = *mon style*
to know a thing or two about = *en savoir long sur* ⟲ to be in the know = *être au parfum*
one's things = *ses affaires* : take your things and let's go ! = *prends tes affaires et allons-y !*
to make a thing of = *faire toute une affaire de* : she made a thing of my coming late = *elle a fait toute une affaire de mon retard* ⟲ to make a big deal of = *faire une maladie de*
not to get a thing out of = *ne pas retirer quoi que ce soit de* : I didn't get a thing out of his class = *je n'ai pas retiré quoi que ce soit de son cours*
not to understand a thing of (what s.o.'s saying) = *ne pas comprendre un mot de (ce que qqn dit)*
the (strange) thing is ... = *ce qu'il y a d'(étrange), c'est ...*

take things as they come = *prenez les choses comme elles viennent* → THAT'S LIFE !
to tell s.o. a thing or two = *dire son fait à qqn* → TO LAMBAST
that's how things are = *c'est comme ça* → THAT'S LIFE !
that's just the thing for me = *c'est exactement ce qu'il me faut*
to see things = *avoir des visions*
those things happen = *ce sont des choses qui arrivent* → THAT'S LIFE !
the thing = *la grande mode* : skiing is the thing in Vermont = *le ski, c'est la grande mode dans le Vermont*
the thing is that (they aren't happy anymore) = *ce qu'il y a, c'est qu'(ils ne sont plus heureux)*
things being as they are = *les choses étant ce qu'elles sont*
things are rough all over = *c'est dur pour tout le monde* → THAT'S LIFE !

> 🕱 *appeler les choses par leur nom* = to call a spade a spade
> — *chose promise, chose due* = a promise is a promise
> — *il y a un truc* = there's a trick

> — *parler de choses et d'autres* = to shoot the breeze
> — *un truc (pour ne pas aller en classe)* = a device (to get out of going to school).

THINGAMABOB (n) *machin* (m) : what a strange thingamabob ! = *quel drôle de machin !* ⓪ doodad = *machin-chose.*

THINGAMAGIG (n) *bidule* (m) : what's this thingamagig? = *qu'est-ce que c'est que ce bidule?* ⓪ whatchamacallit = *machin-truc.*

THINK (to, thought, thought) *penser* : what do you think ? = *qu'en pensez-vous ?,* I think you're right = *je pense que vous avez raison* ⓪ to think over/about = *réfléchir à,* to rack one's brains = *se creuser la cervelle,* to imagine = *imaginer,* to figure = *croire*

let me think ! = *laissez-moi réfléchir !*
one would think so = *il faut croire*
I think so = *je pense que oui* ⓪ I believe so = *je crois bien/que oui*
I thought as much = *je pensais bien*
I thought so = *c'est bien ce que je pensais*
to think ... = *dire que ... :* to think I almost accepted ! = *dire que j'ai failli accepter !*

to think one's it = *ne pas se moucher du pied :* her brother thinks he's it = *son frère ne se mouche pas du pied* ⓪ to think one's hot stuff = *se prendre pour le nombril du monde*
who does he think he is ! = *pour qui se prend-il ?*
who do you think you're talking to ? = *vous savez à qui vous avez affaire ?*

to think about = *penser à :* I often think about my grandfather = *je pense souvent à mon grand-père,* what are you thinking about ? = *à quoi pensez-vous ?*
to think of = 1/ *penser de :* what do you think of her ? = *que pensez-vous d'elle ?* ⓪ what's your opinion of ? = *quelle est votre opinion sur ?* 2/ *penser à :* who thought of that solution ? = *qui a pensé à cette solution ?,* you think of everything = *vous pensez à tout* 3/ *penser (faire) :* I'm thinking of going to Greece this summer

= *je pense aller en Grèce cet été* = to think about ⓪ to envisage = *envisager*
I can't think of (where I met her) = *je n'arrive pas à me rappeler (où je l'ai rencontrée)* ⓪ I can't remember = *je ne me souviens pas*
he never thinks of anyone but imself = *il ne pense qu'à lui*
to think highly/a lot of ≠ ill of s.o. = *penser le plus grand bien/du bien de* ≠ *du mal de qqn* ⓪ **not to think (anything) much of** = *ne pas penser grand-chose de*
I wouldn't think of (asking

her for money) = *l'idée ne me serait pas venue de (lui demander de l'argent)*
to think out/through = *bien réfléchir à :* give me time to think things out/through = *laissez-moi le temps de bien réfléchir à tout cela*
to think up = *imaginer :* he thinks up the zaniest plans = *il imagine les projets les plus loufoques* ⓪ to make up = *fabriquer* 🕱 → to imagine
to think stg over = *réfléchir à qqch :* your offer's interesting ; I'll think it over = *votre offre est intéressante ; j'y réfléchirai.*

> 🕱 *il ne pense qu'à ça* = he has a one-track mind

> — *penses-tu !* = you must be kidding !

THINKABLE (adj) *pensable* : it's just not thinkable that kids are acting in blue movies = *ce n'est pas pensable qu'on fasse jouer des gosses dans des films pornos* ≠ unthinkable = *impensable.*

THINK TANK (n) *structure* (f) *de réflexion* : energy experts gathered in a think tank = *les experts en énergie se sont réunis en structure de réflexion* ⓪ seminar = *séminaire.*

THIN OUT (to, -ned) *se réduire de plus en plus* : the troops are thinning out = *l'effectif se réduit de plus en plus.*

THIN-SKINNED (adj) *sensible* : he's too thin-skinned to be a gangster = *il est trop sensible pour être gangster* ≠ thick-skinned = *qui a la peau dure* 🕱 → sensible.

THIRD (n) *tiers* (m) : a third of the country's population is black = *un tiers de la population du pays est noire* ⓪ quarter = *quart.*

THIRD (adj) *troisième* : her third husband = *son troisième mari*
to give s.o. the third degree = *mettre qqn sur la sellette* ⓪ to give s.o. a rough time of it = *en faire voir de toutes les couleurs à qqn*

a third party = *un tiers/une tierce personne*
the Third World = *le Tiers Monde*
☠ *troisième âge* = senior citizens.

THIRD-RATE (adj) *de troisième ordre* : a third-rate movie/writer = *un film/un écrivain de troisième ordre* ≠ topnotch = *de premier ordre*.

THIRST (n) *soif (f)* : to die of thirst = *mourir de soif* ⓪ hunger = *faim*
a thirst for (knowledge) = *une soif de (connaissances)* ⓪ a craving for = *une folle envie de*
to quench one's thirst = *se désaltérer*
☠ *avoir soif* = to be thirsty.

THIRSTY (adj, -ier, -iest) **to be thirsty** = *avoir soif* : how thirsty I am ! = *ce que j'ai soif !* ≠ to wet one's whistle = *se rincer la dalle*.

THIRTEEN (n, adj) *treize (m)* : number thirteen brings me luck = *le chiffre 13 me porte bonheur* ⓪ thirteenth = *treizième* ☠ *treize à la douzaine* = a baker's dozen.

THIRTY (n, -ies, adj) *trente (m)* : thirty candles on the cake = *trente bougies sur le gâteau* ⓪ thirtieth = *trentième*
to be in one's thirties = *avoir trente ans et quelques* ⓪ to be thirtyish = *avoir la trentaine*
in the thirties = *dans les années trente*
☠ *être sur son trente et un* = to be all spruced up
— *être au trente-sixième dessous* = to be down in the dumps
— *voir trente-six chandelles* = to see stars.

THIS (adj, these) *ce, cette ... (-ci)* : I want this book and that pencil = *je veux ce livre-ci et ce crayon-là* ≠ that = *ce... (-là)*

---

this = *ce, cette... (ci)* ≠ **that** = *ce, cette ... (-là)*
(this book) (that book)
these = *ces ... (-ci)* ≠ **those** = *ces ... (-là)*
(these books) (those books)

☠ one says *"cet ... (-ci)"* in front of a vowel or a silent h : this man = *cet homme(-ci)*, this animal = *cet animal(-ci)*.

THIS (pron, these) *ceci* : this is less expensive than that = *ceci est moins cher que cela*, these are less expensive than those = *ceux-ci sont moins chers que ceux-là* ≠ that = *cela*

---

this = *ceci* ≠ **that** = *cela, ça*
(I want this) (I want that)
these = *ceux-ci,* ≠ **those** = *ceux-là,*
  celles-ci *celles-là*
(I want these) (I want those)

---

this one ≠ **that one** | *celui-là/celle-là* : which
= *celui-ci/celle-ci* ≠ | do you want ? this one

---

or that one ? = *laquelle voulez-vous ? celle-ci ou celle-là ?*
this is (my husband) = *voici (mon mari)* ≠
that is (my husband) | = *voilà (mon mari)*
this is very (expensive/good) = *c'est très (cher/bon)*
what is this ? = *qu'est-ce que c'est ?*

THIS (adv) *à ce point* : I had never been this tired = *je n'avais jamais été fatigué à ce point* ⓪ so = *si*.

THOROUGH (adj) *minutieux, -euse* : she's very thorough in her work = *elle est très minutieuse dans son travail* ⓪ exhaustive = *exhaustif*
a thorough (bastard) = *un (salaud) fini*
thorough cleaning = *nettoyage à fond*
☠ → fastidious.

THOROUGHBRED (n) *pur-sang (m)* : this horse is a thoroughbred = *ce cheval est un pur-sang* **THOROUGHBRED** (adj) *pur sang* : a thoroughbred horse = *un cheval pur sang*.

THOROUGHFARE (n) *route (f) nationale, grande artère (f)* : a dramatic accident on the thoroughfare = *un accident dramatique sur la route nationale* ⓪ highway = *autoroute*.

THOROUGHLY (adv) *entièrement* : I thoroughly agree with you = *je suis entièrement d'accord avec vous* = entirely ⓪ altogether = *tout à fait*.

THOSE (pron, adj) → THAT.

THOUGH (conj) *bien que* : though I love him, I wouldn't marry a guy like that = *bien que je l'aime, jamais je n'épouserais un type comme ça* = tho ⓪ although = *quoique*.

THOUGH (adv) *toutefois* : he hits me ... he loves me though = *il me bat ... toutefois, il m'aime* ⓪ however = *cependant*.

THOUGHT (n) 1/ *pensée (f)* : my thoughts were elsewhere = *mes pensées étaient ailleurs* ⓪ meditation = *méditation* 2/ *idée (f)* : that's an interesting thought = *c'est une idée intéressante* = idea ⓪ concept = ← ☠ → idea
to be lost in thought = *être perdu dans ses pensées* ⓪ to be in the clouds = *être dans les nuages*
to collect one's thoughts = *rassembler ses idées*
give it some thought = *pensez-y* ⓪ think it over = *réfléchissez-y*
it's the thought that counts = *c'est l'intention qui compte*
to read s.o.'s thoughts = *lire dans les pensées de qqn*.

THOUGHTFUL (adj) *attentionné, -e* : a thoughtful husband = *un mari attentionné* ⓪ kind = *gentil* ≠ unthoughtful = *pas attentionné* **THOUGHTFULNESS** (n) *prévenance (f)*.

THOUGHTLESS (adj) *blessant, -e* (to say), *peu attentionné, -e* (to do) : what a thoughtless thing to say/to do

= que c'était blessant de dire ça/peu attentionné de faire ça ≠ thoughtful = attentionné **THOUGHTLESSNESS** (n) manque (m) de prévenance.

THOUGHT-OUT (adj) réfléchi, -e : a well thought-out argument = un argument bien réfléchi.

THOUSAND (n, adj) mille (m inv) : five thousand dollars = cinq mille dollars ⓪ million = ←
thousands (take the train every day) = des milliers de gens (prennent le train quotidiennement)
thousands of (women take the pill) = des milliers de (femmes prennent la pilule)
☠ il ne gagne pas des mille et des cents = he doesn't earn much
— je vous le donne en mille = you'll never guess
— taper/mettre dans le mille = to hit the bull's-eye.

THRASH (to, -ed) rosser : my father used to thrash me = mon père me rossait → TO HIT
to thrash out (a problem) = débattre d'(un problème) ⓪ to work out = trouver une solution.

THRASHING (n) **to give s.o. a (sound) thrashing** = flanquer une (bonne) trempe à qqn → TO HIT.

THREAD (n) fil (m) : red thread = du fil rouge ⓪ thimble = dé à coudre
(his life) is hanging by a thread = (sa vie) ne tient qu'à un fil
to lose the thread = perdre le fil : he lost the thread of his speech = il a perdu le fil de son discours
☠ mince comme un fil = thin as a board
— le fil conducteur = the driving force
— se mettre un fil à la patte = to get hitched
— il n'a pas inventé le fil à couper le beurre = he won't set the world on fire
— au fil des jours = day after day
— donner du fil à retordre à qqn = to give s.o. a headache
— fil de fer = wire
— de fil en aiguille = one thing leading to another.

THREADBARE (adj) élimé, -e : a threadbare coat = un manteau élimé ⓪ in shreds = en lambeaux.

THREAT (n) menace (f) : the threat of blackmail = la menace du chantage ⓪ warning = avertissement ☠ → menace.

THREATEN (to, -ed) menacer : it's no use threatening me = ça ne sert à rien de me menacer ≠ to reassure = rassurer
to threaten to (quit) = menacer de (donner sa démission)
☠ → to menace.

THREATENING (adj) menaçant, -e : a threatening look = un regard menaçant ⓪ alarming = alarmant.

THREE (n, adj) trois (m) : I have three lovers = j'ai trois amants ⓪ third = troisième
☠ haut comme trois pommes = knee-high to a grasshopper

— le trois août = the third of August
— je l'ai acheté pour trois fois rien = I bought it for nothing.

THREE-DIMENSIONAL (adj) à trois dimensions : three dimensional movies = des films à trois dimensions.

THREE-RING CIRCUS (n) vrai cirque (m) : life with her is a three-ring circus = la vie avec elle, c'est un vrai cirque.

THRESHOLD (n) seuil (m) : on the threshold of success = au seuil du succès ⓪ doorway = pas de la porte.

THRIFTY (adj, -ier, -iest) économe : a thrifty housewife = une maîtresse de maison économe ≠ extravagant = dépensier.

THRILL (n) frisson (m) : the thrills of a good detective story = les frissons dus à un bon roman policier ⓪ sensation = ←
sexual thrills = frissons de plaisir/sexuels
it was a thrill to (go to Europe the first time) = ça a été un grand moment d'(aller en Europe pour la première fois)
☠ des frissons de froid = cold shivers.

THRILL (to, -ed) **to be thrilled** = être ravi : he'll be thrilled when he finds out his wife has a lover = il sera ravi quand il apprendra que sa femme a un amant ⓪ to be tickled pink = être aux anges, to be elated = être fou de joie ≠ to be disappointed = être déçu
to be thrilled to death = être fou de joie
to be thrilled to (go) = être ravi de (partir)
to be thrilled with = être ravi de : we were thrilled with the play = nous avons été ravis de cette pièce ⓪ to be delighted with = être enchanté de.

THRILLER (n) thriller (m), film/pièce/roman à suspense : the movie's a thriller = c'est un thriller/un film à suspense ⓪ detective story = histoire policière, whodunit = polar.

THRILLING (adj) passionnant, -e : the movie was thrilling = le film était passionnant ⓪ gripping = palpitant ≠ dull = assommant.

THRIVE (to, -d) être florissant, -e : the economy's thriving = l'économie est florissante ⓪ to prosper = prospérer ≠ to be going to the dogs = battre de l'aile
to thrive on = s'épanouir dans : she thrives on affection = elle s'épanouit dans la tendresse.

THROAT (n) gorge (f) : throat cancer = cancer de la gorge ⓪ windpipe = trachée, tongue = langue, larynx = ←, laryngitis = laryngite
to be at each other's throat = se bouffer le nez ⓪ to be at daggers drawn = être à couteaux tirés
to clear one's throat = s'éclaircir/se racler la gorge
to cut one's own throat = scier la branche sur laquelle on est assis ⓪ to be one's (own) worst enemy = être son (propre) pire ennemi
to jump down s.o.'s throat = sauter sur qqn : he was

so angry he jumped down my throat = *il était tellement en colère qu'il m'a sauté dessus* → TO LAMBAST
☠ *faire des gorges chaudes de qqch* = to comment on stg maliciously
— *rire à gorge déployée* = to laugh one's head off
— *ça lui est resté en travers de la gorge* = he couldn't swallow that
— *prendre qqn à la gorge* = to have s.o. cornered.

THROES (n pl) **to be in the throes of (a breakdown)** = *être dans les affres d'(une dépression).*

THRONE (n) *trône (m) :* to sit on the throne = *s'asseoir sur le trône* ⓧ crown = *couronne.*

THRONG (n) *cohue (f) :* a throng at the beach = *une cohue sur la plage* ⓧ crowd = *foule* ☠ *dans la cohue* = in the crush.

THROUGH (adj) *(qui a) terminé :* are you through with your work ? = *est-ce que vous avez terminé votre travail ?* ⓧ finished = *(qui a) fini.*

THROUGH (prep) *à travers :* through the window = *à travers la fenêtre*
to get/find stg through s.o. = *obtenir/trouver qqch par l'intermédiaire de qqn :* I got the job through my brother = *j'ai obtenu/trouvé ce boulot par l'intermédiaire de mon frère*
through the ... = *pendant tout le ... :* we'll be here through the weekend = *nous serons ici pendant tout le week-end*
☠ for the use of "through" after a verb, see the verb.

THROUGH (adv) **(soaked) through and through** = *(trempé) jusqu'aux os* ⓧ completely = *complètement.*

THROUGHOUT (prep) *d'un bout à l'autre de :* throughout the winter/the United States = *d'un bout à l'autre de l'hiver/des États-Unis* ⓧ everywhere = *partout.*

THROW (to, threw, thrown) **1/** *jeter :* throw me the ball = *jette-moi la balle* ⓧ to hurl = *lancer à toute volée,* to cast = *lancer*

☠ *jeter l'ancre* = to cast anchor	— *jeter un sort* = to cast a spell

---

2/ *perdre délibérément :* the players were accused of throwing the game = *les joueurs ont été accusés d'avoir perdu délibérément la partie* ⓧ to fix = *truquer*

---

to throw (a dinner/a party) = *donner (un dîner/une soirée)* ⓧ to entertain friends = *recevoir des amis*	**to throw s.o.** = *retourner qqn :* what he said threw me = *ce qu'il a dit m'a retourné* ⓧ to shake up = *secouer,* to devastate = *bouleverser*

---

to throw stg at s.o. = *jeter qqch à (la figure de) qqn :* he threw the lamp at me = *il m'a jeté la lampe (à la figure)*
to throw o.s. at s.o. = *se jeter à la tête de qqn :* she threw herself at him = *elle s'est jetée à sa tête*
to throw away = 1/ *jeter :* don't throw your ticket away = *ne jetez pas votre ticket* ⓧ to get rid of = *se débarrasser de* 2/ *gaspiller :* stop throwing your money away = *arrête de gaspiller ton argent,* you threw your only chance away = *tu as gaspillé ton unique chance*
to throw in = *offrir en prime :* they threw in a coffeepot with each sale = *à chaque vente, ils offraient en prime une cafetière*
to throw s.o. into = *jeter qqn dans/en :* they threw him into prison = *ils l'ont jeté en prison*
to throw o.s. into = *se jeter à*

corps perdu dans : after his death, she threw herself into her work = *après sa mort, elle s'est jetée à corps perdu dans son travail*
to throw in with s.o. = *se mettre en cheville avec qqn :* the cop threw in with the Mafia = *ce flic s'est mis en cheville avec la Mafia*
to throw s.o. off = *dérouter qqn :* the new road signs throw drivers off = *les nouveaux panneaux indicateurs déroutent les conducteurs* ⓧ to lead astray = *induire en erreur*
to throw stg on = *enfiler vite qqch :* throw a coat on and let's go for a walk = *enfile vite un manteau et allons nous promener* ⓧ to put on = *mettre*
to throw stg out = *jeter qqch :* the meat's bad, throw it out = *la viande n'est pas bonne, jette-la* ≠ to keep = *garder*

to throw s.o. out = *vider qqn :* they threw him out of school/out of the club = *ils l'ont vidé de l'école/du club* ⓧ to kick out = *ficher à la porte*
to throw over = *jeter bas :* the army threw the government over = *l'armée a jeté bas le gouvernement* ⓧ to bring down = *faire tomber*
to throw s.o. over = *plaquer qqn :* he threw her over for a younger broad = *il l'a plaquée pour une nana plus jeune* ⓧ to dump = *larguer*
to throw up = *dégobiller :* I threw up the whole dinner = *j'ai dégobillé tout le dîner* ⓧ to bring up = *rendre*
to throw stg up to s.o. = *jeter qqch à la figure de qqn :* he threw it up to her that her attitude was selfish = *il lui a jeté à la figure qu'elle avait une attitude égoïste.*

THROWBACK (n) **to be a throwback to** = *remonter à* : her problems with her father are a throwback to her childhood = *ses problèmes avec son père remontent à son enfance.*

THRUST UPON (to, thrust, thrust) *accabler de* : responsibilities were thrust upon her when she was only a teenager = *on l'a accablée de responsabilités alors qu'elle n'était encore qu'adolescente.*

THRUWAY (n) = **THROUGHWAY** *voie* (f) *express* : take the thruway = *prenez la voie express* ⓪ highway = *autoroute.*

THUG (n) *truand* (m) : three thugs held up the bank = *trois truands ont commis un hold-up dans la banque* ⓪ a heavy = *un dur,* hoodlum = *loubard.*

THUMB (n) *pouce* (m) : to suck one's thumb = *sucer son pouce* ⓪ pinky = *petit doigt*
to keep s.o. under one's thumb = *maintenir qqn sous sa coupe* ⓪ to clip s.o.'s wings = *rogner les ailes à qqn*
to twiddle one's thumbs = *se tourner les pouces* ⓪ to goof off = *tirer au flanc*
— *ne pas céder d'un pouce* = not to give an inch
— *manger sur le pouce* = to have a quick snack
— *pouce !* = uncle !

THUMB THROUGH (to, -ed) *lire en diagonale* : to thumb through a book = *lire un livre en diagonale* ⓪ to leaf through = *feuilleter.*

THUNDER (n inv) *tonnerre* (m) : I'm afraid of thunder = *j'ai peur du tonnerre* ⓪ lightning = *éclairs,* thunderbolt = *foudre,* thunderstorm = *orage*
to steal s.o.'s thunder = *couper ses effets à qqn* ⓪ to pull the carpet out from under s.o. = *couper l'herbe sous les pieds de qqn*
— *c'est du tonnerre !* = it's something else !

THUNDER (to, -ed) *tonner* : it thundered all night = *il a tonné toute la nuit* ⓪ it stormed = *il a fait de l'orage.*

THUNDERSTRUCK (adj) *foudroyé, -e* : thunderstruck by the news = *foudroyé par la nouvelle* ⓪ shocked = *choqué.*

THURSDAY (n) *jeudi* (m) : I'll see you Thursday = *je vous verrai jeudi* → WEEK.

THUS (adv) *par conséquent* : we're lacking funds and thus we won't be able to go away this summer = *nous manquons d'argent et par conséquent nous ne pourrons pas partir cet été* ⓪ therefore = *donc.*

THWART (to, -ed) *contrecarrer* : he thwarted my plans = *il a contrecarré mes projets* ⓪ to foil = *déjouer,* to hinder = *gêner.*

THYROID (n) *thyroïde* (f).

TICK (to, -ed) **what makes him tick ?** = *qu'est-ce qui le fait courir ?* : I don't understand what makes him tick = *je ne comprends pas ce qui le fait courir* = what makes him run.

TICKER-TAPE PARADE (n) *accueil d'une personne par une pluie de confettis et de serpentins.*

TICKET (n) **1/** *billet* (m), *ticket* (m) (bus) : get two tickets for the first row = *prends deux billets pour le premier rang,* bus ticket = *ticket d'autobus.*
— *billet (de banque)* = bill (banknote)
— *billet doux* = love letter
— *je vous fiche mon billet que* = I bet my bottom dollar that
— *avoir le ticket avec qqn* = to make a hit with s.o.
2/ *liste* (f) : the Democratic Party ticket = *la liste du Parti démocrate*
split ≠ **straight ticket** = *liste panachée* ≠ *non panachée*
— → list
3/ *contravention* (f), *P.V.* (m) : I got a ticket for speeding = *j'ai eu une contravention/un P.V. pour excès de vitesse.*

TICKLE (to, -d) *chatouiller* : stop tickling my feet = *arrête de me chatouiller les pieds.*

TICKLISH (adj) **1/** *chatouilleux, -euse* : she's ticklish about her weight = *elle est chatouilleuse quand on l'attaque sur son poids* ⓪ touchy = *susceptible* **2/** *épineux, -euse* : a ticklish question = *une question épineuse* ⓪ tricky = *délicat.*

TIDBIT (n) **a (choice) tidbit** = *une nouvelle croustillante (de choix)* ⓪ dirt = *ragots.*

TIDE (n) *marée* (f) ⓪ the ebb and flow = *le flux et le reflux*
the tide's coming in ≠ **going out** = *la marée monte* ≠ *descend*
to go against ≠ **with the tide** = *aller à contre-courant* ≠ *suivre le courant* : his ideas go against the tide = *ses idées vont à contre-courant*
high ≠ **low tide** = *marée haute* ≠ *basse*
to stem the tide of (immigration) = *endiguer le flot de (l'immigration)*
the tide will turn = *le vent va tourner* ⓪ the shoe will be on the other foot = *les rôles pourraient bien être inversés*
— *marée noire* = oil slick
— *marée humaine* = throng
— *arriver comme marée en carême* = to happen inevitably.

TIDE (to, -d) **to tide s.o. over** = *dépanner qqn* : can you lend me some money to tide me over until next week ? = *est-ce que tu peux me prêter de l'argent pour me dépanner jusqu'à la semaine prochaine ?*

TIDY (adj, -ier, -iest) *bien rangé, -e* : a tidy room = *une chambre bien rangée* ⓪ neat = *net* ≠ untidy = *en désordre*
a tidy sum = *une somme rondelette* ⓪ sizeable = *considérable.*

TIDY UP (to, -ied) *ranger* : help me tidy up the living room = *aidez-moi à ranger la salle de séjour* ≠ to make a mess = *ficher la pagaille*
☠ *se ranger (après une vie dissolue)* = (after living it up) to get married and settle down
— *rangez vos affaires* = put away your things
— *où ranges-tu le whisky ?* = where do you keep the Scotch ?
— *se ranger (à l'avis de qqn)* = to come around to (s.o.'s way of thinking)
— *rangez votre voiture sur le bas-côté* = pull your car up on the side of the road.

TIE (n) **1/** *cravate (f)* : I bought Daddy a tie = *j'ai acheté une cravate à papa* = necktie ⅅ tie clip = *pince à cravate*, bow tie = *nœud papillon*, tiepin = *épingle de cravate* ☠ *s'en jeter un derrière la cravate* = to toss down a drink
2/ *attache (f)* : very strong family ties = *des attaches familiales très fortes*

a tie = *à égalité/ex aequo* : the match ended in a tie = *à la fin du match ils étaient à égalité/ex aequo* = *ça s'est terminé par un match nul*

black tie = *tenue de soirée* ≠ white tie = *habit*
to break a tie = *départager des ex aequo*
to sever ties = *cesser toutes relations.*

TIE (to, -d) *attacher* : the terrorists tied his hands to the chair = *les terroristes lui ont attaché les mains à la chaise* ⅅ to bind = *lier* ≠ to untie = *détacher* ☠ → to attach

to be tied (for second place) = *être (deuxième) ex aequo*
to be tied down = *être complètement coincé* : she's tied down with a big house and four kids = *avec une grande maison et ses quatre enfants, elle est complètement coincée* ≠ to be footloose and fancy-free = *être sans attaches*
to tie down to = *contraindre à* : I don't want to be tied down to set hours = *je ne veux pas être contraint à des horaires fixes*
to tie in with = *concorder avec* : his alibi doesn't tie in with the facts = *son alibi ne concorde pas avec les faits* ⅅ to fit in with = *cadrer avec*

to tie up = *ficeler* (package) : tie the package up with a blue ribbon = *ficelez le paquet avec un ruban bleu* ⅅ to wrap up = *emballer*
to be tied up = **1/** *être pris* : I'm very tied up this week = *je suis très pris cette semaine* **2/** *être immobilisé* : his money's tied up in stocks = *son argent est immobilisé en actions*
to tie up with = *se mettre avec* : the French tied up with the British to build the Concorde = *les Français se sont mis avec les Britanniques pour construire le Concorde* ⅅ to team up with = *faire équipe avec.*

TIE-IN (n) *lien (m)* : is there a tie-in between cancer and the pill ? = *est-ce qu'il y a un lien entre le cancer et la pilule ?* = link ⅅ relationship = *rapport* ☠ → link.

TIFF (n) *prise (f) de bec* : I always had tiffs with my brother = *j'ai toujours eu des prises de bec avec mon frère* ⅅ spat = *accrochage.*

TIGER (n) *tigre (m)* ⅅ tigress = *tigresse*, lion = ←.

TIGHT (adj, -er, -est) **1/** *serré, -e* : a tight dress = *une robe serrée* ⅅ closefitting = *ajusté*, clinging = *collant*
(money) is tight = *(l'argent) se fait rare*
to keep a tight rein on = *tenir la bride haute à* ⅅ to crack the whip = *serrer la vis*
what a tight squeeze ! = *ce qu'on était serrés !* : fifty people in the elevator, what a tight squeeze ! = *à cinquante dans l'ascenseur, ce qu'on était serrés !*
☠ *une lutte serrée* = a close fight
— *jouer serré* = to be on one's guards
2/ *gai, -e* : after three drinks I was tight = *après trois verres, j'étais gai* → DRUNK ☠ → gay.

TIGHT (adv) **to sit tight** = *ne pas bouger* : my lawyer advised me to sit tight = *mon avocat m'a conseillé de ne pas bouger* ⅅ to lie low = *se tenir coi*
sleep tight ! = *faites de beaux rêves !*

TIGHTEN (to, -ed) *serrer* : tighten the bolt = *serrez le boulon* ☠ → to clench.

TIGHTFISTED (adj) *près de ses sous* : tightfisted parents = *des parents près de leurs sous* ⅅ miserly = *avare.*

TIGHTROPE (n) **tightrope walker** = *funambule*
to walk on a tightrope = *marcher sur la corde raide* ⅅ to be skating on thin ice = *marcher sur une poudrière.*

TIGHTS (n pl) *collant (m)* : she wore pink tights = *elle portait un collant rose* ⅅ stockings = *bas.*

TIGHTWAD (n) *grigou (m)* : her husband's always been a tightwad = *son mari a toujours été un grigou* ⅅ skinflint = *pingre.*

TILE (n) *carreau (m)*, *tuile (f)* (roof) : there are tiles on the kitchen floor = *le sol de la cuisine est recouvert de carreaux*
☠ *carreau (cartes)* = diamonds (cards)
— *se tenir à carreau* = to stay in line
— *rester sur le carreau* = to be killed on the spot
— *une robe à carreaux* = a checkered dress
— *une tuile (malchance)* = rough luck.

TILL (prep) → UNTIL.

TILT (n) **a tilt to the left/right** = *qui penche vers la gauche/la droite (parti/pays).*

TILT (to, -ed) *incliner :* the tower's tilting = *la tour est inclinée* ☠ *s'incliner devant (les désirs de qqn)* = to bow to (s.o.'s desires).

TIMBER (n) *bois (m) de charpente/de construction :* timber is their main export = *le bois de charpente/de construction est leur principale exportation* ⓪ log = *bûche.*

TIMBUKTU (n) *Trifouillis-les-Oies :* they live very far away in Timbuktu = *ils habitent à Trifouillis-les-Oies* = Podunk ⓪ God's country = *Pétaouchnock.*

TIME (n) **1/** *temps (m) :* I don't have the time = *je n'ai pas le temps,* it'll take a long time = *ça prendra beaucoup de temps*

☠ *le temps présent* = the present tense — *un temps mort (conversation)* = a lull — *le mauvais temps* = bad weather	— *un temps de cinq ans dans l'armée* = a five-year hitch/stint in the army

2/ *fois (f) :* how many times ? = *combien de fois ?,* three times = *trois fois*

☠ *une fois qu'il a décidé* = once he has decided — *pour une fois* = for once	— *une fois n'est pas coutume* = just this once — *une fois pour toutes* = once and for all

3/ *heure (f) :* what time is it please ? = *quelle heure est-il, s'il vous plaît ?* ☠ → hour

---

against time = *contre la montre :* a race against time = *une course contre la montre*
ahead of time = *en avance :* we arrived ahead of time = *nous sommes arrivés en avance* ⓪ early = *tôt*
as time goes by = *à mesure que le temps passe*
at a time = *à la fois :* one person at a time = *une personne à la fois*
at times = *parfois :* we call her at times = *nous lui téléphonons parfois* ⓪ now and then = *de temps à autre*
at the time (of the accident, I was here) = *à l'époque de (l'accident, j'étais ici)*
at this time = *en ce moment :* I can't see you at this time = *je ne peux pas vous voir en ce moment* ⓪ at this point in time = *à l'heure qu'il est*
at that time (we were engaged) = *à cette époque-là (nous étions fiancés)*
at this time of (the year) = *à cette époque de (l'année)*
to be ahead of one's time = *être en avance sur son époque*
to be behind the times = *être en retard sur son époque :* she's really behind the times = *elle est vraiment en retard sur son époque* ≠ to be with it = *être dans le coup*

to bide one's time = *attendre son heure*
to buy on time = *payer à tempérament* ≠ to pay cash on the line = *payer rubis sur l'ongle*
by the time = *le temps que :* by the time the cops came it was too late = *le temps que les flics arrivent, il était trop tard*
to come at the right ≠ **wrong time** = *arriver à point nommé* ≠ *au mauvais moment*
he divides his time between Paris and New York = *il partage son temps entre Paris et New York*
to do time = *faire de la prison/de la taule* (GB)
each/every time = **1/** *à chaque fois :* he calls each/every time = *il téléphone à chaque fois* **2/** *chaque fois que:* each/every time I see him, we fight = *chaque fois que je le vois, nous disputons*
for a long ≠ **short time** = *depuis longtemps* ≠ *peu de temps*
for the time being = *pour le moment :* she's studying in New York for the time being = *pour le moment, elle fait des études à New York* ⓪ just now = *en ce moment*
from time to time = *de temps en temps* ⓪ occasionally = *de temps à autre*

from time immemorial = *depuis la nuit des temps* ⓪ since the beginning of time = *depuis que le monde est monde*
to gain time = *gagner du temps :* she tried to gain time by beating around the bush = *elle a essayé de gagner du temps en tournant autour du pot* ⓪ to stall = *atermoyer*
to get time off for good behavior = *obtenir une remise de peine pour bonne conduite*
to give s.o. a hard/rough time of it = *en faire voir de dures/de toutes les couleurs à qqn* ≠ to have a hard/rough time of it = *en voir de dures*
to go through hard/rough times = *tirer le diable par la queue* → POOR
to go/move with the times = *évoluer avec son époque*
to have a hard/rough time = *avoir bien du mal à :* she had a hard/rough time getting a job = *elle a eu bien du mal à trouver un travail*
to have time off = *avoir du temps libre :* I have no time off this week = *je n'ai pas de temps libre cette semaine*
to have time on one's hands = *avoir du temps à ne savoir qu'en faire* ⓪ to have spare time = *avoir du temps disponible*

to have the time of one's life = *s'amuser comme un fou* : we had the time of our lives at the gala = *nous nous sommes amusés comme des fous au gala* ⓪ **to have a ball** = *bien se marrer*

to have a wild time = *faire la noce* ⓪ **to go on a binge** = *faire la java*

how many times does (4) go into (24) ? = *en (24) combien de fois (4) ?*

in next to no time = *en moins de temps qu'il n'en faut pour le dire* ⓪ **in the bat of an eye** = *en un tour de main*

in no time = *en un rien de temps* : he did it in no time = *il l'a fait en un rien de temps* ⓪ **in a jiffy** = *en un clin d'œil,* **before you could say Jack Robinson** = *avant d'avoir pu dire ouf*

in one's time = *de son temps* : he was quite a playboy in his time = *c'était un vrai play-boy de son temps* ⓪ **in one's day** = *à son époque*

in time = 1/ *à temps* : he didn't arrive in time to save them = *il n'est pas arrivé à temps pour les sauver* 2/ *avec le temps* : we'll understand each other in time = *avec le temps, nous finirons par nous comprendre*

it's about high time (you tell me the truth) = *il est grand temps (que vous me disiez la vérité)*

it's time that (we got married) = *il est temps qu'(on se marie)*

(my watch) keeps (good) time = *(ma montre) a l'heure (exacte)*

to keep up with the times = *vivre avec son temps*

to kill time = *tuer le temps*

to make time with (the boss's wife) = *faire du gringue à (la femme du patron)* = **to make a play for**

to mark time = *rester là à attendre* : I'm just marking time waiting for the results of the exam = *je reste là à attendre les résultats de l'examen*

once upon a time = *il fut un temps* : once upon a time gays were considered mad = *il fut un temps où les homosexuels étaient considérés comme fous*

once upon a time there was ... = *il était une fois ...*

(only) time will tell = *l'avenir (seul) le dira* ⓪ **whatever will be will be** = *ce qui doit arriver arrivera*

on time = *à l'heure* : he never comes on time = *il n'arrive jamais à l'heure* ≠ **late** = *en retard*

to pass the time of day = *parler de la pluie et du beau temps* ⓪ **to chew the fat** = *discuter le bout de gras*

to play for time = *chercher à gagner du temps* : the President's playing for time with the terrorists = *le Président cherche à gagner du temps avec les terroristes*

remember the time (we made love in the kitchen) = *tu te souviens de la fois où (on a fait l'amour dans la cuisine) ?*

to save time = *gagner du temps* : you can save time by taking a taxi = *vous pouvez gagner du temps en prenant un taxi*

a short ≠ long time ago = *il y a peu de temps ≠ il y a long-temps* ⓪ **ages ago** = *il y a belle lurette*

to spend time = *passer du temps à* : she spends a lot of time reading = *il passe beaucoup de temps à lire*

to take time out (to relax) = *faire une pause (pour se reposer)*

take your time = *prenez votre temps*

the time has come (to ask for a raise) = *le moment est venu (de demander une augmentation)*

the time is (exactly 3 o'clock) = *il est (exactement 3 heures)*

there's a time and a place for everything = *il y a un temps pour tout* ⓪ **everything in good time** = *chaque chose en son temps*

there's no time to (eat now) = *on n'a pas le temps de (manger maintenant)*

these are hard/rough times = *les temps sont durs/difficiles*

time and again = *à plusieurs reprises* : he lied to me time and again = *il m'a menti à plusieurs reprises* = **repeatedly** ⓪ **time after time** = *à maintes reprises*

time and a half = *cinquante pour cent de plus* : to be paid time and a half for overtime = *être payé cinquante pour cent de plus pour les heures supplémentaires*

time and tide wait for no man = *on n'arrête pas le temps qui passe* → THAT'S LIFE !

time difference = *décalage horaire*

(his) time has come = *(son) heure est venue*

time is money = *le temps, c'est de l'argent*

time is on our side = *le temps travaille pour nous*

a time limit = *une limite de temps* : there's a time limit for the offer = *il y a une limite de temps pour répondre à cette offre*

time passes so quickly = *le temps passe si vite*

the time's ripe = *la poire est mûre*

times are rough = *les temps sont durs*

time's up ! = *c'est l'heure !*

up to the time that = *jusqu'au moment où* : they were happy up to the time that the second child came along = *ils ont été heureux jusqu'au moment où ils ont eu un second enfant*

to waste one's time = *perdre son temps* : you're wasting your time trying to get the job = *vous perdez votre temps en essayant d'avoir ce poste* ⓪ **to be to no avail** = *être/rester sans effet*

I wouldn't give him the (right) time of day = *il peut se l'accrocher* ⓪ he can whistle for it = *il peut toujours courir.*

TIME (adj) **a time bomb** = *une bombe à retardement*

to be sitting on a time bomb = *être assis sur un* volcan

time zone = *fuseau horaire* ⓪ **jet lag** = *(troubles dus au) décalage horaire.*

> **TIME** (to, -d) **1/** *chronométrer* : to time a race = *chronométrer une course* **2/** *choisir son moment* : you really timed it ! = *tu as vraiment choisi ton moment !*

TIME-CONSUMING (adj) *qui prend du temps* : kids are time-consuming = *les gosses prennent du temps.*

TIMELESS (adj) *qui remonte à la nuit des temps* : a timeless tradition = *une tradition qui remonte à la nuit des temps.*

TIMELY (adj) *opportun, -e* : a timely check = *une vérification opportune* ⓄⒹ apropos = *à propos* ☙ *il serait opportun de* = it would be advisable to.

TIMEOUT (n) *arrêt (m) de jeu* : to ask for a timeout = *demander un arrêt de jeu* ⓄⒹ break = *pause.*

TIMESAVING (adj) *qui fait gagner du temps* : time-saving measures = *des mesures qui font gagner du temps.*

TIMETABLE (n) = SCHEDULE.

TIMID (adj, -er, -est) *timide* : a timid nice guy = *un type sympa et timide* ⓄⒹ people shy = *sauvage* ≠ outgoing = *liant* **TIMIDITY** (n) *timidité (f)* = shyness **TIMIDLY** (adv) *timidement.*

TIMING (n) *moment (m)* : when it comes to love, timing is crucial = *en amour, il faut bien choisir son moment* **it's bad** ≠ **good timing** = *ça tombe mal* ≠ *bien* **your timing is off** = *votre moment est mal choisi* ☙ → moment.

TIN (n inv) **1/** *fer (m) blanc* ⓄⒹ pewter = *étain* **2/** (GB) *boîte (f) de conserve* = can **tin foil** = *papier d'aluminium* **tin soldier** = *soldat de plomb.*

TINKER WITH (to, -ed) *tripoter* : stop tinkering with the clock = *arrête de tripoter la pendule.*

TINSEL (n) *clinquant (m)* : Hollywood's a world of tinsel = *Hollywood est le royaume du clinquant.*

TINY (adj, -ier, -iest) *minuscule* : a tiny room = *une pièce minuscule* ⓄⒹ teeny = *tout petit* ≠ huge = *immense.*

TIP (n) **1/** *pourboire (m)* : he never leaves good tips = *il ne laisse jamais de bons pourboires* **tip included** = *service compris* **2/** *tuyau (m)* : he gave me good tips on where to eat in Paris = *il m'a donné de bons tuyaux pour bien manger à Paris* ⓄⒹ lead = *piste* ≠ bum steer = *tuyau crevé* **3/** *bout (m)* : there's a lighthouse at the tip of the land = *il y a un phare au bout du terrain* **to have stg on the tip of one's tongue** = *avoir qqch sur le bout de la langue* ⓄⒹ to draw a blank = *avoir un trou* **from tip to toe** = *de la tête aux pieds* : well-dressed from tip to toe = *bien habillé de la tête aux pieds* ☙ *connaître qqch sur le bout du doigt* = to have stg down pat
— *au bout d'une heure* = after an hour

— *être (femme) jusqu'au bout des ongles* = to be every inch (a woman)
— *mener qqn par le bout du nez* = to lead s.o. by the nose
— *être à bout* = to be worn out
— *mettons les bouts* = let's get the show on the road
— *venir à bout de* = to get to the end of
— *du bout des lèvres* = halfheartedly
— *un bout de papier* = a scrap of paper
— *à bout de souffle* = out of breath
— *montrer le bout de son nez* = to dash in (and out)
— *le bout de la route* = the end of the road
— *de bout en bout* = from start to finish
— *être au bout du rouleau* = to be at the end of one's rope
— *manger du bout des dents* = to toy with one's food
— *un bout de (chemin)* = a bit of (the way).

TIP (to, -ped) **1/** *pencher* : the boat's tipping = *le bateau penche* ☙ → to lean **2/** *donner un pourboire à* : don't forget to tip the waiter = *n'oublie pas de donner un pourboire au garçon*
to tip off = *tuyauter* : who tipped off the cops ? = *qui a tuyauté les flics ?*, the brothel was tipped off that there was going to be a raid = *on a tuyauté le bordel sur la rafle qu'il devait y avoir*
to tip over = *se renverser* : the glass tipped over = *le verre s'est renversé* ☙ → to spill.

TIPPER (n) *quelqu'un qui donne des pourboires* : a big tipper = *quelqu'un qui donne de gros pourboires.*

TIPSY (adj, -ier, -iest) *pompette* : I was tipsy after two drinks = *j'étais pompette après deux verres* → DRUNK.

TIPTOE (n) **on tiptoe** = *sur la pointe des pieds* ⓄⒹ on all fours = *à quatre pattes* **TIPTOE** (to, -d) *marcher sur la pointe des pieds* : I tiptoed out of the room = *je suis sorti de la pièce sur la pointe des pieds.*

TIP-TOP (adj) *hors pair* : tip-top working conditions = *des conditions de travail hors pair* ⓄⒹ first-rate = *de premier ordre.*

TIRE (n) *pneu (m)* : a flat tire = *un pneu crevé (une crevaison)* = tyre (GB) ⓄⒹ spare wheel = *roue de secours.*

TIRE (to, -d) *fatiguer* : his constant talking tires me = *ça me fatigue qu'il parle tout le temps* ⓄⒹ to wear out = *exténuer*
to be tired of = *être fatigué de* : I'm tired of your criticisms = *je suis fatigué de vos critiques* ⓄⒹ to be fed up with = *en avoir marre de.*

TIRED (adj) *fatigué, -e* : tired children = *des enfants fatigués* ⓄⒹ beat = *crevé* ≠ tireless = *infatigable.*

TIRESOME (adj) *fatigant, -e* : tiresome questioning = *interrogatoire fatigant* ⓄⒹ tedious = *fastidieux* ☙ *tu es fatigant !* = you're a pain !

TISSUE (n) *tissu (m)* : cell tissue = *tissu cellulaire* ☠ *un tissu de mensonges* = a pack of lies
— *tissu (étoffe)* = material.

TIT (n) *nichon (m), téton (m)* : he likes big tits = *il aime les gros nichons/tétons* ⬙ boobs = *nénés*, knockers = *doudounes*
tit for tat = 1/ *du tac au tac* : he answered tit for tat = *il a répondu du tac au tac* 2/ *un prêté pour un rendu* : he did it tit for tat = *c'était un prêté pour un rendu* ⬙ an eye for an eye, a tooth for a tooth = *œil pour œil, dent pour dent*.

TITLE (n) *titre (m)* : what's the title of the book you're reading ? = *quel est le titre du livre que vous lisez ?*
the title role = *le rôle principal*
☠ *les gros titres* = the headlines
— *à ce titre* = as such
— *à titre personnel* = in a private capacity
— *à titre officiel* = officially
— *acheter des titres* = to buy securities.

TO (prep) 1/ *à (au)* : I'm going to Paris/the country/the zoo = *je vais à Paris/à la campagne/au zoo*

be nice/kind to her = *soyez gentil/bon avec elle*
happy/glad to see/talk to you = *heureux/content de vous voir/de vous parler*
it's (ten) to (five) = *il est (cinq) heures moins (dix)*
to go to s.o.'s house/the beauty parlor = *aller chez qqn/le coiffeur*
(to walk) to and fro = *(marcher) de long en large*
to me = *à mon avis* : to me the Beatles were the greatest = *à mon avis, les Beatles étaient les plus grands* ⬙ to my mind = *à mon sens*
you were wrong ≠ right to (come) = *vous avez eu tort ≠ raison de (venir)*

☠ *à six heures* = at six o'clock	— *être payé à l'heure/à la journée* = to be paid by the hour/the day
— *il est au bureau* = he's at the office	— *à condition que* = on condition that
— *à ce soir/à tout à l'heure/à demain* = see you tonight/later/tomorrow	— *à moins que* = unless
— *habiter à New York* = to live in New York	— *penser à qqn* = to think of/about s.o.
— *à deux kilomètres* = two kilometers away	— *tenir à* = to be set on
— *à l'avenir* = in the future	— *à cause de* = because of
	— *à vendre* = for sale

2/ *pour* : too young to go to school = *trop jeune pour aller à l'école*, I did it to help you = *je l'ai fait pour t'aider* ⬙ in order to = *afin de* ☠ → for

☠ for the use of ''to'' after a verb, see the verb.

TOADY (to, -ied) *fayot(t)er* : to toady to the boss = *fayotter auprès du patron* ⬙ to brownnose = *faire de la lèche*.

TOAST (n inv) *toast (m), pain (m) grillé* : jam and toast = *de la confiture et des toasts/et du pain grillé* ⬙ toaster = *grille-pain*
a piece of toast = *un toast/une tartine grillée*
to propose a toast = *porter un toast*
(she's) the toast of (New York) = *(c'est) la coqueluche de (New York)* ⬙ darling = *enfant chéri*.

TOBACCO (n, -s or -es) *tabac (m)* : to export tobacco = *exporter du tabac* ⬙ pipe = ←
☠ *passer qqn à tabac* = to beat s.o. up
— *faire un tabac* = to be a hit.

TO-BE (adj) *futur, -e* : this is my husband to-be = *voilà mon futur mari*.

TOBOGGAN (n) *luge (f)* ☠ *un toboggan* = a slide.

TODAY (n) *aujourd'hui (m)* : women of today use contraception = *les femmes d'aujourd'hui utilisent la contraception*
from today onwards = *dorénavant* ⬙ **as of today** = *à partir d'aujourd'hui*.

TODAY (adv) 1/ *aujourd'hui* : let's go out to have lunch today = *si on déjeunait dehors aujourd'hui* ≠ tomorrow = *demain* 2/ *aujourd'hui* : a lot of men help with the housework today = *aujourd'hui beaucoup d'hommes aident à la maison* ⬙ nowadays = *de nos jours*.

TO-DO (n) *affaire (f) d'État* : stop making a whole to-do about it = *n'en fais pas une affaire d'État* ⬙ fuss = *histoires*.

TOE (n) *doigt (m) de pied, orteil (m)* : my shoes hurt my toes = *mes chaussures me font mal aux doigts de pied/aux orteils*, big toe = *gros orteil* ⬙ foot = *pied*
to be on one's toes = *rester vigilant* : working with him, you've got to be on your toes = *quand on travaille avec lui, il faut rester vigilant* ⬙ to be on the ball = *être dégourdi*
to step/tread on s.o.'s toes = *marcher sur les pieds de qqn*.

TOGETHER (adv) *ensemble* : they came together = *ils sont venus ensemble* ⬙ both = *tous les deux*
☠ for the use of ''together'' after a verb, see the verb.

TOIL (to, -ed) *peiner* : to toil in the fields = *peiner dans les champs* ⬙ to sweat = *trimer* ☠ *cela me peine que ...* = it pains me that ...

TOILET (n) *toilettes (f pl)* : I want to go to the toilet = *je voudrais aller aux toilettes* ⬙ comfort station = *lieu d'aisances*, the john = *le petit coin/les W.-C.*, the can = *les gogues*, toilet paper = *papier hygiénique*
toilet trained (child) = *propre (enfant)* ☠ → clean
☠ *faire sa toilette* = to wash up.

TOKEN (n) 1/ *gage (m)* : he gave him a ring as a token of friendship = *il lui a donné une bague en gage d'amitié*

Ⓞ gesture = *geste*
☠ *tueur à gages* = hired killer
— *mettre en gage* = to pawn
— *gages (salaire)* = earnings/wages
2/ jeton *(m)* : a phone token = *un jeton de téléphone*
☠ *avoir les jetons* = to have the willies
— *un vieux jeton* = an old schnook.

TOKEN (adj) *symbolique* : token payment of one dollar = *paiement symbolique d'un dollar.*

TOLERABLE (adj) *tolérable* : his temper is barely tolerable = *son mauvais caractère est à peine tolérable* Ⓞ bearable = *supportable* ≠ intolerable = *intolérable.*

TOLERANCE (n) *tolérance (f)* : he showed a lot of tolerance = *il a montré beaucoup de tolérance* ≠ intolerance = *intolérance* ☠ *maison de tolérance* = brothel.

TOLERANT (adj) *tolérant, -e* : a tolerant attitude = *une attitude tolérante* Ⓞ liberal = *libéral* ≠ intolerant = *intolérant.*

TOLERATE (to, -d) *tolérer* : I won't tolerate his drinking = *je ne tolérerai pas qu'il boive.*

TOLL (n) **1/** *péage (m)* : there are tolls to pay at every bridge = *il y a un péage à chaque pont*
2/ *bilan (m)* : the toll was a hundred people dead = *le bilan a été de cent morts*
to take a (heavy) toll on = *ébranler sérieusement* : the divorce took a heavy toll on her = *le divorce l'a sérieusement ébranlée*
toll call = *communication interurbaine* = trunk call (GB)
☠ *bilan (entreprise)* = balance sheet
— *déposer son bilan* = to file for bankruptcy
— *bilan de santé* = medical checkup
— *le bilan (d'un homme politique)* = a (politician's) record
— *faire le bilan* = to take stock.

TOMATO (n, -es) **1/** *tomate (f)* : a tomato salad = *une salade de tomates* **2/** *belle plante (f)* : Jane's quite a tomato = *Jane est une belle plante* Ⓞ built like a brick shithouse = *vachement bien foutue.*

TOMB (n) *tombeau (m)* : tombs made of marble = *des tombeaux en marbre* Ⓞ grave = *tombe*, tombstone = *pierre tombale*, mausoleum = *mausolée* ☠ *rouler à tombeau ouvert* = to drive at breakneck speed.

TOMBOY (n) *garçon (m) manqué* : my daughter's a real tomboy = *ma fille est un vrai garçon manqué* ≠ pinup = *pin-up.*

TOMMY GUN (n) *mitraillette (f)* : a tommy gun was found in his suitcase = *on a trouvé une mitraillette dans sa valise* Ⓞ machine gun = *mitrailleuse.*

TOMORROW (n) *demain (m)* : tomorrow is my birthday = *demain, c'est mon anniversaire*
never put off till tomorrow what you can do today = *il ne faut pas remettre au lendemain ce qu'on peut faire le jour même*
tomorrow's another day = *demain, il fera jour* Ⓞ let's call it a day = *à chaque jour suffit sa peine*
who knows what tomorrow may bring ? = *qui sait de quoi demain sera fait ?* → THAT'S LIFE !
☠ *ce n'est pas demain la veille* = don't hold your breath.

TOMORROW (adv) *demain* : I'll see you tomorrow = *je vous verrai demain* ≠ yesterday = *hier*
see you tomorrow ! = *à demain !*
tomorrow morning/night = *demain matin/soir.*

TON (n) *tonne (f)* : a ton of potatoes = *une tonne de pommes de terre* Ⓞ kilo = ←
tons of (people) = *des masses de (gens)* → MANY
☠ *en faire des tonnes* = to pile it on.

TONE (n) **1/** *ton (m)* : a tone of blue = *un ton bleu* Ⓞ shade = *teinte* **2/** *ton (m)* : I didn't like his aggressive tone = *je n'ai pas aimé son ton agressif*
to set the tone = *donner le ton* Ⓞ to set the fashion = *donner le la*
☠ *hausser le ton* = to raise one's voice
— *changer de ton* = to change one's tune
— *si tu le prends sur ce ton* = if you take it that way.

TONE DOWN (to, -d) *atténuer* : your article's too aggressive, tone it down = *votre article est trop agressif, atténuez-le un peu* ☠ *atténuer une douleur* = to ease a pain.

TONGUE (n) *langue (f)* : I burnt my tongue = *je me suis brûlé la langue* Ⓞ teeth = *dents*
bite your tongue ! = *ne parle pas de malheur !* Ⓞ keep your fingers crossed ! = *croise les doigts !*
have you lost your tongue ? = *tu as avalé ta langue ?*
hold your tongue ! = *tiens ta langue !* Ⓞ hush up ! = *tais-toi !*
to set tongues wagging = *faire jaser* : their divorce set tongues wagging = *leur divorce a fait jaser* Ⓞ to gossip = *potiner*
to stick one's tongue out = *tirer la langue*
tongue in cheek = *avec un humour à froid* : he's very tongue in cheek = *il a un humour à froid* Ⓞ deadpan = *impassible*
tongue twister = *mot ou phrase difficile à prononcer* Ⓞ jawbreaker = *nom à coucher dehors*
☠ *avoir la langue bien pendue* = to have the gift of gab
— *la langue anglaise* = the English language
— *la langue verte* = slang
— *(dis-moi) je donne ma langue au chat !* = (tell me,) I give up !
— *délier la langue à qqn* = to make s.o. talk.

TONGUE-TIED (adj) *qui n'arrive plus à parler* : I was so embarrassed I was tongue-tied = *j'étais tellement embarrassé que je n'arrivais plus à parler.*

TONIGHT (adv) *ce soir* : we're eating at home tonight = *ce soir, nous dînons à la maison* ≠ last night = *hier soir.*

TONSIL (n) *amygdale (f)* **TONSILLITIS** (n, -es) *amygdalite (f).*

TOO (adv) **1/** *aussi* : me too = *moi aussi*, she's French too = *elle est Française aussi* = she's French also, he's rich and bright too = *il est riche et intelligent aussi* ⓐ in addition = *en plus* ☠ → also
2/ *trop* : too soon/late/big = *trop tôt/tard/gros* ☠ *je ne sais trop que faire* = I really don't know what to do

(the film) was too much ! = *(ce film,) c'était trop !*	**it's too bad (she's sick again)** = *c'est navrant (qu'elle soit encore malade)*
to carry too far = *dépasser les bornes* : a fur coat and who knows what's next ? don't you think you're carrying it too far ? = *un manteau de fourrure et puis quoi encore ? tu ne trouves pas que tu dépasses les bornes ?*	**too bad !** = *tant pis !* → THAT'S LIFE ! ≠ so much the better ! = *tant mieux !*
	too much for = *trop pour* : this work's too much for me = *ce travail, c'est trop pour moi*
to go too far = *y aller un peu trop fort* : with that remark you went a little too far = *vous y êtes allé un peu trop fort en faisant cette remarque* ⓐ to overdo it = *en faire trop*	**(he's) too much of (a coward)** = *(il est) vraiment trop (lâche)*
	you're expecting too much of him = *vous attendez trop de lui*
I am too ! = *si, je le suis !* : I know you're not happy with him — I am too ! = *je sais que tu n'es pas heureuse avec lui — si, je le suis !*	**you're making too much of it !** = *ce n'est pas la peine d'en faire tout un plat !*
	you're too much ! = *tu es un cas !/c'est trop !*

TOOL (n) *outil (m)* : I don't have the proper tools to repair my bike = *je n'ai pas les outils appropriés pour réparer mon vélo* ⓐ instrument = ← hammer = *marteau*, screwdriver = *tournevis*.

TOOTH (n, teeth) *dent (f)* : I often forget to brush my teeth = *j'oublie souvent de me brosser les dents*

baby teeth = *dents de lait*	**fang** = *croc*	**toothache** = *mal/rage de dents*
braces = *appareil (dentaire)*	**filling** = *plombage*	**toothbrush** = *brosse à dents*
cavity = *carie*	**jaw** = *mâchoire*	**toothless** = *édenté*
dental plate = *dentier/râtelier*	**mouthwash** = *bain de bouche*	**toothpaste** = *dentifrice*
dentist = *dentiste*	**stomatologist** = *stomatologiste*	**toothpick** = *cure-dents*
false teeth = *fausses dents*		**wisdom teeth** = *dents de sagesse*

to cut a tooth = *percer une dent*	*vail) à bras-le-corps*
to fight stg tooth and nail = *combattre qqch avec acharnement* : Congress is fighting the bill tooth and nail = *le Congrès combat le projet de loi avec acharnement*	**to lie in one's teeth** = *mentir comme un arracheur de dents* ≠ to tell the truth = *dire la vérité*
	like pulling teeth = *la croix et la bannière* ≠ easy as pie = *facile comme bonjour*
to get one's teeth into (a job) = *prendre (un tra-*	**to pull a tooth** = *extraire une dent*

☠ *n'avoir rien à se mettre sous la dent* = not to have a bite of food to eat	— *avoir la dent dure* = to be malicious
— *avoir une dent contre qqn* = to have a grudge against s.o.	— *avoir les dents longues* = to be power-/money-hungry
	— *être sur les dents* = to be on the go
— *se casser les dents (sur qqch)* = to come a cropper (over stg)	— *montrer les dents* = to snap at s.o.

TOP (n) **1/** *haut (m)* : the top of the page/mountain = *le haut de la page/de la montagne* ≠ bottom = *bas*
2/ *haut (m)* : I have to buy a top for my skirt = *il faut que j'achète un haut pour aller avec ma jupe* ⓐ halter = *bustier*, blouse = ←

at the top of = *en tête de* : she's at the top of her class = *elle est en tête de sa classe*	*s'est mis dans une colère noire quand il s'est rendu compte de la gaffe que nous avions faite* → ANGRY	psychological ones = *leurs problèmes financiers sont venus s'ajouter à leurs problèmes psychologiques*
to blow one's top = *se mettre dans une colère noire* : he blew his top when he found out about the blunder we had made = *il*	**to come on top of** = *venir s'ajouter à* : their financial problems came on top of their	**to feel on top of the world** = *être aux anges* ≠ to be blue = *avoir le cafard*

from top to bottom = *de haut en bas*
off the top of one's head = *comme ça* : I'm not sure but off the top of my head I'd say it will cost $ 100 = *je n'en suis pas sûr, mais comme ça, je dirais que ça coûtera 100 dollars*
on top of = 1/ *qui maîtrise bien* : she was depressed but she's on top of the situation now = *elle était déprimée, mais*

maintenant elle maîtrise bien la situation 2/ *au-dessus de* : they live on top of us = *ils habitent au-dessus de nous* = above
on top of it = *par-dessus le marché* : he botched up his car, he lost his job and on top of it, his girlfriend walked out = *il a bousillé sa voiture, perdu son boulot et par-dessus le marché sa petite amie s'est tirée* ⓪ to crown it all = *pour couronner le tout*

to see the man/woman at the top = *s'adresser à Dieu plutôt qu'à ses saints* : you'd better see the man at the top = *il vaut mieux s'adresser à Dieu plutôt qu'à ses saints*
to shout at the top of one's lungs = *s'époumoner* ⓪ **to shout at the top of one's voice** = *crier à tue-tête* ⓪ to yell bloody murder = *gueuler comme un putois*

☠ *la haute* (LV) = the upper crust
— *tenir le haut du pavé* = to be a big-timer

— *avoir des hauts et des bas* = to have ups and downs.

TOP (adj) 1/ *du haut* : they live on the top floor = *ils habitent à l'étage du haut*
2/ *hors catégorie* : a top journalist = *un journaliste hors catégorie* ⓪ leading = *de premier plan*

---

top banana = *caïd* : he's a top banana in Hollywood = *c'est un caïd d'Hollywood* ≠ light-weight = *poids léger*
the top brass = *les huiles* ⓪ the bigwigs = *les ténors* ≠ small fry = *menu fretin*
top dog = *quelqu'un qui fait la*

pluie et le beau temps : he's the top dog in the party = *c'est lui qui fait la pluie et le beau temps dans le parti* ⓪ big wheel = *grand manitou*
top man/woman = *grand chef* : he's top man in the company = *c'est lui le grand chef*

dans l'entreprise ⓪ big shot = *grand ponte*
top secret = *top secret* : the report on nuclear research is top secret = *le rapport sur les recherches nucléaires est top secret* ⓪ hush-hush = *ultrasecret*, classified = *secret*.

TOP (to, -ped) *dépasser* : last year's sales topped this year's = *les ventes de l'année dernière ont dépassé celles de cette année* ⓪ to surpass = *surclasser* ☠ → to overtake

---

that tops it ! = *ça couronne le tout !* → GOSH !
to top it all = *pour couronner le tout* = **to top it off** ⓪ to boot = *de surcroît* : he walked out and took all the money to top it all = *il s'est tiré et, pour*

couronner le tout, il a pris tout le fric
to top off (with) = *couronner (par)* : we topped off dinner with a glass of brandy = *on a couronné le dîner par un verre de cognac.*

TOPFLIGHT (adj) *de haut vol* : a topflight lawyer = *un avocat de haut vol* ≠ two-bit = *à la manque.*

TOP-HEAVY (adj) **(she's) top-heavy** = *(il y a) du monde au balcon* ⓪ chesty = *qui a une poitrine avantageuse*
a top-heavy (broad) = *(une nana) qui a une forte poitrine.*

TOPIC (n) *sujet (m)* : the topic of his speech = *le sujet de son discours* ⓪ theme = *thème* ☠ → subject.

TOPLESS (adj) *topless, torse nu* : to dance topless = *danser topless* ⓪ barebreasted = *les seins nus.*

TOP-LEVEL (adj) *au plus haut niveau* : top-level talks = *des entretiens au plus haut niveau.*

TOPNOTCH (adj) *de premier ordre* : a topnotch lawyer = *un avocat de premier ordre* ⓪ topflight = *de haut vol* → WONDERFUL.

TOPPLE (to, -d) *faire chuter* : to topple the government = *faire chuter le gouvernement* ⓪ to bring down = *faire tomber.*

TOPS (adj) *le meilleur/la meilleure qui soit* : my doctor's tops = *j'ai le meilleur médecin qui soit* → WONDERFUL
he's tops in (his field) = *c'est une sommité dans (son domaine)* ⓪ the cream of the crop = *la fine fleur.*

TOPSY-TURVY (adj) *sens dessus dessous* : my room/the world is topsy-turvy = *ma chambre/le monde est sens dessus dessous* ⓪ a mess = *la pagaille.*

TORCH (n, -es) *torche (f), flambeau (m)* : all the skiers were carrying torches = *tous les skieurs portaient une torche/un flambeau* ⓪ flame = *flamme*
to carry a torch for s.o. = *avoir qqn dans la peau* : she's still carrying a torch for him = *elle l'a toujours dans la peau* ⓪ to be hooked on = *être accroché à* ☠ *une torche électrique* = a flashlight.

TORMENT (n) *tourment (m)* : the torments of the abandoned wife = *les tourments de l'épouse abandonnée* ⓪ anguish = *angoisse* **TORMENT** (to, -ed) *tourmenter* : the child keeps tormenting the cat = *l'enfant passe son temps à tourmenter le chat* ⓪ to harass = *harceler.*

TORNADO (n, -(e)s) *tornade (f)* : a violent tornado destroyed the village = *une violente tornade a détruit le village* ○D cyclone = ←.

TORPEDO (n, -es) *torpille (f)* : the torpedo exploded too early = *la torpille a explosé trop tôt* ○D submarine = *sous-marin*.

TORRID (adj) *torride* : torrid heat = *chaleur torride*.

TORSO (n, -s or -si) *torse (m)* ○D thorax = ←.

TORTURE (n) 1/ *torture (f)* : Amnesty International's fighting against torture = *Amnesty International se bat contre la torture* ○D brainwashing = *lavage de cerveau* 2/ *supplice (m)* : going out with my in-laws is a real torture = *c'est un véritable supplice de sortir avec mes beaux-parents* **TORTURE** (to, -d) *torturer* : they tortured the hostage = *ils ont torturé l'otage* ○D to torment = *tourmenter* **TORTURER** (n) *tortionnaire (m)*.

TOSS (to, -ed) *envoyer* : toss me a pencil, will you ? = *tu peux m'envoyer un crayon ?* ○D to throw = *jeter*
to toss and turn (all night) = *se tourner et se retourner dans son lit (toute la nuit)* ≠ to sleep around the clock = *faire le tour du cadran*
to toss down (5 Scotches) = *s'envoyer (5 whiskies) (derrière la cravate)* ○D to guzzle = *siffler* ☠ → to send.

TOSS-UP (n) it's a toss-up whether (she'll call or not) = *on ne peut vraiment pas dire si (elle appellera ou non)*.

TOT (n) *bambin, -e* : their child is still a tot = *leur enfant est encore un bambin* ○D toddler = *tout-petit*, infant = *enfant en bas âge*.

TOTAL (n) *total (m)* : it costs a total of $ 1 000 = *ça fait un total de 1 000 dollars*.

TOTAL (adj) *total, -e* : we're in total agreement = *notre accord est total*
a total loss = *un échec total* : our trip was a total loss = *notre voyage a été un échec total* ○D a dead loss = *une perte sèche*.

TOTAL (to, -(l)ed) *s'élever à* : our bill totaled $ 200 = *notre addition s'est élevée à 200 dollars* ○D to amount to = *se monter à*.

TOTALITARIAN (adj) *totalitaire* : totalitarian regimes = *les régimes totalitaires* ○D tyrannical = *tyrannique* **TOTALITARIANISM** (n) *totalitarisme (m)* ≠ democracy = *démocratie*.

TOTALITY (n, -ies) *totalité (f)*.

TOTALLY (adv) *totalement* : you're totally wrong = *vous avez totalement tort* → VERY.

TOTTER (to, -ed) *chanceler* : the drunkard tottered and fell = *l'ivrogne a chancelé et est tombé* ○D to stumble = *trébucher* ☠ → to falter.

TOUCH (n, -es) *toucher (m)* : the soft touch of satin = *le doux toucher du satin*		
a touch of (curry/brandy) = *un soupçon de (curry/cognac)* ○D a speck of = *un chouia de*, a dot of = *une pointe de* **to be out of touch** = *ne plus être au courant* : the doctor's out of touch with modern treatments = *le docteur n'est plus au courant des traitements modernes* **(he has) a marvelous touch with (animals)** = *(il a) un contact merveilleux avec (les animaux)* **to be/get in touch with** = *être*	en/prendre contact avec : if you go to San Francisco, get in touch with my brother = *si tu vas à San Francisco, prends contact avec mon frère* **to keep in touch** = *rester en contact* : I moved to California but kept in touch with all my friends = *j'ai déménagé en Californie, mais je suis resté en contact avec tous mes amis* **to lose one's touch** = *perdre la main* : since he started drinking the tennis champ has lost his touch = *depuis qu'il s'est mis à*	boire le champion de tennis a perdu la main ○D to be rusty = *être rouillé* **to lose touch with** = *perdre contact avec* : since she left New York, she's lost touch with everyone = *depuis qu'elle a quitté New York, elle a perdu contact avec tout le monde* ≠ to be in touch with = *être en contact avec* **to put the finishing touches to (a painting/a text)** = *mettre la dernière main à (un tableau/un texte)*
☠ *touches (de piano)* = keys — *j'ai fait une touche avec mon prof* = I made a hit with my teacher	— *être sur la touche* = to be on the sidelines — *elle a une drôle de touche* = she surely looks weird.	
TOUCH (to, -ed) *toucher (à)* : touch the wall and see if it's dry = *touche le mur pour voir s'il est sec*, she hardly touched her food = *elle a à peine touché à ce qu'il y avait dans son assiette*		
I never touch it ! = *je n'y touche jamais !* : no liquor for me, I never touch it ! = *pas d'alcool pour moi, je n'y touche jamais !* ○D that's not my thing ! = *ce n'est pas mon truc !*	**not to touch** = *être loin d'égaler* : American wines can't touch French wines = *les vins américains sont loin d'égaler les vins français* ○D not to be compared with = *ne pas être comparable à*	

to touch off = *faire éclater* : new violence was touched off by the President's remarks = *les remarques du Président ont fait éclater de nouveaux troubles* ⏀ to trigger off = *déclencher* **to touch on (a sticky subject)** = *effleurer (un*	*sujet brûlant)* ☠ → to skim **to touch s.o.** = *toucher qqn* : your letter touched me immensely = *ta lettre m'a énormément touché* **to touch up (a photo/an article)** = *retoucher (une photo/un article)*
☠ *toucher à sa fin* = to draw to an end — *toucher à (la photo)* = to dabble in (photography)	— *cette remarque l'a touché au vif* = the remark hit home — *toucher son salaire* = to get paid.

TOUCH-AND-GO (adj) *de justesse* : getting the contract was touch-and-go = *nous avons eu le contrat de justesse*, whether he's going to live or die is touch-and-go = *s'il survit, ce sera de justesse* ⏀ it was a close shave = *il était moins une.*

TOUCHDOWN (n) 1/ *atterrissage* (m) : the touchdown is planned for 4 pm = *l'atterrissage est prévu à 4 heures de l'après-midi* 2/ *essai* (m) (au football américain) : it's the team's third touchdown = *c'est le troisième essai marqué par l'équipe* ⏀ goal = *but* ☠ → essay.

TOUCHED (adj) 1/ *touché, -e* : I was touched by his letter = *j'ai été touché par sa lettre* ⏀ moved = *ému* 2/ *piqué, -e* : the whole family's a little touched = *toute la famille est un peu piquée* → CRAZY.

TOUCHING (adj) *touchant, -e* : a touching letter = *une lettre touchante* ⏀ moving = *émouvant.*

TOUCHY (adj, -ier, -iest) *susceptible* : she's touchy about her acne = *elle est susceptible au sujet de son acné* ⏀ hypersensitive = *hypersensible*
 a touchy subject = *un sujet délicat* ⏀ a sticky question = *une question épineuse* ☠ → susceptible.

TOUGH (adj, -er, -est) 1/ *dur, -e* : the meat's tough = *la viande est dure* ≠ tender = *tendre* 2/ *dur, -e, coriace* : a tough businessman/foreign policy = *un homme d'affaires coriace/une politique étrangère dure* 3/ *dur, -e* : a tough test = *un examen dur* ≠ easy as pie = *facile comme bonjour* ☠ → hard 4/ *rude* : a tough life/day = *une vie rude/une rude journée* ≠ easy = *facile* ☠ → rough	
to be tough on = *être dur pour* : the divorce was very tough on the kids = *le divorce a été très dur pour les gosses* ⏀ to be rough on = *être un coup dur pour* **to get tough with (the terrorists)** = *durcir sa position face (aux terroristes)* ⏀ to crack down on = *mettre le*	*holà à* **to play the tough guy** = *jouer les durs* **that's tough !** = *tant pis !* → THAT'S LIFE ! **a tough customer/cookie/guy** = *un dur à cuire/un coriace* ≠ a softy = *un tendre* **tough shit !** = *j'en ai rien à branler !*

TOUGHIE (n) 1/ *dur, -e* : her husband's a toughie = *son mari est un dur* ⏀ hard egg = *un dur à cuire* 2/ *casse-tête* (m inv) : the problem is a real toughie = *ce problème est un vrai casse-tête* ⏀ a corker = *quelque chose de pas piqué des vers.*

TOUPEE (n) *postiche* (m) : he wears a toupee = *il porte un postiche* ⏀ wig = *perruque.*

TOUR (n) a tour of (Europe) = *un voyage en (Europe)*
 a guided tour = *une visite guidée*
 to be on tour (show) = *être en tournée (spectacle)*
 tour operator = *organisateur de voyages (organisés)/tour-operator.*

TOUR (to, -ed) 1/ *visiter* : to tour France = *visiter la France* ☠ → to visit 2/ *faire une tournée (dans/en)* : the circus is touring the Southern States = *le cirque fait une tournée dans les États du sud.*

TOURIST (n) *touriste* (m, f) : tourists walking around Times Square = *des touristes se promenant à Times Square* ⏀ to go sightseeing = *faire du tourisme*
 tourist trap = *piège à touristes* : this restaurant's a tourist trap = *ce restaurant est un piège à touristes* ⏀ highway robbery = *vol organisé.*

TOURNAMENT (n) *tournoi* (m) : a chess tournament = *un tournoi d'échecs.*

TOW (n) in tow = *dans (son) sillage* : he always has a beautiful girl in tow = *il a toujours une belle fille dans son sillage*
 to take s.o. in tow = *prendre qqn en main* : he was taken in tow by a senior Senator = *il a été pris en main par un sénateur chevronné* ≠ to fend for o.s. = *se dépatouiller tout seul.*

TOW (to, -ed) *remorquer* : the tugboat towed the liner = *le remorqueur a remorqué le paquebot.*

TOWARD(S) (prep) 1/ *vers* : walk toward(s) me = *avancez vers moi* 2/ *envers* : a strange attitude towards women's lib = *une attitude étrange envers le MLF* 3/ *vers* : towards the end of the year = *vers la fin de l'année* ⏀ around = *environ*
 ☠ for the use of "towards" after a verb, see the verb.

TOWEL (n) *serviette* (f) : clean towels for the bathroom = *des serviettes propres pour la salle de bains* ⏀ dish towel = *torchon*, terrycloth towel = *serviette-éponge*, washcloth = *gant de toilette*

☙ *serviette hygiénique* = sanitary napkin
— *serviette (porte-documents)* = briefcase
— *serviette de table* = napkin.

TOWER (n) *tour (f)* : where is the Eiffel tower ? = *où est la tour Eiffel ?* ☙ → turn.

TOWER ABOVE/OVER (to, -ed) **1/** *dominer par la taille* : she towers above/over her husband = *elle domine son mari par la taille* **2/** *surpasser de beaucoup* : his movies tower above/over all others = *ses films surpassent de beaucoup tous les autres.*

TOWN (n) *(petite) ville (f)* : they live in a very small town = *ils habitent dans une toute petite ville* ⓪ a one-horse town = *un trou*, village = ←
to go out on the town = *faire une virée en ville* : we went out on the town to celebrate = *nous avons fait une virée en ville pour fêter ça* ⓪ to live it up = *faire les quatre cents coups*
to go to town = *ne pas y aller avec le dos de la cuillère/s'en donner à cœur joie* : he really went to town criticizing the play = *il n'y est pas allé avec le dos de la cuillère pour critiquer la pièce*, she went shopping in Paris and really went to town = *elle est allée faire des courses à Paris et elle s'en est vraiment donné à cœur joie*
a man/woman about town = *un homme/une femme du monde* ⓪ a socialite = *un mondain*
out of town = *en déplacement* : my husband's out of town this week = *mon mari est en déplacement cette semaine* ⓪ on the road = *en tournée*
to paint the town red = *faire la bringue* ⓪ to hit the high spots = *faire la tournée des grands ducs*, to have a whale of a time = *s'amuser comme des petits fous*
to skip town = *quitter la ville en douce* : he skipped town without paying his debts = *il a quitté la ville en douce sans payer ses dettes*
town council = *conseil municipal*
town hall = *hôtel de ville*
town planning = *urbanisme*.

TOWNHOUSE (n) *hôtel (m) particulier* ⓪ apartment house = *immeuble d'habitation.*

TOXIC (adj) *toxique* : toxic medicine = *médicament toxique* ≠ harmless = *inoffensif.*

TOY (n) *jouet (m)* : buy some toys for the kids = *achète des jouets pour les gosses* ⓪ plaything = *joujou*
toy dog = *chien nain*
☙ *être le jouet d'(une illusion)* = to be the victim of (an illusion).

TOY WITH (to, -ed) **1/** *caresser* : I've been toying with the idea of going to China = *j'ai caressé l'idée d'aller en Chine* ☙ → to caress **2/** *manger du bout des dents* : she always toys with her food = *elle mange toujours du bout des dents* **3/** *se jouer de* : he says he's serious but I think he's only toying with her = *il dit qu'il est sérieux, mais je pense qu'il se joue d'elle.*

TRACE (n) *trace (f)* : no trace of civilization = *aucune*

trace de civilisation ⓪ sign = *signe*
☙ *être sur la trace de* = to be on the trail of
— *les traces d'un meurtrier* = the tracks of a killer
— *marcher sur les traces de qqn* = to follow in s.o.'s footsteps.

TRACE (to, -d) **1/** *retracer* : the book traces the beginning of the women's movement = *le livre retrace les débuts du mouvement féministe* **2/** *décalquer* : can you trace the sketch so I can keep it ? = *pouvez-vous me décalquer le croquis pour que je puisse le garder ?*
to trace s.o. to = *suivre la trace de qqn jusqu'à* : the cops traced him to Miami = *les flics ont suivi sa trace jusqu'à Miami* ⓪ to trail = *filer.*

TRACK (n) *trace (f)* : tracks in the snow = *des traces dans la neige* ⓪ print = *empreinte* ☙ → trace
to be off the beaten track = *être hors des sentiers battus* : this restaurant's off the beaten track = *ce restaurant est hors des sentiers battus* ⓪ out of the way = *au diable vauvert*
to be on s.o.'s track = *être sur la piste de qqn* : the cops are on his tracks = *les flics sont sur sa piste*
to keep track of = *garder trace de* : who can keep track of all the men in her life ?/of all our expenses ? = *qui peut garder trace de tous les hommes de sa vie ?/de toutes nos dépenses ?* ≠ **to lose track of** = *perdre la trace de*
in its track = *sur son passage* : the tornado destroyed everything in its track = *la tornade a tout détruit sur son passage*
the (railway/subway) tracks = *la voie (ferrée)/les rails* : he fell on the subway tracks = *il est tombé sur la voie/sur les rails du métro*
to have a (good) track record = *avoir eu des (bons) résultats*
to keep ≠ **lose track of time** = *garder* ≠ *perdre la notion du temps*
to stop (dead) in one's tracks = *rester cloué sur place*
on the right ≠ **wrong track** = *sur la bonne* ≠ *mauvaise piste*
to throw s.o. off the track = **1/** *brouiller les pistes à qqn* : the murderer threw them off the track = *le meurtrier leur a brouillé les pistes* ⓪ to shake off = *semer* **2/** *faire faire fausse route à qqn* : your answer threw me off the track = *votre réponse m'a fait faire fausse route.*

TRACK (to, -ed) *suivre la piste de* : to track a wolf = *suivre la piste d'un loup*
to track s.o. down = *dépister qqn* : they tracked down the killer = *on a dépisté le tueur* ⓪ to be on the heels of = *être sur les talons de.*

TRACTOR (n) *tracteur (m)* : we need a new tractor = *nous avons besoin d'un nouveau tracteur* ⓪ plow = *charrue*, bulldozer = ←.

TRADE (n) **1/** (inv) *commerce (m)* : the two countries do a lot of trade = *les deux pays font beaucoup de commerce* ⓪ industry = *industrie* ☙ → commerce **2/** *métier (m) manuel* : the electrician's trade = *le métier d'électricien* ⓪ profession = ←

to **the trade** = *aux gens du métier* : they only sell to the trade = *ils ne vendent qu'aux gens du métier*
trade fair = *foire commerciale*
trade union = *syndicat* ☠ → syndicate.

TRADE (to, -d) *échanger* : I like your sweater, you like mine, let's trade = *tu aimes bien mon pull, j'aime bien le tien, on n'a plus qu'à échanger*
to trade stg for stg = *échanger qqch contre qqch* : I wouldn't trade my life for hers = *je n'échangerais pas ma vie contre la sienne*
to trade in = *rapporter pour échanger* : each year he trades in his car for a bigger one = *chaque année, il rapporte sa voiture pour l'échanger contre une plus grosse.*

TRADEMARK (n) *marque* (f) *(de fabrique)* : Kleenex is a trademark = *Kleenex est une marque*
registered trademark = *marque déposée/nom déposé*
☠ → mark.

TRADITION (n) *tradition* (f) : getting married is a tradition = *c'est une tradition de se marier* ⓪ habit = *habitude.*

TRADITIONAL (adj) *traditionnel, -elle* : we're having a traditional Christmas dinner = *nous ferons un dîner de Noël traditionnel* **TRADITIONALLY** (adv) *traditionnellement.*

TRAFFIC (n inv) **1/** *circulation* (f) : there's a lot of traffic today = *il y a beaucoup de circulation aujourd'hui*
traffic is light ≠ **heavy** = *on roule bien* ≠ *mal*
traffic jam = *embouteillage* ⓪ jam = *encombrement,* bumper-to-bumper = *pare-chocs contre pare-chocs*
traffic light = *feu de signalisation*
☠ → circulation
2/ *trafic* (m) : drug traffic = *trafic de drogue* ☠ *trafic d'armes* = arms smuggling/gunrunning.

TRAGEDY (n, -ies) *tragédie* (f) : the death of her dog was a real tragedy = *la mort de son chien a été une vraie tragédie* ⓪ drama = *drame,* disaster = *désastre.*

TRAGIC (adj) *tragique* : a tragic outcome = *une issue tragique* ≠ comic = *comique* ☠ *prendre au tragique* = to dramatize.

TRAIL (n) *piste* (f) : a trail in the forest = *une piste dans la forêt* ⓪ lane = *allée*
to be on s.o.'s trail = *être sur la piste de qqn* = to be in s.o.'s tracks
a trail of (blood) = *une traînée (de sang)*
☠ → lead.

TRAIL (to, -ed) *être à la traîne (de)* : he's trailing the other three candidates = *il est à la traîne des trois autres candidats*
to trail on (the floor) = *traîner sur (le sol)*
to trail s.o. to (a hiding place) = *suivre la piste de qqn jusqu'à (sa cachette)* ⓪ to track s.o. to = *suivre la trace de qqn jusqu'à.*

TRAILBLAZER (n) *pionnier, -ère* : a trailblazer in solar

energy = *un pionnier de l'énergie solaire* ⓪ precursor = *précurseur* ☠ → pioneer.

TRAILER (n) *roulotte* (f) : I live in a trailer = *j'habite une roulotte* ⓪ van = *caravane.*

TRAIN (n) *train* (m) : I missed my train = *j'ai raté mon train* ⓪ dining car = *wagon-restaurant,* locomotive = ←, sleeping car = *wagon-lit*
I lost my train of thought = *j'ai perdu le fil de mes idées*
by train = *par le/en train*
☠ *train de vie* = lifestyle
— *être en train de (manger)* = to be (eat)ing
— *ne pas être en train* = not to feel up to par
— *à ce train-là* = at this rate
— *le train-train* = the daily-grind
— *prendre le train en marche* = to jump on the bandwagon.

TRAIN (to, -ed) **1/** *former* : the boss is training a new assistant = *le patron est en train de former un nouvel assistant* ⓪ to teach = *enseigner* ☠ → to form
2/ *dresser* (animal), *apprendre à* (child) : cats are impossible to train = *il est impossible de dresser les chats,* to train a child to be polite = *apprendre à un enfant à être poli*
☠ *dresser l'oreille* = to prick up one's ears
— *dresser une liste* = to draw up a list
— *se dresser contre qqn* = to turn against s.o.
3/ *(s') entraîner* : the athletes are training in Vermont = *les athlètes s'entraînent dans le Vermont.*

TRAINEE (n) *stagiaire* (m, f) : a computer trainee = *un stagiaire en informatique* ⓪ apprentice = *apprenti.*

TRAINING (n inv) *formation* (f) : she got her training in England = *elle a acquis sa formation en Angleterre*
a training period = *un stage*
in ≠ **out of training** = *qui a de l'entraînement* ≠ *qui manque d'entraînement*
☠ → formation.

TRAIPSE (n) *bout* (m) *de chemin* : it's a traipse from here to the subway = *ça fait un bout de chemin d'ici au métro* ⓪ schlepp = *trotte.*

TRAIPSE (to, -d) *traîner ses guêtres* : we traipsed around Times Square all afternoon = *nous avons traîné nos guêtres dans Times Square tout l'après-midi* ⓪ to walk around = *se promener.*

TRAIT (n) *trait* (m) : generosity is not her finest trait = *la générosité n'est pas son trait dominant* ⓪ peculiarity = *particularité*
☠ *d'un trait* = at one go
— *avoir trait à* = to refer to
— *tirer un trait sur qqch* = to kiss stg goodbye
— *traits (visage)* = features
— *trait d'union* = hyphen.

TRAITOR (n) *traître, -esse* : the traitors were executed = *les traîtres ont été exécutés* ⓪ turncoat = *faux frère,* two-timer = *vendu*

☠ *prendre qqn en traître* = to make an insidious attack on s.o.
— *il est traître* = he's a sneak.

TRAMP (n) 1/ *clodo* (m) : tramps sleeping under the bridge = *des clodos qui dorment sous le pont* ⓓ hobo = *chemineau*
2/ *traînée* (f) : years ago, if you slept with a guy, you would have been called a tramp = *il y a quelques années, si on couchait avec un type on se faisait traiter de traînée* ⓓ floozy = *poufiasse*, tart = *poule*, trollop = *grue*
☠ *une traînée de sang* = a trail of blood
— *se répandre comme une traînée de poudre* = to spread like wildfire.

TRAMPLE (to, -d) *piétiner* : the child was trampled by the crowd = *l'enfant a été piétiné par la foule* ☠ *on piétine* = we're floundering.

TRAMPOLINE (n) *trampoline* (m), *tremplin* (m) *(de gymnastique)*.

TRANCE (n) *transe* (f) : to fall into a trance = *entrer en transe*.

TRANQUIL(L)IZER (n) *tranquillisant* (m) : he absorbed a full bottle of tranquilizers = *il a avalé un plein tube de tranquillisants* ⓓ sedative = *sédatif*, painkiller = *calmant*.

TRANSACT (to, -ed) *traiter* : to transact business = *traiter des affaires* ☠ → to treat.

TRANSACTION (n) *transaction* (f) : a dishonest transaction = *une transaction malhonnête* ⓓ bargaining = *marchandage*.

TRANSCEND (to, -ed) *transcender* : love hopefully transcends pettiness = *il faut espérer que l'amour transcende la mesquinerie*.

TRANSFER (n) *transfert* (m) : transfer of power = *transfert de pouvoir*.

TRANSFER (to, -red) *transférer* : to transfer money/troops = *transférer de l'argent/des troupes*
he transferred to (a college) = *il a été transféré dans (un collège)*.

TRANSFORM (to, -ed) *transformer* : the pill transformed women's lives = *la pilule a transformé la vie des femmes* **TRANSFORMATION** (n) *transformation* (f) : the transformation of the house into a small hotel = *la transformation de la maison en un petit hôtel*.

TRANSFORMER (n) *transformateur* (m).

TRANSFUSION (n) *transfusion* (f) : blood transfusion = *transfusion sanguine*.

TRANSGRESS (to, -ed) *transgresser* : to transgress a taboo = *transgresser un tabou* **TRANSGRESSION** (n) *transgression* (f).

TRANSIENT (adj) *passager, -ère* : a transient period of peace/beauty = *une période de paix/une beauté passagère*
transient guests = *des hôtes de passage*
☠ *rue passagère* = busy street.

TRANSISTOR (n) *transistor* (m) : no transistors allowed on the beach = *les transistors ne sont pas autorisés sur la plage* ⓓ radio = ←.

TRANSIT (n) **in transit** = *en transit*.

TRANSITION (n) *transition* (f) : the transition from the old to the new regime = *la transition de l'ancien au nouveau régime* **TRANSITIONAL** (adj) *de transition* : a transitional period = *une période de transition*.

TRANSITORY (adj) *transitoire* : a transitory government = *un gouvernement transitoire* ⓓ temporary = *temporaire*.

TRANSLATE (to, -d) *traduire* : who translated the novel ? = *qui a traduit le roman ?* **TRANSLATION** (n) *traduction* (f) : there are many translations of the Bible = *il y a de nombreuses traductions de la Bible* **TRANSLATOR** (n) *traducteur, -trice*.

TRANSMIT (to, -ted) *transmettre* : to transmit a message = *transmettre un message* ⓓ to pass on = *faire passer*, to convey = *communiquer*
☠ *la coutume s'est transmise* = the custom was handed down
— *il a transmis l'affaire à son fils* = he turned the business over to his son.

TRANSPARENT (adj) *transparent, -e* : a transparent blouse = *un chemisier transparent* ≠ opaque = ←.

TRANSPIRE (to, -d) *avoir lieu* : a lot has transpired since you were here last = *beaucoup de choses ont eu lieu depuis ta dernière visite* ⓓ to happen = *arriver*.

TRANSPLANT (n) *transplantation* (f), *greffe* (f) : kidney transplant = *transplantation rénale/greffe d'un rein* ☠ *greffe* → graft.

TRANSPLANT (to, -ed) *transplanter*, *faire une greffe de* : to transplant an organ = *transplanter un organe/faire une greffe d'organe*.

TRANSPORT (to, -ed) *transporter* : the victim was transported to the hospital = *la victime a été transportée à l'hôpital* ⓓ to transfer = *transférer*.

TRANSPORTATION (n inv) *transport* (m) : planes are a quick means of transportation = *l'avion est un moyen de transport rapide*.

TRANSVESTITE (n) *travesti* (m), *travelo* (m) (LV) : the restaurant's owned by two transvestites = *les propriétaires du restaurant sont deux travestis/travelos* ⓓ drag show = *spectacle de travelos*.

TRAP (n) *piège* (m) : the whole thing was a trap = *ce n'était qu'un piège* ⓓ lure = *leurre*, trick = *ruse*
to set a trap = *tendre un piège* → TO HUSTLE

shut your trap ! = *ferme ton clapet !* → BUZZ OFF !

to walk into the trap = *tomber dans le piège/dans le panneau* ⓓ **to play right into s.o.'s hands** = *faire le jeu de qqn*
☠ *une question piège* = a trick question
— *les pièges d'une langue* = the pitfalls of a language
— *où est le piège ?* = where is the trick/catch ?

TRAP (to, -ped) *prendre au piège* : they trapped the terrorist on the roof = *le terroriste a été pris au piège sur le toit* ⓓ **to corner** = *coincer.*

TRAPDOOR (n) *trappe* (f) : the Nazis didn't find the trapdoor = *les nazis n'ont pas trouvé la trappe.*

TRAPPINGS (n pl) **the trappings of (success)** = *les signes extérieurs de (la réussite).*

TRASH (n inv) **1/** *saletés* (f pl) : I bought a lot of trash at the flea market = *j'ai acheté des tas de saletés au marché aux puces* ⓓ **dreck** = *saloperies* ☠ → dirt **2/** *quelque chose qui vole très bas* : his films are all trash = *ses films volent vraiment très bas* **TRASHY** (adj, -ier, -iest) *qui vole très bas* : trashy talk = *des propos qui volent très bas.*

TRAUMA (n) *traumatisme* (m) : her death was a trauma for the children = *sa mort a été un traumatisme pour les enfants* **TRAUMATIC** (adj) *traumatisant, -e* : a traumatic experience = *une expérience traumatisante* **TRAUMATIZE** (to, -d) *traumatiser* : being raped traumatized her = *son viol l'a traumatisée.*

TRAVEL (n) **one's travels** = *ses voyages* : a book about his travels = *un livre relatant ses voyages* **travel agency** = *agence de voyages.*

TRAVEL (to, -(l)ed) *voyager* : he travels a lot = *il voyage beaucoup.*

TRAVEL(L)ER (n) *voyageur, -euse* : he's a restless travel(l)er = *c'est un grand voyageur* **traveler's check** = *traveller's check/chèque de voyage.*

TRAVELING (adj) **traveling circus** = *cirque ambulant*
traveling salesman = *représentant de commerce/VRP*
traveling companion = *compagnon de route*
traveling expenses = *frais de déplacement*
☠ *un travelling* = a travel shot.

TRAY (n) *plateau* (m) : the waitress dropped the tray = *la serveuse a laissé tomber le plateau*
☠ *plateau (cinéma)* = set (film)
— *il voudrait qu'on lui apporte tout sur un plateau* = he wants everything brought to him on a silver platter.

TREACHEROUS (adj) *traître, -esse* : treacherous roads = *des routes traîtresses* ⓓ **perilous** = *périlleux*
☠ *l'alcool est traître* = alcohol sneaks up on you
— *pas un traître mot* = not a bloody word.

TREAD ON (to, trod, trodden) *fouler aux pieds* : the government's treading on human rights = *le gouvernement foule aux pieds les droits de l'homme* ≠ **to respect** = *respecter.*

TREASON (n) *trahison* (f) : hanged for treason = *pendu pour trahison* ☠ → betrayal.

TREASURE (n) *trésor* (m) : it's my only treasure = *c'est mon seul trésor* ⓓ **riches** = *richesse*
☠ *mon trésor* = my darling
— *le Trésor (public)* = the Treasury
— *tu es un trésor* = you're a gem.

TREASURE (to, -d) *attacher une grande valeur à* : I treasure my father's letters/our relationship = *j'attache une grande valeur aux lettres de mon père/à nos rapports* ⓓ **to cherish** = *chérir.*

TREASURER (n) *trésorier, -ère* : he's been the treasurer of the club for five years = *il est trésorier du club depuis cinq ans.*

TREASURY (n -ies) **the Treasury** = *le ministère des Finances* = the Exchequer (GB).

TREAT (n) **a treat** = *un régal* : the dinner was quite a treat = *ce dîner a été un vrai régal* ⓓ **a delight** = *un délice*
it's my treat = *c'est moi qui régale* ⓓ **I'm buying** = *c'est moi qui paie.*

TREAT (to, -ed) **1/** *traiter* : he never treated his parents well = *il n'a jamais bien traité ses parents* **2/** *traiter de* : the film treats teenagers' prostitution = *le film traite de la prostitution des adolescents*
☠ *traiter (affaires)* = to handle/to transact
— *traiter qqn de (menteur)* = to call s.o. a (liar)
3/ *inviter* : I'm treating tonight = *ce soir, c'est moi qui invite* ☠ → to invite
to treat o.s. to = *s'offrir* : let's treat ourselves to a good dinner ! = *offrons-nous un bon dîner !* ☠ → to offer
to treat s.o. to = *offrir à qqn* : I'll treat you to a good lunch = *je t'offre un bon déjeuner* ⓓ **to buy** = *payer.*

TREATMENT (n) *traitement* (m) : we got preferential treatment = *nous avons eu droit à un traitement de faveur* ⓓ **care** = *soin*
to give s.o. the treatment = **1/** *sortir le grand jeu à qqn* : it was a five-star hotel and they really gave us the treatment = *c'était un hôtel cinq étoiles et ils nous ont vraiment sorti le grand jeu* ⓓ **to go all out** = *mettre les petits plats dans les grands* **2/** *en faire voir de rudes à qqn* : the cops gave him the treatment = *les flics lui en ont fait voir de rudes* ⓓ **to give s.o. a hard time of it** = *en faire voir de dures à qqn*
☠ *traitement (salaire)* = salary.

TREATY (n, -ies) *traité* (m) : a multilateral treaty = *un traité multilatéral* ⓓ **pact** = *pacte* ☠ *traité (livre)* = treatise.

TREE (n) *arbre* (m) : a beautiful tree in the backyard = *un bel arbre dans le jardin derrière* ⓓ **trunk** = *tronc*, **branch** = *branche*, **bark** = *écorce*, **leaf** = *feuille*

apple tree = *pommier*	**bush** = *buisson*
birch = *bouleau*	**cherry tree** = *cerisier*

chestnut tree = châtaignier **elm** = *orme* **fig tree** = *figuier* **fir** = *sapin* **oak** = *chêne*	**pine tree** = *pin* **weeping willow** = *saule pleureur* **maple tree** = *érable* **redwood** = *séquoia* **shrub** = *arbuste*

to be up a tree = *être bien embarrassé* : I don't know what to do, I'm really up a tree = *je ne sais pas quoi faire, je suis vraiment bien embarrassé* ☺ to be in a predicament = *être dans une situation difficile.*

TREK (n) *bout (m) de chemin* : it's a long trek to your place = *ça fait un sacré bout de chemin pour aller chez toi* ☺ schlepp = *trotte* **TREK** (to, -ked) *se traîner à pied* : the refugees trekked to the border = *les réfugiés se sont traînés à pied jusqu'à la frontière.*

TREMBLE (to, -d) *trembler* : she was so cold she was trembling = *elle avait si froid qu'elle en tremblait* ☺ to shudder = *frémir.*

TREMBLING (n) *tremblement (m)* ☺ shivering = *frissonnement*
☠ *tremblement de terre* = earthquake
— *et tout le tremblement* = and the whole shebang
— *des tremblements dans la jambe* = tremors in her leg.

TREMENDOUS (adj) 1/ *énorme* : a tremendous success/house = *un succès/une maison énorme* = enormous ≠ tiny = *minuscule* 2/ *prodigieux, -euse* : that movie/dinner was tremendous = *ce film/dîner était prodigieux* → WONDERFUL ≠ lousy = *dégueulasse* ☠ → prodigious.

TREMENDOUSLY (adv) *prodigieusement* : tremendously rich = *prodigieusement riche* → VERY.

TREMOR (n) *tremblement (m)* : tremors in her leg = *des tremblements dans la jambe* ☠ → trembling.

TRENCH (n, -es) *tranchée (f)* : he was killed in the trenches = *il a été tué dans les tranchées*
trench coat = *trench-coat.*

TREND (n) *tendance (f)* : the trend of public opinion = *la tendance de l'opinion publique* ☺ drift = *courant* ☠ *une tendance au suicide* = a suicidal tendency.

TRENDSETTER (n) *personne qui lance la vogue* : the First Lady is the trendsetter for Washington = *la femme du Président lance la vogue à Washington.*

TRENDY (adj, -ier, -iest) *très à la page* : trendy clothes = *des vêtements très à la page* ☺ hip = *branché* ≠ old hat = *vieux jeu.*

TRESPASS (to, -ed) **no trespassing** = *défense d'entrer/propriété privée.*

TRESPASSER (n) **trespassers will be prosecuted** = *défense d'entrer sous peine de poursuites.*

TRIAL (n) *procès (m)* : the trial will be held on Monday = *le procès aura lieu lundi* ☺ jury = ←
to stand trial = *passer en jugement* ≠ to try a case = *entendre une affaire*
trial period = *période d'essai*
on trial = *à l'essai* : taken on trial = *pris à l'essai*
by trial and error = *par tâtonnements* : to learn by trial and error = *apprendre par tâtonnements*
the trials and tribulations of (life) = *les vicissitudes de (l'existence)* ☺ ordeals = *épreuves*
☠ → lawsuit.

TRIAL (adj) *d'essai, à l'essai* : a trial offer/marriage = *une offre d'essai/un mariage à l'essai*
trial balloon = *ballon d'essai* : the congressmen sent out the idea as a trial balloon = *les parlementaires ont lancé cette idée comme ballon d'essai.*

TRIANGLE (n) *triangle (m)* : Nazis made homosexuals wear pink triangles = *les nazis forçaient les homosexuels à porter un triangle rose* ☺ rectangle = ←.

TRIBE (n) *tribu (f)* : our whole tribe will visit grandma on Sunday = *dimanche, notre petite tribu au grand complet ira voir mamie* **TRIBAL** (adj) *tribal, -e* : tribal life = *la vie tribale.*

TRIBUTE (n) **to pay a tribute to** = *rendre hommage à* : the country will pay a tribute to its murdered President = *le pays rendra hommage à son Président assassiné.*

TRICK (n) 1/ *ruse (f)* : it was a trick to get money from him = *c'était une ruse pour lui soutirer de l'argent* ☺ maneuver = *manœuvre*, gimmick = *astuce*
2/ *tour (m)* : some dogs do tricks = *certains chiens font des tours* ☺ feat = *prouesse* ☠ → turn
a cute/sexy trick = *une adorable souris/une souris sexy* ☺ a good-looking tomato = *une belle plante*
he never misses a trick = *rien ne lui échappe* ☺ he's on the ball = *il est dégourdi*
how are tricks ? = *ça biche ?* ☺ what's cooking ? = *ça gaze ?*
to play a trick on s.o. = *jouer un tour à qqn* ☺ to play a prank on = *faire une niche à*
that'll do the trick = *ça fera l'affaire* ☺ that's just what the doctor ordered = *c'est exactement ce qu'il me faut*
the trick is (not to get pregnant) = *le tout c'est (de ne pas tomber enceinte)*
the tricks of the trade = *les ficelles du métier*
3/ *passe (f)* : hookers on that street get 100 bucks a trick = *dans cette rue, les putes touchent 100 dollars par passe*
to turn tricks = *faire des passes* : how many tricks does she turn in one evening ? = *combien de passes fait-elle en une soirée ?*
☠ *être dans une bonne* ≠ *mauvaise passe* = to have a streak of good ≠ bad luck
— *hôtel/maison de passe* = brothel
— *un passe* = a passkey.

TRICK (adj) *truqué, -e* : trick photography/cards = *photographie truquée/cartes truquées* ☠ *élections truquées* = rigged elections.

TRICK (to, -ed) *faire des passes* : she's been tricking to pay for college = *elle faisait des passes pour se payer l'université* ⓐ to solicit = *racoler*
trick or treat ! = *des bonbons ou je te joue des tours* ! *(phrase traditionnellement prononcée par les enfants qui sonnent à votre porte, surtout le jour de Halloween, pour vous demander des friandises)*
to trick s.o. = *avoir qqn* : the salesman tricked me = *le vendeur m'a eu* → TO HUSTLE
to trick s.o. into = *amener qqn par la ruse à* : he tricked me into buying a new machine = *il m'a amené par la ruse à acheter une nouvelle machine*
to trick s.o. out of = *refaire qqn de* : he tricked me out of two hundred bucks = *il m'a refait de deux cents dollars* → TO HUSTLE.

TRICKERY (n, -ies) *roublardise* (f) : to win by trickery = *gagner par roublardise*.

TRICKLE (to, -d) *dégouliner* : the rain trickled down the pane = *la pluie dégoulinait le long de la vitre* ⓐ to flow = *couler*.

TRICKSTER (n) *filou* (m) : the cardsharp was a real trickster = *le tricheur professionnel était un véritable filou* ⓐ sharpie = *aigrefin*.

TRICKY (adj, -ier, -iest) 1/ *rusé, -e* : a tricky person = *une personne rusée* ⓐ sly = *sournois* 2/ *délicat, -e* : getting the hostages out alive was a tricky problem = *faire sortir les otages vivants a été un problème délicat* ☠ → delicate.

TRIFLE (n) *bagatelle* (f) : to worry about trifles = *se faire de la bile pour des bagatelles* ⓐ petty detail = *vétille* ☠ *la bagatelle* = monkey business
— *être porté sur la bagatelle* = to have a one-track mind.

TRIGGER (n) **to pull the trigger** = *appuyer sur la gâchette/la détente*.

TRIGGER (OFF) (to, -ed) *déclencher* : the rigged elections triggered (off) a revolt = *le truquage des élections a déclenché une révolte* ⓐ to cause = *causer* ☠ *déclencher une attaque* = to launch an attack
— *la bombe ne s'est pas déclenchée* = the bomb didn't go off.

TRIGGER-HAPPY (adj) *qui a la gâchette facile* : a trigger-happy cop = *un flic qui a la gâchette facile*.

TRILLION (n) *billion* (m), *trillion* (m) (GB).

TRIM (adj, -mer, -mest) *menu, -e* : a trim figure = *une silhouette menue* ≠ stout = *costaud*
☠ *dans les menus détails* = in the smallest details
— *menue monnaie* = small change
— *menu fretin* = small fry.

TRIM (to, -med) *rafraîchir* : I'm going to have my hair trimmed today = *aujourd'hui, je me fais rafraîchir les cheveux* ☠ → to freshen up.

TRIMMINGS (n pl) **the trimmings (of a turkey)** = *la garniture (d'une dinde)*.

TRINKET (n) *babiole* (f) : unusual trinkets from Japan = *des babioles originales venant du Japon* ⓐ knickknack = *bibelot*.

TRIO (n) *trio* (m) ⓐ duo = ←.

TRIP (n) 1/ *voyage* (m) : we're taking a trip to France = *nous allons faire un voyage en France* ⓐ jaunt = *virée*, stay = *séjour* ☠ → voyage 2/ *trip* (m) : jazz isn't my trip = *le jazz, c'est pas mon trip* ⓐ it isn't my cup of tea = *ce n'est pas mon genre*.

TRIP (to, -ped) 1/ *buter* : I tripped and fell = *j'ai buté sur quelque chose et je suis tombé* ⓐ to slip = *glisser*
☠ *buter qqn* = to knock/bump s.o. off
— *buter sur une difficulté* = to come up against a difficulty
2/ *faire un croche-pied/un croc-en-jambe à* : the kid tripped the old man = *le gosse a fait un croche-pied/un croc-en-jambe au vieil homme*
to trip over = *buter sur* : I tripped over the cat = *j'ai buté sur le chat*
to trip up = *faire une gaffe* : I tripped up badly mistaking his mistress for his wife = *j'ai fait une grosse gaffe en prenant sa maîtresse pour sa femme*
to trip s.o. up = *prendre qqn en défaut* : his questions tripped me up = *ses questions m'ont pris en défaut*.

TRIPLE (to, -d) *tripler* : prices have tripled over the last year = *les prix ont triplé depuis l'année dernière* ⓐ to quadruple = *quadrupler*.

TRIPLET (n) *triplé, -e* : triplets are rare = *les triplés, c'est rare*.

TRITE (adj, -r, -st) *bateau* : a trite theme = *un thème bateau* ⓐ hackneyed = *rebattu* ☠ → boat.

TRIUMPH (n) *triomphe* (m) : his last play was a triumph = *sa dernière pièce a été un triomphe* ≠ fiasco = ←
TRIUMPH (to, -ed) *triompher* : she didn't only win, she triumphed = *elle n'a pas seulement gagné, elle a triomphé* ⓐ to win = *gagner* **TRIUMPHAL** (adj) *triomphal, -e* : he received a triumphal welcome = *il a reçu un accueil triomphal*.

TRIUMPHANT (adj) *triomphant, -e* : a triumphant smile = *un sourire triomphant* **TRIUMPHANTLY** (adv) *triomphalement*.

TRIVIAL (adj) *insignifiant, -e* : it's a trivial matter = *c'est une affaire insignifiante* ≠ important = ← ☠ *une remarque triviale* = a base remark.

TROLLEY (n) *trolley(bus)* (m), *tram* (m) : the trolleys of San Francisco = *les trolleybus de San Francisco* **trolley car** = *tramway*.

TROOPER (n) **to swear like a trooper** = *jurer comme un charretier*.

671

TROOPS (n pl) *troupes (f pl)* : our troops withdrew = *nos troupes se sont retirées* ① army = *armée*, soldier = *soldat*.

TROPHY (n, -ies) *trophée (m)* : to win a trophy = *gagner un trophée* ① prize = *prix*.

TROPIC (n) **the Tropic of Capricorn/Cancer** = *le tropique du Capricorne/du Cancer*
the tropics = *les tropiques.*

TROPICAL (adj) *tropical, -e* : a tropical storm = *un orage tropical.*

TROT (to, -ted) *trotter* : a horse trots = *un cheval trotte* ① to canter = *aller au petit galop.*

TROUBLE (n) **1/** *ennui (m)* : she's having troubles with her kids = *elle a des ennuis avec ses gosses* ① hassles = *pépins*, tsuris = *tracas* ☠ → boredom
2/ (inv) *troubles (m pl)* : there's been a lot of trouble in our country recently = *il y a eu pas mal de troubles dans notre pays ces derniers temps* ☠ *troubles du langage* = speech defects

---

to be in trouble with = *avoir des ennuis avec* : I'm in trouble with my landlord = *j'ai des ennuis avec mon propriétaire* ① to be in a pickle = *être frais*
to get into trouble = *s'attirer des ennuis* : your son's going to get into trouble if he continues dealing = *votre fils va s'attirer des ennuis s'il continue à faire du trafic de drogue*
to give s.o. a lot of trouble = *donner beaucoup de mal à qqn* : the kids gave me a lot of trouble = *les gosses m'ont donné beaucoup de mal*
to go to a lot of trouble (to help) = *se donner beaucoup de mal pour (aider)* ① to stand on one's head = *faire des pieds et des mains*
to have trouble (doing stg) = *avoir du mal à (faire qqch)* : I'm having trouble getting myself understood = *j'ai du mal à me faire comprendre*
to have (heart/stomach) trouble = *avoir des ennuis (cardiaques/gastriques)*

it's no trouble ! = *ce n'est rien du tout !* : don't bother to make me coffee ! — it's no trouble ! = *ne vous donnez pas le mal de me faire du café ! — mais ce n'est rien du tout !*
it isn't worth the trouble = *ça n'en vaut pas la peine*
I smell trouble ! = *ça sent le roussi !*
keep out of trouble ! = *soyez sages !*
to make trouble for s.o. = *causer des ennuis à qqn* : his ex-wife's making trouble for him = *son ex-femme lui cause des ennuis*
to put s.o. to trouble = *donner du mal à qqn* : I'm sorry, I didn't want to put you to so much trouble = *je suis désolé, je ne voulais pas vous donner tout ce mal* ① to put s.o. out = *déranger qqn*
to run into trouble = *avoir des difficultés* : I ran into trouble getting a passport on such short notice = *j'ai eu des difficultés à obtenir un passeport dans un*

délai si bref
to take the trouble to = *prendre la peine de* : take the trouble to do it right the first time = *prenez la peine de le faire correctement la première fois* ① to take pains to = *se donner du mal pour*
that saved me a lot of trouble ! = *ça m'a évité/épargné beaucoup d'ennuis !*
my troubles aren't over yet = *je ne suis pas encore sorti de l'auberge*
the trouble is that (it costs too much money) = *l'ennui, c'est que (ça coûte trop cher)* ① the snag is that = *l'os, c'est que*
trouble spot = *poudrière* : trouble spots in South America = *des poudrières en Amérique du Sud* ① hot spot = *point chaud*
what's the trouble ? = *qu'est-ce qui ne va pas ?* ① what's the matter ? = *qu'est-ce qu'il y a ?*
you're looking/asking for trouble = *tu cherches des ennuis.*

TROUBLE (to, -d) *troubler* : what troubles you ? = *qu'est-ce qui vous trouble ?* ① to worry = *inquiéter*

---

may I trouble you for (a light) ? = *puis-je vous demander du (feu) ?*

to trouble s.o. = *déranger qqn* : I don't want to trouble you with my problems = *je ne veux pas vous déranger avec mes problèmes*

☠ *ne vous troublez pas* = keep calm
— *troubler l'ordre public* = to disturb public order

— *les films pornos me troublent* = porn movies excite me.

TROUBLED (adj) *troublé, -e* : troubled times = *une époque troublée*
to fish in troubled waters = *pêcher en eau trouble*
☠ *troublé (sexuellement)* = aroused.

TROUBLEMAKER (n) *fauteur (m) de troubles* : a few troublemakers interrupted the speech = *quelques fauteurs de troubles ont interrompu le discours* ① agitator = *trublion.*

TROUBLESHOOTER (n) *conciliateur, -trice* : he's the President's troubleshooter in the Middle East = *c'est le* *conciliateur du Président au Moyen-Orient* ① mediator = *médiateur.*

TROUBLESOME (adj) *tracassant, -e* : a troublesome situation = *une situation tracassante* ① worrisome = *inquiétant.*

TROUPE (n) *troupe (f)* : a theater troupe = *une troupe de théâtre* ① company = *compagnie* ☠ *les troupes (armée)* = the troops (army).

TROUSERS (n pl) *pantalon (m)(pour hommes surtout)* : he just bought a pair of black trousers = *il vient d'acheter un pantalon noir* ① overalls = *salopette.*

TROUSSEAU (n, -x or -s) *trousseau (m)* : she made her own trousseau = *elle a fait son propre trousseau* ① dowry = *dot.*

TROUT (n) *truite (f)* : smoked trout = *truite fumée,* salmon trout = *truite saumonée.*

TRUCE (n) *trêve (f)* : they signed a truce for Christmas = *ils ont signé une trêve pour Noël* ① cease-fire = *cessez-le-feu* ☠ *trêve de plaisanterie !* = stop kidding around !

TRUCK (n) *camion (m)* : women also drive trucks = *les femmes aussi conduisent des camions* ① van = *poids lourd*
truck driver = *camionneur* ① teamster = *routier.*

TRUE (adj, -r, -st) *vrai, -e* : what you're saying is true = *ce que vous dites est vrai* ① exact = *←* ≠ untrue = *pas vrai*
a true friend/artist = *un vrai ami/artiste*
to come true = *se réaliser* : I hope your dreams come true = *j'espère que vos rêves se réaliseront* ☠ → to realize
how true ! = *c'est bien vrai !*
to hold true = *rester valable* : the law holds true for everyone = *la loi reste valable pour tous*
(his) true self = *(son) vrai moi*
many a true word is spoken in jest = *sous couvert de plaisanteries, on peut faire passer beaucoup de vérités*
to ring true = *sonner juste* : his story didn't ring true = *son histoire ne sonnait pas juste*
to show one's true colors = *se montrer sous son vrai jour*
true to life = *conforme à la réalité* : the film was true to life = *le film était conforme à la réalité*
to be true to (one's wife) = *être fidèle à (sa femme)*
☠ *c'est pas vrai !* = you've got to be kidding !
— *un vrai diamant* = a real diamond.

TRUE-LIFE (adj) *vécu, -e* : a true-life story = *une histoire vécue.*

TRUELOVE (n) *cher, chère et tendre* : she's my true-love = *c'est ma chère et tendre* ① beloved = *bien-aimé.*

TRUISM (n) *truisme (m)* ① saying = *dicton.*

TRULY (adv) *réellement* : she's truly bright = *elle est réellement intelligente* → VERY.

TRUMP (n) **trump card** = *atout* : her brains are her

main trump card = *son intelligence est son principal atout* ≠ drawback = *inconvénient* ☠ → asset.

TRUMPED-UP (adj) *forgé, -e de toutes pièces* : trumped-up charges = *des accusations forgées de toutes pièces.*

TRUMPET (n) *trompette (f)* : I'm learning to play the trumpet = *j'apprends à jouer de la trompette* ① horn = cor.

TRUMP UP (to, -ed) *forger de toutes pièces* : they trumped up the case against him = *ils ont forgé cette affaire de toutes pièces pour lui nuire.*

TRUNK (n) 1/ *malle (f)* : the trunks will be shipped by boat = *les malles seront expédiées par bateau* ① valise = *←*
☠ *se faire la malle* = to escape
— *faire ses malles* = to pack up and leave
2/ *coffre (m)* : our car's trunk is too small for all our luggage = *le coffre de notre voiture est trop petit pour tous nos bagages*
☠ *un coffre (banque)* = a safe-deposit box
— *avoir du coffre* = to have a strong voice.

TRUST (n) 1/ (inv) *confiance (f)* : there must be trust between a lawyer and his client = *il doit y avoir de la confiance entre un avocat et son client*
to have trust in s.o. = *avoir confiance en qqn*
2/ *trust (m)(patrimoine qui rapporte à un bénéficiaire et qui est géré par une personne qui n'en est pas le propriétaire)* : a trust of one million dollars for each child = *un trust d'un million de dollars pour chaque enfant* 3/ *trust (m)* : several companies forming a trust = *plusieurs sociétés qui forment un trust* ① monopoly = *monopole.*

TRUST (to, -ed) *faire confiance à* : I don't trust my old car/you = *je ne fais pas confiance à ma vieille voiture/je ne vous fais pas confiance* ① to rely on = *se fier à* ≠ to distrust = *se défier de*
to trust s.o. with stg = *confier qqch à qqn* : I wouldn't trust him with my money = *je ne lui confierais pas mon argent* = I wouldn't entrust him with my money
I trust that (you're feeling better) = *j'espère que (vous vous sentez mieux).*

TRUSTEE (n) *trustee (m)(gestionnaire d'un patrimoine affecté)* : my husband is a trustee of the university = *mon mari est trustee de l'université.*

TRUSTING (adj) *confiant, -e* : trusting young girls = *des jeunes filles confiantes* ≠ distrustful = *défiant.*

TRUSTWORTHY (adj) *digne de confiance* : a trustworthy lawyer = *un avocat digne de confiance* ≠ unreliable = *sur qui l'on ne peut pas compter.*

TRUTH (n) *vérité (f)* : he never tells the truth = *il ne dit jamais la vérité* ≠ lie = *mensonge*
in truth = *en vérité* : he told me he was divorced, but in truth he's still married = *il m'a dit qu'il était divorcé, mais en vérité il est encore marié* ① in fact = *en fait*
there's some truth in (what he says) = *il y a du vrai dans (ce qu'il dit)*

to stretch the truth = *déformer la vérité*
to tell the truth = *à vrai dire* : to tell the truth, I don't care = *à vrai dire, je m'en fiche*
the truth of the matter is (I don't care) = *à dire vrai (je m'en fiche)* ⓓ the fact of the matter is = *le fait est que*
the truth, the whole truth and nothing but the truth = *la vérité, toute la vérité, rien que la vérité*
truth is stranger than fiction = *la réalité dépasse la fiction*
truth will out = *la vérité finira par sortir (du puits)* ☠ *la vérité sort de la bouche des enfants* = out of mouths of babes
— *c'est une vérité première* = it's self-evident.

TRY (n, -ies) *essai* *(m)* : I did it on the first try = *j'ai réussi à le faire au premier essai* ⓓ stab = *coup d'essai*
give it a try = *faites un essai* ⓓ have a shot = *tentez le coup*
☠ → essay.

TRY (to, -ied) **1/** *essayer* : it's not difficult, try = *ce n'est pas difficile, essaye* ⓓ to make an effort = *faire un effort,* to strive to = *s'efforcer de*
who are you trying to kid ? = *de qui se moque-t-on ?*
→ BUZZ OFF !
to try stg on = *essayer qqch (vêtement)* : what nice dress, try it on ! =*quelle jolie robe, essayez-la !*
to try out = *essayer* : to try out a new machine = *essayer une nouvelle machine* ⓓ to test = *tester*
to try out for = *passer une audition pour* : she's trying out for the part = *elle passe une audition pour le rôle*
to try to = *essayer/tâcher de* : try to come = *essaie/tâche de venir* = try and come ⓓ to endeavour = *s'efforcer de*
2/ *juger* : the criminals will be tried next week = *les criminels seront jugés la semaine prochaine* ⓓ to pass sentence = *prononcer une sentence* ☠ → to judge.

TRYING (adj) *éprouvant, -e* : a trying day = *une journée éprouvante* ⓓ tough = *dur,* nerveracking = *éprouvant pour les nerfs.*

TRYOUT (n) *audition* *(f)* : tryouts will be held on Friday = *les auditions auront lieu vendredi* = audition ⓓ casting = *distribution* ☠ → audition.

TRYST (n) *cinq à sept* *(m)* : a tryst with her lover = *un cinq à sept avec son amant* ⓓ liaison = ←, heavy date = *rancard d'amoureux.*

T-SHIRT (n) *T-shirt* *(m)* : even T-shirts can be sexy = *même les T-shirts peuvent être sexy* = tee-shirt.

TSURIS (n inv) *tracas* *(m pl)* : she has nothing but tsuris from the kids = *elle n'a que des tracas avec les gosses* ⓓ worry = *souci.*

TUB (n) *baignoire* *(f)* : soaking in the tub = *en train de faire trempette dans la baignoire* = bathtub ⓓ shower = *douche.*

TUBE (n) **1/** (GB) *métro* *(m)* = subway **2/** *tube* *(m)* : tubes in her nose = *des tubes dans le nez*
the tube = *le petit écran*

☠ *un tube (chanson)* = a hit song
— *déconner à pleins tubes* = to be full of it.

TUBERCULOSIS (n, -es) *tuberculose* *(f)* = TB ⓓ pneumonia = *pneumonie.*

TUCK (to, -ed) **to tuck s.o. in** = *border qqn* : my mother tucked me in every evening = *ma mère me bordait tous les soirs*
to tuck stg in = *rentrer qqch* : your shirt's sticking out, tuck it in = *ta chemise dépasse, rentre-la.*

TUESDAY (n) *mardi* *(m)* : I see my shrink on Tuesdays = *je vois mon psy le mardi* → WEEK.

TUG (n) **a tug of war** = *une lutte acharnée.*

TUG (to, -ged) **1/** *remorquer* : to tug a boat = *remorquer un bateau* = to tow ⓓ tugboat = *remorqueur* **2/** *tirer fort sur* : stop tugging my coat = *arrête de tirer aussi fort sur mon manteau* ⓓ to pull = *tirer.*

TUITION (n inv) *frais* *(m pl)* *de scolarité* : tuition is very high in American colleges = *les frais de scolarité sont très élevés dans les universités américaines.*

TULIP (n) *tulipe* *(f)* ⓓ flower = *fleur.*

TUMBLE (n) **not to give s.o. a tumble** = *ne pas accorder un regard à qqn* : he never gave her a tumble = *il ne lui a jamais accordé un regard* ≠ to be crazy about = *être fou de.*

TUMBLE DOWN (to, -d) *dégringoler* : the books tumbled down = *les livres ont dégringolé* ⓓ to fall down = *tomber par terre.*

TUMMY (n, -ies) « *petit* » *ventre* *(m)* : his tummy hurts = *il a mal à son petit ventre* ⓓ stomach = *estomac.*

TUMOR (n) *tumeur* *(f)* : a malignant/benign tumor = *une tumeur maligne/bénigne.*

TUMULT (n inv) *tumulte* *(m)* : tumult in the city during the strikes = *le tumulte dans la ville pendant les grèves.*

TUMULTUOUS (adj) *tumultueux, -euse* : a tumultuous relationship = *une liaison tumultueuse.*

TUNA (n) *thon* *(m)* : a tuna sandwich = *un sandwich au thon.*

TUNE (n) *air* *(m)* : I know the words but I don't remember the tune = *je connais les paroles, mais je ne me souviens pas de l'air* ☠ → air
to call the tune = *donner le la* ⓓ to run the show = *mener la danse*
to carry a tune = *chanter juste* ⓓ to have an ear for music = *avoir de l'oreille*
to change one's tune = *changer de ton*
to the tune of = *d'une somme de* : I was taken to the tune of a grand = *je me suis fait avoir d'une somme de mille dollars.*

TUNE (to, -d) **to tune in** ≠ **out** = *écouter* ≠ *ne pas écouter* : when he talks too much, I tune out = *quand il*

parle trop, je n'écoute pas, are you tuned in ? = *tu m'écoutes ?* ☠ → to listen
to be tuned into = *être à l'écoute de :* the Senator is not tuned into young people's needs = *le sénateur n'est pas à l'écoute des besoins des jeunes.*

TUNISIA (n) *Tunisie* (f) Arabia = *Arabie* **TUNISIAN** (n, adj) *Tunisien, -enne.*

TUNNEL (n) *tunnel* (m) : the light at the end of the tunnel = *la lumière au bout du tunnel* Ⓞ bridge = *pont.*

TURF (n) **stay off my turf !** = *ne marchez pas sur mes plates-bandes !*

TURKEY (n) **1/** *dinde* (f) : to eat turkey = *manger de la dinde* Ⓞ fowl = *volaille* ☠ *quelle dinde ! =* what a dummy ! **2/** *navet* (m) (film), quelque chose qui n'est pas une réussite : the film was a turkey = *ce film était un navet,* what a turkey your idea turned out to be = *ton idée, ce n'était pas une réussite* Ⓞ fiasco = ← ☠ *man-*

ger des navets = to eat turnips
to talk turkey = *parler sérieusement :* if you really want to sign the contract, let's talk turkey = *si vous voulez vraiment signer le contrat, parlons sérieusement* Ⓞ to mean business = *ne pas plaisanter.*

TURKEY (n) *Turquie* (f) **TURK** (n) *Turc, Turque* ☠ *fort comme un Turc =* strong as an ox.

TURKISH (adj) *turc, turque :* Turkish bath = *bain turc.*

TURMOIL (n inv) *perturbations* (f pl) : there is great turmoil in her love life/in the Middle East = *il y a de grandes perturbations dans sa vie amoureuse/au Moyen-Orient* Ⓞ shambles = *capharnaüm,* havoc = *chambardement*
to be in turmoil = *être en ébullition :* the faculty is in turmoil over whether to accept the donation = *les professeurs sont en ébullition : doivent-ils accepter la donation ?*

TURN (n) **1/** *tour* (m) : whose turn is it ? = *à qui le tour ?,* it's my turn = *c'est mon tour*

☠ *un tour de cochon =* a dirty trick — *en un tour de main =* in two shakes of a lamb's tail — *attraper le tour de main =* to get the hang of it — *aller faire un tour =* to go for a walk/ride — *faire le tour d'un problème =* to go over a problem — *faire le tour du cadran =* to sleep around the	clock — *un tour de passe-passe =* a sleight of hand — *le tour est joué =* that's the ball game — *un tour de force =* a feat — *avoir plus d'un tour dans son sac =* to have more than one trick up one's sleeve — *une tour (de contrôle) =* a (control) tower — *habiter dans une tour =* to live in a high-rise

2/ *tournure* (f) : the situation in the Middle East is taking a tragic turn = *la situation au Moyen-Orient prend une tournure tragique*

☠ *ça commence à prendre tournure =* it's shaping up	— *donner une nouvelle tournure à une vieille histoire =* to give a new twist to an old tale

at the turn of the century = *au début/à la fin du siècle* **to give s.o. a turn** = *donner un coup à qqn :* hearing a voice in the dark gave me a turn = *ça m'a donné un coup d'entendre une voix dans le noir* Ⓞ to give s.o. a start = *faire sursauter qqn* **in turn** = *à son tour :* he hit his wife and she, in turn, hit the	kids = *il a battu sa femme, et à son tour elle a battu les gosses* **it's my turn to (wash the dishes)** = *c'est mon tour de (faire la vaisselle)* **let's take turns** = *chacun son tour* **to make a left ≠ right turn** = *tourner à gauche ≠ à droite* **to talk/speak out of turn** =	*commettre une indiscrétion* **to take a turn for the better ≠ worse (health)** = *aller mieux ≠ aller plus mal (santé)* **to take turns** = *se relayer* **(an unusual) turn of events** = *(une) tournure (inattendue) des événements* **the turn of the tide** = *un renversement (de la situation).*

TURN (to, -ed) **1/** *(se) tourner :* turn the page = *tournez la page* Ⓞ to spin = *tournoyer*

☠ *tourner autour de qqn =* to hang around s.o. — *tourner une difficulté =* to get round/to circumvent a difficulty	— *tourner bien ≠ mal =* to end well ≠ badly — *se tourner les pouces =* to twiddle one's thumbs — *tourner un film =* to shoot a movie

2/ *se retourner :* he turned and smiled = *il s'est retourné et il a souri* ☠ → to return
3/ *tourner :* the milk turned = *le lait a tourné* Ⓞ to curdle = *cailler*

to turn left ≠ right = *tourner à gauche ≠ à droite*	**she turned (twenty)** = *elle a eu (vingt ans)*

to turn against s.o. = *(se) retourner contre qqn* : when their parents got divorced, the kids turned against their father = *quand leurs parents ont divorcé, les enfants se sont retournés contre leur père*

to turn s.o. against s.o. = *monter qqn contre qqn* : he turned the kids against their mother = *il a monté les enfants contre leur mère* = he set the kids against their mother

to turn around = *se retourner* : I whistled and he turned around = *j'ai sifflé et il s'est retourné* ☠ → to return

to turn around and ... = *en guise de remerciement* : after all she did for him, he turned around and left her = *après tout ce qu'elle a fait pour lui, en guise de remerciement il l'a quittée*

to turn away = *se détourner* : when I looked at him he turned away = *quand je l'ai regardé, il s'est détourné* ☠ → to deter

to turn back = *rebrousser chemin* : he realized he had gone too far and turned back = *il s'est rendu compte qu'il était allé trop loin et il a rebroussé chemin*

to turn down = 1/ *refuser* : I applied for the job but I was turned down = *j'ai posé ma candidature pour le poste mais on m'a refusé* ≠ to accept = *accepter* ☠ → to refuse 2/ *baisser* : turn the radio down = *baisse la radio* ≠ to turn up = *mettre plus fort* ☠ → to lower

to turn in = *aller se coucher* : it's late, I'm going to turn in = *il est tard, je vais aller me coucher* ≠ to get up = *se lever*

to turn o.s. in = *se livrer* : when he realized his goose was cooked, the killer turned himself in = *le meurtrier s'est livré, quand il s'est rendu compte qu'il était cuit* ☠ → to deliver

to turn into = 1/ *(se) transformer en* : the frog turned into a prince = *la grenouille s'est transformée en prince* Ⓞ to become = *devenir* 2/ *devenir* :

after their divorce, he turned into an alcoholic = *après leur divorce, il est devenu alcoolique* ☠ → to become

to turn off = *fermer* : turn the light/gas off = *ferme la lumière/le gaz* ≠ to turn on = *allumer* ☠ → to close

to turn s.o. off = *refroidir qqn* : the price of the apartment turned me off = *le prix de l'appartement m'a refroidi*, his lack of brains turns me off = *son manque d'intelligence me refroidit*

☠ *le temps se refroidit* = the weather's getting cooler

— *refroidir qqn* = to do s.o. in

to turn s.o. on = 1/ *brancher qqn* : his religious talk doesn't turn voters on = *son discours religieux ne branche pas les électeurs* Ⓞ to dig = *botter* ≠ to repel = *repousser* 2/ *exciter qqn* : young men turn her on = *les hommes jeunes l'excitent* Ⓞ to be hot and bothered = *être tout chose*

to turn on = 1/ *allumer* : turn the light on = *allume la lumière* ☠ → to light 2/ *se camer* : they all turned on at the party = *ils se sont tous camés à la soirée* Ⓞ to get high = *planer* 3/ *dépendre de* : everything turns on his decision = *tout dépend de sa décision* = to depend on

to turn on s.o. = *s'attaquer à qqn* : dogs rarely turn on their masters = *les chiens s'attaquent rarement à leur maître*

to turn it on = *faire son numéro de charme* : when he met her parents, he turned it on = *quand il a rencontré ses parents, il leur a fait son numéro de charme* Ⓞ to put on an act = *jouer la comédie*

to turn s.o. onto = *brancher qqn sur* : he turned me onto drugs = *c'est lui qui m'a branché sur la drogue* Ⓞ to put s.o. onto stg = *faire connaître qqch à qqn*

to turn out = 1/ *produire* : they turn out a thousand cars a week = *ils produisent mille voitures par semaine* ☠ → to pro-

duce 2/ *venir* : a lot of people turned out for the demonstration = *beaucoup de gens sont venus à la manifestation* ☠ → to come 3/ *éteindre* : turn out the light = *éteins la lumière* ≠ to turn on = *allumer* ☠ → to extinguish 4/ *finir* : don't worry, it will turn out well = *ne vous inquiétez pas, ça finira bien* ☠ → to finish

to turn out to be = *se révéler* : the film turned out to be excellent = *le film s'est révélé excellent* ☠ → to reveal

it turned out that (you were right) = *il s'est avéré que (vous aviez raison)*

to turn over = *se retourner* : the car turned over = *la voiture s'est retournée* = to overturn ☠ → to return

to turn stg over = *retourner qqch* : turn the book over = *retournez le livre*

to turn stg over to s.o. = *transmettre qqch à qqn* : he turned the business over to his son = *il a transmis l'affaire à son fils*

to turn to s.o. = *se tourner vers qqn* : you can always turn to me if you need help = *vous pouvez toujours vous tourner vers moi si vous avez besoin d'aide*

to turn towards = *(se) tourner vers* : he turned towards me = *il s'est tourné vers moi*

to turn to (page 21) = *se reporter à (la page 21)*

to turn up = 1/ *réapparaître* : the cops lost track of him but he turned up in Florida = *les flics ont perdu sa piste, mais il a réapparu en Floride* Ⓞ to wind up in = *échouer en* 2/ *mettre plus fort* : turn up the radio = *mets la radio plus fort* 3/ *se radiner* : she turned up at the last moment = *elle s'est radinée au dernier moment* Ⓞ to blow in = *débarquer* 4/ *se présenter* : I'm looking for work and I hope something turns up soon = *je cherche du travail et j'espère que quelque chose va bientôt se présenter* ☠ → to present.

TURNABOUT (n) **to do a turnabout** = *retourner sa veste* : he used to be a Republican but he did a turnabout and became a Democrat = *il était républicain, mais il a retourné sa veste et est devenu démocrate.*

TURNCOAT (n) *faux frère* (m) : he turned out to be a turncoat = *il s'est avéré être un faux frère* ⑩ renegade = *renégat.*

TURN-ON (n) *quelque chose qui excite* : for me, brains/black stockings are a turn-on = *l'intelligence m'excite/les bas noirs m'excitent* ≠ turnoff = *quelque chose qui rebute.*

TURNOUT (n) *participation* (f) : a huge turnout = *une participation énorme* ⑩ public = ← ☠ → *participation.*

TURNOVER (n) *chiffre* (m) *d'affaires* : they have a tremendous turnover in that restaurant = *ils font un chiffre d'affaires énorme dans ce restaurant* ⑩ gross = *recette brute.*

TURNPIKE (n) *autoroute* (f) *à péage* ⑩ expressway = *voie express.*

TURQUOISE (n, adj) *turquoise* (f) : a turquoise dress = *une robe turquoise* ⑩ blue = *bleu.*

TURTLE (n) *tortue* (f) : a pet turtle = *une tortue domestique* ⑩ snail = *escargot* ☠ *c'est une vraie tortue* = she goes at a snail's pace.

TURTLEDOVES (n pl) *tourtereaux* (m pl) : what turtledoves those two are ! = *quels tourtereaux, ces deux-là !* ⑩ sweethearts = *amoureux.*

TURTLENECK (n) *col* (m) *roulé* ⑩ V neck = *col en V.*

TUSHY (n, -ies) « *petites* » *fesses* (f pl) : a rash on her tushy = *une éruption de boutons sur ses petites fesses* ⑩ fanny = *popotin/lune.*

TUTOR (n) *précepteur, -trice* : the tutor's giving me private lessons = *le précepteur me donne des leçons particulières.*

TUXEDO (n, -es) *smoking* (m) : all the men were wearing tuxedoes = *tous les hommes étaient en smoking* = tux ⑩ black tie = *tenue de soirée.*

TV (n) *télé* (f) : she watches TV a lot = *elle regarde beaucoup la télé*
a TV special = *une émission spéciale*
TV dinner = *plateau télé (surgelé).*

TWANG (n) *voix* (f) *nasillarde* : to speak with a twang = *parler avec une voix nasillarde.*

TWEEZERS (n pl) *pince* (f) *à épiler* ⑩ to pluck = *épiler.*

TWELVE (n, adj) *douze* (m) : twelve children = *douze enfants* ⑩ twelfth = *douzième*, dozen = *douzaine.*

TWENTY (n, -ies, adj) *vingt* (m) : twenty cigarettes in a pack = *vingt cigarettes dans un paquet* ⑩ twentieth = *vingtième*

the roaring twenties = *les années folles* ⑩ the Gay Nineties = *la Belle Époque*
the twenties = *les années vingt*
to be in one's twenties = *avoir vingt ans et quelques* ⑩ to be twentyish = *avoir une vingtaine d'années*
twenty-four hours a day = *vingt-quatre heures sur vingt-quatre* = around the clock
to have twenty-twenty vision = *avoir dix aux deux yeux.*

TWICE (adv) *deux fois* : I was divorced twice = *j'ai divorcé deux fois*
to think twice = *y regarder à deux fois* : I'll think twice before doing that again = *j'y regarderai à deux fois avant de recommencer*
twice as much = *deux fois plus*
twice a week = *deux fois par semaine*
you won't have to ask me twice = *je ne vais pas me faire prier* ⑩ I'm game = *je suis partant.*

TWIG (n) *brindille* (f) : we need twigs to start the fire = *il faut des brindilles pour allumer le feu* ⑩ branch = *branche.*

TWILIGHT (n) *entre chien et loup* : vampires came out at twilight = *les vampires apparaissaient entre chien et loup* ⑩ dusk = *crépuscule.*

TWIN (n, adj) *jumeau, jumelle* : she just had twins = *elle vient d'avoir des jumeaux* ⑩ triplets = *des triplés*, quadruplets = *des quadruplés*
Siamese twins = *frères siamois/sœurs siamoises* ☠ *des jumelles* = binoculars.

TWINE (n) *grosse ficelle* (f) ⑩ string = *corde.*

TWINKLE (to, -d) *scintiller* : the star's twinkling = *l'étoile scintille* ⑩ to sparkle = *étinceler.*

TWIRL (to, -ed) *tournoyer* : leaves twirling in the wind = *des feuilles tournoyant dans le vent* ⑩ to whirl = *tourbillonner.*

TWIST (n) *tournure* (f) : to give the story a new twist = *donner une nouvelle tournure à l'histoire* ☠ → turn
(an unexpected) twist of events = *(un) rebondissement (inattendu)* ⑩ (an unexpected) turn of events = *(une) tournure (inattendue) des événements.*

TWIST (to, -ed) **1/** *fausser* : they twisted my statement = *ils ont faussé ma déclaration* ⑩ to misconstrue = *mal interpréter*
☠ *fausser les comptes* = to doctor the books
— *fausser le jeu* = to throw the game
— *ses opinions sont faussées par le racisme* = his opinions are colored by his racism
2/ *(se) tordre* : you twisted my bracelet = *tu as tordu mon bracelet*
☠ *se tordre de douleur/de rire* = to double up with pain/laughter
— *tordre une barre de fer* = to bend an iron rod.

TWITCH (n, -es) *tic* (m) : a nervous twitch = *un tic nerveux.*

TWO (n, adj) *deux* (m) : I have two kids = *j'ai deux gosses* ⓄⒹ second = *deuxième/second*

to be like two peas in a pod = *se ressembler comme deux gouttes d'eau* ≠ as different as night and day = *le jour et la nuit*
to be two of a kind = *être du même bois* ⓄⒹ to be of the same ilk = *être du même acabit*
to have two left feet = *danser comme un pied*
I can't do two things at the same time/at once = *je ne peux pas faire deux choses en même temps*
it takes two to tango = *on est tous les deux responsables* : it's not only my fault, it takes two to tango = *ce n'est pas uniquement de ma faute, on est tous les deux responsables*
in two shakes of a lamb's tail = *en deux coups de cuiller à pot*

ⓄⒹ **in a jiffy** = *en un clin d'œil*
to kill two birds with one stone = *faire d'une pierre deux coups*
don't put/stick your two cents in ! = *ne mets pas ton grain de sel là-dedans !* ⓄⒹ don't butt in ! = *ne ramène pas ta fraise !*
there are no two ways about it = *il n'y a pas à tortiller* ⓄⒹ it's no use shilly-shallying = *pas de tergiversations*
there are two sides to every story = *qui n'entend qu'une cloche n'entend qu'un son*
two can play at that game = *moi aussi, je pourrais te faire le même coup* ⓄⒹ what's good for the goose is good for the gander = *il n'y a pas deux poids et deux mesures*

two's company, three's a crowd = *on n'a besoin de personne pour tenir la chandelle*
two heads are better than one = *deux avis valent mieux qu'un*
two wrongs don't make a right = *ce n'est pas une raison* : don't tell me you smoke because I do, two wrongs don't make a right = *ne me dis pas que tu fumes parce que je fume, ce n'est pas une raison*
to put two and two together = *en tirer ses propres conclusions* : now that you know the story, I'll let you put two and two together = *maintenant que vous connaissez l'histoire, tirez-en vos propres conclusions*

☠ *de deux choses l'une* = there aren't a million ways to consider it
— *entre les deux* = in between
— *la vie à deux* = life together
— *prendre son courage à deux mains* = to gather one's courage
— *y regarder à deux fois* = to think twice
— *aussi sûr que deux et deux font quatre* = as sure as shooting

— *deux poids, deux mesures* = double standards
— *être plié en deux* = to be in stitches
— *c'est à deux pas d'ici* = it's a stone's throw from here
— *deux points* = colon
— *le deux juillet* = the second of July
— *des deux côtés* = on both sides
— *entre deux vins* = drunk
— *entre deux âges* = middle-aged.

TWO-BIT (adj) *à la manque* : a two-bit lawyer = *un avocat à la manque* ⓄⒹ big-time = *qui tient le haut du pavé*.

TWO-FACED (adj) *faux jeton* : a crooked, two-faced politician = *un politicien malhonnête et faux jeton* ≠ straightforward = *sans détour*.

TWO-TIME (adj) **a two-time loser** = *un repris de justice* ⓄⒹ old offender = *cheval de retour*.

TWO-TIME (to, -d) 1/ *faire des infidélités à* : he's two-timing his second wife = *il fait des infidélités à sa seconde femme* ⓄⒹ to cheat on = *tromper* 2/ *jouer (un) double jeu avec* : he two-timed the gang = *il a joué (un) double jeu avec le gang* → TO HUSTLE.

TWO-TIMER (n) 1/ *quelqu'un qui fait des infidélités* : her husband's always been a two-timer = *son mari lui a toujours fait des infidélités* 2/ *vendu, -e* : you lousy two-timer !* = *espèce de vendu !* = double-crosser.

TWO-WAY (adj) *où l'on circule dans les deux sens* : a two-way street = *une rue où l'on circule dans les deux sens*.

TYCOON (n) *magnat* (m) : oil tycoons = *les magnats du pétrole* ⓄⒹ baron = ←.

TYPE (n) *type* (m) : I don't like that type of food = *je n'aime pas ce type de nourriture*, he's not my type = *ce n'est pas mon type* ⓄⒹ kind = *genre*
☠ *un type* = a guy/chap/fellow
— *elle a le type sud-américain* = she's a typical South American.

TYPE (to, -d) *taper (à la machine)* : I don't know how to type = *je ne sais pas taper (à la machine)* ⓄⒹ to take shorthand = *prendre en sténo*.

TYPEWRITER (n) *machine* (f) *à écrire* : an electric typewriter = *une machine à écrire électrique* ⓄⒹ key = *touche*, keyboard = *clavier*, ribbon = *ruban*.

TYPHOID (n) *typhoïde* (f) : typhoid fever = *fièvre typhoïde* ⓄⒹ malaria = ←.

TYPHOON (n) *typhon* (m) : a typhoon off the coast = *un typhon au large de la côte* ⓄⒹ hurricane = *ouragan*.

TYPHUS (n) *typhus* (m) ⓄⒹ yellow fever = *fièvre jaune*.

TYPICAL (adj) *typique* : he's a typical American = *c'est un Américain typique* ⓄⒹ normal = ← ≠ atypical = *atypique*
it's typical of him (to forget my birthday) = *c'est*

typiquement lui (d'oublier mon anniversaire) ① it's just like him = *ça lui ressemble.*

TYPICALLY (adv) *typiquement :* her cooking's typically French = *sa cuisine est typiquement française.*

TYPIFY (to, -ied) *être le type même de :* he typifies the French lover = *c'est le type même de l'amant français* ① to exemplify = *être l'exemple de.*

TYPIST (n) *dactylo (f, m) :* we're looking for a new typist = *nous cherchons une nouvelle dactylo* ① shorthand typist = *sténodactylo.*

TYRANNICAL (adj) *tyrannique :* tyrannical parents = *des parents tyranniques* ① despotic = *despotique.*

TYRANNIZE (to, -d) *tyranniser :* he tyrannizes his kids = *il tyrannise ses gosses* ① to bully = *brutaliser.*

TYRANNY (n, -ies) *tyrannie (f) :* the tyranny of passion = *la tyrannie de la passion* ① despotism = *despotisme.*

TYRANT (n) *tyran (m) :* his kids think he's a tyrant = *ses enfants pensent que c'est un tyran* ① dictator = *dictateur,* despot = *despote.*

UFO (abbr) = Unidentified Flying Object = *OVNI (m)* = *objet volant non identifié.*

UGLINESSS (n) *laideur (f)* : repulsive ugliness = *laideur repoussante.*

UGLY (adj, -ier, -iest) *laid, -e* : what an ugly guy ! = *que ce type est laid !* ⓓ plain = *quelconque* ≠ stunning = *sublime*
to be ugly as sin = *être laid comme un pou* ≠ to be pretty as a picture = *être joli comme un cœur*
the ugly duckling = *le vilain petit canard.*

UK (abbr) = United Kingdom = *Royaume-Uni (m)* ⓓ Commonwealth = ←.

ULCER (n) *ulcère (m)* : he has an ulcer = *il a un ulcère* ⓓ stress = ←

ULTERIOR (adj) **ulterior motive** = *arrière-pensée.*

ULTIMATE (n) **the ultimate in (luxury)** = *le summum en matière de (luxe)* ⓓ the last word = *le dernier cri.*

ULTIMATE (adj) *ultime* : the ultimate weapon = *l'arme ultime* ⓓ final = *définitif.*

ULTIMATELY (adv) *en fin de compte* : I considered a lot of countries but ultimately, I decided to go to India = *j'ai pensé à pas mal de pays, mais en fin de compte je me suis décidé pour l'Inde* ⓓ in the end = *finalement.*

ULTIMATUM (n, -s or -ta) *ultimatum (m)* : to give s.o. an ultimatum = *adresser un ultimatum à qqn.*

ULTRA (prep) *ultra-* : ultrarich = *ultra-riche* → VERY.

UMBILICAL CORD (n) *cordon (m) ombilical.*

UMBRELLA (n) *parapluie (m), pépin (m)* (LV) : take your umbrella = *prenez votre parapluie/pépin* ⓓ parasol = ← ☠ *pépin* → hassle.

UMPIRE (n) *arbitre (m)* (base-ball) ☠ → arbitrator.

UMPTEEN (adj) *des centaines de* : I've told you that umpteen times = *je vous ai répété ça des centaines de fois* → MANY.

UMPTEENTH (adj) **for the umpteenth time** = *pour la énième fois.*

UN (abbr) = United Nations = *ONU (f)* = *Nations unies* ⓓ UNESCO = ←.

UNABLE (adj) **to be unable to (come/help)** = *être dans l'impossibilité de (venir)/d'(aider).*

UNACCOUNTED-FOR (adj) *manquant, -e* : an unaccounted-for sum of money/an unaccounted-for POW = *une somme d'argent manquante/un prisonnier de guerre manquant (à l'appel).*

UNADULTERATED (adj) *pur, -e et simple* : what unadulterated stupidity ! = *c'est de la stupidité pure et simple !* ⓓ utter = *parfait.*

UNALIKE (adj) *qui ne se ressemblent pas* : the two brothers are very unalike = *les deux frères ne se ressemblent pas du tout* ⓓ different = *différent.*

UNANIMOUS (adj) *unanime* : a unanimous decision = *une décision unanime* ≠ divided = *divisé.*

UNANIMITY (n) *unanimité (f)* **UNANIMOUSLY** (adv) *unanimement, à l'unanimité.*

UNARMED (adj) *pas armé, -e* : the hijacker was unarmed = *le pirate de l'air n'était pas armé.*

UNASKED FOR (adj) *non sollicité, -e* : unasked for advice = *conseils non sollicités.*

UNASSUMING (adj) *sans prétention* : an unassuming guy = *un type sans prétention* ≠ pretentious = *prétentieux.*

UNATTACHED (adj) *non marié, -e* : there are many unattached guys among her friends = *il y a pas mal de types non mariés parmi ses amis* ≠ married = *marié.*

UNAVOIDABLE (adj) *inéluctable* : an unavoidable accident = *un accident inéluctable* ⓓ inevitable = *inévitable.*

UNAWARE OF (adj) *inconscient, -e de* : unaware of the difficulties involved = *inconscient des difficultés que cela implique* = unconscious of ⓓ oblivious to = *ignorant de.*

UNAWARES (adv) **to catch** ≠ **be caught unawares** = *prendre* ≠ *être pris de court* ⓓ to catch s.o. off guard = *prendre qqn au dépourvu.*

UNBALANCED (adj) *déséquilibré, -e :* an unbalanced budget/guy = *un budget/un type déséquilibré* ≠ balanced = *équilibré.*

UNBEARABLE (adj) *insupportable :* unbearable heat = *une chaleur insupportable* ≠ bearable = *supportable.*

UNBEATABLE (adj) *imbattable :* unbeatable prices = *des prix imbattables.*

UNBECOMING (adj) *peu seyant, -e :* an unbecoming outfit = *un ensemble peu seyant* ≠ comely = *seyant.*

UNBELIEVABLE (adj) *incroyable :* he won an unbelievable amount of money at the races = *il a gagné une incroyable somme d'argent aux courses* ⓓ unreal = *pas possible.*

UNBIASED (adj) *sans parti pris :* an unbiased opinion = *une opinion sans parti pris* ⓓ objective = *objectif.*

UNBREAKABLE (adj) *incassable :* unbreakable glasses = *des verres incassables.*

UNBUTTON (to, -ed) *déboutonner :* unbutton your coat = *déboutonnez votre manteau.*

UNCALLED-FOR (adj) *déplacé, -e :* an uncalled-for remark = *une remarque déplacée* ≠ well-founded = *fondé.*

UNCANNY (adj) *déconcertant, -e :* he has an uncanny way of knowing what you're going to say = *il a la faculté déconcertante de prévoir ce que vous allez dire.*

UNCERTAIN (adj) *pas certain, -e :* it's uncertain whether he's going to come = *il n'est pas certain qu'il vienne* ≠ sure = *sûr*
in no uncertain terms = *en des termes on ne peut plus clairs* ⓓ not to mince words = *ne pas mâcher ses mots*
uncertain weather = *temps incertain/indécis.*

UNCERTAINTY (n, -ies) *incertitude (f) :* the uncertainties of the future = *les incertitudes de l'avenir.*

UNCLE (n) *oncle (m), tonton (m)* (LV) : I have two uncles = *j'ai deux oncles* ≠ aunt = *tante*
(to say) uncle = *(dire) pouce*
Uncle Sam = *l'Oncle Sam (symbole du gouvernement des États-Unis)* ⓓ John Bull = *homme qui symbolise l'Angleterre*
Uncle Tom = *un Noir fayot avec les Blancs* ⓓ the Man = *l'homme blanc.*

UNCOMFORTABLE (adj) **1/** *inconfortable :* an uncomfortable armchair = *un fauteuil inconfortable* **2/** *pas à l'aise :* I'm uncomfortable with my in-laws = *je ne suis pas à l'aise avec mes beaux-parents* ≠ at ease = *à l'aise.*

UNCOMMITTED (adj) *non engagé, -e :* an uncommitted position = *une position non engagée.*

UNCOMMON (adj) *peu commun, -e :* uncommon intelligence = *une intelligence peu commune.*

UNCOMPROMISING (adj) *intransigeant, -e :* an uncompromising person/attitude = *une personne/attitude intransigeante* ⓓ unyielding = *inébranlable,* tough = *dur.*

UNCONDITIONAL (adj) *inconditionnel, -elle :* unconditional support = *soutien inconditionnel* ⓓ absolute = *absolu.*

UNCONNECTED (adj) *sans rapport :* two unconnected killings = *deux meurtres sans rapport* ≠ linked = *lié.*

UNCONSCIOUS (n) *inconscient (m) :* Freud studied the unconscious = *Freud a étudié l'inconscient* ⓓ subconscious = *subconscient.*

UNCONSCIOUS (adj) *inconscient, -e :* the patient's unconscious = *le malade est inconscient* ≠ conscious = *conscient* ☠ *il est inconscient* = he just isn't aware of what he's doing.

UNCONSTITUTIONAL (adj) *inconstitutionnel, -elle :* this new law's unconstitutional = *cette nouvelle loi est inconstitutionnelle* ⓓ illegal = *illégal.*

UNCONVENTIONAL (adj) *peu conventionnel, -elle :* unconventional behavior = *comportement peu conventionnel* ⓓ nonconformist = *non-conformiste.*

UNCOUTH (adj) *fruste :* an uncouth guy = *un type fruste* ⓓ oafish = *rustre.*

UNCOVER (to, -ed) *découvrir :* the police have uncovered new evidence = *la police a découvert de nouvelles preuves* = to discover.

UNDAUNTED (adj) **to be undaunted by (a threat)** = *ne pas être impressionné par (une menace)* ≠ to be fazed by = *être démonté par.*

UNDECIDED (adj) *indécis, -e :* a large number of undecided voters = *un grand nombre d'électeurs indécis* ☠ *un temps indécis* = uncertain weather.

UNDENIABLE (adj) *indéniable :* that he loves her is undeniable = *il est indéniable qu'il l'aime* ≠ dubious = *douteux* **UNDENIABLY** (adv) *indéniablement :* undeniably intelligent = *indéniablement intelligent.*

UNDER (prep) **1/** *sous :* the cat's under the table = *le chat est sous la table* ⓓ beneath = *au-dessous de* ☠ *(marcher) sous la pluie* = (to walk) in the rain
— *sous la main* = at hand
— *sous son sourire, c'est une salope* = underneath her smile, she's a bitch
2/ *moins de :* it costs under a dollar = *ça coûte moins d'un dollar* = less than ≠ more than = *plus de*
☠ for the use of ''under'' after a verb, see the verb.

UNDER (adv) **1/** *en dessous :* the fence was so high we had to crawl under = *la barrière était tellement haute que nous avons dû ramper en dessous*

2/ *moins* : it will cost $ 100 or under = *ça coûtera 100 dollars ou moins,* children of 10 and under = *les enfants de 10 ans et moins* ☠ → less.

UNDERAGE (adj) *qui n'a pas atteint sa majorité* : her daughter's still underage = *sa fille n'a pas encore atteint sa majorité* ⓪ minor = *mineur.*

UNDERCOVER (adj) **an undercover agent** = *un agent secret* = a secret agent.

UNDERCURRENT (n) *quelque chose de sous-jacent* : an undercurrent of hostility = *une hostilité sous-jacente.*

UNDERCUT (to, -cut, -cut) *casser les prix* : discount stores undercut the others = *les magasins de discount cassent les prix du marché* ⓪ to undersell = *vendre moins cher (que).*

UNDERDEVELOPED (adj) *sous-développé, -e* : underdeveloped countries = *pays sous-développés* ≠ expanding = *en pleine expansion.*

UNDERDOG (n) *laissé, -e-pour-compte* : every society has its underdogs = *chaque société a ses laissés-pour-compte* ⓪ the oppressed = *les opprimés.*

UNDERESTIMATE (to, -d) *sous-estimer* : to underestimate s.o.'s ability = *sous-estimer les capacités de qqn* ≠ to exaggerate = *exagérer.*

UNDERGO (to, -went, -gone) *subir* : to undergo an operation = *subir une opération* ⓪ to go through = *traverser* ☠ *subir des attaques* = to come under attack.

UNDERGRADUATE (n) *étudiant, -e (non encore diplômé, -e)* : my daughter's an undergraduate at Yale = *ma fille est étudiante à Yale.*

UNDERGROUND (n) (GB) *métro (m)* = subway.

UNDERGROUND (adj) **1/** *souterrain, -e* : an underground passage = *un passage souterrain* **2/** *clandestin, -e* : an underground organization = *une organisation clandestine* = clandestine ≠ official = *officiel* **3/** *underground* : underground movies/press = *les films underground/la presse underground* ⓪ avant-garde = *d'avant-garde.*

UNDERGROUND (adv) **to go underground** = *prendre le maquis* ⓪ to go into hiding = *entrer dans la clandestinité.*

UNDERHAND(ED) (adj) *fourbe* : underhanded methods = *des méthodes fourbes* ⓪ devious = *tortueux,* sneaky = *sournois* **UNDERHANDEDLY** (adv) *par en dessous.*

UNDERLINE (to, -d) *souligner* : I want to underline the importance of this idea = *je veux souligner l'importance de cette idée* ⓪ to call attention to = *attirer l'attention sur* ☠ → to underscore.

UNDERLING (n) *subalterne (m, f)* : I'm your assistant, not your underling = *je suis votre assistant, pas votre subalterne* ⓪ lackey = *laquais.*

UNDERLYING (adj) *sous-jacent, -e* : the underlying reason = *la raison sous-jacente* ⓪ fundamental = *fondamental.*

UNDERMINE (to, -d) *miner* : the strikes are undermining the government's policy = *les grèves sont en train de miner la politique gouvernementale* ⓪ to sabotage = *saboter* ☠ → to mine.

UNDERNEATH (adv) **1/** *du dessous* : the apartment underneath = *l'appartement du dessous* = the apartment beneath **2/** *en dessous* : they live underneath = *ils habitent en dessous* = they live beneath.

UNDERNEATH (prep) **1/** *sous* : look underneath the table = *regarde sous la table* = under ≠ on top of = *au-dessus de* **2/** *sous* : underneath her smile she's a bitch = *sous son sourire, c'est une salope* ☠ → under.

UNDERNOURISHED (adj) *sous-alimenté, -e* : undernourished children = *des enfants sous-alimentés* ≠ overnourished = *suralimenté.*

UNDERPANTS (n pl) *slip (m)* : she wasn't wearing underpants = *elle ne portait pas de slip* ⓪ underwear = *sous-vêtements.*

UNDERPAY (to, -paid, -paid) *sous-payer* : I'm really underpaid for the work I do = *je suis vraiment sous-payée pour le travail que je fais* ≠ to be well paid = *être bien payé.*

UNDERPRIVILEGED (adj) *défavorisé, -e* : too many children come from underprivileged backgrounds = *trop d'enfants sortent de milieux défavorisés* ⓪ impoverished = *appauvri.*

UNDERRATE (to, -d) *mésestimer* : to underrate s.o.'s talent = *mésestimer le talent de qqn* ⓪ to underestimate = *sous-estimer.*

UNDERSCORE (to, -d) *souligner* : the leak underscored the danger of a nuclear catastrophe = *la fuite a souligné le danger d'une catastrophe nucléaire* ⓪ to lay emphasis on = *mettre l'accent sur* ☠ *je veux souligner que* = I want to underline that.

UNDERSELL (to, -sold, -sold) *vendre moins cher (que)* : they're making a pile underselling their competitors = *ils font fortune en vendant moins cher que leurs concurrents* ⓪ to cut prices = *réduire les prix.*

UNDERSTAFFED (adj) *à court de personnel* : understaffed offices = *des bureaux à court de personnel* ⓪ skeleton staff = *personnel réduit.*

UNDERSTAND (to, -stood, -stood) *comprendre* : do you understand ? = *est-ce que vous comprenez ?* ⓪ to catch on = *piger,* to fathom = *arriver à comprendre* **I can't make myself understood** = *je n'arrive pas à me faire comprendre* **I understand that (they're getting a divorce)** = *j'ai cru comprendre qu'(ils étaient en train de divorcer)* ⓪ it seems that = *il semble que*

it's understood that (we'll go dutch) = *il est entendu que (chacun paie son écot)*
☠ *il ne comprend pas la plaisanterie* = he can't take a joke
— *le prix comprend les boissons* = the price includes the drinks
— *j'ai compris qu'(il voulait se barrer)* = I realized (he wanted to split)
— *l'appartement comprend quatre pièces* = the apartment comprises four rooms.

UNDERSTANDABLE (adj) *compréhensible* : his anger is understandable = *sa colère est compréhensible* = comprehensible ≠ incomprehensible = *incompréhensible.*

UNDERSTANDABLY (adv) *et cela se comprend* : she's understandably upset = *elle est inquiète, et cela se comprend.*

UNDERSTANDING (n) **1/** *arrangement (m)* : I have an understanding with my husband : he cooks, I do the dishes = *j'ai un accord avec mon mari : il fait la cuisine, je fais la vaisselle* = arrangement **2/** *compréhension (f)* : she has no understanding of children = *elle n'a aucune compréhension des enfants* **3/** *entente (f)* : there's a good understanding between France and Germany = *il y a une bonne entente entre la France et l'Allemagne*
to come to/to reach an understanding = *parvenir à une entente.*

UNDERSTANDING (adj) *compréhensif, -ive* : understanding parents = *des parents compréhensifs* ⓄⒹ compassionate = *compatissant* ☠ → comprehensive.

UNDERSTATE (to, -d) *minimiser* : the Prime Minister understated the gravity of the situation = *le Premier ministre a minimisé la gravité de la situation* = to minimize ≠ to blow up = *grossir.*

UNDERSTATEMENT (n) *euphémisme (m)* : to say that he's rich is an understatement = *c'est un euphémisme de dire qu'il est riche* ≠ overstatement = *exagération*
that's the understatement of the year ! = *c'est le moins qu'on puisse dire !*

UNDERSTUDY (n, -ies) *doublure (f)* : the understudy knows the part well = *la doublure connaît bien le rôle* ☠ → lining.

UNDERTAKE (to, -took, -taken) *entreprendre* : she always undertakes more than she can do = *elle entreprend toujours plus de choses qu'elle n'en peut faire.*

UNDERTAKER (n) *entrepreneur (m) de pompes funèbres, croque-mort (m)* (LV).

UNDERTAKING (n) *entreprise (f)* : what a difficult undertaking ! = *quelle difficile entreprise !* = enterprise ⓄⒹ task = *tâche.*

UNDERTONE (n) **an undertone of (jealousy/bitterness)** = *un accent de (jalousie)/d'(amertume).*

UNDERWEAR (n inv) *sous-vêtements (m pl), dessous*

(m pl) : she doesn't wear any underwear = *elle ne porte pas de sous-vêtements/de dessous* ⓄⒹ panties = *(petite) culotte*, bra = *soutien-gorge*, briefs = *caleçon*, long johns = *caleçons longs*, trunks = *caleçon américain* = shorts, undershirt = *chemise de corps*
☠ *les dessous (d'une affaire)* = the dope/the lowdown
— *un dessous-de-table* = a kickback.

UNDERWEIGHT (adj) *trop maigre* : 10 pounds underweight = *trop maigre de 5 kilos.*

UNDERWORLD (n) *milieu (m)* : drugs and prostitution are controlled by the underworld = *la drogue et la prostitution sont sous le contrôle du milieu* ⓄⒹ Mafia = ←.

UNDERWRITE (to, -wrote, -written) *assurer le financement de* : the government is underwriting the student scholarships = *l'État assure le financement des bourses.*

UNDESIRABLE (adj) *indésirable* : undesirable neighbors = *des voisins indésirables.*

UNDIVIDED (adj) **you have my undivided attention** = *vous avez toute mon attention* ⓄⒹ I'm all eyes and ears = *je suis tout yeux, tout oreilles.*

UNDO (to, -did, -done) *défaire* : she undid her hair/the package = *elle a défait sa coiffure/le paquet*
☠ *se défaire d'une mauvaise habitude* = to break o.s. of a bad habit
— *se défaire de* = to dispose of.

UNDOING (n) *perte (f)* : drink was his undoing = *l'alcool a causé sa perte* ⓄⒹ downfall = *chute* ☠ → loss.

UNDOUBTEDLY (adv) *indubitablement* : you're undoubtedly right = *vous avez indubitablement raison* ⓄⒹ without a doubt = *sans aucun doute.*

UNDREAMED-OF (adj) *qui dépasse l'imagination* : an undreamed-of fortune = *une fortune qui dépasse l'imagination.*

UNDRESSED (adj) **to get undressed** = *se déshabiller* : get undressed and go to bed = *déshabille-toi et va au lit* ⓄⒹ to strip = *se mettre à poil.*

UNDULY (adv) *exagérément* : unduly worried = *exagérément inquiet.*

UNEARTH (to, -ed) *déterrer* : to unearth new evidence = *déterrer de nouvelles preuves* ⓄⒹ to find = *trouver.*

UNEASY (adj) *pas tranquille* : I feel uneasy about the kids driving so late = *je ne suis pas tranquille quand les enfants sont sur la route si tard* ⓄⒹ upset = *inquiet*
an uneasy peace = *une paix incertaine.*

UNEMPLOYED (adj) *au chômage* : in her skill many people are unemployed = *dans sa branche, beaucoup sont au chômage* ⓄⒹ out of work = *sans emploi.*

UNEMPLOYMENT (n inv) *chômage (m)* : measures to cut unemployment = *des mesures pour réduire le chômage*

on unemployment = *inscrit au chômage* = on the dole (GB)
he's getting unemployment (benefit) = *il touche l'allocation (de) chômage.*

UNEQUALED (adj) *inégalé, -e* : she's unequaled as a tennis player = *elle est inégalée comme joueuse de tennis* ⟳ unparalleled = *hors pair.*

UNEQUIVOCAL (adj) *sans équivoque* : an unequivocal refusal = *un refus sans équivoque* ⟳ plain = *clair.*

UNESCO (abbr) = United Nations Educational, Scientific and Cultural Organization = *UNESCO (m)* ⟳ IMF = *FMI.*

UNEVEN (adj) **1/** *inégal, -e* : her work's uneven = *son travail est inégal* ≠ reliable = *fiable* ☠ *quantités inégales* = unequal quantities **2/** *irrégulier, -ère* : your hem's uneven = *ton ourlet est irrégulier* ☠ → irregular.

UNEVENTFUL (adj) *sans incident* : an uneventful trip = *un voyage sans incident* ⟳ calm = *calme.*

UNEXCITING (adj) *pas très excitant, -e* : making love with him was unexciting = *ce n'était pas très excitant de faire l'amour avec lui* ⟳ blah = *sans intérêt* ≠ thrilling = *passionnant.*

UNEXPECTED (adj) *inattendu, -e* : an unexpected answer = *une réponse inattendue* ⟳ unforeseen = *imprévu* **UNEXPECTEDLY** (adv) *à l'improviste* : she came unexpectedly = *elle est venue à l'improviste* ⟳ without warning = *sans prévenir.*

UNFAIR (adj) *injuste* : what you're saying's unfair = *ce que vous dites est injuste* = unjust ⟳ not right = *pas juste*
unfair competition = *concurrence déloyale.*

UNFAITHFUL (adj) *infidèle* : an unfaithful husband = *un mari infidèle* ≠ loyal = ←.

UNFAMILIAR (adj) *pas familier, -ère* : I'm unfamiliar with that kind of subject = *je ne suis pas familier de ce genre de sujet.*

UNFASHIONABLE (adj) *pas à la mode* : miniskirts were unfashionable =*les mini-jupes n'étaient pas à la mode* ≠ trendy = *à la page.*

UNFASTEN (to, ed) *détacher* : unfasten your seatbelts ! = *détachez vos ceintures !*

UNFAVORABLE (adj) *défavorable* : unfavorable write-ups = *des critiques défavorables* ⟳ negative = *négatif.*

UNFINISHED BUSINESS (n) *affaires (f pl) non réglées* : there is a lot of unfinished business between her and her ex = *il y a pas mal d'affaires non réglées entre elle et son ex.*

UNFOLD (to, -ed) **1/** *déplier* : to unfold a map/a napkin = *déplier une carte/une serviette* **2/** *se dérouler* : as the story unfolds, suspense increases = *au fur et à mesure que l'histoire se déroule, le suspense augmente.*

UNFORESEEN (adj) *imprévu, -e* : unforeseen problems = *des problèmes imprévus* ⟳ sudden = *soudain.*

UNFORGETTABLE (adj) *inoubliable* : an unforgettable love affair = *une aventure sentimentale inoubliable* → WONDERFUL.

UNFORTUNATE (adj) *malheureux, -euse* : an unfortunate mistake = *une erreur malheureuse* ⟳ regrettable = ← ☠ *elle est très malheureuse* = she's very unhappy/miserable.

UNFORTUNATELY (adv) *malheureusement* : unfortunately, we don't have enough money to buy a new car = *malheureusement, nous n'avons pas assez d'argent pour acheter une nouvelle voiture.*

UNFOUNDED (adj) *non fondé, -e* : unfounded suspicions = *soupçons non fondés* ≠ justified = *justifié.*

UNFRIENDLY (adj) *inamical, -e* : an unfriendly attitude = *une attitude inamicale* ⟳ hostile = ←.

UNFURNISHED (adj) *non meublé, -e* : an unfurnished pad = *un appart non meublé* ⟳ empty = *vide.*

UNGAINLY (adj) *disgracieux, -euse* : tall and ungainly = *grand et disgracieux* ⟳ awkward = *maladroit.*

UNGODLY (adj) *indu, -e* : what an ungodly hour to call me ! = *quelle heure indue pour m'appeler !* ⟳ outrageous = *scandaleux.*

UNGRATEFUL (adj) *ingrat, -e* : don't be so ungrateful ! = *ne soyez pas si ingrat !* ≠ appreciative = *reconnaissant*
☠ *avoir un physique ingrat* = to be plain-looking
— *l'âge ingrat* = the awkward age
— *tâche ingrate* = thankless task.

UNHAPPILY (adv) *par malheur* : unhappily we weren't home when the accident happened = *par malheur nous n'étions pas à la maison quand l'accident est arrivé* ⟳ unfortunately = *malheureusement* ≠ fortunately = *heureusement.*

UNHAPPINESS (n inv) *malheur (m)* : there is so much unhappiness in the world = *il y a tant de malheur dans le monde*
☠ *le malheur, c'est que ...* = the trouble is that ...
— *les malheurs économiques (d'un pays)* = economic woes (of a country)
— *ne parle pas de malheur !* = bite your tongue !
— *faire un malheur* = to be a smash (success)
— *c'est dans le malheur qu'on reconnaît ses amis* = a friend in need is a friend indeed.

UNHAPPY (adj, -ier, -iest) *malheureux, -euse* : when he left, I was very unhappy = *quand il est parti, j'ai été très malheureuse* ⟳ miserable = *malheureux comme les pierres*, dejected = *abattu* ≠ riding high = *aux anges* ☠ → unfortunate.

UNHARMED (adj) *indemne* : he got out of the accident unharmed = *il est sorti indemne de l'accident* ≠ injured = *blessé.*

UNHEALTHY (adj, -ier, -iest) *mauvais, -e pour la santé :* is smoking unhealthy ? = *le tabac est-il mauvais pour la santé ?*

UNHEARD-OF (adj) **1/** *impensable :* getting a legal abortion a hundred years ago was unheard-of = *c'était impensable de se faire avorter légalement il y a une centaine d'années* = unthinkable **2/** *dont on n'a jamais entendu parler :* unheard-of poets = *des poètes dont on n'a jamais entendu parler* ⓓ unknown = *inconnu.*

UNHOOK (to, -ed) *dégrafer :* can you unhook my dress ? = *peux-tu me dégrafer ma robe ?*

UNHOPED-FOR (adj) *inespéré, -e :* the raise was unhoped-for = *cette augmentation était inespérée.*

UNICEF (abbr) = United Nations International Children's Emergency Fund = *UNICEF (m).*

UNIDENTIFIED (adj) *non identifié, -e :* an unidentified body = *un corps non identifié* ≠ identified = *identifié* **an unidentified flying object** = *un objet volant non identifié.*

UNIFICATION (n) *(ré)unification (f) :* the unification of Berlin = *la réunification de Berlin.*

UNIFORM (n) *uniforme (m) :* in uniform = *en uniforme* ≠ in civvies = *en civil* **UNIFORM** (adj) *uniforme :* uniform tastes = *des goûts uniformes* **UNIFORMITY** (n) *uniformité (f)* ⓓ monotony = *monotonie.*

UNIFY (to, -ied) *unifier :* to unify a country = *unifier un pays* ≠ to divide = *diviser.*

UNILATERAL (adj) *unilatéral, -e :* a unilateral decision = *une décision unilatérale* ≠ bilateral = ←.

UNINTENTIONAL (adj) *involontaire :* if I hurt you, it was unintentional = *si je vous ai fait mal, c'était involontaire* **UNINTENTIONALLY** (adv) *involontairement* ≠ deliberately = *délibérément.*

UNION (n) **1/** *syndicat (m) :* to join a union = *adhérer à un syndicat* ⓓ to unionize = *se syndiquer,* to strike = *faire la grève,* labor and management = *les travailleurs et le patronat* ☠ → syndicate **2/** *union (f) :* the union of popular forces = *l'union des forces populaires* ⓓ confederation = *confédération,* federation = *fédération* ☠ *l'union fait la force* = united we stand, divided we fall — *union libre* = free love.

UNIONIZE (to, -d) *se syndiquer :* most mine-workers unionized = *la plupart des mineurs se sont syndiqués.*

UNIQUE (adj) **1/** *unique :* what a unique apartment ! = *quel appartement unique !* ⓓ exceptional = *exceptionnel* **2/** *unique :* a unique copy of the original magazine = *une copie unique du magazine original* ⓓ single = *seul* ☠ *un enfant unique* = an only child — *elle est l'unique personne qui puisse le faire* = she's the one person who can do it.

UNISEX (adj) *unisexe :* unisex clothes = *des vêtements unisexes.*

UNIT (n) *unité (f) :* an army unit = *une unité militaire* ☠ *unité (de vues)* = unity (of views).

UNITE (to, -d) *(s')unir :* hookers of the world, unite ! = *putains de tous les pays, unissez-vous !*

UNITED (adj) *uni, -e :* a united family = *une famille unie* ≠ disunited = *désuni* **United Kingdom** = *Royaume-Uni* ⓓ Great Britain = *Grande-Bretagne* **United Nations** = *les Nations unies* **the United States** = *les États-Unis* ⓓ the US = *les USA* **united we stand, divided we fall** = *l'union fait la force* ☠ *(couleur) unie* = solid (color).

UNITY (n, -ies) *unité (f) :* the party lacks unity = *le parti manque d'unité* ⓓ harmony = *harmonie* ☠ → unit.

UNIVERSAL (adj) *universel, -elle :* famine is a universal problem = *la famine est un problème universel* ⓓ international = ← **UNIVERSALLY** (adj) *universellement.*

UNIVERSE (n) *univers (m) :* our universe is going to hell = *notre univers fout le camp* ⓓ cosmos = ←.

UNIVERSITY (n, -ies) *université (f) :* she's going to university = *elle va à l'université* ⓓ high school = *lycée,* campus = ←.

UNJUST (adj) *injuste :* unjust laws = *des lois injustes* ⓓ inequitable = *inéquitable.*

UNJUSTIFIED (adj) *injustifié, -e :* unjustified criticisms = *des critiques injustifiées* ⓓ gratuitous = *gratuit.*

UNKEMPT (adj) *peu soigné, -e (de sa personne) :* an unkempt appearance = *une apparence peu soignée* ⓓ sloppy = *négligé.*

UNKIND (adj) *pas gentil, -ille :* it was unkind of you to tell her makeup was too heavy = *ce n'était pas gentil de votre part de lui dire qu'elle était trop maquillée* ⓓ mean = *méchant* **the unkindest cut of all** = *le coup de pied de l'âne.*

UNKNOWINGLY (adv) *sans le savoir :* I made a blunder unknowingly = *j'ai fait une gaffe sans le savoir* ≠ deliberately = *délibérément.*

UNKNOWN (adj) *inconnu, -e :* the unknown soldier = *le soldat inconnu* ⓓ obscure = *obscur* ≠ illustrious = *illustre* **unknown to (me)** = *à (mon) insu* **an unknown factor** = *une inconnue.*

UNLEARN (to, -ed) *désapprendre :* to unlearn a bad habit = *désapprendre une mauvaise habitude.*

UNLESS (conj) *à moins que :* don't come unless I call you = *ne venez pas à moins que je ne vous appelle* ⓓ except if = *sauf si.*

UNLIKE (adj) *qui ne se ressemblent pas* : they're very unlike = *ils ne se ressemblent pas du tout* ⓓ dissimilar = *dissemblable.*

UNLIKE (prep) *contrairement à* : the French, unlike the Americans, drink a lot of wine = *les Français, contrairement aux Américains, boivent beaucoup de vin* **it's unlike (him) (to drink so much)** = *ça ne (lui) ressemble pas (de boire tant).*

UNLIKELIHOOD (n) *improbabilité (f)* : the unlikelihood of getting pregnant with the pill = *l'improbabilité de tomber enceinte avec la pilule.*

UNLIKELY (adj) **1/** *peu probable* : it's unlikely that he'll come = *il est peu probable qu'il vienne* ≠ probable = ← **2/** *invraisemblable* : we met in the most unlikely place = *nous nous sommes rencontrés dans l'endroit le plus invraisemblable qui soit* ⓓ wild = *dément.*

UNLIMITED (adj) *illimité, -e* : unlimited power/funds = *un pouvoir illimité/des fonds illimités* ⓓ boundless = *sans bornes.*

UNLOAD (to, -ed) *décharger* : to unload a truck = *décharger un camion.*

UNLOCK (to, -ed) *ouvrir (une porte) fermée à clef* : I can't unlock the door = *je n'arrive pas à ouvrir la porte.*

UNLUCKY (adj, -ier, -iest) *qui n'a pas de chance* : an unlucky guy = *un type qui n'a pas de chance* **UNLUCKILY** (adv) *par malchance* : unluckily, I arrived too late = *par malchance, je suis arrivé trop tard* ⓓ unfortunately = *malheureusement.*

UNMARRIED (adj) *non marié, -e* : she has two unmarried brothers = *elle a deux frères non mariés* **unmarried mother/father** = *mère/père célibataire.*

UNMASK (to, -ed) *démasquer* : to unmask a criminal = *démasquer un criminel.*

UNMISTAKABLE (adj) *indubitable* : her hatred for him is unmistakable = *sa haine pour lui est indubitable* ⓓ manifest = *manifeste.*

UNMOVED (adj) *insensible* : unmoved by misery = *insensible à la misère.*

UNNATURAL (adj) **1/** *qui manque de naturel* : an unnatural way of talking = *une façon de parler qui manque de naturel* ⓓ affected = *affecté* **2/** *contre nature* : so-called unnatural practices = *des pratiques soi-disant contre nature* ⓓ perverse = *pervers.*

UNNECESSARY (adj) *pas nécessaire* : there were many unnecessary questions = *il y a eu beaucoup de questions qui n'étaient pas nécessaires* ≠ required = *requis* **UNNECESSARILY** (adv) *inutilement* : you're worrying unnecessarily = *vous vous inquiétez inutilement.*

UNNERVE (to, -d) *dérouter* : his questions unnerved me = *ses questions m'ont dérouté* ≠ to be flustered = *être démonté* **UNNERVING** (adj) *déroutant, -e* ⓓ unsettling = *déconcertant.*

UNOFFICIAL (adj) *officieux, -euse* : unofficial talks = *des pourparlers officieux* **UNOFFICIALLY** (adv) *officieusement.*

UNPACK (to, -ed) *défaire ses bagages* : I've just arrived and have to unpack = *je viens d'arriver et il faut que je défasse mes bagages.*

UNPAID (adj) *impayé, -e* : an unpaid bill = *une facture impayée* ≠ settled = *réglé.*

UNPARALLELED (adj) *hors pair* : unparalleled stupidity = *une stupidité hors pair* ⓓ incomparable = ←, matchless = *sans pareil.*

UNPLEASANT (adj) *déplaisant, -e* : an unpleasant experience = *une expérience déplaisante* ≠ delightful = *délicieux.*

UNPOPULAR (adj) *impopulaire* : he's very unpopular with young people = *il est très impopulaire parmi les jeunes* ≠ well-liked = *apprécié.*

UNPRECEDENTED (adj) *sans précédent* : unprecedented cruelty = *une cruauté sans précédent.*

UNPREDICTABLE (adj) *imprévisible* : my wife's unpredictable = *ma femme est imprévisible* ⓓ sudden = *soudain* **UNPREDICTABLY** (adv) *d'une façon imprévisible.*

UNPRINCIPLED (adj) *peu scrupuleux, -euse* : an unprincipled lawyer = *un avocat peu scrupuleux* ⓓ unscrupulous = *sans scrupules.*

UNPRINTABLE (adj) *pas racontable, impubliable* (text) : unprintable text/joke = *un texte impubliable/une plaisanterie pas racontable* ⓓ smutty = *cochon.*

UNPROFITABLE (adj) *qui ne rapporte pas* : an unprofitable business : *une affaire qui ne rapporte pas.*

UNPUBLISHED (adj) *inédit, -e* : unpublished poems = *des poèmes inédits.*

UNQUALIFIED (adj) *inqualifiable* : an unqualified lie = *un mensonge inqualifiable.*

UNQUESTIONABLE (adj) *incontestable* : her sincerity's unquestionable = *sa sincérité est incontestable* ⓓ indisputable = *indiscutable* **UNQUESTIONABLY** (adv) *incontestablement* ⓓ undoubtedly = *indubitablement.*

UNRAVEL (to, -ed) *débrouiller, démêler* : to unravel a mystery/a ball of wool = *débrouiller un mystère/démêler une pelote de laine* 🐾 *débrouiller* → to manage.

UNREAL (adj) **1/** *irréel, -elle* : she lives in an unreal world = *elle vit dans un monde irréel* **2/** *pas possible* : your clothes are unreal, man ! = *t'as des vêtements pas possibles, mon vieux !* ⓓ far-out = *dément.*

UNREASONABLE (adj) *déraisonnable* : unreasonable demands = *des exigences déraisonnables.*

UNRELATED (adj) *sans aucun rapport* : two unrelated facts = *deux faits sans aucun rapport* ≠ connected = *qui a un rapport.*

UNRELENTING (adj) *implacable* : unrelenting struggles/opposition = *des luttes implacables/une opposition implacable* = implacable.

UNRELIABLE (adj) *sur qui l'on ne peut pas compter* : she/the machine is unreliable = *on ne peut pas compter sur elle/sur cette machine* = undependable ≠ dependable = *sur qui l'on peut compter.*

UNREMITTING (adj) *incessant, -e* : unremitting attacks = *des attaques incessantes* ⓓ continual = *continuel.*

UNREST (n) *agitation (f)* : labor unrest = *agitation ouvrière* ⓓ turmoil = *bouleversement* 🐾 *une grande agitation (à l'aéroport)* = a big commotion (at the airport).

UNRIVALED (adj) *sans égal, -e* : the unrivaled quality of his cooking = *la qualité sans égale de sa cuisine* ⓓ matchless = *sans pareil.*

UNRUFFLED (adj) *imperturbable* : the criticism was severe but he remained unruffled = *la critique était sévère, mais il est resté imperturbable* ≠ rattled = *dérouté.*

UNRULY (adj) *turbulent, -e* (s.o.), *indiscipliné, -e* (s.o., stg)* : unruly child/hair = *enfant turbulent, indiscipliné/cheveux indisciplinés* = undisciplined.

UNSAFE (adj) *dangereux* : it's unsafe to ride a motorbike without a helmet = *il est dangereux de rouler en moto sans casque* = dangerous
to feel unsafe = *se sentir en danger.*

UNSATISFACTORY (adj) *peu satisfaisant, -e* : unsatisfactory work = *un travail peu satisfaisant* ⓓ poor = *médiocre.*

UNSCATHED (adj) *sans une égratignure* : he got out of the scandal unscathed = *il s'est sorti du scandale sans une égratignure.*

UNSCRUPULOUS (adj) *sans scrupules* : an unscrupulous businessman = *un homme d'affaires sans scrupules* ⓓ crooked = *malhonnête.*

UNSEAT (to, -ed) *faire perdre son siège* : the gun lobby tried to unseat two Senators in the last election = *aux dernières élections, le lobby des marchands de canons a essayé de faire perdre leur siège à deux sénateurs* ⓓ to remove = *destituer (de ses fonctions).*

UNSELFISH (adj) *altruiste* : an unselfish attitude = *une attitude altruiste* ≠ egoistic = *égoïste.*

UNSETTLE (to, -ed) *décontenancer* : his hostility unsettled me = *son hostilité m'a décontenancé* ⓓ to unnerve = *dérouter.*

UNSETTLED (adj) 1/ *pas réglé, -e* : an unsettled bill =

une facture pas réglée ⓓ up in the air = *en suspens*
2/ *perturbé, -e* : an unsettled political situation = *une situation politique perturbée* ⓓ troubled = *troublé.*

UNSETTLING (adj) *déconcertant, -e* : older people find changes in the world unsettling = *les gens âgés trouvent déconcertants les changements dans le monde* ⓓ upsetting = *affolant.*

UNSKILLED (adj) *non qualifié, -e* : unskilled labor = *main-d'œuvre non qualifiée.*

UNSOCIABLE (adj) *peu sociable* : shy and unsociable = *timide et peu sociable* ⓓ people shy = *sauvage.*

UNSOPHISTICATED (adj) *peu sophistiqué, -e* : unsophisticated methods/people = *des méthodes peu sophistiquées/des gens peu sophistiqués.*

UNSOUND (adj) *peu sûr, -e* : unsound judgement/investment = *un jugement/un investissement peu sûr* ≠ solid = *solide.*

UNSPEAKABLE (adj) *indicible* : unspeakable cruelty = *une cruauté indicible* ⓓ unmentionable = *inqualifiable.*

UNSTABLE (adj) *instable* : an unstable personality/economic situation = *une personnalité/une situation économique instable* ⓓ changeable = *changeant.*

UNSUCCESSFUL (adj) *infructueux, -euse* (stg), *qui ne réussit pas* (s.o.) : unsuccessful businessmen/undertakings = *des hommes d'affaires qui ne réussissent pas/des entreprises infructueuses*
to be unsuccessful in (raising the money) = *ne pas réussir à (collecter les fonds).*

UNSUCCESSFULLY (adv) *sans succès* : they unsuccessfully tried to put out the fire = *ils ont essayé sans succès d'éteindre le feu.*

UNSUITABLE (adj) *qui ne convient pas* : an unsuitable moment/dress = *un moment/une robe qui ne convient pas* ⓓ inapt = *peu approprié.*

UNSURE (adj) *peu sûr, -e* : he's unsure of himself = *il est peu sûr de lui.*

UNTHINKABLE (adj) *impensable* : that he would hit her is unthinkable = *il est impensable qu'il la batte* ⓓ inconceivable = *inconcevable.*

UNTIE (to, -d) *délier* : to untie the prisoner's hands = *délier les mains du prisonnier*
🐾 *délier qqn de* = to release s.o. from
— *délier la langue de qqn* = to make s.o. talk.

UNTIL (conj) *jusqu'à* : I was unhappy until I met you = *j'étais malheureux jusqu'à ce que je vous rencontre* = till ⓓ up to the time that = *jusqu'au moment où.*

UNTIL (prep) *jusqu'à* : we'll work until ten = *nous travaillerons jusqu'à dix heures*, wait until tomorrow = *attends jusqu'à demain* = till

not until = *pas avant* : he won't come until ten = *il ne viendra pas avant dix heures*
until now (I thought he was single) = *jusqu'à maintenant (je pensais qu'il était célibataire)* ⓒ up to now = *jusqu'ici*
until then = *jusque-là* : he's coming at five and we'll work until then = *il vient à cinq heures et nous travaillerons jusque-là*
until when ? = *jusqu'à quand ?* : until when are you staying here ? = *jusqu'à quand restez-vous ici ?*
☠ *compter jusqu'à dix* = to count up to ten
— *(il a couru) jusqu'à la maison* = (he ran) all the way home.

UNTIMELY (adj) *qui tombe mal* : an untimely meeting = *une réunion qui tombe mal* ⓒ ill-timed = *malvenu.*

UNTOLD (adj) *indescriptible* : untold riches = *des richesses indescriptibles.*

UNTRUE (adj) *faux, fausse* : untrue rumor = *fausse rumeur* ☠ → false
untrue to (her lover) = *infidèle à (son amant).*

UNUSED (adj) **to be unused to (getting up early)** = *ne pas être habitué à (se lever tôt).*

UNUSUAL (adj) 1/ *inhabituel, -elle* : an unusual pastime/guy = *un passe-temps/type inhabituel* ⓒ strange = *étrange* ≠ common = *courant*
it isn't unusual for (him) to (call me late) = *c'est dans (ses) habitudes de (m'appeler tard)*
there's nothing unusual about that ! = *ça n'a rien d'étrange !*
2/ *original, -e* : what an unusual ring ! = *quelle bague originale !* ⓒ peculiar = *singulier* ☠ → original.

UNUSUALLY (adv) *exceptionnellement* : she's un-usually intelligent = *elle est exceptionnellement intelligente* → VERY.

UNWANTED (adj) *non désiré, -e, non voulu, -e* : an unwanted child = *un enfant non désiré/non voulu.*

UNWARRANTED (adj) *injustifié, -e* : unwarranted criticisms = *des critiques injustifiées* = unjustified ⓒ unfounded = *non fondé.*

UNWAVERING (adj) *inébranlable* : unwavering convictions/beliefs = *convictions/croyances inébranlables* ⓒ unfaltering = *ferme.*

UNWED (adj) **unwed mother/father** = *mère/père célibataire* = unmarried mother/father.

UNWELL (adj) **she's unwell** = *elle est indisposée* ⓒ to have one's period = *avoir ses règles.*

UNWILLING TO (adj) *peu disposé, -e à* : unwilling to help = *peu disposé à aider* ⓒ reluctant to = *réticent à.*

UNWIND (to, -wound, -wound) *se détendre* : have a drink and unwind = *bois un verre et détends-toi* ⓒ to loosen up = *se dégeler* ☠ *la situation s'est détendue* = the situation has eased.

UNWISE (adj) *peu sage* : it's an unwise thing to say = *il est peu sage de dire cela* ⓒ stupid = *stupide.*

UNWITTINGLY (adv) *par mégarde* : I made the blunder unwittingly = *j'ai fait la gaffe par mégarde* ≠ on purpose = *exprès.*

UNWORTHY (adj) *indigne* : this remark was unworthy of you = *cette remarque était indigne de vous.*

UNWRAP (to, -ped) *défaire* : to unwrap a package = *défaire un paquet* ☠ → to undo.

UNYIELDING (adj) *inébranlable* : an unyielding will/stance = *une volonté/position inébranlable* ⓒ inflexible = ←.

UP (n) **to be on the up** = *être en hausse* : inflation/unemployment is on the up = *l'inflation/le chômage est en hausse.*
on the up and up = *en tout bien tout honneur* : his offer is on the up and up = *il a fait cette proposition en tout bien tout honneur* ≠ not kosher = *pas très catholique*
ups and downs = *des hauts et des bas* : like everyone he has his ups and downs = *comme tout le monde, il a des hauts et des bas.*

UP (adj) *levé, -e* : is he up yet ? = *est-ce qu'il est déjà levé ?* ⓒ awake = *réveillé* ≠ asleep = *endormi* ☠ *la séance est levée* = the meeting's adjourned

up and about = *sur pied* : two days after the operation, she was up and about = *deux jours après l'opération, elle était sur pied* ≠ laid up = *alité*
I'm not feeling up to par = *je ne suis pas en train* ⓒ I don't feel like my usual self = *je ne suis pas dans mon assiette*

not up to the mark = *pas à la hauteur* : your work isn't up to the mark = *votre travail n'est pas à la hauteur*
not up to par/scratch/snuff = *pas encore ça* : his work isn't up to par/scratch/snuff = *son travail, ce n'est pas encore ça.*

UP (adv) *plus haut* : they live two floors up = *ils habitent deux étages plus haut* ≠ down = *plus bas*
☠ for the use of "up" after a verb, see the verb

... it up ! = *ce que ... ! : we laughed it up* ! = *ce qu'on a ri* ! ⓪ *like crazy* = *vachement*

up close = *de près :* take the photograph up close = *prenez la photo de près,* up close, she shows her age = *de près, elle fait son âge*

up for grabs = *à qui veut le prendre :* now that he's dead his job's up for grabs = *maintenant qu'il est mort, son poste est à qui veut le prendre*

to be up to no good = *ne rien*

faire de bien

he's up to his old tricks again = *il recommence à faire des siennes*

(it's) up to you ! = *à toi de décider* !

to run/walk up and down = *aller et venir :* I walked up and down on Fifth Avenue = *j'allais et venais sur la Cinquième Avenue* ⓪ *to walk to and fro* = *marcher de long en large*

up to = *jusqu'à :* it can cost up to $ 500 a day = *ça peut coûter*

jusqu'à 500 dollars par jour

up to here ! = *j'en ai jusque-là* ! ⓪ I've had it ! = *j'en ai plein le dos* !

up to now = *jusqu'à présent :* we haven't had any problems up to now = *jusqu'à présent, nous n'avons eu aucun problème* ⓪ *so far* = *jusque-là*

up to then (we were getting on well) = *jusqu'alors (nous nous entendions bien)*

up yours ! = *je t'emmerde* ! → BUZZ OFF !

UP (to, -ped) *faire monter :* they upped their prices = *ils ont fait monter leurs prix* ⓪ *to hike* = *augmenter fortement* ≠ *to drop* = *(faire) chuter*

to up and do stg = *faire qqch aussi sec :* he upped and left = *il est parti aussi sec.*

UP-AND-COMING (adj) *qui a le vent en poupe :* an up-and-coming actress = *une actrice qui a le vent en poupe* ⓪ *rising* = *qui monte.*

UPBEAT (adj) *rose :* an upbeat time in my life = *une période rose de ma vie* ≠ *downbeat* = *morose* ☠ → pink.

UPBRINGING (n) *éducation (f) :* a strict upbringing = *une éducation stricte* ☠ → education.

UPCOMING (adj) *très prochain, -e :* the upcoming release of the film = *la sortie très prochaine du film.*

UPDATE (to, -d) *mettre à jour :* to update a report/a dictionary = *mettre un rapport/un dictionnaire à jour* = to bring up to date.

UP-FRONT (adj) *clair, -e et net, nette :* they both have lovers but everything's up-front = *ils ont tous les deux des amants, mais tout est clair et net entre eux* ⓪ straightforward = *sans détours* ≠ on the sly = *en douce.*

UPGRADE (to, -d) *revaloriser :* to upgrade the quality of the hotel = *revaloriser la qualité du service de l'hôtel* ⓪ to improve = *améliorer.*

UPHEAVAL (n) *bouleversement (m) :* political/emotional upheavals = *des bouleversements politiques/affectifs* ⓪ commotion = *agitation.*

UPHILL (adj) **an uphill fight** = *un rude combat* ≠ plain sailing = *qui marche comme sur des roulettes.*

UPHOLD (to, -held, -held) **1/** *garantir :* the Constitution upholds the principle of freedom of speech = *la Constitution garantit le principe de la liberté de parole* = to guarantee ⓪ to defend = *défendre* **2/** *maintenir :* the lower court's decision was upheld = *la décision du tribunal de première instance a été maintenue* ☠ → to maintain.

UPKEEP (n) *entretien (m) :* the upkeep of a house/car = *l'entretien d'une maison/d'une voiture* ⓪ repairs ☠ → maintenance.

UPLIFT (n) *coup (m) de fouet :* the good news gave me an uplift = *la bonne nouvelle m'a donné un coup de fouet* ⓪ pick-me-up = *remontant.*

UPON (prep) → ON.

UPPER (adj) **the upper half** = *la moitié supérieure*
the upper classes = *les classes supérieures*
the upper crust = *le gratin :* a party for the upper crust of Hollywood = *une soirée pour le gratin d'Hollywood* ⓪ **the upper brackets** = *les tranches supérieures*
to have the upper hand = *avoir le dessus* ⓪ to run the show = *mener la danse.*

UPPERCLASSMAN (n, -men) *étudiant, -e des deux dernières années* ≠ freshman = *bizut.*

UPPERMOST (adj) **uppermost in one's mind** = *primordial dans son esprit* ⓪ essential = *essentiel.*

UPPITY (adj) *bêcheur, -euse :* what an uppity girl he's going out with ! = *il sort avec une fille sacrément bêcheuse* ! = uppish (GB) ⓪ snooty = *snobinard.*

UPRIGHT (adj) *intègre :* an upright lawyer/businessman = *un avocat/un homme d'affaires intègre* ≠ corrupt = *corrompu.*

UPRISING (n) *soulèvement (m) :* a student uprising = *un soulèvement d'étudiants* = rising ⓪ rebellion = *rébellion.*

UPROAR (n) *effervescence (f) :* the uproar created by his proposal = *l'effervescence créée par sa proposition* ⓪ pandemonium = *tohu-bohu*
in an uproar = *en effervescence :* the Senate was in an uproar after the President's speech = *le Sénat était en effervescence après le discours du Président.*

UPROOT (to, -ed) *déraciner* : many people were uprooted during last war = *beaucoup de gens ont été déracinés pendant la dernière guerre* ⓪ to transplant = *transplanter*.

UPSET (adj) 1/ *inquiet, -ète* : I'm upset about my father's health = *je suis inquiet pour la santé de mon père* = worried ⓪ in anguish about = *angoissé de* 2/ *bouleversé, -e* : she was so upset she couldn't do anything but cry = *elle était si bouleversée qu'elle ne pouvait que pleurer* ⓪ in a state = *dans tous ses états*
an upset stomach = *l'estomac barbouillé*.

UPSET (to, -set, -set) *bouleverser* : the change of dates upsets my plans = *le changement de dates bouleverse tous mes plans*, you upset everything by coming so late = *tu as tout bouleversé en arrivant si tard*, her crying upset the kids = *les gosses étaient bouleversés de la voir pleurer* ⓪ to mess up = *ficher en l'air*
it upsets me to (see you like that) = *ça me fait de la peine de (vous voir comme ça)*.

UPSETTING (adj) *bouleversant, -e, angoissant, -e* : an upsetting world/family situation = *une situation internationale/familiale angoissante* ⓪ disturbing = *préoccupant*, alarming = *alarmant*.

UPSHOT (n) *aboutissement* (m) : what was the upshot of the talks ? = *quel a été l'aboutissement des pourparlers ?* ⓪ result = *résultat*.

UPSIDE DOWN (adv) *sens dessus dessous* : everything's upside down = *tout est sens dessus dessous* ⓪ topsy-turvy = *en fouillis*
to turn (the room) upside down = *mettre (la chambre) sens dessus dessous* ⓪ to ransack = *saccager*.

UPSTAGE (to, -d) *éclipser* : the Secretary of State often upstages the President = *le secrétaire d'État éclipse souvent le Président* ⓪ to steal the show = *voler la vedette* ☠ *s'éclipser* = to slip out.

UPSTAIRS (adv) *en haut* : to go upstairs = *aller en haut* ≠ downstairs = *en bas*.

UPSTART (n) *jeune loup* (m) : young upstarts out for power = *de jeunes loups à l'affût du pouvoir* ⓪ go-getter = *ambitieux*.

UPSURGE (n) *recrudescence* (f) : an upsurge of violence = *une recrudescence de la violence* ≠ decline = *déclin*.

UPTAKE (n) **to be quick** ≠ **slow on the uptake** = *avoir l'esprit vif* ≠ *lent* ⓪ to be sharp as a tack = *être malin comme un singe*.

UPTIGHT (adj) 1/ *coincé, -e* : she comes from an uptight family = *elle vient d'une famille coincée* ≠ laidback = *décontracté* 2/ *complexé, -e* : she's uptight about her acne = *elle est complexée à cause de son acné* ⓪ a hang-up = *un complexe*.

UP-TO-DATE (adj) *à jour* (books, etc.), *au goût du jour* (fashion, etc.) : an up-to-date encyclopedia = *une encyclopédie à jour*, up-to-date methods/clothes = *des méthodes/des vêtements au goût du jour* ≠ out-of-date = *démodé*, old hat = *vieux jeu*.

UP-TO-THE-MINUTE (adj) *de dernière heure* (news), *le/la plus récent, -e* : up-to-the-minute news/computers = *des nouvelles de dernière heure/les ordinateurs les plus récents* ≠ outdated = *périmé*.

UPTOWN (n, adv) *quartier* (m) *résidentiel* : I live uptown = *j'habite dans le quartier résidentiel* ≠ downtown = *centre ville*.

UPTURN (n) *relance* (f) : an economic upturn = *une relance économique* ≠ recession = *récession*.

UPWARD(S) (adv) **upwards of ($ 100)** = *à partir de (100 dollars)*.

URANIUM (n) *uranium* (m) ⓪ radioactivity = *radioactivité*.

URBAN (adj) *urbain, -e* : urban life = *la vie urbaine* ≠ rural = ← **URBANISM** (n) *urbanisme* (m).

URCHIN (n) *petit, -e va-nu-pieds* : the urchins of Bogota sleep under heaps of newspapers = *les petits va-nu-pieds de Bogota dorment sous des piles de journaux* ⓪ ragamuffin = *gavroche*.

URGE TO (to, -d) *pousser à* : he urged me to go = *il m'a poussé à y aller* ⓪ to exhort to = *exhorter à*.

URGENCY (n inv) *urgence* (f) : the urgency of finding a solution = *l'urgence de trouver une solution*
☠ *service des urgences* (hôpital) = emergency room (hospital)
— *transporté d'urgence à (l'hôpital)* = rushed to (hospital).

URGENT (adj) *urgent, -e* : I must see you, it's urgent = *il faut que je vous voie, c'est urgent* ⓪ pressing = *pressant*.

URINATE (to, -d) *uriner* ⓪ bladder = *vessie*, to move one's bowels = *aller à la selle* **URINE** (n) *urine* (f) ⓪ piss = *pisse*, bedpan = *bassin*.

US (pron) *nous* (object) : she brought us food = *elle nous a apporté de la nourriture*, can you see us ? = *est-ce que tu nous vois ?*, come with us = *viens avec nous* → I ☠ → we.

USA (abbr) = United States of America = *USA* (m pl) : we're going to the USA = *nous allons aux USA* ⓪ the Star-Spangled Banner = *la bannière étoilée*.

USE (n) *usage* (m) : she lost the use of an eye = *elle a perdu l'usage d'un œil*, the current use of a word = *l'usage courant d'un mot* ⓪ usage = *emploi*, utilization = *utilisation*

to be of great use = *être d'une grande utilité* **can I be of any use ?** = *puis-je me rendre utile ?*	**I have no use for (someone like him)** = *je n'ai pas besoin de (quelqu'un comme lui)*

for my (own) use = *pour (mon) usage personnel*
it's no use (asking him again) = *ça ne sert à rien de (lui redemander ça)* ⓓ **it's useless** = *c'est inutile*
it's no use crying in your beer = *il est trop tard pour pleurer*
it's no use crying over spilt milk = *ce qui est fait est fait* ⓓ **it's too late now** = *il est trop tard*

in ≠ out of use = *usité ≠ pas usité*
to put to (good) use = *faire (bon) usage de* : I'll put the money to good use = *je ferai bon usage de cet argent*
what's the use of (repeating the same thing)? = *à quoi ça sert de (répéter la même chose)?* ⓓ **what's the good?** = *à quoi bon?*

USE (to, -d) **1/** *se servir de* : I don't know how to use your vacuum cleaner = *je ne sais pas me servir de votre aspirateur* ⓓ **to utilize** = *utiliser* **2/** *se servir de* : he used his mistress to get ahead = *il s'est servi de sa maîtresse pour faire son chemin* ⓓ **to exploit** = *exploiter* **3/** *user* : the machine uses too much power = *la machine use trop de courant* ⓓ **to consume** = *consommer*
I could use (a drink) = *je (boirais) bien quelque chose*

🕱 *user de son droit* = to exercise one's right

— *user (chaussures)* = to wear (shoes) out

to use up = *ne plus avoir* : I used up all my money/all the coffee = *je n'ai plus d'argent/de café*
as (I) used to = *qu'avant* : I can't run as fast as I used to = *je ne peux plus courir aussi vite qu'avant*

to get used to = *s'habituer à* : I'll never get used to getting up early = *je ne m'habituerai jamais à me lever tôt* ⓓ **to get accustomed to** = *s'accoutumer à.*

USED TO : *autrefois ... (sous-entendu une action qu'on ne fait plus, se traduit par l'imparfait)*

— did you use to drink a lot?
= *est-ce que vous buviez beaucoup (autrefois)?*

— yes, I did
— yes, I used to drink a lot
= *oui*
= *oui, je buvais beaucoup*

— no, I didn't
— no, I didn't use to drink a lot
= *non*
= *non, je ne buvais pas beaucoup (autrefois).*

USED TO : **to be used to (+ ING)** = *avoir l'habitude de*

— are you used to going to bed early?
= *avez-vous l'habitude de vous coucher tôt?*

— yes, I am
— yes, I'm used to going to bed early
= *oui*
= *oui, j'ai l'habitude de me coucher tôt*

— no, I'm not
— no, I'm not used to going to bed early
= *non,*
= *non, je n'ai pas l'habitude de me coucher tôt.*

USED (adj) **used cars/clothing** = *voitures/vêtements d'occasion* = secondhand.

USEFUL (adj) *utile* : take an umbrella, it could be useful = *prenez un parapluie, ça pourrait bien être utile* ⓓ handy = *commode*
🕱 *en temps utile* = in due time
— *ne pas juger utile de* = to see no point in
— *elle est utile* = she's helpful.

USELESS (adj) *inutile* : it's useless asking him = *il est inutile de le lui demander* ≠ useful = *utile* 🕱 *inutile de dire que* = needless to say that.

USHER (n) *ouvreur* (m) **USHERETTE** (n) *ouvreuse* (f).

USHER IN (to, -ed) *voir le début de* : his election ushered in a period of optimism = *son élection a vu le début d'une période d'optimisme* ⓓ to inaugurate = *inaugurer.*

USSR (n) *URSS* (f) ⓓ Soviet Union = *Union soviétique.*

USUAL (adj) *habituel, -elle* : he said it with his usual frankness = *il l'a dit avec sa franchise habituelle* ⓓ customary = *coutumier* ≠ unusual = *inhabituel*
it's not usual to (drink wine with meals in the United States) = *ce n'est pas courant de (boire du vin aux repas aux États-Unis)*
not to feel like one's usual self = *ne pas être dans son assiette* ≠ to be raring to go = *péter le feu*
🕱 *l'anglais usuel* = everyday English.

USUALLY (adj) *d'habitude, habituellement* : they usually have dinner late = *d'habitude/habituellement ils dînent tard* ⓓ ordinarily = *d'ordinaire*, commonly = *communément.*

USURP (to, -ed) *usurper :* to usurp power = *usurper le pouvoir* ⓓ to seize = *saisir.*

USURY (n, -ies) *usure (f)* ⓓ usurer = *usurier,* usurious = *usuraire.*

UTENSIL (n) *ustensile (m) :* kitchen utensils = *ustensiles de cuisine* ⓓ tool = *outil.*

UTERUS (n, -i or -es) *utérus (m)* ⓓ vagina = *vagin.*

UTILIZE (to, -d) *utiliser :* to utilize solar energy = *utiliser l'énergie solaire* ⓓ to exploit = *exploiter* ☠ *elle utilise son nom de jeune fille* = she goes by/uses her maiden name.

UTMOST (n) **at the (very) utmost** = *(tout) au plus :* it'll cost $ 100 at the utmost = *ça coûtera au plus 100 dollars* ⓓ at the maximum = *au maximum,* at the very most = *à tout casser*
to do one's utmost = *faire tout son possible :* he did his utmost to help us = *il a fait tout son possible pour nous aider* ⓓ to do one's best = *faire de son mieux.*

UTMOST (adj) *le plus grand, la plus grande :* it's of utmost importance = *c'est de la plus grande importance* ≠ minor = *mineur.*

UTOPIA (n) *utopie (f) :* a world without war seems to be an utopia = *un monde sans guerre semble être une utopie* **UTOPIAN** (adj) *utopique :* utopian ideas = *des idées utopiques.*

UTTER (adj) *parfait, -e :* he's an utter idiot = *c'est un parfait idiot,* an utter stranger = *un parfait inconnu* ⓓ perfect ⓓ unmitigated = *consommé,* rank = *fieffé* **UTTERLY** (adv) *complètement :* you're utterly mistaken = *tu te trompes complètement* ⓓ fully = *pleinement.*

U-TURN (n) *demi-tour (m) :* he made a U-turn = *il a fait demi-tour.*

VACANCY (n, -ies) *vacance (f)* : a job vacancy = *une vacance de poste*
☠ *prendre des vacances* = to take a vacation
— *vacances parlementaires* = (Congress) recess.

VACANT (adj) *vacant, -e* : a vacant apartment = *un appartement vacant* ⓪ empty = *vide*
vacant lot = *terrain vague.*

VACATE (to, -d) *libérer* : all rooms must be vacated before noon = *toutes les chambres doivent être libérées avant midi* ☠ → to liberate.

VACATION (n) *vacances (f pl)* : where are you going on vacation ? = *où partez-vous en vacances ?* ☠ → vacancy.

VACCINATE (to, -d) *vacciner* **VACCINATION** (n) *vaccination (f)* **VACCINE** (n) *vaccin (m).*

VACILLATE (to, -d) *balancer* : he keeps vacillating on the question = *il ne cesse de balancer sur cette question* ⓪ to waver = *tergiverser* ☠ → to chuck.

VACUUM (n) *vide (m)* : his leaving left a vacuum in my life = *son départ a laissé un vide dans ma vie*
vacuum cleaner = *aspirateur* ⓪ carpet sweeper = *balai mécanique,* broom = *balai*
☠ → emptiness.

VACUUM (to, -ed) *passer l'aspirateur.*

VAGABOND (n) *vagabond, -e* : to lead the life of a vagabond = *mener une existence de vagabond* ⓪ gypsy = *gitan.*

VAGINA (n) *vagin (m)* ⓪ womb = *matrice.*

VAGRANT (n) *vagabond, -e, mendiant, -e* : vagrants wandering all over the country = *des vagabonds/des mendiants qui parcourent le pays* ⓪ bum = *clochard.*

VAGUE (adj, -r, -st) *vague* : a vague answer = *une réponse vague* ⓪ hazy = *flou* ≠ clear = *net* **VAGUELY** (adv) *vaguement.*

VAIN (adj, -er, -est) **1/** *vain, -e* : a vain attempt = *une tentative vaine* ⓪ useless = *inutile* **2/** *vaniteux, -euse* : a vain person = *une personne vaniteuse* ⓪ pretentious = *prétentieux*

in vain = *en vain* : our efforts were in vain = *nous avons fait tous ces efforts en vain* ⓪ to no end = *qui ne sert à rien.*

VALEDICTORIAN (n) *lauréat, -e qui fait un discours à la sortie d'une promotion.*

VALENTINE'S DAY (n) *la Saint-Valentin* ⓪ sweethearts = *amoureux.*

VALET (n) *valet (m) de chambre* ⓪ servant = *domestique,* lady's maid = *femme de chambre* ☠ *valet (de cœur)* = jack (of hearts).

VALID (adj) **1/** *valable* : a valid argument/reason = *un argument/une raison valable* ≠ farfetched = *tiré par les cheveux* ☠ *quelqu'un de valable/une cause valable* = a worthy person/cause **2/** *valide* : a valid passport = *un passeport valide* ≠ out-of-date = *périmé* ☠ *des hommes valides* = able-bodied men.

VALIDATE (to, -d) *prouver la valeur de* : that validates his alibi = *cela prouve la valeur de son alibi.*

VALISE (n) *valise (f)* : my valise is heavy = *ma valise est lourde* ⓪ overnight case = *baise-en-ville,* hand luggage = *bagage à main*
☠ *faire sa valise* = to pack
— *valise diplomatique* = diplomatic pouch
— *des valises sous les yeux* = bags under the eyes.

VALLEY (n) *vallée (f)* : Death Valley = *la Vallée de la Mort* ⓪ canyon = ← ≠ hill = *colline.*

VALUABLE (adj) *de grande valeur* : a valuable ring = *une bague de grande valeur* ≠ valueless = *sans valeur.*

VALUABLES (n pl) *objets (m pl) de valeur* : leave your valuables in the safe = *laissez vos objets de valeur au coffre* ⓪ jewels = *bijoux.*

VALUE (n) *valeur (f)* : the value of his estate has doubled = *la valeur de sa propriété a doublé* ⓪ price = *prix* ☠ *valeurs en Bourse* = stocks and securities.

VALUE (to, -d) *tenir à* : I value your friendship = *je tiens à votre amitié* ⓪ to prize = *attacher du prix à.*

VALUE-ADDED TAX (n, -es) *taxe (f) à la valeur ajoutée, TVA (f).*

VALUES (n pl) *valeurs (f pl)* : old-fashioned values = *des valeurs démodées.*

VALVE (n) *valve (f)* ⓪ pipe = *tuyau.*

VAMP (n) *vamp (f)* : she plays the part of a vamp = *elle joue le rôle d'une vamp* ⓪ siren = *femme fatale.*

VAMPIRE (n) *vampire (m)* ⓪ blood = *sang.*

VAN (n) **1/** *poids lourd (m)* : lots of vans on the highway = *beaucoup de poids lourds sur l'autoroute*
moving van = *camion de déménagement*
☠ *poids lourd (boxe)* = heavyweight
2/ *caravane (f)* : to travel in a van = *voyager en caravane* ⓪ trailer = *roulotte.*

VANDAL (n) *vandale (m, f)* : vandals broke the shop-windows = *des vandales ont brisé les vitrines des magasins* ⓪ hoodlum = *loubard*, trasher = *casseur* **VANDAL-ISM** (n) *vandalisme (m)* ⓪ riots = *émeutes.*

VANGUARD (n) **in the vanguard of (experimental theater)** = *à l'avant-garde du (théâtre expérimental).*

VANILLA (n) *vanille (f)* ⓪ flavor = *parfum.*

VANISH (to, -ed) *disparaître* : cigarette advertising has vanished from TV = *la publicité pour les cigarettes a disparu de la télé* = to disappear.

VANITY (n, -ies) *vanité (f)* : what vanity ! = *quelle vanité !* ⓪ conceit = *suffisance* ☠ *tirer vanité de* = to take great pride in.

VANQUISH (to, -ed) *vaincre* : to vanquish one's fear = *vaincre sa peur* = to conquer ⓪ to overcome = *surmonter* ☠ *l'armée a été vaincue* = the army was defeated *(« to defeat » est plus utilisé que « to vanquish »).*

VARIANCE (n) **at variance with (professional ethics)** = *en désaccord avec (l'éthique de la profession).*

VARIATION (n) **1/** *variation (f)* : price/temperature variations = *des variations de prix/de température* ⓪ change = *changement* **2/** *variante (f)* : all his speeches are only variations on the same theme = *tous ses discours ne sont que des variantes du même thème.*

VARIED (adj) *varié, -e* : varied meals = *des repas variés* ⓪ diverse = *divers.*

VARIETY (n, -ies) *variété (f)* : a great variety of dishes on the menu = *une grande variété de plats au menu* ⓪ diversity = *diversité*
variety is the spice of life = *tout nouveau tout beau/l'ennui naquit un jour de l'uniformité*
variety show = *spectacle de variétés.*

VARIOUS (adj) *divers, -e* : various kinds of ice cream = *diverses sortes de glaces*, for various reasons = *pour diverses raisons* ⓪ several = *plusieurs* ☠ → diverse.

VARY (to, -ied) *varier* : the price of gas varies from one country to another = *le prix de l'essence varie d'un pays à l'autre* ⓪ to differ = *différer.*

VASE (n) *vase (m)* : put the flowers in a vase = *mettez les fleurs dans un vase* ☠ *vivre en vase clos* = to live cut off from the world.

VAST (adj, -er, -est) *vaste (place)*, *énorme* : vast rooms/differences = *de vastes pièces/des différences énormes* = enormous ⓪ immense = ← **VASTLY** (adv) *infiniment* ⓪ immensely = *immensément.*

VATICAN (n) *Vatican (m)* ⓪ Pope = *pape.*

VAUDEVILLE (n) *vaudeville (m)* : a vaudeville show = *un spectacle de vaudeville.*

VAULT (n) *chambre (f) forte* : the bank's vault = *la chambre forte de la banque.*

VD (abbr) = venereal disease = *maladie (f) vénérienne* ⓪ AIDS = *SIDA.*

VEAL (n) *veau (m)* : veal cutlets = *escalopes de veau*, veal chop = *côtelette de veau* ⓪ meat = *viande* ☠ *veau (animal)* = calf
— *cette voiture est un veau* = this car's a dud.

VEEP (n) *vice-président, -e* = VP.

VEER (to, -ed) *virer* : the party veered to the left = *le parti a viré à gauche* ☠ *virer qqn* = to can s.o.

VEGETABLE (n) *légume (m)* : vegetable soup = *soupe aux légumes* ☠ *une grosse légume* = a big shot	
artichoke = *artichaut*	**leek** = *poireau*
asparagus = *asperge*	**lettuce** = *laitue*
bean sprouts = *soja*	**mushroom** = *champignon*
beet = *betterave*	
broccoli = *brocoli*	**onion** = *oignon*
Brussels sprouts = *choux de Bruxelles*	**peas** = *petits pois*
	potato = *pomme de terre*
cabbage = *chou*	
carrot = *carotte*	**spinach** = *épinard*
cauliflower = *chou-fleur*	**squash** = *courge*
	string beans = *haricots verts*
celery = *céleri*	
cucumber = *concombre*	**tomato** = *tomate*
	turnip = *navet*
eggplant = *aubergine*	**zucchini** = *courgette.*

VEGETARIAN (n, adj) *végétarien, -enne* : vegetarians don't eat meat = *les végétariens ne mangent pas de viande* ≠ carnivore = ←.

VEGETATE (to, -d) *végéter* : I'm not really living, just vegetating = *je ne vis pas vraiment, je végète* ⓪ to stagnate = *stagner.*

VEHEMENCE (n) *véhémence (f)* : to answer with vehemence = *répondre avec véhémence* ⓪ violence = ←.

VEHEMENT (adj) *véhément, -e* : a vehement reply = *une réplique véhémente* ⓪ fervid = *fervent* **VEHEM-**

ENTLY (adv) *avec véhémence :* to deny vehemently = *il a nié avec véhémence avoir couché avec sa belle-sœur.*

VEHICLE (n) 1/ *véhicule (m) :* cars are vehicles = *les voitures sont des véhicules* 2/ *moyen (m) de mettre qqn/qqch en valeur :* his movies are vehicles for his wife = *ses films sont des moyens de mettre sa femme en valeur.*

VEIL (n) *voile (f) :* Arab women still have to wear veils = *les femmes arabes doivent encore porter le voile* ☠ *voile (de bateau)* = sail
— *on met les voiles !* = let's split !

VEIN (n) *veine (f) :* to cut one's veins = *se taillader les veines* ⓓ artery = *artère,* blood vessel = *vaisseau sanguin*
a vein of (pessimism) = *un fond de (pessimisme)* ☠ *quelle veine !* = what good luck !

VELVET (n, adj) *velours (m) :* a velvet skirt = *une jupe de velours* ⓓ corduroy = *velours côtelé*
☠ *faire des yeux de velours à* = to make sheep's eyes at
— *jouer sur du velours* = to play it safe.

VELVETY (adj) *velouté, -e* ⓓ silky = *soyeux.*

VENEER (n) *vernis (m) :* a veneer of sophistication = *un vernis de sophistication* ⓓ appearance = *apparence* ☠ → polish.

VENEREAL (adj) **venereal disease** = *maladie vénérienne* = VD ⓓ gonorrhea = *blennorragie.*

VENEZUELA (n) *Venezuela (m)* **VENEZUELAN** (n, adj) *Vénézuélien, -enne.*

VENGEANCE (n) *vengeance (f) :* a terrible vengeance = *une vengeance terrible* ⓓ reprisals = *représailles*
(to get back) with a vengeance = *la vengeance est un plat qui se mange froid* ⓓ to take one's revenge = *prendre sa revanche.*

VENGEFUL (adj) *revanchard, -e :* a vengeful, bitter woman = *une femme amère et revancharde* ⓓ revengeful = *vengeur.*

VENOM (n) *venin (m) :* a snake's venom = *le venin d'un serpent* ⓓ poison = ← **VENOMOUS** (adj) *venimeux, -euse.*

VENT (n) **to give vent to (one's anger)** = *donner libre cours à (sa colère)* ≠ to hold back = *refouler.*

VENTILATE (to, -d) *ventiler :* the room is badly ventilated = *la pièce est mal ventilée* ⓓ to air = *aérer* **VENTILATION** (n) *ventilation (f)* ☠ *ventilation des coûts* = breakdown of the costs.

VENTRILOQUIST (n) *ventriloque (m, f) :* Bergen was a famous ventriloquist = *Bergen était un ventriloque célèbre* ⓓ puppet = *pantin.*

VENTURE (n) *entreprise (f) risquée :* a wild business venture = *une entreprise commerciale vachement risquée* ⓓ risk = *risque.*

VENTURE (to, -d) *hasarder :* he ventured a question = *il a hasardé une question* ⓓ to chance = *risquer*
to venture to = *se hasarder à :* he ventured to ask her age = *il s'est hasardé à lui demander son âge.*

VERB (n) *verbe (m) :* "to die" is a verb = « *mourir* » *est un verbe* ⓓ infinitive = *infinitif,* participle = *participe,* tense = *temps.*

VERBAL (adj) *verbal, -e :* a verbal agreement = *un accord verbal* ≠ written = *écrit* **VERBALLY** (adv) *verbalement.*

VERBALIZE (to, -d) *traduire en paroles :* to verbalize one's feelings = *traduire ses sentiments en paroles* ⓓ to express = *exprimer.*

VERBATIM (adv) *textuellement :* he said that verbatim = *il a dit ça textuellement* ⓓ word for word = *mot pour mot.*

VERBOSE (adj) *verbeux, -euse :* a verbose orator = *un orateur verbeux* ⓓ prolix = *prolixe* ≠ concise = *concis.*

VERDICT (n) *verdict (m) :* a verdict of guilty = *un verdict de culpabilité* ⓓ sentence = ←.

VERGE (n) **on the verge of (a breakdown/tears)** = *au bord de (la dépression nerveuse)/des (larmes)* ⓓ on the brink of = *à deux doigts de.*

VERIFY (to, -ied) *vérifier :* they'll have to verify his alibi = *il va falloir qu'ils vérifient son alibi* = to check ⓓ to confirm = *confirmer* **VERIFICATION** (n) *vérification (f).*

VERSATILE (adj) *aux talents multiples :* a versatile entertainer = *un artiste de variétés aux talents multiples* ⓓ all-around = *complet* ☠ *elle est très versatile* = she's very mercurial.

VERSE (n) *vers (m) :* a play in verse = *une pièce en vers* ⓓ stanza = *strophe/stance* ☠ → worm.

VERSION (n) *version (f) :* that's my version of the story = *voilà ma version de l'affaire* ⓓ account = *compte rendu.*

VERSUS (adv) *contre :* the pill versus the IUD = *la pilule contre le stérilet,* Hamburg versus Liverpool = *Hambourg contre Liverpool* = vs ⓓ opposed to = *opposé à* ☠ → against.

VERTEBRA (n, -e) *vertèbre (f)* ⓓ spine = *colonne vertébrale.*

VERTICAL (adj) *vertical, -e :* a vertical line = *une ligne verticale* ⓓ perpendicular = *perpendiculaire.*

VERY (adv) *très :* he's very tired/happy/rich = *il est très fatigué/heureux/riche* ≠ a bit = *un peu,* hardly = *à peine*

---

the very best ≠ **worst (restaurant)** = *le meilleur (restaurant)* ≠ *le pire des (restaurants)*
very much = *beaucoup* : I like Chinese food/him very much = *j'aime beaucoup la cuisine chinoise/je l'aime beaucoup*
very much like (his father) = *tout à fait comme (son père)*
very much more (intelligent) = *beaucoup plus (intelligent)*
very much so ! = *et comment !*

very nearly = *bien faillir* : we very nearly had an accident = *nous avons bien failli avoir un accident* ⓪ just about = *quasiment*
the very same (day/month/guy) = *le (jour/mois/type) même*
very soon = *très bientôt* : I hope he'll come very soon = *j'espère qu'il viendra très bientôt*
very well = *très bien* : she writes very well = *elle écrit très bien*
you know that very well ! = *tu le sais très bien !*

--- GROUP : VERY = TRÈS ---

abominably = *abominablement*
absolutely = *absolument*
abundantly = *abondamment*
as ... as anything = *comme tout* = **as ... as can be/as ... as they come**
as hell = *sacrément*
awfully = *drôlement/affreusement*
bad = *méchamment* = **badly**
beyond belief = *c'est à ne pas le croire*
bloody = *salement*
completely = *complètement*
considerably = *considérablement*
damned = *vachement*
darned = *bigrement*
decidedly = *décidément*
dreadfully = *terriblement*
enormously = *extrêmement/ énormément*
entirely = *entièrement*
ever so = *tellement*
exceedingly = *excessivement*
exceptionally = *exceptionnellement*
excessively = *excessivement*
extraordinarily = *extraordinairement*
extremely = *extrêmement*
fabulously = *fabuleusement*
fantastically = *formidablement*

fiercely = *farouchement*
frightfully = *effroyablement*
fucking = *putain ce que*
genuinely = *véritablement*
goddamn = *foutrement*
good and = *bel et bien*
greatly = *grandement*
highly = *hautement*
a hundred percent = *à cent pour cent*
hyper = ←
immensely = *immensément*
impossibly = *incroyablement* = **incredibly**
infinitely = *infiniment*
inordinately = *démesurément*
insanely = *follement*
intensely = *intensément*
jolly = *bien*
keenly = *vivement*
like anything = *vachement* = **like crazy**
like I don't know what = *comme je ne sais quoi*
like mad = *vachement* = **like nobody's business**
mighty = *bougrement*
most = *fort*
nice and = *agréablement*
outrageously = *horriblement (outrageusement)*
phenomenally = *phénoménalement*

plenty = *très très*
positively = *absolument*
pretty = *drôlement*
quite = *tout à fait*
quite simply = *tout bonnement*
real = *rudement*
really = *vraiment*
really and truly = *vraiment très*
remarkably = *remarquablement*
simply = *tout simplement*
so = *tellement/si*
so very = *vraiment très*
super = ←
sure = *archi-*
terribly = *terriblement* = **terrifically**
to a fault = *à l'excès*
totally = *totalement*
tremendously = *prodigieusement*
truly = *réellement*
ultra = *ultra-*
unbelievably = *incroyablement*
unusually = *exceptionnellement*
vitally = *excessivement*
way too = *bien trop*
wildly = *follement.*

VERY (adj) *même* : I stayed in that very hotel = *j'ai séjourné dans cet hôtel même* ☠ → same.

---

at that very moment = *au moment même*
at the very beginning ≠ **end** = *tout au début/au tout début* ≠ *tout à la fin*
for that very reason (I won't go) = *pour cela même (je n'irai pas)*
the very best = *ce qu'il y a de mieux* : they only buy the very best = *ils n'achètent que ce qu'il y a de mieux*
that's the very thing (I was looking for) = *c'est*

tout à fait ce que (je cherchais)
the very thought of him/mention of his name = *rien que de penser à lui/rien que de mentionner son nom* ⓪ the mere ... = *le simple (fait de) ...*
this very moment = *à l'instant même* : I'm leaving this very moment = *je pars à l'instant même* ⓪ just now = *dès maintenant*
to the very end = *jusqu'au bout* : we stayed to the very end = *nous sommes restés jusqu'au bout.*

VESSEL (n) *vaisseau (m)* : blood vessel = *vaisseau sanguin*, vessels at sea = *des vaisseaux en mer* ⓪ ship = *bateau*.

VEST (n) *gilet (m)* = waistcoat (GB) ⓪ jacket = *veste* ☠ *gilet de sauvetage* = life jacket.

VESTIGE (n) *vestige (m)* : vestiges of old civilizations = *des vestiges d'anciennes civilisations* ⓪ trace = ←.

VET (n) **1/** *véto (m, f)* ⓪ veterinarian = *vétérinaire* **2/** *ancien combattant (m)*.

VETERAN (n) *ancien combattant (m), vétéran (m)* : a pension for veterans = *une pension pour les anciens combattants* = vet/ex-serviceman ⓪ disabled ex-servicemen = *invalides de guerre*.

VETERINARIAN (n) *vétérinaire (m, f)* : he's an excellent veterinarian = *c'est un excellent vétérinaire*.

VETO (n inv) *veto (m)* : Congress is trying to overrule the President's veto = *le Congrès essaie de casser le veto du Président* **VETO** (to, -ed) *opposer son veto à* : the President might veto the bill = *le Président pourrait opposer son veto au projet de loi*.

VEX (to, -ed) *contrarier* : you'll vex him with your questions = *vous allez le contrarier avec vos questions* ⓪ to aggravate = *agacer*
☠ *contrarier* → to frustrate
— *vexer qqn* = to hurt/offend s.o.

VIA (prep) *via* : we flew to Boston via London = *nous avons pris l'avion pour Boston via Londres*.

VIABLE (adj) *envisageable* : a viable solution = *une solution envisageable* ⓪ feasible = *faisable*.

VIBES (n pl) *(bonne) ambiance (f)* : what great vibes in that jazz club ! = *quelle super-ambiance dans ce club de jazz !*
there are good ≠ bad vibes between us = *le courant passe ≠ ne passe pas entre nous* ⓪ it's a question of chemistry = *c'est une question de peau*.

VIBRATE (to, -d) *vibrer* : the plane was vibrating = *l'avion vibrait* ⓪ to shake = *secouer* **VIBRATION** (n) *vibration (f)* **VIBRATOR** (n) *vibromasseur (m)*.

VICARIOUS (adj) *par personne interposée* : porn films give him vicarious thrills = *les films pornos lui donnent des frissons par personne interposée*.

VICE (n) *vice (m)* : I have no minor vices = *je n'ai pas de vices mineurs* ⓪ perversity = *perversité*
the vice squad = *la (brigade) mondaine/la brigade des mœurs*
☠ *c'est du vice !* = it's sheer perversion !
— *vice de fabrication* = manufacturing defect.

VICE-PRESIDENT (n) *vice-président, -e* = veep.

VICE VERSA (adv) *vice versa* : parents should be patient with children and vice versa = *les parents devraient être patients avec les enfants et vice versa* ⓪ conversely = *inversement*.

VICINITY (n inv) **(to earn) in the vicinity of ($ 50,000)** = *(gagner) autour de (50 000 dollars)*
(to live) in the vicinity = *(habiter) à proximité* ⓪ in the neighborhood = *dans le voisinage*.

VICIOUS (adj) *malveillant, -e* : what a vicious thing to say ! = *que c'est malveillant de dire ça !* ⓪ hateful = *haïssable*
vicious circle = *cercle vicieux* ⓪ to go round in circles = *tourner en rond*
☠ *il est vicieux* = he's perverse
— *une femme vicieuse* = a lecherous woman.

VICIOUSLY (adv) *avec malveillance* **VICIOUSNESS** (n) *malveillance (f), malfaisance (f)*.

VICISSITUDES (n pl) *vicissitudes (f pl)* : the vicissitudes of life = *les vicissitudes de la vie* ⓪ ups and downs = *les hauts et les bas*.

VICTIM (n) *victime (f)* : the victims of the accident = *les victimes de l'accident*.

VICTIMIZE (to, -d) *martyriser* : he's victimized by his elder brother = *son grand frère le martyrise* ⓪ to persecute = *persécuter*.

VICTORIOUS (adj) *victorieux, -euse* : a victorious army = *une armée victorieuse* ≠ defeated = *vaincu*.

VICTORY (n, -ies) *victoire (f)* : a GOP victory = *une victoire du Parti républicain* ⓪ triumph = *triomphe*.

VIDEO (n) *vidéo (f)* : video tape = *vidéocassette* ⓪ VCR = *magnétoscope*.

VIE FOR (to, -d) *être en compétition pour* : swimmers from every country were vying for the title = *des nageurs de tous les pays étaient en compétition pour le titre* ⓪ to rival = *rivaliser*.

VIETNAM (n) *Viêt-nam (m)* **VIETNAMESE** (n, adj) *Vietnamien, -enne*.

VIEW (n) *vue (f)* : my room has a splendid view = *ma chambre a une vue splendide*
in view = *en vue* : she has no job in view = *elle n'a aucun boulot en vue*
in view of = *en raison de* : in view of the weather the game was called off = *la partie a été annulée en raison du temps* ⓪ because of = *à cause de*
on view = *exposé* : the crown jewels are on view = *les joyaux de la couronne sont exposés*
in my view (you should call her) = *à mon avis (vous devriez l'appeler)* ⓪ to my mind = *à mon sens*
what are his views on (feminism) ? = *quelles sont ses idées sur (le féminisme) ?* ⓪ standpoint = *point de vue*
with a view to = *en vue de* : I'm saving money with a view to buying a car = *j'économise de l'argent en vue d'acheter une voiture* ⓪ with a mind to = *dans la perspective de*
☠ *à vue d'œil/de nez* = at a rough guess
— *elle maigrit à vue d'œil* = you can virtually see her getting thinner and thinner

— *avoir des vues sur* = to have designs on
— *une vue d'ensemble (du problème)* = a general idea (of the problem)
— *perdre qqch de vue* = to lose sight of stg
— *connaître qqn de vue* = to know s.o. on sight
— *une bonne vue* = good vision/good eyesight.

VIEWPOINT (n) *point (m) de vue* : from the consumer's viewpoint = *du point de vue du consommateur* = point of view ⓓ way of thinking = *avis*.

VIGIL (n) *veille (f)* : exhausted after a long vigil = *épuisé après une longue veille*
she kept a vigil (at his bedside the whole night) = *elle a veillé (à son chevet toute la nuit)*
☠ → eve.

VIGOR (n) *vigueur (f)* : full of vigor = *plein de vigueur* = vigour (GB) ⓓ spunk = *nerf* ☠ *entrer en vigueur* = to come into effect.

VIGOROUS (adj) *vigoureux, -euse* : a vigorous effort/style = *un effort/style vigoureux* ⓓ energetic = *énergique*.

VILE (adj, -r, -st) *vil, -e (s.o.), infect, -e* : vile language = *langage vil*, the food was vile = *la cuisine était infecte* → AWFUL ☠ *à vil prix* = at a ridiculously low price.

VILLA (n) *villa (f)* : a villa in Cannes = *une villa à Cannes* ⓓ estate = *propriété*.

VILLAGE (n) *village (m)* : a fishing village = *un village de pêche* ⓓ community = *communauté* **VILLAGER** (n) *villageois, -e*.

VILLAIN (n) *méchant, -e* : he's the villain of the story = *c'est le méchant de l'histoire* ⓓ knave = *gredin*.

VIM (n) *entrain (m)* : full of vim = *plein d'entrain* ⓓ punch = ←.

VINDICATE (to, -d) **1/** *justifier* : all my efforts were vindicated = *tous mes efforts ont été justifiés* = to justify **2/** *innocenter* : the defendant was vindicated = *l'accusé a été innocenté* ⓓ to clear = *disculper*.

VINDICTIVE (adj) *vindicatif, -ive* : she's spiteful and vindictive = *elle est rancunière et vindicative* ≠ forgiving = *indulgent*.

VINE (n) *vigne (f)* : grapes grow on vines = *les raisins poussent sur les vignes* ⓓ vineyard = *vignoble*.

VINEGAR (n) *vinaigre (m)* ⓓ oil = *huile* ☠ *tourner au vinaigre* = to turn sour.

VIOLATE (to, -d) *violer* : to violate the law = *violer la loi* ⓓ to infringe = *enfreindre* ☠ → to rape **VIOLATION** (n) *violation (f)* : violation of the law = *violation de la loi* ⓓ infringement = *transgression*.

VIOLENCE (n) *violence (f)* : the escalation of violence = *l'escalade de la violence* ≠ nonviolence = *non-violence*.

VIOLENT (adj) *violent, -e* : a violent woman/reaction = *une femme/réaction violente* ⓓ brutal = ← **VIOLENTLY** (adv) *violemment*.

VIOLET (n, adj) *violet, -ette* : a violet dress = *une robe violette* ⓓ mauve = ←.

VIOLIN (n) *violon (m)* : to play the violin = *jouer du violon* ⓓ cello = *violoncelle*, fiddle = *crincrin* ☠ *c'est comme si on pissait dans un violon* = it's like pulling your pecker
— *un violon d'Ingres* = a hobby
— *accorder ses violons* = to get one's signals straight
— *passer une nuit au violon* = to spend a night in the clink.

VIOLINIST (n) *violoniste (m, f)* ⓓ fiddler = *violoneux*.

VIP (abbr) = very important person = *personnage (m) de marque* ≠ small fry = *menu fretin*.

VIRGIN (n) *vierge (f)* : she was still a virgin at 32 = *elle était encore vierge à 32 ans* ⓓ maiden = *pucelle* ≠ to deflower = *déflorer*
the Virgin Mary = *la Sainte Vierge*.

VIRGINITY (n, -ies) *virginité (f)* ⓓ hymen = ←.

VIRILE (adj) *viril, -e* : he doesn't like virile men = *il n'aime pas les hommes virils* ⓓ masculine = *masculin* **VIRILITY** (n, -ies) *virilité (f)*.

VIRTUAL (adj) *en fait* : I've lived with him for a year, but we're still virtual strangers = *même si je vis avec lui depuis un an, en fait nous sommes encore des étrangers*.

VIRTUALLY (adj) *quasiment* : he's virtually unknown in America = *il est quasiment inconnu en Amérique* ⓓ practically = *pratiquement*.

VIRTUE (n) *vertu (f)* : is virginity a virtue ? = *est-ce que la virginité est une vertu ?* ≠ vice = ←
by/in virtue of (his diplomatic status) = *en vertu de (son statut diplomatique)* ⓓ by reason of = *en raison de*
to make a virtue of necessity = *faire de nécessité vertu*.

VIRTUOSO (n) *virtuose (m, f)* ≠ novice = ←.

VIRTUOUS (adj) *vertueux, -euse* : a virtuous life = *une vie vertueuse* ≠ debauched = *débauché*.

VIRULENT (adj) *virulent, -e* : a virulent attack = *une attaque virulente* ⓓ harmful = *nuisible*.

VIRUS (n, -es) *virus (m)* : to catch a virus = *attraper un virus* ⓓ microbe = ← ☠ *il a le virus de ...* = he has a mania for ...

VISA (n) *visa (m)* : you need a visa to go to the USSR = *il faut un visa pour aller en URSS* ⓓ passport = *passeport*.

VISCERAL (adj) *viscéral, -e* : a visceral reaction = *une réaction viscérale* ⓓ instinctive = *instinctif*.

VISIBILITY (n, -ies) *visibilité (f)* : poor visibility = *une visibilité médiocre*.

VISIBLE (adj) *visible* : a visible dislike for her mother-in-law = *une aversion visible pour sa belle-mère* ≠ invisible = ← **VISIBLY** (adv) *visiblement* : she was visibly angry = *visiblement, elle était en colère* ⓪ obviously = *de toute évidence*.

VISION (n) *vue* (f) : my eyes are good and my vision is perfect = *j'ai de bons yeux et ma vue est parfaite*
to have visions = *avoir des visions*
she's a vision (in her new dress) = *elle est belle comme tout (dans sa nouvelle robe)*
☠ → view.

VISIT (n) *visite* (f) : she's too sick to have visits = *elle est trop malade pour recevoir des visites*
to pay a visit to (one's family) = *rendre visite à (sa famille)*
☠ *carte de visite* = calling card.

VISIT (to, -ed) *rendre visite à* : to visit friends = *rendre visite à des amis*
☠ *visiter un musée* = to go to a museum
— *visiter une ville* = to go round/to tour a city/to go sight-seeing.

VISITING (adj) *de visite* : visiting hours/rights = *heures/droit de visite*.

VISITOR (n) *visiteur, -euse* : no visitors before one o'clock = *pas de visiteur avant une heure* ⓪ guest = *invité*, company = *du monde*.

VISUALIZE (to, -d) *imaginer* : I can't visualize him doing a striptease = *je ne l'imagine pas en train de faire un strip-tease* = to imagine ☠ → to imagine.

VITAL (adj) *vital, -e* : the vital organs = *les organes vitaux* ⓪ essential = *essentiel*
what are her vital statistics ? = *quelles sont ses mensurations ?*

VITALITY (n, -ies) *vitalité* (f) : full of vitality = *plein de vitalité* ⓪ vigor = *vigueur*.

VITALLY (adv) *excessivement* : vitally important = *excessivement important* = excessively → VERY.

VITAMIN (n) *vitamine* (f) : she lacks vitamins = *elle manque de vitamines*.

VIVACIOUS (adj) *pétulant, -e* : a vivacious guy = *un type pétulant* ⓪ lively = *plein de vie*.

VIVID (adj) **1/** *éclatant, -e* : vivid pink = *rose éclatant* ⓪ bright = *vif* ☠ *une victoire éclatante* = a brilliant victory **2/** *vivant, -e* : a vivid description = *une description vivante* ☠ → live **VIVIDLY** (adv) *d'une manière vivante*.

VIVISECTION (n) *vivisection* (f) : a campaign against vivisection = *une campagne contre la vivisection*.

VOCABULARY (n, -ies) *vocabulaire* (m) : a basic vocabulary of 5 000 words = *un vocabulaire de base de 5 000 mots*.

VOCALIST (n) *chanteur, -euse (d'un groupe)*.

VOCATION (n) *vocation* (f) : teaching is her vocation = *sa vocation, c'est l'enseignement*.

VOCATIONAL (adj) **vocational guidance/training** = *orientation/formation professionnelle*.

VODKA (n) *vodka* (f) : Russian vodka = *vodka russe*.

VOGUE (n) *vogue* (f) : disco music is a vogue = *la musique disco est une vogue* ⓪ fashion = *mode*
in vogue = *en vogue* ⓪ in fashion = *à la mode*.

VOICE (n) *voix* (f) : I didn't recognize your voice = *je n'ai pas reconnu votre voix* ⓪ voiceless = *sans voix*
her voice cracked = *sa voix s'est brisée*
male ≠ female voice = *voix masculine ≠ féminine*
to raise one's voice = *élever la voix*
☠ *voix (élections)* = votes
— *ne pas avoir voix au chapitre* = to have no say in the matter.

VOICE (to, -d) *formuler tout haut* : to voice an opinion = *formuler une opinion tout haut* ⓪ to express = *exprimer*.

VOID (n) *vide* (m) : his death left a void = *sa mort a laissé un vide* ☠ → emptiness.

VOID (adj) *nul, nulle* : to declare a contract void = *déclarer un contrat nul*
void of (all meaning/kindness) = *dépourvu de (toute signification/gentillesse)* ⓪ lacking in = *manquant de*
☠ *être nul en maths* = to be hopeless at math.

VOID (to, -ed) *rendre nul (et non avenu)* : to void a contract = *rendre un contrat nul (et non avenu)* ⓪ to annul = *annuler*.

VOLATILE (adj) *explosif, -ive* : a volatile political situation/personality = *une situation politique/personnalité explosive* ⓪ volcanic = *volcanique*.

VOLCANO (n, -(e)s) *volcan* (m) : a volcano eruption = *l'éruption d'un volcan* ⓪ lava = *lave*.

VOLLEYBALL (n) *volley-ball* (m) : to play volleyball = *jouer au volley-ball*.

VOLUME (n) *volume* (m), *tome* (m) : an autobiography in two volumes = *une autobiographie en deux volumes/tomes*.

VOLUNTARY (adj) **1/** *bénévole* : voluntary nurse/work = *infirmière/travail bénévole* ≠ paid = *payé* **2/** *volontaire* : a voluntary mistake = *une faute volontaire* ☠ *elle est volontaire* = she's very willful **VOLUNTARILY** (adv) *bénévolement*.

VOLUNTEER (n) *volontaire (m, f), bénévole (m, f)* : they're asking for volunteers = *on demande des volontaires* ⓪ draftee = *appelé* **VOLUNTEER** (to, -ed) *se porter volontaire* : he volunteered to help/for the army 3 *il s'est porté volontaire pour aider/pour l'armée*.

VOLUPTUOUS (adj) *voluptueux, -euse* : a voluptuous body = *un corps voluptueux* ⓪ sensual = *sensuel*.

VOMIT (to, -ed) *vomir :* I vomited all night = *j'ai vomi toute la nuit* ⓓ to throw up = *dégobiller.*

VOODOO (n) *vaudou (m) :* do you believe in voodoo ? = *est-ce que vous croyez au vaudou ?* ⓓ sorcery = *sorcellerie.*

VOTE (n) 1/ *vote (m) :* the labor vote = *le vote travailliste* ⓓ ballot = *bulletin de vote,* referendum = *référendum* 2/ *voix (f) :* the socialist candidate got 5 000 votes = *le candidat socialiste a obtenu 5 000 voix* ☠ → voice
to count the votes = *dépouiller le scrutin*
a vote of no confidence = *une motion de censure.*

VOTE (to, -d) *voter :* who are you going to vote for ? = *pour qui allez-vous voter ?* ⓓ to elect = *élire*
to vote down = *rejeter :* the bill was voted down = *le projet de loi a été rejeté* ⓓ to veto = *opposer son veto à* ☠ → to reject
to be voted in ≠ **out** = *être élu* ≠ *battu :* Smith was voted in ≠ out by ten votes = *Smith a été élu* ≠ *battu à dix voix près*
to vote on stg = *mettre qqch aux voix :* let's vote on the project = *mettons le projet aux voix*
I vote that (we go to dinner now) = *je propose que (nous allions dîner maintenant)*
☠ *voter une loi* = to pass a law.

VOTER (n) *électeur, -trice, votant, -e :* many voters abstained = *beaucoup d'électeurs se sont abstenus/il y a eu peu de votants* ≠ candidate = *candidat.*

VOUCH (to, -ed) **to vouch for** = *se porter garant de :* I'll vouch for his honesty = *je me porte garant de son honnêteté* ⓓ to answer for = *répondre de.*

VOW (n) *vœu (m) :* she made a vow to stop smoking = *elle a fait le vœu d'arrêter de fumer* ⓓ resolution = *résolution,* pledge = *engagement*
to take (one's) vows = *prononcer ses vœux*
☠ *meilleurs vœux* = best wishes
— *vœu pieux* = wishful thinking.

VOW (to, -ed) *faire (le) vœu de :* she vowed to get back on him = *elle a fait (le) vœu de se venger de lui* ⓓ to swear = *jurer.*

VOWEL (n) *voyelle (f)* ≠ consonant = *consonne.*

VOYAGE (n) *voyage (m) (espace, temps) :* a voyage into space = *un voyage dans l'espace* ⓓ journey = *trajet*
☠ *un voyage organisé* = a package tour
— *agence de voyages* = travel agency
— *faire un voyage* = to take a trip.

VOYEUR (n) *mateur (m) :* there are a lot of voyeurs at swings = *il y a beaucoup de mateurs dans les partouzes* ⓓ peeping tom = *voyeur (qui se cache).*

VP (abbr) = vice-president = *vice-président, -e.*

VULGAR (adj) *vulgaire :* a vulgar broad = *une nana vulgaire* ⓓ coarse = *grossier,* obscene = *obscène* **VULGARITY** (n, -ies) *vulgarité (f)* ≠ refinement = *raffinement.*

VULNERABILITY (n inv) *vulnérabilité (f).*

VULNERABLE (adj) *vulnérable :* a vulnerable personality/fortress = *une personnalité/une forteresse vulnérable* ⓓ fragile = ←.

VULTURE (n) *vautour (m)* ⓓ sparrowhawk = *épervier.*

WAC (abbr) = Women's Army Corps = *CFA (Corps féminin des armées)* : she's a WAC = *elle appartient au CFA.*

WACKY (adj, -ier, -iest) *loufoque :* a wacky guy/wacky ideas = *un type loufoque/des idées loufoques* → CRAZY.

WAD (n) **a wad of (bills)** = *une liasse de (billets)* **wads of (money)** = *(de l'argent) à profusion* → MANY.

WADE (to, -d) *patauger :* the kids were wading in the lake = *les gosses pataugeaient dans le lac* ☠ → to flounder.

WAFFLE (n) *(genre de) gaufre (f) (qu'on mange surtout au petit déjeuner).*

WAGES (n pl) *salaire (m) :* low monthly wages = *salaires mensuels bas* ☠ → salary
wage dispute = *conflit salarial/sur les salaires*
wage freeze = *blocage/gel des salaires.*

WAGON (n) *chariot (m) :* the donkey pulled the wagon = *l'âne tirait le chariot* ⓪ cart = *charrette*
to be on the wagon = *être au régime sec :* he's been on the wagon since his accident = *il est au régime sec depuis son accident*
that'll fix his wagon ! = *c'est bien fait pour lui !* ⓪ that'll teach him ! = *ça lui apprendra !*
☠ *wagon(-lit)* = (sleeping) car.

WAIF (n) *enfant (m) des rues* ⓪ ragamuffin = *gavroche.*

WAIL (to, -ed) *brailler :* the baby wailed all night = *le bébé a braillé toute la nuit* ⓪ to blubber = *chialer* ☠ → to holler.

WAIST (n) *taille (f) :* she has a small waist = *elle a la taille fine* ☠ → size.

WAIT (n) *attente (f) :* a three-hour wait = *une attente de trois heures* ☠ *répondre à l'attente* = to come up to expectations.

WAIT (to, -ed) *attendre :* how long have you been waiting ? = *depuis combien de temps attendez-vous ?*

wait and see ! = *on verra bien !*
to wait for = *attendre :* wait for me/my answer = *attendez-moi/attendez ma réponse*
to wait on = *s'occuper de :* she's the saleswoman who waited on us last week = *c'est la vendeuse qui s'est occupé de nous la semaine dernière* ⓪ to help = *servir*
I can't wait to (leave)/for (Tuesday) = *j'ai hâte de (partir)/qu'on soit (mardi)*
don't wait up for me = *ne m'attendez pas pour aller vous coucher*
he kept me waiting = *il m'a fait attendre* ☠ → to expect.

WAITER (n) *garçon (m) :* waiter ! = *garçon !* ⓪ head-waiter = *maître d'hôtel,* busboy = *aide-serveur* ☠ → boy **WAITRESS** (n, -es) *serveuse (f).*

WAIVE (to, -d) *renoncer à :* he waived his rights = *il a renoncé à ses droits.*

WAKE (n) **in the wake of (the war/the storm)** = *à la suite de (la guerre/l'orage).*

WAKE (to, woke, woken) *réveiller :* the noise woke me = *le bruit m'a réveillé*	
to wake = *réveiller :* go wake your father = *allez réveiller votre père* **to wake up** = 1/ *se réveiller :* I woke up very early = *je me suis réveillé très tôt* ⓪ to get up = *se lever* 2/ *réveiller :* you woke	me up = *tu m'as réveillé* **to awake** = *(se) réveiller :* I awoke at 4 am = *je me suis réveillé à 4 heures du matin* **to (a)waken** = *réveiller :* the noise (a)wakened us = *le bruit nous a réveillés.*

WALES (n) *pays (m) de Galles :* Prince of Wales = *prince de Galles* ⓪ Welsh = *Gallois.*

WALK (n) *promenade (f) :* a long walk = *une longue promenade* ⓪ drive = *promenade en voiture*	
to go for a walk = *aller se promener :* do you want to go for a walk ? = *voulez-vous aller vous prome-*	*ner ?* ⓪ to go for a stroll = *aller se balader* **it's a (five-minute) walk from here** = *c'est à*

(cinq minutes) à pied d'ici
a (sexy) walk = *une façon (sexy) de marcher* ⓪ | gait = *démarche*
to take a walk = *faire une promenade.*

WALK (to, -ed) **1/** *marcher* : I really like to walk = *j'aime vraiment marcher* ⓪ to stroll = *se balader*

☠ *je ne marche pas !* = no way !
— *faire marcher qqn* = to pull s.o.'s leg
— *ce bus ne marche pas le dimanche* = this bus doesn't run on Sundays
— *l'affaire marche* = the deal is on
— *ça a marché ?* = how did it go ? | — *ça a marché ≠ ça n'a pas marché* = it worked out ≠ it didn't work out
— *(la machine) marche* = the (machine) works
— *comment les choses marchent-elles ?* = how are things coming along ?
— *il n'a pas marché !* = he didn't bite !

2/ *aller à pied* : it's not far, we can walk there = *ce n'est pas loin, on peut y aller à pied* ⓪ to hoof it = *y aller à pinces*

---

to walk across (the border) = *traverser (la frontière) à pied*
to walk around = *se promener* : we walked around the left bank all day = *nous nous sommes promenés sur la rive gauche toute la journée* ⓪ to wander = *flâner*
to walk away from s.o./stg = *laisser tomber qqn/qqch* : he was fed up and walked away from the whole problem = *il en avait marre et a totalement laissé tomber le problème*
to walk away with/off with = *remporter dans un fauteuil* : he walked away/off with the elec- | *tion* = *il a remporté l'élection dans un fauteuil* ⓪ to win hands down = *gagner haut la main*
to walk backwards = *marcher à reculons*
to walk down = *descendre à pied* : to walk down 5th Avenue/the stairs = *descendre la 5ᵉ Avenue/les escaliers à pied* ≠ to walk up = *(re)monter à pied*
anyone can walk in ! = *on y entre comme dans un moulin !*
to walk into = *tomber dans* : you walked right into it ! = *vous êtes tombé en plein dedans !* ⓪ to fall for = *tomber dans le* | *panneau*
to walk out (of) = *partir en claquant la porte* : he was angry and walked out (of the meeting) = *il était en colère et il est parti (de la réunion) en claquant la porte* ⓪ to leave = *quitter*
to walk out on = *plaquer* : he walked out on his wife = *il a plaqué sa femme* ☠ → to jilt
to walk up = **1/** *monter à pied* : the elevator was out of order so we had to walk up = *l'ascenseur était en panne, et nous avons dû monter à pied* **2/** *remonter à pied* : to walk up 5th Avenue = *remonter à pied la 5ᵉ Avenue.*

WALKAWAY (n) **(the elections) were a walkaway for (Smith)** = *(Smith) a gagné (les élections) dans un fauteuil.*

WALKIE-TALKIE (n) *talkie-walkie (m).*

WALKING (adj) **to be within walking distance** = *ne pas être loin à pied*
she gave him his walking papers = *elle l'a envoyé promener* ⓪ she sent him packing = *elle l'a envoyé sur les roses*
a walking encyclopedia = *un dictionnaire ambulant*
walking shoes = *chaussures de marche.*

WALKMAN (n, -s) *Walkman (m), baladeur (m)* : he's running with his walkman on his ears = *il court avec son Walkman sur les oreilles.*

WALK-ON (n, adj) **to have a walk-on part** = *jouer les utilités* ⓪ to have a bit part = *avoir un rôle accessoire.*

WALKOUT (n) *grève (f) surprise* : the workers staged a walkout = *les ouvriers ont organisé une grève surprise* ⓪ wildcat strike = *grève sauvage.*

WALKUP (n) *appartement (m) sans ascenseur* : to live in a sixth-floor walkup = *habiter (un appartement) au sixième sans ascenseur.*

WALL (n) *mur (m)* : a concrete wall = *un mur de béton* ⓪ partition = *cloison*
to drive s.o. up the wall = *rendre qqn chèvre* : the kids are driving me up the wall = *les gosses me rendent chèvre* ⓪ to be the death of s.o. = *avoir la peau de qqn*
to go over the wall = *faire le mur/se faire la paire/se faire la belle* : three prisoners went over the wall = *trois prisonniers ont fait le mur/se sont fait la belle/la paire* ⓪ to bust out = *jouer la fille de l'air*
to hug the wall = *raser les murs*
to talk to a (brick) wall = *parler à un mur* : talking to you is like talking to a (brick) wall = *quand on te parle, c'est comme si on parlait à un mur*
walls have ears = *les murs ont des oreilles*
Wall Street = *centre financier de New York* ⓪ the stock market = *la Bourse*
☠ *le mur du son* = the sound barrier.

WALLET (n) *portefeuille (m)* : a leather wallet = *un portefeuille en cuir* = billfold ⓪ change purse = *porte-monnaie*
☠ *portefeuille (ministère)* = (ministerial) portfolio
— *un lit en portefeuille* = a frenched bed
— *jupe portefeuille* = wraparound skirt.

WALLFLOWER (n) **to be a wallflower** = *faire tapis-*

serie : I was the only wallflower at the party = *j'étais la seule à faire tapisserie à la soirée* ≠ to be the life of the party = *être le boute-en-train de la soirée.*

WALLOP (n) *châtaigne (f)* : a wallop on the nose = *une châtaigne sur le pif* ⊕ bash = *marron,* walloping = *rossée* 💀 *une châtaigne (fruit)* = a chestnut **WALLOP** (to, -ed) *flanquer une châtaigne à* : he walloped the guy = *il a flanqué une châtaigne au type* → TO HIT.

WALLOPING (adj) *de première* : a walloping mistake/lie = *une faute/un mensonge de première* ⊕ a hell of a = *un sacré.*

WALLOW IN (to, -ed) *se complaire dans* : to wallow in guilt feelings = *se complaire dans des sentiments de culpabilité* ⊕ to indulge in = *se laisser aller à.*

WALLPAPER (n) *papier (m) peint* ⊕ paint = *peinture.*

WALRUS (n, -es) *morse (m)* ⊕ seal = *phoque* 💀 *le morse* = the morse code.

WALTZ (n, -es) *valse (f)* ⊕ tango = *←* 💀 *la valse des prix/des étiquettes* = price fluctuations.

WALTZ (to, -ed) *valser* ⊕ to dance = *danser*
to waltz through (an exam) = *réussir (un examen) les*

doigts dans le nez ⊕ to breeze through = *réussir dans un fauteuil.*

WAN (adj, -ner, -nest) *blafard, -e* : a wan complexion = *un teint blafard* ⊕ sallow = *cireux.*

WAND (n) *baguette (f)* : a magical wand = *une baguette magique* 💀 → chopstick.

WANDER (to, -ed) *flâner* : we wandered around/about the left bank = *nous avons flâné sur la rive gauche* ⊕ to roam = *baguenauder,* to saunter = *déambuler.*

WANDERLUST (n) *envie (f) de bouger, bougeotte (f)* : a constant wanderlust keeps him away from his family = *une constante envie de bouger l'éloigne de sa famille.*

WANE (n) **to be on the wane** = *être sur le déclin* : their interest was on the wane = *leur attention était sur le déclin* = to wane/to ebb.

WANGLE (to, -d) *se dépatouiller pour avoir* : I wangled an invitation = *je me suis dépatouillé pour avoir une invitation* ⊕ to finagle = *ruser pour avoir.*

WANNA BE (n) *pseudo-* : the Madonna wanna bes all cut their hair = *les pseudo-Madonna se sont toutes fait couper les cheveux* ⊕ spitting image = *portrait craché.*

WANT (n) **want ad** = *petite annonce (demande)* ⊕ the classified ads = *les petites annonces*	**for want of (anything better)** = *faute de (mieux)* ⊕ for lack of = *à défaut de.*
WANT (to, -ed) *vouloir* : do you want some coffee ? = *voulez-vous du café ?* ⊕ to crave for = *mourir d'envie de,* to wish = *souhaiter*	
to be wanted (by the police/for murder) = *être recherché (par la police/pour meurtre)* **I know when I'm not wanted** = *je vois bien que*	*je suis de trop* **you're wanted (in the office/on the phone)** = *on vous demande (au bureau/au téléphone)*
to want out = *vouloir se tirer* : he can't stand her anymore and wants out = *il ne peut plus la supporter et il veut se tirer* ⊕ to be fed up = *en avoir ras le bol* **to want to** = *vouloir* : I want to go with you = *je*	*veux y aller avec vous* **to want s.o. to ...** = *vouloir que qqn ...* : do you want me to leave/give you a lift ? = *est-ce que vous voulez que je m'en aille/que je vous dépose ?*
💀 *que voulez-vous dire ?* = what do you mean ? — *veux-tu (te taire) !* = will you (shut up) ! — *vouloir, c'est pouvoir* = where there's a will there's a way — *je lui en veux* = I have it in for him — *je veux bien !* = I'm willing !	— *je voudrais un café* = I'd like a coffee — *vouloir du bien* ≠ *du mal à qqn* = to wish ≠ not to wish s.o. well — *où veux-tu en venir ?* = what are you getting at ? — *il en veut* = he's really ambitious.

WANTING (adj) **to be wanting in** = *manquer de* : the least I can say is that my boss is wanting in patience = *le moins qu'on puisse dire c'est que mon patron manque de patience.*

WANTON (adj) **1/** *dévergondé, -e* : a wanton life = *une vie dévergondée* ⊕ debauched = *débauché* **2/** *gratuit, -e* : wanton killings/cruelty = *des meurtres gratuits/une cruauté gratuite* ≠ justified = *justifié* 💀 → gratuitous.

WAR (n) *guerre (f)* : to declare war = *déclarer la guerre*		
atomic war = *guerre atomique* **bomb** = *bombe*	**cease-fire** = *cessez-le-feu* **civil war** = *guerre civile*	**cold war** = *guerre froide* **guerrilla warfare** = *guérilla*

705

holy war = *guerre sainte* **nuclear war** = *guerre nu- cléaire* **prisoner of war** = POW = *prisonnier de guerre* **psychological war** = *guerre psychologique* **treaty** = *traité*	truce = *trêve* **war baby** = *enfant de la guerre* **war bride** = *mariée de guerre* **war correspondent** = *corres- pondant de guerre* **war crime** = *crime de guerre* **war cry** = *cri de guerre* **war memorial** = *monument*	*aux morts* **war of nerves** = *guerre des nerfs* **in wartime** = *en temps de guerre* **weapons** = *armes* **World War I/II** = *Pre- mière/Seconde Guerre mondiale*
to be at war = *être en guerre* : the two countries are at war = *les deux pays sont en guerre* **to go to war** = *entrer en guerre*		**to serve in the war** = *faire la guerre (qqn)* **to wage war** = *faire la guerre (pays)* ≠ to make peace = *faire la paix*
💀 *à la guerre comme à la guerre* = that's the way it goes — *faire la guerre à qqn pour que* = to be constantly		after s.o. because — *(j'ai cédé) de guerre lasse* = (I gave in) I was worn out.

WARD (n) *salle(f)* : there are no private rooms in the hospital, only wards = *il n'y a pas de chambres individuelles dans cet hôpital, il n'y a que des salles (communes)*
ward of the state = *pupille de la nation*
💀 *salle de bains/de bal/salle à manger* = bath-
room/ballroom/dining room
— *faire salle comble* = to pack them in (theater).

WARDEN (n) *directeur, -trice de prison* ⓓ prisoner =
prisonnier.

WARD OFF (to, -ed) *parer* : to ward off a blow/a catastrophe = *parer un coup/une catastrophe* ⓓ to fend off
= *repousser* 💀 *parer au plus pressé* = to do the most
urgent things first.

WARDROBE (n) *garde-robe (f)* : a new wardrobe = *une
nouvelle garde-robe.*

WAREHOUSE (n) *entrepôt (m)* : we bought our furniture directly from the warehouse = *nous avons acheté
nos meubles directement à l'entrepôt* ⓓ storage = *em-
magasinage.*

WARES (n pl) **to push one's wares** = *vanter la marchandise* : the hooker was pushing her wares = *la pute
était en train de vanter la marchandise.*

WARM (adj, -er, -est) **1/** *chaud, -e* : a warm day = *une
journée chaude* ⓓ lukewarm = *tiède* = tepid ≠ ice-
cold = *glacial* 💀 → hot
to be warm = *avoir chaud* : I'm very warm = *j'ai très
chaud*
you're getting warm ! = *tu brûles !* ⓓ guess ! =
devine !
it's warm (today) = *il fait chaud (aujourd'hui)*
2/ *chaleureux, -euse* : a warm person/voice = *une per-
sonne/voix chaleureuse* ≠ cold = *froid.*

WARMONGER (n) *belliciste (m, f)* ≠ dove = *colombe.*

WARMTH (n) *chaleur (f)* : the warmth of his words/the
fire = *la chaleur de ses paroles/du feu* 💀 *être en chaleur*
= to be in heat (animal).

WARM UP (to, -ed) **1/** *faire réchauffer* : I'll warm up the
chicken = *je vais faire réchauffer le poulet* **2/** *s'échauffer* : the team's warming up = *l'équipe s'échauffe* **3/** *se
réchauffer* : the weather's warming up = *le temps se
réchauffe.*

WARN (to, -ed) *prévenir* : I warn you, if you hit me
again, I'll split = *je te préviens, si tu me frappes encore,
je me tire* ⓓ to forewarn = *avertir* 💀 *prévenir (une
maladie)* = to prevent (a disease).

WARNING (n) *avertissement (m)* : this is my last warning
= *c'est mon dernier avertissement*
without warning = *sans prévenir* : he quit without
warning = *il a démissionné sans prévenir.*

WARP (to, -ed) *gauchir* : the wood's warped = *le bois est
gauchi*
a warped mind = *un esprit tordu*
a warped sense of humor = *un sens de l'humour
morbide.*

WARPATH (n) **to be on the warpath** = *être sur le
sentier de la guerre* → ANGRY.

WARRANT (n) *mandat (m)* : cops can't search a house
without a warrant = *les flics ne peuvent pas fouiller une
maison sans mandat* 💀 → mandate.

WARRANT (to, -ed) *légitimer* : nothing warrants such
violence = *rien ne légitime une telle violence* ⓓ to
excuse = *excuser.*

WARRIOR (n) *guerrier, -ère* ⓓ soldier = *soldat.*

WART (n) *verrue (f)* : she has an ugly wart on her hand =
elle a une vilaine verrue sur la main.

WARY (adj, -ier, -iest) **to be wary of (s.o.'s intentions)**
= *se méfier des (intentions de qqn)* = to be leery of.

WASH (n inv) *lessive (f)* : I have to do the wash today = *il
faut que je fasse la lessive aujourd'hui*
it'll come out in the wash = *la vérité finira par sortir
du puits*

to hang out the wash = *étendre le linge/la lessive*
a wash and set = *un shampooing (et) mise en plis.*

WASH (to, -ed) *(se) laver* : wash your hands/the floor = *lavez-vous les mains/lavez le sol* ⓪ to clean = *nettoyer*, to scour = *récurer*
to get washed = *aller se laver* : you should get washed now = *tu devrais aller te laver maintenant*
(her story) won't wash = *(son histoire) ne prendra pas* ≠ not to hold water = *ne pas tenir debout*
washing machine = *machine à laver*
wash and wear = *repassage superflu* ⓪ dripdry = *qui ne se repasse pas*
to wash down = *arroser* : we washed down the dinner with a good wine = *nous avons arrosé le dîner d'un bon vin* ☠ → to water
to wash up = *aller se laver* = to get washed ⓪ to freshen up = *se rafraîchir*
to be washed up = *être fichu* : our couple's washed up = *notre couple est fichu* ⓪ to be through = *être fini* ☠ *laver qqn d'une accusation* = to clear s.o. of an accusation.

WASHABLE (adj) *lavable* : washable fabric = *tissu lavable.*

WASHCLOTH (n) *gant (m) de toilette* ⓪ towel = *serviette de toilette.*

WASHED-OUT (adj) *lessivé, -e* : truly washed-out after the show = *vraiment lessivé après son show* ⓪ wiped-out = *anéanti*, dead beat = *harassé.*

WASHOUT (n) 1/ *bide (m) intégral* : the play was a washout = *la pièce a été un bide intégral* ⓪ bomb = *bide* 2/ *nullité (f)* : as a lawyer, she's a washout = *comme avocate, c'est une nullité* ⓪ a dud = *quelqu'un à la noix.*

WASHROOM (n) *cabinets (m pl)* : where's the washroom ? = *où sont les cabinets ?* ⓪ toilet = *toilettes.*

WASP (n) *guêpe (f)* : bit by a wasp = *piqué par une guêpe* ⓪ bee = *abeille.*

WASP (n) = White Anglo-Saxon Protestant = *blanc, anglo-saxon et protestant (correspondant plus ou moins à la HSP).*

WASTE (n) *gaspillage (m)* : too much waste in this house = *trop de gaspillage dans cette maison*

it's a waste of time = *c'est une perte de temps/c'est du temps perdu* → AWFUL
it's a waste of time and energy = *c'est peine perdue*
it's a waste of money = *c'est de l'argent fichu en l'air*
so much (food) going to waste = *tant de (nourriture) en train de se gaspiller.*

WASTE (to, -d) 1/ *gaspiller* : you're wasting your money buying all these gadgets = *tu gaspilles ton argent à acheter tous ces gadgets* ⓪ to squander = *dilapider* ≠ to conserve = *conserver* 2/ *perdre* : I wasted a whole month looking for an apartment = *j'ai perdu un mois à chercher un appartement* ☠ → to lose
to waste away (from cancer) = *être miné (par un cancer).*

WASTEPAPER BASKET (n) *corbeille (f) à papier.*

WATCH (n, -es) *montre (f)* : my watch has stopped = *ma montre s'est arrêtée* ⓪ wristwatch = *montre-bracelet*, stopwatch = *chrono*, to be ten minutes slow ≠ fast = *retarder* ≠ *avancer de dix minutes* ☠ *(course) contre la montre* = (race) against the clock.

WATCH (to, -ed) 1/ *surveiller* : watch the kids = *surveillez les enfants* ⓪ to mind = *garder* ☠ *il surveille tout* = he oversees everything
if you don't watch it (you'll get in trouble with the boss) = *si vous ne faites pas gaffe (vous allez avoir des ennuis avec le patron)*
watch out ! = *fais gaffe !* ⓪ be careful ! = *fais attention !*
2/ *regarder* : to watch TV = *regarder la télé*, if you want to learn how to do it, watch me = *si tu veux savoir comment on fait, regarde-moi*
☠ *regarde-moi !* = look at me !
— *ça ne te regarde pas !* = it's none of your business !
— *tu ne t'es pas regardé !* = look who's talking !

WATCHDOG (n) *chien, -enne de garde* ⓪ Cerberus = *Cerbère.*

WATCHMAN (n, -men) *gardien (m)* : the watchman was asleep at the time of the robbery = *le gardien était endormi quand le vol a eu lieu* ⓪ guard = *garde* ☠ *un ange gardien* = a guardian angel
— *gardien de but* = goalkeeper
— *gardien de la paix* = policeman
— *gardien d'immeuble/de propriété* = caretaker/custodian/superintendent.

WATER (n) *eau (f)*, *flotte (f)* (LV) : could I have some water please ? = *est-ce que je peux avoir de l'eau, s'il vous plaît ?*

drinking water = *eau potable*	*minérale*	**Seltzer/soda water** = *eau de Seltz/eau gazeuse*
fresh water = *eau douce*	**running water** = *eau courante*	
mineralized water = *eau*	**salt water** = *eau de mer*	**tap water** = *eau du robinet*

that doesn't hold water = *ça ne tient pas debout* ⓪ it's groundless = *c'est sans fondement* **(my criticisms) rolled off him like water off a duck's back** = *(j'ai beau critiquer) les chiens aboient, la caravane passe*	**a lot of water has flowed under the bridge (since then)** = *beaucoup d'eau a passé sous les ponts (depuis lors)* ⓪ it's ancient history = *c'est de l'histoire ancienne*

707

☠ *clair comme de l'eau de roche* = as clear as daylight — *(une histoire) à l'eau de rose* = (a) hearts-and-flowers (story) — *tomber à l'eau* = to fall through — *mettre de l'eau dans son vin* = to tone down/to mellow — *se jeter à l'eau* = to jump in	— *(mille dollars) ou dans ces eaux-là* = (a thousand dollars) or round about — *une goutte d'eau dans la mer* = a drop in the bucket — *une eau-forte* = an etching — *apporter de l'eau au moulin de qqn* = to back up s.o.'s argument	— *rester le bec dans l'eau* = to be left high and dry — *il y a de l'eau dans le gaz* = there's a fly in the ointment — *se terminer en eau de boudin* = to fizzle out — *flotte* → fleet.

WATER (to, -ed) *arroser* : water the flowers twice a week = *arrosez les fleurs deux fois par semaine* ⑩ to sprinkle = *asperger*

☠ *on a arrosé le dîner d'un bon vin* = we washed down the dinner with a good wine — *arroser qqn* (LV) = to pay s.o. off	— *arroser (une victoire)* = to drink to celebrate (a victory).

WATERCOLOR (n) *aquarelle (f)* : he sells watercolors = *il vend des aquarelles.*

WATERED-DOWN (adj) *édulcoré, -e* : a watered-down speech = *un discours édulcoré.*

WATERFALL (n) *chute (f) d'eau* ⑩ cascade = ←.

WATERMELON (n) *pastèque (f)* ⑩ cantaloup = ←.

WATERPROOF (adj) *imperméable* : my parka is waterproof = *ma parka est imperméable* ⑩ watertight = *étanche* ☠ *imperméable aux critiques* = impervious to criticism.

WATER-SKI (to, -ed) *faire du ski nautique* : I don't know how to water-ski = *je n'ai jamais fait de ski nautique.*

WAVE (n) 1/ *vague (f)* : ocean waves = *les vagues de l'océan* ⑩ breaker = *rouleau* 2/ *vague (f)* : a wave of violence/immigration = *une vague de violence/d'immigration* ⑩ flare-up = *poussée*
don't make waves ! = *ne faites pas de vagues !* ⑩ let sleeping dogs lie = *il ne faut pas réveiller le chat qui dort*

☠ *avoir du vague à l'âme* = to feel melancholy
— *une vague de froid* = a cold spell
— *une vague d'immigrants* = a surge of immigrants.

WAVE (to, -d) *faire un signe de la main* : when she saw me, she waved = *quand elle m'a vu, elle a fait un signe de la main.*

WAVELENGTH (n) **on the same ≠ on a different wavelength** = *sur la même ≠ pas sur la même longueur d'onde.*

WAVER (to, -ed) *vaciller (stg), tergiverser (s.o.)* : his determination never wavered = *sa détermination n'a jamais vacillé*, he wavered between getting a divorce and taking a mistress = *il a tergiversé entre demander le divorce et prendre une maîtresse* ⑩ to hesitate = *hésiter* ☠ *(le vieil homme) vacillait* = (the old man) was wobbling.

WAVY (adj, -ier, -iest) *ondulé, -e* : wavy hair = *des cheveux ondulés.*

WAX (n, -es) *cire (f)* : wax museum = *musée de cire.*

WAY (n) 1/ *façon (f)* : that's not the way to do it = *ce n'est pas de cette façon qu'il faut procéder* ⑩ method = *méthode*

☠ *de façon générale* = generally speaking — *faire des façons* = to stand on ceremony	— *dire à qqn sa façon de penser* = to give s.o. a piece of one's mind

2/ *chemin (m)* : which is the shortest way to the next big city ? = *quel est le chemin le plus court pour se rendre à la grande ville la plus proche ?* ⑩ road = *route*

☠ *chemin de fer* = railroad	— *tous les chemins mènent à Rome* = all roads lead to Rome

to ask one's way = *demander son chemin* **to be in s.o.'s way** = *être sur le chemin de qqn* : it' no good to be in his way = *il ne fait pas bon*	*être sur son chemin* **to do things the easy ≠ hard way** = *choisir la facilité ≠ la difficulté* **to do things one's (own) way**	= *n'en faire qu'à sa tête* : she's stubborn and does everything her own way = *elle est têtue et n'en fait qu'à sa tête* **to elbow one's way through**

(the crowd) = *se frayer un chemin à travers (la foule) à coups de coude* ⓪ **to make one's way through (the crowd)** = *se frayer un chemin à travers (la foule)*

to feel one's way = *y aller à tâtons* : I recently began this job and I'm feeling my way = *je viens de commencer ce boulot et j'y vais à tâtons*

to find a way = *trouver un moyen* : we must find a way to get him sign the contract = *nous devons trouver un moyen de lui faire signer le contrat*

to force one's way in = *pénétrer de force dans*

to get in the way of = *être une entrave à* : her love life gets in the way of her studies = *sa vie sentimentale est une entrave à ses études*

to get one's (own) way = *obtenir ce qu'on veut* : she's used to getting her own way = *elle est habituée à obtenir ce qu'elle veut* ⓪ to do as one pleases = *faire comme bon vous semble*

get out of the way ! = *ôte-toi de là !*

to give way = *céder* : the dam gave way = *la digue a cédé* ⓪ to collapse = *s'effondrer* ≠ to hold = *tenir* 🐝 → to give in

to go (fly, etc.) by way of = *passer par* : we went by way of Boston = *nous sommes passés par Boston* ⓪ to go via = *aller via*

to go out of one's way = *se donner un mal de chien* : he went out of his way to help us = *il s'est donné un mal de chien pour nous aider* ⓪ to leave no stone unturned = *remuer ciel et terre*

to go the way of all flesh = *rendre l'âme* ⓪ to kick the bucket = *passer l'arme à gauche*

to have a way about (one) = *avoir un petit je ne sais quoi* : she's not pretty but has a way about her = *elle n'est pas jolie, mais elle a un petit je ne sais quoi* ⓪ to have got it = *avoir du chien*

to have a way with = *savoir s'y prendre avec* : he has a way with kids = *il sait s'y prendre*

avec les gosses

have it your (own) way ! = *faites ce que vous voulez !* ⓪ do as you please ! = *faites comme bon vous semble !*

in a way = *en un sens* : you're right, in a way = *en un sens, vous avez raison* ⓪ so to speak = *pour ainsi dire*

in no way = *en aucune façon* : he's in no way the guy for her = *ce n'est en aucune façon un type pour elle* ⓪ not at all = *pas du tout*

in the way of = *dans le genre* : do you have anything in the way of electronic toys ? = *est-ce que vous avez quelque chose dans le genre jouet électronique ?*

I must be on my way = *il faut que je m'en aille* → TO LEAVE

it's a long ≠ short way from here (to the bank) = *(la banque) est loin ≠ n'est pas loin d'ici*

it was a parting of the ways = *on a pris des chemins différents* ≠ a coming-together = *un rapprochement*

keep/stay out of my way ! = *tu n'as pas intérêt à te trouver sur mon chemin !*

to know one's way around = *savoir se débrouiller (dans un lieu)* : I know my way around New York = *je sais me débrouiller dans New York*

to lead the way = *montrer le chemin* : you lead the way and I'll follow = *montrez le chemin et je vous suis*

let me put it another way = *en d'autres termes* : I don't think he's nice to her ; let me put it another way, he's a bastard ! = *je ne pense pas qu'il soit gentil avec elle ; en d'autres termes, c'est un salaud !* ⓪ in other words = *autrement dit*

let me put it this way = *si vous voulez mon avis*

to lie/joke one's way out = *s'en sortir par des mensonges/des plaisanteries*

to make one's way = *faire son chemin* : don't worry about Jack, he'll make his way = *ne t'en fais pas pour Jack, il fera son chemin*

to make way for = 1/ *laisser*

passer : make way for the President's car ! = *laissez passer la voiture du Président !* 2/ *ouvrir la voie à* : they're tearing down buildings to make way for a highway = *ils démolissent des immeubles pour ouvrir la voie à une autoroute*

to mend one's ways = *rentrer dans le droit chemin* : if she doesn't mend her ways, she'll be sacked = *si elle ne rentre pas dans le droit chemin, elle va être mise à la porte*

not to know which way to turn = *ne plus savoir à quel saint se vouer* ⓪ to be at loose ends = *ne plus savoir où on en est*

not to know which way is up = *perdre les pédales* ⓪ to be beside oneself = *être dans tous ses états*

on the way = *en chemin* : we'll stop on the way for a quick lunch = *nous nous arrêterons en chemin pour déjeuner rapidement*

on the way (home/to school) = *sur le chemin de (la maison/l'école)*

on the way out = *qui passe de mode* : are one-piece bathing suits on the way out ? = *les maillots de bain une pièce sont-ils passés de mode ?*

out of one's way = *pas sur le chemin* : I can't drop you off at the bank, it's out of my way = *je ne peux pas vous déposer à la banque, ce n'est pas sur mon chemin*

out of the way = *au diable (vauvert)* : the restaurant's great but it's out of the way = *le restaurant est génial mais il est au diable (vauvert)*

to pave the way (for) = *préparer le terrain (pour)* : the talks paved the way for the treaty = *les pourparlers ont préparé le terrain pour le traité* ⓪ to set the stage = *ouvrir la voie*

to pay one's own way = *payer son écot* : everybody paid his own way = *chacun a payé son écot* ⓪ to go dutch = *payer chacun sa part*

to see one's way clear to = *voir comment* : I don't see my way clear to getting away this weekend = *je ne vois pas comment je pourrais partir ce weekend*

to send s.o. on his way = *envoyer qqn aux fraises* : the boss sent him on his way = *le patron l'a envoyé aux fraises* Ⓦ **to send s.o. packing** = *envoyer qqn sur les roses*

to shove/push one's way through (the crowd) = *se frayer un chemin dans (la foule)*

to show s.o. the way = *montrer le chemin à qqn* : can you show me the way ? = *est-ce que vous pouvez me montrer le chemin ?*

to split ... ways = *diviser en ...* : let's split the check three ways = *divisons l'addition en trois*

to stand in the way (of) = *se mettre en travers du chemin (de)* : she wants to get married but her parents are standing in her way = *elle veut se marier mais ses parents se mettent en travers de son chemin* Ⓦ **to throw in a monkey wrench** = *mettre des bâtons dans les roues*

to take the short ≠ long way = *prendre le chemin le plus court ≠ long*

to talk one's way out = *s'en tirer par de belles paroles* : the cop's writing up a fine, you can't talk your way out of this = *le flic est en train de remplir la contravention, tu ne pourras pas*

t'en tirer par de belles paroles

that's the best ≠ worst way (of doing it/to do it) = *c'est la meilleure ≠ la pire façon de (le faire)*

that's the way I am = *je suis comme ça*

that's the way to do it = *c'est comme ça qu'il faut (le) faire*

that's the way the ball bounces ! = *ainsi va la vie !* Ⓦ **that's the way the cookie crumbles !** = *on ne fait pas d'omelette sans casser des œufs !* Ⓦ **that's the way things are !** = *c'est comme ça !* Ⓦ **that's the way it goes !** = *qu'est-ce que tu veux !* → THAT'S LIFE !

that's the wrong ≠ right way of (doing it) = *ce n'est pas ≠ c'est comme ça qu'il faut (faire)*

the (American) way of life = *le mode de vie (américain)*

the way in ≠ the way out = *l'entrée ≠ la sortie* : I'm looking for the way in ≠ the way out = *je cherche l'entrée ≠ la sortie* ☠ *entrée* → entrance, *sortie* → exit

the ways and means = *les moyens* : if you want to buy a diamond, you must have the ways and means = *si vous voulez acheter un diamant, il faut en avoir les moyens* → RICH

the way things are going (we'll be broke by the end of the month) = *au train où vont les choses (nous serons fauchés à la fin du mois)*

this way/that way = 1/ *par ici/par là* : I'll go this way and you'll go that way = *j'irai par ici et tu iras par là* 2/ *comme ceci/comme cela* : do it this way and not that way = *faites comme ceci et non comme cela*

to my way of thinking (he's a louse) = *à mon avis (c'est un salaud)* Ⓦ **to my mind** = *à mon sens*

under way = *en train* : negotiations for the treaty are under way = *les négociations concernant le traité sont en train*

way off = *loin du compte* : your guess is way off = *vous êtes loin du compte* Ⓦ **you're all off** = *vous n'y êtes pas du tout*

way out = *porte de sortie* : her marriage is bad and she's looking for a way out = *son ménage ne marche pas bien et elle cherche une porte de sortie*

which way (should we go) ? = *par où (faut-il passer) ?*

which way is (the zoo) ? = *dans quelle direction est (le zoo) ?*

to work one's way through (school) = *travailler pour payer (ses études)*

to work one's way up (in a company) = *gravir les échelons (dans une entreprise)* : he began as a clerk and worked his way up = *il a commencé comme simple employé et a gravi les échelons.*

WAY (adv) **way ahead of** = *loin devant* : France's social services are way ahead of America's = *la France est loin devant les États-Unis en matière de* services sociaux

way too (sophisticated) = *bien trop (sophistiqué)* → VERY.

WAY-OUT (adj) *délirant, -e* : way-out clothes/ideas = *des vêtements délirants/des idées délirantes* Ⓦ **preposterous** = *abracadabrant.*

WE (pron) *nous* : we want to eat something = *nous voulons manger quelque chose* → I
☠ *c'est à nous* = it's ours
— *il nous a vus* = he saw us.

WEAK (adj, -er, -est) 1/ *faible* : a weak man/argument = *un homme/argument faible* Ⓦ **frail** = *frêle*

to be weak in (math) = *être faible en (maths)* ≠ to be good at = *être bon en*

the weaker sex = *le sexe faible* Ⓦ **the fair sex** = *le beau sexe*

(chocolate) is her weak spot = *elle a un faible pour (le chocolat)*

☠ *une faible quantité* = a small quantity
— *une faible chance* = a faint chance

2/ *léger, -ère* : weak tea/coffee = *café/thé léger* ☠ → light.

WEAKEN (to, -ed) *(s')affaiblir* : dissension's weakening the alliance = *les dissensions affaiblissent l'alliance* ≠ to strengthen = *renforcer.*

WEAKLING (n) *mauviette (f)* : she's married to a weakling = *elle a épousé une mauviette.*

WEAKLY (adv) *faiblement* : she smiled weakly = *elle a faiblement souri.*

WEAKNESS (n, -es) *faiblesse* (f) : the weakness of his argument = *la faiblesse de son argument.*

WEALTH (n inv) *richesse* (f) : the cultural wealth of the country = *la richesse culturelle du pays* ≠ poverty = *pauvreté* ☠ *la richesse d'une langue* = the richness of a language.

WEALTHY (adj, -ier, -iest) *très aisé, -e* : a wealthy family = *une famille très aisée* → RICH.

WEAN (to, -ed) *sevrer* : to wean a puppy = *sevrer un chiot* ≠ to nurse = *allaiter.*

WEAPON (n) *arme* (f) : anyone can carry a weapon in the United States = *n'importe qui peut porter une arme aux États-Unis* ⓪ weaponry = *armement* ☠ → arms.

WEAR (n inv) **men's/women's wear** = *vêtements pour hommes/pour femmes.*

WEAR (to, wore, worn) *porter, être en* : what did you wear last night ? = *que portiez-vous hier soir ?*, the women wore long dresses last night = *les femmes étaient en robe longue hier soir* ⓪ to don = *se vêtir* ☠ → to carry **I have nothing to wear** = *je n'ai rien à me mettre (sur le dos)*
to wear off = *passer* : she really fell for him but it wore off quickly = *elle était vraiment très amoureuse de lui, mais ça lui a vite passé*, the action of the sedative is wearing off = *l'action du sédatif commence à passer* ☠ → to pass
to wear out = 1/ *s'user* : kids' clothes wear out quickly = *les vêtements des gosses s'usent vite* ☠ → to use 2/ *exténuer* : this work's wearing me out = *ce travail m'exténue* ⓪ to be pooped = *être raplapla.*

WEARY (adj, -ier, -iest) *las, lasse* : I'm weary of always repeating the same thing = *je suis lasse de toujours répéter la même chose* ≠ refreshed = *reposé.*

WEARY OF (to, -ied) *se lasser de* : one never wearies of good books = *on ne se lasse jamais des bons livres* ⓪ to tire of = *se fatiguer de.*

WEASEL (n) *belette* (f) ⓪ squirrel = *écureuil.*

WEATHER (n) *temps* (m) : what lousy weather ! = *quel temps dégueulasse !* ⓪ weatherman = *météorologue*
I'm feeling under the weather = *je me sens mal fichu* ⓪ I don't feel like my usual self = *je ne suis pas dans mon assiette*
it's nice/fine weather for ducks ! = *il fait un temps à ne pas mettre un chien dehors !* ⓪ it's raining cats and dogs = *il tombe des hallebardes*
to talk about the weather = *parler de tout et de rien* ⓪ to shoot the breeze = *parler de la pluie et du beau temps*
weather forecast = *prévisions météorologiques*
weather permitting = *si le temps le permet*
weather report = *bulletin météo*

what's the weather like ? = *quel temps fait-il ?* ☠ → time.

WEATHER (to, -ed) *réchapper de* : if they weather this crisis, their marriage will hold up = *s'ils réchappent de cette crise, leur ménage tiendra le coup* ⓪ to hold out = *tenir.*

WEAVE (to, wove, wove or woven) *tisser* : to weave a rug = *tisser un tapis* ⓪ loom = *métier à tisser.*

WED (to, -ded or wed) *épouser* : he wed the boss's daughter = *il a épousé la fille du patron* ☠ → to marry.

WEDDING (n) *mariage* (m) : I went to their wedding = *je suis allé à leur mariage* ⓪ the nuptials = *la noce*, bridal procession = *cortège nuptial*, honeymoon = *lune de miel*, bridesmaid = *demoiselle d'honneur*, best man = *témoin (homme)*, maid of honor = *témoin (femme)*
golden/silver wedding anniversary = *noces d'or/d'argent*
wedding anniversary = *anniversaire de mariage*
wedding cake = *gâteau de mariage*
wedding day = *jour du mariage*
wedding night = *nuit de noces*
wedding present/gift = *cadeau de mariage*
wedding ring = *alliance*
☠ → marriage.

WEDLOCK (n) **to be born out of wedlock** = *être un enfant naturel* ⓪ shotgun marriage = *mariage précipité.*

WEDNESDAY (n) *mercredi* (m) : Ash Wednesday = *Mercredi des cendres* → WEEK.

WEE (adj, -r, -st) **a wee bit of (salt)** = *un tout petit peu de (sel)* ⓪ a speck of = *un chouïa de*
the wee hours = *le petit matin* : he came home in the wee hours (of the morning) = *il est rentré à la maison au petit matin* ⓪ at the crack of dawn = *au lever du jour.*

WEED (n) *mauvaise herbe* (f) : I have to pull out the weeds = *il faut que j'arrache les mauvaises herbes* ⓪ weedkiller = *herbicide.*

WEED OUT (to, -ed) *éliminer* : we'll have to weed out the bad players = *il faut que nous éliminions les mauvais joueurs* = to eliminate.

WEEK (n) *semaine* (f) : it'll take a week = *ça prendra une semaine* ⓪ month = *mois*	
Monday = *lundi* **Tuesday** = *mardi* **Wednesday** = *mercredi*	**Thursday** = *jeudi* **Friday** = *vendredi* **Saturday** = *samedi* **Sunday** = *dimanche*
a week from today = *aujourd'hui en huit* **the week after next** = *pas la semaine qui vient, celle d'après*	
☠ *la semaine des quatre jeudis* = in a month of Sundays.	

WEEKDAYS (adv) *en semaine* : he doesn't take his car weekdays = *il ne prend pas sa voiture en semaine.*

WEEKEND (n) *week-end (m), fin (f) de semaine* : I don't work weekends = *je ne travaille pas le week-end*
over the weekend = *ce week-end.*

WEEKLY (n, -ies) *hebdomadaire (m), hebdo (m)* : this magazine's a weekly = *ce magazine est un hebdomadaire/un hebdo* ⓌⒹ monthly = *mensuel* **WEEKLY** (adj) *hebdomadaire* : weekly meetings = *des réunions hebdomadaires* ⓌⒹ monthly = *mensuel* **WEEKLY** (adv) *toutes les semaines* : the newspaper appears weekly = *le journal paraît toutes les semaines* ⓌⒹ monthly = *tous les mois.*

WEEP (to, wept, wept) *pleurer à chaudes larmes* : the child started weeping as soon as his mother closed the door = *l'enfant s'est mis à pleurer à chaudes larmes dès que sa mère a fermé la porte* ⓌⒹ to wail = *brailler*
to weep for (joy) = *pleurer de (joie).*

WEIGH (to, -ed) **1/** *peser* : how much do you weigh ? = *combien pesez-vous ?* **2/** *peser (le pour et le contre)* : I'm weighing the idea of going to Europe this summer = *j'hésite à partir en Europe cet été, je pèse le pour et le contre* ⓌⒹ to think over = *réfléchir à*
to be weighed down with (financial problems) = *ployer sous (les problèmes financiers)* ⓌⒹ to be saddled with = *être accablé de*
to weigh on s.o. = *peser à qqn* : his silence is weighing on me = *son silence me pèse* ⓌⒹ to worry = *inquiéter* ☠ *un silence pesait sur la réunion* = a silence hung over the meeting.

WEIGHT (n) *poids (m)* : what's his weight ? = *quel poids fait-il ?*
to be worth one's weight in gold = *valoir son pesant d'or*
to carry weight = *avoir du poids* : his opinion carries no weight in the company = *son opinion n'a aucun poids dans la société* ≠ to cut no ice = *compter pour du beurre*
to gain weight = *grossir* : you've gained too much weight = *tu as trop grossi* ☠ → to blow up
to put on weight = *prendre du poids*
to give weight to (an argument) = *donner du poids à (un argument)*
to lift weights = *faire des haltères*
to lose weight = *maigrir* ⓌⒹ to reduce = *mincir*
to pull one's weight = *faire sa part* : he doesn't pull his weight at the office = *il ne fait pas sa part de travail au bureau*
to throw one's weight around = *jouer les fiers-à-bras* ⓌⒹ to show off = *faire de l'esbroufe* ☠ *avoir un poids sur la conscience* = to have stg on one's conscience
— *un poids lourd* = a large truck/a van.

WEIRD (adj, -er, -est) *singulier, -ère* : a weird noise/guy = *un bruit/type singulier* ⓌⒹ odd = *étrange*
you're weird, man ! = *tu es taré, mon vieux !* → CRAZY.

WEIRDO (n) *spécimen (m)* : what a weirdo ! = *quel spécimen !* ⓌⒹ weirdy = *hurluberlu,* kook = *farfelu* ☠ → specimen.

WELCOME (n) *accueil (m)* : a warm/cold welcome = *un accueil chaleureux/froid* ⓌⒹ reception = *réception*
to wear out one's welcome = *abuser de l'hospitalité de quelqu'un* ⓌⒹ to be like the man who came to dinner = *s'incruster chez quelqu'un* ☠ *la pièce a reçu un bon* ≠ *mauvais accueil* = the play got a good ≠ bad reception.

WELCOME ! (interj) *bienvenue !* ≠ go away ! = *va-t'en !*
welcome back !/home ! = *on est bien content de vous revoir !/bienvenue chez nous !*

WELCOME (adj) *bienvenu, -e* : you'll always be welcome here = *vous serez toujours (le) bienvenu ici*
you're welcome ! = *de rien !/je vous en prie !* : thank you very much ! — you're welcome ! = *merci beaucoup ! — de rien !/je vous en prie !*
to be welcome to = *ne pas hésiter à* : you're welcome to come with us/to take what you want = *n'hésitez pas à venir avec nous/à prendre ce que vous voulez.*

WELCOME (to, -d) *accueillir* : to welcome people at the airport = *accueillir des gens à l'aéroport,* his suggestion wasn't welcomed = *sa suggestion n'a pas été bien accueillie.*

WELFARE (n) *aide (f) sociale* : a cut in welfare = *une réduction de l'aide sociale* ⓌⒹ food stamps = *bons d'alimentation*
to be on welfare = *vivre de l'aide sociale*
it's for your (own) welfare ! = *c'est pour ton bien !*
the Welfare State = *l'État-providence.*

WELFARE (adj) **Welfare agency** = *bureau d'aide sociale.*

WELL (n) *puits (m)* : to dig a well = *creuser un puits,* an oil well = *un puits de pétrole*	
a well of (information) = *une mine de (renseignements)*	**leave well enough alone !** = *le mieux est l'ennemi du bien !*
WELL (adj) *qui va bien* : my father's well, thank you = *mon père va bien, merci* ⓌⒹ healthy = *en bonne santé* ≠ sick = *malade*	
to feel well = *se sentir bien* = to feel good	**to look** ≠ **not to look well** = *avoir bonne* ≠ *mauvaise mine*

🕱 *les gens bien* = the right kind of people	— *(ce livre) est très bien* = (this book) is very good.

WELL (adv) *bien* : he plays well = *il joue bien* ⓐ great = *merveilleusement* ≠ poorly = *médiocrement*

as well = *ainsi que* : he came to the party and his wife as well = *il est venu à la soirée ainsi que sa femme*
as well as = 1/ *aussi bien que* : she sings as well as she dances = *elle chante aussi bien qu'elle danse* 2/ *non seulement ... mais en plus* : they have cats as well as dogs = *non seulement ils ont des chats, mais en plus ils ont des chiens* ⓐ in addition = *en plus*
(we might) as well (leave now) = *(nous ferions) aussi bien de (partir maintenant)*
to be well into one's (sixties) = *avoir bien entamé (la soixantaine)*
to do well = 1/ *marcher fort* : his business is doing well = *son affaire marche fort* ⓐ to flour-

ish = *être florissant* 2/ *bien s'en sortir* : the patient's doing well = *le malade s'en sort bien*
you did well to (call) = *vous avez bien fait d'(appeler)*
everything's going well = *tout va bien*
to go well = *bien se passer* : the exam went well = *l'examen s'est bien passé* ⓐ to work out = *marcher*
it's well past (2 o'clock) = *il est bien plus de (2 heures)*
to mean well = *être plein de bonnes intentions* : what she said was harsh but she meant well = *c'était dur de dire ça, mais elle était pleine de bonnes intentions*
not to sit well with = *ne pas être apprécié de* : the President's comments didn't sit well with

Congress = *les commentaires du Président n'ont pas été appréciés du Congrès* ⓐ not to go down with = *ne pas être bien reçu par*
that may/might well be but (I'm not sure) = *cela se peut/pourrait bien mais (je n'en suis pas sûr)*
to wear well = *faire de l'usage* : these shoes wear well = *ces chaussures me font de l'usage*
well done ! = *bravo !*
well over (500 people) = *bien plus de (500 personnes)*
well put = *bien envoyé* : her remark was well put = *sa réflexion était bien envoyée*
well said ! = *bien dit !*
I wish her well = *je ne lui souhaite que du bien*

🕱 *c'est bien lui !* = that's him all over ! — *elle est bien jolie/trop jeune* = she's quite pretty/far too young	— *c'est bien fait pour elle !* = that serves her right ! — *c'est bien ça !* = that's right/fine ! — *on verra bien !* = we'll see !

WELL ! (interj) *eh bien !* : well ! what do you think of it ? = *eh bien, qu'est-ce que vous en pensez ?* ⓐ so ! = *alors !*
well, well ! = *tiens donc !* → GOSH !

WELL-ADJUSTED (adj) *(bien) équilibré, -e* : well-adjusted children = *des enfants bien équilibrés* ≠ maladjusted = *mal équilibré*.

WELL-ADVISED (adj) *qui fait bien* : you'd be well-advised to do what he says = *tu ferais bien de faire ce qu'il dit*.

WELL-BEHAVED (adj) *bien élevé, -e* : well-behaved children = *des enfants bien élevés* ⓐ polite =*poli*.

WELL-BEING (n) *bien-être (m)* : a feeling of well-being = *un sentiment de bien-être*.

WELL-BRED (adj) *bien élevé, -e* = well-behaved.

WELL-BUILT (adj) *bien bâti, -e* : she's well-built = *elle est bien bâtie* ⓐ well-proportioned = *bien proportionné*.

WELL-CONNECTED (adj) *qui a ses entrées* : he's well-connected in the administration = *il a ses entrées au gouvernement* ⓐ to have an in = *avoir du piston*.

WELL-DEVELOPED (adj) *bien fait, -e* : she's well-developed for a fourteen-year-old girl = *elle est bien*

faite pour une fille de quatorze ans ⓐ stacked = *bien foutue*.

WELL-DONE (adj) *bien cuit, -e* : I like my meat well-done = *j'aime la viande bien cuite* ≠ rare = *saignant*.

WELL-DRESSED (adj) *bien habillé, -e* : sexy and well-dressed = *sexy et bien habillée* ≠ sloppy = *négligé*.

WELL-FIXED (adj) *fortuné, -e* : he comes from a well-fixed family = *il vient d'une famille fortunée* → RICH ≠ broke = *fauché*.

WELL-FOUNDED (adj) *(bien) fondé, -e* : a well-founded argument = *un argument (bien) fondé* ≠ unfounded = *non fondé*.

WELL-GROOMED (adj) *soigné, -e* : she's always well-groomed = *elle est toujours soignée* ≠ unkempt = *négligé* 🕱 → careful.

WELL-HEELED (adj) *plein, -e aux as* : his father-in-law's well-heeled = *son beau-père est plein aux as* → RICH.

WELL-HUNG (adj) *bien monté* : a well-hung lover = *un amant bien monté*.

WELL-INFORMED (adj) *bien informé, -e :* a well-informed public = *un public bien informé* ≠ misinformed = *mal renseigné.*

WELL-KEPT (adj) 1/ *bien entretenu, -e :* a well-kept house = *une maison bien entretenue* 2/ *bien gardé, -e :* a well-kept secret = *un secret bien gardé.*

WELL-KNOWN (adj) *connu, -e :* a well-known novelist = *un romancier connu* ⓪ renowned = *renommé* ≠ unknown = *inconnu.*

WELL-LIKED (adj) *très apprécié, -e :* she's well-liked in the office = *elle est très appréciée au bureau* ⓪ popular = *populaire.*

WELL-MADE (adj) *bien fait, -e :* well-made cars/clothes = *des voitures bien faites/des vêtements bien faits.*

WELL-MANNERED (adj) *bien éduqué, -e :* well-mannered children = *des enfants bien éduqués* ≠ ill-mannered = *mal éduqué.*

WELL-MATCHED (adj) *bien assorti, -e :* my sister and her husband are well-matched = *ma sœur et son mari sont bien assortis.*

WELL-MEANING (adj) *bien intentionné, -e :* a well-meaning gesture = *un geste bien intentionné.*

WELL-OFF (adj) *aisé, -e :* my family's well-off = *j'ai une famille aisée* → RICH ≠ without a cent = *sans le sou* **(stop complaining) you don't know when you're well-off** = *(arrête de te plaindre) tu ne connais pas ta chance* ⓪ you never had it so good = *ça n'a jamais été aussi bien pour vous* ☠ *un travail aisé* = easy work.

WELL-PLACED (adj) *haut placé, -e :* well-placed in the administration = *haut placé au gouvernement* ⓪ well-connected = *qui a ses entrées.*

WELL-PRESERVED (adj) *bien conservé, -e :* he's well-preserved for his age = *il est bien conservé pour son âge.*

WELL-READ (adj) *qui a des lettres :* a well-read man = *un homme qui a des lettres* ⓪ learned = *savant.*

WELL-THOUGHT-OF (adj) *bien vu, -e :* well-thought-of in the company = *bien vu dans l'entreprise.*

WELL-TIMED (adj) *qui tombe bien :* the check came yesterday ; it was well-timed = *le chèque est arrivé hier ; il tombait bien* ≠ ill-timed = *qui tombe mal.*

WELL-TO-DO (adj) *à son aise :* a well-to-do family = *une famille à son aise* → RICH.

WELL-WISHER (n) *quelqu'un qui veut témoigner sa sympathie :* when he was in hospital, the Pope got hundreds of letters from well-wishers = *quand il était à l'hôpital, le pape a reçu des centaines de lettres de gens qui voulaient lui témoigner leur sympathie.*

WELSH ON (to, -ed) *se dérober :* they reached an agreement but he welshed on it = *ils sont arrivés à un accord* mais il s'est dérobé ⓪ to go back on = *revenir sur* ☠ *dérober qqch à qqn* = to steal stg from s.o.

WEST (n) *ouest (m) :* the West of the United States = *l'ouest des États-Unis* ≠ East = *est* **the West** = *l'Occident.*

WEST (adv) **to go west** = *aller vers l'ouest.*

WEST (adj) *ouest, de l'Ouest :* West Berlin = *Berlin-Ouest,* West Germany = *Allemagne de l'Ouest* **the West Indies** = *les Antilles* **West Point** = *école militaire américaine qui correspond à Saint-Cyr.*

WESTERN (n) *western (m) :* the movie's a western = *ce film est un western.*

WESTERN (adj) *ouest, de l'Ouest :* Western Europe = *Europe de l'Ouest.*

WET (adj, -ter, -test) *mouillé, -e :* my hair's wet = *j'ai les cheveux mouillés* ⓪ soggy = *détrempé,* damp = *humide* **to be all wet** = *se mettre/se fourrer le doigt dans l'œil :* if you think I married him for his money you're all wet = *tu te mets/fourres le doigt dans l'œil si tu penses que je l'ai épousé pour son argent* ⓪ to be off base = *être à côté de la plaque* **he's still wet behind the ears** = *on lui presserait le nez, il en sortirait du lait* ⓪ innocent young thing = *oie blanche* **to be wet through** = *être trempé jusqu'à la moelle* ⓪ to be soaking wet = *être dégoulinant,* to look like a drowned rat = *avoir l'air d'un chien mouillé* **wet blanket** = *bonnet de nuit :* she's married to a wet blanket = *elle a épousé un bonnet de nuit* ⓪ spoilsport = *trouble-fête* **to have wet dreams** = *faire des rêves humides/faire une carte de France* **wet nurse** = *nourrice* **wet paint** = *peinture fraîche.*

WETBACK (n) *ouvrier mexicain entré illégalement aux États-Unis.*

WHACK (n) *gnon (m)* ⓪ wallop = *châtaigne* **WHACK** (to, -ed) *flanquer des gnons à* → TO HIT.

WHALE (n) *baleine (f) :* a tame whale = *une baleine apprivoisée* ⓪ shark = *requin* ☠ *rire comme une baleine* = to split one's sides laughing.

WHAM ! (interj) **wham, bam, thank you ma'am !** = *crac ! boum ! hue ! :* with him sex is wham, bam, thank you ma'am ! = *quand on baise avec lui, c'est crac ! boum ! hue !*

WHARF (n, -ves) *quai (m) :* the passengers got off on the wharf = *les passagers sont descendus sur le quai* ⓪ pier = *jetée* ☠ *le Quai-d'Orsay* = French State Department — *quai (de gare)* = platform (station) — *les quais de la Seine* = the banks of the Seine.

WHAT (pron) **1/** *qu'est-ce que ? :* what are you looking for ? = *qu'est-ce que vous cherchez ?* **2/** *ce que :* do you know what I think ? = *tu sais ce que je pense ?*

to give s.o. what for = *sonner les cloches à qqn* → TO LAMBAST

(that's my advice) take it for what it's worth = *(voilà le conseil que je vous donne,) il vaut ce qu'il vaut*

what about ? = **1/** *et ? :* what about the dough I lent you ? = *et le fric que je t'ai prêté ?* = and the dough I lent you ? **2/** *et si ? :* what about a coffee ? = *et si on prenait un café ?* **3/** *à quel propos/sujet ? :* the boss wants to see you — what about ? = *le patron veut vous voir — à quel propos/sujet ?*

what are you afraid of ? = *de quoi avez-vous peur ?*

what were you talking about ? = *de quoi parliez-vous ?*

what are you thinking about ? = *à quoi pensez-vous ?*

what else ? = *quoi d'autre ?*

what for ? = *pour quoi (faire) ? :* all these tools ? what for ? = *tous ces outils ? pour quoi (faire) ?*

what if ? = *et si ? :* what if he finds out ? = *et s'il découvre la vérité ?*

what is it ? = *qu'est-ce que c'est ?*

what's it for ? = *à quoi ça sert ?*

what's more = *qui plus est :* he smokes a lot and what's more most of it is pot = *il fume énormément, et qui plus est en général de la marie* ⑩ moreover = *du reste*

what's new ? = *quoi de neuf ?* ⑩ **what's cooking ?** = *ça gaze ?,* **what's up ?** = *qu'est-ce qui se passe ?,* **what's doing ?** = *qu'est-ce que vous devenez ?*

what of it ? = *et alors ?* = **so what ?**

what's that ? = *c'est quoi ? :* I know what he wants for Xmas — what's that ? = *je sais ce qu'il veut pour Noël — c'est quoi ?*

what then ? = *et après ?*

what's it to you ? = *qu'est-ce que ça peut te faire ?* ⑩ mind your own business ! = *occupe-toi de tes affaires !*

what's up with (your brother) ? = *qu'est-ce qui se passe avec (ton frère) ?*

what's with you ? = *qu'est-ce qui vous prend ?* ⑩ what's eating you ? = *quelle mouche te pique ?*

what's (the problem/your name) ? = *quel est (le problème/votre nom) ?*

what's it worth to you ? = *qu'est-ce que tu me donnes ? :* what's it worth to you to know whether he's still interested or not ? = *qu'est-ce que tu me donnes pour savoir si ça l'intéresse encore ou non ?*

what with ... and ... = *entre ... et ... :* what with inflation and higher taxes, I can't afford to buy anything = *entre l'inflation et la hausse des impôts, je ne peux rien m'acheter*

what's wrong ? = *qu'est-ce qui ne va pas ?* ⑩ **what's the matter ?** = *qu'est-ce qu'il y a ?*

what's wrong with ... ? = **1/** *qu'est-ce que ... a ? :* what's wrong with the radio/you ? = *qu'est-ce qu'elle a, la radio ?/qu'est-ce que tu as ?* **2/** *quel mal y a-t-il à :* what's wrong with two guys sleeping together ? = *quel mal y a-t-il à ce que deux types couchent ensemble ?*

do you know what ? = *tu sais quoi ?*

he knows what's what = *il sait de quoi il retourne* ⑩ he knows the score = *il connaît la musique*

I'll tell you what ! = *dis donc ! :* I'll tell you what, let's eat Chinese food ! = *dis donc, si on allait dans un restaurant chinois !*

Mr/Mrs what's his/her name = *M./Mme machin chose*

what ! = *quoi !* → GOSH !

WHAT (adj) *quel, quelle :* what kind of man is he ? = *quel genre d'homme est-ce ?,* what nerve ! = *quel toupet !* ☠ *quel frère préfères-tu ?* = which brother do you like best ?

what a (bastard/wonderful guy) ! = *quel (salaud/type merveilleux) !*

what time is it ? = *quelle heure est-il ?* ⑩ **what day is it ?** = *quel jour sommes-nous ?*

WHATCHAMACALLIT (n) *machin(-truc) (m) :* I need a whatchamacallit like yours to open cans = *j'ai besoin d'un machin(-truc) comme le tien pour ouvrir les boîtes de conserve* ⑩ gizmo = *bidule/truc.*

WHATEVER (pron) **1/** *(tout) ce que :* take whatever you want = *prenez (tout) ce que vous voulez* = take anything that you want **2/** *quoi que :* whatever you decide the boss will agree = *quoi que vous décidiez, le patron sera d'accord*

or whatever = *ou n'importe quoi :* let's have a hamburger or whatever = *prenons un hamburger ou n'importe quoi*

whatever happens (call me) = *quoi qu'il arrive (appelez-moi)*

whatever you say = *comme vous voulez* = as you like

whatever will be, will be = *ce qui doit arriver arrivera* → THAT'S LIFE !

WHATEVER (adj) *quel, quelle que soit :* whatever girl he tries to sleep with, he strikes out = *quelle que soit la fille avec qui il essaie de coucher, il fait toujours chou blanc.*

WHATNOT (n) *bricole (f) :* I bought a few little whatnots at the flea market = *j'ai acheté quelques petites bricoles au marché aux puces* ⑩ trinket = *babiole.*

WHATSOEVER (adj, pron) = WHATEVER
☠ « whatsoever » *est moins employé que* « whatever ».

WHEAT (n) *blé (m) :* wheat fields = *champs de blé*
☠ *manger son blé en herbe* = to spend one's money before one gets it
— *t'as du blé ?* = do you have any bread/dough ?

WHEEDLE OUT (OF) (to, -d) *obtenir de (par des cajoleries) :* she wheedled a hundred bucks out of her father = *elle a obtenu cent dollars de son père par des cajoleries.*

WHEEL (n) *roue (f) :* a car has four wheels = *une voiture a quatre roues*
(killed) at the wheel = *(tué) au volant*
to take the wheel = *prendre le volant*
☠ *faire la roue* = to do a cartwheel.

WHEEL AND DEAL (to, -ed) *magouiller* (PEJ), *brasser des affaires :* the Mafia's wheeling and dealing before the elections = *la Mafia magouille avant les élections*, my brother's wheeling and dealing = *mon frère brasse des affaires* → TO HUSTLE.

WHEELBARROW (n) *brouette (f).*

WHEELCHAIR (n) *fauteuil (m) roulant* ⓓ crutches = *béquilles.*

WHEELER-DEALER (n) *brasseur (m) d'affaires, magouilleur (m) :* he's one of Hollywood's top wheeler-dealers = *c'est un des plus gros brasseurs d'affaires d'Hollywood* ⓓ hustler = *combinard.*

WHEN (adv) *quand :* when will you come ? = *quand viendrez-vous ?*
when is it ? = *quand est-ce ?*

WHEN (conj) 1/ *quand :* I don't know when she's coming = *je ne sais pas quand elle va venir* 2/ *quand, lorsque :* the phone rang when he came in = *le téléphone a sonné quand/lorsqu'il est entré* ⓓ the moment that = *au moment où*
the (day) when = *le (jour) où*
when and if = *si jamais :* call me when and if you get to New York = *appelez-moi si jamais vous venez à New York.*

WHENEVER (adv, conj) 1/ *(n'importe) quand :* come whenever you like = *venez quand vous voulez* 2/ *à chaque fois que :* whenever I see my parents, we fight = *à chaque fois que je vois mes parents, nous nous disputons* ⓓ every time = *toutes les fois que.*

WHERE (adv) *où :* where do you live ? = *où habitez-vous ?*, I don't know where their house is = *je ne sais pas où est leur maison*
where else ? = *à quel autre endroit ? :* where else can we eat after midnight ? = *à quel autre endroit peut-on manger après minuit ?*
where is it ? = *où est-ce ?*

WHERE (conj) *où :* I'll go where he tells me to go = *j'irai où il me dira d'aller*
that's where it's at/things are at = *voilà où ça en est/où en sont les choses*
that's where (you're wrong) = *c'est là que (vous avez tort)*
☠ *le jour où* = the day when
— *toi ou moi* = you or me.

WHEREABOUTS (n pl) *endroit où se trouve :* the murderer's whereabouts are unknown = *on ne sait pas à quel endroit se trouve le meurtrier.*

WHEREAS (conj) *tandis que :* an ordinary bomb destroys everything whereas the neutron bomb only kills living beings ! = *une bombe ordinaire détruit tout, tandis que la bombe à neutrons tue uniquement les êtres vivants !* ⓓ while = *alors que.*

WHEREVER (adv) *où donc ? :* wherever did you find a restaurant open so late ? = *où avez-vous donc trouvé un restaurant ouvert si tard ?*

WHEREVER (conj) 1/ *où que :* she'll find you wherever you go = *elle te trouvera où que tu ailles* 2/ *(là) où :* sit wherever you want = *asseyez-vous (là) où vous voulez.*

WHEREWITHAL (n) **to have the wherewithal (to buy a new car)** = *avoir de quoi (acheter une nouvelle voiture)* → RICH.

WHETHER (conj) *si :* I don't know whether I should say yes = *je ne sais pas si je dois dire oui* ☠ → if
whether ... or not = 1/ *si ... ou non :* I don't know whether he's coming or not = *je ne sais pas s'il vient ou non* 2/ *que ... ou non :* whether you agree or not, I couldn't care less = *que vous soyez d'accord ou non, je m'en fiche.*

WHEW ! (interj) *ouf !* → GOSH ! ☠ *avant d'avoir eu le temps de dire ouf !* = before you had the time to say Jack Robinson.

WHICH (pron) 1/ *lequel, laquelle :* I'm not sure which I like the best = *je ne sais pas lequel je préfère*
which is which ! = *qui est qui ?/lequel est lequel ? :* the twins/the two houses are so much alike that I don't know which is which = *les jumeaux/les deux maisons se ressemblent tant que je ne sais pas qui est qui/laquelle est laquelle*
which of (these men/the two) ? = *lequel de (ces hommes)/des (deux) ?*
2/ *qui, que (pronom relatif ; choses) :* the car which they bought is red = *la voiture qu'ils ont achetée est rouge* = that, I took the bus which was the closest = *j'ai pris le bus qui était le plus proche* = that ☠ *qui* → who, *que* → that
3/ *ce qui :* he told me he was divorced, which wasn't true = *il m'a dit qu'il était divorcé, ce qui n'était pas vrai.*

WHICH (adj) *quel, quelle* : which brother/color do you like best ? = *quel frère/quelle couleur préfères-tu ?*
which one ? = *lequel, laquelle ? :* which one do you want ? = *lequel voulez-vous ?*
which ones ? = *lesquels, lesquelles ? :* which ones did he buy ? = *lesquels a-t-il achetés ?*
☠ → what.

WHICHEVER (pron) *quel, quelle que soit :* whichever you chose is OK with me = *quel que soit votre choix, je suis d'accord.*

WHICHEVER (adj) *quel, quelle que soit :* whichever day he comes = *quel que soit le jour où il arrive*
whichever one = *celui que, celle que :* take whichever one you want = *prenez celui que vous voulez.*

WHILE (n) **after a while** = *au bout d'un moment :* after a while, I realized she was lying = *après un moment, je me suis rendu compte qu'elle mentait*
a (little) while = *un (petit) moment :* stay a (little) while = *restez un (petit) moment*
a (little) while after (I got pregnant) = *peu de temps après (je me suis retrouvée enceinte)*
a (little) while ago = 1/ *tout à l'heure :* he called a (little) while ago = *il a appelé tout à l'heure* ⓐ not long ago = *il y a peu de temps* 2/ *il y a quelque temps :* they got married a (little) while ago = *ils se sont mariés il y a quelque temps*
a (little) while longer = *encore un (petit) peu :* stay a (little) while longer = *restez encore un (petit) peu*
I'll make it worth your while = *je ne vous oublierai pas :* if you help me to get an apartment, I'll make it worth your while = *si vous m'aidez à trouver un appartement, je ne vous oublierai pas* ⓐ to get a commission = *toucher une commission*
in a (little) while = *tout à l'heure :* he'll call back in a (little) while = *il rappellera tout à l'heure* ⓐ shortly = *sous peu*
it is ≠ isn't worth your while = *ça vaut ≠ ça ne vaut pas le coup*
quite a while = *un bon bout de temps :* they lived in the Far East quite a while = *ils ont vécu en Extrême-Orient un bon bout de temps.*

WHILE (conj) 1/ *pendant que :* he called while you were out = *il a appelé pendant que vous étiez sorti* ⓐ when = *quand* 2/ *alors que :* she prefers to stay at home while her sisters are real businesswomen = *elle préfère rester à la maison alors que ses sœurs sont de véritables femmes d'affaires*
(buy me one) while you're at it = *(achète-m'en un) pendant que tu y es*
not while (I'm alive) ! = *pas tant que (je vivrai) !* ⓐ not as long as = *pas aussi longtemps que.*

WHILE (to, -d) **to while away (the afternoon/the time)** = *passer agréablement (l'après-midi/le temps).*

WHIM (n) *lubie (f) :* his latest whim is to make love in the kitchen = *sa dernière lubie, c'est de faire l'amour dans la cuisine* ⓐ caprice = ←.

WHIMPER (to, -ed) *pleurnicher* ⓐ to cry bitterly = *pleurer comme une Madeleine.*

WHIMSICAL (adj) *fantasque :* a whimsical personality = *une personnalité fantasque* ⓐ mercurial = *versatile.*

WHINE (to, -d) *geindre :* stop whining and tell me what's wrong = *arrêtez de geindre et dites-moi ce qui ne va pas* ⓐ to whimper = *pleurnicher* ☠ → to moan.

WHIP (n) *fouet (m)* ⓐ lash = *coup de fouet,* cat-o'-nine-tails = *martinet*
to crack the whip = *serrer la vis :* the teacher's going to crack the whip in the fall = *le professeur va nous serrer la vis en automne* ⓐ to put one's foot down = *faire acte d'autorité*
the Senate whip = *le whip du Sénat (chargé de la discipline de vote d'un parti).*

WHIP (to, -ped) 1/ *fouetter :* his father whipped him = *son père l'a fouetté* → TO HIT 2/ *flanquer une pile à :* their team whipped ours = *leur équipe nous a flanqué une pile*
to whip up (a snack) = *préparer (un casse-croûte) vite fait.*

WHIPPING (n) *pile (f) :* to give s.o. a whipping = *flanquer une pile à qqn* → TO HIT ☠ → pile
whipping boy = *souffre-douleur* ⓐ scapegoat = *bouc émissaire.*

WHIRL (n) *tourbillon (m) :* a whirl of social activities = *un tourbillon de mondanités*
give it a whirl ! = *essaie un coup !* ⓐ have a crack at it ! = *essaie de le faire !*

WHISKERS (n pl) *moustaches (f pl) :* you shouldn't cut a cat's whiskers = *il ne faut pas couper les moustaches d'un chat* ☠ → mustache.

WHISKEY (n, -s or -ies) *whisky (m)* ⓐ Scotch = ←.

WHISPER (to, -ed) *chuchoter ≠* to yell = *hurler* **WHISPERING** (n) *chuchotement (m).*

WHISTLE (n) *sifflet (m) :* buy me a whistle = *achète-moi un sifflet*
to blow the whistle on = *découvrir le pot aux roses :* he sold coke to the students till the cops blew the whistle on him = *il a vendu de la coke aux étudiants jusqu'à ce que les flics découvrent le pot aux roses*
to wet one's whistle = *se rincer la dalle* ⓐ to quench one's thirst = *se désaltérer*
☠ *ça m'a coupé le sifflet* = I was completely dumbfounded
— *des sifflets* = catcalls.

WHISTLE (to, -d) *siffler :* I don't know how to whistle = *je ne sais pas siffler*
you can whistle for it ! = *tu peux toujours courir !* ⓐ you should live so long ! = *tu peux toujours te brosser !*

WHITE

you're not just whistling Dixie ! = *je ne te le fais pas dire !* Ⓞ you know it ! = *tu parles !*
☠ *siffler un acteur* = to boo/to hiss an actor
— *siffler (boire)* = to guzzle (drink).

WHITE (n) *blanc (m)* : she wears a lot of white = *elle porte beaucoup de blanc*
the Whites = *les Blancs* : three Whites were killed = *trois Blancs ont été tués* ≠ colored people = *gens de couleur*
☠ *un chèque en blanc* = a blank check
— *laisser un blanc* = to leave a blank
— *balle à blanc* = blank bullet
— *un Blanc* = a white person.

WHITE (adj, -r, -st) *blanc, blanche* : a white coat = *un manteau blanc* Ⓞ off-white = *blanc cassé,* beige = ←
to be as white as a sheet = *être blanc comme un linge/comme un cachet d'aspirine*
a white elephant = *un gouffre (financier)* : many people think that the Concorde is a white elephant = *beaucoup de gens pensent que le Concorde est un gouffre (financier)*
the White House = *la Maison-Blanche*

a white lie = *un pieux mensonge*
a white man/woman = *un Blanc/une Blanche*
white as snow = *blanc comme neige*
white trash = *les petits Blancs*
☠ *c'est bonnet blanc et blanc bonnet* = it's six of one, half a dozen of the other
— *un blanc-bec* = a greenhorn
— *une nuit blanche* = a sleepless night
— *cheveux blancs* = gray hair.

WHITE-COLLAR (adj) *de col blanc* : a white-collar job = *un travail de col blanc*
white-collar worker = *employé de bureau/col blanc.*

WHITEWASH (to, -ed) *blanchir* : the suspect was whitewashed = *le suspect a été blanchi* Ⓞ to exonerate = *mettre hors de cause,* to clear = *disculper* ☠ *ses cheveux blanchissent* = his hair's turning white.

WHIT(E)Y (n, -ies) *sale Blanc, Blanche* = honky ≠ darkie = *bamboula.*

W(H)IZ (n, -zes) a whiz at (physics) = *un as en (physique)* = a wizard at (physics) Ⓞ crackshot = *crack.*

WHO (pron) 1/ (subject) *qui (personne)* : who is she ? = *qui est-elle ?,* I know who did it = *je sais qui a fait ça*
2/ (relative pronoun) *qui, que (personne)* : the man who's looking at you = *l'homme qui vous regarde,* the guy who she's sleeping with = *le type avec qui elle couche*

who is it ? = *qui est-ce ?*
who else (was there) ? = *qui d'autre (était là) ?*
the who's who = *le Who's Who/le Gotha* : he's

part of the who's who of Hollywood = *il fait partie du Gotha d'Hollywood/du Who's Who d'Hollywood* Ⓞ the upper crust = *le gratin*

☠ *le livre qui est sur la table* = the book which is/that's on the table

— *c'est la femme de qui ?* = whose wife is she ?
— *que* → that.

WHO *(complément, usage parlé)*

who did you see ? = *qui avez-vous vu ?*
who did you give it to ? = *à qui l'avez-vous donné ?*
who is it for ? = *pour qui est-ce ?*
who did you come with ? = *avec qui êtes-vous venu ?*

WHOM *(complément, anglais soigné)*

whom did you see ? = *qui avez-vous vu ?*
to whom did you give it ? = *à qui l'avez-vous donné ?*
for whom is it ? = *pour qui est-ce ?*
with whom did you come ? = *avec qui êtes-vous venu ?*

☠ *c'est l'homme qu'elle a épousé* = that's the man whom/that/who she married
— « whom » = *anglais soigné.*

WHODUNIT (n) *polar (m)* : the book is a good whodunit = *ce livre est un bon polar* Ⓞ cloak-and-dagger story = *roman de cape et d'épée.*

WHOEVER (pron) 1/ *quiconque* : whoever sells hard

drugs is a criminal = *quiconque vend des drogues dures est un criminel* Ⓞ the one who = *celui qui* 2/ *quel que soit celui, quelle que soit celle* : whoever he marries, he won't be happy = *quelle que soit celle qu'il épouse, il ne sera pas heureux.*

WHOLE (n) as a whole = *dans son ensemble* : the group as a whole is for free abortion = *le groupe dans son ensemble est pour l'avortement libre*
a whole = *un tout* : two halves make a whole = *deux moitiés font un tout*

on the whole = *dans l'ensemble* : on the whole he's a nice guy = *dans l'ensemble c'est un type sympa*
the whole of (New York is talking about it) = *le tout (New York en parle).*

WHOLE (adj) *entier, -ère* : the whole cake = *le gâteau entier,* I spent my whole salary = *j'ai dépensé mon salaire entier* ≠ partial = *partiel* ☠ → entire

the whole ... = *... en entier* : I didn't see the whole movie = *je n'ai pas vu le film en entier*
the whole business = *toute cette histoire* : the whole business is a pain in the neck = *toute cette histoire est bien casse-pieds*
to go the whole hog = *mettre le paquet* : they went the whole hog on the dinner = *ils ont mis le paquet pour le dîner* ⓪ to go all out = *mettre les petits plats dans les grands*
the whole kit and caboodle = 1/ *toute la smala* : he came with his folks and the whole kit and caboodle = *il est venu avec sa famille et toute la smala* 2/ *tout le truc* : I bought the whole kit and caboodle for a hundred bucks = *j'ai acheté tout le truc pour cinq cent balles*
the whole lot = 1/ *le tout* : the whole lot costs a grand = *le tout coûte mille dollars* 2/ *tout le tremblement* : I'll take the shoes, the bag and the whole lot = *je vais prendre les chaussures, le sac et tout le tremblement*
a whole lot of = *tout plein de* : there were a whole lot of people at the meeting = *il y avait tout plein de gens à la réunion* → MANY
the whole shebang = *tout le bastringue* : he's the head of the French company, the German company and the whole shebang = *il est à la tête de la société française, de la société allemande et de tout le bastringue*
the whole shooting match = *tout le bataclan* : he bought the factory, the machines and the whole shooting match = *il a acheté l'usine, les machines et tout le bataclan*
that's not the whole story ! = *et ce n'est pas tout !* ⓪ you haven't heard anything yet ! = *et tu n'as encore rien entendu !*
that's the whole truth ! = *voilà la vérité tout entière !*
the whole works = *tout le bazar* : the cook left with the china, the TV and the whole works = *la cuisinière est partie avec la porcelaine, la télé et tout le bazar*
(it's the best restaurant) in the whole world = *(c'est le meilleur restaurant) du monde*
the whole world (knows they're sleeping together) = *le monde entier (sait qu'ils couchent ensemble)*
the whole (year/week) = *toute (l'année/la semaine)* = all (year/week).

WHOLEHEARTED (adj) *sans réserve* : you have my wholehearted support = *vous avez mon soutien sans réserve.*

WHOLESALE (adv) *en gros* : they sell furniture wholesale = *ils vendent des meubles en gros* ≠ retail = *au détail* **WHOLESALER** (n) *grossiste (m, f).*

WHOLESOME (adj) *sain, -e* : a wholesome attitude = *une attitude saine* ≠ unwholesome = *malsain* ☠ *sain et sauf* = safe and sound
— *une politique saine* = a sane policy.

WHOLLY (adv) *entièrement* : I'm wholly convinced = *je suis entièrement convaincu* ≠ not at all = *pas du tout.*

WHOM (pron) → WHO.

WHOOP (to, -ed) **to whoop it up** = *faire la fête* : the team whooped it up after the match = *l'équipe a fait la fête après le match* ⓪ to paint the town red = *faire la bringue.*

WHOOPING COUGH (n) *coqueluche (f)* ☠ *la coqueluche de New York* = the toast of New York.

WHOOPS ! (interj) *hop là !*

WHOPPING (adj) *faramineux, -euse* : a whopping mistake/blunder = *une faute/gaffe faramineuse.*

WHORE (n) *pute (f)* : a lot of whores on Times Square = *beaucoup de putes à Times Square* ⓪ tramp = *traînée*

☠ *fils de pute* = son of a bitch **WHOREHOUSE** (n) *boxon (m), lupanar (m)* ⓪ cathouse = *claque.*

WHOSE (pron) 1/ *à qui* : whose car is this ? = *à qui est cette voiture ?,* whose is it ? = *à qui est-ce ?* 2/ *duquel, de laquelle* : one of my brothers' houses — whose ? = *la maison de l'un de mes frères — duquel ?*

WHOSE (adj) *dont* : isn't that the girl whose husband committed suicide ? = *est-ce que ce n'est pas la fille dont le mari s'est suicidé ?*
☠ *dont* = of whom/of which : *ils ont trois enfants, dont deux sont mariés* = they have three kids two of whom are married, *il a écrit plusieurs livres, dont l'un est un best-seller* = he wrote several books, one of which is a best seller
— *la façon dont elle s'habille/écrit* = the way that/in which she dresses/writes.

WHY (n) **the whys and wherefores** = *le pourquoi et le comment.*

WHY (adv) *pourquoi* : why are you staring at me like that ? = *pourquoi me regardez-vous comme ça ?* ⓪ how come ? = *comment se fait-il que ?*
why is it that (there's so much violence in the world) ? = *comment se fait-il qu'(il y ait tant de violence dans le monde) ?*
why not ? = *pourquoi pas ?*

WHY (conj) *pourquoi* : I don't know why you didn't tell me what happened = *je ne sais par pourquoi vous ne m'avez pas dit ce qui s'était passé.*

WICKED (adj) *méchant, -e* : a wicked woman = *une méchante femme*
☠ « wicked » *est moins employé que* « mean »
— → mean.

WIDE (adj, -r, -st) *large* : a wide avenue = *une avenue large* ≠ narrow = *étroit* ☠ → large
to be wide of the mark = *être complètement à côté de la plaque* ⓪ to be off = *ne pas y être*
(2 feet) wide = *large de (60 cm).*

WIDE (adv) **wide open** = *grand ouvert* : the door's wide open = *la porte est grand ouverte* ≠ ajar = *entrebâillé.*

WIDE-AWAKE (adj) *complètement réveillé, -e* : the baby's wide-awake now = *le bébé est complètement réveillé maintenant* ≠ sound asleep = *qui dort à poings fermés.*

WIDE-EYED (adj) *candide* : wide-eyed innocence = *innocence candide* ⓪ naive = *naïf* ☠ → candid.

WIDESPREAD (adj) *largement répandu, -e* : widespread inflation = *une inflation largement répandue* ≠ limited = *limité.*

WIDOW (n) *veuve (f)* : he married a rich widow = *il a épousé une riche veuve*
bridge/golf widow = *femme délaissée par un mari qui passe son temps à jouer au bridge/au golf*
☠ *défendre la veuve et l'orphelin* = to be a do-gooder.

WIDOWER (n) *veuf (m)* ⓪ wife = *femme.*

WIDTH (n) *largeur (f)* : the width of the room = *la largeur de la pièce* ≠ length = *longueur.*

WIELD (to, -ed) *exercer* : to wield influence/power = *exercer une influence/le pouvoir* ☠ → to exert.

WIFE (n, wives) *femme (f), épouse (f)* : I'd like you to meet my wife = *j'aimerais vous présenter ma femme/mon épouse* ⓪ spouse = *conjoint*, the missus = *la baronne*, better half = *moitié* ≠ husband = *mari* ☠ → woman.

WIG (n) *perruque (f)* : she wears a wig = *elle porte une perruque* ⓪ hairpiece = *postiche*, toupee = *(faux) toupet.*

WIGGLE (n) **to walk with a wiggle** = *marcher en se trémoussant* ⓪ to waddle = *se dandiner.*

WILD (adj, -er, -est) **1/** *sauvage* : wild animals = *des animaux sauvages* ≠ tame = *apprivoisé* ☠ → savage **2/** *dément, -e* : a wild hairdo = *une coiffure démente* = far-out ⓪ way-out = *délirant* **3/** *hors de soi* : I was so late the boss was wild ! = *j'étais tellement en retard que le patron était hors de lui !* → ANGRY
to be wild about = *être dingue de* : I'm wild about him/Chinese food = *je suis dingue de lui/de cuisine chinoise* ⓪ to be mad about = *être fou de*
to drive s.o. wild = *rendre qqn fou* : the kids drove me

wild today = *les gosses m'ont rendue folle aujourd'hui* ⓪ to drive s.o. up the wall = *rendre qqn chèvre*
to go wild = *devenir fou* : he went wild when he discovered the theft = *il est devenu fou quand il a découvert le vol*
(I wouldn't have thought of that) in my wildest dreams = *jamais je n'aurais osé penser/imaginer une chose pareille*
to sow one's wild oats = *jeter sa gourme* ⓪ to knock around = *rouler sa bosse*
wild horses couldn't stop me = *un régiment ne m'arrêterait pas.*

WILD (adv) **to be running wild** = *être déchaîné* : the kids are running wild = *les gosses sont déchaînés.*

WILDERNESS (n, -es) *région (f) sauvage* ⓪ desert = *désert.*

WILDFIRE (n) **to spread like wildfire** = *se répandre comme une traînée de poudre* ⓪ to spread = *s'étendre.*

WILD-GOOSE CHASE (n) **(to be (on)/to go on) a wild-goose chase** = *(être/y aller) pour des prunes* : I spent all day looking for a bag like yours, but it was a wild-goose chase ! = *j'ai passé la journée à chercher un sac comme le vôtre, pour des prunes !* ⓪ to go for nothing = *y aller pour rien.*

WILDLY (adv) *follement* : wildly happy = *follement heureux* → VERY.

WILES (n pl) *manigances (f pl)* : feminine wiles = *manigances féminines* ⓪ trick = *ruse.*

WILL (n) **1/** *testament (m)* : he died without leaving a will = *il est mort sans laisser de testament* ⓪ inheritance = *héritage*, executor = *exécuteur testamentaire*
to cut s.o. out of a will = *éliminer qqn d'un testament* ⓪ to disinherit = *déshériter*
2/ *volonté (f)* : she has a very strong will = *elle a énormément de volonté* ☠ *la volonté d'arrêter de fumer* = the willpower to stop smoking
against s.o.'s will = *contre la volonté de qqn* : they sold the house against his will = *ils ont vendu la maison contre sa volonté*
good ≠ ill will = *bonne ≠ mauvaise volonté* : he showed good ≠ ill will = *il a montré de la bonne ≠ mauvaise volonté*
where there's a will there's a way = *vouloir, c'est pouvoir.*

WILLFUL (adj) *volontaire* : a willful child = *un enfant volontaire* ⓪ stubborn = *têtu* ☠ → voluntary.

WILLIES (n pl) *trouille (f)* : this dark alley gives me the willies = *cette ruelle sombre me fiche la trouille* ⓪ the jitters = *la frousse.*

WILLINGLY (adv) *volontiers* : I'll help you willingly = *je vous aiderai volontiers* ≠ unwillingly = *de mauvais gré* ☠ *un whisky ? — volontiers !* = a Scotch ? — gladly !

WILLING TO (adj) *disposé, -e à* : I'm willing to help

you = *je suis disposé à vous aider* ≠ unwilling to = *peu disposé à.*

WILLPOWER (n) *volonté* (f) : you need a lot of willpower to stop smoking = *il faut beaucoup de volonté pour arrêter de fumer* ☠ → will.

WILT (to, -ed) *se faner* : flowers wilt in the heat = *les fleurs se fanent à la chaleur* ≠ to bloom = *fleurir.*

WIMP (n) *ringard, -e* : she's married to a wimp = *elle a épousé un ringard* ⑩ drip = *minus.*

WIN (to, won, won) *gagner* : he won first prize = *il a gagné le premier prix* ⑩ to carry the day = *remporter la victoire* ≠ to fall on one's face = *se casser la gueule*
to win s.o. over to (a cause) = *gagner qqn à (une cause)*
☠ *il gagne à être connu* = he grows on you
— *gagner de l'argent* = to earn/make money
— *elle n'a rien à y gagner* = she has nothing to gain by that.

WINCE (to, -d) *(se) crisper* : the pain made him wince = *il s'est crispé sous la douleur* ☠ *elle me crispe !* = she's really getting on my nerves !

WIND (n) *vent* (m) : strong winds = *des vents forts* ⑩ gale = *coup de vent,* it's windy = *il y a du vent*
to break/pass wind = *faire des vents*
to get wind of = *avoir vent de* : he got wind of the plot = *il a eu vent du complot* ⑩ to hear of = *entendre parler de*
to see how the wind blows = *voir d'où vient le vent* ⑩ to see how the land lies = *tâter le terrain*
to take the wind out of s.o.'s sails = *couper l'herbe sous les pieds de qqn*
to throw (caution) to the winds = *faire fi de toute (prudence)*
☠ *être dans le vent* = to be hip
— *contre vents et marées* = come hell or high water
— *ce qu'il raconte, c'est du vent* = what he says is a lot of hot air.

WIND (to, wound, wound) *remonter* : to wind a clock/a watch = *remonter une pendule/une montre*
to wind around = *enrouler autour de* : she wound the rope around her waist = *elle s'est enroulé la corde autour de la taille*
to wind down = *liquider graduellement* : the company's winding down its European operations = *l'entreprise est en train de liquider graduellement ses opérations européennes*
to wind through = *serpenter* : this road winds through the countryside = *cette route serpente à travers la campagne*
to wind up = 1/ *boucler* : I'm winding up my work = *je boucle mon travail* ≠ to start up = *démarrer*
☠ *boucle-la !* = shut up !
— *boucler (criminel/maison)* = to lock up (criminal/house)
2/ *finir par* : she wound up pregnant = *elle a fini par être enceinte*

3/ *prendre fin* : the meeting's winding up = *la réunion prend fin* ⑩ to draw to a close = *toucher à sa fin*
to be wound up = *avoir les nerfs en boule/en pelote* : why is she always so wound up ? = *pourquoi a-t-elle toujours tellement les nerfs en boule ?/en pelote ?* ⑩ to be under pressure = *être sous pression*
to wind up in = *échouer en/à* : to wind up in jail = *échouer en prison* ⑩ to end up in = *finir en*
☠ *remonter qqn* = to pick s.o. up
— *remonter une affaire* = to get a business back on its feet
— *lui remonter le moral* = to boost his morale
— *ça remonte à deux ans* = that goes back two years.

WINDBAG (n) *pie-jacasse* (f) : don't listen to that windbag = *n'écoutez pas cette pie-jacasse* ⑩ parrot = *perroquet.*

WINDED (adj) *essoufflé, -e* : winded after an hour of jogging = *essoufflé après une heure de jogging* ⑩ out of breath = *à bout de souffle.*

WINDFALL (n) *manne* (f) *(céleste)* : the money I earned this year in stocks is a windfall = *l'argent que m'ont rapporté mes actions cette année est une manne céleste* ⑩ godsend = *aubaine.*

WINDING (adj) *sinueux, -euse* : a winding road = *une route sinueuse* ≠ straight = *droit.*

WINDMILL (n) *moulin* (m) *à vent* ⑩ Don Quixote = Don Quichotte.

WINDOW (n) *fenêtre* (f), *vitrine* (f) (store) : the kids broke the window = *les gosses ont brisé la fenêtre/la vitrine* ⑩ stained-glass window = *vitrail,* windowsill = *rebord de fenêtre,* awning = *store extérieur,* blinds = *stores intérieurs,* pane = *carreau/vitre*
to be window dressing = *être pour la galerie* : the Senator's speech came out for Women's Lib, but it was window dressing = *le sénateur a fait un discours en faveur du MLF, mais c'était pour la galerie*
☠ *servir de vitrine* = to be a showcase.

WINDOW-SHOPPING (n) **to go window-shopping** = *faire du lèche-vitrines.*

WINDSHIELD (n) *pare-brise* (m) ⑩ wipers = *essuie-glaces.*

WINDSURF (n) *planche* (f) *à voile* **WINDSURFER** (n) *véliplanchiste* (m, f).

WINDUP (n) *résultat* (m) : the windup was that she walked out on him = *le résultat, c'est qu'elle l'a plaqué* = result ⑩ upshot = *aboutissement.*

WINDY (adj, -ier, -iest) *venteux, -euse* : a windy beach = *une plage venteuse* ≠ sheltered = *protégé.*

WINE (n) *vin* (m), *pinard* (m) (LV) : let's have some red wine = *prenons un peu de vin rouge* ⑩ cork = *bouchon,* house wine = *vin ordinaire/de table,* vintage wine = *grand cru*
wine bar = *bistro à vins*

wine cellar = *cave à vins*
☠ *avoir le vin gai* ≠ *triste* = to be a good ≠ bad drinker
— *quand le vin est tiré, il faut le boire* = it's too late now, there's no going back
— *cuver son vin* = to sleep it off.

WINE AND DINE (to, -d) *sortir le grand jeu* : they wined and dined him to get the contract signed = *ils lui ont sorti le grand jeu pour lui faire signer le contrat* ⊕ to give the red-carpet treatment = *recevoir en grande pompe.*

WING (n) *aile* (f) : the wing of a bird/a chicken/a house = *l'aile d'un oiseau/d'un poulet/d'une maison*
to clip s.o.'s wings = *rogner les ailes à qqn* ⊕ to make s.o. toe the line = *mettre qqn au pas*
in the wings = *dans les coulisses*
on a wing and a prayer = *si les dieux sont avec (nous)*
the right ≠ **left wing (of the party)** = *l'aile droite* ≠ *gauche (du parti)*
to take s.o. under one's wing = *prendre qqn sous son aile (protectrice)* ⊕ to take s.o. in tow = *prendre qqn en main*
☠ *aile (voiture)* = (car) fender
— *battre de l'aile* = to be going to the dogs
— *vouloir voler avant d'avoir des ailes* = to want to run before one can walk.

WINGDING (n) *pince-fesse(s)* (m) : there's a wingding at the embassy tonight = *il y a un pince-fesses à l'ambassade ce soir* ⊕ bash = *raout.*

WINK (n) *clin* (m) *d'œil* ⊕ blink = *battement de paupières*
I didn't sleep a wink (last night) = *je n'ai pas pu fermer l'œil (de la nuit)* ≠ I slept like a log = *j'ai dormi comme une souche.*

WINK AT (to, -ed) *faire un clin d'œil à* : why did you wink at that guy ? = *pourquoi as-tu fait un clin d'œil à ce type ?* ⊕ to flirt with = *faire du charme à.*

WINNER (n) **1/** *gagnant, -e, gagneur, -euse* : in life, she's a winner = *dans la vie, c'est une gagnante/une gagneuse* ≠ failure = *raté*
winner take all = *le gagnant prend tout*
2/ *quelque chose de chouette* : the movie was a winner = *le film était chouette* ≠ a washout = *un bide intégral.*

WINNING (adj) **1/** *gagnant, -e* : winning number = *numéro gagnant* ≠ losing = *perdant* **2/** *charmeur, -euse* : a winning personality = *une personnalité charmeuse* ⊕ sweet = *délicieux.*

WINO (n) *poivrot, -e* : winos sleeping in the streets = *des poivrots endormis dans les rues* → DRUNK.

WINTER (n) *hiver* (m) : it's cold in winter = *il fait froid en hiver* ⊕ season = *saison.*

WIPE (to, -d) *essuyer* : wipe the table = *essuie la table*
to wipe out = **1/** *anéantir* : so much work wiped me out = *tout ce travail m'a anéanti* ⊕ to wear out = *exténuer*

2/ *anéantir* : they wiped out the enemy = *ils ont anéanti l'ennemi* ⊕ to exterminate = *exterminer* **3/** *extirper* : can crime be wiped out ? = *est-ce qu'on peut extirper le crime ?* **4/** *anéantir* : the fire wiped out our profits = *l'incendie a anéanti nos bénéfices*
☠ *essuyer un refus* = to meet with a refusal
— *essuyer la vaisselle* = to dry the dishes.

WIRE (n) **1/** *fil* (m) *de fer* : barbed wire = *fil de fer barbelé* **2/** *télégramme* (m) : to send a wire = *envoyer un télégramme* = telegram ⊕ telex = *télex.*

WIRE (to, -d) **1/** *envoyer un télégramme* : he wired that he was arriving tonight = *il a envoyé un télégramme disant qu'il arrivait ce soir* ⊕ to cable = *câbler* **2/** *mettre sur table d'écoute* : his phone's wired = *son téléphone est (mis) sur table d'écoute* ⊕ to bug = *poser des micros (clandestins).*

WIRELESS (n, -es) (GB) *radio* (f) = ←.

WIRETAP (to, -ped) *mettre sur table d'écoute* = to tap.

WISDOM (n) *sagesse* (f) : wisdom, alas, doesn't come with age ! = *la sagesse, hélas, ne vient pas avec l'âge !* ≠ folly = *folie.*

WISE (adj, -r, -st) *sage* : a wise decision = *une sage décision* ⊕ sensible = *sensé*
I'm wise to you/to your little game = *je vois clair dans ton petit jeu* ⊕ I have your number = *je te connais, mon bonhomme*
don't be so wise ! = *ne fais pas le malin !* = don't be so smart !
to get wise to = *ouvrir les yeux sur* : it's time to get wise to/to wise up to his carryings-on = *il est temps d'ouvrir les yeux sur ses agissements* = **to wise up to**
to put s.o. wise to = *mettre la puce à l'oreille de qqn* : his gifts put me wise to his cheating = *quant à ses infidélités, ses cadeaux m'ont mis la puce à l'oreille* ⊕ to open s.o.'s eyes = *ouvrir les yeux à qqn*
I'm none the wiser = *je ne suis pas plus avancé pour autant*
a wise guy = *un petit malin* ⊕ a little snot = *un petit morveux*
☠ *sois sage !* = be a good boy !
— *une sage-femme* = a midwife
— *sage comme une image* = as good as gold.

WISE (suff) *pour ce qui est de* : workwise/moneywise = *pour ce qui est du travail/pour ce qui est de l'argent* ⊕ as for = *quant à.*

WISECRACK (n) *vanne* (f) : he was making wisecracks about his in-laws = *il lançait des vannes sur ses beaux-parents* = crack ⊕ quip = *boutade.*

WISELY (adv) *sagement.*

WISH (n, -es) *souhait* (m) : it's my dearest wish = *c'est mon souhait le plus cher* ⊕ desire = *désir*, hope = *espoir* ☠ *à vos souhaits !* = God bless you !
to make a wish = *faire un vœu.*

WISH (to, -ed) *souhaiter* : I wish you would come with us = *je souhaite que vous veniez avec nous* ⓓ to desire = *désirer*
to wish stg on s.o. = *souhaiter qqch à qqn* : I wouldn't wish that on my worst enemy = *je ne souhaiterais pas ça à mon pire ennemi*
(New York is wonderful) wish you were here ! = *(New York est fantastique,) on pense bien à toi* !

WISHFUL (adj) **that's wishful thinking** = *vous prenez vos désirs pour des réalités* ⓓ pipedreams = *des plans sur la comète.*

WISHY-WASHY (adj) *fadasse* : a wishy-washy personality = *une personnalité fadasse* ⓓ insipid = *insipide.*

WIT (n) *esprit* *(m)* : a book full ot wit = *un livre plein d'esprit* ⓓ irony = *ironie* ☠ → spirit
at wit's end = *fou d'inquiétude* : the kids haven't come back yet, she's at wit's end = *les gosses ne sont pas encore rentrés, elle est folle d'inquiétude* ⓓ to be beside oneself = *être dans tous ses états*
to keep one's wits about one = *ne pas perdre son calme* : the passengers kept their wits about them when the plane had to make an emergency landing = *les passagers n'ont pas perdu leur calme quand l'avion a dû faire un atterrissage forcé* ⓓ to keep one's cool = *garder son sang-froid*
to live by one's wits = *vivre d'expédients.*

WITCH (n, -es) *sorcière* *(f)* : they don't burn witches any longer = *on ne brûle plus les sorcières* ⓓ witchcraft = *sorcellerie*
witch doctor = *sorcier* = medicine man ☠ *ce n'est pas sorcier* = it's a cinch.

WITCH-HUNT (n) *chasse* *(f)* *aux sorcières.*

WITH (prep) *avec* : come with me = *venez avec moi* ≠ without = *sans*
with that = *là-dessus* : he hit her, and with that she split = *il l'a battue, et là-dessus elle s'est barrée* ⓓ and then = *et puis* = thereupon
☠ for the use of ''with'' after a verb, see the verb
— *elle est mariée avec un médecin* = she's married to a doctor
— *il a été gentil avec moi* = he's been nice to me.

WITHDRAW (to, -drew, -drawn) *(se) retirer* : I withdrew a lot of money from the bank = *j'ai retiré beaucoup d'argent de la banque,* the troops are withdrawing = *les troupes se retirent*
☠ *les invités se sont retirés* = the guests have retired
— *se faire retirer (son permis de conduire)* = to have (one's driving license) taken away
— *retirer son manteau* = to take off one's coat
— *qu'est-ce que tu en retireras ?* = what will you get out of it ?

WITHDRAWAL (n) *retrait* *(m)* : a withdrawal of money/troops = *un retrait d'argent/de troupes*
withdrawal symptoms = *symptômes d'état de manque* ⓓ addiction = *accoutumance*

☠ *retrait de permis* = suspension of driving license
— *rester en retrait* = to stay in the background.

WITHDRAWN (adj) *renfermé, -e* : shy and withdrawn = *timide et renfermé* ≠ gregarious = *grégaire.*

WITHER (to, -ed) *(se) flétrir* : flowers wither = *les fleurs se flétrissent* ⓓ to wilt = *se faner.*

WITHHOLD (to, -held, -held) *retenir* : they're withholding 10 percent from my salary each month = *ils retiennent 10 pour cent de mon salaire tous les mois* ☠ → to restrain.

WITHIN (prep) **1/** *d'ici* (future) : it'll be done within an hour = *ce sera fait d'ici une heure* **2/** *en moins de* : the cops came within ten minutes = *les flics sont arrivés en moins de dix minutes* **3/** *au sein de* : quarrels within the party = *des querelles au sein du parti.*

WITH-IT (adj) *dans le coup* : a with-it family = *une famille dans le coup* ≠ old hat = *vieux jeu.*

WITHOUT (prep) *sans* : I went without him = *j'y suis allé sans lui* ≠ with = *avec*
without (+ ing) = *sans (+ inf)* : he left without eating = *il est parti sans manger*
without even (saying ·hello) = *sans même (dire bonjour)*
☠ *sans le sou/sans abri* = penniless/homeless
— *sans arrêt* = nonstop
— *sans quoi* = otherwise.

WITHSTAND (to, -stood, -stood) *résister à* : to withstand an attack = *résister à une attaque* ≠ to capitulate = *capituler.*

WITNESS (n, -es) *témoin* *(m)* : two witnesses saw the accident = *deux témoins ont vu l'accident* ⓓ bystander = *badaud,* witness-box = *barre des témoins*
to bear witness to = *témoigner de*
witness for the defense ≠ **prosecution** = *témoin à décharge* ≠ *à charge*
☠ *appartement témoin* = model apartment
— *témoin (mariage)* = best man.

WITNESS (to, -ed) *être témoin de* : he witnessed the accident = *il a été témoin de l'accident.*

WITTINGLY (adv) *sciemment* : did you wittingly lie ? = *est-ce que vous avez menti sciemment ?* ≠ unwittingly = *involontairement.*

WITTY (adj, -ier, -iest) *spirituel, -elle* : a witty conversation/guy = *une conversation spirituelle/un type spirituel* ⓓ clever = *malin,* funny = *drôle* ☠ *vie spirituelle* = religious life.

WIZARD (n) *magicien* *(m)* : the wizard of Oz = *le magicien d'Oz* ⓓ witch = *sorcière*
a wizard at (math) = *un as en (maths).*

WOBBLE (to, -d) *vaciller* (s.o.), *branler* (stg) : the table/the guy is wobbling = *la table branle/le type vacille*

☠ *vaciller* → to waver
— *se branler* = to masturbate /to jerk off (man)
— *je n'en ai rien à branler !* = I don't give a fuck !
— *qu'est-ce que tu branles ?* = what the fuck are you doing ?

WOBBLY (adj, -ier, -iest) *vacillant, -e* (s.o.), *branlant, -e* (stg) : wobbly on her legs = *vacillante sur ses jambes*, a wobbly table = *une table branlante*.

WOE (n) *malheur* (m) : today's economic woes = *les malheurs économiques de notre époque* ○○ tribulation = ←
☠ → unhappiness.

WOLF (n, wolves) **1/** *loup* (m) : a pack of wolves = *une horde de loups* ○○ Little Red Riding Hood = *le Petit Chaperon Rouge*
to cry wolf = *crier au loup* ○○ help ! = *au secours !*
a wolf in sheep's clothing = *un loup déguisé en brebis*
☠ *hurler avec les loups* = to follow the pack
— *quand on parle du loup, on en voit la queue !* = speak of the devil !
— *être connu comme le loup blanc* = to be a regular (at a club, etc.)
— *les loups ne se mangent pas entre eux* = there's honor among thieves
— *faire entrer le loup dans la bergerie* = to set the fox to mind the geese
2/ *dragueur* (m) : what a wolf her brother is ! = *son frère, quel dragueur !* ○○ fast talker = *baratineur*.

WOLF DOWN (to, -ed) *engouffrer* : to wolf down one's meal = *engouffrer son repas* ○○ to gobble up = *ne faire qu'une bouchée de* ☠ *s'engouffrer dans le bus* = to rush into the bus.

WOMAN (n, -men) *femme* (f) : women's rights = *les droits des femmes* ○○ broad = *nana*, businesswoman = *femme d'affaires*, lady = *dame* ≠ man = *homme*
Women's Lib(eration Movement) = *MLF* ○○ feminist = *féministe*
☠ *elle est très femme* = she's very womanly
— *ma femme* = my wife
— *femme de chambre* = chambermaid.

WOMAN (adj) *femme* : a woman doctor/plumber = *une femme médecin/plombier*.

WOMANIZER (n) *coureur* (m) ○○ philanderer = *cavaleur* ☠ → runner **WOMANIZING** (n) *(le fait de) courir le jupon*.

WOMANLY (adj) *femme* : she's very womanly = *elle est très femme* ○○ feminine = *féminin* ≠ manly = *hommasse*.

WOMB (n) *matrice* (f) ○○ uterus = *utérus*, ovary = *ovaire*, embryo = *embryon*.

WONDER (n) **filled with wonder** = *rempli d'émerveillement*
it's a wonder that (she didn't die) = *c'est un miracle qu'(elle ne soit pas morte)*
no wonder ! = *pas étonnant !*
to work/do wonders = *faire merveille* : the medicine worked/did wonders = *le médicament a fait merveille*
you're a wonder ! = *tu es une (petite/vraie) merveille !*

WONDER (adj) *miracle* : a wonder product = *un produit miracle* ○○ miraculous = *miraculeux*.

WONDER (to, -ed) *se demander* : I wonder why he didn't come = *je me demande pourquoi il n'est pas venu* ○○ to speculate on = *s'interroger sur* ☠ → to ask.

WONDERFUL (adj) *merveilleux, -euse* : a wonderful film = *un film merveilleux* ≠ awful = *affreux*

—————— **GROUP : WONDERFUL = MERVEILLEUX** ——————

admirable = ←
amazing = *stupéfiant*
A-one = *hors ligne*
astonishing = *étonnant*
astounding = *époustouflant*
it's the cat's meow = *c'est bath*
cool = *extra*
delightful = *délicieux*
divine = *divin*
dynamite = *génial*
excellent = ←
exceptional = *exceptionnel*
extraordinary = *extraordinaire*
fabulous = *fabuleux*
fantastic = *fantastique*
fine = *très bon*
fine and dandy = *on ne peut mieux*

first-class = *de première classe*
first-rate = *de premier ordre*
glorious = *sensationnel*
good = *bon*
gorgeous = *splendide*
grand = *épatant*
great = *formidable*
groovy = *sensass*
heavenly = *divin*
incomparable = ←
incredible = *incroyable*
just right/fine = *impeccable*
lovely = *charmant*
magnificent = *magnifique*
marvelous = *merveilleux*
neat = *sympa*
next to none = *incomparable*
nice = *sympathique/gentil*
nifty = *super*
out of sight = *dément*

out of this world = *inouï*
outstanding = *hors pair*
phenomenal = *phénoménal*
pleasant = *agréable*
pretty good = *pas mal*
prodigious = *prodigieux*
remarkable = *remarquable*
second to none = *à nul autre pareil*
sensational = *sensationnel*
smashing = *fameux*
something else = *du tonnerre*
spectacular = *spectaculaire*
splendid = *splendide*
stupendous = *époustouflant*
sublime = ←
sumptuous = *somptueux*
super = ←
superb = *superbe*
swell = *chouette*

swinging = *sensass* **terrific** = *terrible* **topnotch** = *de premier ordre*	**tops** = *le meilleur qui soit* **tough** = *super* **tremendous** = *prodigieux*	**unforgettable** = *inoubliable.*

WOO (to, -ed) *courtiser* : the Senator's wooing the feminist vote = *le sénateur courtise l'électorat féministe* ⓒⒹ to give s.o. a line = *baratiner qqn.*

WOOD (n) *bois (m)* : the chair's wood = *la chaise est en bois* ⓒⒹ mahogany = *acajou*, oak = *chêne*, pine = *pin*, walnut = *noyer*, chestnut = *châtaignier*, teak = *te(c)k*, log = *bûche*, carpenter = *charpentier/menuisier*
touch wood ! = *touchons du bois !*
☠ *bois de charpente* = timber
— *bois de planches* = lumber
— *il va voir de quel bois je me chauffe !* = he'll see what I'm made of !

WOOD (adj) *de/en bois* : a wood table/chair = *une table/chaise de/en bois* = wooden.

WOODS (n pl) *bois (m pl)* : they built a house in the woods = *ils ont construit une maison dans les bois*
we're not out of the woods ! = *on n'est pas sorti de l'auberge !*
☠ → wood.

WOOL (n) *laine (f)* : a ball of wool = *une pelote de laine* ⓒⒹ camel hair = *poil de chameau*, flannel = *flanelle*, jersey = ←, cashmere = *cachemire*, mohair = ←, lamb's wool = *lambswool/laine d'agneau*
to pull the wool over s.o.'s eyes = *en faire accroire à qqn* → TO HUSTLE.

WOP (n) *rital, -e* : she married a wop = *elle a épousé un rital* ⓒⒹ dago = *macaroni.*

WORD (n) 1/ *mot (m)* : a sentence is made of words = *une phrase se compose de mots*

☠ *avoir son mot à dire* = to have one's say in the matter — *mot d'ordre* = slogan/catchword — *qui ne dit mot consent* = silence means consent	— *avoir le mot pour rire* = to be a good one for a joke — *mots croisés* = crossword puzzle

2/ *parole (f)* : it's his word against mine = *c'est sa parole contre la mienne*, I wrote the music and he wrote the words = *j'ai écrit la musique et il a écrit les paroles*

☠ *prendre la parole* = to take the floor — *adresser la parole à qqn* = to address s.o.	— *parole d'Évangile !* = Gospel truth !

---

to break one's word = *manquer à sa parole*
by word of mouth = *de bouche à oreille* : the news got around by word of mouth = *la nouvelle s'est transmise de bouche à oreille* ⓒⒹ by hearsay = *par ouï-dire*
(beautiful) beyond words = *(beau) au-delà des mots*
you can take my word for it ! = *vous pouvez me croire sur parole !*
I can't put (my feelings) into words = *je ne trouve pas les mots pour exprimer (ce que je ressens)*
I couldn't get a word out of her = *je n'ai pas pu en tirer un mot*
I don't believe a word of (what he told me) = *je ne crois pas un mot de (ce qu'il m'a dit)*
don't breathe a word ! = *n'en soufflez pas mot !* ⓒⒹ mum's the

word ! = *motus et bouche cousue !*
I'll eat my words if ... = *je veux bien être pendu si ...*
from the word go = *au vrai sens du terme* : he's a bastard from the word go = *c'est un salaud au vrai sens du terme*
to give one's word = *donner sa parole*
you give the word (and we'll split) = *à ton signal (on se barre)*
to hang on s.o.'s every word = *être suspendu à chacune des paroles de qqn* ⓒⒹ to drink in what s.o. says = *boire les paroles de qqn*
to have a word with = *dire un mot à* : if you have a few minutes, I'd like to have a word with you = *si vous avez quelques minutes, j'aimerais vous dire un mot*
to have words with s.o. =

avoir des mots avec qqn ⓒⒹ to have it out with s.o. = *engueuler qqn*
in a word = *bref* : in a word, I think you're all wet = *bref, je crois que vous mettez le doigt dans l'œil* ⓒⒹ in a nutshell = *en un mot*
I couldn't get a word in edgeways/edgewise = *je n'ai pas pu en placer une*
in so many words = *aussi explicitement* : she hinted she was going to have an abortion, but she didn't say it in so many words = *elle a laissé entendre qu'elle allait se faire avorter, mais elle ne l'a pas dit aussi explicitement*
just say the word (and I split) = *vous n'avez qu'un mot à dire (et je me tire)*
to keep one's word = *tenir parole*
to leave word for s.o. = *lais-*

ser un mot pour qqn ① to leave a message = *laisser un message*
to look for one's words = *chercher ses mots*
a man/woman of one's word = *un homme/une femme de parole*
mark my words ! = *je vous aurai prévenu !* ① I warn you ! = *je vous préviens !*
not to mince one's words = *ne pas mâcher ses mots* ① to speak one's mind = *dire ce qu'on pense*
not to say a word = *ne pas dire mot :* he didn't say a word to me = *il ne m'en a pas dit mot* ① not to say boo = *ne pas piper mot*
(expensive) that's not the word for it ! = *(cher) c'est peu dire !*
to put in a (good) word for s.o. = *dire un mot en faveur de*

qqn : can you put in a word for me with the boss ? = *est-ce que vous pouvez dire un mot au patron en ma faveur ?*
to send word that = *envoyer un mot pour dire que :* he sent word that he couldn't come = *il a envoyé un mot pour dire qu'il ne pouvait pas venir*
stop putting words into my mouth = *ne me faites pas dire ce que je n'ai pas dit*
I took him at his word = *je l'ai pris au mot*
you took the words (right) out of my mouth = *j'allais (juste) le dire*
(he's) too (stupid) for words = *il n'y a pas de mots pour dire à quel point (il est stupide)*
(upon) my word ! = *ma parole !* → GOSH !
to utter a word = *prononcer un mot :* he didn't utter a word

all evening = *il n'a pas prononcé un mot de la soirée*
to weigh one's words = *peser ses mots*
without a word of warning = *sans crier gare*
word has it that (he's dead) = *le bruit circule qu'(il est mort)*
word of honor = *parole d'honneur*
word-processor = *machine de traitement de texte* ① word-processing = *traitement de texte*
his word is law = *sa parole fait loi*
a word to the wise is sufficient ! = *à bon entendeur, salut !* ① forewarned is forearmed = *un homme averti en vaut deux*
word for word = *mot à/pour mot :* tell me what he said word for word = *répétez-moi mot à/pour mot ce qu'il a dit.*

WORD (to, -ed) *rédiger :* he worded his letter carefully = *il a rédigé sa lettre avec soin* ☠ *rédiger un contrat/projet de loi* = to draw up/draft a contract/bill.

WORDY (adj, -ier, -iest) *verbeux, -euse :* I don't like this kind of wordy editorial = *je n'aime pas ce genre d'éditorial verbeux* = verbose ① lengthy = *très long* ≠ succinct = ←.

WORK (n inv) *travail (m), boulot (m)* (LV) : I have a lot of work to do today = *j'ai beaucoup de travail/de boulot aujourd'hui,* what kind of work does he do ? = *quel genre de travail/de boulot fait-il ?* ① job = ←, position = situation

to go to work = *aller travailler/à son travail/au boulot :* what time does your husband go to work ? = *à quelle heure votre mari va-t-il travailler/à son travail/au boulot ?*
I have my work cut out for me = *j'ai du pain sur la planche*
to look for work = *chercher du*

travail/du boulot
to make work for = *donner du travail/du boulot à :* the kids make a lot of work for me = *les gosses me donnent beaucoup de travail/de boulot*
out of work = *sans emploi :* he's been out of work for six months = *cela fait six mois qu'il*

est sans emploi
to put a lot of work into = *fournir un travail énorme pour :* they put a lot of work into their last book = *ils ont fourni un travail énorme pour écrire leur dernier livre*
a work of art = *une œuvre d'art*

☠ *travaux forcés* = hard labor | — *j'ai perdu mon travail* = I lost my job.

WORK (to, -ed) 1/ *travailler, bosser* (LV) : I work everyday = *je travaille/je bosse tous les jours* ① to slave = *boulonner,* to toil = *peiner* ≠ to goof off = *tirer au flanc* ☠ *ça me travaille* = it's bugging me
2/ *marcher :* my car doesn't work = *ma voiture ne marche pas* ① to function = *fonctionner*
3/ *marcher :* our plan worked = *notre plan a marché* ① to succeed = *réussir* ☠ → to walk
4/ *faire marcher :* I can't work this machine = *je n'arrive pas à faire marcher cette machine*
to work it = *s'arranger pour :* can you work it so only half what I'm paid is declared ? = *pouvez-vous vous arranger pour que seulement la moitié de ce que je gagne soit déclarée ?*

to work against = *travailler contre :* time's working against us = *le temps travaille contre*

nous
to work at = *y mettre du sien :* marriage isn't easy, you have to

work at it = *le mariage n'est pas une chose facile, il faut y mettre du sien*

to work s.o. in = *trouver une petite place pour qqn* : my schedule's very busy, but I'll try to work you in = *mon emploi du temps est très chargé, mais je vais essayer de vous trouver une petite place*
to work off = *travailler pour rembourser* : I'm working off the debt/the bank loan = *je travaille pour rembourser la dette/l'emprunt bancaire*
to work on = 1/ *travailler* : I'm working on him to buy me a new car = *je le travaille pour qu'il m'achète une nouvelle voiture* ⓪ to persuade = *persuader* 2/ *travailler sur/à* : he's working on a novel = *il travaille à/sur un roman*
to work out = 1/ *s'entraîner* :

the athletes are working out = *les athlètes s'entraînent* ☠ → to entail 2/ *marcher* : the project didn't work out = *le projet n'a pas marché*, I hope everything works out = *j'espère que tout va (bien) marcher* ⓪ to pan out = *se concrétiser* ☠ → to walk 3/ *trouver une solution* : were you able to work things out with your boss ? = *est-ce que vous avez pu trouver une solution avec votre patron ?*
to work s.o. over = *passer qqn à tabac* : the gang worked him over = *le gang l'a passé à tabac* → TO HIT
to work up = 1/ *développer* : to work up a business/an idea = *développer une affaire/une idée* = to develop ⓪ to enlarge on =

approfondir 2/ *chauffer à blanc* : to work up the masses = *chauffer les masses à blanc* ⓪ to stir up = *attiser*
to be/get worked up (about) = *être énervé/s'énerver* : what are you so worked up about ? = *pourquoi es-tu si énervé ?*, what are you getting so worked up about ? = *pourquoi t'énerves-tu comme ça ?* → ANGRY
to work up to (+ ing) = *préparer le terrain pour* : he's working up to asking the boss for a raise = *il prépare le terrain pour demander une augmentation au patron*
to work with = *marcher avec* : tantrums don't work with me = *les crises de rage ne marchent pas avec moi.*

WORKAHOLIC (n) *bourreau (m) de travail* : being married to a workaholic's no fun = *ce n'est pas drôle d'être marié avec un bourreau de travail* ⓪ workhorse = *bête de somme.*

WORKDAY (n) 1/ *journée (f) de travail* : the unions want a six-hour workday = *les syndicats réclament une journée de travail de six heures* ⓪ working day = *jour de travail* 2/ *jour (m) ouvrable* : Christmas is not a workday = *le jour de Noël n'est pas un jour ouvrable.*

WORKER (n) 1/ *ouvrier, -ère, travailleur, -euse* : problems between workers and management = *les problèmes entre les ouvriers/les travailleurs et la direction*, manual worker = *travailleur manuel* ⓪ blue-collar worker = *col bleu*, union = *syndicat*, labor leaders = *dirigeants syndicaux*
highly skilled worker = *ouvrier hautement qualifié*
skilled worker = *ouvrier qualifié* ≠ **unskilled worker** = *ouvrier spécialisé/O.S.*
2/ *travailleur, -euse* : she's the hardest worker at the office = *c'est la plus travailleuse de tout le bureau* ≠ goof-off = *tire-au-flanc.*

WORKHORSE (n) *bête (f) de somme* ≠ lazybones = *fainéant.*

WORKING (adj) **working class** = *classe ouvrière*
working day = *jour de travail*
in working order = *en état de marche.*

WORKOUT (n) *séance (f) d'entraînement* : a three-hour workout every day = *une séance d'entraînement de trois heures tous les jours* ⓪ exercise = *exercice.*

WORKS (n pl) **to get caught up in the works** = *être pris dans l'engrenage*
to give s.o. the works = *faire passer un mauvais quart d'heure à qqn* : the cops gave him the works = *les flics lui ont fait passer un mauvais quart d'heure* ⓪ to give s.o. the treatment = *en faire voir de rudes à qqn*
in the works = *en cours* : the shooting's in the works = *le tournage est en cours* ⓪ under way = *en train*
public works = *travaux publics*
to shoot the works = *faire des folies* : let's shoot the works and order some caviar = *faisons des folies et prenons du caviar*
the works = *le grand jeu* : I want a cut, a permanent and a coloring : the works ! = *je veux une coupe, une permanente et une coloration : le grand jeu !*
the works of (Henry Miller) = *l'œuvre/les œuvres d'(Henry Miller).*

WORKSHOP (n) 1/ *stage (m) de travail* : a theater workshop = *un stage de théâtre* 2/ *atelier (m)* : the work's done in the workshop = *le travail se fait à l'atelier.*

WORKSHY (adj) *qui a un poil dans la main* : her husband's workshy = *son mari a un poil dans la main* ≠ hardworking = *bûcheur.*

WORLD (n) *monde (m)* : the biggest country in the world = *le plus grand pays du monde* ⓪ globe = ←, planet = *planète*, universe = *univers*

to be s.o.'s world = *ne voir que par qqn* : John's her world = *elle ne voit que par John*
to bring into the world =

mettre au monde ⓪ to give birth = *donner naissance*
she/he lives in a world of her/his own = *elle/il vit dans*

un monde à elle/lui
(it will do you) a world of good = *(ça vous fera) un bien fou*

(love/money) makes the world go round = (l'amour/l'argent) fait tourner le monde
man ≠ woman of the world = homme ≠ femme du monde ⓦ socialite = mondain
(he)'ll never set the world on fire = (il) n'a pas inventé la poudre/le fil à couper le beurre
not to be long for this world = ne plus en avoir pour longtemps
not for the world = pour rien au monde : I wouldn't hurt you for the world = je ne voudrais vous blesser pour rien au monde
out of this world = inouï : his last play was out of this world = sa dernière pièce était inouïe → WONDERFUL
that makes a world of difference = ça fait une sacrée diffé-rence
he thinks the world of her = il pense le plus grand bien d'elle ≠ he looks down on her = il la regarde de haut
what/who in the world ! = pourquoi/qui diable ! → GOSH !
what's the world coming to ? = où va le monde ?
we're worlds apart = il y a un monde entre nous

☠ il s'en fait un monde = he makes a fuss about it
— il y a du monde au balcon = she's top-heavy
— il se fiche du monde = he's going a little too far
— pas le moins du monde = not in the least
— nous avons du monde ce soir = we're having company tonight

— il y a du monde ≠ peu de monde = there are a lot of people ≠ very few people
— vieux comme le monde = as old as the hills
— depuis que le monde est monde = since the beginning of time.

WORLD (adj) mondial, -e : a world government = un gouvernement mondial ☠ → worldwide

the world series = la coupe américaine de base-ball

world fair = exposition universelle
world war = guerre mondiale.

WORLDLY (adj, -ier, -iest) tourné, -e vers le monde : a worldly sophisticated man = un homme sophistiqué et tourné vers le monde ⓦ cosmopolitan = cosmopolite.

WORLDWIDE (adj) mondial, -e : worldwide inflation = inflation mondiale ⓦ universal = universel ☠ une guerre mondiale = a world war.

WORM (n) ver (m) : birds eat worms = les oiseaux mangent des vers ⓦ tapeworm = ver solitaire
☠ nu comme un ver = stark-naked
— c'est pas piqué des vers ! = that takes some doing !
— vers (poème) = verse.

WORM (to, -ed) to worm stg out of s.o. = tirer les vers du nez à qqn ⓦ to drag stg out of s.o. = arracher qqch à qqn.

WORN-OUT (adj) 1/ exténué, -e : worn-out from all this work = exténué après tout ce travail ⓦ dead-tired = fourbu, all in = pompé 2/ usé, -e : worn-out shoes = des chaussures usées = worn ≠ brand-new = flambant neuf.

WORRIED (adj) inquiet, -ète : worried parents = des parents inquiets ≠ reassured = rassuré.

WORRISOME (adj) inquiétant, -e : a worrisome situa-tion = une situation inquiétante ⓦ disturbing = préoc-cupant ☠ des bruits inquiétants = eerie sounds.

WORRY (n, -ies) souci (m) : being broke is not my only worry = être fauché n'est pas mon seul souci ⓦ trouble = ennui
full of worry = rempli d'inquiétude
(your) worries are over ! = finis les soucis !

☠ son seul souci est de bien élever ses enfants = her concern is that her children are well-educated.

WORRY (to, -ied) s'inquiéter : you worry too much = tu t'inquiètes trop ⓦ to fret = se tracasser
don't worry ! = ne vous inquiétez pas !/ne vous en fai-tes pas ! ⓦ stay loose ! = te frappe pas !
to be worried (about) = être inquiet (pour) : I'm wor-ried about my father's health = je suis inquiet pour la santé de mon père ⓦ to be concerned about = se faire du souci pour, to be sick about = être malade de
to be worried to death = se faire du mauvais sang/un sang d'encre ⓦ to be worried sick = être aux cent coups.

WORRYWART (n) bileux, -euse : my mother's such a worrywart = ma mère est tellement bileuse ≠ happy-go-lucky = joyeux drille.

WORSE (n) if worse comes to worst = dans le pire des cas ≠ at best = au mieux.

WORSE (adj, comp) pire, plus mal (health) : it would have been worse to tell her the truth = cela aurait été pire de lui dire la vérité, the patient looks worse = le malade a l'air d'aller plus mal ≠ better = mieux/meilleur
it could have been worse = ça aurait pu être pire
to get worse = empirer : the patient/the situation is getting worse = l'état du malade/la situation empire ≠ to get better = s'améliorer
to make things/matters worse = pour comble de malheur
what's worse (an abortion or an unwanted child) ? = qu'est-ce qui est pire (un avortement ou un enfant non voulu) ?
what's worse is that (she took all the money) = le

pire/ce qu'il y a de pire, c'est qu'(elle a embarqué tout l'argent)
worse than = *pire/plus mal que* : you're worse than your sister = *tu es pire que ta sœur*, the patient's worse than yesterday = *le malade va plus mal qu'hier*
worse still = *et pis encore* : he lost his job, worse still, one of his children died = *il a perdu son boulot et, pis encore, un de ses enfants est mort*
☠ *il n'est pire eau que l'eau qui dort* = be wary of still waters.

WORSE (adv, comp) *plus mal* : he doesn't cook well, but she cooks even worse = *il ne cuisine pas bien, mais elle cuisine encore plus mal*
worse than = *plus mal que* : she cooks worse than I do = *elle cuisine plus mal que moi*
to be worse off = *être encore pire* : she's worse off with her second husband = *c'est encore pire pour elle avec son second mari*.

WORSEN (to, -ed) *(faire) empirer* : the economic crisis has worsened the relations between the two countries = *la crise économique a fait empirer les relations entre les deux pays*.

WORSHIP (to, -(p)ed) *vénérer* (people), *adorer* (religion) : they worship idols = *ils adorent des idoles*, she worships her teacher = *elle vénère son professeur* ⓪ to idolize = *idolâtrer* ☠ *adorer* → to adore.

WORST (n) *le pire* : the worst that could happen would be his saying no = *le pire qui pourrait arriver serait qu'il dise non* ≠ the best = *le mieux/le meilleur*
to expect the worst = *s'attendre au pire*
to get the worst of stg = *faire les frais de qqch* : he got the worst of the fight = *il a fait les frais de la bagarre*
at worst (the plane will be delayed an hour) = *au pire (l'avion aura une heure de retard)*
the worst is yet to come = *le pire est encore à venir*.

WORST (adj, superl) *le/la pire, le plus mauvais, la plus mauvaise* : he's the worst lover I've ever had = *c'est le pire/le plus mauvais amant que j'aie jamais eu*
the worst (thing to do) = *la pire des (choses à faire)*
in the worst way = *vraiment terriblement* : I need this document in the worst way = *j'ai vraiment terriblement besoin de ce document* → VERY
you're your (own) worst enemy = *vous êtes votre pire ennemi* ⓪ to cut off one's nose to spite one's face = *tendre les verges pour se faire fouetter*.

WORTH (n) **(a dollar's) worth of (chocolate)** = *pour (un dollar) de (chocolat)*.

WORTH (prep) **to be worth** = *valoir* : the ring's worth a million = *cette bague vaut un million*, what's it worth ? = *qu'est-ce que ça vaut ?/combien ça vaut ?*
to be worth (+ ing) = *valoir la peine de (+ inf)* : the movie's worth seeing = *le film vaut la peine d'être vu*
it's ≠ it isn't worth it = *ça vaut ≠ ça ne vaut pas la peine*
☠ *(moins il parle) mieux ça vaut* = (the less he speaks) the better it is

— *ils se valent* = they're on the same level
— *il vaut mieux ne pas (y aller)* = it would be better (not to go)
— *ça ne m'a valu que des embêtements* = it only got me into trouble.

WORTHLESS (adj) *qui n'a aucune valeur* : her jewelry's worthless = *ses bijoux n'ont aucune valeur* ≠ valuable = *de grande valeur*.

WORTHWHILE (adj) *qui en vaut la peine* : a worthwhile trip/experience = *un voyage/une expérience qui en vaut la peine*.

WORTHY (adj, -ier, -iest) *valable* : a worthy cause/opponent = *une cause/un adversaire valable* ☠ → valid
that wasn't worthy of you = *ce n'était pas digne de vous* ⓪ it was unworthy of you = *c'était indigne de vous*.

WOULD (aux) *auxiliaire du conditionnel* : what would you like to eat ? = *qu'aimeriez-vous manger ?*

she **says** she'll come = *elle dit qu'elle viendra*
she **said** she'd (she **would**) come = *elle a dit qu'elle viendrait*

> I would = I'd
> you would = you'd
> he/she would = he'd/she'd
> we would = we'd
> they would = they'd

☠ *en anglais* (GB), *on remplace parfois* « would » *par* « should » *à la première personne du singulier et du pluriel du conditionnel.*

WOULD-BE (adj) *prétendu, -e* : a would-be actress = *une prétendue actrice* ⓪ so-called = *soi-disant*.

WOUND (n) *blessure (f)* : a deep wound = *une blessure profonde* ⓪ scar = *cicatrice*, bruise = *ecchymose*, bandage = *pansement*
to lick one's wounds = *panser ses blessures/plaies* : it took me a long time to lick my wounds = *ça m'a pris du temps pour panser mes blessures/plaies*.

WOUND (to, -ed) *blesser* : he was wounded in the war = *il a été blessé à la guerre* ☠ → to injure.

WOUNDED (n pl) **the wounded** = *les blessés* : the wounded were evacuated = *on a évacué les blessés* ⓪ casualties = *les accidentés*.

WOW ! (interj) *holà !* → GOSH !

WRANGLE (n) *chicane (f)* ⓪ squabble = *chamaille*
WRANGLE (to, -d) *(se) chicaner* : they wrangled over the price = *ils ont chicané sur le prix* ⓪ to squabble = *se chamailler*.

WRAP (n) *petite laine (f)* : it's cold, take a wrap = *il fait froid, prenez une petite laine* ⓪ shawl = *châle*.

WRAP (to, -ped) **to wrap around** = *enrouler autour de :* wrap the scarf around your ankle = *enroulez le foulard autour de votre cheville*

to wrap in = 1/ *envelopper dans :* I wrapped the gift in pretty paper = *j'ai enveloppé le cadeau dans du joli papier* 2/ *envelopper de :* the affair was wrapped in mystery = *l'affaire était enveloppée de mystère*

to wrap up = 1/ *faire un paquet/emballer :* I'll buy this vase, can you wrap it up for me ? = *je vais prendre ce vase, pouvez-vous me faire un paquet/me l'emballer ?* ☠ *ça ne m'emballe pas* = it doesn't turn me on — *t'emballe pas !* = stay cool ! 2/ *tout régler :* he wants to wrap up the deal and go on vacation = *il veut avoir tout réglé avant de partir en vacances* ⓪ to sew up = *mener à bonne fin*

to be wrapped up in (one's work/a love affair) = *être absorbé par (son travail/une aventure sentimentale)* ⓪ to be taken up with = *être pris par.*

WRATH (n) *courroux (m) :* the wrath of a jealous woman = *le courroux d'une femme jalouse* ⓪ fury = *fureur.*

WREATH (n) *couronne (f) (mortuaire) :* hundreds of wreaths at his funeral = *des centaines de couronnes à son enterrement* ☠ → crown.

WRECK (n) 1/ *épave (f) :* the wreck of a car/ship = *l'épave d'une voiture/d'un navire* ⓪ wreckage = *débris* 2/ *épave (f) :* he's a wreck since he started drinking = *c'est une épave depuis qu'il s'est mis à boire* ⓪ lost soul = *âme en peine.*

WRECK (to, -ed) *ficher en l'air :* money problems wrecked their marriage = *les problèmes d'argent ont fichu leur ménage en l'air* ⓪ to destroy = *détruire.*

WRECKER (n) *naufrageur (m)* (ships), *démolisseur (m)* (cars, buildings).

WRESTLE (to, -d) *faire de la lutte :* few women wrestle = *peu de femmes font de la lutte*

to wrestle with (a problem) = *être aux prises avec (un problème)* ⓪ to grapple with = *se débattre avec.*

WRESTLER (n) *lutteur (m),* catcheur *(m)* ☠ *lutteur* → fighter **WRESTLING** (n inv) *lutte (f) :* I don't like wrestling = *je n'aime pas la lutte* ☠ → struggle.

WRETCHED (adj) *sale :* a wretched existence/cold = *une sale existence/un sale rhume* → AWFUL ☠ → dirty.

WRING (to, wrung, wrung) *essorer :* wring the sweater after you wash it = *essorez le pull après l'avoir lavé.*

WRINGER (n) **to put s.o. through the wringer** = *en*

faire voir de toutes les couleurs à qqn ⓪ to give s.o. a hard time of it = *en faire voir de dures à qqn.*

WRINKLE (n) *ride (f)* (face) : her face is covered with wrinkles = *son visage est couvert de rides* **WRINKLE** (to, -d) *se friper :* this material doesn't wrinkle = *ce tissu ne se fripe pas* ⓪ to iron = *repasser,* to crease = *se froisser.*

WRINKLED (adj) *ridé, -e* (face), *fripé, -e* (clothes) : a wrinkled face/shirt = *un visage ridé/une chemise fripée* ⓪ creased = *qui a des faux plis.*

WRIST (n) *poignet (m) :* a small wrist = *un poignet fin* ⓪ hand = *main*

she slashed her wrist = *elle s'est tailladé le poignet.*

WRISTWATCH (n, -es) *montre-bracelet (f).*

WRIT (n) **writ of habeas corpus** = *writ d'habeas corpus.*

WRITE (to, wrote, written) *écrire :* write your name on the paper = *écrivez votre nom sur le papier* ⓪ to rewrite = *réécrire,* to scribble = *gribouiller*

to write about (Women's Lib) = *écrire sur (le MLF)*

to write back = *répondre (par écrit) :* he wrote back that he wouldn't come = *il a répondu qu'il ne viendrait pas* = to answer

to write down = *marquer :* write it down so that you don't forget = *marquez-le afin de ne pas oublier* ⓪ to take note = *prendre note* ☠ → to mark

to write off = *passer aux profits et pertes :* they wrote the investment off = *ils ont passé l'investissement aux profits et pertes*

to write up = *faire un article sur :* the journalist wrote up the story for a weekly = *le journaliste a fait un article sur cette histoire pour un hebdomadaire.*

WRITER (n) *écrivain (m) :* she married a writer = *elle a épousé un écrivain* ⓪ ghostwriter = *nègre,* hack = *écrivaillon,* man/woman of letters = *homme/femme de lettres,* novelist = *romancier,* author/authoress = *auteur,* historian = *historien,* biographer = *biographe,* playwright = *dramaturge/auteur dramatique,* scriptwriter = *scénariste.*

WRITE-UP (n) *critique (f) :* the play got a great write-up = *la pièce a eu une critique formidable* ⓪ notices = *critiques* ☠ → criticism.

WRITING (n) *écriture (f) :* I recognized her writing = *j'ai reconnu son écriture* ☠ → handwriting

put it in writing = *mettez-le par écrit* ⓪ put it in black and white = *mettez-le noir sur blanc.*

WRONG (n) **to right a wrong** = *réparer un tort.*		
WRONG (adj) *mauvais, -e :* a wrong analysis of the situation = *une mauvaise analyse de la situation,* a wrong translation = *une mauvaise traduction* ≠ right = *bon,* correct = ← ☠ → bad		
to back the wrong horse = *miser sur le mauvais cheval*	**you're barking up the wrong tree** = *vous faites fausse route*	⓪ you're on the right ≠ wrong track = *vous êtes sur la bonne*

≠ *mauvaise piste*
to be born on the wrong side of the tracks = *venir de la zone*
to be wrong = *avoir tort* : I think you're wrong = *je pense que vous avez tort* ⓓ to be in error = *être dans l'erreur*, to be sadly mistaken = *se tromper lourdement*
to get up on the wrong side of the bed = *se lever du pied gauche*
to go about things the wrong way = *s'y prendre mal (pour faire quelque chose)* : you're going about it the wrong way = *vous vous y prenez mal (pour le faire)*
to go the wrong (place) = *se tromper d'(endroit)*
I was wrong about (him) =

j'ai eu tort à (son sujet)
it's the wrong time to (ask her for that) = *ce n'est pas le moment de (lui demander ça)*
to laugh out of the wrong side of one's mouth = *rire jaune*
(lying) is wrong = *c'est mal de (mentir)* = **it's wrong (to lie)**
to rub s.o. the wrong way = *prendre qqn à rebrousse-poil*
to see nothing ≠ something wrong with = *ne voir aucun mal à ≠ voir du mal à* : she sees nothing wrong with getting an abortion = *elle ne voit aucun mal à se faire avorter*
to take the wrong (door/ train) = *se tromper de (porte/ train)*
to take stg the wrong way =

mal prendre qqch : he took what I said the wrong way = *il a mal pris ce que j'ai dit*
that's/there's where you're wrong = *c'est là que vous avez tort*
what's wrong ? = *qu'est-ce qui ne va pas ?* **nothing's wrong** = *tout va bien* ≠ **something's wrong** = *il y a quelque chose qui ne va pas*
that's the wrong (door/answer) = *ce n'est pas la bonne (porte/réponse)*
the wrong ... = *pas ... qu'il faut* : she married the wrong guy = *elle n'a pas épousé le type qu'il lui fallait*
the wrong number = *le mauvais numéro* ≠ **the right number** = *le bon numéro.*

WRONG (adv) *mal* : you wrote my name wrong = *vous avez mal écrit mon nom* ☠ → badly

---

to do stg (all) wrong = *(très) mal faire qqch* : you did your homework wrong = *tu as mal fait tes devoirs*
to go wrong = 1/ *aller de travers/mal* : everything's going wrong today = *tout va de travers/mal aujourd'hui* 2/ *tourner mal* : their son went wrong = *leur fils a mal tourné* ≠ to follow the straight and narrow = *suivre le droit chemin*
don't get me wrong ! = *comprenez-moi bien !*

where I went wrong was in (believing everything he said) = *là où j'ai eu tort, c'est de (croire tout ce qu'il a dit)*
you've got it (all) wrong ! = *vous n'y êtes pas (du tout) !* ⓓ you misunderstood me ! = *vous m'avez mal compris !*
you can't go wrong ! = *vous ne pouvez pas vous tromper !*

WRY (adj, -ier, -iest) *grinçant, -e* : my parents don't appreciate his wry sense of humor = *mes parents n'apprécient pas son sens de l'humour grinçant* ⓓ witty = *spirituel.*

XMAS (n) *Noël* (m) : Xmas greetings = *vœux de Noël* = Christmas greetings.

X-RATED (adj) **an X-rated film** = *un film interdit aux moins de dix-huit ans* ⓐ blue movie = *film porno.*

X-RAY (n) *rayon X* (m) **X-RAY** (to, -ed) *radiographer, faire une radio de.*

YACHT (n) *yacht* (m) ⓐ boat = *bateau.*

YAK (to, -ked) *blablater* : some women can yak all day long = *il y a des femmes qui peuvent blablater toute la journée* = to yackety-yak ⓐ to chatter = *jacasser* **YAK-KING** (n) *blablabla* (m) ⓐ chatter = *jacasserie.*

YANKEE (n) *Yankee* (m, f) ⓐ yank = *ricain, gringo* = *amerloque.*

YANK OUT OF (to, -ed) *arracher de* : he yanked the bill out of my hand = *il m'a arraché la facture des mains* ⓐ to pull = *tirer*
☠ *arracher un aveu à qqn* = to draw a confession out of s.o.
— *c'était tellement intéressant que je n'ai pas pu m'en arracher* = it was so interesting that I couldn't tear myself away
— *elles s'arrachaient les soldes* = they snapped up the items on sale
— *arracher une dent/une page* = to extract a tooth/to tear out a page.

YARD (n) **1/** *jardin* (m) : each house in the area has a small yard = *toutes les maisons du coin ont un petit jardin* ⓐ front yard = *jardin de devant*, backyard = *jardin de derrière*, courtyard = *cour*
(prison) yard = *cour (de prison)*
☠ *jardin soigné* = garden
— *jardin d'enfants* = kindergarten
2/ yard (m) = 0,914 m.

YARN (n) **to spin a yarn** = *raconter des craques* ⓐ to tell stories = *raconter des histoires.*

YAWN (n) *bâillement* (m) **YAWN** (to, -ed) *bâiller* : he kept yawning throughout the movie = *il a bâillé pendant tout le film* ⓐ to snore = *ronfler.*

YEAR (n) *an* (m), *année* (f) : I was married for 5 years = *j'ai été marié pendant 5 ans* ⓐ month = *mois*
to be (10) years old = *avoir (10) ans*
he's getting on in years = *il prend de l'âge* ⓐ he's no spring chicken = *il n'est plus tout jeune*
in years/for years = *depuis des années* : I haven't seen him for/in years = *je ne l'ai pas vu depuis des années*
this ≠ last year = *cette année ≠ l'année dernière*
(to earn $ 20,000) a year = *gagner (20 000 dollars) par an*
☠ *les années trente/vingt* = the thirties/the twenties
— *je m'en moque comme de l'an quarante* = I don't give a hoot.

YEARBOOK (n) *annuaire* (m) *(de fin d'année d'une université/d'un lycée).*

YEARLY (adj) *annuel, -elle* : yearly income/meeting = *revenu annuel/réunion annuelle* **YEARLY** (adv) *tous les ans* : to go to Europe yearly = *aller tous les ans en Europe.*

YEARN FOR/TO (to, -ed) *désirer vivement* : she's yearning to have a child = *elle désire vivement avoir un enfant* ⓐ to long for = *avoir grande envie de.*

YELL (to, -ed) *hurler* : he couldn't hear me so I had to yell = *il ne pouvait pas m'entendre, et j'ai dû hurler* ⓐ to shout = *crier*
don't yell at me ! = *ne crie pas après moi !* → TO LAMBAST.

YELLOW (n) *jaune* (m) : she wears a lot of yellow = *elle s'habille souvent en jaune* ☠ *un jaune (grève)* = a scab.

YELLOW (adj) **1/** *jaune* : yellow fever/curtains = *fièvre jaune/rideaux jaunes* ⓐ white = *blanc*
the yellow pages = *les pages jaunes (annuaire par professions)*
☠ *rire jaune* = to laugh the wrong side of one's mouth
2/ *trouillard, -e* : you're too yellow to fight = *tu es trop trouillard pour te battre* ⓐ chicken = *froussard ≠* fearless = *intrépide*
to have a yellow streak = *avoir un côté lâche.*

YEN (n) **to have a yen for (Chinese food)** = *avoir très envie de (cuisine chinoise)* ⓐ to yearn for = *désirer vivement.*

YENTA (n) *pipelette (f)* : I hate yentas and their gossip = *je déteste les pipelettes et leurs commérages* ⓪ busybody = *mouche du coche*.

YES (adv) *oui* : are you American ? — yes = *êtes-vous américain ? — oui* ⓪ yeah = *ouais* ≠ no = *non*
yes, I am/she is/... = *si* (to correct something that was negatively stated) : he isn't American, is he ? — yes, he is = *il n'est pas américain, n'est-ce pas ? — si* ☠ → *il* ☠ *(il se met en colère) pour un oui, pour un non* = (he gets mad) for anything at all.

YES-MAN (n, -men) *béni-oui-oui (m)* : the President's surrounded by yes-men = *le Président est entouré de béni-oui-oui* ⓪ lackey = *laquais*.

YESTERDAY (adv) *hier* : he left yesterday = *il est parti hier* ≠ tomorrow = *demain*
she wasn't born yesterday = *elle n'est pas née d'hier*
yesterday morning = *hier matin*
☠ *hier soir* = last night.

YET (adv) **1/** *déjà* : has he come yet ? = *est-ce qu'il est déjà arrivé ?* = has he already come ? **2/** *jusqu'à présent* : she's the sexiest girl he met yet = *c'est la fille la plus sexy qu'il ait rencontrée jusqu'à présent*

not yet = *pas encore* : has he come ? — no, not yet ! = *est-ce qu'il est arrivé ? — non, pas encore !*, no, he hasn't come yet = *non, il n'est*	*pas encore arrivé* **you may/might yet (hear from me)** = *vous pouvez/pourriez bien encore (entendre parler de moi)*.

YET (conj) *pourtant* : he's young, yet mature = *il est jeune, pourtant il est mûr* ⓪ nevertheless = *néanmoins*.

YID (n) *youpin, -e* = kike ⓪ sheeny = *youtre*.

YIELD (n) *rendement (m)* : a low yield for this kind of stock = *un faible rendement pour ce genre d'actions* ☠ → output.

YIELD (to, -ed) **1/** *rapporter* : the investment yields 20 per cent = *l'investissement rapporte 20 pour cent* = to bring in ≠ to lose = *perdre*
☠ *rapporter un livre* = to bring/to take back a book
— *rapporter un fait* = to report a fact
— *rapporter (un décret)* = to rescind (a decree)
— *les enfants rapportent* = children tattle
— *se rapporter à* = to pertain to
2/ *(se laisser) fléchir* : he refused to yield = *il a refusé de se laisser fléchir* ⓪ to give in = *céder* ≠ to withstand = *résister* ☠ → to bend.

YMCA (abbr) = Young Men's Christian Association = *Association des jeunes chrétiens* ⓪ YMHA = Young Men's Hebrew Association = *Association de la jeunesse juive*.

YOGA (n) *yoga (m)* ⓪ zen = ←.

YOGURT (n) *yaourt (m)* : fruit yogurt = *yaourt aux fruits*.

YOU (pron) **1/** (subject) *vous, tu* (for friends, lovers, etc.) : are you French ? = *est-ce que vous êtes/tu es français ?* **2/** (object) *vous, te* : I don't see you = *je ne vous/te vois pas* → I
for/with you = *pour/avec vous/toi*
☠ *(un ami) à vous/toi* = (a friend) of yours
— *être à tu et à toi avec qqn* = to be on a first name basis with s.o.

YOUNG (adj, -er, -est) *jeune* : I'm still young = *je suis encore jeune* ⓪ juvenile = *juvénile* ≠ elderly = *âgé* ☠ *nom de jeune fille* = maiden name.

he's not as young as he used to be = *il n'a plus (ses jambes de) vingt ans* ⓪ to be getting on in years = *prendre de l'âge* **to be young at heart**	= *être jeune de cœur* **young man** ≠ **young lady** = *jeune homme* ≠ *jeune fille* **young people (like music)** = *les jeunes (aiment la musique)*

YOUNGER (adj) *plus jeune* : he's very young but she's still younger = *il est très jeune, mais elle est plus jeune encore* ≠ older = *plus vieux*

younger than = *plus jeune que* : he's younger than me = *il est plus jeune que moi*	**my younger brother/sister** = *mon frère cadet/ma sœur cadette*.

YOUNGEST (adj, n) *le plus, la plus jeune* : he's the youngest child in the family = *c'est le plus jeune (enfant) de la famille*.

YOUNGISH (adj) *assez jeune* : her parents are youngish = *ses parents sont assez jeunes* ≠ oldish = *assez vieux*.

YOUNGSTER (n) *gamin, -e* : he has two youngsters = *il a deux gamins* ⓪ tot = *bambin*.

YOUR (adj) *votre, vos, ton, ta, tes* : your car = *votre/ta voiture*, your kids = *vos/tes gosses* → MY.

YOURS (pron) *le/la vôtre, les vôtres (à vous), le tien, la tienne, les tiens, tiennes (à toi)* : that car's yours = *cette voiture est la vôtre/est à vous/est la tienne/est à toi* → MY
☠ *à la tienne/vôtre !* = here's mud in your eye !
— *je suis des vôtres* = count me in.

YOURSELF (pron, -selves) **1/** *vous-même, toi-même* : do it yourself! = *faites-le vous-même/fais-le toi-même !*, do it yourselves! = *faites-le vous-mêmes !* **2/** (reflexive form) *vous/te* : did you hurt yourself? = *est-ce que vous vous êtes/tu t'es fait mal ?* → MYSELF.

YOUTH (n) *jeunesse (f)* : today's youth = *la jeunesse d'aujourd'hui* ⓊⒹ young people = *les jeunes*
in my youth = *dans ma jeunesse*
youth hostel = *auberge de jeunesse*
youth is wasted on the young = *si jeunesse savait, si vieillesse pouvait*
☠ *il faut que jeunesse se passe* = boys will be boys.

YOUTHFUL (adj) **youthful looking** = *qui a l'air jeune.*

YUGOSLAVIA (n) *Yougoslavie (f)* **YUGOSLAV(IAN)** (n, adj) *Yougoslave (m, f).*

YUMMY (adj, -ier, -iest) *miam, miam* : the cake's yummy = *miam, miam ce gâteau* ⓊⒹ scrumptious = *exquis.*

YUPPIE (n, -ies) = young urban professional = *yuppie (m, f) (jeune cadre citadin)* : they are trying to get the yuppie vote = *ils essaient de décrocher les voix des yuppies/des jeunes cadres* ⓊⒹ yumpie = young upwardly mobile professional = *jeune cadre montant*, buppie = black urban professional = *cadre urbain noir.*

ZANY (adj, -ier, -iest) *louf* : a zany film = *un film louf* → CRAZY.

ZEAL (n) *zèle (m)* : he did the work with zeal = *il a fait le travail avec zèle* ≠ apathy = *apathie*
☠ *faire du zèle* = to overdo stg
— *grève du zèle* = work-to-rule strike.

ZEALOT (n) *exalté, -e* : the Ku Klux Klan is full of zealots = *le Ku Klux Klan est plein d'exaltés.*

ZEBRA (n) *zèbre (m)* ⓊⒹ antelope = *antilope* ☠ *un drôle de zèbre* = a queer duck.

ZENITH (n) *zénith (m)* : at the zenith of his career = *au zénith de sa carrière* ⓊⒹ peak = *apogée.*

ZERO (n, -(e)s) **1/** *zéro (m)* : temperature below zero = *température au-dessous de zéro* **2/** *zéro (m)* : her husband's a zero = *son mari est un zéro* ⓊⒹ nebbish = *minus*
to be zero in (math) = *être zéro en (maths)*
☠ *repartir à zéro* = to start again from scratch.

ZERO HOUR (n) *l'heure H* ⓊⒹ D-day = *le jour J.*

ZERO IN ON (to, -ed) *être sur le point de découvrir* : to zero in on a cure for cancer/a murderer = *être sur le point de découvrir un traitement pour le cancer/un meurtrier.*

ZEST (n) *piment (m)* : add some zest to your life = *mettez un peu de piment dans votre vie* ☠ *piment (rouge)* = red pepper.

ZIGZAG (n) *zigzag (m)* ⓊⒹ turn = *virage* **ZIGZAG** (to, -ged) *zigzaguer.*

ZILCH (n inv) *que dalle* : I know as much about him as he knows about me, which is zilch = *j'en sais autant sur lui qu'il en sait sur moi, c'est-à-dire que dalle* ≠ tons = *des tonnes.*

ZIP CODE (n) *code (m) postal* ⓊⒹ post-office box = *boîte postale.*

ZIPPER (n) *fermeture (f) Éclair* **ZIP UP** (to, -ped) *remonter (sa) fermeture Éclair.*

ZONE (n) *zone (f)* : the city's divided into zones = *la ville est divisée en zones* ⓊⒹ area = *région* ☠ *venir de la zone* = to be born on the wrong side of the tracks.

ZONKED (adj) *pété, -e* (drugs/drink) ⓊⒹ stoned = *défoncé* → DRUNK.

ZOO (n) *zoo (m)* : let's go to the zoo! = *allons au zoo !* ⓊⒹ animals = *animaux*, cage = ←.

ZOOM (n) *montée (f) en flèche* : a zoom in unemployment = *une montée en flèche du chômage* ≠ slump = *baisse brutale* **ZOOM** (to, -ed) *monter en flèche* : prices are zooming = *les prix montent en flèche* = to soar.

ZUCCHINI (n) *courgette (f)* ⓊⒹ squash = *courge.*